UNIVERSITY CASEBOOK SERIES®

THE CONSTITUTION OF THE UNITED STATES

by

MICHAEL STOKES PAULSEN
University Chair and Professor of Law
The University of St. Thomas

STEVEN G. CALABRESI
Professor of Law
Northwestern University

MICHAEL W. MCCONNELL
Richard and Frances Mallery Professor of Law
Stanford University

SAMUEL L. BRAY
Assistant Professor of Law
University of California, Los Angeles

SECOND EDITION

FOUNDATION PRESS

© 2010 By THOMSON REUTERS/FOUNDATION PRESS
© 2013 by LEG, Inc. d/b/a West Academic Publishing
    610 Opperman Drive
    St. Paul, MN 55123
    1–800–313–9378

Printed in the United States of America

ISBN: 978–1–60930–271–9

Mat #41381187

To Kristen, love of my life (MSP)

To Mimi, whose love is patient and kind (SGC)

To the next generation of constitutionalists (MWM)

To Abigail (SLB)

PREFACE

The second edition of this casebook continues the organizing principles and central themes of the first edition. As we said in the preface to that edition,

> Why another casebook in the field of constitutional law? The existing casebooks are valuable. They offer a diverse array of approaches, and they are excellent compendia of cases. They tend, though, to focus *only* on cases—and almost exclusively U.S. Supreme Court decisions—as the source of constitutional law. They also emphasize present doctrine more than constitutional history. And they offer more attention to judicial discourse about the Constitution than to the document's own words and phrases and organization.
>
> On each of these points, this casebook offers a different emphasis. It considers how the Constitution is interpreted and applied not only by the Court but also by Congress, the executive branch, lower federal courts, and all branches of state governments. It offers more detail on the history of the formation of the Constitution and more treatment of its principles in our nation's first 150 years. And in keeping with the premise that the document itself is the source of constitutional law, this book will emphasize the Constitution's text and structure. . . .
>
> Our aim is that students should learn how to think about constitutional issues, rather than learn every fine detail of what the Court's most recent thinking is. We should not be in the business of producing law school graduates whose constitutional sophistication has a built-in obsolescence. We should be in the business of training future lawyer-citizens to be able to think about their Constitution, to deal with the constitutional law issues that will arise during their lifetimes, and to be able to place those issues in a broader context.

As in the first edition, four features are especially prominent. First, the organization largely tracks the Constitution's own structure. Second, emphasis is placed on constitutional history. The history is *not* mere background. Rather, it reveals how other interpreters have addressed enduring questions; it shows the path-dependence of constitutional law; and it offers students a chance to interpret the Constitution a few steps removed from contemporary politics. Third, the focus is on "Great Cases." These include not only the great good cases but also the great tragic ones (such as *Dred Scott*), and they include great "cases" of constitutional interpretation outside the courts (such as President Lincoln's First Inaugural Address). Fourth, the casebook lays stress on questions of interpretive methodology. Throughout the book, attention is given to five types of constitutional argument: text, structure, historical purpose, practice and precedent, and policy. The relative merits of these types of constitutional argument, and their inevitable conflicts, are considered in many contexts.

Yet there are also refinements in the second edition. Materials have been added, both old and new—from James Madison's speech in the House on the constitutionality of the Bank of the United States to the judicial opinions in *The Health Care Cases*. Greater attention is given to procedural due process, to the affirmative role of the federal judiciary, and to the First Amendment. (Indeed, the breadth of materials on the First Amendment will make the book a suitable core for some courses on that subject.) Other cases have been cut or trimmed, especially ones that professors adopting the book rarely chose to assign. And the entire text has been revised for concision and clarity. In all, the book is substantially shorter than the first edition.

We appreciate the suggestions from professors and students who used the first edition. We are also grateful for the contributions of Hannah Dubina, Paul Harold, Joshua Hawley, the reference librarians of the UCLA School of Law, and the production team at Foundation Press. Their efforts have made the book a clearer and more useful introduction to the Constitution of the United States.

MSP
SGC
MWM
SLB

May 2013

SUMMARY OF CONTENTS

TABLE OF CONTENTS

PART 2. RIGHTS AGAINST THE GOVERNMENT

UNIVERSITY CASEBOOK SERIES ®

THE CONSTITUTION OF THE UNITED STATES

SECOND EDITION

THE CONSTITUTION
OF THE UNITED STATES

Preamble

We the People of the United States, in Order to form a more perfect Union, establish Justice, insure domestic Tranquillity, provide for the common defence, promote the general Welfare, and secure the Blessings of Liberty to ourselves and our Posterity, do ordain and establish this Constitution for the United States of America.

Article I

Section 1. All legislative Powers herein granted shall be vested in a Congress of the United States, which shall consist of a Senate and House of Representatives.

Section 2. The House of Representatives shall be composed of Members chosen every second Year by the People of the several States, and the Electors in each State shall have the Qualifications requisite for Electors of the most numerous Branch of the State Legislature.

No Person shall be a Representative who shall not have attained to the age of twenty five Years, and been seven Years a Citizen of the United States, and who shall not, when elected, be an Inhabitant of that State in which he shall be chosen.

Representatives and direct Taxes shall be apportioned among the several States which may be included within this Union, according to their respective Numbers, which shall be determined by adding to the whole Number of free Persons, including those bound to Service for a Term of Years, and excluding Indians not taxed, three fifths of all other Persons. The actual Enumeration shall be made within three Years after the first Meeting of the Congress of the United States, and within every subsequent Term of ten Years, in such Manner as they shall by Law direct. The Number of Representatives shall not exceed one for every thirty Thousand, but each State shall have at Least one Representative; and until such enumeration shall be made, the State of New Hampshire shall be entitled to chuse three, Massachusetts eight, Rhode Island and Providence Plantations one, Connecticut five, New York six, New Jersey four, Pennsylvania eight, Delaware one, Maryland six, Virginia ten, North Carolina five, South Carolina five, and Georgia three.

When vacancies happen in the Representation from any State, the Executive Authority thereof shall issue Writs of Election to fill such Vacancies.

The House of Representatives shall chuse their Speaker and other Officers; and shall have the sole Power of Impeachment.

Section 3. The Senate of the United States shall be composed of two Senators from each State, chosen by the Legislature thereof, for six Years; and each Senator shall have one Vote.

Immediately after they shall be assembled in Consequence of the first Election, they shall be divided as equally as may be into three Classes. The Seats of the Senators of the first Class shall be vacated at the Expiration of the second Year, of the second Class at the Expiration of the fourth Year, and of the third Class at the Expiration of the sixth Year, so that one third

1

may be chosen every second Year; and if Vacancies happen by Resignation, or otherwise, during the Recess of the Legislature of any State, the Executive thereof may make temporary Appointments until the next Meeting of the Legislature, which shall then fill such Vacancies.

No Person shall be a Senator who shall not have attained to the Age of thirty Years, and been nine Years a Citizen of the United States, and who shall not, when elected, be an Inhabitant of that State for which he shall be chosen.

The Vice President of the United States shall be President of the Senate but shall have no Vote, unless they be equally divided.

The Senate shall chuse their other Officers, and also a President pro tempore, in the Absence of the Vice President, or when he shall exercise the Office of President of the United States.

The Senate shall have the sole Power to try all Impeachments. When sitting for that Purpose, they shall be on Oath or Affirmation. When the President of the United States is tried the Chief Justice shall preside: And no Person shall be convicted without the Concurrence of two thirds of the Members present.

Judgment in Cases of Impeachment shall not extend further than to removal from Office, and disqualification to hold and enjoy any Office of honor, Trust or Profit under the United States: but the Party convicted shall nevertheless be liable and subject to Indictment, Trial, Judgment and Punishment, according to Law.

Section 4. The Times, Places and Manner of holding Elections for Senators and Representatives, shall be prescribed in each State by the Legislature thereof; but the Congress may at any time by Law make or alter such Regulations, except as to the Places of chusing Senators.

The Congress shall assemble at least once in every Year, and such Meeting shall be on the first Monday in December, unless they shall by Law appoint a different Day.

Section 5. Each House shall be the Judge of the Elections, Returns and Qualifications of its own Members, and a Majority of each shall constitute a Quorum to do Business; but a smaller Number may adjourn from day to day, and may be authorized to compel the Attendance of absent Members, in such Manner, and under such Penalties as each House may provide.

Each House may determine the Rules of its Proceedings, punish its Members for disorderly Behaviour, and, with the Concurrence of two thirds, expel a Member.

Each House shall keep a Journal of its Proceedings, and from time to time publish the same, excepting such Parts as may in their Judgment require Secrecy; and the Yeas and Nays of the Members of either House on any question shall, at the Desire of one fifth of those Present, be entered on the Journal.

Neither House, during the Session of Congress, shall, without the Consent of the other, adjourn for more than three days, nor to any other Place than that in which the two Houses shall be sitting.

Section 6. The Senators and Representatives shall receive a Compensation for their Services, to be ascertained by Law, and paid out of the Treasury of the United States. They shall in all Cases, except Treason, Felony and Breach of the Peace, be privileged from Arrest during their Attendance at the Session of their respective Houses, and in going to and returning from the same; and for any Speech or Debate in either House, they shall not be questioned in any other Place.

No Senator or Representative shall, during the Time for which he was elected, be appointed to any civil Office under the Authority of the United States, which shall have been created, or the Emoluments whereof shall have been encreased during such time; and no Person holding any Office under the United States, shall be a Member of either House during his Continuance in Office.

Section 7. All Bills for raising Revenue shall originate in the House of Representatives; but the Senate may propose or concur with amendments as on other Bills.

Every Bill which shall have passed the House of Representatives and the Senate, shall, before it become a law, be presented to the President of the United States: If he approve he shall sign it, but if not he shall return it, with his Objections to that House in which it shall have originated, who shall enter the Objections at large on their Journal, and proceed to reconsider it. If after such Reconsideration two thirds of that House shall agree to pass the Bill, it shall be sent, together with the Objections, to the other House, by which it shall likewise be reconsidered, and if approved by two thirds of that House, it shall become a Law. But in all such Cases the Votes of both Houses shall be determined by Yeas and Nays, and the Names of the Persons voting for and against the Bill shall be entered on the Journal of each House respectively. If any Bill shall not be returned by the President within ten Days (Sundays excepted) after it shall have been presented to him, the Same shall be a Law, in like Manner as if he had signed it, unless the Congress by their Adjournment prevent its Return, in which Case it shall not be a Law.

Every Order, Resolution, or Vote to which the Concurrence of the Senate and House of Representatives may be necessary (except on a question of Adjournment) shall be presented to the President of the United States; and before the Same shall take Effect, shall be approved by him, or being disapproved by him, shall be repassed by two thirds of the Senate and House of Representatives, according to the Rules and Limitations prescribed in the Case of a Bill.

Section 8. The Congress shall have Power

To lay and collect Taxes, Duties, Imposts and Excises, to pay the Debts and provide for the common Defence and general Welfare of the United States; but all Duties, Imposts and Excises shall be uniform throughout the United States;

To borrow Money on the credit of the United States;

To regulate Commerce with foreign Nations, and among the several States, and with the Indian Tribes;

To establish an uniform Rule of Naturalization, and uniform Laws on the subject of Bankruptcies throughout the United States;

To coin Money, regulate the Value thereof, and of foreign Coin, and fix the Standard of Weights and Measures;

To provide for the Punishment of counterfeiting the Securities and current Coin of the United States;

To establish Post Offices and post Roads;

To promote the Progress of Science and useful Arts, by securing for limited Times to Authors and Inventors the exclusive Right to their respective Writings and Discoveries;

To constitute Tribunals inferior to the supreme Court;

To define and punish Piracies and Felonies committed on the high Seas, and Offences against the Law of Nations;

To declare War, grant Letters of Marque and Reprisal, and make Rules concerning Captures on Land and Water;

To raise and support Armies, but no Appropriation of Money to that Use shall be for a longer Term than two Years;

To provide and maintain a Navy;

To make Rules for the Government and Regulation of the land and naval Forces;

To provide for calling forth the Militia to execute the Laws of the Union, suppress Insurrections and repeal Invasions;

To provide for organizing, arming, and disciplining, the Militia, and for governing such Part of them as may be employed in the Service of the United States, reserving to the States respectively, the Appointment of the Officers, and the Authority of training the Militia according to the discipline prescribed by Congress;

To exercise exclusive Legislation in all Cases whatsoever, over such District (not exceeding ten Miles square) as may, by Cession of Particular States, and the Acceptance of Congress, become the Seat of the Government of the United States, and to exercise like Authority over all Places purchased by the Consent of the Legislature of the State in which the Same shall be, for the Erection of Forts, Magazines, Arsenals, dock Yards and other needful Buildings;—And

To make all Laws which shall be necessary and proper for carrying into Execution the foregoing Powers and all other Powers vested by this Constitution in the Government of the United States, or in any Department or Officer thereof.

Section 9. The Migration or Importation of such Persons as any of the States now existing shall think proper to admit, shall not be prohibited by the Congress prior to the Year one thousand eight hundred and eight, but a Tax or duty may be imposed on such Importation, not exceeding ten dollars for each Person.

The Privilege of the Writ of Habeas Corpus shall not be suspended, unless when in Cases or Rebellion or Invasion the public Safety may require it.

No Bill of Attainder or ex post facto Law shall be passed.

No Capitation, or other direct, Tax shall be laid, unless in Proportion to the Census of Enumeration herein before directed to be taken.

No Tax or Duty shall be laid on Articles exported from any State.

No Preference shall be given by any Regulation of Commerce or Revenue to the Ports of one State over those of another: nor shall Vessels bound to, or from, one State, be obliged to enter, clear or pay Duties in another.

No Money shall be drawn from the Treasury, but in Consequence of Appropriations made by Law; and a regular Statement and Account of the Receipts and Expenditures of all public Money shall be published from time to time.

No Title of Nobility shall be granted by the United States: And no Person holding any Office of Profit or Trust under them, shall, without the Consent of the Congress, accept of any present, Emolument, Office, or Title, of any kind whatever, from any King, Prince or foreign State.

Section 10. No State shall enter into any Treaty, Alliance, or Confederation; grant Letters of Marque and Reprisal; coin Money; emit Bills of Credit; make any Thing but gold and silver Coin a Tender in Payment of Debts; pass any Bill of Attainder, ex post facto Law, or Law impairing the Obligation of Contracts, or grant any Title of Nobility.

No State shall, without the Consent of the Congress, lay any Imposts or Duties on Imports or Exports, except what may be absolutely necessary for executing it's inspection Laws: and the net Produce of all Duties and Imposts, laid by any State on Imports or Exports, shall be for the Use of the Treasury of the United States; and all such Laws shall be subject to the Revision and Controul of the Congress.

No State shall, without the Consent of Congress, lay any Duty of Tonnage, keep Troops, or Ships of War in time of Peace, enter into any Agreement or Compact with another State, or with a foreign Power, or engage in War, unless actually invaded, or in such imminent Danger as will not admit of delay.

Article II

Section 1. The executive Power shall be vested in a President of the United States of America. He shall hold his Office during the Term of four Years, and, together with the Vice President, chosen for the same Term, be elected, as follows:

Each State shall appoint, in such Manner as the Legislature thereof may direct, a Number of Electors, equal to the whole Number of Senators and Representatives to which the State may be entitled in the Congress: but no Senator or Representative, or Person holding an Office of Trust or Profit under the United States, shall be appointed an Elector.

The Electors shall meet in their respective States, and vote by Ballot for two Persons, of whom one at least shall not be an Inhabitant of the same State with themselves. And they shall make a List of all the Persons voted for, and of the Number of Votes for each; which List they shall sign and certify, and transmit sealed to the Seat of the Government of the United States, directed to the President of the Senate. The President of the Senate shall, in the Presence of the Senate and House of Representatives, open all the Certificates, and the Votes shall then be counted. The Person having the greatest Number of Votes shall be the President, if such Number be a Majority of the whole Number of Electors appointed; and if there be more than one who have such Majority, and have an equal Number of Votes, then the House of Representatives shall immediately chuse by Ballot one of them for President; and if no Person have a Majority, then from the five highest on the List the said House shall in like Manner chuse the President. But in chusing the President, the Votes shall be taken by States, the Representatives from each State having one Vote; a quorum for this Purpose shall consist of a Member or Members from two thirds of the States, and a Majority of all the States shall be necessary to a Choice. In every

Case, after the Choice of the President, the Person having the greatest Number of Votes of the Electors shall be the Vice President. But if there should remain two or more who have equal Votes, the Senate shall chuse from them by Ballot the Vice President.

The Congress may determine the Time of chusing the Electors, and the Day on which they shall give their Votes; which Day shall be the same throughout the United States.

No Person except a natural born Citizen, or a Citizen of the United States, at the time of the Adoption of this Constitution, shall be eligible to the Office of President; neither shall any person be eligible to that Office who shall not have attained to the Age of thirty five Years, and been fourteen Years a Resident within the United States.

In Case of the Removal of the President from Office, or of his Death, Resignation, or Inability to discharge the Powers and Duties of the said Office, the Same shall devolve on the Vice President, and the Congress may by Law provide for the Case of Removal, Death, Resignation or Inability, both of the President and Vice President, declaring what Officer shall then act as President, and such Officer shall act accordingly, until the Disability be removed, or a President shall be elected.

The President shall, at stated Times, receive for his Services, a Compensation, which shall neither be encreased nor diminished during the Period for which he shall have been elected, and he shall not receive within that Period any other Emolument from the United States, or any of them.

Before he enter on the Execution of his Office, he shall take the following Oath or Affirmation:—"I do solemnly swear (or affirm) that I will faithfully execute the Office of President of the United States, and will to the best of my Ability, preserve, protect and defend the Constitution of the United States."

Section 2. The President shall be Commander in Chief of the Army and Navy of the United States, and of the Militia of the several States, when called into the actual Service of the United States; he may require the Opinion, in writing, of the principal Officer in each of the executive Departments, upon any Subject relating to the Duties of their respective Offices, and he shall have Power to Grant Reprieves and Pardons for Offences against the United States, except in Cases of Impeachment.

He shall have Power, by and with the Advice and Consent of the Senate, to make Treaties, provided two thirds of the Senators present concur; and he shall nominate, and by and with the Advice and Consent of the Senate, shall appoint Ambassadors, other public Ministers and Consuls, Judges of the supreme Court, and all other Officers of the United States, whose Appointments are not herein otherwise provided for, and which shall be established by Law: but the Congress may by Law vest the Appointment of such inferior Officers, as they think proper, in the President alone, in the Courts of Law, or in the Heads of Departments.

The President shall have Power to fill up all Vacancies that may happen during the Recess of the Senate, by granting Commissions which shall expire at the End of their next Session.

Section 3. He shall from time to time give to the Congress Information on the State of the Union, and recommend to their Consideration such Measures as he shall judge necessary and expedient; he may, on extraordinary Occasions, convene both Houses, or either of them, and in Case of Disagreement between them, with Respect to the Time of Adjournment, he may adjourn them to such Time as he shall think proper; he shall receive Ambassadors and other public Ministers; he shall take Care that the Laws be faithfully executed, and shall Commission all the Officers of the United States.

Section 4. The President, Vice President and all Civil Officers of the United States, shall be removed from Office on Impeachment for and Conviction of, Treason, Bribery, or other high Crimes and Misdemeanors.

Article III

Section 1. The judicial Power of the United States, shall be vested in one supreme Court, and in such inferior Courts as the Congress may from time to time ordain and establish. The Judges, both of the supreme and inferior Courts, shall hold their Offices during good Behaviour, and shall, at stated Times, receive for their Services, a Compensation, which shall not be diminished during their Continuance in Office.

Life tenure

Section 2. The judicial Power shall extend to all Cases, in Law and Equity, arising under this Constitution, the Laws of the United States, and Treaties made, or which shall be made, under their Authority;—to all Cases affecting Ambassadors, other public ministers and Consuls;—to all Cases of admiralty and maritime Jurisdiction;—to Controversies to which the United States shall be a Party;—to Controversies between two or more States;—between a State and Citizens of another State;—between Citizens of different States;—between Citizens of the same State claiming Lands under Grants of different States, and between a State, or the Citizens thereof, and foreign States, Citizens or Subjects.

In all Cases affecting Ambassadors, other public Ministers and Consuls, and those in which a State shall be Party, the supreme Court shall have original Jurisdiction. In all the other Cases before mentioned, the supreme Court shall have appellate Jurisdiction, both as to Law and Fact, with such Exceptions, and under such Regulations as the Congress shall make.

The Trial of all Crimes, except in Cases of Impeachment, shall be by Jury; and such Trial shall be held in the State where the said Crimes shall have been committed; but when not committed within any State, the Trial shall be at such Place or Places as the Congress may by Law have directed.

Section 3. Treason against the United States, shall consist only in levying War against them, or in adhering to their Enemies, giving them Aid and Comfort. No Person shall be convicted of Treason unless on the Testimony of two Witnesses to the same overt Act, or on Confession in open Court.

The Congress shall have Power to declare the Punishment of Treason, but no Attainder of Treason shall work Corruption of Blood, or Forfeiture except during the Life of the Person attainted.

Article IV

Section 1. Full Faith and Credit shall be given in each State to the public Acts, Records, and judicial Proceedings of every other State. And the Congress may by general Laws prescribe the Manner in which such Acts, Records and Proceedings shall be proved, and the Effect thereof.

Federal-State relationship

Section 2. The Citizens of each State shall be entitled to all Privileges and Immunities of Citizens in the several States.

A Person charged in any State with Treason, Felony, or other Crime, who shall flee from Justice, and be found in another State, shall on Demand of the executive Authority of the State from which he fled, be delivered up, to be removed to the State having Jurisdiction of the Crime.

No Person held to Service or Labour in one State, under the Laws thereof, escaping into another, shall, in Consequence of any Law or Regulation therein, be discharged from such Service or Labour, but shall be delivered up on Claim of the Party to whom such Service or Labour may be due.

Section 3. New States may be admitted by the Congress into this Union; but no new State shall be formed or erected within the Jurisdiction of any other State; nor any State be formed by the Junction of two or more States, or Parts of States, without the Consent of the Legislatures of the States concerned as well as of the Congress.

The Congress shall have Power to dispose of and make all needful Rules and Regulations respecting the Territory or other Property belonging to the United States; and nothing in this Constitution shall be so construed as to Prejudice any Claims of the United States, or of any particular State.

Section 4. The United States shall guarantee to every State in this Union a Republican Form of Government, and shall protect each of them against Invasion; and on Application of the Legislature, or of the Executive (when the Legislature cannot be convened) against domestic Violence.

Article V

The Congress, whenever two thirds of both Houses shall deem it necessary, shall propose Amendments to this Constitution, or, on the Application of the Legislatures of two thirds of the several States, shall call a Convention for proposing Amendments, which, in either Case, shall be valid to all Intents and Purposes, as Part of this Constitution, when ratified by the Legislatures of three fourths of the several States, or by Conventions in three fourths thereof, as the one or the other Mode of Ratification may be proposed by the Congress; Provided that no Amendment which may be made prior to the Year One thousand eight hundred and eight shall in any Manner affect the first and fourth Clauses in the Ninth Section of the first Article; and that no State, without its Consent, shall be deprived of its equal Suffrage in the Senate.

Article VI

All Debts contracted and Engagements entered into, before the Adoption of this Constitution, shall be as valid against the United States under this Constitution, as under the Confederation.

This Constitution, and the Laws of the United States which shall be made in Pursuance thereof; and all Treaties made, or which shall be made, under the Authority of the United States, shall be the supreme Law of the Land; and the Judges in every State shall be bound thereby, any Thing in the Constitution or Laws of any state to the Contrary notwithstanding.

The Senators and Representatives before mentioned, and the Members of the several State Legislatures, and all executive and judicial Officers, both of the United States and of the several States, shall be bound by Oath or Affirmation, to support this Constitution; but no religious Test shall ever be required as a Qualification to any Office or public Trust under the United States.

Article VII

The Ratification of the Conventions of nine States, shall be sufficient for the Establishment of this Constitution between the States so ratifying the same.

Articles in addition to, and amendments of, the Constitution of the United States of America, proposed by Congress, and ratified by the legislatures of the several states, pursuant to the Fifth Article of the original Constitution.

Amendment I (1791)

Congress shall make no law respecting an establishment of religion, or prohibiting the free exercise thereof; or abridging the freedom of speech, or of the press; or the right of the people peaceably to assemble, and to petition the Government for a redress of grievances.

Amendment II (1791)

A well regulated Militia, being necessary to the security of a free State, the right of the people to keep and bear Arms, shall not be infringed.

Amendment III (1791)

No Soldier shall, in time of peace be quartered in any house, without the consent of the Owner, nor in time of war, but in a manner to be prescribed by law.

Amendment IV (1791)

The right of the people to be secure in their persons, houses, papers, and effects, against unreasonable searches and seizures, shall not be violated, and no Warrants shall issue, but upon probable cause, supported by Oath or affirmation, and particularly describing the place to be searched, and the persons or things to be seized.

Amendment V (1791)

No person shall be held to answer for a capital, or otherwise infamous crime, unless on a presentment or indictment of a Grand Jury, except in cases arising in the land or naval forces, or in the Militia, when in actual service in time of War or public danger; nor shall any person be subject for the same offence to be twice put in jeopardy of life or limb; nor shall be compelled in any criminal case to be a witness against himself, nor be deprived of life, liberty, or property, without due process of law; nor shall private property be taken for public use, without just compensation.

Amendment VI (1791)

In all criminal prosecutions, the accused shall enjoy the right to a speedy and public trial, by an impartial jury of the State and district wherein the crime shall have been committed, which district shall have been previously ascertained by law, and to be informed of the nature and cause of the accusation; to be confronted with the witnesses against him; to have compulsory process for obtaining witnesses in his favor, and to have the Assistance of Counsel for his defence.

Amendment VII (1791)

In Suits at common law, where the value in controversy shall exceed twenty dollars, the right of trial by jury shall be preserved, and no fact tried by a jury, shall be otherwise re-examined in any Court of the United States, than according to the rules of the common law.

Amendment VIII (1791)

Excessive bail shall not be required, nor excessive fines imposed, nor cruel and unusual punishments inflicted.

Amendment IX (1791)

The enumeration in the Constitution, of certain rights, shall not be construed to deny or disparage others retained by the people.

Amendment X (1791)

The powers not delegated to the United States by the Constitution, nor prohibited by it to the States, are reserved to the States respectively, or to the people.

Amendment XI (1798)

The Judicial power of the United States shall not be construed to extend to any suit in law or equity, commenced or prosecuted against one of the United States by Citizens of another State, or by Citizens or Subjects of any Foreign State.

Amendment XII (1804)

The Electors shall meet in their respective states, and vote by ballot for President and Vice President, one of whom, at least, shall not be an inhabitant of the same state with themselves; they shall name in their ballots the person voted for as President, and in distinct ballots the person voted for as Vice-President, and they shall make distinct lists of all persons voted for as President, and of all persons voted for as Vice-President, and of the number of votes for each, which lists they shall sign and certify, and transmit sealed to the seat of the government of the United States, directed to the President of the Senate;—The President of the Senate shall, in the presence of the Senate and House of Representatives, open all the certificates and the votes shall then be counted;—The person having the greatest number of votes for President, shall be the President, if such number be a majority of the whole number of Electors appointed; and if no person have such majority, then from the persons having the highest numbers not exceeding three on the list of those voted for as President, the House of Representatives shall choose immediately, by ballot, the President. But in choosing the President, the votes shall be taken by states, the representation from each state having one vote; a quorum for this purpose shall consist of a member or members from two-thirds of the states, and a majority of all the states shall be necessary to a choice. And if the House of Representatives shall not choose a President whenever the right of choice shall devolve upon them, before the fourth day of March next following, then the Vice-President shall act as President, as in the case of the death or other constitutional disability of the President.—The person having the greatest number of votes as Vice-President, shall be the Vice-President, if such number be a majority of the whole number of Electors appointed, and if no person have a majority, then from the two highest numbers on the list, the Senate shall choose the Vice-President; a quorum for the purpose shall consist of two-thirds of the whole number of Senators, and a majority of the whole number shall be necessary to a choice. But no person constitutionally ineligible to the office of President shall be eligible to that of Vice-President of the United States.

Amendment XIII (1865)

Section 1. Neither slavery nor involuntary servitude, except as a punishment for crime whereof the party shall have been duly convicted, shall exist within the United States, or any place subject to their jurisdiction.

Section 2. Congress shall have power to enforce this article by appropriate legislation.

Amendment XIV (1868)

Section 1. All persons born or naturalized in the United States, and subject to the jurisdiction thereof, are citizens of the United States and of the State wherein they reside. No State shall make or enforce any law which shall abridge the privileges or immunities of citizens of the United States; nor shall any State deprive any person of life, liberty, or property, without due process of law; nor deny to any person within its jurisdiction the equal protection of the laws.

Section 2. Representatives shall be apportioned among the several States according to their respective numbers, counting the whole number of persons in each State, excluding Indians not taxed. But when the right to vote at any election for the choice of electors for President and Vice President of the United States, Representatives in Congress, the Executive and Judicial officers of a State, or the members of the Legislature thereof, is denied to any of the male inhabitants of such State, being twenty-one years of age, and citizens of the United States, or in any way abridged, except for participation in rebellion, or other crime, the basis of representation therein shall be reduced in the proportion which the number of such male citizens shall bear to the whole number of male citizens twenty-one years of age in such State.

Section 3. No person shall be a Senator or Representative in Congress, or elector of President and Vice President, or hold any office, civil or military, under the United States, or under any State, who, having previously taken an oath, as a member of Congress, or as an officer of the United States, or as a member of any State legislature, or as an executive or judicial officer of any State, to support the Constitution of the United States, shall have engaged in insurrection or rebellion against the same, or given aid or comfort to the enemies thereof. But Congress may by a vote of two-thirds of each House, remove such disability.

Section 4. The validity of the public debt of the United States, authorized by law, including debts incurred for payment of pensions and bounties for services in suppressing insurrection or rebellion, shall not be questioned. But neither the United States nor any State shall assume or pay any debt or obligation incurred in aid of insurrection or rebellion against the United States, or any claim for the loss or emancipation of any slave; but all such debts, obligations and claims shall be held illegal and void.

Section 5. The Congress shall have power to enforce, by appropriate legislation, the provisions of this article.

Amendment XV (1870)

Section 1. The right of citizens of the United States to vote shall not be denied or abridged by the United States or by any State on account of race, color, or previous condition of servitude.

Section 2. The Congress shall have power to enforce this article by appropriate legislation.

Amendment XVI (1913)

The Congress shall have power to lay and collect taxes on incomes, from whatever source derived, without apportionment among the several States, and without regard to any census or enumeration.

Amendment XVII (1913)

The Senate of the United States shall be composed of two Senators from each State, elected by the people thereof, for six years; and each Senator shall have one vote. The electors in each State shall have the qualifications requisite for electors of the most numerous branch of the State legislatures.

When vacancies happen in the representation of any State in the Senate, the executive authority of such State shall issue writs of election to fill such vacancies: Provided, That the legislature of any State may empower the executive thereof to make temporary appointments until the people fill the vacancies by election as the legislature may direct.

This amendment shall not be so construed as to affect the election or term of any Senator chosen before it becomes valid as part of the Constitution.

Amendment XVIII (1919)

Section 1. After one year from the ratification of this article the manufacture, sale, or transportation of intoxicating liquors within, the importation thereof into, or the exportation thereof from the United States and all territory subject to the jurisdiction thereof for beverage purposes is hereby prohibited.

Section 2. The Congress and the several States shall have concurrent power to enforce this article by appropriate legislation.

Section 3. This article shall be inoperative unless it shall have been ratified as an amendment to the Constitution by the legislatures of the several States, as provided in the Constitution, within seven years from the date of the submission hereof to the States by the Congress.

Amendment XIX (1920)

The right of citizens of the United States to vote shall not be denied or abridged by the United States or by any State on account of sex.

Congress shall have power to enforce this article by appropriate legislation.

Amendment XX (1933)

Section 1. The terms of the President and Vice President shall end at noon on the 20th day of January, and the terms of Senators and Representatives at noon on the 3d day of January, of the years in which such terms would have ended if this article had not been ratified; and the terms of their successors shall then begin.

Section 2. The Congress shall assemble at least once in every year, and such meeting shall begin at noon on the 3d day of January, unless they shall by law appoint a different day.

Section 3. If, at the time fixed for the beginning of the term of the President, the President elect shall have died, the Vice President elect shall become President. If a President shall not have been chosen before the time fixed for the beginning of his term, or if the President elect shall have failed to qualify, then the Vice President elect shall act as President until a President shall have qualified; and the Congress may by law provide for the case wherein neither a President elect nor a Vice President elect shall have qualified, declaring who shall then act as President, or the manner in which one who is to act shall be selected, and such person shall act accordingly until a President or Vice President shall have qualified.

Section 4. The Congress may by law provide for the case of the death of any of the persons from whom the House of Representatives may choose a President whenever the right of choice shall have devolved upon them, and for the case of the death of any of the persons from whom the Senate may choose a Vice President whenever the right of choice shall have devolved upon them.

Section 5. Sections 1 and 2 shall take effect on the 15th day of October following the ratification of this article.

Section 6. This article shall be inoperative unless it shall have been ratified as an amendment to the Constitution by the legislatures of three-fourths of the several States within seven years from the date of its submission.

Amendment XXI (1933)

Section 1. The eighteenth article of amendment to the Constitution of the United States is hereby repealed.

Section 2. The transportation or importation into any State, Territory, or possession of the United States for delivery or use therein of intoxicating liquors, in violation of the laws thereof, is hereby prohibited.

Section 3. This article shall be inoperative unless it shall have been ratified as an amendment to the Constitution by conventions in the several States, as provided in the Constitution, within seven years from the date of the submission hereof to the States by the Congress.

Amendment XXII (1951)

Section 1. No person shall be elected to the office of the President more than twice, and no person who has held the office of President, or acted as President, for more than two years of a term to which some other person was elected President shall be elected to the office of the President more than once. But this article shall not apply to any person holding the office of President when this article was proposed by the Congress, and shall not prevent any person who may be holding the office of President, or acting as President, during the term within which this article becomes operative from holding the office of President or acting as President during the remainder of such term.

Section 2. This article shall be inoperative unless it shall have been ratified as an amendment to the Constitution by the legislatures of three-fourths of the several states within seven years from the date of its submission to the states by the Congress.

Amendment XXIII (1961)

Section 1. The District constituting the seat of government of the United States shall appoint in such manner as the Congress may direct:

A number of electors of President and Vice President equal to the whole number of Senators and Representatives in Congress to which the District would be entitled if it were a state, but in no event more than the least populous state; they shall be in addition to those appointed by the states, but they shall be considered, for the purposes of the election of President and Vice President, to be electors appointed by a state; and they shall meet in the District and perform such duties as provided by the twelfth article of amendment.

Section 2. The Congress shall have power to enforce this article by appropriate legislation.

Amendment XXIV (1964)

Section 1. The right of citizens of the United States to vote in any primary or other election for President or Vice President, for electors for President or Vice President, or for Senator or Representative in Congress, shall not be denied or abridged by the United States or any state by reason of failure to pay any poll tax or other tax.

Section 2. The Congress shall have power to enforce this article by appropriate legislation.

Amendment XXV (1967)

Section 1. In case of the removal of the President from office or of his death or resignation, the Vice President shall become President.

Section 2. Whenever there is a vacancy in the office of the Vice President, the President shall nominate a Vice President who shall take office upon confirmation by a majority vote of both Houses of Congress.

Section 3. Whenever the President transmits to the President pro tempore of the Senate and the Speaker of the House of Representatives his written declaration that he is unable to discharge the powers and duties of his office, and until he transmits to them a written declaration to the contrary, such powers and duties shall be discharged by the Vice President as Acting President.

Section 4. Whenever the Vice President and a majority of either the principal officers of the executive departments or of such other body as Congress may by law provide, transmit to the President pro tempore of the Senate and the Speaker of the House of Representatives their written declaration that the President is unable to discharge the powers and duties of his office, the Vice President shall immediately assume the powers and duties of the office as Acting President.

Thereafter, when the President transmits to the President pro tempore of the Senate and the Speaker of the House of Representatives his written declaration that no inability exists, he shall resume the powers and duties of his office unless the Vice President and a majority of either the principal officers of the executive department or of such other body as Congress may by law provide, transmit within four days to the President pro tempore of the Senate and the Speaker of the House of Representatives their written declaration that the President is unable to discharge the powers and duties of his office. Thereupon Congress shall decide the issue, assembling within forty-eight hours for that purpose if not in session. If the Congress, within twenty-one days after receipt of the latter written declaration, or, if Congress is not in session, within twenty-one days after Congress is required to assemble, determines by two-thirds vote of both Houses that the President is unable to discharge the powers and duties of his office, the Vice President shall continue to discharge the same as Acting President; otherwise, the President shall resume the powers and duties of his office.

Amendment XXVI (1971)

Section 1. The right of citizens of the United States, who are 18 years of age or older, to vote, shall not be denied or abridged by the United States or any state on account of age.

Section 2. The Congress shall have the power to enforce this article by appropriate legislation.

Amendment XXVII (1992)

No law varying the compensation for the services of the Senators and Representatives shall take effect until an election of Representatives shall have intervened.

PART 1

STRUCTURE AND POWERS OF THE NATIONAL GOVERNMENT

CHAPTER 1

INTRODUCTION TO THE CONSTITUTION OF THE UNITED STATES

[*Assignment 1*]

I. THE FORMATION OF THE CONSTITUTION

A. THE ADOPTION OF THE CONSTITUTION

The Constitution of the United States is a distinctively American innovation and achievement: a *written* charter of government, deliberately considered and adopted by the people, and designed to be binding as supreme law on all who exercise governmental power under it. In the famous case of *Marbury v. Madison*, 5 U.S. (1 Cranch) 137, 178 (1803), Chief Justice John Marshall commented approvingly on "what we have deemed the greatest improvement on political institutions—a written constitution."

The Constitution has features that have been copied in many other constitutions over time and around the world. These features include: (1) the separation of powers among independent, co-equal branches of government, each being able to "check and balance" the others; (2) federalism, in the sense of a division of government power between a central government and the governments of several states; (3) a written Bill of Rights to protect certain fundamental liberties against government interference; and (4) popular sovereignty expressed through representative, republican government. Each of these features of the Constitution had antecedents, but the signature American contribution was the decision to embody them in a written document and give that written charter the status of "supreme law of the land," binding and authoritative as against all other sources of law, traditions, or political actions.

The Constitution, of course, did not spring to life out of nothing. Its arrangements of powers and rights had many sources. The immediate sources from the American experience included the colonial "charter" governments, the ideologically transforming crucible of the American War for Independence, the experiments of the first state constitutions, and the lessons of a largely failed government under the Articles of Confederation. The Articles were actually the first national "constitution," proposed by the Continental Congress in 1777 and ratified in 1781. The defects of the Articles led to the call for a constitutional convention. That convention, held in Philadelphia in 1787, proposed an entirely new governing document. That document is the Constitution we have today (with twenty-seven amendments). The debate in 1787 and 1788 over ratification of the Constitution was heated, and the vote to ratify was very close in many states. Ratification ultimately depended on promises to propose the Bill of Rights, which was adopted as part of the Constitution in 1791, two years after the new national government had come into existence under the Constitution.

The Constitution thus gestated for fifteen years, from the start of the American War for Independence in 1776 until the ratification of the Bill of Rights in 1791. (This is a sobering fact for emerging democracies trying to quickly write a new constitution.) And the roots of the Constitution lie deeper still, in events of the century and a half between the Jamestown settlement in 1607 and the Declaration of Independence in 1776. Before 1776 Americans were Englishmen, and so to understand the Constitution they drafted it is necessary to examine the English constitutional tradition.

English and American Constitutionalism

Americans were heirs to an English constitutional tradition that had emerged over centuries. In that tradition, a central "constitutional" event—one that at the time of the founding of the United States had happened only a century before—was the Glorious Revolution of 1688. In that revolution, the English overthrew the Stuart dynasty of King James II and established the supremacy of Parliament. The following year, Parliament enacted a statute that recognized a set of individual rights against the king, a statute known as the English Bill of Rights of 1689. Among the rights protected by this statute were the rights to be governed by law, to be tried by a jury, to petition for a writ of habeas corpus, and to be represented in any legislative body that possessed the power to enact taxes.

To compress drastically, the Glorious Revolution thus restored fundamental individual rights against executive authority, established the supremacy of representative government, and proclaimed that legitimate government must ultimately depend on the consent of the governed. This last principle was understood in 1688 (and again by the Americans in 1776) as implying a constitutional right of the people to alter or abolish their form of government and to create a new social contract. The chief defender of the Glorious Revolution was English political philosopher John Locke, especially in his TWO TREATISES OF GOVERNMENT (1690). The justifications he gave for the Glorious Revolution were taken to heart by the Americans: it was Lockean theories of the social contract and the consent of the governed that animated the American Declaration of Independence in 1776, and the Constitution of 1787 became the world's first formal effort to enact an express Lockean social contract. The rights that had been secured by the Glorious Revolution—the individual rights protected by the English Bill of Rights and even the right to revolution to preserve those individual rights—were all features of the English constitutional tradition as it was known to *American* Englishmen in the late eighteenth century.

Although that tradition was largely unwritten, it did contain several important documents. These included (1) the Charter of Liberties of King Henry I of 1100, establishing that there was no Norman royal power to suspend the Anglo–Saxon laws of the pre-Norman realm; (2) Magna Carta ("Great Charter") of 1215, declaring the settlement that the king had no royal power to deprive freeholders of life, liberty, or property except by "the law of the land"; (3) the Petition of Right of 1628, holding that there was no royal power of taxation without action by Parliament and no royal power to imprison subjects without trial by jury; (4) the Habeas Corpus Act of 1679, declaring that there was no royal power to imprison without trial by jury; (5) the English Bill of Rights of 1689, protecting individual rights (as described above); and (6) the Act of Settlement of 1701, providing life tenure for English judges.

As important as these documents were as elements of the English "constitution" (understood as a collection of written and unwritten traditions and practices), none of these documents purported to establish a comprehensive, supreme written constitution as the definitive instrument of government. None of them recognized the sovereignty of the people. The earlier documents were agreements by the king to limit or restrain his own sovereignty, and the later ones were agreements embodying a division of sovereignty between the king and Parliament. None purported to be the one supreme law of the land, and it is even doubtful that most of them were enforceable in court.

Nor did the great written documents of English constitutional history limit the power of the English Parliament. The king, the House of Lords, and the House of Commons were said to represent the three great estates of the realm (the monarchy, the aristocracy, and the common people).[1] Thus, when the king and Parliament acted together, they embodied the entire sovereignty of the English nation, and they were not limited by the English constitutional tradition. They could even alter that tradition by passing an ordinary law—as they did in passing the English Bill of Rights of 1689.

The premise of the U.S. Constitution is quite different. Sovereignty rests not in a king or legislative body but in the people. As its preamble says, "We the People . . . do ordain and establish this Constitution." The Constitution is a delegation of power from the people, enumerating all of the government's powers. Thus all government actions must find their root in some grant of power it contains. It is the supreme law of the land, and it cannot be changed by an agreement of Congress, the president, and the courts. Instead, the Constitution can be amended only by the people, acting through the amendment procedures of Article V.

One consequence of these differences in English and American constitutionalism is a change in burdens of proof. In England, where the starting point was royal power, a subject who asserted a right against the king had to prove it. And a subject had no remedy at all against an act of Parliament. But under the U.S. Constitution, at least in theory, the burden of proof is on the national government and its officers to show that they are acting under a delegation of power from the people.

Another consequence is a change in the relative importance of text and tradition. Both constitutional systems rely on text and on tradition. In England, the written constitutional documents are islands of text in a sea of unwritten tradition. In the United States, the written constitutional text—of the original Constitution and the twenty-seven amendments—is like a great continent, a land mass with scattered lakes and ponds and rivers of tradition.

American Antecedents to the Constitution

On the American side of the Atlantic, the antecedents to the Constitution included colonial charters, the Declaration of Independence, and the Articles of Confederation.

Colonial corporate charters marked out the powers of governors and proprietors and the rights of colonists. They were contracts in one sense

---

[1] Because this traditional English regime included these three estates, it was what political philosophers such as Aristotle and Polybius would have called a "mixed regime."

and early prototypes for written constitutions in another. Some of these charters were issued by the king of England and functioned like articles of incorporation for the societies that colonized certain settlements. Other charters, like the Mayflower Compact, were drafted by the settlers themselves as they disembarked and as colonial life unfolded.

These charters were antecedents of the Constitution in at least two respects. First, they divided power horizontally between royal governors and the popularly elected lower houses of colonial legislatures—a proto-separation of powers. Second, they divided power vertically between the imperial government in London and the colonial governments in the thirteen original colonies—a proto-federalism, with London making decisions about foreign policy, defense, and the regulation of colonial trade while more local powers were devolved to the colonies.[2] As grants from the king, however, colonial charters did not recognize the sovereignty of the people.

From the settling of Jamestown in 1607 to the writing of the Declaration of Independence in 1776, colonial Americans considered themselves English people with the rights of English people, including in extreme circumstances a right to alter and abolish forms of government by a solemn public act. This is what they thought had been done in the Glorious Revolution of 1688, when royal Stuart absolutism had been overthrown. They saw the Glorious Revolution as reinstating and protecting traditional rights—as a "revolution" in the sense of coming full circle, restoring the way things had always been. (This was not exactly true, though eighteenth-century Americans believed it to be true.)

In the 1760s, tensions rose between the thirteen colonies and England. In the French and Indian War, England conquered French Canada, adding the province of Quebec to the empire. But defending the American colonists in the war had been costly. The new king, George III, sought to tax the American colonies in part to pay for the costs of defending them. The colonists had largely avoided English taxation until the 1760s and were determined not to acquiesce.

By 1776, the American colonists were outraged about what they perceived as imperial and royal tyranny. They thought that the English government was taxing them improperly because they were not represented in Parliament, and they accused King George III of Stuart-style despotism. The impetus of the American Revolution of 1776 was thus strongly against the power of the central government in London and for the power of the peripheral governments in the thirteen rebelling colonies, which saw themselves as bastions of traditional Anglo–Saxon liberty.

The impetus of the Revolution was also strongly against royal executive power and for legislative-parliamentary power. The colonial legislatures were seen as the defenders of freedom against the threat of executive tyranny—much like Parliament in the Glorious Revolution. Colonists increasingly saw the local legislatures as checks on royal governors, a hint of the separation of powers to come in the U.S. Constitution. When these grievances led to the American Revolution, the Declaration of Independence proclaimed not only the existence of "self-evident" natural rights to "life, liberty, and the pursuit of happiness" bestowed by the Creator, but also the right of the people to abolish a government that had become abu-

---

[2] In the period before the Revolution, Benjamin Franklin strenuously urged, and worked unsuccessfully to achieve, a federal relationship between England and the colonies. See Edmund S. Morgan, BENJAMIN FRANKLIN 71–103 (2002).

sive and tyrannical. To prove that the English government was in fact tyrannical, the Declaration recites a long train of abuses committed by King George III. Strikingly, the Declaration does not mention abuses of power by Parliament. (In addition to reflecting the colonists' greater concern over royal executive tyranny, this was in part because the colonists denied that Parliament had any power over them since they were not represented in it.)

The Declaration is clear on the point that the right to alter and abolish old governments could only be accomplished through a solemn public act—which is what the Declaration was. In the words of its conclusion, the "Representatives of the united States of America" were undertaking to "solemnly publish and declare, That these United Colonies are, and of Right ought to be, Free and Independent States."

And the Declaration asserted the powers of these "Independent States" to "levy War, conclude Peace, contract Alliances, establish Commerce, and to do all other Acts and Things which Independent States may of right do." What this apparently meant in practice was that these powers could be exercised by *each* of the newly independent states. An actual framework for a common, continental government was not proposed until 1777 in the form of "the Act of Confederation of the United States of America," commonly referred to as the Articles of Confederation. It did not receive the approval of all of the new states until 1781, after General Cornwallis had surrendered to General Washington at Yorktown, Virginia. And independence was not recognized formally until the Treaty of Paris was signed in 1783 and ratified by Congress in 1784.

To appreciate the structure established by the Articles of Confederation, it is helpful to know a little about the state constitutions of the time. Between 1776 and the writing of the Constitution in 1787, eleven of the thirteen newly independent states drew up constitutions, and all of them did so while keeping in mind the 1776 problem of executive tyranny. In many of these constitutions, governors lost their veto, appointment, and pardon powers, and they often served only short terms. Power was concentrated in the state legislatures, which were seen as closer to the people.

These trends are evident in the Articles of Confederation, which you should now read. (It is printed in the appendix to this book.) As you read it, ask yourself how the government it sets up differs from the government of the United States today. List the ways. Are there features of the government under the Articles of Confederation that you think the Constitution should have kept but did not? What defects can you detect in the government set up by the Articles of Confederation? Are you surprised that it was eventually replaced?

* * *

In reading the Articles of Confederation, you probably noticed that the text begins as if it were a treaty among thirteen sovereigns. Indeed, it explicitly states that "[e]ach state retains its sovereignty, freedom, and independence, and every Power, Jurisdiction and right, which is not by this confederation *expressly* delegated to the United States, in Congress assembled" (Article II) and that the states "hereby severally enter into a firm league of friendship with each other" (III). The Articles provided for travel and trade between states (IV). And it established a framework for a general government consisting of a unicameral Congress in which each of the thirteen states received one vote, no matter how large the state and no matter how large its congressional delegation (V). Members of Congress were paid by, and could be recalled by, the state governments they represented. The Articles also regulated treaties and duties and war expenses (VI, VII, VIII)—but revenue was raised through the collection of taxes by the states, an arrangement that proved greatly problematic as it made the "common treasury" of the nation dependent on the separate action, authority, and good faith of each of the states. The Articles also described the powers of the "united states in congress assembled" (IX). And the Articles concluded by declaring that "the union shall be perpetual" and providing for amendments (XIII).

In the fight for independence, the deficiencies of the central government, first under the Continental Congress and then under the Articles of Confederation, became evident. The rule that each state had a single vote made Congress more like an assembly of independent nations—an eighteenth-century United Nations—than a representative legislature for the nation. Combined with the requirement that nine out of thirteen states agree on most significant matters, this meant that Congress could be at the mercy of a small minority and often could not act. Moreover, there was little practical authority of the central government to enforce its enactments even where Congress could agree on measures. The central government was completely dependent on the states, which had all of the real power. The commands of the Articles of Confederation were not "inviolably observed by every state" but were in fact frequently disregarded. And as provided in Article XIII, no changes could be made to the Articles of Confederation without the approval not only of Congress but also of every one of the state legislatures.

A number of striking failures of government occurred under the Articles of Confederation. General Washington had trouble fighting the Revolutionary War because Congress second-guessed his decisions on troop movements and strategy. Congress failed to pay Washington's soldiers because, even though it could request money from the thirteen states, it could not tax them or the American people directly. And Congress lacked the power to regulate trade between the thirteen states or with foreign powers. Declining trade in the war and its aftermath led to an economic crisis. In this crisis, many debtors faced foreclosure and utter economic ruin (not to mention very high court costs). Outbursts of violence against debt collection, such as Shays' Rebellion in Massachusetts, frightened property owners. One response by Congress and the states—printing paper money—led to severe inflation, which worsened the economic situation still further. Many merchants found themselves ruined, while some debtors were effectively absolved of their debts by the inflation. And state legislatures threatened to abuse their nearly absolute powers by cancelling debts and further inflating the currency, dashing the hopes of those who thought that legislatures would always be friendly to liberty. Many feared that the bankrupt, incompetent central government under the Articles of Confederation would even be too weak to prevent invasion by a foreign power.

By 1786—a mere decade after the Declaration of Independence—it seemed that the experiment of American independence was on the verge of failure. At last Congress agreed to call for a special convention of representatives from each state to consider revisions to the Articles of Confederation.[3] The call produced a convention that met in Philadelphia in 1787.

---

[3] For a summary, see Jack N. Rakove, ORIGINAL MEANINGS: POLITICS AND IDEAS IN THE MAKING OF THE CONSTITUTION 23–34 (1997).

The Convention and Ratification

The Constitution of the United States was drafted by a convention of fifty-five distinguished citizens assembled in Philadelphia during the hot summer of 1787. The Philadelphia Convention was chaired by (retired) General George Washington. The delegates agreed to keep their proceedings secret—something almost inconceivable today—to enable more vigorous debate and to present a façade of unanimity by concealing their disagreements. Accordingly, what we know about the proceedings comes from a few journals kept by those present, especially the notes of James Madison (called NOTES OF DEBATES IN THE FEDERAL CONVENTION OF 1787), which were published after his death, nearly forty years later. The authoritative collection of these journals and records is Max Farrand's four-volume THE RECORDS OF THE FEDERAL CONVENTION OF 1787 (Max Farrand ed. 1911).

The Philadelphia Convention was called for the seemingly narrow purpose of proposing only revisions to the Articles of Confederation. But what it produced was dramatically different: a proposal for an entirely new "Constitution of the United States." The document proposed by the Philadelphia Convention stated in its concluding Article that "[t]he Ratification of the Conventions of nine States, shall be sufficient for the Establishment of this Constitution between the States so ratifying the same." The document thus proposed a different form of national government than had existed under the Articles of Confederation and specified that it would take effect in a manner different from what the Articles of Confederation required for amendment—the *unanimous* concurrence of the *legislatures* of each state.

In many ways the Constitution was a compromise. In the eleven years between 1776 and 1787, attitudes had changed enormously. Where Americans once feared executive and national tyranny, many now feared legislative and local tyranny, and the solution seemed to be a strengthened national government and greater executive power. The Constitution was shaped by these cross-cutting fears. It created a powerful national government, and yet that government was given only limited and enumerated powers; it created an executive more powerful than any executive under state constitutions or the Articles of Confederation, and yet that executive was not nearly as powerful as King George III.

At Philadelphia the framers made at least five major decisions. First, they greatly expanded national power. For example, they gave the proposed government the power to regulate commerce and the power to tax and spend to promote the general welfare. The framers decided that members of Congress under the new Constitution would be officers of the national government, with fixed terms and salaries paid by the national treasury. And Congress could legislate upon and directly tax citizens.

Second, in a decision called The Great Compromise, the framers agreed that the new government would have a bicameral legislature with each state having equal representation in the Senate and with representation in the House of Representatives based on each state's population. This was a deal between the more populous states, such as Virginia, which wanted representation based on population; and the less populous ones, such as New Jersey, which wanted a rule of "one state, one vote" as under the Articles of Confederation.

Third, the framers voted to create separate executive and judicial branches of the national government. It was decided that the executive branch would be led by a single president of the United States who was to be selected independently of Congress and guaranteed a four-year term. The president was even given a veto, which English monarchs effectively lacked. With respect to the judiciary, the framers voted to create a national Supreme Court, and Congress was given the power to create inferior courts. (No permanent national courts had existed in the government under the Articles of Confederation.)

Fourth, the framers wrangled over and finally reached an unhappy compromise with respect to slavery. Southern states disenfranchised their large slave populations but nonetheless wanted the slaves to count for apportioning seats in the House of Representatives and for votes for the president in the Electoral College. Northern states objected. The compromise adopted was that a slave would be counted as three-fifths of a person, and a clause would be added that imposed a duty to return fugitive slaves. The appeasement of slaveholders was the great tragedy in the work of the framers at Philadelphia.

Fifth, as mentioned above, the framers wrote the Constitution so that it would go into effect upon ratification by only nine of the original thirteen states. This provision in Article VII was explicitly contrary to the Articles of Confederation, which could be amended only by unanimous agreement. And Article V specified that, going forward, the Constitution would be amendable by a two-thirds vote of both houses of Congress coupled with ratification by three-quarters of the states. Even though this was a step toward easier amendment, it is today regarded as one of the most difficult amendment processes of any constitution in the world.

The Convention began on May 25, 1787. It adjourned on September 17. The final text incorporating these five fundamental decisions was drafted by a Committee of Detail and by a Committee of Style and Arrangement which included among others Gouverneur Morris, Alexander Hamilton, and James Madison. Given the amount of work accomplished by the fifty-five delegates in this short time and the impact it would have on the United States and the world, the Convention has been called the Miracle at Philadelphia. It bears remembering, though, that the framers were building on a centuries-old constitutional tradition in England and the colonies, and also on the experience since 1776.

The Convention's proposal of the Constitution spurred debate in the thirteen states over whether it should be adopted. The most famous contribution to this debate was *The Federalist*, a series of eighty-five newspaper articles written by Alexander Hamilton, James Madison, and John Jay under the pen name "Publius," which urged the people of the state of New York to ratify the Constitution. (These were then collected in rough book form and sent to Virginia for that critical state's ratification debates.) Written in a rush of time and as explicit advocacy documents, *The Federalist* has nonetheless come to be regarded as one of the most important and influential treatises on the meaning of the Constitution. Below are excerpts from *The Federalist No. 1*, which is Hamilton's famous call for careful and honest deliberation over the defects of the Articles of Confederation and the need for this new Constitution; and *The Federalist Nos. 40* and *43*, which are Madison's defense of the Convention's proposal of a document that went beyond mere revision of the Articles and departed from the unanimity rule for amendment.

As you read these passages, consider the legality of the Constitution's adoption. Did it violate the rules for amendment specified by the Articles of

Confederation? Was it an exercise of the right to abolish government of the type that produced the Glorious Revolution of 1688 and the American Revolution of 1776? If so, was the Constitution actually an act of revolution? Or was it more like states withdrawing from a treaty agreement and then forming a new nation? Thankfully, these are no longer live questions. The Constitution was eventually ratified by all the states and is now accepted by all as the United States' fundamental governing document. Still, in thinking about how it came into being, it is useful to consider the legal arguments for its validity that *The Federalist* advances.

The Federalist No. 1

Alexander Hamilton, October 27, 1787

To the People of the State of New York:

AFTER an unequivocal experience of the inefficacy of the subsisting federal government, you are called upon to deliberate on a new Constitution for the United States of America. The subject speaks its own importance; comprehending in its consequences nothing less than the existence of the UNION, the safety and welfare of the parts of which it is composed, the fate of an empire in many respects the most interesting in the world. It has been frequently remarked that it seems to have been reserved to the people of this country, by their conduct and example, to decide the important question, whether societies of men are really capable or not of establishing good government from reflection and choice, or whether they are forever destined to depend for their political constitutions on accident and force. If there be any truth in the remark, the crisis at which we are arrived may with propriety be regarded as the era in which that decision is to be made; and a wrong election of the part we shall act may, in this view, deserve to be considered as the general misfortune of mankind. . . .

Among the most formidable of the obstacles which the new Constitution will have to encounter may readily be distinguished the obvious interest of a certain class of men in every State to resist all changes which may hazard a diminution of the power, emolument, and consequence of the offices they hold under the State establishments; and the perverted ambition of another class of men, who will either hope to aggrandize themselves by the confusions of their country, or will flatter themselves with fairer prospects of elevation from the subdivision of the empire into several partial confederacies than from its union under one government. . . .

I propose, in a series of papers, to discuss the following interesting particulars:—*The utility of the UNION to your political prosperity—The insufficiency of the present Confederation to preserve that Union—The necessity of a government at least equally energetic with the one proposed, to the attainment of this object—The conformity of the proposed Constitution to the true principles of republican government—Its analogy to your own State constitution—and lastly,*

The additional security which its adoption will afford to the preservation of that species of government, to liberty, and to property.

In the progress of this discussion I shall endeavor to give a satisfactory answer to all the objections which shall have made their appearance, that may seem to have any claim to your attention.

It may perhaps be thought superfluous to offer arguments to prove the utility of the UNION, a point, no doubt, deeply engraved on the hearts of the great body of the people in every State, and one, which it may be imagined, has no adversaries. But the fact is, that we already hear it whispered in the private circles of those who oppose the new Constitution, that the thirteen States are of too great extent for any general system, and that we must of necessity resort to separate confederacies of distinct portions of the whole. This doctrine will, in all probability, be gradually propagated, till it has votaries enough to countenance an open avowal of it. For nothing can be more evident, to those who are able to take an enlarged view of the subject, than the alternative of an adoption of the new Constitution or a dismemberment of the Union. It will therefore be of use to begin by examining the advantages of that Union, the certain evils, and the probable dangers, to which every State will be exposed from its dissolution. This shall accordingly constitute the subject of my next address.

The Federalist No. 40

James Madison, January 18, 1788

To the People of the State of New York:

THE *second* point to be examined is, whether the convention were authorized to frame and propose this mixed Constitution . . .

The act from Annapolis recommends the "appointment of commissioners to take into consideration the situation of the United States; to devise *such further provisions* as shall appear to them necessary to render the Constitution of the federal government *adequate to the exigencies of the Union*; and to report such an act for that purpose, to the United States in Congress assembled, as when agreed to by them, and afterwards confirmed by the legislature of every State, will effectually provide for the same."

The recommendatory act of Congress is in the words following: "Whereas, there is provision in the articles of Confederation and perpetual Union, for making alterations therein, by the assent of a Congress of the United States, and of the legislatures of the several States; and whereas experience hath evinced, that there are defects in the present Confederation; as a mean to remedy which, several of the States, and *particularly the State of New York*, by express instructions to their delegates in Congress, have suggested a convention for the purposes expressed in the following resolution; and such convention appearing to be the most probable mean of establishing in these States *a firm national government*:

"Resolved—That in the opinion of Congress it is expedient, that on the second Monday of May next a convention of delegates, who shall have been appointed by the several States, be held at Philadelphia, for the sole and express purpose *of revising the articles of Confederation*, and reporting to Congress and the several legislatures such *alterations and provisions therein*, as shall, when agreed to in Congress, and confirmed by the States, render the federal Constitution *adequate to the exigencies of government and the preservation of the Union.*"

From these two acts, it appears, 1st, that the object of the convention was to establish, in these States, a *firm national government*; 2d, that this government was to be such as would be *adequate to the exigencies of government* and *the preservation of the Union*; 3d, that these purposes were to be effected by *alterations and provisions in the articles of Confederation*, as it is expressed in the act of Congress, or by *such further provisions as should appear necessary*, as it stands in the recommendatory act from Annapolis; 4th, that the alterations and provisions were to be reported to Congress, and to the States, in order to be agreed to by the former and confirmed by the latter.

From a comparison and fair construction of these several modes of expression, is to be deduced the authority under which the convention acted. They were to frame a *national government*, adequate to the exigencies of government, and *of the Union*; and to reduce the articles of Confederation into such form as to accomplish these purposes. . . .

No stress, it is presumed, will, in this case, be laid on the *title*; a change of that could never be deemed an exercise of ungranted power. *Alterations* in the body of the instrument are expressly authorized. *New provisions* therein are also expressly authorized. Here then is a power to change the title; to insert new articles; to alter old ones. Must it of necessity be admitted that this power is infringed, so long as a part of the old articles remain? Those who maintain the affirmative ought at least to mark the boundary between authorized and usurped innovations; between that degree of change which lies within the compass of *alterations and further provisions*, and that which amounts to a *transmutation* of the government. Will it be said that the alterations ought not to have touched the substance of the Confederation? The States would never have appointed a convention with so much solemnity, nor described its objects with so much latitude, if some *substantial* reform had not been in contemplation. Will it be said that the *fundamental principles* of the Confederation were not within the purview of the convention, and ought not to have been varied? I ask, What are these principles? Do they require that, in the establishment of the Constitution, the States should be regarded as distinct and independent sovereigns? They are so regarded by the Constitution proposed. Do they require that the members of the government should derive their appointment from the legislatures, not from the people of the States? One branch of the new government is to be appointed by these legislatures; and under the Confederation, the delegates to Congress *may all* be appointed immediately by the people, and in two States are actually so appointed. Do they require that the powers of the government should act on the States, and not immediately on individuals? In some instances, as has been shown, the powers of the new government will act on the States in their collective characters. In some instances, also, those of the existing government act immediately on individuals. . . .

We have seen that in the new government, as in the old, the general powers are limited; and that the States, in all unenumerated cases, are left in the enjoyment of their sovereign and independent jurisdiction.

The truth is, that the great principles of the Constitution proposed by the convention may be considered less as absolutely new, than as the expansion of principles which are found in the articles of Confederation. The misfortune under the latter system has been, that these principles are so feeble and confined as to justify all the charges of inefficiency which have been urged against it, and to require a degree of enlargement which gives to the new system the aspect of an entire transformation of the old.

In one particular it is admitted that the convention have departed from the tenor of their commission. Instead of reporting a plan requiring the confirmation *of the legislatures of all the States*, they have reported a plan which is to be confirmed by the PEOPLE, and may be carried into effect by *nine States only*. It is worthy of remark that this objection, though the most plausible, has been the least urged in the publications which have swarmed against the convention. The forbearance can only have proceeded from an irresistible conviction of the absurdity of subjecting the fate of twelve States to the perverseness or corruption of a thirteenth; from the example of inflexible opposition given by a *majority* of one sixtieth of the people of America to a measure approved and called for by the voice of twelve States, comprising fifty-nine sixtieths of the people—an example still fresh in the memory and indignation of every citizen who has felt for the wounded honor and prosperity of his country. As this objection, therefore, has been in a manner waived by those who have criticised the powers of the convention, I dismiss it without further observation. . . .

[A]s the plan to be framed and proposed was to be submitted *to the people themselves*, the disapprobation of this supreme authority would destroy it forever; its approbation blot out antecedent errors and irregularities. . . .

But that the objectors may be disarmed of every pretext, it shall be granted for a moment that the convention were neither authorized by their commission, nor justified by circumstances in proposing a Constitution for their country: does it follow that the Constitution ought, for that reason alone, to be rejected? If, according to the noble precept, it be lawful to accept good advice even from an enemy, shall we set the ignoble example of refusing such advice even when it is offered by our friends? The prudent inquiry, in all cases, ought surely to be, not so much *from whom* the advice comes, as whether the advice be *good*. . . .

The Federalist No. 43

James Madison, January 23, 1788

The express authority of the people alone could give due validity to the Constitution. To have required the unanimous ratification of the thirteen States, would have subjected the essential interests of the whole to the caprice or corruption of a single member. It would have marked a want of foresight in the convention, which our own experience would have rendered inexcusable.

Two questions of a very delicate nature present themselves on this occasion: 1. On what principle the Confederation, which stands in the solemn form of a compact among the States, can be superseded without the unanimous consent of the parties to it? 2. What relation is to subsist between the nine or more States ratifying the Constitution, and the remaining few who do not become parties to it?

The first question is answered at once by recurring to the absolute necessity of the case; to the great principle of self-preservation; to the transcendent law of nature and of nature's God, which declares that the safety and happiness of society are the objects at which all political institutions aim, and to which all such institutions must be sacrificed. PERHAPS, also, an answer may be found without searching beyond the principles of the compact itself. . . .

A compact between independent sovereigns, founded on ordinary acts of legislative authority, can pretend to no higher validity than a league or treaty between the parties. It is an established doctrine on the subject of treaties, that all the articles are mutually conditions of each other; that a breach of any one article is a breach of the whole treaty; and that a breach, committed by either of the parties, absolves the others, and authorizes them, if they please, to pronounce the compact violated and void. Should it unhappily be necessary to appeal to these delicate truths for a justification for dispensing with the consent of particular States to a dissolution of the federal pact, will not the complaining parties find it a difficult task to answer the MULTIPLIED and IMPORTANT infractions with which they may be confronted? The time has been when it was incumbent on us all to veil the ideas which this paragraph exhibits. The scene is now changed, and with it the part which the same motives dictate.

The second question is not less delicate; and the flattering prospect of its being merely hypothetical forbids an overcurious discussion of it. It is one of those cases which must be left to provide for itself. . . .

NOTES

1. Using legal arguments, evaluate James Madison's claim that the Convention did not exceed its mandate. What do you think of the argument that if the Convention did go too far, subsequent ratification by the people cures the irregularity? Consider Madison's argument (briefly in *No. 40*, more extensively in *No. 43*) that the necessity of the situation required abandonment of the Articles of Confederation's rule of unanimity for alterations. Is this a legal argument? And consider the quite different argument that the nature of the "government" under the Articles of Confederation was more like a "league" of sovereignties than a government proper, so that the violation of its requirements on all sides left it with essentially the status of a breached treaty, no longer binding on anyone. Is that the regime the Articles of Confederation created?

2. What difference does it make whether the Constitution was adopted legally? Could anyone seriously argue that we are still governed by the Articles of Confederation rather than the Constitution of 1787? Does it matter in any way to interpreting today's document—"the Constitution of the United States"—whether or not that document was legitimately adopted in the 1780s?

3. Think about the last question more broadly. Suppose one did regard the Constitution as illegitimate because it was adopted by a mild-mannered *coup d'état*. Or suppose one regards it as illegitimate because it was adopted by undemocratic or unrepresentative bodies. Or suppose one simply regards it as a very bad constitution, full of foolish or unjust provisions. Or suppose one thinks it illegitimate as a matter of principle for one generation to bind another—for the work of dead, white, propertied slave-holders to govern us from the grave, more than two hundred years later. Do these suppositions affect what the Constitution, as a legal document, means? In other words, does its legitimacy or illegitimacy affect its interpretation?

4. The Constitution requires officers of the United States and of the states to swear an oath "to support this Constitution" (Article VI). For those who have done so, the question of whether it is good or bad, legitimate or illegitimate, is presumably closed. But what about the rest of us? Should we replace the Constitution with something better, just as the Philadelphia Convention and the ratifying conventions scrapped the Articles of Confederation? In *Marbury*, Chief Justice Marshall warned, "The exercise of this original right is a very great exertion; nor can it, nor ought it to be frequently repeated." Do you agree?

[*Assignment 2*]

B. The Nature of the Constitution: Purposes, Features, and Themes

You should now carefully read the text of the Constitution and its twenty-seven amendments. (It begins on p. 1 of this book.) As you read the Constitution, as well as the following selection from James Madison, ask what type of political order is being established. Is it a democracy in the style of ancient Athens, or an oligarchy of a few wealthy leaders, or a tyranny of a single executive? Or, as Madison argues, is it a republic? How did the framers distinguish a republic from other forms of political order?

The Federalist No. 39

James Madison, January 16, 1788

To the People of the State of New York:

THE last paper having concluded the observations which were meant to introduce a candid survey of the plan of government reported by the convention, we now proceed to the execution of that part of our undertaking.

The first question that offers itself is, whether the general form and aspect of the government be strictly republican. It is evident that no other form would be reconcilable with the genius of the people of America; with the fundamental principles of the Revolution; or with that honorable determination which animates every votary of freedom, to rest all our political experiments on the capacity of mankind for self-government. If the plan of the convention, therefore, be found to depart from the republican character, its advocates must abandon it as no longer defensible.

What, then, are the distinctive characters of the republican form . . . ?

If we resort for a criterion to the different principles on which different forms of government are established, we may define a republic to be, or at least may bestow that name on, a government which derives all its powers directly or indirectly from the great body of the people, and is administered by persons holding their offices during pleasure, for a limited period, or during good behavior. It is *essential* to such a government that it be derived from the great body of the society, not from an inconsiderable proportion, or a favored class of it; otherwise a handful of tyrannical nobles, exercising their oppressions by a delegation of their powers, might aspire to the rank of republicans, and claim for their government the honorable title of republic. It is *sufficient* for such a government that the persons administering it be appointed, either directly or indirectly, by the people; and that they hold their appointments by either of the tenures just specified; otherwise every government in the United States, as well as every other popular government that has been or can be well organized or well executed, would be degraded from the republican character. . . .

"[I]t was not sufficient," say the adversaries of the proposed Constitution, "for the convention to adhere to the republican form. They ought, with equal care, to have preserved the *federal* form, which regards the Union as a *confederacy* of sovereign states; instead of which, they have framed a *national* government, which regards the Union as a *consolidation* of the States." And it is asked by what authority this bold and radical innovation was undertaken? The handle which has been made of this objection requires that it should be examined with some precision.

Without inquiring into the accuracy of the distinction on which the objection is founded, it will be necessary to a just estimate of its force, first, to ascertain the real character of the government in question; secondly, to inquire how far the convention were authorized to propose such a government; and thirdly, how far the duty they owed to their country could supply any defect of regular authority.

First. In order to ascertain the real character of the government, it may be considered in relation to the foundation on which it is to be established; to the sources from which its ordinary powers are to be drawn; to the operation of those powers; to the extent of them; and to the authority by which future changes in the government are to be introduced.

On examining the first relation, it appears, on one hand, that the Constitution is to be founded on the assent and ratification of the people of America, given by deputies elected for the special purpose; but, on the other, that this assent and ratification is to be given by the people, not as individuals composing one entire nation, but as composing the distinct and independent States to which they respectively belong. It is to be the assent and ratification of the several States, derived from the supreme authority in each State—the authority of the people themselves. The act, therefore, establishing the Constitution, will not be a national, but a federal act.

That it will be a federal and not a national act, as these terms are understood by the objectors; the act of the people, as forming so many independent States, not as forming one aggregate nation, is obvious from this single consideration, that it is to result neither from the decision of a *majority* of the people of the Union, nor from that of a *majority* of the States. It must result from the *unanimous* assent of the several States that are parties to it, differing no otherwise from their ordinary assent than in its being expressed, not by the legislative authority, but by that of the people themselves. Were the people regarded in this transaction as forming one nation, the will of the majority of the whole people of the United States would bind the minority, in the same manner as the majority in each State must bind the minority; and the will of the majority must be determined either by a comparison of the individual votes, or by considering the will of the majority of the States as evidence of the will of a majority of the people of the United States. Neither of these rules have been adopted. Each State, in ratifying the Constitution, is considered as a sovereign body, independent of all others, and only to be bound by its own voluntary act. In this relation, then, the new Constitution will, if established, be a *federal*, and not a *national* constitution. . . .

The difference between a federal and national government, as it relates to the *operation of the Government*, is supposed to consist in this, that in the former the powers operate on the political bodies composing the Confederacy, in their political capacities; in the latter, on the individual citizens composing the nation, in their individual capacities. On trying the Constitution by this criterion, it falls under the national, not the federal character; though perhaps not so completely as has been understood. In several cases, and particularly in the trial of controversies to which States may be parties, they must be viewed and proceeded against in their collective and political capacities only. So far the national countenance of the government on this side seems to be disfigured by a few federal features. But this blemish is perhaps unavoidable in any plan; and the operation of the government on the people, in their individual capacities, in its ordinary and most essential proceedings, may, on the whole, designate it, in this relation, a national government.

But if the government be national with regard to the *operation* of its powers, it changes its aspect again when we contemplate it in relation to the *extent* of its powers. The idea of a national government involves in it, not only an authority over the individual citizens, but an indefinite supremacy over all persons and things, so far as they are objects of lawful government. Among a people consolidated into one nation, this supremacy is completely vested in the national legislature. Among communities united for particular purposes, it is vested partly in the general and partly in the municipal legislatures. In the former case, all local authorities are subordinate to the supreme; and may be controlled, directed, or abolished by it at pleasure. In the latter, the local or municipal authorities form distinct and independent portions of the supremacy, no more subject, within their respective spheres, to the general authority, than the general authority is subject to them, within its own sphere. In this relation, then, the proposed government cannot be deemed a *national* one; since its jurisdiction extends to certain enumerated objects only, and leaves to the several States a residuary and inviolable sovereignty over all other objects. It is true that in controversies relating to the boundary between the two jurisdictions, the tribunal which is ultimately to decide, is to be established under the general government. But this does not change the principle of the case. The decision is to be impartially made, according to the rules of the Constitution; and all the usual and most effectual precautions are taken to secure this impartiality. Some such tribunal is clearly essential to prevent an appeal to the sword and a dissolution of the compact; and that it ought to be established under the general rather than under the local governments, or, to speak more properly, that it could be safely established under the first alone, is a position not likely to be combated.

If we try the Constitution by its last relation to the authority by which amendments are to be made, we find it neither wholly *national* nor wholly *federal*. Were it wholly national, the supreme and ultimate authority would reside in the *majority* of the people of the Union; and this authority would be competent at all times, like that of a majority of every national society, to alter or abolish its established government. Were it wholly federal, on the other hand, the concurrence of each State in the Union would be essential to every alteration that would be binding on all. The mode provided by the plan of the convention is not founded on either of these principles. In requiring more than a majority, and principles. In requiring more than a majority, and particularly in computing the proportion by *States*, not by *citizens*, it departs from the *national* and advances towards the *federal* character; in rendering the concurrence of less than the whole number of States sufficient, it loses again the *federal* and partakes of the *national* character.

The proposed Constitution, therefore, is, in strictness, neither a national nor a federal Constitution, but a composition of both. In its foundation it is federal, not national; in the sources from which the ordinary powers of the government are drawn, it is partly federal and partly national; in the operation of these powers, it is national, not federal; in the extent of them, again, it is federal, not national; and, finally, in the authoritative mode of introducing amendments, it is neither wholly federal, nor wholly national.

Six Broad Themes of the Constitution

James Madison's *The Federalist No. 39* identifies several prominent features of the Constitution in the course of explaining how the government structure created by the document is partly national and partly federal. Stepping back from that discussion and viewing the Constitution at an even more general level, one can discern six broad themes, themes that recur throughout this book.

1. *A Written Constitution.* The first thing to notice about the Constitution is that it is a written text. As discussed earlier in this chapter, it was the first instance of a nation putting into writing its governing structure and according to that written document the status of "supreme Law." (The phrase "supreme Law" is found in Article VI, Section 2, in what is called the Supremacy Clause.) Closely linked, then, to the idea of a written constitution was constitutional supremacy: The Constitution prevails over any contrary law or action by a state or federal government. This supremacy is the foundation for judicial review of legislative and executive action.

As a written text, the Constitution must be interpreted. How should judges and other officials decide exactly what it means? The Constitution itself does not answer this question, though it does say that what is "the supreme Law of the land" is "this Constitution." The task of constitutional interpretation, therefore, is determining what "this Constitution" means. Throughout this book, five types of constitutional argument, or modes of interpretation, are considered. First, there are arguments based on the text of the Constitution—that is, the meaning the words would have had, in context, to speakers and readers of the English language when the text was enacted or adopted. Second, there are arguments based on the structure or internal logic of the document. These arguments draw inferences from the relationship of provisions to each other, their locations within the Constitution, and the structures of government necessarily framed by the text as a whole. Third, there are arguments from historical purpose, which draw on a provision's historical background, emphasizing not the particular words of the text but the intentions underlying them, as evidenced by statements of its drafters or ratifiers. These statements might be found, for example, in *The Federalist* or in the records of the debates at the Constitutional Convention. Arguments from purpose are frequently resorted to when the linguistic meaning of a constitutional provision remains ambiguous. Fourth, there are arguments from precedent and practice. Here the focus is on previous interpretations, whether by the judiciary or by other branches of government, that have become sufficiently settled to "fix" or "liquidate" the meaning of an ambiguous constitutional provision. Fifth, there are arguments based on policy. These arguments look to consequences, and they ask which interpretation produces the best results according to a specific notion of what is best—for example, asking which interpretation would maximize egalitarian justice, individual autonomy, or economic efficiency. (This list of the types of constitutional argument is adapted from Philip Bobbitt's work on modalities of constitutional interpretation. See, e.g., Philip Bobbitt, CONSTITUTIONAL INTERPRETATION 11–22 (1991).) Which of these types of constitutional argument should be given the most force? Which types would seem to generate the most controversy and disagreement?

2. *Republicanism and Popular Sovereignty.* From its first three words, the Constitution proclaims that it is an act of and for "We the People of the United States." In contrast to the Articles of Confederation, the states are not sovereign (though this point would remain disputed for decades, and

ultimately lead to attempted secession and the Civil War). Nor is the national government sovereign. The people are sovereign.

To be sure, the people of the United States ordinarily exercise their sovereignty through representative institutions. Madison notes this fact in *The Federalist No. 39* when defending the "strictly republican" character of the government under the Constitution. Yet all government power proceeds, ultimately if sometimes indirectly, from the great body of the people, acting either through their national institutions or through their state institutions. Thus, the government is "partly national" and "partly federal."

As Madison notes, the Constitution was adopted by the collective decision of the people of the United States, acting through the separate decisions of the people in three-fourths of the states. Likewise, constitutional change—the adoption of amendments, pursuant to Article V—ultimately requires the ratification of the sovereign "people of the United States," also acting through the separate decision-making processes of three-fourths of the states.

Thus popular sovereignty, achieved through representative, republican institutions, pervades the Constitution, though imperfectly. In the original Constitution, it is present in the schemes of representation in Congress and in the system for election of the president (though both arrangements were tainted by accommodation of slavery). It is also present indirectly in the role of elected officials in the selection of the judiciary, as well as in Article IV's guarantee by the nation as a whole that each state will always have "a Republican Form of Government."

Later amendments reinforced popular sovereignty and republicanism by protecting the right to vote and by increasing the representativeness and accountability of national institutions. This is true of the Fifteenth, Seventeenth, Nineteenth, Twenty-third, Twenty-fourth, Twenty-sixth, and Twenty-seventh Amendments, all of which are discussed below in "A Map of the Constitution."

3. *Separation of Powers.* The next most obvious feature of the Constitution is its division and separation of powers among three branches of the national government—the legislative, executive, and judicial—represented by Congress, the president, and the federal courts. Each branch is, to a substantial degree, independent of the others, and each possesses powers to check or balance the powers of the others.

In America the government would not be a "mixed regime" divided among a king, an aristocracy, and the people (as in the English model of king, House of Lords, and House of Commons). A different division was necessary, and the one the framers employed was functional. Subject to certain exceptions, the legislative function was for Congress, the executive function was for the president, and the judicial function was for the federal courts. The functional separation of powers had been endorsed by John Locke and William Blackstone, and especially by Montesquieu in THE SPIRIT OF THE LAWS (1748, first published in English in 1750).[4]

---

[4] Montesquieu thought this had been achieved in England after the Glorious Revolution of 1688, but he was almost certainly wrong. On his counsel continental Europe and Latin America tended to adopt a rigid functional separation of powers. As a result, until 1945 most civil law countries made no provision for judicial review of legislation, thinking that this would give the judiciary a share in the legislative power. On Enlightenment thinking about separation of powers, see generally M.J.C. Vile, CONSTITUTIONALISM AND THE SEPARATION OF POWERS (1998).

The idea of a functional separation of powers influenced even the critics of the Constitution, the Anti–Federalists, who argued that the Constitution's system of checks and balances actually intermingled the legislative, executive, and judicial powers that Montesquieu had said should be kept separate. And it should be noted that some supporters of the new Constitution, such as John Adams, never accepted the idea of a functional separation of powers. Adams would have preferred a democratic variation of the "mixed regime" where there were three components—the One (the president or governor), the Few (the upper house and the courts), and the many (the lower house)—but all were elected directly or indirectly by the people. In this confused mass of different views about what kind of separation of powers was desirable, and what kind would actually be effected by the Constitution, the defense of the new proposed government for the United States fell to James Madison. Today the system of checks and balances in the Constitution is often called "Madisonian" because of his work in devising and defending it.

In *The Federalist Nos. 47* to *51*, Madison discusses the separation of powers and argues that the Constitution of the United States is consistent with Montesquieu's insights. Madison explains that under the Constitution each branch is given different responsibilities and only a partial role in the selection of the members of the others. The president, senators, and representatives are chosen in different ways by different electorates. A rolling six-year electoral cycle is set up before all the elected officers of the government can be replaced in three staggered elections. Political movements must usually sweep at least two national elections in a row, held two years apart, before they can accomplish much. Even then it may be years before the courts are transformed.

Moreover, each branch is made as independent of the others as possible and is given a "will" of its own so that it does not become subject to one of the others. And vitally important powers—such as the power of warmaking—are divided, requiring joint action by separate branches. The framers insisted on a separation of powers for the national government at the same time they were greatly expanding its strength.

4. *Federalism.* A fourth broad theme of the Constitution lies in its division of power between the national government and the governments of the states. The Constitution itself is the supreme law, and, under the Supremacy Clause of Article VI, any constitutionally valid actions of the national government prevail over actions of the states. But the national government remains, in theory at least, a government of limited, enumerated powers, with the states and the people retaining all the powers not expressly delegated to the national government. Of course, there remains plenty of room for argument over how broadly or narrowly to construe the enumerated powers of the national government, including especially the power to regulate "commerce" among the states, the taxing power, the spending power, and the power to pass laws "necessary and proper" for carrying into execution the other enumerated powers.

Federalism is a division of labor. Ideally, the central government will solve the collective-action problems of local governments. Without the central government, local governments may engage in a destructive race to the bottom, they may be unable to realize economies of scale, and the actions of one local government may generate negative externalities, or costs, for other states (e.g., the installation of coal plants in one state can affect the air quality in a neighboring state). Or a local government may be trampling on the rights of a minority in its jurisdiction. At the same time, a federal system is supposed to allow local governments to address situations for which they are better suited. These include questions for which there is geographic variation in tastes and preferences, where competition can spur a race to the top, or where economic or social experimentation is valuable. And it may be easier for the people to control a local government than a distant one. In practice, however, this division is complicated, and the local governments will often think a question is best resolved at the local level even though the central government disagrees. As a result, in the United States and the nations influenced by its federal system,[5] written constitutional federalism tends to lead to the creation of judicial review, because a court will often be needed to play umpire in disputes between the central and local governments.

5. *Individual Rights.* The Constitution is also designed to promote liberty. The original Constitution of 1787 had some provisions protecting individual rights (e.g., Article I, Sections 9 and 10), but most of the explicit guarantees of such rights have come in subsequent amendments. The increasing protection of individual rights is a major theme in America's constitutional history.

As a general matter, the Bill of Rights, ratified in 1791, protected individual rights from abridgement by the *national* government. The Reconstruction Amendments (the Thirteenth, Fourteenth, and Fifteenth Amendments, ratified after the Civil War) protected rights from abridgement by *state* governments. Indeed, the Reconstruction Amendments so radically transformed our Constitution that they have been described as a Second Founding of the Republic. The Bill of Rights and the Reconstruction Amendments together protect rights such as the freedom of speech and the freedom of religion, and they impose important constraints on the federal and state governments, such as a prohibition on the government taking life, liberty, or property without due process of law.

A related theme of the amendments to the Constitution is the steady expansion of national power to protect these rights. Each of the three Reconstruction Amendments authorized Congress to pass enforcing legislation and in effect gave the federal courts more power against the states. And two constitutional amendments in the early twentieth century made the national government much more powerful. The Sixteenth Amendment (1913), allowing for the taxation of income, gave the federal government an enormous increase in revenue—revenue which it could itself use or return to the states with strings attached. The Seventeenth Amendment (1913), providing for the direct election of U.S. senators (who had previously been elected by the state legislatures), also made the federal government more independent from the states. And, as noted above, a number of amendments have expanded voting rights. Taken together, and read in light of the Declaration of Independence's statement that "All men are created equal," these amendments commit the nation to recognition of equal political and civil rights.

6. *The Imperfect Congruence of the Constitution with Justice.* A final feature of the Constitution is imperfection. It does not forbid all bad things; nor does it require all good things (even assuming there could be complete agreement on what these are). Instead, on many questions the Constitution

---

[5] Since the adoption of the first written constitution embodying federalism—the U.S. Constitution—federal constitutions have been adopted in Australia, Austria, Argentina, Brazil, Canada, Germany, India, Mexico, and Switzerland, as well as the European Union.

permits a wide diversity of answers. It offers a framework in which different political choices can be made.

Although the Constitution is in many ways a magnificent triumph, one cannot be blind to its shortcomings—including the atrocities that it originally permitted and rewarded (especially slavery) and the injustices that since then have been done in its name. When studying the Constitution and its interpretation by judges, presidents, and members of Congress, do not ignore the ways the document and its interpretation have produced grave wrongs. Imperfection should not be celebrated like the other themes identified here—written constitutionalism, popular sovereignty, separation of powers, federalism, and the promotion of individual rights—but it is just as essential to understanding the Constitution.

A Map of the Constitution

In studying the Constitution, it is useful to start with a map, or overview, of its parts. As you read this section, flip back and forth to the text of the Constitution at the start of this book.

The Original Constitution

The Preamble states the purposes of the Constitution, and the authority from which it claims to emanate—the collective, deliberate action of "We the People of the United States" in their exercise of popular sovereignty.

Article I of the Constitution concerns the legislative powers of Congress. It says that Congress consists of a House of Representatives and a Senate, specifies how members are chosen, prescribes the qualifications for each office, and provides rules for lawmaking. Much of Article I (specifically, Section 8) lists the legislative powers of Congress. Article I vests in Congress "all legislative powers *herein granted*," which in theory creates a federal government of limited and enumerated powers. Much of this book's discussion of Article I addresses the question of how broadly or narrowly to construe these listed powers. Article I, Section 9 lists things Congress may not do, and Article I, Section 10 lists things states may not do. (One might think of each of these sections as a mini-Bill of Rights, limiting national and state power, respectively.) Each house of Congress has the sole power to prescribe its own rules of procedure and to punish and expel its own members. Article I also gives Congress the power to remove executive and judicial officers who have committed "high crimes and misdemeanors" (a term that appears in Article II). The House has the power of impeachment, and the Senate has the power, acting by two-thirds vote, to convict and thereby remove an executive or judicial officer found guilty of the impeachment charges. Article I, Section 6 prohibits members of Congress from simultaneously holding executive or judicial offices. (This seemingly obscure clause forecloses parliamentary government in the United States.)

Article II vests "the executive Power" in "a President of the United States." Unlike Congress, whose powers are listed and specifically limited to those "herein granted," the "executive Power" appears to be granted in its entirety to the president and not specifically defined (though this was a subject of early debate and remains highly contested). Article II creates a single, independent chief executive rather than a plural executive or a prime minister, and it describes a procedure for election for a four-year term. It also details certain presidential powers—a move probably made necessary because the framers did not want the president to have some traditional executive powers of the English king and wanted to share some of the president's powers with the Senate. Finally, Article II makes clear that the president and vice president are subject to impeachment (unlike English monarchs). All executive and judicial officers of the United States—but not members of Congress—may be impeached.

Article III vests "the judicial Power" of the United States in a Supreme Court and any inferior courts Congress chooses to create. Each judge is appointed by the president with the Senate's advice and consent, and the appointment is for life (in context, this is what the term "good behaviour" means). The judicial power is not defined, but it is limited to "cases" and "controversies" of certain descriptions, typically disputes involving federal law, ones crossing state lines, or ones implicating some other national interest. It provides for some measure of congressional control over courts' the courts' jurisdiction, the extent of which remains a matter of dispute. No explicit clause in Article III grants a power of "judicial review." That power is an inference from the supremacy of the Constitution and the duty of judges to follow that supreme law as they decide cases and controversies.

Article IV defines certain relationships among the states. The states must recognize and enforce each other's judgments and judicial decrees. They must accord citizens of other states the same "Privileges and Immunities" of citizenship they give to their own citizens. And fugitives—and originally fugitive slaves—escaping from one state to another must be "delivered up" and returned. The Fugitive Slave Clause became a source of much interstate and political friction. So too did the Article IV power of Congress to govern the "Territory" of the United States and to admit new states into the Union—disputes about this power led to the infamous *Dred Scott* case and contributed to the Civil War. Finally, and somewhat cryptically, Article IV provides that the national government shall "guarantee" to every state "a Republican Form of Government" and protect each from invasion and insurrection.

Article V prescribes the procedures for amending the Constitution, the only way the Constitution itself authorizes constitutional change. Amendment was deliberately made difficult. It requires a proposal, either by two-thirds vote of both houses or by a special constitutional convention requested by two-thirds of the states, *plus* ratification by three-fourths of the states. Article V purports to make unamendable two provisions that were critical to securing ratification of the Constitution: the equal representation of small and large states in the Senate, and the restriction on Congress's ability to outlaw the importation of slaves before 1808.

Article VI specifies the authority of the Constitution. It is "the supreme Law of the Land," and it binds the judges of every state, trumping anything to the contrary in state law. Furthermore, all federal officers—and even all state officers—are required to swear an oath "to support this Constitution."

Article VII declared that the Constitution would become operative upon ratification by nine of the thirteen original states.

The Amendments

The original Constitution lacked a Bill of Rights, an omission that became a source of extensive opposition to its ratification. The supporters of ratification, the Federalists, argued that no declaration of rights was needed, because the government would have only the limited powers that the Constitution specified. A Bill of Rights, they contended, would imply that the government had broader powers than it actually did. The opponents of ratification, the Anti–Federalists, argued that the Constitution's powers might be construed in such a broad fashion as to impinge on individual rights and that more should be done to secure those rights. Yielding to political reality, the Federalists agreed that they would propose a Bill of Rights—*after* ratification.

Though there was much new business for the First Congress, it did propose twelve amendments, ten of which were soon ratified. (Another one, discussed below, is now the Twenty-seventh Amendment.) The Bill of Rights originally applied only to actions of the new national government. Later, after the Civil War, the Fourteenth Amendment made much of the Bill of Rights applicable to actions of states governments as well. As a consequence, many modern cases interpreting and applying the Bill of Rights are actually cases under the Fourteenth Amendment.

The First Amendment protects freedom of speech, freedom of the press, freedom of religion, and the right to petition for redress of grievances. It also prohibits Congress from making any law respecting an establishment of religion. These provisions are vital to our national life and have been sources of major constitutional disputes.

The Second Amendment protects the right of citizens to "keep and bear arms" in order to provide for a "well-regulated militia," a right that remains hotly debated. *The Third Amendment* prohibits the government from quartering soldiers in private homes, except in times of war and in a manner prescribed by law.

The Fourth, Fifth, Sixth, and Eighth Amendments mostly concern the rights of criminal suspects and defendants, including the rights to be free from unreasonable searches and seizures and from double prosecution or punishment for the same crime ("double jeopardy"); the right to trial by a jury and indictment by a grand jury; the privilege against self-incrimination; the guarantee of "due process of law"; the right to a speedy and public trial; the right to confront adverse witnesses and present one's own; the right to assistance of counsel; and freedom from excessive bail, excessive fines, and cruel and unusual punishments. *The Fifth Amendment* also protects private property from being taken by the government without compensation. *The Seventh Amendment* preserves the right to trial by jury in civil lawsuits in federal courts.

The Ninth and Tenth Amendments appear to be clarifying provisions made necessary by the Federalists' initial argument that having a Bill of Rights would imply that all rights and powers were assigned into the hands of the national government. *The Ninth Amendment* provides that the enumeration of rights in the Bill of Rights should not be construed to "deny or disparage" other rights "retained by the people." At a minimum, this clarifies that the Bill of Rights does not repeal state constitutional rights. *The Tenth Amendment* confirms that powers not delegated to the national government "are reserved to the States respectively, or to the people." This amendment appears designed to guard against an inference that adopting the Bill of Rights meant that the federal government now had a general power to legislate on anything unless there was a specific right to the contrary—an inference that would have reversed the principle that the federal government is one of limited, enumerated powers.

The Eleventh Amendment, ratified in 1798, removes a category of jurisdiction from the federal courts—suits brought by citizens of one state against a different state—that had become controversial after an early Supreme Court decision. Today, the amendment is at the center of disputes over states' immunity from suit.

The Twelfth Amendment, ratified in 1804, was designed to solve an unforeseen problem with presidential elections, exposed by the development of political parties and the election of 1800, in which Thomas Jefferson and Aaron Burr, running as a "ticket," received the same number of electoral votes—a tie, even though Jefferson had been the intended presidential candidate. The Twelfth Amendment provides that the president and vice president are voted for separately.

The Thirteenth, Fourteenth, and Fifteenth Amendments were ratified after the end of the Civil War (in 1865, 1868, and 1870, respectively). *The Thirteenth Amendment* abolishes slavery. *The Fourteenth Amendment* prohibits states from discriminating against classes of citizens (especially the newly freed slaves) by denying them due process or the equal protection of the laws. The Fourteenth Amendment also prohibits states from abridging the privileges and immunities of U.S. citizenship. The meaning of these provisions has proved enduringly controversial and has framed some of the most important constitutional debates of the past 150 years. Whatever else these provisions might mean, it has come to be widely accepted that the Fourteenth Amendment makes much of the Bill of Rights applicable as limitations on what state governments may do. *The Fifteenth Amendment* forbids denial of the right to vote based on race or previous condition of servitude. Each of these amendments in the wake of the Civil War gave Congress the power of enforcement against state governments.

The early part of the twentieth century produced several constitutional amendments. *The Sixteenth Amendment*, ratified in 1913, formally placed in the Constitution the power of Congress to tax individual incomes directly. *The Seventeenth Amendment*, also ratified in 1913, provides for direct election of U.S. senators, replacing election by state legislatures. *The Eighteenth Amendment*, ratified in 1919, created Prohibition, which was repealed in 1933 by the *Twenty-first Amendment* (now the name of a bar in Washington, D.C.)—the only amendments that canceled each other out. *The Nineteenth Amendment*, ratified in 1920, gave women the right to vote in every state and federal election. *The Twentieth Amendment*, ratified in 1933, advanced the start of the president's term by two months, shortening the "lame duck" period after an election.

Several other electoral and voting reforms became amendments in the second half of the twentieth century. *The Twenty-second Amendment*, ratified in 1951, limits presidents to two terms—only Franklin Roosevelt was ever elected to more than two (1932, 1936, 1940, 1944). *The Twenty-third Amendment*, ratified in 1961, gave the District of Columbia three electoral votes. *The Twenty-fourth Amendment*, ratified in 1964, forbids imposing a tax on voting. *The Twenty-fifth Amendment*, ratified in 1967, provides an elaborate scheme addressing the problem of temporary presidential disability. *The Twenty-sixth Amendment*, ratified in 1971, gave those over eighteen the right to vote.

The Twenty-seventh Amendment, ratified in 1992, forbids alterations in congressional pay from taking effect without an intervening election for the House of Representatives. This amendment was proposed as part of the original Bill of Rights in 1789, but it was ratified 202 years later! Its ratification raises important and entertaining questions of constitutional interpretation, which are considered in Chapter 5.

[Assignment 3]

C. THE ADDITION OF THE BILL OF RIGHTS

One of the most contentious issues surrounding the ratification of the Constitution was the absence in the document of a statement of the rights that the people held against the government—in other words, a "Bill of Rights." Those who championed the new Constitution denied that one was necessary or even desirable. Federalists such as Alexander Hamilton, James Madison, and James Wilson argued that the Constitution would create a federal government of only limited, enumerated powers. To include a Bill of Rights, they maintained, would wrongly imply that the government had more powers than were intended and that all of the many individual rights that were not enumerated could be invaded at will by the national government. It would flip the presumption of the Constitution, because now everything the federal government did would be presumptively constitutional unless it contravened the Bill of Rights. The Anti–Federalist opponents of the Constitution, such as George Mason and Richard Henry Lee, replied that the powers of the federal government, even though enumerated, might still be construed broadly. In particular, the Anti–Federalists called the Necessary and Proper Clause "the Sweeping Clause," and they said that without a Bill of Rights it would sweep away all of the people's liberties.

The Anti–Federalists won the political argument, and the Federalists agreed to propose amendments in the First Congress—after ratification of the Constitution. Based in part on these assurances, the critical states of Massachusetts, New Hampshire, Virginia, and New York ratified the Constitution while also calling for amendments in the nature of a Bill of Rights. Representative James Madison of Virginia took the lead in drafting a series of proposed amendments. Eventually, Congress sent to the states twelve proposed amendments. Ten of these were promptly ratified, and it is these ten amendments that are called the Bill of Rights.

But who was right in this struggle over the interpretation of the original Constitution? Were the Anti–Federalists' fears exaggerated? Were the Federalists' assurances too confident? As you read the following passages from *The Federalist No. 84* and an essay called "What the Anti–Federalists Were *For*," evaluate the contending positions. What insights do you draw about the powers granted to the federal government?

The Federalist No. 84

Alexander Hamilton, May 28, 1788

. . . The most considerable of the remaining objections is that the plan of the convention contains no bill of rights. . . .

It has been several times truly remarked that bills of rights are, in their origin, stipulations between kings and their subjects, abridgements of prerogative in favor of privilege, reservations of rights not surrendered to the prince. Such was MAGNA CHARTA, obtained by the barons, sword in hand, from King John. Such were the subsequent confirmations of that charter by succeeding princes. Such was the *petition of right* assented to by Charles I., in the beginning of his reign. Such, also, was the Declaration of Right presented by the Lords and Commons to the Prince of Orange in 1688, and afterwards thrown into the form of an act of parliament called the Bill of Rights. It is evident, therefore, that, according to their primitive signification, they have no application to constitutions professedly founded upon the power of the people, and executed by their immediate representatives and servants. Here, in strictness, the people surrender nothing; and as they retain every thing they have no need of particular reservations. "WE, THE PEOPLE of the United States, to secure the blessings of liberty to ourselves and our posterity, do ORDAIN and ESTABLISH this Constitution for the United States of America." Here is a better recognition of popular rights, than volumes of those aphorisms which make the principal figure in several of our State bills of rights, and which would sound much better in a treatise of ethics than in a constitution of government.

But a minute detail of particular rights is certainly far less applicable to a Constitution like that under consideration, which is merely intended to regulate the general political interests of the nation, than to a constitution which has the regulation of every species of personal and private concerns.

I go further, and affirm that bills of rights, in the sense and to the extent in which they are contended for, are not only unnecessary in the proposed Constitution, but would even be dangerous. They would contain various exceptions to powers not granted; and, on this very account, would afford a colorable pretext to claim more than were granted. For why declare that things shall not be done which there is no power to do? Why, for instance, should it be said that the liberty of the press shall not be restrained, when no power is given by which restrictions may be imposed? I will not contend that such a provision would confer a regulating power; but it is evident that it would furnish, to men disposed to usurp, a plausible pretense for claiming that power. They might urge with a semblance of reason, that the Constitution ought not to be charged with the absurdity of providing against the abuse of an authority which was not given, and that the provision against restraining the liberty of the press afforded a clear implication, that a power to prescribe proper regulations concerning it was intended to be vested in the national government. This may serve as a specimen of the numerous handles which would be given to the doctrine of constructive powers, by the indulgence of an injudicious zeal for bills of rights.

On the subject of the liberty of the press, as much as has been said, I cannot forbear adding a remark or two: in the first place, I observe, that there is not a syllable concerning it in the constitution of this State; in the next, I contend, that whatever has been said about it in that of any other State, amounts to nothing. What signifies a declaration, that "the liberty of the press shall be inviolably preserved"? What is the liberty of the press? Who can give it any definition which would not leave the utmost latitude for evasion? I hold it to be impracticable; and from this I infer, that its security, whatever fine declarations may be inserted in any constitution respecting it, must altogether depend on public opinion, and on the general spirit of the people and of the government. And here, after all, as is intimated upon another occasion, must we seek for the only solid basis of all our rights.

There remains but one other view of this matter to conclude the point. The truth is, after all the declamations we have heard, that the Constitution is itself, in every rational sense, and to every useful purpose, A BILL OF RIGHTS. The several bills of rights in Great Britain form its Constitution, and conversely the constitution of each State is its bill of rights. And the proposed Constitution, if adopted, will be the bill of rights of the Union. Is it one object of a bill of rights to declare and specify the political privileges of the citizens in the structure and administration of the government? This is done in the most ample and precise manner in the plan of the convention; comprehending various precautions for the public security, which are not to be found in any of the State constitutions. Is another object of a bill of rights to define certain immunities and modes of proceeding, which are relative to personal and private concerns? This we have seen has also been attended to, in a variety of cases, in the same plan. Adverting therefore to the substantial meaning of a bill of rights, it is absurd to allege that it is not to be found in the work of the convention. It may be said that it does not go far enough, though it will not be easy to make this appear; but it can with no propriety be contended that there is no such thing. It certainly must be immaterial what mode is observed as to the order of declaring the rights of the citizens, if they are to be found in any part of the instrument which establishes the government. And hence it must be apparent, that much of what has been said on this subject rests merely on verbal and nominal distinctions, entirely foreign from the substance of the thing.

Herbert Storing, What the Anti–Federalists Were *For*

1 The Complete Anti–Federalist 64–70 (1981)

It is often said that the major legacy of the Anti–Federalists is the Bill of Rights. Many of their suggestions found their way into the proposals for amendments made by state ratifying conventions and thence into the first ten amendments adopted in 1791. Three kinds of rights were stressed: the usual common law procedural rights in criminal prosecutions, liberty of conscience, and liberty of the press. The Anti–Federalists insisted that the Constitution should explicitly recognize the traditional procedural rights: to be safe from general search and seizure, to be indicted by grand jury, to trial by jury, to confront witnesses, and to be protected against cruel and unusual punishments. The most important of these was the trial by jury, and one of the most widely uttered objections against the Constitution was that it did not provide for (and therefore effectively abolished) trial by jury in civil cases. The Federalists' claim that practice among the states in this respect varied too much to provide a general rule was either denied by the Anti–Federalists or used as a further argument against the feasibility of consolidation. Regarding liberty of conscience, the Anti–Federalists' position was complex. Typically they favored both governmental encouragement of religion and liberty of individual conscience. The first proposal of the minority of the Pennsylvania convention was that rights of conscience shall be held inviolable and that no state provision regarding liberty of conscience shall be abridged by the federal government. Some Anti–Federalists professed to see in the prohibition against a religious test for officers of the United States a power to regulate religious beliefs in general, to which this prohibition was an exception. The rights of conscience should be secured, even though there was no immediate threat. Times change, and "the seeds of superstition, bigotry and enthusiasm, are too deeply implanted in our minds, ever to be eradicated. . . ." The third area of concern was liberty of the press, often declaimed by the Anti–Federalists as the palladium of American liberties. "It is the opinion of some great writers," Centinel argued, "that if the liberty of the press, by an institution of religion, or otherwise, could be rendered sacred, even in *Turkey*, that despotism would fly before it." "I say," another Anti–Federalist insisted, "that a declaration of those inherent and political rights out to be made in a BILL OF RIGHTS, that the people may never lose their liberties by construction. If the liberty of the press by an inherent political right, let it be so declared, that no despot however great shall *dare to gain say it*." All of these concerns were pressed with enough vigor so that the Constitution was adopted only on the understanding that one of the first items of business in the new government would be the framing of amendments.

While the Federalists gave us the Constitution, then, the legacy of the Anti–Federalists was the Bill of Rights. But it is an ambiguous legacy, as can be seen by studying the debate. Indeed, in one sense, the success of the Bill of Rights reflects the failure of the Anti–Federalists. The whole emphasis on reservations of rights of individuals implied a fundamental acceptance of the "consolidated" character of the new government. A truly federal government needs no bill of rights. Indeed, there were some Federalists who tried to use the Anti–Federalists' federalism to destroy the Anti–Federalists argument for a bill of rights (incidentally undermining their own position). One Alfredus contended, for example, that a bill or rights was not necessary because the Constitution was a compact not between individuals but between sovereign and independent societies. This argument is easy enough to answer, and the Anti–Federalists often answered it: the government under the Constitution was not a mere compact of sovereign states—at least not in its operation—and it was not exempt from the need for a bill of rights on that account. But in making this reply the Anti–Federalists decisively abandoned the doctrine of strict federalism.

A more substantial "federal" argument against a bill of rights was made by James Wilson in his famous "State house speech" on 4 October 1787. Wilson acknowledge that maxim often put forward by the Anti–Federalists that in establishing governments all powers not expressly reserved are presumed to be granted, but he denied that it applied to the proposed general government, because that was to be a government of specifically enumerated powers. Whereas in the state constitutions the people "invested their representatives with every right and authority which they did not in explicit terms reserve," under the proposed Constitution "the congressional power is to be collected, not from tacit implication, but from the positive grant expressed in the instrument of the union. Hence, it is evident, that in the former case, everything which is not reserved is given; but in the latter the reverse of the proposition prevails, and everything which is not given is reserved." Thus, Wilson concluded, "it would have been superfluous and absurd to have stipulated with a federal body of our own creation, that we should enjoy those privileges of which we are not divested, either by the intention or the act that has brought the body into existent." This is a substantial argument; it was heavily relied on by defenders of the Constitution; and the basis theory on which it rests has become a part of American constitutional orthodoxy. Yet it has some serious difficulties, especially when applied to the question of a bill of rights.

Wilson's position depends on the assumption that the "powers" delegated to the government are fairly easily identifiable and unambiguous. Thus, for example, he contended that there is no "power" granted to the federal government "to regulate literary publications" and therefore no need for a reservation in favor of the liberty of the press. If Congress should enact such a law, the judges would declare it null and void because "inconsistent with those powers vested by this instrument in Congress. . . ." But (even leaving aside the question of libel and seditious libel) the general government is given authority to lay and collect taxes and to regulate commerce, for example, and could not either of these be used to stifle the press? More generally, does not the general government, in the pursuit of its delegated powers, have implied powers that need to be limited for the sake of individual liberties? Cannot the federal government define crimes and criminal procedures, in connection with federal postal regulations, for example; and not is there not therefore a need for procedural restraints of the traditional kind? Brutus made the argument thus: "The powers, rights, and authority, granted to the general government by this constitution, are as complete, with respect to every object to which they extend, as that of any state government—It reaches to every thing which concerns human happiness—Life, liberty, and property, are under its controul. There is the same reason, therefore, that the exercise of power, in this case, should be restrained within proper limits, as in that of the state governments."

The constitutional grant of power to Congress—so laconic and broad—is an argument in favor of a bill of rights, not against it. . . . The inadequacy of Wilson's argument is further demonstrated by the presence in the Constitution of a truncated bill of rights. Why was there any need to restrict the suspension of the writ of habeus corpus or to prohibit granting titles of nobility? Where were such powers granted? The very few Federalists who made any attempt to meet this objection sought to show that these were exceptions to implied powers, but this only reenforced the contention that the "powers" granted are anything but simple and unambiguous—that they are in fact complex and doubtful and capable of great extension. . . .

Even if it were granted that a bill of rights was, strictly speaking, unnecessary, the Anti–Federalists asked, why not be safe? What is the harm? Would it, Patrick Henry asked, have taken too much paper? One answer was that a bill of rights would be positively dangerous, because, as Wilson explained, "it would imply that whatever is not expressed was given, which is not the principle of the proposed constitution." There is some basis for this view. Yet the Anti–Federalists could forcefully contend that any harm of this kind had already been done by the reservations in behalf of individual rights included in the Constitution. And, all things considered, this Federalist argument seemed a bit sophistical.

Did the Bill of Rights Bind the States?

The Bill of Rights originally applied only to the federal government's actions. This is understandable, given its origins in Anti–Federalist concerns about the national government using its powers to violate individual rights or intrude on the states. It was not until the adoption of the Fourteenth Amendment, after the Civil War, that provisions of the Bill of Rights were made applicable to actions taken by state governments. But even before the adoption of the Fourteenth Amendment, some argued that the Bill of Rights actually applied to state governments, too.[6] A famous case presenting this issue, *Barron v. Baltimore*, was decided by the U.S. Supreme Court in 1833. The case is worthy of study for Chief Justice Marshall's sophisticated textual analysis and for the light it sheds on the structure of the original Constitution—the relationship between the national government and the states, and the relationship between powers and rights.

---

[6] The theory was that the Bill of Rights did not create new rights but instead simply declared what the ancient rights of English people (and thus of Americans) had always been—ancient rights that would apply against any government, whether English or American, national or state.

Barron is the first case in this book, and it provides a good occasion to consider systematically how to interpret and apply the Constitution. As you read Chief Justice Marshall's opinion, consider how he uses and prioritizes the five types of constitutional arguments noted above: (1) the text of the Constitution; (2) inferences from the structure of the Constitution and the relationship of its provisions; (3) the historical purpose that underlies a provision; (4) the use of practice or precedent that resolves ambiguities in the meaning of a provision; and (5) policy considerations.

Barron v. Baltimore

32 U.S. 243 (1833)

■ MR. CHIEF JUSTICE MARSHALL delivered the opinion of the Court.

[John Barron owned a commercial wharf in the Baltimore harbor. His ability to make money from that wharf was impaired when the City of Baltimore took actions that made the water near the wharf too shallow for most ships. Barron sued the city in the Maryland state courts, claiming that the state and city had taken his property without just compensation, in violation of the Fifth Amendment to the U.S. Constitution, which provides, in relevant part: "nor shall private property be taken for public use, without just compensation." Barron won $4,500 in the trial court, but that judgment was reversed on appeal. He then appealed to the U.S. Supreme Court.—Editors]

. . . The plaintiff in error contends that [this case] comes within that clause in the fifth amendment to the constitution, which inhibits the taking of private property for public use, without just compensation. He insists that this amendment, being in favour of the liberty of the citizen, ought to be so construed as to restrain the legislative power of a state, as well as that of the United States. If this proposition be untrue, the court can take no jurisdiction of the cause.

The question thus presented is, we think, of great importance, but not of much difficulty.

The constitution was ordained and established by the people of the United States for themselves, for their own government, and not for the government of the individual states. Each state established a constitution for itself, and, in that constitution, provided such limitations and restrictions on the powers of its particular government as its judgment dictated. The people of the United States framed such a government for the United States as they supposed best adapted to their situation, and best calculated to promote their interests. The powers they conferred on this government were to be exercised by itself; and the limitations on power, if expressed in general terms, are naturally, and, we think, necessarily applicable to the government created by the instrument. They are limitations of power granted in the instrument itself; not of distinct governments, framed by different persons and for different purposes.

 If these propositions be correct, the fifth amendment must be understood as restraining the power of the general government, not as applicable to the states. In their several constitutions they have imposed such restrictions on their respective governments as their own wisdom suggested; such as they deemed most proper for themselves. It is a subject on which they judge exclusively, and with which others interfere no farther than they are supposed to have a common interest.

The counsel for the plaintiff in error insists that the constitution was intended to secure the people of the several states against the undue exercise of power by their respective state governments; as well as against that which might be attempted by their general government. In support of this argument he relies on the inhibitions contained in the tenth section of the first article.

We think that section affords a strong if not a conclusive argument in support of the opinion already indicated by the court.

The preceding section contains restrictions which are obviously intended for the exclusive purpose of restraining the exercise of power by the departments of the general government. Some of them use language applicable only to congress: others are expressed in general terms. The third clause, for example, declares that "no bill of attainder or ex post facto law shall be passed." No language can be more general; yet the demonstration is complete that it applies solely to the government of the United States. In addition to the general arguments furnished by the instrument itself, some of which have been already suggested, the succeeding section, the avowed purpose of which is to restrain state legislation, contains in terms the very prohibition. It declares that "no state shall pass any bill of attainder or ex post facto law." This provision, then, of the ninth section, however comprehensive its language, contains no restriction on state legislation.

The ninth section having enumerated, in the nature of a bill of rights, the limitations intended to be imposed on the powers of the general government, the tenth proceeds to enumerate those which were to operate on the state legislatures. These restrictions are brought together in the same section, and are by express words applied to the states. "No state shall enter into any treaty," & c. Perceiving that in a constitution framed by the people of the United States for the government of all, no limitation of the action of government on the people would apply to the state government, unless expressed in terms; the restrictions contained in the tenth section are in direct words so applied to the states.

It is worthy of remark, too, that these inhibitions generally restrain state legislation on subjects entrusted to the general government, or in which the people of all the states feel an interest.

A state is forbidden to enter into any treaty, alliance or confederation. If these compacts are with foreign nations, they interfere with the treaty making power which is conferred entirely on the general government; if with each other, for political purposes, they can scarcely fail to interfere with the general purpose and intent of the constitution. To grant letters of marque and reprisal, would lead directly to war; the power of declaring which is expressly given to congress. To coin money is also the exercise of a power conferred on congress. It would be tedious to recapitulate the several limitations on the powers of the states which are contained in this section. They will be found, generally, to restrain state legislation on subjects entrusted to the government of the union, in which the citizens of all the states are interested. In these alone were the whole people concerned. The question of their application to states is not left to construction. It is averred in positive words.

If the original constitution, in the ninth and tenth sections of the first article, draws this plain and marked line of discrimination between the limitations it imposes on the powers of the general government, and on those of the states; if in every inhibition intended to act on state power, words are employed which directly express that intent; some strong reason must be assigned for departing from this safe and judicious course in framing the amendments, before that departure can be assumed.

We search in vain for that reason. . . . Had the people of the several states, or any of them, required changes in their constitutions; had they required additional safeguards to liberty from the apprehended encroachments of their particular governments: the remedy was in their own hands, and would have been applied by themselves. A convention would have been assembled by the discontented state, and the required improvements would have been made by itself. The unwieldy and cumbrous machinery of procuring a recommendation from two-thirds of congress, and the assent of three-fourths of their sister states, could never have occurred to any human being as a mode of doing that which might be effected by the state itself. Had the framers of these amendments intended them to be limitations on the powers of the state governments, they would have imitated the framers of the original constitution, and have expressed that intention. Had congress engaged in the extraordinary occupation of improving the constitutions of the several states by affording the people additional protection from the exercise of power by their own governments in matters which concerned themselves alone, they would have declared this purpose in plain and intelligible language.

But it is universally understood, it is a part of the history of the day, that the great revolution which established the constitution of the United States, was not effected without immense opposition. Serious fears were extensively entertained that those powers which the patriot statesmen, who then watched over the interests of our country, deemed essential to union, and to the attainment of those invaluable objects for which union was sought, might be exercised in a manner dangerous to liberty. In almost every convention by which the constitution was adopted, amendments to guard against the abuse of power were recommended. These amendments demanded security against the apprehended encroachments of the general government—not against those of the local governments.

In compliance with a sentiment thus generally expressed, to quiet fears thus extensively entertained, amendments were proposed by the required majority in congress, and adopted by the states. These amendments contain no expression indicating an intention to apply them to the state governments. This court cannot so apply them.

We are of opinion that the provision in the fifth amendment to the constitution, declaring that private property shall not be taken for public use without just compensation, is intended solely as a limitation on the exercise of power by the government of the United States, and is not applicable to the legislation of the states. We are therefore of opinion that there is no repugnancy between the several acts of the general assembly of Maryland, given in evidence by the defendants at the trial of this cause, in the court of that state, and the constitution of the United States. . . .

NOTES

1. Recall the five types of constitutional argument, which can be roughly summarized as text, structure, historical purpose, precedent and practice, and policy. Which ones does Chief Justice Marshall use in *Barron v. Baltimore*?

He does not start with the text of the Takings Clause: "[N]or shall private property be taken for public use, without just compensation." After all, the text itself does not say whether it limits state governments. (The verb is in the passive voice—"shall be taken" by whom?—a voice often frowned upon by legal writing instructors precisely because it creates ambiguity.)

Instead, after stating Barron's position, Chief Justice Marshall begins with first principles of the Constitution (as he understands them) and locates the Fifth Amendment within those principles: The Constitution was established by the people of the United States for the government of the United States as a whole, and not for the government of the individual states. The powers the Constitution confers are for this government of the nation; and the limitations on those powers, where expressed in general terms, are naturally understood to be limits on the government of the nation rather than the governments of the states. In a sense, this is an argument from the Constitution's *text*, but in the enlarged sense of seeking to ascertain the meaning the words have within the context of the entire document. One might characterize this as an argument from the Constitution's *structure*, a more inferential (and somewhat less definite) type of textual argument.

2. Next Chief Justice Marshall turns one of Barron's arguments around on him as a *textual argument*. Barron had said (in effect): "look here, the Constitution does sometimes limit state governments—look at Article I, Section 10." Chief Justice Marshall responds by pointing out the differences between Article I, *Section 9* and Article I, *Section 10*. Section 9 limits the powers of the national government. Several times, its prohibitions are stated in general terms. But each time they limit the power of only the national government. Chief Justice Marshall notes that some of these limitations are repeated in Section 10 as limitations on the powers of the states. But whenever the limitations are meant to apply to the states, the Constitution says so specifically: "No state shall."

This argument is central to Chief Justice Marshall's analysis and merits careful attention. Reread carefully Sections 9 and 10 of Article I and look at their context. Note that Section 9—limiting congressional power—appears right after Section 8, which has eighteen clauses, each granting Congress a power. Note also that Article I, Section 10 forbids the states from doing things over which the Constitution appears to give the federal government *exclusive* power. Thus Article I, Section 10 forbids the states from waging war or making treaties—powers that are exclusively federal. But it does not forbid the states from imposing and collecting taxes, even though Section 8 allows Congress to do this. The power of taxation is thus a concurrent power—a power that the states and the federal government may exercise separately.

Chief Justice Marshall notes that each prohibition on the states in Article I, Section 10 begins with the words "No State shall." The limits on Congress in Article I, Section 9 appear with no label limiting them to Congress. He then looks at the Bill of Rights and notes that none of the first eight amendments contain the "No State shall" formula. He concludes that the prohibitions in the Bill of Rights are more like those in Article I, Section 9 than they are like those in Article I, Section 10. Accordingly, he concludes that the Bill of Rights applies only to the federal government and not to the states.

Note how, in making this textual argument, Chief Justice Marshall does not read the words of the Fifth Amendment in isolation, but takes into account their relationship to other provisions of the Constitution. He reads the words in the context of the entire document. Do his arguments from text and structure persuade you? What would you guess might be the strengths and weaknesses of these types of constitutional arguments?

(An aside from later constitutional history: The framers of the Fourteenth Amendment took Chief Justice Marshall's reasoning into account and included these words in that amendment: "*No State shall* make or enforce any law which shall abridge the privileges or immunities of citizens of the United States; *nor shall any State* deprive any person of life, liberty, or property without due process of law; nor deny to any person the equal protection of the laws." Mimicking Article I, Section 10's prohibitions made clear that the Fourteenth Amendment was directed at abridgment of civil rights by states.)

3. Chief Justice Marshall also turns to evidence of *historical purpose* to buttress his textual and structural arguments. It is "part of the history of the day"—well understood by all, he says—that the Bill of Rights was added to limit the actions of the national government, not out of a concern over the actions of the state governments. He says, quite rightly, that the immediate intent of the framers of the Bill of Rights was to limit the power of the national government rather than that of the states. What do you think the strengths and weaknesses might be of appeals to the historical purpose behind a constitutional provision?

A variation is an argument that identifies the purpose of a provision at a fairly high level of abstraction and then applies that more abstract purpose in different circumstances. One might have said in *Barron*, for example, (1) the purpose of the Bill of Rights in 1791 was to protect certain liberties; (2) therefore the Bill of Rights is about protecting liberty; (3) this purpose would be served by construing the Bill of Rights to apply against the states; (4) therefore the Bill of Rights does in fact apply against the states. What do you think are the strengths and weaknesses of this sort of argument?

4. Largely absent from *Barron* is any argument from *precedent and practice*. There are no arguments from case law in *Barron* because it appears to have presented a question of first impression in 1833. Of course, the mere fact that no one tried to argue that the Bill of Rights bound the states during the first forty-two years of its existence strongly suggests that it did not do so. For this reason, Chief Justice Marshall does seem to be aware that applying the Bill of Rights to the states would be a greater change than holding that it applies only to the federal government. Even though they do not appear in *Barron*, these kinds of precedential argument are important for constitutional interpretation. For example, when does a long series of judicial precedents or longstanding practice by the legislative or executive branch determine the meaning of the Constitution? These questions will be considered in many of the following cases.

5. Finally, Chief Justice Marshall makes a policy argument: It would be cumbersome to have state officials bound by the federal Bill of Rights because the whole country would have to agree pursuant to Article V if a state changed its mind about wanting to be bound by a right. How much simpler, he says, to let each state be bound only by its own Bill of Rights. Such a system encourages the states to compete and experiment with one another to produce optimal levels and kinds of protections for liberty. (As it happens, Chief Justice Marshall's policy argument has not been widely accepted. The conventional wisdom in constitutional law is that state governments often insufficiently protect minority rights, and that some minimum level of fundamental rights should be pro-

tected uniformly throughout the country.) The policy argument made by Chief Justice Marshall sounds in pragmatism, but other policy arguments draw on theories of justice or the natural law tradition. What are the strengths and weaknesses of policy arguments in constitutional interpretation?

6. As you think about the types of constitutional argument, consider the characteristics of federal judges. They are trained as lawyers, and once appointed they remain on the bench for life. Do these facts affect which types of constitutional argument are most legitimate for judges? Do they affect which types of argument judges are most likely to use skillfully?

[*Assignment 4*]

II. EARLY CONTROVERSIES UNDER THE CONSTITUTION

Not surprisingly, the first dozen years under the new Constitution of the United States (1789–1801) generated fundamental questions about its meaning and application. Some of the most famous ones are considered here. These are *not* presented as historical background. Instead, these controversies are a way of introducing questions about constitutional law and interpretation that are inevitable and that even today, in various forms, are mainstays of the Supreme Court's docket. These questions include federal versus state power, war, race, freedom of speech, and the authority to decide the meaning of the Constitution.

Four early controversies are considered, and each began in the 1790s:

(1) The question of Congress's power to create a "Bank of the United States."

(2) The power and duties of the federal government with respect to slavery.

(3) The Neutrality Controversy involving war and foreign affairs.

(4) The Alien and Sedition Acts of 1798 and the resolutions by two states that declared those federal statutes unconstitutional.

A. THE FIRST BANK OF THE UNITED STATES

One of the earliest and most persistent constitutional controversies of the young republic concerned the power of Congress to incorporate a "Bank of the United States" for developing the country's financial system. The fight over the constitutionality of the Bank of the United States went on from 1791, when the Bank was created, until the 1830s, when it was abolished by President Andrew Jackson. The Bank was a federally chartered corporation governed by private directors. It could receive deposits, provide savings accounts, manage trusts, and issue "reserve notes"—paper notes supported by deposits on reserve with the Bank. These reserve notes functioned as a form of paper currency before the printing of dollar bills, which did not begin in the United States until the Civil War.

The creation of the Bank was a cornerstone of Secretary of the Treasury Alexander Hamilton's ambitious economic plans to transform the United States from a nation of farmers into a commercial power. Hamilton drew inspiration from the huge success enjoyed by the first central government bank, the Bank of England, which had been created in 1694 and which over the next century made England the world's financial leader. Thomas Jefferson, James Madison, and the other leaders of the nascent Democratic–

Republican Party wanted America to remain an agrarian society and were suspicious, and even contemptuous, of commerce. A career in business, producing goods for consumers, was considered unworthy of gentlemen. Jefferson and Madison thought land ownership promoted civic virtue and concern for the long-term interest of the country. The fight over the Bank was thus not only a constitutional dispute but also, at least in the minds of those waging it, a social one: a fight over what kind of nation America would become.

Read the enumeration of Congress's legislative powers in Article I, Section 8 of the Constitution. Does Congress have power to charter a corporation for a "Bank of the United States"? To charter any corporations at all? Which enumerated power most plausibly supports such an enactment? Think through the issue on your own, before you read the conflicting opinions that President George Washington received. As you are engaging in this exercise, ask yourself: How should the Constitution be interpreted?

* * *

You may be interested to know before you read the following materials that the Constitutional Convention of 1787 specifically considered whether to give Congress the enumerated power to charter or incorporate entities. This had been a power of the king of England, and the king had chartered at one point or another all of the thirteen original colonies. After independence, the states chartered corporations. There were at this time no general incorporation laws, and so corporate charters were handed out one at a time as government grants. Delegates to the Convention debated whether to give Congress a power to charter corporations, especially to deal with matters that the states could not handle on their own. At the time Madison favored giving Congress such a power, but doing so would have raised opposition to ratification from the New York and Philadelphia commercial interests who feared new competitors. Accordingly, no specific enumerated power was written into the Constitution. A proposal to instead give Congress power to charter corporations for the construction of canals was voted down eight to three. As you will see, Jefferson alludes to this fact in his opinion. (Even though Jefferson was not himself present at the Convention, and the Convention's proceedings were unpublished and supposedly secret, he apparently knew of these debates from Madison, his close friend and political ally.)

The bill creating the Bank passed Congress and was sent to President Washington for his signature or veto. Because of the controversy in Congress over whether the Bank was constitutional, President Washington asked for the opinions of Attorney General Edmund Randolph, Secretary of State Jefferson, and Secretary of the Treasury Hamilton on the constitutional issue. Randolph and Jefferson thought the Bank was unconstitutional. Hamilton defended it. President Washington ended up siding with Hamilton and signed the bill. Was President Washington right to take a position on the constitutionality of the Bank before signing it into law? In the selections below from Madison, Jefferson, and Hamilton, who do you think gets the better of the argument? (Note that the selections are not in strict chronological order, but instead they begin with the contribution by Madison to the congressional debate, which is then followed by the deliberations within the executive branch.)

Representative Madison, Speech
on the Constitutionality of the Bank

The House of Representatives, February 2, 1791

Mr. Madison:

[Initial comments on the policy of the bill are omitted.—Editors]

. . . In making these remarks on the merits of the bill, he had reserved to himself, he said, the right to deny the authority of Congress to pass it. He had entertained this opinion from the date of the Constitution. His impression might perhaps be the stronger because he well recollected that a power to grant charters of incorporation had been proposed in the general convention and rejected.

Is the power of establishing an *incorporated bank* among the powers vested by the Constitution in the legislature of the United States? This is the question to be examined. After some general remarks on the limitations of all political power, he took notice of the peculiar manner in which the federal government is limited. It is not a general grant, out of which particular powers are excepted—it is a grant of particular powers only, leaving the general mass in other hands. So it had been understood by its friends and its foes, and so it was to be interpreted.

As preliminaries to a right interpretation, he laid down the following rules:

An interpretation that destroys the very characteristic of the government cannot be just.

Where a meaning is clear, the consequences, whatever they may be, are to be admitted—where doubtful, it is fairly triable by its consequences.

In controverted cases, the meaning of the parties to the instrument, if to be collected by reasonable evidence, is a proper guide.

Cotemporary and concurrent expositions are reasonable evidence of the meaning of the parties.

In admitting or rejecting a constructive authority, not only the degree of its incidentality to an express authority is to be regarded, but the degree of its importance also, since on this will depend the probability or improbability of its being left to construction.

Reviewing the Constitution with an eye to these positions, it was not possible to discover in it the power to incorporate a Bank. The only clauses under which such a power could be pretended, are either—1. The power to lay and collect taxes to pay the debts and provide for the common defence and general welfare; Or, 2. The power to borrow money on the credit of the United States; Or, 3. The power to pass all laws necessary and proper to carry into execution those powers.

The bill did not come within the first power. It laid no tax to pay the debts, or provide for the general welfare. It laid no tax whatever. It was altogether foreign to the subject.

No argument could be drawn from the terms "common defence and general welfare." The power as to these general purposes was limited to acts laying taxes for them; and the general purposes themselves were limited and explained by the particular enumeration subjoined. To understand these terms in any sense that would justify the power in question would give to Congress an unlimited power; would render nugatory the enumeration of particular powers; would supercede all the powers reserved to the state governments. These terms are copied from the Articles of Confederation; had it ever been pretended that they were to be understood otherwise than as here explained?

It had been said that "general welfare" meant cases in which a general power might be exercised by Congress without interfering with the powers of the States; and that the establishment of a National Bank was of this sort. There were, he said, several answers to this novel doctrine.

1. The proposed Bank would interfere so as indirectly to defeat a State Bank at the same place. 2. It would directly interfere with the rights of the states *to prohibit* as well as to establish banks and the circulation of bank notes. He mentioned a law of Virginia, actually prohibiting the circulation of notes payable to bearer. 3. Interference with the power of the states was no constitutional criterion of the power of Congress. If the power was not given, Congress could not exercise it; if given, they might exercise it, altho it should interfere with the laws or even the constitution of the states. 4. If Congress could incorporate a Bank, merely because the act would leave the states free to establish banks also, any other incorporations might be made by Congress. They could incorporate companies of manufacturers, or companies for cutting canals, or even religious societies, leaving similar incorporations by the states, like state banks, to themselves. Congress might even establish religious teachers in every parish and pay them out of the Treasury of the United States, leaving other teachers unmolested in their functions. These inadmissible consequences condemned the controverted principle.

The case of the Bank established by the former Congress had been cited as a precedent. This was known, he said, to have been the child of necessity. It never could be justified by the regular powers of the Articles of Confederation. Congress betrayed a consciousness of this in recommending to the states to incorporate the Bank also. They did not attempt to protect the Bank Notes by penalties against counterfeiters. These were reserved wholly to the authority of the states.

The second clause to be examined is that which empowers Congress to borrow money. Is this a bill to borrow money? It does not borrow a shilling. Is there any fair construction by which the bill can be deemed an exercise of the power to borrow money? The obvious meaning of the power to borrow money is that of accepting it from and stipulating payments to those who are *able* and *willing* to lend.

To say that the power to borrow involves a power of creating the ability, where there may be the will, to lend is not only establishing a dangerous principle, as will be immediately shewn, but is as forced a construction as to say that it involves the power of compelling the will, where there may be the ability, to lend.

The third clause is that which gives the power to pass all laws necessary and proper to execute the specified powers.

Whatever meaning this clause may have, none can be admitted that would give an unlimited discretion to Congress.

Its meaning must, according to the natural and obvious force of the terms and the context, be limited to means *necessary* to the *end* and *incident* to the *nature* of the specified powers.

The clause is in fact merely declaratory of what would have resulted by unavoidable implication, as the appropriate, and as it were, technical means of executing those powers. In this sense it had been explained by the friends of the Constitution and ratified by the state conventions.

The essential characteristic of the government, as composed of limited and enumerated powers, would be destroyed: If instead of direct and incidental means, any means could be used which, in the language of the preamble to the bill, "might be conceived to be conducive to the successful conducting of the finances; or might be *conceived* to *tend* to give *facility* to the obtaining of loans." He urged an attention to the diffuse and ductile terms which had been found requisite to cover the stretch of power contained in the bill. He compared them with the terms *necessary* and *proper,* used in the Constitution, and asked whether it was possible to view the two descriptions as synonimous, or the one as a fair and safe commentary on the other.

If, proceeded he, Congress, by virtue of the power to borrow, can create the means of lending, and in pursuance of these means, can incorporate a Bank, they may do any thing whatever creative of like means.

The East–India Company has been a lender to the British government, as well as the Bank, and the South–Sea Company is a greater creditor than either. Congress then may incorporate similar companies in the United States, and that too not under the idea of regulating trade, but under that of borrowing money.

Private capitals are the chief resources for loans to the British government. Whatever then may be conceived to favor the accumulation of capitals may be done by Congress. They may incorporate manufactures. They may give monopolies in every branch of domestic industry.

If, again, Congress by virtue of the power to borrow money can create the ability to lend, they may by virtue of the power to levy money create the ability to pay it. The ability to pay taxes depends on the general wealth of the society, and this on the general prosperity of agriculture, manufactures and commerce. Congress then may give bounties and make regulations on all of these objects.

The states have, it is allowed on all hands, a concurrent right to lay and collect taxes. This power is secured to them not by its being expressly reserved, but by its not being ceded by the Constitution. The reasons for the bill cannot be admitted because they would invalidate that right; why may it not be *conceived* by Congress that a uniform and exclusive imposition of taxes would, not less than the proposed Banks, be *conducive* to the successful conducting of the national finances, and *tend* to *give facility* to the obtaining of revenue, for the use of the government?

The doctrine of implication is always a tender one. The danger of it has been felt in other governments. The delicacy was felt in the adoption of our own; the danger may also be felt, if we do not keep close to our chartered authorities.

Mark the reasoning on which the validity of the bill depends. To borrow money is made the *end* and the accumulation of capitals *implied* as the *means.* The accumulation of capitals is then the *end* and a bank *implied* as the *means.* The bank is then the *end* and a charter of incorporation, a monopoly, capital punishments, etc. *implied* as the *means.*

If implications thus remote and thus multiplied can be linked together, a chain may be formed that will reach every object of legislation, every object within the whole compass of political economy.

The latitude of interpretation required by the bill is condemned by the rule furnished by the constitution itself.

Congress have power "to regulate the value of money"; yet it is expressly added, not left to be implied, that counterfeitors may be punished.

They have the power "to declare war," to which armies are more incident than incorporated Banks to borrowing; yet is expressly added, the power "to raise and support armies"; and to this again, the express power "to make rules and regulations for the government of armies"; a like remark is applicable to the powers as to a navy.

The regulation and calling out of the militia are more appurtenant to war than the proposed bank to borrowing; yet the former is not left to construction.

The very power to borrow money is a less remote implication from the power of war than an incorporated monopoly bank from the power of borrowing—yet the power to borrow is not left to implication.

It is not pretended that every insertion or omission in the constitution is the effect of systematic attention. This is not the character of any human work, particularly the work of a body of men. The examples cited, with others that might be added, sufficiently inculcate nevertheless a rule of interpretation very different from that on which the bill rests. They condemn the exercise of any power, particularly a great and important power, which is not evidently and necessarily involved in an express power.

It cannot be denied that the power proposed to be exercised is an important power.

As a charter of incorporation the bill creates an artificial person previously not existing in law. It confers important civil rights and attributes which could not otherwise be claimed. It is, though not precisely similar, at least equivalent to the naturalization of an alien, by which certain new civil characters are acquired by him. Would Congress have had the power to naturalize if it had not been expressly given?

In the power to make bylaws, the bill delegated a sort of legislative power, which is unquestionably an act of a high and important nature. He took notice of the only restraint on the bylaws, that they were not to be contrary to the law and the constitution of the bank; and asked what law was intended; if the law of the United States, the scantiness of their code would give a power never before given to a corporation—and obnoxious to the states, whose laws would then be superceded not only by the laws of Congress, but by the bylaws of a corporation within their own jurisdiction. If the law intended was the law of the state, then the state might make laws that would destroy an institution of the United States.

The bill gives a power to purchase and hold lands; Congress themselves could not purchase lands within a state "without the consent of its legislature." How could they delegate a power to others which they did not possess themselves?

It takes from our successors, who have equal rights with ourselves, and with the aid of experience will be more capable of deciding on the subject, an opportunity of exercising that right for an immoderate term.

It takes from our constituents the opportunity of deliberating on the untried measure, although their hands are also to be tied by it for the same term.

It involves a monopoly, which affects the equal rights of every citizen.

It leads to a penal regulation, perhaps capital punishments, one of the most solemn acts of sovereign authority.

From this view of the power of incorporation exercised in the bill, it could never be deemed an accessary or subaltern power, to be deduced by implication, as a means of executing another power; it was in its nature a distinct, an independent and substantive prerogative, which not being enumerated in the Constitution could never have been meant to be included in it, and not being included could never be rightfully exercised.

He here adverted to a distinction which he said had not been sufficiently kept in view, between a power necessary and proper for the government or union and a power necessary and proper for executing the enumerated powers. In the latter case, the powers included in each of the enumerated powers were not expressed, but to be drawn from the nature of each. In the former, the powers composing the government were expressly enumerated. This constituted the peculiar nature of the government; no power therefore not enumerated could be inferred from the general nature of government. Had the power of making treaties, for example, been omitted, however necessary it might have been, the defect could only have been lamented or supplied by an amendment of the Constitution.

But the proposed bank could not even be called necessary to the government; at most it could be but convenient. Its uses to the government could be supplied by keeping the taxes a little in advance—by loans from individuals—by the other banks over which the government would have equal command, nay greater, as it may grant or refuse to these the privilege, made a free and irrevocable gift to the proposed bank, of using their notes in the federal revenue.

He proceeded next to the cotemporary expositions given to the Constitution.

The defence against the charge founded on the want of a bill of rights presupposed, he said, that the powers not given were retained and that those given were not to be extended by remote implications. On any other supposition, the power of Congress to abridge the freedom of the press, or the rights of conscience, etc. could not have been disproved.

The explanations in the state conventions all turned on the same fundamental principle, and on the principle that the terms necessary and proper gave no additional powers to those enumerated. (Here he read sundry passages from the debates of the Pennsylvania, Virginia and North–Carolina conventions, shewing the grounds on which the Constitution had been vindicated by its principal advocates against a dangerous latitude of its powers, charged on it by its opponents.) He did not undertake to vouch for the accuracy or authenticity of the publications which he quoted—he thought it probable that the sentiments delivered might in many instances have been mistaken or imperfectly noted; but the complexion of the whole, with what he himself and many others must recollect, fully justified the use he had made of them.

The explanatory declarations and amendments accompanying the ratifications of the several states formed a striking evidence wearing the same complexion. He referred those who might doubt on the subject to the several acts of ratification.

The explanatory amendments proposed by Congress themselves, at least, would be good authority with them; all these renunciations of power proceeded on a rule of construction excluding the latitude now contended for. These explanations were the more to be respected, as they had not only been proposed by Congress, but ratified by nearly three-fourths of the states. He read several of the articles proposed, remarking particularly on the 11th and 12th *[our 9th and 10th—Editors]*: the former, as guarding against a latitude of interpretation—the latter, as excluding every source of power not within the constitution itself.

With all this evidence of the sense in which the Constitution was understood and adopted, will it not be said, if the bill should pass, that its adoption was brought about by one set of arguments and that it is now administered under the influence of another set; and this reproach will have the keener sting, because it is applicable to so many individuals concerned in both the adoption and administration.

In fine, if the power were in the Constitution, the immediate exercise of it cannot be essential—if not there, the exercise of it involves the guilt of usurpation, and establishes a precedent of interpretation leveling all the barriers which limit the powers of the general government and protect those of the state governments. If the point be doubtful only, respect for ourselves, who ought to shun the appearance of precipitancy and ambition; respect for our successors, who ought not lightly to be deprived of the opportunity of exercising the rights of legislation; respect for our constituents who have had no opportunity of making known their sentiments and who are themselves to be bound down to the measure for so long a period: all these considerations require that the irrevocable decision should at least be suspended until another session.

It appeared on the whole, he concluded, that the power exercised by the bill was condemned by the silence of the Constitution; was condemned by the rule of interpretation arising out of the Constitution; was condemned by its tendency to destroy the main characteristic of the Constitution; was condemned by the expositions of the friends of the Constitution whilst depending before the public; was condemned by the apparent intention of the parties which ratified the Constitution; was condemned by the explanatory amendments proposed by Congress themselves to the Constitution; and he hoped it would receive its final condemnation, by the vote of this house.

Secretary of State Jefferson, Opinion on the Constitutionality of the Bank

February 15, 1791

. . . I consider the foundation of the Constitution as laid on this ground: That "all powers not delegated to the United States, by the Constitution, nor prohibited by it to the States, are reserved to the States or to the people." [Tenth Amendment.] To take a single step beyond the boundaries thus specially drawn around the powers of Congress, is to take possession of a boundless field of power, no longer susceptible of any definition.

The incorporation of a bank, and the powers assumed by this bill, have not, in my opinion, been delegated to the United States, by the Constitution.

I. They are not among the powers specially enumerated: for these are:

1st. A power to lay taxes for the purpose of paying the debts of the United States; but no debt is paid by this bill, nor any tax laid. Were it a bill to raise money, its origination in the Senate would condemn it by the Constitution.

2d. "To borrow money." But this bill neither borrows money nor ensures the borrowing it. The proprietors of the bank will be just as free as any other money holders, to lend or not to lend their money to the public. The operation proposed in the bill first, to lend them two millions, and then to borrow them back again, cannot change the nature of the latter act, which will still be a payment, and not a loan, call it by what name you please.

3d. To "regulate commerce with foreign nations, and among the States, and with the Indian tribes." To erect a bank, and to regulate commerce, are very different acts. He who erects a bank, creates a subject of commerce in its bills, so does he who makes a bushel of wheat, or digs a dollar out of the mines; yet neither of these persons regulates commerce thereby. To make a thing which may be bought and sold, is not to prescribe regulations for buying and selling. Besides, if this was an exercise of the power of regulating commerce, it would be void, as extending as much to the internal commerce of every State, as to its external. For the power given to Congress by the Constitution does not extend to the internal regulation of the commerce of a State, (that is to say of the commerce between citizen and citizen,) which remain exclusively with its own legislature; but to its external commerce only, that is to say, its commerce with another State, or with foreign nations, or with the Indian tribes. Accordingly the bill does not propose the measure as a regulation of trade, but as "productive of considerable advantages to trade." Still less are these powers covered by any other of the special enumerations.

II. Nor are they within either of the general phrases, which are the two following:

1st. To lay taxes to provide for the general welfare of the United States, that is to say, "to lay taxes for *the purpose of* providing for the general welfare." For the laying of taxes is the *power*, and the general welfare the *purpose* for which the power is to be exercised. They are not to lay taxes *ad libitum for any purpose they please*; but only *to pay the debts or provide for the welfare of the Union*. In like manner, they are not *to do anything they please* to provide for the general welfare, but only to *lay taxes* for that purpose. To consider the latter phrase, not as describing the purpose of the first, but as giving a distinct and independent power to do any act they please, which might be for the good of the Union, would render all the preceding and subsequent enumerations of power completely useless.

It would reduce the whole instrument to a single phrase, that of instituting a Congress with power to do whatever would be for the good of the United States; and, as they would be the sole judges of the good or evil, it would be also a power to do whatever evil they please.

It is an established rule of construction where a phrase will bear either of two meanings, to give it that which will allow some meaning to the other parts of the instrument, and not that which would render all the others useless. Certainly no such universal power was meant to be given them. It was intended to lace them up straitly within the enumerated powers, and those without which, as means, these powers could not be carried into effect. It is known that the very power now proposed *as a means* was rejected as *an end* by the Convention which formed the Constitution. A proposition was made to them to authorize Congress to open canals, and an amendatory one to empower them to incorporate. But the whole was rejected, and one of the reasons for rejection urged in debate was, that then they would have a power to erect a bank, which would render the great cities, where there were prejudices and jealousies on the subject, adverse to the reception of the Constitution.

2. The second general phrase is, "to make all laws *necessary* and proper for carrying into execution the enumerated powers." But they can all be carried into execution without a bank. A bank therefore is not *necessary*, and consequently not authorized by this phrase.

It has been urged that a bank will give great facility or convenience in the collection of taxes, Suppose this were true: yet the Constitution allows only the means which are "*necessary*," not those which are merely "convenient" for effecting the enumerated powers. If such a latitude of construction be allowed to this phrase as to give any non-enumerated power, it will go to everyone, for there is not one which ingenuity may not torture into a *convenience* in some instance *or other*, to *some one* of so long a list of enumerated powers. It would swallow up all the delegated powers, and reduce the whole to one power, as before observed. Therefore it was that the Constitution restrained them to the *necessary* means, that is to say, to those means without which the grant of power would be nugatory. . . .

The negative of the President [the veto] is the shield provided by the Constitution to protect against the invasions of the legislature. . . . The present is the case of a right remaining exclusively with the States, and consequently one of those intended by the Constitution to be placed under its protection. . . .

It must be added, however, that unless the President's mind on a view of everything which is urged for and against this bill, is tolerably clear that it is unauthorized by the Constitution; if the pro and the con hang so even as to balance his judgment, a just respect for the wisdom of the legislature would naturally decide the balance in favor of their opinion. It is chiefly for cases where they are clearly misled by error, ambition, or interest, that the Constitution has placed a check in the negative of the President.

————

After receiving Secretary of State Jefferson's opinion and a similar report from the attorney general, President Washington wrote the following in a letter to Secretary of the Treasury Hamilton:

An act to incorporate the Subscribers to the Bank of the United States' is now before my consideration. The constitutionality of it is objected to. It therefore becomes more particularly my duty to examine the ground on w[hi]ch the objection is built. As a means of investigation I have called upon the Attorney General . . . [whose] report is, that the Constitution does not warrant the Act. I then applied to the Secretary of State for his sentiments on the subject. These coincide with the Attorney Generals. . . . I now require, in like manner, yours on the validity & propriety of the above recited Act.

Hamilton responded with the following report.

Secretary of the Treasury Hamilton, Opinion on the Constitutionality of the Bank

February 23, 1791

The Secretary of the Treasury having perused with attention the papers containing the opinions of the Secretary of State and Attorney General, concerning the constitutionality of the bill for establishing a National Bank, proceeds, according to the order of the President, to submit the reasons which have induced him to entertain a different opinion.

It will naturally have been anticipated, that in performing this task, he would feel uncommon solicitude. Personal considerations alone, arising from the reflection that the measure [the proposal to create a Bank] originated with him [Hamilton], would be sufficient to produce it. The sense which he [Hamilton] has manifested of the great importance of such an institution to the successful administration of the department under his particular care, and an expectation of serious ill consequences to result from a failure of the measure, do not permit him to be without anxiety on public accounts. But the chief solicitude arises from a firm persuasion, that principles of construction like those espoused by the Secretary of State and Attorney General, would be fatal to the just and indispensable authority of the United States.

In entering upon the argument, it ought to be premised that the objections of the Secretary of State and Attorney General are founded on a general denial of the authority of the United States to erect corporations. The latter, indeed, expressly admits, that if there be anything in the bill which is not warranted by the Constitution, it is the clause of incorporation.

Now it appears to the Secretary of the Treasury that this general principle is inherent in the very definition of government, and essential to every step of progress to be made by that of the United States, namely: That every power vested in a government is in its nature sovereign, and includes, by force of the term, a right to employ all the means requisite and fairly applicable to the attainment of the ends of such power, and which are not precluded by restrictions and exceptions specified in the Constitution, or not immoral, or not contrary to the essential ends of political society.

This principle, in its application to government in general, would be admitted as an axiom; and it will be incumbent upon those who may incline to deny it, to prove a distinction, and to show that a rule which, in the general system of things, is essential to the preservation of the social order, is inapplicable to the United States.

The circumstance that the powers of sovereignty are in this country divided between the National and State governments, does not afford the distinction required. It does not follow from this, that each of the portion of powers delegated to the one or to the other, is not sovereign with regard to its proper objects. It will only follow from it, that each has sovereign power as to certain things, and not as to other things. To deny that the government of the United States has sovereign power, as to its declared purposes and trusts, because its power does not extend to all cases would be equally to deny that the State governments have sovereign power in any case, because their power does not extend to every case. The tenth section of the first article of the Constitution exhibits a long list of very important things which they may not do. And thus the United States would furnish the singular spectacle of a political society without sovereignty, or of a people governed, without government.

If it would be necessary to bring proof to a proposition so clear, as that which affirms that the powers of the federal government, as to its objects, were sovereign, there is a clause of its Constitution which would be decisive. It is that which declares that the Constitution, and the laws of the United States made in pursuance of it, and all treaties made, or which shall be made, under their authority, shall be the supreme law of the land. The power which can create the supreme law of the land in any case, is doubtless sovereign as to such case.

This general and indisputable principle puts at once an end to the abstract question, whether the United States have power to erect a corporation; that is to say, to give a legal or artificial capacity to one or more persons, distinct from the natural. For it is unquestionably incident to sovereign power to erect corporations, and consequently to that of the United States, in relation to the objects intrusted to the management of the government. The difference is this: where the authority of the government is general, it can create corporations in all cases, where it is confined to certain branches of legislation, it can create corporations only in those cases. . . .

To this mode of reasoning respecting the right of employing all the means requisite to the execution of the specified powers of the government, it is objected, that none but necessary and proper means are to be employed; and the Secretary of State maintains, that no means are to be considered as necessary but those without which the grant of the power would be nugatory. Nay, so far does he go in his restrictive interpretation of the word, as even to make the case of necessity which shall warrant the constitutional exercise of the power to depend on casual and temporary circumstances; an idea which alone refutes the construction. The expediency of exercising a particular power, at a particular time, must, indeed depend on circumstances, but the constitutional right of exercising it must be uniform and invariable, the same to-day as to-morrow. . . .

It is certain that neither the grammatical nor popular sense of the term requires that construction. According to both, necessary often means no more than needful, requisite, incidental, useful, or conducive to. It is a common mode of expression to say, that it is necessary for a government or a person to do this or that thing, when nothing more is intended or understood, than that the interests of the government or person require, or will be promoted by, the doing of this or that thing. The imagination can be at no loss for exemplifications of the use of the word in this sense. And it is the true one in which it is to be understood as used in the Constitution. The whole turn of the clause containing it indicates, that it was the intent of the Convention, by that clause, to give a liberal latitude to the exercise of the specified powers. The expressions have peculiar comprehensiveness. They are thought to make all laws necessary and proper for carrying into execution the foregoing powers, and all other powers vested by the Constitution in the government of the United States, or in any department or officer thereof.

To understand the word as the Secretary of State does, would be to depart from its obvious and popular sense, and to give it a restrictive operation, an idea never before entertained. It would be to give it the same force as if the word absolutely or indispensably had been prefixed to it.

Such a construction would beget endless uncertainty and embarrassment. The cases must be palpable and extreme, in which it could be pronounced, with certainty, that a measure was absolutely necessary, or one, without which, the exercise of a given power would be nugatory. There are few measures of any government which would stand so severe a test. To insist upon it, would be to make the criterion of the exercise of any implied power, a case of extreme necessity; which is rather a rule to justify the overleaping of the bounds of constitutional authority, than to govern the ordinary exercise of it. . . .

This restrictive interpretation of the word necessary is also contrary to this sound maxim of construction, namely, that the powers contained in a constitution of government, especially those which concern the general administration of the affairs of a country, its finances, trade, defense, etc., ought to be construed liberally in advancement of the public good. This rule does not depend on the particular form of a government, or on the particular demarcation of the boundaries of its powers, but on the nature and object of government itself. The means by which national exigencies are to be provided for, national inconveniences obviated, national prosperity promoted, are of such infinite variety, extent, and complexity, that there must of necessity be great latitude of discretion in the selection and application of those means. Hence, consequently, the necessity and propriety of exercising the authorities intrusted to a government on principles of liberal construction. . . .

It is no valid objection to the doctrine to say, that it is calculated to extend the power of the government throughout the entire sphere of State legislation. The same thing has been said, and may be said, with regard to every exercise of power by implication or construction.

The moment the literal meaning is departed from, there is a chance of error and abuse. And yet an adherence to the letter of its powers would at once arrest the motions of government. It is not only agreed, on all hands, that the exercise of constructive powers is indispensable, but every act which has been passed, is more or less an exemplification of it. One has been already mentioned that relating to lighthouses, etc. that which declares the power of the President to remove officers at pleasure, acknowledges the same truth in another and a signal instance.

The truth is, that difficulties on this point are inherent in the nature of the Federal Constitution; they result inevitably from a division of the legislative power. The consequence of this division is, that there will be cases clearly within the power of the national government; others, clearly without its powers; and a third class, which will leave room for controversy and difference of opinion, and concerning which a reasonable latitude of judgment must be allowed.

But the doctrine which is contended for is not chargeable with the consequences imputed to it. It does not affirm that the national government is sovereign in all respects, but that it is sovereign to a certain extent; that is, to the extent of the objects of its specified powers.

It leaves, therefore, a criterion of what is constitutional, and of what is not so. This criterion is the end, to which the measure relates as a mean. If the end be clearly comprehended within any of the specified powers, and if the measure have an obvious relation to that end, and is not forbidden by any particular provision of the Constitution, it may safely be deemed to come within the compass of the national authority. There is also this further criterion, which may materially assist the decision: Does the proposed measure abridge a pre-existing right of any State or of any individual? If it does not, there is a strong presumption in favor of its constitutionality, and slighter relations to any declared object of the Constitution may be permitted to turn the scale. . . .

A hope is entertained that it has, by this time, been made to appear, to the satisfaction of the President, that a bank has a natural relation to the power of collecting taxes—to that of regulating trade—to that of providing for the common defense and that, as the bill under consideration contemplates the government in the light of a joint proprietor of the stock of the bank, it brings the case within the provision of the clause of the Constitution which immediately respects the property of the United States.

Under a conviction that such a relation subsists, the Secretary of the Treasury, with all deference, conceives that it will result as a necessary consequence from the position that all the special powers of government are sovereign, as to the proper objects that the incorporation of a bank is a constitutional measure, and that the objections taken to the bill, in this respect, are ill-founded. . . .

The Bank of the United States, 1791 to 1832

President Washington sided with Hamilton and signed the bill to charter the Bank for twenty years (from 1791 to 1811). By 1811, the political scene had changed markedly. Washington and Hamilton were dead, Jefferson was a former president, and his closest friend Madison was president. The Jeffersonians were riding high in Congress and in the government. A bill was proposed in 1811 to create a Second Bank of the United States for another twenty years but was voted down. Apparently, twenty years of practice begun by President Washington and the First Congress had not yet, in 1811, settled the issue of the constitutionality of the Bank in everyone's minds.

In 1816, Congress changed course and voted to recharter the Bank for another twenty years because of economic problems growing out of the War of 1812. President Madison vetoed the Second Bank bill for policy reasons while stating explicitly that he thought the constitutional question had been settled in favor of the Bank by practice and precedent. Madison said that he was waiving "the question of the constitutional authority of the Legislature to establish an incorporated bank, as being precluded, in my judgment, by the repeated recognition under varied circumstances of the validity of such an institution, in acts of the Legislative, Executive, and Judicial branches of the Government, accompanied by indications, in different modes, of a concurrence of the general will of the nation." (Note that as a member of the House in the First Congress, Madison had opposed the Bank's constitutionality!) Within a year, another Bank bill was presented to President Madison and this time he signed it, creating the Second Bank of the United States, which existed from 1816 to 1836 (another twenty-year term).

It is worth pausing here to think about the implications of these events for the project of constitutional interpretation. If Congress considers and vigorously debates the constitutionality of a bill, and decides that the bill is constitutional and passes it, does that settle the constitutional issue for a future Congress? Did the acceptance of the Bank's constitutionality by President Washington oblige President Madison to accept it, despite his prior views? Does the existence of the Bank for a number of years settle the question of its constitutionality? As a general proposition, if the Constitution says one thing but practice under the Constitution has diverged, which one is controlling?

Several states responded to the 1816 re-creation of the Bank of the United States with opposition. In particular, Maryland imposed a special tax on the Bank that did not apply to any other banks doing business in the state. The Supreme Court considered the constitutionality of the Maryland tax in 1819 in *McCulloch v. Maryland*. *McCulloch* is considered one of the two most important Supreme Court decisions written by Chief Justice John Marshall (the other being *Marbury v. Madison*). The Court held, first, that Congress had the power under the Necessary and Proper Clause to create the Bank; and, second, that the Maryland tax on only the Bank and not on Maryland banks was preempted by the Constitution itself—that is, Maryland's state tax on a national bank was an unconstitutional interference with the operation of a lawful national power. *McCulloch* is presented in Chapter 3. For now, you should know that it triggered enormous antipathy to the Bank in the states. Serious proposals were made in the wake of *McCulloch* to amend the jurisdictional statute governing the Supreme Court in order to take away its jurisdiction to review appeals from state supreme courts on questions of federal law. None of these post-*McCulloch* jurisdiction-stripping bills ever passed.

In 1832, however, the Bank found itself in yet another fight over its constitutionality—this time with a determined and implacable foe. President Andrew Jackson came to the White House in 1829 with a vendetta against banks in general (based on his past dealings with them) and an ardent devotion to federalism and the principle that the national government has limited and enumerated powers. The Second Bank's charter was not set to expire until 1836, but the Bank sought renewal for another twenty years in the election year of 1832. This time, more than forty years after the creation of the Bank during the Washington administration, President Jackson vetoed the Bank bill, and he did so *on the grounds that the Bank was unconstitutional.*

This constitutional event—President Jackson's veto on constitutional grounds that had been previously rejected by all three branches of the national government—is also worth considering for its implications for constitutional interpretation. What do you think of President Jackson's analysis? Was he obliged to accept the constitutionality of the Bank because President Washington and President Madison already had? Because the Supreme Court had in *McCulloch v. Maryland*? Or was he right to stick to his convictions about the Constitution? Here is a letter from former President Madison explaining his position on the Bank, and a veto message from President Jackson explaining his.

James Madison, Letter to Lafayette

November 1826

Dear Friend:

. . . As I have been charged with inconsistency, in not putting a veto on the last act of Congress establishing a Bank, a power to do which was denied in the Report, a word of explanation may not be improper. My construction of the Constitution on this point is not changed. But I regarded the reiterated sanctions given to the power by the exercise of it, thro' a long period of time, in every variety of form, and in some form or other, under every administration preceding mine, with the general concurrence of the State authorities, and acquiescence of the people at large, and without a glimpse of change in the public opinion, but evidently with a growing confirmation of it; all this I regarded as a construction put on the Constitution by the Nation, which having made it had the supreme right to declare its meaning, and regarding moreover, the establishment of a Bank under the existing circumstances as the only expedient for substituting a sound currency in place of the viciated one working so much mischief, I did not feel myself, as a public man, at liberty, to sacrifice all these public considerations to my private opinion.

President Jackson, Veto Message

July 10, 1832

To the Senate.

The bill "to modify and continue" the act entitled "An act to incorporate the subscribers to the Bank of the United States" was presented to me on the 4th July instant. Having considered it with that solemn regard to the principles of the Constitution which the day was calculated to inspire, and come to the conclusion that it ought not to become a law, I herewith return it to the Senate, in which it originated, with my objections. . . .

It is maintained by the advocates of the bank that its constitutionality in all its features ought to be considered as settled by precedent and by the decision of the Supreme Court. To this conclusion I can not assent. Mere precedent is a dangerous source of authority, and should not be regarded as deciding questions of constitutional power except where the acquiescence of the people and the States can be considered as well settled. So far from this being the case on this subject, an argument against the bank might be based on precedent. One Congress, in 1791, decided in favor of a bank; another, in 1811, decided against it. One Congress, in 1815, decided against a bank; another, in 1816, decided in its favor. Prior to the present Congress, therefore, the precedents drawn from that source were equal. If we resort to the States, the expressions of legislative, judicial, and executive opinions against the bank have been probably to those in its favor as 4 to 1. There is nothing in precedent, therefore, which, if its authority were admitted, ought to weigh in favor of the act before me.

If the opinion of the Supreme Court covered the whole ground of this act, it ought not to control the coordinate authorities of this Government. The Congress, the Executive, and the Court must each for itself be guided by its own opinion of the Constitution. Each public officer who takes an oath to support the Constitution swears that he will support it as he understands it, and not as it is understood by others. It is as much the duty of the House of Representatives, of the Senate, and of the President to decide upon the constitutionality of any bill or resolution which may be presented to them for passage or approval as it is of the supreme judges when it may be brought before them for judicial decision. The opinion of the judges has no more authority over Congress than the opinion of Congress has over the judges, and on that point the President is independent of both. The authority of the Supreme Court must not, therefore, be permitted to control the Congress or the Executive when acting in their legislative capacities, but to have only such influence as the force of their reasoning may deserve.

But in the case relied upon the Supreme Court have not decided that all the features of this corporation are compatible with the Constitution. It is true that the court have said that the law incorporating the bank is a constitutional exercise of power by Congress; but taking into view the whole opinion of the court and the reasoning by which they have come to that conclusion, I understand them to have decided that inasmuch as a bank is an appropriate means for carrying into effect the enumerated powers of the General Government, therefore the law incorporating it is in accordance with that provision of the Constitution which declares that Congress shall have power "to make all laws which shall be necessary and proper for carrying those powers into execution." Having satisfied themselves that the word "*necessary*" in the Constitution means *needful*, "*requisite*," "*essential*," "*conducive to*," and that "a bank" is a convenient, a useful, and essential instrument in the prosecution of the Government's "fiscal operations," they conclude that to "use one must be within the discretion of Congress" and that "the act to incorporate the Bank of the United States is a law made in pursuance of the Constitution"; "but," say they, "*where the law is not prohibited and is really calculated to effect any of the objects intrusted to the Government, to undertake here to inquire into the degree of its necessity would be to pass the line which circumscribes the judicial department and to tread on legislative ground.*"

The principle here affirmed is that the "degree of its necessity," involving all the details of a banking institution, is a question exclusively for legislative consideration. A bank is constitutional, but it is the province of the Legislature to determine whether this or that particular power, privilege, or exemption is "necessary and proper" to enable the bank to discharge its duties to the Government, and from their decision there is no appeal to the courts of justice. Under the decision of the Supreme Court, therefore, it is the exclusive province of Congress and the President to decide whether the particular features of this act are *necessary* and *proper* in order to enable the bank to perform conveniently and efficiently the public duties assigned to it as a fiscal agent, and therefore constitutional, or *unnecessary* and *improper*, and therefore unconstitutional.

Without commenting on the general principle affirmed by the Supreme Court, let us examine the details of this act in accordance with the rule of legislative action which they have laid down. It will be found that many of the powers and privileges conferred on it can not be supposed necessary for the purpose for which it is proposed to be created, and are not, therefore, means necessary to attain the end in view, and consequently not justified by the Constitution. . . .

This act authorizes and encourages transfers of its stock to foreigners and grants them an exemption from all State and national taxation. So far from being "*necessary and proper*" that the bank should possess this power to make it a safe and efficient agent of the Government in its fiscal operations, it is calculated to convert the Bank of the United States into a foreign bank, to impoverish our people in time of peace, to disseminate a foreign influence through every section of the Republic, and in war to endanger our independence. . . .

If our power over means is so absolute that the Supreme Court will not call in question the constitutionality of an act of Congress the subject of which "is not prohibited, and is really calculated to effect any of the objects intrusted to the Government," although, as in the case before me, it takes away powers expressly granted to Congress and rights scrupulously reserved to the States, it becomes us to proceed in our legislation with the utmost caution. Though not directly, our own powers and the rights of the States may be indirectly legislated away in the use of means to execute substantive powers. We may not enact that Congress shall not have the power of exclusive legislation over the District of Columbia, but we may pledge the faith of the United States that as a means of executing other powers it shall not be exercised for twenty years or forever. We may not pass an act prohibiting the States to tax the banking business carried on within their limits, but we may, as a means of executing our powers over other objects, place that business in the hands of our agents and then declare it exempt from State taxation in their hands. Thus may our own powers and the rights of the States, which we can not directly curtail or invade, be frittered away and extinguished in the use of means employed by us to execute other powers. That a bank of the United States, competent to all the duties which may be required by the Government, might be so organized as not to infringe on our own delegated powers or the reserved rights of the States I do not entertain a doubt. Had the Executive been called upon to furnish the project of such an institution, the duty would have been cheerfully performed. In the absence of such a call it was obviously proper that he should confine himself to pointing out those prominent features in the act presented which in his opinion make it incompatible with the Constitution and sound policy. A general discussion will now take place, eliciting new light and settling important principles; and a new Congress, elected in the midst of such discussion, and furnishing an equal representation of the people according to the last census, will bear to the Capitol the verdict of public opinion, and, I doubt not, bring this important question to a satisfactory result. . . .

Nor is our Government to be maintained or our Union preserved by invasions of the rights and powers of the several States. In thus attempting to make our General Government strong we make it weak. Its true strength consists in leaving individuals and States as much as possible to themselves—in making itself felt, not in its power, but in its beneficence; not in its control, but in its protection; not in binding the States more closely to the center, but leaving each to move unobstructed in its proper orbit. . . .

I have now done my duty to my country. If sustained by my fellow citizens, I shall be grateful and happy; if not, I shall find in the motives which impel me ample grounds for contentment and peace. In the difficulties which surround us and the dangers which threaten our institutions there is cause for neither dismay nor alarm. For relief and deliverance let us firmly rely on that kind Providence which I am sure watches with peculiar care over the destinies of our Republic, and on the intelligence and wisdom of our countrymen. Through His abundant goodness and their patriotic devotion our liberty and Union will be preserved.

The Death of the Bank of the United States

President Jackson's veto set off a titanic struggle with the Senate. After winning re-election, President Jackson directed the secretary of the treasury to withdraw the federal government's deposits from the Bank (to destroy it). When the secretary of the treasury refused, President Jackson fired him for insubordination, appointing in his place Attorney General Roger Taney—a fiercely partisan ally whom President Jackson would later appoint to be chief justice. Secretary of the Treasury Taney promptly withdrew all federal deposits from the Bank, and the outraged Senate adopted a resolution censuring the president. The Bank tried to save itself by triggering a financial panic, but President Jackson succeeded in persuading the public that the panic was not his fault but the Bank's. The issue was taken to the public in the 1834 midterm elections, in which the president's allies won a major victory—leading the reconstituted Senate to expunge the resolution censuring the president from its records. President Jackson helped get Martin Van Buren, his second vice president, elected to succeed him, and his anti-Bank, limited-federal-power views predominated until the Civil War in 1861. Although Congress did twice pass bills recreating the Bank in the 1840s, President John Tyler vetoed them on the same grounds of unconstitutionality that had been cited by President Jackson.[7] No institution remotely resembling the Bank of the United States was to be created until the passage of the Federal Reserve Act in 1913.

The debate over the constitutionality of the Bank eventually faded into history. Today, its main legacy is the strongly pro-national-power opinion of Chief Justice Marshall in *McCulloch v. Maryland*. Yet this is not how the matter seemed to be settled in the nineteenth century. President Jackson won the Bank War, killing the Bank for the next seventy years. Thus, the resolution of one of the most contentious of the early controversies under the Constitution seemed to reaffirm the Jeffersonian view of more limited national government powers.

Constitutional Interpretation in the Bank Controversy

The Bank controversy is an important early case for considering the who and how of constitutional interpretation. The first question—who interprets the Constitution—is considered presently. Consider here the question of how the Constitution should be read and applied. Ask whether Congress had the power under the Constitution to create the Bank in light of the five types of constitutional argument discussed above.

What *textual* arguments do Madison, Jefferson, Hamilton, and Jackson make? In understanding the text, should an interpreter look to how the text would be understood when it was enacted (or ratified), or rather to how it is understood today? In deciding how the text would be understood— whether then or now—what sorts of evidence should count? For example, would it make sense to look at the leading dictionary at the founding, Dr. Johnson's DICTIONARY OF THE ENGLISH LANGUAGE (1755), which says that *necessary* means "indispensible"? Or does using dictionaries introduce too much indeterminacy and subjectivity, because the interpreter has to choose which dictionary to consult and which meaning to use?

Next consider the following *structural* arguments from the text:

(1) The Necessary and Proper Clause must enhance the powers of Congress because it appears with the list of congressional powers in Article I, Section 8 instead of with the restraints on congressional power in Article I, Section 9.

(2) The Clause cannot be read as a catch-all power that would justify most of what the national government does, because otherwise there would be no point in enumerating the national government's other powers.

---

[7] Had those bills been signed by President Tyler, the Supreme Court—the membership of which had been completely transformed by Presidents Jackson and Van Buren—might well have overruled *McCulloch*. See Gerard Magliocca, ANDREW JACKSON AND THE CONSTITUTION: THE RISE AND FALL OF GENERATIONAL REGIMES (2007).

(3) Article I, Section 10, Paragraph 3 at one point uses the phrase "absolutely necessary." If the word "necessary" in the Constitution means "indispensible," wouldn't "absolutely" be redundant? Does that imply that "necessary" means "convenient" or "useful?"

(4) Jefferson mentions the text of the Tenth Amendment in determining whether Congress had the power to create the Bank. That amendment reserves for the states all powers not delegated to the federal government— but it does not reserve all powers not *expressly* delegated. Is the omission of the word "expressly" in the Tenth Amendment, given its inclusion in the Articles of Confederation, an indication that Congress has implied powers under the Constitution? If Congress does have implied powers, is the power to charter a Bank one of them? Is it a useful means toward the ends of taxing and spending to promote the general welfare, regulating commerce, raising armies and navies, and borrowing money?

Now consider the argument from *historical purpose* that Jefferson offers, alluding to the fact that the Philadelphia Convention considered giving Congress a power to charter corporations and deliberately decided not to do so. Is this persuasive? Also, what purpose was the Necessary and Proper Clause intended to have, and does that purpose shed light on how the clause ought to be interpreted? Is the point to keep the national government from having all of its other powers frustrated? Would that suggest a broad or narrow reading of the text?

And what about *practice and precedent*? Once the First Congress and President Washington construed the word "necessary" to mean "convenient" or "useful," should later interpreters have fallen into line as President Madison did? Should *McCulloch* have simply affirmed in a few sentences because of settled practice?

Finally, consider arguments from *policy*. Would a narrow reading of the Necessary and Proper Clause hobble the national government's ability to solve problems the states could not solve by themselves? Or would a broad reading risk concentrating all governmental power in the national government? And consider another form of policy argument about the judiciary as an institution—the argument for judicial restraint. It could be said that once Congress and the president have determined that an institution such as the Bank is "necessary," the courts should defer to their judgment unless they have made a "clear mistake." (This idea is associated with a late-nineteenth century legal scholar, James Bradley Thayer.) Should the courts have deferred to the judgment of the other branches about what was necessary and proper?

Before considering these kinds of arguments, if you looked only at the text (and perhaps Dr. Johnson's definition), the claim that *necessary* means "convenient" or "useful" would be weak. But once all five types of constitutional argument are considered, the claim is stronger: Reading the text of the Necessary and Proper Clause *in context* supports Hamilton's view that it was an augmenting grant of power, because it was placed within Article I's enumeration of granted powers and contrasts with other language connoting stricter conceptions of "necessity." The problem is that this construction seems to sweep away the idea of limited, enumerated powers— conferring incredibly broad powers on Congress. (Recall that this is why the Anti–Federalists reviled the Necessary and Proper Clause as the "Sweeping Clause.")

One final question about constitutional interpretation is raised by the Bank controversy. *Who* interprets the Constitution? It is obvious that courts must interpret it. Article III gives to the Supreme Court and other federal courts "the judicial Power," and it defines the kinds of cases and controversies that the federal courts could hear, including all cases "arising under this Constitution." When deciding these cases, a federal court will often have to decide what the Constitution means and how it applies to the case at hand. But are courts the only government actors who may interpret the Constitution? How should each branch respond to the interpretations made by other branches? And when does a decision by the Supreme Court finally settle a constitutional question? The various actors in the controversy over the First and Second Banks had to answer these important questions for themselves, and they often disagreed. Start thinking about how these questions should be answered, and they will be considered in more detail in Chapter 2.

[Assignment 5]

B. SLAVERY

Was the antebellum Constitution a pro-slavery document? Some have argued that the compromises over slavery in the Constitution made it, in the words of one abolitionist, "a covenant with death" and "an agreement with Hell." Others have argued that those compromises were essential to forming a national government that would be strong enough to someday eliminate slavery entirely. Although the antebellum Constitution never uses the word *slavery*, it does have some provisions that contemplate slavery, or that create powers or limitations related to it. Look again at the Constitution as it stood before the Civil War, and see for yourself what it says on the subject.

* * *

After you have reviewed what the Constitution says about slavery, consider the following questions that bedeviled our nation during its first century and that ultimately led to the Civil War, answering them as if you were a member of Congress in the 1790s:

(1) Did the Constitution prohibit slavery? Could any provision of the Constitution have been legitimately interpreted to require abolition? (Remember, this is before the Civil War and the Thirteenth Amendment.)

(2) Did the Constitution guarantee slavery, in the sense of providing an affirmative constitutional right of some persons to own others as slaves?

(3) To what government did the Constitution allocate the power to make decisions about whether slavery was prohibited or required? If there was any room for states to make decisions about slavery within their borders, were there any limits on those decisions?

(4) What were the powers of *Congress* with respect to slavery? In particular, consider the following questions about Congress before the Civil War, and ask yourself on which interpretive premises you are relying:

(a) Could Congress have passed a "Fugitive Slave Act" providing a procedure for capturing slaves that escaped into states where slavery was illegal?

(b) Could Congress have abolished the international slave trade? Could it have prohibited the slave trade between the states of the Union? Within a single state?

(c) Could Congress have prohibited slavery within the United States?

(d) Could Congress have prohibited slavery in the "territories" of the United States? Could it have required, as a condition for the entry of any new state into the union, that it prohibit slavery in its own constitution?

(e) Could Congress have prohibited slavery within the District of Columbia? Could it have permitted slavery slavery there?

(5) Summing up: Taking into account all of the provisions in the antebellum Constitution that touch on slavery, do you think their net effect was to protect or to frustrate the institution of slavery in the United States?

In a moment, you will consider two abolitionist petitions to Congress in 1790. As background, it may help to know a little about the history of the abolitionist movement in America during the 1770s and 1780s. One fascinating account is Charles Rappleye's SONS OF PROVIDENCE: THE BROWN BROTHERS, THE SLAVE TRADE, AND THE AMERICAN REVOLUTION (2006), which tells the story of two of the brothers who founded Brown University in Providence, Rhode Island. One brother, John, was a slave trader. The other, Moses, was a Quaker and a leading abolitionist. Even as they fought vigorously over slavery, the brothers remained friends.

Moses had converted to Quakerism in 1773 on the death of his beloved first wife. That autumn, he freed six household slaves. He seemingly regarded the loss of his wife as a divine punishment for his family's and his own involvement in the slave trade—which included a disastrous venture with his brother on a slave ship called *The Sally* on which 109 slaves died. Moses offered his freed slaves employment and shelter.

Moses began lobbying the Rhode Island General Assembly to curtail slavery—or at least the slave trade—to no avail. He and other New England Quakers had more success, however, with the First Continental Congress, which was meeting in Philadelphia to debate American relations with England. In 1774, "the second article of the Continental Association," as the agreement to ban the importation of slaves from England was called, said explicitly: "We will neither import nor purchase, any slave imported after the first of December next; after which time we will wholly discontinue the slave trade, and will neither be concerned in it ourselves, nor will we hire our vessels, nor sell our commodities or manufactures to those who are concerned in it." This was an astonishing step toward abolition by a "legislature" which lacked constitutional powers and even a country of its own at the time. (Evidently, some of those fighting for liberty from England in the 1770s appreciated that there was something incongruous in their enslaving others.) After the adoption of this resolution, the slavery issue would not resurface in government until after peace with England was achieved in the 1780s.

The mid–1780s saw progress and setbacks for the abolitionist cause. A number of societies to promote the manumission of slaves were formed, and public opinion began to shift against slavery. Moses and other Quakers petitioned the Continental Congress in 1783 to ban the slave trade. It received the petitions but referred them to committee, where they were forgotten. Congress was too weak under the Articles of Confederation to take real action against the slave trade; it was beset by other problems.

In 1787, however, the Continental Congress was persuaded to ban slavery in the huge Northwest Territory, which eventually would become the free states of Ohio, Indiana, Illinois, Michigan, and Wisconsin (and part of Minnesota). And in the fall of 1787, Moses persuaded the Rhode Island legislature and governor to outlaw the slave trade—a momentous step, given the importance in the slave trade of merchants from Rhode Island and other New England states. The law made it illegal for any citizen of the state to "directly or indirectly import or transport, buy or sell, or receive on board their vessel . . . any of the natives or inhabitants of any state or kingdom in that part of the world called Africa, as slaves or without their voluntary consent." The penalty was one hundred pounds for each slave imported and one thousand pounds for each ship engaged in the slave trade, with the fines to be divided between the state and the person who filed the complaint.

But 1787 also brought discouraging news for abolitionists and Quakers when the text of the proposed new Constitution drafted in Philadelphia was published. No one knew then of the impassioned debates over slavery in which the drafters had engaged, but the text of the Constitution nowhere limited slavery, and several clauses in fact condoned it. First, the Three–Fifths Clause in Article I counted slaves as three-fifths of a person for apportioning representatives in the House of Representatives, in effect providing the states with large slave populations a representation "bonus" in the new government. Second, Article I, Section 9 forbade Congress from banning the international slave trade until 1808. And, finally, Article IV included a Fugitive Slave Clause that imposed a duty on *all* federal and state governments to arrest fugitive slaves and return them to their masters. The South insisted on these provisions as a condition of agreeing to a government that gave the new nation the powers over commerce that New England's delegates desired. Southerners also wanted the greater representation in the House of Representatives—and thus also in the Electoral College—that came from counting slaves, who could not vote, as three-fifths of a person. This system led to white Southerners "voting their slaves" and gave the South a huge advantage in Congress and in presidential elections. In part due to this advantage, Southerners—and particularly Virginians—dominated the presidency from 1789 until 1861, and with domination of the presidency came Southern domination of the Supreme Court.

Would the new government created by the Constitution restrict slavery? Or would it protect slavery and enable its expansion? This became one of the most contentious issues in America's constitutional history from 1789 through the Civil War of 1861–1865. A great many of the constitutional arguments in that seventy-five-year debate were made in 1790 when the First Congress considered two petitions for legislation.

The Quaker Anti–Slavery Petitions of 1790

In February 1790, Quaker societies presented petitions to Congress proposing abolition of the foreign slave trade and consideration of measures to abolish slavery in America. One petition was presented under the signature of Benjamin Franklin.

What follows are excerpts from the congressional debates over those petitions, which eventually led to the petitions being referred to a committee (as proposed by Representative James Madison). The committee produced a report, which was then amended by the House of Representatives as a whole. The committee version and the full House report are, in essence, constitutional interpretations concerning Congress's power with respect to slavery. Evaluate the reports. Are they right? The outcome, known as the Decision of 1790, later came to be treated by Congress as a "precedent" establishing the impropriety of any congressional action to abolish slavery in the states. See Joseph Ellis, FOUNDING BROTHERS 118 (2001).

The Petition of the Quakers of Pennsylvania, New Jersey, and Other States

Presented in the House of Representatives, February 11, 1790

To the Senate and House of Representatives of the United States.

The Address of the people called Quakers, in their annual assembly convened.

Firmly believing that unfeigned righteousness in public as well as private stations, is the only sure ground of hope for the Divine blessing, whence alone rulers can derive true honor, establish sincere confidence in the hearts of the people, and feeling their minds animated with the ennobling principle of universal good-will to men, find a conscious dignity and felicity in the harmony and success attending the exercise of a solid uniform virtue, short of which the warmest pretensions to public spirit, zeal for our country, and the rights of men, are fallacious and illusive.

Under this persuasion, as professors of faith in that ever blessed allperfect Lawgiver, whose injunctions remain of undiminished obligation on all who profess to believe in him, "whatsoever ye would that men should do unto you, do you even so unto them"; we apprehend ourselves religiously bound to request your serious Christian attention, to the deeply interesting subject whereon our religious society, in their annual assembly, on the tenth month, 1783, addressed the then Congress, who, thought the Christian rectitude of the concern was by the Delegates generally acknowledged, yet not being vested with the powers of Legislation, they declined promoting any public remedy against the gross national iniquity of trafficking in the persons of fellow-men; but divers of the Legislative bodies of the different States, on the Continent, have since manifested their sense of the public detestation due to the licentious wickedness of the African trade for slaves, and the inhuman tyranny and blood guiltiness inseparable from it: the debasing influence whereof most certainly tends to lay waste the virtue, and, of course, the happiness of the people.

Many are the enormities abhorrent to common humanity, and common honesty; which, under the Federal countenance given to this abominable commerce, are practiced in some of the United States, which we judge it not needful to particularize to a body of men, chosen as eminently distinguished for wisdom as extensive information. But we find it indispensably incumbent on us, as a religious body, assuredly believing that both the true temporal interest of nations, and eternal well-being of individuals, depend on doing justly, loving mercy, and walking humbly before God, the creator, preserver, and benefactor of men, thus to attempt to excite your attention to the affecting subject; earnestly desiring that the infinite Father of Spirits may so enrich your minds with his love and truth, and so influence your understandings, by that pure wisdom which is full of mercy and good fruits, as that a sincere and impartial inquiry may take place, whether it be not an essential part of the duty of your exalted station, to exert upright endeavors, to the full extent of your power, to remove every obstruction to public righteousness, which the influence of artifice of particular persons, governed by the narrow mistaken views of self-interest, has occasioned, and whether, notwithstanding such seeming impediments, it be not in reality within your power to exercise justice and mercy, which, if adhered to, we cannot doubt, must produce the abolition of the slave trade.

We consider this subject so essentially and extensively important, as to warrant a hope, that the liberty we now take will be understood, as it really is, a compliance with a sense of religious duty; and that your Christian endeavors to remove reproach from the land may be efficacious to sweeten the labor, and lessen the difficulties incident to the discharge of your important trust.

Signed in and on behalf of the Yearly Meeting, for Pennsylvania, New Jersey, Delaware, and the Western parts of Maryland and Virginia; held by adjournments from the twenty-eighth day of the ninth month, to the third day of the tenth month, inclusive, 1789, by NICHOLAS WALN, Clerk to the meeting this year.

The Petition of the Pennsylvania Society for Promoting the Abolition of Slavery

Presented in the House of Representatives, February 12, 1790

The following memorial of the Pennsylvania Society for promoting the Abolition of Slavery, the relief of free negroes unlawfully held in bondage, and the improvement of the condition of the African race, was presented and read:

The memorial respectfully showeth,

That from a regard for the happiness of mankind, as association was formed several years since in this State, by a number of her citizens, of various religious denominations, for promoting the abolition of slavery, and for the relief of those unlawfully held in bondage. A just and acute conception of the true principles of liberty, as it spread through the land, produced accessions to their numbers, many friends to their cause, and a Legislative co-operation with their views, which, by the blessing of Divine Providence, have been successfully directed to the relieving from bondage a large number of their fellow-creatures of the African race. They have also the satisfaction to observe, that in consequence of that spirit of philanthropy and genuine liberty which is generally diffusing its beneficial influence, similar institutions are forming at home and abroad.

That mankind are all formed by the same Almighty Being, alike objects of his care, and equally designed for the enjoyment of happiness, the Christian religion teaches us to believe, and the political creed of Americans fully coincides with the position. Your memorialists, particularly engaged in attending to the distresses arising from slavery, believe it their indispensable duty to present this subject to your notice. They have observed, with real satisfaction, that many important and salutary powers are vested in you for "promoting the welfare and securing the blessings of liberty to the people of the United States"; and as they conceive that these blessings ought rightfully to be administered, without distinction of color, to all descriptions of people, so they indulge themselves in the pleasing expectation, that nothing which can be done for the relief of the unhappy objects of their care will be either omitted or delayed.

From a persuasion that equal liberty was originally the portion, and is still the birth-right of all men; and influenced by the strong ties of humanity, and the principles of their institution, your memorialists conceive themselves bound to use all justifiable endeavors to loosen the bands of slavery, and promoted a general enjoyment of the blessings of freedom. Under these impressions, they earnestly entreat you serious attention to the subject of slavery; that you will be pleased to countenance the restoration of liberty to those unhappy men, who alone, in this land of freedom are degraded into perpetual bondage, and who, amidst the general joy of surrounding free-men, are groaning in servile subjections; that you will devise means for re-moving this inconsistency from the character of the American people; that you will promote mercy and justice towards this distressed races, and that you will step to the very verge of the power vested in you for discouraging every species of traffic in the persons of our fellow-men.

BENJ. FRANKLIN, *President.*

Slave Trade Debates

The House of Representatives, February 12, 1790

. . . Mr. TUCKER was sorry the petition had a second reading, as he conceived it contained an unconstitutional request, and from that consider-ation he wished it thrown aside. He feared the commitment of it would be a very alarming circumstance to the Southern States; for, if the object was to engage Congress in an unconstitutional measure, it would be considered as an interference with their rights, the people would become very uneasy un-der the Government, and lament that they ever put additional powers into their hands. He was surprised to see another memorial on the same sub-ject, and that signed by a man who ought to have know the Constitution better: He thought it a mischievous attempt, as it respected the persons in whose favor it was intended. It would buoy them up with hopes, without a foundation, and as they could not reason on the subject, as more enlight-ened men would, they might be led to what they would be punished for, and the owners of them, in their own defence, would be compelled to exercise over them a severity they were not accustomed to. Do these men expect a general emancipation of slaves by law? This would never be submitted to by the Southern States without a civil war. Do they mean to purchase their freedom? He believed their money would fall short of the price. But how is it they are more concerned in this business than others? Are they the only persons who possess religion and morality? If the people are not so exem-plary, certainly they will admit, the clergy are; why then do we not find them uniting in the body, praying us to adopt measures for the promotion of religion and piety, or any moral object? They know it would be an im-proper interference; and, to say the best of this memorial, it is an act of im-prudence, which he hoped would receive no countenance from the house.

Mr. SENEY denied that there was any thing unconstitutional in the memorial; at least, if there was, it had escaped his attention, and he should be obliged to the gentleman to point it out. Its only object was, that Con-gress should exercise their constitutional authority, to abate the horrors of slavery, as far as they could; indeed, he considered that all altercation on the subject of commitment was at an end, as the house had impliedly de-termined yesterday that it should be committed.

Mr. BURKE saw the disposition of the House, and he feared it would be referred to a committee, maugre [*i.e., "in spite of"*—*Editors*] all their opposition; but he must insist, that it prayed for an unconstitutional measure; did it not desire Congress to interfere and abolish the slave trade, while the Constitution expressly stipulated that Congress should exercise no such power? He was certain the commitment would sound an alarm, and blow the trumpet of sedition in the Southern States. He was sorry to see the petitioners paid more attention to than the Constitution; however, he would do his duty, and opposed the business totally; and if it was referred to a committee, as mentioned yesterday, consisting of a member from each State, and he was appointed, he would decline serving.

Mr. SCOTT.—I cannot entertain a doubt but the memorial is strictly agreeable to the Constitution; it respects of part of the duty particularly assigned to us by that instrument, and I hope we may be inclined to take it into consideration. We can, at present, lay our hands upon a small duty of ten dollars; I would take this, and if it is all we can do, we must be content: but I am sorry that the framers of the Constitution did not go farther, and enable us to interdict the traffic entirely; for I look upon the slave trade to be one of the most abominable things on earth; and if there was neither God nor devil, I should oppose it upon the principles of humanity, and the law of nature. I cannot, for my part, conceive how any person can be said to acquire a property in another; is it by virtue of conquest? What are the rights of conquest? Some have dared to advance this monstrous principle, that the conqueror is absolute master of his conquest; that he may dispose of it as his property, and treat it as he pleases; but, enough of those who reduce man to the state of transferable goods, or use them like beasts of burthen, who deliver them up as the property or patrimony to others. Let us argue on principles countenanced by reason and becoming humanity; the petitioners view the subject in a religious light, but I do not stand in need of religious motives to induce me to reprobate the traffic in human flesh; other considerations weigh with me to support the commitment of the memorial, and to support every constitutional measure likely to bring about its total abolition. Perhaps, in our legislative capacity, we can go no further than to impose a duty of ten dollars, but I do not know how far I might go, if I was one of the Judges of the United States, and those people were to come before me and claim their emancipation; but I am sure I would go as far as I could.

Mr. JACKSON differed with the gentleman last up, and supposed the master had a qualified property in his slave. He said the contrary doctrine would go to the destruction of every species of personal service. The gentleman said, he did not stand in need of religion to induce him to reprobate slavery, but if he is guided by that evidence upon which the christian system is founded, he will find that religion is not against it. He will see, from Genesis to Revelations, the current setting strong that way. There never was a Government on the face of the earth, but what permitted slavery. The purest sons of freedom in the Grecian Republics, the citizens of Athens and Lacedaemon all held slaves. On this principle, the nations of Europe are associated; it is the basis of the feudal system. But suppose all this to have been wrong, let me ask the gentleman if it is policy to bring forward a business at this moment, likely to light up the flame of civil discord; for the people of the Southern States will resist one tyranny as soon as another? The other parts of the Continent may bear them down by force of arms, but they will never suffer themselves to be divested of their property without a struggle. The gentleman says, if he was a Federal Judge, he does not know to what length he would go in emancipating these people; but, I believe his judgment would be of short duration in Georgia, perhaps even the existence of such a Judge might be in danger.

Mr. SHERMAN could see no difficulty in committing the memorial; because it was probable the committee would understand their business, and perhaps they might bring in such a report as would be satisfactory to gentlemen on both sides of the House.

Mr. BALDWIN was sorry the subject had ever been brought before Congress, because it was of a delicate nature as it respected some of the States. Gentlemen who had been present at the formation of this Constitution could not avoid the recollection of the pain and difficulty which the subject caused in that body. The members from the Southern States were so tender upon this point, that they had well nigh broken up without coming to any determination; however, from the extreme desire of preserving the Union, and obtaining an efficient Government, they were induced mutually to concede, and the Constitution jealously guarded what they agreed to. If gentlemen look over the footsteps of that body, they will find the greatest degree of caution used to imprint them, so as not to be easily eradicated; but the moment we go to jostle on that ground, said he, I fear we shall feel it tremble under our feet. Congress have no power to interfere with the importation of slaves beyond what is in the ninth section of the 1st article of the Constitution; every thing else is interdicted to them in the strongest terms. If we examine the constitution, we shall find the expressions relative to this subject cautiously expressed, and more punctiliously guarded than any other part, "The migration or importation of such persons shall not be prohibited by Congress." But lest this should not have secured the object sufficiently, it is declared, in the same section, "That no capitation or direct tax shall be laid, unless in proportion to the census"; this was intended to prevent Congress from laying any special tax upon negro slaves, as they might, in this way, so burthen the possessors of them as to induce a general emancipation. If we go on to the fifth article, we shall find the first and fifth clauses of the ninth section of the first article restrained from being altered before the year 1808.

Gentlemen have said, that this petition does not pray for an abolition of the slave trade. I think, sir, it prays for nothing else, and therefore we have no more to do with it than if it prayed us to establish an order of nobility, or a national religion.

Mr. SYLVESTER said, that he had always been in the habit of respecting the society called Quakers; he respected them for their exertions in the cause of humanity; but he thought the present was not a time to enter into a consideration of the subject, especially as he conceived it to be a business within the province of the State Legislatures.

Mr. LAWRENCE observed, that the subject would undoubtedly come under the consideration of the House; and he thought, as it was now before them, that the present time was as proper as any; he was therefore for committing the memorial, and when the prayer of it had been properly examined, they could see how far Congress may, constitutionally, interfere; as they knew the limits of their power on this, as well as on every other occasion, there was no just apprehension to be entertained that they would go beyond it.

Mr. SMITH, of South Carolina, insisted that it was not in the power of the House to grant the prayer of the petition, which went to the total abolishment of the slave trade, and it was therefore unnecessary to commit it.

He observed, that in the Southern States, difficulties had arisen on adopting the Constitution, inasmuch as it was apprehended that Congress might
take measures under it for abolishing the slave trade.

Perhaps the petitioners, when they applied to this House, did not
think their object unconstitutional, but now they are told that it is they will
be satisfied with the answer, and press it no further. If their object had
been for Congress to lay a duty of ten dollars per head on the importation of
slaves, they would have said so, but that does not appear to have been the
case. The commitment of the petition, on that ground, cannot be contended.
If they will not be content with that, shall it be committed to investigate
facts? The petition speaks of none. For what purpose, then, shall it be
committed? If gentlemen can assign no good reason for the measure, they
will not support it, when they are told that it will create great jealousies
and alarm in the Southern States; for I can assure them that there is no
point on which they are more jealous and suspicious than on a business
with which they think the government has nothing to do.

When we entered into this confederacy, we did it from political, not
from moral motives, and I do not think my constituents want to learn morals from the petitioners; I do not believe they want improvement in their
moral system; if they do, they can get it at home.

The gentleman from Georgia has justly stated the jealousy of the
Southern States. On entering into this Government, they apprehend that
the other States, not knowing the necessity the citizens of the Southern
States were under to hold this species of property, would, from motives of
humanity and benevolence, be led to vote for a general emancipation; and
had they not seen that the constitution provided against the effect of such a
disposition, I may be bold to say they never would have adopted it. And,
notwithstanding all the calmness with which some gentlemen have viewed
the subject, they will find that the discussion alone will create great alarm.
We have been told, that if this would be the case, we ought to have avoided
it, by saying nothing; but it was not for that purpose that we were sent
here. We look to this measure as an attack upon the palladium of the property of our country; it is therefore our duty to oppose it by every means in
our power. Gentlemen should consider, that when we entered into a political connexion with other States, that this property was there; it was acquired under a former Government, conformably to the laws and constitution, therefore, any thing that will tend to deprive them of that property,
must be an *ex post facto* law, and, as such, is forbidden by our political
compact.

I said the States would never have entered into the Confederation, unless their property had been guaranteed to them, for such is the state of
agriculture in that country, that without slaves it must be abandoned. Why
will these people, then, make use of arguments to induce the slave to turn
his hand against his master? We labor under difficulties enough from the
ravages of the late war. A gentleman can hardly come from that country
with a servant or two, either to this place or Philadelphia, but there are
persons trying to seduce his servants to leave him; and, when they have
done this, the poor wretches are obliged to rob their master, in order to obtain a subsistence; all those, therefore, who are concerned in this seduction,
are accessaries to the robbery.

The reproaches which they cast upon the owners of negro property, is
charging them with the want of humanity. I believe the proprietors have as
much humanity as persons in any part of the continent, and are as conspic-

uous for their good morals as their neighbors. It was said yesterday, that the Quakers are a society known to the laws and the constitution, but they are no more so than other religious societies; they stand exactly in the same situation; their memorial, therefore, relates to a matter in which they are no more interested than any other sect, and can only be considered as a piece of advice, which it is not customary to refer to a committee, but if it is supposed to pray for what they think a moral purpose, is that sufficient to induce us to commit it? What may appear a moral virtue in their eyes, may not be so in reality. I have heard of a sect of Shaking Quakers, who, I presume, suppose their tenets of a moral tendency. I am informed one of them forbids to intermarry, yet you may see them with a numerous offspring about them. Now, if these people were to petition Congress to pass a law prohibiting matrimony, would gentlemen agree to refer such a petition? I think if they would reject one of that nature, as improper, they ought also to reject this.

Mr. PAGE was in favor of the commitment. He hoped that the designs of the respectable memorialists would not be stopped at the threshold, in order to preclude a fair discussion of the prayer of the memorial. He observed, that gentlemen had founded their arguments upon a misrepresentation; for the object of the memorial is not declared to be the total abolition of the slave trade; but that Congress will consider whether it be not in reality within their power to exercise justice and mercy, which, if adhered to, they cannot doubt must produce the abolition of the slave trade. If, then, the prayer contained nothing unconstitutional, he trusted the meritorious effort would not be frustrated.

With respect to the alarm that was apprehended, he conjectured there was none; but there might be just cause if the memorial was not taken into consideration. He placed himself in the case of a slave, and said, that, on hearing that Congress had refused to listen to the decent suggestions of a respectable part of the community, he should infer that the General Government (from which was expected great good would result to every class of citizens) had shut their ears against the voice of humanity, and he should despair of any alleviation of the miseries he and his posterity had in prospect; if any thing could induce him to rebel, it must be a stroke like this, impressing on his mind all the horrors of despair. But if he was told that application was made in his behalf, and that Congress was willing to hear what could be urged in favor of discouraging the practice of importing his fellow-wretches, he would trust in their justice and humanity, and wait the decision patiently. He presumed that these unfortunate people would reason in the same way, and he, therefore, conceived the most likely way to prevent danger was to commit the petition. He lived in a State which had the misfortune of having in her bosom a great number of slaves; he held many of them himself, and was as much interested in the business, as any gentleman in South Carolina or Georgia, yet, if he was determined to hold them in eternal bondage, he should feel no uneasiness or alarm on account of the present measure, because he should rely upon the virtue of Congress that they would not exercise any unconstitutional authority.

Mr. MADISON.—The debate has taken a serious turn, and it will be owing to this alone if an alarm is created; for had the memorial been treated in the usual way, it would have been considered as a matter of course, and a report might have been made so as to have given general satisfaction.

If there was the slightest tendency by the commitment to break in upon the Constitution, he would object to it; but he did not see upon what ground such an event was to be apprehended. The petition prayed, in general terms, for the interference of Congress, so far as they were constitutionally authorized; but even if its prayer was in some degree, unconstitutional, it might be committed, as was the case on Mr. Churchman's petition, one part of which was supposed to apply for an unconstitutional interference by the General Government. He admitted, that Congress is restricted by the Constitution from taking measures to abolish the slave trade; yet there are a variety of ways by which it could countenance the abolition, and regulations might be made in relation to the introduction of them into the new States to be formed out of the Western Territory. He thought the object well worthy of consideration.

Mr. GERRY thought the interference of Congress fully compatible with the constitution, and could not help lamenting the miseries to which the natives of Africa were exposed by this inhuman commerce. He never contemplated the subject, without reflecting what his own feelings would be, in case himself, his children, or friends were placed in the same deplorable circumstances. He then adverted to the flagrant acts of cruelty which are committed in carrying on that traffic; and asked, whether it can be supposed that Congress has no power to prevent such abuses? He then referred to the Constitution, and pointed out the restrictions laid on the General Government respecting the importation of slaves. It was not, he presumed, in the contemplation of any gentleman in this House to violate that part of the Constitution; but that we have a right to regulate this business, is as clear as that we have any rights whatever; nor has the contrary been shown by any person who has spoken on the occasion. Congress can, agreeably to the Constitution, lay a duty of ten dollars on imported slaves; they may do this immediately. He made a calculation of the value of the slaves in the Southern States, and supposed they may be worth ten millions of dollars. Congress have a right, if they see proper, to make a proposal to the Southern States to purchase the whole of them, and their resources in the Western Territory might furnish them with the means: He did not intend to suggest a measure of this kind; he only instanced these particulars to show that Congress certainly has the right to intermeddle in the business. He though that no objection had been offered of any force to prevent the commitment of the memorial.

Mr. BOUDINOT had carefully examined the petition and found nothing like what was complained of by gentlemen contained in it; he, therefore, hoped they would withdraw their opposition and suffer it to be committed.

Mr. SMITH, of South Carolina, said, that, as the petitioners had particularly prayed Congress to take measures for the annihilation of the slave trade; and as that was admitted, on all hands, to be beyond their power; and as the petitioners would not be gratified by a tax of ten dollars per head, which was all that was within their power, there was, of consequence, no occasion for committing it. . . .

Slave Trade Debates:
Report of the Special Committee

The House of Representatives, March 23, 1790

The committee to whom were referred sundry memorials from the people called Quakers; and also a memorial from the Pennsylvania Society for promoting the Abolition of Slavery, submit the following report:

That from the nature of the matters contained in those memorials, they were induced to examine the powers vested in Congress, under the present constitution, relating to the abolition of slavery, and are clearly of opinion,

First. THAT the General Government is expressly restrained from prohibiting the importation of such persons "as any of the States now existing shall think proper to admit, until the year one thousand eight hundred and eight."

Secondly. THAT Congress, by a fair construction of the Constitution, are equally restrained from interfering in the emancipation of slaves, who already are, or who may, within the period mentioned, be imported into, or born within any of the said States.

Thirdly. THAT Congress have no authority to interfere in the internal regulations of particular States, relative to the instruction of slaves in the principles of morality and religion; to their comfortable cloathing, accommodations and subsistence; to the regulation of their marriages, and the prevention of the violation of the rights thereof, or to the separation of children from their parents; to a comfortable provision in cases of sickness, age or infirmity; or to the seizure, transportation or sale of free negroes; but have the fullest confidence in the wisdom and humanity of the Legislatures of the several States, that they will revise their laws from time to time, when necessary, and promote the objects mentioned in the memorials, and every other measure that may tend to the happiness of slaves.

Fourthly. THAT nevertheless Congress have authority, if they shall think it necessary, to lay at any time a tax or duty, not exceeding ten dollars for each person of any description, the importation of whom shall be by any of the States admitted as aforesaid.

Fifthly. THAT Congress have authority to interdict, or (so far as it is or may be carried on by citizens of the united States for supplying foreigners) to regulate the African trade, and to make provision for the humane treatment of slaves, in all cases while on their passage to the United States, or to foreign ports, as far as it respects the citizens of the United States.

Sixthly. THAT Congress have also authority to prohibit foreigners from fitting out vessels, in any port of the United States, for transporting persons from Africa to any foreign port.

Seventhly. THAT the memorialists be informed, that in all cases, to which the authority of Congress extends, they will exercise it for the humane objects of the memorialists, so far as they can be promoted on the principles of justice, humanity and good policy.

Slave Trade Debates:
Report of the Committee of the Whole House

The House of Representatives, March 23, 1790

The committee of the whole House, to whom was committed the report of the committee on the memorials of the people called Quakers, and of the Pennsylvania Society for promoting the Abolition of Slavery, report the following amendments:

STRIKE out the first clause, together with the recital thereto, and in lieu thereof insert, "That the migration or importation of such persons as any of the States now existing shall think proper to admit, cannot be prohibited by Congress, prior to the year one thousand eight hundred and eight."

Strike out the second and third clauses, and in lieu thereof insert, "That congress have no authority to interfere in the emancipation of slaves, or in the treatment of them within any of the States; it remaining with the several States alone to provide any regulations therein, which humanity and true policy may require."

Strike out the fourth and fifth clauses, and in lieu thereof insert, "That Congress have authority to restrain the citizens of the United States from carrying on the African trade, for the purpose of supplying foreigners with slaves, and of providing by proper regulations for the humane treatment, during their passage, of slaves imported by the said citizens into the states admitting such importation."

Strike out the seventh clause.

ORDERED, That the said report of the committee of the whole House do lie on the table. . . .

————

In the wake of this fiasco, the Quakers tried again to petition Congress to act to discourage slavery. They met with Representative James Madison about the question of congressional power to inhibit slavery under the new Constitution. After considering the question closely, Madison pronounced that under the Constitution "Congress has the power to suppress all immoralities." Rappleye, SONS OF PROVIDENCE at 295. The new government, with Representative Madison's blessing, could take steps to curtail slavery. On March 22, 1794, the Senate approved a bill, already passed by the House, entitled "an Act to prohibit the carrying on of the slave trade from the United States to any foreign place or country" with substantial enforcement penalties. This bill was constitutional because it did not restrict the importation of slaves into the United States. President Washington signed the bill into law the same day it passed Congress. And in 1807, President Jefferson—himself a slaveowner—signed into law an "Act to prohibit the importation of slaves into any port or place within the jurisdiction of the United States," which took effect at the earliest constitutionally allowed date. That same year, Parliament passed "An Act for the Abolition of the Slave Trade," and other nations of Europe soon did the same. (The slave trade continued illegally, however.)

But the cotton gin was coming. It made slavery in the American South far more profitable than before, and the institution spread westward, eventually reaching as far as Texas. The opportunity for slavery to be checked in the early Republic had come and gone. The next chance to stop it would not come until the election of Abraham Lincoln in 1860—and the Civil War.

NOTES

1. In 1820, Congress addressed the question of slavery in the territories with what was called the Missouri Compromise. An imaginary line was drawn across the North American continent, from the Atlantic Ocean going west along the northern edge of Maryland, the so-called Mason–Dixon Line. Slavery would be excluded from territories north of the line (except for Missouri itself, which was admitted as a slave state). This accord held until 1857 when the Supreme Court in *Dred Scott v. Sandford* said the Missouri Compromise was unconstitu-

tional because slave owners had a right to settle with their slaves in the Northern territories. *Dred Scott* made it impossible for the federal government to stop the spread of slavery anywhere, inflaming sectional tensions and leading to the Civil War. *Dred Scott* also held that free blacks were not, and could not ever become, citizens of the United States. The case is presented in Chapter 4.

2. Consider again whether the original Constitution was a pro-slavery document. It was abolitionist William Lloyd Garrison who in 1844 called the Constitution "a covenant with death" and "an agreement with Hell" and publicly burned a copy of it (on the Fourth of July no less) in front of a huge crowd in Boston. Was Garrison right? The Constitution contains compromises with the slave states that acknowledge the existence of slavery. Does it thus condone and protect slavery? Is its great moral defect its failure to eradicate slavery? The document put in place a national government of sufficient power to destroy the institution of slavery—but it also tilted the composition of that government in favor of stronger representation of the slaveholding states. Isn't it painful to see the framers' failure to do almost any of the things they could have done in the 1790s to more firmly put slavery on the road toward extinction?

C. THE NEUTRALITY CONTROVERSY

Where does the Constitution allocate power over foreign affairs? In the Congress created by Article I? Or in the president created by Article II? (This is not a federalism question about the distribution of power between the national government and the states, but rather a separation of powers question about the distribution of power between the branches of the national government.)

When the Constitution was adopted, the traditional understanding was that the formulation and conduct of the nation's relations with other nations was an aspect of "the executive Power," which Article II vests in the president. This understanding was especially shaped by two political theorists, the English John Locke and the French Montesquieu. They had somewhat different ways of separating governmental powers: Locke distinguished the legislative, executive, and federative (or foreign affairs) powers, and Montesquieu distinguished the legislative, judicial, and executive powers. They agreed that power over foreign affairs was committed to the executive. But in England the executive was a king. When the United States had to decide where to allocate the foreign affairs power, would it be considered part of the executive power given to the president, or would it be considered a *royal* power that did not belong to any one branch of the U.S. government?

Article I vests important powers related to foreign affairs in Congress, which is given the powers "to declare war," to define and punish piracies "and Offences against the Law of Nations," to "regulate commerce with foreign Nations," and to "establish an uniform Rule of Naturalization." Indeed, fully one-third of Congress's enumerated powers involve foreign affairs in some respect. In addition, the Senate is given a role in treaty-making: two-thirds of the members present must consent before a treaty made by the president with a foreign nation can become law. But no specific Article I provision governs abrogating or terminating treaties, nor is there any mention of a general power over foreign relations.

Article II begins with the Vesting Clause's grant of "the executive Power" to the president. Then Sections 2 and 3 mention specific presidential foreign relations powers: the power to make treaties (by and with the advice and consent of two-thirds of the Senate); the power of being the commander in chief of the nation's armed forces; and the duty to receive ambassadors and other public ministers.

But who has the remainder of the foreign affairs powers that are not specified? Do they inhere in the general grant of "the executive Power" to the president, in accordance with the traditional understanding from Locke and Montesquieu? (On that view, the foreign-affairs-related powers given to Congress would be exceptions, or carve-outs, from the general power given to the executive.) Or are unspecified foreign-affairs powers to be allocated between the legislative and executive branch by analogy to the powers that are specified? Or are the unspecified powers reserved to the states?

One of the first major tests of the Constitution's allocation of foreign affairs powers came in 1793, during the Washington administration. France and England were again at war with one another. During the American Revolution, France had come to the aid of the colonies. Benjamin Franklin had negotiated treaties of alliance and of commerce with France, and these had been absolutely critical to the colonists' victory. Did those treaties now oblige the new United States to join France in its war against England? Or had the French Revolution changed the obligations of the United States?

Americans divided sharply in their opinions about the French Revolution. Thomas Jefferson considered it a continuation of the democratic changes swept in by the American Revolution in 1776. To Jefferson, James Madison, and other prominent American supporters of the French Revolution, it seemed only just and right for America to stand by its treaty of alliance with France from the 1770s and join the French in fighting the English monarchy. More conservative Americans, such as Alexander Hamilton, saw the French Revolution as disorderly and violent. In January 1793, King Louis XVI was executed; by the end of that year France was in the grip of a "Reign of Terror" in which as many as 50,000 people lost their lives, many to the guillotine. Hamilton came to consider Jefferson a dangerous revolutionary whose ideas threatened true liberty, while Jefferson considered Hamilton a closet monarchist. Throughout the 1790s, the United States was sharply divided between pro-English elements (which became the "Federalist" party) and pro-French elements (which became Jefferson's "Democratic–Republican" party).

President George Washington stood squarely between these factions. He faced an immediate legal and political dilemma: deciding whether the United States was bound by its treaty of alliance from the 1770s to give military aid to Revolutionary France. Washington thought that such action would be disastrous for America, which had little to add to France's power and much to lose by entangling itself in a European war.

After consulting his cabinet, President Washington settled on a policy of neutrality and issued a proclamation to that effect. He interpreted the treaty of alliance to be either inapplicable or, if applicable, not an obligation that the United States should continue to honor. In making this decision, Washington claimed for the executive the foreign affairs power, including the power to interpret or abrogate a treaty of the United States and the power in effect to declare *peace*. The Neutrality Proclamation of 1793 went further than a mere declaration of neutrality, however, for Washington also claimed the power to prosecute Americans who violated the neutrality: "I have given instructions to those officers, to whom it belongs, to cause prosecutions to be instituted against all persons, who shall, within the cognizance of the courts of the United States, violate the law of nations, with respect to the Powers at war, or any of them."

The proclamation was challenged by some American defenders of France, such as Representative James Madison, as being beyond the president's power and instead falling squarely within Congress's power to declare war. Below are printed President Washington's proclamation, Alexander Hamilton's pseudonymous defense of it as "Pacificus," and James Madison's pseudonymous objections to it as "Helvidius." Also included is the Neutrality Act of 1794. The Neutrality Controversy raises fascinating questions of constitutional law concerning foreign affairs and executive power. These questions, and the answers ventured by the various parties involved, have proven to be of enduring importance to the life of the nation and they remain as debated in the twenty-first century as they were in the eighteenth.

President Washington,
The Proclamation of Neutrality
April 22, 1793

Whereas it appears that a state of war exists between Austria, Prussia, Sardinia, Great Britain, and the United Netherlands, on the one part, and France on the other; and the duty and interest of the United States require, that they should with sincerity and good faith adopt and pursue a conduct friendly and impartial toward the belligerent Powers;

I have therefore thought fit by these presents to declare the disposition of the United States to observe the conduct aforesaid towards those Powers respectfully; and to exhort and warn the citizens of the United States carefully to avoid all acts and proceedings whatsoever, which may in any manner tend to contravene such disposition.

And I do hereby also make known, that whatsoever of the citizens of the United States shall render himself liable to punishment or forfeiture under the law of nations, by committing, aiding, or abetting hostilities against any of the said Powers, or by carrying to any of them those articles which are deemed contraband by the modern usage of nations, will not receive the protection of the United States, against such punishment or forfeiture; and further, that I have given instructions to those officers, to whom it belongs, to cause prosecutions to be instituted against all persons, who shall, within the cognizance of the courts of the United States, violate the law of nations, with respect to the Powers at war, or any of them.

In testimony whereof, I have caused the seal of the United States of America to be affixed to these presents, and signed the same with my hand. Done at the city of Philadelphia, the twenty-second day of April, one thousand seven hundred and ninety-three, and of the Independence of the United States of America the seventeenth.

Pacificus, No. 1
Alexander Hamilton, June 29, 1793

... The objections which have been raised against the Proclamation of Neutrality lately issued by the President have been urged in a spirit of acrimony and invective, which demonstrates, that more was in view than merely a free discussion of an important public measure; that the discussion covers a design of weakening the confidence of the People in the author of the measure; in order to remove or lessen a powerful obstacle to the success of an opposition to the Government, which however it may change its form, according to circumstances, seems still to be adhered to and pursued with persevering Industry. . . .

The objections in question fall under these heads—

1 That the Proclamation was without authority

2 That it was contrary to our treaties with France

3 That it was contrary to the gratitude, which is due from this to that country; for the succours rendered us in our own Revolution.

4 That it was out of time & unnecessary.

In order to judge of the solidity of the first of these objection[s], it is necessary to examine what is the nature and design of a proclamation of neutrality.

The true nature & design of such an act is—to *make known* to the powers at War and to the Citizens of the Country, whose Government does the Act that such country is in the condition of a Nation at Peace with the belligerent parties, and under no obligations of Treaty, to become an *associate in the war* with either of them; that this being its situation its intention is to observe a conduct conformable with it and to perform towards each the duties of neutrality; and as a consequence of this state of things, to give warning to all within its jurisdiction to abstain from acts that shall contravene those duties, under the penalties which the laws of the land (of which the law of Nations is a part) annexes to acts of contravention. . . .

It will not be disputed that the management of the affairs of this country with foreign nations is confided to the Government of the U[nited] States.

It can as little be disputed, that a Proclamation of Neutrality, where a Nation is at liberty to keep out of a War in which other Nations are engaged and means so to do, is a *usual* and a *proper* measure. *Its main object and effect are to prevent the Nation being immediately responsible for acts done by its citizens, without the privity or connivance of the Government, in contravention of the principles of neutrality.*

An object this of the greatest importance to a Country whose true interest lies in the preservation of peace.

The inquiry then is—what department of the Government of the U[nited] States is the proper one to make a declaration of Neutrality in the cases in which the engagements of the Nation permit and its interests require such a declaration.

A correct and well informed mind will discern at once that it can belong neither to the Legislative nor Judicial Department and of course must belong to the Executive.

The Legislative Department is not the *organ* of intercourse between the U[nited] States and foreign Nations. It is charged neither with *making* nor *interpreting* Treaties. It is therefore not naturally that Organ of the Government which is to pronounce the existing condition of the Nation, with regard to foreign Powers, or to admonish the Citizens of their obligations and duties as founded upon that condition of things. Still less is it charged with enforcing the execution and observance of these obligations and those duties.

It is equally obvious that the act in question is foreign to the Judiciary Department of the Government. The province of that Department is to decide litigations in particular cases. It is indeed charged with the interpretation of treaties; but it exercises this function only in the litigated cases; that is where contending parties bring before it a specific controversy. It has no concern with pronouncing upon the external political relations of Treaties between Government and Government. This position is too plain to need being insisted upon.

It must then of necessity belong to the Executive Department to exercise the function in Question—when a proper case for the exercise of it occurs.

It appears to be connected with that department in various capacities, as the *organ* of intercourse between the Nation and foreign Nations—as the interpreter of the National Treaties in those cases in which the Judiciary is not competent, that is in the cases between Government and Government— as that Power, which is charged with the Execution of the Laws, of which Treaties form a part—as that Power which is charged with the command and application of the Public Force.

This view of the subject is so natural and obvious—so analogous to general theory and practice—that no doubt can be entertained of its justness, unless such doubt can be deduced from particular provisions of the Constitution of the United States.

Let us see then if cause for such doubt is to be found in that constitution.

The second Article of the Constitution of the U[nited] States, section 1st, establishes this general Proposition, That "The Executive Power shall be vested in a President of the United States of America."

The same article in a succeeding Section proceeds to designate particular cases of Executive Power. It declares among other things that the President shall be Commander in Chief of the army and navy of the U[nited] States and of the Militia of the several states when called into the actual service of the U[nited] States, that he shall have power by and with the advice of the senate to make treaties; that it shall be his duty to receive ambassadors and other public Ministers and to take care that the laws be faithfully executed. . . .

The general doctrine then of our constitution is, that the Executive Power of the Nation is vested in the President; subject only to the *exceptions* and *qualifications* which are expressed in the instrument.

Two of these have been already noticed—the participation of the Senate in the appointment of Officers and the making of Treaties. A third remains to be mentioned the right of the Legislature "to declare war and grant letters of marque and reprisal."

With these exceptions the Executive Power of the Union is completely lodged in the President. This mode of construing the Constitution has indeed been recognized by Congress in formal acts, upon full consideration and debate. The power of removal from office is an important instance.

And since upon general principles for reasons already given, the issuing of a proclamation of neutrality is merely an Executive Act; since also the general Executive Power of the Union is vested in the President, the conclusion is, that the step, which has been taken by him, is liable to no just exception on the score of authority.

It may be observed that this Inference would be just if the power of declaring war had not been vested in the Legislature, but that this power naturally includes the right of judging whether the Nation is under obligations to make war or not.

The answer to this is, that however true it may be, that the right of the Legislature to declare war includes the right of judging whether the Nation be under obligations to make War or not—it will not follow that the Executive is in any case excluded from a similar right of Judgment, in the execution of its own functions.

If the Legislature have a right to make war on the one hand—it is on the other the duty of the Executive to preserve Peace till war is declared; and in fulfilling that duty, it must necessarily possess a right of judging what is the nature of the obligations which the treaties of the Country impose on the Government; and when in pursuance of this right it has concluded that there is nothing in them inconsistent with a *state* of neutrality, it becomes both its province and its duty to enforce the laws incident to that state of the Nation. The Executive is charged with the execution of all laws, the laws of Nations as well as the Municipal law, which recognises and adopts those laws. It is consequently bound, by faithfully executing the laws of neutrality, when that is the state of the Nation, to avoid giving a cause of war to foreign Powers. . . .

In this distribution of powers the wisdom of our constitution is manifested. It is the province and duty of the Executive to preserve to the Nation the blessings of peace. The Legislature alone can interrupt those blessings, by placing the Nation in a state of War. . . .

The President is the constitutional Executor of the laws. Our Treaties and the laws of Nations form a part of the law of the land. He who is to execute the laws must first judge for himself of their meaning. In order to the observance of that conduct, which the laws of nations combined with our treaties prescribed to this country, in reference to the present War in Europe, it was necessary for the President to judge for himself whether there was any thing in our treaties incompatible with an adherence to neutrality. Having judged that there was not, he had a right, and if in his opinion the interests of the Nation required it, it was his duty, as Executor of the laws, to proclaim the neutrality of the Nation, to exhort all persons to observe it, and to warn them of the penalties which would attend its non observance.

The Proclamation has been represented as enacting some new law. This is a view of it entirely erroneous. It only proclaims a *fact* with regard to the *existing state* of the Nation, informs the citizens of what the laws previously established require of them in that state, & warns them that these laws will be put in execution against the Infractors of them.

Helvidius, Nos. 1 & 2

James Madison, August 24, 28, & 31, 1793

No. 1

Several pieces with the signature of Pacificus were lately published, which have been read with singular pleasure and applause, by the foreigners and degenerate citizens among us, who hate our republican government, and the French revolution; whilst the publication seems to have been too little regarded, or too much despised by the steady friends to both.

Had the doctrines inculcated by the writer, with the natural consequences from them, been nakedly presented to the public, this treatment might have been proper. Their true character would then have struck every eye, and been rejected by the feelings of every heart. But they offer themselves to the reader in the dress of an elaborate dissertation; they are mingled with a few truths that may serve them as a passport to credulity; and they are introduced with professions of anxiety for the preservation of peace, for the welfare of the government, and for the respect due to the present head of the executive, that may prove a snare to patriotism. . . .

The basis of the reasoning is, we perceive, the extraordinary doctrine, that the powers of making war, and treaties, are in their nature executive; and therefore comprehended in the general grant of executive power, where not especially and strictly excepted out of the grant.

Let us examine this doctrine: and that we may avoid the possibility of mistaking the writer, it shall be laid down in his own words; a precaution the more necessary, as scarce any thing else could outweigh the improbability, that so extravagant a tenet should be hazarded at so early a day, in the face of the public.

His words are—"Two of these [exceptions and qualifications to the executive powers] have been already noticed—the participation of the senate in the *appointment of officers,* and the *making of treaties.* A *third* remains to be mentioned—the right of the legislature to *declare war, and grant letters of marque and reprisal.*"

Again—"It deserves to be remarked, that as the participation of the senate in the *making of treaties,* and the power of the legislature to *declare war,* are *exceptions* out of the general *executive power,* vested in the president; they are to be construed *strictly,* and ought to be extended no further than is *essential* to their execution. . . ."

If we consult, for a moment, the nature and operation of the two powers to declare war and to make treaties, it will be impossible not to see, that they can never fall within a proper definition of executive powers. The natural province of the executive magistrate is to execute laws, as that of the legislature is to make laws. All his acts, therefore, properly executive, must presuppose the existence of the laws to be executed. A treaty is not an execution of laws: it does not presuppose the existence of laws. It is, on the contrary, to have itself the force of a *law,* and to be carried into *execution,* like all *other laws,* by the *executive magistrate.* To say then that the power of making treaties, which are confessedly laws, belongs naturally to the department which is to execute laws, is to say, that the executive department naturally includes a legislative power. In theory this is an absurdity—in practice a tyranny.

The power to declare war is subject to similar reasoning. A declaration that there shall be war, is not an execution of laws: it does not suppose pre-existing laws to be executed: it is not, in any respect, an act merely executive. It is, on the contrary, one of the most deliberate acts that can be performed; and when performed, has the effect of *repealing* all the *laws* operating in a state of peace, so far as they are inconsistent with a state of war; and of *enacting,* as a *rule for the executive, a new code* adapted to the relation between the society and its foreign enemy. In like manner, a conclusion of peace *annuls* all the *laws* peculiar to a state of war, and *revives* the general *laws* incident to a state of peace.

These remarks will be strengthened by adding, that treaties, particularly treaties of peace, have sometimes the effect of changing not only the external laws of the society, but operate also on the internal code, which is purely municipal, and to which the legislative authority of the country is of itself competent and complete.

From this view of the subject it must be evident, that although the executive may be a convenient organ of preliminary communications with foreign governments, on the subjects of treaty or war; and the proper agent for carrying into execution the final determinations of the competent authority; yet it can have no pretensions, from the nature of the powers in question compared with the nature of the executive trust, to that essential agency which gives validity to such determinations. . . .

3. It remains to be inquired, whether there be any thing in the constitution itself, which shows, that the powers of making war and peace are considered as of an executive nature, and as comprehended within a general grant of executive power.

It will not be pretended, that this appears from any *direct* position to be found in the instrument.

If it were *deducible* from any particular expressions, it may be presumed, that the publication would have saved us the trouble of the research.

Does the doctrine, then, result from the actual distribution of powers among the several branches of the government? or from any fair analogy between the powers of war and treaty, and the enumerated powers vested in the executive alone?

Let us examine:

In the general distribution of powers, we find that of declaring war expressly vested in the congress, where every other legislative power is declared to be vested; and without any other qualification than what is common to every other legislative act. The constitutional idea of this power would seem then clearly to be, that it is of a legislative and not an executive nature.

This conclusion becomes irresistible, when it is recollected, that the constitution cannot be supposed to have placed either any power legislative in its nature, entirely among executive powers, or any power executive in its nature, entirely among legislative powers, without charging the constitution, with that kind of intermixture and consolidation of different powers, which would violate a fundamental principle in the organization of free governments. If it were not unnecessary to enlarge on this topic here, it could be shown, that the constitution was originally vindicated, and has been constantly expounded, with a disavowal of any such intermixture.

The power of treaties is vested jointly in the president and in the senate, which is a branch of the legislature. From this arrangement merely, there can be no inference that would necessarily exclude the power from the executive class: since the senate is joined with the president in another power, that of appointing to offices, which, as far as relate to executive offices at least, is considered as of an executive nature. Yet on the other hand, there are sufficient indications that the power of treaties is regarded by the constitution as materially different from mere executive power, and as having more affinity to the legislative than to the executive character.

One circumstance indicating this, is the constitutional regulation under which the senate give their consent in the case of treaties. In all other cases, the consent of the body is expressed by a majority of voices. In this particular case, a concurrence of two-thirds at least is made necessary, as a substitute or compensation for the other branch of the legislature, which, on certain occasions, could not be conveniently a party to the transaction.

But the conclusive circumstance is, that treaties, when formed according to the constitutional mode, are confessedly to have force and operation of *laws,* and are to be a rule for the courts in controversies between man and man, as much as any *other laws.* They are even emphatically declared by the constitution to be "the supreme law of the land."

So far the argument from the constitution is precisely in opposition to the doctrine. As little will be gained in its favour from a comparison of the two powers, with those particularly vested in the president alone.

As there are but few, it will be most satisfactory to review them one by one.

"The president shall be commander in chief of the army and navy of the United States, and of the militia when called into the actual service of the United States."

There can be no relation worth examining between this power and the general power of making treaties. And instead of being analogous to the power of declaring war, it affords a striking illustration of the incompatibility of the two powers in the same hands. Those who are to *conduct a war* cannot in the nature of things, be proper or safe judges, whether *a war ought* to be *commenced, continued,* or *concluded.* They are barred from the latter functions by a great principle in free government, analogous to that which separates the sword from the purse, or the power of executing from the power of enacting laws. . . .

"He shall take care that the laws shall be faithfully executed, and shall commission all officers of the United States." To see the laws faithfully executed constitutes the essence of the executive authority. But what relation has it to the power of making treaties and war, that is, of determining what the *laws shall be* with regard to other nations? No other certainly than what subsists between the powers of executing and enacting laws; no other, consequently, than what forbids a coalition of the powers in the same department. . . .

Thus it appears that by whatever standard we try this doctrine, it must be condemned as no less vicious in theory than it would be dangerous in practice. It is countenanced neither by the writers on law; nor by the nature of the powers themselves; nor by any general arrangements, or particular expressions, or plausible analogies, to be found in the constitution. . . .

No. 2

. . . The declaring of war is expressly made a legislative function. The judging of the obligations to make war, is admitted to be included as a legislative function. Whenever, then, a question occurs, whether war shall be declared, or whether public stipulations require it, the question necessarily belongs to the department to which those functions belong—and no other department can be *in the execution of its proper functions,* if it should undertake to decide such a question.

There can be no refuge against this conclusion, but in the pretext of a *concurrent* right in both departments to judge of the obligations to declare war; and this must be intended by the writer, when he says, "It will not follow, that the executive is excluded *in any case* from a *similar right* of judging," & c. . . .

It has been seen, that the idea of a *concurrent* right is at variance with other ideas, advanced or admitted by the writer. Laying aside, for the present, that consideration, it seems impossible to avoid concluding, that if the executive, as such, has a concurrent right with the legislature to judge of obligations to declare war, and the right to judge be essentially included in the right to declare, it must have the same concurrent right to declare, as it has to judge; and, by another analogy, the same right to judge of other causes of war, as of the particular cause found in a public stipulation. So that whenever the executive, *in the course of its functions,* shall meet with these cases, it must either infer an equal authority in all, or acknowledge its want of authority in any.

If any doubt can remain, or rather if any doubt could ever have arisen, which side of the alternative ought to be embraced, it can be with those only who overlook or reject some of the most obvious and essential truths in political science.

Not very nice

The power to judge of the causes of war, as involved in the power to declare war, is expressly vested, where all other legislative powers are vested, that is, in the congress of the United States. It is consequently determined by the constitution to be a *legislative power.* Now, omitting the inquiry here, in what respects a compound power may be partly legislative, and partly executive, and accordingly vested *partly* in the one, and *partly* in the other department, or *jointly* in both; a remark used on another occasion is equally conclusive on this, that the same power cannot belong, *in the whole* to *both* departments, or be properly so vested as to operate *separately* in *each.* Still more evident is it, that the same *specific function or act,* cannot possibly belong to the *two* departments, and be *separately* exerciseable by *each.*

Veto

Legislative power may be *concurrently* vested in different legislative bodies. Executive powers may be concurrently vested in different executive magistrates. In legislative acts the executive may have a participation, as in the qualified negative on the laws. In executive acts, the legislature, or at least a branch of it, may participate, as in the appointment to offices. Arrangements of this sort are familiar in theory, as well as in practice. But an independent exercise of an *executive act* by the legislature *alone,* or of a *legislative* act by the executive *alone,* one or other of which must happen in every case where the same act is exerciseable by each, and the latter of which would happen in the case urged by the writer, is contrary to one of the first and best maxims of a well-organized government, and ought never to be founded in a forced construction, much less in opposition to a fair one. Instances, it is true, may be discovered among ourselves, where this maxim has not been faithfully pursued; but being generally acknowledged to be errors, they confirm, rather than impeach the truth and value of the maxim.

It may happen also, that different independent departments, the legislative and executive, for example, may, in the exercise of their functions, interpret the constitution differently, and thence lay claim to the same power. This difference of opinion is an inconvenience not entirely to be avoided. It results from what may be called, if it be thought fit, a *concurrent* right to expound the constitution. But this *species* of concurrence is obviously and radically different from that in question. The former supposes the constitution to have given the power to one department only; and the doubt to be, to which it has been given. The latter supposes it to belong to both; and that it may be exercised by either or both, according to the course of exigencies.

A concurrent authority in two independent departments, to perform the same function with respect to the same thing, would be as awkward in practice, as it is unnatural in theory.

If the legislature and executive have both a right to judge of the obligations to make war or not, it must sometimes happen, though not at present, that they will judge differently. The executive may proceed to consider the question to-day; may determine that the United States are not bound to take part in a war, and, *in the execution of its functions,* proclaim that determination to all the world. Tomorrow, the legislature may follow in the consideration of the same subject; may determine that the obligations impose war on the United States, and, *in the execution of its functions* enter into a *constitutional declaration,* expressly contradicting the *constitutional proclamation.*

In what light does this present the constitution to the people who established it? In what light would it present to the world a nation, thus speaking, through two different organs, equally constitutional and authentic, two opposite languages, on the same subject, and under the same existing circumstances?

The Neutrality Act of 1794

June 5, 1794

CHAP. L.—*An Act in addition to the act for the punishment of certain crimes against the United States.*

SEC. 1. *Be it enacted and declared by the Senate and House of Representatives of the United States of America in Congress assembled,* That if any citizen of the United States shall, within the territory or jurisdiction of the same, accept and exercise a commission to serve a foreign prince or state in war by land or sea, the person so offending shall be deemed guilty of a high misdemeanor, and shall be fined no more than two thousand dollars, and shall be imprisoned not exceeding three years. . . .

SEC. 3. *And be it further enacted and declared,* That if any person shall within any of the ports, harbors, bays, rivers or other waters of the United States, fit out and arm or attempt to fit out and arm or procure to be fitted out and armed . . . with intent that such ship or vessel shall be employed in the service of any foreign prince or state to cruise or commit hostilities upon the subjects, citizens or property of another foreign prince or state with whom the United States are at peace . . . shall upon conviction be adjudged guilty of a high misdemeanor, and shall be fined and imprisoned at the discretion of the court. . . .

SEC. 8. *And be it further enacted and declared,* That it shall be lawful for the President of the United States, or such other person as he shall have empowered for that purpose, to employ such part of the land or naval forces of the United States or of the militia thereof, as shall be necessary to compel any foreign ship or vessel to depart the United States, in all cases in which, by the laws of nations or the treaties of the United States, they ought not to remain within the United States. . . .

NOTES

1. Consider some of the questions raised by the Hamilton–Madison debate over the Neutrality Proclamation. If the grant of "the executive Power" to the president in Article II, Section 1 means what Hamilton says, why isn't Article II only one sentence long? Aside from the election provisions, why list additional powers? Does the reference in Article II, Sections 2 and 3 to the president's commander-in-chief power, treaty-making power, and power to receive ambassadors suggest that the Executive Power Vesting Clause is not as sweeping as Hamilton claims? Is there a different way of understanding *why* the specific provisions of Sections 2 and 3 might have been included in Article II that is reconcilable with the idea that the Vesting Clause's grant of "the executive Power" is an actual grant of the executive power? Can the provisions of Sections 2 and 3 be understood as clarifications or elaborations? Can they be explained as having been made necessary by grants of powers to Congress that touch on foreign affairs?

2. The Neutrality Controversy raises the question of war powers. Where does the Constitution vest the power to declare war? If there is a war, who conducts it? Who determines when the war is over? Who concludes terms of peace? What about the power of "not war"? In other words, does the Constitution give the president power to declare neutrality? Is there a difference between the power to declare and maintain neutrality as a matter of foreign policy and the power to establish penalties or punishments if a private citizen violates that neutrality? What do you think of President Washington's statement that it is a prosecutable crime for any U.S. citizen to violate his Neutrality Proclamation?

[*Assignment 6*]

D. THE ALIEN AND SEDITION ACT CONTROVERSIES

Problems with France and England continued for the young United States. The Jay Treaty of 1795, which was negotiated by President Washington's envoy, Chief Justice John Jay, resolved lingering disputes with England but further strained relations with France. By the time John Adams succeeded President Washington in 1797, France was interfering with the United States' shipping rights as a neutral country. A failed diplomatic mission produced only an outrageous French demand for bribes or tribute (the "XYZ Affair"). By 1798, the United States and France were on the brink of war.

Congress, narrowly controlled by a Federalist Party majority (supporting President Adams) over a Democratic–Republican Party minority (supporting Vice President Jefferson) enacted a series of measures popularly known as the Alien and Sedition Acts. These measures were designed to prepare the nation for war with France, its former ally, and to guard against suspected subversion by aliens and those opposed to (and harshly critical of) the administration of President Adams.

As you read the following materials, ask yourself who gets to decide what the Constitution means: Congress? The president? The courts? Juries in criminal cases? All of the above? Did Congress have the power under Article I to pass the Alien and Sedition Acts? May Congress delegate sweeping powers of deportation of aliens to the president acting without a judge or jury? And is the Sedition Act consistent with the First Amendment's protection against laws that abridge the freedom of speech?

The Alien Friends Act

June 25, 1798

SECTION 1. *Be it enacted by the Senate and House of Representatives of the United States of America in Congress assembled*, That it shall be lawful for the President of the United States at any time during the continuance of this act, to *order* all such *aliens* as he shall judge dangerous to the peace and safety of the United States, or shall have reasonable grounds to suspect are concerned in any treasonable or secret machinations against the government thereof, to depart out of the territory of the United States, within such time as shall be expressed in such order. . . . And in case any alien, so ordered to depart, shall be found at large within the United States after the time limited in such order for his departure, and not having obtained a *license* shall not have conformed thereto, every such alien shall, on conviction thereof, be imprisoned for a term not exceeding three years, and shall never after be admitted to become a citizen of the United States. *Provided always, and be it further enacted*, that if any alien so ordered to depart shall prove to the satisfaction of the President, by evidence to be taken before such person or persons as the President shall direct, who are for that purpose hereby authorized to administer oaths, that no injury or danger to the United States will arise from suffering such alien to reside therein, the President may grant a *license* to such alien to remain within the United States for such time as he shall judge proper, and at such place as he may designate. . . .

SEC. 2. *And be it further enacted*, That it shall be lawful for the President of the United States, whenever he may deem it necessary for the public safety, to order to be removed out of the territory thereof, any alien who may or shall be in prison in pursuance of this act; and to cause to be arrested and sent out of the United States such of those aliens as shall have been ordered to depart therefrom and shall not have obtained a license as aforesaid, in all cases where, in the opinion of the President, the public safety requires a speedy removal. And if any alien so removed or sent out of the United States by the President shall voluntarily return thereto, unless by permission of the President of the United States, such alien on conviction thereof, shall be imprisoned so long as, in the opinion of the President, the public safety may require. . . .

The Alien Enemies Act

July 6, 1798

SECTION 1. *Be it enacted by the Senate and House of Representatives of the United States of America in Congress assembled*, That whenever there shall be a declared war between the United States and any foreign nation or government, or any invasion or predatory incursion shall be perpetrated, attempted, or threatened against the territory of the United States, by any foreign nation or government, and the President of the United States shall make public proclamation of the event, all natives, citizens, denizens, or subjects of the hostile nation or government, being males of the age of fourteen years and upwards, who shall be within the United States, and not actually naturalized, shall be liable to be apprehended, restrained, secured and removed, as alien enemies. And the President of the United States shall be, and he is hereby authorized, in any event, as aforesaid, by his proclamation thereof, or other public act, to direct the conduct to be observed, on the part of the United States, towards the aliens who shall become liable, as aforesaid; the manner and degree of the restraint to which they shall be subject, and in what cases, and upon what security their residence shall be permitted, and to provide for the removal of those, who, not being permitted to reside within the United States, shall refuse or neglect to depart therefrom; and to establish any other regulations which shall be found necessary in the premises and for the public safety: Provided, that aliens resident within the United States, who shall become liable as enemies, in the manner aforesaid, and who shall not be chargeable with actual hostility, or other crime against the public safety, shall be allowed, for the recovery, disposal, and removal of their goods and effects, and for their departure, the full time which is, or shall be stipulated by any treaty, where any shall have been between the United States, and the hostile nation or government, of which they shall be natives, citizens, denizens or subjects: and where no such treaty shall have existed, the President of the United States may ascertain and declare such reasonable time as may be consistent with the public safety, and according to the dictates of humanity and national hospitality.

———

Immediately after passing the Alien Acts, Congress passed the Sedition Act, over the objections of the minority Democratic–Republican Party. The Sedition Act established criminal penalties for conspiracy to oppose the government and for writing or voicing false or scandalous statements about the president and Congress. As you read the Sedition Act, keep in mind that the Bill of Rights had been ratified only seven years earlier. There had, however, been significant turnover in the House and Senate: "Of the ninety-five senators and representatives who served in the First Congress, only eighteen remained when the Sedition Act was enacted in July 1798, and of those only ten voted 'aye.' " David A. Anderson, *The Origins of the Press Clause*, 30 UCLA L. Rev. 455, 517 (1983).

The Sedition Act
July 14, 1798

SECTION 1. *Be it enacted by the Senate and House of Representatives of the United States of America, in Congress assembled*, That if any persons shall unlawfully combine or conspire together, with intent to oppose any measure or measures of the government of the United States, which are or shall be directed by proper authority, or to impede the operation of any law of the United States, or to intimidate or prevent any person holding a place or office in or under the government of the United States, from undertaking, performing or executing his trust or duty, and if any person or persons, with intent as aforesaid, shall counsel, advise or attempt to procure any insurrection, riot, unlawful assembly, or combination, whether such conspiracy, threatening, counsel, advice, or attempt shall have the proposed effect or not, he or they shall be deemed guilty of a high misdemeanor, and on conviction, before any court of the United States having jurisdiction thereof, shall be punished by a fine not exceeding five thousand dollars, and by imprisonment during a term not less than six months nor exceeding five years; and further, at the discretion of the court may be holden to find sureties for his good behaviour in such sum, and for such time, as the said court may direct.

SEC. 2. *And be it further enacted*, That if any person shall write, print, utter or publish, or shall cause or procure to be written, printed, uttered or published, or shall knowingly and willingly assist or aid in writing, printing, uttering or publishing any false, scandalous and malicious writing or writings against the government of the United States, or either house of the Congress of the United States, or the President of the United States, with intent to defame the said government, or either house of the said Congress, or the said President, or to bring them, or either of them, into contempt or disrepute; or to excite against them, or either or any of them, the hatred of the good people of the United States, or to stir up sedition within the United States, or to excite any unlawful combinations therein, for opposing or resisting any law of the United States, or any act of the President of the United States, done in pursuance of any such law, or of the powers in him vested by the constitution of the United States, or to resist, oppose, or defeat any such law or act, or to aid, encourage or abet any hostile designs of any foreign nation against United States, their people or government, then such person, being thereof convicted before any court of the United States having jurisdiction thereof, shall be punished by a fine not exceeding two thousand dollars, and by imprisonment not exceeding two years.

SEC. 3. *And be it further enacted and declared*, That if any person shall be prosecuted under this act, for the writing or publishing any libel aforesaid, it shall be lawful for the defendant, upon the trial of the cause, to give in evidence in his defence, the truth of the matter contained in the publication charged as a libel. And the jury who shall try the cause, shall have a right to determine the law and the fact, under the direction of the court, as in other cases. . . .

NOTES

1. Are Sections 1 and 2 of the Alien Friends Act constitutional? Does Congress have an enumerated power to legislate with respect to aliens and their presence in, or exclusion from, the United States? It has the power to naturalize aliens and make them citizens, but is this the same thing as a power to expel resident aliens or to bar them from entering the country? Congress also has extensive defense-related powers, but again, not an enumerated power to expel or bar aliens. Does the Necessary and Proper Clause, as construed in the Bank controversy, give Congress the power to regulate the admission (or expulsion) of aliens? Or would such a power be an incident of the war power (and thus within the Necessary and Proper Clause power to provide for the execution of the war power)?

Immigration was originally considered an area of state authority. Consider carefully the language of the Slave Importation clauses of Article I, Section 9 and Article V's proviso with respect to the unamendability of this rule until 1808. Did they in effect confer a plenary power on states, rather than the national government, with respect to what could be euphemistically termed "immigration" policy? Did they render the Alien Friends and Alien Enemies acts unconstitutional? It was not until Congress enacted the Chinese Exclusion Act in 1882 (with openly racist motives) that the federal government began to seriously regulate the admission of aliens into the United States. In the 1920s,

Congress passed new and more sweeping immigration acts designed to keep immigrants from Southern and Eastern Europe out of the United States while favoring admission of immigrants from Northern Europe. Again the reasons given were explicitly racist. It was not until President Lyndon Johnson's administration in the 1960s that immigration law was significantly reformed. More recently, immigration has been seen by the Supreme Court as primarily an area for federal regulation. See, e.g., *Arizona v. United States*, 132 S.Ct. 2492 (2012) (striking down several provisions of an Arizona immigration statute, including one making it a crime for a person to be in the state without valid immigration papers, as preempted by federal law).

2. The Alien Acts assigned broad discretion to the president to exclude or expel certain aliens from the United States. If Congress does possess legislative power in this area, may it *delegate* to the president the power to carry out an immigration policy in accordance with highly abstract criteria? If it did, would the president be exercising "legislative" power or "executive" power? What due process rights do aliens have under the Fifth Amendment with respect to their continued presence in or exclusion from the United States? Suppose someone is caught on American soil having just crossed over the Canadian border. Is there a constitutional reason why that person cannot be immediately expelled by customs officials without going to court?

3. Next think about the constitutionality of Section 2 of the Sedition Act. Was it within the enumerated powers of Congress to pass such an act? Wasn't it "convenient" or "useful" to the carrying out of the president's foreign policy for there to be a ban on criticizing both him and Congress? Recall the Federalists' argument that a Bill of Rights was unnecessary, because no power to regulate the press was granted to Congress in its enumerated powers—and recall the Anti–Federalists' response. How does that argument look in light of the Federalists' support for the Sedition Act?

4. Even if the Sedition Act would otherwise fall within Congress's enumerated legislative powers, does it violate the First Amendment? Does it help matters that under Section 3 truth is a defense and juries may determine truth? (Note that the Sedition Act did not ban seditious speech directed against the *vice president*—Thomas Jefferson, a Democratic–Republican and a political opponent of the rest of the Adams administration!)

5. Should a jury be permitted to acquit a defendant charged with violating the Sedition Act on the ground that it is unconstitutional? If Congress, the president, and the federal courts all have a duty to follow the Constitution, why not also a jury? In the famous Trial of the Seven Bishops in London in 1688, seven bishops of the Church of England had been ordered by King James II to read from their pulpits his Declaration of Indulgence giving equal civil rights to Catholics. The seven bishops petitioned the king to change his mind, and the king had them prosecuted for seditious libel based on the statements in their petitions. The seven bishops were tried by a jury, which acquitted them in an act of jury nullification for constitutional reasons. The jurors believed, as was affirmed the next year in the English Bill of Rights of 1689, that the bishops had a constitutional right to petition the king for a redress of their grievances. Compare trials under the Sedition Act—would a jury be right to acquit on grounds of unconstitutionality? Even if the judge had instructed the jury that the act was constitutional?

Judicial Enforcement of the Sedition Act

The United States government brought a number of criminal proceedings under the Sedition Act—fourteen in all. Indeed, "five of the six most influential Republican papers were ultimately prosecuted under the new laws by a Federalist-dominated judiciary." Ron Chernow, ALEXANDER HAMILTON 575 (2004). The following is the report of the trial proceedings in the prosecution of Matthew Lyon, an irascible Democratic–Republican congressman from Vermont.

United States v. Lyon

15 F. Cas. 1183 (D. Vt. 1798)

The indictment which was found on October 5, 1798, contained three counts, the first of which, after averring the intent to be "to stir up sedition, and to bring the President and the government of the United States into contempt," laid the following libellous matter:

As to the Executive, when I shall see the efforts of that power bent on the promotion of the comfort, the happiness, and accommodation of the people, that executive shall have my zealous and uniformed support: but whenever I shall, on the part of the Executive, see every consideration of the public welfare swallowed up in a continual grasp for power, in an unbounded thirst for ridiculous pomp, foolish adulation, and selfish avarice; when I shall behold men of real merit daily turned out of office, for no other cause but independency of sentiment; when I shall see men of firmness, merit, years, abilities, and experience, discarded in their applications for office, for fear they possess that independence, and men of meanness preferred for the case with which they know but little of—when I shall see the sacred name of religion employed as a state engine to make mankind hate and persecute one another, I shall not be their humble advocate.

The second consisted of having maliciously, & c., and with intent, & c., published a letter, said to be a letter from a diplomatic character in France, containing two paragraphs, in the words following:

The misunderstanding between the two government (France and the United States), has become extremely alarming; confidence is completely destroyed, mistrusts, jealousy, and a disposition to a wrong attribution of motives, are so apparent, as to require the utmost caution in every word and action that are to come from your Executive. I mean, if your object is to avoid hostilities. Had this truth been understood with you before the recall of Monroe, before the coming and second coming of Pinckney; had it guided the pens that wrote the bullying speech of your President, and stupid answer of your Senate, at the opening of Congress in November last, I should probably had no occasion to address you this letter.

But when we found him borrowing the language of Edmund Burke, and telling the world that although he should succeed in treating with the French, there was no dependence to be placed on any of their engagements, that their religion and morality were at an end, that they would turn pirates and plunderers; and it would be necessary to be perpetually armed against them, though you were at peace: we wondered that the answer of both Houses had not been an order to send him to a mad house. Instead of this the Senate have echoed the speech with more servility than ever George III. experienced from either House of Parliament.

The third count was for assisting, counseling, aiding, and abetting the publication of the same.

Saturday, Oct. 7. The defendant, being still in custody, (having been arrested on a bench warrant immediately after the finding of the bill,) pleaded not guilty, and put in bail for his appearance on Monday, October 9.

Monday, Oct. 9 . . . [t]he box having been filled, and the jury sworn, the defendant interposed an additional plea, to the effect that the sedition law was unconstitutional, which plea was stricken by the court. The district attorney having opened the case, produced a letter from the same defendant, dated Philadelphia, July 7, 1798, and post marked on the same day, which was printed in Vermont on July 23. The authorship of the letter and the fact of the publication were admitted by the defendant. It was further proved that the defendant had several times read at public meetings in Vermont the letter (known at the time as the "Barlow" letter) from which the libellous matter in the second count was taken.

Several witnesses were called to show that the defendant, both in public and in private, had extensively used the letter for political purposes, and in doing so had frequently made use of language highly disrespectful to the administration. On cross examination, it appeared that on one occasion he had endeavored to prevent it from being printed.

The prosecution having closed its case, the defendant stated his defence to consist of three points: first, that the court had no jurisdiction of the offence, the act of Congress being unconstitutional and void, if not so generally, at least, as to writings composed before its passage; second, that the publication was innocent; and third, that the contents were true.

On the first two points he offered no testimony, but on the third, he proposed to call Judge Paterson, the presiding judge, and Judge Israel Smith.

Judge Paterson being then on the bench, was then asked by the defendant, whether he had frequently "dined with the President, and observed his ridiculous pomp and parade?"

Judge Paterson replied, that he had sometimes, though rarely, dined with the President, but that he had never seen any pomp or parade; he had seen, on the contrary, a great deal of plainness and simplicity.

The defendant then asked whether he (the judge) had not seen at the President's more pomp and servants there, than at the tavern at Rutland? To this no answer was given.

No other witness was called.

Mr. Marsh, district attorney, addressed the jury at length, urging, (1) the libellous nature of the offensive passages, which were clearly within the act of Congress, and (2) the declared intentions with which they had been used by the defendant, which expressly same up to the innuendoes:

Judge Smith, (the then Chief Justice of Vermont,) who then appeared as counsel for the defendant, declining to reply, in consequence of the shortness of time allowed him for preparation, he having been called into the case at bar, the defendant addressed the jury at great length, insisting on the unconstitutionality of the law, and the insufficiency of the evidence to show anything more than a legitimate opposition.

■ PATERSON, J. CIRCUIT JUDGE, with whom was HITCHCOCK, J., DISTRICT JUDGE, charged the jury substantially as follows:

> You have nothing whatsoever to do with the constitutionality or unconstitutionality of the sedition law. Congress has said that the author and publisher of seditious libels is to be punished: and until this law is declared null and void by a tribunal competent for the purpose, its validity cannot be disputed. Great would be the abuses were the constitutionality of every statute to be submitted to a jury, in each case where the statute is to be applied. The only question you are to determine is, that which the record submits to you. Did Mr. Lyon publish the writing given in the indictment? Did he do so seditiously? On the first point, the evidence is undisputed, and in fact, he himself concedes the fact of publication as to a large portion of libellous matter. As to the second point, you will have to consider whether language such as that here complained of could have been uttered with any other intent that that of making odious or contemptible the President and government, and bringing them both into disrepute. If you find such is the case, the offence is made out, and you must render a verdict of guilty. Nor should the political rank of the defendant, his past services, or the dependent condition of his family, deter you from this duty. Such considerations are for the court alone in adjusting the penalty they will bestow. The fact of guilt is for you, for the court, the grade of punishment. As to yourselves, one point, in addition, in exercising the functions allotted to you, you must keep in mind: and that is, that in order to render a verdict of guilty, you must be satisfied beyond all reasonable substantial doubt that the hypothesis of innocence is unsustainable. Keeping these instructions in your mind, you will proceed to deliberate on your verdict.

At about eight o'clock in the evening of the same day, after about an hour's absence, the jury returned with a verdict of guilty.

The defendant being called up for sentence, a postponement was obtained till the next morning, when, after a representation of his circumstances, it appearing that he was almost insolvent. Judge Paterson addressed him as follows:

> Matthew Lyon, as a member of the federal legislature, you must be well acquainted with the mischiefs which flow from an unlicensed abuse of government, and of the motives which led to the passage of the act under which this indictment is framed. No one, also, can be better acquainted than yourself with the existence and nature of the act. You position, so far from making the case one which might slip with a nominal fine through the hands of the court, would make impunity conspicuous should such a fine alone be imposed. What however, has tended to mitigate the sentence which would otherwise have been imposed, is, what I am sorry to hear of, the reduced condition of your estate. The judgment of the court is, that you stand imprisoned four months, pay the costs of prosecution, and a fine of one thousand dollars, and stand committed until this sentence be complied with.

———

Consider a second famous example of a prosecution for violation of the Sedition Act, *United States v. Callender*, 25 Fed. Cas. 239 (1800). James Callender, a scandal-mongering Democratic–Republican journalist, was convicted for publishing the following statement:

> The reign of Mr. Adams has been one continued tempest of malignant passion. As President, he has never opened his lips, or lifted his pen without threatening and scolding; the grand object of his administration has been to exasperate the rage of contending parties, to calumniate and destroy every man who differs from his opinions. Mr. Adams has laboured, and with melancholy success, to break up the bonds of social affection, and under the ruins of confidence and friendship, to extinguish the only gleam of happiness that glimmers through the dark and despicable farce of life.

Callender was forced to pay a fine of $200 and was sentenced to nine months in prison, a portion of which he served before being pardoned by Jefferson after his ascent to the presidency.

NOTES

1. If you thought the Sedition Act was unconstitutional, does the fact that the federal courts upheld the convictions of Lyon, Callender, and many others change your mind? There were no successful appeals challenging the constitutionality of the Sedition Act as it was being enforced. Despite the seemingly evident unconstitutionality of the Sedition Act, Congress passed it, the president signed it and brought prosecutions under it, and the federal courts upheld its constitutionality. All three branches of the federal government—the whole Madisonian system of checks and balances—agreed. What should one do in a situation like this? (Consider the Jeffersonians' response below.)

2. Lyon and Callender were not exactly reputable characters. Lyon was court-martialed for cowardice during the Revolutionary War and was reportedly sentenced by General Gates to carry a wooden sword as a symbol of shame. He then left the army before independence was achieved and engaged in land speculation and political machinations in Vermont. A perennial candidate for Congress, Lyon was finally elected, narrowly (by 396 votes), in a 1797 run-off election, and he immediately made a pest of himself and developed a reputation as a demagogue. Once, when he proclaimed himself a champion for the common man, a Federalist congressman, Roger Griswold, asked whether Lyon would be fighting with his wooden sword. Lyon spat in Griswold's face, and a motion to expel Lyon from the House for "gross indecency" failed to obtain the necessary two-thirds vote. Griswold then purchased a large wooden cane and used it thrash Lyon. Most other members of Congress felt he deserved the thrashing. Lyon's reputation at home received its greatest boost from his conviction (and prison term) for violation of the Sedition Act. He became something of a martyr, ran his re-election campaign from prison, and won by a more substantial margin that he had obtained in 1796. For a brief, entertaining account, from which this one is drawn, see Stanley Elkins & Eric McKitrick, THE AGE OF FEDERALISM: THE EARLY AMERICAN REPUBLIC, 1788–1800 706–711 (1993).

3. Callender was a journalist in an era of highly partisan newspapers, and his publications were secretly financed by Vice President Jefferson. Later, though, Callender turned his scandal-mongering in Jefferson's direction, exposing the affair between Jefferson and his slave Sally Hemmings and their having several children together. The accusation, hotly disputed at the time, has

since been proved by DNA evidence. See Joseph Ellis, AMERICAN SPHINX: THE CHARACTER OF THOMAS JEFFERSON 363–367 (1998). Callender ended up hated by all sides. As Ellis puts it, Callender's "only consistency was a perverse flair for treachery." *Id.* at 260.

The Virginia and Kentucky Resolutions and the Northern Responses

Opposition to the Alien and Sedition Acts gave rise to one of the most famous constitutional debates in our nation's history. The states of Virginia and Kentucky, in resolutions drafted by James Madison and Thomas Jefferson, respectively, argued with vigor that these statutes were unconstitutional. (Jefferson's original draft was softened considerably before being adopted by the Kentucky legislature.)

Northern states adopted resolutions defending the laws and arguing that Virginia and Kentucky had no business declaring acts of Congress unconstitutional, because questions of constitutional interpretation were reserved for the courts. (There is some irony here, in that the Northern states' argument that only courts may interpret the Constitution is itself an interpretation of the Constitution.) Virginia responded with an elaborate defense of the resolutions, reiterating its argument that the Alien and Sedition Acts were unconstitutional and defending the propriety of a state legislature making such a declaration. Madison wrote this response, called the Report of 1800.

As you read these documents, consider again the constitutionality of the Alien and Sedition Acts, looking at the arguments made by Virginia (Madison) and Kentucky (Jefferson) about whether Congress possessed an enumerated power to pass the acts and whether they violated the First Amendment. Note, especially with the Kentucky Resolutions, how Jefferson is re-fighting the old battles he lost to Hamilton earlier in the decade over the Bank, the scope of enumerated powers generally, and national-versus-state power.

In addition, join the debate over who may and must interpret the Constitution. Are the Northern states right that constitutional questions are reserved for the courts? Is the Report of 1800 right in defending the propriety of states interpreting the Constitution? If so, what are the implications of such a position? May a state that is fully convinced that a federal law, upheld by the federal courts, is unconstitutional purport to "nullify" the law within its borders or "interpose" state power against its enforcement? Is this a recipe for anarchy, secession, and civil war? How far do Madison and Jefferson press the argument?

Finally, ask yourself whether the people have a role in constitutional interpretation. One reading of the election of 1800 was that it was an act of constitutional interpretation by the electorate, siding with the Democratic–Republicans on the constitutionality of the Alien and Sedition Acts (and overruling the Federalist-dominated federal courts). Do "We the People" possess the power of constitutional interpretation? If so, how may that power be exercised?

The Virginia Resolutions of 1798

James Madison, December 24, 1798

RESOLVED, That the General Assembly of Virginia, doth unequivocally express a firm resolution to maintain and defend the Constitution of the United States, and the Constitution of this State, against every aggression either foreign or domestic, and that they will support the government of the United States in all measures warranted by the former.

That this assembly most solemnly declares a warm attachment to the Union of the States, to maintain which it pledges all its powers; and that for this end, it is their duty to watch over and oppose every infraction of those principles which constitute the only basis of that Union, because a faithful observance of them, can alone secure it's existence and the public happiness.

That this Assembly doth explicitly and peremptorily declare, that it views the powers of the federal government, as resulting from the compact, to which the states are parties; as limited by the plain sense and intention of the instrument constituting the compact; as no further valid that they are authorized by the grants enumerated in that compact; and that in case of a deliberate, palpable, and dangerous exercise of other powers, not granted by the said compact, the states who are parties thereto, have the right, and are in duty bound, to interpose for arresting the progress of the evil, and for maintaining within their respective limits, the authorities, rights and liberties appertaining to them.

That the General Assembly doth also express its deep regret, that a spirit has in sundry instances, been manifested by the federal government, to enlarge its powers by forced constructions of the constitutional charter which defines them; and that implications have appeared of a design to expound certain general phrases (which having been copied from the very limited grant of power, in the former articles of confederation were the less liable to be misconstrued) so as to destroy the meaning and effect, of the particular enumeration which necessarily explains and limits the general phrases; and so as to consolidate the states by degrees, into one sovereignty, the obvious tendency and inevitable consequence of which would be, to transform the present republican system of the United States, into an absolute, or at best a mixed monarchy.

That the General Assembly doth particularly protest against the palpable and alarming infractions of the Constitution, in the two late cases of the "Alien and Sedition Acts" passed at the last session of Congress; the first of which exercises a power no where delegated to the federal government, and which by uniting legislative and judicial powers to those of executive, subverts the general principles of free government; as well as the particular organization, and positive provisions of the federal constitution; and the other of which acts, exercises in like manner, a power not delegated by the constitution, but on the contrary, expressly and positively forbidden by one of the amendments thereto; a power, which more than any other, ought to produce universal alarm, because it is levelled against that right of freely examining public characters and measures, and of free communication among the people thereon, which has ever been justly deemed, the only effectual guardian of every other right.

That this state having by its Convention, which ratified the federal Constitution, expressly declared, that among other essential rights, "the Liberty of Conscience and of the Press cannot be cancelled, abridged, restrained, or modified by any authority of the United States," and from its extreme anxiety to guard these rights from every possible attack of sophistry or ambition, having with other states, recommended an amendment for that purpose, which amendment was, in due time, annexed to the Constitution; it would mark a reproachable inconsistency, and criminal degeneracy, if an indifference were now shewn, to the most palpable violation of one of the Rights, thus declared and secured; and to the establishment of a precedent which may be fatal to the other.

That the good people of this commonwealth, having ever felt, and continuing to feel, the most sincere affection for their brethren of the other states; the truest anxiety for establishing and perpetuating the union of all; and the most scrupulous fidelity to that constitution, which is the pledge of mutual friendship, and the instrument of mutual happiness; the General Assembly doth solemnly appeal to the like dispositions of the other states, in confidence that they will concur with this commonwealth in declaring, as it does hereby declare, that the acts aforesaid, are unconstitutional; and that the necessary and proper measures will be taken by each, for co-operating with this state, in maintaining the Authorities, Rights, and Liberties, referred to the States respectively, or to the people.

That the Governor be desired, to transmit a copy of the foregoing Resolutions to the executive authority of each of the other states, with a request that the same may be communicated to the Legislature thereof; and that a copy be furnished to each of the Senators and Representatives representing this state in the Congress of the United States.

The Kentucky Resolutions of 1798

Thomas Jefferson's Draft, November 10, 1798

1. *Resolved*, That the several States composing, the United States of America, are not united on the principle of unlimited submission to their general government; but that, by a compact under the style and title of a Constitution for the United States, and of amendments thereto, they constituted a general government for special purposes—delegated to that government certain definite powers, reserving, each State to itself, the residuary mass of right to their own self-government; and that whensoever the general government assumes undelegated powers, its acts are unauthoritative, void, and of no force: that to this compact each State acceded as a State, and is an integral part, its co-States forming, as to itself, the other party: that the government created by this compact was not made the exclusive or final judge of the extent of the powers delegated to itself; since that would have made its discretion, and not the Constitution, the measure of its powers; but that, as in all other cases of compact among powers having no common judge, each party has an equal right to judge for itself, as well of infractions as of the mode and measure of redress.

2. *Resolved*, That the Constitution of the United States, having delegated to Congress a power to punish treason, counterfeiting the securities and current coin of the United States, piracies, and felonies committed on the high seas, and offenses against the law of nations, and no other crimes, whatsoever; and it being true as a general principle, and one of the amendments to the Constitution having also declared, that "the powers not delegated to the United States by the Constitution, not prohibited by it to the States, are reserved to the States respectively, or to the people," therefore the act of Congress, passed on the 14th day of July, 1798, and intitled

"An Act in addition to the act intitled An Act for the punishment of certain crimes against the United States," as also the act passed by them on the—day of June, 1798, intitled "An Act to punish frauds committed on the bank of the United States," (and all their other acts which assume to create, define, or punish crimes, other than those so enumerated in the Constitution,) are altogether void, and of no force; and that the power to create, define, and punish such other crimes is reserved, and, of right, appertains solely and exclusively to the respective States, each within its own territory.

3. *Resolved*, That it is true as a general principle, and is also expressly declared by one of the amendments to the Constitutions, that "the powers not delegated to the United States by the Constitution, our prohibited by it to the States, are reserved to the States respectively, or to the people"; and that no power over the freedom of religion, freedom of speech, or freedom of the press being delegated to the United States by the Constitution, nor prohibited by it to the States, all lawful powers respecting the same did of right remain, and were reserved to the States or the people: that thus was manifested their determination to retain to themselves the right of judging how far the licentiousness of speech and of the press may be abridged without lessening their useful freedom, and how far those abuses which cannot be separated from their use should be tolerated, rather than the use be destroyed. And thus also they guarded against all abridgment by the United States of the freedom of religious opinions and exercises, and retained to themselves the right of protecting the same, as this State, by a law passed on the general demand of its citizens, had already protected them from all human restraint or interference. And that in addition to this general principle and express declaration, another and more special provision has been made by one of the amendments to the Constitution, which expressly declares, that "Congress shall make no law respecting an establishment of religion, or prohibiting the free exercise thereof, or abridging the freedom of speech or of the press": thereby guarding in the same sentence, and under the same words, the freedom of religion, of speech, and of the press: insomuch, that whatever violated either, throws down the sanctuary which covers the others, arid that libels, falsehood, and defamation, equally with heresy and false religion, are withheld from the cognizance of federal tribunals. That, therefore, the act of Congress of the United States, passed on the 14th day of July, 1798, intituled "An Act in addition to the act intituled An Act for the punishment of certain crimes against the United States," which does abridge the freedom of the press, is not law, but is altogether void, and of no force.

4. *Resolved*, That alien friends are under the jurisdiction and protection of the laws of the State wherein they are: that no power over them has been delegated to the United States, nor prohibited to the individual States, distinct from their power over citizens. And it being true as a general principle, and one of the amendments to the Constitution having also declared, that "the powers not delegated to the United States by the Constitution, nor prohibited by it to the States, are reserved to the States respectively, or to the people," the act of the Congress of the United States, passed on the—day of July, 1798, intituled "An Act concerning aliens," which assumes powers over alien friends, not delegated by the Constitution, is not law, but is altogether void, and of no force.

5. *Resolved.* That in addition to the general principle, as well as the express declaration, that powers not delegated are reserved, another and more special provision, inserted in the Constitution from abundant caution,

has declared that "the migration or importation of such persons as any of the States now existing shall think proper to admit, shall not be prohibited by the Congress prior to the year 1808" that this commonwealth does admit the migration of alien friends, described as the subject of the said act concerning aliens: that a provision against prohibiting their migration, is a provision against all acts equivalent thereto, or it would be nugatory: that to remove them when migrated, is equivalent to a prohibition of their migration, and is, therefore, contrary to the said provision of the Constitution, and void.

6. *Resolved*, That the imprisonment of a person under the protection of the laws of this commonwealth, on his failure to obey the simple order of the President to depart out of the United States, as is undertaken by said act intitled "An Act concerning aliens" is contrary to the Constitution, one amendment to which has provided that "no person shalt be deprived of liberty without due process of law"; and that another having provided that "in all criminal prosecutions the accused shall enjoy the right to public trial by an impartial jury, to be informed of the nature and cause of the accusation, to be confronted with the witnesses against him, to have compulsory process for obtaining witnesses in his favor, and to have the assistance of counsel for his defense"; the same act, undertaking to authorize the President to remove a person out of the United States, who is under the protection of the law, on his own suspicion, without accusation, without jury, without public trial, without confrontation of the witnesses against him, without heating witnesses in his favor, without defense, without counsel, is contrary to the provision also of the Constitution, is therefore not law, but utterly void, and of no force: that transferring the power of judging any person, who is under the protection of the laws from the courts, to the President of the United States, as is undertaken by the same act concerning aliens, is against the article of the Constitution which provides that "the judicial power of the United States shall be vested in courts, the judges of which shall hold their offices during good behavior"; and that the said act is void for that reason also. And it is further to be noted, that this transfer of judiciary power is to that magistrate of the general government who already possesses all the Executive, and a negative on all Legislative powers.

7. *Resolved*, That the construction applied by the General Government (as is evidenced by sundry of their proceedings) to those parts of the Constitution of the United States which delegate to Congress a power "to lay and collect taxes, duties, imports, and excises, to pay the debts, and provide for the common defense and general welfare of the United States," and "to make all laws which shall be necessary and proper for carrying into execution, the powers vested by the Constitution in the government of the United States, or in any department or officer thereof," goes to the destruction of all limits prescribed to their powers by the Constitution: that words meant by the instrument to be subsidiary only to the execution of limited powers, ought not to be so construed as themselves to give unlimited powers, nor a part to be so taken as to destroy the whole residue of that instrument: that the proceedings of the General Government under color of these articles, will be a fit and necessary subject of revisal and correction, at a time of greater tranquillity, while those specified in the preceding resolutions call for immediate redress.

8. *Resolved*, That a committee of conference and correspondence be appointed, who shall have in charge to communicate the preceding resolutions to the Legislatures of the several States: to assure them that this common-

wealth continues in the same esteem of their friendship and union which it has manifested from that moment at which a common danger first suggested a common union: that it considers union, for specified national purposes, and particularly to those specified in their late federal compact, to be friendly, to the peace, happiness and prosperity of all the States: that faithful to that compact, according to the plain intent and meaning in which it was understood and acceded to by the several parties, it is sincerely anxious for its preservation: that it does also believe, that to take from the States all the powers of self-government and transfer them to a general and consolidated government, without regard to the special delegations and reservations solemnly agreed to in that compact, is not for the peace, happiness or prosperity of these States; and that therefore this commonwealth is determined, as it doubts not its co-States are, to submit to undelegated, and consequently unlimited powers in no man, or body of men on earth: that in cases of an abuse of the delegated powers, the members of the general government, being chosen by the people, a change by the people would be the constitutional remedy; but, where powers are assumed which have not been delegated, a nullification of the act is the rightful remedy: that every State has a natural right in cases not within the compact, (*casus non foederis*) to nullify of their own authority all assumptions of power by others within their limits: that without this right, they would be under the dominion, absolute and unlimited, of whosoever might exercise this right of judgment for them: that nevertheless, this commonwealth, from motives of regard and respect for its co States, has wished to communicate with them on the subject: that with them alone it is proper to communicate, they alone being parties to the compact, and solely authorized to judge in the last resort of the powers exercised under it, Congress being not a party, but merely the creature of the compact, and subject as to its assumptions of power to the final judgment of those by whom, and for whose use itself and its powers were all created and modified. . . .

As noted, the Kentucky legislature toned down Jefferson's draft considerably, shortening it and deleting the potentially explosive references to "nullification" as the "rightful remedy." As it happened, the Virginia and Kentucky Resolutions were explosive enough. The legislatures of many Northern states responded aggressively. Six actively opposed, and none supported, the positions of Virginia and Kentucky. Included below are responses from the states of Rhode Island and New York.

The Response of the State of Rhode Island and Providence Plantations

February 1799

Certain resolutions of the legislature of Virginia, passed on the 21st of December last, being communicated to this Assembly,—

1. *Resolved*, That in the opinion of this legislature, the second section of third article of the Constitution of the United States, in these words, to wit,—"The judicial power shall extend to all cases arising under the laws of the United States,"—vests in the federal courts, exclusively, and in the Supreme Court of the United States, ultimately, the authority of deciding on the constitutionality of an act or law of the Congress of the United States.

2. *Resolved*, That for any state legislature to assume that authority would be—

1st. Blending together legislative and judicial powers;

2d. Hazarding an interruption of the peace of the states by civil discord, in case of a diversity of opinions among the state legislatures; each state having, in that case, no resort, for vindicating its own opinions, but the strength of its own arms;—

3d. Submitting most important questions of law to less competent tribunals; and,

4th. An infraction of the Constitution of the United States, expressed in plain terms.

3. *Resolved*, That although, for the above reasons, this legislature, in their public capacity, do not feel themselves authorized to consider and decide on the constitutionality of the Sedition and Alien laws, (so called,) yet they are called upon, by the exigency of this occasion, to declare that, in their private opinions, these laws are within the powers delegated to Congress, and promotive of the welfare of the United States.

4. *Resolved*, That the governor communicate these resolutions to the supreme executive of the State of Virginia, and at the same time express to him that this legislature cannot contemplate, without extreme concern and regret, the many evil and fatal consequences which may flow from the very unwarrantable resolutions aforesaid of the legislature of Virginia, passed on the twenty-first day of December laws.

The Response of the State of New York

March 5, 1799

Whereas the people of the United States have established for themselves a free and independent national government: And whereas it is essential to the existence of every government, that it have authority to defend and preserve its constitutional powers inviolate, inasmuch as every infringement thereof tends to its subversion: And whereas the judicial power extends expressly to all cases of law and equity arising under the Constitution and the laws of the United States, whereby the interference of the legislatures of the particular states in those cases is manifestly excluded: And whereas our peace, prosperity, and happiness, eminently depend on the preservation of the Union, in order to which a reasonable confidence in the constituted authorities and chosen representatives of the people is indispensable: And whereas every measure calculated to weaken that confidence has a tendency to destroy the usefulness of our public functionaries, and to excite jealousies equally hostile to rational liberty, and the principles of a good republican government: And whereas the Senate, not perceiving that the rights of the particular states have been violated, nor any unconstitutional powers assumed by the general government, cannot forbear to express the anxiety and regret with which they observe the inflammatory and pernicious sentiments and doctrines which are contained in the resolutions of the legislatures of Virginia and Kentucky—sentiments and doctrines no less repugnant to the Constitution of the United States, and the principles of their union, than destructive to the federal government, and unjust to those whom the people have elected to administer it;—wherefore

Resolved, That while the Senate feel themselves constrained to bear unequivocal testimony against such sentiments and doctrines, they deem it a duty no less indispensable explicitly to declare their incompetency, as a branch of the legislature of this state, to supervise the acts of the general government.

Resolved, That his excellency, the governor, be, and he is hereby, requested to transmit a copy of the foregoing resolution to the executives of the states of Virginia and Kentucky, to the end that the same may be communicated to the legislatures thereof.

James Madison's Report
on the Virginia Resolutions

Virginia House of Delegates, approved January 7, 1800

Report of the Committee to whom were referred the Communications of various States, relative to the Resolutions of the last General Assembly of this State, concerning the Alien and Sedition Laws[.]

Whatever room might be found in the proceedings of some of the states, who have disapproved of the resolutions of the General Assembly of this commonwealth, passed on the 21st day of December, 1798, for painful remarks on the spirit and manner of those proceedings, it appears to the committee most consistent with the duty, as well as dignity, of the General Assembly, to hasten an oblivion of every circumstance which might be construed into a diminution of mutual respect, confidence, and affection, among the members of the Union.

The committee have deemed it a more useful task to revise, with a critical eye, the resolutions which have met with their disapprobation; to examine fully the several objections and arguments which have appeared against them; and to inquire whether there can be any errors of fact, of principle, or of reasoning, which the candor of the General Assembly ought to acknowledge and correct. . . .

It appears to your committee to be a plain principle, founded in common sense, illustrated by common practice, and essential to the nature compacts, that, where resort can be had to no tribunal superior to the authority of the parties, the parties themselves must be the rightful judges, in the last resort, whether the bargain made has been pursued or violated. The Constitution of the United States was formed by the sanction of the states, given by each in its sovereign capacity. It adds to the stability and dignity, as well as to the authority, of the Constitution, that it rests on this legitimate and solid foundation. The states, then, being the parties to the constitutional compact, and in their sovereign capacity, it follows of necessity that there can be no tribunal, above their authority, to decide, in the last resort, whether the compact made by them be violated; and consequently, that, as the parties to it, they must themselves decide, in the last resort, such questions as may be of sufficient magnitude to require their interposition. . . .

But it is objected, that the judicial authority is to be regarded as the sole expositor of the Constitution in the last resort; and it may be asked for what reason the declaration by the General Assembly, supposing it to be theoretically true, could be required at the present day, and in so solemn a manner.

On this objection it might be observed, first, that there may be instances of usurped power, which the forms of the Constitution would never draw within the control of the judicial department; secondly, that, if the decision of the judiciary be raised above the authority of the sovereign parties to the Constitution, the decisions of the other departments, not carried by the forms of the Constitution before the judiciary, must be equally authoritative and final with the decisions of that department. But the proper answer to the objection is, that the resolution of the General Assembly relates to those great and extraordinary cases, in which all the forms of the Constitution may prove ineffectual against infractions dangerous to the essential rights of the parties to it. The resolution supposes that dangerous powers, not delegated, may not only be usurped and executed by the other departments, but that the judicial department, also, may exercise or sanction dangerous powers beyond the grant of the Constitution; and, consequently, that the ultimate right of the parties to the Constitution, to judge whether the compact has been dangerously violated, must extend to violations by one delegated authority as well as by another—by the judiciary as well as by the executive, or the legislature.

However true, therefore, it may be, that the judicial department is, in all questions submitted to it by the forms of the Constitution, to decide in the last resort, this resort must necessarily be deemed the last in relation to the authorities of the other departments of the government; not in relation to the rights of the parties to the constitutional compact, from which the judicial, as well as the other departments, hold their delegated trusts. On any other hypothesis, the delegation of judicial power would annul the authority delegating it; and the concurrence of this department with the others in usurped powers, might subvert forever, and beyond the possible reach of any rightful remedy, the very Constitution which all were instituted to preserve. . . .

However difficult it maybe to mark, in every case, with clearness and certainty, the line which divides legislative power from the other departments of power, all will agree that the powers referred to these departments may be so general and undefined, as to be of a legislative, not of an executive or judicial nature, and may for that reason be unconstitutional. Details, to a certain degree, are essential to the nature and character of law; and on criminal subjects, it is proper that details should leave as little as possible to the discretion of those who are to apply and execute the law. If nothing more were required, in exercising a legislative trust, than a general conveyance of authority—without laying down any precise rules by which the authority conveyed should be carried into effect—it would follow that the whole power of legislation might be transferred by the legislature from itself, and proclamations might become substitutes for laws. A delegation of power in this latitude would not be denied to be a union of the different powers.

To determine, then, whether the appropriate powers of the distinct departments are united by the act authorizing the executive to remove aliens, it must be inquired whether it contains such details, definitions, and rules, as appertain to the true character of a law; especially a law by which personal liberty is invaded, property deprived of its value to the owner, and life itself indirectly exposed to danger.

The Alien Act declares "that it shall be lawful for the President to order all such aliens as he shall judge dangerous to the peace and safety of the United States, or shall have reasonable ground to suspect are concerned in any treasonable or secret machinations against the government thereof, to depart," & c. Could a power be well given in terms less definite, less particular, and less precise? To be dangerous to the public safety—to be suspected of secret machination against the government; these can never be mistaken for legal rules or certain definitions. They leave every thing to the President. His will is the law.

But it is not a legislative power only that is given to the President. He is to stand in the place of the judiciary also. His suspicion is the only evidence which is to convict; his order, the only judgment which is to be executed.

Thus it is the President whose will is to designate the offensive conduct; it is his will that is to ascertain the individuals on whom it is charged; and it is his will that is to cause the sentence to be executed. It is rightly affirmed, therefore, that the act unites legislative and judicial powers to those of the executive. . . .

It has been said that it belongs to the judiciary of the United States, and not the state legislatures, to declare the meaning of the Federal Constitution.

But a declaration that proceedings of the federal government are not warranted by the Constitution, is a novelty neither among the citizens nor among the legislatures of the states; nor are the citizens or the legislature of Virginia singular in the example of it.

Nor can the declarations of either, whether affirming or denying the constitutionality of measures of the federal government, or whether made before or after judicial decisions thereon, be deemed, in any point of view, an assumption of the office of the judge. The declarations in such cases are expressions of opinion, unaccompanied with any other effect than what they may produce on opinion, by exciting reflection. The expositions of the judiciary, on the other hand, are carried into immediate effect by force, The former may lead to a change in the legislative expression of the general will—possibly to a change in the opinion of the judiciary; the latter enforces the general will, whilst that will and that opinion continue unchanged.

Resolutions are just opinion

And if there be no impropriety in declaring the unconstitutionality of proceedings in the federal government, where can there be the impropriety of communicating the declaration to other states, and inviting their concurrence in a like declaration? What is allowable for one, must be allowable for all; and a free communication among the states, where the Constitution imposes no restraint, is as allowable among the state governments as among other public bodies or private citizens. This consideration derives a weight that cannot be denied to it, from the relation of the state legislatures to the federal legislature as the immediate constituents of one of its branches. . . .

Resolved, That the General Assembly, having carefully and respectfully attended to the proceedings of a number of the states, in answer to the resolutions of December 21, 1798, and having accurately and fully reexamined and reconsidered the latter, find it to be their indispensable duty to adhere to the same, as founded in truth, as consonant with the Constitution, and as conducive to its preservation; and more especially to be their duty to renew, as they do hereby renew, their PROTEST against Alien and Sedition Acts, as palpable and alarming infractions of the Constitution.

NOTES

1. Evaluate the arguments in the Virginia and Kentucky Resolutions regarding the constitutionality of the Alien and Sedition Acts. Do these arguments cause you to revise your original views? If Jefferson and Madison make a persuasive case that the Sedition Act was unconstitutional, on what ground do they do so—the lack of an enumerated federal legislative power, an improper "delegation" to the executive, or a violation of the First Amendment freedom of speech and of the press?

2. As noted, the federal courts regularly upheld the validity of prosecutions under the Sedition Act. (No case presenting the issue went to the Supreme Court, chiefly because of limitations at that time on appeals and because the act expired in 1801.) Does this render the position taken by the Virginia and Kentucky Resolutions illegitimate or improper? What happens when the courts are simply wrong? Does the fact that courts upheld the constitutionality of the Sedition Act transform an unconstitutional act into a constitutional act?

3. Who was right about the power to interpret the Constitution—the legislatures of Virginia and Kentucky or the legislatures of the Northern states? Is it legitimate for a state to resist what it considers unconstitutional enactments of the national government? How far may it go in such resistance? May it purport to "nullify" those acts? May it "interpose" state power—including force—to resist what it regards as an unconstitutional enactment? Are states the *supreme* interpreters of the Constitution? Is there a difference between Madison's arguments (for Virginia) and Jefferson's (for Kentucky) in this regard? Were the Northern states right that the federal judicial branch has the *sole* power to interpret the Constitution and that every other political actor must adhere to its rulings?

4. The idea that states may use their powers to guard against federal violations of the Constitution has some support in early defenses of the Constitution, such as *The Federalist*. Consider the following excerpts:

> If the representatives of the people betray their constituents, there is then no resource left but in the exertion of that original right of self-defense which is paramount to all positive forms of government, and which against the usurpations of the national rulers, may be exerted within infinitely better prospect of success than against those of the rulers of an individual state. . . . Power being almost always the rival of power, the general government will at all times stand ready to check the usurpations of the state governments, and these will have the same disposition towards the general government. The people, by throwing themselves into either scale, will infallibly make it preponderate. If their rights are invaded by either, they can make use of the other as the instrument of redress. . . . It may safely be received as an axiom in our political system, that the State governments will, in all possible contingencies, afford complete security against invasions of the public liberty by the national authority. . . . [P]ossessing all the organs of civil power, and the confidence of the people, they can at once adopt a regular plan of opposition, in which they can combine all the resources of the community.[8]

---

[8] *The Federalist No. 28* (Alexander Hamilton).

But it will not follow from this doctrine [i.e., the supremacy of federal law over state law] that acts of the larger society which are *not pursuant* to its constitutional powers, but which are invasions of the residuary authorities of the smaller societies, will become the supreme law of the land. These will be merely acts of usurpation, and will deserve to be treated as such.[9]

If it be asked, what is to be the consequence, in case the Congress shall misconstrue this part of the Constitution, and exercise powers not warranted by its true meaning? I answer the same as if they should misconstrue or enlarge any other power vested in them. . . . In the first instance, the success of the usurpation will depend on the executive and judiciary departments, which are to expound and give effect to the legislative acts; and in the last resort, a remedy must be obtained from the people, who can by the election of more faithful representatives, annul the acts of the usurpers. The truth is, that this ultimate redress may be more confided in against unconstitutional acts of the federal than of the State Legislatures, for this plain reason, that as every such act of the former, will be an invasion of the rights of the latter, these will be ever ready to mark the innovation, to sound the alarm to the people, and to exert their local influence in effecting a change of federal representatives.[10]

But ambitious encroachments of the Federal Government, on the authority of the State governments, would not excite the opposition of a single State or of a few States only. They would be signals of general alarm. Every Government would espouse the common cause. A correspondence would be opened. Plans of resistance would be concerted. One spirit would animate and conduct the whole. The same combination in short would result from an apprehensive of the federal, as was produced by the dread of a foreign yoke; and unless the projected innovations should be voluntarily renounced, the same appeal to a trial of force would be made in the one case, as was made in the other. But what degree of madness could ever drive the Federal Government to such an extremity? . . . The only refuge left for those who prophecy the downfall of the State Governments, is the visionary supposition that the Federal Government may previously accumulate a military force for the projects of ambition. . . . [But such an army] would be opposed [by] a militia amounting to nearly half a million of citizens with arms in their hands, officered by men chosen from among themselves, fighting for their common liberties, and united and conducted by governments possessing their affections and confidence. . . . Beside the advantage of being armed, which the Americans possess over the people of almost every other nation, the existence of subordinate governments to which the people are attached, and by which the militia officers are appointed, forms a barrier against the enterprizes of ambition, more insurmountable than any which a simple government of any form can admit of.[11]

---

[9] *The Federalist No. 33* (Alexander Hamilton).

[10] *The Federalist No. 44* (James Madison).

[11] *The Federalist No. 46* (James Madison).

The executive and legislative bodies of each State will be so many sentinels over the persons employed in every department of the national administration.[12]

5. If a state could nullify a federal law within its own borders, wouldn't the country be back to the regime under the Articles of Confederation, where the unanimous agreement of the states was necessary to do anything? Doesn't this create a hold-up problem, where one state can try to extract huge concessions before it is willing to agree to anything? Doesn't the federal government need to be able to overcome such problems with the states?

6. What do you think of Jefferson and Madison's arguments that the Constitution is a "Compact" among the states? Here you might compare the Preamble of the Constitution with the Preamble of the Articles of Confederation. In 1860 and 1861, Southern secessionists, citing as authority "the Spirit of '98" and the Virginia and Kentucky Resolutions, tried to secede from the United States. They called special conventions in the Southern states like the ones that had ratified the Constitution, and then they had those conventions rescind their ratification of the Constitution and declare independence unilaterally (that is, without the approval of the rest of the nation). Was secession permitted by the Constitution?

Does the argument by Jefferson and Madison in their drafts of the Virginia and Kentucky Resolutions lead inexorably to a constitutional right of states to *secede* (at least for a sufficiently serious breach of the Constitution by the organs of the national government)? Is there any stopping-off point in the logic of their arguments that would permit "interposition" or "nullification" but not "secession"? What do you think of the view, expressed by historian Ron Chernow, that the Virginia and Kentucky Resolutions were "as inimical" to the Constitution "as the Alien and Sedition Acts themselves"? Ron Chernow, ALEXANDER HAMILTON 574 (2004). Or the similar view of historian Garry Wills that Jefferson and Madison's "nullification effort, if others had picked it up, would have been a greater threat to freedom" than the Alien and Sedition Acts? Garry Wills, JAMES MADISON 49 (2002).

Note that late in his life, when the issues of the day were different, Madison's views shifted in favor of the federal government's interpretive supremacy, and he argued that the Virginia Resolutions and the Report of 1800 did not support South Carolina's purported "nullification" of a federal tariff during the Jackson administration.

The Election of 1800: We the People Speak

Thomas Jefferson defeated John Adams in the election of 1800, and a major issue in the election was the Alien and Sedition Acts. Jefferson took presidential oath of office on March 4, 1801. He believed, of course, that the Sedition Act was unconstitutional. Had it not expired by the time Jefferson was inaugurated, would it have been appropriate for him to refuse to enforce it?

The main Sedition Act prosecution pending on March 4, 1801, was a federal case brought against William Duane, the editor of a Philadelphia newspaper, the *Aurora*. Jefferson ordered the U.S. attorney who had brought the case, Edward Livingston, to cease any prosecutions under the

---

[12] *The Federalist No. 84* (Alexander Hamilton).

Sedition Act. Jefferson wrote to him, "I affirm that act to be no law, because in opposition to the constitution; and I shall treat it as a nullity, wherever it comes in the way of my functions." Jefferson told Livingston that he could prosecute Duane on any other grounds that might be available, but, because there were none, the case was dropped. Jefferson explained his position to Livingston: "The President is to have the laws executed. He may order an offense then to be prosecuted. If he sees a prosecution put into a train which is not lawful, he may order it to be discontinued and put into a legal train."

Was Jefferson within his rights to order the Sedition Act prosecution of Duane dropped? In doing so, was he suspending an act of Congress—the Sedition Act—in contravention of the Take Care Clause in Article II, Section 3 that imposes on the president the duty to "take care that the laws be faithfully executed"? What is the relevant law that Jefferson was sworn to follow—the Sedition Act or the Constitution itself? If the president may decline to execute laws that he thinks are unconstitutional, is there anything left of the Take Care Clause's effort to make clear that the president has no power to suspend the laws?

The rule that the executive has no "dispensing power" to suspend a law dates back to King James II's effort to dispense with The Test Act, which was an act of Parliament that barred Catholics from holding many political and military offices in England. (It was the proclamation dispensing with the Test Act that the Seven Bishops refused to read from their pulpits.) After James II was overthrown, the English Bill of Rights of 1689 made it clear that future monarchs would have no dispensing power and that they would be bound to execute the laws faithfully. It is from these antecedents that the Take Care Clause is descended.

Jefferson's Pardons and His Defense of Presidential Interpretation

In addition to dismissing the prosecution of Duane and allowing the Sedition Act to expire, President Jefferson also granted pardons to persons already convicted under the Sedition Act. He did this on the grounds that the Sedition Act was unconstitutional. Was this proper? What if the Supreme Court had held it to be constitutional? Press the point one step further: What if the courts were to hold that it is unconstitutional for the president to grant pardons on constitutional grounds rejected by the courts as incorrect interpretations of the Constitution?

In September 1804, in a letter to Abigail Adams, Jefferson justified his pardons of those who had been convicted under the Sedition Act during the Adams administration. For authority he relied on the president's duty of constitutional interpretation in the course of performing duties committed to him, including the pardon power. Jefferson further argued that judicial decisions contrary to the Constitution could not control the president in the exercise of his constitutional responsibilities. He said:

> You seem to think it devolved on the judges to decide on the validity of the sedition law. But nothing in the Constitution has given them a right to decide for the Executive, more than to the Executive to decide for them. Both magistracies are equally independent in the sphere of action assigned to them. The judges, believing the law constitutional, had a right to pass a sentence of fine and imprisonment; because that power was placed in their hands by the Constitution. But the Execu-

tive, believing the law to be unconstitutional, was bound to remit the execution of it; because that power has been confided to him by the Constitution. That instrument meant that its co-ordinate branches should be checks on each other. But the opinion which gives to the judges the right to decide what laws are constitutional, and what not, not only for themselves in their own sphere of action, but for the Legislature & Executive also, in their spheres, would make the judiciary a despotic branch.

NOTES

1. Do you agree with President Jefferson? If the president thinks a law is unconstitutional, can anything be done?

2. May the Supreme Court review a presidential pardon? If the Supreme Court concluded that the president's interpretation of the Constitution was wrong, could it somehow "reverse" the pardon? If the judiciary made such a ruling, would the president actually be obliged to arrest and imprison the previously pardoned offender?

3. If the president may decline to enforce statutes, asserting that they are unconstitutional—whether or not the courts would agree—may the president likewise decline to enforce decisions of the courts, asserting that they rest on unfaithful interpretations of the Constitution? In *The Federalist No. 49*, James Madison stated that "[t]he several departments being perfectly co-ordinate by the terms of their common commission, neither of them, it is evident, can pretend to an exclusive or superior right of settling the boundaries between their respective powers." And in *The Federalist No. 78*, Alexander Hamilton, in the course of explaining and defending the authority of the courts to interpret and apply the Constitution, famously described the judiciary as being the "least dangerous" branch of government and even seemed to imply that the president might decline to enforce its judgments: "The judiciary on the contrary has no influence over either the sword or the purse, no direction either of the strength or of the wealth of the society, and can take no active resolution whatever. It may truly be said to have neither Force nor Will, merely judgment; and must ultimately depend upon the aid of the executive arm even for the efficacy of its judgments."

Do these statements of Madison and Hamilton suggest that it is proper for all three branches of the government to interpret the Constitution and that none is bound by the interpretations of any of the others—and that this, too, is part of the separation of powers? Is this view also suggested by the actions of President Jefferson in granting pardons for persons duly convicted under the Sedition Act, in stopping pending prosecutions, and by his defense of these actions? This view was embraced by President Andrew Jackson in his veto of the Bank and in other actions, and by President Abraham Lincoln on many occasions. (For more on these occasions, see Chapter 2.) Both Jackson and Lincoln often cited and quoted Jefferson. Does it surprise you that strong presidents have taken strong positions in favor of independent executive branch interpretive authority? What dangers can you foresee from these positions?

4. If all three branches of the national government possess an independent power to interpret the Constitution within the operation of their respective powers, does it follow that the states likewise may interpret the Constitution independently and are not bound by the interpretations of the national gov-

ernment (as argued in the Virginia and Kentucky Resolutions)? Are there principled distinctions between the two situations? Does the logic of the analogy suggest that states may interpret the Constitution but that their interpretations do not bind the institutions of the national government? If so, how would a dispute about the Constitution between the national government and (some) state governments be resolved? By force of arms? President Jackson thought so. When South Carolina sought to "nullify" a federal tariff law in 1832, President Jackson, backed by Congress, threatened coercion and prevailed. And when states of the South attempted to secede in 1861, President Lincoln ordered the use of force—and eventually prevailed. Have fundamental questions of constitutional interpretation been resolved on the battlefield?

5. Were President Jefferson's pardons constitutionally proper because of something peculiar to the pardon power? Could one argue that those pardons (and President Jackson's veto) do not support a general proposition that the president possesses the independent authority to interpret the Constitution?

Are there any limits on the president's pardon power? If so, where do they come from? Some pardons have been offers of forgiveness to those engaged in military-related controversies. For example, President Washington pardoned some who participated in the Whiskey Rebellion, and both President Lincoln and President Johnson pardoned former Confederate soldiers. More recently, President Ford pardoned Vietnam-era draft evaders, and President George H. W. Bush pardoned a former defense secretary who was being investigated in connection with the "Iran–Contra" scandal. What if the pardon power were used to forgive executive branch personnel who had engaged in waterboarding? Or to free al-Qaeda terrorists? Does the justice of the reason for the pardon affect the *scope* of the constitutional power?

6. Consider the proposition that, in the end, it is "We the People of the United States" who are the ultimate judges and interpreters of the Constitution. It may be interesting for you to know that the Supreme Court's decisions do, over time, tend to follow broad political trends, in part because of the eventual turnover of justices on the Court and the inescapably political process specified for appointment of Supreme Court justices. In an election campaign, is it always (ever?) legitimate to "appeal" to the people a seemingly wrong court decision, like the ones upholding convictions under the Sedition Act? After all, the constitutional question of the Alien and Sedition Acts was "decided" (after a fashion), and the judgments of the courts sustaining their constitutionality were "reversed" (in a sense), by the American people in the Election of 1800.

As a practical matter, the largest and most important constitutional controversies in American history have eventually been settled by the American people acting through the medium of their presidents, their senators, and the judges selected by those presidents and senators. The Madisonian system of checks and balances guarantees that in the long run the people are the interpreters and enforcers of the Constitution. Is this a good thing? Would a strict rule that only judges could interpret the Constitution, and that judicial independence would be fortified by letting judges pick their successors, be better? If "We the People" are the ultimate interpreters of the Constitution, and if the very reason to have a constitution is to restrain the people, then is our effort to establish constitutional government inevitably bound to fail? Or is "constitutional government" aided, and not subverted, by letting the people, acting through multiple agents, interpret *their* Constitution?

CHAPTER 2

THE POWER OF CONSTITUTIONAL INTERPRETATION

[*Assignment 7*]

> *Article III, Section 2: The judicial Power shall extend to all Cases, in Law and Equity, arising under this Constitution . . . .*
>
> *Article VI, Clause 2: This Constitution, and the Laws of the United States which shall be made in Pursuance thereof; and all Treaties made, or which shall be made, under the Authority of the United States, shall be the supreme Law of the Land; and the Judges in every State shall be bound thereby, any Thing in the Constitution or Laws of any State to the Contrary notwithstanding.*
>
> *Clause 3: The Senators and Representatives before mentioned, and the Members of the several State Legislatures, and all executive and judicial Officers, both of the United States and of the several States, shall be bound by Oath or Affirmation, to support this Constitution . . . .*

I. CONSTITUTIONAL SUPREMACY AND INTERPRETATION

The Constitution declares itself to be the "supreme Law of the Land." For all who agree to be governed by the Constitution—and especially for those who exercise government power under it, all of whom are required by Article VI to swear an oath "to support this Constitution"—the Constitution trumps any other law, policy, or action of federal or state government that comes into conflict with it. But who has the power to decide what the Constitution means?

Most Americans would quickly answer: "the courts." The power to interpret the Constitution arises from the judicial duty to follow and apply the law, which includes the Constitution, when deciding a case or controversy within a court's jurisdiction. What about the other branches of the national government? What is their role in constitutional interpretation? What about the states?

Some answers to these questions are at least implicit in constitutional interpretations already presented in Chapter 1. You have read constitutional views about the Bank of the United States from Representative (and later by President) James Madison, Secretary of the Treasury Alexander Hamilton, Secretary of State Thomas Jefferson, and President Andrew Jackson. There are answers implicit in the actions of President Jefferson, who dismissed pending prosecutions under the Sedition Act because he believed it unconstitutional, and granted pardons to those already convicted for the same reason—even though the federal courts had been united in sustaining the statute's constitutionality. And there was the claim by Kentucky and Virginia of a right to interpret the Constitution and declare the Alien and Sedition Acts unconstitutional, and the Northern states' assertions that such action was illegitimate because all constitutional questions are committed exclusively to the courts.

What does the Constitution itself say on this point? The Supremacy Clause of Article VI provides that the Constitution is "the supreme law of the Land" that binds "the Judges in every State." Article III extends "the judicial Power" to "all Cases, in Law and Equity, arising under this Constitution." The Oath Clause of Article VI requires "Senators and Representatives," "and the Members of the several State Legislatures, and all executive and judicial Officers, both of the United States and of the several States," to "be bound by Oath or Affirmation, to support this Constitution." And Article II instructs the president to "preserve, protect, and defend the Constitution of the United States."

Do these provisions give, or imply, answers to the questions about who has the power to interpret the Constitution? Are there any other provisions that are relevant? Does the structure of the Constitution suggest any answers? Does the constitutional theme of separation of powers? Does the written character of the Constitution?

In addition to the question of *who* has the power to interpret the Constitution, there is the equally fundamental question of *how* that power may be exercised. Are there any general principles or rules of construction for constitutional interpretation that can be derived from the document itself? Or is the Constitution entirely silent as to how it should be interpreted and applied? If it is silent, does that mean that it may be interpreted (by whoever has the power to interpret it) in whatever manner the interpreter thinks is most fitting or desirable? Or are there any implicit "default rules" about the appropriate way to interpret a formal, written legal text that is supreme law for the nation?

This chapter explores these questions. It begins with the framers' conception of how each branch is checked by others, and the debate in the Founding Era over the power of the courts under the Constitution. It then turns to *Marbury v. Madison*, the first case in which the Supreme Court held an act of Congress unconstitutional and declined to enforce it. The chapter concludes with questions about judicial review and judicial supremacy—questions raised in the fierce debates over slavery and the Civil War, and again in the wake of *Brown v. Board of Education*.

A. SEPARATION OF POWERS AND CONSTITUTIONAL SUPREMACY

How is the Constitution supposed to be enforced? *The Federalist Nos. 47, 48,* and *51,* written by James Madison, suggest that the separation of powers under the Constitution, with its resulting checks and balances, is a major part of the answer. What is the role of the judiciary within the scheme of separation of powers? In considering these materials, distinguish between two different issues: whether the courts may interpret the Constitution for themselves and give legal weight to that interpretation even in the face of contrary legislation, and whether the court's interpretive authority is exclusive or supreme.

The Federalist No. 47

James Madison, February 1, 1788

To the People of the State of New York:

HAVING reviewed the general form of the proposed government and the general mass of power allotted to it, I proceed to examine the particular structure of this government, and the distribution of this mass of power among its constituent parts.

One of the principal objections inculcated by the more respectable adversaries to the Constitution, is its supposed violation of the political maxim, that the legislative, executive, and judiciary departments ought to be separate and distinct. In the structure of the federal government, no regard, it is said, seems to have been paid to this essential precaution in favor of liberty. The several departments of power are distributed and blended in such a manner as at once to destroy all symmetry and beauty of form, and to expose some of the essential parts of the edifice to the danger of being crushed by the disproportionate weight of other parts.

No political truth is certainly of greater intrinsic value, or is stamped with the authority of more enlightened patrons of liberty, than that on which the objection is founded. The accumulation of all powers, legislative, executive, and judiciary, in the same hands, whether of one, a few, or many, and whether hereditary, self appointed, or elective, may justly be pronounced the very definition of tyranny. Were the federal Constitution, therefore, really chargeable with the accumulation of power, or with a mixture of powers, having a dangerous tendency to such an accumulation, no further arguments would be necessary to inspire a universal reprobation of the system. I persuade myself, however, that it will be made apparent to every one, that the charge cannot be supported, and that the maxim on which it relies has been totally misconceived and misapplied. In order to form correct ideas on this important subject, it will be proper to investigate the sense in which the preservation of liberty requires that the three great departments of power should be separate and distinct.

The oracle who is always consulted and cited on this subject is the celebrated Montesquieu. . . . The reasons on which Montesquieu grounds his maxim are a further demonstration of his meaning. "When the legislative and executive powers are united in the same person or body," says he, "there can be no liberty, because apprehensions may arise lest THE SAME monarch or senate should ENACT tyrannical laws to EXECUTE them in a tyrannical manner." Again: "Were the power of judging joined with the legislative, the life and liberty of the subject would be exposed to arbitrary control, for THE JUDGE would then be THE LEGISLATOR. Were it joined to the executive power, THE JUDGE might behave with all the violence of AN OPPRESSOR." Some of these reasons are more fully explained in other passages; but briefly stated as they are here, they sufficiently establish the meaning which we have put on this celebrated maxim of this celebrated author.

If we look into the constitutions of the several States, we find that, notwithstanding the emphatical and, in some instances, the unqualified terms in which this axiom has been laid down, there is not a single instance in which the several departments of power have been kept absolutely separate and distinct. . . .

In citing these cases, in which the legislative, executive, and judiciary departments have not been kept totally separate and distinct, I wish not to be regarded as an advocate for the particular organizations of the several State governments. . . . What I have wished to evince is, that the charge brought against the proposed Constitution, of violating the sacred maxim of free government, is warranted neither by the real meaning annexed to that maxim by its author, nor by the sense in which it has hitherto been understood in America. This interesting subject will be resumed in the ensuing paper.

The Federalist No. 48

James Madison, February 1, 1788

To the People of the State of New York:

IT WAS shown in the last paper that the political apothegm there examined does not require that the legislative, executive, and judiciary departments should be wholly unconnected with each other. I shall undertake, in the next place, to show that unless these departments be so far connected and blended as to give to each a constitutional control over the others, the degree of separation which the maxim requires, as essential to a free government, can never in practice be duly maintained.

It is agreed on all sides, that the powers properly belonging to one of the departments ought not to be directly and completely administered by either of the other departments. It is equally evident, that none of them ought to possess, directly or indirectly, an overruling influence over the others, in the administration of their respective powers. It will not be denied, that power is of an encroaching nature, and that it ought to be effectually restrained from passing the limits assigned to it. After discriminating, therefore, in theory, the several classes of power, as they may in their nature be legislative, executive, or judiciary, the next and most difficult task is to provide some practical security for each, against the invasion of the others. What this security ought to be, is the great problem to be solved.

Will it be sufficient to mark, with precision, the boundaries of these departments, in the constitution of the government, and to trust to these parchment barriers against the encroaching spirit of power? This is the security which appears to have been principally relied on by the compilers of most of the American constitutions. But experience assures us, that the efficacy of the provision has been greatly overrated; and that some more adequate defense is indispensably necessary for the more feeble, against the more powerful, members of the government. The legislative department is everywhere extending the sphere of its activity, and drawing all power into its impetuous vortex. . . .

In a government where numerous and extensive prerogatives are placed in the hands of an hereditary monarch, the executive department is very justly regarded as the source of danger, and watched with all the jealousy which a zeal for liberty ought to inspire. In a democracy, where a multitude of people exercise in person the legislative functions, and are continually exposed, by their incapacity for regular deliberation and concerted measures, to the ambitious intrigues of their executive magistrates, tyranny may well be apprehended, on some favorable emergency, to start up in the same quarter. But in a representative republic, where the executive magistracy is carefully limited; both in the extent and the duration of its power; and where the legislative power is exercised by an assembly, which is inspired, by a supposed influence over the people, with an intrepid confidence in its own strength; which is sufficiently numerous to feel all the passions which actuate a multitude, yet not so numerous as to be incapable of pursuing the objects of its passions, by means which reason prescribes; it is against the enterprising ambition of this department that the people ought to indulge all their jealousy and exhaust all their precautions. . . .

I have appealed to our own experience for the truth of what I advance on this subject. Were it necessary to verify this experience by particular proofs, they might be multiplied without end. I might find a witness in every citizen who has shared in, or been attentive to, the course of public administrations. I might collect vouchers in abundance from the records and archives of every State in the Union. But as a more concise, and at the same time equally satisfactory, evidence, I will refer to the example of [Virginia] attested by [an] unexceptionable [authority]

. . . Virginia [is] a State which, as we have seen, has expressly declared in its constitution, that the three great departments ought not to be intermixed. The authority [I cite here] is Mr. Jefferson, who, besides his other advantages for remarking the operation of the government, was himself the [Governor] of it. In order to convey fully the ideas with which his experience had impressed him on this subject, it will be necessary to quote a passage of some length from his very interesting "Notes on the State of Virginia," p. 195. "All the powers of government, legislative, executive, and judiciary, result to the legislative body. The concentrating these in the same hands, is precisely the definition of despotic government. It will be no alleviation, that these powers will be exercised by a plurality of hands, and not by a single one. One hundred and seventy-three despots would surely be as oppressive as one. Let those who doubt it, turn their eyes on the republic of Venice. As little will it avail us, that they are chosen by ourselves. An ELECTIVE DESPOTISM was not the government we fought for; but one which should not only be founded on free principles, but in which the powers of government should be so divided and balanced among several bodies of magistracy, as that no one could transcend their legal limits, without being effectually checked and restrained by the others. For this reason, that convention which passed the ordinance of government, laid its foundation on this basis, that the legislative, executive, and judiciary departments should be separate and distinct, so that no person should exercise the powers of more than one of them at the same time. BUT NO BARRIER WAS PROVIDED BETWEEN THESE SEVERAL POWERS. The judiciary and the executive members were left dependent on the legislative for their subsistence in office, and some of them for their continuance in it. If, therefore, the legislature assumes executive and judiciary powers, no opposition is likely to be made; nor, if made, can be effectual; because in that case they may put their proceedings into the form of acts of Assembly, which will render them obligatory on the other branches. They have accordingly, IN MANY instances, DECIDED RIGHTS which should have been left to JUDICIARY CONTROVERSY, and THE DIRECTION OF THE EXECUTIVE, DURING THE WHOLE TIME OF THEIR SESSION, IS BECOMING HABITUAL AND FAMILIAR." . . .

The conclusion which I am warranted in drawing from these observations is, that a mere demarcation on parchment of the constitutional limits of the several departments, is not a sufficient guard against those encroachments which lead to a tyrannical concentration of all the powers of government in the same hands.

The Federalist No. 51

James Madison, February 8, 1788

To the People of the State of New York:

TO WHAT expedient, then, shall we finally resort, for maintaining in practice the necessary partition of power among the several departments, as laid down in the Constitution? The only answer that can be given is, that as all these exterior provisions are found to be inadequate, the defect must be supplied, by so contriving the interior structure of the government as that its several constituent parts may, by their mutual relations, be the means of keeping each other in their proper places. Without presuming to undertake a full development of this important idea, I will hazard a few general observations, which may perhaps place it in a clearer light, and enable us to form a more correct judgment of the principles and structure of the government planned by the convention.

In order to lay a due foundation for that separate and distinct exercise of the different powers of government, which to a certain extent is admitted on all hands to be essential to the preservation of liberty, it is evident that each department should have a will of its own; and consequently should be so constituted that the members of each should have as little agency as possible in the appointment of the members of the others. Were this principle rigorously adhered to, it would require that all the appointments for the supreme executive, legislative, and judiciary magistracies should be drawn from the same fountain of authority, the people, through channels having no communication whatever with one another. Perhaps such a plan of constructing the several departments would be less difficult in practice than it may in contemplation appear. Some difficulties, however, and some additional expense would attend the execution of it. Some deviations, therefore, from the principle must be admitted. In the constitution of the judiciary department in particular, it might be inexpedient to insist rigorously on the principle: first, because peculiar qualifications being essential in the members, the primary consideration ought to be to select that mode of choice which best secures these qualifications; secondly, because the permanent tenure by which the appointments are held in that department, must soon destroy all sense of dependence on the authority conferring them.

It is equally evident, that the members of each department should be as little dependent as possible on those of the others, for the emoluments annexed to their offices. Were the executive magistrate, or the judges, not independent of the legislature in this particular, their independence in every other would be merely nominal.

But the great security against a gradual concentration of the several powers in the same department, consists in giving to those who administer each department the necessary constitutional means and personal motives to resist encroachments of the others. The provision for defense must in this, as in all other cases, be made commensurate to the danger of attack. Ambition must be made to counteract ambition. The interest of the man must be connected with the constitutional rights of the place. It may be a reflection on human nature, that such devices should be necessary to control the abuses of government. But what is government itself, but the greatest of all reflections on human nature? If men were angels, no government would be necessary. If angels were to govern men, neither external nor internal controls on government would be necessary. In framing a government which is to be administered by men over men, the great difficulty lies in this: you must first enable the government to control the governed; and in the next place oblige it to control itself. A dependence on the people is, no doubt, the primary control on the government; but experience has taught mankind the necessity of auxiliary precautions.

This policy of supplying, by opposite and rival interests, the defect of better motives, might be traced through the whole system of human affairs, private as well as public. We see it particularly displayed in all the subordinate distributions of power, where the constant aim is to divide and arrange the several offices in such a manner as that each may be a check on the other that the private interest of every individual may be a sentinel over the public rights. These inventions of prudence cannot be less requisite in the distribution of the supreme powers of the State. . . .

NOTES

1. Under James Madison's conception of the separation of powers, how is power to be kept limited and checked? How are the written allocations of power in the Constitution to be preserved?

2. What do you make of the fact that Madison never mentions judicial review in his discussion (in *The Federalist No. 51*) of how the Constitution would be enforced? Is it part of the Madisonian system of checks and balances? If so, how is it related to the other checks and balances?

B. THE DEBATE OVER JUDICIAL POWER

The Anti–Federalist writer "Brutus" (probably Robert Yates) was a strong New York critic of the proposed Constitution, who saw in the proposed federal judiciary the seeds of despotism and judicial oligarchy. The very name "Brutus" is one that connotes opposition to despotism, tyranny, and oligarchy. It was the name of two ancient Roman citizens of great fame. Lucius Junius Brutus was a leader in overthrowing the Roman monarchy in 509 BC and establishing the Roman Republic, which lasted for over 400 years. One of his descendants, Marcus Junius Brutus, assassinated Julius Caesar in 44 BC, when Caesar had replaced the Roman Republic with his own rule as a dictator. The American "Brutus" was thus a self-styled opponent of despotism.

Examine Brutus's arguments below carefully. Was Brutus right to fear that adopting the Constitution would lead to federal judicial despotism and oligarchy? (An oligarchy can be thought of as an aristocracy that has become corrupt with power.) Then consider the arguments of Alexander Hamilton in *The Federalist Nos. 78* and *81*, which immediately follow. *The Federalist No. 78* was written largely in response to Brutus. Is Brutus or Hamilton more persuasive?

Brutus, No. 11
January 31, 1788

The nature and extent of the judicial power of the United States, proposed to be granted by this constitution, claims our particular attention. . . . Much has been said and written upon the subject of this new system on both sides, but I have not met with any writer, who has discussed the judicial powers with any degree of accuracy. And yet it is obvious, that we can form but very imperfect ideas of the manner in which this government will work, or the effect it will have in changing the internal police and mode of distributing justice at present subsisting in the respective states, without a thorough investigation of the powers of the judiciary and of the manner in which they will operate. This government is a complete system, not only for making, but for executing laws. And the courts of law, which will be constituted by it, are not only to decide upon the constitution and the laws made in pursuance of it, but by officers subordinate to them to execute all their decisions. The real effect of this system of government, will therefore be brought home to the feelings of the people, through the medium of the judicial power. It is, moreover, of great importance, to examine with care the nature and extent of the judicial power, because those who are to be vested with it, are to be placed in a situation altogether unprecedented in a free country. They are to be rendered totally independent, both of the people and the legislature, both with respect to their offices and salaries. No errors they may commit can be corrected by any power above them, if any such power there be, nor can they be removed from office for making ever so many erroneous adjudications.

The only causes for which they can be displaced, is, conviction of treason, bribery, and high crimes and misdemeanors. . . . This part of the plan is so modelled, as to authorise the courts, not only to carry into execution the powers expressly given, but where these are wanting or ambiguously expressed, to supply what is wanting by their own decisions. . . . That we may be enabled to form a just opinion on this subject, [let us] 1st. Examine the nature and extent of the judicial powers—and 2d. Enquire, whether the courts who are to exercise them, are so constituted as to afford reasonable ground of confidence, that they will exercise them for the general good.

With a regard to the nature and extent of the judicial powers, I have to regret my want of capacity to give that full and minute explanation of them that the subject merits. To be able to do this, a man should be possessed of a degree of law knowledge far beyond what I pretend to. A number of hard words and technical phrases are used in this part of the system, about the meaning of which gentlemen learned in the law differ. . . . Its advocates know how to avail themselves of these phrases. In a number of instances, where objections are made to the powers given to the judicial, they give such an explanation to the technical terms as to avoid them. . . . Though I am not competent to give a perfect explanation of the powers granted to this department of the government, I shall yet attempt to trace some of the leading features of it, from which I presume it will appear, that they will operate to a total subversion of the state judiciaries, if not, to the legislative authority of the states.

In article 3d, sect. 2d, it is said, "The judicial power shall extend to all cases in law and equity arising under this constitution, the laws of the United States, and treaties made, or which shall be made, under their authority, & c." . . . The first article to which this power extends, is, all cases in law and equity arising under this constitution. . . . What latitude of construction this clause should receive, it is not easy to say. At first view, one would suppose, that it meant no more than this, that the courts under the general government should exercise, not only the powers of courts of law, but also that of courts of equity, in the manner in which those powers are usually exercised in the different states. But this cannot be the meaning, because the next clause authorises the courts to take cognizance of all cases in law and equity arising under the laws of the United States; this last article, I conceive, conveys as much power to the general judicial as any of the state courts possess. . . . The cases arising under the constitution must be different from those arising under the laws, or else the two clauses mean exactly the same thing. . . . The cases arising under the constitution must include such, as bring into question its meaning, and will require an explanation of the nature and extent of the powers of the different departments under it. . . . This article, therefore, vests the judicial with a power to resolve all questions that may arise on any case on the construction of the constitution, either in law or in equity.

1st. They are authorised to determine all questions that may arise upon the meaning of the constitution in law. This article vests the courts with authority to give the constitution a legal construction, or to explain it according to the rules laid down for construing a law.—These rules give a certain degree of latitude of explanation. According to this mode of construction, the courts are to give such meaning to the constitution as comports best with the common, and generally received acceptation of the words in which it is expressed, regarding their ordinary and popular use, rather than their grammatical propriety. Where words are dubious, they will be explained by the context. The end of the clause will be attended to, and the words will be understood, as having a view to it; and the words will not be so understood as to bear no meaning or a very absurd one.

2d. The judicial are not only to decide questions arising upon the meaning of the constitution in law, but also in equity. . . . By this they are empowered, to explain the constitution according to the reasoning spirit of it, without being confined to the words or letter. "From this method of interpreting laws (says Blackstone) by the reason of them, arises what we call equity;" which is thus defined by Grotius, "the correction of that, wherein the law, by reason of its universality, is deficient["]; for since in laws all cases cannot be foreseen, or expressed, it is necessary, that when the decrees of the law cannot be applied to particular cases, there should some where be a power vested of defining those circumstances, which had they been foreseen the legislator would have expressed; and these are the cases, which according to Grotius, ["]lex non exacte definit, sed arbitrio boni viri permittet." *[Roughly, "the law does not define exactly, but permits arbitration by a good man."—Editors]* . . . The same learned author observes, "That equity, thus depending essentially upon each individual case, there can be no established rules and fixed principles of equity laid down, without destroying its very essence, and reducing it to a positive law."

From these remarks, the authority and business of the courts of law, under this clause, may be understood. . . . They will give the sense of every article of the constitution, that may from time to time come before them. And in their decisions they will not confine themselves to any fixed or established rules, but will determine, according to what appears to them, the reason and spirit of the constitution. The opinions of the supreme court, whatever they may be, will have the force of law; because there is no power provided in the constitution, that can correct their errors, or controul their adjudications. From this court there is no appeal. And I conceive the legislature themselves, cannot set aside a judgment of this court, because they are authorised by the constitution to decide in the last resort. The legislature must be controuled by the constitution, and not the constitution by them. They have therefore no more right to set aside any judgment pronounced upon the construction of the constitution, than they have to take from the president, the chief command of the army and navy, and commit it to some other person. The reason is plain; the judicial and executive derive their authority from the same source, that the legislature do theirs; and therefore in all cases, where the constitution does not make the one responsible to, or controulable by the other, they are altogether independent of each other.

The judicial power will operate to effect, in the most certain, but yet silent and imperceptible manner, what is evidently the tendency of the constitution:—I mean, an entire subversion of the legislative, executive and judicial powers of the individual states. Every adjudication of the supreme court, on any question that may arise upon the nature and extent of the general government, will affect the limits of the state jurisdiction. In proportion as the former enlarge the exercise of their powers, will that of the latter be restricted.

That the judicial power of the United States, will lean strongly in favour of the general government, and will give such an explanation to the constitution, as will favour an extension of its jurisdiction, is very evident from a variety of considerations. . . . 1st. The constitution itself strongly countenances such a mode of construction. Most of the articles in this system, which convey powers of any considerable importance, are conceived in general and indefinite terms, which are either equivocal, ambiguous, or which require long definitions to unfold the extent of their meaning. The two most important powers committed to any government, those of raising money, and of raising and keeping up troops, have already been considered, and shewn to be unlimitted by any thing but the discretion of the legislature. The clause which vests the power to pass all laws which are proper and necessary, to carry the powers given into execution, it has been shewn, leaves the legislature at liberty, to do every thing, which in their judgment is best. It is said, I know, that this clause confers no power on the legislature, which they would not have had without it—though I believe this is not the fact, yet, admitting it to be, it implies that the constitution is not to receive an explanation strictly, according to its letter; but more power is implied than is expressed. And this clause, if it is to be considered, as explanatory of the extent of the powers given, rather than giving a new power, is to be understood as declaring, that in construing any of the articles conveying power, the spirit, intent and design of the clause, should be attended to, as well as the words in their common acceptation.

This constitution gives sufficient colour for adopting an equitable construction, if we consider the great end and design it professedly has in view—these appear from its preamble to be, "to form a more perfect union, establish justice, insure domestic tranquility, provide for the common defence, promote the general welfare, and secure the blessings of liberty to ourselves and posterity." The design of this system is here expressed, and it is proper to give such a meaning to the various parts, as will best promote the accomplishment of the end; this idea suggests itself naturally upon reading the preamble, and will countenance the court in giving the several articles such a sense, as will the most effectually promote the ends the constitution had in view—how this manner of explaining the constitution will operate in practice, shall be the subject of future enquiry.

2d. Not only will the constitution justify the courts in inclining to this mode of explaining it, but they will be interested in using this latitude of interpretation. Every body of men invested with office are tenacious of power; they feel interested, and hence it has become a kind of maxim, to hand down their offices, with all its rights and privileges, unimpared to their successors; the same principle will influence them to extend their power, and increase their rights; this of itself will operate strongly upon the courts to give such a meaning to the constitution in all cases where it can possibly be done, as will enlarge the sphere of their own authority. Every extension of the power of the general legislature, as well as of the judicial powers, will increase the powers of the courts; and the dignity and importance of the judges, will be in proportion to the extent and magnitude of the powers they exercise. I add, it is highly probable the emolument of the judges will be increased, with the increase of the business they will have to transact and its importance. From these considerations the judges will be interested to extend the powers of the courts, and to construe the constitution as much as possible, in such a way as to favour it; and that they will do it, appears probable.

3d. Because they will have precedent to plead, to justify them in it. It is well known, that the courts in England, have by their own authority, extended their jurisdiction far beyond the limits set them in their original institution, and by the laws of the land. . . . The court of exchequer is a remarkable instance of this. It was originally intended principally to recover the king's debts, and to order the revenues of the crown. It had a common law jurisdiction, which was established merely for the benefit of the king's accomptants. We learn from Blackstone, that the proceedings in this court are grounded on a writ called quo minus, in which the plaintiff suggests, that he is the king's farmer or debtor, and that the defendant hath done him the damage complained of, by which he is less able to pay the king. These suits, by the statute of Rutland, are expressly directed to be confined to such matters as specially concern the king, or his ministers in the exchequer. And by the articuli super cartas, it is enacted, that no common pleas be thenceforth held in the exchequer contrary to the form of the great charter: but now any person may sue in the exchequer. The surmise of being debtor to the king being matter of form, and mere words of course; and the court is open to all the nation.

When the courts will have a precedent before them of a court which extended its jurisdiction in opposition to an act of the legislature, is it not to be expected that they will extend theirs, especially when there is nothing in the constitution expressly against it? and they are authorised to construe its meaning, and are not under any controul? . . . This power in the judicial [branch], will enable them to mould the government, into almost any shape they please. . . .

The Federalist No. 78

Alexander Hamilton, May 28, 1788

To the People of the State of New York:

WE PROCEED now to an examination of the judiciary department of the proposed government. . . . In unfolding the defects of the existing Confederation, the utility and necessity of a federal judicature have been clearly pointed out. It is the less necessary to recapitulate the considerations there urged, as the propriety of the institution in the abstract is not disputed; the only questions which have been raised being relative to the manner of constituting it, and to its extent. To these points, therefore, our observations shall be confined.

The manner of constituting it seems to embrace these several objects: 1st. The mode of appointing the judges. 2d. The tenure by which they are to hold their places. 3d. The partition of the judiciary authority between different courts, and their relations to each other. . . .

First. As to the mode of appointing the judges; this is the same with that of appointing the officers of the Union in general, and has been so fully discussed in the two last numbers, that nothing can be said here which would not be useless repetition.

Second. As to the tenure by which the judges are to hold their places; this chiefly concerns their duration in office; the provisions for their support; the precautions for their responsibility. . . . According to the plan of the convention, all judges who may be appointed by the United States are to hold their offices DURING GOOD BEHAVIOR; which is conformable to the most approved of the State constitutions and among the rest, to that of this State. Its propriety having been drawn into question by the adversaries of that plan, is no light symptom of the rage for objection, which disorders their imaginations and judgments. The standard of good behavior for the continuance in office of the judicial magistracy, is certainly one of the most valuable of the modern improvements in the practice of government. In a monarchy it is an excellent barrier to the despotism of the prince; in a republic it is a no less excellent barrier to the encroachments and oppressions of the representative body. And it is the best expedient which can be devised in any government, to secure a steady, upright, and impartial administration of the laws.

Whoever attentively considers the different departments of power must perceive, that, in a government in which they are separated from each other, the judiciary, from the nature of its functions, will always be the least dangerous to the political rights of the Constitution; because it will be least in a capacity to annoy or injure them. The Executive not only dispenses the honors, but holds the sword of the community. The legislature not only commands the purse, but prescribes the rules by which the duties and rights of every citizen are to be regulated. The judiciary, on the contrary, has no influence over either the sword or the purse; no direction either of the strength or of the wealth of the society; and can take no active resolution whatever. It may truly be said to have neither FORCE nor WILL, but merely judgment; and must ultimately depend upon the aid of the executive arm even for the efficacy of its judgments.

This simple view of the matter suggests several important consequences. It proves incontestably, that the judiciary is beyond comparison the weakest of the three departments of power; that it can never attack with success either of the other two; and that all possible care is requisite to enable it to defend itself against their attacks. It equally proves, that though individual oppression may now and then proceed from the courts of justice, the general liberty of the people can never be endangered from that quarter; I mean so long as the judiciary remains truly distinct from both the legislature and the Executive. For I agree, that "there is no liberty, if the power of judging be not separated from the legislative and executive powers." . . . And it proves, in the last place, that as liberty can have nothing to fear from the judiciary alone, but would have every thing to fear from its union with either of the other departments; that as all the effects of such a union must ensue from a dependence of the former on the latter, notwithstanding a nominal and apparent separation; that as, from the natural feebleness of the judiciary, it is in continual jeopardy of being overpowered, awed, or influenced by its co-ordinate branches; and that as nothing can contribute so much to its firmness and independence as permanency in office, this quality may therefore be justly regarded as an indispensable ingredient in its constitution, and, in a great measure, as the citadel of the public justice and the public security.

The complete independence of the courts of justice is peculiarly essential in a limited Constitution. By a limited Constitution, I understand one which contains certain specified exceptions to the legislative authority; such, for instance, as that it shall pass no bills of attainder, no ex-post-facto laws, and the like. Limitations of this kind can be preserved in practice no other way than through the medium of courts of justice, whose duty it must be to declare all acts contrary to the manifest tenor of the Constitution void. Without this, all the reservations of particular rights or privileges would amount to nothing.

Some perplexity respecting the rights of the courts to pronounce legislative acts void, because contrary to the Constitution, has arisen from an imagination that the doctrine would imply a superiority of the judiciary to the legislative power. It is urged that the authority which can declare the acts of another void, must necessarily be superior to the one whose acts may be declared void. As this doctrine is of great importance in all the American constitutions, a brief discussion of the ground on which it rests cannot be unacceptable.

There is no position which depends on clearer principles, than that every act of a delegated authority, contrary to the tenor of the commission under which it is exercised, is void. No legislative act, therefore, contrary to the Constitution, can be valid. To deny this, would be to affirm, that the deputy is greater than his principal; that the servant is above his master; that the representatives of the people are superior to the people themselves; that men acting by virtue of powers, may do not only what their powers do not authorize, but what they forbid.

If it be said that the legislative body are themselves the constitutional judges of their own powers, and that the construction they put upon them is conclusive upon the other departments, it may be answered, that this cannot be the natural presumption, where it is not to be collected from any particular provisions in the Constitution. It is not otherwise to be supposed, that the Constitution could intend to enable the representatives of the people to substitute their WILL to that of their constituents. It is far more rational to suppose, that the courts were designed to be an intermediate body between the people and the legislature, in order, among other things, to keep the latter within the limits assigned to their authority. The interpretation of the laws is the proper and peculiar province of the courts. A constitution is, in fact, and must be regarded by the judges, as a fundamental law. It therefore belongs to them to ascertain its meaning, as well as the meaning of any particular act proceeding from the legislative body. If there should happen to be an irreconcilable variance between the two, that which has the superior obligation and validity ought, of course, to be preferred; or, in other words, the Constitution ought to be preferred to the statute, the intention of the people to the intention of their agents.

Nor does this conclusion by any means suppose a superiority of the judicial to the legislative power. It only supposes that the power of the people is superior to both; and that where the will of the legislature, declared in its statutes, stands in opposition to that of the people, declared in the Constitution, the judges ought to be governed by the latter rather than the former. They ought to regulate their decisions by the fundamental laws, rather than by those which are not fundamental.

This exercise of judicial discretion, in determining between two contradictory laws, is exemplified in a familiar instance. It not uncommonly happens, that there are two statutes existing at one time, clashing in whole or in part with each other, and neither of them containing any repealing clause or expression. In such a case, it is the province of the courts to liquidate and fix their meaning and operation. So far as they can, by any fair construction, be reconciled to each other, reason and law conspire to dictate that this should be done; where this is impracticable, it becomes a matter of necessity to give effect to one, in exclusion of the other. The rule which has obtained in the courts for determining their relative validity is, that the last in order of time shall be preferred to the first. But this is a mere rule of construction, not derived from any positive law, but from the nature and reason of the thing. It is a rule not enjoined upon the courts by legislative provision, but adopted by themselves, as consonant to truth and propriety, for the direction of their conduct as interpreters of the law. They thought it reasonable, that between the interfering acts of an EQUAL authority, that which was the last indication of its will should have the preference.

But in regard to the interfering acts of a superior and subordinate authority, of an original and derivative power, the nature and reason of the thing indicate the converse of that rule as proper to be followed. They teach us that the prior act of a superior ought to be preferred to the subsequent act of an inferior and subordinate authority; and that accordingly, whenever a particular statute contravenes the Constitution, it will be the duty of the judicial tribunals to adhere to the latter and disregard the former.

It can be of no weight to say that the courts, on the pretense of a repugnancy, may substitute their own pleasure to the constitutional intentions of the legislature. This might as well happen in the case of two contradictory statutes; or it might as well happen in every adjudication upon any single statute. The courts must declare the sense of the law; and if they should be disposed to exercise WILL instead of JUDGMENT, the consequence would equally be the substitution of their pleasure to that of the legislative body. The observation, if it prove any thing, would prove that there ought to be no judges distinct from that body.

If, then, the courts of justice are to be considered as the bulwarks of a limited Constitution against legislative encroachments, this consideration will afford a strong argument for the permanent tenure of judicial offices, since nothing will contribute so much as this to that independent spirit in the judges which must be essential to the faithful performance of so arduous a duty.

This independence of the judges is equally requisite to guard the Constitution and the rights of individuals from the effects of those ill humors, which the arts of designing men, or the influence of particular conjunctures, sometimes disseminate among the people themselves, and which, though they speedily give place to better information, and more deliberate reflection, have a tendency, in the meantime, to occasion dangerous innovations in the government, and serious oppressions of the minor party in the community. Though I trust the friends of the proposed Constitution will never concur with its enemies, . . . in questioning that fundamental principle of republican government, which admits the right of the people to alter or abolish the established Constitution, whenever they find it inconsistent with their happiness, yet it is not to be inferred from this principle, that the representatives of the people, whenever a momentary inclination happens to lay hold of a majority of their constituents, incompatible with the provisions in the existing Constitution, would, on that account, be justifiable in a violation of those provisions; or that the courts would be under a greater obligation to connive at infractions in this shape, than when they had proceeded wholly from the cabals of the representative body. Until the people have, by some solemn and authoritative act, annulled or changed the established form, it is binding upon themselves collectively, as well as individually; and no presumption, or even knowledge, of their sentiments, can warrant their representatives in a departure from it, prior to such an act. But it is easy to see, that it would require an uncommon portion of fortitude in the judges to do their duty as faithful guardians of the Constitution, where legislative invasions of it had been instigated by the major voice of the community.

But it is not with a view to infractions of the Constitution only, that the independence of the judges may be an essential safeguard against the effects of occasional ill humors in the society. These sometimes extend no farther than to the injury of the private rights of particular classes of citizens, by unjust and partial laws. Here also the firmness of the judicial magistracy is of vast importance in mitigating the severity and confining the operation of such laws. It not only serves to moderate the immediate mischiefs of those which may have been passed, but it operates as a check upon the legislative body in passing them; who, perceiving that obstacles to the success of iniquitous intention are to be expected from the scruples of the courts, are in a manner compelled, by the very motives of the injustice they meditate, to qualify their attempts. This is a circumstance calculated to have more influence upon the character of our governments, than but few may be aware of. The benefits of the integrity and moderation of the judiciary have already been felt in more States than one; and though they may have displeased those whose sinister expectations they may have disappointed, they must have commanded the esteem and applause of all the virtuous and disinterested. Considerate men, of every description, ought to prize whatever will tend to beget or fortify that temper in the courts: as no man can be sure that he may not be to-morrow the victim of a spirit of injustice, by which he may be a gainer to-day. And every man must now feel, that the inevitable tendency of such a spirit is to sap the foundations of public and private confidence, and to introduce in its stead universal distrust and distress.

That inflexible and uniform adherence to the rights of the Constitution, and of individuals, which we perceive to be indispensable in the courts of justice, can certainly not be expected from judges who hold their offices by a temporary commission. Periodical appointments, however regulated, or by whomsoever made, would, in some way or other, be fatal to their necessary independence. If the power of making them was committed either to the Executive or legislature, there would be danger of an improper complaisance to the branch which possessed it; if to both, there would be an unwillingness to hazard the displeasure of either; if to the people, or to persons chosen by them for the special purpose, there would be too great a disposition to consult popularity, to justify a reliance that nothing would be consulted but the Constitution and the laws.

There is yet a further and a weightier reason for the permanency of the judicial offices, which is deducible from the nature of the qualifications they require. It has been frequently remarked, with great propriety, that a voluminous code of laws is one of the inconveniences necessarily connected with the advantages of a free government. To avoid an arbitrary discretion in the courts, it is indispensable that they should be bound down by strict rules and precedents, which serve to define and point out their duty in every particular case that comes before them; and it will readily be conceived from the variety of controversies which grow out of the folly and wickedness of mankind, that the records of those precedents must unavoidably swell to a very considerable bulk, and must demand long and laborious study to acquire a competent knowledge of them. Hence it is, that there can be but few men in the society who will have sufficient skill in the laws to qualify them for the stations of judges. And making the proper deductions for the ordinary depravity of human nature, the number must be still smaller of those who unite the requisite integrity with the requisite knowledge. These considerations apprise us, that the government can have no great option between fit character; and that a temporary duration in office, which would naturally discourage such characters from quitting a lucrative line of practice to accept a seat on the bench, would have a tendency to throw the administration of justice into hands less able, and less well qualified, to conduct it with utility and dignity. In the present circumstances of this country, and in those in which it is likely to be for a long time to come, the disadvantages on this score would be greater than they may at first sight appear; but it must be confessed, that they are far inferior to those which present themselves under the other aspects of the subject.

Upon the whole, there can be no room to doubt that the convention acted wisely in copying from the models of those constitutions which have established GOOD BEHAVIOR as the tenure of their judicial offices, in point of duration; and that so far from being blamable on this account, their plan would have been inexcusably defective, if it had wanted this important feature of good government. The experience of Great Britain affords an illustrious comment on the excellence of the institution.

The Federalist No. 81

Alexander Hamilton, May 28, 1788

To the People of the State of New York:

. . . The arguments, or rather suggestions, upon which this charge is founded, are to this effect: "The authority of the proposed Supreme Court of the United States, which is to be a separate and independent body, will be superior to that of the legislature. The power of construing the laws according to the SPIRIT of the Constitution, will enable that court to mould them into whatever shape it may think proper; especially as its decisions will not be in any manner subject to the revision or correction of the legislative body. This is as unprecedented as it is dangerous. In Britain, the judicial power, in the last resort, resides in the House of Lords, which is a branch of the legislature; and this part of the British government has been imitated in the State constitutions in general. The Parliament of Great Britain, and the legislatures of the several States, can at any time rectify, by law, the exceptionable decisions of their respective courts. But the errors and usurpations of the Supreme Court of the United States will be uncontrollable and remediless." This, upon examination, will be found to be made up altogether of false reasoning upon misconceived fact.

In the first place, there is not a syllable in the plan under consideration which DIRECTLY empowers the national courts to construe the laws according to the spirit of the Constitution, or which gives them any greater latitude in this respect than may be claimed by the courts of every State. I admit, however, that the Constitution ought to be the standard of construction for the laws, and that wherever there is an evident opposition, the laws ought to give place to the Constitution. But this doctrine is not deducible from any circumstance peculiar to the plan of the convention, but from the general theory of a limited Constitution; and as far as it is true, is equally applicable to most, if not to all the State governments. . . .

It may in the last place be observed that the supposed danger of judiciary encroachments on the legislative authority, which has been upon many occasions reiterated, is in reality a phantom. Particular misconstructions and contraventions of the will of the legislature may now and then happen; but they can never be so extensive as to amount to an inconvenience, or in any sensible degree to affect the order of the political system. This may be inferred with certainty, from the general nature of the judicial power, from the objects to which it relates, from the manner in which it is exercised, from its comparative weakness, and from its total incapacity to support its usurpations by force. And the inference is greatly fortified by the consideration of the important constitutional check which the power of instituting impeachments in one part of the legislative body, and of determining upon them in the other, would give to that body upon the members of the judicial department. This is alone a complete security. There never can be danger that the judges, by a series of deliberate usurpations on the authority of the legislature, would hazard the united resentment of the body entrusted with it, while this body was possessed of the means of punishing their presumption, by degrading them from their stations. While this ought to remove all apprehensions on the subject, it affords, at the same time, a cogent argument for constituting the Senate a court for the trial of impeachments. . . .

The amount of the observations hitherto made on the authority of the judicial department is this: that it has been carefully restricted to those causes which are manifestly proper for the cognizance of the national judicature; that in the partition of this authority a very small portion of original jurisdiction has been preserved to the Supreme Court, and the rest consigned to the subordinate tribunals; that the Supreme Court will possess an appellate jurisdiction, both as to law and fact, in all the cases referred to them, both subject to any EXCEPTIONS and REGULATIONS which may be thought advisable; that this appellate jurisdiction does, in no case, ABOLISH the trial by jury; and that an ordinary degree of prudence and integrity in the national councils will insure us solid advantages from the establishment of the proposed judiciary, without exposing us to any of the inconveniences which have been predicted from that source. . . .

NOTES

1. Analyze the structure of Alexander Hamilton's argument for the power of judicial review in *The Federalist No. 78*. Is the argument responsive to the concerns of Brutus? Does Hamilton's argument embrace judicial supremacy?

2. What checks exist on the exercise of judicial power? Does Hamilton persuasively counter Brutus's charges on this point? Can he point to any checks on judicial power exercised by the other branches? Or does he merely assert that the judiciary would never overstep the bounds of its legitimate authority? What does Hamilton say about the executive's power with respect to the enforcement of judicial decrees? Is that a check on the judiciary? Does Hamilton's argument in *The Federalist No. 81* suggest that it would be proper for Congress to im-

peach and remove federal judges if they overstep (in Congress's judgment) the bounds of their legitimate authority?

3. Is Hamilton's argument for judicial review, as an inference from the function of courts and the nature of the Constitution as law, consistent with the separation of powers as explicated by Madison in *The Federalist Nos. 47, 48,* and *51*?

4. Today in the United Kingdom and Canada there is a form of judicial review. But a simple majority of the legislature may overturn a constitutional ruling of the highest court as long as the legislature explicitly indicates it is acting notwithstanding the charters protecting fundamental rights. Judicial review in the United Kingdom and Canada thus forces the legislature to take a second look at constitutional issues, but the legislature can always prevail by explicitly overruling the courts. What are the advantages and disadvantages of that approach to judicial review relative to the American approach?

[*Assignment 8*]

C. ARTICULATING THE DOCTRINE OF JUDICIAL REVIEW

The most famous exposition of the power of judicial review is the Supreme Court's decision in *Marbury v. Madison*, 5 U.S. (1 Cranch) 137 (1803). Before *Marbury* the Supreme Court had already taken a stand on constitutional principle against another branch: it had declined to give advice to President Washington about constitutional questions that were not before it in a case, on the ground that doing so would violate the judiciary's proper role under Article III of the Constitution. (This exchange, called the Correspondence of the Justices, is presented in Chapter 3.) Even before that, the justices, in circuit court opinions collected in *Hayburn's Case*, 2 U.S. 408 (1792) (also presented in Chapter 3), had objected, on constitutional grounds, to a statute requiring them to adjudicate veterans' pension claims but making those judicial determinations subject to revision by executive branch officers. And in *Hylton v. United States*, 3 U.S. 171 (1796), the Court had *upheld* an act of Congress—a tax on carriages—against a serious constitutional challenge. In that case, no one questioned the power of judicial review. Nonetheless, *Marbury* is the first time that the entire Court explicitly held an act of Congress unconstitutional while issuing an opinion that laid claim to this power.

Before you read the case itself, some background information would be helpful. *Marbury* had its roots in the hotly contested election of 1800, which matched President John Adams and his Federalist supporters against Vice President Thomas Jefferson and the new Democratic–Republican opposition party. Jefferson narrowly defeated Adams, with his margin of victory being supplied by the "slavery bonus" in the Electoral College afforded to the Southern states by the Three–Fifths Clause. Jefferson and Aaron Burr, who was intended to have been his vice president, tied in the Electoral College, and the choice between them was made by the lame-duck House of Representatives, with Jefferson being elected on the thirty-sixth ballot. (For more on this election, see the note on the Twelfth Amendment in Chapter 6.)

Meanwhile, the lame-duck Congress, which was dominated by defeated Federalists, passed the Judiciary Act of 1801, which replaced the antiquated system of having Supreme Court justices "ride circuit" and sit as members, with district judges, of a "circuit court." In its place, the statute created a new system of circuit courts—and of course new judgeships—and it greatly extended the statutory scope of federal jurisdiction. The abolition of circuit riding was of intense interest to the Federalist Supreme Court justices because it required them to spend as much as six months of the year away from their families travelling through huge sections of the United States on horseback. (The rigors of circuit riding may have contributed to the health problems, and death at age forty-eight, of Justice James Iredell in 1799.) However desirable these judicial reforms may have been, and some of them were probably good ideas, the Democratic–Republicans could not help but see the whole package as a last-ditch Federalist attempt to ensconce themselves in the life-tenured judiciary. Jefferson wrote: "The Federalists have retired into the judiciary as a stronghold and from that battery all the works of republicanism are to be beaten down and erased." Indeed, in February 1801 President John Adams nominated and the lame-duck Federalist Senate confirmed sixteen new life-tenured federal—and, of course, Federalist—circuit court judges.

Of more lasting importance, outgoing President Adams nominated John Marshall to be the fourth chief justice of the United States. He was nominated on January 20, 1801, and was confirmed by the lame-duck Senate fourteen days later. (Prior to the adoption of the Twentieth Amendment, presidential and congressional terms did not begin until March 4th— a full four months after the November election.) The vacancy in the office had been created when former Chief Justice Oliver Ellsworth resigned because of poor health. But Ellsworth's resignation had also been strategically timed to give the outgoing president the ability to pick a new chief justice. President Adams initially wanted John Jay, one author of *The Federalist* and the first chief justice, to again serve in that office. But Jay refused, thinking the job irksome and unimportant. Reluctantly, Adams then turned to Marshall, who was his trusted forty-five-year-old secretary of state (as well as a friend and biographer of George Washington). Marshall would become one of the greatest, if not the greatest, of all the chief justices of the Supreme Court.

Finally, on February 27, 1801—only a week before Jefferson would take office—Congress passed the Organic Act for the District of Columbia. Among other things, this act created more than forty justices of the peace for the new district. This was not a petty office, but neither were the justices "judges" in the Article III sense of the term. They were more like local government officials, partly judicial but also partly administrative, and they had five-year terms. President Adams quickly nominated persons to fill the offices, but this time the nominees were a more bipartisan group. One was William Marbury.

On March 3, 1801—the day before Jefferson and the new Congress took office—the lame-duck Federalist Senate confirmed President Adams's nominees. On the night of March 3, 1801, Secretary of State John Marshall affixed the Great Seal of the United States to the commissions of the newly appointed justices of the peace in his office at the State Department. (By this time, Marshall had already been appointed chief justice, but he had not yet resigned as secretary of state, and he actually held both offices for almost a month. The Constitution forbids any member of Congress from also holding an executive or judicial office, but it does not prohibit joint executive and judicial office-holding.) President Adams signed the commissions before going to bed. He woke early on March 4, and made a speedy exit from the capital at 3 AM so as not to "witness the awful event of Jefferson's inauguration," but in the confusion of the transition

> [p]recisely what happened to the commissions is not clear. Some were delivered. Marshall's younger brother James—himself a newly commissioned Circuit Judge for the District of Columbia—delivered a few to appointees in Alexandria, where there were concerns about the possibility of disruptive political celebrations. Other commissions lay undelivered. Later, John Marshall explained that he was short-handed that night because two State Department aides were assisting the President. Besides, he considered delivery legally inconsequential, once they had been signed and sealed. That was a fateful error.

Michael W. McConnell, "The Story of *Marbury v. Madison*: Making Defeat Look Like Victory," in CONSTITUTIONAL LAW STORIES 17 (Michael Dorf, ed. 2004). William Marbury's commission to be a justice of the peace was not delivered. When President Jefferson took office on March 4, he directed his new secretary of state, James Madison, not to deliver any commissions still in the possession of the State Department.

Marbury eventually filed a suit in the Supreme Court to compel Madison to deliver his commission as a justice of the peace. Marbury's lawyer was Charles Lee, who had served as attorney general under Presidents Washington and Adams. Lee requested a writ of mandamus from the Supreme Court—essentially, an order directing Madison to appear before the Court and defend his non-delivery of the commissions. That was on December 16, 1801. The suit was filed in the Court's original rather than appellate jurisdiction. This means that the case originated or started in the Supreme Court itself, not in a lower federal court or state court. Article III, Section 2, Paragraph 2 regulates the original and the appellate jurisdiction of the Supreme Court. Is this a case within the Supreme Court's original jurisdiction as it is described in Article III?

As the developments surrounding Marbury's lawsuit against Madison were unfolding, the Jeffersonians were rapidly setting about to dismantle the new judicial structure enacted by the Federalists. They voted to repeal the Judiciary Act of 1801, thus abolishing the newly created circuit courts (and with them the judgeships of the newly confirmed judges). This statute again imposed on the justices the onerous duty of circuit riding. Both the abolition of sixteen life-tenured circuit-court judgeships and the reimposition of circuit riding were acts of dubious constitutionality. The nation waited to see how the Federalist-dominated Supreme Court would respond. The Jeffersonians even took the extraordinary step of abolishing by statute the Supreme Court's 1802 session, so Marbury's case was not heard until 1803. By doing this, they ensured that any Supreme Court ruling on the constitutionality of their various actions would not occur until after the 1802 midterm elections.

The constitutional debate over repeal of the Judiciary Act of 1801 was intense. See David P. Currie, THE CONSTITUTION IN CONGRESS: THE JEFFERSONIANS, 1801–1829 10–22 (2001). But at the time no one thought that the case about William Marbury's commission would be of much consequence. Instead, attention was fixed on a different case pending before the Supreme Court, *Stuart v. Laird*, in which the constitutionality of the Repeal Act was indirectly at issue. Could Congress constitutionally abolish federal judgeships and re-impose the duty of circuit riding? Would the Supreme Court defy the Jeffersonians—who had already begun impeachment proceedings against some Federalist judges—by actually holding that the

Repeal Act was unconstitutional? That was the issue of the day. To give away the ending: one week after deciding *Marbury*, the Court upheld the Repeal Act in *Stuart*. In fact, one could even say that "*Marbury* must be understood as the product of a defeated and demoralized Court." McConnell, "The Story of *Marbury v. Madison*," at 22.

As you read *Marbury* and *Stuart*, consider the constitutional arguments made by the Court. In particular, how does the Court see its role in the constitutional structure?

Marbury v. Madison

5 U.S. (1 Cranch) 137 (1803)

■ The following opinion of the court was delivered by [CHIEF JUSTICE MARSHALL].

. . . In the order in which the court has viewed this subject, the following questions have been considered and decided.

1st. Has the applicant a right to the commission he demands?

2dly. If he has a right, and that right has been violated, do the laws of his country afford him a remedy?

3dly. If they do afford him a remedy, is it a *mandamus* issuing from this court?

The first object of inquiry is,

1st. Has the applicant a right to the commission he demands?

His right originates in an act of congress passed in February, 1801, concerning the district of Columbia.

After dividing the district into two counties, the 11th section of this law, enacts, "that there shall be appointed in and for each of the said counties, such number of discreet persons to be justices of the peace as the president of the United States shall, from time to time, think expedient, to continue in office for five years."

It appears, from the affidavits, that in compliance with this law, a commission for William Marbury as a justice of the peace for the county of Washington, was signed by John Adams, then president of the United States; after which the seal of the United States was affixed to it; but the commission has never reached the person for whom it was made out.

In order to determine whether he is entitled to this commission, it becomes necessary to inquire whether he has been appointed to the office. For if he has been appointed, the law continues him in office for five years, and he is entitled to the possession of those evidences of office, which, being completed, become his property.

The 2d section of the 2d article of the constitution, declares that "the president shall nominate, and, by and with the advice and consent of the senate, shall appoint ambassadors, other public ministers and consuls, and all other officers of the United States, whose appointments are not otherwise provided for."

The third section declares, that "he shall commission all the officers of the United States."

An act of congress directs the secretary of state to keep the seal of the United States, "to make out and record, and affix the said seal to all civil commissions to officers of the United States, to be appointed by the President, by and with the consent of the senate, or by the President alone; provided, that the said seal shall not be affixed to any commission before the same shall have been signed by the President of the United States." . . .

The acts of appointing to office, and commissioning the person appointed, can scarcely be considered as one and the same; since the power to perform them is given in two separate and distinct sections of the constitution. . . . This is an appointment made by the President, by and with the advice and consent of the senate, and is evidenced by no act but the commission itself. In such a case therefore the commission and the appointment seem inseparable; it being almost impossible to shew an appointment otherwise than by proving the existence of a commission; still the commission is not necessarily the appointment, though conclusive evidence of it. . . .

The last act to be done by the President, is the signature of the commission. He has then acted on the advice and consent of the senate to his own nomination. The time for deliberation has then passed. He has decided. His judgment, on the advice and consent of the senate concurring with his nomination, has been made, and the officer is appointed. This appointment is evidenced by an open, unequivocal act; and being the last act required from the person making it, necessarily excludes the idea of its being, so far as respects the appointment, an inchoate and incomplete transaction.

Some point of time must be taken when the power of the executive over an officer, not removable at his will, must cease. That point of time must be when the constitutional power of appointment has been exercised. And this power has been exercised when the last act, required from the person possessing the power, has been performed. This last act is the signature of the commission. . . .

The signature is a warrant for affixing the great seal to the commission; and the great seal is only to he affixed to an instrument which is complete. It attests, by an act supposed to be of public notoriety, the verity of the presidential signature.

It is never to be affixed till the commission is signed, because the signature, which gives force and effect to the commission, is conclusive evidence that the appointment is made.

The commission being signed, the subsequent duty of the secretary of state is prescribed by law, and not to be guided by the will of the President. He is to affix the seal of the United States to the commission, and is to record it.

This is not a proceeding which may be varied, if the judgment of the executive shall suggest one more eligible; but is a precise course as accurately marked out by law, and is to be strictly pursued. It is the duty of the secretary of state to conform to the law, and in this he is an officer of the United States, bound to obey the laws. He acts, in this respect, as has been very properly stated at the bar, under the authority of law, and not by the instructions of the President. It is a ministerial act which the law enjoins on a particular officer for a particular purpose. . . .

It has also occurred as possible, and barely possible, that the transmission of the commission, and the acceptance thereof, might be deemed necessary to complete the right of the plaintiff.

The transmission of the commission is a practice directed by convenience, but not by law. . . . It may have some tendency to elucidate this point, to enquire whether the possession of the original commission be indispensably necessary to authorize a person, appointed to any office, to perform the duties of that office. If it was necessary, then a loss of the commission would lose the office. Not only negligence, but accident or fraud, fire or theft, might deprive an individual of his office. In such a case, I presume it could not be doubted but that a copy from the record of the office of the secretary of state would be, to every intent and purpose, equal to the original. The act of congress has expressly made it so. . . .

In the case of commissions, the law orders the secretary of state to record them. When therefore they are signed and sealed, the order for their being recorded is given; and whether inserted in the book or not, they are in law recorded. . . .

It is therefore decidedly the opinion of the court, that when a commission has been signed by the President, the appointment is made; and that the commission is complete, when the seal of the United States has been affixed to it by the Secretary of State.

Where an officer is removable at the will of the executive, the circumstance which completes his appointment is of no concern; because the act is at any time revocable; and the commission may be arrested, if still in the office. But when the officer is not removable at the will of the executive, the appointment is not revocable, and cannot be annulled. It has conferred legal rights which cannot be resumed.

The discretion of the executive is to be exercised until the appointment has been made. But having once made the appointment, his power over the office is terminated in all cases where by law the officer is not removable by him. The right to the office is *then* in the person appointed, and he has the absolute, unconditional, power of accepting or rejecting it.

Mr. Marbury, then, since his commission was signed by the President, and sealed by the secretary of state, was appointed; and as the law creating the office, gave the officer a right to hold for five years, independent of the executive, the appointment was not revocable; but vested in the officer legal rights, which are protected by the laws of his country.

To withhold his commission, therefore, is an act deemed by the court not warranted by law, but violative of a vested legal right.

This brings us to the second inquiry; which is,

2dly. If he has a right, and that right has been violated, do the laws of this country afford him a remedy?

The very essence of civil liberty certainly consists in the right of every individual to claim the protection of the laws, whenever he receives an injury. One of the first duties of government is to afford that protection. In Great Britain the king himself is sued in the respectful form of a petition, and he never fails to comply with the judgment of his court. . . .

The government of the United States has been emphatically termed a government of laws, and not of men. It will certainly cease to deserve this high appellation, if the laws furnish no remedy for the violation of a vested legal right.

If this obloquy is to be cast on the jurisprudence of our country, it must arise from the peculiar character of the case.

It behooves us, then, to inquire whether there be in its composition any ingredient which shall exempt it from legal investigations or exclude the injured party from legal redress. In pursuing this enquiry the first question which presents itself, is, whether this can be arranged with that class of cases which come under the description of *damnum absque injuria*—a loss without an injury.

This description of cases never has been considered, and it is believed never can be considered, as comprehending offices of trust, of honor or of profit. The office of justice of peace in the district of Columbia is such an office; it is therefore worthy of the attention and guardianship of the laws. It has received that attention and guardianship. It has been created by special act of congress, and has been secured, so far as the laws can give security to the person appointed to fill it, for five years. It is not, then, on account of the worthlessness of the thing pursued, that the injured party can be alleged to be without remedy.

Is it in the nature of the transaction? Is the act of delivering or withholding a commission to be considered as a mere political act, belonging to the executive department alone, for the performance of which entire confidence is placed by our constitution in the supreme executive; and for any misconduct respecting which, the injured individual has no remedy?

That there may be such cases is not to be questioned; but that every act of duty, to be performed in any of the great departments of government, constitutes such a case, is not to be admitted. . . .

It follows then that the question, whether the legality of an act of the head of a department be examinable in a court of justice or not, must always depend on the nature of that act.

If some acts be examinable, and others not, there must be some rule of law to guide the court in the exercise of its jurisdiction. . . .

By the constitution of the United States, the President is invested with certain important political powers in the exercise of which he is to use his own discretion, and is accountable only to his country in his political character, and to his own conscience. To aid him in the performance of these duties, he is authorized to appoint certain officers, who act by his authority, and in conformity with his orders.

In such cases, their acts are his acts; and whatever opinion may be entertained of the manner in which executive discretion may be used, still there exists, and can exist, no power to control that discretion. The subjects are political. They respect the nation, not individual rights, and being entrusted to the executive, the decision of the executive is conclusive. . . .

But when the legislature proceeds to impose on that officer other duties; when he is directed peremptorily to perform certain acts; when the rights of individuals are dependent on the performance of those acts; he is so far the officer of the law; is amenable to the laws for his conduct; and cannot at his discretion sport away the vested rights of others.

The conclusion from this reasoning is, that where the heads of departments are the political or confidential agents of the executive, merely to execute the will of the President, or rather to act in cases in which the executive possesses a constitutional or legal discretion, nothing can be more perfectly clear than that their acts are only politically examinable. But where a specific duty is assigned by law, and individual rights depend upon the performance of that duty, it seems equally clear that the individual who considers himself injured, has a right to resort to the laws of his country for a remedy.

If this be the rule, let us inquire how it applies to the case under the consideration of the court.

The power of nominating to the senate, and the power of appointing the person nominated, are political powers, to be exercised by the President according to his own discretion. When he has made an appointment, he has exercised his whole power, and his discretion has been completely applied to the case. If, by law, the officer be removable at the will of the President, then a new appointment may be immediately made, and the rights of the officer are terminated. But as a fact which has existed cannot be made never to have existed, the appointment cannot be annihilated; and consequently, if the officer is by law not removable at the will of the President, the rights he has acquired are protected by the law, and are not resumable by the President. They cannot be extinguished by executive authority, and he has the privilege of asserting them in like manner as if they had been derived from any other source.

The question whether a right has vested or not, is, on its nature, judicial, and must be tried by the judicial authority. If, for example, Mr. Marbury had taken the oaths of a magistrate, and proceeded to act as one; in consequence of which a suit had been instituted against him, in which his defence had depended on his being a magistrate; the validity of his appointment must have been determined by judicial authority.

So, if he conceives that, by virtue of his appointment, he has a legal right, either to the commission which has been made out for him, or to a copy of that commission, it is equally a question examinable in a court, and the decision of the court upon it must depend on the opinion entertained of his appointment.

That question has been discussed, and the opinion is, that the latest point of time which can be taken as that at which the appointment was complete, and evidenced, was when, after the signature of the president, the seal of the United States was affixed to the commission.

It is, then, the opinion of the court,

1st. That by signing the commission of Mr. Marbury, the president of the United States appointed him a justice of peace for the county of Washington in the district of Columbia; and that the seal of the United States, affixed thereto by the secretary of state, is conclusive testimony of the verity of the signature, and of the completion of the appointment, and that the appointment conferred on him a legal right to the office for the space of five years.

2dly. That, having this legal title to the office, he has a consequent right to the commission; a refusal to deliver which, is a plain violation of that right, for which the laws of his country afford him a remedy.

It remains to be inquired whether,

3dly. He is entitled to the remedy for which he applies. This depends on,

1st. The nature of the writ applied for, and,

2dly. The power of this court.

1st. The nature of the writ.

Blackstone, in the 3d volume of his commentaries, page 110, defines a mandamus to be "a command issuing in the king's name from the court of king's bench, and directed to any person, corporation, or inferior court of judicature within the king's dominions, requiring them to do some particular thing therein specified, which appertains to their office and duty, and which the court of king's bench has previously determined, or at least supposes, to be consonant to right and justice." . . .

This writ, if awarded, would be directed to an officer of government, and its mandate to him would be, to use the words of Blackstone, "to do a particular thing therein specified, which appertains to his office and duty, and which the court has previously determined, or at least supposes, to be consonant to right and justice." . . .

These circumstances certainly concur in this case.

Still, to render the mandamus a proper remedy, the other to whom it is to be directed, must be one to whom, on legal principles, such writ may be directed; and the person applying for it must be without any other specific and legal remedy.

. . . The intimate political relation subsisting between the president of the United States and the heads of departments, necessarily renders any legal investigation of the acts of one of those high officers peculiarly irksome, as well as delicate; and excites some hesitation with respect to the propriety of entering into such investigation. Impressions are often received without much reflection or examination, and it is not wonderful that in such a case as this, the assertion, by an individual, of his legal claims in a court of justice; to which claims it is the duty of that court to attend; should at first view be considered by some, as an attempt to intrude into the cabinet, and to intermeddle with the prerogatives of the executive.

It is scarcely necessary for the court to disclaim all pretensions to such a jurisdiction. An extravagance, so absurd and excessive, could not have been entertained for a moment. The province of the court is, solely, to decide on the rights of individuals, not to enquire how the executive, or executive officers, perform duties in which they have a discretion. Questions, in their nature political, or which are, by the constitution and laws, submitted to the executive, can never be made in this court.

But, if this be not such a question; if, so far from being an intrusion into the secrets of the cabinet, it respects a paper, which, according to law, is upon record, and to a copy of which the law gives a right, on the payment of ten cents; if it be no intermeddling with a subject over which the executive can be considered as having exercised any control; what is there in the exalted station of the officer, which shall bar a citizen from asserting, in a court of justice, his legal rights, or shall forbid a court to listen to the claim; or to issue a mandamus, directing the performance of a duty, not depending on executive discretion, but on particular acts of congress and the general principles of law?

If one of the heads of departments commits any illegal act, under color of his office, by which an individual sustains an injury, it cannot be pretended that his office alone exempts him from being sued in the ordinary mode of proceeding, and being compelled to obey the judgment of the law. How, then, can his office exempt him from this particular mode of deciding on the legality of his conduct, if the case be such a case as would, were any other individual the party complained of, authorize the process?

. . . Where the head of a department . . . is directed by law to do a certain act affecting the absolute rights of individuals, in the performance of which he is not placed under the particular direction of the President, and the performance of which the President cannot lawfully forbid, and therefore is never presumed to have forbidden; . . . it is not perceived on what ground the courts of the country are farther excused from the duty of giving judgment, that right be done to an injured individual, then if the same services were to be performed by a person not the head of a department. . . .

It is true that the mandamus, now moved for, is not for the performance of an act expressly enjoined by statute.

It is to deliver a commission; on which subject the acts of Congress are silent. This difference is not considered as affecting the case. It has already been stated that the applicant has, to that commission, a vested legal right, of which the executive cannot deprive him. He has been appointed to an office, from which he is not removable at the will of the executive; and being so appointed, he has a right to the commission which the secretary has received from the president for his use. . . .

This, then, is a plain case for a mandamus, either to deliver the commission, or a copy of it from the record; and it only remains to be enquired,

Whether it can issue from this court.

The act to establish the judicial courts of the United States authorizes the Supreme Court "to issue writs of mandamus in cases warranted by the principles and usages of law, to any courts appointed, or persons holding office, under the authority of the United States."

The secretary of state, being a person holding an office under the authority of the United States, is precisely within the letter of the description; and if this court is not authorized to issue a writ of mandamus to such an officer, it must be because the law is unconstitutional, and therefore absolutely incapable of conferring the authority, and assigning the duties which its words purport to confer and assign.

The constitution vests the whole judicial power of the United States in one supreme court, and such inferior courts as congress shall, from time to time, ordain and establish. This power is expressly extended to all cases arising under the laws of the United States; and, consequently, in some form, may be exercised over the present case; because the right claimed is given by a law of the United States.

In the distribution of this power it is declared that "the supreme court shall have original jurisdiction in all cases affecting ambassadors, other public ministers and consuls, and those in which a state shall be a party. In all other cases, the supreme court shall have appellate jurisdiction."

It has been insisted, at the bar, that if the original grant of jurisdiction, to the supreme and inferior courts, is general, and the clause, assigning original jurisdiction to the supreme court, contains no negative or restrictive words; the power remains to the legislature, to assign original jurisdiction to that court in other cases than those specified in the article which has been recited; provided those cases belong to the judicial power of the United States.

If it had been intended to leave it in the discretion of the legislature to apportion the judicial power between the supreme and inferior courts according to the will of that body, it would certainly have been useless to have proceeded further than to have defined the judicial power, and the tribunals in which it should be vested. The subsequent part of the section is mere surplusage, is entirely without meaning, if such is to be the construction. If congress remains at liberty to give this court appellate jurisdiction, where the constitution has declared their jurisdiction shall be original; and original jurisdiction where the constitution has declared it shall be appellate; the distribution of jurisdiction, made in the constitution, is form without substance.

Affirmative words are often, in their operation, negative of other objects than those affirmed; and in this case, a negative or exclusive sense must be given to them, or they have no operation at all.

It cannot be presumed that any clause in the constitution is intended to be without effect; and, therefore, such a construction is inadmissible unless the words require it. . . .

When an instrument organizing fundamentally a judicial system, divides it into one supreme, and so many inferior courts as the legislature may ordain and establish; then enumerates its powers, and proceeds so far to distribute them, as to define the jurisdiction of the supreme court by declaring the cases in which it shall take original jurisdiction, and that in others it shall take appellate jurisdiction; the plain import of the words seems to be, that in one class of cases its jurisdiction is original, and not appellate; in the other it is appellate, and not original. If any other construction would render the clause inoperative, that is an additional reason for rejecting such other construction, and for adhering to their obvious meaning.

To enable this court then to issue a mandamus, it must be shewn to be an exercise of appellate jurisdiction, or to be necessary to enable them to exercise appellate jurisdiction. . . .

It is the essential criterion of appellate jurisdiction, that it revises and corrects the proceedings in a cause already instituted, and does not create that cause. Although, therefore, a mandamus may be directed to courts, yet to issue such a writ to an officer for the delivery of a paper, is in effect the same as to sustain an original action for that paper, and therefore seems not to belong to appellate, but to original jurisdiction. Neither is it necessary in such a case as this to enable the court to exercise its appellate jurisdiction.

The authority, therefore, given to the supreme court, by the act establishing the judicial courts of the United States, to issue writs of mandamus to public officers, appears not to be warranted by the constitution; and it becomes necessary to enquire whether a jurisdiction, so conferred, can be exercised.

The question, whether an act, repugnant to the constitution, can become the law of the land, is a question deeply interesting to the United States; but, happily, not of an intricacy proportioned to its interest. It seems only necessary to recognize certain principles, supposed to have been long and well established, to decide it.

That the people have an original right to establish, for their future government, such principles as, in their opinion, shall most conduce to their own happiness, is the basis, on which the whole American fabric has been erected. The exercise of this original right is a very great exertion; nor can it, nor ought it to be frequently repeated. The principles, therefore, so established, are deemed fundamental. And as the authority, from which they proceed, is supreme, and can seldom act, they are designed to be permanent.

This original and supreme will organizes the government, and assigns, to different departments, their respective powers. It may either stop here; or establish certain limits not to be transcended by those departments.

The government of the United States is of the latter description. The powers of the legislature are defined, and limited; and that those limits may not be mistaken, or forgotten, the constitution is written. To what purpose are powers limited, and to what purpose is that limitation committed to writing, if these limits may, at any time, be passed by those intended to be restrained? The distinction, between a government with limited and unlimited powers, is abolished, if those limits do not confine the persons on whom they are imposed, and if acts prohibited and acts allowed, are of equal obligation. It is a proposition too plain to be contested, that the constitution controls any legislative act repugnant to it; or, that the legislature may alter the constitution by an ordinary act.

Between these alternatives there is no middle ground. The constitution is either a superior, paramount law, unchangeable by ordinary means, or it is on a level with ordinary legislative acts, and, like other acts, is alterable when the legislature shall please to alter it.

If the former part of the alternative be true, then a legislative act contrary to the constitution is not law: if the latter part be true, then written constitutions are absurd attempts, on the part of the people, to limit a power, in its own nature illimitable.

Certainly all those who have framed written constitutions contemplate them as forming the fundamental and paramount law of the nation, and consequently the theory of every such government must be, that an act of the legislature, repugnant to the constitution, is void.

This theory is essentially attached to a written constitution, and is consequently to be considered, by this court, as one of the fundamental principles of our society. It is not therefore to be lost sight of in the further consideration of this subject.

If an act of the legislature, repugnant to the constitution, is void, does it, notwithstanding its invalidity, bind the courts, and oblige them to give it effect? Or, in other words, though it be not law, does it constitute a rule as operative as if it was a law? This would be to overthrow in fact what was established in theory; and would seem, at first view, an absurdity too gross to be insisted on. It shall, however, receive a more attentive consideration.

It is emphatically the province and duty of the judicial department to say what the law is. Those who apply the rule to particular cases, must of necessity expound and interpret that rule. If two laws conflict with each other, the courts must decide on the operation of each.

So if a law be in opposition to the constitution; if both the law and the constitution apply to a particular case, so that the court must either decide that case conformably to the law, disregarding the constitution; or conformably to the constitution, disregarding the law; the court must determine which of these conflicting rules governs the case. This is of the very essence of judicial duty.

If then the courts are to regard the constitution; and the constitution is superior to any ordinary act of the legislature; the constitution, and not such ordinary act, must govern the case to which they both apply.

Those then who controvert the principle that the constitution is to be considered, in court, as a paramount law, are reduced to the necessity of maintaining that courts must close their eyes on the constitution, and see only the law.

This doctrine would subvert the very foundation of all written constitutions. It would declare that an act, which, according to the principles and theory of our government is entirely void; is yet, in practice, completely obligatory. It would declare that if the legislature shall do what is expressly forbiden, such act, notwithstanding the express prohibition, is in reality effectual. It would be giving to the legislature a practical and real omnipotence, with the same breath which professes to restrict their powers within narrow limits. It is prescribing limits, and declaring that those limits may be passed at pleasure.

That it thus reduces to nothing what we have deemed the greatest improvement on political institutions—a written constitution—would of itself be sufficient, in America, where written constitutions have been viewed with so much reverence, for rejecting the construction. But the peculiar expressions of the constitution of the United States furnish additional arguments in favour of its rejection.

The judicial power of the United States is extended to all cases arising under the constitution.

Could it be the intention of those who gave this power, to say that, in using it, the constitution should not be looked into? That a case arising under the constitution should be decided without examining the instrument under which it arises?

This is too extravagant to be maintained.

In some cases then, the constitution must be looked into by the judges. And it they can open it at all, what part of it are they forbidden to read, or to obey?

There are many other parts of the constitution which serve to illustrate this subject.

It is declared that "no tax or duty shall be laid on articles exported from any state." Suppose a duty on the export of cotton, of tobacco, or of flour; and a suit instituted to recover it. Ought judgment to be rendered in such a case? ought the judges to close their eyes on the constitution, and only see the law?

The constitution declares "that no bill of attainder or *ex post facto* law shall be passed."

If, however, such a bill should be passed and a person should be prosecuted under it; must the court condemn to death those victims whom the constitution endeavours to preserve?

"No person," says the constitution, "shall be convicted of treason unless on the testimony of two witnesses to the same overt act, or on confession in open court."

Here the language of the constitution is addressed especially to the courts. It prescribes, directly for them, a rule of evidence not to be departed from. If the legislature should change that rule, and declare *one* witness, or a confession *out* of court, sufficient for conviction, must the constitutional principle yield to the legislative act?

From these, and many other selections which might be made, it is apparent, that the framers of the constitution contemplated that instrument, as a rule for the government of *courts*, as well as of the legislature.

Why otherwise does it direct the judges to take an oath to support it? This oath certainly applies, in an especial manner, to their conduct in their official character. How immoral to impose it on them, if they were to be used as the instruments, and the knowing instruments, for violating what they swear to support!

The oath of office, too, imposed by the legislature, is completely demonstrative of the legislative opinion on this subject. It is in these words, "I do solemnly swear that I will administer justice without respect to persons, and do equal right to the poor and to the rich; and that I will faithfully and impartially discharge all the duties incumbent on me as ____, according to the best of my abilities and understanding, agreeably to *the constitution*, and laws of the United States."

Why does a judge swear to discharge his duties agreably to the constitution of the United States, if that constitution forms no rule for his government? if it is closed upon him, and cannot be inspected by him?

If such be the real state of things, this is worse than solemn mockery. To prescribe, or to take this oath, becomes equally a crime.

It is also not entirely unworthy of observation, that in declaring what shall be the *supreme* law of the land, the *constitution* itself is first mentioned; and not the laws of the United States generally, but those only which shall be made in *pursuance* of the constitution, have that rank.

Thus, the particular phraseology of the constitution of the United States confirms and strengthens the principle, supposed to be essential to all written constitutions, that a law repugnant to the constitution is void; and that *courts*, as well as other departments, are bound by that instrument.

The rule must be discharged.

NOTES

1. What does *Marbury* hold, and which parts of the opinion are dicta? Chief Justice Marshall's decision is often described as being politically ingenious, given his ultimate conclusion that the Court was without jurisdiction to issue a writ of mandamus. It is sometimes said that Chief Justice Marshall went out of his way in the first half of the opinion to provoke President Jefferson, and that he then went out of his way in the second half of the opinion to decline to issue an order to deliver the judicial commission to William Marbury (an order that would probably have been disregarded anyway). Is that a fair characterization? How do you see the relationship between the different parts of the Court's opinion?

2. What does Chief Justice Marshall say about whether Congress had sought to add to the original jurisdiction of the Supreme Court? Did the Judiciary Act of 1789 purport to confer "original jurisdiction" on the Supreme Court whenever someone seeks a writ of mandamus? Or did it provide that, whenever the Supreme Court already has appellate jurisdiction, mandamus is a writ that it is authorized to employ as a remedy? Here is Section 13 of the act:

And be it further enacted, That the Supreme court shall have exclusive jurisdiction of all controversies of a civil nature, where a state is a party, except between a state and its citizens; and except also between a state and citizens of other states, or aliens, in which latter case it shall have original but not exclusive jurisdiction. And shall have exclusively all such jurisdiction of suits or proceedings against ambassadors, or other public minister, or their domestics, or domestic servants, as a court of law can have or exercise consistently with the law of nations; and original, but not exclusive jurisdiction of all suits brought by ambassadors, or other public ministers, or in which a consul, or vice consul, shall be a party. And the trial of issues of fact in the Supreme Court, in all actions at law against citizens of the United States, shall be by jury. The Supreme Court shall also have appellate jurisdiction from the circuit courts and courts of the several states, in the cases herein after specially provided for; and shall have power to issue writs of prohibition to the district courts, when proceeding as courts of admiralty and maritime jurisdiction, and writs of mandamus, in cases warranted by the principles and usages of law, to any courts appointed, or persons holding office, under the authority of the United States.

Judiciary Act of 1789, 1 Stat. 73, Section 13.

3. Article III, Section 2, clause 2, says: "In all Cases affecting Ambassadors, other public Ministers and Consuls, and those in which a State shall be Party, the supreme Court shall have original Jurisdiction. In all the other Cases before mentioned, the supreme Court shall have appellate Jurisdiction, both as to Law and Fact, with such Exceptions, and under such Regulations as the Congress shall make." How does Chief Justice Marshall interpret this language? Is he right that Congress may not increase the Supreme Court's original jurisdiction? Is there any other plausible reading? What reading seems best?

4. Must the courts have authority to refuse to give effect to legislative acts that contravene the Constitution, when the issue is properly presented in a case or controversy? How does Chief Justice Marshall's analysis resemble or differ from Alexander Hamilton's in *The Federalist No. 78*? Does Chief Justice Marshall's analysis suggest anything about whether the other branches have a power or duty to interpret the Constitution? About which branch's decision is supreme when there is a conflict?

5. Recall the types of constitutional argument, or modes of interpretation, discussed in Chapter 1. Which ones does Chief Justice Marshall employ in *Marbury*? Which ones are most central to his argument?

6. As noted above, part of the political context of *Marbury* involved the Repeal of the Judiciary Act of 1801 and the Democratic–Republicans' attack on the Federalist-appointed judiciary. The case that, at the time, looked like it would be the big confrontation was *Stuart v. Laird*. This case concerned the reassignment of cases from the Federalist-created circuit courts with life-tenured circuit court of appeals judges to the reconstituted circuit courts of one district judge and one Supreme Court justice riding circuit. *Stuart* was thus a case about the constitutionality of re-imposing circuit riding and abolishing federal judgeships. It was decided just a week after *Marbury*. The Court's decision in *Stuart* proved a disappointment, even though the constitutional issues were serious. Does Congress have power to eliminate a layer of lower federal courts entirely—and thereby remove Article III judges from office—and reassign the affected cases, either to new courts or to existing ones? Does Congress have power to require Supreme Court justices to "ride circuit" and hear lower court cases? Ironically, *Stuart* was an appeal to the Supreme Court from a deci-

sion by a circuit court decision of—John Marshall! Chief Justice Marshall therefore recused himself. Was the Court's decision a capitulation? A wise tactical retreat? When deciding whether to confront another branch, should the Court consider the risk to its institutional standing and authority? Or is that an improper consideration?

Stuart v. Laird

5 U.S. (1 Cranch) 299 (1803)

■ PATERSON, JUSTICE, (Judge Cushing being absent on account of ill health,) delivered the opinion of the court.

On an action instituted by John Laird against Hugh Stuart, a judgment was entered in a court for the fourth circuit in the eastern district of Virginia, in December term 1801. On this judgment, an execution was issued, returnable to April term 1802, in the same court. In the term of December 1802, John Laird obtained judgment at a court for the fifth circuit in the Virginia district, against Hugh Stuart and Charles L. Carter, upon their bond for the forthcoming and delivery of certain property therein mentioned, which had been levied upon by virtue of the above execution against the said Hugh Stuart.

Two reasons have been assigned by counsel for reversing the judgment on the forthcoming bond. 1. That as the bond was given for the delivery of property levied on by virtue of an execution issuing out of, and returnable to a court for the fourth circuit, no other court could legally proceed upon the said bond. This is true, if there be no statutable provision to direct and authorize such proceeding. Congress have constitutional authority to establish from time to time such inferior tribunals as they may think proper; and to transfer a cause from one such tribunal to another. In this last particular, there are no words in the constitution to prohibit or restrain the exercise of legislative power.

The present is a case of this kind. It is nothing more than the removal of the suit brought by Stuart against Laird from the court of the fourth circuit to the court of the fifth circuit, which is authorized to proceed upon and carry it into full effect. This is apparent from the ninth section of the act entitled, "an act to amend the judicial system of the United States," passed the 29th of April, 1802. The forthcoming bond is an appendage to the cause, or rather a component part of the proceedings.

2d. Another reason for reversal is, that the judges of the supreme court have no right to sit as circuit judges, not being appointed as such, or in other words, that they ought to have distinct commissions for that purpose. To this objection, which is of recent date, it is sufficient to observe, that practice and acquiescence under it for a period of several years, commencing with the organization of the judicial system, affords an irresistible answer, and has indeed fixed the construction. It is a contemporary interpretation of the most forcible nature. This practical exposition is too strong and obstinate to be shaken or controlled. Of course, the question is at rest, and ought not now to be disturbed.

———

Twenty-eight years after the Court's decision in *Marbury*, Alexis de Tocqueville visited the United States. In his account of American society and institutions, he included a description of the courts and their power of judicial review. What does he say about the powers of American courts? And about the circumstances in which those powers are exercised?

Alexis de Tocqueville on the American Judiciary

From Democracy in America, volume 1 (1835)

I have thought it essential to devote a separate chapter to the judicial authorities of the United States, lest their great political importance should be lessened in the reader's eyes by a merely incidental mention of them. Confederations have existed in other countries beside America, and republics have not been established upon the shores of the New World alone; the representative system of government has been adopted in several States of Europe, but I am not aware that any nation of the globe has hitherto organized a judicial power on the principle now adopted by the Americans. The judicial organization of the United States is the institution which a stranger has the greatest difficulty in understanding. He hears the authority of a judge invoked in the political occurrences of every day, and he naturally concludes that in the United States the judges are important political functionaries; nevertheless, when he examines the nature of the tribunals, they offer nothing which is contrary to the usual habits and privileges of those bodies, and the magistrates seem to him to interfere in public affairs of chance, but by a chance which recurs every day.

When the Parliament of Paris remonstrated, or refused to enregister an edict, or when it summoned a functionary accused of malversation to its bar, its political influence as a judicial body was clearly visible; but nothing of the kind is to be seen in the United States. The Americans have retained all the ordinary characteristics of judicial authority, and have carefully restricted its action to the ordinary circle of its functions.

The first characteristic of judicial power in all nations is the duty of arbitration. But rights must be contested in order to warrant the interference of a tribunal; and an action must be brought to obtain the decision of a judge. As long, therefore, as the law is uncontested, the judicial authority is not called upon to discuss it, and it may exist without being perceived. When a judge in a given case attacks a law relating to that case, he extends the circle of his customary duties, without however stepping beyond it; since he is in some measure obliged to decide upon the law in order to decide the case. But if he pronounces upon a law without resting upon a case, he clearly steps beyond his sphere, and invades that of the legislative authority.

The second characteristic of judicial power is that it pronounces on special cases, and not upon general principles. If a judge in deciding a particular point destroys a general principle, by passing a judgment which tends to reject all the inferences from that principle, and consequently to annul it, he remains within the ordinary limits of his functions. But if he directly attacks a general principle without having a particular case in view, he leaves the circle in which all nations have agreed to confine his authority, he assumes a more important, and perhaps a more useful, influence than that of the magistrate, but he ceases to be a representative of the judicial power.

The third characteristic of the judicial power is its inability to act unless it is appealed to, or until it has taken cognizance of an affair. This characteristic is less general than the other two; but, notwithstanding the exceptions, I think it may be regarded as essential. The judicial power is by its nature devoid of action; it must be put in motion in order to produce a result. When it is called upon to repress a crime, it punishes the criminal; when a wrong is to be redressed, it is ready to redress it; when an act requires interpretation, it is prepared to interpret it; but it does not pursue criminals, hunt out wrongs, or examine into evidence of its own accord. A judicial functionary who should open proceedings, and usurp the censorship of the laws, would in some measure do violence to the passive nature of his authority.

The Americans have retained these three distinguishing characteristics of the judicial power; an American judge can only pronounce a decision when litigation has arisen, he is only conversant with special cases, and he cannot act until the cause has been duly brought before the court. His position is therefore perfectly similar to that of the magistrate of other nations; and he is nevertheless invested with immense political power. If the sphere of his authority and his means of action are the same as those of other judges, it may be asked whence he derives a power which they do not possess. The cause of this difference lies in the simple fact that the Americans have acknowledged the right of the judges to found their decisions on the constitution rather than on the laws. In other words, they have left them at liberty not to apply such laws as may appear to them to be unconstitutional.

I am aware that a similar right has been claimed—but claimed in vain—by courts of justice in other countries; but in America it is recognized by all authorities; and not a party, nor so much as an individual, is found to contest it. This fact can only be explained by the principles of the American constitution. In France the constitution is (or at least is supposed to be) immutable; and the received theory is that no power has the right of changing any part of it. In England the Parliament has an acknowledged right to modify the constitution; as, therefore, the constitution may undergo perpetual changes, it does not in reality exist; the Parliament is at once a legislative and a constituent assembly. The political theories of America are more simple and more rational. An American constitution is not supposed to be immutable as in France, nor is it susceptible of modification by the ordinary powers of society as in England. It constitutes a detached whole, which, as it represents the determination of the whole people, is no less binding on the legislator than on the private citizen, but which may be altered by the will of the people in predetermined cases, according to established rules. In America the constitution may therefore vary, but as long as it exists it is the origin of all authority, and the sole vehicle of the predominating force.

. . . It would be . . . unreasonable to invest the English judges with the right of resisting the decisions of the legislative body, since the Parliament which makes the laws also makes the constitution; and consequently a law emanating from the three powers of the State can in no case be unconstitutional. But neither of these remarks is applicable to America. . . . In the United States the constitution governs the legislator as much as the private citizen; as it is the first of laws it cannot be modified by a law, and it is therefore just that the tribunals should obey the constitution in preference to any law. This condition is essential to the power of the judicature, for to select that legal obligation by which he is most strictly bound is the natural right of every magistrate. . . .

Whenever a law which the judge holds to be unconstitutional is argued in a tribunal of the United States he may refuse to admit it as a rule; this power is the only one which is peculiar to the American magistrate, but it gives rise to immense political influence. Few laws can escape the searching analysis of the judicial power for any length of time, for there are few which are not prejudicial to some private interest or other, and none which may not be brought before a court of justice by the choice of parties, or by the necessity of the case. But from the time that a judge has refused to apply any given law in a case, that law loses a portion of its moral cogency. The persons to whose interests it is prejudicial learn that means exist of evading its authority, and similar suits are multiplied, until it becomes powerless. One of two alternatives must then be resorted to: the people must alter the constitution, or the legislature must repeal the law. The political power which the Americans have entrusted to their courts of justice is therefore immense, but the evils of this power are considerably diminished by the obligation which has been imposed of attacking the laws through the courts of justice alone. If the judge had been empowered to contest the laws on the ground of theoretical generalities, if he had been enabled to open an attack or to pass a censure on the legislator, he would have played a prominent part in the political sphere; and as the champion or the antagonist of a party, he would have arrayed the hostile passions of the nation in the conflict. But when a judge contests a law applied to some particular case in an obscure proceeding, the importance of his attack is concealed from the public gaze, his decision bears upon the interest of an individual, and if the law is slighted it is only collaterally. Moreover, although it is censured, it is not abolished; its moral force may be diminished, but its cogency is by no means suspended, and its final destruction can only be accomplished by the reiterated attacks of judicial functionaries. It will readily be understood that by connecting the censorship of the laws with the private interests of members of the community, and by intimately uniting the prosecution of the law with the prosecution of an individual, legislation is protected from wanton assailants, and from the daily aggressions of party spirit. The errors of the legislator are exposed whenever their evil consequences are most felt, and it is always a positive and appreciable fact which serves as the basis of a prosecution.

I am inclined to believe this practice of the American courts to be at once the most favorable to liberty as well as to public order. . . . [T]he American judge is brought into the political arena independently of his own will. He only judges the law because he is obliged to judge a case. The political question which he is called upon to resolve is connected with the interest of the suitors, and he cannot refuse to decide it without abdicating the duties of his post. He performs his functions as a citizen by fulfilling the precise duties which belong to his profession as a magistrate. It is true that upon this system the judicial censorship which is exercised by the courts of justice over the legislation cannot extend to all laws indiscriminately, inasmuch as some of them can never give rise to that exact species of contestation which is termed a lawsuit; and even when such a contestation is possible, it may happen that no one cares to bring it before a court of justice. The Americans have often felt this disadvantage, but they have left the remedy incomplete, lest they should give it an efficacy which might in some cases prove dangerous. Within these limits the power vested in the American courts of justice of pronouncing a statute to be unconstitutional forms one of the most powerful barriers which has ever been devised against the tyranny of political assemblies. . . .

[*Assignment 9*]

II. THE CONSTITUTIONAL DILEMMA OF JUDICIAL SUPREMACY

Does judicial review imply judicial supremacy? Does the power of courts to independently judge the constitutionality of actions of the political branches, defended by Hamilton in *The Federalist No. 78*, and deployed by Marshall in *Marbury v. Madison*, imply a superiority of the judiciary over the other branches as to any question of interpretation of the Constitution? Would that be consistent with the vision of separation of powers created by the framers and defended in *The Federalist*? Or would it be the nightmare envisioned by Brutus? Is judicial supremacy a contradiction of the principle of constitutional supremacy—and of the reasoning of *Marbury* itself? Or is judicial supremacy the only way to vindicate the supremacy of the Constitution? Is it essential to the maintenance of the constitutional order that the courts have the final say on the constitutionality of government action?

These questions are explored in the following readings. These readings begin with statements by several presidents of what is sometimes called the "departmentalist" view, i.e., that each branch is free to interpret the Constitution independently within the sphere of its own operations, and they conclude with two case studies that test the idea of judicial supremacy in practice.

A. DO THE SUPREME COURT'S DECISIONS CONTROL THE CONSTITUTIONAL JUDGMENT OF ALL OTHER ACTORS?

In thinking about whether the Supreme Court's interpretations of the Constitution are supreme over the other branches of the federal government, begin by considering the following statements by Presidents Jefferson, Madison, Jackson, and Lincoln. (For more such statements, see Michael Stokes Paulsen, *The Most Dangerous Branch: Executive Power to Say What the Law Is*, 83 Geo. L.J. 217, 241–283 (1993).)

Thomas Jefferson, Letter to Abigail Adams
September 11, 1804

You seem to think it devolved on the judges to decide on the validity of the sedition law. But nothing in the Constitution has given them a right to decide for the Executive, more than to the Executive to decide for them. Both magistrates are equally independent in the sphere of action assigned to them. The judges, believing the law constitutional, had a right to pass a sentence of fine and imprisonment; because the power was placed in their hands by the Constitution. But the executive, believing the law to be unconstitutional, were bound to remit the execution of it; because that power has been confided to them by the Constitution. That instrument meant that its coordinate branches should be checks on each other. But the opinion which gives to the judges the right to decide what laws are constitutional, and what are not, not only for themselves in their own sphere of action, but for the legislature and executive also, in their spheres, would make the judiciary a despotic branch. . . .

Thomas Jefferson, Letter to William Charles Jarvis
September 28, 1820

You seem . . . to consider the judges as the ultimate arbiters of all constitutional questions; a very dangerous doctrine indeed, and one that would place us under the despotism of an oligarchy. Our judges are as honest as other men, and not more so. They have, with others, the same passions for party, power, and the privilege of their corps. Their maxim is "*boni judicis est ampliare jurisdictionem*," and their power the more dangerous as they are in office for life, and not responsible, as the other functionaries are, to the elective control. The Constitution has erected no such single tribunal, knowing that to whatever hands confided, with the corruptions of time and party; its members would become despots. It has more wisely made all the departments co-equal and co-sovereign within themselves. If the legislature fails to pass laws for a census, for paying the judges and other officers of government, for establishing a militia, for naturalization as prescribed by the Constitution, or if they fail to meet in Congress, the judges cannot issue their mandamus to them; if the President fails to supply the place of a judge. To appoint other civil or military officers, to issue requisite commissions, the judges cannot force him. They can issue their mandamus . . . to no executive or legislative officer to enforce the fulfillment of their official duties, any more than the President or legislature may issue orders to the judges or their officers. . . . When the legislative or executive functionaries act unconstitutionally, they are responsible to the people in their elective capacity. The exemption of the judges from that is quite dangerous enough. I know no safe depository of the of the ultimate powers of society but the people themselves; and if we think them not enlightened enough to exercise their control with an wholesome discretion, the remedy is not to take it from them, but to inform their discretion by education. . . .

James Madison, Letter to Unknown Addressee
Written in 1834; published in 4 Letters and Other Writings of
James Madison 349–50 (1884)

DEAR SIR,—Having alluded to the Supreme Court of the United States as a constitutional resort in deciding questions of jurisdiction between the United States and the individual States, a few remarks may be proper, showing the sense and degree in which that character is more particularly ascribed to that department of the government.

As the Legislative, Executive, and Judicial departments of the United States are coordinate, and each equally bound to support the Constitution, it follows that each must, in the exercise of its functions, be guided by the text of the Constitution according to its own interpretation of it; and consequently; that in the event of irreconcilable interpretations, the prevalence of the one or the other department must depend on the nature of the case, as receiving its final decision from the one or the other, and passing from that decision into effect, without involving the functions of any other.

It is certainly due from the functionaries of the several departments to pay much respect to the opinions of each other; and as far as official independence and obligation will permit, to consult the means of adjusting differences and avoiding practical embarrassments growing out of them, as must be done in like cases between the different co-ordinate branches of the legislative department.

But notwithstanding this abstract view of the co-ordinate and independent right of the three departments to expound the Constitution, the Judicial department most familiarizes itself to the public attention as the expositor; by the *order* of its functions in relation to the other departments; and attracts most the public confidence by the composition of the tribunal.

It is the judicial department in which questions of constitutionality, as well as of legality, generally, find their ultimate discussion and operative decision; and the public deference to and confidence in the judgment of the body are peculiarly inspired by the qualities implied in its members; by the gravity and deliberation of their proceedings; and by the advantage their plurality gives them over the unity of the Executive department, and their fewness over the multitudinous composition of the Legislative department.

Without losing sight, therefore, of the co-ordinate relations of the three departments to each other, it may always be expected that the judicial bench, when happily filled, will, for the reasons suggested, most engage the respect and reliance of the public as the surest expositor of the Constitution, as well in questions within its cognizance concerning the boundaries between the several departments of the Government as in those between the Union and its members.

Abraham Lincoln, Speech at the Sixth Lincoln–Douglas Debate

October 13, 1858

. . . We oppose the *Dred Scott* decision in a certain way. [We] do not propose that when Dred Scott has been decided to be a slave by the court, we, as a mob, will decide him to be free. We do not propose that, when any other one, or one thousand, shall be decided by that court to be slaves, we will in any violent way disturb the rights of property thus settled; but we nevertheless do oppose that decision as a political rule which shall be binding on the voter, to vote for nobody who thinks it wrong, which shall be binding on the members of Congress or the President to favor no measure that does not actually concur with the principles of that decision. [We] propose so resisting it as to have it reversed if we can, and a new judicial rule established upon this subject. . . .

President Lincoln, First Inaugural Address

March 4, 1861

. . . From questions of this class [*i.e.,* issues on which the Constitution does not expressly supply an answer] spring all our constitutional controversies, and we divide upon them into majorities and minorities. If the minority will not acquiesce, the majority must, or the government must cease. . . . Unanimity is impossible; the rule of a minority, as a permanent arrangement, is wholly inadmissible; so that, rejecting the majority principle, anarchy, or despotism in some form, is all that is left.

I do not forget the position assumed by some, that constitutional questions are to be decided by the Supreme Court; nor do I deny that such decisions must be binding in any case, upon the parties to a suit, as to the object of that suit, while they are also entitled to very high respect and consideration, in all parallel cases, by all other departments of the government. And while it is obviously possible that such decision may be erroneous in any given case, still the evil effect following it, begin limited to that particular case, with the chance that it may be over-ruled, and never become a precedent for other cases, can better be borne than could the evils of a different practice. At the same time the candid citizen must confess that if the policy of the government, upon vital questions, affecting the whole people, is to be irrevocably fixed by decisions of the Supreme court, the instant they are made, in ordinary litigation between parties, in personal actions, the people will have ceased to be their own rulers, having, to that extent, practically resigned their government into the hands of that eminent tribunal. . . .

NOTES

1. The position that each of the three departments of government can independently interpret and enforce the Constitution as they perform their own distinctive functions is often called "departmentalism." Which of the preceding opinions take this view? Which ones address what happens if the different "departments," or branches, of the national government conflict in how they interpret the Constitution? Which opinion is most persuasive?

2. If President Jefferson is right about the president's duty to interpret the Constitution, does it follow that the implicit criticism of *Marbury* in his letter to William Charles Jarvis is also right? Assuming that English courts could issue a writ of mandamus to executive officers to compel them to follow the clear letter of the law, why would the federal courts not have the very same power under the Constitution?

3. In his 1834 letter, James Madison concedes that the text of the Constitution makes no single branch the ultimate interpreter of the Constitution. But he nonetheless makes a functional argument that "ordinarily," and when "the judicial bench is happily filled," the courts will and should have the last word on questions of constitutional meaning. What are the factual premises embedded in Madison's argument?

4. Does the attractiveness of departmentalism depend on the kind of legal question that is being presented? For example, how well does departmentalism work for the question of whether the Constitution allows certain conduct to be criminally punished? If each of the three branches had a duty to exercise independent constitutional judgment, then someone would be convicted and punished only if Congress thought the criminal statute it was enacting was constitutional, *and* the president or other executive-branch officers thought that prosecution under the statute was constitutional, *and* the courts thought that convicting this particular defendant was constitutional. For that kind of legal question would departmentalism provide an important check on government power? What about other kinds of legal questions, such as a debate over whether the president or Congress has power over some aspect of foreign affairs? Or a dispute between the judiciary and Congress about whether the Constitution lets Congress remove all funding for federal courthouses? What are the features of the legal questions for which departmentalism is best suited? Or does the attractiveness of departmentalism depend on which branch of the government you trust most? Are the branches likely to differ in how much weight they give to each of the types of constitutional argument? Are the branches likely to differ in how skillfully they use each type of argument?

5. President Lincoln is the most famous figure in American history to embrace a departmentalist approach. In his First Inaugural address, quoted above, he attacks the notion of judicial supremacy but carves out an exception for actual *judgments* rendered by courts, at least as between the parties to the litigation that produced the judgment. (That exception will be considered next.) Are you persuaded by Lincoln's position? Are you willing to accept it only because of the exception for specific judgments? Or does that exception undermine his general principle?

B. JUDICIAL SUPREMACY AS TO SPECIFIC JUDGMENTS?

Consider two dramatic constitutional confrontations, almost exactly a century apart, with sharply contrasting facts and outcomes. The modern one is presented first—the Supreme Court's claim to judicial supremacy in the face of the massive resistance to *Brown v. Board of Education*, 347 U.S. 483 (1954). The second, older case study is a conflict between President Lincoln and the Court during the Civil War, in *Ex parte Merryman*, 17 F. Cas. 144 (D. Md., April Term 1861).

A Case Study in Judicial Supremacy: *Cooper v. Aaron*

In *Brown v. Board of Education*, the Supreme Court held that racial segregation in public schools violated the Equal Protection Clause of the Fourteenth Amendment. (*Brown* is presented in Chapter 7.) Throughout the South, many officials resisted the Court's decision. The governor of Arkansas, Orville Faubus, refused to comply with a federal court's desegregation decree and even called out the National Guard to block integration. The school district then sought a postponement of integration, because of the turmoil and the potential for violence. The case reached the Supreme Court, which offered its first clear-cut claim to judicial supremacy in constitutional interpretation in *Cooper v. Aaron*, 358 U.S. 1 (1958). The Court's *per curiam* decision was unanimous. It reaffirmed the principles of *Brown* and the obligation of state and local officials to abide by it. Appealing to *Marbury*, the Court claimed for its decisions the status of "supreme law of the land" under Article VI. In the words of the Court:

> The constitutional rights of respondents are not to be sacrificed or yielded to the violence and disorder which have followed upon the actions of the Governor and Legislature. . . .
>
> The controlling legal principles are plain. The command of the Fourteenth Amendment is that no "State" shall deny to any person within its jurisdiction the equal protection of the laws. "A State acts by its legislative, its executive, or its judicial authorities. It can act in no other way. The constitutional provision, therefore, must mean that no agency of the State, or of the officers or agents by whom its powers are exerted, shall deny to any person within its jurisdiction the equal protection of the laws." . . . In short, the constitutional rights of children not to be discriminated against in school admission on grounds of race or color declared by this Court in the *Brown* case can neither be nullified indirectly by them through evasive schemes for segregation whether attempted "ingeniously or ingenuously."
>
> What has been said, in the light of the facts developed, is enough to dispose of the case. However, we should answer the premise of the actions of the Governor and Legislature that they are not bound by our

holding in the *Brown* case. It is necessary only to recall some basic constitutional propositions which are settled doctrine.

Article VI of the Constitution makes the Constitution the "supreme Law of the Land." In 1803, Chief Justice Marshall, speaking for a unanimous Court, referring to the Constitution as "the fundamental and paramount law of the nation," declared in the notable case of *Marbury v. Madison*, 1 Cranch 137, 177, that "It is emphatically the province and duty of the judicial department to say what the law is." This decision declared the basic principle that the federal judiciary is supreme in the exposition of the law of the Constitution, and that principle has ever since been respected by this Court and the Country as a permanent and indispensable feature of our constitutional system. It follows that the interpretation of the Fourteenth Amendment enunciated by this Court in the *Brown* case is the supreme law of the land, and Art. VI of the Constitution makes it of binding effect on the States "any Thing in the Constitution or Laws of any State to the Contrary notwithstanding." Every state legislator and executive and judicial officer is solemnly committed by oath taken pursuant to Art. VI, cl. 3 "to support this Constitution." Chief Justice Taney, speaking for a unanimous Court in 1859, said that this requirement reflected the framers' "anxiety to preserve it [the Constitution] in full force, in all its powers, and to guard against resistance to or evasion of its authority, on the part of a State." *Abelman v. Booth*, 21 How. 506, 524.

No state legislator or executive or judicial officer can war against the Constitution without violating his undertaking to support it. Chief Justice Marshall spoke for unanimous Court in saying that: "If the legislatures of the several states may, at will, annul the judgments of the courts of the United States, and destroy the rights acquired under those judgments, the constitution itself becomes a solemn mockery." *United States v. Peters*, 5 Cranch 115, 136. A Governor who asserts a power to nullify a federal court order is similarly restrained. If he had such power, said Chief Justice Hughes, in 1932, also for a unanimous Court, "it is manifest that the fiat of a state Governor, and not the Constitution of the United States, would be the supreme law of the land; that the restrictions of the Federal Constitution upon the exercise of state power would be but impotent phrases." *Sterling v. Constantin*, 287 U.S. 378, 397–398.

. . . The principles announced in [*Brown*] and the obedience of the States to them according to the command of the Constitution, are indispensable for the protection of the freedoms guaranteed by our fundamental charter for all of us. Our constitutional ideal of equal justice under law is thus made a living truth.

A Case Study in Judicial Supremacy: *Ex parte Merryman*

Now consider the dramatic case of *Ex parte Merryman*, 17 F. Cas. 144 (D. Md., April Term 1861), in which Chief Justice Roger Taney held that President Abraham Lincoln's suspension of the writ of habeas corpus was unconstitutional and that the Union military's detention of armed secessionists suspected of engaging in acts of rebellion in Maryland was illegal. President Lincoln defied the judicial order. On the question of judicial authority, who was right—President Lincoln or Chief Justice Taney? Were President Lincoln's actions inconsistent with the reasoning of *Cooper v. Aaron* a century later?

First, some crucial background: In response to Lincoln's election as president in 1860, several Southern states purported to secede from the Union. In April 1861, secessionist forces fired on and captured a federal fort in the harbor of Charleston, South Carolina—Fort Sumter. In response, President Lincoln by executive decree called for troops to suppress the rebellion, and he imposed a blockade on shipping directed toward the ports of the seceding states. While his decree was largely supported in the North, it led to the secession of states in the Upper South, including the important state of Virginia. Secessionist activity was also pervasive in several "border slave states," including Maryland, Kentucky, Missouri, and Delaware. The capital of the United States, Washington, D.C., was essentially surrounded by secessionist sympathizers. Virginia had seceded, and Maryland was poised to join her. When federal troops attempted to pass through Baltimore to defend the capital, they were attacked by a mob. On April 27, in a private order, President Lincoln authorized General Winfield Scott to suspend the privilege of the writ of habeas corpus for the "public safety" if he deemed it necessary to permit troops to travel through Maryland or to suppress secessionist violence. It was impossible at this time to convene Congress safely in Washington, D.C., in order to ask it to vote on the suspension of the writ of habeas corpus. (President Lincoln himself was probably in some danger in Washington, D.C.) Yet convening Congress outside of the capital would have been humiliating to the national government and might have strengthened the rebel cause.

Pursuant to President Lincoln's suspension of the writ, U.S. Army officers arrested a number of secessionist sympathizers. One was John Merryman, a prominent farmer, state legislator, and lieutenant in a secessionist cavalry unit that had burned bridges and ripped down telegraph wires. Merryman was held in Fort McHenry, Baltimore, yet (somehow) obtained access to legal counsel, who presented a petition for a writ of habeas corpus to Chief Justice Roger Taney, in his capacity as circuit justice for Maryland. Chief Justice Taney issued a writ to the commanding officer at Fort McHenry, General Cadwaladar, directing him to produce Merryman in court in Baltimore the next day, so the lawfulness of Merryman's detention could be determined. General Cadwalader declined to produce Merryman, instead sending a subordinate to appear and inform Chief Justice Taney of President Lincoln's order and request a postponement pending further instructions from Washington. The chief justice was displeased, and he issued an attachment against General Cadwalader for contempt, returnable the next day. Service of the writ was refused at Fort McHenry, and the next day, May 28, 1861, Chief Justice Taney issued the following ruling from the bench, holding Lincoln's suspension of the writ unconstitutional.

Ex parte Merryman

17 F. Cas. 144 (D. Md., April Term 1861)

■ TANEY, CIRCUIT JUSTICE.

. . . The case, then, is simply this: a military officer, residing in Pennsylvania, issues an order to arrest a citizen of Maryland, upon vague and indefinite charges, without any proof, so far as appears; under this order, his house is entered in the night, he is seized as a prisoner, and conveyed to Fort McHenry, and there kept in close confinement; and when a habeas corpus is served on the commanding officer, requiring him to produce the prisoner before a justice of the supreme court, in order that he may examine into the legality of the imprisonment, the answer of the officer, is that he is authorized by the president to suspend the writ of habeas corpus at his discretion, and in the exercise of that discretion, suspends it in this case, and on that ground refuses obedience to the writ.

As the case comes before me, therefore, I understand that the president not only claims the right to suspend the writ of habeas corpus himself, at his discretion, but to delegate that discretionary power to a military officer, and to leave it to him to determine whether he will or will not obey judicial process that may be served upon him. No official notice has been given to the courts of justice, or to the public, by proclamation or otherwise, that the president claimed this power, and had exercised it in the manner stated in the return. And I certainly listened to it with some surprise, for I had supposed it to be one of those points of constitutional law upon which there was no difference of opinion, and that it was admitted on all hands, that the privilege of the writ could not be suspended, except by act of congress. . . .

[B]eing thus officially notified that the privilege of the writ has been suspended, under the orders, and by the authority of the president, and believing, as I do, that the president has exercised a power which he does not possess under the constitution, a proper respect for the high office he fills, requires me to state plainly and fully the grounds of my opinion, in order to show that I have not ventured to question the legality of his act, without a careful and deliberate examination of the whole subject. . . .

The constitution provides, as I have before said, that "no person shall be deprived of life, liberty or property, without due process of law." It declares that "the right of the people to be secure in their persons, houses, papers and effects, against unreasonable searches and seizures, shall not be violated; and no warrant shall issue, but upon probable cause, supported by oath or affirmation, and particularly describing the place to be searched, and the persons or things to be seized." It provides that the party accused shall be entitled to a speedy trial in a court of justice.

These great and fundamental laws, which congress itself could not suspend, have been disregarded and suspended, like the writ of habeas corpus, by a military order, supported by force of arms. Such is the case now before me, and I can only say that if the authority which the constitution has confided to the judiciary department and judicial officers, may thus, upon any pretext or under any circumstances, be usurped by the military power, at its discretion, the people of the United States are no longer living under a government of laws, but every citizen holds life, liberty and property at the will and pleasure of the army officer in whose military district he may happen to be found.

In such a case, my duty was too plain to be mistaken. I have exercised all the power which the constitution and laws confer upon me, but that power has been resisted by a force too strong for me to overcome. It is possible that the officer who has incurred this grave responsibility may have misunderstood his instructions, and exceeded the authority intended to be given him; I shall, therefore, order all the proceedings in this case, with my opinion, to be filed and recorded in the circuit court of the United States for the district of Maryland, and direct the clerk to transmit a copy, under seal, to the president of the United States. It will then remain for that high officer, in fulfilment of his constitutional obligation to "take care that the laws be faithfully executed," to determine what measures he will take to cause the civil process of the United States to be respected and enforced.

———

President Lincoln did not obey Chief Justice Taney's order. Instead, he responded to Congress and to the American public. In a special session of Congress, President Lincoln began his message with an account of events since his inauguration and then proceeded to explain the measures that he has taken as president, including suspension of habeas corpus. In two critical paragraphs, he responded to Chief Justice Taney (without naming him) and defended his actions as consistent with the Suspension Clause of Article I, Section 9. President Lincoln did not address the argument that he must obey Chief Justice Taney's order. He simply announced his disagreement with the constitutional judgment that the chief justice had rendered. The administration's argument about the duty of the president to obey judicial decrees was then advanced the next day by Attorney General Edward Bates, who issued the formal attorney general opinion presented below.

President Lincoln, Message to Congress

July 4, 1861

Fellow-citizens of the Senate and House of Representatives:

Having been convened on an extraordinary occasion, as authorized by the Constitution, your attention is not called to any ordinary subject of legislation. . . . At the beginning of the present Presidential term, four months ago, the functions of the Federal Government were found to be generally suspended within the several States of South Carolina, Georgia, Alabama, Mississippi, Louisiana, and Florida, excepting only those of the Post Office Department. . . .

Soon after the first call for militia, it was considered a duty to authorize the Commanding General, in proper cases, according to his discretion, to suspend the privilege of the writ of habeas corpus; or, in other words, to arrest, and detain, without resort to the ordinary processes and forms of law, such individuals as he might deem dangerous to the public safety. This authority has purposely been exercised but very sparingly. Nevertheless, the legality and propriety of what has been done under it, are questioned; and the attention of the country has been called to the proposition that one who is sworn to "take care that the laws be faithfully executed," should not himself violate them. Of course some consideration was given to the questions of power, and propriety, before this matter was acted upon. The whole of the laws which were required to be faithfully executed, were being resisted, and failing of execution, in nearly one-third of the States. Must they be allowed to finally fail of execution, even had it been perfectly clear, that by the use of the means necessary to their execution, some single law, made in such extreme tenderness of the citizen's liberty, that practically, it relieves more of the guilty, than of the innocent, should, to a very limited extent, be violated? To state the question more directly, are all the laws, but one, to go unexecuted, and the government itself go to pieces, lest that one be violated? Even in such a case, would not the official oath be broken, if the government should be overthrown, when it was believed that disregarding the single law, would tend to preserve it? But it was not believed that this question was presented. It was not believed that any law was violated. The provision of the Constitution that "The privilege of the writ of habeas corpus, shall not be suspended unless when, in cases of rebellion or invasion, the public safety may require it," is equivalent to a provision—is a provision—that such privilege may be suspended when, in cases of rebellion, or invasion, the public safety does require it. It was decided that we have a case of rebellion, and that the public safety does require the qualified suspension of the privilege of the writ which was authorized to be made. Now it is insisted that Congress, and not the Executive, is vested with this power. But the Constitution itself, is silent as to which, or who, is to exercise the power; and as the provision was plainly made for a dangerous emergency, it cannot be believed the framers of the instrument intended, that in every case, the danger should run its course, until Congress could be called together; the very assembling of which might be prevented, as was intended in this case, by the rebellion.

No more extended argument is now offered; as an opinion, at some length, will probably be presented by the Attorney General. Whether there shall be any legislation upon the subject, and if any, what, is submitted entirely to the better judgment of Congress. . . . *[President Lincoln then called upon Congress to take several actions, including appropriations to support the war effort. He concluded by attacking the lawfulness of secession and contesting the South's characterization of it.—Editors]*

Attorney General Bates, Opinion on the Suspension of the Privilege of the Writ of Habeas Corpus

10 Op. Att'y Gen. 74 (July 5, 1861)

[To the President:]

SIR: You have required my opinion in writing upon the following questions:

1. In the present time of a great and dangerous insurrection, has the President the discretionary power to cause to be arrested and held in custody, persons known to have criminal intercourse with the insurgents, or persons against whom there is probable cause for suspicion of such criminal complicity?

2. In such cases of arrest, is the President justified in refusing to obey a writ of habeas corpus issued by a court or a judge, requiring him or his agent to produce the body of the prisoner, and show the cause of his caption and detention, to be adjudged and disposed of by such court or judge?

. . . In the formation of our national government, our fathers [were] actuated by a special dread of the unity of power. . . . Hence, keeping the sovereignty always out of sight, they adopted the plan of "checks and balances," forming separate departments of Government, and giving to each department separate and limited powers. These departments are co-ordinate and coequal—that is, neither being sovereign, each is independent in its sphere, and not subordinate to the others, either of them or both of them together. We have three of these co-ordinate departments. Now, if we allow one of the three to determine the extent of its own powers, and also the extent of the powers of the other two, that one can control the whole government, and has in fact achieved the sovereignty.

. . . [H]aving divided the government into co-ordinate departments, [the framers of the Constitution] did not even try . . . to create an arbiter among them to adjudge their conflicts and keep them within their respective bounds. They were left, by design, I suppose, each independent and free, to act out its own granted powers, without any ordained or legal superior possessing the power to revise and reverse its action. And this with the hope that the three departments, mutually coequal and independent, would keep each other within their proper spheres by their mutual antagonism—that is, by the system of checks and balances, to which our fathers were driven at the beginning by their fear of the unity of power.

In this view of the subject it is quite possible for the same identical question (not case) to come up legitimately before each one of the three departments, and be determined in three different ways, and each decision stand irrevocable, binding upon the parties to each case; and that, for the simple reason that the departments are co-ordinate, and there is no ordained legal superior, with power to revise and reverse their decisions.

To say that the departments of our government are co-ordinate, is to say that the judgment of one of them is not binding upon the other two, as to the arguments and principles involved in the judgment. It binds only the parties to the case decided. But if, admitting that the departments of government are co-ordinate, it be still contended that the principles adopted by one department, in deciding a case properly before it, are binding upon another department, that obligation must of necessity be reciprocal—that is, if the President be bound by the principles laid down by the judiciary, so also is the judiciary bound by the principles laid down by the President. And thus we shall have a theory of constitutional government flatly contradicting itself. Departments co-ordinate and coequal, and yet reciprocally subordinate to each other! That cannot be. The several departments, though far from sovereign, are free and independent, in the exercise of the limited powers granted to them respectively by the Constitution. . . . Indeed, [the judicial department] is not itself bound by its own decisions, for it can and often does overrule and disregard them, as, in common honesty, it ought to do, whenever it finds, by its after and better lights, that its former judgments were wrong. . . .

While the judiciary and the President, as departments of the general government, are co-ordinate, equal in dignity and power, and equally trusted by the law, in their respective spheres, there is, nevertheless, a marked diversity in the character of their functions and their modes of action. The judiciary is, for the most part, passive. It rarely, if ever, takes the initiative; it seldom or never begins an operation. Its great function is judgment, and, in the exercise of that function, it is confined almost exclusively to cases not selected by itself, but made and submitted by others. The President, on the contrary, by the very nature of his office, is active; he must often take the initiative; he must begin operations. His great function is execution, for he is required by the Constitution, (and he is the only department that is so required,) to "take care that the laws (all the laws) be faithfully executed;" and in the exercise of that function, his duties are coextensive with the laws of the land. Often, he comes to the aid of the judiciary, in the execution of its judgments; and this is only a part, and a small part, of his constitutional duty, to take care that the laws be faithfully executed. . . .

As to the first question: I am clearly of opinion that, in a time like the present, when the very existence of the nation is assailed, by a great and dangerous insurrection, the President has the lawful discretionary power to arrest and hold in custody persons known to have criminal intercourse with the insurgents, or persons against whom there is probable cause for suspicion of such criminal complicity. . . . The Constitution requires the President, before he enters upon the execution of his office, to take an oath that he "will faithfully execute the office of President of the United States, and will, to the best of his ability, preserve, protect and defend the Constitution of the United States." . . . And then follows the broad and compendious injunction to "take care that the laws be faithfully executed." And this injunction, embracing as it does all the laws—Constitution treaties, statutes—is addressed to the President alone, and not to any other department or officer of the Government. And this constitutes him, in a peculiar manner, and above all other officers, the guardian of the Constitution—its preserver, protector, and defender. . . .

As to the second question: . . . If it be true, as I have assumed, that the President and the judiciary are co-ordinate departments of government, and the one not subordinate to the other, I do not understand how it can be legally possible for a judge to issue a command to the President to come before him *ad subjiciendum*—that is, to submit implicitly to his judgment—and, in case of disobedience, treat him as a criminal, in contempt of a superior authority, and punish him as for a misdemeanor, by fine and imprisonment. . . .

[The President's power to suspend the writ of habeas corpus] is no part of his ordinary duty in time of peace; it is temporary and exceptional, and was intended only to meet a pressing emergency. . . . [S]hall it be said that when he has fought and captured the insurgent army, and has seized their secret spies and emissaries, he is bound to bring their bodies before any judge who may send him a writ of habeas corpus, "to do, submit to, and receive whatever the said judge shall consider in that behalf?

I deny that he is under any obligation to obey such a writ, issued under such circumstances. . . . The power to do these things is in the hand of the President, placed there by the Constitution and the statute law, as a sacred trust, to be used by him, in his best discretion, in the performance of his great first duty—to preserve, protect, and defend the Constitution. And for any breach of that trust he is responsible before the high court of impeachment, and before no other human tribunal. . . .

NOTES

1. Evaluate the constitutional arguments made by the Supreme Court in *Cooper v. Aaron*, by Chief Justice Taney in *Ex parte Merryman*, and by President Lincoln and Attorney General Bates in their responses. Which modes of interpretation is each one using? Which is most persuasive?

2. Would a power of the president to decline, on constitutional grounds, to enforce the final judgments of the federal judiciary render the federal courts powerless? Is that a separation-of-powers problem? Would it imply that every judicial decision was a mere advisory opinion, in violation of Article III? Alternatively, does the argument of *Cooper* and *Merryman* imply that the president and Congress can be forced to take actions that they think are violations of the Constitution? How could that be squared the Supremacy Clause, the Oath Clause, and the Take Care Clause?

3. Did President Lincoln commit an impeachable offense in refusing to comply with the judicial decision? If the idea of independent constitutional judgment for each branch is taken seriously, would that mean the House of Representatives could have exercised its constitutional judgment that what President Lincoln had done was a violation of the Take Care Clause, and thus impeached him? If not, why not?

4. If President Lincoln had the power and duty not to follow a court judgment he thought was unconstitutional, did Governor Faubus have a similar

right? Does it matter what the strength of their positions was on the merits? Is the case for independent interpretive authority—"departmentalism" no longer seems quite the right word—weaker for states interpreting the national Constitution? Why or why not?

CHAPTER 3

THE DISTRIBUTION AND SEPARATION OF POWERS OF THE NATIONAL GOVERNMENT

[*Assignment 10*]

Preamble: We the People of the United States, in Order to form a more perfect Union, establish Justice, insure domestic Tranquility, provide for the common defense, promote the general Welfare, and secure the Blessings of Liberty to ourselves and our Posterity, do ordain and establish this Constitution for the United States of America.

The text of the Constitution begins with an emphatic declaration of popular sovereignty: the Constitution is established by "We the People of the United States." The Preamble is also a statement of the broad purposes for which this new frame of popular government has been created.

The Constitution then proceeds in its first three Articles to lay out the structure and powers of the three branches of government under the U.S. Constitution. Article I vests "all legislative powers herein granted" in Congress. Article II vests "the executive Power" of the government in "a President of the United States." And Article III vests "the judicial Power" of the United States in a Supreme Court and in the inferior courts that Congress chooses to establish. Each branch is, to a substantial degree, independent of the others. Each checks the others—and is, in turn, checked by the others. Each has its separate functions. None is superior. All derive their authority to act by a constitutional grant of power from the people.

This chapter considers the structure, nature, and functions of Congress, the president, and the judicial branch, and the relationships among them. This chapter is therefore addressed primarily to the *separation of powers*—the distribution of power among the branches of the national government. The next chapter considers *federalism*—the distribution of power between the national government and the states.

We begin with an overview of separation of powers and then examine each of the branches in turn, taking them up in the order of their appearance within the Constitution: Congress, the president, and the courts.

An Introduction to Separation of Powers

Article I, Section 1: All legislative Powers herein granted shall be vested in a Congress of the United States, which shall consist of a Senate and House of Representatives. . . .

Article II, Section 1: The executive Power shall be vested in a President of the United States of America. . . .

Article III, Section 1: The judicial Power of the United States, shall be vested in one supreme Court, and in such inferior Courts as the Congress may from time to time ordain and establish.

Here in a nutshell is the textual commitment of the Constitution to separation of powers. We the People—recall the Preamble—have granted limited and enumerated powers to three branches of the federal government. Each branch may exercise only the powers given to it, not the powers given to the other branches.

The separation of powers in the Constitution ensures that each branch will check and balance the others. Note that this separation of powers is not absolutely pure, for sometimes the Constitution actually allocates some powers to *two* branches working in coordination. (This intermingling of powers was inspired by how the framers understood the largely unwritten English constitution and leading political theorists of the Enlightenment.) But even these shared allocations of power serve the purpose of ensuring that each branch is checked by the others. Consider just a few of the checks and balances established by the Constitution.

Congress can check the president with its most formidable power—the power to raise revenues (often called "the power of the purse"). It can shut down a war, for example, by cutting off funding. Congress can also check the president by enacting laws over a veto with a two-thirds majority in each house. The Senate can hobble the executive branch by refusing to confirm the president's nominees. It can refuse to ratify the treaties the president signs. Each house of Congress can hold oversight hearings, requiring the appearance of officials from the executive branch. Congress can check the judiciary by altering its jurisdiction (though this power is greater for the lower federal courts than for the Supreme Court). It can hamper the judiciary by constraining its funding and allowing inflation to erode judicial salaries. Congress can overturn the judiciary's construction of a statute by enacting new legislation, which it frequently does. And with the cooperation of the states, it can even overturn the Supreme Court's construction of the Constitution by passing a constitutional amendment (something it has done four times in American history). Most strikingly, Congress can impeach and remove any executive or judicial officer—including the president and the justices—by a majority of the House and a two-thirds majority of the Senate.

The president can check Congress by vetoing its bills. And the president's party will almost always have enough votes in Congress to defeat an effort to override the veto. The president can also check Congress by setting priorities in law enforcement and execution. Congress can enact laws, but its will can be frustrated if the executive branch does not enforce them. The president may direct, control, and if necessary even remove policy-making subordinates in the executive branch. As commander in chief of the armed forces, the president can check Congress in the conduct of foreign affairs. In the long run, the president has a powerful check over the judiciary through choosing new judges for the lower courts and new justices for the Supreme Court. The executive branch also influences the issues that the courts are able to decide, because any case involving presidential power can be settled before there is a judicial decision.

The federal courts can check Congress and the president in only one way, but it is a fundamental check that constrains every action they take: the courts may decide that what the legislative or executive branch has done violates the Constitution.

These ways the branches of the national government check each other can be seen in one of the most important cases ever decided by the Supreme Court: *Youngstown Sheet & Tube Co. v. Sawyer*, 343 U.S. 579 (1952), also known as *The Steel Seizure Case*. At the height of the Korean War, President Harry Truman ordered a government seizure of the nation's steel mills, in order to avert a threatened strike that he believed would cripple the war effort.

The seizure of the steel mills was done by unilateral presidential order. Congress had not authorized—and did not subsequently authorize—President Truman's actions by legislation. Thus the steel seizure raised a question as to whether the president possesses either an inherent legislative power or a power to act in emergencies. *Youngstown* went to the Supreme Court in a tremendous rush, yet it produced important and enduring opinions by several Supreme Court justices.

The opinions in *Youngstown* illustrate the five types of constitutional argument, or modes of interpretation, discussed above in Chapter 1: (1) the Constitution's text; (2) inferences from the Constitution's structure and the relationship of its provisions; (3) the historical purpose underlying a provision; (4) precedent or consistent practice that resolves or "liquidates" ambiguities in the meaning of a provision; and (5) policy. As you read each opinion, look for the modes of interpretation it employs.

Youngstown Sheet & Tube Co. v. Sawyer

343 U.S. 579 (1952)

■ MR. JUSTICE BLACK delivered the opinion of the Court.

We are asked to decide whether the President was acting within his constitutional power when he issued an order directing the Secretary of Commerce to take possession of and operate most of the Nation's steel mills. The mill owners argue that the President's order amounts to lawmaking, a legislative function which the Constitution has expressly confided to the Congress and not to the President. The Government's position is that the order was made on findings of the President that his action was necessary to avert a national catastrophe which would inevitably result from a stoppage of steel production, and that in meeting this grave emergency the President was acting within the aggregate of his constitutional powers as the Nation's Chief Executive and the Commander in Chief of the Armed Forces of the United States. The issue emerges here from the following series of events:

In the latter part of 1951, a dispute arose between the steel companies and their employees over terms and conditions that should be included in new collective bargaining agreements. Long-continued conferences failed to resolve the dispute. . . . On April 4, 1952, the Union gave notice of a nationwide strike called to begin at 12:01 a.m. April 9. The indispensability of steel as a component of substantially all weapons and other war materials led the President to believe that the proposed work stoppage would immediately jeopardize our national defense and that governmental seizure of the steel mills was necessary in order to assure the continued availability of steel. Reciting these considerations for his action, the President, a few hours before the strike was to begin, issued Executive Order 10340. The order directed the Secretary of Commerce to take possession of most of the steel mills and keep them running. The Secretary immediately issued his own possessory orders, calling upon the presidents of the various seized companies to serve as operating managers for the United States. They were directed to carry on their activities in accordance with regulations and directions of the Secretary. The next morning the President sent a message to Congress reporting his action. Twelve days later he sent a second message.

Obeying the Secretary's orders under protest, the companies brought proceedings against him in the District Court. Their complaints charged that the seizure was not authorized by an act of Congress or by any constitutional provisions. The District Court was asked to declare the orders of the President and the Secretary invalid and to issue preliminary and permanent injunctions restraining their enforcement. Opposing the motion for preliminary injunction, the United States asserted that a strike disrupting steel production for even a brief period would so endanger the well-being and safety of the Nation that the President had "inherent power" to do what he had done—power "supported by the Constitution, by historical precedent, and by court decisions." Holding against the Government on all points, the District Court on April 30 issued a preliminary injunction restraining the Secretary from "continuing the seizure and possession of the plant . . . and from acting under the purported authority of Executive Order No. 10340." On the same day the Court of Appeals stayed the District Court's injunction. Deeming it best that the issues raised be promptly decided by this Court, we granted certiorari on May 3 and set the cause for argument on May 12. . . .

The President's power, if any, to issue the order must stem either from an act of Congress or from the Constitution itself. There is no statute that expressly authorizes the President to take possession of property as he did here. Nor is there any act of Congress to which our attention has been directed from which such a power can fairly be implied. Indeed, we do not understand the Government to rely on statutory authorization for this seizure. There are two statutes which do authorize the President to take both personal and real property under certain conditions. However, the Government admits that these conditions were not met and that the President's order was not rooted in either of the statutes. The Government refers to the seizure provisions of one of these statutes (s 201(b) of the Defense Production Act) as "much too cumbersome, involved, and time-consuming for the crisis which was at hand."

Moreover, the use of the seizure technique to solve labor disputes in order to prevent work stoppages was not only unauthorized by any congressional enactment; prior to this controversy, Congress had refused to adopt that method of settling labor disputes. When the Taft–Hartley Act was under consideration in 1947, Congress rejected an amendment which would have authorized such governmental seizures in cases of emergency. Apparently it was thought that the technique of seizure, like that of compulsory arbitration, would interfere with the process of collective bargaining. Consequently, the plan Congress adopted in that Act did not provide for seizure under any circumstances. Instead, the plan sought to bring about settlements by use of the customary devices of mediation, conciliation, investigation by boards of inquiry, and public reports. In some instances temporary injunctions were authorized to provide cooling-off periods. All this failing, unions were left free to strike after a secret vote by employees as to whether they wished to accept their employers' final settlement offer.

It is clear that if the President had authority to issue the order he did, it must be found in some provisions of the Constitution. And it is not claimed that express constitutional language grants this power to the President. The contention is that presidential power should be implied from the aggregate of his powers under the Constitution. Particular reliance is placed on provisions in Article II which say that "the executive Power shall be vested in a President . . ."; that "he shall take Care that the Laws be faithfully executed"; and that he "shall be Commander in Chief of the Army and Navy of the United States."

The order cannot properly be sustained as an exercise of the President's military power as Commander in Chief of the Armed Forces. The Government attempts to do so by citing a number of cases upholding broad powers in military commanders engaged in day-to-day fighting in a theater of war. Such cases need not concern us here. Even though "theater of war" be an expanding concept, we cannot with faithfulness to our constitutional system hold that the Commander in Chief of the Armed Forces has the ultimate power as such to take possession of private property in order to keep labor disputes from stopping production. This is a job for the Nation's lawmakers, not for its military authorities.

Nor can the seizure order be sustained because of the several constitutional provisions that grant executive power to the President. In the framework of our Constitution, the President's power to see that the laws are faithfully executed refutes the idea that he is to be a lawmaker. The Constitution limits his functions in the lawmaking process to the recommending of laws he thinks wise and the vetoing of laws he thinks bad. And the Constitution is neither silent nor equivocal about who shall make laws which the President is to execute. The first section of the first article says that "All legislative Powers herein granted shall be vested in a Congress of the United States. . . ." After granting many powers to the Congress, Article I goes on to provide that Congress may "make all Laws which shall be necessary and proper for carrying into Execution the foregoing Powers and all other Powers vested by this Constitution in the Government of the United States, or in any Department or Officer thereof."

The President's order does not direct that a congressional policy be executed in a manner prescribed by Congress—it directs that a presidential policy be executed in a manner prescribed by the President. The preamble of the order itself, like that of many statutes, sets out reasons why the President believes certain policies should be adopted, proclaims these policies as rules of conduct to be followed, and again, like a statute, authorizes a government official to promulgate additional rules and regulations consistent with the policy proclaimed and needed to carry that policy into execution. The power of Congress to adopt such public policies as those proclaimed by the order is beyond question. It can authorize the taking of private property for public use. It can makes laws regulating the relationships between employers and employees, prescribing rules designed to settle labor disputes, and fixing wages and working conditions in certain fields of our economy. The Constitution did not subject this law-making power of Congress to presidential or military supervision or control.

It is said that other Presidents without congressional authority have taken possession of private business enterprises in order to settle labor disputes. But even if this be true, Congress has not thereby lost its exclusive constitutional authority to make laws necessary and proper to carry out the powers vested by the Constitution "in the Government of the United States, or in any Department or Officer thereof."

The Founders of this Nation entrusted the law making power to the Congress alone in both good and bad times. It would do no good to recall the historical events, the fears of power and the hopes for freedom that lay behind their choice. Such a review would but confirm our holding that this seizure order cannot stand.

■ MR. JUSTICE FRANKFURTER, [concurring].

. . . The issue before us can be met, and therefore should be, without attempting to define the President's powers comprehensively. . . . We must therefore put to one side consideration of what powers the President would have had if there had been no legislation whatever bearing on the authority asserted by the seizure, or if the seizure had been only for a short, explicitly temporary period, to be terminated automatically unless Congressional approval were given. These and other questions, like or unlike, are not now here. I would exceed my authority were I to say anything about them.

The question before the Court comes in this setting. Congress has frequently—at least 16 times since 1916—specifically provided for executive seizure of production, transportation, communications, or storage facilities. In every case it has qualified this grant of power with limitations and safeguards. . . . The power to seize has uniformly been given only for a limited period or for a defined emergency, or has been repealed after a short period. . . . Congress also has not left to implication that just compensation be paid: it has usually legislated in detail regarding enforcement of this litigation-breeding general requirement. . . .

In adopting the provisions which it did, by the Labor Management Relations Act of 1947, for dealing with a "national emergency" arising out of a breakdown in peaceful industrial relations, Congress was very familiar with Government seizure as a protective measure. On a balance of considerations Congress chose not to lodge this power in the President. It chose not to make available in advance a remedy to which both industry and labor were fiercely hostile. . . . [N]othing can be plainer than that Congress made a conscious choice of policy in a field full of perplexity and peculiarly within legislative responsibility for choice. In formulating legislation for dealing with industrial conflicts, Congress could not more clearly and emphatically have withheld authority than it did in 1947. . . .

It cannot be contended that the President would have had power to issue this order had Congress explicitly negated such authority in formal legislation. Congress has expressed its will to withhold this power from the President as though it had said so in so many words. . . . By the Labor Management Relations Act of 1947, Congress said to the President, "You may not seize. Please report to us and ask for seizure power if you think it is needed in a specific situation." . . .

It is one thing to draw an intention of Congress from general language and to say that Congress would have explicitly written what is inferred, where Congress has not addressed itself to a specific situation. It is quite impossible, however, when Congress did specifically address itself to a problem, as Congress did to that of seizure, to find secreted in the interstices of legislation the very grant of power which Congress consciously withheld. To find authority so explicitly withheld is not merely to disregard in a particular instance the clear will of Congress. It is to disrespect the whole legislative process and the constitutional division of authority between President and Congress. . . .

Apart from his vast share of responsibility for the conduct of our foreign relations, the embracing function of the President is that "he shall take Care that the Laws be faithfully executed. . . ." Art. II, § 3. The nature of that authority has for me been comprehensively indicated by Mr. Justice Holmes. "The duty of the President to see that the laws be executed is a duty that does not go beyond the laws or require him to achieve more than Congress sees fit to leave within his power." *Myers v. United States*, 272 U.S. 52, 177. The powers of the President are not as particularized as are those of Congress. But unenumerated powers do not mean undefined powers. The separation of powers built into our Constitution gives essential content to undefined provisions in the frame of our government.

To be sure, the content of the three authorities of government is not to be derived from an abstract analysis. The areas are partly interacting, not wholly disjointed. The Constitution is a framework for government. Therefore the way the framework has consistently operated fairly establishes that it has operated according to its true nature. Deeply embedded traditional ways of conducting government cannot supplant the Constitution or legislation, but they give meaning to the words of a text or supply them. It is an inadmissibly narrow conception of American constitutional law to confine it to the words of the Constitution and to disregard the gloss which life has written upon them. In short, a systematic, unbroken, executive practice, long pursued to the knowledge of the Congress and never before questioned, engaged in by Presidents who have also sworn to uphold the Constitution, making as it were such exercise of power part of the structure of our government, may be treated as a gloss on "executive Power" vested in the President by § 1 of Art. II.

Such was the case of *United States v. Midwest Oil Co.*, 236 U.S. 459. . . . In the *Midwest Oil* case, lands which Congress had opened for entry were, over a period of 80 years and in 252 instances, and by Presidents learned and unlearned in the law, temporarily withdrawn from entry so as to enable Congress to deal with such withdrawals. No remotely comparable practice can be vouched for executive seizure of property at a time when this country was not at war, in the only constitutional way in which it can be at war. It would pursue the irrelevant to reopen the controversy over the constitutionality of some acts of Lincoln during the Civil War. Suffice it to say that he seized railroads in territory where armed hostilities had already interrupted the movement of troops to the beleaguered Capital, and his order was ratified by the Congress. . . .

[T]he list of executive assertions of the power of seizure in circumstances comparable to the present reduces to three in the six-month period from June to December of 1941. We need not split hairs in comparing those actions to the one before us, though much might be said by way of differentiation. Without passing on their validity, it suffices to say that these three isolated instances do not add up, either in number, scope, duration or contemporaneous legal justification, to the kind of executive construction of the Constitution revealed in the *Midwest Oil* case. Nor do they come to us sanctioned by long-continued acquiescence of Congress giving decisive weight to a construction by the Executive of its powers.

A scheme of government like ours no doubt at times feels the lack of power to act with complete, all-embracing, swiftly moving authority. No doubt a government with distributed authority, subject to be challenged in the courts of law, at least long enough to consider and adjudicate the challenge, labors under restrictions from which other governments are free. It has not been our tradition to envy such governments. . . . I know no more impressive words on this subject than those of Mr. Justice Brandeis:

"The doctrine of the separation of powers was adopted by the Convention of 1787, not to promote efficiency but to preclude the exercise of arbitrary power. The purpose was, not to avoid friction, but . . . by means of the inevitable friction incident to the distribution of the governmental powers among three departments, to save the people from autocracy." *Myers*, at 240, 293. . . .

■ MR. JUSTICE DOUGLAS, concurring.

There can be no doubt that the emergency which caused the President to seize these steel plants was one that bore heavily on the country. But the emergency did not create power; it merely marked an occasion when power should be exercised. And the fact that it was necessary that measures be taken to keep steel in production does not mean that the President, rather than the Congress, had the constitutional authority to act. . . .

The legislative nature of the action taken by the President seems to me to be clear. When the United States takes over an industrial plant to settle a labor controversy, it is condemning property. The seizure of the plant is a taking in the constitutional sense. A permanent taking would amount to the nationalization of the industry. A temporary taking falls short of that goal. But though the seizure is only for a week or a month, the condemnation is complete and the United States must pay compensation for the temporary possession.

The power of the Federal Government to condemn property is well established. It can condemn for any public purpose; and I have no doubt but that condemnation of a plant, factory, or industry in order to promote industrial peace would be constitutional. But there is a duty to pay for all property taken by the Government. The command of the Fifth Amendment is that no "private property be taken for public use, without just compensation." That constitutional requirement has an important bearing on the present case.

The President has no power to raise revenues. That power is in the Congress by Article I, Section 8 of the Constitution. The President might seize and the Congress by subsequent action might ratify the seizure. But until and unless Congress acted, no condemnation would be lawful. The branch of government that has the power to pay compensation for a seizure is the only one able to authorize a seizure or make lawful one that the President had effected. . . .

We pay a price for our system of checks and balances, for the distribution of power among the three branches of government. It is a price that today may seem exorbitant to many. Today a kindly President uses the seizure power to effect a wage increase and to keep the steel furnaces in production. Yet tomorrow another President might use the same power to prevent a wage increase, to curb trade unionists, to regiment labor as oppressively as industry thinks it has been regimented by this seizure.

■ MR. JUSTICE JACKSON, concurring in the judgment and opinion of the court.

That comprehensive and undefined presidential powers hold both practical advantages and grave dangers for the country will impress anyone who has served as legal adviser to a President in time of transition and public anxiety. *[Justice Jackson had served in President Franklin Roose-*

velt's administration as solicitor general and attorney general.—Editors]
While an interval of detached reflection may temper teachings of that experience, they probably are a more realistic influence on my views than the conventional materials of judicial decision which seem unduly to accentuate doctrine and legal fiction. . . .

A judge, like an executive adviser, may be surprised at the poverty of really useful and unambiguous authority applicable to concrete problems of executive power as they actually present themselves. Just what our forefathers did envision, or would have envisioned had they foreseen modern conditions, must be divined from materials almost as enigmatic as the dreams Joseph was called upon to interpret for Pharaoh. A century and a half of partisan debate and scholarly speculation yields no net result but only supplies more or less apt quotations from respected sources on each side of any question. They largely cancel each other. And court decisions are indecisive because of the judicial practice of dealing with the largest questions in the most narrow way.

The actual art of governing under our Constitution does not and cannot conform to judicial definitions of the power of any of its branches based on isolated clauses or even single Articles torn from context. While the Constitution diffuses power the better to secure liberty, it also contemplates that practice will integrate the dispersed powers into a workable government. It enjoins upon its branches separateness but interdependence, autonomy but reciprocity. Presidential powers are not fixed but fluctuate, depending upon their disjunction or conjunction with those of Congress. We may well begin by a somewhat over-simplified grouping of practical situations in which a President may doubt, or others may challenge, his powers, and by distinguishing roughly the legal consequences of this factor of relativity.

1. When the President acts pursuant to an express or implied authorization of Congress, his authority is at its maximum, for it includes all that he possesses in his own right plus all that Congress can delegate. In these circumstances, and in these only, may he be said (for what it may be worth), to personify the federal sovereignty. If his act is held unconstitutional under these circumstances, it usually means that the Federal Government as an undivided whole lacks power. A seizure executed by the President pursuant to an Act of Congress would be supported by the strongest of presumptions and the widest latitude of judicial interpretation, and the burden of persuasion would rest heavily upon any who might attack it.

2. When the President acts in absence of either a congressional grant or denial of authority, he can only rely upon his own independent powers, but there is a zone of twilight in which he and Congress may have concurrent authority, or in which its distribution is uncertain. Therefore, congressional inertia, indifference or quiescence may sometimes, at least as a practical matter, enable, if not invite, measures on independent presidential responsibility. In this area, any actual test of power is likely to depend on the imperatives of events and contemporary imponderables rather than on abstract theories of law.

3. When the President takes measures incompatible with the expressed or implied will of Congress, his power is at its lowest ebb, for then he can rely only upon his own constitutional powers minus any constitutional powers of Congress over the matter. Courts can sustain exclusive Presidential control in such a case only be disabling the Congress from act-

ing upon the subject. Presidential claim to a power at once so conclusive and preclusive must be scrutinized with caution, for what is at stake is the equilibrium established by our constitutional system.

Into which of these classifications does this executive seizure of the steel industry fit? It is eliminated from the first by admission, for it is conceded that no congressional authorization exists for this seizure. That takes away also the support of the many precedents and declarations which were made in relation, and must be confined, to this category.

Can it then be defended under flexible tests available to the second category? It seems clearly eliminated from that class because Congress has not left seizure of private property an open field but has covered it by three statutory policies inconsistent with this seizure. . . .

This leaves the current seizure to be justified only by the severe tests under the third grouping, where it can be supported only by any remainder of executive power after subtraction of such powers as Congress may have over the subject. In short, we can sustain the President only by holding that seizure of such strike-bound industries is within his domain and beyond control by Congress. Thus, this Court's first review of such seizures occurs under circumstances which leave Presidential power most vulnerable to attack and in the least favorable of possible constitutional postures.

I did not suppose, and I am not persuaded, that history leaves it open to question, at least in the courts, that the executive branch, like the Federal Government as a whole, possesses only delegated powers. The purpose of the Constitution was not only to grant power, but to keep it from getting out of hand. However, because the President does not enjoy unmentioned powers does not mean that the mentioned ones should be narrowed by a niggardly construction. Some clauses could be made almost unworkable, as well as immutable, by refusal to indulge some latitude of interpretation for changing times. I have heretofore, and do now, give to the enumerated powers the scope and elasticity afforded by what seem to be reasonable practical implications instead of the rigidity dictated by a doctrinaire textualism.

The Solicitor General seeks the power of seizure in three clauses of the Executive Article, the first reading, "The executive Power shall be vested in a President of the United States of America." Lest I be thought to exaggerate, I quote the interpretation which his brief puts upon it: "In our view, this clause constitutes a grant of all the executive powers of which the Government is capable." If that be true, it is difficult to see why the forefathers bothered to add several specific items, including some trifling ones.

The example of such unlimited executive power that must have most impressed the forefathers was the prerogative exercised by George III, and the description of its evils in the Declaration of Independence leads me to doubt that they were creating their new Executive in his image. Continental European examples were no more appealing. And if we seek instruction from our own times, we can match it only from the executive powers in those governments we disparagingly describe as totalitarian. I cannot accept the view that this clause is a grant in bulk of all conceivable executive power but regard it as an allocation to the presidential office of the generic powers thereafter stated.

The clause on which the Government next relies is that "The President shall be Commander in Chief of the Army and Navy of the United States. . . ." These cryptic words have given rise to some of the most persistent controversies in our constitutional history. Of course, they imply something more than an empty title. But just what authority goes with the name has plagued Presidential advisers who would not waive or narrow it by nonassertion yet cannot say where it begins or ends. It undoubtedly puts the Nation's armed forces under Presidential command. Hence, [T]his loose appellation is sometimes advanced as support for any Presidential action, internal or external, involving use of force, the idea being that it vests power to do anything, anywhere, that can be done with an army or navy.

That seems to be the logic of an argument tendered at our bar—that the President having, on his own responsibility, sent American troops abroad derives from that act "affirmative power" to seize the means of producing a supply of steel for them. To quote, "Perhaps the most forceful illustrations of the scope of Presidential power in this connection is the fact that American troops in Korea, whose safety and effectiveness are so directly involved here, were sent to the field by an exercise of the President's constitutional powers." Thus, it is said he has invested himself with "war powers."

I cannot foresee all that it might entail if the Court should indorse this argument. Nothing in our Constitution is plainer than that declaration of a war is entrusted only to Congress. Of course, a state of war may in fact exist without a formal declaration. But no doctrine that the Court could promulgate would seem to me more sinister and alarming than that a President whose conduct of foreign affairs is so largely uncontrolled, and often even is unknown, can vastly enlarge his mastery over the internal affairs of the country by his own commitment of the Nation's armed forces to some foreign venture. I do not, however, find it necessary or appropriate to consider the legal status of the Korean enterprise to discountenance argument based on it.

Assuming that we are in a war *de facto*, whether it is or is not a war *de jure*, does that empower the Commander-in-Chief to seize industries he thinks necessary to supply our army? The Constitution expressly places in Congress power "to raise and *support* Armies" and "to *provide* and *maintain* a Navy." (Emphasis supplied.) This certainly lays upon Congress primary responsibility for supplying the armed forces. Congress alone controls the raising of revenues and their appropriation and may determine in what manner and by what means they shall be spent for military and naval procurement. I suppose no one would doubt that Congress can take over war supply as a Government enterprise. On the other hand, if Congress sees fit to rely on free private enterprise collectively bargaining with free labor for support and maintenance of our armed forces can the Executive because of lawful disagreements incidental to that process, seize the facility for operation upon Government-imposed terms?

There are indications that the Constitution did not contemplate that the title Commander-in-Chief *of the Army and Navy* will constitute him also Commander-in-Chief of the country, its industries and its inhabitants. He has no monopoly of "war powers," whatever they are. While Congress cannot deprive the President of the command of the army and navy, only Congress can provide him an army or navy to command. It is also empowered to make rules for the "Government and Regulation of land and naval forces," by which it may to some unknown extent impinge upon even command functions.

That military powers of the Commander-in-Chief were not to supersede representative government of internal affairs seems obvious from the

Constitution and from elementary American history. Time out of mind, and even now in many parts of the world, a military commander can seize private housing to shelter his troops. Not so, however, in the United States, for the Third Amendment says, "No Soldier shall, in time of peace be quartered in any house, without the consent of the Owner, nor in time of war, but in a manner to be prescribed by law." Thus, even in war time, his seizure of needed military housing must be authorized by Congress. . . .

We should not use this occasion to circumscribe, much less to contract, the lawful role of the President as Commander-in-Chief. I should indulge the widest latitude of interpretation to sustain his exclusive function to command the instruments of national force, at least when turned against the outside world for the security of our society. But, when it is turned inward, not because of rebellion but because of a lawful economic struggle between industry and labor, it should have no such indulgence. . . .

The third clause in which the Solicitor General finds seizure powers is that "he shall take Care that the Laws be faithfully executed. . . ." That authority must be matched against words of the Fifth Amendment that "No person shall be . . . deprived of life, liberty, or property, without due process of law. . . ." One gives a governmental authority that reaches so far as there is law, the other gives a private right that authority shall go no farther. These signify about all there is of the principle that ours is a government of laws, not of men, and that we submit ourselves to rulers only if under rules.

The Solicitor General lastly grounds support of the seizure upon nebulous, inherent powers never expressly granted but said to have accrued to the office from the customs and claims of preceding administrations. The plea is for a resulting power to deal with a crisis or an emergency according to the necessities of the case, the unarticulated assumption being that necessity knows no law.

Loose and irresponsible use of adjectives colors all non-legal and much legal discussion of presidential powers. "Inherent" powers, "implied" powers, "incidental" powers, "plenary" powers, "war" powers and "emergency" powers are used, often interchangeably and without fixed or ascertainable meanings.

The vagueness and generality of the clauses that set forth presidential powers afford a plausible basis for pressures within and without an administration for presidential action beyond that supported by those whose responsibility it is to defend his actions in court. The claim of inherent and unrestricted presidential powers has long been a persuasive dialectical weapon in political controversy. . . .

The appeal, however, that we declare the existence of inherent powers *ex necessitate* to meet an emergency asks us to do what many think would be wise, although it is something the forefathers omitted. They knew what emergencies were, knew the pressures they engender for authoritative action, knew, too, how they afford a ready pretext for usurpation. We may also suspect that they suspected that emergency powers would tend to kindle emergencies. Aside from suspension of the privilege of the writ of habeas corpus in time of rebellion or invasion, when the public safety may require it, they made no express provision for exercise of extraordinary authority because of a crisis. I do not think we rightfully may so amend their work, and, if we could, I am not convinced it would be wise to do so, although many modern nations have forthrightly recognized that war and economic crises may upset the normal balance between liberty and authority. Their experience with emergency powers may not be irrelevant to the argument here that we should say that the Executive, of his own volition, can invest himself with undefined emergency powers.

Germany, after the First World War, framed the Weimar Constitution, designed to secure her liberties in the Western tradition. However, the President of the Republic, without concurrence of the Reichstag, was empowered temporarily to suspend any or all individual rights if public safety and order were seriously disturbed or endangered. This proved a temptation to every government, whatever its shade of opinion, and in 13 years suspension of rights was invoked on more than 250 occasions. Finally, Hitler persuaded President Von Hindenberg to suspend all such rights, and they were never restored. . . .

In view of the ease, expedition and safety with which Congress can grant and has granted large emergency powers, certainly ample to embrace this crisis, I am quite unimpressed with the argument that we should affirm possession of them without statute. Such power either has no beginning or it has no end. If it exists, it need submit to no legal restraint. I am not alarmed that it would plunge us straightway into dictatorship, but it is at least a step in that wrong direction. . . .

Executive power has the advantage of concentration in a single head in those choice the whole Nation has a part, making him the focus of public hopes and expectations. In drama, magnitude and finality his decisions so far overshadow any others that almost alone he fills the public eye and ear. No other personality in public life can begin to compete with him in access to the public mind through modern methods of communications. By his prestige as head of state and his influence upon public opinion he exerts a leverage upon those who are supposed to check and balance his power which often cancels their effectiveness. . . .

I have no illusion that any decision by this Court can keep power in the hands of Congress if it is not wise and timely in meeting its problems. A crisis that challenges the President equally, or perhaps primarily, challenges Congress. If not good law, there was worldly wisdom in the maxim attributed to Napoleon that "The tools belong to the man who can use them." We may say that power to legislate for emergencies belongs in the hands of Congress, but only Congress itself can prevent power from slipping through its fingers. . . .

The Executive, except for recommendation and veto, has no legislative power. The executive action we have here originates in the individual will of the President and represents an exercise of authority without law. No one, perhaps not even the President, knows the limits of the power he may seek to exert in this instance and the parties affected cannot learn the limit of their rights. We do not know today what powers over labor or property would be claimed to flow from Government possession if we should legalize it, what rights to compensation would be claimed or recognized, or on what contingency it would end. With all its defects, delays and inconveniences, men have discovered no technique for long preserving free government except that the Executive be under the law, and that the law be made by parliamentary deliberations.

Such institutions may be destined to pass away. But it is the duty of the Court to be last, not first, to give them up.

■ [JUSTICE BURTON's concurring opinion is omitted.]

■ MR. JUSTICE CLARK, concurring in the judgment of the Court.

One of this Court's first pronouncements upon the powers of the President under the Constitution was made by Mr. Chief Justice John Marshall some one hundred and fifty years ago. In *Little v. Barreme*, 2 Cranch 170 (1804), he used this characteristically clear language in discussing the power of the President to instruct the seizure of the *Flying Fish*, a vessel bound from a French port:

> It is by no means clear that the president of the United States whose high duty it is to "take care that the laws be faithfully executed" and who is commander in chief of the armies and navies of the United States, might not, without any special authority for that purpose, in the then-existing state of things, have empowered the officers commanding the armed vessels of the United States to seize, and send into port for adjudication, American vessels which were forfeited by being engaged in this illicit commerce. But when it is observed that [an act of Congress] gives a special authority to seize on the high seas, and limits that authority to the seizure of vessels bound or sailing to a French port, the legislature seem to have prescribed that the manner in which this law shall be carried into execution, was to exclude a seizure of any vessel *not* bound to a French port.

Accordingly, a unanimous Court held that the President's instructions had been issued without authority, and that they could not "legalize an act which, without those instructions, would have been a plain trespass." I know of no subsequent holding of this Court to the contrary.[3] . . .

In my view—taught me not only by the decision of Mr. Chief Justice Marshall in *Little* v. *Barreme*, but also by a score of other pronouncements of distinguished members of this bench—the Constitution does grant to the President extensive authority in times of grave and imperative national emergency. . . .

I conclude that where Congress has laid down specific procedures to deal with the type of crisis confronting the President, he must follow those procedures in meeting the crisis; but that in the absence of such action by Congress, the President's independent power to act depends upon the gravity of the situation confronting the nation. I cannot sustain the seizure in question because here, as in *Little v. Barreme*, Congress had prescribed methods to be followed by the President in meeting the emergency at hand. . . .

■ MR. CHIEF JUSTICE VINSON, with whom MR. JUSTICE REED and MR. JUSTICE MINTON join, dissenting.

---

[3] Decisions of this Court which have upheld the exercise of presidential power include the following: *Prize Cases*, 2 Black 635 (1863) (subsequent ratification of President's acts by Congress); *In re Neagle*, 135 U.S. 1 (1890) (protection of federal officials from personal violence while performing official duties); *In re Debs*, 158 U.S. 564 (1895) (injunction to prevent forcible obstruction of interstate commerce and the mails); *United States v. Midwest Oil Co.*, 236 U.S. 459 (1915) (acquiescence by Congress in more than 250 instances of exercise of same power by various Presidents over period of 80 years); *Myers v. United States*, 272 U.S. 52 (1926) (control over subordinate officials in executive department) [but see *Humphrey's Executor v. United States*, 295 U.S. 602, 626–628 (1935)]; *Hirabayashi v. United States*, 320 U.S. 81 (1943), and *Korematsu v. United States*, 323 U.S. 214 (1944) (express congressional authorization); cf. *United States v. Russell*, 13 Wall. 623 (1871) (imperative military necessity in area of combat during war); *United States v. Curtiss–Wright Export Corp.*, 299 U.S. 304 (1936) (power to negotiate with foreign governments); *United States v. United Mine Workers*, 330 U.S. 258 (1947) (seizure under specific statutory authorization).

. . . In passing upon the question of Presidential powers in this case, we must first consider the context in which those powers were exercised.

Those who suggest that this is a case involving extraordinary powers should be mindful that these are extraordinary times. A world not yet recovered from the devastation of World War II has been forced to face the threat of another and more terrifying global conflict.

Accepting in full measure its responsibility in the world community, the United States was instrumental in securing adoption of the United Nations Charter, approved by the Senate by a vote of 89 to 2. The first purpose of the United Nations is to "maintain international peace and security, and to that end: to take effective collective measures for the prevention and removal of threats to the peace, and for the suppression of acts of aggression or other breaches of the peace. . . ." In 1950, when the United Nations called upon member nations "to render every assistance" to repel aggression in Korea, the United States furnished its vigorous support. For almost two full years, our armed forces have been fighting in Korea, suffering casualties of over 108,000 men. Hostilities have not abated. . . . Congressional support of the action in Korea has been manifested by provisions for increased military manpower and equipment and for economic stabilization, as hereinafter described. . . .

Congress also directed the President to build up our own defenses. Congress, recognizing the "grim fact . . . that the United States is now engaged in a struggle for survival" and that "it is imperative that we now take those necessary steps to make our strength equal to the peril of the hour," granted authority to draft men into the armed forces. As a result, we now have over 3,500,000 men in our armed forces. . . .

The President has the duty to execute the foregoing legislative programs. Their successful execution depends upon continued production of steel and stabilized prices for steel. Accordingly, when the collective bargaining agreements between the Nation's steel producers and their employees, represented by the United Steel Workers, were due to expire on December 31, 1951, and a strike shutting down the entire basic steel industry was threatened, the President acted to avert a complete shutdown of steel production. . . .

After bargaining had failed to avert the threatened shutdown of steel production, the President issued [an] Executive Order [describing the emergency the country faced as he directed seizure of the steel mills.] . . . The next morning, April 9, 1952, the President addressed [a] Message to Congress[. It concluded]:

> On the basis of the facts that are known to me at this time, I do not believe that immediate congressional action is essential; but I would, of course, be glad to cooperate in developing any legislative proposals which the Congress may wish to consider.

If the Congress does not deem it necessary to act at this time, I shall continue to do all that is within my power to keep the steel industry operating and at the same time make every effort to bring about a settlement of the dispute so the mills can be returned to their private owners as soon as possible.

Twelve days passed without action by Congress. On April 21, 1952, the President sent a letter to the President of the Senate in which he again described the purpose and need for his action and again stated his position that "The Congress can, if it wishes, reject the course of action I have followed in this matter." Congress has not so acted to this date. . . .

Secretary of Defense Lovett swore that "a work stoppage in the steel industry will result immediately in serious curtailment of production of essential weapons and munitions of all kinds." He illustrated by showing that 84% of the national production of certain alloy steel is currently used for production of military-end items and that 35% of total production of another form of steel goes into ammunition, 80% of such ammunition now going to Korea. The Secretary of Defense stated that: "We are holding the line [in Korea] with ammunition and not with the lives of our troops." . . . Even ignoring for the moment whatever confidential information the President may possess as "the Nation's organ for foreign affairs," the uncontroverted affidavits in this record amply support the finding that "a work stoppage would immediately jeopardize and imperil our national defense." . . .

A review of executive action demonstrates that our Presidents have on many occasions exhibited the leadership contemplated by the framers when they made the President Commander in Chief, and imposed upon him the trust to "take Care that the Laws be faithfully executed." With or without explicit statutory authorization, Presidents have at such times dealt with national emergencies by acting promptly and resolutely to enforce legislative programs, at least to save those programs until Congress could act. Congress and the courts have responded to such executive initiative with consistent approval. . . .

[Chief Justice Vinson then invoked presidential precedents, such as President Washington's Neutrality Proclamation, President Jefferson's Louisiana Purchase, the Monroe Doctrine, actions by President Lincoln including the seizure of rail and telegraph lines around the capital, President Hayes's use of federal troops to suppress the Railroad Strike of 1877, President Wilson's establishment of a War Labor Board to prevent strikes, and actions by President Franklin Roosevelt including the seizure of an aviation plant in California six months before Pearl Harbor and the seizure of coal mines in 1943.—Editors]

This is but a cursory summary of executive leadership. But it amply demonstrates that Presidents have taken prompt action to enforce the laws and protect the country whether or not Congress happened to provide in advance for the particular method of execution. At the minimum, the executive actions reviewed herein sustain the action of the President in this case. And many of the cited examples of Presidential practice go far beyond the extent of power necessary to sustain the President's order to seize the steel mills. The fact that temporary executive seizures of industrial plants to meet an emergency have not been directly tested in this Court furnishes not the slightest suggestion that such actions have been illegal. Rather, the fact that Congress and the courts have consistently recognized and given their support to such executive action indicates that such a power of seizure has been accepted throughout our history.

History bears out the genius of the Founding Fathers, who created a Government subject to law but not left subject to inertia when vigor and initiative are required.

Focusing now on the situation confronting the President on the night of April 8, 1952, we cannot but conclude that the President was performing his duty under the Constitution to "take Care that the Laws be faithfully executed"—a duty described by President Benjamin Harrison as "the central idea of the office." . . .

Whatever the extent of Presidential power on more tranquil occasions, and whatever the right of the President to execute legislative programs as he sees fit without reporting the mode of execution to Congress, the single Presidential purpose disclosed on this record is to faithfully execute the laws by acting in an emergency to maintain the status quo, thereby preventing collapse of the legislative programs until Congress could act. The President's action served the same purposes as a judicial stay entered to maintain the status quo in order to preserve the jurisdiction of a court. In his Message to Congress immediately following the seizure, the President explained the necessity of his action in executing the military procurement and anti-inflation legislative programs and expressed his desire to cooperate with any legislative proposals approving, regulating or rejecting the seizure of the steel mills. Consequently, there is no evidence whatever of any Presidential purpose to defy Congress or act in any way inconsistent with the legislative will. . . .

The Framers knew, as we should know in these times of peril, that there is real danger in Executive weakness. There is no cause to fear Executive tyranny so long as the laws of Congress are being faithfully executed. Certainly there is no basis for fear of dictatorship when the Executive acts, as he did in this case, only to save the situation until Congress could act. . . .

The broad executive power granted by Article II to an officer on duty 365 days a year cannot, it is said, be invoked to avert disaster. Instead, the President must confine himself to sending a message to Congress recommending action. Under this messenger-boy concept of the Office, the President cannot even act to preserve legislative programs from destruction so that Congress will have something left to act upon. . . .

Seizure of plaintiffs' property is not a pleasant undertaking. Similarly unpleasant to a free country are the draft which disrupts the home and military procurement which causes economic dislocation and compels adoption of price controls, wage stabilization and allocation of materials. The President informed Congress that even a temporary Government operation of plaintiffs' properties was "thoroughly distasteful" to him, but was necessary to prevent immediate paralysis of the mobilization program. . . . A sturdy judiciary should not be swayed by the unpleasantness or unpopularity of necessary executive action, but must independently determine for itself whether the President was acting was acting, as required by the Constitution, to "take Care that the Laws be faithfully executed."

. . . . No basis for claims of arbitrary action, unlimited powers or dictatorial usurpation of congressional power appears from the facts of this case. On the contrary, judicial, legislative and executive precedents throughout our history demonstrate that in this case the President acted in full conformity with his duties under the Constitution. Accordingly, we would reverse the order of the District Court.

NOTES

1. What is the dominant mode of interpretation in each opinion? Which opinions are more flexible and which are more categorical? (In their own ways the opinions of Justice Black and Justice Jackson are each quite categorical—the former categorizing powers as executive or legislative and the latter catego-

rizing situations in which the president acts with Congress's support, in the face of Congress's silence, or over Congress's disapproval.) Which opinion is most persuasive to you? Why?

2. Justice Black reads the three vesting clauses literally and functionally. He thinks the grant of the executive power to the president and of all legislative power to Congress means that the president has no inherent power to respond to emergencies or to deal with foreign affairs. There is in his view no presidential prerogative power. Is Justice Black right in his reading of the text? Compare his reading with two earlier constructions of presidential power that you may already have read: Alexander Hamilton's reading of the Vesting Clauses in the controversy over President Washington's Neutrality Proclamation (see *Pacificus, No. 1*, printed in Chapter 1), and Chief Justice Taney's construction of presidential power during the Civil War in *Ex Parte Merryman* (printed in Chapter 2). Which of these does Justice Black's opinion most closely resemble?

3. Both Justice Frankfurter and Chief Justice Vinson cite past practice, but it leads them to different conclusions. Who has the better argument? How useful is practice as a guide when humanity seems to be teetering on the edge of another world war and even a nuclear apocalypse? Every emergency is unique, and the president who had access to all our military and intelligence secrets thought this one was really bad. Should the Court have deferred to the president because he had more information?

4. If the Constitution had a clause granting the executive "emergency powers," would that make the nation more secure in a crisis, or would it be inimical to the very idea of constitutional governance? The constitution of the Weimar Republic had an emergency-powers clause, and its abuse helped bring Adolf Hitler to power. Would such a clause be less dangerous if there had to be a resolution by two-thirds of both houses of Congress declaring a state of emergency? Is the U.S. Constitution's studied ambiguity on emergency power a good thing? Is the threat of eventual impeachment and removal from office a sufficient check on the executive?

5. *Youngstown* was qualified somewhat by *Dames & Moore v. Regan*, 453 U.S. 654 (1981), in which the Supreme Court upheld a unilateral property seizure by Presidents Jimmy Carter and Ronald Reagan as part of an elaborate settlement to the Iranian hostage crisis. The seizure was not specifically authorized by statute. *Dames & Moore* is discussed later in this chapter. What is relevant here is that cases like *Youngstown* are not uncommon. How they are resolved is critical to the separation of powers created by the Constitution.

[*Assignment 11*]

I. ARTICLE I: THE LEGISLATIVE POWER

A Map of Article I

> *Section 1: All legislative Powers herein granted shall be vested in a Congress of the United States, which shall consist of a Senate and House of Representatives.*

The first section of Article I is an introduction and a statement of substantive principles. Each part of it gives rise to important issues of constitutional structure.

First, Congress is granted only enumerated legislative powers—those "herein granted"—not a general legislative power over everything and everyone. Most of those enumerated legislative powers are specified in Article I, Section 8. The last one is a power to make laws "necessary and proper" for carrying into execution the other legislative powers (or the powers of any other branch of government).

Second, the vesting of these powers in Congress raises the question of delegation. Can Congress give its legislative powers to another actor? Does it matter whether Congress gives instructions to the actor it is delegating power to? How detailed do those instructions need to be? Those sorts of questions are involved in what is today known as the "non-delegation doctrine."

Third, this section introduces bicameralism. As described more fully in Section 7, Article I requires, in order to become law, that a bill must pass both houses of Congress and be presented to the president (who has a qualified veto).

Section 2: The House of Representatives . . . .

This section describes the House: its mode of election, the qualifications its members must have, the method for determining how representation is apportioned among the states, and the power of the House to "chuse" its "Speaker" and other officers. It also provides that the House shall have "the sole power of impeachment."

Section 3: The Senate of the United States . . . .

This section describes the Senate: its composition, the term of office, the mode of selection (until changed by the Seventeenth Amendment), qualifications, the Senate's officers, and its power to "try all Impeachments."

Section 4: The Times, Places and Manner of holding Elections for Senators and Representatives . . . .

This section provides that each state will prescribe the procedures for the election of its own representatives and senators, but subject to Congress's alterations.

Section 5: Each House shall . . . .

This section provides that each house judges the elections and qualifications of its members, determines its own rules of proceedings, and may punish and expel its members. Each house must keep a journal of its proceedings, and neither can adjourn for more than three days without the consent of the other.

Section 6: The Senators and Representatives shall receive a Compensation . . . .

This section provides that senators and representatives receive a salary "ascertained by law." (The Twenty-seventh Amendment provides that no law varying compensation may take effect without an intervening election.) They may not be arrested while going back and forth to Congress, except for "Treason, Felony and Breach of the Peace." Nor may they be appointed to any executive or judicial office that was created (or which had its "Emoluments" increased) during the term for which they were elected. No executive or judicial officer may be a member of Congress.

Section 7: All Bills . . . .

This section prescribes how Congress may enact laws. Bills for raising revenue must originate in the House of Representatives. Every bill must pass both houses and be approved or vetoed by the president. A veto may be overridden by a two-thirds vote of both houses.

Section 8: The Congress shall have Power . . . .

This section contains the famous enumeration of Congress's legislative powers in eighteen separate paragraphs. (These powers often raise questions of federalism, and are considered in detail in Chapter 4.) These eighteen clauses limit and define federal power, but some of the enumerations are sweeping and broad. This is especially true of the eighteenth enumeration: the Necessary and Proper Clause.

Section 9: No Bill . . . . No Preference . . . No Title of Nobility . . . .

This section lists some things that Congress may *not* do with its enumerated but sweeping legislative powers. It may not prevent states from importing "such Persons as any of the States now existing shall think proper to admit" until 1808 (an implicit but unmistakable reference to the slave trade, as discussed in Chapter 1). It may not suspend the privilege of the writ of habeas corpus except in times of invasion or rebellion when the public safety requires it. It may not enact bills of attainder and ex post facto laws. Nor may it enact any laws taxing exports from a state, or preferring the commerce or ports of a particular state. It may not spend money without lawful appropriations. Finally, and somewhat anticlimactically, it may not grant any "Title of Nobility."

Section 10: No State shall . . . .

This section might seem to be a departure from the scheme of Article I, because it lists things that may not be done by *states*: enter into treaties or alliances, coin money, pass bills of attainder or ex post facto laws, impair the obligation of contracts, grant titles of nobility, and tax imports or exports. It also lists things that states may do only with the consent of Congress: keep troops or ships of war, enter into compacts with other states, or engage in war unless actually invaded or in such imminent danger as will not admit of delay. In addition to the discussion of congressional consent, this section's placement in Article I can be explained by the fact that many of the things this section forbids the states to do are the very things that Congress is authorized to do by Article I, Section 8 (e.g., coin money). Section 10 can be helpful in determining which powers under the Constitution are exclusively national and which are held concurrently by the national government and the states.

A. ENUMERATED POWERS AND FEDERAL SUPREMACY: "ALL LEGISLATIVE POWERS HEREIN GRANTED"

Article I, Section 1: All legislative Powers herein granted shall be vested in a Congress of the United States, which shall consist of a Senate and House of Representatives.

A fundamental principle of the Constitution is that the national government is one of limited and enumerated powers. According to Article I, Section 1, the powers that Congress has are "[a]ll legislative powers *herein granted.*" So long as Congress acts within the scope of its enumerated powers and other constitutional constraints, the statutes it enacts are "the supreme law of the Land." Art. VI, Sec. 2.

The scope of national legislative powers was much debated at the founding, and it is addressed in a number of essays in *The Federalist*—especially *Nos. 23, 33, 34, 44,* and *45.* As discussed in Chapter 1, one of the most important early controversies over the scope of national legislative powers—a controversy sustained for decades—concerned the Bank of the United States. The Supreme Court finally weighed in on the issue in 1819 in *McCulloch v. Maryland*, which has become a foundational decision on national legislative powers. It is one of the few constitutional decisions that every nineteenth century attorney was, and every twenty-first century attorney is, expected to know. Consider carefully Chief Justice Marshall's arguments about the scope of the Necessary and Proper Clause. Do they establish a principle of broad, even unrestricted, national legislative powers? Or do they set concrete limits?

McCulloch v. Maryland
17 U.S. (4 Wheat.) 316 (1819)

■ MR. CHIEF JUSTICE MARSHALL delivered the opinion of the Court.

In the case now to be determined, the defendant, a sovereign State, denies the obligation of a law enacted by the legislature of the Union, and the plaintiff, on his part, contests the validity of an act which has been passed by the legislature of that State. The constitution of our country, in its most interesting and vital parts, is to be considered; the conflicting powers of the government of the Union and of its members, as marked in that constitution, are to be discussed; and an opinion given, which may essentially influence the great operations of the government. No tribunal can approach such a question without a deep sense of its importance, and of the awful responsibility involved in its decision. But it must be decided peacefully, or remain a source of hostile legislation, perhaps, of hostility of a still more serious nature; and if it is to be so decided, by this tribunal alone can the decision be made. On the Supreme Court of the United States has the constitution of our country devolved this important duty.

The first question made in the cause is, has Congress power to incorporate a bank?

It has been truly said, that this can scarcely be considered as an open question, entirely unprejudiced by the former proceedings of the nation respecting it. The principle now contested was introduced at a very early period of our history, has been recognised by many successive legislatures, and has been acted upon by the judicial department, in cases of peculiar delicacy, as a law of undoubted obligation.

It will not be denied, that a bold and daring usurpation might be resisted, after an acquiescence still longer and more complete than this. But it is conceived, that a doubtful question, one on which human reason may pause, and the human judgment be suspended, in the decision of which the great principles of liberty are not concerned, but the respective powers of those who are equally the representatives of the people, are to be adjusted; if not put at rest by the practice of the government, ought to receive a considerable impression from that practice. An exposition of the constitution, deliberately established by legislative acts, on the faith of which an immense property has been advanced, ought not to be lightly disregarded.

The power now contested was exercised by the first Congress elected under the present constitution. The bill for incorporating the bank of the United States did not steal upon an unsuspecting legislature, and pass unobserved. Its principle was completely understood, and was opposed with equal zeal and ability. After being resisted, first, in the fair and open field of debate, and afterwards, in the executive cabinet, with as much persevering talent as any measure has ever experienced, and being supported by arguments which convinced minds as pure and as intelligent as this country can boast, it became a law. The original act was permitted to expire; but a short experience of the embarrassments to which the refusal to revive it exposed the government, convinced those who were most prejudiced against the measure of its necessity, and induced the passage of the present law. It would require no ordinary share of intrepidity, to assert that a measure adopted under these circumstances, was a bold and plain usurpation, to which the constitution gave no countenance.

These observations belong to the cause; but they are not made under the impression, that, were the question entirely new, the law would be found irreconcilable with the constitution.

In discussing this question, the counsel for the State of Maryland have deemed it of some importance, in the construction of the constitution, to consider that instrument, not as emanating from the people, but as the act of sovereign and independent States. The powers of the general government, it has been said, are delegated by the States, who alone are truly sovereign; and must be exercised in subordination to the States, who alone possess supreme dominion.

It would be difficult to sustain this proposition. The Convention which framed the constitution was indeed elected by the State legislatures. But the instrument, when it came from their hands, was a mere proposal, without obligation, or pretensions to it. It was reported to the then existing Congress of the United States, with a request that it might be "submitted to a Convention of Delegates, chosen in each State by the people thereof, under the recommendation of its Legislature, for their assent and ratification." This mode of proceeding was adopted; and by the Convention, by Congress, and by the State Legislatures, the instrument was submitted to the people. They acted upon it in the only manner in which they can act safely, effectively and wisely, on such a subject, by assembling in Convention. It is true, they assembled in their several States—and where else should they have assembled? No political dreamer was wild enough to think of breaking down the lines which separate the States, and of compounding the American people into one common mass. Of consequence, when they act, they act in their States. But the measures they adopt do not, on that account, cease to be the measures of the people themselves, or become the measures of the State governments.

From these Conventions, the constitution derives its whole authority. The government proceeds directly from the people; is "ordained and established" in the name of the people; and is declared to be ordained, "in order to form a more perfect union, establish justice, insure domestic tranquility, and secure the blessings of liberty to themselves and to their posterity." The assent of the States, in their sovereign capacity, is implied, in calling a Convention, and thus submitting that instrument to the people. But the people were at perfect liberty to accept or reject it; and their act was final. It required not the affirmance, and could not be negatived, by the State governments. The constitution, when thus adopted, was of complete obligation, and bound the State sovereignties.

It has been said, that the people had already surrendered all their powers to the State sovereignties, and had nothing more to give. But, surely, the question whether they may resume and modify the powers granted to government, does not remain to be settled in this country. Much more might the legitimacy of the general government be doubted, had it been created by the States. The powers delegated to the State sovereignties were to be exercised by themselves, not by a distinct and independent sovereignty, created by themselves. To the formation of a league, such as was the confederation, the State sovereignties were certainly competent. But when, "in order to form a more perfect union," it was deemed necessary to change this alliance into an effective government, possessing great and sovereign powers, and acting directly on the people, the necessity of referring it to the people, and of deriving its powers directly from them, was felt and acknowledged by all.

The government of the Union, then (whatever may be the influence of this fact on the case), is, emphatically, and truly, a government of the people. In form, and in substance, it emanates from them. Its powers are granted by them, and are to be exercised directly on them, and for their benefit.

This government is acknowledged by all to be one of enumerated powers. The principle, that it can exercise only the powers granted to it, would seem too apparent to have required to be enforced by all those arguments which its enlightened friends, while it was depending before the people, found it necessary to urge. That principle is now universally admitted. But the question respecting the extent of the powers actually granted, is perpetually arising, and will probably continue to arise, so long as our system shall exist.

In discussing these questions, the conflicting powers of the general and State governments must be brought into view, and the supremacy of their respective laws, when they are in opposition, must be settled.

If any one proposition could command the universal assent of mankind, we might expect it would be this—that the government of the Union, though limited in its powers, is supreme within its sphere of action. This would seem to result necessarily from its nature. It is the government of all; its powers are delegated by all; it represents all, and acts for all. Though any one State may be willing to control its operations, no State is willing to allow others to control them. The nation, on those subjects on which it can act, must necessarily bind its component parts. But this question is not left to mere reason: the people have, in express terms, decided it, by saying, "this constitution, and the laws of the United States, which shall be made in pursuance thereof," "shall be the supreme law of the land," and by requiring that the members of the State legislatures, and the officers of the executive and judicial departments of the States, shall take the oath of fidelity to it.

The government of the United States, then, though limited in its powers, is supreme; and its laws, when made in pursuance of the constitution, form the supreme law of the land, "anything in the constitution or laws of any State to the contrary notwithstanding."

Among the enumerated powers, we do not find that of establishing a bank or creating a corporation. But there is no phrase in the instrument which, like the articles of confederation, excludes incidental or implied powers; and which requires that everything granted shall be expressly and minutely described. Even the 10th amendment, which was framed for the purpose of quieting the excessive jealousies which had been excited, omits the word "expressly," and declares only, that the powers "not delegated to the United States, nor prohibited to the States, are reserved to the States or to the people;" thus leaving the question, whether the particular power which may become the subject of contest, has been delegated to the one government, or prohibited to the other, to depend on a fair construction of the whole instrument. The men who drew and adopted this amendment had experienced the embarrassments resulting from the insertion of this word in the articles of confederation, and probably omitted it to avoid those embarrassments. A constitution, to contain an accurate detail of all the subdivisions of which its great powers will admit, and of all the means by which they may be carried into execution, would partake of the prolixity of a legal code, and could scarcely be embraced by the human mind. It would, probably, never be understood by the public. Its nature, therefore, requires, that only its great outlines should be marked, its important objects designated, and the minor ingredients which compose those objects, be deduced from the nature of the objects themselves. That this idea was entertained by the framers of the American constitution, is not only to be inferred from the nature of the instrument, but from the language. Why else were some of the limitations, found in the ninth section of the 1st article, introduced? It is also, in some degree, warranted, by their having omitted to use any restrictive term which might prevent its receiving a fair and just interpretation. In considering this question, then, we must never forget that it is *a constitution* we are expounding.

Although, among the enumerated powers of government, we do not find the word "bank" or "incorporation," we find the great powers to lay and collect taxes; to borrow money; to regulate commerce; to declare and conduct a war; and to raise and support armies and navies. The sword and the purse, all the external relations, and no inconsiderable portion of the industry of the nation, are entrusted to its government. It can never be pretended, that these vast powers draw after them others of inferior importance, merely because they are inferior. Such an idea can never be advanced. But it may with great reason be contended, that a government, entrusted with such ample powers, on the due execution of which the happiness and prosperity of the nation so vitally depends, must also be entrusted with ample means for their execution. The power being given, it is the interest of the nation to facilitate its execution. It can never be their interest, and cannot be presumed to have been their intention, to clog and embarrass its execution by withholding the most appropriate means. Throughout this vast republic, from the St. Croix to the Gulph of Mexico, from the Atlantic to the Pacific, revenue is to be collected and expended, armies are to be marched and supported. The exigencies of the nation may require, that the treasure raised in the north should be transported to the south, *that* raised in the east conveyed to the west, or that this order should be reversed. Is that construction of the constitution to be preferred which would render these operations difficult, hazardous, and expensive? Can we adopt that construction (unless the words imperiously require it), which would impute to the framers of that instrument, when granting these powers for the public good, the intention of impeding their exercise by withholding a choice of means? If, indeed, such be the mandate of the constitution, we have only to obey; but that instrument does not profess to enumerate the means by which the powers it confers may be executed; nor does it prohibit the creation of a corporation, if the existence of such a being be essential to the beneficial exercise of those powers. It is, then, the subject of fair inquiry, how far such means may be employed.

It is not denied, that the powers given to the government imply the ordinary means of execution. That, for example, of raising revenue, and applying it to national purposes, is admitted to imply the power of conveying money from place to place, as the exigencies of the nation may require, and of employing the usual means of conveyance. But it is denied that the government has its choice of means; or, that it may employ the most convenient means, if, to employ them, it be necessary to erect a corporation.

On what foundation does this argument rest? On this alone: The power of creating a corporation, is one appertaining to sovereignty, and is not expressly conferred on Congress. This is true. But all legislative powers appertain to sovereignty. The original power of giving the law on any subject whatever, is a sovereign power; and if the government of the Union is restrained from creating a corporation, as a means for performing its functions, on the single reason that the creation of a corporation is an act of sovereignty; if the sufficiency of this reason be acknowledged, there would be some difficulty in sustaining the authority of Congress to pass other laws for the accomplishment of the same objects.

The government which has a right to do an act, and has imposed on it the duty of performing that act, must, according to the dictates of reason, be allowed to select the means; and those who contend that it may not select any appropriate means, that one particular mode of effecting the object is excepted, take upon themselves the burden of establishing that exception.

The creation of a corporation, it is said, appertains to sovereignty. This is admitted. But to what portion of sovereignty does it appertain? Does it belong to one more than to another? In America, the powers of sovereignty are divided between the government of the Union, and those of the States. They are each sovereign, with respect to the objects committed to it, and neither sovereign, with respect to the objects committed to the other. We cannot comprehend that train of reasoning which would maintain, that the extent of power granted by the people is to be ascertained, not by the nature and terms of the grant, but by its date. Some State constitutions were formed *before*, some *since* that of the United States. We cannot believe that their relation to each other is in any degree dependent upon this circumstance. Their respective powers must, we think, be precisely the same as if they had been formed at the same time. Had they been formed at the same time, and had the people conferred on the general government the power contained in the constitution, and on the States the whole residuum of power, would it have been asserted that the government of the Union was not sovereign with respect to those objects which were entrusted to it, in relation to which its laws were declared to be supreme? If this could not have been asserted, we cannot well comprehend the process of reasoning which maintains, that a power appertaining to sovereignty cannot be connected with that vast portion of it which is granted to the general government, so far as it is calculated to subserve the legitimate objects of that government. The power of creating a corporation, though appertaining to sovereignty, is not, like the power of making war, or levying taxes, or of regulating commerce, a great substantive and independent power, which cannot be implied as incidental to other powers, or used as a means of executing them. It is never the end for which other powers are exercised, but a means by which other objects are accomplished. No contributions are made to charity for the sake of an incorporation, but a corporation is created to administer the charity; no seminary of learning is instituted in order to be incorporated, but the corporate character is conferred to subserve the purposes of education. No city was ever built with the sole object of being incorporated, but is incorporated as affording the best means of being well governed. The power of creating a corporation is never used for its own sake, but for the purpose of effecting something else. No sufficient reason is, therefore, perceived, why it may not pass as incidental to those powers which are expressly given, if it be a direct mode of executing them.

But the constitution of the United States has not left the right of Congress to employ the necessary means, for the execution of the powers conferred on the government, to general reasoning. To its enumeration of powers is added that of making "all laws which shall be necessary and proper, for carrying into execution the foregoing powers, and all other powers vested by this constitution, in the government of the United States, or in any department thereof."

The counsel for the State of Maryland have urged various arguments, to prove that this clause, though in terms a grant of power, is not so in effect; but is really restrictive of the general right, which might otherwise be implied, of selecting means for executing the enumerated powers.

In support of this proposition, they have found it necessary to contend, that this clause was inserted for the purpose of conferring on Congress the power of making laws. That, without it, doubts might be entertained, whether Congress could exercise its powers in the form of legislation.

But could this be the object for which it was inserted? A government is created by the people, having legislative, executive, and judicial powers. Its legislative powers are vested in a Congress, which is to consist of a Senate and House of Representatives. Each house may determine the rule of its proceedings; and it is declared that every bill which shall have passed both houses, shall, before it becomes a law, be presented to the President of the United States. The 7th section describes the course of proceedings, by which a bill shall become a law; and, then, the 8th section enumerates the powers of Congress. Could it be necessary to say, that a legislature should exercise legislative powers, in the shape of legislation? After allowing each house to prescribe its own course of proceeding, after describing the manner in which a bill should become a law, would it have entered into the mind of a single member of the Convention, that an express power to make laws was necessary to enable the legislature to make them? That a legislature, endowed with legislative powers, can legislate, is a proposition too self-evident to have been questioned.

But the argument on which most reliance is placed, is drawn from that peculiar language of this clause. Congress is not empowered by it to make all laws, which may have relation to the powers conferred on the government, but such only as may be "*necessary and proper*" for carrying them into execution. The word "*necessary*," is considered as controlling the whole sentence, and as limiting the right to pass laws for the execution of the granted powers, to such as are indispensable, and without which the power would be nugatory. That it excludes the choice of means, and leaves to Congress, in each case, that only which is most direct and simple.

Is it true, that this is the sense in which the word "necessary" is always used? Does it always import an absolute physical necessity, so strong, that one thing, to which another may be termed necessary, cannot exist without that other? We think it does not. If reference be had to its use, in the common affairs of the world, or in approved authors, we find that it frequently imports no more than that one thing is convenient, or useful, or essential to another. To employ the means necessary to an end, is generally understood as employing any means calculated to produce the end, and not as being confined to those single means, without which the end would be entirely unattainable. Such is the character of human language, that no word conveys to the mind, in all situations, one single definite idea; and nothing is more common than to use words in a figurative sense. Almost all compositions contain words, which, taken in their rigorous sense, would convey a meaning different from that which is obviously intended. It is essential to just construction, that many words which import something excessive, should be understood in a more mitigated sense—in that sense which common usage justifies. The word "necessary" is of this description. It has not a fixed character peculiar to itself. It admits of all degrees of comparison; and is often connected with other words, which increase or diminish the impression the mind receives of the urgency it imports. A thing may be necessary, very necessary, absolutely or indispensably necessary. To no mind would the same idea be conveyed, by these several phrases. This comment on the word is well illustrated, by the passage cited at the bar, from the 10th section of the 1st article of the constitution. It is, we think, impossible to compare the sentence which prohibits a State from laying "imposts, or duties on imports or exports, except what may be *absolutely* necessary for executing its inspection laws," with that which authorizes Congress "to make all laws which shall be necessary and proper for carrying into execution" the powers of the general government, without feeling a conviction that the convention understood itself to change materially the meaning of the word "necessary," by prefixing the word "absolutely." This word, then, like others, is used in various senses; and, in its construction, the subject, the context, the intention of the person using them, are all to be taken into view.

Let this be done in the case under consideration. The subject is the execution of those great powers on which the welfare of a nation essentially depends. It must have been the intention of those who gave these powers, to insure, so far as human prudence could insure, their beneficial execution. This could not be done by confiding the choice of means to such narrow limits as not to leave it in the power of Congress to adopt any which might be appropriate, and which were conducive to the end. This provision is made in a constitution intended to endure for ages to come, and, consequently, to be adapted to the various *crises* of human affairs. To have prescribed the means by which government should, in all future time, execute its powers, would have been to change, entirely, the character of the instrument, and give it the properties of a legal code. It would have been an unwise attempt to provide, by immutable rules, for exigencies which, if foreseen at all, must have been seen dimly, and which can be best provided for as they occur. To have declared that the best means shall not be used, but those alone without which the power given would be nugatory, would have been to deprive the legislature of the capacity to avail itself of experience, to exercise its reason, and to accommodate its legislation to circumstances. If we apply this principle of construction to any of the powers of the government, we shall find it so pernicious in its operation that we shall be compelled to discard it. The powers vested in Congress may certainly be carried into execution, without prescribing an oath of office. The power to exact this security for the faithful performance of duty, is not given, nor is it indispensably necessary. The different departments may be established; taxes may be imposed and collected; armies and navies may be raised and maintained; and money may be borrowed, without requiring an oath of office. It might be argued, with as much plausibility as other incidental powers have been assailed, that the Convention was not unmindful of this subject. The oath which might be exacted—that of fidelity to the constitution—is prescribed, and no other can be required. Yet, he would be charged with insanity who should contend, that the legislature might not superadd, to the oath directed by the constitution, such other oath of office as its wisdom might suggest.

So, with respect to the whole penal code of the United States: whence arises the power to punish in cases not prescribed by the constitution? All admit, that the government may, legitimately, punish any violation of its laws; and yet, this is not among the enumerated powers of Congress. The right to enforce the observance of law, by punishing its infraction, might be denied with the more plausibility, because it is expressly given in some cases. Congress is empowered "to provide for the punishment of counterfeiting the securities and current coin of the United States," and "to define and punish piracies and felonies committed on the high seas, and offences against the law of nations." The several powers of Congress may exist, in a very imperfect state to be sure, but they may exist and be carried into execution, although no punishment should be inflicted in cases where the right to punish is not expressly given.

Take, for example, the power "to establish post offices and post roads." This power is executed by the single act of making the establishment. But, from this has been inferred the power and duty of carrying the mail along the post road, from one post office to another. And from this implied power, has again been inferred the right to punish those who steal letters from the post office, or rob the mail. It may be said, with some plausibility, that the right to carry the mail, and to punish those who rob it, is not indispensably necessary to the establishment of a post office and post road. This right is indeed essential to the beneficial exercise of the power, but not indispensably necessary to its existence. So, of the punishment of the crimes of stealing or falsifying a record or process of a Court of the United States, or of perjury in such Court. To punish these offences is certainly conducive to the due administration of justice. But courts may exist, and may decide the causes brought before them, though such crimes escape punishment.

The baneful influence of this narrow construction on all the operations of the government, and the absolute impracticability of maintaining it without rendering the government incompetent to its great objects, might be illustrated by numerous examples drawn from the constitution, and from our laws. The good sense of the public has pronounced, without hesitation, that the power of punishment appertains to sovereignty, and may be exercised, whenever the sovereign has a right to act, as incidental to his constitutional powers. It is a means for carrying into execution all sovereign powers, and may be used, although not indispensably necessary. It is a right incidental to the power, and conducive to its beneficial exercise.

If this limited construction of the word "necessary" must be abandoned in order to punish, whence is derived the rule which would reinstate it, when the government would carry its powers into execution by means not vindictive in their nature? If the word "necessary" means "needful," "requisite," "essential," "conducive to," in order to let in the power of punishment for the infraction of law; why is it not equally comprehensive when required to authorize the use of means which facilitate the execution of the powers of government without the infliction of punishment?

In ascertaining the sense in which the word "necessary" is used in this clause of the constitution, we may derive some aid from that with which it is associated. Congress shall have power "to make all laws which shall be necessary and *proper* to carry into execution" the powers of the government. If the word "necessary" was used in that strict and rigorous sense for which the counsel for the State of Maryland contend, it would be an extraordinary departure from the usual course of the human mind, as exhibited in composition, to add a word, the only possible effect of which is to qualify that strict and rigorous meaning; to present to the mind the idea of some choice of means of legislation not straitened and compressed within the narrow limits for which gentlemen contend.

But the argument which most conclusively demonstrates the error of the construction contended for by the counsel for the State of Maryland, is founded on the intention of the Convention, as manifested in the whole clause. To waste time and argument in proving that, without it, Congress might carry its powers into execution, would be not much less idle than to hold a lighted taper to the sun. As little can it be required to prove, that in the absence of this clause, Congress would have some choice of means. That it might employ those which, in its judgment, would most advantageously effect the object to be accomplished. That any means adapted to the end, any means which tended directly to the execution of the constitutional powers of the government, were in themselves constitutional. This clause, as construed by the State of Maryland, would abridge, and almost annihilate this useful and necessary right of the legislature to select its means. That this could not be intended, is, we should think, had it not been already controverted, too apparent for controversy. We think so for the following reasons:

1st. The clause is placed among the powers of Congress, not among the limitations on those powers.

2d. Its terms purport to enlarge, not to diminish the powers vested in the government. It purports to be an additional power, not a restriction on those already granted. No reason has been, or can be assigned for thus concealing an intention to narrow the discretion of the national legislature, under words which purport to enlarge it. The framers of the constitution wished its adoption, and well knew that it would be endangered by its strength, not by its weakness. Had they been capable of using language which would convey to the eye one idea, and, after deep reflection, impress on the mind, another, they would rather have disguised the grant of power, than its limitation. If, then, their intention had been, by this clause, to restrain the free use of means which might otherwise have been implied, that intention would have been inserted in another place, and would have been expressed in terms resembling these. "In carrying into execution the foregoing powers, and all others," & c. "no laws shall be passed but such as are necessary and proper." Had the intention been to make this clause restrictive, it would unquestionably have been so in form as well as in effect.

The result of the most careful and attentive consideration bestowed upon this clause is, that if it does not enlarge, it cannot be construed to restrain the powers of Congress, or to impair the right of the legislature to exercise its best judgment in the selection of measures to carry into execution the constitutional powers of the government. If no other motive for its insertion can be suggested, a sufficient one is found in the desire to remove all doubts respecting the right to legislate on that vast mass of incidental powers which must be involved in the constitution, if that instrument be not a splendid bauble.

We admit, as all must admit, that the powers of the government are limited, and that its limits are not to be transcended. But we think the sound construction of the constitution must allow to the national legislature that discretion, with respect to the means by which the powers it confers are to be carried into execution, which will enable that body to perform the high duties assigned to it, in the manner most beneficial to the people. Let the end be legitimate, let it be within the scope of the constitution, and all means which are appropriate, which are plainly adapted to that end, which are not prohibited, but consist with the letter and spirit of the constitution, are constitutional.

That a corporation must be considered as a means not less usual, not of higher dignity, not more requiring a particular specification than other means, has been sufficiently proved. If we look to the origin of corporations, to the manner in which they have been framed in that government from which we have derived most of our legal principles and ideas, or to the uses to which they have been applied, we find no reason to suppose that a constitution, omitting, and wisely omitting, to enumerate all the means for carrying into execution the great powers vested in government, ought to have specified this. Had it been intended to grant this power as one which should be distinct and independent, to be exercised in any case whatever, it would have found a place among the enumerated powers of the government. But being considered merely as a means, to be employed only for the purpose of carrying into execution the given powers, there could be no motive for particularly mentioning it.

The propriety of this remark would seem to be generally acknowledged by the universal acquiescence in the construction which has been uniformly put on the 3rd section of the 4th article of the constitution. The power to "make all needful rules and regulations respecting the territory or other property belonging to the United States," is not more comprehensive, than the power "to make all laws which shall be necessary and proper for carrying into execution" the powers of the government. Yet all admit the constitutionality of a territorial government, which is a corporate body.

If a corporation may be employed, indiscriminately with other means, to carry into execution the powers of the government, no particular reason can be assigned for excluding the use of a bank, if required for its fiscal operations. To use one, must be within the discretion of Congress, if it be an appropriate mode of executing the powers of government. That it is a convenient, a useful, and essential instrument in the prosecution of its fiscal operations, is not now a subject of controversy. All those who have been concerned in the administration of our finances, have concurred in representing its importance and necessity; and so strongly have they been felt, that statesmen of the first class, whose previous opinions against it had been confirmed by every circumstance which can fix the human judgment, have yielded those opinions to the exigencies of the nation. Under the confederation, Congress, justifying the measure by its necessity, transcended perhaps its powers to obtain the advantage of a bank; and our own legislation attests the universal conviction of the utility of this measure. The time has passed away when it can be necessary to enter into any discussion in order to prove the importance of this instrument, as a means to effect the legitimate objects of the government.

But, were its necessity less apparent, none can deny its being an appropriate measure; and if it is, the degree of its necessity, as has been very justly observed, is to be discussed in another place. Should Congress, in the execution of its powers, adopt measures which are prohibited by the constitution; or should Congress, under the pretext of executing its powers, pass laws for the accomplishment of objects not entrusted to the government; it would become the painful duty of this tribunal, should a case requiring such a decision come before it, to say that such an act was not the law of the land. But where the law is not prohibited, and is really calculated to effect any of the objects entrusted to the government, to undertake here to inquire into the decree of its necessity, would be to pass the line which circumscribes the judicial department, and to tread on legislative ground. This court disclaims all pretensions to such a power.

After this declaration, it can scarcely be necessary to say, that the existence of State banks can have no possible influence on the question. No trace is to be found in the constitution of an intention to create a dependence of the government of the Union on those of the States, for the execution of the great powers assigned to it. Its means are adequate to its ends; and on those means alone was it expected to rely for the accomplishment of its ends. To impose on it the necessity of resorting to means which it cannot control, which another government may furnish or withhold, would render its course precarious, the result of its measures uncertain, and create a dependence on other governments, which might disappoint its most important designs, and is incompatible with the language of the constitution. But were it otherwise, the choice of means implies a right to choose a national bank in preference to State banks, and Congress alone can make the election.

After the most deliberate consideration, it is the unanimous and decided opinion of this Court, that the act to incorporate the Bank of the United States is a law made in pursuance of the constitution, and is a part of the supreme law of the land.

The branches, proceeding from the same stock, and being conducive to the complete accomplishment of the object, are equally constitutional. It would have been unwise to locate them in the charter, and it would be unnecessarily inconvenient to employ the legislative power in making those subordinate arrangements. The great duties of the bank are prescribed; those duties require branches; and the bank itself may, we think, be safely trusted with the selection of places where those branches shall be fixed; reserving always to the government the right to require that a branch shall be located where it may be deemed necessary.

It being the opinion of the Court, that the act incorporating the bank is constitutional; and that the power of establishing a branch in the State of Maryland might be properly exercised by the bank itself, we proceed to inquire—

2. Whether the State of Maryland may, without violating the constitution, tax that branch?

That the power of taxation is one of vital importance; that it is retained by the States; that it is not abridged by the grant of a similar power to the government of the Union; that it is to be concurrently exercised by the two governments: are truths which have never been denied. But, such is the paramount character of the constitution, that its capacity to withdraw any subject from the action of even this power, is admitted. The States are expressly forbidden to lay any duties on imports or exports, except what may be absolutely necessary for executing their inspection laws. If the obligation of this prohibition must be conceded—if it may restrain a

State from the exercise of its taxing power on imports and exports; the same paramount character would seem to restrain, as it certainly may restrain, a State from such other exercise of this power, as is in its nature incompatible with, and repugnant to, the constitutional laws of the Union. A law, absolutely repugnant to another, as entirely repeals that other as if express terms of repeal were used.

On this ground the counsel for the bank place its claim to be exempted from the power of a State to tax its operations. There is no express provision for the case, but the claim has been sustained on a principle which so entirely pervades the constitution, is so intermixed with the materials which compose it, so interwoven with its web, so blended with its texture, as to be incapable of being separated from it, without rending it into shreds.

This great principle is, that the constitution and the laws made in pursuance thereof are supreme; that they control the constitution and laws of the respective States, and cannot be controlled by them. From this, which may be almost termed an axiom, other propositions are deduced as corollaries, on the truth or error of which, and on their application to this case, the cause has been supposed to depend. These are, 1st. that a power to create implies a power to preserve. 2nd. That a power to destroy, if wielded by a different hand, is hostile to, and incompatible with these powers to create and to preserve. 3d. That where this repugnancy exists, that authority which is supreme must control, not yield to that over which it is supreme.

These propositions, as abstract truths, would, perhaps, never be controverted. Their application to this case, however, has been denied; and, both in maintaining the affirmative and the negative, a splendor of eloquence, and strength of argument, seldom, if ever, surpassed, have been displayed.

The power of Congress to create, and of course to continue, the bank, was the subject of the preceding part of this opinion; and is no longer to be considered as questionable.

That the power of taxing it by the States may be exercised so as to destroy it, is too obvious to be denied. But taxation is said to be an absolute power, which acknowledges no other limits than those expressly prescribed in the constitution, and like sovereign power of every other description, is trusted to the discretion of those who use it. But the very terms of this argument admit that the sovereignty of the State, in the article of taxation itself, is subordinate to, and may be controlled by the constitution of the United States. How far it has been controlled by that instrument must be a question of construction. In making this construction, no principle not declared, can be admissible, which would defeat the legitimate operations of a supreme government. It is of the very essence of supremacy to remove all obstacles to its action within its own sphere, and so to modify every power vested in subordinate governments, as to exempt its own operations from their own influence. This effect need not be stated in terms. It is so involved in the declaration of supremacy, so necessarily implied in it, that the expression of it could not make it more certain. We must, therefore, keep it in view while construing the constitution.

The argument on the part of the State of Maryland, is, not that the States may directly resist a law of Congress, but that they may exercise their acknowledged powers upon it, and that the constitution leaves them this right in the confidence that they will not abuse it.

Before we proceed to examine this argument, and to subject it to test of the constitution, we must be permitted to bestow a few considerations on the nature and extent of this original right of taxation, which is acknowledged to remain with the States. It is admitted that the power of taxing the people and their property is essential to the very existence of government, and may be legitimately exercised on the objects to which it is applicable, to the utmost extent to which the government may chuse to carry it. The only security against the abuse of this power, is found in the structure of the government itself. In imposing a tax the legislature acts upon its constituents. This is in general a sufficient security against erroneous and oppressive taxation.

The people of a State, therefore, give to their government a right of taxing themselves and their property, and as the exigencies of government cannot be limited, they prescribe no limits to the exercise of this right, resting confidently on the interest of the legislator, and on the influence of the constituent over their representative, to guard them against its abuse. But the means employed by the government of the Union have no such security, nor is the right of a State to tax them sustained by the same theory. Those means are not given by the people of a particular State, not given by the constituents of the legislature, which claim the right to tax them, but by the people of all the States. They are given by all, for the benefit of all—and upon theory, should be subjected to that government only which belongs to all.

It may be objected to this definition, that the power of taxation is not confined to the people and property of a State. It may be exercised upon every object brought within its jurisdiction.

This is true. But to what source do we trace this right? It is obvious, that it is an incident of sovereignty, and is co-extensive with that to which it is an incident. All subjects over which the sovereign power of a State extends, are objects of taxation; but those over which it does not extend, are, upon the soundest principles, exempt from taxation. This proposition may almost be pronounced self-evident.

The sovereignty of a State extends to every thing which exists by its own authority, or is introduced by its permission; but does it extend to those means which are employed by Congress to carry into execution powers conferred on that body by the people of the United States? We think it demonstrable that it does not. Those powers are not given by the people of a single State. They are given by the people of the United States, to a government whose laws, made in pursuance of the constitution, are declared to be supreme. Consequently, the people of a single State cannot confer a sovereignty which will extend over them.

If we measure the power of taxation residing in a State, by the extent of sovereignty which the people of a single State possess, and can confer on its government, we have an intelligible standard, applicable to every case to which the power may be applied. We have a principle which leaves the power of taxing the people and property of a State unimpaired; which leaves to a State the command of all its resources, and which places beyond its reach, all those powers which are conferred by the people of the United States on the government of the Union, and all those means which are given for the purpose of carrying those powers into execution. We have a principle which is safe for the States, and safe for the Union. We are relieved, as we ought to be, from clashing sovereignty; from interfering powers; from a repugnancy between a right in one government to pull down what there is an acknowledged right in another to build up; from the incompatibility of a right in one government to destroy what there is a right in another to preserve. We are not driven to the perplexing inquiry, so unfit for the judicial department, what degree of taxation is the legitimate use, and what degree may amount to the abuse of the power. The attempt to use it on the means employed by the government of the Union, in pursuance of the constitution, is itself an abuse, because it is the usurpation of a power which the people of a single State cannot give.

We find, then, on just theory, a total failure of this original right to tax the means employed by the government of the Union, for the execution of its powers. The right never existed, and the question whether it has been surrendered, cannot arise.

But, waiving this theory for the present, let us resume the inquiry, whether this power can be exercised by the respective States, consistently with a fair construction of the constitution?

That the power to tax involves the power to destroy; that the power to destroy may defeat and render useless the power to create; that there is a plain repugnance, in conferring on one government a power to control the constitutional measures of another, which other, with respect to those very measures, is declared to be supreme over that which exerts the control, are propositions not to be denied. But all inconsistencies are to be reconciled by the magic of the word CONFIDENCE. Taxation, it is said, does not necessarily and unavoidably destroy. To carry it to the excess of destruction would be an abuse, to presume which, would banish that confidence which is essential to all government.

But is this a case of confidence? Would the people of any one State trust those of another with a power to control the most insignificant operations of their State government? We know they would not. Why, then, should we suppose that the people of any one State should be willing to trust those of another with a power to control the operations of a government to which they have confided their most important and most valuable interests? In the legislature of the Union alone, are all represented. The legislature of the Union alone, therefore, can be trusted by the people with the power of controlling measures which concern all, in the confidence that it will not be abused. This, then, is not a case of confidence, and we must consider it is as it really is.

If we apply the principle for which the State of Maryland contends, to the constitution generally, we shall find it capable of changing totally the character of that instrument. We shall find it capable of arresting all the measures of the government, and of prostrating it at the foot of the States. The American people have declared their constitution, and the laws made in pursuance thereof, to be supreme; but this principle would transfer the supremacy, in fact, to the States.

If the States may tax one instrument, employed by the government in the execution of its powers, they may tax any and every other instrument. They may tax the mail; they may tax the mint; they may tax patent rights; they may tax the papers of the custom-house; they may tax judicial process; they may tax all the means employed by the government, to an excess which would defeat all the ends of government. This was not intended by the American people. They did not design to make their government dependent on the States.

Gentlemen say, they do not claim the right to extend State taxation to these objects. They limit their pretensions to property. But on what principle is this distinction made? Those who make it have furnished no reason for it, and the principle for which they contend denies it. They contend that the power of taxation has no other limit than is found in the 10th section of the 1st article of the constitution; that, with respect to every thing else, the power of the States is supreme, and admits of no control. If this be true, the distinction between property and other subjects to which the power of taxation is applicable, is merely arbitrary, and can never be sustained. This is not all. If the controlling power of the States be established; if their supremacy as to taxation be acknowledged; what is to restrain their exercising this control in any shape they may please to give it? Their sovereignty is not confined to taxation. That is not the only mode in which it might be displayed. The question is, in truth, a question of supremacy; and if the right of the States to tax the means employed by the general government be conceded, the declaration that the constitution, and the laws made in pursuance thereof, shall be the supreme law of the land, is empty and unmeaning declamation.

In the course of the argument, the *Federalist* has been quoted; and the opinions expressed by the authors of that work have been justly supposed to be entitled to great respect in expounding the constitution. No tribute can be paid to them which exceeds their merit; but in applying their opinions to the cases which may arise in the progress of our government, a right to judge of their correctness must be retained; and, to understand the argument, we must examine the proposition it maintains, and the objections against which it is directed. The subject of those numbers, from which passages have been cited, is the unlimited power of taxation which is vested in the general government. The objection to this unlimited power, which the argument seeks to remove, is stated with fullness and clearness. It is, "that an indefinite power of taxation in the latter (the government of the Union) might, and probably would, in time, deprive the former (the government of the States) of the means of providing for their own necessities; and would subject them entirely to the mercy of the national legislature. As the laws of the Union are to become the supreme law of the land; as it is to have power to pass all laws that may be necessary for carrying into execution the authorities with which it is proposed to vest it; the national government might at any time abolish the taxes imposed for State objects, upon the pretence of an interference with its own. It might allege a necessity for doing this, in order to give efficacy to the national revenues; and thus, all the resources of taxation might, by degrees, become the subjects of federal monopoly, to the entire exclusion and destruction of the State governments."

The objections to the constitution which are noticed in these numbers, were to the undefined power of the government to tax, not to the incidental privilege of exempting its own measures from State taxation. The consequences apprehended from this undefined power were, that it would absorb all the objects of taxation, "to the exclusion and destruction of the State governments." The arguments of the *Federalist* are intended to prove the fallacy of these apprehensions; not to prove that the government was incapable of executing any of its powers, without exposing the means it employed to the embarrassments of State taxation. Arguments urged against these objections, and these apprehensions, are to be understood as relating to the points they mean to prove. Had the authors of those excellent essays been asked, whether they contended for that construction of the constitution, which would place within the reach of the States those measures which the government might adopt for the execution of its powers; no man, who has read their instructive pages, will hesitate to admit, that their answer must have been in the negative.

It has also been insisted, that, as the power of taxation in the general and State governments is acknowledged to be concurrent, every argument which would sustain the right of the general government to tax banks chartered by the States, will equally sustain the right of the States to tax banks chartered by the general government.

But the two cases are not on the same reason. The people of all the States have created the general government, and have conferred upon it the general power of taxation. The people of all the States, and the States themselves, are represented in Congress, and, by their representatives, exercise this power. When they tax the chartered institutions of the States, they tax their constituents; and these taxes must be uniform. But, when a State taxes the operations of the government of the United States, it acts upon institutions created, not by their own constituents, but by people over whom they claim no control. It acts upon the measures of a government created by others as well as themselves, for the benefit of others in common with themselves. The difference is that which always exists, and always must exist, between the action of the whole on a part, and the action of a part on the whole—between the laws of a government declared to be supreme, and those of a government which, when in opposition to those laws, is not supreme.

But if the full application of this argument could be admitted, it might bring into question the right of Congress to tax the State banks, and could not prove the rights of the States to tax the Bank of the United States.

The Court has bestowed on this subject its most deliberate consideration. The result is a conviction that the States have no power, by taxation or otherwise, to retard, impede, burden, or in any manner control, the operations of the constitutional laws enacted by Congress to carry into execution the powers vested in the general government. This is, we think, the unavoidable consequence of that supremacy which the constitution has declared.

We are unanimously of opinion, that the law passed by the legislature of Maryland, imposing a tax on the Bank of the United States, is unconstitutional and void.

This opinion does not deprive the States of any resources which they originally possessed. It does not extend to a tax paid by the real property of the bank, in common with the other real property within the State, nor to a tax imposed on the interest which the citizens of Maryland may hold in this institution, in common with other property of the same description throughout the State. But this is a tax on the operations of the bank, and is, consequently, a tax on the operation of an instrument employed by the government of the Union to carry its powers into execution. Such a tax must be unconstitutional. . . .

NOTES

1. Compare Chief Justice Marshall's defense of the constitutionality of the act of Congress creating the Bank of the United States in *McCulloch* with Alexander Hamilton's defense of the Bank in Chapter 1. Do you find them to be strikingly similar? Recall that Chief Justice Marshall's famous defense of judi-

cial review in *Marbury v. Madison* drew heavily on arguments made by Hamilton in *The Federalist No. 78*. Hamilton and Marshall were military aides to General George Washington during the Revolutionary War, including the cold, cruel winter of 1777 to 1778 when Washington's army was camped at Valley Forge, Pennsylvania. Marshall never forgot the weakness of the national government under the Articles of Confederation, and he was consistent in broadly construing national power under the Constitution. In doing so, he often disagreed with his cousin Thomas Jefferson (whose criticism of the Bank is also printed in Chapter 1).

2. Marshall's opinion in *McCulloch* was handed down in 1819, more than twenty-eight years after the Bank had first been created. Marshall begins his opinion by acknowledging that practice and precedent support the Bank's constitutionality, but he does not regard these arguments as dispositive. To the contrary, Marshall engages in something like a *de novo* review of the constitutional issues surrounding the creation of the Bank. He defends the bank with all the types of constitutional argument, or modes of interpretation, including arguments from text, structure, historical purpose, practice and precedent, and policy. See if you can outline the arguments he made, first, for the scope of federal legislative power, and, second, for the proposition that a state law may not interfere with or burden the operation of a legitimate federal law or governmental operation (the two principal holdings of the case). Which of Marshall's structural arguments strike you as most clever? As most correct?

3. Consider carefully as well the second part of Chief Justice Marshall's opinion, addressing Maryland's legislation that purported to impose state-law requirements in the form of a special tax on the operation of the nationally chartered Bank—a tax that ordinary banks in Maryland did not have to pay. Do you agree with his analysis that Maryland could not single out the Bank of the United States for a special tax? Could a state impose a special tax on the incomes of federal officials living within its borders, a tax that state citizens working in the private sector did not have to pay? If a state did enact such a special tax, either on federal officers or instrumentalities within its borders, what remedy would the Constitution afford to the federal government? Is the tax forbidden simply by a structural inference from the federal Constitution, which arguably preempts the state tax? Or, must Congress act affirmatively by passing a law that trumps the discriminatory tax?

If the Constitution does not of its own force preempt discriminatory state taxes on federal officers and instrumentalities, then one could expect them to proliferate like dandelions. Who would have paid the cost of Maryland's special tax on the Bank if it had been upheld by the Court? Would the burden have fallen on the other states? That would make this a popular step for Maryland to take: state officials would in effect be spending the tax revenue raised by the federal government from voters in other states. Would such a result resemble taxation without representation?

Consider an extension of the *McCulloch* holding that the Constitution preempts action by the states that discriminates against federal officers, instrumentalities, and powers. Suppose a plaintiff sues a federal military contractor in tort for the faulty design of escape hatches in military helicopters. The suit is brought in state court, and a jury awards massive damages. Would the award be preempted by the Constitution? See *Boyle v. United Technologies,* 487 U.S. 500 (1988) (finding such an award preempted).

[*Assignment 12*]

B. LEGISLATIVE SPECIFICITY AND DELEGATION: "SHALL BE VESTED IN A CONGRESS OF THE UNITED STATES"

Article I, Section 1: All legislative Powers herein granted shall be vested in a Congress of the United States, which shall consist of a Senate and House of Representatives.

Does Article I's assignment to Congress of the enumerated legislative powers preclude it from delegating the exercise of those powers to the executive branch? The body of law answering this question is sometimes referred to as the "non-delegation doctrine." There are many conceivable answers to this riddle, and it seems that Congress, the courts, and commentators have embraced, at different times, nearly every possible variation.

Consider this riddle for yourself, using the following two case studies. The first is a debate from 1791 in the second session of Congress. The debate concerned whether Congress, in implementing its power under Article I, Section 8 to "establish Post Offices and post Roads," could assign to the president the task of specifying the particular post offices and roads to be built. The second case study is *Mistretta v. United States*, 488 U.S. 361 (1989), which represents the modern near-full retreat from the non-delegation doctrine. *Mistretta* upheld a broad delegation by Congress to the U.S. Sentencing Commission and announced the modern rule: As long as Congress provides an "intelligible principle" to guide the discretion of the delegatee, it may do as it pleases. As you read the positions in the Post Roads Debate and the opinions in *Mistretta*, ask yourself which (if any) of these views make sense. Is there a better one?

The Post Roads Debate

House of Representatives, December 6–8, 1791 (3 Annals of Cong. 229–41)

The House resolved itself into a Committee of the Whole House on the bill for establishing the Post Office and Post Roads within the United States. . . .

Mr. SEDGWICK moved to strike out all that clause of the bill which designated the roads, and to insert, instead thereof, these words, *"by such route as the President of the United States shall, from time to time, cause to be established."* . . . It had appeared, he said, to be the sense of the House, when this subject was formerly under consideration, that the demarkation of the particular roads should be intrusted to the Executive; the only difference had been with respect to the mode of expression—but the effect was still to have been the same—some gentlemen thinking it best to leave the details of this business entirely to the supreme Executive, others wishing to name the Postmaster General. The members of the House could not be supposed to possess every information that might be requisite on this subject, and their opinions were liable to be biassed by local interests. He had ever considered it as highly incumbent on the house to give the people every possible information on public concerns; but in this, as in every other subject, he thought it sufficient that the House should establish the principle, and then leave it to the Executive to carry it into effect.

Mr. LIVERMORE observed that the Legislative body being empowered by the Constitution "to establish post offices and post roads," it is as clearly their duty to designate the roads as to establish the offices; and he did not think they could with propriety delegate that power, which they were themselves appointed to exercise. Some gentlemen, he knew, were of opinion that the business of the United States could be better transacted by a single person than by many; but this was not the intention of the Constitution. It was provided that the Government should be administered by Representatives, of the people's choice; so that every man, who has the right of voting, shall be in some measure concerned in making every law for the United States. The establishment of post roads he considered as a very important object. . . . If the post office were to be regulated by the will of a single person, the dissemination of intelligence might be impeded, and the people kept entirely in the dark with respect to the transactions of Government; or the Postmaster, if vested with the whole power, might branch out the offices to such a degree as to make them prove a heavy burden to the United States. . . . The most material point, in his opinion, was to determine the road itself; if the House gave up that, they might as well leave all the rest of the business to the discretion of the Postmaster, and permit him to settle the rates of postage, and every other particular relative to the post office, by saying, at once, "there shall be a Postmaster General, who shall have the whole government of the post office, under such regulations as he from time to time shall be pleased to enact."

Mr. SEDGWICK felt himself by no means disposed to resign all the business of the House to the President, or to any one else; but he thought that the Executive part of the business ought to be left to Executive officers. He did not, for his part, know the particular circumstances of population, geography, & c., which had been taken into the calculation by the select committee, when they pointed out the roads delineated in the bill; but he would ask, whether they understood the subject so thoroughly as the Executive officer would, who being responsible to the people for the proper discharge of the trust reposed in him, must use his utmost diligence in order to a satisfactory execution of the delegated power? As to the constitutionality of this delegation, it was admitted by the committee themselves who brought in the bill. . . .

Congress, he observed, are authorized not only to establish post offices and post roads, but also to borrow money; but is it understood that Congress are to go in a body to borrow every sum that may he requisite? Is it not rather their office to determine the principle on which the business is to be conducted, and then delegate the power of carrying their resolves into execution? They are also empowered to coin money, and if no part of their power be delegable, he did not know but they might be obliged to turn coiners, and work in the Mint themselves. Nay, they must even act the part of executioners, in punishing piracies committed on the high seas. In the delegation of power, the whole purpose, in his opinion, is answered, when the rules by which the business is to be conducted are pointed out by law; nor could he discover anything in the Constitution to restrict the House from adopting this mode of conducting business.

Mr. HARTLEY.—I cannot agree with the gentleman from Massachusetts, that as often as this business had been agitated, there had been a majority in the House in favor of leaving it to the Executive to designate the post roads. Nay, so far as my recollection (which is perhaps not so good as that gentleman's) serves me, we uniformly have had a majority for Congress to point out the post roads. . . . The Constitution seems to have intended that we should exercise all the powers respecting the establishing [of] post roads we are capable of; but the gentleman says we are not competent to this duty, that it must be intrusted to the Executive. . . . Sir, in many questions concerning the property or geography of the United States, we had full information on this floor from every quarter. The people's interests and circumstances have been known, however distinctly or differently situated. . . . We represent the people[;] we are constitutionally vested with the power of determining upon the establishment of post roads; and, as I understand at present, ought not to delegate the power to any other person.

A General Post Office is intended to be established by the bill, and the collection of the revenue is put under the superintendence of a Postmaster General; the minutiae is submitted to him. I should imagine there ought to be a limitation of the law in point of time, say three, four, or five years; when we come to the proper place, a motion to that purpose may be made. No one in the United States has a greater respect for the President than myself, and I hold that the several Departments are filled with gentlemen of the first abilities and fitness, but we are not to confine ourselves to a view of the moment. This bill has the complexion of a perpetual law; we must have some regard to consequences. If the amendment takes place, the office as well as revenue will be thrown into the power of the Executive, who may increase the roads and offices as far as the revenues go. The revenue of the post office is at present not great, but if proper seeds are now sown, it may hereafter be productive. In Great Britain, much has been obtained from the post office, and most of the European nations count upon it as a considerable branch of revenue. Will it be prudent for us to grant this power to the Executive, in the latitude contended for? We must not suppose that this country will always remain incorrupt; we shall share the fate of other nations. Through the medium of the post office a weighty influence may be obtained by the Executive; this is guarded against in England by prohibiting officers in the Post Office Department from interfering at elections. There is no such guard or caution in the present bill. . . . This is a law of experiment, let us try it a few years. If, upon experience, we find ourselves incompetent to the duty, we must (if the Constitution will admit) grant the power to the Executive; or, if the Constitution will not allow such a delegation, submit the article for amendment in a constitutional way. I am against the amendment.

Mr. B. BOURNE was in favor of the amendment, which he thought both expedient and constitutional. In speaking of *post offices and post roads* the Constitution, he observed, speaks in general terms, as it does of *a mint, excises, & c.* In passing the excise law, the House, not thinking themselves possessed of sufficient information, empowered the President to mark out the districts and surveys; and if they had a right to delegate such power to the Executive, the further delegation of the power of marking out the roads for the conveyance of the mail, could hardly be thought dangerous. The Constitution meant no more than that Congress should possess the exclusive right of doing that, by themselves or by any other person, which amounts to the same thing. The business he thought much more likely to be well executed by the President, or the Postmaster General, than by Congress. He had himself been of the committee who framed the bill, but could not tell whether the roads marked out in it were better than any other, except so far as relates to the State which he represents; and he imagined the other members of the committee were in a similar predicament. The President having opportunities of obtaining information from the different members of the House, from the Postmaster General, and from others, will be more competent to determine the proper road. It will be occasionally necessary to change the route, and lay out new roads, and he could see no inconvenience from intrusting either the President or the Postmaster General with the necessary powers for these purposes. At all events, the House could guard against any apprehended danger, by the insertion of such a clause as had been proposed [by Mr. HARTLEY], limiting the operation of the bill to three, four, or five years. At the expiration of that term, the power would revert to Congress, and they might then retain the exercise of it in their own hands, if they found that any improper use had been made of it.

Mr. WHITE made several observations on the expediency and constitutionality of the measure. No individual could possess an equal share of information with that House on the subject of the geography of the United States. He disapproved of the amendment for many other reasons, and particularly its approximation to the custom of England. Such advances towards Monarchy, if not checked in season, he was apprehensive would tend to unhinge the present Government. If this Government retains its present Republican form, it will be owing to the members of this House. It is easy to see what hand could be made of the post offices, if ever they are under the direction of an improper person. At the time of a general election, for instance, how easy would it be for this man to dictate to particular towns and villages, "If you do not send such a man to Congress, you shall have no post office; but if you elect my friend, you shall have a post office, and the roads shall be run agreeably to your wishes." Another improper use may be made of this power by the interception of letters, and checking the regular channel of information throughout the country. Upon the whole, he was clearly for rejecting the motion for striking out the words in the bill. . . .

Mr. PAGE.—If the motion before the committee succeeds, I shall make one which will save a deal of time and money, by making a short session of it; for if this House can, with propriety, leave the business of the post office to the President, it may leave to him any other business of legislation; and I may move to adjourn and leave all the objects of legislation to his sole consideration and direction. But how the President should be better acquainted with the proper places for post offices and post roads than the Representatives of the people, I cannot conceive. In Virginia, for instance, cannot the ten Representatives say, with more certainty, what post roads would be proper in that State than any one man? I look upon the motion as unconstitutional, and if it were not so, as having a mischievous tendency, which I am willing to believe the member who made it is not aware of. . . .

Mr. STEELE would not take up the time of the House in considering whether the motion was constitutional or not; but he was apprehensive it would be burdensome to impose the duty on the President, who must feel very disagreeable to hear that after he had exerted his utmost abilities to give satisfaction, discontents had taken place. . . .

Mr. VINING said, that since this subject had been before the last House, during the recess, he had seen many lights thrown on it, and he was convinced that the members were as fully competent to judge of the matter as any one man could be; this, he thought a fact not now to be disputed, as well as that more satisfaction would be given to the country in general. There is no analogy between the United States and Great Britain, when the subject of the post roads and post offices are to be considered. This country, from its great extent and uncultivated state, as well as from a thousand other causes, is not at all similar to the situation of Great Britain; therefore, any attempt to imitate their regulations would be improper. With regard to the regulation being given to the President, two things should be considered; to a good President it would be a burden; to a bad President, a dangerous power of esstablishing [sic] offices and roads in those places only where his interest would be promoted, and removing others of long standing, in order to harrass [sic] those he might suppose inimical to his ambitious views. The Constitution has certainly given us the power of establishing posts and roads, and it is not even implied that it should be transferred to the President; his powers are well defined; we create offices, and he fills them with such persons as he approves of, with the advice of the Senate. . . .

Mr. BARNWELL was not surprised that a diversity of opinions should prevail on such a subject; but that there should be any question respecting the constitutionality of the amendment astonished him. It was very natural to suppose members from the same State would differ in opinion, and this showed the greater degree of necessity there was to vest the power in the hands of a high responsible officer to determine upon it; for, by doing so, there would be less partiality exhibited in the delineation of the roads, & c. But, if left to the House, it would be almost impossible to reconcile any line to all parties; for the members from each State would probably be guided more by the principle of domestic convenience than by a sense of general good. In reply to Mr. V.'s argument, that it would be a burden to a good President, he thought it would be a pleasure to him to render service to his country. Upon the whole, he was in favor of Mr. SEDGWICK'S motion. . . .

Mr. BENSON observed, that the constitutionality of the amendment is denied, and it is said that the Legislature alone is competent to establish post offices and post roads; notwithstanding this, there is not a single post office designated by the bill. Much has been observed respecting the Legislative and Executive powers, and the committee are cautioned against delegating the powers of the Legislature to the Supreme Executive. Without attempting a definition of their powers, or determining their respective limits, which he conceived it was extremely difficult to do, he would only observe that much must necessarily be left to the discretion of the Legislature. He was very doubtful whether it would ever be in the power of the House to form any bill that would give satisfaction. This he spoke from experience; for it had been often tried in the old Congress, and was as often defeated by the partial and local clauses proposed by the different members. For these reasons, he believed it would be better to delegate the power, and let the regulations be made by the President, than to be enacting supplementary laws year after year, at the instance of individual members.

The Committee now rose, and obtained leave to sit again. . . .

Wednesday, December 7. . . .

The House again resolved itself into a Committee of the Whole House on the bill establishing the Post Office and Post Roads, within the United States. Mr. SEDGWICK'S motion being under consideration—. . .

Mr. MADISON said, that the arguments which are offered by the gentleman who are in favor of the amendment, appear to be drawn rather from theory than any line of practice which had hitherto governed the House. However difficult it may be to determine with precision the exact boundaries of the Legislative and Executive powers, he was of opinion that those arguments were not well founded, for they admit of such construction as will lead to blending those powers so as to leave no line of separation whatever. The greatest obstacle to the due exercise of the powers vested in the Legislature by the bill, which has been mentioned, is the difficulty of accommodating the regulations to the various interests of the different parts of the Union; and this is said to be almost impracticable. But it may be remembered, that similar embarrassments appeared when the impost and tonnage bills were under consideration; on those subjects, the members were obliged to be governed, in a great degree, by mutual information and reciprocal confidence. In respect to the establishment and arrangements of the different ports of entry and clearance, and other objects, that was a business of much greater importance and difficulty than this; but it was accomplished. . . . Where is the necessity of departing from the principles of the Constitution in respect to the post office and post roads, more than in all other cases? The subject is expressly committed to Legislative determination by the Constitution. If the second section of the bill requires amendment, it can be rectified when it comes before us; and with respect to future cases, should there be a necessity for additional post roads, they can be provided for by supplementary laws; and therefore no reason on that account can be urged for delaying the provision proposed by the bill. He concluded by saying, that there did not appear to be any necessity for alienating the powers of the House; and that if this should take place, it would be a violation of the Constitution.

Mr. SEDGWICK would make a few observations, which he felt himself obliged to submit to the consideration of the Committee as well to defend himself as his motion from the unwarrantable attacks which gentlemen had made on both. . . . The powers of the Constitution, he was sorry to say, were made in debate to extend or contract, as seemed, for the time being, to suit the convenience of the arguments of gentlemen. . . . It was true, as had been observed by his friend from New York, [Mr. BENSON] that it was impossible precisely to define a boundary line between the business of Legislative and Executive; but from his own experience, as a public man, and from reflection, he was induced to believe, that as a general rule, the establishment of principles was the peculiar province of the former, and the execution of them, that of the latter. He would, therefore, at least, generally, as much, as possible, avoid going into detail. . . . From the nature of the business to be transacted, he had drawn his conclusion; he thought an Executive officer, responsible to the public for the performance of an important and interesting trust, would inquire with more scrupulous caution, and decide with more justice, than could be expected from a popular assembly, who, from the nature of things, would be more remiss than consisted with a just determination; and he appealed to those gentlemen who were members of the last House, for a recollection of that apathy and torpor which prevailed on a former attempt to demark the post roads. . . . Gentlemen had spoken in strong terms of the disinterestedness, information, and respectability of the members of the House, and of the popular confidence which resulted therefrom. No man had a more respectable opinion of the Representatives of the people than himself; he need not, however, observe to them, that they were men, subject to like passions and imperfections with their fellow-citizens. It could not have escaped the reflection of the committee, that the gentlemen who composed it, had a very important interest in establishing the directions of the post; that on the declarations of men thus interested, we must rely for the justness of our ultimate conclusions; on evidence of interested individuals, individuals who are, by their relation to the subject of inquiry, excluded, on principles of law, from all credit, must we rely for a knowledge of those facts which are to direct our judgment.

Mr. BOUDINOT and Mr. GERRY made some remarks, and then the question being taken, Mr. SEDGWICK'S motion was negatived.

Mistretta v. United States
488 U.S. 361 (1989)

■ JUSTICE BLACKMUN delivered the opinion of the Court.

In this litigation, we granted certiorari . . . to consider the constitutionality of the Sentencing Guidelines promulgated by the United States Sentencing Commission. The Commission is a body created under the Sentencing Reform Act of 1984 . . .

The Commission is established "as an independent commission in the judicial branch of the United States." It has seven voting members (one of whom is the Chairman) appointed by the President "by and with the advice and consent of the Senate." "At least three of the members shall be Federal judges selected after considering a list of six judges recommended to the President by the Judicial Conference of the United States." No more than four members of the Commission shall be members of the same political party. The Attorney General, or his designee, is an ex officio nonvoting member. The Chairman and other members of the Commission are subject to removal by the President "only for neglect of duty or malfeasance in office or for other good cause shown." Except for initial staggering of terms, a voting member serves for six years and may not serve more than two full terms. . . .

Petitioner argues that in delegating the power to promulgate sentencing guidelines for every federal criminal offense to an independent Sentencing Commission, Congress has granted the Commission excessive legislative discretion in violation of the constitutionally based nondelegation doctrine. We do not agree.

The nondelegation doctrine is rooted in the principle of separation of powers that underlies our tripartite system of Government. The Constitution provides that "[a]ll legislative Powers herein granted shall be vested in a Congress of the United States," U.S. Const., Art. I, § 1, and we long have insisted that "the integrity and maintenance of the system of government ordained by the Constitution" mandate that Congress generally cannot delegate its legislative power to another Branch. *Field v. Clark*, 143 U.S. 649, 692 (1892). We also have recognized, however, that the separation-of-powers principle, and the nondelegation doctrine in particular, do not prevent Congress from obtaining the assistance of its coordinate Branches. In a passage now enshrined in our jurisprudence, Chief Justice Taft, writing for the Court, explained our approach to such cooperative ventures: "In determining what [Congress] may do in seeking assistance from another branch, the extent and character of that assistance must be fixed according to common sense and the inherent necessities of the government coordination." *J. W. Hampton, Jr., & Co. v. United States*, 276 U.S. 394, 406 (1928). So long as Congress "shall lay down by legislative act an intelligible principle to which the person or body authorized to [exercise the delegated authority] is directed to conform, such legislative action is not a forbidden delegation of legislative power." *Id.*, at 409.

Applying this "intelligible principle" test to congressional delegations, our jurisprudence has been driven by a practical understanding that in our increasingly complex society, replete with ever changing and more technical problems, Congress simply cannot do its job absent an ability to delegate power under broad general directives. . . .

Until 1935, this Court never struck down a challenged statute on delegation grounds. After invalidating in 1935 two statutes as excessive delegations, see *A.L.A. Schechter Poultry Corp. v. United States*, 295 U.S. 495, and *Panama Refining Co. v. Ryan*, 293 U.S. 388, we have upheld, again without deviation, Congress' ability to delegate power under broad standards.

In light of our approval of these broad delegations, we harbor no doubt that Congress' delegation of authority to the Sentencing Commission is sufficiently specific and detailed to meet constitutional requirements. Congress charged the Commission with three goals: to "assure the meeting of the purposes of sentencing as set forth" in the Act; to "provide certainty and fairness in meeting the purposes of sentencing, avoiding unwarranted sentencing disparities among defendants with similar records . . . while maintaining sufficient flexibility to permit individualized sentences," where appropriate; and to "reflect, to the extent practicable, advancement in knowledge of human behavior as it relates to the criminal justice process." Congress further specified four "purposes" of sentencing that the Commission must pursue in carrying out its mandate: "to reflect the seriousness of the offense, to promote respect for the law, and to provide just punishment for the offense"; "to afford adequate deterrence to criminal conduct"; "to protect the public from further crimes of the defendant"; and "to provide the defendant with needed . . . correctional treatment."

In addition, Congress prescribed the specific tool—the guidelines system—for the Commission to use in regulating sentencing. More particularly, Congress directed the Commission to develop a system of "sentencing ranges" applicable "for each category of offense involving each category of defendant." Congress instructed the Commission that these sentencing ranges must be consistent with pertinent provisions of Title 18 of the United States Code and could not include sentences in excess of the statutory maxima. Congress also required that for sentences of imprisonment, "the maximum of the range established for such a term shall not exceed the minimum of that range by more than the greater of 25 percent or 6 months, except that, if the minimum term of the range is 30 years or more, the maximum may be life imprisonment." Moreover, Congress directed the Commission to use current average sentences "as a starting point" for its structuring of the sentencing ranges.

To guide the Commission in its formulation of offense categories, Congress directed it to consider seven factors: the grade of the offense; the aggravating and mitigating circumstances of the crime; the nature and degree of the harm caused by the crime; the community view of the gravity of the offense; the public concern generated by the crime; the deterrent effect that a particular sentence may have on others; and the current incidence of the offense. Congress set forth 11 factors for the Commission to consider in establishing categories of defendants. These include the offender's age, education, vocational skills, mental and emotional condition, physical condition (including drug dependence), previous employment record, family ties and responsibilities, community ties, role in the offense, criminal history, and degree of dependence upon crime for a livelihood. Congress also prohibited the Commission from considering the "race, sex, national origin, creed, and socioeconomic status of offenders," and instructed that the guidelines should reflect the "general inappropriateness" of considering certain other factors, such as current unemployment, that might serve as proxies for forbidden factors.

In addition to these overarching constraints, Congress provided even more detailed guidance to the Commission about categories of offenses and offender characteristics. . . .

We cannot dispute petitioner's contention that the Commission enjoys significant discretion in formulating guidelines. The Commission does have discretionary authority to determine the relative severity of federal crimes and to assess the relative weight of the offender characteristics that Congress listed for the Commission to consider. See §§ 994(c) and (d) (Commission instructed to consider enumerated factors as it deems them to be relevant). The Commission also has significant discretion to determine which crimes have been punished too leniently, and which too severely. Congress has called upon the Commission to exercise its judgment about which types of crimes and which types of criminals are to be considered similar for the purposes of sentencing.

But our cases do not at all suggest that delegations of this type may not carry with them the need to exercise judgment on matters of policy. In *Yakus v. United States*, 321 U.S. 414 (1944), the Court upheld a delegation to the Price Administrator to fix commodity prices that "in his judgment will be generally fair and equitable and will effectuate the purposes of this Act" to stabilize prices and avert speculation. In *National Broadcasting Co. v. United States*, 319 U.S. 190 (1943), we upheld a delegation to the Federal Communications Commission granting it the authority to promulgate regulations in accordance with its view of the "public interest." . . .

Congress has met [the applicable] standard here. The Act sets forth more than merely an "intelligible principle" or minimal standards. One court has aptly put it: "The statute outlines the policies which prompted establishment of the Commission, explains what the Commission should do and how it should do it, and sets out specific directives to govern particular situations." *United States v. Chambless*, 680 F. Supp. 793, 796 (E.D. La. 1988).

Developing proportionate penalties for hundreds of different crimes by a virtually limitless array of offenders is precisely the sort of intricate, labor-intensive task for which delegation to an expert body is especially appropriate. Although Congress has delegated significant discretion to the Commission to draw judgments from its analysis of existing sentencing practice and alternative sentencing models, "Congress is not confined to that method of executing its policy which involves the least possible delegation of discretion to administrative officers." *Yakus v. United States*, 321 U.S., at 425–426. We have no doubt that in the hands of the Commission "the criteria which Congress has supplied are wholly adequate for carrying out the general policy and purpose" of the Act. *Sunshine Coal Co. v. Adkins*, 310 U.S. 381, 398 (1940). . . .

■ JUSTICE SCALIA, dissenting.

While the products of the Sentencing Commission's labors have been given the modest name "Guidelines," they have the force and effect of laws, prescribing the sentences criminal defendants are to receive. A judge who disregards them will be reversed. I dissent from today's decision because I can find no place within our constitutional system for an agency created by Congress to exercise no governmental power other than the making of laws.

There is no doubt that the Sentencing Commission has established significant, legally binding prescriptions governing application of governmental power against private individuals—indeed, application of the ultimate governmental power, short of capital punishment.[1] Statutorily permissible sentences for particular crimes cover as broad a range as zero years to life, see, *e.g.*, 18 U.S.C. § 1201 (1982 ed. and Supp. IV) (kidnapping), and within those ranges the Commission was given broad discretion to prescribe the "correct" sentence. Average prior sentences were to be a starting point for the Commission's inquiry, but it could and regularly did deviate from those averages as it thought appropriate. It chose, for example, to prescribe substantial increases over average prior sentences for white-collar crimes such as public corruption, antitrust violations, and tax evasion. For antitrust violations, before the Guidelines, only 39% of those convicted served any imprisonment, and the average imprisonment was only 45 days, whereas the Guidelines prescribe base sentences (for defendants with no prior criminal conviction) ranging from 2–to–8 months to 10–to–16 months, depending upon the volume of commerce involved.

The Commission also determined when probation was permissible, imposing a strict system of controls because of its judgment that probation had been used for an "inappropriately high percentage of offenders guilty of certain economic crimes." Moreover, the Commission had free rein in determining whether statutorily authorized fines should be imposed in addition to imprisonment, and if so, in what amounts. It ultimately decided that every nonindigent offender should pay a fine according to a schedule devised by the Commission. Congress also gave the Commission discretion to determine whether 7 specified characteristics of offenses, and 11 specified characteristics of offenders, "have any relevance," and should be included among the factors varying the sentence. Of the latter, it included only three among the factors required to be considered, and declared the remainder not ordinarily relevant.

It should be apparent from the above that the decisions made by the Commission are far from technical, but are heavily laden (or ought to be) with value judgments and policy assessments. This fact is sharply reflected in the Commission's product, as described by the dissenting Commissioner:

> Under the guidelines, the judge could give the same sentence for abusive sexual contact that puts the child in fear as for unlawfully entering or remaining in the United States. Similarly, the guidelines permit equivalent sentences for the following pairs of offenses: drug trafficking and a violation of the Wild Free–Roaming Horses and Burros Act; arson with a destructive device and failure to surrender a cancelled naturalization certificate; operation of a common carrier under the influence of drugs that causes injury and alteration of one motor vehicle identification number; illegal trafficking in explosives and trespass; interference with a flight attendant and unlawful conduct relating to contraband cigarettes; aggravated assault and smuggling $11,000 worth of fish.

---

[1] It is even arguable that the Commission has authority to establish guidelines and procedures for imposing the death penalty, thus reinstituting that sanction under federal statutes for which (by reason of our recent decisions) it has been thought unusable because of constitutionally inadequate procedures. The Justice Department believes such authority exists, and has encouraged the Commission to exercise it.

Dissenting View of Commissioner Paul H. Robinson on the Promulgation of the Sentencing Guidelines by the United States Sentencing Commission 6–7 (May 1, 1987).

Petitioner's most fundamental and far-reaching challenge to the Commission is that Congress' commitment of such broad policy responsibility to any institution is an unconstitutional delegation of legislative power. It is difficult to imagine a principle more essential to democratic government than that upon which the doctrine of unconstitutional delegation is founded: Except in a few areas constitutionally committed to the Executive Branch, the basic policy decisions governing society are to be made by the Legislature. Our members of Congress could not, even if they wished, vote all power to the President and adjourn *sine die*.

But while the doctrine of unconstitutional delegation is unquestionably a fundamental element of our constitutional system, it is not an element readily enforceable by the courts. Once it is conceded, as it must be, that no statute can be entirely precise, and that some judgments, even some judgments involving policy considerations, must be left to the officers executing the law and to the judges applying it, the debate over unconstitutional delegation becomes a debate not over a point of principle but over a question of degree. As Chief Justice Taft expressed the point for the Court in the landmark case of *J. W. Hampton, Jr., & Co. v. United States*, 276 U.S. 394, 406 (1928), the limits of delegation "must be fixed according to common sense and the inherent necessities of the governmental coordination." Since Congress is no less endowed with common sense than we are, and better equipped to inform itself of the "necessities" of government; and since the factors bearing upon those necessities are both multifarious and (in the nonpartisan sense) highly political—including, for example, whether the Nation is at war, see *Yakus v. United States*, 321 U.S. 414 (1944), or whether for other reasons "emergency is instinct in the situation"—it is small wonder that we have almost never felt qualified to second-guess Congress regarding the permissible degree of policy judgment that can be left to those executing or applying the law. As the Court points out, we have invoked the doctrine of unconstitutional delegation to invalidate a law only twice in our history, over half a century ago. See *Panama Refining Co. v. Ryan*, 293 U.S. 388 (1935); *A.L.A. Schechter Poultry Corp. v. United States*, 295 U.S. 495 (1935). What legislated standard, one must wonder, can possibly be too vague to survive judicial scrutiny, when we have repeatedly upheld, in various contexts, a "public interest" standard?

In short, I fully agree with the Court's rejection of petitioner's contention that the doctrine of unconstitutional delegation of legislative authority has been violated because of the lack of intelligible, congressionally prescribed standards to guide the Commission.

Precisely because the scope of delegation is largely uncontrollable by the courts, we must be particularly rigorous in preserving the Constitution's structural restrictions that deter excessive delegation. The major one, it seems to me, is that the power to make law cannot be exercised by anyone other than Congress, except in conjunction with the lawful exercise of executive or judicial power.

The whole theory of *lawful* congressional "delegation" is not that Congress is sometimes too busy or too divided and can therefore assign its responsibility of making law to someone else; but rather that a certain degree of discretion, and thus of lawmaking, *inheres* in most executive or judicial action, and it is up to Congress, by the relative specificity or generality of its statutory commands, to determine—up to a point—how small or how large that degree shall be. Thus, the courts could be given the power to say precisely what constitutes a "restraint of trade" or to adopt rules of procedure, or to prescribe by rule the manner in which their officers shall execute their judgments, because that "lawmaking" was ancillary to their exercise of judicial powers. And the Executive could be given the power to adopt policies and rules specifying in detail what radio and television licenses will be in the "public interest, convenience or necessity," because that was ancillary to the exercise of its executive powers in granting and policing licenses and making a "fair and equitable allocation" of the electromagnetic spectrum.[2] Or to take examples closer to the case before us: Trial judges could be given the power to determine what factors justify a greater or lesser sentence within the statutorily prescribed limits because that was ancillary to their exercise of the judicial power of pronouncing sentence upon individual defendants. And the President, through the Parole Commission subject to his appointment and removal, could be given the power to issue Guidelines specifying when parole would be available, because that was ancillary to the President's exercise of the executive power to hold and release federal prisoners.

As Justice Harlan wrote for the Court in *Field v. Clark*, 143 U.S. 649 (1892) (emphasis added):

> The true distinction . . . is between the delegation of power to make the law, which necessarily involves a discretion as to what it shall be, and conferring authority or discretion *as to its execution*, to be exercised under and in pursuance of the law. The first cannot be done; to the latter no valid objection can be made.

> Half the statutes on our books are in the alternative, depending on the discretion of some person or persons to whom is confided the duty of determining *whether the proper occasion exists for executing them*. But it cannot be said that the exercise of such discretion is the making of the law.

. . . The focus of controversy, in the long line of our so-called excessive delegation cases, has been whether the *degree* of generality contained in the authorization for exercise of executive or judicial powers in a particular field is so unacceptably high as to *amount to* a delegation of legislative powers. I say "so-called excessive delegation" because although that convenient terminology is often used, what is really at issue is whether there has been *any* delegation of legislative power, which occurs (rarely) when Congress authorizes the exercise of executive or judicial power without adequate standards. Strictly speaking, there is *no* acceptable delegation of legislative power. As John Locke put it almost 300 years ago, "[t]he power of the *legislative* being derived from the people by a positive voluntary grant and institution, can be no other, than what the positive grant conveyed, which being only to make *laws*, and not to make *legislators*, the *legislative* can have no power to transfer their authority of making laws, and place it in other hands." J. Locke, Second Treatise of Government 87 (R. Cox ed. 1982) (emphasis added). Or as we have less epigrammatically said: "That Congress cannot delegate legislative power to the President is a principle universally recognized as vital to the integrity and maintenance of the

---

[2] An executive agency can, of course, be created with no power other than the making of rules, as long as that agency is subject to the control of the President and the President has executive authority related to the rulemaking. In such circumstances, the rulemaking is ultimately ancillary to the President's executive powers.

system of government ordained by the Constitution." *Field v. Clark, supra,* at 692. In the present case, however, a pure delegation of legislative power is precisely what we have before us. It is irrelevant whether the standards are adequate, because they are not standards related to the exercise of executive or judicial powers; they are, plainly and simply, standards for further legislation.

The lawmaking function of the Sentencing Commission is completely divorced from any responsibility for execution of the law or adjudication of private rights under the law. It is divorced from responsibility for execution of the law not only because the Commission is not said to be "located in the Executive Branch" (as I shall discuss presently, I doubt whether Congress can "locate" an entity within one Branch or another for constitutional purposes by merely saying so); but, more importantly, because the Commission neither exercises any executive power on its own, nor is subject to the control of the President who does. The only functions it performs, apart from prescribing the law, conducting the investigations useful and necessary for prescribing the law, and clarifying the intended application of the law that it prescribes, are data collection and intragovernmental advice giving and education. These latter activities—similar to functions performed by congressional agencies and even congressional staff—neither determine nor affect private rights, and do not constitute an exercise of governmental power. See *Humphrey's Executor v. United States,* 295 U.S. 602, 628 (1935). And the Commission's lawmaking is completely divorced from the exercise of judicial powers since, not being a court, it has no judicial powers itself, nor is it subject to the control of any other body with judicial powers. The power to make law at issue here, in other words, is not ancillary but quite naked. The situation is no different in principle from what would exist if Congress gave the same power of writing sentencing laws to a congressional agency such as the General Accounting Office, or to members of its staff.

The delegation of lawmaking authority to the Commission is, in short, unsupported by any legitimating theory to explain why it is not a delegation of legislative power. To disregard structural legitimacy is wrong in itself—but since structure has purpose, the disregard also has adverse practical consequences. In this case, as suggested earlier, the consequence is to facilitate and encourage judicially uncontrollable delegation. Until our decision last Term in *Morrison v. Olson,* 487 U.S. 654 (1988), it could have been said that Congress could delegate lawmaking authority only at the expense of increasing the power of either the President or the courts. Most often, as a practical matter, it would be the President, since the judicial process is unable to conduct the investigations and make the political assessments essential for most policymaking. Thus, the need for delegation would have to be important enough to induce Congress to aggrandize its primary competitor for political power, and the recipient of the policymaking authority, while not Congress itself, would at least be politically accountable. But even after it has been accepted, pursuant to *Morrison,* that those exercising executive power need not be subject to the control of the President, Congress would still be more reluctant to augment the power of even an independent executive agency than to create an otherwise powerless repository for its delegation. Moreover, assembling the full-time senior personnel for an agency exercising executive powers is more difficult than borrowing other officials (or employing new officers on a short-term basis) to head an organization such as the Sentencing Commission.

By reason of today's decision, I anticipate that Congress will find delegation of its lawmaking powers much more attractive in the future. If rulemaking can be entirely unrelated to the exercise of judicial or executive powers, I foresee all manner of "expert" bodies, insulated from the political process, to which Congress will delegate various portions of its lawmaking responsibility. How tempting to create an expert Medical Commission (mostly M.D.'s, with perhaps a few Ph.D.'s in moral philosophy) to dispose of such thorny, "no win" political issues as the withholding of life-support systems in federally funded hospitals, or the use of fetal tissue for research. This is an undemocratic precedent that we set—not because of the scope of the delegated power, but because its recipient is not one of the three Branches of Government. The only governmental power the Commission possesses is the power to make law; and it is not the Congress. . . .

Today's decision follows the regrettable tendency of our recent separation-of-powers jurisprudence to treat the Constitution as though it were no more than a generalized prescription that the functions of the Branches should not be commingled too much—how much is too much to be determined, case-by-case, by this Court. The Constitution is not that. Rather, as its name suggests, it is a prescribed structure, a framework, for the conduct of government. In designing that structure, the Framers *themselves* considered how much commingling was, in the generality of things, acceptable, and set forth their conclusions in the document. That is the meaning of the statements concerning acceptable commingling made by Madison in defense of the proposed Constitution, and now routinely used as an excuse for disregarding it. When he said . . . that separation of powers "d[oes] not mean that these [three] departments ought to have no *partial agency* in, or no *controul* over the acts of each other," The Federalist No. 47, pp. 325–326 (J. Cooke ed. 1961), his point was that the commingling specifically provided for in the structure that he and his colleagues had designed—the Presidential veto over legislation, the Senate's confirmation of executive and judicial officers, the Senate's ratification of treaties, the Congress' power to impeach and remove executive and judicial officers—did not violate a proper understanding of separation of powers. He would be aghast, I think, to hear those words used as justification for ignoring that carefully designed structure so long as, in the changing view of the Supreme Court from time to time, "too much commingling" does not occur. Consideration of the degree of commingling that a particular disposition produces may be appropriate at the margins, where the outline of the framework itself is not clear; but it seems to me far from a marginal question whether our constitutional structure allows for a body which is not the Congress, and yet exercises no governmental powers except the making of rules that have the effect of laws.

I think the Court errs, in other words, not so much because it mistakes the degree of commingling, but because it fails to recognize that this case is not about commingling, but about the creation of a new Branch altogether, a sort of junior varsity Congress. It may well be that in some circumstances such a Branch would be desirable; perhaps the agency before us here will prove to be so. But there are many desirable dispositions that do not accord with the constitutional structure we live under. And in the long run the improvisation of a constitutional structure on the basis of currently perceived utility will be disastrous.

NOTES

1. Does the non-delegation doctrine have a sound basis in the language of the Constitution? On the one hand, consider the following proposition: There is no non-delegation doctrine in the Constitution, at least not one properly enforceable by courts, for nothing in the Constitution says that Congress may not legislate by announcing general standards and letting the executive branch carry them into effect (even by making more specific regulations). On the other hand, consider this hypothetical: Congress delegates its power to make laws to the staff of the National Zoo. Constitutional?

2. If Congress makes a delegation of authority, must it delegate to the president or some officer subject to the president's direction and control? Or can it delegate quasi-legislative authority to an independent commission or body composed of persons who are not accountable to the president? What do you make of Justice Scalia's objection to the U.S. Sentencing Commission as being a body with no authority to do anything other than "make laws"—a "Junior Varsity Congress"?

3. There is a vast academic literature on the non-delegation doctrine. Some argue that there is no limitation on Congress's discretion to delegate its powers. As long as Congress is able to repeal or rescind the delegation by a new statute, it is not as if Congress has really given away its legislative power—it retains the power and can exercise it differently in the future by passing a new statute. For a defense of this position, see Eric A. Posner & Adrian Vermeule, *Interring the Nondelegation Doctrine*, 69 U. Chi. L. Rev. 1721 (2002); cf. Jerry Mashaw, *Pro–Delegation: Why Administrators Should Make Political Decisions*, 1 J. L. Econ. & Org. 81 (1985) (criticizing the non-delegation doctrine on policy grounds). For a rebuttal, arguing that Congress may not assign core policy decisionmaking concerning matters within its legislative powers, see Larry Alexander & Saikrishna Prakash, *Reports of the Nondelegation Doctrine's Death Are Greatly Exaggerated*, 70 U. Chi. L. Rev. 1297 (2003). For yet another variation, see Gary Lawson, *The Rise and Rise of the Administrative State*, 107 Harv. L. Rev. 1231, 1239 (1994) (arguing seriously, but with self-conscious irony, that the non-delegation doctrine requires that Congress make those decisions that are sufficiently important that Congress should make them).

4. In a post–*Mistretta* case later in this chapter, *Clinton v. City of New York*, 524 U.S. 417 (1998), the Supreme Court struck down a statute that purported to delegate to the president a line-item-veto authority. The delegation in question was especially sweeping and would arguably have affected the balance of power between the president and Congress. The Court went out of its way to deny that its holding in that case was a non-delegation holding, though it seems to have been one. Perhaps *Mistretta* will not be the Court's last word on the non-delegation doctrine.

[*Assignment 13*]

C. THE COMPOSITION OF CONGRESS: "THE HOUSE OF REPRESENTATIVES . . . AND THE SENATE OF THE UNITED STATES SHALL BE COMPOSED . . ."

Article I, Section 2: . . . No Person shall be a Representative who shall not have attained to the Age of twenty-five years, and been seven Years a Citizen of the United States, and who shall not, when elected, be an Inhabitant of that State in which he shall be chosen. . . .

Section 3: . . . No Person shall be a Senator who shall not have attained to the Age of thirty Years, and been nine Years a Citizen of the United States, and who shall not, when elected, be an Inhabitant of that State for which he shall be chosen. . . .

Section 5: Each House shall be the Judge of the Elections, Returns and Qualifications of its own Members. . . . Each House may . . . punish its Members for disorderly behaviour, and, with the Concurrence of two thirds, expel a Member. . . .

As you have seen, the Vesting Clause of Article I gives the enumerated legislative powers to Congress, which consists of a House of Representatives and a Senate. The next question that Article I addresses is the length of terms and eligibility requirements for members of these two bodies. The text is clear on the first question: a fixed term of two years for representatives and six years for senators. Once elected, representatives and senators cannot be recalled. They become officers of the national government and are paid a fixed salary out of the national treasury as prescribed in Article I, Section 6. In this respect, representatives and senators are radically different from the members of the Continental Congress who served under the Articles of Confederation government. The members of that body were almost like ambassadors from their home states: their states paid them and they were subject to recall at any time. Notice how under the Constitution the fixed terms of representatives and senators make them independent not only of the states but also of the president. They can be fired only by their constituents.

Read carefully the constitutional text printed above, which specifies the only qualifications for being a representative or a senator. Article I, Section 5 then goes on to say, in what has been called the Exclusion Clause, that each house is the judge of whether individuals elected to that house have satisfied the three requirements. Section 5 adds, in what has been called the Expulsion Clause, that each house may by a two-thirds vote expel a member for misconduct. These two provisions seem clear, but in the 1960s they became the subject of a famous case, which appears below. As you read it, consider why the issues it addresses are fundamental to the existence of democracy and even freedom. Was the Supreme Court right to decide the case, or should it have treated the case as a non-justiciable political question? Is intervention by the judiciary in cases like this one essential to safeguard the republic, or is it a dangerous threat to the republic? Or is it both?

Powell v. McCormack

395 U.S. 486 (1969)

■ MR. CHIEF JUSTICE WARREN delivered the opinion of the Court.

In November 1966, petitioner Adam Clayton Powell, Jr., was duly elected from the 18th Congressional District of New York to serve in the United States House of Representatives for the 90th Congress. However, pursuant to a House resolution, he was not permitted to take his seat. Powell (and some of the voters in his district) then filed suit in Federal District Court, claiming that the House could exclude him only if it found he failed to meet the standing requirements of age, citizenship, and residence contained in Art. I, § 2, of the Constitution—requirements the House specifically found Powell met—and thus had excluded him unconstitutionally. . . . Powell is entitled to a declaratory judgment that he was unlawfully excluded from the 90th Congress.

During the 89th Congress, a Special Subcommittee on Contracts of the Committee on House Administration conducted an investigation into the expenditures of the Committee on Education and Labor, of which petitioner Adam Clayton Powell, Jr., was chairman. The Special Subcommittee issued a report concluding that Powell and certain staff employees had deceived the House authorities as to travel expenses. The report also indicated there was strong evidence that certain illegal salary payments had been made to Powell's wife at his direction. No formal action was taken during the 89th Congress. However, prior to the organization of the 90th Congress, the Democratic members-elect met in caucus and voted to remove Powell as chairman of the Committee on Education and Labor.

When the 90th Congress met to organize in January 1967, Powell was asked to step aside while the oath was administered to the other members-elect. Following the administration of the oath to the remaining members, the House discussed the procedure to be followed in determining whether Powell was eligible to take his seat. After some debate, by a vote of 363 to 65 the House adopted House Resolution No. 1, which provided that the Speaker appoint a Select Committee to determine Powell's eligibility. Although the resolution prohibited Powell from taking his seat until the House acted on the Select Committee's report, it did provide that he should receive all the pay and allowances due a member during the period.

The Select Committee, composed of nine lawyer-members, . . . [held hearings with testimony from Powell and others.] The Committee recommended that Powell be sworn and seated as a member of the 90th Congress but that he be censured by the House, fined $40,000 and be deprived of his seniority.

The report was presented to the House on March 1, 1967, and the House debated the Select Committee's proposed resolution. At the conclusion of the debate, by a vote of 222 of 202 the House rejected a motion to bring the resolution to a vote. An amendment to the resolution was then offered; it called for the exclusion of Powell and a declaration that his seat was vacant. The Speaker ruled that a majority vote of the House would be sufficient to pass the resolution if it were so amended. After further debate, the amendment was adopted by a vote of 248 to 176. Then the House adopted by a vote of 307 to 116 House Resolution No. 278 in its amended form, thereby excluding Powell and directing that the Speaker notify the Governor of New York that the seat was vacant.

Powell and 13 voters of the 18th Congressional District of New York subsequently instituted this suit in the United States District Court for the District of Columbia. Five members of the House of Representatives were named as defendants individually and "as representatives of a class of citizens who are presently serving . . . as members of the House of Representatives." John W. McCormack was named in his official capacity as Speaker, and the Clerk of the House of Representatives, the Sergeant at Arms and the Doorkeeper were named individually and in their official capacities. The complaint alleged that House Resolution No. 278 violated the Constitution, specifically Art. I, § 2, cl. 1, because the resolution was inconsistent with the mandate that the members of the House shall be elected by the people of each state, and Art. I, § 2, cl. 2, which, petitioners alleged, sets forth the exclusive qualifications for membership. . . . The complaint further alleged that the Clerk of the House threatened to refuse to perform the service for Powell to which a duly elected Congressman is entitled, that the Sergeant at Arms refused to pay Powell his salary, and that the Doorkeeper threatened to deny Powell admission to the House chamber.

. . . [Powell] requested that the District Court grant a permanent injunction restraining respondents from executing the House Resolution, and enjoining the Speaker from refusing to administer the oath, the Clerk from refusing to perform the duties due a Representative, the Sergeant at Arms from refusing to pay Powell his salary, and the Doorkeeper from refusing to admit Powell to the Chamber. The complaint also requested a declaratory judgment that Powell's exclusion was unconstitutional.

The District Court granted respondents' motion to dismiss the complaint "for want of jurisdiction of the subject matter." The Court of Appeals for the District of Columbia Circuit affirmed on somewhat different grounds, with each judge of the panel filing a separate opinion. We granted certiorari. While the case was pending on our docket, the 90th Congress officially terminated and the 91st Congress was seated. In November 1968, Powell was again elected as the representative of the 18th Congressional District of New York, and he was seated by the 91st Congress. The resolution seating Powell also fined him $25,000. Respondents then filed a suggestion of mootness. We postponed further consideration of this suggestion to a hearing on the merits . . . . .

The resolution excluding petitioner Powell was adopted by a vote in excess of two-thirds of the 434 Members of Congress—307 to 116. Article I, § 5, grants the House authority to expel a member "with the Concurrence of two thirds." Respondents assert that the House may expel a member for any reason whatsoever and that, since a two-thirds vote was obtained, the procedure by which Powell was denied his seat in the 90th Congress should be regarded as an expulsion, not an exclusion. . . .

Although respondents repeatedly urge this Court not to speculate as to the reasons for Powell's exclusion, their attempt to equate exclusion with expulsion would require a similar speculation that the House would have voted to expel Powell had it been faced with that question. Powell had not been seated at the time House Resolution No. 278 was debated and passed. After a motion to bring the Select Committee's proposed resolution to an immediate vote had been defeated, an amendment was offered which mandated Powell's exclusion. Mr. Celler, chairman of the Select Committee, then posed a parliamentary inquiry to determine whether a two-thirds vote was necessary to pass the resolution if so amended "in the sense that it might amount to an expulsion." The Speaker replied that "action by a majority vote would be in accordance with the rules." Had the amendment been regarded as an attempt to expel Powell, a two-thirds vote would have been constitutionally required. The Speaker ruled that the House was voting to exclude Powell, and we will not speculate what the result might have been if Powell had been seated and expulsion proceedings subsequently instituted.

Nor is the distinction between exclusion and expulsion merely one of form. The misconduct for which Powell was charged occurred prior to the convening of the 90th Congress. On several occasions the House has debated whether a member can be expelled for actions taken during a prior Congress and the House's own manual of procedure applicable in the 90th Congress states that "both Houses have distrusted their power to punish in such cases." The House rules manual reflects positions taken by prior Congresses. . . . Members of the House having expressed a belief that such strictures apply to its own power to expel, we will not assume that two-thirds of its members would have expelled Powell for his prior conduct had the Speaker announced that House Resolution No. 278 was for expulsion rather than exclusion.

Finally, the proceedings which culminated in Powell's exclusion cast considerable doubt upon respondents' assumption that the two-thirds vote necessary to expel would have been mustered. . . .

[W]e turn to the question whether the case is justiciable. Two determinations must be made in this regard. First, we must decide whether the claim presented and the relief sought are of the type which admit of judicial resolution. Second, we must determine whether the structure of the Federal Government renders the issue presented a "political question"—that is, a question which is not justiciable in federal court because of the separation of powers provided by the Constitution.

In deciding generally whether a claim is justiciable, a court must determine whether "the duty asserted can be judicially identified and its breach judicially determined, and whether protection for the right asserted can be judicially molded." Respondents do not seriously contend that the duty asserted and its alleged breach cannot be judicially determined. If petitioners are correct, the House had a duty to seat Powell once it determined he met the standing requirements set forth in the Constitution. It is undisputed that he met those requirements and that he was nevertheless excluded.

Respondents do maintain, however, that this case is not justiciable because, they assert, it is impossible for a federal court to "mold effective relief for resolving this case." Respondents emphasize that petitioners asked for coercive relief against the officers of the House, and, they contend, federal courts cannot issue mandamus or injunctions compelling officers or employees of the House to perform specific official acts. Respondents rely primarily on the Speech or Debate Clause to support this contention.

We need express no opinion about the appropriateness of coercive relief in this case, for petitioners sought a declaratory judgment, a form of relief the District Court could have issued. The Declaratory Judgment Act, 28 U.S.C. § 2201, provides that a district court may "declare the rights . . . of any interested party . . . whether or not further relief is or could be sought." The availability of declaratory relief depends on whether there is a live dispute between the parties, and a request for declaratory relief may be considered independently of whether other forms of relief are appropriate.

We thus conclude that in terms of the general criteria of justiciability, this case is justiciable.

Respondents maintain that even if this case is otherwise justiciable, it presents only a political question. It is well established that the federal courts will not adjudicate political questions. In *Baker v. Carr*, 369 U.S. 186 (1962), we noted that political questions are not justiciable primarily because of the separation of powers within the Federal Government. After reviewing our decisions in this area, we concluded that on the surface of any case held to involve a political question was at least one of the following formulations:

> a textually demonstrable constitutional commitment of the issue to a co-ordinate political department; or a lack of judicially discoverable and manageable standards for resolving it; or the impossibility of deciding without an initial policy determination of a kind clearly for nonjudicial discretion; or the impossibility of a court's undertaking independent resolution without expressing lack of the respect due co-ordinate branches of government; or an unusual need for unquestioning adherence to a political decision already made; or the potentiality of embarrassment from multifarious pronouncements by various departments on one question.

Respondents first contention is that this case presents a political question because under Art. I, § 5, there has been a "textually demonstrable constitutional commitment" to the House of the "adjudicatory power" to determine Powell's qualifications. Thus it is argued that the House, and the House alone, has power to determine who is qualified to be a member.

In order to determine whether there has been a textual commitment to a coordinate department of the Government, we must interpret the Constitution. . . . In other words, whether there is a "textually demonstrable constitutional commitment of the issue to a coordinate political department" of government and what is the scope of such commitment are questions we must resolve for the first time in this case. For, as we pointed out in *Baker v. Carr*, "[d]eciding whether a matter has in any measure been committed by the Constitution to another branch of government, or whether the action of that branch exceeds whatever authority has been committed, is itself a delicate exercise in constitutional interpretation, and is a responsibility of this Court as ultimate interpreter of the Constitution."

In order to determine the scope of any "textual commitment" under Art. I, § 5, we necessarily must determine the meaning of the phrase to "be the Judge of the Qualifications of its own Members." . . . Our examination of the relevant historical materials leads us to the conclusion that petitioners are correct and that the Constitution leaves the House without authority to *exclude* any person, duly elected by his constituents, who meets all the requirements for membership expressly prescribed in the Constitution. . . .

[The Court then reviewed and discussed the eighteenth-century English experience with qualifications for membership in Parliament, focusing in particular on the case of John Wilkes. While serving as a member of Parliament, Wilkes publicly attacked a peace treaty with France, was convicted of seditious libel, received a 22–month prison sentence, and was expelled from Parliament. He was reelected several times, but Parliament refused to seat him. Wilkes's exclusion from Parliament eventually came to be seen as having been highly improper, and so his case came to stand for the proposi-

tion that Parliament had no authority to exclude properly elected members for misconduct. See 16 Parl. Hist. Eng. 589, 590 (1769).—Editors]

Relying heavily on Charles Warren's analysis of the Convention debates, petitioners argue that the proceedings manifest the Framers' unequivocal intention to deny either branch of Congress the authority to add to or otherwise vary the membership qualifications expressly set forth in the Constitution.... [W]e have concluded that the records of the debates, viewed in the context of the bitter struggle for the right to freely choose representatives which had recently concluded in England and in light of the distinction the Framers made between the power to expel and the power to exclude, indicate that petitioners' ultimate conclusion is correct....

The debates at the state [ratification] conventions also demonstrate the Framers' understanding that the qualifications for members of Congress had been fixed in the Constitution. Before the New York convention, for example, Hamilton emphasized: "[T]he true principle of a republic is, that he people should choose whom they please to govern them. Representation is imperfect in proportion as the current of popular favor is checked. This great source of free government, popular election, should be perfectly pure, and the most unbounded liberty allowed." 2 Debates on the Federal Constitution 257 (J. Elliot ed. 1876)....

As clear as these statements appear, respondents dismiss them as "general statements . . . directed to other issues." They suggest that far more relevant is Congress' own understanding of its power to judge qualifications as manifested in post-ratification exclusion cases. Unquestionably, both the House and the Senate have excluded members-elect for reasons other than their failure to meet the Constitution's standing qualifications. For almost the first 100 years of its existence, however, Congress strictly limited its power to judge the qualifications of its members to those enumerated in the Constitution....

There was no significant challenge to these principles for . . . several decades. They came under heavy attack, however, "during the stress of civil war [but initially] the House of Representatives declined to exercise the power [to exclude], even under circumstances of great provocation." The abandonment of such restraint, however, was among the casualties of the general upheaval produced in war's wake. In 1868, the House voted for the first time in its history to exclude a member-elect. It refused to seat two duly elected representatives for giving aid and comfort to the Confederacy. "This change was produced by the North's bitter enmity toward those who failed to support the Union cause during the war, and was effected by the Radical Republican domination of Congress. It was a shift brought about by the naked urgency of power and was given little doctrinal support." From that time until the present, congressional practice has been erratic; and on the few occasions when a member-elect was excluded although he met all the qualifications set forth in the Constitution, there were frequently vigorous dissents. Even the annotations to the official manual of procedure for the 90th Congress manifest doubt as to the House's power to exclude a member-elect who has met the constitutionally prescribed qualifications.

Had these congressional exclusion precedents been more consistent, their precedential value still would be quite limited. That an unconstitutional action has been taken before surely does not render that same action any less unconstitutional at a later date.... [W]hat evidence we have of Congress' early understanding confirms our conclusion that the House is without power to exclude any member-elect who meets the Constitution's requirements for membership.

Had the intent of the Framers emerged from these materials with less clarity, we would nevertheless have been compelled to resolve any ambiguity in favor of a narrow construction of the scope of Congress' power to exclude members-elect. A fundamental principle of our representative democracy is, in Hamilton's words, "that the people should choose whom they please to govern them." 2 Elliot's Debates 257. As Madison pointed out at the Convention, this principle is undermined as much by limiting whom the people can select as by limiting the franchise itself. In apparent agreement with this basic philosophy, the Convention adopted his suggestion limiting the power to expel. To allow essentially that same power to be exercised under the guise of judging qualifications, would be to ignore Madison's warning, borne out in the Wilkes case and some of Congress' own post–Civil War exclusion cases, against "vesting an improper & dangerous power in the Legislature." 2 Farrand 249. Moreover, it would effectively nullify the Convention's decision to require a two-thirds vote for expulsion. Unquestionably, Congress has an interest in preserving its institutional integrity, but in most cases that interest can be sufficiently safeguarded by the exercise of its power to punish its members for disorderly behavior and, in extreme cases, to expel a member with the concurrence of two-thirds. In short, both the intention of the Framers, to the extent it can be determined, and an examination of the basic principles of our democratic system persuade us that the Constitution does not vest in the Congress a discretionary power to deny membership by a majority vote.

For these reasons, we have concluded that Art. I, § 5, is at most a "textually demonstrable commitment" to Congress to judge only the qualifications expressly set forth in the Constitution. Therefore, the "textual commitment" formulation of the political question doctrine does not bar federal courts from adjudicating petitioners' claims. . . .

Petitioners seek additional forms of equitable relief, including mandamus for the release of petitioner Powell's back pay. The propriety of such remedies, however, is more appropriately considered in the first instance by the courts below. Therefore, as to respondents McCormack, Albert, Ford, Celler, and Moore, the judgment of the Court of Appeals for the District of Columbia Circuit is affirmed. As to respondents Jennings, Johnson, and Miller, the judgment of the Court of Appeals for the District of Columbia Circuit is reversed and the case is remanded to the United States District Court for the District of Columbia with instructions to enter a declaratory judgment and for further proceedings consistent with this opinion.

■ [The concurring opinion of JUSTICE DOUGLAS and the dissenting opinion of JUSTICE STEWART are omitted.]

NOTES

1. Was *Powell v. McCormack* rightly decided? Doesn't Article I, Section 5 delegate to each house of Congress the sole power to judge the qualifications of its members? If so, is this a political question that cannot be decided by the Supreme Court? But does that mean that each house of Congress can add additional qualifications beyond the three enumerated in Article I, Sections 2 and 3? Does the text of the Constitution clearly speak to the issues raised by this case? If not, what other modes of interpretation are helpful? Does the structure of the document answer the question? Does practice since the Founding "liqui-

date" any ambiguity in the text? In which direction does the practice cut? And what policy concerns are implicated here, and how much weight would you give them?

2. What should the role of the Supreme Court be in cases like these? Suppose the House or Senate expels a member by a two-thirds vote under Article I, Section 5. Could the expelled member appeal to the Court, claiming that the expulsion was a punishment for political views in violation of the First Amendment? Would that raise a political question? Is *Powell* different?

3. Assume that the Court was right to decide the case (i.e., the case was justiciable), and that the Court correctly decided the case on the merits (i.e., it correctly held that Powell was unlawfully excluded). What remedy should the Court have been willing to give? The Court gave a declaratory judgment, which is typically a remedy that resolves legal uncertainty about future conduct. See, e.g., *N.H. Hemp Council v. Marshall*, 203 F.3d 1 (1st Cir. 2000) (resolving uncertainty about whether growing industrial hemp would violate federal law). It is not typically used for retrospective adjudication, for decisions about whether past actions were legal. Why do you think the Court gave a declaratory judgment in this case? Based on the Court's reasoning about justiciability and the merits, do you think it would have been willing to award any other remedies—such as damages or an injunction—if the House of Representatives had ignored the declaratory judgment? Would awarding any other remedies have been constitutional?

———

Now that you have read *Powell v. McCormack*'s discussion of congressional power to enforce the Qualifications Clauses, consider a case, a quarter century later, that addresses the issue of state power relative to those clauses. Before reading this case, review the Qualifications Clauses and examine the Tenth Amendment.

Do the states have a reserved power under the Tenth Amendment to add qualifications to federal office? To what extent are members of Congress the representatives of their states and of their congressional district, and to what extent are they officers of the entire nation? Does it matter here that the Constitution specifically provides that members of Congress shall be paid their salaries out of the national treasury and that they serve a fixed term without the possibility of recall? Remember how the framers of the Constitution deliberately departed from the practice under the Articles of Confederation, according to which members of the Continental Congress were paid and subject to recall by their states. Remember also that the Articles of Confederation provided for congressional term limits, while the Constitution did not. These issues are at the core of this fascinating and hard case.

U.S. Term Limits, Inc. v. Thornton
514 U.S. 779 (1995)

■ JUSTICE STEVENS delivered the opinion of the Court.

The Constitution sets forth qualifications for membership in the Congress of the United States. Article I, § 2, cl. 2, which applies to the House of Representatives, provides:

No Person shall be a Representative who shall not have attained to the Age of twenty five Years, and been seven Years a Citizen of the United States, and who shall not, when elected, be an Inhabitant of that State in which he shall be chosen.

Article I, § 3, cl. 3, which applies to the Senate, similarly provides:

No Person shall be a Senator who shall not have attained to the Age of thirty Years, and been nine Years a Citizen of the United States, and who shall not, when elected, be an Inhabitant of that State for which he shall be chosen.

Today's cases present a challenge to an amendment to the Arkansas State Constitution that prohibits the name of an otherwise-eligible candidate for Congress from appearing on the general election ballot if that candidate has already served three terms in the House of Representatives or two terms in the Senate. The Arkansas Supreme Court held that the amendment violates the Federal Constitution. We agree with that holding. Such a state-imposed restriction is contrary to the "fundamental principle of our representative democracy," embodied in the Constitution, that "the people should choose whom they please to govern them." *Powell v. McCormack*, 395 U.S. 486, 547 (1969). Allowing individual States to adopt their own qualifications for congressional service would be inconsistent with the Framers' vision of a uniform National Legislature representing the people of the United States. If the qualifications set forth in the text of the Constitution are to be changed, that text must be amended.

I

At the general election on November 3, 1992, the voters of Arkansas adopted Amendment 73 to their State Constitution. Proposed as a "Term Limitation Amendment," its preamble stated:

The people of Arkansas find and declare that elected officials who remain in office too long become preoccupied with reelection and ignore their duties as representatives of the people. Entrenched incumbency has reduced voter participation and has led to an electoral system that is less free, less competitive, and less representative than the system established by the Founding Fathers. Therefore, the people of Arkansas, exercising their reserved powers, herein limit the terms of elected officials.

. . . Section 3, the provision at issue in these cases, applies to the Arkansas Congressional Delegation. It provides:

(a) Any person having been elected to three or more terms as a member of the United States House of Representatives from Arkansas shall not be certified as a candidate and shall not be eligible to have his/her name placed on the ballot for election to the United States House of Representatives from Arkansas.

(b) Any person having been elected to two or more terms as a member of the United States Senate from Arkansas shall not be certified as a candidate and shall not be eligible to have his/her name placed on the ballot for election to the United States Senate from Arkansas. . . .

On November 13, 1992, respondent Bobbie Hill, on behalf of herself, similarly situated Arkansas "citizens, residents, taxpayers and registered voters," and the League of Women Voters of Arkansas, filed a complaint in the Circuit Court for Pulaski County, Arkansas, seeking a declaratory judgment that § 3 of Amendment 73 is "unconstitutional and void." . . .

II

As the opinions of the Arkansas Supreme Court suggest, the constitutionality of Amendment 73 depends critically on the resolution of two distinct issues. The first is whether the Constitution forbids States to add to or alter the qualifications specifically enumerated in the Constitution. The second is, if the Constitution does so forbid, whether the fact that Amendment 73 is formulated as a ballot access restriction rather than as an outright disqualification is of constitutional significance. Our resolution of these issues draws upon our prior resolution of a related but distinct issue: whether Congress has the power to add to or alter the qualifications of its Members.

Twenty-six years ago, in *Powell v. McCormack,* we reviewed the history and text of the Qualifications Clauses in a case involving an attempted exclusion of a duly elected Member of Congress. . . . [*Powell*] establishes two important propositions: first, that the "relevant historical materials" compel the conclusion that, at least with respect to qualifications imposed by Congress, the Framers intended the qualifications listed in the Constitution to be exclusive; and second, that that conclusion is equally compelled by an understanding of the "fundamental principle of our representative democracy . . . that the people should choose whom they please to govern them." . . .

III

. . . [P]etitioners argue that whatever the constitutionality of additional qualifications for membership imposed by Congress, the historical and textual materials discussed in *Powell* do not support the conclusion that the Constitution prohibits additional qualifications imposed by States. In the absence of such a constitutional prohibition, petitioners argue, the Tenth Amendment and the principle of reserved powers require that States be allowed to add such qualifications.

Before addressing these arguments, we find it appropriate to take note of the striking unanimity among the courts that have considered the issue. . . . Courts have struck down state-imposed qualifications in the form of term limits, district residency requirements, loyalty oath requirements, and restrictions on those convicted of felonies. Prior to *Powell,* the commentators were similarly unanimous. This impressive and uniform body of judicial decisions and learned commentary indicates that the obstacles confronting petitioners are formidable indeed.

Petitioners argue that the Constitution contains no express prohibition against state-added qualifications, and that Amendment 73 is therefore an appropriate exercise of a State's reserved power to place additional restrictions on the choices that its own voters may make. We disagree for two independent reasons. First, we conclude that the power to add qualifications is not within the "original powers" of the States, and thus is not reserved to the States by the Tenth Amendment. Second, even if States possessed some original power in this area, we conclude that the Framers intended the Constitution to be the exclusive source of qualifications for Members of Congress, and that the Framers thereby "divested" States of any power to add qualifications.

The "plan of the convention" as illuminated by the historical materials, our opinions, and the text of the Tenth Amendment draws a basic distinction between the powers of the newly created Federal Government and the powers retained by the pre-existing sovereign States. As Chief Justice Marshall explained, "it was neither necessary nor proper to define the powers retained by the States. These powers proceed, not from the people of America, but from the people of the several States; and remain, after the adoption of the constitution, what they were before, except so far as they may be abridged by that instrument." *Sturges v. Crowninshield,* 4 Wheat. 122, 193 (1819).

This classic statement by the Chief Justice endorsed Hamilton's reasoning in *The Federalist No. 32* that the plan of the Constitutional Convention did not contemplate "[a]n entire consolidation of the States into one complete national sovereignty," but only a partial consolidation in which "the State governments would clearly retain all the rights of sovereignty which they before had, and which were not, by that act, *exclusively* delegated to the United States." *The Federalist No. 32,* at 198. The text of the Tenth Amendment unambiguously confirms this principle:

> The powers not delegated to the United States by the Constitution, nor prohibited by it to the States, are reserved to the States respectively, or to the people.

As we have frequently noted, "[t]he States unquestionably do retain a significant measure of sovereign authority. They do so, however, *only to the extent that the Constitution has not divested them of their original powers* and transferred those powers to the Federal Government."

Contrary to petitioners' assertions, the power to add qualifications is not part of the original powers of sovereignty that the Tenth Amendment reserved to the States. Petitioners' Tenth Amendment argument misconceives the nature of the right at issue because that Amendment could only "reserve" that which existed before. As Justice Story recognized, "the states can exercise no powers whatsoever, which exclusively spring out of the existence of the national government, which the constitution does not delegate to them. . . . No state can say, that it has reserved, what it never possessed." 1 Story § 627.

Justice Story's position thus echoes that of Chief Justice Marshall in *McCulloch v. Maryland,* 4 Wheat. 316 (1819). In *McCulloch,* the Court rejected the argument that the Constitution's silence on the subject of state power to tax corporations chartered by Congress implies that the States have "reserved" power to tax such federal instrumentalities. As Chief Justice Marshall pointed out, an "original right to tax" such federal entities "never existed, and the question whether it has been surrendered, cannot arise." In language that presaged Justice Story's argument, Chief Justice Marshall concluded: "This opinion does not deprive the States of any resources which they originally possessed."

With respect to setting qualifications for service in Congress, no such right existed before the Constitution was ratified. The contrary argument overlooks the revolutionary character of the Government that the Framers conceived. Prior to the adoption of the Constitution, the States had joined together under the Articles of Confederation. In that system, "the States retained most of their sovereignty, like independent nations bound together only by treaties." After the Constitutional Convention convened, the Framers were presented with, and eventually adopted a variation of, "a plan not merely to amend the Articles of Confederation but to create an entirely new National Government with a National Executive, National Judiciary, and a

National Legislature." In adopting that plan, the Framers envisioned a uniform national system, rejecting the notion that the Nation was a collection of States, and instead creating a direct link between the National Government and the people of the United States. . . . In that National Government, representatives owe primary allegiance not to the people of a State, but to the people of the Nation. As Justice Story observed, each Member of Congress is "an officer of the union, deriving his powers and qualifications from the constitution, and neither created by, dependent upon, nor controllable by, the states. . . . Those officers owe their existence and functions to the united voice of the whole, not of a portion, of the people." 1 Story § 627. Representatives and Senators are as much officers of the entire Union as is the President. States thus "have just as much right, and no more, to prescribe new qualifications for a representative, as they have for a president. . . . It is no original prerogative of state power to appoint a representative, a senator, or president for the union." *Ibid.*

We believe that the Constitution reflects the Framers' general agreement with the approach later articulated by Justice Story. For example, Art. I, § 5, cl. 1, provides: "Each House shall be the Judge of the Elections, Returns and Qualifications of its own Members." The text of the Constitution thus gives the representatives of all the people the final say in judging the qualifications of the representatives of any one State. For this reason, the dissent falters when it states that "the people of Georgia have no say over whom the people of Massachusetts select to represent them in Congress."

Two other sections of the Constitution further support our view of the Framers' vision. First, consistent with Story's view, the Constitution provides that the salaries of representatives should "be ascertained by Law, and paid out of the Treasury of the United States," Art. I, § 6, rather than by individual States. The salary provisions reflect the view that representatives owe their allegiance to the people, and not to the States. Second, the provisions governing elections reveal the Framers' understanding that powers over the election of federal officers had to be delegated to, rather than reserved by, the States. It is surely no coincidence that the context of federal elections provides one of the few areas in which the Constitution expressly requires action by the States, namely that "[t]he Times, Places and Manner of holding Elections for Senators and Representatives, shall be prescribed in each State by the Legislature thereof." Art. I, § 4, cl. 1. This duty parallels the duty under Article II that "Each State shall appoint, in such Manner as the Legislature thereof may direct, a Number of Electors." Art. II, § 1, cl. 2. These Clauses are express delegations of power to the States to act with respect to federal elections.

This conclusion is consistent with our previous recognition that, in certain limited contexts, the power to regulate the incidents of the federal system is not a reserved power of the States, but rather is delegated by the Constitution. Thus, we have noted that "[w]hile, in a loose sense, the right to vote for representatives in Congress is sometimes spoken of as a right derived from the states, . . . this statement is true only in the sense that the states are authorized by the Constitution, to legislate on the subject as provided by § 2 of Art. I."

In short, as the Framers recognized, electing representatives to the National Legislature was a new right, arising from the Constitution itself. . . . In the absence of any constitutional delegation to the States of power to add qualifications to those enumerated in the Constitution, such a power does not exist. . . .

We find further evidence of the Framers' intent in Art. I, § 5, cl. 1, which provides: "Each House shall be the Judge of the Elections, Returns and Qualifications of its own Members." That Art. I, § 5, vests a federal tribunal with ultimate authority to judge a Member's qualifications is fully consistent with the understanding that those qualifications are fixed in the Federal Constitution, but not with the understanding that they can be altered by the States. If the States had the right to prescribe additional qualifications—such as property, educational, or professional qualifications—for their own representatives, state law would provide the standard for judging a Member's eligibility. . . .

We also find compelling the complete absence in the ratification debates of any assertion that States had the power to add qualifications. In those debates, the question whether to require term limits, or "rotation," was a major source of controversy. The draft of the Constitution that was submitted for ratification contained no provision for rotation.[22] In arguments that echo in the preamble to Arkansas' Amendment 73, opponents of ratification condemned the absence of a rotation requirement, noting that "there is no doubt that senators will hold their office perpetually; and in this situation, they must of necessity lose their dependence, and their attachments to the people." Even proponents of ratification expressed concern about the "abandonment in every instance of the necessity of rotation in office." At several ratification conventions, participants proposed amendments that would have required rotation.

The Federalists' responses to those criticisms and proposals addressed the merits of the issue, arguing that rotation was incompatible with the people's right to choose. . . .

Regardless of which side has the better of the debate over rotation, it is most striking that nowhere in the extensive ratification debates have we found any statement by either a proponent or an opponent of rotation that the draft constitution would permit States to require rotation for the representatives of their own citizens. If the participants in the debate had believed that the States retained the authority to impose term limits, it is inconceivable that the Federalists would not have made this obvious response to the arguments of the pro-rotation forces. The absence in an otherwise freewheeling debate of any suggestion that States had the power to impose additional qualifications unquestionably reflects the Framers' common understanding that States lacked that power. . . .

Congress' subsequent experience with state-imposed qualifications provides further evidence of the general consensus on the lack of state power in this area. . . . Congress first confronted the issue in 1807 when it faced a challenge to the qualifications of William McCreery, a Representative from Maryland who allegedly did not satisfy a residency requirement imposed by that State. In recommending that McCreery be seated, the Report of the House Committee on Elections noted:

> The committee proceeded to examine the Constitution, with relation to the case submitted to them, and find that *qualifications of members are therein determined, without reserving any authority to the State Legislatures to change, add to, or diminish those qualifications;* and

---

[22] A proposal requiring rotation for Members of the House was proposed at the Convention, but was defeated unanimously.

that, by that instrument, Congress is constituted the sole judge of the qualifications prescribed by it, and are obliged to decide agreeably to the Constitutional rules.

Powell, 395 U.S., at 542, quoting 17 Annals of Cong. 871 (1807) (emphasis added). . . .

Though the House Debate may be inconclusive, commentators at the time apparently viewed the seating of McCreery as confirmation of the States' lack of power to add qualifications. . . . The Senate experience with state-imposed qualifications further supports our conclusions. In 1887, for example, the Senate seated Charles Faulkner of West Virginia, despite the fact that a provision of the West Virginia Constitution purported to render him ineligible to serve. The Senate Committee on Privileges and Elections unanimously concluded that "no State can prescribe any qualification to the office of United States Senator in addition to those declared in the Constitution of the United States." . . . We recognize, as we did in *Powell*, that "congressional practice has been erratic" and that the precedential value of congressional exclusion cases is "quite limited." Nevertheless, those incidents lend support to the result we reach today.

Our conclusion that States lack the power to impose qualifications vindicates the same "fundamental principle of our representative democracy" that we recognized in *Powell,* namely, that "the people should choose whom they please to govern them."

. . . [T]he *Powell* Court recognized that an egalitarian ideal—that election to the National Legislature should be open to all people of merit—provided a critical foundation for the constitutional structure. This egalitarian theme echoes throughout the constitutional debates. . . .

Finally, state-imposed restrictions, unlike the congressionally imposed restrictions at issue in *Powell,* violate a third idea central to this basic principle: that the right to choose representatives belongs not to the States, but to the people. From the start, the Framers recognized that the "great and radical vice" of the Articles of Confederation was "the principle of LEGISLATION for STATES or GOVERNMENTS, in their CORPORATE or COLLECTIVE CAPACITIES, and as contradistinguished from the INDIVIDUALS of whom they consist." The Federalist No. 15, at 108 (Hamilton). Thus the Framers, in perhaps their most important contribution, conceived of a Federal Government directly responsible to the people, possessed of direct power over the people, and chosen directly, not by States, but by the people. . . .

Permitting individual States to formulate diverse qualifications for their representatives would result in a patchwork of state qualifications, undermining the uniformity and the national character that the Framers envisioned and sought to ensure. Such a patchwork would also sever the direct link that the Framers found so critical between the National Government and the people of the United States.

Petitioners attempt to overcome this formidable array of evidence against the States' power to impose qualifications by arguing that the practice of the States immediately after the adoption of the Constitution demonstrates their understanding that they possessed such power. One may properly question the extent to which the States' own practice is a reliable indicator of the contours of restrictions that the Constitution imposed on States, especially when no court has ever upheld a state-imposed qualification of any sort. But petitioners' argument is unpersuasive even on its own terms. At the time of the Convention, "[a]lmost all the State Constitutions required members of their Legislatures to possess considerable property." Despite this near uniformity, only one State, Virginia, placed similar restrictions on Members of Congress, requiring that a representative be, *inter alia*, a "freeholder." Just 15 years after imposing a property qualification, Virginia replaced that requirement with a provision requiring that representatives be only "qualified according to the constitution of the United States." Moreover, several States, including New Hampshire, Georgia, Delaware, and South Carolina, revised their Constitutions at around the time of the Federal Constitution. In the revised Constitutions, each State retained property qualifications for its own state elected officials yet placed no property qualification on its congressional representatives.

The contemporaneous state practice with respect to term limits is similar. At the time of the Convention, States widely supported term limits in at least some circumstances. The Articles of Confederation contained a provision for term limits. As we have noted, some members of the Convention had sought to impose term limits for Members of Congress. In addition, many States imposed term limits on state officers, four placed limits on delegates to the Continental Congress, and several States voiced support for term limits for Members of Congress. Despite this widespread support, no State sought to impose any term limits on its own federal representatives. Thus, a proper assessment of contemporaneous state practice provides further persuasive evidence of a general understanding that the qualifications in the Constitution were unalterable by the States.[341]

In sum, the available historical and textual evidence, read in light of the basic principles of democracy underlying the Constitution and recognized by this Court in *Powell,* reveal the Framers' intent that neither Congress nor the States should possess the power to supplement the exclusive qualifications set forth in the text of the Constitution. . . .

IV

Petitioners argue that, even if States may not add qualifications, Amendment 73 is constitutional because it is not such a qualification, and because Amendment 73 is a permissible exercise of state power to regulate the "Times, Places and Manner of holding Elections." We reject these contentions.

Unlike §§ 1 and 2 of Amendment 73, which create absolute bars to service for long-term incumbents running for state office, § 3 merely provides that certain Senators and Representatives shall not be certified as candidates and shall not have their names appear on the ballot. They may run as write-in candidates and, if elected, they may serve. . . . In our view, Amendment 73 is an indirect attempt to accomplish what the Constitution prohibits Arkansas from accomplishing directly. . . .

Petitioners make the related argument that Amendment 73 merely regulates the "Manner" of elections, and that the amendment is therefore a permissible exercise of state power under Article I, § 4, cl. 1 (the Elections Clause). . . . A necessary consequence of petitioners' argument is that Con-

---

[41] . . . Nor are we persuaded by the more recent state practice involving qualifications such as those that bar felons from being elected. As we have noted, the practice of States is a poor indicator of the effect of restraints on the States, and no court has ever upheld one of these restrictions. Moreover, as one moves away from 1789, it seems to us that state practice is even less indicative of the Framers' understanding of state power. Finally, it is important to reemphasize that the dissent simply has no credible explanation as to why almost every State imposed property qualifications on state representatives but not on federal representatives. . . .

gress itself would have the power to "make or alter" a measure such as Amendment 73. Art. I, § 4, cl. 1. That the Framers would have approved of such a result is unfathomable. As our decision in *Powell* and our discussion above make clear, the Framers were particularly concerned that a grant to Congress of the authority to set its own qualifications would lead inevitably to congressional self-aggrandizement and the upsetting of the delicate constitutional balance. . . .

V

The merits of term limits, or "rotation," have been the subject of debate since the formation of our Constitution, when the Framers unanimously rejected a proposal to add such limits to the Constitution. The cogent arguments on both sides of the question that were articulated during the process of ratification largely retain their force today. Over half the States have adopted measures that impose such limits on some offices either directly or indirectly, and the Nation as a whole, notably by constitutional amendment, has imposed a limit on the number of terms that the President may serve. Term limits, like any other qualification for office, unquestionably restrict the ability of voters to vote for whom they wish. On the other hand, such limits may provide for the infusion of fresh ideas and new perspectives, and may decrease the likelihood that representatives will lose touch with their constituents. It is not our province to resolve this longstanding debate.

We are, however, firmly convinced that allowing the several States to adopt term limits for congressional service would effect a fundamental change in the constitutional framework. Any such change must come not by legislation adopted either by Congress or by an individual State, but rather—as have other important changes in the electoral process—through the amendment procedures set forth in Article V. . . .

■ JUSTICE KENNEDY, concurring.

I join the opinion of the Court[,] . . . and it seems appropriate to add these few remarks to explain why that course of argumentation runs counter to fundamental principles of federalism.

Federalism was our Nation's own discovery. The Framers split the atom of sovereignty. It was the genius of their idea that our citizens would have two political capacities, one state and one federal, each protected from incursion by the other. The resulting Constitution created a legal system unprecedented in form and design, establishing two orders of government, each with its own direct relationship, its own privity, its own set of mutual rights and obligations to the people who sustain it and are governed by it. It is appropriate to recall these origins, which instruct us as to the nature of the two different governments created and confirmed by the Constitution.

A distinctive character of the National Government, the mark of its legitimacy, is that it owes its existence to the act of the whole people who created it. It must be remembered that the National Government, too, is republican in essence and in theory. . . .

In one sense it is true that "the people of each State retained their separate political identities," for the Constitution takes care both to preserve the States and to make use of their identities and structures at various points in organizing the federal union. It does not at all follow from this that the sole political identity of an American is with the State of his or her residence. It denies the dual character of the Federal Government which is its very foundation to assert that the people of the United States do not have a political identity as well, one independent of, though consistent with, their identity as citizens of the State of their residence. It must be recognized that "[f]or all the great purposes for which the Federal government was formed, we are one people, with one common country." *Shapiro v. Thompson,* 394 U.S. 618, 630 (1969) (quoting *Passenger Cases,* 7 How. 283, 492 (1849) (Taney, C.J., dissenting)).

It might be objected that because the States ratified the Constitution, the people can delegate power only through the States or by acting in their capacities as citizens of particular States. But in *McCulloch v. Maryland,* the Court set forth its authoritative rejection of this idea:

> The Convention which framed the constitution was indeed elected by the State legislatures. But the instrument ... was submitted to the people. ... It is true, they assembled in their several States—and where else should they have assembled? No political dreamer was ever wild enough to think of breaking down the lines which separate the States, and of compounding the American people into one common mass. Of consequence, when they act, they act in their States. But the measures they adopt do not, on that account, cease to be the measures of the people themselves, or become the measures of the State governments.

4 Wheat., at 403. . . .

It is maintained by our dissenting colleagues that the State of Arkansas seeks nothing more than to grant its people surer control over the National Government, a control, it is said, that will be enhanced by the law at issue here. The arguments for term limitations (or ballot restrictions having the same effect) are not lacking in force; but the issue, as all of us must acknowledge, is not the efficacy of those measures but whether they have a legitimate source, given their origin in the enactments of a single State. There can be no doubt, if we are to respect the republican origins of the Nation and preserve its federal character, that there exists a federal right of citizenship, a relationship between the people of the Nation and their National Government, with which the States may not interfere. Because the Arkansas enactment intrudes upon this federal domain, it exceeds the boundaries of the Constitution.

■ JUSTICE THOMAS, with whom THE CHIEF JUSTICE, JUSTICE O'CONNOR, and JUSTICE SCALIA join, dissenting.

It is ironic that the Court bases today's decision on the right of the people to "choose whom they please to govern them." Under our Constitution, there is only one State whose people have the right to "choose whom they please" to represent Arkansas in Congress. The Court holds, however, that neither the elected legislature of that State nor the people themselves (acting by ballot initiative) may prescribe any qualifications for those representatives. The majority therefore defends the right of the people of Arkansas to "choose whom they please to govern them" by invalidating a provision that won nearly 60% of the votes cast in a direct election and that carried every congressional district in the State.

I dissent. Nothing in the Constitution deprives the people of each State of the power to prescribe eligibility requirements for the candidates who seek to represent them in Congress. The Constitution is simply silent on this question. And where the Constitution is silent, it raises no bar to action by the States or the people.

I

Because the majority fundamentally misunderstands the notion of "reserved" powers, I start with some first principles. Contrary to the majority's suggestion, the people of the States need not point to any affirmative grant of power in the Constitution in order to prescribe qualifications for their representatives in Congress, or to authorize their elected state legislators to do so.

Our system of government rests on one overriding principle: All power stems from the consent of the people. To phrase the principle in this way, however, is to be imprecise about something important to the notion of "reserved" powers. The ultimate source of the Constitution's authority is the consent of the people of each individual State, not the consent of the undifferentiated people of the Nation as a whole.

The ratification procedure erected by Article VII makes this point clear. The Constitution took effect once it had been ratified by the people gathered in convention in nine different States. But the Constitution went into effect only "between the States so ratifying the same," Art. VII; it did not bind the people of North Carolina until they had accepted it. In Madison's words, the popular consent upon which the Constitution's authority rests was "given by the people, not as individuals composing one entire nation, but as composing the distinct and independent States to which they respectively belong." The Federalist No. 39. . . .

In each State, the remainder of the people's powers—"[t]he powers not delegated to the United States by the Constitution, nor prohibited by it to the States," Amdt. 10—are either delegated to the state government or retained by the people. . . . As far as the Federal Constitution is concerned, then, the States can exercise all powers that the Constitution does not withhold from them. The Federal Government and the States thus face different default rules: Where the Constitution is silent about the exercise of a particular power—that is, where the Constitution does not speak either expressly or by necessary implication—the Federal Government lacks that power and the States enjoy it.

These basic principles are enshrined in the Tenth Amendment, which declares that all powers neither delegated to the Federal Government nor prohibited to the States "are reserved to the States respectively, or to the people." With this careful last phrase, the Amendment avoids taking any position on the division of power between the state governments and the people of the States: It is up to the people of each State to determine which "reserved" powers their state government may exercise. . . .

The Constitution simply does not recognize any mechanism for action by the undifferentiated people of the Nation. Thus, the amendment provision of Article V calls for amendments to be ratified not by a convention of the national people, but by conventions of the people in each State or by the state legislatures elected by those people. Likewise, the Constitution calls for Members of Congress to be chosen State by State, rather than in nationwide elections. Even the selection of the President—surely the most national of national figures—is accomplished by an electoral college made up of delegates chosen by the various States, and candidates can lose a Presidential election despite winning a majority of the votes cast in the Nation as a whole.

In short, the notion of popular sovereignty that undergirds the Constitution does not erase state boundaries, but rather tracks them. . . .

Any ambiguity in the Tenth Amendment's use of the phrase "the people" is cleared up by the body of the Constitution itself. Article I begins by providing that the Congress of the United States enjoys "[a]ll legislative Powers herein granted," § 1, and goes on to give a careful enumeration of Congress' powers, § 8. It then concludes by enumerating certain powers that are *prohibited* to the States. The import of this structure is the same as the import of the Tenth Amendment: If we are to invalidate Arkansas' Amendment 73, we must point to something in the Federal Constitution that deprives the people of Arkansas of the power to enact such measures.

The majority disagrees that it bears this burden, . . . and begins by announcing an enormous and untenable limitation on the principle expressed by the Tenth Amendment. According to the majority, the States possess only those powers that the Constitution affirmatively grants to them or that they enjoyed before the Constitution was adopted; the Tenth Amendment "could only 'reserve' that which existed before." . . .

But it was not the state governments that were doing the reserving. The Constitution derives its authority instead from the consent of *the people* of the States. Given the fundamental principle that all governmental powers stem from the people of the States, it would simply be incoherent to assert that the people of the States could not reserve any powers that they had not previously controlled.

The Tenth Amendment's use of the word "reserved" does not help the majority's position. If someone says that the power to use a particular facility is reserved to some group, he is not saying anything about whether that group has previously used the facility. He is merely saying that the people who control the facility have designated that group as the entity with authority to use it. . . .

The majority also seeks support for its view of the Tenth Amendment in *McCulloch v. Maryland*. But this effort is misplaced. *McCulloch* did make clear that a power need not be "expressly" delegated to the United States or prohibited to the States in order to fall outside the Tenth Amendment's reservation; delegations and prohibitions can also arise by necessary implication. True to the text of the Tenth Amendment, however, *McCulloch* indicated that all powers as to which the Constitution does not speak (whether expressly or by necessary implication) are "reserved" to the state level. Thus, in its only discussion of the Tenth Amendment, *McCulloch* observed that the Amendment "leav[es] the question, whether the particular power which may become the subject of contest has been delegated to the one government, or prohibited to the other, to depend on a fair construction of the whole [Constitution]." *McCulloch* did not qualify this observation by indicating that the question also turned on whether the States had enjoyed the power before the framing. To the contrary, *McCulloch* seemed to assume that the people had "conferred on the general government the power contained in the constitution, and on the States the whole residuum of power." *Id.* . . .

For the past 175 years, *McCulloch* has been understood to rest on the proposition that the Constitution affirmatively barred Maryland from imposing its tax on the bank's operations. See, *e.g., Osborn v. Bank of United States,* 9 Wheat. 738, 859–868 (1824) (reaffirming *McCulloch*'s conclusion that by operation of the Supremacy Clause, the federal statute incorporating the bank impliedly pre-empted state laws attempting to tax the bank's operations); *Maryland v. Louisiana,* 451 U.S. 725, 746 (1981) (citing *McCulloch* for the proposition that the Supremacy Clause deprives the States of the power to pass laws that conflict with federal statutes). For the majority, however, *McCulloch* apparently turned on the fact that before the Constitution was adopted, the States had possessed no power to tax the instrumentalities of the governmental institutions that the Constitution created. This understanding of *McCulloch* makes most of Chief Justice Marshall's opinion irrelevant; according to the majority, there was no need to inquire into whether federal law deprived Maryland of the power in question, because the power could not fall into the category of "reserved" powers anyway. [6]

. . . [T]he only true support for [the majority's] view of the Tenth Amendment comes from Joseph Story's 1833 treatise on constitutional law. Justice Story was a brilliant and accomplished man, and one cannot casually dismiss his views. On the other hand, he was not a member of the Founding generation, and . . . they represent only his own understanding. In a range of cases concerning the federal/state relation, moreover, this Court has deemed positions taken in Story's commentaries to be more nationalist than the Constitution warrants. . . .

The majority also sketches out what may be an alternative (and narrower) argument. Again citing Story, the majority suggests that it would be inconsistent with the notion of "national sovereignty" for the States or the people of the States to have any reserved powers over the selection of Members of Congress. The majority apparently reaches this conclusion in two steps. First, it asserts that because Congress as a whole is an institution of the National Government, the individual Members of Congress "owe primary allegiance not to the people of a State, but to the people of the Nation." Second, it concludes that because each Member of Congress has a nationwide constituency once he takes office, it would be inconsistent with the Framers' scheme to let a single State prescribe qualifications for him.

Political scientists can debate about who commands the "primary allegiance" of Members of Congress once they reach Washington. From the framing to the present, however, the *selection* of the Representatives and Senators from each State has been left entirely to the people of that State or to their state legislature. See Art. I, § 2, cl. 1 (providing that Members of the House of Representatives are chosen "by the People of the several States"); Art. I, § 3, cl. 1 (originally providing that the Senators from each State are "chosen by the Legislature thereof"); Amdt. 17 (amending § 3 to provide that the Senators from each State are "elected by the people thereof"). The very name "congress" suggests a coming together of representatives from distinct entities.[7] In keeping with the complexity of our federal system, once the representatives chosen by the people of each State assemble in Congress, they form a national body and are beyond the control of the individual States until the next election. But the selection of representa-

---

[6] . . . Marshall did go on to argue that the power to tax the operations of the Bank of the United States simply was not susceptible to control by the people of a single State. But that theory is perfectly consistent with my position. Marshall reasoned that the people of a single State may not tax the instrumentalities employed by the people of all the States through the National Government, because such taxation would effectively subject the people of the several States to the taxing power of a single State. This sort of argument proves that the people of a single State may not prescribe qualifications for the President of the United States; the selection of the President, like the operation of the Bank of the United States, is not up to the people of any single State. It does not follow, however, that the people of a single State may not prescribe qualifications for their own representatives in Congress. . . .

[7] See 1 S. Johnson, A Dictionary of the English Language 393 (4th ed. 1773) (defining "congress" as "[a]n appointed meeting for settlement of affairs between different nations: as, the *congress* of Cambray").

tives in Congress is indisputably an act of the people of each State, not some abstract people of the Nation as a whole. . . .

In a final effort to deny that the people of the States enjoy "reserved" powers over the selection of their representatives in Congress, the majority suggests that the Constitution expressly delegates to the States certain powers over congressional elections. Such delegations of power, the majority argues, would be superfluous if the people of the States enjoyed reserved powers in this area.

Only one constitutional provision—the Times, Places and Manner Clause of Article I, § 4—even arguably supports the majority's suggestion. It reads:

> The Times, Places and Manner of holding Elections for Senators and Representatives, shall be prescribed in each State by the Legislature thereof; but the Congress may at any time by Law make or alter such Regulations, except as to the Places of chusing Senators.

Contrary to the majority's assumption, however, this Clause does not delegate any authority to the States. Instead, it simply imposes a duty upon them. . . . Constitutional provisions that impose affirmative duties on the States are hardly inconsistent with the notion of reserved powers.

Of course, the second part of the Times, Places and Manner Clause does grant a power rather than impose a duty. . . . [H]owever, the Clause grants power exclusively to Congress, not to the States. If the Clause did not exist at all, the States would still be able to prescribe the times, places, and manner of holding congressional elections; the deletion of the provision would simply deprive Congress of the power to override these state regulations. . . .

II

. . . Whatever one might think of the wisdom of [the Arkansas] arrangement, we may not override the decision of the people of Arkansas unless something in the Federal Constitution deprives them of the power to enact such measures.

The majority settles on "the Qualifications Clauses" as the constitutional provisions that Amendment 73 violates. Because I do not read those provisions to impose any unstated prohibitions on the States, it is unnecessary for me to decide whether the majority is correct to identify Arkansas' ballot-access restriction with laws fixing true term limits or otherwise prescribing "qualifications" for congressional office. . . . [T]he Qualifications Clauses are merely straightforward recitations of the minimum eligibility requirements that the Framers thought it essential for every Member of Congress to meet. They restrict state power only in that they prevent the States from *abolishing* all eligibility requirements for membership in Congress. . . .

III

It is radical enough for the majority to hold that the Constitution implicitly precludes the people of the States from prescribing any eligibility requirements for the congressional candidates who seek their votes. This holding, after all, does not stop with negating the term limits that many States have seen fit to impose on their Senators and Representatives. . . . Today's decision also means that no State may disqualify congressional candidates whom a court has found to be mentally incompetent, see, *e.g.*, Fla. Stat. § 97.041(2) (1991), who are currently in prison, see, *e.g.*, Ill.

Comp. Stat. Ann., ch. 10, §§ 5/3–5 (1993), or who have past vote-fraud convictions, see, *e.g.*, Ga. Code Ann. § 21–2–2(25) (1993). Likewise, after today's decision, the people of each State must leave open the possibility that they will trust someone with their vote in Congress even though they do not trust him with *a* vote in the election for Congress. See, *e.g.*, R.I. Gen. Laws § 17–14–1.2 (1988) (restricting candidacy to people "qualified to vote").

. . . Current federal law (enacted, of course, by congressional incumbents) confers numerous advantages on incumbents, and these advantages are widely thought to make it "significantly more difficult" for challengers to defeat them. For instance, federal law gives incumbents enormous advantages in building name recognition and good will in their home districts. See, *e.g.*, 39 U.S.C. § 3210 (permitting Members of Congress to send "franked" mail free of charge); 2 U.S.C. §§ 61–1, 72a, 332 (permitting Members to have sizable taxpayer-funded staffs); 2 U.S.C. § 123b (establishing the House Recording Studio and the Senate Recording and Photographic Studios). At the same time that incumbent Members of Congress enjoy these in-kind benefits, Congress imposes spending and contribution limits in congressional campaigns that "can prevent challengers from spending more . . . to overcome their disadvantage in name recognition." Many observers believe that the campaign-finance laws also give incumbents an "enormous fund-raising edge" over their challengers by giving a large financing role to entities with incentives to curry favor with incumbents. In addition, the internal rules of Congress put a substantial premium on seniority, with the result that each Member's already plentiful opportunities to distribute benefits to his constituents increase with the length of his tenure. In this manner, Congress effectively "fines" the electorate for voting against incumbents. . . .

The voters of Arkansas evidently believe that incumbents would not enjoy such overwhelming success if electoral contests were truly fair—that is, if the government did not put its thumb on either side of the scale. The majority offers no reason to question the accuracy of this belief. Given this context, petitioners portray § 3 of Amendment 73 as an effort at the state level to offset the electoral advantages that congressional incumbents have conferred upon themselves at the federal level. . . .

For me, this suggests only two possibilities. Either the majority's holding is wrong and Amendment 73 does not violate the Qualifications Clauses, or (assuming the accuracy of petitioners' factual claims) the electoral system that exists without Amendment 73 is no less unconstitutional than the electoral system that exists with Amendment 73.

. . . [T]oday's decision reads the Qualifications Clauses to impose substantial implicit prohibitions on the States and the people of the States. I would not draw such an expansive negative inference from the fact that the Constitution requires Members of Congress to be a certain age, to be inhabitants of the States that they represent, and to have been United States citizens for a specified period. Rather, I would read the Qualifications Clauses to do no more than what they say.

NOTES

1. Are you persuaded by the majority or by the dissent? Do you find the question in *U.S. Term Limits, Inc. v. Thornton* a close one? Think again of the types of constitutional argument, or modes of interpretation. What is the best

argument as to what the text says about state-imposed term limits on members of Congress? What structural arguments do you think are persuasive? What was the historical purpose of the Qualifications Clauses? Does the history recounted in this case and in *Powell v. McCormack* affect your view of the correct outcome? To what extent do the last two centuries of practice settle this question? Is it dispositive that we have not had state-imposed term limits on federal office? Or, to the contrary, is it dispositive that many states have, for example, disqualified felons from voting or running for office? Do policy concerns cause you to side with the majority or the dissent? Or do you think they are irrelevant?

2. Is it just as appropriate for the Court to decide the constitutional question presented in *Thornton* as it was for the Court to decide the question presented in *Powell*? Or should the Court have a different role when a constitutional provision is being construed by the states rather than by Congress? If so, should the Court's role in a *Thornton* situation be more deferential or less?

3. Think about the questions of the meaning of the Qualifications Clauses raised by William Marbury's argument that the written Constitution is "law"— indeed the supreme law of the land. Is there enough clear law in *Powell* and in *Thornton* to justify the Court's invalidation in those two cases of the actions of the House of Representatives and the state of Arkansas? James Bradley Thayer famously argued that the federal courts should exercise the power of judicial review only when the political branches have made "a clear mistake" in construing the Constitution. James Bradley Thayer, *The Origin and Scope of the American Doctrine of Constitutional Law*, 7 Harv. L. Rev. 129 (1893). Is that exacting standard of proof met here? How much law should the Court need to invalidate a congressional or state action?

4. Justices Stevens and Thomas disagree sharply over the implications of *McCulloch v. Maryland* for the case. Who gets the better of that argument? Does the Tenth Amendment reserve to the states only those powers they possessed prior to the writing of the Constitution or does it reserve all powers not enumerated? Do the text and structure of the Constitution imply that the states cannot burden federal officers, instrumentalities, and powers? If so, are the states preempted from legislating as to qualifications for holding a national office (and not just any national office but membership in a body which is after all the Congress of *the United States*)? If *McCulloch* arose today, would it split the Supreme Court 5 to 4?

5. In the wake of *Thornton*, can the states constitutionally disqualify felons from being elected to and serving in Congress? What if a felon will remain in prison for years and cannot perform the duties of a member of Congress?

[Assignment 14]

D. LEGISLATIVE PROCEDURE AND PREROGATIVES: "EACH HOUSE MAY DETERMINE THE RULES OF ITS PROCEEDINGS"

Article I, Section 5: . . . Each House may determine the Rules of its Proceedings, punish its Members for disorderly Behaviour, and, with the Concurrence of two thirds, expel a Member. . . .

Section 6: The Senators and Representatives shall ... in all Cases, except Treason, Felony, and Breach of the Peace, be privileged from Arrest during their attendance at the Session of their respective Houses, and in going to and returning from the same; and for any Speech or Debate in either House, they shall not be questioned in any other Place. ...

Article I, Section 5 grants to each house the power to determine the rules of its own proceedings. Consider two cases involving this provision. The first, *Kilbourn v. Thompson*, arose out of an investigation by the House of Representatives into a bank that had sold millions of dollars in U.S. government bonds before going bankrupt in the Panic of 1873. A bankruptcy proceeding began in federal district court (the United States was a major creditor). At roughly the same time, a House committee began investigating, and it issued a subpoena to Hallet Kilbourn. He refused to testify, and he was taken into custody by John Thompson, the House sergeant-at-arms. The House voted to hold Kilbourn in custody for contempt until he testified, but the Supreme Court ruled that the House lacked the constitutional power to punish for contempt where it was invading a matter within the jurisdiction of a federal court and where the punishment was not ancillary to the enactment of legislation. *Kilbourn* is important today because of its discussion of the historical origins and limits on congressional power to punish for contempt while conducting a legislative committee investigation. *Kilbourn* was narrowed and distinguished by the second case, *McGrain v. Daugherty*, which grew out of the scandals that engulfed the Harding administration. *McGrain* substantially broadened Congress's ability to conduct investigations and hold oversight hearings. Investigations and oversight hearings have become potent congressional weapons, and they have been used both famously and infamously—contrast the House Judiciary Committee's famous investigation of the Nixon administration with the infamous era of Senator Joseph McCarthy and the House Committee on Un–American Activities.

As you read these cases, ask whether they can be reconciled; if not, which one is right? The Constitution gives Congress only the "legislative power." To what extent does that include a power to investigate, oversee, and punish? Do the different types of constitutional argument, or modes of interpretation, point in different directions?

Kilbourn v. Thompson

103 U.S. 168 (1880)

■ MR. JUSTICE MILLER, after stating the case, delivered the opinion of the court.

The argument before us has assumed a very wide range, and includes the discussion of almost every suggestion that can well be conceived on the subject. The two extremes of the controversy are the proposition on the part of the plaintiff that the House of Representatives has no power whatever to punish for a contempt of its authority, and, on the part of defendants, that such power undoubtedly exists, and when that body has formally exercised it, it must be presumed that it was right fully exercised. ...

The powers of Congress itself, when acting through the concurrence of both branches, are dependent solely on the Constitution. Such as are not conferred by that instrument, either expressly or by fair implication from what is granted, are "reserved to the States respectively, or to the people."

. . . No general power of inflicting punishment by the Congress of the United States is found in that instrument. It contains in the provision that no "person shall be deprived of life, liberty, or property, without due process of law" the strongest implication against punishment by order of the legislative body. It has been repeatedly decided by this court, and by others of the highest authority, that this means a trial in which the rights of the party shall be decided by a tribunal appointed by law, which tribunal is to be governed by rules of law previously established. An act of Congress which proposed to adjudge a man guilty of a crime and inflict the punishment would be conceded by all thinking men to be unauthorized by anything in the Constitution. That instrument, however, is not wholly silent as to the authority of the separate branches of Congress to inflict punishment. It authorizes each House to punish its own members. By the second clause of the fifth section of the first article, "each House may determine the rules of its proceedings, punish its members for disorderly behavior, and, with the concurrence of two-thirds, expel a member," and by the clause immediately preceding, it "may be authorized to compel the attendance of absent members, in such manner and under such penalties as each House may provide." These provisions are equally instructive in what they authorize and in what they do not authorize. There is no express power in that instrument conferred on either House of Congress to punish for contempts.

The advocates of this power have, therefore, resorted to an implication of its existence founded on two principal arguments. These are, 1, its exercise by the House of Commons of England, from which country we, it is said, have derived our system of parliamentary law; and 2d, the necessity of such a power to enable the two Houses of Congress to perform the duties and exercise the power which the Constitution has conferred on them.

That the power to punish for contempt has been exercised by the House of Commons in numerous instances is well known to the general student of history, and is authenticated by the rolls of the Parliament. And there is no question but that this has been upheld by the courts of Westminster Hall. . . . It is important, however, to understand on what principle this power in the House of Commons rests, that we may see whether it is applicable to the two Houses of Congress, and, if it be, whether there are limitations to its exercise.

While there is, in the adjudged cases in the English courts, little agreement of opinion as to the extent of this power and the liability of it[s] exercise to be inquired into by the courts, there is no difference of opinion as to its origin. This goes back to the period when the bishops, the lords, and the knights and burgesses met in one body, and were, when so assembled, called the High Court of Parliament.

They were not only called so, but the assembled Parliament exercised the highest function of a court of judicature, representing in that respect the judicial authority of the king in his Court of Parliament. While this body enacted laws, it also rendered judgments in matters of private right which, when approved by the king, were recognized a[s] valid. Upon the separation of the Lords and Commons into two separate bodies, holding their sessions in different chambers, and hence called the House of Lords and the House of Commons, the judicial function of reviewing by appeal the decisions of the courts of Westminster Hall passed to the House of Lords, where it has been exercised without dispute ever since. To the Commons was left the power of impeachment, and perhaps others of a judicial character, and jointly they exercised, until a very recent period, the power of passing bills of attainder for treason and other high crimes which are in their nature punishment for crime declared judicially by the High Court of Parliament of the Kingdom of England.

It is upon this idea that the two Houses of Parliament were each courts of judicature originally which, though divested by usage and by statute, probably, of many of their judicial functions, have yet retained so much of that power as enables them, like any other court, to punish for a contempt of these privileges and authority that the power rests. . . . *[The Court then cited English cases decided by Lord Ellenborough, Chief Justice Gray, Justice Blackstone, and Justice Gould, as well as Coke's Instruments, in which the great Chief Justice Sir Edward Coke said that each house of Parliament had a power to hold in contempt.—Editors]*

[But] the powers and privileges of the House of Commons of England, on the subject of punishment for contempts, rest on principles which have no application to other legislative bodies, and certainly can have none to the House of Representatives of the United States—a body which is in no sense a court, which exercises no functions derived from its once having been a part of the highest court of the realm, and whose functions, so far as they partake in any degree of that character, are limited to punishing its own members and determining their election. . . .

We are of opinion that the right of the House of Representatives to punish the citizen for a contempt of its authority or a breach of its privileges can derive no support from the precedents and practices of the two Houses of the English Parliament, nor from the adjudged cases in which the English courts have upheld these practices. Nor . . . is much aid given to the doctrine that this power exists as one necessary to enable either House of Congress to exercise successfully their function of legislation.

This latter proposition is one which we do not propose to decide in the present case, because we are able to decide [the present case] without passing upon the existence or nonexistence of such [contempt] power in aid of the legislative function.

As we have already said, the Constitution expressly empowers each House to punish its own members for disorderly behavior. We see no reason to doubt that this punishment may, in a proper case, be imprisonment, and that it may be for refusal to obey some rule on that subject made by the House for the preservation of order. . . .

Whether the power of punishment in either House by fine or imprisonment goes beyond this or not, we are sure that no person can be punished for contumacy as a witness before either House unless his testimony is required in a matter into which that House has jurisdiction to inquire, and we feel equally sure that neither of these bodies possesses the general power of making inquiry into the private affairs of the citizen.

It is believed to be one of the chief merits of the American system of written constitutional law that all the powers intrusted to government, whether State or national, are divided into the three grand departments, the executive, the legislative, and the judicial. . . . [It is] essential to the successful working of this system that the persons intrusted with power in any one of these branches shall not be permitted to encroach upon the powers confided to the others, but that each shall, by the law of its creation, be limited to the exercise of the powers appropriate to its own department, and no other. To these general propositions there are in the Constitution of the United States some important exceptions. One of these is, that the

President is so far made a part of the legislative power, that his assent is required to the enactment of all statutes and resolutions of Congress. . . .

In looking to the preamble and resolution under which the committee acted, before which Kilbourn refused to testify, we are of opinion that the House of Representatives not only exceeded the limit of its own authority, but assumed a power which could only be properly exercised by another branch of the government, because it was, in its nature, clearly judicial.

The Constitution declares that the judicial power of the United States shall be vested in one Supreme Court and in such inferior courts as the Congress may from time to time ordain and establish. If what we have said of the division of the powers of the government among the three departments be sound, this is equivalent to a declaration that no judicial power is vested in the Congress or either branch of it, save in the cases specifically enumerated to which we have referred. . . .

[W]e do not concede that the Houses of Congress possess [a] general power of punishing for contempt. The cases in which they can do this are very limited, as we have already attempted to show. If they are proceeding in a matter beyond their legitimate cognizance, we are of opinion that this can be shown, and we cannot give our assent to the principle that, by the mere act of asserting a person to be guilty of a contempt, they thereby establish their right to fine and imprison him, beyond the power of any court or any other tribunal whatever to inquire into the grounds on which the order was made. . . .

[W]e have found no better expression of the true principle on this subject than in the following language of Mr. Justice Hoar, in the Supreme Court of Massachusetts, in the case of *Burnham v. Morrissey*, 14 Gray, 226 . . . [:]

> The house of representatives is not the final judge of its own power and privilege in cases in which the rights and liberties of the subject are concerned, but the legality of its action may be examined and determined by this court. That house is not the legislature, but only a part of it, and is therefore subject in its action to the laws, in common with all other bodies, officers, and tribunals within the Commonwealth. Especially is it competent and proper for this court to consider whether its proceedings are in conformity with the Constitution and laws, because, living under a written constitution, no branch or department of the government is supreme; and it is the province and duty of the judicial department to determine in cases regularly brought before them, whether the powers of any branch of the government, and even those of the legislature in the enactment of laws, have been exercised in conformity to the Constitution; and if they have not, to treat their acts as null and void. The house of representatives has the power under the Constitution to imprison for contempt; but the power is limited to cases expressly provided for by the Constitution, or to cases where the power is necessarily implied from those constitutional functions and duties, to the proper performance of which it is essential.

In this statement of the law, and in the principles there laid down, we fully concur.

We must, therefore, hold . . . that the resolution of the House of Representatives finding Kilbourn guilty of contempt, and the warrant of its speaker for his commitment to prison, are not conclusive in this case, and, in fact, are no justification, because, as the whole plea shows, the House was without authority in the matter. . . .

McGrain v. Daugherty

273 U.S. 135 (1927)

■ MR. JUSTICE VAN DEVANTER delivered the opinion of the court.

This is an appeal from the final order in a proceeding in *habeas corpus* discharging a recusant witness held in custody under process of attachment issued from the United States Senate in the course of an investigation which it was making of the administration of the Department of Justice. A full statement of the case is necessary.

The Department of Justice is one of the great executive departments established by congressional enactment. . . . Harry M. Daugherty became the Attorney General March 5, 1921, and held that office until March 28, 1924, when he resigned. Late in that period various charges of misfeasance and nonfeasance in the Department of Justice after he became its supervising head were brought to the attention of the Senate by individual senators and made the basis of an insistent demand that the department be investigated to the end that the practices and deficiencies which, according to the charges, were operating to prevent or impair its right administration might be definitely ascertained and that appropriate and effective measures might be taken to remedy or eliminate the evil. The Senate . . . [and House passed] two measures taking important litigation then in immediate contemplation out of the control of the Department of Justice and placing the same in charge of a special counsel to be appointed by the President; and also adopted a resolution authorizing and directing a select committee of five senators "to investigate . . . the alleged failure of Harry M. Daugherty, Attorney General of the United States, to prosecute properly violators of the Sherman Anti-trust Act[.]" . . .

In the course of the investigation the committee issued and caused to be duly served on Mally S. Daugherty—who was a brother of Harry M. Daugherty and president of the Midland National Bank of Washington Court House, Ohio—a subpoena commanding him to appear before the committee. . . . The witness failed to appear. . . .

The committee then made a report to the Senate stating that the subpoenas had been issued, that . . . the witness was personally served; and that he had failed and refused to appear. After a reading of the report, the Senate adopted a resolution reciting these facts and proceeding as follows:

> . . . Resolved, That the President of the Senate pro tempore issue his warrant commanding the Sergeant at Arms or his deputy to take into custody the body of the said M. S. Daugherty wherever found, and to bring the said M. S. Daugherty before the bar of the Senate, then and there to answer such questions pertinent to the matter under inquiry as the Senate may order the President of the Senate pro tempore to propound; and to keep the said M. S. Daugherty in custody to await the further order of the Senate.

It will be observed from the terms of the resolution that the warrant was to be issued in furtherance of the effort be obtain the personal testimony of the witness. . . . The warrant was issued agreeably to the resolution and was addressed simply to the Sergeant at Arms. That officer, on receiving the warrant, endorsed thereon a direction that it be executed by John J. McGrain, already his deputy, and delivered it to him for execution.

The deputy, proceeding under the warrant, took the witness into custody at Cincinnati, Ohio, with the purpose of bringing him before the bar of the Senate as commanded, whereupon the witness petitioned the federal District Court in Cincinnati for a writ of *habeas corpus*. . . .

We have given the case earnest and prolonged consideration because the principal questions involved are of unusual importance and delicacy. They are (a) whether the Senate—or the House of Representatives, both being on the same plane in this regard—has power, through its own process, to compel a private individual to appear before it or one of its committees and give testimony needed to enable it efficiently to exercise a legislative function belonging to it under the Constitution; and (b) whether it sufficiently appears that the process was being employed in this instance to obtain testimony for that purpose. . . .

The Constitution provides for a Congress, consisting of a Senate and House of Representatives, and invests it with "all legislative powers" granted to the United States, and with power "to make all laws which shall be necessary and proper" for carrying into execution these powers and "all other powers" vested by the Constitution in the United States or in any department or officer thereof. Article 1, §§ 1, 8. Other provisions show that, while bills can become laws only after being considered and passed by both houses of Congress, each house is to be distinct from the other, to have its own officers and rules, and to exercise its legislative function independently. But there is no provision expressly investing either house with power to make investigations and exact testimony, to the end that it may exercise its legislative function advisedly and effectively. So the question arises whether this power is so far incidental to the legislative function as to be implied.

In actual legislative practice power to secure needed information by such means has long been treated as an attribute of the power to legislate. It was so regarded in the British Parliament and in the colonial Legislatures before the American Revolution, and a like view has prevailed and been carried into effect in both houses of Congress and in most of the state legislatures.

This power was both asserted and exerted by the House of Representatives in 1792, when it appointed a select committee to inquire into the St. Clair expedition and authorized the committee to send for necessary persons, papers and records. Mr. Madison, who had taken an important part in framing the Constitution only five years before, and four of his associates in that work, were members of the House of Representatives at the time, and all voted for the inquiry. Other exertions of the power by the House of Representatives, as also by the Senate, are shown. . . .

The state courts quite generally have held that the power to legislate carries with it by necessary implication ample authority to obtain information needed in the rightful exercise of that power, and to employ compulsory process for the purpose. . . .

We have referred to the practice of the two houses of Congress; and we now shall notice some significant congressional enactments. . . .

While [our] cases are not decisive of the question we are considering, they definitely settle two propositions which we recognize as entirely sound and having a bearing on its solution: One, that the two houses of Congress, in their separate relations, possess not only such powers as are expressly granted to them by the Constitution, but such auxiliary powers as are necessary and appropriate to make the express powers effective; and, the other, that neither house is invested with "general" power to inquire into private affairs and compel disclosures, but only with such limited power of inquiry as is shown to exist when the rule of constitutional interpretation just stated is rightly applied. . . .

We are of opinion that the power of inquiry—with process to enforce it—is an essential and appropriate auxiliary to the legislative function. It was so regarded and employed in American Legislatures before the Constitution was framed and ratified. Both houses of Congress took this view of it early in their history—the House of Representatives with the approving votes of Mr. Madison and other members whose service in the convention which framed the Constitution gives special significance to their action—and both houses have employed the power accordingly up to the present time. . . . So, when their practice in the matter is appraised according to the circumstances in which it was begun and to those in which it has been continued, it falls nothing short of a practical construction, long continued, of the constitutional provisions respecting their powers, and therefore should be taken as fixing the meaning of those provisions, if otherwise doubtful.

. . . A legislative body cannot legislate wisely or effectively in the absence of information respecting the conditions which the legislation is intended to affect or change; and where the legislative body does not itself possess the requisite information—which not infrequently is true—recourse must be had to others who do possess it. Experience has taught that mere requests for such information often are unavailing, and also that information which is volunteered is not always accurate or complete; so some means of compulsion are essential to obtain what is needed. All this was true before and when the Constitution was framed and adopted. In that period the power of inquiry—with enforcing process—was regarded and employed as a necessary and appropriate attribute of the power to legislate—indeed, was treated as inhering in it. Thus there is ample warrant for thinking, as we do, that the constitutional provisions which commit the legislative function to the two houses are intended to include this attribute to the end that the function may be effectively exercised.

The contention is earnestly made on behalf of the witness that this power of inquiry, if sustained, may be abusively and oppressively exerted. If this be so, it affords no ground for denying the power. The same contention might be directed against the power to legislate, and of course would be unavailing. We must assume, for present purposes, that neither house will be disposed to exert the power beyond its proper bounds, or with out due regard to the rights of witnesses. But if, contrary to this assumption, controlling limitations or restrictions are disregarded, the decisions in *Kilbourn v. Thompson* and *Marshall v. Gordon* point to admissible measures of relief. And it is a necessary deduction from the decisions in *Kilbourn v. Thompson* and *In re Chapman* that a witness rightfully may refuse to answer where the bounds of the power are exceeded or the questions are not pertinent to the matter under inquiry. . . .

We are of opinion that the court's ruling on this question was wrong, and that it sufficiently appears, when the proceedings are rightly interpreted, that the object of the investigation and of the effort to secure the witness' testimony was to obtain information for legislative purposes.

It is quite true that the resolution directing the investigation does not in terms avow that it is intended to be in aid of legislation; but it does show that the subject to be investigated was the administration of the Department of Justice—whether its functions were being properly discharged or were being neglected or misdirected, and particularly whether the Attorney General and his assistants were performing or neglecting their duties in respect of the institution and prosecution of proceedings to punish crimes and enforce appropriate remedies against the wrongdoers—specific instances of alleged neglect being recited. Plainly the subject was one on which legislation could be had and would be materially aided by the information which the investigation was calculated to elicit. This becomes manifest when it is reflected that the functions of the Department of Justice, the powers and duties of the Attorney General, and the duties of his assistants are all subject to regulation by congressional legislation, and that the department is maintained and its activities are carried on under such appropriations as in the judgment of Congress are needed from year to year. . . .

NOTES

1. What enumerated power is Congress relying on in the two cases which you have just read? Is it Congress's power to adopt rules to govern its own proceedings? Yet surely Congress can adopt the equivalent of Robert's Rules of Order without issuing subpoenas and holding unwilling witnesses in contempt. Is there any other enumerated power Congress could be exercising? Is there any enumerated power for which compelling the appearance of a witness might be "necessary and proper"?

2. What do you make of the claim in *Kilbourn* that just because the House of Lords and the House of Commons had adjudicative as well as legislative powers in seventeenth and eighteenth century England, it does not follow that Congress or any other body that is given only the "function" of legislating has such powers? Does the fact revealed by *McGrain* that Congress wields an almost-adjudicative investigatory power suggest that the framers' effort to divide and separate power functionally has not completely succeeded?

3. The statute Congress passed in 1857 giving each house the power to subpoena witnesses is today codified as 2 U.S.C. § 192:

> Every person who having been summoned as a witness by the authority of either House of Congress to give testimony or to produce papers upon any matter under inquiry before either House, or any joint committee established by a joint or concurrent resolution of the two Houses of Congress, or any committee of either House of Congress, willfully makes default, or who, having appeared, refuses to answer any question pertinent to the question under inquiry, shall be deemed guilty of a misdemeanor, punishable by a fine of not more than $1,000 nor less than $100 and imprisonment in a common jail for not less than one month nor more than twelve months.

Since World War II, Congress has abandoned its efforts to prosecute contempt of Congress itself and has instead referred such cases to the U.S. attorneys' offices pursuant to this statute. As long as contempt of Congress is prosecuted by the executive branch and adjudicated by the judiciary, are all constitutional concerns eliminated?

4. In *Watkins v. United States*, 354 U.S. 178 (1957), John Watkins was prosecuted and convicted in federal court for contempt of Congress in violation of 2 U.S.C. § 192. Watkins had refused, in 1954, to answer several questions posed to him by a subcommittee of the House Un–American Activities Committee (HUAC). Although Watkins testified before the subcommittee at length, he nonetheless refused to answer a few questions about the possible Communist Party membership of people he had associated with in the past but did not know to be Communist Party members. Chief Justice Earl Warren's opinion for the Court said:

> The power of the Congress to conduct investigations is inherent in the legislative process. That power is broad. It encompasses inquiries concerning the administration of existing laws, as well as proposed or possibly needed statutes. It includes surveys of defects in our social, economic or political system for the purpose of enabling the Congress to remedy them. It comprehends probes into departments of the Federal Government to expose corruption, inefficiency or waste. But, broad as is this power of inquiry, it is not unlimited. There is no general authority to expose the private affairs of individuals without justification in terms of the functions of the Congress. . . . Nor is the Congress a law enforcement or trial agency. These are functions of the executive and judicial departments of government. No inquiry is an end in itself; it must be related to, and in furtherance of, a legitimate task of the Congress. Investigations conducted solely for the personal aggrandizement of the investigators or to "punish" those investigated are indefensible.

Chief Justice Warren concluded that the committee's questions were not pertinent to its mandate. Justice Clark dissented.

Two years later, in *Barenblatt v. United States,* 360 U.S. 109 (1959), the Supreme Court reversed course and by a 5–to–4 vote upheld broad congressional investigatory powers in the pursuit of alleged communists. Lloyd Barenblatt had been indicted and convicted under 2 U.S.C. § 192 for refusing to answer HUAC subcommittee questions about whether he was a member of the Communist Party or knew of Communist Party activities in U.S. educational institutions. Justice Harlan wrote for the Court that the resolution of the House of Representatives setting up HUAC had authorized the subcommittee to ask the particular questions it did, that the subcommittee's questions were pertinent to its investigation, and that it was not attempting to punish Barenblatt. Justices Black, Warren, Douglas, and Brennan dissented, arguing that the subcommittee was in fact trying to punish Barenblatt by making him unemployable. Justice Black's dissent was a blistering attack on the activities and purposes of HUAC:

> [T]he Court today fails to see what is here for all to see—that exposure and punishment is the aim of this Committee and the reason for its existence. To deny this is to ignore the Committee's own claims and the reports it has issued ever since it was established. I cannot believe that the nature of our judicial office requires us to be so blind, and must conclude that the Un–American Activities Committee's "identification" and "exposure" of Communists and suspected Communists, like the activities of the Committee in *Kilbourn v. Thompson*, amount to an encroachment on the judiciary which bodes ill for the liberties of the people of this land. . . . Ultimately, all the questions in this case really boil down to one—whether we as a

people will try fearfully and futilely to preserve democracy by adopting to-talitarian methods or whether, in accordance with our traditions and our Constitution, we will have the confidence and courage to be free.

Is there an enumerated power under which the House of Representatives could establish the House Committee on Un–American Activities, giving it a vague mission and empowering it to humiliate and ostracize ordinary citizens? Did the committee's activities violate the First Amendment?

5. The division of the Senate and the House of Representatives into many committees and sub-committees has become an important part of the operation of our constitutional system. Committee membership is determined by a mix of seniority, party loyalty, and member preference. The last of these considerations means that members of Congress will gravitate toward the committees that allow them to protect the interests of their constituents and local industries. The congressional committees serve as gatekeepers for new bills in their respective areas, and they can investigate and hold oversight hearings for their respective sections of the executive branch. The rise and proliferation of congressional committees and subcommittees—like the rise of political parties—is not explicitly addressed in the Constitution but has become a dominant feature of our system of government.

A Case Study in Congressional Procedure: The Filibuster

Both the Senate and the House of Representatives have adopted rules to govern their proceedings that are of constitutional magnitude. An obvious example is the Senate rule that debates (and thus filibusters) can be stopped only by a three-fifths majority of the Senate, which today means sixty votes. The Senate is thus the only legislative body in the world where a super-majority can routinely be required for important decisions.

The most famous use of the filibuster came in the 1960s when Southern segregationists sought to use it to stop the adoption of the Civil Rights of Act of 1964. The segregationists were defeated, and the threshold to get cloture was lowered from two-thirds of those voting to three-fifths of the Senate (at least for Senate actions other than rules changes). This liberalization of cloture rules, however, did not lead to a reduction in the number of filibusters. Instead, filibusters have become more common, due in part to the fact that Senate leaders no longer make filibustering senators stay up and talk all night. The practice today is that once a filibuster is threatened and the leadership fails to end it with sixty votes on a cloture motion, the Senate simply discards the filibustered bill and goes on to other business. There is thus no practical cost to threatening to filibuster because one does not actually need to follow through on the threat to stop a bill. And it has now become routine for the president's nominees, including judicial nominees, to be filibustered by the senators of the opposing party.

Could a simple majority of the Senate abolish the filibuster, either in whole or in part? If so, must the majority act at the start of a session rather than in the middle of the session? Is the Senate bound by prior Senates, which adopted the filibuster rule? Can any legislative body bind itself as to actions in the future? (Is the answer different for the House and the Senate, since at each new session of the Senate two-thirds of the senators from the prior session continue to sit?)

Here is one set of criticisms of filibusters in judicial nominations. Identify and evaluate the arguments being made. Do you agree?

The U.S. Constitution was written to establish majority rule. The historical reasons for this are clear. A major defect with the Constitution's precursor, the Articles of Confederation, was that it required super majorities for making many important decisions. The Framers deliberately set out to remedy this defect by empowering Congress to make most decisions by a simple majority. The only exceptions to this principle are in seven express situations where a two-thirds vote is required. Each house of Congress does have the power by majority vote to establish the rules of its proceedings but there's no evidence this clause was originally meant to authorize filibusters. From 1789 to 1806, the Senate's rules allowed for cutting off debate by moving the previous question, a motion which required only a simple majority to pass.

The filibuster of legislation did not originate until 1841, when it was employed by Senator John C. Calhoun to defend slavery and an extreme vision of minority rights. Calhoun was called a filibusterer from a Dutch word for pirate, or as we would say today terrorist, because he was subverting majority rule. From 1841 to the present, the principle use of the filibuster has been to defend Jim Crow laws oppressing African Americans. Now for the first time in 214 years a minority of senators are seeking to extend filibustering from legislation to the whole new area of judicial nominees—nominees who they know enjoy the support of a majority of the Senate.

This is a bad idea for three reasons. First, such filibusters weaken the power of the president, who is one of only two officers of government who is elected to represent all of the American people. Second, filibusters of judges undermine judicial independence by giving a minority of senators led by special interest groups a veto over who can become a judge. It's already hard enough for talented and capable individuals to be appointed judges without a minority of senators imposing a litmus test. Third, the filibuster of legislation can at least be defended on the ground that federal legislation ought to be considered with extraordinary care. In contrast, the confirmation of one out of one hundred and seventy-five appellate judges is a much less momentous matter. . . .

The Senate can always change its rules by majority vote. To the extent that Senate Rule Twenty–Two purports to require a two-thirds majority for rules changes, Rule Twenty–Two is unconstitutional. It is an ancient principle of Anglo–American constitutional law that one session of a legislature cannot bind a succeeding session of the same legislature. This principle goes back to the great William Blackstone, who said in his commentaries "Acts of Parliament derogatory from the power of subsequent parliaments be naught." Three vice presidents of the United States presiding over the Senate, Richard Nixon, Hubert Humphrey, and Nelson Rockefeller, have all ruled that the Senate rules can be changed by a simple majority of the Senate. Lloyd Cutler, White House Counsel to Presidents Jimmy Carter and Bill Clinton, has written in the Washington Post that Senate Rule Twenty–Two is plainly unconstitutional. The Senate can and should now amend Rule Twenty–Two by simple majority vote to ban filibusters of judicial nominations.

Testimony of Professor Steven G. Calabresi, Senate Judiciary Committee Hearing on Judicial Nominations and Filibusters, May 6, 2003.

NOTES

1. The text of the Constitution requires a two-thirds majority for the following seven actions: passing constitutional amendments, overriding presidential vetoes, ratifying treaties (Senate only), convicting impeached officials (Senate only), expelling a member of either house, lifting by either house of the ineligibility for service of an individual who "engaged in insurrection or rebellion," and joint action by the House and Senate to remove from office a president who is disabled (upon petition by the vice president and a majority of the Cabinet). A majority voting rule is expressly required by the Constitution for law-making pursuant to Article I, Section 7; admitting new states into the Union pursuant to Article IV, Section 3; and calling a new constitutional convention pursuant to Article V. What structural inferences can we draw from these voting rules? Is a majority voting rule the default? May each house of Congress decide whether and when to use a different voting rule?

2. Is there a stronger or a weaker case for super-majority rules for the confirmation of federal judges, especially Supreme Court justices? Note that the Federal Republic of Germany requires a two-thirds vote of a committee of the lower house of its legislature to pick half the justices on the German Constitutional Court, while the other half are picked by a two-thirds vote of the upper house of the legislature which represents the German states. Is it better for the power of judicial review to be entrusted only to nominees who can muster a legislative super-majority, because they have wider support from the representatives of the people? Or would a super-majority requirement for judicial nominees (whether *de jure* or *de facto*) produce a bland and overly cautious Court?

A NOTE ON ARTICLE I, SECTION 6

The Speech or Debate Clause of Article I, Section 6 broadly protects members of Congress with respect to comments they make during a speech or a debate (including in committee). It protects them, for example, against federal or state prosecution and libel suits by private parties. This clause complements the preceding clause, which protects members of Congress from arrest when they are attending a session of Congress except in cases of treason, felony, and breach of the peace. That clause, the Privilege from Arrest Clause, has its roots in seventeenth century England where it was one of the ancient parliamentary privileges claimed by enemies of King James I and his son, King Charles I, who violated the privilege by briefly arresting several of his parliamentary opponents on the floor of the House of Commons. Although they were quickly released, this event contributed to the English Civil War, which ended with Charles's beheading. The English Bill of Rights of 1689 confirmed both a parliamentary privilege from arrest and protection for comments made in speeches and debates in Parliament. From these English roots, the two privileges found their way into the U.S. Constitution in Article I, Section 6.

The Speech or Debate Clause is of practical importance given the voluminous congressional record and the testimony and proceedings of all of Congress's many committees and subcommittees. The ability of members of Congress to say or publish anything free of legal consequence both in the congressional record and in committee encourages a free flow of information to the public. If read narrowly, the clause would appear to apply only to members of Congress themselves. But the Supreme Court has read the clause to extend to legislative aides. See *Gravel v. United States*, 408 U.S. 606 (1972). Strikingly, the Speech or Debate Clause applies only to Congress and not to executive branch officers or federal judges. Nevertheless, the president and the courts have endorsed an implied doctrine of executive privilege, which accomplishes much the same object for the executive branch as the Speech or Debate Clause does for Congress.

Gravel is the leading modern case on the Speech or Debate Clause. In addition to holding that the clause applies to legislative aides, the Court held that the clause did *not* protect a member of Congress from being forced to testify before a grand jury about sources of information used in preparation for legislative acts. Four justices dissented.

A more recent situation involving the Speech or Debate Clause occurred in 2006. Agents working for the Federal Bureau of Investigation raided the Capitol Hill offices of Representative William Jefferson, who was suspected of taking bribes. He was later indicted and convicted. Did the FBI raid violate any of Representative Jefferson's rights under the Speech or Debate Clause? Since he could be arrested for the felony of taking bribes, does that mean that his office and files could be raided without there being any violation of the Speech or Debate Clause? The raid on Representative Jefferson's Capitol Hill office led to a sharp war of words between the president and Congress (with members of Congress from both parties indignant at the intrusion), including threats of resignation by executive officials and threats of executive budget reductions by members of the House. The scope of the Speech or Debate Clause is of more than academic interest.

[Assignment 15]

E. BICAMERALISM AND PRESENTMENT: "EVERY BILL WHICH SHALL HAVE PASSED THE HOUSE OF REPRESENTATIVES AND THE SENATE, SHALL . . . BE PRESENTED TO THE PRESIDENT"

Article I, Section 7: . . . Every Bill which shall have passed the House of Representatives and the Senate, shall, before it become a law, be presented to the President of the United States: If he approve he shall sign it. . . .

The modern era of broad delegations to executive branch agencies spawned a new development: the so-called "legislative veto." Congress sought to control, or check, its own delegations to the executive by adding the condition that one house or both houses could veto any actions that the executive branch took pursuant to the delegation. Was this a constitutional (and sensible) way to address the problems created by the need to delegate in sometimes sweeping terms? Or was this a case of "two wrongs do not make a right"? If legislative vetoes are unconstitutional, why? Is it because they interfere with *executive* power, on the theory that once broad statutory authority is conferred, the power to execute, or carry out that authority, should be the president's alone (under Article II's grant to the president of the "executive Power")? Or are legislative veto provisions unconstitutional because they are congressional lawmaking that does not comply with Article I, Section 7's rules for how a bill becomes law? The latter theory became the ground on which the Supreme Court eventually held legislative vetoes unconstitutional in *INS v. Chadha*, presented below.

Chadha is a good opportunity to think about Article I's provisions governing the lawmaking procedure. As you just saw, Section 5 provides that each house acting unilaterally has the power to adopt rules for its own proceedings. Section 7 provides a different and more onerous requirement for how a bill becomes law: action by both houses of Congress and presentment to the president for signature or veto. Presidential vetoes may be overridden, but only by a two-thirds majority of both houses. *Chadha* holds that Congress may not accomplish a change in the law other than through Article I, Section 7's procedures.

But why couldn't Congress—each house using its Article I, Section 5 power to make its own rules of proceedings—formally satisfy but practically circumvent the rule of *Chadha* by providing for "bicameral" passage of a bill under certain expedited procedures? Could Congress delegate broad authority to executive agencies, but specify that the agencies' actions be treated merely as proposals for further legislative action—and then deem those proposals "passed" by both houses and presented to the president (pursuant to the rules-making power) unless affirmatively rejected? Such fast-track legislative procedures are used in other contexts, most commonly international trade and tariff legislation, where the president is delegated broad negotiating authority and Congress commits itself to a straight up or down vote on whatever the president has achieved pursuant to that authority. Consider these types of issues as you read *Chadha* and the case that follows it, *Clinton v. City of New York*, where Congress attempted to give the president a form of line-item-veto authority, pursuant to a procedural arrangement of this sort.

INS v. Chadha

462 U.S. 919 (1983)

■ CHIEF JUSTICE BURGER delivered the opinion of the Court.

We granted certiorari . . . [to consider] a challenge to the constitutionality of the provision in § 244(c)(2) of the Immigration and Nationality Act, authorizing one House of Congress, by resolution, to invalidate the decision of the Executive Branch, pursuant to authority delegated by Congress to the Attorney General of the United States, to allow a particular deportable alien to remain in the United States.

Chadha is an East Indian who was born in Kenya and holds a British passport. He was lawfully admitted to the United States in 1966 on a nonimmigrant student visa. His visa expired on June 30, 1972. On October 11, 1973, the District Director of the Immigration and Naturalization Service ordered Chadha to show cause why he should not be deported for having "remained in the United States for a longer time than permitted." . . . Chadha conceded that he was deportable . . . [and filed] an application for suspension of deportation under § 244(a)(1) of the Act. . . . *[The application was granted through an immigration judge subject to veto by one House of Congress.—Editors]*

On December 12, 1975, Representative Eilberg, Chairman of the Judiciary Subcommittee on Immigration, Citizenship, and International Law, introduced a resolution opposing "the granting of permanent residence in the United States to [six] aliens," including Chadha. . . . The resolution was passed without debate or recorded vote. Since the House action was pursuant to § 244(c)(2), the resolution was not treated as an Art. I legislative act; it was not submitted to the Senate or presented to the President for his action.

After the House veto of the Attorney General's decision to allow Chadha to remain in the United States, the Immigration Judge reopened the deportation proceedings to implement the House order deporting Chadha. Chadha moved to terminate the proceedings on the ground that § 244(c)(2) is unconstitutional. . . .

[A deportation order resulted, which Chadha eventually appealed to] the United States Court of Appeals for the Ninth Circuit. The Immigration and Naturalization Service agreed with Chadha's position before the Court of Appeals and joined him in arguing that § 244(c)(2) is unconstitutional. In light of the importance of the question, the Court of Appeals invited both the Senate and the House of Representatives to file briefs *amici curiae*. . . . [The Ninth Circuit ruled for Chadha.] . . .

[The Court first held that it had appellate jurisdiction to hear the case, and it then turned to the issue of severability.—Editors]

Congress . . . contends that the provision for the one-House veto in § 244(c)(2) cannot be severed from [the delegation of power to suspend deportations in] § 244. Congress argues that if the provision for the one-House veto is held unconstitutional, [then] all of § 244 [including the delegation of power to suspend deportations] must fall. If § 244 in its entirety is violative of the Constitution, it follows that the Attorney General has no authority to suspend Chadha's deportation under § 244(a)(1), and Chadha would be deported. From this, Congress argues that Chadha lacks standing to challenge the constitutionality of the one-House veto provision, because he could receive no relief even if his constitutional challenge proves successful.

. . . [W]e need not [inquire into legislative intent here, however,] since Congress itself has provided the answer to the question of severability in § 406 of the Immigration and Nationality Act, note following 8 U.S.C. § 1101, which provides:

If *any* particular provision of this Act, or the application thereof to *any* person or circumstance, is held invalid, *the remainder of the Act and the application of such provision to other persons or circumstances shall not be affected thereby.* (Emphasis added.)

This language is unambiguous and gives rise to a presumption that Congress did not intend the validity of the Act as a whole, or of any part of the Act, to depend upon whether the veto clause of § 244(c)(2) was invalid. . . . Congress could not have more plainly authorized the presumption that the provision for a one-House veto in § 244(c)(2) is severable from the remainder of § 244 and the Act of which it is a part. . . .

We turn now to the question whether action of one House of Congress under § 244(c)(2) violates strictures of the Constitution. We begin, of course, with the presumption that the challenged statute is valid. Its wisdom is not the concern of the courts; if a challenged action does not violate the Constitution, it must be sustained. . . .

By the same token, the fact that a given law or procedure is efficient, convenient, and useful in facilitating functions of government, standing alone, will not save it if it is contrary to the Constitution. Convenience and efficiency are not the primary objectives—or the hallmarks—of democratic government and our inquiry is sharpened rather than blunted by the fact that congressional veto provisions are appearing with increasing frequency in statutes which delegate authority to executive and independent agencies:

> Since 1932, when the first veto provision was enacted into law, 295 congressional veto-type procedures have been inserted in 196 different statutes as follows: from 1932 to 1939, five statutes were affected; from 1940–49, nineteen statutes; between 1950–59, thirty-four statutes; and from 1960–69, forty-nine. From the year 1970 through 1975, at least one hundred sixty-three such provisions were included in eighty-nine laws.

Abourezk, The Congressional Veto: A Contemporary Response to Executive Encroachment on Legislative Prerogatives, 52 Ind. L. Rev. 323, 324 (1977).

Justice WHITE undertakes to make a case for the proposition that the one-House veto is a useful "political invention," and we need not challenge that assertion. We can even concede this utilitarian argument although the long-range political wisdom of this "invention" is arguable. It has been vigorously debated, and it is instructive to compare the views of the protagonists. But policy arguments supporting even useful "political inventions" are subject to the demands of the Constitution which defines powers and, with respect to this subject, sets out just how those powers are to be exercised.

Explicit and unambiguous provisions of the Constitution prescribe and define the respective functions of the Congress and of the Executive in the legislative process. Since the precise terms of those familiar provisions are critical to the resolution of these cases, we set them out verbatim. Article I provides:

> All legislative Powers herein granted shall be vested in a Congress of the United States, which shall consist of a Senate *and* House of Representatives. Art. I, § 1. (Emphasis added.)
>
> Every Bill which shall have passed the House of Representatives *and* the Senate, *shall*, before it become a law, be presented to the President of the United States. Art. I, § 7, cl. 2. (Emphasis added.)
>
> *Every* Order, Resolution, or Vote to which the Concurrence of the Senate and House of Representatives may be necessary (except on a question of Adjournment) *shall be* presented to the President of the United States; and before the Same shall take Effect, *shall be* approved by him, or being disapproved by him, *shall be* repassed by two thirds of the Senate and House of Representatives, according to the Rules and Limitations prescribed in the Case of a Bill. Art. I, § 7, cl. 3. (Emphasis added.)

These provisions of Art. I are integral parts of the constitutional design for the separation of powers. We have recently noted that "[t]he principle of separation of powers was not simply an abstract generalization in the minds of the Framers: it was woven into the document that they drafted in Philadelphia in the summer of 1787." *Buckley v. Valeo*, 424 U.S. at 124. Just as we relied on the textual provision of Art. II, § 2, cl. 2, to vindicate the principle of separation of powers in *Buckley*, we see that the purposes underlying the Presentment Clauses, Art. I, § 7, cls. 2, 3 and the bicameral requirement of Art. I, § 1, and § 7, cl. 2, guide our resolution of the important question presented in these cases. The very structure of the Articles delegating and separating powers under Arts. I, II, and III exemplifies the concept of separation of powers, and we now turn to Art. I.

The records of the Constitutional Convention reveal that the requirement that all legislation be presented to the President before becoming law was uniformly accepted by the Framers. Presentment to the President and the Presidential veto were considered so imperative that the draftsmen took special pains to assure that these requirements could not be circumvented. During the final debate on Art. I, § 7, cl. 2, James Madison expressed concern that it might easily be evaded by the simple expedient of calling a proposed law a "resolution" or "vote," rather than a "bill." 2 Farrand 301–302. As a consequence, Art. I, § 7, cl. 3 was added.

The decision to provide the President with a limited and qualified power to nullify proposed legislation by veto was based on the profound conviction of the Framers that the powers conferred on Congress were the powers to be most carefully circumscribed. It is beyond doubt that lawmaking was a power to be shared by both Houses and the President . . .

The bicameral requirement of Art. I, §§ 1, 7, was of scarcely less concern to the Framers than was the Presidential veto and indeed the two concepts are interdependent. By providing that no law could take effect without the concurrence of the prescribed majority of the Members of both Houses, the Framers reemphasized their belief, already remarked upon in connection with the Presentment Clauses, that legislation should not be enacted unless it has been carefully and fully considered by the Nation's elected officials. . . .

We see therefore that the Framers were acutely conscious that the bicameral requirement and the Presentment Clauses would serve essential constitutional functions. The President's participation in the legislative process was to protect the Executive Branch from Congress and to protect the whole people from improvident laws. The division of the Congress into two distinctive bodies assures that the legislative power would be exercised only after opportunity for full study and debate in separate settings. The President's unilateral veto power, in turn, was limited by the power of two-thirds of both Houses of Congress to overrule a veto thereby precluding final arbitrary action of one person. It emerges clearly that the prescription for legislative action in Art. I, §§ 1, 7, represents the Framers' decision that the legislative power of the Federal Government be exercised in accord with a single, finely wrought and exhaustively considered, procedure.

The Constitution sought to divide the delegated powers of the new Federal Government into three defined categories, Legislative, Executive, and Judicial, to assure, as nearly as possible, that each Branch of government would confine itself to its assigned responsibility. The hydraulic pressure inherent within each of the separate Branches to exceed the outer limits of its power, even to accomplish desirable objectives, must be resisted.

Although not "hermetically" sealed from one another, the powers delegated to the three Branches are functionally identifiable. When any Branch acts, it is presumptively exercising the power the Constitution has delegated to it. When the Executive acts, he presumptively acts in an executive or administrative capacity as defined in Art. II. And when, as here, one House of Congress purports to act, it is presumptively acting within its assigned sphere.

Beginning with this presumption, we must nevertheless establish that the challenged action under § 244(c)(2) is of the kind to which the procedural requirements of Art. I, § 7, apply. Not every action taken by either House is subject to the bicameralism and presentment requirements of Art. I. Whether actions taken by either House are, in law and fact, an exercise of legislative power depends not on their form but upon "whether they contain matter which is properly to be regarded as legislative in its character and effect."

Examination of the action taken here by one House pursuant to § 244(c)(2) reveals that it was essentially legislative in purpose and effect. In purporting to exercise power defined in Art. I, § 8, cl. 4, to "establish an uniform Rule of Naturalization," the House took action that had the purpose and effect of altering the legal rights, duties, and relations of persons, including the Attorney General, Executive Branch officials and Chadha, all outside the Legislative Branch. . . .

The legislative character of the one-House veto in these cases is confirmed by the character of the congressional action it supplants. Neither the House of Representatives nor the Senate contends that, absent the veto provision in § 244(c)(2), either of them, or both of them acting together, could effectively require the Attorney General to deport an alien once the Attorney General, in the exercise of legislatively delegated authority, had determined the alien should remain in the United States. Without the challenged provision in § 244(c)(2), this could have been achieved, if at all, only by legislation requiring deportation. Similarly, a veto by one House of Congress under § 244(c)(2) cannot be justified as an attempt at amending the standards set out in § 244(a)(1), or as a repeal of § 244 as applied to Chadha. Amendment and repeal of statutes, no less than enactment, must conform with Art. I. . . .

Finally, we see that when the Framers intended to authorize either House of Congress to act alone and outside of its prescribed bicameral legislative role, they narrowly and precisely defined the procedure for such action. There are four provisions in the Constitution, explicit and unambiguous, by which one House may act alone with the unreviewable force of law, not subject to the President's veto:

(a) The House of Representatives alone was given the power to initiate impeachments. Art. I, § 2, cl. 5;

(b) The Senate alone was given the power to conduct trials following impeachment on charges initiated by the House and to convict following trial. Art. I, § 3, cl. 6;

(c) The Senate alone was given final unreviewable power to approve or to disapprove Presidential appointments. Art. II, § 2, cl. 2;

(d) The Senate alone was given unreviewable power to ratify treaties negotiated by the President. Art. II, § 2, cl. 2.

Clearly, when the Draftsmen sought to confer special powers on one House, independent of the other House, or of the President, they did so in explicit, unambiguous terms. . . .

Since it is clear that the action by the House under § 244(c)(2) was not within any of the express constitutional exceptions authorizing one House to act alone, and equally clear that it was an exercise of legislative power, that action was subject to the standards prescribed in Art. I. . . . To accomplish what has been attempted by one House of Congress in this case requires action in conformity with the express procedures of the Constitution's prescription for legislative action: passage by a majority of both Houses and presentment to the President.

The veto authorized by § 244(c)(2) doubtless has been in many respects a convenient shortcut; the "sharing" with the Executive by Congress of its authority over aliens in this manner is, on its face, an appealing compromise. In purely practical terms, it is obviously easier for action to be taken by one House without submission to the President; but it is crystal clear from the records of the Convention, contemporaneous writings and debates, that the Framers ranked other values higher than efficiency. The records of the Convention and debates in the states preceding ratification underscore the common desire to define and limit the exercise of the newly created federal powers affecting the states and the people. There is unmistakable expression of a determination that legislation by the national Congress be a step-by-step, deliberate and deliberative process.

The choices we discern as having been made in the Constitutional Convention impose burdens on governmental processes that often seem clumsy, inefficient, even unworkable, but those hard choices were consciously made by men who had lived under a form of government that permitted arbitrary governmental acts to go unchecked. There is no support in the Constitution or decisions of this Court for the proposition that the cumbersomeness and delays often encountered in complying with explicit constitutional standards may be avoided, either by the Congress or by the President. See *Youngstown Sheet & Tube Co. v. Sawyer*, 343 U.S. 579 (1952). With all the obvious flaws of delay, untidiness, and potential for abuse, we have not yet found a better way to preserve freedom than by making the exercise of power subject to the carefully crafted restraints spelled out in the Constitution.

We hold that the congressional veto provision in § 244(c)(2) is severable from the Act and that it is unconstitutional.

■ JUSTICE POWELL, concurring in the judgment.

The Court's decision, based on the Presentment Clauses, Art. I, § 7, cls. 2 and 3, apparently will invalidate every use of the legislative veto. The breadth of this holding gives one pause. Congress has included the veto in literally hundreds of statutes, dating back to the 1930's. Congress clearly views this procedure as essential to controlling the delegation of power to administrative agencies. One reasonably may disagree with Congress' assessment of the veto's utility, but the respect due its judgment as a coordinate branch of Government cautions that our holding should be no more extensive than necessary to decide these cases. In my view, the cases may be decided on a narrower ground. When Congress finds that a particular person does not satisfy the statutory criteria for permanent residence in this country it has assumed a judicial function in violation of the principle of separation of powers. Accordingly, I concur only in the judgment. . . .

■ JUSTICE WHITE, dissenting.

Today the Court not only invalidates § 244(c)(2) of the Immigration and Nationality Act, but also sounds the death knell for nearly 200 other statutory provisions in which Congress has reserved a "legislative veto." For this reason, the Court's decision is of surpassing importance. And it is for this reason that the Court would have been well advised to decide the cases, if possible, on the narrower grounds of separation of powers, leaving for full consideration the constitutionality of other congressional review statutes operating on such varied matters as war powers and agency rule-making, some of which concern the independent regulatory agencies.

The prominence of the legislative veto mechanism in our contemporary political system and its importance to Congress can hardly be overstated. It has become a central means by which Congress secures the accountability of executive and independent agencies. Without the legislative veto, Congress is faced with a Hobson's choice: either to refrain from delegating the necessary authority, leaving itself with a hopeless task of writing laws with the requisite specificity to cover endless special circumstances across the entire policy landscape, or in the alternative, to abdicate its law-making function to the Executive Branch and independent agencies. To choose the former leaves major national problems unresolved; to opt for the latter risks unaccountable policymaking by those not elected to fill that role. Accordingly, over the past five decades, the legislative veto has been placed in nearly 200 statutes. The device is known in every field of governmental concern: reorganization, budgets, foreign affairs, war powers, and regulation of trade, safety, energy, the environment, and the economy. . . . *[Justice White proceeds to recount the history of the legislative veto, beginning with its origins in the Hoover administration.—Editors]*

Even this brief review suffices to demonstrate that the legislative veto is more than "efficient, convenient, and useful." It is an important if not indispensable political invention that allows the President and Congress to resolve major constitutional and policy differences, assures the accountability of independent regulatory agencies, and preserves Congress' control over lawmaking. Perhaps there are other means of accommodation and accountability, but the increasing reliance of Congress upon the legislative veto suggests that the alternatives to which Congress must now turn are not entirely satisfactory.

The history of the legislative veto also makes clear that it has not been a sword with which Congress has struck out to aggrandize itself at the expense of the other branches—the concerns of Madison and Hamilton. Rather, the veto has been a means of defense, a reservation of ultimate authority necessary if Congress is to fulfill its designated role under Art. I as the Nation's lawmaker. While the President has often objected to particular legislative vetoes, generally those left in the hands of congressional Committees, the Executive has more often agreed to legislative review as the price for a broad delegation of authority. To be sure, the President may have preferred unrestricted power, but that could be precisely why Congress thought it essential to retain a check on the exercise of delegated authority.

. . . [T]he constitutionality of the legislative veto is anything but clearcut. The issue divides scholars, courts, Attorneys General, and the two other branches of the National Government. If the veto devices so flagrantly disregarded the requirements of Art. I as the Court today suggests, I find it incomprehensible that Congress, whose Members are bound by oath to uphold the Constitution, would have placed these mechanisms in nearly 200 separate laws over a period of 50 years.

. . . We should not find the lack of a specific constitutional authorization for the legislative veto surprising, and I would not infer disapproval of the mechanism from its absence. From the summer of 1787 to the present the Government of the United States has become an endeavor far beyond the contemplation of the Framers. Only within the last half century has the complexity and size of the Federal Government's responsibilities grown so greatly that the Congress must rely on the legislative veto as the most effective if not the only means to insure its role as the Nation's lawmaker. But the wisdom of the Framers was to anticipate that the Nation would grow and new problems of governance would require different solutions. Accordingly, our Federal Government was intentionally chartered with the flexibility to respond to contemporary needs without losing sight of fundamental democratic principles. This was the spirit in which Justice Jackson penned his influential concurrence in the *Steel Seizure Case*. . . .

When the Convention did turn its attention to the scope of Congress' lawmaking power, the Framers were expansive. The Necessary and Proper Clause, Art. I, § 8, cl. 18, vests Congress with the power "[t]o make all Laws which shall be necessary and proper for carrying into Execution the foregoing Powers [the enumerated powers of § 8] and all other Powers vested by this Constitution in the Government of the United States, or in any Department or Officer thereof." It is long settled that Congress may "exercise its best judgment in the selection of measures, to carry into execution the constitutional powers of the government," and "avail itself of experience, to exercise its reason, and to accommodate its legislation to circumstances." *McCulloch v. Maryland*, 4 Wheat. 316, 415–416, 420 (1819).

The Court heeded this counsel in approving the modern administrative state. The Court's holding today that all legislative-type action must be enacted through the lawmaking process ignores that legislative authority is routinely delegated to the Executive Branch, to the independent regulatory agencies, and to private individuals and groups:

> The rise of administrative bodies probably has been the most significant legal trend of the last century. . . . They have become a veritable fourth branch of the Government, which has deranged our three-branch legal theories . . . .

FTC v. Ruberoid Co., 343 U.S. 470, 487 (1952) (Jackson, J. dissenting). This Court's decisions sanctioning such delegations make clear that Art. I does not require all action with the effect of legislation to be passed as a law.

Theoretically, agencies and officials were asked only to "fill up the details," and the rule was that "Congress cannot delegate any part of its legislative power except under the limitation of a prescribed standard." . . . In practice, however, restrictions on the scope of the power that could be delegated diminished and all but disappeared. In only two instances did the Court find an unconstitutional delegation. *Panama Refining Co. v. Ryan*, 293 U.S. 388 (1935); *A.L.A. Schechter Poultry Corp. v. United States*, 295 U.S. 495 (1935). . . .

If Congress may delegate lawmaking power to independent and Executive agencies, it is most difficult to understand Art. I as prohibiting Congress from also reserving a check on legislative power for itself. . . .

The Court also takes no account of perhaps the most relevant consideration: However resolutions of disapproval under § 244(c)(2) are formally characterized, in reality, a departure from the status quo occurs only upon the concurrence of opinion among the House, Senate, and President. . . .

The central concern of the presentment and bicameralism requirements of Art. I is that when a departure from the legal status quo is undertaken, it is done with the approval of the President and both Houses of Congress—or, in the event of a Presidential veto, a two-thirds majority in both Houses. This interest is fully satisfied by the operation of § 244(c)(2). The President's approval is found in the Attorney General's action in recommending to Congress that the deportation order for a given alien be suspended. The House and the Senate indicate their approval of the Executive's action by not passing a resolution of disapproval within the statutory period. Thus, a change in the legal status quo—the deportability of the alien—is consummated only with the approval of each of the three relevant actors. . . . Thus understood, § 244(c)(2) fully effectuates the purposes of the bicameralism and presentment requirements. . . .

I do not suggest that all legislative vetoes are necessarily consistent with separation-of-powers principles. A legislative check on an inherently executive function, for example, that of initiating prosecutions, poses an entirely different question. But the legislative veto device here—and in many other settings—is far from an instance of legislative tyranny over the Executive. It is a necessary check on the unavoidably expanding power of the agencies, both Executive and independent, as they engage in exercising authority delegated by Congress. . . .

Today's decision strikes down in one fell swoop provisions in more laws enacted by Congress than the Court has cumulatively invalidated in its history. I fear it will now be more difficult to "insur[e] that the fundamental policy decisions in our society will be made not by an appointed official but by the body immediately responsible to the people." I must dissent.

■ JUSTICE REHNQUIST, with whom JUSTICE WHITE joins, dissenting.

A severability clause creates a presumption that Congress intended the valid portion of the statute to remain in force when one part is found to be invalid. A severability clause does not, however, conclusively resolve the issue. "[T]he determination, in the end, is reached by" asking "[w]hat was the intent of the lawmakers," and "will rarely turn on the presence or absence of such a clause." Because I believe that Congress did not intend the one-House veto provision of § 244(c)(2) to be severable, I dissent. . . .

The Court finds that the legislative history of § 244 shows that Congress intended § 244(c)(2) to be severable because Congress wanted to relieve itself of the burden of private bills. But the history elucidated by the Court shows that Congress was unwilling to give the Executive Branch permission to suspend deportation on its own. Over the years, Congress consistently rejected requests from the Executive for complete discretion in this area. Congress always insisted on retaining ultimate control, whether by concurrent resolution . . . or by [the] one-House veto, as in the present Act. Congress has never indicated that it would be willing to permit suspensions of deportation unless it could retain some sort of veto.

. . . Congress' continued insistence on retaining control of the suspension process indicates that it has never been disposed to give the Executive Branch a free hand. . . .

Because I do not believe that § 244(c)(2) is severable, I would reverse the judgment of the Court of Appeals.

NOTES

1. Chief Justice Burger's majority opinion in *INS v. Chadha* has often been described as formalistic, like Justice Black's majority opinion in *Youngstown*, while Justice White's dissent in *Chadha* is openly functionalist or purposive like Justice Jackson's *Youngstown* concurrence. Chief Justice Burger's majority is formalist in that it asks which of the three powers of government Congress is exercising when it adopts a legislative veto. Burger concludes that here

Congress is trying to exercise its legislative power, but it can do that only through bicameralism and presentment. Congress cannot in *Chadha* exercise executive power since the Constitution gives all of the executive power to the president (who can delegate it). Congress also cannot in *Chadha* exercise judicial power because the Constitution vests that in the federal courts. So what power is Congress trying to exercise in this case? Hasn't Congress, in essence, delegated legislative power to a portion of itself here? That is, instead of sweepingly delegating the ultimate power to suspend deportations to the INS, Congress has instead delegated that power to either one of the two houses should they choose to act? Does that explain the outcome in *INS v. Chadha*? Justice White says Congress is not aggrandizing power to itself with the legislative veto. Is it? If Congress can delegate power to regulate broadcasting "in the public interest" to the Federal Communications Commission (as it has done), then why can't it delegate a similar power to just the Senate or just the House? Why not delegate it to one committee or subcommittee of one of the two houses? Indeed, why not just delegate all the legislative power to the Speaker of the House of Representatives? But if so, what would be left of the separation of powers?

2. Is the legislative veto really "legislative action" in the same sense as the enacting of a new statute or the repealing of an old one? Is this really a problem with Article I, Section 7 as the Court's opinion claims? Or is the true problem one of Congress attempting to control the executive branch's *execution* of delegated authority on a case by case basis? Or is the problem that Congress, by doing this, is exercising *judicial* power as Justice Powell believed? Interestingly, applying the requirements of a law to a particular situation might be a way of characterizing *execution* of the law or *adjudication*, depending on who is doing it and at what stage of the proceedings. Which characterization of the constitutional issue seems most accurate? Why did the Court treat *Chadha* as a case of procedurally defective attempted exercise of legislative power rather than an interference with law execution? Does it matter which power is characterized as having been at issue in *Chadha*?

3. The executive branch has long regarded legislative vetoes as unconstitutional. When a private party challenged the legislative veto in *Chadha*, the Department of Justice agreed with the challenge. But if the government and Chadha are on the same side, why is this case in court? The unusual procedural answer is that the Senate and House of Representatives were allowed to "intervene" as parties in the court of appeals in order to defend their respective interests in having the legislative veto upheld (since the executive branch was arguing that this provision was unconstitutional). In the Supreme Court, the solicitor general (the officer in the Department of Justice who usually argues cases before the Supreme Court) argued that the statute was unconstitutional, and attorneys for the Senate and House of Representatives argued that it was constitutional. Does this make sense? Or should the Department of Justice be required to defend the constitutionality of Congress's acts when challenged by a private party? And if the president believes some aspect of a law is unconstitutional, should the executive branch decline to enforce it?

4. The severability issue in *Chadha* is interesting. Would Congress have intended to delegate to the attorney general the authority to make determinations that would "suspend deportation" of an otherwise deportable alien, *without* the string attached that one house of Congress could override that determination? Maybe. Maybe not. When a court strikes down a provision within a law

as unconstitutional, should the whole law fall? Should it be presumed that the unconstitutional part is severable if the rest of the act is constitutional and can operate in a sensible fashion without the unconstitutional part? How can one tell what Congress would have chosen to do, if it knew it could not have the unconstitutional part of the statute? Is Justice Rehnquist right to let congressional intent trump the severability clause that Congress actually passed?

5. Should the mere presence of a legislative veto in an act of Congress suggest that members think they are delegating legislative power to the executive branch in violation of the non-delegation doctrine? Congress has only legislative and not executive power. Therefore any federal statute that reserved to one house the power to veto an executive action would imply that the power being delegated is in the view of Congress "legislative." One difficulty courts face in enforcing the non-delegation doctrine is that it is almost impossible to draw a line between what is "legislative" and what is "executive" power. How about a presumption that whenever Congress includes a legislative veto in a statute it must *ipso facto* think it is delegating legislative power? If so, the non-delegation doctrine ought to apply and be judicially enforced—but only when Congress attempts to reserve power to itself with a legislative veto!

6. A hypothetical: Congress passes a statute delegating to the attorney general the power to propose all laws and rules governing immigration policy in the United States and provides, pursuant to each house's rules power (Article I, Section 5) that such proposals shall automatically be deemed "passed" thirty days after submission, unless a member calls for a vote and the proposal is defeated by a simple majority of each house. The measure provides for presentment to the president of any immigration law or rule thus "passed." Constitutional? Does it get around the rule of *Chadha* in a way that satisfies the Constitution's requirements of bicameralism and presentment? If the answer to the last question is *yes*, how different is this hypothetical situation from the scheme struck down in *Chadha*?

7. Article I, Section 7 provides the president with veto authority, subject to a congressional override if two-thirds of the members of each house vote to pass the bill again. What is a "bill" as that word is used in Article I, Section 7? As illustrated by the severability issue in *INS v. Chadha*, a single legislative enactment can contain many provisions, both related and unrelated. Does anything in the Constitution restrict Congress's authority to "bundle" items together? Is such bundling permitted by each house's Article I, Section 5 authority to enact rules to govern its own proceedings? What if the effect of such bundling is to present the president with one enormous "bill" with all of the government's appropriations in it—leaving a dreadful all-or-nothing decision as to whether to veto the bill? Is that unconstitutional? May the president veto specific *items* within bills and sign the rest? Does Congress, not the president, get to define what is a "bill" for Article I, Section 7 purposes? Why?

8. Could Congress pass a statute delegating the power to line-item veto appropriations provisions and tax breaks for only a few people while allowing the rest of the bill to become law? This would give the president the authority to decline to spend congressionally appropriated funds. Could Congress provide that whenever the president exercised that authority, Congress would then take up (pursuant to its own rules and internal processes) a bill to reconsider the appropriation and perhaps pass it again as a new bill, with the president's discretion not to spend the funds being removed the second time around?

Would that violate any formal requirement of bicameralism, presentment, non-delegation, or presidential veto authority? What if Congress *called* its new enactment a delegation to the president of line-item-veto authority? Consider the next case, *Clinton v. City of New York*, which involves essentially this situation.

Clinton v. City of New York
524 U.S. 417 (1998)

■ JUSTICE STEVENS delivered the opinion of the Court.

The Line Item Veto Act was enacted in April 1996 and became effective on January 1, 1997. . . . [Later that year] the President exercised his authority to cancel one [spending] provision in the Balanced Budget Act of 1997, and two [limited tax relief benefit] provisions in the Taxpayer Relief Act of 1997. Appellees, claiming that they had been injured by two of those cancellations, filed these cases in the District Court. That Court . . . held the statute invalid, and we . . . expedited our review. We now hold that these appellees have standing to challenge the constitutionality of the Act and, reaching the merits, we agree that the cancellation procedures set forth in the Act violate the Presentment Clause, Art. I, § 7, cl. 2, of the Constitution. . . .

[The Supreme Court began by concluding it had jurisdiction and that the parties had standing to sue.—Editors]

The Line Item Veto Act gives the President the power to "cancel in whole" three types of provisions that have been signed into law: "(1) any dollar amount of discretionary budget authority; (2) any item of new direct spending; or (3) any limited tax benefit." It is undisputed that the New York case involves an "item of new direct spending" and that the Snake River case involves a "limited tax benefit" as those terms are defined in the Act. It is also undisputed that each of those provisions had been signed into law pursuant to Article I, § 7, of the Constitution before it was canceled.

The Act requires the President to adhere to precise procedures whenever he exercises his cancellation authority. In identifying items for cancellation he must consider the legislative history, the purposes, and other relevant information about the items. He must determine, with respect to each cancellation, that it will "(i) reduce the Federal budget deficit; (ii) not impair any essential Government functions; and (iii) not harm the national interest." Moreover, he must transmit a special message to Congress notifying it of each cancellation within five calendar days (excluding Sundays) after the enactment of the canceled provision. It is undisputed that the President meticulously followed these procedures in these cases.

A cancellation takes effect upon receipt by Congress of the special message from the President. If, however, a "disapproval bill" pertaining to a special message is enacted into law, the cancellations set forth in that message become "null and void." The Act sets forth a detailed expedited procedure for the consideration of a "disapproval bill," . . . but no such bill was passed for either of the cancellations involved in these cases. A majority vote of both Houses is sufficient to enact a disapproval bill. The Act does not grant the President the authority to cancel a disapproval bill, but he does, of course, retain his constitutional authority to veto such a bill.

The effect of a cancellation is . . . [that it] prevents the item "from having legal force or effect." Thus, under the plain text of the statute, the two actions of the President that are challenged in these cases prevented one section of the Balanced Budget Act of 1997 and one section of the Taxpayer Relief Act of 1997 "from having legal force or effect." The remaining provisions of those statutes, with the exception of the second canceled item in the latter, continue to have the same force and effect as they had when signed into law.

In both legal and practical effect, the President has amended two Acts of Congress by repealing a portion of each. "[R]epeal of statutes, no less than enactment, must conform with Art. I." *INS v. Chadha*, 462 U.S. 919, 954 (1983). There is no provision in the Constitution that authorizes the President to enact, to amend, or to repeal statutes. Both Article I and Article II assign responsibilities to the President that directly relate to the lawmaking process, but neither addresses the issue presented by these cases. . . .

There are important differences between the President's "return" of a bill pursuant to Article I, § 7, and the exercise of the President's cancellation authority pursuant to the Line Item Veto Act. The constitutional return takes place before the bill becomes law; the statutory cancellation occurs after the bill becomes law. The constitutional return is of the entire bill; the statutory cancellation is of only a part. Although the Constitution expressly authorizes the President to play a role in the process of enacting statutes, it is silent on the subject of unilateral Presidential action that either repeals or amends parts of duly enacted statutes.

There are powerful reasons for construing constitutional silence on this profoundly important issue as equivalent to an express prohibition. The procedures governing the enactment of statutes set forth in the text of Article I were the product of the great debates and compromises that produced the Constitution itself. Familiar historical materials provide abundant support for the conclusion that the power to enact statutes may only "be exercised in accord with a single, finely wrought and exhaustively considered, procedure." *Chadha*, 462 U.S., at 951. Our first President understood the text of the Presentment Clause as requiring that he either "approve all the parts of a Bill, or reject it in toto." What has emerged in these cases from the President's exercise of his statutory cancellation powers, however, are truncated versions of two bills that passed both Houses of Congress. They are not the product of the "finely wrought" procedure that the Framers designed. . . .

The Line Item Veto Act authorizes the President himself to effect the repeal of laws, for his own policy reasons, without observing the procedures set out in Article I, § 7. The fact that Congress intended such a result is of no moment. . . . Congress cannot alter the procedures set out in Article I, § 7, without amending the Constitution.

Neither are we persuaded by the Government's contention that the President's authority to cancel new direct spending and tax benefit items is no greater than his traditional authority to decline to spend appropriated funds. The Government has reviewed in some detail the series of statutes in which Congress has given the Executive broad discretion over the expenditure of appropriated funds. For example, the First Congress appropriated "sum[s] not exceeding" specified amounts to be spent on various Government operations. In those statutes, as in later years, the President was given wide discretion with respect to both the amounts to be spent and how the money would be allocated among different functions. It is argued that the Line Item Veto Act merely confers comparable discretionary authority over the expenditure of appropriated funds. The critical difference between this statute and all of its predecessors, however, is that unlike any of them, this Act gives the President the unilateral power to change the text of duly enacted statutes. None of the Act's predecessors could even arguably have been construed to authorize such a change.

... [A]lthough appellees challenge the validity of the Act on alternative grounds, the only issue we address concerns the "finely wrought" procedure commanded by the Constitution. *Chadha*, 462 U.S., at 951. We have been favored with extensive debate about the scope of Congress' power to delegate law-making authority, or its functional equivalent, to the President. The excellent briefs filed by the parties and their *amici curiae* have provided us with valuable historical information that illuminates the delegation issue but does not really bear on the narrow issue that is dispositive of these cases. Thus, because we conclude that the Act's cancellation provisions violate Article I, § 7, of the Constitution, we find it unnecessary to consider the District Court's alternative holding that the Act "impermissibly disrupts the balance of powers among the three branches of government."

[O]ur decision rests on the narrow ground that the procedures authorized by the Line Item Veto Act are not authorized by the Constitution. The Balanced Budget Act of 1997 is a 500–page document that became "Public Law 105–33" after three procedural steps were taken: (1) a bill containing its exact text was approved by a majority of the members of the House of Representatives; (2) the Senate approved precisely the same text; and (3) that text was signed into law by the President. The Constitution explicitly requires that each of those three steps be taken before a bill may "become a law." Art. I, § 7. If one paragraph of that text had been omitted at any one of those three stages, Public Law 105–33 would not have been validly enacted. If the Line Item Veto Act were valid, it would authorize the President to create a different law—one whose text was not voted on by either House of Congress or presented to the President for signature. ...

If there is to be a new procedure in which the President will play a different role in determining the final text of what may "become a law," such change must come not by legislation but through the amendment procedures set forth in Article V of the Constitution. Cf. *U.S. Term Limits, Inc. v. Thornton*, 514 U.S. 779, 837 (1995). ...

■ JUSTICE KENNEDY, concurring.

... [M]y colleague JUSTICE BREYER ... observes that the statute does not threaten the liberties of individual citizens, a point on which I disagree. The argument is related to his earlier suggestion that our role is lessened here because the two political branches are adjusting their own powers between themselves. To say the political branches have a somewhat free hand to reallocate their own authority would seem to require acceptance of two premises: first, that the public good demands it, and second, that liberty is not at risk. The former premise is inadmissible. The Constitution's structure requires a stability which transcends the convenience of the moment. The latter premise, too, is flawed. Liberty is always at stake when one or more of the branches seek to transgress the separation of powers.

Separation of powers was designed to implement a fundamental insight: concentration of power in the hands of a single branch is a threat to liberty. The Federalist states the axiom in these explicit terms: "The accumulation of all powers, legislative, executive, and judiciary, in the same hands ... may justly be pronounced the very definition of tyranny." The

Federalist No. 47. So convinced were the Framers that liberty of the person inheres in structure that at first they did not consider a Bill of Rights necessary. The Federalist No. 84; G. Wood, The Creation of the American Republic 1776–1787, pp. 536–543 (1969). It was at Madison's insistence that the First Congress enacted the Bill of Rights. It would be a grave mistake, however, to think a Bill of Rights in Madison's scheme then or in sound constitutional theory now renders separation of powers of lesser importance.

In recent years, perhaps, we have come to think of liberty as defined by that word in the Fifth and Fourteenth Amendments and as illuminated by the other provisions of the Bill of Rights. The conception of liberty embraced by the Framers was not so confined. They used the principles of separation of powers and federalism to secure liberty in the fundamental political sense of the term, quite in addition to the idea of freedom from intrusive governmental acts. . . .

The principal object of the statute, it is true, was not to enhance the President's power to reward one group and punish another, to help one set of taxpayers and hurt another, to favor one State and ignore another. Yet these are its undeniable effects. The law establishes a new mechanism which gives the President the sole ability to hurt a group that is a visible target, in order to disfavor the group or to extract further concessions from Congress. The law is the functional equivalent of a line item veto and enhances the President's powers beyond what the Framers would have endorsed.

It is no answer, of course, to say that Congress surrendered its authority by its own hand; nor does it suffice to point out that a new statute, signed by the President or enacted over his veto, could restore to Congress the power it now seeks to relinquish. That a congressional cession of power is voluntary does not make it innocuous. The Constitution is a compact enduring for more than our time, and one Congress cannot yield up its own powers, much less those of other Congresses to follow. Abdication of responsibility is not part of the constitutional design. . . .

The citizen has a vital interest in the regularity of the exercise of governmental power. If this point was not clear before *Chadha*, it should have been so afterwards. . . . By increasing the power of the President beyond what the Framers envisioned, the statute compromises the political liberty of our citizens, liberty which the separation of powers seeks to secure. . . .

■ JUSTICE BREYER, with whom JUSTICE O'CONNOR and JUSTICE SCALIA join as to Part III, dissenting.

I agree with the Court that the parties have standing, but I do not agree with its ultimate conclusion. In my view the Line Item Veto Act does not violate any specific textual constitutional command, nor does it violate any implicit Separation of Powers principle. Consequently, I believe that the Act is constitutional.

I approach the constitutional question before us with three general considerations in mind. *First*, the Act represents a legislative effort to provide the President with the power to give effect to some, but not to all, of the expenditure and revenue-diminishing provisions contained in a single massive appropriations bill. And this objective is constitutionally proper.

When our Nation was founded, Congress could easily have provided the President with this kind of power. In that time period, our population was less than four million, federal employees numbered fewer than 5,000, annual federal budget outlays totaled approximately $4 million, and the entire operative text of Congress's first general appropriations law read as follows:

> Be it enacted . . . [t]hat there be appropriated for the service of the present year, to be paid out of the monies which arise, either from the requisitions heretofore made upon the several states, or from the duties on import and tonnage, the following sums, viz. A sum not exceeding two hundred and sixteen thousand dollars for defraying the expenses of the civil list, under the late and present government; a sum not exceeding one hundred and thirty-seven thousand dollars for defraying the expenses of the department of war; a sum not exceeding one hundred and ninety thousand dollars for discharging the warrants issued by the late board of treasury, and remaining unsatisfied; and a sum not exceeding ninety-six thousand dollars for paying the pensions to invalids.

Act of Sept. 29, 1789, ch. 23, § 1, 1 Stat. 95.

At that time, a Congress, wishing to give a President the power to select among appropriations, could simply have embodied each appropriation in a separate bill, each bill subject to a separate Presidential veto.

Today, however, our population is about 250 million, the Federal Government employs more than four million people, the annual federal budget is $1.5 trillion, and a typical budget appropriations bill may have a dozen titles, hundreds of sections, and spread across more than 500 pages of the Statutes at Large. Congress cannot divide such a bill into thousands, or tens of thousands, of separate appropriations bills, each one of which the President would have to sign, or to veto, separately. Thus, the question is whether the Constitution permits Congress to choose a particular novel *means* to achieve this same, constitutionally legitimate, *end*.

Second, the case in part requires us to focus upon the Constitution's generally phrased structural provisions, provisions that delegate all "legislative" power to Congress and vest all "executive" power in the President. The Court, when applying these provisions, has interpreted them generously in terms of the institutional arrangements that they permit. . . . *McCulloch v. Maryland*, 4 Wheat. 316, 415 (1819). . . .

Third, we need not here referee a dispute among the other two branches. . . .

These three background circumstances mean that, when one measures the literal words of the Act against the Constitution's literal commands, the fact that the Act may closely resemble a different, literally unconstitutional, arrangement is beside the point. To drive exactly 65 miles per hour on an interstate highway closely resembles an act that violates the speed limit. But it does not violate that limit, for small differences matter when the question is one of literal violation of law. No more does this Act literally violate the Constitution's words. . . .

When the President "canceled" the two appropriation measures now before us, he did not *repeal* any law nor did he *amend* any law. He simply *followed* the law, leaving the statutes, as they are literally written, intact. . . .

Because I disagree with the Court's holding of literal violation, I must consider whether the Act nonetheless violates Separation of Powers principles—principles that arise out of the Constitution's vesting of the "executive Power" in "a President," U.S. Const., Art. II, § 1, and "[a]ll legislative Powers" in "a Congress," Art. I, § 1. There are three relevant Separation of Powers questions here: (1) Has Congress given the President the wrong kind of power, i.e., "non-Executive" power? (2) Has Congress given the President the power to "encroach" upon Congress' own constitutionally reserved territory? (3) Has Congress given the President too much power, violating the doctrine of "nondelegation?" These three limitations help assure "adequate control by the citizen's representatives in Congress," upon which Justice KENNEDY properly insists. And with respect to this Act, the answer to all these questions is "no."

Viewed conceptually, the power the Act conveys is the right kind of power. It is "executive." As explained above, an exercise of that power "executes" the Act. Conceptually speaking, it closely resembles the kind of delegated authority—to spend or not to spend appropriations, to change or not to change tariff rates—that Congress has frequently granted the President, any differences being differences in degree, not kind.

The fact that one could also characterize this kind of power as "legislative," say, if Congress itself (by amending the appropriations bill) prevented a provision from taking effect, is beside the point. This Court has frequently found that the exercise of a particular power, such as the power to make rules of broad applicability, . . . can fall within the constitutional purview of more than one branch of Government. . . .

The Act does not undermine what this Court has often described as the principal function of the separation-of-powers, which is to maintain the tripartite structure of the Federal Government—and thereby protect individual liberty—by providing a "safeguard against the encroachment or aggrandizement of one branch at the expense of the other." See The Federalist No. 51 (J. Madison) (separation of powers confers on each branch the means "to resist encroachments of the others").

. . . [O]ne cannot say that the Act "encroaches" upon Congress' power, when Congress retained the power to insert, by simple majority, into any future appropriations bill, into any section of any such bill, or into any phrase of any section, a provision that says the Act will not apply. . . . And it is Congress that drafts and enacts the appropriations statutes that are subject to the Act in the first place—and thereby defines the outer limits of the President's cancellation authority. Thus this Act is not the sort of delegation "without . . . sufficient check" that concerns Justice KENNEDY. . . .

Nor can one say the Act's grant of power "aggrandizes" the Presidential office. The grant is limited to the context of the budget. It is limited to the power to spend, or not to spend, particular appropriated items, and the power to permit, or not to permit, specific limited exemptions from generally applicable tax law from taking effect. These powers . . . resemble those the President has exercised in the past on other occasions. The delegation of those powers to the President may strengthen the Presidency, but any such change in Executive Branch authority seems minute when compared with the changes worked by delegations of other kinds of authority that the Court in the past has upheld. . . .

In sum, I recognize that the Act before us is novel. In a sense, it skirts a constitutional edge. But that edge has to do with means, not ends. The means chosen do not amount literally to the enactment, repeal, or amendment of a law. Nor, for that matter, do they amount literally to the "line item veto" that the Act's title announces. Those means do not violate any basic Separation of Powers principle. They do not improperly shift the constitutionally foreseen balance of power from Congress to the President. Nor, since they comply with Separation of Powers principles, do they threaten the liberties of individual citizens. They represent an experiment that may, or may not, help representative government work better. The Constitution, in my view, authorizes Congress and the President to try novel methods in this way. Consequently, with respect, I dissent.

■ JUSTICE SCALIA, with whom JUSTICE O'CONNOR joins, and with whom JUSTICE BREYER joins as to Part III, concurring in part and dissenting in part.

III

. . . The Presentment Clause requires, in relevant part, that "[e]very Bill which shall have passed the House of Representatives and the Senate, shall, before it becomes a Law, be presented to the President of the United States; If he approve he shall sign it, but if not he shall return it," U.S. Const., Art. I, § 7, cl. 2. There is no question that enactment of the Balanced Budget Act complied with these requirements: the House and Senate passed the bill, and the President signed it into law. It was only after the requirements of the Presentment Clause had been satisfied that the President exercised his authority under the Line Item Veto Act to cancel the spending item. Thus, the Court's problem with the Act is not that it authorizes the President to veto parts of a bill and sign others into law, but rather that it authorizes him to "cancel"—prevent from "having legal force or effect"—certain parts of duly enacted statutes.

Article I, § 7, of the Constitution obviously prevents the President from cancelling a law that Congress has not authorized him to cancel. Such action cannot possibly be considered part of his execution of the law, and if it is legislative action, as the Court observes, "repeal of statutes, no less than enactment, must conform with Art. I." But that is not this case. It was certainly arguable, as an original matter, that Art. I, § 7, also prevents the President from cancelling a law which itself authorizes the President to cancel it. But as the Court acknowledges, that argument has long since been made and rejected. In 1809, Congress passed a law authorizing the President to cancel trade restrictions against Great Britain and France if either revoked edicts directed at the United States. Joseph Story regarded the conferral of that authority as entirely unremarkable in *The Orono*, 18 F. Cas. 830 (No. 10,585) (CCD Mass. 1812). The Tariff Act of 1890 authorized the President to "suspend, by proclamation to that effect" certain of its provisions if he determined that other countries were imposing "reciprocally unequal and unreasonable" duties. This Court upheld the constitutionality of that Act in *Field v. Clark*, 143 U. S. 649 (1892).

As much as the Court goes on about Art. I, § 7, therefore, that provision does not demand the result the Court reaches. It no more categorically prohibits the Executive reduction of congressional dispositions in the course of implementing statutes that authorize such reduction, than it categorically prohibits the Executive *augmentation* of congressional dispositions in the course of implementing statutes that authorize such augmentation—generally known as substantive rulemaking. There are, to be sure, limits upon the former just as there are limits upon the latter—and I am prepared to acknowledge that the limits upon the former may be much more severe. Those limits are established, however, not by some categorical prohibition of Art. I, § 7, which our cases conclusively disprove, but by what has come to be known as the doctrine of unconstitutional delegation of legislative authority: When authorized Executive reduction or augmentation is allowed to go too far, it usurps the nondelegable function of Congress and violates the separation of powers.

It is this doctrine, and not the Presentment Clause, that was discussed in the *Field* opinion, and it is this doctrine, and not the Presentment Clause, that is the issue presented by the statute before us here. . . . [The issue here has] nothing to do with whether the details of Art. I, § 7, have been complied with, but everything to do with whether the authorizations went too far by transferring to the Executive a degree of political, lawmaking power that our traditions demand be retained by the Legislative Branch.

I turn, then, to the crux of the matter: whether Congress's authorizing the President to cancel an item of spending gives him a power that our history and traditions show must reside exclusively in the Legislative Branch. I may note, to begin with, that the Line Item Veto Act is not the first statute to authorize the President to "cancel" spending items. . . .

Insofar as the degree of political, "lawmaking" power conferred upon the Executive is concerned, there is not a dime's worth of difference between Congress's authorizing the President to *cancel* a spending item, and Congress's authorizing money to be spent on a particular item at the President's discretion. And the latter has been done since the Founding of the Nation. From 1789–1791, the First Congress made lump-sum appropriations for the entire Government—"sum[s] not exceeding" specified amounts for broad purposes. From a very early date Congress also made permissive individual appropriations, leaving the decision whether to spend the money to the President's unfettered discretion. In 1803, it appropriated $50,000 for the President to build "not exceeding fifteen gun boats, to be armed, manned and fitted out, and employed for such purposes as in his opinion the public service may require." President Jefferson reported that "[t]he sum of fifty thousand dollars appropriated by Congress for providing gun boats remains unexpended. The favorable and peaceable turn of affairs on the Mississippi rendered an immediate execution of that law unnecessary." Examples of appropriations committed to the discretion of the President abound in our history. During the Civil War, an Act appropriated over $76 million to be divided among various items "as the exigencies of the service may require." During the Great Depression, Congress appropriated $950 million "for such projects and/or purposes and under such rules and regulations as the President in his discretion may prescribe," and $4 billion for general classes of projects, the money to be spent "in the discretion and under the direction of the President." The constitutionality of such appropriations has never seriously been questioned. Rather, "[t]hat Congress has wide discretion in the matter of prescribing details of expenditures for which it appropriates must, of course, be plain. Appropriations and other acts of Congress are replete with instances of general appropriations of large amounts, to be allotted and expended as directed by designated government agencies." *Cincinnati Soap Co. v. United States*, 301 U.S. 308, 321–322 (1937).

Certain Presidents have claimed Executive authority to withhold appropriated funds even *absent* an express conferral of discretion to do so. In 1876, for example, President Grant reported to Congress that he would not spend money appropriated for certain harbor and river improvements, because "[u]nder no circumstances [would he] allow expenditures upon works not clearly national," and in his view, the appropriations were for "works of purely private or local interest, in no sense national." President Franklin D. Roosevelt impounded funds appropriated for a flood control reservoir and levee in Oklahoma. President Truman ordered the impoundment of hundreds of millions of dollars that had been appropriated for military aircraft. President Nixon, the Mahatma Gandhi of all impounders, asserted at a press conference in 1973 that his "constitutional right" to impound appropriated funds was "absolutely clear." Our decision two years later in *Train v. City of New York*, 420 U.S. 35 (1975), proved him wrong, but it implicitly confirmed that Congress may confer discretion upon the executive to withhold appropriated funds, even funds appropriated for a specific purpose. The statute at issue in *Train* authorized spending "not to exceed" specified sums for certain projects, and directed that such "[s]ums authorized to be appropriated . . . shall be allotted" by the Administrator of the Environmental Protection Agency, 33 U.S.C. §§ 1285, 1287 (1970 ed., Supp. III). Upon enactment of this statute, the President directed the Administrator to allot no more than a certain part of the amount authorized. This Court held, as a matter of statutory interpretation, that the statute *did not grant* the Executive discretion to withhold the funds, but required allotment of the full amount authorized.

The short of the matter is this: Had the Line Item Veto Act authorized the President to "decline to spend" any item of spending contained in the Balanced Budget Act of 1997, there is not the slightest doubt that authorization would have been constitutional. What the Line Item Veto Act does instead—authorizing the President to "cancel" an item of spending—is technically different. But the technical difference does *not* relate to the technicalities of the Presentment Clause, which have been fully complied with; and the doctrine of unconstitutional delegation, which is at issue here, is preeminently not a doctrine of technicalities. The title of the Line Item Veto Act, which was perhaps designed to simplify for public comprehension, or perhaps merely to comply with the terms of a campaign pledge, has succeeded in faking out the Supreme Court. The President's action it authorizes in fact is not a line-item veto and thus does not offend Art. I, § 7; and insofar as the substance of that action is concerned, it is no different from what Congress has permitted the President to do since the formation of the Union. . . .

NOTES

1. Does the result in *Clinton v. City of New York* follow inexorably from the holding of *INS v. Chadha*? Why exactly is the line-item veto unconstitutional given that there is nothing to stop Congress from inserting boilerplate language in every statute authorizing the president to, for example, spend between $300 billion and $0.00 on national defense in any given year? As the dissents point out, the first budget of the United States for the Washington administration read like this. Is the delegation of spending-power control to the president more problematic when the federal government spends almost 25% of the Gross Domestic Product rather than 1% or 2%? Is this a non-delegation doctrine case masquerading as a bicameralism and presentment case?

2. Note Justice Kennedy's observation in his concurrence that a president armed with a line-item veto will have a powerful tool when negotiating with senators or representatives about other matters. Is this the real alteration in the balance of power that the Court fears in *Clinton v. City of New York*? Is Justice Kennedy too cynical about the log-rolling and horse-trading that he

thinks goes on between the president and Congress? What weight, if any, should the Supreme Court give to this concern in deciding whether the delegation of power went too far?

3. You are advising Congress. May it re-enact a statute essentially like the Line Item Veto Act in substance by making some changes? What would you recommend? What exactly did the Court find wrong with the statute? If the problem is capable of correction by changing the form or label of the statute, was the Court wrong to have struck it down? Is Justice Scalia correct when he says Congress succeeded inadvertently in "faking out the Supreme Court" by passing a law that looked as if it was unconstitutional when it wasn't?

A NOTE ON EXCLUSIVE AND CONCURRENT POWERS IN ARTICLE I, SECTION 8

The "herein granted" language of Article I, Section 1 is made operational by the listing of limited and enumerated powers in the remainder of Article I and the rest of the Constitution. In particular, Article I, Section 8 contains eighteen clauses, each granting a different enumerated power to Congress. It operates in tandem with Article I, Section 10, which forbids the states from doing most of the things Congress is empowered to do. When read together, Article I, Sections 8 and 10 explicitly give Congress the following *exclusive* legislative powers: (1) the power to lay uniform duties, imposts, and excise taxes for the purpose of raising revenue; (2) the power to coin money, emit bills of credit, or make anything but gold and silver coin a tender in payment of debts; (3) the power to declare war, issue letters of marque and reprisal, keep troops or ships of war in time of peace, and to define and punish piracies and offense against the law of nations; and (4) the power to legislate for the District of Columbia. (Note that Article II, Section 2 reserves the power to make treaties to the president acting with the concurrence of two-thirds of the Senate.)

Article I, Section 8 gives Congress other powers which would seem implicitly to be exclusive. These include: (1) the power to borrow money on the credit of the United States; (2) the power to adopt a uniform rule of naturalization; (3) the power to fix the standard of weights and measures; (4) the power to punish the counterfeiters of U.S. coins; (5) the power to establish post offices and post roads; (6) the power to protect copyrights and patents; (7) the power to constitute tribunals inferior to the Supreme Court; (8) the power to provide rules and regulations for the armed forces of the United States; and (9) the power to provide for the organizing, arming and disciplining of the militias. Some of these powers were exercised by the states after 1789 for some time. See, e.g., Gerald L. Neuman, STRANGERS TO THE CONSTITUTION: IMMIGRANTS, BORDERS, AND FUNDAMENTAL LAW (1996) (discussing the power of naturalization). One might have thought that Congress's power to establish uniform bankruptcy laws was an exclusive federal power, but the Supreme Court ruled otherwise in *Sturges v. Crowninshield*, 17 U.S. 122 (1819). (Note, however, that Chief Justice Marshall and Justice Story later took a position in dissent in another case, *Ogden v. Saunders*, 25 U.S. 213 (1827), which suggests they thought the power to enact bankruptcy laws was exclusively federal.)

Congress's Article I, Section 8 powers are augmented by the following limited and enumerated powers: (1) the implied power to legislate to protect full faith and credit being given in each state to the public acts, records, and judicial proceedings of every other state; (2) the implied power to pass laws dealing with the recovery of fugitives from justice from one state into another; (3) the implied power to pass laws dealing with the recovery of fugitive slaves; (4) the explicit power to admit new states into the union; (5) the explicit power to make all needful rules and regulations respecting the territory and property of the United States; (6) the implied power to guarantee to every state a "Republican Form of Government" and to protect the states against invasion and "domestic Violence"; (7) the explicit power of two-thirds of both houses, when acting with three-quarters of the states, to amend the Constitution; and (8) the implied powers to secure all debts of the United States, to effectuate the supremacy of federal law, and to specify an oath of allegiance to the Constitution and laws of the United States.

Many of these additional powers of Congress suggested by Articles IV, V, and VI are also necessarily exclusive federal powers. The Supreme Court, for example, even held that the power to recover fugitive slaves was an exclusive federal power in *Prigg v. Pennsylvania*, 41 U.S. 539 (1842). If that is right then obviously the power to admit new states into the union, the power to govern the territories and property of the United States, the power to guarantee to the states a republican form of government, and the power to effectuate duties imposed by Article VI must be exclusively federal powers. And a number of constitutional amendments give Congress power to enforce them by enacting appropriate legislation: the Thirteenth, Fourteenth, Fifteenth, Sixteenth, Nineteenth, Twentieth, Twenty–first, Twenty–third, Twenty–fourth, Twenty–fifth, and Twenty–sixth Amendments. The grants of power to Congress in these amendments are sometimes exclusive; more often these are grants to Congress of concurrent enforcement power.

What powers are left over then from Article I, Section 8 that are held concurrently with the states? The Supreme Court has identified two powers that are at least partly concurrent: (1) Congress's power to regulate commerce, whether with foreign nations, among the several states, or with the Indian tribes; and (2) Congress's power to make all laws which shall be necessary and proper for carrying into execution its other powers. The tricky thing, however, is that the Supreme Court has also said that sometimes the Commerce Clause power is exclusively federal, at least when state regulations and laws unreasonably burden the "commerce among the several States" or with foreign nations and Indian tribes. The Supreme Court identifies case by case which state regulations it thinks are unconstitutionally burdensome and which it thinks are not.

The Necessary and Proper Clause power would seem on its face to be concurrent. But sometimes the Supreme Court finds, as it did in *McCulloch v. Maryland*, and as it has done in the new federal common law cases, that the Constitution of its own force preempts state laws and executive or judicial actions that are unreasonably burdensome to or discriminatory against federal powers, officials, or institutions (such as the Bank of the United States).

The bottom line is that Article I, Section 8 creates a formidably powerful federal government whose powers have been greatly augmented by subsequent constitutional amendments. The federal government is one of limited and enumerated powers, but many of those powers are exclusive and many more powers have been implied. There is not much that Congress now lacks the power to do. It cannot discriminate against the institutions or instrumentalities of state governance since doing so is not "necessary and proper," and it cannot force a state which outlaws alcohol to legalize it (as will be discussed in Chapter 4). But there is not much else that is today beyond the scope of federal power. That raises insistently the question of what limits Article I, Section 9 puts on congressional power, the question considered next.

[*Assignment 16*]

F. QUASI–JUDICIAL LEGISLATION: "NO . . . BILL OF ATTAINDER, EX POST FACTO LAW, OR LAW IMPAIRING THE OBLIGATION OF CONTRACTS"

Article I, Section 9: . . . The Privilege of the Writ of Habeas Corpus shall not be suspended, unless when in Cases or Rebellion or Invasion the public Safety may require it. No Bill of Attainder or ex post facto Law shall be passed. . . .

Section 10: No State shall . . . pass any Bill of Attainder, ex post facto Law, or Law impairing the Obligation of Contracts. . . .

In Article I, the rule of recognition for federal lawmaking (Section 7) is followed by a sweeping list of eighteen enumerated powers for the federal government (Section 8), which is followed in turn by limits on federal power (Section 9) and clarification about which federal powers are exclusive and which are shared concurrently with the states (Section 10).

The Suspension Clause, which is found in Article I, Section 9, prevents Congress from suspending the writ of habeas corpus except in cases of rebellion or invasion where the public safety requires doing so. The Suspension Clause is discussed below in the materials on Article II, but it is an important starting point for the various restrictions on Congress and state legislatures found in Sections 9 and 10, because it preserves a longstanding protection at common law—the writ of habeas corpus.

Similarly, each of the other provisions in Section 9 and Section 10 quoted above ensures a kind of procedural regularity. Each one is rooted in common law notions of due process and in the separation of powers required by the U.S. Constitution. Three kinds of lawmaking are prohibited: (1) bills of attainder, (2) ex post facto laws, and (3) laws impairing the obligation of contracts. As you can tell by reading these sections carefully, Congress and the state legislatures are both forbidden to pass bills of attainder or ex post facto laws, while the restriction on laws impairing the obligation of contracts applies only to state legislatures.

Begin with bills of attainder. What are they, and what is so dangerous about them that the framers would prohibit their enactment by the national or state governments? A bill of attainder is a legislative act targeted at only one or a few individuals that declares them to be guilty of a crime and specifies the punishment that they must suffer. When a legislature passes a bill of attainder, there are two essential problems. First, by declaring someone already to be guilty of a crime, the legislature is circumventing all of the protections of a criminal trial (such as trial by jury and the right to confront opposing witnesses). Second, the legislature is not really acting like a legislature, but is instead acting as if it were a court that could adjudicate a specific case.

Bills of attainder are an old problem, but they have recurred with disturbing frequency throughout American history. Consider the following case, and evaluate the types of constitutional argument, or modes of interpretation, that the opinions use to decide whether the challenged statute was a bill of attainder.

United States v. Brown
381 U.S. 437 (1965)

■ MR. CHIEF JUSTICE WARREN delivered the opinion of the Court.

In this case we review for the first time a conviction under § 504 of the Labor–Management Reporting and Disclosure Act of 1959, which makes it a crime for a member of the Communist Party to serve as an officer or . . . an employee of a labor union.[1] . . .

Respondent has been a working longshoreman on the San Francisco docks, and an open and avowed Communist, for more than a quarter of a century. He was elected to the Executive Board of Local 10 of the International Longshoremen's and Warehousemen's Union for consecutive one-year terms in 1959, 1960, and 1961. On May 24, 1961, respondent was charged in a one-count indictment returned in the Northern District of California with "knowingly and willfully serv[ing] as a member of an executive board of a labor organization . . . while a member of the Communist Party, in willful violation of Title 29, United States Code, Section 504." It was neither charged nor proven that respondent at any time advocated or suggested illegal activity by the union, or proposed a political strike. The jury found respondent guilty, and he was sentenced to six months' imprisonment. The Court of Appeals for the Ninth Circuit, sitting *en banc*, reversed and remanded with instructions to set aside the conviction and dismiss the indictment, holding that § 504 violates the First and Fifth Amendments to the Constitution. We granted certiorari.

Respondent urges—in addition to the grounds relied on by the court below—that the statute under which he was convicted is a bill of attainder, and therefore violates Art. I, § 9, of the Constitution. We agree that § 504 is void as a bill of attainder and affirm the decision of the Court of Appeals on that basis. We therefore find it unnecessary to consider the First and Fifth Amendment arguments.

I

The provisions outlawing bills of attainder were adopted by the Constitutional Convention unanimously, and without debate.

"No Bill of Attainder or ex post facto Law shall be passed [by the Congress]." Art. I, § 9, cl. 3.

"No State shall . . . pass any Bill of Attainder, ex post facto Law, or Law impairing the Obligation of Contracts. . . ." Art. I, § 10.

A logical starting place for an inquiry into the meaning of the prohibition is its historical background. The bill of attainder, a parliamentary act

---

[1] The section, which took effect on September 14, 1959, provides, in pertinent part:

(a) No person who is or has been a member of the Communist Party . . . shall serve—

(1) as an officer, director, trustee, member of any executive board or similar governing body, business agent, manager, organizer, or other employee (other than as an employee performing exclusively clerical or custodial duties) of any labor organization . . . during or for five years after the termination of his membership in the Communist Party. . . .

(b) Any person who willfully violates this section shall be fined not more than $10,000 or imprisoned for not more than one year, or both.

sentencing to death one or more specific persons, was a device often resorted to in sixteenth, seventeenth and eighteenth century England for dealing with persons who had attempted, or threatened to attempt, to overthrow the government. In addition to the death sentence, attainder generally carried with it a "corruption of blood," which meant that the attainted party's heirs could not inherit his property. The "bill of pains and penalties" was identical to the bill of attainder, except that it prescribed a penalty short of death, *e.g.*, banishment, deprivation of the right to vote, or exclusion of the designated party's sons from Parliament. Most bills of attainder and bills of pains and penalties named the parties to whom they were to apply; a few, however, simply described them. While some left the designated parties a way of escaping the penalty, others did not. The use of bills of attainder and bills of pains and penalties was not limited to England. During the American Revolution, the legislatures of all thirteen States passed statutes directed against the Tories; among these statutes were a large number of bills of attainder and bills of pains and penalties.

While history thus provides some guidelines, the wide variation in form, purpose and effect of ante-Constitution bills of attainder indicates that the proper scope of the Bill of Attainder Clause, and its relevance to contemporary problems, must ultimately be sought by attempting to discern the reasons for its inclusion in the Constitution, and the evils it was designed to eliminate. The best available evidence, the writings of the architects of our constitutional system, indicates that the Bill of Attainder Clause was intended not as a narrow, technical (and therefore soon to be outmoded) prohibition, but rather as an implementation of the separation of powers, a general safeguard against legislative exercise of the judicial function, or more simply—trial by legislature.

The Constitution divides the National Government into three branches—Legislative, Executive and Judicial. This "separation of powers" was obviously not instituted with the idea that it would promote governmental efficiency. It was, on the contrary, looked to as a bulwark against tyranny. For if governmental power is fractionalized, if a given policy can be implemented only by a combination of legislative enactment, judicial application, and executive implementation, no man or group of men will be able to impose its unchecked will. James Madison wrote:

> The accumulation of all powers, legislative, executive, and judiciary, in the same hands, whether of one, a few, or many, and whether hereditary, self-appointed, or elective, may justly be pronounced the very definition of tyranny.

The Federalist, No. 47. . . .

The authors of the Federalist Papers took the position that although under some systems of government (most notably the one from which the United States had just broken), the Executive Department is the branch most likely to forget the bounds of its authority, "in a representative republic . . . where the legislative power is exercised by an assembly . . . which is sufficiently numerous to feel all the passions which actuate a multitude; yet not so numerous as to be incapable of pursuing the objects of its passions . . .," barriers had to be erected to ensure that the legislature would not overstep the bounds of its authority and perform the functions of the other departments. The Bill of Attainder Clause was regarded as such a barrier. . . .

Thus the Bill of Attainder Clause not only was intended as one implementation of the general principle of fractionalized power, but also reflected the Framers' belief that the Legislative Branch is not so well suited as politically independent judges and juries to the task of ruling upon the blameworthiness, of, and levying appropriate punishment upon, specific persons. . . . By banning bills of attainder, the Framers of the Constitution sought to guard against such dangers by limiting legislatures to the task of rule-making. "It is the peculiar province of the legislature to prescribe general rules for the government of society; the application of those rules to individuals in society would seem to be the duty of other departments." *Fletcher v. Peck*, 6 Cranch 87, 136.

II

It is in this spirit that the Bill of Attainder Clause was consistently interpreted by this Court. . . . In 1810, Chief Justice Marshall, speaking for the Court in *Fletcher*, stated that "[a] bill of attainder may affect the life of an individual, or may confiscate his property, or may do both." This means, of course, that what were known at common law as bills of pains and penalties are outlawed by the Bill of Attainder Clause. The Court's pronouncement therefore served notice that the Bill of Attainder Clause was not to be given a narrow historical reading (which would exclude bills of pains and penalties), but was instead to be read in light of the evil the Framers had sought to bar: legislative punishment, of any form or severity, of specifically designated persons or groups.

The approach which Chief Justice Marshall had suggested was followed in the twin post–Civil War cases of *Cummings v. State of Missouri*, 4 Wall. 277, and *Ex parte Garland*, 4 Wall. 333. *Cummings* involved the constitutionality of amendments to the Missouri Constitution of 1865 which provided that no one could engage in a number of specified professions (Cummings was a priest) unless he first swore that he had taken no part in the rebellion against the Union. At issue in *Garland* was a federal statute which required attorneys to take a similar oath before they could practice in federal courts. This Court struck down both provisions as bills of attainder on the ground that they were legislative acts inflicting punishment on a specific group: clergymen and lawyers who had taken part in the rebellion and therefore could not truthfully take the oath. . . .

The next extended discussion of the Bill of Attainder Clause came in 1946, in *United State v. Lovett*, 328 U. S. 303, where the Court invalidated § 304 of the Urgent Deficiency Appropriation Act, which prohibited payment of further salary to three named federal employees, as a bill of attainder. . . .

III

Under the line of cases just outlined, § 504 of the Labor–Management Reporting and Disclosure Act plainly constitutes a bill of attainder. Congress undoubtedly possesses power under the Commerce Clause to enact legislation designed to keep from positions affecting interstate commerce persons who may use such positions to bring about political strikes. In § 504, however, Congress has exceeded the authority granted it by the Constitution. The statute does not set forth a generally applicable rule decreeing that any person who commits certain acts or possesses certain characteristics (acts and characteristics which, in Congress' view, make them likely to initiate political strikes) shall not hold union office, and leave to courts and juries the job of deciding what persons have committed the specified acts or possess the specified characteristics. Instead, it designates in no uncertain terms the persons who possess the feared characteristics and therefore cannot hold union office without incurring criminal liability—members of the Communist Party. . . .

The Solicitor General points out that in *Board of Governors v. Agnew*, 329 U.S. 441, this Court applied § 32 of the Banking Act of 1933, which provides:

> No officer, director, or employee of any corporation or unincorporated association, no partner or employee of any partnership, and no individual, primarily engaged in the issue, flotation, underwriting, public sale, or distribution, at wholesale or retail, or through syndicate participation, of stocks, bonds, or other similar securities, shall serve the same time as an officer, director, or employee of any member bank. . . .

He suggests that for purposes of the Bill of Attainder Clause, such conflict-of-interest laws are not meaningfully distinguishable from the statute before us. We find this argument without merit. First, we note that § 504, unlike § 32 of the Banking Act, inflicts its deprivation upon the members of a political group thought to present a threat to the national security. As we noted above, such groups were the targets of the overwhelming majority of English and early American bills of attainder. Second, § 32 incorporates no judgment censuring or condemning any man or group of men. In enacting it, Congress relied upon its general knowledge of human psychology, and concluded that the concurrent holding of the two designated positions would present a temptation to *any* man—not just certain men or members of a certain political party. Thus insofar as § 32 incorporates a condemnation, it condemns all men. Third, we cannot accept the suggestion that § 32 constitutes an exercise in specification rather than rule-making. It seems to us clear that § 32 establishes an objective standard of conduct. . . .

It is argued, however, that in § 504 Congress did no more than it did in enacting § 32: it promulgated a general rule to the effect that persons possessing characteristics which make them likely to incite political strikes should not hold union office, and simply inserted in place of a list of those characteristics an alternative, shorthand criterion—membership in the Communist Party. Again, we cannot agree. The designation of Communists as those persons likely to cause political strikes is not the substitution of a semantically equivalent phrase; on the contrary, it rests . . . upon an empirical investigation by Congress of the acts, characteristics and propensities of Communist Party members. In a number of decisions, this Court has pointed out the fallacy of the suggestion that membership in the Communist Party, or any other political organization, can be regarded as an alternative, but equivalent, expression for a list of undesirable characteristics. For, as the Court noted in *Schneiderman v. United States*, 320 U.S. 118, 136, "under our traditions beliefs are personal and not a matter of mere association, and . . . men in adhering to a political party or other organization notoriously do not subscribe unqualifiedly to all of its platforms or asserted principles." . . .

IV

The Solicitor General argues that § 504 is not a bill of attainder because the prohibition it imposes does not constitute "punishment." In support of this conclusion, he urges that the statute was enacted for preventive rather than retributive reasons—that its aim is not to punish Communists for what they have done in the past, but rather to keep them from positions where they will in the future be able to bring about undesirable events. . . .

Section 504 . . . disqualifies from the holding of union office not only present members of the Communist Party, but also anyone who has within the past five years been a member of the Party. However, even if we make the assumption that the five-year provision was inserted not out of desire to visit retribution but purely out of a belief that failure to include it would lead to *pro forma* resignations from the Party which would not decrease the threat of political strikes, it still clearly appears that § 504 inflicts "punishment" within the meaning of the Bill of Attainder Clause. It would be archaic to limit the definition of "punishment" to "retribution." Punishment serves several purposes; retributive, rehabilitative, deterrent—and preventive. One of the reasons society imprisons those convicted of crimes is to keep them from inflicting future harm, but that does not make imprisonment any the less punishment.

Historical considerations by no means compel restriction of the bill of attainder ban to instances of retribution. A number of English bills of attainder were enacted for preventive purposes—that is, the legislature made a judgment, undoubtedly based largely on past acts and associations (as § 504 is) that a given person or group was likely to cause trouble (usually, overthrow the government) and therefore inflicted deprivations upon that person or group in order to keep it from bringing about the feared event. It is also clear that many of the early American bills attainting the Tories were passed in order to impede their effectively resisting the Revolution. . . . Thus Justice Iredell was on solid historical ground when he observed, in *Calder v. Bull*, 3 Dall. 386, 399–400, that "attainders, *on the principle of retaliation and proscription*, have marked all the vicissitudes of party triumph." (Emphasis supplied.) . . .

The Solicitor General urges us to distinguish *Lovett* on the ground that the statute struck down there "singled out three identified individuals." It is of course true that § 504 does not contain the words "Archie Brown," and that it inflicts its deprivation upon more than three people. However, the decisions of this Court, as well as the historical background of the Bill of Attainder Clause, make it crystal clear that these are distinctions without a difference. It was not uncommon for English acts of attainder to inflict their deprivations upon relatively large groups of people, sometimes by description rather than name. Moreover, the statutes voided in *Cummings* and *Garland* were of this nature. We cannot agree that the fact that § 504 inflicts its deprivation upon the membership of the Communist Party rather than upon a list of named individuals takes it out of the category of bills of attainder.

We do not hold today that Congress cannot weed dangerous persons out of the labor movement, any more than the Court held in *Lovett* that subversives must be permitted to hold sensitive government positions. Rather, we make again the point made in *Lovett*: that Congress must accomplish such results by rules of general applicability. It cannot specify the people upon whom the sanction it prescribes is to be levied. Under our Constitution, Congress possesses full legislative authority, but the task of adjudication must be left to other tribunals. . . .

■ MR. JUSTICE WHITE, with whom MR. JUSTICE CLARK, MR. JUSTICE HARLAN, and MR. JUSTICE STEWART join, dissenting.

"A bill of attainder is a legislative act which inflicts punishment without a judicial trial." *Cummings v. State of Missouri*, 4 Wall. 277, 323. When an enactment is challenged as an attainder, the central inquiry must be whether the disability imposed by the act is "punishment" (i.e., is directed at an individual or a group of individuals) or is "regulation" (i.e., is directed at controlling future conduct). Whether a punitive purpose would be inferred has depended in past cases on a number of circumstances, including the nature of the disability, whether it was traditionally regarded as punishment, whether it is rationally connected to a permissible legislative objective, as well as the specificity of the legislature's designation of the persons to be affected.

In this case, however, the Court discards this meticulous multifold analysis that has been deemed necessary in the past. Instead the Court places the burden of separating attainders from permissible regulation on an examination of the legislative findings implied by the nature of the class designated. The Bill of Attainder Clause, the Court says, was intended to implement the separation of powers by confining the legislature to rule-making and preventing legislative invasion of a function left exclusively to the courts—fact-finding connected with applications of a general rule to individuals or groups. Section 504 of the Labor–Management Reporting and Disclosure Act is therefore a bill of attainder because in pursuit of its purpose of preventing political strikes, it has specified the persons—Communist Party members—who are to be disqualified from holding union office, rather than excluding all persons who might engage in the undesirable conduct. The vice in § 504 is that it does not set forth a rule generally applicable to "any person who commits certain acts or possesses certain characteristics (acts and characteristics which, in Congress' view, make them likely to initiate political strikes)" but has instead designated "the persons who possess the feared characteristics," members of the Communist Party.

At this point the Court implies that legislation is sufficiently general if it specifies a characteristic that makes it *likely* that individuals falling within the group designated will engage in conduct Congress may prohibit. But the Court then goes on to reject the argument that Communist Party membership is in itself a characteristic raising such a likelihood. . . .

Similarly invalidated [by the Court's decision today] are statutes denying positions of public importance to groups of persons identified by their business affiliations, commonly known as conflict-of-interest statutes. . . . The majority in the case now before us likewise recognizes the pertinency of such statutes and, in its discussion of *Board of Governors v. Agnew*, 329 U.S. 441, strenuously—and unsuccessfully—attempts to distinguish them. . . .

In terms of the Court's analysis of the Bill of Attainder Clause, no meaningful distinction may be drawn between § 32 of the Banking Act and § 504. Both sections disqualify a specifically described group, officers and employees of underwriting firms in the one case and members of the Communist Party in the other. Both sections may be said to be underinclusive: others besides underwriters may have business interests conflicting with the duties of a bank director and others than Communists may call political strikes. Equally, both sections may be deemed overinclusive: neither section finds that all members of the group affected would violate their obligations to the office from which they are disqualified; some members would and perhaps others would not. Both sections are based on a probability or likelihood that this would occur. Both sections leave to the courts the task of determining whether particular persons are members of the designated groups and occupy the specified positions. . . .

Other legislative enactments relevant here are those statutes disqualifying felons from occupying certain positions. The leading case is *Hawker v. People of State of New York*, 170 U.S. 189, which upheld a provision prohibiting convicted felons from practicing medicine against a claim that, as applied to one convicted before its enactment, it was an *ex post facto* law. The Court noted that a legislature may establish qualifications for the practice of medicine, and character may be such a qualification. Conviction of a felony, the Court reasoned, may be evidence of character. . . .

Section 504 is said to impose punishment on specific individuals because it has disqualified all Communist Party members without providing for a judicial determination as to each member that he will call a political strike. A likelihood of doing so based on membership is not enough. By the same token, a statute disqualifying Communists (or authorizing the Executive Branch to do so) from holding sensitive positions in the Government would be automatically infirm, as would a requirement that employees of the Central Intelligence Agency or the National Security Agency disclaim membership in the Communist Party, unless in each case it is proved by evidence other than membership in the Communist Party, the nature of which has already been adjudicated, that the individual would commit acts of disloyalty or subordinate his official undertakings to the interests of the Party.

But how does one prove that a person would be disloyal? The Communist Party's illegal purpose and its domination by a foreign power have already been adjudicated, both administratively and judicially. If this does not in itself provide a sufficient probability with respect to the individual who persists in remaining a member of the Party, or if a probability is in any event insufficient, what evidence with regard to the individual will be sufficient to disqualify him? If he must be apprehended in the act of calling one political strike or in one act of disloyalty before steps can be taken to exclude him from office, there is little or nothing left of the preventive or prophylactic function of § 504 or of the statutes such as the Court had before it in *Hawker* and *Agnew*.

Examples of statutes that will now be suspect because of the Court's opinion but were, until today, unanimously accepted as legitimate exercises of legislative power could easily be multiplied. Such a catalogue in itself would lead one to inquire whether the Court's reasoning does not contain some flaw that explains such perverse results.

One might well begin by challenging the Court's premise that the Bill of Attainder Clause was intended to provide a general dividing line between legislative and judicial functions and thereby to operate as the chief means of implementing the separation of powers. While it must be conceded that our system of government is based on the separation of powers and that the prohibition on bills of attainder is a judicially enforceable restraint on legislative power and therefore constitutes one among the many mechanisms implementing the separation of powers, that conclusion is the most that can be gleaned from the authorities cited by the Court. . . .

On the other hand, there are substantial reasons for concluding that the Bill of Attainder Clause may not be regarded as enshrining any general rule distinguishing between the legislative and judicial functions. Congress may pass legislation affecting specific persons in the form of private bills. It may also punish persons who commit contempt before it. So too, one may note that if Art. I, § 9, cl. 3, immortalizes some notion of the separation of powers at the federal level, then Art. I, § 10, necessarily does the same for the States. But it has long been recognized by this Court that "[w]hether the legislative, executive, and judicial powers of a state shall be kept altogether distinct and separate, or whether persons or collections of persons belonging to one department may, in respect to some matters, exert powers which, strictly speaking, pertain to another department of government, is for the determination of the State."

The basic flaw in the Court's reasoning, however, is its too narrow view of the legislative process. The Court is concerned to separate the legislative and judicial functions by ensuring that the legislature does not infringe the judicial function of applying general rules to specific circumstances. Congress is held to have violated the Bill of Attainder Clause here because, on the one hand, § 504 does not encompass the whole class of persons having characteristics that would make them likely to call political strikes and, on the other hand, § 504 does single out a particular group, members of the Communist Party, not all of whom possess such characteristics. Because of this combination of underinclusiveness and overinclusiveness the Court concludes that Communist Party members were singled out for punishment, thus rejecting the Government's contention that § 504 has solely a regulatory aim.

The Court's conclusion that a statute which is both underinclusive and overinclusive must be deemed to have been adopted with a punitive purpose assumes that legislatures normally deal with broad categories and attack all of an evil at a time. Or if partial measures are undertaken, a legislature singles out a particular group for regulation only because the group label is a "shorthand phrase" for traits that are characteristic of the broader evil. But this Court has long recognized in equal protection cases that a legislature may prefer to deal with only part of an evil. And it is equally true that a group may be singled out for regulation without any punitive purpose even when not all members of the group would be likely to engage in the feared conduct. . . . [M]any regulatory measures are enacted after investigation into particular incidents or the practices of particular groups and after findings by the legislature that the practices disclosed are inimical to the public interest and should be prevented in the future. Not surprisingly, the resulting legislation may reflect in its specificity the specificity of the preceding legislative inquiry. But the fact that it does should not be taken, in itself, to be conclusive that the legislature's purpose is punitive. Admittedly the degree of specificity is a relevant factor—as when individuals are singled out by name—but because in many instances specificity of the degree here held impermissible may be wholly consistent with a regulatory, rather than a punitive purpose, the Court's per se approach cuts too broadly and invalidates legitimate legislative activity.

Putting aside the Court's *per se* approach based on the nature of the classification specified by the legislation, we must still test § 504 against the traditional definition of the bill of attainder as legislative punishment of particular individuals. In my view, § 504 does not impose punishment and is not a bill of attainder.

We have said that "only the clearest proof could suffice" to establish that Congress' purpose was punitive rather than regulatory. *Flemming v. Nestor*, 363 U.S. 603, 617. A punitive purpose has been found when it could be said that a statute passed amid the fierce passions aroused by the Civil War bore no rational connection to any permissible legislative purpose. *Cummings v. State of Missouri*, 4 Wall. 277, 319, 322. The imposition of a particularly harsh deprivation without any discernible legitimate legislative purpose has similarly been characterized as penal. Similarly a punitive purpose has been found when such a purpose clearly appeared in the legislative history. In other cases the analysis is more difficult. We summarized the relevant considerations in *Kennedy v. Mendoza–Martinez*, 372 U. S., at 168–169:

> Whether the sanction involves an affirmative disability or restraint, whether it has historically been regarded as a punishment, whether it comes into play only on a finding of *scienter*, whether its operation will promote the traditional aims of punishment—retribution and deterrence, whether the behavior to which it applies is already a crime, whether an alternative purpose to which it may rationally be connected is assignable for it, and whether it appears excessive in relation to the alternative purpose assigned are all relevant to the inquiry, and may often point in differing directions.

An application of these criteria to § 504 compels the conclusion that it is regulatory rather than punitive.

Congress' concern with the possibility of political strikes is not simply a fictional concern advanced to mask a punitive purpose. Congress has sought to forestall political strikes since 1947, when it adopted § 9(h) of the National Labor Relations Act. . . .

Nor can it be denied that § 504 is reasonably related to a permissible legislative objective. In *American Communications Ass'n v. Douds*, we held that "Congress could rationally find that the Communist Party is not like other political parties in its utilization of positions of union leadership as means by which to being about strikes . . .," and therefore Congress could rationally infer that members of the Communist Party were likely to call political strikes. In 1956 the Subversive Activities Control Board found, after a trial-type hearing, that the Party's principal leaders and a substantial number of its members recognize the disciplinary power of the Soviet Union. Without question the findings previously made by Congress and the Subversive Activities Control Board afforded a rational basis in 1959 for Congress to conclude that Communists were likely to call political strikes, and sufficiently more likely than others to do so that special measures could appropriately be enacted to deal with the particular threat posed.

In view of Congress' demonstrated concern in preventing future conduct—political strikes—and the reasonableness of the means adopted to that end, I cannot conclude that § 504 had a punitive purpose or that it constitutes a bill of attainder. I intimate no opinion on the issues that the Court does not reach.

NOTES

1. What modes of interpretation does each opinion use? Which opinion do you find most persuasive in its use of these modes of interpretation? Does the majority opinion, though rich in history, move too quickly to draw from the history a highly abstract purpose? Does the dissent show too much deference to Congress?

2. Imagine that the statute was passed not by Congress but by the New York legislature. Should the analysis and result be identical?

3. In 2009, Congress defunded a community organizing group, the Association of Community Organizations for Reform Now (ACORN), after several of its employees were surreptitiously videotaped approving the disbursement of federal funds for what purported to be a child prostitution ring. Congress passed a series of riders to appropriations bills specifying that no federal money could go to ACORN: "None of the funds made available by this joint resolution or any prior Act may be provided to . . . ACORN[], or any of its affiliates, subsidiaries, or allied organizations." Is withdrawing federal grant money in this fashion, from one named organization, a bill of attainder? The Second Circuit held that it was not. See *ACORN v. United States*, 618 F.3d 125 (2010). Although there was evidence in the legislative record that members of Congress intended to punish ACORN, the court found that withholding federal grant money from a corporation was not historically considered a punishment. In addition, the court noted that there were non-punitive purposes for the action, such as protecting taxpayer money from waste and fraud. Do you agree that withholding federal grant money from a named organization is not a bill of attainder?

4. Congress and Parliament have long passed and continue to pass special bills that benefit private individuals or small groups of individuals. There are no constitutional constraints on *benefiting* one or a few individuals except the Constitution's rule that neither Congress nor a state can confer "Titles of Nobility." Prior to the creation of the Court of Claims in 1855, all persons seeking compensation for a taking of property by the federal government or any other form of money damages had to get a private bill passed for their relief (because the U.S. government was immune from suit). Even today, Congress regularly passes "earmarks" which spend federal money for the benefit of one or a few individuals. Should there be a constitutional limit on the legislature, not only when it imposes bill-of-attainder-like punishments, but also when it confers benefits with insufficient generality? Note that some state constitutions require that laws be "general" in scope, though such requirements are rarely enforceable in court.

5. The Court revisited the scope of the Bill of Attainder Clauses in *Nixon v. General Services Administration,* 433 U.S. 425 (1977). This case involved control over the records and presidential papers of former President Richard Nixon. At issue were 42 million pages of documentary material and 880 tape recordings that he had secretly made of himself and others while he was serving in the White House. A month after President Nixon's resignation under threat of certain impeachment and removal by the Senate, the administrator of the General Services Administration announced that he and Nixon had signed an agreement highly favorable to Nixon over the custody of these materials. The administrator argued persuasively that all presidents prior to Nixon had been recognized as having total rights of ownership and custody of their personal papers accumulated during their presidencies. Congress responded to news of the Nixon–GSA agreement by passing a new law, which President Gerald Ford signed, that applied *only* to Richard Nixon's papers and official records. Under this law, Nixon's records were seized including any documents or tape recordings that "involve former President Richard M. Nixon or other individuals who, at the time of the conversation, were employed by the Federal Government." The law thus mentioned Nixon by name on the face of the statute. Nixon challenged the constitutionality of this law on multiple grounds, including that it

was a constitutionally forbidden bill of attainder. Justice Brennan, writing for a majority of the Court, disagreed:

> However expansive the prohibition against bills of attainder, it surely was not intended to serve as a variant of the equal protection doctrine, invalidating every Act of Congress or the States that legislatively burdens some persons or groups, but not all other plausible individuals. In short, while the Bill of Attainder Clause serves as an important bulwark against tyranny, it does not do so by limiting Congress to the choice of legislating for the universe, or legislating only benefits, or not legislating at all.
>
> Thus, in the present case, the Act's specificity—the fact that it refers to appellant by name—does not automatically offend the Bill of Attainder Clause. . . . Congress had reason for concern solely with the preservation of appellant's materials, for he alone had entered into a depository agreement [with the GSA] which by its terms called for the destruction of certain of the materials. . . . [A]ppellant constituted a legitimate class of one, and this provides a basis for Congress' decision to proceed with dispatch with respect to his materials while accepting the status of his predecessors' papers and ordering the further consideration of generalized standards to govern his successors.

How strong was former President Nixon's bill of attainder claim in *Nixon v. GSA*? Was Nixon "a legitimate class of one"? If so, is there anything left of the Bill of Attainder Clause? Is *Nixon v. GSA* consistent with *Brown*?

Ex Post Facto Laws

In addition to forbidding Congress and the states from passing bills of attainder, Article I, Sections 9 and 10 also forbid Congress and the states from passing "ex post facto Laws." The leading case on the meaning of this prohibition is *Calder v. Bull*, 3 U.S. 386 (1798), presented below in Chapter 7. There the Court held that the clause prohibits retroactive criminal laws, but not retroactive civil laws. The examples of ex post facto laws given by the Court included laws that criminalize past innocent conduct or increase the criminal penalty for past conduct. As with bills of attainder, an ex post facto law involves a violation of basic procedural norms and separation of powers.

More recently, in *Smith v. Doe*, 538 U.S. 84 (2003), the Supreme Court considered the constitutionality of an Alaska statute that required among other things that people convicted of sex offenses register in the Alaska Sex Offender Registration Act—even people who were convicted before the Act was passed. The law in question was a "Megan's Law," one of the many state laws enacted in the wake of a gruesome child rape and murder. Under the terms of the Alaska Act, all sex offenders who moved to Alaska were required to register within one day of entering the state. The Act also required that information about the registered sex offenders—including their names, addresses, places of employment, and driver's license numbers—be posted online. The issues raised by the case were (1) whether the law in question was civil or criminal and (2) whether it was punitive in intent or effect.

The Supreme Court upheld the Act against a challenge under the Ex Post Facto Laws Clause. Writing for the Court, Justice Kennedy argued that the Alaska law was not punitive in intent or effect, and that as a result it was a civil law not covered by the Ex Post Facto Laws Clause. Justices

Stevens, Ginsburg, and Breyer dissented, saying the law was obviously punitive and was a clear violation of the Ex Post Facto Laws Clause. Justice Souter concurred only in the judgment, saying the case was so difficult that he simply could not say that the state of Alaska had erred. In other words, for Justice Souter, the presumption of constitutionality carried the day. Based on this brief sketch, who has the better of the argument between Justice Kennedy and the dissenters? Does the Alaska statute make past innocent conduct a crime? Does it increase the punishment for crimes already committed?

The Contracts Clause

An Article I, Section 10 restriction that applies only to state legislatures, not to Congress, is the prohibition on passing laws impairing the obligation of contracts. An example is a state law releasing debtors from repaying their debts. The framers' concern about this was hardly academic—many state legislatures had passed such laws in the years immediately preceding the ratification of the Constitution. Like the restrictions on bills of attainder and ex post facto laws, the Contracts Clause was a requirement rooted in separation of powers and an understanding of the need for legislative action to be sufficiently general and prospective.

Although rarely litigated today, the Contracts Clause gave rise to more constitutional challenges than any other in the first several decades of the United States. The explanation is rooted in the structure of the procedural requirements of the original Constitution and the Bill of Rights. There was a Due Process Clause in the Fifth Amendment, but it applied only to the federal government. And there were restrictions on bills of attainder and ex post facto laws, but those applied only to criminal laws (at least after *Calder v. Bull*). Thus anyone who wanted to bring a constitutional challenge to a non-criminal state statute would need to frame it as somehow impairing the obligation of contracts.

In two major cases the Marshall Court struck down state statutes under the Contracts Clause, one a Georgia statute that rescinded land sales previously approved by the legislature and the other a New Hampshire statute that altered the membership of the board of trustees for Dartmouth College. See *Fletcher v. Peck,* 10 U.S. 87 (1810); *Dartmouth College v. Woodward*, 17 U.S. 518 (1819). Subsequently, however, the Court gradually retreated from vigorous enforcement of the Contracts Clause. The most important cases are *Ogden v. Saunders*, 25 U.S. 213 (1827), reading the clause as restricting only statutes that impair already existing contracts; *Charles River Bridge v. Warren Bridge,* 36 U.S. 420 (1837), concluding that the Massachusetts legislature did not violate the clause when it awarded a charter to build a bridge in substantially the same location as another bridge it had previously authorized; and *Home Building and Loan Association v. Blaisdell*, 290 U.S. 398 (1934), deciding that the emergency of the Great Depression justified a Minnesota statute that effectively allowed judges to stop banks from foreclosing on mortgagees who failed to make the required payments.

Thus the Contracts Clause has gone from a great bustling seaport of constitutional litigation to a quiet backwater. But its basic principles that legislative activity should be sufficiently general and prospective have not disappeared from constitutional law. They are central to the jurisprudence of the Due Process Clauses and the Equal Protection Clause, which are examined in Chapter 7.

[Assignment 17]

II. ARTICLE II: THE EXECUTIVE POWER

The president of the United States is the commander in chief of the world's most formidable army. As the chief law enforcement officer of the national government, the president is in charge of more than two million executive-branch employees. Yet the president cannot buy a light bulb for the Oval Office without an appropriation from Congress. The president is simultaneously very powerful and very constrained—by Congress and its committees, the federal courts, the fifty state governors (who tend to be from the opposite political party), and the press. The president is more powerful than most prime ministers in parliamentary regimes, but lacks the powers that some Russian, French, and Latin American presidents have had to rule by decree, to make appointments to office without legislative confirmation, to suspend the courts, or to abolish elected governorships. In short, the president is what one scholar has called "a tamed prince." See Harvey C. Mansfield, Jr., TAMING THE PRINCE: THE AMBIVALENCE OF MODERN EXECUTIVE POWER (1989).

The finely balanced role of the president is all the more remarkable given that the Constitution creating this office was written just eleven years after the formal start of the American Revolution, a revolution largely directed at grievances attributed to the tyranny of the king of England. How did we evolve this strange hybrid figure at the center of our political life who is both so powerful and so constrained? This section addresses the major issues concerning the constitutional powers of the president. We start with a "map" of the structure and content of Article II of the Constitution, and then proceed to cases that illustrate the meaning in context of the assignment of "The executive Power" to "a President of the United States."

A Map of Article II

Article II of the Constitution contains four sections. Section 1 assigns all of "The executive Power" of the new national government to one "President of the United States." It goes on to explain how the president is to be chosen, the length of term, and the oath of office. This grant of power is immediately qualified by Article II, Section 2, which specifies, describes, and limits certain presidential powers (e.g., the pardon power, the commander-in-chief power), thus giving substantial content to the grant of executive power in Section 1. Section 3 further describes and limits presidential executive power by imposing a series of duties on the president. The president must (1) give a State of the Union address, (2) recommend new laws to Congress, (3) receive ambassadors from foreign countries, (4) take care that the laws are faithfully executed, and (5) commission all officers of the United States. These duties further inform the grant of "The executive Power" to the president in the Vesting Clause of Section 1. Section 4 concludes by providing that the president and vice president, unlike the king of England, are subject to impeachment. This section is critical because it makes clear that the president must act according to law.

Consider briefly four themes about presidential power under Article II.

First, Article II provides for *energy* in the executive. The president is given enough power to partially overcome the special interests that frequently command a majority in Congress but not the supermajority needed to override a veto, and enough power to protect the country from foreign attack and domestic insurrection. Presidential leadership has been important for military success in numerous wars, including the Civil War, two World Wars, and the Cold War. If, as Franklin Delano Roosevelt said, America is the Arsenal of Democracy, the president gets much of the credit.

Second, Article II makes the president *independent* of Congress. In parliamentary systems, the prime minister is a member of parliament and is dependent on his or her party's success in the legislature for continuance in office. By contrast, the president is elected indirectly by We the People for a fixed four-year term in office. The president cannot be booted out of office by Congress on a vote of no confidence. Indeed, the president's own democratic mandate is just as good as Congress's—or even better, since the president and vice president are the only officials who are elected (albeit indirectly) by the entire nation. Presidential independence is reinforced by a guaranteed salary and by the oath that presidents take that they "will faithfully execute the Office of President of the United States, and will to the best of [their] Ability, preserve, protect and defend the Constitution of the United States."

Third, Article II creates *one* executive. The framers of the Constitution made a deliberate choice to vest the executive power in a single individual, rejecting the options of a plural executive or an executive council or cabinet that would limit the president's freedom. Unity can be destroyed by having a Roman Republic-style Triumvirate of three co-equal executives. Modern debates over executive power often raise the question whether unity can be destroyed in other ways, such as by creating entities in the executive branch that are independent of the president.

Fourth, the presidency created by Article II is *accountable* to the people, the Congress, and the courts. The president is constrained by having a short four-year term, and not being able to serve more than two terms. Congressional appropriations and oversight committees further constrain the president, and Congress usually becomes less supportive of the president, since the president's party usually loses seats in the mid-term election. And the media cover every presidential error or embarrassment. In extreme cases, presidents can be and have been impeached by the House. A further constraint is that the president and other executive-branch officials must obey the judgments of the courts.

Consider these themes as you read the following excerpts from *The Federalist* and *In re Neagle*, a case on the scope of executive power under the Constitution.

A. THE NATURE OF EXECUTIVE POWER

The Federalist No. 67

Alexander Hamilton, March 11, 1788

THE constitution of the executive department of the proposed government, claims next our attention.

There is hardly any part of the system which could have been attended with greater difficulty in the arrangement of it than this; and there is, perhaps, none which has been inveighed against with less candor or criticised with less judgment.

Here the writers against the Constitution seem to have taken pains to signalize their talent of misrepresentation. Calculating upon the aversion of the people to monarchy, they have endeavored to enlist all their jealousies and apprehensions in opposition to the intended President of the United States; not merely as the embryo, but as the full-grown progeny, of that detested parent. To establish the pretended affinity, they have not scrupled to draw resources even from the regions of fiction. The authorities of a magistrate, in few instances greater, in some instances less, than those of a governor of New York, have been magnified into more than royal prerogatives. He has been decorated with attributes superior in dignity and splendor to those of a king of Great Britain. He has been shown to us with the diadem sparkling on his brow and the imperial purple flowing in his train. He has been seated on a throne surrounded with minions and mistresses, giving audience to the envoys of foreign potentates, in all the supercilious pomp of majesty. The images of Asiatic despotism and voluptuousness have scarcely been wanting to crown the exaggerated scene. We have been taught to tremble at the terrific visages of murdering janizaries, and to blush at the unveiled mysteries of a future seraglio.

Attempts so extravagant as these to disfigure or, it might rather be said, to metamorphose the object, render it necessary to take an accurate view of its real nature and form: in order as well to ascertain its true aspect and genuine appearance, as to unmask the disingenuity and expose the fallacy of the counterfeit resemblances which have been so insidiously, as well as industriously, propagated. . . .

The Federalist No. 68

Alexander Hamilton, March 12, 1788

To the People of the State of New York:

THE mode of appointment of the Chief Magistrate of the United States is almost the only part of the system, of any consequence, which has escaped without severe censure . . . from its opponents. . . .

It was desirable that the sense of the people should operate in the choice of the person to whom so important a trust was to be confided. This end will be answered by committing the right of making it, not to any preestablished body, but to men chosen by the people for the special purpose, and at the particular conjuncture. . . .

Nothing was more to be desired than that every practicable obstacle should be opposed to cabal, intrigue, and corruption. These most deadly adversaries of republican government might naturally have been expected to make their approaches from more than one quarter, but chiefly from the desire in foreign powers to gain an improper ascendant in our councils. How could they better gratify this, than by raising a creature of their own to the chief magistracy of the Union? But the convention have guarded against all danger of this sort, with the most provident and judicious attention. They have not made the appointment of the President to depend on any preexisting bodies of men, who might be tampered with beforehand to prostitute their votes; but they have referred it in the first instance to an immediate act of the people of America, to be exerted in the choice of persons for the temporary and sole purpose of making the appointment. . . .

The Federalist No. 69

Alexander Hamilton, March 14, 1788

I PROCEED now to trace the real characters of the proposed Executive, as they are marked out in the plan of the convention. This will serve to place in a strong light the unfairness of the representations which have been made in regard to it.

The first thing which strikes our attention is, that the executive authority, with few exceptions, is to be vested in a single magistrate. This will scarcely, however, be considered as a point upon which any comparison can be grounded; for if, in this particular, there be a resemblance to the king of Great Britain, there is not less a resemblance to the Grand Seignior, to the khan of Tartary, to the Man of the Seven Mountains, or to the governor of New York.

That magistrate is to be elected for FOUR years; and is to be re-eligible as often as the people of the United States shall think him worthy of their confidence. In these circumstances there is a total dissimilitude between HIM and a king of Great Britain, who is an HEREDITARY monarch, possessing the crown as a patrimony descendible to his heirs forever; but there is a close analogy between HIM and a governor of New York, who is elected for THREE years, and is re-eligible without limitation or intermission. . . .

The President of the United States would be liable to be impeached, tried, and, upon conviction of treason, bribery, or other high crimes or misdemeanors, removed from office; and would afterwards be liable to prosecution and punishment in the ordinary course of law. The person of the king of Great Britain is sacred and inviolable; there is no constitutional tribunal to which he is amenable; no punishment to which he can be subjected without involving the crisis of a national revolution. In this delicate and important circumstance of personal responsibility, the President of Confederated America would stand upon no better ground than a governor of New York, and upon worse ground than the governors of Maryland and Delaware.

The President of the United States is to have power to return a bill, which shall have passed the two branches of the legislature, for reconsideration; and the bill so returned is to become a law, if, upon that reconsideration, it be approved by two thirds of both houses. The king of Great Britain, on his part, has an absolute negative upon the acts of the two houses of Parliament. . . . The qualified negative of the President differs widely from this absolute negative of the British sovereign; and tallies exactly with the revisionary authority of the council of revision of this State, of which the governor is a constituent part. In this respect the power of the President would exceed that of the governor of New York, . . . but it would be precisely the same with that of the governor of Massachusetts, whose constitution, as to this article, seems to have been the original from which the convention have copied.

The President is to be the "commander-in-chief of the army and navy of the United States, and of the militia of the several States, when called into the actual service of the United States. He is to have power to grant reprieves and pardons for offenses against the United States, EXCEPT IN CASES OF IMPEACHMENT; to recommend to the consideration of Congress such measures as he shall judge necessary and expedient; to convene, on extraordinary occasions, both houses of the legislature, or either of them . . . ; to take care that the laws be faithfully executed; and to commission all officers of the United States." In most of these particulars, the power of the President will resemble equally that of the king of Great Britain and of the governor of New York.

The President is to have power, with the advice and consent of the Senate, to make treaties, provided two thirds of the senators present concur. The king of Great Britain is the sole and absolute representative of the nation in all foreign transactions. He can of his own accord make treaties of peace, commerce, alliance, and of every other description. . . . In this respect, therefore, there is no comparison between the intended power of the President and the actual power of the British sovereign. The one can perform alone what the other can do only with the concurrence of a branch of the legislature.

The President is also to be authorized to receive ambassadors and other public ministers. This, though it has been a rich theme of declamation, is more a matter of dignity than of authority. . . .

The President is to nominate, and, WITH THE ADVICE AND CONSENT OF THE SENATE, to appoint ambassadors and other public ministers, judges of the Supreme Court, and in general all officers of the United States established by law, and whose appointments are not otherwise provided for by the Constitution. The king of Great Britain is emphatically and truly styled the fountain of honor. He not only appoints to all offices, but can create offices. He can confer titles of nobility at pleasure; and has the disposal of an immense number of church preferments. There is evidently a great inferiority in the power of the President, in this particular, to that of the British king; nor is it equal to that of the governor of New York, if we are to interpret the meaning of the constitution of the State by the practice which has obtained under it. . . .

The President of the United States would be an officer elected by the people for FOUR years; the king of Great Britain is a perpetual and HEREDITARY prince. The one would be amenable to personal punishment and disgrace; the person of the other is sacred and inviolable. The one would have a QUALIFIED negative upon the acts of the legislative body; the other has an ABSOLUTE negative. The one would have a right to command the military and naval forces of the nation; the other, in addition to this right, possesses that of DECLARING war, and of RAISING and REGULATING fleets and armies by his own authority. The one would have a concurrent power with a branch of the legislature in the formation of treaties; the other is the SOLE POSSESSOR of the power of making treaties. The one would have a like concurrent authority in appointing to offices; the other is the sole author of all appointments. The one can confer no privileges whatever; the other can make denizens of aliens, noblemen of commoners; can erect corporations with all the rights incident to corporate bodies. The one can prescribe no rules concerning the commerce or currency of the nation; the other is in several respects the arbiter of commerce, and in this capacity can establish markets and fairs, can regulate weights and measures, can lay embargoes for a limited time, can coin money, can authorize or prohibit the circulation of foreign coin. The one has no particle of spiritual jurisdiction; the other is the supreme head and governor of the national church! What answer shall we give to those who would persuade us that things so unlike resemble each other? The same that ought to be given to those who tell us that a government, the whole power of which would be in the hands of the elective and periodical servants of the people, is an aristocracy, a monarchy, and a despotism.

The Federalist No. 70

Alexander Hamilton, March 15, 1788

THERE is an idea, which is not without its advocates, that a vigorous Executive is inconsistent with the genius of republican government. The enlightened well-wishers to this species of government must at least hope that the supposition is destitute of foundation; since they can never admit its truth, without at the same time admitting the condemnation of their own principles. Energy in the Executive is a leading character in the definition of good government. It is essential to the protection of the community against foreign attacks; it is not less essential to the steady administration of the laws; to the protection of property against those irregular and high-handed combinations which sometimes interrupt the ordinary course of justice; to the security of liberty against the enterprises and assaults of ambition, of faction, and of anarchy. Every man the least conversant in Roman story, knows how often that republic was obliged to take refuge in the absolute power of a single man, under the formidable title of Dictator, as well against the intrigues of ambitious individuals who aspired to the tyranny, and the seditions of whole classes of the community whose conduct threatened the existence of all government, as against the invasions of external enemies who menaced the conquest and destruction of Rome.

There can be no need, however, to multiply arguments or examples on this head. A feeble Executive implies a feeble execution of the government. A feeble execution is but another phrase for a bad execution; and a government ill executed, whatever it may be in theory, must be, in practice, a bad government.

Taking it for granted, therefore, that all men of sense will agree in the necessity of an energetic Executive, it will only remain to inquire, what are the ingredients which constitute this energy? How far can they be combined with those other ingredients which constitute safety in the republican sense? And how far does this combination characterize the plan which has been reported by the convention?

The ingredients which constitute energy in the Executive are, first, unity; secondly, duration; thirdly, an adequate provision for its support; fourthly, competent powers.

The ingredients which constitute safety in the republican sense are, first, a due dependence on the people, secondly, a due responsibility.

Those politicians and statesmen who have been the most celebrated for the soundness of their principles and for the justice of their views, have declared in favor of a single Executive and a numerous legislature. They have with great propriety, considered energy as the most necessary qualification of the former, and have regarded this as most applicable to power in a single hand, while they have, with equal propriety, considered the latter as best adapted to deliberation and wisdom, and best calculated to conciliate the confidence of the people and to secure their privileges and interests.

That unity is conducive to energy will not be disputed. Decision, activity, secrecy, and despatch will generally characterize the proceedings of one man in a much more eminent degree than the proceedings of any greater number; and in proportion as the number is increased, these qualities will be diminished.

This unity may be destroyed in two ways: either by vesting the power in two or more magistrates of equal dignity and authority; or by vesting it ostensibly in one man, subject, in whole or in part, to the control and co-operation of others, in the capacity of counsellors to him. Of the first, the two Consuls of Rome may serve as an example; of the last, we shall find examples in the constitutions of several of the States. New York and New Jersey, if I recollect right, are the only States which have intrusted the executive authority wholly to single men. . . . Both these methods of destroying the unity of the Executive have their partisans; but the votaries of an executive council are the most numerous. They are both liable, if not to equal, to similar objections, and may in most lights be examined in conjunction. . . .

Wherever two or more persons are engaged in any common enterprise or pursuit, there is always danger of difference of opinion. If it be a public trust or office, in which they are clothed with equal dignity and authority, there is peculiar danger of personal emulation and even animosity. From either, and especially from all these causes, the most bitter dissensions are apt to spring. Whenever these happen, they lessen the respectability, weaken the authority, and distract the plans and operation of those whom they divide. If they should unfortunately assail the supreme executive magistracy of a country, consisting of a plurality of persons, they might impede or frustrate the most important measures of the government, in the most critical emergencies of the state. And what is still worse, they might split the community into the most violent and irreconcilable factions, adhering differently to the different individuals who composed the magistracy.

Men often oppose a thing, merely because they have had no agency in planning it, or because it may have been planned by those whom they dislike. But if they have been consulted, and have happened to disapprove, opposition then becomes, in their estimation, an indispensable duty of self-love. They seem to think themselves bound in honor, and by all the motives of personal infallibility, to defeat the success of what has been resolved upon contrary to their sentiments. . . .

Upon the principles of a free government, inconveniences from the source just mentioned must necessarily be submitted to in the formation of the legislature; but it is unnecessary, and therefore unwise, to introduce them into the constitution of the Executive. It is here too that they may be most pernicious. . . . [A lack of unity in the executive will] serve to embarrass and weaken the execution of [any] plan or measure . . . which [is undertaken], from the first step to the final conclusion of it. [A lack of unity will] constantly counteract those qualities in the Executive which are the most necessary ingredients in its composition—vigor and expedition, and this without any counterbalancing good. In the conduct of war, in which the energy of the Executive is the bulwark of the national security, every thing would be to be apprehended from its plurality.

It must be confessed that these observations apply with principal weight to the first case supposed—that is, to a plurality of magistrates of equal dignity and authority a scheme, the advocates for which are not likely to form a numerous sect; but they apply, though not with equal, yet with considerable weight to the project of a council, whose concurrence is made constitutionally necessary to the operations of the ostensible Executive. An artful cabal in that council would be able to distract and to enervate the whole system of administration. If no such cabal should exist, the mere diversity of views and opinions would alone be sufficient to tincture the exercise of the executive authority with a spirit of habitual feebleness and dilatoriness.

But one of the weightiest objections to a plurality in the Executive, and which lies as much against the last as the first plan, is, that it tends to conceal faults and destroy responsibility. Responsibility is of two kinds—to censure and to punishment. The first is the more important of the two, especially in an elective office. Man, in public trust, will much oftener act in such a manner as to render him unworthy of being any longer trusted, than in such a manner as to make him obnoxious to legal punishment. But the multiplication of the Executive adds to the difficulty of detection in either case. It often becomes impossible, amidst mutual accusations, to determine on whom the blame or the punishment of a pernicious measure, or series of pernicious measures, ought really to fall. It is shifted from one to another with so much dexterity, and under such plausible appearances, that the public opinion is left in suspense about the real author. The circumstances which may have led to any national miscarriage or misfortune are sometimes so complicated that, where there are a number of actors who may have had different degrees and kinds of agency, though we may clearly see upon the whole that there has been mismanagement, yet it may be impracticable to pronounce to whose account the evil which may have been incurred is truly chargeable. "I was overruled by my council. The council were so divided in their opinions that it was impossible to obtain any better resolution on the point." These and similar pretexts are constantly at hand, whether true or false. And who is there that will either take the trouble or incur the odium, of a strict scrutiny into the secret springs of the transaction? Should there be found a citizen zealous enough to undertake the unpromising task, if there happen to be collusion between the parties concerned, how easy it is to clothe the circumstances with so much ambiguity, as to render it uncertain what was the precise conduct of any of those parties? . . .

It is evident from these considerations, that the plurality of the Executive tends to deprive the people of the two greatest securities they can have for the faithful exercise of any delegated power, first, the restraints of public opinion, which lose their efficacy, as well on account of the division of the censure attendant on bad measures among a number, as on account of the uncertainty on whom it ought to fall; and, secondly, the opportunity of discovering with facility and clearness the misconduct of the persons they trust, in order either to their removal from office or to their actual punishment in cases which admit of it. . . . I clearly concur in opinion, in this particular, with a writer whom the celebrated Junius pronounces to be "deep, solid, and ingenious," that "the executive power is more easily confined when it is ONE"; . . . that it is far more safe there should be a single object for the jealousy and watchfulness of the people; and, in a word, that all multiplication of the Executive is rather dangerous than friendly to liberty. . . . I will only add that, prior to the appearance of the Constitution, I rarely met with an intelligent man from any of the States, who did not admit, as the result of experience, that the UNITY of the executive of this State was one of the best of the distinguishing features of our constitution.

The Federalist No. 71

Alexander Hamilton, March 18, 1788

DURATION in office has been mentioned as the second requisite to the energy of the Executive authority. This has relation to two objects: to the personal firmness of the executive magistrate, in the employment of his constitutional powers; and to the stability of the system of administration which may have been adopted under his auspices. . . .

There are some who would be inclined to regard the servile pliancy of the Executive to a prevailing current, either in the community or in the legislature, as its best recommendation. But such men entertain very crude notions, as well of the purposes for which government was instituted, as of the true means by which the public happiness may be promoted. The republican principle demands that the deliberate sense of the community should govern the conduct of those to whom they intrust the management of their affairs; but it does not require an unqualified complaisance to every sudden breeze of passion, or to every transient impulse which the people may receive from the arts of men, who flatter their prejudices to betray their interests. . . .

The tendency of the legislative authority to absorb every other, has been fully displayed and illustrated by examples in some preceding numbers. In governments purely republican, this tendency is almost irresistible. The representatives of the people, in a popular assembly, seem sometimes to fancy that they are the people themselves, and betray strong symptoms of impatience and disgust at the least sign of opposition from any other quarter; as if the exercise of its rights, by either the executive or judiciary, were a breach of their privilege and an outrage to their dignity. They often appear disposed to exert an imperious control over the other departments; and as they commonly have the people on their side, they always act with such momentum as to make it very difficult for the other members of the government to maintain the balance of the Constitution.

. . . It may be asked . . . whether a duration of four years would answer the end proposed; and if it would not, whether a less period, which would at least be recommended by greater security against ambitious designs, would not, for that reason, be preferable to a longer period, which was, at the same time, too short for the purpose of inspiring the desired firmness and independence of the magistrate.

It cannot be affirmed, that a duration of four years, or any other limited duration, would completely answer the end proposed; but it would contribute towards it in a degree which would have a material influence upon the spirit and character of the government. Between the commencement and termination of such a period, there would always be a considerable interval, in which the prospect of annihilation would be sufficiently remote, not to have an improper effect upon the conduct of a man indued with a tolerable portion of fortitude. . . .

The Federalist No. 72

Alexander Hamilton, March 19, 1788

. . . [An ill effect of imposing a term limit on the President] would be, the depriving the community of the advantage of the experience gained by the chief magistrate in the exercise of his office. That experience is the parent of wisdom, is an adage the truth of which is recognized by the wisest as well as the simplest of mankind. What more desirable or more essential than this quality in the governors of nations? Where more desirable or more essential than in the first magistrate of a nation? . . . [Another] ill effect of the exclusion would be the banishing men from stations in which, in certain emergencies of the state, their presence might be of the greatest moment to the public interest or safety. There is no nation which has not, at one period or another, experienced an absolute necessity of the services of particular men in particular situations; perhaps it would not be too strong to say, to the preservation of its political existence. . . . [Yet another] ill effect of the exclusion would be, that it would operate as a constitutional interdiction of stability in the administration. By NECESSITATING a change of men, in the first office of the nation, it would necessitate a mutability of measures. . . . These are some of the disadvantages which would flow from the principle of exclusion. . . .

The Federalist No. 73

Alexander Hamilton, March 21, 1788

. . . The last of the requisites to energy, which have been enumerated, are competent powers. Let us proceed to consider those which are proposed to be vested in the President of the United States. . . . The first thing that offers itself to our observation, is the qualified negative of the President upon the acts or resolutions of the two houses of the legislature; or, in other words, his power of returning all bills with objections, to have the effect of preventing their becoming laws, unless they should afterwards be ratified by two thirds of each of the component members of the legislative body.

The propensity of the legislative department to intrude upon the rights, and to absorb the powers, of the other departments, has been already suggested and repeated; the insufficiency of a mere parchment delineation of the boundaries of each, has also been remarked upon; and the necessity of furnishing each with constitutional arms for its own defense, has been inferred and proved. From these clear and indubitable principles results the propriety of a negative, either absolute or qualified, in the Executive, upon the acts of the legislative branches. Without the one or the other, the former would be absolutely unable to defend himself against the depredations of the latter. He might gradually be stripped of his authorities by successive resolutions, or annihilated by a single vote. And in the one mode or the other, the legislative and executive powers might speedily come to be blended in the same hands. If even no propensity had ever discovered itself in the legislative body to invade the rights of the Executive, the rules of just reasoning and theoretic propriety would of themselves teach us, that the one ought not to be left to the mercy of the other, but ought to possess a constitutional and effectual power of selfdefense.

But the power in question has a further use. It not only serves as a shield to the Executive, but it furnishes an additional security against the enaction of improper laws. It establishes a salutary check upon the legislative body, calculated to guard the community against the effects of faction, precipitancy, or of any impulse unfriendly to the public good, which may happen to influence a majority of that body. . . .

It may perhaps be said that the power of preventing bad laws includes that of preventing good ones; and may be used to the one purpose as well as to the other. But this objection will have little weight with those who can properly estimate the mischiefs of that inconstancy and mutability in the laws, which form the greatest blemish in the character and genius of our governments. They will consider every institution calculated to restrain the excess of law-making, and to keep things in the same state in which they happen to be at any given period, as much more likely to do good than harm; because it is favorable to greater stability in the system of legislation. The injury which may possibly be done by defeating a few good laws, will be amply compensated by the advantage of preventing a number of bad ones.

Nor is this all. The superior weight and influence of the legislative body in a free government, and the hazard to the Executive in a trial of strength with that body, afford a satisfactory security that the negative would generally be employed with great caution; and there would oftener be room for a charge of timidity than of rashness in the exercise of it. . . .

But the convention have pursued a mean in this business, which will both facilitate the exercise of the power vested in this respect in the executive magistrate, and make its efficacy to depend on the sense of a considerable part of the legislative body. Instead of an absolute negative, it is proposed to give the Executive the qualified negative already described. This is a power which would be much more readily exercised than the other. A man who might be afraid to defeat a law by his single VETO, might not scruple to return it for reconsideration; subject to being finally rejected only in the event of more than one third of each house concurring in the sufficiency of his objections. . . .

The Federalist No. 77

Alexander Hamilton, April 2, 1788

IT HAS been mentioned as one of the advantages to be expected from the co-operation of the Senate, in the business of appointments, that it would contribute to the stability of the administration. The consent of that body would be necessary to displace as well as to appoint. A change of the Chief Magistrate, therefore, would not occasion so violent or so general a revolution in the officers of the government as might be expected, if he were the sole disposer of offices. . . .

. . . We have now completed a survey of the structure and powers of the executive department, which, I have endeavored to show, combines, as far as republican principles will admit, all the requisites to energy. The remaining inquiry is: Does it also combine the requisites to safety, in a republican sense, a due dependence on the people, a due responsibility? The answer to this question has been anticipated in the investigation of its other characteristics, and is satisfactorily deducible from these circumstances; from the election of the President once in four years by persons immediately chosen by the people for that purpose; and from his being at all times liable to impeachment, trial, dismission from office, incapacity to serve in any other, and to forfeiture of life and estate by subsequent prosecution in the common course of law. . . . What more could be desired by an enlightened and reasonable people?

NOTES

1. *The Federalist Nos. 67, 69,* and *77* all address the Anti–Federalist concern that the president would be a tyrant, a democratically elected king. For example, in *The Federalist No. 69,* Alexander Hamilton goes out of his way to assure New Yorkers that the president's powers are more analogous to those of their governor than to the powers of King George III. Is Hamilton's argument persuasive? As discussed in Chapter 1, once the Constitution had been ratified Hamilton immediately began arguing that the president's executive power in foreign affairs was comparable to that of the king of England. Were Hamilton's

views in the Neutrality Controversy consistent with the assurances made in *The Federalist No. 69*?

2. In *The Federalist No. 71*, Hamilton defends the presidency's fixed four-year term on the ground that this would make the president independent. Is four years too long or too short? Is the limitation that the president can serve only two consecutive terms a good idea? Some have proposed that the president should serve a single six-year term with a ban on re-election. Would this make every president a lame duck and unresponsive to public opinion? Others have criticized the American system of fixed terms, saying elections should be held when there is a big issue for the public to decide and not at arbitrary intervals. Would such a system give excessive weight to the passions of the moment rather than the views the public expresses over time?

3. How important is it that the framers created one executive instead of an executive council of two or three or more leaders? In *The Federalist No. 70*, Hamilton argues that unitariness is essential if there is to be an energetic and accountable executive. Is he right? What doctrinal implications flow from the framers' decision to give all of the executive power to the president? Can one infer that the president must have the power to control subordinate officers in the executive branch? Can the president remove them at will? Or is the right view that executive officers appointed with the consent of the Senate can only be removed with the same consent? The idea that Senate consent was required for removal was rejected by the First Congress in an episode called the Decision of 1789, and since then every president has agreed that senatorial consent is not required for removal. Today it would be hard to imagine that an incoming president could be saddled with a predecessor's cabinet or even subcabinet officials. (Note that Hamilton took the position in *The Federalist* that senatorial consent was necessary to remove, though he later recanted this view.)

4. The veto is perhaps the most formidable power the Constitution gives the president. Hamilton defends it in *The Federalist No. 73* by saying that it would prevent "the mischiefs of that inconstancy and mutability in the laws, which form the greatest blemish in the character and genius of our governments." Is he right? What are the long-term consequences of the veto and the rest of the Madisonian system of checks and balances? For example, do they strengthen or endanger the financial soundness of the government of the United States?

5. After reading these essays, think back to President Truman's claim in *Youngstown* that the president had an unenumerated power to seize steel mills, which were private property, in the absence of legislative approval simply because of a foreign policy emergency. How plausible does that claim now seem?

6. A majority of American political scientists believe that presidential-style constitutions are outmoded, and instead they prefer parliamentary government with an independent constitutional court that has the power of judicial review. See, e.g., Bruce Ackerman, *The New Separation of Powers*, 113 Harv. L. Rev. 633 (2000). What do you think are the advantages and disadvantages of the American system? Some fear that all presidential democracies will become dictatorships. Note, though, that unlike some other legal systems with presidents, in the United States (1) the president needs Senate consent to make appointments; (2) the president's appointees are scrutinized by Senate and House subcommittees armed with the subpoena power; and (3) the president has only two years before there is a midterm election in which the entire House of Repre-

sentatives and one-third of the Senate must face re-election. (The party out of power in the White House almost always gains seats in the midterm; and only 11 of the 50 state governors come up for re-election in the same year as presidential elections are held. As a result, the party out of power in the White House usually comes to hold the governorship in a majority of the states.)

Inherent Executive Powers?

Does the president's "executive Power" include any inherent powers over foreign policy and war-making that in England had belonged to the king? Does the "executive Power" include inherent powers of direction and removal because without them the president could not "execute" the laws? What about an inherent power to protect federal officers and instrumentalities when they are violently attacked?

Alexander Hamilton's argument during the Neutrality Controversy that the "executive Power" includes inherent foreign policy and warmaking, or self-defense, powers is a little bit of a stretch. (His argument, under the name *Pacificus*, is presented in Chapter 1.) As *Youngstown* points out, one does not literally "execute" a statute or the Constitution by making foreign policy or seizing steel mills. The case for inherent presidential foreign policy powers grows out of the Presidential Oath of Office Clause and an analogy between presidential power and the royal powers of King George III. The president arguably cannot keep the oath "to preserve, protect, and defend the Constitution" without power to defend it from foreign or domestic attacks. But if the grant of the "executive Power" gives the president these arguably "royal" powers to make foreign policy and to wage war, then what other "royal" powers might the president possess? Is the Constitution's effort to create a *functional* separation of legislative, executive, and judicial power undone if we start saying that the "executive" power in our separation of powers regime corresponds to the king's power in the very different English system, where powers were separated between the king, the House of Lords, and the House of Commons?

This issue is raised with particular urgency in cases where the president claims an inherent power to act, such as *In re Neagle*, which is presented next. As you read this case, ask yourself what law the president was "executing"—the Constitution or a statute? This is the question posed so sharply in *Youngstown*. Is *Neagle* consistent with *Youngstown*? If not, which case is right?

In re Neagle

135 U.S. 1 (1890)

■ MILLER, J.

[Deputy U.S. Marshal David Neagle was arrested for murdering a man while guarding U.S. Supreme Court Justice Stephen J. Field, who was riding circuit in California. The state police arrested Neagle and imprisoned him pending trial in state court. Neagle petitioned for habeas corpus in federal court.—Editors]

This is an appeal by Cunningham, sheriff of the county of San Joaquin, in the state of California, from a judgment of the circuit court of the United States for the northern district of California, discharging David Neagle from the custody of said sheriff, who held him a prisoner on a charge of murder. . . .

The petition . . . recites the circumstances of [an encounter] between said Neagle and David S. Terry, in which the latter was instantly killed by two shots from a revolver in the hands of the former. . . . The main allegation of this petition is that Neagle, as United States deputy-marshal, acting under the orders of . . . and in pursuance of instructions from the attorney general of the United States, had, in consequence of an anticipated attempt at violence on the part of Terry against the Honorable STEPHEN J. FIELD, a justice of the supreme court of the United States, been in attendance upon said justice, and was sitting by his side at a breakfast table when a murderous assault was made by Terry on Judge FIELD, and in defense of the life of the judge the homicide was committed for which Neagle was held by Cunningham. . . . The allegation is also . . . that Marshal Neagle, in killing Terry under the circumstances, was in the discharge of his duty as an officer of the United States, and was not, therefore, guilty of a murder, and that his imprisonment under the warrant held by Sheriff Cunningham is in violation of the laws and constitution of the United States, and that he is in custody for an act done in pursuance of the laws of the United States. . . .

On the 3d of September the court rendered its decision . . . against Sarah Althea Terry and her husband, David S. Terry. The opinion was delivered by Mr. Justice FIELD, and during its delivery a scene of great violence occured in the court-room. . . . Mrs. Terry arose from her seat, and, addressing the justice who was delivering the opinion, asked, in an excited manner, whether he was going to order her to give up the marriage contract to be canceled. Mr. Justice FIELD said: "Be seated, madam." She repeated the question, and was again told to be seated. She then said in a very excited and violent manner, that Justice FIELD had been bought, and wanted to know the price he had sold himself for . . . . Mr. Justice FIELD then directed the marshal to remove her from the court-room. She asserted that she would not go from the room, and that no one could take her from it. [A marshal who was present] proceeded to carry out the order of the court by attempting to compel her to leave, when Terry, her husband, arose from his seat under great excitement, exclaiming that no man living should touch his wife, and struck the marshal a blow in his face so violent as to knock out a tooth. He then unbuttoned his coat, thrust his hand under his vest, apparently for the purpose of drawing a bowie-knife, when he was seized by persons present, and forced down on his back. In the meantime Mrs. Terry was removed from the court-room by the marshal, and Terry was allowed to rise, and was accompanied by officers to the door leading to the marshal's office. As he was about leaving the room, or immediately after being out of it, he succeeded in drawing a bowie-knife, when his arms were seized by a Deputy-marshal and others present to prevent him from using it; and they were able to wrench it from him only after a severe struggle. The most prominent person engaged in wresting the knife from Terry was Neagle, the prisoner now in court. For this conduct both Terry and his wife were sentenced by the court to imprisonment for contempt,— Mrs. Terry for one month, and Terry for six months; and these sentences were immediately carried into effect. . . .

From that time until his death the denunciations by Terry and his wife of Mr. Justice FIELD were open, frequent, and of the most vindictive and malevolent character. While being transported from San Francisco to Alameda, where they were imprisoned, Mrs. Terry repeated a number of times that she would kill . . . Judge FIELD and Terry said that after he got out of jail he would horsewhip Judge FIELD, and that he did not believe he would ever return to California, but this earth was not large enough to keep him from finding Judge FIELD and horsewhipping him; and, in reply to a re-mark that this would be a dangerous thing to do, and that Judge FIELD would resent it, he said: "If Judge FIELD resents it, I will kill him." . . .

It is useless to go over the testimony on this subject more particularly. It is sufficient to say that the evidence is abundant that both Terry and wife contemplated some attack upon Judge FIELD during his official visit to California in the summer of 1889, which they intended should result in his death. Many of these matters were published in the newspapers, and the press of California was filled with the conjectures of a probable attack by Terry on Justice FIELD as soon as it became known that he was going to attend the circuit court in that year.

So much impressed were the friends of Judge FIELD, and of public jus-tice, both in California and in Washington, with the fear that he would fall a sacrifice to the resentment of Terry and his wife, that application was made to the attorney general of the United States suggesting the propriety of his furnishing some protection to the judge while in California. . . .

The result of this correspondence was that . . . Mr. Neagle [was ap-pointed] a deputy-marshal for the northern district of California, [with] special instructions to attend upon Judge FIELD both in court and while going from one court to another, and protect him from any assault that might be attempted upon him by Terry and wife. Accordingly, when Judge FIELD went from San Francisco to Los Angeles, to hold the circuit court of the United States at that place, Mr. Neagle accompanied him, remained with him for the few days that he was engaged in the business of that court, and returned with him to San Francisco.

It appears from the uncontradicted evidence in the case that, while the sleeping-car in which were Justice FIELD and Mr. Neagle stopped a mo-ment, in the early morning, at Fresno, Terry and wife got on the train. . . . [Judge FIELD] and Neagle got out of the car, and went into the dining-room, and took seats beside each other in the place assigned them by the person in charge of the breakfast-room; and very shortly after this Terry and wife came into the room, and Mrs. Terry, recognizing Judge FIELD, turned and left in great haste, while Terry passed beyond where Judge FIELD and Neagle were, and took his seat at another table. It was afterwards ascer-tained that Mrs. Terry went to the car, and took from it a satchel in which was a revolver. Before she returned to the eating-room, Terry arose from his seat, and, passing around the table in such a way as brought him be-hind Judge FIELD, who did not see him or notice him, came up where he was sitting with his feet under the table, and struck him a blow on the side of his face, which was repeated on the other side. He also had his arm drawn back and his fist doubled up, apparently to strike a third blow, when Neagle, who had been observing him all this time, arose from his seat with his revolver in his hand, and in a very loud voice shouted out: "Stop! stop! I am an officer!" Upon this Terry turned his attention to Neagle, and, as Neagle testifies, seemed to recognize him, and immediately turned his hand to thrust it in his bosom, as Neagle felt sure, with the purpose of drawing a bowie-knife. At this instant Neagle fired two shots from his re-volver into the body of Terry, who immediately sank down, and died in a few minutes.

Mrs. Terry entered the room, with the satchel in her hand, just after Terry sank to the floor. She rushed up to the place where he was, threw herself upon his body, made loud exclamations and moans, and commenced inviting the spectators to avenge her wrong upon Field and Neagle. . . .

Without a more minute discussion of this testimony, it produces upon us the conviction of a settled purpose on the part of Terry and his wife, amounting to a conspiracy, to murder Justice FIELD; and we are quite sure that if Neagle had been merely a brother or a friend of Judge FIELD, ... he would have been justified in what he did in defense of Mr. Justice FIELD's life, and possibly of his own.

But such a justification would be a proper subject for consideration on a trial of the case for murder in the courts of the state of California; and there exists no authority in the courts of the United States to discharge the prisoner while held in custody by the state authorities for this offense, unless there be found in aid of the defense of the prisoner some element of power and authority asserted under the government of the United States. This element is said to be found in the facts that Mr. Justice FIELD, when attacked, was in the immediate discharge of his duty as judge of the circuit courts of the United States within California; that the assault upon him grew out of the animosity of Terry and wife, arising out of the previous discharge of his duty as circuit justice in the case, for which they were committed for contempt of court; and that the deputy-marshal of the United States who killed Terry in defense of Field's life, was charged with a duty, under the law of the United States, to protect Field from the violence which Terry was inflicting, and which was intended to lead to Field's death. . . .

We have no doubt that Mr. Justice FIELD, when attacked by Terry, was engaged in the discharge of his duties as circuit justice of the ninth circuit, and was entitled to all the protection, under those circumstances, which the law could give him.

It is urged, however, that there exists no statute authorizing any such protection as that which Neagle was instructed to give Judge FIELD in the present case, and, indeed, no protection whatever against a vindictive or malicious assault growing out of the faithful discharge of his official duties . . . . *[The Court concluded that the statute that authorized the writ of habeas corpus for a person "in custody for an act done or omitted in pursuance of a law of the United States" should be read expansively enough to include Neagle.—Editors]* This view of the subject is confirmed by the alternative provision that he must be in custody "for an act done or omitted in pursuance of a law of the United States, or of an order, process, or decree of a court or a judge thereof, or is in custody in violation of the constitution or of a law or treaty of the United States."

In the view we take of the constitution of the United States, any obligation fairly and properly inferable from that instrument, or any duty of the marshal to be derived from the general scope of his duties under the laws of the United States, is a "law," within the meaning of this phrase. It would be a great reproach to the system of government of the United States, declared to be within its sphere sovereign and supreme, if there is to be found within the domain of its powers no means of protecting the judges, in the conscientious and faithful discharge of their duties, from the malice and hatred of those upon whom their judgments may operate unfavorably. . . .

If a person in the situation of Judge FIELD could have no other guaranty of his personal safety while engaged in the conscientious discharge of a disagreeable duty than the fact that, if he was murdered, his murderer would be subject to the laws of a state, and by those laws could be punished, the security would be very insufficient. The plan which Terry and wife had in mind, of insulting him and assaulting him, and drawing him into a defensive physical contest, in the course of which they would slay him, shows the little value of such remedies. We do not believe that the government of the United States is thus inefficient, or that its constitution and laws have left the high officers of the government so defenseless and unprotected.... Where, then, are we to look for the protection which we have shown Judge FIELD was entitled to when engaged in the discharge of his official duties? Not to the courts of the United States, because, as has been more than once said in this court, in the division of the powers of government between the three great departments, executive, legislative, and judicial, the judicial is the weakest for the purposes of self-protection, and for the enforcement of the powers which it exercises. The ministerial officers through whom its commands must be executed are marshals of the United States, and belong emphatically to the executive department of the government. They are appointed by the president, with the advice and consent of the senate. They are removable from office at his pleasure. They are subjected by act of congress to the supervision and control of the department of justice, in the hands of one of the cabinet officers of the president, and their compensation is provided by acts of congress. The same may be said of the district attorneys of the United States who prosecute and defend the claims of the government in the courts.

The legislative branch of the government can only protect the judicial officers by the enactment of laws for that purpose, and the argument we are now combating assumes that no such law has been passed by congress.

If we turn to the executive department of the government, we find a very different condition of affairs. The constitution, § 3, art. 2, declares that the president "shall take care that the laws be faithfully executed;" and he is provided with the means of fulfilling this obligation by his authority to commission all the officers of the United States, and, by and with the advice and consent of the senate, to appoint the most important of them, and to fill vacancies. He is declared to be the commander in chief of the army and navy of the United States. The duties which are thus imposed upon him he is further enabled to perform by the recognition in the constitution, and the creation by acts of congress, of executive departments, which have varied in number from four or five to seven or eight, who are familiarly called "cabinet ministers." These aid him in the performance of the great duties of his office, and represent him in a thousand acts to which it can hardly be supposed his personal attention is called; and thus he is enabled to fulfill the duty of his great department, expressed in the phrase that "he shall take care that the laws be faithfully executed."

Is this duty limited to the enforcement of acts of congress or of treaties of the United States according to their *express terms*; or does it include the rights, duties, and obligations growing out of the constitution itself, our international relations, and all the protection implied by the nature of the government under the constitution? . . .

So, if the president or the postmaster general is advised that the mails of the United States, possibly carrying treasure, are liable to be robbed, and the mail carriers assaulted and murdered, in any particular region of country, who can doubt the authority of the president, or of one of the executive departments under him, to make an order for the protection of the mail, and of the persons and lives of its carriers, by doing exactly what was done in the case of Mr. Justice FIELD, namely, providing a sufficient guard, whether it be by soldiers of the army or by marshals of the United States . . . to secure the safe performance of the duty of carrying the mail wherever it may be intended to go? The United States is the owner of millions of acres of valuable public land, and has been the owner of much more, which it has sold. Some of these lands owe a large part of their value to the forests which grow upon them. These forests are liable to depredations by people living in the neighborhood, known as "timber thieves," who make a living by cutting and selling such timber, and who are trespassers. But until quite recently, even if there be one now, there was no statute authorizing any preventive measures for the protection of this valuable public property. Has the president no authority to place guards upon the public territory to protect its timber? . . . Has he no power to take any measures to protect this vast domain? Fortunately, we find this question answered by this court in the case of *Wells v. Nickles,* 104 U.S. 444[,] . . . which upheld the authority of the secretary of the interior to make [certain] rules and regulations for the protection of the public lands. . . .

We cannot doubt the power of the president to take measures for the protection of a judge of one of the courts of the United States who, while in the discharge of the duties of his office, is threatened with a personal attack which may probably result in his death; and we think it clear that where this protection is to be afforded through the civil power, the department of justice is the proper one to set in motion the necessary means of protection. The correspondence, already recited in this opinion, between the marshal of the northern district of California and the attorney general and the district attorney of the United States for that district, although prescribing no very specific mode of affording this protection by the attorney general, is sufficient, we think, to warrant the marshal in taking the steps which he did take, in making the provisions which he did make, for the protection and defense of Mr. Justice FIELD. . . .

But, all these questions being conceded, it is urged against the relief sought by this writ of *habeas corpus* that the question of the guilt of the prisoner of the crime of murder is a question to be determined by the laws of California, and to be decided by its courts, and that there exists no power in the government of the United States to take away the prisoner from the custody of the proper authorities of the state of California. . . .

[But t]he enactments now found in the Revised Statutes of the United States on the subject of the writ of *habeas corpus* are the result of a long course of legislation forced upon congress by the attempt of the states of the Union to exercise the power of imprisonment over officers and other persons asserting rights under the federal government or foreign governments, which the states denied. . . .

The result at which we have arrived upon this examination is that, in the protection of the person and the life of Mr. Justice FIELD while in the discharge of his official duties, Neagle was authorized to resist the attack of Terry upon him; that Neagle was correct in the belief that, without prompt action on his part, the assault of Terry upon the judge would have ended in the death of the latter; that, such being his well-founded belief, he was justified in taking the life of Terry, as the only means of preventing the death of the man who was intended to be his victim; that in taking the life of Terry, under the circumstances, he was acting under the authority of the law of the United States, and was justified in so doing; and that he is not liable to answer in the courts of California on account of his part in that transaction.

■ LAMAR, J. [joined by FULLER, C.J., dissenting].

The chief justice and myself are unable to assent to the conclusion reached by the majority of the court. Our dissent is not based on any conviction as to the guilt or innocence of the appellee. The view which we take renders that question immaterial to the inquiry presented by this appeal. . . .

We recognize that the powers of the government, "within its sphere," as defined by the constitution and interpreted by the well-settled principles which have resulted from a century of wise and patriotic analysis, are supreme; that these supreme powers extend to the protection of itself and all of its agencies, as well as to the preservation and the perpetuation of its usefulness; and that these powers may be found not only in the express authorities conferred by the constitution, but also in necessary and proper implications. But, while that is all true, it is also true that the powers must be exercised not only by the organs, but also in conformity with the modes, prescribed by the constitution itself. These great federal powers, whose existence in all their plenitude and energy is incontestable, are not autocratic and lawless. They are organized powers committed by the people to the hands of their servants for their own government, and distributed among the legislative, executive, and judicial departments. They are not extra the Constitution . . . .

The president is sworn to "preserve, protect, and defend the constitution." That oath has great significance. The sections which follow that prescribing the oath (sections 2 and 3 of article 2) prescribe the duties and fix the powers of the president. But one very prominent feature of the constitution which he is sworn to preserve, and which the whole body of the judiciary are bound to enforce, is the closing paragraph of section 8, art. 1, in which it is declared that "the congress shall have power . . . to make all laws which shall be necessary and proper for carrying into execution the foregoing powers, and all other powers vested by this constitution in the government of the United States, or in any department or officer thereof."

This clause is that which contains the germ of all the implication of powers under the constitution. It is that which has built up the congress of the United States into the most august and imposing legislative assembly in the world, and which has secured vigor to the practical operations of the government, and at the same time tended largely to preserve the equilibrium of its various powers among its co-ordinate departments, as partitioned by that instrument. And that clause alone conclusively refutes the assertion of the attorney general that it was "the duty of the executive department of the United States to guard and protect at any hazard the life of Mr. Justice FIELD in the discharge of his duty, because such protection is essential to the existence of the government." Waiving the question of the essentiality of any such protection to the existence of the government, the manifest answer is that the protection needed and to be given must proceed not from the president, but primarily from congress. Again, while it is the president's duty to take care that the laws be faithfully executed, it is not his duty to make laws or a law of the United States. The laws he is to see executed are manifestly those contained in the constitution and those enacted by congress, whose duty it is to make all laws necessary and proper for carrying into execution the powers of those tribunals. . . . Indeed, it has passed such laws in reference to elections, expressly directing the United States marshals to attend places of election, to act as peace-officers, to arrest with and without process, and to protect the supervisors of election in the discharge of their duties; and there was not the slightest legal necessity out of which to imply any such power in the president. . . .

The *gravamen* of this case is in the assertion that Neagle slew Terry in pursuance of a law of the United States. He who claims to have committed a homicide by authority must show the authority. If he claims the authority of law, then what law? And if a law, how came it to be a law? Somehow and somewhere it must have had an origin. Is it a law because of the existence of a special and private authority issued from one of the executive departments? So, in almost these words, it is claimed in this case. Is it a law because of some constitutional investiture of sovereignty in the persons of judges, who carry that sovereignty with them wherever they may go? Because of some power inherent in the judiciary to create for others a rule or law of conduct outside of legislation, which shall extend to the death penalty? So, also, in this case, *in totidem verbis*, it is claimed. We dissent from both these claims. There can be no such law from either of those sources. The right claimed must be traced to legislation of congress, else it cannot exist. . . .

■ FIELD, J., did not sit at the hearing of this case, and took no part in its decision.

NOTES

1. Does the president, along with the attorney general, have an inherent constitutional right to defend with force the life of a Supreme Court justice without an authorizing statute? Does the president's oath "to preserve, protect, and defend the Constitution of the United States" mean that the president has a power to "protect" federal officials, instrumentalities (or even, as President Lincoln argued, to protect the Union itself)? See Henry Monaghan, *The Protective Power of the Presidency*, 93 Colum. L. Rev. 1 (1993).

2. *In re Neagle* defers to the president's executive power in the context of a federalism problem. The issue is whether California may prosecute a U.S. marshal for following the orders of the attorney general to defend the life of a federal justice. If the states were not preempted by the Constitution from doing such things, then presumably they would also be able to tax the Bank of the United States (contrary to *McCulloch v. Maryland*) or impose term limits on members of the U.S. Congress (contrary to *U.S. Term Limits, Inc. v. Thornton*). If the majority is right that there is a protective power, is it an exclusive federal power, or is it one exercised concurrently with the states?

3. In another case, *In re Debs*, 158 U.S. 564 (1895), the Supreme Court upheld the imprisonment of Eugene V. Debs and other labor leaders who had violated a federal injunction ordering striking employees to return to work. The justices unanimously found that the judiciary had an inherent equitable power to enjoin the strike absent a statute because the strike threatened the U.S. mail and interstate commerce. Is there any relevant difference between this inherent judicial power and the inherent executive power sustained by *In re Neagle*? The injunction had been sought by the Cleveland administration. Without statutory authority, the administration also used U.S. troops and marshals to restore order and break the strike. (Controversy over the matter doomed any chance President Cleveland might have had of being nominated in 1896 for a third term.) Was President Cleveland's use of force a valid exercise of the protective power?

4. In *United States v. Midwest Oil Co.*, 236 U.S. 459 (1915), the Supreme Court addressed the question whether the president could withdraw federal land from development and oil drilling in order to protect oil wells on adjacent land owned by the federal government. The oil in question was needed to fuel the Navy. Even though there was an explicit federal statute opening the lands at issue to development, the Court concluded that Congress had for many years acquiesced in the existence of a presidential power to withdraw federal lands from development. Such a longstanding practice, in which Congress had acquiesced, was enough to trump the text of a statute. (Interestingly, this pro-presidential power opinion was written by another Justice Lamar, a cousin of the Justice Lamar who dissented in *In re Neagle*.) Was *Midwest Oil* rightly decided? How important should practice be in these cases?

5. If the president has a protective power, how far does it go? Could President Obama order the invasion of Iran to disable its nuclear weapons program without congressional authorization on the grounds that doing so protects New York City and other parts of the United States from nuclear attack? If so, would anything be left of separation of powers?

[Assignment 18]

B. THE LAW-EXECUTING POWER:
"HE SHALL TAKE CARE THAT THE LAWS BE FAITHFULLY EXECUTED"

Article II, Section 1: The executive Power shall be vested in a President of the United States of America.

Section 3: . . . he shall take Care that the Laws be faithfully executed. . . .

As you have seen in the preceding materials, the Vesting Clause of Article I gives "all legislative powers herein granted" to Congress. The Vesting Clause of Article II, in contrast, gives all of the executive power—not merely those executive powers *herein granted*—to a single officer: the president of the United States. It might as well be phrased to read "The President of the United States shall have the executive power."

Why did the framers use the word *vested*? It comes from the Latin *vestis*, which means clothes or vestments. When judges or executive officials assume their offices and powers, the ceremony is called an investiture. Indeed, judges physically put on the clothes of their office—their robes—as they assume their powers. By "vesting" the president with the executive power, Article II, Section 1 clothes the president with powers that are not legislative or judicial. What those powers are has been the subject of great debate.

Recall that Justice Jackson's concurring opinion in *Youngstown* denied that the Vesting Clause of Article I was a grant of power. Justice Jackson took the view that Article I, Section 1 simply specified the president's title and the fact that we have only one president. Yet the Vesting Clause of Article II is structured like the Vesting Clause of Article III, which is most certainly a grant of power to the judiciary. Is there any way to distinguish the Vesting Clause of Article II? If not, does that mean that it is a grant of the executive power to the president?

But an objection could be raised: if Article II, Section 1 is a grant of the executive power to the president, then why doesn't Article II just stop right there? Why does Article II go on in Section 2 to declare that the president is the commander in chief of the army and navy, has the power to pardon, has the power to make treaties with the concurrence of two-thirds of the Senate, and has the power of appointment subject to Senate confirmation?

Several answers are possible. One is that Section 2 defines, explicates, and limits the general grant of the executive power in the Vesting Clause. It makes clear that the president does not have the executive powers that English monarchs had, such as the power to raise armies (and not just command them), the power to make treaties without legislative consent, and the power to appoint officers without legislative confirmation. On this view, Section 2 would qualify the general grant of the executive power in the Vesting Clause in important ways, even though it does not describe every one of the president's powers. (For example, it does not expressly mention presidential powers to execute the laws or to regulate foreign affairs—powers that have been claimed and exercised by every president.) Thus Section 2 does not purport to be a comprehensive list of presidential powers the way Article I, Section 8 is a comprehensive list of congressional powers. That is consistent with the fact that the Vesting Clause of Article II does not vest the president with "All executive Powers *herein granted.*"

And what about Article II, Sections 3 and 4? What role do they play in the constitutional system? Section 3 imposes a series of duties on the president. The president "shall"—i.e., "must"—deliver a State of the Union message to Congress, receive ambassadors and other public ministers, and "take care that the laws be faithfully executed." (This last duty means that the president is not permitted to dispense with or suspend statutes the way King James II did before the Glorious Revolution of 1688.) Where does the president's power to fulfill the "take care" duty come from? Presumably, it comes from the Vesting Clause of Article II.

Article II, Section 4 makes the president and vice president impeachable from office and removable by the Senate for treason, bribery, and other high crimes and misdemeanors. English monarchs could not be impeached by Parliament; only the royal ministers could be. In contrast, Section 4 makes clear that the president is under the law. This is another major way the president has less power than English sovereigns.

Some presidential powers are not so easily explained by the account just given. One is Article II, Section 2's grant to the president of power to "require the Opinion, in writing, of the principal Officer in each of the executive Departments, upon any Subject relating to the Duties of their respective Offices." Why wouldn't the president be assumed to have that power as a general implication of the grant of "the executive Power"? Or, put differently, if the president can direct executive branch subordinates in everything they do, why would the president need a special power to direct them to give their opinions in writing? *The Federalist No. 74* suggests that the clause may have been added in an excess of caution. Is that persuasive? Is there another way to reconcile the Opinion Clause with the other textual evidence? Another objection might be raised: why was it necessary to say that the president "shall take Care that the Laws be faithfully executed," if that is the core of "the executive Power"? Here an answer could be given that it is at the core of the executive power, but the Take Care Clause goes further and lays on the president an affirmative duty: the president *must* "take Care" that the laws be faithfully executed.

These questions about the meaning of the Vesting Clause of Article II and the scope of executive power are hotly disputed by scholars and courts. But however they are answered, it is generally agreed that the president's "executive Power" consists of two main branches: first, the law-executing power; and second, a power over foreign affairs that extends at least to treaty-making, diplomatic relations, and the command of the nation's armed forces. We begin with the law-execution power.

The Power to Direct Non–Prosecution

President George Washington took office on April 30, 1789, and he immediately asserted control over all the executive entities of the government under the Articles of Confederation, even though Congress had not yet given him any statutory authority over those entities. President Washington issued directives to the acting secretary of war, the board of treasury, the acting postmaster general, and the acting secretaries of war and of foreign affairs. He continued throughout his presidency to issue hundreds of written communications approving plans and actions, conveying directions about administrative operations, and making requests. Specifically, President Washington started and ended criminal prosecutions by federal district attorneys (the forerunners of today's U.S. attorneys). And his Neutrality Proclamation was a major exercise of presidential power, guiding foreign policy and ordering prosecutions.

President Washington's immediate successors, John Adams and Thomas Jefferson, also started and ended prosecutions. President Adams personally directed that a prosecution be brought against newspaper editor William Duane even though no statute purported to give the president the power to do that. He must have thought that his power to start this case was conferred by the Constitution. The Senate asked President Adams to see to it that Duane was prosecuted, thus confirming that senators too thought the president had the power to direct the district attorneys. On two other occasions he specifically ordered that prosecutions be dropped, just as President Washington had done. When President Jefferson took office, he directed the district attorneys not to bring any new prosecutions under the Alien and Sedition Acts (which he thought unconstitutional). He also directed that the prosecution of Duane under the Sedition Act be dropped. He wrote:

> The President is to have the laws executed. He may order an offense then to be prosecuted. If he sees a prosecution put into a train which is not lawful, he may order it to be discontinued and put into a legal train. . . . There appears to be no weak part in any of these positions or inferences.

He also urged the secretary of the treasury to bring a prosecution in a case involving a schooner called *Sally*, and he directed that all federal common law prosecutions for libel be discontinued because he thought them unconstitutional as well. President Jefferson was even minutely involved in controlling the government's prosecution of his first vice president, Aaron Burr, for treason. In sum, the early practice shows that Presidents Washington, Adams, and Jefferson believed that Article II made them the nation's prosecutor in chief. For extensive discussion of more than two centuries of presidential practice, see Steven G. Calabresi & Christopher S. Yoo, THE UNITARY EXECUTIVE: PRESIDENTIAL POWER FROM WASHINGTON TO BUSH (2008).

Consider next an opinion for President Andrew Jackson by Attorney General Roger Taney (later Chief Justice Taney); and *United States v. Cox*, a modern case in which a federal judge ordered the jailing of a federal prosecutor who declined to bring a prosecution. What position on the president's power to direct non-prosecution is constitutionally sound? Which types of constitutional argument, or modes of interpretation, are most helpful in deciding this question?

Attorney General Taney, Opinion on the Jewels of the Princess of Orange

December 28, 1831

To the SECRETARY OF STATE.

I have, according to your request, read your argument on the questions which have grown out of the seizure of the jewels said to have been stolen from the Princess of Orange; and I concur with you in the conclusion to which you have come, although I do not place my opinion on precisely the same grounds.

The main question, and the only one about which there seems to be much difficulty, is, whether the President may lawfully direct the district attorney to discontinue the libel now pending against these jewels in the district court of New York. The libel is in the name of the United States; it was filed by their attorney, in their behalf, and claims to have the property condemned as forfeited to the United States, for an offence alleged to have been committed against their revenue laws.

Having been absent from Washington when this subject was under consideration, I have seen none of the papers or documents in the case, and I take the facts as I find them set forth (no doubt correctly) in your argument. I understand them to be as follows:

The jewels were brought to New York by Polari, and the violation of the revenue laws was committed by him; and, as soon as they were known to be in this country, the minister of the King of the Netherlands, acting under the direction of his government, claimed them as the property of the Princess of Orange, who is one of the family of the King.

Polari does not pretend that the property seized belongs to him. On the contrary, his confessions show that he was either concerned in the theft, or obtained the jewels, knowing them to be stolen; and there is no claimant but the Princess of Orange; and a friendly sovereign, through his minister here, asserts that they belong to her. . . .

The fact that jewels of this description were stolen some time ago from the Princess of Orange, is notorious, and may now be regarded as a matter of history. The jewels which have been seized at New York are of very great value. The seizure of this property has been publicly known for several months; and it is in a high degree improbable that any one who supposed himself entitled to it would neglect, for so long a time, to put in his claim. And as none is made, except that on behalf of the Princess of Orange, the circumstances above stated furnish sufficient evidence to conclude that the jewels in question belong to her, and will justify the President in treating them as her property. . . .

Taking this to be the true state of the case, it is, I think, very clear that the jewels are not liable to condemnation under the laws of the United

States. The real owner has done no act that can rightfully subject the property to forfeiture. The party who imported them into this country obtained the possession fraudulently, and without her knowledge, and brought them here against her will. It was not in her power to prevent it; for she did not know who had the possession of them, or where they were to be found, until they were seized. And property thus obtained, and thus introduced against the consent of the owner, stands on the same footing with that which is cast upon our shores by the violence of the winds and waves, and is entitled to the same protection. It is not liable to forfeiture in either case; and the innocent owner will not be visited with that penalty for an act which it was out of his power to prevent.

There being, then, sufficient evidence to show that these jewels are the property of the Princess of Orange, and therefore not liable to forfeiture,— are the officers of the government, from the nature of our institutions, bound to carry on a prosecution against them, and endeavor to have them condemned, when they are fully convinced that they are not justly liable to condemnation? Must the distant owner be put to the trouble and expense of proving her title, according to the strict and technical rules of evidence which prevail in judicial proceedings?

. . . [W]here an offence has been actually committed, and the penalty of the law unquestionably incurred, no doubt can be entertained of the power of the President to absolve the party from the penalty or forfeiture to which he is liable. And if a prosecution is pending in court, the President may, by his pardon, enable the party to stop the proceedings, without going to trial. And the power to grant a *nolle prosequi* in such a case, is necessarily embraced in the power to pardon an offender.

It would be a singular anomaly in our law, if the power is given thus to put an end to a prosecution against one admitted to be guilty, and yet there should be no power vested anywhere to save a party admitted to be innocent, from a harassing and expensive litigation with the United States, and which, from the distance of its witnesses and the difficulty of collecting his proofs, may often be oppressive and ruinous to him. The men who framed the constitution have not, however, committed this oversight. And in cases of the latter description, the power to interpose appears to me to be evidently embraced by that clause of the constitution which makes it his duty "to take care that the laws be faithfully executed." I proceed to show how that power applies to the case in hand. . . .

[The attorney general proceeds to show that federal district attorneys had discretion not to prosecute cases like this one. The attorney general then considers whether the president can direct and control the exercise of that discretion.—Editors]

I think the President does possess the power. The interest of the country and the purposes of justice manifestly require that he should possess it; and its existence is necessarily implied by the duties imposed upon him in that clause of the constitution before referred to, which enjoins him to take care that the laws be faithfully executed. Cases readily suggest themselves which show the necessity of such a power to enable him to discharge this duty. . . .

If it should be said that, the district attorney having the power to discontinue the prosecution, there is no necessity for inferring a right in the President to direct him to exercise it,—I answer, that the direction of the President is not required to communicate any new authority to the district attorney, but to direct him or aid him in the execution of the power he is admitted to possess. It might, indeed, happen that a district attorney was prosecuting a suit in the name of the United States, against their interest and against justice, and for the purpose of oppressing an individual: such a prosecution would not be a faithful execution of the law; and upon the President being satisfied that the forms of law were abused for such a purpose, and being bound to take care that the law was faithfully executed, it would become his duty to take measures to correct the procedure. And the most natural and proper measure to accomplish that object would be, to order the district attorney to discontinue the prosecution. . . .

I have put the case of a district attorney who wilfully violates his duty, in order to show the necessity of the power in the President for which I am contending. But another class of cases frequently occur, in which the district attorney himself may believe that the prosecution ought to be discontinued, but feels that it would be indiscreet and rash in him to incur the whole responsibility of dismissing it. And no case would better illustrate this class of cases than the one which has given rise to this discussion. The amount of property claimed to be forfeited to the United States is very large. The collector insists that a great part of it is liable to condemnation. It is known to have attracted the attention of the President, and to have become the subject of a correspondence with the minister of a foreign power. It would be indiscreet in the highest degree in Mr. Hamilton, the district attorney, to dismiss such a prosecution on his own responsibility, without first obtaining the approbation of the President; . . .

. . . Upon the whole, I consider the district attorney as under the control and direction of the President, in the institution and prosecution of suits in the name and on behalf of the United States; and that it is within the legitimate power of the President to direct him to institute or to discontinue a pending suit, and to point out to him, his duty, whenever the interest of the United States is directly or indirectly concerned. And I find, on examination, that the practice of the government has conformed to this opinion; and that, in many instances where the interference of the Executive was asked for, the cases have been referred to the Attorney General, and, in every case, the right to interfere and direct the district attorney is assumed or asserted. . . . If the President possesses this power, the remaining inquiry is, whether this is a fit case for its exercise. My opinion on this point is sufficiently indicated by the remarks I have already made. . . .

United States v. Cox

342 F.2d 167 (5th Cir. 1965)

■ Before TUTTLE, CHIEF JUDGE, and RIVES, JONES, BROWN, WISDOM, GEWIN and BELL, CIRCUIT JUDGES.

■ JONES, CIRCUIT JUDGE:

On October 22, 1964, an order of the United States District Court for the Southern District of Mississippi, signed by Harold Cox, a judge of that Court, was entered. The order, with caption and formal closing omitted, is as follows:

THE GRAND JURY, duly elected, impaneled and organized, for the Southern District of Mississippi, reconvened on order of the Court at 9:00 A.M., October 21, 1964, in Court Room Number 2 in Jackson, Mississippi, for the general dispatch of its business. The grand jury was fully instructed as to their duties, powers and responsibilities and retired to the grand jury room number 538 in the Federal Building at Jackson to do its work. The United States Attorney (and one of his assistants) sat with the grand jury throughout the day on October 21 and explained in detail to the grand jury the perjury laws and the Court's construction of such laws for their information. The grand jury heard witnesses throughout the day on October 21, 1964. On the morning of October 22, 1964, the grand jury, through its foreman, made known to the Court in open court that they had requested Robert E. Hauberg, United States Attorney, to prepare certain indictments which they desired to bring against some of the persons under consideration and about which they had heard testimony, and the United States Attorney refused to draft or sign any such indictments on instructions of the Acting Attorney General of the United States; whereupon the Court ordered and directed said United States Attorney to draft such true bills or no bills as the grand jury may have duly voted and desired to report and to sign such instruments as required by law under penalty of contempt. The United States Attorney was afforded one hour within which to decide as to whether or not he would abide by the instructions and order of the Court in such respect. At the end of such time, the Court re-convened and the United States Attorney was specifically asked in open court as to whether or not he intended to conform with the order and direction of the Court in said respects whereupon the United States Attorney answered that he respectfully declined to do so on instructions from Nicholas deB. Katzenbach, Acting Attorney General. He was thereupon duly adjudged by the Court to be in civil contempt of the Court and was afforded an opportunity to make any statement which he desired to make to the Court before sentence; whereupon the United States Attorney reiterated his inability to comply with the order of the Court upon express and direct instructions from Nicholas deB. Katzenbach, Acting Attorney General of the United States.

WHEREFORE, IT IS ORDERED AND ADJUDGED by the Court that Robert E. Hauberg, United States Attorney, is guilty of civil contempt of this Court and in the presence of the Court for his said refusal to obey its said order and he is ordered into custody of the United States Marshal to be confined by him in the Hinds County, Mississippi, jail, there to remain until he purges himself of this contempt by agreeing to conform to said order by performing his official duty for the grand jury as requested in the several (about five) pending cases before them on October 21 and October 22, 1964.

IT IS FURTHER ORDERED by the Court that a citation issue to Nicholas deB. Katzenbach, Acting Attorney General of the United States, directing him to appear before this Court and show cause why he should not be adjudged guilty of contempt of this Court for his instructions and directions to the United States Attorney to disregard and disobey the orders of this Court in the respects stated.

The United States Attorney requested a stay of enforcement of this order and further proceedings herein for five days after this date to enable him to apply to the United States Court of Appeals for the Fifth Circuit for a writ of prohibition and such request is granted; and these proceedings and enforcement of this order in its entirety is stayed for five days, subject to the further orders of the United States

Court of Appeals on said application; and for the enforcement of all of which, let proper process issue.

The United States Attorney, Robert E. Hauberg, and the Acting Attorney General, Nicholas deB. Katzenbach, have appealed from the order and they, joined by the United States, seek a writ of prohibition against the District Judge from enforcing the Court's order, and from asserting jurisdiction to require the Attorney General or the United States Attorney "to institute criminal prosecutions or to take any steps in regard thereto." . . .

The constitutional requirement of an indictment . . . as a predicate to a prosecution for capital or infamous crimes has for its primary purpose the protection of the individual from jeopardy except on a finding of probable cause by a group of his fellow citizens, and is designed to afford a safeguard against oppressive actions of the prosecutor or a court. The constitutional provision is not to be read as conferring on or preserving to the grand jury, as such, any rights or prerogatives. The constitutional provision is, as has been said, for the benefit of the accused. The constitutional provision is not to be read as precluding, as essential to the validity of an indictment, the inclusion of requisites which did not exist at common law. . . .

The judicial power of the United States is vested in the federal courts, and extends to prosecutions for violations of the criminal laws of the United States. The executive power is vested in the President of the United States, who is required to take care that the laws be faithfully executed. The Attorney General is the hand of the President in taking care that the laws of the United States in legal proceedings and in the prosecution of offenses, be faithfully executed. The role of the grand jury is restricted to a finding as to whether or not there is probable cause to believe that an offense has been committed. The discretionary power of the attorney for the United States in determining whether a prosecution shall be commenced or maintained may well depend upon matters of policy wholly apart from any question of probable cause. Although as a member of the bar, the attorney for the United States is an officer of the court, he is nevertheless an executive official of the Government, and it is as an officer of the executive department that he exercises a discretion as to whether or not there shall be a prosecution in a particular case. It follows, as an incident of the constitutional separation of powers, that the courts are not to interfere with the free exercise of the discretionary powers of the attorneys of the United States in their control over criminal prosecutions. . . . If the attorney refuses to sign, as he has the discretionary power of doing, we conclude that there is no valid indictment. . . .

Judges Tuttle, Jones, Brown and Wisdom join in the conclusion that the signature of the United States Attorney is essential to the validity of an indictment. . . . The order before us for review is in the conjunctive; it requires the United States Attorney to prepare and sign. A majority of the court, having decided that the direction to sign is erroneous, the order on appeal will be reversed. . . .

■ [The opinion of CIRCUIT JUDGES RIVES, GEWIN, and GRIFFIN B. BELL, concurring in part and dissenting in part, is omitted.]

■ JOHN R. BROWN, CIRCUIT JUDGE (concurring specially):

Mine is a middle course. I agree with the opinion written by Judge Jones that the District Attorney may not be compelled to sign the formal indictment which the Grand Jury has voted to return. . . . But I do not agree that the District Attorney may ignore the efforts of the Grand Jury to the point of declining to prepare in proper legal form the indictment they have voted to return. On the contrary, I am of the view that the Court may properly compel the District Attorney to act as legal scrivener to the Grand Jury. The Court may, therefore, order the District Attorney to prepare the indictment in legal form. . . .

Responsibility for determining whether a prosecution is to be commenced or maintained must be clearly fixed. The power not to initiate is indeed awesome. But it has to reside somewhere. And the more clearly pinpointed it is, the more the public interest is served through the focus of relentless publicity upon that decision. It may not, with safety, be left to a body whose great virtue is the combination of anonymity, transitory authority, and political unresponsibility.

All must be aware now that there are times when the interests of the nation require that a prosecution be foregone. These instances will most often be in the area of state secrets and national security. With stakes so high, the safety of our country, and hence the security of the world, ought not to be imperiled by leaving the important decision to a body having no definitive political responsibility. And it is hardly realistic to suggest, as do the dissenters, that these factors may be evaluated by the Grand Jury. What will be the source of their information? How extensive will it be? How close will a Grand Jury session approach a presidential cabinet meeting? How will essential government secrets be kept when disclosed to persons none of whom as Grand Jurors will have been subjected to customary security clearance checks?

And even in less sensitive areas, the practical operation of the prosecutorial function makes imperative the need for executive determination. The familiar example is the deliberate choice between those to be prosecuted and those who, often equally guilty, are named as co-conspirators but not as defendants, or others not named who are used as star government witnesses. And in other situations, of which the instant case may well be typical, the executive's purpose to effectuate specific policies thought to be of major importance would be frustrated or encumbered were a Grand Jury given the sole prerogative of determining when a prosecution is to be effectively commenced. . . .

But while I am firm that signature is a vital and significant act which reflects the exercise of an executive discretion to initiate prosecution—a thing here lacking—I am equally positive that the District Attorney has the duty to prepare the indictment when requested to do so by the Grand Jury. If this lacks logical consistency, I can only urge that an institution as old as the Grand Jury, implanted in the structure as idealistic as the Constitution, is one born, not out of logic, but out of the needs of history's rich experience. . . .

The powers of the Executive are so awesome in determining those whom it will not prosecute, that where there is a difference between the Grand Jury and the Executive, this determination and the resulting conflict of views should be revealed in open court. With great power comes great responsibility. Disclosure of this difference of view and the resulting impasse would subject this decision of the Executive to the scrutiny of an informed electorate. . . .

■ WISDOM, CIRCUIT JUDGE (concurring specially):

Too many opinion-writers are like too many cooks. I brave the danger of spoiling *our* broth only because the savory aroma of the competing dish the dissenters offer conceals its indigestible ingredients.

The dissenters show judicial craftsmanship of the highest order in writing persuasively about "the traditional sphere" of the grand jury while not turning up one case holding that a court may compel a prosecutor to prepare and sign a bill of indictment requested by a grand jury. Not one case in all the years between 1166 and 1965! I submit that the result reached in the dissent is the product of a misunderstanding of the historical meaning of "presentment and indictment", a failure to give effect to the difference between the sword and the shield of the grand jury,[1] and an abstract approach that disregards the factual setting in which the issue is presented.

Nothing in the position of any of the judges in the majority "ignores" or tends to diminish the purely inquisitorial role of the federal grand jury. But when that role goes beyond inquiry and report and becomes accusatorial, no aura of traditional or constitutional sanctity surrounds the grand jury. The Grand Jury earned its place in the Bill of Rights by its shield, not by its sword.

The Fifth Amendment requires the grand jury's "presentment or indictment" as a prerequisite to trial for a "capital, or otherwise infamous crime". This language provides no aid and comfort to the notion that either the grand jury or the court has the power to compel prosecution once the grand jury has exercised its accusatorial function. . . . "Federal statutes are silent on the relationship which is to exist between a federal grand jury, the district court which summons it, and the United States attorney's office in the district. From 1789 to the present, Congress has made no definitive statement concerning grand jury powers." Comment, Powers of Federal Grand Juries, 4 Stan.L.Rev. 69 (1951). There is, however, "every reason to believe that our constitutional grand jury was intended to operate substantially like its English progenitor". . . .

Historians usually trace the English grand jury back to the Assize of Clarendon issued by Henry II in 1166, based not on Anglo–Saxon antecedents but on Norman–French inquests. The function of the early grand juries was "to discover and present facts in answer to enquiries addressed to them by the King". 1 Holdsworth, History of English Laws (1956), 321. The primary purpose was to furnish the King with the names of those who were defamed by common repute, *fama publica*, an institution historically analogous to the *infamia* in Roman law, both of which add content to the meaning of the phrase "infamous crimes" in the Fifth Amendment. The "whole principle" of the early grand jury "was to get information useful to the Crown from those most likely to have it—the principle of the ancient inquisition." Plucknett, History of the Common Law (1956), 111–120.

---

[1] The Federal Grand Jury Handbook, p. 8, describes the functions of the Grand Jury in these words:

> The Grand Jury is both a sword and a shield of justice—a sword because it is the terror of criminals, a shield because it is the protection of the innocent against unjust prosecution. But these important powers obviously create equally grave responsibilities to see that such powers are in no wise perverted or abused. With its almost limitless powers, a Grand Jury might, unless motivated by the highest sense of justice, find indictments not warranted by the evidence and thus become a source of oppression to our citizens.

From its beginning until its abolition by Parliament in 1933, the English common law presenting jury could act on its own knowledge, or on the information of others, or on the Crown's written bill of indictment. *But only when this bill was preferred to the grand jury by the Crown and endorsed as a "true bill" was the accusation known as an indictment.* This was the accepted usage when the Fifth Amendment was adopted. Blackstone explained:

> ... An *indictment* is a written accusation of one or more persons of a crime or misdemeanor, preferred to, and presented upon oath by, a grand jury.... When the grand jury have heard the evidence, if they think it a groundless accusation, they used formerly to endorse on the back of the bill, '*ignoramus*'; or, we know nothing of it; intimating, that though the facts might possibly be true, that truth did not appear to them: but now, they assert in English, more absolutely, 'not a true bill;' or (which is the better way) 'not found;' and then the party is discharged without farther answer.... If they are satisfied of the truth of the accusation, they then endorse upon it, 'a true bill,' antiently, '*billa vera.*' The indictment is then said to be found, and the party stands indicted.

Blackstone's Commentaries, Vol. IV, C. XXIII, pp. 301, 302, 305. (Italics supplied by the Editor, St. George Tucker, in the First American edition, 1803).

... Unless there is a bill of indictment preferred to the grand jury at the instance of the Government, there can be no indictment. It is entirely in the hands of the Government whether to submit an accusation to the grand jury leading to presentment in the form of an indictment and serving as the initial pleading in a criminal prosecution....

In sum, there is nothing in my view or in that of the other judges in the majority that would, as the dissenting judges assert, authorize Government counsel to "radically reduce the powers of the grand jury". *The grand jury never had a plenary power to indict. It had a limited power to indict.* It had a limited power to indict—after accusation by the Crown or the Government in the form of a bill of indictment preferred to the grand jury....

Because recognition of the grand jury's shield-like function is lodged in the Bill of Rights, the bedrock of basic rights, it is fair to say that national policy favors a liberal construction of the power of the grand jury to protect the individual against official tyranny. No such policy favors the grand jury in its accusatorial role. Accordingly, we look for and should expect to find a check on its unjust accusations similar to the grand jury's check on the government's unjust accusations....

The prosecution of offenses against the United States is an executive function within the exclusive prerogative of the Attorney General. "There shall be at the seat of government an executive department to be known as the Department of Justice, and an Attorney General, who shall be the head thereof." 5 U.S.C. § 291. That official, the chief law-enforcement officer of the Federal Government is "the hand of the president in taking care that the laws of the United States in protection of the interests of the United States in legal proceedings and in the prosecution of offenses be faithfully executed." Ponzi v. Fessenden, 258 U.S. 254 (1922). He "has the authority, and it is made his duty, to supervise the conduct of all suits brought by or against the United States", including the authority "to begin criminal prosecution". United States v. San Jacinto Tin Co., 125 U.S. 273, 278–279. He "is invested with the general superintendence of all such suits, and all the district attorneys who do bring them in the various courts in the country are placed under his immediate direction and control." Id., p. 279 and see In re Neagle, 135 U.S. 1. . . .

The reason for vesting discretion to prosecute in the Executive, acting through the Attorney General is two-fold. First, in the interests of justice and the orderly, efficient administration of the law, some person or agency should be able to prevent an unjust prosecution. The freedom of the petit jury to bring in a verdict of not guilty and the progressive development of the law in the direction of making more meaningful the guarantees of an accused person's constitutional rights give considerable protection to the individual before and after trial. They do not protect against a baseless prosecution. This is a harassment to the accused and an expensive strain on the machinery of justice. The appropriate repository for authority to prevent a baseless prosecution is the chief law-enforcement officer whose duty, *unlike the grand jury's duty, is to collect evidence on both sides of a case.*

Second, when, within the context of law-enforcement, national policy is involved, because of national security, conduct of foreign policy, or a conflict between two branches of government, the appropriate branch to decide the matter is the executive branch. The executive is charged with carrying out national policy on law-enforcement and, generally speaking, is informed on more levels than the more specialized judicial and legislative branches. In such a situation, a decision not to prosecute is analogous to the exercise of executive privilege. The executive's absolute and exclusive discretion to prosecute may be rationalized as an illustration of the doctrine of separation of powers, but it would have evolved without the doctrine and exists in countries that do not purport to accept this doctrine.

This brings me to the facts. They demonstrate, better than abstract principles or legal dicta, the imperative necessity that the United States, through its Attorney General, have uncontrollable discretion to prosecute.

The crucial fact here is that Goff and Kendrick, two Negroes, testified in a suit by the United States against the Registrar of Clarke County, Mississippi, and the State of Mississippi, to enforce the voting rights of Negroes under the Fourteenth Amendment and the Civil Rights Act.

Goff and Kendrick testified that some seven years earlier at Stonewall, Mississippi, the registrar had refused to register them or give them application forms. They said that they had seen white persons registering, one of whom was a B. Floyd Jones. Ramsey, the registrar, testified that Jones had not registered at that time or place, but had registered the year before in Enterprise, Mississippi. He testified also that he had never discriminated against Negro applicants for registration. Jones testified that he was near the registration table in Stonewall in 1955, had talked with the registrar, and had shaken hands with him. The presiding judge, Judge W. Harold Cox, stated from the bench that Goff and Kendrick should be "bound over to await the action of the grand jury for perjury".

In January 1963 attorneys of the Department of Justice requested the Federal Bureau of Investigation to investigate the possible perjury. The FBI completed a full investigation in March 1963 and referred the matter to the Department's Criminal Division. In June 1963 the Criminal Division advised the local United States Attorney, Mr. Hauberg, that the matter presented "no basis for a perjury prosecution". Mr. Hauberg informed Judge Cox of the Department's decision. Judge Cox stated that in his view the matter was clearly one for the grand jury and that he would be inclined, if necessary, to appoint an outside attorney to present the matter to the grand jury. (I find no authority for a federal judge to displace the United States Attorney by appointing a special prosecutor.) On receiving this information, the Criminal Division again reviewed its files and concluded that the charge of perjury could not be sustained. General Katzenbach, then Deputy Attorney General, after reviewing the files, concurred in the Criminal Division's decision. In September 1963 General Katzenbach called on Judge Cox as a courtesy to explain why the Department had arrived at the conclusion that no perjury was involved. Judge Cox, unconvinced, requested the United States Attorney to present to the grand jury the Goff and Kendrick cases, which he regarded as cases of "palpable perjury".

In October 1963 Goff and Kendrick were arrested, jailed for two days, and placed on a $3,000 bond for violations of State law for falsely testifying in federal court. After their indictment by a state grand jury, the Department of Justice filed suit against the State District Attorney, United States v. Warner, (Civ. No. 1219, S.D.Miss.), seeking to enjoin the state prosecution on the grounds that: (1) the States have no authority to prosecute for alleged perjury committed while testifying in a federal court; (2) the purpose and effect of the State's prosecution was to threaten and intimidate Goff and Kendrick and to inhibit them and other Negroes from registering to vote. . . .

The Federal Grand Jury, originally convened on September 9, 1963, was reconvened on September 21, 1964. September 28, 1964, the Foreman of the Grand Jury advised the Government Attorney who was presenting matters to the Grand Jury that Judge Cox had asked the Foreman to hear several witnesses. September 29, 1964, Mr. Riddell, attorney for the Registrar, and the district attorney for the Second Circuit District for the State of Mississippi, Mr. Holleman, came to the courthouse to appear before the Grand Jury. Judge Mize, in a special charge to the Grand Jury stated—in open court—that Judge Cox had informed him, before leaving for his vacation, that:

> . . . he wanted the Grand Jury to call before it Mr. Boyce Holleman of Gulfport, Mississippi and Mr. Talley Riddell of Quitman, Mississippi as witnesses, because it was his impression that they had some matters that ought to be investigated at least and that they should be permitted to appear.

Judge Mize stated that he was not familiar with the matters "other than just what Judge Cox requested me to do, to see to it that these two witnesses had an opportunity to appear before the Grand Jury." Judge Mize advised the Grand Jury that they had a right to hear the testimony of Messrs. Riddell and Holleman, but requested them not to do so until October 21, 1964, the day after Judge Cox was to return from his vacation.

October 20 Mr. Katzenbach talked with Judge Cox by telephone, reiterating the Department's position. He also instructed Mr. Hauberg not to prepare or sign indictments. October 22 the foreman of the grand jury in open court informed Judge Cox that Mr. Hauberg had declined to assist in preparing true bills. The United States Attorney stated that "the Department of Justice and the United States felt as if that the law and the fact was not sufficient to constitute perjury and that an indictment thereon would be no good." Judge Cox said:

I here and now order and direct you to disregard your instructions from the Department of Justice and to prepare true bills or no bills as this Grand Jury may direct you to do and to sign those bills or no bills, as the Grand Jury may decide under penalty of contempt . . . .

Judge Cox recessed court for one hour. During this recess Mr. Hauberg and Mr. Katzenbach conferred by telephone; the Attorney General directed the United States Attorney not to prepare or sign perjury indictments of Goff and Kendrick. Court reopened. Mr. Hauberg respectfully declined to comply with the court's order. Judge Cox forthwith adjudged him "guilty of civil contempt", ordered him confined to a jail in Hinds County, ordered the issuance of a citation to the Acting Attorney General to appear before the court to show cause why he should not be held in contempt; and stayed the order for a period of five days.

Against the backdrop of Mississippi versus the Nation in the field of civil rights, we have a heated but bona fide difference of opinion between Judge Cox and the Attorney General as to whether two Negroes, Goff and Kendrick, should be prosecuted for perjury. Taking a narrow view of the case, we would be justified in holding that the Attorney General's implied powers, by analogy to the express powers of Rule 48(a), give him discretion to prosecute. Here there was a bona fide, reasonable exercise of discretion made after a full investigation and long consideration of the case—both sides of the case, not just the evidence tending to show guilt. If the grand jury is dissatisfied with that administrative decision, it may exercise its inquisitorial power and make a presentment in open court. It could be said, that is all there is to the case. But there is more to the case.

This Court, along with everyone else, knows that Goff and Kendrick, if prosecuted, run the risk of being tried in a climate of community hostility. They run the risk of a punishment that may not fit the crime. The Registrar, who provoked the original litigation, runs no risk, notwithstanding the fact that the district court, in effect, found that Ramsay did not tell the truth on the witness stand. In these circumstances, the very least demands of justice require that the discretion to prosecute be lodged with a person or agency insulated from local prejudices and parochial pressures. This is not the hard case that makes bad law. This is the type of case that comes up, in one way or another, whenever the customs, beliefs, or interests of a region collide with national policy as fixed by the Constitution or by Congress. It is not likely that the men who devised diversity jurisdiction expected to turn over to local juries the discretionary power to bring federal prosecutions. This case is unusual only for the clarity with which the facts, speaking for themselves, illuminate the imperative necessity in American Federalism that the discretion to prosecute be lodged in the Attorney General of United States.

The decision not to prosecute represents the exercise of a discretion analogous to the exercise of executive privilege. As a matter of law, the Attorney General has concluded that there is not sufficient evidence to prove perjury. As a matter of fact, the Attorney General has concluded, as he pleaded in United States v. Warner, that trial for perjury would have the effect of inhibiting not only Goff and Kendrick but other Negroes in Mississippi from registering to vote. There is a conflict, therefore, between society's interest in law enforcement (diluted in this case by the Attorney General's conclusion that the evidence does not support the charge of guilt) and the national policy, set forth in the Constitution and the Civil Rights Acts, of outlawing racial discrimination. It is unthinkable that resolution of this important conflict affecting the whole Nation should lie with a majority of twenty-three members of a jury chosen from the Southern District of Mississippi. The nature of American Federalism, looking to the differences between the Constitution and the Articles of Confederation, requires that the power to resolve this question lie in the unfettered discretion of the President of United States or his deputy for law enforcement, the Attorney General.

My memory, too, goes back to the days, pointedly referred to by the dissenters, when we had "an Attorney General suspected of being corrupt." But I am not aware that we have had more lawless Attorneys General than lawless juries.

NOTES

1. What do you think of *United States v. Cox*? Does a grand jury exercise judicial power or executive power or is it *sui generis*? What about a regular trial court petit jury? Juries of both kinds were developed by the Plantagenet kings of England only to advise them in criminal cases. Does that suggest that the majority is right in *United States v. Cox*? Think back to Alexander Hamilton's discussion of the executive power in *The Federalist*. How do you think Hamilton would come down in *United States v. Cox*? What does each type of constitutional argument suggest for whether there is a presidential power to prevent or stop a prosecution?

2. The concurrence in *United States v. Cox* would hold that a U.S. attorney has a duty to write up an indictment if a grand jury requests it but that the U.S. attorney has sole discretion as to whether to launch the prosecution by preferring the indictment. Does this make sense? It guarantees that the decision not to indict will be public, which may guard against corruption. But it subjects the individuals who are not indicted to stigma and grave suspicion, even if no prosecution is ever brought.

The Take Care Clause

Article II, Section 3 imposes a series of duties on the president, including the duty to "take Care" that the laws are faithfully executed. The Take Care Clause had its origins in the English Glorious Revolution of 1688. King James II had claimed an absolute power to "dispense" with, or suspend, the laws. (The act of Parliament that he chose to dispense with was one forbidding Roman Catholics from holding office and participating in public life.) When he was overthrown in 1688, part of the settlement that the English revolutionaries insisted on was that his successors agree that no future monarch would ever have or claim a dispensing power. The Take Care Clause of Article II reflects this understanding. It clarifies that the president has no dispensing power with respect to acts of Congress. In this sense, the clause was originally understood as limiting, not augmenting, the executive power of the president. Ironically, American presidents immediately began claiming the Take Care Clause granted them power.

The existence of the Take Care Clause raises problems in constitutional law. One, which is taken up later in this chapter, is the possibility of presidential abrogation of treaties. But what about domestic law? If the president thinks a law is unconstitutional even though it has been upheld by federal courts, may the president decline to execute it? As discussed in Chapter 1, President Jefferson did precisely this with the Sedition Act. Did he act unconstitutionally in "dispensing" with the Sedition Act? Does it matter that the president, unlike the king of England, is bound when executing the laws to follow the supreme law of the Constitution? Presidents have generally been skittish about not executing acts of Congress that they think are unconstitutional but which Congress and the federal courts think pass constitutional muster. And Congress has required notification from the Department of Justice whenever it fails to defend the constitutionality of an act of Congress in court, so Congress can hire its own counsel to defend the act.

By the time of the Monroe administration it was an established practice that presidents could control subordinates in the executive branch. Nonetheless, it was at this time that the first suggestions arose of some Take Care Clause limits on presidential power to direct and control. Attorney General William Wirt expressed some hesitance in a famous case involving presidential control of the decisions of accounting officers as to whether the president could direct and control quasi-adjudicative and ministerial acts taken by lower-level executive employees. Attorney General Wirt's opinion was rejected by some of his successors as limiting presidential powers of direction too much; it was embraced by others. As you read the opinion below, ask yourself whether, and if so how, presidential direction of accounting officers is different from presidential direction to stop or start a prosecution.

Attorney General Wirt, Opinion on the President and Accounting Officers

October 20, 1823

[Accounting officers in the Department of the Treasury made a decision that displeased Major Joseph Wheaton. He sought presidential review, and President James Monroe referred the matter to the attorney general.— Editors]

SIR: I have examined the case of Major Joseph Wheaton, submitted by you for my opinion; and would proceed at once to the expression of an opinion on the merits of his claims, but that there is a preliminary inquiry which must be first made, and as to which I beg leave to ask your direction; and that is, whether it is proper for you to interfere in this case at all? I will suggest the considerations which strike me as rendering it improper.

I. It appears to me that you have no power to interfere.

The constitution of the United States requires the President, in general terms, to take care that the laws be faithfully executed; that is, it places the officers engaged in the execution of the laws under his general superintendence: he is to see that they do their duty faithfully; and on their failure, to cause them to be displaced, prosecuted, or impeached, according to the nature of the case. In case of forcible resistance to the laws, too, [so] as to require the interposition of the power of the government to overcome the illegal resistance, he is to see that that power be furnished. But it could never have been the intention of the constitution, in assigning this general power to the President to take care that the laws be executed, that he should in person execute the laws himself. For example: if a marshal should either refuse to serve process altogether, or serve it irregularly, that the President should correct the irregularity, or supply the omission, by executing the process in person. To interpret this clause of the constitution so as to throw upon the President the duty of a personal interference in every specific case of an alleged or defective execution of the laws, and to call upon him to perform such duties himself, would be not only to require him to perform an impossibility himself, but to take upon himself the responsibility of all the subordinate executive officers of the government—a construction too absurd to be seriously contended for. But the requisition of the constitution is, that he shall take care that the laws be executed. If the laws, then, require a particular officer by name to perform a duty, not only is that officer bound to perform it, but no other officer can perform it without a violation of the law; and were the President to perform it, he would not only be not taking care that the laws were faithfully executed, but he would be violating them himself. The constitution assigns to Congress the power of designating the duties of particular officers: the President is only required to take care that they execute them faithfully. . . .

Let us carry this principle to the laws which regulate the settlement of public accounts. In the original organization of the Treasury Department . . . the duties of the officers are designated specifically. There was one Auditor and one Comptroller. The duty of the Auditor is declared to be to receive all public accounts; and, after examination, to certify the balance, and transmit the accounts, with the vouchers and certificate, to the Comptroller, for his decision thereon; with this proviso: that if any person be dissatisfied therewith, he may within six months appeal to the Comptroller against such settlement. Here the right of appeal stops; there is no proviso for an appeal to the President. . . .

So also the act of 3d March, 1817, which introduces the present organization of the Treasury Department, and under which Major Wheaton's accounts have been settled, assigns to [specific Treasury Department personnel the settling of Major Wheaton's accounts with no statutory right of appeal to the president]. . . . Were it the intention of Congress to subject these accounts to the farther revision and decision of the President, that intention would have been expressed. The truth of this position is illustrated by the act of the last session, "to provide for the settlement of the accounts of Daniel D. Tompkins, late governor of the State of New York." This act expressly provides that the proper accounting officers of the Treasury be authorized to adjust and settle the accounts and claims of Daniel D. Tompkins on principles of equity and justice, "subject to the revision and final decision of the President of the United States." Where was the necessity of this express provision, if all the accounts settled by those officers were already subject to the revision and final decision of the President of the United States? . . . The authority is confined to the accounting officers of the Treasury Department. . . . [T]he President has no authority to interfere.

It would be strange, indeed, if it were otherwise. The office of President is ordained for very different purposes than that of settling individual accounts. The constitution has committed to him the care of the great interests of the nation, in all its foreign and domestic relations. . . . How will it be possible for the President to perform these great duties, if he is also to exercise the appellate power of revising and correcting the settlement of all the individual accounts which pass through the hands of the accounting officers? Let it be remembered that, out of the vest multitude of these accounts which are annually settled by these officers, there are very few which are settled to the entire satisfaction of the claimants; and if every dissatisfied claimant has a right to appeal to the President, and call upon him to revise and correct the settlement, the President would be constrained to abandon the great national objects which are committed to his peculiar care, and become the accountant general of the government. . . .

My opinion is, that the settlement made of the accounts of individuals by the accounting officers appointed by law is final and conclusive, so far as the executive department of the government is concerned. If an individual conceives himself injured by such settlement, his recourse must be one of the other two branches of government—the legislative or judicial. . . .

II. If you do possess the power of revising and correcting the settlements made by the accounting officers of the government, this is not a proper case for the exercise of that power. . . .

I have the honor to remain, sir, very respectfully, your obedient servant.

NOTES

1. What enumerated power is Congress exercising when it gives to accounting officers the final decision in a case? Presumably Congress has power to create accounting officers in the Treasury Department with a power to resolve claims because doing so is "necessary and proper for carrying into execution" the executive power of the president. The power being exercised by the accounting officers is not legislative power: there is no bicameralism and presentment. Nor is it judicial power: the accounting officers who make the final decisions are not Article III judges. Accordingly, the accounting officers must be exercising executive power, which the Constitution gives to the president, who can then delegate that power to the accounting officers. If the president delegates power to the accounting officers, and then disagrees with what they have done, why can't he countermand their decision? Is a statute passed by Congress that purports to insulate exercises of executive power by accounting officers from presidential control a statute that "carries into execution" the executive power? Is it bad as a policy matter for the president to review and alter the actions of the accounting officers and similar appointees? Is the president constitutionally barred from doing that?

2. Attorney General Taney argued in The Jewels of the Princess of Orange that the president can always stop a prosecution by a federal prosecutor. What if Congress were by statute to give a special prosecutor the final decision to prosecute in a case the way it gave accounting officers the final decision in the case Attorney General Wirt discusses? Would the president's obligation to take care that the laws be faithfully executed require him to let an unjust prosecution go forward, because Congress had left final decision-making power to a presidential subordinate? How can the two attorney general opinion letters be squared? What checks exist on presidential power here?

3. If the president has a power of direction and control under the Vesting Clause of Article II and the Take Care Clause, can the president issue executive orders forbidding discrimination in government hiring and contracting? The consensus is yes. Such orders have been issued for more than half a century by Democrats and Republicans alike. Presidents have also issued executive orders directing and supervising executive branch subordinates involved in regulation. Entire agencies, such as the Office of Management and Budget (OMB) and the Office of Information and Regulatory Affairs (OIRA), have even been created to make it easier for presidents to control the vast number of executive branch officials. For discussion of the history of presidential efforts at

supervising and controlling the executive branch, see Steven G. Calabresi & Christopher S. Yoo, THE UNITARY EXECUTIVE: PRESIDENTIAL POWER FROM WASHINGTON TO BUSH (2008).

[Assignment 19]

C. THE APPOINTMENT POWER:
"HE . . . SHALL APPOINT"

Article II, Section 2: . . . [The President] shall nominate, and by and with the Advice and Consent of the Senate, shall appoint Ambassadors, other public Ministers and Consuls, Judges of the Supreme Court, and all other Officers of the United States, whose Appointments are not herein otherwise provided for, and which shall be established by Law: but the Congress may by Law vest the Appointment of such inferior Officers, as they think proper, in the President alone, in the Courts of Law, or in the Heads of Departments.

Consider next another tool of control which the president has over the executive branch: the appointment power. Under Article II, Section 2, the president has the power to appoint executive and judicial officers by and with the advice and consent of the Senate. In addition, Congress can by law vest the power to appoint inferior officers in the president alone, in the heads of departments, or in the courts. What is the scope of the president's appointments power and what limits does the clause that grants it impose on Congress? For answers to these questions, it is helpful again to look to English history and more than two centuries of American practice.

One of the most formidable powers of the king of England in 1787 was the power to create offices with rents accruing to them and to appoint individuals unilaterally to those offices. English kings could thus raise up individuals from nothing and make them rich and prominent by conferring offices upon them. Thus the monarch was described as the "fountain of honors." After the English Revolution of 1688, monarchical power was limited by the principle of parliamentary supremacy. Parliament was empowered to pass laws that would bind the king, laws the king could not suspend or dispense with. From 1688 to 1776, English monarchs responded by creating lucrative offices and appointing members of parliament to them to buy their favor and their votes. There grew up a Court Party of officeholder members of parliament who could be counted on to do the king's bidding, and a Country Party of those whose power came from outside London and who opposed the king.

The American Revolutionaries were repulsed by the practice of kings essentially bribing members of Parliament to vote their way on legislation. They came to see the royal appointment power as an instrument of corruption. The first American state constitutions after 1776 thus took the appointment power away from governors and vested it in either an executive council or the legislature. This led to weak and ineffective state governors and all-powerful legislative bodies. By 1787, Americans had begun to think that their governors were too weak to keep the peace or to enforce the law. They say that legislative favoritism and patronage in the making of appointments could also be corrupting. Plural executive councils with the appointment power were now viewed as weak and unaccountable. As Alexander Hamilton was to argue in *The Federalist*, energy in the executive was essential to good government and energy was promoted by having a single executive who controlled all appointments to office and was accountable for how the appointees governed.

The Philadelphia Convention wrestled at length with the problem of the appointment power and considered vesting it in Congress, the Senate, or the president alone, before settling on the compromise we are so familiar with today: presidential nomination and senatorial advice and consent. This history is recounted at more length below in *Buckley v. Valeo*. The framers decided to deal with the problem of the executive bribing members of the legislature with appointments by forbidding members of Congress from simultaneously serving as officers of the United States. This rule, which is embodied in the Incompatibility Clause of Article I, Section 6, is single-handedly responsible for ensuring that parliamentary government would be unconstitutional in the United States (at the federal level, though not at the state level). Absent the Incompatibility Clause, it is likely that congressional committee chairs would regularly be appointed to cabinet positions. The Incompatibility Clause, which was an ethics rule in its original motivation, is important for the separation of powers system we have today.

The Federalist No. 76

Alexander Hamilton, April 1, 1788

. . . It has been observed in a former paper, that "the true test of a good government is its aptitude and tendency to produce a good administration." If the justness of this observation be admitted, the mode of appointing the officers of the United States contained in the foregoing clauses, must, when examined, be allowed to be entitled to particular commendation. It is not easy to conceive a plan better calculated than this to promote a judicious choice of men for filling the offices of the Union; and it will not need proof, that on this point must essentially depend the character of its administration.

It will be agreed on all hands, that the power of appointment, in ordinary cases, ought to be modified in one of three ways. It ought either to be vested in a single man, or in a SELECT assembly of a moderate number; or in a single man, with the concurrence of such an assembly. The exercise of it by the people at large will be readily admitted to be impracticable; as waiving every other consideration, it would leave them little time to do anything else. . . .

Those who have themselves reflected upon the subject, or who have attended to the observations made in other parts of these papers, in relation to the appointment of the President, will, I presume, agree to the position, that there would always be great probability of having the place supplied by a man of abilities, at least respectable. Premising this, I proceed to lay it down as a rule, that one man of discernment is better fitted to analyze and estimate the peculiar qualities adapted to particular offices, than a body of men of equal or perhaps even of superior discernment.

The sole and undivided responsibility of one man will naturally beget a livelier sense of duty and a more exact regard to reputation. He will, on this account, feel himself under stronger obligations, and more interested to investigate with care the qualities requisite to the stations to be filled, and to prefer with impartiality the persons who may have the fairest pretensions to them. He will have FEWER personal attachments to gratify, than a body of men who may each be supposed to have an equal number; and will be so much the less liable to be misled by the sentiments of friendship and of affection. A single well-directed man, by a single understanding, cannot be distracted and warped by that diversity of views, feelings, and interests, which frequently distract and warp the resolutions of a collective body. There is nothing so apt to agitate the passions of mankind as personal considerations whether they relate to ourselves or to others, who are to be the objects of our choice or preference. Hence, in every exercise of the power of appointing to offices, by an assembly of men, we must expect to see a full display of all the private and party likings and dislikes, partialities and antipathies, attachments and animosities, which are felt by those who compose the assembly. . . . "Give us the man we wish for this office, and you shall have the one you wish for that." This will be the usual condition of the bargain. And it will rarely happen that the advancement of the public service will be the primary object either of party victories or of party negotiations.

The truth of the principles here advanced seems to have been felt by the most intelligent of those who have found fault with the provision made, in this respect, by the convention. They contend that the President ought solely to have been authorized to make the appointments under the federal government. But it is easy to show, that every advantage to be expected from such an arrangement would, in substance, be derived from the power of NOMINATION, which is proposed to be conferred upon him; while several disadvantages which might attend the absolute power of appointment in the hands of that officer would be avoided. In the act of nomination, his judgment alone would be exercised; and as it would be his sole duty to point out the man who, with the approbation of the Senate, should fill an office, his responsibility would be as complete as if he were to make the final appointment. . . .

There can, in this view, be no difference between nominating and appointing. The same motives which would influence a proper discharge of his duty in one case, would exist in the other. And as no man could be appointed but on his previous nomination, every man who might be appointed would be, in fact, his choice.

But might not his nomination be overruled? I grant it might, yet this could only be to make place for another nomination by himself. The person ultimately appointed must be the object of his preference, though perhaps not in the first degree. It is also not very probable that his nomination would often be overruled. The Senate could not be tempted, by the preference they might feel to another, to reject the one proposed; because they could not assure themselves, that the person they might wish would be brought forward by a second or by any subsequent nomination. They could not even be certain, that a future nomination would present a candidate in any degree more acceptable to them; and as their dissent might cast a kind of stigma upon the individual rejected, and might have the appearance of a reflection upon the judgment of the chief magistrate, it is not likely that their sanction would often be refused, where there were not special and strong reasons for the refusal.

To what purpose then require the co-operation of the Senate? I answer, that the necessity of their concurrence would have a powerful, though, in general, a silent operation. It would be an excellent check upon a spirit of favoritism in the President, and would tend greatly to prevent the appointment of unfit characters from State prejudice, from family connection, from personal attachment, or from a view to popularity. In addition to this, it would be an efficacious source of stability in the administration.

It will readily be comprehended, that a man who had himself the sole disposition of offices, would be governed much more by his private inclinations and interests, than when he was bound to submit the propriety of his choice to the discussion and determination of a different and independent body, and that body an entire branch of the legislature. The possibility of rejection would be a strong motive to care in proposing. . . . He would be both ashamed and afraid to bring forward, for the most distinguished or lucrative stations, candidates who had no other merit than that of coming from the same State to which he particularly belonged, or of being in some way or other personally allied to him, or of possessing the necessary insignificance and pliancy to render them the obsequious instruments of his pleasure. . . .

NOTES

1. In *The Federalist No. 76*, Hamilton makes the case for appointment by presidential nomination and senatorial confirmation. Is Hamilton right that if the appointment power were given to the president alone there would likely be abuse? Is Hamilton right that giving the appointment power to a legislative body would result in log-rolling and capture by special interests? Is executive nomination with senatorial confirmation an ingenious solution to the appointments dilemma?

2. The Court handed down its most important separation-of-powers decision since *Youngstown* in *Buckley v. Valeo*, which is presented next. The case involved the constitutionality of the Federal Election Campaign Act, which regulates and publicizes contributions to political campaigns for federal office. The act created the Federal Election Commission, with the power to make rules and to enforce the statute. The commission was described as being in the legislative branch of the government and the statute setting it up provided that two members would be nominated by the president pro tempore of the Senate; another two members would be nominated by the Speaker of the House of Representatives; and two members would be nominated by the president. All six nominations required confirmation by a majority of both houses of Congress. The Court addressed the constitutionality of these provisions in its decision.

Buckley v. Valeo

424 U.S. 1 (1976)

■ PER CURIAM. . . .

Appellants urge that since Congress has given the [Federal Election] Commission wide-ranging rulemaking and enforcement powers with respect to the substantive provisions of the Act, Congress is precluded under the principle of separation of powers from vesting in itself the authority to appoint those who will exercise such authority. Their argument is based on the language of Art. II, § 2, cl. 2, of the Constitution, which provides in pertinent part as follows:

> [The President] shall nominate, and by and with the Advice and Consent of the Senate, shall appoint . . . all other Officers of the United States, whose Appointments are not herein otherwise provided for, and which shall be established by Law: but the Congress may by Law vest

the Appointment of such inferior Officers, as they think proper, in the President alone, in the Courts of Law, or in the Heads of Departments.

Appellants' argument is that this provision is the exclusive method by which those charged with executing the laws of the United States may be chosen. Congress, they assert, cannot have it both ways. If the Legislature wishes the Commission to exercise all of the conferred powers, then its members are in fact "Officers of the United States" and must be appointed under the Appointments Clause. But if Congress insists upon retaining the power to appoint, then the members of the Commission may not discharge those many functions of the Commission which can be performed only by "Officers of the United States," as that term must be construed within the doctrine of separation of powers. . . .

We do not think appellants' arguments based upon Art. II, § 2, cl. 2, of the Constitution may be . . . easily dismissed. . . . Our inquiry of necessity touches upon the fundamental principles of the Government established by the Framers of the Constitution, and all litigants and all of the courts which have addressed themselves to the matter start on common ground in the recognition of the intent of the Framers that the powers of the three great branches of the National Government be largely separate from one another. . . .

The Framers regarded the checks and balances that they had built into the tripartite Federal Government as a self-executing safeguard against the encroachment or aggrandizement of one branch at the expense of the other. . . . This Court has not hesitated to enforce the principle of separation of powers embodied in the Constitution when its application has proved necessary for the decisions of cases or controversies properly before it. . . .

The principle of separation of powers was not simply an abstract generalization in the minds of the Framers: it was woven into the document that they drafted in Philadelphia in the summer of 1787. . . . The Appointments Clause could . . . be read as merely dealing with etiquette or protocol in describing "Officers of the United States," but the drafters had a less frivolous purpose in mind. . . .

We think that the term "Officers of the United States" as used in Art. II, defined to include "all persons who can be said to hold an office under the government" in *United States v. Germaine, supra,* is a term intended to have substantive meaning. We think its fair import is that any appointee exercising significant authority pursuant to the laws of the United States is an "Officer of the United States," and must, therefore, be appointed in the manner prescribed by § 2, cl. 2, of that Article. . . .

Although two members of the Commission are initially selected by the President, his nominations are subject to confirmation not merely by the Senate, but by the House of Representatives as well. The remaining four voting members of the Commission are appointed by the President pro tempore of the Senate and by the Speaker of the House. While the second part of the Clause authorizes Congress to vest the appointment of the officers described in that part in "the Courts of Law, or in the Heads of Departments," neither the Speaker of the House nor the President pro tempore of the Senate comes within this language. . . .

The Appointments Clause specifies the method of appointment only for "Officers of the United States" whose appointment is not "otherwise provided for" in the Constitution. But there is no provision of the Constitution remotely providing any alternative means for the selection of the members of the Commission or for anybody like them. . . .

An interim version of the draft Constitution had vested in the Senate the authority to appoint Ambassadors, public Ministers, and Judges of the Supreme Court, and the language of Art. II as finally adopted is a distinct change in this regard. We believe that it was a deliberate change made by the Framers with the intent to deny Congress any authority itself to appoint those who were "Officers of the United States." The debates on the floor of the Convention reflect at least in part the way the change came about.

On Monday, August 6, 1787, the Committee on Detail to which had been referred the entire draft of the Constitution reported its draft to the Convention, including the following two articles that bear on the question before us: . . .

Article IX, § 1: "The Senate of the United States shall have power . . . to appoint Ambassadors, and Judges of the Supreme Court."

Article X, § 2: "(The President) shall commission all the officers of the United States; and shall appoint officers in all cases not otherwise provided for by this Constitution."

It will be seen from a comparison of these two articles that the appointment of Ambassadors and Judges of the Supreme Court was confided to the Senate, and that the authority to *appoint*—not merely nominate, but to actually appoint—all other officers was reposed in the President.

During a discussion of a provision in the same draft from the Committee on Detail which provided that the "Treasurer" of the United States should be chosen by both Houses of Congress, Mr. Read moved to strike out that clause, "leaving the appointment of the Treasurer *as of other officers* to the Executive." Opposition to Read's motion was based, not on objection to the principle of executive appointment, but on the particular nature of the office of the "Treasurer." . . .

Meanwhile, on Friday, August 31, a motion had been carried without opposition to refer such parts of the Constitution as had been postponed or not acted upon to a Committee of Eleven. Such reference carried with it both Arts. IX and X. The following week the Committee of Eleven made its report to the Convention, in which the present language of Art. II, § 2, cl. 2, dealing with the authority of the President to nominate is found, virtually word for word, as § 4 of Art. X. The same Committee also reported a revised article concerning the Legislative Branch to the Convention. The changes are obvious. In the final version, the Senate is shorn of its power to appoint Ambassadors and Judges of the Supreme Court. The President is given, not the power to appoint public officers of the United States, but only the right to nominate them, and a provision is inserted by virtue of which Congress may require Senate confirmation of his nominees.

It would seem a fair surmise that a compromise had been made. But no change was made in the concept of the term "Officers of the United States," which since it had first appeared in Art. X had been taken by all concerned to embrace all appointed officials exercising responsibility under the public laws of the Nation. . . .

[The Federal Elections Commission] contend[s], and the majority of the Court of Appeals agreed . . . , that whatever shortcomings the provisions for the appointment of members of the Commission might have under

Art. II, Congress had ample authority under the Necessary and Proper Clause of Art. I to effectuate this result. We do not agree. The proper inquiry when considering the Necessary and Proper Clause is not the authority of Congress to create an office or a commission, which is broad indeed, but rather its authority to [specify] that its own officers may make appointments to such office or commission.

So framed, the claim that Congress may provide for this manner of appointment under the Necessary and Proper Clause of Art. I stands on [a weak] footing. . . . Congress could not, merely because it concluded that such a measure was "necessary and proper" to the discharge of its substantive legislative authority, pass a bill of attainder or *ex post facto* law contrary to the prohibitions contained in § 9 of Art. I. No more may it vest in itself, or in its officers, the authority to appoint officers of the United States when the Appointments Clause by clear implication prohibits it from doing so. . . .

We hold that these provisions of the Act, vesting in the Commission primary responsibility for conducting civil litigation in the courts of the United States for vindicating public rights, violate Art. II, § 2, cl. 2, of the Constitution. Such functions may be discharged only by persons who are "Officers of the United States" within the language of that section.

■ MR. JUSTICE WHITE, concurring in part and dissenting in part. . . .

[T]he FEC, in defending the legality of its members' appointments, does not deny that they are "officers of the United States" as that term is used in the Appointments Clause of Art. II. Instead, for reasons the Court outlines, its position appears to be that even if its members are officers of the United States, Congress may nevertheless appoint a majority of the FEC without participation by the President. . . .

The language of the Appointments Clause was . . . debated by the Framers [at length]. . . . The decision to give the President the exclusive power to initiate appointments was thoughtful and deliberate. . . . Under Art. II as finally adopted, law enforcement authority was not to be lodged in elected legislative officials subject to political pressures. Neither was the Legislative Branch to have the power to appoint those who were to enforce and administer the law. . . .

Congress clearly has the power to create federal offices and to define the powers and duties of those offices, *Myers v. United States*, 272 U.S. 52, 128–129 (1926), but no case in this Court even remotely supports the power of Congress to appoint an officer of the United States aside from those officers each House is authorized by Art. I to appoint to assist in the legislative processes. . . .

There is no doubt that the development of the administrative agency in response to modern legislative and administrative need has placed severe strain on the separation-of-powers principle in its pristine formulation. See *Kilbourn v. Thompson*, 103 U.S. 168, 191 (1881). Any notion that the Constitution bans any admixture of powers that might be deemed legislative, executive, and judicial has had to give way. The independent agency has survived attacks from various directions: that it exercises invalidly delegated legislative power, *Sunshine Coal Co. v. Adkins*, 310 U.S. 381 (1940); that it invalidly exercises judicial power, *ibid.*; and that its functions are so executive in nature that its members must be subject to Presidential control, *Humphrey's Executor v. United States*, 295 U.S. 602 (1935). Until now, however, it has not been insisted that the commands of the Appointments

Clause must also yield to permit congressional appointments of members of a major agency. With the Court, I am not convinced that we should create a broad exception to the requirements of that Clause that all officers of the United States be appointed in accordance with its terms. . . .

NOTES

1. What difference do you think it makes that the framers opted for presidential nomination and senatorial advice and consent to nominations rather than giving the appointment power to the Senate or to the Congress as a whole? Would it have been better to let the Senate appoint federal judges and Supreme Court justices? Should the president have been empowered to choose them without confirmation by the Senate? In Germany, the equivalents to our Supreme Court justices are elected by a two-thirds vote of each house of the legislature. Would that be better than the American system?

2. How far can Congress go in adding new duties to a pre-existing office before it violates the Appointments Clause? That question was considered in *Weiss v. United States*, 510 U.S. 163 (1994). Congress had specified that the Court of Military Appeals could impose military discipline on those who violated the Uniform Code of Military Justice. Did the judges on that court, who had already been appointed by the president, need another presidential appointment now that Congress had increased their duties? The Court concluded that the Appointments Clause did not require a new appointment. A key consideration for the Court, drawing on *Shoemaker v. United States*, 147 U.S. 282 (1893), was whether the duties of the new office were "germane": Since "all military officers, consistent with a long tradition, play a role in the operation of the military justice system," the Court concluded that "the role of military judge is 'germane' to that of military officer." How should courts decide whether the new duties Congress has added to an office are germane to the old ones?

———

The offices in question in *Buckley v. Valeo* and in *Weiss v. United States* were principal offices to which the officers were nominated by the president and confirmed by the Senate. But the Appointments Clause also contemplates that Congress can by law vest the power to appoint inferior officers in the president, the heads of departments, or the courts. Is an independent counsel or special prosecutor unimportant enough to count as being only an "inferior" officer who does not need to be confirmed by the Senate? Can the courts of law be given the power to make a cross-branch appointment of an inferior executive branch officer? These questions are considered next.

Morrison v. Olson

487 U.S. 654 (1988) (Appointments Issue)

■ CHIEF JUSTICE REHNQUIST delivered the opinion of the Court.

. . . Title VI of the Ethics in Government Act (the Act) allows for the appointment of an "independent counsel" to investigate and, if appropriate, prosecute certain high-ranking Government officials for violations of federal criminal laws. The Act requires the Attorney General, upon receipt of information that he determines is "sufficient to constitute grounds to investigate whether any person [covered by the Act] may have violated any Federal criminal law," to conduct a preliminary investigation of the matter. When the Attorney General has completed this investigation, or 90 days has elapsed, he is required to report to a special court (the Special Division) [consisting of life tenured Article III judges] created by the Act "for the purpose of appointing independent counsels." . . . The Attorney General's application to the court "shall contain sufficient information to assist the [court] in selecting an independent counsel and in defining that independent counsel's prosecutorial jurisdiction." Upon receiving this application, the Special Division "shall appoint an appropriate independent counsel and shall define that independent counsel's prosecutorial jurisdiction."

With respect to all matters within the independent counsel's jurisdiction, the Act grants the counsel "full power and independent authority to exercise all investigative and prosecutorial functions and powers of the Department of Justice, the Attorney General, and any other officer or employee of the Department of Justice." The functions of the independent counsel include conducting grand jury proceedings and other investigations, participating in civil and criminal court proceedings and litigation, and appealing any decision in any case in which the counsel participates in an official capacity. Under [the Act], the counsel's powers include "initiating and conducting prosecutions in any court of competent jurisdiction, framing and signing indictments, filing informations, and handling all aspects of any case, in the name of the United States." The counsel may appoint employees, may request and obtain assistance from the Department of Justice, and may accept referral of matters from the Attorney General if the matter falls within the counsel's jurisdiction as defined by the Special Division. The Act also states that an independent counsel "shall, except where not possible, comply with the written or other established policies of the Department of Justice respecting enforcement of the criminal laws." In addition, whenever a matter has been referred to an independent counsel under the Act, the Attorney General and the Justice Department are required to suspend all investigations and proceedings regarding the matter. An independent counsel has "full authority to dismiss matters within [his or her] prosecutorial jurisdiction without conducting an investigation or at any subsequent time before prosecution, if to do so would be consistent" with Department of Justice policy.

. . . The parties do not dispute that "[t]he Constitution for purposes of appointment . . . divides all its officers into two classes." . . . The initial question is, accordingly, whether appellant is an "inferior" or a "principal" officer. If she is the latter, as the Court of Appeals concluded, then the Act is in violation of the Appointments Clause.

The line between "inferior" and "principal" officers is one that is far from clear, and the Framers provided little guidance into where it should be drawn. We need not attempt here to decide exactly where the line falls between the two types of officers, because in our view appellant clearly falls on the "inferior officer" side of that line. Several factors lead to this conclusion.

First, appellant is subject to removal by a higher Executive Branch official. Although appellant may not be "subordinate" to the Attorney General (and the President) insofar as she possesses a degree of independent discretion to exercise the powers delegated to her under the Act, the fact that she can be removed by the Attorney General indicates that she is to some degree "inferior" in rank and authority. Second, appellant is empowered by the Act to perform only certain, limited duties. An independent counsel's role is restricted primarily to investigation and, if appropriate, prosecution for certain federal crimes. Admittedly, the Act delegates to appellant "full power and independent authority to exercise all investigative and prosecutorial functions and powers of the Department of Justice," but this grant of authority does not include any authority to formulate policy for the Government or the Executive Branch, nor does it give appellant any administrative duties outside of those necessary to operate her office. The Act specifically provides that in policy matters appellant is to comply to the extent possible with the policies of the Department.

Third, appellant's office is limited in jurisdiction. Not only is the Act itself restricted in applicability to certain federal officials suspected of certain serious federal crimes, but an independent counsel can only act within the scope of the jurisdiction that has been granted by the Special Division pursuant to a request by the Attorney General. Finally, appellant's office is limited in tenure. There is concededly no time limit on the appointment of a particular counsel. Nonetheless, the office of independent counsel is "temporary" in the sense that an independent counsel is appointed essentially to accomplish a single task, and when that task is over the office is terminated, either by the counsel herself or by action of the Special Division. Unlike other prosecutors, appellant has no ongoing responsibilities that extend beyond the accomplishment of the mission that she was appointed for and authorized by the Special Division to undertake. In our view, these factors relating to the "ideas of tenure, duration . . . and duties" of the independent counsel, are sufficient to establish that appellant is an "inferior" officer in the constitutional sense. . . .

This does not, however, end our inquiry under the Appointments Clause. Appellees argue that even if appellant is an "inferior" officer, the Clause does not empower Congress to place the power to appoint such an officer outside the Executive Branch. They contend that the Clause does not contemplate congressional authorization of "interbranch appointments," in which an officer of one branch is appointed by officers of another branch. The relevant language of the Appointments Clause . . . reads: ". . . but the Congress may by Law vest the Appointment of such inferior Officers, as they think proper, in the President alone, in the courts of Law, or in the Heads of Departments." On its face, the language of this "excepting clause" admits of no limitation on interbranch appointments. Indeed, the inclusion of "as they think proper" seems clearly to give Congress significant discretion to determine whether it is "proper" to vest the appointment of, for example, executive officials in the "courts of Law." . . . We also note that the history of the Clause provides no support for appellees' position. . . .

We do not mean to say that Congress' power to provide for interbranch appointments of "inferior officers" is unlimited. In addition to separation-of-powers concerns, which would arise if such provisions for appointment had the potential to impair the constitutional functions assigned to one of the branches, . . . Congress' decision to vest the appointment power in the courts would be improper if there was some "incongruity" between the functions normally performed by the courts and the performance of their duty to appoint. In this case, however, we do not think it impermissible for Congress to vest the power to appoint independent counsel in a specially created federal court. We thus disagree with the Court of Appeals' conclusion that there is an inherent incongruity about a court having the power to appoint prosecutorial officers. . . . Congress, of course, was concerned when it created the office of independent counsel with the conflicts of interest that could arise in situations when the Executive Branch is called upon to investigate its own high-ranking officers. If it were to remove the appointing authority from the Executive Branch, the most logical place to put it was in the Judicial Branch. In the light of the Act's provision making the judges of the Special Division ineligible to participate in any matters relating to an independent counsel they have appointed, we do not think that appointment of the independent counsel by the court runs afoul of the constitutional limitation on "incongruous" interbranch appointments. . . .

■ JUSTICE SCALIA, dissenting.

. . . Because appellant (who all parties and the Court agree is an officer of the United States) was not appointed by the President with the advice and consent of the Senate, but rather by the Special Division of the United States Court of Appeals, her appointment is constitutional only if (1) she is an "inferior" officer within the meaning of the above Clause, and (2) Congress may vest her appointment in a court of law.

As to the first of these inquiries, the Court does not attempt to "decide exactly" what establishes the line between principal and "inferior" officers, but is confident that, whatever the line may be, appellant "clearly falls on the 'inferior officer' side" of it. The Court gives three reasons: *First,* she "is subject to removal by a higher Executive Branch official," namely, the Attorney General. *Second,* she is "empowered by the Act to perform only certain, limited duties." *Third,* her office is "limited in jurisdiction" and "limited in tenure."

The first of these lends no support to the view that appellant is an inferior officer. Appellant is removable only for "good cause" or physical or mental incapacity. By contrast, most (if not all) *principal* officers in the Executive Branch may be removed by the President *at will.* I fail to see how the fact that appellant is more difficult to remove than most principal officers helps to establish that she is an inferior officer. And I do not see how it could possibly make any difference to her superior or inferior status that the President's limited power to remove her must be exercised through the Attorney General. If she were removable at will by the Attorney General, then she would be subordinate to him and thus properly designated as inferior; but the Court essentially admits that she is not subordinate. If it were common usage to refer to someone as "inferior" who is subject to removal for cause by another, then one would say that the President is "inferior" to Congress.

The second reason offered by the Court—that appellant performs only certain, limited duties—may be relevant to whether she is an inferior officer, but it mischaracterizes the extent of her powers. As the Court states: "Admittedly, the Act delegates to appellant [the] *'full power and independent authority to exercise all investigative and prosecutorial functions and powers of the Department of Justice'* (emphasis added)." Moreover, in addition to this general grant of power she is given a broad range of specifically enumerated powers, including a power not even the Attorney General possesses: to "contes[t] in court . . . any claim of privilege or attempt to withhold evidence on grounds of national security." Once all of this is "admitted," it seems to me impossible to maintain that appellant's authority is so "limited" as to render her an inferior officer. The Court seeks to brush this away by asserting that the independent counsel's power does not include any authority to "formulate policy for the Government or the Executive

Branch." But the same could be said for all officers of the Government, with the single exception of the President. All of them only formulate policy within their respective spheres of responsibility—as does the independent counsel, who must comply with the policies of the Department of Justice only to the extent possible.

The final set of reasons given by the Court for why the independent counsel clearly is an inferior officer emphasizes the limited nature of her jurisdiction and tenure. Taking the latter first, I find nothing unusually limited about the independent counsel's tenure. To the contrary, unlike most high-ranking Executive Branch officials, she continues to serve until she (or the Special Division) decides that her work is substantially completed. This particular independent prosecutor has already served more than two years, which is at least as long as many Cabinet officials. As to the scope of her jurisdiction, there can be no doubt that is small (though far from unimportant). But within it she exercises more than the full power of the Attorney General. The Ambassador to Luxembourg is not anything less than a principal officer, simply because Luxembourg is small. And the federal judge who sits in a small district is not for that reason "inferior in rank and authority." If the mere fragmentation of executive responsibilities into small compartments suffices to render the heads of each of those compartments inferior officers, then Congress could deprive the President of the right to appoint his chief law enforcement officer by dividing up the Attorney General's responsibilities among a number of "lesser" functionaries.

. . . I think it preferable to look to the text of the Constitution and the division of power that it establishes. These demonstrate, I think, that the independent counsel is not an inferior officer because she is not *subordinate* to any officer in the Executive Branch (indeed, not even to the President). Dictionaries in use at the time of the Constitutional Convention gave the word "inferiour" two meanings which it still bears today: (1) "[l]ower in place, . . . station, . . . rank of life, . . . value or excellency," and (2) "[s]ubordinate." S. Johnson, Dictionary of the English Language (6th ed. 1785). In a document dealing with the structure (the constitution) of a government, one would naturally expect the word to bear the latter meaning—indeed, in such a context it would be unpardonably careless to use the word *unless* a relationship of subordination was intended. If what was meant was merely "lower in station or rank," one would use instead a term such as "lesser officers." At the only other point in the Constitution at which the word "inferior" appears, it plainly connotes a relationship of subordination. Article III vests the judicial power of the United States in "one supreme Court, and in such *inferior* Courts as the Congress may from time to time ordain and establish." U.S. Const., Art. III, § 1 (emphasis added). In Federalist No. 81, Hamilton pauses to describe the "inferior" courts authorized by Article III as inferior in the sense that they are "subordinate" to the Supreme Court.

That "inferior" means "subordinate" is also consistent with what little we know about the evolution of the Appointments Clause. . . . Of course one is not a "superior officer" without some supervisory responsibility, just as, I suggest, one is not an "inferior officer" within the meaning of the provision under discussion unless one is subject to supervision by a "superior officer." . . .

To be sure, it is not a *sufficient* condition for "inferior" officer status that one be subordinate to a principal officer. Even an officer who is subordinate to a department head can be a principal officer. . . . But it is surely a *necessary* condition for inferior officer status that the officer be subordinate to another officer.

The independent counsel is not even subordinate to the President. The Court essentially admits as much, noting that "appellant may not be 'subordinate' to the Attorney General (and the President) insofar as she possesses a degree of independent discretion to exercise the powers delegated to her under the Act." In fact, there is no doubt about it. As noted earlier, the Act specifically grants her the "*full* power and *independent* authority to exercise *all* investigative and prosecutorial functions of the Department of Justice," and makes her removable only for "good cause," a limitation specifically intended to ensure that she be *independent* of, not *subordinate* to, the President and the Attorney General.

Because appellant is not subordinate to another officer, she is not an "inferior" officer and her appointment other than by the President with the advice and consent of the Senate is unconstitutional. . . .

NOTES

1. In a subsequent case, *Edmond v. United States,* 520 U.S. 651 (1997), the Court considered whether Congress had authorized the secretary of transportation to appoint civilian members of the Coast Guard Court of Criminal Appeals; and if so, whether this authorization was constitutional under the Appointments Clause. The Coast Guard Court of Criminal Appeals is an intermediate court within the military justice system with both military and civilian judges. The appointment of the military judges was clearly constitutional under *Weiss v. United States,* 510 U.S. 163 (1994), but the appointment of the two civilian judges by the secretary of transportation was constitutional only if the judges were inferior officers within the meaning of the Appointments Clause. Writing for the Court in *Edmond*, Justice Scalia set forth the following test for determining inferior officer status:

> Generally speaking, the term "inferior officer" connotes a relationship with some higher ranking officer or officers below the President: Whether one is an "inferior" officer depends on whether he has a superior. It is not enough that other officers may be identified who formally maintain a higher rank, or possess responsibilities of a greater magnitude. If that were the intention, the Constitution might have used the phrase "lesser officer." Rather, in the context of a Clause designed to preserve political accountability relative to important Government assignments, we think it evident that "inferior officers" are officers whose work is directed and supervised at some level by others who were appointed by Presidential nomination with the advice and consent of the Senate. . . .

Applying that test, the Court held that the judicial appointments were valid. The work of the judges on the Court of Criminal Appeals is supervised by the judge advocate general (who is subordinate to the secretary of transportation) as well as the Court of the Appeals for the Armed Forces. Although seven justices joined Justice Scalia's opinion in *Edmond*, Justice Souter wrote separately, saying: "Because the term 'inferior officer' implies an official superior, one who has no superior is not an inferior officer. . . . It does not follow, however, that if one is subject to some supervision and control, one is an inferior officer. Having a superior officer is necessary for inferior officer status, but not sufficient to establish it." Justice Souter was unwilling to join Justice Scalia in saying that even an officer with tremendous power would be an inferior officer so long as he or she had a supervisor. Since *Edmond* did not overrule *Morrison* there are effectively two tests for determining whether someone is an inferior officer. The *Morrison* test of officer inferiority looks at how important the officer in question is, while the *Edmond* test asks if the officer has a boss who supervises and controls what the officer does.

The issue arose again in *Free Enterprise Fund v. Public Co. Accounting Oversight Bd.,* 130 S. Ct. 3138 (2010). The members of the Public Company Accounting Oversight Board (PCAOB) were appointed by the Securities and Exchange Commission and were removable by the SEC only for cause. It was claimed that they were inferior officers who did not need Senate confirmation because the SEC was said to be the "Head" of a department, and it supervised the PCAOB loosely. Both of these claims were disputed, however. The issue was whether the members of the PCAOB were principal officers or inferior officers (in the wake of the Court's conclusion in another part of that case that the PCAOB officers were actually removable at will by the president and not only for cause as the statute setting up the PCAOB had said). The Supreme Court had little difficulty in concluding that the officers in question were inferior officers since they were removable at will by the SEC, which also had broad powers of supervision over their activities. The majority opinion emphasized the *Edmond* test.

2. The federal courts of appeals and district courts are described in Article I, Section 8, Clause 9 as being "inferior to" the Supreme Court, and it is certainly the case that the Supreme Court exercises some supervisory power over them. Could Congress constitutionally give the Supreme Court the power to appoint federal court of appeals and district judges by claiming they were inferior officers and not principal officers whose appointment must be made by the president with the advice and consent of the Senate? Or are some officers just so important, such as federal court of appeals and trial court judges, that they just have to be principal officers even if they have a supervisor? What about the deputy attorney general or the deputy secretary of state, both of whom have bosses who can control what they do? Can officers this powerful be inferior officers? Should officials this powerful need Senate confirmation?

3. Presidents and cabinet secretaries are always looking for ways to circumvent the Senate confirmation process. This is illustrated by the history of the Office of Management and Budget (OMB) in the White House, which has become a powerful tool for presidential control over the bureaucracy. Presidents from Warren Harding to Richard Nixon appointed directors of OMB as inferior officers without Senate confirmation. This changed during the Nixon administration when Congress demanded and got a requirement that OMB directors be confirmed by the Senate. In the Reagan administration, a significant portion of OMB's power devolved to the Office of Information and Regulatory Affairs (OIRA), the head of which was not Senate-confirmed. Eventually the Senate demanded that heads of OIRA be confirmed, too. The administration of President George H. W. Bush responded by creating a Council on Competitiveness under the vice president, who would push for deregulation more actively than would a Senate-confirmed OIRA director. As a general matter, the president often trusts the unconfirmed White House counsel over the attorney general, the unconfirmed national security advisor over the secretary of state, and the unconfirmed White House chief of staff over everyone else. This shows that the requirement that presidential nominees be confirmed by the Senate really does make them more independent of the president. Often presidents find them-

selves stuck with a high official they dislike because no better replacement could be confirmed. For example, President Bill Clinton reportedly wished he could fire Attorney General Janet Reno, but he could not have done so without risking a brutal confirmation process in what by then was a Republican-controlled Senate.

4. One tool the Constitution gives to the President is the power to make recess appointments. On March 27, 2010, an exasperated President Obama made fifteen recess appointments to the executive branch. President George W. Bush had done much the same thing. Recess appointees serve until the end of the Congress during which they were appointed. Presidents can make recess appointments not only to executive branch positions but also to the federal judiciary. Presidents from George Washington down to the present day have all recess-appointed federal Article III judges. A recess-appointed judge holds office, however, only until the end of the next session of the Senate during the recess of which they were appointed. Recess-appointed judges do not hold office during good behavior the way ordinary federal judges do. Litigants have repeatedly challenged the constitutionality of recess-appointed judges and the courts have consistently rejected such challenges, saying the practice of recess appointment for judges goes back to the Founding. The Recess Appointment Clause in Article II, Section 2 is thus said to trump the Judicial Tenure During Good Behavior Clause in Article III, Section 1. What should a conscientious constitutional interpreter do when faced with such a conflict? Consider the majority and dissenting opinions in *United States v. Woodley*, 751 F.2d 1008 (9th Cir. 1985), which eloquently address this issue. Are two centuries of practice dispositive here? If so, why should practice govern here but not in *INS v. Chadha*?

[*Assignment 20*]

D. THE POWER TO REMOVE EXECUTIVE-BRANCH OFFICERS

Article II, Section 1: The executive Power shall be vested in a President of the United States of America.

Section 3: . . . he shall take Care that the Laws be faithfully executed. . . .

A recurring question throughout American history is the existence and scope of a presidential power to remove non-congressional and non-Article III officers of the federal government. As considered above, Article II makes rules for the *appointment* of executive branch officers. But it says nothing expressly about their *removal* (except via impeachment). How should this silence be resolved? Is the right inference that the president may remove any executive branch officer for malfeasance, incompetence, or even simply policy disagreement? Do any provisions of Article II imply a need for unfettered presidential removal power? The Vesting Clause, or perhaps the Take Care Clause? Or does the role of the Senate in the appointment process suggest that it has a role in removal, too?

There was a heated debate in the First Congress over where the Constitution placed the removal power, and it culminated in what came to be known as the Decision of 1789. With Representative Madison's strong encouragement, the House voted in favor of the presidential removal power, and when the Senate divided evenly on the question, the tie-breaking vote in the president's favor was cast by Vice President John Adams. Some early evidence goes the other way, suggesting that Congress can limit the removal of executive-branch officers—statements by Alexander Hamilton in *The Federalist*, and dicta in *Marbury v. Madison* to the effect that Congress could give justices of the peace a fixed five-year term during which they could not be removed by the president. But for the first seventy years of the nation, presidents invoked the Decision of 1789 and consistently asserted that it was settled practice that Congress could not interfere with their power to remove at will executive-branch subordinates.

For example, in the 1830s, President Andrew Jackson fired a secretary of the treasury who refused to obey a presidential order to remove government deposits from the Bank of the United States. The Senate censured President Jackson for misconduct, and he responded with a document he called a Protest: It argued that the grant of the executive power to the president gave him unlimited power to remove executive branch subordinates. The issue was taken to the country, and President Jackson's party won the next election so decisively that the Senate voted to expunge its resolution of censure from the public records.

The issue of presidential removal power arose again in the 1860s when President Andrew Johnson attempted to derail Reconstruction by firing executive officials he had inherited from the Lincoln administration. Congress responded by passing a statute called the Tenure of Office Act, which required senatorial consent before removals could be made permanent. The president denounced this statute as unconstitutional, and in violation of the statute he tried to fire Secretary of War Edwin Stanton (another Lincoln holdover). The House of Representatives impeached President Johnson for doing this, and the Senate came within one vote of removing him from office. A major factor in his acquittal was the belief by some senators that the Tenure of Office Act was unconstitutional. The act was diluted in the Grant administration and repealed in the first Cleveland administration. By the time of its repeal, the act had become widely viewed as unwise and unconstitutional.

In several late nineteenth and early twentieth century cases, the Supreme Court assumed that the Constitution gave the president the removal power and that that question had been settled by the practice of the government since the Decision of 1789. In 1926, the Supreme Court endorsed that view in a sweeping opinion in *Myers v. United States*, 272 U.S. 52 (1926). The Court's decision, which is presented below, was written by Chief Justice William Howard Taft—the only chief justice who also served as president. *Myers* disapproved of *Marbury*'s statements on removal, and it established the general principle that the president has a constitutional power of removal.

In the 1930s, President Franklin D. Roosevelt and a heavily Democratic Congress found themselves in a huge battle with the Supreme Court over the constitutionality of New Deal legislation. During the height of this battle, President Roosevelt decided to remove—i.e., fire—William Humphrey as chairman of the Federal Trade Commission (FTC). Humphrey was a conservative Republican holdover from prior administrations. Humphrey sued claiming the FTC was an independent regulatory commission and that he could be removed only for cause, i.e., for misconduct in office. Humphrey died while the suit was pending, but the executor of his estate seeking back pay took the case up to the Supreme Court. In *Humphrey's Executor v. United States*, 295 U.S. 602 (1935), the Court announced an important exception to the rule of presidential removal power. The Court read the Federal Trade Commission Act as forbidding removal except where there was cause (a somewhat doubtful reading as a matter of statutory construction), and it then held that Congress could limit presidential removal power by creating "independent agencies," such as the FTC. Congress subsequently conferred independence on the Federal Reserve Board and the Securities Exchange Commission, and it created other independent agencies, such as the National Labor Relations Board. It was still assumed, however, that core executive functions could be undertaken only by officers the president could remove.

In the 1970s, in the Nixon administration, the attorney general hired a special prosecutor, Archibald Cox, to investigate the break-in at the Watergate Hotel. When Cox's investigation began to get too close, President Nixon demanded that the attorney general fire Cox. In what came to be known as the Saturday Night Massacre, the attorney general resigned rather than obey the president's order, and the deputy attorney general was removed by the president when he too refused to fire Cox. The third-ranking official in the Department of Justice, Solicitor General Robert Bork, fired Cox. In the ensuing uproar it was clear that unless a new and fiercely independent special prosecutor was appointed, President Nixon would be immediately impeached. Such a prosecutor was appointed, and nine months later he uncovered the evidence that forced President Nixon to resign from office.

Eager to prevent any future Saturday Night Massacres. Congress proposed turning the entire Justice Department into an independent agency, but Griffin Bell, the attorney general in the Carter administration, argued that this would be unconstitutional under *Myers* because prosecution was a core executive function. Congress settled instead for a system of temporary independent special prosecutors set up in a statute called the Ethics In Government Act (EIGA). Under this act, whenever allegations of wrongdoing were raised against certain high-level executive branch officials, the attorney general would be essentially obligated to refer the matter to a special three-judge court, the members of which would be picked by the chief justice of the United States. That court would then appoint a special prosecutor to investigate the relevant official. Between 1978 and the expiration of the EIGA in 1999, over twenty high-level government officials were investigated by such independent counsels. These counsels were removable only for cause and not at will, just like the Federal Trade Commission chairman in *Humphrey's Executor*.

President Carter signed the EIGA. Its constitutionality was challenged, however, by the Reagan administration, on the grounds that it vested a core executive power—the power over prosecutions—in an unremovable official in violation of *Myers*. In the enthusiasm of the moment, the Reagan administration even challenged *Humphrey's Executor*, and Attorney General Edwin Meese said in a widely publicized speech that independent agencies were unconstitutional.

During the Reagan administration, there were two major cases that challenged congressional power to create independent agencies and counsels. The first, *Bowsher v. Synar*, 478 U.S. 714 (1986), involved the constitutionality of the Gramm–Rudman–Hollings Deficit Reduction Act, which gave executive powers to an official who was not removable at will by the president but who was removable by Congress. The Court held the act unconstitutional. The Court's opinion was careful, however, not to call into question the constitutionality of all independent agencies. The second case,

Morrison v. Olson, 487 U.S. 654 (1988), arose when an assistant attorney general in the Department of Justice, Theodore Olson, was accused of wrongfully withholding documents from Congress. The attorney general referred the investigation to the three-judge special court, which appointed Alexia Morrison as an independent counsel. Olson objected that he was being prosecuted unconstitutionally because the independent prosecutor was unaccountable to the president or to anyone else. His case went up to the Supreme Court, which upheld the EIGA (over a blistering lone dissent by Justice Scalia).

During the Clinton administration, Kenneth Starr was appointed by the three-judge special court to investigate the Whitewater investment scandal in which President Clinton and First Lady Hillary Clinton were alleged to be implicated. Starr's investigation expanded to cover more and more allegations, including that officials in the White House travel office were illegally fired and even that a deputy White House counsel who had appeared to have committed suicide had in fact been murdered. Starr, who had no prior prosecutorial experience, kept expanding his investigation to cover new topics and failed to close out the earlier topics referred to him. Eventually, the investigation collided with a lawsuit brought against President Clinton by Paula Jones, who alleged that he had sexually harassed her when he was governor of Arkansas. In a deposition in that civil suit, President Clinton denied that he had ever had sexual relations with White House intern Monica Lewinsky. This was not true. Starr concluded that the president had committed perjury and obstruction of justice. President Clinton was impeached by the Republican majority in the House of Representatives, but he was overwhelmingly acquitted by the Senate. The EIGA came up for renewal a year later, and by this point Republicans and Democrats alike were willing to let it expire, on both policy and constitutional grounds.

Presented below are all three of the great Supreme Court opinions on the scope of the president's removal power—*Myers v. United States*, *Humphrey's Executor*, and *Morrison v. Olson*. As you read these cases, ask yourself where the Constitution places the removal power. Do text, structure, historical purpose, practice and precedent, and policy suggest that the president has the power to remove any officer who is not an Article III judge? Or does Congress have the power to create independent entities?

Myers v. United States
272 U.S. 52 (1926)

■ MR. CHIEF JUSTICE TAFT delivered the opinion of the Court.

This case presents the question whether under the Constitution the President has the exclusive power of removing executive officers of the United States whom he has appointed by and with the advice and consent of the Senate.

Myers . . . was on July 21, 1917, appointed by the President, by and with the advice and consent of the Senate, to be a postmaster of the first class at Portland, Oregon, for a term of four years. On January 20, 1920, Myers' resignation was demanded. He refused the demand. On February 2, 1920, he was removed from office by order of the Postmaster General, acting by direction of the President. On . . . February 10th, Myers sent a petition to the President and another to the Senate committee on post offices, asking to be heard, if any charges were filed. He protested to the department against his removal, and continued to do so until the end of his term. He pursued no other occupation and drew compensation for no other service during the interval. On April 21, 1921, he brought this suit in the Court of Claims for his salary from the date of his removal, which, as claimed by supplemental petition filed after July 21, 1921, the end of his term, amounted to $8,838.71. In August, 1920, the President made a recess appointment of one Jones, who took office September 19, 1920. . . . *[The Court of Claims ruled against Myers, and he appealed to the Supreme Court.—Editors]*

By the 6th section of the Act of Congress of July 12, 1876, under which Myers was appointed with the advice and consent of the Senate as a first-class postmaster, it is provided that

> Postmasters of the first, second, and third classes shall be appointed and may be removed by the President by and with the advice and consent of the Senate, and shall hold their offices for four years unless sooner removed or suspended according to law.

The Senate did not consent to the President's removal of Myers during his term. If this statute in its requirement that his term should be four years unless sooner removed by the President by and with the consent of the Senate is valid, the appellant, Myers' administratrix, is entitled to recover his unpaid salary for his full term and the judgment of the Court of Claims must be reversed. The Government maintains that the [statute is unconstitutional because] under Article II of the Constitution the President's power of removal of executive officers appointed by him with the advice and consent of the Senate is full and complete without consent of the Senate. . . . We are therefore confronted by the constitutional question and cannot avoid it. . . .

The question where the power of removal of executive officers appointed by the President by and with the advice and consent of the Senate was vested, was presented early in the first session of the First Congress. There is no express provision respecting removals in the Constitution, except as Section 4 of Article II . . . provides for removal from office by impeachment. The subject was not discussed in the Constitutional Convention. Under the Articles of Confederation, Congress was given the power of appointing certain executive officers of the Confederation, and during the Revolution and while the Articles were given effect, Congress exercised the power of removal. . . .

In the House of Representatives of the First Congress, on Tuesday, May 18, 1789, Mr. Madison moved . . . that there should be established three executive departments—one of Foreign Affairs, another of the Treasury, and a third of War—at the head of each of which there should be a Secretary, to be appointed by the President by and with the advice and consent of the Senate, and to be removable by the President. . . . On June 22, in the . . . discussion,

> Mr. Benson stated that his objection to the clause 'to be removable by the President' arose from an idea that the power of removal by the President hereafter might appear to be exercised by virtue of a legislative grant only, and consequently be subjected to legislative instability, when he was well satisfied in his own mind that it was fixed by a fair legislative construction of the Constitution.

1 Annals of Congress, 579.

Mr. Madison admitted the objection made by the gentleman near him (Mr. Benson) to the words in the bill. He said:

> ... Gentlemen have all along proceeded on the idea that the Constitution vests the power in the President; and what arguments were brought forward respecting the convenience or inconvenience of such disposition the power, were intended only to throw light upon what was meant by the compilers of the Constitution. Now, as the words proposed by the gentleman from New York expressed to his mind the meaning of the Constitution, he should be in favor of them, and would agree to strike out those agreed to in the committee.

1 Annals of Congress, 578, 579.

Mr. Benson's ... amendment was then approved by a vote of thirty to eighteen. Mr. Benson then moved to strike out in the first clause the words "to be removable by the President," in pursuance of the purpose he had already declared, and this second motion of his was carried by a vote of thirty–one to nineteen. . . .

It is very clear from this history that the exact question which the House voted upon was whether it should recognize and declare the power of the President under the Constitution to remove the Secretary of Foreign Affairs without the advice and consent of the Senate. That was what the vote was taken for. Some effort has been made to question whether the decision carries the result claimed for it, but there is not the slightest doubt, after an examination of the record, that the vote was, and was intended to be, a legislative declaration that the power to remove officers appointed by the President and the Senate vested in the President alone, and until the Johnson impeachment trial in 1868 its meaning was not doubted, even by those who questioned its soundness.

The discussion [in the House of Representatives] was a very full one. . . . After the bill as amended had passed the House, it was sent to the Senate, where it was discussed in secret session, without report. The critical vote there was upon the striking out of the clause recognizing and affirming the unrestricted power of the President to remove. The Senate divided by ten to ten, requiring the deciding vote of the Vice President, John Adams, who voted against striking out, and in favor of the passage of the bill as it had left the House. . . . The bill, having passed as it came from the House, was signed by President Washington and became a law.

It is convenient in the course of our discussion of this case to review the reasons advanced by Mr. Madison and his associates for their conclusion. . . .

First. Mr. Madison insisted that Article II by vesting the executive power in the President was intended to grant to him the power of appointment and removal of executive officers except as thereafter expressly provided in that article. He pointed out that one of the chief purposes of the convention was to separate the legislative from the executive functions. . . .

Accordingly the Constitution was so framed as to vest in the Congress all legislative powers therein granted, to vest in the President the executive power, and to vest in one Supreme Court and such inferior courts as Congress might establish the judicial power. From this division on principle, the reasonable construction of the Constitution must be that the branches should be kept separate in all cases in which they were not expressly blended, and the Constitution should be expounded to blend them no more than it affirmatively requires. Madison, 1 Annals of Congress, 497. . . .

The debates in the Constitutional Convention indicated an intention to create a strong executive, and after a controversial discussion the executive power of the government was vested in one person and many of his important functions were specified so as to avoid the humiliating weakness of the Congress during the Revolution and under the Articles of Confederation.

Mr. Madison . . . dwelt at length upon the necessity there was for construing Article II to give the President the sole power of removal in his responsibility for the conduct of the executive branch, and enforced this by emphasizing his duty expressly declared in the third section of the article to "take care that the laws be faithfully executed."

The vesting of the executive power in the President was essentially a grant of the power to execute the laws. But the President alone and unaided could not execute the laws. He must execute them by the assistance of subordinates. This view has since been repeatedly affirmed by this Court. *[In re] Neagle*, 135 U.S. 1, 63. As he is charged specifically to take care that they be faithfully executed, the reasonable implication, even in the absence of express words, was that as part of his executive power he should select those who were to act for him under his direction in the execution of the laws. The further implication must be, in the absence of any express limitation respecting removals, that as his selection of administrative officers is essential to the execution of the laws by him, so must be his power of removing those for whom he cannot continue to be responsible. It was urged that the natural meaning of the term "executive power" granted the President included the appointment and removal of executive subordinates. If such appointments and removals were not an exercise of the executive power, what were they? They certainly were not the exercise of legislative or judicial power in government as usually understood. . . .

The requirement of the second section of Article II that the Senate should advise and consent to the presidential appointments, was to be strictly construed. The words of section 2, following the general grant of executive power under section 1, were either an enumeration and emphasis of specific functions of the executive, not all inclusive, or were limitations upon the general grant of the executive power, and as such, being limitations, should not be enlarged beyond the words used. Madison, 1 Annals, 462, 463, 464. The executive power was given in general terms strengthened by specific terms where emphasis was regarded as appropriate, and was limited by direct expressions where limitation was needed, and the fact that no express limit was placed on the power of removal by the executive was convincing indication that none was intended. This is the same construction of Article II as that of Alexander Hamilton quoted *infra*.

Second. The view of Mr. Madison . . . was that not only did the grant of executive power to the President in the first section of Article II carry with it the power of removal, but the express recognition of the power of appointment in the second section enforced this view on the well approved principle of constitutional and statutory construction that the power of removal of executive officers was incident to the power of appointment. . . .

Under section 2 of Article II, however, the power of appointment by the executive is restricted in its exercise by the provision that the Senate, a part of the legislative branch of the government, may check the action of the executive by rejecting the officers he selects. Does this make the Senate part of the removing power? . . .

The history of the clause by which the Senate was given a check upon the President's power of appointment makes it clear that it was not prompted by any desire to limit removals. As already pointed out, the important purpose of those who brought about the restriction was to lodge in the Senate, where the small States had equal representation with the larger States, power to prevent the President from making too many appointments from the larger States. . . .

It was pointed out in this great debate that the power of removal, though equally essential to the executive power is different in its nature from that of appointment. A veto by the Senate—a part of the legislative branch of the government—upon removals is a much greater limitation upon the executive branch, and a much more serious blending of the legislative with the executive, than a rejection of a proposed appointment. It is not to be implied. The rejection of a nominee of the President for a particular office does not greatly embarrass him in the conscientious discharge of his high duties in the selection of those who are to aid him, because the President usually has an ample field from which to select for office, according to his preference, competent and capable men. The Senate has full power to reject newly proposed appointees whenever the President shall remove the incumbents. Such a check enables the Senate to prevent the filling of offices with bad or incompetent men or with those against whom there is a tenable objection.

The power to prevent the removal of an officer who has served under the President is different from the authority to consent to or reject his appointment. When a nomination is made, it may be presumed that the Senate is, or may become, as well advised as to the fitness of the nominee as the President, but in the nature of things the defects in ability or intelligence or loyalty in the administration of the laws of one who has served as an officer under the President are facts as to which the President, or his trusted subordinates, must be better informed than the Senate, and the power to remove him may therefore be regarded as confined for very sound and practical reasons, to the governmental authority which has administrative control. The power of removal is incident to the power of appointment, not to the power of advising and consenting to appointment, and when the grant of the executive power is enforced by the express mandate to take care that the laws be faithfully executed, it emphasizes the necessity for including within the executive power as conferred the exclusive power of removal. . . .

In the discussion in the First Congress fear was expressed that such a constitutional rule of construction as was involved in the passage of the bill would expose the country to tyranny through the abuse of the exercise of the power of removal by the President. Underlying such fears was the fundamental misconception that the President's attitude in his exercise of power is one of opposition to the people, while the Congress is their only defender in the government. . . . This view was properly contested by Mr. Madison in the discussion, by Mr. Hartley, by Mr. Lawrence, and by Mr. Scott. The President is a representative of the people, just as the members of the Senate and of the House are, and it may be at some times, on some subjects, that the President, elected by all the people, is rather more representative of them all than are the members of either body of the Legislature, whose constituencies are local and not countrywide. . . .

Another argument advanced in the First Congress against implying the power of removal in the President alone from its necessity in the proper administration of the executive power was that all embarrassment in this respect could be avoided by the President's power of suspension of officers, disloyal or incompetent, until the Senate could act. . . .

In the case before us, the same suggestion has been made. . . . [But t]he implication of removal by the President alone is no more a strained construction of the Constitution than that of suspension by him alone and the broader power is much more needed and more strongly to be implied.

Third. Another argument urged against the constitutional power of the President alone to remove executive officers appointed by him with the consent of the Senate is that, in the absence of an express power of removal granted to the President, power to make provision for removal of all such officers is vested in the Congress by section 8 of Article I. . . .

A reference of the whole power of removal to general legislation by Congress is quite out of keeping with the plan of government devised by the framers of the Constitution. It could never have been intended to leave to Congress unlimited discretion to vary fundamentally the operation of the great independent executive branch of government and thus most seriously to weaken it. It would be a delegation by the Convention to Congress of the function of defining the primary boundaries of another of the three great divisions of government. . . .

It is reasonable to suppose also that had it been intended to give to Congress power to regulate or control removals in the manner suggested, it would have been included among the specifically enumerated legislative powers in Article I, or in the specified limitations on the executive power in Article II. The difference between the grant of legislative power under Article I to Congress which is limited to powers therein enumerated, and the more general grant of the executive power to the President under Article II is significant. The fact that the executive power is given in general terms strengthened by specific terms where emphasis is appropriate, and limited by direct expressions where limitation is needed, and that no express limit is placed on the power of removal by the executive is a convincing indication that none was intended. . . .

Fourth. Mr. Madison . . . pointed out with great force the unreasonable character of the view that the convention intended, without express provision, to give to Congress or the Senate, in case of political or other differences, the means of thwarting the executive in the exercise of his great powers and in the bearing of his great responsbility, by fastening upon him, as subordinate executive officers, men who by their inefficient service under him, by their lack of loyalty to the service, or by their different views of policy might make his taking care that the laws be faithfully executed most difficult or impossible.

As Mr. Madison said in the debate in the First Congress:

> Vest this power in the Senate jointly with the President, and you abolish at once that great principle of unity and responsibility in the executive department, which was intended for the security of liberty and the public good. If the President should possess alone the power of removal from office, those who are employed in the execution of the law will be in their proper situation, and the chain of dependence be preserved; the lowest officers, the middle grade, and the highest will depend, as they ought, on the President, and the President on the community. . . .

Made responsible under the Constitution for the effective enforcement of the law, the President needs as an indispensable aid to meet it the disciplinary influence upon those who act under him of a reserve power of removal. . . .

[The President] must place in each member of his official family, and his chief executive subordinates, implicit faith. The moment that he loses confidence in the intelligence, ability, judgment, or loyalty of any one of them, he must have the power to remove him without delay. To require him to file charges and submit them to the consideration of the Senate might make impossible that unity and co-ordination in executive administration essential to effective action. . . .

We have devoted much space to this discussion and decision of the question of the Presidential power of removal in the First Congress, not because a Congressional conclusion on a constitutional issue is conclusive, but, first, because of our agreement with the reasons upon which it was avowedly based; second, because this was the decision of the First Congress, on a question of primary importance in the organization of the Government, made within two years after the Constitutional Convention and within a much shorter time after its ratification; and, third, because that Congress numbered among its leaders those who had been members of the convention. It must necessarily constitute a precedent upon which many future laws supplying the machinery of the new government would be based and, if erroneous, would be likely to evoke dissent and departure in future Congresses. It would come at once before the executive branch of the Government for compliance and might well be brought before the judicial branch for a test of its validity. [I]t was soon accepted as a final decision of the question by all branches of the Government. . . .

The words of a . . . great constitutional authority quoted as in conflict with the Congressional decision, are those of Chief Justice Marshall. They were used by him in his opinion in *Marbury v. Madison*, 1 Cranch, 137 (1803). The judgment in that case is one of the great landmarks in the history of the construction of the Constitution of the United States, and is of supreme authority, first, in respect to the power and duty of the Supreme Court and other courts to consider and pass upon the validity of acts of Congress enacted in violation of the limitations of the Constitution, when properly brought before them in cases in which the rights of the litigating parties require such consideration and decision, and, second, in respect to the lack of power of Congress to vest in the Supreme Court original jurisdiction to grant the remedy of mandamus in cases in which by the Constitution it is given only appellate jurisdiction. But it is not to be regarded as such authority in respect of the power of the President to remove officials appointed by the advice and consent of the Senate, for that question was not before the Court.

. . . [T]he Chief Justice proceeded to express an opinion on the question whether the appointee was removable by the President. He said:

> As the law creating the office gave the officer a right to hold it for five years, independent of the executive, the appointment was not revocable; but vested in the officer legal rights, which are protected by the laws of his country.

. . . [T]he whole statement was certainly *obiter dictum* with reference to the judgment actually reached. The question whether the officer was removable was not argued to the court by any counsel contending for that view. Counsel for the relator, who made the only argument, contended that the officer was not removable by the President, because he held a judicial office and under the Constitution could not be deprived of his office for the five years of his term by Presidential action. The opinion contains no wider discussion of the question than that quoted above. . . .

Congress in a number of acts, followed and enforced the legislative decision of 1789 for seventy-four years. . . . The acquiescence in the legislative decision of 1789 for nearly three-quarters of a century by all branches of the Government has been affirmed by this Court in unmistakable terms. . . . *[The Court adduced quotations from Chancellor Kent and Justice Story, as well as from attorneys general in the Tyler, Polk, Fillmore, and Buchanan administrations.—Editors]*

We come now to consider an argument, advanced and strongly pressed on behalf of the complainant, that this case concerns only the removal of a postmaster; that a postmaster is an inferior officer; and that such an office was not included within the legislative decision of 1789, which related only to superior officers to be appointed by the President by and with the advice and consent of the Senate. . . .

The very heated discussions during General Jackson's administration, except as to the removal of Secretary Duane, related to the distribution of offices, which were most of them inferior offices, and it was the operation of the legislative decision of 1789 upon the power of removal of incumbents of such offices that led the General to refuse to comply with the request of the Senate that he give his reasons for the removals therefrom. . . .

Section 2 of Article II, after providing that the President shall nominate and with the consent of the Senate appoint ambassadors, other public ministers, consuls, judges of the Supreme Court and all other officers of the United States whose appointments are not herein otherwise provided for, and which shall be established by law, contains the proviso "but the Congress may be law vest the appointment of such inferior officers, as they think proper, in the President alone, in the courts of law or in the heads of departments." . . .

The power to remove inferior executive officers, like that to remove superior executive officers, in an incident of the power to appoint them, and is in its nature an executive power. The authority of Congress given by the excepting clause to vest the appointment of such inferior officers in the heads of departments carries with it authority incidentally to invest the heads of departments with power to remove. It has been the practice of Congress to do so and this Court has recognized that power. The Court also has recognized in the *Perkins* case that Congress, in committing the appointment of such inferior officers to the heads of departments, may prescribe incidental regulations controlling and restricting the latter in the exercise of the power of removal. But the court never has held, nor reasonably could hold, . . . that the excepting clause enables Congress to draw to itself, or to either branch of it, the power to remove or the right to participate in the exercise of that power. To do this would be to go beyond the words and implications of that clause, and to infringe the constitutional principle of the separation of governmental powers. . . .

Summing up, then, the facts as to acquiescence by all branches of the government in the legislative decision of 1789 as to executive officers, whether superior or inferior, we find that from 1789 until 1863, a period of seventy-four years, there was no act of Congress, no executive act, and no decision of this court at variance with the declaration of the First Congress; but there was, as we have seen, clear affirmative recognition of it by each branch of the Government.

Our conclusion on the merits, sustained by the arguments before stated, is that Article II grants to the President the executive power of the Government—i.e., the general administrative control of those executing the laws, including the power of appointment and removal of executive officers—a conclusion confirmed by his obligation to take care that the laws be faithfully executed. . . .

We come now to a period in the history of the Government when both Houses of Congress attempted to reverse this constitutional construction, and to subject the power of removing executive officers appointed by the President and confirmed by the Senate to the control of the Senate—indeed, finally, to the assumed power in Congress to place the removal of such officers anywhere in the Government.

This reversal grew out of the serious political difference between the two Houses of Congress and President Johnson. There was a two-thirds majority of the Republican party, in control of each House of Congress, which resented what it feared would be Mr. Johnson's obstructive course in the enforcement of the reconstruction measures, in respect of the States whose people had lately been at war against the National Government. This led the two Houses to enact legislation to curtail the then acknowledged powers of the President. . . . [T]he Tenure of Office Act of March 2, 1867, provid[ed] that all officers appointed by and with the consent of the Senate should hold their offices until their successors should have in like manner been appointed and qualified, and that certain heads of departments, including the Secretary of War, should hold their offices during the term of the President by whom appointed and one month thereafter subject to removal by consent of the Senate. The Tenure of Office Act was vetoed, but it was passed over the veto. The House of Representatives preferred articles of impeachment against President Johnson for refusal to comply with, and for conspiracy to defeat, the legislation above referred to, but he was acquitted for lack of a two-thirds vote for conviction in the Senate. . . .

The extreme provisions of all this legislation were a full justification for the considerations so strongly advanced by Mr. Madison and his associates in the First Congress for insisting that the power of removal of executive officers by the President alone was essential in the division of powers between the executive and the legislative bodies. It exhibited in a clear degree the paralysis to which a partisan Senate and Congress could subject the executive arm and destroy the principle of executive responsibility and separation of powers, sought for by the framers of our Government, if the President had no power of removal save by consent of the Senate. It was an attempt to redistribute the powers and minimize those of the President.

After President Johnson's term ended, the injury and invalidity of the Tenure of Office Act in its radical innovation were immediately recognized by the executive and objected to. General Grant, succeeding Mr. Johnson in the presidency, earnestly recommended in his first message the total repeal of the act . . . .

While in response to this a bill for repeal of that act passed the House, it failed in the Senate, and, though the law was changed, it still limited the presidential power of removal . . . until 1887, when it was repealed. . . . In 1876 the act here under discussion was passed, making the consent of the

Senate necessary both to the appointment and removal of first, second, and third class postmasters.

[I]n March, 1886, President Cleveland, in discussing the requests which the Senate had made for his reasons for removing officials, and the assumption that the Senate had the right to pass upon those removals and thus to limit the power of the President, said:

> I believe the power to remove or suspend such officials is vested in the President alone by the Constitution, which in express terms provides that "the executive power shall be vested in a President of the United States of America," and that 'he shall take care that the laws be faithfully executed.
>
> The Senate belongs to the legislative branch of the government. When the Constitution by express provision superadded to its legislative duties the right to advise and consent to appointments to office and to sit as a court of impeachment, it conferred upon that body all the control and regulation of Executive action supposed to be necessary for the safety of the people; and this express and special grant of such extraordinary powers, not in any way related to or growing out of general senatorial duties, and in itself a departure from the general plan of our government, should be held, under a familiar maxim of construction, to exclude every other right of interference with Executive functions.

11 Messages and Papers of the Presidents, 4964.

The attitude of the Presidents on this subject has been unchanged and uniform to the present day whenever an issue has clearly been raised. . . .

In spite of the foregoing Presidential declarations, it is contended that, since the passage of the Tenure of Office Act, there has been general acquiescence by the executive in the power of Congress to forbid the President alone to remove executive officers, an acquiescence which has changed any formerly accepted constitutional construction to the contrary. Instances are cited of the signed approval by President Grant and other Presidents of legislation in derogation of such construction. We think these are all to be explained, not by acquiescence therein, but by reason of the otherwise valuable effect of the legislation approved. Such is doubtless the explanation of the executive approval of the act of 1876, which we are considering, for it was an appropriation act on which the section here in question was imposed as a rider. . . .

Other acts of Congress are referred to which contain provisions said to be inconsistent with the 1789 decision. Since the provision for an Interstate Commerce Commission in 1887, many administrative boards have been created whose members are appointed by the President, by and with the advice and consent of the Senate, and in the statutes creating them have been provisions for the removal of the members for specified causes. Such provisions are claimed to be inconsistent with the independent power of removal by the President. This, however, is shown to be unfounded by the case of *Shurtleff v. United States*, 189 U.S. 311 (1903). . . .

There are other later acts pointed out in which doubtless the inconsistency with the independent power of the President to remove is clearer, but these cannot be said to have really received the acquiescence of the executive branch of the Government. Whenever there has been a real issue made in respect to the question of presidential removals, the attitude of the executive in Congressional message has been clear and positive against the validity of such legislation. The language of Mr. Cleveland in 1886, twenty years after the Tenure of Office Act, in his controversy with the Senate in respect to his independence of that body in the matter of removing inferior officers appointed by him and confirmed by the Senate, was quite as pronounced as that of General Jackson in a similar controversy in 1835. Mr. Wilson in 1920 and Mr. Coolidge in 1924 were quite as all-embracing in their views of the power of removal as General Grant in 1869, and as Mr. Madison and Mr. John Adams in 1789. . . .

An argument *ab inconvenienti [i.e., from inconvenience or hardship— Editors]* has been made against our conclusion in favor of the executive power of removal by the President, without the consent of the Senate, that it will open the door to a reintroduction of the spoils system. The evil of the spoils system aimed at in the Civil Service Law and its amendments is in respect to inferior offices. It has never been attempted to extend that law beyond them. Indeed Congress forbids its extension to appointments confirmed by the Senate, except with the consent of the Senate. . . .

What, then, are the elements that enter into our decision of this case? We have, first, a construction of the Constitution made by a Congress which was to provide by legislation for the organization of the government in accord with the Constitution which had just then been adopted, and in which there were, as Representatives and Senators, a considerable number of those who had been members of the convention that framed the Constitution and presented it for ratification. . . . This Court has repeatedly laid down the principle that a contemporaneous legislative exposition of the Constitution, when the founders of our government and framers of our Constitution were actively participating in public affairs, acquiesced in for a long term of years, fixes the construction to be given its provisions.

We are now asked to set aside this construction, thus buttressed, and adopt an adverse view, because the Congress of the United States did so during a heated political difference of opinion between the then President and the majority leaders of Congress over the reconstruction measures . . . at the time of the Civil War. . . . Without animadverting on the character of the measures taken, we are certainly justified in saying that they should not be given the weight affecting proper constitutional construction to be accorded to that reached by the First Congress of the United States during a political calm and acquiesced in by the whole Government for three-quarters of a century, especially when the new construction contended for has never been acquiesced in by either the executive or the judicial departments. . . . When, on the merits, we find our conclusion strongly favoring the view which prevailed in the First Congress, we have no hesitation in holding that conclusion to be correct; and it therefore follows that the Tenure of Office Act of 1867, in so far as it attempted to prevent the President from removing executive officers who had been appointed by him by and with the advice and consent of the Senate, was invalid, and that subsequent legislation of the same effect was equally so.

For the reasons given, we must therefore hold that the provision of the law of 1876 by which the unrestricted power of removal of first-class postmasters is denied to the President is in violation of the Constitution and invalid. . . .

■ MR. JUSTICE HOLMES, dissenting.

My Brothers MCREYNOLDS and BRANDEIS have discussed the question before us with exhaustive research and I say a few words merely to emphasize my agreement with their conclusion.

The arguments drawn from the executive power of the President, and from his duty to appoint officers of the United States (when Congress does not vest the appointment elsewhere), to take care that the laws be faithfully executed, and to commission all officers of the United States, seem to me spiders' webs inadequate to control the dominant facts.

We have to deal with an office that owes its existence to Congress and that Congress may abolish to-morrow. Its duration and the pay attached to it while it lasts depend on Congress alone. Congress alone confers on the President the power to appoint to it and at any time may transfer the power to other hands. With such power over its own creation, I have no more trouble in believing that Congress has power to prescribe a term of life for it free from any interference than I have in accepting the undoubted power of Congress to decree its end. I have equally little trouble in accepting its power to prolong the tenure of an incumbent until Congress or the Senate shall have assented to his removal. The duty of the President to see that the laws be executed is a duty that does not go beyond the laws or require him to achieve more than Congress sees fit to leave within his power.

■ [The dissenting opinion of JUSTICE MCREYNOLDS is omitted.]

■ MR. JUSTICE BRANDEIS, dissenting.

In 1833 Mr. Justice Story, after discussing in his Commentaries on the Constitution the much debated question concerning the President's power of removal, said:

> If there has been any aberration from the true constitutional exposition of the power of removal (which the reader must decide for himself), it will be difficult, and perhaps impracticable, after forty years' experience, to recall the practice to the correct theory. But, at all events, it will be a consolation to those who love the Union, and honor a devotion to the patriotic discharge of duty, that in regard to "inferior officers" (which appellation probably includes ninety-nine out of a hundred of the lucrative offices in the government), the remedy for any permanent abuse is still within the power of Congress, by the simple expedient of requiring the consent of the Senate to removals in such cases.

Postmasters are inferior officer. Congress might have vested their appointment in the head of the department. . . . [The challenged] statute has been in force unmodified for half a century. Throughout the period, it has governed a large majority of all civil officers to which appointments are made by and with the advice and consent of the Senate. May the President, having acted under the statute in so far as it creates the office and authorizes the appointment, ignore, while the Senate is in session, the provision which prescribes the condition under which a removal may take place?

It is this narrow question, and this only. which we are required to decide. We need not consider what power the President, being Commander-in-Chief, has over officers in the Army and the Navy. We need not determine whether the President, acting alone, may remove high political officers. We need not even determine whether, acting alone, he may remove inferior civil officers when the Senate is not in session. It was in session when the President purported to remove Myers, and for a long time thereafter. . . .

The contention that Congress is powerless to make consent of the Senate a condition of removal by the President from an executive office rests mainly upon the clause in § 1 of Article II which declares that "the executive Power shall be vested in a President." The argument is that appointment and removal of officials are executive prerogatives; that the grant to the President of "the executive power" confers upon him, as inherent in the office, the power to exercise these two functions without restriction by Congress, except in so far as the power to restrict his exercise of then is expressly conferred upon Congress by the Constitution; that in respect to appointment certain restrictions of the executive power are so provided for; but that in respect to removal there is no express grant to Congress of any power to limit the President's prerogative. The simple answer to the argument is this: The ability to remove a subordinate executive officer, being an essential of effective government, will, in the absence of express constitutional provision to the contrary, be deemed to have been vested in some person or body. But it is not a power inherent in a chief executive. The President's power of removal from statutory civil inferior offices, like the power of appointment to them, comes immediately from Congress. It is true that the exercise of the power of removal is said to be an executive act, and that when the Senate grants or withholds consent to a removal by the President, it participates in an executive act. But the Constitution has confessedly granted to Congress the legislative power to create offices, and to prescribe the tenure thereof; and it has not in terms denied to Congress the power to control removals. . . . .

It is also argued that the clauses in Article II, § 3, of the Constitution, which declare that the President "shall take Care that the Laws be faithfully executed, and shall Commission all the Officers of the United States" imply a grant to the President of the alleged uncontrollable power of removal. I do not find in either clause anything which supports this claim. The provision that the President "shall Commission all the Officers of the United States" clearly bears no such implication. Nor can it be spelled out of the direction that "he shall take Care that the Laws be faithfully executed." There is no express grant to the President of incidental powers resembling those conferred upon Congress by clause 18 of Article I, § 8. . . . A power essential to protection against pressing dangers incident to disloyalty in the civil service may well be deemed inherent in the executive office. But that need, and also insubordination and neglect of duty, are adequately provided against by implying in the President the constitutional power of suspension. . . . Power to remove, as well as to suspend, a high political officer, might conceivably be deemed indispensable to democratic government and, hence, inherent in the President. But power to remove an inferior administrative officer appointed for a fixed term cannot conceivably be deemed an essential of government.

To imply a grant to the President of the uncontrollable power of removal from statutory inferior executive offices involves an unnecessary and indefensible limitation upon the constitutional power of Congress to fix the tenure of the inferior statutory offices. That such a limitation cannot be justified on the ground of necessity is demonstrated by the practice of our governments, state and national. In none of the original 13 states did the chief executive possess such power at the time of the adoption of the federal Constitution. In none of the 48 states has such power been conferred at any time since by a state constitution, with a single possible exception. In a few states the Legislature has granted to the Governor, or other appointing power, the absolute power of removal. The legislative practice of most states reveals a decided tendency to limit, rather than to extend, the Governor's power of removal. The practice of the Federal Government will be set forth in detail.

Over removal from inferior civil offices, Congress has, from the foundation of our Government, exercised continuously some measure of control by legislation. The instances of such laws are many. Some of the statutes were directory in character. Usually, they were mandatory. Some of them, comprehensive in scope, have endured for generations. During the first 40 years of our Government, there was no occasion to curb removals. Then, the power of Congress was exerted to ensure removals. . . .

In the later period, which began after the spoils system had prevailed for a generation, the control of Congress over inferior offices was exerted to prevent removals. The removal clause here in question was first introduced by the Currency Act of February 25, 1863, which was approved by President Lincoln. That statute provided for the appointment of the Comptroller, and that he "shall hold his office for the term of five years unless sooner removed by the President, by and with the advice and consent of the Senate." In 1867 this provision was inserted in the Tenure of Office Act of March 2, 1867, which applied, in substance, to all presidential offices. It was passed over President Johnson's veto. . . .

By Act of June 8, 1872, a consolidation and revision of the postal laws was made. The removal clause was inserted in section 63 in the precise form in which it had first appeared in the Currency Act of 1863. . . . [This] postal statute[was] approved by President Grant. When President Cleveland secured, by Act of March 3, 1887, the repeal of the [Tenure of Office Act], he made no attempt to apply the repeal to postmasters, although postmasters constituted then, as they have ever since, a large majority of all presidential appointees. The removal clause, which had become operative as to them by specific legislation, was continued in force. For more than half a century this postal law has stood unmodified. No President has recommended to Congress that it be repealed. A few proposals for repeal have been made by bills introduced in the House. Not one of them has been considered by it. . . .

The assertion that the mere grant by the Constitution of executive power confers upon the President as a prerogative the unrestricted power of appointment and of removal from executive offices, except so far as otherwise expressly provided by the Constitution, is clearly inconsistent also with those statutes which restrict the exercise by the President of the power of nomination. . . . [A] multitude of laws have been enacted which limit the President's power to make nominations, and which through the restrictions imposed, may prevent the selection of the person deemed by him best fitted. . . .

Thus Congress has, from time to time, restricted the President's selection by the requirement of citizenship. It has limited the power of nomination by providing that the office may be held only by a resident of the United States; of a state; of a particular state; of a particular district; of a particular territory; of the District of Columbia; of a particular foreign country. It has limited the power of nomination further by prescribing specific professional attainments, or occupational experience. It has, in other cases, prescribed the test of examinations. It has imposed the requirement of age; of sex; of races; of property; and of habitual temperance in the use of intoxicating liquors. Congress has imposed like restrictions on the power of nomination by requiring political representation; or that the selection be made on a nonpartisan basis. It has required, in some cases, that the representation be industrial; in others, that it be geographic. It has at times required that the President's nominees be taken from, or include representatives from, particular branches or departments of the government. By still other statutes, Congress has confined the President's selection to a small number of persons to be named by others. . . .

The historical data submitted present a legislative practice, established by concurrent affirmative action of Congress and the President, to make consent of the Senate a condition of removal from statutory inferior, civil, executive offices to which the appointment is made for a fixed term by the President with such consent. They show that the practice has existed, without interruption, continuously for the last fifty-eight years; that throughout this period, it has governed a great majority of all such offices; that the legislation applying the removal clause specifically to the office of postmaster was enacted more than half a century ago; and that recently the practice has, with the President's approval, been extended to several newly created offices. . . . A persistent legislative practice which involves a delimitation of the respective powers of Congress and the President, and which has been so established and maintained, should be deemed tantamount to judicial construction, in the absence of any decision by any court to the contrary. *United States v. Midwest Oil Co.*, 236 U.S. 459, 469.

. . . The action taken by Congress in 1789 after the great debate does not [support the Court's holding]. The vote then taken did not involve a decision that the President had uncontrollable power. It did not involve a decision of the question whether Congress could confer upon the Senate the right, and impose upon it the duty, to participate in removals. It involved merely the decision that the Senate does not, in the absence of legislative grant thereof, have the right to share in the removal of an officer appointed with its consent, and that the President has, in the absence of restrictive legislation, the constitutional power of removal without such consent. Moreover, as Chief Justice Marshall recognized, the debate and the decision related to a high political office, not to inferior ones. . . .

It is true that several Presidents have asserted that the Constitution conferred a power of removal uncontrollable by Congress. But of the many statutes enacted since the foundation of our government which in express terms controlled the power of removal, either by the clause here in question or otherwise, only two were met with a veto: The Tenure of Office Act of 1867, which related to high political officers among others, and the Budget Act of 1921, which denied to the President any participation in the removal of the Comptroller and Assistant Comptroller. One was passed over the President's veto; the other was approved by the succeeding President. It is true also that several Presidents have at times insisted that for the exercise of their power they were not accountable to the Senate. But even these Presidents have at other times complied with requests that the ground of removal of inferior officers be stated. Many of the Presidents have furnished the desired information without questioning the right to request it. And neither the Senate nor the House has at any time receded from the claim that Congress has power both to control by legislation removal from inferior offices and to require the President to report to it the reasons for removals made therefrom. . . . A construction given to the Constitution by the concurrent affirmative action of Congress and the President continued throughout a long period without interruption should be followed despite the isolated utterances, made in the heat of political controversies not involving the question here in issue by individual Presidents supported only by the advice of the Attorney General. . . .

NOTES

1. Myers was appointed a postmaster after being nominated by the president and confirmed by the Senate. Does this mean he was a principal officer of the United States under the Appointments Clause and not an inferior officer appointed by the president or the head of a department? Is there a stronger constitutional case for presidential power to remove principal officers than to remove inferior officers? Suppose the Tenure of Office Act had been in effect on January 20, 2009. Would that mean President Barack Obama was stuck with President George W. Bush's cabinet and subcabinet officials unless sixty senators agreed to confirm replacements? Would this affect the meaningfulness of presidential elections?

2. The opinions in *Myers* focus heavily on practice from the Decision of 1789 to the Tenure of Office Act on down to the present day. How much weight should be given to constitutional arguments from practice? Should they be given more weight or less weight on questions of the separation of powers? What conclusions about presidential removal are suggested by the other types of constitutional argument?

3. How broad is the holding of *Myers* as opposed to its dicta? May the president fire not only a postmaster but also a federal trade commissioner or a special prosecutor? Note that Chief Justice Taft is the only person to have served as both president and chief justice. Could this explain his passionate support in *Myers* for presidential removal power? A major event in Taft's presidency was his controversial firing of Gifford Pinchot, the first chief of the United States Forest Service and a leading conservationist. Pinchot had accused the secretary of the interior of favoring industry, and he called for and got an investigation by a congressional committee. President Taft then fired Pinchot for insubordination.

Humphrey's Executor v. United States
295 U.S. 602 (1935)

■ MR. JUSTICE SUTHERLAND delivered the opinion of the Court.

Plaintiff brought suit in the Court of Claims against the United States to recover a sum of money alleged to be due the deceased for salary as a Federal Trade Commissioner from October 8, 1933, when the President undertook to remove him from office, to the time of his death on February 14, 1934. The court below has certified to this court two questions in respect of the power of the President to make the removal. . . .

William E. Humphrey, the decedent, on December 10, 1931, was nominated by President Hoover to succeed himself as a member of the Federal Trade Commission, and was confirmed by the United States Senate. He was duly commissioned for a term of seven years, expiring September 25, 1938; and, after taking the required oath of office, entered upon his duties. On July 25, 1933, President Roosevelt addressed a letter to the commissioner asking for his resignation, on the ground "that the aims and purposes of the Administration with respect to the work of the Commission can be carried out most effectively with personnel of my own selection," but disclaiming any reflection upon the commissioner personally or upon his services. The commissioner replied, asking time to consult his friends. After some further correspondence upon the subject, the President on August 31, 1933, wrote the commissioner expressing the hope that the resignation would be forthcoming, and saying: "You will, I know, realize that I do not feel that your mind and my mind go along together on either the policies or the administering of the Federal Trade Commission, and, frankly, I think it is best for the people of this country that I should have a full confidence."

The commissioner declined to resign; and on October 7, 1933, the President wrote him: "Effective as of this date you are hereby removed from the office of Commissioner of the Federal Trade Commission."

Humphrey never acquiesced in this action, but continued thereafter to insist that he was still a member of the commission, entitled to perform its duties and receive the compensation provided by law at the rate of $10,000 per annum. . . .

[The Court first construed Section 1 of the Federal Trade Commission Act—which states that "any commissioner may be removed by the President for: (1) inefficiency, (2) neglect of duty, or (3) malfeasance in office"—as if it allowed the president to remove a commissioner only for those three reasons.—Editors]

We conclude that the intent of the act is to limit the executive power of removal to the causes enumerated, the existence of none of which is claimed here; and we pass to the [constitutional] question.

[T]o support its contention that the removal provision of section 1, as we have just construed it, is an unconstitutional interference with the executive power of the President, the government's chief reliance is *Myers v. United States,* 272 U.S. 52. That case has been so recently decided, and the prevailing and dissenting opinions so fully review the general subject of the power of executive removal, that further discussion would add little of value to the wealth of material there collected. These opinions examine at length the historical, legislative, and judicial data bearing upon the question, beginning with what is called "the decision of 1789" in the first Congress and coming down almost to the day when the opinions were delivered. They occupy 243 pages of the volume in which they are printed. Nevertheless, the narrow point actually decided was only that the President had power to remove a postmaster of the first class, without the advice and consent of the Senate as required by act of Congress. In the course of the opinion of the court, expressions occur which tend to sustain the government's contention, but these are beyond the point involved and, therefore, do not come within the rule of *stare decisis.* In so far as they are out of harmony with the views here set forth, these expressions are disapproved. . . .

The office of a postmaster is so essentially unlike the office now involved that the decision in the *Myers* case cannot be accepted as controlling our decision here. A postmaster is an executive officer restricted to the performance of executive functions. He is charged with no duty at all related to either the legislative or judicial power. The actual decision in the *Myers* case finds support in the theory that such an officer is merely one of the units in the executive department and, hence, inherently subject to the exclusive and illimitable power of removal by the Chief Executive, whose subordinate and aid he is. Putting aside *dicta,* which may be followed if sufficiently persuasive but which are not controlling, the necessary reach of the decision goes far enough to include all purely executive officers. It goes no farther; much less does it include an officer who occupies no place in the executive department and who exercises no part of the executive power vested by the Constitution in the President.

The Federal Trade Commission is an administrative body created by Congress to carry into effect legislative policies embodied in the statute in accordance with the legislative standard therein prescribed, and to perform other specified duties as a legislative or as a judicial aid. Such a body cannot in any proper sense be characterized as an arm or an eye of the executive. Its duties are performed without executive leave and, in the contemplation of the statute, must be free from executive control. In administering the provisions of the statute in respect of "unfair methods of competition," that is to say, in filling in and administering the details embodied by that general standard, the commission acts in part quasi legislatively and in part quasi judicially. In making investigations and reports thereon for the information of Congress under section 6, in aid of the legislative power, it acts as a legislative agency. Under section 7, which authorizes the commission to act as a master in chancery under rules prescribed by the court, it acts as an agency of the judiciary. To the extent that it exercises any executive function, as distinguished from executive power in the constitutional sense, it does so in the discharge and effectuation of its quasi legislative or quasi judicial powers, or as an agency of the legislative or judicial departments of the government.

If Congress is without authority to prescribe causes for removal of members of the trade commission and limit executive power of removal accordingly, that power at once becomes practically all-inclusive in respect of civil officers with the exception of the judiciary provided for by the Constitution. The Solicitor General, at the bar, apparently recognizing this to be true, with commendable candor, agreed that his view in respect of the removability of members of the Federal Trade Commission necessitated a like view in respect of the Interstate Commerce Commission and the Court of Claims. We are thus confronted with the serious question whether not only the members of these quasi legislative and quasi judicial bodies, but the judges of the legislative Court of Claims, exercising judicial power (*Williams v. United States,* 289 U.S. 553, 565–567), continue in office only at the pleasure of the President.

We think it plain under the Constitution that illimitable power of removal is not possessed by the President in respect of officers of the character of those just named. The authority of Congress, in creating quasi legislative or quasi judicial agencies, to require them to act in discharge of their duties independently of executive control cannot well be doubted; and that authority includes, as an appropriate incident, power to fix the period during which they shall continue, and to forbid their removal except for cause in the meantime. For it is quite evident that one who holds his office only during the pleasure of another cannot be depended upon to maintain an attitude of independence against the latter's will. . . .

The power of removal here claimed for the President . . . threatens the independence of a commission, which is not only wholly disconnected from the executive department, but which, as already fully appears, was created by Congress as a means of carrying into operation legislative and judicial powers, and as an agency of the legislative and judicial departments.

In the light of the question now under consideration, we have reexamined the precedents referred to in the *Myers* case, and find nothing in them to justify a conclusion contrary to that which we have reached. The so-called "decision of 1789" had relation to a bill proposed by Mr. Madison to establish an executive Department of Foreign Affairs. . . . We shall not discuss the subject further, since it is so fully covered by the opinions in the *Myers* case, except to say that the office under consideration by Congress was not only purely executive, but the officer one who was responsible to the President, and to him alone, in a very definite sense. A reading of the debates shows that the President's illimitable power of removal was not considered in respect of other than executive officers. And it is pertinent to observe that when, at a later time, the tenure of office for the Comptroller of the Treasury was under consideration, Mr. Madison quite evidently thought that, since the duties of that office were not purely of an executive nature but partook of the judiciary quality as well, a different rule in respect of executive removal might well apply.

In *Marbury v. Madison*, it is made clear that Chief Justice Marshall was of opinion that a justice of the peace for the District of Columbia was not removable at the will of the President; and that there was a distinction between such an officer and officers appointed to aid the President in the performance of his constitutional duties. In the latter case, the distinction he saw was that "their acts are his acts" and his will, therefore, controls; and, by way of illustration, he adverted to the act establishing the Department of Foreign Affairs, which was the subject of the "decision of 1789."

The result of what we now have said is this: Whether the power of the President to remove an officer shall prevail over the authority of Congress to condition the power by fixing a definite term and precluding a removal except for cause will depend upon the character of the office; the *Myers* decision, affirming the power of the President alone to make the removal, is confined to purely executive officers; and as to officers of the kind here under consideration, we hold that no removal can be made during the prescribed term for which the officer is appointed, except for one or more of the causes named in the applicable statute.

To the extent that, between the decision in the *Myers* case, which sustains the unrestrictable power of the President to remove purely executive officers, and our present decision that such power does not extend to an office such as that here involved, there shall remain a field of doubt, we leave such cases as may fall within it for future consideration and determination as they may arise.

■ MR. JUSTICE MCREYNOLDS agrees [for reasons stated in his dissent] in *Myers v. United States.* . . .

NOTES

1. What kind of power did Humphrey exercise as an FTC commissioner: legislative power, judicial power, or executive power? Could it have been legislative power, since the Constitution vests all the granted legislative powers in Congress? Could it have been judicial power, since the Constitution vests all the judicial power in Article III judges? Is the conclusion inescapable that Humphrey exercised executive power? If so, does the Constitution require that he be under presidential control?

2. Can *Humphrey's Executor* be reconciled with *Myers*? If the president may remove a postmaster, does it follow that the president should be able to remove a policy-making official like Humphrey? Among the most important independent agencies today are the Federal Reserve Board and the Securities

and Exchange Commission. On January 20, 2009, when President Obama took office in the middle of a financial crisis, he did not inherit President George W. Bush's cabinet. But he *did* inherit President Bush's appointees to these two agencies, which were central to the government's response to the crisis. Does that make sense? As a presidential candidate, Obama had faulted the Bush administration for economic mismanagement and regulatory laxness. Should President Obama have been able to choose an entirely new financial regulatory team?

3. The strongest argument in *Humphrey's Executor* is that there are many quasi-judicial officials, including administrative law judges, who are technically executive branch officials but who in effect exercise judicial power. Think back to the Accounting Officers controversy. The Court in *Humphrey's Executor* says it doesn't want to politicize these offices. Are you persuaded? Or is the solution for Congress to give life tenure to executive officials who are exercising judicial power? Congress and the federal bench have both been reluctant to have the life-tenured Article III judiciary expanded.

Morrison v. Olson

487 U.S. 654 (1988) (Removal Issue)

■ CHIEF JUSTICE REHNQUIST delivered the opinion of the Court.

This case presents us with a challenge to the independent counsel provisions of the Ethics in Government Act of 1978. . . .

We now turn to consider whether the Act is invalid under the constitutional principle of separation of powers. Two related issues must be addressed: The first is whether the provision of the Act restricting the Attorney General's power to remove the independent counsel to only those instances in which he can show "good cause," taken by itself, impermissibly interferes with the President's exercise of his constitutionally appointed functions. The second is whether, taken as a whole, the Act violates the separation of powers by reducing the President's ability to control the prosecutorial powers wielded by the independent counsel.

Two Terms ago we had occasion to consider whether it was consistent with the separation of powers for Congress to pass a statute that authorized a Government official who is removable only by Congress to participate in what we found to be "executive powers." *Bowsher v. Synar,* 478 U.S. 714, 730 (1986). We held in *Bowsher* that "Congress cannot reserve for itself the power of removal of an officer charged with the execution of the laws except by impeachment." *Id.,* at 726. A primary antecedent for this ruling was our 1926 decision in *Myers v. United States,* 272 U.S. 52 (1926). . . .

Unlike both *Bowsher* and *Myers,* this case does not involve an attempt by Congress itself to gain a role in the removal of executive officials other than its established powers of impeachment and conviction. The Act instead puts the removal power squarely in the hands of the Executive Branch; an independent counsel may be removed from office, "only by the personal action of the Attorney General, and only for good cause." . . . There is no requirement of congressional approval of the Attorney General's removal decision, though the decision is subject to judicial review. . . . In our view, the removal provisions of the Act make this case more analogous to *Humphrey's Executor,* 295 U.S. 602 (1935), and *Wiener v. United States,* 357 U.S. 349 (1958), than to *Myers* or *Bowsher.* . . . In

Humphrey's Executor, the issue was whether a statute restricting the President's power to remove the Commissioners of the Federal Trade Commission (FTC) only for "inefficiency, neglect of duty, or malfeasance in office" was consistent with the Constitution. . . .

Appellees contend that *Humphrey's Executor* and *Wiener* are distinguishable from this case because they did not involve officials who performed a "core executive function." They argue that our decision in *Humphrey's Executor* rests on a distinction between "purely executive" officials and officials who exercise "quasi-legislative" and "quasi-judicial" powers. In their view, when a "purely executive" official is involved, the governing precedent is *Myers,* not *Humphrey's Executor.* See *Humphrey's Executor, supra,* 295 U.S., at 628. And, under *Myers,* the President must have absolute discretion to discharge "purely" executive officials at will. See *Myers,* 272 U.S., at 132–134. . . .

We undoubtedly did rely on the terms "quasi-legislative" and "quasi-judicial" to distinguish the officials involved in *Humphrey's Executor* and *Wiener* from those in *Myers,* but our present considered view is that the determination of whether the Constitution allows Congress to impose a "good cause"-type restriction on the President's power to remove an official cannot be made to turn on whether or not that official is classified as "purely executive." . . . The analysis contained in our removal cases is designed not to define rigid categories of those officials who may or may not be removed at will by the President, . . . but to ensure that Congress does not interfere with the President's exercise of the "executive power" and his constitutionally appointed duty to "take care that the laws be faithfully executed" under Article II. *Myers* was undoubtedly correct in its holding, and in its broader suggestion that there are some "purely executive" officials who must be removable by the President at will if he is to be able to accomplish his constitutional role.[29] See 272 U.S., at 132–134. But as the Court noted in *Wiener*:

> The assumption was short-lived that the *Myers* case recognized the President's inherent constitutional power to remove officials no matter what the relation of the executive to the discharge of their duties and no matter what restrictions Congress may have imposed regarding the nature of their tenure. . . . 357 U.S., at 352.

At the other end of the spectrum from *Myers,* the characterization of the agencies in *Humphrey's Executor* and *Wiener* as "quasi-legislative" or "quasi-judicial" in large part reflected our judgment that it was not essential to the President's proper execution of his Article II powers that these agencies be headed up by individuals who were removable at will. . . . We do not mean to suggest that an analysis of the functions served by the officials at issue is irrelevant. But the real question is whether the removal restrictions are of such a nature that they impede the President's ability to perform his constitutional duty, and the functions of the officials in question must be analyzed in that light.

---

[29] The dissent says that the language of Article II vesting the executive power of the United States in the President requires that every officer of the United States exercising any part of that power must serve at the pleasure of the President and be removable by him at will. Post, at 2626. This rigid demarcation—a demarcation incapable of being altered by law in the slightest degree, and applicable to tens of thousands of holders of offices neither known nor foreseen by the Framers—depends upon an extrapolation from general constitutional language which we think is more than the text will bear. It is also contrary to our holding in *United States v. Perkins,* decided more than a century ago.

Considering for the moment the "good cause" removal provision in isolation from the other parts of the Act at issue in this case, we cannot say that the imposition of a "good cause" standard for removal by itself unduly trammels on executive authority. There is no real dispute that the functions performed by the independent counsel are "executive" in the sense that they are law enforcement functions that typically have been undertaken by officials within the Executive Branch. . . . Although the counsel exercises no small amount of discretion and judgment in deciding how to carry out his or her duties under the Act, we simply do not see how the President's need to control the exercise of that discretion is so central to the functioning of the Executive Branch as to require as a matter of constitutional law that the counsel be terminable at will by the President. . . . We do not think that this limitation as it presently stands sufficiently deprives the President of control over the independent counsel to interfere impermissibly with his constitutional obligation to ensure the faithful execution of the laws. . . .

The final question to be addressed is whether the Act, taken as a whole, violates the principle of separation of powers by unduly interfering with the role of the Executive Branch. . . .

We observe first that this case does not involve an attempt by Congress to increase its own powers at the expense of the Executive Branch. . . . Unlike some of our previous cases, most recently *Bowsher v. Synar,* this case simply does not pose a "dange[r] of congressional usurpation of Executive Branch functions." . . . Indeed, with the exception of the power of impeachment—which applies to all officers of the United States—Congress retained for itself no powers of control or supervision over an independent counsel. The Act does empower certain Members of Congress to request the Attorney General to apply for the appointment of an independent counsel, but the Attorney General has no duty to comply with the request, although he must respond within a certain time limit. . . . Other than that, Congress' role under the Act is limited to receiving reports or other information and oversight of the independent counsel's activities . . . , functions that we have recognized generally as being incidental to the legislative function of Congress. See *McGrain v. Daugherty,* 273 U.S. 135, 174 (1927). . . .

Finally, we do not think that the Act "impermissibly undermine[s]" the powers of the Executive Branch . . . or "disrupts the proper balance between the coordinate branches [by] prevent [ing] the Executive Branch from accomplishing its constitutionally assigned functions," *Nixon v. Administrator of General Services,* . . . 433 U.S., at 443. It is undeniable that the Act reduces the amount of control or supervision that the Attorney General and, through him, the President exercises over the investigation and prosecution of a certain class of alleged criminal activity. The Attorney General is not allowed to appoint the individual of his choice; he does not determine the counsel's jurisdiction; and his power to remove a counsel is limited. . . . Nonetheless, the Act does give the Attorney General several means of supervising or controlling the prosecutorial powers that may be wielded by an independent counsel. Most importantly, the Attorney General retains the power to remove the counsel for "good cause," a power that we have already concluded provides the Executive with substantial ability to ensure that the laws are "faithfully executed" by an independent counsel. No independent counsel may be appointed without a specific request by the Attorney General, and the Attorney General's decision not to request appointment if he finds "no reasonable grounds to believe that further investigation is warranted" is committed to his unreviewable discretion. The Act thus gives the Executive a degree of control over the power to initiate an investigation by the independent counsel. In addition, the jurisdiction of the independent counsel is defined with reference to the facts submitted by the Attorney General, and once a counsel is appointed, the Act requires that the counsel abide by Justice Department policy unless it is not "possible" to do so. Notwithstanding the fact that the counsel is to some degree "independent" and free from executive supervision to a greater extent than other federal prosecutors, in our view these features of the Act give the Executive Branch sufficient control over the independent counsel to ensure that the President is able to perform his constitutionally assigned duties. . . .

■ JUSTICE KENNEDY took no part in the consideration or decision of this case.

■ JUSTICE SCALIA, dissenting.

It is the proud boast of our democracy that we have "a government of laws and not of men." Many Americans are familiar with that phrase; not many know its derivation. It comes from Part the First, Article XXX, of the Massachusetts Constitution of 1780, which reads in full as follows:

> In the government of this Commonwealth, the legislative department shall never exercise the executive and judicial powers, or either of them: The executive shall never exercise the legislative and judicial powers, or either of them: The judicial shall never exercise the legislative and executive powers, or either of them: to the end it may be a government of laws and not of men.

The framers of the Federal Constitution similarly viewed the principle of separation of powers as the absolutely central guarantee of a just Government. In *No. 47* of *The Federalist*, Madison wrote that "[n]o political truth is certainly of greater intrinsic value, or is stamped with the authority of more enlightened patrons of liberty." *The Federalist No. 47*, p. 301 (C. Rossiter ed. 1961) (hereinafter Federalist). Without a secure structure of separated powers, our Bill of Rights would be worthless, as are the bills of rights of many nations of the world that have adopted, or even improved upon, the mere words of ours. . . . The principle of separation of powers is expressed in our Constitution in the first section of each of the first three Articles.

[T]his suit is about . . . [p]ower. The allocation of power among Congress, the President, and the courts in such fashion as to preserve the equilibrium the Constitution sought to establish—so that "a gradual concentration of the several powers in the same department," Federalist No. 51, p. 321 (J. Madison), can effectively be resisted. Frequently an issue of this sort will come before the Court clad, so to speak, in sheep's clothing: the potential of the asserted principle to effect important change in the equilibrium of power is not immediately evident, and must be discerned by a careful and perceptive analysis. But this wolf comes as a wolf. . . .

If to describe this case is not to decide it, the concept of a government of separate and coordinate powers no longer has meaning. The Court devotes most of its attention to such relatively technical details as the Appointments Clause and the removal power, addressing briefly and only at the end of its opinion the separation of powers. . . . I think that has it backwards. Our opinions are full of the recognition that it is the principle of separation of powers, and the inseparable corollary that each department's "defense must . . . be made commensurate to the danger of attack," *Federalist No. 51*, p. 322 (J. Madison), which gives comprehensible content to . . . and determines the appropriate scope of the removal power. Thus, while I will subsequently discuss why our appointments and removal jurisprudence does not support today's holding, I begin with a consideration of the fountainhead of that jurisprudence, the separation and equilibration of powers. . . .

Article II, § 1, cl. 1, of the Constitution provides:

The executive Power shall be vested in a President of the United States.

As I described at the outset of this opinion, this does not mean *some of* the executive power, but *all of* the executive power. It seems to me, therefore, that the decision of the Court of Appeals invalidating the present statute must be upheld on fundamental separation-of-powers principles if the following two questions are answered affirmatively: (1) Is the conduct of a criminal prosecution (and of an investigation to decide whether to prosecute) the exercise of purely executive power? (2) Does the statute deprive the President of the United States of exclusive control over the exercise of that power? Surprising to say, the Court appears to concede an affirmative answer to both questions, but seeks to avoid the inevitable conclusion that since the statute vests some purely executive power in a person who is not the President of the United States it is void.

The Court concedes that "[t]here is no real dispute that the functions performed by the independent counsel are 'executive,' " though it qualifies that concession by adding "in the sense that they are law enforcement functions that typically have been undertaken by officials within the Executive Branch." . . . The qualifier adds nothing but atmosphere. In what *other* sense can one identify "the executive Power" that is supposed to be vested in the President (unless it includes everything the Executive Branch is given to do) *except* by reference to what has always and everywhere—if conducted by government at all—been conducted never by the legislature, never by the courts, and always by the executive. There is no possible doubt that the independent counsel's functions fit this description. She is vested with the "full power and independent authority to exercise all *investigative and prosecutorial* functions and powers of the Department of Justice [and] the Attorney General." 28 U.S.C. § 594(a) (1982 ed., Supp. V) (emphasis added). Governmental investigation and prosecution of crimes is a quintessentially executive function. . . .

As for the second question, whether the statute before us deprives the President of exclusive control over that quintessentially executive activity: The Court does not, and could not possibly, assert that it does not. That is indeed the whole object of the statute. Instead, the Court points out that the President, through his Attorney General, has at least *some* control. That concession is alone enough to invalidate the statute, but I cannot refrain from pointing out that the Court greatly exaggerates the extent of that "some" Presidential control. "Most importan[t]" among these controls, the Court asserts, is the Attorney General's "power to remove the counsel for good cause." . . . This is somewhat like referring to shackles as an effective means of locomotion. . . . What we in *Humphrey's Executor* found to be a means of eliminating Presidential control, the Court today considers the "most importan[t]" means of assuring Presidential control. Congress, of course, operated under no such illusion when it enacted this statute, describing the "good cause" limitation as "protecting the independent counsel's ability to act independently of the President's direct control" since it permits removal only for "misconduct." . . .

Moving on to the presumably "less important" controls that the President retains, the Court notes that no independent counsel may be appointed without a specific request from the Attorney General. . . . [T]he condition that renders such a request mandatory (inability to find "no reasonable grounds to believe" that further investigation is warranted) is so insubstantial that the Attorney General's discretion is severely confined. And once the referral is made, it is for the Special Division to determine the scope and duration of the investigation. . . . And in any event, the limited power over referral is irrelevant to the question whether, *once appointed,* the independent counsel exercises executive power free from the President's control. Finally, the Court points out that the Act directs the independent counsel to abide by general Justice Department policy, except when not "possible." . . . The exception alone shows this to be an empty promise. Even without that, however, one would be hard put to come up with many investigative or prosecutorial "policies" (other than those imposed by the Constitution or by Congress through law) that are absolute. Almost all investigative and prosecutorial decisions including the ultimate decision whether, after a technical violation of the law has been found, prosecution is warranted—involve the balancing of innumerable legal and practical considerations. Indeed, even political considerations (in the nonpartisan sense) must be considered, as exemplified by the recent decision of an independent counsel to subpoena the former Ambassador of Canada, producing considerable tension in our relations with that country. . . . Another preeminently political decision is whether getting a conviction in a particular case is worth the disclosure of national security information that would be necessary. The Justice Department and our intelligence agencies are often in disagreement on this point, and the Justice Department does not always win. The present Act even goes so far as specifically to take the resolution of that dispute away from the President and give it to the independent counsel. . . . In sum, the balancing of various legal, practical, and political considerations, none of which is absolute, is the very essence of prosecutorial discretion. To take this away is to remove the core of the prosecutorial function, and not merely "some" Presidential control.

As I have said, however, it is ultimately irrelevant *how much* the statute reduces Presidential control. The case is over when the Court acknowledges, as it must, that "[i]t is undeniable that the Act reduces the amount of control or supervision that the Attorney General and, through him, the President exercises over the investigation and prosecution of a certain class of alleged criminal activity." . . . It effects a revolution in our constitutional jurisprudence for the Court, once it has determined that (1) purely executive functions are at issue here, and (2) those functions have been given to a person whose actions are not fully within the supervision and control of the President, nonetheless to proceed further to sit in judgment of whether "the President's need to control the exercise of [the independent counsel's] discretion is *so central* to the functioning of the Executive Branch" as to require complete control, . . . (emphasis added), whether the conferral of his powers upon someone else "*sufficiently* deprives the President of control over the independent counsel to interfere impermissibly with [his] constitutional obligation to ensure the faithful execution of the laws," . . . (emphasis added), and whether "the Act give[s] the Executive Branch *sufficient* control over the independent counsel to ensure that the President is able to perform his constitutionally assigned duties," . . . (emphasis added). It is not for us to determine, and we have never presumed to determine, how much of the purely executive powers of government must be within the full control of the President. The Constitution prescribes that they *all* are. . . .

. . . We should say here that the President's constitutionally assigned duties include *complete* control over investigation and prosecution of violations of the law, and that the inexorable command of Article II is clear and definite: the executive power must be vested in the President of the United States. . . . Is it unthinkable that the President should have such exclusive power, even when alleged crimes by him or his close associates are at issue? No more so than that Congress should have the exclusive power of legislation, even when what is at issue is its own exemption from the burdens of certain laws. . . . No more so than that this Court should have the exclusive power to pronounce the final decision on justiciable cases and controversies, even those pertaining to the constitutionality of a statute reducing the salaries of the Justices. . . . A system of separate and coordinate powers necessarily involves an acceptance of exclusive power that can theoretically be abused. . . . While the separation of powers may prevent us from righting every wrong, it does so in order to ensure that we do not lose liberty. The checks against any branch's abuse of its exclusive powers are twofold: First, retaliation by one of the other branch's use of *its* exclusive powers: Congress, for example, can impeach the executive who willfully fails to enforce the laws; the executive can decline to prosecute under unconstitutional statutes . . .; and the courts can dismiss malicious prosecutions. Second, and ultimately, there is the political check that the people will replace those in the political branches (the branches more "dangerous to the political rights of the Constitution," Federalist No. 78, p. 465) who are guilty of abuse. Political pressures produced special prosecutors—for Teapot Dome and for Watergate, for example—long before this statute created the independent counsel. . . .

The Court has, nonetheless, replaced the clear constitutional prescription that the executive power belongs to the President with a "balancing test." What are the standards to determine how the balance is to be struck, that is, how much removal of Presidential power is too much? Many countries of the world get along with an executive that is much weaker than ours—in fact, entirely dependent upon the continued support of the legislature. Once we depart from the text of the Constitution, just where short of that do we stop? The most amazing feature of the Court's opinion is that it does not even purport to give an answer. It simply *announces,* with no analysis, that the ability to control the decision whether to investigate and prosecute the President's closest advisers, and indeed the President himself, is not "so central to the functioning of the Executive Branch" as to be constitutionally required to be within the President's control. Apparently that is so because we say it is so. Having abandoned as the basis for our decision-making the text of Article II that "the executive Power" must be vested in the President, the Court does not even attempt to craft a *substitute* criterion—a "justiciable standard," . . . however remote from the Constitution—that today governs, and in the future will govern, the decision of such questions. Evidently, the governing standard is to be what might be called the unfettered wisdom of a majority of this Court, revealed to an obedient people on a case-by-case basis. This is not only not the government of laws that the Constitution established; it is not a government of laws at all.

In my view, moreover, even as an ad hoc, standardless judgment the Court's conclusion must be wrong. Before this statute was passed, the President, in taking action disagreeable to the Congress, or an executive officer giving advice to the President or testifying before Congress concerning one of those many matters on which the two branches are from time to time at odds, could be assured that his acts and motives would be adjudged—insofar as the decision whether to conduct a criminal investigation and to prosecute is concerned—in the Executive Branch, that is, in a forum attuned to the interests and the policies of the Presidency. That was one of the natural advantages the Constitution gave to the Presidency, just as it gave Members of Congress (and their staffs) the advantage of not being prosecutable for anything said or done in their legislative capacities. See U.S. Const., Art. I, § 6, cl. 1; *Gravel v. United States,* 408 U.S. 606 (1972). It is the very object of this legislation to eliminate that assurance of a sympathetic forum. Unless it can honestly be said that there are "no reasonable grounds to believe" that further investigation is warranted, further investigation must ensue; and the conduct of the investigation, and determination of whether to prosecute, will be given to a person neither selected by nor subject to the control of the President—who will in turn assemble a staff by finding out, presumably, who is willing to put aside whatever else they are doing, for an indeterminate period of time, in order to investigate and prosecute the President or a particular named individual in his administration. The prospect is frightening ... even outside the context of a bitter, interbranch political dispute. Perhaps the boldness of the President himself will not be affected—though I am not even sure of that. (How much easier it is for Congress, instead of accepting the political damage attendant to the commencement of impeachment proceedings against the President on trivial grounds—or, for that matter, how easy it is for one of the President's political foes outside of Congress—simply to trigger a debilitating criminal investigation of the Chief Executive under this law.) But as for the President's high-level assistants, who typically have no political base of support, it is as utterly unrealistic to think that they will not be intimidated by this prospect, and that their advice to him and their advocacy of his interests before a hostile Congress will not be affected, as it would be to think that the Members of Congress and their staffs would be unaffected by replacing the Speech or Debate Clause with a similar provision. It deeply wounds the President, by substantially reducing the President's ability to protect himself and his staff. That is the whole object of the law, of course, and I cannot imagine why the Court believes it does not succeed.

Besides weakening the Presidency by reducing the zeal of his staff, it must also be obvious that the institution of the independent counsel enfeebles him more directly in his constant confrontations with Congress, by eroding his public support. Nothing is so politically effective as the ability to charge that one's opponent and his associates are not merely wrongheaded, naive, ineffective, but, in all probability, "crooks." And nothing so effectively gives an appearance of validity to such charges as a Justice Department investigation and, even better, prosecution. The present statute provides ample means for that sort of attack, assuring that massive and lengthy investigations will occur, not merely when the Justice Department in the application of its usual standards believes they are called for, but whenever it cannot be said that there are "no reasonable grounds to believe" they are called for. The statute's highly visible procedures assure, moreover, that unlike most investigations these will be widely known and prominently displayed. Thus, in the 10 years since the institution of the independent counsel was established by law, there have been nine highly publicized investigations, a source of constant political damage to two administrations. That they could not remotely be described as merely the application of "normal" investigatory and prosecutory standards is demonstrated by, in addition to the language of the statute ("no reasonable grounds to believe"), the following facts: Congress appropriates approximately $50 million annually for general legal activities, salaries, and expenses of the Criminal Division of the Department of Justice. . . . This money is used to support "[f]ederal appellate activity," "[o]rganized crime prosecution," "[p]ublic integrity" and "[f]raud" matters, "[n]arcotic & dangerous drug prosecution," "[i]nternal security," "[g]eneral litigation and legal advice," "special investigations," "[p]rosecution support," "[o]rganized crime drug enforcement," and "[m]anagement & administration." *Id.,* at 284. By comparison, between May 1986 and August 1987, four independent counsel (not all of whom were operating for that entire period of time) spent almost $5 million (1/10th of the amount annually appropriated to the entire Criminal Division), spending almost $1 million in the month of August 1987 alone. . . . For fiscal year 1989, the Department of Justice has requested $52 million for the entire Criminal Division, DOJ Budget Request 285, and $7 million to support the activities of independent counsel, *id.,* at 25.

In sum, this statute does deprive the President of substantial control over the prosecutory functions performed by the independent counsel, and it does substantially affect the balance of powers. That the Court could possibly conclude otherwise demonstrates both the wisdom of our former constitutional system, in which the degree of reduced control and political impairment were irrelevant, since *all* purely executive power had to be in the President; and the folly of the new system of standardless judicial allocation of powers we adopt today. . . .

There is, of course, no provision in the Constitution stating who may remove executive officers, except the provisions for removal by impeachment. Before the present decision it was established, however, . . . that the President's power to remove principal officers who exercise purely executive powers could not be restricted, see *Myers v. United States,* 272 U.S. 52, 127 (1926). . . . [In] our 1935 decision in *Humphrey's Executor v. United States,* 295 U.S. 602—which was considered by many at the time the product of an activist, anti-New Deal Court bent on reducing the power of President Franklin Roosevelt—it [was further] established that the line of permissible restriction upon removal of principal officers lies at the point at which the powers exercised by those officers are no longer purely executive. Thus, removal restrictions have been generally regarded as lawful for so-called "independent regulatory agencies," such as the Federal Trade Commission, . . . the Interstate Commerce Commission, . . . and the Consumer Product Safety Commission, . . . which engage substantially in what has been called the "quasi-legislative activity" of rulemaking, and for members of Article I courts, such as the Court of Military Appeals, . . . who engage in the "quasi-judicial" function of adjudication. It has often been observed, correctly in my view, that the line between "purely executive" functions and "quasi-legislative" or "quasi-judicial" functions is not a clear one or even a rational one. . . . But at least it permitted the identification of certain officers, and certain agencies, whose functions were entirely within the control of the President. Congress had to be aware of that restriction in its legislation. Today, however, *Humphrey's Executor* is swept into the dustbin of repudiated constitutional principles. . . .

One can hardly grieve for the shoddy treatment given today to *Humphrey's Executor,* which, after all, accorded the same indignity (with much less justification) to Chief Justice Taft's opinion 10 years earlier in *Myers v. United States,* 272 U.S. 52 (1926)—gutting, in six quick pages devoid of textual or historical precedent for the novel principle it set forth, a carefully researched and reasoned 70–page opinion. It is in fact comforting to witness the reality that he who lives by the *ipse dixit* dies by the *ipse dixit.* But one must grieve for the Constitution. *Humphrey's Executor* at least had the decency formally to observe the constitutional principle that the President had to be the repository of *all* executive power, see 295 U.S., at 627–628, which, as *Myers* carefully explained, necessarily means that he must be able to discharge those who do not perform executive functions according to his liking. . . . By contrast, "our present considered view" is simply that *any* executive officer's removal can be restricted, so long as the President remains "able to accomplish his constitutional role." . . . There are now no lines. If the removal of a prosecutor, the virtual embodiment of the power to "take care that the laws be faithfully executed," can be restricted, what officer's removal cannot? This is an open invitation for Congress to experiment. What about a special Assistant Secretary of State, with responsibility for one very narrow area of foreign policy, who would not only have to be confirmed by the Senate but could also be removed only pursuant to certain carefully designed restrictions? Could this possibly render the President "[un]able to accomplish his constitutional role"? Or a special Assistant Secretary of Defense for Procurement? The possibilities are endless, and the Court does not understand what the separation of powers, what "[a]mbition . . . counteract [ing] ambition," Federalist No. 51, p. 322 (Madison), is all about, if it does not expect Congress to try them. As far as I can discern from the Court's opinion, it is now open season upon the President's removal power for all executive officers, with not even the superficially principled restriction of *Humphrey's Executor* as cover. The Court essentially says to the President: "Trust us. We will make sure that you are able to accomplish your constitutional role." I think the Constitution gives the President—and the people—more protection than that. . . .

The purpose of the separation and equilibration of powers in general, and of the unitary Executive in particular, was not merely to assure effective government but to preserve individual freedom. Those who hold or have held offices covered by the Ethics in Government Act are entitled to that protection as much as the rest of us, and I conclude my discussion by considering the effect of the Act upon the fairness of the process they receive.

Only someone who has worked in the field of law enforcement can fully appreciate the vast power and the immense discretion that are placed in the hands of a prosecutor with respect to the objects of his investigation. Justice Robert Jackson, when he was Attorney General under President Franklin Roosevelt, described it in a memorable speech to United States Attorneys. . . . Under our system of government, the primary check against prosecutorial abuse is a political one. The prosecutors who exercise this awesome discretion are selected and can be removed by a President, whom the people have trusted enough to elect. Moreover, when crimes are not investigated and prosecuted fairly, nonselectively, with a reasonable sense of proportion, the President pays the cost in political damage to his administration. If federal prosecutors "pick people that [they] thin[k] [they] should get, rather than cases that need to be prosecuted," if they amass many more resources against a particular prominent individual, or against a particular class of political protesters, or against members of a particular political party, than the gravity of the alleged offenses or the record of successful prosecutions seems to warrant, the unfairness will come home to roost in the Oval Office. . . .

That is the system of justice the rest of us are entitled to, but what of that select class consisting of present or former high-level Executive Branch officials? . . . What if [politically partisan judges choose a likeminded independent counsel?] There is no remedy for that, not even a political one. Judges, after all, have life tenure, and appointing a surefire enthusiastic prosecutor could hardly be considered an impeachable offense. So if there is anything wrong with the selection, there is effectively no one to blame. The independent counsel thus selected proceeds to assemble a staff. As I observed earlier, in the nature of things this has to be done by finding lawyers who are willing to lay aside their current careers for an indeterminate amount of time, to take on a job that has no prospect of permanence and little prospect for promotion. One thing is certain, however: it involves investigating and perhaps prosecuting a particular individual. Can one imagine a less equitable manner of fulfilling the executive responsibility to investigate and prosecute? What would be the reaction if, in an area not covered by this statute, the Justice Department posted a public notice inviting applicants to assist in an investigation and possible prosecution of a certain prominent person? . . . [And] even if it were entirely evident that unfairness was in fact the result—the judges hostile to the administration, the independent counsel an old foe of the President, the staff refugees from the recently defeated administration—*there would be no one accountable to the public to whom the blame could be assigned.* . . .

[A]n additional advantage of the unitary Executive [is] that it can achieve a more uniform application of the law. Perhaps that is not always achieved, but the mechanism to achieve it is there. The mini-Executive that is the independent counsel, however, operating in an area where so little is law and so much is discretion, is intentionally cut off from the unifying influence of the Justice Department, and from the perspective that multiple responsibilities provide. What would normally be regarded as a technical violation (there are no rules defining such things), may in his or her small world assume the proportions of an indictable offense. What would normally be regarded as an investigation that has reached the level of pursuing such picayune matters that it should be concluded, may to him or her be an investigation that ought to go on for another year. How frightening it must be to have your own independent counsel and staff appointed, with nothing else to do but to investigate you until investigation is no longer worthwhile—with whether it is worthwhile not depending upon what such judgments usually hinge on, competing responsibilities. And to have that counsel and staff decide, with no basis for comparison, whether what you have done is bad enough, willful enough, and provable enough, to warrant an indictment. How admirable the constitutional system that provides the means to avoid such a distortion. And how unfortunate the judicial decision that has permitted it. . . .

The notion that every violation of law should be prosecuted, including—indeed, *especially*—every violation by those in high places, is an attractive one, and it would be risky to argue in an election campaign that that is not an absolutely overriding value. *Fiat justitia, ruat coelum.* Let justice be done, though the heavens may fall. The reality is, however, that it is not an absolutely overriding value, and it was with the hope that we would be able to acknowledge and apply such realities that the Constitution spared us, by life tenure, the necessity of election campaigns. . . . By its shortsighted action today, I fear the Court has permanently encumbered the Republic with an institution that will do it great harm.

Worse than what it has done, however, is the manner in which it has done it. A government of laws means a government of rules. Today's decision on the basic issue of fragmentation of executive power is ungoverned by rule, and hence ungoverned by law. It extends into the very heart of our most significant constitutional function the "totality of the circumstances" mode of analysis that this Court has in recent years become fond of. Taking all things into account, we conclude that the power taken away from the President here is not really *too* much. The next time executive power is assigned to someone other than the President we may conclude, taking all things into account, that it *is* too much. That opinion, like this one, will not be confined by any rule. . . .

The ad hoc approach to constitutional adjudication has real attraction, even apart from its work-saving potential. It is guaranteed to produce a result, in every case, that will make a majority of the Court happy with the law. The law is, by definition, precisely what the majority thinks, taking all things into account, it *ought* to be. I prefer to rely upon the judgment of the wise men who constructed our system, and of the people who approved it, and of two centuries of history that have shown it to be sound. Like it or not, that judgment says, quite plainly, that "[t]he executive Power shall be vested in a President of the United States."

NOTES

1. How should the problem of high-level executive branch malfeasance be addressed? Note that although in England impeachment was used almost exclusively against high-level executive officials, it has been never been used in the United States to try to force the resignation of a cabinet secretary or undersecretary. Even though two presidents and over a dozen federal judges have been impeached, none of the various cabinet officers who have eventually been convicted of felonies committed while they were in office were ever impeached. Should the House of Representatives set up a special committee on impeachments with a large staff of highly trained public integrity prosecutors to investigate with House subpoenas any evidence of cabinet-level or White House "high crimes and misdemeanors"? Is the House of Representatives shy about using its impeachment power? If so, why?

2. The majority in *Morrison v. Olson* says that Congress was not aggrandizing power to itself when it authorized an independent counsel because the counsel did not work for or report to Congress. As Justice Scalia's dissent notes, however, Congress did pay for these investigations. And it was the members of a House committee who launched the investigation into Olson. Who has the better of the argument, the majority or the dissent?

3. Is the authorization of a independent counsel to investigate one named person a bill of attainder?

4. The most recent major case on the removal power is *Free Enterprise Fund v. Public Co. Accounting Oversight Bd.*, 130 S. Ct. 3138 (2010), in which the Court considered the constitutionality of the removal limitation in the statute establishing the Public Company Accounting Oversight Board. The PCAOB

was created in the wake of accounting scandals at major public companies such as Enron and WorldCom. Its board was subject to two layers of protection against presidential removal: the Securities and Exchange Commission is an independent agency whose commissioners can be removed by the president only for cause; the members of the PCAOB could be removed by the Securities and Exchange Commission, again only for cause. Writing for the majority, Chief Justice Roberts summed up the Court's jurisprudence on the removal power this way. *Myers* states the principle that the president may remove executive branch officers, but *Humphrey's Executor* and *Morrison* limit this principle: *Humphrey's Executor* by allowing Congress to create independent agencies with principal officers the president can remove only for cause, and *Morrison* by allowing Congress to restrict the power of principal officers to remove *their* subordinates. The question in *Free Enterprise Fund*, Chief Justice Roberts said, was whether the "separate layers of protection" in *Humphrey's Executor* and *Morrison* "may be combined." In other words, "[m]ay the President be restricted in his ability to remove a principal officer, who is in turn restricted in his ability to remove an inferior officer, even though that inferior officer determines the policy and enforces the laws of the United States?" The Court held that this kind of double-layer insulation from removal violated Article II's assignment to the president of the executive power, because it could prevent the president from "tak[ing] Care that the Laws be faithfully executed." The Court severed the for-cause removal provision from the rest of the statute, leaving the PCAOB in place (and not invalidating all of its earlier acts). Although the Court chose not to extend *Humphrey's Executor* and *Morrison*, it did not reconsider them (noting pointedly that it had not been asked to by the parties).

Writing in dissent for himself and three other justices, Justice Breyer emphasized that both the president and Congress wanted the PCAOB structured in this way. And he argued that the double-layer insulation was not in practical effect any more of a limitation on presidential powers than a single layer of insulation from removal. Like the majority in *Morrison*, the dissenting justices in *PCAOB* were convinced that Congress had not limited presidential removal power in order to aggrandize its own power—and in their view only self-aggrandizing congressional restrictions on presidential removal were unconstitutional. Does double-layer insulation from presidential removal seem any different to you, as a constitutional matter, than single-layer insulation? How should the Court decide a question like that? Which of the types of constitutional argument, or modes of interpretation, are most useful? Does it matter whether the limitation on presidential removal is an aggrandizement of congressional power? Is *every* decrease in presidential power over an agency automatically an increase in congressional power over the same agency? And what does this line of cases—*Myers, Humphrey's Executor, Morrison*, and *Free Enterprise Fund*—suggest about the constitutional status of political accountability? Under the Constitution, must every government official be subject to control by an elected representative of the people? If so, how tight must this control be? Is this kind of accountability to the people always a good thing? If it can be a bad thing, is it a necessary evil?

[Assignment 21]

E. EXECUTIVE POWER AND FOREIGN AFFAIRS: "HE SHALL HAVE POWER, BY AND WITH THE ADVICE AND CONSENT OF THE SENATE, TO MAKE TREATIES"

Article II, Section 2: The President shall be Commander in Chief of the Army and Navy of the United States, and of the Militia of the several States, when called into the actual Service of the United States. . . . He shall have Power, by and with the Advice and Consent of the Senate, to make Treaties, provided two thirds of the Senators present concur; and he shall nominate, and by and with the Advice and Consent of the Senate, shall appoint Ambassadors, other public Ministers and Consuls, Judges of the supreme Court, and all other Officers of the United States, whose Appointments are not herein otherwise provided for. . . .

Section 3: . . . he shall receive Ambassadors and other public Ministers. . . .

Where does the Constitution assign the power of foreign affairs? It is widely taken for granted that the foreign affairs power is the president's, at least in the main. Why might that be so? No single clause of the Constitution specifically assigns a "foreign affairs power." The text does vest the "executive Power" in the president, and there is at least some strong historical basis for concluding that the public understanding of "executive Power" at the time the Constitution was adopted included a comprehensive, general power over foreign affairs—including all the powers of war, peace, treaties, and alliances. (More on that historical understanding presently.)

If this is correct—if the vesting of the "executive Power" is in effect the general grant of foreign affairs powers to the president, what is the significance of the other provisions of the Constitution that discuss foreign affairs? The clause giving the president the power to make treaties with the concurrence of two thirds of the Senate is not the *source* of the foreign affairs power of the president but a *limitation* on it—a check on the president's ability to make a treaty obligation that would have the force of U.S. domestic law. Similarly, the power to appoint ambassadors subject to the Senate's consent operates as a check on, rather than the source of, the executive's power over foreign affairs. Most significantly of all, Article I, Section 8's grant of the power to declare war to Congress relocates what historically might have been understood as an executive power (in a monarchy) to the legislative branch. And the Commander-in-Chief Clause is a necessary clarification that, even though Congress has the power to declare war, the president retains the traditional executive power to conduct war. Does this view make sense of the entire constitutional text? Is it a sound exposition of its structure? If not, is there an alternative basis for the assumption that the power over foreign affairs belongs primarily to the president?

The historical background of the foreign affairs powers may assist you in answering these questions. Under the Articles of Confederation, all powers of the Union were vested in the Congress because there essentially was no executive. Eventually, the Articles Congress created several departments that appeared to be executive in nature—Finance, Foreign Affairs, Marine, etc.—but these were for administrative convenience. They were subordinate to Congress and had no independent constitutional status. The Virginia Plan, the blueprint on which the deliberations at the Constitutional Convention were based, called for creation of an executive that was independent of Congress but chosen by it. The Virginia Plan provided that "the National Legislature ought to be impowered to enjoy the Legislative Rights vested in Congress by the Confederation" and that the "National Executive . . . ought to enjoy the Executive rights vested in Congress by the Confederation." 1 Farrand 21 (May 29, 1787). This suggests that the terms "Legislative" and "Executive" were substantive rather than mere descriptions of the powers that happened to be allocated to one branch or the other.

June 1, 1787, was the second day that the Constitutional Convention discussed the meaning of these general points. After the resolution concerning the executive was read, Charles Pinckney of South Carolina made the first remark, as recounted in Madison's Notes: "Mr. Pinkney was for a vigorous Executive but was afraid the Executive powers of [the existing] Congress might extend to peace & war [etc.] which would render the Executive a Monarchy, of the worst kind, to wit an elective one." 1 Farrand 64–65 (June 1) (first set of brackets in original). John Rutledge agreed that "he was for vesting the Executive power in a single person, tho' he was not for giving him the power of war and peace." *Id.* at 65.

The delegates may have assumed that the "Executive rights" under the Articles included those of "war and peace" because English constitutional practice gave the monarch power to declare war, to make war, to send and receive ambassadors, to make treaties, and to raise and deploy armies and navies (though Parliament held the purse strings and limited standing armies), as well as command of the army and navy. See William Blackstone, COMMENTARIES ON THE LAWS OF ENGLAND 1:250–280, 334, 408–421; 4:394–402. According to Madison's Notes, James Wilson disagreed: "He did not consider the Prerogatives of the British Monarch as a proper guide in defining the Executive powers. Some of these prerogatives were of a Legislative nature. Among others that of war & peace & c. The only powers he conceived strictly Executive were those of executing the laws, and appointing officers." 1 Farrand 65–66 (June 1). Still others in the framing generation were influenced by John Locke's taxonomy of powers. Instead of our familiar tripartite division of powers as legislative, executive, or judicial, Locke divided them into legislative, executive, and "federative" (regarding judicial powers as a sub-branch of the executive). See John Locke, SECOND TREATISE OF GOVERNMENT, ch. XII, at 82–84 (T. Peardon, ed. 1952) [1690]. Federative powers included "the power of war and peace, leagues and alliances, and all the transactions with all persons and communities without the commonwealth." Yet even Locke noted that "[t]hese two powers, executive and federative, though they be really distinct in themselves, . . . yet they are almost always united" in the executive. This is because the "security and interest" of the nation in external relations are "much less capable to be directed by antecedent, standing, positive laws than [by] the executive" and must be "left to the prudence of those who have this power committed to them."

The delegates to the Convention made several significant decisions with respect to the general principles outlined in the Virginia Plan regarding the foreign affairs power. First, they assigned many of the specific powers relating to war and peace explicitly to one branch or the other. Congress was given the powers to regulate commerce with foreign nations, to "define and punish . . . Offenses against the Law of Nations," to "declare war," to raise and support armies and navies, and to "provide for organizing and calling forth the militia." It also received the power to make laws "necessary and proper" for "carrying into Execution" not only its own powers but those vested in the executive and judiciary. The president was made the commander in chief of the military and was assigned the power to make treaties, the power to appoint ambassadors, and the duty to "receive Ambassadors and other public Ministers." And, as noted, two of the powers vested in the president were made subject to the advice and consent of the Senate (majority approval for appointments and two-thirds approval for treaties). Finally, the initial allocation formula of the Virginia Plan was retained, but with a significant tweak: in Article I, Section 1, Congress was vested with "[a]ll legislative Powers herein granted"; while in Article II, Section 1, the president was vested with "the executive Power"—without express limitation to the subsequent enumeration. What could be the significance of that difference?

We postpone until the next assignment the perennial issues of the Constitution's allocation of war powers between Congress and the president. What follows here are three cases and a famous attorney general opinion on the scope of and justification for the president's presumed constitutional foreign affairs power: *United States v. Curtiss–Wright* (1936) rested the foreign affairs power in general notions of sovereignty and located that power in the president, largely on the basis of tradition and practicality. Attorney General Robert Jackson (later Justice Jackson) wrote an opinion letter, a year before the entry of the United States into World War II, that upheld the propriety of an executive agreement to supply the United Kingdom with aging destroyers (a kind of small fast warship). *Dames & Moore v. Regan* (1980) upheld the domestic law effect of President Carter's executive agreement securing the release of U.S. citizens held hostage in Iran, partially in exchange for relinquishing U.S. companies' claims against Iranian assets seized in the United States. Finally, *Goldwater v. Carter* (1979) is a case from the D.C. Circuit Court of Appeals on the scope of the president's power to make—and even unmake—treaties. The D.C. Circuit upheld President Carter's unilateral power to terminate a mutual defense treaty with Taiwan. (The case reached the Supreme Court but was not decided on the merits.)

United States v. Curtiss–Wright
Export Corporation
299 U.S. 304 (1936)

■ MR. JUSTICE SUTHERLAND delivered the opinion of the Court.

On January 27, 1936, an indictment was returned in the court below, the first count of which charges that appellees, beginning with the 29th day of May, 1934, conspired to sell in the United States certain arms of war, namely, fifteen machine guns, to Bolivia, a country then engaged in armed conflict in the Chaco, in violation of the Joint Resolution of Congress approved May 28, 1934, and the provisions of a proclamation issued on the same day by the President of the United States pursuant to authority conferred by section 1 of the resolution. . . .

Whether, if the Joint Resolution had related solely to internal affairs, it would be open to the challenge that it constituted an unlawful delegation of legislative power to the Executive, we find it unnecessary to determine. The whole aim of the resolution is to affect a situation entirely external to the United States, and falling within the category of foreign affairs. . . . In other words, assuming (but not deciding) that the challenged delegation, if it were confined to internal affairs, would be invalid, may it nevertheless be sustained on the ground that its exclusive aim is to afford a remedy for a hurtful condition within foreign territory?

It will contribute to the elucidation of the question if we first consider the differences between the powers of the federal government in respect of foreign or external affairs and those in respect of domestic or internal affairs. That there are differences between them, and that these differences are fundamental, may not be doubted.

The two classes of powers are different, both in respect of their origin and their nature. The broad statement that the federal government can exercise no powers except those specifically enumerated in the Constitution, and such implied powers as are necessary and proper to carry into effect the enumerated powers, is categorically true only in respect of our internal affairs. In that field, the primary purpose of the Constitution was to carve from the general mass of legislative powers *then possessed by the states* such portions as it was thought desirable to vest in the federal government, leaving those not included in the enumeration still in the states. *Carter v. Carter Coal Co.*, 298 U.S. 238, 294 (1936). That this doctrine applies only to powers which the states had is self-evident. And since the states severally never possessed international powers, such powers could not have been carved from the mass of state powers but obviously were transmitted to the United States from some other source. During the Colonial period, those powers were possessed exclusively by and were entirely under the control of the Crown. By the Declaration of Independence, "the Representatives of the United States of America" declared the United (not the several) Colonies to be free and independent states, and as such to have "full Power to levy War, conclude Peace, contract Alliances, establish Commerce and to do all other Acts and Things which Independent States may of right do."

As a result of the separation from Great Britain by the colonies, acting as a unit, the powers of external sovereignty passed from the Crown not to the colonies severally, but to the colonies in their collective and corporate capacity as the United States of America. Even before the Declaration, the colonies were a unit in foreign affairs, acting through a common agency—namely, the Continental Congress, composed of delegates from the thirteen colonies. That agency exercised the powers of war and peace, raised an army, created a navy, and finally adopted the Declaration of Independence. Rulers come and go; governments end and forms of government change; but sovereignty survives. A political society cannot endure without a supreme will somewhere. Sovereignty is never held in suspense. When, therefore, the external sovereignty of Great Britain in respect of the colonies ceased, it immediately passed to the Union. That fact was given practical application almost at once. The treaty of peace, made on September 3, 1783, was concluded between his Brittanic Majesty and the "United States of America."

The Union existed before the Constitution, which was ordained and established among other things to form "a more perfect Union." . . . The Framers' Convention was called and exerted its powers upon the irrefutable postulate that though the states were several their people in respect of foreign affairs were one. . . .

It results that the investment of the federal government with the powers of external sovereignty did not depend upon the affirmative grants of the Constitution. The powers to declare and wage war, to conclude peace, to make treaties, to maintain diplomatic relations with other sovereignties, if they had never been mentioned in the Constitution, would have vested in the federal government as necessary concomitants of nationality. Neither the Constitution nor the laws passed in pursuance of it have any force in foreign territory unless in respect of our own citizens; and operations of the nation in such territory must be governed by treaties, international understandings and compacts, and the principles of international law. As a member of the family of nations, the right and power of the United States in that field are equal to the right and power of the other members of the international family. Otherwise, the United States is not completely sovereign. The power to acquire territory by discovery and occupation, the power to expel undesirable aliens, the power to make such international agreements as do not constitute treaties in the constitutional sense, none of which is expressly affirmed by the Constitution, nevertheless exist as inherently inseparable from the conception of nationality. . . .

Not only, as we have shown, is the federal power over external affairs in origin and essential character different from that over internal affairs, but participation in the exercise of the power is significantly limited. In this vast external realm, with its important, complicated, delicate and manifold problems, the President alone has the power to speak or listen as a representative of the nation. He *makes* treaties with the advice and consent of the Senate; but he alone negotiates. Into the field of negotiation the Senate cannot intrude; and Congress itself is powerless to invade it. As Marshall said in his great argument of March 7, 1800, in the House of Representatives, "The President is the sole organ of the nation in its external relations, and its sole representative with foreign nations." Annals, 6th Cong., col. 613. The Senate Committee on Foreign Relations at a very early day in our history (February 15, 1816), reported to the Senate, among other things, as follows:

> The President is the constitutional representative of the United States with regard to foreign nations. He manages our concerns with foreign nations and must necessarily be most competent to determine when, how, and upon what subjects negotiation may be urged with the greatest prospect of success. For his conduct he is responsible to the Constitution. The committee considers this responsibility the surest pledge for the faithful discharge of his duty. They think the interference of the Senate in the direction of foreign negotiations calculated to diminish that responsibility and thereby to impair the best security for the national safety. The nature of transactions with foreign nations, moreover, requires caution and unity of design, and their success frequently depends on secrecy and dispatch.

It is important to bear in mind that we are here dealing not alone with an authority vested in the President by an exertion of legislative power, but with such an authority plus the very delicate, plenary and exclusive power of the President as the sole organ of the federal government in the field of international relations—a power which does not require as a basis for its exercise an act of Congress, but which, of course, like every other governmental power, must be exercised in subordination to the applicable provisions of the Constitution. It is quite apparent that if, in the maintenance of our international relations, embarrassment—perhaps serious embarrassment—is to be avoided and success for our aims achieved, congressional legislation which is to be made effective through negotiation and inquiry within the international field must often accord to the President a degree of discretion and freedom from statutory restriction which would not be admissible were domestic affairs alone involved. Moreover, he, not Congress, has the better opportunity of knowing the conditions which prevail in foreign countries, and especially is this true in time of war. He has his confidential sources of information. He has his agents in the form of diplomatic, consular and other officials. Secrecy in respect of information gathered by them may be highly necessary, and the premature disclosure of it productive of harmful results. Indeed, so clearly is this true that the first President refused to accede to a request to lay before the House of Representatives the instructions, correspondence and documents relating to the negotiation of the Jay Treaty—a refusal the wisdom of which was recognized by the House itself and has never since been doubted. . . .

Practically every volume of the United States Statutes contains one or more acts or joint resolutions of Congress authorizing action by the President in respect of subjects affecting foreign relations, which either leave the exercise of the power to his unrestricted judgment, or provide a standard far more general than that which has always been considered requisite with regard to domestic affairs. . . .

The result of holding that the joint resolution here under attack is void and unenforceable as constituting an unlawful delegation of legislative power would be to stamp this multitude of comparable acts and resolutions as likewise invalid. And while this court may not, and should not, hesitate to declare acts of Congress, however many times repeated, to be unconstitutional if beyond all rational doubt it finds them to be so, an impressive array of legislation such as we have just set forth, enacted by nearly every Congress from the beginning of our national existence to the present day, must be given unusual weight in the process of reaching a correct determination of the problem. A legislative practice such as we have here, evidenced not by only occasional instances, but marked by the movement of a steady stream for a century and a half of time, goes a long way in the direction of proving the presence of unassailable ground for the constitutionality of the practice, to be found in the origin and history of the power involved, or in its nature, or in both combined. . . .

The judgment of the court below must be reversed and the cause remanded for further proceedings in accordance with the foregoing opinion. . . .

■ MR. JUSTICE MCREYNOLDS does not agree. He is of opinion that the court below reached the right conclusion and its judgment ought to be affirmed.

■ MR. JUSTICE STONE took no part in the consideration or decision of this case.

NOTES

1. The statute at issue in *Curtiss–Wright* delegated power to the president with respect to prohibiting international arms trade. It was challenged on "nondelegation" grounds (a vigorous interpretation of the non-delegation doctrine prevailed at the time). The Court held *this* delegation permissible, however, in large part because it involved the sphere of foreign affairs. It is helpful to try to disentangle the question of the presidential foreign affairs power from the non-delegation issue. In this case, the president was acting pursuant to legislative authority. (*Youngstown* was of course decided later, in 1952, but this would appear to be a situation involving the strongest possible claim for presidential

authority.) But could the president *alone* impose an arms-trade prohibition, with a criminal sanction, as an exercise of a foreign affairs power? Is *Curtiss–Wright,* despite its statements of broad presidential power, really a case where the congressional statute was essential to enforcing a criminal prohibition?

2. Where does Justice Sutherland's opinion locate the constitutional source of the foreign affairs power? Does he identify a particular clause or article? Does he find a textual basis for the power at all? If the foreign affairs power is simply an inference from national sovereignty, what justifies (under Justice Sutherland's approach) his conclusion that the power is almost exclusively a presidential one? For purposes of determining whether the delegation of power to the executive in this case was excessive, what difference does it make whether sovereignty devolved upon the Union or the states after the Revolutionary War? Assuming the Court is correct that the powers of war and peace devolved upon the Union, why does that have any bearing on the allocation of powers between Congress and the executive? And if the foreign affairs power really is an inference from sovereignty, what other powers not mentioned in the Constitution might be inferred in the same way?

3. Recall the controversy surrounding the validity of President George Washington's Neutrality Proclamation of 1793, discussed in Chapter 1. Secretary of the Treasury Alexander Hamilton (who was President Washington's leading adviser) located the foreign affairs power in the president, too, but attributed that power to Article II's general grant of the executive power. Considering all of the types of constitutional argument, or modes of interpretation, is the view of Hamilton in the Neutrality Controversy or the view of Justice Sutherland in *Curtiss–Wright* more persuasive? Where *does* the Constitution vest the power of foreign affairs? Is it an inference from national sovereignty? Or is it an aspect of the "executive Power"? What are the implications of each view?

4. Note that the functional reasons the Court gives for why the president should have "a degree of discretion and freedom from statutory restriction which would not be admissible were domestic affairs alone involved" strongly resemble Locke's reasons for why the "federative powers" are usually vested in the executive. Are these reasons convincing? Is presidential primacy in foreign affairs constitutionally justifiable simply on the grounds that it is efficient, sensible, and useful? Is it actually true that presidential primacy in foreign affairs is all of these things?

5. What is the function of Article II's specific shared grant of a treaty-making power to the president *and* the Senate? Is this grant of the treaty-making power a textual *refutation* of a general presidential foreign affairs power? Or is it simply a *qualification* of any such power—a check on the president's ability to use the foreign affairs power to create binding international obligations with the force of U.S. law under Article VI's Supremacy Clause? Under either view, what (if anything) supports the president's ability to make non-treaty "executive agreements"—that is, deals with other nations that are neither authorized by statute nor consented to by the Senate as formal treaties? Are such agreements (which are common and often quite significant, as the following materials demonstrate) utterly unconstitutional? Or are they constitutional, but only if one accepts some theory of a general executive foreign affairs power (either Hamilton's theory or the *Curtiss–Wright* theory) to which the treaty-making power is a relatively limited exception?

Attorney General Jackson, Opinion on Acquisition of Naval and Air Bases in Exchange for Over-Age Destroyers

39 U.S. Op. Att'y Gen. 484 (August 27, 1940)

MY DEAR MR. PRESIDENT: In accordance with your request I have considered your constitutional and statutory authority to proceed by Executive agreement with the British Government immediately to acquire for the United States certain off-shore naval and air bases in the Atlantic Ocean without awaiting the inevitable delays which would accompany the conclusion of a formal treaty.

The essential characteristics of the proposal are:

(*a*) The United States to acquire rights for immediate establishment and use of naval and air bases in Newfoundland, Bermuda, the Bahamas, Jamaica, St. Lucia, Trinidad, and British Guiana; such rights to endure for a period of 99 years and to include adequate provisions for access to, and defense of, such bases and appropriate provisions for their control.

(*b*) In consideration it is proposed to transfer to Great Britain the title and possession of certain over-age ships and obsolescent military materials now the property of the United States, and certain other small patrol boats which though nearly completed are already obsolescent.

(*c*) Upon such transfer all obligation of the United States is discharged. The acquisition consists only of rights, which the United States may exercise or not at its option, and if exercised may abandon without consent. The privilege of maintaining such bases is subject only to limitations necessary to reconcile United States' use with the sovereignty retained by Great Britain. Our Government assumes no responsibility for civil administration of any territory. It makes no promise to erect structures, or maintain forces at any point. It undertakes no defense of the possessions of any country. In short it acquires optional bases which may be developed as Congress appropriates funds therefor, but the United States does not assume any continuing or future obligation, commitment, or alliance.

The questions of constitutional and statutory authority, with which alone I am concerned, seem to be these:

FIRST. May such an acquisition be concluded by the President under an Executive agreement or must it be negotiated as a treaty subject to ratification by the Senate?

SECOND. Does authority exist in the President to alienate the title to such ships and obsolescent materials, and if so, on what conditions?

THIRD. Do the statutes of the United States limit the right to deliver the so-called "mosquito boats" now under construction or the over-age destroyers by reason of the belligerent status of Great Britain?

I

There is, of course, no doubt concerning the authority of the President to negotiate with the British Government for the proposed exchange. The only questions that might be raised in connection therewith are (1) whether the arrangement must be put in the form of a treaty and await ratification by the Senate or (2) whether there must be additional legislation by the Congress. Ordinarily (and assuming the absence of enabling legislation) the question whether such an agreement can be concluded under Presidential authority or whether it must await ratification by a two-thirds vote of the United States Senate involves consideration of two powers which the Constitution vests in the President.

One of these is the power of the Commander in Chief of the Army and Navy of the United States, which is conferred upon the President by the Constitution but is not defined or limited. Happily, there has been little occasion in our history for the interpretation of the powers of the President as Commander in Chief of the Army and Navy. I do not find it necessary to rest upon that power alone to sustain the present proposal. But it will hardly be open to controversy that the vesting of such a function in the President also places upon him a responsibility to use all constitutional authority which he may possess to provide adequate bases and stations for the utilization of the naval and air weapons of the United States at their highest efficiency in our defense. It seems equally beyond doubt that present world conditions forbid him to risk any delay that is constitutionally avoidable.

The second power to be considered is that control of foreign relations which the Constitution vests in the President as a part of the Executive function. The nature and extent of this power has recently been explicitly and authoritatively defined by Mr. Justice Sutherland, writing for the Supreme Court . . . in *United States v. Curtiss-Wright Export Corp.*, 299 U.S. 304, 319 . . . .

The President's power over foreign relations while "delicate, plenary, and exclusive" is not unlimited. Some negotiations involve commitments as to the future which would carry an obligation to exercise powers vested in the Congress. Such Presidential arrangements are customarily submitted for ratification by a two-thirds vote of the Senate before the future legislative power of the country is committee. However, the acquisitions which you are proposing to accept are without express or implied promises on the part of the United States to be performed in the future. . . .

There are precedents which might be cited, but not all strictly pertinent. The proposition falls far short in magnitude of the acquisition by President Jefferson of the Louisiana Territory from a belligerent during a European War, the Congress later appropriating the consideration and the Senate later ratifying a treaty embodying the agreement. . . .

It is not believed, however, that it is necessary here to rely exclusively upon your constitutional power. . . . I think there is also ample statutory authority to support the acquisition of these bases. . . . I therefore advise that acquisition by Executive agreement of the rights proposed to be conveyed to the United States by Great Britain will not require ratification by the Senate.

II

The right of the President to dispose of vessels of the Navy and unneeded naval material finds clear recognition in at least two enactments of the Congress and a decision of the Supreme Court—and any who assert that the authority does not exist must assume the burden of establishing that both the Congress and the Supreme Court meant something less than the clear import of seemingly plain language. . . .

I am informed that the destroyers involved here are the survivors of a fleet of over 100 built at about the same time and under the same design. During the year 1930, 58 of these were decommissioned with a view toward scrapping . . . The surviving destroyers now under consideration have been reconditioned and are in service, but all of them are over-age, most of them by several years. . . . In view of this legislative history it is clear that the Congress did not intend to prevent the certification for transfer, exchange, sale or disposition of property merely because it is still used or usable or of possible value for future use. . . .

III

[Attorney General Jackson next considered whether transfer of the "so-called 'mosquito boats' now under construction or the over-age destroyers" would violate provisions of the Neutrality Act of 1917. He concluded that the act was intended to reflect international law at the time and should be construed to forbid sale or transfer of armed vessels built "with the intent that they should enter the service of a belligerent" in a war in which the United States is a neutral nation. This barred transfer of the "mosquito boats" under construction, for their completion would then be with the intention of being transferred to Great Britain during a time when it was at war with Germany. However, this did not bar transfer of the over-age destroyers, "which were not built, armed, equipped as, or converted into vessels of war with the intent that they should enter the service of a belligerent."—Editors]

. . .

IV

Accordingly, you are respectfully advised:

(*a*) That the proposed arrangement may be concluded as an Executive agreement, effective without awaiting ratification.

(*b*) That there is Presidential power to transfer title and possession of the proposed considerations upon certification by appropriate staff officers.

(*c*) That the dispatch of the so-called "mosquito boats" would constitute a violation of the statute law of the United States, but with that exception there is no legal obstacle to the consummation of the transaction, in accordance, of course, with the applicable provisions of the Neutrality Act as to delivery.

Dames & Moore v. Regan

453 U.S. 654 (1981)

■ JUSTICE REHNQUIST delivered the opinion of the Court.

. . . On November 4, 1979, the American Embassy in Tehran was seized and our diplomatic personnel were captured and held hostage. . . .

On December 19, 1979, petitioner Dames & Moore filed suit in the United States District Court for the Central District of California against the Government of Iran, the Atomic Energy Organization of Iran, and a number of Iranian banks. In its complaint, petitioner alleged that its wholly owned subsidiary, Dames & Moore International, S. R. L., was a party to a written contract with the Atomic Energy Organization, and that the subsidiary's entire interest in the contract had been assigned to petitioner. Under the contract, the subsidiary was to conduct site studies for a proposed nuclear power plant in Iran. As provided in the terms of the contract, the Atomic Energy Organization terminated the agreement for its own convenience on June 30, 1979. Petitioner contended, however, that it was owed $3,436,694.30 plus interest for services performed under the contract prior to the date of termination. The District Court issued orders of attachment directed against property of the defendants, and the property of certain Iranian banks was then attached to secure any judgment that might be entered against them.

On January 20, 1981, the Americans held hostage were released by Iran pursuant to an Agreement entered into the day before. . . . The Agreement stated that "[i]t is the purpose of [both the United States and Iran] . . . to terminate all litigation as between the Government of each party and the nationals of the other, and to bring about the settlement and termination of all such claims through binding arbitration." In furtherance of this goal, the Agreement called for the establishment of an Iran–United States Claims Tribunal which would arbitrate any claims not settled within six months. Awards of the Claims Tribunal are to be "final and binding" and "enforceable . . . in the courts of any nation in accordance with its laws." Under the Agreement, the United States is obligated

> to terminate all legal proceedings in United States courts involving claims of United States persons and institutions against Iran and its state enterprises, to nullify all attachments and judgments obtained therein, to prohibit all further litigation based on such claims, and to bring about the termination of such claims through binding arbitration.

In addition, the United States must "act to bring about the transfer" by July 19, 1981, of all Iranian assets held in this country by American banks. One billion dollars of these assets will be deposited in a security account in the Bank of England, to the account of the Algerian Central Bank, and used to satisfy awards rendered against Iran by the Claims Tribunal. . . .

On February 24, 1981, President Reagan issued an Executive Order in which he "ratified" the January 19th Executive Orders. Moreover, he "suspended" all "claims which may be presented to the . . . Tribunal" and provided that such claims "shall have no legal effect in any action now pending in any court of the United States." The suspension of any particular claim terminates if the Claims Tribunal determines that it has no jurisdiction over that claim; claims are discharged for all purposes when the Claims Tribunal either awards some recovery and that amount is paid, or determines that no recovery is due.

Meanwhile, on January 27, 1981, petitioner moved for summary judgment in the District Court against the Government of Iran and the Atomic Energy Organization, but not against the Iranian banks. The District Court granted petitioner's motion and awarded petitioner the amount claimed under the contract plus interest. Thereafter, petitioner attempted to execute the judgment by obtaining writs of garnishment and execution in state court in the State of Washington, and a sheriff's sale of Iranian property in Washington was noticed to satisfy the judgment. . . .

On April 28, 1981, petitioner filed this action in the District Court for declaratory and injunctive relief against the United States and the Secretary of the Treasury, seeking to prevent enforcement of the Executive Orders and Treasury Department regulations implementing the Agreement with Iran. In its complaint, petitioner alleged that the actions of the President and the Secretary of the Treasury implementing the Agreement with Iran were beyond their statutory and constitutional powers and, in any event, were unconstitutional to the extent they adversely affect petitioner's final judgment against the Government of Iran and the Atomic Energy Organization, its execution of that judgment in the State of Washington, its prejudgment attachments, and its ability to continue to litigate against the Iranian banks. . . .

The parties and the lower courts, confronted with the instant questions, have all agreed that much relevant analysis is contained in *Youngstown Sheet & Tube Co. v. Sawyer,* 343 U.S. 579 (1952). Justice Black's opinion for the Court in that case, involving the validity of President Truman's effort to seize the country's steel mills in the wake of a nationwide strike, recognized that "[t]he President's power, if any, to issue the order must stem either from an act of Congress or from the Constitution itself." *Id.,* at 585. Justice Jackson's concurring opinion elaborated in a general way the consequences of different types of interaction between the two democratic branches in assessing Presidential authority to act in any given case. When the President acts pursuant to an express or implied authorization from Congress, he exercises not only his powers but also those delegated by Congress. In such a case the executive action "would be supported by the strongest of presumptions and the widest latitude of judicial interpretation, and the burden of persuasion would rest heavily upon any who might attack it." *Id.,* at 637. When the President acts in the absence of congressional authorization he may enter "a zone of twilight in which he and Congress may have concurrent authority, or in which its distribution is uncertain." *Ibid.* In such a case the analysis becomes more complicated, and the validity of the President's action, at least so far as separation-of-powers principles are concerned, hinges on a consideration of all the circumstances which might shed light on the views of the Legislative Branch toward such action, including "congressional inertia, indifference or quiescence." *Ibid.* Finally, when the President acts in contravention of the will of Congress, "his power is at its lowest ebb," and the Court can sustain his actions "only by disabling the Congress from acting upon the subject." *Id.,* at 637–638. . . .

[The Court concluded that President Carter's nullification of the attachments and order transferring Iranian assets were authorized by the International Emergency Economic Powers Act (IEEPA), 91 Stat. 1626, 50 U.S.C. § 1702(a)(1).—Editors]

. . . [T]here remains the question of the President's authority to suspend claims pending in American courts. Such claims have, of course, an existence apart from the attachments which accompanied them. In terminating these claims through Executive Order No. 12294 the President purported to act under authority of both the IEEPA and 22 U.S.C. § 1732, the so-called "Hostage Act."

We conclude that although the IEEPA authorized the nullification of the attachments, it cannot be read to authorize the suspension of the claims. The claims of American citizens against Iran are not in themselves transactions involving Iranian property or efforts to exercise any rights with respect to such property. An in personam lawsuit, although it might eventually be reduced to judgment and that judgment might be executed upon, is an effort to establish liability and fix damages and does not focus on any particular property within the jurisdiction. The terms of the IEEPA therefore do not authorize the President to suspend claims in American courts. This is the view of all the courts which have considered the question. . . . *[The Court also rejected the argument that the presidential order was authorized by the Hostage Act.—Editors]*

Concluding that neither the IEEPA nor the Hostage Act constitutes specific authorization of the President's action suspending claims, however, is not to say that these statutory provisions are entirely irrelevant to the question of the validity of the President's action. We think both statutes highly relevant in the looser sense of indicating congressional acceptance of a broad scope for executive action in circumstances such as those presented in this case. [T]he IEEPA delegates broad authority to the President to act in times of national emergency with respect to property of a foreign country. The Hostage Act similarly indicates congressional willingness that the President have broad discretion when responding to the hostile acts of foreign sovereigns. . . .

Congress cannot anticipate and legislate with regard to every possible action the President may find it necessary to take or every possible situation in which he might act. Such failure of Congress specifically to delegate authority does not, "especially . . . in the areas of foreign policy and national security," imply "congressional disapproval" of action taken by the Executive. On the contrary, the enactment of legislation closely related to the question of the President's authority in a particular case which evinces legislative intent to accord the President broad discretion may be considered to "invite" "measures on independent presidential responsibility," *Youngstown*, 343 U.S., at 637 (Jackson, J., concurring). At least this is so where there is no contrary indication of legislative intent and when, as here, there is a history of congressional acquiescence in conduct of the sort engaged in by the President. It is to that history which we now turn.

Not infrequently in affairs between nations, outstanding claims by nationals of one country against the government of another country are "sources of friction" between the two sovereigns. To resolve these difficulties, nations have often entered into agreements settling the claims of their respective nationals. As one treatise writer puts it, international agreements settling claims by nationals of one state against the government of another "are established international practice reflecting traditional international theory." L. Henkin, *Foreign Affairs and the Constitution* 262 (1972). Consistent with that principle, the United States has repeatedly exercised its sovereign authority to settle the claims of its nationals against foreign countries. Though those settlements have sometimes been made by treaty, there has also been a longstanding practice of settling such claims by executive agreement without the advice and consent of the Senate. Under such agreements, the President has agreed to renounce or extinguish claims of United States nationals against foreign governments in return for lump-sum payments or the establishment of arbitration procedures. To be sure, many of these settlements were encouraged by the United States claimants themselves, since a claimant's only hope of obtaining any payment at all might lie in having his Government negotiate a diplomatic settlement on his behalf. But it is also undisputed that the "United States has sometimes disposed of the claims of its citizens without their consent, or even without consultation with them, usually without exclusive regard for their interests, as distinguished from those of the nation as a whole." Henkin, *supra*, at 262–263. Accord, Restatement (Second) of Foreign Relations Law of the United States § 213 (1965) (President "may waive or settle a claim against a foreign state . . . [even] without the consent of the [injured] national"). It is clear that the practice of settling claims continues today. Since 1952, the President has entered into at least 10 binding settlements with foreign nations, including an $80 million settlement with the People's Republic of China.

Crucial to our decision today is the conclusion that Congress has implicitly approved the practice of claim settlement by executive agreement. This is best demonstrated by Congress' enactment of the International Claims Settlement Act of 1949, 22 U.S.C. § 1621 *et seq.* The Act had two purposes: (1) to allocate to United States nationals funds received in the course of an executive claims settlement with Yugoslavia, and (2) to provide a procedure whereby funds resulting from future settlements could be distributed. To achieve these ends Congress created the International Claims Commission, now the Foreign Claims Settlement Commission, and gave it jurisdiction to make final and binding decisions with respect to claims by United States nationals against settlement funds. 22 U.S.C. § 1623(a). By creating a procedure to implement future settlement agreements, Congress placed its stamp of approval on such agreements. Indeed, the legislative history of the Act observed that the United States was seeking settlements with countries other than Yugoslavia and that the bill contemplated settlements of a similar nature in the future. H. R. Rep. No. 770, 81st Cong., 1st Sess., 4, 8 (1949).

. . . In addition to congressional acquiescence in the President's power to settle claims, prior cases of this Court have also recognized that the President does have some measure of power to enter into executive agreements without obtaining the advice and consent of the Senate. In *United States v. Pink*, 315 U.S. 203 (1942), for example, the Court upheld the validity of the Litvinov Assignment, which was part of an Executive Agreement whereby the Soviet Union assigned to the United States amounts owed to it by American nationals so that outstanding claims of other American nationals could be paid. The Court explained that the resolution of such claims was integrally connected with normalizing United States' relations with a foreign state:

> Power to remove such obstacles to full recognition as settlement of claims of our nationals . . . certainly is a modest implied power of the President. . . . No such obstacle can be placed in the way of rehabilitation of relations between this country and another nation, unless the historic conception of the powers and responsibilities . . . is to be drastically revised.

Id., at 229–230. . . .

In light of all of the foregoing—the inferences to be drawn from the character of the legislation Congress has enacted in the area, such as the IEEPA and the Hostage Act, and from the history of acquiescence in executive claims settlement—we conclude that the President was authorized to suspend pending claims pursuant to Executive Order No. 12294. As Justice Frankfurter pointed out in *Youngstown*, 343 U.S., at 610–611, "a systematic, unbroken, executive practice, long pursued to the knowledge of the Congress and never before questioned . . . may be treated as a gloss on 'Executive Power' vested in the President by § 1 of Art. II." Past practice does not, by itself, create power, but "long-continued practice, known to and acquiesced in by Congress, would raise a presumption that the [action] had been [taken] in pursuance of its consent. . . ." *United States v. Midwest Oil Co.*, 236 U.S. 459, 474 (1915). Such practice is present here and such a presumption is also appropriate. In light of the fact that Congress may be considered to have consented to the President's action in suspending claims, we cannot say that action exceeded the President's powers.

Our conclusion is buttressed by the fact that the means chosen by the President to settle the claims of American nationals provided an alternative forum, the Claims Tribunal, which is capable of providing meaningful relief. The Solicitor General also suggests that the provision of the Claims Tribunal will actually *enhance* the opportunity for claimants to recover their claims, in that the Agreement removes a number of jurisdictional and procedural impediments faced by claimants in United States courts. Although being overly sanguine about the chances of United States claimants before the Claims Tribunal would require a degree of naiveté which should not be demanded even of judges, the Solicitor General's point cannot be discounted. . . .

Just as importantly, Congress has not disapproved of the action taken here. Though Congress has held hearings on the Iranian Agreement itself, Congress has not enacted legislation, or even passed a resolution, indicating its displeasure with the Agreement. Quite the contrary, the relevant Senate Committee has stated that the establishment of the Tribunal is "of vital importance to the United States." S. Rep. No. 97–71, p. 5 (1981). We are thus clearly not confronted with a situation in which Congress has in some way resisted the exercise of Presidential authority.

Finally, we re-emphasize the narrowness of our decision. We do not decide that the President possesses plenary power to settle claims, even as against foreign governmental entities. As the Court of Appeals for the First Circuit stressed, "[t]he sheer magnitude of such a power, considered against the background of the diversity and complexity of modern international trade, cautions against any broader construction of authority than is necessary." *Chas T. Main Int'l, Inc. v. Khuzestan Water & Power Authority*, 651 F.2d, at 814. But where, as here, the settlement of claims has been determined to be a necessary incident to the resolution of a major foreign policy dispute between our country and another, and where, as here, we can conclude that Congress acquiesced in the President's action, we are not prepared to say that the President lacks the power to settle such claims. . . .

NOTES

1. What constitutional authority supports the power of the president to conclude non-treaty "executive agreements" with foreign nations? What authority does Attorney General Jackson rely on in his opinion supporting the validity of the Destroyers for Bases Agreement concluded by President Roosevelt? What authority does Justice Rehnquist rely on in *Dames & Moore*? If the president has the constitutional power to make such agreements, what is the extent of that power? May the president make an executive agreement that alters vested rights under U.S. domestic law? Or is that tantamount to a unilateral presidential legislative power? What legal authority gives the president the power to make binding international agreements that "settle" the property rights of U.S. citizens out from under them? Is there a difference in this regard between the Destroyers for Bases Agreement and the Algiers Accords (settling the Iranian hostage situation)?

2. How is President Carter's action (ratified by President Reagan) any different from President Truman's actions in seizing the steel mills? In each case, the president acted on his own authority, without congressional participation, and effectively took away the property of some U.S. citizens in order to accomplish a stated foreign policy goal. Is *Dames & Moore* consistent with *Youngstown*? Is it because the relevant statutes (the IEEPA and the Hostage Act, respectively) come close to authorizing the action? Is it because Congress had authorized similar actions in the past? Is it because there was support for the ac-

tion in Congress? Is it because of the seeming necessity as a matter of international public affairs of not upending the agreements? (Consider the last paragraph of *Dames & Moore*: is the holding limited to the case's facts?) Are any of these good justifications for presidential action?

3. Was there anything to stop President Carter or President Reagan from requesting that Congress enact implementing legislation for the executive agreement at issue in *Dames & Moore*? Couldn't the agreement have been submitted to the Senate for ratification as a treaty (and become binding U.S. law that way)? In the next chapter, we will study the leading case holding that Congress possesses the legislative power under the Necessary and Proper Clause to execute all powers vested in the national government, including the executive branch, and thus may enact laws for implementing treaties or executive agreements even if it otherwise might lack the authority to pass such laws. See *Missouri v. Holland*, 252 U.S. 416 (1920). Why do you suppose neither President Carter nor President Reagan pursued these routes?

4. A more recent case, *Medellin v. Texas*, 128 S. Ct. 1346 (2008), involved a state prosecution of a Mexican national for the gang-rape and murder of two teenage girls in Texas. Under an international treaty to which the United States was a party, the Vienna Convention on Consular Relations, a foreign national accused of a crime has the right to contact his nation's consul. Medellin was not advised of his right to contact his embassy. An international tribunal interpreted the Vienna Convention to require judicial reconsideration of criminal convictions where a defendant was not so advised, and President George W. Bush issued an executive order accepting this ruling and directing state courts to comply with it. (An interesting aside: was President Bush required to do so, or does the president's foreign affairs power permit him to judge the extent to which the United States will be bound by prior agreements? Consider in this regard *Goldwater v. Carter*, the next principal case.) The Supreme Court held that the president's foreign affairs power did not include a power to make binding, as a matter of U.S. domestic law, an international obligation assumed as a matter of the president's power over the nation's foreign affairs:

> [T]he terms of a non-self-executing treaty can become domestic law only in the same way as any other law—through passage of legislation by both Houses of Congress, combined with either the President's signature or a congressional override of a presidential veto. . . . As Madison explained in The Federalist No. 47, under our constitutional system of checks and balances, "[t]he magistrate in whom the whole executive power resides cannot of himself make a law." That would, however, seem an apt description of the asserted executive authority unilaterally to give the effect of domestic law to obligations under a non-self-executing treaty.

The Court did not challenge, but instead distinguished, *Dames & Moore*. But if *Medellin* is right on this point—that the president does not have power to interpret international treaty obligations so as to alter U.S. domestic law obligations (for example, by issuing binding directives to state governments)—why wouldn't the same principle apply to the executive agreements the president makes unilaterally? If there is tension, which principle is right?

5. In addition to *Medellin*, several recent Supreme Court decisions have considered whether, under Article VI's Supremacy Clause, the presidential foreign affairs power can preempt state laws touching on foreign affairs. The issue

is complex, and the decisions are not uniform. Clearly, a treaty is binding U.S. law that, under the Supremacy Clause, preempts inconsistent state laws. But what about executive agreements, which are not enacted as U.S. law? What about the *unexercised* foreign affairs power? Compare *Medellin* (rejecting preemption) with *American Insurance Ass'n v. Garamendi*, 539 U.S. 396 (2003) (finding implied preemption of a California law requiring European affiliates of insurance companies doing business in California to divulge information related to unpaid Holocaust-era insurance policies for the purpose of facilitating lawsuits in California, on the grounds that the law was inconsistent with the president's foreign affairs powers even though not in conflict with any extant treaty or executive agreement) and *Crosby v. National Foreign Trade Council*, 530 U.S. 363 (2000) (finding Massachusetts law forbidding state agencies from buying goods or services from companies that do business with the government of Burma [Myanmar] preempted because the state law was an obstacle to achieving the purposes of a congressional enactment designed to put pressure on the Burmese regime by authorizing the president to reduce sanctions).

6. If a president may unilaterally make an executive agreement, at least for foreign affairs purposes, may a subsequent president unilaterally rescind it? Why or why not? Is it because the executive agreement does not have the status of enacted U.S. domestic law? Or is it because of the breadth of the general presidential foreign affairs power? If a president makes a *treaty*, by and with the advice and consent of two-thirds of the Senate, can a subsequent president terminate that treaty unilaterally? Why or why not? That is the issue presented by the following classic case, which presents fundamental questions concerning the scope of the president's general power with respect to foreign affairs and that power's relationship to the specific powers of treaty-making and treaty-termination.

Goldwater v. Carter

617 F.2d 697 (D.C. Cir. 1979)

■ PER CURIAM:

[This paragraph has been relocated from later in the opinion.—Editors]
In the aftermath of the Chinese Revolution and the Korean War, the United States and the Republic of China (ROC) negotiated a Mutual Defense Treaty, primarily directed against the perceived threat from the People's Republic of China (PRC). The Treaty was signed by representatives of both nations on December 2, 1954. It was approved by the Senate, and finally signed by the President on February 11, 1955. Article V of the Treaty provided that, in the event of an attack on Taiwan, the Pescadores, or United States territories in the western Pacific, each nation "would act to meet the common danger in accordance with its constitutional processes." Article X of the Treaty provided that it would remain in force "indefinitely," but said that "[e]ither Party may terminate it one year after notice has been given to the other Party."

[In 1979, President Carter decided to recognize the People's Republic of China as the government of the entire Chinese nation and thus to withdraw recognition from the government of Taiwan. He also notified the Taiwanese government that the United States was terminating their Mutual Defense Treaty. A group of senators and representatives, led by former presidential candidate Barry Goldwater, sued.—Editors]

The court *en banc* has before it for review the judgment of the District Court that the notice of termination given by the President pursuant to the terms of the Mutual Defense Treaty with the Republic of China is ineffective absent either (1) a manifestation of the consent of the Senate to such termination by a two-thirds vote or (2) an approving majority vote therefor by both houses of Congress. The preliminary questions we confront are, first, whether the District Court was without jurisdiction because appellees lacked standing, and, second, whether it should in any event have declined to exercise jurisdiction by reason of the political nature of the question it was called upon to decide. Since a majority of the court does not exist to dispose of the appeal on either of these bases, we reach the merits and reverse.

In doing so, however, we think it important at the outset to stress that the Treaty, as it was presented to the Senate in 1954 and consented to by it, contained an explicit provision for termination by either party on one year's notice. The Senate, in the course of giving its consent, exhibited no purpose and took no action to reserve a role for itself—by amendment, reservation, or condition—in the effectuation of this provision. Neither has the Senate, since the giving of the notice of termination, purported to take any final or decisive action with respect to it, either by way of approval or disapproval. The constitutional issue we face, therefore, is solely and simply the one of whether the President in these precise circumstances is, on behalf of the United States, empowered to terminate the Treaty in accordance with its terms. It is our view that he is, and that the limitations which the District Court purported to place on his action in this regard have no foundation in the Constitution. . . .

Various considerations enter into our determination that the President's notice of termination will be effective on January 1, 1980. The result we reach draws upon their totality, but in listing them hereinafter we neither assign them hierarchical values nor imply that any one factor or combination of factors is determinative.

1. We turn first to the argument, embraced by the District Court, drawn from the language of Article II, § 2, of the Constitution. It is that, since the President clearly cannot enter into a treaty without the consent of the Senate, the inference is inescapable that he must in all circumstances seek the same senatorial consent to terminate that treaty. As a matter of language alone, however, the same inference would appear automatically to obtain with respect to the termination by the President of officers appointed by him under the same clause of the Constitution and subject to Senate confirmation. But the Supreme Court has read that clause as not having such an inevitable effect in any and all circumstances. *Compare Myers v. United States*, 272 U.S. 52 (1926) *with In re Humphrey's Executor v. United States*, 295 U.S. 602 (1935). In the area of foreign relations in particular, where the constitutional commitment of powers to the President is notably comprehensive, it has never been suggested that the services of Ambassadors—appointed by the President, confirmed by the Senate, and of critical importance as they are to the successful conduct of our foreign relations— may not be terminated by the President without the prior authorization of that body.

Expansion of the language of the Constitution by sequential linguistic projection is a tricky business at best. Virtually all constitutional principles have unique elements and can be distinguished from one another. As the Supreme Court has recognized with respect to the clause in question, it is not abstract logic or sterile symmetry that controls, but a sensible and realistic ascertainment of the meaning of the Constitution in the context of the specific action taken.

2. The District Court's declaration, in the alternative, that the necessary authority in this instance may be granted by a majority of each house of Congress presumably has its source in the Supremacy Clause of Article VI. The argument is that a treaty, being a part of the "supreme Law of the Land," can only be terminated at the least by a subsequent federal statute.

The central purpose of the Supremacy Clause has been accepted to be that of causing each of the designated supreme laws Constitution, statute, and treaty—to prevail, for purposes of domestic law, over state law in any form. Article VI speaks explicitly to the judges to assure that this is so. But these three types of supreme law are not necessarily the same in their other characteristics, any more than are the circumstances and terms of their creation the same. Certainly the Constitution is silent on the matter of treaty termination. And the fact that it speaks to the common characteristic of supremacy over state law does not provide any basis for concluding that a treaty must be unmade either by (1) the same process by which it was made, or (2) the alternative means by which a statute is made or terminated.

3. The constitutional institution of advice and consent of the Senate, provided two-thirds of the Senators concur, is a special and extraordinary condition of the exercise by the President of certain specified powers under Article II. It is not lightly to be extended in instances not set forth in the Constitution. Such an extension by implication is not proper unless that implication is unmistakably clear.

The District Court's absolutist extension of this limitation to termination of treaties, irrespective of the particular circumstances involved, is not sound. The making of a treaty has the consequences of an entangling alliance for the nation. Similarly, the amending of a treaty merely continues such entangling alliances, changing only their character, and therefore also requires the advice and consent of the Senate. It does not follow, however, that a constitutional provision for a special concurrence (two-thirds of the Senators) prior to entry into an entangling alliance necessarily applies to its termination in accordance with its terms.

4. The Constitution specifically confers no power of treaty termination on either the Congress or the Executive. We note, however, that the powers conferred upon Congress in Article I of the Constitution are specific, detailed, and limited, while the powers conferred upon the President by Article II are generalized in a manner that bespeaks no such limitation upon foreign affairs powers. "Section 1. The executive Power shall be vested in a President. . . ."[17] Although specific powers are listed in Section 2 and Section 3, these are in many instances not powers necessary to an Executive, while "The executive Power" referred to in Section 1 is nowhere defined. There is no required two-thirds vote of the Senate conditioning the exercise of any power in Section 1. . . .

The President is the constitutional representative of the United States with respect to external affairs. It is significant that the treaty power appears in Article II of the Constitution, relating to the executive branch, and

---

[17] Contrastingly, Article I, Section 1 provides: "All legislative Powers *herein granted* shall be vested in a Congress of the United States . . ." (emphasis supplied).

not in Article I, setting forth the powers of the legislative branch. It is the President as Chief Executive who is given the constitutional authority to enter into a treaty; and even after he has obtained the consent of the Senate it is for him to decide whether to ratify a treaty and put it into effect. Senatorial confirmation of a treaty concededly does not obligate the President to go forward with a treaty if he concludes that it is not in the public interest to do so.

Thus, in contrast to the lawmaking power, the constitutional initiative in the treaty-making field is in the President, not Congress. It would take an unprecedented feat of judicial construction to read into the Constitution an absolute condition precedent of congressional or Senate approval for termination of all treaties, similar to the specific one relating to initial approval. And it would unalterably affect the balance of power between the two Branches laid down in Articles I and II.

5. . . . The recognized powers of Congress to implement (or fail to implement) a treaty by an appropriation or other law essential to its effectuation, or to supersede for all practical purposes the effect of a treaty on domestic law, are legislative powers, not treaty-making or treaty-termination powers. The issue here, however, is not Congress' legislative powers to supersede or affect the domestic impact of a treaty; the issue is whether the Senate (or Congress) must in this case give its prior consent to discontinue a treaty which the President thinks it desirable to terminate in the national interest and pursuant to a provision in the treaty itself. The existence, in practical terms, of one power does not imply the existence, in constitutional terms, of the other.

6. If we were to hold that under the Constitution a treaty could only be terminated by exactly the same process by which it was made, we would be locking the United States into all of its international obligations, even if the President and two-thirds of the Senate minus one firmly believed that the proper course for the United States was to terminate a treaty. Many of our treaties in force, such as mutual defense treaties, carry potentially dangerous obligations. These obligations are terminable under international law upon breach by the other party or change in circumstances that frustrates the purpose of the treaty. In many of these situations the President must take immediate action. The creation of a constitutionally obligatory role in all cases for a two-thirds consent by the Senate would give to one-third plus one of the Senate the power to deny the President the authority necessary to conduct our foreign policy in a rational and effective manner.

7. Even as to the formal termination of treaties, as the District Court pointed out, "a variety of means have been used to terminate treaties."[18] There is much debate among the historians and scholars as to whether in some instances the legislature has been involved at all; they are agreed that, when involved, that involvement with the President has taken many different forms. It appears moreover that the Senate may wish to continue to determine the nature of its involvement on a case by case basis.

---

[18] Since the first treaty to which the United States was a party was terminated in 1798 by an act of Congress, a variety of means have been used to terminate treaties: by statute directing the President to deliver notice of termination; by the President acting pursuant to a joint resolution of Congress or otherwise acting with the concurrence of both houses of Congress; by the President acting with senatorial consent; and by the President acting alone

Goldwater v. Carter, 481 F.Supp. At 959 (D.D.C. 1979).

The District Court concluded that the diversity of historical precedents left an inconclusive basis on which to decide the issue of whether the President's power to terminate a treaty must always be "shared" in some way by the Senate or Congress. We agree. Yet we think it is not without significance that out of all the historical precedents brought to our attention, in no situation has a treaty been continued in force over the opposition of the President.

There is on the other hand widespread agreement that the President has the power as Chief Executive under many circumstances to exercise functions regarding treaties which have the effect of either terminating or continuing their vitality. Prominent among these is the authority of the President as Chief Executive (1) to determine whether a treaty has terminated because of a breach, *Charlton v. Kelly*, 229 U.S. 447, 473–476 (1913); and (2) to determine whether a treaty is at an end due to changed circumstances. . . .

8. . . . We cannot find an implied role in the Constitution for the Senate in treaty termination for some but not all treaties in terms of their relative importance. There is no judicially ascertainable and manageable method of making any distinction among treaties on the basis of their substance, the magnitude of the risk involved, the degree of controversy which their termination would engender, or by any other standards. We know of no standards to apply in making such distinctions. The facts on which such distinctions might be drawn may be difficult of ascertainment; and the resolution of such inevitable disputes between the two Branches would be an improper and unnecessary role for the courts. To decide whether there was a breach or changed circumstances, for example, would involve a court in making fundamental decisions of foreign policy and would create insuperable problems of evidentiary proof. This is beyond the acceptable judicial role. All we decide today is that two-thirds Senate consent or majority consent in both houses is not necessary to terminate this treaty in the circumstances before us now.

9. The circumstances involved in the termination of the Mutual Defense Treaty with the Republic of China include a number of material and unique elements. Prominent is assertion by the officials of both the Republic of China and the People's Republic of China that each of them is the government of China, intending the term China to comprehend both the mainland of China and the island of Taiwan. In the 1972 Shanghai Communique, the United States acknowledged that position and did not challenge it. . . . It is in this context that the recent Joint Communique set forth as of January 1, 1979 that the United States recognizes the People's Republic of China as "the sole legal government of China." This action made reference to "the people of Taiwan," stating that the peoples of the United States and Taiwan "will maintain cultural, commercial and other unofficial relations." This formulation was confirmed by the Taiwan Relations Act.

It is undisputed that the Constitution gave the President full constitutional authority to recognize the PRC and to derecognize the ROC. What the United States has evolved for Taiwan is a novel and somewhat indefinite relationship, namely, of unofficial relations with the people of Taiwan. The subtleties involved in maintaining amorphous relationships are often the very stuff of diplomacy—a field in which the President, not Congress, has responsibility under our Constitution. The President makes a responsible claim that he has authority as Chief Executive to determine that there is no meaningful vitality to a mutual defense treaty when there is no recognized state. That is not to say that the recognition power automatically gives the President authority to take any action that is required or requested by the state being recognized. We do not need to reach this question. Nevertheless, it remains an important ingredient in the case at bar that the President has determined that circumstances have changed so as to preclude continuation of the Mutual Defense Treaty with the ROC; diplomatic recognition of the ROC came to an end on January 1, 1979, and now there exists only "cultural, commercial and other unofficial relations" with the "people on Taiwan."

10. Finally, and of central significance, the treaty here at issue contains a termination clause. The existence of Article X of the ROC treaty, permitting termination by either party on one year's notice, is an overarching factor in this case, which in effect enables all of the other considerations to be knit together.

Without derogating from the executive power of the President to decide to act contrary to the wording of a treaty—for example, because of a breach by the other party, or because of a doctrine of fundamental change of circumstances (*rebus sic stantibus*)—the President's authority as Chief Executive is at its zenith when the Senate has consented to a treaty that expressly provides for termination on one year's notice, and the President's action is the giving of notice of termination.

As already noted, we have no occasion to decide whether this factor would be determinative in a case lacking other factors identified above, *e.g.*, under a notice of withdrawal from the NATO treaty unaccompanied by derecognition of the other signatories. No specific restriction or condition on the President's action is found within the Constitution or this treaty itself. The termination clause is without conditions and without designation as to who shall act to terminate it. No specific role is spelled out in either the Constitution or this treaty for the Senate or the Congress as a whole. That power consequently devolves upon the President, and there is no basis for a court to imply a restriction on the President's power to terminate not contained in the Constitution, in this treaty, or in any other authoritative source.

While under the termination clause of this and similar treaties the power of the President to terminate may appear theoretically absolute, to think that this is so would be to ignore all historical practices in treaty termination and past and current reciprocal relationships between the Chief Executive and Congress. The wide variety of roles played by the Executive and the Congress (or the Senate alone) in the past termination of treaties teaches us nothing conclusive as to constitutional theory, but it instructs us as to what may fairly be contemplated as to the President's future exercise of the treaty termination power. Treaty termination is a political act, but political acts are not customarily taken without political support. Even if formal advice and consent is not constitutionally required as a prerequisite to termination, it might be sought. If the Congress is completely ignored, it has its arsenal of weapons, as previous Chief Executives have on occasion been sharply reminded.

Thus, the court is not to be taken as minimizing the role of the legislature in foreign affairs. The legislature's powers, including prominently its dominant status in the provision of funds, and its authority to investigate the Executive's functioning, establish authority for appropriate legislative participation in foreign affairs. The question of whether the Senate may be able to reserve to itself in particular treaties, at the time of their original submission, a specific role in their termination is not presented by the record in this appeal and we decide nothing with respect to it. The matter before us is solely one of whether the Constitution nullifies the procedure followed by the President in this instance. We find the President did not exceed his authority when he took action to withdraw from the ROC treaty, by giving notice under Article X of the Treaty, without the consent of the Senate or other legislative concurrences.

In our holding in this case we do not ignore the question of justiciability. We regard the only issue here to be whether the constitutional allocation of governmental power between two branches requires prior legislative consent to the termination of this treaty under the circumstances presented by this record. Viewing the issue before us so narrowly and in the circumstances of this treaty and its history to date, we see no reason which we could in good conscience invoke to refrain from judgment, and conclude that it is the duty of the court to confront and decide that issue.

■ MACKINNON, CIRCUIT JUDGE, dissenting in part and concurring in part.

. . . My interpretation is based on the admitted fact that the termination of treaties is not one of the enumerated powers of the Constitution. Rather it is an implied power vested in the government. As such, under the "Necessary and Proper" clause of Article I, Section 8, which the majority decision avoids like the plague, power is conferred upon "*[t]he Congress*" to pass a law to terminate treaties. Since the Constitution makes treaties along with other laws the "Law of the Land", Article II, Section 2, a treaty is to be terminated in the same manner as any other "law"—by a formal act of Congress approved by the President. The language of the Constitution, its interpretation by the Framers, and historical precedent overwhelmingly support such a conclusion. . . .

It is significant that Thomas Jefferson interpreted the Constitution as placing the power to terminate treaties in Congress and so declared in his "Manual," which as a guide for Congressional procedure persists to this day:

> Treaties being declared, equally with the laws of the United States, to be the supreme law of the land, it is understood that an act of the legislature *alone* can declare them infringed and rescinded. This was accordingly the process adopted in the case of France in 1798.

Jefferson's Manual, Rules and Practices, House of Representatives, 96th Congress, § 599, at 274 (1979). (Emphasis added). . . .

These interpretations and our historical practice, hereinafter set forth, consider treaties and statutes to be of equal dignity. It is the Supremacy Clause that directs this result because of the necessity that treaties be supreme over state laws the same as Acts of Congress. Hence, the Constitution, acts of Congress and treaties are the "supreme law of the land". . . .

[T]he sworn declaration of J. Terry Emerson, which is part of the record of this case, claims many more instances of Congressional participation in treaty termination:

> I have identified at least 52 separate treaties or provisions thereof which have been terminated with legislative authority. Four of these 52 have been terminated with legislative approval granted after Presidential request was made for such authority through the mechanism of

the Presidential Message. . . . The remaining 48 have been terminated with legislative authority in the manner [indicated in the declaration].

. . . The first treaty terminated by the United States was abrogated by an Act of *Congress* of July 7, 1798, 1 Stat. 578. By this act, entitled "An Act to Declare the Treaties Heretofore Concluded with France No Longer Obligatory on the United States", Congress pronounced the United States freed and exonerated from Treaties of 1778 with France. As this act occurred just slightly less than ten years after ratification of the Constitution on September 13, 1788, it can be viewed as a reasonably contemporaneous construction that treaty termination was a legislative act. . . .

The President argues that the termination was necessary to his recognition of the People's Republic of China. In making that argument, the President, in effect, asks the courts of this nation to choose between upholding his right to recognize foreign governments and Congress' right to approve the termination of United States' treaties. . . .

The President's objective can be achieved merely by inviting Congress to pass a Joint Resolution authorizing the termination of the Taiwan Treaty. Or he can receive the Ambassador from the Peoples Republic of China without the treaty being terminated. There is nothing inherent in the President's constitutional power to receive the Ambassador from the People's Republic that compels terminating the Taiwan Treaty. What creates the complication that bothers the President is that there are *actually* two Chinas. The President wants to act in some respects as though there is only one China and in other respects, as indicated by the Taiwan Relations Act, as though there are two. This attempt to carry water on both shoulders is the basic cause of the President's problem and he asks this court to distort the Constitution to accomplish his objective without Congressional approval. He should not look to the courts to distort or violate the Constitution in an effort to avoid his obligation to secure congressional action on the suggested termination as the Constitution requires.

The linchpin in the President's argument, and it is completely fallacious, is that he must be recognized as having the power, acting alone, to terminate the treaty because the position of the Mainland Chinese Government was that "termination of the Defense Treaty with Taiwan was a prerequisite to [normalization]" of relations between that government and the United States (Appellant's Br. 6–7). But it is a logical *non sequitur* to conclude from the premise that because the *People's Republic* requires termination of the Taiwan Treaty that therefore the President must be recognized under our Constitution as having the *absolute power alone* to terminate that treaty. Such a conclusion is completely unjustified by the premise. . . .

Finally, this case dramatizes the necessity for contemporary reaffirmation of the Framers' wisdom in designing our constitutional system of checks and balances. Without a congressional check on the President's power to sever our treaty obligations, the President would possess a very dangerous power in some instances to affect our substantive international commitments. Presidents change, and courts should be mindful of that fact. . . .

If the President has absolute power to terminate the Mutual Defense Treaty with Taiwan he likewise has absolute power under similar circumstances to terminate the NATO Treaty, our Japanese Security Treaty, the SALT Treaty and any other Defense Treaty that the Senate might have concurred in by a two-thirds vote. But when the Constitution explicitly requires the vote of two-thirds of the Senators present to ratify a treaty already fully negotiated by the President, a contention that the same Constitution would vest *absolute power* in one official to terminate that treaty is clearly contrary to the constitutional design.

Maintenance of a constitutional balance in treaty termination assumes even greater importance as our nation becomes increasingly oriented toward global affairs. The practicalities of power, and abuse of power, present persuasive arguments for retention of the practice of sharing the treaty termination power. Distance from the days of the Framers of the Constitution should not sever us from their constitutional scheme of checks and balances, any more than it can overcome the logic inherent in the magnificent document they bequeathed to us. . . .

Goldwater v. Carter
444 U.S. 996 (1979)

On petition for writ of certiorari to the United States Court of Appeals for the District of Columbia Circuit.

ORDER

The petition for a writ of certiorari is granted. The judgment of the Court of Appeals is vacated and the case is remanded to the District Court with directions to dismiss the complaint.

Mr. Justice MARSHALL concurs in the result.

Mr. Justice POWELL concurs in the judgment and has filed a statement.

Mr. Justice REHNQUIST concurs in the judgment and has filed a statement in which Mr. Chief Justice BURGER, Mr. Justice STEWART, and Mr. Justice STEVENS join.

Mr. Justice WHITE and Mr. Justice BLACKMUN join in the grant of the petition for a writ of certiorari but would set the case for argument and give it plenary consideration. Mr. Justice BLACKMUN has filed a statement in which Mr. Justice WHITE joins.

Mr. Justice BRENNAN would grant the petition for certiorari and affirm the judgment of the Court of Appeals and has filed a statement.

■ MR. JUSTICE POWELL, concurring.

Although I agree with the result reached by the Court, I would dismiss the complaint as not ripe for judicial review.

This Court has recognized that an issue should not be decided if it is not ripe for judicial review. Prudential considerations persuade me that a dispute between Congress and the President is not ready for judicial review unless and until each branch has taken action asserting its constitutional authority. Differences between the President and the Congress are commonplace under our system. The differences should, and almost invariably do, turn on political rather than legal considerations. The Judicial Branch should not decide issues affecting the allocation of power between the President and Congress until the political branches reach a constitutional impasse. Otherwise, we would encourage small groups or even individual Members of Congress to seek judicial resolution of issues before the normal political process has the opportunity to resolve the conflict.

In this case, a few Members of Congress claim that the President's action in terminating the treaty with Taiwan has deprived them of their constitutional role with respect to a change in the supreme law of the land. Congress has taken no official action. In the present posture of this case, we do not know whether there ever will be an actual confrontation between the Legislative and Executive Branches. Although the Senate has considered a resolution declaring that Senate approval is necessary for the termination of any mutual defense treaty, no final vote has been taken on the resolution. Moreover, it is unclear whether the resolution would have retroactive effect. It cannot be said that either the Senate or the House has rejected the President's claim. If the Congress chooses not to confront the President, it is not our task to do so. I therefore concur in the dismissal of this case. . . .

■ Mr. Justice Rehnquist, with whom the Chief Justice, Mr. Justice Stewart, and Mr. Justice Stevens join, concurring in the judgment.

I am of the view that the basic question presented by the petitioners in this case is "political" and therefore nonjusticiable because it involves the authority of the President in the conduct of our country's foreign relations and the extent to which the Senate or the Congress is authorized to negate the action of the President. . . .

In light of the absence of any constitutional provision governing the termination of a treaty, and the fact that different termination procedures may be appropriate for different treaties (see, *e.g.*, n. 1, *infra*), the instant case in my view also "must surely be controlled by political standards." . . .

■ [The partially dissenting opinion of Justice Blackmun, joined by Justice White, is omitted.]

■ Mr. Justice Brennan, dissenting.

I respectfully dissent from the order directing the District Court to dismiss this case, and would affirm the judgment of the Court of Appeals insofar as it rests upon the President's well-established authority to recognize, and withdraw recognition from, foreign governments.

In stating that this case presents a nonjusticiable "political question," Mr. Justice Rehnquist, in my view, profoundly misapprehends the political-question principle as it applies to matters of foreign relations. Properly understood, the political-question doctrine restrains courts from reviewing an exercise of foreign policy judgment by the coordinate political branch to which authority to make that judgment has been "constitutional[ly] commit[ted]." *Baker v. Carr*, 369 U.S. 186, 211–213, 217 (1962). But the doctrine does not pertain when a court is faced with the antecedent question whether a particular branch has been constitutionally designated as the repository of political decisionmaking power. Cf. *Powell v. McCormack*, 395 U.S. 486, 519–521 (1969). The issue of decisionmaking authority must be resolved as a matter of constitutional law, not political discretion; accordingly, it falls within the competence of the courts.

The constitutional question raised here is prudently answered in narrow terms. Abrogation of the defense treaty with Taiwan was a necessary incident to Executive recognition of the Peking Government, because the defense treaty was predicated upon the now-abandoned view that the Taiwan Government was the only legitimate political authority in China. Our cases firmly establish that the Constitution commits to the President alone the power to recognize, and withdraw recognition from, foreign regimes. That mandate being clear, our judicial inquiry into the treaty rupture can go no further.

NOTES

1. What is the correct answer on the merits: where does the Constitution vest the power of treaty termination? Treaty interpretation? Is the answer that treaty termination is part of the general executive power over foreign affairs, as the D.C. Circuit believed—in other words, that the power of treaty *making* is a specific and limited exception to the otherwise general power of the president over foreign affairs, and that the requirement of supermajority Senate consent to treaty making does not justify the inference of a mirror-image requirement with respect to terminating or limiting treaty obligations?

2. The Supreme Court's "decision"—no majority agreed on a rationale for deciding the case—produced the result of a dismissal of Senator Goldwater's complaint, leaving President Carter's termination of the treaty intact. What is the legal difference between that and a decision for President Carter on the merits? Is there any practical difference? Subsequent to the D.C. Circuit's decision in *Goldwater* (and the Supreme Court's non-decision in *Goldwater*), the executive branch has embraced the view that the president possesses the power to terminate, abrogate, suspend, and interpret U.S. treaty obligations as an aspect of his foreign affairs power. On December 13, 2001, President George W. Bush's administration announced that it was terminating the Anti–Ballistic Missile (ABM) treaty with (the remnants of) the Soviet Union. Office of the Press Secretary, The White House Announcement of Withdrawal from the ABM Treaty (Dec. 13, 2001). See Memorandum from John C. Yoo, Deputy Assistant Att'y Gen., Office of Legal Counsel, & Robert J. Delahunty, Special Counsel, Office of Legal Counsel, to John Bellinger, III, Senior Assoc. Counsel to the President & Legal Adviser to the Nat'l Sec. Counsel (Nov. 15, 2001). Did the Supreme Court's failure to invalidate President Carter's treaty termination—and its collective decision, on various differing grounds, that it lacked power to decide the case—effectively give the green light to such presidential interpretations? Should courts stay out of foreign affairs constitutional controversies altogether? What would be the effect of such an approach? Is it consistent with Article III's assignment of jurisdiction extending to cases arising under the Constitution, statutes, and treaties of the United States to the courts?

3. Is there any constitutional restriction on the topics about which the president may make a treaty (provided two-thirds of the senators present consent) or on what results may be enacted thereby as a matter of U.S. domestic law? What if a treaty violates some other part of the Constitution, such as the First Amendment? Is it still supreme law or is the delegation of the power to make treaties to the president implicitly a delegation only to make treaties that comport with the rest of the Constitution? Can a treaty constitutionally take away Congress's power to declare war? Commit Congress to declare war in a given circumstance (e.g., by treaty of alliance)? In general, can a treaty ever foreclose or irrevocably commit the exercise of a constitutional power? Can it repeal a constitutional right? Can it create new rights as a matter of U.S. law? Suppose a future president and Senate approved a treaty giving every citizen a guaranteed minimum income, or giving every a fetus a right to be free from sex-selective abortion, or giving every person on Death Row immunity from execution? What would be the legal effect of these treaties within the United States?

Does the treaty power allow the president to do things by treaty that Congress lacks the enumerated power to do by legislation? Or does that in itself violate some constitutional provision, such as the Constitution's seeming limitation of the national government's powers to specifically enumerated powers or the Tenth Amendment's reservation of the remainder to the states? Put differently, can the president and Senate, acting together by treaty, effectively alter what otherwise is the balance of federalism—the Constitution's allocation of powers between the national government and the states? (We return to these issues in the next chapter, when studying the cases of *Missouri v. Holland,* 252 U.S. 416 (1920), and *Reid v. Covert,* 354 U.S. 1 (1957).)

Perhaps the most consequential use of the treaty power in America's history was the Louisiana Purchase of 1803. President Thomas Jefferson found himself with the amazing opportunity to acquire the territory of Louisiana from Napoleon, who was eager to sell it to pay for his wars. Congress had no enumerated power to buy land or territory, and President Jefferson generally advocated a narrow construction of national powers. Could a president by treaty acquire land that would double the size of the United States? President Jefferson had his doubts at first, thinking that this could only be done by a constitutional amendment. In the end, however, the deal was too good to refuse. President Jefferson retreated from his initial scruples, the Senate consented to the treaty, and Congress by statute appropriated the needed funds. In retrospect, does the Louisiana Purchase seem like a wise and defensible use of the Treaty Power? If so, what implications does it have for other topics on which treaties might constitutionally be made? Note also that the example of the Louisiana Purchase suggests that there are at least some types of treaties the content of which preclude, as a practical matter, unilateral presidential termination. Surely the president could not unilaterally revoke the Louisiana Purchase!

A NOTE ON INTERNATIONAL LAW AND THE STATUS OF TREATIES AS U.S. LAW

What is the status of international law under the U.S. Constitution? What is international law? The answers to these questions are endlessly complex and much-debated, but a rough summary is possible for purposes of a survey course on the U.S. Constitution. The Constitution's Supremacy Clause designates only three categories of "supreme Law of the land": The Constitution, statutes passed pursuant to the Constitution, and treaties under the authority of the United States. Thus, a U.S. treaty, enacted by the process specified in Article II of the Constitution, becomes part of U.S. law. But many treaties are not "self-executing." That is, they may require further implementing legislation before they have full legal effect. In addition, it is well settled that a U.S. treaty may be superseded by a subsequent statute enacted by Congress and signed by the president. The traditional view is that treaties and statutes are of equal force, so that whichever is enacted most recently supersedes what was enacted before to the extent of any inconsistency. Some recent scholarship contests this consensus, arguing that statutes are always of superior force. See Vasan Kesavan, *The Three Tiers of Federal Law,* 100 Nw. U. L. Rev. 1479 (2006).

What about customary international law, such as norms and principles or the actions of international bodies that are *not* pursuant to any treaty to which the United States is a party? This is much more controversial, because such non-treaty international law is nowhere mentioned in Article VI of the Constitution. Congress possesses an enumerated power to "define and punish Offences against the Laws of Nations," but that contemplates Congress acting through the ordinary legislative process to reduce certain general international law principles into concrete U.S. law. Nonetheless, many international law scholars argue that general principles of international law, not incorporated into any treaty, are binding on the United States. Compare Louis Henkin, *International Law As Law in the United States*, 82 Mich. L. Rev. 1555 (1984) (arguing that customary international law is part of U.S. law), with Curtis Bradley & Jack L. Goldsmith, *Customary International Law As Federal Common Law: A Critique of the Modern Position*, 110 Harv. L. Rev. 815 (1997) (contesting this view). International law might be binding on nations as a matter of *international law* principles, but is it binding as a matter of *U.S. constitutional law*? In the event that these conflict, what is the supreme legal authority in the United States? If the conflict is between international law norms and acts of Congress? Executive decisions? Federal regulations? State law?

[*Assignment 22*]

F. THE WAR POWER: "CONGRESS SHALL HAVE POWER . . . TO DECLARE WAR" BUT "THE PRESIDENT SHALL BE COMMANDER IN CHIEF"

How does the Constitution allocate the enormously important powers of war and peace? From the beginning, this has been one of the most enduring of constitutional controversies, with different views prevailing at different times. While there have been noteworthy judicial decisions in this area, the primary interpretive battleground has been in the political sphere, with Congress and the president each advancing their own constitutional views and struggling for primacy.

We begin with a survey of the text of the Constitution's provisions concerning war powers, the history of their drafting and early interpretation, and a summary of modern practice. We then proceed to explore these issues by examining, roughly chronologically, a series of illustrative situations involving the exercise of war powers throughout America's history: the Civil War; World War II; the Korean War; the Vietnam War; the First Gulf War; the Kosovo War; the "War on Terror" following the attacks of September 11, 2001; the recent American military actions in Libya; and the Seal Team Six raid resulting in the killing of Osama bin Laden.

As to each situation, consider the recurring constitutional questions: What is the scope of Congress's power "to declare War"? What is the scope of the president's power as "Commander in Chief"? Who has the power to initiate a war? What about defensive actions in immediate response to attacks? Who has the power to *conduct* war (and what does this include)? What happens where the several war powers of Congress and the president may intersect and overlap? What constitutes a "war" in the first place: Do all uses of American military force constitute a war that must be declared? And finally: Has America's actual constitutional *practice* with respect to war been consistent with the Constitution's allocation of war powers? If not, what does that say about America's constitutional practice?

The Text

The Constitution appears to vest both Congress and the president with a share of the war power of the nation. Congress has a number of quite specific Article I, Section 8 powers relevant to declaring and waging war. Here are the most relevant provisions:

The Congress shall have power . . .

[10] To define and punish Piracies and Felonies committed on the high Seas, and Offences against the Law of Nations;

[11] To declare War, grant Letters of Marque and Reprisal, and make Rules concerning Captures on Land and Water;

[12] To raise and support Armies, but no Appropriation of Money to that Use shall be for a longer Term than two Years;

[13] To provide and maintain a Navy;

[14] To make Rules for the Government and Regulation of the land and naval Forces;

[15] To provide for calling forth the Militia to execute the Laws of the Union, suppress Insurrections and repel Invasions;

[16] To provide for organizing, arming, and disciplining, the Militia, and for governing such Part of them as may be employed in the Service of the United States, reserving to the States respectively, the Appointment of the Officers, and the Authority of training the Militia according to the discipline prescribed by Congress. . . .

In addition, Congress possesses the taxing and spending power (Article I, Section 8, clause 1) and the Necessary and Proper Clause power "[t]o make all Laws which shall be necessary and proper for carrying into Execution the foregoing Powers, and all other Powers vested by this Constitution in the Government of the United States, or in any Department or Officer thereof" (Article I, Section 8, clause 18).

At the same time, however, the president is given several general and specific powers with respect to war. The president possesses "[t]he executive Power" of the United States (Article II, Section 1), and is specifically made "Commander in Chief of the Army and Navy of the United States, and of the Militia of the several States, when called into the actual Service of the United States" (Article II, Section 2, clause 1). And the president is charged by oath to "preserve, protect, and defend the Constitution of the United States."

These powers—the executive power, the Commander-in-Chief power, and the implications of the oath—have formed the basis for the claimed authority of the president to send the nation's armed forces into combat even when Congress has not declared or authorized war.

Another section of the Constitution limits the war-making powers of *states*. Article I, Section 10, Clause 3 reads: "No State shall, without the Consent of Congress, . . . keep Troops, or ships of War in time of Peace, . . . or engage in War, unless actually invaded, or in such imminent Danger as will not admit of delay."

History

The Constitution's provisions were written against a background understanding of "executive power" as embracing the complete power to manage a nation's external relations, including war and peace. That understanding was embraced by Blackstone and others, and Montesquieu's formulation differed only slightly. See generally Saikrishna B. Prakash & Michael D. Ramsey, *The Executive Power Over Foreign Affairs*, 111 Yale L.J. 231 (2001). Obviously, the Constitution departs from this understanding.

Specifically, it relocates to the legislative branch the power "to declare War" and to raise and support armies and navies, while retaining for the president the role of Commander-in-Chief and whatever else remains of the "executive power."

A portion of the debate at the Constitutional Convention at Philadelphia provides some possible illumination—or, at least, a great many people have thought so. The debate, recorded in Madison's Notes, focused on a proposal to change the language from a grant of power to Congress to "*make* War" to a power to "*declare* War." As you read this somewhat cryptic record of the debates (the entirety of the discussion of the provision), ask yourself what inferences can be drawn for interpreting the Constitution.

Madison's Notes, "To Make War"
August 17, 1787

Mr. Pinkney opposed the vesting this power in the Legislature. Its proceedings were too slow. It wd. meet but once a year. The Hs. of Reps. would be too numerous for such deliberations. The Senate would be the best depositary, being more acquainted with foreign affairs, and most capable of proper resolutions. If the States are equally represented in Senate, so as to give no advantage to large States, the power will notwithstanding be safe, as the small have their all at stake in such cases as well as the large States. It would be singular for one authority to make war, and another peace.

Mr. Butler. The objections agst the Legislature lie in great degree agst the Senate. He was for vesting the power in the President, who will have all the requisite qualities, and will not make war but when the Nation will support it.

Mr. Madison and Mr. Gerry moved to insert "*declare*," striking out "*make*" war; leaving to the Executive the power to repel sudden attacks.

Mr. Sharman thought it stood very well. The executive shd be able to repel and not to commence war. "Make" better than "declare" the latter narrowing the power too much.

Mr. Gerry never expected to hear in a republic a motion to empower the Executive alone to declare war.

Mr. Elseworth. there is a material difference between the cases of making *war* and making *peace*. It shd be more easy to get out of war, than into it. War also is a simple and overt declaration. peace attended with intricate & secret negociations.

Mr. Mason was agst giving the power of war to the Executive, because not safely to be trusted with it; or to the Senate, because not so constructed as to be entitled to it. He was for clogging rather than facilitating war; but for facilitating peace. He preferred "*declare*" to "*make*."

On the motion to insert *declare*—in place of *make*, it was agreed to.

N.H. no. Mas. abst. Cont. no. * Pa. ay. Del. ay. Md. ay. Va. ay. N.C. ay. S.C. ay. Geo. ay.

[* On the remark by Mr. King that "*make*" war might be understood to "*conduct*" it which was an Executive function, Mr. Elseworth gave up his objection, and the vote of Cont. was changed to—ay.]

Mr. Pinkney's motion to strike out whole clause, disagd to without call of States.

Mr. Butler moved to give the Legislature power of peace, as they were to have that of war.

Mr. Gerry 2d him. 8 Senators may possibly exercise the power if vested in that body, and 14 if all should be present; and may consequently give up part of the U. States. The Senate are more liable to be corrupted by an Enemy than the whole Legislature.

On the motion for adding "and peace" after "war"

N. H. no. Mas. no. Ct. no. Pa. no. Del. no. Md. no. Va. No. N.C. no S.C. no. Geo. no.

––––––

Debates in the state ratifying conventions, and early practice, seem to suggest that at the founding most understood the Declare War Clause to have vested in Congress (and not the president) the power to decide to take the nation into a condition of war. See Michael D. Ramsey, *Textualism and War Powers*, 69 U. Chi. L. Rev. 1543 (2002); Charles A. Lofgren, *War–Making Under the Constitution: The Original Understanding*, 81 Yale L.J. 672 (1972). Others see the historical evidence differently, however, reading the text and history as preserving the executive power to wage war as an aspect of the president's foreign affairs power, with the Declare War Clause serving a lesser role of providing formal recognition to such a state of affairs and triggering certain national and international legal relationships that come with a formal state of war. On that view, it would be Congress's power over appropriations, and not the Declare War Clause, that serves as a check on presidential war-making. See John C. Yoo, *The Continuation of Politics by Other Means: The Original Understanding of War Powers*, 84 Cal. L. Rev. 167 (1996); John C. Yoo & Robert J. Delahunty, *The President's Constitutional Authority to Conduct Military Operations Against Terrorist Organizations and the Nations that Harbor or Support Them*, 25 Harv. J. L. & Pub. Pol'y 488 (2002).

If Congress's power to declare war requires congressional authorization for the initiation of military hostilities, there remain questions about whether the president may engage in use of military force *defensively*—to "repel sudden attacks" in the words of the Philadelphia Convention debate—and how far such a defensive power can be pushed (especially in a world where technology permits increasingly quick "sudden attacks"). Also, there is the question of what presidential uses of military power actually constitute "war" in the constitutional sense of the word. Since the early twentieth century, use of military force to rescue or protect Americans abroad has increasingly been understood to be an executive power.

This is one possible synthesis:

> The several constitutional provisions suggest a clear but crude division of power: Congress has the power to initiate or create a state of war and the President does not. The President has the remainder of the "executive" power with respect to war—and Congress does not. This includes the Commander-in-Chief power to conduct war: the power to "execute," as it were, any authorized war; the power to decide whether, when, and how to employ the Nation's armed force in carrying out Congress's authorization to use such force; and the power to decide

when to cease such use of force. In addition, the President has the traditional executive power to defend the Nation against sudden attacks and respond to such attacks or imminent threats as will not admit of delay. Congress does not possess any of these executive war powers.

The obvious problem is that the respective constitutional war powers of Congress and the President overlap. How they apply to particular instances is, therefore, not always clear. Where, for example, does the President's traditional executive power to defend the nation and repel attacks leave off and Congress's power "to declare War" begin? May a President initiate military hostilities against another nation, for the purpose of defending the United States against an anticipated attack? Or is such exercise of force essentially offensive, falling within Congress's exclusive power to declare war? Similarly, how does the Commander-in-Chief power to wage a congressionally-authorized war interact with Congress's control of the scope of authorization? May Congress limit the objectives or means of war? Or is this an interference with the President's exclusive power to direct and command the use of military force?

Michael Stokes Paulsen, Youngstown *Goes to War*, 19 Const. Comm. 215, 239 (2002) (emphasis omitted).

Practice and Precedent

It should not be surprising that this has been an area of conflict between the political branches. Predictably, the executive branch has tended to take a pro-executive view while the legislative branch has adopted a pro-legislative view. Often, though, the two branches are in agreement. (World War II, following the attack on Pearl Harbor, is an obvious case.) And yet the two branches frequently disagree as well. (The later stages of the Vietnam War are an example.) Frequently, disputes focus on the wording of congressional resolutions, like the Gulf of Tonkin Resolution, that are ambiguous endorsements or quasi-authorizations of presidential authority to wage war, or on the still more ambiguous implications of congressional appropriations for support of military operations already underway.

In general, since the end of World War II, with the rise of the Cold War and nuclear weapons, more of the initiative in war-making powers has been seized by the president. President Truman sent troops to Korea on his own authority. He quickly obtained both international support (from the United Nations) and congressional support through funding for the war effort, but the four-year Korean War was never formally authorized by Congress (unless the funding decisions count). The Vietnam War was waged on the authority of the Gulf of Tonkin Resolution, a less than crystalline authorization for war. Numerous other military engagements in the second half of the twentieth century were the result of essentially unilateral presidential action. Without great exaggeration, it might be said that the practice of war powers has rearranged the initial constitutional roles, with the president serving as the primary decision-maker on the question of use of military force and Congress reduced to the role of providing an uncertain "check" on unilateral presidential military action.

A great many of major armed conflicts involving the United States were not authorized by a declaration of war. Indeed, there have been only five formal declarations of war in U.S. history: The War of 1812, the Mexican–American War, the Spanish–American War, World War I, and World War II. (Six, if one counts the American Declaration of Independence, part of the purpose of which was to attempt to clothe American forces with the status of legitimate armed belligerents entitled to the protections of the law of war.) Must Congress "declare" "war"—use those magic words—in order to exercise its war-initiating power under the Declare War Clause? The Clause has never been thought to require the use of particular words. (For a powerful dissenting view, see J. Gregory Sidak, *To Declare War*, 41 Duke L.J. 27 (1991).) If magic words do not need to be used, what instances of U.S. military action amount to "war": Rescue operations? Humanitarian actions? Deployment of troops for peacekeeping? Limited armed interventions to effect an arrest of a war criminal? Are any of these governed by the Declare War Clause? How should a court decide?

What is the value of practice and precedent in resolving questions like these? The courts have rarely been involved in these disputes. (A couple of judicial decisions that are exceptions to the rule are considered below.) Does practice "liquidate" the meaning of the Constitution, as Madison said in *The Federalist No. 37*? Or must we conclude, if practice is inconsistent with the Constitution, that a great deal of the nation's practice with respect to war powers has been *unconstitutional*? Consider these questions as you read the following case studies.

The Prize Cases
67 U.S. 635 (1863)

[In 1861, after the South attacked Fort Sumter, President Lincoln proclaimed a blockade of Southern ports. Under the terms of the blockade, and in accordance with common principles of the "law of nations" at the time, vessels violating the blockade were subject to being captured and seized as "prizes." The owners of several seized ships challenged the legality of the blockade. Congress had not declared war on the states of the Confederacy—and never did. Indeed, President Lincoln's justification for waging the Civil War was that the states of the South could not legally secede, that the "Confederacy" did not truly exist as a lawful entity, and that the actions of the Union were those of putting down a domestic insurrection—thus, no declaration of war was necessary.—Editors]

■ MR. JUSTICE GRIER.

. . . Had the President a right to institute a blockade of ports in possession of persons in armed rebellion against the Government, on the principles of international law, as known and acknowledged among civilized States? . . . Neutrals have a right to challenge the existence of a blockade de facto, and also the authority of the party exercising the right to institute it. They have a right to enter the ports of a friendly nation for the purposes of trade and commerce, but are bound to recognize the rights of a belligerent engaged in actual war, to use this mode of coercion, for the purpose of subduing the enemy.

. . . To legitimate the capture of a neutral vessel or property on the high seas, a war must exist de facto, and the neutral must have a knowledge or notice of the intention of one of the parties belligerent to use this mode of coercion against a port, city, or territory, in possession of the other. Let us enquire whether, at the time this blockade was instituted, a state of war existed which would justify a resort to these means of subduing the hostile force.

War has been well defined to be, "That state in which a nation prosecutes its right by force." The parties belligerent in a public war are independent nations. But it is not necessary to constitute war, that both parties should be acknowledged as independent nations or sovereign States. A war may exist where one of the belligerents, claims sovereign rights as against the other.

Insurrection against a government may or may not culminate in an organized rebellion, but a civil war always begins by insurrection against the lawful authority of the Government. A civil war is never solemnly declared; it becomes such by its accidents—the number, power, and organization of the persons who originate and carry it on. When the party in rebellion occupy and hold in a hostile manner a certain portion of territory; have declared their independence; have cast off their allegiance; have organized armies; have commenced hostilities against their former sovereign, the world acknowledges them as belligerents, and the contest a war. They claim to be in arms to establish their liberty and independence, in order to become a sovereign State, while the sovereign party treats them as insurgents and rebels who owe allegiance, and who should be punished with death for their treason.

The laws of war, as established among nations, have their foundation in reason, and all tend to mitigate the cruelties and misery produced by the scourge of war. Hence the parties to a civil war usually concede to each other belligerent rights. They exchange prisoners, and adopt the other courtesies and rules common to public or national wars. . . .

By the Constitution, Congress alone has the power to declare a national or foreign war. It cannot declare was against a State, or any number of States, by virtue of any clause in the Constitution. The Constitution confers on the President the whole Executive power. He is bound to take care that the laws be faithfully executed. He is Commander-in-chief of the Army and Navy of the United States, and of the militia of the several States when called into the actual service of the United States. He has no power to initiate or declare a war either against a foreign nation or a domestic State. But by the Acts of Congress of February 28th, 1795, and 3d of March, 1807, he is authorized to called out the militia and use the military and naval forces of the United States in case of invasion by foreign nations, and to suppress insurrection against the government of a State or of the United States. . . .

This greatest of civil wars was not gradually developed by popular commotion, tumultuous assemblies, or local unorganized insurrections. However long may have been its previous conception, it nevertheless sprung forth suddenly from the parent brain, a Minerva in the full panoply of war. The President was bound to meet it in the shape it presented itself, without waiting for Congress to baptize it with a name; and no name given to it by him or them could change the fact.

It is not the less a civil war, with belligerent parties in hostile array, because it may be called an "insurrection" by one side, and the insurgents be considered as rebels or traitors. It is not necessary that the independence of the revolted province or State be acknowledged in order to constitute it a party belligerent in a war according to the law of nations. Foreign nations acknowledge it as war by a declaration of neutrality. . . .

The law of nations is also called the law of nature; it is founded on the common consent as well as the common sense of the world. It contains no such anomalous doctrine as that which this Court are now for the first time desired to pronounce, to wit: That insurgents who have risen in rebellion against their sovereign, expelled her Courts, established a revolutionary government, organized armies, and commenced hostilities, are not enemies because they are traitors; and a war levied on the Government by traitors, in order to dismember and destroy it, is not a war because it is an "insurrection."

Whether the President in fulfilling his duties, as Commander in-chief, in suppressing an insurrection, has met with such armed hostile resistance, and a civil war of such alarming proportions as will compel him to accord to them the character of belligerents, is a question to be decided by him, and this Court must be governed by the decisions and acts of the political department of the Government to which this power was entrusted. "He must determine what degree of force the crisis demands." The proclamation of blockade is itself official and conclusive evidence to the Court that a state of war existed which demanded and authorized a recourse to such a measure, under the circumstances peculiar to the case.

. . . If it were necessary to the technical existence of a war, that it should have a legislative sanction, we find it in almost every act passed at the extraordinary session of the Legislature of 1861, which was wholly employed in enacting laws to enable the Government to prosecute the war with vigor and efficiency. And finally, in 1861, we find Congress "ex major cautela" and in anticipation of such astute objections, passing an act "approving, legalizing, and making valid all the acts, proclamations, and orders of the President, & c., as if they had been issued and done under the previous express authority and direction of the Congress of the United States."

. . . On this first question therefore we are of the opinion that the President had a right, jure belli, to institute a blockade of ports in possession of the States in rebellion, which neutrals are bound to regard. . . . *[The Court next raises a second question: the meaning of "enemies' property."— Editors]*

The appellants contend that the term "enemy" is properly applicable to those only who are subjects or citizens of a foreign State at war with our own. . . .

They insist, moreover, that the President himself, in his proclamation, admits that great numbers of the persons residing within the territories in possession of the insurgent government, are loyal in their feelings, and forced by compulsion and the violence of the rebellious and revolutionary party and its "de facto government" to submit to their laws and assist in their scheme of revolution; that the acts of the usurping government cannot legally sever the bond of their allegiance; they have, therefore, a correlative right to claim the protection of the government for their persons and property, and to be treated as loyal citizens, till legally convicted of having renounced their allegiance and made war against the Government by treasonably resisting its laws.

They contend, also, that insurrection is the act of individuals and not of a government or sovereignty; that the individuals engaged are subjects of law. That confiscation of their property can be effected only under a municipal law. That by the law of the land such confiscation cannot take place without the conviction of the owner of some offence, and finally that the secession ordinances are nullities and ineffectual to release any citizen from his allegiance to the national Government, and consequently that the

Constitution and Laws of the United States are still operative over persons in all the States for punishment as well as protection.

This argument rests on the assumption of two propositions, each of which is without foundation on the established law of nations. It assumes that where a civil war exists, the party belligerent claiming to be sovereign, cannot, for some unknown reason, exercise the rights of belligerents, although the revolutionary party may. Being sovereign, he can exercise only sovereign rights over the other party. The insurgent may be killed on the battle-field or by the executioner; his property on land may be confiscated under the municipal law; but the commerce on the ocean, which supplies the rebels with means to support the war, cannot be made the subject of capture under the laws of war, because it is *"unconstitutional"!!!* Now, it is a proposition never doubted, that the belligerent party who claims to be sovereign, may exercise both belligerent and sovereign rights. . . . Treating the other party as a belligerent and using only the milder modes of coercion which the law of nations has introduced to mitigate the rigors of war, cannot be a subject of complaint by the party to whom it is accorded as a grace or granted as a necessity, We have shown that a civil war such as that now waged between the Northern and Southern States is properly conducted according to the humane regulations of public law as regards capture on the ocean.

. . . [I]n organizing this rebellion, they have acted as States claiming to be sovereign over all persons and property within their respective limits, and asserting a right to absolve their citizens from their allegiance to the Federal Government. Several of these States have combined to form a new confederacy, claiming to be acknowledged by the world as a sovereign State. Their right to do so is now being decided by wager of battle. The ports and territory of each of these States are held in hostility to the General Government. It is no loose, unorganized insurrection, having no defined boundary or possession. It has a boundary marked by lines of bayonets, and which can be crossed only by force—south of this line is enemies' territory, because it is claimed and held in possession by an organized, hostile and belligerent power.

All persons residing within this territory whose property may be used to increase the revenues of the hostile power are, in this contest, liable to be treated as enemies, though not foreigners. They have cast off their allegiance and made war on their Government, and are none the less enemies because they are traitors. . . .

Whether property be liable to capture as "enemies' property" does not in any manner depend on the personal allegiance of the owner. "It is the illegal traffic that stamps it as 'enemies' property.' It is of no consequence whether it belongs to an ally or a citizen. The owner, pro hac vice, is an enemy." *3 Wash. C.C.R., 183.*

The produce of the soil of the hostile territory, as well as other property engaged in the commerce of the hostile power, as the source of its wealth and strength, are always regarded as legitimate prize, without regard to the domicil of the owner, and much more so if he reside and trade within their territory.

. . . We now proceed to notice the facts peculiar to the several cases submitted for our consideration. The principles which have just been stated apply alike to all of them. . . . The case of the brig Amy Warwick. . . .

■ MR. JUSTICE NELSON, dissenting.

. . . Another objection taken to the seizure of this vessel and cargo is, that there was no existing war between the United States and the States in insurrection within the meaning of the law of nations, which drew after it the consequences of a public or civil war. A contest by force between independent sovereign States is called a public war; and, when duly commenced by proclamation or otherwise, it entitles both of the belligerent parties to all the rights of war against each other, and as respects neutral nations. Chancellor Kent observes, "Though a solemn declaration, or previous notice to the enemy, be now laid aside, it is essential that some formal public act, proceeding directly from the competent source, should announce to the people at home their new relations and duties growing out of a state of war, and which should equally apprize neutral nations of the fact, to enable them to conform their conduct to the rights belonging to the new state of things." "Such an official act operates from its date to legalize all hostile acts, in like manner as a treaty of peace operates from its date to annul the." He further observes, "as war cannot lawfully be commenced on the part of the United States without an act of Congress, such act is, of course, a formal notice to all the world, and equivalent to the most solemn declaration."

The legal consequences resulting from a state of war between two countries at this day are well understood, and will be found described in every approved work on the subject of international law. The people of the two countries become immediately the enemies of each other—all intercourse commercial or otherwise between then unlawful—all contracts existing at the commencement of the war suspended, and all made during its existence utterly void. . . . All the property of the people of the two countries on land or sea are subject to capture and confiscation by the adverse party as enemies' property, with certain qualifications as it respects property on land (*Brown v. United States, 8 Cranch, 110*), all treaties between the belligerent parties are annulled, The ports of the respective countries may be blockaded, and letters of marque and reprisal granted as rights of war, and the law of prizes as defined by the law of nations comes into full and complete operation, resulting from maritime captures, jur belli. War also effects a change in the mutual relations of all States or countries, not directly, as in the case of the belligerents, but immediately and indirectly, though they take no part in the contest, but remain neutral.

This great and pervading change in the existing condition of a country, and in the relations of all her citizens or subjects, external and internal, from a state of peace, is the immediate effect and result of a state of war: and hence the same code which has annexed to the existence of a war all these disturbing consequences has declared that the right of making war belongs exclusively to the supreme or sovereign power of the State.

This power in all civilized nations is regulated by the fundamental laws or municipal constitution of the country.

By our Constitution this power is lodged in Congress. Congress shall have power "to declare war, grant letters of marque and reprisal, and make rules concerning captures on land and water."

We have thus far been considering the status of the citizens or subjects of a country at the breaking out of a public war when recognized or declared by the competent power.

In the case of a rebellion or resistance of a portion of the people of a country against the established government, there is no doubt, if in its progress and enlargement the government thus sought to be overthrown sees fit, it may by the competent power recognize, or declare the existence of a state of civil war, which will draw after it all the consequences and rights of war between the contending parties as in the case of a public war. . . . But before this insurrection against the established Government can be dealt with on the footing of a civil war, within the meaning of the law of nations and the Constitution of the United States, and which will draw after it belligerent rights, it must be recognized or declared by the war-making power of the Government. No power short of this can change the legal status of the Government or the relations of its citizens from that of peace to a state of war, or bring into existence all those duties and obligations to neutral third parties growing out of a state of war. The war power of the Government must be exercised before this changed condition of the Government and people and of neutral third parties can be admitted. There is no difference in this respect between a civil or a public war.

The [Militia] Acts of 1795 and 1807 did not, and could not under the Constitution, confer on the President the power of declaring war against a State of this Union, or of deciding that war existed, and upon that ground authorize the capture and confiscation of the property of every citizen of the State whenever it was found on the waters. The laws of war, whether the war be civil or inter gentes, as we have seen, convert every citizen of the hostile State into a public enemy, and treat him accordingly, whatever may have been his previous conduct. This great power over the business and property of the citizen is reserved to the legislative department by the express words of the Constitution. It cannot be delegated or surrendered to the Executive. Congress alone can determine whether war exists or should be declared; and until they have acted, no citizen of the State can be punished in his person or property, unless he had committed some offence against a law of Congress passed before the act was committed, which made it a crime, and defined the punishment. The penalty of confiscation for the acts of others with which he had no concern cannot lawfully be inflicted. . . .

Congress assembled on the call for an extra session the 4th of July, 1861, and among the first acts passed was one in which the President was authorized by proclamation to interdict all trade and intercourse between all the inhabitants of States in insurrection and the rest of the United States, subjecting vessel and cargo to capture and condemnation as prize, and also to direct the capture of any ship or vessel belonging in whole or in part to any inhabitant of a State whose inhabitants are declared by the proclamation to be in a state of insurrection, found at sea or in any part of the rest of the United States. Act of Congress of 13th of July, 1861, secs. 5, 6. The 4th section also authorized the President to close any port in a Collection District obstructed so that the revenue could not be collected, and provided for the capture and condemnation of any vessel attempting to enter. . . .

This Act of Congress, we think, recognized a state of civil war between the Government and the Confederate States, and made it territorial. . . .

Upon the whole, after the most careful consideration of this case which the pressure of other duties has admitted, I am compelled to the conclusion that no civil war existed between this Government and the States in insurrection till recognized by the Act of Congress 13th of July, 1861; that the President does not possess the power under the Constitution to declare war or recognize its existence within the meaning of the law of nations, which carries with it belligerent rights, and thus change the country and all its citizens from a state of peace to a state of war; that this power belongs exclusively to the Congress of the United States, and, consequently, that the President had no power to set on foot a blockade under the law of nations, and that the capture of the vessel and cargo in this case, and in all cases before us in which the capture occurred before the 13th of July, 1861, for breach of blockade, or as enemies' property, are illegal and void, and that the decrees of condemnation should be reversed and the vessel and cargo restored.

■ MR. CHIEF JUSTICE TANEY, MR. JUSTICE CATRON and MR. JUSTICE CLIFFORD, concurred in the dissenting opinion of MR. JUSTICE NELSON.

———

Next consider excerpts from the two executive orders called, collectively, "The Emancipation Proclamation." As the basis for these orders, President Lincoln appealed to his authority as commander in chief.

President Lincoln, The Preliminary Emancipation Proclamation

A draft released to the public on September 22, 1862

I, ABRAHAM LINCOLN, President of the United States of America, and Commander-in-Chief of the Army and Navy thereof, etc., hereby proclaim and declare, that hereafter, as heretofore, the war will be prosecuted for the object of practically restoring the constitutional relation between the United States and the people thereof in which States that relation is or may be suspended or disturbed. . . .

That on the first day of January in the year of our Lord, one thousand eight hundred and sixty-three, all persons held as slaves within any state, or designated part of a state, the people whereof shall then be in rebellion against the United States shall be then, thenceforward, and forever free; and the executive government of the United States, including the military and naval authority thereof, will recognize and maintain the freedom of such persons, and will do no act or acts to repress such persons, or any of them, in any efforts they make for their actual freedom.

That the executive will, on the first day of January aforesaid, by proclamation, designate the States, and parts of states, if any, in which the people thereof respectively, shall than be in rebellion against the United States; . . .

That attention is hereby called to an act of Congress entitled "An act to make an additional Article of War" approved March 13, 1862 . . . *[prohibiting use of the military to return fugitive slaves.—Editors]* Also to the ninth and tenth sections of an act entitled "An Act to suppress Insurrection, to punish Treason and Rebellion, to seize and confiscate property of rebels, and for other purposes," approved July 17, 1862 . . . *[proclaiming that slaves of persons engaged in rebellion who escape and take refuge within the lines of the Union army would be free, and further requiring that fugitive slaves not be returned except upon an oath that their owner "has not borne arms against the United States in the present rebellion, nor in any way given aid and comfort thereto."—Editors]*

And I do hereby enjoin upon and order all persons engaged in the military and naval service of the United States, to observe, obey, and enforce, within their respective spheres of service, the act and sections above recited. . . .

President Lincoln, The Final Emancipation Proclamation

January 1, 1863

Whereas, on the twentysecond day of September, in the year of our Lord one thousand eight hundred and sixty two, a proclamation was issued by the President of the United States . . . *[President Lincoln then quoted at length from the Preliminary Emancipation Proclamation.—Editors]*

Now, therefore I, Abraham Lincoln, President of the United States, by virtue of the power in me vested as Commander-in-Chief, of the Army and Navy of the United States in time of actual armed rebellion against the authority and government of the United States, and as a fit and necessary war measure for suppressing said rebellion, do, on this first day of January, in the year of our Lord one thousand eight hundred and sixty-three, and in accordance with my purpose so to do publicly proclaimed for the full period of one hundred days, from the day first above mentioned, order and designate as the States and parts of States wherein the people thereof respectively, are this day in rebellion against the United States, the following, to wit:

Arkansas, Texas, Louisiana, (except the Parishes of St. Bernard, Plaquemines, Jefferson, St. John, St. Charles, St. James Ascension, Assumption, Terrebonne, Lafourche, St. Mary, St. Martin, and Orleans, including the City of New Orleans) Mississippi, Alabama, Florida, Georgia, South Carolina, North Carolina, and Virginia, (except the forty-eight counties designated as West Virginia, and also the counties of Berkley, Accomac, Northampton, Elizabeth City, York, Princess Ann, and Norfolk, including the cities of Norfolk and Portsmouth[)], and which excepted parts, are for the present, left precisely as if this proclamation were not issued.

And by virtue of the power, and for the purpose aforesaid, I do order and declare that all persons held as slaves within said designated States, and parts of States, are, and henceforward shall be free; and that the Executive government of the United States, including the military and naval authorities thereof, will recognize and maintain the freedom of said persons.

And I hereby enjoin upon the people so declared to be free to abstain from all violence, unless in necessary self-defence; and I recommend to them that, in all cases when allowed, they labor faithfully for reasonable wages.

And I further declare and make known, that such persons of suitable condition, will be received into the armed service of the United States to garrison forts, positions, stations, and other places, and to man vessels of all sorts in said service.

And upon this act, sincerely believed to be an act of justice, warranted by the Constitution, upon military necessity, I invoke the considerate judgment of mankind, and the gracious favor of Almighty God. . . .

NOTES

1. The Civil War was not a declared "war," in large part because President Lincoln's view was that the use of force against the Southern states was not a *war* within the meaning of the Constitution (as against a foreign enemy), but rather the suppression by force of a rebellion. Indeed, for one part of the United States to "declare war" against another would have been regarded as improper. Nor was President Lincoln prepared to recognize the "Confederate States of America" as a legitimate sovereign entity, let alone a foreign nation—that would have been inconsistent with the constitutional theory underlying the Union's prosecution of the war. Nevertheless, in practical terms the suppression of the rebellion plainly involved the application of the war power of the United States. What do you think: was the Civil War "unconstitutional"?

More specifically, was the Emancipation Proclamation constitutional? What was President Lincoln's constitutional justification for it? Was it the war powers of the president as commander in chief? Can the president take "property" (offensive as the characterization is for persons) without its owner's consent in order to more effectively wage war? Isn't that the issue presented a century later in *Youngstown Sheet & Tube*, or can the two situations be distinguished? In answering these questions, does it matter whether the president offers compensation? Note that the Emancipation Proclamation applied only to areas in rebellion and controlled at the time by Confederate forces. It freed no slaves in the border slave states that remained in the Union (Kentucky, Maryland, Delaware, and Missouri) or in areas of the South already under the control of the Union army. Does this matter? At all events, does the validity of President Lincoln's Emancipation Proclamation—surely the most significant executive order in all of American constitutional history—depend on the premise that the war power of the United States was validly invoked?

2. How would you describe the theory of *The Prize Cases* concerning the Constitution's allocation of war powers? Does it embrace a version of the president's inherent defensive power to "repel sudden attacks," suggested as one of the reasons for the Constitutional Convention's use of the term "declare" rather than "make" war? Or is the Court's theory something different yet? Is the opinion persuasive? Note finally that though the case was decided after President Lincoln's Emancipation Proclamation, it appears to strongly support the constitutionality of President Lincoln's military order. Did the justices have the Emancipation Proclamation in mind when they made their decision? President Lincoln's Proclamation, while noting the existence of congressional acts indirectly supportive of his action, went considerably beyond any specific congressional authorization.

3. *The Prize Cases* was a pivotal judicial decision concerning the Constitution's allocation of war powers, but it was not the only early judicial decision concerning these issues. The Court's earliest decisions on war powers emphasize congressional control over the use of force rather than presidential power to respond to emergencies and the use of force by others. Several of these cases involved (like *The Prize Cases*) issues concerning the capture of vessels and claimed property rights, some of which arose in the ambiguous situation created by the so-called "Quasi–War" with France in the late 1790s (when Congress passed several statutes essentially putting the nation on a war footing without formally declaring war). For an early judicial statement embracing Congress's complete power over the decision to go to war and the extent of such war, but

also noting that authorization of war brings into play the laws of war, see *Talbot v. Seeman*, 5 U.S. 1, 28 (1801) ("The whole powers of war being, by the constitution of the United States, vested in congress, the acts of that body can alone be resorted to as our guides in this enquiry. It is not denied, nor in the course of the argument has it been denied, that congress may authorize general hostilities, in which case the general laws of war apply to our situation; or partial hostilities, in which case the laws of war, so far as they actually apply to our situation, must be noticed."). See also *Bas v. Tingy*, 4 U.S. 37 (1800) (discussing the legal status of the "quasi-war" with France as governed by Congress's enactments); *Little v. Barreme*, 6 U.S. 170 (1804) (Marshall, C.J.) (rules of "capture" and seizure of ships in prize cases governed by congressional enactment, not presidential military orders); *Brown v. United States*, 12 U.S. 110 (1814) (Marshall, C.J.) (authority of president to confiscate enemy property in United States during War of 1812 governed by Congress's statutes, not executive action); cf. *Durand v. Hollins*, 8 F. Cas. 111 (Circuit Court S.D.N.Y 1860) (sustaining unilateral presidential military order of bombardment of Greytown, Nicaragua, in response to attacks on U.S. property and persons, against damages action for destruction of property).

4. A hypothetical: You are President Lincoln. The year is 1864. A lawsuit is brought challenging the constitutionality of the Emancipation Proclamation, and the Supreme Court rules against you and orders the return of liberated slaves to their former masters in states in rebellion against the Union. You consider the decision badly wrong as a constitutional matter, extraordinarily harmful to the nation as a practical matter, and deeply offensive as a moral matter. Do you nonetheless comply?

Declaring War

If the power "to declare War" vests in Congress control over the decision to initiate sustained military action against an enemy force or nation, what counts as a legally effective authorization of such action? Does Congress need to formally and literally "declare" war, or is it sufficient that it enact legislation authorizing the use of military force? (Why might Congress choose the latter rather than the former?) May Congress enact a limited authorization? May Congress enact a statute prospectively limiting the use of force that it has not specifically authorized, or specifying situations in which its laws should *not* be construed as authorizing the use of force?

What follows are four enactments of Congress in the modern era, for comparison and constitutional analysis: the explicit Declaration of War against Japan, marking America's formal entry into World War II; the more ambiguous Gulf of Tonkin Resolution of 1964, cited as authorization for the Vietnam War; the War Powers Resolution of 1973, passed over President Nixon's veto and purporting to regulate the use of force in a variety of situations; and the Authorization for Use of Military Force of September 18, 2001, conferring and recognizing sweeping authority for the War on Terror.

Declaration of War Against Japan
December 8, 1941

Joint Resolution. Declaring that a state of war exists between the Imperial Government of Japan and the Government and the people of the United States and making provisions to prosecute the same.

Whereas the Imperial Government of Japan has committed unprovoked acts of war against the Government and the people of the United States of America: Therefore be it Resolved by the Senate and House of Representatives of the United States of America in Congress assembled,

That the state of war between the United States and the Imperial Government of Japan which has thus been thrust upon the United States is hereby formally declared; and the President is hereby authorized and directed to employ the entire naval and military forces of the United States and the resources of the Government to carry on war against the Imperial Government of Japan; and, to bring the conflict to a successful termination, all of the resources of the country are hereby pledged by the Congress of the United States.

The Gulf of Tonkin Resolution
August 7, 1964

Resolved by the Senate and House of Representatives of the United States of America in Congress assembled,

[Section 1.] That the Congress approves and supports the determination of the President, as Commander in Chief, to take all necessary measures to repel any armed attack against the forces of the United States and to prevent further aggression.

Section 2. The United States regards as vital to its national interest and to world peace the maintenance of international peace and security in southeast Asia. Consonant with the Constitution of the United States and the Charter of the United Nations and in accordance with its obligations under the Southeast Asia Collective Defense Treaty, the United States is, therefore, prepared, as the President determines, to take all necessary steps, including the use of armed force, to assist any member or protocol state of the Southeast Asia Collective Defense Treaty requesting assistance in defense of its freedom.

Section 3. This resolution shall expire when the President shall determine that the peace and security of the area is reasonably assured by international conditions created by action of the United Nations or otherwise, except that it may be terminated earlier by concurrent resolution of the Congress.

NOTES

1. The Declaration of War Against Japan is a classic instance of a direct, unequivocal, and formal declaration of war. (Germany then declared war on the United States, and the United States then formally declared war on Germany.) Was a declaration of war legally necessary for the president to deploy military force against Japan following the attacks on Pearl Harbor? If not, what legal force does a declaration of war add?

2. After World War II, America's next major military conflict was in Korea. Was the Korean War constitutional? The facts in brief: Following World War II, Korea was partitioned into two zones of allied occupation: the northern zone, under the auspices of Soviet forces; and the southern zone, under the auspices of U.S. forces (eventually these zones became North Korea and South Korea, respectively). In 1950, North Korea attacked South Korea. President Truman unilaterally sent in U.S. forces. The United Nations Security Council soon thereafter supported President Truman's actions and called on U.N. members to support the collective defense of South Korea. (The Soviet Union was boycotting the Security Council, but otherwise would have vetoed the action.) Congress never declared war and never specifically authorized it, but it nonetheless continued to appropriate funds for the military. The United States, by treaty, was of course a member of the United Nations. The U.N. treaty does not itself commit member nations to use military force when requested to assist in enforcement of Security Council actions. (Would a treaty obligation committing the United States to war be consistent with the U.S. Constitution?) Did President Truman possess independent constitutional authority to commit U.S. troops to war in South Korea? Was it part of his executive power over foreign affairs? Was it his duty to faithfully execute U.S. treaty obligations? Does U.N. support suffice for U.S. constitutional purposes? Does it dispense with the necessity of a congressional declaration of war?

3. Was the Vietnam War constitutional? Did the Gulf of Tonkin Resolution constitute sufficient constitutional authorization for the president to wage war in Southeast Asia? (Was authorization needed?) Congress eventually voted to repeal the resolution, but it was the decision to withhold funds for military operations in Southeast Asia past a defined date that ultimately led to the U.S. military's withdrawal from, and the fall of, South Vietnam. Is control of funding the real constitutional power of Congress with respect to war? May Congress implicitly authorize war-making by its funding of the military? How specific must such funding decisions be in order to constitute authorization? Or is control over funding simply an ancillary way of *enforcing* Congress's power to authorize (or not to authorize) war-making? Are *Youngstown*'s categories (or its other principles) relevant here?

The Vietnam War generated numerous legal challenges and lower court decisions. See, e.g., Orlando v. Laird, 443 F.2d 1039 (2d Cir. 1971) (finding the question properly justiciable but rejecting a constitutional challenge, noting that "[t]he Congress and the Executive have taken mutual and joint action in the prosecution and support of military operations in Southeast Asia from the beginning of those operations" and noting, among other things, the Tonkin Gulf Resolution). But the constitutionality of the war was never decided on the merits by the Supreme Court, though many opportunities were presented for such decision. Are constitutional issues of war and peace nonjusticiable political questions best left to the executive and legislative branches to decide? As long as a proper case with proper parties exists, where resolution of the dispute turns on an interpretation of the respective war powers of Congress and the president, is there any constitutional bar to judicial decision of such issues?

4. What about the following military actions:

    a.   President Kennedy ordered a military "quarantine" of Cuba (essentially a blockade) at the time of the Cuban Missile Crisis, when the Soviet Union was attempting to set up short- and intermediate-range missiles in Cuba. Congress did not authorize the action. Constitutional?

b.   President Carter ordered a military commando raid (ultimately unsuccessful) to attempt to rescue U.S. hostages held in Iran following the Iranian seizure of the U.S. Embassy in Tehran in 1979. Congress did not authorize the action. Constitutional?

c.   In 1989, President George H. W. Bush ordered a military invasion of Panama in order to seize the country's dictator, General Manuel Noriega, and protect U.S. citizens in the Canal Zone. Congress did not authorize the action. Constitutional?

5. What about U.S. secret "covert operations" that involve spying, sabotage, or the use of lethal force? What is the constitutionality of such covert operations? Does Congress need to authorize them? Are they part of the war power? Currently, such operations appear authorized, generally, by the "Intelligence Authorization Act of 1991," which permits covert operations in the form of "activities of the United States Government to influence political, economic, or military conditions abroad, where it is intended that the role of the United States Government will not be apparent or acknowledged publicly." The president must determine that "such an action is necessary to support identifiable foreign policy objectives of the United States and is important to the national security of the United States," set forth this determination in writing within 48 hours, and report this information to the intelligence committees of each house of Congress (or, if the president thinks it necessary to withhold such information, report it only to eight designated high-ranking members of Congress).

6. As the Vietnam War became increasingly unpopular politically, concern over the drift of war-making power toward the president led Congress in 1973 to pass the War Powers Resolution (WPR) over President Nixon's veto. The WPR purports to presents Congress's constitutional views concerning the respective war powers of Congress and the president, along with a framework for enforcing those views. As you read the materials on the WPR, ask yourself whether the WPR is constitutional and whether it can be given meaningful enforcement by either Congress or the courts. Subsequent presidents have taken the position that the WPR is an unconstitutional attempt by Congress to limit the presidential authority as commander in chief. Even so, presidents have consistently reported military actions to Congress in a manner consistent with the WPR's requirements, seeking to avoid direct confrontations.

The War Powers Resolution of 1973

Initially passed by Congress in October 1973;
repassed over President Nixon's veto in November 1973

Resolved by the Senate and House of Representatives of the United States of America in Congress assembled,

Section 1. *Short Title.* This joint resolution may be cited as the "War Powers Resolution."

Section 2. *Purpose and Policy.*

(a) It is the purpose of this joint resolution to fulfill the intent of the framers of the Constitution of the United States and insure that the collective judgment of both the Congress and the President will apply to the introduction of United States Armed Forces into hostilities, or into situations where imminent involvement in hostilities is clearly indicated by the circumstances, and to the continued use of such forces . . .

(c) The constitutional powers of the President as Commander-in-Chief to introduce United States Armed Forces into hostilities, or into situations where imminent involvement in hostilities is clearly indicated by the circumstances, are exercised only pursuant to (1) a declaration of war, (2) specific statutory authorization, or (3) a national emergency created by attack upon the United States, its territories or possessions, or its armed forces.

Section 3. *Consultation* [President required to consult Congress "in every possible instance"]

Section 4. *Reporting* [President required to report military action to Congress within 48 hours]

Section 5. *Congressional Action.* . . .

(b) Within sixty calendar days after a report is submitted or is required to be submitted pursuant to section 4(a)(1), whichever is earlier, the President shall terminate any use of United States Armed Forces with respect to which such report was submitted . . . unless the Congress (1) has declared war or enacted a specific authorization for such use of the United States Armed Forces, (2) has extended by law such sixty-day period, or (3) is physically unable to meet as a result of an armed attack upon the United States. Such sixty-day period shall be extended for not more than an additional thirty days if the President determines and certifies to the Congress in writing that unavoidable military necessity respecting the safety of United States Armed Forces requires the continued use of such armed forces in the course of bringing about a prompt removal of such forces.

(c) Notwithstanding subsection (b), at any time that United States Armed Forces are engaged in hostilities outside the territory of the United States, its possessions and territories without a declaration of war or specific statutory authorization, such forces shall be removed by the President if the Congress so directs by concurrent resolution. . . .

Section 8. *Interpretation of Joint Resolution*

(a) Authority to introduce United States Armed Forces into hostilities or into situations wherein involvement in hostilities is clearly indicated by the circumstances shall not be inferred—

    (1) from any provision of law . . ., including any provision contained in an appropriation Act, unless such provision specifically authorizes the introduction of United States Armed Forces into hostilities or into such situations and states that it is intended to constitute specific statutory authorization within the meaning of this joint resolution; or

    (2) from any treaty heretofore or hereafter ratified unless such treaty is implemented by legislation specifically authorizing the introduction of United States Armed Forces into hostilities or into such situations and stating that it is intended to constitute specific statutory authorization within the meaning of this joint resolution.

. . .

(c) Nothing in this joint resolution—

(1) is intended to alter the constitutional authority of the Congress or of the President, or the provisions of existing treaties; or

(2) shall be construed as granting any authority to the President with respect to the introduction of United States Armed Forces . . . which authority he would not have had in the absence of this joint resolution. . . .

President Nixon, Statement Vetoing the War Powers Resolution

October 24, 1973

To the House of Representatives:

I hereby return without my approval House Joint Resolution 542—the War Powers Resolution. While I am in accord with the desire of the Congress to assert its proper role in the conduct of our foreign affairs, the restrictions which this resolution would impose upon the authority of the President are both unconstitutional and dangerous to the best interests of our Nation.

The proper roles of the Congress and the Executive in the conduct of foreign affairs have been debated since the founding of our country. Only recently, however, has there been a serious challenge to the wisdom of the Founding Fathers in choosing not to draw a precise and detailed line of demarcation between the foreign policy powers of the two branches.

The Founding Fathers understood the impossibility of foreseeing every contingency that might arise in this complex area. They acknowledged the need for flexibility in responding to changing circumstances. They recognized that foreign policy decisions must be made through close cooperation between the two branches and not through rigidly codified procedures.

These principles remain as valid today as they were when our Constitution was written. Yet House Joint Resolution 542 would violate those principles by defining the President's powers in ways which would strictly limit his constitutional authority.

Clearly Unconstitutional

House Joint Resolution 542 would attempt to take away, by a mere legislative act, authorities which the President has properly exercised under the Constitution for almost 200 years. One of its provisions would automatically cut off certain authorities after sixty days unless the Congress extended them. Another would allow the Congress to eliminate certain authorities merely by the passage of a concurrent resolution—an action which does not normally have the force of law, since it denies the President his constitutional role in approving legislation.

I believe that both these provisions are unconstitutional. The only way in which the constitutional powers of a branch of the Government can be altered is by amending the Constitution—and any attempt to make such alterations by legislation alone is clearly without force.

Undermining Our Foreign Policy

While I firmly believe that a veto of House Joint Resolution 542 is warranted solely on constitutional grounds, I am also deeply disturbed by the practical consequences of this resolution. For it would seriously undermine this Nation's ability to act decisively and convincingly in times of international crisis. As a result, the confidence of our allies in our ability to assist them could be diminished and the respect of our adversaries for our deterrent posture could decline. A permanent and substantial element of unpredictability would be injected into the world's assessment of American behavior, further increasing the likelihood of miscalculation and war.

If this resolution had been in operation, America's effective response to a variety of challenges in recent years would have been vastly complicated or even made impossible. We may well have been unable to respond in the way we did during the Berlin crisis of 1961, the Cuban missile crisis of 1962, the Congo rescue operation in 1964, and the Jordanian crisis of 1970—to mention just a few examples. In addition, our recent actions to bring about a peaceful settlement of the hostilities in the Middle East would have been seriously impaired if this resolution had been in force.

While all the specific consequences of House Joint Resolution 542 cannot yet be predicted, it is clear that it would undercut the ability of the United States to act as an effective influence for peace. For example, the provision automatically cutting off certain authorities after 60 days unless they are extended by the Congress could work to prolong or intensify a crisis. Until the Congress suspended the deadline, there would be at least a chance of United States withdrawal and an adversary would be tempted therefore to postpone serious negotiations until the 60 days were up. Only after the Congress acted would there be a strong incentive for an adversary to negotiate. In addition, the very existence of a deadline could lead to an escalation of hostilities in order to achieve certain objectives before the 60 days expired.

The measure would jeopardize our role as a force for peace in other ways as well. It would, for example, strike from the President's hand a wide range of important peace-keeping tools by eliminating his ability to exercise quiet diplomacy backed by subtle shifts in our military deployments. It would also cast into doubt authorities which Presidents have used to undertake certain humanitarian relief missions in conflict areas, to protect fishing boats from seizure, to deal with ship or aircraft hijackings, and to respond to threats of attack. Not the least of the adverse consequences of this resolution would be the prohibition contained in section 8 against fulfilling our obligations under the NATO treaty as ratified by the Senate. Finally, since the bill is somewhat vague as to when the 60 day rule would apply, it could lead to extreme confusion and dangerous disagreements concerning the prerogatives of the two branches, seriously damaging our ability to respond to international crises.

Failure to Require Positive Congressional Action

I am particularly disturbed by the fact that certain of the President's constitutional powers as Commander in Chief of the Armed Forces would terminate automatically under this resolution. 60 days after they were invoked. No overt Congressional action would be required to cut off these powers—they would disappear automatically unless the Congress extended them. In effect, the Congress is here attempting to increase its policy-making role through a provision which requires it to take absolutely no action at all.

In my view, the proper way for the Congress to make known its will on such foreign policy questions is through a positive action, with full debate on the merits of the issue and with each member taking the responsibility of casting a yes or no vote after considering those merits. The authorization and appropriations process represents one of the ways in which such influence can be exercised. I do not, however, believe that the Congress can responsibly contribute its considered, collective judgment on such grave questions without full debate and without a yes or no vote. Yet this is precisely what the joint resolution would allow. It would give every future Congress the ability to handcuff every future President merely by doing nothing and sitting still. In my view, one cannot become a responsible partner unless one is prepared to take responsible action.

Strengthening Cooperation between The Congress and the Executive Branches

The responsible and effective exercise of the war powers requires the fullest cooperation between the Congress and the Executive and the prudent fulfillment by each branch of its constitutional responsibilities. House Joint Resolution 542 includes certain constructive measures which would foster this process by enhancing the flow of information from the executive branch to the Congress. Section 3, for example, calls for consultations with the Congress before and during the involvement of the United States forces in hostilities abroad. This provision is consistent with the desire of this Administration for regularized consultations with the Congress in an even wider range of circumstances.

I believe that full and cooperative participation in foreign policy matters by both the executive and the legislative branches could be enhanced by a careful and dispassionate study of their constitutional roles. Helpful proposals for such a study have already been made in the Congress. I would welcome the establishment of a non-partisan commission on the constitutional roles of the Congress and the President in the conduct of foreign affairs. This commission could make a thorough review of the principal constitutional issues in Executive–Congressional relations, including the war powers, the international agreement powers, and the question of Executive privilege, and then submit its recommendations to the President and the Congress. The members of such a commission could be drawn from both parties—and could represent many perspectives including those of the Congress, the executive branch, the legal profession, and the academic community.

This Administration is dedicated to strengthening cooperation between the Congress and the President in the conduct of foreign affairs and to preserving the constitutional prerogatives of both branches of our Government. I know that the Congress shares that goal. A commission on the constitutional roles of the Congress and the President would provide a useful opportunity for both branches to work together toward that common objective.

NOTES

1. Is the War Powers Resolution constitutional? Read it carefully: Does it authorize use of force? Does it implicitly invite unilateral presidential action in certain circumstances? Are its "legislative veto" provisions constitutional? Is its interpretation of the Constitution's allocation of war powers correct? Are its rules of interpretation for applying statutes (and treaties) within Congress's constitutional powers? Every subsequent president through President George W. Bush has maintained that the War Powers Resolution unconstitutionally interferes with the president's power as commander in chief. A definitive posi-

tion has not been taken by President Obama. See Transcript, White House Press Conference with President Obama (June 29, 2011) (answering a journalist's question, President Obama described the consultation required by the War Powers Resolution as "entirely appropriate" but also noted that at some point "[t]here may be a time in which there was a serious question" about its constitutionality, and expressly reserving that question). The issue has never been judicially resolved by the Supreme Court.

2. A case study: In late 1990, Iraq's leader, Saddam Hussein, invaded the nation of Kuwait, a nation friendly to the United States. In an operation known as Operation Desert Shield, President George H. W. Bush sent American troops to Saudi Arabia to guard against invasion of that nation. A first set of questions: Does that action fall within the president's constitutional military power as commander in chief? Does it require a declaration of war or its legal equivalent? Is it subject to the requirements of the War Powers Resolution? The United Nations then authorized the use of force to expel Iraqi forces from Kuwait. President Bush enlarged the U.S. troop presence in the Persian Gulf region, explicitly stating that he was preparing an *offensive* military option. There followed a period of constitutional debate between Congress and President Bush, with many in Congress insisting that President Bush could not launch an attack against Iraqi forces without congressional authorization, and with President Bush insisting that he did not need such authorization in light of U.N. approval and his own constitutional power as commander in chief. Who was right? Is the issue affected by Congress's approval of funding specifically for Operation Desert Shield?

Two U.S. district court opinions in the District of Columbia found the issue nonjusticiable, but for different reasons. In *Dellums v. Bush,* 752 F. Supp. 1141 (D.D.C. 1990), the court found that the issue was not "ripe" because Congress had not acted one way or the other and because there was no certainty of an attack; however, the court did not think the issue a "political question" outside of judicial purview because the Constitution provided a clear standard requiring congressional authorization. In *Ange v. Bush,* 752 F. Supp. 509 (D.D.C. 1990), a different district judge of the same district found the case nonjusticiable because the Constitution failed to provide a basis for resolving the dispute between Congress's and the president's war powers and that the issue was therefore a political question to be worked out by those two branches. Which view do you think is right? In the end, Congress *did* authorize the use of force, mooting the constitutional and War Powers Resolution questions. (Later in this chapter we will return to these cases as an illustration of constitutional limitations on "the judicial Power" of Article III.)

3. Another case study: In 1999, America was involved in armed conflict in Kosovo and other states of the former nation of Yugoslavia. The facts in brief: in March 1999, President Clinton involved the United States in the NATO bombing of Yugoslavia without prior congressional authorization. The Senate quickly voted a resolution of support. In April 1999, all on the same day, the House of Representatives (a) failed, on a tie vote, to join the Senate's resolution; (b) rejected overwhelmingly a resolution to declare war; (c) defeated a resolution pursuant to section 5(c) of the War Powers Act to "veto" the president's action; and (d) passed a resolution stating that the president must get Congress's authorization before sending any ground troops to Yugoslavia. Subsequently, Congress voted a supplemental appropriation for the military action. The Senate tabled a resolution that would have authorized the president to use

"all necessary force" in Yugoslavia. What do you make of these conflicting actions by Congress? Was the Kosovo engagement constitutional? Was it consistent with the War Powers Resolution? Is such consistency necessary?

4. With the attacks on September 11, 2001, the war powers pendulum swung once again. Consider the Authorization for Use of Military Force of September 18, 2001, which follows. Is it the functional equivalent of a declaration of war? Does it repudiate (or revise) Congress's view of the Constitution's allocation of war powers?

Authorization for Use of Military Force
September 18, 2001, Public Law 107–40

JOINT RESOLUTION

To authorize the use of United States Armed Forces against those responsible for the recent attacks launched against the United States.

Whereas, on September 11, 2001, acts of treacherous violence were committed against the United States and its citizens; and

Whereas, such acts render it both necessary and appropriate that the United States exercise its rights to self-defense and to protect United States citizens both at home and abroad; and

Whereas, in light of the threat to the national security and foreign policy of the United States posed by these grave acts of violence; and

Whereas, such acts continue to pose an unusual and extraordinary threat to the national security and foreign policy of the United States; and

Whereas, the President has authority under the Constitution to take action to deter and prevent acts of international terrorism against the United States: Now, therefore, be it

Resolved by the Senate and House of Representatives of the United States of America in Congress assembled,

SECTION 1. SHORT TITLE.

. . . "Authorization for Use of Military Force."

SECTION 2. AUTHORIZATION FOR USE OF UNITED STATES ARMED FORCES.

(a) IN GENERAL—That the President is authorized to use all necessary and appropriate force against those nations, organizations, or persons he determines planned, authorized, committed or aided the terrorist attacks that occurred on September 11, 2001, or harbored such organizations or persons, in order to prevent any future acts of international terrorism against the United States by such nations, organizations, or persons.

(b) WAR POWERS RESOLUTION REQUIREMENTS—

(1) SPECIFIC STATUTORY AUTHORIZATION.—Consistent with section 8(a)(1) of the War Powers Resolution, the Congress declares that this section is intended to constitute specific statutory authorization within the meaning of section 5(b) of the War Powers Resolution.

(2) APPLICABILITY OF OTHER REQUIREMENTS.—Nothing in this resolution supercedes any requirement of the War Powers Resolution.

NOTES

1. Was the AUMF the legal equivalent of a declaration of war? If so, what exactly did it authorize? What was its duration? Was it legally necessary in order for the president to wage war against al Qaeda and its affiliates? Was it legally sufficient to justify the subsequent war against Iraq? (The Iraq War was supported by a later, specific authorization for the use of force.) Does the president, under the AUMF, possess lawful authority to use military force against any nation that "harbors" or fails to expel known terrorists? And what if the persons are only suspected to be terrorists (or potential terrorists)? What sort of "showing" of probable guilt (if any) is required before the president may act pursuant to the AUMF? Who is charged with making this determination? Did the AUMF authorize the American commando raid in Pakistan to capture and kill Osama bin Laden? Could the president have ordered such a raid without the AUMF? Is there any limitation on the persons or nations against whom U.S. military force may be employed pursuant to this authorization?

2. What view of the relative constitutional powers of Congress and the president does the AUMF take? Does it essentially embrace the strongly pro-presidential view that the president "has authority" under the Constitution to take action on his own? Is this surprising? Is this view consistent with the approach of the War Powers Resolution? Does the AUMF constitute a "repeal" of the constitutional approach of Congress enacted in the War Powers Resolution? Or does the specific citation to the WPR negate any such inference?

The War Powers Debate Continues: The Intervention in Libya and the Killing of Osama bin Laden

Perhaps the most significant recent development in the constitutional debate over war powers was President Obama's decision to employ military force against Libya to prevent Libyan dictator Colonel Muammar Qaddafi from massacring rebel forces. The U.S. Department of Justice's Office of Legal Counsel produced a legal opinion justifying unilateral presidential authority to use armed force. See Memorandum for the Attorney General Re Authority to Use Military Force in Libya (April 1, 2011) ("OLC Memorandum").

The OLC Memorandum said that the president had "constitutional authority to direct the use of force in Libya because he could reasonably determine that such use of force was in the national interest." *Id.* at 1. The president had determined "that the use of military force in Libya serves important U.S. interests in preventing instability in the Middle East and preserving the credibility and effectiveness of the United Nations Security Council." *Id.* at 6. Although "not required to direct the use of military force simply because the [U.N. Security Council] has authorized it," the president could use such authorization to justify military action on the ground that it served " 'a substantial national foreign policy objective.' " *Id.* at 12 (quoting *Military Forces in Somalia*, 16 Op. O.L.C. at 12). Because the goal of military action was to implement a U.N. Security Council resolution by enforcing a "no-fly zone" with military action, and because "no U.S. ground forces would be deployed," "the use of military force in Libya was supported by sufficiently important national interests to fall within the President's constitutional power." *Id.* at 6, 12. Thus, "the President had constitutional authority, as Commander in Chief and Chief Executive and pursuant to his foreign affairs powers, to direct such limited military operations abroad, even without prior specific congressional approval." *Id*. at 6.

The Declare War Clause did not limit this unilateral presidential military action, the OLC Memorandum continued: "We have acknowledged one possible constitutionally-based limit on this presidential authority to employ military force in defense of important national interests—a planned military engagement that constitutes a 'war' within the meaning of the Declaration of War Clause may require prior congressional authorization." *Id*. at 8. Nevertheless, "[t]he historical practice of presidential military action without congressional approval precludes any suggestion that Congress's authority to declare war covers every military engagement, however limited, that the President initiates." *Id*. "In our view," the OLC Memorandum continued, "determining whether a particular planned engagement constitutes a 'war' for constitutional purposes instead requires a fact-specific assessment of the 'anticipated nature, scope, and duration' of the planned military operations. This standard generally will be satisfied only by prolonged and substantial military engagements, typically involving exposure of U.S. military personnel to significant risk over a substantial period." *Id*. (quoting *Haiti Deployment*, 18 Op. O.L.C. at 179). Since, at the time President Obama decided to use armed force, the "anticipated nature, scope and duration" of the military engagement was "limited," the use of force by the U.S. in Libya did not "r[i]se to the level of a 'war' in the constitutional sense, requiring the President to seek a declaration of war or other prior authorization from Congress." *Id*. at 13.

At several points in its analysis, the OLC Memorandum relied on earlier OLC opinions defending the lawfulness of presidential military interventions, ranging from rescue operations and goodwill missions to sustained bombing campaigns or commitments of thousands of ground troops. The memorandum specifically cited an earlier bombing of Libya (1986); an intervention in Panama (1989); troop deployments to Somalia (1992), Bosnia (1995), and Haiti (1994 and 2004); air strikes in Bosnia (1993–95); and the bombing campaign in Yugoslavia (1999). "This historical practice is an important indication of constitutional meaning, because it reflects the two political branches' practical understanding, developed since the founding of the Republic, of their respective roles with respect to national defense." *Id*. at 7. Quoting its earlier opinions, OLC concluded that the "pattern of executive conduct, made under claim of right, extended over many decades and engaged in by Presidents of both parties, evidences the existence of broad constitutional power." *Id*. at 7.

The OLC Memorandum also argued that the War Powers Resolution of 1973 "implicitly recognized" unilateral presidential military authority, even though it "does not itself provide affirmative statutory authority for military operations." *Id*. at 8. Quoting earlier OLC opinions, the Memorandum concluded that, notwithstanding section 1547(d)(2)'s directive that nothing in the War Powers Resolution be construed as authorizing military action, the "structure" of the Resolution, by purporting to impose length-of-time cut-offs for any unilateral presidential use of armed force, "recognizes and presupposes the existence of unilateral presidential authority to deploy armed forces into hostilities." *Id*. at 8.

The OLC Memorandum with respect to Libya presents the following questions about the Constitution's allocation of war powers:

1. Note how broad the April 1, 2011 OLC Memorandum's position is on unilateral presidential war powers: The president, acting alone, may initi-

ate offensive military action against an enemy force or nation whenever it is "in the national interest." What provision of the Constitution confers that power? The Commander-in-Chief Clause? The "foreign affairs" power (flowing from the "executive Power" generally)? What are the practical limits on what presidents may identify as the "national interest"?

The Obama administration's position appears to go further than previous administrations. In the past, presidential administrations typically defended unilateral presidential military action, where not authorized by Congress, as falling either within (1) a sometimes-aggressive understanding of the residual executive war power to "repel sudden attacks" (even preemptively or preventively) or to respond to attacks upon the nation or its citizens; or (2) a power to rescue or protect U.S. citizens abroad, derived from some understanding of the general duty of the president as chief executive of the nation to provide such protection to U.S. nationals. But it is not clear that any prior administration has asserted a general presidential war power in order to effectuate foreign policy goals or other general national interests.

2. Note that there are historical precedents of presidential war-making that appear to extend beyond these exceptional categories, as discussed above. The Korean War and the bombing of Kosovo might well be examples of presidential wars not authorized by Congress's exercise of the power to declare war. The Libyan intervention raises again the question of the relationship between the constitutional text and historical practice. In addition, it raises the question of whether the Constitution's allocation of war powers can be affected by institutional acquiescence or waiver. Does it matter whether Congress has acquiesced in the historical practice of the executive branch? (Note that the OLC Memorandum cites both the "historical gloss on the 'executive power' " language of Justice Frankfurter's *Youngstown* concurrence and the "Category II/congressional quiescence" language of Justice Jackson's concurrence in the same case.) And what constitutes such acquiescence? Did Congress, by enacting the War Powers Resolution (unwittingly) acquiesce to a unilateral presidential war-making power for sixty days, even though the Resolution itself states that nothing in it should be construed as granting the president any additional authority? When the sixty-day War Powers Resolution runs out, does that mean that acquiescence expires?

3. The OLC Memorandum acknowledges that Congress's power under the Declare War Clause might limit unilateral presidential war-making— that this clause was a "possible" limitation. However, the Memorandum argued that the Declare War Clause applied only to military actions fitting the meaning of the word "war."

The issue is thus raised once again: What is the constitutional meaning of the word "war"? In the Libyan military engagement, the United States initiated sustained, armed attacks on forces and targets of an enemy nation with whom it was not already engaged in hostilities and which had engaged in no attack on American forces or citizens. Is this not a "war"? But might not the same question be asked of other military actions that never received congressional authorization? (Does that matter?) Consider two factors emphasized in the OLC Memorandum: First, is the *absence of ground troops* controlling? In other words, does it matter to the constitutional understanding of "war" whether the object of an attack is bombed from the air or invaded with ground forces? Second, is the expected *duration* of hostilities controlling? If a military engagement is short and discrete, does it fall outside the category of "war" that Congress must authorize? What effect does an engagement's change over time have on its classification as "war"? A brief and tidy operation can grow into a sustained and messy one. Does that mean that a "non-war" military action can *become* a "war"? (Does the OLC Memorandum admit of this possibility?)

4. What is the effect of a U.N. Security Council resolution on the Constitution's allocation of war powers? May a treaty commitment substitute for a declaration of war (or equivalent legislative authorization for the use of force) if one is otherwise required? May a decision of an ally or an international body, pursuant to a U.S. treaty, trigger a presidential power or duty to use armed force? (The question recalls the situation of the Korean War in certain respects.)

5. Does it matter to the constitutional analysis whether an armed military intervention is for humanitarian purposes, such as preventing a massacre in a civil war?

The military intervention in Libya is not the only recent incident sparking debate over war powers. On May 1, 2011, American forces killed Osama bin Laden, the head of al Qaeda, at a compound in Pakistan. Bin Laden was a legitimate military target under the terms of the AUMF. Does it matter that he was hiding in Pakistan? Was the use of military force within Pakistan authorized by the AUMF? If Pakistan was "harboring" bin Laden, does the AUMF authorize military force against the nation itself?

There were various reports as to precisely what occurred in the raid; one account is that bin Laden was unarmed but in reasonably close proximity to a weapon. What if these facts on the ground matter for international law purposes or U.S. treaty law purposes (such as the Geneva Conventions, a treaty to which the United States is a party)? *If* this was an intentional, targeted killing of an enemy commander known to be unarmed at the time, *and* if such a killing is proscribed by international law (including the customary law of war), does that operate as a constraint on U.S. constitutional power to use armed force? If the United States were a party to a treaty that proscribed such killings, would that operate as a constraint?

On Terminating War

The Constitution gives Congress the power to declare war, but how is war terminated? May a state of war be ended by a presidential proclamation, legislation, or a treaty? The question of how to terminate a war was considered during the Constitutional Convention, where the delegates debated the requirements for concluding a "treaty of peace." Madison argued that a treaty of peace should be easier to approve than other kinds of treaties: a two-thirds majority in the Senate should not be required, and even presidential concurrence was unnecessary. 2 Farrand, RECORDS OF THE FEDERAL CONVENTION 540. In the end, though, the Convention decided that treaties of peace should be subject to the same requirements as other treaties. *Id.* at 544.

The Supreme Court addressed the question of war termination in *Ludecke v. Watkins*, 335 U.S. 160 (1948). The Court held:

War does not cease with a cease-fire order, and power to be exercised by the President such as that conferred by the Act of 1798 is a process which begins when war is declared but is not exhausted when the shooting stops. 'The state of war' may be terminated by treaty or legislation or Presidential proclamation. Whatever the modes, its termination is a political act.

In January of 1971, Congress, in response to growing public resistance to the Vietnam War, repealed the Gulf of Tonkin Resolution of 1964. However, President Nixon continued the war effort based on his authority as commander in chief, and Congress continued to fund the war effort for several more years. Is congressional legislation really an effective means to terminate a war that the executive is determined to pursue? Congress, empowered by the Constitution with the spending power (Article I, Section 8), has the authority to "defund" a war, effectively forcing the United States to withdraw. Is this Congress's most effective tool for ending a war? But is this a politically viable option for legislators seeking reelection? Will a president determined to carry on the war effort, even without continued funding from Congress, always win the inter-branch showdown? If so, are there any effective checks on the president?

[*Assignment 23*]

G. PRISONERS OF WAR AND CIVILIAN DETENTIONS

Where the war power has been constitutionally invoked, how far does it go in allowing the capture, detention, interrogation, and punishment of enemy combatants? Are such powers intrinsically an aspect of the president's Commander in Chief Clause power to conduct war? Or are they subject to Congress's power to direct and control—and, if so, by virtue of which of Congress's powers? The power to prescribe general rules for the armed forces? The power to define and punish offenses against the law of nations? The power to "make Rules concerning Captures on Land and Water"? The Necessary and Proper Clause?

Against whom can such auxiliary war powers be brought to bear? "Unlawful enemy combatants" (subject to capture and detention and potentially punishable by military authorities for war crimes)? "Lawful enemy combatants" (subject to capture and detention but not punishment)? All enemy combatants? Even American citizens? What about civilian non-combatants? Which of these persons can be detained and held as prisoners? On what basis? Who makes the judgment concerning into which category a person fits and whether a sufficient basis exists for military detention or punishment? Who decides whether someone is a spy, a saboteur and terrorist, or merely an innocent bystander? Does it matter whether a detainee is a U.S. citizen? And how bold should a court be in constraining the executive during a time of war?

These questions have arisen many times in America's history, with important judicial decisions arising from the Civil War to World War II to the War on Terror. We present here some key cases in this area: *Ex parte Milligan*, 71 U.S. 2 (1866), held, shortly after the Civil War, that military tribunals could not be used in lieu of civilian courts for treason trials of suspected plotters of sabotage and kidnapping who were not otherwise affiliated with enemy armed forces. *Ex parte Quirin,* 317 U.S. 1 (1942), qualified and limited *Milligan* and unanimously upheld the World War II use of presidentially ordered military trial and punishment of Nazi spies and saboteurs (including a U.S. citizen) for war crimes. *Korematsu v. United States*, 323 U.S. 214 (1944), is the well-known—even notorious—World War II-era case upholding a military order removing Japanese–Americans from their homes and relocating them in detention camps on the basis of ethnicity and suspicion predicated on ethnicity rather than on the basis of any hostile acts actually committed (as had been the case in *Milligan* and *Quirin*). Finally, *Hamdi v. Rumsfeld,* 542 U.S. 507 (2004), upheld the president's power to capture and detain enemy combatants, including American citizens, as part of the war power, but also held that American citizens have a limited due process right to a hearing in which to contest their status as enemy combatants. As you read through the cases, try to sort out what you think are the correct constitutional rules for each situation: When does the war power authorize detention or military punishment under military jurisdiction? Who must (or may) exercise that authority? And when does the Constitution exclude or otherwise limit that authority?

Ex parte Milligan
71 U.S. 2 (1866)

■ MR. JUSTICE DAVIS delivered the opinion of the court.

. . . The importance of the main question presented by this record cannot be overstated; for it involves the very framework of the government and the fundamental principles of American liberty.

During the late wicked Rebellion, the temper of the times did not allow that calmness in deliberation and discussion so necessary to a correct conclusion of a purely judicial question. *Then*, considerations of safety were mingled with the exercise of power; and feelings and interests prevailed which are happily terminated. *Now* that the public safety is assured, this question, as well as all others, can be discussed and decided without passion or the admixture of any element not required to form a legal judgment. We approach the investigation of this case, fully sensible of the magnitude of the inquiry and the necessity of full and cautious deliberation. . . .

The controlling question in the case is this: Upon the *facts* stated in Milligan's petition, and the exhibits filed, had the military commission mentioned in it *jurisdiction*, legally, to try and sentence him? Milligan, not a resident of one of the rebellious states, or a prisoner of war, but a citizen of Indiana for twenty years past, and never in the military or naval service, is, while at his home, arrested by the military power of the United States, imprisoned, and, on certain criminal charges preferred against him, tried, convicted, and sentenced to be hanged by a military commission, organized under the direction of the military commander of the military district of Indiana. Had this tribunal the *legal* power and authority to try and punish this man?

No graver question was ever considered by this court, nor one which more nearly concerns the rights of the whole people; for it is the birthright of every American citizen when charged with crime, to be tried and punished according to law. . . . The Constitution of the United States is a law for rulers and people, equally in war and in peace, and covers with the shield of its protection all classes of men, at all times, and under all circumstances. No doctrine, involving more pernicious consequences, was ever invented by the wit of man than that any of its provisions can be suspended during any of the great exigencies of government. Such a doctrine leads directly to anarchy or despotism, but the theory of necessity on which it is based is false; for the government, within the Constitution, has all the powers granted to it, which are necessary to preserve its existence; as has been happily proved by the result of the great effort to throw off its just authority.

Have any of the rights guaranteed by the Constitution been violated in the case of Milligan? and if so, what are they?

Every trial involves the exercise of judicial power; and from what source did that military commission that tried him derive their authority? Certainly no part of judicial power of the country was conferred on them; because the Constitution expressly vests it "in one supreme court and such inferior courts as the Congress may from time to time ordain and establish," and it is not pretended that the commission was a court ordained and established by Congress. They cannot justify on the mandate of the President; because he is controlled by law, and has his appropriate sphere of duty, which is to execute, not to make, the laws; and there is "no unwritten criminal code to which resort can be had as a source of jurisdiction."

But it is said that the jurisdiction is complete under the "laws and usages of war."

It can serve no useful purpose to inquire what those laws and usages are, whence they originated, where found, and on whom they operate; they can never be applied to citizens in states which have upheld the authority of the government, and where the courts are open and their process unobstructed. This court has judicial knowledge that in Indiana the Federal authority was always unopposed, and its courts always open to hear criminal accusations and redress grievances; and no usage of war could sanction a military trial there for any offence whatever of a citizen in civil life, in nowise connected with the military service. Congress could grant no such power; and to the honor of our national legislature be it said, it has never been provoked by the state of the country even to attempt its exercise. One of the plainest constitutional provisions was, therefore, infringed when Milligan was tried by a court not ordained and established by Congress, and not composed of judges appointed during good behavior. . . .

Another guarantee of freedom was broken when Milligan was denied a trial by jury. . . . *[T]his right*—one of the most valuable in a free country—is preserved to every one accused of crime who is not attached to the army, or navy, or militia in actual service. The sixth amendment affirms that "in all criminal prosecutions the accused shall enjoy the right to a speedy and public trial by an impartial jury," language broad enough to embrace all persons and cases; but the fifth, recognizing the necessity of an indictment, or presentment, before any one can be held to answer for high crimes, "*excepts* cases arising in the land or naval forces, or in the militia, when in actual service, in time of war or public danger"; and the framers of the Constitution, doubtless, meant to limit the right of trial by jury, in the sixth amendment, to those persons who were subject to indictment or presentment in the fifth.

The discipline necessary to the efficiency of the army and navy, required other and swifter modes of trial than are furnished by the common law courts; and, in pursuance of the power conferred by the Constitution, Congress has declared the kinds of trial, and the manner in which they shall be conducted, for offences committed while the party is in the military or naval service. . . . *All other persons*, citizens of states where the courts are open, if charged with crime, are guaranteed the inestimable privilege of trial by jury. This privilege is a vital principle, underlying the whole administration of criminal justice; it is not held by sufference, and cannot be frittered away on any plea of state or political necessity. . . .

It is claimed that martial law covers with its broad mantle the proceedings of this military commission. The proposition is this: that in a time of war the commander of an armed force (if in his opinion the exigencies of the country demand it, and of which he is to judge), has the power, within the lines of his military district, to suspend all civil rights and their remedies, and subject citizens as well as soldiers to the rule of *his will;* and in the exercise of his lawful authority cannot be restrained, except by his superior officer or the President of the United States. . . .

The statement of this proposition shows its importance; for, if true, republican government is a failure, and there is an end of liberty regulated by law. Martial law, established on such a basis, destroys every guarantee of the Constitution, and effectually renders the "military independent of and superior to the civil power"—the attempt to do which by the King of Great Britain was deemed by our fathers such an offence, that they assigned it to the world as one of the causes which impelled them to declare their independence. Civil liberty and this kind of martial law cannot endure together; the antagonism is irreconcilable; and, in the conflict, one or the other must perish. . . .

It is essential to the safety of every government that, in a great crisis, like the one we have just passed through, there should be a power somewhere of suspending the writ of *habeas corpus.* In every war, there are men of previously good character, wicked enough to counsel their fellow-citizens to resist the measures deemed necessary by a good government to sustain its just authority and overthrow its enemies; and their influence may lead to dangerous combinations. In the emergency of the times, an immediate public investigation according to law may not be possible; and yet, the period to the country may be too imminent to suffer such persons to go at large. Unquestionably, there is then an exigency which demands that the government, if it should see fit in the exercise of a proper discretion to make arrests, should not be required to produce the persons arrested in answer to a writ of *habeas corpus.* The Constitution goes no further. It does not say after a writ of *habeas corpus* is denied a citizen, that he shall be tried otherwise than by the course of the common law; if it had intended this result, it was easy by the use of direct words to have accomplished it. The illustrious men who framed that instrument were guarding the foundations of civil liberty against the abuses of unlimited power; they were full of wisdom, and the lessons of history informed them that a trial by an established court, assisted by an impartial jury, was the only sure way of protecting the citizen against oppression and wrong. Knowing this, they limited the suspension to one great right, and left the rest to remain forever inviolable. But, it is insisted that the safety of the country in time of war demands that this broad claim for martial law shall be sustained. If this were true, it could be well said that a country, preserved at the sacrifice of all the cardinal principles of liberty, is not worth the cost of preservation. . . .

It follows, from what has been said on this subject, that there are occasions when martial rule can be properly applied. If, in foreign invasion or civil war, the courts are actually closed, and it is impossible to administer criminal justice according to law, *then*, on the theatre of active military operations, where war really prevails, there is a necessity to furnish a substitute for the civil authority, thus overthrown, to preserve the safety of the army and society; and as no power is left but the military, it is allowed to govern by martial rule until the laws can have their free course. As necessity creates the rule, so it limits its duration; for, if this government is continued *after* the courts are reinstated, it is a gross usurpation of power. Martial rule can never exist where the courts are open, and in the proper and unobstructed exercise of their jurisdiction. It is also confined to the locality of actual war. Because, during the late Rebellion it could have been enforced in Virginia, where the national authority was overturned and the courts driven out, it does not follow that it should obtain in Indiana, where that authority was never disputed, and justice was always administered. And so in the case of a foreign invasion, martial rule may become a necessity in one state, when, in another, it would be "mere lawless violence." . . .

But it is insisted that Milligan was a prisoner of war, and, therefore, excluded from the privileges of the statute. It is not easy to see how he can be treated as a prisoner of war, when he lived in Indiana for the past twenty years, was arrested there, and had not been, during the late troubles, a resident of any of the states in rebellion. If in Indiana he conspired with bad men to assist the enemy, he is punishable for it in the courts of Indiana; but, when tried for the offence, he cannot plead the rights of war; for he was not engaged in legal acts of hostility against the government, and only such persons, when captured, are prisoners of war. If he cannot enjoy the immunities attaching to the character of a prisoner of war, how can he be subject to their pains and penalties? . . .

■ The CHIEF JUSTICE delivered the following opinion [joined by JUSTICES WAYNE, SWAYNE, and MILLER].

Four members of the court, concurring with their brethren in the order heretofore made in this cause, but unable to concur in some important particulars with the opinion which has just been read, think it their duty to make a separate statement of their views of the whole case. . . .

We think that Congress had power, though not exercised, to authorize the military commission which was held in Indiana. . . .

Congress has power to raise and support armies; to provide and maintain a navy; to make rules for the government and regulation of the land and naval forces; and to provide for governing such part of the militia as may be in the service of the United States.

It is not denied that the power to make rules for the government of the army and navy is a power to provide for trial and punishment by military courts without a jury. It has been so understood and exercised from the adoption of the Constitution to the present time.

Nor, in our judgment, does the fifth, or any other amendment, abridge that power. "Cases arising in the land and naval forces, or in the militia in actual service in time of war or public danger," are expressly excepted from the fifth amendment, "that no person shall be held to answer for a capital or otherwise infamous crime, unless on a presentment or indictment of a grand jury," and it is admitted that the exception applies to the other amendments as well as to the fifth. . . .

But we do not put our opinion, that Congress might authorize such a military commission as was held in Indiana, upon the power to provide for the government of the national forces.

Congress has the power not only to raise and support and govern armies but to declare war. It has, therefore, the power to provide by law for carrying on war. This power necessarily extends to all legislation essential to the prosecution of war with vigor and success, except such as interferes with the command of the forces and the conduct of campaigns. That power and duty belong to the President as commander-in-chief. Both these powers are derived from the Constitution, but neither is defined by that instrument. Their extent must be determined by their nature, and by the principles of our institutions. . . .

We by no means assert that Congress can establish and apply the laws of war where no war has been declared or exists.

Where peace exists the laws of peace must prevail. What we do maintain is, that when the nation is involved in war, and some portions of the country are invaded, and all are exposed to invasion, it is within the power of Congress to determine in what states or district such great and imminent public danger exists as justifies the authorization of military tribunals for the trial of crimes and offences against the discipline or security of the army or against the public safety. . . .

Ex parte Quirin

317 U.S. 1 (1944)

■ MR. CHIEF JUSTICE STONE delivered the opinion of the Court.

These cases are brought here by petitioners' several applications for leave to file petitions for habeas corpus in this Court, and by their petitions for certiorari to review orders of the District Court for the District of Columbia, which denied their applications for leave to file petitions for habeas corpus in that court.

The question for decision is whether the detention of petitioners by respondent for trial by Military Commission, appointed by Order of the President of July 2, 1942, on charges preferred against them purporting to set out their violations of the law of war and of the Articles of War, is in conformity to the laws and Constitution of the United States.

After denial of their applications by the District Court, 47 F. Supp. 431, petitioners asked leave to file petitions for habeas corpus in this Court. In view of the public importance of the questions raised by their petitions and of the duty which rests on the courts, in time of war as well as in time of peace, to preserve unimpaired the constitutional safeguards of civil liberty, and because in our opinion the public interest required that we consider and decide those questions without any avoidable delay, we directed that petitioners' applications be set down for full oral argument at a special term of this Court, convened on July 29, 1942. . . .

On July 31, 1942, after hearing argument of counsel and after full consideration of all questions raised, this Court affirmed the orders of the District Court and denied petitioners' applications for leave to file petitions for habeas corpus. By per curiam opinion, we announced the decision of the Court, and that the full opinion in the causes would be prepared and filed with the Clerk.

The following facts appear from the petitions or are stipulated. Except as noted they are undisputed.

All the petitioners were born in Germany; all have lived in the United States. All returned to Germany between 1933 and 1941. All except petitioner Haupt are admittedly citizens of the German Reich, with which the United States is at war. Haupt came to this country with his parents when he was five years old; it is contended that he became a citizen of the United States by virtue of the naturalization of his parents during his minority and that he has not since lost his citizenship. The Government, however, takes the position that on attaining his majority he elected to maintain German allegiance and citizenship or in any case that he has by his conduct renounced or abandoned his United States citizenship. For reasons presently to be stated we do not find it necessary to resolve these contentions.

After the declaration of war between the United States and the German Reich, petitioners received training at a sabotage school near Berlin, Germany, where they were instructed in the use of explosives and in methods of secret writing. Thereafter petitioners, with a German citizen, Dasch, proceeded from Germany to a seaport in Occupied France, where petitioners Burger, Heinck and Quirin, together with Dasch, boarded a German submarine which proceeded across the Atlantic to Amagansett Beach on Long Island, New York. The four were there landed from the submarine in the hours of darkness, on or about June 13, 1942, carrying with them a supply of explosives, fuses and incendiary and timing devices. While landing they wore German Marine Infantry uniforms or parts of uniforms. Immediately after landing they buried their uniforms and the other articles mentioned and proceeded in civilian dress to New York City.

The remaining four petitioners at the same French port boarded another German submarine, which carried them across the Atlantic to Ponte Vedra Beach, Florida. On or about June 17, 1942, they came ashore during the hours of darkness wearing caps of the German Marine Infantry and carrying with them a supply of explosives, fuses, and incendiary and timing devices. They immediately buried their caps and the other articles mentioned and proceeded in civilian dress to Jacksonville, Florida, and thence to various points in the United States. All were taken into custody in New York or Chicago by agents of the Federal Bureau of Investigation. All had received instructions in Germany from an officer of the German High Command to destroy war industries and war facilities in the United States, for which they or their relatives in Germany were to receive salary payments from the German Government. They also had been paid by the German Government during their course of training at the sabotage school and had received substantial sums in United States currency, which were in their possession when arrested. The currency had been handed to them by an officer of the German High Command, who had instructed them to wear their German uniforms while landing in the United States.

The President, as President and Commander in Chief of the Army and Navy, by Order of July 2, 1942, appointed a Military Commission and directed it to try petitioners for offenses against the law of war and the Articles of War, and prescribed regulations for the procedure on the trial and for review of the record of the trial and of any judgment or sentence of the Commission. On the same day, by Proclamation, the President declared that "all persons who are subjects, citizens or residents of any nation at war with the United States or who give obedience to or act under the direction of any such nation, and who during time of war enter or attempt to enter the United States ... through coastal or boundary defenses, and are charged with committing or attempting or preparing to commit sabotage, espionage, hostile or warlike acts, or violations of the law of war, shall be subject to the law of war and to the jurisdiction of military tribunals". . . .

On July 3, 1942, the Judge Advocate General's Department of the Army prepared and lodged with the Commission the following charges against petitioners, supported by specifications:

1. Violation of the law of war.

2. Violation of Article 81 of the Articles of War, defining the offense of relieving or attempting to relieve, or corresponding with or giving intelligence to, the enemy.

3. Violation of Article 82, defining the offense of spying.

4. Conspiracy to commit the offenses alleged in charges 1, 2 and 3.

The Commission met on July 8, 1942, and proceeded with the trial, which continued in progress while the causes were pending in this Court. . . .

Petitioners' main contention is that the President is without any statutory or constitutional authority to order the petitioners to be tried by military tribunal for offenses with which they are charged; that in consequence they are entitled to be tried in the civil courts with the safeguards, including trial by jury, which the Fifth and Sixth Amendments guarantee to all persons charged in such courts with criminal offenses. In any case it is urged that the President's Order, in prescribing the procedure of the Commission and the method for review of its findings and sentence, and the proceedings of the Commission under the Order, conflict with Articles of War adopted by Congress . . . and are illegal and void.

The Government challenges each of these propositions. But regardless of their merits, it also insists that petitioners must be denied access to the courts, both because they are enemy aliens or have entered our territory as enemy belligerents, and because the President's Proclamation undertakes in terms to deny such access to the class of persons defined by the Proclamation, which aptly describes the character and conduct of petitioners. It is urged that if they are enemy aliens or if the Proclamation has force no court may afford the petitioners a hearing. But there is certainly nothing in the Proclamation to preclude access to the courts for determining its applicability to the particular case. And neither the Proclamation nor the fact that they are enemy aliens forecloses consideration by the courts of petitioners' contentions that the Constitution and laws of the United States constitutionally enacted forbid their trial by military commission. As announced in our per curiam opinion we have resolved those questions by our conclusion that the Commission has jurisdiction to try the charge preferred against petitioners. There is therefore no occasion to decide contentions of the parties unrelated to this issue. We pass at once to the consideration of the basis of the Commission's authority.

We are not here concerned with any question of the guilt or innocence of petitioners. Constitutional safeguards for the protection of all who are charged with offenses are not to be disregarded in order to inflict merited punishment on some who are guilty. But the detention and trial of petitioners—ordered by the President in the declared exercise of his powers as Commander in Chief of the Army in time of war and of grave public danger—are not to be set aside by the courts without the clear conviction that they are in conflict with the Constitution or laws of Congress constitutionally enacted.

Congress and the President, like the courts, possess no power not derived from the Constitution. But one of the objects of the Constitution, as declared by its preamble, is to "provide for the common defence". As a means to that end the Constitution gives to Congress the power to "provide for the common Defence", Art. I, § 8, cl. 1; "To raise and support Armies", "To provide and maintain a Navy", Art. I, § 8, cls. 12, 13; and "To make Rules for the Government and Regulation of the land and naval Forces", Art. I, § 8, cl. 14. Congress is given authority "To declare War, grant Letters of Marque and Reprisal, and make Rules concerning Captures on Land and Water", Art. I, § 8, cl. 11; and "To define and punish Piracies and Felonies committed on the high Seas, and Offenses against the Law of Nations", Art. I, § 8, cl. 10. And finally the Constitution authorizes Congress "To make all Laws which shall be necessary and proper for carrying into Execution the foregoing Powers, and all other Powers vested by this Constitution in the Government of the United States, or in any Department or Officer thereof." Art. I, § 8, cl. 18.

The Constitution confers on the President the "executive Power", Art II, § 1, cl. 1, and imposes on him the duty to "take Care that the Laws be faithfully executed". Art. II, § 3. It makes him the Commander in Chief of the Army and Navy, Art. II, § 2, cl. 1, and empowers him to appoint and commission officers of the United States. Art. II, § 3, cl. 1.

The Constitution thus invests the President as Commander in Chief with the power to wage war which Congress has declared, and to carry into effect all laws passed by Congress for the conduct of war and for the government and regulation of the Armed Forces, and all laws defining and punishing offences against the law of nations, including those which pertain to the conduct of war.

By the Articles of War, 10 U.S.C. §§ 1471–1593, Congress has provided rules for the government of the Army. It has provided for the trial and punishment, by courts martial, of violations of the Articles by members of the armed forces and by specified classes of persons associated or serving with the Army. Arts. 1, 2. But the Articles also recognize the "military commission" appointed by military command as an appropriate tribunal for the trial and punishment of offenses against the law of war not ordinarily tried by court martial. See Arts. 12, 15. Articles 38 and 46 authorize the President, with certain limitations, to prescribe the procedure for military commissions. Articles 81 and 82 authorize trial, either by court martial or military commission, of those charged with relieving, harboring or corresponding with the enemy and those charged with spying. And Article 15 declares that "the provisions of these articles conferring jurisdiction upon courts-martial shall not be construed as depriving military commissions . . . or other military tribunals of concurrent jurisdiction in respect of offenders or offenses that by statute or by the law of war may be triable by such military commissions . . . or other military tribunals". Article 2 includes among those persons subject to military law the personnel of our own military establishment. But this, as Article 12 provides, does not exclude from that class "any other person who by the law of war is subject to trial by military tribunals" and who under Article 12 may be tried by court martial or under Article 15 by military commission. . . .

From the very beginning of its history this Court has recognized and applied the law of war as including that part of the law of nations which prescribes, for the conduct of war, the status, rights and duties of enemy nations as well as of enemy individuals. By the Articles of War, and especially Article 15, Congress has explicitly provided, so far as it may constitutionally do so, that military tribunals shall have jurisdiction to try offenders or offenses against the law of war in appropriate cases. Congress, in addition to making rules for the government of our Armed Forces, has thus exercised its authority to define and punish offenses against the law of nations by sanctioning, within constitutional limitations, the jurisdiction of military commissions to try persons for offenses which, according to the rules and precepts of the law of nations, and more particularly the law of war, are cognizable by such tribunals. And the President, as Commander in Chief, by his Proclamation in time of war his invoked that law. By his Order creating the present Commission he has undertaken to exercise the authority conferred upon him by Congress, and also such authority as the Constitution itself gives the Commander in Chief, to direct the performance of those functions which may constitutionally be performed by the military arm of the nation in time of war.

An important incident to the conduct of war is the adoption of measures by the military command not only to repel and defeat the enemy, but to seize and subject to disciplinary measures those enemies who in their attempt to thwart or impede our military effort have violated the law of war. It is unnecessary for present purposes to determine to what extent the President as Commander in Chief has constitutional power to create military commissions without the support of Congressional legislation. For here Congress has authorized trial of offenses against the law of war before such commissions. We are concerned only with the question whether it is within the constitutional power of the national government to place petitioners upon trial before a military commission for the offenses with which they are charged. . . .

It is no objection that Congress in providing for the trial of such offenses has not itself undertaken to codify that branch of international law or to mark its precise boundaries, or to enumerate or define by statute all the acts which that law condemns. An Act of Congress punishing "the crime of piracy as defined by the law of nations" is an appropriate exercise of its constitutional authority, Art. I, § 8, cl. 10, "to define and punish" the offense since it has adopted by reference the sufficiently precise definition of international law. Similarly by the reference in the 15th Article of War to "offenders or offenses that . . . by the law of war may be triable by such military commissions", Congress has incorporated by reference, as within the jurisdiction of military commissions, all offenses which are defined as such by the law . . . and which may constitutionally be included within that jurisdiction. Congress had the choice of crystallizing in permanent form and in minute detail every offense against the law of war, or of adopting the system of common law applied by military tribunals so far as it should be recognized and deemed applicable by the courts. It chose the latter course.

By universal agreement and practice the law of war draws a distinction between the armed forces and the peaceful populations of belligerent nations and also between those who are lawful and unlawful combatants. Lawful combatants are subject to capture and detention as prisoners of war by opposing military forces. Unlawful combatants are likewise subject to capture and detention, but in addition they are subject to trial and punishment by military tribunals for acts which render their belligerency unlawful. The spy who secretly and without uniform passes the military lines of a belligerent in time of war, seeking to gather military information and communicate it to the enemy, or an enemy combatant who without uniform comes secretly through the lines for the purpose of waging war by destruction of life or property, are familiar examples of belligerents who are generally deemed not to be entitled to the status of prisoners of war, but to be offenders against the law of war subject to trial and punishment by military tribunals.

Such was the practice of our own military authorities before the adoption of the Constitution, and during the Mexican and Civil Wars. . . .

These and related provisions have been continued in substance by the Rules of Land Warfare promulgated by the War Department for the guidance of the Army. Paragraph 357 of the 1940 Rules provides that "All war crimes are subject to the death penalty although a lesser penalty may be imposed". Paragraph 8 (1940) divides the enemy population into "armed forces" and "peaceful population", and Paragraph 9 names as distinguishing characteristics of lawful belligerents that they "carry arms openly" and "have a fixed distinctive emblem". Paragraph 348 declares that "persons who take up arms and commit hostilities" without having the means of identification prescribed for belligerents are punishable as "war criminals". Paragraph 351 provides that "men and bodies of men, who, without being lawful belligerents" "nevertheless commit hostile acts of any kind" are not entitled to the privileges of prisoners of war if captured and may be tried by military commission and punished by death or lesser punishment. . . . The definition of lawful belligerents by Paragraph 9 is that adopted by Article 1, Annex to Hague Convention No. IV . . .

Our Government, by thus defining lawful belligerents entitled to be treated as prisoners of war, has recognized that there is a class of unlawful belligerents not entitled to that privilege, including those who though combatants do not wear "fixed and distinctive emblems". And by Article 15 of the Articles of War Congress has made provision for their trial and punishment by military commission, according to "the law of war".

By a long course of practical administrative construction by its military authorities, our Government has likewise recognized that those who during time of war pass surreptitiously from enemy territory into our own, discarding their uniforms upon entry, for the commission of hostile acts involving destruction of life or property, have the status of unlawful combatants punishable as such by military commission. This precept of the law of war has been so recognized in practice both here and abroad, and has so generally been accepted as valid by authorities on international law that we think it must be regarded as a rule or principle of the law of war recognized by this Government by its enactment of the Fifteenth Article of War.

Specification 1 of the first charge is sufficient to charge all the petitioners with the offense of unlawful belligerency, trial of which is within the jurisdiction of the Commission, and the admitted facts affirmatively show that the charge is not merely colorable or without foundation.

Specification 1 states that petitioners "being enemies of the United States and acting for . . . the German Reich, a belligerent enemy nation, secretly and covertly passed, in civilian dress, contrary to the law of war, through the military and naval lines and defenses of the United States . . . and went behind such lines, contrary to the law of war, in civilian dress . . . for the purpose of committing . . . hostile acts, and, in particular, to destroy certain war industries, war utilities and war materials within the United States."

This specification so plainly alleges violation of the law of war as to require but brief discussion of petitioners' contentions. As we have seen, entry upon our territory in time of war by enemy belligerents, including those acting under the direction of the armed forces of the enemy, for the purpose of destroying property used or useful in prosecuting the war, is a hostile and war-like act. It subjects those who participate in it without uniform to the punishment prescribed by the law of war for unlawful belligerents. It is without significance that petitioners were not alleged to have borne conventional weapons or that their proposed hostile acts did not necessarily contemplate collision with the Armed Forces of the United States. Paragraphs 351 and 352 of the Rules of Land Warfare, already referred to, plainly contemplate that the hostile acts and purposes for which unlawful belligerents may be punished are not limited to assaults on the Armed Forces of the United States. Modern warfare is directed at the destruction of enemy war supplies and the implements of their production and transportation quite as much as at the armed forces. Every consideration which makes the unlawful belligerent punishable is equally applicable whether his objective is the one or the other. The law of war cannot rightly treat those agents of enemy armies who enter our territory, armed with explosives intended for the destruction of war industries and supplies, as any the less belligerent enemies than are agent similarly entering for the purpose of destroying fortified places or our Armed Forces. By passing our boundaries for such purposes without uniform or other emblem signifying their belligerent status, or by discarding that means of identification after entry, such enemies become unlawful belligerents subject to trial and punishment.

Citizenship in the United States of an enemy belligerent does not relieve him from the consequences of a belligerency which is unlawful because in violation of the law of war. Citizens who associate themselves with the military arm of the enemy government, and with its aid, guidance and direction enter this country bent on hostile acts are enemy belligerents within the meaning of the Hague Convention and the law of war. It is as an enemy belligerent that petitioner Haupt is charged with entering the United States, and unlawful belligerency is the gravamen of the offense of which he is accused.

Nor are petitioners any the less belligerents if, as they argue, they have not actually committed or attempted to commit any act of depredation or entered the theatre or zone of active military operations. The argument leaves out of account the nature of the offense which the Government charges and which the Act of Congress, by incorporating the law of war, punishes. It is that each petitioner, in circumstances which gave him the status of an enemy belligerent, passed our military and naval lines and defenses or went behind those lines, in civilian dress and with hostile purpose. The offense was complete when with that purpose they entered—or, having so entered, they remained upon—our territory in time of war without uniform or other appropriate means of identification. For that reason, even when committed by a citizen, the offense is distinct from the crime of treason defined in Article III, § 3 of the Constitution, since the absence of uniform essential to one is irrelevant to the other.

But petitioners insist that even if the offenses with which they are charged are offenses against the law of war, their trial is subject to the requirement of the Fifth Amendment that no person shall be held to answer for a capital or otherwise infamous crime unless on a presentment or indictment of a grand jury, and that such trials by Article III, § 2, and the Sixth Amendment must be by jury in a civil court. Before the Amendments,

§ 2 of Article III, the Judiciary Article, had provided: "The Trial of all Crimes, except in Cases of Impeachment, shall be by Jury", and had directed that "such Trial shall be held in the State where the said Crimes shall have been committed."

Presentment by a grand jury and trial by a jury of the vicinage where the crime was committed were at the time of the adoption of the Constitution familiar parts of the machinery for criminal trials in the civil courts. But they were procedures unknown to military tribunals, which are not courts in the sense of the Judiciary Article, *Ex parte Vallandigham*, 1 Wall. 243, and which in the natural course of events are usually called upon to function under conditions precluding resort to such procedures. As this Court has often recognized, it was not the purpose or effect of § 2 of Article III, read in the light of the common law, to enlarge the then existing right to a jury trial. The object was to preserve unimpaired trial by jury in all those cases in which it had been recognized by the common law and in all cases of a like nature as they might arise in the future, but not to bring within the sweep of the guaranty those cases in which it was then well understood that a jury trial could not be demanded as of right.

The Fifth and Sixth Amendments, while guaranteeing the continuance of certain incidents of trial by jury which Article III, § 2 had left unmentioned, did not enlarge the right to jury trial as it had been established by that Article. Hence petty offenses triable at common law without a jury may be tried without a jury in the federal courts, notwithstanding Article III, § 2, and the Fifth and Sixth Amendments. Trial by jury of criminal contempts may constitutionally be dispensed with in the federal courts in those cases in which they could be tried without a jury at common law. . . .

All these are instances of offenses committed against the United States, for which a penalty is imposed, but they are not deemed to be within Article III, § 2 or the provisions of the Fifth and Sixth Amendments relating to "crimes" and "criminal prosecutions". In the light of this long-continued and consistent interpretation we must conclude that § 2 of Article III and the Fifth and Sixth Amendments cannot be taken to have extended the right to demand a jury to trials by military commission, or to have required that offenses against the law of war not triable by jury at common law be tried only in the civil courts.

The fact that "cases arising in the land or naval forces" are excepted from the operation of the Amendments does not militate against this conclusion. Such cases are expressly excepted from the Fifth Amendment, and are deemed excepted by implication from the Sixth. *Ex parte Milligan, supra*, 4 Wall. 123, 138. It is argued that the exception, which excludes from the Amendment cases arising in the armed forces, has also by implication extended its guaranty to all other cases; that since petitioners, not being members of the Armed Forces of the United States, are not within the exception, the Amendment operates to give to them the right to a jury trial. But we think this argument misconceives both the scope of the Amendment and the purpose of the exception.

We may assume, without deciding, that a trial prosecuted before a military commission created by military authority is not one "arising in the land . . . forces", when the accused is not a member of or associated with those forces. But even so, the exception cannot be taken to affect those trials before military commissions which are neither within the exception nor within the provisions of Article III, § 2, whose guaranty the Amendments did not enlarge. No exception is necessary to exclude from the operation of these provisions cases never deemed to be within their terms. . . .

. . . It has not hitherto been challenged, and so far as we are advised it has never been suggested in the very extensive literature of the subject that an alien spy, in time of war, could not be tried by military tribunal without a jury.[14]

The exception from the Amendments of "cases arising in the land or naval forces" was not aimed at trials by military tribunals, without a jury, of such offenses against the law of war. Its objective was quite different—to authorize the trial by court martial of the members of our Armed Forces for all that class of crimes which under the Fifth and Sixth Amendments might otherwise have been deemed triable in the civil courts. The cases mentioned in the exception are not restricted to those involving offenses against the law of war alone, but extend to trial of all offenses, including crimes which were of the class traditionally triable by jury at common law.

Since the Amendments, like § 2 of Article III, do not preclude all trials of offenses against the law of war by military commission without a jury when the offenders are aliens not members of our Armed Forces, it is plain that they present no greater obstacle to the trial in like manner of citizen enemies who have violated the law of war applicable to enemies. Under the original statute authorizing trial of alien spies by military tribunals, the offenders were outside the constitutional guaranty of trial by jury, not because they were aliens but only because they had violated the law of war by committing offenses constitutionally triable by military tribunal.

We cannot say that Congress in preparing the Fifth and Sixth Amendments intended to extend trial by jury to the cases of alien or citizen offenders against the law of war otherwise triable by military commission, while withholding it from members of our own armed forces charged with infractions of the Articles of War punishable by death. It is equally inadmissible to construe the Amendments—whose primary purpose was to continue unimpaired presentment by grand jury and trial by petit jury in all those cases in which they had been customary—as either abolishing all trials by military tribunals, save those of the personnel of our own armed forces, or what in effect comes to the same thing, as imposing on all such tribunals the necessity of proceeding against unlawful enemy belligerents only on presentment and trial by jury. We conclude that the Fifth and Sixth Amendments did not restrict whatever authority was conferred by the Constitution to try offenses against the law of war by military commission, and that petitioners, charged with such an offense not required to be tried by jury at common law, were lawfully placed on trial by the Commission without a jury.

Petitioners, and especially petitioner Haupt, stress the pronouncement of this Court in the *Milligan* case, 4 Wall. page 121, that the law of war

---

[14] In a number of cases during the Revolutionary War enemy spies were tried and convicted by military tribunals: (1) Major John Andre, Sept. 29, 1780. (2) Thomas Shanks was convicted by a "Board of General Officers" at Valley Forge on June 3, 1778, for "being a Spy in the Service of the Enemy" and sentenced to be hanged. 12 Writings of Washington (Bicentennial Comm'n ed.) 14. (3) Matthias Colbhart was convicted of "holding a Correspondence with the Enemy" and "living as a Spy among the Continental Troops" by a General Court Martial convened by order of Major General Putnam on Jan. 13, 1778; General Washington, the Commander in Chief, ordered the sentence of death to be executed, 12 *Id.* 449–50. *[The Court then gives nine other Revolutionary War examples, and dozens from the War of 1812 and the Civil War.—Editors]*

"can never be applied to citizens in states which have upheld the authority of the government, and where the courts are open and their process unobstructed". Elsewhere in its opinion, the Court was at pains to point out that Milligan, a citizen twenty years resident in Indiana, who had never been a resident of any of the states in rebellion, was not an enemy belligerent either entitled to the status of a prisoner of war or subject to the penalties imposed upon unlawful belligerents. We construe the Court's statement as to the inapplicability of the law of war to Milligan's case as having particular reference to the facts before it. From them the Court concluded that Milligan, not being a part of or associated with the armed forces of the enemy, was a non-belligerent, not subject to the law of war save as—in circumstances found not there to be present and not involved here—martial law might be constitutionally established.

The Court's opinion is inapplicable to the case presented by the present record. We have no occasion now to define with meticulous care the ultimate boundaries of the jurisdiction of military tribunals to try persons according to the law of war. It is enough that petitioners here, upon the conceded facts, were plainly within those boundaries, and were held in good faith for trial by military commission, charged with being enemies who, with the purpose of destroying war materials and utilities, entered or after entry remained in our territory without uniform—an offense against the law of war. We hold only that those particular acts constitute an offense against the law of war which the Constitution authorizes to be tried by military commission.

Since the first specification of Charge I set forth a violation of the law of war, we have no occasion to pass on the adequacy of the second specification of Charge I, or to construe the 81st and 82nd Articles of War for the purpose of ascertaining whether the specifications under Charges II and III allege violations of those Articles or whether if so construed they are constitutional. . . .

We need not inquire whether Congress may restrict the power of the Commander in Chief to deal with enemy belligerents. For the Court is unanimous in its conclusion that the Articles in question could not at any stage of the proceedings afford any basis for issuing the writ. But a majority of the full Court are not agreed on the appropriate grounds for decision. Some members of the Court are of opinion that Congress did not intend the Articles of War to govern a Presidential military commission convened for the determination of questions relating to admitted enemy invaders and that the context of the Articles makes clear that they should not be construed to apply in that class of cases. Others are of the view that—even though this trial is subject to whatever provisions of the Articles of War Congress has in terms made applicable to "commissions"—the particular Articles in question, rightly construed, do not foreclose the procedure prescribed by the President or that shown to have been employed by the Commission in a trial of offenses against the law of war and the 81st and 82nd Articles of War, by a military commission appointed by the President.

Accordingly, we conclude that Charge I, on which petitioners were detained for trial by the Military Commission, alleged an offense which the President is authorized to order tried by military commission; that his Order convening the Commission was a lawful order and that the Commission was lawfully constituted; that the petitioners were held in lawful custody and did not show cause for their discharge. It follows that the orders of the

District Court should be affirmed, and that leave to file petitions for habeas corpus in this Court should be denied. . . .

NOTES

1. Was *Milligan* rightly decided? Was *Quirin* rightly decided? Can the two cases be reconciled? In what ways does *Quirin* modify, qualify, or distinguish *Milligan*? Is its reasoning persuasive?

2. Should Nazi saboteurs—or Al Qaeda terrorists—be tried in *civilian* courts for war crimes? Is the only alternative that they may be tried by military tribunals? Should the German saboteurs have been given *Miranda* warnings when they were captured? Did the Fourth Amendment apply to searches and seizures of the saboteurs? Does it matter for these questions whether there is a declared state of war? Does it matter whether the saboteurs or terrorists are affiliated with a foreign state?

3. Although the Court announced the result in *Quirin* on July 21, 1942—which was one week before the execution of six of the saboteurs—the Court did not issue its full opinion until October 29, 1944. Does this make the Court's decision seem less authoritative? More authoritative?

4. The evidence against the German saboteurs was strong. Does that matter? The evidence came not from FBI surveillance, but rather from two defectors among the German saboteurs. Is that relevant in understanding *Quirin's* lessons?

5. Lloyd Cutler, who later served as White House counsel in the Carter and Clinton administrations, was a young attorney in the Office of Legal Counsel when the capture of the German saboteurs was announced to the public. He described the setting:

> One Sunday afternoon in June I was called and asked to report to the Justice Department, where for three months I worked as the youngest of 10 lawyers who tried the saboteurs. In the days after [FBI Director J. Edgar] Hoover's announcement, I helped draft a proclamation for Roosevelt that created a military commission to try foreign spies and saboteurs, and denied them the right to judicial review and the right to trial in nonmilitary U.S. courts. They would, instead, be tried by a military tribunal of seven generals, none a trained lawyer, in a conference room in the FBI headquarters, on the fifth floor of the Justice Department, away from the press, a civilian jury and civilian judges.

Lloyd Cutler, "What I Saw at a Military Tribunal," TIME (Nov. 19, 2001). When a military tribunal is used, who should be the judges?

Korematsu v. United States

323 U.S. 214 (1944)

■ Mr. Justice BLACK delivered the opinion of the Court.

The petitioner, an American citizen of Japanese descent, was convicted in a federal district court for remaining in San Leandro, California, a "Military Area", contrary to Civilian Exclusion Order No. 34 of the Commanding General of the Western Command, U.S. Army, which directed that after May 9, 1942, all persons of Japanese ancestry should be excluded from that area. No question was raised as to petitioner's loyalty to the United States. The Circuit Court of Appeals affirmed, and the importance of the constitutional question involved caused us to grant certiorari.

It should be noted, to begin with, that all legal restrictions which curtail the civil rights of a single racial group are immediately suspect. That is not to say that all such restrictions are unconstitutional. It is to say that courts must subject them to the most rigid scrutiny. Pressing public necessity may sometimes justify the existence of such restrictions; racial antagonism never can.

In the instant case prosecution of the petitioner was begun by information charging violation of an Act of Congress, of March 21, 1942, 56 Stat. 173, which provides that ". . . whoever shall enter, remain in, leave, or commit any act in any military area or military zone prescribed, under the authority of an Executive order of the President, by the Secretary of War, or by any military commander designated by the Secretary of War, contrary to the restrictions applicable to any such area or zone or contrary to the order of the Secretary of War or any such military commander, shall, if it appears that he knew or should have known of the existence and extent of the restrictions or order and that his act was in violation thereof, be guilty of a misdemeanor and upon conviction shall be liable to a fine of not to exceed $5,000 or to imprisonment for not more than one year, or both, for each offense."

Exclusion Order No. 34, which the petitioner knowingly and admittedly violated was one of a number of military orders and proclamations, all of which were substantially based upon Executive Order No. 9066, 7 Fed. Reg. 1407. That order, issued after we were at war with Japan, declared that "the successful prosecution of the war requires every possible protection against espionage and against sabotage to national-defense material, national-defense premises, and national-defense utilities. . . ."

One of the series of orders and proclamations, a curfew order, which like the exclusion order here was promulgated pursuant to Executive Order 9066, subjected all persons of Japanese ancestry in prescribed West Coast military areas to remain in their residences from 8 p.m. to 6 a.m. As is the case with the exclusion order here, that prior curfew order was designed as a "protection against espionage and against sabotage." In *Hirabayashi v. United States*, we sustained a conviction obtained for violation of the curfew order. The *Hirabayashi* conviction and this one thus rest on the same 1942 Congressional Act and the same basic executive and military orders, all of which orders were aimed at the twin dangers of espionage and sabotage.

The 1942 Act was attacked in the *Hirabayashi* case as an unconstitutional delegation of power; it was contended that the curfew order and other orders on which it rested were beyond the war powers of the Congress, the military authorities and of the President, as Commander in Chief of the Army; and finally that to apply the curfew order against none but citizens of Japanese ancestry amounted to a constitutionally prohibited discrimination solely on account of race. To these questions, we gave the serious consideration which their importance justified. We upheld the curfew order as an exercise of the power of the government to take steps necessary to prevent espionage and sabotage in an area threatened by Japanese attack.

In the light of the principles we announced in the *Hirabayashi* case, we are unable to conclude that it was beyond the war power of Congress and the Executive to exclude those of Japanese ancestry from the West Coast war area at the time they did. True, exclusion from the area in which one's home is located is a far greater deprivation than constant confinement to the home from 8 p.m. to 6 a.m. Nothing short of apprehension by the proper military authorities of the gravest imminent danger to the public safety can constitutionally justify either. But exclusion from a threatened area, no less than curfew, has a definite and close relationship to the prevention of espionage and sabotage. The military authorities, charged with the primary responsibility of defending our shores, concluded that curfew provided inadequate protection and ordered exclusion. They did so, as pointed out in our *Hirabayashi* opinion, in accordance with Congressional authority to the military to say who should, and who should not, remain in the threatened areas.

In this case the petitioner challenges the assumptions upon which we rested our conclusions in the *Hirabayashi* case. He also urges that by May 1942, when Order No. 34 was promulgated, all danger of Japanese invasion of the West Coast had disappeared. After careful consideration of these contentions we are compelled to reject them.

Here, as in the *Hirabayashi* case, ". . . we cannot reject as unfounded the judgment of the military authorities and of Congress that there were disloyal members of that population, whose number and strength could not be precisely and quickly ascertained. We cannot say that the war-making branches of the Government did not have ground for believing that in a critical hour such persons could not readily be isolated and separately dealt with, and constituted a menace to the national defense and safety, which demanded that prompt and adequate measures be taken to guard against it."

Like curfew, exclusion of those of Japanese origin was deemed necessary because of the presence of an unascertained number of disloyal members of the group, most of whom we have no doubt were loyal to this country. It was because we could not reject the finding of the military authorities that it was impossible to bring about an immediate segregation of the disloyal from the loyal that we sustained the validity of the curfew order as applying to the whole group. In the instant case, temporary exclusion of the entire group was rested by the military on the same ground. The judgment that exclusion of the whole group was for the same reason a military imperative answers the contention that the exclusion was in the nature of group punishment based on antagonism to those of Japanese origin. That there were members of the group who retained loyalties to Japan has been confirmed by investigations made subsequent to the exclusion. Approximately five thousand American citizens of Japanese ancestry refused to swear unqualified allegiance to the United States and to renounce allegiance to the Japanese Emperor, and several thousand evacuees requested repatriation to Japan.

We uphold the exclusion order as of the time it was made and when the petitioner violated it. In doing so, we are not unmindful of the hardships imposed by it upon a large group of American citizens. But hardships are part of war, and war is an aggregation of hardships. All citizens alike, both in and out of uniform, feel the impact of war in greater or lesser measure. Citizenship has its responsibilities as well as its privileges, and in time of war the burden is always heavier. Compulsory exclusion of large groups of citizens from their homes, except under circumstances of direst emergency and peril, is inconsistent with our basic governmental institutions. But when under conditions of modern warfare our shores are threatened by hostile forces, the power to protect must be commensurate with the threatened danger.

It is argued that on May 30, 1942, the date the petitioner was charged with remaining in the prohibited area, there were conflicting orders outstanding, forbidding him both to leave the area and to remain there. Of course, a person cannot be convicted for doing the very thing which it is a crime to fail to do. But the outstanding orders here contained no such contradictory commands.

There was an order issued March 27, 1942, which prohibited petitioner and others of Japanese ancestry from leaving the area, but its effect was specifically limited in time "until and to the extent that a future proclamation or order should so permit or direct." 7 Fed. Reg. 2601. That "future order," the one for violation of which petitioner was convicted, was issued May 3, 1942, and it did "direct" exclusion from the area of all persons of Japanese ancestry, before 12 o'clock noon, May 9; furthermore it contained a warning that all such persons found in the prohibited area would be liable to punishment under the March 21, 1942 Act of Congress. Consequently, the only order in effect touching the petitioner's being in the area on May 30, 1942, the date specified in the information against him, was the May 3 order which prohibited his remaining there, and it was that same order, which he stipulated in his trial that he had violated, knowing of its existence. There is therefore no basis for the argument that on May 30, 1942, he was subject to punishment, under the March 27 and May 3 orders, whether he remained in or left the area.

It does appear, however, that on May 9, the effective date of the exclusion order, the military authorities had already determined that the evacuation should be effected by assembling together and placing under guard all those of Japanese ancestry, at central points, designated as "assembly centers," in order "to insure the orderly evacuation and resettlement of Japanese voluntarily migrating from military area No. 1 to restrict and regulate such migration." Public Proclamation No. 4, 7 Fed. Reg. 2601. And on May 19, 1942, eleven days before the time petitioner was charged with unlawfully remaining in the area, Civilian Restrictive Order No. 1, 8 Fed. Reg. 982, provided for detention of those of Japanese ancestry in assembly or relocation centers. It is now argued that the validity of the exclusion order cannot be considered apart from the orders requiring him, after departure from the area, to report and to remain in an assembly or relocation center. The contention is that we must treat these separate orders as one and inseparable; that, for this reason, if detention in the assembly or relocation center would have illegally deprived the petitioner of his liberty, the exclusion order and his conviction under it cannot stand.

We are thus being asked to pass at this time upon the whole subsequent detention program in both assembly and relocation centers, although the only issues framed at the trial related to petitioner's remaining in the prohibited area in violation of the exclusion order. Had petitioner here left the prohibited area and gone to an assembly center we cannot say either as a matter of fact or law that his presence in that center would have resulted in his detention in a relocation center. Some who did report to the assembly center were not sent to relocation centers, but were released upon condition that they remain outside the prohibited zone until the military orders were modified or lifted. This illustrates that they pose different problems and may be governed by different principles. The lawfulness of one does not necessarily determine the lawfulness of the others. This is made clear when we analyze the requirements of the separate provisions of the separate orders. These separate requirements were that those of Japanese ancestry (1) depart from the area; (2) report to and temporarily remain in an assembly center; (3) go under military control to a relocation center there to remain for an indeterminate period until released conditionally or unconditionally by the military authorities. Each of these requirements, it will be noted, imposed distinct duties in connection with the separate steps in a complete evacuation program. Had Congress directly incorporated into one Act the language of these separate orders, and provided sanctions for their violations, disobedience of any one would have constituted a separate offense. There is no reason why violations of these orders, insofar as they were promulgated pursuant to congressional enactment, should not be treated as separate offenses. . . .

It is sufficient here for us to pass upon the order which petitioner violated. . . .

The Assembly Center was conceived as a part of the machinery for group evacuation. The power to exclude includes the power to do it by force if necessary. And any forcible measure must necessarily entail some degree of detention or restraint whatever method of removal is selected. But whichever view is taken, it results in holding that the order under which petitioner was convicted was valid.

It is said that we are dealing here with the case of imprisonment of a citizen in a concentration camp solely because of his ancestry, without evidence or inquiry concerning his loyalty and good disposition towards the United States. Our task would be simple, our duty clear, were this a case involving the imprisonment of a loyal citizen in a concentration camp because of racial prejudice. Regardless of the true nature of the assembly and relocation centers—and we deem it unjustifiable to call them concentration camps with all the ugly connotations that term implies—we are dealing specifically with nothing but an exclusion order. To cast this case into outlines of racial prejudice, without reference to the real military dangers which were presented, merely confuses the issue. Korematsu was not excluded from the Military Area because of hostility to him or his race. He was excluded because we are at war with the Japanese Empire, because the properly constituted military authorities feared an invasion of our West Coast and felt constrained to take proper security measures, because they decided that the military urgency of the situation demanded that all citizens of Japanese ancestry be segregated from the West Coast temporarily, and finally, because Congress, reposing its confidence in this time of war in our military leaders—as inevitably it must—determined that they should have the power to do just this. There was evidence of disloyalty on the part of some, the military authorities considered that the need for action was great, and time was short. We cannot—by availing ourselves of the calm perspective of hindsight—now say that at that time these actions were unjustified.

■ MR. JUSTICE FRANKFURTER, concurring.

According to my reading of Civilian Exclusion Order No. 34, it was an offense for Korematsu to be found in Military Area No. 1, the territory wherein he was previously living, except within the bounds of the established Assembly Center of that area. Even though the various orders issued by General DeWitt be deemed a comprehensive code of instructions, their tenor is clear and not contradictory. They put upon Korematsu the obligation to leave Military Area No. 1, but only by the method prescribed in the instructions, i.e., by reporting to the Assembly Center. I am unable to see how the legal considerations that led to the decision in *Hirabayashi v. United States* fail to sustain the military order which made the conduct now in controversy a crime. And so I join in the opinion of the Court, but should like to add a few words of my own.

The provisions of the Constitution which confer on the Congress and the President powers to enable this country to wage war are as much part of the Constitution as provisions looking to a nation at peace. And we have had recent occasion to quote approvingly the statement of former Chief Justice Hughes that the war power of the Government is "the power to wage war successfully." Therefore, the validity of action under the war power must be judged wholly in the context of war. That action is not to be stigmatized as lawless because like action in times of peace would be lawless. To talk about a military order that expresses an allowable judgment of war needs by those entrusted with the duty of conducting war as "an unconstitutional order" is to suffuse a part of the Constitution with an atmosphere of unconstitutionality. The respective spheres of action of military authorities and of judges are of course very different. But within their sphere, military authorities are no more outside the bounds of obedience to the Constitution than are judges within theirs. "The war power of the United States, like its other powers . . . is subject to applicable constitutional limitations." To recognize that military orders are "reasonably expedient military precautions" in time of war and yet to deny them constitutional legitimacy makes of the Constitution an instrument for dialectic subtleties not reasonably to be attributed to the hard-headed Framers, of whom a majority had had actual participation in war. If a military order such as that under review does not transcend the means appropriate for conducting war, such action by the military is as constitutional as would be any authorized action by the Interstate Commerce Commission within the limits of the constitutional power to regulate commerce. And being an exercise of the war power explicitly granted by the Constitution for safeguarding the national life by prosecuting war effectively, I find nothing in the Constitution which denies to Congress the power to enforce such a valid military order by making its violation an offense triable in the civil courts. To find that the Constitution does not forbid the military measures now complained of does not carry with it approval of that which Congress and the Executive did. That is their business, not ours.

■ MR. JUSTICE ROBERTS, dissenting.

I dissent, because I think the indisputable facts exhibit a clear violation of Constitutional rights.

This is not a case of keeping people off the streets at night as was *Hirabayashi v. United States*, nor a case of temporary exclusion of a citizen from an area for his own safety or that of the community, nor a case of offering him an opportunity to go temporarily out of an area where his presence might cause danger to himself or to his fellows. On the contrary, it is the case of convicting a citizen as a punishment for not submitting to imprisonment in a concentration camp, based on his ancestry, and solely because of his ancestry, without evidence or inquiry concerning his loyalty and good disposition towards the United States. If this be a correct statement of the facts disclosed by this record, and facts of which we take judicial notice, I need hardly labor the conclusion that Constitutional rights have been violated.

The Government's argument, and the opinion of the court, in my judgment, erroneously divide that which is single and indivisible and thus make the case appear as if the petitioner violated a Military Order, sanctioned by Act of Congress, which excluded him from his home, by refusing voluntarily to leave and, so, knowingly and intentionally, defying the order and the Act of Congress. . . .

The predicament in which the petitioner thus found himself was this: He was forbidden, by Military Order, to leave the zone in which he lived; he was forbidden, by Military Order, after a date fixed, to be found within that zone unless he were in an Assembly Center located in that zone. General DeWitt's report to the Secretary of War concerning the programme of evacuation and relocation of Japanese makes it entirely clear . . . that an Assembly Center was a euphemism for a prison. No person within such a center was permitted to leave except by Military Order. . . .

We cannot shut our eyes to the fact that had the petitioner attempted to violate Proclamation No. 4 and leave the military area in which he lived he would have been arrested and tried and convicted for violation of Proclamation No. 4. The two conflicting orders, one which commanded him to stay and the other which commanded him to go, were nothing but a cleverly devised trap to accomplish the real purpose of the military authority, which was to lock him up in a concentration camp. . . .

These stark realities are met by the suggestion that it is lawful to compel an American citizen to submit to illegal imprisonment on the assumption that he might, after going to the Assembly Center, apply for his discharge by suing out a writ of habeas corpus. . . . The answer, of course, is that where he was subject to two conflicting laws he was not bound, in order to escape violation of one or the other, to surrender his liberty for any period. Nor will it do to say that the detention was a necessary part of the process of evacuation, and so we are here concerned only with the validity of the latter.

Again it is a new doctrine of constitutional law that one indicted for disobedience to an unconstitutional statute may not defend on the ground of the invalidity of the statute but must obey it though he knows it is no law and, after he has suffered the disgrace of conviction and lost his liberty by sentence, then, and not before, seek, from within prison walls, to test the validity of the law. . . .

I would reverse the judgment of conviction.

■ MR. JUSTICE MURPHY, dissenting.

This exclusion of "all persons of Japanese ancestry, both alien and non-alien," from the Pacific Coast area on a plea of military necessity in the absence of martial law ought not to be approved. Such exclusion goes over "the very brink of constitutional power" and falls into the ugly abyss of racism.

In dealing with matters relating to the prosecution and progress of a war, we must accord great respect and consideration to the judgments of the military authorities who are on the scene and who have full knowledge of the military facts. The scope of their discretion must, as a matter of necessity and common sense, be wide. And their judgments ought not to be overruled lightly by those whose training and duties ill-equip them to deal intelligently with matters so vital to the physical security of the nation.

At the same time, however, it is essential that there be definite limits to military discretion, especially where martial law has not been declared. Individuals must not be left impoverished of their constitutional rights on a plea of military necessity that has neither substance nor support. Thus, like other claims conflicting with the asserted constitutional rights of the individual, the military claim must subject itself to the judicial process of having its reasonableness determined and its conflicts with other interests reconciled. "What are the allowable limits of military discretion, and whether or not they have been overstepped in a particular case, are judicial questions."

The judicial test of whether the Government, on a plea of military necessity, can validly deprive an individual of any of his constitutional rights is whether the deprivation is reasonably related to a public danger that is so "immediate, imminent, and impending" as not to admit of delay and not to permit the intervention of ordinary constitutional processes to alleviate the danger. Civilian Exclusion Order No. 34, banishing from a prescribed area of the Pacific Coast "all persons of Japanese ancestry, both alien and non-alien," clearly does not meet that test. Being an obvious racial discrimination, the order deprives all those within its scope of the equal protection of the laws as guaranteed by the Fifth Amendment. It further deprives these individuals of their constitutional rights to live and work where they will, to establish a home where they choose and to move about freely. In excommunicating them without benefit of hearings, this order also deprives them of all their constitutional rights to procedural due process. Yet no reasonable relation to an "immediate, imminent, and impending" public danger is evident to support this racial restriction which is one of the most sweeping and complete deprivations of constitutional rights in the history of this nation in the absence of martial law.

It must be conceded that the military and naval situation in the spring of 1942 was such as to generate a very real fear of invasion of the Pacific Coast, accompanied by fears of sabotage and espionage in that area. The military command was therefore justified in adopting all reasonable means necessary to combat these dangers. In adjudging the military action taken in light of the then apparent dangers, we must not erect too high or too meticulous standards; it is necessary only that the action have some reasonable relation to the removal of the dangers of invasion, sabotage and espionage. But the exclusion, either temporarily or permanently, of *all* persons with Japanese blood in their veins has no such reasonable relation. And that relation is lacking because the exclusion order necessarily must rely for its reasonableness upon the assumption that all persons of Japanese ancestry may have a dangerous tendency to commit sabotage and espionage and to aid our Japanese enemy in other ways. It is difficult to believe that reason, logic or experience could be marshalled in support of such an assumption.

That this forced exclusion was the result in good measure of this erroneous assumption of racial guilt rather than bona fide military necessity is evidenced by the Commanding General's Final Report on the evacuation from the Pacific Coast area. In it he refers to all individuals of Japanese descent as "subversive," as belonging to "an enemy race" whose "racial strains are undiluted," and as constituting "over 112,000 potential enemies . . . at large today" along the Pacific Coast. In support of this blanket condemnation of all persons of Japanese descent, however, no reliable evidence is cited to show that such individuals were generally disloyal, or had generally so conducted themselves in this area as to constitute a special menace to defense installations or war industries, or had otherwise by their behavior furnished reasonable ground for their exclusion as a group.

Justification for the exclusion is sought, instead, mainly upon questionable racial and sociological grounds not ordinarily within the realm of expert military judgment, supplemented by certain semi-military conclusions drawn from an unwarranted use of circumstantial evidence. Individuals of Japanese ancestry are condemned because they are said to be "a large, unassimilated, tightly knit racial group, bound to an enemy nation by strong ties of race, culture, custom and religion." They are claimed to be given to "emperor worshipping ceremonies" and to "dual citizenship." Japanese language schools and allegedly pro-Japanese organizations are cited as evidence of possible group disloyalty, together with facts as to certain persons being educated and residing at length in Japan. It is intimated that many of these individuals deliberately resided "adjacent to strategic points," thus enabling them "to carry into execution a tremendous program of sabotage on a mass scale should any considerable number of them have been inclined to do so." The need for protective custody is also asserted. The report refers without identity to "numerous incidents of violence" as well as to other admittedly unverified or cumulative incidents. From this, plus certain other events not shown to have been connected with the Japanese Americans, it is concluded that the "situation was fraught with danger to the Japanese population itself" and that the general public "was ready to take matters into its own hands." Finally, it is intimated, though not directly charged or proved, that persons of Japanese ancestry were responsible for three minor isolated shellings and bombings of the Pacific Coast area, as well as for unidentified radio transmissions and night signaling.

The main reasons relied upon by those responsible for the forced evacuation, therefore, do not prove a reasonable relation between the group characteristics of Japanese Americans and the dangers of invasion, sabotage and espionage. The reasons appear, instead, to be largely an accumulation of much of the misinformation, half-truths and insinuations that for years have been directed against Japanese Americans by people with racial and economic prejudices—the same people who have been among the foremost advocates of the evacuation. A military judgment based upon such racial and sociological considerations is not entitled to the great weight ordinarily given the judgments based upon strictly military considerations. . . .

No adequate reason is given for the failure to treat these Japanese Americans on an individual basis by holding investigations and hearings to separate the loyal from the disloyal, as was done in the case of persons of German and Italian ancestry. It is asserted merely that the loyalties of this group "were unknown and time was of the essence." Yet nearly four months elapsed after Pearl Harbor before the first exclusion order was issued; nearly eight months went by until the last order was issued; and the last of these "subversive" persons was not actually removed until almost eleven months had elapsed. Leisure and deliberation seem to have been more of the essence than speed. And the fact that conditions were not such as to warrant a declaration of martial law adds strength to the belief that the factors of time and military necessity were not as urgent as they have been represented to be.

Moreover, . . . not one person of Japanese ancestry was accused or convicted of espionage or sabotage after Pearl Harbor while they were still free, a fact which is some evidence of the loyalty of the vast majority of these individuals and of the effectiveness of the established methods of combatting these evils. It seems incredible that under these circumstances it would have been impossible to hold loyalty hearings for the mere 112,000 persons involved—or at least for the 70,000 American citizens—especially when a large part of this number represented children and elderly men and women. Any inconvenience that may have accompanied an attempt to conform to procedural due process cannot be said to justify violations of constitutional rights of individuals.

I dissent, therefore, from this legalization of racism. Racial discrimination in any form and in any degree has no justifiable part whatever in our democratic way of life. It is unattractive in any setting but it is utterly revolting among a free people who have embraced the principles set forth in the Constitution of the United States. All residents of this nation are kin in some way by blood or culture to a foreign land. Yet they are primarily and necessarily a part of the new and distinct civilization of the United States. They must accordingly be treated at all times as the heirs of the American experiment and as entitled to all the rights and freedoms guaranteed by the Constitution.

■ MR. JUSTICE JACKSON, dissenting.

Korematsu was born on our soil, of parents born in Japan. The Constitution makes him a citizen of the United States by nativity and a citizen of California by residence. No claim is made that he is not loyal to this country. There is no suggestion that apart from the matter involved here he is not law-abiding and well disposed. Korematsu, however, has been convicted of an act not commonly a crime. It consists merely of being present in the state whereof he is a citizen, near the place where he was born, and where all his life he has lived.

Even more unusual is the series of military orders which made this conduct a crime. They forbid such a one to remain, and they also forbid him to leave. They were so drawn that the only way Korematsu could avoid violation was to give himself up to the military authority. This meant submission to custody, examination, and transportation out of the territory, to be followed by indeterminate confinement in detention camps.

A citizen's presence in the locality, however, was made a crime only if his parents were of Japanese birth. Had Korematsu been one of four—the others being, say, a German alien enemy, an Italian alien enemy, and a citizen of American-born ancestors, convicted of treason but out on parole—only Korematsu's presence would have violated the order. The difference between their innocence and his crime would result, not from anything he did, said, or thought, different than they, but only in that he was born of different racial stock.

Now, if any fundamental assumption underlies our system, it is that guilt is personal and not inheritable. Even if all of one's antecedents had been convicted of treason, the Constitution forbids its penalties to be visited upon him, for it provides that "no Attainder of Treason shall work Corruption of Blood, or Forfeiture except during the Life of the Person attainted." But here is an attempt to make an otherwise innocent act a crime merely because this prisoner is the son of parents as to whom he had no choice, and belongs to a race from which there is no way to resign. If Congress in peace-time legislation should enact such a criminal law, I should suppose this Court would refuse to enforce it.

But the "law" which this prisoner is convicted of disregarding is not found in an act of Congress, but in a military order. Neither the Act of Congress nor the Executive Order of the President, nor both together, would afford a basis for this conviction. It rests on the orders of General DeWitt. And it is said that if the military commander had reasonable military grounds for promulgating the orders, they are constitutional and become law, and the Court is required to enforce them. There are several reasons why I cannot subscribe to this doctrine.

It would be impracticable and dangerous idealism to expect or insist that each specific military command in an area of probable operations will conform to conventional tests of constitutionality. When an area is so beset that it must be put under military control at all, the paramount consideration is that its measures be successful, rather than legal. The armed services must protect a society, not merely its Constitution. The very essence of the military job is to marshal physical force, to remove every obstacle to its effectiveness, to give it every strategic advantage. Defense measures will not, and often should not, be held within the limits that bind civil authority in peace. No court can require such a commander in such circumstances to act as a reasonable man; he may be unreasonably cautious and exacting. Perhaps he should be. But a commander in temporarily focusing the life of a community on defense is carrying out a military program; he is not making law in the sense the courts know the term. He issues orders, and they may have a certain authority as military commands, although they may be very bad as constitutional law.

But if we cannot confine military expedients by the Constitution, neither would I distort the Constitution to approve all that the military may deem expedient. That is what the Court appears to be doing, whether consciously or not. I cannot say, from any evidence before me, that the orders of General DeWitt were not reasonably expedient military precautions, nor could I say that they were. But even if they were permissible military procedures, I deny that it follows that they are constitutional. If, as the Court holds, it does follow, then we may as well say that any military order will be constitutional and have done with it.

The limitation under which courts always will labor in examining the necessity for a military order are illustrated by this case. How does the Court know that these orders have a reasonable basis in necessity? No evidence whatever on that subject has been taken by this or any other court. There is sharp controversy as to the credibility of the DeWitt report. So the Court, having no real evidence before it, has no choice but to accept General DeWitt's own unsworn, self-serving statement, untested by any cross-examination, that what he did was reasonable. And thus it will always be when courts try to look into the reasonableness of a military order.

In the very nature of things, military decisions are not susceptible of intelligent judicial appraisal. They do not pretend to rest on evidence, but are made on information that often would not be admissible and on assumptions that could not be proved. Information in support of an order could not be disclosed to courts without danger that it would reach the enemy. Neither can courts act on communications made in confidence. Hence courts can never have any real alternative to accepting the mere declaration of the authority that issued the order that it was reasonably necessary from a military viewpoint.

Much is said of the danger to liberty from the Army program for deporting and detaining these citizens of Japanese extraction. But a judicial construction of the due process clause that will sustain this order is a far more subtle blow to liberty than the promulgation of the order itself. A military order, however unconstitutional, is not apt to last longer than the military emergency. Even during that period a succeeding commander may revoke it all. But once a judicial opinion rationalizes such an order to show that it conforms to the Constitution, or rather rationalizes the Constitution to show that the Constitution sanctions such an order, the Court for all time has validated the principle of racial discrimination in criminal procedure and of transplanting American citizens. The principle then lies about like a loaded weapon ready for the hand of any authority that can bring forward a plausible claim of an urgent need. Every repetition imbeds that principle more deeply in our law and thinking and expands it to new purposes. All who observe the work of courts are familiar with what Judge Cardozo described as "the tendency of a principle to expand itself to the limit of its logic." A military commander may overstep the bounds of constitutionality, and it is an incident. But if we review and approve, that passing incident becomes the doctrine of the Constitution. There it has a generative power of its own, and all that it creates will be in its own image. Nothing better illustrates this danger than does the Court's opinion in this case.

It argues that we are bound to uphold the conviction of Korematsu because we upheld one in *Hirabayashi v. United States*, when we sustained these orders in so far as they applied a curfew requirement to a citizen of Japanese ancestry. I think we should learn something from that experience.

In that case we were urged to consider only the curfew feature, that being all that technically was involved, because it was the only count necessary to sustain Hirabayashi's conviction and sentence. We yielded, and the Chief Justice guarded the opinion as carefully as language will do. . . . However, in spite of our limiting words we did validate a discrimination on the basis of ancestry for mild and temporary deprivation of liberty. Now the principle of racial discrimination is pushed from support of mild measures to very harsh ones, and from temporary deprivations to indeterminate ones. And the precedent which it is said requires us to do so is *Hirabayashi*. The Court is now saying that in *Hirabayashi* we did decide the very things we there said we were not deciding. . . .

I should hold that a civil court cannot be made to enforce an order which violates constitutional limitations even if it is a reasonable exercise of military authority. The courts can exercise only the judicial power, can apply only law, and must abide by the Constitution, or they cease to be civil courts and become instruments of military policy.

Of course the existence of a military power resting on force, so vagrant, so centralized, so necessarily heedless of the individual, is an inherent threat to liberty. But I would not lead people to rely on this Court for a review that seems to me wholly delusive. The military reasonableness of these orders can only be determined by military superiors. If the people ever let command of the war power fall into irresponsible and unscrupulous hands, the courts wield no power equal to its restraint. The chief restraint upon those who command the physical forces of the country, in the future as in the past, must be their responsibility to the political judgments of their contemporaries and to the moral judgments of history.

My duties as a justice as I see them do not require me to make a military judgment as to whether General DeWitt's evacuation and detention program was a reasonable military necessity. I do not suggest that the courts should have attempted to interfere with the Army in carrying out its task. But I do not think they may be asked to execute a military expedient that has no place in law under the Constitution. I would reverse the judgment and discharge the prisoner.

NOTES

1. The internment of Japanese-Americans and lawful Japanese resident aliens—by the order of President Franklin D. Roosevelt, enforced by a criminal statute that was enacted by Congress and upheld by the Supreme Court—is widely regarded as one of the great injustices in America's constitutional history. For excellent treatments, see Peter Irons, JUSTICE AT WAR (1983); Greg Robinson, BY ORDER OF THE PRESIDENT: FDR AND THE INTERNMENT OF JAPANESE AMERICANS (2001). Four decades after the Supreme Court upheld Fred Korematsu's conviction, a federal district court, with the government's consent, granted a writ of *coram nobis* vacating his conviction. *Korematsu v. United States*, 584 F. Supp. 1406 (N.D. Cal. 1984). The ground for vacating the conviction was that evidence the government had submitted, in the form of military officers' evaluation of the dangers from sabotage and espionage, had misrepresented the true known facts. (Indeed, it appears that the Department of Justice's earlier draft briefs in *Korematsu* had disavowed General DeWitt's report in important respects.) In 1988, Congress appropriated funds for reparations.

2. The *Hirabayashi* case, discussed in the *Korematsu* opinions, had been decided by the Supreme Court just the year before. It unanimously upheld a race-based evening-to-daylight hours curfew on Japanese nationals and Japanese–American citizens within the military district. The Court did so on the basis of the need to defer to military authorities' judgment about the demands of military necessity in time of war or threatened invasion. Is there a principled basis for distinguishing *Hirabayashi* and *Korematsu*? Is it the magnitude of the intrusion on individual liberty ("stay in your house after dark" versus "leave your house and be relocated to a detention camp")? Is the question of deference to military judgment about matters of asserted military necessity any different? If the two cases are not distinguishable, should the Court have followed or overruled *Hirabayashi*?

3. Would it really have been possible for the Court to rule against the military and invalidate its judgments during World War II? Were *Hirabayashi* and *Korematsu* inevitable? Consider Justice Jackson's dissent in this regard. He argues that law cannot, as a practical matter, prevail over perceptions of military necessity and perhaps should not even try, but that the Court should not validate the military's action. Is this position principled? Is it wise? What would have been the consequence for Korematsu himself? Would it make a difference if the case had been before the Court on a motion for an *injunction* ordering the military to close the internment camps?

4. On the same day the Court decided *Korematsu*, it decided *Ex parte Endo*, 323 U.S. 283 (1944). *Endo* was a habeas corpus challenge, not to the initial exclusion order but to continued detention once time had allowed for the determination that an internee was loyal and not a threat. The Court held that continued detention under such circumstances was not authorized by statute. The case has a strong aura of quasi-constitutional considerations. See Patrick O. Gudridge, *Remember* Endo?, 116 Harv. L. Rev. 1933 (2003). Does *Endo*— which in practical effect required the closing of the internment camps—affect

how you think about *Korematsu*? Was the Court trying to "split the difference" by simultaneously upholding the principle of military authority even while ending the internment program?

5. What explains *Korematsu*? Racism? Wartime hysteria? Principled deference to the military and to the national security judgments of the executive? Lack of an applicable constitutional prohibition? Adherence to *Hirabayashi*?

6. Construct the best facts you can in support of the *Hirabayashi–Korematsu* approach: Suppose there exists a substantial threat of a West Coast invasion by Japan; suppose there have been proven instances of sabotage and espionage by some Japanese nationals living in America; suppose that a military order restricts the liberty of non-citizens who are nationals of an enemy nation without any removal from their homes or internment. The consequences of too little caution might be invasion, loss of life, and loss of the war. Time is short. The generals say these measures are essential to military success. Would you sustain the military's actions? If so, how different is the situation in *Korematsu* as it was presented to the Court? Which of these hypothetical facts could be different and still justify a conclusion supporting the military's judgment?

7. Consider a more recent hypothetical: On September 12, 2001, could the U.S. government have used heightened security-screening procedures (in whatever context) against persons of Arabic ethnicity or against Muslims? Would it have mattered whether the people who were profiled this way were American citizens? Would it have mattered whether they had expressed support for Al Qaeda?

8. It is often said that our Constitution is flexible and capable of being adapted to circumstances. Does the Constitution's meaning change during a crisis? Many constitutions contain clauses that allow for the declaration of states of emergency during which actions like those in *Korematsu* can be taken without setting a precedent for times of peace. Do these clauses run the risk of begetting more emergencies? Remember Justice Jackson's concurrence in *Youngstown*, which discussed how the existence of an emergency powers clause in the constitution of the Weimar Republic helped pave the way for the rise of Hitler. If formal emergency powers clauses are risky, is there something to be said for the elasticity of reading the U.S. Constitution to let presidential powers expand during emergencies and contract when people feel safe? Or is this dangerous, too?

9. The law in the area of war prisoners and military commissions has not stood still. Indeed, it is fair to say that, since September 11, 2001, the Supreme Court has been extraordinarily active in this area, issuing a large number of significant decisions concerning presidential and congressional military authority. A full treatment of these decisions is impossible in a general constitutional law survey course. Three recent cases, however, stand out as being especially important.

a. In *Hamdi v. Rumsfeld*, presented next, the Court, by a divided vote and without a controlling opinion (and dividing differently on different questions), held that (1) the war power generally (and the AUMF of September 18, 2001, specifically) authorizes the president as commander in chief to capture and hold enemy combatants as war prisoners, including American citizens fighting for enemy forces and captured in the course of waging an authorized war; and

(2) that American citizens nonetheless possess the right, under the Fifth Amendment's Due Process Clause, to contest the propriety of their classification as war prisoners through some form of hearing, perhaps including an informal military hearing.

b. In *Hamdan v. Rumsfeld,* 548 U.S. 557 (2006), in what appeared to be a significant departure from the tenor of the unanimous World War II-era decision in *Quirin,* the Court, by a vote of 5–3 (Chief Justice Roberts had ruled on the case as a court of appeals judge and thus did not participate), held that neither the AUMF nor the president's power as commander in chief authorized the use of a military tribunal to try an alleged enemy war criminal captured in Afghanistan and held at Guantanamo Bay, Cuba. Justice Stevens' wide-ranging opinion suggested a narrow reading of the Commander in Chief Clause powers (in considerable tension with prior decisions) and a broad reading of international law as constraining such power. A one-paragraph concurrence by Justice Breyer, joined by four of the five justices comprising the majority (all except Justice Stevens) embraced a more focused rationale, emphasizing that all that was required was congressional action in support of the president's position. Congress indeed responded quickly, with the Military Commissions Act of 2006 ("MCA"), Pub. L. No. 109–366, 120 Stat. 2600, which comprehensively defined punishable war crimes, specified the jurisdiction and procedures of military commissions, and essentially enacted as statutory law the positions that the Bush administration had advocated concerning the effect of international law and the military powers of the president as commander in chief. Did the MCA essentially transform the question of the president's power to prescribe military tribunals from a *Youngstown* "Category III" situation to a *Youngstown* "Category I" situation (where the president's powers are at their height, combining Article II powers with all the powers Congress could delegate)?

c. The MCA provided that challenges to detention and military punishment must proceed through the procedures prescribed for military tribunals, with judicial review thereafter in the U.S. Court of Appeals for the D.C. Circuit and, ultimately, in the U.S. Supreme Court. In *Boumediene v. Bush,* 553 U.S. 723 (2008), the Court held 5–4 that this procedure unconstitutionally deprived enemy alien combatants of their U.S. constitutional right to the writ of habeas corpus to challenge their military detentions abroad and that judicial review of military determinations was an inadequate legal substitute for the writ of habeas corpus. This enormously significant decision addressed the scope of Congress's powers to prescribe the jurisdiction of federal courts and to suspend the writ of habeas corpus, as well as the rights of persons captured in war. It is discussed in more detail later in this chapter in the materials on Article III.

Hamdi v. Rumsfeld

542 U.S. 507 (2004)

■ JUSTICE O'CONNOR announced the judgment of the Court and delivered an opinion, in which THE CHIEF JUSTICE, JUSTICE KENNEDY, and JUSTICE BREYER join.

At this difficult time in our Nation's history, we are called upon to consider the legality of the Government's detention of a United States citizen on United States soil as an "enemy combatant" and to address the process that is constitutionally owed to one who seeks to challenge his classification as such. . . . We hold that although Congress authorized the detention of combatants in the narrow circumstances alleged here, due process demands that a citizen held in the United States as an enemy combatant be given a meaningful opportunity to contest the factual basis for that detention before a neutral decisionmaker.

I

On September 11, 2001, the al Qaeda terrorist network used hijacked commercial airliners to attack prominent targets in the United States. Approximately 3,000 people were killed in those attacks. One week later, in response to these "acts of treacherous violence," Congress passed a resolution [the "Authorization for Use of Military Force" (AUMF)] authorizing the President to "use all necessary and appropriate force against those nations, organizations, or persons he determines planned, authorized, committed, or aided the terrorist attacks" or "harbored such organizations or persons, in order to prevent any future acts of international terrorism against the United States by such nations, organizations or persons." . . .

This case arises out of the detention of a man whom the Government alleges took up arms with the Taliban during this conflict. . . . Born in Louisiana in 1980, Hamdi moved with his family to Saudi Arabia as a child. By 2001, the parties agree, he resided in Afghanistan. At some point that year, he was seized by members of the Northern Alliance, a coalition of military groups opposed to the Taliban government, and eventually was turned over to the United States military. . . . The Government contends that Hamdi is an "enemy combatant," and that this status justifies holding him in the United States indefinitely—without formal charges or proceedings—unless and until it makes the determination that access to counsel or further process is warranted. . . .

II

The threshold question before us is whether the Executive has the authority to detain citizens who qualify as "enemy combatants." . . . [W]e agree with the Government's position, that Congress has in fact authorized Hamdi's detention, through the AUMF. . . .

There can be no doubt that individuals who fought against the United States in Afghanistan as part of the Taliban, an organization known to have supported the al Qaeda terrorist network responsible for those attacks, are individuals Congress sought to target in passing the AUMF. We conclude that detention of individuals falling into the limited category we are considering, for the duration of the particular conflict in which they were captured, is so fundamental and accepted an incident to war as to be an exercise of the "necessary and appropriate force" Congress has authorized the President to use.

The capture and detention of lawful combatants and the capture, detention, and trial of unlawful combatants, by "universal agreement and practice," are "important incident[s] of war." *Ex Parte Quirin*, supra, at 28. The purpose of detention is to prevent captured individuals from returning to the field of battle and taking up arms once again.

There is no bar to this Nation's holding one of its own citizens as an enemy combatant. In *Quirin*, one of the detainees, Haupt, alleged that he was a naturalized United States citizen. We held that "[c]itizens who associate themselves with the military arm of the enemy government, and with its aid, guidance and direction enter this country bent on hostile acts, are enemy belligerents within the meaning of . . . the law of war." While Haupt was tried for violations of the law of war, nothing in *Quirin* suggests that his citizenship would have precluded his mere detention for the duration of the relevant hostilities. . . .

It is a clearly established principle of the law of war that detention may last no longer than active hostilities. . . . The United States may detain, for the duration of these hostilities, individuals legitimately determined to be Taliban combatants who "engaged in an armed conflict against the United States." If the record establishes that United States troops are still involved in active combat in Afghanistan, those detentions are part of the exercise of "necessary and appropriate force," and therefore are authorized by the AUMF. . . .

[O]ur opinion only finds legislative authority to detain under the AUMF once it is sufficiently clear that the individual is, in fact, an enemy combatant; whether that is established by concession or by some other process that verifies this fact with sufficient certainty seems beside the point. . . .

III

Even in cases in which the detention of enemy combatants is legally authorized, there remains the question of what process is constitutionally due to a citizen who disputes his enemy-combatant status. . . .

It is beyond question that substantial interests lie on both sides of the scale in this case. . . . [A]s critical as the Government's interest may be in detaining those who actually pose an immediate threat to the national security of the United States during ongoing international conflict, history and common sense teach us that an unchecked system of detention carries the potential to become a means for oppression and abuse of others who do not present that sort of threat. . . . We reaffirm today the fundamental nature of a citizen's right to be free from involuntary confinement by his own government without due process of law, and we weigh the opposing governmental interests against the curtailment of liberty that such confinement entails. . . .

We . . . hold that a citizen-detainee seeking to challenge his classification as an enemy combatant must receive notice of the factual basis for his classification, and a fair opportunity to rebut the Government's factual assertions before a neutral decisionmaker. . . .

At the same time, the exigencies of the circumstances may demand that, aside from these core elements, enemy-combatant proceedings may be tailored to alleviate their uncommon potential to burden the Executive at a time of ongoing military conflict. Hearsay, for example, may need to be accepted as the most reliable available evidence from the Government in such a proceeding. Likewise, the Constitution would not be offended by a presumption in favor of the Government's evidence, so long as that presumption remained a rebuttable one and fair opportunity for rebuttal were provided. . . .

We think it unlikely that this basic process will have the dire impact on the central functions of warmaking that the Government forecasts. The parties agree that initial captures on the battlefield need not receive the process we have discussed here; that process is due only when the determination is made to *continue* to hold those who have been seized. . . . While we accord the greatest respect and consideration to the judgments of military authorities in matters relating to the actual prosecution of a war, and recognize that the scope of that discretion necessarily is wide, it does not infringe on the core role of the military for the courts to exercise their own time-honored and constitutionally mandated roles of reviewing and resolving claims like those presented here.

In sum, while the full protections that accompany challenges to detentions in other settings may prove unworkable and inappropriate in the enemy-combatant setting, the threats to military operations posed by a basic system of independent review are not so weighty as to trump a citizen's core rights to challenge meaningfully the Government's case and to be heard by an impartial adjudicator.

In so holding, we necessarily reject the Government's assertion that separation of powers principles mandate a heavily circumscribed role for the courts in such circumstances. Indeed, the position that the courts must forgo any examination of the individual case and focus exclusively on the legality of the broader detention scheme cannot be mandated by any reasonable view of separation of powers, as this approach serves only to *condense* power into a single branch of government. We have long since made clear that a state of war is not a blank check for the President when it comes to the rights of the Nation's citizens. *Youngstown Sheet & Tube*, 343 U.S., at 587. Whatever power the United States Constitution envisions for the Executive in its exchanges with other nations or with enemy organizations in times of conflict, it most assuredly envisions a role for all three branches when individual liberties are at stake. . . .

There remains the possibility that the standards we have articulated could be met by an appropriately authorized and properly constituted military tribunal. Indeed, it is notable that military regulations already provide for such process in related instances, dictating that tribunals be made available to determine the status of enemy detainees who assert prisoner-of-war status under the Geneva Convention. In the absence of such process, however, a court that receives a petition for a writ of habeas corpus from an alleged enemy combatant must itself ensure that the minimum requirements of due process are achieved. . . .

■ JUSTICE SOUTER, with whom JUSTICE GINSBURG joins, concurring in part, dissenting in part, and concurring in the judgment.

[Justice Souter would have found Hamdi's detention forbidden by the "Non–Detention Act," 18 U.S.C. § 4001(a), which bars imprisonment or detention of U.S. citizens "except pursuant to an Act of Congress." Justice Souter did not believe that the Authorization for Use of Military Force (AUMF) was an act authorizing detention. Justices Souter and Ginsburg thus joined neither the plurality's holding that the AUMF authorized detention nor the plurality's due process analysis. Nonetheless, because of "the need to give practical effect to the conclusions of eight members of the Court rejecting the Government's position," they joined in the order of remand for a hearing.—Editors]

■ JUSTICE SCALIA, with whom JUSTICE STEVENS joins, dissenting.

Petitioner Yaser Hamdi, a presumed American citizen, has been imprisoned without charge or hearing in the Norfolk and Charleston Naval Brigs for more than two years, on the allegation that he is an enemy combatant who bore arms against his country for the Taliban. His father claims to the contrary, that he is an inexperienced aid worker caught in the wrong place at the wrong time. . . .

Where the Government accuses a citizen of waging war against it, our constitutional tradition has been to prosecute him in federal court for treason or some other crime. Where the exigencies of war prevent that, the

Constitution's Suspension Clause, Art. I, § 9, cl. 2, allows Congress to relax the usual protections temporarily. Absent suspension, however, the Executive's assertion of military exigency has not been thought sufficient to permit detention without charge. No one contends that the congressional Authorization for Use of Military Force, on which the Government relies to justify its actions here, is an implementation of the Suspension Clause. Accordingly, I would reverse the judgment below. . . .

The gist of the Due Process Clause, as understood at the founding and since, was to force the Government to follow those common-law procedures traditionally deemed necessary before depriving a person of life, liberty, or property. When a citizen was deprived of liberty because of alleged criminal conduct, those procedures typically required committal by a magistrate followed by indictment and trial. . . .

The allegations here, of course, are no ordinary accusations of criminal activity. Yaser Esam Hamdi has been imprisoned because the Government believes he participated in the waging of war against the United States. The relevant question, then, is whether there is a different, special procedure for imprisonment of a citizen accused of wrongdoing *by aiding the enemy in wartime.* . . .

[I]n *Ex Parte Milligan,* [77 U.S. (4 Wall.) 2 (1866)], . . . the Court issued the writ to an American citizen who had been tried by military commission for offenses that included conspiring to overthrow the Government, seize munitions, and liberate prisoners of war. The Court rejected in no uncertain terms the Government's assertion that military jurisdiction was proper "under the laws and usages of war." . . .

[T]he reasoning and conclusion of *Milligan* logically cover the present case. The Government justifies imprisonment of Hamdi on principles of the law of war and admits that, absent the war, it would have no such authority. But if the law of war cannot be applied to citizens where courts are open, then Hamdi's imprisonment without criminal trial is no less unlawful than Milligan's trial by military tribunal. . . .

The Government argues that our more recent jurisprudence ratifies its indefinite imprisonment of a citizen within the territorial jurisdiction of federal courts. It places primary reliance upon *Ex parte Quirin,* 317 U.S. 1 (1942), a World War II case upholding the trial by military commission of eight German saboteurs, one of whom, Herbert Haupt, was a U.S. citizen. The case was not this Court's finest hour. . . .

In my view [*Quirin*] seeks to revise *Milligan* rather than describe it. . . .

It follows from what I have said that Hamdi is entitled to a habeas decree requiring his release unless (1) criminal proceedings are promptly brought, or (2) Congress has suspended the writ of habeas corpus. A suspension of the writ could, of course, lay down conditions for continued detention, similar to those that today's opinion prescribes under the Due Process Clause. . . .

Having found a congressional authorization for detention of citizens where none clearly exists; and having discarded the categorical procedural protection of the Suspension Clause; the plurality then proceeds, under the guise of the Due Process Clause, to prescribe what procedural protections *it* thinks appropriate. It "weigh[s] the private interest . . . against the Government's asserted interest" . . . and—just as though writing a new Constitution—comes up with an unheard-of system in which the citizen rather than the Government bears the burden of proof, testimony is by hearsay rather than live witnesses, and the presiding officer may well be a "neutral" military officer rather than judge and jury. . . .

Many think it not only inevitable but entirely proper that liberty give way to security in times of national crisis—that, at the extremes of military exigency, *inter arma silent leges*. Whatever the general merits of the view that war silences law or modulates its voice, that view has no place in the interpretation and application of a Constitution designed precisely to confront war and, in a manner that accords with democratic principles, to accommodate it. Because the Court has proceeded to meet the current emergency in a manner the Constitution does not envision, I respectfully dissent.

■ JUSTICE THOMAS, dissenting.

The Executive Branch, acting pursuant to the powers vested in the President by the Constitution and with explicit congressional approval, has determined that Yaser Hamdi is an enemy combatant and should be detained. This detention falls squarely within the Federal Government's war powers, and we lack the expertise and capacity to second-guess that decision. As such, petitioners' habeas challenge should fail, and there is no reason to remand the case. . . .

The Founders intended that the President have primary responsibility—along with the necessary power—to protect the national security and to conduct the Nation's foreign relations. They did so principally because the structural advantages of a unitary Executive are essential in these domains. "Energy in the executive is a leading character in the definition of good government. It is essential to the protection of the community against foreign attacks." [The Federalist], No. 70 (A. Hamilton). The principle "ingredien[t]" for "energy in the executive" is "unity." This is because "[d]ecision, activity, secrecy, and dispatch will generally characterise the proceedings of one man, in a much more eminent degree, than the proceedings of any greater number."

These structural advantages are most important in the national-security and foreign-affairs contexts. "Of all the cares or concerns of government, the direction of war most peculiarly demands those qualities which distinguish the exercise of power by a single hand." *Id.*, No. 74 (A. Hamilton). . . .

This Court has long recognized these features and has accordingly held that the President has *constitutional* authority to protect the national security and that this authority carries with it broad discretion. . . .

I agree with the plurality that the Federal Government has power to detain those that the Executive Branch determines to be enemy combatants. But I do not think that the plurality has adequately explained the breadth of the President's authority to detain enemy combatants, an authority that includes making virtually conclusive factual findings. . . .

In this context, due process requires nothing more than a good-faith executive determination. To be clear: The Court has held that an Executive, acting pursuant to statutory and constitutional authority, may, consistent with the Due Process Clause, unilaterally decide to detain an individual if the Executive deems this necessary for the public safety *even if he is mistaken*. . . .

The Government's asserted authority to detain an individual that the President has determined to be an enemy combatant, at least while hostilities continue, comports with the Due Process Clause. . . . I therefore cannot agree with Justice SCALIA's conclusion that the Government must choose between using standard criminal processes and suspending the writ. . . .

By detaining Hamdi, the President, in the prosecution of a war and authorized by Congress, has acted well within his authority. Hamdi thereby received all the process to which he was due under the circumstances. I therefore believe that this is no occasion to balance the competing interests, as the plurality unconvincingly attempts to do. . . .

NOTES

1. First, sort out the holdings and the alignment of the justices. On the power to capture and hold a U.S. citizen pursuant to the war power: Five justices—the four justices joining Justice O'Connor's plurality opinion, plus Justice Thomas in dissent—agreed that the government had authority to hold Hamdi, a U.S. citizen, pursuant to the war power to hold enemy prisoners triggered by the AUMF and the president's power as Commander in Chief. In what ways does Justice Thomas's legal position on this issue differ from that of the plurality? Why did he not join the plurality opinion on this point? Note that Justice Thomas's dissent is a dissent precisely because he disagrees with the ultimate disposition of the case: he would uphold the president's power to detain Hamdi, without more. In his view, presidential wartime determinations (through military subordinates) as to a captured person's status are all the process that is due captured war prisoners. Justices Souter and Ginsburg disagreed with this holding on the ground that Hamdi's detention was not authorized by congressional act—the AUMF was not sufficient. Justices Scalia and Stevens—a rather unusual pairing—disagreed with this holding on the ground that a *U.S. citizen* may never be held by military authorities, but instead must be charged with a civilian crime or released, unless Congress has exercised the power to suspend the privilege of the writ of habeas corpus. This argument explicitly disagreed with the unanimous holding in *Quirin* and sought a return to the language of *Milligan*. Which view on this point is right—the position of the majority, or the positions of Justices Souter and Scalia?

2. On the requirement of a hearing: The plurality finds that, notwithstanding the president's authority to capture and hold enemy prisoners, a *U.S. citizen* has a due process right to some sort of hearing to challenge the validity of his detention as a war prisoner. (Why U.S. citizens only? Does the Fifth Amendment's Due Process Clause, which says that no "person" can be deprived of liberty without due process of law, draw this distinction? What is the source of the balancing test the plurality employs?) But the plurality appears to leave considerable room for informal procedures. What form of hearing does the plurality opinion require? What do you think of its resolution of this issue? Is it principled? Is it a compromise? If so, is it a sensible compromise? Is there a good alternative? No other justice appears to agree with the plurality on this point, though Justice Souter's opinion concurs in the disposition because it is the next closest thing to what he would have held. Again: What do you think is the correct resolution of this issue?

3. Justice Thomas's dissent is far different from that of Justices Scalia and Stevens. Both positions warrant careful study. To compress drastically: Justice Thomas finds that the original meaning of the Constitution commits to the

president the ultimate authority to make decisions concerning the capture and detention of enemies, including U.S. citizens, in times of war. Justice Scalia finds that the original meaning of the Constitution forbids national authorities ever to hold a U.S. citizen under military authority without civilian charges being brought, subject only to the exception provided in the Writ Suspension Clause. Who is right (if either of them)? Does the sharp disagreement between two committed adherents to original meaning provide a potent argument against originalism, because it can yield divergent conclusions? Is any approach to constitutional interpretation immune from good-faith disagreement about its application?

4. Is the plurality opinion superior to the other opinions in seeking to strike a balance between competing extremes? What should a collective judicial body do when there are multiple divergent views and multiple issues in a case? Should it try to craft a consensus opinion? Should it allow each view to be expressed and then count noses for each distinct holding? Which approach does *Hamdi* more closely resemble?

[*Assignment 24*]

H. IMPEACHMENT: "THE PRESIDENT . . . SHALL BE REMOVED FROM OFFICE ON IMPEACHMENT . . . AND CONVICTION"

Article II, Section 4: The President, Vice President and all civil Officers of the United States, shall be removed from Office on Impeachment for, and Conviction of, Treason, Bribery, or other high Crimes and Misdemeanors.

Article I, Section 3, Clause 7: Judgment in Cases of Impeachment shall not extend further than to removal from Office, and disqualification to hold any Office of honor, Trust or Profit under the United States: but the Party convicted shall nevertheless be liable and subject to Indictment, Trial, Judgment, and Punishment, according to Law.

As noted above, the Impeachment Clause of Article II, Section 4 makes clear that the president, unlike the king of England, is removable from office by impeachment. The only methods for getting rid of the English king were to kill him, force him to abdicate, or drive him into exile. These methods were used from time to time, but none was free of inconvenience.

The following sources consider impeachment, and especially the debate during the impeachment of President Clinton over the standards that should apply in determining what is a "high Crime" or "Misdemeanor." They offer the diverging views of legal scholars and one member of the House of Representatives. As you read them, ask yourself what the circumstances are in which Congress has (1) a duty to impeach and remove the president, (2) discretion to impeach and remove the president, or (3) no constitutional authority to impeach and remove the president.

Law Professors' Letter on the Clinton Impeachment

November 6, 1998

Dear Mr. Speaker, Mr. Gephardt, Mr. Hyde and Mr. Conyers:

Did President Clinton commit "high Crimes and Misdemeanors" warranting impeachment under the Constitution? We, the undersigned professors of law, believe that the misconduct alleged in the report of the Independent Counsel, and in the statement of Investigative Counsel David Schippers, does not cross that threshold.

We write neither as Democrats nor as Republicans. Some of us believe that the President has acted disgracefully, some that the Independent Counsel has. This letter has nothing to do with any such judgments. Rather, it expresses the one judgment on which we all agree: that the allegations detailed in the Independent Counsel's referral and summarized in Counsel Schippers's statement do not justify presidential impeachment under the Constitution.

No existing judicial precedents bind Congress's determination of the meaning of "high Crimes and Misdemeanors." But it is clear that Members of Congress would violate their constitutional responsibilities if they sought to impeach and remove the President for misconduct, even criminal misconduct, that fell short of the high constitutional standard required for impeachment.

The President's independence from Congress is fundamental to the American structure of government. It is essential to the separation of powers. It is essential to the President's ability to discharge such constitutional duties as vetoing legislation that he considers contrary to the nation's interests. And it is essential to governance whenever the White House belongs to a party different from that which controls the Capitol. The lower the threshold for impeachment, the weaker the President. If the President could be removed for any conduct of which Congress disapproved, this fundamental element of our democracy—the President's independence from Congress—would be destroyed. It is not enough, therefore, that Congress strongly disapprove of the President's conduct. Under the Constitution, the President cannot be impeached unless he has committed "Treason, Bribery, or other high Crimes and Misdemeanors."

Some of the charges raised against the President fall so far short of this high standard that they strain good sense: for example, the charge that the President repeatedly declined to testify voluntarily or pressed a debatable privilege claim that was later judicially rejected. Such litigation "offenses" are not remotely impeachable. With respect, however, to other allegations, careful consideration must be given to the kind of misconduct that renders a President constitutionally unfit to remain in office.

Neither history nor legal definitions provide a precise list of high crimes and misdemeanors. Reasonable people have differed in interpreting these words. We believe that the proper interpretation of the Impeachment Clause must begin by recognizing treason and bribery as core or paradigmatic instances, from which the meaning of "other high Crimes and Misdemeanors" is to be extrapolated. The constitutional standard for impeachment would be very different if different offenses had been specified. The clause does not read, "Treason, Felony, or other Crime" (as does Article IV, Section 2 of the Constitution), so that any violation of a criminal statute would be impeachable. Nor does it read, "Arson, Larceny, or other high Crimes and Misdemeanors," implying that any serious crime, of whatever nature, would be impeachable. Nor does it read, "Adultery, Fornication, or other high Crimes and Misdemeanors," implying that any conduct deemed to reveal serious moral lapses might be an impeachable offense.

When a President commits treason, he exercises his *executive powers*, or uses information obtained by virtue of his *executive powers*, deliberately to aid an enemy. When a President is bribed, he exercises or offers to exercise his *executive powers* in exchange for corrupt gain. Both acts involve the criminal exercise of presidential powers, converting those awful powers into an instrument either of enemy interests or of purely personal gain. We believe that the critical, distinctive feature of treason and bribery is grossly derelict exercise of official power (or, in the case of bribery to obtain or retain office, gross criminality in the pursuit of official power). Non-indictable conduct might rise to this level. For example, a President might be properly impeached if, as a result of drunkenness, he recklessly and repeatedly misused executive authority.

Much of the misconduct of which the President is accused does not involve the exercise of executive powers at all. *If* the President committed perjury regarding his sexual conduct, this perjury involved no exercise of presidential power as such. *If* he concealed evidence, this misdeed too involved no exercise of executive authority. By contrast, *if* he sought wrongfully to place someone in a job at the Pentagon, or lied to subordinates hoping they would repeat his false statements, these acts could have involved a wrongful use of presidential influence, but we cannot believe that the President's alleged conduct of this nature amounts to the grossly derelict exercise of executive power sufficient for impeachment.

Perjury and obstructing justice can without doubt be impeachable offenses. A President who corruptly used the Federal Bureau of Investigation to obstruct an investigation would have criminally exercised his presidential powers. Moreover, covering up a crime furthers or aids the underlying crime. Thus a President who committed perjury to cover up his subordinates' criminal exercise of executive authority would also have committed an impeachable offense. But making false statements about sexual improprieties is not a sufficient constitutional basis to justify the trial and removal from office of the President of the United States.

It goes without saying that lying under oath is a very serious offense. But even if the House of Representatives had the constitutional authority to impeach for any instance of perjury or obstruction of justice, a responsible House would not exercise this awesome power on the facts alleged in this case. The House's power to impeach, like a prosecutor's power to indict, is discretionary. This power must be exercised not for partisan advantage, but only when circumstances genuinely justify the enormous price the nation will pay in governance and stature if its President is put through a long, public, voyeuristic trial. The American people understand this price. They demonstrate the political wisdom that has held the Constitution in place for two centuries when, even after the publication of Mr. Starr's report, with all its extraordinary revelations, they oppose impeachment for the offenses alleged therein.

We do not say that a "private" crime could never be so heinous as to warrant impeachment. Congress might responsibly take the position that an individual who by the law of the land cannot be permitted to remain at large, need not be permitted to remain President. But if certain crimes such as murder warrant removal of a President from office because of their unspeakable heinousness, the offenses alleged in the Independent Counsel's report or the Investigative Counsel's statement are not among them. Short of heinous criminality, impeachment demands convincing evidence of grossly derelict exercise of official authority. In our judgment, Mr. Starr's report contains no such evidence.

Sincerely,

[Signatures of 430 law professors]

Michael Stokes Paulsen, Impeachment

3 Encyclopedia of the American Constitution
(L. Levy & K. Karst, eds. 2d ed. 2000).

. . . The Constitution's impeachment provisions have produced much scholarly and political debate, especially in recent years by virtue of President Bill Clinton's impeachment, trial, and acquittal in 1998 and 1999. The most important question is the meaning of the term "high Crimes and Misdemeanors" for which officials may be impeached and removed. The Clinton impeachment produced numerous arguments on this score, some of them obviously tinged with partisan bias. The best answer, confirmed by recent and perennial debates over the point, is simply that the term does not have a clear, fixed, or determinate meaning, and that application of this general standard was deliberately committed to the judgment of Congress in making the decision whether to impeach (by the House) and convict (by the Senate).

As Alexander Hamilton wrote in *The Federalist* No. 65, explaining the justification for vesting the impeachment power in Congress rather than the courts or some other body, "the nature of the proceeding" is such that it "can never be tied down by such strict rules, either in the delineation of the offence by the prosecutors, or in the construction of it by the Judges, as in common cases serve to limit the discretion of courts in favor of personal security." Rather, the Constitution recognizes "[t]he awful discretion; which a court of impeachments must have, to doom to honor or to infamy. . . ." The Supreme Court has apparently endorsed this view, ruling unanimously in a case involving the impeachment of federal judge Walter Nixon that the Constitution's assignment of "sole Power" to impeach and try to the House and Senate respectively constitutes a textual commitment of all (or nearly all) impeachment questions to the judgment of these bodies, where the Constitution does not provide a clear answer to the contrary. (*Nixon v. United States*, 1993)

Congress's constitutional power to interpret and apply the "high Crimes and Misdemeanors standard" is broad, but not limitless. Certain guidelines are clear from history or implicit in the structure of the Constitution as a whole. First, it is clear that misconduct need not be a crime in the ordinary sense of the term in order to justify impeachment and removal, but may include "political crimes" in the sense of perceived offenses against the Constitution or the People—such as violation of one's oath of office or breach of a public trust. Hamilton in *The Federalist* No. 65, for example, said that proper grounds for impeachment and removal included "offenses which proceed from the misconduct of public men, or in other words from the abuse or violation of some public trust." Such offenses, Hamilton wrote, constitute "injuries done immediately to the society itself."

At the same time, however, it is implicit in our constitutional structure of separate, independent Legislative, Executive, and Judicial branches that impeachment must be more than simply a policy vote of "no confidence" in the Executive, leading to the fall of his administration (akin to parliamentary systems of government) or, in the case of judges, attempted removal from office because of disapproval of a judge's rulings, made in good faith. The narrow impeachment-acquittal of President Andrew Johnson by a reconstruction Congress strongly opposed to Johnson's policies, but with flimsy charges of "high Crimes and Misdemeanors," has been taken by many as a precedent against impeachment even for strongly-felt reasons of policy felt to be of vital concern to the future of the Nation. The impeachment-acquittal of Justice Samuel Chase, early in our nation's history, has been taken by many as a precedent against impeachment of judges merely because of disagreement (however intense and perhaps justified) with their judgments and demeanor.

While conduct need not be a crime in order to constitute an impeachable offence, it is clear that criminal acts in the ordinary sense of the term may themselves be "high Crimes and Misdemeanors" sufficient to warrant removal from office, if Congress judges them to be of sufficient seriousness. The misconduct need not be a felony—high "Misdemeanors" fall within the standard—but the commission of felonies is a classic case in which the Constitution contemplates, and Congress's practice over the centuries confirms, that federal officers should be impeached and removed. (Moreover, Congress is not bound by the "proof beyond a reasonable doubt" standard that applies in a criminal prosecution in which an individual may be imprisoned or fined if found guilty; Congress indeed has impeached and removed a federal judge who was *acquitted* of essentially the same charges in a federal criminal prosecution.) Thus, federal judges have been removed for bribery and tax evasion. President Richard Nixon resigned rather than face near-certain impeachment (and probable conviction) for obstruction of justice. President Bill Clinton was impeached for perjury and obstruction of justice, both serious federal felonies carrying substantial prison terms, but acquitted largely on the basis of votes of senators of his own party who concluded that such misconduct, even if proved, did not constitute "high Crimes and Misdemeanors."

Once again (as the Clinton case confirms), the question of what is sufficiently "high" criminal misconduct—sufficiently serious, important, weighty—is committed to the "awful discretion" (in Alexander Hamilton's terms) of Congress, and Congress may exercise that judgment for good or for ill and need not be consistent or principled in its actions. It seems highly unlikely, for example, that Congress in 1974 would have judged obstruction of justice not to be an impeachable offense, in the case of President Nixon. (A scholarly report of the House Judiciary Committee indeed concluded the contrary.)

One possible ground for distinguishing the Clinton and Nixon cases, advanced by Clinton's defenders (including numerous academics), is that Clinton's misconduct was of a "private" nature and that "private" crimes are not included within the meaning of "high Crimes and Misdemeanors." There must exist a nexus, the argument goes, between the criminal act and the official's public office. Nothing in the text of the Constitution supports this distinction, however, and Alexander Hamilton's argument that the impeachment power characteristically is directed at breaches of a public trust does not imply that the power may not be exercised to remove an official for crimes for which any citizen guilty of such offence might well be sent to prison. (Clinton's prosecutors, and the 50 senators who voted to convict him, additionally maintained that there is no such thing as "private" perjury or obstruction of justice; that such crimes committed by the chief law enforcement officer of the nation *do* relate to the performance of his duties; that perjury is strongly akin to "Bribery," which is explicitly a ground for removal; and that Clinton's misconduct in any event involved a violation of his oath of office and a breach of trust with the People.)

There is a further flaw with the nexus-to-office limitation. Taken seriously, it would require the absurdity of permitting a federal officer to remain in office following commission of a "private" first-degree murder if that homicide was unrelated to the performance of his or her office. In an attempt to avoid this problem, a letter signed by law professors sympathetic to President Clinton argued that private criminal conduct does not warrant impeachment unless the crime is a "heinous" one. Again, however, the "heinous" standard does not appear in the Constitution, nor is it mentioned in the framers' discussions and debates over impeachment. The standard chosen was *"high"* crimes and misdemeanors. It has been plausibly argued that "high" in this context denotes the rank or office of the alleged miscreant, but the better answer is that it creates a general standard of seriousness or importance (as judged by Congress). A crime can be serious without being "heinous" and the Constitution clearly imposes no such limitation on the scope of the impeachment power.

A final argument advanced during the Clinton case was that, for purposes of impeachment, the President should be held to a lower standard of conduct than federal judges and other federal officers; that is, that the height of "high" crimes needs to be higher in the case of the President, before Congress is constitutionally justified in removing him from office. There is no basis for this argument in the text of the Constitution. Article III's provision that judges serve "during good behaviour" is a description of judges' tenure (life), not a substitute for Article II's statement of the impeachment-removal standard applicable to "all civil officers of the United States," a term that embraces Article III judges. While removal of a sitting President is obviously a more serious matter that removal of a single federal judge, this political reality does not alter the meaning of the Constitution's terms. Nor does the claim that removal of a President would "upset" the result of a national election change the Constitution's standard. Presidential impeachment will nearly always remove an elected leader; the framers, in creating an impeachment standard that explicitly mentions the President and Vice President, obviously contemplated such a possibility.

Though the Constitution does not require it, a practical necessity for removal of the President is that he *both* has committed serious offences *and* lost popular political support, extending to members of his own party in the Senate. Experience has shown that the two-thirds majority requirement makes it extremely difficult to convict a sitting President, regardless of the merits of the charges. As the acquittal of President Johnson shows, even large partisan majorities strongly opposed to an unpopular President on policy grounds encounter principled defections of senators opposed removal on such constitutionally dubious grounds. Conversely, as the acquittal of President Clinton shows, a popular president retaining the unified, partisan, support of senators of his party may avoid removal from office even when few (in either party) question that he has committed serious criminal offenses. (President Nixon resigned, rather than face impeachment, once it became clear that he had lost the support even of his own political party.)

A related issue that arose in the Clinton impeachment is whether Congress has the power to punish presidential misconduct by "censure." Censure, in the form of a resolution of disapproval (without further penalty), is neither mentioned in nor prohibited by the Constitution. Whatever its propriety, censure is a remedy outside the impeachment process. . . .

The proviso that "the party convicted shall, nevertheless, be subject to indictment, trial, judgment, and punishment, according to law" has traditionally been thought to imply that the President must be removed from office before he may be indicted. But if this is so, it must be because of some other constitutional provision, not the punishment proviso, which in form merely holds that Congress's judgment is separate from, and not preclusive of, criminal prosecution: It does not dictate that impeachment precede indictment. Prosecution has preceded impeachment in the case of some removed federal judges. It is probably the case that the framers *expected,* in the case of the President at least, that removal would precede prosecution, for the simple reason that federal prosecutors are subordinates of the President within the executive branch and might be expected not to indict the Chief–Executive. State prosecutions of a sitting President or other federal officer, while also theoretically possible, may not be practically enforceable without federal judicial or congressional approval (through impeachment). But where an "independent counsel" serves as federal prosecutor acting on behalf of the executive branch (an arrangement constitutionally problematic in its own right Under Article II, but upheld by the Supreme Court in 1988 in the case of *Morrison v. Olson*), or where a federal prosecutor is not otherwise countermanded by the President, the Constitution would not seem to bar those stages of a criminal case—indictment, trial, entry of judgment—that do not effect the equivalent of removal of a President from office (arrest, imprisonment). Removal is the exclusive province of impeachment. But otherwise the President is not above the requirements and burdens of the law that apply to any other citizen, taking into account the needs of the nation, as the Supreme Court has twice held, unanimously, in different contexts. (*United States v. Nixon* (1974) (President not immune to subpoenas for evidence in federal criminal case); *Clinton v. Jones* (1997) (President not immune from private civil litigation concerning his personal conduct).)

It has been suggested that Article I section 3's mandate of removal upon conviction for "high Crimes and Misdemeanors" does not necessarily imply that Congress lacks power to impeach and, in the Senate's *discretion,* remove or impose some lesser punishment (like censure) for perceived *lesser* offenses. Otherwise, the argument goes, what remedy would have existed (prior to adoption of the Twenty-fifth Amendment in 1967) for removing an incapacitated or incompetent President? The argument has some serious problems, however. First, it imports into the word "impeachment" a broader power than appears supported by the language of the various clauses of the Constitution, and one that would seem inconsistent with other structural provisions of the Constitution. . . . [Further], the apparent point-of-departure for this argument—the problem of presidential incapacity—is exactly the reason the Twenty-fifth Amendment was adopted. . . . If [present] needs are sufficiently great, the amendment process exists to address them.

Indeed, with respect to the power of impeachment, one can even detect an embarrassing glitch that begs for a remedy: While the Chief Justice, rather than the Vice President, serves as presiding officer of the Senate when the President is tried (to remove obvious conflict-of-interest problems), no such substitution is prescribed in the case when the Vice President is put on trial. The framers no doubt erred in permitting the Vice President to preside over his own impeachment trial!

In every other respect, however, the Constitution's impeachment provisions contain a sufficient and balanced constitutional check against lawlessness and misconduct by executive and judicial officers, if—and it has proven at various points in our history, including during the Clinton presidency, to be a big "if"—Congress is prepared to employ that check in a consistent, principled, serious way. The Clinton trial has led to the same concerns expressed by Thomas Jefferson, who, as President, bemoaned the impeachment power as exercised in his day as a mere "scarecrow." But Jefferson's remark, as with Clinton's acquittal, simply highlights the fact that the practical application of the awesome constitutional power of impeachment depends on the fortitude and judgment of Congress and thus, for good or for ill, the politics of the moment.

Cass Sunstein, Impeachment?
The Framers Wouldn't Buy It

Op-ed, Washington Post, October 4, 1998

We all now know that, under the Constitution, the president can be impeached for "Treason, Bribery, or other high Crimes and Misdemeanors." But what did the framers intend us to understand with these words? Evidence of the phrase's evolution is extensive—and it strongly suggests that, if we could solicit the views of the Constitution's authors, the current allegations against President Clinton would not be impeachable offenses.

When the framers met in Philadelphia during the stifling summer of 1787, they were seeking not only to design a new form of government, but to outline the responsibilities of the president who would head the new nation. They shared a commitment to disciplining public officials through a system of checks and balances. But they disagreed about the precise extent of presidential power and, in particular, about how, if at all, the president might be removed from office. If we judge by James Madison's characteristically detailed accounts of the debates, this question troubled and divided the members of the Constitutional Convention.

The initial draft of the Constitution took the form of resolutions presented before the 30-odd members on June 13. One read that the president could be impeached for "malpractice, or neglect of duty," and, on July 20, this provision provoked extensive debate. The notes of Madison, who was representing Virginia, show that three distinct positions dominated the day's discussion. One extreme view, represented by Roger Sherman of Connecticut, was that "the National Legislature should have the power to remove the Executive at pleasure." Charles Pinckney of South Carolina, Rufus King of Massachusetts and Gouverneur Morris of Pennsylvania opposed, with Pinckney arguing that the president "ought not to be impeachable whilst in office." The third position, which ultimately carried the day, was that the president should be impeachable, but only for a narrow category of abuses of the public trust.

It was George Mason of Virginia who took a lead role in promoting this more moderate course. He argued that it would be necessary to counter the risk that the president might obtain his office by corrupting his electors. "Shall that man be above" justice, he asked, "who can commit the most extensive injustice?" The possibility of the new president becoming a near-monarch led the key votes—above all, Morris—to agree that impeachment might be permitted for (in Morris's words) "corruption & some few other offences." Madison concurred, and Edmund Randolph of Virginia captured the emerging consensus, favoring impeachment on the grounds that the executive "will have great opportunitys of abusing his power; particularly in time of war when the military force, and in some respect the public money, will be in his hands." The clear trend of the discussion was toward allowing a narrow impeachment power by which the president could be removed only for gross abuses of public authority.

To Pinckney's continued protest that the separation of powers should be paramount, Morris argued that "no one would say that we ought to expose ourselves to the danger of seeing the first Magistrate in foreign pay without being able to guard against it by displacing him." At the same time, Morris insisted, "we should take care to provide some mode that will not make him dependent on the Legislature." Thus, led by Morris, the framers moved toward a position that would maintain the separation between president and Congress, but permit the president to be removed in extreme situations.

A fresh draft of the Constitution's impeachment clause, which emerged two weeks later on Aug. 6, permitted the president to be impeached, but only for treason, bribery and corruption (exemplified by the president's securing his office by unlawful means). With little additional debate, this provision was narrowed on Sept. 4 to "treason and bribery." But a short time later, the delegates took up the impeachment clause anew. Mason complained that the provision was too narrow, that "maladministration" should be added, so as to include "attempts to subvert the Constitution" that would not count as treason or bribery.

But Madison, the convention's most careful lawyer, insisted that the term "maladministration" was "so vague" that it would "be equivalent to a tenure during pleasure of the Senate," which is exactly what the framers were attempting to avoid. Hence, Mason withdrew "maladministration" and added the new terms "other high Crimes and Misdemeanors against the State"—later unanimously changed to, according to Madison, "against the United States" to "remove ambiguity." The phrase itself was taken from English law, where it referred to a category of distinctly political offenses against the state.

There is a further wrinkle in the clause's history. On Sept. 10, the entire Constitution was referred to the Committee on Style and Arrangement. When that committee's version appeared two days later, the words "against the United States" had been dropped, probably on the theory that they were redundant, although we have no direct evidence. It would be astonishing if this change were intended to have a substantive effect, for the committee had no authority to change the meaning of any provision, let alone the impeachment clause on which the framers had converged. The Constitution as a whole, including the impeachment provision, was signed by the delegates and offered to the nation on Sept. 17.

These debates support a narrow understanding of "high Crimes and Misdemeanors," founded on the central notions of bribery and treason. The early history tends in the same direction. The Virginia and Delaware constitutions, providing a background for the founders' work, generally allowed impeachment for acts "by which the safety of the State may be endangered." And consider the words of the highly respected (and later Supreme Court Justice) James Iredell, speaking in the North Carolina ratifying convention: "I suppose the only instances, in which the President would be liable to impeachment, would be where he had received a bribe, or had acted from some corrupt motive or other." By way of explanation, Iredell referred to a situation in which "the President has received a bribe . . . from a foreign power, and, under the influence of that bribe, had address enough with the Senate, by artifices and misrepresentations, to seduce their consent to a pernicious treaty."

James Wilson, a convention delegate from Pennsylvania, wrote similarly in his 1791 "Lectures on Law": "In the United States and in Pennsylvania, impeachments are confined to political characters, to political crimes and misdemeanors, and to political punishments." Another early commentator went so far as to say that "the legitimate causes of impeachment . . . can have reference only to public character, and official duty. . . . In general, those offenses, which may be committed equally by a private person, as a public officer, are not the subjects of impeachment."

This history casts new light on the famous 1970 statement of Gerald Ford, then a representative from Michigan, that a high crime and misdemeanor "is whatever a majority of the House of Representatives considers it to be." In a practical sense, of course, Ford was right; no court would review a decision to impeach. But in a constitutional sense, he was quite wrong; the framers were careful to circumscribe the power of the House of Representatives by sharply limiting the category of legitimately impeachable offenses.

The Constitution is not always read to mean what the founders intended it to mean, and Madison's notes hardly answer every question. But under any reasonable theory of constitutional interpretation, the current allegations against Clinton fall far short of the permissible grounds for removing a president from office. Of course, perjury and obstruction of justice could be impeachable offenses if they involved, for example, lies about unlawful manipulation of elections. It might even be possible to count as impeachable "corruption" the extraction of sexual favors in return for public benefits of some kind. But nothing of this kind has been alleged thus far.

. . . A decision to impeach President Clinton would not and should not be subject to judicial review. But for those who care about the Constitution's words, and the judgment of its authors, there is a good argument that it would nonetheless be unconstitutional.

Representative Canady,
Statement on Impeachment of President Clinton

House of Representatives, December 19, 1998

. . . The argument has been made that in essence, we in the House should, in carrying out our responsibility, look to the Senate, and make a guess about how the proceedings would turn out in the Senate, to determine how we exercise our responsibility under the Constitution.

I would suggest to you, I don't think that's a proper way for us to proceed. I believe that we have an independent responsibility, under the Constitution, to make a judgment concerning the conduct of the president, and whether he should be impeached or not. And it would be in derogation of our constitutional responsibility to attempt to count noses in the Senate. I will have to say that it's a very difficult thing to count noses in the Senate anyway, and in a proceeding like this, it's hard to predict the outcome.

But aside from that, I just don't think that's a proper undertaking for us to be involved in. And I'd also point out that the very structure of the Constitution indicates that. In the Constitution, the framers provided that the House could impeach with a simple majority. They provided that conviction in the Senate would have to be by a two-thirds majority.

Now, I would suggest to you that that structural feature of the Constitution suggests that the framers would have contemplated circumstances in which the House might very well impeach, but the Senate would not convict. Now, I think that's obvious on the face of the documents. Some of these arguments I think have to be brought back to the text of the Constitution and evaluated in that light.

But on this issue of prosecutorial discretion, let me pose a scenario here, which I think is very analogous to what we have before us. Suppose the chief executive of a Fortune 500 corporation, a major national corporation in the United States, was accused of sexual harassment, and the corporation had been sued—sexual harassment or any other civil rights offense. And in the course of the discovery in that case, the chief executive of that major national corporation lied under oath to impede that civil rights action.

Now, I believe that the fact that the chief executive of a major national corporation was engaged in that type of conduct, would be a relevant consideration for the prosecutors who were evaluating the case and whether to bring it, because of the impact of that conduct.

Now, I do believe that bringing prosecutions have a deterrent impact. And that is one of the considerations that has to be factored into prosecutorial discretion.

So, I think if we step back from this situation—and again, we can argue about the weight of the facts, and I understand you disagree with the evaluation some of us may have made about the weight of the facts here. But if the president of the United States did engage in obstruction of justice, and committed multiple acts of lying under oath, I think that we have to look at that conduct, in light of the consequences that it has, and the message it sends, just as we would look at the conduct of the chief executive of a major national corporation who was the defendant in a civil rights case brought against that corporation.

NOTES

1. Well before he was obliged as chief justice to preside over the Senate's trial of President Clinton, William Rehnquist wrote book and a law review article on the subject of impeachment. See William H. Rehnquist, GRAND INQUESTS: THE HISTORIC IMPEACHMENTS OF JUSTICE SAMUEL CHASE AND PRESIDENT ANDREW JOHNSON (1992); William H. Rehnquist, *The Impeachment Clause: A Wild Card in the Constitution*, 85 Nw. U. L. Rev. 903 (1991). His thesis was that modern ideas of the separation of powers depend on the understanding that impeachment will be rarely, if ever, used. Chief Justice Rehnquist noted that the impeachment of Federalist Supreme Court Justice Samuel Chase on

flimsy grounds by the Jeffersonians helped establish the idea that judges cannot be impeached just because Congress disagrees with their judicial philosophy. Since then, no federal judge has been impeached except where there has been criminal misconduct. Chief Justice Rehnquist also discussed the failed effort to impeach President Andrew Johnson. Here, again, the effort stemmed mainly from opposition to President Johnson's policy views rather than from any malfeasance in office. Do you think judges should be impeachable on account of their judicial philosophies, or that presidents should be impeachable for policy reasons? If a judge declares, "I do not believe in law and do not feel bound by it," would that be an impeachable offense? Suppose a president commits no crime but goes on vacation for a year. Would that be a gross dereliction of duty for which the president may be impeached?

2. In the sources presented above, what positions are taken about when impeachment and conviction are permissible? About when they are required? Which types of constitutional argument, or modes of interpretation, are most helpful in resolving these questions?

3. Should the House of Representatives ever impeach an executive or judicial officer when it is clear that the Senate will not remove the official?

4. At the time of President Clinton's impeachment, there were some who thought Congress ought to adopt a resolution censuring President Clinton instead of impeaching him. Others argued that Congress has no enumerated power to censure and that its authority on such matters is carefully confined to impeachment. What do you think? (As noted in Chapter 1, in the 1830s the Senate censured President Andrew Jackson, but it repealed its resolution of censure after the Jacksonians won the next election.)

[*Assignment 25*]

III. ARTICLE III: THE JUDICIAL POWER

We turn next to Article III of the Constitution, the article vesting "the judicial Power" of the United States in federal courts, describing the structure of the federal judiciary, and enumerating the categories of "cases" and "controversies" to which the federal judicial power extends.

A Map of Article III

Section 1: The judicial Power of the United States, shall be vested . . . .

Section 2: The judicial Power shall extend to all Cases, in Law and Equity, arising under this Constitution, the Laws of the United States, and Treaties made, or which shall be made, under their Authority;—to all Cases affecting Ambassadors, other public ministers and Consuls;—to all Cases of admiralty and maritime Jurisdiction;—to Controversies to which the United States shall be a Party;—to Controversies between two or more States;—between a State and Citizens of another State;—between Citizens of different States;—between Citizens of the same State claiming Lands under Grants of different States, and between a State, or the Citizens thereof, and foreign States, Citizens or Subjects. . . .

Article III (like Article I and Article II) begins with a Vesting Clause that directly vests power in a Department of the national government. Section 1 vests "[t]he judicial Power of the United States" in a system of federal courts—in "one supreme Court, and in such inferior Courts as the Congress shall from time to time ordain and establish." But the first and most fundamental question of Article III is this: Exactly what is "the judicial Power" that Article III vests in the national court system?

That large question entails a series of propositions and issues. Classically, the judicial power was simply the authority to decide cases of a judicial character in accordance with pre-existing governing law. The governing law would be set forth in the Constitution, federal laws and treaties, the laws of the states, or some other source (such as the common law, the principles of equity, or admiralty law). In this sense, the judicial power was thought of as a law-applying power, not a law-making power. Of course, this distinction can mask the problem that courts, in applying law, frequently appear to be making rules as much as applying them. Nonetheless, as a general matter, the starting point for the judicial power is the idea of deciding cases in accordance with existing law.

The judicial power, then, is a power to decide *cases*—lawsuits, disputes of a classically judicial character. (This idea is reinforced in Article III, Section 2's specification of federal judicial jurisdiction as extending to "cases" and "controversies" of certain description.) But what makes a case a "case"? What are the outer boundaries of "the judicial Power"? Are there limitations inherent in the notion of what "the judicial power" *is*? Over the years the federal courts have developed a series of sub-doctrines attempting to mark the boundaries of the legitimate exercise of judicial authority: First, courts will not render *advisory opinions* outside the context of an actual dispute between parties with something at issue. Second, and building on the rule against advisory opinions, the parties in a case must have a real legal interest at stake, giving them *standing* to sue. In other words, something must turn on the court's decision. Third, the dispute must be sufficiently immediate, not remote and distant—in legal parlance, the case must be *ripe*. Fourth, the dispute must remain a live one at all stages of the proceeding; if the conflict between the parties ever disappears, the case is *moot*. The ripeness and mootness requirements also flow out of the rule against advisory opinions: if a court were speculating about a question that was entirely in the future or the past, it would merely be giving advice. Finally, the parties' legal interests must be genuinely in conflict, or *adverse*, and the legal dispute must not be contrived, feigned, or collusive.

A further long-standing restriction on "the judicial Power" of Article III is that it does not extend to "*political questions*"—that is, matters that the Constitution appears to leave to political judgment or discretion, either by assigning policy discretion or final constitutional judgment concerning a topic Congress or the president, or simply by not supplying any rule of law that would provide judges a principled basis for invalidating what a political actor has done. The precise scope and content—and even the legitimacy—of the "political question doctrine" has long been disputed. Is it a principled doctrine of judicial restraint, commanded by the Constitution's separation of powers? Or is it an unprincipled, *ad hoc* doctrine of strategic non-decision—in effect a form of "activist judicial restraint"?

Another enduring question concerning the meaning of "the judicial Power" concerns its relationship and authority vis-à-vis the other branches of government. Does the power to interpret and apply the law, in specific cases, make the judiciary the supreme branch of the national government? As discussed in Chapter 2, the framers of the Constitution denied this to be the case. As Madison wrote in *The Federalist No. 49*: "The several departments being perfectly co-ordinate by the terms of their commission, neither of them, it is evident, can pretend to an exclusive or superior right of settling the boundaries between their respective powers." And as Hamilton wrote in *The Federalist No. 78*: "Whoever attentively considers the different departments of power must perceive that, in a government in which they are separate from each other, the judiciary, from the nature of its functions, will always be the least dangerous to the political rights of the Constitution; because it will be least in a capacity to annoy or injure them. . . . It may truly be said to have neither FORCE nor WILL but merely judgment; and must ultimately depend upon the aid of the executive arm even for the efficacy of its judgments." Nonetheless, judicial supremacy—the proposed binding character of the federal courts' decisions on other branches of government—remains a recurrent issue in understanding the scope of "the judicial Power." (See Chapter 2.)

> *Section 1: The judicial Power of the United States, shall be vested in one supreme Court, and in such inferior Courts as the Congress may from time to time ordain and establish. . . .*
>
> *Section 2: . . . In all Cases affecting Ambassadors, other public Ministers and Consuls, and those in which a State shall be Party, the supreme Court shall have original Jurisdiction. In all the other Cases before mentioned, the supreme Court shall have appellate Jurisdiction, both as to Law and Fact, with such Exceptions, and under such Regulations as the Congress shall make.*

As noted, Article III vests the judicial Power in a system in "one supreme Court, and in such inferior Courts as the Congress shall from time to time ordain and establish." Article III thus leaves it to Congress whether to have any lower federal courts at all and, if so, to prescribe or limit their jurisdiction. This was part of a compromise—commonly called the "Madisonian Compromise," for James Madison, who proposed it at the Constitutional Convention—between those who favored a complete system of national courts and those who wished only one supreme Court, with the rest of the judicial power left to existing state court systems. From the beginning, Congress has chosen to create at least some lower federal courts. The Judiciary Act of 1789 created sixteen district court judgeships. Today, we have roughly a thousand lower federal trial and appellate judges. Congress is free under Article III to change that number at any time.

A consequence of the Madisonian Compromise is that some or all of "the judicial Power of the United States" could be left to the exercise of *state* courts. Apparently to that end, Article I, Section 8 includes as one of Congress's specific enumerated powers the power "To constitute Tribunals inferior to the supreme Court," a seeming cross-reference to Article III that recognizes Congress's powers not only to create lower federal courts but also to designate that state courts may serve as national courts in the first instance. (That is, state courts may be "constituted" as inferior tribunals for that purpose, even though they are not created by Congress.) An early, important decision upheld the propriety of the U.S. Supreme Court's exercise of appellate review of the decisions of state supreme courts in cases falling within Article III's menu of cases within the appellate jurisdiction of the U.S. Supreme Court. *Martin v. Hunter's Lessee,* 14 U.S. (1 Wheat.) 304 (1816); see also *Cohens v. Virginia*, 19 U.S. 264 (1821).

Note that Article III also does not specify the size of the Supreme Court, implicitly leaving that decision to Congress, too. The Supreme Court initially had six justices. Congress has adjusted the size of the Court several times, and the number of justices has ranged from six to ten. For much of the past century the number of justices has stood steady at nine. (In 1937, President Franklin D. Roosevelt proposed enlarging the Supreme Court to as many as fifteen justices, but his effort to thus "pack" the Court produced a political backlash, and no president or Congress has sought to adjust the size of the Court since that time.)

As noted, Article III's Vesting Clause itself directly vests the judicial power in the Supreme Court and whatever other federal courts Congress chooses to create. The words "The judicial Power ... *shall be vested*" in the federal courts are thus the equivalent of saying "The federal court created by this Article shall have the judicial power." Some interpreters read the Vesting Clause as *commanding Congress* to vest the judicial power in the courts it creates—and Congress has since 1789 enacted statutes designing the federal court system and sometimes rather elaborately prescribing federal court jurisdiction and procedural powers. As a constitutional matter, however, these statutes are probably better understood as Congress's exercise of its Necessary and Proper Clause power to carry into execution the judicial power as vested by Article III. (In addition, as we discuss presently, Article III, Section 2 specifies that the Supreme Court's appellate jurisdiction is subject to "Exceptions" and "Regulations" made by Congress.)

Article III, Section 2 lists nine categories of "cases" and "controversies" to which the federal judicial power extends. The first three categories, denominated "cases," consist of lawsuits concerning *national law or national authority*—presenting issues of federal statutory, treaty, or constitutional law; cases affecting ambassadors; and matters of "admiralty and maritime Jurisdiction." The next six categories, denominated "controversies," are defined not by the legal issues presented but by *the parties to the suit*. These controversies all have some interstate aspect, such as suits between citizens of different states, or an international aspect, such as suits involving "foreign States."

Is Article III, Section 2's listing of cases and controversies within federal jurisdiction a command that federal courts must hear all such cases? Or is it a menu of cases in which federal courts can be permitted to exercise jurisdiction, if Congress so decides? Is it some of each? This question has engaged the attention of lawyers, judges, and scholars since the Constitution's creation.

The answer would seem to depend on two related features of Article III's design. First, the Madisonian Compromise, reflected in Article III, Section 1: If Congress need not create lower federal courts in the first place, surely it may create lower federal courts with limited jurisdiction—with some portion of the Article III "menu," or with different lower federal courts having different portions. (There is contrary dicta, though, in *Martin v. Hunter's Lessee* (1816), referred to above.) And until 1875 there was no jurisdiction in lower federal courts to hear cases simply because they presented issues of federal law. Most statutory lower federal court jurisdiction consisted of diversity-of-state-citizenship controversies—and even these were limited to suits involving a minimum amount in controversy. The Supreme Court eventually made clear that lower federal courts' jurisdiction is within Congress's discretion to grant, withhold, or limit as it sees fit. See *Sheldon v. Sill*, 49 U.S. 441 (1850) ("Congress, having the power to establish the [lower federal] courts, must define their respective jurisdictions. . . . Congress may withhold from any court of its creation jurisdiction of any of the enumerated controversies. Courts created by statute can have no jurisdiction but such as the statute confers.").

The second feature of Article III bearing on the extent to which the jurisdiction of the federal courts is subject to Congress's control is this passage describing the Supreme Court's jurisdiction: "In all Cases affecting Ambassadors, other public Ministers and Consuls, and those in which a State shall be Party, the supreme Court shall have original Jurisdiction. In all the other Cases before mentioned, the supreme Court shall have appellate Jurisdiction, both as to Law and Fact, with such Exceptions, and under such Regulations as the Congress shall make." The apparent import of this passage is that Congress could withdraw entirely some types of cases from the Supreme Court's appellate jurisdiction—a rather surprising conclusion, but one seemingly accepted by the Court in the landmark Reconstruction-era case of *Ex parte McCardle*, 74 U.S. 506 (1868). If this were correct, would it mean that some cases might receive their final resolution by *state* courts, if Congress so directs—with the attendant possibility of multiple different "final" conclusions by multiple different state judiciaries, even on issues of federal law? Does that prospect mean that Congress may withdraw appellate jurisdiction from the Supreme Court but only if it also creates, and vests final jurisdiction in, some other federal court?

Where authorized by the Constitution and as regulated by Congress in accordance with Article III's provisions, *jurisdiction* creates a power of federal courts to hear and decide cases. But a grant of jurisdiction does not ordinarily confer a power to create the substantive law governing those cases. Such law is supplied by the Constitution, by federal statutes, and by treaties of the United States (at least for the first three categories of cases). Where federal courts have jurisdiction on the basis of party-identity— "diversity of citizenship" jurisdiction being the classic example—what is the governing source of law? Do the federal courts have power themselves to create the governing substantive rules, a kind of federal common law? The answer for most of the last century has been that such cases are governed by *state* law; the federal courts do not have power to create their own body of substantive law simply because they possess jurisdiction to resolve a particular type of dispute. See *Erie Railroad Co. v. Tompkins*, 304 U.S. 64 (1938).

> *Section 1: . . . The Judges, both of the supreme and inferior Courts, shall hold their Offices during good Behaviour, and shall, at stated Times, receive for their Services, a Compensation, which shall not be diminished during their Continuance in Office.*

A singular feature of Article III, Section 1 is that all federal judges— Supreme Court justices and lower federal court judges—serve "during good Behaviour," a term of art that means indefinitely: i.e., for life, unless a judge voluntarily retires. (Recall that federal judges are appointed by the president, subject to the Senate's advice and consent. See Art. II, Sec. 2, cl. 2.) Further, Article III provides that the judges can never have their salaries reduced. These provisions were considered essential to the independence of federal judges in the exercise of their constitutional duties. (For more on this point, see *The Federalist No. 78*, Alexander Hamilton's defense of judicial independence and the courts' power of independent constitutional judgment, which is presented above in Chapter 2.)

At the same time, *The Federalist No. 81* appears to contemplate the possibility of impeachment of judges, including Supreme Court justices, for perceived abuse of the judicial power. Referring to the judiciary's "total incapacity to support its usurpations by force," Hamilton states that this inference

> is greatly fortified by the consideration of the important constitutional check which the power of instituting impeachments in one part of the legislative body and determining them in the other, would give to that body upon the members of the judicial department. This is alone a complete security. There never can be danger that the judges, by a series of deliberate usurpations of the authority of the legislature, would hazard the united resentment of the body intrusted with it, while this body was possessed of the means of punishing their presumption by degrading them from their stations.

In short, the independence and energy of the judiciary is ensured by life tenure. The primary checks possessed by the other branches of the national government consist of the front-end check supplied by the political process of appointment (presidential nomination and Senate confirmation); Congress's control to some degree of the courts' jurisdiction; Congress's control over the creation of lower courts and the size of the Supreme Court (itself subject to political checks); and the blunt, difficult, rarely used, and controversial last resort of impeachment.

A. THE NATURE AND ROLE OF THE FEDERAL JUDICIARY: FORMATIVE INTERPRETATIONS

We begin with early, formative explanations of the meaning and nature of "the judicial Power" of the national courts, including the very first Supreme Court cases—and correspondence—on that power and its limits. *The Federalist No. 80* is Alexander Hamilton's description of the nature and structure of the judicial power under the judicial structure created by the Constitution. We follow this with an excerpt on the nature of judicial power from James Wilson's "Of Government," one of his lectures on law from the winter of 1790–1791. Wilson, a key participant at the Constitutional Convention, was the principal drafter of Article III of the Constitution and one of the first justices of the Supreme Court. We then turn to two early controversies presented to the Supreme Court that raised fundamental questions about the nature, purpose, and appropriate role of the judiciary within a constitutional system of separation of powers: *Hayburn's Case* (1792) and the "Correspondence of the Justices" (1793). Both controversies have become foundational for subsequent understanding of the nature of "the judicial Power" under the Constitution.

The Federalist No. 80

Alexander Hamilton, June 21, 1788

To JUDGE with accuracy of the proper extent of the federal judicature, it will be necessary to consider, in the first place, what are its proper objects.

It seems scarcely to admit of controversy, that the judiciary authority of the Union ought to extend to these several descriptions of cases: 1st, to all those which arise out of the laws of the United States, passed in pursuance of their just and constitutional powers of legislation; 2d, to all those which concern the execution of the provisions expressly contained in the articles of Union; 3d, to all those in which the United States are a party; 4th, to all those which involve the PEACE of the CONFEDERACY, whether they relate to the intercourse between the United States and foreign nations, or to that between the States themselves; 5th, to all those which originate on the high seas, and are of admiralty or maritime jurisdiction; and, lastly, to all those in which the State tribunals cannot be supposed to be impartial and unbiased.

The first point depends upon this obvious consideration, that there ought always to be a constitutional method of giving efficacy to constitutional provisions. What, for instance, would avail restrictions on the authority of the State legislatures, without some constitutional mode of enforcing the observance of them? The States, by the plan of the convention, are prohibited from doing a variety of things, some of which are incompatible with the interests of the Union, and others with the principles of good government. The imposition of duties on imported articles, and the emission of paper money, are specimens of each kind. No man of sense will believe, that such prohibitions would be scrupulously regarded, without some effectual power in the government to restrain or correct the infractions of them. This power must either be a direct negative on the State laws, or an authority in the federal courts to overrule such as might be in manifest contravention of the articles of Union. There is no third course that I can imagine. The latter appears to have been thought by the convention preferable to the former, and, I presume, will be most agreeable to the States.

As to the second point, it is impossible, by any argument or comment, to make it clearer than it is in itself. If there are such things as political axioms, the propriety of the judicial power of a government being coextensive with its legislative, may be ranked among the number. The mere necessity of uniformity in the interpretation of the national laws, decides the question. Thirteen independent courts of final jurisdiction over the same causes, arising upon the same laws, is a hydra in government, from which nothing but contradiction and confusion can proceed.

Still less need be said in regard to the third point. Controversies between the nation and its members or citizens, can only be properly referred to the national tribunals. Any other plan would be contrary to reason, to precedent, and to decorum.

The fourth point rests on this plain proposition, that the peace of the WHOLE ought not to be left at the disposal of a PART. The Union will undoubtedly be answerable to foreign powers for the conduct of its members. And the responsibility for an injury ought ever to be accompanied with the faculty of preventing it. As the denial or perversion of justice by the sentences of courts, as well as in any other manner, is with reason classed among the just causes of war, it will follow that the federal judiciary ought to have cognizance of all causes in which the citizens of other countries are concerned. This is not less essential to the preservation of the public faith, than to the security of the public tranquillity. A distinction may perhaps be imagined between cases arising upon treaties and the laws of nations and those which may stand merely on the footing of the municipal law. The former kind may be supposed proper for the federal jurisdiction, the latter for that of the States. But it is at least problematical, whether an unjust sentence against a foreigner, where the subject of controversy was wholly relative to the lex loci, would not, if unredressed, be an aggression upon his sovereign, as well as one which violated the stipulations of a treaty or the general law of nations. And a still greater objection to the distinction would result from the immense difficulty, if not impossibility, of a practical discrimination between the cases of one complexion and those of the other. So great a proportion of the cases in which foreigners are parties, involve national questions, that it is by far most safe and most expedient to refer all those in which they are concerned to the national tribunals.

The power of determining causes between two States, between one State and the citizens of another, and between the citizens of different States, is perhaps not less essential to the peace of the Union than that which has been just examined. History gives us a horrid picture of the dissensions and private wars which distracted and desolated Germany prior to the institution of the Imperial Chamber by Maximilian, towards the close of the fifteenth century; and informs us, at the same time, of the vast influence of that institution in appeasing the disorders and establishing the tranquillity of the empire. This was a court invested with authority to decide finally all differences among the members of the Germanic body.

A method of terminating territorial disputes between the States, under the authority of the federal head, was not unattended to, even in the imperfect system by which they have been hitherto held together. But there are many other sources, besides interfering claims of boundary, from which bickerings and animosities may spring up among the members of the Union. To some of these we have been witnesses in the course of our past experience. It will readily be conjectured that I allude to the fraudulent laws which have been passed in too many of the States. And though the proposed Constitution establishes particular guards against the repetition of those instances which have heretofore made their appearance, yet it is warrantable to apprehend that the spirit which produced them will assume new shapes, that could not be foreseen nor specifically provided against. Whatever practices may have a tendency to disturb the harmony between the States, are proper objects of federal superintendence and control.

It may be esteemed the basis of the Union, that "the citizens of each State shall be entitled to all the privileges and immunities of citizens of the several States." And if it be a just principle that every government OUGHT TO POSSESS THE MEANS OF EXECUTING ITS OWN PROVISIONS BY ITS OWN AUTHORITY, it will follow, that in order to the inviolable maintenance of that equality of privileges and immunities to which the citizens of the Union will be entitled, the national judiciary ought to preside in all cases in which one State or its citizens are opposed to another State or its citizens. To secure the full effect of so fundamental a provision against all evasion and subterfuge, it is necessary that its construction should be committed to that tribunal which, having no local attachments, will be likely to be impartial between the different States and their citizens, and which, owing its official existence to the Union, will never be likely to feel any bias inauspicious to the principles on which it is founded.

The fifth point will demand little animadversion. The most bigoted idolizers of State authority have not thus far shown a disposition to deny the national judiciary the cognizances of maritime causes. These so generally depend on the laws of nations, and so commonly affect the rights of foreigners, that they fall within the considerations which are relative to the public peace. The most important part of them are, by the present Confederation, submitted to federal jurisdiction.

The reasonableness of the agency of the national courts in cases in which the State tribunals cannot be supposed to be impartial, speaks for itself. No man ought certainly to be a judge in his own cause, or in any cause in respect to which he has the least interest or bias. This principle has no inconsiderable weight in designating the federal courts as the proper tribunals for the determination of controversies between different States and their citizens. And it ought to have the same operation in regard to some cases between citizens of the same State. Claims to land under grants of different States, founded upon adverse pretensions of boundary, are of this description. The courts of neither of the granting States could be expected to be unbiased. The laws may have even prejudged the question, and tied the courts down to decisions in favor of the grants of the State to which they belonged. And even where this had not been done, it would be natural that the judges, as men, should feel a strong predilection to the claims of their own government.

Having thus laid down and discussed the principles which ought to regulate the constitution of the federal judiciary, we will proceed to test, by these principles, the particular powers of which, according to the plan of the convention, it is to be composed. It is to comprehend "all cases in law and equity arising under the Constitution, the laws of the United States, and treaties made, or which shall be made, under their authority; to all cases affecting ambassadors, other public ministers, and consuls; to all cases of admiralty and maritime jurisdiction; to controversies to which the United States shall be a party; to controversies between two or more States; between a State and citizens of another State; between citizens of different States; between citizens of the same State claiming lands and grants of different States; and between a State or the citizens thereof and foreign states, citizens, and subjects." This constitutes the entire mass of the judicial authority of the Union. Let us now review it in detail. It is, then, to extend:

First. To all cases in law and equity, ARISING UNDER THE CONSTITUTION and THE LAWS OF THE UNITED STATES. This corresponds with the two first classes of causes, which have been enumerated, as proper for the jurisdiction of the United States. It has been asked, what is meant by "cases arising under the Constitution," in contradiction from those "arising under the laws of the United States"? The difference has been already explained. All the restrictions upon the authority of the State legislatures furnish examples of it. They are not, for instance, to emit paper money; but the interdiction results from the Constitution, and will have no connection with any law of the United States. Should paper money, notwithstanding, be emited, the controversies concerning it would be cases arising under the Constitution and not the laws of the United States, in the ordinary signification of the terms. This may serve as a sample of the whole.

It has also been asked, what need of the word "equity"? What equitable causes can grow out of the Constitution and laws of the United States? There is hardly a subject of litigation between individuals, which may not involve those ingredients of FRAUD, ACCIDENT, TRUST, or HARDSHIP, which would render the matter an object of equitable rather than of legal jurisdiction, as the distinction is known and established in several of the States. It is the peculiar province, for instance, of a court of equity to relieve against what are called hard bargains: these are contracts in which, though there may have been no direct fraud or deceit, sufficient to invalidate them in a court of law, yet there may have been some undue and unconscionable advantage taken of the necessities or misfortunes of one of the parties, which a court of equity would not tolerate. In such cases, where foreigners were concerned on either side, it would be impossible for the federal judicatories to do justice without an equitable as well as a legal jurisdiction. Agreements to convey lands claimed under the grants of different States, may afford another example of the necessity of an equitable jurisdiction in the federal courts. This reasoning may not be so palpable in those States where the formal and technical distinction between LAW and EQUITY is not maintained, as in this State, where it is exemplified by every day's practice.

The judiciary authority of the Union is to extend:

Second. To treaties made, or which shall be made, under the authority of the United States, and to all cases affecting ambassadors, other public ministers, and consuls. These belong to the fourth class of the enumerated cases, as they have an evident connection with the preservation of the national peace.

Third. To cases of admiralty and maritime jurisdiction. These form, altogether, the fifth of the enumerated classes of causes proper for the cognizance of the national courts.

Fourth. To controversies to which the United States shall be a party. These constitute the third of those classes.

Fifth. To controversies between two or more States; between a State and citizens of another State; between citizens of different States. These belong to the fourth of those classes, and partake, in some measure, of the nature of the last.

Sixth. To cases between the citizens of the same State, *claiming lands under grants from different States.* These fall within the last class, and *are the only instances in which the proposed Constitution directly contemplates the cognizance of disputes between the citizens of the same State.*

Seventh. To cases between a State and the citizens thereof, and foreign States, citizens, or subjects. These have been already explained to belong to the fourth of the enumerated classes, and have been shown to be, in a peculiar manner, the proper subjects of the national judicature.

From this review of the particular powers of the federal judiciary, as marked out in the Constitution, it appears that they are all conformable to the principles which ought to have governed the structure of that department, and which were necessary to the perfection of the system. If some partial inconveniences should appear to be connected with the incorporation of any of them into the plan, it ought to be recollected that the national legislature will have ample authority to make such EXCEPTIONS, and to prescribe such regulations as will be calculated to obviate or remove these inconveniences. The possibility of particular mischiefs can never be viewed, by a well informed mind, as a solid objection to a general principle, which is calculated to avoid general mischiefs and to obtain general advantages.

James Wilson on the Judicial Power
From "Of Government," a lecture delivered in the winter of 1790–1791

The third great division of the powers of government is the judicial authority. It is sometimes considered as a branch of the executive power; but inaccurately. When the decisions of courts of justice are made, they must, it is true, be executed; but the power of executing them is ministerial, not judicial. The judicial authority consists in applying, according to the principles of right and justice, the constitution and laws to facts and transactions in cases, in which the manner or principles of this application are disputed by the parties interested in them.

The very existence of a dispute is presumptive evidence, that the application is not altogether without intricacy or difficulty. When intricacy or difficulty takes place in the application, it cannot be properly made without the possession of skill in the science of jurisprudence, and the most unbiassed behaviour in the exercise of that skill. Clear heads, therefore, and honest hearts are essential to good judges.

As all controversies in the community respecting life, liberty, reputation, and property, must be influenced by their judgments; and as their judgments ought to be calculated not only to do justice, but also to give general satisfaction, to inspire general confidence, and to take even from disappointed suiters—for in every cause disappointment must fall on one side—the slightest pretence of complaint; they ought to be placed in such a situation, as not only to be, but likewise to appear superiour to every extrinsick circumstance, which can be supposed to have the smallest operation upon their understandings or their inclinations. In their salaries, and in their offices, they ought to be completely independent: in other words, they should be removed from the most distant apprehension of being affected, in their judicial character and capacity, by any thing, except their own behaviour and its consequences.

"We are," says a very sensible writer on political subjects, "to look upon all the vast apparatus of government as having ultimately no other object or purpose, but the distribution of justice. All men are sensible of the necessity of justice to maintain peace and order; and all men are sensible of the necessity of peace and order for the maintenance of society." "The pure, and wise, and equal administration of the laws," says Mr. Paley, "forms the first end and blessing of social union." But how can society be maintained—how can a state expect to enjoy peace and order, unless the administration of justice is able and impartial? Can such an administration be expected, unless the judges can maintain dignified and independent characters? Can dignity and independence be expected from judges, who are liable to be tossed about by every veering gale of politicks, and who can be secured from destruction, only by dexterously swimming along with every successive tide of party? Is there not reason to fear, that in such a situation, the decisions of courts would cease to be the voice of law and justice, and would become the echo of faction and violence?

Hayburn's Case
2 U.S. 408 (1792)

THIS was a motion for a mandamus, to be directed to the circuit court for the district of Pennsylvania, commanding the said court to proceed in a certain petition of William Hayburn, who had applied to be put on the pension list of the United States, as an invalid pensioner. The principal case arose upon the act of congress passed the 23d of March 1792.

The Attorney–General (Randolph), who made the motion for the mandamus, having premised that it was done ex officio, without an application from any particular person, but with a view to procure the execution of an act of congress, particularly interesting to a meritorious and unfortunate class of citizens, THE COURT declared, that they entertained great doubt upon his right, under such circumstances, and in a case of this kind, to proceed ex officio; and directed him to state the principles on which he attempted to support the right. The Attorney–General, accordingly, entered into an elaborate description of the powers and duties of his office:

BUT THE COURT being divided in opinion on that question, the motion, made ex officio, was not allowed. The Attorney–General then changed the ground of his interposition, declaring it to be at the instance, and on behalf of Hayburn, a party interested; and he entered into the merits of the case, upon the act of congress, and the refusal of the judges to carry it into effect. THE COURT observed, that they would hold the motion under advisement, until the next term; but no decision was ever pronounced, as the legislature, at an intermediate session, provided, in another way, for the relief of the pensioners.

[The following was then added by the Court reporter as an extended footnote to the above report of the argument and disposition of the case.—Editors]

*As the reasons assigned by the judges, for declining to execute the first act of Congress, involve a great constitutional question, it will not be thought improper to subjoin them, in illustration of Hayburn's case.

The Circuit Court for the district of New York (consisting of JAY, CHIEF JUSTICE, CUSHING, JUSTICE, and DUANE, DISTRICT JUDGE) . . . [unanimously agreed as follows:]

"That by the Constitution of the United States, the government thereof is divided into *three* distinct and independent branches, and that it is the duty of each to abstain from, and to oppose, encroachments on either. That neither the *Legislative* nor the *Executive* branches, can constitutionally assign to the *Judicial* any duties, but such as are properly judicial, and to be performed in a judicial manner.

"That the duties assigned to the Circuit courts, by this act, are not of that description, and that the act itself does not appear to contemplate them as such; inasmuch as it subjects the decisions of these courts, made pursuant to those duties, first to the consideration and suspension of the secretary at war, and then to the revision of the legislature; whereas, by the constitution, neither the Secretary at war, nor any other Executive officer, nor even the legislature, are authorized to sit as a court of errors on the judicial acts or opinions of this court.

"As, therefore, the business assigned to this court, by the act, is not judicial, nor directed to be performed judicially, the act can only be considered as appointing commissioners for the purposes mentioned in it, by *official* instead of *personal* description. That the *Judges* of this court regard themselves as being the commissioners designated by the act, and therefore, as being at liberty to accept or decline that office. That as the objects of this act are exceedingly benevolent, and do real honor to the humanity and justice of congress; and as the judges desire to manifest, on all proper occasions, and in every proper manner, their high respect for the national legislature, they will execute this act in the capacity of commissioners. . . ."

The Circuit court for the district of Pennsylvania (consisting of WILSON and BLAIR, Justices, and PETERS, District Judge) made the following representation, in a letter jointly addressed to the president of the United States, on the 18th of April 1792.

"To you it officially belongs to 'take care that the laws' of the United States 'be faithfully executed.' Before you, therefore, we think it our duty to lay the sentiments, which, on a late painful occasion, governed us with regard to an act passed by the legislature of the Union. . . .

"It is a principle important to freedom, that in government, the judicial should be distinct from, and independent of, the legislative department. To this important principle, the people of the United States, in forming their constitution, have manifested the highest regard. They have placed their judicial power, not in congress, but in 'courts.' They have ordained that the 'judges of those courts shall hold their offices during good behavior,' and that 'during their continuance in office, their salaries shall not be diminished.'

"Congress have lately passed an act, to regulate, among other things, 'the claims to invalid pensions.' Upon due consideration, we have been unanimously of opinion, that, under this act, the circuit court held for the Pennsylvania district could not proceed.

"1st. Because the business directed by this act is not of a judicial nature. It forms no part of the power vested by the Constitution in the courts of the United States; the Circuit court must, consequently, have proceeded *without* constitutional authority. 2d. Because, if, upon that business, the court had proceeded, its *judgments* (for its *opinions* are its judgments) might, under the same act, have been revised and controuled by the legislature, and by an officer in the executive department. Such revision and control we deemed radically inconsistent with the independence of that judicial power which is vested in the courts; and consequently, with that important principle which is so strictly observed by the constitution of the United States. . . ."

The circuit court for the district of North Carolina (consisting of IREDELL, Justice, and SITGREAVES, District Judge) made the following representation, in a letter jointly addressed to the President of the United States, on the 8th of June 1792.

"We, the judges now attending at the circuit court of the United States for the district of North Carolina, conceive it our duty to lay before you some important observations which have occurred to us in the consideration of an act of congress lately passed, entitled, 'An act to provide for the settlement of the claims of widows and orphans, barred by the limitations heretofore established, and to regulate the claims to invalid pensions.' . . . We therefore, Sir, submit to you the following:

"1. That the Legislative, Executive and Judicial departments are each formed in a separate and independent manner; and that the ultimate basis of each is the Constitution only, within the limits of which each department can alone justify any act of authority.

"2. That the Legislature, among other important powers, unquestionably possess that of establishing courts in such a manner as to their wisdom shall appear best, limited by the terms of the constitution only; and to whatever extent that power may be exercised, or however severe the duty they may think proper to require, the judges, when appointed in virtue of any such establishment, owe implicit and unreserved obedience to it.

"3. That, at the same time, such courts cannot be warranted, as we conceive, by virtue of that part of the constitution delegating *Judicial power*, for the exercise of which any act of the legislature is provided, in exercising (even under the authority of another act) any power not in its nature *judicial*, or, if *judicial*, not provided for upon the terms the Constitution requires.

"4. That whatever doubt may be suggested, whether the power in question is properly of a judicial nature, yet, inasmuch as the decision of the court is not made final, but may be at least suspended in its operation, by the Secretary at War, if he shall have cause to suspect imposition or mistake; this subjects the decision of the court to a mode of revision, which we consider to be unwarranted by the Constitution; for though Congress may certainly establish, in instances not yet provided for, courts of appellate jurisdiction, yet such courts must consist of judges appointed in the manner the Constitution requires, and holding their offices by no other tenure than that of their good behavior, by which tenure the office of Secretary at War is not held. And we beg leave to add, with all due deference, that no decision of any court of the United States can, under any circumstances, in our opinion, agreeable to the constitution, be liable to a rev[i]sion or even suspension, by the Legislature itself, in whom no judicial power of any kind appears to be vested, but the important one relative to impeachments.

"These, Sir, are our reasons for being of opinion, as we are at present, that this circuit court cannot be justified in the execution of that part of the act, which requires it to examine and report an opinion on the unfortunate cases of officers and soldiers disabled in the service of the United States. . . .

"The high respect we entertain for the legislature, our feelings, as men, for persons whose situation requires the earliest, as well as the most effectual relief, and our sincere desire to promote, whether officially or otherwise, the just and benevolent views of congress, so conspicuous on the present as well as on many other occasions, have induced us to reflect, whether we could be justified in acting, under this act, personally, in the character of commissioners, during the session of a court; and could we be satisfied that we had authority to do so, we would cheerfully devote such part of our time as might be necessary for the performance of the service. But we confess we have great doubts on this head. The power appears to be given to the court only, and not to the judges of it; . . . We do not mean, however, to preclude ourselves from a very deliberate consideration, whether we can be warranted in executing the purposes of the act in that manner, in case an application should be made.

"No application has yet been made to the court, or to ourselves individually, and therefore, we have had some doubts as to the propriety of giving an opinion in a case which has not yet come regularly and judicially before us. None can be more sensible than we are of the necessity of judges being, in general, extremely cautious in not intimating an opinion, in any case, extra-judicially, because we well know how liable the best minds are, notwithstanding their utmost care, to a bias, which may arise from a preconceived opinion, even unguardedly, much more, deliberately, given: but in the present instance, as many unfortunate and meritorious individuals, whom Congress have justly thought proper objects of immediate relief, may suffer great distress, even by a short delay, and may be utterly ruined, by a long one, we determined; at all events, to make our sentiments known as early as possible . . .

Notes

1. The "case" styled as *Hayburn's Case* presents nearly every foundational issue concerning the nature, independence, and limits of the judicial power under Article III. It is arguably the first instance in the Court's history of the Court's exercise of what is now called judicial review: the independent power and duty of the judicial branch to refuse to give judicial sanction and effect to a statute or executive action it judges to be unconstitutional, and to refuse itself to take action that would be contrary to the Constitution. (*Hayburn's Case* occurred more than a decade before *Marbury v. Madison* and a year before the Correspondence of the Justices, which is considered next.)

2. The first issue presented by the case is one that would today be called "standing"—the fundamental idea that the judicial power may only be exercised in a *case* or *controversy* between parties possessing a genuine stake in the outcome. At first, Hayburn—who had a real stake in the outcome, in the form of his claim for a pension being granted—was not a party to the case. Whom did Attorney General Randolph represent (at first)? What legal interest did he purport to be representing? Can a party legitimately assert a legal interest simply in having some government officer comply with his or her assigned duties? Can one branch of government "sue" another branch directly? Was the Court right to be dubious of Randolph's mandamus petition? What was the Court's resolution of the issue of Randolph's (or the government's) standing?

3. Randolph then shifts his representation to that of essentially being a private attorney for Hayburn. (Can he do that? What do you think of this move?) Does this maneuver, if otherwise proper, cure the "standing" problem and turn the matter into a genuine "case" appropriate for the Court to resolve? In the end, the Court still does not resolve the underlying question of the constitutionality of requiring federal judges to decide on veterans' pension eligibility, subject to revision by the secretary of war, because a new statute intervened. Was this appropriate? In today's terms, the Court apparently thought that the underlying dispute had become "moot"—that is, that it *no longer* presented a live case or controversy, and that deciding the issue presented would be in effect to give a legal opinion and judgment in a situation in which the rights of no party properly before it would be affected. As noted above, mootness is related to standing in the sense that both doctrines implement the notion that federal courts decide legal questions only in the context of resolving actual cases and controversies.

4. The merits issue of the constitutionality of the law requiring judicial determination of pension eligibility is then discussed in the reporter's footnote discussing three circuit court "cases" (two of which were actually correspondence with the president) addressing this issue. Evaluate each of the "opinions." Note the emphasis in each on the independence and separation of the branches of the national government. Note also the asserted inconsistency with "the judicial Power" of having decisions of the Article III branch being subjected to review and revision by executive branch officers—or, put different, the objection that the judiciary would not truly be resolving cases. Were the judges essentially being asked to be subordinate bureaucrats to the secretary of war? Is that consistent with the function of courts? *Hayburn's Case* has been taken as the basis for later judicial doctrine that the exercise of the judicial power—in order to be the judicial power—cannot be made subject to official revision by the legislature or the executive. *See, e.g., Plaut v. Spendthrift Farm, Inc.*, 514 U.S. 211

(1995) (unconstitutional for statute to direct the re-opening of final judicial decrees of dismissal). Hamilton made this same point in *The Federalist No. 81*: "The theory, neither of the British, nor the State constitutions, authorizes the revisal of a judicial sentence by a legislative act. . . . A legislature, without exceeding its province, cannot reverse a determination once made in a particular case; though it may prescribe a new rule for future cases."

Some of the opinions collected in *Hayburn's Case* seem concerned that the secretary of war was essentially being given judicial power himself. What do you think of this argument? Article III requires that federal judges exercising the judicial power of the United States be appointed in a certain manner, and possess life tenure and salary guarantees. Does this mean that the judicial power may not be exercised by anyone else? What about state court judges? In addition, could Congress pass a statute providing that veterans' pension claims are to be "judged" by subordinate government bureaucrats, before being reviewed by the secretary of war—and leaving the federal courts out of it altogether? Could executive branch officials exercise administrative functions, in a quasi-judicial fashion, without having to be appointed as Article III judges? (There are now thousands of "administrative law judges" working for agencies of the national government, applying statutory schemes of various sorts to individual cases. Are such arrangements constitutional?) What makes "the judicial Power" the *judicial* power, distinctively?

5. Several of the circuit court opinions suggest the willingness of the judges to serve, in their individual capacities, as "commissioners," performing the described functions. Is there anything wrong with that? Is there any prohibition in Article III on a federal judge *also* performing some administrative function? Recall that at one point Chief Justice John Marshall was simultaneously serving as secretary of state, that Chief Justice John Jay was an emissary for the Washington administration to negotiate a treaty with England, that Justice Robert Jackson served after World War II as chief war crimes prosecutor for the United States at the Nuremburg Trials, and that Chief Justice Earl Warren led the "Warren Commission" investigating the assassination of President John F. Kennedy.

Note that some of the judges in the cases and correspondence noted in the report of *Hayburn's Case* were willing to construe the statute requiring the performance of evaluating pension claims as if it were a request to them in their individual capacities, rather than a command. Others were not. Which approach was more appropriate?

The Correspondence of the Justices

The Neutrality Controversy of 1793, discussed in Chapter 1, in which President Washington sought to keep the United States out of any involvement in the war between France and England, gave rise to another important separation of powers precedent concerning the nature and limits of the judicial power under Article III of the Constitution: the question of whether the president may call upon the justices of the Supreme Court for guidance when facing difficult legal questions. Secretary of State Thomas Jefferson wrote to Chief Justice John Jay asking the Supreme Court twenty-nine legal questions arising out of America's relationship with France. The experience proved a significant precedent not because of the justices' answers to the questions, but rather because of the justices' *refusal* to answer them and their declaration that the judicial power was constitutionally limited to deciding cases and controversies between actual parties in litigation. Consider the following exchange of letters.

Secretary of State Jefferson, Letter to the Justices of the Supreme Court
July 18, 1793

The war which has taken place among the powers of Europe produces frequent transactions within our ports and limits, on which questions arise of considerable difficulty, and of greater importance to the peace of the US. These questions depend on their solution on the construction of our treaties, on the laws of nature and nations, and on the laws of the land; and are often presented under circumstances which do not give cognisance of them to the tribunals of the country. Yet their decision is so little analogous to the ordinary functions of the Executive as to occasion much embarrassment and difficulty to them. The president would be much relieved if he found himself free to refer to questions of this description to the opinions of the Judges of the Supreme Court of the US whose knowledge of the subject would secure us against errors dangerous to the peace of the US and their authority insure the respect of all parties. He has therefore asked the attendance of such of the judges as could be collected in time for the occasion, to know, in the first place, their opinion, Whether the public may, without propriety, be availed of their advice on these questions? and if they may, to present for their advice, the abstract questions which have already occurred, or may soon occur, from which they will themselves strike out such as any circumstances might, in their opinion, forbid them to pronounce on.

The Justices of the Supreme Court, Letter to President Washington
Philadelphia, August, 8, 1793

Sir: We have considered the previous question stated in a letter written by your direction to us by the Secretary of State in the 18th of last month, [regarding] the lines of separation drawn by the Constitution between the three departments of the government. These being in certain respects checks upon each other, and our being judges of a court in the last resort, are considerations which afford strong arguments against the propriety of our extra-judicially deciding the question alluded to, especially as the power given by the Constitution to the president, of calling on the heads of the departments for opinions, seems to have been *purposely* as well as expressly united to the *executive* departments.

We exceedingly regret every event that may cause embarrassment to your administration, but we derive consolation from the reflection that your judgment will discern what is right, and that your usual prudence, decision, and firmness will surmount every obstacle to the preservation of the rights, peace, and dignity of the United States.

We have the honour to be, with perfect respect, sir, your most obedient and most humble servants.

NOTES

1. The Correspondence of the Justices has become foundational to our conception of the judicial power under Article III. Consider President Washington's request (through Secretary of State Jefferson) for legal advice from the Supreme Court. Was the Court correct to refuse it? Why or why not? Is it within the constitutional province of the Court to render "advisory opinions"? Upon what type of constitutional argument, or mode of interpretation, does the Court rest its judgment on this point?

2. Under Article III, Section 2, the federal courts may exercise "the judicial Power of the United States" when a matter falls within one of nine enumerated kinds of "Cases" or "Controversies." This gives the federal courts a limited jurisdiction. But what is a "case" or "controversy" within the meaning of Article III? The answer the justices give in the Correspondence of the Justices is that a "case" is a traditional lawsuit between two competing parties, presenting a dispute over something real and concrete. Asking the courts for legal advice does not present the courts with a case or controversy within the scope of "the judicial Power."

3. It is clear from the debates at Philadelphia that the framers considered giving federal judges and justices the power to issue advisory opinions and decided not to. Does this evidence of original intent together with more than two centuries of the federal courts not issuing advisory opinions resolve the question whether they are constitutional? How meaningful is it to say that federal judges cannot render advisory opinions in light of the expansive dicta in some opinions?

4. In a sense, the Correspondence of the Justices is one of the earliest exercises by the Supreme Court of the power of judicial review—the power of the courts, on constitutional grounds, to refuse to give legal effect to an unconstitutional action by a coordinate branch of the federal government. And it preceded by a decade the famous case of *Marbury v. Madison* in 1803, in which the Court would refuse to give effect to an act of Congress that the Court thought improperly enlarged the Court's jurisdiction on the ground that the jurisdiction was forbidden by the Constitution. In both the Correspondence of the Justices and *Marbury*, the Court refused to decide a particular issue on the merits, saying instead that it did not have jurisdiction.

5. Is it a bit ironic that the justices were in effect providing an advisory opinion (of sorts) to the president on the inadvisability, or outright unconstitutionality, of the Justices offering advisory opinions to the president? Or did the administration's request for legal advice from the justices essentially present a "case" that at least raised the question of the Court's jurisdiction to answer such requests? Is the rendering of this opinion, in the form of a letter, merely an illustration of the proposition that every court properly has jurisdiction at least to determine whether it has jurisdiction?

[Assignment 26]

B. ADJUDICATION OF GENUINE DISPUTES: "THE JUDICIAL POWER SHALL EXTEND TO . . . CASES [AND] CONTROVERSIES"

The first paragraph of Article III, Section 2 says that the judicial power granted by Section 1's Vesting Clause "shall extend to" nine categories of "cases" or "controversies." What is a "case" or a "controversy" for purposes of this language? We have already seen in the Correspondence of the Justices that the Supreme Court decided in the early 1790s that it did not have the power to issue advisory opinions. Madison's notes taken at the Philadelphia Convention show that proposals were made to give the courts power to issue advisory opinions and they were rejected. A proposal to vest the veto power jointly in the president and the justices in what was called a Council of Revision was also rejected. The framers felt the justices ought not to be involved in policy making or in giving advice in any way.

The prohibition against advisory opinions was thus understood in the Correspondence of the Justices as requiring first that for the judicial power to be invoked there had to be an actual dispute between adverse litigants. This requirement has been understood as also precluding collusive, feigned lawsuits. *Hayburn's Case* can be understood as a variation on the same basic theme. First, the Court was skeptical of the proposition that the attorney general could rightfully seek, on the behalf of the United States, a judicial order (mandamus) that judges perform the statutory duty of adjudicating pension claims. Only a party whose actual legal rights were affected could invoke the judicial power and receive a ruling. Second, once the statute was altered to no longer present the legal question at issue, the Court simply dismissed the petition for mandamus, illustrating the principle that courts will not decide moot cases. Finally, the idea that, where the judicial power is invoked to decide a legal question, the courts' decision on a legal question must not be subject to legislative or executive revision can also be seen as a variation on the rule against advisory opinions.

At a bare minimum, then, the case or controversy requirement of Article III, Section 2, Paragraph 1 requires an actual dispute, between adverse litigants, and a substantial likelihood that a federal court decision will have an effect in the real world.

These principles are given force today by three doctrines that help to define what is a case or controversy for purposes of Article III: (1) standing; (2) mootness; and (3) ripeness. Standing doctrine asks whether a particular person is a proper party to raise an issue in federal court for adjudication. In order to have standing, a plaintiff must show: first, that he or she has suffered a concrete, present injury to a cognizable legal interest; second, that the injury is fairly attributable to the defendant's conduct; and third, that a favorable federal court ruling will redress the injury. Standing thus deals with the "who" question in litigation. The doctrines of mootness and ripeness deal with the "when" of litigation. A case is moot when the requisite personal injury that gave rise to the case or controversy ceases for some reason to exist. Ripeness doctrine is concerned with the other end of timing, when the case is being brought too early for judicial decision, because the alleged legal injury is remote and speculative.

The Supreme Court has built up an elaborate and in many ways arcane case law on standing, mootness, and ripeness. Nonetheless, these doctrines are vital for a lawyer trying to get a case into federal court, and so questions about them frequently arise in private practice—more frequently than any other constitutional law issue. Here are a few key points about these doctrines:

Standing Doctrine: The Supreme Court has repeatedly said that ordinary citizens or taxpayers do not have standing to raise just any constitutional issue that they feel strongly about. If they did, the federal courts would be empowered to issue advisory opinions and to decide matters that would not have been considered cases or controversies in "law" or "equity" before the royal courts of justice at Westminster in England in 1787 when the Constitution was written. For someone to raise a constitutional issue, therefore, the Supreme Court has said that the person must show a concrete personal injury to a legal right. Of course, whether or not someone has a "legal right" is a question of the underlying substantive law—and this is not always so clear. Moreover, Congress can create new legal rights, the invasion of which would constitute a cognizable injury, even if a nontraditional one. The (fuzzy) line remains whether one has suffered a discrete injury to a personal legal interest; there is no general "right" to require that the government act in conformance with the Constitution, with laws in general, or with one's preferences. Thus, for example, if the government punishes a citizen for speech in violation of the First Amendment, that counts as personal legal injury. But if the government spends money in violation of its enumerated powers, but doing so does not injure a specific legal interest of an individual, that does not count as a sufficiently personal legal injury to constitute a case or controversy. Remember here that *Marbury v. Madison* said that the power of judicial review is triggered by the obligation and duty of the federal courts to decide cases or controversies. The Supreme Court's standing rules, which define what is a case or controversy, thus also mark the outer boundaries of judicial review.

Mootness Doctrine: A change in the facts giving rise to a case that ends the immediate actual controversy will moot a case. The death of a party, the settlement of a case, or the repeal or expiration of a governmental action that is being challenged (recall *Hayburn's Case*) could each under some circumstances render a case moot. Recall that in *Powell v. McCormack*, presented earlier in this chapter, it was argued that the case was moot because the session of Congress that Adam Clayton Powell had been elected to serve in had ended, Powell had been re-elected to a new Congress, and the new Congress had seated him. The Supreme Court quite rightly said the case was not moot because Powell was still entitled to sue for his salary and backpay for the session of Congress from which he had allegedly been unconstitutionally excluded. Another illustrative mootness case is *DeFunis v. Odegaard*, 416 U.S. 312 (1974), involving a lawsuit challenging affirmative action racial preferences in state law school admissions. The plaintiff, Marco DeFunis, had been denied admission to the University of Washington allegedly on the basis of race—a real, concrete injury—and had won a preliminary injunction in the lower courts. He was provisionally admitted, and by the time the case was argued before the U.S. Supreme Court, he was in his last semester of law school and scheduled to graduate. The Court decided that the case was moot because nothing concrete turned on resolving the constitutional issue. (The dissenters argued that something might still go wrong—failing a final, perhaps?—and that the issue of DeFunis's legal entitlement to finish law school remained live.) There are exceptions to the mootness doctrine: where collateral consequences to an injury remain (the back-pay situation in *Powell*); where the legal injury is capable of repetition as to that party, but likely to evade final judicial review; where a defendant has voluntarily ceased its alleged wrongful conduct but remains free to resume it later; and where a case has been certified as a class action. But there is no exception to mootness simply because an issue was *once* a real dispute, or because it is especially interesting or important (as in *DeFunis*).

Ripeness Doctrine: A case is considered "unripe" where the claimed injury has not occurred and its occurrence is thought too speculative or contingent to constitute a real, present dispute. The Supreme Court has announced a two-part test for determining whether a case is ripe under the Constitution. First, federal courts should look to the hardship to the parties from withholding court consideration. This element is usually satisfied whenever there is a likelihood of prosecution with substantial consequences unless a plaintiff forgoes engaging in allegedly lawful behavior; or the enforcement of a statute is certain but enforcement proceedings have not yet begun; or there is substantial hardship from collateral injuries. The second element of the ripeness test is establishing the fitness of the issues and of the record for judicial review. The more a question is purely legal, and the less development of a factual record matters, the more likely it is that a case will be deemed ripe for review.

Law professors and dissenting Supreme Court justices have had a field day over the last forty years with the Supreme Court's variable case law on the justiciability doctrines, which is riddled with clumsy formulations and seemingly inconsistent results. One common criticism is that in order to determine whether a plaintiff has suffered a legal, personal injury a court must look at the merits of the plaintiff's case. If so, why not just let the court decide the case on the merits? See William A. Fletcher, *The Structure of Standing*, 98 Yale L.J. 221 (1988). For all their problems, the doctrines of standing, mootness, and ripeness at some level guard against advisory opinions and contrived pseudo-cases. These doctrines are meant to ensure that the courts resolve real disputes brought by genuinely injured parties, rather than allowing courts to pick the constitutional issues they wish to decide. A justice may want to hear a Second Amendment case, but if there is not a plaintiff with a concrete, personal injury to a legal interest protected by the Second Amendment, no such case can be heard. Thus the executive and legislative branches can be proactive in making policy, but the judicial branch is more reactive and limited to the function of deciding actual cases.

More than forty years ago Alexander Bickel argued in a famous book, THE LEAST DANGEROUS BRANCH: THE SUPREME COURT AT THE BAR OF POLITICS (1962), that judges ought to use (or manipulate?) standing, mootness, and ripeness doctrine to maximize their institutional power and effectiveness. What do you think of Bickel's view? Is it prudent and deeply, structurally constitutional? Or is it cynical and political, even a violation of the judicial oath?

We present three illustrative cases on standing, ranging from the wonderfully simple to the frustratingly complex: *Ex parte Levitt*, 302 U.S. 633 (1937), is a one-paragraph Supreme Court opinion rejecting a lawyer's claim that the appointment of Justice Hugo Black to the Court was a violation of the Emoluments Clause of the Constitution. *Massachusetts v. Mellon* and *Frothingham v. Mellon*, 262 U.S. 447 (1923) is a combined early case rejecting state standing and taxpayer standing to challenge a federal program for allegedly exceeding the constitutional powers of Congress. Finally, *Summers v. Earth Island Institute,* 555 U.S. 488 (2009), is a case involving a suit brought by an environmental group challenging U.S. Forest Service regulations and the procedures by which they were adopted. *Summers* presents standing doctrine in its full modern complexity and within a modern administrative-law statutory and regulatory context involving rights, and claimed injuries to them, very different from traditional causes of action at common law.

Ex parte Levitt
302 U.S. 633 (1937)

■ PER CURIAM.

[This was an original motion in the Supreme Court brought by Albert Levitt for leave to file a petition for an order requiring Mr. Justice Black to show cause why he should be permitted to serve as a justice of the Court.—Editors]

The grounds of this motion are that the appointment of Mr. Justice Black by the President and the confirmation thereof by the Senate of the United States were null and void by reason of his ineligibility under article 1, § 6, cl. 2, of the Constitution of the United States, and because there was no vacancy for which the appointment could lawfully be made. The motion papers disclose no interest upon the part of the petitioner other than that of a citizen and a member of the bar of this Court. That is insufficient. It is an established principle that to entitle a private individual to invoke the judicial power to determine the validity of executive or legislative action he must show that he has sustained, or is immediately in danger of sustaining, a direct injury as the result of that action and it is not sufficient that he has merely a general interest common to all members of the public. . . . Fairchild v. Hughes, 258 U.S. 126 [1922]; Massachusetts v. Mellon, 262 U.S. 447, 488 [1923].

NOTES

1. *Ex parte Levitt* is a refreshingly short and simple case. Levitt, an attorney, challenged the constitutionality of Hugo Black's appointment to the Supreme Court, on the ground that while Black was a U.S. Senator, the "emoluments" (salary) of justices had been increased, and that this made Black's appointment unconstitutional under Article I, Section 6 of the Constitution, which says: "No Senator or Representative shall, during the Time for which he was elected, be appointed to any civil Office under the Authority of the United States, which shall have been created, or the Emoluments whereof shall have been increased during such time." The Court denied his motion, saying he had "no interest" aside from being a citizen and lawyer. Why is that not enough? What would be enough? Would someone have standing as a taxpayer? As a litigant before the Court? Would *anyone* have standing to sue to challenge such an allegedly unconstitutional appointment? If not, is that troubling? Or are there some constitutional provisions that simply do not give rise to direct, individual, personal injuries sufficient to make something a proper "case" within traditional understandings of the judicial power? For a discussion of the interpretive issues surrounding the Emoluments Clause, including the question of standing

to sue, see Michael Stokes Paulsen, *Is Lloyd Bentsen Unconstitutional?* 46 Stan. L. Rev. 907 (1994).

2. *Fairchild v. Hughes,* 258 U.S. 126 (1922), cited by the Court in *Ex parte Levitt*, was a suit by "taxpayers and members of the American Constitutional League," a private group interested in constitutional issues, alleging that the Nineteenth Amendment, granting women the right to vote, was not properly ratified and seeking to enjoin the secretary of state from enforcing it. The group's members claimed an interest in not having "the effectiveness of their votes" diminished and in the government not incurring election expenses. The Court said that the plaintiff lacked standing: "Plaintiff has only the right, possessed by every citizen, to require that the government be administered according to law and that the public moneys be not wasted. Obviously this general right does not entitle a private citizen to institute in the federal courts a suit to secure by indirection a determination whether a statute, if passed, or a constitutional amendment, about to be adopted, will be valid." Do you agree?

3. *Massachusetts v. Mellon,* 262 U.S. 447 (1923), also cited by the Court (and which we present next), was a suit challenging a federal government program as being beyond the powers of the national government to enact and thus in violation of the Tenth Amendment. Who has standing to raise a judicial challenge on such grounds? A state? Taxpayers? Everyone? No one?

Massachusetts v. Mellon; Frothingham v. Mellon
262 U.S. 447 (1923)

■ MR. JUSTICE SUTHERLAND delivered the opinion of the Court.

These cases were argued and will be considered and disposed of together. The first is an original suit in this court. The other was brought in the Supreme Court of the District of Columbia. That court dismissed the bill and its decree was affirmed by the District Court of Appeals. Thereupon the case was brought here by appeal. Both cases challenge the constitutionality of [a statute] commonly called the Maternity Act. Briefly, it provides for an initial appropriation and thereafter annual appropriations for a period of five years, to be apportioned among such of the several states as shall accept and comply with its provisions, for the purpose of co-operating with them to reduce maternal and infant mortality and protect the health of mothers and infants. It creates a bureau to administer the act in co-operation with state agencies, which are required to make such reports concerning their operations and expenditures as may be prescribed by the federal bureau. Whenever that bureau shall determine that funds have not been properly expended in respect of any state, payments may be withheld.

It is asserted that these appropriations are for purposes not national, but local to the states, and together with numerous similar appropriations constitute an effective means of inducing the states to yield a portion of their sovereign rights. It is further alleged that the burden of the appropriations provided by this act and similar legislation falls unequally upon the several states, and rests largely upon the industrial states, such as Massachusetts; that the act is a usurpation of power not granted to Congress by the Constitution—an attempted exercise of the power of local self-government reserved to the states by the Tenth Amendment; and that the defendants are proceeding to carry the act into operation. In the Massachusetts Case it is alleged that the plaintiff's rights and powers as a sovereign state and the rights of its citizens have been invaded and usurped by these expenditures and acts, and that, although the state has not accepted the act, its constitutional rights are infringed by the passage thereof and the imposition upon the state of an illegal and unconstitutional option either to yield to the federal government a part of its reserved rights or lose the share which it would otherwise be entitled to receive of the moneys appropriated. In the Frothingham Case plaintiff alleges that the effect of the statute will be to take her property, under the guise of taxation, without due process of law.

We have reached the conclusion that the cases must be disposed of for want of jurisdiction, without considering the merits of the constitutional questions.

In the first case, the state of Massachusetts presents no justiciable controversy, either in its own behalf or as the representative of its citizens. The appellant in the second suit has no such interest in the subject-matter, nor is any such injury inflicted or threatened, as will enable her to sue.

First. The state of Massachusetts in its own behalf, in effect, complains that the act in question invades the local concerns of the state, and is a usurpation of power, viz. the power of local self-government, reserved to the states.

Probably it would be sufficient to point out that the powers of the state are not invaded, since the statute imposes no obligation but simply extends an option which the state is free to accept or reject. But we do not rest here. Under article 3, § 2, of the Constitution, the judicial power of this court extends "to controversies . . . between a state and citizens of another state" and the court has original jurisdiction "in all cases . . . in which a state shall be a party." The effect of this is not to confer jurisdiction upon the court merely because a state is a party, but only where it is a party to a proceeding of judicial cognizance. Proceedings not of a justiciable character are outside the contemplation of the constitutional grant. . . .

[We have previously recognized state standing to sue] . . . in *Texas v. White*, 7 Wall. 700, *The State of Florida v. Anderson*, 91 U.S. 667, and *Alabama v. Burr*, 115 U.S. 413, because proprietary rights were involved; in *Georgia v. Tennessee Copper Co.*, 206 U.S. 230, 237, because the right of dominion of the state over the air and soil within its dominion was affected; in *Missouri v. Holland*, 252 U.S. 416, because, as asserted, there was an invasion, by acts done and threatened, of the quasi sovereign right of the state to regulate the taking of wild game within its borders; and in other cases because boundaries were in dispute. It is not necessary to cite additional cases. The foregoing for present purposes sufficiently indicate the jurisdictional line of demarcation.

What, then, is the nature of the right of the state here asserted and how is it affected by this statute? Reduced to its simplest terms, it is alleged that the statute constitutes an attempt to legislate outside the powers granted to Congress by the Constitution and within the field of local powers exclusively reserved to the states. Nothing is added to the force or effect of this assertion by the further incidental allegations that the ulterior purpose of Congress thereby was to induce the states to yield a portion of their sovereign rights; that the burden of the appropriations falls unequally upon the several states; and that there is imposed upon the states an illegal and unconstitutional option either to yield to the federal government a part of their reserved rights or lose their share of the moneys appropriated. But what burden is imposed upon the states, unequally or otherwise? Certainly there is none, unless it be the burden of taxation, and that falls upon their inhabitants, who are within the taxing power of Congress as well as that of the states where they reside. Nor does the statute require the states to do or to yield anything. If Congress enacted it with the ulterior purpose of tempting them to yield, that purpose may be effectively frustrated by the simple expedient of not yielding.

In the last analysis, the complaint of the plaintiff state is brought to the naked contention that Congress has usurped the reserved powers of the several states by the mere enactment of the statute, though nothing has been done and nothing is to be done without their consent; and it is plain that that question, as it is thus presented, is political, and not judicial in character, and therefore is not a matter which admits of the exercise of the judicial power. . . .

It follows that, in so far as the case depends upon the assertion of a right on the part of the state to sue in its own behalf, we are without jurisdiction. In that aspect of the case we are called upon to adjudicate, not rights of person or property, not rights of dominion over physical domain, not quasi sovereign rights actually invaded or threatened, but abstract questions of political power, of sovereignty, of government. No rights of the state falling within the scope of the judicial power have been brought within the actual or threatened operation of the statute, and this court is . . . without authority to pass abstract opinions upon the constitutionality of acts of Congress. . . .

We come next to consider whether the suit may be maintained by the state as the representative of its citizens. To this the answer is not doubtful. We need not go so far as to say that a state may never intervene by suit to protect its citizens against any form of enforcement of unconstitutional acts of Congress; but we are clear that the right to do so does not arise here. Ordinarily, at least, the only way in which a state may afford protection to its citizens in such cases is through the enforcement of its own criminal statutes, where that is appropriate, or by opening its courts to the injured persons for the maintenance of civil suits or actions. But the citizens of Massachusetts are also citizens of the United States. It cannot be conceded that a state, as parens patriae, may institute judicial proceedings to protect citizens of the United States from the operation of the statutes thereof. While the state, under some circumstances, may sue in that capacity for the protection of its citizens, it is no part of its duty or power to enforce their rights in respect of their relations with the federal government. In that field it is the United States, and not the state, which represents them as parens patriae, when such representation becomes appropriate; and to the former, and not to the latter, they must look for such protective measures as flow from that status.

Second. The attack upon the statute in the Frothingham Case is, generally, the same, but this plaintiff alleges, in addition that she is a taxpayer of the United States; and her contention, though not clear, seems to be that the effect of the appropriations complained of will be to increase the burden of future taxation and thereby take her property without due process of law. The right of a taxpayer to enjoin the execution of a federal appropriation act, on the ground that it is invalid and will result in taxation for illegal purposes, has never been passed upon by this court. In cases where it was presented, the question has either been allowed to pass sub silentio or the determination of it expressly withheld. [One, Bradfield v. Roberts,] came here from the Court of Appeals of the District of Columbia, and that court sustained the right of the plaintiff to sue by treating the case as one directed against the District of Columbia, and therefore subject to the rule, frequently stated by this court, that resident taxpayers may sue to enjoin an illegal use of the moneys of a municipal corporation. . . . But the relation of a taxpayer of the United States to the federal government is very different. His interest in the moneys of the treasury—partly realized from taxation and partly from other sources—is shared with millions of others, is comparatively minute and indeterminable, and the effect upon future taxation, of any payment out of the funds, so remote, fluctuating and uncertain, that no basis is afforded for an appeal to the preventive powers of a court of equity.

The administration of any statute, likely to produce additional taxation to be imposed upon a vast number of taxpayers, the extent of whose several liability is indefinite and constantly changing, is essentially a matter of public and not of individual concern. If one taxpayer may champion and litigate such a cause, then every other taxpayer may do the same, not only in respect of the statute here under review, but also in respect of every other appropriation act and statute whose administration requires the outlay of public money, and whose validity may be questioned. The bare suggestion of such a result, with its attendant inconveniences, goes far to sustain the conclusion which we have reached, that a suit of this character cannot be maintained. It is of much significance that no precedent sustaining the right to maintain suits like this has been called to our attention, although, since the formation of the government, as an examination of the acts of Congress will disclose, a large number of statutes appropriating or involving the expenditure of moneys for nonfederal purposes have been enacted and carried into effect.

The functions of government under our system are apportioned. To the legislative department has been committed the duty of making laws, to the executive the duty of executing them, and to the judiciary the duty of interpreting and applying them in cases properly brought before the courts. The general rule is that neither department may invade the province of the other and neither may control, direct, or restrain the action of the other. We are not now speaking of the merely ministerial duties of officials. We have no power per se to review and annul acts of Congress on the ground that they are unconstitutional. That question may be considered only when the justification for some direct injury suffered or threatened, presenting a justiciable issue, is made to rest upon such an act. Then the power exercised is that of ascertaining and declaring the law applicable to the controversy. It amounts to little more than the negative power to disregard an unconstitutional enactment, which otherwise would stand in the way of the enforcement of a legal right. The party who invokes the power must be able to show, not only that the statute is invalid, but that he has sustained or is immediately in danger of sustaining some direct injury as the result of its enforcement, and not merely that he suffers in some indefinite way in common with people generally. If a case for preventive relief be presented, the court enjoins, in effect, not the execution of the statute, but the acts of the official, the statute notwithstanding. Here the parties plaintiff have no such case. Looking through forms of words to the substance of their complaint, it is merely that officials of the executive department of the government are executing and will execute an act of Congress asserted to be unconstitutional; and this we are asked to prevent. To do so would be, not to decide a judicial controversy, but to assume a position of authority over plainly we do not possess. . . .

NOTES

1. If no citizen and no state has standing to challenge the constitutionality of the federal law at issue in these cases, then who will enforce the constitutional limits on Congress's spending and taxing power? Should we conclude that Congress and the president are to enforce the limits on their own power? Since the *Mellon* cases were decided in the 1920s, there has been an explosion in Congress's use of the spending and taxing power to make policy in all areas of American life. Does that change your view of these cases at all?

2. The general rule against taxpayer standing to raise constitutional changes was abandoned in lawsuits alleging a violation of the Establishment Clause in a case called *Flast v. Cohen*, 392 U.S. 83 (1968), which many at the time saw as the Court's first step toward a broad recognition of taxpayer standing and the overruling of the *Mellon* cases you just read. The Court in *Flast* rationalized taxpayer standing for Establishment Clause cases as being uniquely warranted because, the Court said, the evil the Establishment Clause was aimed at was the injury to conscience that comes from obliging a person to pay even the smallest amount in taxes to support a faith with which the person disagrees. The Court has drastically limited *Flast*, so that it now constitutes a tightly confined, and nearly discarded, exception to the general rule of *Frothingham*. See, e.g., *Arizona Christian School Tuition Organization v. Winn*, 131 S. Ct. 1436 (2011).

3. The no-state-standing rule of *Massachusetts v. Mellon* also remains dominant, though at least one recent case seems to be an exception. In *Massachusetts v. Environmental Protection Agency*, 549 U.S. 497 (2007), the Court, by vote of 5–4, upheld a state's standing to challenge the Environmental Protection Agency's failure to regulate greenhouse gas emissions from new motor vehicles under the Clean Air Act, alleging that such inaction on global warming threatened harm to state citizen landowners and to the state itself as a landowner, because global warming threatens "a precipitate rise in sea levels by the end of the century," "severe and irreversible changes to natural ecosystems," and other environmental, economic, and storm-related injuries. The majority stated that Massachusetts' "sovereign interests" entitled it to "special solicitude in our standing analysis." The four dissenters, citing *Massachusetts v. Mellon,* argued against "[r]elaxing Article III standing requirements because asserted injuries are pressed by a State." Which approach strikes you as more correct? Why?

Massachusetts v. Environmental Protection Agency is one of many recent cases involving claims of new types of legal interests and injuries, conferred by statutes, often in the area of environmental regulation and species protection. In addition, many other recent cases involve statutes that recognize various types of administrative, procedural, or informational injuries and appear to confer (or purport to confer) on a broad class of "aggrieved" persons the right to challenge violations of the statute. And many such statutes arguably recognize attenuated injuries and causation. These cases present some of the most complex and difficult questions under modern standing law. The next case, *Summers v. Earth Island Institute,* is representative of the Article III standing issues presented in such cases.

Summers v. Earth Island Institute

555 U.S. 488 (2009)

■ JUSTICE SCALIA delivered the opinion of the Court.

Respondents are a group of organizations dedicated to protecting the environment. (We will refer to them collectively as "Earth Island.") They seek to prevent the United States Forest Service from enforcing regulations that exempt small fire-rehabilitation and timber-salvage projects from the notice, comment, and appeal process used by the Forest Service for more significant land management decisions. We must determine whether respondents have standing to challenge the regulations in the absence of a live dispute over a concrete application of those regulations.

I

In 1992, Congress enacted the Forest Service Decisionmaking and Appeals Reform Act (Appeals Reform Act or Act). Among other things, this required the Forest Service to establish a notice, comment, and appeal process for "proposed actions of the Forest Service concerning projects and activities implementing land and resource management plans developed under the Forest and Rangeland Renewable Resources Planning Act of 1974."

The Forest Service's regulations implementing the Act provided that certain of its procedures would not be applied to projects that the Service considered categorically excluded from the requirement to file an environmental impact statement (EIS) or environmental assessment (EA). Later amendments to the Forest Service's manual ... provided that fire-rehabilitation activities on areas of less than 4,200 acres, and salvage-timber sales of 250 acres or less, did not cause a significant environmental impact and thus would be categorically exempt from the requirement to file an EIS or EA. This had the effect of excluding these projects from the notice, comment, and appeal process.

In the summer of 2002, fire burned a significant area of the Sequoia National Forest. In September 2003, the Service issued a decision memo approving the Burnt Ridge Project, a salvage sale of timber on 238 acres damaged by that fire. Pursuant to its categorical exclusion of salvage sales of less than 250 acres, the Forest Service did not provide notice in a form consistent with the Appeals Reform Act, did not provide a period of public comment, and did not make an appeal process available.

In December 2003, respondents filed a complaint in the Eastern District of California, challenging [these actions].... The District Court granted a preliminary injunction against the Burnt Ridge salvage-timber sale. Soon thereafter, the parties settled their dispute over the Burnt Ridge Project and the District Court concluded that "the Burnt Ridge timber sale is not at issue in this case." The Government argued that, with the Burnt Ridge dispute settled, and with no other project before the court in which respondents were threatened with injury in fact, respondents lacked standing to challenge the regulations; and that absent a concrete dispute over a particular project a challenge to the regulations would not be ripe. The District Court proceeded, however, to adjudicate the merits of Earth Island's challenges. It invalidated five of the regulations ... and entered a nationwide injunction against their application....

II

In limiting the judicial power to "Cases" and "Controversies," Article III of the Constitution restricts it to the traditional role of Anglo–American courts, which is to redress or prevent actual or imminently threatened injury to persons caused by private or official violation of law. Except when necessary in the execution of that function, courts have no charter to review and revise legislative and executive action. See *Lujan v. Defenders of Wildlife*, 504 U.S. 555, 559–560 (1992); *Los Angeles v. Lyons*, 461 U.S. 95, 111–112 (1983). This limitation "is founded in concern about the proper—and properly limited—role of the courts in a democratic society." *Warth v. Seldin*, 422 U.S. 490, 498 (1975).

The doctrine of standing is one of several doctrines that reflect this fundamental limitation. It requires federal courts to satisfy themselves that "the plaintiff has alleged such a personal stake in the outcome of the controversy as to warrant *his* invocation of federal-court jurisdiction." 422 U.S., at 498–499. He bears the burden of showing that he has standing for each type of relief sought. To seek injunctive relief, a plaintiff must show that he is under threat of suffering "injury in fact" that is concrete and particularized; the threat must be actual and imminent, not conjectural or hypothetical; it must be fairly traceable to the challenged action of the defendant; and it must be likely that a favorable judicial decision will prevent or redress the injury. This requirement assures that "there is a real need to exercise the power of judicial review in order to protect the interests of the complaining party," *Schlesinger v. Reservists Comm. to Stop the War*, 418 U.S. 208, 221 (1974). . . .

The regulations under challenge here neither require nor forbid any action on the part of respondents. The standards and procedures that they prescribe for Forest Service appeals govern only the conduct of Forest Service officials engaged in project planning. "[W]hen the plaintiff is not himself the object of the government action or inaction he challenges, standing is not precluded, but it is ordinarily 'substantially more difficult' to establish." *Defenders of Wildlife, supra*, at 562. Here, respondents can demonstrate standing only if application of the regulations by the Government will affect *them* in the manner described above.

It is common ground that the respondent organizations can assert the standing of their members. To establish the concrete and particularized injury that standing requires, respondents point to their members' recreational interests in the National Forests. While generalized harm to the forest or the environment will not alone support standing, if that harm in fact affects the recreational or even the mere esthetic interests of the plaintiff, that will suffice. *Sierra Club v. Morton*, 405 U.S. 727, 734–736 (1972).

Affidavits submitted to the District Court alleged that organization member Ara Marderosian had repeatedly visited the Burnt Ridge site, that he had imminent plans to do so again, and that his interests in viewing the flora and fauna of the area would be harmed if the Burnt Ridge Project went forward without incorporation of the ideas he would have suggested if the Forest Service had provided him an opportunity to comment. The Government concedes this was sufficient to establish Article III standing with respect to Burnt Ridge. Marderosian's threatened injury with regard to that project was originally one of the bases for the present suit. After the District Court had issued a preliminary injunction, however, the parties settled their differences on that score. Marderosian's injury in fact with regard to that project has been remedied, and it is, as the District Court pronounced, "not at issue in this case." 376 F.Supp.2d, at 999. We know of no precedent for the proposition that when a plaintiff has sued to challenge the lawfulness of certain action or threatened action but has settled that suit, he retains standing to challenge the basis for that action (here, the regulation in the abstract), apart from any concrete application that threatens imminent harm to his interests. Such a holding would fly in the face of Article III's injury-in-fact requirement. See *Lyons, supra,* at 111.

Respondents have identified no other application of the invalidated regulations that threatens imminent and concrete harm to the interests of their members. The only other affidavit relied on was that of Jim Bensman. He asserted, first, that he had suffered injury in the past from development on Forest Service land. That does not suffice for several reasons: because it was not tied to application of the challenged regulations, because it does not identify any particular site, and because it relates to past injury rather than imminent future injury that is sought to be enjoined.

Bensman's affidavit further asserts that he has visited many National Forests and plans to visit several unnamed National Forests in the future. Respondents describe this as a mere failure to "provide the name of each timber sale that affected [Bensman's] interests" It is much more (or much less) than that. It is a failure to allege that any particular timber sale or other project claimed to be unlawfully subject to the regulations will impede a specific and concrete plan of Bensman's to enjoy the National Forests. The National Forests occupy more than 190 million acres, an area larger than Texas. There may be a chance, but is hardly a likelihood, that Bensman's wanderings will bring him to a parcel about to be affected by a project unlawfully subject to the regulations. Indeed, without further specification it is impossible to tell *which* projects are (in respondents' view) unlawfully subject to the regulations. The allegations here present a weaker likelihood of concrete harm than that which we found insufficient in *Lyons*, 461 U.S. 95, where a plaintiff who alleged that he had been injured by an improper police chokehold sought injunctive relief barring use of the hold in the future. We said it was "no more than conjecture" that Lyons would be subjected to that chokehold upon a later encounter. *Id.*, at 108. Here we are asked to assume not only that Bensman will stumble across a project tract unlawfully subject to the regulations, but also that the tract is about to be developed by the Forest Service in a way that harms his recreational interests, and that he would have commented on the project but for the regulation. Accepting an intention to visit the National Forests as adequate to confer standing to challenge any Government action affecting any portion of those forests would be tantamount to eliminating the requirement of concrete, particularized injury in fact.

The Bensman affidavit does refer specifically to a series of projects in the Allegheny National Forest that are subject to the challenged regulations. It does not assert, however, any firm intention to visit their locations, saying only that Bensman "want[s] to" go there. This vague desire to return is insufficient to satisfy the requirement of imminent injury: "Such 'some day' intentions—without any description of concrete plans, or indeed any specification of when the some day will be—do not support a finding of the 'actual or imminent' injury that our cases require." *Defenders of Wildlife*, 504 U.S., at 564.

Respondents argue that they have standing to bring their challenge because they have suffered procedural injury, namely that they have been denied the ability to file comments on some Forest Service actions and will continue to be so denied. But deprivation of a procedural right without some concrete interest that is affected by the deprivation—a procedural right *in vacuo*—is insufficient to create Article III standing. . . .

It makes no difference that the procedural right has been accorded by Congress. That can loosen the strictures of the redressability prong of our standing inquiry—so that standing existed with regard to the Burnt Ridge Project, for example, despite the possibility that Earth Island's allegedly guaranteed right to comment would not be successful in persuading the Forest Service to avoid impairment of Earth Island's concrete interests. See *Ibid.* Unlike redressability, however, the requirement of injury in fact is a hard floor of Article III jurisdiction that cannot be removed by statute.

> "[I]t would exceed [Article III's] limitations if, at the behest of Congress and in the absence of any showing of concrete injury, we were to entertain citizen suits to vindicate the public's nonconcrete interest in the proper administration of the laws. . . . [T]he party bringing suit must show that the action injures him in a concrete and personal way." *Id.*, at 580–581 (KENNEDY, J., concurring in part and concurring in judgment).

III

The dissent proposes a hitherto unheard-of test for organizational standing: whether, accepting the organization's self-description of the activities of its members, there is a statistical probability that some of those members are threatened with concrete injury. Since, for example, the Sierra Club asserts in its pleadings that it has more than "700,000 members nationwide, including thousands of members in California" who "use and enjoy the Sequoia National Forest," it is probable (according to the dissent) that some (unidentified) members have planned to visit some (unidentified) small parcels affected by the Forest Service's procedures and will suffer (unidentified) concrete harm as a result. This novel approach to the law of organizational standing would make a mockery of our prior cases, which have required plaintiff-organizations to make specific allegations establishing that at least one identified member had suffered or would suffer harm. . . .

A major problem with the dissent's approach is that it accepts the organizations' self-descriptions of their membership, on the simple ground that "no one denies" them. But it is well established that the court has an independent obligation to assure that standing exists, regardless of whether it is challenged by any of the parties. Without individual affidavits, how is the court to assure itself that the Sierra Club, for example, has "thousands of members" who "use and enjoy the Sequoia National Forest"? And, because to establish standing plaintiffs must show that they "use the area affected by the challenged activity and not an area roughly in the vicinity of" a project site, *Defenders of Wildlife*, 504 U.S., at 566, how is the court to assure itself that some of these members plan to make use of the specific sites upon which projects may take place? Or that these same individuals will find their recreation burdened by the Forest Service's use of the challenged procedures? While it is certainly possible—perhaps even likely—that one individual will meet all of these criteria, that speculation does not suffice. "Standing," we have said, "is not 'an ingenious academic exercise in the conceivable' . . . [but] requires . . . a factual showing of perceptible harm." *Ibid.* In part because of the difficulty of verifying the facts upon which such probabilistic standing depends, the Court has required plaintiffs claiming an organizational standing to identify members who have suffered the requisite harm—surely not a difficult task here, when so many thousands are alleged to have been harmed.

The dissent would have us replace the requirement of "imminent" harm, which it acknowledges our cases establish with the requirement of " 'a *realistic* threat' that reoccurrence of the challenged activity would cause [the plaintiff] harm 'in the reasonably near future.' " That language is taken, of course, from an opinion that did not find standing, so the seeming expansiveness of the test made not a bit of difference. The problem for the dissent is that the timely affidavits no more meet that requirement than they meet the usual formulation. They fail to establish that the affiants' members will ever visit one of the small parcels at issue. . . .

Since we have resolved this case on the ground of standing, we need not reach the Government's contention that plaintiffs have not demonstrated that the regulations are ripe for review under the Administrative Procedure Act. We likewise do not reach the question whether, if respondents prevailed, a nationwide injunction would be appropriate. And we do not disturb the dismissal of respondents' challenge to the remaining regulations, which has not been appealed.

■ JUSTICE KENNEDY, concurring.

I join in full the opinion of the Court. As the opinion explains, "deprivation of a procedural right without some concrete interest that is affected by the deprivation—a procedural right *in vacuo*—is insufficient to create Article III standing." The procedural injury must "impair a separate concrete interest." *Lujan v. Defenders of Wildlife*, 504 U.S. 555, 572 (1992).

This case would present different considerations if Congress had sought to provide redress for a concrete injury "giv[ing] rise to a case or controversy where none existed before." *Id.*, at 580 (KENNEDY, J., concurring in part and concurring in judgment). Nothing in the statute at issue here, however, indicates Congress intended to identify or confer some interest separate and apart from a procedural right.

■ JUSTICE BREYER, with whom JUSTICE STEVENS, JUSTICE SOUTER, and JUSTICE GINSBURG join, dissenting.

The Court holds that the Sierra Club and its members (along with other environmental organizations) do not suffer any "concrete injury" when the Forest Service sells timber for logging on "many thousands" of small (250–acre or less) woodland parcels without following legally required procedures—procedures which, if followed, could lead the Service to cancel or to modify the sales. Nothing in the record or the law justifies this counter-intuitive conclusion. . . .

The plaintiffs, respondents in this case, are five environmental organizations. . . .

These five organizations point to a federal law that says the Forest Service "shall establish a notice and comment process," along with a procedure for filing administrative "appeals," for "proposed actions . . . concerning projects and activities implementing land and resource management plans". . . . They add that the Service has exempted from "notice, comment, and appeal" processes its decisions that allow, among other things, salvage-timber sales on burned forest lands of less than 250 acres in size. And they claim that the Service's refusal to provide notice, comment, and appeal procedures violates the statute.

The majority says that the plaintiffs lack *constitutional* standing to raise this claim. It holds that the dispute between the five environmental groups and the Forest Service consists simply of an abstract challenge; it does not amount to the concrete "Cas[e]" or "Controvers[y]" that the Constitution grants federal courts the power to resolve. Art. III, § 2, cl. 1. I cannot agree that this is so.

To understand the *constitutional* issue that the majority decides, it may prove helpful to imagine that Congress enacted a *statutory* provision that expressly permitted environmental groups like the respondents here to bring cases just like the present one, provided (1) that the group has members who have used salvage-timber parcels in the past and are likely to do so in the future, and (2) that the group's members have opposed Forest Service timber sales in the past (using notice, comment, and appeal procedures to do so) and will likely use those procedures to oppose salvage-timber sales in the future. The majority cannot, and does not, claim that such a statute would be unconstitutional. How then can it find the present case constitutionally unauthorized?

I believe the majority answers this question as follows: It recognizes, as this Court has held, that a plaintiff has constitutional standing if the plaintiff demonstrates (1) an "injury in fact," (2) that is "fairly traceable" to the defendant's "challenged action," and which (3) a "favorable [judicial] decision" will likely prevent or redress. The majority does not deny that the plaintiffs meet the latter two requirements. It focuses only upon the first, the presence of "actual," as opposed to "conjectural or hypothetical," injury. In doing so, it properly agrees that the "organizations" here can "assert the standing of their members." It points out that injuries to the "members' recreational" or even "mere esthetic interests . . . will suffice." It does not claim that the *procedural* nature of the plaintiffs' claim makes the difference here, for it says only that "deprivation of a procedural right *without some concrete interest*" thereby affected, *i.e.*, "a procedural right *in vacuo*" would prove "insufficient to create Article III standing." The majority assumes, as do I, that these unlawful Forest Service procedures will lead to substantive actions, namely the sales of salvage timber on burned lands, that might not take place if the proper procedures were followed. But the majority then finds that the plaintiffs have not sufficiently demonstrated that these salvage-timber sales cause plaintiffs an actual injury, that is, harm to the recreational, aesthetic, or other environmental interests of organization members. To put the matter in terms of my hypothetical statute, the majority holds that the plaintiff organizations, while showing that they have members who have used salvage-timber sale parcels in the past (*i.e.*, parcels that the Service does not subject to the notice, comment, and appeal procedures required by law), have failed to show that they have members likely to use such parcels in the future.

How can the majority credibly claim that salvage-timber sales, and similar projects, are unlikely to harm the asserted interests of the members of these environmental groups? . . . [A] threat of future harm may be realistic even where the plaintiff cannot specify precise times, dates, and GPS coordinates. . . .

The Forest Service admits that it intends to conduct thousands of further salvage-timber sales and other projects exempted under the challenged regulations "in the reasonably near future." How then can the Court deny that the plaintiffs have shown a "realistic" threat that the Forest Service will continue to authorize (without the procedures claimed necessary) salvage-timber sales, and other Forest Service projects, that adversely affect the recreational, aesthetic, and environmental interests of the plaintiffs' members? . . .

NOTES

1. How should the case-or-controversy language of Article III be construed when Congress has determined that a new harm ought to be recognized? Are you more persuaded by Justice Scalia's majority opinion or by Justice Breyer's dissent?

2. Is there any limit at all on Congress's power to create new legal injuries that give rise to standing? Can Congress give citizens standing to challenge the lawfulness of the procedures government agencies follow in cases where they have suffered no particularized injury? Could Congress pass a law giving anyone who is displeased with the president's exercise of prosecutorial discretion standing to go to federal court to get a judge to order that federal law be enforced a certain way? Or could Congress authorize anyone to sue who is displeased with the president's decision to pardon someone? Would there be anything left of presidential power in those situations?

[*Assignment 27*]

C. THE POLITICAL QUESTION DOCTRINE

Even where Article III's prerequisites for a "case" or "controversy" falling within the traditional understanding of the judicial power are satisfied—there is a genuine controversy and not a request for an advisory opinion; the parties have legal interests conferring standing; the case is adversarial and not contrived, feigned, or collusive; the dispute is ripe and not moot—there may remain a further question: whether the *legal issue presented* is appropriate for judicial resolution at all or is instead, a matter the Constitution leaves to the resolution of the political branches of government. This is referred to as the "political question doctrine."

Are there some constitutional issues that are, by the text, structure, and logic of the Constitution, simply exempt from judicial decision because the Constitution commits them to Congress or the president? Are there some constitutional issues for which the Constitution simply does not supply an answer, so that there are no standards by which the judiciary could rule in a principled fashion? Are there practical or pragmatic reasons that might make it extraordinarily inappropriate for the courts to interfere with some types of decisions made by the political branches of the national government? If so, what types of decisions, on what issues, should the courts refrain from deciding—and are there principled criteria for making those judgments?

We have already seen one case, *Goldwater v. Carter*, 444 U.S. 996 (1979), presenting the question of whether the Senate must consent to treaty termination, where a plurality of the Court invoked the political question doctrine to hold that it lacked authority to decide the constitutional question on the merits. (Recall also that Justice Powell disagreed with this conclusion, but invoked the "ripeness" doctrine to reach the same conclusion.) Is a decision to refrain from decision on the merits, on the basis of the political question doctrine, really just a different form of decision on the merits?

The content, and even the legitimacy, of the political question doctrine remains hotly disputed. We present here two cases concerning the political question doctrine. *Luther v. Borden*, 48 U.S. 1 (1849), is an early case, predating the modern doctrine, but in many ways it is the leading case contributing to the development of that doctrine. *Nixon v. United States*, 506

U.S. 224 (1993), is a modern case presenting, distilling, and debating the application of the current political question doctrine in the context of a judicial impeachment proceeding. As you study these cases, seek to identify the various strands of the political question doctrine and evaluate them. Is the doctrine principled and coherent? Are decisions under the political question doctrine simply roundabout decisions on the merits? Are there cases involving constitutional issues that courts just should not decide? If so, what are they: Matters involving war and foreign affairs? Matters involving impeachment? Matters involving national authority to assure that the states maintain "a republican form of government"? What else (and why)?

Luther v. Borden
48 U.S. 1 (1849)

■ MR. CHIEF JUSTICE TANEY delivered the opinion of the court.

This case has arisen out of the unfortunate political differences which agitated the people of Rhode Island in 1841 and 1842.

It is an action of trespass brought by Martin Luther, the plaintiff in error, against Luther M. Borden and others, the defendants, in the Circuit Court of the United States for the District of Rhode Island, for breaking and entering the plaintiff's house. The defendants justify upon the ground that large numbers of men were assembled in different parts of the State for the purpose of overthrowing the government by military force, and were actually levying war upon the State; that, in order to defend itself from this insurrection, the State was declared by competent authority to be under martial law; that the plaintiff was engaged in the insurrection; and that the defendants, being in the military service of the State, by command of their superior officer, broke and entered the house and searched the rooms for the plaintiff, who was supposed to be there concealed, in order to arrest him, doing as little damage as possible. . . .

The existence and authority of the government under which the defendants acted was called in question; and the plaintiff insists, that, before the acts complained of were committed, that government had been displaced and annulled by the people of Rhode Island, and that the plaintiff was engaged in supporting the lawful authority of the State, and the defendants themselves were in arms against it.

This is a new question in this court, and certainly a very grave one; and at the time when the trespass is alleged to have been committed it had produced a general and painful excitement in the State, and threatened to end in bloodshed and civil war.

The evidence shows that the defendants, in breaking into the plaintiff's house and endeavouring to arrest him, as stated in the pleadings, acted under the authority of the government which was established in Rhode Island at the time of the Declaration of Independence, and which is usually called the charter government. For when the separation from England took place, Rhode Island did not, like the other States, adopt a new constitution, but continued the form of government established by the charter of Charles the Second in 1663; making only such alterations, by acts of the legislature, as were necessary to adapt it to their condition and rights as an independent State. It was under this form of government that Rhode Island united with the other States in the Declaration of Independence, and afterwards ratified the Constitution of the United States and became a member of this Union; and it continued to be the established and unquestioned government of the State until the difficulties took place which have given rise to this action.

In this form of government no mode of proceeding was pointed out by which amendments might be made. It authorized the legislature to prescribe the qualification of voters, and in the exercise of this power the right of suffrage was confined to freeholders, until the adoption of the constitution of 1843.

For some years previous to the disturbances of which we are now speaking, many of the citizens became dissatisfied with the charter government, and particularly with the restriction upon the right of suffrage. Memorials were addressed to the legislature upon this subject, urging the justice and necessity of a more liberal and extended rule. But they failed to produce the desired effect. And thereupon meetings were held and associations formed by those who were in favor of a more extended right of suffrage, which finally resulted in the election of a convention to form a new constitution to be submitted to the people for their adoption or rejection. . . . The persons chosen as above mentioned came together and framed a constitution, by which the right of suffrage was extended to every male citizen of twenty-one years of age, who had resided in the State for one year, and in the town in which he offered to vote for six months, next preceding the election. The convention also prescribed the manner in which this constitution should be submitted to the decision of the people,— permitting every one to vote on that question who was an American citizen, twenty-one years old, and who had a permanent residence or home in the State, and directing the votes to be returned to the convention.

Upon the return of the votes, the convention declared that the constitution was adopted and ratified by a majority of the people of the State, and was the paramount law and constitution of Rhode Island. And it communicated this decision to the governor under the charter government, for the purpose of being laid before the legislature; and directed elections to be held for a governor, members of the legislature, and other officers under the new constitution. These elections accordingly took place, and the governor, lieutenant-governor, secretary of state, and senators and representatives thus appointed assembled at the city of Providence on May 3d, 1842, and immediately proceeded to organize the new government, by appointing the officers and passing the laws necessary for that purpose.

The charter government did not, however, admit the validity of these proceedings, nor acquiesce in them. On the contrary, in January, 1842, when this new constitution was communicated to the governor, and by him laid before the legislature, it passed resolutions declaring all acts done for the purpose of imposing that constitution upon the State to be an assumption of the powers of government, in violation of the rights of the existing government and of the people at large; and that it would maintain its authority and defend the legal and constitutional rights of the people.

In adopting this measure, as well as in all others taken by the charter government to assert its authority, it was supported by a large number of the citizens of the State, claiming to be a majority, who regarded the proceedings of the adverse party as unlawful and disorganizing, and maintained that, as the existing government had been established by the people of the State, no convention to frame a new constitution could be called without its sanction; and that the times and places of taking the votes, and the officers to receive them, and the qualification of voters, must be previously regulated and appointed by law.

But, notwithstanding the determination of the charter government, and of those who adhered to it, to maintain its authority, Thomas W. Dorr, who had been elected governor under the new constitution, prepared to assert the authority of that government by force, and many citizens assembled in arms to support him. The charter government thereupon passed an act declaring the State under martial law, and at the same time proceeded to call out the militia, to repel the threatened attack and to subdue those who were engaged in it. In this state of the contest, the house of the plaintiff, who was engaged in supporting the authority of the new government, was broken and entered in order to arrest him. The defendants were, at the time, in the military service of the old government, and in arms to support its authority.

It appears, also, that the charter government at its session of January, 1842, took measures to call a convention to revise the existing form of government; and after various proceedings, which it is not material to state, a new constitution was formed by a convention elected under the authority of the charter government, and afterwards adopted and ratified by the people; the times and places at which the votes were to be given, the persons who were to receive and return them, and the qualification of the voters, having all been previously authorized and provided for by law passed by the charter government. This new government went into operation in May, 1843, at which time the old government formally surrendered all its powers; and this constitution has continued ever since to be the admitted and established government of Rhode Island.

The difficulties with the government of which Mr. Dorr was the head were soon over. They had ceased before the constitution was framed by the convention elected by the authority of the charter government. For after an unsuccessful attempt made by Mr. Dorr in May, 1842, at the head of a military force, to get possession of the State arsenal at Providence, in which he was repulsed, and an assemblage of some hundreds of armed men under his command at Chepatchet in the June following, which dispersed upon the approach of the troops of the old government, no further effort was made to establish it; and until the constitution of 1843 went into operation the charter government continued to assert its authority and exercise its powers, and to enforce obedience, throughout the State, arresting and imprisoning, and punishing in its judicial tribunals, those who had appeared in arms against it.

We do not understand from the argument that the constitution under which the plaintiff acted is supposed to have been in force after the constitution of May, 1843, went into operation. The contest is confined to the year preceding. The plaintiff contends that the charter government was displaced, and ceased to have any lawful power, after the organization, in May, 1842, of the government which he supported, and although that government never was able to exercise any authority in the State, nor to command obedience to its laws or to its officers, yet he insists that it was the lawful and established government, upon the ground that it was ratified by a large majority of the male people of the State of the age of twenty-one and upwards, and also by a majority of those who were entitled to vote for general officers under the then existing laws of the State. The fact that it was so ratified was not admitted; and at the trial in the Circuit Court he offered to prove it by the production of the original ballots, and the original registers of the persons voting, verified by the oaths of the several moderators and clerks of the meetings, and by the testimony of all the persons so voting, and by the said constitution; and also offered in evidence, for the same purpose, that part of the census of the United States for the year 1840 which applies to Rhode Island; and a certificate of the secretary of state of the charter government, showing the number of votes polled by the freemen of the State for the ten years then last past.

The Circuit Court rejected this evidence, and instructed the jury that the charter government and laws under which the defendants acted were, at the time the trespass is alleged to have been committed, in full force and effect as the form of government and paramount law of the State, and constituted a justification of the acts of the defendants as set forth in their pleas.

It is this opinion of the Circuit Court that we are now called upon to review. It is set forth more at large in the exception, but is in substance as above stated; and the question presented is certainly a very serious one: For, if this court is authorized to enter upon this inquiry as proposed by the plaintiff, and it should be decided that the charter government had no legal existence during the period of time above mentioned,—if it had been annulled by the adoption of the opposing government,—then the laws passed by its legislature during that time were nullities; its taxes wrongfully collected; its salaries and compensation to its officers illegally paid; its public accounts improperly settled; and the judgments and sentences of its courts in civil and criminal cases null and void, and the officers who carried their decisions into operation answerable as trespassers, if not in some cases as criminals.

When the decision of this court might lead to such results, it becomes its duty to examine very carefully its own powers before it undertakes to exercise jurisdiction.

Certainly, the question which the plaintiff proposed to raise by the testimony he offered has not heretofore been recognized as a judicial one in any of the State courts. In forming the constitutions of the different States, after the Declaration of Independence, and in the various changes and alterations which have since been made, the political department has always determined whether the proposed constitution or amendment was ratified or not by the people of the State, and the judicial power has followed its decision. In Rhode Island, the question has been directly decided. Prosecutions were there instituted against some of the persons who had been active in the forcible opposition to the old government. And in more than one of the cases evidence was offered on the part of the defence similar to the testimony offered in the Circuit Court, and for the same purpose; that is, for the purpose of showing that the proposed constitution had been adopted by the people of Rhode Island, and had, therefore, become the established government, and consequently that the parties accused were doing nothing more than their duty in endeavouring to support it.

But the courts uniformly held that the inquiry proposed to be made belonged to the political power and not to the judicial; that it rested with the political power to decide whether the charter government had been displaced or not; and when that decision was made, the judicial department would be bound to take notice of it as the paramount law of the State, without the aid of oral evidence or the examination of witnesses; that, according to the laws and institutions of Rhode Island, no such change had been recognized by the political power; and that the charter government was the lawful and established government of the State during the period in contest, and that those who were in arms against it were insurgents, and liable to punishment. This doctrine is clearly and forcibly stated in the opinion of the Supreme Court of the State in the trial of Thomas W. Dorr, who was the governor elected under the opposing constitution, and headed the armed force which endeavoured to maintain its authority.

Indeed, we do not see how the question could be tried and judicially decided in a State court. Judicial power presupposes an established government capable of enacting laws and enforcing their execution, and of appointing judges to expound and administer them. The acceptance of the judicial office is a recognition of the authority of the government from which it is derived. And if the authority of that government is annulled and overthrown, the power of its courts and other officers is annulled with it. And if a State court should enter upon the inquiry proposed in this case, and should come to the conclusion that the government under which it acted had been put aside and displaced by an opposing government, it would cease to be a court, and be incapable of pronouncing a judicial decision upon the question it undertook to try. If it decides at all as a court, it necessarily affirms the existence and authority of the government under which it is exercising judicial power.

It is worthy of remark, however, when we are referring to the authority of State decisions, that the trial of Thomas W. Dorr took place after the constitution of 1843 went into operation. The judges who decided that case held their authority under that constitution; and it is admitted on all hands that it was adopted by the people of the State, and is the lawful and established government. It is the decision, therefore, of a State court, whose judicial authority to decide upon the constitution and laws of Rhode Island is not questioned by either party to this controversy, although the government under which it acted was framed and adopted under the sanction and laws of the charter government.

The point, then, raised here has been already decided by the courts of Rhode Island. The question relates, altogether, to the constitution and laws of that State; and the well settled rule in this court is, that the courts of the United States adopt and follow the decisions of the State courts in questions which concern merely the constitution and laws of the State[.]

Upon what ground could the Circuit Court of the United States which tried this case have departed from this rule, and disregarded and overruled the decisions of the courts of Rhode Island? Undoubtedly the courts of the United States have certain powers under the Constitution and laws of the United States which do not belong to the State courts. But the power of determining that a State government has been lawfully established, which the courts of the State disown and repudiate, is not one of them. Upon such a question the courts of the United States are bound to follow the decisions of the State tribunals, and must therefore regard the charter government as the lawful established government during the time of this contest.

Besides, if the Circuit Court had entered upon this inquiry, by what rule could it have determined the qualification of voters upon the adoption or rejection of the proposed constitution, unless there was some previous law of the State to guide it? It is the province of a court to expound the law, not to make it. And certainly it is no part of the judicial functions of any court of the United States to prescribe the qualification of voters in a State, giving the right to those to whom it is denied by the written and established constitution and laws of the State, or taking it away from those to whom it is given; nor has it the right to determine what political privileges the citizens of a State are entitled to, unless there is an established constitution or law to govern its decision. . . .

Moreover, the Constitution of the United States, as far as it has provided for an emergency of this kind, and authorized the general government to interfere in the domestic concerns of a State, has treated the subject as political in its nature, and placed the power in the hands of that department.

The fourth section of the fourth article of the Constitution of the United States provides that the United States shall guarantee to every State in the Union a republican form of government, and shall protect each of them against invasion; and on the application of the legislature or of the executive (when the legislature cannot be convened) against domestic violence.

Under this article of the Constitution it rests with Congress to decide what government is the established one in a State. For as the United States guarantee to each State a republican government, Congress must necessarily decide what government is established in the State before it can determine whether it is republican or not. And when the senators and representatives of a State are admitted into the councils of the Union, the authority of the government under which they are appointed, as well as its republican character, is recognized by the proper constitutional authority. And its decision is binding on every other department of the government, and could not be questioned in a judicial tribunal. It is true that the contest in this case did not last long enough to bring the matter to this issue; and as no senators or representatives were elected under the authority of the government of which Mr. Dorr was the head, Congress was not called upon to decide the controversy. Yet the right to decide is placed there, and not in the courts.

So, too, as relates to the clause in the above-mentioned article of the Constitution, providing for cases of domestic violence. It rested with Congress, too, to determine upon the means proper to be adopted to fulfil this guarantee. They might, if they had deemed it most advisable to do so, have placed it in the power of a court to decide when the contingency had happened which required the federal government to interfere. But Congress thought otherwise, and no doubt wisely; and by the act of February 28, 1795, provided, that, "in case of an insurrection in any State against the government thereof, it shall be lawful for the President of the United States, on application of the legislature of such State or of the executive (when the legislature cannot be convened), to call forth such number of the militia of any other State or States, as may be applied for, as he may judge sufficient to sufficient to suppress such insurrection."

By this act, the power of deciding whether the exigency had arisen upon which the government of the United States is bound to interfere, is given to the President. He is to act upon the application of the legislature or of the executive, and consequently he must determine what body of men constitute the legislature, and who is the governor, before he can act. The fact that both parties claim the right to the government cannot alter the case, for both cannot be entitled to it. If there is an armed conflict, like the one of which we are speaking, it is a case of domestic violence, and one of the parties must be in insurrection against the lawful government. And the President must, of necessity, decide which is the government, and which party is unlawfully arrayed against it, before he can perform the duty imposed upon him by the act of Congress.

After the President has acted and called out the militia, is a Circuit Court of the United States authorized to inquire whether his decision was right? Could the court, while the parties were actually contending in arms for the possession of the government, call witnesses before it and inquire which party represented a majority of the people? If it could, then it would become the duty of the court (provided it came to the conclusion that the President had decided incorrectly) to discharge those who were arrested or detained by the troops in the service of the United States or the government which the President was endeavouring to maintain. If the judicial power extends so far, the guarantee contained in the Constitution of the United States is a guarantee of anarchy, and not of order. Yet if this right does not reside in the courts when the conflict is raging, if the judicial power is at that time bound to follow the decision of the political, it must be equally bound when the contest is over. It cannot, when peace is restored, punish as offences and crimes the acts which it before recognized, and was bound to recognize, as lawful.

It is true that in this case the militia were not called out by the President. But upon the application of the governor under the charter government, the President recognized him as the executive power of the State, and took measures to call out the militia to support his authority if it should be found necessary for the general government to interfere; and it is admitted in the argument, that it was the knowledge of this decision that put an end to the armed opposition to the charter government, and prevented any further efforts to establish by force the proposed constitution. The interference of the President, therefore, by announcing his determination, was as effectual as if the militia had been assembled under his orders. And it should be equally authoritative. For certainly no court of the United States, with a knowledge of this decision, would have been justified in recognizing the opposing party as the lawful government; or in treating as wrongdoers or insurgents the officers of the government which the President had recognized, and was prepared to support by an armed force. In the case of foreign nations, the government acknowledged by the President is always recognized in the courts of justice. And this principle has been applied by the act of Congress to the sovereign States of the Union.

It is said that this power in the President is dangerous to liberty, and may be abused. All power may be abused if placed in unworthy hands. But it would be difficult, we think, to point out any other hands in which this power would be more safe, and at the same time equally effectual. When citizens of the same State are in arms against each other, and the constituted authorities unable to execute the laws, the interposition of the United States must be prompt, or it is of little value. The ordinary course of proceedings in courts of justice would be utterly unfit for the crisis. And the elevated office of the President, chosen as he is by the people of the United States, and the high responsibility he could not fail to feel when acting in a case of so much moment, appear to furnish as strong safeguards against a wilful abuse of power as human prudence and foresight could well provide. At all events, it is conferred upon him by the Constitution and laws of the United States, and must therefore be respected and enforced in its judicial tribunals. . . .

The remaining question is whether the defendants, acting under military orders issued under the authority of the government, were justified in breaking and entering the plaintiff's house. In relation to the act of the legislature declaring martial law, it is not necessary in the case before us to inquire to what extent, nor under what circumstances, that power may be exercised by a State. Unquestionably a military government, established as the permanent government of the State, would not be a republican government, and it would be the duty of Congress to overthrow it. But the law of Rhode Island evidently contemplated no such government. It was intended merely for the crisis, and to meet the peril in which the existing government was placed by the armed resistance to its authority. It was so understood and construed by the State authorities. And, unquestionably, a State may use its military power to put down an armed insurrection, too strong to be controlled by the civil authority. The power is essential to the existence of every government, essential to the preservation of order and free institutions, and is as necessary to the States of this Union as to any other government. The State itself must determine what degree of force the crisis demands. And if the government of Rhode Island deemed the armed opposition so formidable, and so ramified throughout the State, as to require the use of its military force and the declaration of martial law, we see no ground upon which this court can question its authority. It was a state of war; and the established government resorted to the rights and usages of war to maintain itself, and to overcome the unlawful opposition. And in that state of things the officers engaged in its military service might lawfully arrest any one, who, from the information before them, they had reasonable grounds to believe was engaged in the insurrection; and might order a house to be forcibly entered and searched, when there were reasonable grounds for supposing he might be there concealed. Without the power to do this, martial law and the military array of the government would be mere parade, and rather encourage attack than repel it. No more force, however, can be used than is necessary to accomplish the object. And if the power is exercised for the purposes of oppression, or any injury wilfully done to person or property, the party by whom, or by whose order, it is committed would undoubtedly be answerable. . . .

Upon the whole, we see no reason for disturbing the judgment of the Circuit Court. . . . Much of the argument on the part of the plaintiff turned upon political rights and political questions, upon which the court has been urged to express an opinion. We decline doing so. The high power has been conferred on this court of passing judgment upon the acts of the State sovereignties, and of the legislative and executive branches of the federal government, and of determining whether they are beyond the limits of power marked out for them respectively by the Constitution of the United States. This tribunal, therefore, should be the last to overstep the boundaries which limit its own jurisdiction. And while it should always be ready to meet any question confided to it by the Constitution, it is equally its duty not to pass beyond its appropriate sphere of action, and to take care not to involve itself in discussions which properly belong to other forums. No one, we believe, has ever doubted the proposition, that, according to the institutions of this country, the sovereignty in every State resides in the people of the State, and that they may alter and change their form of government at their own pleasure. But whether they have changed it or not by abolishing an old government, and establishing a new one in its place, is a question to be settled by the political power. And when that power has decided, the courts are bound to take notice of its decision, and to follow it.

■ [JUSTICE WOODBURY's dissent is omitted.]

NOTES

1. At the start of the twentieth century, popular referenda and initiatives were introduced in many states by progressives. Some opponents said that government by referendum was not "a Republican Form of Government" because it did not provide the filter that is offered by representative democracy. But the Supreme Court refused to hear a Guarantee Clause challenge to because of the political question doctrine. Was the Court right?

2. In the late 1940s many states had failed to reapportion their congressional and state legislative districts for decades, leading to a situation where some districts had far more constituents than others. This malapportionment was challenged as violating the right of the people to "a Republican Form of Government." Again the Supreme Court refused to hear the case because of the political question doctrine. Was the Court right? A decade and a half later, the Supreme Court heard a challenge to the constitutionality of malapportionment under the Equal Protection Clause, and a majority of the justices ruled that the case did not raise a political question (over the spirited dissent of Justice Felix Frankfurter). Is malapportionment any different when challenged as a deprivation of equal protection than when it is challenged as a deprivation of a republican form of government? The case allowing the challenge to malapportionment to go forward was *Baker v. Carr*, 369 U.S. 186 (1962), and it is presented below in Chapter 8. It has become one of the most cited cases on the modern formulation of the political question doctrine, as you will see in the next case.

(Walter) Nixon v. United States

506 U.S. 224 (1993)

■ CHIEF JUSTICE REHNQUIST delivered the opinion of the Court.

Petitioner Walter L. Nixon, Jr., asks this Court to decide whether Senate Rule XI, which allows a committee of Senators to hear evidence against an individual who has been impeached and to report that evidence to the full Senate, violates the Impeachment Trial Clause, Art. I, § 3, cl. 6. That Clause provides that the "Senate shall have the sole Power to try all Impeachments." But before we reach the merits of such a claim, we must decide whether it is "justiciable," that is, whether it is a claim that may be resolved by the courts. We conclude that it is not.

Nixon, a former Chief Judge of the United States District Court for the Southern District of Mississippi, was convicted by a jury of two counts of making false statements before a federal grand jury and sentenced to prison. The grand jury investigation stemmed from reports that Nixon had accepted a gratuity from a Mississippi businessman in exchange for asking a local district attorney to halt the prosecution of the businessman's son. Because Nixon refused to resign from his office as a United States District Judge, he continued to collect his judicial salary while serving out his prison sentence.

On May 10, 1989, the House of Representatives adopted three articles of impeachment for high crimes and misdemeanors. The first two articles charged Nixon with giving false testimony before the grand jury and the third article charged him with bringing disrepute on the Federal Judiciary.

After the House presented the articles to the Senate, the Senate voted to invoke its own Impeachment Rule XI, under which the presiding officer appoints a committee of Senators to "receive evidence and take testimony." Senate Impeachment Rule XI. The Senate committee held four days of hearings, during which 10 witnesses, including Nixon, testified. Pursuant to Rule XI, the committee presented the full Senate with a complete transcript of the proceeding and a Report stating the uncontested facts and summarizing the evidence on the contested facts. Nixon and the House impeachment managers submitted extensive final briefs to the full Senate and delivered arguments from the Senate floor during the three hours set aside for oral argument in front of that body. Nixon himself gave a personal appeal, and several Senators posed questions directly to both parties. The Senate voted by more than the constitutionally required two-thirds majority to convict Nixon on the first two articles. The presiding officer then entered judgment removing Nixon from his office as United States District Judge.

Nixon thereafter commenced the present suit, arguing that Senate Rule XI violates the constitutional grant of authority to the Senate to "try" all impeachments because it prohibits the whole Senate from taking part in the evidentiary hearings. See Art. I, § 3, cl. 6. Nixon sought a declaratory judgment that his impeachment conviction was void and that his judicial salary and privileges should be reinstated. The District Court held that his claim was nonjusticiable, and the Court of Appeals for the District of Columbia Circuit agreed. We granted certiorari.

A controversy is nonjusticiable—*i.e.,* involves a political question— where there is "a textually demonstrable constitutional commitment of the issue to a coordinate political department; or a lack of judicially discoverable and manageable standards for resolving it. . . ." *Baker v. Carr,* 369 U.S. 186, 217 (1962). But the courts must, in the first instance, interpret the text in question and determine whether and to what extent the issue is textually committed. As the discussion that follows makes clear, the concept of a textual commitment to a coordinate political department is not completely separate from the concept of a lack of judicially discoverable and manageable standards for resolving it; the lack of judicially manageable standards may strengthen the conclusion that there is a textually demonstrable commitment to a coordinate branch.

In this case, we must examine Art. I, § 3, cl. 6, to determine the scope of authority conferred upon the Senate by the Framers regarding impeachment. It provides:

> The Senate shall have the sole Power to try all Impeachments. When sitting for that Purpose, they shall be on Oath or Affirmation. When the President of the United States is tried, the Chief Justice shall preside: And no Person shall be convicted without the Concurrence of two thirds of the Members present.

The language and structure of this Clause are revealing. The first sentence is a grant of authority to the Senate, and the word "sole" indicates that this authority is reposed in the Senate and nowhere else. The next two sentences specify requirements to which the Senate proceedings shall conform: The Senate shall be on oath or affirmation, a two-thirds vote is required to convict, and when the President is tried the Chief Justice shall preside.

Petitioner argues that the word "try" in the first sentence imposes by implication an additional requirement on the Senate in that the proceedings must be in the nature of a judicial trial. From there petitioner goes on to argue that this limitation precludes the Senate from delegating to a select committee the task of hearing the testimony of witnesses, as was done pursuant to Senate Rule XI. " '[T]ry' means more than simply 'vote on' or 'review' or 'judge.' In 1787 and today, trying a case means hearing the evidence, not scanning a cold record." Petitioner concludes from this that courts may review whether or not the Senate "tried" him before convicting him.

There are several difficulties with this position which lead us ultimately to reject it. The word "try," both in 1787 and later, has considerably broader meanings than those to which petitioner would limit it. Older dictionaries define try as "[t]o examine" or "[t]o examine as a judge." See 2 S. Johnson, A Dictionary of the English Language (1785). In more modern usage the term has various meanings. For example, try can mean "to examine or investigate judicially," "to conduct the trial of," or "to put to the test by experiment, investigation, or trial." Webster's Third New International Dictionary 2457 (1971). Petitioner submits that "try," as contained in T. Sheridan, Dictionary of the English Language (1796), means "to examine as a judge; to bring before a judicial tribunal." Based on the variety of definitions, however, we cannot say that the Framers used the word "try" as an implied limitation on the method by which the Senate might proceed in trying impeachments. . . .

The conclusion that the use of the word "try" in the first sentence of the Impeachment Trial Clause lacks sufficient precision to afford any judicially manageable standard of review of the Senate's actions is fortified by the existence of the three very specific requirements that the Constitution does impose on the Senate when trying impeachments: The Members must be under oath, a two-thirds vote is required to convict, and the Chief Justice presides when the President is tried. These limitations are quite precise, and their nature suggests that the Framers did not intend to impose additional limitations on the form of the Senate proceedings by the use of the word "try" in the first sentence.

Petitioner devotes only two pages in his brief to negating the significance of the word "sole" in the first sentence of Clause 6. As noted above, that sentence provides that "[t]he Senate shall have the sole Power to try all Impeachments." We think that the word "sole" is of considerable significance. Indeed, the word "sole" appears only one other time in the Constitution—with respect to the House of Representatives' *sole* Power of Impeachment." Art. I, § 2, cl. 5 (emphasis added). The commonsense meaning of the word "sole" is that the Senate alone shall have authority to determine whether an individual should be acquitted or convicted. The dictionary definition bears this out. "Sole" is defined as "having no companion," "solitary," "being the only one," and "functioning . . . independently and without assistance or interference." Webster's Third New International Dictionary 2168 (1971). If the courts may review the actions of the Senate in order to determine whether that body "tried" an impeached official, it is difficult to see how the Senate would be "functioning . . . independently and without assistance or interference."

Nixon asserts that the word "sole" has no substantive meaning. To support this contention, he argues that the word is nothing more than a mere "cosmetic edit" added by the Committee of Style after the delegates had approved the substance of the Impeachment Trial Clause. There are two difficulties with this argument. First, accepting as we must the proposition that the Committee of Style had no authority from the Convention to alter the meaning of the Clause, we must presume that the Committee's reorganization or rephrasing accurately captured what the Framers meant in their unadorned language. See *Powell v. McCormack,* 395 U.S., at 538– 539. That is, we must presume that the Committee did its job. This presumption is buttressed by the fact that the Constitutional Convention voted on, and accepted, the Committee of Style's linguistic version. We agree with the Government that "the word 'sole' is entitled to no less weight than any other word of the text, because the Committee revision perfected what 'had been agreed to.' " Second, carrying Nixon's argument to its logical conclusion would constrain us to say that the *second to last draft* would govern in every instance where the Committee of Style added an arguably substantive word. Such a result is at odds with the fact that the Convention passed the Committee's version, and with the well-established rule that the plain language of the enacted text is the best indicator of intent. . . .

Petitioner finally argues that even if significance be attributed to the word "sole" in the first sentence of the Clause, the authority granted is to the Senate, and this means that "the Senate—not the courts, not a lay jury, not a Senate Committee—shall try impeachments." It would be possible to read the first sentence of the Clause this way, but it is not a natural reading. Petitioner's interpretation would bring into judicial purview not merely the sort of claim made by petitioner, but other similar claims based on the conclusion that the word "Senate" has imposed by implication limitations on procedures which the Senate might adopt. . . .

The history and contemporary understanding of the impeachment provisions support our reading of the constitutional language. The parties do not offer evidence of a single word in the history of the Constitutional Convention or in contemporary commentary that even alludes to the possibility of judicial review in the context of the impeachment powers. This silence is quite meaningful in light of the several explicit references to the availability of judicial review as a check on the Legislature's power with respect to bills of attainder, *ex post facto* laws, and statutes. See The Federalist No. 78, p. 524 (J. Cooke ed. 1961).

The Framers labored over the question of where the impeachment power should lie. Significantly, in at least two considered scenarios the power was placed with the Federal Judiciary. See 1 Farrand 21–22 (Virginia Plan); *id.,* at 244 (New Jersey Plan). Indeed, James Madison and the Committee of Detail proposed that the Supreme Court should have the power to determine impeachments. Despite these proposals, the Convention ultimately decided that the Senate would have "the sole Power to try all Impeachments." Article I, § 3, cl. 6. According to Alexander Hamilton, the Senate was the "most fit depositary of this important trust" because its Members are representatives of the people. See The Federalist No. 65, p. 440 (J. Cooke ed. 1961). The Supreme Court was not the proper body because the Framers "doubted whether the members of that tribunal would, at all times, be endowed with so eminent a portion of fortitude as would be called for in the execution of so difficult a task" or whether the Court "would possess the degree of credit and authority" to carry out its judgment if it conflicted with the accusation brought by the Legislature—the people's representative. See *id.,* at 441. In addition, the Framers believed the Court was too small in number: "The awful discretion, which a court of impeachments must necessarily have, to doom to honor or to infamy the most confidential and the most distinguished characters of the community, forbids the commitment of the trust to a small number of persons." *Id.,* at 441–442.

There are two additional reasons why the Judiciary, and the Supreme Court in particular, were not chosen to have any role in impeachments. First, the Framers recognized that most likely there would be two sets of proceedings for individuals who commit impeachable offenses—the impeachment trial and a separate criminal trial. In fact, the Constitution explicitly provides for two separate proceedings. See Art. I, § 3, cl. 7. The Framers deliberately separated the two forums to avoid raising the specter of bias and to ensure independent judgments. . . .

Second, judicial review would be inconsistent with the Framers' insistence that our system be one of checks and balances. In our constitutional system, impeachment was designed to be the *only* check on the Judicial Branch by the Legislature. . . . Judicial involvement in impeachment proceedings, even if only for purposes of judicial review, is counterintuitive because it would eviscerate the "important constitutional check" placed on the Judiciary by the Framers. Nixon's argument would place final reviewing authority with respect to impeachments in the hands of the same body that the impeachment process is meant to regulate.

Nevertheless, Nixon argues that judicial review is necessary in order to place a check on the Legislature. Nixon fears that if the Senate is given unreviewable authority to interpret the Impeachment Trial Clause, there is a grave risk that the Senate will usurp judicial power. The Framers anticipated this objection and created two constitutional safeguards to keep the Senate in check. The first safeguard is that the whole of the impeachment power is divided between the two legislative bodies, with the House given the right to accuse and the Senate given the right to judge. This split of authority "avoids the inconvenience of making the same persons both accusers and judges; and guards against the danger of persecution from the prevalency of a factious spirit in either of those branches." The second safeguard is the two-thirds supermajority vote requirement. Hamilton explained that "[a]s the concurrence of two-thirds of the senate will be requisite to a condemnation, the security to innocence, from this additional circumstance, will be as complete as itself can desire."

In addition to the textual commitment argument, we are persuaded that the lack of finality and the difficulty of fashioning relief counsel against justiciability. See *Baker v. Carr,* 369 U.S., at 210. We agree with the Court of Appeals that opening the door of judicial review to the procedures used by the Senate in trying impeachments would "expose the political life of the country to months, or perhaps years, of chaos." This lack of finality would manifest itself most dramatically if the President were impeached. The legitimacy of any successor, and hence his effectiveness, would be impaired severely, not merely while the judicial process was running its course, but during any retrial that a differently constituted Senate might conduct if its first judgment of conviction were invalidated. Equally uncertain is the question of what relief a court may give other than simply setting aside the judgment of conviction. Could it order the reinstatement of a convicted federal judge, or order Congress to create an additional judgeship if the seat had been filled in the interim?

Petitioner finally contends that a holding of nonjusticiability cannot be reconciled with our opinion in *Powell v. McCormack,* 395 U.S. 486 (1969). The relevant issue in *Powell* was whether courts could review the House of Representatives' conclusion that Powell was "unqualified" to sit as a Member because he had been accused of misappropriating public funds and abusing the process of the New York courts. We stated that the question of justiciability turned on whether the Constitution committed authority to the House to judge its Members' qualifications, and if so, the extent of that commitment. Article I, § 5, provides that "Each House shall be the Judge of the Elections, Returns and Qualifications of its own Members." In turn, Art. I, § 2, specifies three requirements for membership in the House: The candidate must be at least 25 years of age, a citizen of the United States for no less than seven years, and an inhabitant of the State he is chosen to represent. We held that, in light of the three requirements specified in the Constitution, the word "qualifications"—of which the House was to be the Judge—was of a precise, limited nature. . . .

In the case before us, there is no separate provision of the Constitution that could be defeated by allowing the Senate final authority to determine the meaning of the word "try" in the Impeachment Trial Clause. We agree with Nixon that courts possess power to review either legislative or executive action that transgresses identifiable textual limits. As we have made clear, "whether the action of [either the Legislative or Executive Branch] exceeds whatever authority has been committed, is itself a delicate exercise in constitutional interpretation, and is a responsibility of this Court as ultimate interpreter of the Constitution." *Baker v. Carr*, *supra*, 369 U.S., at 211. But we conclude, after exercising that delicate responsibility, that the word "try" in the Impeachment Trial Clause does not provide an identifiable textual limit on the authority which is committed to the Senate.

■ JUSTICE STEVENS, concurring.

For me, the debate about the strength of the inferences to be drawn from the use of the words "sole" and "try" is far less significant than the central fact that the Framers decided to assign the impeachment power to the Legislative Branch. The disposition of the impeachment of Samuel Chase in 1805 demonstrated that the Senate is fully conscious of the profound importance of that assignment, and nothing in the subsequent history of the Senate's exercise of this extraordinary power suggests otherwise. See generally 3 A. Beveridge, The Life of John Marshall 169–222 (1919); W. Rehnquist, Grand Inquests 275–278 (1992). Respect for a coordinate branch of the Government forecloses any assumption that improbable hypotheticals like those mentioned by Justice WHITE and Justice SOUTER will ever occur. Accordingly, the wise policy of judicial restraint, coupled with the potential anomalies associated with a contrary view, provide a sufficient justification for my agreement with the views of THE CHIEF JUSTICE.

■ JUSTICE WHITE, with whom JUSTICE BLACKMUN joins, concurring in the judgment.

Petitioner contends that the method by which the Senate convicted him on two articles of impeachment violates Art. I, § 3, cl. 6, of the Constitution, which mandates that the Senate "try" impeachments. The Court is of the view that the Constitution forbids us even to consider his contention. I find no such prohibition and would therefore reach the merits of the claim. I concur in the judgment because the Senate fulfilled its constitutional obligation to "try" petitioner.

It should be said at the outset that, as a practical matter, it will likely make little difference whether the Court's or my view controls this case. This is so because the Senate has very wide discretion in specifying impeachment trial procedures and because it is extremely unlikely that the Senate would abuse its discretion and insist on a procedure that could not be deemed a trial by reasonable judges. Even taking a wholly practical approach, I would prefer not to announce an unreviewable discretion in the Senate to ignore completely the constitutional direction to "try" impeachment cases. When asked at oral argument whether that direction would be satisfied if, after a House vote to impeach, the Senate, without any procedure whatsoever, unanimously found the accused guilty of being "a bad guy," counsel for the United States answered that the Government's theory "leads me to answer that question yes." Especially in light of this advice from the Solicitor General, I would not issue an invitation to the Senate to find an excuse, in the name of other pressing business, to be dismissive of its critical role in the impeachment process. . . .

[T]he issue in the political question doctrine is *not* whether the constitutional text commits exclusive responsibility for a particular governmental function to one of the political branches. There are numerous instances of this sort of textual commitment, *e.g.*, Art. I, § 8, and it is not thought that disputes implicating these provisions are nonjusticiable. Rather, the issue is whether the Constitution has given one of the political branches final responsibility for interpreting the scope and nature of such a power. . . .

The courts therefore are usually left to infer the presence of a political question from the text and structure of the Constitution. In drawing the inference that the Constitution has committed final interpretive authority to one of the political branches, courts are sometimes aided by textual evidence that the Judiciary was not meant to exercise judicial review—a coordinate inquiry expressed in *Baker*'s "lack of judicially discoverable and manageable standards" criterion.

The majority finds a clear textual commitment in the Constitution's use of the word "sole" in the phrase "[t]he Senate shall have the sole Power to try all Impeachments." It attributes "considerable significance" to the fact that this term appears in only one other passage in the Constitution. The Framers' sparing use of "sole" is thought to indicate that its employment in the Impeachment Trial Clause demonstrates a concern to give the Senate exclusive interpretive authority over the Clause.

. . . The significance of the Constitution's use of the term "sole" lies not in the infrequency with which the term appears, but in the fact that it appears exactly twice, in parallel provisions concerning impeachment. That the word "sole" is found only in the House and Senate Impeachment Clauses demonstrates that its purpose is to emphasize the distinct role of each in the impeachment process. As the majority notes, the Framers, following English practice, were very much concerned to separate the prosecutorial from the adjudicative aspects of impeachment. *Ante,* at 739 (citing The Federalist No. 66, p. 446 (J. Cooke ed. 1961)). Giving each House "sole" power with respect to its role in impeachments effected this division of labor. . . .

The majority's review of the historical record . . . explains why the power to try impeachments properly resides with the Senate. It does not explain, however, the sweeping statement that the Judiciary was "not chosen to have any role in impeachments." Not a single word in the historical materials cited by the majority addresses judicial review of the Impeachment Trial Clause. . . .

What the relevant history mainly reveals is deep ambivalence among many of the Framers over the very institution of impeachment, which, by its nature, is not easily reconciled with our system of checks and balances. As they clearly recognized, the branch of the Federal Government which is possessed of the authority to try impeachments, by having final say over the membership of each branch, holds a potentially unanswerable power over the others. In addition, that branch, insofar as it is called upon to try not only members of other branches, but also its own, will have the advantage of being the judge of its own members' causes. . . .

The historical evidence reveals above all else that the Framers were deeply concerned about placing in any branch the "awful discretion, which a court of impeachments must necessarily have." The Federalist No. 65, p. 441 (J. Cooke ed. 1961). . . .

The majority also contends that the term "try" does not present a judicially manageable standard. It notes that in 1787, as today, the word "try" may refer to an inquiry in the nature of a judicial proceeding, or, more generally, to experimentation or investigation. In light of the term's multiple senses, the Court finds itself unable to conclude that the Framers used the word "try" as "an implied limitation on the method by which the Senate might proceed in trying impeachments." . . .

To begin with, one would intuitively expect that, in defining the power of a political body to conduct an inquiry into official wrongdoing, the Framers used "try" in its legal sense. That intuition is borne out by reflection on the alternatives. The third Clause of Art. I, § 3, cannot seriously be read to mean that the Senate shall "attempt" or "experiment with" impeachments. It is equally implausible to say that the Senate is charged with "investigating" impeachments given that this description would substantially overlap with the House of Representatives' "sole" power to draw up articles of impeachment. That these alternatives are not realistic possibilities is finally evidenced by the use of "tried" in the third sentence of the Impeachment Trial Clause ("[w]hen the President of the United States is tried . . ."), and by Art. III, § 2, cl. 3 ("[t]he Trial of all Crimes, except in Cases of Impeachment . . .").

The other variant of the majority position focuses not on which sense of "try" is employed in the Impeachment Trial Clause, but on whether the legal sense of that term creates a judicially manageable standard. The majority concludes that the term provides no "identifiable textual limit." Yet, as the Government itself conceded at oral argument, the term "try" is hardly so elusive as the majority would have it. Were the Senate, for example, to adopt the practice of automatically entering a judgment of conviction whenever articles of impeachment were delivered from the House, it is quite clear that the Senate will have failed to "try" impeachments.[2] Indeed in this respect, "try" presents no greater, and perhaps fewer, interpretive difficulties than some other constitutional standards that have been found amenable to familiar techniques of judicial construction, including, for example, "Commerce . . . among the several States."

The majority's conclusion that "try" is incapable of meaningful judicial construction is not without irony. One might think that if any class of concepts would fall within the definitional abilities of the Judiciary, it would be that class having to do with procedural justice. . . .

■ JUSTICE SOUTER, concurring in the judgment.

---

[2] It is not a sufficient rejoinder to this example to say, with one of the Court of Appeals judges below, that it postulates a "monstrous hypothetical abuse." The unlikelihood of the example being realized does not undermine the point that "try" has a definable meaning and thus ought to be regarded as judicially manageable.

I agree with the Court that this case presents a nonjusticiable political question. Because my analysis differs somewhat from the Court's, however, I concur in its judgment by this separate opinion.

As we cautioned in *Baker v. Carr,* 369 U.S. 186, 210–211 (1962), "the 'political question' label" tends "to obscure the need for case-by-case inquiry." The need for such close examination is nevertheless clear from our precedents, which demonstrate that the functional nature of the political question doctrine requires analysis of "the precise facts and posture of the particular case," and precludes "resolution by any semantic cataloguing," *id.,* at 217:

> Prominent on the surface of any case held to involve a political question is found a textually demonstrable constitutional commitment of the issue to a coordinate political department; or a lack of judicially discoverable and manageable standards for resolving it; or the impossibility of deciding without an initial policy determination of a kind clearly for nonjudicial discretion; or the impossibility of a court's undertaking independent resolution without expressing lack of the respect due coordinate branches of government; or an unusual need for unquestioning adherence to a political decision already made; or the potentiality of embarrassment from multifarious pronouncements by various departments on one question.

Whatever considerations feature most prominently in a particular case, the political question doctrine is "essentially a function of the separation of powers," *ibid.,* existing to restrain courts "from inappropriate interference in the business of the other branches of Government," and deriving in large part from prudential concerns about the respect we owe the political departments. Not all interference is inappropriate or disrespectful, however, and application of the doctrine ultimately turns, as Learned Hand put it, on "how importunately the occasion demands an answer." L. Hand, The Bill of Rights 15 (1958).

This occasion does not demand an answer. . . . It seems fair to conclude that the Clause contemplates that the Senate may determine, within broad boundaries, such subsidiary issues as the procedures for receipt and consideration of evidence necessary to satisfy its duty to "try" impeachments. . . . As the Court observes, judicial review of an impeachment trial would under the best of circumstances entail significant disruption of government.

One can, nevertheless, envision different and unusual circumstances that might justify a more searching review of impeachment proceedings. If the Senate were to act in a manner seriously threatening the integrity of its results, convicting, say, upon a coin toss, or upon a summary determination that an officer of the United States was simply "a bad guy," judicial interference might well be appropriate. In such circumstances, the Senate's action might be so far beyond the scope of its constitutional authority, and the consequent impact on the Republic so great, as to merit a judicial response despite the prudential concerns that would ordinarily counsel silence. . . .

NOTES

1. Which of the opinions above do you agree with? Is the answer that practice has established that Congress has the last word on impeachments? It is true that whoever has the last word can do something monstrous. Is there any more reason to fear the Court having the last word on impeachments, given

that this is one of the few constitutional checks that the Constitution gives the political branches against the federal courts?

2. What is the practical difference between the holding of the majority in *Nixon* that the case presents a "nonjusticiable" political question and a holding "on the merits" that the Senate's action was within the scope of its constitutional powers? Is there any? Are all (or many) political question holdings really just merits holdings in disguise? Consider in this regard the first two aspects of the political question doctrine. How is a holding that an issue is "textually committed" to a political branch any different from a straightforward holding on the merits that the action of the political branch was not unconstitutional, because within the sphere of its discretion to act? How is a holding that there are no "judicially discoverable and manageable standards" for resolving an issue any different from a straightforward holding, on the merits, that the Constitution does not supply a rule invalidating the decision of the political branches and thus was not unconstitutional?

3. What about the other factors listed in standard formulations of the political question doctrine: "the impossibility of a court's undertaking independent resolution without expressing lack of the respect due coordinate branches of government; or an unusual need for unquestioning adherence to a political decision already made; or the potentiality of embarrassment from multifarious pronouncements by various departments on one question." *Baker v. Carr,* 369 U.S. 186, 217 (1962). Are these considerations appropriate grounds for refusal to decide a case on the merits, where the issue is (by hypothesis) *not* textually committed to the judgment of the political branches and where the Constitution *does* supply a rule or standard that the political branches action violates?

[*Assignment 28*]

D. STRUCTURE AND JURISDICTION OF THE FEDERAL COURTS:
"SHALL BE VESTED IN . . . WITH SUCH EXCEPTIONS"

So far we have been considering the nature of "the judicial Power" under the Constitution, the independence of the judiciary, and limitations on the proper scope of the judicial power to cases and controversies of a judicial nature. We turn now to a second set of structural questions concerning Article III: What is the constitutionally prescribed *jurisdiction* of the federal courts? To what types of cases does "the judicial Power of the United States" extend? What is the scope of Congress's power to structure the system of national courts and to prescribe or limit the federal courts' jurisdiction? What is the relationship between state courts and federal courts?

We begin with Alexander Hamilton's treatment of the structure of the federal judiciary under the Constitution, set forth in *The Federalist No. 81,* then turn to questions of Congress's power to prescribe, regulate, and make exceptions to—and perhaps manipulate—the jurisdiction of the lower federal courts and the appellate jurisdiction of the U.S. Supreme Court.

The Federalist No. 81

Alexander Hamilton, June 25 & 28, 1788

LET US now return to the partition of the judiciary authority between different courts, and their relations to each other,

"The judicial power of the United States is" (by the plan of the convention) "to be vested in one Supreme Court, and in such inferior courts as the Congress may, from time to time, ordain and establish." [Article III, Section 1]

That there ought to be one court of supreme and final jurisdiction, is a proposition which is not likely to be contested. The reasons for it have been assigned in another place, and are too obvious to need repetition. The only question that seems to have been raised concerning it, is, whether it ought to be a distinct body or a branch of the legislature. The same contradiction is observable in regard to this matter which has been remarked in several other cases. The very men who object to the Senate as a court of impeachments, on the ground of an improper intermixture of powers, advocate, by implication at least, the propriety of vesting the ultimate decision of all causes, in the whole or in a part of the legislative body.

The arguments, or rather suggestions, upon which this charge is founded, are to this effect: "The authority of the proposed Supreme Court of the United States, which is to be a separate and independent body, will be superior to that of the legislature. The power of construing the laws according to the SPIRIT of the Constitution, will enable that court to mould them into whatever shape it may think proper; especially as its decisions will not be in any manner subject to the revision or correction of the legislative body. This is as unprecedented as it is dangerous. In Britain, the judicial power, in the last resort, resides in the House of Lords, which is a branch of the legislature; and this part of the British government has been imitated in the State constitutions in general. The Parliament of Great Britain, and the legislatures of the several States, can at any time rectify, by law, the exceptionable decisions of their respective courts. But the errors and usurpations of the Supreme Court of the United States will be uncontrollable and remediless." This, upon examination, will be found to be made up altogether of false reasoning upon misconceived fact.

In the first place, there is not a syllable in the plan under consideration which DIRECTLY empowers the national courts to construe the laws according to the spirit of the Constitution, or which gives them any greater latitude in this respect than may be claimed by the courts of every State. I admit, however, that the Constitution ought to be the standard of construction for the laws, and that wherever there is an evident opposition, the laws ought to give place to the Constitution. But this doctrine is not deducible from any circumstance peculiar to the plan of the convention, but from the general theory of a limited Constitution; and as far as it is true, is equally applicable to most, if not to all the State governments. There can be no objection, therefore, on this account, to the federal judicature which will not lie against the local judicatures in general, and which will not serve to condemn every constitution that attempts to set bounds to legislative discretion.

But perhaps the force of the objection may be thought to consist in the particular organization of the Supreme Court; in its being composed of a distinct body of magistrates, instead of being one of the branches of the legislature, as in the government of Great Britain and that of the State. To insist upon this point, the authors of the objection must renounce the meaning they have labored to annex to the celebrated maxim, requiring a separation of the departments of power. It shall, nevertheless, be conceded to them, agreeably to the interpretation given to that maxim in the course of these papers, that it is not violated by vesting the ultimate power of judging in a PART of the legislative body. But though this be not an absolute violation of that excellent rule, yet it verges so nearly upon it, as on this account alone to be less eligible than the mode preferred by the convention. From a body which had even a partial agency in passing bad laws, we could rarely expect a disposition to temper and moderate them in the application. The same spirit which had operated in making them, would be too apt in interpreting them; still less could it be expected that men who had infringed the Constitution in the character of legislators, would be disposed to repair the breach in the character of judges. Nor is this all. Every reason which recommends the tenure of good behavior for judicial offices, militates against placing the judiciary power, in the last resort, in a body composed of men chosen for a limited period. There is an absurdity in referring the determination of causes, in the first instance, to judges of permanent standing; in the last, to those of a temporary and mutable constitution. And there is a still greater absurdity in subjecting the decisions of men, selected for their knowledge of the laws, acquired by long and laborious study, to the revision and control of men who, for want of the same advantage, cannot but be deficient in that knowledge. The members of the legislature will rarely be chosen with a view to those qualifications which fit men for the stations of judges; and as, on this account, there will be great reason to apprehend all the ill consequences of defective information, so, on account of the natural propensity of such bodies to party divisions, there will be no less reason to fear that the pestilential breath of faction may poison the fountains of justice. The habit of being continually marshalled on opposite sides will be too apt to stifle the voice both of law and of equity.

These considerations teach us to applaud the wisdom of those States who have committed the judicial power, in the last resort, not to a part of the legislature, but to distinct and independent bodies of men. Contrary to the supposition of those who have represented the plan of the convention, in this respect, as novel and unprecedented, it is but a copy of the constitutions of New Hampshire, Massachusetts, Pennsylvania, Delaware, Maryland, Virginia, North Carolina, South Carolina, and Georgia; and the preference which has been given to those models is highly to be commended.

It is not true, in the second place, that the Parliament of Great Britain, or the legislatures of the particular States, can rectify the exceptionable decisions of their respective courts, in any other sense than might be done by a future legislature of the United States. The theory, neither of the British, nor the State constitutions, authorizes the revisal of a judicial sentence by a legislative act. Nor is there any thing in the proposed Constitution, more than in either of them, by which it is forbidden. In the former, as well as in the latter, the impropriety of the thing, on the general principles of law and reason, is the sole obstacle. A legislature, without exceeding its province, cannot reverse a determination once made in a particular case; though it may prescribe a new rule for future cases. This is the principle, and it applies in all its consequences, exactly in the same manner and extent, to the State governments, as to the national government now under consideration. Not the least difference can be pointed out in any view of the subject.

It may in the last place be observed that the supposed danger of judiciary encroachments on the legislative authority, which has been upon many occasions reiterated, is in reality a phantom. Particular misconstructions and contraventions of the will of the legislature may now and then happen; but they can never be so extensive as to amount to an inconvenience, or in any sensible degree to affect the order of the political system. This may be inferred with certainty, from the general nature of the judicial power, from the objects to which it relates, from the manner in which it is exercised, from its comparative weakness, and from its total incapacity to support its usurpations by force. And the inference is greatly fortified by the consideration of the important constitutional check which the power of instituting impeachments in one part of the legislative body, and of determining upon them in the other, would give to that body upon the members of the judicial department. This is alone a complete security. There never can be danger that the judges, by a series of deliberate usurpations on the authority of the legislature, would hazard the united resentment of the body intrusted with it, while this body was possessed of the means of punishing their presumption, by degrading them from their stations. While this ought to remove all apprehensions on the subject, it affords, at the same time, a cogent argument for constituting the Senate a court for the trial of impeachments.

Having now examined, and, I trust, removed the objections to the distinct and independent organization of the Supreme Court, I proceed to consider the propriety of the power of constituting inferior courts,[2] and the relations which will subsist between these and the former.

The power of constituting inferior courts is evidently calculated to obviate the necessity of having recourse to the Supreme Court in every case of federal cognizance. It is intended to enable the national government to institute or AUTHORIZE, in each State or district of the United States, a tribunal competent to the determination of matters of national jurisdiction within its limits.

But why, it is asked, might not the same purpose have been accomplished by the instrumentality of the State courts? This admits of different answers. Though the fitness and competency of those courts should be allowed in the utmost latitude, yet the substance of the power in question may still be regarded as a necessary part of the plan, if it were only to empower the national legislature to commit to them the cognizance of causes arising out of the national Constitution. To confer the power of determining such causes upon the existing courts of the several States, would perhaps be as much "to constitute tribunals," as to create new courts with the like power. But ought not a more direct and explicit provision to have been made in favor of the State courts? There are, in my opinion, substantial reasons against such a provision: the most discerning cannot foresee how far the prevalency of a local spirit may be found to disqualify the local tribunals for the jurisdiction of national causes; whilst every man may discover, that courts constituted like those of some of the States would be improper channels of the judicial authority of the Union. State judges, holding

---

[2] This power has been absurdly represented as intended to abolish all the county courts in the several States, which are commonly called inferior courts. But the expressions of the Constitution are, to constitute "tribunals INFERIOR TO THE SUPREME COURT"; and the evident design of the provision is to enable the institution of local courts, subordinate to the Supreme, either in States or larger districts. It is ridiculous to imagine that county courts were in contemplation.

their offices during pleasure, or from year to year, will be too little independent to be relied upon for an inflexible execution of the national laws. And if there was a necessity for confiding the original cognizance of causes arising under those laws to them there would be a correspondent necessity for leaving the door of appeal as wide as possible. In proportion to the grounds of confidence in, or distrust of, the subordinate tribunals, ought to be the facility or difficulty of appeals. And well satisfied as I am of the propriety of the appellate jurisdiction, in the several classes of causes to which it is extended by the plan of the convention. I should consider every thing calculated to give, in practice, an UNRESTRAINED COURSE to appeals, as a source of public and private inconvenience.

I am not sure, but that it will be found highly expedient and useful, to divide the United States into four or five or half a dozen districts; and to institute a federal court in each district, in lieu of one in every State. The judges of these courts, with the aid of the State judges, may hold circuits for the trial of causes in the several parts of the respective districts. Justice through them may be administered with ease and despatch; and appeals may be safely circumscribed within a narrow compass. This plan appears to me at present the most eligible of any that could be adopted; and in order to it, it is necessary that the power of constituting inferior courts should exist in the full extent in which it is to be found in the proposed Constitution.

These reasons seem sufficient to satisfy a candid mind, that the want of such a power would have been a great defect in the plan. Let us now examine in what manner the judicial authority is to be distributed between the supreme and the inferior courts of the Union.

The Supreme Court is to be invested with original jurisdiction, only "in cases affecting ambassadors, other public ministers, and consuls, and those in which A STATE shall be a party." Public ministers of every class are the immediate representatives of their sovereigns. All questions in which they are concerned are so directly connected with the public peace, that, as well for the preservation of this, as out of respect to the sovereignties they represent, it is both expedient and proper that such questions should be submitted in the first instance to the highest judicatory of the nation. Though consuls have not in strictness a diplomatic character, yet as they are the public agents of the nations to which they belong, the same observation is in a great measure applicable to them. In cases in which a State might happen to be a party, it would ill suit its dignity to be turned over to an inferior tribunal.

Though it may rather be a digression from the immediate subject of this paper, I shall take occasion to mention here a supposition which has excited some alarm upon very mistaken grounds. It has been suggested that an assignment of the public securities of one State to the citizens of another, would enable them to prosecute that State in the federal courts for the amount of those securities; a suggestion which the following considerations prove to be without foundation.

It is inherent in the nature of sovereignty not to be amenable to the suit of an individual WITHOUT ITS CONSENT. This is the general sense, and the general practice of mankind; and the exemption, as one of the attributes of sovereignty, is now enjoyed by the government of every State in the Union. Unless, therefore, there is a surrender of this immunity in the plan of the convention, it will remain with the States, and the danger intimated must be merely ideal. The circumstances which are necessary to produce an alienation of State sovereignty were discussed in considering the article of taxation, and need not be repeated here. A recurrence to the principles there established will satisfy us, that there is no color to pretend that the State governments would, by the adoption of that plan, be divested of the privilege of paying their own debts in their own way, free from every constraint but that which flows from the obligations of good faith. The contracts between a nation and individuals are only binding on the conscience of the sovereign, and have no pretensions to a compulsive force. They confer no right of action, independent of the sovereign will. To what purpose would it be to authorize suits against States for the debts they owe? How could recoveries be enforced? It is evident, it could not be done without waging war against the contracting State; and to ascribe to the federal courts, by mere implication, and in destruction of a pre-existing right of the State governments, a power which would involve such a consequence, would be altogether forced and unwarrantable.

Let us resume the train of our observations. We have seen that the original jurisdiction of the Supreme Court would be confined to two classes of causes, and those of a nature rarely to occur. In all other cases of federal cognizance, the original jurisdiction would appertain to the inferior tribunals; and the Supreme Court would have nothing more than an appellate jurisdiction, "with such EXCEPTIONS and under such REGULATIONS as the Congress shall make."

The propriety of this appellate jurisdiction has been scarcely called in question in regard to matters of law; but the clamors have been loud against it as applied to matters of fact. Some well-intentioned men in this State, deriving their notions from the language and forms which obtain in our courts, have been induced to consider it as an implied supersedure of the trial by jury, in favor of the civil-law mode of trial, which prevails in our courts of admiralty, probate, and chancery. A technical sense has been affixed to the term "appellate," which, in our law parlance, is commonly used in reference to appeals in the course of the civil law. But if I am not misinformed, the same meaning would not be given to it in any part of New England. There an appeal from one jury to another, is familiar both in language and practice, and is even a matter of course, until there have been two verdicts on one side. The word "appellate," therefore, will not be understood in the same sense in New England as in New York, which shows the impropriety of a technical interpretation derived from the jurisprudence of any particular State. The expression, taken in the abstract, denotes nothing more than the power of one tribunal to review the proceedings of another, either as to the law or fact, or both. The mode of doing it may depend on ancient custom or legislative provision (in a new government it must depend on the latter), and may be with or without the aid of a jury, as may be judged advisable. If, therefore, the re-examination of a fact once determined by a jury, should in any case be admitted under the proposed Constitution, it may be so regulated as to be done by a second jury, either by remanding the cause to the court below for a second trial of the fact, or by directing an issue immediately out of the Supreme Court.

But it does not follow that the re-examination of a fact once ascertained by a jury, will be permitted in the Supreme Court. Why may not it be said, with the strictest propriety, when a writ of error is brought from an inferior to a superior court of law in this State, that the latter has jurisdiction of the fact as well as the law? It is true it cannot institute a new inquiry concerning the fact, but it takes cognizance of it as it appears upon the record, and pronounces the law arising upon it.[3] This is jurisdiction of both fact and law; nor is it even possible to separate them. Though the common-law courts of this State ascertain disputed facts by a jury, yet they unquestionably have jurisdiction of both fact and law; and accordingly when the former is agreed in the pleadings, they have no recourse to a jury, but proceed at once to judgment. I contend, therefore, on this ground, that the expressions, "appellate jurisdiction, both as to law and fact," do not necessarily imply a re-examination in the Supreme Court of facts decided by juries in the inferior courts.

The following train of ideas may well be imagined to have influenced the convention, in relation to this particular provision. The appellate jurisdiction of the Supreme Court (it may have been argued) will extend to causes determinable in different modes, some in the course of the COMMON LAW, others in the course of the CIVIL LAW. In the former, the revision of the law only will be, generally speaking, the proper province of the Supreme Court; in the latter, the re-examination of the fact is agreeable to usage, and in some cases, of which prize causes are an example, might be essential to the preservation of the public peace. It is therefore necessary that the appellate jurisdiction should, in certain cases, extend in the broadest sense to matters of fact. It will not answer to make an express exception of cases which shall have been originally tried by a jury, because in the courts of some of the States ALL CAUSES are tried in this mode[4]; and such an exception would preclude the revision of matters of fact, as well where it might be proper, as where it might be improper. To avoid all inconveniencies, it will be safest to declare generally, that the Supreme Court shall possess appellate jurisdiction both as to law and FACT, and that this jurisdiction shall be subject to such EXCEPTIONS and regulations as the national legislature may prescribe. This will enable the government to modify it in such a manner as will best answer the ends of public justice and security.

This view of the matter, at any rate, puts it out of all doubt that the supposed ABOLITION of the trial by jury, by the operation of this provision, is fallacious and untrue. The legislature of the United States would certainly have full power to provide, that in appeals to the Supreme Court there should be no re-examination of facts where they had been tried in the original causes by juries. This would certainly be an authorized exception; but if, for the reason already intimated, it should be thought too extensive, it might be qualified with a limitation to such causes only as are determinable at common law in that mode of trial.

The amount of the observations hitherto made on the authority of the judicial department is this: that it has been carefully restricted to those causes which are manifestly proper for the cognizance of the national judicature; that in the partition of this authority a very small portion of original jurisdiction has been preserved to the Supreme Court, and the rest consigned to the subordinate tribunals; that the Supreme Court will possess an appellate jurisdiction, both as to law and fact, in all the cases referred to them, both subject to any EXCEPTIONS and REGULATIONS which may be thought advisable; that this appellate jurisdiction does, in no case, ABOLISH the trial by jury; and that an ordinary degree of prudence and integrity in the national councils will insure us solid advantages from the establish-

---

[3] This word is composed of JUS and DICTIO, juris dictio or a speaking and pronouncing of the law.

[4] I hold that the States will have concurrent jurisdiction with the subordinate federal judicatories, in many cases of federal cognizance, as will be explained in my next paper.

ment of the proposed judiciary, without exposing us to any of the inconveniences which have been predicted from that source.

PUBLIUS.

NOTES

1. In this paper, Hamilton is (in part) responding to the arguments of the Anti–Federalist writer "Brutus" that the Supreme Court's jurisdiction and authority will give it complete power to "mould" the Constitution "into whatever shape it may think proper" and that its decisions will be subject to no constraints. (Recall the discussion of this issue in Chapter 2.) How does Hamilton answer this charge? What does he say about the *manner* in which the Constitution should be construed by courts? What does he say about the *checks* that exist on perceived abuse of judicial power? Does *The Federalist No. 81* actually contemplate impeachment of judges for abuse of judicial power?

2. *The Federalist No. 81* lays out the structure of the national judiciary and the ways in which Article III permits Congress a degree of discretion over the existence and precise arrangement of federal courts, as well as over their jurisdiction. (This theme is continued in *The Federalist No. 82.*) What does Hamilton say about lower federal courts and their relationship to state courts? What does he say about the jurisdiction of the Supreme Court? About the scope of Congress's power to make "Exceptions" to that jurisdiction?

3. You may have noticed discussion of the question of appellate jurisdiction over both "law and fact"—a controversial issue at the time, as many feared the power of appellate courts to undo the verdicts of juries, which were regarded as important checks on overweening government power. The concerns that Hamilton was trying to calm ultimately became the subject of the Seventh Amendment, preserving jury trial in many civil cases and prohibiting judicial re-examination of certain facts determined by juries.

4. Finally, note Hamilton's self-conscious digression into a discussion of traditional doctrines of state "sovereign immunity" from suit. His argument appears to be that a grant of *jurisdiction* over certain types of suits—including suits where states are a party—does not itself alter common law rules of *substantive law* concerning principles of sovereign immunity. Does this seem right? Confusion over this question produced one of the Supreme Court's most controversial decisions concerning the jurisdiction and power of the national courts, *Chisholm v. Georgia,* 2 U.S. 419 (1793), and the Eleventh Amendment, which was the very first amendment to the Constitution after the Bill of Rights. These issues will be considered later in this chapter.

A NOTE ON CONGRESS'S AUTHORITY OVER FEDERAL JURISDICTION

The power of Congress with respect to the jurisdiction of the federal courts has long been a source of controversy. Efforts to pass so-called "jurisdiction-stripping" bills have been around for a long time. In the 1820s, some congressional Democrats noisily argued that the Supreme Court should be stripped of its power to hear appeals from the highest court of a state because those members of Congress disapproved of the Marshall Court's decisions emphasizing federal power. After the Civil War, congressional Republicans became very concerned that Reconstruction might be held unconstitutional in a case that was before the Supreme Court, *Ex parte McCardle*. The case had already been briefed and argued, but Congress stripped the Court of jurisdiction to decide the case (even overriding a veto of President Johnson in order to do so). You will see what result Congress's actions had when you read *McCardle*, which is presented below. Jurisdiction-stripping bills have been introduced in Congress in the modern era as well. Southern segregationist members of Congress tried to strip the federal courts of jurisdiction in school desegregation cases. And conservatives such as former Senator Jesse Helms tried in the late 1970s and 1980s to strip the federal courts of jurisdiction to hear abortion and school prayer cases. None of the modern measures ever passed, in part because of serious doubts as to their constitutionality.

In analyzing congressional power over jurisdiction, it is necessary to separate congressional power over the jurisdiction of the inferior federal courts from congressional power over the Supreme Court's jurisdiction. We take up each issue separately in this introductory note, then turn to the two leading Supreme Court cases that best illustrate each of these areas. We then conclude with an extensive note on a major recent case in which the Court struck down a congressional statute eliminating the federal courts' jurisdiction to issue writs of habeas corpus for enemy alien war combatants detained by the U.S. military outside of the United States, *Boumediene v. Bush*, 553 U.S. 723 (2008).

a. *Congressional Power Over Lower Federal Court Jurisdiction.* The overwhelming consensus among scholars and judges is that Congress has very broad power to strip the inferior federal courts of jurisdiction. Article I, Section 8, clause 9 specifically gives Congress the power to "constitute" the inferior courts—the only place in the Constitution where the verb "constitute" appears. Article III, Section 1 vests the judicial power "in such inferior Courts as the Congress may from time to time ordain and establish." The conclusion that has been almost unanimously drawn from these clauses is that since Congress had no obligation to create any inferior federal courts at all, it must also have the power to create those courts but limit their jurisdiction in some way. Congress could under the Constitution have chosen to create only inferior courts that would have heard admiralty cases or cases to which a foreign nation was a party. Beginning with the Judiciary Act of 1789, however, Congress has always chosen to create some inferior federal courts with broader jurisdiction. But it was not until 1875 that Congress gave the inferior federal courts jurisdiction to hear cases arising under the Constitution, laws, and treaties of the United States. Prior to that time, the inferior federal courts heard a few criminal cases and a lot of "diversity suits"—controversies between the citizens of one state and the citizens of another.

The question whether Congress could limit the jurisdiction of the inferior federal courts reached the U.S. Supreme Court in *Sheldon v. Sill*, 49 U.S. (8 How.) 441 (1850). The Court had no trouble concluding that Congress had plenary power over inferior federal court jurisdiction: the greater power not to create any such courts included the lesser power to create them but with limited jurisdiction. *Sheldon v. Sill* remains good law. Obviously, Congress cannot use its plenary power over inferior federal court jurisdiction in some way that violates another constitutional command, such as the First Amendment. But subject to the restrictions imposed by other constitutional provisions, Congress's power over the jurisdiction of lower federal courts is plenary.

Note that the assumption that scholars in this area make is that the state courts are always open to hear cases involving federal law should Congress choose not to create any inferior federal courts. Article III itself does not mention the state courts, but, as noted above, Congress's power to "constitute tribunals" inferior to the Supreme Court might be taken to embrace authority to have state courts decide issues of federal law in the first instance, either in addition to or instead of the jurisdiction of lower federal courts. (That is our familiar arrangement today.) The Supremacy Clause of Article VI also appears to contemplate that state courts will be called on to decide cases involving federal law, as it proclaims that the Constitution, laws, and treaties are the "supreme Law of the Land" and says that "the Judges in every State shall be bound thereby, any Thing in the Constitution or Laws of any state to the Contrary notwithstanding." State court interpretations of federal law are reviewable by the U.S. Supreme Court in the exercise of its appellate jurisdiction, a principle firmly established since the Supreme Court's decision in the case of *Martin v. Hunter's Lessee*, 14 U.S. (1 Wheat.) 304 (1816), which upheld such jurisdiction against a claim that it violated state sovereignty.

One final point about Congress's plenary power to create or not to create inferior federal courts: Justice Joseph Story, who was a leading member of the Marshall Court and also a professor of law at Harvard Law School, argued that Congress had an obligation in good faith to create at least some inferior federal courts. He noted that the Vesting Clause of Article III commands that the judicial power "shall," i.e. "must," be vested and that it must extend to all cases arising under federal law. Justice Story's argument was set forth at great length in dicta in *Martin v. Hunter's Lessee*. What do you think of this argument?

b. *Congressional Power over the Supreme Court's Appellate Jurisdiction.* What about congressional power over the Supreme Court's jurisdiction? The Supreme Court is created by the Constitution itself, and its jurisdiction appears to flow directly from the words of Article III. Consider the following clauses, all of which bear on this question:

> *The judicial Power of the United States, shall be vested in one supreme Court, and in such inferior Courts as the Congress may from time to time ordain and establish. . . . .*

> *The judicial Power shall extend to all Cases, in Law and Equity, arising under this Constitution, the Laws of the United States, and Treaties made, or which shall be made, under their Authority . . .*

> *In all Cases affecting Ambassadors, other public Ministers and Consuls, and those in which a State shall be Party, the supreme Court shall have original Jurisdiction. In all the other Cases before mentioned, the supreme Court shall have appellate Jurisdiction, both as to Law and Fact, with such Exceptions and under such Regulations as the Congress shall make.*

What do these provisions, read individually and together, say about the jurisdiction that the U.S. Supreme Court *must* possess? What is the scope of Congress's power over the Supreme Court's jurisdiction? To what extent does the Vesting Clause directly confer an irreducible minimum of jurisdiction in the federal judiciary? To what extent is Article III's menu of jurisdiction, or some part of it, best understood as mandatory? To what extent does the Exceptions Clause recognize a power of Congress to decide the scope of the Supreme

Court's appellate jurisdiction, including the power to eliminate certain cases from the Court's jurisdiction entirely? There are several competing views—and each view has certain difficulties associated with it.

First, Article III could be read to give Congress plenary control over the Supreme Court's appellate jurisdiction, by virtue of the Exceptions Clause. In certain ways, this seems a natural and straightforward reading of the language. But it creates problems. Does this mean that Congress could remove the Supreme Court's appellate jurisdiction entirely—leaving nothing but the Supreme Court's mandated original jurisdiction in a narrow category of cases—or carve up the Court's appellate jurisdiction by removing certain categories of cases or issues, and leave final resolution of whatever matters are removed from the Supreme Court's jurisdiction to fifty different state court systems? Is that plausible as a structural matter? Is it in some tension with the idea of the supremacy of the "one supreme Court" created by Article III? The Supreme Court's decision in *Ex parte McCardle*, presented below, could be read as embracing this view, but the opinion is not perfectly clear on the exact scope of the Exceptions Clause power to strip the Supreme Court of appellate jurisdiction. For a comprehensive defense of this position, often thought of as the "traditional" view, see John Harrison, *The Power of Congress to Limit the Jurisdiction of Federal Courts and the Text of Article III*, 64 U. Chi. L. Rev. 203 (1997).

Second, Article III could be read to give Congress power to remove cases from the Supreme Court's appellate jurisdiction, by virtue of the Exceptions Clause, but only if Congress assigns that jurisdiction to *lower* federal courts. This would give effect to the apparently mandatory language of the Vesting Clause—"The judicial Power of the United States," described to include the cases listed in Section 2, "*shall* be vested in one supreme Court, *and* in such inferior Courts as the Congress may from time to time ordain and establish"— by saying that Congress must vest all Article III jurisdiction somewhere within the Article III federal judiciary. It may limit lower federal court jurisdiction *or* remove cases from the Supreme Court's appellate jurisdiction; it may not do both simultaneously. It may not remove *all* jurisdiction over Article III's menu of cases and controversies from both lower federal courts and the Supreme Court. This view shares some of the problems with the traditional view, in that it allows Congress to allow some matters to be finally resolved by lower courts (albeit lower *federal* courts). It also is inconsistent with much historical practice, in that Congress has never in its judiciary acts vested the full menu of Article III jurisdiction in the federal courts. But does it make better sense of the text and structure of Article III? For a defense of this position, see Akhil Amar, *A Neo–Federalist View of Article III: Separating the Two Tiers of Federal Jurisdiction*, 65 B.U. L. Rev. 205 (1985).

Third, the Exceptions Clause might be read as *not* permitting Congress to remove cases from the Supreme Court's jurisdiction, but only as permitting Congress to shift cases from the Court's *appellate* jurisdiction to its *original* jurisdiction (and vice versa). On this view, the Constitution grants the Supreme Court original jurisdiction in specified cases, states that in all others "before mentioned" the Court will have appellate jurisdiction, but that Congress may make exceptions to this baseline starting point, moving cases of certain description from one category of the Court's jurisdiction to another—appellate to original or original to appellate. For a defense of this position, see Steven G. Calabresi & Gary Lawson, *The Unitary Executive, Jurisdiction Stripping, and the Hamdan Opinions: A Textualist Response to Justice Scalia*, 107 Colum. L.

Rev. 1002 (2007). This reading of the text has much to commend it as a linguistic and structural matter, and avoids certain of the problems of the first two views. It gives full effect both to the Vesting Clause and the Exceptions Clause, and also accommodates the interest in maintaining the supreme character of the Supreme Court by holding that the Court ultimately may exercise jurisdiction over all federal law cases—with Congress given the choice between original and appellate jurisdiction. But this position has the distinct problem of being directly contrary to *Marbury v. Madison* (1803), which held that Congress could not add cases to the Supreme Court's original jurisdiction beyond those listed in the Original Jurisdiction Clause. (But might *Marbury* have been wrong on this point, as on some others?)

Finally, the Exceptions Clause could be read to permit Congress to remove Supreme Court appellate jurisdiction over certain types of cases and permit final resolution in state or lower federal courts (as with the first and second options), but limited by a notion of what is necessary to maintain the Supreme Court's supremacy within the federal judicial system or a notion of the Court's "essential role." In other words, the "Exceptions" that Congress makes should not be allowed to swallow the rule. For a defense of this position, see Leonard G. Ratner, *Congressional Power Over the Appellate Jurisdiction of the Supreme Court*, 109 U. Pa. L. Rev. 157 (1960). The difficulties with this position are, first, that it interpolates an "essential role" exception into the Exceptions Clause and, second, that it can be difficult to decide what exactly is required by the Court's essential role.

Which view is right? Is there another, superior reading of the text?

So far, we have looked at textual and structural arguments about congressional power over federal court jurisdiction. What about arguments from historical purpose or practice and precedent? What does Alexander Hamilton say on the subject in *The Federalist Nos. 80* and *81*, presented above? Does his discussion supply a clear answer? From the Judiciary Act of 1789 to the present, the practice of Congress has been to pass statutes regulating the Supreme Court's appellate jurisdiction in both incidental and major substantive respects. The Judiciary Act of 1789 did not assign the entirety of Article III's allowable appellate jurisdiction to the Supreme Court, either over federal questions presented in state court cases or over decisions of lower federal courts. Indeed, for more than a century under the Constitution, Congress did not grant the Supreme Court appellate jurisdiction over all cases presenting federal law issues. Is this longstanding practice indicative of the meaning of the Constitution, with respect to Congress's powers over the Supreme Court's jurisdiction? Finally, there is judicial precedent: *Marbury v. Madison* and practice have made it settled law that Congress cannot add to the Supreme Court's original jurisdiction. And in 1869, the Supreme Court upheld the action of Congress in withdrawing appellate jurisdiction over a case pending before the Court—*Ex parte McCardle*. And what policy arguments could be made for and against the various views about the limits of congressional power to regulate the jurisdiction of the federal courts?

Sheldon v. Sill

49 U.S. 441 (1850)

■ MR. JUSTICE GRIER delivered the opinion of the court.

The only question which it will be necessary to notice in this case is, whether the Circuit Court had jurisdiction.

Sill, the complainant below, a citizen of New York, filed his bill in the Circuit Court of the United States for Michigan, against Sheldon, claiming to recover the amount of a bond and mortgage, which had been assigned to him by Hastings, the President of the Bank of Michigan.

Sheldon, in his answer, among other things, pleaded that "the bond and mortgage in controversy, having been originally given by a citizen of Michigan to another citizen of the same State, and the complainant being assignee of them, the Circuit Court had no jurisdiction."

The eleventh section of the Judiciary Act, which defines the jurisdiction of the Circuit Courts, restrains them from taking "cognizance of any suit to recover the contents of any promissory note or other chose in action, in favor of an assignee, unless a suit might have been prosecuted in such court to recover the contents, if no assignment had been made, except in cases of foreign bills of exchange."

The third article of the Constitution declares that "the judicial power of the United States shall be vested in one Supreme Court, and such inferior courts as the Congress may, from time to time, ordain and establish." The second section of the same article enumerates the cases and controversies of which the judicial power shall have cognizance, and, among others, it specifies "controversies between citizens of different States."

It has been alleged, that this restriction of the Judiciary Act, with regard to assignees of choses in action, is in conflict with this provision of the Constitution, and therefore void.

It must be admitted, that if the Constitution had ordained and established the inferior courts, and distributed to them their respective powers, they could not be restricted or divested by Congress. But as it has made no such distribution, one of two consequences must result,—either that each inferior court created by Congress must exercise all the judicial powers not given to the Supreme Court, or that Congress, having the power to establish the courts, must define their respective jurisdictions. The first of these inferences has never been asserted, and could not be defended with any show of reason, and if not, the latter would seem to follow as a necessary consequence. And it would seem to follow, also, that, having a right to prescribe, Congress may withhold from any court of its creation jurisdiction of any of the enumerated controversies. Courts created by statute can have no jurisdiction but such as the statute confers. No one of them can assert a just claim to jurisdiction exclusively conferred on another, or withheld from all.

The Constitution has defined the limits of the judicial power of the United States, but has not prescribed how much of it shall be exercised by the Circuit Court; consequently, the statute which does prescribed the limits of their jurisdiction, cannot be in conflict with the Constitution, unless it confers powers not enumerated therein.

Such has been the doctrine held by this court since its first establishment. To enumerate all the cases in which it has been either directly advanced or tacitly assumed would be tedious and unnecessary.

In the case of *Turner v. Bank of North America*, 4 Dall. 10, it was contended, as in this case, that, as it was a controversy between citizens of different States, the Constitution gave the plaintiff a right to sue in the Circuit Court, notwithstanding he was an assignee within the restriction of the eleventh section of the Judiciary Act. But the court said,—"The political truth is, that the disposal of the judicial power (except in a few specified instances) belongs to Congress: and Congress is not bound to enlarge the jurisdiction of the Federal courts to every subject, in every form which the Constitution might warrant." This decision was made in 1799; since that time, the same doctrine has been frequently asserted by this court, as may be seen in *McIntire v. Wood*, 7 Cranch, 506; *Kendall v. United States*, 12 Peters, 616; *Cary v. Curtis*, 3 Howard, 245.

The only remaining inquiry is, whether the complainant in this case is the assignee of a "chose in action," within the meaning of the statute. The term "chose in action" is one of comprehensive import. It includes the infinite variety of contracts, covenants, and promises, which confer on one party a right to recover a personal chattel or a sum of money from another, by action. . . .

The complainant in this case is the purchaser and assignee of a sum of money, a debt, a chose in action, not of a tract of land. He seeks to recover by this action a debt assigned to him. He is therefore the "assignee of a chose in action," within the letter and spirit of the act of Congress under consideration, and cannot support this action in the Circuit Court of the United States, where his assignor could not.

The judgment of the Circuit Court must therefore be reversed, for want of jurisdiction. . . .

Background to *Ex parte McCardle*

Because the opinion in *Ex parte McCardle* is cryptic, some background information may be helpful. The case concerns the availability of the ancient writ of habeas corpus by which anyone who has been unlawfully imprisoned can petition a judge to order his release. The right to petition for writs of habeas corpus was referred to by William Blackstone as being as important to English liberties as Magna Carta itself, and it was codified in English statutory law in the Habeas Corpus Act of 1679. The writ was widely understood to be available in the United States prior to independence. Article I, Section 9, Clause 2 of the Constitution provides that "The Privilege of the Writ of Habeas Corpus shall not be suspended, unless when in Cases of Rebellion or Invasion the public Safety may require it." President Lincoln suspended the right to the writ in 1861 without congressional authorization, but it seems highly likely that in what might be called ordinary emergencies only Congress, and not the president acting alone, has the power to suspend the writ. Presumably this is why a limitation on Congress's power to suspend the writ is placed in Article I, Section 9, right after the enumeration of Congress's powers in Article I, Section 8.

The First Congress in the Judiciary Act of 1789 provided that federal courts would have jurisdiction to issue writs of habeas corpus upon petition for anyone being detained by federal officials in a federal jail. As late as 1867, state prisoners held in state jails had no statutory right to petition for federal habeas relief even if they claimed they were being held unlawfully in violation of their federal constitutional or civil rights. In the wake of the Civil War, the inability of state prisoners to petition federal courts for habeas relief when state officials unlawfully detained them became a major issue. As a result, the Reconstruction Congress passed the Habeas Corpus Act of 1867 that gave federal judges the power to issue writs of habeas corpus in all cases of detention where custody was challenged on the basis of federal law. This statute worked a revolution in federal criminal law because it allowed for collateral review by federal district judges of the legality under federal law of state detentions. The 1867 Act provided a broad right to appeal decisions in these cases to the U.S. Supreme Court.

William McCardle was a newspaper publisher and former Confederate soldier who was publishing seditious articles in a Mississippi newspaper called *The Vicksburg Times* shortly after the end of the Civil War. He was imprisoned by a U.S. military commander for violating the Military Reconstruction Act of 1867. McCardle filed a petition for a writ of habeas corpus under the 1867 statute saying that his First Amendment rights of freedom of speech and of the press had been violated and that he was being illegally imprisoned. McCardle argued for good measure that the Military Reconstruction Act of 1867 was unconstitutional. McCardle denied that Congress had power under the Republican Form of Government Clause of Article IV, Section 4 to reconstruct the South. McCardle's habeas petition threatened to use the Republicans' 1867 Habeas Corpus Act to destroy their 1867 Military Reconstruction Act.

The Republicans in Congress were very concerned that McCardle's case could lead the Supreme Court to rule that some or all of Reconstruction was unconstitutional. The Court during this period did rule against Congress in *Ex parte Milligan* and in a case involving whether the government had had the wartime power to issue paper money. Congress responded by attaching a rider to an appropriations bill that purported to repeal the 1867 Habeas Corpus Act in circumstances like those faced by McCardle. The bill was vetoed by President Johnson and was passed over his veto by a two-thirds majority of both houses of Congress. The repeal act went into effect after *Ex parte McCardle* had been briefed and argued, but before a decision was announced. The justices responded with the following opinion.

Ex parte McCardle
74 U.S. 506 (1868)

APPEAL from the Circuit Court for the Southern District of Mississippi.

The case was this:

The Constitution of the United States ordains as follows:

> § 1. The judicial power of the United States shall be vested *in one Supreme Court*, and in such inferior courts as the Congress may from time to time ordain and establish.'

> § 2. The judicial power shall extend to all cases in law or equity arising *under this Constitution, the laws of the United States*, & c.

And in these last cases the Constitution ordains that,

The Supreme Court shall have appellate jurisdiction, both as to law and fact, *with such exceptions, and under such regulations, as the Congress shall make.*

With these constitutional provisions in existence, Congress, on the 5th February, 1867, by "An act to amend an act to establish the judicial courts of the United States, approved September 24, 1789," provided that the several courts of the United States, and the several justices and judges of such courts, within their respective jurisdiction, in addition to the authority already conferred by law, should have power to grant writs of *habeas corpus* in all cases where any person may be restrained of his or her liberty in violation of the Constitution, or of any treaty or law of the United States. And that, from the final decision of any judge, justice, or court inferior to the Circuit Court, appeal might be taken to the Circuit Court of the United States for the district in which the cause was heard, and *from the judgment of the said Circuit Court to the Supreme Court of the United States.*

This statute being in force, one McCardle, alleging unlawful restraint by military force, preferred a petition in the court below, for the writ of *habeas corpus.*

The writ was issued, and a return was made by the military commander, admitting the restraint, but denying that it was unlawful.

It appeared that the petitioner was not in the military service of the United States, but was held in custody by military authority for trial before a military commission, upon charges founded upon the publication of articles alleged to be incendiary and libellous, in a newspaper of which he was editor. The custody was alleged to be under the authority of certain acts of Congress.

Upon the hearing, the petitioner was remanded to the military custody; but, upon his prayer, an appeal was allowed him to this court, and upon filing the usual appeal bond, for costs, he was admitted to bail upon recognizance, with sureties, conditioned for his future appearance in the Circuit Court, to abide by and perform the final judgment of this court. The appeal was taken under the above-mentioned act of February 5, 1867.

A motion to dismiss this appeal was made at the last term, and, after argument, was denied.

Subsequently, on the 2d, 3d, 4th, and 9th March, the case was argued very thoroughly and ably upon the merits, and was taken under advisement. While it was thus held, and before conference in regard to the decision proper to be made, an act was passed by Congress, returned with objections by the President, and, on the 27th March, repassed by the constitutional majority, the second section of which was as follows:

And be it further enacted, That so much of the act approved February 5, 1867, entitled 'An act to amend an act to establish the judicial courts of the United States, approved September 24, 1789,' as authorized an appeal from the judgment of the Circuit Court to the Supreme Court of the United States, or the exercise of any such jurisdiction by said Supreme Court, on appeals which have been, or may hereafter be taken, be, and the same is hereby repealed.

The attention of the court was directed to this statute at the last term, but counsel having expressed a desire to be heard in argument upon its effect, and the Chief Justice being detained from his place here, by his duties in the Court of Impeachment, the cause was continued under advisement. Argument was now heard upon the effect of the repealing act.

■ The CHIEF JUSTICE delivered the opinion of the court.

The first question necessarily is that of jurisdiction; for, if the act of March, 1868, takes away the jurisdiction defined by the act of February, 1867, it is useless, if not improper, to enter into any discussion of other questions.

It is quite true, as was argued by the counsel for the petitioner, that the appellate jurisdiction of this court is not derived from acts of Congress. It is, strictly speaking, conferred by the Constitution. But it is conferred "with such exceptions and under such regulations as Congress shall make."

It is unnecessary to consider whether, if Congress had made no exceptions and no regulations, this court might not have exercised general appellate jurisdiction under rules prescribed by itself. For among the earliest acts of the first Congress, at its first session, was the act of September 24th, 1789, to establish the judicial courts of the United States. That act provided for the organization of this court, and prescribed regulations for the exercise of its jurisdiction.

The source of that jurisdiction, and the limitations of it by the Constitution and by statute, have been on several occasions subjects of consideration here. In the case of *Durousseau* v. *The United States*, particularly, the whole matter was carefully examined, and the court held, that while "the appellate powers of this court are not given by the judicial act, but are given by the Constitution," they are, nevertheless, "limited and regulated by that act, and by such other acts as have been passed on the subject." The court said, further, that the judicial act was an exercise of the power given by the Constitution to Congress "of making exceptions to the appellate jurisdiction of the Supreme Court." "They have described affirmatively," said the court, "its jurisdiction, and this affirmative description has been understood to imply a negation of the exercise of such appellate power as is not comprehended within it."

The principle that the affirmation of appellate jurisdiction implies the negation of all such jurisdiction not affirmed having been thus established, it was an almost necessary consequence that acts of Congress, providing for the exercise of jurisdiction, should come to be spoken of as acts granting jurisdiction, and not as acts making exceptions to the constitutional grant of it.

The exception to appellate jurisdiction in the case before us, however, is not an inference from the affirmation of other appellate jurisdiction. It is made in terms. The provision of the act of 1867, affirming the appellate jurisdiction of this court in cases of *habeas corpus* is expressly repealed. It is hardly possible to imagine a plainer instance of positive exception.

We are not at liberty to inquire into the motives of the legislature. We can only examine into its power under the Constitution; and the power to make exceptions to the appellate jurisdiction of this court is given by express words.

What, then, is the effect of the repealing act upon the case before us? We cannot doubt as to this. Without jurisdiction the court cannot proceed at all in any cause. Jurisdiction is power to declare the law, and when it ceases to exist, the only function remaining to the court is that of announcing the fact and dismissing the cause. And this is not less clear upon authority than upon principle.

Several cases were cited by the counsel for the petitioner in support of the position that jurisdiction of this case is not affected by the repealing act. But none of them, in our judgment, afford any support to it. They are all cases of the exercise of judicial power by the legislature, or of legislative interference with courts in the exercising of continuing jurisdiction.

On the other hand, the general rule, supported by the best elementary writers, is, that "when an act of the legislature is repealed, it must be considered, except as to transactions past and closed, as if it never existed." And the effect of repealing acts upon suits under acts repealed, has been determined by the adjudications of this court. The subject was fully considered in *Norris* v. *Crecker*, and more recently in *Insurance Company* v. *Ritchie*. In both of these cases it was held that no judgment could be rendered in a suit after the repeal of the act under which it was brought and prosecuted.

It is quite clear, therefore, that this court cannot proceed to pronounce judgment in this case, for it has no longer jurisdiction of the appeal; and judicial duty is not less fitly performed by declining ungranted jurisdiction than in exercising firmly that which the Constitution and the laws confer.

Counsel seem to have supposed, if effect be given to the repealing act in question, that the whole appellate power of the court, in cases of *habeas corpus*, is denied. But this is an error. The act of 1868 does not except from that jurisdiction any cases but appeals from Circuit Courts under the act of 1867. It does not affect the jurisdiction which was previously exercised.

The appeal of the petitioner in this case must be DISMISSED FOR WANT OF JURISDICTION.

NOTES

1. The last full paragraph of *Ex parte McCardle* says obliquely that the 1867 Habeas Corpus Act did "not affect the jurisdiction which was previously exercised." The Court is referring here to its habeas jurisdiction under the Judiciary Act of 1789. The effect of this paragraph is to say that when there are two avenues to the Supreme Court for the same case, Congress can cut off *one* of them, depriving the Supreme Court of jurisdiction on that basis (but not necessarily removing the other avenue). By itself, this conclusion is unremarkable. What the Court is saying is that the *McCardle* case does not present the extreme situation of Congress totally stripping the Supreme Court of its appellate jurisdiction over a case. This was confirmed in *Ex parte Yerger*, 75 U.S. (8 Wall.) 85 (1869), where the Court concluded it could still hear habeas appeals in cases from the occupied South under the Judiciary Act of 1789. Is all the emphatic language about Congress's great power over the Supreme Court's appellate jurisdiction in *Ex parte McCardle* mere dicta? *McCardle* arguably did not quite hold, although the opinion implies, that Congress can use the Exceptions Clause to totally eliminate a litigant's right of appeal to the Supreme Court.

2. Is the power to remove cases from the Supreme Court's appellate jurisdiction an appropriate check the political branches have on the judiciary? Or is it merely an illegitimate backdoor way for Congress to dictate to the judiciary how to decide cases, "or else"?

3. What about other ways of checking the Supreme Court? Would it be a good idea for Congress to be able to overrule the Supreme Court by a majority vote, a three-fifths vote, or a two-thirds vote of one or both houses? What about term limits for Supreme Court justices? Supreme Court justices' average tenure on the Court has shot up from about 15 years to more than 25 years. This results from the fact that while the average age of appointment has consistently hovered around 53, the average age of departure from the Court is now nearly 80; before 1970 it was at about age 69. For a proposed cure—a fixed non-renewable eighteen-year term for Supreme Court justices—see Steven G. Calabresi & James Lindgren, *Term Limits for the Supreme Court: Life Tenure Reconsidered*, 29 Harv. J. L. & Pub. Pol'y 769 (2006).

4. *Ex parte McCardle* holds (at minimum) that Congress may eliminate one avenue of federal judicial review—review by writ of habeas corpus—where an alternative avenue for judicial relief exists. A recent decision of the Supreme Court stands in at least some considerable tension with that holding.

In *Boumediene v. Bush*, 553 U.S. 723 (2008), the Court considered the constitutionality of a provision of the Military Commissions Act of 2006 providing that no court of the United States could issue a writ of habeas corpus to consider a challenge brought by a captured enemy alien combatant in military custody outside the territorial jurisdiction of the United States. But the MCA provided for judicial review in the U.S. Court of Appeals for the D.C. Circuit (with Supreme Court review on writ of certiorari) of military determinations of prisoner status and final decisions by military tribunals in prosecutions for violations of the law of war. In an opinion by Justice Kennedy, a 5–4 majority struck down the provision withdrawing habeas corpus jurisdiction, holding that the provision was "an unconstitutional suspension of the writ" and that the alternative procedure was not a constitutionally adequate substitute. The majority held that the petitioners were not "barred from seeking the writ or invoking the protections of the Suspension Clause either because of their status, i.e., petitioners' designation by the Executive Branch as enemy combatants, or their physical location, i.e., their presence at Guantanamo Bay." The Court held that the privilege of the writ of habeas corpus extended to aliens and that the U.S. naval base at Guantanamo Bay, while "not formally part of the United States" was under its "practical sovereignty."

Chief Justice Roberts, joined by three other justices, dissented: "Today the Court strikes down as inadequate the most generous set of procedural protections ever afforded aliens detained by this country as enemy combatants." Even assuming that petitioners could claim the protections of the writ of habeas corpus, Chief Justice Roberts wrote, the alternative procedures fashioned by Congress, including full judicial appellate review of the relevant military decisions, were a perfectly adequate alternative.

Justice Scalia, also joined by three justices, dissented on the ground that the writ of habeas corpus did not extend to alien enemies held abroad by military authorities:

> Today, for the first time in our Nation's history, the Court confers a constitutional right to habeas corpus on alien enemies detained abroad by our military forces in the course of an ongoing war. The Chief Justice's dissent, which I join, shows that the procedures prescribed by Congress in the Detainee Treatment Act provide the essential protections that habeas corpus guarantees; there has thus been no suspension of the writ, and no basis

exists for judicial intervention beyond what the Act allows. My problem with today's opinion is more fundamental still: The writ of habeas corpus does not, and never has, run in favor of aliens abroad; the Suspension Clause thus has no application, and the Court's intervention in this military matter is entirely ultra vires.

Justice Scalia noted that the Court's decision was contrary to "our settled precedent in *Johnson v. Eisentrager*, 339 U.S. 763 (1950)," which had rejected habeas corpus jurisdiction to consider challenges to detention brought by captured enemy combatants who had been convicted by military tribunal for spying and who were being held in custody at an allied military base in post-war Germany. *Eisentrager* was a "conclusive precedent" directly on point. Moreover, it was "clear that the original understanding of the Suspension Clause was that habeas corpus was not available to aliens abroad." Justice Scalia even said the Court's decision "will make the war harder on us. It will almost certainly cause more Americans to be killed . . . The Nation will live to regret what the Court has done today."

The case to which Justice Scalia referred, *Johnson v. Eisentrager*, 339 U.S. 763 (1950), arose out of the capture of two German nationals who had been spying for the Japanese government. After being captured in China, they were tried by military commission for violation of the laws of war, were convicted, and were imprisoned in U.S.-occupied Germany. They filed a petition for writ of habeas corpus in federal court. The Court rejected the petition:

> We are cited to no instance where a court, in this or any other country where the writ is known, has issued it on behalf of an alien enemy who, at no relevant time and in no stage of his captivity, has been within its territorial jurisdiction. Nothing in the text of the Constitution extends such a right, nor does anything in our statutes. . . . We hold that the Constitution does not confer a right of personal security or an immunity from military trial and punishment upon an alien enemy engaged in the hostile service of a government at war with the United States." If aliens captured and held abroad had habeas rights, the Court said, it "would hamper the war effort and bring aid and comfort to the enemy.

Can *Boumediene* be reconciled with *Eisentrager*? If not, which case is right? Do enemy aliens, captured in wartime and held in military custody abroad, have U.S. constitutional rights, including the privilege of the writ of habeas corpus? On the theory of the majority in *Boumediene*, could any prisoner of war, held in military custody in any area within U.S. control (such as an overseas army base) bring a petition for a writ of habeas corpus, challenging the lawfulness of their detention in U.S. domestic court?

A necessary premise of the majority's opinion in *Boumediene* was that Congress had not properly exercised its power to suspend the privilege of the writ of habeas corpus, pursuant to its power to do so under the Writ Suspension Clause of Article I, Section 9. Is that premise necessarily correct? Could Congress's enactment of the Military Commissions Act of 2006, including the provisions withdrawing habeas corpus relief for enemy combatants, be understood as an exercise of that power (if not in precisely such terms)? The Writ Suspension Clause requires a situation of rebellion or "invasion." Do the attacks of September 11, 2001 constitute an "invasion" of the United States by enemy forces? Could Congress suspend the writ during the ensuing global war against al Qaeda, its affiliates, and persons, nations, and groups assisting or harboring the same? Who makes the judgment as to whether there has been an "invasion"? Who makes the judgment as to whether "the public Safety may require" suspension of the writ? Are such matters "political questions" committed to Congress's (or the president's) judgment? See Amanda Tyler, *Is Suspension a Political Question?*, 59 Stan. L. Rev. 333 (2006).

[*Assignment 29*]

E. SOVEREIGN IMMUNITY AND THE *ERIE* PROBLEM: "THE JUDICIAL POWER . . . SHALL NOT . . . EXTEND TO"

Where Article III confers jurisdiction in cases not themselves governed by federal law in the form of the Constitution, federal statutes, and treaties—as it does in the various grants of party-defined jurisdiction—does that grant of *jurisdiction* carry with it the power of federal courts to formulate rules of *substantive law*, in the form of federal common law or judge-made "general" law, with which to decide cases falling within such jurisdiction? In the field of admiralty and maritime law (one of the categories of enumerated federal jurisdiction), this has long been the practice. But outside of that context, the usual rule is that a grant of jurisdiction is only that—a grant of *jurisdiction*—in the sense of authority to apply the governing law to the case at hand, and not a grant of law-making power.

But it was not always so understood. Or, at least, in earlier times the question of jurisdiction (the power "to say what the law is" in the sense of authority to adjudicate a matter) was not always kept so strictly separate from the question of law-making power (the power "to say what the law is" in the sense of authority to prescribe or determine the substantive law governing a matter). Where written federal law governed, there was no confusion. But where there was no written federal law, the two questions often became conflated or intermingled.

Consider two important illustrations of such a problem.

The first is the question of the "sovereign immunity" of states from suits for damages. Article III authorized federal court jurisdiction over suits against states brought by citizens of different states, as one of the categories of diversity jurisdiction. Did that authorization constitute a repudiation of common law principles of state sovereign immunity? The question produced one of the first instances of a decision of the Supreme Court that provoked broad public outcry: *Chisholm v. Georgia,* 2 U.S. 419 (1793). *Chisholm* recognized jurisdiction and rejected Georgia's defense of state sovereign immunity. This led to the adoption of the Eleventh Amendment, designed to overturn the result in *Chisholm*, which reads: "The Judicial power of the United States shall not be construed to extend to any suit in law or equity, commenced or prosecuted against one of the United States by Citizens of another State, or by Citizens or Subjects of any Foreign State." Does the Eleventh Amendment remove a category of federal court subject matter jurisdiction? Or does it repudiate *Chisholm*'s substantive law holding and in effect (re-?) adopt a rule of state sovereign immunity as a matter of federal constitutional law? The issue has remained enduringly controversial.

The second illustration may be familiar to you from Civil Procedure, and it, too, presents significant constitutional questions: Does Article III's grant of diversity-of-citizenship jurisdiction mean that in these cases federal courts may develop and apply common law substantive rules? Or are federal courts bound by *state* common law and statutory law? One answer to these questions goes by the name "the *Erie* doctrine," after the Supreme Court's decision in *Erie Railroad Co. v. Tompkins,* 304 U.S. 64 (1938), which is presented below.

The Eleventh Amendment and Sovereign Immunity

At common law, the king could not be subjected to a suit in his own courts. Recall Alexander Hamilton's aside in *The Federalist No. 81:* "It is inherent in the nature of sovereignty not to be amenable to the suit of an individual *without its consent.* This is the general sense and the general practice of mankind; and the exemption, as one of the attributes of sovereignty, is now enjoyed by the government of every State in the Union. Unless, therefore, there is a surrender of this immunity in the plan of the convention, it will remain with the States."

But how did that common law doctrine translate to the United States under the Constitution—where sovereignty does not reside in a king? After all, the whole theory of the Constitution is that "We the People" are sovereign: the president and Congress are not sovereign, so suing them is *not* like suing the king. Moreover, the Diversity Clause of Article III, Section 2, seemed to expressly allow suits against states, for it extends federal jurisdiction to "controversies . . . between a State and a citizen of another State." These questions are not absolutely free from doubt, though, because the federal courts exercise only judicial power, and as noted the judicial power in England did not extend to suits against the king. Yet it seems strained to confine the judicial power in the United States by a doctrine of sovereign immunity.

As it happens, a lawsuit was brought almost immediately after the Constitution went into effect litigating this very issue. The case of *Chisholm v. Georgia* was brought in South Carolina by Alexander Chisholm, the executor of the estate of Robert Farquhar, who sued the state of Georgia for money damages over a debt that dated back to the Revolutionary War. Georgia refused to appear in court, claiming that as a sovereign state it was immune from suit. Chisholm was represented before the Supreme Court by U.S. Attorney General Edmund Randolph. The case excited great interest because many out-of-state citizens, including some foreigners, had claims for money damages against various state governments arising out of Revolutionary War debts. The Supreme Court ruled 4 to 1 that Georgia's sovereign immunity had been abrogated by the Diversity Clause in Article III. Accordingly, Chisholm's lawsuit could go forward and sovereign immunity did not bar it. The lone dissent was filed by Justice Iredell. At the time, 1793—before John Marshall established a different practice when he arrived at the Court in 1800—the justices delivered *seriatim* opinions, each justice stating his individual views, with no "Opinion of the Court." Thus, Justice Iredell's dissent appears *first* in the U.S. Reports.

Chisholm v. Georgia

2 U.S. 419 (1793)

■ IREDELL, JUSTICE.

. . . The action is an action of assumpsit. The particular question then before the Court, is, will an action of assumpsit lie against a State? . . . . If it will, it must be in virtue of the Constitution of the United States, and of some law of Congress conformable thereto. The part of the Constitution concerning the Judicial Power, is as follows, viz: Art.3. sect. 2. The Judicial Power shall extend . . . To controversies between . . . a State and citizens of another State. . . .

The words of the general judicial act, conveying the authority of the Supreme Court, under the Constitution, so far as they concern this question, are as follow:—Sect. 13. "That the Supreme Court shall have exclusive jurisdiction of all controversies of a civil nature, where a State is a party, except between . . . a State and citizens of other States, or aliens, in which latter case it shall have original, but not exclusive jurisdiction. . . ." The suit now before the Court (if maintainable at all) comes within the latter description, it being a suit against a State by a citizen of another State. . . .

I conceive, that all the Courts of the United States must receive, not merely their organization as to the number of Judges of which they are to consist; but all their authority, as to the manner of their proceeding, from the Legislature only. This appears to me to be one of those cases, with many others, in which an article of the Constitution cannot be effectuated without the intervention of the Legislative authority. . . .

[I]n instances like this before the Court, this Court hath a concurrent jurisdiction only; the present being one of those cases where by the judicial act this Court hath original but not exclusive jurisdiction. This Court, therefore, under that act, can exercise no authority in such instances, but such authority as from the subject matter of it may be exercised in some other Court. . . . [S]uch a jurisdiction . . . could be only concurrent with the Courts of the several States. It follows, therefore, unquestionably, I think, that looking at the act of Congress, which I consider is on this occasion the limit of our authority (whatever further might be constitutiona[l]ly, enacted) we can exercise no authority in the present instance consistently with the clear intention of the act, but such as a proper State Court would have been at least competent to exercise at the time the act was passed.

It therefore . . . is incumbent upon us to enquire, whether previous to the adoption of the Constitution . . . an action of the nature like this before the Court could have been maintained against one of the States in the Union upon the principles of the common law. . . . If it could, I think it is now maintainable here; If it could not, I think, as the law stands at present, it is not maintainable; whatever opinion may be entertained; upon the construction of the Constitution, as to the power of Congress to authorize such a one. Now I presume it will not be denied, that in every State in the Union, previous to the adoption of the Constitution, the only common law principles in regard to suits that were in any manner admissible in respect to claims against the State, were those which in England apply to claims against the crown; there being certainly no other principles of the common law which, previous to the adoption of this Constitution could, in any manner, or upon any colour apply to the case of a claim against a State in its own Courts, where it was solely and completely sovereign in respect to such cases at least. Whether that remedy was strictly applicable or not, still I apprehend there was no other. The only remedy in a case like that before the Court, by which, by any possibility, a suit can be maintained against the crown in England, or could be at any period from which the common law, as in force in America, could be derived, I believe is that which is called a Petition of right. . . . [I]n all cases the remedy to come at it was by petition to the person of the King: and no other method can be shown to have been practised at common law." . . .

[I]t appears, that in England even in case of a private debt contracted by the King, in his own person, there is no remedy but by petition, which must receive his express sanction, otherwise there can be no proceeding upon it. . . .

I have now, I think, established the following particulars. 1st. That the Constitution, so far as it respects the judicial authority, can only be carried into effect by acts of the Legislature appointing Courts, and prescribing their methods of proceeding. 2nd. That Congress has provided no new law in regard to this case, but expressly referred us to the old. 3rd. That there are no principles of the old law, to which, we must have recourse, that in any manner authorise the present suit, either by precedent or by analogy. The consequence of which, in my opinion, clearly is, that the suit in question cannot be maintained . . . .

■ BLAIR, JUSTICE.

In considering this important case, I have thought it best to pass over all the strictures which have been made on the various European confederations; because, as, on the one hand, their likeness to our own is not sufficiently close to justify any analogical application; so, on the other, they are utterly destitute of any binding authority here. The Constitution of the United States is the only fountain from which I shall draw; the only authority to which I shall appeal. Whatever be the true language of that, it is obligatory upon every member of the Union; for, no State could have become a member, but by an adoption of it by the people of that State. What then do we find there requiring the submission of individual States to the judicial authority of the United States? This is expressly extended, among other things, to controversies between a State and citizens of another State. Is then the case before us one of that description? Undoubtedly it is. . . . [I]f sovereignty be an exemption from suit in any other than the sovereign's own Courts, it follows that when a State, by adopting the Constitution, has agreed to be amenable to the judicial power of the United States, she has, in that respect, given up her right of sovereignty. . . .

■ WILSON, JUSTICE.

This is a case of uncommon magnitude. One of the parties to it is a State; certainly respectable, claiming to be sovereign. The question to be determined is, whether this State, so respectable, and whose claim soars so high, is amenable to the jurisdiction of the Supreme Court of the United States? This question, important in itself, will depend on others, more important still; and, may, perhaps, be ultimately resolved into one, no less radical than this "do the people of the United States form a Nation?" . . .

To the Constitution of the United States the term SOVEREIGN, is totally unknown. There is but one place where it could have been used with propriety. But, even in that place it would not, perhaps, have comported with the delicacy of those, who ordained and established that Constitution. They might have announced themselves SOVEREIGN people of the United States: But serenely conscious of the fact, they avoided the ostentatious declaration. . . .

Man, fearfully and wonderfully made, is the workmanship of his all perfect Creator: A State; useful and valuable as the contrivance is, is the inferior contrivance of man; and from his native dignity derives all its acquired importance. . . .

I am . . . chiefly, to examine the important question now before us, by the Constitution of the United States, and the legitimate result of that valuable instrument. Under this view, the question is naturally subdivided into two others. 1. Could the Constitution of the United States vest a jurisdiction over the State of Georgia? 2. Has that Constitution vested such jurisdiction in this Court? . . .

Concerning the prerogative of Kings, and concerning the sovereignty of States, much has been said and written; but little has been said and written concerning a subject much more dignified and important, the majesty of the people. . . . With the strictest propriety, therefore, classical and political, our national scene opens with the most magnificent object, which the nation could present. "The PEOPLE of the United States" are the first personages introduced. . . . In order, therefore, to form a more perfect union, to establish justice, to ensure domestic tranquillity, to provide for common defence, and to secure the blessings of liberty, those people, among whom were the people of Georgia, ordained and established the present Constitution. By that Constitution Legislative power is vested, Executive power is vested, Judicial power is vested.

. . . The inference, which necessarily results, is, that the Constitution ordained and established by those people; and, still closely to apply the case, in particular by the people of Georgia, could vest jurisdiction or judicial power over those States and over the State of Georgia in particular.

The next question under this head, is, Has the Constitution done so? . . . Whoever considers, in a combined and comprehensive view, the general texture of the Constitution, will be satisfied, that the people of the United States intended to form themselves into a nation for national purposes. They instituted, for such purposes, a national Government, complete in all its parts, with powers Legislative, Executive and Judiciary; and, in all those powers, extending over the whole nation. Is it congruous, that, with regard to such purposes, any man or body of men, any person natural or artificial, should be permitted to claim successfully an entire exemption from the jurisdiction of the national Government? Would not such claims, crowned with success, be repugnant to our very existence as a nation? . . .

But, in my opinion, this doctrine rests not upon the legitimate result of fair and conclusive deduction from the Constitution: It is confirmed, beyond all doubt, by the direct and explicit declaration of the Constitution itself. "The judicial power of the United States shall extend, to controversies between *two* States." Two States are supposed to have a controversy between them: This controversy is supposed to be brought before those vested with the judicial power of the United States: Can the most consummate degree of professional ingenuity devise a mode by which this "controversy between two States" can be brought before a Court of law; and yet neither of those States be a Defendant? "The judicial power of the United States shall extend to controversies, between a state and citizens of another State." Could the strictest legal language; could even that language, which is peculiarly appropriated to an art, deemed, by a great master, to be one of the most honorable, laudable, and profitable things in our law; could this strict and appropriated language, describe, with more precise accuracy, the cause now depending before the tribunal? Causes, and not parties to causes, are weighed by justice, in her equal scales: On the former solely, her attention is fixed: To the latter, she is, as she is painted, blind. . . .

■ CUSHING, JUSTICE.

The grand and principal question in this case is, whether a State can, by the Federal Constitution, be sued by an individual citizen of another State?

The point turns not upon the law or practice of England, although perhaps it may be in some measure elucidated thereby, nor upon the law of any other country whatever; but upon the Constitution established by the people of the United States; and particularly upon the extent of powers given to the Federal Judicial in the second section of the third article of the Constitution. . . . The judicial power . . . is expressly extended to "controversies between a State and citizens of another State." When a citizen makes a demand against a State, of which he is not a citizen, it is as really a controversy between a State and a citizen of another State, as if such State made a demand against such citizen. The case, then, seems clearly to fall within the letter of the Constitution. It may be suggested that it could not be intended to subject a State to be a Defendant, because it would effect the sovereignty of States. If that be the case, what shall we do with the immediate preceding clause; "controversies between two or more States,' where a State must of necessity be Defendant" If it was not the intent, in the very next clause also, that a State might be made Defendant, why was it so expressed as naturally to lead to and comprehend that idea? Why was not an exception made if one was intended? . . .

■ JAY, CHIEF JUSTICE.

The question we are now to decide has been accurately stated, viz. Is a State suable by individual citizens of another State?

It is said, that Georgia refuses to appear and answer to the Plaintiff in this action, because she is a sovereign State, and therefore not liable to such actions. In order to ascertain the merits of this objection, let us enquire, 1st. In what sense Georgia is a sovereign State. 2nd. Whether suability is incompatable with such sovereignty. 3rd. Whether the Constitution (to which Georgia is a party) authorises such an action against her. . . .

1st. . . . [T]he people, in their collective and national capacity, established the present Constitution. It is remarkable that in establishing it, the people exercised their own rights, and their own proper sovereignty, and conscious of the plenitude of it, they declared with becoming dignity, "We the people of the United States, do ordain and establish this Constitution." Here we see the people acting as sovereigns of the whole country; and in the language of sovereignty, establishing a Constitution by which it was their will, that the State Governments should be bound, and to which the State Constitutions should be made to conform. . . .

Sovereignty is the right to govern; a nation or State-sovereign is the person or persons in whom that resides. In Europe the sovereignty is generally ascribed to the Prince; here it rests with the people; there, the sovereign actually administers the Government; here, never in a single instance; our Governors are the agents of the people, and at most stand in the same relation to their sovereign, in which regents in Europe stand to their sovereigns. Their Princes have personal powers, dignities, and pre-eminences, our rulers have none but official; nor do they partake in the sovereignty otherwise, or in any other capacity, than as private citizens.

2nd. The second object of enquiry now presents itself, viz. whether suability is compatible with State sovereignty. . . . If there be any such incompatability as is pretended, whence does it arise? In what does it consist? There is at least one strong undeniable fact against this incompatibility, and that is this, any one State in the Union may sue another State, in this Court, that is, all the people of one State may sue all the people of another State. It is plain then, that a State may be sued, and hence it plainly follows, that suability and state sovereignty are not incompatible. As one State may sue another State in this Court, it is plain that no degradation to a State is thought to accompany her appearance in this Court. . . .

Let us now turn to the Constitution. . . . The question now before us renders it necessary to pay particular attention to that part of the second section [of Article III], which extends the judicial power "to controversies between a state and citizens of another state." It is contended, that this ought to be construed to reach none of these controversies, excepting those in which a State may be Plaintiff. The ordinary rules for construction will easily decide whether those words are to be understood in that limited sense. . . .

If we attend to the words, we find them to be express, positive, free from ambiguity, and without room for such implied expressions: "The judicial power of the United States shall extend to controversies between a state and citizens of another state." If the Constitution really meant to extend these powers only to those controversies in which a State might be Plaintiff, to the exclusion of those in which citizens had demands against a State, it is inconceivable that it should have attempted to convey that meaning in words, not only so incompetent, but also repugnant to it; if it meant to exclude a certain class of these controversies, why were they not expressly excepted; on the contrary, not even an intimation of such intention appears in any part of the Constitution. It cannot be pretended that where citizens urge and insist upon demands against a State, which the State refuses to admit and comply with, that there is no controversy between them. If it is a controversy between them, then it clearly falls not only within the spirit, but the very words of the Constitution. What is it to the cause of justice, and how can it effect the definition of the word controversy, whether the demands which cause the dispute, are made by a State against citizens of another State, or by the latter against the former? When power is thus extended to a controversy, it necessarily, as to all judicial purposes, is also extended to those, between whom it subsists.

The exception contended for, would contradict and do violence to the great and leading principles of a free and equal national government, one of the great objects of which is, to ensure justice to all. . . . For my own part, I am convinced that the sense in which I understand and have explained the words "controversies between States and citizens of another State," is the true sense. The extension of the judiciary power of the United States to such controversies, appears to me to be wise, because it is honest, and because it is useful. . . .

NOTES

1. Was the majority right or wrong in finding that the case was within the jurisdiction contemplated by Article III? Was the majority right or wrong in finding that state sovereign immunity was abrogated by the Constitution? Are these two separate questions, or one and the same? Can the answers be different?

2. The decision in *Chisholm* that the states could be sued in federal court provoked surprise and outrage. The case was almost immediately overruled by the Eleventh Amendment, which provides that:

The Judicial power of the United States shall not be construed to extend to any suit in law or equity, commenced or prosecuted against one of the United States by Citizens of another State, or by Citizens or Subjects of any Foreign State.

Did the Eleventh Amendment withdraw a sub-category of diversity jurisdiction only, or did it confer (or restore) state sovereign immunity? What does the text say? Assuming the intention underlying the amendment was, more broadly, to repudiate *Chisholm*, does that affect how it should be interpreted? The Eleventh Amendment through its plain words overrules *Chisholm*'s holding that Article III's grant to the federal courts of diversity jurisdiction was meant to authorize citizens to sue states notwithstanding considerations of sovereign immunity. But, in terms, it does not do so by enacting a rule concerning sovereign immunity but a rule concerning the scope of the judicial power. Moreover, the words of the Eleventh Amendment do not say anything at all about whether a citizen of a state could sue that citizen's *own state* under the Federal Question Clause of Article III, which authorizes the federal courts to hear "all Cases, in Law and Equity, arising under this Constitution, the Laws of the United States, and Treaties made, or which shall be made under their Authority." As we shall see, there is a huge present-day controversy over this very question. In sum, the Eleventh Amendment re-established state sovereign immunity in cases where federal jurisdiction was based on diversity of citizenship but not necessarily in federal question cases, which are in practice much more important.

3. What types of constitutional argument are used in each of the separate opinions in *Chisholm v. Georgia*? The majority opinions make a powerful textual case that since under the Constitution sovereignty resides in "We the People," and since Article III specifically contemplates suits between one state and another state, it simply cannot be the case that the original Constitution contemplated state sovereign immunity. Famous members of the framing generation—including Hamilton, Madison, and Marshall—expressly declared during the ratification debates that the Diversity Clause would only allow states to sue out-of-state citizens and not the other way around. Is that consistent with the text? If text and (powerful evidence of) original intention or understanding diverge, which controls? Justice Iredell's dissent argues for sovereign immunity on the grounds that: (1) he doubts Congress meant to confer jurisdiction to hear suits against states, and (2) he doubts such a grant would be constitutional if made. Justice Iredell has no answer, however, to the majority's arguments about the sovereignty of We the People and the implications of Article III's authorizing suits *between* states. Nevertheless, the Iredell view has become our governing law through a combination of the enactment of the Eleventh Amendment and the decision you will read next, *Hans v. Louisiana*.

4. How powerful is the argument by Justice Wilson and Chief Justice Jay that it is unrepublican to think of states as sovereign—that only the People are sovereign? If Georgia is sued and has to pay, who would ultimately have to foot the bill? If the officials of the state violate their oath of office in the course of their duties, inflict injury, and are successfully sued, who should pay? Why should the sovereign People have to pay through taxes for the misconduct of their agents? Note that the proposition that *the United States* has sovereign immunity has never been questioned, and to this day any waiver of the national government's sovereign immunity by Congress must be express and will be

narrowly construed by the courts. Why is that not equally inconsistent with republicanism?

5. When Congress set up the federal courts in the Judiciary Act of 1789, it created one Supreme Court of six justices and sixteen district court judgeships. Congress gave the federal courts jurisdiction to hear all admiralty cases and cases between citizens of different states, as well as other diversity cases, where there was a substantial amount of money at stake. Congress, however, chose *not* to give the lower federal courts any jurisdiction at all over federal question cases—cases which arose under the Constitution, federal law, or federal treaties. The Supreme Court was given limited jurisdiction to hear appeals with respect to federal questions from state supreme courts where there was a decision against the federal claim of right. Because the lower federal courts from 1789 to 1875 had no federal question jurisdiction at all, no case arose in federal court until 1890 that raised the question whether a state enjoyed sovereign immunity when it was sued by one of its own citizens for violating federal law. Technically, the Eleventh Amendment says nothing about federal question suits brought against a state by its own citizens so perhaps such a case ought to be governed by *Chisholm*.

6. A federal question suit by a state's own citizen on a question of federal law can be heard in federal court under Article III because the judicial power extends to "all Cases in Law and Equity, arising under the Constitution, the Laws of the United States, and Treaties made, or which shall be made, under their Authority." Is a suit for money damages or injunctive relief by a private citizen against his or her own state government or against the federal government without its consent a "Case in Law or Equity" to which the judicial power of the United States extends? Arguably it is not. The phrase "Cases in Law and Equity" was a specialized legal term of art in 1787 with important English background. The law courts at this time included the Court of King's Bench, the Court of Common Pleas, and the Court of Exchequer; the only court of equity was the Court of Chancery. There was at this time in England a separate Court of Admiralty, and matters of family law were also handled outside the royal court system by ecclesiastical courts.

The framers deliberately gave the Article III federal courts limited and enumerated judicial power over all "Cases in Law and Equity" and over "all Cases in Admiralty," which subject they apparently thought not covered by the "Law and Equity" label. The framers also considered extending the judicial power to cases of impeachment, but they deliberately decided against doing that, leaving sole jurisdiction over those cases with the House of Representatives and the Senate. So what exactly are the Cases in Law and Equity which the Article III courts have power to hear if they are not admiralty suits and they are not impeachment cases? The answer is almost certainly that Cases in Law and Equity included all of those matters or forms of action that could be heard in the Court of King's Bench, the Court of Common Pleas, the Court of Exchequer, or the Court of Chancery in 1787. These forms of actions, and maybe others closely analogous to them, are the only matters arising under federal law that fall under the "Cases in Law and Equity" grant of power to the courts.

If suits for money damages or injunctive relief could not be brought against the king, his officers, or the houses of Parliament in 1787, does this then suggest that such suits were not within the contemplation of the term "Cases, in Law and Equity"? If you had a claim for money damages in England in 1787, your remedy was to petition Parliament to pass a private bill for your relief. Was that understanding implicitly carried forward in the U.S. Constitution, even with respect to non-diversity suits? If *Chisholm* rejected that understanding, but the Eleventh Amendment rejected *Chisholm,* does that restore sovereign immunity?

In 1890, the Supreme Court finally addressed this question in *Hans v. Louisiana*, which is excerpted below. Was *Hans* rightly decided?

Hans v. Louisiana
134 U.S. 1 (1890)

■ BRADLEY, J.

This is an action brought in the circuit court of the United States, in December, 1884, against the state of Louisiana, by Hans, a citizen of that state, to recover the amount of certain coupons annexed to bonds of the state, issued under the provisions of an act of the legislature approved January 24, 1874. The bonds are known and designated as the "consolidated bonds of the state of Louisiana," and the coupons sued on are for interest which accrued January 1, 1880. . . . [The State breached its contract by adopting a new constitution, and Hans sued in federal court alleging] that said provisions of said constitution are in contravention of said contract, and their adoption was an active violation thereof, and that said state thereby sought to impair the validity thereof with your petitioner, in violation of article 1, section 10, of the constitution of the United States, and the effect so given to said state constitution does impair said contract. [Hans asked] that the state of Louisiana be cited to answer this demand, and that after due proceedings she be condemned to pay . . . $87,500 . . . with legal interest. . . .

[The State of Louisiana claimed the federal court was] without jurisdiction. . . . By the judgment of the court this exception was sustained, and the suit was dismissed. . . . To this judgment the present writ of error is brought; and the question is presented whether a state can be sued in a circuit court of the United States by one of its own citizens upon a suggestion that the case is one that arises under the constitution or laws of the United States.

The ground taken is that under the constitution, as well as under the act of congress passed to carry it into effect, a case is within the jurisdiction of the federal courts, without regard to the character of the parties, if it arises under the constitution or laws of the United States, or, which is the same thing, if it necessarily involves a question under said constitution or laws. The language relied on is that clause of the third article of the constitution, which declares that "the judicial power of the United States shall extend to all cases in law and equity arising under this constitution, the laws of the United States, and treaties made, or which shall be made, under their authority;" and the corresponding clause of the act conferring jurisdiction upon the circuit court, which, as found in the act of March 3, 1875, is as follows, to-wit: "That the circuit courts of the United States shall have original cognizance, concurrent with the courts of the several states, of all suits of a civil nature, at common law or in equity, . . . arising under the constitution or laws of the United States, or treaties made, or which shall be made, under their authority." It is said that these jurisdictional clauses make no exception arising from the character of the parties, and therefore that a state can claim no exemption from suit, if the case is really one arising under the constitution, laws, or treaties of the United States. . . .

In the present case the plaintiff in error contends that he, being a citizen of Louisiana, is not embarrassed by the obstacle of the eleventh amendment, inasmuch as that amendment only prohibits suits against a state which are brought by the citizens of another state, or by citizens or subjects of a foreign state. It is true the amendment does so read, and, if there were no other reason or ground for abating his suit, it might be maintainable; and then we should have this anomalous result, that, in cases arising under the constitution or laws of the United States, a state may be sued in the federal courts by its own citizens, though it cannot be sued for a like cause of action by the citizens of other states, or of a foreign state; and may be thus sued in the federal courts, although not allowing itself to be sued in its own courts. If this is the necessary consequence of the language of the constitution and the law, the result is no less startling and unexpected than was the original decision of this court, that, under the language of the constitution and of the judiciary act of 1789, a state was liable to be sued by a citizen of another state or of a foreign country. That decision was made in the case of *Chisholm v. Georgia*, 2 Dall. 419, and created such a shock of surprise throughout the country that, at the first meeting of congress thereafter, the eleventh amendment to the constitution was almost unanimously proposed, and was in due course adopted by the legislatures of the states. This amendment, expressing the will of the ultimate sovereignty of the whole country, superior to all legislatures and all courts, actually reversed the decision of the supreme court. It did not in terms prohibit suits by individuals against the states, but declared that the constitution should not be construed to import any power to authorize the bringing of such suits. The language of the amendment is that "the judicial power of the United States shall not be construed to extend to any suit, in law or equity, commenced or prosecuted against one of the United States by citizens of another state, or by citizens or subjects of any foreign state." The supreme court had construed the judicial power as extending to such a suit, and its decision was thus overruled. The court itself so understood the effect of the amendment. . . .

This view of the force and meaning of the amendment is important. It shows that, on this question of the suability of the states by individuals, the highest authority of this country was in accord rather with the minority than with the majority of the court in the decision of the case of *Chisholm v. Georgia*; and this fact lends additional interest to the able opinion of Mr. Justice IREDELL on that occasion. The other justices were more swayed by a close observance of the letter of the constitution, without regard to former experience and usage; and because the letter said that the judicial power shall extend to controversies "between a state and citizens of another state;" and "between a state and foreign states, citizens or subjects," they felt constrained to see in this language a power to enable the individual citizens of one state, or of a foreign state, to sue another state of the Union in the federal courts. Justice IREDELL, on the contrary, contended that it was not the intention to create new and unheard of remedies, by subjecting sovereign states to actions at the suit of individuals, (which he conclusively showed was never done before,) but only, by proper legislation, to invest the federal courts with jurisdiction to hear and determine controversies and cases, between the parties designated, that were properly susceptible of litigation in courts. Looking back from our present stand-point at the decision in *Chisholm v. Georgia*, we do not greatly wonder at the effect which it had upon the country. Any such power as that of authorizing the federal judiciary to entertain suits by individuals against the states had been expressly disclaimed, and even resented, by the great defenders of the constitution while it was on its trial before the American people. . . .

It seems to us that these views of those great advocates and defenders of the constitution were most sensible and just, and they apply equally to the present case as to that then under discussion. The letter is appealed to now, as it was then, as a ground for sustaining a suit brought by an individual against a state. The reason against it is as strong in this case as it was in that. It is an attempt to strain the constitution and the law to a construction never imagined or dreamed of. Can we suppose that, when the eleventh amendment was adopted, it was understood to be left open for citizens of a state to sue their own state in the federal courts, while the idea of suits by citizens of other states, or of foreign states, was indignantly repelled? Suppose that congress, when proposing the eleventh amendment, had appended to it a proviso that nothing therein contained should prevent a state from being sued by its own citizens in cases arising under the constitution or laws of the United States, can we imagine that it would have been adopted by the states? The supposition that it would is almost an absurdity on its face.

The truth is that the cognizance of suits and actions unknown to the law, and forbidden by the law, was not contemplated by the constitution when establishing the judicial power of the United States. Some things, undoubtedly, were made justifiable which were not known as such at the common law; such, for example, as controversies between states as to boundary lines, and other questions admitting of judicial solution. . . .

The suability of a state, without its consent, was a thing unknown to the law. This has been so often laid down and acknowledged by courts and jurists that it is hardly necessary to be formally asserted. It was fully shown by an exhaustive examination of the old law by Mr. Justice IREDELL in his opinion in *Chisholm v. Georgia*; and it has been conceded in every case since, where the question has, in any way, been presented, even in the cases which have gone furthest in sustaining suits against the officers or agents of states. . . .

Undoubtedly a state may be sued by its own consent. . . . But besides the presumption that no anomalous and unheard-of proceedings or suits were intended to be raised up by the constitution,—anomalous and unheard of when the constitution was adopted,—an additional reason why the jurisdiction claimed for the circuit court does not exist is the language of the act of congress by which its jurisdiction is conferred. The words are these: "The circuit courts of the United States shall have original cognizance, concurrent with the courts of the several states, of all suits of a civil nature, at common law or in equity, . . . arising under the constitution or laws of the United States, or treaties," etc. "Concurrent with the courts of the several states." Does not this qualification show that congress, in legislating to carry the constitution into effect, did not intend to invest its courts with any new and strange jurisdictions? The state courts have no power to entertain suits by individuals against a state without its consent. . . .

To avoid misapprehension, it may be proper to add that, although the obligations of a state rest for their performance upon its honor and good faith, and cannot be made the subjects of judicial cognizance unless the state consents to be sued or comes itself into court, yet, where property or rights are enjoyed under a grant or contract made by a state, they cannot wantonly be invaded. While the state cannot be compelled by suit to perform its contracts, any attempt on its part to violate property or rights acquired under its contracts may be judicially resisted, and any law impairing the obligation of contracts under which such property or rights are held is void and powerless to affect their enjoyment. It is not necessary that we should enter upon an examination of the reason or expediency of the rule which exempts a sovereign state from prosecution in a court of justice at the suit of individuals. This is fully discussed by writers on public law. It is enough for us to declare its existence. The legislative department of a state represents its polity and its will, and is called upon by the highest demands of natural and political law to preserve justice and judgment, and to hold inviolate the public obligations. Any departure from this rule, except for reasons most cogent, (of which the legislature, and not the courts, is the judge,) never fails in the end to incur the odium of the world, and to bring lasting injury upon the state itself. But to deprive the legislature of the power of judging what the honor and safety of the state may require, even at the expense of a temporary failure to discharge the public debts, would be attended with greater evils than such failure can cause.

■ HARLAN, J.

I concur with the court in holding that a suit directly against a state by one of its own citizens is not one to which the judicial power of the United States extends, unless the state itself consents to be sued. Upon this ground alone I assent to the judgment. But I cannot give my assent to many things said in the opinion. The comments made upon the decision in *Chisholm v. Georgia* do not meet my approval. They are not necessary to the determination of the present case. Besides, I am of opinion that the decision in that case was based upon a sound interpretation of the constitution as that instrument then was.

NOTES

1. Was *Hans* rightly decided? What is the Court's argument? Is there a better argument for the conclusion that states are immune from suits for damages even in federal question cases? One way to approach the question is to look to the 1875 statute granting federal question jurisdiction, under which Hans sued: "The circuit courts of the United States shall have original cognizance, concurrent with the courts of the several states, of all suits of a civil nature, at common law or in equity, . . . arising under the constitution or laws of the United States, or treaties." Was this suit for money damages a suit "of a civil nature, at common law or in equity"? Recall the argument that English common law did not include suits against the government, without the government's consent, as fitting within the judicial power. Is there an argument that that is the view adopted in 1875 by statute?

2. The question of state sovereign immunity continues to be hotly contested and vigorously litigated. In recent years, the Supreme Court has divided in a series of sovereign immunity cases over whether Congress has the power in a clear statute to abrogate state sovereign immunity and subject the states to suit for money damages in federal question cases. The issue was thus raised not only as to whether *Hans* was correctly decided but also as to whether it was of a constitutional dimension such that Congress could not displace it. In *Seminole Tribe of Florida v. Florida*, 517 U.S. 44 (1996), a 5 to 4 majority reaffirmed *Hans* and held that Congress may not constitutionally subject a state to suit in

federal court without its consent. This holding was extended by the same 5 to 4 majority to forbid Congress from subjecting states to suit without their consent in *state* courts in *Alden v. Maine*, 527 U.S. 706 (1999). But the Court has also held that Congress may abrogate state sovereignty, by statute, when acting pursuant to its power to enforce the Fourteenth Amendment—which was adopted *after* the Eleventh—but not when acting pursuant to powers granted in the original Constitution *before* adoption of the Eleventh Amendment. See, e.g., *Fitzpatrick v. Bitzer*, 427 U.S. 445 (1976). Does this make sense?

3. The significance of *Hans* and more generally of sovereign immunity is limited somewhat by the doctrine associated with *Ex parte Young*, 209 U.S. 123 (1908). In that case the Court allowed a railroad to sue a state official and obtain an injunction forbidding that official from bringing a enforcement action. (The case could be brought in federal court because the railroad claimed the threatened enforcement action would violate the Fourteenth Amendment of the U.S. Constitution.) The case seems to have been a somewhat conventional suit for an anti-suit injunction, a kind of suit in equity that allows a person who might imminently be a *defendant* to instead start the legal process and raise as claims what the person would otherwise have raised as defenses. The modern Court has read *Ex parte Young* as a foundational decision that created an exception to sovereign immunity for suits seeking relief against state officers in their private capacity. See generally John C. Harrison, *Ex parte Young*, 60 Stan. L. Rev. 989 (2008).

Does Diversity Jurisdiction Confer Common Law–Making Power?

A final question raised by the text of Article III is what power the federal courts acquire once they assume jurisdiction over a case. The word *jurisdiction* comes from two Latin words: *juris*, which means law, and *diction*, which means to speak. To have jurisdiction over a case is thus to have the power to say what the law is as to that case. If the law is clearly codified in a constitution or statute, the power to say what the law is may be relatively straightforward. But what if the area of law in question is an area of common law? Should the federal courts in such a case apply the judge-made common law of the state in which the case arises, or should they instead apply the general principles of the common law as they understand them? Does the grant to federal courts of diversity jurisdiction, or admiralty jurisdiction, or jurisdiction to resolve disputes between two states over their boundary carry with it a power to "discover" or "make" federal common law?

The Supreme Court famously went from a rule that federal courts could fashion federal common law in diversity cases, announced by Justice Joseph Story in *Swift v. Tyson,* 41 U.S. 1 (1842), to a rule that they could not fashion federal common law but were bound to apply *state* substantive law (including applicable *state* common law), announced by Justice Louis Brandeis in *Erie Railroad Co. v. Tompkins*, 304 U.S. 64 (1938). The federal common law of *Swift v. Tyson* played an important role in the nineteenth century in creating a uniform national market and probably helped to fuel the economic growth of the nation, but by the 1930s there was extensive forum-shopping because a case would be decided under different rules in federal and state courts.

Erie Railroad Co. v. Tompkins

304 U.S. 64 (1938)

■ MR. JUSTICE BRANDEIS delivered the opinion of the Court.

The question for decision is whether the oft-challenged doctrine of *Swift v. Tyson* shall now be disapproved.

Tompkins, a citizen of Pennsylvania, was injured on a dark night by a passing freight train of the Erie Railroad Company while walking along its right of way at Hughestown in that state. He claimed that the accident occurred through negligence in the operation, or maintenance, of the train. . . . To enforce that claim he brought an action in the federal court for Southern New York, which had jurisdiction because the company is a corporation of that state. . . .

The Erie insisted that its duty to Tompkins was no greater than that owed to a trespasser. It contended, among other things, that its duty to Tompkins, and hence its liability, should be determined in accordance with the Pennsylvania law; that under the law of Pennsylvania, as declared by its highest court, persons who use pathways along the railroad right of way . . . are to be deemed trespassers; and that the railroad is not liable for injuries to undiscovered trespassers resulting from its negligence, unless it be wanton or willful. . . .

The trial judge refused to rule that the applicable law precluded recovery. The jury brought in a verdict of $30,000; and the judgment entered thereon was affirmed by the Circuit Court of Appeals, which held that it was unnecessary to consider whether the law of Pennsylvania was as contended, because the question was one not of local, but of general, law, and that "upon questions of general law the federal courts are free, in absence of a local statute, to exercise their independent judgment as to what the law is; and it is well settled that the question of the responsibility of a railroad for injuries caused by its servants is one of general law." . . .

The Erie had contended that application of the Pennsylvania rule was required, among other things, by section 34 of the Federal Judiciary Act of September 24, 1789, 28 U.S.C. § 725, which provides: "The laws of the several States, except where the Constitution, treaties, or statutes of the United States otherwise require or provide, shall be regarded as rules of decision in trials at common law, in the courts of the United States, in cases where they apply."

Because of the importance of the question whether the federal court was free to disregard the alleged rule of the Pennsylvania common law, we granted certiorari.

First. *Swift v. Tyson*, 16 Pet. 1, 18, held that federal courts exercising jurisdiction on the ground of diversity of citizenship need not, in matters of general jurisprudence, apply the unwritten law of the State as declared by its highest court; that they are free to exercise an independent judgment as to what the common law of the State is—or should be; and that, as there stated by Mr. Justice Story:

> the true interpretation of the thirty-fourth section limited its application to state laws strictly local, that is to say, to the positive statutes of the state, and the construction thereof adopted by the local tribunals, and to rights and titles to things having a permanent locality, such as the rights and titles to real estate, and other matters immovable and

intraterritorial in their nature and character. It never has been supposed by us, that the section did apply, or was intended to apply, to questions of a more general nature, not at all dependent upon local statutes or local usages of a fixed and permanent operation, as, for example, to the construction of ordinary contracts or other written instruments, and especially to questions of general commercial law, where the state tribunals are called upon to perform the like functions as ourselves, that is, to ascertain upon general reasoning and legal analogies, what is the true exposition of the contract or instrument, or what is the just rule furnished by the principles of commercial law to govern the case.

The Court in applying the rule of § 34 to equity cases, in *Mason v. United States*, 260 U.S. 545, 559, said: "The statute, however, is merely declarative of the rule which would exist in the absence of the statute." The federal courts assumed, in the broad field of "general law," the power to declare rules of decision which Congress was confessedly without power to enact as statutes. Doubt was repeatedly expressed as to the correctness of the construction given § 34, and as to the soundness of the rule which it introduced. But it was the more recent research of a competent scholar, who examined the original document, which established that the construction given to it by the Court was erroneous; and that the purpose of the section was merely to make certain that, in all matters except those in which some federal law is controlling, the federal courts exercising jurisdiction in diversity of citizenship cases would apply as their rules of decision the law of the State, unwritten as well as written.

Criticism of the doctrine became widespread after the decision of *Black & White Taxicab Co. v. Brown & Yellow Taxicab Co.*, 276 U.S. 518. There, Brown and Yellow, a Kentucky corporation owned by Kentuckians, and the Louisville and Nashville Railroad, also a Kentucky corporation, wished that the former should have the exclusive privilege of soliciting passenger and baggage transportation at the Bowling Green, Kentucky, railroad station; and that the Black and White, a competing Kentucky corporation, should be prevented from interfering with that privilege. Knowing that such a contract would be void under the common law of Kentucky, it was arranged that the Brown and Yellow reincorporate under the law of Tennessee, and that the contract with the railroad should be executed there. The suit was then brought by the Tennessee corporation in the federal court for western Kentucky to enjoin competition by the Black and White; an injunction issued by the District Court was sustained by the Court of Appeals; and this Court, citing many decisions in which the doctrine of *Swift v. Tyson* had been applied, affirmed the decree.

Second. Experience in applying the doctrine of *Swift v. Tyson*, had revealed its defects, political and social; and the benefits expected to flow from the rule did not accrue. Persistence of state courts in their own opinions on questions of common law prevented uniformity; and the impossibility of discovering a satisfactory line of demarcation between the province of general law and that of local law developed a new well of uncertainties.

On the other hand, the mischievous results of the doctrine had become apparent. Diversity of citizenship jurisdiction was conferred in order to prevent apprehended discrimination in state courts against those not citizens of the State. *Swift v. Tyson* introduced grave discrimination by noncitizens against citizens. It made rights enjoyed under the unwritten "general law" vary according to whether enforcement was sought in the state or in the federal court; and the privilege of selecting the court in which the right should be determined was conferred upon the non-citizen. Thus, the doctrine rendered impossible equal protection of the law. In attempting to promote uniformity of law throughout the United States, the doctrine had prevented uniformity in the administration of the law of the State.

The discrimination resulting became in practice far-reaching. This resulted in part from the broad province accorded to the so-called "general law" as to which federal courts exercised an independent judgment. In addition to questions of purely commercial law, "general law" was held to include the obligations under contracts entered into and to be performed within the State, the extent to which a carrier operating within a State may stipulate for exemption from liability for his own negligence or that of his employee; the liability for torts committed within the State upon persons resident or property located there, even where the question of liability depended upon the scope of a property right conferred by the State; and the right to exemplary or punitive damages. Furthermore, state decisions construing local deeds, mineral conveyances, and even devises of real estate were disregarded.

In part the discrimination resulted from the wide range of persons held entitled to avail themselves of the federal rule by resort to the diversity of citizenship jurisdiction. Through this jurisdiction individual citizens willing to remove from their own State and become citizens of another might avail themselves of the federal rule. And, without even change of residence, a corporate citizen of the State could avail itself of the federal rule by re-incorporating under the laws of another State, as was done in the *Taxicab* case.

The injustice and confusion incident to the doctrine of *Swift v. Tyson* have been repeatedly urged as reasons for abolishing or limiting diversity of citizenship jurisdiction. Other legislative relief has been proposed. If only a question of statutory construction were involved, we should not be prepared to abandon a doctrine so widely applied throughout nearly a century. But the unconstitutionality of the course pursued has now been made clear and compels us to do so.

Third. Except in matters governed by the Federal Constitution or by Acts of Congress, the law to be applied in any case is the law of the State. And whether the law of the State shall be declared by its Legislature in a statute or by its highest court in a decision is not a matter of federal concern. There is no federal general common law. Congress has no power to declare substantive rules of common law applicable in a State whether they be local in their nature or "general," be they commercial law or a part of the law of torts. And no clause in the Constitution purports to confer such a power upon the federal courts. As stated by Mr. Justice Field when protesting in *Baltimore & Ohio R. Co. v. Baugh*, 149 U.S. 368, 401, against ignoring the Ohio common law of fellow servant liability:

> I am aware that what has been termed the general law of the country—which is often little less than what the judge advancing the doctrine thinks at the time should be the general law on a particular subject—has been often advanced in judicial opinions of this court to control a conflicting law of a State. I admit that learned judges have fallen into the habit of repeating this doctrine as a convenient mode of brushing aside the law of a State in conflict with their views. And I confess that, moved and governed by the authority of the great names of those judges, I have, myself, in many instances, unhesitatingly and confi-

dently, but I think now erroneously, repeated the same doctrine. But, notwithstanding the great names which may be cited in favor of the doctrine, and notwithstanding the frequency with which the doctrine has been reiterated, there stands, as a perpetual protest against its repetition, the Constitution of the United States, which recognizes and preserves the autonomy and independence of the States—independence in their legislative and independence in their judicial departments. Supervision over either the legislative or the judicial action of the States is in no case permissible except as to matters by the Constitution specifically authorized or delegated to the United States. Any interference with either, except as thus permitted, is an invasion of the authority of the State and, to that extent, a denial of its independence.

The fallacy underlying the rule declared in *Swift v. Tyson* is made clear by Mr. Justice Holmes. The doctrine rests upon the assumption that there is "a transcendental body of law outside of any particular State but obligatory within it unless and until changed by statute," that federal courts have the power to use their judgment as to what the rules of common law are; and that in the federal courts "the parties are entitled to an independent judgment on matters of general law":

> but law in the sense in which courts speak of it today does not exist without some definite authority behind it. The common law so far as it is enforced in a State, whether called common law or not, is not the common law generally but the law of that State existing by the authority of that State without regard to what it may have been in England or anywhere else. . . .

> The authority and only authority is the State, and if that be so, the voice adopted by the State as its own [whether it be of its Legislature or of its Supreme Court] should utter the last word.

Thus the doctrine of *Swift v. Tyson* is, as Mr. Justice Holmes said, "an unconstitutional assumption of powers by courts of the United States which no lapse of time or respectable array of opinion should make us hesitate to correct." In disapproving that doctrine we do not hold unconstitutional § 34 of the Federal Judiciary Act of 1789 or any other Act of Congress. We merely declare that in applying the doctrine this Court and the lower courts have invaded rights which in our opinion are reserved by the Constitution to the several States.

Fourth. The defendant contended that by the common law of Pennsylvania as declared by its highest court in *Falchetti v. Pennsylvania R. Co.*, 307 Pa. 203, the only duty owed to the plaintiff was to refrain from wilful or wanton injury. The plaintiff denied that such is the Pennsylvania law. . . . The Circuit Court of Appeals ruled that the question of liability is one of general law; and on that ground declined to decide the issue of state law. As we hold this was error, the judgment is reversed and the case remanded to it for further proceedings in conformity with our opinion.

■ MR. JUSTICE CARDOZO took no part in the consideration or decision of this case.

■ MR. JUSTICE BUTLER[, whose dissenting opinion was joined by MR. JUSTICE McREYNOLDS].

The case presented by the evidence is a simple one. Plaintiff was severely injured in Pennsylvania. While walking on defendant's right of way along a much-used path at the end of the cross-ties of its main track, he came into collision with an open door swinging from the side of a car in a train going in the opposite direction. Having been warned by whistle and headlight, he saw the locomotive approaching and had time and space enough to step aside and so avoid danger. To justify his failure to get out of the way, he says that upon many other occasions he had safely walked there while trains passed. . . .

No constitutional question was suggested or argued below or here. And as a general rule, this Court will not consider any question not raised below and presented by the petition. Here it does not decide either of the questions presented, but, changing the rule of decision in force since the foundation of the government, remands the case to be adjudged according to a standard never before deemed permissible.

The opinion just announced states that: "The question for decision is whether the oft-challenged doctrine of *Swift v. Tyson* shall now be disapproved." . . .

The doctrine of that case has been followed by this Court in an unbroken line of decisions. So far as appears, it was not questioned until more than 50 years later, and then by a single judge. . . .

While amendments to section 34 have from time to time been suggested, the section stands as originally enacted. Evidently Congress has intended throughout the years that the rule of decision as construed should continue to govern federal courts in trials at common law. The opinion just announced suggests that Mr. Warren's research has established that from the beginning this Court has erroneously construed section 34. But that author's "New Light on the History of the Federal Judiciary Act of 1789" does not purport to be authoritative, and was intended to be no more than suggestive. The weight to be given to his discovery has never been discussed at this bar. Nor does the opinion indicate the ground disclosed by the research. In his dissenting opinion in the *Taxicab* Case, Mr. Justice Holmes referred to Mr. Warren's work, but failed to persuade the Court that "laws" as used in section 34 included varying and possibly ill-considered rulings by the courts of a state on questions of common law. . . . It is hard to foresee the consequences of the radical change so made. Our opinion in the *Taxicab* Case cites numerous decisions of this Court which serve in part to indicate the field from which it is now intended forever to bar the federal courts. It extends to all matters of contracts and torts not positively governed by state enactments. Counsel searching for precedent and reasoning to disclose common-law principles on which to guide clients and conduct litigation are by this decision told that as to all of these questions the decisions of this Court and other federal courts are no longer anywhere authoritative.

This Court has often emphasized its reluctance to consider constitutional questions and that legislation will not be held invalid as repugnant to the fundamental law if the case may be decided upon any other ground. In view of grave consequences liable to result from erroneous exertion of its power to set aside legislation, the Court should move cautiously, seek assistance of counsel, act only after ample deliberation, show that the question is before the Court, that its decision cannot be avoided by construction of the statute assailed or otherwise, indicate precisely the principle or provision of the Constitutional held to have been transgressed, and fully disclose the reasons and authorities found to warrant the conclusion of invalidity. These safeguards against the improvident use of the great power to invalidate legislation are so well-grounded and familiar that statement of reasons or citation of authority to support them is no longer necessary. . . .

I am of opinion that the constitutional validity of the rule need not be considered, because under the law, as found by the courts of Pennsylvania and generally throughout the country, it is plain that the evidence required a finding that plaintiff was guilty of negligence that contributed to cause his injuries, and that the judgment below should be reversed upon that ground.

■ [The concurring opinion of JUSTICE REED is omitted.]

NOTES

1. In a sense, the question presented in *Erie* is a different version of the question presented in *Chisholm*: Does a grant of jurisdiction over a type of case include a power for courts to decide—and even fashion—the substantive law applicable to the case? What is the answer in *Erie*? Is it different in the two contexts? Why or why not?

2. Which types of constitutional argument does Justice Brandeis employ? What weight does he give to the text? To the new historical research by Charles Warren? To *Swift*, a precedent that was almost a century old and on which the entire commercial establishment of the country had relied? What weight does Justice Butler give to each type of constitutional argument? When should courts be willing to rethink basic premises of our constitutional jurisprudence? Does it matter whether the parties want a court to rethink those premises? In *Erie* the stakes could hardly have been higher—in terms of the number of cases that depend on the choice of a legal rule, the switch from *Swift* to *Erie* was the most consequential in the history of the Supreme Court, affecting the controlling substantive law in thousands of diversity suits brought every year in federal court. When the stakes are that high, does it change the weight that should be given to the different types of constitutional argument? Does stability matter more, meaning that additional weight should be given to practice and precedent and to policy? Or is it even more important than ever to get the answer right as a matter of constitutional text and structure? Whichever answer you give, how would you apply it in *Erie*?

CHAPTER 4

FEDERALISM

[Assignment 30]

Federalism, the general term for the division of power between two levels of government, and the relationships among states and between the states and the national government, is in large measure America's distinctive contribution to political theory. Before America, there had been many successful democracies on a small scale: ancient Athens, the Roman Republic, the Venetian Republic, the Netherlands, England and Switzerland. But before America, there had never been a successful democratic government on an *extended* scale. The history of the world is full of the stories of the rise and fall of empires, but a truly republican "empire" had never before succeeded. Confederations had existed, but they tended either to collapse into disarray or become consolidated under centralized government and tyranny. (Many thoughtful observers in 1787 denied that it was possible to create an extended democratic republic. They believed that democracy would flourish only in small homogeneous states. They feared that if the thirteen free colonies on the Atlantic seaboard formed a strong central government, freedom and democracy would perish. Most of the people who thought this way became Anti-Federalist opponents of the new Constitution of 1787.)

The framers' proposed answer was a compound *federal* republic with a division of powers between the autonomous governments of the states and a collective government for the whole—for a true *union* of states—with the two levels of government serving in some respects as checks on one another. The framers thus sought to turn the traditional conception on its head and *exploit* the advantages of size and geographical extent to create a structure where pluralism flourished and where both freedom and effective government could prevail at both at the national and local levels. Political necessity was the mother of constitutional invention. The framers had little practical choice but to devise some kind of a working federal system. States were a given. America's federal system had its origins in the federalism of the British Empire, in which thirteen chartered royal colonies were created as independent and partially self-governing entities on the North American continent. By the time of the American Revolution, the existence of these polities as distinct governing entities with separate identities was fairly well entrenched. The Revolution had sought the independence of a group of (lowercase-u) "united States." But by 1787, the need for a stronger national government had become clear. The Constitution was thus designed to form a "more perfect Union" of the (uppercase-U) United States of America—a nation of distinct states, each with its own constitution and republican form of government, but a nation nonetheless.

And so the practical problems of structure and power were presented to the framers at Philadelphia: What would be the powers of each level of government? What would be the relationship between these levels of government? Which would be "sovereign," or would sovereignty in some sense be "divided"? And should each government be thought of as simply a different set of "agents" of the sovereign people? What would be the relationship *between* states within this union?

These are some of the great questions of American federalism, framed by the Constitution, which proclaims itself—not the national government and not the state governments, to be supreme. In this chapter, we start with the Constitution's allocation of powers between the national and state governments: the Constitution's structure of enumerated powers and reservation of remaining powers to the states. We have already seen some of this in the debate over the Bank of the United States, and in the Supreme Court's decision in *McCulloch v. Maryland*. The major controversies in this area have concerned the scope of Congress's powers under Article I, Section 8, especially the powers to regulate "commerce among the states," to tax, to spend money, and to enact laws necessary and proper for carrying into execution of every other enumerated legislative power plus the powers of any other department or officer of the United States government. A related series of controversies concerns what types of legislative enactments might be thought of as *impliedly* forbidden *to the states*, simply as a consequence of the assignment of legislative powers to the national government.

We then turn to questions of nation-state and state-state relationships under the Constitution's structures of federalism—questions that historically have been perhaps the most significant in our nation's history, ultimately leading to the Civil War. We have already had an extended glimpse of such issues in the context of the Alien and Sedition Act controversies and the arguments over the meaning, and propriety, of the Virginia and Kentucky Resolutions against them. While the Civil War resolved the question of sovereignty and supremacy in favor of the power of the people acting through the national government, over the claims of state governments, these questions are not of mere historical interest: they continue to pose difficult and to a certain extent unresolved constitutional issues today.

This chapter begins with an introductory overview of the Constitution's federalism provisions and a brief look at the framers' political theory of federalism—as famously discussed in James Madison's brilliant *The Federalist No. 10*. We then examine in detail two broad features of America's constitutional federalism: The first part of the chapter concerns the allocation of powers between the national and state governments, and it emphasizes questions of Congress's power under the Commerce Clause, Necessary and Proper Clause, Taxing Clause, spending power, and a sampling of other national legislative powers under Article I, Section 8. The second part of the chapter concerns the questions of national-versus-state sovereignty and the state-state relationships within our federal system, which are primarily governed by Article IV of the Constitution. This part emphasizes questions that deeply troubled the early republic and culminated in the Civil War.

A Map of the Constitution's Federalism Provisions

There is, of course, no "Federalism Clause" in the Constitution. Federalism is, rather, the descriptive label attached to the pattern that emerges from several key structural features of the Constitution.

First, the states continue to exist and function as states, with their own autonomous powers and sphere of authority. While they are states within a larger union, governed by a single Constitution that in important respects limits the powers of the states, the states are not merely subordinate administrative districts of the national government. Much of Article IV of the Constitution governs the relationship of the states to the national government, and to each other. (A map of Article IV's provisions is presented later in this chapter.)

Second, the powers of the national government are specifically enumerated and limited, and the states have the remaining, "reserved" powers, except where prohibited by the Constitution or in conflict with the exercise of national power. This will be the major theme of the first half of this chapter: What is the division of powers between the national government and the governments of the states?

The text and structure of the Constitution provide that the legislative powers of Congress are not plenary, but are limited to those listed in Article I, Section 8—an itemized listing of eighteen specific powers—and contained in other provisions of the Constitution, including Article IV and Article V and the enforcement clauses of numerous constitutional amendments. While those powers are sometimes written in broad, sweeping terms, it remains the case that the legislative powers of the national government are not unlimited. They are limited to the powers specifically listed.

In addition to national legislative powers, the Constitution in Article II grants the president "the executive Power" of the nation. As discussed in Chapter 3, Article II grants specific presidential powers, such as being commander in chief of the military, making treaties and appointments (powers shared with the Senate), and issuing pardons. Article III grants "the judicial Power" to a system of national and state courts. The scope of these powers was also discussed in Chapter 3.

Where Congress possesses national legislative power pursuant to one of the Constitution's grants of such power, this does not necessarily mean that the states *lack* legislative power to act. Sometimes national and state legislative power is concurrent: both the federal and state governments may act. In certain circumstances, however, the Constitution specifically excludes or limits states' powers. Article I, Section 10 is intricately interlocked with Article I, Section 8, in that almost all the things it forbids states to do are things that Section 8 expressly empowers the federal government to do. Thus, the states may not on their own authority (1) enter into treaties; (2) wage war unless invaded; (3) coin money; (4) emit bills of credit; (5) print paper money; (6) tax imports or exports; (7) lay duties of tonnage; (8) keep troops or ships of war in peacetime; or (9) enter into compacts with another state without Congress's consent. Thus, Article I, Section 10 makes clear that the national legislative powers over foreign policy, monetary policy, and tariffs are exclusive. Only the federal government may act in these areas; the states are expressly preempted from acting by the Constitution.

Where exercise of a state power conflicts with the exercise of a national power, the Supremacy Clause of the Constitution (in Article VI) makes clear that national power prevails: "This Constitution, and the Laws of the United States which shall be made in Pursuance thereof; and all Treaties made, or which shall be made, under the Authority of the United States, shall be the supreme Law of the Land; and the Judges in every States shall be bound thereby, any Thing in the Constitution or Laws of any state to the Contrary notwithstanding." (You have seen this principle at work in *McCulloch v. Maryland*, in Chapter 3: Maryland's law taxing the operations of the Bank of the United States was held to be in conflict with Congress's exercise of national legislative power in creating the Bank.)

In addition, the Supreme Court has long held that the very existence of certain national powers can, in some circumstances, impliedly exclude states' power in such areas, even where Congress has not exercised its national powers in a way that conflicts with a state's action and even where the power is not specifically prohibited by Article I, Section 10. This doctrine, referred to as "implied pre-emption" or sometimes "dormant pre-emption" is presented in two early cases discussed in this chapter: *Gibbons v. Ogden* (1824), addressing the issue of whether a state law regulating commerce might be forbidden because the Commerce Clause of Article I, Section 8 grants Congress power to act (whether or not Congress has not acted in conflict with the state's law); and *Prigg v. Pennsylvania* (1842), a case under the Fugitive Slave Clause of Article IV presenting the issue whether a state law forbidding seizure and taking of alleged fugitive slaves without legal process impliedly conflicted with national authority under the Constitution.

The Tenth Amendment confirms the principles of limited, enumerated national powers and the reserved authority of the states in matters where the Constitution does not grant power to the national government. It provides: "The powers not delegated to the United States by the Constitution, nor prohibited by it to the States, are reserved to the States respectively, or to the People." But as many have pointed out, this does not answer the question of how broadly or narrowly to construe powers that *are* "delegated to the United States." The Ninth Amendment might also be thought of as a kind of federalism provision, by stating that the adoption of a federal Bill of Rights limiting the powers of the national government does not thereby negate rights retained by the people in their state constitutions, common law, or some other unspecified source: "The enumeration in the Constitution, of certain rights, shall not be construed to deny or disparage others retained by the people."

As noted, several constitutional amendments explicitly enlarge the powers of the national government. Most striking is a fact about the three amendments known as the Reconstruction Amendments—the Thirteenth, which abolishes slavery; the Fourteenth, which limits the powers of states to deprive persons of certain privileges and immunities, due process, and the equal protection of the laws; and the Fifteenth, which prohibits denial of the right to vote on the basis of race. All three of the Reconstruction Amendments grant Congress sweeping power to "enforce" their requirements by "appropriate" legislation. (The scope of these powers is considered below in Chapter 7.) There are similar grants of congressional enforcement authority in the Nineteenth Amendment, guaranteeing sex equality in voting, and the Twenty-third, and Twenty-fourth, and Twenty-sixth Amendments, also concerning voting rights. The Sixteenth Amendment was arguably a major expansion of congressional power, giving Congress specific authority to impose a direct tax on personal incomes.

A third and distinct feature of the Constitution's federalism is that it is built into the very structure of the national government. The Senate explicitly represents the states as states, with each state entitled to two senators, irrespective of population. (And the state-oriented representative nature of the Senate was strongly reinforced by the original mode of selecting senators, as discussed in the next paragraph.) The House of Representatives, while based primarily on population, nonetheless is structured along state lines and provides that each state is entitled to at least one representative regardless of population. Finally, the Electoral College for selecting the president is based on state-chosen means for selecting electors and assigns the number of electors based on a state's combined representation in the House and Senate, a formula that builds on the federalism embodied in those provisions. (The Constitution's provisions about representation and voting are considered in Chapter 8.)

One way federalism pervaded the national government's structure has been emphatically changed from the original design. The Constitution originally provided for selection of a state's senators by its state legislature. This arrangement was seen by the framers as an important check on the power of the national government. Writing to John Adams in 1789, Roger Sherman put it this way: "The senators, being eligible by the legislatures of the several states, and dependent on them for re-election, will be vigilant in supporting their rights against infringement by the legislative or executive of the United States." That arrangement persisted until the Seventeenth Amendment, which was ratified in 1913. This amendment required the direct election of senators. See generally Ralph A. Rossum, FEDERALISM, THE SUPREME COURT, AND THE SEVENTEENTH AMENDMENT: THE IRONY OF CONSTITUTIONAL DEMOCRACY (2001). It seems that the Seventeenth Amendment changed the political composition of the U.S. Senate (which had previously been controlled by whichever party controlled the most state legislatures), and it encouraged much longer terms of service by senators. Critically, the amendment eliminated the intense incentives of the senators to protect the interests of their state governments, because their reelection was no longer in the hands of the state legislature. The amendment also undermined the state legislatures' practice of "instruction" of their state's senators on how they should vote on important questions. Previously, state legislatures had instructed senators about their votes on major pending legislation, on the ratification of treaties, and (less frequently) on key nominations to executive-branch or judicial office. Although the effects are hard to measure precisely, it would be hard to overstate the significance of the Seventeenth Amendment's removal of this critical state check on the exercise of national power.

The Political Theory of American Federalism

The starting point for thinking about America's constitutional federalism is what may well be the most important essay on political theory ever written by an American—*The Federalist No. 10*, by James Madison.

The Federalist No. 10

James Madison, November 22, 1787

To the People of the State of New York:

AMONG the numerous advantages promised by a well constructed Union, none deserves to be more accurately developed than its tendency to break and control the violence of faction. The friend of popular governments never finds himself so much alarmed for their character and fate, as when he contemplates their propensity to this dangerous vice. He will not fail, therefore, to set a due value on any plan which, without violating the principles to which he is attached, provides a proper cure for it. The instability, injustice, and confusion introduced into the public councils, have, in truth, been the mortal diseases under which popular governments have everywhere perished; as they continue to be the favorite and fruitful topics from which the adversaries to liberty derive their most specious declamations. The valuable improvements made by the American constitutions on the popular models, both ancient and modern, cannot certainly be too much admired; but it would be an unwarrantable partiality, to contend that they have as effectually obviated the danger on this side, as was wished and expected. Complaints are everywhere heard from our most considerate and virtuous citizens, equally the friends of public and private faith, and of public and personal liberty, that our governments are too unstable, that the public good is disregarded in the conflicts of rival parties, and that measures are too often decided, not according to the rules of justice and the rights of the minor party, but by the superior force of an interested and overbearing majority. However anxiously we may wish that these complaints had no foundation, the evidence, of known facts will not permit us to deny that they are in some degree true. It will be found, indeed, on a candid review of our situation, that some of the distresses under which we labor have been erroneously charged on the operation of our governments; but it will be found, at the same time, that other causes will not alone account for many of our heaviest misfortunes; and, particularly, for that prevailing and increasing distrust of public engagements, and alarm for private rights, which are echoed from one end of the continent to the other. These must be chiefly, if not wholly, effects of the unsteadiness and injustice with which a factious spirit has tainted our public administrations.

By a faction, I understand a number of citizens, whether amounting to a majority or a minority of the whole, who are united and actuated by some common impulse of passion, or of interest, adversed to the rights of other citizens, or to the permanent and aggregate interests of the community.

There are two methods of curing the mischiefs of faction: the one, by removing its causes; the other, by controlling its effects.

There are again two methods of removing the causes of faction: the one, by destroying the liberty which is essential to its existence; the other, by giving to every citizen the same opinions, the same passions, and the same interests.

It could never be more truly said than of the first remedy, that it was worse than the disease. Liberty is to faction what air is to fire, an aliment without which it instantly expires. But it could not be less folly to abolish liberty, which is essential to political life, because it nourishes faction, than it would be to wish the annihilation of air, which is essential to animal life, because it imparts to fire its destructive agency.

The second expedient is as impracticable as the first would be unwise. As long as the reason of man continues fallible, and he is at liberty to exercise it, different opinions will be formed. As long as the connection subsists between his reason and his self-love, his opinions and his passions will have a reciprocal influence on each other; and the former will be objects to which the latter will attach themselves. The diversity in the faculties of men, from which the rights of property originate, is not less an insuperable obstacle to a uniformity of interests. The protection of these faculties is the first object of government. From the protection of different and unequal faculties of acquiring property, the possession of different degrees and kinds of property immediately results; and from the influence of these on the sentiments and views of the respective proprietors, ensues a division of the society into different interests and parties.

The latent causes of faction are thus sown in the nature of man; and we see them everywhere brought into different degrees of activity, according to the different circumstances of civil society. A zeal for different opinions concerning religion, concerning government, and many other points, as well of speculation as of practice; an attachment to different leaders ambitiously contending for pre-eminence and power; or to persons of other descriptions whose fortunes have been interesting to the human passions, have, in turn, divided mankind into parties, inflamed them with mutual animosity, and rendered them much more disposed to vex and oppress each other than to co-operate for their common good. So strong is this propensity of mankind to fall into mutual animosities, that where no substantial occasion presents itself, the most frivolous and fanciful distinctions have been sufficient to kindle their unfriendly passions and excite their most violent conflicts. But the most common and durable source of factions has been the various and unequal distribution of property. Those who hold and those who are without property have ever formed distinct interests in society. Those who are creditors, and those who are debtors, fall under a like discrimination. A landed interest, a manufacturing interest, a mercantile interest, a moneyed interest, with many lesser interests, grow up of necessity in civilized nations, and divide them into different classes, actuated by different sentiments and views. The regulation of these various and interfering interests forms the principal task of modern legislation, and involves the spirit of party and faction in the necessary and ordinary operations of the government.

No man is allowed to be a judge in his own cause, because his interest would certainly bias his judgment, and, not improbably, corrupt his integrity. With equal, nay with greater reason, a body of men are unfit to be both judges and parties at the same time; yet what are many of the most important acts of legislation, but so many judicial determinations, not indeed concerning the rights of single persons, but concerning the rights of large bodies of citizens? And what are the different classes of legislators but advocates and parties to the causes which they determine? Is a law proposed concerning private debts? It is a question to which the creditors are parties on one side and the debtors on the other. Justice ought to hold the balance between them. Yet the parties are, and must be, themselves the judges; and the most numerous party, or, in other words, the most powerful faction must be expected to prevail. Shall domestic manufactures be encouraged, and in what degree, by restrictions on foreign manufactures? are questions which would be differently decided by the landed and the manufacturing classes, and probably by neither with a sole regard to justice and the public good. The apportionment of taxes on the various descriptions of property is an act which seems to require the most exact impartiality; yet there is, perhaps, no legislative act in which greater opportunity and temptation are given to a predominant party to trample on the rules of justice. Every shilling with which they overburden the inferior number, is a shilling saved to their own pockets.

It is in vain to say that enlightened statesmen will be able to adjust these clashing interests, and render them all subservient to the public good. Enlightened statesmen will not always be at the helm. Nor, in many cases, can such an adjustment be made at all without taking into view indirect and remote considerations, which will rarely prevail over the immediate interest which one party may find in disregarding the rights of another or the good of the whole.

The inference to which we are brought is, that the CAUSES of faction cannot be removed, and that relief is only to be sought in the means of controlling its EFFECTS.

If a faction consists of less than a majority, relief is supplied by the republican principle, which enables the majority to defeat its sinister views by regular vote. It may clog the administration, it may convulse the society; but it will be unable to execute and mask its violence under the forms of the Constitution. When a majority is included in a faction, the form of popular government, on the other hand, enables it to sacrifice to its ruling passion or interest both the public good and the rights of other citizens. To secure the public good and private rights against the danger of such a faction, and at the same time to preserve the spirit and the form of popular government, is then the great object to which our inquiries are directed. Let me add that it is the great desideratum by which this form of government can be rescued from the opprobrium under which it has so long labored, and be recommended to the esteem and adoption of mankind.

By what means is this object attainable? Evidently by one of two only. Either the existence of the same passion or interest in a majority at the same time must be prevented, or the majority, having such coexistent passion or interest, must be rendered, by their number and local situation, unable to concert and carry into effect schemes of oppression. If the impulse and the opportunity be suffered to coincide, we well know that neither moral nor religious motives can be relied on as an adequate control. They are not found to be such on the injustice and violence of individuals, and lose their efficacy in proportion to the number combined together, that is, in proportion as their efficacy becomes needful.

From this view of the subject it may be concluded that a pure democracy, by which I mean a society consisting of a small number of citizens, who assemble and administer the government in person, can admit of no cure for the mischiefs of faction. A common passion or interest will, in almost every case, be felt by a majority of the whole; a communication and concert result from the form of government itself; and there is nothing to check the inducements to sacrifice the weaker party or an obnoxious individual. Hence it is that such democracies have ever been spectacles of turbulence and contention; have ever been found incompatible with personal security or the rights of property; and have in general been as short in their lives as they have been violent in their deaths. Theoretic politicians, who have patronized this species of government, have erroneously supposed that by reducing mankind to a perfect equality in their political rights, they would, at the same time, be perfectly equalized and assimilated in their possessions, their opinions, and their passions.

A republic, by which I mean a government in which the scheme of representation takes place, opens a different prospect, and promises the cure for which we are seeking. Let us examine the points in which it varies from pure democracy, and we shall comprehend both the nature of the cure and the efficacy which it must derive from the Union.

The two great points of difference between a democracy and a republic are: first, the delegation of the government, in the latter, to a small number of citizens elected by the rest; secondly, the greater number of citizens, and greater sphere of country, over which the latter may be extended.

The effect of the first difference is, on the one hand, to refine and enlarge the public views, by passing them through the medium of a chosen body of citizens, whose wisdom may best discern the true interest of their country, and whose patriotism and love of justice will be least likely to sacrifice it to temporary or partial considerations. Under such a regulation, it may well happen that the public voice, pronounced by the representatives of the people, will be more consonant to the public good than if pronounced by the people themselves, convened for the purpose. On the other hand, the effect may be inverted. Men of factious tempers, of local prejudices, or of sinister designs, may, by intrigue, by corruption, or by other means, first obtain the suffrages, and then betray the interests, of the people. The question resulting is, whether small or extensive republics are more favorable to the election of proper guardians of the public weal; and it is clearly decided in favor of the latter by two obvious considerations:

In the first place, it is to be remarked that, however small the republic may be, the representatives must be raised to a certain number, in order to guard against the cabals of a few; and that, however large it may be, they must be limited to a certain number, in order to guard against the confusion of a multitude. Hence, the number of representatives in the two cases not being in proportion to that of the two constituents, and being proportionally greater in the small republic, it follows that, if the proportion of fit characters be not less in the large than in the small republic, the former will present a greater option, and consequently a greater probability of a fit choice.

In the next place, as each representative will be chosen by a greater number of citizens in the large than in the small republic, it will be more difficult for unworthy candidates to practice with success the vicious arts by which elections are too often carried; and the suffrages of the people being more free, will be more likely to centre in men who possess the most attractive merit and the most diffusive and established characters.

It must be confessed that in this, as in most other cases, there is a mean, on both sides of which inconveniences will be found to lie. By enlarging too much the number of electors, you render the representatives too little acquainted with all their local circumstances and lesser interests; as by reducing it too much, you render him unduly attached to these, and too little fit to comprehend and pursue great and national objects. The federal Constitution forms a happy combination in this respect; the great and aggregate interests being referred to the national, the local and particular to the State legislatures.

The other point of difference is, the greater number of citizens and extent of territory which may be brought within the compass of republican than of democratic government; and it is this circumstance principally which renders factious combinations less to be dreaded in the former than in the latter. The smaller the society, the fewer probably will be the distinct parties and interests composing it; the fewer the distinct parties and interests, the more frequently will a majority be found of the same party; and the smaller the number of individuals composing a majority, and the smaller the compass within which they are placed, the more easily will they concert and execute their plans of oppression. Extend the sphere, and you take in a greater variety of parties and interests; you make it less probable that a majority of the whole will have a common motive to invade the rights of other citizens; or if such a common motive exists, it will be more difficult for all who feel it to discover their own strength, and to act in unison with each other. Besides other impediments, it may be remarked that, where there is a consciousness of unjust or dishonorable purposes, communication is always checked by distrust in proportion to the number whose concurrence is necessary.

Hence, it clearly appears, that the same advantage which a republic has over a democracy, in controlling the effects of faction, is enjoyed by a large over a small republic,—is enjoyed by the Union over the States composing it. Does the advantage consist in the substitution of representatives whose enlightened views and virtuous sentiments render them superior to local prejudices and schemes of injustice? It will not be denied that the representation of the Union will be most likely to possess these requisite endowments. Does it consist in the greater security afforded by a greater variety of parties, against the event of any one party being able to outnumber and oppress the rest? In an equal degree does the increased variety of parties comprised within the Union, increase this security. Does it, in fine, consist in the greater obstacles opposed to the concert and accomplishment of the secret wishes of an unjust and interested majority? Here, again, the extent of the Union gives it the most palpable advantage.

The influence of factious leaders may kindle a flame within their particular States, but will be unable to spread a general conflagration through the other States. A religious sect may degenerate into a political faction in a part of the Confederacy; but the variety of sects dispersed over the entire face of it must secure the national councils against any danger from that source. A rage for paper money, for an abolition of debts, for an equal division of property, or for any other improper or wicked project, will be less apt to pervade the whole body of the Union than a particular member of it; in the same proportion as such a malady is more likely to taint a particular county or district, than an entire State.

In the extent and proper structure of the Union, therefore, we behold a republican remedy for the diseases most incident to republican government. And according to the degree of pleasure and pride we feel in being republicans, ought to be our zeal in cherishing the spirit and supporting the character of Federalists.

NOTES

1. Is Madison right or is he overly pessimistic in saying that the causes of faction are sown in the nature of man? Are human beings inherently good, so that if private property were abolished everyone would behave like angels and factions would disappear? Are human beings so inherently prone to wage a Hobbesian war of all against all that only an absolute monarchy or a dictatorship can prevent disaster? Is the truth about human nature somewhere between utopianism and despair? What ground does Madison occupy?

2. Is Madison right that permanently entrenched majorities engaged in self-dealing will be less likely in a transcontinental Congress than in a small city-state (more like, say, Rhode Island)? Has the federal government in fact had a better record than the states in protecting the rights of racial minorities?

3. Why does democracy work so well in Switzerland, a small country divided among German, French, and Italian speakers and between Protestants and Catholics? One answer may be that the various social divisions cross cut each other so that half the German speakers are Protestant and half are Catholic; half the French speakers are Protestant and half are Catholic; and half of each language group dwells in urban areas while the other half live in rural areas. In addition, the accidents of history divided the Swiss Federation up into

26 cantons and half cantons, adding to the multiplicity of interest groups. Cross-cutting social divisions and the creation of 26 federal subunits has produced a *Federalist No. 10* effect. Contrast the Swiss federation with the Canadian federation, where almost all the French speakers and Catholics live in one large province (Quebec) and the other nine provinces are populated overwhelmingly with English-speaking Protestants. Is it surprising that secession is a real threat in Canada but not in Switzerland?

4. Does the Constitution's system of electing the president reflect, in certain ways, Madison's political theory in *The Federalist No. 10*? The president of the United States is elected by a majority of the Electoral College, which usually (but not always) means a majority of the U.S. population. A winning presidential coalition typically requires a national popular majority made up of a variety of interests and perspectives. At present, both the Republicans and the Democrats have a base vote for their national electoral coalitions of about 40% of the American people. Presidential elections are thus won or lost on who gets a majority of the middle 20%. Both party's presidential candidates face powerful pressure to moderate their views to win a majority of the middle 20% of the vote that is up for grabs. Once elected, presidents need to maintain broad popular support if they are to be effective in dealing with Congress, or if they want to be re-elected (or see friendly successors replace them). The net result is that presidents must constantly try to shepherd together a national popular majority of the kind Madison talks about in *The Federalist No. 10*. Does this explain why presidents often adopt relatively moderate policies in office?

The federal system of presidential election also has the effect of requiring that a successful candidate generally must appeal to multiple, diverse constituencies throughout the nation; overwhelming support that is concentrated in a few states or a particular region will usually not translate into an Electoral College majority. (An important historical counter-example is the election of Abraham Lincoln in 1860, whose electoral majority was concentrated exclusively in Northern and Western states, but that was possible only because it was a four-way race.) Is this a desirable arrangement or an undesirable one? Is your view affected by reflecting on *The Federalist No. 10*?

5. In light of *The Federalist No. 10* (and in light of the materials in Chapter 3 on the separation of powers), what kind of constitutional framework would you recommend to a new democracy in another country? What does *The Federalist No. 10* imply about the desirability of a world government or at least of a united government of all the democracies? Is there some point at which a democratic "empire" might become so big that it would collapse? At present, some benefits of size and scope in self-defense and free-trade are provided by transnational entities like NATO and the WTO, while the benefits of decentralization remain in the roughly two hundred largely sovereign nations. But some collective-action problems, such as those involving climate change, remain to be solved, and local minorities continue to be oppressed in some parts of the world—much as *The Federalist No. 10* predicts. Do decentralized global structures offer a solution to these problems? To what extent are the questions presented by the possibility of "federal" arrangements different at the transnational level than they are within the United States? Is American federalism a model for world government, or something unique to the American situation? Federalists of the World Unite?

I. NATIONAL POWERS IN ARTICLE I, SECTION 8

A. FORMATIVE DECISIONS ABOUT THE COMMERCE, TAXING, SPENDING, AND NECESSARY AND PROPER POWERS

Article I, Section 8: The Congress shall have Power

To lay and collect Taxes, Duties, Imposts and Excises, to pay the Debts and provide for the common Defence and general Welfare of the United States; . . .

To regulate Commerce with foreign Nations, and among the several States, and with the Indian tribes; . . .

To make all Laws which shall be necessary and proper for carrying into Execution the foregoing Powers and all other Powers vested by this Constitution in the Government of the United States, or in any Department or Officer thereof.

We turn now to the broad issue of the Constitution's division of power between the national government and the governments of the states. The question of the scope of national legislative powers under the Constitution is as old as the earliest days of the Washington administration and as current as the Supreme Court's decision in *National Federation of Independent Business v. Sebelius* (2012), upholding in part and invalidating in part the Affordable Care Act. That case is presented later in this section.

The most persistent and insistent of such questions have involved the scope of Congress's enumerated Article I, Section 8 powers: (a) to "regulate Commerce . . . among the several States"; (b) to "lay and collect Taxes, Duties, Imposts and Excises, to pay the Debts and provide for the common Defence and general Welfare of the United States"; (c) to spend money so raised, for various purposes; and (d) to "make all Laws which shall be necessary and proper for carrying into Execution the foregoing Powers" and all other powers vested in the national government. What follows is a brisk general history of these areas of controversy, from the formative early controversies to the new forms in which these age-old questions are presented today.

Early Disputes Over National Power: Banks, Debts, Taxes, and Commerce

1. *The Bank of the United States.* Early constitutional controversies swirled concerning the scope of each of these powers. We have already seen how the issue of the power to create a national bank was vigorously debated by Alexander Hamilton, Thomas Jefferson, and James Madison in 1791, and eventually led to the Supreme Court's decision in *McCulloch v. Maryland* (1819) sustaining a broad construction of the Necessary and Proper Clause and national legislative powers generally. Those crucial, formative debates are presented in Chapter 1, and *McCulloch* in Chapter 3. It is nearly impossible to understand the historic, and even the modern, debates over the scope of Congress's legislative powers without understanding the foundations of those debates and their earliest resolutions. They are worth reviewing at this juncture.

2. *The Assumption Controversy.* Another early controversy over the scope of the new national government's power, predating by a year even the issue of the power to create a Bank of the United States, was the issue of

"assumption." In 1790, Treasury Secretary Alexander Hamilton proposed that the national government assume (i.e., take over) the vast remaining debts that the state governments had incurred in the Revolutionary War. The national government would then finance the debt through credit and interest payments on bonds, which would be backed by revenue from national excise taxes, including taxes on coffee and tea and on wine and spirits distilled in the United States. The result would be to free the states of their debts, to establish a national system of credit and public finance, to provide what was essentially a form of currency in bonds, and thus to secure the economic and political supremacy of the national government. For a lucid historical treatment, see Stanley Elkins & Eric McKitrick, THE AGE OF FEDERALISM: THE EARLY AMERICAN REPUBLIC, 1788–1800 114–123 (1993); see also Ron Chernow, ALEXANDER HAMILTON 297–306 (2004).

A version of Hamilton's assumption plan was eventually enacted, though not without resistance. James Madison objected that funding the bonds would reward speculators. Virginia, which claimed to have paid most of its debt, objected to what in effect was a bailout for the other states. And there were constitutional undercurrents to some of these objections: The assumption plan, it was said, would tend to consolidate power in the national government and subordinate the states. Was such a scheme consistent with the Constitution's vision of the national government as one of limited, enumerated powers? Was national assumption of (varying) state debt—and the indirect burdens this placed on other parts of the nation—consistent with the Constitution's principles of federalism? The controversy highlights questions of the scope of the national government's powers to impose taxes to pay debts (Art. I, Sec. 8, cl. 1); to borrow money on the credit of the United States (Art. I, Sec. 8, cl. 2); to *spend* money in ways that might affect different states differently; and—as with the Bank controversy—to make laws deemed "necessary and proper" for executing these other powers (Art. I, Sec. 8, cl. 18). What specific grant of power, if any, supports the power of the national government to assume state government debt? To issue bonds at stated interest rates? To impose taxes on products? May the national government spend money (and borrow money) in ways that affect different states differently? May it impose taxes that have different effects on different states?

3. *The Taxing Power and Carriage Tax Case: Hylton v. United States (1796).* The scope of the taxing power, and specifically the question of what is a "direct" versus an "indirect" tax, was presented in one of the Supreme Court's very first cases involving judicial review of the constitutionality of an act of Congress, decided seven years before *Marbury v. Madison: Hylton v. United States,* 3 U.S. 171 (1796). Under Article I, Section 9, any "direct" or "capitation" tax must be apportioned among the states on the basis of population, in accordance with Article I, Section 2 (including, originally, the notorious Three-fifths Clause). Under Article I, Section 8, an "indirect" tax—an excise, duty, or impost—is subject only to the requirement that it be "uniform" throughout the United States. The question presented was whether a congressional tax on carriages, which was not apportioned on the basis of population, was a direct or indirect tax. The case came before the Supreme Court on the basis of stipulated facts, and with an arrangement of parties that may well have been contrived to create a (probably illegitimate) test case rather than a genuinely adversarial dispute. (The United States apparently paid Hylton's attorneys, and the parties stipulated that Hylton owned 125 carriages, which was almost certainly untrue, in order to satisfy jurisdictional requirements.) The case featured an argument on one

side by Alexander Hamilton and on the other by Luther Martin, a prominent Anti–Federalist. The background of the case is discussed in David P. Currie, THE CONSTITUTION IN THE SUPREME COURT: THE FIRST HUNDRED YEARS, 1789–1888, 31–37 (1985).

All three justices participating in *Hylton* (Chase, Paterson, and Iredell), in seriatim opinions, upheld the tax as an indirect tax, not requiring apportionment but only uniformity. (Justice Wilson had upheld the tax while sitting as a judge on the circuit court, Justice Cushing did not participate because he had been ill at the time of argument, and Chief Justice Ellsworth had just been sworn in that day.) In his opinion for himself, Justice Paterson, who had been an active delegate at the Constitutional Convention, located the direct-indirect distinction in a desire to protect the Southern states against a direct per-person tax on slaves or a per-acre tax on property:

> What are direct taxes within the meaning of the Constitution? The Constitution declares that a capitation tax is a direct tax; and, both in theory and practice, a tax on land is deemed to be a direct tax. . . . Whether direct taxes, in the sense of the Constitution, comprehend any other tax than a capitation tax, and tax on land, is a questionable point. . . . Local considerations, and the particular circumstances, and relative situation of the states, naturally lead to this view of the subject. The provision was made in favor of the southern States. They possessed a large number of slaves; they had extensive tracts of territory, thinly settled, and not very productive. A majority of the states had but few slaves, and several of them a limited territory, well settled, and in a high state of cultivation. The southern states, if no provision had been introduced in the Constitution, would have been wholly at the mercy of the other states. Congress in such case, might tax slaves, at discretion or arbitrarily, and land in every part of the Union after the same rate or measure: so much a head in the first instance, and so much an acre in the second. To guard against imposition in these particulars, was the reason of introducing the clause in the Constitution, which directs that representatives and direct taxes shall be apportioned among the states, according to their respective numbers.

3 U.S. at 176–177. The clarity of the direct-indirect distinction has remained elusive to this day. (As you will see, the issue was presented in the Supreme Court's 2012 decision in *National Federation of Independent Business*, discussed below, which upheld the individual mandate in the Affordable Care Act as a valid exercise of the taxing power.) Nonetheless, *Hylton* became an early, longstanding precedent on the direct-indirect taxation distinction, effectively permitting broad national power to impose "indirect" taxes on commodities, consumption, and conduct—all without the troublesome requirement of apportionment on the basis of state population. Note that now the Sixteenth Amendment explicitly authorizes the national government to tax incomes without any requirement of apportionment.

Note that there was no issue in *Hylton* as to the bare power of Congress to impose a tax on carriages in the first place. The only issue was whether the tax imposed was direct as opposed to indirect and thus in need of being apportioned on the basis of population. Consider the implications of this for the Taxing Clause power generally: May Congress impose a tax on essentially anything it likes (or, perhaps, that it *doesn't* like), with the only constraints being apportionment for direct taxes and geographical uniformity for all others? The power to tax is a freestanding, independent national legislative power—indeed, it is the very first power listed in Article I, Section 8. But what is the scope of that power, and for what purposes may it be employed? May Congress impose a tax in part to achieve a regulatory or policy purpose apart from raising revenue—such as to express disfavor for the carriage industry (or, alternatively, to protect a favored industry by imposing tariffs or excises on competing products from abroad)? May it impose a tax, for regulatory purposes, even where it might not have the express power to regulate that activity directly? (Would Congress otherwise have power to regulate a purely intra-state carriage business?) Is there any limitation on how large such a tax may be before it becomes in effect a regulation of something Congress lacks power to regulate, or are there no such limits because the taxing power is its own, independent power?

4. *Gibbons v. Ogden and early interpretation of the Commerce Clause.* Along with *McCulloch v. Maryland*, decided in 1819, one of the earliest and most important Supreme Court cases concerning the scope of Congress's legislative powers was *Gibbons v. Ogden*, an 1824 decision of Chief Justice John Marshall interpreting the Commerce Clause and the Supremacy Clause:

Gibbons v. Ogden

22 U.S. (9 Wheat.) 1 (1824)

[The New York legislature enacted a statute granting Robert Fulton and Robert Livingston the exclusive right to operate steamboats in New York waters. The purpose of this statute was to encourage investment in the development of steamboat technology. Fulton and Livingston licensed Aaron Ogden to operate a ferry between New York City and Elizabethtown, New Jersey. Thomas Gibbons, once Ogden's partner, began operating a competing ferry service that, because it necessarily entered New York waters, violated the grant given to Fulton and Livingston. Ogden obtained an injunction from the New York courts that ordered Gibbons to stop operating his vessels in New York waters. On appeal, Gibbons argued that his "vessels" were enrolled and licensed to be employed in carrying on the coasting trade under the act of Congress, passed on February 18, 1793. Gibbons claimed that this congressional act preempted the New York statute, and thus he was entitled to navigate the waters of New York.—Editors]

■ MR. CHIEF JUSTICE MARSHALL delivered the opinion of the Court, and, after stating the case, proceeded as follows:

The appellant contends that . . . the [New York] laws which purport to give the exclusive privilege . . . are repugnant to the constitution and laws of the United States. They are said to be repugnant—

1st. To that clause in the constitution which authorizes Congress to regulate commerce. . . .

As preliminary to the very able discussions of the constitution, which we have heard from the bar, and as having some influence on its construction, reference has been made to the political situation of these States, anterior to its formation. It has been said, that they were sovereign, were completely independent, and were connected with each other only by a league. This is true. But, when these allied sovereigns converted their league into a government, when they converted their Congress of Ambassadors, deputed to deliberate on their common concerns, and to recommend measures of general utility, into a Legislature, empowered to enact laws on the most interesting subjects, the whole character in which the States appear, underwent a change, the extent of which must be determined by a fair consideration of the instrument by which that change was effected.

This instrument contains an enumeration of powers expressly granted by the people to their government. It has been said, that these powers ought to be construed strictly. But why ought they to be so construed? Is there one sentence in the constitution which gives countenance to this rule? In the last of the enumerated powers, that which grants, expressly, the means for carrying all others into execution, Congress is authorized 'to make all laws which shall be necessary and proper' for the purpose. But this limitation on the means which may be used, is not extended to the powers which are conferred; nor is there one sentence in the constitution, which has been pointed out by the gentlemen of the bar, or which we have been able to discern, that prescribes this rule. We do not, therefore, think ourselves justified in adopting it. What do gentlemen mean, by a strict construction? If they contend only against that enlarged construction, which would extend words beyond their natural and obvious import, we might question the application of the term, but should not controvert the principle. If they contend for that narrow construction which, in support or some theory not to be found in the constitution, would deny to the government those powers which the words of the grant, as usually understood, import, and which are consistent with the general views and objects of the instrument; for that narrow construction, which would cripple the government, and render it unequal to the object for which it is declared to be instituted, and to which the powers given, as fairly understood, render it competent; then we cannot perceive the propriety of this strict construction, nor adopt it as the rule by which the constitution is to be expounded. As men, whose intentions require no concealment, generally employ the words which most directly and aptly express the ideas they intend to convey, the enlightened patriots who framed our constitution, and the people who adopted it, must be understood to have employed words in their natural sense, and to have intended what they have said. If, from the imperfection of human language, there should be serious doubts respecting the extent of any given power, it is a well settled rule, that the objects for which it was given, especially when those objects are expressed in the instrument itself, should have great influence in the construction. We know of no reason for excluding this rule from the present case. . . .

The subject to be regulated is commerce; and our constitution being, as was aptly said at the bar, one of enumeration, and not of definition, to ascertain the extent of the power, it becomes necessary to settle the meaning of the word. The counsel for the appellee would limit it to traffic, to buying and selling, or the interchange of commodities, and do not admit that it comprehends navigation. This would restrict a general term, applicable to many objects, to one of its significations. Commerce, undoubtedly, is traffic, but it is something more: it is intercourse. It describes the commercial intercourse between nations, and parts of nations, in all its branches, and is regulated by prescribing rules for carrying on that intercourse. The mind can scarcely conceive a system for regulating commerce between nations, which shall exclude all laws concerning navigation, which shall be silent on the admission of the vessels of the one nation into the ports of the other, and be confined to prescribing rules for the conduct of individuals, in the actual employment of buying and selling, or of barter.

If commerce does not include navigation, the government of the Union has no direct power over that subject, and can make no law prescribing what shall constitute American vessels, or requiring that they shall be navigated by American seamen. Yet this power has been exercised from the commencement of the government, has been exercised with the consent of all, and has been understood by all to be a commercial regulation. All America understands, and has uniformly understood, the word "commerce," to comprehend navigation. It was so understood, and must have been so understood, when the constitution was framed. The power over commerce, including navigation, was one of the primary objects for which the people of America adopted their government, and must have been contemplated in forming it. . . .

The subject to which the power is next applied, is to commerce "among the several States." The word "among" means intermingled with. A thing which is among others, is intermingled with them. Commerce among the States, cannot stop at the external boundary line of each State, but may be introduced into the interior.

It is not intended to say that these words comprehend that commerce, which is completely internal, which is carried on between man and man in a State, or between different parts of the same State, and which does not extend to or affect other States. Such a power would be inconvenient, and is certainly unnecessary.

Comprehensive as the word "among" is, it may very properly be restricted to that commerce which concerns more States than one. The phrase is not one which would probably have been selected to indicate the completely interior traffic of a State, because it is not an apt phrase for that purpose; and the enumeration of the particular classes of commerce, to which the power was to be extended, would not have been made, had the intention been to extend the power to every description. The enumeration presupposes something not enumerated; and that something, if we regard the language or the subject of the sentence, must be the exclusively internal commerce of a State. The genius and character of the whole government seem to be, that its action is to be applied to all the external concerns of the nation, and to those internal concerns which affect the States generally; but not to those which are completely within a particular State, which do not affect other States, and with which it is not necessary to interfere, for the purpose of executing some of the general powers of the government. The completely internal commerce of a State, then, may be considered as reserved for the State itself.

But, in regulating commerce with foreign nations, the power of Congress does not stop at the jurisdictional lines of the several States. It would be a very useless power, if it could not pass those lines. The commerce of the United States with foreign nations, is that of the whole United States. Every district has a right to participate in it. The deep streams which penetrate our country in every direction, pass through the interior of almost every State in the Union, and furnish the means of exercising this right. If Congress has the power to regulate it, that power must be exercised whenever the subject exists. If it exists within the States, if a foreign voyage may commence or terminate at a port within a State, then the power of Congress may be exercised within a State.

This principle is, if possible, still more clear, when applied to commerce "among the several States." They either join each other, in which case they are separated by a mathematical line, or they are remote from each other, in which case other States lie between them. What is commerce "among" them; and how is it to be conducted? Can a trading expedition between two adjoining States, commence and terminate outside of each? And if the trading intercourse be between two States remote from each other, must it not commence in one, terminate in the other, and probably pass through a third? Commerce among the States must, of necessity, be commerce with the States. . . .

We are now arrived at the inquiry—What is this power?

It is the power to regulate; that is, to prescribe the rule by which commerce is to be governed. This power, like all others vested in Congress, is complete in itself, may be exercised to its utmost extent, and acknowledges no limitations, other than are prescribed in the constitution. These are expressed in plain terms, and do not affect the questions which arise in this case, or which have been discussed at the bar. If, as has always been understood, the sovereignty of Congress, though limited to specified objects, is plenary as to those objects, the power over commerce with foreign nations, and among the several States, is vested in Congress as absolutely as it would be in a single government, having in its constitution the same restrictions on the exercise of the power as are found in the constitution of the United States. The wisdom and the discretion of Congress, their identity with the people, and the influence which their constituents possess at elections, are, in this, as in many other instances, as that, for example, of declaring war, the sole restraints on which they have relied, to secure them from its abuse. They are the restraints on which the people must often rely solely, in all representative governments.

The power of Congress, then, comprehends navigation, within the limits of every State in the Union; so far as that navigation may be, in any manner, connected with "commerce with foreign nations, or among the several States, or with the Indian tribes." It may, of consequence, pass the jurisdictional line of New–York, and act upon the very waters to which the prohibition now under consideration applies.

But it has been urged with great earnestness, that, although the power of Congress to regulate commerce with foreign nations, and among the several States, be co-extensive with the subject itself, and have no other limits than are prescribed in the constitution, yet the States may severally exercise the same power, within their respective jurisdictions. In support of this argument, it is said, that they possessed it as an inseparable attribute of sovereignty, before the formation of the constitution, and still retain it, except so far as they have surrendered it by that instrument; that this principle results from the nature of the government, and is secured by the tenth amendment; that an affirmative grant of power is not exclusive, unless in its own nature it be such that the continued exercise of it by the former possessor is inconsistent with the grant, and that this is not of that description.

The grant of the power to lay and collect taxes is, like the power to regulate commerce, made in general terms, and has never been understood to interfere with the exercise of the same power by the State; and hence has been drawn an argument which has been applied to the question under consideration. But the two grants are not, it is conceived, similar in their terms or their nature. Although many of the powers formerly exercised by the States, are transferred to the government of the Union, yet the State governments remain, and constitute a most important part of our system. The power of taxation is indispensable to their existence, and is a power which, in its own nature, is capable of residing in, and being exercised by, different authorities at the same time. . . . [A] power in one to take what is necessary for certain purposes, is not, in its nature, incompatible with a power in another to take what is necessary for other purposes. Congress is authorized to lay and collect taxes, and to pay the debts, and provide for the common defense and general welfare of the United States. This does not interfere with the power of the States to tax for the support of their own governments; nor is the exercise of that power by the States, an exercise of any portion of the power that is granted to the United States. In imposing taxes for State purposes, they are not doing what Congress is empowered to do. Congress is not empowered to tax for those purposes which are within the exclusive province of the States. When, then, each government exercises the power of taxation, neither is exercising the power of the other. But, when a State proceeds to regulate commerce with foreign nations, or among the several States, it is exercising the very power that is granted to Congress, and is doing the very thing which Congress is authorized to do. There is no analogy, then, between the power of taxation and the power of regulating commerce. . . .

It is obvious, that the government of the Union, in the exercise of its express powers, that, for example, of regulating commerce with foreign nations and among the States, may use means that may also be employed by a State, in the exercise of its acknowledged powers; that, for example, of regulating commerce within the State. If Congress license vessels to sail from one port to another, in the same State, the act is supposed to be, necessarily, incidental to the power expressly granted to Congress, and implies no claim of a direct power to regulate the purely internal commerce of a State, or to act directly on its system of police. So, if a State, in passing laws on subjects acknowledged to be within its control, and with a view to those subjects, shall adopt a measure of the same character with one which Congress may adopt, it does not derive its authority from the particular power which has been granted, but from some other, which remains with the State, and may be executed by the same means. All experience shows, that the same measures, or measures scarcely distinguishable from each other, may flow from distinct powers; but this does not prove that the powers themselves are identical. Although the means used in their execution may sometimes approach each other so nearly as to be confounded, there are other situations in which they are sufficiently distinct to establish their individuality. . . .

Since, however, in exercising the power of regulating their own purely internal affairs, whether of trading or police, the States may sometimes enact laws, the validity of which depends on their interfering with, and being contrary to, an act of Congress passed in pursuance of the constitution, the Court will enter upon the inquiry, whether the laws of New–York, as expounded by the highest tribunal of that State, have, in their application to this case, come into collision with an act of Congress, and deprived a citizen of a right to which that act entitles him. Should this collision exist, it will be immaterial whether those laws were passed in virtue of a concurrent power "to regulate commerce with foreign nations and among the several States," or, in virtue of a power to regulate their domestic trade and police. In one case and the other, the acts of New–York must yield to the law of Congress; and the decision sustaining the privilege they confer, against a right given by a law of the Union, must be erroneous. . . .

[I]t has been contended, that if a law passed by a State, in the exercise of its acknowledged sovereignty, comes into conflict with a law passed by Congress in pursuance of the constitution, they affect the subject, and each other, like equal opposing powers.

But the framers of our constitution foresaw this state of things, and provided for it, by declaring the supremacy not only of itself, but of the laws made in pursuance of it. The nullity of any act, inconsistent with the constitution, is produced by the declaration, that the constitution is the supreme law. The appropriate application of that part of the clause which confers the same supremacy on laws and treaties, is to such acts of the State Legislatures as do not transcend their powers, but, though enacted in the execution of acknowledged State powers, interfere with, or are contrary to the laws of Congress, made in pursuance of the constitution, or some treaty made under the authority of the United States. In every such case, the act of Congress, or the treaty, is supreme; and the law of the State, though enacted in the exercise of powers not controverted, must yield to it.

[Chief Justice Marshall then found that the New York law conflicted with the federal laws licensing those engaged in the coastal trade and was thus invalid under the Supremacy Clause. The injunction against Gibbons was dissolved.—Editors]

NOTES

1. *Gibbons's Two Aspects.* Chief Justice Marshall's opinion in *Gibbons* has two primary parts. The first examines the meaning and scope of Congress's power under the Commerce Clause. The second examines the issue of conflicting federal and state laws affecting commerce. In this respect, the structure of his opinion (though not its length) parallels the opinion in *McCulloch,* which first looked to the question of *national power* to create a Bank of the United States and then looked to whether a *state law affecting the exercise of that national power* was unconstitutional because it conflicted with national authority.

2. *Congress's Power to "Regulate" "Commerce" "Among the States."* On the first broad point—the scope of the Commerce Clause power—Chief Justice Marshall breaks down the analysis largely according to the words of the text, and it is worth identifying the discussion in his opinion of each word or phrase: First, how does he understand "commerce"? Is his conception of "commerce" broad or narrow? Is it persuasive? Second, Marshall examines "among the several states." How does he describe the meaning of this phrase? What are its implications? Is the opinion persuasive on this point? Third, he addresses "regulate." According to the opinion, what does the power to "regulate" contain? How broadly should it be construed? Each of these questions, and the Court's discussion of each in *Gibbons,* has had an enduring influence on subsequent decisions of the Court construing the scope of the Commerce Clause power, continuing up to today.

3. *State Laws Interfering with Congress's Regulations of Commerce.* On the second broad point—the effect of conflicting federal and state laws—*Gibbons'* discussion merits untangling. First, there is the question of what happens when a state law, otherwise within the states' general legislative powers, conflicts with a federal law enacted within the scope of the national government's enumerated powers. In form, this is essentially the same question as was presented in *McCulloch*: If Congress validly possesses power to create a national bank, may states, which otherwise possess a general power to tax entities oper-

ating within their borders, impose a tax on this nationally-chartered institution? In *Gibbons*: If Congress's power to regulate commerce among the states
includes the power to grant licenses to coasting vessels, may a state grant a
steamboat monopoly that apparently conflicts with operations pursuant to such
a license? *Gibbons* says *no*. Is there any reason to doubt the correctness of this
analysis? Is the structure of the argument sound? Is there a colorable argument
that the federal and state laws are *not* actually in conflict? The principle in
Gibbons seems sound as a matter of applying the Supremacy Clause: Where a
valid federal law conflicts with a state law, the federal law prevails. (This principle also extends to the Constitution, to federal treaties, and to actions by the
president exercising the powers granted to the executive branch.) But determining *when* this principle is violated—in other words, when there is such an
actual conflict or interference—is not always an easy question. Over the years,
the Supreme Court has developed an extensive body of doctrine concerning this
issue of "preemption," including the concepts of "express preemption," "conflict
preemption" and "field preemption."

4. *The Roots of the Dormant Commerce Clause. Gibbons* also introduced
(albeit in dicta) another variation on the question of federal-versus-state authority. It suggests that the grant of power to Congress over commerce among
the states—"commerce which concerns more states than one"—is *exclusive*, so
that states are divested of power to regulate commerce which concerns more
states than one: "But, when a State proceeds to regulate commerce with foreign
nations, or among the several States, it is exercising the very power that is
granted to Congress, and is doing the very thing which Congress is authorized
to do." Put differently, the proposition is that the grant of power to Congress to
regulate interstate commerce negates, to the very same extent, the power of the
states. (Note that Marshall's opinion does *not* draw this conclusion with respect
to the taxing power: federal and state taxing power may exist concurrently.)
This dictum in *Gibbons* has given rise to what has come to be known as
"dormant Commerce Clause" doctrine. This line of cases says, in essence, that
states may not regulate commerce that falls within the scope of congressional
power to regulate interstate commerce. Are the two questions really the strict
inverse of each other?

A Look Ahead: Enumerated Powers and Federalism in a New Context

McCulloch, *Gibbons*, and *Hylton* were landmarks establishing early
patterns of interpretation, and they have had an enduring influence on interpretation of the scope of the commerce, taxing, spending, and necessary
and proper powers of Congress. But they of course did not resolve all questions of interpretation and application of these powers. New situations have
continually arisen testing the understanding and correctness of the early
doctrines.

Indeed, the scope of each of these powers—commerce, taxing, spending, and necessary and proper—was vigorously contested in the landmark
2012 decision of the Court in *National Federation of Independent Business
v. Sebelius,* involving a challenge to the constitutionality of the Affordable
Care Act's individual mandate requiring all persons to purchase health insurance (or else pay a tax penalty) and its Medicaid expansion provisions,
which conditioned continued federal Medicaid funding to states on dramatic expansions in state-law coverage. You will read this case at length

just a little later in this chapter. But based upon the principles you have seen so far, and anticipating the issues presented in *NFIB v. Sebelius*, what are your intuitions about each of the following questions (no peeking ahead!):

(1) Does Congress's power to regulate commerce include, under the reasoning of *Gibbons*, the power to require individuals to purchase a commercial product, like health insurance, from a private provider—that is, to *engage* in commerce? How broad is the power to "regulate"?

(2) Does Congress's power to regulate commerce "among the states" include the power to regulate conduct that, albeit local, substantially affects interstate commerce when considered in the aggregate? If not sustainable under the Commerce Clause alone, is such power sustainable (under the reasoning of *McCulloch*) as a measure "necessary and proper" to accomplishing an interstate commercial-regulation ends? Is compelled participation in a national commercial market for health insurance within the scope of such power?

(3) Does Congress's power to tax include a power to impose taxation in order to accomplish essentially regulatory purposes as long as the tax actually functions as a tax? Is there any restriction on the objects or activities that Congress can constitutionally tax (like carriages)? If Congress's requirement that all persons purchase health insurance is not sustainable as a regulation of commerce (or as necessary and proper to a regulation of commerce), may Congress accomplish essentially the same ends by using the power to tax to impose a penalty on the *non*-purchase of health insurance? Does the amount of the tax affect the validity of the purported exercise of such power? Does the existence of a given power under the Taxing Clause depend on whether Congress calls an exaction a "tax" or characterizes it instead as a "penalty" for non-compliance with a requirement styled as a direct regulation of conduct?

(4) May Congress enact laws *requiring states* to enact certain laws, or does that violate some necessary structural requirement of federalism? (If so, what provision of the Constitution identifies such a violation?) In other words, if some regulatory law is otherwise within the constitutional power of Congress to enact, may it accomplish such an end indirectly by requiring states to undertake the desired regulation?

(5) What is the scope (and constitutional source) of Congress's power to spend money? May Congress leverage whatever constitutional power it has to spend money by attaching substantive conditions to the receipt of federal funds that essentially require states receiving the funds to enact particular legislation? If not, why not? If so, what are the limits (if any) on such a power? May Congress compel states to expand Medicaid coverage in state laws, as a condition of receipt of federal Medicaid funds?

[*Assignment 31*]

A History of the Commerce and Necessary and Proper Clauses in the Supreme Court

The Commerce and Necessary and Proper Clauses have had a long history. The place to begin is with a brief overview of the Supreme Court's cases that have framed the interpretive issues that continue today. As you read these materials, ask yourself what the words of these two clauses mean when they are read together.

It was not until after the Civil War that Congress passed legislation that seriously began to test the limits of its regulatory power under the Commerce Clause, beginning with the Interstate Commerce Act of 1887 and continuing with the Sherman Antitrust Act of 1890.

1. *United States v. E.C. Knight Co.*, 156 U.S. 1 (1895) (5–4), adopted a restrictive interpretation of "commerce." The United States invoked the Sherman Act when the American Sugar Refining Company acquired the stock of four other refineries. This acquisition gave the company control of 98% of the country's sugar supply. The Supreme Court refused to apply the Sherman Antitrust Act to defeat the monopolization of sugar *manufacturing* because "Manufacturing" was not included within the meaning of "Commerce." Chief Justice Fuller's majority opinion stated:

> Doubtless the power to control the manufacture of a given thing involves in a certain sense the control of its disposition, but this is a secondary and not the primary sense; and although the exercise of that power may result in bringing the operation of commerce into play, it does not control it, and affects it only incidentally and indirectly. Commerce succeeds to manufacture and is not a part of it.

Fearing that the control of manufacturing would give Congress too much power under the Commerce Clause and would consequently deprive the states of all regulatory power in this area, the Court said:

> If it be held that the [the Commerce power] includes the regulation of all such manufactures as are intended to be the subject of commercial transactions in the future [the] result would be that Congress would be invested, to the exclusion of the States, with the power to regulate, not only manufactures, but also agriculture, horticulture, stock raising, domestic fisheries, mining—in short every branch of human industry.

(This holding was effectively repudiated in favor of a broader reading of the commerce power in a series of cases in the late 1930s and early 1940s that are described below: *National Labor Relations Board v. Jones & Laughlin Steel*, 301 U.S. 1 (1937); *United States v. Darby*, 312 U.S. 100 (1941); and *Wickard v. Filburn*, 317 U.S. 111 (1942).)

2. *Champion v. Ames (The Lottery Case)*, 188 U.S. 321 (1903) (5–4), leaned in the opposite direction from *E.C. Knight,* adopting an expansive interpretation of the commerce power. In this case, a man was indicted for shipping a box of Paraguayan lottery tickets from Texas to California despite the Federal Lottery Act of 1895, which prohibited importing, mailing, or interstate transporting of lottery tickets. The Court found that the transportation of lottery tickets from one state to another was "commerce." Writing for the majority, Justice Harlan held: "[T]he carrying from one state to another by independent carriers of things or commodities that are ordinary subjects of traffic, and which have in themselves a recognized value of money, constitutes interstate commerce." The Court also held that the power "to regulate" commerce included the power "to prohibit" commerce in noxious goods, like lottery tickets. The power to regulate commerce is more than the power to make it regular by eliminating trade barriers: Congress can also ban certain categories of commerce altogether.

The Court further stated: "[Congress] has not assumed to interfere with the completely internal affairs of any State, and has only legislated in respect of a matter which concerns the people of the United States. As a State may, for the purpose of guarding the morals of its own people, forbid all sales of lottery tickets within its limits, so Congress, for the purpose of guarding the people of the United States against the 'widespread pestilence of lotteries' and to protect the commerce which concerns all the States, may prohibit the carrying of lottery tickets from one State to another."

Champion has come to stand for the proposition that Congress has broad power to regulate the "channels" of interstate commerce as well as any articles moving "in" commerce, even for "police power"-like reasons: Congress may employ its commerce power by *excluding* from interstate commerce things or conduct of which it disapproves. Is this sound or unsound? Must the power to regulate interstate commerce be employed for a commercial-regulatory purpose? Or is the power complete in itself, so that it can be used for any policy purpose Congress desires? Is a prohibition on the shipment of a certain good a "regulation" of commerce?

3. *Shreveport Rate Case (Houston E. & W. T. Ry. Co. v. United States)*, 234 U.S. 342 (1914), also adopted an expansive interpretation of the power to regulate the "instrumentalities" of commerce—including their *intra*state activities. The Interstate Commerce Commission was regulating intrastate railroad rates because it found that several railroads were "discriminating" against shipments to and from Shreveport, Louisiana. For example, shipments by the railroads from Dallas to Marshall, Texas, a distance of 148 miles, cost 37 cents; but the railroads' shipments from Shreveport, Louisiana to Marshall, a distance of 42 miles, cost 56 cents. The Court held that the ICC may regulate even intrastate railroad rates because Congress has the power to regulate the "instrumentalities" of commerce, including intrastate activities that may injure interstate commerce.

Justice Hughes, writing the majority opinion, stated: "The fact that carriers are instruments of intrastate commerce, as well as of interstate commerce, does not derogate from the complete and paramount authority of Congress over the latter, or preclude the Federal power from being exerted to prevent the intrastate operations of such carriers from being made a means of injury to that which has been confided to Federal Care. . . . Congress in the exercise of its paramount power may prevent the common instrumentalities of interstate and intrastate commercial intercourse from being used in their intrastate operations to the injury of interstate commerce. This is not to say that Congress possesses the authority to regulate the internal commerce of a state, as such, but that it does possess the power to foster and protect interstate commerce, and to take all measures necessary or appropriate to that end, although intrastate transactions of interstate carriers may thereby be controlled."

Note Justice Hughes' reference to congressional power "to take all measures necessary and appropriate" to the protection of interstate commerce—even if in doing so intrastate commerce gets regulated. Is it the Necessary and Proper Clause, more than the Commerce Clause, that is doing the real work here?.

4. *Caminetti v. United States*, 242 U.S. 470 (1917), rested on a broad interpretation of the Commerce Clause power along the lines of that employed in *Champion*. In *Caminetti*, three men were convicted of violating the so-called White Slave Traffic Act of 1910. Specifically, the men were charged with "transporting and causing to be transported, and aiding and assisting in obtaining transportation for certain women in interstate commerce, for the purpose of debauchery, and for an immoral purpose." (They drove mistresses from Sacramento, California, to Reno, Nevada, and from Oklahoma City, Oklahoma, to Wichita, Kansas.) The three men argued that "the act of Congress is intended to reach only 'commercialized vice,' or

the traffic in women for gain." Thus, they claimed that the statute did not apply to them because "in none of the cases was it charged or proved that the transportation was for gain or for the purpose of furnishing women for prostitution or for hire."

Although the Court conceded that the acts of the men did not constitute a "commercial activity," the Court upheld the convictions. The Court concluded: "The transportation of passengers in interstate commerce, it has long been settled, is within the regulatory power of Congress, under the Commerce Clause of the Constitution, and the authority of Congress to keep the channels of interstate commerce free from immoral and injurious uses has been frequently sustained, and is no longer open to question."

5. *Hammer v. Dagenhart*, 247 U.S. 251 (1918) (5–4), took a more restrictive view of the Commerce Clause power. At issue was a federal law banning the interstate shipment of goods produced in violation of certain restrictions on the use of child labor. The majority struck down the regulation, distinguishing *Champion*, *Caminetti*, and other cases upholding interstate transportation restrictions, on the ground that "[i]n each of these instances the use of interstates transportation was necessary to the accomplishment of harmful results" and that this element "is wanting in the present case." The federal law "does not regulate transportation among the states, but aims to standardize the ages at which children may be employed in mining and manufacturing within the states. The goods shipped are themselves harmless." The majority added that "[t]he grant of power of Congress over the subject of interstate commerce was to enable it to regulate such commerce, and not to give it authority to control the states in their exercise of the police power over local trade and manufacture. . . . The grant of authority over a purely federal matter was not intended to destroy the local power always existing and carefully reserved to the states in the Tenth Amendment to the Constitution."

Was *Hammer*'s distinction of *Champion* and *Caminetti* persuasive? Should the existence of a constitutional power to regulate or prohibit items in interstate commerce depend on whether the prohibition is because Congress regards the items themselves as harmful (and therefore wishes to prohibit them) or because it regards the manner of their production or manufacture as harmful (and therefore wishes to prohibit the interstate shipment of goods so produced)? Was the Court's decision in *Hammer* influenced by its view that permitting such an exercise of the federal commerce power would impair state power? Is such reasoning sound?

Justice Holmes's dissent emphasized that "the statute in question is within the power expressly given to Congress if considered only as to its immediate effects and that if invalid it is so only upon some collateral ground." In other words, the statute clearly and directly regulated interstate commerce; Congress's purpose and motivation was irrelevant in determining whether the statute fell within the literal terms of that constitutional power. Justice Holmes also disapproved of the notion that recognizing such a federal power interfered "with anything belonging to the States. They may regulate their internal affairs and their domestic commerce as they like. But when they seek to send their products across the State line they are no longer within their rights. If there were no Constitution and no Congress their power to cross the line would depend upon their neighbors. Under the Constitution such commerce belongs not to the States but to Congress to regulate. It may carry out its views of public policy whatever indirect effect that may have upon the activities of the States." Are you persuaded by the reasoning of the majority, or by that of the dissent?

Hammer was overruled twenty-two years later in *United States v. Darby*, 312 U.S. 100 (1941), a decision presented below.

6. Meanwhile, on the Taxing Clause front, in *Bailey v. Drexel Furniture Co.* (*The Child Labor Tax Case*), 259 U.S. 20 (1922), the Court considered a challenge to Congress's use of the taxing power to try to accomplish the very policy objective that the Court had held was beyond Congress's commerce-regulating power in *Hammer*. The law at issue in *Bailey* imposed an "excise tax equivalent to 10 per centum of the entire net profits received or accrued" in a year on mills, canneries, workshops, factories, or other manufacturing establishments employing child labor in violation of prescribed standards. Relying on *Hammer*, the Court struck down the tax on the ground that it operated as a regulatory law that exceeded Congress's power to regulate commerce: "Grant the validity of this law, and all that Congress would need to do, hereafter, in seeking to take over to its control any one of the great number of subjects of public interest, jurisdiction of which the states have never parted with, and which are reserved to them by the Tenth Amendment, would be to enact a detailed measure of complete regulation of the subject and enforce it by a so called tax upon departures from it. To give such magic to the word 'tax' would be to break down all constitutional limitations of the powers of Congress and completely wipe out the sovereignty of the states." The Court distinguished between a true "tax" and what it thought a "penalty" for violating a regulatory law. While it was true that taxes could have the "incidental motive" of discouraging certain conduct or products—"[t]hey do not lose their character as taxes because of the incidental motive"—the Court held that "there comes a time in the extension of the penalizing features of the so-called tax when it loses its character as such and becomes a mere penalty, with the characteristics of regulation and punishment." The tax on profits from child had such a character, the Court found.

We will return to *Bailey* when considering the scope of the taxing power. But for now, several questions seem evident, in connection with the relationship between the commerce power and the taxing power. If the taxing power may be employed to accomplish (at least in part) non-revenue-raising purposes, much as the commerce power may be used to accomplish noncommercial purposes, what are the limits of each power? In particular, does it follow that Congress may not constitutionally use the taxing power to accomplish a regulatory end if such end would not be within the scope of the Commerce Clause power? Are they two entirely different powers, or do the limitations on each operate as implicit restrictions on the scope of the other? Is *Bailey*'s distinction between a permitted "tax" and a mere "penalty" a persuasive one? If so, how does one draw a principled line between permissible and impermissible uses of the taxing power? If not, is there any answer to Chief Justice Taft's objection in *Bailey* that the taxing power could be used to "break down all constitutional limitations of the powers of Congress"?

There is, of course, another major case presenting the question of whether the taxing power might enable the national government to enact a measure going beyond the scope of what the Court concludes are the limits to the commerce power: *National Federation of Independent Business v. Sebelius* (2012), where five justices sustained the individual insurance-purchase mandate of the Affordable Care Act on the ground that a provision requiring payment of a penalty as part of income taxes if one did *not* purchase health insurance could be sustained as an exercise of the Taxing Clause power, even if it could not be sustained as an exercise of the Commerce Clause power (as a different five justices held). *NFIB* is presented as a principal case below.

7. *A.L.A. Schechter Poultry Corp. v. United States*, 295 U.S. 435 (1935), took a more restrictive approach to the Commerce Clause power. The National Industrial Recovery Act of 1933 authorized the president to approve "codes of fair competition." (The case is also famous for its other holding, invalidating the act as an improper "delegation" of legislative power. For more discussion of the non-delegation doctrine, see Chapter 3.) President Roosevelt approved codes establishing a forty-hour work week and a minimum wage of fifty cents an hour, applicable to the Schecters' slaughterhouse in Brooklyn. The Schecter company purchased chickens that had been shipped to New York from other states and then used the poultry for slaughter and resale to butchers within the state of New York. The Schecters were convicted for violating the wage and hour provisions of the code. (They were also prosecuted for selling improperly inspected poultry, giving rise to the case's nickname as "the sick chicken case.")

The Court struck down the regulations fixing the hours and wages of individuals employed by an intrastate business because the activity being regulated was related to interstate commerce only "indirectly": "Where the effect of intrastate transactions upon interstate commerce is merely indirect, such transactions remain within the domain of state power." The Court further stated that "[the regulations] are imposed in order to govern the details of defendants' management of their local business. The persons employed in slaughtering and selling in local trade are not employed in interstate commerce. Their hours and wages have no direct relation to interstate commerce ... [and] if the federal government may determine the wages and hours of employees in the internal commerce of a State, because of their relation to costs and prices and their indirect effect on interstate commerce, it would seem that a similar control might be exerted over other elements of cost, also affecting prices." This case, too, was later repudiated by the rulings in *Jones & Laughlin Steel* (1937) and *Darby* (1941).

8. *Carter v. Carter Coal Co.*, 293 U.S. 238 (1936), was another case interpreting the scope of the Commerce Clause restrictively. The Bituminous Coal Conservation Act of 1935 regulated the maximum hours and minimum wages of coal mine workers. A stockholder in Carter Coal sued to enjoin the company from complying with the provisions of the code. The Court struck down the regulations, finding that mining (like "manufacturing") is not itself "commerce." Writing for the majority, Justice Sutherland held that "[t]he effect of the labor provisions falls upon production and not upon commerce. ... Production is a purely local activity. It follows that none of these essential antecedents of production constitutes a transaction in or forms any part of interstate commerce." (This case, too, was effectively repudiated by *Jones & Laughlin Steel* and *Darby*.)

9. *"The New Deal Revolution": A Switch in Time?* Around this time, President Franklin D. Roosevelt, reelected in a landslide and displeased by the decisions of the Court's "Nine Old Men" invalidating New Deal legislation, proposed his famous "court-packing" plan. It would have allowed the number of Supreme Court justices to increase to as many as fifteen depending on how many sitting justices were over age seventy. The practical effect of this in 1937 would have been to give Roosevelt six new seats to fill on the

Supreme Court. Although the proposal was defeated, the Court's decisions beginning in 1937 upheld a broader interpretation of Congress's legislative powers under the Commerce Clause. One of the justices formerly in the majority against a broad interpretation of Congress's powers (Justice Roberts) began voting more consistently with the justices favoring such broad interpretations, leading to the quip—not necessarily justified—that there had been a "switch in time that saved nine."

10. *National Labor Relations Board v. Jones & Laughlin Steel Corp.,* 301 U.S. 1 (1937), was a watershed, marking the Court's change to a more expansive interpretation of the Commerce Clause power of Congress—a change that has proved enduring. The opinion was written by Chief Justice Charles Evans Hughes, who had been the author of *The Shreveport Rate Case* (1914) twenty-three years earlier. (Chief Justice Hughes left the Court in 1916 and was the Republican presidential nominee, narrowly losing to incumbent Woodrow Wilson. He later served as secretary of state before returning to the Court as chief justice in 1930.) In *Jones & Laughlin Steel,* the Court upheld the National Labor Relations Act, which comprehensively regulated labor practices and relationships. The decision rejected the "direct" versus "indirect" effects on interstate commerce approach of *Schecter Poultry,* at least where intrastate activities have "such a close and substantial relation to interstate commerce that their control is essential or appropriate to protect that commerce from burdens and obstructions." Additionally, the Court downplayed the "production" distinction of *Carter Coal Co.,* stating that "[i]t is the effect upon commerce, not the source of the injury, which is the criterion. . . . [T]he fact that the employees here concerned were engaged in production is not determinative." The Court held that "the National Labor Relations Act may be construed so as to operate within the sphere of constitutional authority. The grant of authority to the Board does not purport to extend to the relationship between all industrial employees ad employers. Its terms do not impose collective bargaining upon all industry regardless of effects upon interstate or foreign commerce. It purports to reach only what may be deemed to burden or obstruct commerce and, thus qualified, it must be construed as contemplating the exercise of control within constitutional bounds."

Was *Jones & Laughlin Steel* right or wrong? Does the power to regulate commerce extend to the power to regulate labor practices in industries that have substantial effects on interstate commerce? If so, does such power flow directly from the Commerce Clause, or should it be understood as flowing from the Necessary and Proper Clause in combination with the Commerce Clause? (Does it make any difference as a practical matter? Does it make a difference as an analytical matter?)

Jones & Laughlin Steel was a narrowly written decision by a narrow 5–4 majority of the Court. Within five years, however, its principles had been reaffirmed and dramatically expanded. The "New Deal Revolution" (or "restoration"?) in interpretation of the Commerce Clause was cemented by two significant—and unanimous—decisions adopting very broad interpretations of the scope of Congress's powers under the Commerce and Necessary and Proper Clauses, which are presented below as principal cases. *United States v. Darby* (1941) explicitly overruled *Hammer v. Dagenhart.* *Wickard v. Filburn* (1942) adopted the most expansive view of Congress's powers the Court ever embraced, upholding Congress's power to regulate purely intrastate activities—the production of wheat for home consumption—as part of a comprehensive regulation of a national market in the production of agricultural commodities. Both decisions were unanimous. Both decisions were landmarks. Both decisions continue to be embraced by the Court today. But are both decisions right?

United States v. Darby

312 U.S. 100 (1941)

■ MR. JUSTICE STONE delivered the opinion of the Court.

The two principal questions raised by the record in this case are, *first*, whether Congress has constitutional power to prohibit the shipment in interstate commerce of lumber manufactured by employees whose wages are less than a prescribed minimum or whose weekly hours of labor at that wage are greater than a prescribed maximum, and, *second*, whether it has power to prohibit the employment of workmen in the production of goods "for interstate commerce" at other than prescribed wages and hours. . . .

The Fair Labor Standards Act set up a comprehensive legislative scheme for preventing the shipment in interstate commerce of certain products and commodities produced in the United States under labor conditions as respects wages and hours which fail to conform to standards set up by the Act. . . .

While manufacture is not, of itself, interstate commerce, the shipment of manufactured goods interstate is such commerce, and the prohibition of such shipment by Congress is indubitably a regulation of the commerce. The power to regulate commerce is the power "to prescribe the rule by which commerce is governed." *Gibbons v. Ogden*, 9 Wheat. 1, 196. It extends not only to those regulations which aid, foster and protect the commerce, but embraces those which prohibit it. It is conceded that the power of Congress to prohibit transportation in interstate commerce includes noxious articles, stolen articles, kidnapped persons, and articles such as intoxicating liquor or convict made goods, traffic in which is forbidden or restricted by the laws of the state of destination.

But it is said that the present prohibition falls within the scope of none of these categories; that, while the prohibition is nominally a regulation of the commerce, its motive or purpose is regulation of wages and hours of persons engaged in manufacture, the control of which has been reserved to the states and upon which Georgia and some of the states of destination have placed no restriction; that the effect of the present statute is not to exclude the proscribed articles from interstate commerce in aid of state regulation, but instead, under the guise of a regulation of interstate commerce, it undertakes to regulate wages and hours within the state contrary to the policy of the state which has elected to leave them unregulated.

The power of Congress over interstate commerce "is complete in itself, may be exercised to its utmost extent, and acknowledges no limitations other than are prescribed in the Constitution." *Gibbons v. Ogden, supra*, 196. That power can neither be enlarged nor diminished by the exercise or nonexercise of state power. . . .

Such regulation is not a forbidden invasion of state power merely because either its motive or its consequence is to restrict the use of articles of commerce within the states of destination, and is not prohibited unless by other Constitutional provisions. It is no objection to the assertion of the power to regulate interstate commerce that its exercise is attended by the same incidents which attend the exercise of the police power of the states.

The motive and purpose of the present regulation are plainly to make effective the Congressional conception of public policy that interstate commerce should not be made the instrument of competition in the distribution of goods produced under substandard labor conditions, which competition is injurious to the commerce and to the states from and to which the commerce flows. The motive and purpose of a regulation of interstate commerce are matters for the legislative judgment upon the exercise of which the Constitution places no restriction, and over which the courts are given no control. . . . Whatever their motive and purpose, regulations of commerce which do not infringe some constitutional prohibition are within the plenary power conferred on Congress by the Commerce Clause. Subject only to that limitation, presently to be considered, we conclude that the prohibition of the shipment interstate of goods produced under the forbidden substandard labor conditions is within the constitutional authority of Congress.

In the more than a century which has elapsed since the decision of *Gibbons v. Ogden*, these principles of constitutional interpretation have been so long and repeatedly recognized by this Court as applicable to the Commerce Clause that there would be little occasion for repeating them now were it not for the decision of this Court twenty-two years ago in *Hammer v. Dagenhart*, 247 U.S. 251. In that case, it was held by a bare majority of the Court, over the powerful and now classic dissent of Mr. Justice Holmes setting forth the fundamental issues involved, that Congress was without power to exclude the products of child labor from interstate commerce. The reasoning and conclusion of the Court's opinion there cannot be reconciled with the conclusion which we have reached, that the power of Congress under the Commerce Clause is plenary to exclude any article from interstate commerce subject only to the specific prohibitions of the Constitution.

Hammer v. Dagenhart has not been followed. The distinction on which the decision was rested, that Congressional power to prohibit interstate commerce is limited to articles which in themselves have some harmful or deleterious property—a distinction which was novel when made and unsupported by any provision of the Constitution—has long since been abandoned. The thesis of the opinion—that the motive of the prohibition or its effect to control in some measure the use or production within the states of the article thus excluded from the commerce can operate to deprive the regulation of its constitutional authority—has long since ceased to have force. . . .

The conclusion is inescapable that *Hammer v. Dagenhart* was a departure from the principles which have prevailed in the interpretation of the Commerce Clause both before and since the decision, and that such vitality, as a precedent, as it then had, has long since been exhausted. It should be, and now is, overruled. . . .

There remains the question whether such restriction on the production of goods for commerce is a permissible exercise of the commerce power. The power of Congress over interstate commerce is not confined to the regulation of commerce among the states. It extends to those activities intrastate which so affect interstate commerce or the exercise of the power of Congress over it as to make regulation of them appropriate means to the attainment of a legitimate end, the exercise of the granted power of Congress to regulate interstate commerce. See *McCulloch v. Maryland*, 4 Wheat. 316, 421. . . .

Congress, having by the present Act adopted the policy of excluding from interstate commerce all goods produced for the commerce which do not conform to the specified labor standards, it may choose the means reasonably adapted to the attainment of the permitted end even though they involve control of intrastate activities. Such legislation has often been sustained with respect to powers other than the commerce power granted to the national government when the means chosen, although not themselves within the granted power, were nevertheless deemed appropriate aids to the accomplishment of some purpose within an admitted power of the national government. . . .

As we have said, the evils aimed at by the Act are the spread of substandard labor conditions through the use of the facilities of interstate commerce for competition by the goods so produced with those produced under the prescribed or better labor conditions, and the consequent dislocation of the commerce itself caused by the impairment or destruction of local businesses by competition made effective through interstate commerce. The Act is thus directed at the suppression of a method or kind of competition in interstate commerce which it has, in effect, condemned as "unfair," as the Clayton Act has condemned other "unfair methods of competition" made effective through interstate commerce.

Our conclusion is unaffected by the Tenth Amendment, which provides: "The powers not delegated to the United States by the Constitution, nor prohibited by it to the States, are reserved to the States respectively, or to the people." The amendment states but a truism that all is retained which has not been surrendered. There is nothing in the history of its adoption to suggest that it was more than declaratory of the relationship between the national and state governments as it had been established by the Constitution before the amendment, or that its purpose was other than to allay fears that the new national government might seek to exercise powers not granted, and that the states might not be able to exercise fully their reserved powers.

From the beginning and for many years, the amendment has been construed as not depriving the national government of authority to resort to all means for the exercise of a granted power which are appropriate and plainly adapted to the permitted end. . . .

Wickard v. Filburn

317 U.S. 111 (1942)

■ MR. JUSTICE JACKSON delivered the opinion of the Court.

The appellee filed his complaint against the Secretary of Agriculture of the United States, three members of the County Agricultural Conservation Committee for Montgomery County, Ohio, and a member of the State Agricultural Conservation Committee for Ohio. He sought to enjoin enforcement against himself of the marketing penalty imposed by the amendment of May 26, 1941, to the Agricultural Adjustment Act of 1938, upon that part of his 1941 wheat crop which was available for marketing in excess of the marketing quota established for his farm. He also sought a declaratory judgment that the wheat marketing quota provisions of the Act as amended and applicable to him were unconstitutional because not sustainable under the Commerce Clause or consistent with the Due Process Clause of the Fifth Amendment. . . .

The appellee for many years past has owned and operated a small farm in Montgomery County, Ohio, maintaining a herd of dairy cattle, selling milk, raising poultry, and selling poultry and eggs. It has been his practice to raise a small acreage of winter wheat, sown in the Fall and harvested in the following July; to sell a portion of the crop; to feed part to poultry and livestock on the farm, some of which is sold; to use some in making flour for home consumption; and to keep the rest for the following seeding. The intended disposition of the crop here involved has not been expressly stated.

In July of 1940, pursuant to the Agricultural Adjustment Act of 1938, as then amended, there were established for the appellee's 1941 crop a wheat acreage allotment of 11.1 acres and a normal yield of 20.1 bushels of wheat an acre. He was given notice of such allotment in July of 1940 before the Fall planting of his 1941 crop of wheat, and again in July of 1941, before it was harvested. He sowed, however, 23 acres, and harvested from his 11.9 acres of excess acreage 239 bushels, which under the terms of the Act as amended on May 26, 1941, constituted farm marketing excess, subject to a penalty of 49 cents a bushel, or $117.11 in all. The appellee has not paid the penalty and he has not postponed or avoided it by storing the excess under regulations of the Secretary of Agriculture, or by delivering it up to the Secretary. The Committee, therefore, refused him a marketing card, which was, under the terms of Regulations promulgated by the Secretary, necessary to protect a buyer from liability to the penalty and upon its protecting lien.

The general scheme of the Agricultural Adjustment Act of 1938 as related to wheat is to control the volume moving in interstate and foreign commerce in order to avoid surpluses and shortages and the consequent abnormally low or high wheat prices and obstructions to commerce. Within prescribed limits and by prescribed standards the Secretary of Agriculture is directed to ascertain and proclaim each year a national acreage allotment for the next crop of wheat, which is then apportioned to the states and their counties, and is eventually broken up into allotments for individual farms. Loans and payments to wheat farmers are authorized in stated circumstances. . . .

It is urged that under the Commerce Clause of the Constitution, Article I, § 8, clause 3, Congress does not possess the power it has in this instance sought to exercise. The question would merit little consideration since our decision in *United States v. Darby*, 312 U.S. 100, sustaining the federal power to regulate production of goods for commerce except for the fact that this Act extends federal regulation to production not intended in any part for commerce but wholly for consumption on the farm. The Act includes a definition of "market" and its derivatives so that as related to wheat in addition to its conventional meaning it also means to dispose of "by feeding (in any form) to poultry or livestock which, or the products of which, are sold, bartered, or exchanged, or to be so disposed of." Hence, marketing quotas not only embrace all that may be sold without penalty but also what may be consumed on the premises. Wheat produced on excess acreage is designated as "available for marketing" as so defined and the penalty is imposed thereon. Penalties do not depend upon whether any part of the wheat either within or without the quota is sold or intended to be sold. The sum of this is that the Federal Government fixes a quota including all that the farmer may harvest for sale or for his own farm needs, and declares that wheat produced on excess acreage may neither be disposed of nor used except upon payment of the penalty or except it is stored as required by the Act or delivered to the Secretary of Agriculture.

Appellee says that this is a regulation of production and consumption of wheat. Such activities are, he urges, beyond the reach of Congressional power under the Commerce Clause, since they are local in character, and their effects upon interstate commerce are at most "indirect." In answer the Government argues that the statute regulates neither production nor consumption, but only marketing; and, in the alternative, that if the Act does go beyond the regulation of marketing it is sustainable as a "necessary and proper" implementation of the power of Congress over interstate commerce.

The Government's concern lest the Act be held to be a regulation of production or consumption rather than of marketing is attributable to a few dicta and decisions of this Court which might be understood to lay it down that activities such as "production," "manufacturing," and "mining" are strictly "local" and, except in special circumstances which are not present here, cannot be regulated under the commerce power because their effects upon interstate commerce are, as matter of law, only "indirect." Even today, when this power has been held to have great latitude, there is no decision of this Court that such activities may be regulated where no part of the product is intended for interstate commerce or intermingled with the subjects thereof. We believe that a review of the course of decision under the Commerce Clause will make plain, however, that questions of the power of Congress are not to be decided by reference to any formula which would give controlling force to nomenclature such as "production" and "indirect" and foreclose consideration of the actual effects of the activity in question upon interstate commerce.

At the beginning Chief Justice Marshall described the Federal commerce power with a breadth never yet exceeded. *Gibbons v. Ogden*, 9 Wheat. 1, 194, 195. He made emphatic the embracing and penetrating nature of this power by warning that effective restraints on its exercise must proceed from political rather than from judicial processes. 9 Wheat. at page 197. . . .

It was not until 1887 with the enactment of the Interstate Commerce Act that the interstate commerce power began to exert positive influence in American law and life. This first important federal resort to the commerce power was followed in 1890 by the Sherman Anti–Trust Act and, thereafter, mainly after 1903, by many others. These statutes ushered in new phases of adjudication, which required the Court to approach the interpretation of the Commerce Clause in the light of an actual exercise by Congress of its power thereunder. . . .

The Court's recognition of the relevance of the economic effects in the application of the Commerce Clause . . . has made the mechanical application of legal formulas no longer feasible. Once an economic measure of the reach of the power granted to Congress in the Commerce Clause is accepted, questions of federal power cannot be decided simply by finding the activity in question to be "production" nor can consideration of its economic effects be foreclosed by calling them "indirect." . . .

Whether the subject of the regulation in question was "production," "consumption," or "marketing" is, therefore, not material for purposes of deciding the question of federal power before us. That an activity is of local character may help in a doubtful case to determine whether Congress intended to reach it. The same consideration might help in determining whether in the absence of Congressional action it would be permissible for the state to exert its power on the subject matter, even though in so doing it to some degree affected interstate commerce. But even if appellee's activity be local and though it may not be regarded as commerce, it may still, whatever its nature, be reached by Congress if it exerts a substantial economic effect on interstate commerce and this irrespective of whether such effect is what might at some earlier time have been defined as "direct" or "indirect."

The parties have stipulated a summary of the economics of the wheat industry. Commerce among the states in wheat is large and important. Although wheat is raised in every state but one, production in most states is not equal to consumption. Sixteen states on average have had a surplus of wheat above their own requirements for feed, seed, and food. Thirty-two states and the District of Columbia, where production has been below consumption, have looked to these surplus-producing states for their supply as well as for wheat for export and carryover.

The wheat industry has been a problem industry for some years. Largely as a result of increased foreign production and import restrictions, annual exports of wheat and flour from the United States during the ten-year period ending in 1940 averaged less than 10 per cent of total production, while during the 1920s they averaged more than 25 per cent. The decline in the export trade has left a large surplus in production which in connection with an abnormally large supply of wheat and other grains in recent years caused congestion in a number of markets; tied up railroad cars; and caused elevators in some instances to turn away grains, and railroads to institute embargoes to prevent further congestion. . . .

The effect of consumption of homegrown wheat on interstate commerce is due to the fact that it constitutes the most variable factor in the disappearance of the wheat crop. Consumption on the farm where grown appears to vary in an amount greater than 20 per cent of average production. The total amount of wheat consumed as food varies but relatively little, and use as seed is relatively constant.

The maintenance by government regulation of a price for wheat undoubtedly can be accomplished as effectively by sustaining or increasing the demand as by limiting the supply. The effect of the statute before us is to restrict the amount which may be produced for market and the extent as well to which one may forestall resort to the market by producing to meet his own needs. That appellee's own contribution to the demand for wheat may be trivial by itself is not enough to remove him from the scope of federal regulation where, as here, his contribution, taken together with that of many others similarly situated, is far from trivial. *National Labor Relations Board v. Fainblatt*, 306 U.S. 601, 606, et seq., 307 U.S. 609; *United States v. Darby, supra*, 312 U.S. at page 123.

It is well established by decisions of this Court that the power to regulate commerce includes the power to regulate the prices at which commodities in that commerce are dealt in and practices affecting such prices. One of the primary purposes of the Act in question was to increase the market price of wheat and to that end to limit the volume thereof that could affect the market. It can hardly be denied that a factor of such volume and variability as home-consumed wheat would have a substantial influence on price and market conditions. This may arise because being in marketable condition such wheat overhangs the market and if induced by rising prices tends to flow into the market and check price increases. But if we assume that it is never marketed, it supplies a need of the man who grew it which would otherwise be reflected by purchases in the open market. Home-grown wheat in this sense competes with wheat in commerce. The stimulation of commerce is a use of the regulatory function quite as definitely as prohibitions or restrictions thereon. This record leaves us in no doubt that Congress may properly have considered that wheat consumed on the farm where grown if wholly outside the scheme of regulation would have a substantial effect in defeating and obstructing its purpose to stimulate trade therein at increased prices.

It is said, however, that this Act, forcing some farmers into the market to buy what they could provide for themselves, is an unfair promotion of the markets and prices of specializing wheat growers. It is of the essence of regulation that it lays a restraining hand on the self interest of the regulated and that advantages from the regulation commonly fall to others. The conflicts of economic interest between the regulated and those who advantage by it are wisely left under our system to resolution by the Congress under its more flexible and responsible legislative process. Such conflicts rarely lend themselves to judicial determination. And with the wisdom, workability, or fairness, of the plan of regulation we have nothing to do. . . .

[The Court's analysis of the due process claim is omitted.—Editors]

NOTES

1. Consider first *Darby*. Is the Court's reasoning persuasive? The Court upheld the Fair Labor Standards Act of 1938, which prohibited the shipment in interstate commerce of goods produced by employees who were paid less than a set minimum wage or who worked more than a prescribed maximum number of hours: "The power of Congress over interstate commerce . . . extends to those activities intrastate which so affect interstate commerce . . . as to make regulation of them appropriate means to the attainment of a legitimate end." Is this an interpretation of the Commerce Clause power, or is it once again the Necessary and Proper Clause, more than the Commerce Clause alone, that is the true source of this power?

2. Consider next *Wickard v. Filburn*. Is the Court's reasoning persuasive? Is the regulation of homegrown wheat, for home consumption, a regulation of "interstate commerce"? If not, is the decision wrong? Is regulation of purely local production and consumption of a product that, considered in the aggregate, substantially affects interstate commerce "necessary and proper" to carrying into execution a regulation of an interstate commercial market? If so, is there any limit to the types of regulations of commercial or economic activity—even of intrastate activity—that Congress may enact?

3. The key doctrinal innovation of *Wickard v. Filburn* is the aggregation principle: the idea that one should look at all the homegrown wheat in the country and its effect on commerce and not just at the homegrown wheat of the farmer in this case. Is the aggregation principle sound? Is it sound as a matter of text? Is it relevant whether the framers of the Constitution would have envisaged such an expansive application of the Commerce Clause power (even when teamed with the Necessary and Proper Clause power)? Surely one cannot imagine that the framing generation would have thought such national power acceptable. But are the framers' intentions—or subjective expectations—controlling as to the meaning of constitutional language?

4. Recall the Court's admonition in *Gibbons v. Ogden* that the Constitution's enumeration of powers "presupposes something not enumerated." In light of the Supreme Court's jurisprudence as it emerged from the New Deal era, is there any thing that Congress cannot do pursuant to its power to regulate commerce, as aided by the Necessary and Proper Clause? (Set to one side laws that would violate some specific *prohibition* on Congress's power, like the First Amendment or the Second Amendment.) It might be a useful exercise—and perhaps even entertaining—to try to imagine laws that Congress lacks power to enact, given the decisions in *Darby* and *Wickard*. Can you come up with any? If so, what are the defining characteristics of laws that Congress lacks any enumerated power to enact? If not, does that prove that *Darby* and *Wickard* were unanimously wrong? Or would it show that the characterization of Congress's powers as "limited" and "enumerated" is illusory, or meaningless, given the breadth with which those powers can be interpreted? Consider, before going on to more recent cases, some envelope-pushing hypotheticals: May Congress nationalize education, taking over that function from state and local governments? May Congress mandate a universal compulsory national exercise regime for all citizens? May Congress require everybody to wash his or her laundry once a week? Brush his or her teeth? Buy broccoli?

[*Assignment 32*]

The Modern Debate

In large measure, the consensus forged in the New Deal era concerning the broad scope of national legislative power—right or wrong—has continued to endure. What follows are two cases about the outer boundaries of congressional power under the Commerce Clause. In the first, *Heart of Atlanta Motel v. United States* (1964), the Court upheld the Civil Rights Act of 1964 as an exercise of the Commerce Clause power. In this case the Court relied on a broad understanding of that power and the uses to which it could be put. In the second, *United States v. Lopez* (1995), the Court struck down, by a 5–4 vote, the Gun–Free School Zones Act. *Lopez* was the first major decision in nearly six decades to find an enforceable limit on the scope of the Commerce Clause power. It is an important case not only for its contested holding but also for its distilling of the Court's case law from the previous two centuries.

Heart of Atlanta Motel v. United States

379 U.S. 241 (1964)

■ MR. JUSTICE CLARK delivered the opinion of the Court.

This is a declaratory judgment action attacking the constitutionality of Title II of the Civil Rights Act of 1964. . . .

The case comes here on admissions and stipulated facts. Appellant owns and operates the Heart of Atlanta Motel which has 216 rooms available to transient guests. The motel . . . is readily accessible to interstate highways 75 and 85 and state highways 23 and 41. Appellant solicits patronage from outside the State of Georgia through various national advertising media, including magazines of national circulation; it maintains over 50 billboards and highway signs within the State, soliciting patronage for the motel; it accepts convention trade from outside Georgia and approximately 75% of its registered guests are from out of state. Prior to passage of the

Act the motel had followed a practice of refusing to rent rooms to Negroes, and it alleged that it intended to continue to do so. In an effort to perpetuate that policy this suit was filed.

The appellant contends that Congress in passing this Act exceeded its power to regulate commerce under Art. I, § 8, cl. 3, of the Constitution of the United States; that the Act violates the Fifth Amendment because appellant is deprived of the right to choose its customers and operate its business as it wishes, resulting in a taking of its liberty and property without due process of law and a taking of its property without just compensation; and, finally, that by requiring appellant to rent available rooms to Negroes against its will, Congress is subjecting it to involuntary servitude in contravention of the Thirteenth Amendment.

The appellees counter that the unavailability to Negroes of adequate accommodations interferes significantly with interstate travel, and that Congress, under the Commerce Clause, has power to remove such obstructions and restraints; that the Fifth Amendment does not forbid reasonable regulation and that consequential damage does not constitute a "taking" within the meaning of that amendment; that the Thirteenth Amendment claim fails because it is entirely frivolous to say that an amendment directed to the abolition of human bondage and the removal of widespread disabilities associated with slavery places discrimination in public accommodations, beyond the reach of both federal and state law.

. . . The legislative history of the Act indicates that Congress based the Act on § 5 and the Equal Protection Clause of the Fourteenth Amendment as well as its power to regulate interstate commerce under Art. I, § 8, cl. 3, of the Constitution.

The Senate Commerce Committee made it quite clear that the fundamental object of Title II was to vindicate "the deprivation of personal dignity that surely accompanies denials of equal access to public establishments." At the same time, however, it noted that such an objective has been and could be readily achieved 'by congressional action based on the commerce power of the Constitution.' Our study of the legislative record, made in the light of prior cases, has brought us to the conclusion that Congress possessed ample power in this regard, and we have therefore not considered the other grounds relied upon. This is not to say that the remaining authority upon which it acted was not adequate, a question upon which we do not pass, but merely that since the commerce power is sufficient for our decision here we have considered it alone. . . .

While the Act as adopted carried no congressional findings the record of its passage through each house is replete with evidence of the burdens that discrimination by race or color places upon interstate commerce. This testimony included the fact that our people have become increasingly mobile with millions of people of all races traveling from State to State; that Negroes in particular have been the subject of discrimination in transient accommodations, having to travel great distances to secure the same; that often they have been unable to obtain accommodations and have had to call upon friends to put them up overnight; and that these conditions had become so acute as to require the listing of available lodging for Negroes in a special guidebook which was itself "dramatic testimony to the difficulties" Negroes encounter in travel. These exclusionary practices were found to be nationwide, the Under Secretary of Commerce testifying that there is "no question that this discrimination in the North still exists to a large degree" and in the West and Midwest as well. This testimony indicated a qualita-

tive as well as quantitative effect on interstate travel by Negroes. The former was the obvious impairment of the Negro traveler's pleasure and convenience that resulted when he continually was uncertain of finding lodging. As for the latter, there was evidence that this uncertainty stemming from racial discrimination had the effect of discouraging travel on the part of a substantial portion of the Negro community. This was the conclusion not only of the Under Secretary of Commerce but also of the Administrator of the Federal Aviation Agency who wrote the Chairman of the Senate Commerce Committee that it was his "belief that air commerce is adversely affected by the denial to a substantial segment of the traveling public of adequate and desegregated public accommodations." We shall not burden this opinion with further details since the voluminous testimony presents overwhelming evidence that discrimination by hotels and motels impedes interstate travel.

The power of Congress to deal with these obstructions depends on the meaning of the Commerce Clause. Its meaning was first enunciated 140 years ago by the great Chief Justice John Marshall in Gibbons v. Ogden, 9 Wheat. 1 (1824) . . . .

In short, the determinative test of the exercise of power by the Congress under the Commerce Clause is simply whether the activity sought to be regulated is "commerce which concerns more States than one" and has a real and substantial relation to the national interest. Let us now turn to this facet of the problem.

That the "intercourse" of which the Chief Justice spoke included the movement of persons through more States than one was settled as early as 1849, in the *Passenger Cases* (Smith v. Turner), 7 How. 283. . . .

Nor does it make any difference whether the transportation is commercial in character. *Caminetti v. United States*, 242, U.S. 470, 484–486. . . .

The same interest in protecting interstate commerce which led Congress to deal with segregation in interstate carriers and the white-slave traffic has prompted it to extend the exercise of its power to gambling, *Lottery Case (Champion v. Ames)*, 188 U.S. 321 (1903); to criminal enterprises, *Brooks v. United States*, 267 U.S. 432 (1925); to deceptive practices in the sale of products, *Federal Trade Comm. v. Mandel Bros., Inc.*, 359 U.S. 385 (1959); to fraudulent security transactions, *Securities & Exchange Comm. v. Ralston Purina Co.*, 346 U.S. 119 (1953); to misbranding of drugs, *Weeks v. United States*, 245 U.S. 618 (1918); to wages and hours, *United States v. Darby*, 312 U.S. 100 (1941); to members of labor unions, *National Labor Relations Board v. Jones & Laughlin Steel Corp.*, 301 U.S. 1 (1937); to crop control, *Wickard v. Filburn*, 317 U.S. 111 (1942); to discrimination against shippers, *United States v. Baltimore & Ohio R. Co.*, 333 U.S. 169 (1948); to the protection of small business from injurious price cutting, *Moore v. Mead's Fine Bread Co.*, 348 U.S. 115 (1954); to resale price maintenance, *Hudson Distributors, Inc. v. Eli Lilly & Co.*, 377 U.S. 386 (1964), *Schwegmann Bros. v. Calvert Distillers Corp.*, 341 U.S. 384 (1951); to professional football, *Radovich v. National Football League*, 352 U.S. 445 (1957); and to racial discrimination by owners and managers of terminal restaurants, *Boynton v. Com. of Virginia*, 364 U.S. 454 (1960).

That Congress was legislating against moral wrongs in many of these areas rendered its enactments no less valid. In framing Title II of this Act Congress was also dealing with what it considered a moral problem. But that fact does not detract from the overwhelming evidence of the disruptive effect that racial discrimination has had on commercial intercourse. It was this burden which empowered Congress to enact appropriate legislation, and, given this basis for the exercise of its power, Congress was not restricted by the fact that the particular obstruction to interstate commerce with which it was dealing was also deemed a moral and social wrong.

It is said that the operation of the motel here is of a purely local character. But, assuming this to be true, "[i]f it is interstate commerce that feels the pinch, it does not matter how local the operation which applies the squeeze." *United States v. Women's Sportswear Mfg. Ass'n*, 336 U.S. 460, 464 (1949). . . .

Thus the power of Congress to promote interstate commerce also includes the power to regulate the local incidents thereof, including local activities in both the States of origin and destination, which might have a substantial and harmful effect upon that commerce. One need only examine the evidence which we have discussed above to see that Congress may—as it has—prohibit racial discrimination by motels serving travelers, however "local" their operations may appear. . . .

[The Court also rejected individual-rights claims by the motel owner under the Fifth Amendment.—Editors]

We, therefore, conclude that the action of the Congress in the adoption of the Act as applied here to a motel which concededly serves interstate travelers is within the power granted it by the Commerce Clause of the Constitution, as interpreted by this Court for 140 years. It may be argued that Congress could have pursued other methods to eliminate the obstructions it found in interstate commerce caused by racial discrimination. But this is a matter of policy that rests entirely with the Congress not with the courts. How obstructions in commerce may be removed—what means are to be employed—is within the sound and exclusive discretion of the Congress. It is subject only to one caveat—that the means chosen by it must be reasonably adapted to the end permitted by the Constitution. We cannot say that its choice here was not so adapted. The Constitution requires no more.

NOTES

1. Is the prohibition of racial discrimination by inns, motels, and hotels a regulation of "commerce"? Is it a regulation of commerce involving more than one state? (The statute defined inns, motels, hotels, and other places of public accommodation as per se affecting interstate commerce.) How does the Court answer these questions? Does the Court defer to the factual findings of Congress? Do those findings affect its decision on the constitutional question? Should they affect its decision? Are there any limits on the conduct that Congress could find substantially affects interstate commerce? Keep these questions in mind—they will return—as you consider the Court's opinion in the next case, *United States v. Lopez*.

2. In *Heart of Atlanta Motel's* companion case, *Katzenbach v. McClung*, 379 U.S. 241 (1964), the Court unanimously upheld the Civil Rights Act as applied to almost wholly intrastate restaurants—in that case, the famous "Ollie's Barbecue" in Birmingham, Alabama. The Court, relying on congressional testimony, upheld the act on the basis that discrimination in restaurants had a direct and highly restrictive effect upon interstate travel by black Americans:

This resulted ... because discriminatory practices prevent [them] from buying prepared food served on the premises while on a trip, except in isolated and unkempt restaurants and under most unsatisfactory and often unpleasant conditions. This obviously discourages travel and obstructs interstate commerce for one can hardly travel without eating. Likewise, [Congress] said that discrimination deterred professional, as well as skilled, people from moving into areas where such practices occurred and thereby caused industry to be reluctant to establish there.

The Court then gave a second reason why the Civil Rights Act was constitutional—namely that the restaurant used supplies that may have been produced in or traveled in interstate commerce:

The only remaining question—one answered in the affirmative by the court below—is whether the particular restaurant either serves or offers to serve interstate travelers or serves food a substantial portion of which has moved in interstate commerce. We must conclude that [Congress] had a rational basis for finding that racial discrimination in restaurants had a direct and adverse effect on the free flow of interstate commerce. Insofar as the sections of the Act here relevant are concerned, Congress prohibited discrimination only in those establishments having a close tie to interstate commerce, i.e., those, like the McClungs', serving food that has come from out of the State. We think in so doing that Congress acted well within its power to protect and foster commerce in extending the coverage of Title II only to those restaurants offering to serve interstate travelers or serving food, a substantial portion of which has moved in interstate commerce.

Katzenbach v. McClung introduced the rational-basis test into the enumerated powers case law: all Congress needs is a rational basis for thinking that its regulation of interstate commerce is convenient and useful to the promotion of interstate commerce.

3. In *Perez v. United States*, 402 U.S. 146 (1971), the Court upheld the constitutionality of a statute making "extortionate credit transactions" (loan sharking) a federal crime. The Court held that even when extortion is wholly intrastate, it directly affects interstate commerce because loan sharking "provides organized crime with its second most lucrative source of revenue, exacts millions from the pockets of people, coerces its victims into the commission of crimes against property, and causes the takeover by racketeers of legitimate businesses.... [L]oan sharking in its national setting is one way organized interstate crime holds its guns to the heads of the poor and the rich alike and syphons funds from numerous localities to finance its national operations." The defendant was convicted even though there was no showing that his individual loan sharking involved interstate commerce.

4. By the 1970s and 1980s, it was widely believed that there were essentially no limits on the scope of Congress's constitutional power under the Commerce Clause, combined with the Necessary and Proper Clause. For a short period, the Court wrestled with the question of whether the Tenth Amendment might limit the ability of Congress, acting pursuant to the Commerce Power, to regulate the activities *of states* that affect commerce. Compare *National League of Cities v. Usery*, 426 U.S. 833 (1976) (finding such implied federalism limitations), with *Garcia v. San Antonio Metropolitan Transit Authority*, 469 U.S. 528 (1985) (rejecting such implied limitations). But the Commerce Clause power

itself was not disputed. The only question was whether the Tenth Amendment, or some principle implied by it, cut across that power and trumped it—with respect to commercial activity engaged in by state governments.

But was there any practical limit to the scope of the Commerce Clause power itself? *United States v. Lopez* (1995), the next principal case, was the first case in nearly six decades to invalidate an act of Congress as being in excess of the commerce power. In the course of doing so, the Court distilled—and distinguished—nearly two hundred years of constitutional experience.

United States v. Lopez

514 U.S. 549 (1995)

■ CHIEF JUSTICE REHNQUIST delivered the opinion of the Court.

In the Gun–Free School Zones Act of 1990, Congress made it a federal offense "for any individual knowingly to possess a firearm at a place that the individual knows, or has reasonable cause to believe, is a school zone." The Act neither regulates a commercial activity nor contains a requirement that the possession be connected in any way to interstate commerce. We hold that the Act exceeds the authority of Congress "[t]o regulate Commerce . . . among the several States. . . ."

On March 10, 1992, respondent, who was then a 12th–grade student, arrived at Edison High School in San Antonio, Texas, carrying a concealed .38–caliber handgun and five bullets. Acting upon an anonymous tip, school authorities confronted respondent, who admitted that he was carrying the weapon. He was arrested and charged under Texas law with firearm possession on school premises. The next day, the state charges were dismissed after federal agents charged respondent by complaint with violating the Gun–Free School Zones Act of 1990.[1] . . .

[Lopez was indicted and convicted]. On appeal, [he] challenged his conviction based on his claim that [the Act] exceeded Congress' power to legislate under the Commerce Clause. The Court of Appeals for the Fifth Circuit agreed and reversed respondent's conviction. . . . Because of the importance of the issue, we granted certiorari, and we now affirm.

We start with first principles. The Constitution creates a Federal Government of enumerated powers. See Art. I, § 8. As James Madison wrote: "The powers delegated by the proposed Constitution to the federal government are few and defined. Those which are to remain in the State governments are numerous and indefinite." The Federalist No. 45, pp. 292–293 (C. Rossiter ed. 1961). This constitutionally mandated division of authority "was adopted by the Framers to ensure protection of our fundamental liberties." "Just as the separation and independence of the coordinate branches of the Federal Government serve to prevent the accumulation of excessive power in any one branch, a healthy balance of power between the States and the Federal Government will reduce the risk of tyranny and abuse from either front."

The Constitution delegates to Congress the power "[t]o regulate Commerce with foreign Nations, and among the several States, and with the Indian Tribes." Art. I, § 8, cl. 3. The Court, through Chief Justice Marshall,

---

[1] The term "school zone" is defined as "in, or on the grounds of, a public, parochial or private school" or "within a distance of 1,000 feet from the grounds of a public, parochial or private school." § 921(a)(25).

first defined the nature of Congress' commerce power in *Gibbons v. Ogden*, 9 Wheat. 1, 189–190 (1824):

> Commerce, undoubtedly, is traffic, but it is something more: it is intercourse. It describes the commercial intercourse between nations, and parts of nations, in all its branches, and is regulated by prescribing rules for carrying on that intercourse.

The commerce power "is the power to regulate; that is, to prescribe the rule by which commerce is to be governed. This power, like all others vested in congress, is complete in itself, may be exercised to its utmost extent, and acknowledges no limitations, other than are prescribed in the constitution." *Id.,* at 196. The *Gibbons* Court, however, acknowledged that limitations on the commerce power are inherent in the very language of the Commerce Clause.

> It is not intended to say that these words comprehend that commerce, which is completely internal, which is carried on between man and man in a State, or between different parts of the same State, and which does not extend to or affect other States. Such a power would be inconvenient, and is certainly unnecessary.

> Comprehensive as the word "among" is, it may very properly be restricted to that commerce which concerns more States than one. . . . The enumeration presupposes something not enumerated; and that something, if we regard the language, or the subject of the sentence, must be the exclusively internal commerce of a State.

Id., at 194–195.

For nearly a century thereafter, the Court's Commerce Clause decisions dealt but rarely with the extent of Congress' power, and almost entirely with the Commerce Clause as a limit on state legislation that discriminated against interstate commerce. Under this line of precedent, the Court held that certain categories of activity such as "production," "manufacturing," and "mining" were within the province of state governments, and thus were beyond the power of Congress under the Commerce Clause.

In 1887, Congress enacted the Interstate Commerce Act, and in 1890, Congress enacted the Sherman Antitrust Act. These laws ushered in a new era of federal regulation under the commerce power. When cases involving these laws first reached this Court, we imported from our negative Commerce Clause cases the approach that Congress could not regulate activities such as "production," "manufacturing," and "mining." See, *e.g.,* *United States v. E.C. Knight Co.,* 156 U.S. 1, 12 (1895) ("Commerce succeeds to manufacture, and is not part of it"); *Carter v. Carter Coal Co.,* 298 U.S. 238, 304 (1936) ("Mining brings the subject matter of commerce into existence. Commerce disposes of it"). Simultaneously, however, the Court held that, where the interstate and intrastate aspects of commerce were so mingled together that full regulation of interstate commerce required incidental regulation of intrastate commerce, the Commerce Clause authorized such regulation. See, *e.g.,* *Shreveport Rate Cases,* 234 U.S. 342 (1914).

In *A.L.A. Schechter Poultry Corp. v. United States,* 295 U.S. 495, 550 (1935), the Court struck down regulations that fixed the hours and wages of individuals employed by an intrastate business because the activity being regulated related to interstate commerce only indirectly. In doing so, the Court characterized the distinction between direct and indirect effects of intrastate transactions upon interstate commerce as "a fundamental one, essential to the maintenance of our constitutional system." *Id.,* at 548. Activities that affected interstate commerce directly were within Congress' power; activities that affected interstate commerce indirectly were beyond Congress' reach. *Id.,* at 546. The justification for this formal distinction was rooted in the fear that otherwise "there would be virtually no limit to the federal power and for all practical purposes we should have a completely centralized government." *Id.,* at 548.

Two years later, in the watershed case of *NLRB v. Jones & Laughlin Steel Corp.,* 301 U.S. 1 (1937), the Court upheld the National Labor Relations Act against a Commerce Clause challenge, and in the process, departed from the distinction between "direct" and "indirect" effects on interstate commerce. *Id.,* at 36–38 ("The question [of the scope of Congress' power] is necessarily one of degree"). The Court held that intrastate activities that "have such a close and substantial relation to interstate commerce that their control is essential or appropriate to protect that commerce from burdens and obstructions" are within Congress' power to regulate. *Id.,* at 37.

In *United States v. Darby,* 312 U.S. 100 (1941), the Court upheld the Fair Labor Standards Act, stating:

> The power of Congress over interstate commerce is not confined to the regulation of commerce among the states. It extends to those activities intrastate which so affect interstate commerce or the exercise of the power of Congress over it as to make regulation of them appropriate means to the attainment of a legitimate end, the exercise of the granted power of Congress to regulate interstate commerce.

Id., at 118. . . .

In *Wickard v. Filburn,* the Court upheld the application of amendments to the Agricultural Adjustment Act of 1938 to the production and consumption of homegrown wheat. 317 U.S., at 128–129. The *Wickard* Court explicitly rejected earlier distinctions between direct and indirect effects on interstate commerce. . . . The *Wickard* Court emphasized that although Filburn's own contribution to the demand for wheat may have been trivial by itself, that was not "enough to remove him from the scope of federal regulation where, as here, his contribution, taken together with that of many others similarly situated, is far from trivial."

Jones & Laughlin Steel, Darby, and *Wickard* ushered in an era of Commerce Clause jurisprudence that greatly expanded the previously defined authority of Congress under that clause. In part, this was a recognition of the great changes that had occurred in the way business was carried on in this country. Enterprises that had once been local or at most regional in nature had become national in scope. But the doctrinal change also reflected a view that earlier Commerce Clause cases artificially had constrained the authority of Congress to regulate interstate commerce.

But even these modern-era precedents which have expanded congressional power under the Commerce Clause confirm that this power is subject to outer limits. In *Jones & Laughlin Steel,* the Court warned that the scope of the interstate commerce power "must be considered in the light of our dual system of government and may not be extended so as to embrace effects upon interstate commerce so indirect and remote that to embrace them, in view of our complex society, would effectually obliterate the distinction between what is national and what is local and create a completely centralized government." 301 U.S., at 37; see also *Darby, supra,* 312 U.S., at 119–120 (Congress may regulate intrastate activity that has a "substantial effect" on interstate commerce); *Wickard, supra,* at 125 (Congress may regulate activity that "exerts a substantial economic effect on interstate commerce"). Since that time, the Court has heeded that warning and undertaken to decide whether a rational basis existed for concluding that a regulated activity sufficiently affected interstate commerce. . . .

[W]e have identified three broad categories of activity that Congress may regulate under its commerce power. First, Congress may regulate the use of the channels of interstate commerce. See, *e.g., Darby*, 312 U.S., at 114; *Heart of Atlanta Motel, supra*, at 256 (" '[T]he authority of Congress to keep the channels of interstate commerce free from immoral and injurious uses has been frequently sustained, and is no longer open to question.' " (quoting *Caminetti v. United States*, 242 U.S. 470, 491 (1917))). Second, Congress is empowered to regulate and protect the instrumentalities of interstate commerce, or persons or things in interstate commerce, even though the threat may come only from intrastate activities. See, *e.g., Shreveport Rate Cases*, 234 U.S. 342 (1914); *Southern R. Co. v. United States*, 222 U.S. 20 (1911) (upholding amendments to Safety Appliance Act as applied to vehicles used in intrastate commerce); *Perez, supra*, at 150 ("[F]or example, the destruction of an aircraft (18 U.S.C. § 32), or . . . thefts from interstate shipments (18 U.S.C. § 659)"). Finally, Congress' commerce authority includes the power to regulate those activities having a substantial relation to interstate commerce, *Jones & Laughlin Steel*, 301 U.S., at 37, *i.e.,* those activities that substantially affect interstate commerce, *Wirtz, supra*, at 196, n. 27.

Within this final category, admittedly, our case law has not been clear whether an activity must "affect" or "substantially affect" interstate commerce in order to be within Congress' power to regulate it under the Commerce Clause. Compare *Preseault v. ICC*, 494 U.S. 1, 17 (1990), with *Wirtz, supra*, at 196, n. 27 (the Court has never declared that "Congress may use a relatively trivial impact on commerce as an excuse for broad general regulation of state or private activities"). We conclude, consistent with the great weight of our case law, that the proper test requires an analysis of whether the regulated activity "substantially affects" interstate commerce.

We now turn to consider the power of Congress, in the light of this framework, to enact [the Gun–Free School Zones Act]. The first two categories of authority may be quickly disposed of: the Act is not a regulation of the use of the channels of interstate commerce, nor is it an attempt to prohibit the interstate transportation of a commodity through the channels of commerce; nor can [the Act] be justified as a regulation by which Congress has sought to protect an instrumentality of interstate commerce or a thing in interstate commerce. Thus, if [the Act] is to be sustained, it must be under the third category as a regulation of an activity that substantially affects interstate commerce.

First, we have upheld a wide variety of congressional Acts regulating intrastate economic activity where we have concluded that the activity substantially affected interstate commerce. Examples include the regulation of intrastate coal mining; *Hodel, supra*, intrastate extortionate credit transactions, *Perez, supra*, restaurants utilizing substantial interstate supplies, *McClung, supra*, inns and hotels catering to interstate guests, *Heart of Atlanta Motel, supra*, and production and consumption of homegrown wheat, *Wickard v. Filburn*, 317 U.S. 111 (1942). These examples are by no means exhaustive, but the pattern is clear. Where economic activity substantially affects interstate commerce, legislation regulating that activity will be sustained.

Even *Wickard,* which is perhaps the most far reaching example of Commerce Clause authority over intrastate activity, involved economic activity in a way that the possession of a gun in a school zone does not. Roscoe Filburn operated a small farm in Ohio, on which, in the year involved, he raised 23 acres of wheat. It was his practice to sow winter wheat in the fall, and after harvesting it in July to sell a portion of the crop, to feed part of it to poultry and livestock on the farm, to use some in making flour for home consumption, and to keep the remainder for seeding future crops. The Secretary of Agriculture assessed a penalty against him under the Agricultural Adjustment Act of 1938 because he harvested about 12 acres more wheat than his allotment under the Act permitted. The Act was designed to regulate the volume of wheat moving in interstate and foreign commerce in order to avoid surpluses and shortages, and concomitant fluctuation in wheat prices, which had previously obtained. . . .

[The Act] is a criminal statute that by its terms has nothing to do with "commerce" or any sort of economic enterprise, however broadly one might define those terms. [The Act] is not an essential part of a larger regulation of economic activity, in which the regulatory scheme could be undercut unless the intrastate activity were regulated. It cannot, therefore, be sustained under our cases upholding regulations of activities that arise out of or are connected with a commercial transaction, which viewed in the aggregate, substantially affects interstate commerce.

Second, [the Act] contains no jurisdictional element which would ensure, through case-by-case inquiry, that the firearm possession in question affects interstate commerce. For example, in *United States v. Bass,* 404 U.S. 336 (1971), the Court interpreted former 18 U.S.C. § 1202(a), which made it a crime for a felon to "receiv[e], posses[s], or transpor[t] in commerce or affecting commerce . . . any firearm." 404 U.S., at 337. . . . Unlike the statute in *Bass,* [the Act] has no express jurisdictional element which might limit its reach to a discrete set of firearm possessions that additionally have an explicit connection with or effect on interstate commerce.

Although as part of our independent evaluation of constitutionality under the Commerce Clause we of course consider legislative findings, and indeed even congressional committee findings, regarding effect on interstate commerce, see, *e.g., Preseault v. ICC,* 494 U.S., at 17, (1990), the Government concedes that "[n]either the statute nor its legislative history contain[s] express congressional findings regarding the effects upon interstate commerce of gun possession in a school zone." We agree with the Government that Congress normally is not required to make formal findings as to the substantial burdens that an activity has on interstate commerce. See *McClung,* 379 U.S., at 304; see also *Perez,* 402 U.S., at 156 ("Congress need [not] make particularized findings in order to legislate"). But to the extent that congressional findings would enable us to evaluate the legislative judgment that the activity in question substantially affected interstate commerce, even though no such substantial effect was visible to the naked eye, they are lacking here.[4]

---

[4] We note that on September 13, 1994, President Clinton signed into law the Violent Crime Control and Law Enforcement Act of 1994, Pub.L. 103–322, 108 Stat. 1796. Section 320904 of that Act, *id.,* at 2125, amends § 922(q) to include congressional findings regarding the effects of firearm possession in and around schools upon interstate and foreign commerce. The Government does not rely upon these subsequent findings as a substitute for the absence of findings in the first instance. Tr. of Oral Arg. 25 ("[W]e're not relying on them in the strict sense of the word, but we think that at a very minimum they indicate that reasons can be identified for why Congress wanted to regulate this particular activity").

The Government's essential contention, *in fine,* is that we may determine here that [the Act] is valid because possession of a firearm in a local school zone does indeed substantially affect interstate commerce. The Government argues that possession of a firearm in a school zone may result in violent crime and that violent crime can be expected to affect the functioning of the national economy in two ways. First, the costs of violent crime are substantial, and, through the mechanism of insurance, those costs are spread throughout the population. Second, violent crime reduces the willingness of individuals to travel to areas within the country that are perceived to be unsafe. Cf. *Heart of Atlanta Motel,* 379 U.S., at 253. The Government also argues that the presence of guns in schools poses a substantial threat to the educational process by threatening the learning environment. A handicapped educational process, in turn, will result in a less productive citizenry. That, in turn, would have an adverse effect on the Nation's economic well-being. As a result, the Government argues that Congress could rationally have concluded that [the Act] substantially affects interstate commerce.

We pause to consider the implications of the Government's arguments. The Government admits, under its "costs of crime" reasoning, that Congress could regulate not only all violent crime, but all activities that might lead to violent crime, regardless of how tenuously they relate to interstate commerce. Tr. of Oral Arg. 8–9. Similarly, under the Government's "national productivity" reasoning, Congress could regulate any activity that it found was related to the economic productivity of individual citizens: family law (including marriage, divorce, and child custody), for example. Under the theories that the Government presents in support of [the Act], it is difficult to perceive any limitation on federal power, even in areas such as criminal law enforcement or education where States historically have been sovereign. Thus, if we were to accept the Government's arguments, we are hard pressed to posit any activity by an individual that Congress is without power to regulate.

Although Justice BREYER argues that acceptance of the Government's rationales would not authorize a general federal police power, he is unable to identify any activity that the States may regulate but Congress may not. Justice BREYER posits that there might be some limitations on Congress' commerce power, such as family law or certain aspects of education. These suggested limitations, when viewed in light of the dissent's expansive analysis, are devoid of substance.

Justice BREYER focuses, for the most part, on the threat that firearm possession in and near schools poses to the educational process and the potential economic consequences flowing from that threat. Specifically, the dissent reasons that (1) gun-related violence is a serious problem; (2) that problem, in turn, has an adverse effect on classroom learning; and (3) that adverse effect on classroom learning, in turn, represents a substantial threat to trade and commerce. This analysis would be equally applicable, if not more so, to subjects such as family law and direct regulation of education.

For instance, if Congress can, pursuant to its Commerce Clause power, regulate activities that adversely affect the learning environment, then, *a fortiori,* it also can regulate the educational process directly. Congress could determine that a school's curriculum has a "significant" effect on the extent of classroom learning. As a result, Congress could mandate a federal curriculum for local elementary and secondary schools because what is taught in local schools has a significant "effect on classroom learning," and that, in turn, has a substantial effect on interstate commerce.

Justice BREYER rejects our reading of precedent and argues that "Congress . . . could rationally conclude that schools fall on the commercial side of the line." Again, Justice BREYER's rationale lacks any real limits because, depending on the level of generality, any activity can be looked upon as commercial. Under the dissent's rationale, Congress could just as easily look at child rearing as "fall[ing] on the commercial side of the line" because it provides a "valuable service—namely, to equip [children] with the skills they need to survive in life and, more specifically, in the workplace." We do not doubt that Congress has authority under the Commerce Clause to regulate numerous commercial activities that substantially affect interstate commerce and also affect the educational process. That authority, though broad, does not include the authority to regulate each and every aspect of local schools.

Admittedly, a determination whether an intrastate activity is commercial or noncommercial may in some cases result in legal uncertainty. But, so long as Congress' authority is limited to those powers enumerated in the Constitution, and so long as those enumerated powers are interpreted as having judicially enforceable outer limits, congressional legislation under the Commerce Clause always will engender "legal uncertainty." . . . Any possible benefit from eliminating this "legal uncertainty" would be at the expense of the Constitution's system of enumerated powers.

In *Jones & Laughlin Steel,* 301 U.S., at 37, we held that the question of congressional power under the Commerce Clause "is necessarily one of degree." To the same effect is the concurring opinion of Justice Cardozo in *Schechter Poultry:*

> There is a view of causation that would obliterate the distinction between what is national and what is local in the activities of commerce. Motion at the outer rim is communicated perceptibly, though minutely, to recording instruments at the center. A society such as ours "is an elastic medium which transmits all tremors throughout its territory; the only question is of their size."

295 U.S., at 554.

These are not precise formulations, and in the nature of things they cannot be. But we think they point the way to a correct decision of this case. The possession of a gun in a local school zone is in no sense an economic activity that might, through repetition elsewhere, substantially affect any sort of interstate commerce. Respondent was a local student at a local school; there is no indication that he had recently moved in interstate commerce, and there is no requirement that his possession of the firearm have any concrete tie to interstate commerce.

To uphold the Government's contentions here, we would have to pile inference upon inference in a manner that would bid fair to convert congressional authority under the Commerce Clause to a general police power of the sort retained by the States. Admittedly, some of our prior cases have taken long steps down that road, giving great deference to congressional action. The broad language in these opinions has suggested the possibility of additional expansion, but we decline here to proceed any further. To do so would require us to conclude that the Constitution's enumeration of powers does not presuppose something not enumerated, cf. *Gibbons v. Ogden, supra,* at 195, and that there never will be a distinction between what is truly national and what is truly local, cf. *Jones & Laughlin Steel, supra,* at 30. This we are unwilling to do.

■ JUSTICE KENNEDY, with whom JUSTICE O'CONNOR joins, concurring.

The history of the judicial struggle to interpret the Commerce Clause during the transition from the economic system the Founders knew to the single, national market still emergent in our own era counsels great restraint before the Court determines that the Clause is insufficient to support an exercise of the national power. That history gives me some pause about today's decision, but I join the Court's opinion with these observations on what I conceive to be its necessary though limited holding. . . .

The case that seems to mark the Court's definitive commitment to the practical conception of the commerce power is *NLRB v. Jones & Laughlin Steel Corp.,* 301 U.S. 1 (1937), where the Court sustained labor laws that applied to manufacturing facilities, making no real attempt to distinguish *Carter Coal* and *Schechter Poultry.* The deference given to Congress has since been confirmed. *United States v. Darby,* 312 U.S. 100, 116–117 (1941), overruled *Hammer v. Dagenhart, supra.* And in *Wickard v. Filburn,* 317 U.S. 111 (1942), the Court disapproved *E.C. Knight* and the entire line of direct-indirect and manufacture-production cases, explaining that "broader interpretations of the Commerce Clause [were] destined to supersede the earlier ones," at 122, and "[w]hatever terminology is used, the criterion is necessarily one of degree and must be so defined. This does not satisfy those who seek mathematical or rigid formulas. But such formulas are not provided by the great concepts of the Constitution," *id.,* at 123, n. 24. Later examples of the exercise of federal power where commercial transactions were the subject of regulation include *Heart of Atlanta Motel, Inc. v. United States,* 379 U.S. 241 (1964), *Katzenbach v. McClung,* 379 U.S. 294 (1964), and *Perez v. United States,* 402 U.S. 146 (1971). These and like authorities are within the fair ambit of the Court's practical conception of commercial regulation and are not called in question by our decision today.

. . . [T]he Court as an institution and the legal system as a whole have an immense stake in the stability of our Commerce Clause jurisprudence as it has evolved to this point. *Stare decisis* operates with great force in counseling us not to call in question the essential principles now in place respecting the congressional power to regulate transactions of a commercial nature. That fundamental restraint on our power forecloses us from reverting to an understanding of commerce that would serve only an 18th–century economy, dependent then upon production and trading practices that had changed but little over the preceding centuries; it also mandates against returning to the time when congressional authority to regulate undoubted commercial activities was limited by a judicial determination that those matters had an insufficient connection to an interstate system. Congress can regulate in the commercial sphere on the assumption that we have a single market and a unified purpose to build a stable national economy. . . .

The statute before us upsets the federal balance to a degree that renders it an unconstitutional assertion of the commerce power, and our intervention is required. As THE CHIEF JUSTICE explains, unlike the earlier cases to come before the Court here neither the actors nor their conduct has a commercial character, and neither the purposes nor the design of the statute has an evident commercial nexus. The statute makes the simple possession of a gun within 1,000 feet of the grounds of the school a criminal offense. In a sense any conduct in this interdependent world of ours has an ultimate commercial origin or consequence, but we have not yet said the commerce power may reach so far. If Congress attempts that extension, then at the least we must inquire whether the exercise of national power seeks to intrude upon an area of traditional state concern. . . .

■ JUSTICE THOMAS, concurring.

The Court today properly concludes that the Commerce Clause does not grant Congress the authority to prohibit gun possession within 1,000 feet of a school, as it attempted to do in the Gun–Free School Zones Act of 1990. Although I join the majority, I write separately to observe that our case law has drifted far from the original understanding of the Commerce Clause. In a future case, we ought to temper our Commerce Clause jurisprudence in a manner that both makes sense of our more recent case law and is more faithful to the original understanding of that Clause.

We have said that Congress may regulate not only "Commerce . . . among the several States," U.S. Const., Art. I, § 8, cl. 3, but also anything that has a "substantial effect" on such commerce. This test, if taken to its logical extreme, would give Congress a "police power" over all aspects of American life. Unfortunately, we have never come to grips with this implication of our substantial effects formula. Although we have supposedly applied the substantial effects test for the past 60 years, we *always* have rejected readings of the Commerce Clause and the scope of federal power that would permit Congress to exercise a police power; our cases are quite clear that there are real limits to federal power. . . .

While the principal dissent concedes that there are limits to federal power, the sweeping nature of our current test enables the dissent to argue that Congress can regulate gun possession. But it seems to me that the power to regulate "commerce" can by no means encompass authority over mere gun possession, any more than it empowers the Federal Government to regulate marriage, littering, or cruelty to animals, throughout the 50 States. Our Constitution quite properly leaves such matters to the individual States, notwithstanding these activities' effects on interstate commerce. Any interpretation of the Commerce Clause that even suggests that Congress could regulate such matters is in need of reexamination.

In an appropriate case, I believe that we must further reconsider our "substantial effects" test with an eye toward constructing a standard that reflects the text and history of the Commerce Clause without totally rejecting our more recent Commerce Clause jurisprudence. . . .

At the time the original Constitution was ratified, "commerce" consisted of selling, buying, and bartering, as well as transporting for these purposes. See 1 S. Johnson, A Dictionary of the English Language 361 (4th ed. 1773) (defining commerce as "Intercour[s]e; exchange of one thing for another; interchange of any thing; trade; traffick"); N. Bailey, An Universal Etymological English Dictionary (26th ed. 1789) ("trade or traffic"); T. Sheridan, A Complete Dictionary of the English Language (6th ed. 1796) ("Exchange of one thing for another; trade, traffick"). This understanding finds support in the etymology of the word, which literally means "with merchandise." See 3 Oxford English Dictionary 552 (2d ed. 1989) (com—"with"; merci—"merchandise"). In fact, when Federalists and Anti–Federalists discussed the Commerce Clause during the ratification period, they often used trade (in its selling/bartering sense) and commerce interchangeably. See The Federalist No. 4, p. 22 (J. Jay) (asserting that countries will cultivate our friendship when our "trade" is prudently regulated by Federal Government); *id.*, No. 7, at 39–40 (A. Hamilton) (discussing "competitions of commerce" between States resulting from state "regulations of trade"); *id.*, No. 40, at 262 (J. Madison) (asserting that it was an "acknowledged object of the Convention . . . that the regulation of trade should be submitted to the general government"); Lee, Letters of a Federal Farmer No. 5, in Pamphlets on the Constitution of the United States 319 (P. Ford ed. 1888); Smith, An Address to the People of the State of New York, in *id.*, at 107.

As one would expect, the term "commerce" was used in contradistinction to productive activities such as manufacturing and agriculture. Alexander Hamilton, for example, repeatedly treated commerce, agriculture, and manufacturing as three separate endeavors. See, *e.g.*, The Federalist No. 36, at 224 (referring to "agriculture, commerce, manufactures"); *id.*, No. 21, at 133 (distinguishing commerce, arts, and industry); *id.*, No. 12, at 74 (asserting that commerce and agriculture have shared interests). The same distinctions were made in the state ratification conventions. . . .

The Constitution not only uses the word "commerce" in a narrower sense than our case law might suggest, it also does not support the proposition that Congress has authority over all activities that "substantially affect" interstate commerce. The Commerce Clause does not state that Congress may "regulate matters that substantially affect commerce with foreign Nations, and among the several States, and with the Indian Tribes." In contrast, the Constitution itself temporarily prohibited amendments that would "affect" Congress' lack of authority to prohibit or restrict the slave trade or to enact unproportioned direct taxation. Art. V. Clearly, the Framers could have drafted a Constitution that contained a "substantially affects interstate commerce" Clause had that been their objective.

In addition to its powers under the Commerce Clause, Congress has the authority to enact such laws as are "necessary and proper" to carry into execution its power to regulate commerce among the several States. U.S. Const., Art. I, § 8, cl. 18. But on this Court's understanding of congressional power under these two Clauses, many of Congress' other enumerated powers under Art. I, § 8, are wholly superfluous. After all, if Congress may regulate all matters that substantially affect commerce, there is no need for the Constitution to specify that Congress may enact bankruptcy laws, cl. 4, or coin money and fix the standard of weights and measures, cl. 5, or punish counterfeiters of United States coin and securities, cl. 6. Likewise, Congress would not need the separate authority to establish post offices and post roads, cl. 7, or to grant patents and copyrights, cl. 8, or to "punish Piracies and Felonies committed on the high Seas," cl. 10. It might not even need the power to raise and support an Army and Navy, cls. 12 and 13, for fewer people would engage in commercial shipping if they thought that a foreign power could expropriate their property with ease. Indeed, if Congress could regulate matters that substantially affect interstate commerce, there would have been no need to specify that Congress can regulate international trade and commerce with the Indians. As the Framers surely understood, these other branches of trade substantially affect interstate commerce.

Put simply, much if not all of Art. I, § 8 (including portions of the Commerce Clause itself), would be surplusage if Congress had been given authority over matters that substantially affect interstate commerce. An interpretation of cl. 3 that makes the rest of § 8 superfluous simply cannot be correct. Yet this Court's Commerce Clause jurisprudence has endorsed just such an interpretation: The power we have accorded Congress has swallowed Art. I, § 8.

Indeed, if a "substantial effects" test can be appended to the Commerce Clause, why not to every other power of the Federal Government? There is no reason for singling out the Commerce Clause for special treatment. Accordingly, Congress could regulate all matters that "substantially affect" the Army and Navy, bankruptcies, tax collection, expenditures, and so on. In that case, the Clauses of § 8 all mutually overlap, something we can assume the Founding Fathers never intended.

Our construction of the scope of congressional authority has the additional problem of coming close to turning the Tenth Amendment on its head. Our case law could be read to reserve to the United States all powers not expressly *prohibited* by the Constitution. Taken together, these fundamental textual problems should, at the very least, convince us that the "substantial effects" test should be reexamined.

The exchanges during the ratification campaign reveal the relatively limited reach of the Commerce Clause and of federal power generally. . . .

Hamilton, for instance, acknowledged that the Federal Government could not regulate agriculture and like concerns:

The administration of private justice between the citizens of the same State, the supervision of agriculture and of other concerns of a similar nature, all those things in short which are proper to be provided for by local legislation, can never be desirable cares of a general jurisdiction.

The Federalist No. 17, at 106. . . .

The comments of Hamilton and others about federal power reflected the well-known truth that the new Government would have only the limited and enumerated powers found in the Constitution. See, *e.g.*, 2 Debates 267–268 (A. Hamilton at New York Convention) (noting that there would be just cause for rejecting the Constitution if it would enable the Federal Government to "alter, or abrogate . . . [a State's] civil and criminal institutions [or] penetrate the recesses of domestic life, and control, in all respects, the private conduct of individuals"); The Federalist No. 45, at 313 (J. Madison). . . .

Apart from its recent vintage and its corresponding lack of any grounding in the original understanding of the Constitution, the substantial effects test suffers from the further flaw that it appears to grant Congress a police power over the Nation. When asked at oral argument if there were *any* limits to the Commerce Clause, the Government was at a loss for words. Tr. of Oral Arg. 5. Likewise, the principal dissent insists that there are limits, but it cannot muster even one example. Indeed, the dissent implicitly concedes that its reading has no limits when it criticizes the Court for "threaten[ing] legal uncertainty in an area of law that . . . seemed reasonably well settled." The one advantage of the dissent's standard is certainty: It is certain that under its analysis everything may be regulated under the guise of the Commerce Clause.

The substantial effects test suffers from this flaw, in part, because of its "aggregation principle." Under so-called "class of activities" statutes, Congress can regulate whole categories of activities that are not themselves either "interstate" or "commerce." In applying the effects test, we ask whether the class of activities *as a whole* substantially affects interstate commerce, not whether any specific activity within the class has such effects when considered in isolation. See *Maryland v. Wirtz,* 392 U.S., at 192–193 (if class of activities is "within the reach of federal power," courts may not excise individual applications as trivial).

The aggregation principle is clever, but has no stopping point. Suppose all would agree that gun possession within 1,000 feet of a school does not substantially affect commerce, but that possession of weapons generally (knives, brass knuckles, nunchakus, etc.) does. Under our substantial effects doctrine, even though Congress cannot single out gun possession, it can prohibit weapon possession generally. But one *always* can draw the circle broadly enough to cover an activity that, when taken in isolation, would not have substantial effects on commerce. Under our jurisprudence, if Congress passed an omnibus "substantially affects interstate commerce" statute, purporting to regulate every aspect of human existence, the Act apparently would be constitutional. Even though particular sections may govern only trivial activities, the statute in the aggregate regulates matters that substantially affect commerce.

This extended discussion of the original understanding and our first century and a half of case law does not necessarily require a wholesale abandonment of our more recent opinions.[8] It simply reveals that our substantial effects test is far removed from both the Constitution and from our early case law and that the Court's opinion should not be viewed as "radical" or another "wrong turn" that must be corrected in the future. The analysis also suggests that we ought to temper our Commerce Clause jurisprudence.

Unless the dissenting Justices are willing to repudiate our long-held understanding of the limited nature of federal power, I would think that they, too, must be willing to reconsider the substantial effects test in a future case. If we wish to be true to a Constitution that does not cede a police power to the Federal Government, our Commerce Clause's boundaries simply cannot be "defined" as being "commensurate with the national needs" or self-consciously intended to let the Federal Government "defend itself against economic forces that Congress decrees inimical or destructive of the national economy." See *post* (BREYER, J., dissenting). Such a formulation of federal power is no test at all: It is a blank check.

At an appropriate juncture, I think we must modify our Commerce Clause jurisprudence. Today, it is easy enough to say that the Clause certainly does not empower Congress to ban gun possession within 1,000 feet of a school.

■ JUSTICE STEVENS, dissenting.

. . . Guns are both articles of commerce and articles that can be used to restrain commerce. Their possession is the consequence, either directly or indirectly, of commercial activity. In my judgment, Congress' power to regulate commerce in firearms includes the power to prohibit possession of guns at any location because of their potentially harmful use; it necessarily follows that Congress may also prohibit their possession in particular markets. The market for the possession of handguns by school-age children is, distressingly, substantial. Whether or not the national interest in eliminat-

---

[8] Although I might be willing to return to the original understanding, I recognize that many believe that it is too late in the day to undertake a fundamental reexamination of the past 60 years. Consideration of *stare decisis* and reliance interests may convince us that we cannot wipe the slate clean.

ing that market would have justified federal legislation in 1789, it surely does today.

■ [The dissenting opinion of JUSTICE SOUTER is omitted.]

■ JUSTICE BREYER, with whom JUSTICE STEVENS, JUSTICE SOUTER, and JUSTICE GINSBURG join, dissenting.

The issue in this case is whether the Commerce Clause authorizes Congress to enact a statute that makes it a crime to possess a gun in, or near, a school. In my view, the statute falls well within the scope of the commerce power as this Court has understood that power over the last half century.

In reaching this conclusion, I apply three basic principles of Commerce Clause interpretation. First, the power to "regulate Commerce . . . among the several States" encompasses the power to regulate local activities insofar as they significantly affect interstate commerce. As the majority points out, the Court, in describing how much of an effect the Clause requires, sometimes has used the word "substantial" and sometimes has not. . . . I use the word "significant" because the word "substantial" implies a somewhat narrower power than recent precedent suggests. But to speak of "substantial effect" rather than "significant effect" would make no difference in this case.

Second, in determining whether a local activity will likely have a significant effect upon interstate commerce, a court must consider, not the effect of an individual act (a single instance of gun possession), but rather the cumulative effect of all similar instances (*i.e.,* the effect of all guns possessed in or near schools). See, *e.g., Wickard, supra,* 317 U.S., at 127– 128. . . .

Third, the Constitution requires us to judge the connection between a regulated activity and interstate commerce, not directly, but at one remove. Courts must give Congress a degree of leeway in determining the existence of a significant factual connection between the regulated activity and interstate commerce—both because the Constitution delegates the commerce power directly to Congress and because the determination requires an empirical judgment of a kind that a legislature is more likely than a court to make with accuracy. The traditional words "rational basis" capture this leeway. Thus, the specific question before us, as the Court recognizes, is not whether the "regulated activity sufficiently affected interstate commerce," but, rather, whether Congress could have had *"a rational basis"* for so concluding. . . .

Applying these principles to the case at hand, we must ask whether Congress could have had a *rational basis* for finding a significant (or substantial) connection between gun-related school violence and interstate commerce. Or, to put the question in the language of the *explicit* finding that Congress made when it amended this law in 1994: Could Congress rationally have found that "violent crime in school zones," through its effect on the "quality of education," significantly (or substantially) affects "interstate" or "foreign commerce"? As long as one views the commerce connection, not as a "technical legal conception," but as "a practical one," *Swift & Co. v. United States,* 196 U.S. 375, 398 (1905) (Holmes, J.), the answer to this question must be yes. Numerous reports and studies—generated both inside and outside government—make clear that Congress could reasonably have found the empirical connection that its law, implicitly or explicitly, asserts.

For one thing, reports, hearings, and other readily available literature make clear that the problem of guns in and around schools is widespread and extremely serious. These materials report, for example, that four percent of American high school students (and six percent of inner-city high school students) carry a gun to school at least occasionally; that 20 percent of those students have been threatened with guns; and that, in any 6-month period, several hundred thousand schoolchildren are victims of violent crimes in or near their schools. And, they report that this widespread violence in schools throughout the Nation significantly interferes with the quality of education in those schools.... Congress could therefore have found a substantial educational problem—teachers unable to teach, students unable to learn—and concluded that guns near schools contribute substantially to the size and scope of that problem.

Having found that guns in schools significantly undermine the quality of education in our Nation's classrooms, Congress could also have found, given the effect of education upon interstate and foreign commerce, that gun-related violence in and around schools is a commercial, as well as a human, problem. Education, although far more than a matter of economics, has long been inextricably intertwined with the Nation's economy....

Finally, there is evidence that, today more than ever, many firms base their location decisions upon the presence, or absence, of a work force with a basic education....

The economic links I have just sketched seem fairly obvious....

The majority's holding—that [the Act] falls outside the scope of the Commerce Clause—creates three serious legal problems. First, the majority's holding runs contrary to modern Supreme Court cases that have upheld congressional actions despite connections to interstate or foreign commerce that are less significant than the effect of school violence....

The second legal problem the Court creates comes from its apparent belief that it can reconcile its holding with earlier cases by making a critical distinction between "commercial" and noncommercial "transaction[s]." That is to say, the Court believes the Constitution would distinguish between two local activities, each of which has an identical effect upon interstate commerce, if one, but not the other, is "commercial" in nature. As a general matter, this approach fails to heed this Court's earlier warning not to turn "questions of the power of Congress" upon "formula[s]" that would give

> controlling force to nomenclature such as "production" and "indirect" and foreclose consideration of the actual effects of the activity in question upon interstate commerce.

Wickard, supra, 317 U.S., at 120....

The third legal problem created by the Court's holding is that it threatens legal uncertainty in an area of law that, until this case, seemed reasonably well settled....

Upholding this legislation would do no more than simply recognize that Congress had a "rational basis" for finding a significant connection between guns in or near schools and (through their effect on education) the interstate and foreign commerce they threaten.

NOTES

1. *Is Lopez Surprising?* The Supreme Court's decision in *Lopez* in 1995 was something of a shock to the legal community because it represented the first time since 1937 that the Supreme Court had found a congressional exercise of power to exceed the permissible scope of the Commerce Clause. Yet the majority opinion does not overrule any prior precedent of the Court. Rather, it collates the Court's prior cases upholding statutes as within the Commerce Clause power and places them in three broad categories: (1) laws regulating the *use* of the "channels of interstate commerce," including the decisions in cases like *Champion*, *Caminetti*, and *Heart of Atlanta Motel*; (2) laws regulating the "instrumentalities" of commerce or "persons or things in interstate commerce," even if the regulation focuses on intrastate activities, including the decisions in *Shreveport Rate Cases* and the *Perez* anti-loansharking case; and (3) laws regulating activities, including intrastate conduct, that, considered in the aggregate, "substantially affect" interstate commerce, such as the Court's decisions in *Jones & Laughlin Steel, Darby, Wickard v. Filburn*, and several other cases. Is there anything dramatic (or counter-revolutionary) in the Court's categorizations? Is there anything surprising about the majority opinion, other than the result—that an act of Congress, passed under the Commerce Clause, was held not to fit any of these categories? The outcome in *Lopez* appears to turn on (1) whether wholly intrastate activities must "substantially" affect interstate commerce to fall within the scope of the Commerce Clause power (the view of the majority) or merely "significantly" affect interstate commerce (the view of the dissent), and (2) who gets to make that determination: Congress (even without specifically considering the issue) or the Court. What do you think: Was the case rightly decided or wrongly decided? Why?

2. *"Commerce" or "Necessary and Proper"?* Does it make a difference to the analysis whether the claimed national power to enact the Gun–Free School Zones Act is thought to flow from the Commerce Clause itself or from the Necessary and Proper Clause? Congress has the power "To make all Laws which shall be necessary and proper for carrying into Execution" its power to regulate commerce among the several states. As interpreted in *McCulloch v. Maryland* this is a power "To make all Laws which shall be *convenient or useful* for carrying into Execution" its power to regulate commerce among the several states. Is the Necessary and Proper Clause what provides the foundation for the "substantially affecting interstate commerce" prong of the three-part *Lopez* test? If so, how does this affect the argument (if at all)? Is the law in *Lopez* "convenient" or "useful" to regulating the interstate market in guns? To promoting better learning in schools? (Is regulation of education a regulation of "commerce"? A regulation of interstate commerce?) Is *Lopez,* in rejecting the invitation to "pile inference upon inference" in order to sustain the law implicitly a holding about the limits of Congress's use of the Necessary and Proper Clause to justify intrastate non-commercial regulations in the name of regulating interstate commerce?

3. *The Lopez Opinions.* Consider the various opinions in *Lopez* and their different approaches to the issue. Which do you find more persuasive? Why?

a. The majority opinion of Chief Justice Rehnquist strives to connect the dots of all the Court's prior cases, synthesize their holdings, and derive certain general principles from them—and especially limitations on the scope of the Commerce Clause power of Congress. It starts from the premise (in the words of Chief Justice Marshall's opinion in *Gibbons v. Ogden*) that the enumeration of powers "presupposes something not enumerated." The majority opinion thus takes as its starting point that the one interpretation not open to the Court is that the Commerce Clause confers essentially unlimited legislative power on Congress. How sound is this as an interpretive starting point? The opinion then seeks to accommodate the Court's precedents within this broader framework and derive certain limiting principles and standards consistent with this first premise. Does it succeed? Note how the majority opinion holds together the positions of the concurring justices (Kennedy and O'Connor, who emphasized the narrowness of the majority's holding; and Thomas, who would have been open to a more fundamental reexamination of the Court's Commerce Clause jurisprudence).

b. The concurring opinion of Justices Kennedy and O'Connor—who joined the majority opinion—conducts a similar enterprise, emphasizing the narrowness of the Court's ruling and offering the reassurance that principles of *stare decisis* foreclose any general reconsideration of the Court's Commerce Clause jurisprudence since 1937. Is this reassurance persuasive? *Should* principles of *stare decisis* foreclose reexamination of the Court's earlier Commerce Clause decisions?

c. Justice Thomas's concurring opinion—and he also joined the majority opinion—is more far-reaching. It is unabashedly "originalist," looking to what Justice Thomas believed to be the original meaning of the Commerce Clause and finding that the Court's New Deal era decisions had expanded the scope of Congress's powers in a way not justified by the Constitution's text, as originally understood. Thomas would be willing to reopen the entire area of Commerce Clause interpretation, but concurred with the majority's opinion as an accurate and sound description and limitation of the scope of the Court's own precedents. Is Justice Thomas right that the Supreme Court went too far when it recognized a federal power under the Commerce Clause to regulate wholly intrastate activities that substantially affect interstate commerce? How does Justice Thomas respond to the argument that the law in *Lopez* can be justified as being within Congress's power under the Necessary and Proper Clause even if it is not within congressional power under the Commerce Clause?

d. The dissenting opinions—four justices—would have upheld an even broader power of Congress to reach intrastate activity, on the basis of Congress's judgment (or what the Court might assume could have been Congress's judgment) about its indirect effects on interstate commerce. The approach is broadly deferential to Congress's judgments. Is this the better approach? How would you describe the interpretive methodology of the dissents?

4. *"We start with first principles."* As noted, Chief Justice Rehnquist's majority opinion begins by laying down two markers: first, the legislative powers of the national government are enumerated, and therefore limited; second, the enumeration "presupposes something not enumerated" (quoting *Gibbons*). The conclusion suggested is that any interpretation of the Commerce Clause (and the Necessary and Proper Clause) which would produce a national government of essentially unlimited powers must be wrong. Is this a sound starting point? At all events, this premise appears to have been significant to the majority. Justice Thomas's concurring opinion notes what many observers of the oral argument in *Lopez* have said may have been a critical turning point in the Court's deliberation: When justices asked Solicitor General Drew Days wheth-

er, under the government's position, he could think of anything that Congress would not have the power to regulate in the name of the Commerce Clause, he had considerable difficulty—indeed, no success—in identifying any such areas. The majority balked at this as being inconsistent with the Constitution's first premise of establishing a government of limited, enumerated powers. (The majority also seemed concerned that the government's interpretation of the Commerce Clause would render the other enumerated powers essentially superfluous. How important is it to the correct interpretation of the Commerce Clause that a broad interpretation would essentially swallow up several more specific powers? Or are overlap and redundancy, generality and specificity, not a problem?)

Justice Breyer's dissent argues for a broad view of national power under the Commerce and Necessary and Proper Clauses, building on the consensus that prevailed from 1937 to 1995. But would not the position of the dissent press this consensus yet further than such cases as *Darby*, *Wickard*, and *Heart of Atlanta Motel* in extending what types of activities could be regulated as an incident of the commerce power? Under Justice Breyer's view, is there anything that Congress cannot do, in the name of regulating things that, in the aggregate, affect commerce?

5. *The Economics of Federalism?* At the time *Lopez* was decided, more than forty states already had laws against carrying guns in or near schools. Recently there has been renewed scholarly attention to the economics of federalism. See, e.g., Robert D. Cooter & Neil S. Siegel, *Collective Action Federalism: A General Theory of Article I, Section 8*, 63 Stan. L. Rev. 115 (2010). A central idea is that a federal system allows the states to compete with each other, making every state better off, but the national government can step in to solve collective-action problems—the kind of problems where each state by acting in its own self-interest will make all of the states collectively worse off. Was the statute in *Lopez* solving a problem that the states were unable to resolve by themselves? When one state decided to, or not to, restrict gun possession near a school, did that decision impose "negative externalities," or costs, on *other* states? The statute in *Lopez* is hard to understand as a solution to a collective-action problem among the states.

Related questions were actually considered at the Philadelphia Convention. One of the delegates, Gunning Bedford of Delaware, put forward the following resolution: "the national Legislature ought to possess the legislative rights vested in Congress by the confederation [and the right] to legislate in all cases for the general interests of the Union, and also *in those to which the States are separately incompetent*, or in which the harmony of the United States may be interrupted by the exercise of individual legislation." 2 Max Farrand, THE RECORDS OF THE FEDERAL CONVENTION OF 1787 21, 27 (emphasis added). The Bedford Resolution was approved, and the Committee of Detail was charged with writing this outcome into the text of the Constitution. The result, however, was Article I, Section 8—the single very long sentence that has eighteen clauses enumerating the national legislative powers. How is the approach of the Bedford Resolution similar to and different from the text that was actually adopted? If the text of the Constitution had included the Bedford Resolution instead of Article I, Section 8, would it have strengthened the argument of the majority or the dissent in *Lopez*? Should the solving-collective-action-problems conception of federalism affect the interpretation of Article I, Section 8?

6. *Burdens of Proof.* In cases involving federalism and enumerated powers, who has the burden of proof? In *Proving the Law*, 86 Nw. U. L. Rev. 859 (1992), Gary Lawson argues that the federal government has the burden of proving that it has the power to act. If it is unclear whether there is federal power to act, then there is no clear constitutional "law" which the courts can apply to alter the private distribution of liberty and property. In Bill of Rights and Fourteenth Amendment cases, Lawson argues, ambiguity means there is no clear constitutional "law" trumping state power. Accordingly, any ambiguity over whether a federal power to act exists must be resolved in favor of the states' power to act. Since *McCulloch v. Maryland,* arguably, and since the New Deal, certainly, the Court's actual practice has been almost the opposite. Who do you think has the burden of proving that a law is necessary and proper or that it substantially affects interstate commerce: the federal government, or the individual challenging a federal action?

7. *Jurisdictional Elements.* Could Congress accomplish the Gun–Free School Zone Act's objectives by including a "jurisdictional" element—a requirement of proof that a gun has traveled in interstate commerce, or was manufactured using materials or supplies derived from interstate commerce? Could it make a statutory *finding* concerning the national handgun industry or market? What deference should be accorded to these factual findings by Congress? While *Lopez* was pending before the Court, Congress in fact amended the statute to include the following findings: that "crime, particularly [crime committed with] guns, is a pervasive nationwide problem"; that "crime at the local level is exacerbated by" the interstate movement of guns; that guns and ammunition "move easily in interstate commerce and have been found in increasing numbers in and around schools"; that the "component parts, ammunition, and raw materials" from which firearms are made "have considerably moved in interstate commerce"; that people "may fear to travel to or through certain parts of the country due to concern about violent crime and gun violence, and parents may decline to send their children to school for the same reason"; that "crime in school zones has resulted in a decline in the quality of education," with the result that this "decline . . . has an adverse impact on interstate commerce"; and that states and localities find it impossible to handle all such gun-related crime by themselves.

Should this alter the constitutional outcome? Following *Lopez*, Congress further amended the statute to provide: "It shall be unlawful for any individual knowingly to possess a firearm that has moved in or that otherwise affects interstate commerce at a place that the individual knows, or has reasonable cause to believe, is a school zone." Constitutional?

8. *The Debate Continues: Significant Post–Lopez Commerce Clause Cases.* As significant as it was, *Lopez* was, of course, hardly the last word in the Court's Commerce Clause jurisprudence. Consider the following noteworthy cases between *Lopez* and the Court's 2012 decision in *National Federation of Independent Business v. Sebelius.*

a. *United States v. Morrison*, 529 U.S. 598 (2000). In *Morrison*, the Court held, 5–4 (with the same alignment of justices as in *Lopez*), that the Commerce Clause did not empower Congress to enact the Violence Against Women Act ("VAWA"), which made certain acts of domestic violence federal crimes and torts. (In a separate holding, the Court held that Congress lacked power to enact VAWA as a measure to enforce the Fourteenth Amendment, on reasoning similar to that in the *Civil Rights Cases'* holding that the Fourteenth Amendment does not authorize Congress to regulate private conduct directly, but only "state action." This part of the case is printed in Chapter 7.) Building on *Lopez,* the *Morrison* Court held that the Commerce Clause could not be leveraged into a power to regulate purely intrastate noncommercial activity: "Gender-motivated crimes of violence are not, in any sense of the phrase, economic activity. . . . We accordingly reject the argument that Congress may regulate noneconomic, violent criminal conduct based solely on that conduct's aggregate effect on interstate commerce." The fact that Congress had made factual findings that gender-motivated violence had a substantial impact on commerce made no difference: "[T]he existence of congressional findings is not sufficient, by itself, to sustain the constitutionality of Commerce Clause legislation. As we stated in *Lopez,* '[s]imply because Congress may conclude that a particular activity substantially affects interstate commerce does not necessarily make it so.' " The Court reasoned that to completely defer to Congress's findings would permit Congress to "use the Commerce Clause to completely obliterate the Constitution's distinction between national and local authority. . . . The reasoning that petitions advance seeks to follow the bur-for causal chain from the initial occurrence of violent crime (the suppression of which has always been the prime object of the States' police power) to every attenuated effect upon interstate commerce. If accepted, petitioners' reasoning would allow Congress to regulate any crime as long as the nationwide, aggregated impact of that crime has substantial effects on employment, production, transit, or consumption." Congress could regulate murder or any other crime directly under the Commerce Clause, as well as "family law and other areas of traditional state regulation since the aggregate effect of marriage, divorce, and childrearing on the national economy is undoubtedly significant."

Does *Morrison* follow *a fortiori* from *Lopez*? Is the connection-to-commerce justification stronger in one case than the other? How attenuated must the chain of causation be before Congress is denied the power to regulate? Was the Court in *Morrison* correct or incorrect in discounting the significance of congressional findings concerning these matters?

b. *Gonzales v. Raich,* 545 U.S. 1 (2005). California passed a law in 1996 permitting the seriously ill to use marijuana for medicinal purposes. That law conflicted with federal drug laws. Angel Raich and others seeking to use marijuana to alleviate symptoms of illness challenged the constitutionality of the federal statute on the ground, among others, that it exceeded Congress's power under the Commerce Clause. A 6-3 majority upheld the federal statute. Justice Stevens's majority opinion relied heavily on the reasoning of *Wickard v. Filburn*: *Wickard* "establishes that Congress can regulate purely intrastate activity that is not itself 'commercial,' in that it is not produced for sale, if it concludes that failure to regulate that class of activity would undercut the regulation of the interstate market in that commodity." Since it was clear that Congress could prohibit all interstate commerce in marijuana (under the line of cases permitting Congress to ban such commerce in specific goods, see *Champion v. Ames* and *United States v. Darby*), it also could ban purely intrastate production and consumption of marijuana (just as it could regulate Farmer Filburn's production of wheat for home consumption in *Wickard*). Justice Scalia concurred in the judgment, on the ground that such power was located in the Necessary and Proper Clause: "Where necessary to make a regulation of interstate commerce effective, Congress may regulate even those intrastate activities that do not themselves substantially affect interstate commerce." Justice O'Connor, joined by Chief Justice Rehnquist and Justice Thomas, dissented, arguing that the Court's decision "allows Congress to regulate intrastate activity without heck, so long as there is some implication by legislative design that regulating intrastate activity is essential . . . to the interstate regulatory scheme."

Was *Gonzales v. Raich* rightly or wrongly decided? Is it consistent with *Lopez* and *Morrison*? Is there a principled difference among these three cases that explains why Justice Scalia and Justice Kennedy voted for federal power in *Raich*, but not in *Lopez* or *Morrison*? Are you persuaded by the majority's analysis that the case is nearly identical to *Wickard v. Filburn*? Is there a sense in which the growing of marijuana is not "commercial" in the same sense that the growing of wheat, even for farm consumption, is? Both *Raich* and *Wickard* appear predicated on the idea that the government can use the Commerce Clause to prohibit the private growing of commodities that might "overhang" the national market and thereby affect interstate commerce with respect to that commodity. On that reasoning, could Congress outlaw church bingo games or private poker nights because they "overhang" the market of interstate commercial gambling?

c. *Of Rare Flies and Hapless Toads: The Commerce Clause and Environmental Law.* Is the federal Endangered Species Act constitutional? Does the Commerce Clause enable Congress to enact a law prohibiting or restricting commercial activity that adversely affects the existence or habitat of a particular species? What if that habitat and species exist only in one state? For an entertaining and enlightening discussion, see John C. Nagle, *The Commerce Clause Meets the Delhi Sands Flower–Loving Fly,* 97 Mich. L. Rev. 174 (1998).

In *Rancho Viejo, LLC v. Norton*, 323 F.2d 1062 (D.C. Cir. 2003), the D.C. Circuit upheld the application of the Endangered Species Act to prohibit a construction project deemed "likely to jeopardize the continued existence of the arroyo southwestern toad, which the Secretary of the Interior has listed as an endangered species since 1994." The court concluded that "the regulated activity"—that is, commercial development—"substantially affects interstate commerce" and so was within Congress's Commerce Clause power, as interpreted in *Lopez*. "This conclusion," the court said, "is not diminished by the fact that the arroyo toad, like the Flower–Loving Fly, does not travel outside of California, or that Rancho Viejo's development, like the San Bernardino hospital, is located wholly within the state." The relevant regulated activity was "Rancho Viejo's planned commercial development, not the arroyo toad that it threatens." And that commercial development had substantial effects on interstate commerce.

The D.C. Circuit voted 8–2 not to rehear the case en banc. In dissent, then-Judge—and now Chief Justice—John Roberts observed that "[t]he panel's approach in this case leads to the result that regulating the taking of a hapless toad that, for reasons of its own, lives its entire life in California constitutes regulating 'Commerce among the several states.' " *Rancho Viejo LLC v. Norton*, 334 F.3d 1158, 1160 (D.C. Cir. 2003) (Roberts, J., dissenting from denial of rehearing en banc). He insisted that the panel wrongly asked "whether the challenged *regulation* substantially affects interstate commerce, rather than whether the *activity* being regulated does so." Judge Roberts believed that the proper question was whether "the incidental taking of arroyo toads can be said to be interstate commerce," not whether the proposed development constituted interstate commerce. What is the difference? Which focus is correct?

In the case referred to by the D.C. Circuit panel in *Rancho Viejo*, involving a similar issue concerning the Delhi Sands Flower-Loving Fly, *National Association of Home Builders v. Babbitt,* three D.C. Circuit judges has split three different ways on the proper question presented. Judge Wald asked whether there was a sufficient relationship between the protection of endangered species generally and interstate commerce. Judge Henderson asked whether there was a sufficient relationship between the hospital construction project and interstate commerce. Judge Sentelle asked whether there was a sufficient relationship between the Delhi Sands Flower–Loving Fly and interstate commerce. Who asked the right question? See Nagle, 97 Mich. L. Rev. 174.

9. The Supreme Court's next, and most recent, major decision interpreting the Commerce Clause came in *National Federation of Independent Business v. Sebelius,* in 2012. That case, however, also presented major issues of interpretation concerning the scope of Congress's powers under the Taxing Clause and pursuant to the national government's power to spend money—and to attach conditions to such expenditures. Before turning to that decision, then, we pause to consider the major modern-era decisions concerning the taxing and spending powers of Congress, prior to *NFIB*.

[*Assignment 33*]

B. THE TAXING POWER, THE SPENDING POWER, AND TENTH AMENDMENT LIMITATIONS ON NATIONAL POWER

The emphasis in the Supreme Court's cases on the scope of Congress's Commerce Clause power has led to a relative lack of attention to two other vitally important, closely-linked national legislative powers: the power to tax, and the power to spend. Any thorough account of federalism and national legislative power must pay significant attention to these powers. This is especially true in light of the Supreme Court's reliance on these powers to sustain in part, and to invalidate in part, the Affordable Care Act in *National Federation of Independent Business v. Sebelius* (2012).

In this assignment, we first discuss the course of the Court's decisions concerning the Taxing Clause power prior to the decision in *NFIB*. Next, we take up the Court's decisions concerning the scope of Congress's spending power—a related power sometimes thought to be located in the Taxing Clause power itself but arguably flowing from other constitutional provisions. The Court's modern cases have focused on the question of Congress's power to attach regulatory mandates to the receipt of federal funds and whether such arrangements improperly leverage the power to spend into a power to coerce compliance with federal mandates that could not be imposed directly. We include two principal cases presenting this issue: *South Dakota v. Dole*, 483 U.S. 203 (1987), involving the conditioning of federal highway funds on a requirement that states raise their minimum drinking age to twenty-one; and *New York v. United States*, 505 U.S. 144 (1992), involving a combination of tax-imposition, spending incentives, and direct regulation to induce states to adopt federal policies concerning the disposal of radioactive waste. The latter case also presents important, related structural issues of federalism: Does the Tenth Amendment, or the structure of American federalism generally, bar the national government from coercing the states to adopt or enforce nationally mandated policies? If so, do some exercises of the taxing and spending powers amount to such forbidden coercion or "commandeering" of the states by the national government? We also include as a principal case, *Printz v. United States*, 521 U.S. 898 (1997), which considered whether the anti-commandering principle of *New York v. United States* extended not only to state legislatures but also to state and local law enforcement officers.

The Taxing Power

As Chief Justice John Marshall colorfully put it in *McCulloch v. Maryland*, "the power to tax is the power to destroy." And Congress has the power to tax. Indeed, it is the first power listed in the Article I, Section 8 enumeration of 18 specific national legislative powers. To what extent may the power to tax constitutionally be employed to pursue regulatory policy objectives?

Article I, Section 8, Clause 1 provides: "The Congress shall have Power To lay and collect Taxes, Duties, Imposts and Excises, to pay the Debts and provide for the common Defence and general Welfare of the United States; but all Duties, Imposts and Excises shall be uniform throughout the United States." Article I, Section 9, Clause 4 imposes a further limitation: "No Capitation, or other direct, Tax shall be laid, unless in Proportion to the Census or Enumeration herein before directed to be taken." That limitation references Article I, Section 2's original representation and taxation formula—the infamous Three-fifths Clause—which provides that "Representatives and direct Taxes shall be apportioned among the several States . . . according to their respective Numbers, which shall be determined by adding to the whole Number of free Persons, including those bound to Service for a Term of Years, and excluding Indians not taxed, three fifths of all other Persons." Article I, Section 9, Clause 5 provides a separate constraint on the taxing power: "No Tax or Duty shall be laid on Articles exported from any State." The combination of these provisions appears to have been designed to prevent Congress from imposing a per-slave "head tax" (a "capitation" tax) on slaveholding or from taxing the interstate slave trade. On the direct-versus-indirect distinction and apportionment, recall also the very early decision of the Court in *Hylton v. United States* (1796).

Aside from these limitations, what is the scope of Congress's power to impose uniform taxes? Can it impose such taxes for reasons apart from simply raising revenue? That is, can it use the taxing power for essentially regulatory or other public policy purposes (such as we have seen with the Commerce Clause power to bar interstate commerce in certain articles)? For example, can Congress impose a high duty on imports of certain goods for a protectionist purpose, such as avoiding or limiting competition to a domestic industry? Can Congress tax a product heavily in order to discourage its sale and use? Historically, the answer has been yes to both questions. (Think of protective tariffs throughout our nation's history and steep excise taxes on items like cigarettes.) But just how far can such a power be pressed? Specifically, can it be employed to accomplish regulatory objectives *otherwise beyond* Congress's powers?

The Supreme Court's cases have charted an uncertain path on this question, as the following brief survey illustrates, but generally the Court has held—with notable exceptions and uncertain qualifications—that the Taxing Clause power is an independent power that can be used to achieve

policy goals not attainable under the Commerce Clause or any other separately enumerated legislative power.

1. *The License Tax Cases (1866)*. In the *License Tax Cases*, 72 U.S. 462
(1866), the Court upheld a federal license and fee requirement, the Internal
Revenue Act, for selling lottery tickets and retailing liquor, even as to purely intrastate activities. The taxpayers challenging the exaction argued that
Congress lacked such taxing authority as to activities carried on purely
within a state. The Court said that Congress would have had "no power of
regulation nor any direct control" over the businesses at issue, and could
not even actually authorize businesses to sell lottery tickets or retail liquor.
But the Court nonetheless found that Congress could impose a license requirement *as a tax*: "The power to tax is not questioned, nor the power to
impose penalties for non-payment of taxes. The granting of a license, therefore, must be regarded as nothing more than a mere form of imposing a tax,
and of implying nothing except that the licensee shall be subject to no penalties under national law, if he pays it." The *License Tax Cases* are thus
early authority for the proposition that Congress can tax activities that it
has no authority to directly regulate under the Commerce Clause. (Does
this seem correct or incorrect? Why?)

2. *Veazie Bank v. Fenno (1869)*. Not long after the *License Tax Cases,*
in *Veazie Bank v. Fenno*, 75 U.S. 533 (1869), the Court upheld a federal tax
on state bank notes against a charge that it was "excessive." That did not
disable the Taxing Clause power, the Court held, but was a matter for political judgment: "[T]he judicial cannot prescribe to the legislative departments of the government limitations upon the exercise of its acknowledged
powers. The power to tax may be exercised oppressively upon persons, but
the responsibility of the Legislature is not to the courts, but to the people
by whom its members are elected." The Court added in dicta, however, that
there are "certain virtual limitations" on the taxing power, "arising from
the principles of the Constitution itself. It would undoubtedly be an abuse
of the power if so exercised as to impair the separate existence and independent self-government of the states, or if exercised for ends inconsistent
with the limited grants of power in the Constitution." Was the Court correct in saying that the size of a tax is for legislative judgment? Is there anything in the Constitution that would supply a principled basis for distinguishing between when a tax is excessive and when it is not? What about
Veazie's dicta? Do you agree that a tax would be unconstitutional if it impaired the "separate existence" or "independent self-government" of the
states? What is the basis for such a principle? How would one know whether or not it has been violated? What about the assertion that the taxing
power may not be used for "ends inconsistent with the limited grants of
power in the Constitution"? Was the Court suggesting that the taxing power could only be used to accomplish regulatory ends already within the
scope of other constitutional powers? Do you agree? Is such a position consistent with the Taxing Clause being its own separate, enumerated power?

3. *McCray v. United States—the "Oleomargarine Case."* The next notable taxing power case was *McCray v. United States*, 195 U.S. 27 (1904),
which involved an excise tax on oleomargarine, a product competing with
butter. The tax was almost certainly enacted to benefit butter producers.
The Court sustained the validity of the tax, noting that while the courts
possessed the duty of upholding the Constitution, this did not include "the
responsibility of correcting every possible abuse arising from the exercise
by the other departments of their conceded authority." To so hold would

"overthrow the entire distinction between the legislative, judicial, and executive departments of the government, upon which our system is founded, and would be a mere act of judicial usurpation." The Court explicitly disclaimed any power to invalidate a tax simply because of the policy motivations that might have prompted it:

> It is, however, argued, if a lawful power may be exerted for an unlawful purpose, and thus, by abusing the power, it may be made to accomplish a result not intended by the Constitution, all limitations of power must disappear, and the grave function lodged in the judiciary, to confine all the departments within the authority conferred by the Constitution, will be of no avail. This, when reduced to its last analysis, comes to this: that, because a particular department of the government may exert its lawful powers with the object or motive of reaching an end not justified, therefore it becomes the duty of the judiciary to restrain the exercise of a lawful power wherever it seems to the judicial mind that such lawful power has been abused. But this reduces itself to this contention that, under our constitutional system, the abuse by one department of the government of its lawful powers is to be corrected by the abuse of its powers by another department.

The remedy for an alleged abuse of the taxing power, the Court said, "lies, not in the abuse by the judicial authority of its functions, but in the people, upon whom, after all, under our institutions, reliance must be placed for the correction of abuses committed in the exercise of a lawful power." Is *McCray* correct? If so, does this leave Congress with substantial discretion to impose what taxes it will for whatever policy reasons it chooses (so long as the tax does not violate some other constitutional provision)? Is Congress's power to tax truly "the power to destroy" indirectly through taxation what it cannot prohibit by direct command? Or are some policy uses of the taxing power invalid precisely because of those policy purposes?

4. *The Child Labor Tax Case (1922)*. This brings us to *Bailey v. Drexel Furniture Co.*, 259 U.S. 20 (1922), the "*Child Labor Tax Case*." As mentioned earlier in connection with the history of the Court's Commerce Clause jurisprudence, the statute at issue was an attempt by Congress to *tax* goods manufactured using child labor in violation of federal standards. Recall that at the time the Court's Commerce Clause decision in *Hammer v. Dagenhart* (1918) denied Congress the power to regulate the interstate shipment of goods produced by child labor. (That decision was later overruled by *United States v. Darby* (1941), but in the meantime Congress had sought to achieve the same policy end by instead imposing a 10% excise tax on profits from the sale of goods manufactured by child labor.)

The *Child Labor Tax Case* struck down the tax on the ground that it was a regulatory penalty designed to circumvent *Hammer*—a result very much leaning in the opposite direction from the interpretations of the taxing power advanced by *Veazie* and *McCray*, cases the Court distinguished these cases on the ground that they did not involve "the detailed specifications of a regulation of a state concern and business with a heavy exaction to promote the efficacy of such regulation." The Court found that "[t]he case before us . . . cannot be distinguished from that of *Hammer v. Dagenhart*." The Court's reasoning in the *Child Labor Tax Case* bears repeating—and careful examination:

> The law is attacked on the ground that it is a regulation of the employment of child labor in the states—an exclusively state function under the federal Constitution and within the reservations of the Tenth

Amendment. It is defended on the ground that it is a mere excise tax levied by the Congress of the United States under its broad power of taxation conferred by section 8, article 1, of the federal Constitution. . . .

Out of a proper respect for the acts of a co-ordinate branch of the government, this court has gone far to sustain taxing acts as such, even though there has been ground for suspecting, from the weight of the tax, it was intended to destroy its subject. But in the act before us the presumption of validity cannot prevail, because the proof of the contrary is found on the very face of its provisions. Grant the validity of this law, and all that Congress would need to do, hereafter, in seeking to take over to its control any one of the great number of subjects of public interest, jurisdiction of which the states have never parted with, and which are reserved to them by the Tenth Amendment, would be to enact a detailed measure of complete regulation of the subject and enforce it by a so called tax upon departures from it. To give such magic to the word "tax" would be to break down all constitutional limitations of the powers of Congress and completely wipe out the sovereignty of the states.

The difference between a tax and a penalty is sometimes difficult to define, and yet the consequences of the distinction in the required method of their collection often are important. Where the sovereign enacting the law has power to impose both tax and penalty, the difference between revenue production and mere regulation may be immaterial, but not so when one sovereign can impose a tax only, and the power of regulation rests in another. Taxes are occasionally imposed in the discretion of the Legislature on proper subjects with the primary motive of obtaining revenue from them and with the incidental motive of discouraging them by making their continuance onerous. They do not lose their character as taxes because of the incidental motive. But there comes a time in the extension of the penalizing features of the so-called tax when it loses its character as such and becomes a mere penalty, with the characteristics of regulation and punishment. Such is the case in the law before us. Although Congress does not invalidate the contract of employment or expressly declare that the employment within the mentioned ages is illegal, it does exhibit its intent practically to achieve the latter result by adopting the criteria of wrongdoing and imposing its principal consequence on those who transgress its standard.

Is the Court's reasoning persuasive? Is it consistent with the *License Tax Cases, Veazie,* and *McCray*? If not, which states the correct interpretation of the Taxing Clause power? Why? Is the result in the *Child Labor Tax Case* primarily attributable to the Court's narrow reading of the Commerce Clause power at the time? Even if so, might the "anti-circumvention" limitation on the Taxing Clause power be correct? Or is it simply a judicially manufactured limitation on an *independent* enumerated legislative power, committed to Congress's policy discretion to exercise for good or ill as it sees fit?

5. *The Social Security Tax Cases (1937)*. In the important cases of *Steward Machine Company v. Davis,* 301 U.S. 548 (1937), and *Helvering v. Davis,* 301 U.S. 619 (1937), the Court tacked back again in the direction of broad national government power to impose taxes and spend money to further regulatory and social policy purposes. These decisions occurred in the

same year as the Court's decisions in *NLRB v. Jones & Laughlin Steel*, the 5–4 decision adopting a broad construction of Congress's legislative commerce power and rejecting earlier decisions adopting a narrower view (discussed earlier in this chapter), and *West Coast Hotel v. Parrish*, which repudiated earlier cases imposing substantive due process restrictions on state laws regulating economic activity (discussed in Chapter 7). *Steward Machine* and *Helvering* were thus of a piece with the "Revolution of 1937," or the supposed "switch in time that saved nine."

Steward Machine sustained, by vote of 5–4, the unemployment compensation tax provisions of the Social Security Act of 1935, which were designed to induce states to adopt their own unemployment compensation laws—laws that the national government clearly could not directly require states to enact. Title IX of the act imposed a payroll tax on employers but provided a credit of up to 90% of the federal tax for any contributions to a state unemployment fund certified by the federal government as complying with prescribed federal standards. Though the tax and refund scheme was plainly intended to achieve social policy goals, it nonetheless was within the Taxing Clause power. Thus, the core of the challenge in *Steward Machine* was not to the tax itself, but to its supposed effect of "coercing" the states. The Court rejected that challenge: "The statute does not call for a surrender by the states of powers essential to their quasi-sovereign existence." The Court distinguished the *Child Labor Tax Case* as presenting entirely different issues.

Steward Machine raises a variety of questions (to which we will return) in connection with Congress's spending power: Are there principled constitutional limitations on Congress's ability to use its financial powers—the power to tax and the power to spend—to compel or induce action *by states*? Do state-autonomy concerns check what would otherwise be the scope of these congressional powers? For now, it is sufficient to note that *Steward Machine* upheld a broad power to impose taxes in order to achieve social policy objectives, and not merely to raise revenues.

6. *United States v. Kahriger (1953)*. Finally, consider the case of *United States v. Kahriger*, 345 U.S. 22 (1953), which involved a "tax on persons engaged in the business of accepting wagers"—that is, a tax on "bookies." The tax was challenged as unconstitutional on the ground that "Congress, under the pretense of exercising its power to tax has attempted to penalize illegal intrastate gambling through the regulatory features of the Act . . . and has thus infringed the police power which is reserved to the states." The Court upheld the tax, citing the *License Tax Cases*, *Veazie*, *McCray*, and several other cases upholding taxes where "the intent to curtail and hinder, as well as tax," an activity was "manifest." (These included cases imposing taxes on narcotics, firearms, and "marihuana.") The Court in *Kahriger* noted that it was "conceded that a federal excise tax does not cease to be valid merely because it discourages or deters the activities taxed. Nor is the tax invalid because the revenue obtained is negligible. Appellee, however, argues that the sole purpose of the statute is to penalize only illegal gambling in the states through the guise of a tax measure. As with the above excise taxes which we have held to be valid, the instant tax has a regulatory effect. But regardless of its regulatory effect, the wagering tax produces revenue."

Justice Jackson joined the Court's opinion but expressed reservations: "I concur in the judgment and opinion of the Court, but with such doubt that if the minority agreed upon an opinion which did not impair legitimate use of the taxing power I probably would join it." But he observed that "all taxation has a tendency proportioned to its burdensomeness to discourage the activity taxed" and it is not possible to impose principled limitations:

> One cannot formulate a revenue-raising plan that would not have economic and social consequences. Congress may and should place the burden of taxes where it will least handicap desirable activities and bear most heavily on useless or harmless ones. If Congress may tax one citizen to the point of discouragement for making an honest living, it is hard to say that it may not do the same to another just because he makes a sinister living.

Jackson conceded that the tax at issue was "a plan to tax out of existence the professional gambler whom [Congress] has found impossible to prosecute out of existence." Two justices dissented.

A summary question: Based on this whirlwind tour, what do you believe is the correct understanding of the Taxing Clause power? Which of these cases are right, and which are wrong? May Congress impose taxes for policy purposes? If so, are there any limits? If not, how do you tell if a tax is a "real" tax, or if it instead impermissibly seeks to accomplish a collateral purpose? Does one look for legislative motivation? Is the distinction between a permitted "tax" and a regulatory "penalty" a principled and sensible one, or does it lack meaningful constitutional content? Should (or does) how Congress characterizes its financial exactions matter in deciding whether an exercise of its Taxing Clause power is legitimate? Or is it the substance that counts? Must a tax actually raise some revenue to be a tax? If so, how much? Keep these questions—and your preliminary answers—in mind as we return to these issues in *National Federation of Independent Business v. Sebelius* (2012) in the next assignment.

The Spending Power

Congress also has the power to *spend* money. What is the relation between the spending power and the taxing power? Does the power of Congress to spend money come from the Taxing Power Clause of Article I, Section 8? If so, is it subject to the same limitations? Is the power to spend money constrained by the broad purposes for which the Taxing Power Clause says it is designed, "to pay the Debts and provide for the common Defence and general Welfare of the United States"? Are these meaningful limitations? Is the power to spend money limited to spending money for carrying into effect the other enumerated powers listed in Article I, Section 8, as James Madison seems to have thought? (See below "A Note on *United States v. Butler.*") This would make the spending power simply one application of Congress's Necessary and Proper Clause power. Does all federal spending have to be "necessary and proper"? Would the federal government as we know it today be able to survive if its appropriations were subjected to such scrutiny? Or is the spending power a broad power of its own, a power to spend for any "general welfare" common purpose (such as paying debts, providing for defense, furthering the general welfare), as Alexander Hamilton thought? (Recall his plan, as secretary of the treasury, for the national government to assume the states' Revolutionary War debts. Is there any national power, other than a power to spend for the general national welfare, that could justify such action?)

If the Hamiltonian view is right, and the spending power is an independent legislative power—and, as we will see, the Supreme Court has said as much in dicta—what clause of the Constitution confers that power? Is it truly the Taxing Clause (which does not specifically anything about a *power* to spend, but only that spending is a purpose for which taxes may be imposed)? Hamilton himself seems to have viewed the spending power as flowing naturally from the language of the taxing power. Is this the most plausible textual basis for the spending power? Or is the Necessary and Proper Clause the true source of the spending power—appropriations being an obviously useful, conducive means of carrying into execution enumerated-powers ends? Another view, advanced by David Engdahl's interesting historical scholarship, is that the power flows from Article IV, Section 3's broad language: "The Congress shall have Power to dispose of and make all needful Rules and Regulations respecting the Territory or other Property belonging to the United States." That clause—located amidst provisions concerning the governance of territories, the disposition of property, and the admission of new states to the Union—might seem an odd place to locate the power to spend, but Engdahl points out that money and other resources of the United States are, legally, its "property" and that the terms of this clause literally apply. See David Engdahl, *The Spending Power*, 44 Duke L.J. 1 (1994); see also David Engdahl, *The Basis for the Spending Power*, 18 Seattle U. L. Rev. 215 (1995).

Another view might be that the power to spend is simply one that governments have: they may spend the resources that they possess. Since the power to tax is a source of revenue (there might be others), it is expected that Congress may also spend that money. Other provisions of the Constitution seem to assume this. Most clearly, Article I, Section 9, Clause 7 provides that "No Money shall be drawn from the Treasury, but in Consequence of Appropriations made by Law." Could this provision be read as authorizing Congress to make appropriations by law? Or does it constrain Congress and the executive branch to spend money only via appropriations bills and not by other extra-legal means? Note the related provision in Article I, Section 8, Clause 12 that limits appropriations of money for raising and supporting armies to two years.

If the power to spend is a free-standing power, it is a power *only to spend*—not a power to regulate. However, even on this view, Congress has the Necessary and Proper Clause power to pass laws it deems necessary and appropriate for *carrying into effect the spending* of the United States—including, presumably, the terms and conditions of the expenditure. (And on Engdahl's theory of the source of the spending power in Article IV, Section 3, Congress could pass all "needful Rules and Regulations" concerning it—an authorization just as sweeping as the Necessary and Proper Clause, if not more so.) Thus, it could be argued that Congress can, in effect, regulate action by spending money and attaching conditions to the appropriation. What are the limits of this power to attach conditions to spending? Must the conditions attached be "necessary and proper" to effectuating the goal of the particular spending? If so, does that impose a practical requirement of some degree of "germaneness" between the condition and the spending—and, if so, who is to judge the propriety of the relationship? On the other hand, could it be argued that the spending power is different, in that someone who is enticed by a contemplated grant is always free to refuse the money (and thus the strings attached to it), with the consequence that Congress can impose any conditions it wants so long as it does not *coerce* recipients?

We present three paradigm cases for thinking about these questions. The first, *United States v. Butler*, 297 U.S. 1 (1936), is a Note. *Butler* presents a classic confrontation—significantly, occurring before the Court's "Revolution of 1937" in its jurisprudence concerning the commerce and taxing powers—between the narrow, "Madisonian" view of the spending power and the broader, "Hamiltonian" view. The majority adopted the narrower view (even though, curiously, it purported to embrace the Hamiltonian position), and the dissent adopted the broader view (which lost in *Butler* itself but has eventually prevailed). In the seeds sown by the competing views in *Butler*, one can discern the origins of the doctrines that later grew in two more recent cases concerning the scope of the spending power: *South Dakota v. Dole*, 483 U.S. 203 (1987); and *New York v. United States*, 505 U.S. 144 (1992). Each of these later cases presents a wide range of issues concerning the national power to spend—with attached conditions—and its interaction with considerations of the independence and autonomy of the states.

A NOTE ON UNITED STATES V. BUTLER

United States v. Butler, 297 U.S. 1 (1936), was a constitutional challenge to the Agricultural Adjustment Act of 1933 ("AAA"), a New Deal measure designed to stabilize agricultural production and prices during the Great Depression. The AAA authorized the secretary of agriculture to make contracts with farmers to reduce the production of agricultural commodities in exchange for direct benefit payments, financed by a tax on the "first domestic processing" of the particular agricultural commodity. Recall that, at the time, the Court's Commerce Clause jurisprudence would not have sustained such a scheme to regulate production as within Congress's power to regulate directly. The government did not seek to defend the program on such grounds. Rather, the question was whether the program could be sustained under Congress's taxing and spending powers, even though it was not within Congress's power to regulate interstate commerce.

Justice Owen Roberts wrote for the majority, rejecting such a power:

> The clause thought to authorize the [AAA] confers upon the Congress power "to lay and collect Taxes, Duties, Imposts and Excises, to pay the Debts and provide for the common Defense and general Welfare of the United States. . . ." It is not contended that this provision grants power to regulate agricultural production upon the theory that such legislation would promote the general welfare. The Government concedes that the phrase "to provide for the general welfare" qualifies the power "to lay and collect taxes." . . . Nevertheless, the Government asserts that warrant is found in this clause for the adoption of the [AAA]. The argument is that Congress may appropriate and authorize the spending of moneys for the "general welfare"; that the phrase should be liberally construed to cover anything conducive to national welfare; that decision as to what will promote such welfare rests with Congress alone, and that courts may not review the determination; and finally that the appropriation under attack was in fact for the general welfare of the United States.

The Court then explained what it viewed as the historical argument between the Madisonian and Hamiltonian views of the scope of the national government's taxing and spending power to promote the "general welfare" (under Article I, Section 8, clause 1):

Madison asserted it amounted to no more that a reference to the other powers enumerated in the subsequent clauses of the same section; that, as the United States is a government of limited and enumerated powers, the grant of power to tax and spend for the general national welfare must be confined to the enumerated legislative fields committed to the Congress. In this view the phrase is mere tautology, for taxation and appropriation are or may be necessary incidents of the exercise of any of the enumerated powers. Hamilton, on the other hand, maintained the clause confers a power separate and distinct from those later enumerated, is not restricted in meaning by the grant of them, and Congress consequently has a substantive power to tax and to appropriate, limited only by the requirement that it shall be exercised to provide for the general welfare of the United States.

Hamilton's position, not Madison's, the Court said was the correct one: "[T]he power of Congress to authorize expenditure of public moneys for public purposes is not limited by the [other] direct grants of legislative power found in the Constitution."

Nonetheless, the Court said—seemingly reversing course—that "another principle embedded in our Constitution prohibits the enforcement of the [AAA]. The act invades the reserved rights of the states." Citing the *Child Labor Tax Case* and the dictum in *McCulloch v. Maryland* stating that Congress's granted powers could not be used as a "pretext" to achieve improper ends, the *Butler* majority concluded that "[t]he tax, the appropriation of the funds raised, and the direction for their disbursement" were "but parts of the plan" and "means to an unconstitutional end":

> If the taxing power may not be used as the instrument to enforce a regulation of matters of state concern with respect to which Congress has no authority to interfere, may it, as in the present case, be employed to raise the money necessary to purchase a compliance which the Congress is powerless to command? The Government asserts that whatever might be said against the validity of the plan if compulsory, it is constitutionally sound because the end is accomplished by voluntary co-operation. There are two sufficient answers to the contention. The regulation is not in fact voluntary. The farmer, of course, may refuse to comply, but the price of such refusal is the loss of benefits. The amount offered is intended to be sufficient to exert pressure on him to agree to the proposed regulation. The power to confer or withhold unlimited benefits is the power to coerce or destroy. If the cotton grower elects not to accept the benefits, he will receive less for his crops; those who receive payments will be able to undersell him. The result may well be financial ruin. . . . This is coercion by economic pressure. The asserted power of choice is illusory. . . .

> [I]f the plan were one for purely voluntary co-operation it would stand no better so far as federal power is concerned. At best, it is a scheme for purchasing with federal funds submission to federal regulation of a subject reserved to the states. . . . Is a statute less objectionable which authorizes expenditure of federal moneys to induce action in a field in which the United States has no power to intermeddle? The Congress cannot invade state jurisdiction to compel individual action; no more can it purchase such action.

The majority might have accepted "conditional appropriation" where the conditions were designed to assure that funds were spent only for the legitimate purpose for which they were appropriated. But that was not the case with the AAA: "There is an obvious difference between a statute stating the conditions upon which moneys shall be expended and one effective only upon assumption of a contractual obligation to submit to a regulation which otherwise could not be enforced." Sustaining the latter, the majority said, would obliterate all limits on national legislative power: "An affirmance of the authority of Congress so condition the expenditure of an appropriation would tend to nullify all constitutional limitations upon legislative power." Because Congress could not command the farmers' compliance directly, "[i]t must follow that it may not indirectly accomplish those ends by taxing and spending to purchase compliance."

The Court rejected what it considered the premise of the government's argument: that the framers, though intending "sedulously to limit" the national government's powers, "nevertheless by a single clause gave power to the Congress to tear down the barriers, to invade the states' jurisdiction, and to become a parliament of the whole people, subject to no restrictions save such as are self-imposed."

Justice Stone, joined by Justices Brandeis and Cardozo, dissented. "[C]ourts are concerned only with the power to enact statutes, not with their wisdom." The only constitutional limitation on the spending power, he argued, was "that public funds shall be spent for a defined purpose, the promotion of the general welfare." The power to spend was not limited to purposes within other grants of enumerated power, and thus could be used to achieve ends not within Congress's powers of direct regulation:

> The power of Congress to spend is inseparable from persuasion to action over which Congress has no legislative control. Congress may not command that the science of agriculture be taught in state universities. But if it would aid the teaching of that science by grants to state institutions, it is appropriate, if not necessary, that the grant be on the condition . . . that it be used for the intended purpose. . . . It is a contradiction in terms to say that there is power to spend for the national welfare, while rejecting any power to impose conditions reasonably adapted to the attainment of the end which alone would justify the expenditure. . . . If the expenditure is for a national public purpose, that purpose will not be thwarted because payment is on condition which will advance that purpose.

The dissent did acknowledge some limits to the spending power: "The power to tax and spend is not without constitutional restraints. One restriction is that the purpose must be truly national. Another is that it may not be used to coerce action left to state control. Another is the conscience and patriotism of Congress and the Executive. . . . Courts are not the only agency of government that must be assumed to have capacity to govern."

Which view is right? Does the majority opinion, while purporting to adopt Hamilton's position, in fact more closely resemble Madison's position? What is the answer to the objection that taxing and spending, in combination, might effectively coerce compliance just as fully as direct regulation (which both the majority and dissent acknowledge)? What is the answer to the objection that these determinations must be made by Congress? Is there a principled middle ground supported by the text and structure of the Constitution, or must one inevitably slide all the way down one slippery slope or the other?

South Dakota v. Dole

483 U.S. 203 (1987)

■ CHIEF JUSTICE REHNQUIST delivered the opinion of the Court.

Petitioner South Dakota permits persons 19 years of age or older to purchase beer containing up to 3.2% alcohol. In 1984 Congress enacted 23 U.S.C. § 158, which directs the Secretary of Transportation to withhold a percentage of federal highway funds otherwise allocable from States "in which the purchase or public possession . . . of any alcoholic beverage by a person who is less than twenty-one years of age is lawful." The State sued in United States District Court seeking a declaratory judgment that § 158 violates the constitutional limitations on congressional exercise of the spending power and violates the Twenty-first Amendment to the United States Constitution. The District Court rejected the State's claims, and the Court of Appeals for the Eighth Circuit affirmed. 791 F.2d 628 (1986).

In this Court, the parties direct most of their efforts to defining the proper scope of the Twenty-first Amendment. Relying on our statement in *California Retail Liquor Dealers Assn. v. Midcal Aluminum, Inc.*, 445 U.S. 97, 110 (1980), that the "Twenty-first Amendment grants the States virtually complete control over whether to permit importation or sale of liquor and how to structure the liquor distribution system," South Dakota asserts that the setting of minimum drinking ages is clearly within the "core powers" reserved to the States under § 2 of the Amendment.[1] . . . The Secretary in response asserts that the Twenty-first Amendment is simply not implicated by § 158; the plain language of § 2 confirms the States' broad power to impose restrictions on the sale and distribution of alcoholic beverages but does not confer on them any power to *permit* sales that Congress seeks to *prohibit.* . . . .

Despite the extended treatment of the question by the parties, however, we need not decide in this case whether that Amendment would prohibit an attempt by Congress to legislate directly a national minimum drinking age. Here, Congress has acted indirectly under its spending power to encourage uniformity in the States' drinking ages. As we explain below, we find this legislative effort within constitutional bounds even if Congress may not regulate drinking ages directly.

The Constitution empowers Congress to "lay and collect Taxes, Duties, Imposts, and Excises, to pay the Debts and provide for the common Defence and general Welfare of the United States." Art. I, § 8, cl. 1. Incident to this power, Congress may attach conditions on the receipt of federal funds, and has repeatedly employed the power "to further broad policy objectives by conditioning receipt of federal moneys upon compliance by the recipient with federal statutory and administrative directives." *Fullilove v. Klutznick*, 448 U.S. 448, 474 (1980) (opinion of Burger, C.J.). See *Steward Machine Co. v. Davis*, 301 U.S. 548 (1937). The breadth of this power was made clear in *United States v. Butler*, 297 U.S. 1, 66 (1936), where the Court, resolving a longstanding debate over the scope of the Spending

---

[1] Section 2 of the Twenty-first Amendment provides: "The transportation or importation into any State, Territory, or possession of the United States for delivery or use therein of intoxicating liquors, in violation of the laws thereof, is hereby prohibited."

Clause, determined that "the power of Congress to authorize expenditure of public moneys for public purposes is not limited by the direct grants of legislative power found in the Constitution." Thus, objectives not thought to be within Article I's "enumerated legislative fields," *id.*, at 65, may nevertheless be attained through the use of the spending power and the conditional grant of federal funds.

The spending power is of course not unlimited, but is instead subject to several general restrictions articulated in our cases. The first of these limitations is derived from the language of the Constitution itself: the exercise of the spending power must be in pursuit of "the general welfare." See *Helvering v. Davis*, 301 U.S. 619, 640–641 (1937); *United States v. Butler, supra*, at 65. In considering whether a particular expenditure is intended to serve general public purposes, courts should defer substantially to the judgment of Congress. *Helvering v. Davis, supra*, at 640, 645.[2] Second, we have required that if Congress desires to condition the States' receipt of federal funds, it "must do so unambiguously . . ., enabl[ing] the States to exercise their choice knowingly, cognizant of the consequences of their participation." *Pennhurst State School and Hospital v. Halderman, supra*, at 17. Third, our cases have suggested (without significant elaboration) that conditions on federal grants might be illegitimate if they are unrelated "to the federal interest in particular national projects or programs." *Massachusetts v. United States*, 435 U.S. 444, 461 (1978) (plurality opinion). See also *Ivanhoe Irrigation Dist. v. McCracken, supra*, 357 U.S., at 295, ("[T]he Federal Government may establish and impose reasonable conditions relevant to federal interest in the project and to the over-all objectives thereof"). Finally, we have noted that other constitutional provisions may provide an independent bar to the conditional grant of federal funds.

South Dakota does not seriously claim that § 158 is inconsistent with any of the first three restrictions mentioned above. We can readily conclude that the provision is designed to serve the general welfare, especially in light of the fact that "the concept of welfare or the opposite is shaped by Congress. . . ." *Helvering v. Davis, supra,* at 645. Congress found that the differing drinking ages in the States created particular incentives for young persons to combine their desire to drink with their ability to drive, and that this interstate problem required a national solution. The means it chose to address this dangerous situation were reasonably calculated to advance the general welfare. The conditions upon which States receive the funds, moreover, could not be more clearly stated by Congress. And the State itself, rather than challenging the germaneness of the condition to federal purposes, admits that it "has never contended that the congressional action was . . . unrelated to a national concern in the absence of the Twenty-first Amendment." Indeed, the condition imposed by Congress is directly related to one of the main purposes for which highway funds are expended—safe interstate travel. See 23 U.S.C. § 101(b).[3]

---

[2] The level of deference to the congressional decision is such that the Court has more recently questioned whether "general welfare" is a judicially enforceable restriction at all. See *Buckley v. Valeo*, 424 U.S. 1, 90–91 (1976) *(per curiam).*

[3] Our cases have not required that we define the outer bounds of the "germaneness" or "relatedness" limitation on the imposition of conditions under the spending power. *Amici* urge that we take this occasion to establish that a condition on federal funds is legitimate only if it relates directly to the purpose of the expenditure to which it is attached. See Brief for National Conference of State Legislatures et al. as *Amici Curiae* 10. Because petitioner has not sought such a restriction, see Tr. of Oral Arg. 19–21, and because we find any such limitation on conditional federal grants satisfied in this case in any event, we do not address whether condi-

This goal of the interstate highway system had been frustrated by varying drinking ages among the States. A Presidential commission appointed to study alcohol-related accidents and fatalities on the Nation's highways concluded that the lack of uniformity in the States' drinking ages created "an incentive to drink and drive" because "young persons commut[e] to border States where the drinking age is lower." Presidential Commission on Drunk Driving, Final Report 11 (1983). By enacting § 158, Congress conditioned the receipt of federal funds in a way reasonably calculated to address this particular impediment to a purpose for which the funds are expended.

The remaining question about the validity of § 158—and the basic point of disagreement between the parties—is whether the Twenty-first Amendment constitutes an "independent constitutional bar" to the conditional grant of federal funds. Petitioner, relying on its view that the Twenty-first Amendment prohibits *direct* regulation of drinking ages by Congress, asserts that "Congress may not use the spending power to regulate that which it is prohibited from regulating directly under the Twenty-first Amendment." But our cases show that this "independent constitutional bar" limitation on the spending power is not of the kind petitioner suggests. *United States v. Butler, supra,* 297 U.S., at 66, for example, established that the constitutional limitations on Congress when exercising its spending power are less exacting than those on its authority to regulate directly.

We have also held that a perceived Tenth Amendment limitation on congressional regulation of state affairs did not concomitantly limit the range of conditions legitimately placed on federal grants. In *Oklahoma v. Civil Service Comm'n,* 330 U.S. 127 (1947), the Court considered the validity of the Hatch Act insofar as it was applied to political activities of state officials whose employment was financed in whole or in part with federal funds. The State contended that an order under this provision to withhold certain federal funds unless a state official was removed invaded its sovereignty in violation of the Tenth Amendment. Though finding that "the United States is not concerned with, and has no power to regulate, local political activities as such of state officials," the Court nevertheless held that the Federal Government "does have power to fix the terms upon which its money allotments to states shall be disbursed." *Id.,* at 143. The Court found no violation of the State's sovereignty because the State could, and did, adopt "the 'simple expedient' of not yielding to what she urges is federal coercion. The offer of benefits to a state by the United States dependent upon cooperation by the state with federal plans, assumedly for the general welfare, is not unusual." *Id.,* at 143–144.

These cases establish that the "independent constitutional bar" limitation on the spending power is not, as petitioner suggests, a prohibition on the indirect achievement of objectives which Congress is not empowered to achieve directly. Instead, we think that the language in our earlier opinions stands for the unexceptionable proposition that the power may not be used to induce the States to engage in activities that would themselves be unconstitutional. Thus, for example, a grant of federal funds conditioned on invidiously discriminatory state action or the infliction of cruel and unusual punishment would be an illegitimate exercise of the Congress' broad spending power. But no such claim can be or is made here. Were South Dakota to succumb to the blandishments offered by Congress and raise its drinking

---

tions less directly related to the particular purpose of the expenditure might be outside the bounds of the spending power.

age to 21, the State's action in so doing would not violate the constitutional rights of anyone.

Our decisions have recognized that in some circumstances the financial inducement offered by Congress might be so coercive as to pass the point at which "pressure turns into compulsion." *Steward Machine Co. v. Davis, supra,* 301 U.S., at 590. Here, however, Congress has directed only that a State desiring to establish a minimum drinking age lower than 21 lose a relatively small percentage of certain federal highway funds. Petitioner contends that the coercive nature of this program is evident from the degree of success it has achieved. We cannot conclude, however, that a conditional grant of federal money of this sort is unconstitutional simply by reason of its success in achieving the congressional objective.

When we consider, for a moment, that all South Dakota would lose if she adheres to her chosen course as to a suitable minimum drinking age is 5% of the funds otherwise obtainable under specified highway grant programs, the argument as to coercion is shown to be more rhetoric than fact. As we said a half century ago in *Steward Machine Co. v. Davis:*

> [E]very rebate from a tax when conditioned upon conduct is in some measure a temptation. But to hold that motive or temptation is equivalent to coercion is to plunge the law in endless difficulties. The outcome of such a doctrine is the acceptance of a philosophical determinism by which choice becomes impossible. Till now the law has been guided by a robust common sense which assumes the freedom of the will as a working hypothesis in the solution of its problems.

301 U.S., at 589–590.

Here Congress has offered relatively mild encouragement to the States to enact higher minimum drinking ages than they would otherwise choose. But the enactment of such laws remains the prerogative of the States not merely in theory but in fact. Even if Congress might lack the power to impose a national minimum drinking age directly, we conclude that encouragement to state action found in § 158 is a valid use of the spending power.

■ JUSTICE BRENNAN, dissenting.

I agree with Justice O'CONNOR that regulation of the minimum age of purchasers of liquor falls squarely within the ambit of those powers reserved to the States by the Twenty-first Amendment. Since States possess this constitutional power, Congress cannot condition a federal grant in a manner that abridges this right. The Amendment, itself, strikes the proper balance between federal and state authority. I therefore dissent.

■ JUSTICE O'CONNOR, dissenting.

The Court today upholds the National Minimum Drinking Age Amendment, 23 U.S.C. § 158, as a valid exercise of the spending power conferred by Article I, § 8. But § 158 is not a condition on spending reasonably related to the expenditure of federal funds and cannot be justified on that ground. Rather, it is an attempt to regulate the sale of liquor, an attempt that lies outside Congress' power to regulate commerce because it falls within the ambit of § 2 of the Twenty-first Amendment.

My disagreement with the Court is relatively narrow on the spending power issue: it is a disagreement about the application of a principle rather than a disagreement on the principle itself. I agree with the Court that Congress may attach conditions on the receipt of federal funds to further "the federal interest in particular national projects or programs." *Massa-*

chusetts v. United States, 435 U.S. 444, 461 (1978); see *Oklahoma v. Civil Service Comm'n,* 330 U.S. 127, 143–144 (1947); *Steward Machine Co. v. Davis,* 301 U.S. 548 (1937). I also subscribe to the established proposition that the reach of the spending power "is not limited by the direct grants of legislative power found in the Constitution." *United States v. Butler,* 297 U.S. 1, 66 (1936). Finally, I agree that there are four separate types of limitations on the spending power: the expenditure must be for the general welfare, *Helvering v. Davis,* 301 U.S. 619, 640–641 (1937), the conditions imposed must be unambiguous, *Pennhurst State School and Hospital v. Halderman,* 451 U.S. 1, 17 (1981), they must be reasonably related to the purpose of the expenditure, *Massachusetts v. United States, supra,* 435 U.S., at 461, and the legislation may not violate any independent constitutional prohibition, *Lawrence County v. Lead–Deadwood School Dist.,* 469 U.S. 256, 269–270 (1985). Insofar as two of those limitations are concerned, the Court is clearly correct that § 158 is wholly unobjectionable. Establishment of a national minimum drinking age certainly fits within the broad concept of the general welfare and the statute is entirely unambiguous. I am also willing to assume, *arguendo,* that the Twenty-first Amendment does not constitute an "independent constitutional bar" to a spending condition.

But the Court's application of the requirement that the condition imposed be reasonably related to the purpose for which the funds are expended is cursory and unconvincing. We have repeatedly said that Congress may condition grants under the spending power only in ways reasonably related to the purpose of the federal program. *Massachusetts v. United States, supra,* 435 U.S., at 461; *Ivanhoe Irrigation Dist. v. McCracken,* 357 U.S. 275, 295 (1958) (the United States may impose "reasonable conditions relevant to federal interest in the project and to the over-all objectives thereof"); *Steward Machine Co. v. Davis, supra,* 301 U.S. at 590 ("We do not say that a tax is valid, when imposed by act of Congress, if it is laid upon the condition that a state may escape its operation through the adoption of a statute unrelated in subject matter to activities fairly within the scope of national policy and power"). In my view, establishment of a minimum drinking age of 21 is not sufficiently related to interstate highway construction to justify so conditioning funds appropriated for that purpose.

In support of its contrary conclusion, the Court relies on a supposed concession by counsel for South Dakota that the State "has never contended that the congressional action was . . . unrelated to a national concern in the absence of the Twenty-first Amendment." In the absence of the Twenty-first Amendment, however, there is a strong argument that the Congress might regulate the conditions under which liquor is sold under the commerce power, just as it regulates the sale of many other commodities that are in or affect interstate commerce. The fact that the Twenty-first Amendment is crucial to the State's argument does not, therefore, amount to a concession that the condition imposed by § 158 is reasonably related to highway construction. The Court also relies on a portion of the argument transcript in support of its claim that South Dakota conceded the reasonable relationship point. But counsel's statements there are at best ambiguous. Counsel essentially said no more than that he was not prepared to argue the reasonable relationship question discussed at length in the Brief for the National Conference of State Legislatures et al. as *Amici Curiae.*

Aside from these "concessions" by counsel, the Court asserts the reasonableness of the relationship between the supposed purpose of the expenditure—"safe interstate travel"—and the drinking age condition. The Court reasons that Congress wishes that the roads it builds may be used safely, that drunken drivers threaten highway safety, and that young people are more likely to drive while under the influence of alcohol under existing law than would be the case if there were a uniform national drinking age of 21. It hardly needs saying, however, that if the purpose of § 158 is to deter drunken driving, it is far too over and under-inclusive. It is over-inclusive because it stops teenagers from drinking even when they are not about to drive on interstate highways. It is under-inclusive because teenagers pose only a small part of the drunken driving problem in this Nation. See, *e.g.,* 130 Cong. Rec. 18648 (1984) (remarks of Sen. Humphrey) ("Eighty-four percent of all highway fatalities involving alcohol occur among those whose ages exceed 21"); *id.,* at 18651 (remarks of Sen. McClure) ("Certainly, statistically, if you use that one set of statistics, then the mandatory drinking age ought to be raised at least to 30"); *ibid.* (remarks of Sen. Symms) ("[M]ost of the studies point out that the drivers of age 21–24 are the worst offenders").

When Congress appropriates money to build a highway, it is entitled to insist that the highway be a safe one. But it is not entitled to insist as a condition of the use of highway funds that the State impose or change regulations in other areas of the State's social and economic life because of an attenuated or tangential relationship to highway use or safety. Indeed, if the rule were otherwise, the Congress could effectively regulate almost any area of a State's social, political, or economic life on the theory that use of the interstate transportation system is somehow enhanced. If, for example, the United States were to condition highway moneys upon moving the state capital, I suppose it might argue that interstate transportation is facilitated by locating local governments in places easily accessible to interstate highways—or, conversely, that highways might become overburdened if they had to carry traffic to and from the state capital. In my mind, such a relationship is hardly more attenuated than the one which the Court finds supports § 158. Cf. Tr. of Oral Arg. 39 (counsel for the United States conceding that to condition a grant upon adoption of a unicameral legislature would violate the "germaneness" requirement).

There is a clear place at which the Court can draw the line between permissible and impermissible conditions on federal grants. It is the line identified in the Brief for the National Conference of State Legislatures et al. as *Amici Curiae:*

> Congress has the power to *spend* for the general welfare[;] it has the power to *legislate* only for delegated purposes. . . . The appropriate inquiry, then, is whether the spending requirement or prohibition is a condition on a grant or whether it is regulation. The difference turns on whether the requirement specifies in some way how the money should be spent, so that Congress' intent in making the grant will be effectuated. Congress has no power under the Spending Clause to impose requirements on a grant that go beyond specifying how the money should be spent. A requirement that is not such a specification is not a condition, but a regulation, which is valid only if it falls within one of Congress' delegated regulatory powers.

Id., at 19–20.

This approach harks back to *United States v. Butler,* 297 U.S. 1 (1936), the last case in which this Court struck down an Act of Congress as beyond the authority granted by the Spending Clause. There the Court wrote that "[t]here is an obvious difference between a statute stating the conditions upon which moneys shall be expended and one effective only upon assumption of a contractual obligation to submit to a regulation which otherwise could not be enforced." *Id.*, at 73. The *Butler* Court saw the Agricultural Adjustment Act for what it was—an exercise of regulatory, not spending, power. The error in *Butler* was not the Court's conclusion that the act was essentially regulatory, but rather its crabbed view of the extent of Congress' regulatory power under the Commerce Clause. The Agricultural Adjustment Act was regulatory but it was regulation that today would likely be considered within Congress' commerce power. See, *e.g., Katzenbach v. McClung,* 379 U.S. 294 (1964); *Wickard v. Filburn,* 317 U.S. 111 (1942).

While *Butler's* authority is questionable insofar as it assumes that Congress has no regulatory power over farm production, its discussion of the spending power and its description of both the power's breadth and its limitations remain sound. The Court's decision in *Butler* also properly recognizes the gravity of the task of appropriately limiting the spending power. If the spending power is to be limited only by Congress' notion of the general welfare, the reality, given the vast financial resources of the Federal Government, is that the Spending Clause gives "power to the Congress to tear down the barriers, to invade the states' jurisdiction, and to become a parliament of the whole people, subject to no restrictions save such as are self-imposed." *United States v. Butler, supra,* 297 U.S., at 78. This, of course, as *Butler* held, was not the Framers' plan and it is not the meaning of the Spending Clause.

Our later cases are consistent with the notion that, under the spending power, the Congress may only condition grants in ways that can fairly be said to be related to the expenditure of federal funds. . . .

As discussed above, a condition that a State will raise its drinking age to 21 cannot fairly be said to be reasonably related to the expenditure of funds for highway construction. The only possible connection, highway safety, has nothing to do with how the funds Congress has appropriated are expended. Rather than a condition determining how federal highway money shall be expended, it is a regulation determining who shall be able to drink liquor. As such it is not justified by the spending power.

Of the other possible sources of congressional authority for regulating the sale of liquor only the commerce power comes to mind. But in my view, the regulation of the age of the purchasers of liquor, just as the regulation of the price at which liquor may be sold, falls squarely within the scope of those powers reserved to the States by the Twenty-first Amendment. *Capital Cities Cable, Inc. v. Crisp,* 467 U.S. 691 (1984). As I emphasized in *324 Liquor Corp. v. Duffy,* 479 U.S. 335, 356 (1987) (dissenting opinion):

> The history of the Amendment strongly supports Justice Black's view that the Twenty-first Amendment was intended to return absolute control of the liquor trade to the States, and that the Federal Government could not use its Commerce Clause powers to interfere in any manner with the States' exercise of the power conferred by the Amendment.

Accordingly, Congress simply lacks power under the Commerce Clause to displace state regulation of this kind. *Ibid.*

The immense size and power of the Government of the United States ought not obscure its fundamental character. It remains a Government of enumerated powers. *McCulloch v. Maryland,* 4 Wheat. 316, 405 (1819). Because 23 U.S.C. § 158 cannot be justified as an exercise of any power delegated to the Congress, it is not authorized by the Constitution. The Court errs in holding it to be the law of the land, and I respectfully dissent.

NOTES

1. Identify the four-part test the Court uses in *South Dakota v. Dole*. Note that both the majority and the dissenting opinions agree with these criteria in principle; they simply disagree as to their application. Do you agree with these criteria? Consider them each one by one. Do they flow logically from the text of the Constitution? From prior cases? Do they impose principled, sensible limitations on the scope of the spending power?

2. Taking these criteria as given, the point of disagreement between the majority and the dissent concerns the question whether the condition attached to the appropriation is sufficiently related to the expenditure of funds itself and its purposes. (This is sometimes referred to as "germaneness.") Who has the better of the argument? Why? What is the proper standard for judging whether a condition is sufficiently related to an appropriation? Are there any valid criteria? Is Chief Justice Rehnquist's principle correct, that the Court should give substantial deference to Congress in making such judgments? Or is Justice O'Connor's dissent correct in saying that there is a bright-line distinction between a condition and a regulation? What do you make of her argument based on *United States v. Butler*?

3. Is the question whether a spending condition is sufficiently related or germane simply another way of asking whether the condition is "necessary and proper" for carrying into effect the power to spend money? Are such issues really Necessary and Proper Clause issues rather than matters of the scope of the spending power standing alone? Notice the different approaches and formulations of the majority and the dissent concerning this issue in *South Dakota v. Dole*. How similar or different are they from the formulations in *McCulloch v. Maryland*? Does the majority's formulation ensure that strings attached to congressional spending bills are really necessary and proper means for carrying into execution the spending power of the national government? Does the majority's test impose a meaningful limit on the use of strings in spending bills?

4. The author of the Court's sweeping-national-power opinion in *South Dakota v. Dole*, Chief Justice Rehnquist, was also the author of the limited-national-power opinion in *United States v. Lopez*. Are these decisions consistent? Why does Rehnquist think Congress can "induce" the states to raise their drinking ages to twenty-one? One way of approaching this question is to ask whether, under *Lopez*, Rehnquist would have thought that Congress itself had the power to directly outlaw the selling of liquor nationwide to anyone under the age of twenty-one. Selling liquor, after all, is a commercial activity. Would a uniform national drinking age, imposed by direct regulation, fall within the Commerce Clause power under *Lopez* (putting aside for a moment whether the Twenty-first Amendment creates a carve-out from such national power)? What Congress can do directly by regulation it can certainly do indirectly with strings attached to appropriations bills. Is the majority willing to accept spending conditions only because it would have been willing to accept direct regulation? Or is *South Dakota v. Dole* authority for a broad spending power *independent* of the existence of regulatory power?

5. *South Dakota v. Dole* avoided deciding explicitly the question of how the Twenty-first Amendment—which repealed Prohibition under the Eighteenth Amendment—interacts with the Commerce Clause power, and thus did not explicitly decide whether direct regulatory power would exist to impose a nationwide twenty-one-year-old drinking age. How would you answer that constitutional question? Section 2 of the Twenty-first Amendment says: "The transportation or importation into any State, Territory, or possession of the United States for delivery or use therein of intoxicating liquors, in violation of the laws thereof, is hereby prohibited." The Twenty–first Amendment thus gives every state an indefeasible right to be a dry state. Congress cannot force a state to allow the sale of alcohol if it does not want to allow it. But is the converse true? Does the Twenty–first Amendment stop Congress from banning alcohol in states that want to allow it? The plain words of the Twenty–first Amendment repeal the Eighteenth Amendment's ban on alcohol and its special grant of an enumerated power to prohibit alcohol, but does the Twenty–first Amendment withdraw congressional power under the Commerce and Necessary and Proper Clauses to pass nationwide regulations on the sale of alcohol?

6. *The Spending Power and "Commandeering" of States to Enact or Execute Congressional Policies: New York v. United States and the Tenth Amendment.* A recurrent theme running through the taxing power and spending power cases concerns whether a particular use of the power might be so "coercive" as to impair a state's constitutional autonomy with respect to some reserved power, prerogative, or essential attribute of being a state that is guaranteed by the Constitution. With respect to exercises of the taxing and spending powers, the difficult question is *at what point*—if any—the use of such granted powers to accomplish an objective that the national government could not command directly becomes so coercive as to be irresistible (and thus unconstitutional). (Is it possible to draw a principled line?) But before reaching that question, one must first conclude (or assume for the sake of argument) that Congress could not have commanded the desired result directly. In the *Child Labor Tax Case* and *Butler*, for example, the Court assumed that Congress could not, under the Commerce Clause, command by direct regulation the policies it sought to achieve through the taxing and spending powers. Likewise, in *South Dakota v. Dole*, the majority assumed (for the sake of argument) that Congress could not directly command a nationwide minimum drinking age.

The next principal case, *New York v. United States,* presents issues concerning the use of the taxing and spending powers to induce the states to adopt certain policies with respect to the disposal of low-level radioactive waste. It also presents related issues of federalism and national powers under the Commerce Clause (specifically, Congress's power to *authorize states* to exclude or discriminate against commerce in certain products, like radioactive waste) and under the Compact Clause of Article I, Section 9 (which requires Congress's approval of certain agreements between or among states). Finally, it presents a fundamental federalism issue of national power versus a sphere of state autonomy reserved by the Tenth Amendment: whether Congress can in effect *command* the states to adopt certain policies with respect to the disposal of such waste. When financial carrots and sticks fail, can Congress "commandeer" states to enact (as a matter of state law) or to execute (through its state officials) a prescribed national policy? Or does such commandeering of the states violate a Tenth Amendment structural federalism principle protecting states' autonomy as states?

New York v. United States

505 U.S. 144 (1992)

■ JUSTICE O'CONNOR delivered the opinion of the Court.

These cases implicate one of our Nation's newest problems of public policy and perhaps our oldest question of constitutional law. The public policy issue involves the disposal of radioactive waste: In these cases, we address the constitutionality of three provisions of the Low–Level Radioactive Waste Policy Amendments Act of 1985, 42 U.S.C. § 2021b *et seq.* The constitutional question is as old as the Constitution: It consists of discerning the proper division of authority between the Federal Government and the States. We conclude that while Congress has substantial power under the Constitution to encourage the States to provide for the disposal of the radioactive waste generated within their borders, the Constitution does not confer upon Congress the ability simply to compel the States to do so. We therefore find that only two of the Act's three provisions at issue are consistent with the Constitution's allocation of power to the Federal Government.

I

We live in a world full of low level radioactive waste. Radioactive material is present in luminous watch dials, smoke alarms, measurement devices, medical fluids, research materials, and the protective gear and construction materials used by workers at nuclear power plants. Low level radioactive waste is generated by the Government, by hospitals, by research institutions, and by various industries. The waste must be isolated from humans for long periods of time, often for hundreds of years. Millions of cubic feet of low level radioactive waste must be disposed of each year. . . .

Our Nation's first site for the land disposal of commercial low level radioactive waste opened in 1962 . . . . [S]ince 1979 only three disposal sites—those in Nevada, Washington, and South Carolina—have been in operation. Waste generated in the rest of the country must be shipped to one of these three sites for disposal.

In 1979, both the Washington and Nevada sites were forced to shut down temporarily, leaving South Carolina to shoulder the responsibility of storing low level radioactive waste produced in every part of the country. The Governor of South Carolina, understandably perturbed, ordered a 50% reduction in the quantity of waste accepted at the Barnwell site. The Governors of Washington and Nevada announced plans to shut their sites permanently.

Faced with the possibility that the Nation would be left with no disposal sites for low level radioactive waste, Congress responded by enacting the Low–Level Radioactive Waste Policy Act. . . . The 1980 Act authorized States to enter into regional compacts that, once ratified by Congress, would have the authority beginning in 1986 to restrict the use of their disposal facilities to waste generated within member States. The 1980 Act included no penalties for States that failed to participate in this plan.

By 1985, only three approved regional compacts had operational disposal facilities; not surprisingly, these were the compacts formed around South Carolina, Nevada, and Washington, the three sited States. The following year, the 1980 Act would have given these three compacts the ability to exclude waste from nonmembers, and the remaining 31 States would have had no assured outlet for their low level radioactive waste. With this prospect looming, Congress once again took up the issue of waste disposal. The result was the legislation challenged here, the Low–Level Radioactive Waste Policy Amendments Act of 1985.

The 1985 Act was again based largely on a proposal submitted by the National Governors' Association. In broad outline, the Act embodies a compromise among the sited and unsited States. The sited States agreed to extend for seven years the period in which they would accept low level radioactive waste from other States. In exchange, the unsited States agreed to end their reliance on the sited States by 1992.

The mechanics of this compromise are intricate. The Act directs: "Each State shall be responsible for providing, either by itself or in cooperation with other States, for the disposal of . . . low-level radioactive waste generated within the State," 42 U.S.C. § 2021c(a)(1)(A), with the exception of certain waste generated by the Federal Government, §§ 2021c(a)(1)(B), 2021c(b). The Act authorizes States to "enter into such [interstate] compacts as may be necessary to provide for the establishment and operation of regional disposal facilities for low-level radioactive waste." § 2021d(a)(2). For an additional seven years beyond the period contemplated by the 1980 Act, from the beginning of 1986 through the end of 1992, the three existing disposal sites "shall make disposal capacity available for low-level radioactive waste generated by any source," with certain exceptions not relevant here. § 2021e(a)(2). But the three States in which the disposal sites are located are permitted to exact a graduated surcharge for waste arriving from outside the regional compact—in 1986–1987, $10 per cubic foot; in 1988–1989, $20 per cubic foot; and in 1990–1992, $40 per cubic foot. § 2021e(d)(1). After the 7–year transition period expires, approved regional compacts may exclude radioactive waste generated outside the region. § 2021d(c).

The Act provides three types of incentives to encourage the States to comply with their statutory obligation to provide for the disposal of waste generated within their borders.

1. *Monetary incentives.* One quarter of the surcharges collected by the sited States must be transferred to an escrow account held by the Secretary of Energy. § 2021e(d)(2)(A). The Secretary then makes payments from this account to each State that has complied with a series of deadlines. . . . The rest of the account is to be paid out to those States or compacts able to dispose of all low level radioactive waste generated within their borders by January 1, 1993. § 2021e(d)(2)(B)(iv). Each State that has not met the 1993 deadline must either take title to the waste generated within its borders or forfeit to the waste generators the incentive payments it has received. § 2021e(d)(2)(C).

2. *Access incentives.* The second type of incentive involves the denial of access to disposal sites. States that fail to meet the July 1986 deadline may be charged twice the ordinary surcharge for the remainder of 1986 and may be denied access to disposal facilities thereafter. § 2021e(e)(2)(A). States that fail to meet the 1988 deadline may be charged double surcharges for the first half of 1988 and quadruple surcharges for the second half of 1988, and may be denied access thereafter. § 2021e(e)(2)(B). States that fail to meet the 1990 deadline may be denied access. § 2021e(e)(2)(C). Finally, States that have not filed complete applications by January 1, 1992, for a license to operate a disposal facility, or States belonging to compacts that have not filed such applications, may be charged triple surcharges. §§ 2021e(e)(1)(D), 2021e(e)(2)(D).

3. *The take title provision.* The third type of incentive is the most severe. The Act provides:

> If a State (or, where applicable, a compact region) in which low-level radioactive waste is generated is unable to provide for the disposal of all such waste generated within such State or compact region by January 1, 1996, each State in which such waste is generated, upon the request of the generator or owner of the waste, shall take title to the waste, be obligated to take possession of the waste, and shall be liable for all damages directly or indirectly incurred by such generator or owner as a consequence of the failure of the State to take possession of the waste as soon after January 1, 1996, as the generator or owner notifies the State that the waste is available for shipment.

§ 2021e(d)(2)(C). These three incentives are the focus of petitioners' constitutional challenge.

In the seven years since the Act took effect, Congress has approved nine regional compacts, encompassing 42 of the States. All six unsited compacts and four of the unaffiliated States have met the first three statutory milestones.

New York, a State whose residents generate a relatively large share of the Nation's low level radioactive waste, did not join a regional compact. Instead, the State complied with the Act's requirements by enacting legislation providing for the siting and financing of a disposal facility in New York. The State has identified five potential sites, three in Allegany County and two in Cortland County. Residents of the two counties oppose the State's choice of location.

Petitioners—the State of New York and the two counties—filed this suit against the United States in 1990. They sought a declaratory judgment that the Act is inconsistent with the [Tenth Amendment and the Guarantee Clause of Article IV]. . . .

II

A

. . . These questions can be viewed in either of two ways. In some cases the Court has inquired whether an Act of Congress is authorized by one of the powers delegated to Congress in Article I of the Constitution. See, *e.g., Perez v. United States,* 402 U.S. 146 (1971); *McCulloch v. Maryland,* 4 Wheat. 316 (1819). In other cases the Court has sought to determine whether an Act of Congress invades the province of state sovereignty reserved by the Tenth Amendment. See, *e.g., Garcia v. San Antonio Metropolitan Transit Authority*, 469 U.S. 528 (1985). In a case like these, involving the division of authority between federal and state governments, the two inquiries are mirror images of each other. If a power is delegated to Congress in the Constitution, the Tenth Amendment expressly disclaims any reservation of that power to the States; if a power is an attribute of state sovereignty reserved by the Tenth Amendment, it is necessarily a power the Constitution has not conferred on Congress.

It is in this sense that the Tenth Amendment "states but a truism that all is retained which has not been surrendered." *United States v. Darby,* 312 U.S. 100, 124 (1941). As Justice Story put it, "[t]his amendment is a mere affirmation of what, upon any just reasoning, is a necessary rule of interpreting the constitution. Being an instrument of limited and enumerated powers, it follows irresistibly, that what is not conferred, is withheld, and belongs to the state authorities." 3 J. Story, Commentaries on the Constitution of the United States 752 (1833). This has been the Court's consistent understanding: "The States unquestionably do retai[n] a significant measure of sovereign authority ... to the extent that the Constitution has not divested them of their original powers and transferred those powers to the Federal Government." *Garcia v. San Antonio Metropolitan Transit Authority, supra,* 469 U.S., at 549.

Congress exercises its conferred powers subject to the limitations contained in the Constitution. Thus, for example, under the Commerce Clause Congress may regulate publishers engaged in interstate commerce, but Congress is constrained in the exercise of that power by the First Amendment. The Tenth Amendment likewise restrains the power of Congress, but this limit is not derived from the text of the Tenth Amendment itself, which, as we have discussed, is essentially a tautology. Instead, the Tenth Amendment confirms that the power of the Federal Government is subject to limits that may, in a given instance, reserve power to the States. The Tenth Amendment thus directs us to determine, as in this case, whether an incident of state sovereignty is protected by a limitation on an Article I power.

The benefits of this federal structure have been extensively cataloged elsewhere, see, *e.g., Gregory v. Ashcroft, supra,* 501 U.S., at 457–460; Merritt, The Guarantee Clause and State Autonomy: Federalism for a Third Century, 88 Colum.L.Rev. 1, 3–10 (1988); McConnell, Federalism: Evaluating the Founders' Design, 54 U.Chi.L.Rev. 1484, 1491–1511 (1987), but they need not concern us here. Our task would be the same even if one could prove that federalism secured no advantages to anyone. It consists not of devising our preferred system of government, but of understanding and applying the framework set forth in the Constitution. . . .

This framework has been sufficiently flexible over the past two centuries to allow for enormous changes in the nature of government. The Federal Government undertakes activities today that would have been unimaginable to the Framers in two senses; first, because the Framers would not have conceived that *any* government would conduct such activities; and second, because the Framers would not have believed that the *Federal* Government, rather than the States, would assume such responsibilities. Yet the powers conferred upon the Federal Government by the Constitution were phrased in language broad enough to allow for the expansion of the Federal Government's role. Among the provisions of the Constitution that have been particularly important in this regard, three concern us here.

First, the Constitution allocates to Congress the power "[t]o regulate Commerce ... among the several States." Art. I, § 8, cl. 3. . . . As interstate commerce has become ubiquitous, activities once considered purely local have come to have effects on the national economy, and have accordingly come within the scope of Congress' commerce power. See, *e.g., Katzenbach v. McClung,* 379 U.S. 294 (1964); *Wickard v. Filburn,* 317 U.S. 111 (1942).

Second, the Constitution authorizes Congress "to pay the Debts and provide for the ... general Welfare of the United States." Art. I, § 8, cl. 1. . . . While the spending power is "subject to several general restrictions articulated in our cases," these restrictions have not been so severe as to prevent the regulatory authority of Congress from generally keeping up with the growth of the federal budget.

The Court's broad construction of Congress' power under the Commerce and Spending Clauses has of course been guided, as it has with respect to Congress' power generally, by the Constitution's Necessary and Proper Clause, which authorizes Congress "[t]o make all Laws which shall be necessary and proper for carrying into Execution the foregoing Powers." U.S. Const., Art. I, § 8, cl. 18. See, *e.g., Legal Tender Case,* 110 U.S. 421, 449–450 (1884); *McCulloch v. Maryland,* 4 Wheat., at 411–421.

Finally, the Constitution provides that "the Laws of the United States . . . shall be the supreme Law of the Land . . . any Thing in the Constitution or Laws of any State to the Contrary notwithstanding." U.S. Const., Art. VI, cl. 2. . . . We have observed that the Supremacy Clause gives the Federal Government "a decided advantage in th[e] delicate balance" the Constitution strikes between state and federal power. *Gregory v. Ashcroft,* 501 U.S., at 460.

The actual scope of the Federal Government's authority with respect to the States has changed over the years, therefore, but the constitutional structure underlying and limiting that authority has not. In the end, just as a cup may be half empty or half full, it makes no difference whether one views the question at issue in these cases as one of ascertaining the limits of the power delegated to the Federal Government under the affirmative provisions of the Constitution or one of discerning the core of sovereignty retained by the States under the Tenth Amendment. Either way, we must determine whether any of the three challenged provisions of the Low–Level Radioactive Waste Policy Amendments Act of 1985 oversteps the boundary between federal and state authority.

B

Petitioners do not contend that Congress lacks the power to regulate the disposal of low level radioactive waste. Space in radioactive waste disposal sites is frequently sold by residents of one State to residents of another. Regulation of the resulting interstate market in waste disposal is therefore well within Congress' authority under the Commerce Clause. Petitioners likewise do not dispute that under the Supremacy Clause Congress could, if it wished, pre-empt state radioactive waste regulation. Petitioners contend only that the Tenth Amendment limits the power of Congress to regulate in the way it has chosen. Rather than addressing the problem of waste disposal by directly regulating the generators and disposers of waste, petitioners argue, Congress has impermissibly directed the States to regulate in this field.

Most of our recent cases interpreting the Tenth Amendment have concerned the authority of Congress to subject state governments to generally applicable laws. The Court's jurisprudence in this area has traveled an unsteady path. See *Maryland v. Wirtz,* 392 U.S. 183 (1968) (state schools and hospitals are subject to Fair Labor Standards Act); *National League of Cities v. Usery,* 426 U.S. 833 (1976) (overruling *Wirtz*) (state employers are *not* subject to Fair Labor Standards Act); *Garcia v. San Antonio Metropolitan Transit Authority,* 469 U.S. 528 (1985) (overruling *National League of Cities*) (state employers are once again subject to Fair Labor Standards Act). This litigation presents no occasion to apply or revisit the holdings of any of these cases, as this is not a case in which Congress has subjected a State to the same legislation applicable to private parties.

This litigation instead concerns the circumstances under which Congress may use the States as implements of regulation; that is, whether

Congress may direct or otherwise motivate the States to regulate in a particular field or a particular way. Our cases have established a few principles that guide our resolution of the issue.

1

As an initial matter, Congress may not simply "commandee[r] the legislative processes of the States by directly compelling them to enact and enforce a federal regulatory program." *Hodel v. Virginia Surface Mining & Reclamation Assn., Inc.,* 452 U.S. 264, 288 (1981). . . .

While Congress has substantial powers to govern the Nation directly, including in areas of intimate concern to the States, the Constitution has never been understood to confer upon Congress the ability to require the States to govern according to Congress' instructions. See *Coyle v. Smith,* 221 U.S. 559, 565 (1911). The Court has been explicit about this distinction. "Both the States and the United States existed before the Constitution. The people, through that instrument, established a more perfect union by substituting a national government, acting, with ample power, *directly upon the citizens,* instead of the Confederate government, which acted with powers, greatly restricted, only upon the States." *Lane County v. Oregon,* 7 Wall., at 76 (emphasis added). . . .

Indeed, the question whether the Constitution should permit Congress to employ state governments as regulatory agencies was a topic of lively debate among the Framers. Under the Articles of Confederation, Congress lacked the authority in most respects to govern the people directly. In practice, Congress "could not directly tax or legislate upon individuals; it had no explicit 'legislative' or 'governmental' power to make binding 'law' enforceable as such."

The inadequacy of this governmental structure was responsible in part for the Constitutional Convention. Alexander Hamilton observed: "The great and radical vice in the construction of the existing Confederation is in the principle of LEGISLATION for STATES or GOVERNMENTS, in their CORPORATE or COLLECTIVE CAPACITIES, and as contra-distinguished from the INDIVIDUALS of whom they consist." The Federalist No. 15, p. 108 (C. Rossiter ed. 1961). As Hamilton saw it, "we must resolve to incorporate into our plan those ingredients which may be considered as forming the characteristic difference between a league and a government; we must extend the authority of the Union to the persons of the citizens—the only proper objects of government." *Id.,* at 109. . . .

In the end, the Convention opted for a Constitution in which Congress would exercise its legislative authority directly over individuals rather than over States . . .

In providing for a stronger central government, therefore, the Framers explicitly chose a Constitution that confers upon Congress the power to regulate individuals, not States. As we have seen, the Court has consistently respected this choice. We have always understood that even where Congress has the authority under the Constitution to pass laws requiring or prohibiting certain acts, it lacks the power directly to compel the States to require or prohibit those acts. . . .

2

This is not to say that Congress lacks the ability to encourage a State to regulate in a particular way, or that Congress may not hold out incentives to the States as a method of influencing a State's policy choices. Our cases have identified a variety of methods, short of outright coercion, by which Congress may urge a State to adopt a legislative program consistent with federal interests. Two of these methods are of particular relevance here.

First, under Congress' spending power, "Congress may attach conditions on the receipt of federal funds." *South Dakota v. Dole,* 483 U.S., at 206. . . .

Second, where Congress has the authority to regulate private activity under the Commerce Clause, we have recognized Congress' power to offer States the choice of regulating that activity according to federal standards or having state law pre-empted by federal regulation. . . .

By either of these methods, as by any other permissible method of encouraging a State to conform to federal policy choices, the residents of the State retain the ultimate decision as to whether or not the State will comply. If a State's citizens view federal policy as sufficiently contrary to local interests, they may elect to decline a federal grant. . . . Where Congress encourages state regulation rather than compelling it, state governments remain responsive to the local electorate's preferences; state officials remain accountable to the people.

By contrast, where the Federal Government compels States to regulate, the accountability of both state and federal officials is diminished. If the citizens of New York, for example, do not consider that making provision for the disposal of radioactive waste is in their best interest, they may elect state officials who share their view. That view can always be pre-empted under the Supremacy Clause if it is contrary to the national view, but in such a case it is the Federal Government that makes the decision in full view of the public, and it will be federal officials that suffer the consequences if the decision turns out to be detrimental or unpopular. But where the Federal Government directs the States to regulate, it may be state officials who will bear the brunt of public disapproval, while the federal officials who devised the regulatory program may remain insulated from the electoral ramifications of their decision. Accountability is thus diminished when, due to federal coercion, elected state officials cannot regulate in accordance with the views of the local electorate in matters not pre-empted by federal regulation. With these principles in mind, we turn to the three challenged provisions of the Low–Level Radioactive Waste Policy Amendments Act of 1985.

III

. . . Construed as a whole, the Act comprises three sets of "incentives" for the States to provide for the disposal of low level radioactive waste generated within their borders. We consider each in turn.

A

The first set of incentives works in three steps. First, Congress has authorized States with disposal sites to impose a surcharge on radioactive waste received from other States. Second, the Secretary of Energy collects a portion of this surcharge and places the money in an escrow account. Third, States achieving a series of milestones receive portions of this fund.

The first of these steps is an unexceptionable exercise of Congress' power to authorize the States to burden interstate commerce. While the Commerce Clause has long been understood to limit the States' ability to discriminate against interstate commerce, that limit may be lifted, as it has been here, by an expression of the "unambiguous intent" of Congress. Whether or not the States would be permitted to burden the interstate transport of low level radioactive waste in the absence of Congress' approval, the States can clearly do so *with* Congress' approval, which is what the Act gives them.

The second step, the Secretary's collection of a percentage of the surcharge, is no more than a federal tax on interstate commerce, which petitioners do not claim to be an invalid exercise of either Congress' commerce or taxing power. Cf. *Steward Machine Co. v. Davis,* 301 U.S. 548, 581–583 (1937).

The third step is a conditional exercise of Congress' authority under the Spending Clause: Congress has placed conditions—the achievement of the milestones—on the receipt of federal funds. Petitioners do not contend that Congress has exceeded its authority in any of the four respects our cases have identified. See generally *South Dakota v. Dole,* 483 U.S., at 207–208. . . .

The Act's first set of incentives, in which Congress has conditioned grants to the States upon the States' attainment of a series of milestones, is well within the authority of Congress under the Commerce and Spending Clauses. Because the first set of incentives is supported by affirmative constitutional grants of power to Congress, it is not inconsistent with the Tenth Amendment.

B

In the second set of incentives, Congress has authorized States and regional compacts with disposal sites gradually to increase the cost of access to the sites, and then to deny access altogether, to radioactive waste generated in States that do not meet federal deadlines. As a simple regulation, this provision would be within the power of Congress to authorize the States to discriminate against interstate commerce. Where federal regulation of private activity is within the scope of the Commerce Clause, we have recognized the ability of Congress to offer States the choice of regulating that activity according to federal standards or having state law pre-empted by federal regulation. . . .

The Act's second set of incentives thus represents a conditional exercise of Congress' commerce power, along the lines of those we have held to be within Congress' authority. As a result, the second set of incentives does not intrude on the sovereignty reserved to the States by the Tenth Amendment.

C

The take title provision is of a different character. This third so-called "incentive" offers States, as an alternative to regulating pursuant to Congress' direction, the option of taking title to and possession of the low level radioactive waste generated within their borders and becoming liable for all damages waste generators suffer as a result of the States' failure to do so promptly. In this provision, Congress has crossed the line distinguishing encouragement from coercion. . . .

The take title provision offers state governments a "choice" of either accepting ownership of waste or regulating according to the instructions of Congress. Respondents do not claim that the Constitution would authorize Congress to impose either option as a freestanding requirement. On one hand, the Constitution would not permit Congress simply to transfer radioactive waste from generators to state governments. Such a forced transfer, standing alone, would in principle be no different than a congressionally compelled subsidy from state governments to radioactive waste producers. The same is true of the provision requiring the States to become liable for the generators' damages. Standing alone, this provision would be indistinguishable from an Act of Congress directing the States to assume the liabilities of certain state residents. Either type of federal action would "commandeer" state governments into the service of federal regulatory purposes, and would for this reason be inconsistent with the Constitution's division of authority between federal and state governments. On the other hand, the second alternative held out to state governments—regulating pursuant to Congress' direction—would, standing alone, present a simple command to state governments to implement legislation enacted by Congress. As we have seen, the Constitution does not empower Congress to subject state governments to this type of instruction.

Because an instruction to state governments to take title to waste, standing alone, would be beyond the authority of Congress, and because a direct order to regulate, standing alone, would also be beyond the authority of Congress, it follows that Congress lacks the power to offer the States a choice between the two. Unlike the first two sets of incentives, the take title incentive does not represent the conditional exercise of any congressional power enumerated in the Constitution. In this provision, Congress has not held out the threat of exercising its spending power or its commerce power; it has instead held out the threat, should the States not regulate according to one federal instruction, of simply forcing the States to submit to another federal instruction. A choice between two unconstitutionally coercive regulatory techniques is no choice at all. Either way, "the Act commandeers the legislative processes of the States by directly compelling them to enact and enforce a federal regulatory program," *Hodel v. Virginia Surface Mining & Reclamation Assn., Inc., supra,* 452 U.S., at 288, an outcome that has never been understood to lie within the authority conferred upon Congress by the Constitution. . . .

The take title provision appears to be unique. No other federal statute has been cited which offers a state government no option other than that of implementing legislation enacted by Congress. Whether one views the take title provision as lying outside Congress' enumerated powers, or as infringing upon the core of state sovereignty reserved by the Tenth Amendment, the provision is inconsistent with the federal structure of our Government established by the Constitution.

IV

. . . While the Framers no doubt endowed Congress with the power to regulate interstate commerce in order to avoid further instances of the interstate trade disputes that were common under the Articles of Confederation, the Framers did *not* intend that Congress should exercise that power through the mechanism of mandating state regulation. The Constitution established Congress as "a superintending authority over the reciprocal trade" among the States, The Federalist No. 42, p. 268 (C. Rossiter ed. 1961), by empowering Congress to regulate that trade directly, not by authorizing Congress to issue trade-related orders to state governments. As Madison and Hamilton explained, "a sovereignty over sovereigns, a government over governments, a legislation for communities, as contradistinguished from individuals, as it is a solecism in theory, so in practice it is subversive of the order and ends of civil polity." *Id.,* No. 20, at 138.

The sited state respondents focus their attention on the process by which the Act was formulated. They correctly observe that public officials representing the State of New York lent their support to the Act's enactment. A Deputy Commissioner of the State's Energy Office testified in favor of the Act. Senator Moynihan of New York spoke in support of the Act on the floor of the Senate. Respondents note that the Act embodies a bargain among the sited and unsited States, a compromise to which New York was a willing participant and from which New York has reaped much benefit. Respondents then pose what appears at first to be a troubling question: How can a federal statute be found an unconstitutional infringement of state sovereignty when state officials consented to the statute's enactment?

The answer follows from an understanding of the fundamental purpose served by our Government's federal structure. The Constitution does not protect the sovereignty of States for the benefit of the States or state governments as abstract political entities, or even for the benefit of the public officials governing the States. To the contrary, the Constitution divides authority between federal and state governments for the protection of individuals. State sovereignty is not just an end in itself: "Rather, federalism secures to citizens the liberties that derive from the diffusion of sovereign power." "Just as the separation and independence of the coordinate branches of the Federal Government serves to prevent the accumulation of excessive power in any one branch, a healthy balance of power between the States and the Federal Government will reduce the risk of tyranny and abuse from either front." *Gregory v. Ashcroft*, 501 U.S., at 458 (1991). See The Federalist No. 51, p. 323 (C. Rossiter ed. 1961).

Where Congress exceeds its authority relative to the States, therefore, the departure from the constitutional plan cannot be ratified by the "consent" of state officials. An analogy to the separation of powers among the branches of the Federal Government clarifies this point. The Constitution's division of power among the three branches is violated where one branch invades the territory of another, whether or not the encroached-upon branch approves the encroachment. In *Buckley v. Valeo,* 424 U.S. 1, 118–137 (1976), for instance, the Court held that Congress had infringed the President's appointment power, despite the fact that the President himself had manifested his consent to the statute that caused the infringement by signing it into law. In *INS v. Chadha,* 462 U.S. 919, 944–959 (1983), we held that the legislative veto violated the constitutional requirement that legislation be presented to the President, despite Presidents' approval of hundreds of statutes containing a legislative veto provision. The constitutional authority of Congress cannot be expanded by the "consent" of the governmental unit whose domain is thereby narrowed, whether that unit is the Executive Branch or the States.

State officials thus cannot consent to the enlargement of the powers of Congress beyond those enumerated in the Constitution. . . . Where state officials purport to submit to the direction of Congress in this manner, federalism is hardly being advanced.

Nor does the State's prior support for the Act estop it from asserting the Act's unconstitutionality. . . .

[The Court rejected the separate Guarantee Clause challenge to the provisions it had upheld as legitimate exercises of Congress's interstate commerce, taxing, spending, and compact-ratification powers, expressing doubts as to the justiciability of Guarantee Clause challenges but concluding that, in any event, neither the monetary incentives nor the commercial regu-

lations "can reasonably be said to deny any State a republican form of government." In a final substantive section, the Court found that the take-title
provision was severable from the rest of the act, and so upheld the act in
part and invalidated it in part.—Editors]

■ JUSTICE WHITE, with whom JUSTICE BLACKMUN and JUSTICE STEVENS
join, concurring in part and dissenting in part.

[In Part I of his opinion, Justice White described the facts leading to the
arrangement in question at great length, emphasizing that the states had
agreed to this arrangement and that Congress, acting pursuant to its power
to permit "interstate compacts," was encouraging state-state voluntary cooperation.—Editors]

II

To justify its holding that the take title provision contravenes the Constitution, the Court posits that "[i]n this provision, Congress has crossed
the line distinguishing encouragement from coercion." Without attempting
to understand properly the take title provision's place in the interstate bargaining process, the Court isolates the measure analytically and proceeds
to dissect it in a syllogistic fashion. The Court candidly begins with an argument respondents do *not* make: that "the Constitution would not permit
Congress simply to transfer radioactive waste from generators to state governments." "Such a forced transfer," it continues, "standing alone, would in
principle be no different than a congressionally compelled subsidy from
state governments to radioactive waste producers." Since this is *not* an argument respondents make, one naturally wonders why the Court builds its
analysis that the take title provision is unconstitutional around this opening premise. But having carefully built its straw man, the Court proceeds
impressively to knock him down. "As we have seen," the Court teaches, "the
Constitution does not empower Congress to subject state governments to
this type of instruction."

Curiously absent from the Court's analysis is any effort to place the
take title provision within the overall context of the legislation. As the discussion in Part I of this opinion suggests, the 1980 and 1985 statutes were
enacted against a backdrop of national concern over the availability of additional low-level radioactive waste disposal facilities. Congress could have
pre-empted the field by directly regulating the disposal of this waste pursuant to its powers under the Commerce and Spending Clauses, but instead it *unanimously* assented to the States' request for congressional ratification of agreements to which they had acceded. See 131 Cong.Rec. 35252
(1985); *id.*, at 38425. As the floor statements of Members of Congress reveal, the States wished to take the lead in achieving a solution to this problem and agreed among themselves to the various incentives and penalties
implemented by Congress to ensure adherence to the various deadlines and
goals. The chief executives of the States proposed this approach, and I am
unmoved by the Court's vehemence in taking away Congress' authority to
sanction a recalcitrant unsited State now that New York has reaped the
benefits of the sited States' concessions.

In my view, New York's actions subsequent to enactment of the 1980
and 1985 Acts fairly indicate its approval of the interstate agreement process embodied in those laws within the meaning of Art. I, § 10, cl. 3, of the
Constitution, which provides that "[n]o State shall, without the Consent of
Congress, . . . enter into any Agreement or Compact with another State."
. . .

IV

Though I disagree with the Court's conclusion that the take title provision is unconstitutional, I do not read its opinion to preclude Congress from adopting a similar measure through its powers under the Spending or Commerce Clauses. The Court makes clear that its objection is to the alleged "commandeer[ing]" quality of the take title provision. As its discussion of the surcharge and rebate incentives reveals, the spending power offers a means of enacting a take title provision under the Court's standards. Congress could, in other words, condition the payment of funds on the State's willingness to take title if it has not already provided a waste disposal facility. . . . See *South Dakota v. Dole,* 483 U.S. 203, 208–209 (1987).

Similarly, should a State fail to establish a waste disposal facility by the appointed deadline (under the statute as presently drafted, January 1, 1996, § 2021e(d)(2)(C)), Congress has the power pursuant to the Commerce Clause to regulate directly the producers of the waste. . . .

■ JUSTICE STEVENS, concurring in part and dissenting in part.

Under the Articles of Confederation, the Federal Government had the power to issue commands to the States. See Arts. VIII, IX. Because that indirect exercise of federal power proved ineffective, the Framers of the Constitution empowered the Federal Government to exercise legislative authority directly over individuals within the States, even though that direct authority constituted a greater intrusion on state sovereignty. Nothing in that history suggests that the Federal Government may not also impose its will upon the several States as it did under the Articles. The Constitution enhanced, rather than diminished, the power of the Federal Government.

The notion that Congress does not have the power to issue "a simple command to state governments to implement legislation enacted by Congress" is incorrect and unsound. There is no such limitation in the Constitution. The Tenth Amendment surely does not impose any limit on Congress' exercise of the powers delegated to it by Article I. Nor does the structure of the constitutional order or the values of federalism mandate such a formal rule. To the contrary, the Federal Government directs state governments in many realms. The Government regulates state-operated railroads, state school systems, state prisons, state elections, and a host of other state functions. Similarly, there can be no doubt that, in time of war, Congress could either draft soldiers itself or command the States to supply their quotas of troops. I see no reason why Congress may not also command the States to enforce federal water and air quality standards or federal standards for the disposition of low-level radioactive wastes. . . .

For these reasons, as well as those set forth by Justice WHITE, I respectfully dissent.

NOTES

1. *New York v. United States* makes for a good review and summary of several of the powers of Congress we have been studying in this section. What parts of the Low–Level Radioactive Waste Disposal Act did the Court uphold under the Commerce Clause power? Under the taxing power? Under the spending power? Do you agree with the Court's application of those powers in *New York v. United States*? Is Justice O'Connor's majority opinion consistent with

her dissent in *South Dakota v. Dole* with respect to the scope of the spending power? Why or why not?

2. Is the *principle* pursuant to which the Court struck down the "take-title" requirement correct: that Congress may not directly compel states to enact specific state laws? What historical and textual evidence does Justice O'Connor's majority opinion marshal in support of this conclusion? What do you make of the position of Justice Stevens's dissenting opinion: that there is no such prohibition in the Constitution? Is the *application* of that principle correct? Could the "take-title" provision be sustained on the theory that it is simply a "tax" on non-participation in the cooperative waste disposal scheme—i.e., a choice of either participating in a regulatory regime or suffering the financial penalties of being required to "own" and dispose of a state's own privately-produced low-level radioactive waste? Or is this not a "tax," but instead a regulatory penalty that Congress could not impose directly for non-compliance with its attempted commandeering of states to enact congressional policies?

3. The Compact Clause of Article I, Section 9 prohibits states from making certain types of agreements with each other absent Congress's consent. Where states *do* enter into such agreements, however, and Congress exercises its power specifically to approve such arrangements, should the states be considered contractually bound? This appears to be the strong emphasis of Justice White's dissent. Evaluate the majority's response: that the Constitution's structural provisions of federalism, like its structural protections of separation of powers, cannot be bargained away or waived by state officials, because they exist as fundamental limitations on the powers of government, for the ultimate benefit of individuals. Is this response persuasive?

4. *Coyle v. Smith,* 221 U.S. 559 (1911), cited by the Court in *New York v. United States*, is perhaps the paradigmatic illustration of a core, reserved prerogative of states as autonomous political communities. The act of Congress admitting Oklahoma as a new state provided that Oklahoma could not relocate its capital city until 1913. The Court held that this restriction was invalid: "The power to locate its own seat of government, and to determine when and how it shall be changed from one place to another, and to appropriate its own public funds for that purpose, are essentially and peculiarly state powers. That one of the original thirteen states could now be shorn of such powers by an act of Congress would not be for a moment entertained." Neither could Congress impose such a restriction as a condition of admission as a new state. Article IV, Section 3 conferred power to admit "new states into this Union." However:

> "This Union" was and is a union of states, equal in power, dignity, and authority, each competent to exert that residuum of sovereignty not delegated to the United States by the Constitution itself. To maintain otherwise would be to say that the Union, through the power of Congress to admit new states, might come to be a union of states unequal in power, as including states whose powers were restricted only by the Constitution, with others whose powers had been further restricted by an act of Congress accepted as a condition of admission.

If Congress could not condition a state's admission into the Union on would-be state's locating its capital in a specified city, can it impose such a condition as a requirement of receipt of federal funds? (For *any* purpose? What about federal construction grants for building state capitol buildings?) Could it authorize interstate compacts on the condition that the states not relocate their capitals?

5. What is the scope of the anti-commandeering principle? If Congress constitutionally cannot compel state *legislatures* to enact nationally-prescribed policies against their will, can it compel state *executive officers* to execute national laws? Or is that a different matter? Those questions were raised in the following case:

Printz v. United States
521 U.S. 898 (1997)

■ JUSTICE SCALIA delivered the opinion of the Court.

The question presented in these cases is whether certain interim provisions of the Brady Handgun Violence Prevention Act, commanding state and local law enforcement officers to conduct background checks on prospective handgun purchasers and to perform certain related tasks, violate the Constitution.

I

The Gun Control Act of 1968 establishes a detailed federal scheme governing the distribution of firearms. . . . In 1993, Congress amended the GCA by enacting the Brady Act. The Act requires the Attorney General to establish a national instant background-check system by November 30, 1998, and immediately puts in place certain interim provisions until that system becomes operative. Under the interim provisions, a firearms dealer who proposes to transfer a handgun must first receive from the transferee a statement (the Brady Form), containing the name, address, and date of birth of the proposed transferee . . . and provide the "chief law enforcement officer" (CLEO) of the transferee's residence with notice of the contents (and a copy) of the Brady Form. With some exceptions, the dealer must then wait five business days before consummating the sale, unless the CLEO earlier notifies the dealer that he has no reason to believe the transfer would be illegal. . . .

When a CLEO receives the required notice of a proposed transfer from the firearms dealer, the CLEO must "make a reasonable effort to ascertain within 5 business days whether receipt or possession would be in violation of the law, including research in whatever State and local recordkeeping systems are available and in a national system designated by the Attorney General." The Act does not require the CLEO to take any particular action if he determines that a pending transaction would be unlawful; he may notify the firearms dealer to that effect, but is not required to do so. If, however, the CLEO notifies a gun dealer that a prospective purchaser is ineligible to receive a handgun, he must, upon request, provide the would-be purchaser with a written statement of the reasons for that determination. . . . [A]ny person who "knowingly violates [the section of the GCA amended by the Brady Act] shall be fined under this title, imprisoned for not more than 1 year, or both."

Petitioners Jay Printz and Richard Mack, the CLEOs for Ravalli County, Montana, and Graham County, Arizona, respectively, filed separate actions challenging the constitutionality of the Brady Act's interim provisions. In each case, the District Court held that the provision requiring CLEOs to perform background checks was unconstitutional .... A divided panel of the Court of Appeals for the Ninth Circuit reversed. ...

II

From the description set forth above, it is apparent that the Brady Act purports to direct state law enforcement officers to participate, albeit only temporarily, in the administration of a federally enacted regulatory scheme. ... Petitioners here object to being pressed into federal service, and contend that congressional action compelling state officers to execute federal laws is unconstitutional. Because there is no constitutional text speaking to this precise question, the answer to the CLEOs' challenge must be sought in historical understanding and practice, in the structure of the Constitution, and in the jurisprudence of this Court. We treat those three sources, in that order, in this and the next two sections of this opinion. ...

The Government contends ... that "the earliest Congresses enacted statutes that required the participation of state officials in the implementation of federal laws." The Government's contention demands our careful consideration, since early congressional enactments "provid[e] contemporaneous and weighty evidence of the Constitution's meaning." Indeed, such "contemporaneous legislative exposition of the Constitution . . ., acquiesced in for a long term of years, fixes the construction to be given its provisions."
. . .

The Government observes that statutes enacted by the first Congresses required state courts to record applications for citizenship, to transmit abstracts of citizenship applications and other naturalization records to the Secretary of State, and to register aliens seeking naturalization and issue certificates of registry. . . . Other statutes of that era apparently or at least arguably required state courts to perform functions unrelated to naturalization, such as resolving controversies between a captain and the crew of his ship concerning the seaworthiness of the vessel, hearing the claims of slave owners who had apprehended fugitive slaves and issuing certificates authorizing the slave's forced removal to the State from which he had fled, taking proof of the claims of Canadian refugees who had assisted the United States during the Revolutionary War, and ordering the deportation of alien enemies in times of war.

These early laws establish, at most, that the Constitution was originally understood to permit imposition of an obligation on state *judges* to enforce federal prescriptions, insofar as those prescriptions related to matters appropriate for the judicial power. ... It is understandable why courts should have been viewed distinctively in this regard; unlike legislatures and executives, they applied the law of other sovereigns all the time. The principle underlying so-called "transitory" causes of action was that laws which operated elsewhere created obligations in justice that courts of the forum State would enforce. The Constitution itself, in the Full Faith and Credit Clause, Art. IV, § 1, generally required such enforcement with respect to obligations arising in other States.

For these reasons, we do not think the early statutes imposing obligations on state courts imply a power of Congress to impress the state executive into its service. Indeed, it can be argued that the numerousness of these statutes, contrasted with the utter lack of statutes imposing obligations on the States' executive (notwithstanding the attractiveness of that course to Congress), suggests an assumed *absence* of such power. . . .

Not only do the enactments of the early Congresses, as far as we are aware, contain no evidence of an assumption that the Federal Government may command the States' executive power in the absence of a particularized constitutional authorization, they contain some indication of precisely the opposite assumption. On September 23, 1789—the day before its proposal of the Bill of Rights—the First Congress enacted a law aimed at obtaining state assistance of the most rudimentary and necessary sort for the enforcement of the new Government's laws: the holding of federal prisoners in state jails at federal expense. Significantly, the law issued not a command to the States' executive, but a recommendation to their legislatures. . . .

In addition to early legislation, the Government also appeals to other sources we have usually regarded as indicative of the original understanding of the Constitution. It points to portions of The Federalist which . . . [state] that Congress will probably "make use of the State officers and State regulations, for collecting" federal taxes, The Federalist No. 36 (A. Hamilton), and predicted that "the eventual collection [of internal revenue] under the immediate authority of the Union, will generally be made by the officers, and according to the rules, appointed by the several States," No. 45 (J. Madison). The Government also invokes The Federalist's more general observations that the Constitution would "enable the [national] government to employ the ordinary magistracy of each [State] in the execution of its laws," No. 27 (A. Hamilton), and that it was "extremely probable that in other instances, particularly in the organization of the judicial power, the officers of the States will be clothed with the correspondent authority of the Union," No. 45 (J. Madison). But none of these statements necessarily implies—what is the critical point here—that Congress could impose these responsibilities *without the consent of the States*. They appear to rest on the natural assumption that the States would consent to allowing their officials to assist the Federal Government, an assumption proved correct by the extensive mutual assistance the States and Federal Government voluntarily provided one another in the early days of the Republic. . . .

To complete the historical record, we must note that there is not only an absence of executive-commandeering statutes in the early Congresses, but there is an absence of them in our later history as well, at least until very recent years. The Government points to the Act of August 3, 1882, which enlisted state officials "to take charge of the local affairs of immigration in the ports within such State, and to provide for the support and relief of such immigrants therein landing as may fall into distress or need of public aid"; to inspect arriving immigrants and exclude any person found to be a "convict, lunatic, idiot," or indigent; and to send convicts back to their country of origin "without compensation." The statute did not, however, *mandate* those duties, but merely empowered the Secretary of the Treasury "to *enter into contracts* with such State . . . officers as *may be designated* for that purpose *by the governor* of any State." (Emphasis added.)

The Government [also] cites the World War I selective draft law that authorized the President "to utilize the service of any or all departments and any or all officers or agents of the United States *and of the several States,* Territories, and the District of Columbia, and subdivisions thereof, in the execution of this Act," and made any person who refused to comply with the President's directions guilty of a misdemeanor. Act of May 18, 1917 (emphasis added). However, it is far from clear that the authorization "to utilize the service" of state officers was an authorization to *compel* the service of state officers; and the misdemeanor provision surely applied only to refusal to comply with the President's *authorized* directions, which might not have included directions to officers of States whose Governors had not volunteered their services. It is interesting that in implementing the Act President Wilson did not commandeer the services of state officers, but instead requested the assistance of the States' Governors, obtained the consent of each of the Governors, and left it to the Governors to issue orders to their subordinate state officers. It is impressive that even with respect to a wartime measure the President should have been so solicitious of state independence.

The Government points to a number of federal statutes enacted within the past few decades that require the participation of state or local officials in implementing federal regulatory schemes. Some of these are connected to federal funding measures, and can perhaps be more accurately described as conditions upon the grant of federal funding than as mandates to the States; others, which require only the provision of information to the Federal Government, do not involve the precise issue before us here, which is the forced participation of the States' executive in the actual administration of a federal program. . . . Even assuming they represent assertion of the very same congressional power challenged here, they are of such recent vintage that they are no more probative than the statute before us of a constitutional tradition that lends meaning to the text. Their persuasive force is far outweighed by almost two centuries of apparent congressional avoidance of the practice. . . .

III

The constitutional practice we have examined above tends to negate the existence of the congressional power asserted here, but is not conclusive. We turn next to consideration of the structure of the Constitution, to see if we can discern among its "essential postulate[s]," *Principality of Monaco v. Mississippi,* 292 U.S. 313, 322 (1934), a principle that controls the present cases.

A

It is incontestable that the Constitution established a system of "dual sovereignty." *Gregory v. Ashcroft,* 501 U.S. 452, 457 (1991). Although the States surrendered many of their powers to the new Federal Government, they retained "a residuary and inviolable sovereignty," The Federalist No. 39 (J. Madison). This is reflected throughout the Constitution's text, including (to mention only a few examples) the prohibition on any involuntary reduction or combination of a State's territory, Art. IV, § 3; the Judicial Power Clause, Art. III, § 2, and the Privileges and Immunities Clause, Art. IV, § 2, which speak of the "Citizens" of the States; the amendment provision, Article V, which requires the votes of three-fourths of the States to amend the Constitution; and the Guarantee Clause, Art. IV, § 4, which "presupposes the continued existence of the states and . . . those means and instrumentalities which are the creation of their sovereign and reserved rights," *Helvering v. Gerhardt,* 304 U.S. 405, 414–415 (1938). Residual state sovereignty was also implicit, of course, in the Constitution's conferral upon Congress of not all governmental powers, but only discrete, enumerated ones, Art. I, § 8, which implication was rendered express by the Tenth Amendment's assertion that "[t]he powers not delegated to the United States by the Constitution, nor prohibited by it to the States, are reserved to the States respectively, or to the people." . . .

[T]he Framers rejected the concept of a central government that would act upon and through the States, and instead designed a system in which the State and Federal Governments would exercise concurrent authority over the people—who were, in Hamilton's words, "the only proper objects of government," The Federalist No. 15. . . . The great innovation of this design was that "our citizens would have two political capacities, one state and one federal, each protected from incursion by the other"—"a legal system unprecedented in form and design, establishing two orders of government, each with its own direct relationship, its own privity, its own set of mutual rights and obligations to the people who sustain it and are governed by it." *U.S. Term Limits, Inc. v. Thornton,* 514 U.S. 779, 838 (1995) (Kennedy, J., concurring). The Constitution thus contemplates that a State's government will represent and remain accountable to its own citizens. . . .

This separation of the two spheres is one of the Constitution's structural protections of liberty. "Just as the separation and independence of the coordinate branches of the Federal Government serve to prevent the accumulation of excessive power in any one branch, a healthy balance of power between the States and the Federal Government will reduce the risk of tyranny and abuse from either front." *Gregory,* 501 U.S., at 458. . . . The power of the Federal Government would be augmented immeasurably if it were able to impress into its service—and at no cost to itself—the police officers of the 50 States.

B

. . . [F]ederal control of state officers . . . would also have an effect upon the . . . separation and equilibration of powers between the three branches of the Federal Government itself. The Constitution does not leave to speculation who is to administer the laws enacted by Congress; the President, it says, "shall take Care that the Laws be faithfully executed," Art. II, § 3, personally and through officers whom he appoints (save for such inferior officers as Congress may authorize to be appointed by the "Courts of Law" or by "the Heads of Departments" who are themselves Presidential appointees), Art. II, § 2. The Brady Act effectively transfers this responsibility to thousands of CLEOs in the 50 States, who are left to implement the program without meaningful Presidential control. . . . The insistence of the Framers upon unity in the Federal Executive—to ensure both vigor and accountability—is well known. See The Federalist No. 70 (A. Hamilton); see also Calabresi & Prakash, The President's Power to Execute the Laws, 104 Yale L.J. 541 (1994). That unity would be shattered, and the power of the President would be subject to reduction, if Congress could act as effectively without the President as with him, by simply requiring state officers to execute its laws. . . .

C

The dissent of course resorts to the last, best hope of those who defend ultra vires congressional action, the Necessary and Proper Clause. It reasons that the power to regulate the sale of handguns under the Commerce Clause, coupled with the power to "make all Laws which shall be necessary and proper for carrying into Execution the foregoing Powers," Art. I, § 8, conclusively establishes the Brady Act's constitutional validity, because the Tenth Amendment imposes no limitations on the exercise of delegated powers but merely prohibits the exercise of powers "not delegated to the United States." What destroys the dissent's Necessary and Proper Clause argument, however, is not the Tenth Amendment but the Necessary and Proper

Clause itself. When a "La[w] . . . for carrying into Execution" the Commerce Clause violates the principle of state sovereignty reflected in the various constitutional provisions we mentioned earlier, it is not a "La[w] . . . *proper* for carrying into Execution the Commerce Clause," and is thus, in the words of The Federalist, "merely [an] ac[t] of usurpation" which "deserve[s] to be treated as such." The Federalist No. 33 (A. Hamilton). We in fact answered the dissent's Necessary and Proper Clause argument in *New York*: "[E]ven where Congress has the authority under the Constitution to pass laws requiring or prohibiting certain acts, it lacks the power directly to compel the States to require or prohibit those acts. . . . [T]he Commerce Clause, for example, authorizes Congress to regulate interstate commerce directly; it does not authorize Congress to regulate state governments' regulation of interstate commerce." 505 U.S., at 166. . . .

IV

Finally, and most conclusively in the present litigation, we turn to the prior jurisprudence of this Court. . . . [O]pinions of ours have made clear that the Federal Government may not compel the States to implement, by legislation or executive action, federal regulatory programs. In *Hodel v. Virginia Surface Mining & Reclamation Assn., Inc.,* 452 U.S. 264 (1981), and *FERC v. Mississippi,* 456 U.S. 742 (1982), we sustained statutes against constitutional challenge only after assuring ourselves that they did not require the States to enforce federal law. . . .

When we were at last confronted squarely with a federal statute that unambiguously required the States to enact or administer a federal regulatory program, our decision should have come as no surprise. [I]n *New York v. United States,* 505 U.S. 144 (1992), . . . [we held that] "[t]he Federal Government . . . may not compel the States to enact or administer a federal regulatory program."

The Government contends that *New York* is distinguishable on the following ground: Unlike the "take title" provisions invalidated there, the background-check provision of the Brady Act does not require state legislative or executive officials to make policy, but instead issues a final directive to state CLEOs. It is permissible, the Government asserts, for Congress to command state or local officials to assist in the implementation of federal law so long as "Congress itself devises a clear legislative solution that regulates private conduct" and requires state or local officers to provide only "limited, non-policymaking help in enforcing that law." "[T]he constitutional line is crossed only when Congress compels the States to make law in their sovereign capacities." Brief for United States 16.

The Government's distinction between "making" law and merely "enforcing" it, between "policymaking" and mere "implementation," is an interesting one. . . . [But e]xecutive action that has utterly no policymaking component is rare, particularly at an executive level as high as a jurisdiction's chief law enforcement officer. Is it really true that there is no policymaking involved in deciding, for example, what "reasonable efforts" shall be expended to conduct a background check? It may well satisfy the Act for a CLEO to direct that (a) no background checks will be conducted that divert personnel time from pending felony investigations, and (b) no background check will be permitted to consume more than one-half hour of an officer's time. But nothing in the Act *requires* a CLEO to be so parsimonious; diverting at least *some* felony-investigation time, and permitting at least *some* background checks beyond one-half hour would certainly not be *un*reasonable. Is this decision whether to devote maximum "reasonable efforts" or minimum "reasonable efforts" not preeminently a matter of policy? It is quite impossible, in short, to draw the Government's proposed line at "no policymaking," and we would have to fall back upon a line of "not too much policymaking." How much is too much is not likely to be answered precisely; and an imprecise barrier against federal intrusion upon state authority is not likely to be an effective one.

Even assuming, moreover, that the Brady Act leaves no "policymaking" discretion with the States, we fail to see how that improves rather than worsens the intrusion upon state sovereignty. Preservation of the States as independent and autonomous political entities is arguably less undermined by requiring them to make policy in certain fields than (as Judge Sneed aptly described it over two decades ago) by "reduc[ing] [them] to puppets of a ventriloquist Congress," *Brown v. EPA,* 521 F.2d, at 839. It is an essential attribute of the States' retained sovereignty that they remain independent and autonomous within their proper sphere of authority. It is no more compatible with this independence and autonomy that their officers be "dragooned" . . . into administering federal law, than it would be compatible with the independence and autonomy of the United States that its officers be impressed into service for the execution of state laws.

The Government purports to find support for its proffered distinction of *New York* in our decisions in *Testa v. Katt,* 330 U.S. 386 (1947). . . . We [do not find this case] relevant. *Testa* stands for the proposition that state courts cannot refuse to apply federal law—a conclusion mandated by the terms of the Supremacy Clause ("the Judges in every State shall be bound [by federal law]"). As we have suggested earlier, that says nothing about whether state executive officers must administer federal law. . . .

The Government also maintains that requiring state officers to perform discrete, ministerial tasks specified by Congress does not violate the principle of *New York* because it does not diminish the accountability of state or federal officials. This argument fails even on its own terms. By forcing state governments to absorb the financial burden of implementing a federal regulatory program, Members of Congress can take credit for "solving" problems without having to ask their constituents to pay for the solutions with higher federal taxes. And even when the States are not forced to absorb the costs of implementing a federal program, they are still put in the position of taking the blame for its burdensomeness and for its defects. Under the present law, for example, it will be the CLEO and not some federal official who stands between the gun purchaser and immediate possession of his gun. And it will likely be the CLEO, not some federal official, who will be blamed for any error (even one in the designated federal database) that causes a purchaser to be mistakenly rejected.

The dissent makes no attempt to defend the Government's basis for distinguishing *New York,* but instead advances what seems to us an even more implausible theory. The Brady Act, the dissent asserts, is different from the "take title" provisions invalidated in *New York* because the former is addressed to individuals—namely, CLEOs—while the latter were directed to the State itself. That is certainly a difference, but it cannot be a constitutionally significant one. While the Brady Act is directed to "individuals," it is directed to them in their official capacities as state officers; it controls their actions, not as private citizens, but as the agents of the State. The distinction between judicial writs and other government action directed against individuals in their personal capacity, on the one hand, and in their official capacity, on the other hand, is an ancient one, principally because it is dictated by common sense. We have observed that "a suit against a state official in his or her official capacity is not a suit against the official but rather is a suit against the official's office. . . . As such, it is no different from a suit against the State itself." *Will v. Michigan Dept. of State Police,* 491 U.S. 58, 71 (1989). . . .

Finally, the Government puts forward a cluster of arguments that can be grouped under the heading: "The Brady Act serves very important purposes, is most efficiently administered by CLEOs during the interim period, and places a minimal and only temporary burden upon state officers." Assuming *all* the mentioned factors were true, they might be relevant if we were evaluating whether the incidental application to the States of a federal law of general applicability excessively interfered with the functioning of state governments. But where, as here, it is the whole *object* of the law to direct the functioning of the state executive, and hence to compromise the structural framework of dual sovereignty, such a "balancing" analysis is inappropriate. It is the very *principle* of separate state sovereignty that such a law offends, and no comparative assessment of the various interests can overcome that fundamental defect. We expressly rejected such an approach in *New York*. . . .

V

. . . We held in *New York* that Congress cannot compel the States to enact or enforce a federal regulatory program. Today we hold that Congress cannot circumvent that prohibition by conscripting the State's officers directly. The Federal Government may neither issue directives requiring the States to address particular problems, nor command the States' officers, or those of their political subdivisions, to administer or enforce a federal regulatory program. It matters not whether policymaking is involved, and no case-by-case weighing of the burdens or benefits is necessary; such commands are fundamentally incompatible with our constitutional system of dual sovereignty.

■ JUSTICE STEVENS, with whom JUSTICE SOUTER, JUSTICE GINSBURG, and JUSTICE BREYER join, dissenting.

When Congress exercises the powers delegated to it by the Constitution, it may impose affirmative obligations on executive and judicial officers of state and local governments as well as ordinary citizens. This conclusion is firmly supported by the text of the Constitution, the early history of the Nation, decisions of this Court, and a correct understanding of the basic structure of the Federal Government. . . .

Indeed, since the ultimate issue is one of power, we must consider its implications in times of national emergency. Matters such as the enlistment of air raid wardens, the administration of a military draft, the mass inoculation of children to forestall an epidemic, or perhaps the threat of an international terrorist, may require a national response before federal personnel can be made available to respond. If the Constitution empowers Congress and the President to make an appropriate response, is there anything in the Tenth Amendment, "in historical understanding and practice, in the structure of the Constitution, [or] in the jurisprudence of this Court," that forbids the enlistment of state officers to make that response effective? More narrowly, what basis is there in any of those sources for concluding that it is the Members of this Court, rather than the elected representatives of the people, who should determine whether the Constitution contains the unwritten rule that the Court announces today?

Perhaps today's majority would suggest that no such emergency is presented by the facts of these cases. But such a suggestion is itself an expression of a policy judgment. And Congress' view of the matter is quite different from that implied by the Court today.

The Brady Act was passed in response to what Congress described as an "epidemic of gun violence." The Act's legislative history notes that 15,377 Americans were murdered with firearms in 1992, and that 12,489 of these deaths were caused by handguns. Congress expressed special concern that "[t]he level of firearm violence in this country is, by far, the highest among developed nations." The partial solution contained in the Brady Act, a mandatory background check before a handgun may be purchased, has met with remarkable success. Between 1994 and 1996, approximately 6,600 firearm sales each month to potentially dangerous persons were prevented by Brady Act checks; over 70% of the rejected purchasers were convicted or indicted felons. See U.S. Dept. of Justice, Bureau of Justice Statistics Bulletin, A National Estimate: Presale Firearm Checks 1 (Feb. 1997). Whether or not the evaluation reflected in the enactment of the Brady Act is correct as to the extent of the danger and the efficacy of the legislation, the congressional decision surely warrants more respect than it is accorded in today's unprecedented decision.

I

The text of the Constitution provides a sufficient basis for a correct disposition of these cases.

Article I, § 8, grants Congress the power to regulate commerce among the States. Putting to one side the revisionist views expressed by Justice Thomas in his concurring opinion in *United States v. Lopez,* 514 U.S. 549, 584 (1995), there can be no question that that provision adequately supports the regulation of commerce in handguns effected by the Brady Act. Moreover, the additional grant of authority in that section of the Constitution "[t]o make all Laws which shall be necessary and proper for carrying into Execution the foregoing Powers" is surely adequate to support the temporary enlistment of local police officers in the process of identifying persons who should not be entrusted with the possession of handguns. In short, the affirmative delegation of power in Article I provides ample authority for the congressional enactment. . . .

The [Tenth] Amendment confirms the principle that the powers of the Federal Government are limited to those affirmatively granted by the Constitution, but it does not purport to limit the scope or the effectiveness of the exercise of powers that are delegated to Congress. Thus, the Amendment provides no support for a rule that immunizes local officials from obligations that might be imposed on ordinary citizens. Indeed, it would be more reasonable to infer that federal law may impose greater duties on state officials than on private citizens because another provision of the Constitution requires that "all executive and judicial Officers, both of the United States and of the several States, shall be bound by Oath or Affirmation, to support this Constitution." Art. VI, cl. 3. . . .

There is not a clause, sentence, or paragraph in the entire text of the Constitution of the United States that supports the proposition that a local police officer can ignore a command contained in a statute enacted by Congress pursuant to an express delegation of power enumerated in Article I.

II

Under the Articles of Confederation the National Government had the power to issue commands to the several sovereign States, but it had no authority to govern individuals directly. . . . That method of governing proved to be unacceptable, not because it demeaned the sovereign character of the several States, but rather because it was cumbersome and inefficient. . . . The basic change in the character of the government that the Framers conceived was designed to enhance the power of the national government, not to provide some new, unmentioned immunity for state officers. Because indirect control over individual citizens ("the only proper objects of government") was ineffective under the Articles of Confederation, Alexander Hamilton explained that "we must *extend* the authority of the Union to the persons of the citizens." The Federalist No. 15 (emphasis added).

Indeed, the historical materials strongly suggest that the founders intended to enhance the capacity of the Federal Government by empowering it—as a part of the new authority to make demands directly on individual citizens—to act through local officials. Hamilton made clear that the new Constitution, "by extending the authority of the federal head to the individual citizens of the several States, will enable the government to employ the ordinary magistracy of each in the execution of its laws." The Federalist No. 27. Hamilton's meaning was unambiguous; the Federal Government was to have the power to demand that local officials implement national policy programs. . . .

More specifically, during the debates concerning the ratification of the Constitution, it was assumed that state agents would act as tax collectors for the Federal Government. Opponents of the Constitution had repeatedly expressed fears that the new Federal Government's ability to impose taxes directly on the citizenry would result in an overbearing presence of federal tax collectors in the States. Federalists rejoined that this problem would not arise because, as Hamilton explained, "the United States . . . will make use of the State officers and State regulations for collecting" certain taxes. No. 36. . . .

Bereft of support in the history of the founding, the Court rests its conclusion on the claim that there is little evidence the National Government actually exercised such a power in the early years of the Republic. This reasoning is misguided in principle and in fact. While we have indicated that the express consideration and resolution of difficult constitutional issues by the First Congress in particular "provides contemporaneous and weighty evidence of the Constitution's meaning since many of [its] Members . . . had taken part in framing that instrument," we have never suggested that the failure of the early Congresses to address the scope of federal power in a particular area or to exercise a particular authority was an argument against its existence. That position, if correct, would undermine most of our post-New Deal Commerce Clause jurisprudence. . . .

More importantly, the fact that Congress did elect to rely on state judges and the clerks of state courts to perform a variety of executive functions is surely evidence of a contemporary understanding that their status as state officials did not immunize them from federal service. . . .

For example, statutes of the early Congresses required in mandatory terms that state judges and their clerks perform various executive duties with respect to applications for citizenship. . . . Similarly, the First Congress enacted legislation requiring state courts to serve, functionally, like contemporary regulatory agencies in certifying the seaworthiness of vessels. . . . The majority's insistence that this evidence of federal enlistment of state officials to serve executive functions is irrelevant simply because the assistance of "judges" was at issue rests on empty formalistic reasoning of the highest order.

III

The Court's "structural" arguments are not sufficient [either]. . . . As we explained in *Garcia v. San Antonio Metropolitan Transit Authority,* 469 U.S. 528 (1985): "[T]he principal means chosen by the Framers to ensure the role of the States in the federal system lies in the structure of the Federal Government itself. It is no novelty to observe that the composition of the Federal Government was designed in large part to protect the States from overreaching by Congress." *Id.,* at 550–551. Given the fact that the Members of Congress are elected by the people of the several States, with each State receiving an equivalent number of Senators in order to ensure that even the smallest States have a powerful voice in the Legislature, it is quite unrealistic to assume that they will ignore the sovereignty concerns of their constituents. It is far more reasonable to presume that their decisions to impose modest burdens on state officials from time to time reflect a considered judgment that the people in each of the States will benefit therefrom. . . .

Recent developments demonstrate that the political safeguards protecting our Federalism are effective. The majority expresses special concern that were its rule not adopted the Federal Government would be able to avail itself of the services of state government officials "at no cost to itself." But this specific problem of federal actions that have the effect of imposing so-called "unfunded mandates" on the States has been identified and meaningfully addressed by Congress in [the] Unfunded Mandates Reform Act of 1995. . . . Whatever the ultimate impact of the new legislation, its passage demonstrates that unelected judges are better off leaving the protection of federalism to the political process in all but the most extraordinary circumstances.

Perversely, the majority's rule seems more likely to damage than to preserve the safeguards against tyranny provided by the existence of vital state governments. By limiting the ability of the Federal Government to enlist state officials in the implementation of its programs, the Court creates incentives for the National Government to aggrandize itself. In the name of State's rights, the majority would have the Federal Government create vast national bureaucracies to implement its policies. This is exactly the sort of thing that the early Federalists promised would not occur, in part as a result of the National Government's ability to rely on the magistracy of the States. . . .

IV

Finally, the Court advises us that the "prior jurisprudence of this Court" is the most conclusive support for its position. That "prior jurisprudence" is *New York v. United States.* The case involved the validity of a federal statute that provided the States with three types of incentives to encourage them to dispose of radioactive wastes generated within their borders. The Court held that the first two sets of incentives were authorized by affirmative grants of power to Congress, and therefore "not inconsistent with the Tenth Amendment." . . .

The third so-called "incentive" gave the States the option either of adopting regulations dictated by Congress or of taking title to and possession of the low level radioactive waste. The Court concluded that, because Congress had no power to compel the state governments to take title to the waste, the "option" really amounted to a simple command to the States to enact and enforce a federal regulatory program. . . .

After noting that the "take title provision appears to be unique" because no other federal statute had offered "a state government no option other than that of implementing legislation enacted by Congress," the Court concluded that the provision was "inconsistent with the federal structure of our Government established by the Constitution."

Our statements, taken in context, clearly did not decide the question presented here, whether state executive officials—as opposed to state legislators—may in appropriate circumstances be enlisted to implement federal policy. The "take title" provision at issue in New York was beyond Congress' authority to enact because it was "in principle . . . no different than a congressionally compelled subsidy from state governments to radioactive waste producers," almost certainly a legislative Act.

The majority relies upon dictum in *New York* to the effect that "[t]he Federal Government may not compel the States to enact *or administer* a federal regulatory program." But that language was wholly unnecessary to the decision of the case. It is, of course, beyond dispute that we are not bound by the dicta of our prior opinions. To the extent that it has any substance at all, *New York*'s administration language may have referred to the possibility that the State might have been able to take title to and devise an elaborate scheme for the management of the radioactive waste through purely executive policymaking. But despite the majority's effort to suggest that similar activities are required by the Brady Act, it is hard to characterize the minimal requirement that CLEO's perform background checks as one involving the exercise of substantial policymaking discretion on that essentially legislative scale. . . .

Finally, the majority provides an incomplete explanation of our decision in *Testa v. Katt,* 330 U.S. 386 (1947), and demeans its importance. In that case the Court unanimously held that state courts of appropriate jurisdiction must occupy themselves adjudicating claims brought by private litigants under the federal Emergency Price Control Act of 1942, regardless of how otherwise crowded their dockets might be with state-law matters. . . . Even if the Court were correct in its suggestion that it was the reference to judges in the Supremacy Clause, rather than the central message of the entire Clause, that dictated the result in *Testa,* the Court's implied *expressio unius* argument that the Framers therefore did *not* intend to permit the enlistment of other state officials is implausible. Throughout our history judges, state as well as federal, have merited as much respect as executive agents. The notion that the Framers would have had no reluctance to press state judges into federal service against their will but would have regarded the imposition of a similar—indeed, far lesser—burden on town constables as an intolerable affront to principles of state sovereignty can only be considered perverse. If such a distinction had been contemplated by the learned and articulate men who fashioned the basic structure of our government, surely some of them would have said so.

The provision of the Brady Act that crosses the Court's newly defined constitutional threshold is more comparable to a statute requiring local police officers to report the identity of missing children to the Crime Control

Center of the Department of Justice than to an offensive federal command to a sovereign State. If Congress believes that such a statute will benefit the people of the Nation, and serve the interests of cooperative federalism better than an enlarged federal bureaucracy, we should respect both its policy judgment and its appraisal of its constitutional power.

■ [The concurring opinions of JUSTICES O'CONNOR and THOMAS and the dissenting opinions of JUSTICES SOUTER and BREYER are omitted.]

NOTES

1. Recall the five types of constitutional argument, or modes of interpretation: text, structure, historical purpose, practice and precedent, and policy. Which of these does the majority opinion rely on? Which ones does the dissent rely on? Work through each one, asking yourself which of the two opinions is more persuasive:

a. Which provisions of the Constitution does each opinion adduce? As a whole, does the text clearly resolve the case, as Justice Stevens suggests, or is it ambiguous?

b. Are there inferences that can be drawn from the structure of the Constitution? If so, are these general structural inferences, or are they drawn from the interaction of specific textual provisions? And, if so, what is the stopping point, or limiting principle, in applying these structural arguments?

c. Each opinion draws on copious amounts of materials about the intentions of the founders, especially the statements in *The Federalist*. Which side is most persuasive? How specifically do each of the opinions expect the founders to speak about a constitutional question? How specifically should we expect them to speak?

d. *Printz* came on the heels of the Court's decision in *New York*—are the efforts by Justice Stevens to distinguish that case persuasive? What deference, if any, is he giving to the Court's recent decision on the constitutional question in *New York*? What deference should he give?

e. And in which direction do the policy arguments cut? Should the policy decision be left in the hands of Congress? Should the federal courts defer as long as the states speak out in support of the congressional legislation? (If most states *oppose* the constitutionality of a federal statute, should the federal courts defer to that judgment?) Who exactly is federalism supposed to protect?

2. It has long been held that Congress *does* have power to require the state courts to hear and decide issues of federal law. A modern case for this proposition is referenced by both the majority opinion and Justice Stevens's dissent: *Testa v. Katt*, 330 U.S. 386 (1947). It is assumed that Congress must have this power since it need not create lower federal courts at all—Congress could have provided that all federal cases would originate in state court and then be appealable to the Supreme Court. See Art III, Sec. 1; see also Art. I, Sec. 8, cl. 9 (giving Congress power "To *constitute* Tribunals inferior to the Supreme Court"). (The verb "constitute" appears nowhere else in the "Constitution," and there is reason to think it allows Congress to designate preexisting state tribunals as being inferior to the Supreme Court.) Does this essentially mean that Congress can "commandeer" state judicial branches to exercise the federal judicial power? If so, does that undermine the anti-commandeering premises of *New York v. United States* and *Printz v. United States*? Or does it simply mean

that, as a consequence of the specific provisions of Article III with respect to the federal judiciary and the federal government's power to "constitute" inferior tribunals, the situation is different with respect to ordering state judiciaries to decide federal law issues? Are state executive branch officials more like state judges, who can be "commandeered" (after a fashion); or more like state legislatures, which cannot be?

[Assignments 34–35]

We turn now to the Supreme Court's most recent and highly significant decision interpreting the scope of Congress's legislative powers under the Commerce Clause, the Necessary and Proper Clause, the Taxing Clause, and the conditional spending power: the controversial decision of a closely divided Court upholding in part and invalidating in part the Patient Protection and Affordable Care Act of 2010 (colloquially referred to by some as "Obamacare").

National Federation of Independent Business v. Sebelius [The Health Care Cases]

132 S. Ct. 2566 (2012)

■ CHIEF JUSTICE ROBERTS announced the judgment of the Court and delivered the opinion of the Court with respect to Parts I, II, and III–C, an opinion with respect to Part IV, in which JUSTICE BREYER and JUSTICE KAGAN join, and an opinion with respect to Parts III–A, III–B, and III–D.

Today we resolve constitutional challenges to two provisions of the Patient Protection and Affordable Care Act of 2010: the individual mandate, which requires individuals to purchase a health insurance policy providing a minimum level of coverage; and the Medicaid expansion, which gives funds to the States on the condition that they provide specified health care to all citizens whose income falls below a certain threshold. . . .

In our federal system, the National Government possesses only limited powers; the States and the people retain the remainder. Nearly two centuries ago, Chief Justice Marshall observed that "the question respecting the extent of the powers actually granted" to the Federal Government "is perpetually arising, and will probably continue to arise, as long as our system shall exist." *McCulloch v. Maryland,* 4 Wheat. 316, 405 (1819). In this case we must again determine whether the Constitution grants Congress powers it now asserts, but which many States and individuals believe it does not possess. Resolving this controversy requires us to examine both the limits of the Government's power, and our own limited role in policing those boundaries.

The Federal Government "is acknowledged by all to be one of enumerated powers." *Ibid.* That is, rather than granting general authority to perform all the conceivable functions of government, the Constitution lists, or enumerates, the Federal Government's powers. . . . The enumeration of powers is also a limitation of powers, because "[t]he enumeration presupposes something not enumerated." [*Gibbons v. Ogden* (1824)]. The Constitution's express conferral of some powers makes clear that it does not grant others. . . .

Today, the restrictions on government power foremost in many Americans' minds are likely to be affirmative prohibitions, such as contained in the Bill of Rights. These affirmative prohibitions come into play, however, only where the Government possesses authority to act in the first place. If no enumerated power authorizes Congress to pass a certain law, that law may not be enacted, even if it would not violate any of the express prohibitions in the Bill of Rights or elsewhere in the Constitution.

Indeed, the Constitution did not initially include a Bill of Rights at least partly because the Framers felt the enumeration of powers sufficed to restrain the Government. As Alexander Hamilton put it, "the Constitution is itself, in every rational sense, and to every useful purpose, A Bill of Rights." The Federalist No. 84, p. 515 (C. Rossiter ed. 1961). And when the Bill of Rights was ratified, it made express what the enumeration of powers necessarily implied: "The powers not delegated to the United States by the Constitution . . . are reserved to the States respectively, or to the people." U.S. Const., Amdt. 10. The Federal Government has expanded dramatically over the past two centuries, but it still must show that a constitutional grant of power authorizes each of its actions.

The same does not apply to the States, because the Constitution is not the source of their power. The Constitution may restrict state governments—as it does, for example, by forbidding them to deny any person the equal protection of the laws. But where such prohibitions do not apply, state governments do not need constitutional authorization to act. The States thus can and do perform many of the vital functions of modern government—punishing street crime, running public schools, and zoning property for development, to name but a few—even though the Constitution's text does not authorize any government to do so. Our cases refer to this general power of governing, possessed by the States but not by the Federal Government, as the "police power." . . . "State sovereignty is not just an end in itself: Rather, federalism secures to citizens the liberties that derive from the diffusion of sovereign power." *New York v. United States,* 505 U.S. 144, 181 (1992). Because the police power is controlled by 50 different States instead of one national sovereign, the facets of governing that touch on citizens' daily lives are normally administered by smaller governments closer to the governed. The Framers thus ensured that powers which "in the ordinary course of affairs, concern the lives, liberties, and properties of the people" were held by governments more local and more accountable than a distant federal bureaucracy. The Federalist No. 45, at 293 (J. Madison). The independent power of the States also serves as a check on the power of the Federal Government: "By denying any one government complete jurisdiction over all the concerns of public life, federalism protects the liberty of the individual from arbitrary power." *Bond v. United States,* 131 S.Ct. 2355, 2364 (2011).

This case concerns two powers that the Constitution does grant the Federal Government, but which must be read carefully to avoid creating a general federal authority akin to the police power. The Constitution authorizes Congress to "regulate Commerce with foreign Nations, and among the several States, and with the Indian Tribes." Art. I, § 8, cl. 3. Our precedents read that to mean that Congress may regulate "the channels of interstate commerce," "persons or things in interstate commerce," and "those activities that substantially affect interstate commerce." *Morrison,* at 609. . . .

Congress may also "lay and collect Taxes, Duties, Imposts and Excises, to pay the Debts and provide for the common Defence and general Welfare of the United States." U.S. Const., Art. I, § 8, cl. 1. Put simply, Congress may tax and spend. This grant gives the Federal Government considerable influence even in areas where it cannot directly regulate. The Federal Government may enact a tax on an activity that it cannot authorize, forbid, or otherwise control. See, *e.g., License Tax Cases,* 5 Wall. 462, 471 (1867). And in exercising its spending power, Congress may offer funds to the States, and may condition those offers on compliance with specified conditions. These offers may well induce the States to adopt policies that the Federal Government itself could not impose. See, *e.g., South Dakota v. Dole,* 483 U.S. 203, 205–206 (1987) (conditioning federal highway funds on States raising their drinking age to 21).

The reach of the Federal Government's enumerated powers is broader still because the Constitution authorizes Congress to "make all Laws which shall be necessary and proper for carrying into Execution the foregoing Powers." Art. I, § 8, cl. 18. We have long read this provision to give Congress great latitude in exercising its powers: "Let the end be legitimate, let it be within the scope of the constitution, and all means which are appropriate, which are plainly adapted to that end, which are not prohibited, but consist with the letter and spirit of the constitution, are constitutional." *McCulloch,* 4 Wheat., at 421.

Our permissive reading of these powers is explained in part by a general reticence to invalidate the acts of the Nation's elected leaders. . . . Members of this Court are vested with the authority to interpret the law; we possess neither the expertise nor the prerogative to make policy judgments. Those decisions are entrusted to our Nation's elected leaders, who can be thrown out of office if the people disagree with them. It is not our job to protect the people from the consequences of their political choices.

Our deference in matters of policy cannot, however, become abdication in matters of law. "The powers of the legislature are defined and limited; and that those limits may not be mistaken, or forgotten, the constitution is written." *Marbury v. Madison,* 1 Cranch 137, 176 (1803). Our respect for Congress's policy judgments thus can never extend so far as to disavow restraints on federal power that the Constitution carefully constructed. . . . And there can be no question that it is the responsibility of this Court to enforce the limits on federal power by striking down acts of Congress that transgress those limits. . . .

I

. . . The individual mandate requires most Americans to maintain "minimum essential" health insurance coverage. . . . Beginning in 2014, those who do not comply with the mandate must make a "[s]hared responsibility payment" to the Federal Government. That payment, which the Act describes as a "penalty," is calculated as a percentage of household income, subject to a floor based on a specified dollar amount and a ceiling based on the average annual premium the individual would have to pay for qualifying private health insurance. . . . The Act provides that the penalty will be paid to the Internal Revenue Service with an individual's taxes. . . .

II

[The Court first found that the individual mandate, because not denominated a "tax" in the statute, was not subject to the restrictions of the tax Anti–Injunction Act, which forbids suits for injunctive relief against tax statutes. The challenge to the constitutionality of the individual mandate was thus not barred. The Court stated that this statutory holding did not control the constitutional question of whether the mandate was a valid exer-

cise of Congress's taxing power. That issue is considered in part IV of Chief Justice Roberts's opinion.—Editors]

III–A

The Government's first argument is that the individual mandate is a valid exercise of Congress's power under the Commerce Clause and the Necessary and Proper Clause. According to the Government, the health care market is characterized by a significant cost-shifting problem. Everyone will eventually need health care at a time and to an extent they cannot predict, but if they do not have insurance, they often will not be able to pay for it. Because state and federal laws nonetheless require hospitals to provide a certain degree of care to individuals without regard to their ability to pay . . . hospitals end up receiving compensation for only a portion of the services they provide. To recoup the losses, hospitals pass on the cost to insurers through higher rates, and insurers, in turn, pass on the cost to policy holders in the form of higher premiums. . . .

In the Affordable Care Act, Congress addressed the problem of those who cannot obtain insurance coverage because of preexisting conditions or other health issues. It did so through the Act's "guaranteed-issue" and "community-rating" provisions. These provisions together prohibit insurance companies from denying coverage to those with such conditions or charging unhealthy individuals higher premiums than healthy individuals.

The guaranteed-issue and community-rating reforms do not, however, address the issue of healthy individuals who choose not to purchase insurance to cover potential health care needs. In fact, the reforms sharply exacerbate that problem, by providing an incentive for individuals to delay purchasing health insurance until they become sick, relying on the promise of guaranteed and affordable coverage. The reforms also threaten to impose massive new costs on insurers, who are required to accept unhealthy individuals but prohibited from charging them rates necessary to pay for their coverage. This will lead insurers to significantly increase premiums on everyone.

The individual mandate was Congress's solution to these problems. By requiring that individuals purchase health insurance, the mandate prevents cost-shifting by those who would otherwise go without it. In addition, the mandate forces into the insurance risk pool more healthy individuals, whose premiums on average will be higher than their health care expenses. This allows insurers to subsidize the costs of covering the unhealthy individuals the reforms require them to accept. The Government claims that Congress has power under the Commerce and Necessary and Proper Clauses to enact this solution.

1

The Government contends that the individual mandate is within Congress's power because the failure to purchase insurance "has a substantial and deleterious effect on interstate commerce" by creating the cost-shifting problem. The path of our Commerce Clause decisions has not always run smooth, see *United States v. Lopez,* 514 U.S. 549, 552–559 (1995), but it is now well established that Congress has broad authority under the Clause. We have recognized, for example, that "[t]he power of Congress over interstate commerce is not confined to the regulation of commerce among the states," but extends to activities that "have a substantial effect on interstate commerce." *United States v. Darby,* 312 U.S. 100, 118–119 (1941). Congress's power, moreover, is not limited to regulation of an activity that by itself substantially affects interstate commerce, but also extends to activities that do so only when aggregated with similar activities of others. See *Wickard,* 317 U.S., at 127–128.

Given its expansive scope, it is no surprise that Congress has employed the commerce power in a wide variety of ways to address the pressing needs of the time. But Congress has never attempted to rely on that power to compel individuals not engaged in commerce to purchase an unwanted product. . . .

The Constitution grants Congress the power to "*regulate* Commerce." Art. I, § 8, cl. 3 (emphasis added). The power to *regulate* commerce presupposes the existence of commercial activity to be regulated. If the power to "regulate" something included the power to create it, many of the provisions in the Constitution would be superfluous. For example, the Constitution gives Congress the power to "coin Money," in addition to the power to "regulate the Value thereof." *Id.,* cl. 5. And it gives Congress the power to "raise and support Armies" and to "provide and maintain a Navy," in addition to the power to "make Rules for the Government and Regulation of the land and naval Forces." *Id.,* cls. 12–14. If the power to regulate the armed forces or the value of money included the power to bring the subject of the regulation into existence, the specific grant of such powers would have been unnecessary. The language of the Constitution reflects the natural understanding that the power to regulate assumes there is already something to be regulated. See *Gibbons,* 9 Wheat., at 188 ("[T]he enlightened patriots who framed our constitution, and the people who adopted it, must be understood to have employed words in their natural sense, and to have intended what they have said").

Our precedent also reflects this understanding. As expansive as our cases construing the scope of the commerce power have been, they all have one thing in common: They uniformly describe the power as reaching "activity." It is nearly impossible to avoid the word when quoting them. See, *e.g., Lopez,* at 560 ("Where economic activity substantially affects interstate commerce, legislation regulating that activity will be sustained"); *Perez,* 402 U.S., at 154 ("Where the *class of activities* is regulated and that *class* is within the reach of federal power, the courts have no power to excise, as trivial, individual instances of the class" (emphasis in original)); *Wickard,* at 125 ("[E]ven if appellee's activity be local and though it may not be regarded as commerce, it may still, whatever its nature, be reached by Congress if it exerts a substantial economic effect on interstate commerce"); *NLRB v. Jones & Laughlin Steel Corp.,* 301 U.S. 1, 37 (1937) ("Although activities may be intrastate in character when separately considered, if they have such a close and substantial relation to interstate commerce that their control is essential or appropriate to protect that commerce from burdens and obstructions, Congress cannot be denied the power to exercise that control"). . . .

The individual mandate, however, does not regulate existing commercial activity. It instead compels individuals to *become* active in commerce by purchasing a product, on the ground that their failure to do so affects interstate commerce. Construing the Commerce Clause to permit Congress to regulate individuals precisely *because* they are doing nothing would open a new and potentially vast domain to congressional authority. Every day individuals do not do an infinite number of things. In some cases they decide not to do something; in others they simply fail to do it. Allowing Congress to justify federal regulation by pointing to the effect of inaction on commerce would bring countless decisions an individual could *potentially* make within the scope of federal regulation, and—under the Government's theory—empower Congress to make those decisions for him.

Applying the Government's logic to the familiar case of *Wickard v. Filburn* shows how far that logic would carry us from the notion of a government of limited powers. In *Wickard,* the Court famously upheld a federal penalty imposed on a farmer for growing wheat for consumption on his own farm. 317 U.S., at 114–115. That amount of wheat caused the farmer to exceed his quota under a program designed to support the price of wheat by limiting supply. The Court rejected the farmer's argument that growing wheat for home consumption was beyond the reach of the commerce power. It did so on the ground that the farmer's decision to grow wheat for his own use allowed him to avoid purchasing wheat in the market. That decision, when considered in the aggregate along with similar decisions of others, would have had a substantial effect on the interstate market for wheat. *Id.,* at 127–129.

Wickard has long been regarded as "perhaps the most far reaching example of Commerce Clause authority over intrastate activity," *Lopez,* 514 U.S., at 560, but the Government's theory in this case would go much further. Under *Wickard* it is within Congress's power to regulate the market for wheat by supporting its price. But price can be supported by increasing demand as well as by decreasing supply. The aggregated decisions of some consumers not to purchase wheat have a substantial effect on the price of wheat, just as decisions not to purchase health insurance have on the price of insurance. Congress can therefore command that those not buying wheat do so, just as it argues here that it may command that those not buying health insurance do so. The farmer in *Wickard* was at least actively engaged in the production of wheat, and the Government could regulate that activity because of its effect on commerce. The Government's theory here would effectively override that limitation, by establishing that individuals may be regulated under the Commerce Clause whenever enough of them are not doing something the Government would have them do.

Indeed, the Government's logic would justify a mandatory purchase to solve almost any problem. To consider a different example in the health care market, many Americans do not eat a balanced diet. That group makes up a larger percentage of the total population than those without health insurance. The failure of that group to have a healthy diet increases health care costs, to a greater extent than the failure of the uninsured to purchase insurance. Those increased costs are borne in part by other Americans who must pay more, just as the uninsured shift costs to the insured. . . . Under the Government's theory, Congress could address the diet problem by ordering everyone to buy vegetables.

People, for reasons of their own, often fail to do things that would be good for them or good for society. Those failures—joined with the similar failures of others—can readily have a substantial effect on interstate commerce. Under the Government's logic, that authorizes Congress to use its commerce power to compel citizens to act as the Government would have them act.

That is not the country the Framers of our Constitution envisioned. James Madison explained that the Commerce Clause was "an addition which few oppose and from which no apprehensions are entertained." The Federalist No. 45, at 293. . . . Congress already enjoys vast power to regulate much of what we do, fundamentally changing the relation between the citizen and the Federal Government.

To an economist, perhaps, there is no difference between activity and inactivity; both have measurable economic effects on commerce. But the distinction between doing something and doing nothing would not have been lost on the Framers. . . . As we have explained, "the framers of the Constitution were not mere visionaries, toying with speculations or theories, but practical men, dealing with the facts of political life as they understood them, putting into form the government they were creating, and prescribing in language clear and intelligible the powers that government was to take." *South Carolina v. United States,* 199 U.S. 437, 449 (1905). The Framers gave Congress the power to *regulate* commerce, not to *compel* it, and for over 200 years both our decisions and Congress's actions have reflected this understanding. There is no reason to depart from that understanding now.

The Government sees things differently. It argues that because sickness and injury are unpredictable but unavoidable, "the uninsured as a class are active in the market for health care, which they regularly seek and obtain." The individual mandate "merely regulates how individuals finance and pay for that active participation—requiring that they do so through insurance, rather than through attempted self-insurance with the back-stop of shifting costs to others." *Ibid.*

The Government repeats the phrase "active in the market for health care" throughout its brief, but that concept has no constitutional significance. An individual who bought a car two years ago and may buy another in the future is not "active in the car market" in any pertinent sense. The phrase "active in the market" cannot obscure the fact that most of those regulated by the individual mandate are not currently engaged in any commercial activity involving health care, and that fact is fatal to the Government's effort to "regulate the uninsured as a class." *Id.,* at 42. Our precedents recognize Congress's power to regulate "class[es] of *activities*," not classes of *individuals,* apart from any activity in which they are engaged.

The individual mandate's regulation of the uninsured as a class is, in fact, particularly divorced from any link to existing commercial activity. The mandate primarily affects healthy, often young adults who are less likely to need significant health care and have other priorities for spending their money. It is precisely because these individuals, as an actuarial class, incur relatively low health care costs that the mandate helps counter the effect of forcing insurance companies to cover others who impose greater costs than their premiums are allowed to reflect. . . . If the individual mandate is targeted at a class, it is a class whose commercial inactivity rather than activity is its defining feature.

The Government, however, claims that this does not matter. The Government regards it as sufficient to trigger Congress's authority that almost all those who are uninsured will, at some unknown point in the future, engage in a health care transaction. Asserting that "[t]here is no temporal limitation in the Commerce Clause," the Government argues that because "[e]veryone subject to this regulation is in or will be in the health care market," they can be "regulated in advance."

The proposition that Congress may dictate the conduct of an individual today because of prophesied future activity finds no support in our precedent. We have said that Congress can anticipate the *effects* on commerce of an economic activity. . . . Each one of our cases, including those cited by Justice Ginsburg, involved preexisting economic activity. See, *e.g., Wickard,* 317 U.S., at 127–129 (producing wheat); *Raich,* at 25 (growing marijuana).

Everyone will likely participate in the markets for food, clothing, transportation, shelter, or energy; that does not authorize Congress to direct them to purchase particular products in those or other markets today. The Commerce Clause is not a general license to regulate an individual from cradle to grave, simply because he will predictably engage in particular transactions. Any police power to regulate individuals as such, as opposed to their activities, remains vested in the States.

The Government argues that the individual mandate can be sustained as a sort of exception to this rule, because health insurance is a unique product. According to the Government, upholding the individual mandate would not justify mandatory purchases of items such as cars or broccoli because, as the Government puts it, "[h]ealth insurance is not purchased for its own sake like a car or broccoli; it is a means of financing health-care consumption and covering universal risks." But cars and broccoli are no more purchased for their "own sake" than health insurance. They are purchased to cover the need for transportation and food.

The Government says that health insurance and health care financing are "inherently integrated." But that does not mean the compelled purchase of the first is properly regarded as a regulation of the second. No matter how "inherently integrated" health insurance and health care consumption may be, they are not the same thing: They involve different transactions, entered into at different times, with different providers. And for most of those targeted by the mandate, significant health care needs will be years, or even decades, away. The proximity and degree of connection between the mandate and the subsequent commercial activity is too lacking to justify an exception of the sort urged by the Government. The individual mandate forces individuals into commerce precisely because they elected to refrain from commercial activity. Such a law cannot be sustained under a clause authorizing Congress to "regulate Commerce."

2

The Government next contends that Congress has the power under the Necessary and Proper Clause to enact the individual mandate because the mandate is an "integral part of a comprehensive scheme of economic regulation"—the guaranteed-issue and community-rating insurance reforms. Under this argument, it is not necessary to consider the effect that an individual's inactivity may have on interstate commerce; it is enough that Congress regulate commercial activity in a way that requires regulation of inactivity to be effective.

The power to "make all Laws which shall be necessary and proper for carrying into Execution" the powers enumerated in the Constitution, Art. I, § 8, cl. 18, vests Congress with authority to enact provisions "incidental to the [enumerated] power, and conducive to its beneficial exercise," *McCulloch,* 4 Wheat., at 418. Although the Clause gives Congress authority to "legislate on that vast mass of incidental powers which must be involved in the constitution," it does not license the exercise of any "great substantive and independent power[s]" beyond those specifically enumerated. *Id.,* at 411, 421. Instead, the Clause is " 'merely a declaration, for the removal of all uncertainty, that the means of carrying into execution those [powers] otherwise granted are included in the grant.' " *Kinsella v. United States ex rel. Singleton,* 361 U.S. 234, 247 (1960) (quoting VI Writings of James Madison 383 (G. Hunt ed. 1906)).

As our jurisprudence under the Necessary and Proper Clause has developed, we have been very deferential to Congress's determination that a regulation is "necessary." We have thus upheld laws that are " 'convenient, or useful' or 'conducive' to the authority's 'beneficial exercise.' " *Comstock,* 130 S.Ct., at 1965 (quoting *McCulloch,* at 413, 418). But we have also carried out our responsibility to declare unconstitutional those laws that undermine the structure of government established by the Constitution. Such laws, which are not "consist[ent] with the letter and spirit of the constitution," *McCulloch,* at 421, are not *"proper* [means] for carrying into Execution" Congress's enumerated powers. . . .

[T]he individual mandate cannot be sustained under the Necessary and Proper Clause as an essential component of the insurance reforms. Each of our prior cases upholding laws under that Clause involved exercises of authority derivative of, and in service to, a granted power. For example, we have upheld provisions permitting continued confinement of those *already in federal custody* when they could not be safely released; criminalizing bribes involving organizations *receiving federal funds*; and tolling state statutes of limitations while cases are *pending in federal court.* The individual mandate, by contrast, vests Congress with the extraordinary ability to create the necessary predicate to the exercise of an enumerated power.

This is in no way an authority that is "narrow in scope," [*Comstock*], or "incidental" to the exercise of the commerce power, [*McCulloch*]. Rather, such a conception of the Necessary and Proper Clause would work a substantial expansion of federal authority. No longer would Congress be limited to regulating under the Commerce Clause those who by some preexisting activity bring themselves within the sphere of federal regulation. Instead, Congress could reach beyond the natural limit of its authority and draw within its regulatory scope those who otherwise would be outside of it. Even if the individual mandate is "necessary" to the Act's insurance reforms, such an expansion of federal power is not a "proper" means for making those reforms effective.

The Government relies primarily on our decision in *Gonzales v. Raich.* In *Raich,* we considered "comprehensive legislation to regulate the interstate market" in marijuana. 545 U.S., at 22. Certain individuals sought an exemption from that regulation on the ground that they engaged in only intrastate possession and consumption. We denied any exemption, on the ground that marijuana is a fungible commodity, so that any marijuana could be readily diverted into the interstate market. Congress's attempt to regulate the interstate market for marijuana would therefore have been substantially undercut if it could not also regulate intrastate possession and consumption. . . . *Raich* thus did not involve the exercise of any "great substantive and independent power," [*McCulloch*] of the sort at issue here. Instead, it concerned only the constitutionality of "individual *applications* of a concededly valid statutory scheme." *Raich,* at 23 (emphasis added).

Just as the individual mandate cannot be sustained as a law regulating the substantial effects of the failure to purchase health insurance, neither can it be upheld as a "necessary and proper" component of the insurance reforms. The commerce power thus does not authorize the mandate. Accord, *post* (joint opinion of Scalia, Kennedy, Thomas, and Alito, JJ., dissenting).

B

That is not the end of the matter. Because the Commerce Clause does not support the individual mandate, it is necessary to turn to the Government's second argument: that the mandate may be upheld as within Congress's enumerated power to "lay and collect Taxes." Art. I, § 8, cl. 1.

The Government's tax power argument asks us to view the statute differently than we did in considering its commerce power theory. In making its Commerce Clause argument, the Government defended the mandate as a regulation requiring individuals to purchase health insurance. The Government does not claim that the taxing power allows Congress to issue such a command. Instead, the Government asks us to read the mandate not as ordering individuals to buy insurance, but rather as imposing a tax on those who do not buy that product.

The text of a statute can sometimes have more than one possible meaning. . . . [I]t is well established that if a statute has two possible meanings, one of which violates the Constitution, courts should adopt the meaning that does not do so. Justice Story said that 180 years ago: "No court ought, unless the terms of an act rendered it unavoidable, to give a construction to it which should involve a violation, however unintentional, of the constitution." *Parsons v. Bedford,* 3 Pet. 433, 448–449 (1830). Justice Holmes made the same point a century later: "[T]he rule is settled that as between two possible interpretations of a statute, by one of which it would be unconstitutional and by the other valid, our plain duty is to adopt that which will save the Act." *Blodgett v. Holden,* 275 U.S. 142, 148 (1927) (concurring opinion).

The most straightforward reading of the mandate is that it commands individuals to purchase insurance. After all, it states that individuals "shall" maintain health insurance. Congress thought it could enact such a command under the Commerce Clause, and the Government primarily defended the law on that basis. But, for the reasons explained above, the Commerce Clause does not give Congress that power. Under our precedent, it is therefore necessary to ask whether the Government's alternative reading of the statute—that it only imposes a tax on those without insurance— is a reasonable one.

Under the mandate, if an individual does not maintain health insurance, the only consequence is that he must make an additional payment to the IRS when he pays his taxes. . . . [I]f the mandate is in effect just a tax hike on certain taxpayers who do not have health insurance, it may be within Congress's constitutional power to tax.

The question is not whether that is the most natural interpretation of the mandate, but only whether it is a "fairly possible" one. *Crowell v. Benson,* 285 U.S. 22, 62 (1932). As we have explained, "every reasonable construction must be resorted to, in order to save a statute from unconstitutionality." *Hooper v. California,* 155 U.S. 648, 657 (1895). The Government asks us to interpret the mandate as imposing a tax, if it would otherwise violate the Constitution. Granting the Act the full measure of deference owed to federal statutes, it can be so read, for the reasons set forth below.

C

The exaction the Affordable Care Act imposes on those without health insurance looks like a tax in many respects. The "[s]hared responsibility payment," as the statute entitles it, is paid into the Treasury by "taxpayer[s]" when they file their tax returns. It does not apply to individuals who do not pay federal income taxes because their household income is less than the filing threshold in the Internal Revenue Code. For taxpayers who do owe the payment, its amount is determined by such familiar factors as taxable income, number of dependents, and joint filing status. The requirement to pay is found in the Internal Revenue Code and enforced by the IRS, which—as we previously explained—must assess and collect it "in the same manner as taxes." This process yields the essential feature of any tax: it produces at least some revenue for the Government. *United States v. Kahriger,* 345 U.S. 22, 28, n. 4 (1953). Indeed, the payment is expected to raise about $4 billion per year by 2017. . . .

It is of course true that the Act describes the payment as a "penalty," not a "tax." But while that label is fatal to the application of the Anti–Injunction Act, it does not determine whether the payment may be viewed as an exercise of Congress's taxing power. It is up to Congress whether to apply the Anti–Injunction Act to any particular statute, so it makes sense to be guided by Congress's choice of label on that question. That choice does not, however, control whether an exaction is within Congress's constitutional power to tax. . . .

We have . . . held that exactions not labeled taxes nonetheless were authorized by Congress's power to tax. In the *License Tax Cases,* for example, we held that federal licenses to sell liquor and lottery tickets—for which the licensee had to pay a fee—could be sustained as exercises of the taxing power. 5 Wall., at 471. And in *New York v. United States* we upheld as a tax a "surcharge" on out-of-state nuclear waste shipments, a portion of which was paid to the Federal Treasury. 505 U.S., at 171. We thus ask whether the shared responsibility payment falls within Congress's taxing power, "[d]isregarding the designation of the exaction, and viewing its substance and application." *United States v. Constantine,* 296 U.S. 287, 294 (1935); cf. *Quill Corp. v. North Dakota,* 504 U.S. 298, 310 (1992) ("[M]agic words or labels" should not "disable an otherwise constitutional levy").

Our cases confirm this functional approach. For example, in *Drexel Furniture,* we focused on three practical characteristics of the so-called tax on employing child laborers that convinced us the "tax" was actually a penalty. First, the tax imposed an exceedingly heavy burden—10 percent of a company's net income—on those who employed children, no matter how small their infraction. Second, it imposed that exaction only on those who knowingly employed underage laborers. Such scienter requirements are typical of punitive statutes, because Congress often wishes to punish only those who intentionally break the law. Third, this "tax" was enforced in part by the Department of Labor, an agency responsible for punishing violations of labor laws, not collecting revenue. . . .

The same analysis here suggests that the shared responsibility payment may for constitutional purposes be considered a tax, not a penalty: First, for most Americans the amount due will be far less than the price of insurance, and, by statute, it can never be more. It may often be a reasonable financial decision to make the payment rather than purchase insurance, unlike the "prohibitory" financial punishment in *Drexel Furniture.* 259 U.S., at 37. Second, the individual mandate contains no scienter requirement. Third, the payment is collected solely by the IRS through the normal means of taxation—except that the Service is *not* allowed to use those means most suggestive of a punitive sanction, such as criminal prosecution. The reasons the Court in *Drexel Furniture* held that what was called a "tax" there was a penalty support the conclusion that what is called a "penalty" here may be viewed as a tax.

None of this is to say that the payment is not intended to affect individual conduct. Although the payment will raise considerable revenue, it is plainly designed to expand health insurance coverage. But taxes that seek to influence conduct are nothing new. Some of our earliest federal taxes sought to deter the purchase of imported manufactured goods in order to foster the growth of domestic industry. . . . Today, federal and state taxes can compose more than half the retail price of cigarettes, not just to raise more money, but to encourage people to quit smoking. And we have upheld such obviously regulatory measures as taxes on selling marijuana and sawed-off shotguns. . . .

In distinguishing penalties from taxes, this Court has explained that "if the concept of penalty means anything, it means punishment for an unlawful act or omission." *United States v. Reorganized CF & I Fabricators of Utah, Inc.,* 518 U.S. 213, 224 (1996). . . . While the individual mandate clearly aims to induce the purchase of health insurance, it need not be read to declare that failing to do so is unlawful. Neither the Act nor any other law attaches negative legal consequences to not buying health insurance, beyond requiring a payment to the IRS. The Government agrees with that reading . . .

Indeed, it is estimated that four million people each year will choose to pay the IRS rather than buy insurance. . . . We would expect Congress to be troubled by that prospect if such conduct were unlawful. That Congress apparently regards such extensive failure to comply with the mandate as tolerable suggests that Congress did not think it was creating four million outlaws. It suggests instead that the shared responsibility payment merely imposes a tax citizens may lawfully choose to pay in lieu of buying health insurance.

The joint dissenters argue that we cannot uphold § 5000A as a tax because Congress did not "frame" it as such. In effect, they contend that even if the Constitution permits Congress to do exactly what we interpret this statute to do, the law must be struck down because Congress used the wrong labels. An example may help illustrate why labels should not control here. Suppose Congress enacted a statute providing that every taxpayer who owns a house without energy efficient windows must pay $50 to the IRS. The amount due is adjusted based on factors such as taxable income and joint filing status, and is paid along with the taxpayer's income tax return. Those whose income is below the filing threshold need not pay. The required payment is not called a "tax," a "penalty," or anything else. No one would doubt that this law imposed a tax, and was within Congress's power to tax. That conclusion should not change simply because Congress used the word "penalty" to describe the payment. Interpreting such a law to be a tax would hardly "[i]mpos[e] a tax through judicial legislation." Rather, it would give practical effect to the Legislature's enactment. . . .

Even if the taxing power enables Congress to impose a tax on not obtaining health insurance, any tax must still comply with other requirements in the Constitution. Plaintiffs argue that the shared responsibility payment does not do so, citing Article I, § 9, clause 4. That clause provides: "No Capitation, or other direct, Tax shall be laid, unless in Proportion to the Census or Enumeration herein before directed to be taken." This requirement means that any "direct Tax" must be apportioned so that each State pays in proportion to its population. . . .

Even when the Direct Tax Clause was written it was unclear what else, other than a capitation (also known as a "head tax" or a "poll tax"), might be a direct tax. . . . Soon after the framing, Congress passed a tax on ownership of carriages, over James Madison's objection that it was an unapportioned direct tax. *Id.,* at 597. This Court upheld the tax, in part reasoning that apportioning such a tax would make little sense, because it would have required taxing carriage owners at dramatically different rates depending on how many carriages were in their home State. See *Hylton v. United States,* 3 Dall. 171, 174 (1796) (opinion of Chase, J.). The Court was unanimous, and those Justices who wrote opinions either directly asserted or strongly suggested that only two forms of taxation were direct: capitations and land taxes. . . .

That narrow view of what a direct tax might be persisted for a century. . . . In 1895, we expanded our interpretation to include taxes on personal property and income from personal property, in the course of striking down aspects of the federal income tax. *Pollock v. Farmers' Loan & Trust Co.,* 158 U.S. 601, 618 (1895). That result was overturned by the Sixteenth Amendment, although we continued to consider taxes on personal property to be direct taxes.

A tax on going without health insurance does not fall within any recognized category of direct tax. It is not a capitation. Capitations are taxes paid by every person, "without regard to property, profession, or *any other circumstance.*" *Hylton,* at 175 (opinion of Chase, J.) (emphasis altered). The whole point of the shared responsibility payment is that it is triggered by specific circumstances—earning a certain amount of income but not obtaining health insurance. The payment is also plainly not a tax on the ownership of land or personal property. The shared responsibility payment is thus not a direct tax that must be apportioned among the several States.

There may, however, be a more fundamental objection to a tax on those who lack health insurance. Even if only a tax, the payment under § 5000A(b) remains a burden that the Federal Government imposes for an omission, not an act. If it is troubling to interpret the Commerce Clause as authorizing Congress to regulate those who abstain from commerce, perhaps it should be similarly troubling to permit Congress to impose a tax for not doing something.

Three considerations allay this concern. First, and most importantly, it is abundantly clear the Constitution does not guarantee that individuals may avoid taxation through inactivity. A capitation, after all, is a tax that everyone must pay simply for existing, and capitations are expressly contemplated by the Constitution. The Court today holds that our Constitution protects us from federal regulation under the Commerce Clause so long as we abstain from the regulated activity. But from its creation, the Constitution has made no such promise with respect to taxes. See Letter from Benjamin Franklin to M. Le Roy (Nov. 13, 1789) ("Our new Constitution is now established . . . but in this world nothing can be said to be certain, except death and taxes").

Whether the mandate can be upheld under the Commerce Clause is a question about the scope of federal authority. Its answer depends on whether Congress can exercise what all acknowledge to be the novel course of directing individuals to purchase insurance. Congress's use of the Taxing Clause to encourage buying something is, by contrast, not new. Tax incentives already promote, for example, purchasing homes and professional educations. Sustaining the mandate as a tax depends only on whether Congress *has* properly exercised its taxing power to encourage purchasing health insurance, not whether it *can*. Upholding the individual mandate under the Taxing Clause thus does not recognize any new federal power. It determines that Congress has used an existing one.

Second, Congress's ability to use its taxing power to influence conduct is not without limits. A few of our cases policed these limits aggressively, invalidating punitive exactions obviously designed to regulate behavior otherwise regarded at the time as beyond federal authority. See, *e.g., United States v. Butler*, 297 U.S. 1 (1936); *Drexel Furniture*, 259 U.S. 20. More often and more recently we have declined to closely examine the regulatory motive or effect of revenue-raising measures. See *Kahriger*, 345 U.S., at 27–31 (collecting cases). We have nonetheless maintained that " 'there comes a time in the extension of the penalizing features of the so-called tax when it loses its character as such and becomes a mere penalty with the characteristics of regulation and punishment.' " *Kurth Ranch*, 511 U.S., at 779 (quoting *Drexel Furniture*).

We have already explained that the shared responsibility payment's practical characteristics pass muster as a tax under our narrowest interpretations of the taxing power. Because the tax at hand is within even those strict limits, we need not here decide the precise point at which an exaction becomes so punitive that the taxing power does not authorize it. . . .

Third, although the breadth of Congress's power to tax is greater than its power to regulate commerce, the taxing power does not give Congress the same degree of control over individual behavior. . . . Congress's authority under the taxing power is limited to requiring an individual to pay money into the Federal Treasury, no more. If a tax is properly paid, the Government has no power to compel or punish individuals subject to it. We do not make light of the severe burden that taxation—especially taxation motivated by a regulatory purpose—can impose. But imposition of a tax nonetheless leaves an individual with a lawful choice to do or not do a certain act, so long as he is willing to pay a tax levied on that choice.

The Affordable Care Act's requirement that certain individuals pay a financial penalty for not obtaining health insurance may reasonably be characterized as a tax. Because the Constitution permits such a tax, it is not our role to forbid it, or to pass upon its wisdom or fairness. . . .

IV–A

The States also contend that the Medicaid expansion exceeds Congress's authority under the Spending Clause. They claim that Congress is coercing the States to adopt the changes it wants by threatening to withhold all of a State's Medicaid grants, unless the State accepts the new expanded funding and complies with the conditions that come with it. This, they argue, violates the basic principle that the "Federal Government may not compel the States to enact or administer a federal regulatory program." *New York*, 505 U.S., at 188. . . .

The Spending Clause grants Congress the power "to pay the Debts and provide for the . . . general Welfare of the United States." U.S. Const., Art. I, § 8, cl. 1. We have long recognized that Congress may use this power to grant federal funds to the States, and may condition such a grant upon the States' "taking certain actions that Congress could not require them to take." *College Savings Bank*, 527 U.S., at 686. Such measures "encourage a State to regulate in a particular way, [and] influenc[e] a State's policy choices." *New York,* at 166. The conditions imposed by Congress ensure that the funds are used by the States to "provide for the . . . general Welfare" in the manner Congress intended.

At the same time, our cases have recognized limits on Congress's power under the Spending Clause to secure state compliance with federal objectives. "We have repeatedly characterized . . . Spending Clause legislation as 'much in the nature of a *contract.*' " *Barnes v. Gorman,* 536 U.S. 181, 186 (2002) (quoting *Pennhurst State School and Hospital v. Halderman,* 451 U.S. 1, 17 (1981)). The legitimacy of Congress's exercise of the spending power "thus rests on whether the State voluntarily and knowingly accepts the terms of the 'contract.' " *Pennhurst,* at 17. Respecting this limitation is critical to ensuring that Spending Clause legislation does not undermine the status of the States as independent sovereigns in our federal system. . . . "[T]he Constitution has never been understood to confer upon Congress the ability to require the States to govern according to Congress' instructions." *New York,* at 162. . . .

That insight has led this Court to strike down federal legislation that commandeers a State's legislative or administrative apparatus for federal purposes. See, *e.g., Printz,* 521 U.S., at 933 (striking down federal legislation compelling state law enforcement officers to perform federally mandated background checks on handgun purchasers); *New York,* at 174–175 (invalidating provisions of an Act that would compel a State to either take title to nuclear waste or enact particular state waste regulations). It has also led us to scrutinize Spending Clause legislation to ensure that Congress is not using financial inducements to exert a "power akin to undue influence." *Steward Machine Co. v. Davis,* 301 U.S. 548, 590 (1937). Congress may use its spending power to create incentives for States to act in accordance with federal policies. But when "pressure turns into compulsion," *ibid.,* the legislation runs contrary to our system of federalism. "[T]he Constitution simply does not give Congress the authority to require the States to regulate." *New York,* 505 U.S., at 178. That is true whether Congress directly commands a State to regulate or indirectly coerces a State to adopt a federal regulatory system as its own.

. . . As our decision in *Steward Machine* confirms, Congress may attach appropriate conditions to federal taxing and spending programs to preserve its control over the use of federal funds. . . . The States, however, argue that the Medicaid expansion is far from the typical case. They object that Congress has "crossed the line distinguishing encouragement from coercion," *New York,* at 175, in the way it has structured the funding: Instead of simply refusing to grant the new funds to States that will not accept the new conditions, Congress has also threatened to withhold those States' existing Medicaid funds. The States claim that this threat serves no purpose other than to force unwilling States to sign up for the dramatic expansion in health care coverage effected by the Act.

Given the nature of the threat and the programs at issue here, we must agree. We have upheld Congress's authority to condition the receipt of funds on the States' complying with restrictions on the use of those funds, because that is the means by which Congress ensures that the funds are spent according to its view of the "general Welfare." Conditions that do not here govern the use of the funds, however, cannot be justified on that basis. When, for example, such conditions take the form of threats to terminate other significant independent grants, the conditions are properly viewed as a means of pressuring the States to accept policy changes.

In *South Dakota v. Dole,* we considered a challenge to a federal law that threatened to withhold five percent of a State's federal highway funds if the State did not raise its drinking age to 21. The Court found that the condition was "directly related to one of the main purposes for which highway funds are expended—safe interstate travel." 483 U.S., at 208. At the same time, the condition was not a restriction on how the highway funds— set aside for specific highway improvement and maintenance efforts—were to be used.

We accordingly asked whether "the financial inducement offered by Congress" was "so coercive as to pass the point at which 'pressure turns into compulsion.' " *Id.,* at 211 (quoting *Steward Machine,* at 590). By "financial inducement" the Court meant the threat of losing five percent of highway funds; no new money was offered to the States to raise their drinking ages. We found that the inducement was not impermissibly coercive, because Congress was offering only "relatively mild encouragement to the States." *Dole,* 483 U.S., at 211. We observed that "all South Dakota would lose if she adheres to her chosen course as to a suitable minimum drinking age is 5%" of her highway funds. *Ibid.* In fact, the federal funds at stake constituted less than half of one percent of South Dakota's budget at the time. . . . In consequence, "we conclude[d] that [the] encouragement to state action [was] a valid use of the spending power." *Dole,* 483 U.S., at 212. Whether to accept the drinking age change "remain[ed] the prerogative of the States not merely in theory but in fact." *Id.,* at 211–212.

In this case, the financial "inducement" Congress has chosen is much more than "relatively mild encouragement"—it is a gun to the head. . . . A State that opts out of the Affordable Care Act's expansion in health care coverage . . . stands to lose not merely "a relatively small percentage" of its existing Medicaid funding, but *all* of it. Medicaid spending accounts for over 20 percent of the average State's total budget, with federal funds covering 50 to 83 percent of those costs. . . . It is easy to see how the *Dole* Court could conclude that the threatened loss of less than half of one percent of South Dakota's budget left that State with a "prerogative" to reject Congress's desired policy, "not merely in theory but in fact." 483 U.S., at 211–212. The threatened loss of over 10 percent of a State's overall budget, in contrast, is economic dragooning that leaves the States with no real option but to acquiesce in the Medicaid expansion.

Justice Ginsburg claims that *Dole* is distinguishable because here "Congress has not threatened to withhold funds earmarked for any other program." But that begs the question: The States contend that the expansion is in reality a new program and that Congress is forcing them to accept it by threatening the funds for the existing Medicaid program. We cannot agree that existing Medicaid and the expansion dictated by the Affordable Care Act are all one program simply because "Congress styled" them as such. If the expansion is not properly viewed as a modification of the existing Medicaid program, Congress's decision to so title it is irrelevant. . . .

The Court in *Steward Machine* did not attempt to "fix the outermost line" where persuasion gives way to coercion. . . . We have no need to fix a line either. It is enough for today that wherever that line may be, this statute is surely beyond it. . . .

B

Nothing in our opinion precludes Congress from offering funds under the Affordable Care Act to expand the availability of health care, and requiring that States accepting such funds comply with the conditions on their use. What Congress is not free to do is to penalize States that choose not to participate in that new program by taking away their existing Medicaid funding. . . . In light of the Court's holding, the Secretary cannot apply § 1396c to withdraw existing Medicaid funds for failure to comply with the requirements set out in the expansion.

That fully remedies the constitutional violation we have identified. . . .

This is not to say, as the joint dissent suggests, that we are "rewriting the Medicaid Expansion." Instead, we determine, first, that § 1396c is unconstitutional when applied to withdraw existing Medicaid funds from States that decline to comply with the expansion. We then follow Congress's explicit textual instruction to leave unaffected "the remainder of the chapter, and the application of [the challenged] provision to other persons or circumstances." § 1303. When we invalidate an application of a statute because that application is unconstitutional, we are not "rewriting" the statute; we are merely enforcing the Constitution. . . .

The Affordable Care Act is constitutional in part and unconstitutional in part. The individual mandate cannot be upheld as an exercise of Congress's power under the Commerce Clause. That Clause authorizes Congress to regulate interstate commerce, not to order individuals to engage in it. In this case, however, it is reasonable to construe what Congress has done as increasing taxes on those who have a certain amount of income, but choose to go without health insurance. Such legislation is within Congress's power to tax.

As for the Medicaid expansion, that portion of the Affordable Care Act violates the Constitution by threatening existing Medicaid funding. Congress has no authority to order the States to regulate according to its instructions. Congress may offer the States grants and require the States to comply with accompanying conditions, but the States must have a genuine choice whether to accept the offer. The States are given no such choice in this case: They must either accept a basic change in the nature of Medicaid, or risk losing all Medicaid funding. The remedy for that constitutional violation is to preclude the Federal Government from imposing such a sanction. That remedy does not require striking down other portions of the Affordable Care Act.

The Framers created a Federal Government of limited powers, and assigned to this Court the duty of enforcing those limits. The Court does so today. But the Court does not express any opinion on the wisdom of the Affordable Care Act. Under the Constitution, that judgment is reserved to the people. . . .

■ JUSTICE GINSBURG, with whom JUSTICE SOTOMAYOR joins, and with whom JUSTICE BREYER and JUSTICE KAGAN join as to Parts I, II, III, and IV, concurring in part, concurring in the judgment in part, and dissenting in part.

I agree with The Chief Justice that the Anti–Injunction Act does not bar the Court's consideration of this case, and that the minimum coverage provision is a proper exercise of Congress' taxing power. I therefore join Parts I, II, and III–C of The Chief Justice's opinion. Unlike The Chief Justice, however, I would hold, alternatively, that the Commerce Clause authorizes Congress to enact the minimum coverage provision. I would also hold that the Spending Clause permits the Medicaid expansion exactly as Congress enacted it.

I

The provision of health care is today a concern of national dimension, just as the provision of old-age and survivors' benefits was in the 1930's. In the Social Security Act, Congress installed a federal system to provide monthly benefits to retired wage earners and, eventually, to their survivors. Beyond question, Congress could have adopted a similar scheme for health care. Congress chose, instead, to preserve a central role for private insurers and state governments. According to The Chief Justice, the Commerce Clause does not permit that preservation. This rigid reading of the Clause makes scant sense and is stunningly retrogressive. . . .

States cannot resolve the problem of the uninsured on their own. Like Social Security benefits, a universal health-care system, if adopted by an individual State, would be "bait to the needy and dependent elsewhere, encouraging them to migrate and seek a haven of repose." *Helvering v. Davis,* 301 U.S. 619, 644 (1937). . . . States that undertake health-care reforms on their own thus risk "placing themselves in a position of economic disadvantage as compared with neighbors or competitors." *Davis,* 301 U.S., at 644. . . . Facing that risk, individual States are unlikely to take the initiative in addressing the problem of the uninsured, even though solving that problem is in all States' best interests. Congress' intervention was needed to overcome this collective-action impasse.

Aware that a national solution was required, Congress could have taken over the health-insurance market by establishing a tax-and-spend federal program like Social Security. Such a program, commonly referred to as a single-payer system (where the sole payer is the Federal Government), would have left little, if any, room for private enterprise or the States. Instead of going this route, Congress enacted the ACA, a solution that retains a robust role for private insurers and state governments. To make its chosen approach work, however, Congress had to use some new tools, including a requirement that most individuals obtain private health insurance coverage. . . .

A central aim of the ACA is to reduce the number of uninsured U.S. residents. . . . To ensure that individuals with medical histories have access to affordable insurance, Congress devised a three-part solution. First, Congress imposed a "guaranteed issue" requirement, which bars insurers from denying coverage to any person on account of that person's medical condition or history. . . . Second, Congress required insurers to use "community rating" to price their insurance policies. . . . Community rating, in effect, bars insurance companies from charging higher premiums to those with preexisting conditions. But these two provisions, Congress comprehended, could not work effectively unless individuals were given a powerful incentive to obtain insurance. . . .

When insurance companies are required to insure the sick at affordable prices, individuals can wait until they become ill to buy insurance. Pretty soon, those in need of immediate medical care—*i.e.,* those who cost insurers the most—become the insurance companies' main customers. This "adverse selection" problem leaves insurers with two choices: They can either raise premiums dramatically to cover their ever-increasing costs or they can exit the market. . . .

In sum, Congress passed the minimum coverage provision as a key component of the ACA to address an economic and social problem that has plagued the Nation for decades: the large number of U.S. residents who are unable or unwilling to obtain health insurance. Whatever one thinks of the policy decision Congress made, it was Congress' prerogative to make it. Reviewed with appropriate deference, the minimum coverage provision, allied to the guaranteed-issue and community-rating prescriptions, should survive measurement under the Commerce and Necessary and Proper Clauses.

II–B

Consistent with the Framers' intent, we have repeatedly emphasized that Congress' authority under the Commerce Clause is dependent upon "practical" considerations, including "actual experience." *Jones & Laughlin Steel Corp.,* 301 U.S., at 41–42; see *Wickard v. Filburn,* 317 U.S. 111, 122 (1942). . . . We afford Congress the leeway "to undertake to solve national problems directly and realistically." *American Power & Light Co. v. SEC,* 329 U.S. 90, 103 (1946).

Until today, this Court's pragmatic approach to judging whether Congress validly exercised its commerce power was guided by two familiar principles. First, Congress has the power to regulate economic activities "that substantially affect interstate commerce." *Gonzales v. Raich,* 545 U.S. 1, 17 (2005). . . . Second, we owe a large measure of respect to Congress when it frames and enacts economic and social legislation. See *Raich,* 545 U.S., at 17. . . .

C

Straightforward application of these principles would require the Court to hold that the minimum coverage provision is proper Commerce Clause legislation. Beyond dispute, Congress had a rational basis for concluding that the uninsured, as a class, substantially affect interstate commerce. Those without insurance consume billions of dollars of health-care products and services each year. Those goods are produced, sold, and delivered largely by national and regional companies who routinely transact business across state lines. The uninsured also cross state lines to receive care. Some have medical emergencies while away from home. Others, when sick, go to a neighboring State that provides better care for those who have not prepaid for care.

Not only do those without insurance consume a large amount of health care each year; critically, as earlier explained, their inability to pay for a significant portion of that consumption drives up market prices, foists costs on other consumers, and reduces market efficiency and stability. Given these far-reaching effects on interstate commerce, the decision to forgo insurance is hardly inconsequential or equivalent to "doing nothing"; it is, instead, an economic decision Congress has the authority to address under the Commerce Clause. . . .

D

Rather than evaluating the constitutionality of the minimum coverage provision in the manner established by our precedents, The Chief Justice relies on a newly minted constitutional doctrine. The commerce power does not, The Chief Justice announces, permit Congress to "compe[l] individuals to become active in commerce by purchasing a product."

1

The Chief Justice's novel constraint on Congress' commerce power gains no force from our precedent and for that reason alone warrants disapprobation. But even assuming, for the moment, that Congress lacks authority under the Commerce Clause to "compel individuals not engaged in commerce to purchase an unwanted product," such a limitation would be inapplicable here. Everyone will, at some point, consume health-care products and services. Thus, if The Chief Justice is correct that an insurance-purchase requirement can be applied only to those who "actively" consume health care, the minimum coverage provision fits the bill.

The Chief Justice does not dispute that all U.S. residents participate in the market for health services over the course of their lives. . . . But, The Chief Justice insists, the uninsured cannot be considered active in the market for health care, because "[t]he proximity and degree of connection between the [uninsured today] and [their] subsequent commercial activity is too lacking." . . .

This argument has multiple flaws. First, more than 60% of those without insurance visit a hospital or doctor's office each year. . . . Nearly 90% will within five years. An uninsured's consumption of health care is thus quite proximate: It is virtually certain to occur in the next five years and more likely than not to occur this year. . . .

Second, it is Congress' role, not the Court's, to delineate the boundaries of the market the Legislature seeks to regulate. . . . Congress could reasonably have viewed the market from a long-term perspective, encompassing all transactions virtually certain to occur over the next decade, not just those occurring here and now.

Third, contrary to The Chief Justice's contention, our precedent does indeed support "[t]he proposition that Congress may dictate the conduct of an individual today because of prophesied future activity." . . . Our decisions . . . acknowledge Congress' authority, under the Commerce Clause, to direct the conduct of an individual today (the farmer in *Wickard,* stopped from growing excess wheat; the plaintiff in *Raich,* ordered to cease cultivating marijuana) because of a prophesied future transaction (the eventual sale of that wheat or marijuana in the interstate market). Congress' actions are even more rational in this case, where the future activity (the consumption of medical care) is certain to occur, the sole uncertainty being the time the activity will take place.

Maintaining that the uninsured are not active in the health-care market, The Chief Justice draws an analogy to the car market. An individual "is not 'active in the car market,' " The Chief Justice observes, simply because he or she may someday buy a car. The analogy is inapt. The inevitable yet unpredictable need for medical care and the guarantee that emergency care will be provided when required are conditions nonexistent in other markets. . . . Although an individual *might* buy a car or a crown of broccoli one day, there is no certainty she will ever do so. And if she eventually wants a car or has a craving for broccoli, she will be obliged to pay at the counter before receiving the vehicle or nourishment. She will get no free ride or food, at the expense of another consumer forced to pay an inflated price. . . . Upholding the minimum coverage provision on the ground that all are participants or will be participants in the health-care market would therefore carry no implication that Congress may justify under the Commerce Clause a mandate to buy other products and services. . . .

The Chief Justice asserts, "[t]he language of the Constitution reflects the natural understanding that the power to regulate assumes there is already something to be regulated." This argument is difficult to fathom. Requiring individuals to obtain insurance unquestionably regulates the interstate health-insurance and health-care markets, both of them in existence well before the enactment of the ACA. . . . Thus, the "something to be regulated" was surely there when Congress created the minimum coverage provision. . . .

In concluding that the Commerce Clause does not permit Congress to regulate commercial "inactivity," and therefore does not allow Congress to adopt the practical solution it devised for the health-care problem, The Chief Justice views the Clause as a "technical legal conception," precisely what our case law tells us not to do. *Wickard*, 317 U.S., at 122. . . . These line-drawing exercises were untenable, and the Court long ago abandoned them. . . . Failing to learn from this history, The Chief Justice plows ahead with his formalistic distinction between those who are "active in commerce," and those who are not.

It is not hard to show the difficulty courts (and Congress) would encounter in distinguishing statutes that regulate "activity" from those that regulate "inactivity." As Judge Easterbrook noted, "it is possible to restate most actions as corresponding inactions with the same effect." *Archie v. Racine,* 847 F.2d 1211, 1213 (C.A.7 1988) (en banc). Take this case as an example. An individual who opts not to purchase insurance from a private insurer can be seen as actively selecting another form of insurance: self-insurance. See *Thomas More Law Center,* 651 F.3d, at 561 (Sutton, J., concurring in part) ("No one is inactive when deciding how to pay for health care, as self-insurance and private insurance are two forms of action for addressing the same risk."). The minimum coverage provision could therefore be described as regulating activists in the self-insurance market. . . .

2

Underlying The Chief Justice's view that the Commerce Clause must be confined to the regulation of active participants in a commercial market is a fear that the commerce power would otherwise know no limits. . . . This concern is unfounded.

First, The Chief Justice could certainly uphold the individual mandate without giving Congress *carte blanche* to enact any and all purchase mandates. As several times noted, the unique attributes of the health-care market render everyone active in that market and give rise to a significant free-riding problem that does not occur in other markets. . . .

Nor would the commerce power be unbridled, absent The Chief Justice's "activity" limitation. Congress would remain unable to regulate noneconomic conduct that has only an attenuated effect on interstate commerce and is traditionally left to state law. See *Lopez,* 514 U.S., at 567; *Morrison,* 529 U.S., at 617–619. . . .

As an example of the type of regulation he fears, The Chief Justice cites a Government mandate to purchase green vegetables. One could call this concern "the broccoli horrible." Congress, The Chief Justice posits, might adopt such a mandate, reasoning that an individual's failure to eat a healthy diet, like the failure to purchase health insurance, imposes costs on others.

Consider the chain of inferences the Court would have to accept to conclude that a vegetable-purchase mandate was likely to have a substantial effect on the health-care costs borne by lithe Americans. The Court would have to believe that individuals forced to buy vegetables would then eat them (instead of throwing or giving them away), would prepare the vegetables in a healthy way (steamed or raw, not deep-fried), would cut back on unhealthy foods, and would not allow other factors (such as lack of exercise or little sleep) to trump the improved diet. Such "pil[ing of] inference upon inference" is just what the Court refused to do in *Lopez* and *Morrison*.

Other provisions of the Constitution also check congressional over-reaching. A mandate to purchase a particular product would be unconstitutional if, for example, the edict impermissibly abridged the freedom of speech, interfered with the free exercise of religion, or infringed on a liberty interest protected by the Due Process Clause.

Supplementing these legal restraints is a formidable check on congressional power: the democratic process. . . . As the controversy surrounding the passage of the Affordable Care Act attests, purchase mandates are likely to engender political resistance. This prospect is borne out by the behavior of state legislators. Despite their possession of unquestioned authority to impose mandates, state governments have rarely done so. . . .

When contemplated in its extreme, almost any power looks dangerous. The commerce power, hypothetically, would enable Congress to prohibit the purchase and home production of all meat, fish, and dairy goods, effectively compelling Americans to eat only vegetables. . . . Yet no one would offer the "hypothetical and unreal possibilit[y]," *Pullman Co. v. Knott*, 235 U.S. 23, 26 (1914), of a vegetarian state as a credible reason to deny Congress the authority ever to ban the possession and sale of goods. The Chief Justice accepts just such specious logic when he cites the broccoli horrible as a reason to deny Congress the power to pass the individual mandate. Cf. R. Bork, The Tempting of America 169 (1990) ("Judges and lawyers live on the slippery slope of analogies; they are not supposed to ski it to the bottom."). But see, *e.g., post* (joint opinion of Scalia, Kennedy, Thomas, and Alito, JJ.) (asserting, outlandishly, that if the minimum coverage provision is sustained, then Congress could make "breathing in and out the basis for federal prescription"). . . .

III–A

. . . The Necessary and Proper Clause "empowers Congress to enact laws in effectuation of its [commerce] powe[r] that are not within its authority to enact in isolation." *Raich*, 545 U.S., at 39 (Scalia, J., concurring in judgment). Hence, "[a] complex regulatory program . . . can survive a Commerce Clause challenge without a showing that every single facet of the program is independently and directly related to a valid congressional goal." *Indiana*, 452 U.S., at 329, n. 17 ("It is enough that the challenged provisions are an integral part of the regulatory program and that the regulatory scheme when considered as a whole satisfies this test." *Ibid.* (collecting cases).

Recall that one of Congress' goals in enacting the Affordable Care Act was to eliminate the insurance industry's practice of charging higher prices or denying coverage to individuals with preexisting medical conditions. . . . The commerce power allows Congress to ban this practice, a point no one disputes. . . .

Congress knew, however, that simply barring insurance companies from relying on an applicant's medical history would not work in practice. . . . The minimum coverage provision is thus an "essential par[t] of a larger regulation of economic activity"; without the provision, "the regulatory scheme [w]ould be undercut." *Raich*, 545 U.S., at 24–25. Put differently, the minimum coverage provision, together with the guaranteed-issue and community-rating requirements, is "reasonably adapted to the attainment of a legitimate end under the commerce power": the elimination of pricing and sales practices that take an applicant's medical history into account. See *id.,* at 37 (Scalia, J., concurring in judgment).

B

Asserting that the Necessary and Proper Clause does not authorize the minimum coverage provision, The Chief Justice focuses on the word "proper." . . .

The Chief Justice cites only two cases in which this Court concluded that a federal statute impermissibly transgressed the Constitution's boundary between state and federal authority: *Printz v. United States,* 521 U.S. 898 (1997), and *New York v. United States,* 505 U.S. 144 (1992). . . . The statutes at issue in both cases, however, compelled *state officials* to act on the Federal Government's behalf. . . . The minimum coverage provision, in contrast, acts "directly upon individuals, without employing the States as intermediaries." *New York,* 505 U.S., at 164. The provision is thus entirely consistent with the Constitution's design. See *Printz,* 521 U.S., at 920 ("[T]he Framers explicitly chose a Constitution that confers upon Congress the power to regulate individuals, not States."). . . .

Nor does The Chief Justice pause to explain *why* the power to direct either the purchase of health insurance or, alternatively, the payment of a penalty collectible as a tax is more far-reaching than other implied powers this Court has found meet under the Necessary and Proper Clause. These powers include the power to enact criminal laws; the power to imprison, including civil imprisonment; and the power to create a national bank.

In failing to explain why the individual mandate threatens our constitutional order, The Chief Justice disserves future courts. How is a judge to decide, when ruling on the constitutionality of a federal statute, whether Congress employed an "independent power," or merely a "derivative" one[?] Whether the power used is "substantive," or just "incidental"? The instruction The Chief Justice, in effect, provides lower courts: You will know it when you see it. . . .

V

[Justice Ginsburg would have upheld the Medicaid Expansion as an exercise of the spending power.—Editors]

. . . The Chief Justice acknowledges that Congress may "condition the receipt of [federal] funds on the States' complying with restrictions on the use of those funds," but nevertheless concludes that the 2010 expansion is unduly coercive. His conclusion rests on three premises, each of them essential to his theory. First, the Medicaid expansion is, in The Chief Justice's view, a new grant program, not an addition to the Medicaid program existing before the ACA's enactment. Congress, The Chief Justice maintains, has threatened States with the loss of funds from an old program in an effort to get them to adopt a new one. Second, the expansion was unforeseeable by the States when they first signed on to Medicaid. Third, the threatened loss of funding is so large that the States have no real choice but to participate in the Medicaid expansion. The Chief Justice therefore— for the first time ever—finds an exercise of Congress' spending power unconstitutionally coercive.

Medicaid, as amended by the ACA, however, is not two spending programs; it is a single program with a constant aim—to enable poor persons to receive basic health care when they need it. Given past expansions, plus express statutory warning that Congress may change the requirements participating States must meet, there can be no tenable claim that the ACA fails for lack of notice. Moreover, States have no entitlement to receive any Medicaid funds; they enjoy only the opportunity to accept funds on Congress' terms. Future Congresses are not bound by their predecessors' dispositions; they have authority to spend federal revenue as they see fit. The Federal Government, therefore, is not, as The Chief Justice charges, threatening States with the loss of "existing" funds from one spending program in order to induce them to opt into another program. Congress is simply requiring States to do what States have long been required to do to receive Medicaid funding: comply with the conditions Congress prescribes for participation. . . .

Congress' authority to condition the use of federal funds is not confined to spending programs as first launched. The legislature may, and often does, amend the law, imposing new conditions grant recipients henceforth must meet in order to continue receiving funds. Yes, there are federalism-based limits on the use of Congress' conditional spending power. In the leading decision in this area, *South Dakota v. Dole,* 483 U.S. 203 (1987), the Court identified four criteria. The conditions placed on federal grants to States must (a) promote the "general welfare," (b) "unambiguously" inform States what is demanded of them, (c) be germane "to the federal interest in particular national projects or programs," and (d) not "induce the States to engage in activities that would themselves be unconstitutional."

The Court in *Dole* mentioned, but did not adopt, a further limitation, one hypothetically raised a half-century earlier: In "some circumstances," Congress might be prohibited from offering a "financial inducement . . . so coercive as to pass the point at which 'pressure turns into compulsion.' " *Id.,* at 211 (quoting *Steward Machine Co. v. Davis,* 301 U.S. 548, 590 (1937)). Prior to today's decision, however, the Court has never ruled that the terms of any grant crossed the indistinct line between temptation and coercion.

. . . This case does not present the concerns that led the Court in *Dole* even to consider the prospect of coercion. In *Dole,* the condition—set 21 as the minimum drinking age—did not tell the States how to use funds Congress provided for highway construction. Further, in view of the Twenty-First Amendment, it was an open question whether Congress could directly impose a national minimum drinking age.

The ACA, in contrast, relates solely to the federally funded Medicaid program; if States choose not to comply, Congress has not threatened to withhold funds earmarked for any other program. Nor does the ACA use Medicaid funding to induce States to take action Congress itself could not undertake. The Federal Government undoubtedly could operate its own health-care program for poor persons, just as it operates Medicare for seniors' health care.

That is what makes this such a simple case, and the Court's decision so unsettling. Congress, aiming to assist the needy, has appropriated federal money to subsidize state health-insurance programs that meet federal standards. The principal standard the ACA sets is that the state program cover adults earning no more than 133% of the federal poverty line. Enforcing that prescription ensures that federal funds will be spent on health care for the poor in furtherance of Congress' present perception of the general welfare. . . .

■ JUSTICE SCALIA, JUSTICE KENNEDY, JUSTICE THOMAS, and JUSTICE ALITO, dissenting.

... This case is in one respect difficult: it presents two questions of first impression. The first of those is whether failure to engage in economic activity (the purchase of health insurance) is subject to regulation under the Commerce Clause. Failure to act does result in an effect on commerce, and hence might be said to come under this Court's "affecting commerce" criterion of Commerce Clause jurisprudence. But in none of its decisions has this Court extended the Clause that far. The second question is whether the congressional power to tax and spend, U.S. Const., Art. I, § 8, cl. 1, permits the conditioning of a State's continued receipt of all funds under a massive state-administered federal welfare program upon its acceptance of an expansion to that program. Several of our opinions have suggested that the power to tax and spend cannot be used to coerce state administration of a federal program, but we have never found a law enacted under the spending power to be coercive. Those questions are difficult.

The case is easy and straightforward, however, in another respect. What is absolutely clear, affirmed by the text of the 1789 Constitution, by the Tenth Amendment ratified in 1791, and by innumerable cases of ours in the 220 years since, is that there are structural limits upon federal power—upon what it can prescribe with respect to private conduct, and upon what it can impose upon the sovereign States. Whatever may be the conceptual limits upon the Commerce Clause and upon the power to tax and spend, they cannot be such as will enable the Federal Government to regulate all private conduct and to compel the States to function as administrators of federal programs.

That clear principle carries the day here. The striking case of *Wickard v. Filburn*, 317 U.S. 111 (1942), which held that the economic activity of growing wheat, even for one's own consumption, affected commerce sufficiently that it could be regulated, always has been regarded as the *ne plus ultra* of expansive Commerce Clause jurisprudence. To go beyond that, and to say the *failure* to grow wheat (which is *not* an economic activity, or any activity at all) nonetheless affects commerce and therefore can be federally regulated, is to make mere breathing in and out the basis for federal prescription and to extend federal power to virtually all human activity.

I

The Individual Mandate

[The joint dissent agrees with Chief Justice Roberts that the individual mandate is not constitutional under the Commerce Clause and Necessary and Proper Clause.—Editors]

A few respectful responses to Justice Ginsburg's dissent on the issue of the Mandate are in order. That dissent duly recites the test of Commerce Clause power that our opinions have applied, but disregards the premise the test contains. It is true enough that Congress needs only a "rational basis for concluding that the *regulated activity* substantially affects interstate commerce" (emphasis added). But it must be *activity* affecting commerce that is regulated, and not merely the failure to engage in commerce. And one is not now purchasing the health care covered by the insurance mandate simply because one is likely to be purchasing it in the future. ... If all inactivity affecting commerce is commerce, commerce is everything. Ultimately the dissent is driven to saying that there is really no difference between action and inaction, a proposition that has never recommended itself, neither to the law nor to common sense. To say, for example, that the inaction here consists of activity in "the self-insurance market," seems to us wordplay. By parity of reasoning the failure to buy a car can be called participation in the non-private-car-transportation market. Commerce becomes everything. . . .

The dissent's exposition of the wonderful things the Federal Government has achieved through exercise of its assigned powers . . . is quite beside the point. The issue here is whether the federal government can impose the Individual Mandate through the Commerce Clause. And the relevant history is not that Congress has achieved wide and wonderful results through the proper exercise of its assigned powers in the past, but that it has never before used the Commerce Clause to compel entry into commerce. The dissent treats the Constitution as though it is an enumeration of those problems that the Federal Government can address. . . . The Constitution is not that. It enumerates not federally soluble *problems,* but federally available *powers.* The Federal Government can address whatever problems it wants but can bring to their solution only those powers that the Constitution confers, among which is the power to regulate commerce. None of our cases say anything else. Article I contains no whatever-it-takes-to-solve-a-national-problem power. . . .

II

The Taxing Power

As far as § 5000A is concerned, we would stop there. Congress has attempted to regulate beyond the scope of its Commerce Clause authority, and § 5000A is therefore invalid. . . . The provision challenged under the Constitution is either a penalty or else a tax. Of course in many cases what was a regulatory mandate enforced by a penalty *could have been* imposed as a tax upon permissible action; or what was imposed as a tax upon permissible action *could have been* a regulatory mandate enforced by a penalty. But we know of no case, and the Government cites none, in which the imposition was, for constitutional purposes, both. . . . The issue is not whether Congress had the *power* to frame the minimum-coverage provision as a tax, but whether it *did* so. . . . In this case, there is simply no way, "without doing violence to the fair meaning of the words used," *Grenada County Supervisors v. Brogden,* 112 U.S. 261, 269 (1884), to escape what Congress enacted: a mandate that individuals maintain minimum essential coverage, enforced by a penalty.

Our cases establish a clear line between a tax and a penalty. . . . In a few cases, this Court has held that a "tax" imposed upon private conduct was so onerous as to be in effect a penalty. But we have never held—*never*—that a penalty imposed for violation of the law was so trivial as to be in effect a tax. We have never held that *any* exaction imposed for violation of the law is an exercise of Congress' taxing power—even when the statute *calls* it a tax, much less when (as here) the statute repeatedly calls it a penalty. . . .

So the question is, quite simply, whether the exaction here is imposed for violation of the law. It unquestionably is. . . . Eighteen times in § 5000A itself and elsewhere throughout the Act, Congress called the exaction in § 5000A(b) a "penalty."

That § 5000A imposes not a simple tax but a mandate to which a penalty is attached is demonstrated by the fact that some are exempt from the tax who are not exempt from the mandate—a distinction that would make no sense if the mandate were not a mandate. . . .

For all these reasons, to say that the Individual Mandate merely imposes a tax is not to interpret the statute but to rewrite it. . . . We have no doubt that Congress knew precisely what it was doing when it rejected an earlier version of this legislation that imposed a tax instead of a requirement-with-penalty. . . . Imposing a tax through judicial legislation inverts the constitutional scheme, and places the power to tax in the branch of government least accountable to the citizenry.

Finally, we must observe that rewriting § 5000A as a tax in order to sustain its constitutionality would force us to confront a difficult constitutional question: whether this is a direct tax that must be apportioned among the States according to their population. Art. I, § 9, cl. 4. Perhaps it is not (we have no need to address the point); but the meaning of the Direct Tax Clause is famously unclear, and its application here is a question of first impression that deserves more thoughtful consideration than the lick-and-a-promise accorded by the Government and its supporters. The Government's opening brief did not even address the question—perhaps because, until today, no federal court has accepted the implausible argument that § 5000A is an exercise of the tax power. And once respondents raised the issue, the Government devoted a mere 21 lines of its reply brief to the issue. At oral argument, the most prolonged statement about the issue was just over 50 words. One would expect this Court to demand more than fly-by-night briefing and argument before deciding a difficult constitutional question of first impression.

III

The Anti–Injunction Act

[The joint dissent agrees that the Anti–Injunction Act does not apply because the individual mandate is not a tax, but they argue that this reasoning supports the conclusion that it cannot be treated as a tax for constitutional purposes.—Editors]

. . . What the Government would have us believe in these cases is that the very same textual indications that show this is not a tax under the Anti–Injunction Act show that it is a tax under the Constitution. That carries verbal wizardry too far, deep into the forbidden land of the sophists.

IV

The Medicaid Expansion

[The joint dissent agrees with Chief Justice Roberts that the Medicaid Expansion provisions of the ACA exceeded constitutional limitations on Congress's spending power, but they disagreed as to the appropriate remedy.—Editors]

. . . Seven Members of the Court agree that the Medicaid Expansion, as enacted by Congress, is unconstitutional. See Part IV–A to IV–E; Part IV–A (opinion of Roberts, C.J., joined by Breyer and Kagan, JJ.). Because the Medicaid Expansion is unconstitutional, the question of remedy arises. The most natural remedy would be to invalidate the Medicaid Expansion. However, the Government proposes—in two cursory sentences at the very end of its brief—preserving the Expansion. Under its proposal, States would receive the additional Medicaid funds if they expand eligibility, but States would keep their pre-existing Medicaid funds if they do not expand eligibility. We cannot accept the Government's suggestion.

. . . [T]he Government's proposed remedy introduces a new dynamic: States must choose between expanding Medicaid or paying huge tax sums to the federal fisc for the sole benefit of expanding Medicaid in other States. If this divisive dynamic between and among States can be introduced at all, it should be by conscious congressional choice, not by Court-invented interpretation. We do not doubt that States are capable of making decisions when put in a tight spot. We do doubt the authority of this Court to put them there. . . .

V

Severability

[The joint dissent would have held both the individual mandate and the Medicaid Expansion unconstitutional, and would have held that those provisions were so central to the ACA that they required invalidation of the entire act. The joint dissent's lengthy severability analysis is omitted.—Editors]

. . . The Court today decides to save a statute Congress did not write. It rules that what the statute declares to be a requirement with a penalty is instead an option subject to a tax. And it changes the intentionally coercive sanction of a total cut-off of Medicaid funds to a supposedly noncoercive cut-off of only the incremental funds that the Act makes available.

The Court regards its strained statutory interpretation as judicial modesty. It is not. It amounts instead to a vast judicial overreaching. It creates a debilitated, inoperable version of health-care regulation that Congress did not enact and the public does not expect. It makes enactment of sensible health-care regulation more difficult, since Congress cannot start afresh but must take as its point of departure a jumble of now senseless provisions, provisions that certain interests favored under the Court's new design will struggle to retain. And it leaves the public and the States to expend vast sums of money on requirements that may or may not survive the necessary congressional revision. . . .

The values that should have determined our course today are caution, minimalism, and the understanding that the Federal Government is one of limited powers. But the Court's ruling undermines those values at every turn. In the name of restraint, it overreaches. In the name of constitutional avoidance, it creates new constitutional questions. In the name of cooperative federalism, it undermines state sovereignty.

The Constitution, though it dates from the founding of the Republic, has powerful meaning and vital relevance to our own times. The constitutional protections that this case involves are protections of structure. Structural protections—notably, the restraints imposed by federalism and separation of powers—are less romantic and have less obvious a connection to personal freedom than the provisions of the Bill of Rights or the Civil War Amendments. Hence they tend to be undervalued or even forgotten by our citizens. It should be the responsibility of the Court to teach otherwise, to remind our people that the Framers considered structural protections of freedom the most important ones, for which reason they alone were embodied in the original Constitution and not left to later amendment. The fragmentation of power produced by the structure of our Government is central to liberty, and when we destroy it, we place liberty at peril. Today's decision should have vindicated, should have taught, this truth; instead, our judgment today has disregarded it.

For the reasons here stated, we would find the Act invalid in its entirety.

■ [The dissenting opinion of JUSTICE THOMAS is omitted.]

NOTES

1. *Counting Noses.* Start with the holdings and the alignment of the justices: What is the *result* of the case? What parts of the Affordable Care Act were upheld and what parts were struck down? What is the alignment of justices as to each holding? Did invalidation of some parts invalidate the act as a whole? Or did the Court allow the remainder of the act to remain operative?

As to the alignment of votes: Only one justice—Chief Justice John Roberts—joined *every* aspect of the Court's holding and judgment. Was there in fact majority support for all (or nearly all) of the constitutional conclusions set forth in Chief Justice Roberts's opinion? Did a majority of the Court hold that the individual mandate was not within Congress's power under the Commerce Clause and Necessary and Proper Clause—Roberts and the four justices in the joint dissent? Why did the four dissenters not *join* those parts of Roberts's opinion? Was it because they disagreed with the ultimate disposition of the case? Or was it for some other reason? Was there majority support for that part of the opinion upholding the individual mandate provision on Taxing Clause grounds? Does that holding render the holding concerning the Commerce Clause—which the majority opinion at this point *calls* a holding—dictum, because unnecessary to that part of the judgment?

2. *Construing the Statute as a Tax.* As a matter of constitutional interpretive methodology, what do you think of that part of Chief Justice Roberts's opinion holding that the individual mandate could be sustained, in the alternative, as an exercise of the Taxing Clause power, even if not the "most straightforward reading" of the provision? Was this a proper use of the constitutional avoidance doctrine—the idea that a Court should construe a statute, where possible, to conform to the Constitution? Note that it would not have been necessary to construe the mandate as a "tax" if the mandate were constitutional under the Commerce Clause and Necessary and Proper Clause.

3. *The Commerce Clause.* Debate the merits: Considered apart from the Necessary and Proper Clause, is Chief Justice Roberts's (and the joint dissent's) position on the Commerce Clause persuasive, or is Justice Ginsburg's opposing position? Which types of constitutional argument, or modes of interpretation, does each opinion employ? Is there any good answer to the majority's textual arguments that the power to "regulate" commerce presupposes existing commerce to regulate, and therefore does not contain a power to create or mandate commercial activity? Is there any good answer to the majority's argument that, if inactivity can be regulated because it affects commerce, *everything* can be regulated because it affects commerce? Is the majority persuasive in arguing that such a conclusion is inconsistent with the first principles of federalism? On the other hand, is there any good answer to Justice Ginsburg's argument that everyone, in the end (no pun intended), will be a consumer of healthcare services, and that the individual mandate merely regulates the system of payment for these services? Is there any good answer to her argument that the individual mandate regulates conduct (whether characterized as "activity" or "inactivity") with substantial market consequences?

Evaluate the effect of *NFIB v. Sebelius* on Commerce Clause jurisprudence: Is the majority's rejection of the Commerce Clause rationale something hugely important and entirely new? Is it a departure from prior cases? Is it a new limitation on the scope of the Commerce Clause, but one not foreclosed by prior cases? Or is it simply an application (or extension) of principles set forth in earlier cases?

4. *The Necessary and Proper Clause.* Even if the individual mandate cannot be justified solely as a regulation of "commerce," might it be justified as "necessary and proper" to a regulation of commerce? The government argued that the mandate was necessary to enable the enforcement of the "guaranteed issue" and "community rating" rules, which are undoubtedly regulations of commerce. Make sure you understand the logic of that argument. What is Chief Justice Roberts's answer to it? Who has the better of the argument on this point? Is Chief Justice Roberts's line of distinction between permissible and impermissible applications of the Necessary and Proper Clause persuasive? Is it clear? Is it consistent with *McCulloch?* Or does it, as Justice Ginsburg suggests, depart from precedents interpreting the Necessary and Proper Clause broadly? If it is such a departure, is it perhaps a justified one?

a. The Roberts opinion twice quotes *McCulloch* to the effect that the Necessary and Proper Clause does not "license the exercise of any 'great substantive and independent power[s]' beyond those specifically enumerated." The idea was that relatively minor powers could be implied as incidental to the enumerated powers, but that "great substantive and independent powers" must be granted explicitly. There is a rich history to this way of interpreting the clause. See Robert G. Natelson, "The Framing and Adoption of the Necessary and Proper Clause," in Gary Lawson et al., THE ORIGINS OF THE NECESSARY AND PROPER CLAUSE 84, 116–118 (2010); William Baude, *Rethinking the Federal Eminent Domain Power*, 122 Yale L.J. (2013). In effect, the majority holds that the power to mandate individual action is too important and independent a power to be merely incidental. Is this a solution to the centuries-old interpretive dilemma presented by the Necessary and Proper Clause: namely, that the clause can be construed either to permit almost anything or else to add almost nothing to other congressional powers, but it does not seem to easily fit any in-between position? Does the "great substantive and independent powers doctrine" explain why the framers thought it necessary to spell out such powers as taxing and spending, regulating commerce, fixing the standards of weights and measures, and establishing post roads, but not such powers as passing and enforcing criminal laws, conscripting troops, condemning land through eminent domain, printing money, or regulating immigration? Are these latter powers, which Congress has long exercised without controversy, any less great, substantive, and independent than the power to impose an individual mandate?

b. What do you make of Chief Justice Roberts's characterization of the individual mandate as not an "essential component of the insurance reforms"? Is that factually accurate? Is that a determination reserved for Congress? Compare Roberts's "not essential" argument with Jefferson's argument for a restrictive understanding of the word "necessary" in the Bank controversy: Are they similar? (Jefferson's argument is discussed in Chapter 1.)

c. What do you make of Chief Justice Roberts's emphasis on the word "proper" as embracing federalism concerns about the limited power of the national government? How does one answer the objection that, if the Necessary and Proper Clause, when allied with the Commerce Clause, permits Congress to regulate inactivity as well as activity, it is a license for the national government to regulate all activity—and that this is inconsistent with the Constitution's basic design? Does the word "proper" provide a standard for invalidating acts that would otherwise be "necessary" to carry out an enumerated power?

d. Chief Justice Roberts observes that upholding the mandate would "vest[] Congress with the extraordinary ability to create the necessary predicate to the exercise of an enumerated power." Does this mean that Congress can never invoke the Necessary and Proper Clause when the necessity for a particular measure was created by Congress's own predicate acts? Two years before *NFIB*, in *United States v. Comstock*, 130 S. Ct. 1949 (2010), the Court considered a constitutional challenge to a provision of a federal statute authorizing the continued detention of mentally ill, sexually dangerous federal prisoners beyond the date when they would otherwise be released for having served their sentences. (The constitutional challenge was that Congress lacked an enumerated power to enact the law, not a individual-rights challenge.) By a vote of 7–2, the Court upheld the provision on the basis of the Necessary and Proper Clause—i.e., the provision was necessary and proper to carrying into execution a penal system and general enforcement of federal criminal laws (which were in turn necessary and proper to carrying into execution other grants of power). Are *NFIB* and *Comstock* in tension with each other on this point, or are there valid points of distinction? If inconsistent, which one states the correct principle? Is *NFIB* consistent with *Gonzales v. Raich*, 545 U.S. 1 (2005), which held that a prohibition on intrastate production and consumption of marijuana was justified as a necessary part of an effective federal prohibition of interstate commerce in marijuana? Is *NFIB* a landmark limitation on the scope of the Necessary and Proper Clause power—as big a deal, perhaps, as *McCulloch*, and arguably even cutting back on that foundational, 193–year–old precedent?

5. *The Taxing Power.*

a. Who needs the Commerce Clause? If the national government can accomplish its objectives simply by imposing a tax on the activity (or inactivity) it wishes to eliminate (or reduce), what difference does it make? How does Chief Justice Roberts's majority opinion upholding the individual mandate on taxing power grounds respond to this objection?

What distinctions does the Court identify that make the taxing power a *different* power from the Commerce Clause power? What *limitations* does the Court identify on the taxing power? Is such a broad understanding of the taxing power any less objectionable on federalism grounds? Or is the answer to the "federalism" objection that the taxing power sometimes permits an exercise of national authority through incentives and penalties that the commerce power does not permit through direct regulation, and that this is simply part of American federalism? (There is, after all, no "Federalism Clause" in the Constitution.)

Is this view troubling? Is it the Tax Clause power, not the Commerce Clause power, that is really the ultimate national power? Is the Tax Clause power a Trojan horse for federalism? Would Chief Justice Roberts's opinion allow a tax on people who fail to donate a kidney, or refuse to eat broccoli, or refrain from having children? Would it matter for these questions if the tax were small rather than being financially ruinous? The Court likes to say the power to tax is not the power to destroy—"while this Court sits"—but how can it be otherwise?

b. The joint dissenters do not argue that Congress *could not* have enacted the individual mandate as an exercise of the taxing power, but only that Congress *did not* do so. Should this matter? Is there a persuasive answer to Chief Justice Roberts's argument that, if the enactment was validly within Congress's constitutional taxing power, then it should not matter—other than perhaps for political purposes—what Congress called the provision? On the other hand, should Congress be held to its choice of characterizing the individual mandate as a "penalty" for the purpose of determining whether the mandate falls within the power to lay and collect taxes? What do you think of the dissent's argument that the majority had to twist—"rewrite"—the individual mandate provision in order to uphold it, and that this was illegitimate? What do you think of Chief Justice Roberts's argument that the Court has an obligation to construe a statute, if fairly possible, in such a manner as to sustain its constitutionality? Who has the better of the argument here?

c. The dissent questions Chief Justice Roberts's opinion for holding that the healthcare mandate tax is an indirect rather than a direct tax. As noted earlier, indirect taxes, like import taxes and sales taxes, need only be set at a uniform level in each of the states, but direct taxes, like a capitation or head tax, or a tax on real estate, cannot be imposed unless they are apportioned among the states in proportion to the census. U.S. Const., Art. I, § 9, cl. 4. Recall the early case of *Hylton v. United States*, 3 U.S. 171 (1796), in which the Court unanimously held that a tax on the possession of carriages was an excise rather than a direct tax. Does the dissent actually assert that the tax (if a tax) *is* a direct tax, or does it simply raise the question?

Chief Justice Roberts's opinion appears to limit the category of direct taxes to capitation taxes and property taxes and thus holds that the insurance penalty is not a direct tax. Is that a sound interpretation of the constitutional language? The mandate is not a tax on a transaction, like a sales or excise tax, nor does it fall on a third party. The healthcare mandate falls directly on any person who does not have health insurance unless the person's income is below a certain level. Is it essentially a head tax on anyone who does not have health insurance? Can it fairly be characterized as an *income* tax, since it is imposed via the income tax system and because those below a certain income level are exempt? If so, is the tax—even if otherwise characterized as "direct"— authorized by the Sixteenth Amendment?

d. In a portion of the opinion not presented here, the Court held that the individual mandate was not a tax for purposes of applying the tax Anti–Injunction Act, a statutory provision forbidding taxpayers from bringing suits for injunctive relief from the collection of taxes. (In effect, the Anti–Injunction Act requires taxpayers to pay a disputed tax and then sue for a refund.) The Court held that Congress can designate something as not a tax for purposes of applying the Anti–Injunction Act but that this characterization does not foreclose the exaction being a "tax" within the meaning of the scope of Congress's constitutional powers to enact. Is that a contradiction? Or does it mean that Congress is the master of its own statutes, and can repeal, modify, or limit one statute by enacting another one, but that Congress cannot alter the scope of its own constitutional powers by virtue of the labels it uses?

6. *The Spending Power.* A 7–2 majority found that the Medicaid Expansion provisions of the Affordable Care Act exceeded Congress's power to attach conditions to the receipt of federal funds by the states, because the states were essentially coerced to accept the funds and the conditions attached to them. Is the Court's reasoning persuasive? The majority opinion characterized the conditions imposed by the statute as "a gun to the head." What did the Court identify as the essential features of the act's new conditions that make them coercive? Is it the size of the program as a percentage of states' budgets? Is it the fact that the condition involved forfeiture of funds under the existing Medicaid program, if a state did not accept funds for the expanded Medicaid program? Is it a combination of the two? Where is the line?

The Supreme Court held that the remedy for the condition ruled unconstitutional was elimination of the power to impose the condition on the states, not the invalidation of the Medicaid expansion itself. The joint dissenters disagreed, calling this, too, a rewriting of the statute and an improper exercise of judicial power. Who is right? Why?

Is the Court's spending power holding dictated by concerns of federalism—that is, is it specific to the situation of federal spending grants made to states? Or is it a general limitation on the national government's power to spend, such that private recipients of federal government grants and expenditures could argue, based on *NFIB v. Sebelius*, that a particular grant condition was a "gun to the head" to coerce behavior the national government could not command?

[*Assignment 36*]

C. OTHER MAJOR NATIONAL POWERS, ENUMERATED OR INHERENT

Article I, Section 8: The Congress shall have Power . . .

To establish an uniform Rule of Naturalization[;] . . .

To Coin Money, regulate the Value thereof, and of foreign Coin, and fix the Standard of Weights and Measures; . . .

To raise and support Armies, but no Appropriation of Money to that Use shall be for a longer Term than two Years; . . .

In the materials up to now, we have considered the major issues and debates surrounding the interpretation of the provisions most frequently invoked as the source of the national legislative powers of Congress: the Commerce Clause, the Taxing Clause, the spending power, and the Necessary and Proper Clause. But Article I, Section 8 of course contains a much more extensive list of Congress's legislative powers. It would be impossible to treat all of them in the same level of detail, but several deserve attention as representative of the trend toward a broad interpretation of national power: the power to issue *paper money*; the power over *naturalization and immigration*; the power to prescribe a *military draft*; and the power to legislate to carry out *treaty obligations*. Each of these powers in some sense reflects a core attribute of nationhood; each was given a broad judicial construction well before the New Deal Revolution of 1937; in each case the broad construction or application had as much to do with the force supplied by the Necessary and Proper Clause as with the underlying power itself; and in each case the asserted power was controversial at the time.

Paper Money

Paper money was one of the great evils that the framers of the U.S. Constitution liked to inveigh against. If you go back and consult *The Federalist No. 10* at the beginning of this Chapter, you will see that James Madison calls a rage for paper money "a wicked project." Article I, Section 8, Clause 5 gives Congress the power "To coin Money," but no enumerated power to print it. Given the framers' awareness of the existence of paper money during the period of the Articles of Confederation, there can be little doubt that omitting an enumerated power to print paper money was deliberate.

Paper money was first introduced under the Constitution by President Abraham Lincoln during the Civil War. The statute at issue was the Legal Tender Act of 1862, and, at the time it was adopted, the Union's finances and prospects of winning the Civil War seemed dire. If ever there was a time when paper money might seem to be "necessary and proper," 1862 was such a time. In *Hepburn v. Griswold*, 75 U.S. 603 (1869), after the Civil War was safely over and won, the Supreme Court held, by a 4–3 vote, that paper money was unconstitutional. Strikingly, the Court's opinion was written by Chief Justice Salmon P. Chase, who as Abraham Lincoln's treasury secretary had presided over the first issuance of printed dollar bills. Subsequently, President Grant appointed two new justices to the Court, Joseph Bradley and William Strong, thus bringing the Court back up to its full complement of nine members. They then voted to overrule *Hepburn* in *Knox v. Lee*, 79 U.S. 457 (1870), by a 5–4 vote. Thirteen years later, in *Juilliard v. Greenman*, 110 U.S. 421 (1884), the Court found that paper money was "necessary and proper" not only in the Civil War, but also in peacetime. By this point, Americans were so accustomed to federal paper money that only Justice Stephen J. Field dissented. These three cases are known collectively as *The Legal Tender Cases*. Here is only a short excerpt from one of the many very lengthy opinions that the issue of paper money gave rise to, but it indicates the Court's approach.

Knox v. Lee

79 U.S. 457 (1870)

■ MR. JUSTICE STRONG delivered the opinion of the court.

The controlling questions in these cases are the following: Are the acts of Congress, known as the legal tender acts, constitutional when applied to contracts made before their passage; and, secondly, are they valid as applicable to debts contracted since their enactment? . . . It would be difficult to overestimate the consequences which must follow our decision. They will affect the entire business of the country, and take hold of the possible continued existence of the government. If it be held by this court that Congress has no constitutional power, under any circumstances, or in any emergency, to make treasury notes a legal tender for the payment of all debts (a power confessedly possessed by every independent sovereignty other than the United States), the government is without those means of self-preservation which, all must admit, may, in certain contingencies, become indispensable. . . . It is also clear that if we hold the acts invalid as applicable to debts incurred, or transactions which have taken place since their enactment, our decision must cause, throughout the country, great business derangement, widespread distress, and the rankest injustice. . . . Men have bought and sold, borrowed and lent, and assumed every variety of obligations contemplating that payment might be made with such notes. Indeed, legal tender treasury notes have become the universal measure of values. . . . [C]an Congress constitutionally give to treasury notes the character and qualities of money? Can such notes be constituted a legitimate circulating medium, having a defined legal value? . . . [T]hose who hold the legal tender acts unconstitutional when applied to contracts made before February, 1862, find themselves compelled also to hold that the acts are invalid as to debts created after that time, and to hold that both classes of debts alike can be discharged only by gold and silver coin.

The consequences of which we have spoken, serious as they are, must be accepted, if there is a clear incompatibility between the Constitution and the legal tender acts. But we are unwilling to precipitate them upon the country unless such an incompatibility plainly appears. . . .

Nor can it be questioned that, when investigating the nature and extent of the powers conferred by the Constitution upon Congress, it is indispensable to keep in view the objects for which those powers were granted. This is a universal rule of construction applied alike to statutes, wills, contracts, and constitutions. . . . In no other way can the intent of the framers of the instrument be discovered. And there are more urgent reasons for looking to the ultimate purpose in examining the powers conferred by a constitution than there are in construing a statute, a will, or a contract. We do not expect to find in a constitution minute details. It is necessarily brief and comprehensive. . . .

[T]he power to levy and collect taxes, to coin money and regulate its value, to raise and support armies, or to provide for and maintain a navy, are instruments for the paramount object, which was to establish a government, sovereign within its sphere, with capability of self-preservation, thereby forming a union more perfect than that which existed under the old Confederacy.

The same may be asserted also of all the non-enumerated powers included in the authority expressly given "to make all laws which shall be necessary and proper for carrying into execution the specified powers vested in Congress, and all other powers vested by the Constitution in the government of the United States, or in any department or officer thereof." It is impossible to know what those non-enumerated powers are, and what is their nature and extent, without considering the purposes they were intended to subserve. . . . It certainly was intended to confer upon the government the power of self-preservation. . . . That would appear, then, to be a most unreasonable construction of the Constitution which denies to the government created by it, the right to employ freely every means, not prohibited, necessary for its preservation, and for the fulfilment of its acknowledged duties. Such a right, we hold, was given by the last clause of the eighth section of its first article. The means or instrumentalities referred to in that clause, and authorized, are not enumerated or defined. In the nature of things enumeration and specification were impossible. But they were left to the discretion of Congress, subject only to the restrictions that they be not prohibited, and be necessary and proper for carrying into execution the enumerated powers given to Congress, and all other powers vested in the government of the United States, or in any department or officer thereof.

And here it is to be observed it is not indispensable to the existence of any power claimed for the Federal government that it can be found specified in the words of the Constitution, or clearly and directly traceable to some one of the specified powers. Its existence may be deduced fairly from more than one of the substantive powers expressly defined, or from them all combined. It is allowable to group together any number of them and infer from them all that the power claimed has been conferred. Such a treatment of the Constitution is recognized by its own provisions. This is well illustrated in its language respecting the writ of habeas corpus. The power to suspend the privilege of that writ is not expressly given, nor can it be deduced from any one of the particularized grants of power. Yet it is provided that the privileges of the writ shall not be suspended except in certain defined contingencies. This is no express grant of power. It is a restriction. But it shows irresistibly that somewhere in the Constitution power to suspend the privilege of the writ was granted, either by some one or more of the specifications of power, or by them all combined. And, that important powers were understood by the people who adopted the Constitution to have been created by it, powers not enumerated, and not included incidentally in any one of those enumerated, is shown by the amendments. The first ten of these were suggested in the conventions of the States, and proposed at the first session of the first Congress, before any complaint was made of a disposition to assume doubtful powers. . . . They tend plainly to show that, in the judgment of those who adopted the Constitution, there were powers created by it, neither expressly specified nor deducible from any one specified power, or ancillary to it alone, but which grew out of the aggregate of powers conferred upon the government, or out of the sovereignty instituted. Most of these amendments are denials of power which had not been expressly granted, and which cannot be said to have been necessary and proper for carrying into execution any other powers. Such, for example, is the prohibition of any laws respecting the establishment of religion, prohibiting the free exercise thereof, or abridging the freedom of speech or of the press.

And it is of importance to observe that Congress has often exercised, without question, powers that are not expressly given nor ancillary to any single enumerated power. Powers thus exercised are what are called by Judge Story in his Commentaries on the Constitution, resulting powers, arising from the aggregate powers of the government. He instances the right to sue and make contracts. Many others might be given. The oath required by law from officers of the government is one. So is building a capitol or a presidential mansion, and so also is the penal code. This last is worthy of brief notice. Congress is expressly authorized "to provide for the punishment of counterfeiting the securities and current coin of the United States, and to define and punish piracies and felonies committed on the high seas and offences against the laws of nations." It is also empowered to declare the punishment of treason, and provision is made for impeachments. This is the extent of power to punish crime expressly conferred. It might be argued that the expression of these limited powers implies an exclusion of all other subjects of criminal legislation. Such is the argument in the present cases. It is said because Congress is authorized to coin money and regulate its value it cannot declare anything other than gold and silver to be money or make it a legal tender. Yet Congress, by the act of April 30, 1790, entitled "An act more effectually to provide for the punishment of certain crimes against the United States," and the supplementary act of March 3d, 1825, defined and provided for the punishment of a large class of crimes other than those mentioned in the Constitution, and some of the punishments prescribed are manifestly not in aid of any single substantive power.

No one doubts that this was rightfully done, and the power thus exercised has been affirmed by this court in *United States v. Marigold*. . . .

Indeed the whole history of the government and of congressional legislation has exhibited the use of a very wide discretion, even in times of peace and in the absence of any trying emergency, in the selection of the necessary and proper means to carry into effect the great objects for which the government was framed, and this discretion has generally been unquestioned, or, if questioned, sanctioned by this court. . . . Under the power to establish post-offices and post-roads Congress has provided for carrying the mails, punishing theft of letters and mail robberies, and even for transporting the mails to foreign countries. Under the power to regulate commerce, provision has been made by law for the improvement of harbors, the establishment of observatories, the erection of lighthouses, breakwaters, and buoys, the registry, enrolment, and construction of ships, and a code has been enacted for the government of seamen. Under the same power and other powers over the revenue and the currency of the country, for the convenience of the treasury and internal commerce, a corporation known as the United States Bank was early created. . . . [T]his Court, in *McCulloch v. Maryland*, unanimously ruled that in authorizing the bank, Congress had not transcended its powers. . . .

Happily the true meaning of the clause authorizing the enactment of all laws necessary and proper for carrying into execution the express powers conferred upon Congress, and all other powers vested in the government of the United States, or in any of its departments or officers, has long since been settled.

[I]n *McCulloch v. Maryland* . . . the fullest consideration was given to this clause of the Constitution granting auxiliary powers, and a construction adopted that has ever since been accepted as determining its true meaning. . . .

[B]efore we can hold the legal tender acts unconstitutional, we must be convinced they were not appropriate means, or means conducive to the execution of any or all of the powers of Congress, or of the government, not appropriate in any degree (for we are not judges of the degree of appropriateness), or we must hold that they were prohibited. This brings us to the inquiry whether they were, when enacted, appropriate instrumentalities for carrying into effect, or executing any of the known powers of Congress, or of any department of the government. . . .

We do not propose to dilate at length upon the circumstances in which the country was placed, when Congress attempted to make treasury notes a legal tender. They are of too recent occurrence to justify enlarged description. Suffice it to say that a civil war was then raging which seriously threatened the overthrow of the government and the destruction of the Constitution itself. It demanded the equipment and support of large armies and navies, and the employment of money to an extent beyond the capacity of all ordinary sources of supply. Meanwhile the public treasury was nearly empty, and the credit of the government, if not stretched to its utmost tension, had become nearly exhausted. Moneyed institutions had advanced largely of their means, and more could not be expected of them. They had been compelled to suspend specie payments. Taxation was inadequate to pay even the interest on the debt already incurred, and it was impossible to await the income of additional taxes. The necessity was immediate and pressing. The army was unpaid. There was then due to the soldiers in the field nearly a score of millions of dollars. The requisitions from the War and

Navy Departments for supplies exceeded fifty millions, and the current expenditure was over one million per day. The entire amount of coin in the country, including that in private hands, as well as that in banking institutions, was insufficient to supply the need of the government three months, had it all been poured into the treasury. Foreign credit we had none. We say nothing of the overhanging paralysis of trade, and of business generally, which threatened loss of confidence in the ability of the government to maintain its continued existence, and therewith the complete destruction of all remaining national credit.

It was at such a time and in such circumstances that Congress was called upon to devise means for maintaining the army and navy, for securing the large supplies of money needed, and, indeed, for the preservation of the government created by the Constitution. It was at such a time and in such an emergency that the legal tender acts were passed. . . .

But if it be conceded that some other means might have been chosen for the accomplishment of these legitimate and necessary ends, the concession does not weaken the argument. It is urged now, after the lapse of nine years, and when the emergency has passed, that treasury notes without the legal tender clause might have been issued, and that the necessities of the government might thus have been supplied. . . . But admitting it to be true, what does it prove? Nothing more than that Congress had the choice of means for a legitimate end, each appropriate, and adapted to that end, though, perhaps, in different degrees. What then? . . . The degree of the necessity for any congressional enactment, or the relative degree of its appropriateness, if it have any appropriateness, is for consideration in Congress, not here. Said Chief Justice Marshall, in *McCulloch v. Maryland*, . . . "When the law is not prohibited, and is really calculated to effect any of the objects entrusted to the government, to undertake here to inquire into the degree of its necessity, would be to pass the line which circumscribes the judicial department, and to tread on legislative ground." . . .

Concluding, then, that the provision which made treasury notes a legal tender for the payment of all debts other than those expressly excepted, was not an inappropriate means for carrying into execution the legitimate powers of the government, we proceed to inquire whether it was forbidden by the letter or spirit of the Constitution. It is not claimed that any express prohibition exists, but it is insisted that the spirit of the Constitution was violated by the enactment. Here those who assert the unconstitutionality of the acts mainly rest their argument. They claim that the clause which conferred upon Congress power "to coin money, regulate the value thereof, and of foreign coin," contains an implication that nothing but that which is the subject of coinage, nothing but the precious metals can ever be declared by law to be money, or to have the uses of money. If by this is meant that because certain powers over the currency are expressly given to Congress, all other powers relating to the same subject are impliedly forbidden, we need only remark that such is not the manner in which the Constitution has always been construed. On the contrary it has been ruled that power over a particular subject may be exercised as auxiliary to an express power, though there is another express power relating to the same subject, less comprehensive. There an express power to punish a certain class of crimes (the only direct reference to criminal legislation contained in the Constitution), was not regarded as an objection to deducing authority to punish other crimes from another substantive and defined grant of power. There are other decisions to the same effect. To assert, then, that the clause enabling

Congress to coin money and regulate its value tacitly implies a denial of all other power over the currency of the nation, is an attempt to introduce a new rule of construction against the solemn decisions of this court. So far from its containing a lurking prohibition, many have thought it was intended to confer upon Congress that general power over the currency which has always been an acknowledged attribute of sovereignty in every other civilized nation than our own, especially when considered in connection with the other clause which denies to the States the power to coin money, emit bills of credit, or make anything but gold and silver coin a tender in payment of debts. . . . The Constitution was intended to frame a government as distinguished from a league or compact, a government supreme in some particulars over States and people. It was designed to provide the same currency, having a uniform legal value in all the States. It was for this reason the power to coin money and regulate its value was conferred upon the Federal government, while the same power as well as the power to emit bills of credit was withdrawn from the States. The States can no longer declare what shall be money, or regulate its value. Whatever power there is over the currency is vested in Congress. Such a construction, it might be said, would be in close analogy to the mode of construing other substantive powers granted to Congress. They have never been construed literally, and the government could not exist if they were. Thus the power to carry on war is conferred by the power to "declare war." The whole system of the transportation of the mails is built upon the power to establish post-offices and post-roads. The power to regulate commerce has also been extended far beyond the letter of the grant. Even the advocates of a strict literal construction of the phrase, "to coin money and regulate the value thereof," while insisting that it defines the material to be coined as metal, are compelled to concede to Congress large discretion in all other particulars. The Constitution does not ordain what metals may be coined, or prescribe that the legal value of the metals, when coined, shall correspond at all with their intrinsic value in the market. Nor does it even affirm that Congress may declare anything to be a legal tender for the payment of debts. . . . How then can the grant of a power to coin money and regulate its value, made in terms so liberal and unrestrained, coupled also with a denial to the States of all power over the currency, be regarded as an implied prohibition to Congress against declaring treasury notes a legal tender, if such declaration is appropriate, and adapted to carrying into execution the admitted powers of the government? . . .

[W]ithout extending our remarks further, it will be seen that we hold the acts of Congress constitutional as applied to contracts made either before or after their passage. In so holding, we overrule so much of what was decided in *Hepburn v. Griswold*, as ruled the acts unwarranted by the Constitution so far as they apply to contracts made before their enactment. That case was decided by a divided court, and by a court having a less number of judges than the law then in existence provided this court shall have. These cases have been heard before a full court, and they have received our most careful consideration. The questions involved are constitutional questions of the most vital importance to the government and to the public at large. . . . [I]t is no unprecedented thing in courts of last resort, both in this country and in England, to overrule decisions previously made. We agree this should not be done inconsiderately, but in a case of such far-reaching consequences as the present, thoroughly convinced as we are that Congress has not transgressed its powers, we regard it as our duty so to decide and to affirm both these judgments.

NOTES

1. Is Justice Strong's opinion persuasive? What types of constitutional argument, or modes of interpretation, does it employ? Does it follow that because other Western democracies can print paper money, our government of limited and enumerated powers can do so? To what extent does his opinion rely on the idea that such a power is necessary, or essential? To what extent is the opinion influenced by the fact that the power was deemed essential during the Civil War? Are these considerations the driving force behind Justice Strong's opinion? How relevant are such considerations?

2. Note the Court's emphasis on *McCulloch v. Maryland*. Indeed, given *McCulloch*'s upholding of broad congressional power under the Necessary and Proper Clause to choose the means for carrying into effect other granted powers, is the issuance of paper money even a close question? Is there any persuasive argument that Congress, given its power to coin money and regulate value, might not have the ability to choose to issue paper notes as legal tender? Is the fact that Congress is granted a specific power to *coin* money a persuasive argument that Congress must not be able to *print paper* money? Note how Justice Strong actually turns this proposition around: the power to coin implies a necessary and proper power to issue paper currency. Are you persuaded?

3. How would *McCulloch*'s "great substantive and independent powers" doctrine, which is discussed above in Note 4 after *NFIB*, apply to paper money?

Naturalization and Immigration

Article I, Section 8, Clause 4 gives Congress the power to "establish an uniform Rule of Naturalization." Does this specific power imply that Congress may, pursuant to the Necessary and Proper Clause, prescribe laws governing *immigration*? Does it imply a power to exclude aliens? No clause in the Constitution specifically gives Congress the power to exclude aliens from coming into our country, and no clause provides the power to expel them once they are here. Yet the courts have long understood Congress to possess essentially plenary power over immigration. Is this a sound conclusion?

The Alien Act of 1798, which was discussed in Chapter 1, granted President John Adams the power to expel enemy aliens unilaterally, and both James Madison and Thomas Jefferson objected that the act was unconstitutional. The issue of excluding or expelling aliens next became salient in the 1880s, with the immigration of Chinese laborers to California. In *The Chinese Exclusion Case*, 130 U.S. 581 (1889), the Supreme Court addressed the question whether Congress had power to *exclude* aliens from entering the country, upholding such a power. In the case that follows, the Court reviewed that decision and extended it, upholding a power to *expel* resident aliens with no more due process than an order from an executive branch official.

Fong Yue Ting v. United States
149 U.S. 698 (1893)

■ MR. JUSTICE GRAY, after stating the facts, delivered the opinion of the court.

The general principles of public law which lie at the foundation of these cases are clearly established by previous judgments of this court, and by the authorities therein referred to.

In the recent case of *Nishimura Ekiu v. U. S.*, 142 U. S. 651, 659, the court, in sustaining the action of the executive department, putting in force an act of congress for the exclusion of aliens, said: "It is an accepted maxim of international law that every sovereign nation has the power, as inherent in sovereignty, and essential to self-preservation, to forbid the entrance of foreigners within its dominions, or to admit them only in such cases and upon such conditions as it may see fit to prescribe. In the United States this power is vested in the national government, to which the constitution has committed the entire control of international relations, in peace as well as in war. It belongs to the political department of the government, and may be exercised either through treaties made by the president and senate or through statutes enacted by congress."

The same views were more fully expounded in the earlier case of *Chae Chan Ping v. U.S.*, 130 U. S. 581, in which the validity of a former act of congress, excluding Chinese laborers from the United States, under the circumstances therein stated, was affirmed.

In the elaborate opinion delivered by Mr. Justice Field in behalf of the court it was said: "Those laborers are not citizens of the United States; they are aliens. That the government of the United States, through the action of the legislative department, can exclude aliens from its territory, is a proposition which we do not think open to controversy. Jurisdiction over its own territory to that extent is an incident of every independent nation. It is a part of its independence. If it could not exclude aliens, it would be to that extent subject to the control of another power." "The United States, in their relation to foreign countries and their subjects or citizens, are one nation, invested with powers which belong to independent nations, the exercise of which can be invoked for the maintenance of its absolute independence and security throughout its entire territory." 130 U. S. 603, 604.

It was also said, repeating the language of Mr. Justice Bradley in *Knox v. Lee*, 12 Wall. 457, 555: "The United States is not only a government, but it is a national government, and the only government in this country that has the character of nationality. It is invested with power over all the foreign relations of the country, war, peace, and negotiations and intercourse with other nations; all of which are forbidden to the state governments." 130 U. S. 605. And it was added: "For local interests, the several states of the Union exist; but for international purposes, embracing our relations with foreign nations, we are but one people, one nation, one power."

The court then went on to say: "To preserve its independence, and give security against foreign aggression and encroachment, is the highest duty of every nation; and to attain these ends nearly all other considerations are to be subordinated. It matters not in what form such aggression and encroachment come, whether from the foreign nation acting in its national character, or from vast hordes of its people crowding in upon us. . . . If, therefore, the government of the United States, through its legislative department, considers the presence of foreigners of a different race in this country, who will not assimilate with us, to be dangerous to its peace and security, their exclusion is not to be stayed because at the time there are no actual hostilities with the nation of which the foreigners are subjects. . . . The power of the government to exclude foreigners from the country, whenever, in its judgment, the public interests require such exclusion, has been asserted in repeated instances, and never denied by the executive or legislative departments." 130 U. S. 606, 607. . . .

The right of a nation to expel or deport foreigners who have not been naturalized, or taken any steps towards becoming citizens of the country, rests upon the same grounds, and is as absolute and unqualified, as the right to prohibit and prevent their entrance into the country.

This is clearly affirmed in dispatches referred to by the court in *Chae Chan Ping's Case*. The statements of leading commentators on the law of nations are to the same effect. . . .

The right to exclude or to expel all aliens, or any class of aliens, absolutely or upon certain conditions, in war or in peace, being an inherent and inalienable right of every sovereign and independent nation, essential to its safety, its independence, and its welfare, the question now before the court is whether the manner in which congress has exercised this right in sections 6 and 7 of the act of 1892 is consistent with the constitution.

The United States are a sovereign and independent nation, and are vested by the constitution with the entire control of international relations, and with all the powers of government necessary to maintain that control, and to make it effective. The only government of this country which other nations recognize or treat with is the government of the Union, and the only American flag known throughout the world is the flag of the United States. . . .

As long ago said by Chief Justice Marshall, and since constantly maintained by this court: "The sound construction of the constitution must allow to the national legislature that discretion, with respect to the means by which the powers it confers are to be carried into execution, which will enable that body to perform the high duties assigned to it, in the manner most beneficial to the people. Let the end be legitimate, let it be within the scope of the constitution; and all means which are appropriate, which are plainly adapted to that end, which are not prohibited, but consistent with the letter and spirit of the constitution, are constitutional." "Where the law is not prohibited, and is really calculated to effect any of the objects intrusted to the government, to undertake here to inquire into the degree of its necessity would be to pass the line which circumscribes the judicial department, and to tread on legislative ground. This court disclaims all pretensions to such a power." *McCulloch v. Maryland*, 4 Wheat. 316, 421, 423; *Juilliard v. Greenman*, 110 U. S. 421, 440, 450.

The power to exclude or to expel aliens, being a power affecting international relations, is vested in the political departments of the government, and is to be regulated by treaty or by act of congress, and to be executed by the executive authority according to the regulations so established, except so far the judicial department has been authorized by treaty or by statute, or is required by the paramount law of the constitution, to intervene. . . .

The power to exclude aliens, and the power to expel them, rest upon one foundation, are derived from one source, are supported by the same reasons, and are in truth but parts of one and the same power.

The power of congress, therefore, to expel, like the power to exclude, aliens, or any specified class of aliens, from the country, may be exercised entirely through executive officers; or congress may call in the aid of the judiciary to ascertain any contested facts on which an alien's right to be in the country has been made by congress to depend.

Congress, having the right, as it may see fit, to expel aliens of a particular class, or to permit them to remain, has undoubtedly the right to provide a system of registration and identification of the members of that class within the country, and to take all proper means to carry out the system which it provides. . . .

By the law of nations, doubtless, aliens residing in a country, with the intention of making it a permanent place of abode, acquire, in one sense, a domicile there; and, while they are permitted by the nation to retain such a residence and domicile, are subject to its laws, and may invoke its protection against other nations. This is recognized by those publicists who, as has been seen, maintain in the strongest terms the right of the nation to expel any or all aliens at its pleasure.

Chinese laborers, therefore, like all other aliens residing in the United States for a shorter or longer time, are entitled, so long as they are permitted by the government of the United States to remain in the country, to the safeguards of the constitution, and to the protection of the laws, in regard to their rights of person and of property, and to their civil and criminal responsibility. But they continue to be aliens, having taken no steps towards becoming citizens, and incapable of becoming such under the naturalization laws; and therefore remain subject to the power of congress to expel them, or to order them to be removed and deported from the country, whenever, in its judgment, their removal is necessary or expedient for the public interest. . . .

The question whether, and upon what conditions, these aliens shall be permitted to remain within the United States being one to be determined by the political departments of the government, the judicial department cannot properly express an opinion upon the wisdom, the policy, or the justice of the measures enacted by congress in the exercise of the powers confided to it by the constitution over this subject.

The three cases now before us do not differ from one another in any material particular. In the first case the petitioner had wholly neglected, failed, and refused to apply to the collector of internal revenue for a certificate of residence. . . . In the second case the petitioner had likewise neglected, failed, and refused to apply to the collector of internal revenue for a certificate of residence. . . . In the third case the petitioner had, within the year, applied to a collector of internal revenue for a certificate of residence, and had been refused it, because he produced, and could produce, none but Chinese witnesses. . . .

Upon careful consideration of the subject, the only conclusion which appears to us to be consistent with the principles of international law, with the constitution and laws of the United States, and with the previous decisions of this court, is that in each of these cases the judgment of the circuit court dismissing the writ of habeas corpus is right, and must be affirmed.

■ MR. JUSTICE BREWER, dissenting.

. . . I rest my dissent on three propositions: First, that the persons against whom the penalties of section 6 of the act of 1892 are directed are persons lawfully residing within the United States; secondly, that as such they are within the protection of the constitution, and secured by its guaranties against oppression and wrong; and, third, that section 6 deprives them of liberty, and imposes punishment, without due process of law, and in disregard of constitutional guaranties, especially those found in the 4th, 5th, 6th, and 8th articles of the amendments.

. . . [F]irst, these persons are lawfully residing within the limits of the United States. *[The discussion of treaties between the U.S. and China is omitted.—Editors]* . . . [Subsequently], congress passed several acts . . . to restrict the entrance into this country of Chinese laborers, and while the validity of this restriction was sustained in the *Chinese Exclusion Case,* 130 U. S. 581, yet no act has been passed, denying the right of those laborers who had once lawfully entered the country to remain, and they are here not as travelers, or only temporarily. We must take judicial notice of that which is disclosed by the census, and which is also a matter of common knowledge. There are 100,000 and more of these persons living in this country, making their homes here, and striving by their labor to earn a livelihood. They are not travelers, but resident aliens. . . .

That those who have become domiciled in a country are entitled to a more distinct and larger measure of protection than those who are simply passing through, or temporarily in, it, has long been recognized by the law of nations. . . . Indeed, there is force in the contention of counsel for appellants that these persons are "denizens," within the true meaning and spirit of that word as used in the common law. . . . "A denizen is an alien born, but who has obtained ex donatione regis letters patent to make him an English subject. . . . A denizen is in a kind of middle state between an alien and a natural-born subject, and partakes of both of them." 1 Bl. Comm. 374. . . .

[W]hatever rights a resident alien might have in any other nation, here he is within the express protection of the constitution, especially in respect to those guaranties which are declared in the original amendments. It has been repeated so often as to become axiomatic that this government is one of enumerated and delegated powers; and, as declared in article 10 of the amendments, "the powers not delegated to the United States by the constitution, nor prohibited by it to the states, are reserved to the states, respectively, or to the people."

It is said that the power here asserted is inherent in sovereignty. This doctrine of powers inherent in sovereignty is one both indefinite and dangerous. Where are the limits to such powers to be found, and by whom are they to be pronounced? Is it within legislative capacity to declare the limits? If so, then the mere assertion of an inherent power creates it, and despotism exists. May the courts establish the boundaries? Whence do they obtain the authority for this? Shall they look to the practices of other nations to ascertain the limits? The governments of other nations have elastic powers. Ours are fixed and bounded by a written constitution. The expulsion of a race may be within the inherent powers of a despotism. History, before the adoption of this constitution, was not destitute of examples of the exercise of such a power; and its framers were familiar with history, and wisely, and it seems to me, they gave to this government no general power to banish. Banishment may be resorted to as punishment for crime; but among the powers reserved to the people, and not delegated to the government, is that of determining whether whole classes in our midst shall, for no crime but that of their race and birthplace, be driven from our territory.

Whatever may be true as to exclusion,—and as to that see *Chinese Exclusion Case,* 130 U. S. 581, and *Nishimura Ekiu v. United States,* 142 U.S 651,—I deny that there is any arbitrary and unrestrained power to banish residents, even resident aliens. What, it may be asked, is the reason for any difference? The answer is obvious. The constitution has no extraterritorial effect, and those who have not come lawfully within our territory cannot claim any protection from its provisions; and it may be that the national government, having full control of all matters relating to other nations, has the power to build, as it were, a Chinese wall around our borders, and absolutely forbid aliens to enter. But the constitution has potency everywhere within the limits of our territory, and the powers which the national government may exercise within such limits are those, and only those, given to it by that instrument. Now, the power to remove resident aliens is, confessedly, not expressed. Even if it be among the powers implied, yet still it can be exercised only in subordination to the limitations and restrictions imposed by the constitution. . . .

[T]he use of the word "person" in the fourteenth amendment protects all individuals lawfully within the state, [and so] the use of the same word, "person," in the fifth must be equally comprehensive, and secures to all persons lawfully within the territory of the United States the protection named therein; and a like conclusion must follow as to the sixth.

I pass, therefore, to the consideration of my third proposition: [the law we are considering] deprives [persons] of "life, liberty, and property without due process of law." It imposes punishment without a trial, and punishment cruel and severe. It places the liberty of one individual subject to the unrestrained control of another. . . .

[I]t needs no citation of authorities to support the proposition that deportation is punishment. Every one knows that to be forcibly taken away from home and family and friends and business and property, and sent across the ocean to a distant land, is punishment, and that oftentimes most severe and cruel. Apt and just are the words of one of the framers of this constitution,—President Madison,—when he says, (4 Elliot Deb. 555:) "If the banishment of an alien from a country into which he has been invited as the asylum most auspicious to his happiness,—a country where he may have formed the most tender connections; where he may have invested his entire property, and acquired property of the real and permanent, as well as the movable and temporary, kind; where he enjoys, under the laws, a greater share of the blessings of personal security and personal liberty than he can elsewhere hope for;—if a banishment of this sort be not a punishment, and among the severest of punishments, it will be difficult to imagine a doom to which the name can be applied."

But punishment implies a trial: "No person shall be deprived of life, liberty, or property without due process of law." Due process requires that a man be heard before he is condemned, and both heard and condemned in the due and orderly procedure of a trial, as recognized by the common law from time immemorial. . . . [H]ere the Chinese are not arrested and extradited for trial, but arrested, and, without a trial, punished by banishment. . . .

It is true this statute is directed only against the obnoxious Chinese, but, if the power exists, who shall say it will not be exercised to-morrow against other classes and other people? If the guaranties of these amendments can be thus ignored in order to get rid of this distasteful class, what security have others that a like disregard of its provisions may not be resorted to? . . .

■ MR. JUSTICE FIELD, dissenting.

I also wish to say a few words upon these cases, and upon the extraordinary doctrines announced in support of the orders of the court below.

With the treaties between the United States and China, and the subsequent legislation adopted by congress to prevent the immigration of Chinese laborers into this country, resulting in the exclusion act of October 1, 1888, the court is familiar.... The validity of this act was sustained by this court. *Chinese Exclusion Case*, 130 U. S. 581. In the opinion announcing the decision we considered the treaties with China, and also the legislation of congress, and the causes which led to its enactment. The court cited numerous instances in which statesmen and jurists of eminence had held that it was the undoubted right of every independent nation to exclude foreigners from its limits whenever, in its judgment, the public interests demanded such exclusion....

I had the honor to be the organ of the court in announcing this opinion and judgment. I still adhere to the views there expressed, in all particulars; but between legislation for the exclusion of Chinese persons,—that is, to prevent them from entering the country,—and legislation for the deportation of those who have acquired a residence in the country under a treaty with China, there is a wide and essential difference. The power of the government to exclude foreigners from this country,—that is, to prevent them from entering it,—whenever the public interests, in its judgment, require such exclusion, has been repeatedly asserted by the legislative and executive departments of our government, and never denied; but its power to deport from the country persons lawfully domiciled therein by its consent, and engaged in the ordinary pursuits of life, has never been asserted by the legislative or executive departments, except for crime, or as an act of war, in view of existing or anticipated hostilities, unless the alien act of 1798 can be considered as recognizing that doctrine. 1 Stat. p. 570, c. 58.

That act vested in the president power to order all such aliens as he should adjudge dangerous to the peace and safety of the United States, or should have reasonable grounds to suspect were concerned in any treasonable or secret machinations against the government, to depart out of the territory of the United States within such time as should be expressed in his order; and in case any alien when thus ordered to depart should be found at large within the United States after the term limited in the order, not having obtained a license from the president to reside therein, or, having obtained such license, should not have conformed thereto, he should, on conviction thereof, be imprisoned for a term not exceeding three years, and should never afterwards be admitted to become a citizen of the United States....

The passage of this act produced great excitement throughout the country, and was severely denounced by many of its ablest statesmen and jurists as unconstitutional and barbarous, and among them may be mentioned the great names of Jefferson and Madison, who are throughout our country honored and revered for their lifelong devotion to principles of constitutional liberty. It was defended by its advocates as a war measure....

The decision of the court, and the sanction it would give to legislation depriving resident aliens of the guaranties of the constitution, fill me with apprehensions. Those guaranties are of priceless value to every one resident in the country, whether citizen or alien.... How far will its legislation go? The unnaturalized resident feels it to-day, but if congress can disregard the guaranties with respect to any one domiciled in the country with its consent, it may disregard the guaranties with respect to naturalized citizens. What assurance have we that it may not declare that naturalized citizens of a particular country cannot remain in the United States after a certain day, unless they have in their possession a certificate that they are of good moral character, and attached to the principles of our constitution, which certificate they must obtain from a collector of internal revenue upon the testimony of at least one competent witness of a class or nationality to be designated by the government? . . .

■ [The dissenting opinion of CHIEF JUSTICE FULLER is omitted.]

NOTES

1. What do you think of the majority opinion? Is it despicable and indefensible? Or is it simply the logical consequence of Congress's power over "naturalization" as augmented by the Necessary and Proper Clause—that Congress has plenary power over all matters of immigration and admission of aliens into the nation? Shorn of the questions of policy, who has the better argument as to the correct interpretation of the scope of Congress's constitutional power in this area, the majority or the dissents? What do you think of the dissenters' argument that expulsion from the country violates individual constitutional rights to due process of law and trial? Note that this case remains good law in some respects down to the present day: Resident aliens remain subject to expulsion through predominately non-Article III proceedings even if they have long lived with their families in the United States.

2. If the national government does not have plenary power over immigration matters, is that a power that state governments may exercise? Is there any other alternative? And if national legislative power over such matters does not flow from the Naturalization Clause power (plus the Necessary and Proper Clause), where is it located? These issues remain very much the subject of controversy today. In *Arizona v. United States,* 132 S. Ct. 2492 (2012), the Court considered a constitutional challenge to several provisions of an Arizona law making violations of federal immigration law also state law crimes or vesting state law enforcement officers with duties with respect to determining immigration status. The Court struck down most of the challenged provisions as "preempted" by federal law, including a provision that made it a crime under state law for a person to be in Arizona without valid immigration papers. Justice Kennedy emphasized federal power over immigration policy. For the majority, this power was derived from Article I Section 8—which authorizes the national government to "establish an uniform Rule of Naturalization"—and from the national government's "inherent power as a sovereign to control and conduct relations with foreign nations." In partial dissent, Justice Scalia argued that the states had never surrendered the powers they had as sovereigns to regulate immigration. He appealed to the debate over the Alien and Sedition Acts, the historical practice of state regulation of immigration, and several constitutional provisions recognizing state authority over borders.

3. Is excluding or expelling aliens a "great substantive and independent power"?

The Draft

Congress has the power to "raise and support armies." Does that power entail the power to conscript for involuntary military service? The use of a military "draft" was contemplated during the War of 1812, but it was resisted in some quarters as unconstitutional and was never employed. The first military draft in the United States occurred during the height of the

Civil War and led to the worst anti-draft and anti-war (and also anti-emancipation) riots in our nation's history, in New York City. Yet by the time America entered into World War I, the idea that the federal government's power to raise armies encompassed a power to draft soldiers had become widely accepted. Eventually, after the bitter controversies caused by the draft in the Vietnam War, Congress abolished the draft in favor of a professional, volunteer army in the 1970s. This arrangement has worked well ever since. There is, however, still a requirement that males register for the draft when they turn eighteen. It remains possible that at some point in the future the country will again resort to the draft.

Here are two opinions upholding the constitutionality of a compulsory military draft. The first is President Abraham Lincoln's unpublished legal opinion discussing the constitutionality of a military draft. The document was never made public, but elements of it were reprised in public and private letters of Lincoln discussing the issue. The second opinion is the Supreme Court's decision upholding the World War I draft, *The Selective Draft Law Cases.*

President Lincoln, Unpublished Opinion on the Constitutionality of the Draft

circa September 1863

. . . You who do not wish to be soldiers, do not like this law. This is natural; nor does it imply want of patriotism. Nothing can be so just, and necessary, as to make us like it, if it is disagreeable to us. We are prone, too, to find false arguments with which to excuse ourselves for opposing such disagreeable things. In this case those who desire the rebellion to succeed, and others who seek reward in a different way, are very active in accommodating us with this class of arguments. They tell us the law is unconstitutional. It is the first instance, I believe, in which the power of congress to do a thing has ever been questioned, in a case when the power is given by the constitution in express terms. Whether a power can be implied, when it is not expressed, has often been the subject of controversy; but this is the first case in which the degree of effrontery has been ventured upon, of denying a power which is plainly and distinctly written down in the constitution. The constitution declares that "The congress shall have power . . . To raise and support armies; but no appropriation of money to that use shall be for a longer term than two years." The whole scope of the conscription act is "to raise and support armies." There is nothing else in it. It makes no appropriation of money; and hence the money clause just quoted, is not touched by it. The case simply is the constitution provides that the congress shall have power to raise and support armies; and, by this act, the congress has exercised the power to raise and support armies. This is the whole of it. It is a law made in literal pursuance of this part of the United States Constitution; . . .

Do you admit that the power is given to raise and support armies, and yet insist that by this act congress has not exercised the power in a constitutional mode?—has not done the thing, in the right way? Who is to judge of this? The constitution gives congress the power, but it does not prescribe the mode, or expressly declare who shall prescribe it. In such case congress must prescribe the mode, or relinquish the power. There is no alternative. Congress could not exercise the power to do the thing, if it had not the power of providing a way to do it, when no way is provided by the constitution for doing it. . . . If the constitution had prescribed a mode, congress could and must follow that mode; but as it is, the mode necessarily goes to congress, with the power expressly given. The power is given fully, completely, unconditionally. It is not a power to raise armies *if* State authorities consent; nor *if* the men to compose the armies are entirely willing; but it is a power to raise and support armies given to congress by the constitution, without an if. . . .

Selective Draft Law Cases
245 U.S. 366 (1917)

■ MR. CHIEF JUSTICE WHITE delivered the opinion of the court.

We are here concerned with some of the provisions of the Act of May 18, 1917, entitled "An Act to authorize the President to increase temporarily the Military Establishment of the United States." The law, as its opening sentence declares, was intended to supply temporarily the increased military force which was required by the existing emergency, the war then and now flagrant. . . .

The act proposed to raise a national army . . . by subjecting all male citizens between the ages of twenty-one and thirty to duty in the national army for the period of the existing emergency after the proclamation of the President announcing the necessity for their service, and . . . by providing for selecting from the body so called, on the further proclamation of the President, 500,000 enlisted men and a second body of the same number, should the President in his discretion deem it necessary. To carry out its purposes, the act made it the duty of those liable to the call to present themselves for registration on the proclamation of the President, so as to subject themselves to the terms of the act, and provided full federal means for carrying out the selective draft. It gave the President, in his discretion, power to create local boards to consider claims for exemption for physical disability or otherwise made by those called. The act exempted from subjection to the draft designated United States and state officials, as well as those already in the military or naval service of the United States, regular or duly ordained ministers of religion and theological students under the conditions provided for, and, while relieving from military service in the strict sense the members of religious sects as enumerated whose tenets excluded the moral right to engage in war, nevertheless subjected such persons to the performance of service of a noncombatant character to be defined by the President.

The proclamation of the President calling the persons designated within the ages described in the statute was made, and the plaintiffs in error, who were in the class and, under the statute, were obliged to present themselves for registration and subject themselves to the law, failed to do so, and were prosecuted under the statute for the penalties for which it provided. They all defended by denying that there had been conferred by the Constitution upon Congress the power to compel military service by a selective draft, and asserted that, even if such power had been given by the Constitution to Congress, the terms of the particular act for various reasons caused it to be beyond the power and repugnant to the Constitution. The cases are here for review because of the constitutional questions thus raised, convictions having resulted from instructions of the courts that the legal defences were without merit, and that the statute was constitutional.

The possession of authority to enact the statute must be found in the clauses of the Constitution giving Congress power ["]to declare war; . . . to raise and support armies, but no appropriation of money to that use shall be for a longer term than two years; . . . to make rules for the government and regulation of the land and naval forces.["] Article I, § 8. And, of course, the powers conferred by these provisions, like all other powers given, carry with them, as provided by the Constitution, the authority "to make all laws which shall be necessary and proper for carrying into execution the foregoing powers." Article I, § 8.

As the mind cannot conceive an army without the men to compose it, on the face of the Constitution, the objection that it does not give power to provide for such men would seem to be too frivolous for further notice. It is said, however, that since, under the Constitution as originally framed, state citizenship was primary, and United States citizenship but derivative and dependent thereon, therefore the power conferred upon Congress to raise armies was only coterminous with United States citizenship, and could not be exerted so as to cause that citizenship to lose its dependent character and dominate state citizenship. But the proposition simply denies to Congress the power to raise armies which the Constitution gives. That power, by the very terms of the Constitution being delegated, is supreme. Article VI. In truth, the contention simply assails the wisdom of the framers of the Constitution in conferring authority on Congress, and in not retaining it as it was under the Confederation in the several States. Further, it is said, the right to provide is not denied by calling for volunteer enlistments, but it does not and cannot include the power to exact enforced military duty by the citizen. This however but challenges the existence of all power, for a governmental power which has no sanction to it and which therefore can only be exercised provided the citizen consents to its exertion is in no substantial sense a power. It is argued, however, that, although this is abstractly true, it is not concretely so, because, as compelled military service is repugnant to a free government and in conflict with all the great guarantees of the Constitution as to individual liberty, it must be assumed that the authority to raise armies was intended to be limited to the right to call an army into existence counting alone upon the willingness of the citizen to do his duty in time of public need, that is, in time of war. But the premise of this proposition is so devoid of foundation that it leaves not even a shadow of ground upon which to base the conclusion. Let us see if this is not at once demonstrable. It may not be doubted that the very conception of a just government and its duty to the citizen includes the reciprocal obligation of the citizen to render military service in case of need, and the right to compel it. Vattel, Law of Nations, Book III, c. 1 & 2. To do more than state the proposition is absolutely unnecessary in view of the practical illustration afforded by the almost universal legislation to that effect now in force. . . . *[The opinion next reviewed the practice in England dating back to before the Norman Conquest.—Editors]*

In the Colonies before the separation from England, there cannot be the slightest doubt that the right to enforce military service was unquestioned, and that practical effect was given to the power in many cases. Indeed, the brief of the Government contains a list of Colonial acts manifesting the power and its enforcement in more than two hundred cases. And this exact situation existed also after the separation. . . . [I]t is indisputable that the States, in response to the calls made upon them, met the situation when they deemed it necessary by directing enforced military service on the part of the citizens. In fact, the duty of the citizen to render military service and the power to compel him against his consent to do so was expressly sanctioned by the constitutions of at least nine of the States. . . .

When the Constitution came to be formed, it may not be disputed that one of the recognized necessities for its adoption was the want of power in Congress to raise an army and the dependence upon the States for their quotas. In supplying the power, it was manifestly intended to give it all, and leave none to the States, since, besides the delegation to Congress of authority to raise armies, the Constitution prohibited the States, without the consent of Congress, from keeping troops in time of peace or engaging in war. Article I, § 10.

To argue that, as the state authority over the militia prior to the Constitution embraced every citizen, the right of Congress to raise an army should not be considered as granting authority to compel the citizen's service in the army is but to express in a different form the denial of the right to call any citizen to the army. . . .

The fallacy of the argument results from confounding the constitutional provisions concerning the militia with that conferring upon Congress the power to raise armies. It treats them as one, while they are different. This is the militia clause:

> The Congress shall have power . . . To provide for calling forth the militia to execute the laws of the Union, suppress insurrections and repel invasions; To provide for organizing, arming, and disciplining the militia, and for governing such part of them as may be employed in the service of the United States, reserving to the States, respectively, the appointment of the officers, and the authority of training the militia according to the discipline prescribed by Congress.

Article I, § 8.

The line which separates it from the army power is not only inherently plainly marked by the text of the two clauses, but will stand out in bolder relief by considering the condition before the Constitution was adopted and the remedy which it provided for the military situation with which it dealt. The right, on the one hand, of Congress under the Confederation to call on the States for forces, and the duty, on the other, of the States to furnish when called, embraced the complete power of government over the subject. When the two were combined and were delegated to Congress, all governmental power on that subject was conferred, a result manifested not only by the grant made, but by the limitation expressly put upon the States on the subject. The army sphere therefore embraces such complete authority. . . .

And upon this understanding of the two powers, the legislative and executive authority has been exerted from the beginning. From the act of the first session of Congress carrying over the army of the Government under the Confederation to the United States under the Constitution (Act of September 29, 1789, c. 25, 1 Stat. 95) down to 1812, the authority to raise armies was regularly exerted as a distinct and substantive power, the force being raised and recruited by enlistment. . . .

[The opinion describes early practice, including a proposal for a draft in the War of 1812, which encountered political and constitutional objections. A draft was not suggested for the Mexican War.—Editors]

So the course of legislation from that date to 1861 affords no ground for any other than the same conception of legislative power which we have already stated. In that year, when the mutterings of the dread conflict which was to come began to be heard and the Proclamation of the President calling a force into existence was issued, it was addressed to the body organized out of the militia and trained by the States in accordance with the previous acts of Congress. (Proclamation of April 15, 1861, 12 Stat. 1258.) That force being inadequate to meet the situation, an act was passed authorizing the acceptance of 500,000 volunteers by the President to be by him organized into a national army. (Act of July 22, 1861, c. 9, 12 Stat. 268.) This was soon followed by another act increasing the force of the militia to be organized by the States for the purpose of being drawn upon when trained under the direction of Congress (Act of July 29, 1861, c. 25, 12 Stat. 281), the two acts, when considered together, presenting in the clearest possible form the distinction between the power of Congress to raise armies and its authority under the militia clause. But it soon became manifest that more men were required. As a result, the Act of March 3, 1863, c. 75, 12 Stat. 731, was adopted, entitled "An Act for enrolling and calling out the National Forces and for other purposes." By that act, which was clearly intended to directly exert upon all the citizens of the United States the national power which it had been proposed to exert in 1814 on the recommendation of the then Secretary of War, Mr. Monroe, every male citizen of the United States between the ages of twenty and forty-five was made subject by the direct action of Congress to be called by compulsory draft to service in a national army at such time and in such numbers as the President in his discretion might find necessary. In that act, as in the one of 1814 and in this one, the means by which the act was to be enforced were directly federal, and the force to be raised as a result of the draft was therefore typically national, as distinct from the call into active service of the militia as such. And under the power thus exerted, four separate calls for draft were made by the President and enforced, that of July, 1863, of February and March, 1864, of July and December, 1864, producing a force of about a quarter of a million men. It is undoubted that the men thus raised by draft were treated as subject to direct national authority and were used either in filling the gaps occasioned by the vicissitudes of war in the ranks of the existing national forces or for the purpose of organizing such new units as were deemed to be required. It would be childish to deny the value of the added strength which was thus afforded. . . .

Thus sanctioned as is the act before us by the text of the Constitution and by its significance as read in the light of the fundamental principles with which the subject is concerned, by the power recognized and carried into effect in many civilized countries, by the authority and practice of the colonies before the Revolution, of the States under the Confederation, and of the Government since the formation of the Constitution, the want of merit in the contentions that the act in the particulars which we have been previously called upon to consider was beyond the constitutional power of Congress is manifest. . . .

It remains only to consider contentions which, while not disputing power, challenge the act because of the repugnancy to the Constitution supposed to result from some of its provisions. First, we are of opinion that the contention that the act is void as a delegation of federal power to state officials because of some of its administrative features is too wanting in merit to require further notice. Second, we think that the contention that the statute is void because vesting administrative officers with legislative discretion has been so completely adversely settled as to require reference only to some of the decided cases. A like conclusion also adversely disposes of a similar claim concerning the conferring of judicial power. And we pass without anything but statement the proposition that an establishment of a religion or an interference with the free exercise thereof repugnant to the First Amendment resulted from the exemption clauses of the act to which we at the outset referred because we think its unsoundness is too apparent to require us to do more.

Finally, as we are unable to conceive upon what theory the exaction by government from the citizen of the performance of his supreme and noble duty of contributing to the defense of the rights and honor of the nation, as the result of a war declared by the great representative body of the people, can be said to be the imposition of involuntary servitude in violation of the prohibitions of the Thirteenth Amendment, we are constrained to the conclusion that the contention to that effect is refuted by its mere statement.

NOTES

1. President Lincoln's unpublished memorandum contains the simplest argument for the constitutionality of a military draft: the text explicitly gives Congress the power to "raise and support armies" and does not specify the means. The draft is a means of raising armies. Is there any good response to this textual argument? Does it matter how important the implied means is? (Recall the discussion in *McCulloch* and *NFIB* of "great substantive and independent powers"—is the draft one?) Note that President Lincoln says that the result is, of course, distasteful to many, but he carefully separates the legal argument from the political or practical one. Is this proper? What policy arguments—sounding in considerations of military necessity, tradition, justice, and personal freedom—could be made about the draft? What weight should be given to those arguments here? Should they be able to displace what otherwise would appear to be the proper interpretation of the Constitution? Does the Constitution, rightly construed, sometimes permit some unfortunate policy results? (Is the draft one of them? Would *not* having the draft be one of them?)

2. The Court in *The Selective Draft Law Cases* says that there was a long controversy in England over whether the king or the Parliament had the power to draft troops, but that it was always assumed that both of them acting together could do so. Does it follow that in the United States the president and Congress acting together can also draft troops under the Constitution? What types of constitutional argument does the Court draw on? Does the Court emphasize practice more than text? Could a sufficiently clear historical practice properly lead to a conclusion that the text does not mean what it seems to say?

3. Federalism and a balance between state and national power are built into the original Constitution's scheme with respect to the military. The national government had the power to declare and wage war, with the president serving as commander in chief, but most of the troops would be from the state militias, which were essentially state armies. If the president and Congress did not take care, they might find the state militias recalcitrant or disobedient. Congress did have power to raise armies, but the framers probably thought that such a mercenary standing army was inimical to liberty. Note that the Third Amendment reflects this view by forbidding the quartering of troops in peoples' houses—a kind of a draft of property—in time of peace. Even in time of war, any quartering of troops in homes must be done according to law. The framers would probably have thought that any power to draft was a power of the states to compel service in their militias, which could then be "federalized"

under presidential command, but with each soldier serving with his neighbors under officers from his own state. This original military structure resulted in an army that had loyalties to both its home state and to the nation.

4. In the Civil War, eleven state militias banded together and formed the Confederate army. This was the danger inherent in the framers' original scheme of dividing military power between the nation and the states. After the Civil War, the state militias were turned into national guard units, and national control over the officer corps of the army was greatly enhanced. Today, the term "state militia" sounds positively quaint.

In light of this constitutional history, do you think a military draft in World War I was authorized either by the power to raise armies or by Congress's power to adopt "necessary and proper" means for winning the war against Germany? Does the fact that Germany and France had historically imposed a draft have any bearing on whether doing so is "necessary and proper" under the U.S. Constitution?

From time to time politicians talk about imposing on a duty of one or two years of mandatory community service (along the lines of the Peace Corps or Teach for America except, of course, being involuntary). This is obviously analogous to the draft. Does Congress have power under the Constitution to do this?

The Treaty–Executing Power

In Chapter 3, we saw that Article III of the Constitution provides that the president may make treaties that have the force of U.S. law, where consented to by two-thirds vote of the Senate. Congress's legislative power under the Necessary and Proper Clause has long been understood to include the power to enact laws for carrying into execution America's treaty obligations. Does this mean that the president, acting with the Senate, may make a treaty that has the effect, as a practical matter, of enlarging Congress's legislative powers under the Constitution? May a treaty confer upon Congress power to enact laws it otherwise would not have? If so, does the treaty power enable an end-run around the Constitution's principle of limited and enumerated legislative power? A related question is whether a treaty may abridge an individual right protected under the Bill of Rights. For example, could we join an international agreement to prohibit "hate speech" or "laws defaming religion" (as some nations in Europe and the Middle East are currently urging), even though these kinds of speech are broadly protected by the First Amendment?

These questions are important ones—and increasingly so as the United States has assumed, by treaty, broader international legal commitments (and corresponding domestic-law obligations) than ever before. The issue was addressed in the context of federalism in *Missouri v. Holland* (1920), and in the context of individual rights in *Reid v. Covert* (1957).

Missouri v. Holland
252 U.S. 416 (1920)

■ MR. JUSTICE HOLMES delivered the opinion of the Court.

This is a bill in equity brought by the State of Missouri to prevent a game warden of the United States from attempting to enforce the Migratory Bird Treaty Act of July 3, 1918, and the regulations made by the Secretary of Agriculture in pursuance of the same. The ground of the bill is that the statute is an unconstitutional interference with the rights reserved to the States by the Tenth Amendment, and that the acts of the defendant done and threatened under that authority invade the sovereign right of the State and contravene its will manifested in statutes. The State also alleges a pecuniary interest, as owner of the wild birds within its borders. . . .

On December 8, 1916, a treaty between the United States and Great Britain was proclaimed by the President. It recited that many species of birds in their annual migrations traversed many parts of the United States and of Canada, that they were of great value as a source of food and in destroying insects injurious to vegetation, but were in danger of extermination through lack of adequate protection. It therefore provided for specified closed seasons and protection in other forms, and agreed that the two powers would take or propose to their lawmaking bodies the necessary measures for carrying the treaty out. The above mentioned act of July 3, 1918, entitled an act to give effect to the convention, prohibited the killing, capturing or selling any of the migratory birds included in the terms of the treaty except as permitted by regulations compatible with those terms, to be made by the Secretary of Agriculture. . . . [T]he question raised is the general one whether the treaty and statute are void as an interference with the rights reserved to the States. . . .

It is said that a treaty cannot be valid if it infringes the Constitution, that there are limits, therefore, to the treaty-making power, and that one such limit is that what an act of Congress could not do unaided, in derogation of the powers reserved to the States, a treaty cannot do. An earlier act of Congress that attempted by itself and not in pursuance of a treaty to regulate the killing of migratory birds within the States had been held bad in the District Court. *United States v. Shauver*, 214 Fed. 154[;] *United States v. McCullagh*, 221 Fed. 288. Those decisions were supported by arguments that migratory birds were owned by the States in their sovereign capacity for the benefit of their people, and that . . . this control was one that Congress had no power to displace. The same argument is supposed to apply now with equal force.

Whether the two cases cited were decided rightly or not they cannot be accepted as a test of the treaty power. Acts of Congress are the supreme law of the land only when made in pursuance of the Constitution, while treaties are declared to be so when made under the authority of the United States. It is open to question whether the authority of the United States means more than the formal acts prescribed to make the convention. We do not mean to imply that there are no qualifications to the treaty-making power; but they must be ascertained in a different way. It is obvious that there may be matters of the sharpest exigency for the national well being that an act of Congress could not deal with but that a treaty followed by such an act could, and it is not lightly to be assumed that, in matters requiring national action, "a power which must belong to and somewhere reside in every civilized government" is not to be found. *Andrews v. Andrews*, 188 U.S. 14, 33. What was said in that case with regard to the powers of the States applies with equal force to the powers of the nation in cases where the States individually are incompetent to act. We are not yet discussing the particular case before us but only are considering the validity of the test proposed. With regard to that we may add that when we are dealing with words that also are a constituent act, like the Constitution of the United States, we must realize that they have called into life a being the development of which could not have been foreseen completely by the most gifted of its begetters. It was enough for them to realize or to hope that they had created an organism; it has taken a century and has cost their successors much sweat and blood to prove that they created a nation. The case before us must be considered in the light of our whole experience and not merely in that of what was said a hundred years ago. The treaty in question does not contravene any prohibitory words to be found in the Constitution. The only question is whether it is forbidden by some invisible radiation from the general terms of the Tenth Amendment. We must consider what this country has become in deciding what that amendment has reserved.

The State as we have intimated founds its claim of exclusive authority upon an assertion of title to migratory birds, an assertion that is embodied in statute. No doubt it is true that as between a State and its inhabitants the State may regulate the killing and sale of such birds, but it does not follow that its authority is exclusive of paramount powers. To put the claim of the State upon title is to lean upon a slender reed. Wild birds are not in the possession of anyone; and possession is the beginning of ownership. The whole foundation of the State's rights is the presence within their jurisdiction of birds that yesterday had not arrived, tomorrow may be in another State and in a week a thousand miles away. . . .

Here a national interest of very nearly the first magnitude is involved. It can be protected only by national action in concert with that of another power. The subject matter is only transitorily within the State and has no permanent habitat therein. But for the treaty and the statute there soon might be no birds for any powers to deal with. We see nothing in the Constitution that compels the Government to sit by while a food supply is cut off and the protectors of our forests and our crops are destroyed. It is not sufficient to rely upon the States. The reliance is vain, and were it otherwise, the question is whether the United States is forbidden to act. We are of opinion that the treaty and statute must be upheld. . . .

Reid v. Covert

354 U.S. 1 (1957)

■ MR. JUSTICE BLACK delivered the opinion of the Court.

These cases raise basic constitutional issues of the utmost concern. They call into question the role of the military under our system of government. They involve the power of Congress to expose civilians to trial by military tribunals, under military regulations and procedures, for offenses against the United States thereby depriving them of trial in civilian courts, under civilian laws and procedures and with all the safeguards of the Bill of Rights. These cases are particularly significant because for the first time since the adoption of the Constitution wives of soldiers have been denied trial by jury in a court of law and forced to trial before courts-martial. . . .

I

At the beginning we reject the idea that when the United States acts against citizens abroad it can do so free of the Bill of Rights. The United States is entirely a creature of the Constitution. Its power and authority have no other source. It can only act in accordance with all the limitations imposed by the Constitution. When the Government reaches out to punish a citizen who is abroad, the shield which the Bill of Rights and other parts of the Constitution provide to protect his life and liberty should not be stripped away just because he happens to be in another land. . . .

II

At the time of Mrs. Covert's alleged offense, an executive agreement was in effect between the United States and Great Britain which permitted United States' military courts to exercise exclusive jurisdiction over offenses committed in Great Britain by American servicemen or their dependents. . . . Even though a court-martial does not give an accused trial by jury and other Bill of Rights protections, the Government contends that article 2(11) of [Uniform Code of Military Justice], insofar as it provides for the military trial of dependents accompanying the armed forces in Great Britain and Japan, can be sustained as legislation which is necessary and proper to carry out the United States' obligations under the international agreements made with those countries. The obvious and decisive answer to this, of course, is that no agreement with a foreign nation can confer power on the Congress, or on any other branch of Government, which is free from the restraints of the Constitution.

Article VI, the Supremacy Clause of the Constitution, declares:

> This Constitution, and the Laws of the United States which shall be made in Pursuance thereof; and all Treaties made, or which shall be made, under the Authority of the United States, shall be the supreme Law of the Land . . .

There is nothing in this language which intimates that treaties and laws enacted pursuant to them do not have to comply with the provisions of the Constitution. Nor is there anything in the debates which accompanied the drafting and ratification of the Constitution which even suggests such a result. These debates as well as the history that surrounds the adoption of the treaty provision in Article VI make it clear that the reason treaties were not limited to those made in "pursuance" of the Constitution was so that agreements made by the United States under the Articles of Confederation, including the important peace treaties which concluded the Revolutionary War, would remain in effect. It would be manifestly contrary to the objectives of those who created the Constitution, as well as those who were responsible for the Bill of Rights—let alone alien to our entire constitutional history and tradition—to construe Article VI as permitting the United States to exercise power under an international agreement without observing constitutional prohibitions. In effect, such construction would permit amendment of that document in a manner not sanctioned by Article V. The prohibitions of the Constitution were designed to apply to all branches of the National Government and they cannot be nullified by the Executive or by the Executive and the Senate combined.

NOTES

1. How broad is the treaty power of the president and the Senate acting together? For example, could a treaty forbid the fifty American states from having a death penalty if Congress lacks the enumerated power to enact such a federal law? Could the national government by treaty abrogate the First Amendment as well as federalism? Why, in principle, should enumerated-powers limitations on Congress be more easily overcome (if indeed they can be) than the limitations the Bill of Rights puts on the federal government? Can *Missouri v. Holland* and *Reid v. Covert* be reconciled? Why is the Tenth Amendment not as specific a limitation as the Fifth or Sixth Amendments?

Under the logic of these decisions, could a treaty violate the separation of powers, for example by imposing a tax or a law by treaty, without passage of implementing legislation by the full Congress?

2. What, precisely, is the holding of *Missouri v. Holland?* The opinion states: "We do not mean to imply that there are no qualifications to the treaty-making power; but they must be ascertained in a different way." Is that consistent with the Court's argument from the text of the Supremacy Clause? Later in the opinion, the Court comments that the treaty in question involves "a national interest of very nearly the first magnitude" on which the "the States individually are incompetent to act." Should we understand those criteria to be limitations on the treaty power? Where do those limits come from, if they are limits? Is there some natural scope or limit deriving from the nature of treaties? When the Constitution was drafted, the law of nations limited treaties to matters of clashing sovereign interests; more recently treaties commonly limit the powers of governments vis-à-vis their own citizens. Is this modern development legitimate under our constitutional system?

Advocates of various causes, impatient with the limitations on federal authority, have proposed that we enter into treaties on the subjects of their interest, and rely on *Missouri v. Holland* to say that Congress would then have the Necessary and Proper Clause power to implement the treaty. For example, treaties could supply the federal authority found lacking to enforce the Religious Freedom Restoration Act against state governments, the Violence Against Women Act, and protections for wholly intrastate endangered species. In response, a scholar has launched a challenge to *Missouri v. Holland.* See Nicholas Rosenkranz, *Executing the Treaty Power,* 118 Harv. L. Rev. 1867 (2005) (arguing that the treaty power cannot enlarge the legislative power of Congress).

Rosenkranz's argument does not extend to self-executing treaties, about which there is also a lively academic debate. The treaty most important to the framers, the Treaty of Paris ending the Revolutionary War, contained provisions interfering with state laws regarding the debts and other property of English citizens and Tories. These provisions fall outside the enumerated powers of Congress. Federalists nonetheless regarded them as binding on the states, though there was great disagreement about how the states could be compelled to comply with them. See John T. Perry, *Congress, the Supremacy Clause, and the Implementation of Treaties,* 32 Fordham Int'l Law J. 1209 (2009).

3. An international treaty, the Vienna Convention on Consular Relations, requires signatory nations to inform foreign nationals who are arrested that they have the right to have their embassy or consulate notified of their arrest. In *Medellin v. Texas,* 552 U.S. 491 (2008), the state of Texas had neglected to provide this notice to a Mexican national on death row. In prior litigation the Supreme Court had held the treaty was not self-executing. Mexico brought suit in the International Court of Justice ("ICJ"), claiming that the United States was failing to comply with the treaty. The United States, however, had withdrawn from the ICJ many years before. Nevertheless, the ICJ ruled that the United States was in violation of the Vienna Convention. In an attempt to effectuate the ICJ's judgment, President George W. Bush issued a memorandum to the attorney general in which he directed the states to review the convictions and sentences of individuals whose rights under the Vienna Convention had been violated. The Texas court did not change its view that, under applicable

law, Medellin's conviction had been proper. The U.S. Supreme Court then held that President Bush's memorandum had no legal force, basing its judgment on both separation of powers and federalism principles. Do you think the Court's ruling was correct? Can (or should) the interpretation of a treaty by an international body override state law? If so, what is the enforcement mechanism? What is the president's role? What could Congress have done had it wished to comply with the ICJ decision?

4. A pending Supreme Court case, *United States v. Bond*, 681 F.3d 149 (3d Cir. 2012), *cert. granted* 133 S. Ct. 978 (Jan. 18, 2013), resubmits, in part, the question presented in *Missouri v. Holland*. The facts are memorable: Carol Bond learned that her friend Myrlinda Haynes was pregnant and that the father was Ms. Bond's husband. Ms. Bond acquired highly toxic chemicals and put them on Ms. Haynes' mailbox, car door handles, and house doorknob. She was indicted for violating the Chemical Weapons Convention Implementation Act of 1998, which implemented the 1993 Chemical Weapons Convention Act, a treaty to which the United States is a party. Ms. Bond challenged her conviction on the ground that the statute violated the Tenth Amendment. An earlier Supreme Court decision in the case upheld the standing of individuals to raise Tenth Amendment and enumerated-powers constitutional objections to statutes to which they were subject. *Bond v. United States*, 131 S. Ct. 2355 (2011). On remand, the Third Circuit upheld the statute on the authority of *Missouri v. Holland*. What will the Court decide this time?

[*Assignment 37*]

II. ARTICLE IV FEDERALISM: THE RELATIONSHIP OF THE STATES TO EACH OTHER AND TO THE NATION AS A WHOLE

Articles I, II, and III of the Constitution set forth, respectively, the powers of the legislative, executive, and judicial branches of the national government. Article IV is different: its provisions *bind the states to one another as a Union*. Article IV provides for interstate comity—each state must recognize the judgments of other states' court systems, and must to some extent recognize and apply other states' laws (the Full Faith and Credit Clause). Article IV provides for certain reciprocal benefits and privileges for the citizens of each state (the Privileges and Immunities Clause). Article IV requires the rendition of fugitives from one state to another—both fugitives from justice (the Extradition Clause) and, originally, fugitive slaves (the Fugitive Slave Clause). It provides for the admission of new states, and for Congress's power to legislate for the territories unless and until they are admitted as new states (the Statehood Admission Clause and the Territories Clause). And Article IV establishes the Union's power, and duty, to guarantee each state a republican form of government and protect each state's security against foreign invasion or domestic insurrection (the Guarantee Clause).

Several provisions in Article IV were infected by—one was *about*—the original Constitution's protection of slavery. Recall from Chapter 1 that the opponents of slavery at the Philadelphia Convention in 1787 made a grudging decision that its abolition in North America could be accomplished only if they first set up a powerful central government in place of the one existing under the Articles of Confederation, and history offers some support for this judgment. Among the concessions the framers made to slavery was the Fugitive Slave Clause, which, as noted above, obligated the free states to return fugitive slaves. This clause forced the free states to become complicit in the institution of slavery. Nothing did more to inflame Northern opinion against slavery than the efforts in the 1840s and 1850s of slave-catchers to force the extradition to the South of alleged fugitive slaves in the federal and state courts sitting in the free states. Slave-catching and extradition fueled the Abolitionist movement in the North.

The study of major nineteenth century cases involving slavery is fascinating and important in its own right, both historically and as a study of constitutional injustice. And—relevant for the consideration of these cases here—slavery was the theme in many of the early cases arising under Article IV. Those cases show how Article IV works, then and now. They are a constitutional lens through which to view modern controversies, including questions such as whether a same-sex marriage recognized by one state must be recognized in another. We begin with a map of the federalism provisions of Article IV.

A Map of Article IV of the U.S. Constitution

Section 1: Full Faith and Credit shall be given in each State to the public Acts, Records, and judicial Proceedings of every other State. And the Congress may by general Laws prescribe the Manner in which such Acts, Records and Proceedings shall be proved, and the Effect thereof.

Article IV begins with a Full Faith and Credit Clause that provides that the final judicial decrees of each state shall be recognized and enforced by the other states. In addition, the *content* of the laws of each state are to be recognized by the other states; they do not need to be "proved" as facts in a sister state's courts (the traditional rule for introducing the content of the law of a "foreign" jurisdiction). For such purposes, the states are not "foreign" to one another.

Beyond this obligation of giving effect to sister-state judgments and recognizing the content of sister-state laws, the Supreme Court has interpreted the Full Faith and Credit Clause as imposing only the barest minimum of constraints on states' choice-of-law principles and state choices made pursuant to those principles. A state is free to apply its own laws to any matter in its courts where there is some connection to the state, giving rise to sufficient interests in that state's applying its own laws, so that doing so is not regarded as fundamentally unfair. The Court has derived that standard from both the Full Faith and Credit Clause and from the Due Process Clause of the Fourteenth Amendment. See *Allstate Insurance Co. v. Hague*, 449 U.S. 302 (1981).

The Full Faith and Credit Clause gives Congress the power to pass laws about the procedure for states' honoring other states' laws. Congress may thus prescribe national choice-of-law rules. Congress has used this power to require that states give the same "full faith and credit" to judgments rendered by another state that the rendering state's courts would give. 28 U.S.C. Section 1738. More controversially, in the Defense of Marriage Act (DOMA), Congress said that laws or judgments of one state that recognize or confer a status of marriage upon same-sex relationships are *not* binding on other states. 28 U.S.C. Section 1738C.

Section 2, Clause 1: The Citizens of each State shall be entitled to all Privileges and Immunities of Citizens in the several States.

The Privileges and Immunities Clause of Article IV is a bulwark of constitutional federalism. It descends in slightly altered form from a Privileges and Immunities Clause that was in the Articles of Confederation (printed in the appendix to this book). What are the "Privileges and Immunities of Citizens in the several States" and who is a citizen? Were free black men and women in the North "citizens" who were entitled by this Clause to exercise First and Second Amendment freedoms while travelling through the South such that they could hand out abolitionist literature and carry guns? Conversely, did Southern slave owners have a constitutional right to hold their slaves in slavery while they were travelling through free states? Did that mean that slavery could not constitutionally be abolished altogether even in the free states?

The best and most widely accepted reading of the Privileges and Immunities Clause is that it prescribes a rule forbidding states from discriminating against out-of-staters with respect to those fundamental "privileges and immunities" of citizenship or civil rights that it accords its own citizens. Simply put, Rhode Island cannot treat Minnesotans differently from the way it treats Rhode Islanders. Thus, the clause is sometimes called the Comity Clause. Whatever civil rights a state gives to its own citizens, it must give the same civil rights to out-of-state citizens.

Does that mean that a state must treat out-of-staters the same as its own citizens with respect to *everything*? No—or, at least, that is what courts have consistently held. The Privileges and Immunities Clause forbids discrimination against out-of-staters only with respect to fundamental or civil rights. States can discriminate against out-of-staters with respect to the use of state property or political rights, such as the right to vote. Thus, a state may charge out-of-staters higher fees to use state parks or obtain fishing licenses, given that in-staters might have had to pay state taxes to support some of these services. States can also forbid out-of-staters from voting or serving on juries since those are political rights, and out-of-staters are not part of the state's polity. Thus the Privileges and Immunities Clause applies only to "fundamental" rights of citizenship, which are best understood to include civil rights but not political rights or equal access to state property.

Section 2, Clause 2: A Person charged in any State with Treason, Felony, or other Crime, who shall flee from Justice, and be found in another State. . . .

The Extradition Clause of Article IV requires, "on Demand of the executive Authority of the State from which [the person charged] fled," that the charged person "be delivered up, to be removed to the State having Jurisdiction of the Crime." This is an obvious interstate-comity provision. It deals with the federalism problem of criminals who flee the state where they committed their crime.

Section 2, Clause 3: No Person held to Service or Labour in one State, under the Laws thereof, escaping into another, shall . . . be discharged from such Service or Labour, but shall be delivered up on Claim of the Party to whom such Service or Labour may be due.

This is the Fugitive Slave Clause of the Constitution. It, too, is a comity provision, of sorts, akin to the Extradition Clause, which immediately precedes it. One notable difference: It is not the "executive Authority" of the state that demands a fugitive's return. Rather, with alleged fugitive slaves, as opposed to fugitives charged with crimes, the person shall be "delivered up" *"on Claim of the Party"*—the person who says he is the master. Does this require a free state to deliver an accused fugitive slave simply on the say-so of any out-of-state person who claims to be the person's master? May a state pass laws providing due process, or jury trial rights, to guard against improper claims? May Congress pass laws specifying federal procedures, as it did with the Fugitive Slave Acts of 1793 and 1850—hotly contested, bitterly divisive pieces of legislation?

> *Section 3: New States may be admitted by the Congress into this Union. . . . The Congress shall have Power to dispose of and make all needful Rules and Regulations respecting the Territory or other Property belonging to the United States. . . .*

Some of the most important non-judicial constitutional controversies in our nation's early history concerned the scope (and exercise) of the power to admit new states, and the power of Congress to legislate with respect to U.S. territories that are not yet states. Note that new states entering the Union are co-equal with the thirteen original states.

> *Section 4: The United States shall guarantee to every State in this Union a Republican Form of Government, and shall protect each of them against Invasion; and . . . domestic Violence.*

The "Guarantee Clause" (also sometimes called the "Republican Form of Government Clause") is a guarantee by the Union as a whole, extended to every state, that each shall always have a "republican" form of government. It is combined with a pledge of the protection by the Union as a whole of every state, as against invasion or domestic violence. As noted, Lincoln relied in part on this clause for his conclusion that the Constitution does not permit a state to secede from the Union, it then being impossible any longer to guarantee it a republican form of government. (Another good argument against secession might be the fact that Article IV contains a provision for admitting new states to the Union, but *not* for permitting states to leave the Union, suggesting perhaps that secession would require a constitutional amendment; indeed, no provision of the Constitution appears to authorize a state to secede.)

The Guarantee Clause is ambiguous about which branch is primarily responsible for enforcing these "guarantees" and about exactly how far the national power created by the Guarantee Clause extends. Recall that *Luther v. Borden*, 48 U.S. 1 (1849), presented in Chapter 3, found these issues to be "political questions" assigned to the discretion of the political branches of the national government. During the Civil War, the Guarantee Clause was invoked by Congress as a source of *its* authority to take legislative action directed against secessionist governments. And the Guarantee Clause was invoked by President Lincoln as a source of *his* authority to take such actions. The clause's lack of perfect clarity about enforcement permitted each branch to make claims for itself, and to some extent papered over certain tensions between them—tensions that emerged into full-blown interbranch conflict during Reconstruction.

What are the essentials of "republican government"? What is the furthest that the concept can be pushed as a justification for federal power over state governments? These and similar questions have troubled the interpretation of the Guarantee Clause for over two hundred years and are, even today, not fully settled.

A. THE FULL FAITH AND CREDIT AND PRIVILEGES AND IMMUNITIES CLAUSES

The most cited and discussed early case on Article IV is *Corfield v. Coryell*, 6 F.Cas. 546 (C.C.E.D. Pa. 1823), a Circuit Court opinion written by Supreme Court Justice Bushrod Washington (nephew of the first president and the inheritor of his Mount Vernon estate, exclusive of a slave whom George Washington freed in his will).

This Article IV case is of huge importance because the framers of the Fourteenth Amendment, which has a Privileges *or* Immunities Clause, cited it repeatedly as evidence of what the fundamental civil rights (i.e., privileges and immunities) were that they meant the Fourteenth Amendment to protect from state action. Modern debates, such as the debate over whether the Constitution creates abortion rights, thus turn in part on the way Justice Washington memorialized the Privileges and Immunities Clause of Article IV. Unfortunately, for us, Justice Washington's opinion in *Corfield* is almost void for vagueness.

The facts of *Corfield* are picturesque: Some Pennsylvanians rented a boat and sailed it out of Philadelphia into the coastal waters of New Jersey, where they raked for clams in violation of a New Jersey law that restricted clam-raking in New Jersey waters to in-state residents. The penalty was $10 and forfeiture of the offenders' vessel (and the clams). *Corfield* was a federal court lawsuit for "trespass," brought by the Philadelphia boat owner to get his boat back, after the renters had lost it to New Jersey authorities. The plaintiff claimed (1) that the New Jersey law violated the Commerce Clause (on a dormant commerce theory); and (2) that the New Jersey law violated the Privileges and Immunities Clause. The court rejected both claims. With respect to the Privileges and Immunities Clause, Justice Washington had "no hesitation in confining these expressions to those privileges and immunities which are, in their nature, fundamental; which belong, of right, to the citizens of all free governments; and which have, at all times, been enjoyed by the citizens of the several states which compose this Union, from the time of their becoming free, independent and sovereign."

Thus, a state must accord out-of-staters only the "fundamental" privileges and immunities or civil rights of citizens. And just what are those? Justice Washington said it would be "more tedious than difficult" to list them, but then said they would fall

> under the following general heads: Protection by the government; the enjoyment of life and liberty, with the right to acquire and possess property of every kind, and to pursue and obtain happiness and safety; subject nevertheless to such restraints as the government may justly prescribe for the general good of the whole. The right of a citizen of one state to pass through, or to reside in any other state, for purposes of trade, agriculture, professional pursuits, or otherwise; to claim the benefit of the writ of habeas corpus; to institute and maintain actions of any kind in the courts of the state; to take, hold and dispose of property, either real or personal; and an exemption from higher taxes or impositions than are paid by the other citizens of the state; may be mentioned as some of the particular privileges and immunities of citizens, which are clearly embraced by the general description of privileges deemed to be fundamental: to which may be added, the elective franchise, as regulated and established by the laws or constitution of the state in which it is to be exercised. These, and many others which

might be mentioned, are, strictly speaking, privileges and immunities, and the enjoyment of them by the citizens of each state, in every other state, was manifestly calculated (to use the expressions of the preamble of the corresponding provision in the old articles of confederation) "the better to secure and perpetuate mutual friendship and intercourse among the people of the different states of the Union."

What about the right to rake clams along the shore—or, at a higher level of generality, the right to share in state-owned property? Is that a "fundamental" privilege or immunity of citizenship, a civil right like the common law rights to own property and sue in contract or like civil rights under state constitutional law? Certainly not: "[W]e cannot accede to the proposition . . . [that] the citizens of the several states are permitted to participate in all the rights which belong exclusively to the citizens of any other particular state, merely upon the ground that they are enjoyed by those citizens; much less, that in regulating the use of the common property of the citizens of such state, the legislature is bound to extend to the citizens of all the other states the same advantages as are secured to their own citizens."

As noted above, *Corfield* became an influential decision decades later in our constitutional history. The Privileges and Immunities Clause (Comity Clause) of Article IV was the model on which the Privileges *or* Immunities Clause of the Fourteenth Amendment was patterned, four decades later, after the Civil War. *Corfield* was cited by the amendment's congressional sponsors as central to their understanding of the meaning of this provision of the Fourteenth Amendment, suggesting that the meaning of the two provisions is closely related. We will return to that issue—and to *Corfield v. Coryell*—in Chapter 7. You should know that *Corfield*'s iconic status to the framers of the Fourteenth Amendment is somewhat ironic because Justice Washington, like many Southern judges of his time, may have been eager to read the Privileges and Immunities Clause as narrowly as possible for fear that it might confer civil rights—such as the right to own a gun and speak freely—on free black men and women who traveled to the South. Hence his desire to confine "Privileges and Immunities" to rights that are fundamental and that date back to 1776.

To return to the Privileges and Immunities Clause of Article IV, Section 2: Whatever the scope of the "privileges and immunities" or civil rights that a state must accord citizens of other states on the same terms as it gives such privileges to its own citizens, it is clear that out-of-staters do not carry *their* state's rights with them into another state: A Minnesota fishing license is not good in Wisconsin. Wisconsin has to accord Minnesotans only the ("fundamental") civil rights it accords Wisconsinites. The phrase civil rights derives from the same Latin root as the words citizen and city. Civil rights are the rights of citizens. They are often contrasted with the narrower category of so-called political rights like the right to vote, to run for office, or to serve on a jury. In the nineteenth century, men, women, and children all had civil rights but only white men had political rights. The Privileges and Immunities Clause bound the states to give equal civil rights to out-of-staters, but not the political rights of voting or jury service.

A good illustration is the pre-Civil War case of *Lemmon v. The People*, presented below. The question was whether New York was required to recognize a Virginia family's Virginia-law right to own slaves, when that Virginia family traveled through New York en route to another state where slavery was permitted. The case raises questions concerning the meaning of the Full Faith and Credit Clause, the Privileges and Immunities Clause, and even the Commerce Clause.

What about the reverse of the *Lemmon* situation? A master takes his slave to "free soil" and lives there for several years. When he returns to a slave state, the slave sues for his freedom. Is the slave state obliged to apply the law of the free state? In *Scott v. Emerson*, 15 Mo. 576 (1852), the Missouri Supreme Court held that Missouri was permitted to apply Missouri law to determine the status of a Missouri resident as slave or free, in a Missouri court proceeding—at least in the absence of a judgment from a sister state awarding Scott his freedom. (In such a case, the Full Faith and Credit Clause would oblige Missouri to honor the sister-state judgment awarding Scott his freedom; and he would be entitled to return to Missouri as a free man, entitled to the privileges and immunities Missouri accorded its own citizens.) The Missouri decision in *Scott v. Emerson* was the first of two cases involving the slave Scott, eventually culminating in the Supreme Court's *Dred Scott* decision.

In order to understand *Lemmon* it is necessary first that you read *Sommersett's Case*, which is a foundational case for the "law of nations" at the time of the founding. The term "law of nations" embraced aspects of what we would today call "international law" and "natural law." *Sommersett's Case* concerned the duty of one nation to give effect to the laws or legal status conferred by another and the limits of such duty in the name of justice and a nation's own laws. The case formed a crucial part of the baseline legal understandings that informed Article IV, and was a central case in the American understanding of international law on slavery.

Sommersett's Case

English Court of King's Bench, 20 State Tr. 1 (1772)

[In 1769, Charles Steuart, a citizen of Virginia, traveled to England on business, bringing with him a slave, James Sommersett, whom he had purchased in Jamaica. In October 1771, Sommersett escaped from Steuart, but was recaptured and placed aboard a vessel bound for Jamaica, where he was to be resold. Opponents of slavery in England engaged counsel and petitioned the Court of King's Bench for a writ of habeas corpus on Sommersett's behalf. In an initial opinion in the case, the chief justice of the Court of King's Bench (William Murray, commonly known as Lord Mansfield) urged Steuart to "end the question, by discharging or giving freedom to" Sommersett. Lord Mansfield noted that there were 14,000 or 15,000 slaves then present in England, with a total value of over 700,000 pounds. "But if the parties will have it decided, we must give our opinion. Compassion will not, on the one hand, nor inconvenience on the other, be to decide; but the law." The following is Lord Mansfield's final opinion in the case.—Editors]

■ LORD MANSFIELD.

On the part of Sommersett, the case which we gave notice should be decided this day, the Court now proceeds to give its opinion. I shall recite the return to the writ of Habeas Corpus, as ground of our determination; omitting only words of form. The captain of the ship on board of which the negro was taken, makes his return to the writ in terms of signifying that there have been, and still are, slaves to a great number in Africa; and that the trade in them is authorized by the laws and opinions of Virginia and Jamaica; that they are goods and chattels; and, as such, saleable and sold.

That James Sommersett is a negro of Africa, and long before the return of the king's writ was brought to be sold, and was sold to Charles Steuart, esq. then in Jamaica, and has not been manumitted since; that Mr. Steuart, having occasion to transact business, came over hither, with an intention to return; and brought Sommersett at attend and abide with him, and to carry him back as soon as the business should be transacted. That such intention has been, and still continues; and that the negro did remain till the time of his departure in the service of his master Mr. Steuart, and quitted it without his consent; and thereupon, before the return of the king's writ, the said Charles Steuart did commit the slave on board the Anne and Mary, to safe custody, to be kept till he should set sail, and then to be taken with him to Jamaica, and there sold as a slave. And this is the cause why he, captain Knowles, who was then and now is, commander of the above vessel, then and now lying in the river of Thames, did the said negro, committed to his custody, detain; and on which he now renders him to the orders of the Court. . . . The only question before us is, whether the cause on the return is sufficient? If it is, the negro must be remanded; if it is not, he must be discharged. Accordingly, the return states, that the slave departed and refused to serve; whereupon he was kept, to be sold abroad. So high an act of dominion must be recognized by the law of the country where it is used. The power of a master over his slave has been extremely different, in different countries. The state of slavery is of such a nature, that it is incapable of being introduced on any reasons, moral or political, but only by positive law, which preserves its force long after the reasons, occasion, and time itself from whence it was created, is erased from memory. It is so odious, that nothing can be suffered to support it, but positive law. Whatever inconveniences, therefore, may follow from the decision, I cannot say this case is allowed or approved by the law of England; and therefore the black must be discharged.

Lemmon v. The People

20 N.Y. 562 (1860)

[Two slaveowners, Jonathan and Juliet Lemmon, were traveling from Virginia to Texas with eight slaves. Strange as it may seem, the easiest route was to take a ship from Norfolk to New York and then take a larger ship from New York down the east coast and around to the Gulf of Mexico, to New Orleans, and proceed from there to Texas.—Editors]

On the 6th day of November, 1852, [while docked in New York harbor,] Louis Napoleon, a colored citizen of this State, made application . . . for a writ of *habeas corpus* to be directed to one Jonathan Lemmon and the keeper of house No. 3 Carlisle street, New York, requiring them to bring before said justice the bodies of eight colored persons, one man, two women and five children, who on the day preceding were confined and restrained of their liberty on board the steamer City of Richmond, in the harbor of New York, and were taken therefrom on the night of that day to No. 3 Carlisle street, and there detained under the pretence that they were slaves.

. . . Lemmon made a return to the writ under oath, in which he averred that the eight persons named were the slaves and property of Juliet Lemmon his wife, who had been the owner of such persons as slaves . . . under the Constitution and laws of Virginia: "that the said Juliet, with her said slaves, persons or property, is now *in transitu* or transit from the State of Virginia aforesaid to the State of Texas, the ultimate place of destination and another slaveholding State of the United States of America . . . that the said slaves, sailing from the port of Norfolk in the said State of Virginia, on board the steamship City of Richmond, never touched, landed nor came into the harbor or State of New York except for the mere purpose of passage and transit from the State of Virginia, aforesaid, to the State of Texas, aforesaid, and for no other purpose, intention, object or design whatever: that the said Juliet with her said slaves was compelled by necessity or accident to take passage in the steamship City of Richmond . . . for the State of Texas aforesaid, the ultimate place of destination." The return also denied any intention, on the part of Mrs. Lemmon or her husband, of selling the negroes.

To this return the relator orally interposed a general demurrer. Mr. Justice PAINE held the case under advisement until the 13th of November, 1852, when he discharged the colored Virginians. . . . *[Lemmon appealed to the intermediate appellate court, which affirmed, and then to this court.— Editors]*

■ DENIO, J.

. . . I understand the effect of these statements to be that Mrs. Lemmon, being the owner of these slaves, desired to take them from her residence in Norfolk to the State of Texas; and, as a means of effecting that purpose, she embarked . . . for New York, with a view to secure a passage from thence to her place of destination. As nothing is said of any stress of weather, and no marine casualty is mentioned, the necessity of landing, which is spoken of, refers, no doubt, to the exigency of that mode of prosecuting her journey. . . . The question to be decided is whether the bringing the slaves into this State under these circumstances entitled them to their freedom.

The intention, and the effect, of the statutes of this State bearing upon the point are very plain and unequivocal. By an act passed in 1817, it was declared that no person held as a slave should be imported, introduced or brought into this State on any pretence whatever, except [that] . . . "Any person, not being an inhabitant of this State, who shall be traveling to or from, or passing through this State, may bring with him any person lawfully held in slavery, and may take such person with him from this State; but the person so held in slavery shall not reside or continue in this State more than nine months; if such residence be continued beyond that time such person shall be free." In the year 1841, the Legislature repealed this section . . . [making freedom] absolute and unqualified. . . . [T]he meaning of the statute is as plain as though the Legislature had declared in terms that if any person should introduce a slave into this State, in the course of a journey to or from it, or in passing through it, the slave shall be free.

If, therefore, the Legislature had the constitutional power to enact this statute, the law of the State precisely meets the case of the persons who were brought before the judge on the writ of *habeas corpus*, and his order discharging them from constraint was unquestionably correct. Every sovereign State has a right to determine by its laws the condition of all persons who may at any time be within its jurisdiction; to exclude therefrom those whose introduction would contravene its policy, or to declare the conditions upon which they may be received, and what subordination or restraint may lawfully be allowed by one class or description of persons over another. Each State has, moreover, the right to enact such rules as it may see fit respecting the title to property, and to declare what subjects shall, within the State, possess the attributes of property, and what shall be incapable of a proprietary right. . . .

The power which has been mentioned as residing in the States is assumed by the Constitution itself to extend to persons held as slaves by such of the States as allow the condition of slavery. . . . The provision respecting the return of fugitives from service contains a very strong implication to that effect. It declares that no person held to service or labor in one State, under the laws thereof, escaping into another, shall in consequence of any law or regulation therein, be discharged from such service or labor, &c. . . . It was assumed by the authors of the Constitution, that the fact of a Federative Union would not of itself create a duty on the part of the States which should abolish slavery to respect the rights of the owners of slaves escaping thence from the States where it continued to exist. The apprehension was not that any of the States would establish rules or regulations looking primarily to the emancipation of fugitives from labor, but that the abolition of slavery in any State would draw after it the principle that a person held in slavery would immediately become free on arriving, in any manner, within the limits of such State.

. . . The aspect in which the case of fugitive slaves was presented to the authors of the Constitution therefore was this: A number of the States had very little interest in continuing the institution of slavery, and were likely soon to abolish it within their limits. When they should do so, the principle of the laws of England as to personal rights and the remedies for illegal imprisonment, would immediately prevail in such States. The judgment in Somerset's case and the principles announced by Lord MANSFIELD, were standing admonitions that even a temporary restraint of personal liberty by virtue of a title derived under the laws of slavery, could not be sustained where that institution did not exist by positive law. . . . This was not unreasonable, as the owner was free to determine whether he would voluntarily permit his slave to go within a jurisdiction which did not allow him to be held in bondage. That was within his own power, but he could not always prevent his slaves from escaping out of the State in which their servile condition was recognized. The provision was precisely suited to the exigency of the case, and it went no further.

In examining other arrangements of the Constitution, apparently inserted for purposes having no reference to slavery, we ought to bear in mind that when passing the fugitive slave provision the Convention was contemplating the future existence of States which should have abolished slavery, in a political union with other States where the institution would still remain in force. It would naturally be supposed that if there were other cases in which the rights of slave owners ought to be protected in the States which should abolish slavery, they would be adjusted in connection with the provision looking specially to that case, instead of being left to be deduced by construction from clauses intended primarily for cases to which slavery had no necessary relation. . . .

The Constitution declares that the citizens of each State shall be entitled to all privileges and immunities of citizens in the several States. (*Art.* 4, § 2.) No provision in that instrument has so strongly tended to constitute the citizens of the United States one people as this. . . . The question now to be considered is, how far the State jurisdiction . . . is restricted by the provision we are considering; or, to come at once to the precise point in controversy, whether it obliges the State governments to recognize, in any way, within their own jurisdiction, the property in slaves which the citizens of States in which slavery prevails may lawfully claim within their own States—beyond the case of fugitive slaves. The language is that they shall have the privileges and immunities of citizens in the several States. In my opinion the meaning is, that in a given State, every citizen of every other State shall have the same privileges and immunities—that is, the same rights—which the citizens of that State possess. . . . They can hold property by the same titles by which every other citizen may hold it, and by no other. . . . A citizen of Virginia, having his home in that State, and never having been within the State of New York, has the same rights under our laws which a native born citizen, domiciled elsewhere, would have, and no other rights. . . .

The position that a citizen carries with him, into every State into which he may go, the legal institutions of the one in which he was born, cannot be supported. . . .

The Legislature has declared, in effect, that no person shall bring a slave into this State, even in the course of a journey between two slaveholding States, and that if he does, the slave shall be free. Our own citizens are of course bound by this regulation. . . . [T]he [slave]owner cannot lawfully do anything which our laws do not permit to be done by one of our own citizens, and as a citizen of this State cannot bring a slave within its limits except under the condition that he shall immediately become free, the owner of these slaves could not do it without involving herself in the same consequences.

It remains to consider the effect upon this case of the provision by which power is given to Congress to regulate commerce among the several States. . . .

The act under consideration is not in any just sense a regulation of commerce. It does not suggest to me the idea that it has any connection with that subject. It would have an extensive operation altogether independent of commerce. . . . We will concede, for the purpose of the argument, that the transportation of slaves from one slaveholding State to another is an act of inter-state commerce, which may be legally protected and regulated by federal legislation. Acts have been passed to regulate the coasting trade, so that if these slaves had been *in transitu* between Virginia and Texas, in a coasting vessel, at the time the *habeas corpus* was served, they could not have been interfered with while passing through the navigable waters of a free State by the authority of a law of such State. But they were not thus in transit at that time. Congress has not passed any act to regulate commerce between the States when carried on by land, or otherwise than in coasting vessels. But conceding that, in order to facilitate commerce among the States, Congress has power to provide for precisely such a case as the present . . . the unexercised power to enact such a law, to regulate such a transit, would not affect the power of the States to deal with the *status* of all persons within their territory in the meantime, and before the existence of such a law. . . . Upon the whole case, I have come to the conclusion that there is nothing in the National Constitution or the laws of Congress to preclude the State judicial authorities from declaring these slaves thus introduced into the territory of this State, free, and setting them at liberty, according to the direction of the statute referred to. For the foregoing reasons, I am in favor of affirming the judgment of the Supreme Court.

■ WRIGHT, J., concurring.

. . . The question is one affecting the State in her sovereignty. As a sovereign State she may determine and regulate the *status* or social and civil condition of her citizens, and every description of persons within her territory. This power she possesses exclusively; and when she has declared or expressed her will in this respect, no authority or power from without can rightly interfere, except in the single instance of a slave escaping from a State of the Union into her territory; and in this, only because she has, by compact, yielded her right of sovereignty. . . .

The constitutional provision that "the citizens of each State shall be entitled to all the privileges and immunities of citizens in the several States" (*U.S. Const., art.* 4, § 2, subd. 1), is also invoked as having some bearing on the question of the appellant's right. I think this is the first occasion in the juridical history of the country that an attempt has been made to torture this provision into a guaranty of the right of a slave owner to bring his slaves into, and hold them for any purpose in, a non-slaveholding State. The provision was always understood as having but one design and meaning, viz., to secure to the citizens of every State, within every other, the privileges and immunities (whatever they might be) accorded in each to its own citizens. It was intended to guard against a State discriminating in favor of its own citizens. A citizen of Virginia coming into New York was to be entitled to all the privileges and immunities accorded to the citizens of New York. He was not to be received or treated as an alien or enemy in the particular sovereignty.

. . . The State has declared, through her Legislature, that the *status* of African slavery shall not exist, and her laws transform the slave into a freeman the instant he is brought voluntarily upon her soil. . . . She says, in effect, to the foreign slave owner, if you bring your slaves within the State, on any pretence whatever, neither by comity nor in any other way shall the municipal law let in and give place to the foreign law . . . and the persons before held as slaves shall stand upon her soil in their natural relations as men and as freemen. . . . It is the *status*, the unjust and unnatural relation, which the policy of the State aims to suppress, and her policy fails, at least in part, if the *status* be upheld at all. . . .

■ DAVIES, BACON AND WELLES, JS., concurred.

■ CLERKE, J. (Dissenting.)

. . . Whether slavery is agreeable or in opposition to the law of nature; whether it is morally right or wrong; whether it is expedient or inexpedient; whether the African race are adapted, by their physical and moral organization, only to this condition; whether they can be induced to labor only by compulsion; whether the fairest and most fertile portions of the earth—those lying near and within the tropical zones—can alone be cultivated to any extent by that race, and whether, if without their labor, therefore, this large portion of the globe will, contrary to the manifest design of the Creator, continue or become a sterile waste, are questions very interesting within the domain of theology, or ethics, or political economy, but totally inappropriate to the discussion of the purely legal questions now presented for our consideration. Those questions are, 1st, whether the Legislature of this State has declared that all slaves brought by their masters into this State, under any circumstances whatever, even for a moment, shall be free; and 2d, if it has so declared, had it the constitutional power to do so.

1. The act passed in 1817 . . . allows a person, not an inhabitant of this State, traveling to or from, or passing through this State, to bring his slave

here and take him away again; but if the slave continues here more than nine months, he shall be free. These exceptions were repealed by an act passed May 25, 1841. . . . [T]he language of the acts referred to is too plain to admit of any doubt of that intent. It evidently intended to declare that all slaves voluntarily brought into this State, under any circumstances whatever, should become instantly free.

2. But it is a question of much greater difficulty, whether the Legislature had the constitutional power to do so.

New York is a member of a confederacy of free and sovereign States, united for certain specific and limited purposes, under a solemn written covenant. And this covenant not only establishes a confederacy of States, but also, in regard to its most material functions, it gives this confederacy the character of a homogeneous national government. The Constitution is not alone federal or alone national; but, by the almost divine wisdom which presided over its formation, while its framers desired to preserve the independence and sovereignty of each State within the sphere of ordinary domestic legislation, yet they evidently designed to incorporate this people into one nation, not only in its character as a member of the great family of nations, but also in the internal, moral, social and political effect of the Union upon the people themselves. It was essential to this grand design that there should be as free and as uninterrupted an intercommunication between the inhabitants and citizens of the different States, as between the inhabitants and citizens of the same State. The people of the United States, therefore, "in order to form a more perfect union" than had existed under the old Confederacy, declare and provide, among other things in the Constitution under which we have now the privilege of living, that Congress (alone) shall have power to regulate commerce among the several States . . . that full faith or credit shall be given in each State to the public acts, records and judicial proceedings of every other State, and that citizens of each State shall be entitled to all the privileges and immunities of citizens in the several States. The people, in adopting this Constitution, declare in its very preamble that they intended to form a more perfect union than had bound them under the old Articles of Confederation. . . . Most assuredly, the people who adopted the present Constitution did not intend that the intercourse between the people of the different States should be more limited or restricted than the States, in their corporate capacity, provided in the Articles of Confederation. . . .

Is it consistent with this purpose of perfect union, and perfect and unrestricted intercourse, that property which the citizen of one State brings into another State, for the purpose of passing through it to a State where he intends to take up his residence, shall be confiscated in the State through which he is passing, or shall be declared to be no property, and liberated from his control? . . . By the law of nations, the citizens of one government have a right of passage through the territory of another, peaceably, for business or pleasure; and the latter acquires no right over such person or his property. This privilege is yielded between foreign nations towards each other without any express compact. It is a principle of the unwritten law of nations.

Of course this principle is much more imperative on the several States than between foreign nations in their relations towards each other. For it can be clearly deduced, as we have seen, from the compact on which their union is based. Therefore, making this principle of the law of nations applicable to the compact which exists between the several States, we say, that the citizens of any one State have a right of passage through the territory of another, peaceably, for business or pleasure; and the latter acquires no right over such person or his property. . . .

The error into which the judge who decided this case in the first instance fell, consisted in supposing, because the law of nations refused to recognize slaves as property, the several States of this Union were at liberty to do the same; forgetting that the compact, by which the latter are governed in their relation towards each other, modifies the law of nations in this respect; and while each particular State is at liberty to abolish or retain slavery in reference to its own inhabitants and within its own borders, as its sense of right or expediency may dictate, it is not permitted in its dealings or intercourse with other States or their inhabitants to ignore the right to property in the labor and service of persons in transitu from those States. The Supreme Court having fallen into the same error, their order should be reversed. . . .

[Brief statements by Chief Justice Comstock and Justice Selden indicated that neither one had been able to give the case, as the chief justice put it, "the attention which its importance might justify." Nevertheless, Chief Justice Comstock joined, and Justice Selden expressed sympathy with, the dissent.—Editors]

NOTES

1. *Lemmon* is a famous and fascinating case, widely believed to have been headed for the U.S. Supreme Court—and feared by anti-slavery advocates (including Abraham Lincoln) to be a potential "Second *Dred Scott*" decision, in which the Supreme Court might make slavery *national*, by forbidding Northern states to exclude slavery within their territorial limits. *Lemmon* was decided by the New York Court of Appeals (the state's highest court) in 1860. Lincoln was elected president later that year, and in April 1861 the South fired on Fort Sumter, launching the Civil War. *Lemmon* never reached the Supreme Court, and the question of whether it might become a "Second *Dred Scott*" was, of course, overtaken by other events.

2. Was *Lemmon* rightly or wrongly decided, as a matter of U.S. constitutional law? The case raised three main constitutional questions: First, did the Full Faith and Credit Clause of Article IV require New York courts to apply Virginia law to the question of the legal status (slave versus free) of the slaves temporarily present in New York? Second, did the Privileges and Immunities Clause of Article IV require that New York recognize the property rights of the Lemmons in their slaves, in New York, by according them the same rights they possessed in Virginia? Third, did New York's law interfere with commerce among the states and thereby violate an implied constitutional prohibition on such a state law, resulting from the grant to Congress of the power to regulate interstate commerce (a "dormant Commerce Clause" issue)? What were the court's answers? Were they correct?

On the dormant Commerce Clause issue, Justice Wright noted the Court's decision in *Groves v. Slaughter*, 40 U.S. 449 (1841), which considered whether a Mississippi constitutional provision forbidding the importation of slaves into the state for sale interfered with interstate commerce. The majority opinion in *Groves* sidestepped the issue by construing the state constitutional provision as not self-executing. Justice McLean's concurrence found that slaves were persons, not articles of commerce—and so not subject to Congress's power over commerce. Chief Justice Taney's concurrence in *Groves* held that slavery was purely a matter of state law and that "the action of the several States upon this subject[ ] cannot be controlled by Congress, either by virtue of its power to regulate commerce, or by virtue of any other power[.]" Justice Baldwin argued that interstate trade in slavery was subject to national power and that "wherever slavery exists, by the laws of a state, slaves are property in every constitutional sense, and for every purpose" so that states could not interfere with interstate commerce in such property if their own laws recognized slaves as property. Is *Groves* relevant to the issues in *Lemmon*?

3. One can imagine a further possible constitutional issue in *Lemmon*, not clearly addressed in any of the opinions. Did the U.S. Supreme Court's decision in *Dred Scott*, holding that there was a substantive due process right of (white) citizens to own slaves, so that Congress could not prohibit slavery in federal territories, mean that *states* were similarly barred from prohibiting slavery? This was Lincoln's feared "Second *Dred Scott*" decision: "We shall *lie down* pleasantly dreaming that the people of *Missouri* are on the verge of making their State *free*; and we shall *awake* to the *reality*, instead, that the *Supreme* Court has made *Illinois* a *slave* State." Abraham Lincoln, "House Divided" Speech, Springfield, Illinois (June 16, 1858). Once you have read *Dred Scott*, ask yourself whether the Court that rendered that decision might well have held as Lincoln predicted, or feared.

4. Consider *Lemmon* in variation: A family brings its slaves from a slave state to a free state, but *returns to the slave state* with its slaves, without the free state having taken any legal action. Is *Virginia* bound to apply *New York* law and declare the slaves free? Or is it as free to apply its own law as New York was, in *Lemmon*, to apply its? (Wouldn't your answer be different if New York *had* rendered a decision in favor of freedom, and the family returned to Virginia with their slaves in any event?) Interestingly, this fact variation is almost *exactly* the situation presented by the *Dred Scott* case, and the Missouri Supreme Court, in the first round of that litigation (*Scott v. Emerson*), held that Missouri was not obliged to apply the law of free-state Illinois or of free-territory Minnesota, where Captain Emerson had traveled with his slave, Dred Scott.

5. Now consider a modern parallel. A lesbian couple living in Virginia (Miller and Jenkins) traveled to Vermont in 2000 to obtain a civil union. (Virginia did not recognize any such legal status.) In 2002 the two women decided to have a child. Miller became pregnant through artificial insemination, and gave birth to a baby girl in April 2002. The couple then moved to Vermont. In 2003, the couple split up. Miller filed a "Complaint for Civil Union Dissolution" in Vermont. The Vermont court granted the dissolution, but also gave the other partner, Jenkins, visitation rights with respect to the little girl. Miller then moved, with the girl, to Virginia. Must Virginia give effect to the visitation order of the Vermont court, notwithstanding that Virginia law does not recognize civil unions of this sort as having any valid legal status? See *Miller–Jenkins v. Miller–Jenkins*, 661 S.E.2d 822 (Va. 2008) (upholding, on procedural grounds, a lower Virginia court ruling that answered this question "yes"), *cert. denied* 129 S.Ct. 726. If there had *not* been a Vermont court decision, would Virginia have been required to recognize the Vermont civil union as legally valid in Virginia? Is this latter situation any different from the question presented in *Lemmon*? Put generally: when (if ever) is one state constitutionally required to recognize a legal status conferred in another state that is contrary to its own laws?

6. The Supreme Court has permitted states a broad berth in deciding to apply their own law, rather than another state's laws, under the Full Faith and Credit Clause and the Due Process Clause. A leading case is *Allstate Insurance Co. v. Hague*, 449 U.S. 302 (1981). A Wisconsin resident, insured by Allstate in Wisconsin, was hit and killed in Wisconsin by an uninsured Wisconsin driver. His Wisconsin widow moves to Minnesota and sues in Minnesota court. May Minnesota courts constitutionally choose to apply Minnesota law (which permitted triple the recovery on these facts) or are they required to apply Wisconsin law? The Minnesota Supreme Court held that its state's multi-factor choice-of-law rules permitted it to apply Minnesota law—with the tipping factor being that Minnesota had the "better law." Allstate appealed to the U.S. Supreme Court, arguing that this violated the Full Faith and Credit Clause. The Court ruled for the widow, a plurality holding that a state could choose to apply its own substantive law as long as there were "a significant contact or significant aggregation of contacts, creating state interests, such that [the state's] choice of law is neither arbitrary nor unfair"—and that the widow's new residence in Minnesota was sufficient. The full Court embraced this generous constitutional standard in *Phillips Petroleum Co. v. Shutts*, 472 U.S. 797 (1985). The Full Faith and Credit Clause strictly requires the courts of one state to enforce the final judgments and decrees of another state of the Union, but does not very often require one state to apply another state's *laws* in its own courts, absent such a prior valid judgment. Is this right? Is there an alternative, principled standard for applying the Full Faith and Credit Clause?

7. The Full Faith and Credit Clause provides that states must accord full faith and credit to the "public Acts, Records, and judicial Proceedings of every other State." The next sentence reads: "And the Congress may by general Laws prescribe the Manner in which such Acts, Records and Proceedings shall be proved, and the Effect thereof." May Congress employ this power to direct that states do *not* need to give effect, in some respect, to the laws or judicial proceedings of other states? Could it, in essence, enact an *anti*-Full Faith and Credit statute, providing (for example) that states need not give effect to the marriages of same-sex couples in other states, or even to judicial custody decrees based on laws authorizing these marriages? Consider in this regard the Defense of Marriage Act (DOMA), passed by Congress in 1996, which has provisions to this effect. 28 U.S.C. § 1738C ("No State, territory, or possession of the United States, or Indian tribe, shall be required to give effect to any public act, record, or judicial proceeding of any other State, territory, possession, or tribe respecting a relationship between persons of the same sex that is treated as a marriage under the laws of such other State, territory, possession, or tribe, or a right or claim arising from such relationship."). For analysis of state-state conflicts over same-sex marriage laws, see Andrew Koppelman, SAME SEX, DIFFERENT STATES: WHEN SAME–SEX MARRIAGES CROSS STATE LINES (2006); William Baude, *Beyond DOMA: Choice of State Law in Federal Statutes*, 64 Stan. L. Rev. 1371 (2012). For a history of state-state status-recognition issues, see Lynn D. Wardle, *From Slavery to Same–Sex Marriage: Comity Versus Public Policy in Inter-jurisdictional Recognition of Controversial Domestic Relations*, 2008 BYU L. Rev. 1855 (2008).

8. To what types of legal rights or interests does the Privileges and Immunities Clause apply? *Lemmon* rejected the view that it provides a right of Virginians, when in New York, to hold persons in slavery—a civil right that New Yorkers would not have under state law. The clause requires that New

York accord Virginians the same civil rights it would give to New Yorkers— nothing more. But not necessarily nothing *less*: recall that a state may prefer its own citizens over out-of-staters with respect to some things, like political rights or use of state property or natural resources.

9. Modern cases continue to apply the general principle that states may not discriminate against out-of-state citizens, except with respect to state re- sources which are jointly owned by in-state citizens. In *Hicklin v. Orbeck*, 437 U.S. 518 (1978), the Court struck down "Alaska Hire," a state law providing an absolute preference for Alaska residents over out-of-staters for employment in connection with "oil and gas leases, easements . . . for oil or gas pipeline pur- poses . . . or any renegotiation of any of the preceding to which the state is a party[.]" This law clearly gave out-of-staters different civil rights to make con- tracts from the civil rights enjoyed by Alaskans. Justice Brennan's opinion for the Court quoted *Paul v. Virginia*, 8 Wall. 168, 180 (1869), as aptly stating the purpose of the Privileges and Immunities Clause:

> To place the citizens of each State upon the same footing with citizens of other States, so far as the advantages resulting from citizenship in those States are concerned. It relieves them from the disabilities of alienage in other States; it inhibits discriminating legislation against them by other States; it gives them the right of free ingress into other States, and egress from them; it insures to them in other States the same freedom possessed by the citizens of those States in the acquisition and enjoyment of property and in the pursuit of happiness; and it secures to them in other States the equal protection of their laws. It has been justly said that no provision in the Constitution has tended so strongly to constitute the citizens of the United States one people as this.

Alaska contended that oil and gas were resources of the state—state prop- erty—and that the state could give preference to its own citizens with respect to benefits derived from these property resources. (Recall *Corfield v. Coryell*, with respect to New Jersey's exclusion from Pennsylvanians from clam-raking on New Jersey shores.) The Court rejected the argument: "We do not agree that the fact that a State owns a resource, of itself, completely removes a law con- cerning that resource from the prohibitions of the Clause." The reason was "that Alaska has little or no proprietary interest in much of the activity swept within the ambit of Alaska Hire; and the connection of the State's oil and gas with much of the covered activity is sufficiently attenuated so that it cannot justifiably be the basis for requiring private employers to discriminate against nonresidents."

Hicklin has not been the modern Court's last word in this area. In *United Building & Construction Trades Council v. Mayor and Council of Camden*, 465 U.S. 208 (1984), the Court considered a Camden, New Jersey ordinance requir- ing that at least 40% of the employees of contractors and subcontractors work- ing on city construction projects be Camden residents. Justice Rehnquist's ma- jority opinion quoted earlier cases noting that, "like many other constitutional provisions, the privileges and immunities clause is not an absolute," and that "state should have considerable leeway in analyzing local evils and in prescrib- ing appropriate cures." But the Court found it "impossible to evaluate Cam- den's justification on the record as it now stands," and therefore remanded the case for further factual findings. In *Supreme Court of New Hampshire v. Piper*, 470 U.S. 274 (1985), the Court struck down a New Hampshire action denying admission to the bar to a Vermont woman who lived 400 yards from the New Hampshire border as a violation of the Privileges and Immunities Clause, finding that none of the state's reasons for New Hampshire's residency requirement constituted a substantial reason justifying discrimination against nonresidents.

Finally, in the notable recent case of *Saenz v. Roe*, 526 U.S. 489 (1999), the Court relied in part on the Privileges and Immunities Clause of Article IV in support of a "right to travel"—"the right of the newly arrived citizen to the same privileges and immunities enjoyed by other citizens of the same State." The Court struck down a California statute providing lower welfare benefits to residents who had been in the state less than a year. The Court also relied on the Fourteenth Amendment's Citizenship Clause and Privileges *or* Immunities Clause, as supporting such a right to travel: all citizens of the United States "have the right to choose to be citizens 'of the State wherein they reside' " under Section One of the Fourteenth Amendment. "The States, however, do not have any right to select their citizens. The Fourteenth Amendment, like the Constitution itself, was, as Justice Cardozo put it, 'framed upon the theory that the peoples of the several states must sink or swim together; and that in the long run prosperity and salvation are in union and not division.' "

What is the right answer? What *are* "the privileges and immunities of citizens" of the states? Do you agree with *Corfield*'s formulation that the privileges and immunities included within the Article IV Clause are limited to "fundamental" privileges and immunities associated with "citizenship"? Does it make more sense to read the clause as protecting equal civil rights but not equal political rights or equal access to state property? What does this mean for the right of non-residents to practice law? (Technically, a state's lawyers are officers of the state courts, so maybe the right to practice law in a state is a political right, like jury service, about which a state may discriminate against out-of-staters.) What other things may a state give to in-staters but not out-of-staters, consistent with the Privileges and Immunities Clause? In answering these questions about the meaning of the clause, which types of constitutional argument, or modes of interpretation, are you relying on most?

B. THE FUGITIVE SLAVE AND FUGITIVE EXTRADITION CLAUSES

The Fugitive Slave Clause requires that any "persons held to service or labour" under the laws of one state—i.e., "slaves"—who escape to another state "shall be delivered up" on claim of the person to whom that service may be due. Does that clause, which imposes a duty on states, also give Congress legislative *power* to enforce the duty by legislation? Does that clause bar all state laws providing for due process or jury trial, or forbidding kidnapping in the recovery of alleged slaves?

Prigg v. Pennsylvania is a gut-wrenching case, and one that has peculiar facts: Edward Prigg, a professional "slavecatcher" travelled from Maryland to Pennsylvania to capture an alleged fugitive slave woman named Margaret. Margaret had at one time been owned by Marylander John Ashmore. Ashmore had allowed several of his slaves to live freely, and Margaret had married a free black man named James Morgan and moved to Pennsylvania, seemingly with her (former?) master's consent, if not explicit act of emancipation. While living in Pennsylvania, the couple had several children. Enter Prigg, the slavecatcher, acting on behalf of Ashmore's heirs. In defiance of a Pennsylvania law that forbade "self-help" remedies, Prigg essentially kidnapped Margaret *and her children* in the middle of the night, lied to Margaret's husband as to their intentions, and then dragged them back to Maryland, where they apparently were sold to be slaves in the deep South, from which they could not be found or recovered. Pennsylvania prosecuted Prigg (who, interestingly, was delivered to Pennsylvania pursuant to the requirements of the Fugitive *Extradition* Clause). Prigg argued that Pennsylvania's law was unconstitutional.

Prigg v. Pennsylvania
41 U.S. 539 (1842)

[Prigg was indicted by Pennsylvania for violating a state law that made it a felony to recapture an alleged fugitive slave by force. Prigg pleaded not guilty, on the ground that he was acting on behalf of the Ashmore family. The Pennsylvania court found him guilty, and he appealed to the U.S. Supreme Court.—Editors]

■ STORY, J.

Few questions which have ever come before this court involve more delicate and important considerations; and few upon which the public at large may be presumed to feel a more profound and pervading interest.

Before, however, we proceed to the points more immediately before us, it may be well, in order to clear the case of difficulty, to say, that in the exposition of this part of the constitution, we shall limit ourselves to those considerations which appropriately and exclusively belong to it, without laying down any rules of interpretation of a more general nature. It will, indeed, probably, be found, when we look to the character of the constitution itself, the objects which it seeks to attain, the powers which it confers, the duties which it enjoins, and the rights which it secures, as well as the known historical fact, that many of its provisions were matters of compromise of opposing interests and opinions, that no uniform rule of interpretation can be applied to it, which may not allow, even if it does not positively demand, many modifications, in its actual application to particular clauses. And, perhaps, the safest rule of interpretation, after all, will be found to be to look to the nature and objects of the particular powers, duties and rights, with all the lights and aids of contemporary history; and to give to the words of each just such operation and force, consistent with their legitimate meaning, as may fairly secure and attain the ends proposed.

There are two clauses in the constitution upon the subject of fugitives, which stand in juxtaposition with each other, and have been thought mutually to illustrate each other. They are both contained in the second section of the fourth article, and are in the following words: "A person charged in any state with treason, felony or other crime, who shall flee from justice, and be found in another state, shall, on demand of the executive authority of the state from which he fled, be delivered up, to be removed to the state having jurisdiction of the crime." "No person held to service or labor in one state, under the laws thereof, escaping into another, shall, in consequence of any law or regulation therein, be discharged from such service or labor; but shall be delivered up, on claim of the party to whom such service or labor may be due."

The last clause is that, the true interpretation whereof is directly in judgment before us. Historically, it is well known, that the object of this clause was to secure to the citizens of the slave-holding states the complete right and title of ownership in their slaves, as property, in every state in the Union into which they might escape from the state where they were held in servitude. The full recognition of this right and title was indispensable to the security of this species of property in all the slave-holding states; and, indeed, was so vital to the preservation of their domestic interests and institutions, that it cannot be doubted, that it constituted a fundamental article, without the adoption of which the Union could not have been formed. Its true design was, to guard against the doctrines and principles prevalent in the non-slave-holding states, by preventing them from intermeddling with, or obstructing, or abolishing the rights of the owners of slaves.

By the general law of nations, no nation is bound to recognise the state of slavery, as to foreign slaves found within its territorial dominions, when it is in opposition to its own policy and institutions, in favor of the subjects of other nations where slavery is recognised. If it does it, it is as a matter of comity, and not as a matter of international right. The state of slavery is deemed to be a mere municipal regulation, founded upon and limited to the range of the territorial laws. . . . It is manifest, from this consideration, that if the constitution had not contained this clause, every non-slave-holding state in the Union would have been at liberty to have declared free all runaway slaves coming within its limits, and to have given them entire immunity and protection against the claims of their masters; a course which would have created the most bitter animosities, and engendered perpetual strife between the different states. The clause was, therefore, of the last importance to the safety and security of the southern states, and could not have been surrendered by them, without endangering their whole property in slaves. The clause was accordingly adopted into the constitution, by the unanimous consent of the framers of it; a proof at once of its intrinsic and practical necessity.

How, then, are we to interpret the language of the clause? The true answer is, in such a manner as, consistently with the words, shall fully and completely effectuate the whole objects of it. If, by one mode of interpretation, the right must become shadowy and unsubstantial, and without any remedial power adequate to the end, and by another mode, it will attain its just end and secure its manifest purpose, it would seem, upon principles of reasoning, absolutely irresistible, that the latter ought to prevail. No court of justice can be authorized so to construe any clause of the constitution as to defeat its obvious ends, when another construction, equally accordant with the words and sense thereof, will enforce and protect them.

The clause manifestly contemplates the existence of a positive, unqualified right on the part of the owner of the slave, which no state law or regulation can in any way qualify, regulate, control or restrain. The slave is not to be discharged from service or labor, in consequence of any state law or regulation. Now, certainly, without indulging in any nicety of criticism upon words, it may fairly and reasonably be said, that any state law or state regulation, which interrupts, limits, delays or postpones the right of the owner to the immediate possession of the slave, and the immediate command of his service and labor, operates, *pro tanto*, a discharge of the slave therefrom. The question can never be, how much the slave is discharged from; but whether he is discharged from any, by the natural or necessary operation of state laws or state regulations. The question is not one of quantity or degree, but of withholding or controlling the incidents of a positive and absolute right.

. . . We have not the slightest hesitation in holding, that under and in virtue of the constitution, the owner of a slave is clothed with entire authority, in every state in the Union, to seize and recapture his slave, whenever he can do it, without any breach of the peace or any illegal violence. In this sense, and to this extent, this clause of the constitution may properly be said to execute itself, and to require no aid from legislation, state or national.

But the clause of the constitution does not stop here; nor, indeed, consistently with its professed objects, could it do so. Many cases must arise, in which, if the remedy of the owner were confined to the mere right of seizure and recaption, he would be utterly without any adequate redress. He may not be able to lay his hands upon the slave. He may not be able to enforce his rights against persons, who either secrete or conceal, or withhold the slave. He may be restricted by local legislation, as to the mode of proofs of his ownership; as to the courts in which he shall sue, and as to the actions which he may bring; or the process be may use to compel the delivery of the slave. Nay! the local legislation may be utterly inadequate to furnish the appropriate redress, . . . and this may be innocently as well as designedly done, since every state is perfectly competent, and has the exclusive right, to prescribe the remedies in its own judicial tribunals, to limit the time as well as the mode of redress, and to deny jurisdiction over cases, which its own policy and its own institutions either prohibit or discountenance. If, therefore, the clause of the constitution had stopped at the mere recognition of the right, without providing or contemplating any means by which it might be established and enforced, in cases where it did not execute itself, it is plain, that it would have been, in a great variety of cases, a delusive and empty annunciation. . . .

And this leads us to the consideration of the other part of the clause, which implies at once a guarantee and duty. It says, "but he (the slave) shall be delivered up, on claim of the party to whom such service or labor may be due." Now, we think it exceedingly difficult, if not impracticable, to read this language, and not to feel, that it contemplated some further remedial redress than that which might be administered at the hands of the owner himself. . . . If, indeed, the constitution guaranties the right, and if it requires the delivery upon the claim of the owner (as cannot well be doubted), the natural inference certainly is, that the national government is clothed with the appropriate authority and functions to enforce it. The fundamental principle, applicable to all cases of this sort, would seem to be, that where the end is required, the means are given; and where the duty is enjoined, the ability to perform it is contemplated to exist, on the part of the functionaries to whom it is intrusted. The clause is found in the national constitution, and not in that of any state. It does not point out any state functionaries, or any state action, to carry its provisions into effect. The states cannot, therefore, be compelled to enforce them; and it might well be deemed an unconstitutional exercise of the power of interpretation, to insist, that the states are bound to provide means to carry into effect the duties of the national government, nowhere delegated or intrusted to them by the constitution. On the contrary, the natural, if not the necessary, conclusion is, that the national government, in the absence of all positive provisions to the contrary, is bound, through its own proper departments, legislative, judicial or executive, as the case may require, to carry into effect all the rights and duties imposed upon it by the constitution. It is plain, then, that where a claim is made by the owner, out of possession, for the delivery of a slave, it must be made, if at all, against some other person; and inasmuch as the right is a right of property, capable of being recognized and asserted by proceedings before a court of justice, between parties adverse to each other, it constitutes, in the strictest sense, a controversy between the parties, and a case "arising under the constitution" of the United States, within the express delegation of judicial power given by that instrument. Congress, then, may call that power into activity, for the very purpose of giving effect to that right; and if so, then it may prescribe the mode and extent in which it shall be applied, and how, and under what circumstances, the proceedings shall afford a complete protection and guarantee to the right.

Congress has taken this very view of the power and duty of the national government. As early as the year 1791, the attention of congress was drawn to it (as we shall hereafter more fully see), in consequence of some practical difficulties arising under the other clause, respecting fugitives from justice escaping into other states. The result of their deliberations was the passage of the act of the 12th of February 1793, ch. 51, which, after having, in the first and second sections, provided by the case of fugitives from justice, by a demand to be made of the delivery, through the executive authority of the state where they are found, proceeds, in the third section, to provide, that when a person held to labor or service in any of the United States, shall escape into any other of the states or territories, the person to whom such labor or service may be due, his agent or attorney, is hereby empowered to seize or arrest such fugitive from labor, and take him or her before any judge of the circuit or district courts of the United States, residing or being within the state, or before any magistrate of a county, city or town corporate, wherein such seizure or arrest shall be made; and upon proof, to the satisfaction of such judge or magistrate, . . . to give a certificate thereof to such claimant, his agent or attorney, which shall be sufficient warrant for removing the said fugitive from labor, to the state or territory from which he or she fled. The fourth section provides a penalty against any person, who shall knowingly and willingly obstruct or hinder such claimant, his agent or attorney, in so seizing or arresting such fugitive from labor, or rescue such fugitive from the claimant, or his agent or attorney, when so arrested, or who shall harbor or conceal such fugitive, after notice that he is such; and it also saves to the person claiming such labor or service, his right of action for or on account of such injuries.

In a general sense, this act may be truly said to cover the whole ground of the constitution, both as to fugitives from justice, and fugitive slaves . . . because it points out fully all the modes of attaining those objects, which congress, in their discretion, have as yet deemed expedient or proper to meet the exigencies of the constitution. If this be so, then it would seem, upon just principles of construction, that the legislation of congress, if constitutional, must supersede all state legislation upon the same subject; and by necessary implication prohibit it. For, if congress have a constitutional power to regulate a particular subject, and they do actually regulate it in a given manner, and in a certain form, it cannot be, that the state legislatures have a right to interfere, . . . In such a case, the legislation of congress, in what it does prescribe, manifestly indicates, that it does not intend that there shall be any further legislation to act upon the subject-matter. Its silence as to what it does not do, is as expressive of what its intention is, as the direct provisions made by it. . . . [W]here congress have exercised a power over a particular subject given them by the constitution, it is not competent for state legislation to add to the provisions of congress upon that subject; for that the will of congress upon the whole subject is as clearly established by what it has not declared, as by what it has expressed.

But it has been argued, that the act of congress is unconstitutional, because it does not fall within the scope of any of the enumerated powers of legislation confided to that body; and therefore, it is void. Stripped of its artificial and technical structure, the argument comes to this, that although rights are exclusively secured by, or duties are exclusively imposed upon, the national government, yet, unless the power to enforce these rights or to execute these duties, can be found among the express powers of legislation enumerated in the constitution, they remain without any means of giving them effect by any act of congress; and they must operate solely *proprio vigore*, however defective may be their operation; nay! even although, in a practical sense, they may become a nullity, from the want of a proper remedy to enforce them, or to provide against their violation. If this be the true interpretation of the constitution, it must, in a great measure, fail to attain many of its avowed and positive objects, as a security of rights, and recognition of duties. Such a limited construction of the constitution has never yet been adopted as correct, either in theory or practice. No one has ever supposed that congress could, constitutionally, by its legislation, exercise powers, or enact laws, beyond the powers delegated to it by the constitution. But it has, on various occasions, exercised powers which were necessary and proper as means to carry into effect rights expressly given, and duties expressly enjoined thereby. The end being required, it has been deemed a just and necessary implication, that the means to accomplish it are given also; or, in other words, that the power flows as a necessary means to accomplish the end.

. . . [The] nature of the provision and the objects to be attained by it, require that it should be controlled by one and the same will, and act uniformly by the same system of regulations throughout the Union. If, then, the states have a right, in the absence of legislation by congress, to act upon the subject, each state is at liberty to prescribe just such regulations as suit its own policy, local convenience and local feelings. The legislation of one state may not only be different from, but utterly repugnant to and incompatible with, that of another.

It is scarcely conceivable, that the slave-holding states would have been satisfied with leaving to the legislation of the non-slave-holding states, a power of regulation, in the absence of that of congress, which would or might practically amount to a power to destroy the rights of the owner. If the argument, therefore, of a concurrent power in the states to act upon the subject-matter, in the absence of legislation by congress, be well founded; then, if congress had never acted at all, or if the act of congress should be repealed, without providing a substitute, there would be a resulting authority in each of the states to regulate the whole subject, at its pleasure, and to dole out its own remedial justice, or withhold it, at its pleasure, and according to its own views of policy and expediency. Surely, such a state of things never could have been intended, under such a solemn guarantee of right and duty. On the other hand, construe the right of legislation as exclusive in congress, and every evil and every danger vanishes. The right and the duty are then co-extensive and uniform in remedy and operation throughout the whole Union.

These are some of the reasons, but by no means all, upon which we hold the power of legislation on this subject to be exclusive in congress. To guard, however, against any possible misconstruction of our views, it is proper to state, that we are by no means to be understood, in any manner whatsoever, to doubt or to interfere with the police power belonging to the states, in virtue of their general sovereignty. That police power extends over all subjects within territorial limits of the states, and has never been conceded to the United States. It is wholly distinguishable from the right and duty secured by the provision now under consideration; which is exclusively derived from and secured by the constitution of the United States, and owes its whole efficacy thereto. We entertain no doubt whatsoever, that the states, in virtue of their general police power, possesses full jurisdiction to arrest and restrain runaway slaves, and remove them from their borders, and otherwise to secure themselves against their depredations and evil example, as they certainly may do in cases of idlers, vagabonds and paupers. The rights of the owners of fugitive slaves are in no just sense interfered with, or regulated, by such a course; and in many cases, the operations of this police power, although designed generally for other purposes, for protection, safety and peace of the state, may essentially promote and aid the interests of the owners. But such regulations can never be permitted to interfere with, or to obstruct, the just rights of the owner to reclaim his slave, derived from the constitution of the United States, or with the remedies prescribed by congress to aid and enforce the same.

Upon these grounds, we are of opinion, that the act of Pennsylvania upon which this indictment is founded, is unconstitutional and void. It purports to punish as a public offence against that state, the very act of seizing and removing a slave, by his master, which the constitution of the United States was designed to justify and uphold. The special verdict finds this fact, and the state courts have rendered judgment against the plaintiff in error upon that verdict. That judgment must, therefore, be reversed, and the cause remanded to the supreme court of Pennsylvania, with directions to carry into effect the judgment of this court rendered upon the special verdict, in favor of the plaintiff in error.

■ TANEY, CHIEF JUSTICE, concurring.

. . . The opinion of the court maintains, that the power over this subject is so exclusively vested in congress, that no state, since the adoption of the constitution, can pass any law in relation to it. In other words, according to the opinion just delivered, the state authorities are prohibited from interfering, for the purpose of protecting the right of the master, and aiding him in the recovery of his property. I think, the states are not prohibited; and that, on the contrary, it is enjoined upon them as a duty, to protect and support the owner, when he is endeavoring to obtain possession of his property found within their respective territories. The language used in the constitution does not, in my judgment, justify this construction given to it by the court. It contains no words prohibiting the several states from passing laws to enforce this right. They are, in express terms, forbidden to make any regulation that shall impair it; but there the prohibition stops. And according to the settled rules of construction for all written instruments, the prohibition being confined to laws injurious to the right, the power to pass laws to support and enforce it, is necessarily implied. And the words of the article which direct that the fugitive "shall be delivered up," seem evidently designed to impose it as a duty upon the people of the several states, to pass laws to carry into execution, in good faith, the compact into which they thus solemnly entered with each other. . . .

I dissent, therefore, upon these grounds, from that part of the opinion of the court which denies the obligation and the right of the state authorities to protect the master, when he is endeavoring to seize a fugitive from his service, in pursuance of the right given to him by the constitution of the United States; provided the state law is not in conflict with the remedy provided by congress.

■ McLEAN, JUSTICE, dissenting.

As this case involves questions deeply interesting, if not vital, to the permanency of the Union of these states; and as I differ on one point from the opinion of the court, I deem it proper to state my own views on the subject.

The plaintiff, Edward Prigg, was indicted under the first section of an act of Pennsylvania, entitled "an act to give effect to the provisions of the constitution of the United States, relative to fugitives from labor, for the protection of free people of color, and to prevent kidnapping." It provides, "if any person or persons shall, from and after the passing of this act, by force and violence, take and carry away, or cause to be taken or carried away, and shall, by fraud or false pretence seduce, or cause to be seduced, or shall attempt to take, carry away or seduce, any negro or mulatto, from any part or parts of this commonwealth, to any other place or places whatsoever, out of this commonwealth, with a design and intention of selling and disposing of, or of causing to be sold, or of keeping and detaining, or of causing to be kept and detained, such negro or mulatto, as a slave or servant for life, or for any term whatsoever; every such person or persons, his or their aiders or abettors, shall, on conviction thereof, be deemed guilty of felony, and shall be fined in a sum not less than five hundred nor more than one thousand dollars, and shall be sentenced to imprisonment and hard labor not less than seven nor more than twenty-one years."

The plaintiff, being a citizen of Maryland, with others, took Margaret Morgan, a colored woman, and a slave, by force and violence, without the certificate required by the act of congress, from the state of Pennsylvania, and brought her to the state of Maryland. By an amicable arrangement between the two states, judgment was entered against the defendant, in the court where the indictment was found; and on the cause being removed to the supreme court of the state, that judgment, *pro forma*, was affirmed. And the case is now here for our examination and decision. . . .

Does the provision in regard to the reclamation of fugitive slaves, vest the power exclusively in the federal government? This must be determined from the language of the constitution, and the nature of the power. . . . The states are inhibited from passing "any law or regulation which shall discharge a fugitive slave from the service of his master"; and a positive duty is enjoined on them to deliver him up, "on claim of the party to whom his service may be due." . . . Under the confederation, the master had no legal means of enforcing his rights, in a state opposed to slavery. A disregard of rights thus asserted was deeply felt in the south; it produced great excitement, and would have led to results destructive of the Union. To avoid this, the constitutional guarantee was essential. The necessity for this provision was found in the views and feelings of the people of the states opposed to slavery; and who, under such an influence, could not be expected favorably to regard the rights of the master. . . .

It is contended, that the power to execute it rests with the states. The law was designed to protect the rights of the slave-holder against the states opposed to those rights; and yet, by this argument, the effective power is in the hands of those on whom it is to operate. This would produce a strange anomaly in the history of legislation; it would show an inexperience and folly in the venerable framers of the constitution, from which, of all public bodies that ever assembled, they were, perhaps, most exempt. . . . It is, therefore, essential to the uniform efficacy of his constitutional provision, that it should be considered exclusively a federal power. . . . The constitution provides that the fugitive from labor shall be delivered up, on claim being made by the person entitled to such labor; but it is silent as to how and on whom this claim shall be made; the act of congress provides for this defect and uncertainty, by establishing the mode of procedure.

. . . I come now to a most delicate and important inquiry in this case, and that is, whether the claimant of a fugitive from labor may seize and remove him by force, out of the state in which he may be found, in defiance of its laws. I refer not to laws which are in conflict with the constitution, or the act of 1793. Such state laws, I have already said, are void. But I have reference to those laws which regulate the police of the state, maintain the peace of its citizens, and preserve its territory and jurisdiction from acts of violence. . . . In my judgment, there is not the least foundation in the act for the right asserted in the argument, to take the fugitive by force and remove him out of the state.

Such a proceeding can receive no sanction under the act, for it is in express violation of it. The claimant having seized the fugitive, is required by the act, to take him before a federal judge within the state, or a state magistrate within the county, city or town corporate, within which the seizure was made. Now, can there be any pretence, that after the seizure under the statute, the claimant may disregard the other express provision of it, by taking the fugitive, without claim, out of the state. But it is said, the master may seize his slave wherever he finds him, if by doing so, he does not violate the public peace; that the relation of master and slave is not affected by the laws of the state, to which the slave may have fled, and where he is found. If the master has a right to seize and remove the slave, without claim, he can commit no breach of the peace, by using all the force necessary to accomplish his object. . . .

It is very clear, that no power to seize and forcibly remove the slave, without claim, is given by the act of congress. Can it be exercised under the constitution? Congress have legislated on the constitutional power, and have directed the mode in which it shall be executed. The act, it is admitted, covers the whole ground; and that it is constitutional, there seems to be no reason to doubt. Now, under such circumstances, can the provisions of the act be disregarded, and an assumed power set up under the constitution? This is believed to be wholly inadmissible by any known rule of construction. . . .

It appears, in the case under consideration, that the state magistrate before whom the fugitive was brought refused to act. In my judgment, he was bound to perform the duty required of him by a law paramount to any act, on the same subject, in his own state. But this refusal does not justify the subsequent action of the claimant; he should have taken the fugitive before a judge of the United States, two of whom resided within the state. . . .

NOTES

1. It is important to try to untangle the constitutional questions presented and decided in *Prigg*. The Fugitive Slave Clause plainly says that fugitive

slaves must be "delivered up" on claim. But this leaves a few things up for grabs:

First, does the Fugitive Slave Clause, of its own force, invalidate all state legislation, of any kind, that might affect the ability of slave owners to recapture their (alleged) fugitive slaves? Does it invalidate state laws providing for due process—for hearings as to the propriety of the claim of ownership? Does it invalidate state laws providing for jury trial of such claims? (Does it matter in this regard that local juries in some Northern states might never rule for slave owners?) Does the Fugitive Slave Clause, of its own force, invalidate anti-self-help, anti-kidnapping laws, like Pennsylvania's?

Second, does the Fugitive Slave Clause imply—it does not quite say—that there exists *federal legislative power* in Congress to enact federal laws for enforcing the obligation to return fugitives? Is such an inferred power supported by the Necessary and Proper Clause? (Re-read the words of that clause carefully!) Is this question related to whether the Suspension Clause implies the existence of a congressional power to suspend the writ of habeas corpus under the Necessary and Proper Clause? Is the existence of a power to enact national fugitive slave laws impliedly *negated* by the absence of its mention *in Article IV*— and by the specific mention of legislative powers of Congress elsewhere in Article IV, with respect to other clauses (like Full Faith and Credit)? President Lincoln thought the clause fairly open to an interpretation supporting federal legislative power: "Shall fugitives from labor be surrendered by national or by State authority? The Constitution does not expressly say." Lincoln, First Inaugural Address.

Third, assuming that Congress possesses legislative power, is that power exclusive? That is, does federal legislative power preempt all state legislation in the area? Are not most federal powers exclusive? See, in Chapter 3, the Note on Article I, Section 8.

Fourth, even if preemption is not automatic, did Congress's enactment of the Fugitive Slave Act of 1793 preempt all state legislation concerning fugitive slave rendition, including Pennsylvania's anti-kidnapping statute?

How did each of the opinions reprinted here—Justice Story's majority opinion, Chief Justice Taney's concurrence, Justice McLean's dissent—resolve each question? What do you think is the legally correct resolution of each question?

2. Consider Justice Story's interpretive methodology (and whether he is faithful to it). Is his emphasis on the actual text of the Fugitive Slave Clause or the Necessary and Proper Clause? Or is his analysis better described as focused on the perceived historical purpose behind those clauses? If the latter, should that purpose then be the focus of interpretation (so that whatever best fulfills that purpose is the preferred interpretation of the words)? Or is the "purpose" limited by the degree to which the words of the text actually fulfill it (so that courts cannot rightly pursue a text's supposed purpose further than the words themselves support)? Consider the question in its most extreme form: what if the words of a legal text clearly said one thing, yet evidence of the historical purpose of the text clearly said something else entirely? Which one counts? If the Necessary and Proper Clause is the source of all implied powers under the Constitution, and the Fugitive Slave Clause suggests an implied power, then isn't that reason enough to find an implied power in *Prigg*? Does the fact that

Congress passed a Fugitive Slave Law in the 1790s, early in our constitutional history, matter in resolving this question, as it did with the constitutionality of the Bank of the United States?

3. Are there other constitutional issues lurking, unaddressed, in the opinions in *Prigg*? Could the federal government have created fugitive slave "Commissioners"—who were not Article III judges—to hear claims by slave owners? Did alleged slaves have a *federal* constitutional right to trial by jury?

4. How does the text of the Fugitive Slave Clause differ from the text of the Extradition Clause? One difference is that the Fugitive Slave Clause "applied only to those *actually* held to 'service or labour' in marked contrast to the Extradition Clause, which applied to all those 'charged' with crime. So the application of the federal rule required a determination of whether the target was a slave or not—the subject of two fugitive slave statutes and plenty of litigation." Baude, 64 Stan. L. Rev. at 1425. The Extradition Clause is similar to a clause in the Articles of Confederation, and early in our history Congress passed an extradition statute carrying into execution its implied power under this clause. The major early case under the clause was *Kentucky v. Dennison,* 65 U.S. 66 (1860). It involved a free black man, Willis Lago, who had violated Kentucky law by helping a slave girl escape. He fled to Ohio, where the governor refused to extradite him. Chief Justice Taney's opinion came to the astonishing conclusion that while the governor of Ohio was constitutionally obligated to extradite Lago, the Supreme Court lacked the power to issue a writ of mandamus compelling the governor to do so. The decision can be explained only by what were at that time Chief Justice Taney's extreme pro-state power and pro-executive-power views. The Court unanimously overruled *Dennison* in *Puerto Rico v. Branstad*, 483 U.S. 219 (1987).

[Assignment 38]

C. THE TERRITORIES CLAUSE, THE NEW STATES ADMISSION CLAUSE, AND CITIZENSHIP

Article I, Section 3: The Congress shall have Power to dispose of and make all needful Rules and Regulations respecting the Territory or other Property belonging to the United States.

Article IV, Section 2: The Citizens of each State shall be entitled to all Privileges and Immunities of citizens in the several States.

Section 3: New States may be admitted . . . into this Union.

In antebellum American history, the most important constitutional controversies concerned these clauses, and especially Congress's powers under the Territories Clause—the Civil War itself began as a fight over slavery in the territories. The review here cannot be comprehensive. For a much fuller treatment, see Gary Lawson & Guy Seidman, THE CONSTITUTION OF EMPIRE: TERRITORIAL EXPANSION & AMERICAN LEGAL HISTORY (2004).

Consider briefly two important early controversies involving these clauses—the "Louisiana Purchase" and the "Missouri Compromise." The Louisiana Purchase of 1803 was probably the most important event in American constitutional history between the ratification of the Bill of Rights (1789–1791) and the crisis of secession and the Civil War (1860–1865). President Thomas Jefferson was presented with an unexpected opportunity to purchase the entirety of the vast trans-Mississippi territory of "Louisiana" from France, when Napoleon Bonaparte offered to sell the entire territory for the bargain price of $15 million. Jefferson's envoys, Robert Livingston and James Monroe, who had been sent to negotiate the possible purchase of New Orleans only, seized the opportunity. The Purchase doubled the physical size of the United States, and the treaty committed the United States to incorporating the territory and its residents into the nation—over time, eventually accounting for fourteen new states.

Jefferson had doubts about whether it was constitutional to add to the territory of the United States beyond its initial borders, thinking it arguably beyond the Constitution's enumerated powers and requiring a constitutional amendment. Jefferson, Letter to Wilson Nicholas (Sept. 7, 1803). Jefferson's position echoed his "strict construction" position with respect to the Bank.

(Do you agree or disagree that the federal government lacked enumerated power to acquire new territory? Is there any reason why new territory or property may not be added to the United States by treaty or by purchase, provided Congress appropriates the necessary funds? The president and the Senate together have the power to make treaties, and English kings had for centuries acquired and divested themselves of parts of France by treaty. Is there any reason then why Jefferson could not acquire the Louisiana Purchase by treaty? Here the treaty power was even being used to acquire part of France!)

Jefferson thought the purchase so beneficial to the nation's interest that he went forward notwithstanding his constitutional qualms—and without seeking an amendment that might upend the bargain. He later stated: "A strict observance of the written law is doubtless one of the high duties of a good citizen, but it is not the highest. The laws of necessity, of self-preservation, of saving our country when in danger, are of higher obligation. To lose our country by a scrupulous adherence to the written law, would be to lose the law itself, with life, liberty, property and all those who are enjoying them with us; thus absurdly sacrificing the end to the means." Jefferson, Letter to John Colvin (Sept. 20, 1810). Do you agree? If Jefferson was right to be troubled about the constitutional question, was it lawless for him to go forward with the Louisiana Purchase? Does the Constitution contain implied exceptions in favor of "necessity"? For a general treatment of "necessity" in constitutional interpretation, with an emphasis on President Lincoln's invocation of the concept, see Michael Stokes Paulsen, *The Constitution of Necessity*, 79 Notre Dame L. Rev. 1257 (2004).

One constitutional legacy of the Louisiana Purchase was vast new territory in which slavery potentially could expand. The Northwest Ordinance of 1787 (re-enacted by the First Congress in 1789) forever banned slavery in the regions of the old Northwest. But Jefferson and his political allies did not seek such a restriction for the new Louisiana Territory. The battle over whether slavery would be permitted in new territories—or which ones—and whether new slave states would be admitted to the Union was *the* major political-constitutional controversy of the first half of the nineteenth century, dwarfing even the Bank and Nullification controversies of the 1820s and 1830s. The question of the expansion of slavery, and the balance between slave-state and free-state power, eventually produced several tenuous compromises. Most notable among them was the "Missouri Compromise" of 1820, which admitted Maine and Missouri to statehood (one free state for one slave state) and crafted a geographical rule—a line—

concerning where slavery might be allowed in the territories and (by implication) in future states carved out of those territories. North of a line of 36 degrees 30 minutes north latitude (excluding the state of Missouri itself), slavery would be prohibited; below that line, it would be permitted. The Missouri Compromise was invoked by Dred Scott's lawyers in support of his freedom—only to have the Supreme Court (wrongly) declare it unconstitutional in *Dred Scott v. Sandford.*

The *Dred Scott* case involves several aspects of Article IV. First, it involved the question of whether black men and women, suing for their freedom under state or federal law, were "citizens" of the states in which they claimed residence and entitled to the "privileges and immunities of citizens in the several States." The majority's monstrous holding that no black person, whether slave or free, could constitutionally be a "citizen" of the United States—and therefore could not be a citizen of any state—had a lot to do with the majority's view that it would be unthinkable for free blacks to possess the "Privileges and Immunities" or civil rights of citizens in the several states: that probably would mean they had the freedom of speech under the First Amendment and the right to bear arms under the Second Amendment, even in Southern states.

Second, the case had everything to do with Congress's power under the Territories Clause. The case came to the Court in the context of a long and bitter period of territorial expansion and battles between North and South over the admission of new states. Would newly admitted states be free states or slave states? Did Congress have the power to enforce a prohibition on slavery in new states? And did Congress have the power to prohibit slavery in some or all of the *territories,* while they were still territories and before they applied for statehood? The decision famously struck down the important "Missouri Compromise" Act of Congress of 1820, which had forbidden slavery in territories north of a designated line, as part of a compromise assuring a continued balance of slave states and free states. *Dred Scott* declared that compromise unconstitutional, saying that the federal government had no legitimate constitutional power to limit the spread of slavery to new territories and essentially ending all hopes of a political compromise to settle the long-simmering conflict between free states and slave states.

Worse yet was the Court's purported *reason* why the Missouri Compromise was unconstitutional. The Court in *Dred Scott* held that slave owners had a substantive right under the Due Process Clause of the Fifth Amendment to own slaves and to carry their slave "property" into any federal territory and that the national government lacked power under the Constitution to restrict ownership of slaves in the territories. The nature of such a wild claim portended that the Court might hold that *states* could not exclude slavery either. Thus, there was a very real threat that *Dred Scott* would have the effect of requiring Northern states to recognize, even within their own borders, the status of slavery. (Recall *Lemmon v. The People,* which it was feared might become, were it to reach the Supreme Court, in the words of Abraham Lincoln, a "Second *Dred Scott*" decision making slavery *national.*)

It would be overstating matters, at least somewhat, to say that the *Dred Scott* case led to the Civil War. But it was certainly an important link in the chain-of-events leading to the election of Lincoln (who stood opposed to the case), the South's secession (over the election of Lincoln), and the Civil War (because of the South's attempted secession). *Dred Scott* was hugely significant at the time. For a full history, see Don Fehrenbacher's THE DRED SCOTT CASE: ITS SIGNIFICANCE IN AMERICAN LAW AND POLITICS (1978). An edited version of the Supreme Court decision is presented below.

Indeed, the election of Lincoln; the South's secession; and the Civil War all might be said to be a great national re-adjudication of the Supreme Court's atrocious misinterpretation of the Constitution in *Dred Scott.*

To short-circuit the story: the Union eventually won the war; secession was defeated; Lincoln issued the Emancipation Proclamation as a war measure, pursuant to his constitutional power as military commander in chief; and, following the success of the Union armies, the Constitution was amended to abolish slavery and to overrule and repudiate the *Dred Scott* decision. The case is, therefore, also hugely significant in terms of the major constitutional changes that it (indirectly) spawned. The Thirteenth Amendment, abolishing slavery, the Fourteenth Amendment, overruling *Dred Scott*'s citizenship holding and providing for civil rights and the equal protection of the laws, and the Fifteenth Amendment, forbidding racial discrimination in voting, were results of the War and ultimately connect back to the *Dred Scott* decision itself. Thus, much of modern constitutional law—in the form of the three Civil War amendments—is a more or less direct response to, and repudiation of, the *Dred Scott* case.

Something of a roadmap, and a warning, is required before one's first reading of Chief Justice Taney's opinion for the Court: Nearly everything Chief Justice Taney says is wrong—and directed to achieving the firmest possible pro-slavery outcome on every conceivable issue. Read the opinion with a sharply critical eye. He first addresses whether there was proper jurisdiction under the Diversity Clause of the Constitution, and uses that question as a vehicle for considering whether a black person may ever be a citizen of the United States entitled to sue in federal courts. Next, he considers whether the Missouri Compromise statute's prohibition of slavery in the territories could really operate to grant Dred Scott his freedom by virtue of his stay at Fort Snelling, in free federal territory. He concludes it could not have this result, because the statute was an unconstitutional deprivation of slaveholders' property "without due process of law." Finally, he concludes that, in any event, neither the Missouri Compromise law concerning slavery in federal territory, nor Illinois's law as a free state, could operate to make Dred Scott free in Missouri. Neither law had "extraterritorial" effect.

Dred Scott v. Sandford

60 (19 How.) U.S. 393 (1857)

[The facts were agreed to by the parties and are relocated here from where they are set forth midway through Chief Justice Taney's opinion of the Court.—Editors]

In the year 1834, the plaintiff was a negro slave belonging to Dr. Emerson, who was a surgeon in the army of the United States. In that year, 1834, said Dr. Emerson took the plaintiff from the State of Missouri to the military post at Rock Island, in the State of Illinois, and held him there as a slave until the month of April or May, 1836.

[Dr. Emerson then took Dred Scott to Fort Snelling, in present-day Minnesota, then part of the territory known as Upper Louisiana. Slavery in

that territory was banned by the Missouri Compromise federal statute of 1820, which admitted Missouri as a slave state, Maine as a free state, and prohibited slavery in the remainder of the Louisiana Purchase north of the line of thirty-six degrees thirty minutes latitude. In 1836, Dr. Emerson acquired Harriet, a slave.—Editors]

In the year 1836, the plaintiff and said Harriet, at said Fort Snelling, with the consent of said Dr. Emerson, who then claimed to be their master and owner, intermarried. . . . Eliza and Lizzie . . . are the fruit of that marriage. Eliza is about fourteen years old, and was born on board the steamboat Gipsey, north of the north line of the State of Missouri, and upon the river Mississippi. Lizzie is about seven years old, and was born in the State of Missouri, at the military post called Jefferson Barracks.

In the year 1838, said Dr. Emerson removed the plaintiff and said Harriet and their said daughter Eliza, from said Fort Snelling to the State of Missouri, where they have ever since resided.

[The procedural history of the case is famously convoluted. To compress drastically: Dred Scott first brought suit against Dr. Emerson's widow, in Missouri state court, asserting his freedom. He won in the trial court, but the Missouri Supreme Court reversed, overruling its own prior precedents which would have treated Scott's long stay in Illinois, a free state, as sufficient to confer on him freedom. Under the earlier cases, Missouri would have applied Illinois's law to determine Scott's status, as a matter of "comity." The Missouri Supreme Court decided instead to apply Missouri law to Scott's status, and found him to be a slave under Missouri law. Before the judgment became final (apparently), Scott was (apparently) either sold or transferred to Mrs. Emerson's brother, Mr. Sanford, a citizen of New York state. (Sanford's name was misspelled in the official Supreme Court report, giving the case the name Dred Scott v. Sandford.) Scott's lawyers commenced a new suit in federal court, invoking federal diversity jurisdiction, which exists for cases between a citizen of one state and a citizen of another state. Sanford was a citizen of New York; if Scott was a citizen of Missouri, the federal courts would have jurisdiction under Article III of the Constitution to hear his case. But if even free black persons could not be "citizens" as the word is used in Article III, then Scott's case would have to be dismissed and he would have no remedy in federal court. Scott lost in the lower federal court, and appealed to the U.S. Supreme Court.—Editors]

■ MR. CHIEF JUSTICE TANEY delivered the opinion of the court. . . .

There are two leading questions presented by the record:

1. Had the Circuit Court of the United States jurisdiction to hear and determine the case between these parties? And

2. If it had jurisdiction, is the judgment it has given erroneous or not?

The plaintiff in error, . . . was, with his wife and children, held as slaves by the defendant, in the State of Missouri; and he brought this action in the Circuit Court of the United States for that district, to assert the title of himself and his family to freedom. . . .

The defendant pleaded in abatement to the jurisdiction of the court, that the plaintiff was not a citizen of the State of Missouri, as alleged in his declaration, being a negro of African descent, whose ancestors were of pure African blood, and who were brought into this country and sold as slaves. . . .

The question is simply this: Can a negro, whose ancestors were imported into this country, and sold as slaves, become a member of the political community formed and brought into existence by the Constitution of the United States, and as such become entitled to all the rights, and privileges, and immunities, guaranteed by that instrument to the citizen? One of which rights is the privilege of suing in a court of the United States in the cases specified in the Constitution. . . .

The words "people of the United States" and "citizens" are synonymous terms, and mean the same thing. They both describe the political body who, according to our republican institutions, form the sovereignty, and who hold the power and conduct the Government through their representatives. They are what we familiarly call the "sovereign people," and every citizen is one of this people, and a constituent member of this sovereignty. The question before us is, whether [persons of African descent] compose a portion of this people, and are constituent members of this sovereignty? We think they are not, and that they are not included, and were not intended to be included, under the word "citizens" in the Constitution, and can therefore claim none of the rights and privileges which that instrument provides for and secures to citizens of the United States. On the contrary, they were at that time considered as a subordinate and inferior class of beings, who had been subjugated by the dominant race, and, whether emancipated or not, yet remained subject to their authority, and had no rights or privileges but such as those who held the power and the Government might choose to grant them. . . .

In discussing this question, we must not confound the rights of citizenship which a State may confer within its own limits, and the rights of citizenship as a member of the Union. It does not by any means follow, because he has all the rights and privileges of a citizen of a State, that he must be a citizen of the United States. He may have all of the rights and privileges of the citizen of a State, and yet not be entitled to the rights and privileges of a citizen in any other State. For, previous to the adoption of the Constitution of the United States, every State had the undoubted right to confer on whomsoever it pleased the character of citizen, and to endow him with all its rights. But this character of course was confined to the boundaries of the State, and gave him no rights or privileges in other States beyond those secured to him by the laws of nations and the comity of States. Nor have the several States surrendered the power of conferring these rights and privileges by adopting the Constitution of the United States. Each State may still confer them upon an alien, or any one it thinks proper, or upon any class or description of persons; yet he would not be a citizen in the sense in which that word is used in the Constitution of the United States, nor entitled to sue as such in one of its courts, nor to the privileges and immunities of a citizen in the other States. The rights which he would acquire would be restricted to the State which gave them. The Constitution has conferred on Congress the right to establish an uniform rule of naturalization, and this right is evidently exclusive, and has always been held by this court to be so. Consequently, no State, since the adoption of the Constitution, can by naturalizing an alien invest him with the rights and privileges secured to a citizen of a State under the Federal Government, although, so far as the State alone was concerned, he would undoubtedly be entitled to the rights of a citizen, and clothed with all the rights and immunities which the Constitution and laws of the State attached to that character.

It is very clear, therefore, that no State can, by any act or law of its own, passed since the adoption of the Constitution, introduce a new member into the political community created by the Constitution of the United States. It cannot make him a member of this community by making him a member of its own. And for the same reason it cannot introduce any person, or description of persons, who were not intended to be embraced in this new political family, which the Constitution brought into existence, but were intended to be excluded from it.

The question then arises, whether the provisions of the Constitution, in relation to the personal rights and privileges to which the citizen of a State should be entitled, embraced the negro African race, at that time in this country, or who might afterwards be imported, who had then or should afterwards be made free in any State; and to put it in the power of a single State to make him a citizen of the United States, and endue him with the full rights of citizenship in every other State without their consent? Does the Constitution of the United States act upon him whenever he shall be made free under the laws of a State, and raised there to the rank of a citizen, and immediately cloth him with all the privileges of a citizen in every other State, and in its own courts?

The court think the affirmative of these propositions cannot be maintained. And if it cannot, the plaintiff in error could not be a citizen of the State of Missouri, within the meaning of the Constitution of the United States, and, consequently, was not entitled to sue in its courts.

It is true, every person, and every class and description of persons, who were at the time of the adoption of the Constitution recognized as citizens in the several States, became also citizens of this new political body; but none other; it was formed by them, and for them and their posterity, but for no one else. And the personal rights and privileges guarantied to citizens of this new sovereignty were intended to embrace those only who were then members of the several State communities, or who should afterwards by birthright or otherwise become members, according to the provisions of the Constitution and the principles on which it was founded. It was the union of those who were at that time members of distinct and separate political communities into one political family, whose power, for certain specified purposes, was to extend over the whole territory of the United States. And it gave to each citizen rights and privileges outside of his State which he did not before possess, and placed him in every other State upon a perfect equality with its own citizens as to rights of person and rights of property; it made him a citizen of the United States.

It becomes necessary, therefore, to determine who were citizens of the several States when the Constitution was adopted. And in order to do this, we must recur to the Governments and institutions of the thirteen colonies, when they separated from Great Britain and formed new sovereignties, and took their places in the family of independent nations. . . .

In the opinion of the court, the legislation and histories of the times, and the language used in the Declaration of Independence, show, that neither the class of persons who had been imported as slaves, nor their descendants, whether they had become free or not, were then acknowledged as a part of the people, nor intended to be included in the general words used in that memorable instrument.

It is difficult at this day to realize the state of public opinion in relation to that unfortunate race, which prevailed in the civilized and enlightened portions of the world at the time of the Declaration of Independence, and when the Constitution of the United States was framed and adopted. But the public history of every European nation displays it in a manner too plain to be mistaken.

They had for more than a century before been regarded as beings of an inferior order, and altogether unfit to associate with the white race, either in social or political relations; and so far inferior, that they had no rights which the white man was bound to respect; and that the negro might justly and lawfully be reduced to slavery for his benefit. He was bought and sold, and treated as an ordinary article of merchandise and traffic, whenever a profit could be made by it. This opinion was at that time fixed and universal in the civilized portion of the white race. It was regarded as an axiom in morals as well as in politics, which no one thought of disputing, or supposed to be open to dispute; and men in every grade and position in society daily and habitually acted upon it in their private pursuits, as well as in matters of public concern, without doubting for a moment the correctness of this opinion.

And in no nation was this opinion more firmly fixed or more uniformly acted upon than by the English Government and English people. They not only seized them on the coast of Africa, and sold them or held them in slavery for their own use; but they took them as ordinary articles of merchandise to every country where they could make a profit on them, and were far more extensively engaged in this commerce than any other nation in the world.

The opinion thus entertained and acted upon in England was naturally impressed upon the colonies they founded on this side of the Atlantic. And, accordingly, a negro of the African race was regarded by them as an article of property, and held, and bought and sold as such, in every one of the thirteen colonies which united in the Declaration of Independence, and afterwards formed the Constitution of the United States. The slaves were more or less numerous in the different colonies, as slave labor was found more or less profitable. But no one seems to have doubted the correctness of the prevailing opinion of the time.

The legislation of the different colonies furnishes positive and indisputable proof of this fact. *[Chief Justice Taney then proceeds to give illustrations.—Editors]* . . .

The language of the Declaration of Independence is equally conclusive: . . . "We hold these truths to be self-evident: that all men are created equal; that they are endowed by their Creator with certain unalienable rights; that among them is life, liberty, and the pursuit of happiness; that to secure these rights, Governments are instituted, deriving their just powers from the consent of the governed."

The general words above quoted would seem to embrace the whole human family, and if they were used in a similar instrument at this day would be so understood. But it is too clear for dispute, that the enslaved African race were not intended to be included, and formed no part of the people who framed and adopted this declaration; for if the language, as understood in that day, would embrace them, the conduct of the distinguished men who framed the Declaration of Independence would have been utterly and flagrantly inconsistent with the principles they asserted; and instead of the sympathy of mankind, to which they so confidently appeared, they would have deserved and received universal rebuke and reprobation.

Yet the men who framed this declaration were great men—high in literary acquirements—high in their sense of honor, and incapable of asserting principles inconsistent with those on which they were acting. They perfectly understood the meaning of the language they used, and how it would be understood by others; and they knew that it would not in any part of the civilized world be supposed to embrace the negro race, which, by common consent, had been excluded from civilized Governments and the family of nations, and doomed to slavery. They spoke and acted according to the then established doctrines and principles, and in the ordinary language of the day, no one misunderstood them. The unhappy black race were separated from the white by indelible marks, and laws long before established, and were never thought of or spoken of except as property, and when the claims of the owner or the profit of the trader were supposed to need protection. . . .

[T]here are two clauses in the Constitution which point directly and specifically to the negro race as a separate class of persons, and show clearly that they were not regarded as a portion of the people or citizens of the Government then formed.

One of these clauses reserves to each of the thirteen States the right to import slaves until the year 1808, if it thinks proper. . . . *[The other is the Fugitive Slave Clause.—Editors]* By the first above-mentioned clause, therefore, the right to purchase and hold this property is directly sanctioned and authorized for twenty years by the people who framed the Constitution. And by the second, they pledge themselves to maintain and uphold the right of the master in the manner specified, as long as the Government they then formed should endure. And these two provisions show, conclusively, that neither the description of persons therein referred to, not their descendants, were embraced in any of the other provisions of the Constitution; for certainly these two clauses were not intended to confer on them or their posterity the blessings of liberty, or any of the personal rights so carefully provided for the citizen.

No one of that race had ever migrated to the United States voluntarily; all of them had been brought here as articles of merchandise. The number that had been emancipated at that time were but few in comparison with those held in slavery; and they were identified in the public mind with the race to which they belonged, and regarded as a part of the slave population rather than the free. It is obvious that they were not even in the minds of the framers of the Constitution when they were conferring special rights and privileges upon the citizens of a State in every other part of the Union. . . .

A clause similar to the one in the Constitution, in relation to the rights and immunities of citizens of one State in the other States, was contained in the Articles of Confederation. But there is a difference of language, which is worthy of note. The provision in the Articles of Confederation was, "that the *free inhabitants* of each of the States, paupers, vagabonds, and fugitives from justice, excepted, should be entitled to all the privileges and immunities of free citizens in the several States."

. . . The term *free inhabitant*, in the generality of its terms, would certainly include one of the African race who had been manumitted. But . . . notwithstanding the generality of the words "free inhabitants," it is very clear that, according to their accepted meaning in that day, they did not include the African race, whether free or not: for the fifth section of the ninth article provides that Congress should have the power "to agree upon the number of land forces to be raised, and to make requisitions from each State for its quota in proportion to the number of *white* inhabitants in such State, which requisition should be binding."

Words could hardly have been used which more strongly mark the line of distinction between the citizen and the subject; the free and the subjugated races. . . .

The only two provisions [in the Constitution] which point to them and include them, treat them as property, and make it the duty of the Government to protect it; no other power, in relation to this race, is to be found in the Constitution; and as it is a Government of special, delegated, powers, no authority beyond these two provisions can be constitutionally exercised. The Government of the United States had no right to interfere for any other purpose but that of protecting the rights of the owner, leaving it altogether with the several States to deal with this race, whether emancipated or not, as each State may think justice, humanity, and the interests and safety of society, require. The States evidently intended to reserve this power exclusively to themselves.

No one, we presume, supposes that any change in public opinion or feeling, in relation to this unfortunate race, in the civilized nations of Europe or in this country, should induce the court to give to the words of the Constitution a more liberal construction in their favor than they were intended to bear when the instrument was framed and adopted. Such an argument would be altogether inadmissible in any tribunal called on to interpret it. If any of its provisions are deemed unjust, there is a mode prescribed in the instrument itself by which it may be amended; but while it remains unaltered, it must be construed now as it was understood at the time of its adoption. It is not only the same in words, but the same in meaning, and delegates the same powers to the Government, and reserves and secures the same rights and privileges to the citizen; and as long as it continues to exist in its present form, it speaks not only in the same words, but with the same meaning and intent with which it spoke when it came from the hands of its framers, and was voted on and adopted by the people of the United States. Any other rule of construction would abrogate the judicial character of this court, and make it the mere reflex of the popular opinion or passion of the day. This court was not created by the Constitution for such purposes. Higher and graver trusts have been confided to it, and it must not falter in the path of duty.

What the construction was at that time, we think can hardly admit of doubt. We have the language of the Declaration of Independence and of the Articles of Confederation, in addition to the plain words of the Constitution itself; we have the legislation of the different States, before, about the time, and since, the Constitution was adopted; we have the legislation of Congress, from the time of its adoption to a recent period; and we have the constant and uniform action of the Executive Department, all concurring together, and leading to the same result. And if anything in relation to the construction of the Constitution can be regarded as settled, it is that which we now give to the word "citizen" and the word "people."

And upon a full and careful consideration of the subject, the court is of opinion, that, upon the facts stated in the plea in abatement, Dred Scott was not a citizen of Missouri within the meaning of the Constitution of the United States, and not entitled as such to sue in its courts; and, consequently, that the Circuit Court had no jurisdiction of the case . . .

It is true that the result either way, by dismissal or by a judgment for the defendant, makes very little, if any, difference in a pecuniary or personal point of view to either party. But the fact that the result would be very nearly the same to the parties in either form of judgment, would not justify this court in sanctioning an error in the judgment which is patent on the record, and which, if sanctioned, might be drawn into precedent, and lead to serious mischief and injustice in some future suit.

We proceed, therefore, to inquire whether the facts relied on by the plaintiff entitled him to his freedom. *[The opinion then proceeds to lay out the facts as relocated to the beginning of this edited opinion.—Editors]* . . .

Before the commencement of this suit, said Dr. Emerson sold and conveyed the plaintiff, and Harriet, Eliza, and Lizzie, to the defendant, as slaves, and the defendant has ever since claimed to hold them, and each of them, as slaves.

In considering this part of the controversy, two questions arise: 1. Was he, together with his family, free in Missouri by reason of the stay in the territory of the United States hereinbefore mentioned? And 2. If they were not, is Scott himself free by reason of his removal to Rock Island, in the State of Illinois, as stated in the above admissions?

We proceed to examine the first question.

The act of Congress, upon which the plaintiff relies, declares that slavery and involuntary servitude, except as a punishment for crime, shall be forever prohibited in all that part of the territory ceded by France, under the name of Louisiana, which lies north of thirty-six degrees thirty minutes north latitude, and not included within the limits of Missouri. And the difficulty which meets us at the threshold of this part of the inquiry is, whether Congress was authorized to pass this law under any of the powers granted to it by the Constitution; for if the authority is not given by that instrument, it is the duty of this court to declare it void and inoperative, and incapable of conferring freedom upon any one who is held as a slave under the laws of any one of the States.

The counsel for the plaintiff has laid much stress upon that article in the Constitution which confers on Congress the power "to dispose of and make all needful rules and regulations respecting the territory or other property belonging to the United States"; but, in the judgment of the court, that provision has no bearing on the present controversy, and the power there given, whatever it may be, is confined, and was intended to be confined, to the territory which at that time belonged to, or was claimed by, the United States, and was within their boundaries as settled by the treaty with Great Britain, and can have no influence upon a territory afterwards acquired from a foreign Government. It was a special provision for a known and particular territory, and to meet a present emergency, and nothing more. . . .

The language used in the clause, the arrangement and combination of the powers, and the somewhat unusual phraseology it uses, when it speaks of the political power to be exercised in the government of the territory, all indicate the design and meaning of the clause to be such as we have mentioned. It does not speak of *any* territory, nor of *Territories*, but uses language which, according to its legitimate meaning, points to a particular thing. The power is given in relation only to *the* territory of the United States—that is, to a territory then in existence, and then known or claimed as the territory of the United States. It begins its enumeration of powers by that of disposing, in other words, making sale of the lands, or raising money from them, which, as we have already said, was the main object to the cession, and which is accordingly the first thing provided for in the article. It then gives the power which was necessarily associated with the disposition and sale of the lands—that is, the power of making needful rules and regulations respecting the territory. And whatever construction may now be given to these words, every one, we think, must admit that they are not the words usually employed by statesmen in giving supreme power of legislation. They are certainly very unlike the words used in the power granted to legislate over territory which the new Government might afterwards itself obtain by cession from a State, either for its seat of Government, of for forts, magazines, arsenals, dock yards, and other needful buildings.

And the same power of making needful rules respecting the territory is, in precisely the same language, applied to the other property belonging to the United States—associating the power over the territory in this respect with the power over movable or personal property—that is, the ships, arms, and munitions of war, which then belonged in common to the State sovereignties. And it will hardly be said, that this power, in relation to the last-mentioned objects, was deemed necessary to be thus specially given to the new Government, in order to authorize it to make needful rules and regulations respecting the ships it might itself build, or arms and munitions of war it might itself manufacture or provide for the public service.

No one, it is believed, would think a moment of deriving the power of Congress to make needful rules and regulations in relation to property of this kind from this clause of the Constitution. Nor can it, upon any fair construction, be applied to any property but that which the new Government was about to receive from the confederated States. And if this be true as to this property, it must be equally true and limited as to the territory, which is so carefully and precisely coupled with it—and like it referred to as property in the power granted. The concluding words of the clause appear to render this construction irresistible; for, after the provisions we have mentioned, it proceeds to say, "that nothing in the Constitution shall be so construed as to prejudice any claims of the United States, or of any particular State." . . .

The words "needful rules and regulations" would seem, also, to have been cautiously used for some definite object. They are not the words usually employed by statesmen, when they mean to give the powers of sovereignty, or to establish a Government, or to authorize its establishment. Thus, in the law to renew and keep alive the ordinance of 1787, and to reestablish the Government, the title of the law is: "An act to provide for the government of the territory northwest of the river Ohio." And in the Constitution, when granting the power to legislate over the territory that may be selected for the seat of Government independently of a State, it does not say Congress shall have power "to make all needful rules and regulations respecting the territory"; but it declares that "Congress shall have power to exercise exclusive legislation in all cases whatsoever over such District (not exceeding ten miles square) as may, by cession of particular States and the acceptance of Congress, become the seat of the Government of the United States.["] . . .

Whether, therefore, we take the particular clause in question, by itself, or in connection with the other provisions of the Constitution, we think it clear, that it applies only to the particular territory of which we have spoken, and cannot, by any just rule of interpretation, be extended to territory which the new Government might afterwards obtain from a foreign nation. . . .

This brings us to examine by what provision of the Constitution the present Federal Government, under its delegated and restricted powers, is authorized to acquire territory outside of the original limits of the United States, and what powers it may exercise therein over the person or property of a citizen of the United States, while it remains a Territory, and until it shall be admitted as one of the States of the Union. . . .

We do not mean, however, to question the power of Congress in this respect. The power to expand the territory of the United States by the admission of new States is plainly given; and in the construction of this power by all the departments of the Government, it has been held to authorize the acquisition of territory, not fit for admission at the time, but to be admitted as soon as its population and situation would entitle it to admission. It is acquired to become a State, and not to be held as a colony and governed by Congress with absolute authority; and as the propriety of admitting a new State is committed to the sound discretion of Congress, the power to acquire territory for that purpose, to be held by the United States until it is in a suitable condition to become a State upon an equal footing with the other States, must rest upon the same discretion. . . . [W]hatever the political department of the Government shall recognize as within the limits of the United States, the judicial department is also bound to recognize, and to administer in it the laws of the United States, . . . and to maintain in the Territory . . . the personal rights and rights of property of individual citizens, as secured by the Constitution. . . .

Taking this rule to guide us, it may be safely assumed that citizens of the United States who migrate to a Territory belonging to the people of the United States, cannot be ruled as mere colonists, dependent upon the will of the General Government, and to be governed by any laws it may think proper to impose. . . . A power . . . in the General Government to obtain and hold colonies and dependent territories, over which they might legislate without restriction, would be inconsistent with its own existence in its present form. Whatever it acquires, it acquires for the benefit of the people of the several states who created it. It is their trustee acting for them, and charged with the duty of promoting the interests of the whole people of the Union in the exercise of the powers specifically granted.

At the time when the Territory in question was obtained by cession from France, it contained no population fit to be associated together and admitted as a State; and it therefore was absolutely necessary to hold possession of it, as a Territory belonging to the United States, until it was [settled, inhabited, and ready to be admitted as a State]. . . .

But until that time arrives, it is undoubtedly necessary that some Government should be established, in order to organize society, and to protect the inhabitants in their persons and property . . . The power to acquire necessarily carries with it the power to preserve and apply to the purposes for which it was acquired. . . . [S]ome form of civil authority would be absolutely necessary to organize and preserve civilized society, and prepare it to become a State; and what is the best form must always depend on the condition of the Territory at the time, and the choice of the mode must depend upon the exercise of a discretionary power by Congress, acting within the scope of its constitutional authority, and not infringing upon the rights of person or rights of property of the citizen who might go there to reside, or for any other lawful purpose. . . .

But the power of Congress over the person or property of a citizen can never be a mere discretionary power. . . . The powers of the Government and the rights and privileges of the citizen are regulated and plainly defined by the Constitution itself. And when the Territory becomes a part of the United States, the Federal Government enters into possession in the character impressed upon it by those who created it. It enters upon it with its powers over the citizen strictly defined, and limited by the Constitution, from which it derives its own existence, and by virtue of which alone it continues to exist and act as a Government and sovereignty. It has no power of any kind beyond it; and it cannot, when it enters a Territory of the United States, put off its character, and assume discretionary or despotic powers which the Constitution has denied to it. . . . [T]he Government and the citizen both enter it under the authority of the Constitution, with their respective rights defined and marked out; and the Federal Government can exercise no power over his person or property, beyond what that instrument confers, nor lawfully deny any right which it has reserved. . . .

For example, no one, we presume, will contend that Congress can make any law in a Territory respecting that establishment of religion, or the free exercise thereof, or abridging the freedom of speech or of the press, or the right of the people of the Territory peaceably to assemble, and to petition the Government for the redress of grievances.

Nor can Congress deny to the people the right to keep and bear arms, nor the right to trial by jury, nor compel any one to be a witness against himself in a criminal proceeding.

These powers, and others, in relation to rights of person, which it is not necessary here to enumerate, are, in express and positive terms, denied to the General Government; and the rights of private property have been guarded with equal care. Thus the rights of property are united with the rights of person, and placed on the same ground by the Fifth Amendment to the Constitution, which provides that no person shall be deprived of life, liberty, and property, without due process of law. And an act of Congress which deprives a citizen of the United States of his liberty or property, merely because he came himself or brought his property into a particular Territory of the United States, and who had committed no offence against the laws, could hardly be dignified with the name of due process of law.

So, too, it will hardly be contended that Congress could by law quarter a soldier in a house in a Territory . . . [or] take private property for public use without just compensation.

The powers over person and property of which we speak are not only not granted to Congress, but are in express terms denied, and they are forbidden to exercise them. And this prohibition is not confined to the States, but the words are general, and extend to the whole territory over which the Constitution gives it power to legislate, including those portions of it remaining under Territorial Government, as well as that covered by States. It is a total absence of power everywhere within the dominion of the United States, and places the citizens of a Territory, so far as these rights are concerned, on the same footing with citizens of the States, and guards them as firmly and plainly against any inroads which the General Government might attempt, under the plea of implied or incidental powers. And if Congress itself cannot do this—if it is beyond the powers conferred on the Federal Government—it will be admitted, we presume, that it could not authorize a Territorial Government to exercise them. It could confer no power on any local Government, established by its authority, to violate the provisions of the Constitution.

It seems, however, to be supposed, that there is a difference between property in a slave and other property, and that different rules may be applied to it in expounding the Constitution of the United States. And the laws and usages of nations, and the writing of eminent jurists upon the relation of master and slave and their mutual rights and duties, and the powers which Governments may exercise over it, have been dwelt upon in the argument.

But in considering the question before us, it must be borne in mind that there is no law of nations standing between the people of the United States and their Government, and interfering with their relation to each other. The powers of the Government, and the rights of the citizen under it, are positive and practical regulations plainly written down. . . . And if the Constitution recognises the right of property of the master in a slave, and makes no distinction between that description of property and other property owned by a citizen, no tribunal, acting under the authority of the United States, whether it be legislative, executive, or judicial, has a right to draw such a distinction, or deny to it the benefit of the provisions and guarantees which have been provided for the protection of private property against the encroachments of the Government.

Now, as we have already said in an earlier part of this opinion, upon a different point, the right of property in a slave is distinctly and expressly affirmed in the Constitution. The right to traffic in it, like an ordinary article of merchandise and property, was guarantied to the citizens of the United States, in every State that might desire it, for twenty years. And the Government in express terms is pledged to protect it in all future time, if the slave escapes from his owner. This is done in plain words—too plain to be misunderstood. And no word can be found in the Constitution which gives Congress a greater power over slave property, or which entitles property of that kind to less protection than property of any other description. The only power conferred is the power coupled with the duty of guarding and protecting the owner in his rights.

Upon these considerations, it is the opinion of the court that the act of Congress which prohibited a citizen from holding and owning property of this kind in the territory of the United States north of the line therein mentioned, is not warranted by the Constitution, and is therefore void; and that neither Dred Scott himself, nor any of his family, were made free by being carried into this territory; even if they had been carried there by the owner, with the intention of becoming a permanent resident. . . .

But there is another point in the case which depends on State power and State law. And it is contended, on the part of the plaintiff, that he is made free by being taken to Rock Island, in the State of Illinois, independently of his residence in the territory of the United States; and being so made free, he was not again reduced to a state of slavery by being brought back to Missouri.

Our notice of this part of the case will be very brief; for the principle on which it depends was decided . . . in the case of *Strader et al. v. Graham* [10 How. 82]. In that case, the slaves had been taken from Kentucky to Ohio, with the consent of the owner, and afterwards brought back to Kentucky. And this court held that their *status* or condition, as free or slave, depended upon the laws of Kentucky, when they were brought back into that State, and not of Ohio; and that this court had no jurisdiction to revise the judgment of a State court upon its own laws. . . .

So in this case. As Scott was a slave when taken into the State of Illinois by his owner, and was there held as such, and brought back in that character, his *status*, as free or slave, depended on the laws of Missouri, and not of Illinois.

It has, however, been urged in the argument, that by the laws of Missouri he was free on his return, and that this case, therefore, cannot be governed by the case of *Strader et al. v. Graham*, where it appeared, by the laws of Kentucky, that the plaintiffs continued to be slaves on their return from Ohio. But whatever doubts or opinions may, at one time, have been entertained upon this subject, we are satisfied, upon a careful examination of all the cases decided in the State courts of Missouri referred to, that it is now firmly settled by the decisions of the highest court in the State, that Scott and his family upon their return were not free, but were, by the laws of Missouri, the property of the defendant; and that the Circuit Court of the United States had no jurisdiction, when, by the laws of the State, the plaintiff was a slave, and not a citizen.

Moreover, the plaintiff, it appears, brought a similar action against the defendant in the State court of Missouri, claiming the freedom of himself and his family upon the same grounds and the same evidence upon which he relies in the case before the court. The case was carried before the Supreme Court of the State; was fully argued there; and that court decided that neither the plaintiff nor his family were entitled to freedom, and were still the slaves of the defendant; and reversed the judgment of the inferior State court, which had given a different decision. If the plaintiff supposed that this judgment of the Supreme Court of the State was erroneous, and that this court had jurisdiction to revise and reverse it, the only mode by which he could legally bring it before this court was by writ of error directed to the Supreme Court of the State, requiring it to transmit the record to this court. If this had been done, it is too plain for argument that the writ must have been dismissed for want of jurisdiction in this court. The case of Strader and others v. Graham is directly in point; and, indeed, independent of any decision, the language of the 25th section of the act of 1789 is too clear and precise to admit of controversy.

But the plaintiff did not pursue the mode prescribed by law for bringing the judgment of a State court before this court for revision, but suffered the case to be remanded to the inferior State court, where it is still continued, and is, by agreement of parties, to await the judgment of this court on the point. . . .

And while the case is yet open and pending in the inferior State court, the plaintiff goes into the Circuit Court of the United States, upon the same case and the same evidence, and against the same party, and proceeds to judgment, and then brings here the same case from the Circuit Court, which the law would not have permitted him to bring directly from the State court. . . . It would ill become this court to sanction such an attempt to evade the law, or to exercise an appellate power in this circuitous way, which it is forbidden to exercise in the direct and regular and invariable forms of judicial proceedings.

Upon the whole, therefore, it is the judgment of this court, that it appears by the record before us that the plaintiff in error is not a citizen of Missouri, in the sense in which that word is used in the Constitution; and that the Circuit Court of the United States, for that reason, had no jurisdiction in the case, and could give no judgment in it. Its judgment for the defendant must, consequently, be reversed, and a mandate issued, directing the suit to be dismissed for want of jurisdiction.

■ [The concurring opinions of JUSTICES WAYNE, GRIER, DANIEL, CAMPBELL, and CATON are omitted.]

■ MR. JUSTICE NELSON [concurring].

. . . The question upon the merits, in general terms, is, whether or not the removal of the plaintiff, who was a slave, with his master, from the State of Missouri to the State of Illinois . . . works an emancipation.

As appears from an agreed statement of facts, this question has been before the highest court of the State of Missouri, and a judgment rendered that this residence in the free State has no such effect; but, on the contrary, that his original condition continued unchanged. . . .

The argument against these decisions is, that the laws of Illinois, forbidding slavery within her territory, had the effect to set the slave free while residing in that State, and to impress upon him the condition and status of a freeman; and that, by force of these laws, this status and condition accompanied him on his return to the slave State, and of consequence he could not be there held as a slave.

. . . Our opinion is, that the question is one which belongs to each State to decide for itself, either by its Legislature or courts of justice; and hence, in respect to the case before us, to the State of Missouri. . . . In other words, except in cases where the power is restrained by the Constitution of the United States, the law of the State is supreme over the subject of slavery within its jurisdiction.

As a practical illustration of the principle, we may refer to the legislation of the free States in abolishing slavery, and prohibiting its introduction into their territories. Confessedly, except as restrained by the Federal Constitution, they exercised, and rightfully, complete and absolute power over the subject. Upon what principle, then, can it be denied to the State of Missouri? The power flows from the sovereign character of the States of this Union; sovereign, not merely as respects the Federal Government—except as they have consented to its limitation—but sovereign as respects each other. Whether, therefore, the State of Missouri will recognize or give effect to the laws of Illinois within her territories on the subject of slavery, is a question for her to determine. Nor is there any constitutional power in this Government that can rightfully control her.

Every State . . . may regulate the manner and circumstances under which property is held, and the condition, capacity, and state, of all persons therein; and, also, the remedy and modes of administering justice. And it is equally true, that no State or nation can affect or bind property out of its territory, or persons not residing within it. . . . Such laws can have no inherent authority extra-territorially. This is the necessary result of the independence of distinct and separate sovereignties.

Now, it follows from these principles, that whatever force or effect the laws of one State or nation may have in the territories of another, must depend solely upon the laws and municipal regulations of the latter, upon its own jurisprudence and polity, and upon its own express or tacit consent. . . .

Nations, from convenience and comity, and from mutual interest, and a sort of moral necessity to do justice, recognize and administer the laws of other countries. But, of the nature, extent, and utility, of them, respecting property, or the state and condition of persons within her territories, each nation judges for itself; and is never bound, even upon the ground of comity, to recognize them, if prejudicial to her own interests. The recognition is purely from comity, and not from any absolute or paramount obligation. . . .

These principles fully establish, that it belongs to the sovereign State of Missouri to determine by her laws the question of slavery within her jurisdiction, subject only to such limitations as may be found in the Federal Constitution; and, further, that the laws of other States[,] . . . whether enacted by their Legislatures or expounded by their courts, can have no operation within her territory, or affect rights growing out of her own laws on the subject. This is the necessary result of the independent and sovereign character of the State. . . .

In view of these principles, let us examine a little more closely the doctrine of those who maintain that the law of Missouri is not to govern the status and condition of the plaintiff. They insist that the removal and temporary residence with his master in Illinois, where slavery is inhibited, had the effect to set him free, and that the same effect is to be given to the law of Illinois, within the State of Missouri, after his return. Why was he set free in Illinois? Because the law of Missouri, under which he was held as a slave, had no operation by its own force extra-territorially; and the State of Illinois refused to recognize its effect within her limits, upon principles of comity, as a state of slavery was inconsistent with her laws, and contrary to her policy. But, how is the case different on the return of the plaintiff to the State of Missouri? Is she bound to recognize and enforce the law of Illinois? For, unless she is, the status and condition of the slave upon his return remains the same as originally existed. Has the law of Illinois any greater force within the jurisdiction of Missouri, than the laws of the latter within that of the former? Certainly not. They stand upon an equal footing. Neither has any force extra-territorially, except what may be voluntarily conceded to them. . . .

It is perhaps not unfit to notice, in this connection, that many of the most eminent statesmen and jurists of the country entertain the opinion that . . . the act of Congress, even within the territory to which it relates, was not authorized by any power under the Constitution. The doctrine here contended for, not only upholds its validity in the territory, but claims for it effect beyond and within the limits of a sovereign State—an effect, as insisted, that displaces the laws of the State, and substitutes its own provisions in their place.

The consequences of any such construction are apparent. If Congress possesses the power, under the Constitution, to abolish slavery in a Territory, it must necessarily possess the like power to establish it. It cannot be a one-sided power, as may suit the convenience or particular views of the advocates. It is a power, if it exists at all, over the whole subject; and then, upon the process of reasoning which seeks to extend its influence beyond the Territory, and within the limits of a State, if Congress should establish, instead of abolish, slavery, we do not see but that, if a slave should be removed from the Territory into a free State, his status would accompany him, and continue, notwithstanding its laws against slavery. The laws of the free State, according to the argument, would be displaced, and the act of Congress, in its effect, be substituted in their place. We do not see how this conclusion could be avoided, if the construction against which we are contending should prevail. We are satisfied, however, it is unsound, and that the true answer to it is, that even conceding, for the purposes of the argument, that this provision of the act of Congress is valid within the Territory for which it was enacted, it can have no operation or effect beyond its limits, or within the jurisdiction of a State. It can neither displace its laws, nor change the status or condition of its inhabitants.

Our conclusion, therefore, is, upon this branch of the case, that the question involved is one depending solely upon the law of Missouri, and that the Federal court sitting in the State, and trying the case before us, was bound to follow it. . . .

■ MR. JUSTICE MCLEAN dissenting.

. . . In the great and leading case of *Prigg v. The State of Pennsylvania*, (16 Peters, 594; 14 Curtis, 421,) this court say that, by the general law of nations, no nation is bound to recognize the state of slavery, as found within its territorial dominions, where it is in opposition to its own policy and institutions, in favor of the subjects of other nations where slavery is organized. If it does it, it is as a matter of comity, and not as a matter of international right. The state of slavery is deemed to be a mere municipal regulation, founded upon and limited to the range of the territorial laws. This was fully recognized in Somersett's case, which was decided before the American Revolution. . . .

No case in England appears to have been more thoroughly examined than that of Somersett. The judgment pronounced by Lord Mansfield was the judgment of the Court of King's Bench . . . :

> The state of slavery is of such a nature that it is incapable of being introduced on any reasons, moral or political, but only by positive law, which preserves its force long after the reasons, occasion, and time itself, from whence it was created, is erased from the memory; it is of a nature that nothing can be suffered to support it but positive law. . . .

The power of Congress to establish Territorial Governments, and to prohibit the introduction of slavery therein, is the next point to be considered. . . .

[I]f it be admitted that the word territory as used means land, and nothing but land, the power of Congress to organize a temporary Government is clear. It has power to make all needful regulations respecting the public lands, and the extent of those "needful regulations" depends upon the direction of Congress, where the means are appropriate to the end, and do not conflict with any of the prohibitions of the Constitution. . . .

If Congress may establish a Territorial Government in the exercise of its discretion, it is a clear principle that a court cannot control that discretion. This being the case, I do not see on what ground the act is held to be void. It did not purport to forfeit property, or take it for public purposes. It only prohibited slavery; in doing which, it followed the ordinance of 1787. . . .

If the principle laid down in the case of *Prigg v. The State of Pennsylvania* is to be maintained, and it is certainly to be maintained until overruled, as the law of this court, there can be no difficulty on this point. In that case, the court says: "The state of slavery is deemed to be a mere municipal regulation, founded upon and limited to the range of the territorial laws." If this be so, slavery can exist nowhere except under the authority of law, founded on usage having the force of law, or by statutory recognition. And the court further says: "It is manifest, from this consideration, that if the Constitution had not contained the clause requiring the rendition of fugitives from labor, every non-slaveholding State in the Union would have been at liberty to have declared free all runaway slaves coming within its limits, and to have given them entire immunity and protection against the claims of their masters." . . .

By virtue of what law is it, that a master may take his slave into free territory, and exact from him the duties of a slave? The law of the Territory does not sanction it. No authority can be claimed under the Constitution of the United States, or any law of Congress. Will it be said that the slave is taken as property, the same as other property which the master may own? To this I answer, that colored persons are made property by the law of the State, and no such power has been given to Congress. Does the master carry with him the law of the State from which he removes into the Territory? . . .

It is said the Territories are common property of the States, and that every man has a right to go there with his property. This is not controverted. But the courts say a slave is not property beyond the operation of the local law which makes him such. . . .

The States of Missouri and Illinois are bounded by a common line. The one prohibits slavery, the other admits it. This has been done by the exercise of that sovereign power which appertains to each. We are bound to respect the institutions of each. . . . Have the people of either any right to disturb the relations of the other? . . .

Illinois has declared in the most solemn and impressive form that there shall be neither slavery nor involuntary servitude in that State, and that any slave brought into it, with a view of becoming a resident, shall be emancipated. . . . With a full knowledge of these facts, a slave is brought from Missouri to Rock Island, in the State of Illinois, and is retained there as a slave for two years, and then taken to Fort Snelling, where slavery is prohibited by the Missouri compromise act, and there he is detained two years longer in a state of slavery. Harriet, his wife, was also kept at the same place four years as a slave. . . . They were then removed to the State of Missouri, and sold as slaves, and in the action before us they are not only claimed as slaves, but a majority of my brethren have held that on their being returned to Missouri the status of slavery attached to them.

I am not able to reconcile this result with the respect due to the State of Illinois. Having the same rights of sovereignty as the State of Missouri in adopting a Constitution, I can perceive no reason why the institutions of Illinois should not receive the same consideration as those of Missouri. . . . [I]t seems to me the principle laid down will enable the people of a slave State to introduce slavery into a free State, for a longer or shorter time, as may suit their convenience; and by returning the slave to the State whence he was brought, by force or otherwise, the status of slavery attaches, and protects the rights of the master, and defies the sovereignty of the free State. There is no evidence before us that Dred Scott and his family returned to Missouri voluntarily. . . . He was removed; which shows that he was passive, as a slave, having exercised no volition on the subject. He did not resist the master by absconding or force. But that was not sufficient to bring him within Lord Stowell's decision; he must have acted voluntarily. It would be a mockery of law and an outrage on his rights to coerce his return, and then claim that it was voluntary, and on that ground that his former status of slavery attached. . . .

In every decision of a slave case prior to that of *Dred Scott v. Emerson*, the Supreme Court of Missouri considered it as turning upon the Constitution of Illinois, the ordinance of 1787, or the Missouri compromise act of 1820. The court treated these acts as in force, and held itself bound to execute them, by declaring the slave to be free who had acquired a domicile under them with the consent of his master.

The late decision reversed this whole line of adjudication, and held that neither the Constitution and laws of the States, nor acts of Congress in relation to Territories, could be judicially noticed by the Supreme Court of Missouri. This is believed to be in conflict with the decisions of all the courts in the Southern States, with some exceptions of recent cases. . . .

I now come to inquire . . . "whether the decisions of the Supreme Court of Missouri, on the question before us, are binding on this court."

While we respect the learning and high intelligence of the State courts, and consider their decisions, with others, as authority, we follow them only where they give a construction to the State statutes. . . .

For twenty-eight years, the decisions of the Supreme Court of Missouri were consistent on all the points made in this case. But this consistent course was suddenly terminated, whether by some new light suddenly springing up, or an excited public opinion, or both, it is not necessary to say. In the case of *Scott v. Emerson*, in 1852, they were overturned and repudiated. . . .

But there is another ground which I deem conclusive, and which I will re-state.

The Supreme Court of Missouri refused to notice the act of Congress or the Constitution of Illinois, under which Dred Scott, his wife and children, claimed that they are entitled to freedom.

This being rejected by the Missouri court, there was no case before it, or least it was a case with only one side. And this is the case which, in the opinion of this court, we are bound to follow. The Missouri court disregards the express provisions of an act of Congress and the Constitution of a sovereign State, both of which laws for twenty-eight years it had not only regarded, but carried into effect.

If a State court may do this, on a question involving the liberty of a human being, what protection do the laws afford? So far from this being a Missouri question, it is a question, as it would seem, within the twenty-fifth section of the judiciary act, where a right to freedom being set up under the act of Congress, and the decision being against such right, it may be brought for revision before this court, from the Supreme Court of Missouri.

■ MR. JUSTICE CURTIS dissenting.

I dissent from the opinion pronounced by the Chief Justice, and from the judgment which the majority of the court think it proper to render in this case. . . .

[U]nder the allegations contained in this plea, and admitted by the demurrer, the question is, whether any person of African descent, whose ancestors were sold as slaves in the United States, can be a citizen of the United States. If any such person can be a citizen, this plaintiff has the right to the judgment of the court that he is so; for no cause is shown by the

plea why he is not so, except his descent and the slavery of his ancestors. . . .

To determine whether any free persons, descended from Africans held
in slavery, were citizens of the United States under the Confederation, and
consequently at the time of the adoption of the Constitution of the United
States, it is only necessary to know whether any such persons were citizens
of either of the States under the Confederation, at the time of the adoption
of the Constitution.

Of this there can be no doubt. At the time of the ratification of the Articles of Confederation, all free native-born inhabitants of the States of New
Hampshire, Massachusetts, New York, New Jersey, and North Carolina,
though descended from African slaves, were not only citizens of those
States, but such of them as had the other necessary qualifications possessed the franchise of electors, on equal terms with other citizens. . . .

The fourth of the fundamental articles of the Confederation was as follows: "The free inhabitants of each of these States, paupers, vagabonds, and
fugitives from justice, excepted, shall be entitled to all the privileges and
immunities of free citizens in the several States."

The fact that free persons of color were citizens of some of the several
States, and the consequence, that this fourth article of the Confederation
would have the effect to confer on such persons the privileges and immunities of general citizenship, were not only known to those who framed and
adopted those articles, but the evidence is decisive, that the fourth article
was intended to have that effect, and that more restricted language, which
would have excluded such persons, was deliberately and purposely rejected. . . .

Did the Constitution of the United States deprive them or their descendants of citizenship? . . .

I can find nothing in the Constitution which, *proprio vigore*, deprives
of their citizenship any class of persons who were citizens of the United
States at the time of its adoption, or who should be native-born citizens of
any State after its adoption; nor any power enabling Congress to disfranchise persons born on the soil of any State, and entitled to citizenship of
such State by its Constitution and laws. And my opinion is, that, under the
Constitution of the United States, every free person born on the soil of a
State, who is a citizen of that State by force of its Constitution or laws, is
also a citizen of the United States. . . .

The first section of the second article of the Constitution uses the language, "a natural-born citizen." It thus assumes that citizenship may be
acquired by birth. Undoubtedly, this language of the Constitution was used
in reference to that principle of public law, well understood in this country
at the time of the adoption of the Constitution, which referred citizenship to
the place of birth. . . .

That the Constitution itself has defined citizenship of the United
States by declaring what persons, born within the several States, shall or
shall not be citizens of the United States, will not be pretended. . . .

Has it empowered Congress to enact what free persons, born within
the several States, shall or shall not be citizens of the United States? . . .
Among the powers expressly granted to Congress is "the power to establish
a uniform rule of naturalization." It is not doubted that this is a power to
prescribe a rule for the removal of the disabilities consequent on foreign

birth. To hold that it extends further than this, would do violence to the meaning of the term naturalization. . . .

It appears, then, that the only power expressly granted to Congress to legislate concerning citizenship, is confined to the removal of the disabilities of foreign birth. . . .

It has been often asserted that the Constitution was made exclusively by and for the white race. It has already been shown that in five of the thirteen original States, colored persons then possessed the elective franchise, and were among those by whom the Constitution was ordained and established. If so, it is not true, in point of fact, that the Constitution was made exclusively by the white race. And that it was made exclusively for the white race is, in my opinion, not only an assumption not warranted by anything in the Constitution, but contradicted by its opening declaration, that it was ordained and established by the people of the United States, for themselves and their posterity. And as free colored persons were then citizens of at least five States, and so in every sense part of the people of the United States, they were among those for whom and whose posterity the Constitution was ordained and established. . . .

I dissent, therefore, from that part of the opinion of the majority of the court, in which it is held that a person of African descent cannot be a citizen of the United States; and I regret I must go further, and dissent both from what I deem their assumption of authority to examine the constitutionality of the act of Congress commonly called the Missouri compromise act, and the grounds and conclusions announced in their opinion. . . .

The judgment of this court is, that the case is to be dismissed for want of jurisdiction, because the plaintiff was not a citizen of Missouri, as he alleged in his declaration. Into that judgment, according to the settled course of this court, nothing appearing after a plea to the merits can enter. A great question of constitutional law, deeply affecting the peace and welfare of the country, is not, in my opinion, a fit subject to be thus reached.

But as, in my opinion, the Circuit Court had jurisdiction, I am obliged to consider the question whether its judgment on the merits of the case should stand or be reversed. . . .

The general question may be stated to be, whether the plaintiff's *status*, as a slave, was so changed by his residence within [the Wisconsin] territory, that he was not a slave in the State of Missouri, at the time this action was brought.

In such cases, two inquiries arise, which may be confounded, but should be kept distinct.

The first is, what was the law of the Territory into which the master and slave went, respecting the relation between them?

The second is, whether the State of Missouri recognizes and allows the effect of that law of the Territory, on the *status* of the slave, on his return within its jurisdiction.

As to the first of these questions[:] . . . In the *Commonwealth v. Aves*, (18 Pick., 218,) Mr. Chief Justice Shaw said: "From the principle above stated, on which a slave brought here becomes free, to wit: that he becomes entitled to the protection of our laws, it would seem to follow, as a necessary conclusion, that if the slave waives the protection of those laws, and returns to the State where he is held as a slave, his condition is not changed." It was upon this ground, as is apparent from his whole reasoning, that Sir William Scott rests his opinion in the case of the slave Grace. To use one of his expressions, the effect of the law of England was to put the liberty of the slave into a parenthesis. If there had been an act of Parliament declaring that a slave coming to England with his master should thereby be deemed no longer to be a slave, it is easy to see that the learned judge could not have arrived at the same conclusion. . . .

[I]f the acts of Congress on this subject are valid, the law of the Territory of Wisconsin, within whose limits the residence of the plaintiff and his wife, and their marriage and the birth of one or both of their children, took place, . . . is a law operating directly on the *status* of the slave [setting him free and terminating the rights of the master]. By the eighth section of the act of March 6, 1820, it was enacted that, within this Territory, "slavery and involuntary servitude, otherwise than in the punishment of crimes, whereof the parties shall have been duly convicted, shall be, and is hereby, forever prohibited: *Provided, always*, that any person escaping into the same, from whom labor or service is lawfully claimed in any State or Territory of the United States, such fugitive may be lawfully reclaimed, and conveyed to the person claiming his or her labor or service, as aforesaid." . . .

It thus appears that, by these acts of Congress . . . it was positively enacted that slavery and involuntary servitude, with only one exception, specifically described, should not exist there. It is not simply that slavery is not recognized and cannot be aided by the municipal law. It is recognised for the purpose of being absolutely prohibited, and declared incapable of existing within the Territory, save in the instance of a fugitive slave. . . .

I must conclude, therefore, that it was the will of Congress that the state of involuntary servitude of a slave, coming into the Territory with his master, should cease to exist. . . .

But it is a distinct question, whether the law of Missouri recognised and allowed effect to the change wrought in the status of the plaintiff, by force of the laws of the Territory of Wisconsin.

. . . Undoubtedly, every sovereign State may refuse to recognise a change, wrought by the law of a foreign State, on the *status* of a person, while within such foreign State. . . . Its will to refuse such recognition may be manifested by what we term statute law, or by the customary law of the State. It is within the province of its judicial tribunals to inquire and adjudge whether it appears, from the statute or customary law of the State, to be the will of the State to refuse to recognise such changes of *status* by force of foreign law, as the rules of the law of nations require to be recognised. But, in my opinion, it is not within the province of any judicial tribunal to refuse such recognition from any political considerations, or any view it may take of the exterior political relations between the State and one or more foreign States, or any impressions it may have that a change of foreign opinion and action on the subject of slavery may afford a reason why the State should change its own action. To understand and give just effect to such considerations, and to change the action of the State in consequence of them, are functions of diplomatists and legislators, not of judges. . . .

[T]here are other facts stated on the record which should not be passed over. It is agreed that, in the year 1836, the plaintiff, while residing in the Territory, was married, with the consent of Dr. Emerson, to Harriet, . . . and that Eliza and Lizzie were the children of that marriage, the first named having been born on the Mississippi river, north of the line of Missouri, and the other having been born after their return to Missouri. And the inquiry is, whether . . . any other State or Country can, consistently with the settled rules of international law, refuse to recognise and treat him as a free man, when suing for the liberty of himself, his wife, and the children of that marriage. It is in reference to his [and his family's] *status*, as viewed in other States and countries, that the contract of marriage and the birth of children becomes strictly material. . . .

It is a principle of international law, settled beyond controversy in England and America, that a marriage, valid by the law of the place where it was contracted, and not in fraud of the law of any other place, is valid everywhere; and that no technical domicile at the place of the contract is necessary to make it so.

If, in Missouri, the plaintiff were held to be a slave, the validity and operation of his contract of marriage must be denied. . . .

What, then, shall we say of the consent of the master, that the slave may contract a lawful marriage, attended with all the civil rights and duties which belong to that relation; that he may enter into a relation which none but a free man can assume . . . ? In my judgment, there can be no more effectual abandonment of the legal rights of a master over his slave, than by the consent of the master that the slave should enter into a contract of marriage, in a free State, attended by all the civil rights and obligations which belong to that condition.

And any claim by Dr. Emerson, or any one claiming under him, the effect of which is to deny the validity of this marriage, and the lawful paternity of the children born from it, wherever asserted, is, in my judgment, a claim inconsistent with good faith and sound reason, as well as with the rules of international law. And I go further: in my opinion, a law of the State of Missouri, which should thus annul a marriage, lawfully contracted by these parties while resident in Wisconsin, not in fraud of any law of Missouri, or of any right of Dr. Emerson, who consented thereto, would be a law impairing the obligation of a contract, and within the prohibition of the Constitution of the United States. (See [*Trustees of Dartmouth College v. Woodward, 12 U.S.*] 4 Wheat., 629, 695, 696.) . . .

But it is insisted that the Supreme Court of Missouri has settled this case by its decision in *Scott v. Emerson.* . . .

To the correctness of such a decision I cannot assent. In my judgment, the opinion of the majority of the court in that case is in conflict with its previous decisions, with a great weight of judicial authority in other slaveholding States. . . .

When the decisions of the highest court of a State are directly in conflict with each other, it has been repeatedly held, here, that the last decision is not necessarily to be taken as the rule. . . .

I have thus far assumed, merely for the purpose of the argument, that the laws of the United States, respecting slavery in this Territory, were constitutionally enacted by Congress. It remains to inquire whether they are constitutional and binding laws. . . . *[Justice Curtis rejects the proposition that the Territory Clause of Article IV applies only to original territory.—Editors]*

It has been urged that the words "rules and regulations" are not appropriate terms in which to convey authority to make laws for the government of the territory.

But it must be remembered that this is a grant of power to the Congress—that it is therefore necessarily a grant of power to legislate. . . . Power granted to a Legislature to make all needful rules and regulations respecting the territory, is a power to pass all needful laws respecting it. . . .

But it is insisted, that whatever other powers Congress may have respecting the territory of the United States, the subject of negro slavery forms an exception.

The Constitution declares that Congress shall have power to make "*all* needful rules and regulations" respecting the territory belonging to the United States. . . .

There is nothing in the context which qualifies the grant of power. The regulations must be "respecting the territory." An enactment that slavery may or may not exist there, is a regulation respecting the territory. Regulations must be needful; but it is necessarily left to the legislative discretion to determine whether a law be needful. No other clause of the Constitution has been referred to at the bar, or has been seen by me, which imposes any restriction or makes any exception concerning the power of Congress to allow or prohibit slavery in the territory belonging to the United States. . . .

It appears, however, from what has taken place at the bar, that notwithstanding the language of the Constitution, and the long line of legislative and executive precedents under it, three different and opposite views are taken of the power of Congress respecting slavery in the Territories.

One is, that though Congress can make a regulation prohibiting slavery in a Territory, they cannot make a regulation allowing it; another is, that it can neither be established nor prohibited by Congress, but that the people of a Territory, when organized by Congress, can establish or prohibit slavery; while the third is, that the Constitution itself secures to every citizen who holds slaves, under the laws of any State, the indefeasible right to carry them into any Territory, and there hold them as property.

No particular clause of the Constitution has been referred to at the bar in support of either of these views. The first seems to be rested upon general considerations concerning the social and moral evils of slavery, its relations to republican Governments, its inconsistency with the Declaration of Independence and with natural right.

The second is drawn from considerations equally general, concerning the right of self-government, and the nature of the political institutions which have been established by the people of the United States.

While the third is said to rest upon the equal right of all citizens to go with their property upon the public domain, and the inequality of a regulation which would admit the property of some and exclude the property of other citizens. . . .

With the weight of either of these considerations, when presented to Congress to influence its action, this court has no concern. One or the other may be justly entitled to guide or control the legislative judgment upon what is a needful regulation. The question here is, whether they are sufficient to authorize this court to insert into this clause of the Constitution an exception of the exclusion or allowance of slavery, not found therein, nor in any other part of that instrument. . . . To allow this to be done with the Constitution, upon reasons purely political, renders its judicial interpretation impossible—because judicial tribunals, as such, cannot decide upon political considerations. Political reasons have not the requisite certainty to afford rules of juridical interpretation. They are different in different men. They are different in the same men at different times. And when a strict interpretation of the Constitution, according to the fixed rules which govern the interpretation of laws, is abandoned, and the theoretical opinions of individuals are allowed to control its meaning, we have no longer a Constitution; we are under the government of individual men, who for the time being have power to declare what the Constitution is, according to their own views of what it ought to mean. . . .

Looking at the power of Congress over the Territories as of the extent just described, what positive prohibition exists in the Constitution, which restrained Congress from enacting [the Missouri Compromise]?

The only one suggested is that clause in the fifth article of the amendments of the Constitution which declares that no person shall be deprived of his life, liberty, or property, without due process of law. . . .

Is it conceivable that the Constitution has conferred the right on every citizen to become a resident on the territory of the United States with his slaves, and there to hold them as such, but has neither made nor provided for any municipal regulations which are essential to the existence of slavery? . . .

Nor, in my judgment, will the position, that a prohibition to bring slaves into a Territory deprives any one of his property without due process of law, bear examination.

. . . It was certainly understood by the Convention which framed the Constitution, and has been so understood ever since, that, under the power to regulate commerce, Congress could prohibit the importation of slaves; and the exercise of the power was restrained till 1808. A citizen of the United States owns slaves in Cuba, and brings them to the United States, where they are set free by the legislation of Congress. Does this legislation deprive him of his property without due process of law? If so, what becomes of the laws prohibiting the slave trade? If not, how can a similar regulation respecting a Territory violate the fifth amendment of the Constitution? . . .

For these reasons, I am of opinion that so much of the several acts of Congress as prohibited slavery and involuntary servitude within that part of the Territory of Wisconsin lying north of thirty-six degrees thirty minutes north latitude, and west of the river Mississippi, were constitutional and valid laws. . . .

NOTES

1. *The Most Significant Supreme Court Decision Ever?* Dred Scott is arguably the most significant U.S. Supreme Court decision in history. It is also one of the most outrageously, and seemingly deliberately, wrong Supreme Court decisions of all time. The Court seemed to go out of its way to decide as many issues as possible, in the most pro-slavery manner possible. Why? The topic remains one of great historical speculation, but it seems clear that, in the heated political context of the day ("Bleeding Kansas" throughout 1856, Representative Preston Brooks's brutal caning of Senator Charles Sumner on the Senate floor in May of that year, following his provocative anti-slavery speech, the contentious presidential election of November 1856), the Court—and especially Chief Justice Taney—felt it appropriate that it settle the large constitutional issues concerning slavery and national expansion. See Fehrenbacher,

THE DRED SCOTT CASE 285–388. There is evidence that, a year earlier, before the presidential election and re-argument, the Court was prepared to rule against Dred Scott on narrower legal grounds, along the lines of Justice Nelson's concurring opinion (which apparently was originally drafted as the majority opinion of the Court). When it became clear that the dissenting justices would find that Dred Scott was free, on the basis of the Missouri Compromise, Taney decided to write a more comprehensive opinion. He was urged on by President-elect Buchanan, who disgracefully lobbied the Court about a matter that was *sub judice*. A case that had begun nearly eleven years earlier, as a state-court lawsuit seemingly certain to result in Scott's freedom under then-controlling Missouri law, had come to acquire enormous national significance.

2. *Disentangling Chief Justice Taney's Opinion.* It is useful to try to sort out the different holdings in Taney's opinion. While there was much clamoring at the time (and argument today) over whether certain of the holdings were dicta, the fact remains that each holding purports to be part of the Opinion of the Court. See Fehrenbacher, THE DRED SCOTT CASE, 322–334.

a. *The Jurisdiction/"Citizenship" Holding.* The first issue is whether the district court properly had diversity-of-citizenship jurisdiction. John Sanford (Mrs. Emerson's brother) was a resident and citizen of New York state. What was Dred Scott's state citizenship for purposes of federal diversity jurisdiction under Article III's provision authorizing federal court suits between "citizens of different states"? Taney concludes that Dred Scott may not be considered a citizen of Missouri. He has *no* state citizenship—he cannot be a citizen of *any* state, Taney claims, because he cannot be a citizen of the *United States*, given his race.

It is in the course of the citizenship holding that Taney writes some of the most racist rhetoric ever to disgrace a Supreme Court opinion, referring to "beings of an inferior order, . . . altogether unfit to associate with the white race." The Declaration of Independence and the Constitution did nothing to change that status.

How many ways is this wrong? Study Taney's argument and the rejoinder of the dissenters. Justice Curtis points out that, among other flaws, Taney's point is simply false as an historical matter: many free blacks were citizens of states at the time of the founding. What is really going on here? Apparently, Taney simply could not countenance the prospect of free blacks as citizens entitled to the "privileges and immunities" that citizens possess in other states (pursuant to Article IV's Privileges and Immunities Clause).

b. *The Territory Clause Power/Missouri Compromise Holding.* The next question the Court decides is whether Dred Scott could be considered entitled to his freedom by virtue of his master's long sojourn in (present-day) Minnesota, in a federal territory where slavery was prohibited by the Missouri Compromise. By the time *Dred Scott* was decided, the Missouri Compromise limiting slavery in the territories was thirty-seven years old and the Northwest Ordinance banning slavery in the original federal territories was seventy years old. Isn't it astonishing that a majority of the Supreme Court would so cavalierly depart from a practice and constitutional interpretation that dated back to the founding of the Republic?

How did this happen? The answer lies in the Three–Fifths Clause that the North agreed to at the Philadelphia Convention. In 1787, this Clause was important to the South because it gave the South a majority in the House of Representatives. The South soon lost this majority due to westward expansion, but the Three–Fifths Clause still gave it a lock on the Electoral College and therefore on the presidency. This was illustrated in the presidential election of 1800, which scholars now agree was won by Thomas Jefferson over John Adams only because the Three–Fifths Clause allowed Southern slaveholders to "vote their slaves." With Southern domination of the presidency came Southern domination of the Supreme Court, because justices could be nominated only by the president. Of the first fifteen presidents, eight were from the South (Washington, Jefferson, Madison, Monroe, Jackson, Tyler, Polk, and Taylor) and four more have been called "Northern men with Southern sympathies" or "dough faces" (Van Buren, Fillmore, Pierce, and Buchanan). Thus twelve out of the first fifteen presidents were either from slave states or were openly supportive of slavery, and only two—John Adams and his son John Quincy Adams—were Northern opponents of slavery. The first fifteen presidents appointed a total of thirty-five Supreme Court justices. Thirty-one of these justices were appointed by the twelve presidents from the South or sympathetic to it. Only four justices were appointed by the two Adamses. The explanation for the Supreme Court's cavalier decision and opinions in the *Dred Scott* case lies, then, in the Southern domination of the presidency and of the Supreme Court—a direct result of the Three–Fifths Clause.

Note Taney's convoluted (and seemingly irrelevant) holding that it is not the Territory Clause that gives Congress the power to pass laws governing the territories. That clause was meant only for territory possessed by the nation *at the time the Constitution was adopted*, Taney said. (Can you see why that reasoning is flawed? Is the meaning of a constitutional provision the objective meaning of its language or is it limited to factual situations that were present at the time it was enacted or adopted?) Nonetheless, Taney says, the power *to admit new states* gives rise to an *implied power* to legislate for the territories in the interim.

But then Taney says: Surely Congress cannot, in passing laws for the territories, pass a law that violates one of the provisions of the Bill of Rights. Surely Congress could not establish an official territorial religion. Or abolish the freedom of speech in a territory. And likewise, surely Congress could not pass a law depriving someone of their property, could it? Here Taney invoked the Due Process Clause of the Fifth Amendment: "[T]he rights of property are united with the rights of person, and placed on the same ground by the fifth amendment to the Constitution, which provides that no person shall be deprived of life, liberty, and property, without due process of law. *And an act of Congress which deprives a citizen of the United States of his liberty or property, merely because he came himself or brought his property into a particular Territory of the United States, and who had committed no offence against the laws, could hardly be dignified with the name of due process of law*" (emphasis added).

Did you catch the sleight-of-hand? The Due Process Clause plainly does not forbid government from ever depriving someone of life, liberty, or property. It allows all of these deprivations as long as there is "due process of law." Taney seemingly reads those words out of the clause, changing it from a guarantee of procedural regularity into a power for courts to inquire into the substantive fairness of a law. (The Due Process Clauses are discussed in more detail in Chapter 7.) And what he did with that power was truly awful: a judicially invented "individual right" of (white) persons to own slaves. On this point, as with the citizenship holding, Taney's opinion illustrates how constitutional interpretation can go wrong: picking a desired result first, then distorting the Constitution's language to produce that result; reading constitutional texts to mean the opposite of what they say, either by ignoring what they plainly say, or by making up things they plainly do not say; and then predicating such readings on false claims about original intent, history, or precedent.

c. *The State-State Choice of Law Holding.* Taney is not quite finished at this point. There remains the question of whether Dred Scott might be free by virtue of his time in the free *state* of Illinois. Taney's reasoning here is perhaps not entirely indefensible: Illinois law might have made Scott free, but Scott brought his claim in Missouri courts and Missouri might legitimately have determined that Missouri law, not Illinois law, governed Scott's status in such a suit. Illinois law might have operated to free Scott, but it had not been brought to bear in an actual adjudication. So, upon his return to Missouri, his status as a slave might validly re-attach, it never having been *legally* severed.

Recall the discussion, in *Lemmon.* Is Chief Justice Taney's analysis so clearly wrong on this point? Might it have been different if Illinois had *adjudicated* Scott to be free and he then *returned* to Missouri? Might Missouri then have been required to honor and enforce the Illinois judgment under the Full Faith and Credit Clause? Indeed, would not Scott in such an instance then have been entitled, in Missouri, to the "Privileges and Immunities of citizens of the several States"—the same privileges or civil rights that Missouri provided any of its citizens?

This is the argument set forth at greater length (and with greater precision) in Justice Nelson's concurrence, which apparently had been the original draft majority opinion for the Court—a narrower argument for the result that Dred Scott remained, legally, a slave. Is this position right? If it is, wouldn't the same reasoning apply to the legal consequences of Scott's sojourn in federal territory? Perhaps the Missouri Compromise, had it been brought to bear in a suit adjudicating Scott's claim for freedom, would have made him free. But that had never happened. Unless somehow the bare act of *touching* free soil makes a slave (if not a fugitive) free, why was not Missouri permitted to apply Missouri law to determine the legal status of a Missouri domiciliary, in an action brought in courts situated in Missouri?

What is the dissenters' response to this argument? Is it that the Missouri Compromise law really was self-executing? What about the argument that allowing Dred Scott and Harriet to be married constituted an affirmative act of manumission? Do you find any of these arguments persuasive? What should have been the outcome?

3. *Interpretive Methodology in Dred Scott.* How would you describe Chief Justice Taney's interpretive method? Was it "originalist" in some sense— emphasizing history or the intentions (at least of some)? Taney at certain points certainly casts his opinion in such terms. And at least some commentators have used *Dred Scott* as an illustration of the perils of original-intent or original-meaning approaches to constitutional interpretation. See Christopher Eisgruber, *Dred Again: Originalism's Forgotten Past*, 10 Const. Comm. 37 (1993); cf. Mark Graber, DRED SCOTT AND THE PROBLEM OF CONSTITUTIONAL EVIL (2006).

Justice Curtis's dissent certainly did not see the Court's opinion in such terms. He condemned it as showing a willful disregard for faithful interpretation of the Constitution's text, history, and original meaning, in what has become a classic statement of the argument against judicial activism: "Political reasons have not the requisite certainty to afford rules of juridical interpretation. They are different in different men. They are different in the same men at different times. And when a strict interpretation of the Constitution, according to the fixed rules which govern the interpretation of laws, is abandoned, and the theoretical opinions of individuals are allowed to control its meaning, we have no longer a Constitution; we are under the government of individual men, who for the time being have power to declare what the Constitution is, according to their own views of what it ought to mean."

4. *Was the Nation Bound by Dred Scott Unless and Until it was Overruled by the Court itself or by a Constitutional Amendment?* The Court's decision produced the strongest and most sustained backlash against the authority of the Supreme Court's decisions in our nation's history. Editorialists condemned the decision as entitled to "just so much moral weight as would be the judgment of a majority of those congregated in any Washington bar-room." Editorial, *New York Tribune* (March 7, 1857). Abraham Lincoln rose to national prominence in large part based on his attacks on the *Dred Scott* decision. He argued that the decision was not binding on elected officials or on voters. Indeed, he argued that it was legitimate and necessary for the people to repudiate the Court's holding in the upcoming elections, lest it be extended and the Court render a "Second *Dred Scott*" decision nationalizing slavery. In the famous Lincoln–Douglas debates during the Illinois Senate campaign of 1858, incumbent Senator Stephen Douglas excoriated Lincoln's position as being in defiance of the Constitution itself. The Supreme Court had settled the meaning of the Constitution, Douglas argued, and it was horrible to contemplate that mere ignorant country lawyers, or politicians of any sort, should treat that resolution as anything but final. Lincoln's position was nothing less than a betrayal of the Constitution. Hear Douglas (as quoted by Lincoln in his Speech at Springfield, Illinois, on the *Dred Scott* decision, June 26, 1857):

> The courts are the tribunals prescribed by the Constitution and created by the authority of the people to determine, expound and enforce the law. Hence, whoever resists the final decision of the highest judicial tribunal, aims a deadly blow to our whole republican system of government—a blow, which if successful would place all our rights and liberties at the mercy of passion, anarchy and violence. I repeat, therefore, that if resistance to the decisions of the Supreme Court of the United States, in a matter like the points decided in the Dred Scott case, clearly within their jurisdiction as defined by the Constitution, shall be forced upon the country as a political issue, it will become a distinct and naked issue between the friends and the enemies of the Constitution—the friends and the enemies of the supremacy of the laws.

Michael Stokes Paulsen, *Lincoln and Judicial Authority*, 83 Notre Dame L. Rev. 1227, 1240 (2008).

Lincoln consistently, and insistently, defended the propriety of opposition to the Court's decision. He attacked Douglas's position, noting that if the Supreme Court were to hold that the Constitution forbids a state to exclude slavery, Douglas would support it:

This man sticks to a decision which forbids the people of a Territory from excluding slavery, and he does so not because he says it is right in itself—he does not give any opinion on that—but because it has been *decided by the court,* and being decided by the court, he is, and your bound to take it in your political action as *law*—not that he judges at all of its merits, but because a decision of the court is to him a *"Thus saith the Lord."* [Applause.] He places it on that ground alone, and you will bear in mind that thus committing himself unreservedly to this decision, *commits him to the next one* just as firmly as to this. He did not commit himself on account of the merit or demerit of the decision, but it is a *Thus saith the Lord.* The next decision, as much as this, will be a *thus saith the Lord.*

Id. at 1252–53 (quoting Lincoln in First Lincoln–Douglas Debate).

Was Lincoln right or was Douglas right? *Dred Scott* tests one's views about the authority of the Supreme Court. For if the Court's decisions are absolutely authoritative—the final, definitive word on the meaning of the Constitution—then they are absolutely authoritative *even when they are clearly wrong.* Shouldn't the Court's decision have been regarded as settling the matter? Or may political officials rightfully resist what they understand to be a lawless decision of the Supreme Court? When do we need someone to decide the meaning of the Constitution authoritatively?

5. *Dred Scott and the Constitutional Case for Secession.* Lincoln lost the Senate race to Douglas in 1858, but won the rematch: In 1860, Lincoln defeated Douglas and two other candidates in a four-way race for president of the United States. Lincoln's election immediately led several Southern states to enact resolutions purporting to secede from the Union. By the time Lincoln was inaugurated in March 1861, seven states had seceded and organized themselves as the Confederate States of America.

In the next set of materials, we take up the general question of the constitutional (il)legitimacy of secession, along with other questions arising under Article IV's provisions authorizing the federal government to suppress domestic insurrections and requiring the United States to guarantee each state a republican form of government.

But for now, consider this question: Assume for the sake of argument that a sufficiently material breach of the Constitution by all the institutions of the national government would justify a state in withdrawing from the Union. Was Lincoln's declared refusal to be bound by the Supreme Court's decision as a political rule governing his own conduct and policies as president at least *prospectively* a grave breach of the Constitution? Was Lincoln's opposition to the Court's decision the equivalent of opposition to the Constitution itself, and a breach of his constitutional oath?

6. Does Congress have power under the Territories Clause to create non-Article III courts in the territorial governments and confer on them the judicial power of the United States? See Gary Lawson & Guy Seidman, THE CONSTITU-TION OF EMPIRE: TERRITORIAL EXPANSION & AMERICAN LEGAL HISTORY 140–150 (2004). If Congress can circumvent Article III using its power under the Territories Clause, as the Marshall Court effectively held in *American Insurance Company v. Canter,* 26 U.S. 511 (1828), then why could it not violate the Bill of Rights in the territories? Note that the Constitution gives Congress an extraor-

dinarily broad power to "dispose of and make all needful Rules and Regulations respecting the Territory" of the United States.

[*Assignment 39*]

D. THE GUARANTEE CLAUSE: SECESSION AND RECONSTRUCTION

Article IV, Section 4 ends with a clause in which the United States pledges to guarantee to every state a Republican Form of Government. The most nationalist of the framers had high hopes for the Guarantee Clause, but it was not used until Dorr's Rebellion in Rhode Island in the 1840s. In the Civil War and Reconstruction, however, this Clause became extraordinarily important. Did the eleven Confederate states have a Republican Form of Government? And if not, was President Lincoln constitutionally obligated by his oath of office and the Take Care Clause to put down what he termed the War of the Rebellion, and to reconstruct these states to ensure that a Republican Form of Government was established?

We begin with President Abraham Lincoln's First Inaugural Address. It is a masterpiece of constitutional analysis. The speech consists almost entirely of an examination of important constitutional questions, such as the Constitution's treatment of slavery, secession, judicial supremacy, and the duties and powers of the executive.

President Lincoln, First Inaugural Address

March 4, 1861

Fellow citizens of the United States:

In compliance with a custom as old as the Government itself, I appear before you to address you briefly and to take in your presence the oath prescribed by the Constitution of the United States to be taken by the President "before he enters on the execution of this office."

I do not consider it necessary at present for me to discuss those matters of administration about which there is no special anxiety or excitement.

Apprehension seems to exist among the people of the Southern States that by the accession of a Republican Administration their property and their peace and personal security are to be endangered. There has never been any reasonable cause for such apprehension. Indeed, the most ample evidence to the contrary has all the while existed and been open to their inspection. It is found in nearly all the published speeches of him who now addresses you. I do but quote from one of those speeches when I declare that "I have no purpose, directly or indirectly, to interfere with the institution of slavery in the States where it exists. I believe I have no lawful right to do so, and I have no inclination to do so." Those who nominated and elected me did so with full knowledge that I had made this and many similar declarations and had never recanted them; and more than this, they placed in the platform for my acceptance, and as a law to themselves and to me, the clear and emphatic resolution which I now read:

Resolved, That the maintenance inviolate of the rights of the States, and especially the right of each State to order and control its own domestic institutions according to its own judgment exclusively, is essential to that balance of power on which the perfection and endurance of our political fabric depend; and we denounce the lawless invasion by armed force of the soil of any State or Territory, no matter what pretext, as among the gravest of crimes.

I now reiterate these sentiments, and in doing so I only press upon the public attention the most conclusive evidence of which the case is susceptible that the property, peace, and security of no section are to be in any wise endangered by the now incoming Administration. I add, too, that all the protection which, consistently with the Constitution and the laws, can be given will be cheerfully given to all the States when lawfully demanded, for whatever cause—as cheerfully to one section as to another.

There is much controversy about the delivering up of fugitives from service or labor. The clause I now read is as plainly written in the Constitution as any other of its provisions:

> No person held to service or labor in one State, under the laws thereof, escaping into another, shall in consequence of any law or regulation therein be discharged from such service or labor, but shall be delivered up on claim of the party to whom such service or labor may be due.

It is scarcely questioned that this provision was intended by those who made it for the reclaiming of what we call fugitive slaves; and the intention of the lawgiver is the law. All members of Congress swear their support to the whole Constitution—to this provision as much as to any other. To the proposition, then, that slaves whose cases come within the terms of this clause "shall be delivered up" their oaths are unanimous. Now, if they would make the effort in good temper, could they not with nearly equal unanimity frame and pass a law by means of which to keep good that unanimous oath?

There is some difference of opinion whether this clause should be enforced by national or by State authority, but surely that difference is not a very material one. If the slave is to be surrendered, it can be of but little consequence to him or to others by which authority it is done. And should anyone in any case be content that his oath shall go unkept on a merely unsubstantial controversy as to *how* it shall be kept?

Again, in any law upon this subject ought not all the safeguards of liberty known in civilized and humane jurisprudence to be introduced, so that a free man be not in any case surrendered as a slave? And might it not be well at the same time to provide by law for the enforcement of that clause in the Constitution which guarantees that "the citizens of each State shall be entitled to all privileges and immunities of citizens in the several States"?

I take the official oath to-day with no mental reservations and with no purpose to construe the Constitution or laws by any hypercritical rules; and while I do not choose now to specify particular acts of Congress as proper to be enforced, I do suggest that it will be much safer for all, both in official and private stations, to conform to and abide by all those acts which stand unrepealed than to violate any of them trusting to find impunity in having them held to be unconstitutional.

It is seventy-two years since the first inauguration of a President under our National Constitution. During that period fifteen different and greatly distinguished citizens have in succession administered the executive branch of the Government. They have conducted it through many perils, and generally with great success. Yet, with all this scope of precedent, I now enter upon the same task for the brief constitutional term of four years under great and peculiar difficulty. A disruption of the Federal Union, heretofore only menaced, is now formidably attempted.

I hold that in contemplation of universal law and of the Constitution the Union of these States is perpetual. Perpetuity is implied, if not expressed, in the fundamental law of all national governments. It is safe to assert that no government proper ever had a provision in its organic law for its own termination. Continue to execute all the express provisions of our National Constitution, and the Union will endure forever, it being impossible to destroy it except by some action not provided for in the instrument itself.

Again, if the United States be not a government proper, but an association of States in the nature of contract merely, can it, as a contract, be peaceably unmade by less than all the parties who made it? One party to a contract may violate it—break it, so to speak—but does it not require all to lawfully rescind it?

Descending from these general principles, we find the proposition that in legal contemplation the Union is perpetual confirmed by the history of the Union itself. The Union is much older than the Constitution. It was formed, in fact, by the Articles of Association in 1774. It was matured and continued by the Declaration of Independence in 1776. It was further matured, and the faith of all the then thirteen States expressly plighted and engaged that it should be perpetual, by the Articles of Confederation in 1778. And finally, in 1787, one of the declared objects for ordaining and establishing the Constitution was *"to form a more perfect Union."*

But if destruction of the Union by one or by a part only of the States be lawfully possible, the Union is *less* perfect than before the Constitution, having lost the vital element of perpetuity.

It follows from these views that no State upon its own mere motion can lawfully get out of the Union; that *resolves* and *ordinances* to that effect are legally void, and that acts of violence within any State or States against the authority of the United States are insurrectionary or revolutionary, according to circumstances.

I therefore consider that in view of the Constitution and the laws the Union is unbroken, and to the extent of my ability, I shall take care, as the Constitution itself expressly enjoins upon me, that the laws of the Union be faithfully executed in all the States. Doing this I deem to be only a simple duty on my part, and I shall perform it so far as practicable unless my rightful masters, the American people, shall withhold the requisite means or in some authoritative manner direct the contrary. I trust this will not be regarded as a menace, but only as the declared purpose of the Union that it *will* constitutionally defend and maintain itself.

In doing this there needs to be no bloodshed or violence, and there shall be none unless it be forced upon the national authority. The power confided to me will be used to hold, occupy, and possess the property and places belonging to the Government and to collect the duties and imposts; but beyond what may be necessary for these objects, there will be no invasion, no using of force against or among the people anywhere. Where hostility to the United States in any interior locality shall be so great and universal as to prevent competent resident citizens from holding the Federal offices, there will be no attempt to force obnoxious strangers among the people for that object. While the strict legal right may exist in the Government to enforce the exercise of these offices, the attempt to do so would be so irritating and so nearly impracticable withal that I deem it better to forego for the time the uses of such offices.

The mails, unless repelled, will continue to be furnished in all parts of the Union. So far as possible the people everywhere shall have that sense of perfect security which is most favorable to calm thought and reflection. The course here indicated will be followed unless current events and experience shall show a modification or change to be proper, and in every case and exigency my best discretion will be exercised, according to circumstances actually existing and with a view and a hope of a peaceful solution of the national troubles and the restoration of fraternal sympathies and affections.

That there are persons in one section or another who seek to destroy the Union at all events and are glad of any pretext to do it I will neither affirm nor deny; but if there be such, I need address no word to them. To those, however, who really love the Union may I not speak?

Before entering upon so grave a matter as the destruction of our national fabric, with all its benefits, its memories, and its hopes, would it not be wise to ascertain precisely why we do it? Will you hazard so desperate a step while there is any possibility that any portion of the ills you fly from have no real existence? Will you, while the certain ills you fly to are greater than all the real ones you fly from, will you risk the commission of so fearful a mistake?

All profess to be content in the Union if all constitutional rights can be maintained. Is it true, then, that any right plainly written in the Constitution has been denied? I think not. Happily, the human mind is so constituted that no party can reach to the audacity of doing this. Think, if you can, of a single instance in which a plainly written provision of the Constitution has ever been denied. If by the mere force of numbers a majority should deprive a minority of any clearly written constitutional right, it might in a moral point of view justify revolution; certainly would if such right were a vital one. But such is not our case. All the vital rights of minorities and of individuals are so plainly assured to them by affirmations and negations, guaranties and prohibitions, in the Constitution that controversies never arise concerning them. But no organic law can ever be framed with a provision specifically applicable to every question which may occur in practical administration. No foresight can anticipate nor any document of reasonable length contain express provisions for all possible questions. Shall fugitives from labor be surrendered by national or by State authority? The Constitution does not expressly say. *May* Congress prohibit slavery in the Territories? The Constitution does not expressly say. *Must* Congress protect slavery in the Territories? The Constitution does not expressly say.

From questions of this class spring all our constitutional controversies, and we divide upon them into majorities and minorities. If the minority will not acquiesce, the majority must, or the Government must cease. There is no other alternative, for continuing the Government is acquiescence on one side or the other. If a minority in such case will secede rather than acquiesce, they make a precedent which in turn will divide and ruin them, for a minority of their own will secede from them whenever a majority refuses to be controlled by such minority. For instance, why may not any portion of a new confederacy a year or two hence arbitrarily secede again, precisely as portions of the present Union now claim to secede from it? All who cherish disunion sentiments are now being educated to the exact temper of doing this. Is there such perfect identity of interests among the States to compose a new union as to produce harmony only and prevent renewed secession?

Plainly the central idea of secession is the essence of anarchy. A majority held in restraint by constitutional checks and limitations, and always changing easily with deliberate changes of popular opinions and sentiments, is the only true sovereign of a free people. Whoever rejects it does of necessity fly to anarchy or to despotism. Unanimity is impossible. The rule of a minority, as a permanent arrangement, is wholly inadmissible; so that, rejecting the majority principle, anarchy or despotism in some form is all that is left.

I do not forget the position assumed by some that constitutional questions are to be decided by the Supreme Court, nor do I deny that such decisions must be binding in any case upon the parties to a suit as to the object of that suit, while they are also entitled to very high respect and consideration in all parallel cases by all other departments of the Government. And while it is obviously possible that such decision may be erroneous in any given case, still the evil effect following it, being limited to that particular case, with the chance that it may be overruled and never become a precedent for other cases, can better be borne than could the evils of a different practice. At the same time, the candid citizen must confess that if the policy of the Government upon vital questions affecting the whole people is to be irrevocably fixed by decisions of the Supreme Court, the instant they are made in ordinary litigation between parties in personal actions the people will have ceased to be their own rulers, having to that extent practically resigned their Government into the hands of that eminent tribunal. Nor is there in this view any assault upon the court or the judges. It is a duty from which they may not shrink to decide cases properly brought before them, and it is no fault of theirs if others seek to turn their decisions to political purposes.

One section of our country believes slavery is *right* and ought to be extended, while the other believes it is *wrong* and ought not to be extended. This is the only substantial dispute. The fugitive-slave clause of the Constitution and the law for the suppression of the foreign slave trade are each as well enforced, perhaps, as any law can ever be in a community where the moral sense of the people imperfectly supports the law itself. The great body of the people abide by the dry legal obligation in both cases, and a few break over in each. This, I think, can not be perfectly cured, and it would be worse in both cases *after* the separation of the sections than before. The foreign slave trade, now imperfectly suppressed, would be ultimately revived without restriction in one section, while fugitive slaves, now only partially surrendered, would not be surrendered at all by the other.

Physically speaking, we can not separate. We can not remove our respective sections from each other nor build an impassable wall between them. A husband and wife may be divorced and go out of the presence and beyond the reach of each other, but the different parts of our country can not do this. They can not but remain face to face, and intercourse, either amicable or hostile, must continue between them. Is it possible, then, to make that intercourse more advantageous or more satisfactory *after* separation than *before?* Can aliens make treaties easier than friends can make laws? Can treaties be more faithfully enforced between aliens than laws can among friends? Suppose you go to war, you can not fight always; and when, after much loss on both sides and no gain on either, you cease fighting, the identical old questions, as to terms of intercourse, are again upon you.

This country, with its institutions, belongs to the people who inhabit it. Whenever they shall grow weary of the existing Government, they can exercise their *constitutional* right of amending it or their *revolutionary* right to dismember or overthrow it. I can not be ignorant of the fact that many worthy and patriotic citizens are desirous of having the National Constitution amended. While I make no recommendation of amendments, I fully recognize the rightful authority of the people over the whole subject, to be exercised in either of the modes prescribed in the instrument itself; and I should, under existing circumstances, favor rather than oppose a fair opportunity being afforded the people to act upon it. I will venture to add that to me the convention mode seems preferable, in that it allows amendments to originate with the people themselves, instead of only permitting them to take or reject propositions originated by others, not especially chosen for the purpose, and which might not be precisely such as they would wish to either accept or refuse. I understand a proposed amendment to the Constitution—which amendment, however, I have not seen—has passed Congress, to the effect that the Federal Government shall never interfere with the domestic institutions of the States, including that of persons held to service. To avoid misconstruction of what I have said, I depart from my purpose not to speak of particular amendments so far as to say that, holding such a provision to now be implied constitutional law, I have no objection to its being made express and irrevocable.

The Chief Magistrate derives all his authority from the people, and they have referred none upon him to fix terms for the separation of the States. The people themselves can do this if also they choose, but the Executive as such has nothing to do with it. His duty is to administer the present Government as it came to his hands and to transmit it unimpaired by him to his successor.

Why should there not be a patient confidence in the ultimate justice of the people? Is there any better or equal hope in the world? In our present differences, is either party without faith of being in the right? If the Almighty Ruler of Nations, with His eternal truth and justice, be on your side of the North, or on yours of the South, that truth and that justice will surely prevail by the judgment of this great tribunal of the American people.

By the frame of the Government under which we live this same people have wisely given their public servants but little power for mischief, and have with equal wisdom provided for the return of that little to their own hands at very short intervals. While the people retain their virtue and vigilance no Administration by any extreme of wickedness or folly can very seriously injure the Government in the short space of four years.

My countrymen, one and all, think calmly and *well* upon this whole subject. Nothing valuable can be lost by taking time. If there be an object to *hurry* any of you in hot haste to a step which you would never take *deliberately,* that object will be frustrated by taking time; but no good object can be frustrated by it. Such of you as are now dissatisfied still have the old Constitution unimpaired, and, on the sensitive point, the laws of your own framing under it; while the new Administration will have no immediate power, if it would, to change either. If it were admitted that you who are dissatisfied hold the right side in the dispute, there still is no single good reason for precipitate action. Intelligence, patriotism, Christianity, and a firm reliance on Him who has never yet forsaken this favored land are still competent to adjust in the best way all our present difficulty.

In *your* hands, my dissatisfied fellow-countrymen, and not in *mine,* is the momentous issue of civil war. The Government will not assail *you.* You can have no conflict without being yourselves the aggressors. *You* have no oath registered in heaven to destroy the Government, while I shall have the most solemn one to "preserve, protect, and defend it."

I am loath to close. We are not enemies, but friends. We must not be enemies. Though passion may have strained it must not break our bonds of affection. The mystic chords of memory, stretching from every battlefield and patriot grave to every living heart and hearthstone all over this broad land, will yet swell the chorus of the Union, when again touched, as surely they will be, by the better angels of our nature.

NOTES

1. *Slavery.* Lincoln's First Inaugural reviews much of the pre-Civil War constitutional law of slavery, as well as Article IV. According to Lincoln, does the Constitution create a general constitutional right to own slaves? What are the federal government's obligations and powers with respect to slavery? What do you think of Lincoln's willingness to support a constitutional amendment making permanent his understanding that the federal government lacks power to interfere with slavery in the states (the "Corwin Amendment")?

2. *Secession.* Evaluate Lincoln's legal argument for the unconstitutionality of secession. Consider the modes of constitutional argument he employs: text, structure, political theory, history. How is Lincoln's argument related to the position of Madison and Jefferson in the Virginia and Kentucky resolutions (described in Chapter 1)? Does their support for "nullification" and "interposition" lead inexorably to an argument for the constitutionality of secession?

3. *Sovereignty.* Where does "sovereignty" reside under the U.S. Constitution? Lincoln thought that "the central idea of secession, is the essence of anarchy" and that it was inconsistent with the democratic theory of the Constitution for a minority, whenever feeling itself aggrieved, to secede rather than acquiesce. Lincoln amplified this denial of states' sovereignty in a Message to Congress on July 4, 1861 (after the states of the Upper South had seceded and the war had begun). He argued that "secession" should be called "rebellion," conveying the idea of "*violation* of law." He attacked the theory of state sovereignty as a systematic and "insidious debauching of the public mind." Referring to secessionist theorists, he said:

> They invented an ingenious sophism, which, if conceded, was followed by perfectly logical steps, through all the incidents, to the complete destruction of the Union. The sophism itself is, that any state of the Union may, *consistently* with the national Constitution, and therefore *lawfully,* and *peacefully,* withdraw from the Union, without the consent of the Union, or of any other state. The little disguise that the supposed right is to be exercised only for just cause, themselves to be the sole judge of its justice, is too thin to merit any notice....
>
> This sophism derives much—perhaps the whole—of its currency, from the assumption, that there is some omnipotent, and sacred supremacy, pertaining to a *State*—to each State of our Federal Union. Our States have neither more, nor less power, than that reserved to them, in the Un-

ion, by the Constitution—no one of them ever having been a State *out* of the Union. . . . Having never been States, either in substance, or in name, *outside* of the Union, whence this magical omnipotence of "State rights," asserting a claim of power to lawfully destroy the Union itself? Much is said about the "sovereignty" of the States; but the word, even, is not in the national Constitution; nor, as is believed, in any of the State constitutions. What is a "sovereignty," in the political sense of the term? Would it be far wrong to define it "A political community, without a political superior"? Tested by this, no one of our States, except Texas, ever as a sovereignty. And even Texas gave up the character on coming into the Union; by which act, she acknowledged the Constitution of the United States, and the laws and treaties of the United States made in pursuance of the Constitution, to be, for her, the supreme law of the land. The States have their *status* IN the Union, and they have no other *legal status*. If they break from this, they can only do so against law, and by revolution. The Union, and not themselves separately, procured their independence, and their liberty. By conquest or purchase, the Union gave each of them, whatever of independence, and liberty, it has. The Union is older than any of the States; and, in fact, it created them as States. . . . Not one of them ever had a State constitution, independent of the Union. . . .

Unquestionably the States have the powers, and rights, reserved to them in, and by the National Constitution; but among these, surely, are not included all conceivable powers, however mischievous, or destructive; but, at most, such only, as were known in the world, at the time, as governmental powers; and certainly, a power to destroy the government itself, had never been known as a governmental—as a merely administrative powers. This relative matter of National power, and State rights, as a principle, is no other than the principle of *generality*, and *locality*. Whatever concerns the whole should be confided to the whole—to the general government; while, whatever concerns *only* the State, should be left exclusively, to the State. This is all there is of original principle about it.

Do you agree with Lincoln's assessment of the nature of the Union and the location of sovereignty? Lincoln added an argument from the Guarantee Clause of Article IV:

The Constitution provides, and all the States have accepted the provision, that "The United States shall guarantee to every State in this Union a republican form of government." But, if a State may lawfully go out of the Union, having done so, it may also discard the republican form of government; so that to prevent its going out, is an indispensable *means*, to the *end*, of maintaining the guarantee mentioned.

What do you think of this constitutional argument against secession, which Lincoln would also use to justify the use of coercive national force?

4. *Secession, but Without a Theory of State Sovereignty?* Even if you agree with Lincoln's argument against state sovereignty, what of the problem presented if the national government were truly to violate the Constitution, at the expense of the rights of the states? (This problem was presented, in one form, by the Alien and Sedition Acts in 1798–1800.) Imagine, for example, that the rest of the Union, decided to kick a state out; the nation refused to seat its senators or representatives, to grant it protection from invasion, or to honor its citizens with the privileges and immunities of citizenship in any other state.

(Lincoln used a version of this hypothetical in his July 4, 1861 Message, arguing that the logic of "secession" would permit every state to secede except for one, effectively ousting it.) Would the aggrieved state then have the right to secede from a Constitution from which it had been in effect expelled? Is there anything in Lincoln's refutation of the broader Southern argument of "state sovereignty" that weakens the force of this narrower argument for a right to secede for egregious, intentional, irremediable violations of the Constitution itself?

This narrower argument was almost exactly how the "moderate" Southern secessionists justified the lawfulness of secession under the Constitution. (Radical secessionists embraced the "state sovereignty" position that states could secede for whatever reason they chose. Others thought secession was perhaps literally unconstitutional, but nonetheless justifiable as an act of revolution, after the fashion of the American Revolution of 1776.) Consider the speeches of two Southern senators during the secession crisis of the winter of 1860–1861, after Lincoln's election but before his inauguration. Their argument, in a nutshell, was that Lincoln's pledged opposition to *Dred Scott was* a gross violation of the South's constitutional rights. Hear first Senator Nicholson of Tennessee:

> This [Republican] party promises us, as the inducement to our repose, that our rights of property in slaves shall not be interfered with in the States, because the Constitution recognizes those rights. But they refuse to extend that promise to our rights of property in slaves outside of the States, although, upon the authority of the high judicial tribunal of the country for deciding constitutional questions, we have exactly the same rights outside of the States, within the jurisdiction of the Federal Government, as the owners of any other species of property have. They . . . [deny our rights] and, in so doing, repudiate the authoritative adjudication of the Supreme Court. . . . Although this principle has been declared by the Supreme Court to be the true intent and meaning of the Constitution, . . . the Republican party repudiated that solemn adjudication.

And hear Senator Benjamin of Louisiana, explicitly drawing the analogy equating refusal to accede to the Supreme Court's rulings to refusal to seat a state's representatives in Congress:

> [T]he Constitution . . . has provided for a supreme judiciary to determine cases arising in law or equity which may involve the construction of the Constitution. . . .
>
> For the purpose of illustrating the argument upon this subject, let us suppose a clear, palpable case of violation of the Constitution. Let us suppose that the State of South Carolina, having sent two Senators to sit upon this floor, had been met by a resolution of the majority here that, according to her just weight in the Confederacy, one was enough. . . . The Constitution says that each State shall be entitled to two Senators and each Senator shall have one vote. . . . [W]hat man will stand up in this Senate and pretend that if, under these circumstances, the State of South Carolina had declared, "I entered into a Confederacy or a compact by which I was to have my rights guarantied by the constant presence of two Senators upon your floor; you allow me but one; you refuse to repair the injustice; I withdraw," what man would dare say that that was a violation of the Constitution on the part of South Carolina? Who would say that was a revolutionary remedy? Who would deny the plain and palpable proposi-

tion that it was the exercise of a right inherent in her under the very principles of the Constitution, and necessarily so inherent for self-defense?

. . . Suppose this violation occurs under circumstances where it does not appear so plain to you, but where it does appear equally plain to South Carolina. . . . South Carolina says, "You forced me to the expenditure of my treasure, you forced me to the shedding of the blood of my people, by a majority vote, and with my aid you acquired territory; now I have a constitutional right to go into that territory with my property, and to be there secured by your laws against its loss." You say, no, she has not. Now there is this to be said: that right is not put down in the Constitution in quite so clear terms as the right to have two Senators; but it is a right which she asserts . . . in accordance with the opinion expressed by the Supreme Court of the United States.

What is the answer to this argument for the validity of secession?

5. *The Interpretive Supremacy of the Supreme Court?* Why not have the Supreme Court resolve the question of the validity of secession? Lincoln, of course, had denied that the Court's decisions were binding on the policy of the nation: Thus, his famous, carefully hedged denial of judicial supremacy in the First Inaugural, culminating in the conclusion that "if the policy of the government, upon vital questions, affecting the whole people, is to be irrevocably fixed by decisions of the Supreme Court, . . . the people will have ceased, to be their own rulers, having, to that extent, practically resigned their government, into the hands of that eminent tribunal." Lincoln's earlier draft—before advisers convinced him to soften it somewhat—had the concluding phrase read that "the people will have ceased to be their own rulers, *having turned their government over to the despotism of the few life-officers composing the Court.*" The draft original thus explicitly linked the notion of judicial supremacy to the "despotism" of a minority over a majority, in the preceding paragraph.

If Lincoln was *wrong* about judicial supremacy, was the South *right* to secede—acting lawfully, in defense of its constitutional rights, as authoritatively interpreted by the Supreme Court? What if a case presenting the lawfulness of secession had reached the Supreme Court? Imagine the following scenario. South Carolina fires on Fort Sumter, and Lincoln calls up troops to suppress the rebellion. Virginia argues that South Carolina's secession was within its constitutional rights and that national "coercion" is thus unconstitutional. Suppose Virginia brought a suit against the United States, seeking to prohibit the passage of federal armies through its territory to invade a "former" state of the Union. What result? The argument that the national government lacked power to "coerce" the states to remain in the Union was very much part of the discussion at the time. The feckless lame-duck President Buchanan had argued in his December 3, 1860 annual message to Congress that secession was unconstitutional but that the national government had no legitimate power to prevent secession by force, because that would be making war on a state. Republicans ridiculed Buchanan's position as saying, in effect, that no state could secede—unless it wants to—and that the president has a duty to enforce the laws—unless somebody opposes him. There is also evidence that Chief Justice Taney held the same view that the national government lacked power to coerce states to remain in the Union. Suppose then that the Taney Court—essentially the same Court that had decided *Dred Scott* just three years earlier—had ruled in favor of Virginia and ordered the national government to allow the states of the

South to leave the Union. Would Lincoln have been required to obey the order? What if Taney had ordered the White House vacated and the Union government moved to some point north of the Mason–Dixon line. Should Lincoln have packed his bags? (And, later in the war, suppose the Supreme Court had declared the Emancipation Proclamation unconstitutional. Should Lincoln have returned freed slaves to their Southern masters?) Who was right about judicial supremacy—Lincoln, the South, or neither?

6. *Secession, "Coercion," and Civil War.* On the merits, did the national government possess the power to "coerce" the seceding states to remain in the Union? Lincoln's First Inaugural lays out his view that it was his constitutional duty as President to resist what he regarded as a massive violation of the Constitution. What do you think of Lincoln's conception of presidential duty? Could he have negotiated terms for dissolving the Union, consistent with his oath?

Lincoln's theory was that secession was illegal—unconstitutional—and thus of no effect. Accordingly, the Civil War was not a "war" in the constitutional sense that Congress need declare it. It was a massive domestic insurrection, subject to the Guarantee Clause power of the national government to assure republican government and to the duty of the national government to protect each state from "domestic violence." Lincoln consistently referred to the South as "rebels" or "so-called seceding States," never as the "Confederacy" or the "Confederate States of America." Lincoln nonetheless maintained that, as the military power was in operation as a practical matter, he possessed power under the Commander in Chief Clause to employ the law of war to confiscate property and materiel within the control of an enemy force or power—thus, his claimed authority for the Emancipation Proclamation. (Is this position inconsistent?) Lincoln's theory would have other consequences, too: for the conduct of the war, for recognizing temporary or permanent "reconstructed" state governments in the South, and for the constitutional amendment process.

7. *Article IV and Reconstruction.* The central constitutional question of "Reconstruction" during and after the war, in both the Lincoln and Andrew Johnson administrations, was what to do with states that had purported to secede. This question turned on whether those states had in fact left the Union. If they had, then they had ceased to exist as states of the Union. Upon defeat and surrender, the region could be treated as part of the "territory" of the United States, subject to Congress's plenary legislative power under the Territories Clause of Article IV. Similarly, "re-admission" as states would be subject to Congress's plenary legislative power with respect to statehood admissions, also under Article IV. If, however, the states had never legally left, but throughout the War remained technically part of the Union, but simply lacked lawful, loyal governments—Lincoln's theory—then Reconstruction was largely a matter of executive policy, supported by congressional legislation, as to how to restore and recognize lawful state governments, under the Guarantee Clause of Article IV.

Which view is right? Consider the creation of the State of West Virginia. Here are the facts in a nutshell: when Virginia purported to secede from the Union, a convention at Wheeling, in the northwest part of the state, declared itself the lawful (loyal) government of Virginia. The federal government recognized that government as the government of Virginia. The loyal government at Wheeling then gave Virginia's consent to the creation of a new state of West Virginia (which would include Wheeling). In short, essentially the same body gave consent to itself to partition Virginia and form a new state. Does this satisfy the Constitution? Article IV, Section 3, Clause 1 provides: "New States may be admitted by the Congress into this Union; but no new State shall be formed or erected within the Jurisdiction of any other State; nor any State be formed by the Junction of two or more States, or Parts of States, without the Consent of the Legislatures of the States concerned as well as of the Congress." (Read the clause carefully: is it permissible *at all* to carve a new state out of an existing one? Does the "consent" proviso apply only to the creation of a new state from the "junction" of two or more existing states or parts of states?) For an argument that West Virginia probably is a legal state of the Union, see Kesavan & Paulsen, *Is West Virginia Unconstitutional?* 90 Cal. L. Rev. 291 (2002).

8. *Texas v. White.* Several years after the War, a (somewhat) reconstituted Supreme Court considered a case in which the outcome turned in part on whether Texas had or had not left the Union—ceased to be a state of the United States—during the period of the Civil War when Texas purported to secede. In *Texas v. White*, 74 U.S. 700 (1868), in an opinion by Chief Justice Salmon P. Chase (who had been Lincoln's secretary of treasury and at one time a rival for the presidency), the Court famously held that "[t]he Constitution, in all its provisions, looks to an indestructible Union, composed of indestructible States." *Id.* at 725. The case sets forth, in a Supreme Court decision, the essential legal theory of the Lincoln administration (and the Johnson administration) on secession, national authority to combat secession, and reconstruction.

Texas v. White
74 U.S. 700 (1868)

[The specific question in the case concerned the validity of certain United States bonds, issued in 1851 and payable after 1864 to the state of Texas or the bearer, as affected by the intervening legislative acts of Texas seizing such property in the rebellion. The Court began by reciting at length the history of Texas's actions.—Editors]

■ THE CHIEF JUSTICE delivered the opinion of the court.

. . . In all respects, so far as the object [of secession] could be accomplished by ordinances of the convention, by acts of the legislature, and by votes of the citizens, the relations of Texas to the Union were broken up, and new relations to a new government were established by them. . . . Did Texas, in consequence of these acts, cease to be a State? Or, if not, did the State cease to be a member of the Union?

It is needless to discuss, at length, the question whether the right of a State to withdraw from the Union for any cause, regarded by herself as sufficient, is consistent with the Constitution of the United States.

The Union of the States never was a purely artificial and arbitrary relation. It began among the Colonies, and grew out of common origin, mutual sympathies, kindred principles, similar interests, and geographical relations. It was confirmed and strengthened by the necessities of war, and received definite form, and character, and sanction from the Articles of Confederation. By these the Union was solemnly declared to "be perpetual." And when these Articles were found to be inadequate to the exigencies of the country, the Constitution was ordained "to form a more perfect Union." It is difficult to convey the idea of indissoluble unity more clearly than by these words. What can be indissoluble if a perpetual Union, made more perfect, is not?

But the perpetuity and indissolubility of the Union, by no means implies the loss of distinct and individual existence, or of the right of self-government by the States. Under the Articles of Confederation each State retained its sovereignty, freedom, and independence, and every power, jurisdiction, and right not expressly delegated to the United States. Under the Constitution, though the powers of the States were much restricted, still, all powers not delegated to the United States nor prohibited to the States, are reserved to the States respectively, or to the people. And we have already had occasion to remark at this term, that "the people of each State compose a State, having its own government, and endowed with all the functions essential to separate and independent existence," and that "without the States in union, there could be no such political body as the United States." Not only, therefore, can there be no loss of separate and independent autonomy to the States, through their union under the Constitution, but it may be not unreasonably said that the preservation of the States, and the maintenance of their governments, are as much within the design and care of the Constitution as the preservation of the Union and the maintenance of the National government. The Constitution, in all its provisions, looks to an indestructible Union, composed of indestructible States.

When, therefore, Texas became one of the United States, she entered into an indissoluble relation. All the obligations of perpetual union, and all the guaranties of republican government in the Union, attached at once to the State. The act which consummated her admission into the Union was something more than a compact; it was the incorporation of a new member into the political body. And it was final. The union between Texas and the other States was as complete, as perpetual and indissoluble as the union between the original States. There was no place for reconsideration, or revocation, except through revolution, or through consent of the States.

Considered therefore as transactions under the Constitution, the ordinance of secession, adopted by the convention and ratified by a majority of the citizens of Texas, and all the acts of her legislature intended to give effect to that ordinance, were absolutely null. They were utterly without operation in law. The obligations of the State, as a member of the Union, and of every citizen of the State, as a citizen of the United States, remained perfect and unimpaired. It certainly follows that the States did not cease to be a State, nor her citizens to be citizens of the Union. If this were otherwise, the State must have become foreign, and her citizens foreigners. The war must have ceased to be a war for the suppression of rebellion, and must have become a war for conquest and subjugation.

Our conclusion therefore is, that Texas continued to be a State, and a State of the Union, notwithstanding the transactions to which we have referred. . . .

[I]t is by no means a logical conclusion . . . that the governmental relations of Texas to the Union remained unaltered. Obligations often remained unimpaired, while relations are greatly changed. . . . And the same must necessarily be true of the obligations and relations of States and citizens to the Union. No one has been bold enough to contend that, while Texas was controlled by a government hostile to the United States, and in affiliation with a hostile confederation, waging war upon the United States, senators chosen by her legislature, or representatives elected by her citizens, were entitled to seats in Congress; . . . All admit that, during this condition of civil war, the rights of the State as a member, and of her people as citizens of the Union, were suspended. The government and the citizens of the State, refusing to recognize their constitutional obligations, assumed the character of enemies, and incurred the consequences of rebellion.

These new relations imposed new duties upon the United States. The first was that of suppressing the rebellion. The next was that of re-establishing the broken relations of the State with the Union. The first of these duties having been performed, the next necessarily engaged the attention of the National government.

The authority for the performance of the first had been found in the power to suppress insurrection and carry on war; for the performance of the second, authority was derived from the obligation of the United States to guarantee to every State in the Union a republican form of government. The latter, indeed, in the case of a rebellion which involves the government of a State . . . seems to be a necessary complement to the former.

Of this, the case of Texas furnishes a striking illustration. . . . Slaves, in the insurgent States, with certain local exceptions, had been declared free by the Proclamation of Emancipation; and whatever questions might be made as to the effect of that act, under the Constitution, it was clear, from the beginning, that its practical operation, in connection with legislative acts of like tendency, must be complete enfranchisement. Wherever the National forces obtained control, the slaves became freemen. Support to the acts of Congress and the proclamation of the President, concerning slaves, was made a condition of amnesty by President Lincoln, in December 1863, and by President Johnson in May, 1865. And emancipation was confirmed, rather than ordained, in the insurgent States, by the amendment to the Constitution prohibiting slavery throughout the Union, which was proposed by Congress in February 1865, and ratified, before the close of the following autumn, by the requisite three-fourths of the States.

The new freemen necessarily became part of the people, and the people still constituted the State; for States, like individuals, retain their identity, though changed to some extent in their constituent elements. And it was the State, thus constituted, which was now entitled to the benefit of the constitutional guaranty.

There being then no government in Texas in constitutional relations with the Union, it became the duty of the United States to provide for the restoration of such a government. But the restoration of the government which existed before the rebellion, without a new election of officers, was obviously impossible; and before any such election could be properly held, it was necessary that the old constitution should receive such amendments as would conform its provisions to the new conditions created by emancipation, and afford adequate security to the people of the State.

In the exercise of the power conferred by the guaranty clause, as in the exercise of every other constitutional power, a discretion in the choice of means is necessary allowed. It is essential only that the means must be necessary and proper for carrying into execution the power conferred, through the restoration of the State to its constitutional relations, under a republican form of government, and that no acts be done, and no authority exerted, which is either prohibited or unsanctioned by the Constitution.

. . . [A]lmost immediately after the cessation of organized hostilities, and while the war yet smouldered in Texas, the President of the United

States issued his proclamation appointing a provisional governor for the State, and providing for the assembling of a convention, with a view to the re-establishment of a republican government, under an amended constitution, and to the restoration of the State to her proper relations. A convention was accordingly assembled, the constitution amended, elections held, and a State government, acknowledging its obligations to the Union, established.

Whether the action then taken was, in all respects, warranted by the Constitution, it is not now necessary to determine. The power exercised by the President was supposed, doubtless, to be derived from his constitutional functions, as commander-in-chief; and so long as the war continued, it cannot be denied that he might institute temporary government within insurgent districts, occupied by the National forces, or take measures, in any State, for the restoration of State government faithful to the Union. . . .

But, the power to carry into effect the clause of guaranty is primarily a legislative power, and resides in Congress. . . . *[The opinion then quotes the Guarantee Clause and discusses Luther v. Borden.—Editors]*

The action of the President must, therefore, be considered as provisional, and, in that light, it seems to have regarded by Congress. . . . But, it is important to observe that these [Reconstruction Acts of Congress] themselves show that the governments, which had been established and had been in actual operation under executive direction, were recognized by Congress as provisional, as existing, and as capable of continuance. . . .

[Therefore,] the title of the State [to the bonds] was not divested by the act of the insurgent government in entering into this contract.

NOTES

1. Does Article IV explicitly provide for the division of a state? Indeed, as to Texas itself, it may not be that the state as currently constituted is "indestructible." The act of Congress admitting Texas as a state permits it to divide into as many as five states; these terms have never been repealed and under the theory of *Texas v. White* they were not superseded by the Civil War.

2. Article IV, Clause 3 provides a way for new states to join the Union, but it does not provide for any mechanism for states to leave, whether unilaterally or with Congress's consent. Does this mean that before a state—say Alaska or Hawaii—could leave the Union, the Constitution would first have to be amended to provide a way out? *Expressio unius, exclusion alterius*: the specification of a way to enter without the specification of a way to leave implies that leaving has not been authorized. At a minimum, the fact that the text of the Constitution requires Congress's consent before a state can join the union might be read to imply a requirement of congressional consent before a state could leave. Is it plausible that a state could just leave a federation without assuming its share of the national debt and without offering assurances for minority populations in what would become a new nation? The bottom line is that unilateral secession is unconstitutional until and unless a constitutional amendment is passed to provide for it.

3. The Canadian Supreme Court was asked by the government in the 1990s to render an advisory opinion on whether Quebec could unilaterally secede from Canada if the people of that province voted for secession in a popular referendum (as they almost did). The Court concluded, in *Reference re Secession*

of Quebec, 2 S.C.R. 217 (Supreme Court of Canada 1998), that if the people of Quebec voted for secession the central government would be obligated to enter into negotiations with it on the terms of secession, including how to apportion the national debt and where to draw the new nation's boundary lines as well as how effectively to protect the rights of English speakers in Quebec. On the topic of constitutionalism and secession generally, see Cass Sunstein, *Constitutionalism and Secession,* 58 U. Chi. L. Rev. 633 (1991).

CHAPTER 5

THE CONSTITUTIONAL AMENDMENT PROCESS

[*Assignment 40*]

> *Article V: The Congress, whenever two thirds of both Houses shall deem it necessary, shall propose Amendments to this Constitution, or, on the Application of the Legislatures of two thirds of the several States, shall call a Convention for proposing Amendments, which, in either Case, shall be valid to all Intents and Purposes, as Part of this Constitution, when ratified by the Legislatures of three fourths of the several States, or by Conventions in three fourths thereof, as the one or the other Mode of Ratification may be proposed by the Congress; Provided that no Amendment which may be made prior to the Year one thousand eight hundred and eight shall in any Manner affect the first and fourth Clauses in the ninth Section of the first Article; and that no State, without its Consent, shall be deprived of its equal Suffrage in the Senate.*

I. A PERFECT PROBLEM

This short but important chapter considers the process for constitutional amendment, which is set out in Article V of the Constitution. We begin with a situation that raised, directly or indirectly, nearly every issue concerning Article V and the constitutional amendment process. In 1789, as part of the originally proposed Bill of Rights, Congress put forward the following amendment: "No law, varying the compensation for the services of Senators and Representatives, shall take effect, until an election of Representatives shall have intervened." The amendment was declared ratified in *1992*, more than two centuries later, and is now listed as the Twenty-seventh Amendment to the Constitution. But is this amendment, also called the Congressional Pay Amendment, really part of the Constitution? Was it proposed and ratified in accordance with the procedures specified by the Constitution for making amendments?

Here are the rules: Article V provides that amendments to the Constitution may be *proposed* in either of two ways: (1) by two-thirds majorities of both houses of Congress; or (2) by a national convention for proposing amendments, to be called by Congress upon application by two-thirds of the states. A proposed amendment must then be *ratified* by three-fourths of the states, acting either through their state legislatures or through special state ratifying conventions—whichever method Congress chooses in the particular case. (Recall from Chapter 1 that the framers provided that the original Constitution was to be ratified by special state ratifying conventions, thereby circumventing the state legislatures, which were interested in preserving the status quo and their own powers.)

After being proposed by Congress in 1789, the Congressional Pay Amendment gathered only six state ratifications in the period during which the first ten amendments were ratified—well short of the three-fourths required by Article V. Ohio, which had not been a state at the time of the original proposal, purported to ratify the amendment in 1873—still making the number far short of a three-fourths majority of the states. A large number of states purported to ratify the amendment in the 1980s and early 1990s, with Michigan's ratification on May 7, 1992, as the thirty-eighth state (*of fifty*) putting the amendment over the three-fourths mark. Is this valid under Article V?

II. THE RIDDLES OF ARTICLE V

In assessing whether the Twenty–seventh Amendment is part of the Constitution, think about the following questions. This is a rare opportunity for you to engage in constitutional interpretation without the courts having given their view first—very few judicial opinions interpret Article V.

1. Article V does not specify a time limit for a proposed amendment to be ratified. Is it proper to read into the text an implicit requirement? Should adoption of a constitutional amendment require a "contemporaneous consensus" of some sort? See *Dillon v. Gloss*, 256 U.S. 368 (1921) (suggesting such a view in dicta). If so, what is that time limit? Is it a "reasonable" period of time?

2. Could Congress, in the proposed amendment itself, specify a deadline for ratification, after which the proposal would be deemed dead? (Look at the Eighteenth, Twentieth, Twenty–first, and Twenty–second Amendments.) Could Congress specify a deadline not in the text of the proposed amendment (perhaps for stylistic reasons) but rather in the bill or resolution proposing the amendment to the states?

3. Could Congress specify a deadline after an amendment has been proposed? For example, could Congress have "terminated" the proposed Congressional Pay Amendment sometime before Michigan's 1992 ratification, if it thought that the proposal had lingered too long, or if the present Congress no longer favored it? Could Congress impose a deadline after the (purported) scale-tipping state ratification? That is, could Congress judge whether such ratification was timely, after the fact? (Note that Congress voted 414–3 in the House and 99–0 in the Senate to "accept" the Twenty-seventh Amendment as validly ratified.)

4. Could Congress judge other things about the validity of state ratifications—such as whether or not the state legislature acted properly, according to its own rules of procedure, in purporting to ratify an amendment? See *Coleman v. Miller,* 307 U.S. 433 (1939) (suggesting, without a controlling majority opinion, either that Congress possesses this power or that its acceptance of a state ratification is a "political question").

5. How sure are you of your answer to the preceding question? See if it holds up—or whether you might be tempted to reconsider—when you are presented with the following question: Could Congress conclude that a state's failure to ratify a proposed constitutional amendment was illegitimate, replace ("reconstruct") the state government and its legislature so as to produce a body more sympathetic to the attempt, and refuse to seat that state's U.S. representatives and senators in Congress until that state changed its mind and ratified the proposed amendments? This real-life hypothetical is remarkably close to the story of the ratification of the Fourteenth Amendment—perhaps the amendment most central to modern constitutional law. Was the Fourteenth Amendment illegally adopted? (We return to this in question 13.) Note that at least Congress did not out-and-

out declare the amendment *ratified* by the state legislatures when it had in fact been *rejected* by them. Congress at least felt it necessary to replace the state legislatures in question and have them vote to ratify the amendment proposal.

6. Back to the question of the validity of the Twenty-seventh Amendment and whether Article V implies a time limit for ratification (or leaves it up to Congress's judgment, at any time): If Article V does not contain a time limit, and Congress did not specify one in advance as part of the enactment proposing the amendment, does a proposed constitutional amendment live forever—floating around in suspended animation, waiting to be ratified (like the Congressional Pay Amendment)? Or could Congress "recall" a constitutional amendment proposal? If so, should it take the same two-thirds majority vote of both houses of Congress that it took to propose the amendment?

7. Here are some amendments passed by two-thirds of both houses of Congress, but not ratified: First, there is the proposal (also part of the original proposed Bill of Rights) to increase the size of the House of Representatives. (Adoption of that amendment would not affect anything today.) Second, there is a proposal from 1810 that would strip U.S. citizenship from anyone who accepts a title of nobility from any foreign government or who (without Congress's consent) accepts any "emolument" from a foreign nation. (This amendment would have real consequences if adopted, but probably not harmful ones unless its rule were deemed retroactive.) Third, there is the "Corwin Amendment," a proposed amendment passed by Congress during the secession crisis of the winter of 1860–1861 (after Abraham Lincoln's election but before his inauguration) that would have permanently forbidden Congress from making any constitutional amendment interfering with the right of states to maintain the institution of slavery. Had it been ratified at the time, it would have become the Thirteenth Amendment? Query: Does the adoption of the *real* Thirteenth Amendment—abolishing slavery—extinguish this proposal? Finally, there is the "Child Labor Amendment" of the 1920s, intended to overrule Supreme Court decisions of that era finding no power under the Commerce Clause or the Taxing Clause to regulate child labor. (Adoption of that amendment would now merely embrace the rule the Supreme Court subsequently adopted, as a matter of interpretation of those existing provisions.)

8. May an amendment ever prohibit its own repeal, as the Corwin Amendment purported to do? If it did, couldn't a subsequent amendment simply repeal the supposedly un-repealable amendment's no-repeal provision, in the course of repealing it? But if it could, what of the other provisions of the Constitution that Article V itself makes (or purports to make) un-repealable: the prohibition (until 1808) of amendments permitting Congress to restrict the international slave trade and the prohibition of amendments depriving any state of equal representation in the Senate? Could an amendment be adopted changing Article V's no-amendment proviso with respect to the Senate without its consent? Could one *then* pass an amendment changing the representation rule for the Senate? If so, why not do both in one step, in a single amendment?

9. Is there anything in the Constitution (other than the Article V provisos) that limits what a constitutional amendment can say or do? Can there really be such a thing as an *unconstitutional* constitutional amendment, or is such an idea nonsensical? If there is no limit on what an amendment proposal might say, couldn't an "amendment" essentially cre-

ate a whole new system of government, scrapping the Constitution? Is it then no longer an "amendment"? (But isn't that pretty much what happened with the Constitutional Convention and the adoption of the Constitution?) Push the hypothetical a step further: Are there some amendments that would be "out of keeping with" the "spirit" of the Constitution, and thus cannot be adopted? See Jeffrey Rosen, Note, *Was the Flag Burning Amendment Unconstitutional?*, 100 Yale L.J. 1073 (1991) (arguing that a proposed amendment to overturn the Court's decision finding flag-burning to be constitutionally protected by the freedom of speech would violate natural law limitations on the Article V amendment power); see also Laurence H. Tribe, *A Constitution We are Amending: In Defense of a Restrained Judicial Role*, 97 Harv. L. Rev. 433, 438–39 (1983) (suggesting that some amendments would not "fit" the Constitution).

10. Back to the question of time limits on amendment proposals: If Congress did adopt a time limit in an amendment proposal or in the text of the amendment itself, may a later Congress change the time limit? If so, how? This was a major constitutional controversy in the 1970s and early 1980s, when the proposed Equal Rights Amendment ("ERA")—forbidding denial of equal treatment by the federal government or by any state government on the basis of sex—narrowly failed to receive the necessary number of state ratifications. Congress initially enacted a seven-year time limit for ratification, as part of the joint resolution proposing the ERA. As the deadline neared without enough states ratifying, Congress voted to extend the deadline by seven more years. Is this permissible? See Michael Stokes Paulsen, *A General Theory of Article V: The Constitutional Lessons of the Twenty-seventh Amendment*, 103 Yale L.J. 677, 726 (1993) (surveying discussion of the issue and concluding that the original ERA proposal had a "sunset" period of seven years and that Congress would need to enact a new amendment proposal and solicit new ratifications). As it happened, the ERA did not receive the requisite number of state ratifications, even assuming the extension was legitimate. But what is the right answer? Would your answer be different if the substance of the proposal were different? Could Congress resurrect the despicable Corwin Amendment by majority vote, and give the states renewed time to consider it?

11. May a state legislature rescind its ratification of a proposed amendment? Certainly not after the three-fourths threshold has been crossed, right? Once the amendment has been ratified, it remains ratified; the scale-tipping ratification locks the amendment in place. (Unless, of course, the amendment is superseded by another amendment—as the Twenty–first Amendment repealed the Eighteenth Amendment, ending Prohibition.) Were it otherwise, couldn't a state "secede" from some or all of the Constitution, by withdrawing its earlier consent? Now change the situation: What about a state's rescission of its ratification before the scale-tipping ratification that makes an amendment part of the Constitution? Is it a one-way street, or can a state turn its ratification light-switch from on to off? Idaho rescinded its ratification of the ERA while the proposal was still pending, a move upheld by a federal district court before the issue became moot. See *Idaho v. Freeman*, 529 F. Supp. 1107 (D. Idaho 1981), *vacated as moot sub nom. National Organization for Women v. Idaho*, 459 U.S. 809 (1982). Is that the right answer? Ohio and New Jersey rescinded their ratifications of the Fourteenth Amendment before that amendment took effect. While the issue remains disputed as a matter of history, it appears that these ratifications were not counted by the secretary of state in

the three-fourths needed for ratification. (But Congress apparently wanted them counted. Does this make a difference?)

12. May a state ratify an amendment after previously rejecting it? If your answer to the preceding question was that a state may change its ratification light-switch from on to off, surely it may turn its switch from off back to on, right? Or might ratification be a one-way street, rather than an on-off switch? That is, may a state change its mind in one direction but not the other? Does the text of Article V help you?

13. Return now to an issue mentioned in question 5. There, we were concerned with whether Congress had complete control to decide whether an amendment has been validly ratified by the states. Here, we pick up on the question of states changing their minds from "no" to "yes." Several Southern states in fact switched from "no" to "yes" on ratifying the Fourteenth Amendment during Reconstruction—after Congress either *replaced* those state governments or *required* that they ratify the Fourteenth Amendment as a condition of being re-admitted to representation in Congress. Was this permissible? Does the question turn on Article IV issues of Congress's powers of reconstruction, pursuant to the Republican Form of Government Clause, rather than on Article V? See Akhil Amar, AMERICA'S CONSTITUTION: A BIOGRAPHY 364–380 (2005) (arguing that Congress could fairly conclude that the Southern governments in question were not "republican" within the meaning of Article IV, in that they denied the vote to large numbers of their free, male citizens even after slavery had been abolished by the Thirteenth Amendment). A related question involving constitutional amendments and the Civil War: in counting state ratifications of the Thirteenth and Fourteenth Amendments, should you include in the denominator states that have purported to secede from the Union? If your theory is President Lincoln's, that a state may not lawfully leave the Union, don't you need three-fourths of all the states, including the "so-called" seceded states? Isn't that a problem if you don't have operating loyal, *Union* governments in those states? Or can you just set up such governments, provisionally, using military reconstruction powers—and have those governments ratify your proposed amendment? Compare Vasan Kesavan & Michael Stokes Paulsen, *Is West Virginia Unconstitutional?* 90 Cal. L. Rev. 291 (2002) (yes) with Bruce Ackerman, 2 WE THE PEOPLE: TRANSFORMATIONS 99–109 (1998); Bruce A. Ackerman *The Storrs Lectures: Discovering the Constitution*, 93 Yale L.J. 1013 (1984) (no). See generally John Harrison, *The Lawfulness of the Reconstruction Amendments*, 68 U. Chi. L. Rev. 375 (2001).

14. Bruce Ackerman has elaborated a theory of constitutional amendment by virtue of large political events in the life of the nation. He argues that the Fourteenth Amendment was not properly ratified under the rules of Article V but nonetheless is part of the Constitution—the series of dramatic Reconstruction-era events were a "constitutional moment" that could achieve a change in the Constitution without complying with Article V's prescribed process. Ackerman, 2 WE THE PEOPLE: TRANSFORMATIONS at 99–119, 207–34. Ackerman also maintains that the Constitution was illegally adopted, under the rules of the Articles of Confederation. He infers from these incidents a general principle that the Constitution may be amended by events, apart from Article V. The key historical events, for Ackerman, were the adoption of the Constitution, Reconstruction, and the New Deal. What do you think? May the Constitution be amended by great political events? If so, have there been other constitutional moments?

15. Akhil Amar has argued for a rather different theory of extra-Article V constitutional amendment. Unlike Ackerman's approach, Amar's concerns the adoption of an actual constitutional text. Amar merely proposes that Article V should not be read as the *exclusive* mode of adopting textual amendments. His argument is that Congress, or a convention called pursuant to Article V, could propose that an amendment be ratified not by three-fourths of the states (whether legislatures or special ratifying conventions) but by a national referendum. After all, Amar argues, the Constitutional Convention at Philadelphia in 1787 proposed a method of ratification that departed from the rules of the document it was amending. i.e., the Articles of Confederation. It was legitimate for the Convention to do so because the framers were returning to the source of authority that made the Articles—the separate, sovereign "peoples" of each of the individual states. Now, under the Constitution, the legitimate source of authority is "We the People of the United States" taken as a whole. Why not therefore turn to that ultimate popular sovereign as the relevant ratifying authority? Akhil R. Amar, *Philadelphia Revisited: Amending the Constitution Outside Article V*, 55 U. Chi. L. Rev. 1043 (1988). Is Amar's argument sound? Does it require a strained reading of Article V to conclude that it is not the exclusive method of amending the Constitution (at least doing so constitutionally)? Why else would the framers have specified, in reasonably full detail, two amendment proposal methods (two-thirds of both houses of Congress, or proposal by a Convention called in response to the applications of two-thirds of the states) and two ratification methods (three-fourths of state legislatures or state ratifying conventions, whichever mode Congress chooses)? Why go to the bother if the prescribed methods of amendment are not *the* prescribed methods of amendment? Recall James Madison's straightforward explanation in *The Federalist No. 43* for why the Constitution included an amendment article: "That useful alterations will be suggested by experience could not but be foreseen. It was *requisite*, therefore, that a mode for introducing them should be provided. The mode preferred by the convention seems to be stamped with every mark of propriety." Is it possible that Amar's argument is sound as a matter of political theory and sovereignty but not as an interpretation of Article V? Is it an act of revolution or quasi-revolution, perhaps justified as such (like the American Revolution or the adoption of the Constitution), but not justified under the Constitution itself?

16. The convention method of proposing amendments was explicitly contemplated by the framers as an alternative route to proposal by Congress—a way to circumvent Congress if its members were too resistant to constitutional change. (Does this provide some further reason to question whether Congress is the ultimate judge of whether an amendment has been adopted?) The convention method provides that, "The Congress, . . . on the Application of the legislatures of two thirds of the several States shall call a Convention for proposing Amendments."

One problem is whether a constitutional convention could be limited in the topics that it considers for amendments. Certainly Congress could not limit what kind of amendments a convention could propose. That would defeat the purpose of the convention method as an alternative to Congress. But could states apply for a "limited" constitutional convention, and if so, would the convention be bound by the limitation? The Supreme Court has never addressed the question, and scholars are split. The greater weight of scholarly authority (for whatever that might be worth) leans toward the view that any constitutional convention could propose whatever it wants.

Article V's spare language—"a Convention for proposing Amendments"— would seem to contemplate a convention for "proposing such amendments as that convention decides to propose." Charles L. Black, *Amending the Constitution: A Letter to a Congressman*, 82 Yale L.J. 189, 199 (1972). Article V specifies two (and only two) *substantive* restrictions on constitutional amendments (and one of those is moot) and there is little reason to suppose that a convention could not propose anything that Congress could propose, given that the convention mode was designed as an alternative for avoiding Congress. In addition, Article V specifies only two checks on the adoption of amendments proposed by a convention: (1) Congress chooses between state legislatures and state ratifying conventions as to the mode of ratification; (2) three-fourths of the states must ratify. Doesn't this suggest that those are the only restrictions that exist? For those who would fear a "runaway" convention—like the one at Philadelphia in 1787?—Charles Black quipped that the term makes no sense, as "no convention can be called that has anything to run away from." *Id.* at 199.

17. What do you think of Article V's procedure for amending the Constitution? The framers appear to have wanted to make it difficult to amend the Constitution, in order to assure stability and prevent frequent changes. Does Article V permit a small minority of the people to block constitutional change? In theory, all that is needed to defeat even an overwhelmingly popular constitutional amendment proposal is a blocking coalition in one house of a two-house state legislature, in one-fourth (plus one) of the smallest-population states. Isn't that unfair—just a slightly different version of the problem James Madison complained about in *The Federalist No. 43* with respect to the Articles of Confederation, which permitted tiny, obstreperous Rhode Island to block needed reform because of the rule of state unanimity? What do the number of amendments suggest about this concern?

Around the world there is huge variety in constitutional amendment processes. The U.S. Constitution is regarded as among the most difficult to amend, though some other constitutions have substantial parts that may not be amended at all. For example, the modern German constitution begins with an unamendable bill of rights, and its provision declaring Germany a federal and democratic republic is also unamendable. The German Constitutional Court has reviewed constitutional amendments for constitutionality—that is, for conformity with the unamendability requirement. The Supreme Court of India has engaged in a similar review of constitutional amendments. At the other end of the spectrum, Canada and the United Kingdom allow a majority in the legislature to act "notwithstanding" the constitution or overrule constitutional decisions. What are the conditions—whether as a matter of law, politics, or institutions—that make it desirable for constitutional amendment to be difficult or easy? Does the amendment process in Article V fit with, or clash with, the rest of the U.S. Constitution? Should we amend Article V's amendment process?

18. One final set of questions about the amendment process: Does the presence of Article V in the Constitution suggest any general rules for constitutional interpretation? Does the difficulty of amending the Constitution imply that courts should be active in updating it by means of constitutional interpretation? Or does the existence of Article V—by virtue of its rules for making amendments to the text—imply that the Constitution is not to be "amended" by interpretation? Who should update the Constitution?

PART 2

RIGHTS AGAINST THE GOVERNMENT

CHAPTER 6

THE BILL OF RIGHTS

[Assignment 41]

The Bill of Rights—the name customarily given to the first ten amendments to the Constitution—is practically a second Constitution all its own. These amendments set forth important individual and collective liberties against the government. Even where the government might otherwise possess *power* in a certain area, the enumeration of *rights* "trumps" (so to speak) that power and limits what the government may constitutionally do.

Originally, the provisions of the Bill of Rights were intended as limitations only on the actions of the new national government. See *Barron v. Baltimore*, 32 U.S. 243 (1833) (presented in Chapter 1). As you will see, the Fourteenth Amendment, adopted after the Civil War, for the most part incorporated these provisions as limitations on the actions of state and local governments as well, so that it is now fair to say (with a few exceptions) that the substantive provisions contained in the Bill of Rights limit the actions of government at every level.

In this Chapter, we look in depth at the substance of the Bill of Rights and major judicial cases interpreting these amendments. We begin with an extended discussion of the First Amendment (freedoms of speech, press, religion, and petition); proceed through the "Military Amendments" (the Second Amendment right to keep and bear arms and the Third Amendment right against government quartering of soldiers); and then consider briefly the constitutional law of criminal procedure, addressing questions of police search and seizure, the privilege against self-incrimination, and the prohibition on cruel and unusual punishments, covered by the Fourth, Fifth, Sixth, and Eighth Amendments. (And there is a note on the Seventh Amendment.) We then conclude with a brief examination of the provisions of the Ninth, Tenth, Eleventh, and Twelfth Amendments.

A Short History of the Bill of Rights

The Bill of Rights has its origins in English constitutional history. Beginning with Magna Carta in 1215 and continuing with the Petition of Right of 1628, English kings signed written documents that intertwined what we today would call "individual" and "structural" constitutional rights. Thus, the Petition of Right, which Sir Edward Coke and Parliament forced King Charles I to sign in 1628, confirmed that the king could not arrest or detain his subjects without authority of statute and due process of a jury trial; that only Parliament could raise taxes; and that there were limits to the royal power of quartering soldiers in private homes. King Charles reneged on his pledges and was beheaded in the English Civil War that followed. In 1688, Charles's son, King James II, was driven into exile as a result of the Glorious Revolution, and a document called the English Bill of Rights of 1689 was adopted.

This English Bill of Rights was a statute codifying a Declaration of Rights that Parliament presented to James II's successors, William and

Mary. Their succession to the throne was conditioned on their accepting these rights as being absolutely binding on them and their successors. It is almost a constitution, and is binding down to the present day. As you will notice, most of the English Bill of Rights found its way in some form or another into the U.S. Constitution:

The English Bill of Rights of 1689

And whereas the said late King James the Second having abdicated the government, and the throne being thereby vacant . . . the said lords spiritual and temporal, and commons . . . do in the first place (as their ancestors in like case have usually done) for the vindicating and asserting their ancient rights and liberties, declare;

1. That the pretended power of suspending of laws, or the execution of laws, by regal authority, without consent of parliament, is illegal.

2. That the pretended power of dispensing with laws, or the execution of laws, by regal authority, as it hath been assumed and exercised of late, is illegal.

3. That the commission for erecting the late court of commissioners for ecclesiastical causes, and all other commissions and courts of like nature are illegal and pernicious.

4. That levying money for or to the use of the crown, by pretence of prerogative, without grant of parliament, for longer time, or in other manner than the same is or shall be granted, is illegal.

5. That it is the right of the subjects to petition the King, and all commitments and prosecutions for such petitioning are illegal.

6. That the raising or keeping a standing army within the kingdom in time of peace, unless it be with consent of parliament, is against law.

7. That the subjects which are protestants, may have arms for their defence suitable to their conditions, and as allowed by law.

8. That election of members of parliament ought to be free.

9. That the freedom of speech, and debates or proceedings in parliament, ought not to be impeached or questioned in any court or place out of parliament.

10. That excessive bail ought not to be required, nor excessive fines imposed; nor cruel and unusual punishments inflicted.

11. That jurors ought to be duly impaneled and returned, and jurors which pass upon men in trials for high treason ought to be freeholders.

12. That all grants and promises of fines and forfeitures of particular persons before conviction are illegal and void.

13. And that for redress of all grievances, and for the amending, strengthening, and preserving of the laws, parliaments ought to be held frequently.

As we saw in Chapter 1, the Federalists who argued for ratification of the U.S. Constitution did not think a separate Bill of Rights was necessary.

They claimed that Articles I through VII of the proposed Constitution already accomplished the main aims of the English Bill of Rights because they (1) obligated the president to take care that the laws were faithfully executed, (2) gave the power of taxation to Congress, (3) also gave Congress the power to create new federal courts, (4) protected speech and debate in Congress, (5) provided for jury trial in criminal cases, and (6) required that Congress meet at least once a year. More importantly, the Federalists argued, the careful enumeration of national legislative powers in Article I, Section 8 did not invest the federal government with any authority to invade personal rights. It did not, for example, allow any federal regulation of the press or of religion. This argument did not prove persuasive; supporters of a Bill of Rights did not find it hard to show how virtually every grant of power in Section 8 could be abused.[1]

The absence of a Bill of Rights was the Anti–Federalists' most potent argument against the proposed Constitution, and five state conventions demanded a Bill of Rights as the price of ratification. The Anti–Federalist argument for a Bill of Rights was a states-rights argument and an individual-rights argument intertwined as one. The Anti–Federalists rejected Madison's argument in *The Federalist No. 10* and thought that liberty would be best protected by keeping government local and close to the people. Such governments, they thought, would be more vigilant in protecting their rights than a distant and less accountable central government— whether in London or in Washington, D.C. Thus the Anti–Federalists sought and got from Congress a Bill of Rights that protected liberty through localism and through the enumeration of a few important (but at the time largely uncontroversial) individual rights.

This is illustrated by a few key facts you need to know. The Bill of Rights as it originally passed Congress consisted of *twelve* amendments. The first two were not immediately ratified. James Madison's proposed First Amendment dealt with the size of the House of Representatives, and his proposed Second Amendment dealt with pay increases for members of Congress. These are obviously issues of what would now be called structural constitutional law. The Establishment Clause in Madison's Third (our First) Amendment was also structural. It forbade national legislation that would either establish a national church or interfere with state established churches, such as the Congregational establishment in Connecticut. Our Sixth and Seventh Amendments give us rights to jury trial in criminal and civil cases. These amendments, too, can be seen as structural guarantees that empower local juries to protect citizens against government officials— national as well as state. In addition, James Madison's Bill of Rights ends with a federalism guarantee in our Tenth Amendment. Thus the original Bill of Rights of 1791 was partly a structural, even communitarian, document.

Madison also proposed an amendment that would have secured a small set of rights—the "equal rights of conscience," the "freedom of speech, or of the press," and the "right of trial by jury in criminal cases"—against infringement by the *state* governments. But the Senate, which was then elected by state legislators, rejected this proposal. Thus, the Bill of Rights

---

[1] Some have argued that the "necessary and proper" standard would forbid enactment of "improper" laws infringing rights. See Gary Lawson & Patricia B. Granger, *The "Proper" Scope of Federal Power: A Jurisdictional Interpretation of the Sweeping Clause*, 43 Duke L.J. 267 (1993). This is linguistically plausible, but is it consistent with the Necessary and Proper Clause's place in Section 8 as an additional power?

was regarded as applicable only to actions of the federal government, as confirmed by *Barron v. Baltimore.*

Between 1791 and the adoption of the Fourteenth Amendment in 1868, it became increasingly evident that the states—in particular, the slave states—posed as much or more of a danger to individual rights than did the distant federal government. In their defense of slavery, Southern states violated almost every one of the rights addressed by the first eight amendments. Southern states found that they could maintain slavery only by restricting the abolitionist press, punishing clergy who sermonized against slavery, limiting access to guns, denying due process to those alleged to be fugitive slaves, censoring the mail, and restricting travel. After the Civil War, the victorious Republicans imposed the Fourteenth Amendment as the price for readmitting Southern representatives to Congress. Among other things, that amendment protects against state laws the "privileges or immunities of citizens of the United States," and one interpretation of that clause is that it "incorporated" (or applied) the Bill of Rights against the states. If so, the Supreme Court was slow to recognize the meaning. Provisions of the Bill of Rights were applied to the states only selectively, and most of them only after 1940. During these decades, the justices entertained three schools of thought regarding the Bill of Rights and the states.

Total Incorporation—Nothing More, Nothing Less: Justice Hugo Black, who served on the Supreme Court from 1937 until 1971, argued that Section One of the Fourteenth Amendment, and particularly the Privileges or Immunities Clause, incorporated all of the rights in the federal Bill of Rights against the states. In other words, the privileges and immunities of national citizenship *were* the rights in the federal Bill of Rights. No other justice has ever accepted this view.

Fundamental Fairness: At the opposite end of the spectrum, Justice Felix Frankfurter, who served on the Supreme Court from 1939 to 1962, argued that the Fourteenth Amendment did not incorporate any of the Bill of Rights against the states but that it did protect basic principles of fundamental fairness and ordered liberty through another one of its clauses, the Due Process Clause. To Frankfurter (who was born in Vienna, Austria), freedom of speech and of religion were fundamental but Anglo–American criminal procedure with its rights to a jury trial and its protection against self-incrimination was not. Frankfurter was aware that the civil law countries of Europe, Latin America, and Asia got along well without Anglo–American criminal procedure. His view opposing incorporation while protecting fundamental fairness generally prevailed in the 1940s and 1950s, but it was rejected by the Warren Court in the 1960s.

Selective Incorporation: This approach was championed by Justice William J. Brennan, who served on the Supreme Court from 1956 to 1990, and it is the view that has carried the day. Under selective incorporation, the Supreme Court decides whether each right ought to apply against the states on a case-by-case basis. Ultimately the Court has incorporated all parts of the Bill of Rights against the states except the Third Amendment; the Fifth Amendment grand jury right; and the Seventh Amendment right to civil jury trial.

Among legal scholars, there have been arguments for and against incorporation, though the prevailing view is that the Fourteenth Amendment does incorporate the Bill of Rights—though most think the framers of the Fourteenth Amendment accomplished this through the Privileges or Immunities Clause, rather than through the Due Process Clause. The Due Process Clause seems an inapt vehicle for incorporating substantive rights, because by its terms the clause does allow the government to deprive a person of liberty so long as it provides due process of law in doing so. The Privileges or Immunities Clause, by contrast, flatly prohibits any state to "make or enforce any law" abridging the protected rights. Nevertheless, the Court has incorporated almost all of the provisions of the Bill of Rights against the states through the Due Process Clause.

The Bill of Rights cases we are going to study below make no distinction between those against the federal government under the Bill of Rights proper and those against the states under the Fourteenth Amendment. Still, it is worth noting that most of the "Bill of Rights cases" in this chapter are actually Fourteenth Amendment cases because the government action being challenged is action by a state government. *The Federalist No. 10*, which you read in Chapter 4, gives some very good reasons why one might expect the states to be less protective of civil rights than the federal government, and in retrospect it seems prophetic. Justice Oliver Wendell Holmes once said, "I do not think the United States would come to an end if we lost our power to declare an Act of Congress void. I do think the Union would be imperiled if we could not make that declaration as to the laws of the several states." Oliver Wendell Holmes, Jr., COLLECTED LEGAL PAPERS 295–96 (1920). Most observers think Holmes was right, at least on the necessity of federal judicial review of state action.

There is one final wrinkle to keep in mind as you read the federal and state Bill of Rights cases below. Recall the types of constitutional argument, or modes of interpretation, discussed in Chapter 1. One of these, text, considers the meaning that the words had when they were enacted or ratified. When provisions of the Bill of Rights are being applied to the national government, that is the meaning of the words in 1791, the year the Bill of Rights was ratified. When provisions of the Fourteenth Amendment are being applied to the states, the meaning of their words is the meaning they had in 1868. But when applying the Bill of Rights to the states *through the Fourteenth Amendment*, do the words of the Bill of Rights take on a different meaning (an 1868 meaning) rather than the meaning they have when applied to the national government?

I. THE FIRST AMENDMENT AND FREEDOM OF SPEECH

Amendment I: Congress shall make no law respecting an establishment of religion, or prohibiting the free exercise thereof; or abridging the freedom of speech, or of the press, or the right of the people peaceably to assemble, and to petition the Government for the redress of grievances.

Read the First Amendment carefully. What does it mean? What interpretative questions does it raise?

Two quick preliminaries: First, the subject of the First Amendment is "Congress." Does that mean that executive and judicial officials may abridge the freedom of speech? The Supreme Court has never squarely addressed the question, but remember that, according to the Due Process Clause, no person may be deprived of "life, *liberty*, or property" without "due process of *law*." The freedom of speech is presumably a "liberty." The Supremacy Clause in Article VI tells us that "law" refers to statutes passed by Congress, as well as the Constitution and treaties. It follows that persons cannot be deprived of their freedom of speech, even by executive or judicial officers, except pursuant to a law. And if Congress cannot pass such a law, the freedom is thus secured against all three branches. (Is it secured against treaties? That could become an important question in future years, if the United States joins treaties reflecting international norms on matters such as hate speech or the "defamation of religion"—norms that are at odds with American notions of freedom of speech and religion.)

Second, the prohibition of the First Amendment now applies to actions of *state* government bodies, as well as those of the federal government. As discussed above, the Bill of Rights originally applied only to the actions of the national government. But the Due Process Clause of the Fourteenth Amendment has been understood to "incorporate" against the states most of the Bill of Rights, including the freedom of speech.

A Map of the First Amendment

Freedom of Speech and of the Press

The First Amendment Free Speech Clause has generated an enormous body of case law and legal doctrine. There are many outstanding books that synthesize this area of law.[2] Any overview will therefore be reductionist and incomplete. Nevertheless, we offer this "map" in the hope that it will make this huge subject more manageable. It is organized according to the words of the text. Four large questions present themselves:

What is "speech"?

What is meant by "the freedom of" speech?

What is a "law" "abridging" the freedom of speech?

What is meant by "or of the Press"?

1. *What is "speech"?* "Speech" might be, for example, the vocal expression of messages of discernible content. The framers of the Bill of Rights did not discuss the term at length, perhaps assuming that the phrase had a commonly understood meaning in ordinary discourse. Is it confined to oral expression and its close cognates, such as sign language? The framers spoke far more often about the freedom of the press, and evidently regarded it as more important. The freedom of the press protects the publication of ideas and opinions to the general public—originally by means of the printing press, but presumably also through other media of public communications. "Assembly" protects gatherings of individuals for expressive purposes, such as conventions, rallies, and demonstrations. As you will see, the initial controversy over the meaning of the First Amendment concerned whether it protected the right to gather in self-selected groups, or just in spontaneous public meetings. "Petition" protects communications with the officials of government. What protects written communication of a nonpublic nature, like a private letter?

---

[2] Among the best (and most student-friendly) are Daniel A. Farber, THE FIRST AMENDMENT (1998) and Rodney A. Smolla and Melville B. Nimmer, SMOLLA AND NIMMER ON FREEDOM OF SPEECH (1996). Harry Kalven, Jr.'s discussion of Supreme Court cases in the area of free speech, A WORTHY TRADITION, is one of the best books ever written in the field of constitutional law. Two other excellent histories are Michael Kent Curtis, FREE SPEECH, "THE PEOPLE'S DARLING PRIVILEGE": STRUGGLES FOR FREEDOM OF EXPRESSION IN AMERICAN HISTORY (2000) and Geoffrey R. Stone, PERILOUS TIMES: FREE SPEECH IN WARTIME (2004). An excellent comparative treatment of the subject is Ronald J. Krotoszynski, Jr., THE FIRST AMENDMENT IN CROSS–CULTURAL PERSPECTIVE: A COMPARATIVE LEGAL ANALYSIS OF THE FREEDOM OF SPEECH (2006).

And what about expressive *conduct*—actions that communicate a message or idea? Is that "speech"? The received answer is that the government may regulate conduct, including conduct of an expressive nature, if its interest in doing so is unrelated to the suppression of expression; if it has an important, substantial interest in regulating the conduct at issue; and if its regulation involves no greater incidental restriction of *expression* than is necessary to accomplish its legitimate interest in regulating the *conduct* at issue. If this (concededly imperfect) standard is satisfied, it cannot be said that the regulation at issue is a law abridging the freedom of "speech."

2. *What is "the freedom of" speech?* Not everything that seems to be included in the term "speech" is necessarily protected by "the freedom of" speech. In contrast to the Free Exercise Clause, this part of the First Amendment does not say that "Congress shall make no law prohibiting speech," which would be more absolute, nor even that Congress shall make no law "abridging freedom of speech," which would be more abstract— perhaps referring to a philosophical notion of speech freedom. (Someone who says she goes to "university" is saying only that she is getting a college education; someone who says she goes to "the university" is likely referring to a particular local institution. "The" freedom of speech is presumably a particular and familiar instantiation of the idea of freedom of speech.) Use of the definite article seems to indicate that before the First Amendment was passed there existed something called "the" freedom of speech, presumably a legal construct, and that this legal freedom was not be diminished. The language thus suggests reference to legal arrangements prior to 1789, either the formal English precedent or informal American practice (which was broader). The precise boundaries of that understanding—and the degree to which it should be thought controlling—are, however, hotly contested.

There are certain categories of speech that, the Court tells us, have never enjoyed free speech protection, such as true threats, false advertising, and words used to effectuate a criminal act (such as "your money or your life"). We will consider below what these categories are.

Standard doctrine tells us that content-neutral regulations of the time, the place, or the manner of expression do not abridge the freedom of speech, so long as the regulations are (1) "reasonable," (2) justified "without reference to the content of the regulated speech," (3) "narrowly tailored to serve a significant governmental interest," and (4) "leave open ample alternative channels for communication of the information." *Clark v. Community for Creative Non–Violence*, 468 U.S. 288, 293 (1984). Notice the very close resemblance of this test to the test for regulation of expressive conduct mixed with expression. In both instances, the government's interest must be unrelated to regulating speech *content* and must be an important or substantial one.

There are also ways in which "the freedom of" speech may be *broader* in its protections than the universe of "speech" itself. First: The First Amendment protects the freedom *not* to speak—a freedom not to be compelled or coerced by the government to engage in expression or promotion of views not truly one's own. This logical corollary (or flipside) to the freedom to express one's own views has been recognized in such disparate circumstances as the right of schoolchildren not to recite the Pledge of Allegiance, the right of a New Hampshire driver to cover up the "Live Free or Die" slogan on a license plate, and the right of a worker not to have to contribute toward the political advocacy of a labor union—all real cases, presented below.

Second: Since the right to freedom of speech is not limited to individuals acting alone, but also extends to groups acting for common purposes, the First Amendment protects an allied right of "expressive association": the freedom of groups of persons to band together to advance their desired messages, to control their own identity by deciding which speakers or messages represent them, and to exclude messages or speakers they do not wish to include. This corollary to the freedom of speech has produced cases upholding a political party's right to exclude voters who are not party members from its primary elections, the right of the organizers of a parade to exclude contingents they do not wish included, and the right of the Boy Scouts to exclude openly gay scoutmasters (but not a right of a law school religious group to meet on campus if it limits its leaders to Christians, or a right of civic clubs to exclude women members).

3. *What is a law "abridging" the freedom of speech?* The verb "to abridge" means to shorten or diminish—an abridged book is a shortened version of the full text. The most natural meaning of the phrase, then, is that Congress cannot reduce the level of protection for speech that Americans enjoyed before the First Amendment. In other words, the amendment embeds and constitutionalizes a preexisting freedom, protecting it from the future vicissitudes of politics. Note that the question is not what laws "abridge speech"—presumably any laws whatsoever that prohibit, regulate, or punish speech would fall within that term. The question is what laws abridge the "freedom" of speech, meaning the legal protections for speech.

One particularly important question is whether the freedom of speech (or possibly the freedom of assembly) entails a right to use public property, such as the town square, for meetings or demonstrations. For many decades, the answer was "no." But under current doctrine certain areas—streets, sidewalks, public parks—are traditional public fora that the government may not close to all expression. In addition, where the government has *chosen* to make facilities available for a range of expressive purposes, it has created a "limited public forum" and may not then pick and choose among the speakers based on the content of their messages. But what happens when the government is acting as proprietor, educator, patron, publisher, editor, employer, speaker, or program-funder? The answers offered by current cases are not necessarily perfectly clear or consistent.

Is there a general, implied exception to the First Amendment freedom of speech—an all-purpose escape hatch—when the public interest (the *government's* interest?) in suppressing speech is so great that the seemingly absolute terms of the First Amendment ("no law abridging") simply make no sense? The illustration frequently given is Justice Holmes's oft-misquoted aphorism about falsely shouting fire in a crowded theatre. *Schenck v. United States*, 249 U.S. 47, 52 (1919). Does anything in the text of the First Amendment permit this move? And how can the category of overriding interests be cabined so that the exception does not swallow the rule?

4. *What is "the press"?* It is widely agreed that "the press" includes all media of communicating messages to the general public. Virtually all free speech protections apply to the press. But does the "freedom of the press" mean something quite different: a set of additional freedoms belonging not to everyone but only to professional media organizations, however defined? Most such claims have been rejected. See, e.g., *Branzburg v. Hayes*, 408

U.S. 665 (1972) (rejecting a claimed constitutional privilege for reporters to refuse to reveal their sources or provide other evidence in a criminal grand jury investigation); *Zurcher v. The Stanford Daily*, 436 U.S. 547 (1978) (rejecting a claimed *First* Amendment right of newspapers to immunity from searches, where the *Fourth* Amendment's standards for constitutionally valid searches and seizures are satisfied). Is there a workable definition of "the press" for these purposes? Do these special freedoms, not enjoyed by ordinary Americans, extend to bloggers, to authors, to freelancers, to writers of letters to the editor, to pamphleteers?

Freedoms of Assembly and Petition

The Supreme Court has almost completely collapsed assembly and petition into the freedoms of speech and association. See *McDonald v. Smith*, 472 U.S. 479, 485 (1985) (holding that the Petition Clause did not provide absolute immunity for libel contained in a letter to the president and noting that "there is no sound basis for granting greater constitutional protection to statements made in a petition to the President than other First Amendment expressions"); see generally John D. Inazu, *The Forgotten Freedom of Assembly*, 84 Tulane L. Rev. 565 (2010).

Restrictions on assembly are evaluated under the public forum doctrine. In *Cox v. New Hampshire*, 312 U.S. 569 (1941), the Court upheld a conviction for holding a parade without a license, because the licensing system was a reasonable time, place, and manner restriction. In *Clark v. Community for Creative Non–Violence*, 468 U.S. 288 (1984), the National Park Service denied the Community for Creative Non–Violence a permit to sleep in symbolic tent cities erected to call attention to the plight of the homeless. Camping was allowed only in designated campgrounds. The Court upheld the permit denial as a reasonable and content-neutral time, place, and manner restriction.

Freedom of Association

If you read the text of the First Amendment carefully, you noticed that freedom of association is not mentioned. Association is protected because of its expressive elements: "It is beyond debate that freedom to engage in association for advancement of beliefs and ideas is an inseparable aspect of the 'liberty' assured by the Due Process Clause of the Fourteenth Amendment, which embraces freedom of speech." *NAACP v. Alabama*, 357 U.S. 449, 460 (1958). Although freedom of association is most closely linked with freedom of speech, it protects a different set of expressive activities: the right to associate or not associate with other individuals when engaging in or planning protected public speech. Infringements of the right of association must be viewpoint neutral, justified by a compelling interest, and narrowly tailored. Some scholars say the authentic textual home for freedom of association is the Assembly Clause.

Many freedom of association cases involve the application of anti-discrimination laws to private groups. The Supreme Court has upheld the application of these laws to private groups when the discrimination was not related to the group's message and application of the law would not interfere with the group's speech. See *Board of Directors of Rotary International v. Rotary Club of Duarte*, 481 U.S. 537 (1987); *Roberts v. United States Jaycees*, 468 U.S. 609 (1984). But the Court has refused to apply anti-discrimination laws when these conditions were not met. See *Boy Scouts of America v. Dale*, 530 U.S. 640 (2000) (permitting the exclusion of homosexuals from serving as Scout leaders); *Hurley v. Irish–American Gay, Lesbian and Bisexual Group of Boston*, Inc., 515 U.S. 557 (1995) (permitting parade organizers to exclude a group).

In the public-forum context, freedom of association may have been collapsed into freedom of speech. In *Christian Legal Society v. Martinez*, 130 S. Ct. 2971 (2010), the Court upheld a school's "all-comers" policy that required all registered student organizations to allow any student to participate, become a member, or seek leadership positions in the organization. The plaintiffs were a Christian student group that required members and group officers to be Christians; they had been denied status as a registered student organization. The Court applied public-forum analysis, and upheld the all-comers policy as reasonable and viewpoint neutral.

The Religion Clauses

Six large questions are presented by the Religion Clauses:

What is "religion"?

What is "the free exercise of" religion?

What is a law "prohibiting" the free exercise of religion?

What is an "establishment of religion"?

What is a law "respecting" an establishment of religion?

Do Free Exercise accommodations violate the Establishment Clause?

1. *What is "religion"?* The contemporary ambiguity of the term "religion" was less pronounced at the founding, when the great majority of Americans were Protestant Christians. In the Virginia Declaration of Rights, George Mason and James Madison defined religion as "the duty which we owe to our Creator, and the manner of discharging it." This definition works well for the traditional Western monotheistic religions, but not for other religions that lack a creator god to whom duties are owed. While the Supreme Court has never directly addressed the constitutional definition of religion, in the context of statutory protections for conscientious objectors to military conscription it has defined religion broadly to include nontheistic beliefs.

2. *What is "the free exercise of" religion?* At the founding, "the phrase [free exercise of religion] generally connoted various forms of free public religious action—religious speech, religious worship, religious assembly, religious publication, religious education, among others." John Witte, Jr., *The Essential Rights and Liberties of Religion in the American Constitutional Experiment*, 71 Notre Dame L. Rev. 371, 395 (1996). The phrase has been interpreted more narrowly by the Supreme Court. In *Reynolds v. United States*, 98 U.S. 145 (1879), which concerned a law criminalizing the Mormon practice at the time of plural marriage, the Court distinguished between belief and conduct. *Id.* at 164. Belief is fully protected; conduct is not. To protect conduct fully, the Court said, would "make the professed doctrines of religious belief superior to the law of the land" and "permit every citizen to become a law unto himself." *Id.*, at 166–67. In the mid-twentieth century, the Court moved away from *Reynolds*, applying strict scrutiny to neutral laws that substantially burdened religious conduct. But the Court cabined this approach in *Employment Division v. Smith*, 494 U.S. 872, 877–88 (1990). Under *Smith*, "the right of free exercise does not relieve an individual of the obligation to comply with a valid and neutral law of general applicability on the ground that the law proscribes (or prescribes) conduct that his religion prescribes (or proscribes)." *Id.* at 879. Laws that are not neutral and generally applicable still must survive strict scrutiny.

Recently, the Court has recognized a broader freedom for the internal decisions of religious institutions.

3. *What is a law "prohibiting" the free exercise of religion?* Note that while the First Amendment forbids laws "abridging" the freedoms of speech, press, and assembly, it forbids laws "prohibiting" free exercise. Does this mean that the government may abridge free exercise, so long as it does not prohibit it? Or is the choice of verb a reflection of the fact that, under British law, there was no preexisting right of free exercise of religion (unlike speech or press)? Plaintiffs in free exercise cases must demonstrate a constitutionally cognizable burden on their exercise of religion. The issue of burden is often thorny. It may be clear in cases where a law criminalizes religious practice. But what if a government action makes the plaintiff's religious exercise more expensive, or more inconvenient?

4. *What is an "establishment of religion"?* At the time of the founding, there was an established religion in England that had four primary legal features: government control over doctrine and personnel, suppression of alternative faiths, religious tests for office, and compelled church attendance and support. In the colonies, the degree and nature of establishment varied, with an exclusive Anglican establishment in the South, and localized Puritan establishments in the New England colonies.

The Supreme Court has formulated several tests for identifying an establishment of religion. The most well-known is the three-part test of *Lemon v. Kurtzman*, 403 U.S. 602 (1971). Under *Lemon*, a law must (1) have a secular purpose; (2) have a "primary effect" that "neither advances nor inhibits religion"; and (3) not foster an "excessive entanglement" between government and religion. The Court has applied the *Lemon* test in a number of contexts, including aid to religious schools, school prayer and curriculum, government symbolic displays, chaplaincy programs, and many more. Each of the prongs is ambiguous, and while the Court frequently invokes the test, it has not consistently applied it. Another test is the endorsement test articulated by Justice Sandra Day O'Connor in *Lynch v. Donnelly*, 465 U.S. 668, 687–88 (1984) (O'Connor, J., concurring). In her view, the Establishment Clause "prohibits government from making adherence to a religion relevant in any way to a person's standing in the political community," which it may do through "excessive entanglement with religious institutions" or by "endorsement or disapproval of religion." *Id.* This is a reformulation of the *Lemon* test, where the first prong "asks whether government's actual purpose is to endorse or disapprove of religion," and the second prong, "asks whether, irrespective of government's actual purpose, the practice under review in fact conveys a message of endorsement or disapproval." *Id.* at 690. While Justice O'Connor's reformulation has had some influence on the doctrine, it has primarily been confined to cases involving public displays of religious symbols. E.g., *County of Allegheny v. ACLU*, 492 U.S. 573 (1989) (applying the endorsement test to hold that a crèche display was unconstitutional, but not the display of a Hanukkah menorah accompanied by a decorated Christmas tree). Justice Thomas has argued for a return to the original meaning of establishment as government coercion of religion, such as mandatory observance or mandatory payment of taxes supporting ministers. *Elk Grove Unified School Dist. v. Newdow*, 542 U.S. 1, 45–54 (2004) (Thomas, J., concurring). The Court has not adopted this approach.

5. *What is a law "respecting" an establishment of religion?* One of the original purposes of the Establishment Clause was to limit the power of the

federal government to interfere with state establishments. See 1 ANNALS OF CONG. 729–33 (1789) (Joseph Gales ed., 1834). Thus, Congress could make no law "respecting" an establishment, meaning either a law establishing religion or a law disturbing an existing state establishment. See Akhil Amar, THE BILL OF RIGHTS 36–39 (1998). It was not until the Establishment Clause was incorporated against the states through the Fourteenth Amendment, that the clause was held to limit state establishments. Some, notably Justice Thomas, have argued that the Establishment Clause is a federalism provision, rather than a provision protecting an individual right, and because it protects the states it cannot logically be incorporated against them.

6. *Do Free Exercise accommodations violate the Establishment Clause?* The *Lemon* test, if taken literally, might seem to forbid any legislative accommodation of religious exercise. After all, won't accommodations lack a secular purpose, or have the effect of advancing religion, or entangle the government and religion? The Supreme Court upheld one of these accommodations, the Religious Land Use and Institutionalized Persons Act (RLUIPA), but did so without applying the *Lemon* test. See *Cutter v. Wilkinson*, 544 U.S. 709 (2005). Instead, the Court argued that RLUIPA "alleviates exceptional government-created burdens on private religious exercise," "take[s] adequate account of the burdens a requested accommodation may impose on non-beneficiaries," and is "administered neutrally among different faiths." *Id.* at 720.

Procedural Issues in Free Speech Cases

1. *Vagueness.* In theory, any law—especially any criminal law—can be challenged under the Due Process Clauses for vagueness. If a reasonable person can't tell what is prohibited, the "notice" essential to due process is absent. In practice, however, the vagueness doctrine has little bite outside of the First Amendment. In the context of restrictions on speech, however, the vagueness principle has particular force because the vagueness of a law serves to "chill" the exercise of constitutional rights of expression—to avoid risk of punishment, a person might refrain from engaging in entirely lawful expression. See Anthony Amsterdam, *The Void-for-Vagueness Doctrine in the Supreme Court*, 109 U. Pa. L. Rev. 67 (1960). For example, an ordinance forbidding speech that might "annoy" others in a public place is likely void for vagueness: How is a speaker supposed to guess what speech others might find annoying? See *Coates v. Cincinnati*, 402 U.S. 611 (1971). Note that what matters is whether the speaker can tell if his or her intended speech is lawful, not whether the speaker understands every ramification of the law as it might be applied to other conduct.

2. *Overbreadth.* Ordinarily, a person has no standing to challenge laws as they apply to other people, but in the free speech context, the overbreadth doctrine allows a speaker to challenge a law on the grounds that it would be unconstitutional as to others, even if the speech of the person bringing the challenge is not constitutionally protected. See *Gooding v. Wilson*, 405 U.S. 518 (1972). For example, if an anti-abortion protestor grabs the arm of a woman attempting to enter a clinic, that conduct (though expressive) is not protected; but if that protestor is then prosecuted under a law that attempts to ban all anti-abortion protests based on content, the protestor can nevertheless challenge the ordinance on overbreadth grounds. In recent years, recognizing its anomalous nature, the Court has narrowed the overbreadth doctrine, allowing a facial challenge only when the overbreadth is "substantial."

Overbreadth and vagueness are conceptually distinct but often travel together. In *Coates*, the Court struck down a city ordinance that made it illegal for "three or more persons to assemble" on city sidewalks and "conduct themselves in a manner annoying to persons passing by." The Court found the "annoying" standard to be no standard at all (a vagueness problem) and to interfere with too much clearly protected expression (an overbreadth problem). Another example is *Houston v. Hill*, 482 U.S. 451 (1987). Hill, seeing police officers question a friend, said to the officers, "Why don't you pick on somebody your own size?" One of the police officers then asked Hill: "Are you interrupting me in my official capacity as a Houston police officer?" When Hill answered "Yes, why don't you pick on somebody my size?" he was arrested, pursuant to a municipal law making it "unlawful for any person to assault, strike or in any manner *oppose*, molest, abuse, *or interrupt* any policeman in the execution of his duty" (emphases added). The Court found the law unconstitutionally overbroad in that it permitted police "unfettered discretion" to arrest individuals "for words or conduct that annoy or offend them." Was the law unduly vague—or was it clear enough, but too broad?

3. *"Unfettered Discretion."* Joining "vagueness" and "overbreadth" in the lineup of First Amendment procedural doctrines is the problem of enforcement discretion. *Houston v. Hill*, in the passage just quoted, noted the problem that an overbroad law gives those enforcing it "unfettered discretion" which could be employed to abridge rights of free speech. *Board of Airport Commissioners v. Jews for Jesus*, 482 U.S. 569 (1987), involved possibly the most overbroad ordinance in the annals of American law: it purported to forbid all "First Amendment activities" in the Los Angeles airport (LAX). Think of everything that includes! The Court noted that if the airport officials did not actually enforce the rule against all violators (and how could they?), the ordinance would "give LAX officials alone the power to decide in the first instance whether a given activity is" within the purposes of the ordinance. The law would improperly "confer[] on police a virtually unrestrained power" to make arrests. The "opportunity for abuse, especially where a statute has received a virtually open-ended interpretation, is self-evident." Thus laws that permit government officials sweeping discretion to punish or permit speech are generally considered presumptive violations of the Free Speech Clause. See, e.g., *City of Lakewood v. Plain Dealer Publishing Co.*, 486 U.S. 750 (1988) (striking down city ordinance that vested a mayor with essentially "unbridled discretion" to decide which publishers could place newsracks on public property).

A. BACKGROUND AND DRAFTING HISTORY

The eighteenth century English understanding of First Amendment freedoms stands far removed from ours today. Speech, press, assembly, petition, and religion received considerably less protection under the English constitutional tradition (which included written texts and unwritten traditions, as described in Chapter 1). None of the rights codified in the English Bill of Rights of 1689, for example, restricted the powers of Parliament; all were restrictions on the power of the king. As James Madison put it, when discussing the need for a Bill of Rights in the United States, "their Magna Charta does not contain any one provision for the security of those rights, respecting which the people of America are most alarmed. The freedom of the press and rights of conscience, those choicest privileges of the people, are unguarded in the British constitution." 1 ANNALS OF CONG. 453 (1789)

(Joseph Gales ed., 1834). Nonetheless, although providing no constitutional protection vis-à-vis Parliament, the common law in practice made England one of the freest nations on earth. And many people in England argued that their freedoms of speech, press, assembly, and petition were broader than the legal precedents might indicate. In particular, juries often declined to convict in cases involving these freedoms.

1. *Speech.* Freedom of speech under the English constitution was a parliamentary privilege, not a right of the people against the government. The English Bill of Rights of 1689 specified that "the freedom of speech and debates or proceedings in Parliament ought not to be impeached or questioned in any court or place out of Parliament." The right protected members of Parliament against punishment by the king for their conduct in the House of Commons. But it was also used by legislators to punish public critics of Parliament. David S. Bogen, *The Origins of Freedom of Speech and Press*, 42 Md. L. Rev. 429, 431–39 (1983).

In England, sovereignty rested in Parliament, in conjunction with the king. The right of parliamentarians to deliberate among themselves without fear of punishment can be seen as part of their rights as sovereign. In America, however, the People are sovereign. Should they have the same sovereign right to deliberate among themselves? Perhaps the parliamentary freedom of speech, as applied in the different circumstances of a republic, produces a broader principle: the right of all citizens to exchange information and opinion on public matters.

2. *Press.* In England the press operated under a licensing scheme until 1695. The Licensing Act of 1662—its longer title was "The Act for preventing abuses in printing seditious, treasonable, and unlicensed books and pamphlets, and for regulating of printing and printing-presses"—provided for the prepublication censorship of "heretical, seditious, schismatical, or offensive" works. 14 Car. II, c. 33. Every manuscript had to be approved by the licensing authority before printing. The act restricted the number and location of printers and printing presses, and it permitted the king's representatives to search for and seize unauthorized presses and publications. Raymond Astbury, *The Renewal of the Licensing Act in 1693 and its Lapse in 1695*, 33 Libr. 296 (1978). Printers resented the state-licensed monopolies and the delay involved in obtaining licenses. Changes in the religious and political bents of the licensers exposed the arbitrariness of the licensing system. After extensive debate emphasizing the value of press freedom, Parliament allowed the act to lapse in 1695. See Philip Hamburger, *The Development of the Law of Seditious Libel and the Control of the Press*, 37 Stan. L. Rev. 661, 714–25 (1985). After the demise of the licensing system, the Crown relied on the law of seditious libel to punish producers of offensive material, and between 1702 and 1760 at least 115 such prosecutions were brought. *Id.* at 724–25. The legitimacy of these prosecutions was hotly debated.

3. *Assembly.* Freedom of assembly was the least protected. Gatherings of three or more people were regulated by statutes and the common law as early as 1415. If three individuals gathered for a common and illegal purpose, they committed the crime of unlawful assembly. If they acted in furtherance of that purpose, they were guilty of rout or riot, depending on the private or public nature of the purpose. M. Glenn Abernathy, THE RIGHT OF ASSEMBLY AND ASSOCIATION 20–23 (2d. rev. ed. 1981). By the 1715 enactment of the Riot Act, individuals could be said to commit the crime of unlawful assembly whenever they gathered for a common purpose, lawful or

unlawful, in such a manner as to create a reasonable fear of a breach of the peace. 1 William Hawkins, PLEAS OF THE CROWN 513–16 (John Curwood ed., 8th ed. 1824). Authorities used the law to suppress meetings by political opponents and religious minorities.

4. *Petition.* The right to petition enjoyed the most secure protection, perhaps because it was convenient for the Crown to have access to the uncensored complaints of the people about the conduct of nobles and subordinate royal officials. The right to petition was first recognized in Magna Carta (1215), and later reaffirmed in the English Bill of Rights of 1689. Petitions began as "an error-correcting device for a limited set of [private] grievances," where relief would benefit the sovereign. Gregory A. Mark, *The Vestigial Constitution: The History and Significance of the Right of Petition*, 66 Fordham L. Rev. 2153, 2163 (1998). After Magna Carta, petitions developed a public dimension: through petitions, a citizen could request a policy change or the review of an administrative action. *Id.* at 2165–66. Often petitions garnered hundreds of signatures, and were (like assembly) a means of demonstrating the strength and direction of public opinion in a world before opinion polls. In the eighteenth century, though, Parliament limited petitions to relatively small numbers of signatories, just as it limited assemblies to small numbers of participants. Perhaps this is why the framers of the First Amendment specified that these rights—unlike speech, press, and religion—are rights of "the people": to make clear that petition and assembly may be exercised collectively in groups.

5. *Religion.* England also had an array of laws restricting the exercise of religion. The Act of Supremacy of 1534 severed England's connection with the Roman Catholic Church and established the English crown as "the only supreme head on earth of the Church in England." 26 Hen. VIII c. 1. Disavowal of the act was treason, punishable by death. Treasons Act 1534, 26 Hen. VIII c. 13. Any person taking public or church office had to swear the Oath of Supremacy, which affirmed the monarch as the head of the Church of England, and declare the invalidity of the Catholic doctrine of transubstantiation. 25 Car. II. c. 2. The Act of Uniformity made the Book of Common Prayer the only legal form of worship in the Church of England. 2 & 3 Edw. VI c. 1. Various penal laws forbade worship in disfavored churches, such as (at different times) those of Puritans, Quakers, and Catholics. And the Conventicles Act forbade dissenting religious assemblies of more than five people. 16 Car. II c. 4.

6. *A Note on Order.* The provisions of the First Amendment about the freedom of religion come before the provisions about speech, press, assembly, and petition. Originally, while the First Congress was debating the Bill of Rights, these were in separate parts, or "Articles"—numbers Three and Four. (So much for the idea that the First Amendment is the first because it takes priority.) The materials on speech, press, assembly, and petition are presented here before the materials on religion for a practical reason: Much of free speech law applies equally to religious speech and many of the doctrines carry over. To a great extent, the religion clauses take the law of speech, press, and association and add new elements: protections for conduct (the "exercise" of religion) and restrictions on governmental support and control (the "establishment" of religion). It is, therefore, more convenient to study the non-religious parts of the amendment first. The framers of the Bill of Rights do not appear to have attached any significance to the order of these two sets of provisions.

William Blackstone on the Liberty of the Press

4 Commentaries on the Laws of England *151–53 (first published 1756)

In this, and the other instances which we have lately considered, where blasphemous, immoral, treasonable, schismatical, seditious, or scandalous libels are punished by the English law, some with a greater, others with a less degree of severity; the liberty of the press, properly understood, is by no means infringed or violated. The liberty of the press is indeed essential to the nature of a free state: but this consists in laying no previous restraints upon publications, and not in freedom from censure for criminal matter when published. Every freeman has an undoubted right to lay what sentiments he pleases before the public: to forbid this, is to destroy the freedom of the press: but if he publishes what is improper, mischievous, or illegal, he must take the consequence of his own temerity. To subject the press to the restrictive power of a licenser, as was formerly done, both before and since the revolution, is to subject all freedom of sentiment to the prejudices of one man, and make him the arbitrary and infallible judge of all controverted points in learning, religion, and government. But to punish (as the law does at present) any dangerous or offensive writings, which, when published, shall on a fair and impartial trial be adjudged of a pernicious tendency, is necessary for the preservation of peace and good order, of government and religion, the only solid foundations of civil liberty. Thus the will of individuals is still left free; the abuse only of that free will is the object of legal punishment. Neither is any restraint hereby laid upon freedom of thought or enquiry: liberty of private sentiment is still left; the disseminating, or making public, of bad sentiments, destructive of the ends of society, is the crime which society corrects. A man (says a fine writer on this subject) may be allowed to keep poisons in his closet, but not publicly to vend them as cordials. And to this we may add, that the only plausible argument heretofore used for restraining the just freedom of the press, "that it was necessary to prevent the daily abuse of it," will entirely lose its force, when it is shewn (by a seasonable exertion of the laws) that the press cannot be abused to any bad purpose, without incurring a suitable punishment: whereas it never can be used to any good one, when under the control of an inspector. So true will it be found, that to censure the licentiousness, is to maintain the liberty, of the press.

————

Contrast Blackstone's relatively narrow interpretation with that espoused by the radical Whig opposition. The Whigs were regarded as dissidents and malcontents at home in England, but their writings were widely reprinted and commanded widespread agreement and respect in the American colonies. Of all of *Cato's Letters*—political essays by John Trenchard and Thomas Gordon criticizing the political establishment— the following two essays were the most commonly reprinted in the American colonies.

Cato's Letter No. 15, "Of Freedom of Speech: That the same is inseparable from publick Liberty"

Thomas Gordon, February 4, 1720

SIR,

Without freedom of thought, there can be no such thing as wisdom; and no such thing as publick liberty, without freedom of speech: Which is the right of every man, as far as by it he does not hurt and control the right of another; and this is the only check which it ought to suffer, the only bounds which it ought to know.

This sacred privilege is so essential to free government, that the security of property; and the freedom of speech, always go together; and in those wretched countries where a man can not call his tongue his own, he can scarce call any thing else his own. Whoever would overthrow the liberty of the nation, must begin by subduing the freedom of speech; a thing terrible to publick traitors.

This secret was so well known to the court of King Charles I that his wicked ministry procured a proclamation to forbid the people to talk of Parliaments, which those traitors had laid aside. To assert the undoubted right of the subject, and defend his Majesty's legal prerogative, was called disaffection, and punished as sedition. Nay, people were forbid to talk of religion in their families: For the priests had combined with the ministers to cook up tyranny, and suppress truth and the law. While the late King James, when Duke of York, went avowedly to mass; men were fined, imprisoned, and undone, for saying that he was a papist: And, that King Charles II might live more securely a papist, there was an act of Parliament made, declaring it treason to say that he was one.

That men ought to speak well of their governors, is true, while their governors deserve to be well spoken of; but to do publick mischief, without hearing of it, is only the prerogative and felicity of tyranny: A free people will be shewing that they are so, by their freedom of speech.

The administration of government is nothing else, but the attendance of the trustees of the people upon the interest and affairs of the people. And as it is the part and business of the people, for whose sake alone all publick matters are, or ought to be, transacted, to see whether they be well or ill transacted; so it is the interest, and ought to be the ambition, of all honest magistrates, to have their deeds openly examined, and publickly scanned: Only the wicked governors of men dread what is said of them. . . .

Freedom of speech is the great bulwark of liberty; they prosper and die together: And it is the terror of traitors and oppressors, and a barrier against them. It produces excellent writers, and encourages men of fine genius. Tacitus tells us, that the Roman commonwealth bred great and numerous authors, who writ with equal boldness and eloquence: But when it was enslaved, those great wits were no more. . . . The minds of men, terrified by unjust power, degenerated into all the vileness and methods of servitude: Abject sycophancy and blind submission grew the only means of preferment, and indeed of safety; men durst not open their mouths, but to flatter. . . .

All ministers, therefore, who were oppressors, or intended to be oppressors, have been loud in their complaints against freedom of speech, and the licence of the press; and always restrained, or endeavoured to restrain, both. In consequence of this, they have brow-beaten writers, punished them violently, and against law, and burnt their works. By all which they shewed how much truth alarmed them, and how much they were at enmity with truth. . . .

The best princes have ever encouraged and promoted freedom of speech; they knew that upright measures would defend themselves, and that all upright men would defend them. . . .

Cato's Letter No. 38, "The Right and Capacity of the People to Judge of Government"

Thomas Gordon, July 22, 1721

Of all the sciences that I know in the world, that of government concerns us most, and is the easiest to be known, and yet is the least understood. Most of those who manage it would make the lower world believe that there is I know not what difficulty and mystery in it, far above vulgar understandings; which proceeding of theirs is direct craft and imposture: Every ploughman knows a good government from a bad one, from the effects of it: he knows whether the fruits of his labour be his own, and whether he enjoy them in peace and security: And if he do not know the principles of government, it is for want of thinking and enquiry, for they lie open to common sense; but people are generally taught not to think of them at all, or to think wrong of them.

What is government, but a trust committed by all, or the most, to one, or a few, who are to attend upon the affairs of all, that every one may, with the more security, attend upon his own? A great and honourable trust; but too seldom honourably executed; those who possess it having it often more at heart to increase their power, than to make it useful; and to be terrible, rather than beneficent. It is therefore a trust, which ought to be bounded with many and strong restraints, because power renders men wanton, insolent to others, and fond of themselves. . . .

But some have said, It is not the business of private man to meddle with government. A bold, false, and dishonest saying; and whoever says it, either knows not what he says, or cares not, or slavishly speaks the sense of others. It is a cant now almost forgot in England, and which never prevailed but when liberty and the constitution were attacked, and never can prevail but upon the like occasion. . . .

But to the falsehood of the thing: Publick truths ought never to be kept secrets; and they who do it, are guilty of a solecism, and a contradiction: Every man ought to know what it concerns all to know. Now, nothing upon earth is of a more universal nature than government; and every private man upon earth has a concern in it, because in it is concerned, and nearly and immediately concerned, his virtue, his property, and the security of his person: And where all these are best preserved and advanced, the government is best administered; and where they are not, the government is impotent, wicked, or unfortunate; and where the government is so, the people will be so, there being always and every where a certain sympathy and analogy between the nature of the government and the nature of the people. This holds true in every instance. Public men are the patterns of private; and the virtues and vices of the governors become quickly the virtues and vices of the governed. . . .

Such is the difference between one government and another, and of such important concernment is the nature and administration of government to a people. And to say that private men have nothing to do with government, is to say that private men have nothing to do with their own happiness and misery. What is the publick, but the collective body of private men, as every private man is a member of the publick? And as the whole ought to be concerned for the preservation of every private individual, it is the duty of every individual to be concerned for the whole, in which himself is included.

One man, or a few men, have often pretended the publick, and meant themselves, and consulted their own personal interest, in instances essential to its well-being; but the whole people, by consulting their own interest, consult the publick, and act for the publick by acting for themselves: This is particularly the spirit of our constitution, in which the whole nation is represented; and our records afford instances, where the House of Commons have declined entering upon a question of importance, till they had gone into the country, and consulted their principals, the people: So far were they from thinking that private men had no right to meddle with government. In truth, our whole worldly happiness and misery (abating for accidents and diseases) are owing to the order or mismanagement of government; and he who says that private men have no concern with government, does wisely and modestly tell us, that men have no concern in that which concerns them most; it is saying that people ought not to concern themselves whether they be naked or clothed, fed or starved, deceived or instructed, and whether they be protected or destroyed: What nonsense and servitude in a free and wise nation!

For myself, who have thought pretty much of these matters, I am of opinion, that a whole nation are like to be as much attached to themselves, as one man or a few men are like to be, who may by many means be detached from the interest of a nation. It is certain that one man, and several men, may be bribed into an interest opposite to that of the publick; but it is as certain that a whole country can never find an equivalent for itself, and consequently a whole country can never be bribed. It is the eternal interest of every nation, that their government should be good; but they who direct it frequently reason a contrary way and find their own account in plunder and oppression; and while the publick voice is pretended to be declared, by one or a few, for vile and private ends, the publick know nothing of what is done, till they feel the terrible effects of it.

By the Bill of Rights, and the Act of Settlement, at the Revolution; a right is asserted to the people applying to the King and to the Parliament, by petition and address, for a redress of publick grievances and mismanagements, when such there are, of which they are left to judge; and the difference between free and enslaved countries lies principally here, that in the former, their magistrates must consult the voice and interest of the people; but in the latter, the private will, interest, and pleasure of the governors, are the sole end and motives of their administration.

NOTES

Blackstone and Cato's Letters represent the two poles of pre-Independence thinking in England about freedom of speech and press. Do they have anything in common? What, precisely, are the differences between them? Which is the better guide for the meaning of our First Amendment? Why?

Demands for First Amendment Protections

Two delegates to the Constitutional Convention refused to sign the document because it lacked a bill of rights. In the Convention's final days, both Elbridge Gerry and George Mason proposed that a bill of rights be added to the Constitution, but their proposals failed. Anti–Federalist opponents of the Constitution exploited the lack of a bill of rights, arguing that one would be a bulwark of liberty against an encroaching federal government. The Constitution's Federalist supporters responded that a bill of rights would be unnecessary, because the federal government had only limited powers. The Anti–Federalist argument was effective; a handful of key states, including Virginia and New York, attached proposals for amendments to their ratification resolutions. The relevant text of these proposals for what became the First Amendment is as follows:

New Hampshire (June 21, 1788)

Congress shall make no Laws touching Religion, or to infringe the rights of Conscience.

New York (July 26, 1788)

That the People have an equal, natural and unalienable right, freely and peaceably to Exercise their Religion according to the dictates of Conscience, and that no Religious Sect or Society ought to be favoured or established by Law in preference of others. . . .

That the People have a right peaceably to assemble together to consult for their common good, or to instruct their Representatives; and that every person has a right to Petition or apply to the Legislature for redress of Grievances.—That the Freedom of the Press ought not to be violated or restrained.[3]

Virginia (July 26, 1788)[4]

That the people have a right peaceably to assemble together to consult for the common good, or to instruct their Representatives; and that every freeman has a right to petition or apply to the legislature for redress of grievances.

That the people have a right to freedom of speech, and of writing and publishing their Sentiments; but the freedom of the press is one of the greatest bulwarks of liberty and ought not to be violated.

That any person religiously scrupulous of bearing arms ought to be exempted upon payment of an equivalent to employ another to bear arms in his stead.

That religion or the duty which we owe to our Creator, and the manner of discharging it can be directed only by reason and conviction, not by force or violence, and therefore all men have an equal, natural and unalienable right to the free exercise of religion according to the dictates of conscience, and that no particular religious sect or society ought to be favored or established by Law in preference to others.

---

[3] New York did not propose these provisions as amendments, rather it "declar[ed] that the rights aforesaid cannot be abridged or violated, and that the Explanations aforesaid are consistent with the said Constitution . . . ."

[4] North Carolina, which ratified the Constitution more than a year after Virginia, proposed an identical set of amendments. Rhode Island proposed a nearly identical set of amendments, but in slightly different order.

———

Consider next the key sources in the drafting history of the First Amendment: James Madison's initial proposal, the debate in the House of Representatives, and the draft of the First Amendment sent by the House to the Senate.

Madison's Initial Proposal for the Freedoms of Speech, Press, Assembly, and Petition

House of Representatives, June 8, 1789 (1 Annals of Cong. 434)

That in article 1st, section 9, between clauses 3 and 4, be inserted these clauses, to wit:

. . . The people shall not be deprived or abridged of their right to speak, to write, or to publish their sentiments; and the freedom of the press, as one of the great bulwarks of liberty, shall be inviolable.

The people shall not be restrained from peaceably assembling and consulting for their common good; nor from applying to the Legislature by petitions, or remonstrances, for redress of their grievances.

Debate on Speech, Press, Assembly, and Petition

House of Representatives, August 15 & 21, 1789 (1 Annals of Cong. 729–33, 767–68)

The next clause of the fourth proposition was taken into consideration, and was as follows:

"The freedom of speech and of the press, and the right of the people peaceably to assemble and consult for their common good, and to apply to the Government for redress of grievances, shall not be infringed."

Mr. SEDGWICK submitted to those gentlemen who had contemplated the subject, what effect such an amendment as this would have; he feared it would tend to make them appear trifling in the eyes of their constituents; what, said he, shall we secure the freedom of speech, and think it necessary, at the same time, to allow the right of assembling? If people freely converse together, they must assemble for that purpose; it is a self-evident, unalienable right which the people possess; it is certainly a thing that never would be called in question; it is derogatory to the dignity of the House to descend to such minutiae; he therefore moved to strike out "assemble and."

Mr. BENSON. The committee who framed this report proceeded on the principle that these rights belonged to the people; they conceived them to be inherent; and all that they meant to provide against was their being infringed by the Government.

Mr. SEDGWICK replied, that if the committee were governed by that general principle, they might have gone into a very lengthy enumeration of rights; they might have declared that a man should have a right to wear his hat if he pleased; that he might get up when he pleased, and go to bed when he thought proper; but he would ask the gentleman whether he thought it necessary to enter these trifles in a declaration of rights, in a Government where none of them were intended to be infringed.

Mr. TUCKER hoped the words would not be struck out, for lie considered them of importance; besides, they were recommended by the States of

Virginia and North Carolina, though he noticed that the most material part proposed by those States was omitted, which was a declaration that the people should have a right to instruct their representatives. He would move to have those words inserted as soon as the motion for striking out was decided.

Mr. GERRY was also against the words being struck out, because he conceived it to be an essential right; it was inserted in the constitutions of several States; and though it had been abused in the year 1786 in Massachusetts, yet that abuse ought not to operate as an argument against the use of it. The people ought to be secure in the peaceable enjoyment of this privilege, and that can only be done by making a declaration to that effect in the Constitution.

Mr. PAGE. The gentleman from Massachusetts, (Mr. SEDGWICK,) who made this motion, objects to the clause, because the right is of so trivial a nature. He supposes it no more essential than whether a man has a right to wear his hat or not; but let me observe to him that such rights have been opposed, and a man has been obliged to pull off his hat when lie appeared before the face of authority; people have also been prevented from assembling together on their lawful occasions, therefore it is well to guard against such stretches of authority, by inserting the privilege in the declaration of rights. If the people could be deprived of the power of assembling under any pretext whatsoever, they might be deprived of every other privilege contained in the clause.

Mr. VINING said, if the thing were harmless and it would tend to gratify the States that had proposed amendments, he should agree to it.

Mr. HARTLEY observed that it had been asserted in the convention of Pennsylvania, by the friends of the Constitution, that all the rights and powers that were not given to the Government, were retained by the States and the people thereof. This was also his own opinion; but as four or five States had required to be secured in those rights by an express declaration in the Constitution, he is disposed to gratify them; he thought every thing that was not incompatible with the general good, ought to be granted, if it would tend to obtain the confidence of the people in the Government; and, upon the whole, he thought these words were as necessary to be inserted in the declaration of rights as most in the clause.

Mr. GERRY said that his colleague contended for nothing, if he supposed that the people had a right to consult for the common good, because they could not consult unless they met for the purpose.

Mr. SEDGWICK replied, that if they were understood or implied in the word consult, they were utterly unnecessary, and upon that ground he moved to have them struck out.

The question was now put upon Mr. SEDGWICK's motion, and lost by a considerable majority.

House Draft Transmitted to the Senate

1 Senate Journal 70-71 (September 4, 1789)

The freedom of speech, and of the press, and the right of the people peaceably to assemble, and consult for their common good, and to apply to the Government for redress of grievances, shall not be infringed.

B. Early Controversies and Interpretation

The early constitutional controversies—such as those over the Bank of the United States and over the Neutrality Proclamation—cast valuable light on the meaning of the Constitution. Often the early controversies offer more fundamental and perceptive ways of dealing with the Constitution than do the modern cases. They also provide examples of constitutional interpretation outside of the courts. We therefore begin with one of the controversies about the First Amendment that broke out in the first decade of the Republic: over the Democratic–Republican Clubs. Another early controversy that is highly useful for understanding the First Amendment occurred over the Sedition Act. That controversy is discussed in detail in Chapter 1 of this book. Both controversies were resolved politically, but only after extensive debate.

The Democratic–Republican Clubs Controversy

Recall that in the House debate over the First Amendment, Theodore Sedgwick objected to the Assembly Clause on the ground that it was redundant and unnecessary. "If people freely converse together, they must assemble for that purpose," he said. "[I]it is a self-evident, unalienable right which the people possess; it is certainly a thing that never would be called in question." Ironically, the nation's first major civil liberties controversy erupted over precisely that question. In the early years of President Washington's second term, political opponents—perhaps inspired by the Jacobin Clubs of France—created what were called the Democratic–Republican Societies. These were voluntary political associations where self-selected groups of like-minded citizens would gather to discuss—and criticize—policies of the federal government. See Robert M. Chesney, *Democratic–Republican Societies, Subversion, and the Limits of Legitimate Political Dissent in the Early Republic*, 82 N.C. L. Rev. 1525 (2004). In the summer of 1794, opponents of the whiskey excise razed the home of a local Treasury official in western Pennsylvania, and 5,000 armed men marched through Pittsburgh. *Id.* at 1556. A federal army commanded by Washington and Hamilton put down the rebellion. Federalists accused the Democratic–Republican societies of subversive activity and blamed them for instigating the Whiskey Rebellion.

Pay particular attention to Washington's distinction between societies that are "self-created" and "permanent," versus the right of the people "to meet occasionally" to remonstrate against acts of the Congress. Does the freedom of assembly extend to organized associations of self-selected membership, meeting in secret—or does the freedom apply only to occasional gatherings of members of the public at large?

President Washington, Letter to Burgess Ball
September 25, 1794

Dear Sir:

. . . The Insurrection in the Western counties of this State . . . may be considered as the first *ripe fruit* of the Democratic Societies. I did not, I must confess; expect their labours would come to maturity so soon; though I never had a doubt, that such conduct would produce some such issue; if it did not meet the frown of those who were well disposed to order and good government, in time; for can any thing be more absurd, more arrogant, or

more pernicious to the peace of Society, than for self created bodies, forming themselves into *permanent* Censors, and under the shade of Night in a
conclave, resolving that acts of Congress which have undergone the most
deliberate, and solemn discussion by the Representatives of the people,
chosen for the express purpose, and bringing with them from the different
parts of the Union the sense of their Constituents, endeavouring as far as
the nature of the thing will admit, to form *that will* into Laws for the government of the whole; I say, under these circumstances, for a self created,
permanent body, (for no one denies the right of the people to meet occasionally, to petition for, or to remonstrate against, any Act of the Legislature
[etc.]) to declare that *this act* is unconstitutional, and *that* act is pregnant of
mischief; and that all who vote contrary to their dogmas are actuated by
selfish motives, or under foreign influence; nay in plain terms are traitors
to their Country, is such a stretch of arrogant presumption as is not to be
reconciled with laudable motives . . . .

————

In his Sixth Annual Message to Congress, President Washington denounced the Democratic–Republican Clubs, urging their censure. The Fed-
eralist-controlled Senate quickly passed a resolution praising President
Washington's address and censuring the societies. 4 ANNALS OF CONG. 794–
95. The Republican-controlled House debated Washington's address and
the propriety of censuring the societies for five days. The following is a
small sampling of the arguments.

Debate on Self-Created Societies

House of Representatives, November 1794 (4 Annals of Cong. 895–949)

Monday, November 24

Mr. FITZSIMONS then rose and said, that it would seem somewhat incongruous for the House to present an Address to the PRESIDENT which
omitted all notice of so very important an article in his Speech as that referring to the self-created societies. Mr. F. then read an amendment, which
gave rise to a very interesting debate. The amendment was in these words:

> "As part of this subject, we cannot withhold our reprobation of the self-
> created societies, which have risen up in some parts of the Union, mis-
> representing the conduct of the Government, and disturbing the opera-
> tion of the laws, and which, by deceiving and inflaming the ignorant
> and the weak, may naturally be supposed to have stimulated and
> urged the insurrection."

These are "institutions, not strictly unlawful, yet not less fatal to good
order and true liberty; and reprehensible in the degree that our system of
government approaches to perfect political freedom." . . .

Mr. G[ILES] began by declaring that, when he saw, or thought he saw,
the House of Representatives about to erect itself into an office of censorship, he could not sit silent.

. . . He then entered into an examination of the propriety of the expression employed by the PRESIDENT, with regard to self-created societies.
Mr. G. said, that there was not an individual in America, who might not
come under the charge of being a member of someone or other self-created
society. Associations of this kind, religious, political, and philosophical,

were to be found in every quarter of the Continent. The Baptists and Methodists, for example, might be termed self-created societies. The people called the Friends, were of the same kind. Every pulpit in the United States might be included in this vote of censure, since, from every one of them, upon occasion, instructions had been delivered, not only for the eternal welfare, but likewise for the temporal happiness of the people. . . . If the self-created societies act contrary to law, they arc unprotected, and let the law pursue them. That a man is a member of one of these societies will not protect him from an accusation for treason, if the charge is well founded. If the charge is not well founded, if the societies, in their proceedings, keep within the verge of the law, Mr. G. would be glad to learn what was to be the sequel? If the House undertake to censure particular classes of men, who can tell where they will stop? . . . Mr. G. rejected all aiming at a restraint on the opinions of private persons. . . .

Mr. [W.] S[MITH] declared that he was a friend to the freedom of the press; but would any one compare a regular town meeting where deliberations were cool and unruffled, to these societies, to the nocturnal meetings of individuals, after they have dined, where they shut their doors, pass votes in secret, and admit no members into their societies, but those of their own choosing? Mr. S., by way of illustration, observed, that this House had never done much business after dinner. . . .

Tuesday, November 25

. . . Mr. DEXTER believed that such societies were in themselves, wrong, but he was still not for making laws against them. He had, however, numerous objections to their conduct. One of these was, that they erected themselves into a model for the rest of their fellow-citizens to copy. The great principle of Republicanism was, that the minority should submit to the will of the majority. But these people have elevated themselves into tyrants. Such societies are proper in a country where Government is despotic, but it is improper that such societies should exist in a free country like the United States, and hence Mr. D. was a friend to the amendment proposed by Mr. FITZSIMONS. . . .

Wednesday, November 26

[Mr. GILES:] It had yesterday been alleged, as the very worst trait in the character of Democratic societies, that they began their business after dinner, bolted their doors, and voted in the dark. This was a very alarming and detestable species of conduct! Whether the accusation were true, or not, Mr. G. could not tell from personal knowledge, for he knew nothing about these societies, but from report. But, Mr. Chairman, (pointing to the roof of the room,) is there no other place where people bolt their doors, and vote in the dark? Is there not a branch of our Legislature which transacts its business in this way? *[This was a reference to the Senate, whose deliberations were at that time not open to the public, nor published.—Editors]* And, while things are so, does it become us to censure other people for voting in the dark?

Thursday, November 27

. . . [Mr. MADISON] conceived it to be a sound principle, that an action innocent in the eye of the law could not be the object of censure to a Legislative body. When the people have formed a Constitution, they retain those rights which they have not expressly delegated. It is a question whether what is thus retained can be legislated upon. Opinions are not the objects of legislation. You animadvert on the abuse of reserved rights: how far will this go? It may extend to the liberty of speech, and of the press. It is in vain to say that this indiscriminate censure is no punishment. If it falls on classes, or individuals, it will be a severe punishment. He wished it to be considered how extremely guarded the Constitution was in respect to cases not within its limits. Murder, or treason, cannot be noticed by the Legislature. Is not this proposition, if voted, a vote of attainder? To consider a principle, we must try its nature, and see how far it will go: in the present case, he considered the effects of the principle contended for would be pernicious. If we advert to the nature of Republican Government, we shall find that the censorial power is in the people over the Government, and not in the Government over the people. As he had confidence in the good sense and patriotism of the people, he did not anticipate any lasting evil to result from the publications of these societies; they will stand or fall by the public opinion; no line can be drawn in this case. The law is the only rule of right: what is consistent with that, is not punishable; what is not contrary to that, is innocent, or at least not censurable by the Legislative body. . . .

Mr. DEXTER rose in reply to Mr. MADISON. He said that . . . the most certain way to destroy this freedom was, to encourage an unlimited abuse of it; and the way to render a free press useless, was to prostitute it to the base purposes of party and falsehood, until, wearied with constant impositions, the public would reject all information from that source as uncertain and delusive. He said that the most successful weapon used by the enemies of civil freedom over had been, to push the ideas of liberty to such wild extremes as to render it impracticable and ridiculous, and thus to compel the sober part of the community to submit to usurpation as a less evil than utter insecurity and anarchy: he added, if America loses her liberty, this will be the instrument of her destruction. . . . Let men meet for deliberating on public matters; let them freely express their opinions in conversation or in print, but let them do this with a decent respect for the will of the majority, and for the Government and rulers which the people have appointed; let them not become a band of conspirators, to make and propagate falsehood and slander; let them not instigate to the highest crimes against society; and, sir, if any have so done, let not us encourage them in these outrages by calling them the exercise of the inviolable rights of freemen. . . .

[Mr. DEXTER] was no more inclined to infringe rights which the people had reserved than that gentleman; but he did not know any article or principle of the Constitution by which the people had reserved to themselves the precious right of vilifying and misrepresenting their own Government and laws and exciting treason and rebellion with impunity. However inestimable the right of free discussion of public matters, and of a free press, might be, (and no man valued them more highly than himself,) he thought that when they were so abused as to become hostile to liberty, and threaten her destruction, the abuses ought to be corrected; and he argued from the principle of self-preservation, that the Government of every country must have the right to do so. Unless those are more sacred than the very liberty they are designed to secure, this cannot be denied. . . .

———

The Federalist attempt to censure the societies ultimately failed by a handful of votes. The final House resolution contained only a vague reference to "combinations of men." 4 ANNALS OF CONG. 947–48. Madison wrote that Washington's attack on the clubs was the worst mistake of his career. What constitutional principles can you glean from this debate? Do Americans have the right to form permanent societies consisting of "no members, but those of their own choosing"? May they be required to be open to anyone who wishes to participate in their deliberations? May they meet in secret? May they dissent from public measures or organize opposition to laws passed by Congress? Is there anything wrong with the legislature passing statutes criticizing such groups?

[*Assignment 42*]

C. FREEDOM OF THE PRESS

New York Times Co. v. Sullivan

376 U.S. 254 (1964)

■ MR. JUSTICE BRENNAN delivered the opinion of the Court.

We are required in this case to determine for the first time the extent to which the constitutional protections for speech and press limit a State's power to award damages in a libel action brought by a public official against critics of his official conduct.

Respondent L. B. Sullivan is one of the three elected Commissioners of the City of Montgomery, Alabama. . . . He brought this civil libel action against the four individual petitioners, who are Negroes and Alabama clergymen, and against petitioner the New York Times Company, a New York corporation which publishes the New York Times, a daily newspaper. . . .

Respondent's complaint alleged that he had been libeled by statements in a full-page advertisement that was carried in the New York Times on March 29, 1960. Entitled "Heed Their Rising Voices," the advertisement [described the civil rights movement and concluded with an appeal for funds]. . . .

Of the 10 paragraphs of text in the advertisement, the third and a portion of the sixth were the basis of respondent's claim of libel. They read as follows:

> [¶ 3] In Montgomery, Alabama, after students sang "My Country, 'Tis of Thee" on the State Capitol steps, their leaders were expelled from school, and truckloads of police armed with shotguns and tear-gas ringed the Alabama State College Campus. When the entire student body protested to state authorities by refusing to re-register, their dining hall was padlocked in an attempt to starve them into submission.

> [¶ 6] Again and again the Southern violators have answered Dr. King's peaceful protests with intimidation and violence. They have bombed his home almost killing his wife and child. They have assaulted his person. They have arrested him seven times—for "speeding," "loitering" and similar "offenses." And now they have charged him with "perjury"—a *felony* under which they could imprison him for *ten years*. . . .

Although neither of these statements mentions respondent by name, he contended that the word "police" in the third paragraph referred to him as the Montgomery Commissioner who supervised the Police Department, so that he was being accused of "ringing" the campus with police. He further claimed that the paragraph would be read as imputing to the police, and hence to him, the padlocking of the dining hall in order to starve the students into submission. As to the sixth paragraph, he contended that since arrests are ordinarily made by the police, the statement "They have arrested (Dr. King) seven times" would be read as referring to him . . . .

It is uncontroverted that some of the statements contained in the two paragraphs were not accurate descriptions of events which occurred in Montgomery. Although Negro students staged a demonstration on the State Capital steps, they sang the National Anthem and not "My Country, 'Tis of Thee." Although nine students were expelled by the State Board of Education, this was not for leading the demonstration at the Capitol, but for demanding service at a lunch counter in the Montgomery County Courthouse on another day. Not the entire student body, but most of it, had protested the expulsion, not by refusing to register, but by boycotting classes on a single day; virtually all the students did register for the ensuing semester. The campus dining hall was not padlocked on any occasion, and the only students who may have been barred from eating there were the few who had neither signed a preregistration application nor requested temporary meal tickets. Although the police were deployed near the campus in large numbers on three occasions, they did not at any time "ring" the campus, and they were not called to the campus in connection with the demonstration on the State Capitol steps, as the third paragraph implied. Dr. King had not been arrested seven times, but only four; and although he claimed to have been assaulted some years earlier in connection with his arrest for loitering outside a courtroom, one of the officers who made the arrest denied that there was such an assault. . . .

The cost of the advertisement was approximately $4800, and it was published by the Times upon an order from a New York advertising agency acting for the signatory Committee. The agency submitted the advertisement with a letter from A. Philip Randolph, Chairman of the Committee, certifying that the persons whose names appeared on the advertisement had given their permission. Mr. Randolph was known to the Times' Advertising Acceptability Department as a responsible person, and, in accepting the letter as sufficient proof of authorization it followed its established practice. . . . The manager of the Advertising Acceptability Department testified that he had approved the advertisement for publication because he knew nothing to cause him to believe that anything in it was false, and because it bore the endorsement of "a number of people who are well known and whose reputation" he "had no reason to question." Neither he nor anyone else at the Times made an effort to confirm the accuracy of the advertisement, either by checking it against recent Times news stories relating to some of the described events or by any other means.

Alabama law denies a public officer recovery of punitive damages in a libel action brought on account of a publication concerning his official conduct unless he first makes a written demand for a public retraction and the defendant fails or refuses to comply. Respondent served such a demand upon each of the petitioners. . . . The Times did not publish a retraction in response to the demand, but wrote respondent a letter stating, among other things, that "we . . . are somewhat puzzled as to how you think the statements in any way reflect on you," and "you might, if you desire, let us know in what respect you claim that the statements in the advertisement reflect on you." Respondent filed this suit a few days later without answering the letter. . . .

The trial judge submitted the case to the jury under instructions that the statements in the advertisement were "libelous per se" and were not privileged, so that petitioners might be held liable if the jury found that they had published the advertisement and that the statements were made "of and concerning" respondent. . . . The judge rejected petitioners' contention that his rulings abridged the freedoms of speech and of the press that are guaranteed by the First and Fourteenth Amendments.

[The jury returned a verdict for $500,000, the amount requested by the plaintiffs; the Alabama Supreme Court affirmed.—Editors]

. . . We reverse the judgment. We hold that the rule of law applied by the Alabama courts is constitutionally deficient for failure to provide the safeguards for freedom of speech and of the press that are required by the First and Fourteenth Amendments in a libel action brought by a public official against critics of his official conduct. We further hold that under the proper safeguards the evidence presented in this case is constitutionally insufficient to support the judgment for respondent.

I

[The Supreme Court held that the libel judgment was state action and was thus subject to constitutional scrutiny.—Editors]

The second contention is that the constitutional guarantees of freedom of speech and of the press are inapplicable here, at least so far as the Times is concerned, because the allegedly libelous statements were published as part of a paid, "commercial" advertisement. The argument relies on *Valentine v. Chrestensen*, 316 U.S. 52 (1942), where the Court held that a city ordinance forbidding street distribution of commercial and business advertising matter did not abridge the First Amendment freedoms, even as applied to a handbill having a commercial message on one side but a protest against certain official action on the other. The reliance is wholly misplaced. The Court in *Chrestensen* reaffirmed the constitutional protection for "the freedom of communicating information and disseminating opinion"; its holding was based upon the factual conclusions that the handbill was "purely commercial advertising" and that the protest against official action had been added only to evade the ordinance.

The publication here was not a "commercial" advertisement in the sense in which the word was used in *Chrestensen*. It communicated information, expressed opinion, recited grievances, protested claimed abuses, and sought financial support on behalf of a movement whose existence and objectives are matters of the highest public interest and concern. That the Times was paid for publishing the advertisement is as immaterial in this connection as is the fact that newspapers and books are sold. Any other conclusion would discourage newspapers from carrying "editorial advertisements" of this type, and so might shut off an important outlet for the promulgation of information and ideas by persons who do not themselves have access to publishing facilities and who wish to exercise their freedom of speech even though they are not members of the press. The effect would be to shackle the First Amendment in its attempt to secure "the widest possible dissemination of information from diverse and antagonistic sources." To avoid placing such a handicap upon the freedoms of expression, we hold that if the allegedly libelous statements would otherwise be constitutionally protected from the present judgment, they do not forfeit that protection because they were published in the form of a paid advertisement.

II

Under Alabama law as applied in this case, a publication is "libelous per se" if the words "tend to injure a person . . . in his reputation" or to "bring (him) into public contempt"; the trial court stated that the standard

was met if the words are such as to "injure him in his public office, or impute misconduct to him in his office, or want of official integrity, or want of
fidelity to a public trust. . . ." The jury must find that the words were published "of and concerning" the plaintiff, but where the plaintiff is a public
official his place in the governmental hierarchy is sufficient evidence to
support a finding that his reputation has been affected by statements that
reflect upon the agency of which he is in charge. Once "libel per se" has
been established, the defendant has no defense as to stated facts unless he
can persuade the jury that they were true in all their particulars. His privilege of "fair comment" for expressions of opinion depends on the truth of the
facts upon which the comment is based. Unless he can discharge the burden of proving truth, general damages are presumed, and may be awarded
without proof of pecuniary injury. A showing of actual malice is apparently
a prerequisite to recovery of punitive damages, and the defendant may in
any event forestall a punitive award by a retraction meeting the statutory
requirements. Good motives and belief in truth do not negate an inference
of malice, but are relevant only in mitigation of punitive damages if the jury chooses to accord them weight.

The question before us is whether this rule of liability, as applied to an
action brought by a public official against critics of his official conduct,
abridges the freedom of speech and of the press that is guaranteed by the
First and Fourteenth Amendments.

Respondent relies heavily, as did the Alabama courts, on statements of
this Court to the effect that the Constitution does not protect libelous publications. Those statements do not foreclose our inquiry here. None of the
cases sustained the use of libel laws to impose sanctions upon expression
critical of the official conduct of public officials. . . . In deciding the question now, we are compelled by neither precedent nor policy to give any more
weight to the epithet "libel" than we have to other "mere labels" of state
law. Like insurrection, contempt, advocacy of unlawful acts, breach of the
peace, obscenity, solicitation of legal business, and the various other formu-
lae for the repression of expression that have been challenged in this Court,
libel can claim no talismanic immunity from constitutional limitations. It
must be measured by standards that satisfy the First Amendment.

The general proposition that freedom of expression upon public questions is secured by the First Amendment has long been settled by our decisions. The constitutional safeguard, we have said, "was fashioned to assure
unfettered interchange of ideas for the bringing about of political and social
changes desired by the people." "The maintenance of the opportunity for
free political discussion to the end that government may be responsive to
the will of the people and that changes may be obtained by lawful means,
an opportunity essential to the security of the Republic, is a fundamental
principle of our constitutional system." "[I]t is a prized American privilege
to speak one's mind, although not always with perfect good taste, on all
public institutions," and this opportunity is to be afforded for "vigorous advocacy" no less than "abstract discussion." The First Amendment, said
Judge Learned Hand, "presupposes that right conclusions are more likely
to be gathered out of a multitude of tongues, than through any kind of authoritative selection. To many this is, and always will be, folly; but we have
staked upon it our all." . . .

Thus we consider this case against the background of a profound national commitment to the principle that debate on public issues should be
uninhibited, robust, and wide-open, and that it may well include vehement,

caustic, and sometimes unpleasantly sharp attacks on government and public officials. The present advertisement, as an expression of grievance and protest on one of the major public issues of our time, would seem clearly to qualify for the constitutional protection. The question is whether it forfeits that protection by the falsity of some of its factual statements and by its alleged defamation of respondent.

Authoritative interpretations of the First Amendment guarantees have consistently refused to recognize an exception for any test of truth—whether administered by judges, juries, or administrative officials—and especially one that puts the burden of proving truth on the speaker. The constitutional protection does not turn upon "the truth, popularity, or social utility of the ideas and beliefs which are offered." As Madison said, "Some degree of abuse is inseparable from the proper use of every thing; and in no instance is this more true than in that of the press." 4 Elliot's Debates on the Federal Constitution (1876), p. 571. In *Cantwell v. Connecticut*, 310 U.S. 296 (1940), the Court declared:

> In the realm of religious faith, and in that of political belief, sharp differences arise. In both fields the tenets of one man may seem the rankest error to his neighbor. To persuade others to his own point of view, the pleader, as we know, at times, resorts to exaggeration, to vilification of men who have been, or are, prominent in church or state, and even to false statement. But the people of this nation have ordained in the light of history, that, in spite of the probability of excesses and abuses, these liberties are, in the long view, essential to enlightened opinion and right conduct on the part of the citizens of a democracy.

[E]rroneous statement is inevitable in free debate, and . . . must be protected if the freedoms of expression are to have the "breathing space" that they "need . . . to survive." . . .

If neither factual error nor defamatory content suffices to remove the constitutional shield from criticism of official conduct, the combination of the two elements is no less inadequate. This is the lesson to be drawn from the great controversy over the Sedition Act of 1798, 1 Stat. 596, which first crystallized a national awareness of the central meaning of the First Amendment. That statute made it a crime, punishable by a $5,000 fine and five years in prison, "if any person shall write, print, utter or publish . . . any false, scandalous and malicious writing or writings against the government of the United States, or either house of the Congress . . ., or the President . . ., with intent to defame . . . or to bring them, or either of them, into contempt or disrepute; or to excite against them, or either or any of them, the hatred of the good people of the United States." The Act allowed the defendant the defense of truth, and provided that the jury were to be judges both of the law and the facts. Despite these qualifications, the Act was vigorously condemned as unconstitutional in an attack joined in by Jefferson and Madison. . . .

Madison prepared the Report in support of the protest. His premise was that the Constitution created a form of government under which "The people, not the government, possess the absolute sovereignty." The structure of the government dispersed power in reflection of the people's distrust of concentrated power, and of power itself at all levels. This form of government was "altogether different" from the British form, under which the Crown was sovereign and the people were subjects. "Is it not natural and necessary, under such different circumstances," he asked, "that a different degree of freedom in the use of the press should be contemplated?" Earlier, in a debate in the House of Representatives, Madison had said: "If we advert to the nature of Republican Government, we shall find that the censorial power is in the people over the Government, and not in the Government over the people." 4 Annals of Congress, p. 934 (1794). Of the exercise of that power by the press, his Report said: "In every state, probably, in the Union, the press has exerted a freedom in canvassing the merits and measures of public men, of every description, which has not been confined to the strict limits of the common law. On this footing the freedom of the press has stood; on this foundation it yet stands. . . ." 4 Elliot's Debates, *supra*, p. 570. The right of free public discussion of the stewardship of public officials was thus, in Madison's view, a fundamental principle of the American form of government.

Although the Sedition Act was never tested in this Court, the attack upon its validity has carried the day in the court of history. Fines levied in its prosecution were repaid by Act of Congress on the ground that it was unconstitutional. Calhoun, reporting to the Senate on February 4, 1836, assumed that its invalidity was a matter "which no one now doubts." Report with Senate bill No. 122, 24th Cong., 1st Sess., p. 3. Jefferson, as President, pardoned those who had been convicted and sentenced under the Act and remitted their fines, stating: "I discharged every person under punishment or prosecution under the sedition law, because I considered, and now consider, that law to be a nullity, as absolute and as palpable as if Congress had ordered us to fall down and worship a golden image." Letter to Mrs. Adams, July 22, 1804. The invalidity of the Act has also been assumed by Justices of this Court. These views reflect a broad consensus that the Act, because of the restraint it imposed upon criticism of government and public officials, was inconsistent with the First Amendment. . . .

What a State may not constitutionally bring about by means of a criminal statute is likewise beyond the reach of its civil law of libel. The fear of damage awards under a rule such as that invoked by the Alabama courts here may be markedly more inhibiting than the fear of prosecution under a criminal statute. . . . Whether or not a newspaper can survive a succession of such judgments, the pall of fear and timidity imposed upon those who would give voice to public criticism is an atmosphere in which the First Amendment freedoms cannot survive. Plainly the Alabama law of civil libel is "a form of regulation that creates hazards to protected freedoms markedly greater than those that attend reliance upon the criminal law."

The state rule of law is not saved by its allowance of the defense of truth. . . . A rule compelling the critic of official conduct to guarantee the truth of all his factual assertions—and to do so on pain of libel judgments virtually unlimited in amount—leads to a comparable "self-censorship." Allowance of the defense of truth, with the burden of proving it on the defendant, does not mean that only false speech will be deterred. . . . Under such a rule, would-be critics of official conduct may be deterred from voicing their criticism, even though it is believed to be true and even though it is in fact true, because of doubt whether it can be proved in court or fear of the expense of having to do so. They tend to make only statements which "steer far wider of the unlawful zone." The rule thus dampens the vigor and limits the variety of public debate. It is inconsistent with the First and Fourteenth Amendments.

The constitutional guarantees require, we think, a federal rule that prohibits a public official from recovering damages for a defamatory falsehood relating to his official conduct unless he proves that the statement was made with "actual malice"—that is, with knowledge that it was false or with reckless disregard of whether it was false or not. An oft-cited statement of a like rule, which has been adopted by a number of state courts, is found in the Kansas case of *Coleman v. MacLennan*, 78 Kan. 711 (1908).

. . .

We conclude that such a privilege is required by the First and Fourteenth Amendments.

III

We hold today that the Constitution delimits a State's power to award damages for libel in actions brought by public officials against critics of their official conduct. Since this is such an action,[23] the rule requiring proof of actual malice is applicable. . . .

Since respondent may seek a new trial, we deem that considerations of effective judicial administration require us to review the evidence in the present record to determine whether it could constitutionally support a judgment for respondent. . . .

Applying these standards, we consider that the proof presented to show actual malice lacks the convincing clarity which the constitutional standard demands, and hence that it would not constitutionally sustain the judgment for respondent under the proper rule of law. The case of the individual petitioners requires little discussion. Even assuming that they could constitutionally be found to have authorized the use of their names on the advertisement, there was no evidence whatever that they were aware of any erroneous statements or were in any way reckless in that regard. The judgment against them is thus without constitutional support.

As to the Times, we similarly conclude that the facts do not support a finding of actual malice. . . .

We think the evidence against the Times supports at most a finding of negligence in failing to discover the misstatements, and is constitutionally insufficient to show the recklessness that is required for a finding of actual malice.

We also think the evidence was constitutionally defective in another respect: it was incapable of supporting the jury's finding that the allegedly libelous statements were made "of and concerning" respondent. . . .

■ MR. JUSTICE BLACK, with whom MR. JUSTICE DOUGLAS joins (concurring).

. . . I base my vote to reverse on the belief that the First and Fourteenth Amendments not merely "delimit" a State's power to award damages to "public officials against critics of their official conduct" but completely prohibit a State from exercising such a power. The Court goes on to hold that a State can subject such critics to damages if "actual malice" can be proved against them. "Malice," even as defined by the Court, is an elusive, abstract concept, hard to prove and hard to disprove. The requirement that malice be proved provides at best an evanescent protection for the right

---

[23] We have no occasion here to determine how far down into the lower ranks of government employees the 'public official' designation would extend for purposes of this rule, or otherwise to specify categories of persons who would or would not be included. Nor need we here determine the boundaries of the 'official conduct' concept. It is enough for the present case that respondent's position as an elected city commissioner clearly made him a public official, and that the allegations in the advertisement concerned what was allegedly his official conduct as Commissioner in charge of the Police Department.

critically to discuss public affairs and certainly does not measure up to the sturdy safeguard embodied in the First Amendment. Unlike the Court, therefore, I vote to reverse exclusively on the ground that the Times and the individual defendants had an absolute, unconditional constitutional right to publish in the Times advertisement their criticisms of the Montgomery agencies and officials. . . .

While our Court has held that some kinds of speech and writings, such as "obscenity," *Roth v. United States*, 354 U.S. 476 (1957), and "fighting words," *Chaplinsky v. New Hampshire*, 315 U.S. 568 (1942), are not expression within the protection of the First Amendment, freedom to discuss public affairs and public officials is unquestionably, as the Court today holds, the kind of speech the First Amendment was primarily designed to keep within the area of free discussion. To punish the exercise of this right to discuss public affairs or to penalize it through libel judgments is to abridge or shut off discussion of the very kind most needed. This Nation, I suspect, can live in peace without libel suits based on public discussions of public affairs and public officials. But I doubt that a country can live in freedom where its people can be made to suffer physically or financially for criticizing their government, its actions, or its officials. . . . An unconditional right to say what one pleases about public affairs is what I consider to be the minimum guarantee of the First Amendment.

I regret that the Court has stopped short of this holding indispensable to preserve our free press from destruction.

■ [JUSTICE GOLDBERG's opinion concurring in result is omitted.]

NOTES

1. The majority relies on the opposition to the Sedition Act and its ultimate political repudiation. Why? Why was the opposition to the act by the Jeffersonians authoritative, but not support for the act by the Federalists?

2. Note that *Sullivan* involved two different sets of petitioners, with separate petitions for certiorari: (1) The New York Times Co., a corporation in the business of producing and distributing newspapers, which ran a paid advertisement written by others; and (2) a group of Southern clergy and civil rights leaders, not professional journalists, who wrote the ad and contributed money to secure its publication. The Supreme Court treated both as fully protected by the First Amendment, without distinguishing between them. Was that correct? Is a newspaper really "the press" insofar as what is written is not the product of professional journalism, and is published for profit? Do private citizens exercise the freedom of the press when they purchase advertising space in a newspaper? Does it matter whether they are protected under the Speech Clause or the Press Clause?

Assume that the advertisement was published within sixty days of an election, and that Sullivan was running for reelection. Consistent with the First Amendment, could the individual signatories have been prosecuted under the campaign finance laws for making an illegal campaign expenditure? Could the newspaper? Is there more protection for libels than for electioneering?

3. Does the First Amendment preclude suits for defamatory falsehoods against private individuals? In *Rosenbloom v. Metromedia*, 403 U.S. 29 (1971), the Supreme Court produced five different answers. A three-justice plurality, led by Justice Brennan, concluded that the privilege applied when the defama-

tion concerned a private individual's "involvement in an event of public or general interest." *Id.* at 31–32. Justice Black argued that the privilege extended to all discussion of matters of public concern, without regard to the individual's fame, and even if the statements are known to be false. *Id.* at 57. Justice White argued that, absent actual malice, the privilege applied to defamatory falsehoods about private individuals made incident to report and comment about public figures. *Id.* at 62. In dissent, Justice Harlan argued that the privilege for defamatory falsehoods about private individuals limited the jury's authority to award unreasonable punitive damages. *Id.* at 77. And Justice Marshall argued that strict liability could not be used, and punitive damages could not be imposed, for defamation of private individuals. *Id.* at 82–86. Where did these various formulations come from? In *Gertz v. Robert Welch, Inc.*, 418 U.S. 323 (1974), a 5–4 Court ruled that the actual-malice rule does not apply to non-public figures, but that strict liability for defamation was unconstitutional in all cases and that punitive damages require a finding of actual malice.

4. That raises the question: Who is a "public figure"? In *Gertz*, the Court identified two categories of public figures. First, "an individual may achieve such pervasive fame or notoriety that he becomes a public figure for all purposes and in all contexts." 418 U.S. at 351. Second, "an individual [who] voluntarily injects himself or is drawn into a particular public controversy . . . becomes a public figure for a limited range of issues." *Id.* at 351. What do these categories include? A wealthy socialite and her divorce proceedings? *Time Inc. v. Firestone*, 424 U.S. 448 (1975) (no). A scientist's receipt of federal grants and accusations of wasteful government spending? *Hutchinson v. Proxmire*, 442 U.S. 111 (1979) (no). The president of a local teacher's union and contract negotiations? *Bartnicki v. Vopper*, 532 U.S. (2001) (Breyer, J., concurring) (yes).

5. In your opinion, are Justices Black and Douglas right? Should we worry about the potential impact of intentional falsehoods (perhaps disseminated at the last minute before an election) on our political system? Is self-censorship all bad?

New York Times Co. v. United States
[The Pentagon Papers Case]
403 U.S. 713 (1971)

[In 1967, Defense Secretary Robert McNamara commissioned a top-secret study of the Vietnam War, which contained information indicating that successive administrations had misled the public about the war's scope, the probable casualties, and the prospects for success. Dr. Daniel Ellsberg, a Pentagon official with a top-secret security clearance, had access to the papers. After becoming convinced that the war was a mistake, he made copies of the materials (without proper authorization) and shared them with several people outside the Pentagon. He gave a copy to a New York Times reporter under a promise of confidentiality. After several months of study, and consultation with its lawyers, the newspaper started publishing portions of the Pentagon Papers on June 13, 1971. The Nixon administration quickly went to court to restrain further publication. Court orders delayed publication for fifteen days, until the Supreme Court entered the following decision on June 30.—Editors]

■ PER CURIAM.

We granted certiorari in these cases in which the United States seeks to enjoin the New York Times and the Washington Post from publishing the contents of a classified study entitled "History of U.S. Decision–Making Process on Viet Nam Policy."

"Any system of prior restraints of expression comes to this Court bearing a heavy presumption against its constitutional validity." *Bantam Books, Inc. v. Sullivan,* 372 U.S. 58, 70 (1963). The Government "thus carries a heavy burden of showing justification for the imposition of such a restraint." *Organization for a Better Austin v. Keefe,* 402 U.S. 415, 419 (1971). The District Court for the Southern District of New York in the New York Times case and the District Court for the District of Columbia and the Court of Appeals for the District of Columbia Circuit in the Washington Post case held that the Government had not met that burden. We agree....

■ MR. JUSTICE BLACK, with whom MR. JUSTICE DOUGLAS joins, concurring.

I adhere to the view that the Government's case against the Washington Post should have been dismissed and that the injunction against the New York Times should have been vacated without oral argument when the cases were first presented to this Court. I believe that every moment's continuance of the injunctions against these newspapers amounts to a flagrant, indefensible, and continuing violation of the First Amendment.... In my view it is unfortunate that some of my Brethren are apparently willing to hold that the publication of news may sometimes be enjoined. Such a holding would make a shambles of the First Amendment....

In seeking injunctions against these newspapers and in its presentation to the Court, the Executive Branch seems to have forgotten the essential purpose and history of the First Amendment. When the Constitution was adopted, many people strongly opposed it because the document contained no Bill of Rights to safeguard certain basic freedoms. They especially feared that the new powers granted to a central government might be interpreted to permit the government to curtail freedom of religion, press, assembly, and speech. In response to an overwhelming public clamor, James Madison offered a series of amendments to satisfy citizens that these great liberties would remain safe and beyond the power of government to abridge.... The Bill of Rights changed the original Constitution into a new charter under which no branch of government could abridge the people's freedoms of press, speech, religion, and assembly. Yet the Solicitor General argues and some members of the Court appear to agree that the general powers of the Government adopted in the original Constitution should be interpreted to limit and restrict the specific and emphatic guarantees of the Bill of Rights adopted later. I can imagine no greater perversion of history. Madison and the other Framers of the First Amendment, able men that they were, wrote in language they earnestly believed could never be misunderstood: "Congress shall make no law ... abridging the freedom ... of the press...." Both the history and language of the First Amendment support the view that the press must be left free to publish news, whatever the source, without censorship, injunctions, or prior restraints.

In the First Amendment the Founding Fathers gave the free press the protection it must have to fulfill its essential role in our democracy. The press was to serve the governed, not the governors. The Government's power to censor the press was abolished so that the press would remain forever free to censure the Government. The press was protected so that it could bare the secrets of government and inform the people. Only a free and un-restrained press can effectively expose deception in government. And paramount among the responsibilities of a free press is the duty to prevent any part of the government from deceiving the people and sending them off to distant lands to die of foreign fevers and foreign shot and shell. In my view, far from deserving condemnation for their courageous reporting, the New York Times, the Washington Post, and other newspapers should be commended for serving the purpose that the Founding Fathers saw so clearly. In revealing the workings of government that led to the Vietnam war, the newspapers nobly did precisely that which the Founders hoped and trusted they would do.

The Government's case here is based on premises entirely different from those that guided the Framers of the First Amendment. . . . [T]he Government argues in its brief that in spite of the First Amendment, "[t]he authority of the Executive Department to protect the nation against publication of information whose disclosure would endanger the national security stems from two interrelated sources: the constitutional power of the President over the conduct of foreign affairs and his authority as Commander-in-Chief."

In other words, we are asked to hold that despite the First Amendment's emphatic command, the Executive Branch, the Congress, and the Judiciary can make laws enjoining publication of current news and abridging freedom of the press in the name of "national security." The Government does not even attempt to rely on any act of Congress. Instead it makes the bold and dangerously far-reaching contention that the courts should take it upon themselves to "make" a law abridging freedom of the press in the name of equity, presidential power and national security, even when the representatives of the people in Congress have adhered to the command of the First Amendment and refused to make such a law. To find that the President has "inherent power" to halt the publication of news by resort to the courts would wipe out the First Amendment and destroy the fundamental liberty and security of the very people the Government hopes to make "secure." No one can read the history of the adoption of the First Amendment without being convinced beyond any doubt that it was injunctions like those sought here that Madison and his collaborators intended to outlaw in this Nation for all time. . . .

■ [JUSTICE DOUGLAS's concurring opinion, joined by JUSTICE BLACK, is omitted.]

■ MR. JUSTICE BRENNAN, concurring.

I write separately in these cases only to emphasize what should be apparent: that our judgments in the present cases may not be taken to indicate the propriety, in the future, of issuing temporary stays and restraining orders to block the publication of material sought to be suppressed by the Government. So far as I can determine, never before has the United States sought to enjoin a newspaper from publishing information in its possession. The relative novelty of the questions presented, the necessary haste with which decisions were reached, the magnitude of the interests asserted, and the fact that all the parties have concentrated their arguments upon the question whether permanent restraints were proper may have justified at least some of the restraints heretofore imposed in these cases. Certainly it is difficult to fault the several courts below for seeking to assure that the issues here involved were preserved for ultimate review by this Court. But even if it be assumed that some of the interim restraints were proper in the two cases before us, that assumption has no bearing upon the propriety of similar judicial action in the future. To begin with, there has now been ample time for reflection and judgment; whatever values there may be in the preservation of novel questions for appellate review may not support any restraints in the future. More important, the First Amendment stands as an absolute bar to the imposition of judicial restraints in circumstances of the kind presented by these cases.

The error that has pervaded these cases from the outset was the granting of any injunctive relief whatsoever, interim or otherwise. The entire thrust of the Government's claim throughout these cases has been that publication of the material sought to be enjoined "could," or "might," or "may" prejudice the national interest in various ways. But the First Amendment tolerates absolutely no prior judicial restraints of the press predicated upon surmise or conjecture that untoward consequences may result. Our cases, it is true, have indicated that there is a single, extremely narrow class of cases in which the First Amendment's ban on prior judicial restraint may be overridden. Our cases have thus far indicated that such cases may arise only when the Nation "is at war," *Schenck v. United States*, 249 U.S. 47, 52 (1919), during which times "[n]o one would question but that a government might prevent actual obstruction to its recruiting service or the publication of the sailing dates of transports or the number and location of troops." *Near v. Minnesota ex rel. Olson*, 283 U.S. 697, 716 (1931). Even if the present world situation were assumed to be tantamount to a time of war, or if the power of presently available armaments would justify even in peacetime the suppression of information that would set in motion a nuclear holocaust, in neither of these actions has the Government presented or even alleged that publication of items from or based upon the material at issue would cause the happening of an event of that nature. "[T]he chief purpose of [the First Amendment's] guaranty [is] to prevent previous restraints upon publication." *Near v. Minnesota*, [283 U.S.] at 713. Thus, only governmental allegation and proof that publication must inevitably, directly, and immediately cause the occurrence of an event kindred to imperiling the safety of a transport already at sea can support even the issuance of an interim restraining order. In no event may mere conclusions be sufficient: for if the Executive Branch seeks judicial aid in preventing publication, it must inevitably submit the basis upon which that aid is sought to scrutiny by the judiciary. And therefore, every restraint issued in this case, whatever its form, has violated the First Amendment—and not less so because that restraint was justified as necessary to afford the courts an opportunity to examine the claim more thoroughly. Unless and until the Government has clearly made out its case, the First Amendment commands that no injunction may issue.

■ MR. JUSTICE STEWART, with whom MR. JUSTICE WHITE joins, concurring.

In the governmental structure created by our Constitution, the Executive is endowed with enormous power in the two related areas of national defense and international relations. This power, largely unchecked by the Legislative and Judicial branches, has been pressed to the very hilt since the advent of the nuclear missile age. For better or for worse, the simple fact is that a President of the United States possesses vastly greater constitutional independence in these two vital areas of power than does, say, a prime minister of a country with a parliamentary form of government.

In the absence of the governmental checks and balances present in other areas of our national life, the only effective restraint upon executive policy and power in the areas of national defense and international affairs may lie in an enlightened citizenry—in an informed and critical public opinion which alone can here protect the values of democratic government. For this reason, it is perhaps here that a press that is alert, aware, and free most vitally serves the basic purpose of the First Amendment. For without an informed and free press there cannot be an enlightened people.

Yet it is elementary that the successful conduct of international diplomacy and the maintenance of an effective national defense require both confidentiality and secrecy. Other nations can hardly deal with this Nation in an atmosphere of mutual trust unless they can be assured that their confidences will be kept. And within our own executive departments, the development of considered and intelligent international policies would be impossible if those charged with their formulation could not communicate with each other freely, frankly, and in confidence. In the area of basic national defense the frequent need for absolute secrecy is, of course, self-evident.

I think there can be but one answer to this dilemma, if dilemma it be. The responsibility must be where the power is. If the Constitution gives the Executive a large degree of unshared power in the conduct of foreign affairs and the maintenance of our national defense, then under the Constitution the Executive must have the largely unshared duty to determine and preserve the degree of internal security necessary to exercise that power successfully. . . . [I]t is clear to me that it is the constitutional duty of the Executive—as a matter of sovereign prerogative and not as a matter of law as the courts know law—through the promulgation and enforcement of executive regulations, to protect the confidentiality necessary to carry out its responsibilities in the fields of international relations and national defense.

This is not to say that Congress and the courts have no role to play. Undoubtedly Congress has the power to enact specific and appropriate criminal laws to protect government property and preserve government secrets. Congress has passed such laws, and several of them are of very colorable relevance to the apparent circumstances of these cases. And if a criminal prosecution is instituted, it will be the responsibility of the courts to decide the applicability of the criminal law under which the charge is brought. Moreover, if Congress should pass a specific law authorizing civil proceedings in this field, the courts would likewise have the duty to decide the constitutionality of such a law as well as its applicability to the facts proved.

But in the cases before us we are asked neither to construe specific regulations nor to apply specific laws. We are asked, instead, to perform a function that the Constitution gave to the Executive, not the Judiciary. We are asked, quite simply, to prevent the publication by two newspapers of material that the Executive Branch insists should not, in the national interest, be published. I am convinced that the Executive is correct with respect to some of the documents involved. But I cannot say that disclosure of any of them will surely result in direct, immediate, and irreparable damage to our Nation or its people. That being so, there can under the First Amendment be but one judicial resolution of the issues before us. I join the judgments of the Court.

■ MR. JUSTICE WHITE, with whom MR. JUSTICE STEWART joins, concurring.

I concur in today's judgments, but only because of the concededly extraordinary protection against prior restraints enjoyed by the press under our constitutional system. I do not say that in no circumstances would the First Amendment permit an injunction against publishing information about government plans or operations. Nor, after examining the materials the Government characterizes as the most sensitive and destructive, can I deny that revelation of these documents will do substantial damage to public interests. Indeed, I am confident that their disclosure will have that result. But I nevertheless agree that the United States has not satisfied the very heavy burden that it must meet to warrant an injunction against publication in these cases, at least in the absence of express and appropriately limited congressional authorization for prior restraints in circumstances such as these.

The Government's position is simply stated: The responsibility of the Executive for the conduct of the foreign affairs and for the security of the Nation is so basic that the President is entitled to an injunction against publication of a newspaper story whenever he can convince a court that the information to be revealed threatens "grave and irreparable" injury to the public interest; and the injunction should issue whether or not the material to be published is classified, whether or not publication would be lawful under relevant criminal statutes enacted by Congress, and regardless of the circumstances by which the newspaper came into possession of the information.

At least in the absence of legislation by Congress, based on its own investigations and findings, I am quite unable to agree that the inherent powers of the Executive and the courts reach so far as to authorize remedies having such sweeping potential for inhibiting publications by the press. . . . To sustain the Government in these cases would start the courts down a long and hazardous road that I am not willing to travel, at least without congressional guidance and direction. . . .

[T]erminating the ban on publication of the relatively few sensitive documents the Government now seeks to suppress does not mean that the law either requires or invites newspapers or others to publish them or that they will be immune from criminal action if they do. Prior restraints require an unusually heavy justification under the First Amendment; but failure by the Government to justify prior restraints does not measure its constitutional entitlement to a conviction for criminal publication. That the Government mistakenly chose to proceed by injunction does not mean that it could not successfully proceed in another way.

When the Espionage Act was under consideration in 1917, Congress eliminated from the bill a provision that would have given the President broad powers in time of war to proscribe, under threat of criminal penalty, the publication of various categories of information related to the national defense. Congress at that time was unwilling to clothe the President with such far-reaching powers to monitor the press, and those opposed to this part of the legislation assumed that a necessary concomitant of such power was the power to "filter out the news to the people through some man." 55 Cong. Rec. 2008 (remarks of Sen. Ashurst). However, these same members of Congress appeared to have little doubt that newspapers would be subject to criminal prosecution if they insisted on publishing information of the type Congress had itself determined should not be revealed. Senator Ashurst, for example, was quite sure that the editor of such a newspaper "should be punished if he did publish information as to the movements of the fleet, the troops, the aircraft, the location of powder factories, the location of defense works, and all that sort of thing."

The Criminal Code contains numerous provisions potentially relevant to these cases. Section 797 makes it a crime to publish certain photographs or drawings of military installations. Section 798, also in precise language, proscribes knowing and willful publication of any classified information concerning the cryptographic systems or communication intelligence activities of the United States as well as any information obtained from communication intelligence operations. If any of the material here at issue is of this nature, the newspapers are presumably now on full notice of the position of the United States and must face the consequences if they publish. I would have no difficulty in sustaining convictions under these sections on facts that would not justify the intervention of equity and the imposition of a prior restraint.

The same would be true under those sections of the Criminal Code casting a wider net to protect the national defense. Section 793(e) makes it a criminal act for any unauthorized possessor of a document "relating to the national defense" either (1) willfully to communicate or cause to be communicated that document to any person not entitled to receive it or (2) willfully to retain the document and fail to deliver it to an officer of the United States entitled to receive it. The subsection was added in 1950 because pre-existing law provided no penalty for the unauthorized possessor unless demand for the documents was made. "The dangers surrounding the unauthorized possession of such items are self-evident, and it is deemed advisable to require their surrender in such a case, regardless of demand, especially since their unauthorized possession may be unknown to the authorities who would otherwise make the demand." S. Rep. No. 2369, pt. 1, 81st Cong., 2d Sess., 9 (1950). . . .

It is thus clear that Congress has addressed itself to the problems of protecting the security of the country and the national defense from unauthorized disclosure of potentially damaging information. Cf. *Youngstown Sheet & Tube Co. v. Sawyer*, 343 U.S. 579, 585–586 (1952). It has not, however, authorized the injunctive remedy against threatened publication. It has apparently been satisfied to rely on criminal sanctions and their deterrent effect on the responsible as well as the irresponsible press. I am not, of course, saying that either of these newspapers has yet committed a crime or that either would commit a crime if it published all the material now in its possession. That matter must await resolution in the context of a criminal proceeding if one is instituted by the United States. In that event, the issue of guilt or innocence would be determined by procedures and standards quite different from those that have purported to govern these injunctive proceedings.

■ MR. JUSTICE MARSHALL, concurring.

The Government contends that the only issue in these cases is whether in a suit by the United States, "the First Amendment bars a court from prohibiting a newspaper from publishing material whose disclosure would pose a grave and immediate danger to the security of the United States." With all due respect, I believe the ultimate issue in this case is even more basic than the one posed by the Solicitor General. The issue is whether this Court or the Congress has the power to make law.

In these cases there is no problem concerning the President's power to classify information as "secret" or "top secret." Congress has specifically recognized Presidential authority . . . to classify documents and information. See, *e.g.*, 18 U.S.C. § 798. Nor is there any issue here regarding the President's power as Chief Executive and Commander in Chief to protect national security by disciplining employees who disclose information and by taking precautions to prevent leaks.

The problem here is whether in these particular cases the Executive Branch has authority to invoke the equity jurisdiction of the courts to protect what it believes to be the national interest. See *In re Debs*, 158 U.S. 564, 584 (1895). The Government argues that in addition to the inherent power of any government to protect itself, the President's power to conduct foreign affairs and his position as Commander in Chief give him authority to impose censorship on the press to protect his ability to deal effectively with foreign nations and to conduct the military affairs of the country. . . .

It would, however, be utterly inconsistent with the concept of separation of powers for this Court to use its power of contempt to prevent behavior that Congress has specifically declined to prohibit. There would be a similar damage to the basic concept of these co-equal branches of Government if when the Executive Branch has adequate authority granted by Congress to protect "national security" it can choose instead to invoke the contempt power of a court to enjoin the threatened conduct. The Constitution provides that Congress shall make laws, the President execute laws, and courts interpret laws. *Youngstown Sheet & Tube Co. v. Sawyer*, 343 U.S. 579 (1952). It did not provide for government by injunction in which the courts and the Executive Branch can "make law" without regard to the action of Congress. . . .

■ MR. CHIEF JUSTICE BURGER, dissenting.

So clear are the constitutional limitations on prior restraint against expression, that from the time of *Near v. Minnesota ex rel. Olson*, 283 U.S. 697 (1931), until recently in *Organization for a Better Austin v. Keefe*, 402 U.S. 415 (1971), we have had little occasion to be concerned with cases involving prior restraints against news reporting on matters of public interest. There is, therefore, little variation among the members of the Court in terms of resistance to prior restraints against publication. Adherence to this basic constitutional principle, however, does not make these cases simple ones. In these cases, the imperative of a free and unfettered press comes into collision with another imperative, the effective functioning of a complex modern government and specifically the effective exercise of certain constitutional powers of the Executive. Only those who view the First Amendment as an absolute in all circumstances—a view I respect, but reject—can find such cases as these to be simple or easy.

These cases are not simple for another and more immediate reason. We do not know the facts of the cases. No District Judge knew all the facts. No Court of Appeals Judge knew all the facts. No member of this Court knows all the facts.

Why are we in this posture, in which only those judges to whom the First Amendment is absolute and permits of no restraint in any circumstances or for any reason, are really in a position to act?

I suggest we are in this posture because these cases have been conducted in unseemly haste. . . . The prompt settling of these cases reflects our universal abhorrence of prior restraint. But prompt judicial action does not mean unjudicial haste.

Here, moreover, the frenetic haste is due in large part to the manner in which the Times proceeded from the date it obtained the purloined documents. It seems reasonably clear now that the haste precluded reasonable and deliberate judicial treatment of these cases and was not warranted. . . .

An issue of this importance should be tried and heard in a judicial atmosphere conducive to thoughtful, reflective deliberation, especially when haste, in terms of hours, is unwarranted in light of the long period the Times, by its own choice, deferred publication.[4]

It is not disputed that the Times has had unauthorized possession of the documents for three to four months, during which it has had its expert analysts studying them, presumably digesting them and preparing the material for publication. During all of this time, the Times, presumably in its capacity as trustee of the public's "right to know," has held up publication for purposes it considered proper and thus public knowledge was delayed. No doubt this was for a good reason; the analysis of 7,000 pages of complex material drawn from a vastly greater volume of material would inevitably take time and the writing of good news stories takes time. But why should the United States Government, from whom this information was illegally acquired by someone, along with all the counsel, trial judges, and appellate judges be placed under needless pressure? After these months of deferral, the alleged "right to know" has somehow and suddenly become a right that must be vindicated instanter.

Would it have been unreasonable, since the newspaper could anticipate the Government's objections to release of secret material, to give the Government an opportunity to review the entire collection and determine whether agreement could be reached on publication? Stolen or not, if security was not in fact jeopardized, much of the material could not doubt have been declassified, since it spans a period ending in 1968. With such an approach—one that great newspapers have in the past practiced and stated editorially to be the duty of an honorable press—the newspapers and Government might well have narrowed the area of disagreement as to what was and was not publishable, leaving the remainder to be resolved in orderly litigation, if necessary. To me it is hardly believable that a newspaper long regarded as a great institution in American life would fail to perform one of the basic and simple duties of every citizen with respect to the discovery or possession of stolen property or secret government documents. That duty, I had thought—perhaps naively—was to report forthwith, to responsible public officers. This duty rests on taxi drivers, Justices, and the New York Times. . . .

I should add that I am in general agreement with much of what Mr. Justice WHITE has expressed with respect to penal sanctions concerning communication or retention of documents or information relating to the national defense. . . .

■ MR. JUSTICE HARLAN, with whom THE CHIEF JUSTICE and MR. JUSTICE BLACKMUN join, dissenting.

. . . With all respect, I consider that the Court has been almost irresponsibly feverish in dealing with these cases.

---

[4] As noted elsewhere the Times conducted its analysis of the 47 volumes of Government documents over a period of several months and did so with a degree of security that a government might envy. Such security was essential, of course, to protect the enterprise from others. Meanwhile the Times has copyrighted its material and there were strong intimations in the oral argument that the Times contemplated enjoining its use by any other publisher in violation of its copyright. Paradoxically this would afford it a protection, analogous to prior restraint, against all others—a protection the Times denies the Government of the United States.

Both the Court of Appeals for the Second Circuit and the Court of Appeals for the District of Columbia Circuit rendered judgment on June 23. The New York Times' petition for certiorari, its motion for accelerated consideration thereof, and its application for interim relief were filed in this Court on June 24 at about 11 a.m. The application of the United States for interim relief in the Post case was also filed here on June 24 at about 7:15 p.m. This Court's order setting a hearing before us on June 26 at 11 a.m., a course which I joined only to avoid the possibility of even more peremptory action by the Court, was issued less than 24 hours before. The record in the Post case was filed with the Clerk shortly before 1 p.m. on June 25; the record in the Times case did not arrive until 7 or 8 o'clock that same night. The briefs of the parties were received less than two hours before argument on June 26.

This frenzied train of events took place in the name of the presumption against prior restraints created by the First Amendment. Due regard for the extraordinarily important and difficult questions involved in these litigations should have led the Court to shun such a precipitate timetable. In order to decide the merits of these cases properly, some or all of the following questions should have been faced:

1. Whether the Attorney General is authorized to bring these suits in the name of the United States. Compare *In re Debs,* 158 U.S. 564 (1895), with *Youngstown Sheet & Tube Co. v. Sawyer,* 343 U.S. 579 (1952). This question involves as well the construction and validity of a singularly opaque statute—the Espionage Act, 18 U.S.C. § 793(e).

2. Whether the First Amendment permits the federal courts to enjoin publication of stories which would present a serious threat to national security. See *Near v. Minnesota*, ex rel. *Olson*, 283 U.S. 697, 716 (1931) (dictum).

3. Whether the threat to publish highly secret documents is of itself a sufficient implication of national security to justify an injunction on the theory that regardless of the contents of the documents harm enough results simply from the demonstration of such a breach of secrecy.

4. Whether the unauthorized disclosure of any of these particular documents would seriously impair the national security.

5. What weight should be given to the opinion of high officers in the Executive Branch of the Government with respect to questions 3 and 4.

6. Whether the newspapers are entitled to retain and use the documents notwithstanding the seemingly uncontested facts that the documents, or the originals of which they are duplicates, were purloined from the Government's possession and that the newspapers received them with knowledge that they had been feloniously acquired.

7. Whether the threatened harm to the national security or the Government's possessory interest in the documents justifies the issuance of an injunction against publication in light of—

> a. The strong First Amendment policy against prior restraints on publication;

> b. The doctrine against enjoining conduct in violation of criminal statutes; and

> c. The extent to which the materials at issue have apparently already been otherwise disseminated.

These are difficult questions of fact, of law, and of judgment; the potential consequences of erroneous decision are enormous. The time which has been available to us, to the lower courts, and to the parties has been wholly inadequate for giving these cases the kind of consideration they deserve. . . .

Forced as I am to reach the merits of these cases, I dissent from the opinion and judgments of the Court. Within the severe limitations imposed by the time constraints under which I have been required to operate, I can only state my reasons in telescoped form, even though in different circumstances I would have felt constrained to deal with the cases in the fuller sweep indicated above.

. . . It is plain to me that the scope of the judicial function in passing upon the activities of the Executive Branch of the Government in the field of foreign affairs is very narrowly restricted. This view is, I think, dictated by the concept of separation of powers upon which our constitutional system rests.

In a speech on the floor of the House of Representatives, Chief Justice John Marshall, then a member of that body, stated: "The President is the sole organ of the nation in its external relations, and its sole representative with foreign nations." From that time, shortly after the founding of the Nation, to this, there has been no substantial challenge to this description of the scope of executive power. See *United States v. Curtiss–Wright Export Corp.*, 299 U.S. 304, 319–321 (1936).

From this constitutional primacy in the field of foreign affairs, it seems to me that certain conclusions necessarily follow. Some of these were stated concisely by President Washington, declining the request of the House of Representatives for the papers leading up to the negotiation of the Jay Treaty:

> The nature of foreign negotiations requires caution, and their success must often depend on secrecy; and even when brought to a conclusion a full disclosure of all the measures, demands, or eventual concessions which may have been proposed or contemplated would be extremely impolitic; for this might have a pernicious influence on future negotiations, or produce immediate inconveniences, perhaps danger and mischief, in relation to other powers.

J. Richardson, Messages and Papers of the Presidents 194–195 (1896).

The power to evaluate the "pernicious influence" of premature disclosure is not, however, lodged in the Executive alone. I agree that, in performance of its duty to protect the values of the First Amendment against political pressures, the judiciary must review the initial Executive determination to the point of satisfying itself that the subject matter of the dispute does lie within the proper compass of the President's foreign relations power. . . .

But in my judgment the judiciary may not properly redetermine for itself the probable impact of disclosure on the national security.

> [T]he very nature of executive decisions as to foreign policy is political, not judicial. Such decisions are wholly confided by our Constitution to the political departments of the government, Executive and Legislative. They are delicate, complex, and involve large elements of prophecy. They are and should be undertaken only by those directly responsible to the people whose welfare they advance or imperil. They are deci-

sions of a kind for which the Judiciary has neither aptitude, facilities nor responsibility and have long been held to belong in the domain of political power not subject to judicial intrusion or inquiry.

Chicago & Southern Air Lines, Inc. v. Waterman Steamship Corp., 333 U.S. 103, 111 (1948) (Jackson, J.).

Even if there is some room for the judiciary to override the executive determination, it is plain that the scope of review must be exceedingly narrow. I can see no indication in the opinions of either the District Court or the Court of Appeals in the *Post* litigation that the conclusions of the Executive were given even the deference owing to an administrative agency, much less that owing to a co-equal branch of the Government operating within the field of its constitutional prerogative. . . .

Pending further hearings in each case conducted under the appropriate ground rules, I would continue the restraints on publication. I cannot believe that the doctrine prohibiting prior restraints reaches to the point of preventing courts from maintaining the *status quo* long enough to act responsibly in matters of such national importance as those involved here.

■ Mr. Justice Blackmun, dissenting.

. . . The First Amendment, after all, is only one part of an entire Constitution. Article II of the great document vests in the Executive Branch primary power over the conduct of foreign affairs and places in that branch the responsibility for the Nation's safety. Each provision of the Constitution is important, and I cannot subscribe to a doctrine of unlimited absolutism for the First Amendment at the cost of downgrading other provisions. . . .

I therefore would remand these cases to be developed expeditiously, of course, but on a schedule permitting the orderly presentation of evidence from both sides, with the use of discovery, if necessary, as authorized by the rules, and with the preparation of briefs, oral argument, and court opinions of a quality better than has been seen to this point. . . .

The Court, however, decides the cases today the other way. I therefore add one final comment.

I strongly urge, and sincerely hope, that these two newspapers will be fully aware of their ultimate responsibilities to the United States of America. Judge Wilkey, dissenting in the District of Columbia case, after a review of only the affidavits before his court (the basic papers had not then been made available by either party), concluded that there were a number of examples of documents that, if in the possession of the Post, and if published, "could clearly result in great harm to the nation," and he defined "harm" to mean "the death of soldiers, the destruction of alliances, the greatly increased difficulty of negotiation with our enemies, the inability of our diplomats to negotiate. . . ." I, for one, have now been able to give at least some cursory study not only to the affidavits, but to the material itself. I regret to say that from this examination I fear that Judge Wilkey's statements have possible foundation. I therefore share his concern. I hope that damage has not already been done. If, however, damage has been done, and if, with the Court's action today, these newspapers proceed to publish the critical documents and there results therefrom "the death of soldiers, the destruction of alliances, the greatly increased difficulty of negotiation with our enemies, the inability of our diplomats to negotiate," to which list I might add the factors of prolongation of the war and of further delay in the freeing of United States prisoners, then the Nation's people will know where the responsibility for these sad consequences rests.

NOTES

1. *Prior Restraints*. One of the main purposes of the First Amendment was to prohibit prior restraints on speech. As you have seen, Blackstone's COMMEN-TARIES, the leading legal treatise of the founding era, argued that freedom of the press was limited to prohibiting prior restraints. Thus, under one reading of the First Amendment, the freedoms of speech and press protects speakers against prior restraints on their speech, but not against subsequent punishment. *Patterson v. Colorado*, 205 U.S. 454, 462 (1907). This makes distinguishing between prior restraint and punishment essential. According to Justice Kennedy, "In its simple, most blatant form, a prior restraint is a law which requires submission of speech to an official who may grant or deny permission to utter or publish it based upon its contents. . . . In contrast are laws which punish speech or expression only after it has occurred and been found unlawful." *Alexander v. United States*, 509 U.S. 544, 566 (1993). One problem, however, is that "some governmental actions may have the characteristics both of punishment and prior restraint." *Id.* at 567.

While the distinction is difficult to manage, it has a theoretical justification. As the Court stated in *Southeastern Promotions, Ltd. v. Conrad*, "Behind the distinction is a theory deeply etched in our law: a free society prefers to punish the few who abuse rights of speech after they break the law than to throttle them and all others beforehand. It is always difficult to know in advance what an individual will say, and the line between legitimate and illegitimate speech is often so finely drawn that the risks of freewheeling censorship are formidable." 420 U.S. 546, 559 (1975). Perhaps more important are the institutional considerations. Subsequent punishment is put to a jury, while judges or (more commonly) executive officials administer licensing schemes.

2. Prior restraints commonly take two forms. One is a compulsory licensing scheme, in which a speaker must obtain government approval before speaking. The other is a judicial injunction, like the one at issue in *The Pentagon Papers Case*.

The Court first reviewed a licensing law in *Lovell v. City of Griffin*. 303 U.S. 444 (1938). *Lovell* concerned a city ordinance that required pamphleteers to obtain written permission from the city manager before distributing their pamphlets. The plaintiff was a Jehovah's Witness convicted under the ordinance for distributing religious material. The Court struck the ordinance down, declaring that the law "strikes at the very foundation of the freedom of the press by subjecting it to license and censorship." *Id.* at 451. Despite this strong language, the Court has not made licensing systems unconstitutional per se. In *Freedman v. Maryland*, the Court held that certain procedural safeguards would allow a licensing system to avoid constitutional infirmity. 380 U.S. 51, 58–59 (1965) (striking down a state motion picture censorship statute). The burden of proof must be on the censor, there must be judicial review of the censor's decision to deny a license, and there must be a mechanism for a "prompt final judicial decision" to minimize the deterrent effect of a denial of a license. *Id.*

Another line of prior restraint cases involves judicial injunctions. In *Near v. Minnesota*, the Court addressed a Minnesota law that declared any "malicious, scandalous and defamatory newspaper, magazine or other periodical" to be a nuisance, and allowed county attorneys to obtain injunctions against their publication. 283 U.S. 697, 701–02 (1931). The Court considered the function of the law to be "the essence of censorship" and struck it down. *Id.* at 713. Writing for the four dissenters, Justice Butler argued that the regular publication of defamatory material was "an abuse of the right of free press" and that the law was not a prior restraint because it only enjoined further publication of defamatory material. *Id.* at 735–36 (Butler J., dissenting).

3. The Court's brief per curiam opinion in *The Pentagon Papers Case* notes only that there is a "heavy presumption" against the validity of a prior restraint and that the government had failed to carry its burden. Prior restraints are not unconstitutional per se, and may be permissible depending on the content of the speech. Prior restraints involving imminent threats to national security, injunctions necessary to protect a defendant's right to a fair trial, or censorship of obscenity may be permissible. See *Near v. Minnesota*, 283 U.S. 697, 716 (1931). How would this case have come out if, instead of a prior restraint, the government had sought to punish the New York Times after the fact?

4. Do the protections against prior restraints apply to everyone, or just to the institutional press? Suppose the government had become aware that Dr. Ellsberg had made copies of the Pentagon Papers, and it sought an injunction against his disseminating them to the public in any way. Would the legal analysis have been any different?

Branzburg v. Hayes

408 U.S. 665 (1972)

■ Opinion of the Court by MR. JUSTICE WHITE, announced by THE CHIEF JUSTICE.

The issue in these cases is whether requiring newsmen to appear and testify before state or federal grand juries abridges the freedom of speech and press guaranteed by the First Amendment. We hold that it does not.

I

[Paul Branzburg, a staff reporter, wrote two articles for the Courier–Journal about drug manufacturing and use in Kentucky. The first article included a photograph of hashish held in an unidentified person's hands above a laboratory table. The second article included interviews with several marijuana users. To gain access to these sources, Branzburg promised that he would not identify those interviewed. He was subpoenaed by two grand juries but refused to identify his sources. He asserted that he was protected by a reporter's privilege in the First Amendment of the U.S. Constitution. The Supreme Court consolidated Branzburg with cases involving a reporter from the New York Times and a television news reporter, who wrote about Black Panther groups allegedly planning acts of civil disorder.—Editors]

II

Petitioners . . . press First Amendment claims that may be simply put: that to gather news it is often necessary to agree either not to identify the source of information published or to publish only part of the facts revealed, or both; that if the reporter is nevertheless forced to reveal these confidences to a grand jury, the source so identified and other confidential sources of other reporters will be measurably deterred from furnishing publishable information, all to the detriment of the free flow of information protected by the First Amendment. Although the newsmen in these cases do not claim an absolute privilege against official interrogation in all circumstances, they assert that the reporter should not be forced either to appear or to testify before a grand jury or at trial until and unless sufficient grounds are shown for believing that the reporter possesses information relevant to a crime the grand jury is investigating, that the information the reporter has is unavailable from other sources, and that the need for the information is sufficiently compelling to override the claimed invasion of First Amendment interests occasioned by the disclosure. Principally relied upon are prior cases emphasizing the importance of the First Amendment guarantees to individual development and to our system of representative government, decisions requiring that official action with adverse impact on First Amendment rights be justified by a public interest that is "compelling" or "paramount," and those precedents establishing the principle that justifiable governmental goals may not be achieved by unduly broad means having an unnecessary impact on protected rights of speech, press, or association. The heart of the claim is that the burden on news gathering resulting from compelling reporters to disclose confidential information outweighs any public interest in obtaining the information. . . .

The sole issue before us is the obligation of reporters to respond to grand jury subpoenas as other citizens do and to answer questions relevant to an investigation into the commission of crime. Citizens generally are not constitutionally immune from grand jury subpoenas; and neither the First Amendment nor any other constitutional provision protects the average citizen from disclosing to a grand jury information that he has received in confidence. The claim is, however, that reporters are exempt from these obligations because if forced to respond to subpoenas and identify their sources or disclose other confidences, their informants will refuse or be reluctant to furnish newsworthy information in the future. This asserted burden on news gathering is said to make compelled testimony from newsmen constitutionally suspect and to require a privileged position for them.

It is clear that the First Amendment does not invalidate every incidental burdening of the press that may result from the enforcement of civil or criminal statutes of general applicability. Under prior cases, otherwise valid laws serving substantial public interests may be enforced against the press as against others, despite the possible burden that may be imposed. The Court has emphasized that "the publisher of a newspaper has no special immunity from the application of general laws. He has no special privilege to invade the rights and liberties of others." *Associated Press* v. *NLRB*, 301 U.S. 103, 132–133 (1937). It was there held that the Associated Press, a news-gathering and disseminating organization, was not exempt from the requirements of the National Labor Relations Act. The holding was reaffirmed in *Oklahoma Press Publishing Co.* v. *Walling*, 327 U.S. 186, 192–193 (1946), where the Court rejected the claim that applying the Fair Labor Standards Act to a newspaper publishing business would abridge the freedom of press guaranteed by the First Amendment. *Associated Press* v. *United States*, 326 U.S. 1 (1945), similarly overruled assertions that the First Amendment precluded application of the Sherman Act to a newsgathering and disseminating organization. Likewise, a newspaper may be subjected to nondiscriminatory forms of general taxation. *Grosjean* v. *American Press Co.*, 297 U.S. 233, 250 (1936); *Murdock* v. *Pennsylvania*, 319 U.S. 105, 112 (1943). . . .

It has generally been held that the First Amendment does not guarantee the press a constitutional right of special access to information not available to the public generally. In *Zemel* v. *Rusk,* 318 U.S. 1 (1965), for example, the Court sustained the Government's refusal to validate passports to Cuba even though that restriction "render[ed] less than wholly free the flow of information concerning that country." The ban on travel was held constitutional, for "the right to speak and publish does not carry with it the unrestrained right to gather information."

Despite the fact that news gathering may be hampered, the press is regularly excluded from grand jury proceedings, our own conferences, the meetings of other official bodies gathered in executive session, and the meetings of private organizations. Newsmen have no constitutional right of access to the scenes of crime or disaster when the general public is excluded, and they may be prohibited from attending or publishing information about trials if such restrictions are necessary to assure a defendant a fair trial before an impartial tribunal. . . .

It is thus not surprising that the great weight of authority is that newsmen are not exempt from the normal duty of appearing before a grand jury and answering questions relevant to a criminal investigation. At common law, courts consistently refused to recognize the existence of any privilege authorizing a newsman to refuse to reveal confidential information to a grand jury. In 1958, a news gatherer asserted for the first time that the First Amendment exempted confidential information from public disclosure pursuant to a subpoena issued in a civil suit, *Garland* v. *Torre,* 259 F.2d 545 (CA2), cert. denied, 358 U.S. 910 (1958), but the claim was denied, and this argument has been almost uniformly rejected since then. . . .

A number of States have provided newsmen a statutory privilege of varying breadth, but the majority have not done so, and none has been provided by federal statute. Until now the only testimonial privilege for unofficial witnesses that is rooted in the Federal Constitution is the Fifth Amendment privilege against compelled self-incrimination. We are asked to create another by interpreting the First Amendment to grant newsmen a testimonial privilege that other citizens do not enjoy. This we decline to do. Fair and effective law enforcement aimed at providing security for the person and property of the individual is a fundamental function of government, and the grand jury plays an important, constitutionally mandated role in this process. On the records now before us, we perceive no basis for holding that the public interest in law enforcement and in ensuring effective grand jury proceedings is insufficient to override the consequential, but uncertain, burden on news gathering that is said to result from insisting that reporters, like other citizens, respond to relevant questions put to them in the course of a valid grand jury investigation or criminal trial. . . .

The argument that the flow of news will be diminished by compelling reporters to aid the grand jury in a criminal investigation is not irrational, nor are the records before us silent on the matter. But we remain unclear how often and to what extent informers are actually deterred from furnishing information when newsmen are forced to testify before a grand jury. The available data indicate that some newsmen rely a great deal on confidential sources and that some informants are particularly sensitive to the threat of exposure and may be silenced if it is held by this Court that, ordinarily, newsmen must testify pursuant to subpoenas, but the evidence fails to demonstrate that there would be a significant constriction of the flow of news to the public if this Court reaffirms the prior common-law and constitutional rule regarding the testimonial obligations of newsmen. Estimates of the inhibiting effect of such subpoenas on the willingness of informants to make disclosures to newsmen are widely divergent and to a great extent speculative. It would be difficult to canvass the views of the informants themselves; surveys of reporters on this topic are chiefly opinions of predicted informant behavior and must be viewed in the light of the professional self-interest of the interviewees. Reliance by the press on confidential informants does not mean that all such sources will in fact dry up because of the later possible appearance of the newsman before a grand jury. The reporter may never be called and if he objects to testifying, the prosecution may not insist. . . .

Accepting the fact, however, that an undetermined number of informants not themselves implicated in crime will nevertheless, for whatever reason, refuse to talk to newsmen if they fear identification by a reporter in an official investigation, we cannot accept the argument that the public interest in possible future news about crime from undisclosed, unverified sources must take precedence over the public interest in pursuing and prosecuting those crimes reported to the press by informants and in thus deterring the commission of such crimes in the future. . . .

We are admonished that refusal to provide a First Amendment reporter's privilege will undermine the freedom of the press to collect and disseminate news. But this is not the lesson history teaches us. As noted previously, the common law recognized no such privilege, and the constitutional argument was not even asserted until 1958. From the beginning of our country the press has operated without constitutional protection for press informants, and the press has flourished. The existing constitutional rules have not been a serious obstacle to either the development or retention of confidential news sources by the press. . . .

The requirements of those cases which hold that a State's interest must be "compelling" or "paramount" to justify even an indirect burden on First Amendment rights, are also met here. As we have indicated, the investigation of crime by the grand jury implements a fundamental governmental role of securing the safety of the person and property of the citizen, and it appears to us that calling reporters to give testimony in the manner and for the reasons that other citizens are called "bears a reasonable relationship to the achievement of the governmental purpose asserted as its justification." If the test is that the government "convincingly show a substantial relation between the information sought and a subject of overriding and compelling state interest," *Gibson* v. *Florida Legislative Investigation Committee*, U.S. 539, 546 (1963), it is quite apparent (1) that the State has the necessary interest in extirpating the traffic in illegal drugs, in forestalling assassination attempts on the President, and in preventing the community from being disrupted by violent disorders endangering both persons and property; and (2) that, based on the stories [written by the petitioners], the grand jury called these reporters as they would others— because it was likely that they could supply information to help the government determine whether illegal conduct had occurred and, if it had, whether there was sufficient evidence to return an indictment.

Similar considerations dispose of the reporters' claims that preliminary to requiring their grand jury appearance, the State must show that a crime has been committed and that they possess relevant information not available from other sources, for only the grand jury itself can make this determination. The role of the grand jury as an important instrument of effective law enforcement necessarily includes an investigatory function with respect to determining whether a crime has been committed and who committed it. To this end it must call witnesses, in the manner best suited to perform its task. . . . It is only after the grand jury has examined the evidence that a determination of whether the proceeding will result in an indictment can be made. . . .

We are unwilling to embark the judiciary on a long and difficult journey to such an uncertain destination. The administration of a constitutional newsman's privilege would present practical and conceptual difficulties of a high order. Sooner or later, it would be necessary to define those categories of newsmen who qualified for the privilege, a questionable procedure in light of the traditional doctrine that liberty of the press is the right of the lonely pamphleteer who uses carbon paper or a mimeograph just as much as of the large metropolitan publisher who utilizes the latest photocomposition methods. Freedom of the press is a "fundamental personal right" which "is not confined to newspapers and periodicals. It necessarily embraces pamphlets and leaflets. . . . The press in its historic connotation comprehends every sort of publication which affords a vehicle of information and opinion." *Lovell* v. *Griffin*, 303 U.S. 444, 450, 452 (1938). See also *Mills* v. *Alabama*, 384 U.S. 214, 219 (1966); *Murdock* v. *Pennsylvania*, 319 U.S. 105, 111 (1943). The informative function asserted by representatives of the organized press in the present cases is also performed by lecturers, political pollsters, novelists, academic researchers, and dramatists. Almost any author may quite accurately assert that he is contributing to the flow of information to the public, that he relies on confidential sources of information, and that these sources will be silenced if he is forced to make disclosures before a grand jury.[40]

In each instance where a reporter is subpoenaed to testify, the courts would also be embroiled in preliminary factual and legal determinations with respect to whether the proper predicate had been laid for the reporter's appearance: Is there probable cause to believe a crime has been committed? Is it likely that the reporter has useful information gained in confidence? Could the grand jury obtain the information elsewhere? Is the official interest sufficient to outweigh the claimed privilege?

Thus, in the end, by considering whether enforcement of a particular law served a "compelling" governmental interest, the courts would be inextricably involved in distinguishing between the value of enforcing different criminal laws. By requiring testimony from a reporter in investigations involving some crimes but not in others, they would be making a value judgment that a legislature had declined to make, since in each case the criminal law involved would represent a considered legislative judgment, not constitutionally suspect, of what conduct is liable to criminal prosecution. The task of judges, like other officials outside the legislative branch, is not to make the law but to uphold it in accordance with their oaths. . . .

Finally, as we have earlier indicated, news gathering is not without its First Amendment protections, and grand jury investigations if instituted or conducted other than in good faith, would pose wholly different issues for

---

[40] Such a privilege might be claimed by groups that set up newspapers in order to engage in criminal activity and to, therefore, be insulated from grand jury inquiry, regardless of Fifth Amendment grants of immunity. It might appear that such "sham" newspapers would be easily distinguishable, yet the First Amendment ordinarily prohibits courts from inquiring into the content of expression, except in cases of obscenity or libel, and protects speech and publications regardless of their motivation, orthodoxy, truthfulness, timeliness, or taste. By affording a privilege to some organs of communication but not to others, courts would inevitably be discriminating on the basis of content.

resolution under the First Amendment. Official harassment of the press undertaken not for purposes of law enforcement but to disrupt a reporter's relationship with his news sources would have no justification. Grand juries are subject to judicial control and subpoenas to motions to quash. We do not expect courts will forget that grand juries must operate within the limits of the First Amendment as well as the Fifth. . . .

■ MR. JUSTICE STEWART, with whom MR. JUSTICE BRENNAN and MR. JUSTICE MARSHALL join, dissenting.

The Court's crabbed view of the First Amendment reflects a disturbing insensitivity to the critical role of an independent press in our society. The question whether a reporter has a constitutional right to a confidential relationship with his source is of first impression here, but the principles that should guide our decision are as basic as any to be found in the Constitution. While MR. JUSTICE POWELL's enigmatic concurring opinion gives some hope of a more flexible view in the future, the Court in these cases holds that a newsman has no First Amendment right to protect his sources when called before a grand jury. The Court thus invites state and federal authorities to undermine the historic independence of the press by attempting to annex the journalistic profession as an investigative arm of government. Not only will this decision impair performance of the press' constitutionally protected functions, but it will, I am convinced, in the long run, harm rather than help the administration of justice. . . .

■ [The concurring opinion of JUSTICE POWELL and the dissenting opinion of JUSTICE DOUGLAS are omitted.]

NOTES

1. *Who is the Press?* If members of "the press" are to be given special protections not accorded to ordinary members of the public, it is necessary to define who comprises "the press." The Court notes that this definition "would present practical and conceptual difficulties of a high order." This has been borne out in the scholarly debate over the proper interpretation of the Press Clause. One group of scholars has argued that the institutional press receives special protection under the Press Clause. E.g., Randall P. Bezanson, *Whither Freedom of the Press?*, 97 Iowa L. Rev. 1259 (2012); David A. Anderson, *Freedom of the Press*, 80 Tex. L. Rev. 429 (2002). Another group has argued that the clause protects every person's right to use the printing press and analogous technology to disseminate a message. E.g., Eugene Volokh, *Freedom for the Press as an Industry, or for the Press as a Technology? From the Framing to Today*, 160 U. Pa. L. Rev. 459 (2012).

Media stalwarts like the New York Times Company clearly qualify as "the press." What about advocacy journalists? What about student journalists? What about stringers (i.e., people who write occasionally for news media without having a formal contract)? What about writers for news organizations that do not make money and that operate at a loss for purposes of advocacy? What about book authors? Novelists? Pamphleteers? Bloggers? Tweeters? Was "freedom of the press" originally meant to refer to organized news media, or did it guarantee the right of all persons to disseminate their ideas to the public? The Supreme Court has sometimes spoken of the press in broad terms. *Branzburg v. Hayes*, 408 U.S. 665, 703 (1972) ("[L]iberty of the press is the right of the lonely pamphleteer who uses carbon paper or a mimeograph just as much as of the large metropolitan publisher who utilizes the latest photocomposition methods."); *Lovell v. City of Griffin*, 303 U.S. 444, 452 (1938) ("The press in its historic connotation comprehends every sort of publication which affords a vehicle of information and opinion."). Under this view, "the freedom of the press" is not a privilege for a particular industry or profession, but for all persons to disseminate their views to the public through the various media of communications. What are the consequences of defining the press so expansively?

Justice Potter Stewart advocated for robust protections for a much narrower group—the "organized press" comprising "the daily newspapers and other established news media." Potter Stewart, *Or of the Press*, 26 Hastings L.J. 631, 631 (1975). Legislatures responded to *Branzburg* and other decisions by enacting statutes protecting various press privileges and defining the press for the purposes of the statute. Consider New Jersey's journalist's privilege statute: "Subject to [evidentiary rules governing waiver of privilege], a person engaged on, engaged in, connected with, or employed by news media for the purpose of gathering, procuring, transmitting, compiling, editing or disseminating news for the general public or on whose behalf news is so gathered, procured, transmitted, compiled, edited or disseminated has a privilege to refuse to disclose. . . ." N.J. Stat. Ann. § 2A:84A–21 (West 2012). "News media" is defined as "newspapers, magazines, press associations, news agencies, wire services, radio, television or other similar printed, photographic, mechanical or electronic means of disseminating news to the general public." *Id.* Would this protect book authors? Freelance reporters? Would it protect the civil rights leaders who wrote the advertisement at issue in *Sullivan*?

2. The Court analyzes the subpoenaing of a journalist as an "indirect" restraint on the freedom of the press—not a prohibition on publishing, but a generally applicable law that, as applied to journalists, has a restraining effect. We will encounter other indirect restraints in other First Amendment context, also involving the enforcement of generally applicable laws. Among these are the application of criminal laws to expressive conduct and the application of generally applicable laws to acts of religious exercise. When you come to these, think about *Branzburg*, and ask yourself whether the Court is applying a consistent theory.

3. You might compare the arguments for a journalist-source privilege with those for other privileges, such as doctor-patient or husband-wife. The priest-penitent privilege is now recognized as a federal constitutional right; unlike the claimed privilege in *Branzburg*, it is absolute.

[*Assignment 43*]

D. The Rise and Fall of Categorical Exceptions

Chaplinsky v. New Hampshire
315 U.S. 568 (1942)

■ MR. JUSTICE MURPHY delivered the opinion of the Court.

Appellant, a member of the sect known as Jehovah's Witnesses, was convicted in the municipal court of Rochester, New Hampshire, for violation of Chapter 378, § 2, of the Public Laws of New Hampshire:

> No person shall address any offensive, derisive or annoying word to any other person who is lawfully in any street or other public place,

> nor call him by any offensive or derisive name, nor make any noise or exclamation in his presence and hearing with intent to deride, offend or annoy him, or to prevent him from pursuing his lawful business or occupation.

The complaint charged that appellant,

> with force and arms, in a certain public place in said city of Rochester, to-wit, on the public sidewalk on the easterly side of Wakefield Street, near unto the entrance of the City Hall, did unlawfully repeat the words following, addressed to the complainant, that is to say, 'You are a God damned racketeer' and 'a damned Fascist and the whole government of Rochester are Fascists or agents of Fascists,' the same being offensive, derisive and annoying words and names.

Upon appeal, there was a trial *de novo* of appellant before a jury in the Superior Court. He was found guilty, and the judgment of conviction was affirmed by the Supreme Court of the State.

By motions and exceptions, appellant raised the questions that the statute was invalid under the Fourteenth Amendment of the Constitution of the United States in that it placed an unreasonable restraint on freedom of speech, freedom of the press, and freedom of worship, and because it was vague and indefinite. These contentions were overruled, and the case comes here on appeal.

There is no substantial dispute over the facts. Chaplinsky was distributing the literature of his sect on the streets of Rochester on a busy Saturday afternoon. Members of the local citizenry complained to the City Marshal, Bowering, that Chaplinsky was denouncing all religion as a "racket." Bowering told them that Chaplinsky was lawfully engaged, and then warned Chaplinsky that the crowd was getting restless. Some time later, a disturbance occurred and the traffic officer on duty at the busy intersection started with Chaplinsky for the police station, but did not inform him that he was under arrest or that he was going to be arrested. On the way, they encountered Marshal Bowering, who had been advised that a riot was under way and was, therefore, hurrying to the scene. Bowering repeated his earlier warning to Chaplinsky, who then addressed to Bowering the words set forth in the complaint. . . .

It is now clear that "Freedom of speech and freedom of the press, which are protected by the First Amendment from infringement by Congress, are among the fundamental personal rights and liberties which are protected by the Fourteenth Amendment from invasion by state action." *Lovell v. Griffin*, 303 U.S. 444, 450. Freedom of worship is similarly sheltered. *Cantwell v. Connecticut*, 310 U.S. 296, 303.

Appellant assails the statute as a violation of all three freedoms, speech, press and worship, but only an attack on the basis of free speech is warranted. The spoken, not the written, word is involved. And we cannot conceive that cursing a public officer is the exercise of religion in any sense of the term. But even if the activities of the appellant which preceded the incident could be viewed as religious in character, and therefore entitled to the protection of the Fourteenth Amendment, they would not cloak him with immunity from the legal consequences for concomitant acts committed in violation of a valid criminal statute. We turn, therefore, to an examination of the statute itself.

Allowing the broadest scope to the language and purpose of the Fourteenth Amendment, it is well understood that the right of free speech is not absolute at all times and under all circumstances. There are certain well defined and narrowly limited classes of speech, the prevention and punishment of which have never been thought to raise any Constitutional problem.[3] These include the lewd and obscene, the profane, the libelous, and the insulting or "fighting" words—those which, by their very utterance, inflict injury or tend to incite an immediate breach of the peace. It has been well observed that such utterances are no essential part of any exposition of ideas, and are of such slight social value as a step to truth that any benefit that may be derived from them is clearly outweighed by the social interest in order and morality. "Resort to epithets or personal abuse is not in any proper sense communication of information or opinion safeguarded by the Constitution, and its punishment as a criminal act would raise no question under that instrument." *Cantwell v. Connecticut*, 310 U.S. 296, 309–310. . . .

On the authority of its earlier decisions, the state court declared that the statute's purpose was to preserve the public peace, no words being "forbidden except such as have a direct tendency to cause acts of violence by the persons to whom, individually, the remark is addressed." It was further said:

> The word "offensive" is not to be defined in terms of what a particular addressee thinks. . . . The test is what men of common intelligence would understand would be words likely to cause an average addressee to fight. . . . The English language has a number of words and expressions which, by general consent, are "fighting words" when said without a disarming smile. . . . [S]uch words, as ordinary men know, are likely to cause a fight. So are threatening, profane or obscene revilings. Derisive and annoying words can be taken as coming within the purview of the statute as heretofore interpreted only when they have this characteristic of plainly tending to excite the addressee to a breach of the peace. . . . The statute, as construed, does no more than prohibit the face-to-face words plainly likely to cause a breach of the peace by the addressee, words whose speaking constitutes a breach of the peace by the speaker—including "classical fighting words," words in current use less "classical" but equally likely to cause violence, and other disorderly words, including profanity, obscenity and threats.

We are unable to say that the limited scope of the statute as thus construed contravenes the Constitutional right of free expression. It is a statute narrowly drawn and limited to define and punish specific conduct lying within the domain of state power, the use in a public place of words likely to cause a breach of the peace. Cf. *Cantwell v. Connecticut*, 310 U.S. 296, 311; *Thornhill v. Alabama*, 310 U.S. 88, 105. This conclusion necessarily disposes of appellant's contention that the statute is so vague and indefinite as to render a conviction thereunder a violation of due process. A statute punishing verbal acts, carefully drawn so as not unduly to impair liberty of expression, is not too vague for a criminal law. Cf. *Fox v. Washington*, 236 U.S. 273, 277.

Nor can we say that the application of the statute to the facts disclosed by the record substantially or unreasonably impinges upon the privilege of free speech. Argument is unnecessary to demonstrate that the appellations

---

[3] The protection of the First Amendment, mirrored in the Fourteenth, is not limited to the Blackstonian idea that freedom of the press means only freedom from restraint prior to publication. *Near v. Minnesota*, 283 U.S. 697, 714–715.

"damned racketeer" and "damned Fascist" are epithets likely to provoke the average person to retaliation, and thereby cause a breach of the peace. . . .

NOTES

1. Fighting words are "those which by their very utterance inflict injury or tend to incite an immediate breach of the peace." Are these two different theories, or only one? Does the doctrine authorize punishment of speech that "inflicts injury" on others by insulting or degrading them? Or does it only prohibit speech that might inspire a violent response? In thinking about these questions, consider recent episodes of high-profile criticism of Islam.

In 1988, British author Salman Rushdie published *The Satanic Verses*. The title alludes to the so-called Satanic Verses, verses that Mohammed supposedly proclaimed as revelation from God but later renounced as deception by Satan. The book also contains a dream sequence about a prophet named Mahound whose story resembles Mohammed's and several other elements offensive to Muslims. The book sparked outrage. Several bookstores that carried the book were bombed and dozens were threatened. And Ayatollah Khomeini, a Muslim leader, issued a fatwa calling for the death of Rushdie and his publishers. Later, Rushdie said, "I expected a few mullahs would be offended, call me names, and then I could defend myself in public . . . I honestly never expected anything like this." Hunter Davies, *The Real Life Salman Rushdie*, The Independent (Feb. 11, 1993).

In 2005, a Danish newspaper, the *Jyllands–Posten*, published cartoons that depicted Mohammad, including one of him wearing a bomb as a turban. The cartoons were republished in newspapers around the world. Death threats were made against the cartoonists and publishers. Violent demonstrations in predominantly Muslim countries resulted in over two hundred deaths. See Patricia Cohen, *Danish Cartoon Controversy*, N.Y. Times (Aug. 12, 2009).

In 2010, Terry Jones, the pastor of a small Florida church, announced he would burn two hundred Korans on the anniversary of the 9/11 attacks. Media coverage of his plan led to international outrage. Shortly before 9/11, Jones canceled his plan to burn the Korans, but protests in the Middle East and Asia had already resulted in over twenty deaths. In 2011, he held a "trial of the Koran," found the book guilty of "crimes against humanity," and burned a copy in his church's sanctuary. Afterwards, protestors in Afghanistan attacked a United Nations mission, killing twelve people. See Enayat Najafizada and Rod Nordland, *Afghans Avenge Florida Koran Burning, Killing 12*, N.Y. Times (April 1, 2012).

In 2012, an American of Egyptian Coptic descent uploaded to YouTube a fourteen-minute movie trailer entitled *Innocence of Muslims*. The film shows a Muslim mob attacking Egyptian Christians and has several scenes portraying Mohammad as a fraud. A two-minute clip was broadcast on Egyptian television. The clip sparked protests around the world, including attacks on the American embassy in Cairo. Administration officials blamed the film (incorrectly, as it turned out) for inspiring the attack on the diplomatic outpost in Benghazi, Libya, which killed five Americans including the ambassador, and the secretary of state reportedly assured the father of one of the murdered Americans that the filmmaker responsible for causing the attacks would be punished. The filmmaker was arrested and jailed for probation violations in connection with a prior offense for fraud.

Does the speech in any of these episodes "inflict injury" by "its very utterance"? If the purpose of prohibiting "fighting words" is to keep the peace by preventing speech that might precipitate a violent reaction, do these episodes count? The Supreme Court's fighting words cases have all concerned face-to-face speech. But if one rationale for proscribing fighting words is a concern for public safety, why shouldn't mass communication of fighting words be proscribed? Are mass riots causing the murder of hundreds of innocent people less serious than outbreaks of "fisticuffs"? Does it matter if, as in the above episodes, the audience willingly exposed themselves to the speaker's message? Does it matter whether the audience reaction is reasonable? By whose lights? Is it reasonable to riot when someone insults The Prophet?

If inflammatory speech threatens a breach of the peace, should the police arrest the speaker or the hostile audience? Both? Won't speech on important topics often threaten a breach of the peace? Consider the following from *Terminiello v. Chicago*, 337 U.S. 1, 4–5 (1949):

> [A] function of free speech under our system of government is to invite dispute. It may indeed best serve its high purpose when it induces a condition of unrest, creates dissatisfaction with conditions as they are, or even stirs people to anger. Speech is often provocative and challenging. It may strike at prejudices and preconceptions and have profound unsettling effects as it presses for acceptance of an idea. That is why freedom of speech, though not absolute, is nevertheless protected against censorship or punishment, unless shown likely to produce a clear and present danger of a serious substantive evil that rises far above public inconvenience, annoyance, or unrest.

In each of the above episodes, dozens of people were killed. Should we censor speech that produces violent reactions? Speech that leads to deaths? What incentives does this create? Should the fighting words doctrine be overruled?

2. Are there other ways in which such speech may injure? Jeremy Waldron has argued that offensive speech directed at minorities is a form of group libel that undermines the ability of minorities to participate in society. Jeremy Waldron, THE HARM IN HATE SPEECH (2012). In *Beauharnais v. Illinois*, the Supreme Court upheld a state law that criminalized defamation of a race or religion. 343 U.S. 250 (1952). Although it has never explicitly overruled *Beauharnais*, the Court struck down a similar statute in *R.A.V. v. City of St. Paul*, reasoning that the government could proscribe an entire category of unprotected speech but it could not pick favorites. 505 U.S. 377 (1992). Fighting words, the Court held, are not "entirely invisible to the Constitution" and cannot be "vehicles for content discrimination unrelated to their distinctively proscribable content." Id. at 383–384.

Can the fighting words doctrine be stretched to cover speech that insults beliefs, or groups of people? In *Cohen v. California*, presented below, the Supreme Court reversed Cohen's conviction in part because his speech was not "a direct personal insult." 403 U.S. 15, 20 (1971) (reversing a breach of the peace conviction for wearing a jacket bearing the words, "F*** the Draft"). But insulting someone's religion may be more hurtful or inflammatory than a personal insult. Cf. *Texas v. Johnson*, 491 U.S. at 409 (concluding that "[n]o reasonable onlooker would have regarded Johnson's [flag burning] as a direct personal insult"). Why should this matter?

Categorical Content–Based Exclusions from First Amendment Protection

The Court states that "[t]here are certain well defined and narrowly limited classes of speech, the prevention and punishment of which have never been thought to raise any Constitutional problem." Are these "classes" of unprotected speech defined historically, functionally, or in some other way? The Court has identified the following categories. This is not a comprehensive list. Is it possible to compose a comprehensive list?

1. *Fighting words.* As we have just seen, in *Chaplinsky*, the Court recognized an exclusion from the domain of protected expression for "fighting words"—words in the immediate presence of another that would constitute an immediate provocation to "fisticuffs." In cases subsequent to *Chaplinsky*, the decision is often cited, never overruled, but always distinguished. The fighting-words exception thus remains a recognized (though shrinking) categorical exception to "the freedom of" speech. Can you think of contexts where it should be applied? Doesn't this doctrine reward those who respond to speech with violence, by lending the support of the law to the censorship they desire?

2. *True threats.* True threats are not protected expression under the First Amendment. No one has the right to threaten another, whether for extortionate purpose or just to frighten them. But it is not always easy to distinguish between true threats and hateful (but protected) speech. Suppose a political activist tells a businessman that if he takes a certain action there is likely to be a riot at his place of business. Is that a true threat? Suppose someone says that anyone who supports gun rights should be shot. Is that really a threat? What if speech does not literally include a threat, but is reasonably perceived as threatening? "People like you do not belong in this neighborhood." Cross-burnings present a particularly thorny problem. In some contexts, the Court has treated them as protected speech, it has left open the possibility that burning a cross could, under some circumstances, be punishable as a threat. See *Virginia v. Black*, 538 U.S. 343 (2003).

3. *Defamation and false statements of fact.* False statements of fact, injurious to a person's reputation, traditionally have fallen outside the protection of the freedom of speech. Instead, they constitute the common law tort of libel (if in print) or slander (if made orally). Yet as we have seen, in order to provide "breathing space" to First Amendment freedoms, the Court limited the traditional defamation exception in cases involving criticism of public figures to false statements of fact made "knowingly" or in "reckless disregard" of whether they were true or not. Federal courts are divided on whether false statements of opinion are constitutionally protected. See *Ollman v. Evans*, 750 F.2d 970 (D.C. Cir. 1984) (en banc). Scathing, offensive, *satirical* depictions, however, are not "false" statements of *fact*, and do not fit within any exception to the freedom of speech. Other countries have very stringent tort laws (by American standards) that restrict libelous speech. See Vikram David Amar & Mark V. Tushnet, GLOBAL PERSPECTIVES ON CONSTITUTIONAL LAW 228–239 (2009).

In many opinions, the Court seemed to say that false statements of fact in general are unprotected, but recently rejected that broad proposition. *United States v. Alvarez*, 132 S. Ct. 1421 (2012). A divided majority struck down the federal Stolen Valor Act, which made it illegal for anyone to falsely claim he had been awarded a medal of honor. The plurality opinion, by Justice Kennedy, stated that the Court's "prior decisions" had never recognized a categorical exception for false statements of fact. Under *Chaplinsky*, though, isn't that a historical inquiry? Should the Court have sought to determine whether false statements of fact historically enjoyed protection under American law? Justice Breyer, concurring, rejected categorical analysis and argued that the Court should examine "whether the statute works speech-related harm that is out of proportion to its justifications." The three dissenters pointed to "a long line of cases recognizing that the right to free speech does not protect false factual statements that inflict real harm and serve no legitimate interest." Why did that not satisfy *Chaplinsky*? Has the Court simply shut the door on any categorical exemption not already recognized?

False statements of fact about commercial products or services, in advertisements of those products or services, are not protected by the First Amendment. The boundaries of this doctrine are contested. In one famous case, Nike (the shoe manufacturer) defended itself against the charge that its production facilities abroad are sweat shops, and was sued under a California law on the ground that the defense contained inaccuracies. See *Nike, Inc. v. Kasky*, 539 U.S. 654 (2003). Was that commercial speech? May a drug company distribute copies of a scientific paper indicating an off-label use for its drug, if the FDA has not approved the drug for that purpose? If the drug company did so, and the FDA sought to impose punishment, would the government have to prove the scientific study is false?

4. *Commercial speech generally?* In 1942, the Court declared that there had never been protection for commercial speech—speech advertising a product or proposing a commercial transaction—whether or not the speech was "false." *Valentine v. Chrestensen*, 316 U.S. 52 (1942). Thus, governments could regulate advertising content as they saw fit. The historical basis for that holding is contested, and since 1942 the categorical exclusion of commercial speech from First Amendment protection has eroded considerably. Query: Can government legalize the use of a harmful substance like alcohol, cigarettes, or marijuana but forbid the advertising of it?

In *Ford v. Quebec (Attorney General)*, [1988] 2 S.C.R. 712, the Canadian Supreme Court addressed the constitutionality of a law in Quebec Province that prohibited commercial advertising in Quebec in any language other than French. The Court concluded that the protection of freedom of expression in the Canadian Charter of Rights and Freedoms extended fully to commercial speech. The decision set off a political firestorm that greatly aggravated tensions in Quebec–Canada relations. See Vicki C. Jackson & Mark Tushnet, COMPARATIVE CONSTITUTIONAL LAW 1040–1075 (2d. ed. 2006).

5. *Obscenity and child pornography.* The Supreme Court has long held that "obscene" material—"sexually explicit material that violates fundamental notions of decency"—does not fall within the traditional understanding of "the freedom of" speech. *United States v. Williams*, 553 U.S. 285 (2008). But because it is not always clear what material falls on which side of the line, the Court has fashioned a test that provides limited protection even to patently offensive sexually explicit material that may have some serious literary, artistic, or scientific merit. See *id.* (collecting cases and discussing this test). In contrast, the Canadian Supreme Court has upheld government power to prohibit pornography, broadly defined. See *R. v. Butler*, [1992] 1 S.C.R. 452 (Supreme Court of Canada). American law draws the line, though, at sexually explicit visual depictions of children—

including virtually all nudity—which is one reason movies about teenagers commonly employ older actors. Moreover, the government may limit the sale of sexually explicit materials, even those falling far short of being "obscene," to minors.

6. *Crime-facilitating speech.* Although there are not many cases, it is undisputed that speech is not protected if it is used to carry out a crime. If a gang member shouted "The Supreme Court is Awesome" as a signal to confederates to attack another gang, this would not be protected. The government would not be punishing the speech because of its message. Similarly, the government may punish fraud, perjury, extortionate speech, and similar speech acts.

7. *Others?* Are there other exclusions from what is thought embraced by "the freedom of" speech? If not, should there be? And what, if anything, unites the above categorical exclusions? Is it simply the original understanding of the term "the freedom of speech"?

Brown v. Entertainment Merchants Association
131 S. Ct 2729 (2011)

■ JUSTICE SCALIA delivered the opinion of the Court.

We consider whether a California law imposing restrictions on violent video games comports with the First Amendment.

I

California Assembly Bill 1179 (2005), prohibits the sale or rental of "violent video games" to minors, and requires their packaging to be labeled "18." The Act covers games "in which the range of options available to a player includes killing, maiming, dismembering, or sexually assaulting an image of a human being, if those acts are depicted" in a manner that "[a] reasonable person, considering the game as a whole, would find appeals to a deviant or morbid interest of minors," that is "patently offensive to prevailing standards in the community as to what is suitable for minors," and that "causes the game, as a whole, to lack serious literary, artistic, political, or scientific value for minors." § 1746(d)(1)(A). Violation of the Act is punishable by a civil fine of up to $1,000. § 1746.3.

Respondents, representing the video-game and software industries, brought a preenforcement challenge to the Act in the United States District Court for the Northern District of California. That court concluded that the Act violated the First Amendment and permanently enjoined its enforcement. The Court of Appeals affirmed, and we granted certiorari.

II

California correctly acknowledges that video games qualify for First Amendment protection. The Free Speech Clause exists principally to protect discourse on public matters, but we have long recognized that it is difficult to distinguish politics from entertainment, and dangerous to try. "Everyone is familiar with instances of propaganda through fiction. What is one man's amusement, teaches another's doctrine." *Winters* v. *New York*, 333 U.S. 507, 510 (1948). Like the protected books, plays, and movies that preceded them, video games communicate ideas—and even social messages—through many familiar literary devices (such as characters, dialogue, plot, and music) and through features distinctive to the medium (such as the player's interaction with the virtual world). That suffices to confer First

Amendment protection . . . . And whatever the challenges of applying the Constitution to ever-advancing technology, "the basic principles of freedom of speech and the press, like the First Amendment's command, do not vary" when a new and different medium for communication appears. *Joseph Burstyn, Inc. v. Wilson,* 343 U.S. 495, 503 (1952).

The most basic of those principles is this: "[A]s a general matter, . . . government has no power to restrict expression because of its message, its ideas, its subject matter, or its content." *Ashcroft v. American Civil Liberties Union,* 535 U.S. 564, 573 (2002). There are of course exceptions. "From 1791 to the present, . . . the First Amendment has permitted restrictions upon the content of speech in a few limited areas, and has never include[d] a freedom to disregard these traditional limitations." *United States v. Stevens,* 559 U.S. 460, __ (2010). These limited areas—such as obscenity, *Roth v. United States,* 354 U S. 476, 483 (1957), incitement, *Brandenburg v. Ohio,* 395 U.S. 444, 447–449 (1969) (*per curiam*), and fighting words, *Chaplinsky v. New Hampshire,* 315 U.S. 568, 572 (1942)—represent "well-defined and narrowly limited classes of speech, the prevention and punishment of which have never been thought to raise any Constitutional problem," *id.,* at 571–572.

Last Term, in *Stevens,* we held that new categories of unprotected speech may not be added to the list by a legislature that concludes certain speech is too harmful to be tolerated. *Stevens* concerned a federal statute purporting to criminalize the creation, sale, or possession of certain depictions of animal cruelty. See 18 U.S.C. § 48 (amended 2010). The statute covered depictions "in which a living animal is intentionally maimed, mutilated, tortured, wounded, or killed" if that harm to the animal was illegal where the "the creation, sale, or possession t[ook] place," § 48(c)(1). . . . We held that statute to be an impermissible content-based restriction on speech. There was no American tradition of forbidding the *depiction of* animal cruelty—though States have long had laws against *committing* it.

The Government argued in *Stevens* that lack of a historical warrant did not matter; that it could create new categories of unprotected speech by applying a "simple balancing test" that weighs the value of a particular category of speech against its social costs and then punishes that category of speech if it fails the test. We emphatically rejected that "startling and dangerous" proposition. "Maybe there are some categories of speech that have been historically unprotected, but have not yet been specifically identified or discussed as such in our case law." But without persuasive evidence that a novel restriction on content is part of a long (if heretofore unrecognized) tradition of proscription, a legislature may not revise the "judgment [of] the American people," embodied in the First Amendment, "that the benefits of its restrictions on the Government outweigh the costs."

That holding controls this case. As in *Stevens,* California has tried to make violent-speech regulation look like obscenity regulation by appending a saving clause required for the latter. That does not suffice. Our cases have been clear that the obscenity exception to the First Amendment does not cover whatever a legislature finds shocking, but only depictions of "sexual conduct," *Miller, supra,* at 24. . . .

Because speech about violence is not obscene, it is of no consequence that California's statute mimics the New York statute regulating obscenity-for-minors that we upheld in *Ginsberg v. New York,* 390 U.S. 629 (1968). That case approved a prohibition on the sale to minors of *sexual* material that would be obscene from the perspective of a child. We held that the legislature could "adjus[t] the definition of obscenity to social realities by permitting the appeal of this type of material to be assessed in terms of the sexual interests . . . of . . . minors." And because "obscenity is not protected expression," the New York statute could be sustained so long as the legislature's judgment that the proscribed materials were harmful to children "was not irrational." 390 U.S., at 641.

The California Act is something else entirely. It does not adjust the boundaries of an existing category of unprotected speech to ensure that a definition designed for adults is not uncritically applied to children. California does not argue that it is empowered to prohibit selling offensively violent works *to adults*—and it is wise not to, since that is but a hair's breadth from the argument rejected in *Stevens*. Instead, it wishes to create a wholly new category of content-based regulation that is permissible only for speech directed at children.

That is unprecedented and mistaken. "[M]inors are entitled to a significant measure of First Amendment protection, and only in relatively narrow and well-defined circumstances may government bar public dissemination of protected materials to them." *Erznoznik* v. *Jacksonville*, 422 U.S. 205, 212–213 (1975). No doubt a State possesses legitimate power to protect children from harm, *Ginsberg*, *supra*, at 640–641; *Prince* v. *Massachusetts*, 321 U.S. 158, 165 (1944), but that does not include a free-floating power to restrict the ideas to which children may be exposed. "Speech that is neither obscene as to youths nor subject to some other legitimate proscription cannot be suppressed solely to protect the young from ideas or images that a legislative body thinks unsuitable for them." *Erznoznik*, *supra*, at 213–214.

California's argument would fare better if there were a longstanding tradition in this country of specially restricting children's access to depictions of violence, but there is none. Certainly the *books* we give children to read—or read to them when they are younger—contain no shortage of gore. Grimm's Fairy Tales, for example, are grim indeed. As her just deserts for trying to poison Snow White, the wicked queen is made to dance in red hot slippers "till she fell dead on the floor, a sad example of envy and jealousy." The Complete Brothers Grimm Fairy Tales 198 (2006 ed.). Cinderella's evil stepsisters have their eyes pecked out by doves. *Id.*, at 95. And Hansel and Gretel (children!) kill their captor by baking her in an oven. *Id.*, at 54.

High-school reading lists are full of similar fare. Homer's Odysseus blinds Polyphemus the Cyclops by grinding out his eye with a heated stake. In the Inferno, Dante and Virgil watch corrupt politicians struggle to stay submerged beneath a lake of boiling pitch, lest they be skewered by devils above the surface. And Golding's Lord of the Flies recounts how a schoolboy called Piggy is savagely murdered *by other children* while marooned on an island.

This is not to say that minors' consumption of violent entertainment has never encountered resistance. In the 1800's, dime novels depicting crime and "penny dreadfuls" (named for their price and content) were blamed in some quarters for juvenile delinquency. When motion pictures came along, they became the villains instead. "The days when the police looked upon dime novels as the most dangerous of textbooks in the school for crime are drawing to a close. . . . They say that the moving picture machine . . . tends even more than did the dime novel to turn the thoughts of the easily influenced to paths which sometimes lead to prison." For a time, our Court did permit broad censorship of movies because of their capacity to be "used for evil," see *Mutual Film Corp.* v. *Industrial Comm'n of Ohio*,

236 U.S. 230, 242 (1915), but we eventually reversed course, *Joseph Burstyn, Inc.*, 343 U.S., at 502; see also *Erznoznik, supra*, at 212–214 (invalidating a drive-in movies restriction designed to protect children). Radio dramas were next, and then came comic books. Many in the late 1940's and early 1950's blamed comic books for fostering a "preoccupation with violence and horror" among the young, leading to a rising juvenile crime rate. See Note, Regulation of Comic Books, 68 Harv. L. Rev. 489, 490 (1955). But efforts to convince Congress to restrict comic books failed. Brief for Comic Book Legal Defense Fund as *Amicus Curiae* 11–15. And, of course, after comic books came television and music lyrics.

California claims that video games present special problems because they are "interactive," in that the player participates in the violent action on screen and determines its outcome. The latter feature is nothing new: Since at least the publication of The Adventures of You: Sugarcane Island in 1969, young readers of choose-your-own-adventure stories have been able to make decisions that determine the plot by following instructions about which page to turn to. Cf. *Interactive Digital Software Assn.* v. *St. Louis County*, 329 F.3d 954, 957–958 (CA8 2003). As for the argument that video games enable participation in the violent action, that seems to us more a matter of degree than of kind. As Judge Posner has observed, all literature is interactive. "[T]he better it is, the more interactive. Literature when it is successful draws the reader into the story, makes him identify with the characters, invites him to judge them and quarrel with them, to experience their joys and sufferings as the reader's own." *American Amusement Machine Assn.* v. *Kendrick*, 244 F.3d 572, 577 (CA7 2001) (striking down a similar restriction on violent video games).

JUSTICE ALITO has done considerable independent research to identify video games in which "the violence is astounding." "Victims are dismembered, decapitated, disemboweled, set on fire, and chopped into little pieces. . . . Blood gushes, splatters, and pools." JUSTICE ALITO recounts all these disgusting video games in order to disgust us—but disgust is not a valid basis for restricting expression. And the same is true of JUSTICE ALITO's description of those video games he has discovered that have a racial or ethnic motive for their violence—"ethnic cleansing [of] . . . African Americans, Latinos, or Jews." To what end does he relate this? Does it somehow increase the "aggressiveness" that California wishes to suppress? Who knows? But it does arouse the reader's ire, and the reader's desire to put an end to this horrible message. Thus, ironically, JUSTICE ALITO's argument highlights the precise danger posed by the California Act: that the *ideas* expressed by speech—whether it be violence, or gore, or racism—and not its objective effects, may be the real reason for governmental proscription.

III

Because the Act imposes a restriction on the content of protected speech, it is invalid unless California can demonstrate that it passes strict scrutiny—that is, unless it is justified by a compelling government interest and is narrowly drawn to serve that interest. The State must specifically identify an "actual problem" in need of solving, and the curtailment of free speech must be actually necessary to the solution. That is a demanding standard. "It is rare that a regulation restricting speech because of its content will ever be permissible." *Playboy*, 529 U.S., at 818.

California cannot meet that standard. . . . California relies primarily on the research of Dr. Craig Anderson and a few other research psychologists whose studies purport to show a connection between exposure to violent video games and harmful effects on children. These studies have been rejected by every court to consider them, and with good reason: They do not prove that violent video games *cause* minors to *act* aggressively (which would at least be a beginning). Instead, "[n]early all of the research is based on correlation, not evidence of causation, and most of the studies suffer from significant, admitted flaws in methodology." *Video Software Dealers Assn.* 556 F. 3d, at 964. They show at best some correlation between exposure to violent entertainment and minuscule real-world effects, such as children's feeling more aggressive or making louder noises in the few minutes after playing a violent game than after playing a nonviolent game. . . .

The Act is also seriously underinclusive in another respect—and a respect that renders irrelevant the contentions of the concurrence and the dissents that video games are qualitatively different from other portrayals of violence. The California Legislature is perfectly willing to leave this dangerous, mind-altering material in the hands of children so long as one parent (or even an aunt or uncle) says it's OK. And there are not even any requirements as to how this parental or avuncular relationship is to be verified; apparently the child's or putative parent's, aunt's, or uncle's say-so suffices. That is not how one addresses a serious social problem.

California claims that the Act is justified in aid of parental authority: By requiring that the purchase of violent video games can be made only by adults, the Act ensures that parents can decide what games are appropriate. At the outset, we note our doubts that punishing third parties for conveying protected speech to children *just in case* their parents disapprove of that speech is a proper governmental means of aiding parental authority. Accepting that position would largely vitiate the rule that "only in relatively narrow and well-defined circumstances may government bar public dissemination of protected materials to [minors]." *Erznoznik*, 422 U.S., at 212–213.

But leaving that aside, California cannot show that the Act's restrictions meet a substantial need of parents who wish to restrict their children's access to violent video games but cannot do so. The video-game industry has in place a voluntary rating system designed to inform consumers about the content of games. . . . This system does much to ensure that minors cannot purchase seriously violent games on their own, and that parents who care about the matter can readily evaluate the games their children bring home. Filling the remaining modest gap in concerned-parents' control can hardly be a compelling state interest.

And finally, the Act's purported aid to parental authority is vastly overinclusive. Not all of the children who are forbidden to purchase violent video games on their own have parents who *care* whether they purchase violent video games. While some of the legislation's effect may indeed be in support of what some parents of the restricted children actually want, its entire effect is only in support of what the State thinks parents *ought* to want. This is not the narrow tailoring to "assisting parents" that restriction of First Amendment rights requires. . . .

■ JUSTICE ALITO, with whom THE CHIEF JUSTICE joins, concurring in the judgment.

The California statute that is before us in this case represents a pioneering effort to address what the state legislature and others regard as a potentially serious social problem: the effect of exceptionally violent video games on impressionable minors, who often spend countless hours immersed in the alternative worlds that these games create. Although the California statute is well intentioned, its terms are not framed with the precision that the Constitution demands, and I therefore agree with the Court that this particular law cannot be sustained.

I disagree, however, with the approach taken in the Court's opinion. In considering the application of unchanging constitutional principles to new and rapidly evolving technology, this Court should proceed with caution. We should make every effort to understand the new technology. We should take into account the possibility that developing technology may have important societal implications that will become apparent only with time. We should not jump to the conclusion that new technology is fundamentally the same as some older thing with which we are familiar. And we should not hastily dismiss the judgment of legislators, who may be in a better position than we are to assess the implications of new technology. The opinion of the Court exhibits none of this caution.

In the view of the Court, all those concerned about the effects of violent video games—federal and state legislators, educators, social scientists, and parents—are unduly fearful, for violent video games really present no serious problem. Spending hour upon hour controlling the actions of a character who guns down scores of innocent victims is not different in "kind" from reading a description of violence in a work of literature.

The Court is sure of this; I am not. There are reasons to suspect that the experience of playing violent video games just might be very different from reading a book, listening to the radio, or watching a movie or a television show.

I

[Justice Alito argued that the statute's definition of "violent video game" was unconstitutionally vague and that there was thus "no need to reach the broader First Amendment issues addressed by the Court."—Editors]

II

Having outlined how I would decide this case, I will now briefly elaborate on my reasons for questioning the wisdom of the Court's approach. . . .

A

The Court is wrong in saying that the holding in *Stevens* "controls this case." . . . The portion of *Stevens* on which the Court relies rejected the Government's contention that depictions of animal cruelty were categorically outside the range of *any* First Amendment protection. Going well beyond *Stevens*, the Court now holds that any law that attempts to prevent minors from purchasing violent video games must satisfy strict scrutiny instead of the more lenient standard applied in *Ginsberg*, 390 U.S. 629, our most closely related precedent. As a result of today's decision, a State may prohibit the sale to minors of what *Ginsberg* described as "girlie magazines," but a State must surmount a formidable (and perhaps insurmountable) obstacle if it wishes to prevent children from purchasing the most violent and depraved video games imaginable.

. . . *Stevens* expressly left open the possibility that a more narrowly drawn statute targeting depictions of animal cruelty might be compatible with the First Amendment. In this case, the Court's sweeping opinion will likely be read by many, both inside and outside the video-game industry, as suggesting that no regulation of minors' access to violent video games is allowed—at least without supporting evidence that may not be realistically obtainable given the nature of the phenomenon in question.

B

The Court's opinion distorts the effect of the California law. I certainly agree with the Court that the government has no "free-floating power to restrict the ideas to which children may be exposed," but the California law does not exercise such a power. If parents want their child to have a violent video game, the California law does not interfere with that parental pre-rogative. Instead, the California law reinforces parental decisionmaking in exactly the same way as the New York statute upheld in *Ginsberg*. Under both laws, minors are prevented from purchasing certain materials; and under both laws, parents are free to supply their children with these items if that is their wish.

Citing the video-game industry's voluntary rating system, the Court argues that the California law does not "meet a substantial need of parents who wish to restrict their children's access to violent video games but cannot do so." The Court does not mention the fact that the industry adopted this system in response to the threat of federal regulation, a threat that the Court's opinion may now be seen as largely eliminating. Nor does the Court acknowledge that compliance with this system at the time of the enactment of the California law left much to be desired—or that future enforcement may decline if the video-game industry perceives that any threat of gov-ernment regulation has vanished. Nor does the Court note, as JUSTICE BREYER points out, that many parents today are simply not able to monitor their children's use of computers and gaming devices.

C

Finally, the Court is far too quick to dismiss the possibility that the experience of playing video games (and the effects on minors of playing vio-lent video games) may be very different from anything that we have seen before. Any assessment of the experience of playing video games must take into account certain characteristics of the video games that are now on the market and those that are likely to be available in the near future.

Today's most advanced video games create realistic alternative worlds in which millions of players immerse themselves for hours on end. These games feature visual imagery and sounds that are strikingly realistic, and in the near future video-game graphics may be virtually indistinguishable from actual video footage. . . .

Persons who play video games also have an unprecedented ability to participate in the events that take place in the virtual worlds that these games create. Players can create their own video-game characters and can use photos to produce characters that closely resemble actual people. A per-son playing a sophisticated game can make a multitude of choices and can thereby alter the course of the action in the game. In addition, the means by which players control the action in video games now bear a closer rela-tionship to the means by which people control action in the real world. While the action in older games was often directed with buttons or a joy-stick, players dictate the action in newer games by engaging in the same motions that they desire a character in the game to perform. For example, a player who wants a video-game character to swing a baseball bat—either to hit a ball or smash a skull—could bring that about by simulating the mo-tion of actually swinging a bat.

These present-day and emerging characteristics of video games must be considered together with characteristics of the violent games that have already been marketed.

In some of these games, the violence is astounding. Victims by the dozens are killed with every imaginable implement, including machine guns, shotguns, clubs, hammers, axes, swords, and chainsaws. Victims are dismembered, decapitated, disemboweled, set on fire, and chopped into little pieces. They cry out in agony and beg for mercy. Blood gushes, splatters, and pools. Severed body parts and gobs of human remains are graphically shown. In some games, points are awarded based, not only on the number of victims killed, but on the killing technique employed.

It also appears that there is no antisocial theme too base for some in the video-game industry to exploit. There are games in which a player can take on the identity and reenact the killings carried out by the perpetrators of the murders at Columbine High School and Virginia Tech. The objective of one game is to rape a mother and her daughters; in another, the goal is to rape Native American women. There is a game in which players engage in "ethnic cleansing" and can choose to gun down African–Americans, Latinos, or Jews. In still another game, players attempt to fire a rifle shot into the head of President Kennedy as his motorcade passes by the Texas School Book Depository.

If the technological characteristics of the sophisticated games that are likely to be available in the near future are combined with the characteristics of the most violent games already marketed, the result will be games that allow troubled teens to experience in an extraordinarily personal and vivid way what it would be like to carry out unspeakable acts of violence.

The Court is untroubled by this possibility. According to the Court, the "interactive" nature of video games is "nothing new" because "all literature is interactive." Disagreeing with this assessment, the International Game Developers Association (IGDA)—a group that presumably understands the nature of video games and that supports respondents—tells us that video games are "far more concretely interactive." Brief for IGDA et al. as *Amici Curiae* 3. And on this point, the game developers are surely correct. . . .

When all of the characteristics of video games are taken into account, there is certainly a reasonable basis for thinking that the experience of playing a video game may be quite different from the experience of reading a book, listening to a radio broadcast, or viewing a movie. And if this is so, then for at least some minors, the effects of playing violent video games may also be quite different. The Court acts prematurely in dismissing this possibility out of hand. . . .

For all these reasons, I would hold only that the particular law at issue here fails to provide the clear notice that the Constitution requires. I would not squelch legislative efforts to deal with what is perceived by some to be a significant and developing social problem. If differently framed statutes are enacted by the States or by the Federal Government, we can consider the constitutionality of those laws when cases challenging them are presented to us.

■ JUSTICE THOMAS, dissenting.

The Court's decision today does not comport with the original public understanding of the First Amendment. . . . The practices and beliefs of the founding generation establish that "the freedom of speech," as originally understood, does not include a right to speak to minors (or a right of minors to access speech) without going through the minors' parents or guardians.

[Justice Thomas performed a detailed historical analysis of colonial attitudes to childrearing and concludes: "The history clearly shows a founding generation that believed parents to have complete authority over their minor children and expected parents to direct the development of those children."— Editors]

■ JUSTICE BREYER, dissenting.

. . . A facial challenge to this statute based on the First Amendment can succeed only if "a substantial number of its applications are unconstitutional, judged in relation to the statute's plainly legitimate sweep." Moreover, it is more difficult to mount a facial First Amendment attack on a statute that seeks to regulate activity that involves action as well as speech. Hence, I shall focus here upon an area within which I believe the State can legitimately apply its statute, namely sales to minors under the age of 17 (the age cutoff used by the industry's own ratings system), of highly realistic violent video games, which a reasonable game maker would know meet the Act's criteria. That area lies at the heart of the statute. I shall assume that the number of instances in which the State will enforce the statute within that area is comparatively large, and that the number outside that area (for example, sales to 17–year–olds) is comparatively small. And the activity the statute regulates combines speech with action (a virtual form of target practice).

In determining whether the statute is unconstitutional, I would apply both this Court's "vagueness" precedents and a strict form of First Amendment scrutiny. In doing so, the special First Amendment category I find relevant is not (as the Court claims) the category of "depictions of violence," but rather the category of "protection of children." This Court has held that the "power of the state to control the conduct of children reaches beyond the scope of its authority over adults." *Prince* v. *Massachusetts*, 321 U.S. 158, 170 (1944). And the "regulatio[n] of communication addressed to [children] need not conform to the requirements of the [F]irst [A]mendment in the same way as those applicable to adults." *Ginsberg* v. *New York*, 390 U.S. 629, 638, n. 6 (1968) (quoting Emerson, Toward a General Theory of the First Amendment, 72 Yale L.J. 877, 939 (1963)).

The majority's claim that the California statute, if upheld, would create a "new categor[y] of unprotected speech," is overstated. No one here argues that depictions of violence, even extreme violence, *automatically* fall outside the First Amendment's protective scope as, for example, do obscenity and depictions of child pornography. We properly speak of *categories* of expression that lack protection when, like "child pornography," the category is broad, when it applies automatically, and when the State can prohibit everyone, including adults, from obtaining access to the material within it. But where, as here, careful analysis must precede a narrower judicial conclusion (say, denying protection to a shout of "fire" in a crowded theater, or to an effort to teach a terrorist group how to peacefully petition the United Nations), we do not normally describe the result as creating a "new category of unprotected speech."

Thus, in *Stevens*, after rejecting the claim that *all* depictions of animal cruelty (a category) fall outside the First Amendment's protective scope, we went on to decide whether the particular statute at issue violates the First Amendment under traditional standards; and we held that, because the statute was overly broad, it was invalid. Similarly, here the issue is whether, applying traditional First Amendment standards, this statute does, or does not, pass muster.

II

[Justice Breyer argued that the statute was not unconstitutionally vague.—Editors]

III

Video games combine physical action with expression. Were physical activity to predominate in a game, government could appropriately intervene, say by requiring parents to accompany children when playing a game involving actual target practice, or restricting the sale of toys presenting physical dangers to children. But because video games also embody important expressive and artistic elements, I agree with the Court that the First Amendment significantly limits the State's power to regulate. And I would determine whether the State has exceeded those limits by applying a strict standard of review.

Like the majority, I believe that the California law must be "narrowly tailored" to further a "compelling interest," without there being a "less restrictive" alternative that would be "at least as effective." *Reno* v. *American Civil Liberties Union*, 521 U.S. 844, 874, 875, 879 (1997). I would not apply this strict standard "mechanically." Rather, in applying it, I would evaluate the degree to which the statute injures speech-related interests, the nature of the potentially-justifying "compelling interests," the degree to which the statute furthers that interest, the nature and effectiveness of possible alternatives, and, in light of this evaluation, whether, overall, "the statute works speech-related harm . . . out of proportion to the benefits that the statute seeks to provide."

First Amendment standards applied in this way are difficult but not impossible to satisfy. . . . *[Justice Breyer next described cases in which restrictions on speech were upheld under strict scrutiny.—Editors]*

B

The interest that California advances in support of the statute is compelling. As this Court has previously described that interest, it consists of both (1) the "basic" parental claim "to authority in their own household to direct the rearing of their children," which makes it proper to enact "laws designed to aid discharge of [parental] responsibility," and (2) the State's "independent interest in the well-being of its youth." *Ginsberg*, 390 U.S., at 639–640. And where these interests work in tandem, it is not fatally "underinclusive" for a State to advance its interests in protecting children against the special harms present in an interactive video game medium through a default rule that still allows parents to provide their children with what their parents wish.

Both interests are present here. As to the need to help parents guide their children, the Court noted in 1968 that "parental control or guidance cannot always be provided." 390 U.S., at 640. Today, 5.3 million grade-school-age children of working parents are routinely home alone. . . . Thus, it has, if anything, become more important to supplement parents' authority to guide their children's development.

As to the State's independent interest, we have pointed out that juveniles are more likely to show a "lack of maturity" and are "more vulnerable or susceptible to negative influences and outside pressures," and that their "character . . . is not as well formed as that of an adult." *Roper* v. *Simmons*, 543 U.S. 551, 569–570 (2005). And we have therefore recognized "a compelling interest in protecting the physical and psychological well-being of minors." *Sable Communications, supra,* at 126.

At the same time, there is considerable evidence that California's statute significantly furthers this compelling interest. That is, in part, because video games are excellent teaching tools. Learning a practical task often means developing habits, becoming accustomed to performing the task, and receiving positive reinforcement when performing that task well. Video games can help develop habits, accustom the player to performance of the task, and reward the player for performing that task well. Why else would the Armed Forces incorporate video games into its training? . . .

There are many scientific studies that support California's views. Social scientists, for example, have found *causal* evidence that playing these games results in harm. Longitudinal studies, which measure changes over time, have found that increased exposure to violent video games causes an increase in aggression over the same period. . . .

And "meta-analyses," *i.e.,* studies of all the studies, have concluded that exposure to violent video games "was positively associated with aggressive behavior, aggressive cognition, and aggressive affect," and that "playing violent video games is a *causal* risk factor for long-term harmful outcomes." . . .

Some of these studies take care to explain in a common-sense way why video games are potentially more harmful than, say, films or books or television. In essence, they say that the closer a child's behavior comes, not to watching, but to *acting* out horrific violence, the greater the potential psychological harm. . . .

Experts debate the conclusions of all these studies. Like many, perhaps most, studies of human behavior, each study has its critics, and some of those critics have produced studies of their own in which they reach different conclusions. (I list both sets of research in the appendixes.) I, like most judges, lack the social science expertise to say definitively who is right. But associations of public health professionals who do possess that expertise have reviewed many of these studies and found a significant risk that violent video games, when compared with more passive media, are particularly likely to cause children harm. . . .

Unlike the majority, I would find sufficient grounds in these studies and expert opinions for this Court to defer to an elected legislature's conclusion that the video games in question are particularly likely to harm children. This Court has always thought it owed an elected legislature some degree of deference in respect to legislative facts of this kind, particularly when they involve technical matters that are beyond our competence, and even in First Amendment cases. The majority, in reaching its own, opposite conclusion about the validity of the relevant studies, grants the legislature no deference at all. . . .

The industry also argues for an alternative technological solution, namely "filtering at the console level." But it takes only a quick search of the Internet to find guides explaining how to circumvent any such technological controls. . . .

IV

... I add that the majority's different conclusion creates a serious anomaly in First Amendment law. *Ginsberg* makes clear that a State can prohibit the sale to minors of depictions of nudity; today the Court makes clear that a State cannot prohibit the sale to minors of the most violent interactive video games. But what sense does it make to forbid selling to a 13–year–old boy a magazine with an image of a nude woman, while protecting a sale to that 13–year–old of an interactive video game in which he actively, but virtually, binds and gags the woman, then tortures and kills her? What kind of First Amendment would permit the government to protect children by restricting sales of that extremely violent video game *only* when the woman—bound, gagged, tortured, and killed—is also topless?

This anomaly is not compelled by the First Amendment. It disappears once one recognizes that extreme violence, where interactive, and *without literary, artistic, or similar justification*, can prove at least as, if not more, harmful to children as photographs of nudity. And the record here is more than adequate to support such a view. That is why I believe that *Ginsberg* controls the outcome here *a fortiori*. And it is why I believe California's law is constitutional on its face.

This case is ultimately less about censorship than it is about education. Our Constitution cannot succeed in securing the liberties it seeks to protect unless we can raise future generations committed cooperatively to making our system of government work. Education, however, is about choices. Sometimes, children need to learn by making choices for themselves. Other times, choices are made for children—by their parents, by their teachers, and by the people acting democratically through their governments. In my view, the First Amendment does not disable government from helping parents make such a choice here—a choice not to have their children buy extremely violent, interactive video games, which they more than reasonably fear pose only the risk of harm to those children.

NOTES

1. Does *Brown*, together with *Stevens* (the animal cruelty-depiction case discussed in *Brown*) sound the death knell for the categorical approach? Can any "class" of speech ever be added to the list of unprotected categories? What evidence would it take? Does this mean that any new form of content-based regulation of speech will have to satisfy strict scrutiny? You should read Justice Breyer's dissent carefully to appreciate just how strictly the majority interpreted strict scrutiny.

2. Are you persuaded by the majority's reasoning? Consider the following:

a. What is the Court's theory about what constitutional rights fully apply to minors? Do they have the right to bear arms, to own property, to marry, to vote, to enter into contracts, to avoid coercive indoctrination (in the form of public education)? Any idea why this case is about their rights, as opposed to whether profit-making corporations have a right to direct speech *to them*? Is it true that speech directed to minors is fully protected, and subject to strict scrutiny? The Court cites *Erznoznik v. City of Jacksonville* for this proposition, but *Erznoznik* involved an ordinance, a prohibition of nudity in drive-in movies, that was directed to everyone. It is well established that the government may not censor speech for everyone on the ground that there might be minors in the audience. Moreover, the *Erznoznik* Court stated in a footnote:

The First Amendment rights of minors are not "co-extensive with those of adults." *Tinker v. Des Moines School Dist.*, 393 U. S. 503, 515 (1969) (STEWART, J., concurring). "[A] State may permissibly determine that, at least in some precisely delineated areas, a child—like someone in a captive audience—is not possessed of that full capacity for individual choice which is the presupposition of First Amendment guarantees." *Ginsberg v. New York*, 390 U. S. 629, 649–650 (1968) (STEWART, J., concurring). In assessing whether a minor has the requisite capacity for individual choice the age of the minor is a significant factor. See *Rowan v. Post Office Dept.*, 397 U. S., at 741 (BRENNAN, J., concurring).

Isn't that what California thought it was doing?

The Court recounts a series of attempts through American history to censor materials thought harmful to minors, from dime novels to movies, radio dramas, comic books, television, music lyrics. Obviously the majority regards these efforts as having been wrong-headed. But do they not point to a "tradition"—albeit one the majority disapproves of—"of specifically restricting children's access to materials" thought harmful?

b. Is exposure to extreme violence any less harmful to children than exposure to depictions of nudity? In *Ginsberg*, cited in *Brown*, the Court upheld a prosecution for the sale to a 16–year–old boy of what it described as a "girlie magazine," based on the Court's judgment that it was "rational for the legislature to find that the minors' exposure to such material might be harmful." Why is exposure to extreme violence so very different? The Court cites examples of violent material, such as Snow White, the Odyssey, and the Inferno, to which minors are exposed, suggesting that the extremely violent video games are similar in kind. Presumably one could have made the same argument about nudity, pointing to Botticelli's Venus, Michelangelo's David, *Schindler's List*, and a sex education textbook. Children are often exposed to depictions of nudity, just as they are to violence—just not to particular kinds of depictions of nudity (those without redeeming social value) and particular kinds of violence. What do these examples prove?

c. The Court is surely right that violent video games involve speech—messages disseminated by the producers of the games to the gamers. But don't they also involve significant elements of conduct by the gamer—such things as murdering people, raping women, cutting off heads, and torturing victims? Is it crazy to think that engaging in such conduct for hours on end in the fictional world of video games might habituate a young person to such conduct in reality? Should the Court have analyzed the case as one that involved pure speech, rather than speech mixed with conduct?

d. What do you make of the disagreement between the majority and Justice Breyer over the social science evidence? How should judges—who are usually not trained in the methods of empirical social science—treat this kind of evidence?

e. The majority observed that voluntary industry codes provide sufficient protection. But what if those codes were adopted to forestall legislation? Can the industry now repeal those codes, confident that any legislative attempt to replace them will be struck down?

3. It is interesting to compare the two dissents, by Justices Thomas and Breyer. Thomas relies on history; Breyer relies on social science. Which offers the more persuasive reading of the Constitution?

4. For several decades after *Chaplinsky*, the Court's principal approach to interpretation of the First Amendment was to carve out specific, content-based exclusions based on some combination of history (usually without much historical research) and intuition. That approach seems to have come to an end. Now the Court applies strict scrutiny to content-based speech regulation, and lesser scrutiny to speech regulation that is not content-based. As you read the modern cases, you should ask yourself: Is the new approach an improvement? Despite its new approach, the Court has not overruled the old categorical cases. The list has simply been frozen, like an insect in amber, leading to an odd jurisprudence where some regulation based on content is allowed with little or no scrutiny, and other regulation based on content is subject to strict (and if *Brown* is any indication, extremely strict) scrutiny. Is there any logic to this—historical, pragmatic, utilitarian, or otherwise?

5. If "it is difficult to distinguish politics from entertainment, and dangerous to try," as the majority says, do all the doctrines extending protection to speech on "matters of public concern" now apply across the board, even to speech that is merely entertaining?

[*Assignment 44*]

E. CONTENT–BASED AND CONTENT–NEUTRAL RESTRICTIONS

We begin this section with two cases about protesters who were prosecuted. One of the protesters burned a draft card; the other one burned an American flag. But what is more important is the character of the law under which each was prosecuted. As you read the cases, ask yourself what is fundamentally different between the draft-card-burning law and the flag-burning law.

United States v. O'Brien
391 U.S. 367 (1968)

■ MR. CHIEF JUSTICE WARREN delivered the opinion of the Court.

On the morning of March 31, 1966, David Paul O'Brien and three companions burned their Selective Service registration certificates on the steps of the South Boston Courthouse. A sizable crowd, including several agents of the Federal Bureau of Investigation, witnessed the event. Immediately after the burning, members of the crowd began attacking O'Brien and his companions. An FBI agent ushered O'Brien to safety inside the courthouse. After he was advised of his right to counsel and to silence, O'Brien stated to FBI agents that he had burned his registration certificate because of his beliefs, knowing that he was violating federal law. He produced the charred remains of the certificate, which, with his consent, were photographed.

For this act, O'Brien was indicted, tried, convicted, and sentenced in the United States District Court for the District of Massachusetts. He did not contest the fact that he had burned the certificate. He stated in argument to the jury that he burned the certificate publicly to influence others to adopt his antiwar beliefs, as he put it, "so that other people would reevaluate their positions with Selective Service, with the armed forces, and reevaluate their place in the culture of today, to hopefully consider my position."

The indictment upon which he was tried charged that he "willfully and knowingly did mutilate, destroy, and change by burning . . . [his] Registration Certificate . . . in violation of Title 50, App., United States Code, Section 462(b)" . . . of the Universal Military Training and Service Act of 1948. Section 462(b)(3) . . . was amended by Congress in 1965, 79 Stat. 586 (adding the words italicized below), so that at the time O'Brien burned his certificate an offense was committed by any person, "who *forges, alters, knowingly destroys, knowingly mutilates, or* in any manner changes any such certificate. . . ." (Italics supplied.) . . .

[T]he Court of Appeals . . . held the 1965 Amendment unconstitutional as a law abridging freedom of speech. At the time the Amendment was enacted, a regulation of the Selective Service System required registrants to keep their registration certificates in their "personal possession at all times." 32 CFR § 1617.1 (1962). Wilful violations of regulations promulgated pursuant to the Universal Military Training and Service Act were made criminal by statute. 50 U.S.C. App. § 462(b)(6). The Court of Appeals, therefore, was of the opinion that conduct punishable under the 1965 Amendment was already punishable under the nonpossession regulation, and consequently that the Amendment served no valid purpose; further, that in light of the prior regulation, the Amendment must have been "directed at public as distinguished from private destruction." On this basis, the court concluded that the 1965 Amendment ran afoul of the First Amendment by singling out persons engaged in protests for special treatment. . . . We hold that the 1965 Amendment is constitutional both as enacted and as applied. . . .

I

When a male reaches the age of 18, he is required by the Universal Military Training and Service Act to register with a local draft board. He is assigned a Selective Service number, and within five days he is issued a registration certificate. . . . Subsequently, . . . he is assigned a classification denoting his eligibility for induction, and "[a]s soon as practicable" thereafter he is issued a Notice of Classification. . . . Both the registration and classification certificates are small white cards, approximately 2 by 3 inches. . . .

Congress demonstrated its concern that certificates issued by the Selective Service System might be abused well before the 1965 Amendment here challenged. . . . By the 1965 Amendment, Congress added to § 12(b)(3) of the 1948 Act the provision here at issue, subjecting to criminal liability not only one who "forges, alters, or in any manner changes" but also one who "knowingly destroys [or] knowingly mutilates" a certificate. We note at the outset that the 1965 Amendment plainly does not abridge free speech on its face, and we do not understand O'Brien to argue otherwise. Amended § 12(b)(3) on its face deals with conduct having no connection with speech. It prohibits the knowing destruction of certificates issued by the Selective Service System, and there is nothing necessarily expressive about such conduct. The Amendment does not distinguish between public and private destruction, and it does not punish only destruction engaged in for the purpose of expressing views. Compare *Stromberg v. People of State of Califor-*

nia, 283 U.S. 359 (1931). A law prohibiting destruction of Selective Service certificates no more abridges free speech on its face than a motor vehicle law prohibiting the destruction of drivers' licenses, or a tax law prohibiting the destruction of books and records.

O'Brien nonetheless argues that the 1965 Amendment is unconstitutional in its application to him, and is unconstitutional as enacted because what he calls the "purpose" of Congress was "to suppress freedom of speech." We consider these arguments separately.

II

O'Brien first argues that the 1965 Amendment is unconstitutional as applied to him because his act of burning his registration certificate was protected "symbolic speech" within the First Amendment. His argument is that the freedom of expression which the First Amendment guarantees includes all modes of "communication of ideas by conduct," and that his conduct is within this definition because he did it in "demonstration against the war and against the draft."

We cannot accept the view that an apparently limitless variety of conduct can be labeled "speech" whenever the person engaging in the conduct intends thereby to express an idea. However, even on the assumption that the alleged communicative element in O'Brien's conduct is sufficient to bring into play the First Amendment, it does not necessarily follow that the destruction of a registration certificate is constitutionally protected activity. This Court has held that when "speech" and "nonspeech" elements are combined in the same course of conduct, a sufficiently important governmental interest in regulating the nonspeech element can justify incidental limitations on First Amendment freedoms. To characterize the quality of the governmental interest which must appear, the Court has employed a variety of descriptive terms: compelling; substantial; subordinating; paramount; cogent; strong. Whatever imprecision inheres in these terms, we think it clear that a government regulation is sufficiently justified if it is within the constitutional power of the Government; if it furthers an important or substantial governmental interest; if the governmental interest is unrelated to the suppression of free expression; and if the incidental restriction on alleged First Amendment freedoms is no greater than is essential to the furtherance of that interest. We find that the 1965 Amendment to § 12(b)(3) of the Universal Military Training and Service Act meets all of these requirements, and consequently that O'Brien can be constitutionally convicted for violating it.

The constitutional power of Congress to raise and support armies and to make all laws necessary and proper to that end is broad and sweeping. The power of Congress to classify and conscript manpower for military service is "beyond question." Pursuant to this power, Congress may establish a system of registration for individuals liable for training and service, and may require such individuals within reason to cooperate in the registration system. The issuance of certificates indicating the registration and eligibility classification of individuals is a legitimate and substantial administrative aid in the functioning of this system. And legislation to insure the continuing availability of issued certificates serves a legitimate and substantial purpose in the system's administration.

O'Brien's argument to the contrary is necessarily premised upon his unrealistic characterization of Selective Service certificates. He essentially adopts the position that such certificates are so many pieces of paper designed to notify registrants of their registration or classification, to be retained or tossed in the wastebasket according to the convenience or taste of the registrant. . . . We agree that the registration certificate contains much information of which the registrant needs no notification. This circumstance, however, does not lead to the conclusion that the certificate serves no purpose, but that, like the classification certificate, it serves purposes in addition to initial notification. Many of these purposes would be defeated by the certificates' destruction or mutilation. Among these are:

1. The registration certificate serves as proof that the individual described thereon has registered for the draft. The classification certificate shows the eligibility classification of a named but undescribed individual. Voluntarily displaying the two certificates is an easy and painless way for a young man to dispel a question as to whether he might be delinquent in his Selective Service obligations. Correspondingly, the availability of the certificates for such display relieves the Selective Service System of the administrative burden it would otherwise have in verifying the registration and classification of all suspected delinquents. Further, since both certificates are in the nature of "receipts" attesting that the registrant has done what the law requires, it is in the interest of the just and efficient administration of the system that they be continually available, in the event, for example, of a mix-up in the registrant's file. Additionally, in a time of national crisis, reasonable availability to each registrant of the two small cards assures a rapid and uncomplicated means for determining his fitness for immediate induction, no matter how distant in our mobile society he may be from his local board.

2. The information supplied on the certificates facilitates communication between registrants and local boards, simplifying the system and benefiting all concerned. To begin with, each certificate bears the address of the registrant's local board, an item unlikely to be committed to memory. Further, each card bears the registrant's Selective Service number. . . . Finally, a registrant's inquiry, particularly through a local board other than his own, concerning his eligibility status is frequently answerable simply on the basis of his classification certificate; whereas, if the certificate were not reasonably available and the registrant were uncertain of his classification, the task of answering his questions would be considerably complicated.

3. Both certificates carry continual reminders that the registrant must notify his local board of any change of address, and other specified changes in his status. . . . [T]he destruction of certificates deprives the system of a potentially useful notice device.

4. The regulatory scheme involving Selective Service certificates includes clearly valid prohibitions against the alteration, forgery, or similar deceptive misuse of certificates. The destruction or mutilation of certificates obviously increases the difficulty of detecting and tracing abuses such as these. Further, a mutilated certificate might itself be used for deceptive purposes.

The many functions performed by Selective Service certificates establish beyond doubt that Congress has a legitimate and substantial interest in preventing their wanton and unrestrained destruction and assuring their continuing availability by punishing people who knowingly and willfully destroy or mutilate them. And we are unpersuaded that the preexistence of the nonpossession regulations in any way negates this interest.

. . . [A] comparison of the regulations with the 1965 Amendment indicates that they protect overlapping but not identical governmental interests, and that they reach somewhat different classes of wrongdoers. The gravamen of the offense defined by the statute is the deliberate rendering of certificates unavailable for the various purposes which they may serve. Whether registrants keep their certificates in their personal possession at all times, as required by the regulations, is of no particular concern under the 1965 Amendment, as long as they do not mutilate or destroy the certificates so as to render them unavailable. . . .

We think it apparent that the continuing availability to each registrant of his Selective Service certificates substantially furthers the smooth and proper functioning of the system that Congress has established to raise armies. We think it also apparent that the Nation has a vital interest in having a system for raising armies that functions with maximum efficiency and is capable of easily and quickly responding to continually changing circumstances. For these reasons, the Government has a substantial interest in assuring the continuing availability of issued Selective Service certificates.

It is equally clear that the 1965 Amendment specifically protects this substantial governmental interest. We perceive no alternative means that would more precisely and narrowly assure the continuing availability of issued Selective Service certificates than a law which prohibits their wilful mutilation or destruction. Compare *Sherbert v. Verner*, 374 U.S. 398, 407–408 (1963), and the cases cited therein. The 1965 Amendment prohibits such conduct and does nothing more. In other words, both the governmental interest and the operation of the 1965 Amendment are limited to the noncommunicative aspect of O'Brien's conduct. The governmental interest and the scope of the 1965 Amendment are limited to preventing harm to the smooth and efficient functioning of the Selective Service System. When O'Brien deliberately rendered unavailable his registration certificate, he willfully frustrated this governmental interest. For this noncommunicative impact of his conduct, and for nothing else, he was convicted.

The case at bar is therefore unlike one where the alleged governmental interest in regulating conduct arises in some measure because the communication allegedly integral to the conduct is itself thought to be harmful. In *Stromberg v. People of State of California*, 283 U.S. 359 (1931), for example, this Court struck down a statutory phrase which punished people who expressed their "opposition to organized government" by displaying "any flag, badge, banner, or device." Since the statute there was aimed at suppressing communication it could not be sustained as a regulation of noncommunicative conduct.

In conclusion, we find that because of the Government's substantial interest in assuring the continuing availability of issued Selective Service certificates, because amended § 462(b) is an appropriately narrow means of protecting this interest and condemns only the independent noncommunicative impact of conduct within its reach, and because the noncommunicative impact of O'Brien's act of burning his registration certificate frustrated the Government's interest, a sufficient governmental interest has been shown to justify O'Brien's conviction.

III

O'Brien finally argues that the 1965 Amendment is unconstitutional as enacted because what he calls the "purpose" of Congress was "to suppress freedom of speech." We reject this argument because under settled principles the purpose of Congress, as O'Brien uses that term, is not a basis for declaring this legislation unconstitutional.

It is a familiar principle of constitutional law that this Court will not strike down an otherwise constitutional statute on the basis of an alleged illicit legislative motive. As the Court long ago stated:

> The decisions of this court from the beginning lend no support whatever to the assumption that the judiciary may restrain the exercise of lawful power on the assumption that a wrongful purpose or motive has caused the power to be exerted.

McCray v. United States, 195 U.S. 27, 56 (1904). This fundamental principle of constitutional adjudication was reaffirmed and the many cases were collected by Mr. Justice Brandeis for the Court in *State of Arizona v. State of California*, 283 U.S. 423 (1931).

Inquiries into congressional motives or purposes are a hazardous matter. When the issue is simply the interpretation of legislation, the Court will look to statements by legislators for guidance as to the purpose of the legislature, because the benefit to sound decision-making in this circumstance is thought sufficient to risk the possibility of misreading Congress' purpose. It is entirely a different matter when we are asked to void a statute that is, under well-settled criteria, constitutional on its face, on the basis of what fewer than a handful of Congressmen said about it. What motivates one legislator to make a speech about a statute is not necessarily what motivates scores of others to enact it, and the stakes are sufficiently high for us to eschew guesswork. We decline to void essentially on the ground that it is unwise legislation which Congress had the undoubted power to enact and which could be reenacted in its exact form if the same or another legislator made a "wiser" speech about it. . . .

IV

Since the 1965 Amendment to § 12(b)(3) of the Universal Military Training and Service Act is constitutional as enacted and as applied, . . . [we] reinstate the judgment and sentence of the District Court. . . .

■ MR. JUSTICE HARLAN, concurring.

The crux of the Court's opinion . . . is . . . its general statement that:

> a government regulation is sufficiently justified if it is within the constitutional power of the Government; if it furthers an important or substantial governmental interest; if the governmental interest is unrelated to the suppression of free expression; and if the incidental restriction on alleged First Amendment freedoms is no greater than is essential to the furtherance of that interest.

I wish to make explicit my understanding that this passage does not foreclose consideration of First Amendment claims in those rare instances when an "incidental" restriction upon expression, imposed by a regulation which furthers an "important or substantial" governmental interest and satisfies the Court's other criteria, in practice has the effect of entirely preventing a "speaker" from reaching a significant audience with whom he could not otherwise lawfully communicate. This is not such a case, since O'Brien manifestly could have conveyed his message in many ways other than by burning his draft card.

■ MR. JUSTICE DOUGLAS, dissenting.

The Court states that the constitutional power of Congress to raise and support armies is "broad and sweeping" and that Congress' power "to classify and conscript manpower for military service is beyond question." This is undoubtedly true in times when, by declaration of Congress, the Nation is in a state of war. The underlying and basic problem in this case, however, is whether conscription is permissible in the absence of a declaration of war. That question has not been briefed nor was it presented in oral argument; but it is, I submit, a question upon which the litigants and the country are entitled to a ruling. . . .

NOTES

1. *United States v. O'Brien* illustrates a host of First Amendment issues. Does "speech" include *conduct* that has an expressive component? If so, does it include such conduct only when engaged in *for such expressive purposes*? Can it really include *any* and *all* conduct? If not, how does one tell which conduct also can be considered "speech" for First Amendment purposes? Identify the Court's answers.

2. Does the categorization of expressive conduct, either as protected or unprotected, depend on the understandings of the speaker, of the government, or of both? In other words: is conduct protected because the individual sought to convey a message through his conduct, or because the government seeks to regulate it on account of its communicative impact? Or should the outcome depend on balancing the practical impact on speech against the government's interest? Consider the following examples from real cases. (1) The government bans the street distribution of leaflets because of the litter problem they produce. (2) The government requires bands performing in a public park to use the city's audio engineers to prevent excessive decibel levels. (3) The government bans sleeping in urban parks, thus precluding the Occupy Movement from engaging in its characteristic protests. (4) The government bans public nudity, thus preventing both political protests involving nudity and also nude dancing.

3. Try to generalize toward a rule: What should be the test for whether government regulation of *conduct* (that has an identifiable expressive component to it) violates the First Amendment? What is the test that the Court in *O'Brien* employs for this inquiry? This is worth finding, marking, and studying, in the context of the case, for it is a much-repeated formulation in the Court's modern First Amendment law.

4. The classic case of content-discriminatory laws is *Police Dep't of Chicago v. Mosley*, 408 U.S. 92 (1972). It involved a Chicago ordinance forbidding picketing and demonstrations within 150 feet of a school, except in the case of a labor dispute. The exception rendered the ordinance content-discriminatory. The Court held the ordinance unconstitutional; the question was not whether the school district might have a legitimate (even compelling) basis for forbidding demonstrations close to schools, but whether it had such a basis for forbidding some demonstrations and not others. "The central problem with Chicago's ordinance," the Court explained, "is that it describes permissible picketing in terms of its subject matter." The *Mosley* holding is now a staple of First Amendment doctrine. Note two aspects of the holding. First, the carve-out for labor picketing had two ramifications: (1) it entailed a more exacting level of scrutiny, and (2) it called into question the seriousness of any governmental assertion of an interest in preventing the disruption to education that demon-

strations cause. If the government is willing to put up with the disruption in some cases, why not all? Second, the concept of content-neutrality is not limited to viewpoints; it extends to subject matter as well.

5. Why does the Court refuse to consider Congress's motive in enacting the law? In 1965, Representative Mendel Rivers introduced a bill to make willful destruction of a draft card a criminal offense, championing the bill as a "clear answer to those who would make a mockery of our efforts in South Vietnam by engaging in the mass destruction of draft cards." A senator condemned draft-card burning as "treason." See Geoffrey R. Stone, PERILOUS TIMES: FREE SPEECH IN WARTIME; FROM THE SEDITION ACT OF 1798 TO THE WAR ON TERROR-ISM 471–472 (2004). Isn't that the strongest possible evidence that Congress is regulating on the basis of communicative impact rather than the administrative issues involved in destruction of a draft card?

Texas v. Johnson
491 U.S. 397 (1989)

■ JUSTICE BRENNAN delivered the opinion of the Court.

After publicly burning an American flag as a means of political protest, Gregory Lee Johnson was convicted of desecrating a flag in violation of Texas law. This case presents the question whether his conviction is consistent with the First Amendment. We hold that it is not.

I

While the Republican National Convention was taking place in Dallas in 1984, respondent Johnson participated in a political demonstration dubbed the "Republican War Chest Tour." As explained in literature distributed by the demonstrators and in speeches made by them, the purpose of this event was to protest the policies of the Reagan administration and of certain Dallas-based corporations. The demonstrators marched through the Dallas streets, chanting political slogans and stopping at several corporate locations to stage "die-ins" intended to dramatize the consequences of nuclear war. On several occasions they spray-painted the walls of buildings and overturned potted plants, but Johnson himself took no part in such activities. He did, however, accept an American flag handed to him by a fellow protestor who had taken it from a flagpole outside one of the targeted buildings.

The demonstration ended in front of Dallas City Hall, where Johnson unfurled the American flag, doused it with kerosene, and set it on fire. While the flag burned, the protestors chanted: "America, the red, white, and blue, we spit on you." After the demonstrators dispersed, a witness to the flag burning collected the flag's remains and buried them in his backyard. No one was physically injured or threatened with injury, though several witnesses testified that they had been seriously offended by the flag burning.

Of the approximately 100 demonstrators, Johnson alone was charged with a crime. The only criminal offense with which he was charged was the desecration of a venerated object in violation of Tex. Penal Code Ann. § 42.09(a)(3) (1989). After a trial, he was convicted, sentenced to one year in prison, and fined $2,000. ... [T]he Texas Court of Criminal Appeals reversed, 755 S.W.2d 92 (1988), holding that the State could not, consistent with the First Amendment, punish Johnson for burning the flag in these circumstances. . . .

II

. . . We must first determine whether Johnson's burning of the flag constituted expressive conduct, permitting him to invoke the First Amendment in challenging his conviction. See, *e.g., Spence v. Washington,* 418 U.S. 405, 409–411 (1974). If his conduct was expressive, we next decide whether the State's regulation is related to the suppression of free expression. See, *e.g., United States v. O'Brien,* 391 U.S. 367, 377 (1968). If the State's regulation is not related to expression, then the less stringent standard we announced in *O'Brien* for regulations of noncommunicative conduct controls. If it is, then we are outside of *O'Brien*'s test, and we must ask whether this interest justifies Johnson's conviction under a more demanding standard. . . .

The First Amendment literally forbids the abridgment only of "speech," but we have long recognized that its protection does not end at the spoken or written word. While we have rejected "the view that an apparently limitless variety of conduct can be labeled 'speech' whenever the person engaging in the conduct intends thereby to express an idea," [*O'Brien*], we have acknowledged that conduct may be "sufficiently imbued with elements of communication to fall within the scope of the First and Fourteenth Amendments[.]" [*Spence.*]

In deciding whether particular conduct possesses sufficient communicative elements to bring the First Amendment into play, we have asked whether "[a]n intent to convey a particularized message was present, and [whether] the likelihood was great that the message would be understood by those who viewed it." 418 U.S., at 410–411. Hence, we have recognized the expressive nature of students' wearing of black armbands to protest American military involvement in Vietnam, *Tinker v. Des Moines Independent Community School Dist.,* 393 U.S. 503, 505 (1969); of a sit-in by blacks in a "whites only" area to protest segregation, *Brown v. Louisiana,* 383 U.S. 131, 141–142 (1966); of the wearing of American military uniforms in a dramatic presentation criticizing American involvement in Vietnam, *Schacht v. United States,* 398 U.S. 58 (1970); and of picketing about a wide variety of causes, see, *e.g., Food Employees v. Logan Valley Plaza, Inc.,* 391 U.S. 308, 313–314 (1968); *United States v. Grace,* 461 U.S. 171, 176 (1983).

Especially pertinent to this case are our decisions recognizing the communicative nature of conduct relating to flags. Attaching a peace sign to the flag, *Spence, supra,* at 409–410; refusing to salute the flag, *West Virginia Board of Education v. Barnette,* 319 U.S. 624, 632 (1943); and displaying a red flag, *Stromberg v. California,* 283 U.S. 359, 368–369 (1931), we have held, all may find shelter under the First Amendment. See also *Smith v. Goguen,* 415 U.S. 566, 588 (1974) (White, J., concurring in judgment) (treating flag "contemptuously" by wearing pants with small flag sewn into their seat is expressive conduct). That we have had little difficulty identifying an expressive element in conduct relating to flags should not be surprising. The very purpose of a national flag is to serve as a symbol of our country; it is, one might say, "the one visible manifestation of two hundred years of nationhood." *Id.* at 603 (Rehnquist, J., dissenting). . . .

The State of Texas conceded for purposes of its oral argument in this case that Johnson's conduct was expressive conduct and this concession seems to us [prudent]. Johnson burned an American flag as part—indeed, as the culmination—of a political demonstration that coincided with the convening of the Republican Party and its renomination of Ronald Reagan for President. The expressive, overtly political nature of this conduct was both intentional and overwhelmingly apparent. . . . In these circumstances, Johnson's burning of the flag was conduct "sufficiently imbued with elements of communication," *Spence*, 418 U.S., at 409, to implicate the First Amendment.

III

The government generally has a freer hand in restricting expressive conduct than it has in restricting the written or spoken word. It may not, however, proscribe particular conduct *because* it has expressive elements. "[W]hat might be termed the more generalized guarantee of freedom of expression makes the communicative nature of conduct an inadequate *basis* for singling out that conduct for proscription. A law *directed at* the communicative nature of conduct must, like a law directed at speech itself, be justified by the substantial showing of need that the First Amendment requires." *Community for Creative Non–Violence v. Watt*, 227 U.S. App. D.C. 19, 55–56 (1983) (Scalia, J., dissenting) (emphasis in original), rev'd *sub nom. Clark v. Community for Creative Non–Violence*, 468 U.S. 288, 293 (1984). It is, in short, not simply the verbal or nonverbal nature of the expression, but the governmental interest at stake, that helps to determine whether a restriction on that expression is valid.

Thus, although we have recognized that where "speech and nonspeech elements are combined in the same course of conduct, a sufficiently important governmental interest in regulating the nonspeech element can justify incidental limitations on First Amendment freedoms," [*O'Brien*], we have limited the applicability of *O'Brien*'s relatively lenient standard to those cases in which "the governmental interest is unrelated to the suppression of free expression." In stating, moreover, that *O'Brien*'s test "in the last analysis is little, if any, different from the standard applied to time, place, or manner restrictions," *Clark, supra*, at 298, we have highlighted the requirement that the governmental interest in question be unconnected to expression in order to come under *O'Brien*'s less demanding rule.

In order to decide whether *O'Brien*'s test applies here, therefore, we must decide whether Texas has asserted an interest in support of Johnson's conviction that is unrelated to the suppression of expression. If we find that an interest asserted by the State is simply not implicated on the facts before us, we need not ask whether *O'Brien*'s test applies. The State offers two separate interests to justify this conviction: preventing breaches of the peace and preserving the flag as a symbol of nationhood and national unity. We hold that the first interest is not implicated on this record and that the second is related to the suppression of expression.

A

Texas claims that its interest in preventing breaches of the peace justifies Johnson's conviction for flag desecration. However, no disturbance of the peace actually occurred or threatened to occur because of Johnson's burning of the flag. Although the State stresses the disruptive behavior of the protestors during their march toward City Hall, it admits that "no actual breach of the peace occurred at the time of the flagburning or in response to the flagburning." . . . The only evidence offered by the State at trial to show the reaction to Johnson's actions was the testimony of several persons who had been seriously offended by the flag burning.

The State's position, therefore, amounts to a claim that an audience that takes serious offense at particular expression is necessarily likely to disturb the peace and that the expression may be prohibited on this basis. Our precedents do not countenance such a presumption. On the contrary, they recognize that a principal "function of free speech under our system of government is to invite dispute. It may indeed best serve its high purpose when it induces a condition of unrest, creates dissatisfaction with conditions as they are, or even stirs people to anger." *Terminiello v. Chicago*, 337 U.S. 1, 4 (1949). It would be odd indeed to conclude *both* that "if it is the speaker's opinion that gives offense, that consequence is a reason for according it constitutional protection," *FCC v. Pacifica Foundation*, 438 U.S. 726, 745 (1978), *and* that the government may ban the expression of certain disagreeable ideas on the unsupported presumption that their very disagreeableness will provoke violence.

Thus, we have not permitted the government to assume that every expression of a provocative idea will incite a riot, but have instead required careful consideration of the actual circumstances surrounding such expression, asking whether the expression "is directed to inciting or producing imminent lawless action and is likely to incite or produce such action." *Brandenburg v. Ohio*, 395 U.S. 444, 447 (1969) (reviewing circumstances surrounding rally and speeches by Ku Klux Klan). To accept Texas' arguments that it need only demonstrate "the potential for a breach of the peace," and that every flag burning necessarily possesses that potential, would be to eviscerate our holding in *Brandenburg*. This we decline to do.

Nor does Johnson's expressive conduct fall within that small class of "fighting words" that are "likely to provoke the average person to retaliation, and thereby cause a breach of the peace." *Chaplinsky v. New Hampshire*, 315 U.S. 568, 574 (1942). No reasonable onlooker would have regarded Johnson's generalized expression of dissatisfaction with the policies of the Federal Government as a direct personal insult or an invitation to exchange fisticuffs.

We thus conclude that the State's interest in maintaining order is not implicated on these facts. The State need not worry that our holding will disable it from preserving the peace. We do not suggest that the First Amendment forbids a State to prevent "imminent lawless action." *Brandenburg, supra*, at 447. And, in fact, Texas already has a statute specifically prohibiting breaches of the peace, Tex. Penal Code Ann. § 42.01 (1989), which tends to confirm that Texas need not punish this flag desecration in order to keep the peace.

B

The State also asserts an interest in preserving the flag as a symbol of nationhood and national unity. In *Spence*, we acknowledged that the government's interest in preserving the flag's special symbolic value "is directly related to expression in the context of activity" such as affixing a peace symbol to a flag. 418 U.S., at 414, n. 8. We are equally persuaded that this interest is related to expression in the case of Johnson's burning of the flag. The State, apparently, is concerned that such conduct will lead people to believe either that the flag does not stand for nationhood and national unity, but instead reflects other, less positive concepts, or that the concepts reflected in the flag do not in fact exist, that is, that we do not enjoy unity as a Nation. These concerns blossom only when a person's treatment of the flag communicates some message, and thus are related "to the suppression of free expression" within the meaning of *O'Brien*. We are thus outside of *O'Brien*'s test altogether.

IV

It remains to consider whether the State's interest in preserving the flag as a symbol of nationhood and national unity justifies Johnson's conviction.

As in *Spence*, "[w]e are confronted with a case of prosecution for the expression of an idea through activity," and "[a]ccordingly, we must examine with particular care the interests advanced by [petitioner] to support its prosecution." 418 U.S., at 411. Johnson was not, we add, prosecuted for the expression of just any idea; he was prosecuted for his expression of dissatisfaction with the policies of this country, expression situated at the core of our First Amendment values.

Moreover, Johnson was prosecuted because he knew that his politically charged expression would cause "serious offense." If he had burned the flag as a means of disposing of it because it was dirty or torn, he would not have been convicted of flag desecration under this Texas law: federal law designates burning as the preferred means of disposing of a flag "when it is in such condition that it is no longer a fitting emblem for display," 36 U.S.C. § 176(k), and Texas has no quarrel with this means of disposal. The Texas law is thus not aimed at protecting the physical integrity of the flag in all circumstances, but is designed instead to protect it only against impairments that would cause serious offense to others. . . .

Whether Johnson's treatment of the flag violated Texas law thus depended on the likely communicative impact of his expressive conduct. Our decision in *Boos v. Barry, supra*, tells us that this restriction on Johnson's expression is content based. In *Boos*, we considered the constitutionality of a law prohibiting "the display of any sign within 500 feet of a foreign embassy if that sign tends to bring that foreign government into public odium or public disrepute." Rejecting the argument that the law was content neutral because it was justified by "our international law obligation to shield diplomats from speech that offends their dignity," we held that "[t]he emotive impact of speech on its audience is not a 'secondary effect' " unrelated to the content of the expression itself. *Id.* at 321 (plurality opinion).

According to the principles announced in *Boos*, Johnson's political expression was restricted because of the content of the message he conveyed. We must therefore subject the State's asserted interest in preserving the special symbolic character of the flag to "the most exacting scrutiny."

. . . [T]he State's claim is that it has an interest in preserving the flag as a symbol of *nationhood* and *national unity*, a symbol with a determinate range of meanings. According to Texas, if one physically treats the flag in a way that would tend to cast doubt on either the idea that nationhood and national unity are the flag's referents or that national unity actually exists, the message conveyed thereby is a harmful one and therefore may be prohibited.

If there is a bedrock principle underlying the First Amendment, it is that the government may not prohibit the expression of an idea simply because society finds the idea itself offensive or disagreeable. *[The Court then cited a long list of cases for this proposition.—Editors]*

We have not recognized an exception to this principle even where our flag has been involved. In *Street v. New York*, 394 U.S. 576 (1969), we held that a State may not criminally punish a person for uttering words critical of the flag. Rejecting the argument that the conviction could be sustained on the ground that Street had "failed to show the respect for our national symbol which may properly be demanded of every citizen," we concluded that "the constitutionally guaranteed 'freedom to be intellectually . . . diverse or even contrary,' and the 'right to differ as to things that touch the heart of the existing order,' encompass the freedom to express publicly one's opinions about our flag, including those opinions which are defiant or contemptuous." Nor may the government, we have held, compel conduct that would evince respect for the flag. "To sustain the compulsory flag salute we are required to say that a Bill of Rights which guards the individual's right to speak his own mind, left it open to public authorities to compel him to utter what is not in his mind."

In holding in *Barnette* that the Constitution did not leave this course open to the government, Justice Jackson described one of our society's defining principles in words deserving of their frequent repetition: "If there is any fixed star in our constitutional constellation, it is that no official, high or petty, can prescribe what shall be orthodox in politics, nationalism, religion, or other matters of opinion or force citizens to confess by word or act their faith therein." *Id.* at 642. . . .

Texas' focus on the precise nature of Johnson's expression, moreover, misses the point of our prior decisions: their enduring lesson, that the government may not prohibit expression simply because it disagrees with its message, is not dependent on the particular mode in which one chooses to express an idea. If we were to hold that a State may forbid flag burning wherever it is likely to endanger the flag's symbolic role, but allow it wherever burning a flag promotes that role—as where, for example, a person ceremoniously burns a dirty flag—we would be saying that when it comes to impairing the flag's physical integrity, the flag itself may be used as a symbol—as a substitute for the written or spoken word or a "short cut from mind to mind"—only in one direction. We would be permitting a State to "prescribe what shall be orthodox" by saying that one may burn the flag to convey one's attitude toward it and its referents only if one does not endanger the flag's representation of nationhood and national unity.

We never before have held that the Government may ensure that a symbol be used to express only one view of that symbol or its referents. . . . To conclude that the government may permit designated symbols to be used to communicate only a limited set of messages would be to enter territory having no discernible or defensible boundaries. Could the government, on this theory, prohibit the burning of state flags? Of copies of the Presidential seal? Of the Constitution? In evaluating these choices under the First Amendment, how would we decide which symbols were sufficiently special to warrant this unique status? To do so, we would be forced to consult our own political preferences, and impose them on the citizenry, in the very way that the First Amendment forbids us to do.

There is, moreover, no indication—either in the text of the Constitution or in our cases interpreting it—that a separate juridical category exists for the American flag alone. . . . The First Amendment does not guarantee that other concepts virtually sacred to our Nation as a whole—such as the principle that discrimination on the basis of race is odious and destructive—will go unquestioned in the marketplace of ideas. See *Brandenburg v. Ohio*, 395 U.S. 444 (1969). We decline, therefore, to create for the flag an exception to the joust of principles protected by the First Amendment.

It is not the State's ends, but its means, to which we object. It cannot be gainsaid that there is a special place reserved for the flag in this Nation, and thus we do not doubt that the government has a legitimate interest in making efforts to "preserv[e] the national flag as an unalloyed symbol of our country." We reject the suggestion, urged at oral argument by counsel for Johnson, that the government lacks "any state interest whatsoever" in regulating the manner in which the flag may be displayed. Congress has, for example, enacted precatory regulations describing the proper treatment of the flag, see 36 U.S.C. §§ 173–177, and we cast no doubt on the legitimacy of its interest in making such recommendations. To say that the government has an interest in encouraging proper treatment of the flag, however, is not to say that it may criminally punish a person for burning a flag as a means of political protest. "National unity as an end which officials may foster by persuasion and example is not in question. The problem is whether under our Constitution compulsion as here employed is a permissible means for its achievement." *Barnette*, 319 U.S., at 640.

We are fortified in today's conclusion by our conviction that forbidding criminal punishment for conduct such as Johnson's will not endanger the special role played by our flag or the feelings it inspires. To paraphrase Justice Holmes, we submit that nobody can suppose that this one gesture of an unknown man will change our Nation's attitude towards its flag. See *Abrams v. United States*, 250 U.S. 616, 628 (1919) (Holmes, J., dissenting). Indeed, Texas' argument that the burning of an American flag "is an act having a high likelihood to cause a breach of the peace," and its statute's implicit assumption that physical mistreatment of the flag will lead to "serious offense," tend to confirm that the flag's special role is not in danger; if it were, no one would riot or take offense because a flag had been burned.

We are tempted to say, in fact, that the flag's deservedly cherished place in our community will be strengthened, not weakened, by our holding today. Our decision is a reaffirmation of the principles of freedom and inclusiveness that the flag best reflects, and of the conviction that our toleration of criticism such as Johnson's is a sign and source of our strength. . . .

The way to preserve the flag's special role is not to punish those who feel differently about these matters. It is to persuade them that they are wrong. "To courageous, self-reliant men, with confidence in the power of free and fearless reasoning applied through the processes of popular government, no danger flowing from speech can be deemed clear and present, unless the incidence of the evil apprehended is so imminent that it may befall before there is opportunity for full discussion. If there be time to expose through discussion the falsehood and fallacies, to avert the evil by the processes of education, the remedy to be applied is more speech, not enforced silence." *Whitney v. California*, 274 U.S. 357, 377 (1927) (Brandeis, J., concurring). And, precisely because it is our flag that is involved, one's response to the flag burner may exploit the uniquely persuasive power of the flag itself. We can imagine no more appropriate response to burning a flag than waving one's own, no better way to counter a flag burner's message than by saluting the flag that burns, no surer means of preserving the dignity even of the flag that burned than by—as one witness here did—according its remains a respectful burial. We do not consecrate the flag by punishing its desecration, for in doing so we dilute the freedom that this cherished emblem represents.

V

Johnson was convicted for engaging in expressive conduct. The State's interest in preventing breaches of the peace does not support his conviction because Johnson's conduct did not threaten to disturb the peace. Nor does the State's interest in preserving the flag as a symbol of nationhood and national unity justify his criminal conviction for engaging in political expression.

■ [JUSTICE KENNEDY'S concurrence is omitted.]

■ CHIEF JUSTICE REHNQUIST, with whom JUSTICE WHITE and JUSTICE O'CONNOR join, dissenting.

In holding this Texas statute unconstitutional, the Court ignores Justice Holmes' familiar aphorism that "a page of history is worth a volume of logic." . . . *[The dissent gives many examples of the honor attributed to the flag in American history.—Editors]*

The American flag, then, throughout more than 200 years of our history, has come to be the visible symbol embodying our Nation. It does not represent the views of any particular political party, and it does not represent any particular political philosophy. The flag is not simply another "idea" or "point of view" competing for recognition in the marketplace of ideas. Millions and millions of Americans regard it with an almost mystical reverence regardless of what sort of social, political, or philosophical beliefs they may have. I cannot agree that the First Amendment invalidates the Act of Congress, and the laws of 48 of the 50 States, which make criminal the public burning of the flag. . . .

But the Court insists that the Texas statute prohibiting the public burning of the American flag infringes on respondent Johnson's freedom of expression. Such freedom, of course, is not absolute. See *Schenck v. United States*, 249 U.S. 47 (1919). In *Chaplinsky v. New Hampshire*, 315 U.S. 568 (1942), a unanimous Court said:

> Allowing the broadest scope to the language and purpose of the Fourteenth Amendment, it is well understood that the right of free speech is not absolute at all times and under all circumstances. There are certain well-defined and narrowly limited classes of speech, the prevention and punishment of which have never been thought to raise any Constitutional problem. These include the lewd and obscene, the profane, the libelous, and the insulting or "fighting" words—those which by their very utterance inflict injury or tend to incite an immediate breach of the peace. It has been well observed that such utterances are no essential part of any exposition of ideas, and are of such slight social value as a step to truth that any benefit that may be derived from them is clearly outweighed by the social interest in order and morality.

Id. at 571–572.

The Court upheld Chaplinsky's conviction under a state statute that made it unlawful to "address any offensive, derisive or annoying word to any person who is lawfully in any street or other public place." *Id.* at 569. Chaplinsky had told a local marshal, "You are a God damned racketeer" and a "damned Fascist and the whole government of Rochester are Fascists or agents of Fascists." *Ibid.*

Here it may equally well be said that the public burning of the American flag by Johnson was no essential part of any exposition of ideas, and at the same time it had a tendency to incite a breach of the peace. Johnson was free to make any verbal denunciation of the flag that he wished; indeed, he was free to burn the flag in private. He could publicly burn other symbols of the Government or effigies of political leaders. He did lead a march through the streets of Dallas, and conducted a rally in front of the Dallas City Hall. He engaged in a "die-in" to protest nuclear weapons. He shouted out various slogans during the march, including: "Reagan, Mondale which will it be? Either one means World War III"; "Ronald Reagan, killer of the hour, Perfect example of U.S. power"; and "red, white and blue, we spit on you, you stand for plunder, you will go under." Brief for Respondent 3. For none of these acts was he arrested or prosecuted; it was only when he proceeded to burn publicly an American flag stolen from its rightful owner that he violated the Texas statute.

The Court could not, and did not, say that Chaplinsky's utterances were not expressive phrases—they clearly and succinctly conveyed an extremely low opinion of the addressee. The same may be said of Johnson's public burning of the flag in this case; it obviously did convey Johnson's bitter dislike of his country. But his act, like Chaplinsky's provocative words, conveyed nothing that could not have been conveyed and was not conveyed just as forcefully in a dozen different ways. As with "fighting words," so with flag burning, for purposes of the First Amendment: It is "no essential part of any exposition of ideas, and [is] of such slight social value as a step to truth that any benefit that may be derived from [it] is clearly outweighed" by the public interest in avoiding a probable breach of the peace . . .

The result of the Texas statute is obviously to deny one in Johnson's frame of mind one of many means of "symbolic speech." Far from being a case of "one picture being worth a thousand words," flag burning is the equivalent of an inarticulate grunt or roar that, it seems fair to say, is most likely to be indulged in not to express any particular idea, but to antagonize others. . . . The Texas statute deprived Johnson of only one rather inarticulate symbolic form of protest—a form of protest that was profoundly offensive to many—and left him with a full panoply of other symbols and every conceivable form of verbal expression to express his deep disapproval of national policy. Thus, in no way can it be said that Texas is punishing him because his hearers—or any other group of people—were profoundly opposed to the message that he sought to convey. Such opposition is no proper basis for restricting speech or expression under the First Amendment. It was Johnson's use of this particular symbol, and not the idea that he sought to convey by it or by his many other expressions, for which he was punished. . . .

But the Court today will have none of this. The uniquely deep awe and respect for our flag felt by virtually all of us are bundled off under the rubric of "designated symbols" that the First Amendment prohibits the government from "establishing." But the government has not "established" this feeling; 200 years of history have done that. The government is simply recognizing as a fact the profound regard for the American flag created by that history when it enacts statutes prohibiting the disrespectful public burning of the flag. . . .

■ JUSTICE STEVENS, dissenting.

As the Court analyzes this case, it presents the question whether the State of Texas, or indeed the Federal Government, has the power to prohibit the public desecration of the American flag. The question is unique. In my judgment rules that apply to a host of other symbols, such as state flags, armbands, or various privately promoted emblems of political or commercial identity, are not necessarily controlling. Even if flag burning could be considered just another species of symbolic speech under the logical application of the rules that the Court has developed in its interpretation of the First Amendment in other contexts, this case has an intangible dimension that makes those rules inapplicable. . . .

The Court is therefore quite wrong in blandly asserting that respondent "was prosecuted for his expression of dissatisfaction with the policies of this country, expression situated at the core of our First Amendment values." Respondent was prosecuted because of the method he chose to express his dissatisfaction with those policies. Had he chosen to spray-paint—or perhaps convey with a motion picture projector—his message of dissatisfaction on the facade of the Lincoln Memorial, there would be no question about the power of the Government to prohibit his means of expression. The prohibition would be supported by the legitimate interest in preserving the quality of an important national asset. Though the asset at stake in this case is intangible, given its unique value, the same interest supports a prohibition on the desecration of the American flag. . . .

NOTES

1. Identify the "*O'Brien* test" as used by the Court in *Texas v. Johnson*. Does Texas's criminal punishment of flag—burning fit within the set of situations described by that test—government regulation of conduct for reasons unrelated to the suppression of free expression? What is the Court's answer? Do you agree with the Court's analysis or not? Is Texas regulating conduct, and in the process only incidentally restricting the expression of ideas? What do you think of Justice Stevens's analogy, in dissent, to spray-painting the Lincoln Memorial?

2. Even assuming that Johnson's conduct constitutes "speech" falling within the protection of the First Amendment, are there not some interests of the state, and of society, that must prevail over the individual's right to free speech? If so, what might those be? Can you formulate a general proposition from your consideration of those interests that might justify suppression of free speech—something like "The freedom of speech is absolute except. . . ." Except when?

3. When, if ever, should government be able to suppress speech because of the offensiveness of the message being conveyed? What about the offensiveness of the *manner* in which or *means or method* by which it is being conveyed? Are there some ideas that are just so offensive and of so little or even negative value that their expression need never be permitted? Is flag-burning in some such category? Are you persuaded by the dissenters' arguments about the special circumstances of the U.S. flag? If so, are there other things that fit in a similar category?

4. What if the offensiveness of certain speech or expressive conduct is so great that it is likely to produce a violent reaction—start a fight, trigger a riot, lead to murders? May government regulate it in the interest of preserving public peace or saving lives or property? How does the Court in *Texas v. Johnson* deal with this problem? What do you make of the "fighting words" doctrine and precedent? In 2005, the largest circulation paper in Denmark, *Jyllands–Posten*, published a series of cartoon depictions of the Muslim prophet Mohammed. The depictions were considered so offensive that they produced violent demonstra-

tions in response, including the burnings of Danish embassies in Syria and Gaza. The same year, a false Newsweek report (later retracted) that U.S. interrogators had flushed a Koran down a toilet sparked riots that resulted in seventeen deaths. See Katherine Q. Seelye & Neil A. Lewis, *Newsweek Says It Is Retracting Koran Report*, N.Y. Times (May 17, 2005). Should anticipated violence in response to offensive speech permit the government to restrict such speech?

As we noted above, other Western nations' constitutions handle these issues differently. On the one hand, they are often written more broadly, explicitly to protect "freedom of expression" rather than merely "freedom of speech and of the press." On the other hand, they sometimes explicitly say that the right of free expression must be balanced against the need to promote a democratic society, thus permitting more restrictions on speech considered harmful. See generally Vicki C. Jackson & Mark Tushnet, COMPARATIVE CONSTITUTIONAL LAW 1468–1637 (2d ed. 2006). Which approach do you prefer?

5. *Texas v. Johnson* created a political tempest. President George H. W. Bush called for a constitutional amendment to ban flag-burning, which would repudiate the outcome of the case. Congress, controlled by the Democrats, responded instead by passing a federal flag-burning statute that tried (rather feebly) to work around some of the defects of Texas's statute, by eliminating explicit use of the word "desecrate" but punishing anyone who "knowingly mutilates, defaces, physically defiles, burns, maintains on the floor or ground, or tramples upon any flag of the United States." The statute was immediately challenged. Is such a federal law "necessary and proper for carrying into execution" the enumerated powers even if it does not violate the First Amendment? Have We the People delegated to Congress the power to pass laws against flag burning? In *United States v. Eichman*, 496 U.S. 310 (1990), decided the next year, the Supreme Court struck down the federal statute on First Amendment grounds as well—by an identical 5–4 vote—concluding that the government's interest was still not "unrelated to the suppression of free expression" but instead focused on disrespectful treatment of the flag. Should it have been 9–0? Was it proper for the dissenting justices to stick to their positions? Was it improper for Congress to seek to force the Supreme Court to reconsider its prior decision?

Reasonable, Neutral Time, Place, and Manner Regulations

One important subcategory of content-neutral restrictions on speech comprises reasonable, content-neutral, time, place, and manner regulations. Unlike laws regulating expressive conduct, these rules single out speech for particular restrictions, but (1) do not distinguish between different cases on the basis of the content of the speech, (2) do not prohibit the speech, but only confine it to certain reasonable times, places, or manners. What issues does this form of regulation raise?

1. *Some "time, place, and manner" cases.* In *Kovacs v. Cooper*, 336 U.S. 77 (1949), the Court upheld a ban on "sound trucks" (loudspeaker systems). In *Grayned v. Rockford*, 408 U.S. 104 (1972), the Court upheld (against Free Speech Clause challenge) a conviction for violating an "anti-noise" ordinance prohibiting disturbing noise adjacent to a school building when classes are in session—distinguishing situations where similar speech might occur in a public park. In *Heffron v. International Society for Krishna Consciousness (ISKCON)*, 452 U.S. 640 (1981), the Court upheld a Minnesota State Fair regulation requiring anyone wishing to sell, distribute, or

promote anything to do so in a "booth"—as applied to prohibit the Hare Krishna sect's desire to walk around the fairgrounds and distribute literature to fairgoers. In *Frisby v. Schultz*, 487 U.S. 474 (1988), the Court upheld a ban on targeted residential picketing of a person's home. In *Ward v. Rock Against Racism*, 491 U.S. 781 (1989), the Court upheld New York City's regulation requiring use of city-provided sound systems and technicians to control the volume of performances in Central Park. In *City of Ladue v. Gilleo*, 512 U.S. 43 (1994), the Court unanimously struck down an ordinance banning most yard signs in residential neighborhoods (but exempting certain categories—for-sale signs, business signs). The city wanted to avoid "visual clutter." The Court thought this left too few "alternative channels" for persons to express their messages. In *Hill v. Colorado*, 530 U.S. 703 (2000), the Court upheld, 5–4, a law prohibiting persons from "knowingly" approaching within eight feet of another person, in order to present a handbill or leaflet, counsel, or protest, in front of a hospital or other medical facility. Which of these cases do you think were rightly decided?

2. *Time*: May government restrict public demonstrations or rallies to daylight hours? To weekend days? To between 4:00 PM and 5:00 PM on Tuesdays and Thursdays? How is the reasonableness of a "time" restriction to be evaluated?

3. *Place*: May government forbid demonstrations, rallies, picketing, leafleting, or personal advocacy of a point of view within one hundred feet of a school? A church? A cemetery? A hospital? An animal-research facility? A foreign embassy? A military base? In front of all public buildings? Near abortion clinics? In airport corridors? Within public-school hallways? (Many of these are real cases.) Could it do so at certain times of day (combining a time regulation and a place regulation)?

4. *Manner*: May government forbid the use of megaphones or other amplification devices? May it set limits on the total decibel level of speech? May it prohibit group chanting? Subliminal messages during movies? Would such restrictions be content-based or content-neutral? Reasonable? Where is the line between regulating "manner" and regulating a particular type of expressive conduct because of its emotive force (like burning a flag or draft card or sleeping in a "Reaganville" across the street from the White House)? Could you describe the violent video game regulation in *Brown* as a "manner" regulation?

Renton v. Playtime Theaters
475 U.S. 41 (1986)

■ JUSTICE REHNQUIST delivered the opinion of the Court.

This case involves a constitutional challenge to a zoning ordinance . . . that prohibits adult motion picture theaters from locating within 1,000 feet of any residential zone, single- or multiple-family dwelling, church, park, or school. Appellees [sought] a declaratory judgment that the Renton ordinance violated the First and Fourteenth Amendments and a permanent injunction against its enforcement. The District Court ruled in favor of Renton and denied the permanent injunction, but the Court of Appeals for the Ninth Circuit reversed and remanded for reconsideration. We . . . reverse the judgment of the Ninth Circuit . . .

In our view, the resolution of this case is largely dictated by our decision in *Young v. American Mini Theatres*. There, although five Members of the Court did not agree on a single rationale for the decision, we held that the city of Detroit's zoning ordinance, which prohibited locating an adult theater within 1,000 feet of any two other "regulated uses" or within 500 feet of any residential zone, did not violate the First and Fourteenth Amendments. The Renton ordinance, like the one in *American Mini Theatres,* does not ban adult theaters altogether, but merely provides that such theaters may not be located within 1,000 feet of any residential zone, single- or multiple-family dwelling, church, park, or school. The ordinance is therefore properly analyzed as a form of time, place, and manner regulation.

Describing the ordinance as a time, place, and manner regulation is, of course, only the first step in our inquiry. This Court has long held that regulations enacted for the purpose of restraining speech on the basis of its content presumptively violate the First Amendment. On the other hand, so-called "content-neutral" time, place, and manner regulations are acceptable so long as they are designed to serve a substantial governmental interest and do not unreasonably limit alternative avenues of communication.

At first glance, the Renton ordinance, like the ordinance in *American Mini Theatres,* does not appear to fit neatly into either the "content-based" or the "content-neutral" category. To be sure, the ordinance treats theaters that specialize in adult films differently from other kinds of theaters. Nevertheless, as the District Court concluded, the Renton ordinance is aimed not at the *content* of the films shown at "adult motion picture theatres," but rather at the *secondary effects* of such theaters on the surrounding community. The District Court found that the City Council's *"predominate* concerns" were with the secondary effects of adult theaters, and not with the content of adult films themselves. But the Court of Appeals . . . held that this was not enough to sustain the ordinance. According to the Court of Appeals, if *"a motivating factor"* in enacting the ordinance was to restrict respondents' exercise of First Amendment rights the ordinance would be invalid, apparently no matter how small a part this motivating factor may have played in the City Council's decision. This view of the law was rejected in *O'Brien*, [which stated that "an otherwise constitutional statute" is not unconstitutional "on the basis of an alleged illicit legislative motive."]

The District Court's finding as to "predominate" intent, left undisturbed by the Court of Appeals, is more than adequate to establish that the city's pursuit of its zoning interests here was unrelated to the suppression of free expression. The ordinance by its terms is designed to prevent crime, protect the city's retail trade, maintain property values, and generally "protec[t] and preserv[e] the quality of [the city's] neighborhoods, commercial districts, and the quality of urban life," not to suppress the expression of unpopular views. As Justice POWELL observed in *American Mini Theatres,* "[i]f [the city] had been concerned with restricting the message purveyed by adult theaters, it would have tried to close them or restrict their number rather than circumscribe their choice as to location."

In short, the Renton ordinance is completely consistent with our definition of "content-neutral" speech regulations as those that "are *justified* without reference to the content of the regulated speech." The ordinance does not contravene the fundamental principle that underlies our concern about "content-based" speech regulations: that "government may not grant the use of a forum to people whose views it finds acceptable, but deny use to those wishing to express less favored or more controversial views."

It was with this understanding in mind that, in *American Mini Theatres,* a majority of this Court decided that, at least with respect to businesses that purvey sexually explicit materials, zoning ordinances designed to combat the undesirable secondary effects of such businesses are to be reviewed under the standards applicable to "content-neutral" time, place, and manner regulations. Justice STEVENS, writing for the plurality, concluded that the city of Detroit was entitled to draw a distinction between adult theaters and other kinds of theaters "without violating the government's paramount obligation of neutrality in its regulation of protected communication," that "[i]t is th[e] secondary effect which these zoning ordinances attempt to avoid, not the dissemination of 'offensive' speech." Justice POWELL, in concurrence, elaborated:

> "[The] dissent misconceives the issue in this case by insisting that it involves an impermissible time, place, and manner restriction based on the content of expression. It involves nothing of the kind. We have here merely a decision by the city to treat certain movie theaters differently because they have markedly different effects upon their surroundings. . . . Moreover, even if this were a case involving a special governmental response to the content of one type of movie, it is possible that the result would be supported by a line of cases recognizing that the government can tailor its reaction to different types of speech according to the degree to which its special and overriding interests are implicated. See, *e.g., Tinker.*

The appropriate inquiry in this case, then, is whether the Renton ordinance is designed to serve a substantial governmental interest and allows for reasonable alternative avenues of communication. It is clear that the ordinance meets such a standard. As a majority of this Court recognized in *American Mini Theatres,* a city's "interest in attempting to preserve the quality of urban life is one that must be accorded high respect." Exactly the same vital governmental interests are at stake here.

The Court of Appeals ruled, however, that because the Renton ordinance was enacted without the benefit of studies specifically relating to "the particular problems or needs of Renton," the city's justifications for the ordinance were "conclusory and speculative." We think the Court of Appeals imposed on the city an unnecessarily rigid burden of proof. The record in this case reveals that Renton relied heavily on the experience of, and studies produced by, the city of Seattle. In Seattle, as in Renton, the adult theater zoning ordinance was aimed at preventing the secondary effects caused by the presence of even one such theater in a given neighborhood . . .

We hold that Renton was entitled to rely on the experiences of Seattle and other cities, and in particular on the "detailed findings" summarized in the Washington Supreme Court's *Northend Cinema* opinion, in enacting its adult theater zoning ordinance. The First Amendment does not require a city, before enacting such an ordinance, to conduct new studies or produce evidence independent of that already generated by other cities, so long as whatever evidence the city relies upon is reasonably believed to be relevant to the problem that the city addresses. That was the case here. Nor is our holding affected by the fact that Seattle ultimately chose a different method of adult theater zoning than that chosen by Renton, since Seattle's choice of a different remedy to combat the secondary effects of adult theaters does not call into question either Seattle's identification of those secondary effects or the relevance of Seattle's experience to Renton.

We also find no constitutional defect in the method chosen by Renton to further its substantial interests. Cities may regulate adult theaters by dispersing them, as in Detroit, or by effectively concentrating them, as in Renton. "It is not our function to appraise the wisdom of [the city's] decision to require adult theaters to be separated rather than concentrated in the same areas. . . . [T]he city must be allowed a reasonable opportunity to experiment with solutions to admittedly serious problems." *American Mini Theatres*. Moreover, the Renton ordinance is "narrowly tailored" to affect only that category of theaters shown to produce the unwanted secondary effects, thus avoiding the flaw that proved fatal to the regulations [in other cases].

Respondents contend that the Renton ordinance is "under-inclusive," in that it fails to regulate other kinds of adult businesses that are likely to produce secondary effects similar to those produced by adult theaters. On this record the contention must fail. There is no evidence that, at the time the Renton ordinance was enacted, any other adult business was located in, or was contemplating moving into, Renton. In fact, Resolution No. 2368, enacted in October 1980, states that "the City of Renton does not, at the present time, have any business whose primary purpose is the sale, rental, or showing of sexually explicit materials." That Renton chose first to address the potential problems created by one particular kind of adult business in no way suggests that the city has "singled out" adult theaters for discriminatory treatment. We simply have no basis on this record for assuming that Renton will not, in the future, amend its ordinance to include other kinds of adult businesses that have been shown to produce the same kinds of secondary effects as adult theaters. *Lee Optical*.

Finally, turning to the question whether the Renton ordinance allows for reasonable alternative avenues of communication, we note that the ordinance leaves some 520 acres, or more than five percent of the entire land area of Renton, open to use as adult theater sites . . .

Respondents argue [that none of the available land is "commercially viable."] The Court of Appeals accepted these arguments . . . and therefore held that the Renton ordinance "would result in a substantial restriction" on speech.

We disagree with both the reasoning and the conclusion of the Court of Appeals. That respondents must fend for themselves in the real estate market, on an equal footing with other prospective purchasers and lessees, does not give rise to a First Amendment violation. . . . In our view, the First Amendment requires only that Renton refrain from effectively denying respondents a reasonable opportunity to open and operate an adult theater within the city, and the ordinance before us easily meets this requirement.

In sum, we find that the Renton ordinance represents a valid governmental response to the "admittedly serious problems" created by adult theaters. Renton has not used "the power to zone as a pretext for suppressing expression," but rather has sought to make some areas available for adult theaters and their patrons, while at the same time preserving the quality of life in the community at large by preventing those theaters from locating in other areas. This, after all, is the essence of zoning. Here, as in *American*

Mini Theatres, the city has enacted a zoning ordinance that meets these goals while also satisfying the dictates of the First Amendment.

■ JUSTICE BLACKMUN concurs in the result.

■ JUSTICE BRENNAN, with whom JUSTICE MARSHALL joins, dissenting.

Renton's zoning ordinance selectively imposes limitations on the location of a movie theater based exclusively on the content of the films shown there. The constitutionality of the ordinance is therefore not correctly analyzed under standards applied to content-neutral time, place, and manner restrictions. But even assuming that the ordinance may fairly be characterized as content neutral, it is plainly unconstitutional under the standards established by the decisions of this Court. Although the Court's analysis is limited to cases involving "businesses that purvey sexually explicit materials," and thus does not affect our holdings in cases involving state regulation of other kinds of speech, I dissent.

I

"[A] constitutionally permissible time, place, or manner restriction may not be based upon either the content or subject matter of speech." The Court asserts that the ordinance is "aimed not at the *content* of the films shown at 'adult motion picture theatres,' but rather at the *secondary effects* of such theaters on the surrounding community," and thus is simply a time, place, and manner regulation.[1] This analysis is misguided.

The fact that adult movie theaters may cause harmful "secondary" land-use effects may arguably give Renton a compelling reason to regulate such establishments; it does not mean, however, that such regulations are content neutral. Because the ordinance imposes special restrictions on certain kinds of speech on the basis of *content,* I cannot simply accept, as the Court does, Renton's claim that the ordinance was not designed to suppress the content of adult movies . . . In this case, both the language of the ordinance and its dubious legislative history belie the Court's conclusion that "the city's pursuit of its zoning interests here was unrelated to the suppression of free expression."

A

The ordinance discriminates on its face against certain forms of speech based on content . . . Other [types of] motion picture theaters, and other forms of "adult entertainment," such as bars, massage parlors, and adult bookstores, are not subject to the same restrictions. This selective treatment strongly suggests that Renton was interested not in controlling the "secondary effects" associated with adult businesses, but in discriminating against adult theaters based on the content of the films they exhibit. The Court ignores this discriminatory treatment, declaring that Renton is free "to address the potential problems created by one particular kind of adult business," and to amend the ordinance in the future to include other adult enterprises. However, because of the First Amendment interests at stake here, this one-step-at-a-time analysis is wholly inappropriate.

"This Court frequently has upheld underinclusive classifications on the sound theory that a legislature may deal with one part of a problem without addressing all of it. See *e.g., Lee Optical.* This presumption of

---

[1] The Court apparently finds comfort in the fact that the ordinance does not "deny use to those wishing to express less favored or more controversial views." However, content-based discrimination is not rendered "any less odious" because it distinguishes "among entire classes of ideas, rather than among points of view within a particular class." . . .

statutory validity, however, has less force when a classification turns on the subject matter of expression. '[A]bove all else, the First Amendment means that government has no power to restrict expression because of its message, its ideas, its subject matter, or its content.' " *Erznoznik v. City of Jacksonville*, 422 U.S. 205, 215 (1975).

In this case, the city has not justified treating adult movie theaters differently from other adult entertainment businesses. The ordinance's underinclusiveness is cogent evidence that it was aimed at the *content* of the films shown in adult movie theaters.

B

Shortly *after* this lawsuit commenced, the Renton City Council amended the ordinance, adding a provision explaining that its intention in adopting the ordinance had been "to promote the City of Renton's great interest in protecting and preserving the quality of its neighborhoods, commercial districts, and the quality of urban life through effective land use planning." The amended ordinance also lists certain conclusory "findings" concerning adult entertainment land uses that the Council purportedly relied upon in adopting the ordinance. The city points to these provisions as evidence that the ordinance was designed to control the secondary effects associated with adult movie theaters, rather than to suppress the content of the films they exhibit. However, the "legislative history" of the ordinance strongly suggests otherwise.

Prior to the amendment, there was no indication that the ordinance was designed to address any "secondary effects" a single adult theater might create. In addition to the suspiciously coincidental timing of the amendment, many of the City Council's "findings" do not relate to legitimate land-use concerns. As the Court of Appeals observed, "[b]oth the magistrate and the district court recognized that many of the stated reasons for the ordinance were no more than expressions of dislike for the subject matter." That some residents may be offended by the *content* of the films shown at adult movie theaters cannot form the basis for state regulation of speech.

Some of the "findings" added by the City Council do relate to supposed "secondary effects" associated with adult movie theaters. However, the Court cannot, as it does, merely accept these *post hoc* statements at face value . . . *[The Court noted that the City Council "conducted no studies, and heard no expert testimony" and "never considered" less restrictive alternatives. It also did not demonstrate that the experiences of other cities "were relevant to Renton's problems."—Editors]*

Rather than speculate about Renton's motives for adopting such measures, our cases require the conclusion that the ordinance, like any other content-based restriction on speech, is constitutional "only if the [city] can show that [it] is a precisely drawn means of serving a compelling [governmental] interest." Only this strict approach can insure that cities will not use their zoning powers as a pretext for suppressing constitutionally protected expression.

Applying this standard to the facts of this case, the ordinance is patently unconstitutional. Renton has not shown that locating adult movie theaters in proximity to its churches, schools, parks, and residences will necessarily result in undesirable "secondary effects," or that these problems could not be effectively addressed by less intrusive restrictions . . .

NOTES

1. Is there any answer to Justice Brennan's point that the "secondary effects" invoked by the city are nothing other than justifications, to be judged according to the appropriate standard of review (in his view, strict scrutiny)? Is the majority correct to say that an ordinance directed at some movies and not others is "content-neutral"?

2. Perhaps the opinion is best understood as creating an entirely new mode of analysis, rather than as a type of "content-neutrality." Under this view, an ordinance restricting the time, place, or manner of speech is subject to lesser scrutiny if (1) it does not distinguish between types of speech on the basis of content, or (2) if the justification for the restriction is unrelated to the communicative impact of the speech. Does that principle make sense of the purposes of the First Amendment? Is it too broad? Think of the various cases we have encountered. How many of them could be recast as "secondary effects" cases?

3. It is important to keep in mind two restrictions on the application of the secondary-effects analysis. First, it applies only to time, place, and manner regulations, and not to complete prohibitions on speech. Second, it applies only to secondary effects that are not the result of the communicative impact, or message, of the speech. In *Renton*, for example, prostitutes and crime might well be attracted to XXX-rated theaters because of the clientele these theaters attract, which is not a result of the images being conveyed. In *Boos v. Barry* (a case distinguished by the *Renton* Court), the offense to the foreign embassies entailed by hostile demonstrations was a direct result of the messages themselves. Is that a coherent distinction? Is it an important distinction, grounded in genuine First Amendment logic?

[*Assignment 45*]

F. INCITEMENT, SUBVERSIVE ADVOCACY, AND THREATS

As the cases in the preceding section have illustrated, a core principle of the First Amendment's Free Speech Clause is that the government may not prohibit, punish, or penalize speech because of its content or message. But what about where the speech advocates unlawful conduct? What if the speech advocates murder? Overthrow of the government by force or violence? Criminal resistance to the draft? Should the usual free speech answer—the government may not prohibit, punish, or penalize speech based on its content or viewpoint—be different where the speaker is advocating illegal conduct, or trying to "incite" violence or other illegal action? The government certainly may regulate or prohibit the underlying conduct that the speaker is advocating. When, if ever, does this mean that the government should be able to prohibit the advocacy itself?

A Historical Introduction to Incitement, Subversive Advocacy, and Speech Urging Violation of the Law

1. *The Sedition Act of 1798.* Recall the "Sedition Act" of 1798, discussed in Chapter 1. Entitled "An Act for the Punishment of Certain Crimes Against the United States," Section 1 of the Sedition Act made it a crime to "unlawfully combine or conspire together, with *intent to oppose any measure or measures of the government of the United States,* which are or shall be directed by proper authority, *or to impede the operation of any law of the*

United State." It further provided that "if any person or persons, *with intent as aforesaid, shall counsel, advise or attempt to procure* any insurrection, riot, unlawful assembly, or combination, . . . he or they shall be deemed guilty of a high misdemeanor."

Was Section 1 of the Sedition Act unconstitutional? (Recall that it was S*ection 2* of the Sedition Act that punished "false, scandalous and malicious writing" against the government of the United States and that gave rise to the prosecution of journalists, members of Congress, and others for scurrilous public criticism of the Adams administration. Was *that* part of the Sedition Act unconstitutional?)

2. *Lincoln and Vallandigham.* Long before the issue of unlawful advocacy first made its appearance in U.S. Supreme Court cases in the World War I era, there was a fascinating example that occurred during the administration of President Abraham Lincoln in the middle of the Civil War. General Ambrose Burnside had issued "General Order No. 38," which announced that anyone who committed "acts for the benefit of the enemies of our country," including "the habit of declaring sympathies for the enemy," would be arrested.

Former Congressman Clement Vallandigham, an irascible, racist "copperhead" (or "peace") Democratic critic of the administration, decided to test the order. He gave a contentious, anti-war speech against Lincoln and the draft within Burnside's jurisdiction. Vallandigham railed against "King Lincoln," and his "black Republican" policies like the Emancipation Proclamation and urged his fellow Ohio citizens not to cooperate with the administration. The war was "wicked, cruel, and unnecessary," a war "for the freedom of the blacks and the enslavement of the whites," Vallandigham railed. By innuendo, at least, his two-hour tirade suggested that individuals resist military service and the authority of the administration and military officers in the enforcement of the draft. On May 5, 1863, Burnside and Union soldiers arrested Vallandigham and tried him, before a military commission, for violating General Order 38. The action created a small political firestorm, including a public letter from a group of citizens in New York arguing that the action was unconstitutional.

Lincoln was presented with a difficult problem. On the one hand, it was hard to defend General Burnside's action. On the other, releasing Vallandigham and repudiating his own general would have undermined the general's authority and created a host of other problems. Lincoln, in a public letter "To Erastus Corning and Others" (June 12, 1863) made the best defense he could of the constitutional validity of the arrest of Vallandigham—and then commuted his sentence to banishment behind Confederate lines. Lincoln, a shrewd lawyer, laid out versions of arguments that would become the building blocks of Supreme Court doctrine many decades later:

> Take the particular case mentioned by the meeting. It is asserted in substance that Mr. Vallandigham was by a military commander, seized and tried "for no other reason than words addressed to a public meeting, in criticism of the course of the administration, and in condemnation of the military orders of that general." Now, if there be no mistake about this—if this assertion is the truth and the whole truth—if there was no other reason for the arrest, then I concede that the arrest was wrong. But the arrest, as I understand, was made for a very different reason. Mr. Vallandigham avows his hostility to the war on the part of the Union; and his arrest was made because he was la-

boring, with some effect, to prevent the raising of troops, to encourage desertions from the army, and to leave the rebellion without an adequate military force to suppress it. He was not arrested because he was damaging the political prospects of the administration, or the personal interests of the commanding general; but because he was damaging the army, upon the existence, and vigor of which, the life of the nation depends. He was warring upon the military; and this gave the military constitutional jurisdiction to lay hands upon him. If Mr. Vallandigham was not damaging the military power of the country, then his arrest was made on mistake of fact, which I would be glad to correct, on reasonably satisfactory evidence.

I understand the meeting, whose resolutions I am considering, to be in favor of suppressing the rebellion by military force—by armies. Long experience has shown that armies can not be maintained unless desertion shall be punished by the severe penalty of death. The case requires, and the law and the constitution, sanction this punishment. Must I shoot a simple-minded soldier boy who deserts, while I must not touch a hair of a wily agitator who induces him to desert? This is none the less injurious when effected by getting a father, or brother, or friend, into a public meeting, and there working upon his feeling, till he is persuaded to write the soldier boy, that he is fighting in a bad cause, for a wicked administration of a contemptible government, too weak to arrest and punish him if he shall desert. I think that in such a case, to silence the agitator, and save the boy, is not only constitutional, but, withal, a great mercy.

If I be wrong on this question of constitutional power, my error lies in believing that certain proceedings are constitutional when, in cases of rebellion or Invasion, the public Safety requires them, which would not be constitutional when, in absence of rebellion or invasion, the public Safety does not require them—in other words, that the constitution is not in its application in all respects the same, in cases of Rebellion or invasion, involving the public Safety, as it is in times of profound peace and public security. The constitution itself makes the distinction; and I can no more be persuaded that the government can constitutionally take no strong measure in time of rebellion, because it can be shown that the same could not be lawfully taken in time of peace, than I can be persuaded that a particular drug is not good medicine for a sick man, because it can be shown to not be good food for a well one. . . .

And yet, let me say that in my own discretion, I do not know whether I would have ordered the arrest of Mr. V. While I can not shift the responsibility from myself, I hold that, as a general rule, the commander in the field is the better judge of the necessity in any particular case. Of course I must practice a general directory and revisory power in the matter.

One of the resolutions expresses the opinion of the meeting that arbitrary arrests will have the effect to divide and distract those who should be united in suppressing the rebellion; and I am specifically called on to discharge Mr. Vallandigham. I regard this as, at least, a fair appeal to me, on the expediency of exercising a constitutional power which I think exists. In response to such appeal I have to say it gave me pain when I learned that Mr. V. had been arrested, that is, I was pained that there should have seemed to be a necessity for arresting him and that it will afford me great pleasure to discharge him so soon as I can, by any means, believe the public safety will not suffer by it. . . .

What do you make of Lincoln's argument that Vallandigham was arrested for "warring on the military"—for punishable *conduct*, not for his *expression of views* criticizing the government? Lincoln concedes in principle that the latter would not be a constitutional basis for suppressing speech. Is incitement to draft resistance, or even to desertion, punishable conduct or protected speech? What is the appropriate answer to Lincoln's famous rhetorical question: "Must I shoot a simple-minded soldier boy who deserts, while I must not touch a hair of a wily agitator who induces him to desert?" Lincoln also makes an argument from necessity, under the circumstances—that sometimes even the most valued liberties must yield to pressing public necessity. Do you agree?

3. *"Clear and Present Danger": the Wilson Administration, the Espionage Act of 1917, the Sedition Act of 1918, and the Supreme Court's World War I Era and "Red Scare" Cases.* Probably the most severe restrictions of freedom of speech on grounds of its harmful tendencies took place during the administration of President Woodrow Wilson. During World War I, the administration pressed for adoption of the Espionage Age of 1917 and the Sedition Act of 1918, as tools for combating opposition to the war, the draft, and the administration's wartime policies. Congress gave the administration much of what it sought, and the Wilson administration gave these acts the broadest possible readings "in order to suppress a broad range of political dissent." Stone, PERILOUS TIMES at 146. Even after the war was over, the administration continued to arrest and prosecute alleged communists, radicals, and anarchists.

The Espionage Act of 1917 was largely directed at the disclosure of military secrets. But the act also created three new offenses:

[1] Whoever, when the United States is at war, shall willfully make or convey false reports or false statements with intent to interfere with the operation or success of the military or naval forces of the United States or to promote the success of its enemies, and [2] whoever, when the United States is at war, shall willfully cause or attempt to cause insubordination, disloyalty, mutiny, or refusal of duty, in the military or naval forces of the United States, or [3] shall willfully obstruct the recruiting or enlistment service of the United States, to the injury of the service or of the United States, shall be punished by a fine of not more than $10,000 or imprisonment for not more than twenty years, or both.

There were over 2,000 convictions for violations of the act. Were these provisions constitutional? In 1919, a trio of cases reached the Supreme Court. The majority opinion in the lead case, *Schenck v. United States*, 249 U.S. 47 (1919), written by Justice Oliver Wendell Holmes, is famous for its creation of the "clear and present danger" test. The offense consisted of a printed pamphlet arguing that conscription violated the Thirteenth Amendment (prohibiting slavery), championing "your right to assert your opposition to the draft," and denying the power of the government to order troops abroad. "You must do your share to maintain, support and uphold the rights of the people of this country," the pamphlet argued.

Justice Holmes wrote: "Of course the document would not have been sent unless it had been intended to have some effect, and we do not see what effect it could be expected to have upon persons subject to the draft except to influence them to obstruct the carrying of it out. The defendants do not deny that the jury might find against them [in this respect]." As to the defendant's objection on First Amendment grounds, he said:

> We admit that in many places and in ordinary times the defendants in saying all that was said in the circular would have been within their constitutional rights. But ... the most stringent protection of free speech would not protect a man in falsely shouting fire in a theatre and causing a panic.... The question in every case is whether the words used are used in such circumstances and are of such a nature as to create a clear and present danger that they will bring about the substantive evils that Congress has a right to prevent. It is a question of proximity and degree. When a nation is at war many things that might be said in time of peace are such a hindrance to its effort that their utterance will not be endorsed so long as men fight, and that no Court could regard them as protected by any constitutional right.

The Court concluded that if such words had the actual effect of obstructing recruitment, they could be punished. It followed that if the words were spoken with intent to produce such effect, and had such a natural tendency, they could be punished whether or not they had actually obstructed recruitment.

Frohwerk v. United States, 249 U.S. 204 (1919), decided a week after *Schenck*, upheld a conviction for publishing a newspaper that allegedly attempted to cause disloyalty, mutiny, and refusal of duty in the military. There was, "so far as the language of the articles goes," no difference between them and those in *Schenck*. "The first begins by declaring it a monumental and inexcusable mistake to send our soldiers to France, says that it comes no doubt from the great trusts, and later that it appears to be outright murder without serving anything practical; speaks of the unconquerable spirit and undiminished strength of the German nation, and characterizes its own discourse as words of warning to the American people." Holmes again wrote for the Court: "[W]e find ourselves unable to say that the articles could not furnish a basis for a conviction."

But perhaps the most controversial decision of the Court concerning "seditious" speech or incitement was *Debs v. United States,* 249 U.S. 211 (1919). Eugene V. Debs was a Socialist Party presidential candidate, who at one time received over a million votes for the Presidency of the United States. Debs delivered a speech, the "main theme" of which was "Socialism, its growth, and a prophecy of its ultimate success." The Court noted: "With that we have nothing to do, but if a part or the manifest intent of the more general utterances was to encourage those present to obstruct the recruiting service and if in passages such encouragement was directly given, the immunity of the general theme may not be enough to protect the speech." In an opinion by Justice Holmes, the Supreme Court affirmed his conviction under the Espionage Act.

Most of the speech, as summarized in the opinion, consisted of praise for various "loyal comrades" in the struggle for the "working class." One of these men had been convicted of obstructing the recruiting service and attempting to cause insubordination and refusal of duty in the military forces of the United States. In the course of the trial, the defendant addressed the jury himself, and while contending that his speech did not warrant the charges said, "I have been accused of obstructing the war. I admit it. Gentlemen, I abhor war. I would oppose the war if I stood alone." The Court observed that "The statement was not necessary to warrant the jury in finding that one purpose of the speech, whether incidental or not does not matter, was to oppose not only war in general but this war, and that the opposition was so expressed that its natural and intended effect would be to obstruct recruiting. If that was intended and if, in all the circumstances, that would be its probable effect, it would not be protected by reason of its being part of a general program and expressions of a general and conscientious belief." The Court concluded that "the jury were most carefully instructed that they could not find the defendant guilty for advocacy of any of his opinions unless the words used had as their natural tendency and reasonably probable effect to obstruct the recruiting service, & c., and unless the defendant had the specific intent to do so in his mind."

Debs was sentenced to prison for ten years, which he served in a maximum security prison in Georgia. Debs ran again for president in 1920—from prison—and received nearly a million votes, approximately as many as he had received in 1912. Following the election, the lame-duck President Wilson was urged to commute Debs's sentence, because sixty-five-year-old Debs was in poor health and it was feared he might die in prison. Wilson refused. Eventually, on Christmas Day of 1921, President Warren Harding commuted Debs's sentence.

Following *Debs*, the next term, in *Abrams v. United States*, 250 U.S. 616 (1919), the Court again upheld a conviction under the statute for publishing circulars advocating a general strike and urging munitions factory workers to stop producing weapons that might be used against Russian revolutionaries. The majority applied the "clear and present danger" formulation that Justice Holmes set forth in *Schenck*. This time, however, Justice Holmes disagreed with the result, finding insufficient proof of intent to interfere with the war effort. His dissent, joined by Justice Brandeis, began by reaffirming the correctness of the *Schenck–Frohwerk–Debs* trilogy and the "clear and present danger" test he coined:

> I do not doubt for a moment that by the same reasoning that would justify punishing persuasion to murder, the United States constitutionally may punish speech that produces or is intended to produce a clear and imminent danger that it will bring about forthwith certain substantive evils that the United States constitutionally may seek to prevent. The power undoubtedly is greater in time of war than in time of peace because war opens dangers that do not exist at other times. But as against dangers peculiar to war, as against others, the principle of the right to free speech is always the same. It is only the present danger of immediate evil or an intent to bring it about that warrants Congress in setting a limit to the expression of opinion where private rights are not concerned.

But Holmes challenged the *application* of this rule to the pamphlets at issue and the charges against Abrams:

> Now nobody can suppose that the surreptitious publishing of a silly leaflet by an unknown man, without more, would present any immediate danger that its opinion would hinder the success of the government arms or have any appreciable tendency to do so. Publishing those opinions for the very purpose of obstructing, however, might indicate a greater danger and at any rate would have the quality of an attempt . . . [but] I do not see how anyone can find the intent required by the statute in any of the defendants' words.

Is Holmes's disagreement with the majority in *Abrams* simply a factual disagreement as to how dangerous one pamphlet's message is as opposed to another's? How secure is the freedom of speech of an agitator, if he must guess, at his "own peril, subject to a jury's guessing at motive, tendency and possible effect," whether his speech will be protected? Ernst Freund, *The Debs Case and Freedom of Speech*, The New Republic (May 3, 1919). Holmes's *Abrams* dissent ended with stirring words about the value of freedom of speech:

> Persecution for the expression of opinions seems to me perfectly logical. If you have no doubt of your premises or your power and want a certain result with all your heart you naturally express your wishes in law and sweep away all opposition. To allow opposition by speech seems to indicate that you think the speech impotent, as when a man says that he has squared the circle, or that you do not care wholeheartedly for the result, or that you doubt either your power or your premises. But when men have realized that time has upset many fighting faiths, they may come to believe even more than they believe the very foundations of their own conduct that the ultimate good desired is better reached by free trade in ideas—that the best test of truth is the power of the thought to get itself accepted in the competition of the market, and that truth is the only ground upon which their wishes safely can be carried out. That at any rate is the theory of our Constitution. . . . I wholly disagree with the argument of the Government that the First Amendment left the common law as to seditious libel in force. History seems to me against the notion. I had conceived that the United States through many years had shown its repentance for the Sedition Act of 1798, by repaying fines that it imposed. Only the emergency that makes it immediately dangerous to leave the correction of evil counsels to time warrants making any exception to the sweeping command, "Congress shall make no [law] abridging the freedom of speech."

Is this consistent with Holmes's opinion affirming the conviction of Eugene Debs?

Two important successors to the World War I era cases are *Gitlow v. New York*, 268 U.S. 652 (1925), and *Whitney v. California*, 274 U.S. 357 (1927). Unlike the World War I era cases, these arose under the Fourteenth Amendment. The Court upheld state convictions for "criminal anarchy" (*Gitlow*) and "criminal syndicalism" (*Whitney*) based on advocacy, or organization to engage in advocacy, of the "duty, necessity and propriety of overthrowing and overturning organized government by force, violence, and unlawful means." *Gitlow*, 268 U.S. at 654. Justices Holmes, joined by Justice Brandeis, dissented in *Gitlow*:

> If what I think the correct test is applied, it is manifest that there was no present danger of an attempt to overthrow the government by force on the part of the admittedly small minority who shared the defendant's views. It is said that this manifesto was more than a theory, that it was an incitement. Every idea is an incitement. It offers itself for belief and if believed it is acted on unless some other belief outweighs it or some failure of energy stifles the movement at its birth. The only difference between the expression of an opinion and an incitement in the narrower sense is the speaker's enthusiasm for the result. Eloquence may set fire to reason. But whatever may be thought of the redundant discourse before us it had no chance of starting a present conflagration. If in the long run the beliefs ex-

pressed in proletarian dictatorship are destined to be accepted by the dominant forces of the community, the only meaning of free speech is that they should be given their chance and have their way. If the publication of this document had been laid as an attempt to induce an uprising against government at once and not at some indefinite time in the future it would have presented a different question. The object would have been one with which the law might deal, subject to the doubt whether there was any danger that the publication could produce any result, or in other words, whether it was not futile and too remote from possible consequences.

Under the Holmes–Brandeis reasoning, is "incendiary" speech permissible—unless it is likely to be effective?

In *Whitney*, Justice Brandeis, joined by Justice Holmes, concurred in the judgment affirming the conviction. Justice Brandeis's opinion is significant for its refinement of the formulation of the "clear and present danger" test. Elements of this opinion now form part of the Supreme Court's modern doctrine, as set forth in *Brandenburg v. Ohio* (1969). But Brandeis and Holmes nonetheless voted to affirm the conviction of a "radical" for advocating "criminal syndicalism" based on her membership in the Communist Labor Party and its adopted manifesto.

4. *Dennis v. United States.* What if there exists an ideological group committed to engaging in acts of violence for political purposes, and organizing for such common purposes, and the government believes—or fears—that the group may have, or may in due time acquire, the means of actually carrying out its goals? May it punish such an organization as a criminal conspiracy, on the basis of the content of its message? Make the group in question the Communist Party of the United States and you have *Dennis v. United States*, 341 U.S. 494 (1951), a mammoth case involving the criminal prosecution of the leadership of the Communist Party USA during the height of Cold War fears. The Court upheld the conviction for organizing a group to teach and advocate the overthrow of the government of the United States by force and violence. A four-justice plurality, in an opinion by Chief Justice Vinson, applied a version of the "clear and present danger" test to uphold the convictions:

> [T]he words "clear and present danger" cannot mean that before the Government may act, it must wait until the putsch is about to be executed, the plans have been laid and the signal is awaited. If Government is aware that a group aiming at its overthrow is attempting to indoctrinate its members and to commit them to a course whereby they will strike when the leaders feel the circumstances permit, action by the Government is required. . . . Certainly an attempt to overthrow the Government by force, even though doomed from the outset because of inadequate numbers or power of the revolutionists, is a sufficient evil for Congress to prevent. The damage which such attempts create both physically and politically to a nation makes it impossible to measure the validity in terms of the probability of success, or the immediacy of a successful attempt. [We] must therefore reject the contention that success or probability of success is the criterion.

The plurality's analysis provoked the vigorous dissents of Justices Black and Douglas, who argued that the application of the test had severely watered down the original standard.

The majority to affirm the conviction was supplied by the separate concurrences of Justice Frankfurter and of Justice Jackson. Frankfurter's opinion eschewed absolute rules and embraced balancing of interests and deference to legislative judgments:

> [It] is not for us to decide how we would adjust the clash of interests which this case presents were the primary responsibility . . . ours. Congress has determined that the danger created by advocacy of overthrow justifies the ensuing restriction on freedom of speech. [To] make validity of legislation depend on judicial reading of events still in the womb of time—a forecast, that is, of the outcome of forces at best appreciated only with knowledge of the topmost secrets of nations—is to charge the judiciary with duties beyond its [capacity].

Justice Jackson argued that the "clear and present danger" test was more appropriate as a "rule of reason" reserved for the types of cases in which it arose—"criminality of a hotheaded speech on a street corner, or circulation of a few incendiary pamphlets." In Jackson's view, applying the clear-and-present-danger test to organizations advocating violent overthrow would require the Court to

> appraise imponderables, including international and national phenomena which baffle the best informed foreign offices and our most experienced politicians. . . . The judicial process simply is not adequate to a trial of such far-flung issues. The answers given would reflect our own political predilections and nothing more. The authors of the clear and present danger test never applied it to a case like this, nor would I. If applied as it is proposed here, it means that the Communist plotting is protected during its period of incubation; its preliminary stages of organization and preparation are immune from the law; the Government can move only after imminent action is manifest, when it would, of course, be too late.

Dennis is a transitional case in terms of Supreme Court doctrine. No opinion commanded a majority and the clear-and-present danger test governing speech advocating violent action was changed in *Brandenburg*, which we take up next.

It is easy to unthinkingly dismiss the fears of Communist conspiracies in the United States during the Cold War. In THE LOGIC OF PERSECUTION (2005), Martin Redish notes that former Soviet archives show that there really was a form of Communist conspiracy in the United States, involving espionage and subterfuge and including high ranking government officers. If you were confident of those facts, would they justify the prosecution in *Dennis*? It may help to think about a more modern example.

A NOTE ON HOLDER V. HUMANITARIAN LAW PROJECT

Holder v. Humanitarian Law Project, 130 S. Ct. 2705 (2010), raised a facial challenge to a law prohibiting "material support" to foreign terrorist organizations. The central question was whether the national security considerations supporting the statute were sufficiently compelling to justify prohibiting *speech* assisting such organizations—even speech that did not directly facilitate an unlawful act. The Court, 6–3, upheld the statute, as applied, in an opinion by Chief Justice Roberts.

The Court rejected the government's broader position that the law regulated only conduct for reasons unrelated to its message, and thus should be sustained under the standards of *United States v. O'Brien*: "The Government is wrong that the only thing actually at issue in this litigation is conduct, and therefore wrong to argue that *O'Brien* provides the correct standard of review. *O'Brien* does not provide the applicable standard for reviewing a content-based regulation of speech, and [the material-support statute] regulates speech on the basis of its content. Plaintiffs want to speak to the [groups identified by the government as foreign terrorist organizations] and whether they may do so under [the material-support statute] depends on what they say. If plaintiffs' speech to these groups imparts a 'specific skill' or communicates advice derived from 'specialized knowledge'—for example, training on the use of international law or advice on petitioning the United Nations—then it is barred. On the other hand, plaintiffs' speech is not barred if it imparts only general or unspecialized knowledge." Nor did the Court accept the government's argument that the *O'Brien* standard should apply because the statute "*generally* functions as a regulation of conduct." That argument, the Court said, "runs headlong into a number of our precedents, most prominently *Cohen v. California*, 403 U.S. 15 (1971)." *Cohen* involved a general breach of the peace statute; but as applied to Cohen's expression, the relevant standard was the one regulating speech because of its content.

Nevertheless, the Court sustained the statute, even as a content-based regulation of speech, because of the compelling interest in combating terrorism. "Everyone agrees that the Government's interest in combating terrorism is an urgent objective of the highest order," Chief Justice Roberts wrote. The disagreement centered on plaintiffs' contention that the ban on material support to terrorist organizations, as applied to plaintiffs' expression, was not necessary to further that interest. Plaintiffs claimed that their speech-support would advance "only the legitimate activities of the designated terrorist organizations, not their terrorism." The Court disagreed, wryly noting that, "[w]hether foreign terrorist organizations meaningfully segregate support of their legitimate activities from support of terrorism" was "an empirical question," adding that Congress had considered and appropriately rejected such a view. Material support for the ostensibly peaceable conduct of terrorist organizations "can further terrorism in multiple ways. 'Material support' is a valuable resource by definition. Such support frees up other resources within the organization that may be put to violent ends." The Court noted that "[m]oney is fungible," and, furthermore, that assistance given to certain activities of terrorist organizations may serve to "legitimize and further" their terrorist means. Moreover, such material support "furthers terrorism by straining the United States' relationships with its allies."

The Court rejected the dissent's argument that such reasoning has "no natural stopping place" because "Congress has settled on just such a natural stopping place: The statute reaches only material support coordinated with or under the direction of a designated foreign terrorist organization. Independent advocacy that might be viewed as promoting the group's legitimacy is not covered."

The Court continued: "In analyzing whether it is possible in practice to distinguish material support for a foreign terrorist group's violent activities and its nonviolent activities, we do not rely exclusively on our own inferences drawn from the record evidence." Rather, the Court found the assessments of Congress and the executive branch "entitled to deference." "This litigation implicates sensitive and weighty interests of national security and foreign affairs" on which it was vital that the judicial branch not substitute its own evaluation of evidence for the reasonable judgments of the political branches. Although this did not mean "abdication of the judicial role," the courts have a relative lack of competence in collecting and evaluating this evidence. In such matters, "respect for the Government's conclusions is appropriate."

The Court limited its holding: "All this is not to say that any future applications of the material-support statute to speech or advocacy will survive First Amendment scrutiny. It is also not to say that any other statute relating to speech and terrorism would satisfy the First Amendment. In particular, we in no way suggest that a regulation of independent speech would pass constitutional muster, even if the Government were to show that such speech benefits foreign terrorist organizations. We also do not suggest that Congress could extend the same prohibition on material support at issue here to domestic organizations. We simply hold that, in prohibiting the particular forms of support that plaintiffs seeks to provide to foreign terrorist groups, [the statute] does not violate the freedom of speech." The Court also rejected a claim that the statute unconstitutionally interfered with the freedom of association protected by the First Amendment.

Justice Breyer, joined by Justices Ginsburg and Sotomayor, dissented: "I cannot agree with the Court's conclusion that the Constitution permits the Government to prosecute the plaintiffs criminally for engaging in coordinated teaching and advocacy furthering the designated organizations' lawful political objectives." The dissent emphasized that the activities in which plaintiffs wished to engage—training on "how to use humanitarian and international law to peacefully resolve disputes," political advocacy, and teaching about how to petition representative bodies such as the United Nations—"are of a kind that the First Amendment ordinarily protects."

He acknowledged that "[t]he Government does identify a compelling countervailing interest, namely, the interest in protecting the security of the United States and its nationals from the threats that foreign terrorist organizations pose by denying those organizations financial and other fungible resources." But he added: "I do not dispute the importance of this interest. But I do dispute whether the interest can justify the statute's criminal prohibition."

Justice Breyer therefore would have construed the statute to avoid what he considered "serious doubt" as to its constitutionality: "I would "I would read the statute as criminalizing First–Amendment-protected pure speech and association only when the defendant knows or intends that those activities will assist the organization's unlawful terrorist actions. Under this reading, the Government would have to show, at a minimum, that such defendants provided support that they knew was significantly likely to help the organization pursue its unlawful terrorist aims."

Is this case in any way doctrinally different from cases involving association with the Communist Party?

Do you understand why the majority rejects the analogy to *O'Brien*, and thus applies strict scrutiny? According to the Court, the plaintiffs "want to speak" to the terrorist groups, and whether they may do so under the statute "depends on what they say." Why did the Court not apply "secondary effects" analysis? To be sure, the statute targets "what they say," just as the ordinance did in *Renton*. But might it be argued that the reason for the regulation was not based on the communicative impact of the speech? The government does not care whether anyone is persuaded by the plaintiffs' speech, but only about whether that speech helps the terrorist group. Is that covered by *Renton*? If so, does it suggest a better way to analyze the problem in *Humanitarian Law Project*? Or does it suggest that *Renton*'s "secondary effects" theory is alarmingly broad?

Brandenburg v. Ohio
395 U.S. 444 (1969)

■ PER CURIAM.

The appellant, a leader of a Ku Klux Klan group, was convicted under the Ohio Criminal Syndicalism statute for "advocat[ing] . . . the duty, necessity, or propriety of crime, sabotage, violence, or unlawful methods of terrorism as a means of accomplishing industrial or political reform' and for 'voluntarily assembl[ing] with any society, group, or assemblage of persons formed to teach or advocate the doctrines of criminal syndicalism." He was fined $1,000 and sentenced to one to 10 years' imprisonment. . . .

The record shows that a man, identified at trial as the appellant, telephoned an announcer-reporter on the staff of a Cincinnati television station and invited him to come to a Ku Klux Klan "rally" to be held at a farm in Hamilton County. With the cooperation of the organizers, the reporter and a cameraman attended the meeting and filmed the events. Portions of the films were later broadcast on the local station and on a national network.

The prosecution's case rested on the films and on testimony identifying the appellant as the person who communicated with the reporter and who spoke at the rally. The State also introduced into evidence several articles appearing in the film, including a pistol, a rifle, a shotgun, ammunition, a Bible, and a red hood worn by the speaker in the films.

One film showed 12 hooded figures, some of whom carried firearms. They were gathered around a large wooden cross, which they burned. No one was present other than the participants and the newsmen who made the film. Most of the words uttered during the scene were incomprehensible when the film was projected, but scattered phrases could be understood that were derogatory of Negroes and, in one instance, of Jews.[1] Another scene on the same film showed the appellant, in Klan regalia, making a speech. The speech, in full, was as follows:

> This is an organizers' meeting. We have had quite a few members here today which are—we have hundreds, hundreds of members throughout the State of Ohio. I can quote from a newspaper clipping from the Co-

---

[1] The significant portions that could be understood were:
"How far is the nigger going to—yeah."
"This is what we are going to do to the niggers."
"A dirty nigger."
"Send the Jews back to Israel."
"Let's give them back to the dark garden."
"Save America."
"Let's go back to constitutional betterment."
"Bury the niggers."
"We intend to do our part."
"Give us our state rights."
"Freedom for the whites."
"Nigger will have to fight for every inch he gets from now on."

lumbus, Ohio *Dispatch*, five weeks ago Sunday morning. The Klan has more members in the State of Ohio than does any other organization. We're not a revengent organization, but if our President, our Congress, our Supreme Court, continues to suppress the white, Caucasian race, it's possible that there might have to be some revengeance taken.

We are marching on Congress July the Fourth, four hundred thousand strong. From there we are dividing into two groups, one group to march on St. Augustine, Florida, the other group to march into Mississippi. Thank you.

The second film showed six hooded figures one of whom, later identified as the appellant, repeated a speech very similar to that recorded on the first film. The reference to the possibility of "revengeance" was omitted, and one sentence was added: "Personally, I believe the nigger should be returned to Africa, the Jew returned to Israel." Though some of the figures in the films carried weapons, the speaker did not.

The Ohio Criminal Syndicalism Statute was enacted in 1919. From 1917 to 1920, identical or quite similar laws were adopted by 20 States and two territories. E. Dowell, A History of Criminal Syndicalism Legislation in the United States 21 (1939). In 1927, this Court sustained the constitutionality of California's Criminal Syndicalism Act, the text of which is quite similar to that of the laws of Ohio. *Whitney v. California*, 274 U.S. 357 (1927). The Court upheld the statute on the ground that, without more, 'advocating' violent means to effect political and economic change involves such danger to the security of the State that the State may outlaw it. But *Whitney* has been thoroughly discredited by later decisions. See *Dennis v. United States*, 341 U.S. 494, at 507 (1951). These later decisions have fashioned the principle that the constitutional guarantees of free speech and free press do not permit a State to forbid or proscribe advocacy of the use of force or of law violation except where such advocacy is directed to inciting or producing imminent lawless action and is likely to incite or produce such action. As we said in *Noto v. United States*, 367 U.S. 290, 297–298 (1961), "the mere abstract teaching . . . of the moral propriety or even moral necessity for a resort to force and violence, is not the same as preparing a group for violent action and steeling it to such action." A statute which fails to draw this distinction impermissibly intrudes upon the freedoms guaranteed by the First and Fourteenth Amendments. It sweeps within its condemnation speech which our Constitution has immunized from governmental control.

Measured by this test, Ohio's Criminal Syndicalism Act cannot be sustained. The Act punishes persons who "advocate or teach the duty, necessity, or propriety" of violence "as a means of accomplishing industrial or political reform"; or who publish or circulate or display any book or paper containing such advocacy; or who "justify" the commission of violent acts "with intent to exemplify, spread or advocate the propriety of the doctrines of criminal syndicalism"; or who "voluntarily assemble" with a group formed "to teach or advocate the doctrines of criminal syndicalism." Neither the indictment nor the trial judge's instructions to the jury in any way refined the statute's bald definition of the crime in terms of mere advocacy not distinguished from incitement to imminent lawless action.

Accordingly, we are here confronted with a statute which, by its own words and as applied, purports to punish mere advocacy and to forbid, on pain of criminal punishment, assembly with others merely to advocate the described type of action. Such a statute falls within the condemnation of the First and Fourteenth Amendments. The contrary teaching of *Whitney v. California, supra,* cannot be supported, and that decision is therefore overruled. . . .

■ [The concurring opinions of JUSTICE BLACK and JUSTICE DOUGLAS are omitted.]

NOTES

1. The *Brandenburg* test combines some of the features of the old clear-and-present danger test and some of the features of Justice Brandeis's concurrence in *Whitney.* The core of the test is the following: "[T]he constitutional guarantees of free speech and free press do not permit a State to forbid or proscribe advocacy of the use of force or of criminality except where such advocacy is directed to inciting or producing imminent lawless action and is likely to incite or produce such action." Break apart the elements:

(1) *"directed to"* (an intent-of-the-speaker element?)

(2) *"inciting or producing"* (words as triggers to action; not pure advocacy)

(3) *"imminent"* (no time for "answering speech" or intervening reflection?)

(4) *"lawless action"* (of *any* kind? No matter how *harmful* the legal violation may be?)

(5) *"**and** likely to produce such action"* (probability of the harm).

Is this a sound dissection of the test? Is *Brandenburg* a *good* test? Is it likely to be a stable, enduring test? Does it accurately capture the meaning of the First Amendment's *language* as applied to this type of problem? How does it differ from Lincoln's "test"? Holmes's? How does it decide cases like Lincoln's concerning Clement Vallandigham? Eugene Debs's speech? *Dennis?* An al Qaeda sleeper cell?

2. Consider here the European Court of Human Rights' decision in *Zana v. Turkey,* 27 Eur. Ct. H.R. 667 (1997). Mr. Mehdi Zana was a Turkish national who had once served as mayor of a city in the Kurdish southeast of Turkey. Since 1985, more than 8,000 people had been killed in this part of Turkey as a result of conflict between the government and the PKK (Worker's Party of Kurdistan). Mr. Zana had long been a supporter of the Kurdish cause who was opposed to violence. While in a Turkish prison on other charges, he gave an interview to a newspaper. He said: "I support the PKK national liberation movement, on the other hand, I am not in favor of massacres. Anyone can make mistakes, and the PKK kill women and children by mistake." Mr. Zana was charged with the crime of supporting an armed organization, the PKK, whose aim was to break up Turkey's territorial integrity. Zana was accused of inciting people to disobey the law and with stirring up hatred and hostility in a way that endangered the public safety. Mr. Zana argued that his conviction under Turkish law violated Article 10 of the European Convention on Human Rights, which protects "freedom of expression," and Article 9 of the Convention, which protects freedom of thought. Turkey responded that paragraph 2 of Article 10 allows the government to suppress freedom of expression where doing so is "necessary in a democratic society, in the interest of national security, territorial integrity, or public safety, for the prevention of disorder or crime for the protection of public health and morals." The European Court of Human Rights ruled in favor of Turkey and upheld Zana's conviction under the Convention.

Support given to the PKK by a former mayor could be construed as incitement to violence. In any event, the European Court said Turkey was entitled to "a margin of appreciation" such that standards of what might constitute incitement in the whole of Europe might be relaxed in Turkey given its unique history and circumstances. Eight judges dissented, at least in part. Was Zana guilty of incitement? Is the European Convention insufficiently protective of freedom of expression because of the explicit balancing language in the text of Article 10 quoted above? What do you think in this context of the idea of a margin of appreciation? Would the robust protection of freedom of speech Americans enjoy have been appropriate in West Germany in 1949—right after the defeat of Hitler and in a time of conflict with Stalin?

A NOTE ON PLANNED PARENTHOOD OF THE COLUMBIA/WILLAMETTE, INC. V. AMERICAN COALITION OF LIFE ACTIVISTS

Consider the case of *Planned Parenthood of the Columbia/Willamette, Inc. v. American Coalition of Life Activists*, 290 F.3d 1058 (9th Cir. 2002) (en banc). The facts in brief: Plaintiffs were abortion clinics and abortion-performing doctors. Defendants were strident anti-abortion, "pro-life" activists—individuals and an organization called "American Coalition of Life Activists" (ACLA). ACLA maintained a web site called "The Nuremburg Files." The web site identified certain abortion doctors by name, address, and photograph. It described the doctors as murderers who, while not capable of being punished under present law, perhaps could be punished one day, just as Nazi war criminals were punished in the Nuremburg trials following World War II. Where an abortion provider had been killed, the web site put a black X through his picture. Defendants also distributed printed "DEADLY DOZEN" and "WANTED" posters, identifying certain abortion doctors as criminal baby-killers.

As the Ninth Circuit's opinion describes, several abortion-performing doctors had been murdered by anti-abortion extremists—none of whom were the individual defendants in this case or part of the ACLA. The plaintiff abortion clinics and doctors brought a civil suit against defendants, seeking an injunction against the website and the distribution of the posters on the ground that they constituted "true threats" of actual violence against them or (alternatively) "incitement" to violence and murder. The suit was brought pursuant to two federal statutes, the Freedom of Access to Clinics Entrances Act and the Racketeer Influenced and Corrupt Organizations Act.

Following a jury trial, the district court awarded actual and punitive damages against the defendants totaling more than $100 million. The court also issued a permanent injunction restraining defendants from publishing or distributing the "DEADLY DOZEN" poster or other posters identifying any of the plaintiffs with intent to threaten them or from posting such materials on the "Nuremburg Files" website or any other website, or from otherwise publishing or distributing personally identifying information about the plaintiffs. A panel of the Ninth Circuit reversed, but the Ninth Circuit granted rehearing *en banc* and held for the plaintiff abortion clinics and doctors:

> Construing the facts in the light most favorable to physicians, the verdict is supported by substantial evidence. ACLA was aware that a "wanted"-type poster would likely be interpreted as a serious threat of death or bodily harm by a doctor in the reproductive health services community who

was identified on one, given the previous pattern of "WANTED" posters identifying a specific physician followed by that physician's murder. The same is true of the posting about these physicians on that part of the "Nuremberg Files" where lines were drawn through the names of doctors who provided abortion services and who had been killed or wounded. We are independently satisfied that to this limited extent, ACLA's conduct amounted to a true threat and is not protected speech.

Judge Kozinski wrote for himself and four other dissenters (Berzon, Kleinfeld, O'Scannlain, and Reinhardt), emphasizing that the "true threat" exception applied only when the *speaker himself* was the one threatening to do violence to someone. There was no evidence—apart from the defendants' speech itself—from which anyone could find or infer a threat. In addition, the website and posters did not threaten violence against the plaintiffs, but in fact *disclaimed* any such intention. While the website and posters could be construed as potentially *intimidating*, that did not rob the defendants of their constitutional right to free expression; the *Brandenburg* test for incitement was not met. Judge Kozinski said:

> In this case, none of the statements on which liability was premised were overtly threatening. On the contrary, the two posters and the web page, by their explicit terms, foreswore the use of violence and advocated lawful means of persuading plaintiffs to stop performing abortions or punishing them for continuing to do so. Nevertheless, because context matters, the statements could reasonably be interpreted as an effort to intimidate plaintiffs into ceasing their abortion-related activities. If that were enough to strip the speech of First Amendment protection, there would be nothing left to decide. But the Supreme Court has told us that "[s]peech does not lose its protected character . . . simply because it may embarrass others *or coerce them into action*." *NAACP v. Claiborne Hardware Co.*, 458 U.S. 886, 910 (1982) (emphasis added). In other words, some forms of intimidation enjoy constitutional protection. . . .
>
> Even assuming that one could somehow distill a true threat from the posters themselves, the majority opinion is still fatally defective because it contradicts the central holding of *Claiborne Hardware*: Where the speaker is engaged in public political speech, the public statements themselves cannot be the sole proof that they were true threats, unless the speech directly threatens actual injury to identifiable individuals. Absent such an unmistakable, specific threat, there must be evidence *aside from the political statements themselves* showing that the public speaker would himself or in conspiracy with others inflict unlawful harm. 458 U.S. at 932–34. The majority cites not a scintilla of evidence—other than the posters themselves—that plaintiffs or someone associated with them would carry out the threatened harm.
>
> Given this lack of evidence, the posters can be viewed, at most, as a call to arms for *other* abortion protesters to harm plaintiffs. However, the Supreme Court made it clear that under *Brandenburg*, encouragement or even advocacy of violence is protected by the First Amendment: "[M]ere *advocacy* of the use of force or violence does not remove speech from the protection of the First Amendment." *Claiborne Hardware*, 458 U.S. at 927 (citing *Brandenburg*, 395 U.S. at 447) (emphasis in the original). *Claiborne Hardware* in fact goes much farther; it cautions that where liability is

premised on "politically motivated" activities, we must "examine critically the basis on which liability was imposed." *Id.* at 915. As the Court explained, "Since respondents would impose liability on the basis of a public address—which predominantly contained highly charged political rhetoric lying at the core of the First Amendment—we approach this suggested basis for liability with extreme care." *Id.* at 926–27. This is precisely what the majority does *not* do; were it to do so, it would have no choice but to reverse. . . .

The Nuremberg Files website is clearly an expression of a political point of view. The posters and the website are designed both to rally political support for the views espoused by defendants, and to intimidate plaintiffs and others like them into desisting abortion-related activities. This political agenda may not be to the liking of many people—political dissidents are often unpopular—but the speech, including the intimidating message, does not constitute a direct threat because there is no evidence other than the speech itself that the speakers intend to resort to physical violence if their threat is not heeded. . . . While today it is abortion protesters who are singled out for punitive treatment, the precedent set by this court—the broad and uncritical deference to the judgment of a jury—will haunt dissidents of all political stripes for many years to come. [T]his is contrary to the principles of the First Amendment as explicated by the Supreme Court in *Claiborne Hardware* and its long-standing jurisprudence stemming from *Brandenburg v. Ohio*.

R.A.V. v. St. Paul
505 U.S. 377 (1992)

■ JUSTICE SCALIA delivered the opinion of the Court.

In the predawn hours of June 21, 1990, petitioner and several other teenagers allegedly assembled a crudely made cross by taping together broken chair legs. They then allegedly burned the cross inside the fenced yard of a black family that lived across the street from the house where petitioner was staying. Although this conduct could have been punished under any of a number of laws,[1] one of the two provisions under which respondent city of St. Paul chose to charge petitioner (then a juvenile) was the St. Paul Bias–Motivated Crime Ordinance, St. Paul, Minn., Legis. Code § 292.02 (1990), which provides:

> Whoever places on public or private property a symbol, object, appellation, characterization or graffiti, including, but not limited to, a burning cross or Nazi swastika, which one knows or has reasonable grounds to know arouses anger, alarm or resentment in others on the basis of race, color, creed, religion or gender commits disorderly conduct and shall be guilty of a misdemeanor.

Petitioner moved to dismiss this count on the ground that the St. Paul ordinance was substantially overbroad and impermissibly content based

---

[1] The conduct might have violated Minnesota statutes carrying significant penalties. See, *e.g.,* Minn.Stat. § 609.713(1) (1987) (providing for up to five years in prison for terroristic threats); § 609.563 (arson) (providing for up to five years and a $10,000 fine, depending on the value of the property intended to be damaged); § 609.595 (Supp.1992) (criminal damage to property) (providing for up to one year and a $3,000 fine, depending upon the extent of the damage to the property).

and therefore facially invalid under the First Amendment. The trial court granted this motion, but the Minnesota Supreme Court reversed. . . .

I

In construing the St. Paul ordinance, we are bound by the construction given to it by the Minnesota court. Accordingly, we accept the Minnesota Supreme Court's authoritative statement that the ordinance reaches only those expressions that constitute "fighting words" within the meaning of *Chaplinsky*. Petitioner and his *amici* urge us to modify the scope of the *Chaplinsky* formulation, thereby invalidating the ordinance as "substantially overbroad." We find it unnecessary to consider this issue. Assuming, *arguendo*, that all of the expression reached by the ordinance is proscribable under the "fighting words" doctrine, we nonetheless conclude that the ordinance is facially unconstitutional in that it prohibits otherwise permitted speech solely on the basis of the subjects the speech addresses.

The First Amendment generally prevents government from proscribing speech, or even expressive conduct, see, *e.g.*, *Texas v. Johnson*, 491 U.S. 397 (1989), because of disapproval of the ideas expressed. Content-based regulations are presumptively invalid. [Citing *Simon & Schuster* and *Mosley*.] From 1791 to the present, however, our society, like other free but civilized societies, has permitted restrictions upon the content of speech in a few limited areas, which are "of such slight social value as a step to truth that any benefit that may be derived from them is clearly outweighed by the social interest in order and morality." *Chaplinsky*, *supra*, 315 U.S., at 572. We have recognized that "the freedom of speech" referred to by the First Amendment does not include a freedom to disregard these traditional limitations. See, *e.g.*, *Roth v. United States*, 354 U.S. 476 (1957) (obscenity); *Beauharnais v. Illinois*, 343 U.S. 250 (1952) (defamation); *Chaplinsky v. New Hampshire*, *supra* ("fighting words"). Our decisions . . . have narrowed the scope of the traditional categorical exceptions for defamation, see *New York Times Co. v. Sullivan*, 376 U.S. 254 (1964); and for obscenity, see *Miller v. California*, 413 U.S. 15 (1973), but a limited categorical approach has remained an important part of our First Amendment jurisprudence.

We have sometimes said that these categories of expression are "not within the area of constitutionally protected speech," or that the "protection of the First Amendment does not extend" to them. Such statements must be taken in context, however. What they mean is that these areas of speech can, consistently with the First Amendment, be regulated *because of their constitutionally proscribable content* (obscenity, defamation, etc.)—not that they are categories of speech entirely invisible to the Constitution, so that they may be made the vehicles for content discrimination unrelated to their distinctively proscribable content. Thus, the government may proscribe libel; but it may not make the further content discrimination of proscribing *only* libel critical of the government. . . .

The proposition that a particular instance of speech can be proscribable on the basis of one feature (*e.g.*, obscenity) but not on the basis of another (*e.g.*, opposition to the city government) is commonplace and has found application in many contexts. We have long held, for example, that nonverbal expressive activity can be banned because of the action it entails, but not because of the ideas it expresses—so that burning a flag in violation of an ordinance against outdoor fires could be punishable, whereas burning a flag in violation of an ordinance against dishonoring the flag is not. [Citing, among other cases, *Texas v. Johnson* and *United States v. O'Brien*.] Similarly, we have upheld reasonable "time, place, or manner" restrictions, but only if they are "justified without reference to the content of the regulated speech." *Ward v. Rock Against Racism*, 491 U.S. 781, 791 (1989) [upholding a noise ordinance as applied to rock concerts]; see also *Clark v. Community for Creative Non–Violence*, 468 U.S. 288, 298 (1984) (noting that the *O'Brien* test differs little from the standard applied to time, place, or manner restrictions). And just as the power to proscribe particular speech on the basis of a noncontent element (*e.g.*, noise) does not entail the power to proscribe the same speech on the basis of a content element; so also, the power to proscribe it on the basis of *one* content element (*e.g.*, obscenity) does not entail the power to proscribe it on the basis of *other* content elements.

. . . Fighting words are thus analogous to a noisy sound truck. . . . As with the sound truck, however, so also with fighting words: The government may not regulate use based on hostility—or favoritism—towards the underlying message expressed. . . .

II

Applying these principles to the St. Paul ordinance, we conclude that, even as narrowly construed by the Minnesota Supreme Court, the ordinance is facially unconstitutional. Although the phrase in the ordinance, "arouses anger, alarm or resentment in others," has been limited by the Minnesota Supreme Court's construction to reach only those symbols or displays that amount to "fighting words," the remaining, unmodified terms make clear that the ordinance applies only to "fighting words" that insult, or provoke violence, "on the basis of race, color, creed, religion or gender." Displays containing abusive invective, no matter how vicious or severe, are permissible unless they are addressed to one of the specified disfavored topics. Those who wish to use "fighting words" in connection with other ideas—to express hostility, for example, on the basis of political affiliation, union membership, or homosexuality—are not covered. The First Amendment does not permit St. Paul to impose special prohibitions on those speakers who express views on disfavored subjects. *Simon & Schuster*, 502 U.S., at 116. In its practical operation, moreover, the ordinance goes even beyond mere content discrimination, to actual viewpoint discrimination. Displays containing some words—odious racial epithets, for example— would be prohibited to proponents of all views. But "fighting words" that do not themselves invoke race, color, creed, religion, or gender—aspersions upon a person's mother, for example—would seemingly be usable *ad libitum* in the placards of those arguing *in favor* of racial, color, etc., tolerance and equality, but could not be used by those speakers' opponents. One could hold up a sign saying, for example, that all "anti-Catholic bigots" are misbegotten; but not that all "papists" are, for that would insult and provoke violence "on the basis of religion." St. Paul has no such authority to license one side of a debate to fight freestyle, while requiring the other to follow Marquis of Queensberry rules.

What we have here, it must be emphasized, is not a prohibition of fighting words that are directed at certain persons or groups (which would be *facially* valid if it met the requirements of the Equal Protection Clause); but rather, a prohibition of fighting words that contain (as the Minnesota Supreme Court repeatedly emphasized) messages of "bias-motivated" hatred and in particular, as applied to this case, messages "based on virulent notions of racial supremacy." 464 N.W.2d, at 508, 511. One must wholeheartedly agree with the Minnesota Supreme Court that "[i]t is the responsibility, even the obligation, of diverse communities to confront such notions in whatever form they appear," *id.*, at 508, but the manner of that confrontation cannot consist of selective limitations upon speech. St. Paul's brief asserts that a general "fighting words" law would not meet the city's needs because only a content-specific measure can communicate to minority groups that the "group hatred" aspect of such speech "is not condoned by the majority." The point of the First Amendment is that majority preferences must be expressed in some fashion other than silencing speech on the basis of its content. . . .

Finally, St. Paul and its *amici* defend the conclusion of the Minnesota Supreme Court that, even if the ordinance regulates expression based on hostility towards its protected ideological content, this discrimination is nonetheless justified because it is narrowly tailored to serve compelling state interests. Specifically, they assert that the ordinance helps to ensure the basic human rights of members of groups that have historically been subjected to discrimination, including the right of such group members to live in peace where they wish. We do not doubt that these interests are compelling, and that the ordinance can be said to promote them. But the "danger of censorship" presented by a facially content-based statute, requires that that weapon be employed only where it is "*necessary* to serve the asserted [compelling] interest." . . . The dispositive question in this case, therefore, is whether content discrimination is reasonably necessary to achieve St. Paul's compelling interests; it plainly is not. An ordinance not limited to the favored topics, for example, would have precisely the same beneficial effect. In fact the only interest distinctively served by the content limitation is that of displaying the city council's special hostility towards the particular biases thus singled out. That is precisely what the First Amendment forbids. The politicians of St. Paul are entitled to express that hostility—but not through the means of imposing unique limitations upon speakers who (however benightedly) disagree. . . .

Let there be no mistake about our belief that burning a cross in someone's front yard is reprehensible. But St. Paul has sufficient means at its disposal to prevent such behavior without adding the First Amendment to the fire.

■ JUSTICE WHITE, with whom JUSTICE BLACKMUN and JUSTICE O'CONNOR join, and with whom JUSTICE STEVENS joins except as to Part I–A, concurring in the judgment.

I agree with the majority that the judgment of the Minnesota Supreme Court should be reversed. However, our agreement ends there.

This case could easily be decided within the contours of established First Amendment law by holding, as petitioner argues, that the St. Paul ordinance is fatally overbroad because it criminalizes not only unprotected expression but expression protected by the First Amendment. . . .

NOTES

1. *R.A.V.* (the defendant was identified by initials, because he was a minor) is a much-discussed free speech case arising under the Fourteenth Amendment. At bottom, it stands for the proposition that the government may not engage in content- or viewpoint-based regulation of expression, *even within otherwise "unprotected" categories of expression*, like defamation, obscenity, or asserted "fighting words." The result was unanimous, though the four concurring justices disagreed with the breadth of the principle as stated by the majority, and would have preferred to strike down St. Paul's bias-motivated crime

ordinance on the basis of the First Amendment doctrine of "overbreadth"—that is, that the ordinance reached much constitutionally protected speech as well as unprotected expression or conduct. One apparent effect of the Court's decision in *R.A.V.* is to render invalid government laws or rules that prohibit or punish "hate speech" directed at particular groups. Government may not authoritatively pick and choose which messages are too hateful to be communicated; and even within the (increasingly narrow, but not quite dead) category of "fighting words," government may not be selective in imposing punishment only for certain viewpoints or only for certain subcategories of fighting words.

Does *R.A.V.* mean that the government may not prohibit racially discriminatory *conduct* (or other forms of discriminatory conduct)? No: Government may regulate conduct, such as racially discriminatory employment practices, even where such conduct is engaged in for assertedly expressive purposes (recall *United States v. O'Brien*). A racist employer may not discriminate on the basis of race in employment; the government may penalize such conduct. But a racist employer may not be penalized for racist speech alone. Does this distinction make sense? But press the hypotheticals one step further: Certainly a racist employer who expressed racially discriminatory views would find those words used as evidence of his possible motive for taking employment actions that an aggrieved employee might believe were taken because of discrimination on the basis of race. Is there anything wrong with this use of one's expressed views as evidence of the reason for conduct the motives of which are disputed or unclear? (Consider in this regard *Wisconsin v. Mitchell*, discussed in the next note.) One more variation: What about where the alleged discriminatory conduct consists solely or chiefly of a "hostile work environment" attributable to racially (or other) discriminatory or similarly hateful speech? For contrasting views, with excellent analysis, compare Eugene Volokh, Comment, *Freedom of Speech and Workplace Harassment*, 39 UCLA L. Rev. 1791 (1992) (hostile-environment laws constitutionally problematic) with Richard H. Fallon, Jr., *Sexual Harassment, Content–Neutrality, and the First Amendment Dog That Didn't Bark*, 1994 S. Ct. Rev. 1 (1994) (defending such laws).

2. The very next year after *R.A.V.*, in *Wisconsin v. Mitchell*, 508 U.S. 476 (1993), the Court drew a sharp distinction between statutes regulating and punishing certain hateful *speech* (as in *R.A.V.*) and punishing certain hateful *conduct* more severely because of an assertedly aggravating mind-state of racial animus. The Court's opinion was unanimous. The facts of *Mitchell*, as set forth in the Court's opinion, were as follows:

> On the evening of October 7, 1989, a group of young black men and boys, including Mitchell, gathered at an apartment complex in Kenosha, Wisconsin. Several members of the group discussed a scene from the motion picture "Mississippi Burning," in which a white man beat a young black boy who was praying. The group moved outside and Mitchell asked them: "Do you all feel hyped up to move on some white people?" Shortly thereafter, a young white boy approached the group on the opposite side of the street where they were standing. As the boy walked by, Mitchell said: "You all want to fuck somebody up? There goes a white boy; go get him." Mitchell counted to three and pointed in the boy's direction. The group ran towards the boy, beat him severely, and stole his tennis shoes. The boy was rendered unconscious and remained in a coma for four days.

Mitchell was convicted of aggravated battery. Under Wisconsin law, the fact that Mitchell had intentionally selected his victim on the basis of the boy's race was an aggravating factor that increased his maximum sentence from two to seven years. Mitchell was sentenced to four years. Before the U.S. Supreme Court, Mitchell argued that the penalty-enhancement statute was unconstitutional under *R.A.V.* But the Court rejected the argument, concluding that it was not supported by the analysis in *R.A.V.* Motive for a crime, the Court said in *Mitchell*, is a traditional factor that affects the level of punishment in criminal law, and it

> plays the same role under the Wisconsin statute as it does under federal and state antidiscrimination laws, which we have previously upheld against constitutional challenge. Title VII of the Civil Rights Act of 1964], for example, makes it unlawful for an employer to discriminate against an employee "because of such individual's race, color, religion, sex, or national origin." . . . In *R.A.V.* we cited Title VII as an example of a permissible content-neutral regulation of conduct. . . . Whereas the ordinance struck down in *R.A.V.* was explicitly directed at expression (i.e., "speech" or "messages"), the statute in this case is aimed at conduct unprotected by the First Amendment. Moreover, the Wisconsin statute singles out for enhancement bias-inspired conduct because this conduct is thought to inflict greater individual and societal harm.

508 U.S. at 477.

3. The Court confronted cross-burning prosecutions again in *Virginia v. Black*, 538 U.S. 343 (2003), also a Fourteenth Amendment case dealing with free speech principles. In a somewhat convoluted split decision, a majority of the Court held that a state may, notwithstanding *R.A.V.*, "ban cross burning carried out with the intent to intimidate," on the theory that the First Amendment does not protect "true threats" of violence. That holding commanded a majority of six justices of the Court (O'Connor, Rehnquist, Stevens, Breyer, Scalia, and Thomas).

But a different majority was formed by O'Connor, Rehnquist, Stevens, and Breyer (four of the original six), together with the separate concurring opinion of Justices Souter, Kennedy, and Ginsburg, to *strike down* one aspect of Virginia's statute: the provision stating that the fact of burning a cross was itself "prima facie evidence of an intent to intimidate a person or group of persons." Justice O'Connor's plurality opinion on this point said that the prima facie evidence provision could be interpreted and applied (and had been so interpreted and applied by the trial court, in its instructions to the jury) in such a manner as to "create an unacceptable risk of the suppression of ideas": "The act of burning a cross may mean that a person is engaging in constitutionally proscribable intimidation. But that same act may mean only that the person is engaged in core political speech. [The] prima facie provision makes no effort to distinguish among these different types of cross burnings. . . . The prima facie evidence provision in this case ignores all of the contextual factors that are necessary to decide whether a particular cross burning is intended to intimidate. The First Amendment does not permit such a shortcut." Justice Souter's concurring opinion (joined by Justices Kennedy and Ginsburg) did not join in Justice O'Connor's rationale. It was more categorical, rejecting the conviction under *R.A.V.*: "I agree with the majority that the Virginia statute makes a content-based distinction within the category of punishable intimidating or threatening expression, the very type of distinction we considered in *R.A.V.* I disagree that any exception should save Virginia's law from unconstitutionality under the holding in *R.A.V.* or any acceptable variation of it."

Justice Scalia and Justice Thomas joined in the first holding, but disagreed with the (second) majority about the effect of the "prima facie evidence" provision, finding "no justification for the plurality's apparent decision to invalidate" it. Justice Thomas, the only black member of the Court at the time, filed a lone dissent that would have held that cross-burning is simply not protected expression under the First Amendment: "Although I agree with the majority's conclusion that it is constitutionally permissible to 'ban . . . cross burning carried out with intent to intimidate,' I believe that the majority errs in imputing an expressive component to the activity in question. . . . In light of my conclusion that the statute here addresses only conduct, there is no need to analyze it under any of our First Amendment tests."

Thus, a six-justice majority (all joining in the same controlling opinion) agreed that true threats can be punished, without violating the First Amendment, and that cross-burning can be a true threat. A different seven-justice majority (*not* all joining in the same reasoning) agreed that Virginia's law, by treating cross-burning itself as prima facie evidence of an intent to intimidate by threat, was unconstitutional under the First Amendment. Is the result in *Black* coherent?

Nazis in Skokie

In the late 1970s, a group of American neo-Nazis sought to march through the streets of Skokie, Illinois, wearing Nazi uniforms and displaying the swastika. Skokie, a Chicago suburb, at the time had the largest concentration of Holocaust survivors of any community in America. The efforts to resist the Nazis led to a series of noteworthy judicial decisions.

The town of Skokie first sought, and obtained from an Illinois trial court, an *injunction* prohibiting parading in the uniform of the Nazi party, displaying the swastika, and distributing pamphlets that "incite or promote hatred against persons of Jewish faith or ancestry, race or religion." The Illinois Appellate Court declined to stay the injunction, and the Illinois Supreme Court denied expedited review. The Nazi group petitioned the U.S. Supreme Court for a stay. The Court treated the stay as a petition for certiorari and reversed in a per curiam opinion, *National Socialist Party v. Skokie*, 432 U.S. 43 (1977), holding that the First Amendment required, at minimum, procedural safeguards before a judicial injunction could be issued against speech. Injunctions against speech—judicial orders—have long been considered a form of "prior restraint" against speech, an especially severe type of restriction in the Court's view. (The Court had just a few years earlier invalidated injunctions against publication by the press of leaked classified material, in *The Pentagon Papers Case*, 403 U.S. 713 (1971), presented earlier in this chapter.) The Court in *National Socialist Party* started from the premise that such injunctions limiting speech are strongly disfavored, but its holding necessarily touched on the fact that the restriction of speech was obviously based on the content, and offensiveness, of the Nazis' message:

> [T]he outstanding injunction will deprive [petitioners] of rights protected by the First Amendment during the period of appellate review which, in the normal course, may take a year or more to complete. If a

State seeks to impose a restraint of this kind, it must provide strict procedural safeguards including immediate appellate review. . . . Absent such review, the State must instead allow a stay. The order of the Illinois Supreme Court constituted a denial of that right.

On remand, the Illinois courts struck down the injunction, finding it not justified by the "fighting words" doctrine. In light of cases like *Cohen*, the Illinois Supreme Court held, it was not permissible to restrict speech on the basis of the expected hostile reaction of the audience. The offensiveness of the swastika symbol was not a proper basis for banning the group's expression, either, the court said. Rather, it was up to Skokie's offended citizens to "avoid the offensive symbol if they can do so without unreasonable inconvenience." 373 N.E. 2d at 21 (Ill. 1978). In the words of the Illinois Supreme Court:

> The decisions of [the Supreme Court], particularly *Cohen v. California*, . . . in our opinion compel us to permit the demonstration as proposed, including display of the swastika. "It is firmly settled that under our Constitution the public expression of ideas may not be prohibited merely because the ideas are themselves offensive to some of their hearers" (*Bachellar v. Maryland*, 397 U.S. 564, 567 (1970)), and it is entirely clear that the wearing of distinctive clothing can be symbolic expression of a thought or philosophy. The symbolic expression of thought falls within the free speech clause of the First Amendment (*Tinker v. Des Moines Independent Sch. Dist.*, 393 U.S. 503 (1969) [upholding constitutional right of public high school and junior high school students to wear black armbands to school in protest of Vietnam War]) and the plaintiff village has the heavy burden of justifying the imposition of a prior restraint upon defendants' right to freedom of speech. . . .

> Plaintiff urges, and the appellate court has held, that the exhibition of the Nazi symbol, the swastika, addresses to ordinary citizens a message which is tantamount to fighting words. Plaintiff further asks this court to extend *Chaplinsky*, which upheld a statute punishing the use of such words, and hold that the fighting-words doctrine permits a prior restraint on defendants' symbolic speech. In our judgment we are precluded from doing so. . . .

> The display of the swastika, as offensive to the principles of a free nation as the memories it recalls may be, is symbolic political speech intended to convey to the public the beliefs of those who display it. It does not, in our opinion, fall within the definition of "fighting words," and that doctrine cannot be used here to overcome the heavy presumption against the constitutional validity of a prior restraint. Nor can we find that the swastika, while not representing fighting words, is nevertheless so offensive and peace threatening to the public that its display can be enjoined. We do not doubt that the sight of this symbol is abhorrent to the Jewish citizens of Skokie, and that the survivors of the Nazi persecutions, tormented by their recollections, may have strong feelings regarding its display. Yet it is entirely clear that this factor does not justify enjoining defendants' speech. . . .

> In summary, as we read the controlling Supreme Court opinions, use of the swastika is a symbolic form of free speech entitled to First Amendment protections. Its display on uniforms or banners by those engaged in peaceful demonstrations cannot be totally precluded solely because that display may provoke a violent reaction by those who view

it. Particularly is this true where, as here, there has been advance notice by the demonstrators of their plans so that they have become, as the complaint alleges, "common knowledge" and those to whom sight of the swastika banner or uniforms would be offensive are forewarned and need not view them. A speaker who gives prior notice of his message has not compelled a confrontation with those who voluntarily listen.

While the first case was proceeding, Skokie passed several ordinances targeting the Nazi groups' parade requests. One required $300,000 in liability insurance and $50,000 in property insurance before a group could receive a parade permit. A second prohibited "dissemination of . . . materials" in Skokie that "promotes and incites hatred against persons by reason of their race, national origin, or religion." A third prohibited public demonstrations by political groups wearing military-like uniforms. A challenge was quickly brought in federal court, and the district court and Court of Appeals for the Seventh Circuit struck down the ordinances as violating the First Amendment. *Collin v. Smith*, 578 F.2d 1197 (7th Cir. 1978).

This time Skokie sought a stay in the U.S. Supreme Court. The Court denied the stay, with two justices dissenting. The Nazis, having won the right to march, did not do so, but staged rallies in Chicago and in Evanston, another nearby suburb.

Is a Nazi swastika in Skokie, or neo-Nazis marching in uniform through the streets of a community with many Jewish Holocaust survivors, any *less* a "threat" than a Ku Klux Klan cross-burning? Is the cross-burning in *Virginia v. Black* anything other than a different instance of hateful, deeply offensive speech? Is it really possible for courts to draw principled lines among different types of "hate speech" based on social context? Is *Black* wrong? Are the Illinois Nazi cases wrong?

[*Assignment 46*]

G. OFFENSIVE AND DEGRADING SPEECH

Cohen v. California
403 U.S. 15 (1971)

■ MR. JUSTICE HARLAN delivered the opinion of the Court.

This case may seem at first blush too inconsequential to find its way into our books, but the issue it presents is of no small constitutional significance.

Appellant Paul Robert Cohen was convicted in the Los Angeles Municipal Court of violating that part of California Penal Code § 415 which prohibits "maliciously and willfully disturb(ing) the peace or quiet of any neighborhood or person . . . by . . . offensive conduct. . . ." He was given 30 days' imprisonment. The facts upon which his conviction rests . . . are as follows:

> On April 26, 1968, the defendant was observed in the Los Angeles County Courthouse in the corridor outside of division 20 of the municipal court wearing a jacket bearing the words "Fuck the Draft" which were plainly visible. There were women and children present in the corridor. The defendant was arrested. The defendant testified that he wore the jacket knowing that the words were on the jacket as a means

of informing the public of the depth of his feelings against the Vietnam War and the draft.

The defendant did not engage in, nor threaten to engage in, nor did anyone as the result of his conduct in fact commit or threaten to commit any act of violence. The defendant did not make any loud or unusual noise, nor was there any evidence that he uttered any sound prior to his arrest.

1 Cal. App. 3d 94, 97–98 (1969).

In affirming the conviction the Court of Appeal held that "offensive conduct" means "behavior which has a tendency to provoke *others* to acts of violence or to in turn disturb the peace," and that the State had proved this element because, on the facts of this case, "[i]t was certainly reasonably foreseeable that such conduct might cause others to rise up to commit a violent act against the person of the defendant or attempt to forceably remove his jacket." . . . We now reverse. . . .

I

In order to lay hands on the precise issue which this case involves, it is useful first to canvass various matters which this record does not present.

The conviction quite clearly rests upon the asserted offensiveness of the *words* Cohen used to convey his message to the public. The only "conduct" which the State sought to punish is the fact of communication. Thus, we deal here with a conviction resting solely upon "speech," cf. *Stromberg v. California*, 283 U.S. 359 (1931), not upon any separately identifiable conduct which allegedly was intended by Cohen to be perceived by others as expressive of particular views but which, on its face, does not necessarily convey any message and hence arguably could be regulated without effectively repressing Cohen's ability to express himself. Cf. *United States v. O'Brien*, 391 U.S. 367 (1968). Further, the State certainly lacks power to punish Cohen for the underlying content of the message the inscription conveyed. At least so long as there is no showing of an intent to incite disobedience to or disruption of the draft, Cohen could not, consistently with the First and Fourteenth Amendments, be punished for asserting the evident position on the inutility or immorality of the draft his jacket reflected. *Yates v. United States*, 354 U.S. 298 (1957).

Appellant's conviction, then, rests squarely upon his exercise of the "freedom of speech" protected from arbitrary governmental interference by the Constitution and can be justified, if at all, only as a valid regulation of the manner in which he exercised that freedom, not as a permissible prohibition on the substantive message it conveys. This does not end the inquiry, of course, for the First and Fourteenth Amendments have never been thought to give absolute protection to every individual to speak whenever or wherever he pleases or to use any form of address in any circumstances that he chooses. In this vein, too, however, we think it important to note that several issues typically associated with such problems are not presented here.

In the first place, Cohen was tried under a statute applicable throughout the entire State. Any attempt to support this conviction on the ground that the statute seeks to preserve an appropriately decorous atmosphere in the courthouse where Cohen was arrested must fail in the absence of any language in the statute that would have put appellant on notice that certain kinds of otherwise permissible speech or conduct would nevertheless, under California law, not be tolerated in certain places. No fair reading of the phrase "offensive conduct" can be said sufficiently to inform the ordinary person that distinctions between certain locations are thereby created.

In the second place, as it comes to us, this case cannot be said to fall within those relatively few categories of instances where prior decisions have established the power of government to deal more comprehensively with certain forms of individual expression simply upon a showing that such a form was employed. This is not, for example, an obscenity case. Whatever else may be necessary to give rise to the States' broader power to prohibit obscene expression, such expression must be, in some significant way, erotic. *Roth v. United States*, 354 U.S. 476 (1957). It cannot plausibly be maintained that this vulgar allusion to the Selective Service System would conjure up such psychic stimulation in anyone likely to be confronted with Cohen's crudely defaced jacket.

This Court has also held that the States are free to ban the simple use, without a demonstration of additional justifying circumstances, of so-called "fighting words," those personally abusive epithets which, when addressed to the ordinary citizen, are, as a matter of common knowledge, inherently likely to provoke violent reaction. *Chaplinsky v. New Hampshire*, 315 U.S. 568 (1942). While the four-letter word displayed by Cohen in relation to the draft is not uncommonly employed in a personally provocative fashion, in this instance it was clearly not "directed to the person of the hearer." *Cantwell v. Connecticut*, 310 U.S. 296, 309 (1940). No individual actually or likely to be present could reasonably have regarded the words on appellant's jacket as a direct personal insult. Nor do we have here an instance of the exercise of the State's police power to prevent a speaker from intentionally provoking a given group to hostile reaction. Cf. *Feiner v. New York*, 340 U.S. 315 (1951); *Terminiello v. Chicago*, 337 U.S. 1 (1949). There is, as noted above, no showing that anyone who saw Cohen was in fact violently aroused or that appellant intended such a result.

Finally, in arguments before this Court much has been made of the claim that Cohen's distasteful mode of expression was thrust upon unwilling or unsuspecting viewers, and that the State might therefore legitimately act as it did in order to protect the sensitive from otherwise unavoidable exposure to appellant's crude form of protest. Of course, the mere presumed presence of unwitting listeners or viewers does not serve automatically to justify curtailing all speech capable of giving offense. See, *e.g.*, *Organization for a Better Austin v. Keefe*, 402 U.S. 415 (1971). While this Court has recognized that government may properly act in many situations to prohibit intrusion into the privacy of the home of unwelcome views and ideas which cannot be totally banned from the public dialogue, *e.g.*, *Rowan v. United States Post Office Dept.*, 397 U.S. 728 (1970), we have at the same time consistently stressed that "we are often 'captives' outside the sanctuary of the home and subject to objectionable speech." *Id.*, at 738. The ability of government, consonant with the Constitution, to shut off discourse solely to protect others from hearing it is, in other words, dependent upon a showing that substantial privacy interests are being invaded in an essentially intolerable manner. Any broader view of this authority would effectively empower a majority to silence dissidents simply as a matter of personal predilections.

In this regard, persons confronted with Cohen's jacket were in a quite different posture than, say, those subjected to the raucous emissions of sound trucks blaring outside their residences. Those in the Los Angeles courthouse could effectively avoid further bombardment of their sensibilities simply by averting their eyes. And, while it may be that one has a more substantial claim to a recognizable privacy interest when walking through a courthouse corridor than, for example, strolling through Central Park, surely it is nothing like the interest in being free from unwanted expression in the confines of one's own home. Cf. *Keefe, supra.* Given the subtlety and complexity of the factors involved, if Cohen's "speech" was otherwise entitled to constitutional protection, we do not think the fact that some unwilling "listeners" in a public building may have been briefly exposed to it can serve to justify this breach of the peace conviction where, as here, there was no evidence that persons powerless to avoid appellant's conduct did in fact object to it, and where that portion of the statute upon which Cohen's conviction rests evinces no concern, either on its face or as construed by the California courts, with the special plight of the captive auditor, but, instead, indiscriminately sweeps within its prohibitions all "offensive conduct" that disturbs "any neighborhood or person." Cf. *Edwards v. South Carolina, supra.*

II

Against this background, the issue flushed by this case stands out in bold relief. It is whether California can excise, as "offensive conduct," one particular scurrilous epithet from the public discourse, either upon the theory of the court below that its use is inherently likely to cause violent reaction or upon a more general assertion that the States, acting as guardians of public morality, may properly remove this offensive word from the public vocabulary.

The rationale of the California court is plainly untenable. At most it reflects an "undifferentiated fear or apprehension of disturbance (which) is not enough to overcome the right to freedom of expression." *Tinker v. Des Moines Indep. Community School Dist.*, 393 U.S. 503, 508 (1969). We have been shown no evidence that substantial numbers of citizens are standing ready to strike out physically at whoever may assault their sensibilities with execrations like that uttered by Cohen. There may be some persons about with such lawless and violent proclivities, but that is an insufficient base upon which to erect, consistently with constitutional values, a governmental power to force persons who wish to ventilate their dissident views into avoiding particular forms of expression. The argument amounts to little more than the self-defeating proposition that to avoid physical censorship of one who has not sought to provoke such a response by a hypothetical coterie of the violent and lawless, the States may more appropriately effectuate that censorship themselves.

Admittedly, it is not so obvious that the First and Fourteenth Amendments must be taken to disable the States from punishing public utterance of this unseemly expletive in order to maintain what they regard as a suitable level of discourse within the body politic. We think, however, that examination and reflection will reveal the shortcomings of a contrary viewpoint.

At the outset, we cannot overemphasize that, in our judgment, most situations where the State has a justifiable interest in regulating speech will fall within one or more of the various established exceptions, discussed above but not applicable here, to the usual rule that governmental bodies may not prescribe the form or content of individual expression. Equally important to our conclusion is the constitutional backdrop against which our decision must be made. The constitutional right of free expression is powerful medicine in a society as diverse and populous as ours. It is designed and intended to remove governmental restraints from the arena of public discussion, putting the decision as to what views shall be voiced largely into the hands of each of us, in the hope that use of such freedom will ultimately produce a more capable citizenry and more perfect polity and in the belief that no other approach would comport with the premise of individual dignity and choice upon which our political system rests. See *Whitney v. California*, 274 U.S. 357, 375–377 (1927) (Brandeis, J., concurring).

To many, the immediate consequence of this freedom may often appear to be only verbal tumult, discord, and even offensive utterance. These are, however, within established limits, in truth necessary side effects of the broader enduring values which the process of open debate permits us to achieve. That the air may at times seem filled with verbal cacophony is, in this sense not a sign of weakness but of strength. We cannot lose sight of the fact that, in what otherwise might seem a trifling and annoying instance of individual distasteful abuse of a privilege, these fundamental societal values are truly implicated. That is why "(w)holly neutral futilities . . . come under the protection of free speech as fully as do Keats' poems or Donne's sermons," *Winters v. New York*, 333 U.S. 507, 528 (1948) (Frankfurter, J., dissenting), and why "so long as the means are peaceful, the communication need not meet standards of acceptability," *Organization for a Better Austin v. Keefe*, 402 U.S. 415 (1971).

. . . [T]he principle contended for by the State seems inherently boundless. How is one to distinguish this from any other offensive word? Surely the State has no right to cleanse public debate to the point where it is grammatically palatable to the most squeamish among us. Yet no readily ascertainable general principle exists for stopping short of that result were we to affirm the judgment below. For, while the particular four-letter word being litigated here is perhaps more distasteful than most others of its genre, it is nevertheless often true that one man's vulgarity is another's lyric. Indeed, we think it is largely because governmental officials cannot make principled distinctions in this area that the Constitution leaves matters of taste and style so largely to the individual.

Additionally, we cannot overlook the fact, because it is well illustrated by the episode involved here, that much linguistic expression serves a dual communicative function: it conveys not only ideas capable of relatively precise, detached explication, but otherwise inexpressible emotions as well. In fact, words are often chosen as much for their emotive as their cognitive force. We cannot sanction the view that the Constitution, while solicitous of the cognitive content of individual speech has little or no regard for that emotive function which practically speaking, may often be the more important element of the overall message sought to be communicated. Indeed, as Mr. Justice Frankfurter has said, "[o]ne of the prerogatives of American citizenship is the right to criticize public men and measures—and that means not only informed and responsible criticism but the freedom to speak foolishly and without moderation."

Finally, and in the same vein, we cannot indulge the facile assumption that one can forbid particular words without also running a substantial risk of suppressing ideas in the process. Indeed, governments might soon seize upon the censorship of particular words as a convenient guise for banning the expression of unpopular views. We have been able, as noted above, to discern little social benefit that might result from running the risk of opening the door to such grave results.

It is, in sum, our judgment that, absent a more particularized and compelling reason for its actions, the State may not, consistently with the First and Fourteenth Amendments, make the simple public display here involved of this single four-letter expletive a criminal offense. Because that is the only arguably sustainable rationale for the conviction here at issue, the judgment below must be reversed.

■ MR. JUSTICE BLACKMUN, with whom THE CHIEF JUSTICE and MR. JUSTICE BLACK join.

I dissent . . . Cohen's absurd and immature antic, in my view, was mainly conduct and little speech. The California Court of Appeal appears so to have described it, and I cannot characterize it otherwise. Further, the case appears to me to be well within the sphere of *Chaplinsky v. New Hampshire*, 315 U.S. 568 (1942). . . . As a consequence, this Court's agonizing over First Amendment values seems misplaced and unnecessary. . . .

NOTES

1. *Cohen v. California* is a Free Speech Clause classic. Was it rightly decided, or was it a disgraceful tribute to the increasing coarseness of our discourse? Note that the United States is exceptional in its legal protection of "coarse" speech. Our northern neighbor Canada, for example, is much less protective of such speech. Why? One scholar has argued that it is because Canada was populated, after the American Revolution, by Tories who supported the monarchy and the established Church of England, rather than by those who valued dissident speech. See Seymour Martin Lipset, CONTINENTAL DIVIDE: THE VALUES AND INSTITUTIONS OF THE UNITED STATES AND CANADA (1990).

2. Break down the First Amendment question in this Fourteenth Amendment case into some possible component parts: Was Cohen's jacket "speech" or "conduct"? If conduct, was it expressive conduct? If speech or expressive conduct, was it obscene? Did it constitute "fighting words"? What is it that might cause offense to those who see it—is it the particular word used or the message of strong anti-draft/anti-war feeling? Is that offensiveness ground for regulation? Does that provide a legitimate basis for regulating it? Could the government legitimately prohibit the use of particularly offensive words (or images) on the ground that the speaker could just as effectively communicate his message through the use of other words (or images)? Would this be just a limitation on the "manner" of the expression of the speaker's views? Or is it a limitation on its content or message in some meaningful sense?

3. Try a different tack: Cohen's "speech" occurred in a courthouse. Many citizens are there on official business—indeed, many are *required* to be there as witnesses, government employees, or parties in a case. Are they a "captive audience" that the government has a legitimate interest in shielding from exposure to unwanted (and offensive) speech? Is there a "privacy right" of individuals to be free from exposure to the offensive speech of others, at least in public buildings? Does the government have a legitimate interest in protecting unwilling hearers—especially vulnerable or sensitive persons—from messages or words they might strongly wish not to hear? Does the First Amendment permit the government to balance this interest against Cohen's interest in expressing his particular message in a particular way? What if children are likely to be present? Does that provide a ground for regulating or prohibiting Cohen's jacket? If so, how far does that justification extend?

4. Is it possible the decision in Cohen was affected by the obvious political character of the message? Might the Court have thought, without saying, that Cohen was singled out for his anti-war advocacy? What if he had been wearing a t-shirt with a crude but nonpolitical message? Is it really possible that the government cannot maintain some standards of public decorum in public places?

Hustler Magazine v. Falwell
485 U.S. 46 (1988)

■ CHIEF JUSTICE REHNQUIST delivered the opinion of the Court.

Petitioner Hustler Magazine, Inc., is a magazine of nationwide circulation. Respondent Jerry Falwell, a nationally known minister who has been active as a commentator on politics and public affairs, sued petitioner and its publisher, petitioner Larry Flynt, to recover damages for invasion of privacy, libel, and intentional infliction of emotional distress. . . .

The inside front cover of the November 1983 issue of Hustler Magazine featured a "parody" of an advertisement for Campari Liqueur that contained the name and picture of respondent and was entitled "Jerry Falwell talks about his first time." This parody was modeled after actual Campari ads that included interviews with various celebrities about their "first times." Although it was apparent by the end of each interview that this meant the first time they sampled Campari, the ads clearly played on the sexual double entendre of the general subject of "first times." Copying the form and layout of these Campari ads, Hustler's editors chose respondent as the featured celebrity and drafted an alleged "interview" with him in which he states that his "first time" was during a drunken incestuous rendezvous with his mother in an outhouse. The Hustler parody portrays respondent and his mother as drunk and immoral, and suggests that respondent is a hypocrite who preaches only when he is drunk. In small print at the bottom of the page, the ad contains the disclaimer, "ad parody—not to be taken seriously." The magazine's table of contents also lists the ad as "Fiction; Ad and Personality Parody."

Soon after the November issue of Hustler became available to the public, respondent brought this diversity action in the United States District Court against Hustler Magazine, Inc., Larry C. Flynt, and Flynt Distributing Co., Inc. Respondent stated in his complaint that publication of the ad parody in Hustler entitled him to recover damages for libel, invasion of privacy, and intentional infliction of emotional distress. The case proceeded to trial. At the close of the evidence, the District Court granted a directed verdict for petitioners on the invasion of privacy claim. The jury then found against respondent on the libel claim, specifically finding that the ad parody could not "reasonably be understood as describing actual facts about [respondent] or actual events in which [he] participated." The jury ruled for respondent on the intentional infliction of emotional distress claim, however, and stated that he should be awarded $100,000 in compensatory damages, as well as $50,000 each in punitive damages from petitioners. . . .

This case presents us with a novel question involving First Amendment limitations upon a State's authority to protect its citizens from the intentional infliction of emotional distress. We must decide whether a public figure may recover damages for emotional harm caused by the publication of an ad parody offensive to him, and doubtless gross and repugnant in the eyes of most. Respondent would have us find that a State's interest in protecting public figures from emotional distress is sufficient to deny First Amendment protection to speech that is patently offensive and is intended to inflict emotional injury, even when that speech could not reasonably have been interpreted as stating actual facts about the public figure involved. This we decline to do.

At the heart of the First Amendment is the recognition of the fundamental importance of the free flow of ideas and opinions on matters of public interest and concern. "[T]he freedom to speak one's mind is not only an aspect of individual liberty—and thus a good unto itself—but also is essential to the common quest for truth and the vitality of society as a whole." *Bose Corp. v. Consumers Union of United States, Inc.*, 466 U.S. 485, 503–504 (1984). We have therefore been particularly vigilant to ensure that individual expressions of ideas remain free from governmentally imposed sanctions. The First Amendment recognizes no such thing as a "false" idea. *Gertz v. Robert Welch, Inc.*, 418 U.S. 323, 339 (1974). As Justice Holmes wrote, "when men have realized that time has upset many fighting faiths, they may come to believe even more than they believe the very foundations of their own conduct that the ultimate good desired is better reached by free trade in ideas—that the best test of truth is the power of the thought to get itself accepted in the competition of the market. . . ." *Abrams v. United States*, 250 U.S. 616, 630 (1919) (dissenting opinion).

The sort of robust political debate encouraged by the First Amendment is bound to produce speech that is critical of those who hold public office or those public figures who are "intimately involved in the resolution of important public questions or, by reason of their fame, shape events in areas of concern to society at large." *Associated Press v. Walker*, decided with *Curtis Publishing Co. v. Butts*, 388 U.S. 130, 164 (1967) (Warren, C.J., concurring in result). Justice Frankfurter put it succinctly in *Baumgartner v. United States*, 322 U.S. 665, 673–674 (1944), when he said that "[o]ne of the prerogatives of American citizenship is the right to criticize public men and measures." Such criticism, inevitably, will not always be reasoned or moderate; public figures as well as public officials will be subject to "vehement, caustic, and sometimes unpleasantly sharp attacks," *New York Times, supra*, 376 U.S., at 270. "[T]he candidate who vaunts his spotless record and sterling integrity cannot convincingly cry 'Foul!' when an opponent or an industrious reporter attempts to demonstrate the contrary." *Monitor Patriot Co. v. Roy*, 401 U.S. 265, 274 (1971).

Of course, this does not mean that any speech about a public figure is immune from sanction in the form of damages. Since *New York Times Co. v. Sullivan*, 376 U.S. 254 (1964), we have consistently ruled that a public figure may hold a speaker liable for the damage to reputation caused by publication of a defamatory falsehood, but only if the statement was made "with knowledge that it was false or with reckless disregard of whether it was false or not." *Id.*, 376 U.S., at 279–280. False statements of fact are particularly valueless; they interfere with the truth-seeking function of the marketplace of ideas, and they cause damage to an individual's reputation that cannot easily be repaired by counterspeech, however persuasive or effective. See *Gertz*, 418 U.S., at 340, 344, n. 9. But even though falsehoods have little value in and of themselves, they are "nevertheless inevitable in free debate," *id.*, at 340, and a rule that would impose strict liability on a publisher for false factual assertions would have an undoubted "chilling" effect on speech relating to public figures that does have constitutional value. "Freedoms of expression require 'breathing space.' " *Philadelphia Newspapers, Inc. v. Hepps*, 475 U.S. 767, 772 (1986) (quoting *New York Times, supra*, 376 U.S., at 272). This breathing space is provided by a constitutional rule that allows public figures to recover for libel or defamation only when they can prove both that the statement was false and that the statement was made with the requisite level of culpability.

Respondent argues, however, that a different standard should apply in this case because here the State seeks to prevent not reputational damage, but the severe emotional distress suffered by the person who is the subject of an offensive publication. In respondent's view, and in the view of the Court of Appeals, so long as the utterance was intended to inflict emotional distress, was outrageous, and did in fact inflict serious emotional distress, it is of no constitutional import whether the statement was a fact or an opinion, or whether it was true or false. It is the intent to cause injury that is the gravamen of the tort, and the State's interest in preventing emotional harm simply outweighs whatever interest a speaker may have in speech of this type.

Generally speaking the law does not regard the intent to inflict emotional distress as one which should receive much solicitude, and it is quite understandable that most if not all jurisdictions have chosen to make it civilly culpable where the conduct in question is sufficiently "outrageous." But in the world of debate about public affairs, many things done with motives that are less than admirable are protected by the First Amendment. In *Garrison v. Louisiana*, 379 U.S. 64 (1964), we held that even when a speaker or writer is motivated by hatred or illwill his expression was protected by the First Amendment:

> Debate on public issues will not be uninhibited if the speaker must run the risk that it will be proved in court that he spoke out of hatred; even if he did speak out of hatred, utterances honestly believed contribute to the free interchange of ideas and the ascertainment of truth.

Id., at 73. Thus while such a bad motive may be deemed controlling for purposes of tort liability in other areas of the law, we think the First Amendment prohibits such a result in the area of public debate about public figures.

Were we to hold otherwise, there can be little doubt that political cartoonists and satirists would be subjected to damages awards without any showing that their work falsely defamed its subject. Webster's defines a caricature as "the deliberately distorted picturing or imitating of a person, literary style, etc. by exaggerating features or mannerisms for satirical effect." The appeal of the political cartoon or caricature is often based on exploitation of unfortunate physical traits or politically embarrassing events—an exploitation often calculated to injure the feelings of the subject of the portrayal. The art of the cartoonist is often not reasoned or even-handed, but slashing and one-sided. One cartoonist expressed the nature of the art in these words:

> The political cartoon is a weapon of attack, of scorn and ridicule and satire; it is least effective when it tries to pat some politician on the back. It is usually as welcome as a bee sting and is always controversial in some quarters.

... Despite their sometimes caustic nature, from the early cartoon portraying George Washington as an ass down to the present day, graphic depictions and satirical cartoons have played a prominent role in public and political debate . . . Lincoln's tall, gangling posture, Teddy Roosevelt's glasses and teeth, and Franklin D. Roosevelt's jutting jaw and cigarette holder have been memorialized by political cartoons with an effect that could not have been obtained by the photographer or the portrait artist. From the viewpoint of history it is clear that our political discourse would have been considerably poorer without them.

Respondent contends, however, that the caricature in question here was so "outrageous" as to distinguish it from more traditional political cartoons. There is no doubt that the caricature of respondent and his mother published in Hustler is at best a distant cousin of the political cartoons described above, and a rather poor relation at that. If it were possible by laying down a principled standard to separate the one from the other, public discourse would probably suffer little or no harm. But we doubt that there is any such standard, and we are quite sure that the pejorative description "outrageous" does not supply one. "Outrageousness" in the area of political and social discourse has an inherent subjectiveness about it which would allow a jury to impose liability on the basis of the jurors' tastes or views, or perhaps on the basis of their dislike of a particular expression. An "outrageousness" standard thus runs afoul of our longstanding refusal to allow damages to be awarded because the speech in question may have an adverse emotional impact on the audience. See *NAACP v. Claiborne Hardware Co.*, 458 U.S. 886, 910 (1982) ("Speech does not lose its protected character . . . simply because it may embarrass others or coerce them into action"). And, as we stated in *FCC v. Pacifica Foundation*, 438 U.S. 726 (1978):

> [T]he fact that society may find speech offensive is not a sufficient reason for suppressing it. Indeed, if it is the speaker's opinion that gives offense, that consequence is a reason for according it constitutional protection. For it is a central tenet of the First Amendment that the government must remain neutral in the marketplace of ideas.

Id., at 745–746. See also *Street v. New York*, 394 U.S. 576, 592 (1969) ("It is firmly settled that . . . the public expression of ideas may not be prohibited merely because the ideas are themselves offensive to some of their hearers").

Admittedly, these oft-repeated First Amendment principles, like other principles, are subject to limitations. We recognized in *Pacifica Foundation*, that speech that is "vulgar, offensive, and shocking" is "not entitled to absolute constitutional protection under all circumstances." 438 U.S., at 747. In *Chaplinsky v. New Hampshire*, 315 U.S. 568 (1942), we held that a State could lawfully punish an individual for the use of insulting "fighting words—those which by their very utterance inflict injury or tend to incite an immediate breach of the peace." *Id.*, at 571–572. These limitations are but recognition of the observation in *Dun & Bradstreet, Inc. v. Greenmoss Builders, Inc.*, 472 U.S. 749, 758 (1985), that this Court has "long recognized that not all speech is of equal First Amendment importance." But the sort of expression involved in this case does not seem to us to be governed by any exception to the general First Amendment principles stated above.

We conclude that public figures and public officials may not recover for the tort of intentional infliction of emotional distress by reason of publications such as the one here at issue without showing in addition that the publication contains a false statement of fact which was made with "actual malice," *i.e.*, with knowledge that the statement was false or with reckless disregard as to whether or not it was true. This is not merely a "blind application" of the *New York Times* standard, see *Time, Inc. v. Hill*, 385 U.S. 374, 390 (1967), it reflects our considered judgment that such a standard is necessary to give adequate "breathing space" to the freedoms protected by the First Amendment.

Here it is clear that respondent Falwell is a "public figure" for purposes of First Amendment law. The jury found against respondent on his libel claim when it decided that the Hustler ad parody could not "reasonably be understood as describing actual facts about [respondent] or actual events in which [he] participated." The Court of Appeals interpreted the jury's finding to be that the ad parody "was not reasonably believable," 97 F.2d, at 1278, and in accordance with our custom we accept this finding. Respondent is thus relegated to his claim for damages awarded by the jury for the intentional infliction of emotional distress by "outrageous" conduct. But for reasons heretofore stated this claim cannot, consistently with the First Amendment, form a basis for the award of damages when the conduct in question is the publication of a caricature such as the ad parody involved here.

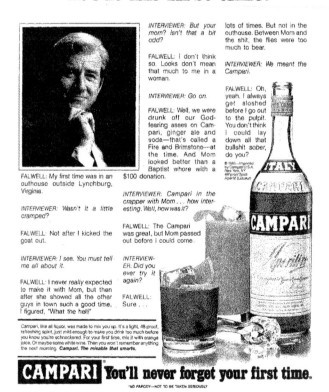

NOTES

1. Presumably no one reading the offensive parody in Hustler thought it was making a claim of fact. So why did the Court talk about "actual malice," which means knowing or reckless falsehood? Every parody meets that stand-

ard. What is the proper First Amendment test for speech that makes no claims of fact but is designed to inflict emotional distress?

2. In *Snyder v. Phelps*, 131 S. Ct. 1207 (2011), the Court held that the First Amendment forbade an award of damages against Fred Phelps and other members of the Westboro Baptist Church for picketing near a soldier's funeral service. As described in Chief Justice Roberts's majority opinion, "[t]he church's congregation believes that God hates and punishes the United States for its tolerance of homosexuality, particularly in America's military," and that "God kills American soldiers as punishment" for the nation's undue toleration of homosexuality. "The church frequently communicates its views by picketing, often at military funerals."

Church members picketed near the memorial service held for Marine Lance Corporal Matthew Snyder, who had been killed in Iraq in the line of duty. The picketing took place on public property, within a 10–by–25–foot plot of land adjacent to a public street. As the Court said, the picketers carried signs saying:

> "God Hates the USA/Thank God for 9/11," "America is Doomed," Don't Pray for the USA," "Thank God for IEDs," "Thank God for Dead Soldiers," "Pope in Hell," "Priests Rape Boys," "God Hates Fags," "You're Going to Hell," and "God Hates You."

Snyder's father sued Phelps and other church members for, among other things, intentional infliction of emotional distress, intrusion upon seclusion, and civil conspiracy. A jury found for Snyder on these claims and awarded damages totaling (after remittitur) $5 million.

The Supreme Court rejected the tort award as inconsistent with the First Amendment, under the reasoning of *Hustler v. Falwell* and other decisions. "[T]he church members had the right to be where they were," the Court held, and "[t]he record confirms that any distress occasioned by Westboro's picketing turned on the content and viewpoint of the message conveyed, rather than any interference with the funeral itself." The Court said:

> Given that Westboro's speech was at a public place on a matter of public concern, that speech is entitled to 'special protection' under the First Amendment. Such speech cannot be restricted simply because it is upsetting or arouses contempt. "If there is a bedrock principle underlying the First Amendment, it is that the government may not prohibit the expression of an idea simply because society finds the idea itself offensive or disagreeable." *Texas v. Johnson*, 491 U.S. 397, 414 (1989). Indeed, "the point of all speech protection . . . is to shield just those choices of content that in someone's eyes are misguided, or even hurtful." *Hurley v. Irish–American Gay, Lesbian and Bisexual Group of Boston, Inc.*, 515 U.S. 557, 574 (1995).

As in *Hustler*, the Court held that "outrageousness" was a "highly malleable standard with 'an inherent subjectiveness about it which would allow a jury to impose liability on the basis of the jurors' tastes or views, or perhaps on the basis of their dislike of a particular expression' " (quoting *Hustler*). The Court noted that its holding was "narrow" and did not implicate laws imposing time, place, or manner restrictions on funeral picketing. "To the extent these laws are content neutral, they raise very different questions from the tort verdict at issue in this case. . . . [W]e have no occasion to consider how [Maryland's such law] might apply to facts such as those before us, or whether it or other similar regulations are constitutional."

The Court concluded:

Westboro believes that America is morally flawed; many Americans might feel the same about Westboro. Westboro's funeral picketing is certainly hurtful and its contribution to public discourse may be negligible. But Westboro addressed matters of public import on public property, in a peaceful manner, in full compliance with the guidance of local officials. . . .

Speech is powerful. It can stir people to action, move them to tears of both joy and sorrow, and—as it did here—inflict great pain. On the facts before us, we cannot react to that pain by punishing the speaker. As a Nation, we have chosen a different course—to protect even hurtful speech on public issues to ensure that we do not stifle public debate. That choice requires that we shield Westboro from tort liability for its picketing in this case.

Only Justice Alito dissented, stating that "[o]ur profound national commitment to free and open debate is not a license for the vicious verbal assault that occurred in this case." He emphasized that Snyder was not a "public figure," and argued that the attack was not truly expression on any issue of public concern, but a "brutal" attack on an individual. "Respondents' outrageous conduct caused petitioner great injury, and the Court now compounds that injury by depriving petitioner of a judgment that acknowledges the wrong he suffered. In order to have a society in which public issues can be openly and vigorously debated, it is not necessary to allow the brutalization of innocent victims like petitioner."

––––––––

What if the offensive speech is degrading to a person on the basis of race, gender, religion, or sexual orientation? May speech be punished on the ground that it communicates a message of subordination? If so, should it be?

American Booksellers Association v. Hudnut
771 F.2d 323 (7th Cir. 1985), aff'd mem. 475 U.S. 1001 (1986)

■ EASTERBROOK, CIRCUIT JUDGE.

Indianapolis enacted an ordinance defining "pornography" as a practice that discriminates against women. "Pornography" is to be redressed through the administrative and judicial methods used for other discrimination. The City's definition of "pornography" is considerably different from "obscenity," which the Supreme Court has held is not protected by the First Amendment.

To be "obscene" under *Miller v. California*, 413 U.S. 15 (1973), "a publication must, taken as a whole, appeal to the prurient interest, must contain patently offensive depictions or descriptions of specified sexual conduct, and on the whole have no serious literary, artistic, political, or scientific value." *Brockett v. Spokane Arcades, Inc.*, 472 U.S. 491 (1985). Offensiveness must be assessed under the standards of the community. Both offensiveness and an appeal to something other than "normal, healthy sexual desires" (*Brockett, supra*,) are essential elements of "obscenity."

"Pornography" under the ordinance is "the graphic sexually explicit subordination of women, whether in pictures or in words, that also includes one or more of the following:

(1) Women are presented as sexual objects who enjoy pain or humiliation; or

(2) Women are presented as sexual objects who experience sexual pleasure in being raped; or

(3) Women are presented as sexual objects tied up or cut up or mutilated or bruised or physically hurt, or as dismembered or truncated or fragmented or severed into body parts; or

(4) Women are presented as being penetrated by objects or animals; or

(5) Women are presented in scenarios of degradation, injury, abasement, torture, shown as filthy or inferior, bleeding, bruised, or hurt in a context that makes these conditions sexual; or

(6) Women are presented as sexual objects for domination, conquest, violation, exploitation, possession, or use, or through postures or positions of servility or submission or display.

The statute provides that the "use of men, children, or transsexuals in the place of women in paragraphs (1) through (6) above shall also constitute pornography under this section." The ordinance as passed in April 1984 defined "sexually explicit" to mean actual or simulated intercourse or the uncovered exhibition of the genitals, buttocks or anus. An amendment in June 1984 deleted this provision, leaving the term undefined.

[Unlike the obscenity standard, the] Indianapolis ordinance does not refer to the prurient interest, to offensiveness, or to the standards of the community. It demands attention to particular depictions, not to the work judged as a whole. It is irrelevant under the ordinance whether the work has literary, artistic, political, or scientific value. The City and many amici point to these omissions as virtues. They maintain that pornography influences attitudes, and the statute is a way to alter the socialization of men and women rather than to vindicate community standards of offensiveness. And as one of the principal drafters of the ordinance has asserted, "if a woman is subjected, why should it matter that the work has other value?" Catharine A. MacKinnon, *Pornography, Civil Rights, and Speech*, 20 Harv.Civ.Rts.–Civ.Lib.L.Rev. 1, 21 (1985).

Civil rights groups and feminists have entered this case as amici on both sides. Those supporting the ordinance say that it will play an important role in reducing the tendency of men to view women as sexual objects, a tendency that leads to both unacceptable attitudes and discrimination in the workplace and violence away from it. Those opposing the ordinance point out that much radical feminist literature is explicit and depicts women in ways forbidden by the ordinance and that the ordinance would reopen old battles. It is unclear how Indianapolis would treat works from James Joyce's *Ulysses* to Homer's *Iliad;* both depict women as submissive objects for conquest and domination.

We do not try to balance the arguments for and against an ordinance such as this. The ordinance discriminates on the ground of the content of the speech. Speech treating women in the approved way—in sexual encounters "premised on equality"—is lawful no matter how sexually explicit.

Speech treating women in the disapproved way—as submissive in matters sexual or as enjoying humiliation—is unlawful no matter how significant the literary, artistic, or political qualities of the work taken as a whole. The state may not ordain preferred viewpoints in this way. The Constitution forbids the state to declare one perspective right and silence opponents.

I

The ordinance contains four prohibitions. People may not "traffic" in pornography, "coerce" others into performing in pornographic works, or "force" pornography on anyone. Anyone injured by someone who has seen or read pornography has a right of action against the maker or seller. . . .

For purposes of all four offenses, it is generally "not . . . a defense that the respondent did not know or intend that the materials were pornography. . . ." But the ordinance provides that damages are unavailable in trafficking cases unless the complainant proves "that the respondent knew or had reason to know that the materials were pornography." . . .

The district court held the ordinance unconstitutional. The court concluded that the ordinance regulates speech rather than the conduct involved in making pornography. The regulation of speech could be justified, the court thought, only by a compelling interest in reducing sex discrimination, an interest Indianapolis had not established. . . .

II

The plaintiffs are a congeries of distributors and readers of books, magazines, and films. The American Booksellers Association comprises about 5,200 bookstores and chains. The Association for American Publishers includes most of the country's publishers. Video Shack, Inc., sells and rents video cassettes in Indianapolis. Kelly Bentley, a resident of Indianapolis, reads books and watches films. There are many more plaintiffs. Collectively the plaintiffs (or their members, whose interests they represent) make, sell, or read just about every kind of material that could be affected by the ordinance, from hard-core films to W.B. Yeats's poem "Leda and the Swan" (from the myth of Zeus in the form of a swan impregnating an apparently subordinate Leda), to the collected works of James Joyce, D.H. Lawrence, and John Cleland. . . .

III

"If there is any fixed star in our constitutional constellation, it is that no official, high or petty, can prescribe what shall be orthodox in politics, nationalism, religion, or other matters of opinion or force citizens to confess by word or act their faith therein." *West Virginia State Board of Education v. Barnette*, 319 U.S. 624, 642 (1943). Under the First Amendment the government must leave to the people the evaluation of ideas. Bald or subtle, an idea is as powerful as the audience allows it to be. A belief may be pernicious—the beliefs of Nazis led to the death of millions, those of the Klan to the repression of millions. A pernicious belief may prevail. Totalitarian governments today rule much of the planet, practicing suppression of billions and spreading dogma that may enslave others. One of the things that separates our society from theirs is our absolute right to propagate opinions that the government finds wrong or even hateful.

The ideas of the Klan may be propagated. *Brandenburg v. Ohio*, 395 U.S. 444 (1969). Communists may speak freely and run for office. *DeJonge v. Oregon*, 299 U.S. 353 (1937). The Nazi Party may march through a city with a large Jewish population. *Collin v. Smith*, 578 F.2d 1197 (7th Cir.), *cert. denied*, 439 U.S. 916 (1978). People may criticize the President by misrepresenting his positions, and they have a right to post their misrepresentations on public property. *Lebron v. Washington Metropolitan Area Transit Authority*, 749 F.2d 893 (D.C.Cir.1984) (Bork, J.). People may teach religions that others despise. People may seek to repeal laws guaranteeing equal opportunity in employment or to revoke the constitutional amendments granting the vote to blacks and women. They may do this because "above all else, the First Amendment means that government has no power to restrict expression because of its message [or] its ideas. . . ." *Police Department v. Mosley*, 408 U.S. 92, 95 (1972).

Under the ordinance graphic sexually explicit speech is "pornography" or not depending on the perspective the author adopts. Speech that "subordinates" women and also, for example, presents women as enjoying pain, humiliation, or rape, or even simply presents women in "positions of servility or submission or display" is forbidden, no matter how great the literary or political value of the work taken as a whole. Speech that portrays women in positions of equality is lawful, no matter how graphic the sexual content. This is thought control. It establishes an "approved" view of women, of how they may react to sexual encounters, of how the sexes may relate to each other. Those who espouse the approved view may use sexual images; those who do not, may not.

Indianapolis justifies the ordinance on the ground that pornography affects thoughts. Men who see women depicted as subordinate are more likely to treat them so. Pornography is an aspect of dominance. It does not persuade people so much as change them. It works by socializing, by establishing the expected and the permissible. In this view pornography is not an idea; pornography is the injury.

There is much to this perspective. Beliefs are also facts. People often act in accordance with the images and patterns they find around them. People raised in a religion tend to accept the tenets of that religion, often without independent examination. People taught from birth that black people are fit only for slavery rarely rebelled against that creed; beliefs coupled with the self-interest of the masters established a social structure that inflicted great harm while enduring for centuries. Words and images act at the level of the subconscious before they persuade at the level of the conscious. Even the truth has little chance unless a statement fits within the framework of beliefs that may never have been subjected to rational study.

Therefore we accept the premises of this legislation. Depictions of subordination tend to perpetuate subordination. The subordinate status of women in turn leads to affront and lower pay at work, insult and injury at home, battery and rape on the streets. . . .

Yet this simply demonstrates the power of pornography as speech. All of these unhappy effects depend on mental intermediation. Pornography affects how people see the world, their fellows, and social relations. If pornography is what pornography does, so is other speech. Hitler's orations affected how some Germans saw Jews. Communism is a worldview, not simply a *Manifesto* by Marx and Engels or a set of speeches. Efforts to suppress communist speech in the United States were based on the belief that the public acceptability of such ideas would increase the likelihood of totalitarian government. Religions affect socialization in the most pervasive way. . . . Many people believe that the existence of television, apart from the content of specific programs, leads to intellectual laziness, to a penchant for violence, to many other ills. The Alien and Sedition Acts passed during the administration of John Adams rested on a sincerely held belief that disrespect for the government leads to social collapse and revolution—a belief with support in the history of many nations. Most governments of the world act on this empirical regularity, suppressing critical speech. In the United States, however, the strength of the support for this belief is irrelevant. Seditious libel is protected speech unless the danger is not only grave but also imminent. See *New York Times Co. v. Sullivan*, 376 U.S. 254 (1964); cf. *Brandenburg v. Ohio, supra; New York Times Co. v. United States*, 403 U.S. 713 (1971).

Racial bigotry, anti-semitism, violence on television, reporters' biases—these and many more influence the culture and shape our socialization. None is directly answerable by more speech, unless that speech too finds its place in the popular culture. Yet all is protected as speech, however insidious. Any other answer leaves the government in control of all of the institutions of culture, the great censor and director of which thoughts are good for us.

Sexual responses often are unthinking responses, and the association of sexual arousal with the subordination of women therefore may have a substantial effect. But almost all cultural stimuli provoke unconscious responses. Religious ceremonies condition their participants. Teachers convey messages by selecting what not to cover; the implicit message about what is off limits or unthinkable may be more powerful than the messages for which they present rational argument. Television scripts contain unarticulated assumptions. People may be conditioned in subtle ways. If the fact that speech plays a role in a process of conditioning were enough to permit governmental regulation, that would be the end of freedom of speech.

It is possible to interpret the claim that the pornography is the harm in a different way. Indianapolis emphasizes the injury that models in pornographic films and pictures may suffer. The record contains materials depicting sexual torture, penetration of women by red-hot irons and the like. These concerns have nothing to do with written materials subject to the statute, and physical injury can occur with or without the "subordination" of women. A state may make injury in the course of producing a film unlawful independent of the viewpoint expressed in the film. . . .

Much of Indianapolis's argument rests on the belief that when speech is "unanswerable," and the metaphor that there is a "marketplace of ideas" does not apply, the First Amendment does not apply either. The metaphor is honored; Milton's *Aeropagitica* and John Stewart Mill's *On Liberty* defend freedom of speech on the ground that the truth will prevail, and many of the most important cases under the First Amendment recite this position. The Framers undoubtedly believed it. As a general matter it is true. But the Constitution does not make the dominance of truth a necessary condition of freedom of speech. To say that it does would be to confuse an outcome of free speech with a necessary condition for the application of the amendment.

A power to limit speech on the ground that truth has not yet prevailed and is not likely to prevail implies the power to declare truth. At some point the government must be able to say (as Indianapolis has said): "We know what the truth is, yet a free exchange of speech has not driven out falsity, so that we must now prohibit falsity." If the government may declare the truth, why wait for the failure of speech? Under the First Amendment, however, there is no such thing as a false idea, *Gertz v. Robert*

Welch, Inc., 418 U.S. 323, 339 (1974), so the government may not restrict speech on the ground that in a free exchange truth is not yet dominant.

At any time, some speech is ahead in the game; the more numerous speakers prevail. Supporters of minority candidates may be forever "excluded" from the political process because their candidates never win, because few people believe their positions. This does not mean that freedom of speech has failed. . . .

We come, finally, to the argument that pornography is "low value" speech, that it is enough like obscenity that Indianapolis may prohibit it. Some cases hold that speech far removed from politics and other subjects at the core of the Framers' concerns may be subjected to special regulation. These cases do not sustain statutes that select among viewpoints, however. . . .

At all events, "pornography" is not low value speech within the meaning of these cases. Indianapolis seeks to prohibit certain speech because it believes this speech influences social relations and politics on a grand scale, that it controls attitudes at home and in the legislature. This precludes a characterization of the speech as low value. . . .

Any rationale we could imagine in support of this ordinance could not be limited to sex discrimination. Free speech has been on balance an ally of those seeking change. Governments that want stasis start by restricting speech. Culture is a powerful force of continuity; Indianapolis paints pornography as part of the culture of power. Change in any complex system ultimately depends on the ability of outsiders to challenge accepted views and the reigning institutions. Without a strong guarantee of freedom of speech, there is no effective right to challenge what is. . . .

NOTES

1. The "speech" in question in this case was not "legally obscene"—it did not fall in that category of wholly unprotected expression. We have seen, several times now, references to "obscenity" and child pornography as categories of expression excluded from First Amendment protection. Justice Scalia's opinion for the Court in *United States v. Williams*, 553 U.S. 285 (2008), provides a concise summary of the Court's doctrines in these areas:

> We have long held that obscene speech—sexually explicit material that violates fundamental notions of decency—is not protected by the First Amendment. But to protect explicit material that has social value, we have limited the scope of the obscenity exception, and have overturned convictions for the distribution of sexually graphic but nonobscene material. . . .
>
> Over the last 25 years, we have confronted a related and overlapping category of proscribable speech: child pornography. See *Ashcroft v. Free Speech Coalition*, 535 U.S. 234 (2002); *Osborne v. Ohio*, 495 U.S. 103 (1990); *New York v. Ferber*, 458 U.S. 747 (1982). This consists of sexually explicit visual portrayals that feature children. We have held that a statute which proscribes the distribution of all child pornography, even material that does not qualify as obscenity, does not on its face violate the First Amendment. . . . Moreover, we have held that the government may criminalize the possession of child pornography, even though it may not crimi-

nalize the mere possession of obscene material involving adults. Compare *Osborne*, supra, at 111, with *Stanley v. Georgia*, 394 U.S. 557, 568 (1969).

2. Judge Easterbrook's opinion is an excellent (if again painful) review and distillation of the First Amendment principle that the government may not prohibit, punish, or penalize speech because of its content. Is the First Amendment freedom of speech really worth all this? Nazis marching through Skokie, Illinois? KKK cross burnings? Porn shops? Is some speech so offensive, and of so little value to meaningful public discourse, that it should just be prohibited as out-of-bounds for a civilized society? Alternatively, can't some such "speech" be deemed "threats" or "assaults" that should be punishable as *unlawful conduct*, irrespective of whether they might flow from the communication of messages?

3. *Hate Speech?* In American law, there has never been an exception to the freedom of speech simply because of the "hateful," discriminatory, or demeaning nature of the expression—though there have been attempts to expand the "fighting words" exception to embrace such types of expression. In the 1990s, some public university campuses promulgated "speech codes" regulating what students could and could not say in public discourse—typically forbidding remarks that were offensive or derogatory on the basis of race, gender, sexual orientation, or some other category. In *R.A.V. v. City of St. Paul*, 505 U.S. 377 (1992), presented above, the Supreme Court unanimously struck down St. Paul, Minnesota's "Bias–Oriented Crime Ordinance" as a violation of the First Amendment, overturning the petitioner's conviction for burning a cross on a black family's lawn. The City could not validly make the alarm or affront caused by a speaker's message, no matter how hateful, the basis for criminal punishment. (There were many statutes under which the City could have punished the petitioner's *conduct* on grounds *not* related to the content of his message.) It is thus reasonably clear under present doctrine that there is no general "hate speech" exception to the First Amendment freedom of speech. The Canadian Supreme Court, however, operating under a much less speech-protective constitution, has upheld laws against hate speech. See *R. v. Keegstra*, 3 S.C.R. 697 (Supreme Court of Canada 1990). The United States is exceptional in finding that hate speech laws are unconstitutional.

4. *Hostile Environment?* May speech that communicates a message that members of a minority racial, gender, religious, or sexual orientation group is inferior be punished if it takes place in a workplace? A university? Or a place of public accommodation, such as a restaurant?

[*Assignment 47*]

H. COMMERCIAL SPEECH

Valentine v. Chrestensen
316 U.S. 52 (1942)

■ MR. JUSTICE ROBERTS delivered the opinion of the Court.

The respondent, a citizen of Florida, owns a former United States Navy submarine which he exhibits for profit. In 1940 he brought it to New York City and moored it at a State pier in the East River. He prepared and printed a handbill advertising the boat and soliciting visitors for a stated admission fee. On his attempting to distribute the bill in the city streets, he was advised by the petitioner, as Police Commissioner, that this activity would violate section 318 of the Sanitary Code which forbids distribution in the streets of commercial and business advertising matter, but was told that he might freely distribute handbills solely devoted to "information or a public protest."

Respondent thereupon prepared and showed to the petitioner, in proof form, a double-faced handbill. On one side was a revision of the original, altered by the removal of the statement as to admission fee but consisting only of commercial advertising. On the other side was a protest against the action of the City Dock Department in refusing the respondent wharfage facilities at a city pier for the exhibition of his submarine, but no commercial advertising. The Police Department advised that distribution of a bill containing only the protest would not violate section 318, and would not be restrained, but that distribution of the double-faced bill was prohibited. The respondent, nevertheless, proceeded with the printing of his proposed bill and started to distribute it. He was restrained by the police.

Respondent then brought this suit to enjoin the petitioner from interfering with the distribution. In his complaint he alleged diversity of citizenship; an amount in controversy in excess of $3,000; the acts and threats of the petitioner under the purported authority of section 318; asserted a consequent violation of section 1 of the Fourteenth Amendment of the Constitution; and prayed an injunction. The District Court granted an interlocutory injunction, and after trial on a stipulation from which the facts appear as above recited, granted a permanent injunction. The Circuit Court of Appeals, by a divided court, affirmed.

The question is whether the application of the ordinance to the respondent's activity was, in the circumstances, an unconstitutional abridgement of the freedom of the press and of speech.

1. This court has unequivocally held that the streets are proper places for the exercise of the freedom of communicating information and disseminating opinion and that, though the states and municipalities may appropriately regulate the privilege in the public interest, they may not unduly burden or proscribe its employment in these public thoroughfares. We are equally clear that the Constitution imposes no such restraint on government as respects purely commercial advertising. Whether, and to what extent, one may promote or pursue a gainful occupation in the streets, to what extent such activity shall be adjudged a derogation of the public right of user, are matters for legislative judgment. The question is not whether the legislative body may interfere with the harmless pursuit of a lawful business, but whether it must permit such pursuit by what it deems an undesirable invasion of, or interference with, the full and free use of the highways by the people in fulfillment of the public use to which streets are dedicated. If the respondent was attempting to use the streets of New York by distributing commercial advertising, the prohibition of the code provision was lawfully invoked against his conduct.

2. The respondent contends that, in truth, he was engaged in the dissemination of matter proper for public information, none the less so because there was inextricably attached to the medium of such dissemination commercial advertising matter. The court below appears to have taken this view since it adverts to the difficulty of apportioning, in a given case, the contents of the communication as between what is of public interest and what is for private profit. We need not indulge nice appraisal based upon

subtle distinctions in the present instance nor assume possible cases not now presented. It is enough for the present purpose that the stipulated facts justify the conclusion that the affixing of the protest against official conduct to the advertising circular was with the intent, and for the purpose, of evading the prohibition of the ordinance. If that evasion were successful, every merchant who desires to broadcast advertising leaflets in the streets need only append a civic appeal, or a moral platitude, to achieve immunity from the law's command.

NOTES

1. Did the Court's decision in *Valentine* depend on the content of the handbill, or on whether the distribution of the handbill was part of a business—a "gainful occupation in the streets"? Would the case have been different if he were selling newspapers? What if the respondent were in the business of distributing political leaflets for hire? What if ideological enthusiasts for a movie—leftwingers inspired by *Fahrenheit 9/11*, rightwingers by *2016: Obama's America*, or Christians by *Chariots of Fire*—circulate leaflets urging people to view these films?

2. The Court provided no citation for the proposition that "the Constitution imposes no such restraint on government as respects purely commercial advertising." The following article, co-written by a legal scholar and a distinguished judge on the Ninth Circuit Court of Appeals, provides some historical context.

Alex Kozinski & Stuart Banner, "The Anti–History and Pre–History of Commercial Speech"
71 Texas L. Rev. 747 (1993)

In at least five cases before *Valentine*, the Court assessed the constitutionality of state regulation of advertising. The earliest was *Halter v. Nebraska*, in 1907, in which a beer bottler intent on placing the American flag on its bottles claimed that a state law barring this practice denied liberty and property without due process. Even in the heyday of substantive due process—*Lochner* had been decided only two years before—the Court wouldn't go for it. Selling beer might be part of liberty, but even "the rights inhering in personal liberty are subject . . . to such reasonable restraints as may be required for the general good," a good which wouldn't tolerate disrespect for the flag. And while the bottler had a property right in the bottle, he had no property right in the representation of the flag, "which, in itself, cannot belong, as property, to an individual.' " No speech-related claim was made in *Halter*, probably because of the murky status of the First Amendment's application to Nebraska, but probably also because the litigants didn't conceive of bottle-labeling as speech.

The following decade, still a period of uncertainty as to whether there was a freedom of speech as against a state, the Court decided three cases involving municipal ordinances banning certain outdoor advertising. *Fifth Avenue Coach Co. v. City of New York* involved an ordinance prohibiting advertising on the outside of buses—still called "stages" in 1911. The other two cases, *Thomas Cusack Co. v. City of Chicago* and *St. Louis Poster Advertising Co. v. City of St. Louis*, involved ordinances limiting the size of billboards. In all three cases, the advertiser raised substantive due process claims; the primary argument in each was that the ordinance deprived the advertiser of property and of the liberty to carry on its business. The advertiser lost in all three. No speech-related issue was raised in any of the cases, again suggesting that advertising at the time was considered to be a business, not a vehicle of expression.

The fifth pre-*Valentine* case involving state regulation of advertising was *Packer Corp. v. Utah*, decided in 1932. By then, as we have seen, it was clear that the Due Process Clause limited a state's power to abridge the freedom of speech. *Packer* involved a state statute implicating what is today one of the quintessential issues of commercial speech—the statute prohibited the advertising of cigarettes on billboards and streetcar signs. The billboard company's lawyers were not ignorant of the Constitution; they claimed that the statute violated the Equal Protection Clause because advertising in newspapers was permitted, that the statute took property without due process because it arbitrarily curtailed the liberty of contract, and that the statute burdened interstate commerce in violation of the Commerce Clause. The Court rejected all three arguments. Relevant for our purposes is a claim the billboard company did not make: despite the incorporation of the First Amendment and what seems today like an obvious limitation on the company's ability to communicate with customers, the company did not make any claim relating to the freedom of speech. While one can come up with any number of possible reasons why this might have been so, the most likely candidate is simply that the Packer Corporation's lawyers didn't think of advertising as speech.

A second group of pre-*Valentine* cases presents an even better opportunity to look at contemporary notions of what we think of today as commercial speech, because this group involved the federal government, and we thus avoid the difficulty posed by the uncertain status of the First Amendment's applicability to the states. While the federal government did little at the time that could potentially abridge speech, it did run the post office. In the late nineteenth and early twentieth centuries, the Court decided three cases involving First Amendment challenges to various aspects of the postal system.

In 1868, Congress banned advertisements for lotteries from the mail. Nine years later, in *Ex parte Jackson*, the Court reasoned that the ban didn't violate the First Amendment, provided that lottery advertisements could still be circulated by other means. "[W]e do not think," wrote Justice Field (speaking of "newspapers and pamphlets"), "that Congress possesses the power to prevent the transportation in other ways, as merchandise, of matter which it excludes from the mails." Such a complete ban on circulation would be "a fatal blow given to the freedom of the press." The petitioner had been convicted of mailing a lottery advertisement; the Court formulated its First Amendment rule by discussing only newspapers and pamphlets, with no indication in the opinion that advertisements are any different from newspapers so far as the First Amendment is concerned. Unless this is just sloppy writing, the *Jackson* Court implicitly considered advertising (or at least printed circulars advertising lotteries) to be speech entitled to the same degree of First Amendment protection as any other.

The sloppy-writing hypothesis is rendered unlikely by the Court's repetition of *Jackson*'s holding fifteen years later, in another lottery case, *In re Rapier*. Citing only *Jackson*, the Court reiterated

> that in excluding various articles from the mails the object of Congress is not to interfere with the freedom of the press or with any other rights of the people, but to refuse the facilities for the distribution of

matter deemed injurious by Congress to the public morals; and that the transportation in any other way of matters excluded from the mails would not be forbidden.

The petitioner does *not* lose because lottery advertisements do not receive First Amendment protection; he loses because the First Amendment protects him only from complete bans on circulation, not the mere refusal to carry his ads in the mail.

The third postal case, *Lewis Publishing Co. v. Morgan*, reinforces the inference that advertising wasn't beyond the coverage of the First Amendment. The Post Office Appropriation Act of 1912 required newspapers and magazines, as a condition of second-class mailing privileges (i.e., cheaper postal rates), to mark all advertisements with the word "advertisement." The Act was upheld against a First Amendment challenge, not because advertising was outside the scope of the Amendment, but simply because the statute didn't concern "any general regulation of what should be published in newspapers." It concerned only "the right on behalf of the publishers to continue to enjoy great privileges and advantages at the public expense," a matter that raised no First Amendment concern. One gets the sense that the opinion could have read just the same had the statute required editorials to be marked "editorial"; the publisher lost its case, but not because the case involved advertising.

A final case from this period deserves its own category. *Mutual Film Corp. v. Industrial Commission*, decided by a unanimous Court in 1915, produced an opinion that is startling to read today. The case concerned a classic prior restraint—Ohio's establishment of a film censorship board, empowered to determine in advance of public exhibition the films that could be shown in the state. But a prior restraint on film exhibition abridges the freedom of speech only if film is speech, and the Court was quite certain that it wasn't. Justice McKenna wrote:

> The first impulse of the mind is to reject the contention. We immediately feel that the argument is wrong or strained which extends the guaranties of free opinion and speech to the multitudinous shows which are advertised on the bill-boards of our cities and towns . . ., and which seeks to bring motion pictures and other spectacles into practical and legal similitude to a free press and liberty of opinion.

Film, like the theater, the circus, and "all other shows and spectacles," was beyond the scope of the First Amendment.

In a particularly striking passage, Justice McKenna continued:

> It cannot be put out of view that the exhibition of moving pictures is a business pure and simple, originated and conducted for profit, like other spectacles, not to be regarded . . . as part of the press of the country or as organs of public opinion. They are mere representations of events, of ideas and sentiments published and known, vivid, useful and entertaining no doubt, but . . . capable of evil, having power for it, the greater because of their attractiveness and manner of exhibition.

This case is fascinating for a number of reasons, not the least of which is the jurisprudential view of the brand new medium of film and the ancient medium of theater—a view which hasn't survived. More to the point, the Court's emphasis on the fact that films are shown for a profit might be read to mean that the First Amendment doesn't protect profit-motivated speech. But this probably wouldn't be an accurate reading. The opinion suggests quite strongly that (1) the publication of the script of a play, even if for profit, would be protected by the First Amendment, even though the actual staging of the play would not; and (2) a film not produced and shown for profit would still not be entitled to the protection of the First Amendment. Despite the sentence about profit motive, it is the medium that is important, not the motive. *Mutual Film* can't plausibly be read as a blanket statement about the constitutional status of profit-motivated speech.

That brings us back to the two groups of pre-*Valentine* advertising cases discussed above. These two groups of cases present two snapshots of the contemporary legal climate that are difficult to reconcile. On one hand, when a state or local government regulated advertising on billboards and public transportation, the advertisers never thought to raise any speech-related claims. On the other hand, when the federal government regulated advertising in the mail, the advertisers did raise claims based on the First Amendment, and although the claims were unsuccessful, that apparently was not because they involved advertisements.

For our purposes, no reconciliation is necessary, as we aren't trying to discern the law—we're trying only to get a sense of what was commonly thought about advertising and the First Amendment in the late nineteenth and early twentieth centuries. And while this set of evidence is admittedly small, we think it excludes the two extreme hypotheses. First, it probably can't be said about this period that advertising was obviously within the scope of the First Amendment. If that had been so, surely one of the state-regulated advertisers would have braved the incorporation question and raised a speech-related claim. Second, it probably can't be said about the period that advertising was obviously not within the scope of the First Amendment. If that had been so, surely one of the three federal postal cases would have been decided on that ground; such a decision would have been far easier to reach and write than the elaborate theory of postal regulation set forth in *Jackson* and *Lewis*.

Eliminate the two extremes, and we're left with a picture of contemporary jurisprudence in which the status of advertising as speech protected by the First Amendment was uncertain. Certainly the Supreme Court had said nothing either way. To answer this question in a less cursory fashion than we have, research into lower court decisions and other indications of contemporary opinion is necessary. From our limited look at what the Supreme Court had to say, and at what litigants chose to present to the Court, we can tentatively conclude that the status of advertising as speech was murky in the decades before *Valentine*.

Virginia State Board of Pharmacy v. Virginia Citizens Consumer Council

425 U.S. 748 (1976)

■ MR. JUSTICE BLACKMUN delivered the opinion of the Court.

The plaintiff-appellees in this case attack, as violative of the First and Fourteenth Amendments, that portion of [the Virginia Code], which provides that a pharmacist licensed in Virginia is guilty of unprofessional conduct if he "(3) publishes, advertises or promotes, directly or indirectly, in any manner whatsoever, any amount, price, fee, premium, discount, rebate or credit terms . . . for any drugs which may be dispensed only by prescription." The three-judge District Court [enjoined the defendant-appellants from enforcing it].

. . . The present [attack] on the statute is one made not by one directly subject to its prohibition, that is, a pharmacist, but by prescription drug consumers who claim that they would greatly benefit if the prohibition were lifted and advertising freely allowed. . . . Their claim is that the First Amendment entitles the user of prescription drugs to receive information that pharmacists wish to communicate to them through advertising and other promotional means, concerning the prices of such drugs. . . .

III

The question first arises whether, even assuming that First Amendment protection attaches to the flow of drug price information, it is a protection enjoyed by the appellees as recipients of the information, and not solely, if at all, by the advertisers themselves who seek to disseminate that information.

Freedom of speech presupposes a willing speaker. But where a speaker exists, as is the case here, the protection afforded is to the communication, to its source and to its recipients both. . . . If there is a right to advertise, there is a reciprocal right to receive the advertising, and it may be asserted by these appellees.

IV

The appellants contend that the advertisement of prescription drug prices is outside the protection of the First Amendment because it is "commercial speech." There can be no question that in past decisions the Court has given some indication that commercial speech is unprotected. In *Valentine v. Chrestensen*, the Court upheld a New York statute that prohibited the distribution of any "handbill, circular . . . or other advertising matter whatsoever in or upon any street." The Court concluded that, although the First Amendment would forbid the banning of all communication by handbill in the public thoroughfares, it imposed "no such restraint on government as respects purely commercial advertising." Further support for a "commercial speech" exception to the First Amendment may perhaps be found in *Breard v. Alexandria*, where the Court upheld a conviction for violation of an ordinance prohibiting door-to-door solicitation of magazine subscriptions. The Court reasoned: "The selling . . . brings into the transaction a commercial feature," and it distinguished *Martin v. Struthers*, where it had reversed a conviction for door-to-door distribution of leaflets publicizing a religious meeting, as a case involving "no element of the commercial." Moreover, the Court several times has stressed that communications to which First Amendment protection was given were not "purely commercial."

Since the decision in *Breard*, however, the Court has never denied protection on the ground that the speech in issue was "commercial speech." [The Court cites *Pittsburgh Press Co. v. Human Relations Comm'n*, which upheld a law banning sex-designated 'help wanted' ads. The *Pittsburgh Press* Court characterized the advertisements as "classic examples of commercial speech," but upheld the law because the discriminatory hirings and their newspaper layout, were themselves illegal.]

Last Term, in *Bigelow v. Virginia*, the notion of unprotected "commercial speech" all but passed from the scene. We reversed a conviction for violation of a Virginia statute that made the circulation of any publication to encourage or promote the processing of an abortion in Virginia a misdemeanor. . . .

[T]he question whether there is a First Amendment exception for "commercial speech" is squarely before us. Our pharmacist does not wish to editorialize on any subject, cultural, philosophical, or political. He does not wish to report any particularly newsworthy fact, or to make generalized observations even about commercial matters. The "idea" he wishes to communicate is simply this: "I will sell you the X prescription drug at the Y price." Our question, then, is whether this communication is wholly outside the protection of the First Amendment.

V

We begin with several propositions that already are settled or beyond serious dispute. It is clear, for example, that speech does not lose its First Amendment protection because money is spent to project it, as in a paid advertisement of one form or another. Speech likewise is protected even though it is carried in a form that is "sold" for profit, and even though it may involve a solicitation to purchase or otherwise pay or contribute money.

If there is a kind of commercial speech that lacks all First Amendment protection, therefore, it must be distinguished by its content. Yet the speech whose content deprives it of protection cannot simply be speech on a commercial subject. No one would contend that our pharmacist may be prevented from being heard on the subject of whether, in general, pharmaceutical prices should be regulated, or their advertisement forbidden. Nor can it be dispositive that a commercial advertisement is noneditorial, and merely reports a fact. Purely factual matter of public interest may claim protection.

Our question is whether speech which does "no more than propose a commercial transaction," is so removed from any "exposition of ideas," and from "truth, science, morality, and arts in general, in its diffusion of liberal sentiments on the administration of Government," that it lacks all protection. Our answer is that it is not.

Focusing first on the individual parties to the transaction that is proposed in the commercial advertisement, we may assume that the advertiser's interest is a purely economic one. That hardly disqualifies him from protection under the First Amendment. The interests of the contestants in a labor dispute are primarily economic, but it has long been settled that both the employee and the employer are protected by the First Amendment when they express themselves on the merits of the dispute in order to influence its outcome. We know of no requirement that, in order to avail themselves of First Amendment protection, the parties to a labor dispute need address themselves to the merits of unionism in general or to any subject beyond their immediate dispute. . . .

As to the particular consumer's interest in the free flow of commercial information, that interest may be as keen, if not keener by far, than his interest in the day's most urgent political debate. Appellees' case in this respect is a convincing one. Those whom the suppression of prescription drug price information hits the hardest are the poor, the sick, and particularly the aged. A disproportionate amount of their income tends to be spent on prescription drugs; yet they are the least able to learn, by shopping from pharmacist to pharmacist, where their scarce dollars are best spent. When drug prices vary as strikingly as they do, information as to who is charging what becomes more than a convenience. It could mean the alleviation of physical pain or the enjoyment of basic necessities.

Generalizing, society also may have a strong interest in the free flow of commercial information. Even an individual advertisement, though entirely "commercial," may be of general public interest. The facts of decided cases furnish illustrations: advertisements stating that referral services for legal abortions are available; that a manufacturer of artificial furs promotes his product as an alternative to the extinction by his competitors of fur-bearing mammals; and that a domestic producer advertises his product as an alternative to imports that tend to deprive American residents of their jobs. Obviously, not all commercial messages contain the same or even a very great public interest element. There are few to which such an element, however, could not be added. Our pharmacist, for example, could cast himself as a commentator on store-to-store disparities in drug prices, giving his own and those of a competitor as proof. We see little point in requiring him to do so, and little difference if he does not.

Moreover, there is another consideration that suggests that no line between publicly "interesting" or "important" commercial advertising and the opposite kind could ever be drawn. Advertising, however tasteless and excessive it sometimes may seem, is nonetheless dissemination of information as to who is producing and selling what product, for what reason, and at what price. So long as we preserve a predominantly free enterprise economy, the allocation of our resources in large measure will be made through numerous private economic decisions. It is a matter of public interest that those decisions, in the aggregate, be intelligent and well informed. To this end, the free flow of commercial information is indispensable. And if it is indispensable to the proper allocation of resources in a free enterprise system, it is also indispensable to the formation of intelligent opinions as to how that system ought to be regulated or altered. Therefore, even if the First Amendment were thought to be primarily an instrument to enlighten public decisionmaking in a democracy, we could not say that the free flow of information does not serve that goal.

Arrayed against these substantial individual and societal interests are a number of justifications for the advertising ban. These have to do principally with maintaining a high degree of professionalism on the part of licensed pharmacists. Indisputably, the State has a strong interest in maintaining that professionalism. It is exercised in a number of ways for the consumer's benefit. . . .

Price advertising, it is argued, will place in jeopardy the pharmacist's expertise and, with it, the customer's health. It is claimed that the aggressive price competition that will result from unlimited advertising will make it impossible for the pharmacist to supply professional services in the compounding, handling, and dispensing of prescription drugs. Such services are time consuming and expensive; if competitors who economize by eliminating them are permitted to advertise their resulting lower prices, the more painstaking and conscientious pharmacist will be forced either to follow suit or to go out of business. It is also claimed that prices might not necessarily fall as a result of advertising. If one pharmacist advertises, others must, and the resulting expense will inflate the cost of drugs. It is further claimed that advertising will lead people to shop for their prescription drugs among the various pharmacists who offer the lowest prices, and the loss of stable pharmacist-customer relationships will make individual attention and certainly the practice of monitoring impossible. Finally, it is argued that damage will be done to the professional image of the pharmacist. This image, that of a skilled and specialized craftsman, attracts talent to the profession and reinforces the better habits of those who are in it. Price advertising, it is said, will reduce the pharmacist's status to that of a mere retailer.

The strength of these proffered justifications is greatly undermined by the fact that high professional standards, to a substantial extent, are guaranteed by the close regulation to which pharmacists in Virginia are subject. And this case concerns the retail sale by the pharmacist more than it does his professional standards. Surely, any pharmacist guilty of professional dereliction that actually endangers his customer will promptly lose his license. At the same time, we cannot discount the Board's justifications entirely. The Court regarded justifications of this type sufficient to sustain the advertising bans challenged on due process and equal protection grounds[.]

The challenge now made, however, is based on the First Amendment. This casts the Board's justifications in a different light, for on close inspection it is seen that the State's protectiveness of its citizens rests in large measure on the advantages of their being kept in ignorance. The advertising ban does not directly affect professional standards one way or the other. It affects them only through the reactions it is assumed people will have to the free flow of drug price information. There is no claim that the advertising ban in any way prevents the cutting of corners by the pharmacist who is so inclined. That pharmacist is likely to cut corners in any event. The only effect the advertising ban has on him is to insulate him from price competition and to open the way for him to make a substantial, and perhaps even excessive, profit in addition to providing an inferior service. The more painstaking pharmacist is also protected but, again, it is a protection based in large part on public ignorance.

It appears to be feared that if the pharmacist who wishes to provide low cost, and assertedly low quality, services is permitted to advertise, he will be taken up on his offer by too many unwitting customers. They will choose the low-cost, low-quality service and drive the "professional" pharmacist out of business. They will respond only to costly and excessive advertising, and end up paying the price. They will go from one pharmacist to another, following the discount, and destroy the pharmacist-customer relationship. They will lose respect for the profession because it advertises. All this is not in their best interests, and all this can be avoided if they are not permitted to know who is charging what.

There is, of course, an alternative to this highly paternalistic approach. That alternative is to assume that this information is not in itself harmful, that people will perceive their own best interests if only they are well enough informed, and that the best means to that end is to open the channels of communication rather than to close them. If they are truly open, nothing prevents the "professional" pharmacist from marketing his own assertedly superior product, and contrasting it with that of the low-cost, high-volume prescription drug retailer. But the choice among these alternative approaches is not ours to make or the Virginia General Assembly's. It is precisely this kind of choice, between the dangers of suppressing information, and the dangers of its misuse if it is freely available, that the First Amendment makes for us. Virginia is free to require whatever professional standards it wishes of its pharmacists; it may subsidize them or protect them from competition in other ways. But it may not do so by keeping the public in ignorance of the entirely lawful terms that competing pharmacists are offering. In this sense, the justifications Virginia has offered for

suppressing the flow of prescription drug price information, far from persuading us that the flow is not protected by the First Amendment, have
reinforced our view that it is. We so hold.

VI

In concluding that commercial speech, like other varieties, is protected, we of course do not hold that it can never be regulated in any way.
Some forms of commercial speech regulation are surely permissible. We
mention a few only to make clear that they are not before us and therefore
are not foreclosed by this case.

There is no claim, for example, that the prohibition on prescription
drug price advertising is a mere time, place, and manner restriction. We
have often approved restrictions of that kind provided that they are justified without reference to the content of the regulated speech, that they
serve a significant governmental interest, and that in so doing they leave
open ample alternative channels for communication of the information.
Whatever may be the proper bounds of time, place, and manner restrictions
on commercial speech, they are plainly exceeded by this Virginia statute,
which singles out speech of a particular content and seeks to prevent its
dissemination completely.

Nor is there any claim that prescription drug price advertisements are
forbidden because they are false or misleading in any way. Untruthful
speech, commercial or otherwise, has never been protected for its own sake.
Obviously, much commercial speech is not provably false, or even wholly
false, but only deceptive or misleading. We foresee no obstacle to a State's
dealing effectively with this problem.[24] The First Amendment, as we construe it today does not prohibit the State from insuring that the stream of
commercial information flow cleanly as well as freely.

Also, there is no claim that the transactions proposed in the forbidden
advertisements are themselves illegal in any way. Finally, the special problems of the electronic broadcast media are likewise not in this case.

What is at issue is whether a State may completely suppress the dissemination of concededly truthful information about entirely lawful activity, fearful of that information's effect upon its disseminators and its recipients. Reserving other questions, we conclude that the answer to this one is
in the negative.

---

[24] In concluding that commercial speech enjoys First Amendment protection, we have not
held that it is wholly undifferentiable from other forms. There are commonsense differences
between speech that does "no more than propose a commercial transaction," and other varieties. Even if the differences do not justify the conclusion that commercial speech is valueless,
and thus subject to complete suppression by the State, they nonetheless suggest that a different degree of protection is necessary to insure that the flow of truthful and legitimate commercial information is unimpaired. The truth of commercial speech, for example, may be more
easily verifiable by its disseminator than, let us say, news reporting or political commentary,
in that ordinarily the advertiser seeks to disseminate information about a specific product or
service that he himself provides and presumably knows more about than anyone else. Also,
commercial speech may be more durable than other kinds. Since advertising is the sine qua
non of commercial profits, there is little likelihood of its being chilled by proper regulation and
forgone entirely.

Attributes such as these, the greater objectivity and hardiness of commercial speech, may
make it less necessary to tolerate inaccurate statements for fear of silencing the speaker. They
may also make it appropriate to require that a commercial message appear in such a form, or
include such additional information, warnings, and disclaimers, as are necessary to prevent its
being deceptive. They may also make inapplicable the prohibition against prior restraints.

■ [The concurring opinions of CHIEF JUSTICE BURGER and JUSTICE STEWART are omitted.]

■ MR. JUSTICE REHNQUIST, dissenting.

The logical consequences of the Court's decision in this case, a decision which elevates commercial intercourse between a seller hawking his wares and a buyer seeking to strike a bargain to the same plane as has been previously reserved for the free marketplace of ideas, are far reaching indeed. Under the Court's opinion the way will be open not only for dissemination of price information but for active promotion of prescription drugs, liquor, cigarettes, and other products the use of which it has previously been thought desirable to discourage. Now, however, such promotion is protected by the First Amendment so long as it is not misleading or does not promote an illegal product or enterprise. In coming to this conclusion, the Court has overruled a legislative determination that such advertising should not be allowed and has done so on behalf of a consumer group which is not directly disadvantaged by the statute in question. This effort to reach a result which the Court obviously considers desirable is a troublesome one, for two reasons. It extends standing to raise First Amendment claims beyond the previous decisions of this Court. It also extends the protection of that Amendment to purely commercial endeavors which its most vigorous champions on this Court had thought to be beyond its pale. . . .

Thus the issue on the merits is not, as the Court phrases it, whether "[o]ur pharmacist" may communicate the fact that he "will sell you the X prescription drug at the Y price." No pharmacist is asserting any such claim to so communicate. The issue is rather whether appellee consumers may override the legislative determination that pharmacists should not advertise even though the pharmacists themselves do not object. In deciding that they may do so, the Court necessarily adopts a rule which cannot be limited merely to dissemination of price alone, and which cannot possibly be confined to pharmacists but must likewise extend to lawyers, doctors, and all other professions.

The Court speaks of the consumer's interest in the free flow of commercial information, particularly in the case of the poor, the sick, and the aged. It goes on to observe that "society also may have a strong interest in the free flow of commercial information." One need not disagree with either of these statements in order to feel that they should presumptively be the concern of the Virginia Legislature, which sits to balance these and other claims in the process of making laws such as the one here under attack. The Court speaks of the importance in a "predominantly free enterprise economy" of intelligent and well-informed decisions as to allocation of resources. While there is again much to be said for the Court's observation as a matter of desirable public policy, there is certainly nothing in the United States Constitution which requires the Virginia Legislature to hew to the teachings of Adam Smith in its legislative decisions regulating the pharmacy profession. . . .

There are undoubted difficulties with an effort to draw a bright line between "commercial speech" on the one hand and "protected speech" on the other, and the Court does better to face up to these difficulties than to attempt to hide them under labels. In this case, however, the Court has unfortunately substituted for the wavering line previously thought to exist between commercial speech and protected speech a no more satisfactory line of its own than between "truthful" commercial speech, on the one hand, and that which is "false and misleading" on the other. The difficulty with this line is not that it wavers, but on the contrary that it is simply too Procrustean to take into account the congeries of factors which I believe could, quite consistently with the First and Fourteenth Amendments, properly influence a legislative decision with respect to commercial advertising.

The Court insists that the rule it lays down is consistent even with the view that the First Amendment is "primarily an instrument to enlighten public decisionmaking in a democracy." I had understood this view to relate to public decisionmaking as to political, social, and other public issues, rather than the decision of a particular individual as to whether to purchase one or another kind of shampoo. It is undoubtedly arguable that many people in the country regard the choice of shampoo as just as important as who may be elected to local, state, or national political office, but that does not automatically bring information about competing shampoos within the protection of the First Amendment. It is one thing to say that the line between strictly ideological and political commentaries and other kinds of commentary is difficult to draw, and that the mere fact that the former may have in it an element of commercialism does not strip it of First Amendment protection. But it is another thing to say that because that line is difficult to draw, we will stand at the other end of the spectrum and reject out of hand the observation of so dedicated a champion of the First Amendment as Mr. Justice Black that the protections of that Amendment do not apply to a "merchant who goes from door to door selling pots." . . .

Both Congress and state legislatures have by law sharply limited the permissible dissemination of information about some commodities because of the potential harm resulting from those commodities, even though they were not thought to be sufficiently demonstrably harmful to warrant outright prohibition of their sale. Current prohibitions on television advertising of liquor and cigarettes are prominent in this category, but apparently under the Court's holding so long as the advertisements are not deceptive they may no longer be prohibited.

. . . Here the rights of the appellees seem to me to be marginal at best. There is no ideological content to the information which they seek and it is freely available to them they may even publish it if they so desire. The only persons directly affected by this statute are not parties to this lawsuit. On the other hand, the societal interest against the promotion of drug use for every ill, real or imaginary, seems to me extremely strong. I do not believe that the First Amendment mandates the Court's "open door policy" toward such commercial advertising.

NOTES

1. Is the lower protection for commercial speech one of those categorical "traditional limitations" recognized in *Chaplinsky* and *Brown*? Does it satisfy *Brown*'s requirement of a "historical warrant" based on "persuasive evidence" of a "long tradition of proscription"? Or is it justified by weighing the value of commercial speech against its cost—an approach the *Brown* Court called "startling and dangerous"? After canvassing the Court's own precedents, from *Valentine* to *Bigelow*, and finding the question of protection for commercial speech unresolved, the Court seemed to draw its own conclusions about the dangers and benefits of restricting commercial speech. Pay careful attention to the "commonsense differences" attributable to commercial speech in footnote 24. Is regulation of commercial speech limited to the implications of these differences, or may the entire field of commercial speech be subject to a lower standard of

scrutiny on account of being of lower value in a democracy? Is the latter what Justice Rehnquist suggests?

2. Did it matter whether the speakers in this case were corporations? Note the Court's statement: "No one would contend that our pharmacist may be prevented from being heard on the subject of whether, in general, pharmaceutical prices should be regulated, or their advertisement forbidden." Is that true? Do profit-making businesses have a First Amendment right to make their opinions about public policy matters known to the public? Do they have a right to spend money to do so, by buying advertising on websites or on television? Think about these questions as you consider the question of campaign finance restrictions presented below.

3. The plaintiffs in this case were consumers who wanted to receive information about drug prices, not pharmacies who wanted to disseminate it. Justice Blackmun's references to "our pharmacist" were therefore entirely hypothetical. Do you see why no pharmacy in Virginia chose to challenge the law? What is the economics of a ban on price advertising? Justice Rehnquist treats the fact that the directly regulated parties were not challenging the law as reason not to question its constitutionality. Does he perhaps have it backwards?

Is this aspect of the decision merely about standing to sue, or does it imply that willing listeners or readers have a constitutional right against laws that ban willing speakers or writers from communicating with them? Is there a constitutional right to hear, view, and read—as well as a constitutional right to speak, write, and publish? What are the implications of that? On the one hand, this seems intuitively correct: *Brown v. Entertainment Merchants* was concerned with the rights of teenage gamers to purchase violent video games; a prisoner presumably has free speech rights to read newspapers or religious materials; a householder may challenge postal regulations preventing the delivery of lewd magazines. But this holding could have a powerful and unsettling consequence: it may render presumptively unconstitutional any speaker-based restrictions on speech, if challenged by a person who wants access to the message. Think about this as you consider presently whether corporations can be prohibited from engaging in the same sort of speech that natural persons and groups have a right to engage in.

A NOTE ON THE CENTRAL HUDSON TEST

In *Central Hudson Gas & Elect. Corp. v. Public Service Comm'n*, 447 U.S. 557, 563–64 (1980), the Supreme Court announced what appeared to be a general test for the regulation of commercial speech:

> In commercial speech cases, then, a four-part analysis has developed. At the outset, we must determine whether the expression is protected by the First Amendment. For commercial speech to come within that provision, it at least must concern lawful activity and not be misleading. Next, we ask whether the asserted governmental interest is substantial. If both inquiries yield positive answers, we must determine whether the regulation directly advances the governmental interest asserted, and whether it is not more extensive than is necessary to serve that interest.

This test is familiar; it is essentially the same as other forms of "intermediate scrutiny": the government's interest need only be "substantial" (not "compelling"); it must "directly advance" that interest (as opposed to being "necessary"); and there must not be a more limited restriction that would serve that interest "as well." This approach is in tension with the idea that commercial speech is fully protected unless it falls within one of the "commonsense differences" that distinguish commercial speech from other forms of expression. Under *Central Hudson*, all governmental justifications are treated the same way and are subject to intermediate scrutiny. Under the alternative approach, only certain justifications warrant regulation. See the way this tension plays out in this subsequent case:

44 Liquormart, Inc. v. Rhode Island

517 U.S. 484 (1996)

[Rhode Island law prohibited "advertising in any manner whatsoever" the price of alcohol, except for price tags and signs inside liquor stores. The Rhode Island Supreme Court had upheld the law against multiple challenges, holding that the law reasonably furthered "the substantial state interest in the promotion of temperance" and was not "more extensive than necessary to further that interest." Two discount liquor stores sought a declaratory judgment in federal court that the advertising ban violated the First Amendment. The Rhode Island Liquor Stores Association intervened as a defendant. The district court found "as a fact that Rhode Island's off-premises liquor price advertising ban has no significant impact on levels of alcohol consumption in Rhode Island." The court of appeals reversed, noting "inherent merit" in the state's submission that competitive price advertising would lower prices and that lower prices would produce more sales."—Editors]

■ JUSTICE STEVENS announced the judgment of the Court and delivered the opinion of the Court with respect to Parts I, II, VII, and VIII, an opinion with respect to Parts III and V, in which JUSTICE KENNEDY, JUSTICE SOUTER, and JUSTICE GINSBURG join, an opinion with respect to Part VI, in which JUSTICE KENNEDY, JUSTICE THOMAS, and JUSTICE GINSBURG join, and an opinion with respect to Part IV, in which JUSTICE KENNEDY and JUSTICE GINSBURG join.

III

Advertising has been a part of our culture throughout our history. Even in colonial days, the public relied on "commercial speech" for vital information about the market. Early newspapers displayed advertisements for goods and services on their front pages, and town criers called out prices in public squares. Indeed, commercial messages played such a central role in public life prior to the founding that Benjamin Franklin authored his early defense of a free press in support of his decision to print, of all things, an advertisement for voyages to Barbados.

In accord with the role that commercial messages have long played, the law has developed to ensure that advertising provides consumers with accurate information about the availability of goods and services. In the early years, the common law, and later, statutes, served the consumers' interest in the receipt of accurate information in the commercial market by prohibiting fraudulent and misleading advertising. It was not until the 1970's, however, that this Court held that the First Amendment protected the dissemination of truthful and nonmisleading commercial messages about lawful products and services. See generally Kozinski & Banner, The

Anti–History and Pre–History of Commercial Speech, 71 Texas L. Rev. 747 (1993).

... At the same time, our early cases recognized that the State may regulate some types of commercial advertising more freely than other forms of protected speech. Specifically, we explained that the State may require commercial messages to "appear in such a form, or include such additional information, warnings, and disclaimers, as are necessary to prevent its being deceptive," *Virginia Bd. of Pharmacy*, and that it may restrict some forms of aggressive sales practices that have the potential to exert "undue influence" over consumers, see *Bates v. State Bar of Ariz.*

Virginia Bd. of Pharmacy attributed the State's authority to impose these regulations in part to certain "commonsense differences" that exist between commercial messages and other types of protected expression. Our opinion noted that the greater "objectivity" of commercial speech justifies affording the State more freedom to distinguish false commercial advertisements from true ones, and that the greater "hardiness" of commercial speech, inspired as it is by the profit motive, likely diminishes the chilling effect that may attend its regulation.

Subsequent cases explained that the State's power to regulate commercial transactions justifies its concomitant power to regulate commercial speech that is "linked inextricably" to those transactions. As one commentator has explained: "The entire commercial speech doctrine, after all, represents an accommodation between the right to speak and hear expression *about* goods and services and the right of government to regulate the sales *of* such goods and services." Nevertheless, as we explained in *Linmark,* the State retains less regulatory authority when its commercial speech restrictions strike at "the substance of the information communicated" rather than the "commercial aspect of [it]—with offerors communicating offers to offerees."

In *Central Hudson*, we took stock of our developing commercial speech jurisprudence. In that case, we considered a regulation "completely" banning all promotional advertising by electric utilities. Our decision acknowledged the special features of commercial speech but identified the serious First Amendment concerns that attend blanket advertising prohibitions that do not protect consumers from commercial harms.

Five Members of the Court recognized that the state interest in the conservation of energy was substantial, and that there was "an immediate connection between advertising and demand for electricity." Nevertheless, they concluded that the regulation was invalid because respondent commission had failed to make a showing that a more limited speech regulation would not have adequately served the State's interest.

In reaching its conclusion, the majority explained that although the special nature of commercial speech may require less than strict review of its regulation, special concerns arise from "regulations that entirely suppress commercial speech in order to pursue a nonspeech-related policy." In those circumstances, "a ban on speech could screen from public view the underlying governmental policy." As a result, the Court concluded that "special care" should attend the review of such blanket bans, and it pointedly remarked that "in recent years this Court has not approved a blanket ban on commercial speech unless the expression itself was flawed in some way, either because it was deceptive or related to unlawful activity."

IV

[Not] *all* commercial speech regulations are subject to a similar form of constitutional review simply because they target a similar category of expression. The mere fact that messages propose commercial transactions does not in and of itself dictate the constitutional analysis that should apply to decisions to suppress them.

When a State regulates commercial messages to protect consumers from misleading, deceptive, or aggressive sales practices, or requires the disclosure of beneficial consumer information, the purpose of its regulation is consistent with the reasons for according constitutional protection to commercial speech and therefore justifies less than strict review. However, when a State entirely prohibits the dissemination of truthful, nonmisleading commercial messages for reasons unrelated to the preservation of a fair bargaining process, there is far less reason to depart from the rigorous review that the First Amendment generally demands.

Sound reasons justify reviewing the latter type of commercial speech regulation more carefully. Most obviously, complete speech bans, unlike content-neutral restrictions on the time, place, or manner of expression, are particularly dangerous because they all but foreclose alternative means of disseminating certain information. . . .

The special dangers that attend complete bans on truthful, nonmisleading commercial speech cannot be explained away by appeals to the "commonsense distinctions" that exist between commercial and non-commercial speech. Regulations that suppress the truth are no less troubling because they target objectively verifiable information, nor are they less effective because they aim at durable messages. As a result, neither the "greater objectivity" nor the "greater hardiness" of truthful, nonmisleading commercial speech justifies reviewing its complete suppression with added deference.

It is the State's interest in protecting consumers from "commercial harms" that provides "the typical reason why commercial speech can be subject to greater governmental regulation than noncommercial speech." Yet bans that target truthful, nonmisleading commercial messages rarely protect consumers from such harms. Instead, such bans often serve only to obscure an "underlying governmental policy" that could be implemented without regulating speech. In this way, these commercial speech bans not only hinder consumer choice, but also impede debate over central issues of public policy.

Precisely because bans against truthful, nonmisleading commercial speech rarely seek to protect consumers from either deception or overreaching, they usually rest solely on the offensive assumption that the public will respond "irrationally" to the truth. The First Amendment directs us to be especially skeptical of regulations that seek to keep people in the dark for what the government perceives to be their own good. That teaching applies equally to state attempts to deprive consumers of accurate information about their chosen products: . . .

V

In this case, there is no question that Rhode Island's price advertising ban constitutes a blanket prohibition against truthful, nonmisleading speech about a lawful product. There is also no question that the ban serves an end unrelated to consumer protection. Accordingly, we must review the price advertising ban with "special care," mindful that speech prohibitions of this type rarely survive constitutional review.

The State argues that the price advertising prohibition should nevertheless be upheld because it directly advances the State's substantial interest in promoting temperance, and because it is no more extensive than necessary. Although there is some confusion as to what Rhode Island means by temperance, we assume that the State asserts an interest in reducing alcohol consumption.

In evaluating the ban's effectiveness in advancing the State's interest, we note that a commercial speech regulation "may not be sustained if it provides only ineffective or remote support for the government's purpose." *Central Hudson.* For that reason, the State bears the burden of showing not merely that its regulation will advance its interest, but also that it will do so "to a material degree." The need for the State to make such a showing is particularly great given the drastic nature of its chosen means-the wholesale suppression of truthful, nonmisleading information. Accordingly, we must determine whether the State has shown that the price advertising ban will *significantly* reduce alcohol consumption.

We can agree that common sense supports the conclusion that a prohibition against price advertising, like a collusive agreement among competitors to refrain from such advertising, will tend to mitigate competition and maintain prices at a higher level than would prevail in a completely free market. Despite the absence of proof on the point, we can even agree with the State's contention that it is reasonable to assume that demand, and hence consumption throughout the market, is somewhat lower whenever a higher, noncompetitive price level prevails. However, without any findings of fact, or indeed any evidentiary support whatsoever, we cannot agree with the assertion that the price advertising ban will significantly advance the State's interest in promoting temperance.

Although the record suggests that the price advertising ban may have some impact on the purchasing patterns of temperate drinkers of modest means, the State has presented no evidence to suggest that its speech prohibition will *significantly* reduce marketwide consumption. Indeed, the District Court's considered and uncontradicted finding on this point is directly to the contrary. Moreover, the evidence suggests that the abusive drinker will probably not be deterred by a marginal price increase, and that the true alcoholic may simply reduce his purchases of other necessities. . . .

As is evident, any conclusion that elimination of the ban would significantly increase alcohol consumption would require us to engage in the sort of "speculation or conjecture" that is an unacceptable means of demonstrating that a restriction on commercial speech directly advances the State's asserted interest. Such speculation certainly does not suffice when the State takes aim at accurate commercial information for paternalistic ends.

The State also cannot satisfy the requirement that its restriction on speech be no more extensive than necessary. It is perfectly obvious that alternative forms of regulation that would not involve any restriction on speech would be more likely to achieve the State's goal of promoting temperance. As the State's own expert conceded, higher prices can be maintained either by direct regulation or by increased taxation. Per capita purchases could be limited as is the case with prescription drugs. Even educational campaigns focused on the problems of excessive, or even moderate, drinking might prove to be more effective.

As a result, even under the less than strict standard that generally applies in commercial speech cases, the State has failed to establish a "reasonable fit" between its abridgment of speech and its temperance goal. It necessarily follows that the price advertising ban cannot survive the more stringent constitutional review that *Central Hudson* itself concluded was appropriate for the complete suppression of truthful, nonmisleading commercial speech.

VI

The State responds by arguing that it merely exercised appropriate "legislative judgment" in determining that a price advertising ban would best promote temperance. [R]hode Island first argues that, because expert opinions as to the effectiveness of the price advertising ban "go both ways," the Court of Appeals correctly concluded that the ban constituted a "reasonable choice" by the legislature. The State next contends that precedent requires us to give particular deference to that legislative choice because the State could, if it chose, ban the sale of alcoholic beverages outright. Finally, the State argues that deference is appropriate because alcoholic beverages are so-called "vice" products. We consider each of these contentions in turn.

The State's first argument fails to justify the speech prohibition at issue. Our commercial speech cases recognize some room for the exercise of legislative judgment. However, Rhode Island errs in concluding that *Edge* and *Posadas* establish the degree of deference that its decision to impose a price advertising ban warrants.

In *United States v. Edge Broadcasting Corp.*, 509 U.S. 418 (1993), we upheld a federal statute [that] was designed to regulate advertising about an activity that had been deemed illegal in the jurisdiction in which the broadcaster was located [lottery advertising]. Here, by contrast, the commercial speech ban targets information about entirely lawful behavior.

Posadas de Puerto Rico v. Tourism Co. of Puerto Rico, 478 U.S. 328 (1986), is more directly relevant. There, a five-Member majority held that, under the *Central Hudson* test, it was "up to the legislature" to choose to reduce gambling by suppressing in-state casino advertising rather than engaging in educational speech. Rhode Island argues that this logic demonstrates the constitutionality of its own decision to ban price advertising in lieu of raising taxes or employing some other less speech-restrictive means of promoting temperance.

The reasoning in *Posadas* does support the State's argument, but, on reflection, we are now persuaded that *Posadas* erroneously performed the First Amendment analysis. The casino advertising ban was designed to keep truthful, nonmisleading speech from members of the public for fear that they would be more likely to gamble if they received it. As a result, the advertising ban served to shield the State's antigambling policy from the public scrutiny that more direct, nonspeech regulation would draw.

Given our longstanding hostility to commercial speech regulation of this type, *Posadas* clearly erred in concluding that it was "up to the legislature" to choose suppression over a less speech-restrictive policy. The *Posadas* majority's conclusion on that point cannot be reconciled with the unbroken line of prior cases striking down similarly broad regulations on truthful, nonmisleading advertising when non-speech-related alternatives were available.

Because the 5–to–4 decision in *Posadas* marked such a sharp break from our prior precedent, and because it concerned a constitutional question about which this Court is the final arbiter, we decline to give force to its highly deferential approach. . . .

We also cannot accept the State's second contention, which is premised entirely on the "greater-includes-the-lesser" reasoning endorsed toward the end of the majority's opinion in *Posadas.* There, the majority stated that "the greater power to completely ban casino gambling necessarily includes the lesser power to ban advertising of casino gambling." It went on to state that "*because* the government could have enacted a wholesale prohibition of [casino gambling] it is permissible for the government to take the less intrusive step of allowing the conduct, but reducing the demand through restrictions on advertising."

Although we do not dispute the proposition that greater powers include lesser ones, we fail to see how that syllogism requires the conclusion that the State's power to regulate commercial *activity* is "greater" than its power to ban truthful, nonmisleading commercial *speech.* Contrary to the assumption made in *Posadas,* we think it quite clear that banning speech may sometimes prove far more intrusive than banning conduct. As a venerable proverb teaches, it may prove more injurious to prevent people from teaching others how to fish than to prevent fish from being sold. Similarly, a local ordinance banning bicycle lessons may curtail freedom far more than one that prohibits bicycle riding within city limits. In short, we reject the assumption that words are necessarily less vital to freedom than actions, or that logic somehow proves that the power to prohibit an activity is necessarily "greater" than the power to suppress speech about it.

As a matter of First Amendment doctrine, the *Posadas* syllogism is even less defensible. The text of the First Amendment makes clear that the Constitution presumes that attempts to regulate speech are more dangerous than attempts to regulate conduct. That presumption accords with the essential role that the free flow of information plays in a democratic society. As a result, the First Amendment directs that government may not suppress speech as easily as it may suppress conduct, and that speech restrictions cannot be treated as simply another means that the government may use to achieve its ends. . . .

That the State has chosen to license its liquor retailers does not change the analysis. Even though government is under no obligation to provide a person, or the public, a particular benefit, it does not follow that conferral of the benefit may be conditioned on the surrender of a constitutional right. In *Perry v. Sindermann,* relying on a host of cases applying that principle during the preceding quarter century, the Court explained that government "may not deny a benefit to a person on a basis that infringes his constitutionally protected interests—especially his interest in freedom of speech." That teaching clearly applies to state attempts to regulate commercial speech, as our cases striking down bans on truthful, nonmisleading speech by licensed professionals attest. . . .

Finally, we find unpersuasive the State's contention that, under *Posadas* and *Edge,* the price advertising ban should be upheld because it targets commercial speech that pertains to a "vice" activity. . . . [T]he scope of any "vice" exception to the protection afforded by the First Amendment would be difficult, if not impossible, to define. Almost any product that poses some threat to public health or public morals might reasonably be characterized by a state legislature as relating to "vice activity." Such characterization, however, is anomalous when applied to products such as alcoholic beverages, lottery tickets, or playing cards, that may be lawfully purchased on the open market. The recognition of such an exception would also have the unfortunate consequence of either allowing state legislatures to justify censorship by the simple expedient of placing the "vice" label on selected lawful activities, or requiring the federal courts to establish a federal common law of vice. For these reasons, a "vice" label that is unaccompanied by a corresponding prohibition against the commercial behavior at issue fails to provide a principled justification for the regulation of commercial speech about that activity.

VII

[The Court held that the Twenty-first Amendment "does not in any way diminish the force" of the First Amendment and thus could not save Rhode Island's ban on liquor price advertising.—Editors]

VIII

Because Rhode Island has failed to carry its heavy burden of justifying its complete ban on price advertising, we conclude that [the Rhode Island statutes] abridge speech in violation of the First Amendment as made applicable to the States by the Due Process Clause of the Fourteenth Amendment.

■ JUSTICE SCALIA, concurring in part and concurring in the judgment.

I share Justice THOMAS's discomfort with the *Central Hudson* test, which seems to me to have nothing more than policy intuition to support it. I also share Justice STEVENS's aversion towards paternalistic governmental policies that prevent men and women from hearing facts that might not be good for them. On the other hand, it would also be paternalism for us to prevent the people of the States from enacting laws that we consider paternalistic, unless we have good reason to believe that the Constitution itself forbids them. I will take my guidance as to what the Constitution forbids, with regard to a text as indeterminate as the First Amendment's preservation of "the freedom of speech," and where the core offense of suppressing particular political ideas is not at issue, from the long accepted practices of the American people. . . .

■ JUSTICE THOMAS, concurring in Parts I, II, VI, and VII, and concurring in the judgment.

In cases such as this, in which the government's asserted interest is to keep legal users of a product or service ignorant in order to manipulate their choices in the marketplace, the balancing test adopted in *Central Hudson*, should not be applied, in my view. Rather, such an "interest" is *per se* illegitimate and can no more justify regulation of "commercial" speech than it can justify regulation of "noncommercial" speech. . . .

II

I do not join the principal opinion's application of the *Central Hudson* balancing test because I do not believe that such a test should be applied to a restriction of "commercial" speech, at least when, as here, the asserted interest is one that is to be achieved through keeping would-be recipients of the speech in the dark. Application of the advancement-of-state-interest prong of *Central Hudson* makes little sense to me in such circumstances. Faulting the State for failing to show that its price advertising ban decreases alcohol consumption "significantly," as Justice STEVENS does, seems to imply that if the State had been *more successful* at keeping consumers ignorant and thereby decreasing their consumption, then the restriction might have been upheld. This contradicts *Virginia Bd. of Pharmacy's* rationale for protecting "commercial" speech in the first instance.

[Justice Thomas points out that the argument (made by Justices Stevens and O'Connor) that the restriction on price advertising is not the least restrictive means of achieving the governmental purpose "would appear to commit the courts to striking down restrictions on speech whenever a direct regulation (i.e., a regulation involving no restriction on speech regarding lawful activity at all) would be an equally effective method of dampening demand by legal users"—which is "virtually always" true.—Editors]

[R]ather than "applying" the fourth prong of *Central Hudson* to reach the inevitable result that all or most such advertising restrictions must be struck down, I would adhere to the doctrine adopted in *Virginia Bd. of Pharmacy* and in Justice Blackmun's *Central Hudson* concurrence, that all attempts to dissuade legal choices by citizens by keeping them ignorant are impermissible.

III

Although the Court took a sudden turn away from *Virginia Bd. of Pharmacy* in *Central Hudson,* it has never explained why manipulating the choices of consumers by keeping them ignorant is more legitimate when the ignorance is maintained through suppression of "commercial" speech than when the same ignorance is maintained through suppression of "noncommercial" speech. The courts, including this Court, have found the *Central Hudson* "test" to be, as a general matter, very difficult to apply with any uniformity. This may result in part from the inherently nondeterminative nature of a case-by-case balancing "test" unaccompanied by any categorical rules, and the consequent likelihood that individual judicial preferences will govern application of the test. Moreover, the second prong of *Central Hudson,* as applied to the facts of that case and to those here, apparently requires judges to delineate those situations in which citizens cannot be trusted with information, and invites judges to decide whether they themselves think that consumption of a product is harmful enough that it *should* be discouraged. In my view, the *Central Hudson* test asks the courts to weigh incommensurables—the value of knowledge versus the value of ignorance—and to apply contradictory premises—that informed adults are the best judges of their own interests, and that they are not. Rather than continuing to apply a test that makes no sense to me when the asserted state interest is of the type involved here, I would return to the reasoning and holding of *Virginia Bd. of Pharmacy.* Under that decision, these restrictions fall.

■ [The concurring opinion by JUSTICE O'CONNOR, which was joined by THE CHIEF JUSTICE and JUSTICES SOUTER and BREYER, is omitted.]

NOTES

1. Do you agree with Justice Thomas that the *Central Hudson* test is unhelpful and should be jettisoned? Why or why not?

2. Do you agree with the Court that it is impermissible for the government to seek to regulate behavior by suppressing speech that might encourage that behavior? Why is this not the least restrictive means? The experience of Prohibition suggests that banning the sale of alcohol may not work very well: among other things it led to an increase in violence and organized crime (though it

reduced some forms of violence, such as domestic violence). Why not adopt the lesser measure of allowing the sale of alcohol but not public promotion of drinking? Agreements between regulators and the relevant industries now sharply restrict television advertising of liquor and cigarettes. Is that a bad thing? Why not allow those restrictions to be imposed legislatively?

3. On the other hand, maybe current doctrine is too permissive about government regulation of commercial speech. Drug companies can be prohibited from disseminating reprints of scholarly articles reporting beneficial uses of their products, if the Food and Drug Administration has not approved those uses. Much of this information is entirely truthful and nonmisleading, and could be of great value to doctors and patients. In effect, the law treats claims by drug manufacturers as "misleading" because they have not been proven to the satisfaction of the regulators. Does this go too far? Who should bear the burden of proof that a claim is misleading—the government or the speaker?

A NOTE ON CINCINNATI V. DISCOVERY NETWORK

In *Cincinnati v. Discovery Network*, 507 U.S. 410 (1993), the Court invalidated a city ordinance barring commercial advertising supplements from using newsracks on public sidewalks. The ordinance's justification was a reduction of visual clutter. "The city argued that since a number of courts had held that a complete ban on the use of newsracks dispensing traditional newspapers would be unconstitutional, and that the 'Constitution . . . accords a lesser protection to commercial speech than to other constitutionally guaranteed expression,' *Central Hudson Gas & Electric Corp. v. Public Serv. Comm'n*, 447 U. S. 557, 563 (1980), its preferential treatment of newspapers over commercial publications was a permissible method of serving its legitimate interest in ensuring safe streets and regulating visual blight. The Court of Appeals disagreed, holding that the lesser status of commercial speech is relevant only when its regulation was designed either to prevent false or misleading advertising, or to alleviate distinctive adverse effects of the specific speech at issue." The Supreme Court affirmed, holding:

> Not only does Cincinnati's categorical ban on commercial newsracks place too much importance on the distinction between commercial and noncommercial speech, but in this case, the distinction bears no relationship whatsoever to the particular interests that the city has asserted. . . . The city has asserted an interest in esthetics, but respondent publishers' newsracks are no greater an eyesore than the newsracks permitted to remain on Cincinnati's sidewalks. Each newsrack, whether containing "newspapers" or "commercial handbills," is equally unattractive. . . . [T]he city's primary concern, as argued to us, is with the aggregate number of newsracks on its streets. On that score, however, all newsracks, regardless of whether they contain commercial or noncommercial publications, are equally at fault. In fact, the newspapers are arguably the greater culprit because of their superior number.

507 U.S. at 424–26.

Does this make sense to you? If the Supreme Court itself can apply a lower standard of scrutiny to commercial speech across the board, why can't a city similarly prefer noncommercial over commercial speech when allocating scarce resources? If it is true that the First Amendment prohibits discriminating against commercial speech except when its commercial character relates to the public policy, does that imply that *Central Hudson* is wrong and the broader approach of *Virginia Pharmacy* is restored?

In *Metromedia, Inc. v. San Diego*, 453 U.S. 490 (1981), a billboard case, the Court held that cities may not favor commercial over noncommercial speech. Does *Discovery Network* mean that the converse is also true (assuming, as is likely, that commercial and noncommercial billboards pose the same safety and aesthetic concerns)? Must billboard ordinances be absolutely neutral as the content of the messages?

[Assignment 48]

I.   CAMPAIGN FINANCE

Speech about matters of "public concern," and particularly candidates, officials, and democratic decisions, are at the core of First Amendment protections, yet advertisements in the course of political campaigns are among the most heavily regulated of all forms of speech. This is because money is involved. Does that make a difference? Should it? Almost all forms of speech involve the expenditure of money. Certainly that was true of the advertisement criticizing the police commissioner, which was the subject of *New York Times v. Sullivan*. Money is not speech. But are regulations limiting the use of money for the dissemination of speech of a particular content regulations on speech? Think about these questions as you read the following cases.

Buckley v. Valeo

424 U.S. 1 (1976)

■ PER CURIAM.

These appeals present constitutional challenges to the key provisions of the Federal Election Campaign Act of 1971 (Act), and related provisions of the Internal Revenue Code of 1954, all as amended in 1974. . . .

The statutes at issue summarized in broad terms, contain the following provisions: (a) individual political contributions are limited to $1,000 to any single candidate per election, with an overall annual limitation of $25,000 by any contributor; independent expenditures by individuals and groups "relative to a clearly identified candidate" are limited to $1,000 a year; campaign spending by candidates for various federal offices and spending for national conventions by political parties are subject to prescribed limits; (b) contributions and expenditures above certain threshold levels must be reported and publicly disclosed; (c) a system for public funding of Presidential campaign activities is established . . .; and (d) a Federal Election Commission is established to administer and enforce the legislation. . . .

The Act's contribution and expenditure limitations operate in an area of the most fundamental First Amendment activities. Discussion of public issues and debate on the qualifications of candidates are integral to the operation of the system of government established by our Constitution. . . . Appellees contend that what the Act regulates is conduct, and that its effect on speech and association is incidental at most. Appellants respond that contributions and expenditures are at the very core of political speech, and that the Act's limitations thus constitute restraints on First Amendment liberty that are both gross and direct.

In upholding the constitutional validity of the Act's contribution and expenditure provisions on the ground that those provisions should be viewed as regulating conduct, not speech, the Court of Appeals relied upon *United States v. O'Brien*, 391 U.S. 367 (1968). . . .

We cannot share the view that the present Act's contribution and expenditure limitations are comparable to the restrictions on conduct upheld in *O'Brien*. The expenditure of money simply cannot be equated with such conduct as destruction of a draft card. Some forms of communication made possible by the giving and spending of money involve speech alone, some involve conduct primarily, and some involve a combination of the two. Yet this Court has never suggested that the dependence of a communication on the expenditure of money operates itself to introduce a nonspeech element or to reduce the exacting scrutiny required by the First Amendment. See *New York Times Co. v. Sullivan*.

Even if the categorization of the expenditure of money as conduct were accepted, the limitations challenged here would not meet the *O'Brien* test because the governmental interests advanced in support of the Act involve "suppressing communication." The interests served by the Act include restricting the voices of people and interest groups who have money to spend and reducing the overall scope of federal election campaigns. Although the Act does not focus on the ideas expressed by persons or groups subject to its regulations, it is aimed in part at equalizing the relative ability of all voters to affect electoral outcomes by placing a ceiling on expenditures for political expression by citizens and groups. Unlike *O'Brien*, where the Selective Service System's administrative interest in the preservation of draft cards was wholly unrelated to their use as a means of communication, it is beyond dispute that the interest in regulating the alleged "conduct" of giving or spending money "arises in some measure because the communication allegedly integral to the conduct is itself thought to be harmful.".

Nor can the Act's contribution and expenditure limitations be sustained, as some of the parties suggest, by reference to . . . the proposition that the government may adopt reasonable time, place, and manner regulations, which do not discriminate among speakers or ideas, in order to further an important governmental interest unrelated to the restriction of communication. . . . The critical difference between this case and those time, place, and manner cases is that the present Act's contribution and expenditure limitations impose direct quantity restrictions on political communication and association by persons, groups, candidates, and political parties in addition to any reasonable time, place, and manner regulations otherwise imposed.[17]

---

[17] The nongovernmental appellees argue that just as the decibels emitted by a sound truck can be regulated consistently with the First Amendment, *Kovacs v. Cooper*, 336 U.S. 77 (1949), the Act may restrict the volume of dollars in political campaigns without impermissibly restricting freedom of speech. This comparison underscores a fundamental misconception. The decibel restriction upheld in *Kovacs* limited the *manner* of operating a soundtruck but not the extent of its proper use. By contrast, the Act's dollar ceilings restrict the *extent* of the reasonable use of virtually every means of communicating information. As the *Kovacs* Court emphasized, the nuisance ordinance only barred sound trucks from broadcasting "in a loud and raucous manner on the streets," and imposed "no restriction upon the communication of ideas or discussion of issues by the human voice, by newspapers, by pamphlets, by dodgers," or by soundtrucks operating at a reasonable volume.

A restriction on the amount of money a person or group can spend on political communication during a campaign necessarily reduces the quantity of expression by restricting the number of issues discussed, the depth of their exploration, and the size of the audience reached. This is because virtually every means of communicating ideas in today's mass society requires the expenditure of money. The distribution of the humblest handbill or leaflet entails printing, paper, and circulation costs. Speeches and rallies generally necessitate hiring a hall and publicizing the event. The electorate's increasing dependence on television, radio, and other mass media for news and information has made these expensive modes of communication indispensable instruments of effective political speech.

By contrast with a limitation upon expenditures for political expression, a limitation upon the amount that any one person or group may contribute to a candidate or political committee entails only a marginal restriction upon the contributor's ability to engage in free communication. A contribution serves as a general expression of support for the candidate and his views, but does not communicate the underlying basis for the support. The quantity of communication by the contributor does not increase perceptibly with the size of his contribution, since the expression rests solely on the undifferentiated, symbolic act of contributing. At most, the size of the contribution provides a very rough index of the intensity of the contributor's support for the candidate. A limitation on the amount of money a person may give to a candidate or campaign organization thus involves little direct restraint on his political communication, for it permits the symbolic expression of support evidenced by a contribution but does not in any way infringe the contributor's freedom to discuss candidates and issues. While contributions may result in political expression if spent by a candidate or an association to present views to the voters, the transformation of contributions into political debate involves speech by someone other than the contributor. . . .

The Act's contribution and expenditure limitations also impinge on protected associational freedoms. Making a contribution, like joining a political party, serves to affiliate a person with a candidate. In addition, it enables like-minded persons to pool their resources in furtherance of common political goals. The Act's contribution ceilings thus limit one important means of associating with a candidate or committee, but leave the contributor free to become a member of any political association and to assist personally in the association's efforts on behalf of candidates. And the Act's contribution limitations permit associations and candidates to aggregate large sums of money to promote effective advocacy. By contrast, the Act's $1,000 limitation on independent expenditures "relative to a clearly identified candidate" precludes most associations from effectively amplifying the voice of their adherents, the original basis for the recognition of First Amendment protection of the freedom of association. . . .

[Accordingly, the Court generally upheld "reasonable" restrictions on contributions to political candidates and political parties, while striking down restrictions on expenditures by those candidates and parties. The Court also struck down restrictions on "independent expenditures" by persons or groups who are not candidates or parties, in support of candidates, so long as those expenditures were not "coordinated" with the campaign. (To avoid vagueness problems, the Court construed this portion of the statute as applying only to messages that clearly identify a candidate.) The Court also struck down limits on expenditures by a candidate from his personal or fam-

ily resources, on the ground that this could not possibly contribute to corruption or the appearance of it. Because of its importance, we provide some of the Court's reasoning as to why independent expenditures enjoy constitutional protection.—Editors]

We find that the governmental interest in preventing corruption and the appearance of corruption is inadequate to justify § 608(e)(1)'s ceiling on independent expenditures. First, assuming, arguendo, that large independent expenditures pose the same dangers of actual or apparent quid pro quo arrangements as do large contributions, § 608(e)(1) does not provide an answer that sufficiently relates to the elimination of those dangers. . . . *[The Court said that because groups are free to disseminate messages that benefit campaigns without clearly identifying the candidate, the restrictions are easily evaded.—Editors]*

Second, quite apart from the shortcomings of § 608(e)(1) in preventing any abuses generated by large independent expenditures, the independent advocacy restricted by the provision does not presently appear to pose dangers of real or apparent corruption comparable to those identified with large campaign contributions. The parties defending § 608(e)(1) contend that it is necessary to prevent would-be contributors from avoiding the contribution limitations by the simple expedient of paying directly for media advertisements or for other portions of the candidate's campaign activities. . . . Unlike contributions, such independent expenditures may well provide little assistance to the candidate's campaign and indeed may prove counterproductive. The absence of prearrangement and coordination of an expenditure with the candidate or his agent not only undermines the value of the expenditure to the candidate, but also alleviates the danger that expenditures will be given as a quid pro quo for improper commitments from the candidate. Rather than preventing circumvention of the contribution limitations, § 608(e)(1) severely restricts all independent advocacy despite its substantially diminished potential for abuse.

While the independent expenditure ceiling thus fails to serve any substantial governmental interest in stemming the reality or appearance of corruption in the electoral process, it heavily burdens core First Amendment expression. . . . Advocacy of the election or defeat of candidates for federal office is no less entitled to protection under the First Amendment than the discussion of political policy generally or advocacy of the passage or defeat of legislation.

It is argued, however, that the ancillary governmental interest in equalizing the relative ability of individuals and groups to influence the outcome of elections serves to justify the limitation on express advocacy of the election or defeat of candidates imposed by § 608(e)(1)'s expenditure ceiling. But the concept that government may restrict the speech of some elements of our society in order to enhance the relative voice of others is wholly foreign to the First Amendment, which was designed "to secure the widest possible dissemination of information from diverse and antagonistic sources," and "to assure unfettered interchange of ideas for the bringing about of political and social changes desired by the people." *New York Times Co. v. Sullivan,* 376 U.S., at 266, 269. The First Amendment's protection against governmental abridgment of free expression cannot properly be made to depend on a person's financial ability to engage in public discussion. . . .

[The Court also uphold the Act's reporting and disclosure requirements, and its public financing of presidential election campaigns.—Editors]

■ MR. JUSTICE STEVENS took no part in the consideration or decision of these cases.

■ MR. CHIEF JUSTICE BURGER, concurring in part and dissenting in part.

. . . I agree fully with that part of the Court's opinion that holds unconstitutional the limitations the Act puts on campaign expenditures which "place substantial and direct restrictions on the ability of candidates, citizens, and associations to engage in protected political expression, restrictions that the First Amendment cannot tolerate." Yet when it approves similarly stringent limitations on contributions, the Court ignores the reasons it finds so persuasive in the context of expenditures. For me contributions and expenditures are two sides of the same First Amendment coin.

. . . The Court's attempt to distinguish the communication inherent in political contributions from the speech aspects of political expenditures simply "will not wash." We do little but engage in word games unless we recognize that people candidates and contributors spend money on political activity because they wish to communicate ideas, and their constitutional interest in doing so is precisely the same whether they or someone else utters the words.

. . . At any rate, the contribution limits are a far more severe restriction on First Amendment activity than the sort of "chilling" legislation for which the Court has shown such extraordinary concern in the past. *[Citing Cohen v. California and the obscenity cases.—Editors]* If such restraints can be justified at all, they must be justified by the very strongest of state interests. . . . After a bow to the "weighty interests" Congress meant to serve, the Court then forsakes this analysis in one sentence: "Congress was surely entitled to conclude that disclosure was only a partial measure, and that contribution ceilings were a necessary legislative concomitant to deal with the reality or appearance of corruption. . . ." In striking down the limitations on campaign expenditures, the Court relies in part on its conclusion that other means namely, disclosure and contribution ceilings will adequately serve the statute's aim. It is not clear why the same analysis is not also appropriate in weighing the need for contribution ceilings in addition to disclosure requirements. Congress may well be entitled to conclude that disclosure was a "partial measure," but I had not thought until today that Congress could enact its conclusions in the First Amendment area into laws immune from the most searching review by this Court.

Finally, it seems clear to me that in approving these limitations on contributions the Court must rest upon the proposition that "pooling" money is fundamentally different from other forms of associational or joint activity. I see only two possible ways in which money differs from volunteer work, endorsements, and the like. Money can be used to buy favors, because an unscrupulous politician can put it to personal use; second, giving money is a less visible form of associational activity. With respect to the first problem, the Act does not attempt to do any more than the bribery laws to combat this sort of corruption. In fact, the Act does not reach at all, and certainly the contribution limits do not reach, forms of "association" that can be fully as corrupt as a contribution intended as a quid pro quo such as the eleventh-hour endorsement by a former rival, obtained for the promise of a federal appointment. . . .

■ MR. JUSTICE WHITE, concurring in part and dissenting in part.

. . . Since the contribution and expenditure limitations are neutral as to the content of speech and are not motivated by fear of the consequences of the political speech of particular candidates or of political speech in general, this case depends on whether the nonspeech interests of the Federal Government in regulating the use of money in political campaigns are sufficiently urgent to justify the incidental effects that the limitations visit upon the First Amendment interests of candidates and their supporters.

Despite its seeming struggle with the standard by which to judge this case, this is essentially the question the Court asks and answers in the affirmative with respect to the limitations on contributions which individuals and political committees are permitted to make to federal candidates. In the interest of preventing undue influence that large contributors would have or that the public might think they would have, the Court upholds the provision that an individual may not give to a candidate, or spend on his behalf if requested or authorized by the candidate to do so, more than $1,000 in any one election. This limitation is valid although it imposes a low ceiling on what individuals may deem to be their most effective means of supporting or speaking on behalf of the candidate[,] i.e., financial support given directly to the candidate. The Court thus accepts the congressional judgment that the evils of unlimited contributions are sufficiently threatening to warrant restriction regardless of the impact of the limits on the contributor's opportunity for effective speech and in turn on the total volume of the candidate's political communications by reason of his inability to accept large sums from those willing to give.

The congressional judgment, which I would also accept, was that other steps must be taken to counter the corrosive effects of money in federal election campaigns. One of these steps is § 608(e), which, aside from those funds that are given to the candidate or spent at his request or with his approval or cooperation limits what a contributor may independently spend in support or denigration of one running for federal office. Congress was plainly of the view that these expenditures also have corruptive potential; but the Court strikes down the provision, strangely enough claiming more insight as to what may improperly influence candidates than is possessed by the majority of Congress that passed this bill and the President who signed it. Those supporting the bill undeniably included many seasoned professionals who have been deeply involved in elective processes and who have viewed them at close range over many years.

It would make little sense to me, and apparently made none to Congress, to limit the amounts an individual may give to a candidate or spend with his approval but fail to limit the amounts that could be spent on his behalf. Yet the Court permits the former while striking down the latter limitation. No more than $1,000 may be given to a candidate or spent at his request or with his approval or cooperation; but otherwise, apparently, a contributor is to be constitutionally protected in spending unlimited amounts of money in support of his chosen candidate or candidates.

. . . It is also important to restore and maintain public confidence in federal elections. It is critical to obviate or dispel the impression that federal elections are purely and simply a function of money, that federal offices are bought and sold or that political races are reserved for those who have the facility and the stomach for doing whatever it takes to bring together those interests, groups, and individuals that can raise or contribute large fortunes in order to prevail at the polls.

The ceiling on candidate expenditures represents the considered judgment of Congress that elections are to be decided among candidates none of whom has overpowering advantage by reason of a huge campaign war chest. At least so long as the ceiling placed upon the candidates is not plainly too low, elections are not to turn on the difference in the amounts of money that candidates have to spend. This seems an acceptable purpose and the means chosen a common-sense way to achieve it. The Court nevertheless holds that a candidate has a constitutional right to spend unlimited amounts of money, mostly that of other people, in order to be elected. The holding perhaps is not that federal candidates have the constitutional right to purchase their election, but many will so interpret the Court's conclusion in this case. I cannot join the Court in this respect. . . .

■ [JUSTICE REHNQUIST's opinion, concurring in part and dissenting in part, is omitted.]

NOTES

1. Do you understand the Court's distinctions between contributions and independent expenditures? From the individual's point of view, according to the Court, limiting the size of a contribution "entails only a marginal restriction" on freedom of speech because the "quantity of communication by the contributor does not increase perceptibly with the size of his contribution, since the expression rests solely on the undifferentiated, symbolic act of contributing." Is that right? Is a $50 contribution not "perceptibly" different from $500? If the purpose of making a contribution is to help persuade the public to vote for a candidate, doesn't the amount matter? Why do some people contribute multiple times? Conversely, why does the Court not apply the same reasoning to independent expenditures in support of the candidates? Why does quantity matter in one context but not the other?

From the government's point of view, according to the Court, independent expenditures are far less likely to result in actual or apparent corruption. Why?

2. Note the practical effect of the Court's holdings. Allowing contribution limits but not independent expenditure limits has the effect of directing campaign money away from candidates and political parties, who arguably are most accountable to the public, toward advocacy groups, including "super-PACS," who can receive and spend essentially unlimited sums of money to support or oppose candidates of their choice. What good does this accomplish? What evils might it magnify? Do you imagine this was Congress's intention?

The Court also struck down limits on expenditures by a candidate from his personal or family resources, on the ground that this could not possibly contribute to corruption or the appearance of it. The logic may be sound, but the effect is to privilege wealthy candidates—so-called "self-funding candidates"—over those who have to raise money in dribs and drabs. Is this a good thing?

Congress's theory was that limiting campaign expenditures would make it unnecessary for candidate to raise so much money, thus freeing them from the need to spend so much of their time fundraising. By striking down expenditure limits while upholding contribution limits, the Court likely *increased* the amount of time needed for fundraising, relative to what it was before the statute was passed. Candidates need just as large a war chest, but it is more time-consuming to raise money in small sums than large sums. Critics also claim that this feature of the decision favors incumbents, whose name recognition and pull with interest groups makes it easier for them to raise money.

Some critics say that, as a result of the combination of holdings in *Buckley*, the campaign finance system makes no sense and pleases no one. Was the Court wrong to apply the "severability" doctrine to "save" only portions of the legislation it thought constitution, leaving the rest in place? Should the Court have struck the statute down completely, leaving it Congress to decide how to replace it? Can you think of ways to reform the campaign finance system that are consistent with the Court's constitutional holdings?

3. *Buckley*'s distinction between contributions and expenditures has few defenders on constitutional grounds and even fewer defenders on policy grounds. But it has never been repudiated and remains in force today. About half the Court believes that contribution limitations should be stuck down, and about half think that expenditure limits should be restored, producing a compromise that seemingly pleases no one. Is there a way out of this quandary?

Nixon v. Shrink Missouri Government PAC

528 U.S. 377 (2000)

[In the majority opinion, the Court upheld Missouri's $1,000 cap on campaign contributions despite the fact that this sum, though approved in Buckley, had greatly diminished in value through inflation. The majority largely deferred to legislative judgments.—Editors]

■ JUSTICE BREYER, with whom JUSTICE GINSBURG joins, concurring.

. . . If the dissent believes that the Court diminishes the importance of the First Amendment interests before us, it is wrong. The Court's opinion does not question the constitutional importance of political speech or that its protection lies at the heart of the First Amendment. Nor does it question the need for particularly careful, precise, and independent judicial review where, as here, that protection is at issue. But this is a case where constitutionally protected interests lie on both sides of the legal equation. For that reason there is no place for a strong presumption against constitutionality, of the sort often thought to accompany the words "strict scrutiny." Nor can we expect that mechanical application of the tests associated with "strict scrutiny"—the tests of "compelling interests" and "least restrictive means"—will properly resolve the difficult constitutional problem that campaign finance statutes pose.

On the one hand, a decision to contribute money to a campaign is a matter of First Amendment concern—not because money is speech (it is not); but because it enables speech. Through contributions the contributor associates himself with the candidate's cause, helps the candidate communicate a political message with which the contributor agrees, and helps the candidate win by attracting the votes of similarly minded voters. *Buckley v. Valeo*, 424 U.S. 1, 24–25 (1976) (*per curiam*). Both political association and political communication are at stake.

On the other hand, restrictions upon the amount any one individual can contribute to a particular candidate seek to protect the integrity of the electoral process—the means through which a free society democratically translates political speech into concrete governmental action. Moreover, by limiting the size of the largest contributions, such restrictions aim to democratize the influence that money itself may bring to bear upon the electoral process. In doing so, they seek to build public confidence in that process and broaden the base of a candidate's meaningful financial support, encouraging the public participation and open discussion that the First Amendment itself presupposes.

In service of these objectives, the statute imposes restrictions of degree. It does not deny the contributor the opportunity to associate with the candidate through a contribution, though it limits a contribution's size. Nor does it prevent the contributor from using money (alone or with others) to pay for the expression of the same views in other ways. Instead, it permits all supporters to contribute the same amount of money, in an attempt to make the process fairer and more democratic.

Under these circumstances, a presumption against constitutionality is out of place. . . . In such circumstances—where a law significantly implicates competing constitutionally protected interests in complex ways—the Court has closely scrutinized the statute's impact on those interests, but refrained from employing a simple test that effectively presumes unconstitutionality. Rather, it has balanced interests. And in practice that has meant asking whether the statute burdens any one such interest in a manner out of proportion to the statute's salutary effects upon the others (perhaps, but not necessarily, because of the existence of a clearly superior, less restrictive alternative). Where a legislature has significantly greater institutional expertise, as, for example, in the field of election regulation, the Court in practice defers to empirical legislative judgments—at least where that deference does not risk such constitutional evils as, say, permitting incumbents to insulate themselves from effective electoral challenge. . . .

Applying this approach to the present case, I would uphold the statute essentially for the reasons stated by the Court. I agree that the legislature understands the problem—the threat to electoral integrity, the need for democratization—better than do we. We should defer to its political judgment that unlimited spending threatens the integrity of the electoral process. But we should not defer in respect to whether its solution, by imposing too low a contribution limit, significantly increases the reputation-related or media-related advantages of incumbency and thereby insulates legislators from effective electoral challenge. The statutory limit here, $1,075 (or 378, 1976 dollars), is low enough to raise such a question. But given the empirical information presented—the type of election at issue; the record of adequate candidate financing postreform; and the fact that the statute indexes the amount for inflation—I agree with the Court that the statute does not work disproportionate harm. The limit may have prevented the plaintiff, Zev David Fredman, from financing his own campaign for office, for Fredman's support among potential contributors was not sufficiently widespread. But any contribution statute will narrow the field of conceivable challengers to some degree. Undue insulation is a practical matter, and it cannot be inferred automatically from the fact that the limit makes ballot access more difficult for one previously unsuccessful candidate. . . .

■ JUSTICE KENNEDY, dissenting.

. . . The justifications for the case system and stare decisis must rest upon the Court's capacity, and responsibility, to acknowledge its missteps. It is our duty to face up to adverse, unintended consequences flowing from our own prior decisions. With all respect, I submit the Court does not accept this obligation in the case before us. Instead, it perpetuates and compounds a serious distortion of the First Amendment resulting from our own intervention in *Buckley*.

The plain fact is that the compromise the Court invented in *Buckley* set the stage for a new kind of speech to enter the political system. It is covert speech. The Court has forced a substantial amount of political speech underground, as contributors and candidates devise ever more elaborate methods of avoiding contribution limits, limits which take no account of rising campaign costs. The preferred method has been to conceal the real purpose of the speech. Soft money may be contributed to political parties in unlimited amounts, see *Colorado Republican Federal Campaign Comm. v. Federal Election Comm'n*, 518 U.S. 604, 616 (1996), and is used often to fund so-called issue advocacy, advertisements that promote or attack a candidate's positions without specifically urging his or her election or defeat. Issue advocacy, like soft money, is unrestricted, while straightforward speech in the form of financial contributions paid to a candidate, speech subject to full disclosure and prompt evaluation by the public, is not. Thus has the Court's decision given us covert speech. This mocks the First Amendment. The current system would be unfortunate, and suspect under the First Amendment, had it evolved from a deliberate legislative choice; but its unhappy origins are in our earlier decree in *Buckley*, which by accepting half of what Congress did (limiting contributions) but rejecting the other (limiting expenditures) created a misshapen system, one which distorts the meaning of speech. . . .

■ JUSTICE THOMAS, with whom JUSTICE SCALIA joins, dissenting.

I begin with a proposition that ought to be unassailable: Political speech is the primary object of First Amendment protection. The Founders sought to protect the rights of individuals to engage in political speech because a self-governing people depends upon the free exchange of political information. And that free exchange should receive the most protection when it matters the most—during campaigns for elective office.

I do not start with these foundational principles because the Court openly disagrees with them—it could not, for they are solidly embedded in our precedents. Instead, I start with them because the Court today abandons them. For nearly half a century, this Court has extended First Amendment protection to a multitude of forms of "speech," such as making false defamatory statements, filing lawsuits, dancing nude, exhibiting drive-in movies with nudity, burning flags, and wearing military uniforms. Not surprisingly, the Courts of Appeals have followed our lead and concluded that the First Amendment protects, for example, begging, shouting obscenities, erecting tables on a sidewalk, and refusing to wear a necktie. In light of the many cases of this sort, today's decision is a most curious anomaly. Whatever the proper status of such activities under the First Amendment, I am confident that they are less integral to the functioning of our Republic than campaign contributions. Yet the majority today, rather than going out of its way to protect political speech, goes out of its way to avoid protecting it. As I explain below, contributions to political campaigns generate essential political speech. And contribution caps, which place a direct and substantial limit on core speech, should be met with the utmost skepticism and should receive the strictest scrutiny. . . .

To justify its decision upholding contribution limitations while striking down expenditure limitations, the Court in *Buckley* explained that expenditure limits "represent substantial rather than merely theoretical restraints on the quantity and diversity of political speech," 424 U.S., at 19, while contribution limits "entai[l] only a marginal restriction upon the contributor's ability to engage in free communication," id., at 20–21. In drawing this distinction, the Court in *Buckley* relied on the premise that contributing to a candidate differs qualitatively from directly spending money. It noted that "[w]hile contributions may result in political expression if spent by a candidate or an association to present views to the voters, the transformation of contributions into political debate involves speech by someone other than the contributor." 424 U.S., at 21. But this was a faulty distinction *ab initio* because it ignored the reality of how speech of all kinds is disseminated:

> "Even in the case of a direct expenditure, there is usually some go-between that facilitates the dissemination of the spender's message—for instance, an advertising agency or a television station. To call a contribution 'speech by proxy' thus does little to differentiate it from an expenditure. The only possible difference is that contributions involve an extra step in the proxy chain. But again, that is a difference in form, not substance." *Colorado Republican*, 518 U.S., at 638–639 (THOMAS, J., concurring in judgment and dissenting in part).

And, insofar as the speech-by-proxy argument was disconnected from the realities of political speech to begin with, it is not surprising that we have firmly rejected it since *Buckley*. In *Federal Election Comm'n v. National Conservative Political Action Comm.*, 470 U.S. 480 (1985), we cast aside the argument that a contribution does not represent the constitutionally protected speech of a contributor, recognizing "that the contributors obviously like the message they are hearing from these organizations and want to add their voices to that message; otherwise they would not part with their money." Id., at 495. Though in that case we considered limitations on expenditures made by associations, our holding that the speech-by-proxy argument fails to diminish contributors' First Amendment rights is directly applicable to this case. In both cases, donors seek to disseminate information by giving to an organization controlled by others. Through contributing, citizens see to it that their views on policy and politics are articulated.

Without the assistance of the speech-by-proxy argument, the remainder of *Buckley*'s rationales founder. Those rationales—that the "quantity of communication by the contributor does not increase perceptibly with the size of his contribution," that "the size of the contribution provides a very rough index of the intensity of the contributor's support for the candidate," and that "[a] contribution serves as a general expression of support for the candidate and his views, but does not communicate the underlying basis for the support," still rest on the proposition that speech by proxy is not fully protected. These contentions simply ignore that a contribution, by amplifying the voice of the candidate, helps to ensure the dissemination of the messages that the contributor wishes to convey. . . .

Citizens United v. Federal Election Commission

130 S. Ct. 876 (2010)

■ JUSTICE KENNEDY delivered the opinion of the Court.

Federal law prohibits corporations and unions from using their general treasury funds to make independent expenditures for speech defined as an "electioneering communication" or for speech expressly advocating the election or defeat of a candidate. 2 U.S.C. § 441b. Limits on electioneering communications were upheld in *McConnell v. Federal Election Comm'n*, 540 U.S. 93, 203–209 (2003). The holding of *McConnell* rested to a large extent on an earlier case, *Austin v. Michigan Chamber of Commerce*, 494 U.S. 652 (1990). *Austin* had held that political speech may be banned based on the speaker's corporate identity.

In this case we are asked to reconsider *Austin* and, in effect, *McConnell*. . . . [We] hold that *stare decisis* does not compel the continued acceptance of *Austin*. The Government may regulate corporate political speech through disclaimer and disclosure requirements, but it may not suppress that speech altogether. . . .

I–A

Citizens United is a nonprofit corporation. . . . [It] has an annual budget of about $12 million. Most of its funds are from donations by individuals; but, in addition, it accepts a small portion of its funds from for-profit corporations.

In January 2008, Citizens United released a film entitled *Hillary: The Movie*. We refer to the film as *Hillary*. It is a 90–minute documentary about then-Senator Hillary Clinton, who was a candidate in the Democratic Party's 2008 Presidential primary elections. *Hillary* mentions Senator Clinton by name and depicts interviews with political commentators and other persons, most of them quite critical of Senator Clinton. *Hillary* was released in theaters and on DVD, but Citizens United wanted to increase distribution by making it available through video-on-demand.

Video-on-demand allows digital cable subscribers to select programming from various menus, including movies, television shows, sports, news, and music. The viewer can watch the program at any time and can elect to rewind or pause the program. In December 2007, a cable company offered, for a payment of $1.2 million, to make *Hillary* available on a video-on-demand channel called "Elections '08." Some video-on-demand services require viewers to pay a small fee to view a selected program, but here the proposal was to make *Hillary* available to viewers free of charge.

To implement the proposal, Citizens United was prepared to pay for the video-on-demand; and to promote the film, it produced two 10–second ads and one 30–second ad for *Hillary*. Each ad includes a short (and, in our view, pejorative) statement about Senator Clinton, followed by the name of the movie and the movie's Website address. Citizens United desired to promote the video-on-demand offering by running advertisements on broadcast and cable television.

B

Before the Bipartisan Campaign Reform Act of 2002 (BCRA), federal law prohibited—and still does prohibit—corporations and unions from using general treasury funds to make direct contributions to candidates or independent expenditures that expressly advocate the election or defeat of a candidate, through any form of media, in connection with certain qualified federal elections. BCRA § 203 amended [the law] to prohibit any "electioneering communication" as well. An electioneering communication is defined as "any broadcast, cable, or satellite communication" that "refers to a clearly identified candidate for Federal office" and is made within 30 days of a primary or 60 days of a general election. § 434(f)(3)(A). The Federal Election Commission's (FEC) regulations further define an electioneering communication as a communication that is "publicly distributed." 11 CFR § 100.29(a)(2) (2009). "In the case of a candidate for nomination for President . . . *publicly distributed* means" that the communication "[c]an be received by 50,000 or more persons in a State where a primary election . . . is being held within 30 days." § 100.29(b)(3)(ii). Corporations and unions are barred from using their general treasury funds for express advocacy or electioneering communications. They may establish, however, a "separate segregated fund" (known as a political action committee, or PAC) for these purposes. The moneys received by the segregated fund are limited to donations from stockholders and employees of the corporation or, in the case of unions, members of the union. . . .

III

. . . The law before us is an outright ban, backed by criminal sanctions. Section 441b makes it a felony for all corporations—including non-profit advocacy corporations—either to expressly advocate the election or defeat of candidates or to broadcast electioneering communications within 30 days of a primary election and 60 days of a general election. Thus, the following acts would all be felonies under § 441b: The Sierra Club runs an ad, within the crucial phase of 60 days before the general election, that exhorts the public to disapprove of a Congressman who favors logging in national forests; the National Rifle Association publishes a book urging the public to vote for the challenger because the incumbent U.S. Senator supports a handgun ban; and the American Civil Liberties Union creates a Web site telling the public to vote for a Presidential candidate in light of that candidate's defense of free speech. These prohibitions are classic examples of censorship.

Section 441b is a ban on corporate speech notwithstanding the fact that a PAC created by a corporation can still speak. A PAC is a separate association from the corporation. So the PAC exemption from § 441b's expenditure ban, § 441b(b)(2), does not allow corporations to speak. Even if a PAC could somehow allow a corporation to speak—and it does not—the option to form PACs does not alleviate the First Amendment problems with § 441b. PACs are burdensome alternatives; they are expensive to administer and subject to extensive regulations. For example, every PAC must appoint a treasurer, forward donations to the treasurer promptly, keep detailed records of the identities of the persons making donations, preserve receipts for three years, and file an organization statement and report changes to this information within 10 days. . . .

Speech is an essential mechanism of democracy, for it is the means to hold officials accountable to the people. The right of citizens to inquire, to hear, to speak, and to use information to reach consensus is a precondition to enlightened self-government and a necessary means to protect it. The First Amendment "has its fullest and most urgent application to speech uttered during a campaign for political office." *Eu v. San Francisco County Democratic Central Comm.*, 489 U.S. 214, 223 (1989); see *Buckley*, at 14 ("Discussion of public issues and debate on the qualifications of candidates are integral to the operation of the system of government established by our Constitution").

For these reasons, political speech must prevail against laws that would suppress it, whether by design or inadvertence. Laws that burden political speech are "subject to strict scrutiny," which requires the Government to prove that the restriction "furthers a compelling interest and is narrowly tailored to achieve that interest." *Federal Election Comm'n v. Wisconsin Right to Life, Inc.*, 551 U.S. 449, 464 (2007) (opinion of ROBERTS, C.J.) [hereinafter *WRTL*]. . . .

Quite apart from the purpose or effect of regulating content, moreover, the Government may commit a constitutional wrong when by law it identifies certain preferred speakers. By taking the right to speak from some and giving it to others, the Government deprives the disadvantaged person or class of the right to use speech to strive to establish worth, standing, and respect for the speaker's voice. The Government may not by these means deprive the public of the right and privilege to determine for itself what speech and speakers are worthy of consideration. The First Amendment protects speech and speaker, and the ideas that flow from each. . . .

A–1

The Court has recognized that First Amendment protection extends to corporations. *Bellotti*, at 778, n. 14, (citing *Linmark Associates, Inc. v. Willingboro*, 431 U.S. (1977); *Time, Inc. v. Firestone*, 424 U.S. 448 (1976); *Doran v. Salem Inn, Inc.*, 422 U.S. 922 (1975); *Southeastern Promotions, Ltd. v. Conrad*, 420 U.S. 546, (1975); *Cox Broadcasting Corp. v. Cohn*, 420 U.S. 469 (1975); *Miami Herald Publishing Co. v. Tornillo*, 418 U.S. 241 (1974); *New York Times Co. v. United States*, 403 U.S. 713 (1971) (*per curiam*); *Time, Inc. v. Hill*, 385 U.S. 374 (1967); *New York Times Co. v. Sullivan*, 376 U.S. 254; *Kingsley Int'l Pictures Corp. v. Regents of Univ. of N. Y.*, 360 U.S. 684(1959); *Joseph Burstyn, Inc. v. Wilson*, 343 U.S. 495 (1952)); see, *e.g.*, *Turner Broadcasting System, Inc. v. FCC*, 520 U.S. 180 (1997); *Denver Area Ed. Telecommunications Consortium, Inc. v. FCC*, 518 U.S. (1996); *Turner*, 512 U.S. 622; *Simon & Schuster*, 502 U.S. 105; *Sable Communications of Cal., Inc. v. FCC*, 492 U.S. 11593 (1989); *Florida Star v. B.J. F.*, 491 U.S. 524 (1989); *Philadelphia Newspapers, Inc. v. Hepps*, 475 U.S. 767 (1986); *Landmark Communications, Inc. v. Virginia*, 435 U.S. (1978); *Young v. American Mini Theatres, Inc.*, 427 U.S. 50 (1976); *Gertz v. Robert Welch, Inc.*, 418 U.S. 323 (1974); *Greenbelt Cooperative Publishing Assn., Inc. v. Bresler*, 398 U.S. 6 (1970). . . .

Under the rationale of these precedents, political speech does not lose First Amendment protection "simply because its source is a corporation." *Bellotti*, at 784; see *Pacific Gas & Elec. Co. v. Public Util. Comm'n of Cal.*, 475 U.S. 1, 8 (1986) (plurality opinion) ("The identity of the speaker is not decisive in determining whether speech is protected. Corporations and other associations, like individuals, contribute to the 'discussion, debate, and the dissemination of information and ideas' that the First Amendment seeks to foster" (quoting *Bellotti*, 435 U.S., at 783)). The Court has thus rejected the argument that political speech of corporations or other associations should be treated differently under the First Amendment simply because such associations are not "natural persons." *Id.*, at 776.

At least since the latter part of the 19th century, the laws of some States and of the United States imposed a ban on corporate direct contributions to candidates. See B. Smith, Unfree Speech: The Folly of Campaign Finance Reform 23 (2001). Yet not until 1947 did Congress first prohibit independent expenditures by corporations and labor unions in § 304 of the Labor Management Relations Act 1947, 61 Stat. 159 (codified at 2 U.S.C. § 251 (1946 ed., Supp. I)). In passing this Act Congress overrode the veto of President Truman, who warned that the expenditure ban was a "dangerous intrusion on free speech." . . .

2

. . . Less than two years after *Buckley*, *Bellotti*, 435 U.S. 765, reaffirmed the First Amendment principle that the Government cannot restrict political speech based on the speaker's corporate identity. *Bellotti* could not have been clearer when it struck down a state-law prohibition on corporate independent expenditures related to referenda issues:

> We thus find no support in the First . . . Amendment, or in the decisions of this Court, for the proposition that speech that otherwise would be within the protection of the First Amendment loses that protection simply because its source is a corporation that cannot prove, to the satisfaction of a court, a material effect on its business or property. . . . [That proposition] amounts to an impermissible legislative prohibition of speech based on the identity of the interests that spokesmen may represent in public debate over controversial issues and a requirement that the speaker have a sufficiently great interest in the subject to justify communication. . . .
>
> In the realm of protected speech, the legislature is constitutionally disqualified from dictating the subjects about which persons may speak and the speakers who may address a public issue.

Id. at 784–785. . . .

3

Thus the law stood until *Austin*. *Austin* "uph[eld] a direct restriction on the independent expenditure of funds for political speech for the first time in [this Court's] history." 494 U.S., at 695 (KENNEDY, J., dissenting). There, the Michigan Chamber of Commerce sought to use general treasury funds to run a newspaper ad supporting a specific candidate. Michigan law, however, prohibited corporate independent expenditures that supported or opposed any candidate for state office. A violation of the law was punishable as a felony. The Court sustained the speech prohibition.

 . . . [T]he *Austin* Court identified a new governmental interest in limiting political speech: an antidistortion interest. *Austin* found a compelling governmental interest in preventing "the corrosive and distorting effects of immense aggregations of wealth that are accumulated with the help of the corporate form and that have little or no correlation to the public's support for the corporation's political ideas." 494 U.S., at 660.

B

 . . . In its defense of the corporate-speech restrictions in § 441b, the Government notes the antidistortion rationale on which *Austin* and its progeny rest in part, yet it all but abandons reliance upon it. It argues instead that two other compelling interests support *Austin*'s holding that corporate expenditure restrictions are constitutional: an anticorruption interest, and a shareholder-protection interest. We consider the three points in turn.

1

As for *Austin*'s antidistortion rationale, the Government does little to defend it. And with good reason, for the rationale cannot support § 441b.

If the First Amendment has any force, it prohibits Congress from fining or jailing citizens, or associations of citizens, for simply engaging in political speech. If the antidistortion rationale were to be accepted, however, it would permit Government to ban political speech simply because the speaker is an association that has taken on the corporate form. The Government contends that *Austin* permits it to ban corporate expenditures for almost all forms of communication stemming from a corporation. If *Austin* were correct, the Government could prohibit a corporation from expressing political views in media beyond those presented here, such as by printing books. The Government responds "that the FEC has never applied this statute to a book," and if it did, "there would be quite [a] good as-applied challenge." Tr. of Oral Arg. 65 (Sept. 9, 2009). This troubling assertion of brooding governmental power cannot be reconciled with the confidence and stability in civic discourse that the First Amendment must secure.

. . . *Austin* sought to defend the antidistortion rationale as a means to prevent corporations from obtaining "an unfair advantage in the political marketplace" by using "resources amassed in the economic marketplace." 494 U.S., at 659. But *Buckley* rejected the premise that the Government has an interest "in equalizing the relative ability of individuals and groups to influence the outcome of elections." *Buckley* was specific in stating that "the skyrocketing cost of political campaigns" could not sustain the governmental prohibition. 424 U.S., at 26. The First Amendment's protections do not depend on the speaker's "financial ability to engage in public discussion." *Id.*, at 49. . . .

Either as support for its antidistortion rationale or as a further argument, the *Austin* majority undertook to distinguish wealthy individuals from corporations on the ground that "[s]tate law grants corporations special advantages—such as limited liability, perpetual life, and favorable treatment of the accumulation and distribution of assets." 494 U.S., at 658–659. This does not suffice, however, to allow laws prohibiting speech. "It is rudimentary that the State cannot exact as the price of those special advantages the forfeiture of First Amendment rights." *Id.*, at 680 (SCALIA, J., dissenting).

It is irrelevant for purposes of the First Amendment that corporate funds may "have little or no correlation to the public's support for the corporation's political ideas." All speakers, including individuals and the media, use money amassed from the economic marketplace to fund their speech. The First Amendment protects the resulting speech, even if it was enabled by economic transactions with persons or entities who disagree with the speaker's ideas.

Austin's antidistortion rationale would produce the dangerous, and unacceptable, consequence that Congress could ban political speech of media corporations. Media corporations are now exempt from § 441b's ban on corporate expenditures. Yet media corporations accumulate wealth with the help of the corporate form, the largest media corporations have "immense aggregations of wealth," and the views expressed by media corporations often "have little or no correlation to the public's support" for those views. Thus, under the Government's reasoning, wealthy media corporations could have their voices diminished to put them on par with other media entities. There is no precedent for permitting this under the First Amendment.

The media exemption discloses further difficulties with the law now under consideration. There is no precedent supporting laws that attempt to distinguish between corporations which are deemed to be exempt as media corporations and those which are not. "We have consistently rejected the proposition that the institutional press has any constitutional privilege beyond that of other speakers." With the advent of the Internet and the decline of print and broadcast media, moreover, the line between the media and others who wish to comment on political and social issues becomes far more blurred. . . .

There is simply no support for the view that the First Amendment, as originally understood, would permit the suppression of political speech by media corporations. The Framers may not have anticipated modern business and media corporations. Yet television networks and major newspapers owned by media corporations have become the most important means of mass communication in modern times. The First Amendment was certainly not understood to condone the suppression of political speech in society's most salient media. It was understood as a response to the repression of speech and the press that had existed in England and the heavy taxes on the press that were imposed in the colonies. The great debates between the Federalists and the Anti–Federalists over our founding document were published and expressed in the most important means of mass communication of that era—newspapers owned by individuals. At the founding, speech was open, comprehensive, and vital to society's definition of itself; there were no limits on the sources of speech and knowledge. . . .

When Government seeks to use its full power, including the criminal law, to command where a person may get his or her information or what distrusted source he or she may not hear, it uses censorship to control thought. This is unlawful. The First Amendment confirms the freedom to think for ourselves.

2

What we have said also shows the invalidity of other arguments made by the Government. For the most part relinquishing the antidistortion rationale, the Government falls back on the argument that corporate political speech can be banned in order to prevent corruption or its appearance. In *Buckley*, the Court found this interest "sufficiently important" to allow limits on contributions but did not extend that reasoning to expenditure limits. 424 U.S., at 25. When *Buckley* examined an expenditure ban, it found "that the governmental interest in preventing corruption and the appearance of corruption [was] inadequate to justify [the ban] on independent expenditures." *Id.*, at 45. . . .

"The absence of prearrangement and coordination of an expenditure with the candidate or his agent not only undermines the value of the expenditure to the candidate, but also alleviates the danger that expenditures will be given as a *quid pro quo* for improper commitments from the candidate." *Buckley*, 424 U.S., at 47; see *ibid.* (independent expenditures have a "substantially diminished potential for abuse"). Limits on independent expenditures, such as § 441b, have a chilling effect extending well beyond the Government's interest in preventing *quid pro quo* corruption. The anticorruption interest is not sufficient to displace the speech here in question. Indeed, 26 States do not restrict independent expenditures by for-profit corporations. The Government does not claim that these expenditures have corrupted the political process in those States. . . .

3

The Government contends further that corporate independent expenditures can be limited because of its interest in protecting dissenting shareholders from being compelled to fund corporate political speech. . . . The First Amendment does not allow that power. There is, furthermore, little evidence of abuse that cannot be corrected by shareholders "through the procedures of corporate democracy." *Bellotti*, 435 U.S., at 794.

Those reasons are sufficient to reject this shareholder-protection interest; and, moreover, the statute is both underinclusive and overinclusive. As to the first, if Congress had been seeking to protect dissenting shareholders, it would not have banned corporate speech in only certain media within 30 or 60 days before an election. A dissenting shareholder's interests would be implicated by speech in any media at any time. As to the second, the statute is overinclusive because it covers all corporations, including non-profit corporations and for-profit corporations with only single shareholders. As to other corporations, the remedy is not to restrict speech but to consider and explore other regulatory mechanisms. The regulatory mechanism here, based on speech, contravenes the First Amendment.

4

We need not reach the question whether the Government has a compelling interest in preventing foreign individuals or associations from influencing our Nation's political process. Cf. 2 U.S.C. § 441e (contribution and expenditure ban applied to "foreign national[s]"). Section 441b is not limited to corporations or associations that were created in foreign countries or funded predominately by foreign shareholders. Section 441b therefore would be overbroad even if we assumed, *arguendo*, that the Government has a compelling interest in limiting foreign influence over our political process. . . .

IV–A

Citizens United next challenges BCRA's disclaimer and disclosure provisions as applied to *Hillary* and the three advertisements for the movie. . . .

[The Court upholds these provisions.—Editors]

B

. . . Citizens United argues that disclosure requirements can chill donations to an organization by exposing donors to retaliation. Some *amici* point to recent events in which donors to certain causes were blacklisted, threatened, or otherwise targeted for retaliation. In *McConnell*, the Court recognized that § 201 would be unconstitutional as applied to an organization if there were a reasonable probability that the group's members would face threats, harassment, or reprisals if their names were disclosed. 540 U.S., at 198. The examples cited by *amici* are cause for concern. Citizens United, however, has offered no evidence that its members may face similar threats or reprisals. To the contrary, Citizens United has been disclosing its donors for years and has identified no instance of harassment or retaliation.

. . . [M]odern technology makes disclosures rapid and informative. A campaign finance system that pairs corporate independent expenditures with effective disclosure has not existed before today. It must be noted, furthermore, that many of Congress' findings in passing BCRA were premised on a system without adequate disclosure. With the advent of the Internet, prompt disclosure of expenditures can provide shareholders and citizens with the information needed to hold corporations and elected officials accountable for their positions and supporters. Shareholders can determine whether their corporation's political speech advances the corporation's interest in making profits, and citizens can see whether elected officials are " 'in the pocket' of so-called moneyed interests." 540 U.S., at 259. The First Amendment protects political speech; and disclosure permits citizens and shareholders to react to the speech of corporate entities in a proper way. This transparency enables the electorate to make informed decisions and give proper weight to different speakers and messages. . . .

V

. . . Modern day movies, television comedies, or skits on Youtube.com might portray public officials or public policies in unflattering ways. Yet if a covered transmission during the blackout period creates the background for candidate endorsement or opposition, a felony occurs solely because a corporation, other than an exempt media corporation, has made the "purchase, payment, distribution, loan, advance, deposit, or gift of money or anything of value" in order to engage in political speech. Speech would be suppressed in the realm where its necessity is most evident: in the public dialogue preceding a real election. Governments are often hostile to speech, but under our law and our tradition it seems stranger than fiction for our Government to make this political speech a crime. Yet this is the statute's purpose and design.

Some members of the public might consider *Hillary* to be insightful and instructive; some might find it to be neither high art nor a fair discussion on how to set the Nation's course; still others simply might suspend judgment on these points but decide to think more about issues and candidates. Those choices and assessments, however, are not for the Government to make. . . .

■ CHIEF JUSTICE ROBERTS, with whom JUSTICE ALITO joins, concurring.

The Government urges us in this case to uphold a direct prohibition on political speech. It asks us to embrace a theory of the First Amendment that would allow censorship not only of television and radio broadcasts, but of pamphlets, posters, the Internet, and virtually any other medium that corporations and unions might find useful in expressing their views on matters of public concern. Its theory, if accepted, would empower the Government to prohibit newspapers from running editorials or opinion pieces supporting or opposing candidates for office, so long as the newspapers were owned by corporations—as the major ones are. First Amendment rights could be confined to individuals, subverting the vibrant public discourse that is at the foundation of our democracy.

The Court properly rejects that theory, and I join its opinion in full. . . .

■ JUSTICE SCALIA, with whom JUSTICE ALITO joins, and with whom JUSTICE THOMAS joins in part, concurring.

I join the opinion of the Court.

I write separately to address Justice STEVENS' discussion of *"Original Understandings."* This section of the dissent purports to show that today's decision is not supported by the original understanding of the First Amendment. The dissent attempts this demonstration, however, in splendid isolation from the text of the First Amendment. It never shows why "the freedom of speech" that was the right of Englishmen did not include the freedom to speak in association with other individuals, including association in the corporate form. To be sure, in 1791 (as now) corporations could pursue only the objectives set forth in their charters; but the dissent provides no evidence that their speech in the pursuit of those objectives could be censored. . . .

. . . The Framers didn't like corporations, the dissent concludes, and therefore it follows (as night the day) that corporations had no rights of free speech. Of course the Framers' personal affection or disaffection for corporations is relevant only insofar as it can be thought to be reflected in the understood meaning of the text they enacted—not, as the dissent suggests, as a freestanding substitute for that text. . . .

Even if we thought it proper to apply the dissent's approach of excluding from First Amendment coverage what the Founders disliked, and even if we agreed that the Founders disliked founding-era corporations; modern corporations might not qualify for exclusion. Most of the Founders' resentment towards corporations was directed at the state-granted monopoly privileges that individually chartered corporations enjoyed. Modern corporations do not have such privileges, and would probably have been favored by most of our enterprising Founders—excluding, perhaps, Thomas Jefferson and others favoring perpetuation of an agrarian society. Moreover, if the Founders' specific intent with respect to corporations is what matters, why does the dissent ignore the Founders' views about other legal entities that have more in common with modern business corporations than the founding-era corporations? At the time of the founding, religious, educational, and literary corporations were incorporated under general incorporation statutes, much as business corporations are today. There were also small unincorporated business associations, which some have argued were the "true progenitors" of today's business corporations. Were all of these silently excluded from the protections of the First Amendment? . . .

Historical evidence relating to the textually similar clause "the freedom of . . . the press" also provides no support for the proposition that the First Amendment excludes conduct of artificial legal entities from the scope of its protection. The freedom of "the press" was widely understood to protect the publishing activities of individual editors and printers. But these individuals often acted through newspapers, which (much like corporations) had their own names, outlived the individuals who had founded them, could be bought and sold, were sometimes owned by more than one person, and were operated for profit. Their activities were not stripped of First Amendment protection simply because they were carried out under the banner of an artificial legal entity. And the notion which follows from the dissent's view, that modern newspapers, since they are incorporated, have free-speech rights only at the sufferance of Congress, boggles the mind. . . .

The dissent says that when the Framers "constitutionalized the right to free speech in the First Amendment, it was the free speech of individual Americans that they had in mind." That is no doubt true. All the provisions of the Bill of Rights set forth the rights of individual men and women—not, for example, of trees or polar bears. But the individual person's right to speak includes the right to speak *in association with other individual persons*. Surely the dissent does not believe that speech by the Republican Party or the Democratic Party can be censored because it is not the speech of "an individual American." It is the speech of many individual Americans, who have associated in a common cause, giving the leadership of the party the right to speak on their behalf. The association of individuals in a business corporation is no different—or at least it cannot be denied the right to speak on the simplistic ground that it is not "an individual American."

But to return to, and summarize, my principal point, which is the conformity of today's opinion with the original meaning of the First Amendment. The Amendment is written in terms of "speech," not speakers. Its text offers no foothold for excluding any category of speaker, from single individuals to partnerships of individuals, to unincorporated associations of individuals, to incorporated associations of individuals—and the dissent offers no evidence about the original meaning of the text to support any such exclusion. We are therefore simply left with the question whether the speech at issue in this case is "speech" covered by the First Amendment. No one says otherwise. A documentary film critical of a potential Presidential candidate is core political speech, and its nature as such does not change simply because it was funded by a corporation. Nor does the character of that funding produce any reduction whatever in the "inherent worth of the speech" and "its capacity for informing the public," Indeed, to exclude or impede corporate speech is to muzzle the principal agents of the modern free economy. We should celebrate rather than condemn the addition of this speech to the public debate.

■ JUSTICE STEVENS, with whom JUSTICE GINSBURG, JUSTICE BREYER, and JUSTICE SOTOMAYOR join, concurring in part and dissenting in part.

The real issue in this case concerns how, not if, the appellant may finance its electioneering. Citizens United is a wealthy nonprofit corporation that runs a political action committee (PAC) with millions of dollars in assets. Under the Bipartisan Campaign Reform Act of 2002 (BCRA), it could have used those assets to televise and promote *Hillary: The Movie* wherever and whenever it wanted to. It also could have spent unrestricted sums to broadcast *Hillary* at any time other than the 30 days before the last primary election. Neither Citizens United's nor any other corporation's speech has been "banned." All that the parties dispute is whether Citizens United had a right to use the funds in its general treasury to pay for broadcasts during the 30–day period. The notion that the First Amendment dictates an affirmative answer to that question is, in my judgment, profoundly misguided. Even more misguided is the notion that the Court must rewrite the law relating to campaign expenditures by *for-profit* corporations and unions to decide this case.

The basic premise underlying the Court's ruling is its iteration, and constant reiteration, of the proposition that the First Amendment bars regulatory distinctions based on a speaker's identity, including its "identity" as a corporation. While that glittering generality has rhetorical appeal, it is not a correct statement of the law. Nor does it tell us when a corporation may engage in electioneering that some of its shareholders oppose. It does not even resolve the specific question whether Citizens United may be required to finance some of its messages with the money in its PAC. The conceit that corporations must be treated identically to natural persons in the political sphere is not only inaccurate but also inadequate to justify the Court's disposition of this case.

In the context of election to public office, the distinction between corporate and human speakers is significant. Although they make enormous contributions to our society, corporations are not actually members of it. They cannot vote or run for office. Because they may be managed and controlled by nonresidents, their interests may conflict in fundamental respects with the interests of eligible voters. The financial resources, legal structure, and instrumental orientation of corporations raise legitimate concerns about their role in the electoral process. Our lawmakers have a compelling constitutional basis, if not also a democratic duty, to take measures designed to guard against the potentially deleterious effects of corporate spending in local and national races.

The majority's approach to corporate electioneering marks a dramatic break from our past. Congress has placed special limitations on campaign spending by corporations ever since the passage of the Tillman Act in 1907, ch. 420, 34 Stat. 864. We have unanimously concluded that this "reflects a permissible assessment of the dangers posed by those entities to the electoral process," *FEC v. National Right to Work Comm.*, 459 U.S. 197 (1982) (*NRWC*), and have accepted the "legislative judgment that the special characteristics of the corporate structure require particularly careful regulation," *id.*, at 209–210. The Court today rejects a century of history when it treats the distinction between corporate and individual campaign spending as an invidious novelty born of *Austin v. Michigan Chamber of Commerce.* . . .

III

Identity–Based Distinctions

The second pillar of the Court's opinion is its assertion that "the Government cannot restrict political speech based on the speaker's . . . identity." The case on which it relies for this proposition is *First Nat. Bank of Boston v. Bellotti*, 435 U.S. 765 (1978). As I shall explain, the holding in that case was far narrower than the Court implies. Like its paeans to unfettered discourse, the Court's denunciation of identity-based distinctions may have rhetorical appeal but it obscures reality.

"Our jurisprudence over the past 216 years has rejected an absolutist interpretation" of the First Amendment. *WRTL*, 551 U.S., at 482 (opinion of ROBERTS, C.J.). The First Amendment provides that "Congress shall make no law . . . abridging the freedom of speech, or of the press." Apart perhaps from measures designed to protect the press, that text might seem to permit no distinctions of any kind. Yet in a variety of contexts, we have held that speech can be regulated differentially on account of the speaker's identity, when identity is understood in categorical or institutional terms. The Government routinely places special restrictions on the speech rights of students, prisoners, members of the Armed Forces, foreigners, and its own employees. When such restrictions are justified by a legitimate governmental interest, they do not necessarily raise constitutional problems. In contrast to the blanket rule that the majority espouses, our cases recognize that the Government's interests may be more or less compelling with respect to different classes of speakers. . . .

The election context is distinctive in many ways, and the Court, of course, is right that the First Amendment closely guards political speech. But in this context, too, the authority of legislatures to enact viewpoint-neutral regulations based on content and identity is well settled. . . .

The same logic applies to this case with additional force because it is the identity of corporations, rather than individuals, that the Legislature has taken into account. As we have unanimously observed, legislatures are entitled to decide "that the special characteristics of the corporate structure require particularly careful regulation" in an electoral context. Not only has the distinctive potential of corporations to corrupt the electoral process long been recognized, but within the area of campaign finance, corporate spending is also "furthest from the core of political expression, since corporations' First Amendment speech and association interests are derived largely from those of their members and of the public in receiving information," *Beaumont*, 539 U.S., at 161, n. 8. Campaign finance distinctions based on corporate identity tend to be less worrisome, in other words, because the "speakers" are not natural persons, much less members of our political community, and the governmental interests are of the highest order. Furthermore, when corporations, as a class, are distinguished from noncorporations, as a class, there is a lesser risk that regulatory distinctions will reflect invidious discrimination or political favoritism.

If taken seriously, our colleagues' assumption that the identity of a speaker has *no* relevance to the Government's ability to regulate political speech would lead to some remarkable conclusions. Such an assumption would have accorded the propaganda broadcasts to our troops by "Tokyo Rose" during World War II the same protection as speech by Allied commanders. More pertinently, it would appear to afford the same protection to multinational corporations controlled by foreigners as to individual Americans: To do otherwise, after all, could "enhance the relative voice" of some (*i.e.*, humans) over others (*i.e.*, nonhumans). Under the majority's view, I suppose it may be a First Amendment problem that corporations are not permitted to vote, given that voting is, among other things, a form of speech.

In short, the Court dramatically overstates its critique of identity-based distinctions, without ever explaining why corporate identity demands the same treatment as individual identity. Only the most wooden approach to the First Amendment could justify the unprecedented line it seeks to draw.

Our First Amendment Tradition

A third fulcrum of the Court's opinion is the idea that *Austin* and *McConnell* are radical outliers, "aberration[s]," in our First Amendment tradition. See infra (professing fidelity to "our law and our tradition"). The Court has it exactly backwards. It is today's holding that is the radical departure from what had been settled First Amendment law. To see why, it is useful to take a long view.

1. *Original Understandings*

Let us start from the beginning. The Court invokes "ancient First Amendment principles," and original understandings, to defend today's ruling, yet it makes only a perfunctory attempt to ground its analysis in the principles or understandings of those who drafted and ratified the Amendment. Perhaps this is because there is not a scintilla of evidence to support the notion that anyone believed it would preclude regulatory distinctions based on the corporate form. To the extent that the Framers' views are discernible and relevant to the disposition of this case, they would appear to cut strongly against the majority's position.

This is not only because the Framers and their contemporaries conceived of speech more narrowly than we now think of it, see Bork, Neutral Principles and Some First Amendment Problems, 47 Ind. L.J. 1, 22 (1971), but also because they held very different views about the nature of the First Amendment right and the role of corporations in society. Those few corporations that existed at the founding were authorized by grant of a special legislative charter. Corporate sponsors would petition the legislature, and the legislature, if amenable, would issue a charter that specified the corporation's powers and purposes and "authoritatively fixed the scope and content of corporate organization," including "the internal structure of the corporation." Corporations were created, supervised, and conceptualized as quasi-public entities, "designed to serve a social function for the state." It was "assumed that [they] were legally privileged organizations that had to be closely scrutinized by the legislature because their purposes had to be made consistent with public welfare."

The individualized charter mode of incorporation reflected the "cloud of disfavor under which corporations labored" in the early years of this Nation. Thomas Jefferson famously fretted that corporations would subvert the Republic. General incorporation statutes, and widespread acceptance of business corporations as socially useful actors, did not emerge until the 1800's.

The Framers thus took it as a given that corporations could be comprehensively regulated in the service of the public welfare. Unlike our colleagues, they had little trouble distinguishing corporations from human beings, and when they constitutionalized the right to free speech in the First Amendment, it was the free speech of individual Americans that they had in mind. While individuals might join together to exercise their speech rights, business corporations, at least, were plainly not seen as facilitating such associational or expressive ends. . . . In light of these background practices and understandings, it seems to me implausible that the Framers believed "the freedom of speech" would extend equally to all corporate speakers, much less that it would preclude legislatures from taking limited measures to guard against corporate capture of elections. . . .

IV

. . . The majority recognizes that *Austin* and *McConnell* may be defended on anticorruption, antidistortion, and shareholder protection rationales. It badly errs both in explaining the nature of these rationales, which overlap and complement each other, and in applying them to the case at hand.

The Anticorruption Interest

Undergirding the majority's approach to the merits is the claim that the only "sufficiently important governmental interest in preventing corruption or the appearance of corruption" is one that is "limited to quid pro quo corruption." . . . While it is true that we have not always spoken about corruption in a clear or consistent voice, the approach taken by the majority cannot be right, in my judgment. It disregards our constitutional history and the fundamental demands of a democratic society.

On numerous occasions we have recognized Congress' legitimate interest in preventing the money that is spent on elections from exerting an "undue influence on an officeholder's judgment" and from creating "the appearance of such influence," beyond the sphere of quid pro quo relationships. Corruption can take many forms. Bribery may be the paradigm case. But the difference between selling a vote and selling access is a matter of degree, not kind. And selling access is not qualitatively different from giving special preference to those who spent money on one's behalf. Corruption operates along a spectrum, and the majority's apparent belief that quid pro quo arrangements can be neatly demarcated from other improper influences does not accord with the theory or reality of politics. It certainly does not accord with the record Congress developed in passing BCRA, a record that stands as a remarkable testament to the energy and ingenuity with which corporations, unions, lobbyists, and politicians may go about scratching each other's backs—and which amply supported Congress' determination to target a limited set of especially destructive practices.

The District Court that adjudicated the initial challenge to BCRA pored over this record. In a careful analysis, Judge Kollar–Kotelly made numerous findings about the corrupting consequences of corporate and union independent expenditures in the years preceding BCRA's passage. As summarized in her own words:

> "The factual findings of the Court illustrate that corporations and labor unions routinely notify Members of Congress as soon as they air electioneering communications relevant to the Members' elections. The record also indicates that Members express appreciation to organizations for the airing of these election-related advertisements. Indeed, Members of Congress are particularly grateful when negative issue advertisements are run by these organizations, leaving the candidates free to run positive advertisements and be seen as 'above the fray.' Political consultants testify that campaigns are quite aware of who is running advertisements on the candidate's behalf, when they are being run, and where they are being run. Likewise, a prominent lobbyist testifies that these organizations use issue advocacy as a means to influence various Members of Congress.
>
> "The Findings also demonstrate that Members of Congress seek to have corporations and unions run these advertisements on their behalf. The Findings show that Members suggest that corporations or individuals make donations to interest groups with the understanding that the money contributed to these groups will assist the Member in a campaign. After the election, these organizations often seek credit for their support. . . . Finally, a large majority of Americans (80%) are of the view that corporations and other organizations that engage in electioneering communications, which benefit specific elected officials, receive special consideration from those officials when matters arise that affect these corporations and organizations." *Id.*, at 623–624.

Many of the relationships of dependency found by Judge Kollar–Kotelly seemed to have a *quid pro quo* basis, but other arrangements were more subtle. Her analysis shows the great difficulty in delimiting the precise scope of the *quid pro quo* category, as well as the adverse consequences that *all* such arrangements may have. There are threats of corruption that are far more destructive to a democratic society than the odd bribe. Yet the majority's understanding of corruption would leave lawmakers impotent to address all but the most discrete abuses. . . .

Quid Pro Quo Corruption

There is no need to take my side in the debate over the scope of the anticorruption interest to see that the Court's merits holding is wrong. Even under the majority's "crabbed view of corruption," *McConnell*, 540 U.S., at 152, the Government should not lose this case. . . .

Although the Court suggests that *Buckley* compels its conclusion, *Buckley* cannot sustain this reading. It is true that, in evaluating FECA's ceiling on independent expenditures by all persons, the *Buckley* Court found the governmental interest in preventing corruption "inadequate." 424 U.S., at 45. But *Buckley* did not evaluate corporate expenditures specifically, nor did it rule out the possibility that a future Court might find otherwise. The opinion reasoned that an expenditure limitation covering only express advocacy (*i.e.*, magic words) would likely be ineffectual, a problem that Congress tackled in BCRA, and it concluded that "the independent advocacy restricted by [FECA § 608(e)(1)] *does not presently appear* to pose dangers of real or apparent corruption comparable to those identified with large campaign contributions." . . .

Corporations, as a class, tend to be more attuned to the complexities of the legislative process and more directly affected by tax and appropriations measures that receive little public scrutiny; they also have vastly more money with which to try to buy access and votes. See Supp. Brief for Appellee 17 (stating that the Fortune 100 companies earned revenues of $13.1 trillion during the last election cycle). Business corporations must engage the political process in instrumental terms if they are to maximize shareholder value. The unparalleled resources, professional lobbyists, and single-minded focus they bring to this effort, I believe, make *quid pro quo* corruption and its appearance inherently more likely when they (or their conduits or trade groups) spend unrestricted sums on elections.

. . . The legislative and judicial proceedings relating to BCRA generated a substantial body of evidence suggesting that, as corporations grew more and more adept at crafting "issue ads" to help or harm a particular candidate, these nominally independent expenditures began to corrupt the political process in a very direct sense. The sponsors of these ads were routinely granted special access after the campaign was over; "candidates and officials knew who their friends were." Many corporate independent expenditures, it seemed, had become essentially interchangeable with direct contributions in their capacity to generate *quid pro quo* arrangements. In an age in which money and television ads are the coin of the campaign realm, it is hardly surprising that corporations deployed these ads to curry favor with, and to gain influence over, public officials. . . .

Austin and Corporate Expenditures

   1. *Antidistortion*

The fact that corporations are different from human beings might seem to need no elaboration, except that the majority opinion almost completely elides it. *Austin* set forth some of the basic differences. Unlike natural persons, corporations have "limited liability" for their owners and managers, "perpetual life," separation of ownership and control, "and favorable treatment of the accumulation and distribution of assets . . . that enhance their ability to attract capital and to deploy their resources in ways that maximize the return on their shareholders' investments." Unlike voters in U.S. elections, corporations may be foreign controlled. Unlike other interest groups, business corporations have been "effectively delegated responsibility for ensuring society's economic welfare"; they inescapably structure the life of every citizen. "[T]he resources in the treasury of a business corporation," furthermore, "are not an indication of popular support for the corporation's political ideas." "They reflect instead the economically motivated decisions of investors and customers. The availability of these resources may make a corporation a formidable political presence, even though the power of the corporation may be no reflection of the power of its ideas."

It might also be added that corporations have no consciences, no beliefs, no feelings, no thoughts, no desires. Corporations help structure and facilitate the activities of human beings, to be sure, and their "personhood" often serves as a useful legal fiction. But they are not themselves members of "We the People" by whom and for whom our Constitution was established. . . .

It is an interesting question "who" is even speaking when a business corporation places an advertisement that endorses or attacks a particular candidate. Presumably it is not the customers or employees, who typically have no say in such matters. It cannot realistically be said to be the shareholders, who tend to be far removed from the day-to-day decisions of the firm and whose political preferences may be opaque to management. Perhaps the officers or directors of the corporation have the best claim to be the ones speaking, except their fiduciary duties generally prohibit them from using corporate funds for personal ends. . . . Take away the ability to use general treasury funds for some of those ads, and no one's autonomy, dignity, or political equality has been impinged upon in the least.

Corporate expenditures are distinguishable from individual expenditures in this respect. I have taken the view that a legislature may place reasonable restrictions on individuals' electioneering expenditures in the service of the governmental interests explained above, and in recognition of the fact that such restrictions are not direct restraints on speech but rather on its financing. But those restrictions concededly present a tougher case, because the primary conduct of actual, flesh-and-blood persons is involved. Some of those individuals might feel that they need to spend large sums of money on behalf of a particular candidate to vindicate the intensity of their electoral preferences. This is obviously not the situation with business corporations, as their routine practice of giving "substantial sums to *both* major national parties" makes pellucidly clear. "[C]orporate participation" in elections, any business executive will tell you, "is more transactional than ideological." Supp. Brief for Committee for Economic Development as *Amicus Curiae* 10.

In this transactional spirit, some corporations have affirmatively urged Congress to place limits on their electioneering communications. These corporations fear that officeholders will shake them down for supportive ads, that they will have to spend increasing sums on elections in an ever-escalating arms race with their competitors, and that public trust in business will be eroded. A system that effectively forces corporations to use their shareholders' money both to maintain access to, and to avoid retribution from, elected officials may ultimately prove more harmful than beneficial to many corporations. It can impose a kind of implicit tax.

. . . Recognizing the weakness of a speaker-based critique of *Austin*, the Court places primary emphasis not on the corporation's right to electioneer, but rather on the listener's interest in hearing what every possible speaker may have to say. The Court's central argument is that laws such as § 203 have "deprived [the electorate] of information, knowledge and opinion vital to its function," and this, in turn, "interferes with the 'open marketplace' of ideas protected by the First Amendment."

There are many flaws in this argument. If the overriding concern depends on the interests of the audience, surely the public's perception of the value of corporate speech should be given important weight. . . .

In a state election such as the one at issue in *Austin*, the interests of nonresident corporations may be fundamentally adverse to the interests of local voters. Consequently, when corporations grab up the prime broadcasting slots on the eve of an election, they can flood the market with advocacy that bears "little or no correlation" to the ideas of natural persons or to any broader notion of the public good. The opinions of real people may be marginalized. "The expenditure restrictions of [2 U.S.C.] § 441b are thus meant to ensure that competition among actors in the political arena is truly competition among ideas."

In addition to this immediate drowning out of noncorporate voices, there may be deleterious effects that follow soon thereafter. Corporate "domination" of electioneering can generate the impression that corporations dominate our democracy. When citizens turn on their televisions and radios before an election and hear only corporate electioneering, they may lose faith in their capacity, as citizens, to influence public policy. A Government captured by corporate interests, they may come to believe, will be neither responsive to their needs nor willing to give their views a fair hearing. The predictable result is cynicism and disenchantment: an increased perception that large spenders "call the tune" and a reduced "willingness of voters to take part in democratic governance." . . . At the least, I stress again, a legislature is entitled to credit these concerns and to take tailored measures in response. . . .

In critiquing *Austin*'s antidistortion rationale and campaign finance regulation more generally, our colleagues place tremendous weight on the example of media corporations. Yet it is not at all clear that *Austin* would permit § 203 to be applied to them. The press plays a unique role not only in the text, history, and structure of the First Amendment but also in facilitating public discourse; as the *Austin* Court explained, "media corporations differ significantly from other corporations in that their resources are devoted to the collection of information and its dissemination to the public," 494 U.S., at 667. Our colleagues have raised some interesting and difficult questions about Congress' authority to regulate electioneering by the press, and about how to define what constitutes the press. *But that is not the case before us.* Section 203 does not apply to media corporations, and even if it did, Citizens United is not a media corporation. . . .

2. Shareholder Protection

There is yet another way in which laws such as § 203 can serve First Amendment values. Interwoven with *Austin*'s concern to protect the integrity of the electoral process is a concern to protect the rights of shareholders from a kind of coerced speech: electioneering expenditures that do not "reflec[t] [their] support." When corporations use general treasury funds to praise or attack a particular candidate for office, it is the shareholders, as the residual claimants, who are effectively footing the bill. Those shareholders who disagree with the corporation's electoral message may find their financial investments being used to undermine their political convictions. . . .

I would affirm the judgment of the District Court.

■ JUSTICE THOMAS, concurring in part and dissenting in part.

I join all but Part IV of the Court's opinion. . . .

I dissent from Part IV of the Court's opinion . . . because the Court's constitutional analysis does not go far enough. The disclosure, disclaimer, and reporting requirements in BCRA §§ 201 and 311 are also unconstitutional.

Congress may not abridge the "right to anonymous speech" based on the "simple interest in providing voters with additional relevant information," *McIntyre v. Ohio Elections Comm'n*, 514 U.S. 334, 348 (1995)). In continuing to hold otherwise, the Court misapprehends the import of "recent events" that some *amici* describe "in which donors to certain causes were blacklisted, threatened, or otherwise targeted for retaliation." The Court properly recognizes these events as "cause for concern," but fails to acknowledge their constitutional significance. . . .

Amici's examples relate principally to Proposition 8, a state ballot proposition that California voters narrowly passed in the 2008 general election. Proposition 8 amended California's constitution to provide that "[o]nly marriage between a man and a woman is valid or recognized in California." Cal. Const., Art. I, § 7.5. Any donor who gave more than $100 to any committee supporting or opposing Proposition 8 was required to disclose his full name, street address, occupation, employer's name (or business name, if self-employed), and the total amount of his contributions. The California Secretary of State was then required to post this information on the Internet.

Some opponents of Proposition 8 compiled this information and created Web sites with maps showing the locations of homes or businesses of Proposition 8 supporters. Many supporters (or their customers) suffered property damage, or threats of physical violence or death, as a result. They cited these incidents in a complaint they filed after the 2008 election, seeking to invalidate California's mandatory disclosure laws. Supporters recounted being told: "Consider yourself lucky. If I had a gun I would have gunned you down along with each and every other supporter," or, "we have plans for you and your friends." Proposition 8 opponents also allegedly harassed the measure's supporters by defacing or damaging their property. Two religious organizations supporting Proposition 8 reportedly received through the mail envelopes containing a white powdery substance.

Those accounts are consistent with media reports describing Proposition 8–related retaliation. The director of the nonprofit California Musical Theater gave $1,000 to support the initiative; he was forced to resign after artists complained to his employer. The director of the Los Angeles Film Festival was forced to resign after giving $1,500 because opponents threatened to boycott and picket the next festival. And a woman who had managed her popular, family-owned restaurant for 26 years was forced to resign after she gave $100, because "throngs of [angry] protesters" repeatedly arrived at the restaurant and "shout[ed] 'shame on you' at customers." The police even had to "arriv[e] in riot gear one night to quell the angry mob" at the restaurant. Some supporters of Proposition 8 engaged in similar tactics; one real estate businessman in San Diego who had donated to a group opposing Proposition 8 "received a letter from the Prop. 8 Executive Committee threatening to publish his company's name if he didn't also donate to the 'Yes on 8' campaign."

The success of such intimidation tactics has apparently spawned a cottage industry that uses forcibly disclosed donor information to *pre-empt* citizens' exercise of their First Amendment rights. Before the 2008 Presidential election, a "newly formed nonprofit group . . . plann[ed] to confront donors to conservative groups, hoping to create a chilling effect that will dry up contributions." Luo, Group Plans Campaign Against G.O.P. Donors, N.Y. Times, Aug. 8, 2008, p. A15. Its leader, "who described his effort as 'going for the jugular,'" detailed the group's plan to send a "warning letter . . . alerting donors who might be considering giving to right-wing groups to a variety of potential dangers, including legal trouble, public exposure and watchdog groups digging through their lives."

These instances of retaliation sufficiently demonstrate why this Court should invalidate mandatory disclosure and reporting requirements. But *amici* present evidence of yet another reason to do so—the threat of retaliation from *elected officials*. As *amici*'s submissions make clear, this threat extends far beyond a single ballot proposition in California. For example, a candidate challenging an incumbent state attorney general reported that some members of the State's business community feared donating to his campaign because they did not want to cross the incumbent; in his words, "I go to so many people and hear the same thing: 'I sure hope you beat [the incumbent], but I can't afford to have my name on your records. He might come after me next.' " Strassel, Challenging Spitzerism at the Polls, Wall Street Journal, Aug. 1, 2008, p. A11. The incumbent won reelection in 2008.

My point is not to express any view on the merits of the political controversies I describe. Rather, it is to demonstrate—using real-world, recent examples—the fallacy in the Court's conclusion that "[d]isclaimer and disclosure requirements . . . impose no ceiling on campaign-related activities, and do not prevent anyone from speaking." Of course they do. Disclaimer and disclosure requirements enable private citizens and elected officials to implement political strategies *specifically calculated* to curtail campaign-related activity and prevent the lawful, peaceful exercise of First Amendment rights. . . .

[T]he Court's promise that as-applied challenges will adequately protect speech is a hollow assurance. Now more than ever, §§ 201 and 311 will chill protected speech because—as California voters can attest—"the advent of the Internet" enables "prompt disclosure of expenditures," which "provide[s]" political opponents "with the information needed" to intimidate and retaliate against their foes. Thus, "disclosure permits citizens . . . to react to the speech of [political opponents] in a proper"—or undeniably *improper*—"way" long before a plaintiff could prevail on an as-applied challenge.

I cannot endorse a view of the First Amendment that subjects citizens of this Nation to death threats, ruined careers, damaged or defaced property, or pre-emptive and threatening warning letters as the price for engaging in "core political speech, the 'primary object of First Amendment protection.' " Accordingly, I respectfully dissent from the Court's judgment upholding BCRA §§ 201 and 311.

NOTES

1. Does either the majority or the dissent offer a coherent theory as to which constitutional rights may be exercised by entities in corporate form, and which may not? Compare these cases—

Berea College v. Kentucky, 211 U.S. 45 (1908) (upholding, against an Equal Protection Clause challenge, criminal penalties for a private religious school that taught black and white students together, on the ground that the school was a corporation);

Late Corporation of Jesus Christ of Latter–Day Saints v. United States, 136 U.S. 1 (1890) (upholding federal statute disbanding the Mormon Church and seizing most of its property, on the ground that it was a corporation);

Western & Southern Life Ins. Co. v. California Bd. of Equalization, 451 U.S. 648, 656 (1981) (holding that the Privileges and Immunities Clause of Article IV does not apply to corporations)

—with these cases—

id. (holding that the Equal Protection and negative Commerce Clauses protect corporations);

Santa Clara County v. Southern Pac. R. Co., 118 U.S. 394 (holding that due process applies to corporations);

44 Liquormart, Inc. v. Rhode Island, 517 U.S. 484 (1996) (protecting the commercial speech of a corporation);

Corporation of Presiding Bishop v. Amos, 483 U.S. 327 (1987) (implicitly holding that Free Exercise Clause protects corporations);

Upjohn Co. v. United States, 449 U.S. 383 (1981) (applying attorney-client privilege to a corporation);

Marshall v. Barlow's, Inc., 436 U.S. 307 (1978) (applying Fourth Amendment protections to corporation);

New York Times v. Sullivan, 376 U.S. 254 (1964) (applying Free Press Clause to a corporation).

Kaiser Aetna v. United States, 444 U. S. 164 (1979) (applying Takings Clause of the Fifth Amendment to corporations).

2. Can the dissent be understood not as resting on the corporate form of the speaker, but on the belief that *Buckley* was wrong to grant free speech protection to so-called "independent expenditures"? Note that the dissent does not appear to deny free speech protection to corporations when they engage in lobbying, genuine issues ads, or other political speech outside the context of elections. Why not? And if it is true, as the dissent says, that "corporate independent expenditures [have] become essentially interchangeable with direct contributions in their capacity to generate *quid pro quo* arrangements," why isn't that equally true of non-corporate independent expenditures? Recall that the distinction between contributions and independent expenditures was drawn in *Buckley v. Valeo*. Is the dissenting position in *Citizens United* predicated on rejecting that distinction? Recall also that the dissenters in *Citizens United* scolded the majority for overturning two precedents, *Austin* and *McConnell*. What is the role for *stare decisis* in this area?

3. What is the dissent's position on non-profit corporations, wholly-owned corporations, limited partnerships, and the like? What about unions?

4. The majority purports not to address foreign-owned corporations. Does the logic of the opinion permit banning their election expenditures? How about election expenditures by foreign governments?

5. The majority leaves in place the ban on corporate contributions to candidates. How, given its logic, can that be justified?

6. The majority stresses that if corporations cannot publish their views about candidates prior to elections, this would interfere with the ability of media corporations, such as newspapers, to publish editorial endorsements, which is clearly constitutionally protected. See *Mills v. Alabama*, 384 U.S. 214 (1966) (striking down state statute forbidding a newspaper owned by a corporation from endorsing or opposing a candidate on election day). How does the dissent respond? One might respond that media corporations have special protection under the Free Press Clause, but is that so? The Court has consistently rejected the claim that media corporations have special rights under the Press Clause, holding instead that the clause protects the right of all persons, including the lonely pamphleteer, to publish their views to the public. See Eugene Volokh, *"The Freedom . . . of the Press," from 1791 to 1868 to Now—Freedom for the*

Press as an Industry, or the Press as a Technology?, 160 U. Pa. L. Rev. 459 (2011). If that is an accurate statement of the law, is the dissent saying that corporations have no constitutional right to own newspapers that endorse or denounce candidates in an election campaign?

For that matter, why wasn't this case litigated under the Free Press Clause? Isn't a documentary a form of "the press"? Suppose the New York Times Company produces a broadcast or video-on-demand version of its editorial page, in which journalists discuss the reasons behind the newspaper's editorial positions, including its candidate endorsements. Could it be prohibited from airing such a program within sixty days of an election? Why is Citizens United any different? Because it is not a "media corporation"? Why isn't it? It makes documentaries. What more is needed to be a "media corporation"?

7. The majority was much criticized for reaching out for the broadest possible holding in this case. The plaintiffs did not ask the Court to overrule *Austin* and *McConnell*. The Court on its own motion ordered reargument on the broader theory. Was that inappropriate?

8. The majority declined to defer to Congress's findings or judgment about campaign finance because of the danger that members of Congress have an incentive to write rules to favor incumbents. The dissent says there is no basis in the record for this fear. What do you think? Do campaign finance laws in general, and the rules against electioneering communications in particular, favor incumbents? What are the obstacles to a relatively unknown challenger raising the money for a successful campaign? Do incumbents experience those obstacles to the same degree? Does this matter to the First Amendment question?

9. Maybe it is a mistake to view campaign contributions primarily as an attempt by the contributions to influence or persuade. Maybe they are a form of extortion by officeholders. "Unless you contribute to my campaign, I will use government power to punish you." See Fred S. McChesney, Money for Nothing: Politics, Rent Extraction, and Political Extortion (1997). If that is so, does it affect your view of the First Amendment issues?

A Note on Campaign Finance Cases in the 2011 Term

The Supreme Court summarily decided two cases related to campaign finance and the First Amendment during the 2011 Term of Court. A summary decision is rendered without oral argument, and generally means that the decision was governed by clear precedent. Often these decisions are issued "per curiam" (a term that means the opinion is not attributed to any particular author), and sometimes without an opinion. If there is no opinion, the holding of the court is the narrowest reading of the lower court decision that would support the judgment.

1. A unanimous Court summarily affirmed the decision of a three-judge district court in *Bluman v. Federal Election Commission*, 800 F. Supp. 2d 281 (D.D.C. 2011), aff'd, 132 S. Ct. 1087 (2011), without an opinion. The lower court had upheld the constitutionality of 2 U.S.C. 441e(a), which prohibits foreign citizens who are not lawful permanent residents of the United States from contributing to candidates for federal political office and making independent expenditures in support of or opposition to such candidates. The lower court relied on what it called the "straightforward principle" that "[i]t is fundamental to the definition of our national political community that foreign citizens do not

have a constitutional right to participate in, and thus may be excluded from, activities of democratic self-government." The court relied on precedents permitting discrimination against non-citizens when the exclusion is related to democratic self-government—such as laws excluding aliens from serving as public school teachers, police officers, or jurors. It also relied on the four-justice dissent in *Citizens United*, which invoked the prohibition on independent expenditures by foreign citizens as an argument against the majority's view that speaker-based exclusions from freedom of speech are generally unconstitutional.

Do you believe the decision in *Bluman* can be squared with the rationale of *Citizens United*? What, precisely, are the free speech rights of foreigners? The lower court stated that it did "not decide whether Congress could prohibit foreign nationals from engaging in speech other than contributions to candidates and parties, express-advocacy expenditures, and donations to outside groups to be used for contributions to candidates and parties and express-advocacy expenditures." What is the answer to that question?

2. Over four dissents, the Court summarily reversed a decision by the Montana Supreme Court upholding a ban on corporate campaign expenditures, stating that "Montana's arguments in support of the judgment below either were already rejected in *Citizens United*, or fail to meaningfully distinguish that case." *American Tradition Partnership v. Bullock*, 132 S. Ct. 2490 (2012). The Montana court held that the state of Montana had a long history of political corruption through corporate influence, which justified the ban. Three *Citizens United* dissenters once again dissented, joined by Justice Kagan (who had taken the place on the Court of the fourth dissenter in *Citizens United*, Justice Stevens). They said that "Montana's experience, like considerable experience elsewhere since the Court's decision in *Citizens United*, casts grave doubt on the Court's supposition that independent expenditures do not corrupt or appear to do so." Was *Citizens United* based on a contrary view? Was *Buckley*?

[*Assignment 49*]

J. PUBLIC FORUM DOCTRINE

A great deal of private speech occurs on public property: street demonstrations, sidewalk protests, prayer services in parks, speeches on the town square. Do Americans have a right to use public property for purposes of assembly, or is this just a privilege the government is entitled to grant or deny?

Commonwealth v. Davis
162 Mass. 510 (1895)

[William Davis was convicted for delivering a sermon on the Boston Common in violation of this city ordinance: "No person shall, in or upon any of the public grounds, make any public address, discharge any cannon or firearm, expose for sale any goods, wares or merchandise, erect or maintain any booth stand, tent, or apparatus for the purposes of public amusement or show, except in accordance with a permit from the mayor."—Editors]

■ HOLMES, J.

... There is no evidence before us to show that the power of the legislature over the common is less than its power over any other park dedicated to the use of the public, or over public streets, the legal title to which is in a city or town. As representative of the public, it may and does exercise control over the use which the public may make of such places, and it may and does delegate more or less of such control to the city or town immediately concerned. For the legislature absolutely or conditionally to forbid public speaking in a highway or public park is no more an infringement of the rights of a member of the public than for the owner of a private house to forbid it in his house. When no proprietary rights interfere, the legislature may end the right of the public to enter upon the public place by putting an end to the dedication to public uses. So it may take the less[er] step of limiting the public use to certain purposes.

... It is argued that the ordinance really is directed especially against free preaching of the gospel in public places, as certain western ordinances, seemingly general, have been held to be directed against the Chinese. But we have no reason to believe, and do not believe, that this ordinance was passed for any other than its ostensible purpose, namely, as a proper regulation of the use of public grounds.

[This decision was affirmed unanimously by the U.S. Supreme Court in Davis v. Massachusetts, 167 U.S. 43 (1897).—Editors]

Hague v. CIO

307 U.S. 496 (1939)

[The Committee for Industrial Organization, which organized workers into labor unions and informed workers of their rights under the National Labor Relations Act, sought to hold outdoor meetings on public property in Jersey City, New Jersey. City ordinances required permits for holding outdoor meetings. City officials refused to issue permits to the CIO, arguing that they were Communists who advocated the overthrow of the government. CIO members proceeded without permits and were arrested. The CIO sued, arguing that the ordinances were facially unconstitutional and that the city had enforced them in a discriminatory fashion. The district court found for the CIO, concluding that the city had no legitimate basis for refusing to issue the permits. The court of appeals affirmed.—Editors]

■ MR. JUSTICE ROBERTS delivered an opinion in which MR. JUSTICE BLACK concurred [and in which MR. CHIEF JUSTICE HUGHES concurred in pertinent part].

By their specifications of error, the petitioners ... assert that the court erred in holding that the street meeting ordinance is unconstitutional on its face, and that it has been unconstitutionally administered ...

[The respondents' rights were infringed by the city] unless, as petitioners contend, the city's ownership of streets and parks is as absolute as one's ownership of his home, with consequent power altogether to exclude citizens from the use thereof, or unless, though the city holds the streets in trust for public use, the absolute denial of their use to the respondents is a valid exercise of the police power.

The findings of fact negative the latter assumption. In support of the former the petitioners rely upon *Davis v. Massachusetts*, 167 U.S. 43 (1897). There it appeared that, pursuant to enabling legislation, the city of Boston adopted an ordinance prohibiting anyone from speaking, discharging fire arms, selling goods, or maintaining any booth for public amusement on any of the public grounds of the city except under a permit from the Mayor. Davis spoke on Boston Common without a permit and without applying to the Mayor for one. He was charged with a violation of the ordinance and moved to quash the complaint, inter alia, on the ground that the ordinance abridged his privileges and immunities as a citizen of the United States and denied him due process of law because it was arbitrary and unreasonable. His contentions were overruled and he was convicted. The judgment was affirmed by the Supreme Court of Massachusetts and by this court.

The decision seems to be grounded on the holding of the State court that the Common 'was absolutely under the control of the legislature', and that it was thus 'conclusively determined there was no right in the plaintiff in error to use the common except in such mode and subject to such regulations as the legislature, in its wisdom, may have deemed proper to prescribe.' The Court added that the Fourteenth Amendment did not destroy the power of the states to enact police regulations as to a subject within their control or enable citizens to use public property in defiance of the constitution and laws of the State.

The ordinance there in question apparently had a different purpose from that of the one here challenged, for it was not directed solely at the exercise of the right of speech and assembly, but was addressed as well to other activities, not in the nature of civil rights, which doubtless might be regulated or prohibited as respects their enjoyment in parks. In the instant case the ordinance deals only with the exercise of the right of assembly for the purpose of communicating views entertained by speakers, and is not a general measure to promote the public convenience in the use of the streets or parks.

We have no occasion to determine whether, on the facts disclosed, [*Davis*] was rightly decided, but we cannot agree that it rules the instant case. Wherever the title of streets and parks may rest, they have immemorially been held in trust for the use of the public and, time out of mind, have been used for purposes of assembly, communicating thoughts between citizens, and discussing public questions. Such use of the streets and public places has, from ancient times, been a part of the privileges, immunities, rights, and liberties of citizens. The privilege of a citizen of the United States to use the streets and parks for communication of views on national questions may be regulated in the interest of all; it is not absolute, but relative, and must be exercised in subordination to the general comfort and convenience, and in consonance with peace and good order; but it must not, in the guise of regulation, be abridged or denied.

We think the court below was right in holding the ordinance quoted in Note 1 void upon its face. It does not make comfort or convenience in the use of streets or parks the standard of official action. It enables the Director of Safety to refuse a permit on his mere opinion that such refusal will prevent 'riots, disturbances or disorderly assemblage.' It can thus, as the record discloses, be made the instrument of arbitrary suppression of free expression of views on national affairs for the prohibition of all speaking will undoubtedly 'prevent' such eventualities. But uncontrolled official suppression of the privilege cannot be made a substitute for the duty to maintain order in connection with the exercise of the right . . .

■ [Concurring opinions by CHIEF JUSTICE HUGHES and JUSTICES STONE and REED, and dissenting opinions by JUSTICES MCREYNOLDS and BUTLER, are omitted.]

NOTES

1. What support is there for the Court's declaration that public streets and parks have been used for purposes of assembly, communication, and discussion "time out of mind"? Was this true in Britain? In light of the unanimous decision in *Davis*, was it true in the United States? Consider two possible alternative explanations for the holding. First, could the Assembly Clause of the First Amendment be understood to imply a right to assemble in public spaces? Where else could "the people" assemble? Second, there is some support for the idea that certain public property is indeed held in trust for use by the public— even if, this right did not extend to assemblies for purposes of speech. This is called "the public trust doctrine." After enactment of the First Amendment, one might argue that a law singling out speech for special prohibition is not a regulation of access to public property, but one abridging the freedom of speech.

2. Did the *Hague* Court properly distinguish *Davis*? Or are the decisions inconsistent?

3. In *Greer v. Spock*, 424 U.S. 828 (1976), the Court upheld a rule barring speeches and demonstrations of a partisan political nature on military bases, such as by candidates for political office. The Court held that military bases are non-public forums, and that the rule was "objectively and evenhandedly applied." In *Lehman v. City of Shaker Heights*, 418 U.S. 298 (1974), the Court upheld a rule allowing private persons to purchase advertising space on public buses, but excluding political advertisements. A four-justice plurality reasoned that the bus advertising space is not a forum for speech, and that the restriction need only be reasonable and viewpoint neutral. A fifth justice—Justice Douglas—reasoned that because bus riders are a captive audience the government had an interest in protecting the right of bus riders "to be free from forced intrusions on their privacy." In *Jones v. North Carolina Prisoners Union*, 433 U.S. 119 (1977), the Court upheld a prison policy that prohibited the solicitation of prisoners to join a labor union, as well as labor union meetings, but allowed meetings by "service organizations" such as the Jaycees, Alcoholics Anonymous, and the Boy Scouts. Then came the following case:

Perry Education Association v. Perry Local Educators Association

460 U.S. 37 (1983)

■ JUSTICE WHITE delivered the opinion of the Court.

Perry Education Association is the duly elected exclusive bargaining representative for the teachers of the Metropolitan School District of Perry Township, Ind. A collective-bargaining agreement with the Board of Education provided that Perry Education Association, but no other union, would have access to the interschool mail system and teacher mailboxes in the Perry Township schools. The issue in this case is whether the denial of similar access to the Perry Local Educators' Association, a rival teacher group, violates the First and Fourteenth Amendments.

I

The Metropolitan School District of Perry Township, Ind., operates a public school system of 13 separate schools. Each school building contains a set of mailboxes for the teachers. Interschool delivery by school employees permits messages to be delivered rapidly to teachers in the district. The primary function of this internal mail system is to transmit official messages among the teachers and between the teachers and the school administration. In addition, teachers use the system to send personal messages and individual school building principals have allowed delivery of messages from various private organizations. Local parochial schools, church groups, YMCAs, and Cub Scout units have used the system. The record does not indicate whether any requests for use have been denied, nor does it reveal whether permission must separately be sought for every message that a group wishes delivered to the teachers.—*[Text relocated from footnote.— Editors]*

Prior to 1977, both the Perry Education Association (PEA) and the Perry Local Educators' Association (PLEA) represented teachers in the school district and apparently had equal access to the interschool mail system. In 1977, [PEA was elected as exclusive representative, as provided by state law.]

The Board permits a school district to provide access to communication facilities to the union selected for the discharge of the exclusive representative duties of representing the bargaining unit and its individual members without having to provide equal access to rival unions. Following the election, PEA and the school district [contracted for] PEA "access to teachers' mailboxes in which to insert material" and the right to use the interschool mail delivery system to the extent that the school district incurred no extra expense by such use. The labor agreement noted that these access rights were being accorded to PEA "acting as the representative of the teachers" and went on to stipulate that these access rights shall not be granted to any other "school employee organization"—a term of art defined by Indiana law to mean "any organization which has school employees as members and one of whose primary purposes is representing school employees in dealing with their employer." . . .

The exclusive access policy applies only to use of the mailboxes and school mail system. PLEA is not prevented from using other school facilities to communicate with teachers. PLEA may post notices on school bulletin boards; may hold meetings on school property after school hours; and may, with approval of the building principals, make announcements on the public address system. Of course, PLEA also may communicate with teachers by word of mouth, telephone, or the United States mail. Moreover, under Indiana law, the preferential access of the bargaining agent may continue only while its status as exclusive representative is insulated from challenge. While a representation contest is in progress, unions must be afforded equal access to such communication facilities. . . .

III

. . . There is no question that constitutional interests are implicated by denying PLEA use of the interschool mail system. "It can hardly be argued that either students or teachers shed their constitutional rights to freedom of speech or expression at the schoolhouse gate." *Tinker v. Des Moines School District.* The First Amendment's guarantee of free speech applies to teacher's mailboxes as surely as it does elsewhere within the school, and on sidewalks outside, *Police Department of Chicago v. Mosley*. But this is not to say that the First Amendment requires equivalent access to all parts of a school building in which some form of communicative activity occurs. "Nowhere [have we] suggested that students, teachers, or anyone else has an absolute constitutional right to use all parts of a school building or its immediate environs for . . . unlimited expressive purposes." The existence of a right of access to public property and the standard by which limitations upon such a right must be evaluated differ depending on the character of the property at issue.

A

In places which by long tradition or by government fiat have been devoted to assembly and debate, the rights of the state to limit expressive activity are sharply circumscribed. At one end of the spectrum are streets and parks which "have immemorially been held in trust for the use of the public, and, time out of mind, have been used for purposes of assembly, communicating thoughts between citizens, and discussing public questions." *Hague v. CIO*. In these quintessential public forums, the government may not prohibit all communicative activity. For the state to enforce a content-based exclusion it must show that its regulation is necessary to serve a compelling state interest and that it is narrowly drawn to achieve that end. The state may also enforce regulations of the time, place, and manner of expression which are content-neutral, are narrowly tailored to serve a significant government interest, and leave open ample alternative channels of communication.

A second category consists of public property which the state has opened for use by the public as a place for expressive activity. The Constitution forbids a state to enforce certain exclusions from a forum generally open to the public even if it was not required to create the forum in the first place. *Widmar v. Vincent* (university meeting facilities); *City of Madison Joint School District v. Wisconsin Public Employment Relations Comm'n* (school board meeting); *Southeastern Promotions, Ltd. v. Conrad* (municipal theater).[7] Although a state is not required to indefinitely retain the open character of the facility, as long as it does so it is bound by the same standards as apply in a traditional public forum. Reasonable time, place and manner regulations are permissible, and a content-based prohibition must be narrowly drawn to effectuate a compelling state interest.

Public property which is not by tradition or designation a forum for public communication is governed by different standards. We have recognized that the "First Amendment does not guarantee access to property simply because it is owned or controlled by the government." In addition to time, place, and manner regulations, the state may reserve the forum for its intended purposes, communicative or otherwise, as long as the regulation on speech is reasonable and not an effort to suppress expression merely because public officials oppose the speaker's view. As we have stated on several occasions, "the State, no less than a private owner of property, has power to preserve the property under its control for the use to which it is lawfully dedicated."

The school mail facilities at issue here fall within this third category. The Court of Appeals recognized that Perry School District's interschool mail system is not a traditional public forum: "We do not hold that a

---

[7] A public forum may be created for a limited purpose such as use by certain groups, or for the discussion of certain subjects.

school's internal mail system is a public forum in the sense that a school board may not close it to all but official business if it chooses." On this point the parties agree. Nor do the parties dispute that, as the District Court observed, the "normal and intended function [of the school mail facilities] is to facilitate internal communication of school related matters to teachers." The internal mail system, at least by policy, is not held open to the general public. It is instead PLEA's position that the school mail facilities have become a "limited public forum" from which it may not be excluded because of the periodic use of the system by private non-school connected groups, and PLEA's own unrestricted access to the system prior to PEA's certification as exclusive representative.

Neither of these arguments is persuasive. The use of the internal school mail by groups not affiliated with the schools is no doubt a relevant consideration. If by policy or by practice the Perry School District has opened its mail system for indiscriminate use by the general public, then PLEA could justifiably argue a public forum has been created. This, however, is not the case. As the case comes before us, there is no indication in the record that the school mailboxes and interschool delivery system are open for use by the general public. Permission to use the system to communicate with teachers must be secured from the individual building principal. There is no court finding or evidence in the record which demonstrates that this permission has been granted as a matter of course to all who seek to distribute material. We can only conclude that the schools do allow some outside organizations such as the YMCA, Cub Scouts, and other civic and church organizations to use the facilities. This type of selective access does not transform government property into a public forum. In *Greer v. Spock*, the fact that other civilian speaker and entertainers had sometimes been invited to appear at Fort Dix did not convert the military base into a public forum. And in *Lehman v. Shaker Heights*, a plurality of the Court concluded that a city transit system's rental of space in its vehicles for commercial advertising did not require it to accept partisan political advertising.

Moreover, even if we assume that by granting access to the Cub Scouts, YMCAs, and parochial schools, the school district has created a "limited" public forum, the constitutional right of access would in any event extend only to other entities of similar character. While the school mail facilities thus might be a forum generally open for use by the Girl Scouts, the local boys' club and other organizations that engage in activities of interest and educational relevance to students, they would not as a consequence be open to an organization such as PLEA, which is concerned with the terms and conditions of teacher employment.

PLEA also points to its ability to use the school mailboxes and delivery system on an equal footing with PEA prior to the collective bargaining agreement signed in 1978. Its argument appears to be that the access policy in effect at that time converted the school mail facilities into a limited public forum generally open for use by employee organizations, and that once this occurred, exclusions of employee organizations thereafter must be judged by the constitutional standard applicable to public forums. The fallacy in the argument is that it is not the forum, but PLEA itself, which has changed. Prior to 1977, there was no exclusive representative for the Perry school district teachers. PEA and PLEA each represented its own members. Therefore the school district's policy of allowing both organizations to use the school mail facilities simply reflected the fact that both unions represented the teachers and had legitimate reasons for use of the system.

PLEA's previous access was consistent with the school district's preservation of the facilities for school-related business, and did not constitute creation of a public forum in any broader sense.

Because the school mail system is not a public forum, the School District had no "constitutional obligation per se to let any organization use the school mail boxes." In the Court of Appeals' view, however, the access policy adopted by the Perry schools favors a particular viewpoint, that of the PEA, on labor relations, and consequently must be strictly scrutinized regardless of whether a public forum is involved. There is, however, no indication that the school board intended to discourage one viewpoint and advance another. We believe it is more accurate to characterize the access policy as based on the *status* of the respective unions rather than their views. Implicit in the concept of the nonpublic forum is the right to make distinctions in access on the basis of subject matter and speaker identity. These distinctions may be impermissible in a public forum but are inherent and inescapable in the process of limiting a nonpublic forum to activities compatible with the intended purpose of the property. The touchstone for evaluating these distinctions is whether they are reasonable in light of the purpose which the forum at issue serves.

B

The differential access provided PEA and PLEA is reasonable because it is wholly consistent with the district's legitimate interest in "preserv[ing] the property . . . for the use to which it is lawfully dedicated." Use of school mail facilities enables PEA to perform effectively its obligations as exclusive representative of *all* Perry Township teachers. Conversely, PLEA does not have any official responsibility in connection with the school district and need not be entitled to the same rights of access to school mailboxes . . . Moreover, exclusion of the rival union may reasonably be considered a means of insuring labor-peace within the schools. The policy "serves to prevent the District's schools from becoming a battlefield for inter-union squabbles."

The Court of Appeals accorded little or no weight to PEA's special responsibilities. In its view these responsibilities, while justifying PEA's access, did not justify denying equal access to PLEA. The Court of Appeals would have been correct if a public forum were involved here. But the internal mail system is not a public forum. As we have already stressed, when government property is not dedicated to open communication the government may—without further justification—restrict use to those who participate in the forum's official business.

Finally, the reasonableness of the limitations on PLEA's access to the school mail system is also supported by the substantial alternative channels that remain open for union-teacher communication to take place. These means range from bulletin boards to meeting facilities to the United States mail. During election periods, PLEA is assured of equal access to all modes of communication. There is no showing here that PLEA's ability to communicate with teachers is seriously impinged by the restricted access to the internal mail system. The variety and type of alternative modes of access present here compare favorably with those in other non-public forum cases where we have upheld restrictions on access. See, *e.g. Greer v. Spock* (servicemen free to attend political rallies off-base); *Pell v. Procunier* (prison inmates may communicate with media by mail and through visitors).

IV

The Court of Appeals also held that the differential access provided the rival unions constituted impermissible content discrimination in violation of the Equal Protection Clause of the Fourteenth Amendment. We have rejected this contention when cast as a First Amendment argument, and it fares no better in equal protection garb. . . .

■ JUSTICE BRENNAN, with whom JUSTICE MARSHALL, JUSTICE POWELL, and JUSTICE STEVENS join, dissenting.

The Court today holds that an incumbent teachers' union may negotiate a collective bargaining agreement with a school board that grants the incumbent access to teachers' mailboxes and to the interschool mail system and denies such access to a rival union. Because the exclusive access provision in the collective bargaining agreement amounts to viewpoint discrimination that infringes the respondents' First Amendment rights and fails to advance any substantial state interest, I dissent.

I

. . . Based on a finding that the interschool mail system is not a "public forum," the Court states that the respondents have no right of access to the system, and that the school board is free "to make distinctions in access on the basis of subject matter and speaker identity," if the distinctions are "reasonable in light of the purpose which the forum at issue serves." According to the Court, the petitioner's status as the exclusive bargaining representative provides a reasonable basis for the exclusive access policy.

The Court fundamentally misperceives the essence of the respondents' claims. . . . This case does not involve an "absolute access" claim. It involves an "equal access" claim. As such it does not turn on whether the internal school mail system is a "public forum." In focusing on the public forum issue, the Court disregards the First Amendment's central proscription against censorship, in the form of viewpoint discrimination, in any forum, public or nonpublic. . . .

Once the government permits discussion of certain subject matter, it may not impose restrictions that discriminate among viewpoints on those subjects whether a nonpublic forum is involved or not. This prohibition is implicit in the *Mosley* line of cases, in *Tinker*, and in those cases in which we have approved content-based restrictions on access to government property that is not a public forum. We have never held that government may allow discussion of a subject and then discriminate among viewpoints on that particular topic, even if the government for certain reasons may entirely exclude discussion of the subject from the forum. In this context, the greater power does not include the lesser because for First Amendment purposes exercise of the lesser power is more threatening to core values. Viewpoint discrimination is censorship in its purest form and government regulation that discriminates among viewpoints threatens the continued vitality of "free speech."

Against this background, it is clear that the Court's approach to this case is flawed. By focusing on whether the interschool mail system is a public forum, the Court disregards the independent First Amendment protection afforded by the prohibition against viewpoint discrimination. This case does not involve a claim of an absolute right of access to the forum to discuss any subject whatever. If it did, public forum analysis might be relevant. This case involves a claim of equal access to discuss a subject that the board has approved for discussion in the forum. In essence, the respondents are not asserting a right of access at all; they are asserting a right to be free from discrimination. The critical inquiry, therefore, is whether the board's grant of exclusive access to the petitioner amounts to prohibited viewpoint discrimination.

II

The Court addresses only briefly the respondents' claim that the exclusive access provision amounts to viewpoint discrimination. In rejecting this claim, the Court starts from the premise that the school mail system is not a public forum and that, as a result, the board has no obligation to grant access to the respondents. The Court then suggests that there is no indication that the board intended to discourage one viewpoint and to advance another. In the Court's view, the exclusive access policy is based on the status of the respective parties rather than on their views. The Court then states that "implicit in the concept of the nonpublic forum is the right to make distinctions in access on the basis of subject matter and speaker identity." According to the Court, "these distinctions may be impermissible in a public forum but are inherent and inescapable in the process of limiting a nonpublic forum to activities compatible with the intended purpose of the property."

As noted, whether the school mail system is a public forum or not the board is prohibited from discriminating among viewpoints on particular subjects. Moreover, whatever the right of public authorities to impose content-based restrictions on access to government property that is a nonpublic forum, once access is granted to one speaker to discuss a certain subject access may not be denied to another speaker based on his viewpoint. Regardless of the nature of the forum, the critical inquiry is whether the board has engaged in prohibited viewpoint discrimination.

The Court responds to the allegation of viewpoint discrimination by suggesting that there is no indication that the board intended to discriminate and that the exclusive access policy is based on the parties' status rather than on their views. In this case, for the reasons discussed below, the intent to discriminate can be inferred from the effect of the policy, which is to deny an effective channel of communication to the respondents, and from other facts in the case. In addition, the petitioner's status has nothing to do with whether viewpoint discrimination in fact has occurred. If anything, the petitioner's status is relevant to the question of whether the exclusive access policy can be justified, not to whether the board has discriminated among viewpoints.

Addressing the question of viewpoint discrimination directly, free of the Court's irrelevant public forum analysis, it is clear that the exclusive access policy discriminates on the basis of viewpoint. The Court of Appeals found that "the access policy adopted by the Perry schools, in form a speaker restriction, favors a particular viewpoint on labor relations in the Perry schools . . . the teachers inevitably will receive from [the petitioner] self-laudatory descriptions of its activities on their behalf and will be denied the critical perspective offered by [the respondents]." This assessment of the effect of the policy is eminently reasonable. Moreover, certain other factors strongly suggest that the policy discriminates among viewpoints.

On a practical level, the only reason for the petitioner to seek an exclusive access policy is to deny its rivals access to an effective channel of communication. No other group is explicitly denied access to the mail system. In fact, as the Court points out, many other groups have been granted access to the system. Apparently, access is denied to the respondents because of the likelihood of their expressing points of view different from the petitioner's on a range of subjects. The very argument the petitioner advances in support of the policy, the need to preserve labor peace, also indicates that the access policy is not viewpoint-neutral.

In short, the exclusive access policy discriminates against the respondents based on their viewpoint. The board has agreed to amplify the speech of the petitioner, while repressing the speech of the respondents based on the respondents' point of view. This sort of discrimination amounts to censorship and infringes the First Amendment rights of the respondents. In this light, the policy can survive only if the petitioner can justify it. . . .

[Justice Brennan's discussion of governmental justifications is omitted.—Editors]

Because the grant to the petitioner of exclusive access to the internal school mail system amounts to viewpoint discrimination that infringes the respondents' First Amendment rights and because the petitioner has failed to show that the policy furthers any substantial state interest, the policy must be invalidated as violative of the First Amendment . . .

NOTES

1. Look carefully at footnote 7. Is it consistent with the three-part forum analysis set forth in the text? In the context of a designated public forum, must limitations based on subject matter satisfy strict scrutiny? What about limitations favoring one group over another? Does this footnote collapse designated forums into nonpublic forums?

Perhaps it would be helpful to use a different vocabulary for the third category—what the Court calls a "non-public forum." Would it be helpful to call this a "selective forum"—one in which the government allows private speech only insofar as that speech affirmatively advances the government's own purposes? A selective forum may be contrasted with a genuine public forum, in which private speakers are entitled to speak on subjects of their own choosing and for their own purposes. What should be the standard for evaluating limits on a genuine "designated public forum"? How would *Perry, Jones, Lehman,* and *Greer* come out under this analysis?

2. Can you tell the difference between speaker-based discrimination and viewpoint-based discrimination? Are those overlapping or separate categories? Which is this?

Rosenberger v. Rector and Visitors
of University of Virginia
515 U.S. 819 (1995)

■ JUSTICE KENNEDY delivered the opinion of the Court.

The University of Virginia, an instrumentality of the Commonwealth for which it is named and thus bound by the First and Fourteenth Amendments, authorizes the payment of outside contractors for the printing costs of a variety of student publications. It withheld any authorization for payments on behalf of petitioners for the sole reason that their student paper "primarily promotes or manifests a particular belie[f] in or about a deity or an ultimate reality." That the paper did promote or manifest views within the defined exclusion seems plain enough. The challenge is to the University's regulation and its denial of authorization, the case raising issues under the Speech and Establishment Clauses of the First Amendment.

I

The public corporation we refer to as the "University" is denominated by state law as "the Rector and Visitors of the University of Virginia," . . . Founded by Thomas Jefferson in 1819, and ranked by him, together with the authorship of the Declaration of Independence and of the Virginia Act for Religious Freedom, as one of his proudest achievements, the University is among the Nation's oldest and most respected seats of higher learning. It has more than 11,000 undergraduate students, and 6,000 graduate and professional students. An understanding of the case requires a somewhat detailed description of the program the University created to support extracurricular student activities on its campus.

Before a student group is eligible to submit bills from its outside contractors for payment by the fund described below, it must become a "Contracted Independent Organization" (CIO). CIO status is available to any group the majority of whose members are students, whose managing officers are fulltime students, and that complies with certain procedural requirements. A CIO must file its constitution with the University; must pledge not to discriminate in its membership; and must include in dealings with third parties and in all written materials a disclaimer, stating that the CIO is independent of the University and that the University is not responsible for the CIO. CIO's enjoy access to University facilities, including meeting rooms and computer terminals. A standard agreement signed between each CIO and the University provides that the benefits and opportunities afforded to CIO's "should not be misinterpreted as meaning that those organizations are part of or controlled by the University, that the University is responsible for the organizations' contracts or other acts or omissions, or that the University approves of the organizations' goals or activities."

All CIO's may exist and operate at the University, but some are also entitled to apply for funds from the Student Activities Fund (SAF). Established and governed by University Guidelines, the purpose of the SAF is to support a broad range of extracurricular student activities that "are related to the educational purpose of the University." The SAF is based on the University's "recogni[tion]" that the availability of a wide range of opportunities" for its students "tends to enhance the University environment." The Guidelines require that it be administered "in a manner consistent with the educational purpose of the University as well as with state and federal law." The SAF receives its money from a mandatory fee of $14 per semester assessed to each full-time student. The Student Council, elected by the students, has the initial authority to disburse the funds, but its actions are subject to review by a faculty body chaired by a designee of the Vice President for Student Affairs.

Some, but not all, CIO's may submit disbursement requests to the SAF. The Guidelines recognize 11 categories of student groups that may seek payment to third-party contractors because they "are related to the educational purpose of the University of Virginia." One of these is "student news, information, opinion, entertainment, or academic communications media groups." The Guidelines also specify, however, that the costs of certain activities of CIO's that are otherwise eligible for funding will not be reimbursed by the SAF. The student activities that are excluded from SAF support are religious activities, philanthropic contributions and activities, political activities, activities that would jeopardize the University's tax-exempt status, those which involve payment of honoraria or similar fees, or social entertainment or related expenses. The prohibition on "political activities" is defined so that it is limited to electioneering and lobbying. The Guidelines provide that "[t]hese restrictions on funding political activities are not intended to preclude funding of any otherwise eligible student organization which . . . espouses particular positions or ideological viewpoints, including those that may be unpopular or are not generally accepted." A "religious activity," by contrast, is defined as any activity that "primarily promotes or manifests a particular belie[f] in or about a deity or an ultimate reality."

The Guidelines prescribe these criteria for determining the amounts of third-party disbursements that will be allowed on behalf of each eligible student organization: the size of the group, its financial self-sufficiency, and the University-wide benefit of its activities. If an organization seeks SAF support, it must submit its bills to the Student Council, which pays the organization's creditors upon determining that the expenses are appropriate. No direct payments are made to the student groups. During the 1990–1991 academic year, 343 student groups qualified as CIO's. One hundred thirty-five of them applied for support from the SAF, and 118 received funding. Fifteen of the groups were funded as "student news, information, opinion, entertainment, or academic communications media groups."

Petitioners' organization, Wide Awake Productions (WAP), qualified as a CIO. Formed by petitioner Ronald Rosenberger and other undergraduates in 1990, WAP was established "[t]o publish a magazine of philosophical and religious expression," "[t]o facilitate discussion which fosters an atmosphere of sensitivity to and tolerance of Christian viewpoints," and "[t]o provide a unifying focus for Christians of multicultural backgrounds." WAP publishes Wide Awake: A Christian Perspective at the University of Virginia. The paper's Christian viewpoint was evident from the first issue, in which its editors wrote that the journal "offers a Christian perspective on both personal and community issues, especially those relevant to college students at the University of Virginia." The editors committed the paper to a two-fold mission: "to challenge Christians to live, in word and deed, according to the faith they proclaim and to encourage students to consider what a personal relationship with Jesus Christ means." The first issue had articles about racism, crisis pregnancy, stress, prayer, C.S. Lewis' ideas about evil and free will, and reviews of religious music. In the next two issues, Wide Awake featured stories about homosexuality, Christian missionary work, and eating disorders, as well as music reviews and interviews with University professors. Each page of Wide Awake, and the end of each article or review, is marked by a cross. The advertisements carried in Wide Awake also reveal the Christian perspective of the journal. For the most part, the advertisers are churches, centers for Christian study, or Christian bookstores. By June 1992, WAP had distributed about 5,000 copies of Wide Awake to University students, free of charge.

WAP had acquired CIO status soon after it was organized. This is an important consideration in this case, for had it been a "religious organization," WAP would not have been accorded CIO status. As defined by the Guidelines, a "[r]eligious [o]rganization" is "an organization whose purpose is to practice a devotion to an acknowledged ultimate reality or deity." At no stage in this controversy has the University contended that WAP is such an organization.

A few months after being given CIO status, WAP requested the SAF to pay its printer $5,862 for the costs of printing its newspaper. The Appropriations Committee of the Student Council denied WAP's request on the ground that Wide Awake was a "religious activity" within the meaning of the Guidelines, *i.e.,* that the newspaper "promote[d] or manifest[ed] a particular belie[f] in or about a deity or an ultimate reality." It made its determination after examining the first issue. WAP appealed the denial to the full Student Council, contending that WAP met all the applicable Guidelines and that denial of SAF support on the basis of the magazine's religious perspective violated the Constitution. The appeal was denied without further comment, and WAP appealed to the next level, the Student Activities Committee. In a letter signed by the Dean of Students, the committee sustained the denial of funding.

Having no further recourse within the University structure, WAP, Wide Awake, and three of its editors and members filed suit in the United States District Court for the Western District of Virginia . . . They alleged that refusal to authorize payment of the printing costs of the publication, solely on the basis of its religious editorial viewpoint, violated their rights to freedom of speech and press, to the free exercise of religion, and to equal protection of the law. They relied also upon Article I of the Virginia Constitution and the Virginia Act for Religious Freedom, but did not pursue those theories on appeal. The suit sought damages for the costs of printing the paper, injunctive and declaratory relief, and attorney's fees.

On cross-motions for summary judgment, the District Court ruled for the University, holding that denial of SAF support was not an impermissible content or viewpoint discrimination against petitioners' speech, and that the University's Establishment Clause concern over its "religious activities" was a sufficient justification for denying payment to third-party contractors . . .

[T]he Fourth Circuit . . . held that the Guidelines did discriminate on the basis of content. It ruled that, while the State need not underwrite speech, there was a presumptive violation of the Speech Clause when viewpoint discrimination was invoked to deny third-party payment otherwise available to CIO's. . . *[Nevertheless, the Court of Appeals affirmed on Establishment Clause grounds.—Editors]*

II

It is axiomatic that the government may not regulate speech based on its substantive content or the message it conveys. Other principles follow from this precept. In the realm of private speech or expression, government regulation may not favor one speaker over another. Discrimination against speech because of its message is presumed to be unconstitutional. These rules informed our determination that the government offends the First Amendment when it imposes financial burdens on certain speakers based on the content of their expression. When the government targets not subject matter, but particular views taken by speakers on a subject, the violation of the First Amendment is all the more blatant. Viewpoint discrimination is thus an egregious form of content discrimination. The government must abstain from regulating speech when the specific motivating ideology or the opinion or perspective of the speaker is the rationale for the restriction.

These principles provide the framework forbidding the State to exercise viewpoint discrimination, even when the limited public forum is one of its own creation. In a case involving a school district's provision of school facilities for private uses, we declared that "[t]here is no question that the District, like the private owner of property, may legally preserve the property under its control for the use to which it is dedicated." *Lamb's Chapel v. Center Moriches Union Free School Dist.*, 508 U.S. 384, 390 (1993). The necessities of confining a forum to the limited and legitimate purposes for which it was created may justify the State in reserving it for certain groups or for the discussion of certain topics. Once it has opened a limited forum, however, the State must respect the lawful boundaries it has itself set. The State may not exclude speech where its distinction is not "reasonable in light of the purpose served by the forum," nor may it discriminate against speech on the basis of its viewpoint. Thus, in determining whether the State is acting to preserve the limits of the forum it has created so that the exclusion of a class of speech is legitimate, we have observed a distinction between, on the one hand, content discrimination, which may be permissible if it preserves the purposes of that limited forum, and, on the other hand, viewpoint discrimination, which is presumed impermissible when directed against speech otherwise within the forum's limitations.

The SAF is a forum more in a metaphysical than in a spatial or geographic sense, but the same principles are applicable. The most recent and most apposite case is our decision in *Lamb's Chapel*. There, a school district had opened school facilities for use after school hours by community groups for a wide variety of social, civic, and recreational purposes. The district, however, had enacted a formal policy against opening facilities to groups for religious purposes. Invoking its policy, the district rejected a request from a group desiring to show a film series addressing various child-rearing questions from a "Christian perspective." There was no indication in the record in *Lamb's Chapel* that the request to use the school facilities was "denied, for any reason other than the fact that the presentation would have been from a religious perspective." Our conclusion was unanimous: "[I]t discriminates on the basis of viewpoint to permit school property to be used for the presentation of all views about family issues and childrearing except those dealing with the subject matter from a religious standpoint."

The University does acknowledge (as it must in light of our precedents) that "ideologically driven attempts to suppress a particular point of view are presumptively unconstitutional in funding, as in other contexts," but insists that this case does not present that issue because the Guidelines draw lines based on content, not viewpoint. As we have noted, discrimination against one set of views or ideas is but a subset or particular instance of the more general phenomenon of content discrimination. And, it must be acknowledged, the distinction is not a precise one. It is, in a sense, something of an understatement to speak of religious thought and discussion as just a viewpoint, as distinct from a comprehensive body of thought. The nature of our origins and destiny and their dependence upon the existence of a divine being have been subjects of philosophic inquiry throughout human history. We conclude, nonetheless, that here, as in *Lamb's Chapel*, viewpoint discrimination is the proper way to interpret the University's objections to Wide Awake. By the very terms of the SAF prohibition, the University does not exclude religion as a subject matter but selects for disfavored treatment those student journalistic efforts with religious editorial viewpoints. Religion may be a vast area of inquiry, but it also provides, as it did here, a specific premise, a perspective, a standpoint from which a variety of subjects may be discussed and considered. The prohibited perspective, not the general subject matter, resulted in the refusal to make third-party payments, for the subjects discussed were otherwise within the approved category of publications.

The dissent's assertion that no viewpoint discrimination occurs because the Guidelines discriminate against an entire class of viewpoints reflects an insupportable assumption that all debate is bipolar and that antireligious speech is the only response to religious speech. Our understanding of the complex and multifaceted nature of public discourse has not embraced such a contrived description of the marketplace of ideas. If the topic of debate is, for example, racism, then exclusion of several views on that problem is just as offensive to the First Amendment as exclusion of only one. It is as objectionable to exclude both a theistic and an atheistic perspective on the debate as it is to exclude one, the other, or yet another political, economic, or social viewpoint. The dissent's declaration that debate is not skewed so long as multiple voices are silenced is simply wrong; the debate is skewed in multiple ways.

The University's denial of WAP's request for third-party payments in the present case is based upon viewpoint discrimination not unlike the discrimination the school district relied upon in *Lamb's Chapel* and that we found invalid. The church group in *Lamb's Chapel* would have been qualified as a social or civic organization, save for its religious purposes. Furthermore, just as the school district in *Lamb's Chapel* pointed to nothing but the religious views of the group as the rationale for excluding its message, so in this case the University justifies its denial of SAF participation to WAP on the ground that the contents of Wide Awake reveal an avowed religious perspective. It bears only passing mention that the dissent's attempt to distinguish *Lamb's Chapel* is entirely without support in the law. Relying on the transcript of oral argument, the dissent seems to argue that we found viewpoint discrimination in that case because the government excluded Christian, but not atheistic, viewpoints from being expressed in the forum there. The Court relied on no such distinction in holding that discriminating against religious speech was discriminating on the basis of viewpoint. There is no indication in the opinion of the Court (which, unlike an advocate's statements at oral argument, is the law) that exclusion or inclusion of other religious or antireligious voices from that forum had any bearing on its decision.

The University tries to escape the consequences of our holding in *Lamb's Chapel* by urging that this case involves the provision of funds rather than access to facilities. The University begins with the unremarkable proposition that the State must have substantial discretion in determining how to allocate scarce resources to accomplish its educational mission. Citing our decisions in *Rust v. Sullivan* (1991), *Regan v. Taxation with Representation of Wash.* (1983), and *Widmar v. Vincent* (1981), the University argues that content-based funding decisions are both inevitable and lawful. Were the reasoning of *Lamb's Chapel* to apply to funding decisions as well as to those involving access to facilities, it is urged, its holding "would become a judicial juggernaut, constitutionalizing the ubiquitous content-based decisions that schools, colleges, and other government entities routinely make in the allocation of public funds."

To this end the University relies on our assurance in *Widmar v. Vincent.* There, in the course of striking down a public university's exclusion of religious groups from use of school facilities made available to all other student groups, we stated: "Nor do we question the right of the University to make academic judgments as to how best to allocate scarce resources."

The quoted language in *Widmar* was but a proper recognition of the principle that when the State is the speaker, it may make content-based choices. When the University determines the content of the education it provides, it is the University speaking, and we have permitted the government to regulate the content of what is or is not expressed when it is the speaker or when it enlists private entities to convey its own message. In the same vein, in *Rust v. Sullivan,* we upheld the government's prohibition on abortion-related advice applicable to recipients of federal funds for family planning counseling. There, the government did not create a program to encourage private speech but instead used private speakers to transmit specific information pertaining to its own program. We recognized that when the government appropriates public funds to promote a particular policy of its own it is entitled to say what it wishes. When the government disburses public funds to private entities to convey a governmental message, it may take legitimate and appropriate steps to ensure that its message is neither garbled nor distorted by the grantee.

It does not follow, however, and we did not suggest in *Widmar,* that viewpoint-based restrictions are proper when the University does not itself speak or subsidize transmittal of a message it favors but instead expends funds to encourage a diversity of views from private speakers. A holding that the University may not discriminate based on the viewpoint of private persons whose speech it facilitates does not restrict the University's own speech, which is controlled by different principles. For that reason, the University's reliance on *Regan v. Taxation with Representation of Wash.* is inapposite as well. *Regan* involved a challenge to Congress' choice to grant tax deductions for contributions made to veterans' groups engaged in lobbying, while denying that favorable status to other charities which pursued lobbying efforts. Although acknowledging that the Government is not required to subsidize the exercise of fundamental rights, we reaffirmed the requirement of viewpoint neutrality in the Government's provision of financial benefits by observing that "[t]he case would be different if Congress were to discriminate invidiously in its subsidies in such a way as to 'ai[m] at the suppression of dangerous ideas,' " *Regan* relied on a distinction based on preferential treatment of certain speakers—veterans' organizations— and not a distinction based on the content or messages of those groups' speech. The University's regulation now before us, however, has a speech-based restriction as its sole rationale and operative principle.

The distinction between the University's own favored message and the private speech of students is evident in the case before us. The University itself has taken steps to ensure the distinction in the agreement each CIO must sign. The University declares that the student groups eligible for SAF support are not the University's agents, are not subject to its control, and are not its responsibility. Having offered to pay the third-party contractors on behalf of private speakers who convey their own messages, the University may not silence the expression of selected viewpoints.

The University urges that, from a constitutional standpoint, funding of speech differs from provision of access to facilities because money is scarce and physical facilities are not. Beyond the fact that in any given case this proposition might not be true as an empirical matter, the underlying premise that the University could discriminate based on viewpoint if demand for space exceeded its availability is wrong as well. The government cannot justify viewpoint discrimination among private speakers on the economic fact of scarcity. Had the meeting rooms in *Lamb's Chapel* been scarce, had the demand been greater than the supply, our decision would have been no different. It would have been incumbent on the State, of course, to ration or allocate the scarce resources on some acceptable neutral principle; but nothing in our decision indicated that scarcity would give the State the right to exercise viewpoint discrimination that is otherwise impermissible.

Vital First Amendment speech principles are at stake here. The first danger to liberty lies in granting the State the power to examine publications to determine whether or not they are based on some ultimate idea and, if so, for the State to classify them. The second, and corollary, danger is to speech from the chilling of individual thought and expression. That danger is especially real in the University setting, where the State acts against a background and tradition of thought and experiment that is at the center of our intellectual and philosophic tradition. In ancient Athens, and, as Europe entered into a new period of intellectual awakening, in places like Bologna, Oxford, and Paris, universities began as voluntary and spontaneous assemblages or concourses for students to speak and to write and to learn. The quality and creative power of student intellectual life to this day remains a vital measure of a school's influence and attainment. For the University, by regulation, to cast disapproval on particular viewpoints of its students risks the suppression of free speech and creative inquiry in one of the vital centers for the Nation's intellectual life, its college and university campuses.

The Guideline invoked by the University to deny third-party contractor payments on behalf of WAP effects a sweeping restriction on student thought and student inquiry in the context of University sponsored publications. The prohibition on funding on behalf of publications that "primarily promot[e] or manifes[t] a particular belie[f] in or about a deity or an ultimate reality," in its ordinary and commonsense meaning, has a vast potential reach. The term "promotes" as used here would comprehend any writing advocating a philosophic position that rests upon a belief in a deity or ultimate reality. See Webster's Third New International Dictionary 1815 (1961) (defining "promote" as "to contribute to the growth, enlargement, or prosperity of: further, encourage"). And the term "manifests" would bring within the scope of the prohibition any writing that is explicable as resting upon a premise that presupposes the existence of a deity or ultimate reality. See *id.,* at 1375 (defining "manifest" as "to show plainly: make palpably evident or certain by showing or displaying"). Were the prohibition applied with much vigor at all, it would bar funding of essays by hypothetical student contributors named Plato, Spinoza, and Descartes. And if the regulation covers, as the University says it does, those student journalistic efforts that primarily manifest or promote a belief that there is no deity and no ultimate reality, then under-graduates named Karl Marx, Bertrand Russell, and Jean–Paul Sartre would likewise have some of their major essays excluded from student publications. If any manifestation of beliefs in first principles disqualifies the writing, as seems to be the case, it is indeed difficult to name renowned thinkers whose writings would be accepted, save perhaps for articles disclaiming all connection to their ultimate philosophy. Plato could contrive perhaps to submit an acceptable essay on making pasta or peanut butter cookies, provided he did not point out their (necessary) imperfections.

Based on the principles we have discussed, we hold that the regulation invoked to deny SAF support, both in its terms and in its application to these petitioners, is a denial of their right of free speech guaranteed by the

First Amendment . . . *[The Court then concluded that the Establishment Clause did not justify the University's viewpoint discrimination.—Editors]*

■ [The concurring opinions of JUSTICES O'CONNOR and THOMAS, and the dissenting opinion of JUSTICE SOUTER, which was joined by JUSTICES STEVENS, GINSBURG, and BREYER, are omitted.]

NOTES

1. Are you persuaded that the same principles should apply to what the Court calls a "metaphysical forum"—meaning cash subsidies—as apply to the use of public real estate? Why or why not?

2. Do you agree that exclusion of "religious activities" is viewpoint-discriminatory? The dissenters essentially argue that a restriction is not viewpoint-discriminatory unless it discriminates *among* religions. So long as Christians, Jews, Buddhists, atheists, and Zoroastrians all are excluded, the dissenters say, there is no problem. Would they take the same position if all religious perspectives were equally *favored*?

3. The majority seems to rely on several details about the University's program: (1) that the funds are paid to the printer rather than to the student group; (2) that the funds come from mandatory student fees rather than from taxes; and (3) that the group was excluded as a religious "activity" rather than as a religious "organization." Do these details matter? Why?

4. The case involved not just free speech questions but also whether funding *Wide Awake* would violate the Establishment Clause. That question will be addressed below.

[Assignment 50]

K. PROTESTS AND DEMONSTRATIONS

Apart from freedom of speech, the Constitution guarantees the "right of the people peaceably to assemble, and to petition for the redress of grievances." The separate clause appears to recognize both the special issues raised by mass public meetings, and the special temptations for government control of this potent method of dissent. Yet the Court's modern cases pay little attention to the Assembly Clause, instead applying (and sometimes modifying) ordinary principles of free speech and press. Recall that in the debate in the First Congress, Representative Sedgwick moved to strike the Assembly Clause, saying that it was unnecessary in light of freedom of speech, but his motion was rejected by a large margin. Has the modern Court done, in effect, what the First Congress declined to do? In the cases that follow, think about whether and why mass public assemblies need special constitutional rules.

Thomas v. Chicago Park District

534 U.S. 316 (2002)

■ SCALIA, J., delivered the opinion for a unanimous Court.

This case presents the question whether a municipal park ordinance requiring individuals to obtain a permit before conducting large-scale events must, consistent with the First Amendment, contain the procedural safeguards described in *Freedman v. Maryland,* 380 U.S. 51 (1965).

I

Respondent, the Chicago Park District (Park District), is responsible for operating public parks and other public property in Chicago. Pursuant to its authority to "establish by ordinance all needful rules and regulations for the government and protection of parks . . . and other property under its jurisdiction," the Park District adopted an ordinance that requires a person to obtain a permit in order to "conduct a public assembly, parade, picnic, or other event involving more than fifty individuals," or engage in an activity such as "creat[ing] or emit[ting] any Amplified Sound." Chicago Park Dist. Code, ch. VII, §§ C.3.a(1), C.3.a(6). The ordinance provides that "[a]pplications for permits shall be processed in order of receipt," § C.5.a, and the Park District must decide whether to grant or deny an application within 14 days unless, by written notice to the applicant, it extends the period an additional 14 days, § C.5.c. Applications can be denied on any of 13 specified grounds. § C.5.e.[1] If the Park District denies an application, it must clearly set forth in writing the grounds for denial and, where feasible, must propose measures to cure defects in the application. When the basis for denial is prior receipt of a competing application for the same time and place, the Park District must suggest alternative times or places. An unsuccessful applicant has seven days to file a written appeal to the General

---

[1] Section C.5.e of the ordinance provides in relevant part:

"To the extent permitted by law, the Park District may deny an application for permit if the applicant or the person on whose behalf the application for permit was made has on prior occasions made material misrepresentations regarding the nature or scope of an event or activity previously permitted or has violated the terms of prior permits issued to or on behalf of the applicant. The Park District may also deny an application for permit on any of the following grounds:

(1) the application for permit (including any required attachments and submissions) is not fully completed and executed;

(2) the applicant has not tendered the required application fee with the application or has not tendered the required user fee, indemnification agreement, insurance certificate, or security deposit within the times prescribed by the General Superintendent;

(3) the application for permit contains a material falsehood or misrepresentation;

(4) the applicant is legally incompetent to contract or to sue and be sued;

(5) the applicant or the person on whose behalf the application for permit was made has on prior occasions damaged Park District property and has not paid in full for such damage, or has other outstanding and unpaid debts to the Park District;

(6) a fully executed prior application for permit for the same time and place has been received, and a permit has been or will be granted to a prior applicant authorizing uses or activities which do not reasonably permit multiple occupancy of the particular park or part hereof;

(7) the use or activity intended by the applicant would conflict with previously planned programs organized and conducted by the Park District and previously scheduled for the same time and place;

(8) the proposed use or activity is prohibited by or inconsistent with the classifications and uses of the park or part thereof designated pursuant to this chapter;

(9) the use or activity intended by the applicant would present an unreasonable danger to the health or safety of the applicant, or other users of the park, of Park District Employees or of the public;

(10) the applicant has not complied or cannot comply with applicable licensure requirements, ordinances or regulations of the Park District concerning the sale or offering for sale of any goods or services;

(11) the use or activity intended by the applicant is prohibited by law, by this Code and ordinances of the Park District, or by the regulations of the General Superintendent. . . ."

Superintendent of the Park District, who must act on the appeal within seven days. If the General Superintendent affirms a permit denial, the applicant may seek judicial review in state court by common-law certiorari.

Petitioners have applied to the Park District on several occasions for permits to hold rallies advocating the legalization of marijuana. The Park District has granted some permits and denied others. Not satisfied, petitioners filed an action pursuant to 42 U.S.C. § 1983 in the United States District Court for the Northern District of Illinois, alleging, *inter alia,* that the Park District's ordinance is unconstitutional on its face. The District Court granted summary judgment in favor of the Park District, and the United States Court of Appeals for the Seventh Circuit affirmed. We granted certiorari.

II

The First Amendment's guarantee of "the freedom of speech, or of the press" prohibits a wide assortment of government restraints upon expression, but the core abuse against which it was directed was the scheme of licensing laws implemented by the monarch and Parliament to contain the "evils" of the printing press in 16th– and 17–century England. The Printing Act of 1662 had "prescribed what could be printed, who could print, and who could sell." It punished the publication of any book or pamphlet without a license and required that all works be submitted for approval to a government official, who wielded broad authority to suppress works that he found to be "heretical, seditious, schismatical, or offensive." The English licensing system expired at the end of the 17th century, but the memory of its abuses was still vivid enough in colonial times that Blackstone warned against the "restrictive power" of such a "licenser"—an administrative official who enjoyed unconfined authority to pass judgment on the content of speech. 4 W. Blackstone, Commentaries on the Laws of England 152 (1769).

In *Freedman v. Maryland,* 380 U.S. 51 (1965), we confronted a state law that enacted a strikingly similar system of prior restraint for motion pictures. It required that every motion picture film be submitted to a Board of Censors before the film was shown anywhere in the State. The board enjoyed authority to reject films that it considered "obscene" or that "tend[ed], in the judgment of the Board, to debase or corrupt morals or incite to crimes," characteristics defined by the statute in broad terms. The statute punished the exhibition of a film not submitted to the board for advance approval, even where the film would have received a license had it been properly submitted. It was no defense that the content of the film was protected by the First Amendment.

We recognized in *Freedman* that a scheme conditioning expression on a licensing body's prior approval of content "presents peculiar dangers to constitutionally protected speech." "[T]he censor's business is to censor," and a licensing body likely will overestimate the dangers of controversial speech when determining, without regard to the film's actual effect on an audience, whether speech is likely "to incite" or to "corrupt [the] morals." In response to these grave "dangers of a censorship system," we held that a film licensing process must contain certain procedural safeguards in order to avoid constituting an invalid prior restraint: "(1) any restraint prior to judicial review can be imposed only for a specified brief period during which the status quo must be maintained; (2) expeditious judicial review of that decision must be available; and (3) the censor must bear the burden of going to court to suppress the speech and must bear the burden of proof once in court."

Petitioners contend that the Park District, like the Board of Censors in *Freedman,* must initiate litigation every time it denies a permit and that the ordinance must specify a deadline for judicial review of a challenge to a permit denial. We reject those contentions. *Freedman* is inapposite because the licensing scheme at issue here is not subject-matter censorship but content-neutral time, place, and manner regulation of the use of a public forum. The Park District's ordinance does not authorize a licensor to pass judgment on the content of speech: None of the grounds for denying a permit has anything to do with what a speaker might say. Indeed, the ordinance (unlike the classic censorship scheme) is not even directed to communicative activity as such, but rather to *all* activity conducted in a public park. The picnicker and soccer player, no less than the political activist or parade marshal, must apply for a permit if the 50–person limit is to be exceeded. And the object of the permit system (as plainly indicated by the permissible grounds for permit denial) is not to exclude communication of a particular content, but to coordinate multiple uses of limited space, to assure preservation of the park facilities, to prevent uses that are dangerous, unlawful, or impermissible under the Park District's rules, and to assure financial accountability for damage caused by the event. As the Court of Appeals well put it: "[T]o allow unregulated access to all comers could easily reduce rather than enlarge the park's utility as a forum for speech."

We have never required that a content-neutral permit scheme regulating speech in a public forum adhere to the procedural requirements set forth in *Freedman.*[5] "A licensing standard which gives an official authority to censor the content of a speech differs *toto coelo* from one limited by its terms, or by nondiscriminatory practice, to considerations of public safety and the like." *Niemotko v. Maryland,* 340 U.S. 268, 282 (1951) (Frankfurter, J., concurring in result). . . . Regulations of the use of a public forum that ensure the safety and convenience of the people are not "inconsistent with civil liberties but . . . [are] one of the means of safeguarding the good order upon which [civil liberties] ultimately depend." *Cox v. New Hampshire,* 312 U.S. 569, 574 (1941). Such a traditional exercise of authority does not raise the censorship concerns that prompted us to impose the extraordinary procedural safeguards on the film licensing process in *Freedman.*

III

Of course even content-neutral time, place, and manner restrictions can be applied in such a manner as to stifle free expression. Where the licensing official enjoys unduly broad discretion in determining whether to grant or deny a permit, there is a risk that he will favor or disfavor speech based on its content. We have thus required that a time, place, and manner regulation contain adequate standards to guide the official's decision and render it subject to effective judicial review. Petitioners contend that the Park District's ordinance fails this test.

We think not. As we have described, the Park District may deny a permit only for one or more of the reasons set forth in the ordinance. See n. 1, *supra.* It may deny, for example, when the application is incomplete or contains a material falsehood or misrepresentation; when the applicant has damaged Park District property on prior occasions and has not paid for the damage; when a permit has been granted to an earlier applicant for the

---

[5] *FW/PBS, Inc. v. Dallas,* 493 U.S. 215, 224, 110 S.Ct. 596, 107 L.Ed.2d 603 (1990), which applied two of the *Freedman* requirements, involved a licensing scheme that "target[ed] businesses purveying sexually explicit speech."

same time and place; when the intended use would present an unreasonable danger to the health or safety of park users or Park District employees; or when the applicant has violated the terms of a prior permit. Moreover, the Park District must process applications within 28 days, and must clearly explain its reasons for any denial. These grounds are reasonably specific and objective, and do not leave the decision "to the whim of the administrator." *Forsyth County,* 505 U.S., at 133. They provide "narrowly drawn, reasonable and definite standards" to guide the licensor's determination. And they are enforceable on review—first by appeal to the General Superintendent of the Park District, and then by writ of common-law certiorari in the Illinois courts, which provides essentially the same type of review as that provided by the Illinois administrative procedure act.

Petitioners contend that the criteria set forth in the ordinance are insufficiently precise because they are described as grounds on which the Park District "may" deny a permit, rather than grounds on which it *must* do so. This, they contend, allows the Park District to waive the permit requirements for some favored speakers, while insisting upon them for others. That is certainly not the intent of the ordinance, which the Park District has reasonably interpreted to permit overlooking only those inadequacies that, under the circumstances, do no harm to the policies furthered by the application requirements. Granting waivers to favored speakers (or, more precisely, denying them to disfavored speakers) would of course be unconstitutional, but we think that this abuse must be dealt with if and when a pattern of unlawful favoritism appears, rather than by insisting upon a degree of rigidity that is found in few legal arrangements. On petitioners' theory, every obscenity law, or every law placing limits upon political expenditures, contains a constitutional flaw, since it merely permits, but does not require, prosecution. The prophylaxis achieved by insisting upon a rigid, no-waiver application of the ordinance requirements would be far outweighed, we think, by the accompanying senseless prohibition of speech (and of other activity in the park) by organizations that fail to meet the technical requirements of the ordinance but for one reason or another pose no risk of the evils that those requirements are designed to avoid. On balance, we think the permissive nature of the ordinance furthers, rather than constricts, free speech. . . .

NOTES

1. Is there a good reason why the requirement of obtaining advance permission is (almost always) impermissible for publications, but permissible for mass meetings in public parks, streets, or sidewalks? What about movies? Was *Freedman v. Maryland* rightly decided? Is showing a film more like an assembly (a gathering of people in a public place) or more like the press (dissemination of a message to the general public)? What was the purpose of the regulatory scheme in *Thomas*? What was the purpose in *Freedman*? The constitutional rules set forth in *Thomas* are similar to content-neutral "time, place, and manner regulations" in substance—especially in their requirement of content-neutrality—but are different in their procedure. Most time, place, and manner regulations are enforced after the fact, not by prior restraint. Is Assembly any different?

2. Can the government require groups to pay the costs generated by mass events on public property? In *Forsyth County v. The Nationalist Movement,* 505 U.S. 123 (1992), the Court held that the government may not charge such fees

if the amount is left to the unbridled discretion of city officials, for fear that groups with different messages might not be treated equally. More interesting is another holding in the case: groups may not be assessed the actual cost of additional police protection needed to maintain public order, where that amount may be affected by the controversial nature of their message and the prospect of counterdemonstrators who threaten public order. The case involved a proposed demonstration by a far-right racist group, to which tens of thousands of civil rights demonstrators planned to respond. In one prior incident involving this group, the police presence needed to maintain the peace between these antagonists cost $670,000.

In 2011, various Tea Party groups complained that they had paid thousands of dollars in fees to city governments for the costs of their rallies, while similar laws were not enforced against the Occupy Movement. See, e.g., Wesley Hester, *Tea party say city favoring occupiers*, Richmond Time–Dispatch, A1 (Oct. 27, 2011). Once the government fails to enforce the law against one group, is it stopped from enforcing that law against anyone else? What is the proper remedy: to give the Tea Party group its money back, or to require the city to assess Occupy the costs they incurred? What if Occupy is too amorphous to pay? Some Tea Partiers pointed to statements by city council members expressing sympathy or support for the Occupiers' objectives (even if not their methods). If true, would that indicate favoritism was in the works? How can favoritism in the exercise of law enforcement discretion be controlled?

3. In a pair of cases in the late 1960s, the Court held that protestors prosecuted for violating an *ordinance* restricting street demonstrations may defend themselves by arguing that it is unconstitutional, *Shuttlesworth v. City of Birmingham*, 394 U.S. 147 (1969); but protestors prosecuted for contempt after violating an *injunction* restricting their demonstration may not challenge the injunction's constitutionality. *Walker v. City of Birmingham*, 388 U.S. 307 (1967). Can you understand the logic? Do you agree with it?

Clark v. Community for Creative Non–Violence
468 U.S. 288 (1984)

■ JUSTICE WHITE delivered the opinion of the Court.

The issue in this case is whether a National Park Service regulation prohibiting camping in certain parks violates the First Amendment when applied to prohibit demonstrators from sleeping in Lafayette Park and the Mall in connection with a demonstration intended to call attention to the plight of the homeless. We hold that it does not and reverse the contrary judgment of the Court of Appeals.

I

The Interior Department, through the National Park Service, is charged with responsibility for the management and maintenance of the National Parks and is authorized to promulgate rules and regulations for the use of the parks in accordance with the purposes for which they were established. The network of National parks includes the National Memorial-core parks, Lafayette Park and the Mall, which are set in the heart of Washington, D.C., and which are unique resources that the Federal Government holds in trust for the American people. Lafayette Park is a roughly 7–acre square located across Pennsylvania Avenue from the White House. . . .

Under the regulations involved in this case, camping in National Parks is permitted only in campgrounds designated for that purpose. 36 CFR § 50.27(a) (1983). No such campgrounds have ever been designated in Lafayette Park or the Mall. Camping is defined as

the use of park land for living accommodation purposes such as sleeping activities, or making preparations to sleep (including the laying down of bedding for the purpose of sleeping), or storing personal belongings, or making any fire, or using any tents or . . . other structure . . . for sleeping or doing any digging or earth breaking or carrying on cooking activities.

These activities, the regulation provides,

constitute camping when it reasonably appears, in light of all the circumstances, that the participants, in conducting these activities, are in fact using the area as a living accommodation regardless of the intent of the participants or the nature of any other activities in which they may also be engaging.

Demonstrations for the airing of views or grievances are permitted in [Lafayette Park and the Mall], but for the most part only by Park Service permits. 36 CFR § 50.19 (1983). Temporary structures may be erected for demonstration purposes but may not be used for camping. 36 CFR § 50.19(e)(8) (1983).

In 1982, the Park Service issued a renewable permit to respondent Community for Creative Non–Violence (CCNV) to conduct a wintertime demonstration in Lafayette Park and the Mall for the purpose of demonstrating the plight of the homeless. The permit authorized the erection of two symbolic tent cities: 20 tents in Lafayette Park that would accommodate 50 people and 40 tents in the Mall with a capacity of up to 100. The Park Service, however, relying on the above regulations, specifically denied CCNV's request that demonstrators be permitted to sleep in the symbolic tents.

CCNV and several individuals then filed an action to prevent the application of the no-camping regulations to the proposed demonstration, which, it was claimed, was not covered by the regulation. It was also submitted that the regulations were unconstitutionally vague, had been discriminatorily applied, and could not be applied to prevent sleeping in the tents without violating the First Amendment. The District Court granted summary judgment in favor of the Park Service. The Court of Appeals, sitting en banc, reversed. *Community for Creative Non–Violence v. Watt*, 703 F.2d 586 (D.C. Cir. 1983). . . . [A 6–5 majority held] that application of the regulations so as to prevent sleeping in the tents would infringe the demonstrators' First Amendment right of free expression. . . . We granted the Government's petition for certiorari, and now reverse.

II

We need not differ with the view of the Court of Appeals that overnight sleeping in connection with the demonstration is expressive conduct protected to some extent by the First Amendment. We assume for present purposes, but do not decide, that such is the case, *cf. United States v. O'Brien*, 391 U.S. 367 (1968), but this assumption only begins the inquiry. Expression, whether oral or written or symbolized by conduct, is subject to reasonable time, place, or manner restrictions. We have often noted that restrictions of this kind are valid provided that they are justified without reference to the content of the regulated speech, that they are narrowly tailored to serve a significant governmental interest, and that they leave open ample alternative channels for communication of the information.

It is also true that a message may be delivered by conduct that is intended to be communicative and that, in context, would reasonably be understood by the viewer to be communicative. *Spence v. Washington*, 418 U.S. 405 (1974); *Tinker v. Des Moines School District*, 393 U.S. 503 (1969). Symbolic expression of this kind may be forbidden or regulated if the conduct itself may constitutionally be regulated, if the regulation is narrowly drawn to further a substantial governmental interest, and if the interest is unrelated to the suppression of free speech. *United States v. O'Brien, supra.*

Petitioners submit . . . that the regulation forbidding sleeping is defensible either as a time, place, or manner restriction or as a regulation of symbolic conduct. We agree with that assessment. The permit that was issued authorized the demonstration but required compliance with 36 CFR § 50.19 (1913), which prohibits "camping" on park lands, that is, the use of park lands for living accommodations, such as sleeping, storing personal belongings, making fires, digging, or cooking. These provisions, including the ban on sleeping, are clearly limitations on the manner in which the demonstration could be carried out. That sleeping, like the symbolic tents themselves, may be expressive and part of the message delivered by the demonstration does not make the ban any less a limitation on the manner of demonstrating, for reasonable time, place, or manner regulations normally have the purpose and direct effect of limiting expression but are nevertheless valid. Neither does the fact that sleeping, *arguendo*, may be expressive conduct, rather than oral or written expression, render the sleeping prohibition any less a time, place, or manner regulation. To the contrary, the Park Service neither attempts to ban sleeping generally nor to ban it everywhere in the parks. It has established areas for camping and forbids it elsewhere, including Lafayette Park and the Mall. Considered as such, we have very little trouble concluding that the Park Service may prohibit overnight sleeping in the parks involved here.

The requirement that the regulation be content-neutral is clearly satisfied. The courts below accepted that view, and it is not disputed here that the prohibition on camping, and on sleeping specifically, is content-neutral and is not being applied because of disagreement with the message presented. Neither was the regulation faulted, nor could it be, on the ground that without overnight sleeping the plight of the homeless could not be communicated in other ways. The regulation otherwise left the demonstration intact, with its symbolic city, signs, and the presence of those who were willing to take their turns in a day-and-night vigil. Respondents do not suggest that there was, or is, any barrier to delivering to the media, or to the public by other means, the intended message concerning the plight of the homeless.

It is also apparent to us that the regulation narrowly focuses on the Government's substantial interest in maintaining the parks in the heart of our Capital in an attractive and intact condition, readily available to the millions of people who wish to see and enjoy them by their presence. To permit camping—using these areas as living accommodations—would be totally inimical to these purposes, as would be readily understood by those who have frequented the National Parks across the country and observed the unfortunate consequences of the activities of those who refuse to confine their camping to designated areas.

It is urged by respondents, and the Court of Appeals was of this view, that if the symbolic city of tents was to be permitted and if the demonstrators did not intend to cook, dig, or engage in aspects of camping other than sleeping, the incremental benefit to the parks could not justify the ban on sleeping, which was here an expressive activity said to enhance the message concerning the plight of the poor and homeless. We cannot agree. In the first place, we seriously doubt that the First Amendment requires the Park Service to permit a demonstration in Lafayette Park and the Mall involving a 24–hour vigil and the erection of tents to accommodate 150 people. Furthermore, although we have assumed for present purposes that the sleeping banned in this case would have an expressive element, it is evident that its major value to this demonstration would be facilitative. Without a permit to sleep, it would be difficult to get the poor and homeless to participate or to be present at all. This much is apparent from the permit application filed by respondents: "Without the incentive of sleeping space or a hot meal, the homeless would not come to the site." The sleeping ban, if enforced, would thus effectively limit the nature, extent, and duration of the demonstration and to that extent ease the pressure on the parks.

Beyond this, however, it is evident from our cases that the validity of this regulation need not be judged solely by reference to the demonstration at hand. *Heffron v. International Society for Krishna Consciousness, Inc.*, 452 U.S. 640, 652–653 (1981). Absent the prohibition on sleeping, there would be other groups who would demand permission to deliver an asserted message by camping in Lafayette Park. Some of them would surely have as credible a claim in this regard as does CCNV, and the denial of permits to still others would present difficult problems for the Park Service. With the prohibition, however, as is evident in the case before us, at least some around-the-clock demonstrations lasting for days on end will not materialize, others will be limited in size and duration, and the purposes of the regulation will thus be materially served. Perhaps these purposes would be more effectively and not so clumsily achieved by preventing tents and 24–hour vigils entirely in [Lafayette Park or the Mall]. But the Park Service's decision to permit nonsleeping demonstrations does not, in our view, impugn the camping prohibition as a valuable, but perhaps imperfect, protection to the parks. If the Government has a legitimate interest in ensuring that the National Parks are adequately protected, which we think it has, and if the parks would be more exposed to harm without the sleeping prohibition than with it, the ban is safe from invalidation under the First Amendment as a reasonable regulation of the manner in which a demonstration may be carried out. . . .

We have difficulty, therefore, in understanding why the prohibition against camping, with its ban on sleeping overnight, is not a reasonable time, place, or manner regulation that withstands constitutional scrutiny. Surely the regulation is not unconstitutional on its face. None of its provisions appears unrelated to the ends that it was designed to serve. Nor is it any less valid when applied to prevent camping in [Lafayette Park and the Mall] by those who wish to demonstrate and deliver a message to the public and the central Government. Damage to the parks as well as their partial inaccessibility to other members of the public can as easily result from camping by demonstrators as by nondemonstrators. In neither case must the Government tolerate it. All those who would resort to the parks must abide by otherwise valid rules for their use, just as they must observe the traffic laws, sanitation regulations, and laws to preserve the public peace.

This is no more than a reaffirmation that reasonable time, place, or manner restrictions on expression are constitutionally acceptable.

Contrary to the conclusion of the Court of Appeals, the foregoing analysis demonstrates that the Park Service regulation is sustainable under the four-factor standard of *United States v. O'Brien*, 391 U.S. 367 (1968), for validating a regulation of expressive conduct, which, in the last analysis is little, if any, different from the standard applied to time, place, or manner restrictions. No one contends that aside from its impact on speech a rule against camping or overnight sleeping in public parks is beyond the constitutional power of the Government to enforce. And for the reasons we have discussed above, there is a substantial Government interest in conserving park property, an interest that is plainly served by, and requires for its implementation, measures such as the proscription of sleeping that are designed to limit the wear and tear on park properties. That interest is unrelated to suppression of expression.

We are unmoved by the Court of Appeals' view that the challenged regulation is unnecessary, and hence invalid, because there are less speech-restrictive alternatives that could have satisfied the Government interest in preserving park lands. There is no gainsaying that preventing overnight sleeping will avoid a measure of actual or threatened damage to Lafayette Park and the Mall. The Court of Appeals' suggestions that the Park Service minimize the possible injury by reducing the size, duration, or frequency of demonstrations would still curtail the total allowable expression in which demonstrators could engage, whether by sleeping or otherwise, and these suggestions represent no more than a disagreement with the Park Service over how much protection the . . . parks require or how an acceptable level of preservation is to be attained. We do not believe, however, that either *United States v. O'Brien* or the time, place, or manner decisions assign to the judiciary the authority to replace the Park Service as the manager of the Nation's parks or endow the judiciary with the competence to judge how much protection of park lands is wise and how that level of conservation is to be attained.

■ [CHIEF JUSTICE BURGER's concurrence is omitted.]

■ JUSTICE MARSHALL, with whom JUSTICE BRENNAN joins, dissenting.

The Court's disposition of this case is marked by two related failings. First, the majority is either unwilling or unable to take seriously the First Amendment claims advanced by respondents. Contrary to the impression given by the majority, respondents are not supplicants seeking to wheedle an undeserved favor from the Government. They are citizens raising issues of profound public importance who have properly turned to the courts for the vindication of their constitutional rights. Second, the majority misapplies the test for ascertaining whether a restraint on speech qualifies as a reasonable time, place, and manner regulation. In determining what constitutes a sustainable regulation, the majority fails to subject the alleged interests of the Government to the degree of scrutiny required to ensure that expressive activity protected by the First Amendment remains free of unnecessary limitations.

I

The proper starting point for analysis of this case is a recognition that the activity in which respondents seek to engage—sleeping in a highly public place, outside, in the winter for the purpose of protesting homelessness—is symbolic speech protected by the First Amendment. The majority assumes, without deciding, that the respondents' conduct is entitled to constitutional protection. The problem with this assumption is that the Court thereby avoids examining closely the reality of respondents' planned expression. The majority's approach denatures respondents' asserted right and thus makes all too easy identification of a Government interest sufficient to warrant its abridgment. A realistic appraisal of the competing interests at stake in this case requires a closer look at the nature of the expressive conduct at issue and the context in which that conduct would be displayed. . . .

The primary purpose for making *sleep* an integral part of the demonstration was "to re-enact the central reality of homelessness," and to impress upon public consciousness, in as dramatic a way as possible, that homelessness is a widespread problem, often ignored, that confronts its victims with life-threatening deprivations. . . .

In a long line of cases, this Court has afforded First Amendment protection to expressive conduct that qualifies as symbolic speech. In light of the surrounding context, respondents' proposed activity meets the qualifications. The Court has previously acknowledged the importance of context in determining whether an act can properly be denominated as "speech" for First Amendment purposes and has provided guidance concerning the way in which courts should "read" a context in making this determination. . . . Here, respondents clearly intended to protest the reality of homelessness by sleeping outdoors in the winter in the near vicinity of the magisterial residence of the President of the United States. In addition to accentuating the political character of their protest by their choice of location and mode of communication, respondents also intended to underline the meaning of their protest by giving their demonstration satirical names. Respondents planned to name the demonstration on the Mall "Congressional Village," and the demonstration in Lafayette Park, "Reaganville II." . . .

II

Although sleep in the context of this case is symbolic speech protected by the First Amendment, it is nonetheless subject to reasonable time, place, and manner restrictions. I agree with the standard enunciated by the majority: "[R]estrictions of this kind are valid provided that they are justified without reference to the content of the regulated speech, that they are narrowly tailored to serve a significant governmental interest, and that they leave open ample alternative channels for communication of the information." I conclude, however, that the regulations at issue in this case, as applied to respondents, fail to satisfy this standard.

According to the majority, the significant Government interest advanced by denying respondents' request to engage in sleep-speech is the interest in "maintaining the parks in the heart of our capital in an attractive and intact condition, readily available to the millions of people who wish to see and enjoy them by their presence." That interest is indeed significant. However, neither the Government nor the majority adequately explains how prohibiting respondents' planned activity will substantially further that interest. . . .

The majority's second argument is comprised of the suggestion that, although sleeping contains an element of expression, "its major value to [respondents'] demonstration would have been facilitative." While this observation does provide a hint of the weight the Court attached to respondents' First Amendment claims, it is utterly irrelevant to whether the Government's ban on sleeping advances a substantial Government interest.

The majority's third argument is based upon two claims. The first is that the ban on sleeping relieves the Government of an administrative burden because, without the flat ban, the process of issuing and denying permits to other demonstrators asserting First Amendment rights to sleep in the parks "would present difficult problems for the Park Service." The second is that the ban on sleeping will increase the probability that "some around-the-clock demonstrations for days on end will not materialize, [that] others will be limited in size and duration, and that the purpose of the regulation will thus be materially served," that purpose being "to limit the wear and tear on park properties."

The flaw in these two contentions is that neither is supported by a factual showing that evinces a real, as opposed to a merely speculative, problem. The majority fails to offer any evidence indicating that the absence of an absolute ban on sleeping would present administrative problems to the Park Service that are substantially more difficult than those it ordinarily confronts. A mere apprehension of difficulties should not be enough to overcome the right to free expression. . . .

The Court's erroneous application of the standard for ascertaining a reasonable time, place, and manner restriction is also revealed by the majority's conclusion that a substantial governmental interest is served by the sleeping ban because it will discourage "around-the-clock demonstrations for days" and thus further the regulation's purpose "to limit wear and tear on park properties." The majority cites no evidence indicating that sleeping engaged in as symbolic speech will cause *substantial* wear and tear on park property. Furthermore, the Government's application of the sleeping ban in the circumstances of this case is strikingly underinclusive. The majority acknowledges that a proper time, place, and manner restriction must be "narrowly tailored." Here, however, the tailoring requirement is virtually forsaken inasmuch as the Government offers no justification for applying its absolute ban on sleeping yet is willing to allow respondents to engage in activities—such as feigned sleeping—that is no less burdensome.

In short, there are no substantial Government interests advanced by the Government's regulations as applied to respondents. All that the Court's decision advances are the prerogatives of a bureaucracy that over the years has shown an implacable hostility toward citizens' exercise of First Amendment rights.

III

The disposition of this case impels me to make two additional observations. First, in this case, as in some others involving time, place, and manner restrictions, the Court has dramatically lowered its scrutiny of governmental regulations once it has determined that such regulations are content-neutral. The result has been the creation of a two-tiered approach to First Amendment cases: while regulations that turn on the content of the expression are subjected to a strict form of judicial review, regulations that are aimed at matters other than expression receive only a minimal level of scrutiny. The minimal scrutiny prong of this two-tiered approach has led to an unfortunate diminution of First Amendment protection. By narrowly limiting its concern to whether a given regulation creates a content-based distinction, the Court has seemingly overlooked the fact that content-neutral restrictions are also capable of unnecessarily restricting protected expressive activity. . . .

Second, the disposition of this case reveals a mistaken assumption regarding the motives and behavior of government officials who create and administer content-neutral regulations. The Court's salutary skepticism of Governmental decisionmaking in First Amendment matters suddenly dissipates once it determines that a restriction is not content-based. The Court evidently assumes that the balance struck by officials is deserving of deference so long as it does not appear to be tainted by content discrimination. What the Court fails to recognize is that public officials have strong incentives to overregulate even in the absence of an intent to censor particular views. This incentive stems from the fact that of the two groups whose interests officials must accommodate—on the one hand, the interests of the general public and, on the other, the interests of those who seek to use a particular forum for First Amendment activity—the political power of the former is likely to be far greater than that of the latter. . . .

NOTES

1. Is sleeping "speech"? (Several of us have known students to have engaged in what might charitably be called "expressive napping" in law-school classrooms. It unquestionably communicates a message to the professor—but is it truly "speech"?) Review the First Amendment test established by the Court's doctrine for this type of issue (the *O'Brien* test). The Court in *Clark* did not decide the case explicitly on this ground, but noted the resemblance of this test to the "time, place, and manner" test. How would you apply *O'Brien*?

2. Is the decision in *Clark v. CCNV* correct? Is the line drawn by the Court's cases principled? Is it capable of consistent application? How would you resolve this type of issue, in a way that is faithful to the text, structure, and history of the First Amendment?

3. As part of the Occupy Movement, mentioned above, in the summer of 2012 large numbers of demonstrators camped overnight in public squares in New York, Washington, Oakland, and many other U.S. cities. Did they have a constitutional right to do so? What were they communicating by sleeping overnight? Is there a communicative difference between the sleeping itself and the maintenance of a 24–7 demonstration? What interests were sufficient for the government to squelch the Occupations? Do other citizens have a right to use public squares to stroll about, have lunch, play chess, or walk dogs?

What if a group planning a large demonstration in Washington can make a persuasive claim that they need to be able to camp in public spaces because there are not enough hotel accommodations within their price range to accommodate all the demonstrators? Do they have a constitutional right to do so? Is their claim any different from that in *CCNV*? If the government chose not to interfere with CCNV's camping or Occupy's occupation, is it stopped from interfering with other groups with different messages, who might also find it convenient to camp in Lafayette Square?

NAACP v. Claiborne Hardware Co.

458 U.S. 886 (1982)

■ JUSTICE STEVENS delivered the opinion of the Court.

The term "concerted action" encompasses unlawful conspiracies and constitutionally protected assemblies. . . . The boycott of white merchants in Claiborne County, Miss., that gave rise to this litigation had such a character; it included elements of criminality and elements of majesty. Evidence that fear of reprisals caused some black citizens to withhold their patronage from respondents' businesses convinced the Supreme Court of Mississippi that the entire boycott was unlawful and that each of the 92 petitioners was liable for all of its economic consequences. Evidence that persuasive rhetoric, determination to remedy past injustices, and a host of voluntary decisions by free citizens were the critical factors in the boycott's success presents us with the question whether the state court's judgment is consistent with the Constitution of the United States.

I

In March 1966, black citizens of Port Gibson, Miss., and other areas of Claiborne County presented white elected officials with a list of particularized demands for racial equality and integration. The complainants did not receive a satisfactory response and, at a local National Association for the Advancement of Colored People (NAACP) meeting at the First Baptist Church, several hundred black persons voted to place a boycott on white merchants in the area. On October 31, 1969, several of the merchants filed suit in state court to recover losses caused by the boycott and to enjoin future boycott activity. . . .

The complaint was filed . . . by 17 white merchants. The merchants named two corporations and 146 individuals as defendants: the NAACP, a New York membership corporation; Mississippi Action for Progress (MAP), a Mississippi corporation that implemented the federal "Head Start" program; Aaron Henry, the President of the Mississippi State Conference of the NAACP; Charles Evers, the Field Secretary of the NAACP in Mississippi; and 144 other individuals who had participated in the boycott. The complaint sought injunctive relief and an attachment of property, as well as damages. . . .

[T]he chancellor issued an opinion and decree finding that "an overwhelming preponderance of the evidence" established the joint and several liability of 130 of the defendants on three separate conspiracy [tort] theories [malicious interference with plaintiffs' businesses; illegal "secondary boycott" in that "defendants' primary dispute was with the governing authorities of Port Gibson and Claiborne County and not with the white merchants at whom the boycott was directed"; and violation of state antitrust law]. . . .

Five of the merchants offered no evidence of business losses. The chancellor found that the remaining 12 had suffered lost business earnings and lost goodwill during a 7-year period from 1966 to 1972 amounting to $944,699. That amount, plus statutory penalties and attorney's fees, produced a final judgment of $1,250,699, plus interest. . . . As noted, the chancellor found all but 18 of the original 148 defendants jointly and severally liable for the entire judgment. The court justified imposing full liability on the national organization of the NAACP on the ground that it had failed to "repudiate" the actions of Charles Evers. . . .

In addition to imposing damages liability, the chancellor entered a broad permanent injunction. He permanently enjoined petitioners from stationing "store watchers" at the respondents' business premises; from "persuading" any person to withhold his patronage from respondents; from "using demeaning and obscene language to or about any person" because that person continued to patronize the respondents; from "picketing or patroling" the premises of any of the respondents; and from using violence against any person or inflicting damage to any real or personal property. . . .

The Mississippi Supreme Court upheld the imposition of liability . . . on the basis of the chancellor's common-law tort theory. After reviewing the chancellor's recitation of the facts, the court quoted the following finding made by the trial court:

> In carrying out the agreement and design, certain of the defendants, acting for all others, engaged in acts of physical force and violence against the persons and property of certain customers and prospective customers. Intimidation, threats, social ostracism, vilification, and traduction were some of the devices used by the defendants to achieve the desired results. Most effective, also, was the stationing of guards ("enforcers," "deacons," or "black hats") in the vicinity of white-owned businesses. Unquestionably, the evidence shows that the volition of many black persons was overcome out of sheer fear, and they were forced and compelled against their personal wills to withhold their trade and business intercourse from the complainants.

On the basis of this finding, the court concluded that the entire boycott was unlawful. "If any of these factors—force, violence, or threats—is present, then the boycott is illegal regardless of whether it is primary, secondary, economical, political, social or other." In a brief passage, the court rejected petitioners' reliance on the First Amendment:

> The agreed use of illegal force, violence, and threats against the peace to achieve a goal makes the present state of facts a conspiracy. We know of no instance, and our attention has been drawn to no decision, wherein it has been adjudicated that free speech guaranteed by the First Amendment includes in its protection the right to commit crime.
> . . .

II–A

The boycott of white merchants at issue in this case took many forms. The boycott was launched at a meeting of a local branch of the NAACP attended by several hundred persons. Its acknowledged purpose was to secure compliance by both civic and business leaders with a lengthy list of demands for equality and racial justice. The boycott was supported by speeches and nonviolent picketing. Participants repeatedly encouraged others to join in its cause.

Each of these elements of the boycott is a form of speech or conduct that is ordinarily entitled to protection under the First and Fourteenth Amendments. The black citizens named as defendants in this action banded together and collectively expressed their dissatisfaction with a social structure that had denied them rights to equal treatment and respect. As we so recently acknowledged in *Citizens Against Rent Control Coalition for Fair Housing v. Berkeley*, 454 U.S. 290, 294, "the practice of persons sharing common views banding together to achieve a common end is deeply embedded in the American political process." We recognized that "by collective effort individuals can make their views known, when, individually, their voices would be faint or lost." *Ibid.* . . .

The right to associate does not lose all constitutional protection merely because some members of the group may have participated in conduct or advocated doctrine that itself is not protected. . . . Of course, the petitioners in this case did more than assemble peaceably and discuss among themselves their grievances against governmental and business policy. Other elements of the boycott, however, also involved activities ordinarily safeguarded by the First Amendment. . . . Speech itself also was used to further the aims of the boycott. Nonparticipants repeatedly were urged to join the common cause, both through public address and through personal solicitation. These elements of the boycott involve speech in its most direct form. In addition, names of boycott violators were read aloud at meetings at the First Baptist Church and published in a local black newspaper. Petitioners admittedly sought to persuade others to join the boycott through social pressure and the "threat" of social ostracism. Speech does not lose its protected character, however, simply because it may embarrass others or coerce them into action. . . .

[T]he boycott clearly involved constitutionally protected activity. . . . Through exercise of these First Amendment rights, petitioners sought to bring about political, social, and economic change. Through speech, assembly, and petition—rather than through riot or revolution—petitioners sought to change a social order that had consistently treated them as second-class citizens.

The presence of protected activity, however, does not end the relevant constitutional inquiry. . . . *[The Court cited United States v. O'Brien in support of the authority of government to regulate conduct for reasons aside from its expressive message.—Editors]* . . . A nonviolent and totally voluntary boycott may have a disruptive effect on local economic conditions. This Court has recognized the strong governmental interest in certain forms of economic regulation, even though such regulation may have an incidental effect on rights of speech and association. . . .

[But w]hile States have broad power to regulate economic activity, we do not find a comparable right to prohibit peaceful political activity such as that found in the boycott in this case. . . . The right of the States to regulate economic activity could not justify a complete prohibition against a nonviolent, politically motivated boycott designed to force governmental and economic change. . . .

We hold that the nonviolent elements of petitioners' activities are entitled to the protection of the First Amendment.

B

. . . The First Amendment does not protect violence. . . . Although the extent and significance of the violence in this case are vigorously disputed by the parties, there is no question that acts of violence occurred. No federal rule of law restricts a State from imposing tort liability for business losses that are caused by violence and by threats of violence. When such conduct occurs in the context of constitutionally protected activity, however, "precision of regulation" is demanded. Specifically, the presence of activity protected by the First Amendment imposes restraints on the grounds that may give rise to damages liability and on the persons who may be held accountable for those damages. . . .

The First Amendment . . . restricts the ability of the State to impose liability on an individual solely because of his association with another. . . . Civil liability may not be imposed merely because an individual belonged to a group, some members of which committed acts of violence. For liability to be imposed by reason of association alone, it is necessary to establish that the group itself possessed unlawful goals and that the individual held a specific intent to further those illegal aims. . . .

III

. . . The opinion of the Mississippi Supreme Court itself demonstrates that all business losses were not proximately caused by the violence and threats of violence found to be present. The court stated that "coercion, intimidation, and threats" formed "*part* of the boycott activity" and "*contributed* to its almost complete success." The court broadly asserted—without differentiation—that "[i]ntimidation, threats, social ostracism, vilification, and traduction" were devices used by the defendants to effectuate the boycott. The court repeated the chancellor's finding that "the volition of *many* black persons was overcome out of sheer fear." These findings are inconsistent with the court's imposition of all damages "resulting from the boycott." To the extent that the court's judgment rests on the ground that "many" black citizens were "intimidated" by "threats" of "social ostracism, vilification, and traduction," it is flatly inconsistent with the First Amendment. The ambiguous findings of the Mississippi Supreme Court are inadequate to assure the "precision of regulation" demanded by that constitutional provision. . . .

[I]n this case, the Mississippi Supreme Court has relied on isolated acts of violence during a limited period to uphold respondents' recovery of *all* business losses sustained over a 7–year span. . . . The court's judgment . . . cannot stand. *[The Court also held, in a footnote, that the permanent injunction "must be dissolved." Alternatively, "the injunction must be modified to restrain only unlawful conduct and the persons responsible for conduct of that character."—Editors] . . .*

Respondents also argue that liability may be imposed on individuals who were either "store watchers" or members of the "Black Hats." There is nothing unlawful in standing outside a store and recording names. Similarly, there is nothing unlawful in wearing black hats, although such apparel may cause apprehension in others. As established above, mere association with either group—absent a specific intent to further an unlawful aim embraced by that group—is an insufficient predicate for liability. At the same time, the evidence does support the conclusion that some members of each of these groups engaged in violence or threats of violence. Unquestionably, these individuals may be held responsible for the injuries that they caused; a judgment tailored to the consequences of their unlawful conduct may be sustained.

Respondents have sought separately to justify the judgment entered against Charles Evers and the national NAACP. . . . For the reasons set forth above, liability may not be imposed on Evers for his presence at NAACP meetings or his active participation in the boycott itself. To the extent that Evers caused respondents to suffer business losses through his organization of the boycott, his emotional and persuasive appeals for unity in the joint effort, or his "threats" of vilification or social ostracism, Evers' conduct is constitutionally protected and beyond the reach of a damages award. Respondents point to Evers' speeches, however, as justification for the chancellor's damages award. . . .

There are three separate theories that might justify holding Evers liable for the unlawful conduct of others. First, a finding that he authorized, directed, or ratified specific tortious activity would justify holding him responsible for the consequences of that activity. Second, a finding that his public speeches were likely to incite lawless action could justify holding him liable for unlawful conduct that in fact followed within a reasonable period. Third, the speeches might be taken as evidence that Evers gave other specific instructions to carry out violent acts or threats.

While many of the comments in Evers' speeches might have contemplated "discipline" in the permissible form of social ostracism, it cannot be denied that references to the possibility that necks would be broken and to the fact that the Sheriff could not sleep with boycott violators at night implicitly conveyed a sterner message. In the passionate atmosphere in which the speeches were delivered, they might have been understood as inviting an unlawful form of discipline or, at least, as intending to create a fear of violence whether or not improper discipline was specifically intended.

It is clear that "fighting words"—those that provoke immediate violence—are not protected by the First Amendment. *Chaplinsky v. New Hampshire*, 315 U.S. 568, 572. . . . This Court has made clear, however, that mere *advocacy* of the use of force or violence does not remove speech from the protection of the First Amendment. [*Brandenburg v. Ohio*, 395 U.S. 444.] . . . The emotionally charged rhetoric of Charles Evers' speeches did not transcend the bounds of protected speech set forth in *Brandenburg*. The lengthy addresses generally contained an impassioned plea for black citizens to unify, to support and respect each other, and to realize the political and economic power available to them. In the course of those pleas, strong language was used. . . . An advocate must be free to stimulate his audience with spontaneous and emotional appeals for unity and action in a common cause. When such appeals do not incite lawless action, they must be regarded as protected speech. . . .

[W]e conclude that Evers' addresses did not exceed the bounds of protected speech. . . . [T]here is no evidence—apart from the speeches themselves—that Evers authorized, ratified, or directly threatened acts of violence. . . . The chancellor made no finding that Charles Evers or any other NAACP member had either actual or apparent authority to commit acts of violence or to threaten violent conduct. The evidence in the record suggests the contrary. . . . To impose liability without a finding that the NAACP authorized—either actually or apparently—or ratified unlawful conduct would impermissibly burden the rights of political association that are protected by the First Amendment. . . .

IV

In litigation of this kind the stakes are high. Concerted action is a powerful weapon. History teaches that special dangers are associated with conspiratorial activity. And yet one of the foundations of our society is the right of individuals to combine with other persons in pursuit of a common goal by lawful means.

At times the difference between lawful and unlawful collective action may be identified easily by reference to its purpose. In this case, however, petitioners' ultimate objectives were unquestionably legitimate. The charge of illegality—like the claim of constitutional protection—derives from the means employed by the participants to achieve those goals. The use of speeches, marches, and threats of social ostracism cannot provide the basis for a damages award. But violent conduct is beyond the pale of constitutional protection.

The taint of violence colored the conduct of some of the petitioners. They, of course, may be held liable for the consequences of their violent deeds. The burden of demonstrating that it colored the entire collective effort, however, is not satisfied by evidence that violence occurred or even that violence contributed to the success of the boycott. A massive and prolonged effort to change the social, political, and economic structure of a local environment cannot be characterized as a violent conspiracy simply by reference to the ephemeral consequences of relatively few violent acts. . . . A court must be wary of a claim that the true color of a forest is better revealed by reptiles hidden in the weeds than by the foliage of countless freestanding trees. . . .

NOTES

1. There are several notable features of the Court's landmark, unanimous decision in *Claiborne Hardware*. First, the Free Speech Clause protects *collective* advocacy—the rights of groups of like-minded persons to band together for joint action in a common cause. Second, the Court strongly reaffirms the Free Speech Clause right of groups to engage in *expressive conduct*—here, conduct that otherwise arguably constituted an economic tort—under the *O'Brien* test, requiring not only that the state's interest be strong but also requiring "precision of regulation" so as not to interfere with legitimate speech. Third, following from these principles, the Court holds that, while the Free Speech Clause does not protect violence, it forbids holding *the group* responsible for the torts of individuals that the other members of the group did not authorize, direct, or ratify. The First Amendment forbids group advocacy from being considered a "conspiracy"—otherwise, all members of the group could be liable for the wrongful acts of anyone in the group. Fourth, and for similar reasons, the Court held that an *injunction* against speech or expressive conduct by members of the group is improper, merely because some members of the group may have engaged in individual wrongful acts. Group advocacy may not be enjoined based on torts committed by some members of the group. Fifth, the Court reaffirmed, emphatically, that speech does not lose its constitutionally protected character simply on account of its "coercive," "intimidating," or "vilifying" nature. The "black hats" looking for boycott-violators; the taking down of names; the reading of names aloud in church—are all protected by the First Amendment, regardless of the fact that they may have a coercive or intimidating effect on others. Sixth, the Court vigorously reaffirmed *Brandenburg's* holding that a speaker may not be punished even for advocacy of violence, absent strong proof of a direct and intentional connection to immediate violence.

2. Do you agree with the Court's holdings? Are they consistent with the terms of the First Amendment, which protects the right to "peaceably" assemble? Does this limitation have any practical application? Every assembly is peaceable until it is not.

A NOTE ON ABORTION CLINIC PROTESTS

Anti-abortion protests at abortion clinics, in the 1980s and 1990s and into the twenty-first century, have presented something like the *Claiborne Hardware* controversies of their day. Like the civil rights movement of the 1960s, anti-abortion advocates have pressed their grievances vigorously, vehemently, vociferously—and sometimes violently. (Recall some of the discussion in *Planned Parenthood of the Columbia/Willamette*.) Methods have included classic exercises of the freedom of speech, such as picketing, marching, chanting, distributing pamphlets, praying, sit-ins, and direct, face-to-face counseling or advocacy. But such protests (again like the civil rights movement) also have involved unlawful activity, including blocking of abortion clinic entrances and driveways, and threatening conduct directed at clinic workers or women seeking abortions. Women seeking abortions, and employees of the abortion provider, have been photographed (as in *Claiborne Hardware*). Some groups, such as "Operation Rescue," have been open about their desire to shut down "abortion businesses" entirely.

As with the civil rights movement, this has led to lawsuits against protesters, seeking damages and injunctive relief on a wide variety of legal theories: asserted violation of state and federal "antitrust" and anti-competitive conduct statutes; common law or statutory tort theories of intentional infliction of emotional distress, outrageous conduct, false imprisonment, and assault; "conspiracy" laws, including federal laws forbidding conspiracies to deny civil rights, 42 U.S.C. Section 1985, and even state and federal anti-racketeering and organized-crime statutes. The Supreme Court rejected the use of Section 1985 as a vehicle for suing anti-abortion groups, in *Bray v. Alexandria Women's Health Clinic*, 506 U.S. 263 (1993) (finding the statute inapplicable because of absence of the element of "class-based animus"; opposition to abortion does not constitute class-based animus against women as a class), but upheld the use of federal RICO (the Racketeer Influenced and Corrupt Organization provisions of a 1970 law) as such a tool in *National Organization for Women, Inc. v. Scheidler*, 510 U.S. 249 (1994).

The Court also has upheld the issuance of injunctions directed against pro-life/anti-abortion advocacy groups' activities at abortion clinics, predicated (sometimes) in part on the occurrence of tortious or other wrongful conduct by some protestors. Sometimes the injunctions run against specific persons, and sometimes against organizations. They also run against anyone "in active concert or participation with" a named person or organization. See Fed. R. Civ. P. 65(d)(2)(C). Does *Claiborne Hardware* permit injunctions against the speech activities of groups seemingly defined by their association in a common cause? Does it permit statutes directed against their speech activities?

As you think about such issues—and the Supreme Court's decisions described in the next two notes, concerning anti-abortion protests—separate your own views about abortion (and about anti-abortion protests) from the analysis of the First Amendment issues. Is the Court's approach consistent in addressing how the First Amendment applies in these two contexts?

1. In *Madsen v. Women's Health Center, Inc.*, 512 U.S. 753 (1994), the Court upheld (in part) a state judge's issuance of an injunction creating a 36–foot "buffer zone" prohibiting anti-abortion protestors from engaging in speech on a public street and sidewalk near an abortion clinic, citing significant government interests as justification for the exclusion zone. (The Court held certain other parts of the injunction unconstitutional.)

The state court initially had issued an injunction against blocking or interfering with access to the abortion clinic, but later expanded the injunction to include the 36–foot no-speech zone and other provisions regulating anti-abortion protestors (some of which the U.S. Supreme Court struck down). The injunction's terms ran against not only named individuals but also against an-ti-abortion advocacy *groups*, including "Operation Rescue, Operation Rescue America, Operation Goliath, their officers, agents, members, employees and servants" and, in addition, "all persons acting in concert or participation with them, or on their behalf." Here is the Supreme Court's description of the events leading to this injunction:

> Respondents operate abortion clinics throughout central Florida. Petition-ers and other groups and individuals are engaged in activities near the site of one such clinic in Melbourne, Florida. They picketed and demon-strated where the public street gives access to the clinic. In September 1992, a Florida state court permanently enjoined petitioners from blocking or interfering with public access to the clinic, and from physically abusing persons entering or leaving the clinic. Six months later, respondents sought to broaden the injunction, complaining that access to the clinic was still impeded by petitioners' activities and that such activities had also discouraged some potential patients from entering the clinic, and had del-eterious physical effects on others. The trial court thereupon issued a broader injunction, which is challenged here.

> The court found that, despite the initial injunction, protesters contin-ued to impede access to the clinic by congregating on the paved portion of the street—Dixie Way—leading up to the clinic, and by marching in front of the clinic's driveways. It found that as vehicles heading toward the clin-ic slowed to allow the protesters to move out of the way, "sidewalk counse-lors" would approach and attempt to give the vehicle's occupants antiabor-tion literature. The number of people congregating varied from a handful to 400, and the noise varied from singing and chanting to the use of loud-speakers and bullhorns.

> The protests, the court found, took their toll on the clinic's patients. A clinic doctor testified that, as a result of having to run such a gauntlet to enter the clinic, the patients "manifested a higher level of anxiety and hy-pertension causing those patients to need a higher level of sedation to un-dergo the surgical procedures, thereby increasing the risk associated with such procedures." . . . The noise produced by the protesters could be heard within the clinic, causing stress in the patients both during surgical pro-cedures and while recuperating in the recovery rooms. And those patients who turned away because of the crowd to return at a later date, the doctor testified, increased their health risks by reason of the delay.

> Doctors and clinic workers, in turn, were not immune even in their homes. Petitioners picketed in front of clinic employees' residences; shout-ed at passersby; rang the doorbells of neighbors and provided literature identifying the particular clinic employee as a "baby killer." Occasionally, the protesters would confront minor children of clinic employees who were home alone.

> This and similar testimony led the state court to conclude that its original injunction had proved insufficient "to protect the health, safety and rights of women in Brevard and Seminole County, Florida and sur-rounding counties seeking access to [medical and counseling] services." . . . The state court therefore amended its prior order, enjoining a broader

array of activities. The amended injunction prohibits petitioners from engaging in the following acts:

(1) At all times on all days, from entering the premises and property of the Aware Woman Center for Choice [the Melbourne clinic]. . . .

(2) At all times on all days, from blocking, impeding, inhibiting, or in any other manner obstructing or interfering with access to, ingress into and egress from any building or parking lot of the Clinic.

(3) At all times on all days, from congregating, picketing, patrolling, demonstrating or entering that portion of public right-of-way or private property within [36] feet of the property line of the Clinic. . . . An exception to the 36 foot buffer zone is the area immediately adjacent to the Clinic on the east. . . . The [petitioners] . . . must remain at least [5] feet from the Clinic's east line. Another exception to the 36 foot buffer zone relates to the record title owners of the property to the north and west of the Clinic . . . and their invitees . . .

(4) During the hours of 7:30 a.m. through noon, on Mondays through Saturdays, during surgical procedures and recovery periods, from singing, chanting, whistling, shouting, yelling, use of bullhorns, auto horns, sound amplification equipment or other sounds or images observable to or within earshot of the patients inside the Clinic.

(5) At all times on all days, in an area within [300] feet of the Clinic, from physically approaching any person seeking the services of the Clinic unless such person indicates a desire to communicate by approaching or by inquiring of the [petitioners] . . .

(6) At all times on all days, from approaching, congregating, picketing, patrolling, demonstrating or using bullhorns or other sound amplification equipment within [300] feet of the residence of any of the [respondents'] employees, staff, owners or agents, or blocking or attempting to block, barricade, or in any other manner, temporarily or otherwise, obstruct the entrances, exits or driveways of the residences of any of the [respondents'] employees, staff, owners or agents. The [petitioners] and those acting in concert with them are prohibited from inhibiting or impeding or attempting to impede, temporarily or otherwise, the free ingress or egress of persons to any street that provides the sole access to the street on which those residences are located.

(7) At all times on all days, from physically abusing, grabbing, intimidating, harassing, touching, pushing, shoving, crowding or assaulting persons entering or leaving, working at or using services at the [respondents'] Clinic or trying to gain access to, or leave, any of the homes of owners, staff or patients of the Clinic . . .

(8) At all times on all days, from harassing, intimidating or physically abusing, assaulting or threatening any present or former doctor, health care professional, or other staff member, employee or volunteer who assists in providing services at the [respondents'] Clinic.

(9) At all times on all days, from encouraging, inciting, or securing other persons to commit any of the prohibited acts listed herein.

Id. at 759–761. Before you read on: which of these provisions of the injunction, as a substantive matter, are consistent with the First Amendment? Which ones abridge the freedom of speech, or the right of the people peaceably to assemble? Under the reasoning of *Claiborne Hardware*, are all of them invalid, as applied to members of the groups named (or others "acting in concert" with them) who never committed any act of blocking or interfering with access to the abortion clinics? Under the reasoning of the *Pentagon Papers Case*, are all of them invalid simply because they are contained in an injunction, a form of prior restraint? Does the occurrence of a disruptive protest that may have involved acts of trespass or other torts provide a sufficient predicate for a judicially crafted injunction regulating such protests generally? (Is this a question of state law, or of First Amendment law?)

Here were the Court's answers: First, the majority held that the injunction was not content-based or viewpoint-based, even though it restricted only the speech of anti-abortion protestors, because "[t]o accept petitioners' claim would be to classify virtually every injunction as content or viewpoint based. An injunction, by its very nature, applies only to a particular group (or individuals) and regulates the activities, and perhaps the speech, of that group." Accordingly, the majority applied an "intermediate" standard of scrutiny for injunctions directed against speech, roughly analogous to the test traditionally applied to content-neutral "time, place, and manner" regulations.

Applying that standard, the majority then *upheld* those parts of the injunction creating the 36–foot "buffer zone" and prohibiting "singing, chanting, whistling, shouting, yelling" that could be heard inside the abortion clinic. The majority *struck down* the prohibition on display of images, however: "The only plausible reason a patient would be bothered by 'images observable' inside the clinic would be if the patient found the expression contained in such images disagreeable. But it is much easier for the clinic to pull its curtains than for a patient to stop up her ears. . . . This provision of the injunction violates the First Amendment." The majority also struck down the 300–foot "no-approach" zone as too broad.

Justice Scalia's emphatic dissent (joined by Kennedy and Thomas) began with a colorful recitation of the facts giving rise to the trial court's injunction order. Scalia then addressed specifically the question of injunctions against speech (as opposed to statutes or ordinances):

> But this is *not* a statute, and it *is* an injunctive order. The Court might just as logically (or illogically) have begun Part III: "If this were a content-based injunction, rather than a non-content-based injunction, its constitutionality would be assessed under the strict scrutiny standard"—and have then proceeded to discuss whether *respondents* can sustain the burden of departing from *that* presumed disposition. The question should be approached, it seems to me, without any such artificial loading of the dice. And the central element of the answer is that a restriction upon speech imposed by injunction (whether nominally content based or nominally content neutral) is *at least* as deserving of strict scrutiny as a statutory, content-based restriction.

That is so for several reasons: The danger of content-based statutory restrictions upon speech is that they may be designed and used precisely to suppress the ideas in question rather than to achieve any other proper governmental aim. But that same danger exists with injunctions. Although a speech-restricting injunction may not attack content *as content* (in the present case, as I shall discuss, even that is not true), it lends itself just as readily to the targeted suppression of particular ideas. When a judge, on the motion of an employer, enjoins picketing at the site of a labor dispute, he enjoins (and he *knows* he is enjoining) the expression of pro-union views. Such targeting of one or the other side of an ideological dispute cannot readily be achieved in speech-restricting general legislation except by making content the basis of the restriction; it is achieved in speech-restricting injunctions almost invariably. The proceedings before us here illustrate well enough what I mean. The injunction was sought against a single-issue advocacy group by persons and organizations with a business or social interest in suppressing that group's point of view.

The second reason speech-restricting injunctions are at least as deserving of strict scrutiny is obvious enough: They are the product of individual judges rather than of legislatures—and often of judges who have been chagrined by prior disobedience of their orders. The right to free speech should not lightly be placed within the control of a single man or woman. And the third reason is that the injunction is a much more powerful weapon than a statute, and so should be subjected to greater safeguards. Normally, when injunctions are enforced through contempt proceedings, only the defense of factual innocence is available. The collateral bar rule of *Walker v. Birmingham*, 388 U.S. 307 (1967), eliminates the defense that the injunction itself was unconstitutional. . . . Thus, persons subject to a speech-restricting injunction who have not the money or not the time to lodge an immediate appeal face a Hobson's choice: They must remain silent, since if they speak their First Amendment rights are no defense in subsequent contempt proceedings. This is good reason to require the strictest standard for issuance of such orders. . . .

2. *Hill v. Colorado*, 530 U.S. 703 (2000). Eighteen years after *Claiborne Hardware*, Justice Stevens again wrote the majority opinion for the Court in a case involving restrictions of organized mass protest activities directed at lawful private businesses. This time the protests involved anti-abortion speakers condemning abortion clinics and seeking to dissuade—or intimidate—women from having abortions. In *Hill v. Colorado*, the Court upheld a law forbidding persons to "knowingly approach" within eight feet of another person "for the purpose of passing a leaflet or handbill to, displaying a sign to, or engaging in oral protest, education, or counseling," without consent of the person approached, within 100 feet of a "health care facility." Is such a law "content-neutral" with respect to speech? Is it a "time, place or manner" regulation?

Justice Stevens said:

The right to free speech, of course, includes the right to attempt to persuade others to change their views, and may not be curtailed simply because the speaker's message may be offensive to his audience. But the protection afforded to offensive messages does not always embrace offensive speech that is so intrusive that the unwilling audience cannot avoid it. The recognizable privacy interest in avoiding unwanted communication varies widely in different settings. . . . While the freedom to communicate is substantial, "the right of every person 'to be let alone' must be placed in the scales with the right of others to communicate." It is that right, as well as the right of "passage without obstruction," that the Colorado statute legitimately seeks to protect.

Justice Stevens then upheld the 8–foot restriction as a narrowly tailed, and content-neutral, "time, place, and manner regulation": it regulated not the content of speech but "the places where some speech may occur" and was neutral as to viewpoints expressed—prohibiting *all* "protest" and *all* "counseling," whether for or against abortion, or whether pro or con on any other topic.

In dissent, Justice Kennedy argued the regulation was content-based:

The Court's holding contradicts more than a half century of well-established First Amendment principles. For the first time, the Court approves a law which bars a private citizen from passing a message, in a peaceful manner and on a profound moral issue, to a fellow citizen on a public sidewalk. If from this time forward the Court repeats its grave errors of analysis, we shall have no longer the proud tradition of free and open discourse in a public forum. . . . Colorado's statute is a textbook example of a law which is content-based. . . .

The law imposes content-based restrictions on speech by reason of the terms it uses, the categories it employs, and the conditions for its enforcement. It is content based, too, by its predictable and intended operation. Whether particular messages violate the statute is determined by their substance. The law is a prime example of a statute inviting screening and censoring of individual speech; and it is serious error to hold otherwise.

. . . Under the Colorado enactment, . . . the State must review content to determine whether a person has engaged in criminal "protest, education, or counseling." When a citizen approaches another on the sidewalk in a disfavored-speech zone, an officer of the State must listen to what the speaker says. If, in the officer's judgment, the speaker's words stray too far toward "protest, education, or counseling"—the boundaries of which are far from clear—the officer may decide the speech has moved from the permissible to the criminal. The First Amendment does not give the government such power.

The statute is content based for an additional reason: It restricts speech on particular topics. Of course, the enactment restricts "oral protest, education, or counseling" on any subject; but a statute of broad application is not content neutral if its terms control the substance of a speaker's message. If oral protest, education, or counseling on every subject within an 8–foot zone present a danger to the public, the statute should apply to every building entrance in the State. It does not. It applies only to a special class of locations: entrances to buildings with health care facilities. We would close our eyes to reality were we to deny that "oral protest, education, or counseling" outside the entrances to medical facilities concern a narrow range of topics—indeed, one topic in particular. By confining the law's application to the specific locations where the prohibited discourse occurs, the State has made a content-based determination. The Court ought to so acknowledge. Clever content-based restrictions are no less offensive than censoring on the basis of content. If, just a few decades ago, a State with a history of enforcing racial discrimination had enacted a statute like this one, regulating "oral protest, education, or counseling" within 100 feet of the entrance to any lunch counter, our predecessors would not have hesitated to hold it was content based or viewpoint based. It should be a profound disappointment to defenders of the First Amendment that the Court today refuses to apply the same structural analysis when the speech involved is less palatable to it.

The Court, in error and irony, validates the Colorado statute because it purports to restrict all of the proscribed expressive activity regardless of the subject. The evenhandedness the Court finds so satisfying, however, is but a disguise for a glaring First Amendment violation. The Court, by citing the breadth of the statute, cannot escape the conclusion that its categories are nonetheless content based. The liberty of a society is measured in part by what its citizens are free to discuss among themselves. Colorado's scheme of disfavored-speech zones on public streets and sidewalks, and the Court's opinion validating them, are antithetical to our entire First Amendment tradition. To say that one citizen can approach another to ask the time or the weather forecast or the directions to Main Street but not to initiate discussion on one of the most basic moral and political issues in all of contemporary discourse, a question touching profound ideas in philosophy and theology, is an astonishing view of the First Amendment. For the majority to examine the statute under rules applicable to content-neutral regulations is an affront to First Amendment teachings.

Does it matter to this analysis that the restrictions at issue in *Hill* were enacted by a legislative body, rather than imposed by a court in the form of an injunction? Does this distinguish *Claiborne Hardware*? Would the Court's opinion in *Claiborne Hardware* have been different if the restrictions imposed on the boycott were imposed by statute rather than by injunction?

3. In general: when may the government restrict public collective speech—assembly—because of its disruptive, annoying, harassing, or intimidating nature? Because of its interference with the privacy of others? As a prophylactic measure to guard against violence or other torts?

[Assignment 51]

L. COMPELLED SPEECH

Does the freedom of speech embrace the freedom *not* to speak—a freedom of individuals and groups from government-compelled expression, and to control the content of their own expression?

West Virginia State Board of Education v. Barnette

319 U.S. 624 (1943)

■ MR. JUSTICE JACKSON delivered the opinion of the Court.

Following the decision by this Court on June 3, 1940, in *Minersville School District v. Gobitis*, 310 U.S. 586, the West Virginia legislature amended its statutes to require all schools therein to conduct courses of instruction in history, civics, and in the Constitutions of the United States and of the State "for the purpose of teaching, fostering and perpetuating the ideals, principles and spirit of Americanism, and increasing the knowledge of the organization and machinery of the government." Appellant Board of Education was directed, with advice of the State Superintendent of Schools, to "prescribe the courses of study covering these subjects" for public schools. The Act made it the duty of private, parochial and denominational schools to prescribe courses of study "similar to those required for the public schools."

The Board of Education on January 9, 1942, adopted a resolution containing recitals taken largely from the Court's *Gobitis* opinion and ordering that the salute to the flag become "a regular part of the program of activities in the public schools," that all teachers and pupils "shall be required to participate in the salute honoring the Nation represented by the Flag; provided, however, that refusal to salute the Flag be regarded as an Act of insubordination, and shall be dealt with accordingly."

 . . . What is now required is the "stiff-arm" salute, the saluter to keep the right hand raised with palm turned up while the following is repeated: "I pledge allegiance to the Flag of the United States of America and to the Republic for which it stands; one Nation, indivisible, with liberty and justice for all."

Failure to conform is "insubordination" dealt with by expulsion. Readmission is denied by statute until compliance. Meanwhile the expelled child is "unlawfully absent" and may be proceeded against as a delinquent. His parents or guardians are liable to prosecution, and if convicted are subject to fine not exceeding $50 and jail term not exceeding thirty days. . . .

This case calls upon us to reconsider a precedent decision, as the Court throughout its history often has been required to do. Before turning to the *Gobitis* case, however, it is desirable to notice certain characteristics by which this controversy is distinguished.

The freedom asserted by these appellees does not bring them into collision with rights asserted by any other individual. It is such conflicts which most frequently require intervention of the State to determine where the rights of one end and those of another begin. But the refusal of these persons to participate in the ceremony does not interfere with or deny rights of others to do so. Nor is there any question in this case that their behavior is peaceable and orderly. The sole conflict is between authority and rights of the individual. The State asserts power to condition access to public education on making a prescribed sign and profession and at the same time to coerce attendance by punishing both parent and child. The latter stand on a right of self-determination in matters that touch individual opinion and personal attitude.

As the present CHIEF JUSTICE said in dissent in the *Gobitis* case, the State may "require teaching by instruction and study of all in our history and in the structure and organization of our government, including the guaranties of civil liberty which tend to inspire patriotism and love of country." Here, however, we are dealing with a compulsion of students to declare a belief. They are not merely made acquainted with the flag salute so that they may be informed as to what it is or even what it means. . . . In the present case attendance is not optional. . . .

There is no doubt that, in connection with the pledges, the flag salute is a form of utterance. Symbolism is a primitive but effective way of communicating ideas. The use of an emblem or flag to symbolize some system, idea, institution, or personality, is a short cut from mind to mind. Causes and nations, political parties, lodges and ecclesiastical groups seek to knit the loyalty of their followings to a flag or banner, a color or design. The State announces rank, function, and authority through crowns and maces, uniforms and black robes; the church speaks through the Cross, the Crucifix, the altar and shrine, and clerical raiment. Symbols of State often convey political ideas just as religious symbols come to convey theological ones. Associated with many of these symbols are appropriate gestures of acceptance or respect: a salute, a bowed or bared head, a bended knee. A person gets from a symbol the meaning he puts into it, and what is one man's comfort and inspiration is another's jest and scorn.

Over a decade ago Chief Justice Hughes led this Court in holding that the display of a red flag as a symbol of opposition by peaceful and legal means to organized government was protected by the free speech guaranties of the Constitution. *Stromberg v. California*, 283 U.S. 359. Here it is the State that employs a flag as a symbol of adherence to government as presently organized. It requires the individual to communicate by word and sign his acceptance of the political ideas it thus bespeaks. Objection to this form of communication when coerced is an old one, well known to the framers of the Bill of Rights.[13]

It is also to be noted that the compulsory flag salute and pledge requires affirmation of a belief and an attitude of mind. . . . It is now a commonplace that censorship or suppression of expression of opinion is tolerated by our Constitution only when the expression presents a clear and present danger of action of a kind the State is empowered to prevent and punish. It would seem that involuntary affirmation could be commanded only on even more immediate and urgent grounds than silence. . . . To sustain the compulsory flag salute we are required to say that a Bill of Rights which guards the individual's right to speak his own mind, left it open to public authorities to compel him to utter what is not in his mind.

Whether the First Amendment to the Constitution will permit officials to order observance of ritual of this nature does not depend upon whether as a voluntary exercise we would think it to be good, bad or merely innocuous. . . . [V]alidity of the asserted power to force an American citizen publicly to profess any statement of belief or to engage in any ceremony of assent to one presents questions of power that must be considered independently of any idea we may have as to the utility of the ceremony in question.

Nor does the issue as we see it turn on one's possession of particular religious views or the sincerity with which they are held. While religion supplies appellees' motive for enduring the discomforts of making the issue in this case, many citizens who do not share these religious views hold such a compulsory rite to infringe constitutional liberty of the individual. It is not necessary to inquire whether non-conformist beliefs will exempt from the duty to salute unless we first find power to make the salute a legal duty.

The *Gobitis* decision, however, *assumed*, as did the argument in that case and in this, that power exists in the State to impose the flag salute discipline upon school children in general. The Court only examined and rejected a claim based on religious beliefs of immunity from an unques-

---

[13] Early Christians were frequently persecuted for their refusal to participate in ceremonies before the statue of the emperor or other symbol of imperial authority. The story of William Tell's sentence to shoot an apple off his son's head for refusal to salute a bailiff's hat is an ancient one. The Quakers, William Penn included, suffered punishment rather than uncover their heads in deference to any civil authority.

tioned general rule. The question which underlies the flag salute controversy is whether such a ceremony so touching matters of opinion and political attitude may be imposed upon the individual by official authority under powers committed to any political organization under our Constitution. We examine rather than assume existence of this power and, against this broader definition of issues in this case, re-examine specific grounds assigned for the *Gobitis* decision.

1. It was said that the flag-salute controversy confronted the Court with "the problem which Lincoln cast in memorable dilemma: 'Must a government of necessity be too *strong* for the liberties of its people, or too *weak* to maintain its own existence?'" and that the answer must be in favor of strength. . . .

It may be doubted whether Mr. Lincoln would have thought that the strength of government to maintain itself would be impressively vindicated by our confirming power of the state to expel a handful of children from school. Such oversimplification, so handy in political debate, often lacks the precision necessary to postulates of judicial reasoning. If validly applied to this problem, the utterance cited would resolve every issue of power in favor of those in authority and would require us to override every liberty thought to weaken or delay execution of their policies.

Government of limited power need not be anemic government. Assurance that rights are secure tends to diminish fear and jealousy of strong government, and by making us feel safe to live under it makes for its better support. Without promise of a limiting Bill of Rights it is doubtful if our Constitution could have mustered enough strength to enable its ratification. To enforce those rights today is not to choose weak government over strong government. It is only to adhere as a means of strength to individual freedom of mind in preference to officially disciplined uniformity for which history indicates a disappointing and disastrous end.

The subject now before us exemplifies this principle. Free public education, if faithful to the ideal of secular instruction and political neutrality, will not be partisan or enemy of any class, creed, party, or faction. If it is to impose any ideological discipline, however, each party or denomination must seek to control, or failing that, to weaken the influence of the educational system. Observance of the limitations of the Constitution will not weaken government in the field appropriate for its exercise.

2. It was also considered in the *Gobitis* case that functions of educational officers in states, counties and school districts were such that to interfere with their authority "would in effect make us the school board for the country."

The Fourteenth Amendment, as now applied to the States, protects the citizen against the State itself and all of its creatures—Boards of Education not excepted. These have, of course, important, delicate, and highly discretionary functions, but none that they may not perform within the limits of the Bill of Rights. That they are educating the young for citizenship is reason for scrupulous protection of Constitutional freedoms of the individual, if we are not to strangle the free mind at its source and teach youth to discount important principles of our government as mere platitudes.

Such Boards are numerous and their territorial jurisdiction often small. . . . There are village tyrants as well as village Hampdens, but none who acts under color of law is beyond reach of the Constitution.

3. The *Gobitis* opinion reasoned that this is a field "where courts possess no marked and certainly no controlling competence,' that it is committed to the legislatures as well as the courts to guard cherished liberties and that it is constitutionally appropriate to "fight out the wise use of legislative authority in the forum of public opinion and before legislative assemblies rather than to transfer such a contest to the judicial arena," since all the "effective means of inducing political changes are left free."

The very purpose of a Bill of Rights was to withdraw certain subjects from the vicissitudes of political controversy, to place them beyond the reach of majorities and officials and to establish them as legal principles to be applied by the courts. One's right to life, liberty, and property, to free speech, a free press, freedom of worship and assembly, and other fundamental rights may not be submitted to vote; they depend on the outcome of no elections. . . . [F]reedoms of speech and of press, of assembly, and of worship . . . are susceptible of restriction only to prevent grave and immediate danger to interests which the state may lawfully protect. . . .

Nor does our duty to apply the Bill of Rights to assertions of official authority depend upon our possession of marked competence in the field where the invasion of rights occurs. . . . But we act in these matters not by authority of our competence but by force of our commissions. We cannot, because of modest estimates of our competence in such specialties as public education, withhold the judgment that history authenticates as the function of this Court when liberty is infringed.

4. Lastly, and this is the very heart of the *Gobitis* opinion, it reasons that "National unity is the basis of national security," that the authorities have "the right to select appropriate means for its attainment," and hence reaches the conclusion that such compulsory measures toward "national unity" are constitutional. Upon the verity of this assumption depends our answer in this case.

National unity as an end which officials may foster by persuasion and example is not in question. The problem is whether under our Constitution compulsion as here employed is a permissible means for its achievement.

Struggles to coerce uniformity of sentiment in support of some end thought essential to their time and country have been waged by many good as well as by evil men. Nationalism is a relatively recent phenomenon but at other times and places the ends have been racial or territorial security, support of a dynasty or regime, and particular plans for saving souls. As first and moderate methods to attain unity have failed, those bent on its accomplishment must resort to an ever-increasing severity. As governmental pressure toward unity becomes greater, so strife becomes more bitter as to whose unity it shall be. Probably no deeper division of our people could proceed from any provocation than from finding it necessary to choose what doctrine and whose program public educational officials shall compel youth to unite in embracing. Ultimate futility of such attempts to compel coherence is the lesson of every such effort from the Roman drive to stamp out Christianity as a disturber of its pagan unity, the Inquisition, as a means to religious and dynastic unity, the Siberian exiles as a means to Russian unity, down to the fast failing efforts of our present totalitarian enemies. Those who begin coercive elimination of dissent soon find themselves exterminating dissenters. Compulsory unification of opinion achieves only the unanimity of the graveyard.

It seems trite but necessary to say that the First Amendment to our Constitution was designed to avoid these ends by avoiding these beginnings. There is no mysticism in the American concept of the State or of the nature or origin of its authority. We set up government by consent of the governed, and the Bill of Rights denies those in power any legal opportunity to coerce that consent. Authority here is to be controlled by public opinion, not public opinion by authority.

The case is made difficult not because the principles of its decision are obscure but because the flag involved is our own. Nevertheless, we apply the limitations of the Constitution with no fear that freedom to be intellectually and spiritually diverse or even contrary will disintegrate the social organization. To believe that patriotism will not flourish if patriotic ceremonies are voluntary and spontaneous instead of a compulsory routine is to make an unflattering estimate of the appeal of our institutions to free minds. We can have intellectual individualism and the rich cultural diversities that we owe to exceptional minds only at the price of occasional eccentricity and abnormal attitudes. When they are so harmless to others or to the State as those we deal with here, the price is not too great. But freedom to differ is not limited to things that do not matter much. That would be a mere shadow of freedom. The test of its substance is the right to differ as to things that touch the heart of the existing order.

If there is any fixed star in our constitutional constellation, it is that no official, high or petty, can prescribe what shall be orthodox in politics, nationalism, religion, or other matters of opinion or force citizens to confess by word or act their faith therein. If there are any circumstances which permit an exception, they do not now occur to us.

We think the action of the local authorities in compelling the flag salute and pledge transcends constitutional limitations on their power and invades the sphere of intellect and spirit which it is the purpose of the First Amendment to our Constitution to reserve from all official control.

The decision of this Court in *Minersville School District v. Gobitis* and the holdings of those few *per curiam* decisions which preceded and foreshadowed it are overruled.

■ MR. JUSTICE ROBERTS and MR. JUSTICE REED adhere to the views expressed by the Court in *Minersville School District v. Gobitis*, 310 U.S. 586, and are of the opinion that the judgment below should be reversed.

■ [The concurring opinions of JUSTICES BLACK, DOUGLAS, and MURPHY are omitted.]

■ MR. JUSTICE FRANKFURTER, dissenting.

One who belongs to the most vilified and persecuted minority in history is not likely to be insensible to the freedoms guaranteed by our Constitution. Were my purely personal attitude relevant I should whole-heartedly associate myself with the general libertarian views in the Court's opinion, representing as they do the thought and action of a lifetime. But as judges we are neither Jew nor Gentile, neither Catholic nor agnostic. We owe equal attachment to the Constitution and are equally bound by our judicial obligations whether we derive our citizenship from the earliest or the latest immigrants to these shores. As a member of this Court I am not justified in writing my private notions of policy into the Constitution, no matter how deeply I may cherish them or how mischievous I may deem their disregard. The duty of a judge who must decide which of two claims before the Court shall prevail, that of a State to enact and enforce laws within its general competence or that of an individual to refuse obedience because of the demands of his conscience, is not that of the ordinary person. It can never be emphasized too much that one's own opinion about the wisdom or evil of a law should be excluded altogether when one is doing one's duty on the bench. The only opinion of our own even looking in that direction that is material is our opinion whether legislators could in reason have enacted such a law. In the light of all the circumstances, including the history of this question in this Court, it would require more daring than I possess to deny that reasonable legislators could have taken the action which is before us for review. Most unwillingly, therefore, I must differ from my brethren with regard to legislation like this. I cannot bring my mind to believe that the "liberty" secured by the Due Process Clause gives this Court authority to deny to the State of West Virginia the attainment of that which we all recognize as a legitimate legislative end, namely, the promotion of good citizenship, by employment of the means here chosen. . . .

NOTES

1. Was *Barnette* rightly decided? Is it a fair understanding of the freedom *of* speech that it embraces more than the freedom *to* speak and includes the freedom *not to* speak? If so, what is the scope of this right, as set forth in *Barnette*?

2. Note that *Barnette* occurs in the context of public schools, and within what the school district claimed to be a matter of its curriculum. Do students have the First Amendment right to refuse to participate in classroom instructional exercises that they regard as requiring them to articulate a view (or engage in expressive conduct) with which they disagree? If so, is there any limit to this principle? If not, what is the scope of *Barnette*'s freedom from compelled expression?

3. Not a hypothetical: Christina Axson–Flynn was a student in the University of Utah's actor training program. She was a member of the Latter–Day Saints and objected on religious grounds to being required to use the "F" word or to "take the Lord's name in vain," in classroom training exercises. School authorities said that she could not continue in the program if she did not perform scripts as written in all classroom exercises. She sued, challenging her *de facto* dismissal under *Barnette* (and the Free Exercise Clause). What result? The Tenth Circuit ruled in Ms. Axson–Flynn's favor, reversing the district court's grant of summary judgment on the ground that the case presented genuine issues of material fact as to whether university officials were motivated by disagreement with Ms. Axson–Flynn's religious beliefs. See *Axson–Flynn v. Johnson*, 356 F.3d 1277 (10th Cir. 2004).

4. Does the freedom from compelled speech include the right not to be forced by the government to make financial contributions to a private organization (like a labor union or a trade association) to support speech one does not wish to endorse or be associated with? In a series of cases, the Court has said *yes*. Thus, union members may be required to pay dues for collective-bargaining negotiations but not for a union's political or ideological advocacy. *Abood v. Detroit Bd. of Education*, 431 U.S. 209 (1977). In *United States v. United Foods, Inc.* 533 U.S. 405 (2001), the Court struck down a federal government-compelled advertising assessment imposed on fresh mushroom handlers to promote mushroom sales, distinguishing (not entirely persuasively) rather than disapproving *Glickman v. Wileman Bros.*, 521 U.S. 457 (1997), which had up-

held (5–4) a California marketing order assessing California fruit growers the costs of generic advertising of certain fruit products. In *Board of Regents of the University of Wisconsin v. Southworth*, 529 U.S. 217 (2000), the Court rejected students' challenge to a compulsory student activities fee that funded student groups, so long as the University's funding decisions observed "the requirement of viewpoint neutrality in the allocation of funding support." In short, if the funding program was itself viewpoint-neutral, then compelled contributions to a fund used to support a broad range of expressive activity by recipients did not present a problem under the *Barnette* and *Abood* line of decisions. (On the requirement of actual viewpoint-neutrality in such situations, see *Rosenberger v. Rector & Visitors of the University of Virginia*, 515 U.S. 819 (1995).)

Wooley v. Maynard

430 U.S. 705 (1977)

■ MR. CHIEF JUSTICE BURGER delivered the opinion of the Court.

The issue on appeal is whether the State of New Hampshire may constitutionally enforce criminal sanctions against persons who cover the motto "Live Free or Die" on passenger vehicle license plates because that motto is repugnant to their moral and religious beliefs.

I

Since 1969 New Hampshire has required that noncommercial vehicles bear license plates embossed with the state motto, "Live Free or Die." Another New Hampshire statute makes it a misdemeanor "knowingly [to obscure] . . . the figures or letters on any number plate." The term "letters" in this section has been interpreted by the State's highest court to include the state motto. . . .

Appellees George Maynard and his wife Maxine are followers of the Jehovah's Witnesses faith. The Maynards consider the New Hampshire State motto to be repugnant to their moral, religious, and political beliefs, and therefore assert it objectionable to disseminate this message by displaying it on their automobiles. Pursuant to these beliefs, the Maynards began early in 1974 to cover up the motto on their license plates. . . .

[Mr. Maynard was issued a first citation for violating § 262:27–c, appeared in court as his own attorney to contest it, explained his religious objections, and was fined $25, the fine suspended on condition of his "good behavior." Later that month, he was charged with another violation and again fought it in court, representing himself. He was again found guilty, fined $50, and sentenced to six months in jail and ordered to pay the $25 fine for the first offense.—Editors] Maynard informed the court that, as a matter of conscience, he refused to pay the two fines. The court thereupon sentenced him to jail for a period of 15 days. He has served the full sentence. . . .

II

. . . The District Court held that by covering up the state motto "Live Free or Die" on his automobile license plate, Mr. Maynard was engaging in symbolic speech and that "New Hampshire's interest in the enforcement of its defacement statute is not sufficient to justify the restriction on [Maynard's] constitutionally protected expression." We find it unnecessary to pass on the "symbolic speech" issue, since we find more appropriate First Amendment grounds to affirm the judgment of the District Court. We turn instead to what in our view is the essence of appellees' objection to the requirement that they display the motto "Live Free or Die" on their automobile license plates. This is succinctly summarized in the statement made by Mr. Maynard in his affidavit filed with the District Court: "I refuse to be coerced by the State into advertising a slogan which I find morally, ethically, religiously and politically abhorrent." We are thus faced with the question of whether the State may constitutionally require an individual to participate in the dissemination of an ideological message by displaying it on his private property in a manner and for the express purpose that it be observed and read by the public. We hold that the State may not do so.

A

We begin with the proposition that the right of freedom of thought protected by the First Amendment against state action includes both the right to speak freely and the right to refrain from speaking at all. See *Board of Education v. Barnette*, 319 U.S. 624, 633–634 (1943). A system which secures the right to proselytize religious, political, and ideological causes must also guarantee the concomitant right to decline to foster such concepts. The right to speak and the right to refrain from speaking are complementary components of the broader concept of "individual freedom of mind," *Id.*, at 637. This is illustrated by the recent case of *Miami Herald Publishing Co. v. Tornillo*, 418 U.S. 241 (1974), where we held unconstitutional a Florida statute placing an affirmative duty upon newspapers to publish the replies of political candidates whom they had criticized. We concluded that such a requirement deprived a newspaper of the fundamental right to decide what to print or omit:

> Faced with the penalties that would accrue to any newspaper that published news or commentary arguably within the reach of the right-of-access statute, editors might well conclude that the safe course is to avoid controversy. Therefore, under the operation of the Florida statute, political and electoral coverage would be blunted or reduced. Government-enforced right of access inescapably "dampens the vigor and limits the variety of public debate," *New York Times Co. v. Sullivan*, 376 U.S. [254,] at 279.

Id., at 257.

The Court in *Barnette*, *supra*, was faced with a state statute which required public school students to participate in daily public ceremonies by honoring the flag both with words and traditional salute gestures. In overruling its prior decision in *Minersville District v. Gobitis*, 310 U.S. 586 (1940), the Court held that "a ceremony so touching matters of opinion and political attitude may [not] be imposed upon the individual by official authority under powers committed to any political organization under our Constitution." Compelling the affirmative act of a flag salute involved a more serious infringement upon personal liberties than the passive act of carrying the state motto on a license plate, but the difference is essentially one of degree. Here, as in *Barnette*, we are faced with a state measure which forces an individual . . . to be an instrument for fostering public adherence to an ideological point of view he finds unacceptable. In doing so, the State "invades the sphere of intellect and spirit which it is the purpose of the First Amendment to our Constitution to reserve from all official control."

New Hampshire's statute in effect requires that appellees use their private property as a "mobile billboard" for the State's ideological message—or suffer a penalty, as Maynard already has. As a condition to driving an automobile—a virtual necessity for most Americans—the Maynards must display "Live Free or Die" to hundreds of people each day. The fact that most individuals agree with the thrust of New Hampshire's motto is not the test; most Americans also find the flag salute acceptable. The First Amendment protects the right of individuals to hold a point of view different from the majority and to refuse to foster, in the way New Hampshire commands, an idea they find morally objectionable.

B

Identifying the Maynards' interests as implicating First Amendment protections does not end our inquiry however. We must also determine whether the State's countervailing interest is sufficiently compelling to justify requiring appellees to display the state motto on their license plates. See, *e.g.*, *United States v. O'Brien*, 391 U.S. 367 (1968). The two interests advanced by the State are that display of the motto (1) facilitates the identification of passenger vehicles, and (2) promotes appreciation of history, individualism, and state pride.

[The Court rejected the first asserted state interest on the basis that it was readily satisfied by the portions of the license plate not covered up.— Editors] . . . The State's second claimed interest is not ideologically neutral. The State is seeking to communicate to others an official view as to proper appreciation of history, state pride, and individualism. Of course, the State may legitimately pursue such interests in any number of ways. However, where the State's interest is to disseminate an ideology, no matter how acceptable to some, such interest cannot outweigh an individual's First Amendment right to avoid becoming the courier for such message.

We conclude that the State of New Hampshire may not require appellees to display the state motto[15] upon their vehicle license plates.

■ [JUSTICE WHITE'S dissent, addressed to the abstention question, is omitted.]

■ Mr. JUSTICE REHNQUIST, with whom MR. JUSTICE BLACKMUN joins, dissenting.

. . . The Court cites *Barnette* for the proposition that there is a constitutional right, in some cases, to "refrain from speaking." What the Court does not demonstrate is that there is any "speech" or "speaking" in the context of this case. . . . For First Amendment principles to be implicated, the State must place the citizen in the position of either apparently to, or actually "asserting as true" the message. This was the focus of *Barnette*, and clearly distinguishes this case from that one.

In holding that the New Hampshire statute does not run afoul of our holding in *Barnette*, the New Hampshire Supreme Court in [another case] aptly articulated why there is no required affirmation of belief in this case: "The defendants' membership in a class of persons required to display plates bearing the State motto carries no implication and is subject to no requirement that they endorse that motto or profess to adopt it as matter of belief."

---

[15] It has been suggested that today's holding will be read as sanctioning the obliteration of the national motto, "In God We Trust" from United States coins and currency. That question is not before us today but we note that currency, which is passed from hand to hand, differs in significant respects from an automobile, which is readily associated with its operator. Currency is generally carried in a purse or pocket and need not be displayed to the public. The bearer of currency is thus not required to publicly advertise the national motto.

As found by the New Hampshire Supreme Court . . ., there is nothing in state law which precludes appellees from displaying their disagreement with the state motto as long as the methods used do not obscure the license plates. Thus appellees could place on their bumper a conspicuous bumper sticker explaining in no uncertain terms that they do not profess the motto "Live Free or Die" and that they violently disagree with the connotations of that motto. Since any implication that they affirm the motto can be so easily displaced, I cannot agree that the state statutory system for motor vehicle identification and tourist promotion may be invalidated under the fiction that appellees are unconstitutionally forced to affirm, or profess belief in, the state motto.

The logic of the Court's opinion leads to startling, and I believe totally unacceptable, results. For example, the mottoes "In God We Trust" and "E Pluribus Unum" appear on the coin and currency of the United States. I cannot imagine that the statutes proscribing defacement of United States currency impinge upon the First Amendment rights of an atheist. The fact that an atheist carries and uses United States currency does not, in any meaningful sense, convey any affirmation of belief on his part in the motto "In God We Trust." Similarly, there is no affirmation of belief involved in the display of state license tags upon the private automobiles involved here.

I would reverse the judgment of the District Court.

NOTES

1. Is "In God We Trust" on the nation's coins and currency a violation of the principle of *Barnette* and *Wooley*?

2. Is *Wooley* persuasive on its facts? Can the state's license plate slogan be defended on the ground that it is *the state's* speech? Compare the analysis in *Pleasant Grove City v. Summum*, 129 S. Ct. 1125 (2009). The municipality of Pleasant Grove maintained a small park in which it displayed a collection of privately donated monuments, including one of the Ten Commandments. A religious group, called Summum, argued that this was a public forum, and that it had a right to erect its own monument, commemorating its version of the Commandments, called "The Seven Aphorisms." In a unanimous decision, the Court held that the monuments in the park, though privately donated, were the government's own speech and did not create a forum. Note that this holding implied that the Establishment Clause would apply to the display. In *Capitol Square Review and Advisory Bd. v. Pinette*, 515 U.S. 753 (1995), the Court had held that signs and symbols displayed by members of the public in a city square in front of the capitol building were private, and constituted a public forum— meaning that a private group (which happened to be the Ku Klux Klan, though its identity was irrelevant to the legal analysis), had the right to erect a large cross. The cross would not be attributed to the state for purposes of the Establishment Clause. All these cases, and many more, hinge on whether the speech in question is private or governmental. Can you tell the difference? Here is an oversimplified statement of the rule: The government must be evenhanded in its regulation of private speech (including religious speech), and may not compel private persons to speak. But the government may speak in its own name and may take sides even on controversial matters without having to give private persons the same opportunity, except that it may not endorse religion.

The Right of Groups to Control Their Own Expressive Messages

Barnette stands for the proposition that the government may not compel individuals to state or affirm messages other than the ones they have chosen. The next case, *Hurley v. Irish–American Gay, Lesbian and Bisexual Group of Boston*, considers a *Barnette*-like problem as applied to a *group*'s desire to control the content of its own expressive messages by excluding messages it does not wish to have mixed with its own. Is "freedom of association" to engage in expression nothing more than the aggregation of individual free speech claims by like-minded individuals?

Hurley provides a good case for reviewing and integrating a number of First Amendment doctrines introduced already in this chapter. The case involves a St. Patrick's Day parade. Is a parade "speech"? May government condition a permit for a parade on certain grounds? Is the condition that the government imposed here a speech-related condition, or is it content neutral? What is the government's interest? What is the "negative free speech" interest here?

Hurley v. Irish–American Gay, Lesbian and Bisexual Group of Boston

515 U.S. 557 (1995)

■ JUSTICE SOUTER delivered the opinion of the Court.

The issue in this case is whether Massachusetts may require private citizens who organize a parade to include among the marchers a group imparting a message the organizers do not wish to convey. We hold that such a mandate violates the First Amendment.

I

March 17 is set aside for two celebrations in South Boston. As early as 1737, some people in Boston observed the feast of the apostle to Ireland, and since 1776 the day has marked the evacuation of royal troops and Loyalists from the city, prompted by the guns captured at Ticonderoga and set up on Dorchester Heights under General Washington's command. Washington himself reportedly drew on the earlier tradition in choosing "St. Patrick" as the response to "Boston," the password used in the colonial lines on evacuation day. Although the General Court of Massachusetts did not officially designate March 17 as Evacuation Day until 1938, the City Council of Boston had previously sponsored public celebrations of Evacuation Day, including notable commemorations on the centennial in 1876, and on the 125th anniversary in 1901, with its parade, salute, concert, and fireworks display.

The tradition of formal sponsorship by the city came to an end in 1947. . . . Every year since that time, the [South Boston Allied War Veterans] Council has applied for and received a permit for the parade, which at times has included as many as 20,000 marchers and drawn up to 1 million watchers. No other applicant has ever applied for that permit. Through 1992, the city allowed the Council to use the city's official seal, and provided printing services as well as direct funding.

In 1992, a number of gay, lesbian, and bisexual descendants of the Irish immigrants joined together with other supporters to form the respondent organization, GLIB, to march in the parade as a way to express pride in their Irish heritage as openly gay, lesbian, and bisexual individuals. . . . Although the Council denied GLIB's application to take part in the 1992 parade, GLIB obtained a state-court order to include its contingent, which marched "uneventfully" among that year's 10,000 participants and 750,000 spectators.

In 1993, after the Council had again refused to admit GLIB to the upcoming parade, the organization and some of its members filed this suit against the Council, the individual petitioner John J. "Wacko" Hurley, and the city of Boston, alleging violations of the State and Federal Constitutions and of the state public accommodations law, which prohibits "any distinction, discrimination or restriction on account of . . . sexual orientation . . . relative to the admission of any person to, or treatment in any place of public accommodation, resort or amusement." Mass. Gen. Laws § 272:98 (1992). . . . [T]he state trial court ruled that the parade fell within the statutory definition of a public accommodation . . . [and] rejected the Council's contention that the parade was "private" (in the sense of being exclusive), holding instead that "the lack of genuine selectivity in choosing participants and sponsors demonstrates that the Parade is a public event." . . .

The court rejected the notion that GLIB's admission would trample on the Council's First Amendment rights since the court understood that constitutional protection of any interest in expressive association would "requir[e] focus on a specific message, theme, or group" absent from the parade. "Given the [Council's] lack of selectivity in choosing participants and failure to circumscribe the marchers' message," the court found it "impossible to discern any specific expressive purpose entitling the Parade to protection under the First Amendment." It concluded that the parade is "not an exercise of [the Council's] constitutionally protected right of expressive association," but instead "an open recreational event that is subject to the public accommodations law."

The court held that because the statute did not mandate inclusion of GLIB but only prohibited discrimination based on sexual orientation, any infringement on the Council's right to expressive association was only "incidental" and "no greater than necessary to accomplish the statute's legitimate purpose" of eradicating discrimination. App. to Pet. for Cert. (citing *Roberts v. United States Jaycees,* 468 U.S. 609, 628–629 (1984)). . . . The Supreme Judicial Court of Massachusetts affirmed . . .

We granted certiorari to determine whether the requirement to admit a parade contingent expressing a message not of the private organizers' own choosing violates the First Amendment. We hold that it does and reverse.

II

. . . *[The Court noted that GLIB did not present any constitutional claim before the Court.—Editors]* [T]heir claim for inclusion in the parade rests solely on the Massachusetts public accommodations law. . . .

III–A

If there were no reason for a group of people to march from here to there except to reach a destination, they could make the trip without expressing any message beyond the fact of the march itself. Some people might call such a procession a parade, but it would not be much of one. . . . [W]e use the word "parade" to indicate marchers who are making some sort of collective point, not just to each other but to bystanders along the way. . . . Parades are thus a form of expression, not just motion, and the inherent expressiveness of marching to make a point explains our cases involving protest marches. In *Gregory v. Chicago,* 394 U.S. 111, 112 (1969), for example, petitioners had taken part in a procession to express their grievances to the city government, and we held that such a "march, if peaceful and orderly, falls well within the sphere of conduct protected by the First Amendment." Similarly, in *Edwards v. South Carolina, supra,* 372 U.S., at 235 where petitioners had joined in a march of protest and pride, carrying placards and singing The Star Spangled Banner, we held that the activities "reflect an exercise of these basic constitutional rights in their most pristine and classic form."

The protected expression that inheres in a parade is not limited to its banners and songs, however, for the Constitution looks beyond written or spoken words as mediums of expression. Noting that "[s]ymbolism is a primitive but effective way of communicating ideas," *West Virginia Bd. of Ed. v. Barnette,* 319 U.S. 624, 632 (1943), our cases have recognized that the First Amendment shields such acts as saluting a flag (and refusing to do so), wearing an armband to protest a war, *Tinker v. Des Moines Independent Community School Dist.,* 393 U.S. 503, 505–506 (1969), displaying a red flag, *Stromberg v. California,* 283 U.S. 359, 369 (1931), and even "[m]arching, walking or parading" in uniforms displaying the swastika, *National Socialist Party of America v. Skokie,* 432 U.S. 43 (1977). As some of these examples show, a narrow, succinctly articulable message is not a condition of constitutional protection. . . .

Not many marches, then, are beyond the realm of expressive parades, and the South Boston celebration is not one of them. Spectators line the streets; people march in costumes and uniforms, carrying flags and banners with all sorts of messages (*e.g.,* "England get out of Ireland," "Say no to drugs"); marching bands and pipers play; floats are pulled along; and the whole show is broadcast over Boston television. To be sure, we agree with the state courts that in spite of excluding some applicants, the Council is rather lenient in admitting participants. But a private speaker does not forfeit constitutional protection simply by combining multifarious voices, or by failing to edit their themes to isolate an exact message as the exclusive subject matter of the speech. Nor, under our precedent, does First Amendment protection require a speaker to generate, as an original matter, each item featured in the communication. . . .

Respondents' participation as a unit in the parade was equally expressive. GLIB was formed for the very purpose of marching in it, as the trial court found, in order to celebrate its members' identity as openly gay, lesbian, and bisexual descendants of the Irish immigrants, to show that there are such individuals in the community, and to support the like men and women who sought to march in the New York parade. The organization distributed a fact sheet describing the members' intentions, and the record otherwise corroborates the expressive nature of GLIB's participation. In 1993, members of GLIB marched behind a shamrock-strewn banner with the simple inscription "Irish American Gay, Lesbian and Bisexual Group of Boston." GLIB understandably seeks to communicate its ideas as part of the existing parade, rather than staging one of its own.

B

The Massachusetts public accommodations law under which respondents brought suit has a venerable history. At common law, innkeepers, smiths, and others who "made profession of a public employment," were prohibited from refusing, without good reason, to serve a customer. As one of the 19th–century English judges put it, the rule was that "[t]he innkeeper is not to select his guests[;] [h]e has no right to say to one, you shall come into my inn, and to another you shall not, as every one coming and conducting himself in a proper manner has a right to be received; and for this purpose innkeepers are a sort of public servants." . . .

As with many public accommodations statutes across the Nation, the legislature continued to broaden the scope of legislation, to the point that the law today prohibits discrimination on the basis of "race, color, religious creed, national origin, sex, sexual orientation . . ., deafness, blindness or any physical or mental disability or ancestry" in "the admission of any person to, or treatment in any place of public accommodation, resort or amusement." Provisions like these are well within the State's usual power to enact when a legislature has reason to believe that a given group is the target of discrimination, and they do not, as a general matter, violate the First or Fourteenth Amendments. Nor is this statute unusual in any obvious way, since it does not, on its face, target speech or discriminate on the basis of its content, the focal point of its prohibition being rather on the act of discriminating against individuals in the provision of publicly available goods, privileges, and services on the proscribed grounds.

C

In the case before us, however, the Massachusetts law has been applied in a peculiar way. Its enforcement does not address any dispute about the participation of openly gay, lesbian, or bisexual individuals in various units admitted to the parade. Petitioners disclaim any intent to exclude homosexuals as such, and no individual member of GLIB claims to have been excluded from parading as a member of any group that the Council has approved to march. Instead, the disagreement goes to the admission of GLIB as its own parade unit carrying its own banner. Since every participating unit affects the message conveyed by the private organizers, the state courts' application of the statute produced an order essentially requiring petitioners to alter the expressive content of their parade. Although the state courts spoke of the parade as a place of public accommodation, once the expressive character of both the parade and the marching GLIB contingent is understood, it becomes apparent that the state courts' application of the statute had the effect of declaring the sponsors' speech itself to be the public accommodation. Under this approach any contingent of protected individuals with a message would have the right to participate in petitioners' speech, so that the communication produced by the private organizers would be shaped by all those protected by the law who wished to join in with some expressive demonstration of their own. But this use of the State's power violates the fundamental rule of protection under the First Amendment, that a speaker has the autonomy to choose the content of his own message.

"Since *all* speech inherently involves choices of what to say and what to leave unsaid," *Pacific Gas & Electric Co. v. Public Utilities Comm'n of Cal.,* 475 U.S. 1, 11 (1986) (plurality opinion) (emphasis in original), one important manifestation of the principle of free speech is that one who chooses to speak may also decide "what not to say," *id.,* at 16. . . . [T]his general rule, that the speaker has the right to tailor the speech, applies not only to expressions of value, opinion, or endorsement, but equally to statements of fact the speaker would rather avoid, *McIntyre v. Ohio Elections Comm'n,* 514 U.S. 334, 341–342 (1995). . . . Nor is the rule's benefit restricted to the press, being enjoyed by business corporations generally and by ordinary people engaged in unsophisticated expression as well as by professional publishers. . . .

Petitioners' claim to the benefit of this principle of autonomy to control one's own speech is as sound as the South Boston parade is expressive. . . . [T]he Council clearly decided to exclude a message it did not like from the communication it chose to make, and that is enough to invoke its right as a private speaker to shape its expression by speaking on one subject while remaining silent on another. The message it disfavored is not difficult to identify. Although GLIB's point (like the Council's) is not wholly articulate, a contingent marching behind the organization's banner would at least bear witness to the fact that some Irish are gay, lesbian, or bisexual, and the presence of the organized marchers would suggest their view that people of their sexual orientations have as much claim to unqualified social acceptance as heterosexuals and indeed as members of parade units organized around other identifying characteristics. The parade's organizers may not believe these facts about Irish sexuality to be so, or they may object to unqualified social acceptance of gays and lesbians or have some other reason for wishing to keep GLIB's message out of the parade. But whatever the reason, it boils down to the choice of a speaker not to propound a particular point of view, and that choice is presumed to lie beyond the government's power to control.

. . . On its face, the object of the [Massachusetts] law is to ensure by statute for gays and lesbians desiring to make use of public accommodations what the old common law promised to any member of the public wanting a meal at the inn, that accepting the usual terms of service, they will not be turned away merely on the proprietor's exercise of personal preference. When the law is applied to expressive activity in the way it was done here, its apparent object is simply to require speakers to modify the content of their expression to whatever extent beneficiaries of the law choose to alter it with messages of their own. But in the absence of some further, legitimate end, this object is merely to allow exactly what the general rule of speaker's autonomy forbids.

It might, of course, have been argued that a broader objective is apparent: that the ultimate point of forbidding acts of discrimination toward certain classes is to produce a society free of the corresponding biases. Requiring access to a speaker's message would thus be not an end in itself, but a means to produce speakers free of the biases, whose expressive conduct would be at least neutral toward the particular classes, obviating any future need for correction. But if this indeed is the point of applying the state law to expressive conduct, it is a decidedly fatal objective. . . . The very idea that a noncommercial speech restriction be used to produce thoughts and statements acceptable to some groups or, indeed, all people, grates on the First Amendment, for it amounts to nothing less than a proposal to limit speech in the service of orthodox expression. The Speech Clause has no more certain antithesis. See, *e.g., Barnette,* 319 U.S., at 642. While the law is free to promote all sorts of conduct in place of harmful behavior, it is not free to interfere with speech for no better reason than promoting an approved message or discouraging a disfavored one, however enlightened either purpose may strike the government. . . .

IV

Our holding today rests not on any particular view about the Council's message but on the Nation's commitment to protect freedom of speech. Disapproval of a private speaker's statement does not legitimize use of the

Commonwealth's power to compel the speaker to alter the message by including one more acceptable to others. . . .

NOTES

1. *Group Barnette Rights.* Is the question of a group's freedom to control the content of its own expression at all different from the question of an individual's freedom?

2. *Hurley and the First Amendment Right of Expressive Association.* *Hurley* is an important, unanimous ruling for the proposition that a speaker—including an organization—has the right to control the content of its own expressive messages. Does a group's First Amendment freedom to control the content of its messages also include a right to exclude members that the group feels do not share the group's views or reflect its self-definition? That is the question presented in several cases below. Does *Hurley* have anything to say about this proposition?

Abood v. Detroit Board of Education
431 U.S. 209 (1977)

■ MR. JUSTICE STEWART delivered the opinion of the Court.

The State of Michigan has enacted legislation authorizing a system for union representation of local governmental employees. A union and a local government employer are specifically permitted to agree to an "agency shop" arrangement, whereby every employee represented by a union—even though not a union member—must pay to the union, as a condition of employment, a service fee equal in amount to union dues. The issue before us is whether this arrangement violates the constitutional rights of government employees who object to public-sector unions as such or to various union activities financed by the compulsory service fees. . . . *[The Court upheld the requirement that unwilling workers pay dues to support the collective-bargaining and grievance-resolution activities of the union, but not their political advocacy.—Editors]*

To compel employees financially to support their collective-bargaining representative has an impact upon their First Amendment interests. An employee may very well have ideological objections to a wide variety of activities undertaken by the union in its role as exclusive representative. His moral or religious views about the desirability of abortion may not square with the union's policy in negotiating a medical benefits plan. One individual might disagree with a union policy of negotiating limits on the right to strike, believing that to be the road to serfdom for the working class, while another might have economic or political objections to unionism itself. An employee might object to the union's wage policy because it violates guidelines designed to limit inflation, or might object to the union's seeking a clause in the collective-bargaining agreement proscribing racial discrimination. The examples could be multiplied. To be required to help finance the union as a collective-bargaining agent might well be thought, therefore, to interfere in some way with an employee's freedom to associate for the advancement of ideas, or to refrain from doing so, as he sees fit. But . . . such interference as exists is constitutionally justified by the legislative assessment of the important contribution of the union shop to the system of labor relations established by Congress. . . .

Our decisions establish with unmistakable clarity that the freedom of an individual to associate for the purpose of advancing beliefs and ideas is protected by the First and Fourteenth Amendments. Equally clear is the proposition that a government may not require an individual to relinquish rights guaranteed him by the First Amendment as a condition of public employment. The appellants argue that they fall within the protection of these cases because they have been prohibited, not from actively associating, but rather from refusing to associate. They specifically argue that they may constitutionally prevent the Union's spending a part of their required service fees to contribute to political candidates and to express political views unrelated to its duties as exclusive bargaining representative. We have concluded that this argument is a meritorious one.

One of the principles underlying the Court's decision in *Buckley v. Valeo*, 424 U.S. 1, was that contributing to an organization for the purpose of spreading a political message is protected by the First Amendment. . . . The fact that the appellants are compelled to make, rather than prohibited from making, contributions for political purposes works no less an infringement of their constitutional rights. For at the heart of the First Amendment is the notion that an individual should be free to believe as he will, and that in a free society one's beliefs should be shaped by his mind and his conscience rather than coerced by the State. . . .

We do not hold that a union cannot constitutionally spend funds for the expression of political views, on behalf of political candidates, or toward the advancement of other ideological causes not germane to its duties as collective-bargaining representative. Rather, the Constitution requires only that such expenditures be financed from charges, dues, or assessments paid by employees who do not object to advancing those ideas and who are not coerced into doing so against their will by the threat of loss of governmental employment. . . .

■ [The concurring opinions of JUSTICES REHNQUIST and STEVENS are omitted.]

■ MR. JUSTICE POWELL, with whom THE CHIEF JUSTICE and MR. JUSTICE BLACKMUN join, concurring in the judgment.

The Court today holds that a State cannot constitutionally compel public employees to contribute to union political activities which they oppose. . . . With this much of the Court's opinion I agree, and I therefore join the Court's judgment remanding this case for further proceedings.

But the Court's holding and judgment are but a small part of today's decision. Working from the novel premise that public employers are under no greater constitutional constraints than their counterparts in the private sector, the Court apparently rules that public employees can be compelled by the State to pay full union dues to a union with which they disagree, subject only to a possible rebate or deduction if they are willing to step forward, declare their opposition to the union, and initiate a proceeding to establish that some portion of their dues has been spent on "ideological activities unrelated to collective bargaining." Such a sweeping limitation of First Amendment rights by the Court is . . . unsupported by either precedent or reason. . . .

The initial question is whether a requirement of a school board that all of its employees contribute to a teachers' union as a condition of employment impinges upon the First Amendment interests of those who refuse to support the union, whether because they disapprove of unionization of public employees or because they object to certain union activities or positions. The Court answers this question in the affirmative.... I agree with the Court as far as it goes, but I would make it more explicit that compelling a government employee to give financial support to a union in the public sector—regardless of the uses to which the union puts the contribution—impinges seriously upon interests in free speech and association protected by the First Amendment.

In *Buckley v. Valeo*, 424 U.S. 1 (1976), we considered the constitutional validity of the Federal Election Campaign Act, which in one of its provisions limited the amounts that individuals could contribute to federal election campaigns. We held that these limitations on political contributions "impinge on protected associational freedoms":

> Making a contribution, like joining a political party, serves to affiliate a person with a candidate. In addition, it enables like-minded persons to pool their resources in furtherance of common political goals. The Act's contribution ceilings thus limit one important means of associating with a candidate or committee.

Id. at 22. That *Buckley* dealt with a contribution limitation rather than a contribution requirement does not alter its importance for this case. An individual can no more be required to affiliate with a candidate by making a contribution than he can be prohibited from such affiliation. The only question after *Buckley* is whether a union in the public sector is sufficiently distinguishable from a political candidate or committee to remove the withholding of financial contributions from First Amendment protection. In my view no principled distinction exists.

The ultimate objective of a union in the public sector, like that of a political party, is to influence public decisionmaking in accordance with the views and perceived interests of its membership. Whether a teachers' union is concerned with salaries and fringe benefits, teacher qualifications and inservice training, pupil-teacher ratios, length of the school day, student discipline, or the content of the high school curriculum, its objective is to bring school board policy and decisions into harmony with its own views. Similarly, to the extent that school board expenditures and policy are guided by decisions made by the municipal, State, and Federal Governments, the union's objective is to obtain favorable decisions—and to place persons in positions of power who will be receptive to the union's viewpoint. In these respects, the public-sector union is indistinguishable from the traditional political party in this country....

Nor is there any basis here for distinguishing "collective-bargaining activities" from "political activities" so far as the interests protected by the First Amendment are concerned. Collective bargaining in the public sector is "political" in any meaningful sense of the word. This is most obvious when public-sector bargaining extends—as it may in Michigan—to such matters of public policy as the educational philosophy that will inform the high school curriculum. But it is also true when public-sector bargaining focuses on such "bread and butter" issues as wages, hours, vacations, and pensions. Decisions on such issues will have a direct impact on the level of public services, priorities within state and municipal budgets, creation of bonded indebtedness, and tax rates. The cost of public education is normally the largest element of a county or municipal budget. Decisions reached through collective bargaining in the schools will affect not only the teachers and the quality of education, but also the taxpayers and the beneficiaries of other important public services. Under our democratic system of government, decisions on these critical issues of public policy have been entrusted to elected officials who ultimately are responsible to the voters.

Disassociation with a public-sector union and the expression of disagreement with its positions and objectives therefore lie at "the core of those activities protected by the First Amendment." *Elrod v. Burns*, 427 U.S. 347, 356 (1976) (plurality opinion). . . .

"Neither the right to associate nor the right to participate in political activities is absolute." *CSC v. Letter Carriers*, 413 U. S. 548, 567 (1973). This is particularly true in the field of public employment, where "the State has interests as an employer in regulating the speech of its employees that differ significantly from those it possesses in connection with regulation of the speech of the citizenry in general." *Pickering v. Board of Education*, 391 U. S. 563, 568 (1968). Nevertheless, even in public employment, "a significant impairment of First Amendment rights must survive exacting scrutiny." *Elrod v. Burns*, 427 U.S., at 362 (plurality opinion).

> The [governmental] interest advanced must be paramount, one of vital importance, and the burden is on the government to show the existence of such an interest. . . . [C]are must be taken not to confuse the interest of partisan organizations with governmental interests. Only the latter will suffice. Moreover, . . . the government must emplo[y] means closely drawn to avoid unnecessary abridgment.

Id., at 362–363 (plurality opinion). . . .

Before today it had been well established that when state law intrudes upon protected speech, the State itself must shoulder the burden of proving that its action is justified by overriding state interests. The Court, for the first time in a First Amendment case, simply reverses this principle. Under today's decision, a nonunion employee who would vindicate his First Amendment rights apparently must initiate a proceedings to prove that the union has allocated some portion of its budget to "ideological activities unrelated to collective bargaining." I would adhere to established First Amendment principles and require the State to come forward and demonstrate, as to each union expenditure for which it would exact support from minority employees, that the compelled contribution is necessary to serve overriding governmental objectives. This placement of the burden of litigation, not the Court's, gives appropriate protection to First Amendment rights without sacrificing ends of government that may be deemed important.

[Assignment 52]

M. COLLECTIVE EXPRESSION: GROUPS AND THE FREEDOM OF "EXPRESSIVE ASSOCIATION"

As we have seen, the freedom of speech includes the right to engage in *collective* speech—for groups of persons to organize, join their voices, pool their resources, and speak or publish together. Does the right to engage in collective expression include a right of a group to define itself and *exclude* persons that the rest of the group believes do not embrace the message of the group or who would make poor exemplars or representatives of the group? In many ways, the right of expressive association resembles the right identified in *Barnette* and *Hurley* for individual speakers—or a group of speakers—to control the content of their own messages, and not to be required to embrace messages they disfavor.

How far does this First Amendment principle extend? Does it matter whether the group involved is a political party or something more like a "business club" or a private law firm? What if the group is a law school? What if the group is the Boy Scouts?

Democratic Party of United States v. Wisconsin
450 U.S. 107 (1981)

■ JUSTICE STEWART delivered the opinion of the Court.

The charter of the appellant Democratic Party of the United States (National Party) provides that delegates to its National Convention shall be chosen through procedures in which only Democrats can participate. Consistently with the charter, the National Party's Delegate Selection Rules provide that only those who are willing to affiliate publicly with the Democratic Party may participate in the process of selecting delegates to the Party's National Convention. The question on this appeal is whether Wisconsin may successfully insist that its delegates to the Convention be seated, even though those delegates are chosen through a process that includes a binding state preference primary election in which voters do not declare their party affiliation. The Wisconsin Supreme Court held that the National Convention is bound by the Wisconsin primary election results, and cannot refuse to seat the delegates chosen in accord with Wisconsin law. . . .

I

The election laws of Wisconsin allow non-Democrats—including members of other parties and independents—to vote in the Democratic primary without regard to party affiliation and without requiring a public declaration of party preference. The voters in Wisconsin's "open" primary express their choice among Presidential candidates for the Democratic Party's nomination; they do not vote for delegates to the National Convention. Delegates to the National Convention are chosen separately, after the primary, at caucuses of persons who have stated their affiliation with the Party. But these delegates, under Wisconsin law, are bound to vote at the National Convention in accord with the results of the open primary election. Accordingly, while Wisconsin's open Presidential preference primary does not itself violate National Party rules, the State's mandate that the results of the primary shall determine the allocation of votes cast by the State's delegates at the National Convention does. . . .

III

The question in this case is . . . whether, once Wisconsin has opened its Democratic Presidential preference primary to voters who do not publicly declare their party affiliation, it may then bind the National Party to honor the binding primary results, even though those results were reached in a manner contrary to National Party rules. . . . [T]his issue was resolved, we believe, in *Cousins v. Wigoda*, 419 U.S. 477.

In *Cousins* the Court reviewed the decision of an Illinois court holding that state law exclusively governed the seating of a state delegation at the 1972 Democratic National Convention, and enjoining the National Party from refusing to seat delegates selected in a manner in accord with state law although contrary to National Party rules. . . . The Court reversed the state judgment, holding that "Illinois' interest in protecting the integrity of its electoral process cannot be deemed compelling in the context of the selection of delegates to the National Party Convention." That disposition controls here.

The *Cousins* Court relied upon the principle that "[t]he National Democratic Party and its adherents enjoy a constitutionally protected right of political association." This First Amendment freedom to gather in association for the purpose of advancing shared beliefs is protected by the Fourteenth Amendment from infringement by any State. And the freedom to associate for the "common advancement of political beliefs" necessarily presupposes the freedom to identify the people who constitute the association, and to limit the association to those people only. "Any interference with the freedom of a party is simultaneously an interference with the freedom of its adherents." *Sweezy v. New Hampshire*, 354 U.S. 234, 250.

Here, the members of the National Party, speaking through their rules, chose to define their associational rights by limiting those who could participate in the processes leading to the selection of delegates to their National Convention. On several occasions this Court has recognized that the inclusion of persons unaffiliated with a political party may seriously distort its collective decisions—thus impairing the party's essential functions—and that political parties may accordingly protect themselves "from intrusion by those with adverse political principles." *Ray v. Blair*, 343 U.S. 214, 221–222. . . .

A political party's choice among the various ways of determining the makeup of a State's delegation to the party's national convention is protected by the Constitution. And as is true of all expressions of First Amendment freedoms, the courts may not interfere on the ground that they view a particular expression as unwise or irrational.[27] . . .

IV

We must consider, finally, whether the State has compelling interests that justify the imposition of its will upon the appellants. . . . The State asserts a compelling interest in preserving the overall integrity of the electoral process, providing secrecy of the ballot, increasing voter participation in primaries, and preventing harassment of voters. But all those interests go to the conduct of the Presidential preference primary—not to the imposition of voting requirements upon those who, in a separate process, are eventually selected as delegates. Therefore, the interests advanced by the State do not justify its substantial intrusion into the associational freedom of members of the National Party. . . .

■ JUSTICE POWELL, with whom JUSTICE BLACKMUN and JUSTICE REHNQUIST join, dissenting.

. . . The question in this case is whether, in light of the National Party's rule that only publicly declared Democrats may have a voice in the nomination process, Wisconsin's open primary law infringes the National Party's First Amendment rights of association. Because I believe that this law does not impose a substantial burden on the associational freedom of the National Party, and actually promotes the free political activity of the citizens of Wisconsin, I dissent. . . .

---

[27] . . . It is for the National Party—and not the Wisconsin Legislature or any court—to determine the appropriate standards for participation in the Party's candidate selection process.

NOTES

1. *Democratic Party of Wisconsin* is the leading modern case in a line of decisions standing for the proposition that a group's collective constitutional rights to free speech and association to engage in expressive activity includes the right to define who is in the group, in order for the group to be able to control the content of its own collective expression. Put in doctrinal terms, the right of "expressive association" includes a right of expressive *dis*association— the right to exclude from the group persons who do not share in the group's message, purposes, beliefs, values, or ideals. (*Hurley v. GLIB* can be seen as a case of this kind as well, in addition to illustrating the more specific problem of government compulsion for a speaker to include a message the speaker does not wish to include with its own message.)

Do you agree with this notion as a general principle? How would you formulate it? Should it extend to the right of a national political party to decide the rules by which delegates to its national convention are selected—overriding state election law procedures to the contrary? That is what the Court held in *Democratic Party of Wisconsin*. Essentially, the majority said: "It's their party; they can decide who gets to come to their party." Do you agree? How far might this principle extend? What kind of groups would or should get the benefit of it?

The First Amendment speech clause basis for the doctrine has been put this way: "if the freedom of speech can be a group freedom, that group freedom means that *the group* gets to decide *what* messages the group wishes to express, *who* is in the group that is deciding what the group 'says' *as a group*, *how* the group will operate to decide these things, and *how* and *through whom* it will communicate the messages it chooses." Michael Stokes Paulsen, *Scouts, Families, and Schools*, 85 Minn. L. Rev. 1917, 1922 (2001).

2. Next consider three cases that test the logic and limits of this doctrine. First, may a private "business club" or "service club" (like the Jaycees, Kiwanis, Rotary, Lions Club) exclude women? In answer to this question, *Roberts v. Jaycees* said *no*, on the ground that the group was primarily commercial in character and was not really seeking to preserve any particular expressive message. Second, may the Boy Scouts of America have a policy or practice of not allowing gay men to serve in leadership positions of troops of young boys, on the basis that this is not consistent with the group's mission and values? *Boy Scouts of America v. Dale* said *yes*, but the Court was bitterly divided (5–4) on this question, notwithstanding *Hurley,* decided unanimously five years earlier. Third, may public and private universities exclude U.S. military recruiters from campus for non-compliance with the universities' non-discrimination (or other?) regulations, and still be constitutionally entitled to receive government funds? *Rumsfeld v. FAIR* unanimously said *no*, on the ground that a statutory requirement of access for the military at any institution receiving federal financial aid interfered with no free speech rights of the universities as institutions.

Roberts v. United States Jaycees

468 U.S. 609 (1984)

■ JUSTICE BRENNAN delivered the opinion of the Court.

This case requires us to address a conflict between a State's efforts to eliminate gender-based discrimination against its citizens and the constitutional freedom of association asserted by members of a private organization. In the decision under review, the Court of Appeals for the Eighth Circuit concluded that, by requiring the United States Jaycees to admit women as full voting members, the Minnesota Human Rights Act violates the First and Fourteenth Amendment rights of the organization's members. We . . . reverse.

I–A

The United States Jaycees [originally the "Junior Chamber of Commerce"] . . . is a nonprofit membership corporation [devoted to]

> such educational and charitable purposes as will promote and foster the growth and development of young men's organizations in the United States, designed to inculcate in the individual membership of such organization a spirit of genuine Americanism and civic interest, and as a supplementary education institution to provide them with opportunity for personal development and achievement and an avenue for intelligent participation by young men in the affairs of their community, state and nation, and to develop true friendship and understanding among young men of all nations.

The organization's bylaws establish seven classes of membership, including individual or regular members, associate individual members, and local chapters. Regular membership is limited to young men between the ages of 18 and 35. . . . [Women may be "associate members."] The bylaws define a local chapter as "[a]ny young men's organization of good repute existing in any community within the United States, organized for purposes similar to and consistent with those" of the national organization. . . . The national organization's executive vice president estimated at trial that women associate members make up about two percent of the Jaycees' total membership. . . .

B

In 1974 and 1975, respectively, the Minneapolis and St. Paul chapters of the Jaycees began admitting women as regular members. Currently, the memberships and boards of directors of both chapters include a substantial proportion of women. As a result, the two chapters have been in violation of the national organization's bylaws for about 10 years. The national organization has imposed a number of sanctions on the Minneapolis and St. Paul chapters. . . .

In December 1978, the president of the national organization advised both chapters that a motion to revoke their charters would be considered at a forthcoming meeting of the national board of directors in Tulsa. Shortly after receiving this notification, members of both chapters filed charges of discrimination with the Minnesota Department of Human Rights. The complaints alleged that the exclusion of women from full membership required by the national organization's bylaws violated the Minnesota Human Rights Act (Act), which provides in part:

> It is an unfair discriminatory practice:

> > To deny any person the full and equal enjoyment of the goods, services, facilities, privileges, advantages, and accommodations of a place of public accommodation because of race, color, creed, religion, disability, national origin or sex.

Minn. Stat. § 363.03, subd. 3 (1982). The term "place of public accommodation" is defined in the Act as "a business, accommodation, refreshment, entertainment, recreation, or transportation facility of any kind, whether licensed or not, whose goods, services, facilities, privileges, advantages or accommodations are extended, offered, sold, or otherwise made available to the public."§ 363.01, subd. 18. . . .

[The procedural history is omitted. The Eighth Circuit ruled that the Jaycees possessed a First Amendment right to exclude women members.— Editors]

II

. . . An individual's freedom to speak, to worship, and to petition the government for the redress of grievances could not be vigorously protected from interference by the State unless a correlative freedom to engage in group effort toward those ends were not also guaranteed. According protection to collective effort on behalf of shared goals is especially important in preserving political and cultural diversity and in shielding dissident expression from suppression by the majority. Consequently, we have long understood as implicit in the right to engage in activities protected by the First Amendment a corresponding right to associate with others in pursuit of a wide variety of political, social, economic, educational, religious, and cultural ends. In view of the various protected activities in which the Jaycees engages, that right is plainly implicated in this case.

Government actions that may unconstitutionally infringe upon this freedom can take a number of forms. Among other things, government may seek to impose penalties or withhold benefits from individuals because of their membership in a disfavored group, *e.g., Healy v. James*, 408 U.S. 169, 180–184 (1972); it may attempt to require disclosure of the fact of membership in a group seeking anonymity, *e.g., Brown v. Socialist Workers '74 Campaign Committee, supra*, 459 U.S. 87, 91–92 (1982); and it may try to interfere with the internal organization or affairs of the group, *e.g., Cousins v. Wigoda*, 419 U.S. 477, 487–488 (1975). By requiring the Jaycees to admit women as full voting members, the Minnesota Act works an infringement of the last type. There can be no clearer example of an intrusion into the internal structure or affairs of an association than a regulation that forces the group to accept members it does not desire. Such a regulation may impair the ability of the original members to express only those views that brought them together. Freedom of association therefore plainly presupposes a freedom not to associate. See *Abood v. Detroit Board of Education*, 431 U.S., at 234–235.

The right to associate for expressive purposes is not, however, absolute. Infringements on that right may be justified by regulations adopted to serve compelling state interests, unrelated to the suppression of ideas, that cannot be achieved through means significantly less restrictive of associational freedoms. We are persuaded that Minnesota's compelling interest in eradicating discrimination against its female citizens justifies the impact that application of the statute to the Jaycees may have on the male members' associational freedoms.

On its face, the Minnesota Act does not aim at the suppression of speech, does not distinguish between prohibited and permitted activity on the basis of viewpoint, and does not license enforcement authorities to administer the statute on the basis of such constitutionally impermissible criteria. Nor does the Jaycees contend that the Act has been applied in this case for the purpose of hampering the organization's ability to express its views. Instead, as the Minnesota Supreme Court explained, the Act reflects the State's strong historical commitment to eliminating discrimination and assuring its citizens equal access to publicly available goods and services. That goal, which is unrelated to the suppression of expression, plainly serves compelling state interests of the highest order. . . .

By prohibiting gender discrimination in places of public accommodation, the Minnesota Act protects the State's citizenry from a number of serious social and personal harms. In the context of reviewing state actions under the Equal Protection Clause, this Court has frequently noted that discrimination based on archaic and overbroad assumptions about the relative needs and capacities of the sexes forces individuals to labor under stereotypical notions that often bear no relationship to their actual abilities. It thereby both deprives persons of their individual dignity and denies society the benefits of wide participation in political, economic, and cultural life. . . . That stigmatizing injury, and the denial of equal opportunities that accompanies it, is surely felt as strongly by persons suffering discrimination on the basis of their sex as by those treated differently because of their race.

Nor is the state interest in assuring equal access limited to the provision of purely tangible goods and services. . . . Thus, in explaining its conclusion that the Jaycees local chapters are "place[s] of public accommodations" within the meaning of the Act, the Minnesota court noted the various commercial programs and benefits offered to members and stated that "[l]eadership skills are 'goods,' [and] business contacts and employment promotions are 'privileges' and 'advantages'. . . ." Assuring women equal access to such goods, privileges, and advantages clearly furthers compelling state interests.

In applying the Act to the Jaycees, the State has advanced those interests through the least restrictive means of achieving its ends. Indeed, the Jaycees has failed to demonstrate that the Act imposes any serious burdens on the male members' freedom of expressive association. See *Hishon v. King & Spalding*, 467 U.S. 69, 78 (1984) (law firm "has not shown how its ability to fulfill [protected] function[s] would be inhibited by a requirement that it consider [a woman lawyer] for partnership on her merits"). . . . Over the years, the national and local levels of the organization have taken public positions on a number of diverse issues, and members of the Jaycees regularly engage in a variety of civic, charitable, lobbying, fundraising, and other activities worthy of constitutional protection under the First Amendment. There is, however, no basis in the record for concluding that admission of women as full voting members will impede the organization's ability to engage in these protected activities or to disseminate its preferred views. The Act requires no change in the Jaycees' creed of promoting the interests of young men, and it imposes no restrictions on the organization's ability to exclude individuals with ideologies or philosophies different from those of its existing members. Moreover, the Jaycees already invites women to share the group's views and philosophy and to participate in much of its training and community activities. Accordingly, any claim that admission of women as full voting members will impair a symbolic message conveyed by the very fact that women are not permitted to vote is attenuated at best.

. . . In the absence of a showing far more substantial than that attempted by the Jaycees, we decline to indulge in the sexual stereotyping that underlies appellee's contention that, by allowing women to vote, application of the Minnesota Act will change the content or impact of the organization's speech.

In any event, even if enforcement of the Act causes some incidental abridgment of the Jaycees' protected speech, that effect is no greater than is necessary to accomplish the State's legitimate purposes. . . .

■ JUSTICE REHNQUIST concurs in the judgment.

■ THE CHIEF JUSTICE and JUSTICE BLACKMUN took no part in the decision of this case. [*Chief Justice Burger had been a chapter president of the St. Paul, Minnesota Jaycees and Justice Blackmun had been a member of the Minneapolis Jaycees.—Editors*]

■ JUSTICE O'CONNOR, concurring in part and concurring in the judgment.

. . . I part company with the Court over its First Amendment analysis. . . . I agree with the Court that application of the Minnesota law to the Jaycees does not contravene the First Amendment, but I reach that conclusion for reasons distinct from those offered by the Court. I believe the Court has adopted a test that unadvisedly casts doubt on the power of States to pursue the profoundly important goal of ensuring nondiscriminatory access to commercial opportunities in our society. At the same time, the Court has adopted an approach to the general problem presented by this case that accords insufficient protection to expressive associations and places inappropriate burdens on groups claiming the protection of the First Amendment.

I

[The Court's test is] both overprotective of activities undeserving of constitutional shelter and underprotective of important First Amendment concerns. The Court declares that the Jaycees' right of association depends on the organization's making a "substantial" showing that the admission of unwelcome members "will change the message communicated by the group's speech." I am not sure what showing the Court thinks would satisfy its requirement of proof of a membership-message connection, but whatever it means, the focus on such a connection is objectionable.

Imposing such a requirement, especially in the context of the balancing-of-interests test articulated by the Court, raises the possibility that certain commercial associations, by engaging occasionally in certain kinds of expressive activities, might improperly gain protection for discrimination. . . . Whether an association is or is not constitutionally protected in the selection of its membership should not depend on what the association says or why its members say it.

The Court's readiness to inquire into the connection between membership and message reveals a more fundamental flaw in its analysis. The Court pursues this inquiry as part of its mechanical application of a "compelling interest" test, under which the Court weighs the interests of the State of Minnesota in ending gender discrimination against the Jaycees' First Amendment right of association. The Court entirely neglects to establish at the threshold that the Jaycees is an association whose activities or purposes should engage the strong protections that the First Amendment extends to expressive associations.

On the one hand, an association engaged exclusively in protected expression enjoys First Amendment protection of both the content of its message and the choice of its members. Protection of the message itself is judged by the same standards as protection of speech by an individual. Protection of the association's right to define its membership derives from the recognition that the formation of an expressive association is the creation of a voice, and the selection of members is the definition of that voice. . . . On the other hand, there is only minimal constitutional protection of the freedom of *commercial* association. . . . The Constitution does not guarantee a right to choose employees, customers, suppliers, or those with whom one engages in simple commercial transactions, without restraint from the State. A shopkeeper has no constitutional right to deal only with persons of one sex.

The dichotomy between rights of commercial association and rights of expressive association is also found in the more limited constitutional protections accorded an association's recruitment and solicitation activities and other dealings with its members and the public. . . . Many associations cannot readily be described as purely expressive or purely commercial. . . . The standard must nevertheless give substance to the ideal of complete protection for purely expressive association, even while it readily permits state regulation of commercial affairs.

In my view, an association should be characterized as commercial, and therefore subject to rationally related state regulation of its membership and other associational activities, when, and only when, the association's activities are not predominantly of the type protected by the First Amendment. It is only when the association is predominantly engaged in protected expression that state regulation of its membership will necessarily affect, change, dilute, or silence one collective voice that would otherwise be heard. An association must choose its market. Once it enters the marketplace of commerce in any substantial degree it loses the complete control over its membership that it would otherwise enjoy if it confined its affairs to the marketplace of ideas.

Determining whether an association's activity is predominantly protected expression will often be difficult, if only because a broad range of activities can be expressive. . . .

In summary, this Court's case law recognizes radically different constitutional protections for expressive and nonexpressive associations. The First Amendment is offended by direct state control of the membership of a private organization engaged exclusively in protected expressive activity, but no First Amendment interest stands in the way of a State's rational regulation of economic transactions by or within a commercial association. The proper approach to analysis of First Amendment claims of associational freedom is, therefore, to distinguish nonexpressive from expressive associations and to recognize that the former lack the full constitutional protections possessed by the latter.

II

Minnesota's attempt to regulate the membership of the Jaycees chapters operating in that State presents a relatively easy case for application of the expressive-commercial dichotomy. . . . Notwithstanding its protected expressive activities, the Jaycees—otherwise known as the Junior Chamber of Commerce—is, first and foremost, an organization that, at both the national and local levels, promotes and practices the art of solicitation and management. The organization claims that the training it offers its members gives them an advantage in business, and business firms do indeed sometimes pay the dues of individual memberships for their employees. Jaycees members hone their solicitation and management skills, under the direction and supervision of the organization, primarily through their active recruitment of new members. . . . Recruitment and selling are commercial activities, even when conducted for training rather than for prof-it. . . .

Boy Scouts of America v. Dale

530 U.S. 640 (2000)

■ CHIEF JUSTICE REHNQUIST delivered the opinion of the Court.

Petitioners are the Boy Scouts of America and the Monmouth Council, a division of the Boy Scouts of America, . . . a private, not-for-profit organization engaged in instilling its system of values in young people. The Boy Scouts asserts that homosexual conduct is inconsistent with the values it seeks to instill. Respondent is James Dale, a former Eagle Scout whose adult membership in the Boy Scouts was revoked when the Boy Scouts learned that he is an avowed homosexual and gay rights activist. The New Jersey Supreme Court held that New Jersey's public accommodations law requires that the Boy Scouts readmit Dale. This case presents the question whether applying New Jersey's public accommodations law in this way violates the Boy Scouts' First Amendment right of expressive association. We hold that it does.

I

[The Court began by reciting the history of Dale's membership in the Boy Scouts, his public homosexuality, and his desire to hold a position as an assistant scoutmaster. The New Jersey courts found that the Boy Scouts' decision to exclude him from such a position violated state law concerning public accommodations and was not protected by the First Amendment right of the Boy Scouts to expressive association.—Editors]

II

In *Roberts v. United States Jaycees*, 468 U.S. 609, 622 (1984), we observed that "implicit in the right to engage in activities protected by the First Amendment" is "a corresponding right to associate with others in pursuit of a wide variety of political, social, economic, educational, religious, and cultural ends." This right is crucial in preventing the majority from imposing its views on groups that would rather express other, perhaps unpopular, ideas. Government actions that may unconstitutionally burden this freedom may take many forms, one of which is "intrusion into the internal structure or affairs of an association" like a "regulation that forces the group to accept members it does not desire." Forcing a group to accept certain members may impair the ability of the group to express those views, and only those views, that it intends to express. Thus, "[f]reedom of association . . . plainly presupposes a freedom not to associate."

The forced inclusion of an unwanted person in a group infringes the group's freedom of expressive association if the presence of that person affects in a significant way the group's ability to advocate public or private viewpoints. But the freedom of expressive association, like many freedoms, is not absolute. We have held that the freedom could be overridden "by regulations adopted to serve compelling state interests, unrelated to the suppression of ideas, that cannot be achieved through means significantly less restrictive of associational freedoms." [*Roberts*, supra, at 623.]

To determine whether a group is protected by the First Amendment's expressive associational right, we must determine whether the group engages in "expressive association." The First Amendment's protection of expressive association is not reserved for advocacy groups. But to come within its ambit, a group must engage in some form of expression, whether it be public or private. . . .

[T]he general mission of the Boy Scouts is clear: "[T]o instill values in young people." The Boy Scouts seeks to instill these values by having its adult leaders spend time with the youth members, instructing and engaging them in activities like camping, archery, and fishing. During the time spent with the youth members, the scoutmasters and assistant scoutmasters inculcate them with the Boy Scouts' values—both expressly and by example. It seems indisputable that an association that seeks to transmit such a system of values engages in expressive activity. See *Roberts, supra,* at 636 (O'CONNOR, J., concurring) ("Even the training of outdoor survival skills or participation in community service might become expressive when the activity is intended to develop good morals, reverence, patriotism, and a desire for self-improvement"). . . . The Boy Scouts asserts that homosexual conduct is inconsistent with the values embodied in the Scout Oath and Law, particularly with the values represented by the terms "morally straight" and "clean." . . .

The New Jersey Supreme Court analyzed the Boy Scouts' beliefs and found that the "exclusion of members solely on the basis of their sexual orientation is inconsistent with Boy Scouts' commitment to a diverse and 'representative' membership . . . [and] contradicts Boy Scouts' overarching objective to reach 'all eligible youth.' " The court concluded that the exclusion of members like Dale "appears antithetical to the organization's goals and philosophy." But our cases reject this sort of inquiry; it is not the role of the courts to reject a group's expressed values because they disagree with those values or find them internally inconsistent. See *Democratic Party of United States v. Wisconsin ex rel. La Follette,* 450 U.S. 107, 124 (1981) ("[A]s is true of all expressions of First Amendment freedoms, the courts may not interfere on the ground that they view a particular expression as unwise or irrational").

The Boy Scouts asserts that it "teach[es] that homosexual conduct is not morally straight," Brief for Petitioners 39, and that it does "not want to promote homosexual conduct as a legitimate form of behavior," Reply Brief for Petitioners 5. We accept the Boy Scouts' assertion. We need not inquire further to determine the nature of the Boy Scouts' expression with respect to homosexuality . . .

Dale, by his own admission, is one of a group of gay Scouts who have "become leaders in their community and are open and honest about their sexual orientation." Dale was the co-president of a gay and lesbian organization at college and remains a gay rights activist. Dale's presence in the Boy Scouts would, at the very least, force the organization to send a message, both to the youth members and the world, that the Boy Scouts accepts homosexual conduct as a legitimate form of behavior.

Hurley is illustrative on this point. There we considered whether the application of Massachusetts' public accommodations law to require the organizers of a private St. Patrick's Day parade to include among the marchers an Irish–American gay, lesbian, and bisexual group, GLIB, violated the parade organizers' First Amendment rights. We noted that the parade organizers did not wish to exclude the GLIB members because of their sexual orientations, but because they wanted to march behind a GLIB banner. We observed:

[A] contingent marching behind the organization's banner would at least bear witness to the fact that some Irish are gay, lesbian, or bisexual, and the presence of the organized marchers would suggest their view that people of their sexual orientations have as much claim to unqualified social acceptance as heterosexuals. . . . The parade's organizers may not believe these facts about Irish sexuality to be so, or they may object to unqualified social acceptance of gays and lesbians or have some other reason for wishing to keep GLIB's message out of the parade. But whatever the reason, it boils down to the choice of a speaker not to propound a particular point of view, and that choice is presumed to lie beyond the government's power to control.

515 U.S., at 574–575. Here, we have found that the Boy Scouts believes that homosexual conduct is inconsistent with the values it seeks to instill in its youth members. . . . As the presence of GLIB in Boston's St. Patrick's Day parade would have interfered with the parade organizers' choice not to propound a particular point of view, the presence of Dale as an assistant scoutmaster would just as surely interfere with the Boy Scouts' choice not to propound a point of view contrary to its beliefs.

The New Jersey Supreme Court determined that the Boy Scouts' ability to disseminate its message was not significantly affected by the forced inclusion of Dale as an assistant scoutmaster because of the following findings:

> Boy Scout members do not associate for the purpose of disseminating the belief that homosexuality is immoral; Boy Scouts discourages its leaders from disseminating *any* views on sexual issues; and Boy Scouts includes sponsors and members who subscribe to different views in respect of homosexuality.

We disagree with the New Jersey Supreme Court's conclusion drawn from these findings.

First, associations do not have to associate for the "purpose" of disseminating a certain message in order to be entitled to the protections of the First Amendment. An association must merely engage in expressive activity that could be impaired in order to be entitled to protection. For example, the purpose of the St. Patrick's Day parade in *Hurley* was not to espouse any views about sexual orientation, but we held that the parade organizers had a right to exclude certain participants nonetheless.

Second, even if the Boy Scouts discourages Scout leaders from disseminating views on sexual issues—a fact that the Boy Scouts disputes with contrary evidence—the First Amendment protects the Boy Scouts' method of expression. If the Boy Scouts wishes Scout leaders to avoid questions of sexuality and teach only by example, this fact does not negate the sincerity of its belief discussed above.

Third, the First Amendment simply does not require that every member of a group agree on every issue in order for the group's policy to be "expressive association." The Boy Scouts takes an official position with respect to homosexual conduct, and that is sufficient for First Amendment purposes. In this same vein, Dale makes much of the claim that the Boy Scouts does not revoke the membership of heterosexual Scout leaders that openly disagree with the Boy Scouts' policy on sexual orientation. But if this is true, it is irrelevant. The presence of an avowed homosexual and gay rights activist in an assistant scoutmaster's uniform sends a distinctly different message from the presence of a heterosexual assistant scoutmaster who is on record as disagreeing with Boy Scouts policy. The Boy Scouts has a First Amendment right to choose to send one message but not the other. The fact that the organization does not trumpet its views from the housetops, or that it tolerates dissent within its ranks, does not mean that its views receive no First Amendment protection.

Having determined that the Boy Scouts is an expressive association and that the forced inclusion of Dale would significantly affect its expression, we inquire whether the application of New Jersey's public accommodations law to require that the Boy Scouts accept Dale as an assistant scoutmaster runs afoul of the Scouts' freedom of expressive association. We conclude that it does. . . .

Justice STEVENS' dissent makes much of its observation that the public perception of homosexuality in this country has changed. Indeed, it appears that homosexuality has gained greater societal acceptance. But this is scarcely an argument for denying First Amendment protection to those who refuse to accept these views. The First Amendment protects expression, be it of the popular variety or not. See, e.g., *Texas v. Johnson*, 491 U.S. 397 (1989); Brandenburg v. Ohio, 395 U.S. 444 (1969). And the fact that an idea may be embraced and advocated by increasing numbers of people is all the more reason to protect the First Amendment rights of those who wish to voice a different view. . . .

■ JUSTICE STEVENS, with whom JUSTICE SOUTER, JUSTICE GINSBURG, and JUSTICE BREYER join, dissenting.

. . . [The Boy Scouts'] claim finds no support in our cases. . . . [W]e have routinely and easily rejected assertions of this right by expressive organizations with discriminatory membership policies, such as private schools, law firms, and labor organizations. In fact, until today, we have never once found a claimed right to associate in the selection of members to prevail in the face of a State's antidiscrimination law. . . .

Several principles are made perfectly clear by *Jaycees* and *Rotary Club*. First, to prevail on a claim of expressive association . . ., it is not enough simply to engage in *some kind* of expressive activity. Both the Jaycees and the Rotary Club engaged in expressive activity protected by the First Amendment, yet that fact was not dispositive. Second, it is not enough to adopt an openly avowed exclusionary membership policy. Both the Jaycees and the Rotary Club did that as well. Third, it is not sufficient merely to articulate *some* connection between the group's expressive activities and its exclusionary policy. . . .

The evidence before this Court makes it exceptionally clear that BSA has, at most, simply adopted an exclusionary membership policy and has no shared goal of disapproving of homosexuality. BSA's mission statement and federal charter say nothing on the matter; its official membership policy is silent; its Scout Oath and Law—and accompanying definitions—are devoid of any view on the topic; its guidance for Scouts and Scoutmasters on sexuality declare that such matters are "not construed to be Scouting's proper area," but are the province of a Scout's parents and pastor; and BSA's posture respecting religion tolerates a wide variety of views on the issue of homosexuality. . . . In short, Boy Scouts of America is simply silent on homosexuality. There is no shared goal or collective effort to foster a belief about homosexuality at all—let alone one that is significantly burdened by admitting homosexuals.

As in *Jaycees,* there is "no basis in the record for concluding that admission of [homosexuals] will impede the [Boy Scouts'] ability to engage in [its] protected activities or to disseminate its preferred views" and New Jersey's law "requires no change in [BSA's] creed." . . .

[The Boy Scouts] has not contended, nor does the record support, that Dale had ever advocated a view on homosexuality to his troop before his membership was revoked. . . . Though *[Hurley v. GLIB]* has a superficial similarity to the present case, a close inspection reveals a wide gulf between that case and the one before us today. First, it was critical to our analysis that GLIB was actually conveying a message by participating in the parade—otherwise, the parade organizers could hardly claim that they were being forced to include any unwanted message at all. . . . Second, we found it relevant that GLIB's message "would likely be perceived" as the parade organizers' own speech. . . . Dale's inclusion in the Boy Scouts is nothing like the case in *Hurley.* His participation sends no cognizable message to the Scouts or to the world. Unlike GLIB, Dale did not carry a banner or a sign; he did not distribute any factsheet; and he expressed no intent to send any message. If there is any kind of message being sent, then, it is by the mere act of joining the Boy Scouts. . . .

The only apparent explanation for the majority's holding, then, is that homosexuals are simply so different from the rest of society that their presence alone—unlike any other individual's—should be singled out for special First Amendment treatment. Under the majority's reasoning, an openly gay male is irreversibly affixed with the label "homosexual." That label, even though unseen, communicates a message that permits his exclusion wherever he goes. His openness is the sole and sufficient justification for his ostracism. . . .

Furthermore, it is not likely that BSA would be understood to send any message, either to Scouts or to the world, simply by admitting someone as a member. . . . The notion that an organization of that size and enormous prestige implicitly endorses the views that each of those adults may express in a non-Scouting context is simply mind boggling. . . .

Unfavorable opinions about homosexuals "have ancient roots." Like equally atavistic opinions about certain racial groups, those roots have been nourished by sectarian [religious] doctrine. . . . That such prejudices are still prevalent and that they have caused serious and tangible harm to countless members of the class New Jersey seeks to protect are established matters of fact that neither the Boy Scouts nor the Court disputes. That harm can only be aggravated by the creation of a constitutional shield for a policy that is itself the product of a habitual way of thinking about strangers. . . .

If we would guide by the light of reason, we must let our minds be bold.

■ [JUSTICE SOUTER's dissent is omitted.]

Rumsfeld v. Forum for Academic and Institutional Rights (FAIR)

547 U.S. 47 (2006)

■ CHIEF JUSTICE ROBERTS delivered the opinion of the Court.

When law schools began restricting the access of military recruiters to their students because of disagreement with the Government's policy on homosexuals in the military, Congress responded by enacting the Solomon Amendment. See 10 U.S.C.A. § 983 (Supp.2005). That provision specifies that if any part of an institution of higher education denies military recruiters access equal to that provided other recruiters, the entire institution would lose certain federal funds. The law schools responded by suing, alleging that the Solomon Amendment infringed their First Amendment freedoms of speech and association. . . .

I

Respondent Forum for Academic and Institutional Rights, Inc. (FAIR), is an association of law schools and law faculties. . . . FAIR members have adopted policies expressing their opposition to discrimination based on, among other factors, sexual orientation. They would like to restrict military recruiting on their campuses because they object to the policy Congress has adopted with respect to homosexuals in the military. The Solomon Amendment, however, forces institutions to choose between enforcing their non-discrimination policy against military recruiters in this way and continuing to receive specified federal funding. . . . FAIR argue[s] that this forced inclusion and equal treatment of military recruiters violated the law schools' First Amendment freedoms of speech and association. . . .

II

The Solomon Amendment denies federal funding to an institution of higher education that "has a policy or practice . . . that either prohibits, or in effect prevents" the military "from gaining access to campuses, or access to students . . . on campuses, for purposes of military recruiting in a manner that is at least equal in quality and scope to the access to campuses and to students that is provided to any other employer." The statute provides an exception for an institution with "a longstanding policy of pacifism based on historical religious affiliation." The Government and FAIR agree on what this statute requires: In order for a law school and its university to receive federal funding, the law school must offer military recruiters the same access to its campus and students that it provides to the nonmilitary recruiter receiving the most favorable access.

Certain law professors participating as *amici,* however, argue that the Government and FAIR misinterpret the statute. According to these *amici,* the Solomon Amendment's equal-access requirement is satisfied when an institution applies to military recruiters the same policy it applies to all other recruiters. On this reading, a school excluding military recruiters would comply with the Solomon Amendment so long as it also excluded any other employer that violates its nondiscrimination policy. . . . Under *amici*'s reading, a military recruiter has the same "access" to campuses and students as, say, a law firm when the law firm is permitted on campus to interview students and the military is not. . . .

The Solomon Amendment does not focus on the *content* of a school's recruiting policy, as the *amici* would have it. Instead, it looks to the *result* achieved by the policy and compares the "access . . . provided" military recruiters to that provided other recruiters. Applying the same policy to all recruiters is therefore insufficient to comply with the statute if it results in a greater level of access for other recruiters than for the military. Law schools must ensure that their recruiting policy operates in such a way that military recruiters are given access to students at least equal to that "*provided* to any other employer." (Emphasis added.) . . . Under the statute, military recruiters must be given the same access as recruiters who comply with the policy.

III

The Constitution grants Congress the power to "provide for the common Defence," "[t]o raise and support Armies," and "[t]o provide and maintain a Navy." Art. I, § 8, cls. 1, 12–13. Congress' power in this area "is broad and sweeping," *O'Brien,* 391 U.S., at 377, and there is no dispute in this case that it includes the authority to require campus access for military recruiters. . . .

Although Congress has broad authority to legislate on matters of military recruiting, it nonetheless chose to secure campus access for military recruiters indirectly, through its Spending Clause power. The Solomon Amendment gives universities a choice: Either allow military recruiters the same access to students afforded any other recruiter or forgo certain federal funds. Congress' decision to proceed indirectly does not reduce the deference given to Congress in the area of military affairs. Congress' choice to promote its goal by creating a funding condition deserves at least as deferential treatment as if Congress had imposed a mandate on universities.

Congress' power to regulate military recruiting under the Solomon Amendment is arguably greater because universities are free to decline the federal funds. In *Grove City College v. Bell,* 465 U.S. 555, 575–576 (1984), we rejected a private college's claim that conditioning federal funds on its compliance with Title IX of the Education Amendments of 1972 violated the First Amendment. We thought this argument "warrant[ed] only brief consideration" because "Congress is free to attach reasonable and unambiguous conditions to federal financial assistance that educational institutions are not obligated to accept." We concluded that no First Amendment violation had occurred—without reviewing the substance of the First Amendment claims—because Grove City could decline the Government's funds.

Other decisions, however, recognize a limit on Congress' ability to place conditions on the receipt of funds. We recently held that "the government may not deny a benefit to a person on a basis that infringes his constitutionally protected . . . freedom of speech even if he has no entitlement to that benefit." *United States v. American Library Assn., Inc.,* 539 U.S. 194, 210 (2003). Under this principle, known as the unconstitutional conditions doctrine, the Solomon Amendment would be unconstitutional if Congress could not directly require universities to provide military recruiters equal access to their students.

This case does not require us to determine when a condition placed on university funding goes beyond the "reasonable" choice offered in *Grove City* and becomes an unconstitutional condition. . . . Because the First Amendment would not prevent Congress from directly imposing the Solomon Amendment's access requirement, the statute does not place an unconstitutional condition on the receipt of federal funds.

A

The Solomon Amendment neither limits what law schools may say nor requires them to say anything. Law schools remain free under the statute to express whatever views they may have on the military's congressionally mandated employment policy, all the while retaining eligibility for federal funds.... As a general matter, the Solomon Amendment regulates conduct, not speech. It affects what law schools must *do*—afford equal access to military recruiters—not what they may or may not *say*....

1

Some of this Court's leading First Amendment precedents have established the principle that freedom of speech prohibits the government from telling people what they must say. In *West Virginia Bd. of Ed. v. Barnette,* 319 U.S. 624, 642 (1943), we held unconstitutional a state law requiring schoolchildren to recite the Pledge of Allegiance and to salute the flag. And in *Wooley v. Maynard,* 430 U.S. 705, 717 (1977), we held unconstitutional another that required New Hampshire motorists to display the state motto—"Live Free or Die"—on their license plates.

The Solomon Amendment does not require any similar expression by law schools. Nonetheless, recruiting assistance provided by the schools often includes elements of speech. For example, schools may send e-mails or post notices on bulletin boards on an employer's behalf. Law schools offering such services to other recruiters must also send e-mails and post notices on behalf of the military to comply with the Solomon Amendment. As FAIR points out, these compelled statements of fact ("The U.S. Army recruiter will meet interested students in Room 123 at 11 a.m."), like compelled statements of opinion, are subject to First Amendment scrutiny.

This sort of recruiting assistance, however, is a far cry from the compelled speech in *Barnette* and *Wooley.* The Solomon Amendment, unlike the laws at issue in those cases, does not dictate the content of the speech at all, which is only "compelled" if, and to the extent, the school provides such speech for other recruiters. There is nothing in this case approaching a Government-mandated pledge or motto that the school must endorse.

The compelled speech to which the law schools point is plainly incidental to the Solomon Amendment's regulation of conduct, and "it has never been deemed an abridgment of freedom of speech or press to make a course of conduct illegal merely because the conduct was in part initiated, evidenced, or carried out by means of language, either spoken, written, or printed." *Giboney v. Empire Storage & Ice Co.,* 336 U.S. 490, 502 (1949). Congress, for example, can prohibit employers from discriminating in hiring on the basis of race. The fact that this will require an employer to take down a sign reading "White Applicants Only" hardly means that the law should be analyzed as one regulating the employer's speech rather than conduct. See *R.A.V. v. St. Paul,* 505 U.S. 377, 389 (1992) ("[W]ords can in some circumstances violate laws directed not against speech but against conduct"). Compelling a law school that sends scheduling e-mails for other recruiters to send one for a military recruiter is simply not the same as forcing a student to pledge allegiance, or forcing a Jehovah's Witness to display the motto "Live Free or Die," and it trivializes the freedom protected in *Barnette* and *Wooley* to suggest that it is.

2

Our compelled-speech cases are not limited to the situation in which an individual must personally speak the government's message. We have also in a number of instances limited the government's ability to force one speaker to host or accommodate another speaker's message. See *Hurley v. Irish–American Gay, Lesbian and Bisexual Group of Boston, Inc.,* 515 U.S. 557, 566 (1995) (state law cannot require a parade to include a group whose message the parade's organizer does not wish to send). . . .

The compelled-speech violation in each of our prior cases, however, resulted from the fact that the complaining speaker's own message was affected by the speech it was forced to accommodate. The expressive nature of a parade was central to our holding in *Hurley* . . . . . [B]ecause "every participating unit affects the message conveyed by the [parade's] private organizers," a law dictating that a particular group must be included in the parade "alter[s] the expressive content of th[e] parade." As a result, we held that the State's public accommodation law, as applied to a private parade, "violates the fundamental rule of protection under the First Amendment, that a speaker has the autonomy to choose the content of his own message." . . .

In this case, accommodating the military's message does not affect the law schools' speech, because the schools are not speaking when they host interviews and recruiting receptions. Unlike a parade organizer's choice of parade contingents, a law school's decision to allow recruiters on campus is not inherently expressive. Law schools facilitate recruiting to assist their students in obtaining jobs. A law school's recruiting services lack the expressive quality of a parade, a newsletter, or the editorial page of a newspaper; its accommodation of a military recruiter's message is not compelled speech because the accommodation does not sufficiently interfere with any message of the school. . . . Nothing about recruiting suggests that law schools agree with any speech by recruiters, and nothing in the Solomon Amendment restricts what the law schools may say about the military's policies. . . .

3

Having rejected the view that the Solomon Amendment impermissibly regulates *speech,* we must still consider whether the expressive nature of the *conduct* regulated by the statute brings that conduct within the First Amendment's protection. . . . [W]e have extended First Amendment protection only to conduct that is inherently expressive. . . . Unlike flag burning, the conduct regulated by the Solomon Amendment is not inherently expressive. Prior to the adoption of the Solomon Amendment's equal-access requirement, law schools "expressed" their disagreement with the military by treating military recruiters differently from other recruiters. But these actions were expressive only because the law schools accompanied their conduct with speech explaining it. . . . An observer who sees military recruiters interviewing away from the law school has no way of knowing whether the law school is expressing its disapproval of the military, all the law school's interview rooms are full, or the military recruiters decided for reasons of their own that they would rather interview someplace else.

The expressive component of a law school's actions is not created by the conduct itself but by the speech that accompanies it. The fact that such explanatory speech is necessary is strong evidence that the conduct at issue here is not so inherently expressive that it warrants protection under *O'Brien.* If combining speech and conduct were enough to create expressive conduct, a regulated party could always transform conduct into "speech" simply by talking about it. For instance, if an individual announces that he intends to express his disapproval of the Internal Revenue Service by refusing to pay his income taxes, we would have to apply *O'Brien* to determine whether the Tax Code violates the First Amendment. Neither *O'Brien* nor its progeny supports such a result. . . .

[In any event, on-campus] recruiting promotes the substantial Government interest in raising and supporting the Armed Forces—an objective that would be achieved less effectively if the military were forced to recruit on less favorable terms than other employers. . . . It suffices that the means chosen by Congress add to the effectiveness of military recruitment. Accordingly, even if the Solomon Amendment were regarded as regulating expressive conduct, it would not violate the First Amendment under *O'Brien*.

B

The Solomon Amendment does not violate law schools' freedom of speech, but the First Amendment's protection extends beyond the right to speak. We have recognized a First Amendment right to associate for the purpose of speaking, which we have termed a "right of expressive association." See, *e.g., Boy Scouts of America v. Dale,* 530 U.S. 640, 644 (2000). The reason we have extended First Amendment protection in this way is clear: The right to speak is often exercised most effectively by combining one's voice with the voices of others. If the government were free to restrict individuals' ability to join together and speak, it could essentially silence views that the First Amendment is intended to protect.

FAIR argues that the Solomon Amendment violates law schools' freedom of expressive association. According to FAIR, law schools' ability to express their message that discrimination on the basis of sexual orientation is wrong is significantly affected by the presence of military recruiters on campus and the schools' obligation to assist them. Relying heavily on our decision in *Dale,* the Court of Appeals agreed.

In *Dale,* we held that the Boy Scouts' freedom of expressive association was violated by New Jersey's public accommodations law, which required the organization to accept a homosexual as a scoutmaster. After determining that the Boy Scouts was an expressive association, that "the forced inclusion of Dale would significantly affect its expression," and that the State's interests did not justify this intrusion, we concluded that the Boy Scout's First Amendment rights were violated. 530 U.S., at 655–659.

The Solomon Amendment, however, does not similarly affect a law school's associational rights. To comply with the statute, law schools must allow military recruiters on campus and assist them in whatever way the school chooses to assist other employers. Law schools therefore "associate" with military recruiters in the sense that they interact with them. But recruiters are not part of the law school. Recruiters are, by definition, outsiders who come onto campus for the limited purpose of trying to hire students—not to become members of the school's expressive association. This distinction is critical. Unlike the public accommodations law in *Dale,* the Solomon Amendment does not force a law school " 'to accept members it does not desire.' " *Id.,* at 648 (quoting *Roberts, supra,* at 623). . . .

Students and faculty are free to associate to voice their disapproval of the military's message; nothing about the statute affects the composition of the group by making group membership less desirable. . . . A military recruiter's mere presence on campus does not violate a law school's right to associate, regardless of how repugnant the law school considers the recruiter's message.

In this case, FAIR has attempted to stretch a number of First Amendment doctrines well beyond the sort of activities these doctrines protect. The law schools object to having to treat military recruiters like other recruiters, but that regulation of conduct does not violate the First Amendment. To the extent that the Solomon Amendment incidentally affects expression, the law schools' effort to cast themselves as just like the schoolchildren in *Barnette,* the parade organizers in *Hurley,* and the Boy Scouts in *Dale* plainly overstates the expressive nature of their activity and the impact of the Solomon Amendment on it, while exaggerating the reach of our First Amendment precedents.

Because Congress could require law schools to provide equal access to military recruiters without violating the schools' freedoms of speech or association, the Court of Appeals erred in holding that the Solomon Amendment likely violates the First Amendment. . . .

NOTES

1. Were these cases rightly decided?

2. What is the line separating protected freedom of expressive association and the authority of government to regulate private groups' membership practices? Is it the commercial/non-commercial distinction? Is that line sustainable? Is it principled? Aren't some *commercial* enterprises "expressive"? Aren't many *expressive associations* "commercial"? (Is a private school a commercial association or an expressive association?) Is the line a function of the strength of the state interest in regulating the type of "discrimination" in question? Is the line a function of how "expressive" the expressive association really is? Is that a sustainable or principled standard?

A NOTE ON CHRISTIAN LEGAL SOCIETY V. MARTINEZ

In *Christian Legal Society v. Martinez,* 130 S. Ct. 2971 (2010), the Court upheld a state university policy that barred official recognition (and with it preferred access to meeting rooms, internal communications channels, and other benefits) to student groups if they restricted their leadership or voting membership to persons who adhered to their fundamental beliefs. The university insisted that all groups adhere to an "all-comers" policy, meaning that they could not exclude anyone on the basis of "status or belief." If evenhandedly applied, this would mean that a Republican club would have to accept Democratic members, and a feminist club would have to accept male chauvinists. The case involved a Christian student group that limited its leaders and voting members to those who signed a "Statement of Beliefs," which included (among many other things) a belief that sexual intimacy should be limited to married heterosexual couples.

How does the "all-comers" policy compare to the position that President Washington took, contra the Democratic–Republican clubs, that there is something wrong with "self-selected" organizations?

How should this case have come out under *Democratic Party of Wisconsin, Roberts,* and *Dale?* The students argued that they could not be denied access to an otherwise available public benefit on account of their exercise of the constitutional right of freedom of association. Before you read the rest of this note, try to come up with plausible doctrinal reasons to reject that argument.

The Court analyzed the case under its "limited public forum" doctrine for freedom of speech. See *Rosenberger v. Rector and Visitors of the University of Virginia*, 515 U.S. 819 (1995) (presented above). Under this doctrine, the government may exclude speakers from public property that has been opened up for speech activities only if it has a reason that is both viewpoint-neutral and "reasonable in light of the purposes served by the forum." The Court held that the university's policy satisfied both of these criteria. (Can you fashion arguments by the students why that might not be so?) The Court thus treated access to the forum as "effectively a state subsidy," and distinguished *Boy Scouts* and *Roberts* as cases that "involved regulations that *compelled* a group to include unwanted members" (emphasis in original). Do you agree that equal access to a forum for speech should be categorized as a "subsidy"? Could the government insist on an all-comers policy as a condition to a group's eligibility for tax exemptions, or use of the post office or roads? If an unrecognized student group were excluded from meeting on campus, would it be "compelled"?

This answered the free speech claim. But what about the freedom of association claim? The students argued they could not be denied a generally available benefit to which they would otherwise be entitled—such as use of meeting rooms and university communications media—on account of their exercise of a constitutional right. The Court rejected the claim, explaining that

> the same considerations that have led us to apply a less restrictive level of scrutiny to speech in limited public forums as compared to other environments, apply with equal force to expressive association occurring in limited public forums. . . . When these intertwined rights arise in exactly the same context, it would be anomalous for a restriction on speech to survive constitutional review under our limited-public-forum test only to be invalidated as an impermissible infringement of expressive association.

Why would it be "anomalous" to apply different constitutional tests to different constitutional rights when they arise in the same context? The Speech Clause protects a group's message, and the viewpoint-neutrality test is relevant to that. But freedom of association protects a group's prior ability to formulate their message by meeting in groups of their own choosing. The relevant constitutional principle for that is not viewpoint-neutrality, but control over group identity. One might argue that the state has a compelling interest in preventing certain kinds of discrimination, but does the state have an interest in preventing religious groups from having leaders of their own choosing?

Critics have argued that the *Martinez* decision eliminates any separate protection for freedom of association, beyond restrictions on freedom of speech. How would other freedom of association cases fare under that approach?

[*Assignment 53*]

II. THE FIRST AMENDMENT AND FREEDOM OF RELIGION

A. BACKGROUND AND DRAFTING HISTORY

The First Amendment expressly protects religious freedom in two distinct but overlapping ways. The Religion Clauses contain first, the Establishment Clause which forbids government from setting up "an establishment of religion," limiting citizens' religious freedom by designating an official church or official articles of faith, coercing church attendance or membership, imposing some punishment or disability for non-attendance or non-membership, or coercing direct tax support for the official church. Initially, the ban on religious "establishment" applied only to the federal government. Many states (at first) retained established churches; indeed, part of the purpose of the Establishment Clause was to forbid the federal government from interfering with—*dis*establishing—state official churches. Today, by virtue of the Fourteenth Amendment's incorporation of the Bill of Rights as a limitation on the powers of state governments, the Establishment Clause is understood to forbid states, as well as the federal government, from coercing religious exercise or observance. As we will see, however, some modern Supreme Court decisions have interpreted the Establishment Clause to prohibit considerably more. Second, the Free Exercise Clause forbids laws "prohibiting the free exercise thereof," meaning of religion. This gives believers the right to determine their religious beliefs for themselves and—what is more—to "exercise" them. By its language, the clause goes beyond belief and beyond speech. What exactly is the scope of its protection?

We begin with a petition written anonymously by James Madison, which garnered thousands of signatures from Virginians in 1785. The petition opposed a proposal by Patrick Henry to force every Virginian to pay a tax for the support of religion. Each taxpayer could direct a payment to the Christian church of the taxpayer's choice (there were no non-Christian churches in Virginia at that time), or if there was no church the taxpayer wished to support, to public "seminaries of learning." Madison's petition is widely regarded as the most powerful and well-reasoned statement of the framing period on the principles of religious freedom. The Henry proposal was voted down, and in its stead, Jefferson's Bill for Establishing Religious Freedom was enacted.

James Madison, Memorial and Remonstrance Against Religious Assessments

June 20, 1785

To the Honorable the General Assembly of the Commonwealth of Virginia A Memorial and Remonstrance

We the subscribers, citizens of the said Commonwealth, having taken into serious consideration, a Bill printed by order of the last Session of General Assembly, entitled "A Bill establishing a provision for Teachers of the Christian Religion," and conceiving that the same if finally armed with the sanctions of a law, will be a dangerous abuse of power, are bound as faithful members of a free State to remonstrate against it, and to declare the reasons by which we are determined. We remonstrate against the said Bill,

1. Because we hold it for a fundamental and undeniable truth, "that religion or the duty which we owe to our Creator and the manner of discharging it, can be directed only by reason and conviction, not by force or violence." *[This is a quotation from the 1776 Virginia Declaration of Rights.—Editors]* The Religion then of every man must be left to the conviction and conscience of every man; and it is the right of every man to exercise it as these may dictate. This right is in its nature an unalienable right. It is unalienable, because the opinions of men, depending only on the evidence contemplated by their own minds cannot follow the dictates of other men: It is unalienable also, because what is here a right towards men, is a

duty towards the Creator. It is the duty of every man to render to the Creator such homage and such only as he believes to be acceptable to him. This duty is precedent, both in order of time and in degree of obligation, to the claims of Civil Society. Before any man can be considered as a member of Civil Society, he must be considered as a subject of the Governour of the Universe: And if a member of Civil Society, do it with a saving of his allegiance to the Universal Sovereign. We maintain therefore that in matters of Religion, no man's right is abridged by the institution of Civil Society and that Religion is wholly exempt from its cognizance. True it is, that no other rule exists, by which any question which may divide a Society, can be ultimately determined, but the will of the majority; but it is also true that the majority may trespass on the rights of the minority. . . .

3. Because it is proper to take alarm at the first experiment on our liberties. We hold this prudent jealousy to be the first duty of Citizens, and one of the noblest characteristics of the late Revolution. The free men of America did not wait till usurped power had strengthened itself by exercise, and entangled the question in precedents. They saw all the consequences in the principle, and they avoided the consequences by denying the principle. We revere this lesson too much soon to forget it. Who does not see that the same authority which can establish Christianity, in exclusion of all other Religions, may establish with the same ease any particular sect of Christians, in exclusion of all other Sects? that the same authority which can force a citizen to contribute three pence only of his property for the support of any one establishment, may force him to conform to any other establishment in all cases whatsoever?

4. Because the Bill violates the equality which ought to be the basis of every law, and which is more indispensible, in proportion as the validity or expediency of any law is more liable to be impeached. If "all men are by nature equally free and independent," all men are to be considered as entering into Society on equal conditions; as relinquishing no more, and therefore retaining no less, one than another, of their natural rights. Above all are they to be considered as retaining an "equal title to the free exercise of Religion according to the dictates of Conscience." Whilst we assert for ourselves a freedom to embrace, to profess and to observe the Religion which we believe to be of divine origin, we cannot deny an equal freedom to those whose minds have not yet yielded to the evidence which has convinced us. If this freedom be abused, it is an offence against God, not against man: To God, therefore, not to man, must an account of it be rendered. . . .

5. Because the Bill implies either that the Civil Magistrate is a competent Judge of Religious Truth; or that he may employ Religion as an engine of Civil policy. The first is an arrogant pretension falsified by the contradictory opinions of Rulers in all ages, and throughout the world: the second an unhallowed perversion of the means of salvation. . . .

We the Subscribers say, that the General Assembly of this Commonwealth have no such authority: And that no effort may be omitted on our part against so dangerous an usurpation, we oppose to it, this remonstrance; earnestly praying, as we are in duty bound, that the Supreme Lawgiver of the Universe, by illuminating those to whom it is addressed, may on the one hand, turn their Councils from every act which would affront his holy prerogative, or violate the trust committed to them: and on the other, guide them into every measure which may be worthy of his blessing, may redound to their own praise, and may establish more firmly the liberties, the prosperity and the happiness of the Commonwealth.

NOTES

1. Note the theological nature of the arguments in the Paragraph 1 of Madison's petition. Is it surprising to see arguments of this sort in support of disestablishment? It may help to know that the leading opponents of Patrick Henry's bill were the Virginia Baptists—the most fervent evangelical sect in the Commonwealth. They were not opposed to the bill because it "advanced" religion but because it invaded a province reserved to the authority of God.

2. The Memorial and Remonstrance is commonly cited in support of disestablishment of religion. But note its implications for the free exercise of religion. If duties to the Creator are "precedent, both in order of time and in degree of obligation, to the claims of Civil Society," what does that say about rights of free exercise?

3. Just four years after the Memorial and Remonstrance, as a Congressman from Virginia, Madison led the effort to amend the Constitution to add a Bill of Rights, including protections for religious liberty. Here are the results of his efforts:

Madison's Initial Proposal for the Religion Clauses

House of Representatives, June 8, 1789 (1 Annals of Cong. 434)

That in article 1st, section 9, between clauses 3 and 4, be inserted these clauses, to wit: The civil rights of none shall be abridged on account of religious belief or worship, nor shall any national religion be established, nor shall the full and equal rights of conscience be in any manner, or on any pretext, infringed.

Debate on Establishment of Religion and Rights of Conscience

House of Representatives, August 15 & 20, 1789 (1 Annals of Cong. 729–33, 767–68)

Saturday, August 15

The fourth proposition being under consideration, as follows:

Article 1. Section 9. Between paragraphs two and three insert "no religion shall be established by law, nor shall the equal rights of conscience be infringed."

Mr. SYLVESTER had some doubts of the propriety of the mode of expression used in this paragraph. He apprehended that it was liable to a construction different from what had been made by the committee. He feared it might be thought to have a tendency to abolish religion altogether.

Mr. VINING suggested the propriety of transposing the two members of the sentence.

Mr. GERRY said it would read better if it was, that no religious doctrine shall be established by law.

Mr. SHERMAN thought the amendment altogether unnecessary, inasmuch as Congress had no authority whatever delegated to them by the Constitution to make religious establishments; he would, therefore, move to have it struck out.

Mr. CARROLL.—As the rights of conscience are, in their nature, of peculiar delicacy, and will little bear the gentlest touch of governmental hand; and as many sects have concurred in opinion that they are not well secured under the present Constitution. He said he was much in favor of adopting the words. He thought it would tend more towards conciliating the minds of the people to the Government than almost any other amendment he had heard proposed. He would not contend with gentlemen about the phraseology, his object was to secure the substance in such a manner as to satisfy the wishes of the honest part of the community.

Mr. MADISON said, he apprehended the meaning of the words to be, that Congress should not establish a religion, and enforce the legal observation of it by law, nor compel men to worship God in any manner contrary to their conscience. Whether the words are necessary or not, he did not mean to say, but they had been required by some of the State Conventions, who seemed to entertain an opinion that under the clause of the Constitution, which gave power to Congress to make all laws necessary and proper to carry into execution the Constitution, and the laws made under it enabled them to make laws of such a nature as might infringe the rights of conscience, and establish a national religion; to prevent these effects he presumed the amendment was intended and he thought it as well expressed as the nature of the language would admit.

Mr. HUNTINGTON said that he feared, with the gentleman first up on this subject, that the words might be taken in such latitude as to be extremely hurtful to the cause of religion. He understood the amendment to mean what had been expressed by the gentleman from Virginia; but others might find it convenient to put another construction upon it. The ministers of their congregations to the Eastward were maintained by the contributions of those who belonged to their society; the expense of building meeting-houses was contributed in the same manner. These things were regulated by by-laws. If an action was brought before a Federal Court on any of these cases, the person who had neglected to perform his engagements could not be compelled to do it; for a support of ministers or building of places of worship might be construed into a religious establishment.

By the charter of Rhode Island, no religion could be established by law; he could give a history of the effects of such a regulation; indeed the people were now enjoying the blessed fruits of it. He hoped, therefore, the amendment would be made in such a way as to secure the rights of conscience, and a free exercise of the rights of religion, but not to patronise those who professed no religion at all.

Mr. MADISON thought, if the word "national" was inserted before religion, it would satisfy the minds of honorable gentlemen. He believed that the people feared one sect might obtain a pre-eminence, or two combine together, and establish a religion to which they would compel others to conform. He thought if the word "national" was introduced, it would point the amendment directly to the object it was intended to prevent.

Mr. LIVERMORE was not satisfied with that amendment; but he did not wish them to dwell long on the subject. He thought it would be better if it were altered, and made to read in this manner, that Congress shall make no laws touching religion, or infringing the rights of conscience.

Mr. GERRY did not like the term national, proposed by the gentleman from Virginia, and he hoped it would not be adopted by the House. It brought to his mind some observations that had taken place in the conventions at the time they were considering the present Constitution. It had been insisted upon by those who were called anti-federalists, that this form of Government consolidated the Union; the honorable gentleman's motion shows that he considers it in the same light. Those who were called anti-federalists at that time, complained that they had injustice done them by the title, because they were in favor of a Federal Government, and the others were in favor of a national one; the federalists were for ratifying the Constitution as it stood, and the others not until amendments were made. Their names then ought not to have been distinguished by federalists and anti-federalists, but rats and anti-rats.

Mr. MADISON withdrew his motion, but observed that the words "no national religion shall be established by law," did not imply that the Government was a national one; the question was then taken on Mr. LIVERMORE's motion, and passed in the affirmative, thirty-one for, and twenty against it. . . .

Thursday, August 20

On motion of Mr. AMES, the fourth amendment was altered so as to read "Congress shall make no law establishing religion or to prevent the free exercise thereof; or to infringe the rights of conscience." This being adopted,

The first proposition was agreed to.

Mr. SCOTT objected to the clause in the sixth amendment, "No person religiously scrupulous shall be compelled to bear arms." He observed that if this becomes part of the Constitution, such persons can neither he called upon for their services, nor can an equivalent be demanded; it is also attended with still further difficulties, for a militia can never be depended upon. This would lead to the violation of another article in the Constitution, which secures to the people the right of keeping arms, and in this case recourse must be had to a standing army. I conceive it, said he, to be a Legislative right altogether. There are many sects I know, who are religiously scrupulous in this respect; I do not mean to deprive them of any indulgence the law affords; my design is to guard against those who are of no religion. It has been urged that religion is on the decline; if so, the argument is more strong in my favor, for when the time comes that religion shall be discarded the generality of persons will have recourse to these pretexts to get excused from bearing arms.

Mr. BOUDINOT thought the provision in the clause, or something similar to it, was necessary. Can any dependence, said he, be placed in men who are conscientious in this respect? or what justice can there be in compelling them to bear arms, when, according to their religious principles, they would rather die than use them? He adverted to several instances of oppression on this point, that occurred during the war. In forming a militia, an effectual defence ought to be calculated, and no characters of this religious description ought to be compelled to take up arms. I hope that in establishing this Government, we may show the world that proper care is taken that the Government may not interfere with the religious sentiments of any person. Now, by striking out the clause, people may be led to believe that there is an intention in the General Government to compel all its citizens to bear arms.

Some further desultory conversation arose, and it was agreed to insert the words "in person," to the end of the clause; after which, it was adopted, as was the fourth, fifth, sixth, seventh, and eighth clauses of the fourth proposition; then the fifth, sixth, and seventh propositions were agreed to, and the House adjourned.

House Draft Transmitted to the Senate

1 Senate Journal 63 (August 24, 1789)

Article the Third

Congress shall make no law establishing Religion, or prohibiting the free exercise thereof, nor shall the rights of conscience be infringed.

Senate Motions

1 Senate Journal 70 (September 3, 1789)

On motion, To amend Article third, and to strike out these words. "Religion or prohibiting the free Exercise thereof," and Insert, "One Religious Sect or Society in preference to others,"

It passed in the Negative.

On motion, For reconsideration,

It passed in the Affirmative.

On motion, That Article the third be striken out,

It passed in the Negative.

On motion, To adopt the following, in lieu of the third Article, "Congress shall not make any law, infringing the rights of conscience or establishing any Religious Sect or Society,"

It passed in the Negative.

On motion, To amend the third Article, to read thus—"Congress shall make no law establishing any particular denomination of religion in preference to another, or prohibiting the free exercise thereof, nor shall the rights of conscience be infringed."

It passed in the Negative.

On the question upon the third Article as it came from the House of Representatives—

It passed in the Negative.

On motion, To adopt the third Article proposed in the Resolve of the House of Representatives, amended by striking out these words—"Nor shall the rights of conscience be infringed."

It passed in the Affirmative. . . .

On motion to amend article the third, to read as follows: "Congress shall make no law establishing articles of faith or a mode of worship, or prohibiting the free exercise of religion, or abridging the freedom of speech, or the press, or the right of the people peaceable to assemble, and petition to the government for the redress of grievances."

It was passed in the affirmative.

NOTES

1. Unfortunately, we do not have records of the debates in the Senate, because its proceedings were not open to the public or the press. (The House de-

bates were recorded unofficially by newspaper reporters sitting in the House galleries taking notes. They are presumably not complete, and they are not official.) Keep track of what the senators were arguing about. There appear to be two main issues. First, would the clause protect the "free exercise of religion," the "rights of conscience," or both? What might be the difference(s) between these terms? What is the significance of the decision to protect the "free exercise of religion" and not the "rights of conscience"? Second, would the clause extend broadly to "establishment of religion," or more narrowly to a prohibition on government-formed "articles of faith" or "modes of worship"? The latter terms referred to English laws prescribing the Church of England's statement of doctrine (the Thirty–Nine Articles) and its liturgy (the Book of Common Prayer) and requiring all ministers to conform to them. The House of Representatives insisted on the broader term, and the Senate acceded to it. What practices are part of the "establishment of religion" that would not have been included in the Senate's version?

2. What did the debates in the House focus on? Note that several members—conspicuously Huntington of Connecticut—feared that the draft amendment would interfere with state and local establishments of religion, such as the one in place in Connecticut. Madison responded that the purpose would be made clear if the amendment used the language "national religion," leaving state establishments to state law, but Gerry objected to the word "national." Eventually, the members settled on a clause that specified that it applied only to "Congress" and prohibited laws "respecting" an establishment, likely meaning laws either establishing a national religion or disturbing state establishments. In other words, they adopted the solution of federalism—local diversity—to the contentious question of religion. Only in the twentieth century, after incorporation of the Establishment Clause, have states been unable to decide for themselves what types of support to provide for religion.

3. Finally, consider the debate over the exemption from compulsory militia service for persons "religiously scrupulous of bearing arms." What does it tell us about free exercise of religion? About the legitimacy of legislative acts accommodating religious exercise? Some say such acts are an unfair form of favoring religion—effectively an establishment. Would the framers have agreed?

B. THE FREE EXERCISE CLAUSE

Amendment I: Congress shall make no law respecting an establishment of religion, or prohibiting the free exercise thereof. . . .

What does it mean to "prohibit" the "free exercise of religion"? Does this mean the government may penalize or inhibit the exercise of religion, so long as it does not "prohibit" it? Or should the term be interpreted to encompass any substantial burden on the exercise of religion, as would be the case for most constitutional freedoms? And what is the "exercise" of religion? Presumably this does not mean only belief. But at the time of adoption of the Fourteenth Amendment, many state constitutions protected only acts of "worship," not all forms of "exercise of religion."[5] Should that be un-

---

[5] In 1868, when the Fourteenth Amendment was ratified, all thirty-seven states protected religious freedom in one way or another in their state Bills of Rights. Steven G. Calabresi & Sarah E. Agudo, *Individual Rights Under State Constitutions when the Fourteenth Amendment Was Ratified in 1868: What Rights Are Deeply Rooted in American History and Tradition?*, 87 Tex. L. Rev. 7, 33–36 (2008). Thirty-five states protected freedom of "worship"; three states protected free "exercise" of religion. *Id.* at 34. In addition, the state Bill of Rights in

derstood as a gloss on the First Amendment language? If so, what would be the consequence? If not, what is the reach of the constitutional term? Does it include any action that the individual believer regards as conducive to a life in accordance with the will of God? Are there any limits? More importantly, perhaps, is the right of free exercise absolute, or may it be defeated by the superior claims of the state? May a believer assert the right to commit murder or trespass in the service of God? If not, why not? How strong must the governmental interest be to interfere with the free exercise of religion, and how may it be evaluated? Finally, what is "religion"? The Virginia Declaration of Rights, on which the First Amendment may have been modeled, defined "religion" as the "duty which we owe to our Creator, and the manner of discharging it." Is that a sound definition today? Is it too narrow? Is it too broad? If you are tempted to adopt a broad definition of "religion" for purposes of the protections of the Free Exercise Clause, ask yourself whether the same definition would work for purposes of the Establishment Clause.

We start with several cases on the Free Exercise Clause. The first is the shortest case you will ever see in a law school casebook: *Stansbury v. Marks*, a 1793 Pennsylvania Supreme Court decision decided under the Pennsylvania constitution of 1790. It can be used to illustrate just about every current issue under the First Amendment's protection of religion. The remaining cases illustrate the modern Supreme Court's approaches to these questions: *Wisconsin v. Yoder* (1972), *Employment Division v. Smith* (1990) and *Hosanna-Tabor Evangelical Lutheran Church and School v. EEOC* (2012).

Stansbury v. Marks
2 Dall. 213 (Pa. 1793)

In this cause (which was tried on *Saturday*, the 5th of *April*), the defendant offered *Jonas Phillips*, a Jew, as a witness; but he refused to be sworn, because it was his *Sabbath*. The Court, therefore, fined him £10; but the defendant, afterwards, waving the benefit of his testimony, he was discharged from the fine.

NOTES

1. *Stansbury*'s facts are cryptic; its reasoning is cryptic. It is not at all clear that the court based its actions on any constitutional provision. The Pennsylvania Constitution of 1790, Art. IX, section 3, in effect at the time of *Stansbury v. Marks*, provided as follows:

> That all men have a natural and indefeasible right to worship Almighty God according to the dictates of their own consciences; that no man can of right be compelled to attend, erect, or support any place of worship, or maintain any ministry, against his consent; that no human authority can, in any case whatever, control or interfere with the rights of conscience; and that no preference shall ever be given, by law, to any religious establishment or modes of worship.

---

twenty-seven states forbade an establishment of religion. *Id.* at 31–33. Is there any significance to the fact that state constitutions used a different formulation than the First Amendment?

What legal and interpretive questions does this raise? How should the case have come out under this provision? Would the result be different under the Free Exercise Clause of the First Amendment?

2. What is the "free exercise" of religion? Does it include freedom of *conduct*, or just freedom of belief? Was Jonas Phillips's stance one of religious "belief" or religious "conduct"—or is this a false dichotomy?

3. What does the First Amendment mean when it bans laws "prohibiting" the free exercise of religion? Does the First Amendment forbid laws that have the *effect* of burdening religious exercise, even if cast in neutral terms? Or is the better reading of the language that it forbids only government laws and practices that are *specifically directed* at religious beliefs or practices? Put differently, is the Free Exercise Clause a substantive immunity from the usual powers of government, or a rule of government nondiscrimination on the basis of religion only?

A related question concerning the meaning of "prohibit": What constitutes a law *prohibiting* religious exercise as opposed to merely *burdening* it? What if a law made Christian worship illegal, but imposed a fine of only $1 per week? Would that "prohibit" the free exercise of religion? Did the fine at issue in *Stansbury* "prohibit" Mr. Phillips's exercise of religion? (After all, he could observe his Sabbath; he merely had to pay the fine.) Does it make a difference if the burden is imposed by a facially neutral law? What if a law imposed a general tax, but payment of that tax conflicted with the individual's, or a religious sect's, sincere beliefs (just as Saturday testimony conflicted with Mr. Phillips's Jewish faith)? Is that a law prohibiting the free exercise of religion? Compare *United States v. Lee*, 455 U.S. 252 (1982) (unanimously rejecting a claimed Free Exercise Clause right of Amish religious employers not to pay Social Security taxes/contributions for their employees on grounds of religious faith requirements to the contrary).

4. What if the issue were conscientious objection to the draft? Should the Free Exercise Clause be understood to require religious-based conscientious objection to and exemption from military service? What about *non*-religious-based conscientious objection? Is there a problem with religious conscience being preferred over non-religious conscience? Draft exemption led to a series of Supreme Court decisions presenting these issues. *United States v. Seeger*, 380 U.S. 163 (1965); *Welsh v. United States*, 398 U.S. 333 (1970); *Gillette v. United States*, 401 U.S. 437 (1971).

5. Assuming the state was not constitutionally required to accommodate Mr. Phillips's religious objection to testifying on his Sabbath, would the Establishment Clause forbid the state from doing so as a matter of legislative policy? Would it establish religion to *excuse* Jonas Phillips from testifying (assuming the Free Exercise Clause does not require such an exception)? Does it violate the Establishment Clause to hold court on Saturdays (thus establishing a religion that does not recognize Saturdays as the Sabbath)? Fridays? Ash Wednesday? Yom Kippur? Would a law professor at a state university violate the Establishment Clause by canceling a Constitutional Law class on Yom Kippur, to accommodate Jewish students, and rescheduling a make-up class on a different day (the regular practice of one of the casebook's authors)?

In general, does government accommodation of religion violate the Establishment Clause? What about government symbolic invocation of religion? Does that violate the Establishment Clause? Are the Free Exercise and Establishment Clauses inconsistent with each other?

This is the central dilemma of the Free Exercise Clause. Is it a mere non-discrimination provision? (Can it really mean so little?) Or does it confer a substantive immunity from society's laws, for all whose religious beliefs conflict with such laws? See Stephen Pepper, *Taking the Free Exercise Clause Seriously*, 1986 BYU L. Rev. 299 (1986). The Supreme Court has vacillated between these two positions. Compare the decisions reached in 1970 in Wisconsin v. Yoder with that reached in 1990 in *Employment Division v. Smith*.

Wisconsin v. Yoder
406 U.S. 205 (1972)

■ CHIEF JUSTICE BURGER delivered the opinion of the Court.

. . . Respondents Jonas Yoder and Wallace Miller are members of the Old Order Amish religion, and respondent Adin Yutzy is a member of the Conservative Amish Mennonite Church. They and their families are residents of Green County, Wisconsin. Wisconsin's compulsory school-attendance law required them to cause their children to attend public or private school until reaching age 16 but the respondents declined to send their children, ages 14 and 15, to public school after they complete the eighth grade. The children were not enrolled in any private school, or within any recognized exception to the compulsory-attendance law, and they are conceded to be subject to the Wisconsin statute.

On complaint of the school district administrator for the public schools, respondents were charged, tried, and convicted of violating the compulsory-attendance law in Green County Court and were fined the sum of $5 each. Respondents defended on the ground that the application of the compulsory-attendance law violated their rights under the First and Fourteenth Amendments. The trial testimony showed that respondents believed, in accordance with the tenets of Old Order Amish communities generally, that their children's attendance at high school, public or private, was contrary to the Amish religion and way of life. They believed that by sending their children to high school, they would not only expose themselves to the danger of the censure of the church community, but, as found by the county court, also endanger their own salvation and that of their children. The State stipulated that respondents' religious beliefs were sincere.

[Members of the Amish faith seek] to return to the early, simple, Christian life de-emphasizing material success, rejecting the competitive spirit, and seeking to insulate themselves from the modern world. . . .

Amish objection to formal education beyond the eighth grade is firmly grounded in these central religious concepts. They object to the high school, and higher education generally, because the values they teach are in marked variance with Amish values and the Amish way of life; they view secondary school education as an impermissible exposure of their children to a "wordly" influence in conflict with their beliefs. The high school tends to emphasize intellectual and scientific accomplishments, self-distinction, competitiveness, worldly success, and social life with other students. Amish society emphasizes informal learning-through-doing; a life of "goodness," rather than a life of intellect; wisdom, rather than technical knowledge; community welfare, rather than competition; and separation from, rather than integration with, contemporary worldly society.

Formal high school education beyond the eighth grade is contrary to Amish beliefs, not only because it places Amish children in an environment hostile to Amish beliefs with increasing emphasis on competition in class work and sports and with pressure to conform to the styles, manners, and ways of the peer group, but also because it takes them away from their community, physically and emotionally, during the crucial and formative adolescent period of life. During this period, the children must acquire Amish attitudes favoring manual work and self-reliance and the specific skills needed to perform the adult role of an Amish farmer or housewife. They must learn to enjoy physical labor. Once a child has learned basic reading, writing, and elementary mathematics, these traits, skills, and attitudes admittedly fall within the category of those best learned through example and "doing" rather than in a classroom.

I

[I]n order for Wisconsin to compel school attendance beyond the eighth grade against a claim that such attendance interferes with the practice of a legitimate religious belief, it must appear either that the State does not deny the free exercise of religious belief by its requirement, or that there is a state interest of sufficient magnitude to override the interest claiming protection under the Free Exercise Clause.... The essence of all that has been said and written on the subject is that only those interests of the highest order and those not otherwise served can overbalance legitimate claims to the free exercise of religion. We can accept it as settled, therefore, that, however strong the State's interest in universal compulsory education, it is by no means absolute to the exclusion or subordination of all other interests.

II

We come then to the quality of the claims of the respondents concerning the alleged encroachment of Wisconsin's compulsory school-attendance statute on their rights and the rights of their children to the free exercise of the religious beliefs they and their forbears have adhered to for almost three centuries. In evaluating those claims we must be careful to determine whether the Amish religious faith and their mode of life are, as they claim, inseparable and interdependent. A way of life, however virtuous and admirable, may not be interposed as a barrier to reasonable state regulation of education if it is based on purely secular considerations; to have the protection of the Religion Clauses, the claims must be rooted in religious belief. Although a determination of what is a "religious" belief or practice entitled to constitutional protection may present a most delicate question, the very concept of ordered liberty precludes allowing every person to make his own standards on matters of conduct in which society as a whole has important interests. Thus, if the Amish asserted their claims because of their subjective evaluation and rejection of the contemporary secular values accepted by the majority, much as Thoreau rejected the social values of his time and isolated himself at Walden Pond, their claims would not rest on a religious basis. Thoreau's choice was philosophical and personal rather than religious, and such belief does not rise to the demands of the Religion Clauses.

Giving no weight to such secular considerations, however, we see that the record in this case abundantly supports the claim that the traditional way of life of the Amish is not merely a matter of personal preference, but one of deep religious conviction, shared by an organized group, and intimately related to daily living. That the Old Order Amish daily life and religious practice stem from their faith is shown by the fact that it is in response to their literal interpretation of the Biblical injunction from the Epistle of Paul to the Romans, "be not conformed to this world. . . ." This command is fundamental to the Amish faith. Moreover, for the Old Order Amish, religion is not simply a matter of theocratic belief. . . .

III

Wisconsin concedes that under the Religion Clauses religious beliefs are absolutely free from the State's control, but it argues that "actions," even though religiously grounded, are outside the protection of the First Amendment But our decisions have rejected the idea that religiously grounded conduct is always outside the protection of the Free Exercise Clause. It is true that activities of individuals, even when religiously based, are often subject to regulation by the States in the exercise of their undoubted power to promote the health, safety, and general welfare, or the Federal Government in the exercise of its delegated powers. But to agree that religiously grounded conduct must often be subject to the broad police power of the State is not to deny that there are areas of conduct protected by the Free Exercise Clause of the First Amendment and thus beyond the power of the State to control, even under regulations of general applicability. . . .

Nor can this case be disposed of on the grounds that Wisconsin's requirement for school attendance to age 16 applies uniformly to all citizens of the State and does not, on its face, discriminate against religions or a particular religion, or that it is motivated by legitimate secular concerns. A regulation neutral on its face may, in its application, nonetheless offend the constitutional requirement for governmental neutrality if it unduly burdens the free exercise of religion. The Court must not ignore the danger that an exception from a general obligation of citizenship on religious grounds may run afoul of the Establishment Clause, but that danger cannot be allowed to prevent any exception no matter how vital it may be to the protection of values promoted by the right of free exercise.

[The Court then rejected the state's argument that its interest in requiring education to age sixteen was compelling, largely on the ground that Amish children received education at home that was adequate for the state's purposes.—Editors]

■ [The concurring opinions joined by JUSTICES STEWART, BRENNAN, AND WHITE are omitted.]

■ JUSTICE DOUGLAS, dissenting in part.

I agree with the Court that the religious scruples of the Amish are opposed to the education of their children beyond the grade schools, yet I disagree with the Court's conclusion that the matter is within the dispensation of parents alone. The Court's analysis assumes that the only interests at stake in the case are those of the Amish parents on the one hand, and those of the State on the other. The difficulty with this approach is that, despite the Court's claim, the parents are seeking to vindicate not only their own free exercise claims, but also those of their high-school-age children. . . .

[In cases where the high-school-age children agree with their parents, Justice Douglas was in accord with the Court that the Free Exercise Clause protects their decision not to attend school. The other justices stated that this issue was not raised in the case.—Editors]

Employment Division v. Smith

494 U.S. 872 (1990)

■ JUSTICE SCALIA delivered the opinion of the Court.

This case requires us to decide whether the Free Exercise Clause of the First Amendment permits the State of Oregon to include religiously inspired peyote use within the reach of its general criminal prohibition on use of that drug, and thus permits the State to deny unemployment benefits to persons dismissed from their jobs because of such religiously inspired use.

I

Oregon law prohibits the knowing or intentional possession of a "controlled substance," [including] . . . the drug peyote, a hallucinogen derived from the plant *Lophophora williamsii Lemaire*.

Respondents Alfred Smith and Galen Black (hereinafter respondents) were fired from their jobs with a private drug rehabilitation organization because they ingested peyote for sacramental purposes at a ceremony of the Native American Church, of which both are members. When respondents applied to petitioner Employment Division (hereinafter petitioner) for unemployment compensation, they were determined to be ineligible for benefits because they had been discharged for work-related "misconduct." . . .

[T]he Oregon Supreme Court held that respondents' religiously inspired use of peyote fell within the prohibition of the Oregon statute, which "makes no exception for the sacramental use" of the drug. It then considered whether that prohibition was valid under the Free Exercise Clause, and concluded that it was not. The court therefore [held] that the State could not deny unemployment benefits to respondents for having engaged in that practice. . . .

II

Respondents' claim for relief rests on our decisions in *Sherbert v. Verner*, 374 U.S. 398 (1963), *Thomas v. Review Bd. of Indiana Employment Security Div.*, 450 U.S. 707 (1981), and *Hobbie v. Unemployment Appeals Comm'n of Florida*, 480 U.S. 136 (1987), in which we held that a State could not condition the availability of unemployment insurance on an individual's willingness to forgo conduct required by his religion. As we observed in [an earlier appeal in this case], however, the conduct at issue in those cases was not prohibited by law. . . . Now that the Oregon Supreme Court has confirmed that Oregon does prohibit the religious use of peyote, we proceed to consider whether that prohibition is permissible under the Free Exercise Clause.

A

The Free Exercise Clause of the First Amendment, which has been made applicable to the States by incorporation into the Fourteenth Amendment, provides that "Congress shall make no law respecting an establishment of religion, or *prohibiting the free exercise thereof*." The free exercise of religion means, first and foremost, the right to believe and profess whatever religious doctrine one desires. Thus, the First Amendment obviously excludes all "governmental regulation of religious *beliefs* as such." *Sherbert v. Verner, supra*, 374 U.S., at 402. The government may not compel affirmation of religious belief, punish the expression of religious doctrines it believes to be false, impose special disabilities on the basis of religious views or religious status; or lend its power to one or the other side in controversies over religious authority or dogma.

But the "exercise of religion" often involves not only belief and profession but the performance of (or abstention from) physical acts: assembling with others for a worship service, participating in sacramental use of bread and wine, proselytizing, abstaining from certain foods or certain modes of transportation. It would be true, we think (though no case of ours has involved the point), that a State would be "prohibiting the free exercise [of religion]" if it sought to ban such acts or abstentions only when they are engaged in for religious reasons, or only because of the religious belief that they display. It would doubtless be unconstitutional, for example, to ban the casting of "statues that are to be used for worship purposes," or to prohibit bowing down before a golden calf.

Respondents in the present case, however, seek to carry the meaning of "prohibiting the free exercise [of religion]" one large step further. They contend that their religious motivation for using peyote places them beyond the reach of a criminal law that is not specifically directed at their religious practice, and that is concededly constitutional as applied to those who use the drug for other reasons. They assert, in other words, that "prohibiting the free exercise [of religion]" includes requiring any individual to observe a generally applicable law that requires (or forbids) the performance of an act that his religious belief forbids (or requires). As a textual matter, we do not think the words must be given that meaning. It is no more necessary to regard the collection of a general tax, for example, as "prohibiting the free exercise [of religion]" by those citizens who believe support of organized government to be sinful, than it is to regard the same tax as "abridging the freedom . . . of the press" of those publishing companies that must pay the tax as a condition of staying in business. It is a permissible reading of the text, in the one case as in the other, to say that if prohibiting the exercise of religion (or burdening the activity of printing) is not the object of the tax but merely the incidental effect of a generally applicable and otherwise valid provision, the First Amendment has not been offended.

Our decisions reveal that the latter reading is the correct one. We have never held that an individual's religious beliefs excuse him from compliance with an otherwise valid law prohibiting conduct that the State is free to regulate. We first had occasion to assert that principle in *Reynolds v. United States,* 98 U.S. 145 (1878), where we rejected the claim that criminal laws against polygamy could not be constitutionally applied to those whose religion commanded the practice. "Laws," we said, "are made for the government of actions, and while they cannot interfere with mere religious belief and opinions, they may with practices. . . . Can a man excuse his practices to the contrary because of his religious belief? To permit this would be to make the professed doctrines of religious belief superior to the law of the land, and in effect to permit every citizen to become a law unto himself." *Id.,* at 166–167. . . .

Our most recent decision involving a neutral, generally applicable regulatory law that compelled activity forbidden by an individual's religion was *United States v. Lee,* 455 U.S. 252, at 258–261 (1982). There, an Amish employer, on behalf of himself and his employees, sought exemption from collection and payment of Social Security taxes on the ground that the Amish faith prohibited participation in governmental support programs. We rejected the claim that an exemption was constitutionally required. There would be no way, we observed, to distinguish the Amish believer's objection to Social Security taxes from the religious objections that others might have to the collection or use of other taxes. "If, for example, a religious adherent believes war is a sin, and if a certain percentage of the federal budget can be identified as devoted to war-related activities, such individuals would have a similarly valid claim to be exempt from paying that percentage of the income tax. The tax system could not function if denominations were allowed to challenge the tax system because tax payments were spent in a manner that violates their religious belief."

The only decisions in which we have held that the First Amendment bars application of a neutral, generally applicable law to religiously motivated action have involved not the Free Exercise Clause alone, but the Free Exercise Clause in conjunction with other constitutional protections, such as freedom of speech and of the press, see *Cantwell*; *Murdock*; or the right of parents, acknowledged in *Pierce v. Society of Sisters,* 268 U.S. 510 (1925), to direct the education of their children, see *Wisconsin v. Yoder,* 406 U.S. 205 (1972) (invalidating compulsory school-attendance laws as applied to Amish parents who refused on religious grounds to send their children to school). Some of our cases prohibiting compelled expression, decided exclusively upon free speech grounds, have also involved freedom of religion, cf. *Wooley v. Maynard*; *West Virginia Bd. of Education v. Barnette*. And it is easy to envision a case in which a challenge on freedom of association grounds would likewise be reinforced by Free Exercise Clause concerns. *Cf. Roberts v. United States Jaycees,* 468 U.S. 609, 622 (1984) ("An individual's freedom to speak, to worship, and to petition the government for the redress of grievances could not be vigorously protected from interference by the State [if] a correlative freedom to engage in group effort toward those ends were not also guaranteed").

The present case does not present such a hybrid situation, but a free exercise claim unconnected with any communicative activity or parental right. Respondents urge us to hold, quite simply, that when otherwise prohibitable conduct is accompanied by religious convictions, not only the convictions but the conduct itself must be free from governmental regulation. We have never held that, and decline to do so now. . . .

B

Respondents argue that even though exemption from generally applicable criminal laws need not automatically be extended to religiously motivated actors, at least the claim for a religious exemption must be evaluated under the balancing test set forth in *Sherbert v. Verner,* 374 U.S. 398 (1963). Under the *Sherbert* test, governmental actions that substantially burden a religious practice must be justified by a compelling governmental interest. . . . We have never invalidated any governmental action on the basis of the *Sherbert* test except the denial of unemployment compensation. Although we have sometimes purported to apply the *Sherbert* test in contexts other than that, we have always found the test satisfied, see *Lee,* 455 U.S. 252 (1982); *Gillette,* 401 U.S. 437 (1971). In recent years we have abstained from applying the *Sherbert* test (outside the unemployment compensation field) at all. . . .

Even if we were inclined to breathe into *Sherbert* some life beyond the unemployment compensation field, we would not apply it to require exemptions from a generally applicable criminal law. The *Sherbert* test, it must be recalled, was developed in a context that lent itself to individualized governmental assessment of the reasons for the relevant conduct. . . .

Whether or not the decisions are that limited, they at least have nothing to do with an across-the-board criminal prohibition on a particular form of conduct. Although . . . we have sometimes used the *Sherbert* test to analyze free exercise challenges to such laws, we have never applied the test to invalidate one. We conclude today that the sounder approach, and the approach in accord with the vast majority of our precedents, is to hold the test inapplicable to such challenges. The government's ability to enforce generally applicable prohibitions of socially harmful conduct, like its ability to carry out other aspects of public policy, "cannot depend on measuring the effects of a governmental action on a religious objector's spiritual development." *Lyng.* To make an individual's obligation to obey such a law contingent upon the law's coincidence with his religious beliefs, except where the State's interest is "compelling"—permitting him, by virtue of his beliefs, "to become a law unto himself," *Reynolds v. United States*—contradicts both constitutional tradition and common sense.

The "compelling government interest" requirement seems benign, because it is familiar from other fields. But using it as the standard that must be met before the government may accord different treatment on the basis of race, . . . or before the government may regulate the content of speech, . . . is not remotely comparable to using it for the purpose asserted here. What it produces in those other fields—equality of treatment and an unrestricted flow of contending speech—are constitutional norms; what it would produce here—a private right to ignore generally applicable laws—is a constitutional anomaly.

Nor is it possible to limit the impact of respondents' proposal by requiring a "compelling state interest" only when the conduct prohibited is "central" to the individual's religion. It is no more appropriate for judges to determine the "centrality" of religious beliefs before applying a "compelling interest" test in the free exercise field, than it would be for them to determine the "importance" of ideas before applying the "compelling interest" test in the free speech field. What principle of law or logic can be brought to bear to contradict a believer's assertion that a particular act is "central" to his personal faith? . . . Repeatedly and in many different contexts, we have warned that courts must not presume to determine the place of a particular belief in a religion or the plausibility of a religious claim.

If the "compelling interest" test is to be applied at all, then, it must be applied across the board, to all actions thought to be religiously commanded. Moreover, if "compelling interest" really means what it says (and watering it down here would subvert its rigor in the other fields where it is applied), many laws will not meet the test. Any society adopting such a system would be courting anarchy, but that danger increases in direct proportion to the society's diversity of religious beliefs, and its determination to coerce or suppress none of them. Precisely because we value and protect religious divergence, we cannot afford the luxury of deeming *presumptively invalid,* as applied to the religious objector, every regulation of conduct that does not protect an interest of the highest order. The rule respondents favor would open the prospect of constitutionally required religious exemptions from civic obligations of almost every conceivable kind. . . . The First Amendment's protection of religious liberty does not require this.

Values that are protected against government interference through enshrinement in the Bill of Rights are not thereby banished from the political process. Just as a society that believes in the negative protection accorded to the press by the First Amendment is likely to enact laws that affirmatively foster the dissemination of the printed word, so also a society that believes in the negative protection accorded to religious belief can be expected to be solicitous of that value in its legislation as well. It is therefore not surprising that a number of States have made an exception to their drug laws for sacramental peyote use. But to say that a nondiscriminatory religious-practice exemption is permitted, or even that it is desirable, is not to say that it is constitutionally required, and that the appropriate occasions for its creation can be discerned by the courts. It may fairly be said that leaving accommodation to the political process will place at a relative disadvantage those religious practices that are not widely engaged in; but that unavoidable consequence of democratic government must be preferred to a system in which each conscience is a law unto itself or in which judges weigh the social importance of all laws against the centrality of all religious beliefs.

Because respondents' ingestion of peyote was prohibited under Oregon law, and because that prohibition is constitutional, Oregon may, consistent with the Free Exercise Clause, deny respondents unemployment compensation when their dismissal results from use of the drug.

■ JUSTICE O'CONNOR, with whom JUSTICE BRENNAN, JUSTICE MARSHALL, and JUSTICE BLACKMUN join as to Parts I and II, concurring in the judgment.

Although I agree with the result the Court reaches in this case, I cannot join its opinion. In my view, today's holding dramatically departs from well-settled First Amendment jurisprudence, appears unnecessary to resolve the question presented, and is incompatible with our Nation's fundamental commitment to individual religious liberty. . . .

II

The Court today . . . interprets the [Free Exercise] Clause to permit the government to prohibit, without justification, conduct mandated by an individual's religious beliefs, so long as that prohibition is generally applicable. But a law that prohibits certain conduct—conduct that happens to be an act of worship for someone—manifestly does prohibit that person's free exercise of his religion. A person who is barred from engaging in religiously motivated conduct is barred from freely exercising his religion. Moreover, that person is barred from freely exercising his religion regardless of whether the law prohibits the conduct only when engaged in for religious reasons, only by members of that religion, or by all persons. . . .

The Court responds that generally applicable laws are "one large step" removed from laws aimed at specific religious practices. The First Amendment, however, does not distinguish between laws that are generally applicable and laws that target particular religious practices. Indeed, few States would be so naive as to enact a law directly prohibiting or burdening a religious practice as such. Our free exercise cases have all concerned generally applicable laws that had the effect of significantly burdening a religious practice. If the First Amendment is to have any vitality, it ought not be construed to cover only the extreme and hypothetical situation in which a State directly targets a religious practice. . . .

To say that a person's right to free exercise has been burdened, of course, does not mean that he has an absolute right to engage in the conduct. Under our established First Amendment jurisprudence, we have recognized that the freedom to act, unlike the freedom to believe, cannot be absolute. Instead, we have respected both the First Amendment's express textual mandate and the governmental interest in regulation of conduct by requiring the government to justify any substantial burden on religiously motivated conduct by a compelling state interest and by means narrowly tailored to achieve that interest. The compelling interest test effectuates the First Amendment's command that religious liberty is an independent liberty, that it occupies a preferred position, and that the Court will not permit encroachments upon this liberty, whether direct or indirect, unless required by clear and compelling governmental interests "of the highest order," *Yoder*, 406 U.S., at 215. . . .

The Court attempts to support its narrow reading of the Clause by claiming that "[w]e have never held that an individual's religious beliefs excuse him from compliance with an otherwise valid law prohibiting conduct that the State is free to regulate." But as the Court later notes, as it must, in cases such as *Cantwell* and *Yoder* we have in fact interpreted the Free Exercise Clause to forbid application of a generally applicable prohibition to religiously motivated conduct. Indeed, in *Yoder* we expressly rejected the interpretation the Court now adopts:

> [O]ur decisions have rejected the idea that religiously grounded conduct is always outside the protection of the Free Exercise Clause. It is true that activities of individuals, even when religiously based, are often subject to regulation by the States in the exercise of their undoubted power to promote the health, safety, and general welfare, or the Federal Government in the exercise of its delegated powers. But to agree that religiously grounded conduct must often be subject to the broad police power of the State is not to deny that there are areas of conduct protected by the Free Exercise Clause of the First Amendment and thus beyond the power of the State to control, *even under regulations of general applicability.* . . .
>
> A regulation neutral on its face may, in its application, nonetheless offend the constitutional requirement for government neutrality if it unduly burdens the free exercise of religion.

Id., at 219–220 (emphasis added).

The Court endeavors to escape from our decisions in *Cantwell* and *Yoder* by labeling them "hybrid" decisions, but there is no denying that both cases expressly relied on the Free Exercise Clause and that we have consistently regarded those cases as part of the mainstream of our free exercise jurisprudence. Moreover, in each of the other cases cited by the Court to support its categorical rule, we rejected the particular constitutional claims before us only after carefully weighing the competing interests. That we rejected the free exercise claims in those cases hardly calls into question the applicability of First Amendment doctrine in the first place. Indeed, it is surely unusual to judge the vitality of a constitutional doctrine by looking to the win-loss record of the plaintiffs who happen to come before us. . . .

In my view . . . the essence of a free exercise claim is relief from a burden imposed by government on religious practices or beliefs, whether the burden is imposed directly through laws that prohibit or compel specific religious practices, or indirectly through laws that, in effect, make abandonment of one's own religion or conformity to the religious beliefs of others the price of an equal place in the civil community. As we explained in *Thomas*:

> Where the state conditions receipt of an important benefit upon conduct proscribed by a religious faith, or where it denies such a benefit

because of conduct mandated by religious belief, thereby putting substantial pressure on an adherent to modify his behavior and to violate
his beliefs, a burden upon religion exists.

450 U.S., at 717–718. A State that makes criminal an individual's religiously motivated conduct burdens that individual's free exercise of religion in
the severest manner possible, for it "results in the choice to the individual
of either abandoning his religious principle or facing criminal prosecution."
. . .

The Court today gives no convincing reason to depart from settled
First Amendment jurisprudence. There is nothing talismanic about neutral
laws of general applicability or general criminal prohibitions, for laws neutral toward religion can coerce a person to violate his religious conscience
or intrude upon his religious duties just as effectively as laws aimed at religion. . . . The Court's parade of horribles not only fails as a reason for discarding the compelling interest test, it instead demonstrates just the opposite: that courts have been quite capable of applying our free exercise jurisprudence to strike sensible balances between religious liberty and competing state interests.

Finally, the Court today suggests that the disfavoring of minority religions is an "unavoidable consequence" under our system of government and
that accommodation of such religions must be left to the political process.
In my view, however, the First Amendment was enacted precisely to protect the rights of those whose religious practices are not shared by the majority and may be viewed with hostility. The history of our free exercise
doctrine amply demonstrates the harsh impact majoritarian rule has had
on unpopular or emerging religious groups such as the Jehovah's Witnesses
and the Amish. . . .

III

The Court's holding today not only misreads settled First Amendment
precedent; it appears to be unnecessary to this case. I would reach the same
result applying our established free exercise jurisprudence.

A

There is no dispute that Oregon's criminal prohibition of peyote places
a severe burden on the ability of respondents to freely exercise their religion. Peyote is a sacrament of the Native American Church and is regarded
as vital to respondents' ability to practice their religion. . . . [M]embers of
the Native American Church must choose between carrying out the ritual
embodying their religious beliefs and avoidance of criminal prosecution.
That choice is, in my view, more than sufficient to trigger First Amendment
scrutiny.

There is also no dispute that Oregon has a significant interest in enforcing laws that control the possession and use of controlled substances by
its citizens. . . .

B

Thus, the critical question in this case is whether exempting respondents from the State's general criminal prohibition "will unduly interfere
with fulfillment of the governmental interest." *Lee*, 455 U.S. at 259. Although the question is close, I would conclude that uniform application of
Oregon's criminal prohibition is "essential to accomplish," *id.*, at 257, its
overriding interest in preventing the physical harm caused by the use of a
Schedule I controlled substance. Oregon's criminal prohibition represents

that State's judgment that the possession and use of controlled substances, even by only one person, is inherently harmful and dangerous. Because the health effects caused by the use of controlled substances exist regardless of the motivation of the user, the use of such substances, even for religious purposes, violates the very purpose of the laws that prohibit them. Moreover, in view of the societal interest in preventing trafficking in controlled substances, uniform application of the criminal prohibition at issue is essential to the effectiveness of Oregon's stated interest in preventing any possession of peyote. Cf. *Jacobson v. Massachusetts,* 197 U.S. 11 (1905) (denying exemption from small pox vaccination requirement).

For these reasons, I believe that granting a selective exemption in this case would seriously impair Oregon's compelling interest in prohibiting possession of peyote by its citizens. Under such circumstances, the Free Exercise Clause does not require the State to accommodate respondents' religiously motivated conduct. . . .

I would therefore adhere to our established free exercise jurisprudence and hold that the State in this case has a compelling interest in regulating peyote use by its citizens and that accommodating respondents' religiously motivated conduct "will unduly interfere with fulfillment of the governmental interest." *Lee,* 455 U.S., at 259. Accordingly, I concur in the judgment of the Court.

■ JUSTICE BLACKMUN, with whom JUSTICE BRENNAN and JUSTICE MARSHALL join, dissenting.

. . . I agree with JUSTICE O'CONNOR's analysis of the applicable free exercise doctrine, and I join parts I and II of her opinion. As she points out, "the critical question in this case is whether exempting respondents from the State's general criminal prohibition will unduly interfere with fulfillment of the governmental interest." I do disagree, however, with her specific answer to that question. . . .

The State's interest in enforcing its prohibition, in order to be sufficiently compelling to outweigh a free exercise claim, cannot be merely abstract or symbolic. The State cannot plausibly assert that unbending application of a criminal prohibition is essential to fulfill any compelling interest, if it does not, in fact, attempt to enforce that prohibition. In this case, the State actually has not evinced any concrete interest in enforcing its drug laws against religious users of peyote. Oregon has never sought to prosecute respondents, and does not claim that it has made significant enforcement efforts against other religious users of peyote. The State's asserted interest thus amounts only to the symbolic preservation of an unenforced prohibition. . . .

Similarly, this Court's prior decisions have not allowed a government to rely on mere speculation about potential harms, but have demanded evidentiary support for a refusal to allow a religious exception. . . . The State proclaims an interest in protecting the health and safety of its citizens from the dangers of unlawful drugs. It offers, however, no evidence that the religious use of peyote has ever harmed anyone. . . .

The carefully circumscribed ritual context in which respondents used peyote is far removed from the irresponsible and unrestricted recreational use of unlawful drugs. The Native American Church's internal restrictions on, and supervision of, its members' use of peyote substantially obviate the State's health and safety concerns. . . .

Finally, the State argues that granting an exception for religious peyote use would erode its interest in the uniform, fair, and certain enforcement of its drug laws. The State fears that, if it grants an exemption for religious peyote use, a flood of other claims to religious exemptions will follow. It would then be placed in a dilemma, it says, between allowing a patchwork of exemptions that would hinder its law enforcement efforts, and risking a violation of the Establishment Clause by arbitrarily limiting its religious exemptions. . . .

The State's apprehension of a flood of other religious claims is purely speculative. Almost half the States, and the Federal Government, have maintained an exemption for religious peyote use for many years, and apparently have not found themselves overwhelmed by claims to other religious exemptions. Allowing an exemption for religious peyote use would not necessarily oblige the State to grant a similar exemption to other religious groups. The unusual circumstances that make the religious use of peyote compatible with the State's interests in health and safety and in preventing drug trafficking would not apply to other religious claims. . . .

NOTES

1. *The Holding.* The Court's current understanding of the Free Exercise Clause is set forth in *Employment Division v. Smith*. What is the standard that *Smith* settles on for identifying when government action violates the clause? What exceptions does *Smith* recognize to its general rule? Why does the Court adopt those exceptions?

2. *Interpretive Methodology and the Resolution of Ambiguity.* The case also raises once again important questions of methodology in interpreting and applying the Constitution: What counts in constitutional interpretation? The text alone? What if the text is ambiguous, as Justice Scalia argues in his majority opinion in *Smith*? (Is the text ambiguous?) Should an ambiguous text protecting individual freedom from government action be viewed from the perspective of the individual ("Does the government's action prohibit me from exercising my religion?") or from the perspective of the government ("Is our rule a rule that prohibits religious exercise or does it prohibit conduct, irrespective of why someone might do it?")? If the text of the Free Exercise Clause is in fact ambiguous, what other type of constitutional argument, or mode of interpretation, is best for resolving the ambiguity? Comparison with how similar types of questions are addressed for other provisions in the Constitution? Evidence of the historical purpose of the provision? Past practice? Prior judicial interpretations? The policy and practical implications of one interpretation versus another? Which of these types of argument do you think is best for the Free Exercise Clause? Why? And whatever type of argument you thought most helpful, is it the type of argument that Justice Scalia turned to?

There has been a considerable amount of scholarship on the historical evidence of the original understanding of the Free Exercise Clause. For contrasting analyses, see Phillip A. Hamburger, *A Constitutional Right of Religious Exemption: An Historical Perspective*, 60 Geo. Wash. L. Rev. 915 (1992), and Michael W. McConnell, *The Origins and Historical Understanding of Free Exercise of Religion*, 103 Harv. L. Rev. 1409 (1990); see also Douglas Laycock, RELIGIOUS LIBERTY: VOLUME I—OVERVIEWS AND HISTORY (2010).

3. *Precedent.* The Court says that "[o]ur decisions reveal" which of the two textually plausible readings is correct: "We have never held that an individual's religious beliefs excuse him from compliance with an otherwise valid law prohibiting conduct that the State is free to regulate." 494 U.S. at 878–879. Can you square that statement with *Wisconsin v. Yoder*? Is *Smith* faithful to precedent?

4. *A Constitutional Anomaly?* Justice Scalia's majority opinion states that what a "strict scrutiny" or "compelling interest" test produces with respect to the Free Exercise Clause (as opposed to in the Free Speech Clause and racial discrimination areas) is not a way of protecting a true constitutional "norm" but is instead a "constitutional anomaly," "a private right to ignore generally applicable laws." Is the charge correct? Is it possible that the charge is correct, but that that is indeed what the Free Exercise Clause is all about—an exemption from the usual rules where they conflict with legitimate religious exercise? Put the matter concretely: Is drug use different, i.e., should it be treated differently by the law, when engaged in as a matter of sincere religious exercise as opposed to simply for the purpose of "getting high"? Does the Free Exercise Clause require a different treatment for religious-exercise drug use? Put the issue in a slightly different (but analogous) context: During Prohibition, did the Free Exercise Clause require an exception for the use of communion wine in Christian worship?

5. *Legislative Accommodation of Religion.* As a matter of history, the Volstead Act exempted the sacramental use of wine from Prohibition—which suggests a few more questions: First, assuming such an exception was *not required* by the Free Exercise Clause, was such statutory accommodation of religion—granting religious use an exception from the rules that govern other uses—*forbidden* by the Establishment Clause? (We will return to that question presently, when we take up the Establishment Clause.) Second, does the fact that such an accommodation *was* made vindicate the majority's assurance, expressed late in the opinion, that society "can be expected to be solicitous" of religious freedom? Or—quite the reverse—is the fact that such accommodations might tend to be made for majority religions and not minority religions (like Native American ritual peyote use) suggest that the democratic process *cannot* be expected to be solicitous of religious freedom, at least not equally so? But *Smith* did prompt passage of the "American Indian Religious Freedom Act Amendments of 1994," in which Congress found that the lack of uniformity in state protections for the ceremonial use of peyote was causing Native Americans to be stigmatized and marginalized. Congress declared that "the use, possession, or transportation of peyote by an Indian for bona fide traditional ceremonial purposes" shall not be prohibited by or in the United States. 42 U.S.C. § 1996a(a)(3), (5) (1994). Is the accommodation of Native American practitioners permitting them—but not others—to use peyote an unconstitutional establishment of religion under the Establishment Clause?

6. *Applications and Extensions.* How would you respond to the following not-so-hypothetical hypotheticals, drawn from actual cases?

a. A state law requires that unemployment compensation benefits are available only to persons who make themselves available for "suitable" work. May a state exclude a Seventh–Day Adventist (a member of a denomination that observes a Saturday Sabbath) from unemployment compensation, where she declines to be available for work on Saturday? *Sherbert v. Verner,* 374 U.S.

398 (1963), held no—and *Smith* retains that case. Could a state exclude a religious person from unemployment benefits when he became unavailable for work because of religious objections to working on armaments manufacturing? *Thomas v. Review Board*, 450 U.S. 707 (1981), held the individual entitled to benefits, notwithstanding the general rule—and *Smith* retains that decision as well. Would it matter if not all members of his sect or denomination held the same conviction? *Thomas* holds that it does not matter—that free exercise is determined by individual beliefs and practices, so long as they are sincere.

b. A particular order of Amish object on sincere religious grounds to participation in Social Security (and payment of Social Security taxes), because the community provides for its own members as a matter of religious duty and obligation. May the government nonetheless require Amish employers to participate in Social Security? *United States v. Lee*, 455 U.S. 252 (1982), said that this requirement did *not* violate the Free Exercise Clause.

c. Does the Free Exercise Clause require accommodating religion-based conscientious objection to military service, and thus an exemption from the draft for religious believers? *Gillette v. United States,* 401 U.S. 437 (1971), said *no*, even under the pre-*Smith* "compelling interest" standard. Could the national government voluntarily accommodate religion-based conscientious objection to military service? Could it do so and not similarly permit secular-conscience exemption from such (otherwise) compulsory service?

d. Does the Free Exercise Clause permit the government to

(1) require claimants to provide a Social Security number in order to obtain welfare benefits, over a sincere religious objection to doing so? *Bowen v. Roy*, 476 U.S. 693 (1986), says *yes*.

(2) forbid a Jewish military officer from wearing a yarmulke, pursuant to a uniform headgear requirement? *Goldman v. Weinberger*, 475 U.S. 503 (1986), says *yes*.

(3) build a logging and construction road, on government land, through a traditional Native American high holy ground? *Lyng v. Northwest Indian Cemetery Protection Assn.*, 485 U.S. 439 (1988), says *yes,* on the ground that it is no longer the Native Americans' land, and that there is no burden on religious exercise (within the meaning of the language "*prohibiting* the free exercise thereof") where a religious adherent seeks to tell the government what it may or may not do, as opposed to where the government seeks to tell the religious adherent what he or she may not do.

e. Going down the slope a little faster: Does the Free Exercise Clause require that religious adherents be excused, on the basis of religious conviction, from otherwise generally applicable (1) child neglect laws? (2) animal mistreatment laws? (3) minimum wage laws? (4) anti-discrimination laws (race, sex, sexual orientation)? (5) environmental protection or endangered species laws (e.g., exempting Native Americans on religious grounds from prohibitions on the taking of bald eagle feathers)? (6) prohibitions of polygamy?

7. *The Religious Freedom Restoration Act.* In the wake of *Smith*, Congress in 1993 enacted the "Religious Freedom Restoration Act," 42 U.S.C. Section 2000bb et seq. ("RFRA"). In essence, RFRA enacted a federal statutory protection of religious freedom comparable to the constitutional approach rejected in *Smith*: requiring the government to justify a burden on religious exercise by showing that it was the "least restrictive means" of furthering a "compelling

governmental interest." In *City of Boerne v. Flores*, 521 U.S. 507 (1997), the Court held RFRA could not constitutionally be applied to actions of state and local governments: it was beyond the national government's legislative powers to enact such a measure, pursuant to Section 5 of the Fourteenth Amendment, because that power is only the power "to enforce" the Fourteenth Amendment's prohibitions of state action. RFRA was not, the Court in *Boerne* held, a measure "to enforce" the Fourteenth Amendment's incorporation of the Free Exercise Clause because it adopted a much broader protection of the free exercise of religion than the Court had held was required (in *Smith*).

RFRA remains valid as Congress's self-restriction on the exercise of powers by the *federal* government. And in *Gonzales v. O Centro Espirita Beneficente Uniao Do Vegetal*, 546 U.S. 418 (2006), a seeming reprise of *Smith*, the Court, in a unanimous opinion written by Chief Justice Roberts, upheld an injunction forbidding the federal government from prosecuting a small religious sect for the use of a hallucinogenic sacramental tea. The government lacked a "compelling interest" in "uniform enforcement" of the Act, the Court held, and RFRA therefore required an exemption from the Controlled Substances Act for this sincere religious practice: "The Government's argument echoes the classic rejoinder of bureaucrats throughout history: If I make an exception for you, I'll have to make one for everybody, so no exceptions. But RFRA operates by mandating consideration, under the compelling interest test, of exceptions to 'rules of general applicability.' " *Id.* at 436. Does *O Centro Espirita* undermine some of the reasoning that informed the Court's interpretation of the Free Exercise Clause in *Smith*—the impracticality and unprincipled nature of having judges make these sorts of decisions? Or are the two situations different because Congress *directed* the courts to make such decisions by enacting RFRA?

Does RFRA violate the Establishment Clause? Once again, the question is one of *permissible* government accommodation of religion. The clear implication of *Cutter v. Wilkinson*, 544 U.S. 709 (2005), presented below, is *no*. *Cutter* upheld a different, somewhat narrower federal statutory requirement that states accommodate religious exercise, passed in the wake of *City of Boerne*, against Establishment Clause challenge. While not directly presenting the issue, *O Centro Espirita* appears implicitly to assume that RFRA's requirement of accommodation does not violate the Establishment Clause.

8. *Comparative Constitutional Law.* Consider the fascinating case and opinions of the European Court of Human Rights in *Kokkinakis v. Greece*, 260 Eur. Ct. H.R. (1993). Greece is a member of the Council of Europe. Article III of the Greek Constitution says: "The dominant religion in Greece is that of the Christian Eastern Orthodox Church. The Greek Orthodox Church, which recognizes as its head Our Lord Jesus Christ, is indissolubly united, doctrinally, with the Great Church of Constantinople and with any other Christian Church in communion with it (*omodoxi*), immutably observing, like the other Churches, the holy apostolic and synodical canons and the holy traditions. . . . The text of the Holy Scripture is unalterable. No official translation into any other form or language may be made without the prior consent of the autocephalous Greek Church and the Greek Christian Church at Constantinople." Article 13 of the Greek Constitution protects freedom of conscience, freedom to practice, and freedom of rites of worship that do not violate public mores. Under Greek law, it is a crime to engage in proselytism.

Minos Kokkinakis became a Jehovah's Witness in 1936. Since then, he has been arrested for proselytism more than sixty times and on several occasions has been imprisoned. (According to Greek courts, proselytism includes, for example, merely saying that the saints are nothing more than figures adorning a wall.) Kokkinakis and his wife were arrested for proselytizing after they knocked on Georgia Kyriakaki's door at night telling her that they had "Good News." She trustingly but reluctantly let them in, and the Kokkinakises proceeded to urge her to become a Jehovah's Witness. Unfortunately, for the Kokkinakises, Mrs. Kyriakaki was the wife of the cantor of the local Orthodox Church. She complained to the police, and Minos Kokkinakis was tried, convicted, and sentenced to three months in prison—a penalty that was later remitted to a fine.

Kokkinakis appealed to the European Court of Human Rights, alleging a violation of Article 9 of the European Convention on Rights and Fundamental Freedoms. Article 9, Section 1 provides: "Everyone has the right to freedom of thought, conscience and religion; this right includes freedom to change his religion or belief and freedom, either alone or in community with others and in public or in private, to manifest his religion or belief, in worship, teaching, practice, and observance." Article 9, Section 2 qualifies this by saying: "Freedom to manifest one's religion or beliefs shall be subject only to such limitations as are prescribed by law and are necessary in a democratic society in the interests of public safety, for the protection of public order, health or morals, or for the protection of the rights and freedoms of others." The European Court of Human rights held by a vote of 6 to 3 that Greece had violated the Convention.

Is there an element of fraud in knocking on an elderly person's door at night and gaining admittance to the house by saying only that you brought "Good News"? Is it appropriate for a government to regulate proselytizing to prohibit fraud? To forbid the offer of money in exchange for a conversion? What about time, place, and manner restrictions for proselytizing? And is the idea of a right to proselytize itself a distinctly Protestant idea? If you believe in the existence of an authoritative religious body or hierarchy (e.g., Roman Catholic, Orthodox, or Islamic), is it really essential that there be a right to proselytize? On the other hand, if you think that each person, whether a believer or nonbeliever, is independently responsible for determining what is true (which is a more characteristically Protestant notion), then to allow proselytizing makes room for the speech that is essential for arriving at the truth. To Protestants, then, proselytizing may seem more benign than it does to others.

A NOTE ON CHURCH OF THE LUKUMI BABALU AYE

Just three years after *Smith*, in *Church of the Lukumi Babalu Aye v. City of Hialeah*, 508 U.S. 520 (1993), the Supreme Court unanimously held that an ordinance outlawing "animal sacrifice" was unconstitutional. The prohibited practice was defined as "unnecessarily" killing an animal in a "public or private ritual or ceremony not for the primary purpose of food consumption." The Court concluded that the ordinance was not neutral because it was directed at the practices of the Santeria religion—an Afro–Cuban syncretistic sect that practiced animal sacrifice to the horror of their neighbors—and that it was not "generally applicable" because the city permitted the killing of animals, sometimes by cruel means, for a large number of purposes, including sport, pest control, and medical experimentation. Moreover, the legal category "unnecessary" required a case-by-case evaluation of whether a particular killing had a legitimate purpose. How is a civil government to decide whether a Santerian sacrifice is "unnecessary"? Santerians do not think so.

Lukumi made apparent that *Smith*'s category of "neutral and generally applicable laws" may not be as all-encompassing as it seemed to be. Many laws, though framed in general terms, with no reference to religion, contain exemptions that shield most secular conduct, or that vest discretionary normal judgments to government officials. *Lukumi* suggests that these legal schemes remain subject to strict scrutiny.

Moreover, the Court strongly endorsed a rule prohibiting discrimination against religion or religious activities. "At a minimum," the Court wrote, "the protections of the Free Exercise Clause pertain if the law at issue discriminates against some or all religious beliefs or regulates or prohibits conduct because it is undertaken for religious reasons." Most real-world examples of such discrimination arise from government exclusions of religious beneficiaries from otherwise neutral benefits because of concerns about separation between church and state—such as exclusion from public speech forums (forbidden in *Widmar v. Vincent*, 454 U.S. 263 (1981), and *Lamb's Chapel v. Center Moriches Union School Dist.*, 508 U.S. 384 (1993)), from unemployment benefits (forbidden in *Sherbert v. Verner*, 374 U.S. 398 (1963)), from receipt of student activities funds (forbidden in *Rosenberger v. University of Virginia*, 515 U.S. 819 (1995)), or from eligibility for government grants or contracts. In *Locke v. Davey*, 540 U.S. 712 (2004), the Court upheld a scholarship program that excluded students pursuing a degree in devotional theology. Was that consistent with *Lukumi*?

Hosanna–Tabor Evangelical Lutheran Church and School v. EEOC

132 S. Ct. 694 (2012)

■ CHIEF JUSTICE ROBERTS delivered the opinion of the Court.

Certain employment discrimination laws authorize employees who have been wrongfully terminated to sue their employers for reinstatement and damages. The question presented is whether the Establishment and Free Exercise Clauses of the First Amendment bar such an action when the employer is a religious group and the employee is one of the group's ministers.

I–A

[Hosanna–Tabor is a church and school in the Lutheran Church Missouri–Synod denomination. Cheryl Perich, a "called" teacher who was a "commissioned minister" in the denomination, took a leave of absence for narcolepsy. When she tried to return to teaching in the middle of the school year, she was told that a replacement teacher had been hired for the year. She threatened to sue, and she was then discharged by Hosanna–Tabor, which cited as grounds for termination her "insubordination and disruptive behavior" as well as the damage she had done to her "working relationship" with the school by "threatening to take legal action." The church congregation also voted to rescind Perich's call as a "commissioned minister."— Editors]

The Synod classifies teachers into two categories: "called" and "lay." "Called" teachers are regarded as having been called to their vocation by God through a congregation. To be eligible to receive a call from a congregation, a teacher must satisfy certain academic Synod district, and pass an oral examination by a faculty committee. A teacher who meets these requirements may be called by a congregation. Once called, a teacher receives the formal title "Minister of Religion, Commissioned." A commissioned minister serves for an open-ended term; at Hosanna–Tabor, a call could be rescinded only for cause and by a supermajority vote of the congregation.

"Lay" or "contract" teachers, by contrast, are not required to be trained by the Synod or even to be Lutheran. At Hosanna–Tabor, they were appointed by the school board, without a vote of the congregation, to one-year renewable terms. Although teachers at the school generally performed the same duties regardless of whether they were lay or called, lay teachers were hired only when called teachers were unavailable. . . .

Perich . . . taught math, language arts, social studies, science, gym, art and music. She also taught a religion class four days a week, led the students in prayer and devotional exercises each day, and attended a weekly school-wide chapel service. Perich led the chapel service herself about twice a year.

B

Perich filed a charge with the Equal Employment Opportunity Commission, alleging that her employment had been terminated in violation of the Americans with Disabilities Act, 104 Stat. 327, 42 U. S. C. § 12101 *et seq.* (1990). The ADA prohibits an employer from discriminating against a qualified individual on the basis of disability. It also prohibits an employer from retaliating "against any individual because such individual has opposed any act or practice made unlawful by [the ADA] or because such individual made a charge, testified, assisted, or participated in any manner in an investigation, proceeding, or hearing under [the ADA]." § 12203(a).

The EEOC brought suit against Hosanna–Tabor, alleging that Perich had been fired in retaliation for threatening to file an ADA lawsuit. Perich intervened in the litigation, claiming unlawful retaliation under both the ADA and the Michigan Persons with Disabilities Civil Rights Act, Mich. Comp. Laws § 37.1602(a) (1979). The EEOC and Perich sought Perich's reinstatement to her former position (or frontpay in lieu thereof), along with backpay, compensatory and punitive damages, attorney's fees, and other injunctive relief.

Hosanna–Tabor moved for summary judgment. Invoking what is known as the "ministerial exception," the Church argued that the suit was barred by the First Amendment because the claims at issue concerned the employment relationship between a religious institution and one of its ministers. According to the Church, Perich was a minister, and she had been fired for a religious reason—namely, that her threat to sue the Church violated the Synod's belief that Christians should resolve their disputes internally.

. . . The Court of Appeals recognized the existence of a ministerial exception barring certain employment discrimination claims against religious institutions—an exception "rooted in the First Amendment's guarantees of religious freedom." The court concluded, however, that Perich did not qualify as a "minister" under the exception, noting in particular that her duties as a called teacher were identical to her duties as a lay teacher. . . .

II

The First Amendment provides, in part, that "Congress shall make no law respecting an establishment of religion, or prohibiting the free exercise thereof." We have said that these two Clauses "often exert conflicting pressures," *Cutter* v. *Wilkinson* (p. 271). . . . Not so here. Both Religion Clauses bar the government from interfering with the decision of a religious group to fire one of its ministers. . . .

[The Court reviewed the history of religious establishment not only in colonial America but also in the Church of England, including government control over the selection of ministers; occasions when James Madison, once as Secretary of State and once President, had determined that the government could not choose religious "functionaries"; the Court's property cases affirming the institutional autonomy of religious organizations; and the lower court precedents that uniformly found that in one form or another there was a "ministerial exception."—Editors]

We agree that there is . . . a ministerial exception. The members of a religious group put their faith in the hands of their ministers. Requiring a church to accept or retain an unwanted minister, or punishing a church for failing to do so, intrudes upon more than a mere employment decision. Such action interferes with the internal governance of the church, depriving the church of control over the selection of those who will personify its beliefs. By imposing an unwanted minister, the state infringes the Free Exercise Clause, which protects a religious group's right to shape its own faith and mission through its appointments. According the state the power to determine which individuals will minister to the faithful also violates the Establishment Clause, which prohibits government involvement in such ecclesiastical decisions.

The EEOC and Perich acknowledge that employment discrimination laws would be unconstitutional as applied to religious groups in certain circumstances. They grant, for example, that it would violate the First Amendment for courts to apply such laws to compel the ordination of women by the Catholic Church or by an Orthodox Jewish seminary. According to the EEOC and Perich, religious organizations could successfully defend against employment discrimination claims in those circumstances by invoking the constitutional right to freedom of association—a right "implicit" in the First Amendment. The EEOC and Perich thus see no need—and no basis—for a special rule for ministers grounded in the Religion Clauses themselves.

We find this position untenable. The right to freedom of association is a right enjoyed by religious and secular groups alike. It follows under the EEOC's and Perich's view that the First Amendment analysis should be the same, whether the association in question is the Lutheran Church, a labor union, or a social club. That result is hard to square with the text of the First Amendment itself, which gives special solicitude to the rights of religious organizations. We cannot accept the remarkable view that the Religion Clauses have nothing to say about a religious organization's freedom to select its own ministers.

The EEOC and Perich also contend that our decision in *Employment Div., Dept. of Human Resources of Ore.* v. *Smith*, precludes recognition of a ministerial exception. In *Smith*, two members of the Native American Church were denied state unemployment benefits after it was determined that they had been fired from their jobs for ingesting peyote, a crime under

Oregon law. We held that this did not violate the Free Exercise Clause, even though the peyote had been ingested for sacramental purposes, because the "right of free exercise does not relieve an individual of the obligation to comply with a valid and neutral law of general applicability on the ground that the law proscribes (or prescribes) conduct that his religion prescribes (or proscribes)."

It is true that the ADA's prohibition on retaliation, like Oregon's prohibition on peyote use, is a valid and neutral law of general applicability. But a church's selection of its ministers is unlike an individual's ingestion of peyote. *Smith* involved government regulation of only outward physical acts. The present case, in contrast, concerns government interference with an internal church decision that affects the faith and mission of the church itself. See *id.*, at 877 (distinguishing the government's regulation of "physical acts" from its "lend[ing] its power to one or the other side in controversies over religious authority or dogma"). The contention that *Smith* forecloses recognition of a ministerial exception rooted in the Religion Clauses has no merit.

III

Having concluded that there is a ministerial exception grounded in the Religion Clauses of the First Amendment, we consider whether the exception applies in this case. We hold that it does.

Every Court of Appeals to have considered the question has concluded that the ministerial exception is not limited to the head of a religious congregation, and we agree. We are reluctant, however, to adopt a rigid formula for deciding when an employee qualifies as a minister. It is enough for us to conclude, in this our first case involving the ministerial exception, that the exception covers Perich, given all the circumstances of her employment. . . .

Because Perich was a minister within the meaning of the exception, the First Amendment requires dismissal of this employment discrimination suit against her religious employer. The EEOC and Perich originally sought an order reinstating Perich to her former position as a called teacher. By requiring the Church to accept a minister it did not want, such an order would have plainly violated the Church's freedom under the Religion Clauses to select its own ministers.

Perich no longer seeks reinstatement, having abandoned that relief before this Court. But that is immaterial. Perich continues to seek frontpay in lieu of reinstatement, backpay, compensatory and punitive damages, and attorney's fees. An award of such relief would operate as a penalty on the Church for terminating an unwanted minister, and would be no less prohibited by the First Amendment than an order overturning the termination. Such relief would depend on a determination that Hosanna–Tabor was wrong to have relieved Perich of her position, and it is precisely such a ruling that is barred by the ministerial exception.

The EEOC and Perich suggest that Hosanna–Tabor's asserted religious reason for firing Perich—that she violated the Synod's commitment to internal dispute resolution—was pretextual. That suggestion misses the point of the ministerial exception. The purpose of the exception is not to safeguard a church's decision to fire a minister only when it is made for a religious reason. The exception instead ensures that the authority to select and control who will minister to the faithful—a matter "strictly ecclesiastical," is the church's alone.

IV

. . . The case before us is an employment discrimination suit brought on behalf of a minister, challenging her church's decision to fire her. Today we hold only that the ministerial exception bars such a suit. We express no view on whether the exception bars other types of suits, including actions by employees alleging breach of contract or tortious conduct by their religious employers. There will be time enough to address the applicability of the exception to other circumstances if and when they arise.

. . . The interest of society in the enforcement of employment discrimination statutes is undoubtedly important. But so too is the interest of religious groups in choosing who will preach their beliefs, teach their faith, and carry out their mission. When a minister who has been fired sues her church alleging that her termination was discriminatory, the First Amendment has struck the balance for us. The church must be free to choose those who will guide it on its way.

■ [The concurring opinions of JUSTICE THOMAS and JUSTICE ALITO, joined by JUSTICE KAGAN, are omitted.]

NOTES

1. *Hosanna–Tabor* contains two holdings—one narrow and one exceptionally broad. The narrow holding is that the antidiscrimination laws must contain a ministerial exception—that religious organizations have the right, free of government regulation, to choose ministers, broadly defined to include all who convey the church's religious message to members and the public. The broad holding is found in the case's distinction of *Smith*. It is that the *Smith* rule that neutral laws of general applicability do not violate the Free Exercise Clause applies only to "outward physical acts" and not to an "internal church decision that affects the faith and mission of the church itself." What does that mean? Is it a persuasive distinction of *Smith*? Does the Free Exercise Clause provide more protection for religious institutions than to religious individuals?

2. Note that the decision rests not just on the Free Exercise Clause but also on the Establishment Clause. The Court says very little about that. What could it mean?

[*Assignment 54*]

C. THE ESTABLISHMENT CLAUSE

Amendment I: Congress shall make no law respecting an establishment of religion. . . .

What does the Establishment Clause mean? Does it require "separation of church and state"? Or government neutrality toward religion? Does it forbid government coercion in religious matters? Or government sponsorship or endorsement of religion? Is government accommodation of religion and religious exercise permissible?

American Jewish Congress v. City of Chicago

827 F.2d 120 (7th Cir. 1987)

■ FLAUM, CIRCUIT JUDGE.

Every winter holiday season for the past thirty years, a crèche has been displayed in the lobby of the Chicago City–County Building. In November, 1985, the American Jewish Congress filed this suit against the City of Chicago and others (collectively referred to as "the city"), contending that the display of the crèche violated the Establishment Clause of the First Amendment. The district court held that the case was controlled by *Lynch v. Donnelly,* 465 U.S. 668 (1984). In *Lynch,* the Supreme Court held that a city-owned holiday display that included a crèche, and that was located in a privately-owned park, was constitutional. The district court therefore granted summary judgment to the defendants. We find that this case is distinguishable from *Lynch,* and we reverse the judgment of the district court.

I–A

The Daley Center Plaza and the City–County Building (better known as "City Hall") form a single unit, divided by Clark Street, but connected by a broad underground corridor. The two buildings house both city and county governmental offices. Each year, from shortly after Thanksgiving Day to New Year's Day, the entire complex is decorated for the winter holiday season. At issue in this case is a nativity scene which, with the city's permission, was on display from December 4, 1985 to January 4, 1986.

The nativity scene was placed at the intersection of the east-west and north-south lobbies of City Hall, slightly north of the center line of the east-west lobby. The scene consisted of several white plaster figures, each under twelve inches in height, representing the infant Jesus, the Virgin Mary, Joseph, the Three Wise Men, and various shepherds and animals. Behind the figures were tree branches strung with miniature holiday lights. The display was arranged on a three-foot-high platform measuring approximately nine feet wide by eight feet deep. At the rear of the platform, and rising from it to a height of ten feet from the lobby floor, was a fabric backdrop, at the top of which was a banner reading "On Earth Peace—Good Will Toward Men." No public funds were expended on the scene for repair, maintenance, rent, or heat. However, a nominal amount of public funds was expended on the electricity required to illuminate the scene. Although the appellants allege that city workers erected and dismantled the display, the city maintains that the workers did so on their own time and were not paid for their work.

In addition to the nativity scene, the City of Chicago erected a number of other displays and decorations in the City Hall lobby for the 1985–86 holiday season. These included: eight Christmas wreaths, each forty-two inches in diameter, hung on the lobby walls above the elevators that service the upper floors of the building; one decorated Christmas tree eighteen feet in height and fifteen feet in diameter, which stood near the LaSalle Street entrance; a mechanical Santa Claus, accompanied by two reindeer and a sleigh that served as a depository for donations to "Share–It", a city program designed to encourage citizens to donate food and supplies to needy persons; and other displays that formed part of the "Share–It" program, such as stacked cartons in the north side of the north-south lobby and a banner strung across and above the intersection of the east-west and north-south lobbies. These decorations and displays were placed from ten to ninety feet away from the nativity scene.

Still further away were other seasonal decorations and displays. For instance, the first-floor window-wells of City Hall contained small Christmas trees with lights; the potted trees along the curb on LaSalle Street were strung with lights; and a ninety-foot, decorated Christmas tree stood in the Daley Center Plaza. As part of the "Share–It" program, the city also erected a large "snowman" and a contribution box display in the plaza.

Finally, the entire complex served as a forum for public performances relating to the holiday season, such as local schoolchildren performing Christmas carols. In addition, recorded holiday music played continuously in the Daley Center Plaza.

B

. . . The [nativity scene] display was built over thirty years ago by the Chicago Plasterer's Institute, a private entity, and donated to the City of Chicago. In 1978, the American Civil Liberties Union and others sued the city, charging that the display violated the Establishment Clause of the First Amendment. That lawsuit ended in a consent order in 1979. Under the consent order, the city was permitted to continue to display the crèche in the City Hall lobby, provided that the city expend no public funds for the display, and that it affix written disclaimer-of-endorsement signs to the display. Consequently, the city attached six rectangular disclaimer signs to the nativity scene, two affixed to the front of the display platform, and two located on each side of the display. Each sign measured approximately seven and one-half inches by ten inches, and read: "Donated by the Chicago Plasterer's Institute—this exhibit is neither sponsored nor endorsed by the Government of the City of Chicago." . . .

In 1984, William Ware, the mayor's chief of staff, ordered that the display be dismantled. However, this decision caused intense public outcry, and Mayor Washington eventually ordered the nativity scene reerected.

The events related to this litigation began in October, 1985, when Sylvia Neil, the Midwest Legal Director of the American Jewish Congress ("AJC"), wrote a letter to Ernest Barefield, the mayor's chief of staff, requesting on behalf of her organization that the city not allow the display of the crèche in City Hall during the 1985–86 holiday season. Barefield responded that the nativity scene would continue to be displayed, because: (1) it had been a traditional part of the city's holiday festivities for many years; (2) the Supreme Court had made clear in *Lynch v. Donnelly,* 465 U.S. 668 (1984) and in *Board of Trustees v. McCreary,* 471 U.S. 83 (1985) that such displays were not unconstitutional; and (3) public sentiment favored such holiday displays. . . .

III–A

The First Amendment provides that "Congress shall make no law respecting an establishment of religion, or prohibiting the free exercise thereof." U.S. Const. Amend. I. It has often been contended that the drafters of the amendment had only two narrow purposes in mind: to prevent the establishment of a national church, and to forbid a national preference of one Christian sect over another. . . .

Over time, however, the courts have come to recognize that the Religion Clauses of the First Amendment signify a broader set of principles. One of these is the principle that government—at all levels—should stay out of religious affairs. This principle has been memorialized in Thomas Jefferson's famous metaphor of a "wall of separation" between church and state. . . . The Religion Clauses have also come to stand for the principle of government neutrality, meaning not only that government should not favor one religion over another, but also that government should not favor religion over nonreligion. . . . Finally, and most importantly, the Religion

Clauses have come to symbolize the principle of liberty and the individual's right to conscience. . . .

Because of these broad, often conflicting visions behind the Religion Clauses, the Establishment Clause erects a " 'blurred, indistinct, and variable barrier depending on all the circumstances of a particular relationship.' " *Lynch,* 465 U.S. at 679 (quoting *Lemon v. Kurtzman,* 403 U.S. 602, 614 (1971)). However, the Supreme Court has provided some guidance. In *Lemon v. Kurtzman,* the Supreme Court adopted a three-part test for analyzing Establishment Clause cases. "First, the legislature must have adopted the law with a secular purpose. Second, the statute's principal or primary effect must be one that neither advances nor inhibits religion. Third, the statute must not result in an excessive entanglement of government with religion." The district court did not analyze this case under the *Lemon* test, because in its view *Lynch* was clearly controlling. We find that *Lynch* is distinguishable, and that the display of the nativity scene violated the second prong of *Lemon.*

B

In *Lynch v. Donnelly,* the Supreme Court considered the constitutionality of a nativity scene that had formed part of an annual Christmas display owned and erected by the city of Pawtucket, Rhode Island. The display was situated "in a park owned by a nonprofit organization and located in the heart of the shopping district." In addition to the nativity scene, the display included, among other things, "a Santa Claus house, reindeer pulling Santa's sleigh, candy-striped poles, a Christmas tree, carolers, cutout figures representing such characters as a clown, an elephant, and a teddy bear, hundreds of colored lights, [and] a large banner that read[ ] SEASONS GREETINGS." . . .

The Court began its analysis by noting that in each Establishment Clause case, "the inquiry calls for line-drawing; no fixed, *per se* rule can be framed." *Lynch,* 465 U.S. at 678. . . . The relevant inquiry, according to the Court, was not whether a nativity scene, considered in the abstract, is a religious symbol, but whether the particular display at issue, considered in its overall context, could be said to advance religion. In the Court's judgment, given the overwhelmingly secular character of the Pawtucket display as a whole, "the inclusion of a single symbol of a particular historic religious event . . . [did not] so 'taint' the city's exhibit as to render it violative of the Establishment Clause."

The district court in this case erred when it concluded that the City Hall nativity scene "matche[d] squarely the Christmas context contemplated by the Supreme Court in *Lynch.*" . . . This case is different. Despite the City of Chicago's contention that the entire City Hall–Daley Center Plaza complex constitutes a single display for purposes of the *Lemon* test, the evidence supports the conclusion that the nativity scene was self-contained, rather than one element of a larger display. For instance, the closest decoration to the nativity scene—the "Share–It" banner ten feet away, suspended above the intersection of the lobbies in City Hall—was thematically related to the other elements of the "Share–It" display (the Santa Claus, reindeer, and sleigh full of donated canned goods), but not to the nativity scene. Similarly, the wreaths on the wall above the elevators, although perhaps visible to an observer standing near the crèche, cannot reasonably be said to have been part of the same "display." Finally, the wording of the disclaimer signs affixed to the platform of the display called attention to the nativity scene as a distinct entity. In this case, therefore, unlike *Lynch,* the secularized decorations in the vicinity of the nativity scene were not clearly part of the same display.

We need not, however, settle the debate over how far a nativity scene must stand from a Christmas tree or Santa Claus to be considered part of the same display, and hence "neutralized" by secular symbols of holiday cheer. In this case, another aspect of the nativity scene's physical setting plainly distinguishes it from *Lynch*: its placement in City Hall.

The Establishment Clause is concerned with the messages the government may send to its citizenry about the significance of religion. *See Lynch*, 465 U.S. at 692 (O'Connor, J., concurring). The crèche in *Lynch*, although sponsored by the City of Pawtucket, was located in a privately-owned park, a setting devoid of the government's presence. But the display in this case was located within a government building—a setting where the presence of government is pervasive and inescapable. The Court's holding in *Lynch* that the inclusion of a crèche in a holiday display located in a private park did not violate the Establishment Clause cannot control this case, where the display was placed inside the "official headquarters building of the municipal government." . . .

C

The first requirement of *Lemon* is that the government action serve a secular purpose. . . . The AJC, in arguing that the purpose of the City Hall nativity scene was to promote Christianity, points out that in October, 1959, Mayor Daley said of the scene, "We are a Christian Nation. I think the more religion we can get in politics, the better off we are." This comment, although perhaps relevant to the original purpose of the nativity scene, reveals little about the purpose behind the 1985–86 display. More pertinent is the affidavit of Ernest Barefield, Mayor Washington's chief of staff at the time this litigation began. Barefield's affidavit reveals several purposes behind Chicago's display: (1) recognition of a city tradition of "taking official note of Christmas"; (2) recognition of public sentiment in favor of the nativity scene; and (3) attraction of visitors to the downtown business district. None of these stated purposes is impermissible.

The city's intention to "take official note of Christmas" by permitting the nativity scene to be displayed in City Hall is not an illegitimate purpose under *Lemon*. . . . Christmas is clearly a public holiday, as well as a day of religious significance to Christians, and the Establishment Clause does not preclude the City of Chicago from acting with the intent to take "official note" of the day.

The city's recognition of public sentiment in favor of the nativity scene was similarly permissible. The AJC points out that in 1984 the Chicago City Council, in voting to affirm the display of the nativity scene, stated that the crèche "symbolized the 'true meaning of Christmas' for hundreds of thousands of Christian Chicagoans." But this recognition and accommodation of religious sentiments is not the same as intending to promote a particular point of view in religious matters. . . . [W]e must conclude that the 1985–86 display had no invidious purpose.

The second inquiry under *Lemon* is whether the government action had the effect of advancing or inhibiting religion. . . . An important concern of the effects test is thus "whether the symbolic union of church and state effected by the challenged governmental action is sufficiently likely to be perceived by adherents of the controlling denominations as an endorsement, and by the nonadherents as a disapproval, of their individual religious choices." *Grand Rapids School Dist. v. Ball,* 473 U.S. 373, 390 (1985). "Every government practice must be judged in its unique circumstances to determine whether it constitutes an endorsement or disapproval of religion." *Lynch,* 465 U.S. at 694 (O'Connor, J., concurring). . . .

We begin with the recognition that "[t]he Nativity scene, with its figures of Mary, Joseph, the infant Jesus, the Magi, shepherds, angels, and animals, is an unequivocal Christian symbol, unlike the Christmas tree and the reindeer and the tinsel and Santa Claus." . . . Thus, "none who sense the origins of the Christmas celebration would fail to be aware of its religious implications." *Lynch,* 465 U.S. at 685. *Lynch* makes clear, however, that our analysis cannot stop with the conclusion that nativity scenes have religious significance. "Even the traditional, purely secular displays extant at Christmas, with or without a crèche, would inevitably recall the religious nature of the holiday." *Id.* Rather, the critical inquiry is whether, considered in its unique physical context, the nativity scene at issue in this case communicates a message of government endorsement. We conclude that it does.

The presence of the government in Chicago's City Hall is unavoidable. . . . Because City Hall is so plainly under government ownership and control, every display and activity in the building is implicitly marked with the stamp of government approval. The presence of a nativity scene in the lobby, therefore, inevitably creates a clear and strong impression that the local government tacitly endorses Christianity.

The message of endorsement is equally powerful on the symbolic level. Like the nativity scene itself, City Hall is a symbol—a symbol of government power. The very phrase "City Hall" is commonly used as a metaphor for government. A crèche in City Hall thus brings together Church and State in a manner that unmistakably suggests their alliance. The display at issue in this case advanced religion by sending a message to the people of Chicago that the city approved of Christianity.

The city has attempted to mitigate the impact of this message by posting six disclaimer signs on the display, two on each side, and two on the front. However, the message of government endorsement generated by this display was too pervasive to be mitigated by the presence of disclaimers. . . .

■ EASTERBROOK, CIRCUIT JUDGE, dissenting.

We must decide whether Chicago violates the Establishment Clause of the first amendment, made applicable to the states by the fourteenth, by displaying a crèche in City Hall during the Christmas season. To do so we must apply *Lynch v. Donnelly,* 465 U.S. 668 (1984). This decision, like others requiring multi-factor balances, gives judges of the inferior federal courts fits. The Court avoided creating a rule about the treatment of religious symbols and instead announced that judges should examine each symbol's context. But which items of the context matter? If different elements cut in different directions, what is to be done? It is discomfiting to think that our fundamental charter of government distinguishes between painted and white figures—a subject the parties have debated—and governs the interaction of elements of a display, thus requiring scrutiny more commonly associated with interior decorators than with the judiciary. When everything matters, when nothing is dispositive, when we must juggle incommensurable factors, a judge can do little but announce his gestalt. . . .

Our case is about symbology—about the images of Christmas and the event that holiday celebrates. Christmas, no less than the date inscribed on the Constitution, marks the religion of most Americans. Unlike Sunday closing laws, indeed unlike the formal holiday, the display of the crèche does not require obedience. People may venerate, disdain, or curse the icons as they please, without reward for the first or reprisal for the last. To hold that Chicago may not use a symbol showing the religious origin and significance of a national holiday is to extend Jefferson's "wall of separation" metaphor beyond its proper scope. . . .

II

Lynch held that Pawtucket, R.I., could include a crèche in an ensemble of other symbols of Christmas. *Lynch* requires us to affirm the district court's judgment. The crèche in *Lynch* had life-sized, painted figures and was the most prominent part of the display in the city's principal park. . . . The Supreme Court thought it significant that the display included reindeer, a tree festooned with lights, and other symbols of Christmas—some religious, some secular, and some (a talking wishing well, for example) irrelevant. The display in Chicago has the same mixture. City Hall and its outdoor plaza contain two trees (18' indoors and 90' outdoors), a mechanical Santa Claus, reindeer and sleigh (the sleigh serving as the depository for donations to the "Share–It" program), many 42" wreaths, and banners asking people to make contributions of food and supplies to the needy. The Santa, sleigh, wreaths, banners, and indoor tree are between 10 and 90 feet from the crèche. On the plaza the City erected the larger tree, a snowman, and more Share–It receptacles. Christmas carols, live or recorded, sound constantly. Chicago's display lacks a talking wishing well, but I doubt that one is constitutionally necessary.

Whether the secular element of the display nearest the crèche is five or twenty feet away is insignificant. In each the crèche is part of a larger ensemble, and anyone walking through the park (or building) will see both the religious and the secular elements. Of course someone standing near enough to the crèche in Chicago will see little else, but that was true in Pawtucket as well; this comes from the law of perspective rather than the law of the land. The important thing, the Court concluded in *Lynch,* is that the government's entire activity celebrate all aspects of the holiday and not just the religious aspect. Chicago has not made religious icons the sole feature of its Christmas display.

The court distinguishes *Lynch* on the ground that Pawtucket's display was in a park, while Chicago's crèche is in City Hall. Its location in City Hall, according to my colleagues, conveys an unmistakable impression that the City is behind Christianity. This finesses the question whether one should look at the crèche alone or at the whole display. *Lynch* holds that the government's stance must be discerned from everything the government chooses to exhibit. *That* principle does not depend on whether the display is in a park or in City Hall. And if the context is conclusive, then this case is, as the district court held, just like *Lynch*. What the City has "endorsed" is Christmas and its collection of symbols—Santa Claus, reindeer, sleighs, generosity, carols, trees, lights, wreaths, and the birth of the figure from whom the holiday takes its name as well as its original significance. *Lynch* holds that a city may display the symbols of Christmas without thereby endorsing Christianity. That is all Chicago has done. *Lynch* has been lampooned for implying that the secular symbols drain the religious symbols of their significance, see William W. Van Alstyne, *Trends in the*

Supreme Court: Mr. Jefferson's Crumbling Wall—A Comment on Lynch v. Donnelly, 1984 Duke L.J. 770, but any doubts we may have about whether a crèche loses its religious significance when surrounded by folderol should not affect our disposition of this case. . . .

III

Although Chicago's crèche is no more an endorsement of Christianity than Pawtucket's, I wonder whether it would matter had Chicago endorsed that family of religions explicitly. A statement of views about religion is not an "establishment" of religion. One can be persuaded (as I am) . . . that the Establishment Clause bars aid to all religions quite as much as it bars preferences among religions—and . . . that the religion clauses together prevent the government from using force or funds to aid or inhibit the practice of religion—yet believe that the government may participate as a speaker in moral debates, including religious ones. Speech is not coercive; the listener may do as he likes.

We must distinguish threats from shadows. . . . When the government expresses views in public debates, all are as free as they were before; that these views may offend some and persuade others is a political rather than a constitutional problem. . . .

State and federal governments have engaged in religious speech since the founding of the Republic. The First Congress established a chaplaincy, and to this day Congress opens with prayer. See *Marsh v. Chambers.* Congress provides the military and prisoners with chapels and chaplains. *Katcoff v. Marsh,* 755 F.2d 223 (2d Cir.1985). President Washington (and all presidents since, other than Jefferson) proclaimed days of thanksgiving. Thanksgiving and Christmas are national holidays. Congress regularly asks the President to issue religious proclamations. E.g., Pub. L. 97–280, calling on the President to proclaim 1983 as the "Year of the Bible"—which he did. Congress has enacted permanent legislation calling for annual National Days of Prayer. . . . The nation's money proclaims "In God We Trust"; the Pledge of Allegiance and National Anthem refer to God; witnesses in our courts take oaths on the Bible; sessions of court open with the cry "God save the United States and this honorable Court." The newest national holiday celebrates the life of a Baptist minister, whose religious message is inseparable from his political message.

These religious acknowledgments and symbols share with Chicago's crèche the absence of coercion. The holder of a nickel need not trust in God, no matter what the coin says, and need not contribute the nickel (or even three pence) to a church. He may labor on Christmas if he likes—though Ebenezer Scrooge had to give Bob Cratchit that day off without governmental compulsion. He may "affirm" rather than "swear" when giving testimony and be silent while others say the Pledge of Allegiance. *Board of Education v. Barnette,* 319 U.S. 624 (1943). He need not study or even own a Bible during the "Year of the Bible". And he may turn his back on the crèche. The holidays, the chaplains, the proclamations, the slogans, the oath, the pledge, and the crèche alike give offense—to those of other faiths (or no faith) who feel slighted, to those of the same faith who believe that governmental involvement with religion diminishes both institutions, to those who see the camel's nose. The display of secular symbols to the exclusion of religious symbols for the same event offends other people. Either way, offense in the raw is not actionable. All speech may offend. There is no heckler's veto. Insult without injury is not even enough to create a case or controversy. . . .

It is essential, of course, to ensure that governmental speech does not restrain. So in *Wooley v. Maynard,* 430 U.S. 705 (1977), the Court held that drivers in New Hampshire may blot out the slogan "Live Free or Die" (the state's motto) on their license plates. The government's right to have a motto does not imply a right to compel anyone to be a billboard. Yet the Court thought it sufficient to give each person control of his own speech; Mr. Maynard could not silence the message blaring from thousands of other license plates. There may be special problems when the audience is young, captive, or both. Sessions of a legislature may open with prayer, *Marsh* holds, but sessions of school may not. *Engel v. Vitale,* 370 U.S. 421 (1962). Children are summoned by law to school; even if told they need not pray, they will be subject to pressure to do so. Children's ridicule and ostracism of their peers for nonconformity may be more compelling than any fine the government could impose. So, too, *Stone v. Graham,* 449 U.S. 39 (1980), which involved the posting of the Ten Commandments in a classroom, dealt with a captive audience. When the audience can avert its eyes, walk away, or talk back, speakers have greater freedom. This principle should apply to governmental as well as private speakers. . . .

Perhaps speech about religion is fundamentally different from speech about communism ("live free or die"). But for a long time the Court has said that the religion clauses deal with governmental compulsion. . . . This emphasis on compulsion as the central concern of the religion clauses has a solid footing. The establishments of Europe and the states were riddled with compulsion: compulsion to pay church taxes, compulsion to attend church, compulsion to accept the tenets of the chosen creed, test oaths, and disqualifications for office. Some states established a single church; some states established all Protestant sects and allowed towns to choose; some states established no religion. But without taxes, test oaths, appointments of ministers, or other acts backed by threat of penalty, it is impossible to speak of "establishment". The use of governmental force and funds is exactly what people meant in 1789 by the word "establishment".

The works of Madison and Jefferson reveal the point. Jefferson wrote the principal draft of Virginia's Act for Establishing Religious Freedom and Madison the *Memorial and Remonstrance* of 1785, which jointly inform the meaning of the religion clauses. These are dominated by complaints about coercion. See generally Michael W. McConnell, *Coercion: The Lost Element of Establishment,* 27 Wm. & Mary L.Rev. 933 (1986).

Jefferson's bill of 1779 (modified slightly and enacted in 1785) objects to three principal elements of establishments: religious taxes, religious tests of office, and attempts to restrain the propagation of religious beliefs. The preamble declares, for example, that "to compel a man to furnish contributions of money for the propagation of opinions which he disbelieves and abhors, is sinful and tyrannical". The bill does not protest government use of persuasion on matters religious; it is concerned with compulsion alone. The substantive rule it establishes is that

> no man shall be compelled to frequent or support any religous [sic] Worship place or Ministry whatsoever, nor shall be enforced, restrained, molested, or burthened in his body or goods, nor shall otherwise suffer on account of his religious opinions or belief, but that all men shall be free to profess, and by argument to maintain their opinion in matters of religion, and that the same shall in no wise diminish, enlarge, or affect their civil capacities.

The preamble to the bill is itself an exercise in religious persuasion. Jefferson begins:

> Well aware that the opinions and belief of men depend not on their own will, but follow involuntarily the evidence proposed to their minds, that Almighty God hath created the mind free, and manifested his Supreme will that free it shall remain, by making it altogether insusceptible of restraint: That all attempts to influence it by temporal punishments or burthens, or by civil incapacitations, tend only to beget habits of hypocrisy and meanness, and are a departure from the plan of the holy author of our religion, who being Lord both of body and mind, yet chose not to propagate it by coercions on either, as was in his Almighty power to do, but to extend it by, its influence on reason alone. . . .

If all endorsement by the state of Christian beliefs is forbidden, then any state that today enacted Jefferson's Bill for Establishing Religious Freedom would be violating the Establishment Clause!

The *Memorial and Remonstrance,* on which the Supreme Court has relied too many times to count, is an objection to a proposed tax for the support of Christian "teachers" in Virginia. Madison wrote that any support of religion "if finally armed with the sanctions of a law, will be a dangerous abuse of power" and expatiated on the evils of coerced support of the church. He held that religion "can be directed only by reason and conviction, not by force or violence". . . .

When introducing and debating the Establishment Clause on the floor of the House in 1789, Madison stated that

> he apprehended the meaning of the words to be, that Congress should not establish a religion, and enforce the legal observation of it by law, nor compel men to worship God in any manner contrary to their conscience.

1 Annals of Congress 730 (J. Gales ed. 1834) (Aug. 15, 1789). Although the language was altered after that remark, none of the changes affects Madison's point: that the government should eschew the business of funding religion or penalizing adherence to any system of beliefs. Madison did not suggest that the Establishment Clause put government out of the business of suasion; neither did anyone else in 1789. That is why the Congress that sent the Establishment Clause to the states thought it permissible simultaneously to call on President Washington to issue a religious proclamation of thanksgiving. . . .

The genesis of the Establishment Clause persuades me that force or funds are essential ingredients of an "establishment". Yet I offer this conclusion in the spirit of constructive criticism, because it is plainly not the law today. *Engel v. Vitale,* 370 U.S. at 430, contains this passage:

> The Establishment Clause, unlike the Free Exercise Clause, does not depend upon any showing of direct governmental compulsion and is violated by the enactment of laws which establish an official religion whether those laws operate directly to coerce nonobserving individuals or not.

The passage is circular: it says that there needn't be coercion, there need only be "establishment". If establishment *means* force or funds, then you can't have one without the other. The passage also is ukase. It is unreasoned, unsupported by history, and irrelevant to the case at hand. The very next passage states: "This is not to say, of course, that [school prayers] do not involve coercion". *Id.* at 430–31. And in this the Court is correct, for the pressure on children to conform, and the shame of ostracism, may be more powerful than the threat of imprisonment. Nonetheless, the dismissal of coercion in *Engel* has been the basis of subsequent decisions including *Lynch,* in which the Court thought it essential to inquire whether the context made the whole display secular. . . .

A judge's obligation to apply the dicta of *Engel* and the rationale of *Lynch* does not mean that he must endorse as well as acquiesce. A judge may, and I do, suggest that the prevailing doctrine could bear reexamination. While declaring that coercion is not part of an establishment of religion, the Court also continues to say that the interpretation of the Establishment Clause is informed by the original meaning of the text. No other part of our jurisprudence under the Bill of Rights contains such extensive discussions of, and reliance on, the background of the text. In some cases, such as *Marsh* (upholding legislative chaplains), the Court has held late 18th Century practices dispositive. In the great majority of cases the Court has assumed that "the line we must draw between the permissible and the impermissible is one which accords with history and faithfully reflects the understanding of the Founding Fathers." *Abington School District v. Schempp,* 374 U.S. 203, 294 (1963) (Brennan, J., concurring). That line is one demarcating force (forbidden) from suasion (tolerable, even if unwelcome). It may be hard to draw, as *Engel* and the cases concerning seals and crosses show. I have not tried to resolve the many hard cases that could arise under this approach. But difficulty in applying the original constitutional rule is not a good reason for expanding the scope of the constitutional prohibition.

IV

The disappearance of coercion from the Establishment Clause in 1962 is an example of a tendency in constitutional reasoning to make the rule more abstract and then take the abstraction to the limit of its logic.

. . . Madison did not propose, and the states did not ratify, a text that terminates all intercourse between church and state. The Establishment Clause expunges a certain kind of relationship, an "establishment"—a term with meaning, denoting a relationship characterized by public funding and legal penalties. To say that a broader prohibition would achieve more of the end in view is true but irrelevant, for it assumes away the character of the Establishment Clause as a *rule*—as a text binding judges today just the way it bound the Congress of 1792. We should not drain constitutional terms of meaning in order to create grand generalities that we can imbue with our own elaborations on the purposes or directions these terms imply. . . .

As a legislator or moral philosopher, I would join Madison in thinking that civil authority should not support religion in any way. . . . But our function is not to pursue Madison's objective as far as it can be pushed, however beneficent that conclusion may be; it is to enforce a text, the limits of which bind us just as they do the political branches. To the extent the Supreme Court today pursues a different conception of the judicial role under the Establishment Clause, it has yet to justify that conception, which is not congruent with the Court's stated view that it is under the sway of history. . . .

This case puts political and moral philosophies in conflict with constitutional history and text. In that contest there can be but one winner.

NOTES

1. Judge Easterbrook's dissent makes a forceful argument that the Establishment Clause is concerned with government *coercion* in matters of religious exercise, a view that harmonizes nicely with the Free Exercise Clause. The clause says that the government may not coerce or induce the exercise of religion, while the Free Exercise Clause says that the government may not prohibit or prevent the exercise of religion. So understood, the two religion clauses are "two sides of the same coin" of religious freedom. See Michael Stokes Paulsen, *Religion, Equality, and the Constitution: An Equal Protection Approach to Establishment Clause Adjudication,* 61 Notre Dame L. Rev. 311, 313 (1986). This "coercion" view has many adherents, and has (sometimes) served as the basis of the Court's decisions in this area. See *Lee v. Weisman,* 505 U.S. 577 (1992).

However, as the *AJC* majority opinion reflects, the Supreme Court's decisions in this area have taken many diverging approaches. They have sounded the theme of "separation of church and state," drawing on Thomas Jefferson's metaphor in a letter he wrote to a church when he was president. They have emphasized the theme of government "neutrality"—which sometimes pulls in the same direction as a strict "separation," and sometimes pushes in the opposite direction (as *Rosenberger* demonstrates). They have sought to harmonize the disparate strands of "separation," "neutrality," and "no coercion" into a multi-factor test: the three-part "*Lemon* test" discussed by the majority, and named for the case of *Lemon v. Kurtzman,* 403 U.S. 602 (1971). They have emphasized historical practice, as in the *Lynch* decision, upholding the Pawtucket, Rhode Island crèche display, and in *Marsh v. Chambers,* 463 U.S. 783 (1983), upholding the practice of chaplaincies and prayer in legislative sessions. They have looked to whether the government action has sent a message of "endorsement" of religion, as in *Grand Rapids School District v. Ball,* 473 U.S. 373 (1985). And they have used some combination of these tests, or simply sought to analogize a new situation to the result of the closest prior precedent, regardless of the test employed, as in *Kiryas Joel v. Grumet,* 512 U.S. 687 (1994).

All of which simply recreates the fundamental question: What is the proper interpretation of the Establishment Clause? Is it the original linguistic meaning of the text, taken in context? Is it the subjective intentions or expectations of the framers? Is it historical practices? Is it the broad purposes of the text, as best one can understand them (the position that Judge Easterbrook warns makes it easy to play a levels-of-generality "trick" on the Establishment Clause)? Is it prior judicial interpretation of the clause?

2. *Equal Inclusion of Religion in Government Programs, Benefits, or Fora.* One seemingly settled proposition flows from the idea of "neutrality." The Establishment Clause does not require that religious speech, religious speakers, religious groups, and religious persons be excluded from public fora or public benefits otherwise available, on account of their religious speech, exercise, or identity. This holds true even if accomplishing such neutrality necessitates some degree of state involvement with religion, and thus a deviation from strict "separation." Equal inclusion of religion in a government benefit program generally does not violate the Establishment Clause, even if such inclusion benefits

the religious person or group in question and indirectly furthers the promotion of religious beliefs.

In *Widmar v. Vincent*, 454 U.S. 263 (1981), a student religious group at the University of Missouri–Kansas City sought to use the state university center for its religious group meetings, on the same terms that the university permitted other student groups to use the facility. University officials said no, on the ground that the students' meetings would be religious in nature. They believed that the Establishment Clause (and parallel provisions of the Missouri Constitution) dictated that they exclude the religious student group. The U.S. Supreme Court held, 8–1, for the students. The exclusion of a religious student group from a designated public forum for student expressive activities, based on the religious content of their expression, was a presumptive violation of the Free Speech Clause, the Court held. Did the Establishment Clause require exclusion otherwise forbidden by the Free Speech Clause? The Court said no. Equal inclusion within a government forum (or other benefit) did not have the purpose or effect of advancing religion specially, but merely afforded neutral, equal treatment. Nor would equal access "entangle" government with religion; to the contrary, it would avoid entanglement by requiring equal treatment, rather than placing the government in the role of roving censor of possible religious expression by student organizations. *Widmar* was an important precedent in establishing the proposition that the Establishment Clause does not require (and the Free Speech Clause does not permit) discriminatory exclusion of religion or religious persons from benefits or fora to which they otherwise would be given access on an equal basis.

3. *Government Use of Religious Symbols: Of Crèches, Crosses, Coins, and City Names. American Jewish Congress* is a good example of the recurrent, perpetually unsettled issue of government use of religious symbols. May governments erect Christmas displays that include explicitly religious images or messages? Does the answer (really?) depend on the presence or proximity of Jumbo Candy Canes, talking wishing wells, elves, and Santa Claus? What about other religious symbols? What about "In God We Trust" on coins?

Is Christmas unconstitutional? Does the government violate the Establishment Clause when it recognizes (and gives government employees the day off for) Christmas? Even the majority in *American Jewish Congress* was not prepared to go so far, stating instead that recognition of the holiday is permissible. (Why? Is this consistent?) May government recognize a religious holiday for its own, secular reasons? As an accommodation of the religious views of its citizens? May government recognize a religious holiday but only if it leaches away the holiday's religious significance?

Judge Easterbrook's dissent raises some other interesting hypotheticals: Is *the Constitution* unconstitutional? Does the document's declaration that the Constitutional Convention submitted the document "in the year of our Lord" 1787 violate the Establishment Clause? What about Thanksgiving as a holiday, presidential Thanksgiving Day proclamations, and presidential prayers or other religious speech in Inaugural addresses? Are these unconstitutional? Was President Lincoln's Second Inaugural—suffused with deep, profound religious themes, inquiries, and theological reflection on the meaning of the Civil War—unconstitutional? Is its inclusion, in full, on a wall of the interior of the Lincoln Memorial unconstitutional?

These types of issues have divided and bedeviled (so to speak) the Supreme Court. Five years after *Lynch* (with the Seventh Circuit's decision in *AJC* falling in between), the Court decided *County of Allegheny v. American Civil Liberties Union*, 492 U.S. 573 (1989). At issue were two seasonal displays in Pittsburgh: a Christmas nativity scene located on a landing of steps in a courthouse, and a large Hanukkah Menorah situated outside the entrance to a city-county building. Three justices (Brennan, Marshall, and Stevens) found both displays unconstitutional promotions of religion, and voted to strike them down. Four justices (Kennedy, Rehnquist, White, and Scalia), applying a "no-coercion" test, found both displays constitutionally proper and voted to uphold both of them. Two justices (Blackmun and O'Connor), applying an "endorsement" test, thought that the Christmas nativity scene impermissibly advanced Christianity but the Hanukkah Menorah did not impermissibly advance Judaism, in part because of the presence of a nearby ("secular") Christmas tree. The two-justice Blackmun–O'Connor position, combined with the three-justice position, resulted in a holding that the nativity scene was unconstitutional. But the two-justice Blackmun–O'Connor position, combined with the four-justice position, resulted in a holding that the menorah was constitutional. This resulted in a disposition of the case that *seven* justices thought was wrong—indeed, the worst possible outcome—that one religion's symbol was struck down and another's was permitted.

A pair of "Ten Commandments Display" cases, decided by the Court in 2005, produced a similarly incoherent (or at least inconclusive) set of decisions. In *McCreary County v. ACLU*, 545 U.S. 844 (2005), the Court struck down a Ten Commandments display included as part of a display of historic legal documents in a Kentucky courthouse. The same day, in *Van Orden v. Perry*, 545 U.S. 677 (2005), the Court *upheld* a freestanding Ten Commandments monument erected on the grounds of the Texas state capitol building. Can these decisions be reconciled? As in *Allegheny*, only two justices voted in the majority in *both* cases of this split doubleheader. One of those justices—Justice Breyer—emphasized the importance of avoiding divisiveness along religious lines and suggested that displays that had existed for long period of time without controversy were likely permissible. *McCreary County* involved a new display; *Van Orden* involved one that was decades old. Is that a practical distinction? Is it theoretically justifiable?

What about the words "under God" in the Pledge of Allegiance? In *Elk Grove Unified School District v. Newdow*, 542 U.S. 1 (2004), the Court avoided deciding the question of whether the inclusion of the words "under God" in the Pledge violate the Establishment Clause. (The Court held that the plaintiff lacked standing to sue.) Recall that in *West Virginia State Board of Education v. Barnette*, 319 U.S. 624 (1943), the Court held, as a matter of Free Speech Clause freedom-from-compelled-expression doctrine, that *no one* may be required to say the Pledge. The challenge in *Newdow* is to the bare fact that the words "under God" are *in* the Pledge, as part of the public school exercise. Consider the question again, after reading the Court's school prayer decision in *Engel v. Vitale*.

————

One of the most controversial Establishment Clause decisions in the Court's history was *Engel v. Vitale*, 370 U.S. 421 (1962), in which the Court held unconstitutional the long-customary practice of public school student recitation of state-written prayers as part of the school instructional program, typically in "opening exercises" for the school day.

Engel v. Vitale

370 U.S. 421 (1962)

■ MR. JUSTICE BLACK delivered the opinion of the Court.

The respondent Board of Education of Union Free School District No. 9, New Hyde Park, New York, acting in its official capacity under state law, directed the School District's principal to cause the following prayer to be said aloud by each class in the presence of a teacher at the beginning of each school day:

> Almighty God, we acknowledge our dependence upon Thee, and we beg Thy blessings upon us, our parents, our teachers and our Country.

This daily procedure was adopted on the recommendation of the State Board of Regents, a governmental agency created by the [New York] State Constitution to which the New York Legislature has granted broad supervisory, executive, and legislative powers over the State's public school system. These state officials composed the prayer which they recommended and published as a part of their "Statement on Moral and Spiritual Training in the Schools."

. . . [T]he parents of ten pupils brought this action in a New York State Court insisting that use of this official prayer in the public schools was contrary to the beliefs, religions, or religious practices of both themselves and their children. Among other things, these parents challenged the constitutionality of both the state law authorizing the School District to direct the use of prayer in public schools and the School District's regulation ordering the recitation of this particular prayer on the ground that these actions [violate the Establishment Clause of the First Amendment]. . . .

We think that by using its public school system to encourage recitation of the Regents' prayer, the State of New York has adopted a practice wholly inconsistent with the Establishment Clause. There can, of course, be no doubt that New York's program of daily classroom invocation of God's blessings as prescribed in the Regents' prayer is a religious activity. It is a solemn avowal of divine faith and supplication for the blessings of the Almighty. The nature of such a prayer has always been religious, none of the respondents has denied this and the trial court expressly so found . . . .

The petitioners contend among other things that the state laws requiring or permitting use of the Regents' prayer must be struck down as a violation of the Establishment Clause because that prayer was composed by governmental officials as a part of a governmental program to further religious beliefs. For this reason, petitioners argue, the State's use of the Regents' prayer in its public school system breaches the constitutional wall of separation between Church and State. We agree with that contention since we think that the constitutional prohibition against laws respecting an establishment of religion must at least mean that in this country it is no part of the business of government to compose official prayers for any group of the American people to recite as a part of a religious program carried on by government.

It is a matter of history that this very practice of establishing governmentally composed prayers for religious services was one of the reasons which caused many of our early colonists to leave England and seek religious freedom in America. . . .

It is an unfortunate fact of history that when some of the very groups which had most strenuously opposed the established Church of England found themselves sufficiently in control of colonial governments in this country to write their own prayers into law, they passed laws making their own religion the official religion of their respective colonies. Indeed, as late as the time of the Revolutionary War, there were established churches in at least eight of the thirteen former colonies and established religions in at least four of the other five. But the successful Revolution against English political domination was shortly followed by intense opposition to the practice of establishing religion by law. . . .

By the time of the adoption of the Constitution, our history shows that there was a widespread awareness among many Americans of the dangers of a union of Church and State. These people knew, some of them from bitter personal experience, that one of the greatest dangers to the freedom of the individual to worship in his own way lay in the Government's placing its official stamp of approval upon one particular kind of prayer or one particular form of religious services. . . . Under that Amendment's prohibition against governmental establishment of religion, as reinforced by the provisions of the Fourteenth Amendment, government in this country, be it state or federal, is without power to prescribe by law any particular form of prayer which is to be used as an official prayer in carrying on any program of governmentally sponsored religious activity.

There can be no doubt that New York's state prayer program officially establishes the religious beliefs embodied in the Regents' prayer. The respondents' argument to the contrary, which is largely based upon the contention that the Regents' prayer is "nondenominational" and the fact that the program, as modified and approved by state courts, does not require all pupils to recite the prayer but permits those who wish to do so to remain silent or be excused from the room, ignores the essential nature of the program's constitutional defects. Neither the fact that the prayer may be denominationally neutral nor the fact that its observance on the part of the students is voluntary can serve to free it from the limitations of the Establishment Clause, as it might from the Free Exercise Clause. . . . Although these two clauses may in certain instances overlap, they forbid two quite different kinds of governmental encroachment upon religious freedom. The Establishment Clause, unlike the Free Exercise Clause, does not depend upon any showing of direct governmental compulsion and is violated by the enactment of laws which establish an official religion whether those laws operate directly to coerce nonobserving individuals or not. This is not to say, of course, that laws officially prescribing a particular form of religious worship do not involve coercion of such individuals. When the power, prestige and financial support of government is placed behind a particular religious belief, the indirect coercive pressure upon religious minorities to conform to the prevailing officially approved religion is plain. But the purposes underlying the Establishment Clause go much further than that. Its first and most immediate purpose rested on the belief that a union of government and religion tends to destroy government and to degrade religion. The history of governmentally established religion, both in England and in this country, showed that whenever government had allied itself with one particular form of religion, the inevitable result had been that it had incurred the hatred, disrespect and even contempt of those who held contrary beliefs. That same history showed that many people had lost their respect for any religion that had relied upon the support for government to spread its faith. The Establishment Clause thus stands as an expression of principle on the part of the Founders of our Constitution that religion is too personal, too sacred, too holy, to permit its "unhallowed perversion" by a civil magistrate. Another purpose of the Establishment Clause rested upon an awareness of the historical fact that governmentally established religions and religious persecutions go hand in hand. . . . It was in large part to get completely away from this sort of systematic religious persecution that the Founders brought into being our Nation, our Constitution, and our Bill of Rights with its prohibition against any governmental establishment of religion. . . .

It has been argued that to apply the Constitution in such a way as to prohibit state laws respecting an establishment of religious services in public schools is to indicate a hostility toward religion or toward prayer. Nothing, or course, could be more wrong. . . .

[T]he First Amendment, which tried to put an end to governmental control of religion and of prayer, was not written to destroy either. . . . [I]t was written to quiet well-justified fears which nearly all of them felt arising out of an awareness that governments of the past had shackled men's tongues to make them speak only the religious thoughts that government wanted them to speak and to pray only to the God that government wanted them to pray to. It is neither sacrilegious nor antireligious to say that each separate government in this country should stay out of the business of writing or sanctioning official prayers and leave that purely religious function to the people themselves and to those the people choose to look to for religious guidance.[21]

■ [The concurring opinion of JUSTICE DOUGLAS has been omitted.]

■ MR. JUSTICE STEWART, dissenting.

A local school board in New York has provided that those pupils who wish to do so may join in a brief prayer at the beginning of each school day, acknowledging their dependence upon God and asking His blessing upon them and upon their parents, their teachers, and their country. The Court today decides that in permitting this brief non-denominational prayer the school board has violated the Constitution of the United States. I think this decision is wrong.

The Court does not hold, nor could it, that New York has interfered with the free exercise of anybody's religion. For the state courts have made clear that those who object to reciting the prayer must be entirely free of any compulsion to do so, including any "embarrassments and pressures." Cf. *West Virginia State Board of Education v. Barnette*, 319 U.S. 624. But the Court says that in permitting school children to say this simple prayer, the New York authorities have established "an official religion."

---

[21] There is of course nothing in the decision reached here that is inconsistent with the fact that school children and others are officially encouraged to express love for our country by reciting historical documents such as the Declaration of Independence which contain references to the Deity or by singing officially espoused anthems which include the composer's professions of faith in a Supreme Being, or with the fact that there are many manifestations in our public life of belief in God. Such patriotic or ceremonial occasions bear no true resemblance to the unquestioned religious exercise that the State of New York has sponsored in this instance.

With all respect, I think the Court has misapplied a great constitutional principle. I cannot see how an "official religion" is established by letting those who want to say a prayer say it. On the contrary, I think that to deny the wish of these school children to join in reciting this prayer is to deny them the opportunity of sharing in the spiritual heritage of our Nation. . . .

D. ACCOMMODATION OF RELIGION: THE INTERSECTION OF FREE EXERCISE AND NON-ESTABLISHMENT

We return now to a question introduced earlier: When may the government "accommodate" religion in ways not required by the Free Exercise Clause, without violating the Establishment Clause? This question is presented in the next case, *Corporation of Presiding Bishop v. Amos*. Title VII of the Civil Rights Act of 1964 generally prohibits employment discrimination on the basis of religion. But the statute contains an exemption that permits religious organizations to "discriminate" (if that is the right word) on the basis of religion in their hiring decisions. In *Amos* the Court unanimously upheld that accommodation—but with some disagreement about exactly why it was permissible, and where the outer bounds lie for government accommodation of religion. As you read the case, ask yourself to what degree the exemption of religious organizations from the no-discrimination-on-the-basis-of-religion rule was required by the Free Exercise Clause. Then consider whether the non-required part (if any) violates the Establishment Clause. See if you can develop a theory of why, and when, such accommodations are permissible.

Corporation of Presiding Bishop of Church of Jesus Christ of Latter–Day Saints v. Amos

483 U.S. 327 (1987)

■ JUSTICE WHITE delivered the opinion of the Court.

Section 702 of the Civil Rights Act of 1964 exempts religious organizations from Title VII's prohibition against discrimination in employment on the basis of religion.[1] The question presented is whether applying the § 702 exemption to the secular nonprofit activities of religious organizations violates the Establishment Clause of the First Amendment. . . .

I

The Deseret Gymnasium (Gymnasium) in Salt Lake City, Utah, is a nonprofit facility, open to the public, run by the Corporation of the Presiding Bishop of The Church of Jesus Christ of Latter-day Saints (CPB), and the Corporation of the President of The Church of Jesus Christ of Latter-day Saints (COP). The CPB and the COP are religious entities associated with The Church of Jesus Christ of Latter-day Saints (Church), an unincorporated religious association sometimes called the Mormon or LDS Church.

---

[1] Section 702 provides in relevant part:

This subchapter [i.e., Title VII of the Civil Rights Act of 1964, shall] not apply . . . to a religious corporation, association, educational institution, or society with respect to the employment of individuals of a particular religion to perform work connected with the carrying on by such corporation, association, educational institution, or society of its activities.

Appellee Mayson worked at the Gymnasium for some 16 years as an assistant building engineer and then as building engineer. He was discharged in 1981 because he failed to qualify for a temple recommend, that is, a certificate that he is a member of the Church and eligible to attend its temples.[4]

Mayson and others purporting to represent a class of plaintiffs brought an action against the CPB and the COP alleging, among other things, discrimination on the basis of religion in violation of § 703 of the Civil Rights Act of 1964, 42 U.S.C. § 2000e–2. The defendants moved to dismiss this claim on the ground that § 702 shields them from liability. The plaintiffs contended that if construed to allow religious employers to discriminate on religious grounds in hiring for nonreligious jobs, § 702 violates the Establishment Clause.

The District Court . . . found: first, that the Gymnasium is intimately connected to the Church financially and in matters of management; second, that there is no clear connection between the primary function which the Gymnasium performs and the religious beliefs and tenets of the Mormon Church or church administration; and third, that none of Mayson's duties at the Gymnasium are "even tangentially related to any conceivable religious belief or ritual of the Mormon Church or church administration." The court concluded that Mayson's case involves nonreligious activity.

The court next considered the plaintiffs' constitutional challenge to § 702. Applying the three-part test set out in *Lemon v. Kurtzman*, 403 U.S. 602 (1971), the court first held that § 702 has the permissible secular purpose of "assuring that the government remains neutral and does not meddle in religious affairs by interfering with the decision-making process in religions. . . ." The court concluded, however, that § 702 fails the second part of the *Lemon* test because the provision has the primary effect of advancing religion.[10] Among the considerations mentioned by the court were: that § 702 singles out religious entities for a benefit, rather than benefiting a broad grouping of which religious organizations are only a part; that § 702 is not supported by long historical tradition; and that § 702 burdens the free exercise rights of employees of religious institutions who work in nonreligious jobs. Finding that § 702 impermissibly sponsors religious organizations by granting them "an exclusive authorization to engage in conduct which can directly and immediately advance religious tenets and practices," the court declared the statute unconstitutional as applied to secular activity. . . .

II

"This Court has long recognized that the government may (and sometimes must) accommodate religious practices and that it may do so without violating the Establishment Clause." *Hobbie v. Unemployment Appeals*

---

[4] JUSTICE STEVENS criticizes us for discussing the prologue last. But if a prologue can be used only to clarify an ambiguous operative provision, surely the first step must be to determine whether the operative provision is ambiguous. It might be argued, we suppose, that the prologue itself should be one of the factors that go into the determination of whether the operative provision is ambiguous—but that would cause the prologue to be used to produce ambiguity rather than just to resolve it. In any event, even if we considered the prologue *along with* the operative provision we would reach the same result we do today, since (as we explain) our interpretation of "the right of the people to keep and bear arms" furthers the purpose of an effective militia no less than (indeed, more than) the dissent's interpretation.

[10] The court rejected the defendants' arguments that § 702 is required both by the need to avoid excessive governmental entanglement with religion and by the Free Exercise Clause.

Comm'n of Fla., 480 U.S. 136, 144–145 (1987). It is well established, too, that "[t]he limits of permissible state accommodation to religion are by no means co-extensive with the noninterference mandated by the Free Exercise Clause." *Walz v. Tax Comm'n,* 397 U.S. 664, 673 (1970). There is ample room under the Establishment Clause for "benevolent neutrality which will permit religious exercise to exist without sponsorship and without interference." *Id.* at 669. At some point, accommodation may devolve into "an unlawful fostering of religion," *Hobbie, supra,* 480 U.S. at 145, but these are not such cases, in our view.

The private appellants contend that we should not apply the three-part *Lemon* approach, which is assertedly unsuited to judging the constitutionality of exemption statutes such as § 702. The argument is that an exemption statute will always have the effect of advancing religion and hence be invalid under the second (effects) part of the *Lemon* test [*Lemon v. Kurtzman,* 411 U.S. 192 (1973)], a result claimed to be inconsistent with cases such as *Walz v. Tax Comm'n, supra,* which upheld property tax exemptions for religious organizations.... [W]e need not reexamine *Lemon* as applied in this context, for the exemption involved here is in no way questionable under the *Lemon* analysis.

Lemon requires first that the law at issue serve a "secular legislative purpose." This does not mean that the law's purpose must be unrelated to religion—that would amount to a requirement "that the government show a callous indifference to religious groups," *Zorach v. Clauson,* 343 U.S. 306, 314 (1952), and the Establishment Clause has never been so interpreted. Rather, *Lemon's* "purpose" requirement aims at preventing the relevant governmental decisionmaker—in this case, Congress—from abandoning neutrality and acting with the intent of promoting a particular point of view in religious matters.

Under the *Lemon* analysis, it is a permissible legislative purpose to alleviate significant governmental interference with the ability of religious organizations to define and carry out their religious missions. Appellees argue that there is no such purpose here because § 702 provided adequate protection for religious employers prior to the 1972 amendment, when it exempted only the religious activities of such employers from the statutory ban on religious discrimination. We may assume for the sake of argument that the pre–1972 exemption was adequate in the sense that the Free Exercise Clause required no more. Nonetheless, it is a significant burden on a religious organization to require it, on pain of substantial liability, to predict which of its activities a secular court will consider religious. The line is hardly a bright one, and an organization might understandably be concerned that a judge would not understand its religious tenets and sense of mission. Fear of potential liability might affect the way an organization carried out what it understood to be its religious mission.

... [T]he District Court concluded that Congress' purpose was to minimize governmental "interfer[ence] with the decision-making process in religions." We agree with the District Court that this purpose does not violate the Establishment Clause.

The second requirement under *Lemon* is that the law in question have "a principal or primary effect ... that neither advances nor inhibits religion." Undoubtedly, religious organizations are better able now to advance their purposes than they were prior to the 1972 amendment to § 702. But religious groups have been better able to advance their purposes on account of many laws that have passed constitutional muster.... A law is not unconstitutional simply because it *allows* churches to advance religion, which is their very purpose. For a law to have forbidden "effects" under *Lemon,* it must be fair to say that the *government itself* has advanced religion through its own activities and influence. As the Court observed in *Walz,* "for the men who wrote the Religion Clauses of the First Amendment the 'establishment' of a religion connoted sponsorship, financial support, and active involvement of the sovereign in religious activity." 397 U.S., at 668.

The District Court appeared to fear that sustaining the exemption would permit churches with financial resources impermissibly to extend their influence and propagate their faith by entering the commercial, profit-making world. The cases before us, however, involve a nonprofit activity instituted over 75 years ago in the hope that "all who assemble here, and who come for the benefit of their health, and for physical blessings, [may] feel that they are in a house dedicated to the Lord." Dedicatory Prayer for the Gymnasium. These cases therefore do not implicate the apparent concerns of the District Court. Moreover, we find no persuasive evidence in the record before us that the Church's ability to propagate its religious doctrine through the Gymnasium is any greater now than it was prior to the passage of the Civil Rights Act in 1964. In such circumstances, we do not see how any advancement of religion achieved by the Gymnasium can be fairly attributed to the Government, as opposed to the Church.[15]

We find unpersuasive the District Court's reliance on the fact that § 702 singles out religious entities for a benefit. Although the Court has given weight to this consideration in its past decisions, it has never indicated that statutes that give special consideration to religious groups are *per se* invalid. That would run contrary to the teaching of our cases that there is ample room for accommodation of religion under the Establishment Clause. Where, as here, government acts with the proper purpose of lifting a regulation that burdens the exercise of religion, we see no reason to require that the exemption comes packaged with benefits to secular entities.

We are also unpersuaded by the District Court's reliance on the argument that § 702 is unsupported by long historical tradition. There was simply no need to consider the scope of the § 702 exemption until the 1964 Civil Rights Act was passed, and the fact that Congress concluded after eight years that the original exemption was unnecessarily narrow is a decision entitled to deference, not suspicion.

. . . It cannot be seriously contended that § 702 impermissibly entangles church and state; the statute effectuates a more complete separation of the two and avoids the kind of intrusive inquiry into religious belief that the District Court engaged in this case. The statute easily passes muster under the third part of the *Lemon* test.[17]

■ JUSTICE BRENNAN, with whom JUSTICE MARSHALL joins, concurring in the judgment.

I write separately to emphasize that my concurrence in the judgment rests on the fact that these cases involve a challenge to the application of § 702's categorical exemption to the activities of a *nonprofit* organization. I believe that the particular character of nonprofit activity makes inappro-

---

[15] Undoubtedly, Mayson's freedom of choice in religious matters was impinged upon, but it was the Church (through the COP and the CPB), and not the Government, who put him to the choice of changing his religious practices or losing his job. . . .

[17] We have no occasion to pass on the argument of the COP and the CPB that the exemption to which they are entitled under § 702 is required by the Free Exercise Clause.

priate a case-by-case determination whether its nature is religious or secular.

These cases present a confrontation between the rights of religious organizations and those of individuals. Any exemption from Title VII's proscription on religious discrimination necessarily has the effect of burdening the religious liberty of prospective and current employees. An exemption says that a person may be put to the choice of either conforming to certain religious tenets or losing a job opportunity, a promotion, or, as in these cases, employment itself. The potential for coercion created by such a provision is in serious tension with our commitment to individual freedom of conscience in matters of religious belief.

At the same time, religious organizations have an interest in autonomy in ordering their internal affairs, so that they may be free to:

> select their own leaders, define their own doctrines, resolve their own disputes, and run their own institutions. Religion includes important communal elements for most believers. They exercise their religion through religious organizations, and these organizations must be protected by the [Free Exercise] [C]lause.

Laycock, Towards a General Theory of the Religion Clauses: The Case of Church Labor Relations and the Right to Church Autonomy, 81 Colum. L. Rev. 1373, 1389 (1981). For many individuals, religious activity derives meaning in large measure from participation in a larger religious community. Such a community represents an ongoing tradition of shared beliefs, an organic entity not reducible to a mere aggregation of individuals. Determining that certain activities are in furtherance of an organization's religious mission, and that only those committed to that mission should conduct them, is thus a means by which a religious community defines itself. Solicitude for a church's ability to do so reflects the idea that furtherance of the autonomy of religious organizations often furthers individual religious freedom as well.

The authority to engage in this process of self-definition inevitably involves what we normally regard as infringement on free exercise rights, since a religious organization is able to condition employment in certain activities on subscription to particular religious tenets. We are willing to countenance the imposition of such a condition because we deem it vital that, if certain activities constitute part of a religious community's practice, then a religious organization should be able to require that only members of its community perform those activities.

This rationale suggests that, ideally, religious organizations should be able to discriminate on the basis of religion *only* with respect to religious activities, so that a determination should be made in each case whether an activity is religious or secular. This is because the infringement on religious liberty that results from conditioning performance of *secular* activity upon religious belief cannot be defended as necessary for the community's self-definition. Furthermore, the authorization of discrimination in such circumstances is not an accommodation that simply enables a church to gain members by the normal means of prescribing the terms of membership for those who seek to participate in furthering the mission of the community. Rather, it puts at the disposal of religion the added advantages of economic leverage in the secular realm. As a result, the authorization of religious discrimination with respect to nonreligious activities goes beyond reasonable accommodation, and has the effect of furthering religion in violation of the Establishment Clause.

What makes the application of a religious-secular distinction difficult is that the character of an activity is not self-evident. As a result, determining whether an activity is religious or secular requires a searching case-by-case analysis. This results in considerable ongoing government entanglement in religious affairs. Furthermore, this prospect of government intrusion raises concern that a religious organization may be chilled in its free exercise activity. While a church may regard the conduct of certain functions as integral to its mission, a court may disagree. A religious organization therefore would have an incentive to characterize as religious only those activities about which there likely would be no dispute, even if it genuinely believed that religious commitment was important in performing other tasks as well. As a result, the community's process of self-definition would be shaped in part by the prospects of litigation. A case-by-case analysis for all activities therefore would both produce excessive government entanglement with religion and create the danger of chilling religious activity.

The risk of chilling religious organizations is most likely to arise with respect to *nonprofit* activities. The fact that an operation is not organized as a profit-making commercial enterprise makes colorable a claim that it is not purely secular in orientation. In contrast to a for-profit corporation, a non-profit organization must utilize its earnings to finance the continued provision of the goods or services it furnishes, and may not distribute any surplus to the owners. See generally Hansmann, The Role of Nonprofit Enterprise, 89 Yale L.J. 835 (1980). This makes plausible a church's contention that an entity is not operated simply in order to generate revenues for the church, but that the activities themselves are infused with a religious purpose. Furthermore, unlike for-profit corporations, nonprofits historically have been organized specifically to provide certain community services, not simply to engage in commerce. Churches often regard the provision of such services as a means of fulfilling religious duty and of providing an example of the way of life a church seeks to foster.

Nonprofit activities therefore are most likely to present cases in which characterization of the activity as religious or secular will be a close question. If there is a danger that a religious organization will be deterred from classifying as religious those activities it actually regards as religious, it is likely to be in this domain. This substantial potential for chilling religious activity makes inappropriate a case-by-case determination of the character of a nonprofit organization, and justifies a categorical exemption for nonprofit activities. . . . While not every nonprofit activity may be operated for religious purposes, the likelihood that many are makes a categorical rule a suitable means to avoid chilling the exercise of religion.

. . . Sensitivity to individual religious freedom dictates that religious discrimination be permitted only with respect to employment in religious activities. Concern for the autonomy of religious organizations demands that we avoid the entanglement and the chill on religious expression that a case-by-case determination would produce. We cannot escape the fact that these aims are in tension. Because of the nature of nonprofit activities, I believe that a categorical exemption for such enterprises appropriately balances these competing concerns. As a result, I concur in the Court's judgment that the nonprofit Deseret Gymnasium may avail itself of an automatic exemption from Title VII's proscription on religious discrimination.

■ [The concurring opinion of JUSTICE BLACKMUN is omitted.]

■ JUSTICE O'CONNOR, concurring in the judgment.

Although I agree with the judgment of the Court, I write separately to note that this action once again illustrates certain difficulties inherent in the Court's use of the test articulated in *Lemon v. Kurtzman,....*

The necessary first step in evaluating an Establishment Clause challenge to a government action lifting from religious organizations a generally applicable regulatory burden is to recognize that such government action *does* have the effect of advancing religion. The necessary second step is to separate those benefits to religion that constitutionally accommodate the free exercise of religion from those that provide unjustifiable awards of assistance to religious organizations. As I have suggested in earlier opinions, the inquiry framed by the *Lemon* test should be "whether government's purpose is to endorse religion and whether the statute actually conveys a message of endorsement." To ascertain whether the statute conveys a message of endorsement, the relevant issue is how it would be perceived by an objective observer, acquainted with the text, legislative history, and implementation of the statute. . . .

The above framework, I believe, helps clarify why the amended § 702 raises different questions as it is applied to nonprofit and for-profit organizations. . . . These cases involve a Government decision to lift from a nonprofit activity of a religious organization the burden of demonstrating that the particular nonprofit activity is religious as well as the burden of refraining from discriminating on the basis of religion. Because there is a probability that a nonprofit activity of a religious organization will itself be involved in the organization's religious mission, in my view the objective observer should perceive the Government action as an accommodation of the exercise of religion rather than as a Government endorsement of religion.

It is not clear, however, that activities conducted by religious organizations solely as profit-making enterprises will be as likely to be directly involved in the religious mission of the organization. . . . I [only] emphasize that under the holding of the Court, and under my view of the appropriate Establishment Clause analysis, the question of the constitutionality of the § 702 exemption as applied to for-profit activities of religious organizations remains open.

NOTES

1. *Amos* was unanimous as to result, but with some differences as to reasoning. All the justices agreed that it was permissible for Congress to exempt religious groups from Title VII's usual prohibition of religious discrimination in employment. The majority opinion of Justice White applied the three-part *Lemon* test we have seen from other cases. *Lemon* remains in use, but is also much-criticized. *Amos* holds that the religious-hiring accommodation does not have an impermissible purpose—that there is nothing constitutionally wrong, in principle, with government's having as its goal the accommodation of religion. But what is the "effect" of an accommodation of religion? Doesn't it (in a certain sense) "advance" religion? Justice O'Connor notes this problem in her concurrence, and instead urges a no-"endorsement" test. But doesn't a special accommodation of religion (in a sense) "endorse" religion in precisely the same way? The majority's answer is that it does not advance religion, in the sense

that the Establishment Clause forbids, for government to allow religious organizations to promote their missions: "A law is not unconstitutional simply because it allows churches to advance religion, which is their very purpose. For a law to have forbidden 'effects' under *Lemon*, it must be fair to say that the government itself has advanced religion through its own activities and influence." Does this distinction make sense?

2. Justice Brennan's concurring opinion takes issue with this approach, contending that *Amos* is a difficult case because it presents "a confrontation between the rights of religious organizations and those of individuals" and that the church's "process of self-definition" (that is, excluding persons who are not church members in good standing from employment) "involves what we normally regard as infringement on free exercise rights, since a religious organization is able to condition employment in certain activities on subscription to particular religious tenets." Is this view right? Does government's act of accommodating a religious institution's self-definition itself impair the rights of non-religious individuals?

3. Justice Brennan's opinion nonetheless defends the rights of religious institutions to define their mission by defining their membership. Note the very strong resemblance of his reasoning on this point to the "expressive association" line of freedom of *speech* cases—cases like *Roberts v. U.S. Jaycees*, 468 U.S. 609, 622–23 (1984):

> An individual's freedom to speak, to worship, and to petition the government for the redress of grievances could not be vigorously protected from interference by the State unless a correlative freedom to engage in group effort toward those ends were not also guaranteed. . . . Government actions that may unconstitutionally infringe upon [the freedom of expressive association] can take a number of forms . . . [including] interfer[ence] with the internal organization or affairs of the group. . . . There can be no clearer example of an intrusion into the internal structure or affairs of an association than a regulation that forces the group to accept members it does not desire.

Justice Brennan wrote the majority opinion in *Roberts*. To what extent do you think Justice Brennan thought the accommodation in this case required by Free Speech Clause principles, derived from the expressive association line of cases?

4. The line Justice Brennan would draw is between the "religious" and the "secular" activities of a religious organization. Nonetheless, he recognizes the difficulty in drawing the line, and therefore would permit an accommodation for the "non-profit" (as opposed to "profit"-making) activities of a religious organization. Does the "religious"/"secular" distinction make sense? (Which one is a church soup kitchen or homeless shelter? Are any of a church's activities "secular"?) Does the "profit"/"non-profit" distinction make sense? (Isn't this just a function of how a business is set up?) How good a proxy is it for the religious-secular line that Brennan is trying to achieve?

5. There have been numerous other "accommodation" decisions of the Supreme Court, tending to point in different directions. Are the results correct or incorrect as applications of the Establishment Clause?

Estate of Thornton v. Caldor, Inc., 472 U.S. 703 (1985). May a state enact a law providing that employers must allow employees who observe a weekly religious sabbath to have that one day per week off? A divided Court (in a pre-*Amos* decision) held that this attempted accommodation violated the Establishment Clause. Rightly or wrongly decided? (Could Pennsylvania in the 1790s have had a statute that excused witnesses from testifying in court on their Sabbath?) Is *Caldor* consistent with *Amos*? Title VII of the Civil Rights Act of 1964 (the statute that contains the religious-employer exemption at issue in *Amos*) also provides that all employers must make "reasonable accommodation" of the religious practices of employees. Is that statute unconstitutional? Is it distinguishable from *Caldor*?

Texas Monthly, Inc. v. Bullock, 489 U.S. 1 (1989). May a state exempt religious periodicals from a sales tax it imposes on other magazines and newspapers? A divided court (6–3) held this to violate the Establishment Clause, emphasizing the fact that the exemption was not available to similarly situated non-religious periodicals. Does this adequately distinguish the *Amos* case? There was no controlling majority opinion. Might the result be correct on Free Speech Clause grounds that the tax exemption discriminates on the basis of a publication's content? Does one need the Establishment Clause for this case?

In *Board of Educ. of Kiryas Joel Village School Dist. v. Grumet,* 512 U.S. 687 (1994). New York created a special public school district to accommodate the special education needs of children of members of the Satmar Hasidim (a Jewish religious sect) that lived in its own community. Constitutional accommodation or unconstitutional establishment of religion? The Court, 6–3, struck down the accommodation because it explicitly accommodated a particular sect and the Court was concerned that there was no assurance the state would similarly accommodate others. (New York re-passed its law in different form, designed to avoid specific reference to the religious group. That accommodation was upheld by New York's highest state court against constitutional challenge.)

The Supreme Court's most recent case concerning accommodation upheld a federal statute broadly requiring that governments accommodate religious exercise in prisons and in land-use regulation. Note carefully the Supreme Court's rationale in *Cutter v. Wilkinson.*

Cutter v. Wilkinson

544 U.S. 709 (2005)

■ JUSTICE GINSBURG delivered the opinion of the Court.

Section 3 of the Religious Land Use and Institutionalized Persons Act of 2000 (RLUIPA) provides in part: "No government shall impose a substantial burden on the religious exercise of a person residing in or confined to an institution," unless the burden furthers "a compelling governmental interest," and does so by "the least restrictive means." Plaintiffs below, petitioners here, are current and former inmates of institutions operated by the Ohio Department of Rehabilitation and Correction and assert that they are adherents of "nonmainstream" religions: the Satanist, Wicca, and Asatru religions, and the Church of Jesus Christ Christian. They complain that Ohio prison officials (respondents here), in violation of RLUIPA, have failed to accommodate their religious exercise . . .

In response, . . . prison officials have mounted a facial challenge to the institutionalized-persons provision of RLUIPA; respondents contend, *inter alia,* that the Act improperly advances religion in violation of the First

Amendment's Establishment Clause.... "This Court has long recognized that the government may ... accommodate religious practices ... without violating the Establishment Clause." ... "At some point, accommodation may devolve into 'an unlawful fostering of religion.'" *Corporation of Presiding Bishop of Church of Jesus Christ of Latter-day Saints v. Amos,* 483 U.S. 327, 334 (1987). But § 3 of RLUIPA, we hold, does not, on its face, exceed the limits of permissible government accommodation of religious practices.

... Responding to *Employment Division v. Smith,* Congress enacted the Religious Freedom Restoration Act of 1993 (RFRA).... In *City of Boerne v. Flores,* 521 U.S. 507 (1997), this Court invalidated RFRA as applied to States and their subdivisions, holding that the Act exceeded Congress' remedial powers under the Fourteenth Amendment.... Congress again responded, this time by enacting RLUIPA. Less sweeping than RFRA, and invoking federal authority under the Spending and Commerce Clauses, RLUIPA targets two areas: Section 2 of the Act concerns land-use regulation; § 3 relates to religious exercise by institutionalized persons. ...

The Religion Clauses of the First Amendment provide: "Congress shall make no law respecting an establishment of religion, or prohibiting the free exercise thereof." The first of the two Clauses, commonly called the Establishment Clause, commands a separation of church and state. The second, the Free Exercise Clause, requires government respect for, and noninterference with, the religious beliefs and practices of our Nation's people. While the two Clauses express complementary values, they often exert conflicting pressures. See *Locke,* 540 U.S., at 718.

Our decisions recognize that "there is room for play in the joints" between the Clauses, *Walz v. Tax Comm'n of City of New York,* 397 U.S. 664, 669 (1970), some space for legislative action neither compelled by the Free Exercise Clause nor prohibited by the Establishment Clause.... [W]e hold that § 3 of RLUIPA fits within the corridor between the Religion Clauses: On its face, the Act qualifies as a permissible legislative accommodation of religion that is not barred by the Establishment Clause.

Foremost, we find RLUIPA's institutionalized-persons provision compatible with the Establishment Clause because it alleviates exceptional government-created burdens on private religious exercise. See *Board of Ed. of Kiryas Joel Village School Dist. v. Grumet,* 512 U.S. 687 (1994) (government need not "be oblivious to impositions that legitimate exercises of state power may place on religious belief and practice"). Furthermore, the Act on its face does not founder on shoals our prior decisions have identified: Properly applying RLUIPA, courts must take adequate account of the burdens a requested accommodation may impose on nonbeneficiaries, see *Estate of Thornton v. Caldor, Inc.,* 472 U.S. 703 (1985); and they must be satisfied that the Act's prescriptions are and will be administered neutrally among different faiths, see *Kiryas Joel,* 512 U.S. 687.

... Section 3 covers state-run institutions—mental hospitals, prisons, and the like—in which the government exerts a degree of control unparalleled in civilian society and severely disabling to private religious exercise. RLUIPA thus protects institutionalized persons who are unable freely to attend to their religious needs and are therefore dependent on the government's permission and accommodation for exercise of their religion.

We note in this regard the Federal Government's accommodation of religious practice by members of the military. ...

We do not read RLUIPA to elevate accommodation of religious observances over an institution's need to maintain order and safety. Our decisions indicate that an accommodation must be measured so that it does not override other significant interests. In *Caldor,* the Court struck down a Connecticut law that "arm[ed] Sabbath observers with an absolute and unqualified right not to work on whatever day they designate[d] as their Sabbath." 472 U.S., at 709. We held the law invalid under the Establishment Clause because it "unyielding[ly] weigh[ted]" the interests of Sabbatarians "over all other interests." *Id.,* at 710.

We have no cause to believe that RLUIPA would not be applied in an appropriately balanced way, with particular sensitivity to security concerns. . . .

Finally, RLUIPA does not differentiate among bona fide faiths. In *Board of Ed. of Kiryas Joel Village School District v. Grumet,* we invalidated a state law that carved out a separate school district to serve exclusively a community of highly religious Jews, the Satmar Hasidim. We held that the law violated the Establishment Clause, 512 U.S., at 690, in part because it "single[d] out a particular religious sect for special treatment," *id.,* at 706. RLUIPA presents no such defect. It confers no privileged status on any particular religious sect, and singles out no bona fide faith for disadvantageous treatment.

The Sixth Circuit misread our precedents to require invalidation of RLUIPA as "impermissibly advancing religion by giving greater protection to religious rights than to other constitutionally protected rights." Our decision in *Amos* counsels otherwise. There, we upheld against an Establishment Clause challenge a provision exempting "religious organizations from Title VII's prohibition against discrimination in employment on the basis of religion." The District Court in *Amos,* reasoning in part that the exemption improperly "single[d] out religious entities for a benefit," had "declared the statute unconstitutional as applied to secular activity." Religious accommodations, we held, need not "come packaged with benefits to secular entities." . . .

■ [The concurring opinion of JUSTICE THOMAS is omitted.]

NOTES

1. Note that the Court does not apply the *Lemon* test. Why not? In past cases, some Justices argued that accommodations of religion necessarily violated all three prongs of the *Lemon* test, and that this was a good reason to revise or abandon it. Does *Cutter* implicitly accept that criticism?

2. In place of *Lemon,* *Cutter* looks to three considerations. Each of them raises new questions. First, the Court notes that the challenged statute "alleviates exceptional government-created burdens on private religious exercise." How exceptional is "exceptional"? In prior decisions, the Court had stated that accommodations must alleviate "substantial" or "significant" burdens. Why the change in vocabulary?

Second, the Court stated that under the statute, "courts must take adequate account of the burdens a requested accommodation may impose on nonbeneficiaries." How adequate is "adequate"? Why should nonbeneficiaries be required to shoulder any part of the cost of another person's religious exercise? On the other hand, if the burden on nonbeneficiaries is not religious in nature—if it involves mere cost or inconvenience—why is that a constitutional problem? Modern social welfare regulation frequently shifts burdens from one person to another—for example, from employees to employers. Why does the Establishment Clause point to a different result?

Third, the Court states that to be constitutional the Act must be "administered neutrally among different faiths." That sounds reasonable, but exactly what does it mean? Suppose there is a law exempting kosher slaughterhouses from certain meat-packing regulations. Perhaps the same exemption must be extended to halal meatpackers. But how can specific accommodations of this sort be neutral in any global sense? Many accommodations are targeted at particular religious practices known to be at odds with the law. Is that permissible under *Cutter*?

3. In the historical materials at the beginning of this section, you read the First Congress's debates over whether to exempt religious conscientious objectors from compulsory service in the militia. Some thought exemptions should be constitutionalized; some thought they should be left to legislative discretion; some thought they would be fair only if those exempted paid for an equivalent. This debate seems to be powerful support for the proposition that the framers of the First Amendment did not regard accommodations as establishments of religion. Why didn't the Court invoke this history in support of its reasoning?

[*Assignment 55*]

Financial Aid to Religious Activities

Everson v. Board of Education
330 U.S. 1 (1947)

■ MR. JUSTICE BLACK delivered the opinion of the Court.

A New Jersey statute authorizes its local school districts to make rules and contracts for the transportation of children to and from schools. The appellee, a township board of education, acting pursuant to this statute authorized reimbursement to parents of money expended by them for the bus transportation of their children on regular busses operated by the public transportation system. Part of this money was for the payment of transportation of some children in the community to Catholic parochial schools. These church schools give their students, in addition to secular education, regular religious instruction conforming to the religious tenets and modes of worship of the Catholic Faith. The superintendent of these schools is a Catholic priest.

The appellant, in his capacity as a district taxpayer, filed suit . . .

The only contention here is that the State statute and the resolution, in so far as they authorized reimbursement to parents of children attending parochial schools, . . . forced inhabitants to pay taxes to help support and maintain schools which are dedicated to, and which regularly teach, the Catholic Faith. This is alleged to be a use of State power to support church schools contrary to the prohibition of the First Amendment which the Fourteenth Amendment made applicable to the states . . .

A large proportion of the early settlers of this country came here from Europe to escape the bondage of laws which compelled them to support and attend government favored churches . . .

These practices became so commonplace as to shock the freedom-loving colonials into a feeling of abhorrence. The imposition of taxes to pay ministers' salaries and to build and maintain churches and church property aroused their indignation. It was these feelings which found expression in the First Amendment ... The people [in Virginia], as elsewhere, reached the conviction that individual religious liberty could be achieved best under a government which was stripped of all power to tax, to support, or otherwise to assist any or all religions, or to interfere with the beliefs of any religious individual or group.

The movement toward this end reached its dramatic climax in Virginia in 1785–86 when the Virginia legislative body was about to renew Virginia's tax levy for the support of the established church ... Madison wrote his great Memorial and Remonstrance against the law. In it, he eloquently argued that a true religion did not need the support of law; that no person, either believer or non-believer, should be taxed to support a religious institution of any kind; that the best interest of a society required that the minds of men always be wholly free; and that cruel persecutions were the inevitable result of government-established religions. Madison's Remonstrance received strong support throughout Virginia, and the Assembly postponed consideration of the proposed tax measure until its next session. When the proposal came up for consideration at that session, it not only died in committee, but the Assembly enacted the famous "Virginia Bill for Religious Liberty" originally written by Thomas Jefferson. The preamble to that Bill stated among other things that

> Almighty God hath created the mind free; that all attempts to influence it by temporal punishments, or burthens, or by civil incapacitations, tend only to beget habits of hypocrisy and meanness, and are a departure from the plan of the Holy author of our religion who being Lord both of body and mind, yet chose not to propagate it by coercions on either ...; that to compel a man to furnish contributions of money for the propagation of opinions which he disbelieves, is sinful and tyrannical; that even the forcing him to support this or that teacher of his own religious persuasion, is depriving him of the comfortable liberty of giving his contributions to the particular pastor, whose morals he would make his pattern. ...

And the statute itself enacted

> That no man shall be compelled to frequent or support any religious worship, place, or ministry whatsoever, nor shall be enforced, restrained, molested, or burthened, in his body or goods, nor shall otherwise suffer on account of his religious opinions or belief. ...

The "establishment of religion clause of the First Amendment means at least this: Neither a state nor the Federal Government can set up a church. Neither can pass laws which aid one religion, aid all religions, or prefer one religion over another. Neither can force nor influence a person to go to or to remain away from church against his will or force him to profess a belief or disbelief in any religion. No person can be punished for entertaining or professing religious beliefs or disbeliefs, for church attendance or non-attendance. No tax in any amount, large or small, can be levied to support any religious activities or institutions, whatever they may be called, or whatever form they may adopt to teach or practice religion. Neither a state nor the Federal Government can, openly or secretly, participate in the affairs of any religious organizations or groups and vice versa. In the words of

Jefferson, the clause against establishment of religion by law was intended to erect "a wall of separation between Church and State."

We must consider the New Jersey statute in accordance with the fore-going limitations imposed by the First Amendment. But we must not strike that state statute down if it is within the state's constitutional power even though it approaches the verge of that power. New Jersey cannot consist-ently with the "establishment of religion" clause of the First Amendment contribute tax-raised funds to the support of an institution which teaches the tenets and faith of any church. On the other hand, other language of the amendment commands that New Jersey cannot hamper its citizens in the free exercise of their own religion. Consequently, it cannot exclude in-dividual Catholics, Lutherans, Mohammedans, Baptists, Jews, Methodists, Non-believers, Presbyterians, or the members of any other faith, because of their faith, or lack of it, from receiving the benefits of public welfare legisla-tion. While we do not mean to intimate that a state could not provide transportation only to children attending public schools, we must be care-ful, in protecting the citizens of New Jersey against state-established churches, to be sure that we do not inadvertently prohibit New Jersey from extending its general State law benefits to all its citizens without regard to their religious belief.

Measured by these standards, we cannot say that the First Amend-ment prohibits New Jersey from spending taxraised funds to pay the bus fares of parochial school pupils as a part of a general program under which it pays the fares of pupils attending public and other schools. It is undoubt-edly true that children are helped to get to church schools. There is even a possibility that some of the children might not be sent to the church schools if the parents were compelled to pay their children's bus fares out of their own pockets when transportation to a public school would have been paid for by the State. The same possibility exists where the state requires a local transit company to provide reduced fares to school children including those attending parochial schools, or where a municipally owned transportation system undertakes to carry all school children free of charge. Moreover, state-paid policemen, detailed to protect children going to and from church schools from the very real hazards of traffic, would serve much the same purpose and accomplish much the same result as state provisions intended to guarantee free transportation of a kind which the state deems to be best for the school children's welfare. And parents might refuse to risk their children to the serious danger of traffic accidents going to and from paro-chial schools, the approaches to which were not protected by policemen. Similarly, parents might be reluctant to permit their children to attend schools which the state had cut off from such general government services as ordinary police and fire protection, connections for sewage disposal, pub-lic highways and sidewalks. Of course, cutting off church schools from these services, so separate and so indisputably marked off from the religious function, would make it far more difficult for the schools to operate. But such is obviously not the purpose of the First Amendment. That Amend-ment requires the state to be a neutral in its relations with groups of reli-gious believers and non-believers; it does not require the state to be their adversary. State power is no more to be used so as to handicap religions, than it is to favor them.

This Court has said that parents may, in the discharge of their duty under state compulsory education laws, send their children to a religious rather than a public school if the school meets the secular educational requirements which the state has power to impose. See *Pierce v. Society of Sisters*, 268 U.S. 510 (1925). It appears that these parochial schools meet New Jersey's requirements. The State contributes no money to the schools. It does not support them. Its legislation, as applied, does no more than provide a general program to help parents get their children, regardless of their religion, safely and expeditiously to and from accredited schools.

The First Amendment has erected a wall between church and state. That wall must be kept high and impregnable. We could not approve the slightest breach. New Jersey has not breached it here.

■ [The dissenting opinion of JUSTICE JACKSON is omitted.]

■ MR. JUSTICE RUTLEDGE, with whom MR. JUSTICE FRANKFURTER, MR. JUSTICE JACKSON and MR. JUSTICE BURTON agree, dissenting.

I

Not simply an established church, but any law respecting an establishment of religion is forbidden. The Amendment was broadly but not loosely phrased. It is the compact and exact summation of its author's views formed during his long struggle for religious freedom . . .

The Amendment's purpose was not to strike merely at the official establishment of a single sect, creed or religion, outlawing only a formal relation such as had prevailed in England and some of the colonies. Necessarily it was to uproot all such relationships. But the object was broader than separating church and state in this narrow sense. It was to create a complete and permanent separation of the spheres of religious activity and civil authority by comprehensively forbidding every form of public aid or support for religion . . .

"Religion" and "establishment" were not used in any formal or technical sense. The prohibition broadly forbids state support, financial or other, of religion in any guise, form or degree. It outlaws all use of public funds for religious purposes.

II

No provision of the Constitution is more closely tied to or given content by its generating history than the religious clause of the First Amendment. It is at once the refined product and the terse summation of that history. The history includes not only Madison's authorship and the proceedings before the First Congress, but also the long and intensive struggle for religious freedom in America, more especially in Virginia, of which the Amendment was the direct culmination . . .

As the Remonstrance discloses throughout, Madison opposed every form and degree of official relation between religion and civil authority. For him religion was a wholly private matter beyond the scope of civil power either to restrain or to support. . . .

In no phase was he more unrelentingly absolute than in opposing state support or aid by taxation. Not even "three pence" contribution was thus to be exacted from any citizen for such a purpose. Remonstrance, Par. 3. Tithes had been the life blood of establishment before and after other compulsions disappeared. Madison and his coworkers made no exceptions or abridgments to the complete separation they created . . . And the principle was as much to prevent "the interference of law in religion" as to restrain religious intervention in political matters. In this field the authors of our freedom would not tolerate "the first experiment on our liberties" or "wait till usurped power had strengthened itself by exercise, and entangled the question in precedents." Remonstrance, Par. 3. Nor should we.

In view of this history no further proof is needed that the Amendment forbids any appropriation, large or small, from public funds to aid or support any and all religious exercises . . .

III

Does New Jersey's action furnish support for religion by use of the taxing power? Certainly it does, if the test remains undiluted as Jefferson and Madison made it, that money taken by taxation from one is not to be used or given to support another's religious training or belief, or indeed one's own. Today as then the furnishing of "contributions of money for the propagation of opinions which he disbelieves" is the forbidden exaction; and the prohibition is absolute for whatever measure brings that consequence and whatever mount may be sought or given to that end.

The funds used here were raised by taxation. The Court does not dispute nor could it that their use does in fact give aid and encouragement to religious instruction. It only concludes that this aid is not "support" in law. But Madison and Jefferson were concerned with aid and support in fact not as a legal conclusion "entangled in precedents." Remonstrance, Par. 3. Here parents pay money to send their children to parochial schools and funds raised by taxation are used to reimburse them. This not only helps the children to get to school and the parents to send them. It aids them in a substantial way to get the very thing which they are sent to the particular school to secure, namely, religious training and teaching.

Believers of all faiths, and others who do not express their feeling toward ultimate issues of existence in any creedal form, pay the New Jersey tax . . . Each [person] thus contributes to "the propagation of opinions which he disbelieves" in so far as their religious differ, as do others who accept no creed without regard to those differences. Each thus pays taxes also to support the teaching of his own religion, an exaction equally forbidden since it denies "the comfortable liberty" of giving one's contribution to the particular agency of instruction he approves.

New Jersey's action therefore exactly fits the type of exaction and the kind of evil at which Madison and Jefferson struck. Under the test they framed it cannot be said that the cost of transportation is no part of the cost of education or of the religious instruction given. That it is a substantial and a necessary element is shown most plainly by the continuing and increasing demand for the state to assume it . . . And the very purpose of the state's contribution is to defray the cost of conveying the pupil to the place where he will receive not simply secular, but also and primarily religious, teaching and guidance . . .

Finally, transportation, where it is needed, is as essential to education as any other element . . . Without buildings, without equipment, without library, textbooks and other materials, and without transportation to bring teacher and pupil together in such an effective teaching environment, there can be not even the skeleton of what our times require. Hardly can it be maintained that transportation is the least essential of these items, or that it does not in fact aid, encourage, sustain and support, just as they do, the very process which is its purpose to accomplish . . .

For me, therefore, the feat is impossible to select so indispensable an item from the composite of total costs, and characterize it as not aiding, contributing to, promoting or sustaining the propagation of beliefs which it is the very end of all to bring about. Unless this can be maintained, and the Court does not maintain it, the aid thus given is outlawed . . . No rational line can be drawn between payment for such larger, but not more necessary, items and payment for transportation. The only line that can be so drawn is one between more dollars and less. Certainly in this realm such a line can be no valid constitutional measure . . .

IV

But we are told that the New Jersey statute is valid in its present application because the appropriation is for a public, not a private purpose, namely, the promotion of education, and the majority accept this idea in the conclusion that all we have here is "public welfare legislation." . . .

If the fact alone be determinative that religious schools are engaged in education, thus promoting the general and individual welfare, together with the legislature's decision that the payment of public moneys for their aid makes their work a public function, then I can see no possible basis, except one of dubious legislative policy, for the state's refusal to make full appropriation for support of private, religious schools, just as is done for public instruction. There could not be, on that basis, valid constitutional objection.

Of course paying the cost of transportation promotes the general cause of education and the welfare of the individual . . .

To say that New Jersey's appropriation and her use of the power of taxation for raising the funds appropriated are not for public purposes but are for private ends, is to say that they are for the support of religion and religious teaching. Conversely, to say that they are for public purposes is to say that they are not for religious ones.

This is precisely for the reason that education which includes religious training and teaching, and its support, have been made matters of private right and function not public, by the very terms of the First Amendment. That is the effect not only in its guaranty of religion's free exercise, but also in the prohibition of establishments. It was on this basis of the private character of the function of religious education that this Court held parents entitled to send their children to private, religious schools. *Pierce.* Now it declares in effect that the appropriation of public funds to defray part of the cost of attending those schools is for a public purpose. If so, I do not understand why the state cannot go father or why this case approaches the verge of its power.

In truth this view contradicts the whole purpose and effect of the First Amendment as heretofore conceived. The "public function"—"public welfare"—"social legislation" argument seeks in Madison's words, to "employ Religion (that is, here, religious education) as an engine of Civil policy." Remonstrance, Par. 5 . . .

Our constitutional policy is exactly the opposite. It does not deny the value or the necessity for religious training, teaching or observance. Rather it secures their free exercise. But to that end it does deny that the state can undertake or sustain them in any form or degree. For this reason the sphere of religious activity, as distinguished from the secular intellectual liberties, has been given the twofold protection and, as the state cannot forbid, neither can it perform or aid in performing the religious function. The dual prohibition makes that function altogether private. It cannot be made a public one by legislative act. This was the very heart of Madison's Remonstrance, as it is of the Amendment itself . . .

[The majority makes two arguments:] one that the aid extended partakes of the nature of a safety measure, the other that failure to provide it would make the state unneutral in religious matters, discriminating against or hampering such children concerning public benefits all others receive . . .

[T]his approach, if valid, supplies a ready method for nullifying the Amendment's guaranty, not only for this case and others involving small grants in aid for religious education, but equally for larger ones. The only thing needed will be for the Court again to transplant the "public welfare-public function" view from its proper nonreligious due process bearing to First Amendment application, holding that religious education is not "supported" though it may be aided by the appropriation, and that the cause of education generally is furthered by helping the pupil to secure that type of training . . .

VI

Short treatment will dispose of what remains. Whatever might be said of some other application of New Jersey's statute, the one made here has no semblance of bearing as a safety measure or, indeed, for securing expeditious conveyance. The transportation supplied is by public conveyance, subject to all the hazards and delays of the highway and the streets incurred by the public generally in going about its multifarious business.

Nor is the case comparable to one of furnishing fire or police protection, or access to public highways. These things are matters of common right, part of the general need for safety.[56] Certainly the fire department must not stand idly by while the church burns. Nor is this reason why the state should pay the expense of transportation or other items of the cost of religious education . . .

Two great drives are constantly in motion to abridge, in the name of education, the complete division of religion and civil authority which our forefathers made. One is to introduce religious education and observances into the public schools. The other, to obtain public funds for the aid and support of various private religious schools. In my opinion both avenues were closed by the Constitution. Neither should be opened by this Court . . .

NOTES

1. The majority opinion is a bit schizophrenic. The first part proclaims the necessity of strict separation; the second part relies on neutral. Which is it?

2. Justice Rutledge relies heavily on the history of the Virginia assessment bill. Is that really so close an analogy? The Virginia bill required taxpayers to pay money to churches for religious uses. The New Jersey statute uses money in the general treasury to defray the costs of transportation of all students to school, no matter where they go. The Virginia statute expressly sought to support religion as such; the New Jersey statute supports education and is neutral about whether that education has a religious element. How would you deal with these issues?

---

[56] The protections are of a nature which does not require appropriations specially made from the public treasury and earmarked, as is New Jersey's here, particularly for religious institutions or uses. The First Amendment does not exclude religious property or activities from protection against disorder or the ordinary accidental incidents of community life. It forbids support, not protection from interference or destruction . . .

3. How far would Justice Rutledge go? Must churches be denied all benefits paid for by taxes? Police protection? Use of the mails or roads?

4. *Pierce v. Society of Sisters*, cited by the majority, struck down a state statute (supported by the Ku Klux Klan) requiring all students to attend public schools. (It is presented in Chapter 7.) If parents have the constitutional right to send their children to schools that educate them in the tenets of their faith, why should they be denied their fair share of the school fund? Why isn't the most neutral polity to allow all families to choose the schools their children will attend, with the government paying the costs and excluding only those that fail to provide a proper education?

Lemon v. Kurtzman

403 U.S. 602 (1971)

■ MR. CHIEF JUSTICE BURGER delivered the opinion of the Court.

These two appeals raise questions as to Pennsylvania and Rhode Island statutes providing state aid to church-related elementary and secondary schools. Both statutes are challenged as violative of the Establishment and Free Exercise Clauses of the First Amendment and the Due Process Clause of the Fourteenth Amendment . . . We hold that both statutes are unconstitutional.

I

The Rhode Island [law] rests on the legislative finding that the quality of education available in nonpublic elementary schools has been jeopardized by the rapidly rising salaries needed to attract competent and dedicated teachers. [It] supplement[s] the salaries of teachers of secular subjects in nonpublic elementary schools by paying directly to a teacher an amount not in excess of 15% of his current annual salary. As supplemented, however, a nonpublic school teacher's salary cannot exceed the maximum paid to teachers in the State's public schools, and the recipient must be certified by the state board of education in substantially the same manner as public school teachers.

In order to be eligible for the Rhode Island salary supplement, the recipient must teach in a nonpublic school at which the average per-pupil expenditure on secular education is less than the average in the State's public schools during a specified period . . . .

The Act also requires that teachers eligible for salary supplements must teach only those subjects that are offered in the State's public schools. They must use "only teaching materials which are used in the public schools." Finally, any teacher applying for a salary supplement must first agree in writing "not to teach a course in religion for so long as or during such time as he or she receives any salary supplements" under the Act . . .

[The Court's description of the Pennsylvania statute is omitted.— Editors]

II

. . . [The First Amendment's] authors did not simply prohibit the establishment of a state church or a state religion, an area history shows they regarded as very important and fraught with great dangers. Instead they commanded that there should be "no law respecting an establishment of religion." A law may be one "respecting" the forbidden objective while falling short of its total realization. A law "respecting" the proscribed result, that is, the establishment of religion, is not always easily identifiable as one violative of the Clause. A given law might not establish a state religion but nevertheless be one "respecting" that end in the sense of being a step that could lead to such establishment and hence offend the First Amendment.

In the absence of precisely stated constitutional prohibitions, we must draw lines with reference to the three main evils against which the Establishment Clause was intended to afford protection: "sponsorship, financial support, and active involvement of the sovereign in religious activity."

Every analysis in this area must begin with consideration of the cumulative criteria developed by the Court over many years. Three such tests may be gleaned from our cases. First, the statute must have a secular legislative purpose; second, its principal or primary effect must be one that neither advances nor inhibits religion; finally, the statute must not foster "an excessive government entanglement with religion."

Inquiry into the legislative purposes of the Pennsylvania and Rhode Island statutes affords no basis for a conclusion that the legislative intent was to advance religion. On the contrary, the statutes themselves clearly state that they are intended to enhance the quality of the secular education in all schools covered by the compulsory attendance laws. There is no reason to believe the legislatures meant anything else . . .

In *Allen* the Court acknowledged that secular and religious teachings were not necessarily so intertwined that secular textbooks furnished to students by the State were in fact instrumental in the teaching of religion. The legislatures of Rhode Island and Pennsylvania have concluded that secular and religious education are identifiable and separable. In the abstract we have no quarrel with this conclusion.

The two legislatures, however, have also recognized that church-related elementary and secondary schools have a significant religious mission and that a substantial portion of their activities is religiously oriented. They have therefore sought to create statutory restrictions designed to guarantee the separation between secular and religious educational functions and to ensure that State financial aid supports only the former. All these provisions are precautions taken in candid recognition that these programs approached, even if they did not intrude upon, the forbidden areas under the Religion Clauses. We need not decide whether these legislative precautions restrict the principal or primary effect of the programs to the point where they do not offend the Religion Clauses, for we conclude that the cumulative impact of the entire relationship arising under the statutes in each State involves excessive entanglement between government and religion.

III

. . . Our prior holdings do not call for total separation between church and state; total separation is not possible in an absolute sense. Some relationship between government and religious organizations is inevitable. Fire inspections, building and zoning regulations, and state requirements under compulsory school-attendance laws are examples of necessary and permissible contacts. Indeed, under the statutory exemption before us in *Walz*, the State had a continuing burden to ascertain that the exempt property was in fact being used for religious worship. Judicial caveats against entanglement must recognize that the line of separation, far from being a "wall," is blurred, indistinct, and variable barrier depending on all the circumstances of a particular relationship . . .

In order to determine whether the government entanglement with religion is excessive, we must examine the character and purposes of the institutions that are benefited, the nature of the aid that the State provides, and the resulting relationship between the government and the religious authority . . . Here we find that both statutes foster an impermissible degree of entanglement.

(a) Rhode Island program

. . . The church schools involved in the program are located close to parish churches. This understandably permits convenient access for religious exercises since instruction in faith and morals is part of the total educational process. The school buildings contain identifying religious symbols such as crosses on the exterior and crucifixes, and religious paintings and statutes either in the classrooms or hallways. Although only approximately 30 minutes a day are devoted to direct religious instruction, there are religiously oriented extracurricular activities. Approximately two-thirds of the teachers in these schools are nuns of various religious orders. Their dedicated efforts provide an atmosphere in which religious instruction and religious vocations are natural and proper parts of life in such schools. Indeed, as the District Court found, the role of teaching nuns in enhancing the religious atmosphere has led the parochial school authorities to attempt to maintain a one-to-one ratio between nuns and lay teachers in all schools rather than to permit some to be staffed almost entirely by lay teachers.

On the basis of these findings the District Court concluded that the parochial schools constituted "an integral part of the religious mission of the Catholic Church." The various characteristics of the schools make them "a powerful vehicle for transmitting the Catholic faith to the next generation." This process of inculcating religious doctrine is, of course, enhanced by the impressionable age of the pupils, in primary schools particularly. In short, parochial schools involve substantial religious activity and purpose.

The substantial religious character of these church-related schools gives rise to entangling church-state relationships of the kind the Religion Clauses sought to avoid. Although the District Court found that concern for religious values did not inevitably or necessarily intrude into the content of secular subjects, the considerable religious activities of these schools led the legislature to provide for careful governmental controls and surveillance by state authorities in order to ensure that state aid supports only secular education.

The dangers and corresponding entanglements are enhanced by the particular form of aid that the Rhode Island Act provides. Our decisions from *Everson* to *Allen* have permitted the States to provide church-related schools with secular, neutral, or nonideological services, facilities, or materials. Bus transportation, school lunches, public health services, and secular textbooks supplied in common to all students were not thought to offend the Establishment Clause. We note that the dissenters in Allen seemed chiefly concerned with the pragmatic difficulties involved in ensuring the truly secular content of the textbooks provided at state expense.

In *Allen* the Court refused to make assumptions, on a meager record, about the religious content of the textbooks that the State would be asked to provide. We cannot, however, refuse here to recognize that teachers have a substantially different ideological character from books. In terms of potential for involving some aspect of faith or morals in secular subjects, a textbook's content is ascertainable, but a teacher's handling of a subject is not. We cannot ignore the danger that a teacher under religious control and discipline poses to the separation of the religious from the purely secular aspects of precollege education. The conflict of functions inheres in the situation. . . .

[The Court notes that the Catholic schools are under the supervision of clergy appointed by the local bishop, and thus "[r]eligious authority necessarily pervades the school system." And that according to diocesan regulations, "[r]eligious formation is not confined to formal courses."—Editors]

Several teachers testified, however, that they did not inject religion into their secular classes. And the District Court found that religious values did not necessarily affect the content of the secular instruction. But what has been recounted suggests the potential if not actual hazards of this form of state aid. The teacher is employed by a religious organization, subject to the direction and discipline of religious authorities, and works in a system dedicated to rearing children in a particular faith. These controls are not lessened by the fact that most of the lay teachers are of the Catholic faith. Inevitably some of a teacher's responsibilities hover on the border between secular and religious orientation.

We need not and do not assume that teachers in parochial schools will be guilty of bad faith or any conscious design to evade the limitations imposed by the statute and the First Amendment. We simply recognize that a dedicated religious person, teaching in a school affiliated with his or her faith and operated to inculcate its tenets, will inevitably experience great difficulty in remaining religiously neutral. Doctrines and faith are not inculcated or advanced by neutrals. With the best of intentions such a teacher would find it hard to make a total separation between secular teaching and religious doctrine. What would appear to some to be essential to good citizenship might well for others border on or constitute instruction in religion. Further difficulties are inherent in the combination of religious discipline and the possibility of disagreement between teacher and religious authorities over the meaning of the statutory restrictions.

We do not assume, however, that parochial school teachers will be unsuccessful in their attempts to segregate their religious beliefs from their secular educational responsibilities. But the potential for impermissible fostering of religion is present . . . To ensure that no trespass occurs, the State has therefore carefully conditioned its aid with pervasive restrictions . . .

A comprehensive, discriminating, and continuing state surveillance will inevitably be required to ensure that these restrictions are obeyed and the First Amendment otherwise respected. Unlike a book, a teacher cannot be inspected once so as to determine the extent and intent of his or her personal beliefs and subjective acceptance of the limitations imposed by the First Amendment. These prophylactic contacts will involve excessive and enduring entanglement between state and church.

There is another area of entanglement in the Rhode Island program that gives concern. The statute excludes teachers employed by nonpublic schools whose average per-pupil expenditures on secular education equal or exceed the comparable figures for public schools. In the event that the total expenditures of an otherwise eligible school exceed this norm, the program requires the government to examine the school's records in order to deter-

mine how much of the total expenditures is attributable to secular education and how much to religious activity. This kind of state inspection and
evaluation of the religious content of a religious organization is fraught
with the sort of entanglement that the Constitution forbids. It is a relationship pregnant with dangers of excessive government direction of church
schools and hence of churches. The Court noted "the hazards of government
supporting churches" in *Walz*, and we cannot ignore here the danger that
pervasive modern governmental power will ultimately intrude on religion
and thus conflict with the Religion Clauses.

(b) Pennsylvania program

[The Court's analysis of the Pennsylvania program is similar.—
Editors]

IV

A broader base of entanglement of yet a different character is presented by the divisive political potential of these state programs. In a community where such a large number of pupils are served by church-related
schools, it can be assumed that state assistance will entail considerable political activity. Partisans of parochial schools, understandably concerned
with rising costs and sincerely dedicated to both the religious and secular
educational missions of their schools, will inevitably champion this cause
and promote political action to achieve their goals. Those who oppose state
aid, whether for constitutional, religious, or fiscal reasons, will inevitably
respond and employ all of the usual political campaign techniques to prevail. Candidates will be forced to declare and voters to choose. It would be
unrealistic to ignore the fact that many people confronted with issues of
this kind will find their votes aligned with their faith.

Ordinarily political debate and division, however vigorous or even partisan, are normal and healthy manifestations of our democratic system of
government, but political division along religious lines was one of the principal evils against which the First Amendment was intended to protect.
The potential divisiveness of such conflict is a threat to the normal political
process ... The history of many countries attests to the hazards of religion's intruding into the political arena or of political power intruding into
the legitimate and free exercise of religious belief.

Of course, as the Court noted in *Walz*, "[a]dherents of particular faiths
and individual churches frequently take strong positions on public issues."
We could not expect otherwise, for religious values pervade the fabric of our
national life. But [h]ere we are confronted with successive and very likely
permanent annual appropriations that benefit relatively few religious
groups. Political fragmentation and divisiveness on religious lines are thus
likely to be intensified ...

V

The merit and benefits of these schools, however, are not the issue before us in these cases. The sole question is whether state aid to these
schools can be squared with the dictates of the Religion Clauses. Under our
system the choice has been made that government is to be entirely excluded
from the area of religious instruction and churches excluded from the affairs of government. The Constitution decrees that religion must be a private matter for the individual, the family, and the institutions of private
choice, and that while some involvement and entanglement are inevitable,
lines must be drawn ...

■ [JUSTICE DOUGLAS's concurring opinion, joined by JUSTICE BLACK, is omitted.]

■ MR. JUSTICE WHITE, dissenting:

No one in these cases questions the constitutional right of parents to satisfy their state-imposed obligation to educate their children by sending them to private schools, sectarian or otherwise, as long as those schools meet minimum standards established for secular instruction. The States are not only permitted, but required by the Constitution, to free students attending private schools from any public school attendance obligation. The States may also furnish transportation for students, and books for teaching secular subjects to students attending parochial and other private as well as public schools; we have also upheld arrangements whereby students are released from public school classes so that they may attend religious instruction. Outside the field of education, we have upheld Sunday closing laws, state and federal laws exempting church property and church activity from taxation, and governmental grants to religious organizations for the purpose of financing improvements in the facilities of hospitals managed and controlled by religious orders.

Our prior cases have recognized the dual role of parochial schools in American society: they perform both religious and secular functions. Our cases also recognize that legislation having a secular purpose and extending governmental assistance to sectarian schools in the performance of their secular functions does not constitute "law[s] respecting an establishment of religion" forbidden by the First Amendment merely because a secular program may incidentally benefit a church in fulfilling its religious mission. That religion may indirectly benefit from governmental aid to the secular activities of churches does not convert that aid into an impermissible establishment of religion . . .

It is enough for me that the States and the Federal Government are financing a separable secular function of overriding importance in order to sustain the legislation here challenged. That religion and private interests other than education may substantially benefit does not convert these laws into impermissible establishments of religion.

It is unnecessary, therefore, to urge that the Free Exercise Clause of the First Amendment at least permits government, in some respects, to modify and mold its secular programs out of express concern for free-exercise values. The Establishment Clause, however, coexists in the First Amendment with the Free Exercise Clause, and the latter is surely relevant in cases such as these. Where a state program seeks to ensure the proper education of its young, in private as well as public schools, free exercise considerations at least counsel against refusing support for students attending parochial schools simply because, in that setting, they are also being instructed in the tenets of the faith they are constitutionally free to practice.

NOTES

1. Think about the way in which the second and third prongs of the *Lemon* test interact. The "effects" test requires the state to be "certain" that its funds do not support religion, but the "entanglement" test renders regulatory efforts to monitor use of the funds unconstitutional. In a later case, the Court called this a "Catch–22."

2. Who is being protected by the decision in *Lemon*? The taxpayers? Assuming the schools are of equal educational quality—and no one denies this—taxpayers are getting full value for their money. Indeed, because religious schools are less expensive than public schools, they may be saving money. The children? Their parents selected these schools, and presumably like the religious education they are getting. The schools themselves? They are the most plausible candidates for recipients of protection. The state statutes effectively provide that they can receive money if and only if they secularize a significant portion of their curriculum. Financially hard-pressed schools may find that difficult to turn down. But why do taxpayers have standing to "protect" schools if the schools do not want to be protected?

3. On the same day as *Lemon*, the Court decided *Tilton v. Richardson*, 403 U.S. 672 (1971), involving public aid to religious colleges and universities. Most of the Justices thought the same principles were involved, but they split between those who thought the aid constitutional and those who thought it unconstitutional. A minority of the Justices thought that higher education was distinguishable, because it was not "pervasively sectarian." Because these recipient institutions were not "pervasively sectarian," the state could rely on their assurances that they would not use public money for religious purposes, thus making entangling "surveillance" unnecessary. Eventually, the same rule spread to religious social welfare organizations. *Bowen v. Kendrick*, 487 U.S. 589 (1988). Although recipients could not use funds for "specifically religious activities," the burden was on plaintiffs to prove a violation—in contrast to *Lemon*, where the need for entangling surveillance was simply assumed. In practice, then, the Catch–22 of the *Lemon* test applied only to "pervasively sectarian" organizations. Only churches and elementary and secondary schools were deemed to fall in this category, which meant that public funds could flow relatively freely to religious organizations other than schools. See Stephen Monsma, WHEN SACRED AND SECULAR MIX: RELIGIOUS NONPROFIT ORGANIZATIONS AND PUBLIC MONEY (2000).

Cases After *Lemon*

1. *Committee for Public Education v. Nyquist*, 413 U.S. 756 (1973). In 1972, New York State created three programs to provide assistance to nonpublic elementary and secondary schools. The first program provided direct money grants to qualifying nonpublic schools for maintenance and repair. The grants, made to schools with many low-income students, were made on a per-pupil basis but could not exceed the prior year's maintenance expenses or 50 percent of the average per-student cost for public schools. The second and third programs were for families using nonpublic schools. Through the second program, low income families could receive tuition grants of $50 or $100 per child depending on grade year, not to exceed half of the child's tuition. Through the third program, higher income families were eligible for a tuition tax credit, which diminished as their taxable income increased. Schools eligible under these programs included schools that imposed religious restrictions on admissions and faculty appointments, required student attendance at religious activities and adherence to doctrines of faith, established curricula consistent with church teaching, and sough the inculcation of religious values. By a 6–3 vote, the Court invalidated all three programs under the effects prong of the *Lemon* test.

Regarding the maintenance and repair grants, the Court noted that the program made no attempt to ensure that the funds were "used exclusively for secular purposes." For instance, the school might use the grant to pay "the salaries of employees who maintain the school chapel" or to "renovat[e] classrooms in which religion is taught." The Court distinguished *Everson*, which dealt with busing, and *Allen*, which dealt with textbooks, on the basis that those were secular functions. The Court rejected the argument that the limitation of 50 percent of per-student public school spending ensured that the program aided only secular functions. Citing *Lemon*, where the Rhode Island salary supplement was invalided even though it provided only 15 percent of a teacher's salary, the Court declared that "a mere statistical judgment will not suffice as a guarantee that state funds will not be used to finance religious education."

The Court also invalidated the tuition grants. Reasoning that the grants could not be given directly to sectarian schools without "an effective means of guaranteeing that the state aid . . . will be used exclusively for secular, neutral, and nonideological purposes," it concluded that the fact that the grants went to parents instead, was merely "one among many factors to be considered." The Court dismissed the argument that the aid to secular education was more substantial than the aid to religious education, and was thus the primary effect of the program under *Lemon*: "We do not think that such metaphysical judgments are either possible or necessary. Our cases simply do not support the notion that a law found to have a 'primary' effect to promote some legitimate end under the State's police power is immune from further examination to ascertain whether it also has the direct and immediate effect of advancing religion." The Court also noted that the tuition grants went only to private-school families, in contrast to *Everson* and *Allen*, where both public- and private-school families benefited. The state maintained that the grants sought to ensure "comparable benefits" to all families, but the Court rejected this argument, reasoning that private-school families received the grants in addition to the right to send their children to public school, and that the state's argument, if accepted, would justify "the complete subsidization of all religious schools" in order "to equalize the position of parents who elect such schools." The Court reserved the question of whether a generally available grant program that did not consider "sectarian-nonsectarian, or public-nonpublic" distinctions would violate the Establishment Clause. The Court also rejected the argument that the grants were necessary "to promote the free exercise of religion" of low-income parents, noting that "tension inevitably exists between the Free Exercise and the Establishment Clause, and . . . it may often not be possible to promote the former without offending the latter."

The Court invalidated the tax credits for similar reasons. Additionally, the Court distinguished New York's tax credits from New York's system of exempting religious organizations from property taxes that had been upheld in *Walz v. Tax Commission*, 397 U.S. 664 (1970). According to the Court, tax exemptions enjoyed "an apparently universal approval" at the time of the adoption of the First Amendment, while tax credits for religious schooling were "a recent innovation." Furthermore, tax exemptions were "a reasonable and balanced attempt to guard against" the dangers of oppressive taxation, while tax credits were "[s]pecial tax benefits" that aided sectarian institutions and "tend to increase rather than limit [church-state] involvement." And, the *Walz* tax exemption was extended to all property "devoted to religious, educational, or charitable purposes."

2. In *Meek v. Pittenger*, 421 U.S. 349 (1975), the Court struck down a Pennsylvania law that provided instructional materials, including periodicals, photographs, maps, charts, recordings, and films. The Court wrote:

[A]s part of general legislation made available to all students, a State may include church-related schools in programs providing bus transportation, school lunches, and public health facilities—secular and non-ideological services unrelated to the primary, religion-oriented educational function of the sectarian school. The indirect and incidental benefits to church-related schools from those programs do not offend the constitutional prohibition against establishment of religion. But the massive aid provided the church-related nonpublic schools of Pennsylvania by Act 195 is neither indirect nor incidental.

For the 1972–1973 school year, the Commonwealth authorized just under $12 million of direct aid to the predominantly church-related nonpublic schools of Pennsylvania through the loan of instructional material and equipment pursuant to Act 195. To be sure, the material and equipment that are the subjects of the loan—maps, charts, and laboratory equipment, for example—are "self-polic[ing], in that, starting as secular, nonideological and neutral, they will not change in use." But faced with the substantial amounts of direct support authorized by Act 195, it would simply ignore reality to attempt to separate secular educational functions from the predominantly religious role performed by many of Pennsylvania's church-related elementary and secondary schools, and to then characterize Act 195 as channeling aid to the secular without providing direct aid to the sectarian. Even though earmarked for secular purposes, "when it flows to an institution in which religion is so pervasive that a substantial portion of its functions are subsumed in the religious mission," state aid has the impermissible primary effect of advancing religion.

Nevertheless, the Court distinguished and reaffirmed *Allen*, which upheld the loaning of secular textbooks to religious school students.

In *Meek*, the Court also struck down Pennsylvania's provision of "auxiliary services," like remedial and therapeutic services, and English as a second language, by public school personnel on religious school premises. According to the Court, any form of educational instruction in a religious school risked the injection of religious content into the teaching.

3. In *Aguilar v. Felton*, 473 U.S. 402 (1985), the Court declared unconstitutional New York City's use of federal funds to pay for public school teachers to provide remedial education to low-income students in religious schools. While New York City adopted a system for monitoring the religious content of the publicly funded classes, the Court held that this system would require "comprehensive surveillance" and thus inevitably result in the excessive entanglement of church and state. *Aguilar* was later overruled by *Agostini v. Felton*, 521 U.S. 203 (1997).

Zelman v. Simmons–Harris

536 U.S. 639 (2002)

■ CHIEF JUSTICE REHNQUIST delivered the opinion of the Court.

The State of Ohio has established a pilot program designed to provide educational choices to families with children who reside in the Cleveland City School District. The question presented is whether this program offends the Establishment Clause of the United States Constitution. We hold that it does not.

There are more than 75,000 children enrolled in the Cleveland City School District. The majority of these children are from low-income and minority families. Few of these families enjoy the means to send their children to any school other than an inner-city public school. For more than a generation, however, Cleveland's public schools have been among the worst performing public schools in the Nation . . .

It is against this backdrop that Ohio enacted, among other initiatives, its Pilot Project Scholarship Program. The program provides financial assistance to families in any Ohio school district that is or has been "under federal court order requiring supervision and operational management of the district by the state superintendent." Cleveland is the only Ohio school district to fall within that category.

The program provides two basic kinds of assistance to parents of children in a covered district. First, the program provides tuition aid for students in kindergarten through third grade, expanding each year through eighth grade, to attend a participating public or private school of their parent's choosing. Second, the program provides tutorial aid for students who choose to remain enrolled in public school.

The tuition aid portion of the program is designed to provide educational choices to parents who reside in a covered district. Any private school, whether religious or nonreligious, may participate in the program and accept program students so long as the school is located within the boundaries of a covered district and meets statewide educational standards. Participating private schools must agree not to discriminate on the basis of race, religion, or ethnic background, or to "advocate or foster unlawful behavior or teach hatred of any person or group on the basis of race, ethnicity, national origin, or religion." Any public school located in a school district adjacent to the covered district may also participate in the program. Adjacent public schools are eligible to receive a $2,250 tuition grant for each program student accepted in addition to the full amount of per-pupil state funding attributable to each additional student. All participating schools, whether public or private, are required to accept students in accordance with rules and procedures established by the state superintendent.

Tuition aid is distributed to parents according to financial need. Families with incomes below 200% of the poverty line are given priority and are eligible to receive 90% of private school tuition up to $2,250. For these lowest income families, participating private schools may not charge a parental copayment greater than $250. For all other families, the program pays 75% of tuition costs, up to $1,875, with no copayment cap. These families receive tuition aid only if the number of available scholarships exceeds the number of low-income children who choose to participate. Where tuition aid is spent depends solely upon where parents who receive tuition aid choose to enroll their child. If parents choose a private school, checks are made payable to the parents who then endorse the checks over to the chosen school . . .

The program has been in operation within the Cleveland City School District since the 1996–1997 school year. In the 1999–2000 school year, 56 private schools participated in the program, 46 (or 82%) of which had a religious affiliation. None of the public schools in districts adjacent to Cleveland have elected to participate. More than 3,700 students participated in

the scholarship program, most of whom (96%) enrolled in religiously affiliated schools. Sixty percent of these students were from families at or below
the poverty line. In the 1998–1999 school year, approximately 1,400 Cleveland public school students received tutorial aid. This number was expected
to double during the 1999–2000 school year.

The program is part of a broader undertaking by the State to enhance
the educational options of Cleveland's schoolchildren in response to the
1995 takeover. That undertaking includes programs governing community
and magnet schools . . . During the 1999–2000 school year, there were 10
startup community schools in the Cleveland City School District with more
than 1,900 students enrolled. For each child enrolled in a community
school, the school receives state funding of $4,518, twice the funding a par-
ticipating program school may receive.

Magnet schools are public schools operated by a local school board that
emphasize a particular subject area, teaching method, or service to students. For each student enrolled in a magnet school, the school district receives $7,746, including state funding of $4,167, the same amount received
per student enrolled at a traditional public school. As of 1999, parents in
Cleveland were able to choose from among 23 magnet schools, which together enrolled more than 13,000 students in kindergarten through eighth
grade . . .

In July 1999, respondents [sued] on the ground that [the program] violated the Establishment Clause of the United States Constitution. . . . *[The
District Court granted summary judgment for the respondents, and a divided Court of Appeals affirmed.—Editors]* We granted certiorari, and now
reverse the Court of Appeals.

The Establishment Clause of the First Amendment, applied to the
States through the Fourteenth Amendment, prevents a State from enacting
laws that have the "purpose" or "effect" of advancing or inhibiting religion.
There is no dispute that the program challenged here was enacted for the
valid secular purpose of providing educational assistance to poor children
in a demonstrably failing public school system. Thus, the question presented is whether the Ohio program nonetheless has the forbidden "effect" of
advancing or inhibiting religion.

To answer that question, our decisions have drawn a consistent distinction between government programs that provide aid directly to religious schools, and programs of true private choice, in which government aid
reaches religious schools only as a result of the genuine and independent
choices of private individuals. While our jurisprudence with respect to the
constitutionality of direct aid programs has "changed significantly" over the
past two decades, our jurisprudence with respect to true private choice programs has remained consistent and unbroken. Three times we have confronted Establishment Clause challenges to neutral government programs
that provide aid directly to a broad class of individuals, who, in turn, direct
the aid to religious schools or institutions of their own choosing. Three
times we have rejected such challenges.

In *Mueller*, we rejected an Establishment Clause challenge to a Minnesota program authorizing tax deductions for various educational expenses, including private school tuition costs, even though the great majority of
the program's beneficiaries (96%) were parents of children in religious
schools . . .

In *Witters*, we used identical reasoning to reject an Establishment Clause challenge to a vocational scholarship program that provided tuition aid to a student studying at a religious institution to become a pastor . . .

Finally, in *Zobrest*, we applied *Mueller* and *Witters* to reject an Establishment Clause challenge to a federal program that permitted sign-language interpreters to assist deaf children enrolled in religious schools . . .

Mueller, *Witters*, and *Zobrest* thus make clear that where a government aid program is neutral with respect to religion, and provides assistance directly to a broad class of citizens who, in turn, direct government aid to religious schools wholly as a result of their own genuine and independent private choice, the program is not readily subject to challenge under the Establishment Clause. A program that shares these features permits government aid to reach religious institutions only by way of the deliberate choices of numerous individual recipients. The incidental advancement of a religious mission, or the perceived endorsement of a religious message, is reasonably attributable to the individual recipient, not to the government, whose role ends with the disbursement of benefits. As a plurality of this Court recently observed:

> "[I]f numerous private choices, rather than the single choice of a government, determine the distribution of aid, pursuant to neutral eligibility criteria, then a government cannot, or at least cannot easily, grant special favors that might lead to a religious establishment."

It is precisely for these reasons that we have never found a program of true private choice to offend the Establishment Clause.

We believe that the program challenged here is a program of true private choice, consistent with *Mueller*, *Witters*, and *Zobrest*, and thus constitutional. As was true in those cases, the Ohio program is neutral in all respects toward religion. It is part of a general and multifaceted undertaking by the State of Ohio to provide educational opportunities to the children of a failed school district. It confers educational assistance directly to a broad class of individuals defined without reference to religion, *i.e.*, any parent of a school-age child who resides in the Cleveland City School District. The program permits the participation of *all* schools within the district, religious or nonreligious. Adjacent public schools also may participate and have a financial incentive to do so. Program benefits are available to participating families on neutral terms, with no reference to religion. The only preference stated anywhere in the program is a preference for low-income families, who receive greater assistance and are given priority for admission at participating schools.

There are no "financial incentive[s]" that "ske[w]" the program toward religious schools. Such incentives "[are] not present . . . where the aid is allocated on the basis of neutral, secular criteria that neither favor nor disfavor religion, and is made available to both religious and secular beneficiaries on a nondiscriminatory basis." The program here in fact creates financial *dis*incentives for religious schools, with private schools receiving only half the government assistance given to community schools and one-third the assistance given to magnet schools. Adjacent public schools, should any choose to accept program students, are also eligible to receive two to three times the state funding of a private religious school. Families too have a financial disincentive to choose a private religious school over other schools. Parents that choose to participate in the scholarship program and then to enroll their children in a private school (religious or nonreligious) must copay a portion of the school's tuition. Families that choose a community school, magnet school, or traditional public school pay nothing. Although such features of the program are not necessary to its constitutionality, they clearly dispel the claim that the program "creates . . . financial incentive[s] for parents to choose a sectarian school."

Respondents suggest that even without a financial incentive for parents to choose a religious school, the program creates a "public perception that the State is endorsing religious practices and beliefs." But we have repeatedly recognized that no reasonable observer would think a neutral program of private choice, where state aid reaches religious schools solely as a result of the numerous independent decisions of private individuals, carries with it the *imprimatur* of government endorsement. The argument is particularly misplaced here since "the reasonable observer in the endorsement inquiry must be deemed aware" of the "history and context" underlying a challenged program. Any objective observer familiar with the full history and context of the Ohio program would reasonably view it as one aspect of a broader undertaking to assist poor children in failed schools, not as an endorsement of religious schooling in general.

There also is no evidence that the program fails to provide genuine opportunities for Cleveland parents to select secular educational options for their school-age children. Cleveland schoolchildren enjoy a range of educational choices: They may remain in public school as before, remain in public school with publicly funded tutoring aid, obtain a scholarship and choose a religious school, obtain a scholarship and choose a nonreligious private school, enroll in a community school, or enroll in a magnet school . . . .

Justice SOUTER speculates that because more private religious schools currently participate in the program, the program itself must somehow discourage the participation of private nonreligious schools. But Cleveland's preponderance of religiously affiliated private schools certainly did not arise as a result of the program; it is a phenomenon common to many American cities . . . It is true that 82% of Cleveland's participating private schools are religious schools, but it is also true that 81% of private schools in Ohio are religious schools. To attribute constitutional significance to this figure, moreover, would lead to the absurd result that a neutral school-choice program might be permissible in some parts of Ohio, such as Columbus, where a lower percentage of private schools are religious schools, but not in inner-city Cleveland, where Ohio has deemed such programs most sorely needed, but where the preponderance of religious schools happens to be greater . . .

Respondents and Justice SOUTER claim that even if we do not focus on the number of participating schools that are religious schools, we should attach constitutional significance to the fact that 96% of scholarship recipients have enrolled in religious schools. They claim that this alone proves parents lack genuine choice, even if no parent has ever said so . . . The constitutionality of a neutral educational aid program simply does not turn on whether and why, in a particular area, at a particular time, most private schools are run by religious organizations, or most recipients choose to use the aid at a religious school. As we said in *Mueller,* "[s]uch an approach would scarcely provide the certainty that this field stands in need of, nor can we perceive principled standards by which such statistical evidence might be evaluated." . . .

Respondents finally claim that we should look to *Nyquist* to decide these cases. We disagree . . . [T]the program in *Nyquist* was quite different from the program challenged here. *Nyquist* involved a New York program that gave a package of benefits exclusively to private schools and the parents of private school enrollees. Although the program was enacted for ostensibly secular purposes, we found that its "function" was "*unmistakably* to provide desired financial support for nonpublic, sectarian institutions." Its genesis, we said, was that private religious schools faced "increasingly grave fiscal problems." The program thus provided direct money grants to religious schools. It provided tax benefits "unrelated to the amount of money actually expended by any parent on tuition," ensuring a windfall to parents of children in religious schools. It similarly provided tuition reimbursements designed explicitly to "offe[r] . . . an incentive to parents to send their children to sectarian schools." Indeed, the program flatly prohibited the participation of any public school, or parent of any public school enrollee. Ohio's program shares none of these features . . .

In sum, the Ohio program is entirely neutral with respect to religion. It provides benefits directly to a wide spectrum of individuals, defined only by financial need and residence in a particular school district. It permits such individuals to exercise genuine choice among options public and private, secular and religious. The program is therefore a program of true private choice. In keeping with an unbroken line of decisions rejecting challenges to similar programs, we hold that the program does not offend the Establishment Clause.

■ [The concurring opinions of JUSTICES O'CONNOR and THOMAS, and the dissenting opinion of JUSTICE STEVENS, are omitted.]

■ JUSTICE SOUTER, with whom JUSTICE STEVENS, JUSTICE GINSBURG, and JUSTICE BREYER join, dissenting.

. . . The majority's statements of Establishment Clause doctrine cannot be appreciated without some historical perspective on the Court's announced limitations on government aid to religious education, and its repeated repudiation of limits previously set . . .

Viewed with the necessary generality, the cases can be categorized in three groups. In the period from 1947 to 1968, the basic principle of no aid to religion through school benefits was unquestioned. Thereafter for some 15 years, the Court termed its efforts as attempts to draw a line against aid that would be divertible to support the religious, as distinct from the secular, activity of an institutional beneficiary. Then, starting in 1983, concern with divertibility was gradually lost in favor of approving aid in amounts unlikely to afford substantial benefits to religious schools, when offered evenhandedly without regard to a recipient's religious character, and when channeled to a religious institution only by the genuinely free choice of some private individual. Now, the three stages are succeeded by a fourth, in which the substantial character of government aid is held to have no constitutional significance, and the espoused criteria of neutrality in offering aid, and private choice in directing it, are shown to be nothing but examples of verbal formalism . . .

II

Although it has taken half a century since *Everson* to reach the majority's twin standards of neutrality and free choice, the facts show that, in the majority's hands, even these criteria cannot convincingly legitimize the Ohio scheme.

A

Consider first the criterion of neutrality . . . In order to apply the neutrality test[,] it makes sense to focus on a category of aid that may be directed to religious as well as secular schools, and ask whether the scheme favors a religious direction. Here, one would ask whether the voucher provisions, allowing for as much as $2,250 toward private school tuition (or a grant to a public school in an adjacent district), were written in a way that skewed the scheme toward benefiting religious schools.

This, however, is not what the majority asks. The majority looks not to the provisions for tuition vouchers, but to every provision for educational opportunity: "The program permits the participation of *all* schools within the district, [as well as public schools in adjacent districts], religious or nonreligious." The majority then finds confirmation that "participation of *all* schools" satisfies neutrality by noting that the better part of total state educational expenditure goes to public schools, thus showing there is no favor of religion.

The illogic is patent. If regular, public schools (which can get no voucher payments) "participate" in a voucher scheme with schools that can, and public expenditure is still predominantly on public schools, then the majority's reasoning would find neutrality in a scheme of vouchers available for private tuition in districts with no secular private schools at all . . .

B

The majority addresses the issue of choice the same way it addresses neutrality, by asking whether recipients or potential recipients of voucher aid have a choice of public schools among secular alternatives to religious schools. Again, however, the majority asks the wrong question and misapplies the criterion. The majority has confused choice in spending scholarships with choice from the entire menu of possible educational placements, most of them open to anyone willing to attend a public school . . . If "choice" is present whenever there is any educational alternative to the religious school to which vouchers can be endorsed, then there will always be a choice and the voucher can always be constitutional, even in a system in which there is not a single private secular school as an alternative to the religious school . . .

It is not, of course, that I think even a genuine choice criterion is up to the task of the Establishment Clause when substantial state funds go to religious teaching; the discussion in Part III, shows that it is not. The point is simply that if the majority wishes to claim that choice is a criterion, it must define choice in a way that can function as a criterion with a practical capacity to screen something out.

If, contrary to the majority, we ask the right question about genuine choice to use the vouchers, the answer shows that something is influencing choices in a way that aims the money in a religious direction: of 56 private schools in the district participating in the voucher program (only 53 of which accepted voucher students in 1999–2000), 46 of them are religious; 96.6% of all voucher recipients go to religious schools, only 3.4% to nonreligious ones . . . Evidence shows, however, that almost two out of three families using vouchers to send their children to religious schools did not embrace the religion of those schools . . .

Even [this] might be consistent with true choice if the students "chose" their religious schools over a wide array of private nonreligious options, or if it could be shown generally that Ohio's program had no effect on educational choices and thus no impermissible effect of advancing religious education. But both possibilities are contrary to fact. First, [there are few, if any, open seats at nonreligious private schools]. Second, the $2,500 cap [discourages students from attending nonreligious private schools that have higher tuition]. By comparison, the average tuition at participating Catholic schools in Cleveland in 1999–2000 was $1,592, almost $1,000 below the cap . . .

And it is entirely irrelevant that the State did not deliberately design the network of private schools for the sake of channeling money into religious institutions. The criterion is one of genuinely free choice on the part of the private individuals who choose, and a Hobson's choice is not a choice, whatever the reason for being Hobsonian.

III

I do not dissent merely because the majority has misapplied its own law, for even if I assumed *arguendo* that the majority's formal criteria were satisfied on the facts, today's conclusion would be profoundly at odds with the Constitution. Proof of this is clear on two levels. The first is circumstantial, in the now discarded symptom of violation, the substantial dimension of the aid. The second is direct, in the defiance of every objective supposed to be served by the bar against establishment.

A

The scale of the aid to religious schools approved today is unprecedented, both in the number of dollars and in the proportion of systemic school expenditure supported. Each measure has received attention in previous cases. On one hand, the sheer quantity of aid, when delivered to a class of religious primary and secondary schools, was suspect on the theory that the greater the aid, the greater its proportion to a religious school's existing expenditures, and the greater the likelihood that public money was supporting religious as well as secular instruction . . .

On the other hand, the Court has found the gross amount unhelpful for Establishment Clause analysis when the aid afforded a benefit solely to one individual, however substantial as to him, but only an incidental benefit to the religious school at which the individual chose to spend the State's money. When neither the design nor the implementation of an aid scheme channels a series of individual students' subsidies toward religious recipients, the relevant beneficiaries for establishment purposes, the Establishment Clause is unlikely to be implicated . . .

The Cleveland voucher program has cost Ohio taxpayers $33 million since its implementation in 1996 ($28 million in voucher payments, $5 million in administrative costs), and its cost was expected to exceed $8 million in the 2001–2002 school year . . .

The gross amounts of public money contributed are symptomatic of the scope of what the taxpayers' money buys for a broad class of religious-school students. In paying for practically the full amount of tuition for thousands of qualifying students, the scholarships purchase everything that tuition purchases, be it instruction in math or indoctrination in faith . . .

B

[This program threatens harms that the Establishment Clause was designed to prevent. First, it violates respect for freedom of conscience and the Jeffersonian idea enshrined in the Bill for Establishing Religious Freedom that no one "shall be compelled to . . . support any religious worship, place or ministry whatsoever." Second, it risks foisting a "corrosive secularism" upon religious schools. These harms are] already being realized. In Ohio, for example, a condition of receiving government money under the program is that participating religious schools may not "discriminate on the basis of . . . religion," which means the school may not give admission preferences to children who are members of the patron faith; children of a parish are generally consigned to the same admission lotteries as non-believers . . . Nor is the State's religious antidiscrimination restriction limited to student admission policies: by its terms, a participating religious school may well be forbidden to choose a member of its own clergy to serve as teacher or principal over a layperson of a different religion claiming equal qualification for the job. Indeed, a separate condition that "[t]he school . . . not . . . teach hatred of any person or group on the basis of . . . religion," could be understood (or subsequently broadened) to prohibit religions from teaching traditionally legitimate articles of faith as to the error, sinfulness, or ignorance of others, if they want government money for their schools . . .

■ Justice Breyer, with whom Justice Stevens and Justice Souter join, dissenting.

[The Religion] Clauses embody an understanding, reached in the 17th century after decades of religious war, that liberty and social stability demand a religious tolerance that respects the religious views of all citizens, permits those citizens to "worship God in their own way," and allows all families to "teach their children and to form their characters" as they wish. The Clauses reflect the Framers' vision of an American Nation free of the religious strife that had long plagued the nations of Europe. Whatever the Framers might have thought about particular 18th–century school funding practices, they undeniably intended an interpretation of the Religion Clauses that would implement this basic First Amendment objective.

In part for this reason, the Court's 20th–century Establishment Clause cases—both those limiting the practice of religion in public schools and those limiting the public funding of private religious education—focused directly upon social conflict, potentially created when government becomes involved in religious education . . .

[A]n earlier American society might have found a less clear-cut church/state separation compatible with social tranquility. Indeed, historians point out that during the early years of the Republic, American schools—including the first public schools—were Protestant in character . . . The 20th–century Court was fully aware, however, that immigration and growth had changed American society dramatically since its early years . . .

The Court appreciated the religious diversity of contemporary American society. It realized that the status quo favored some religions at the expense of others. And it understood the Establishment Clause to prohibit (among other things) any such favoritism. Yet *how* did the Clause achieve that objective? Did it simply require the government to give each religion an equal chance to introduce religion into the primary schools—a kind of "equal opportunity" approach to the interpretation of the Establishment Clause? Or, did that Clause avoid government favoritism of some religions by insisting upon "separation"—that the government achieve equal treatment by removing itself from the business of providing religious education for children? This interpretive choice arose in respect both to religious activities in public schools and government aid to private education.

In both areas the Court concluded that the Establishment Clause required "separation," in part because an "equal opportunity" approach was not workable . . .

With respect to government aid to private education, did not history show that efforts to obtain equivalent funding for the private education of children whose parents did not hold popular religious beliefs only exacerbated religious strife? . . .

The upshot is the development of constitutional doctrine that reads the Establishment Clause as avoiding religious strife, *not* by providing every religion with an *equal opportunity* (say, to secure state funding or to pray in the public schools), but by drawing fairly clear lines of *separation* between church and state—at least where the heartland of religious belief, such as primary religious education, is at issue. . . .

IV

I do not believe that the "parental choice" aspect of the voucher program sufficiently offsets the concerns I have mentioned. Parental choice cannot help the taxpayer who does not want to finance the religious education of children. It will not always help the parent who may see little real choice between inadequate nonsectarian public education and adequate education at a school whose religious teachings are contrary to his own. It will not satisfy religious minorities unable to participate because they are too few in number to support the creation of their own private schools. It will not satisfy groups whose religious beliefs preclude them from participating in a government-sponsored program, and who may well feel ignored as government funds primarily support the education of children in the doctrines of the dominant religions. And it does little to ameliorate the entanglement problems or the related problems of social division that Part II describes. Consequently, the fact that the parent may choose which school can cash the government's voucher check does not alleviate the Establishment Clause concerns associated with voucher programs.

NOTES

1. The majority relies primarily on a formal understanding of neutrality: if the statute makes no distinctions between religious and secular, treating all schools alike, it does not matter for constitutional purposes what choices are actually made. But the majority also argues, seemingly in the alternative, that the Cleveland program has neutral results. The difference between the majority and the dissent on this point hinges on what the denominator is. The majority asks what proportion of the total education fund goes to religious schools. The dissent focuses on the small part of the education scheme for which religious schools are eligible, and complains that religious schools predominate in that part. Which is right?

2. The Court has come a long way from *Lemon*, *Nyquist*, *Meek*, and *Aguilar*, to *Zelman*. Which approach best accords with the language, history, and purposes of the First Amendment? Under which approach do Americans enjoy the widest religious freedom—including freedom not to be religious, and not to support religion? What accounts for the shift?

Rosenberger v. Rector and Visitors of University of Virginia

515 U.S. 819 (1995)

[In another part of this opinion, reproduced above, the Court held that the Free Speech Clause does not allow a public university to exclude a student group from the benefits of the student activities fund on account of the religious viewpoint the group expresses. In this part of the opinion, the Court addresses whether funding the student group is a violation of the Establishment Clause. The lower court had held that the Free Speech and Establishment Clauses led to opposite results, and that Establishment prevailed over Speech.—Editors]

■ JUSTICE KENNEDY delivered the opinion of the Court.

III

. . . The Court of Appeals ruled that withholding SAF support from Wide Awake contravened the Speech Clause of the First Amendment, but proceeded to hold that the University's action was justified by the necessity of avoiding a violation of the Establishment Clause, an interest it found compelling. Recognizing that this Court has regularly "sanctioned awards of direct nonmonetary benefits to religious groups where government has created open fora to which all similarly situated organizations are invited," *Widmar*, 454 U.S. at 257, the Fourth Circuit asserted that direct monetary subsidization of religious organizations and projects is "a beast of an entirely different color." The court declared that the Establishment Clause would not permit the use of public funds to support "a specifically religious activity in an otherwise substantially secular setting." It reasoned that because Wide Awake is "a journal pervasively devoted to the discussion and advancement of an avowedly Christian theological and personal philosophy," the University's provision of SAF funds for its publication would "send an unmistakably clear signal that the University of Virginia supports Christian values and wishes to promote the wide promulgation of such values." . . .

A central lesson of our decisions is that a significant factor in upholding governmental programs in the face of Establishment Clause attack is their neutrality towards religion. We have decided a series of cases addressing the receipt of government benefits where religion or religious views are implicated in some degree. The first case in our modern Establishment Clause jurisprudence was *Everson v. Board of Ed. of Ewing*, 330 U.S. 1 (1947). There we cautioned that in enforcing the prohibition against laws respecting establishment of religion, we must "be sure that we do not inadvertently prohibit [the government] from extending its general state law benefits to all its citizens without regard to their religious belief." We have held that the guarantee of neutrality is respected, not offended, when the government, following neutral criteria and evenhanded policies, extends benefits to recipients whose ideologies and viewpoints, including religious ones, are broad and diverse. [*Mueller v. Allen*; *Widmar*.] More than once have we rejected the position that the Establishment Clause even justifies, much less requires, a refusal to extend free speech rights to religious speakers who participate in broad-reaching government programs neutral in design.

The governmental program here is neutral toward religion. There is no suggestion that the University created it to advance religion or adopted some ingenious device with the purpose of aiding a religious cause. The object of the SAF is to open a forum for speech and to support various student enterprises, including the publication of newspapers, in recognition of the diversity and creativity of student life. The University's SAF Guidelines have a separate classification for, and do not make third-party payments on behalf of, "religious organizations," which are those "whose purpose is to practice a devotion to an acknowledged ultimate reality or deity." The category of support here is for "student news, information, opinion, entertainment, or academic communications media groups," of which Wide Awake was 1 of 15 in the 1990 school year. WAP did not seek a subsidy because of its Christian editorial viewpoint; it sought funding as a student journal, which it was.

The neutrality of the program distinguishes the student fees from a tax levied for the direct support of a church or group of churches. A tax of that sort, of course, would run contrary to Establishment Clause concerns dating from the earliest days of the Republic. The apprehensions of our predecessors involved the levying of taxes upon the public for the sole and exclusive purpose of establishing and supporting specific sects. The exaction here, by contrast, is a student activity fee designed to reflect the reality that student life in its many dimensions includes the necessity of wide-ranging speech and inquiry and that student expression is an integral part of the University's educational mission. The fee is mandatory, and we do not have before us the question whether an objecting student has the First Amendment right to demand a pro rata return to the extent the fee is expended for speech to which he or she does not subscribe. We must treat it, then, as an exaction upon the students. But the $14 paid each semester by the students is not a general tax designed to raise revenue for the University. The SAF cannot be used for unlimited purposes, much less the illegitimate purpose of supporting one religion. Much like the arrangement in *Widmar,* the money goes to a special fund from which any group of students with CIO status can draw for purposes consistent with the University's educational mission; and to the extent the student is interested in speech, withdrawal is permitted to cover the whole spectrum of speech, whether it manifests a religious view, an antireligious view, or neither. Our decision, then, cannot be read as addressing an expenditure from a general tax fund. Here, the disbursements from the fund go to private contractors for the cost of printing that which is protected under the Speech Clause of the First Amendment. This is a far cry from a general public assessment designed and effected to provide financial support for a church.

Government neutrality is apparent in the State's overall scheme in a further meaningful respect. The program respects the critical difference "between *government* speech endorsing religion, which the Establishment Clause forbids, and *private* speech endorsing religion, which the Free Speech and Free Exercise Clauses protect." In this case, "the government has not fostered or encouraged" any mistaken impression that the student newspapers speak for the University. The University has taken pains to disassociate itself from the private speech involved in this case. The Court of Appeals' apparent concern that Wide Awake's religious orientation would be attributed to the University is not a plausible fear, and there is no real likelihood that the speech in question is being either endorsed or coerced by the State.

The Court of Appeals (and the dissent) are correct to extract from our decisions the principle that we have recognized special Establishment

Clause dangers where the government makes direct money payments to sectarian institutions. The error is not in identifying the principle, but in believing that it controls this case. Even assuming that WAP is no different from a church and that its speech is the same as the religious exercises conducted in *Widmar* (two points much in doubt), the Court of Appeals decided a case that was, in essence, not before it, and the dissent would have us do the same. We do not confront a case where, even under a neutral program that includes nonsectarian recipients, the government is making direct money payments to an institution or group that is engaged in religious activity. Neither the Court of Appeals nor the dissent, we believe, takes sufficient cognizance of the undisputed fact that no public funds flow directly to WAP's coffers.

It does not violate the Establishment Clause for a public university to grant access to its facilities on a religion-neutral basis to a wide spectrum of student groups, including groups that use meeting rooms for sectarian activities, accompanied by some devotional exercises. [*Widmar.*] This is so even where the upkeep, maintenance, and repair of the facilities attributed to those uses are paid from a student activities fund to which students are required to contribute. [*Widmar.*] The government usually acts by spending money. Even the provision of a meeting room, as in *Mergens* and *Widmar*, involved governmental expenditure, if only in the form of electricity and heating or cooling costs. The error made by the Court of Appeals, as well as by the dissent, lies in focusing on the money that is undoubtedly expended by the government, rather than on the nature of the benefit received by the recipient. If the expenditure of governmental funds is prohibited whenever those funds pay for a service that is, pursuant to a religion-neutral program, used by a group for sectarian purposes, then *Widmar, Mergens,* and *Lamb's Chapel* would have to be overruled. Given our holdings in these cases, it follows that a public university may maintain its own computer facility and give student groups access to that facility, including the use of the printers, on a religion neutral, say first-come-first-served, basis. If a religious student organization obtained access on that religion-neutral basis and used a computer to compose or a printer or copy machine to print speech with a religious content or viewpoint, the State's action in providing the group with access would no more violate the Establishment Clause than would giving those groups access to an assembly hall. There is no difference in logic or principle, and no difference of constitutional significance, between a school using its funds to operate a facility to which students have access, and a school paying a third-party contractor to operate the facility on its behalf. The latter occurs here. The University provides printing services to a broad spectrum of student newspapers qualified as CIO's by reason of their officers and membership. Any benefit to religion is incidental to the government's provision of secular services for secular purposes on a religion-neutral basis. Printing is a routine, secular, and recurring attribute of student life.

By paying outside printers, the University in fact attains a further degree of separation from the student publication, for it avoids the duties of supervision, escapes the costs of upkeep, repair, and replacement attributable to student use, and has a clear record of costs. As a result, and as in *Widmar,* the University can charge the SAF, and not the taxpayers as a whole, for the discrete activity in question. It would be formalistic for us to say that the University must forfeit these advantages and provide the services itself in order to comply with the Establishment Clause. It is, of course, true that if the State pays a church's bills it is subsidizing it, and we must guard against this abuse. That is not a danger here, based on the considerations we have advanced and for the additional reason that the student publication is not a religious institution, at least in the usual sense of that term as used in our case law, and it is not a religious organization as used in the University's own regulations. It is instead a publication involved in a pure forum for the expression of ideas, ideas that would be both incomplete and chilled were the Constitution to be interpreted to require that state officials and courts scan the publication to ferret out views that principally manifest a belief in a divine being.

Were the dissent's view to become law, it would require the University, in order to avoid a constitutional violation, to scrutinize the content of student speech, lest the expression in question—speech otherwise protected by the Constitution—contain too great a religious content. The dissent, in fact, anticipates such censorship as "crucial" in distinguishing between "works characterized by the evangelism of Wide Awake and writing that merely happens to express views that a given religion might approve." That eventuality raises the specter of governmental censorship, to ensure that all student writings and publications meet some baseline standard of secular orthodoxy. To impose that standard on student speech at a university is to imperil the very sources of free speech and expression. As we recognized in *Widmar*, official censorship would be far more inconsistent with the Establishment Clause's dictates than would governmental provision of secular printing services on a religion-blind basis.

"[T]he dissent fails to establish that the distinction [between 'religious' speech and speech 'about' religion] has intelligible content. There is no indication when 'singing hymns, reading scripture, and teaching biblical principles' cease to be 'singing, teaching, and reading'—all apparently forms of 'speech,' despite their religious subject matter—and become unprotected 'worship.' . . .

"[E]ven if the distinction drew an arguably principled line, it is highly doubtful that it would lie within the judicial competence to administer. Merely to draw the distinction would require the university—and ultimately the courts—to inquire into the significance of words and practices to different religious faiths, and in varying circumstances by the same faith. Such inquiries would tend inevitably to entangle the State with religion in a manner forbidden by our cases. *E.g., Walz v. Tax Comm'n of City of New York,* 397 U.S. 664 (1970).

To obey the Establishment Clause, it was not necessary for the University to deny eligibility to student publications because of their viewpoint. The neutrality commanded of the State by the separate Clauses of the First Amendment was compromised by the University's course of action. The viewpoint discrimination inherent in the University's regulation required public officials to scan and interpret student publications to discern their underlying philosophic assumptions respecting religious theory and belief. That course of action was a denial of the right of free speech and would risk fostering a pervasive bias or hostility to religion, which could undermine the very neutrality the Establishment Clause requires. There is no Establishment Clause violation in the University's honoring its duties under the Free Speech Clause.

■ JUSTICE O'CONNOR, concurring.

. . . The nature of the dispute does not admit of categorical answers, nor should any be inferred from the Court's decision today. Instead, certain considerations specific to the program at issue lead me to conclude that by providing the same assistance to Wide Awake that it does to other publications, the University would not be endorsing the magazine's religious perspective.

First, the student organizations, at the University's insistence, remain strictly independent of the University . . . And the agreement requires that student organizations include in every letter, contract, publication, or other written materials [a] disclaimer. . . . Any reader of Wide Awake would be on notice of the publication's independence from the University.

Second, financial assistance is distributed in a manner that ensures its use only for permissible purposes. A student organization seeking assistance must submit disbursement requests; if approved, the funds are paid directly to the third-party vendor and do not pass through the organization's coffers. This safeguard . . . ensures that the funds are used only to further the University's purpose in maintaining a free and robust marketplace of ideas, from whatever perspective. This feature also makes this case analogous to a school providing equal access to a generally available printing press (or other physical facilities) and unlike a block grant to religious organizations.

Third, assistance is provided to the religious publication in a context that makes improbable any perception of government endorsement of the religious message. Wide Awake does not exist in a vacuum. It competes with 15 other magazines and newspapers for advertising and readership. The widely divergent viewpoints of these many purveyors of opinion, all supported on an equal basis by the University, significantly diminishes the danger that the message of any one publication is perceived as endorsed by the University. Besides the general news publications, for example, the University has provided support to The Yellow Journal, a humor magazine that has targeted Christianity as a subject of satire, and Al–Salam, a publication to "promote a better understanding of Islam to the University Community." Given this wide array of nonreligious, antireligious and competing religious viewpoints in the forum supported by the University, any perception that the University endorses one particular viewpoint would be illogical. This is not the harder case where religious speech threatens to dominate the forum . . .

The Court's decision today therefore neither trumpets the supremacy of the neutrality principle nor signals the demise of the funding prohibition in Establishment Clause jurisprudence. As I observed last Term, "[e]xperience proves that the Establishment Clause, like the Free Speech Clause, cannot easily be reduced to a single test." *Kiryas Joel*, 512 U.S. at 720 (opinion concurring in part and concurring in judgment). When bedrock principles collide, they test the limits of categorical obstinacy and expose the flaws and dangers of a Grand Unified Theory that may turn out to be neither grand nor unified. The Court today does only what courts must do in many Establishment Clause cases—focus on specific features of a particular government action to ensure that it does not violate the Constitution. By withholding from Wide Awake assistance that the University provides generally to all other student publications, the University has discriminated on the basis of the magazine's religious viewpoint in violation of the Free Speech Clause. And particular features of the University's program—such as the explicit disclaimer, the disbursement of funds directly to third-party vendors, the vigorous nature of the forum at issue, and the possibility for objecting students to opt out—convince me that providing such assistance in this case would not carry the danger of impermissible use of public funds to endorse Wide Awake's religious message.

Subject to these comments, I join the opinion of the Court.

■ [The concurring opinion of JUSTICE THOMAS is omitted.]

■ JUSTICE SOUTER, with whom JUSTICE STEVENS, JUSTICE GINSBURG, and JUSTICE BREYER join, dissenting.

The Court today, for the first time, approves direct funding of core religious activities by an arm of the State . . . I would hold that the University's refusal to support petitioners' religious activities is compelled by the Establishment Clause. . . .

The Court's difficulties will be all the more clear after a closer look at Wide Awake than the majority opinion affords. The character of the magazine is candidly disclosed on the opening page of the first issue, where the editor-in-chief announces Wide Awake's mission in a letter to the readership signed, "Love in Christ": it is "to challenge Christians to live, in word and deed, according to the faith they proclaim and to encourage students to consider what a personal relationship with Jesus Christ means." App. 45. The masthead of every issue bears St. Paul's exhortation, that "[t]he hour has come for you to awake from your slumber, because our salvation is nearer now than when we first believed. Romans 13:11."

Each issue of Wide Awake contained in the record makes good on the editor's promise and echoes the Apostle's call to accept salvation: "The only way to salvation through Him is by confessing and repenting of sin. It is the Christian's duty to make sinners aware of their need for salvation. Thus, Christians must confront and condemn sin, or else they fail in their duty of love." Mourad & Prince, A Love/Hate Relationship, Nov./Dec. 1990, p. 3 . . . " 'Go into all the world and preach the good news to all creation.' (Mark 16:15) The Great Commission is the prime-directive for our lives as Christians. . . ." Liu, Christianity and the Five-legged Stool, Sept./Oct. 1991, p. 3.

"The Spirit provides access to an intimate relationship with the Lord of the Universe, awakens our minds to comprehend spiritual truth and empowers us to serve as effective ambassadors for the Lord Jesus in our earthly lives." Buterbaugh, A Spiritual Advantage, Mar./Apr. 1991, p. 21.

There is no need to quote further from articles of like tenor, but one could examine such other examples as religious poetry, religious textual analysis and commentary, and instruction on religious practice . . .

This writing . . . is straightforward exhortation to enter into a relationship with God as revealed in Jesus Christ, and to satisfy a series of moral obligations derived from the teachings of Jesus Christ . . .

Using public funds for the direct subsidization of preaching the word is categorically forbidden under the Establishment Clause, and if the Clause was meant to accomplish nothing else, it was meant to bar this use of public money . . . Four years before the First Congress proposed the First Amendment, Madison gave his opinion on the legitimacy of using public funds for religious purposes, in the Memorial and Remonstrance Against Religious Assessments, which played the central role in ensuring the defeat of the Virginia tax assessment bill in 1786 and framed the debate upon which the Religion Clauses stand: "Who does not see that . . . the same authority which can force a citizen to contribute three pence only of his property for the support of any one establishment, may force him to conform to any other establishment in all cases whatsoever?" . . .

Why does the Court not apply this clear law to these clear facts and conclude, as I do, that the funding scheme here is a clear constitutional violation? The answer must be in part that the Court fails to confront the evidence set out in the preceding section. Throughout its opinion, the Court refers uninformatively to Wide Awake's "Christian viewpoint," or its "religious perspective[.]" . . . The Court does not quote the magazine's adoption of Saint Paul's exhortation to awaken to the nearness of salvation, or any of its articles enjoining readers to accept Jesus Christ, or the religious verses, or the religious textual analyses, or the suggested prayers. And so it is easy for the Court to lose sight of what the University students and the Court of Appeals found so obvious, and to blanch the patently and frankly evangelistic character of the magazine by unrevealing allusions to religious points of view . . . This is a flat violation of the Establishment Clause. . . .

––––––––––

Having read these cases, what is your opinion? Does the government violate the Establishment Clause when it extends aid neutrally to a broad class of beneficiaries, based on criteria unrelated to religion? Does the government violate the Free Exercise Clause when it prohibits conduct pursuant to neutral and generally applicable laws? What rules best serve the interests of religious freedom? What rules best comport with the text and history of the Religion Clauses?

[*Assignment 56*]

III. THE SECOND AND THIRD AMENDMENTS

> *Amendment II: A well regulated Militia, being necessary to the security of a free State, the right of the people to keep and bear Arms, shall not be infringed.*
>
> *Amendment III: No Soldier shall, in time of peace be quartered in any house, without the consent of the Owner, nor in time of war, but in a manner to be prescribed by law.*

The Second Amendment has generated much interpretive debate but little in the way of judicial decisions. The Supreme Court's first major case in this area did not come until *District of Columbia v. Heller*, 128 S. Ct. 2783 (2008). The Third Amendment has generated essentially no interpretive debate or controversy whatsoever: its language and purpose have evidently been so clear, and its resolution of the problem to which it was directed so complete, that it is one of those provisions of the Constitution that has proved successful enough to be ignored. The two amendments share a slight but definite connection, in that both protect rights that early Americans thought essential protections against the dangers of national military power.

The Second Amendment presents fascinating interpretive questions. Consider the language of the amendment carefully. The Second Amendment is somewhat unusual in that it contains a "purpose" statement as a preamble of sorts to its substantive statement of the "right of the people to keep and bear arms." Does this purpose limit the substantive content of the right? Or does it merely state a reason for recognizing the right? If the former, the right to keep and bear arms might be thought limited to potential militia service. If the latter, the right to keep and bear arms is a right to keep and bear arms for any lawful purpose, including hunting and defense of home, as well as defense of the community. Is the right to "keep and bear arms" an individual right or a collective right of the states? As Akhil Amar notes, the text contains some important clues, but they do not necessarily all point in the same direction:

> The states-rights reading slights the fact that the amendment's actual command language—"shall not be infringed"—appeared in the second clause, which enunciated a right of "the people" and not "the States." Surely the Tenth Amendment, which contradistinguished "the States" and "the people" made clear that these two phrases were not identical and that the Founders knew how to say "States" when they meant states. . . . But the individual-rights reading must contend with textual embarrassments of its own. The amendment announced a right of "the people" collectively rather than of "persons" individually. Also, it used a distinctly military phrase: "bear Arms."

Akhil Reed Amar, AMERICA'S CONSTITUTION: A BIOGRAPHY 322 (2005).

For the generation that ratified the Second Amendment, two historical lessons about an armed populace were prominent. First, in seventeenth century England, the Stuart kings came to be associated in the public mind with absolutism and with standing armies. They were ultimately overthrown and executed when ordinary English citizens and nobles rose in armed revolt. After the overthrow of James II, the last Stuart king, the English Bill of Rights of 1689 explicitly forbade standing armies and it guaranteed the right to keep and bear arms of the (Protestant) citizens of the realm. Second, the need for a popular check on royal tyranny was confirmed for the framers in the victories of the Massachusetts Militia over the royal army of King George III at Lexington and Concord. Once again, the colonists told themselves, a king, this time aided eventually by Hessian mercenaries, had tried to take away their freedom only to be stopped by an armed citizenry.

But are these historical lessons still determinative for what the Constitution means today? Should the Second Amendment be considered obsolete and read out of the Constitution? If not, how should its terms apply in a world not of muskets, but of AK–47 assault rifles, hand-held rocket launchers, and nuclear weapons? What are "arms"? Even on the (contestable) assumption that the amendment originally created a right of state governments and not a right of individual citizens forming the militia, does the Fourteenth Amendment give the people of each state a right to keep and bear arms as a check against the powers of state governments as well as federal? Does the Second Amendment's purpose-preamble answer any of these questions? Suppose the First Amendment began with a preamble like the Second's: "The right of the people to express views and ideas freely being essential to republican government, Congress shall make no law . . . abridging the freedom of speech or of the press. . . ." Would that make a difference in how the First Amendment should be interpreted?

Consider these questions as you read excerpts from *The Federalist* that suggest the historical context for the Second Amendment. That amendment was not, of course, part of the Constitution that Publius was writing about, yet Hamilton and Madison appear to contemplate the right to keep and bear arms—and the potential exercise of that right—as a check against an overreaching national government with a standing army. Next is presented the Supreme Court's first thorough discussion of the language and meaning of the Second Amendment, more than two centuries after the amendment was adopted. The question before the Court was whether the Second Amendment protects an individual right to keep and bear arms for purposes that extend beyond potential militia service. Did the Court get the answer right? Consider carefully the interpretive methodology of the opinions.

The Federalist No. 28

Alexander Hamilton, December 26, 1787

If the representatives of the people betray their constituents, there is then no resource left but in the exertion of that original right of self-defense which is paramount to all positive forms of government, and which against the usurpations of the national rulers may be exercised with infinitely better prospect of success than against those of the rulers of an individual state. In a single state, if the persons intrusted with supreme power become usurpers, the different parcels, subdivisions, or districts of which it consists, having no distinct government in each, can take no regular measures for defense. The citizens must rush tumultuously to arms, without concert, without system, without resource; except in their courage and despair. The usurpers, clothed with the forms of legal authority, can too often crush the opposition in embryo. The smaller the extent of the territory, the more difficult will it be for the people to form a regular or systematic plan of opposition, and the more easy will it be to defeat their early efforts. . . .

The obstacles to usurpation and the facilities of resistance increase with the increased extent of the state, provided the citizens understand their rights and are disposed to defend them. . . . But in a confederacy the people, without exaggeration, may be said to be entirely the masters of their own fate. Power being almost always the rival of power, the general government will at all times stand ready to check the usurpations of the state governments, and these will have the same disposition towards the general government. The people, by throwing themselves into either scale, will infallibly make it preponderate.

The Federalist No. 46

James Madison, January 29, 1788

But ambitious encroachments of the federal government on the authority of the State governments would not excite the opposition of a single State, or of a few States only. They would be signals of general alarm. Every government would espouse the common cause. A correspondence would be opened. Plans of resistance would be concerted. One spirit would animate and conduct the whole. The same combinations, in short, would result from an apprehension of the federal, as was produced by the dread of a foreign, yoke; and unless the projected innovations should be voluntarily renounced, the same appeal to a trial of force would be made in the one case as was made in the other. . . .

The only refuge left for those who prophesy the downfall of the State governments is the visionary supposition that the federal government may previously accumulate a military force for the projects of ambition. . . . Extravagant as the supposition is, let it, however, be made. Let a regular army, fully equal to the resources of the country, be formed; and let it be entirely at the devotion of the federal government; still it would not be going too far to say that the State governments with the people on their side would be able to repel the danger. The highest number to which, according to their best computation, a standing army can be carried in any country does not exceed one hundredth part of the whole number of souls; or one twenty-fifth part of the number able to bear arms. . . . To these would be opposed a militia amounting to near half a million of citizens with arms in their hands, officered by men chosen from among themselves, fighting for their common liberties and united and conducted by governments possessing their affections and confidence. It may well be doubted whether a militia thus circumstanced could ever be conquered by such a proportion of regular troops. Those who are best acquainted with the late successful resistance of this country against the British arms will be most inclined to deny the possibility of it. Besides the advantage of being armed, which the Americans possess over the people of almost every other nation, the existence of subordinate governments, to which the people are attached and by which the militia officers are appointed, forms a barrier against the enterprises of ambition, more insurmountable than any which a simple government of any form can admit of. Notwithstanding the military establishments in the several kingdoms of Europe, . . . the governments are afraid to trust the people with arms. . . . But were the people to possess the additional advantages of local governments chosen by themselves, who could collect the national will and direct the national force, and of officers appointed out of the militia by these governments and attached both to them and to the militia, it may be affirmed with the greatest assurance that the throne of every tyranny in Europe would be speedily overturned in spite of the legions which surround it. . . .

District of Columbia v. Heller

128 S. Ct. 2783 (2008)

■ JUSTICE SCALIA delivered the opinion of the Court.

We consider whether a District of Columbia prohibition on the possession of usable handguns in the home violates the Second Amendment to the Constitution.

I

The District of Columbia generally prohibits the possession of handguns. It is a crime to carry an unregistered firearm, and the registration of handguns is prohibited. Wholly apart from that prohibition, no person may carry a handgun without a license, but the chief of police may issue licenses for 1–year periods. District of Columbia law also requires residents to keep their lawfully owned firearms, such as registered long guns, "unloaded and dissembled or bound by a trigger lock or similar device" unless they are located in a place of business or are being used for lawful recreational activities.

Respondent Dick Heller is a D.C. special police officer authorized to carry a handgun while on duty at the Federal Judicial Center. He applied for a registration certificate for a handgun that he wished to keep at home, but the District refused. He thereafter filed a lawsuit in the Federal District Court for the District of Columbia seeking, on Second Amendment grounds, to enjoin the city from enforcing the bar on the registration of handguns, the licensing requirement insofar as it prohibits the carrying of a firearm in the home without a license, and the trigger-lock requirement insofar as it prohibits the use of "functional firearms within the home." . . .

II

We turn first to the meaning of the Second Amendment.

The Second Amendment provides: "A well regulated Militia, being necessary to the security of a free State, the right of the people to keep and bear Arms, shall not be infringed." In interpreting this text, we are guided by the principle that "[t]he Constitution was written to be understood by the voters; its words and phrases were used in their normal and ordinary as distinguished from technical meaning." *United States v. Sprague,* 282 U.S. 716, 731 (1931). Normal meaning may of course include an idiomatic meaning, but it excludes secret or technical meanings that would not have been known to ordinary citizens in the founding generation.

. . . Petitioners and today's dissenting Justices believe that [the Amendment] protects only the right to possess and carry a firearm in connection with militia service. Respondent argues that it protects an individual right to possess a firearm unconnected with service in a militia, and to use that arm for traditionally lawful purposes, such as self-defense within the home.

The Second Amendment is naturally divided into two parts: its prefatory clause and its operative clause. The former does not limit the latter grammatically, but rather announces a purpose. The Amendment could be rephrased, "Because a well regulated Militia is necessary to the security of a free State, the right of the people to keep and bear Arms shall not be infringed." Although this structure of the Second Amendment is unique in our Constitution, other legal documents of the founding era, particularly individual-rights provisions of state constitutions, commonly included a prefatory statement of purpose. See generally Volokh, The Commonplace Second Amendment, 73 N.Y.U. L. Rev. 793, 814–821 (1998).

Logic demands that there be a link between the stated purpose and the command. The Second Amendment would be nonsensical if it read, "A well regulated Militia, being necessary to the security of a free State, the right of the people to petition for redress of grievances shall not be infringed." That requirement of logical connection may cause a prefatory clause to resolve an ambiguity in the operative clause. . . . But apart from that clarifying function, a prefatory clause does not limit or expand the scope of the operative clause. . . . Therefore, while we will begin our textual analysis with the operative clause, we will return to the prefatory clause to ensure that our reading of the operative clause is consistent with the announced purpose.[4]

---

[4] Alexander Hamilton was opposed to a bill of rights on the ground that it was unnecessary because the Federal Government was a government of delegated powers and it was not granted the power to intrude upon fundamental personal rights. The Federalist, No. 84. He also argued, "I go further, and affirm that bills of rights, in the sense and in the extent in which they are contended for, are not only unnecessary in the proposed constitution, but would even be dangerous. They would contain various exceptions to powers which are not granted; and on this very account, would afford a colourable pretext to claim more than were granted. For why declare that things shall not be done which there is no power to do? Why for instance, should it be said, that the liberty of the press shall not be restrained, when no power is given by which restrictions may be imposed? I will not contend that such a provision would confer a regulating power; but it is evident that it would furnish, to men disposed to usurp, a plausible pretence for claiming that power." *Id.,* at 579. The Ninth Amendment and the Tenth Amendment, which provides, "The powers not delegated to the United States by the Constitu-

1. Operative Clause.

a. "Right of the People." The first salient feature of the operative clause is that it codifies a "right of the people." The unamended Constitution and the Bill of Rights use the phrase "right of the people" two other times, in the First Amendment's Assembly and Petition Clause and in the Fourth Amendment's Search and Seizure Clause. The Ninth Amendment uses very similar terminology ("The enumeration in the Constitution, of certain rights, shall not be construed to deny or disparage others retained by the people"). All three of these instances unambiguously refer to individual rights, not "collective" rights, or rights that may be exercised only through participation in some corporate body.

Three provisions of the Constitution refer to "the people" in a context other than "rights"—the famous preamble ("We the people"), § 2 of Article I (providing that "the people" will choose members of the House), and the Tenth Amendment (providing that those powers not given the Federal Government remain with "the States" or "the people"). Those provisions arguably refer to "the people" acting collectively—but they deal with the exercise or reservation of powers, not rights. Nowhere else in the Constitution does a "right" attributed to "the people" refer to anything other than an individual right.

What is more, in all six other provisions of the Constitution that mention "the people," the term unambiguously refers to all members of the political community, not an unspecified subset. As we said in *United States v. Verdugo–Urquidez,* 494 U.S. 259, 265 (1990):

> "[T]he people" seems to have been a term of art employed in select parts of the Constitution. . . . [Its uses] sugges[t] that "the people" protected by the Fourth Amendment, and by the First and Second Amendments, and to whom rights and powers are reserved in the Ninth and Tenth Amendments, refers to a class of persons who are part of a national community or who have otherwise developed sufficient connection with this country to be considered part of that community.

This contrasts markedly with the phrase "the militia" in the prefatory clause. As we will describe below, the "militia" in colonial America consisted of a subset of "the people"—those who were male, able bodied, and within a certain age range. Reading the Second Amendment as protecting only the right to "keep and bear Arms" in an organized militia therefore fits poorly with the operative clause's description of the holder of that right as "the people."

We start therefore with a strong presumption that the Second Amendment right is exercised individually and belongs to all Americans.

b. "Keep and bear Arms." We move now from the holder of the right—"the people"—to the substance of the right: "to keep and bear Arms."

Before addressing the verbs "keep" and "bear," we interpret their object: "Arms." The 18th–century meaning is no different from the meaning today. The 1773 edition of Samuel Johnson's dictionary defined "arms" as "weapons of offence, or armour of defence." 1 Dictionary of the English Language 107 (4th ed.) (hereinafter Johnson). Timothy Cunningham's important 1771 legal dictionary defined "arms" as "any thing that a man

---

tion, nor prohibited by it to the States, are reserved to the States respectively, or to the people," were apparently also designed in part to meet the above-quoted argument of Hamilton.

wears for his defence, or takes into his hands, or useth in wrath to cast at or strike another." 1 A New and Complete Law Dictionary (1771).

The term was applied, then as now, to weapons that were not specifically designed for military use and were not employed in a military capacity. . . . Some have made the argument, bordering on the frivolous, that only those arms in existence in the 18th century are protected by the Second Amendment. We do not interpret constitutional rights that way. Just as the First Amendment protects modern forms of communications, and the Fourth Amendment applies to modern forms of search, the Second Amendment extends, prima facie, to all instruments that constitute bearable arms, even those that were not in existence at the time of the founding. . . .

The phrase "keep arms" was not prevalent in the written documents of the founding period that we have found, but there are a few examples, all of which favor viewing the right to "keep Arms" as an individual right unconnected with militia service. . . . "Keep arms" was simply a common way of referring to possessing arms, for militiamen *and everyone else.*

At the time of the founding, as now, to "bear" meant to "carry." See Johnson 161. When used with "arms," however, the term has a meaning that refers to carrying for a particular purpose—confrontation. . . . From our review of founding-era sources, we conclude that this natural meaning was also the meaning that "bear arms" had in the 18th century. In numerous instances, "bear arms" was unambiguously used to refer to the carrying of weapons outside of an organized militia. The most prominent examples are those most relevant to the Second Amendment: Nine state constitutional provisions written in the 18th century or the first two decades of the 19th, which enshrined a right of citizens to "bear arms in defense of themselves and the state" or "bear arms in defense of himself and the state." It is clear from those formulations that "bear arms" did not refer only to carrying a weapon in an organized military unit. That was also the interpretation of those state constitutional provisions adopted by pre-Civil War state courts. . . .

The phrase "bear Arms" also had at the time of the founding an idiomatic meaning that was significantly different from its natural meaning: "to serve as a soldier, do military service, fight" or "to wage war." See Linguists' Brief 18; *post,* at 2827–2828 (STEVENS, J., dissenting). But it *unequivocally* bore that idiomatic meaning only when followed by the preposition "against," which was in turn followed by the target of the hostilities. See 2 Oxford 21. (That is how, for example, our Declaration of Independence ¶ 28, used the phrase: "He has constrained our fellow Citizens taken Captive on the high Seas to bear Arms against their Country"). . . .

In any event, the meaning of "bear arms" that petitioners and JUSTICE STEVENS propose is *not even* the (sometimes) idiomatic meaning. Rather, they manufacture a hybrid definition, whereby "bear arms" connotes the actual carrying of arms (and therefore is not really an idiom) but only in the service of an organized militia. No dictionary has ever adopted that definition, and we have been apprised of no source that indicates that it carried that meaning at the time of the founding. But it is easy to see why petitioners and the dissent are driven to the hybrid definition. . . . [Under the dissent's reading], the phrase "keep and bear Arms" would be incoherent. The word "Arms" would have two different meanings at once: "weapons" (as the object of "keep") and (as the object of "bear") one-half of an idiom. It would be rather like saying "He filled and kicked the bucket" to mean "He filled the bucket and died." Grotesque.

Petitioners justify their limitation of "bear arms" to the military context by pointing out the unremarkable fact that it was often used in that context. . . . [T]he fact that the phrase was commonly used in a particular context does not show that it is limited to that context, and, in any event, we have given many sources where the phrase was used in nonmilitary contexts. . . .

JUSTICE STEVENS places great weight on James Madison's inclusion of a conscientious-objector clause in his original draft of the Second Amendment: "but no person religiously scrupulous of bearing arms, shall be compelled to render military service in person." . . . It is always perilous to derive the meaning of an adopted provision from another provision deleted in the drafting process. In any case, what JUSTICE STEVENS would conclude from the deleted provision does not follow. . . . [T]he most natural interpretation of Madison's deleted text is that those opposed to carrying weapons for potential violent confrontation would not be "compelled to render military service," in which such carrying would be required.

Finally, JUSTICE STEVENS suggests that "keep and bear Arms" was some sort of term of art, presumably akin to "hue and cry" or "cease and desist." (This suggestion usefully evades the problem that there is no evidence whatsoever to support a military reading of "keep arms.") JUSTICE STEVENS believes that the unitary meaning of "keep and bear Arms" is established by the Second Amendment's calling it a "right" (singular) rather than "rights" (plural). There is nothing to this. State constitutions of the founding period routinely grouped multiple (related) guarantees under a singular "right," and the First Amendment protects the "right [singular] of the people peaceably to assemble, and to petition the Government for a redress of grievances." . . .

c. Meaning of the Operative Clause. Putting all of these textual elements together, we find that they guarantee the individual right to possess and carry weapons in case of confrontation. This meaning is strongly confirmed by the historical background of the Second Amendment. We look to this because it has always been widely understood that the Second Amendment, like the First and Fourth Amendments, codified a *pre-existing* right. The very text of the Second Amendment implicitly recognizes the pre-existence of the right and declares only that it "shall not be infringed."

Between the Restoration and the Glorious Revolution, the Stuart Kings Charles II and James II succeeded in using select militias loyal to them to suppress political dissidents, in part by disarming their opponents. . . . These experiences caused Englishmen to be extremely wary of concentrated military forces run by the state and to be jealous of their arms. They accordingly obtained an assurance from William and Mary, in the Declaration of Right (which was codified as the English Bill of Rights), that Protestants would never be disarmed [.] . . . This right has long been understood to be the predecessor to our Second Amendment. It was clearly an individual right, having nothing whatever to do with service in a militia. . . .

By the time of the founding, the right to have arms had become fundamental for English subjects. Blackstone, whose works, we have said, "constituted the preeminent authority on English law for the founding generation," cited the arms provision of the Bill of Rights as one of the fundamental rights of Englishmen. See 1 Blackstone 136, 139–140 (1765). His description of it cannot possibly be thought to tie it to militia or military service. It was, he said, "the natural right of resistance and self-preservation," and "the right of having and using arms for self-preservation and defence." Other contemporary authorities concurred. Thus, the right secured in 1689 as a result of the Stuarts' abuses was by the time of the founding understood to be an individual right protecting against both public and private violence.

And, of course, what the Stuarts had tried to do to their political enemies, George III had tried to do to the colonists. In the tumultuous decades of the 1760's and 1770's, the Crown began to disarm the inhabitants of the most rebellious areas. That provoked polemical reactions by Americans invoking their rights as Englishmen to keep arms. They understood the right to enable individuals to defend themselves. As the most important early American edition of Blackstone's Commentaries (by the law professor and former Antifederalist St. George Tucker) made clear in the notes to the description of the arms right, Americans understood the "right of self-preservation" as permitting a citizen to "repe[l] force by force" when "the intervention of society in his behalf, may be too late to prevent an injury." 1 Blackstone's Commentaries 145–146, n. 42 (1803).

There seems to us no doubt, on the basis of both text and history, that the Second Amendment conferred an individual right to keep and bear arms. Of course the right was not unlimited, just as the First Amendment's right of free speech was not. Thus, we do not read the Second Amendment to protect the right of citizens to carry arms for *any* sort of confrontation, just as we do not read the First Amendment to protect the right of citizens to speak for *any purpose*. Before turning to limitations upon the individual right, however, we must determine whether the prefatory clause of the Second Amendment comports with our interpretation of the operative clause.

2. Prefatory Clause.

The prefatory clause reads: "A well regulated Militia, being necessary to the security of a free State. . . ."

a. "Well–Regulated Militia." In *United States v. Miller*, 307 U.S. 174, 179 (1939), we explained that "the Militia comprised all males physically capable of acting in concert for the common defense." That definition comports with founding-era sources.

Petitioners take a seemingly narrower view of the militia, stating that "[m]ilitias are the state- and congressionally-regulated military forces described in the Militia Clauses (art. I, § 8, cls. 15–16)." Although we agree with petitioners' interpretive assumption that "militia" means the same thing in Article I and the Second Amendment, we believe that petitioners identify the wrong thing, namely, the organized militia. Unlike armies and navies, which Congress is given the power to create . . ., the militia is assumed by Article I already to be *in existence.* . . . This is fully consistent with the ordinary definition of the militia as all able-bodied men. From that pool, Congress has plenary power to organize the units that will make up an effective fighting force. . . .

Finally, the adjective "well-regulated" implies nothing more than the imposition of proper discipline and training. *Cf.* Va. Declaration of Rights § 13 (1776), in 7 Thorpe 3812, 3814 (referring to "a well-regulated militia, composed of the body of the people, trained to arms").

b. "Security of a Free State." The phrase "security of a free state" meant "security of a free polity," not security of each of the several States as the dissent below argued. . . . It is true that the term "State" elsewhere in the Constitution refers to individual States, but the phrase "security of a free state" and close variations seem to have been terms of art in 18th–century political discourse, meaning a "free country" or free polity. Moreover, the other instances of "state" in the Constitution are typically accompanied by modifiers making clear that the reference is to the several States. . . .

There are many reasons why the militia was thought to be "necessary to the security of a free state." See 3 Story § 1890. First, of course, it is useful in repelling invasions and suppressing insurrections. Second, it renders large standing armies unnecessary—an argument that Alexander Hamilton made in favor of federal control over the militia. The Federalist No. 29. Third, when the able-bodied men of a nation are trained in arms and organized, they are better able to resist tyranny.

3. Relationship between Prefatory Clause and Operative Clause.

We reach the question, then: Does the preface fit with an operative clause that creates an individual right to keep and bear arms? It fits perfectly, once one knows the history that the founding generation knew and that we have described above. That history showed that the way tyrants had eliminated a militia consisting of all the able-bodied men was not by banning the militia but simply by taking away the people's arms, enabling a select militia or standing army to suppress political opponents. This is what had occurred in England that prompted codification of the right to have arms in the English Bill of Rights.

The debate with respect to the right to keep and bear arms, as with other guarantees in the Bill of Rights, was not over whether it was desirable (all agreed that it was) but over whether it needed to be codified in the Constitution. During the 1788 ratification debates, the fear that the federal government would disarm the people in order to impose rule through a standing army or select militia was pervasive in Antifederalist rhetoric. See, *e.g.,* Letters from The Federal Farmer III (Oct. 10, 1787), in 2 The Complete Anti–Federalist 234, 242 (H. Storing ed.1981). . . . Federalists responded that because Congress was given no power to abridge the ancient right of individuals to keep and bear arms, such a force could never oppress the people. It was understood across the political spectrum that the right helped to secure the ideal of a citizen militia, which might be necessary to oppose an oppressive military force if the constitutional order broke down.

It is therefore entirely sensible that the Second Amendment's prefatory clause announces the purpose for which the right was codified: to prevent elimination of the militia. The prefatory clause does not suggest that preserving the militia was the only reason Americans valued the ancient right; most undoubtedly thought it even more important for self-defense and hunting. But the threat that the new Federal Government would destroy the citizens' militia by taking away their arms was the reason that right—unlike some other English rights—was codified in a written Constitution. . . .

We now address how the Second Amendment was interpreted from immediately after its ratification through the end of the 19th century. Before proceeding, however, we take issue with JUSTICE STEVENS' equating of these sources with postenactment legislative history, a comparison that betrays a fundamental misunderstanding of a court's interpretive task. "Legislative history," of course, refers to the pre-enactment statements of those who drafted or voted for a law; it is considered persuasive by some, not because they reflect the general understanding of the disputed terms, but because the legislators who heard or read those statements presumably voted with that understanding. "Postenactment legislative history," a deprecatory contradiction in terms, refers to statements of those who drafted or voted for the law that are made after its enactment and hence could have had no effect on the congressional vote. It most certainly does not refer to the examination of a variety of legal and other sources to determine *the public understanding* of a legal text in the period after its enactment or ratification. That sort of inquiry is a critical tool of constitutional interpretation. As we will show, virtually all interpreters of the Second Amendment in the century after its enactment interpreted the Amendment as we do. . . .

[The majority opinion then examined post-ratification commentary, pre-Civil War case law, post-Civil War legislation, and post-Civil War commentators. Next it discussed two of the Court's Reconstruction Era precedents, United States v. Cruikshank and Presser v. Illinois.—Editors]

JUSTICE STEVENS places overwhelming reliance upon this Court's decision in *United States v. Miller*, 307 U.S. 174 (1939). "[H]undreds of judges," we are told, "have relied on the view of the Amendment we endorsed there," and "[e]ven if the textual and historical arguments on both side of the issue were evenly balanced, respect for the well-settled views of all of our predecessors on this Court, and for the rule of law itself . . . would prevent most jurists from endorsing such a dramatic upheaval in the law." And what is, according to JUSTICE STEVENS, the holding of *Miller* that demands such obeisance? That the Second Amendment "protects the right to keep and bear arms for certain military purposes, but that it does not curtail the legislature's power to regulate the nonmilitary use and ownership of weapons."

Nothing so clearly demonstrates the weakness of JUSTICE STEVENS' case. *Miller* did not hold that and cannot possibly be read to have held that. The judgment in the case upheld against a Second Amendment challenge two men's federal convictions for transporting an unregistered short-barreled shotgun in interstate commerce, in violation of the National Firearms Act. It is entirely clear that the Court's basis for saying that the Second Amendment did not apply was *not* that the defendants were "bear[ing] arms" not "for . . . military purposes" but for "nonmilitary use." Rather, it was that the *type of weapon at issue* was not eligible for Second Amendment protection: "In the absence of any evidence tending to show that the possession or use of a [short-barreled shotgun] at this time has some reasonable relationship to the preservation or efficiency of a well regulated militia, we cannot say that the Second Amendment guarantees the right to keep and bear *such an instrument*." 307 U.S., at 178 (emphasis added). "Certainly," the Court continued, "it is not within judicial notice that this weapon is any part of the ordinary military equipment or that its use could contribute to the common defense." Beyond that, the opinion provided no explanation of the content of the right.

This holding is not only consistent with, but positively suggests, that the Second Amendment confers an individual right to keep and bear arms (though only arms that "have some reasonable relationship to the preservation or efficiency of a well regulated militia"). Had the Court believed that the Second Amendment protects only those serving in the militia, it would have been odd to examine the character of the weapon rather than simply note that the two crooks were not militiamen. JUSTICE STEVENS can say again and again that *Miller* did "not turn on the difference between muskets and sawed-off shotguns, it turned, rather, on the basic difference between the military and nonmilitary use and possession of guns," but the words of the opinion prove otherwise. The most JUSTICE STEVENS can plausibly claim for *Miller* is that it declined to decide the nature of the Second Amendment right. *Miller* stands only for the proposition that the Second Amendment right, whatever its nature, extends only to certain types of weapons. It is particularly wrongheaded to read *Miller* for more than what it said, because the case did not even purport to be a thorough examination of the Second Amendment. . . .

We conclude that nothing in our precedents forecloses our adoption of the original understanding of the Second Amendment. It should be unsurprising that such a significant matter has been for so long judicially unresolved. For most of our history, the Bill of Rights was not thought applicable to the States, and the Federal Government did not significantly regulate the possession of firearms by law-abiding citizens. Other provisions of the Bill of Rights have similarly remained unilluminated for lengthy periods. This Court first held a law to violate the First Amendment's guarantee of freedom of speech in 1931, almost 150 years after the Amendment was ratified, and it was not until after World War II that we held a law invalid under the Establishment Clause. Even a question as basic as the scope of proscribable libel was not addressed by this Court until 1964, nearly two centuries after the founding. It is demonstrably not true that, as JUSTICE STEVENS claims, "for most of our history, the invalidity of Second–Amendment-based objections to firearms regulations has been well settled and uncontroversial." For most of our history the question did not present itself.

III

Like most rights, the right secured by the Second Amendment is not unlimited. From Blackstone through the 19th–century cases, commentators and courts routinely explained that the right was not a right to keep and carry any weapon whatsoever in any manner whatsoever and for whatever purpose. . . . Although we do not undertake an exhaustive historical analysis today of the full scope of the Second Amendment, nothing in our opinion should be taken to cast doubt on longstanding prohibitions on the possession of firearms by felons and the mentally ill, or laws forbidding the carrying of firearms in sensitive places such as schools and government buildings, or laws imposing conditions and qualifications on the commercial sale of arms.

We also recognize another important limitation on the right to keep and carry arms. *Miller* said, as we have explained, that the sorts of weapons protected were those "in common use at the time." 307 U.S., at 179. We think that limitation is fairly supported by the historical tradition of prohibiting the carrying of "dangerous and unusual weapons." See 4 Blackstone 148–149 (1769); 3 B. Wilson, Works of the Honourable James Wilson 79 (1804); J. Dunlap, The New–York Justice 8 (1815); C. Humphreys, A Compendium of the Common Law in Force in Kentucky 482 (1822).

It may be objected that if weapons that are most useful in military service—M–16 rifles and the like—may be banned, then the Second Amendment right is completely detached from the prefatory clause. But as we have said, the conception of the militia at the time of the Second Amendment's ratification was the body of all citizens capable of military service, who would bring the sorts of lawful weapons that they possessed at home to militia duty. It may well be true today that a militia, to be as effective as militias in the 18th century, would require sophisticated arms that are highly unusual in society at large. Indeed, it may be true that no amount of small arms could be useful against modern-day bombers and tanks. But the fact that modern developments have limited the degree of fit between the prefatory clause and the protected right cannot change our interpretation of the right.

IV

We turn finally to the law at issue here. As we have said, the law totally bans handgun possession in the home. It also requires that any lawful firearm in the home be disassembled or bound by a trigger lock at all times, rendering it inoperable.

As the quotations earlier in this opinion demonstrate, the inherent right of self-defense has been central to the Second Amendment right. The handgun ban amounts to a prohibition of an entire class of "arms" that is overwhelmingly chosen by American society for that lawful purpose. The prohibition extends, moreover, to the home, where the need for defense of self, family, and property is most acute. Under any of the standards of scrutiny that we have applied to enumerated constitutional rights, banning from the home "the most preferred firearm in the nation to 'keep' and use for protection of one's home and family" would fail constitutional muster. . . .

It is no answer to say, as petitioners do, that it is permissible to ban the possession of handguns so long as the possession of other firearms (*i.e.*, long guns) is allowed. It is enough to note, as we have observed, that the American people have considered the handgun to be the quintessential self-defense weapon. . . . Whatever the reason, handguns are the most popular weapon chosen by Americans for self-defense in the home, and a complete prohibition of their use is invalid.

We must also address the District's requirement (as applied to respondent's handgun) that firearms in the home be rendered and kept inoperable at all times. This makes it impossible for citizens to use them for the core lawful purpose of self-defense and is hence unconstitutional. . . .

[In his dissent,] JUSTICE BREYER . . . criticizes us for declining to establish a level of scrutiny for evaluating Second Amendment restrictions. He proposes, explicitly at least, none of the traditionally expressed levels (strict scrutiny, intermediate scrutiny, rational basis), but rather a judge-empowering "interest-balancing inquiry" that "asks whether the statute burdens a protected interest in a way or to an extent that is out of proportion to the statute's salutary effects upon other important governmental interests." After an exhaustive discussion of the arguments for and against gun control, JUSTICE BREYER arrives at his interest-balanced answer: because handgun violence is a problem, because the law is limited to an urban area, and because there were somewhat similar restrictions in the founding period (a false proposition that we have already discussed), the interest-balancing inquiry results in the constitutionality of the handgun ban. QED.

We know of no other enumerated constitutional right whose core protection has been subjected to a freestanding "interest-balancing" approach. The very enumeration of the right takes out of the hands of government— even the Third Branch of Government—the power to decide on a case-by-case basis whether the right is *really worth* insisting upon. A constitutional guarantee . . . is the very *product* of an interest-balancing by the people— which JUSTICE BREYER would now conduct for them anew. And whatever else [the Second Amendment] leaves to future evaluation, it surely elevates above all other interests the right of law-abiding, responsible citizens to use arms in defense of hearth and home.

[S]ince this case represents this Court's first in-depth examination of the Second Amendment, one should not expect it to clarify the entire field. . . . In sum, we hold that the District's ban on handgun possession in the home violates the Second Amendment, as does its prohibition against rendering any lawful firearm in the home operable for the purpose of immediate self-defense. Assuming that Heller is not disqualified from the exercise of Second Amendment rights, the District must permit him to register his handgun and must issue him a license to carry it in the home. . . .

We are aware of the problem of handgun violence in this country, and we take seriously the concerns raised by the many *amici* who believe that prohibition of handgun ownership is a solution. The Constitution leaves the District of Columbia a variety of tools for combating that problem, including some measures regulating handguns. But the enshrinement of constitutional rights necessarily takes certain policy choices off the table. These include the absolute prohibition of handguns held and used for self-defense in the home. Undoubtedly some think that the Second Amendment is outmoded in a society where our standing army is the pride of our Nation, where well-trained police forces provide personal security, and where gun violence is a serious problem. That is perhaps debatable, but what is not debatable is that it is not the role of this Court to pronounce the Second Amendment extinct.

■ JUSTICE STEVENS, with whom JUSTICE SOUTER, JUSTICE GINSBURG, and JUSTICE BREYER join, dissenting.

The question presented by this case is not whether the Second Amendment protects a "collective right" or an "individual right." Surely it protects a right that can be enforced by individuals. But a conclusion that the Second Amendment protects an individual right does not tell us anything about the scope of that right. . . . The text of the Amendment, its history, and our decision in *United States v. Miller,* 307 U.S. 174 (1939), provide a clear answer to that question.

The Second Amendment was adopted to protect the right of the people of each of the several States to maintain a well-regulated militia. It was a response to concerns raised during the ratification of the Constitution that the power of Congress to disarm the state militias and create a national standing army posed an intolerable threat to the sovereignty of the several States. Neither the text of the Amendment nor the arguments advanced by its proponents evidenced the slightest interest in limiting any legislature's authority to regulate private civilian uses of firearms. Specifically, there is no indication that the Framers of the Amendment intended to enshrine the common-law right of self-defense in the Constitution.

. . . The view of the Amendment we took in *Miller*—that it protects the right to keep and bear arms for certain military purposes, but that it does not curtail the Legislature's power to regulate the nonmilitary use and ownership of weapons—is both the most natural reading of the Amendment's text and the interpretation most faithful to the history of its adoption.

Since our decision in *Miller,* hundreds of judges have relied on the view of the Amendment we endorsed there. . . . In this dissent I shall first explain why our decision in *Miller* was faithful to the text of the Second Amendment and the purposes revealed in its drafting history. I shall then comment on the postratification history of the Amendment, which makes abundantly clear that the Amendment should not be interpreted as limiting the authority of Congress to regulate the use or possession of firearms for purely civilian purposes.

I

The text of the Second Amendment is brief. It provides: "A well regulated Militia, being necessary to the security of a free State, the right of the people to keep and bear Arms, shall not be infringed."

Three portions of that text merit special focus: the introductory language defining the Amendment's purpose, the class of persons encompassed within its reach, and the unitary nature of the right that it protects.

*"A well regulated Militia, being necessary
to the security of a free State"*

The preamble to the Second Amendment makes three important points. It identifies the preservation of the militia as the Amendment's purpose; it explains that the militia is necessary to the security of a free State; and it recognizes that the militia must be "well regulated." . . . While the need for state militias has not been a matter of significant public interest for almost two centuries, that fact should not obscure the contemporary concerns that animated the Framers. . . .

The preamble thus both sets forth the object of the Amendment and informs the meaning of the remainder of its text. Such text should not be treated as mere surplusage, for "[i]t cannot be presumed that any clause in the constitution is intended to be without effect." *Marbury v. Madison,* 1 Cranch 137, 174 (1803).

The Court today tries to denigrate the importance of this clause of the Amendment by beginning its analysis with the Amendment's operative provision and returning to the preamble merely "to ensure that our reading of the operative clause is consistent with the announced purpose." That is not how this Court ordinarily reads such texts, and it is not how the preamble would have been viewed at the time the Amendment was adopted. While the Court makes the novel suggestion that it need only find some "logical connection" between the preamble and the operative provision, it does acknowledge that a prefatory clause may resolve an ambiguity in the text. Without identifying any language in the text that even mentions civilian uses of firearms, the Court proceeds to "find" its preferred reading in what is at best an ambiguous text, and then concludes that its reading is not foreclosed by the preamble. Perhaps the Court's approach to the text is acceptable advocacy, but it is surely an unusual approach for judges to follow.

"The right of the people"

The centerpiece of the Court's textual argument is its insistence that the words "the people" as used in the Second Amendment must have the same meaning, and protect the same class of individuals, as when they are used in the First and Fourth Amendments. . . .

The Court . . . overlooks the significance of the way the Framers used the phrase "the people" in these constitutional provisions. In the First Amendment, no words define the class of individuals entitled to speak, to publish, or to worship; in that Amendment it is only the right peaceably to assemble, and to petition the Government for a redress of grievances, that is described as a right of "the people." These rights contemplate collective action. While the right peaceably to assemble protects the individual rights of those persons participating in the assembly, its concern is with action engaged in by members of a group, rather than any single individual. Likewise, although the act of petitioning the Government is a right that can be exercised by individuals, it is primarily collective in nature. For if they are to be effective, petitions must involve groups of individuals acting in concert.

Similarly, the words "the people" in the Second Amendment refer back to the object announced in the Amendment's preamble. They remind us that it is the collective action of individuals having a duty to serve in the militia that the text directly protects and, perhaps more importantly, that the ultimate purpose of the Amendment was to protect the States' share of the divided sovereignty created by the Constitution.

As used in the Fourth Amendment, "the people" describes the class of persons protected from unreasonable searches and seizures by Government officials. It is true that the Fourth Amendment describes a right that need not be exercised in any collective sense. But that observation does not settle the meaning of the phrase "the people" when used in the Second Amendment. For, as we have seen, the phrase means something quite different in the Petition and Assembly Clauses of the First Amendment. Although the abstract definition of the phrase "the people" could carry the same meaning in the Second Amendment as in the Fourth Amendment, the preamble of the Second Amendment suggests that the uses of the phrase in the First and Second Amendments are the same in referring to a collective activity. . . .

"To keep and bear Arms"

Although the Court's discussion of these words treats them as two "phrases"—as if they read "to keep" and "to bear"—they describe a unitary right: to possess arms if needed for military purposes and to use them in conjunction with military activities. . . .

When each word in the text is given full effect, the Amendment is most naturally read to secure to the people a right to use and possess arms in conjunction with service in a well-regulated militia. So far as appears, no more than that was contemplated by its drafters or is encompassed within its terms. Even if the meaning of the text were genuinely susceptible to more than one interpretation, the burden would remain on those advocating a departure from the purpose identified in the preamble and from settled law to come forward with persuasive new arguments or evidence. The textual analysis offered by respondent and embraced by the Court falls far short of sustaining that heavy burden. . . .

Indeed, not a word in the constitutional text even arguably supports the Court's overwrought and novel description of the Second Amendment as "elevat[ing] above all other interests" "the right of law-abiding, responsible citizens to use arms in defense of hearth and home."

II

The proper allocation of military power in the new Nation was an issue of central concern for the Framers. The compromises they ultimately reached, reflected in Article I's Militia Clauses and the Second Amendment, represent quintessential examples of the Framers' "split[ting] the atom of sovereignty." . . .

Madison, charged with the task of assembling the proposals for amendments sent by the ratifying States, was the principal draftsman of the Second Amendment. . . . Madison's decision to model the Second Amendment on the distinctly military Virginia proposal is . . . revealing, since it is clear that he considered and rejected formulations that would have unambiguously protected civilian uses of firearms. When Madison prepared his first draft, and when that draft was debated and modified, it is reasonable to assume that all participants in the drafting process were fully aware of the other formulations that would have protected civilian use and possession of weapons and that their choice to craft the Amendment as they did represented a rejection of those alternative formulations. . . .

The history of the adoption of the Amendment thus describes an overriding concern about the potential threat to state sovereignty that a federal standing army would pose, and a desire to protect the States' militias as the means by which to guard against that danger. But state militias could not effectively check the prospect of a federal standing army so long as Congress retained the power to disarm them, and so a guarantee against such disarmament was needed. As we explained in *Miller:* "With obvious purpose to assure the continuation and render possible the effectiveness of such forces the declaration and guarantee of the Second Amendment were made. It must be interpreted and applied with that end in view." The evidence plainly refutes the claim that the Amendment was motivated by the Framers' fears that Congress might act to regulate any civilian uses of weapons. . . .

III

. . . The Court is simply wrong when it intones that *Miller* contained *"not a word"* about the Amendment's history. The Court plainly looked to history to construe the term "Militia," and, on the best reading of *Miller,* the entire guarantee of the Second Amendment. After noting the original Constitution's grant of power to Congress and to the States over the militia, the Court explained:

> With obvious purpose to assure the continuation and render possible the effectiveness of such forces the declaration and guarantee of the Second Amendment were made. It must be interpreted and applied with that end in view.
>
> The Militia which the States were expected to maintain and train is set in contrast with Troops which they were forbidden to keep without the consent of Congress. The sentiment of the time strongly disfavored standing armies; the common view was that adequate defense of country and laws could be secured through the Militia—civilians primarily, soldiers on occasion.

The signification attributed to the term Militia appears from the debates in the Convention, the history and legislation of Colonies and States, and the writings of approved commentators.

Miller, 307 U.S., at 178–179. The majority cannot seriously believe that the *Miller* Court did not consider any relevant evidence; the majority simply does not approve of the conclusion the *Miller* Court reached on that evidence. Standing alone, that is insufficient reason to disregard a unanimous opinion of this Court, upon which substantial reliance has been placed by legislators and citizens for nearly 70 years.

V

The Court concludes its opinion by declaring that it is not the proper role of this Court to change the meaning of rights "enshrine[d]" in the Constitution. But the right the Court announces was not "enshrined" in the Second Amendment by the Framers; it is the product of today's law-changing decision. The majority's exegesis has utterly failed to establish that as a matter of text or history, "the right of law-abiding, responsible citizens to use arms in defense of hearth and home" is "elevate[d] above all other interests" by the Second Amendment.

Until today, it has been understood that legislatures may regulate the civilian use and misuse of firearms so long as they do not interfere with the preservation of a well-regulated militia. The Court's announcement of a new constitutional right to own and use firearms for private purposes upsets that settled understanding, but leaves for future cases the formidable task of defining the scope of permissible regulations. . . .

The Court properly disclaims any interest in evaluating the wisdom of the specific policy choice challenged in this case, but it fails to pay heed to a far more important policy choice—the choice made by the Framers themselves. The Court would have us believe that over 200 years ago, the Framers made a choice to limit the tools available to elected officials wishing to regulate civilian uses of weapons, and to authorize this Court to use the common-law process of case-by-case judicial lawmaking to define the contours of acceptable gun-control policy. Absent compelling evidence that is nowhere to be found in the Court's opinion, I could not possibly conclude that the Framers made such a choice.

For these reasons, I respectfully dissent.

■ [JUSTICE BREYER'S dissenting opinion is omitted.]

NOTES

1. *Methodology.* What is the interpretive methodology used in each of the opinions? Recall the five types of constitutional argument discussed in Chapter 1, as they apply here: (1) the text of the Second Amendment, (2) inferences from the Constitution's structure and the relationship of its provisions, (3) the historical purpose underlying the Second Amendment, (4) precedent (i.e., *Miller*) or consistent practice interpreting the amendment, and (5) policy considerations. What weight does each opinion give to these arguments? Which arguments do you consider most helpful in deciding the case?

2. *Preamble.* Is the purpose for the Second Amendment laid out by the preamble or prefatory clause still relevant today? If so, how should that affect the interpretation of the rest of the amendment? If not, how does that affect the

amendment's interpretation? If the constitutionally stated reason for the Second Amendment vanishes, does the amendment itself vanish?

3. *The Third Amendment.* What about the Third Amendment—has it vanished from the Constitution? Does the modern situation change how it should be interpreted? Or does the fact that the Third Amendment has generated so little controversy over interpretation simply mean that that amendment has been successful in accomplishing its purposes? Would it be appropriate to *expand* the meaning of the Third Amendment in order to effectuate its broader underlying "purpose" of safeguarding the integrity of the home from government intrusion? Would that be more or less appropriate than it would be to *contract* the scope of the Second Amendment if (some of) the purposes for which it was included no longer require private, individual ownership of firearms? Are we stuck with constitutional provisions (absent an amendment) even if they are no longer necessary to serve their purposes?

4. *Criticism.* Back to the Second Amendment. Judge J. Harvie Wilkinson III, of the Fourth Circuit U.S. Court of Appeals, has said that *Heller* rejects the "values of textualism, self-restraint, separation of powers, and federalism" and leaves "only originalism as the foundation of conservative jurisprudence. A set of reasonable tenets each providing a separate check on judicial activism has now been replaced by a singular focus on original understanding." J. Harvie Wilkinson III, *Of Guns, Abortions, and the Unraveling Rule of Law*, 95 Va. L. Rev. 253, 256 (2009). The problem, in Judge Wilkinson's view, is that an unconstrained originalism can be "a theory no less subject to judicial subjectivity and endless argumentation as any other." Do you agree? How much should constitutional interpretation rely on the original understanding of the text (emphasized by Justice Scalia in *Heller*) and how much should it temper that understanding with norms of judicial restraint, deference to the democratic process, and policy considerations (emphasized in Judge Wilkinson's critique)?

5. *Incorporation.* Does the Second Amendment right to keep and bear arms, as interpreted by *Heller*, apply against state governments? In *McDonald v. City of Chicago*, 130 S. Ct. 3020 (2010), the Supreme Court, by vote of 5–4, held that the Second Amendment's individual right to keep and bear arms, recognized in *Heller*, applied against state and local government action as well as against the federal government. The majority held that the Second Amendment right was incorporated by the Fourteenth Amendment as a limitation on the power of state governments. The Court therefore struck down two local ordinances, of Chicago and Oak Park, Illinois, that effectively prohibited private handgun possession by nearly all private citizens.

The majority opinion, by Justice Alito, asked whether "the right to keep and bear arms is fundamental to our scheme of ordered liberty, or . . . 'deeply rooted in this Nation's history and tradition." According to the Court, the "decision in *Heller* points unmistakably to the answer. Self-defense is a basic right, recognized by many legal systems from ancient times to the present day, and in Heller, we held that individual self-defense is 'the *central* component' of the Second Amendment right." Drawing on Fourteenth Amendment's drafting history and evidence from the period immediately following ratification, the Court concluded "that the right to keep and bear arms was considered fundamental." The Court also noted that in 1868 "22 of the 37 States in the Union had constitutional provisions explicitly protecting the right to keep and bear arms." (The source the Court cited for this point is discussed at the end of this note.) Justice

Thomas concurred in part and concurred in the judgment, writing separately to argue that the Privileges or Immunities Clause of the Fourteenth Amendment provided "a more straightforward path" to the Court's conclusion—"one that is more faithful to the Fourteenth Amendment's text and history."

In dissent, Justice Stevens argued that the question of whether the Second Amendment applied to the states had been "squarely" and "correctly resolved" in late nineteenth-century cases. He considered the case to really be about substantive due process, and he would not have recognized the right of individuals to keep and bear arms as a protected substantive due process liberty: "firearms have a fundamentally ambivalent relationship to liberty," and "may be used to kill another person." He also argued that "the experience of other advanced democracies . . . undercuts the notion that an expansive right to keep and bear arms is intrinsic to ordered liberty."

The dissent of Justice Breyer, joined by Justice Ginsburg and Justice Sotomayor, considered the case in terms of the Court's precedents on incorporation of the Bill of Rights, asking the question "whether the Second Amendment right to private self-defense is 'fundamental' so that it applies to the States." Justice Breyer could "find nothing in the Second Amendment's text, history, or underlying rationale that could warrant characterizing it as 'fundamental' insofar as to it seeks to protect the keeping and bearing of arms for private, self-defense purposes." Nor could he find "any justification for interpreting the Constitution as transferring ultimate regulatory authority over the private uses of firearms from democratically elected legislatures to courts or from the States to the Federal Government."

One conceptual puzzle in incorporating the Second Amendment against the states lies in its historical purpose. If that purpose was to check government tyranny at the national level by protecting an individual right to own firearms, that right could easily be incorporated against states (since they, too, could prove tyrannical). But if the purpose was to protect the state militias, on the theory that they would be the strong check on national power, would that be consistent with incorporating the Second Amendment against the states themselves? (This is not the only place in the Bill of Rights where this sort of puzzle arises. Two other provisions are sometimes read—though each reading is contestable—as taking decisionmaking authority about a question away from the national government and giving it to the states, namely the Establishment Clause and the Seventh Amendment's preservation of the right to a jury trial.)

In thinking about the application of the Second Amendment to the states, one source to consider is state constitutions in 1868. What did they say about the right to keep and bear arms? Twenty-two out of thirty-seven states explicitly protected such a right, and in a majority of these states it was made clear that the people had a right to keep and bear arms to protect themselves, as well as to facilitate service in the militia. Steven G. Calabresi & Sarah E. Agudo, *Individual Rights Under State Constitutions when the Fourteenth Amendment Was Ratified in 1868: What Rights Are Deeply Rooted in American History and Tradition?*, 87 Tex. L. Rev. 7, 50–53 (2008). Twenty-seven states had Lockean Provisos that might be relevant: "All men are by nature free and independent, and have certain inalienable rights, among which are those of enjoying *and defending* life and liberty, acquiring, possessing, and *protecting* property: and pursuing and obtaining safety and happiness." *Id.* at 88 (emphasis added). In addition, thirty-five out of thirty-seven states in 1868 had clauses in their state

Bills of Rights which stated that the military was to be subordinate to the civilian power. Twenty-one states had clauses that read: "No standing army shall be kept up without the consent of the legislature." The lessons of Stuart absolutism and of Lexington and Concord continued to influence American constitutionalism in 1868.

[Assignment 57]

IV. THE CONSTITUTION AND CRIMINAL PROCEEDINGS: THE FOURTH, FIFTH, SIXTH, AND EIGHTH AMENDMENTS

At the center of the Bill of Rights stands a cluster of provisions addressing the rights of the people of America against law-enforcement officials and the rights of the accused in criminal cases to fair and reliable proceedings: The right to be free from unreasonable government searches and seizures; the right to trial by jury, following an indictment by a grand jury; the requirement that proceedings be in accordance with "due process of law"; the rights to confront witnesses and to produce one's own; the right to the assistance of counsel; and the prohibitions on cruel and unusual punishments and excessive bail or fines.

These issues form the core of many law school courses on Criminal Procedure. But they are also part of the Constitution. Here is a brief sketch of these constitutional provisions, with two cases that illustrate important questions of constitutional interpretation.

A. THE FOURTH AMENDMENT

Amendment IV: The right of the people to be secure in their persons, houses, papers, and effects, against unreasonable searches and seizures, shall not be violated, and no Warrants shall issue, but upon probable cause, supported by Oath or Affirmation, and particularly describing the place to be searched, and the persons or things to be seized.

The Fourth Amendment prohibits searches and seizures that are "unreasonable." How does one determine whether a search is reasonable or unreasonable? Is that a determination of law for a judge to make? Is it a judgment committed to a jury, much as tort law questions of reasonableness sometimes call for judgment by juries? Are there certain categorical rules? Where do they come from?

What is the relationship between the prohibition of "unreasonable" searches and the requirement that warrants be supported by "probable cause"? Is a search always *unreasonable* if it is not based on "probable cause"? Is a search always *reasonable* if it *is* supported by probable cause? Do all searches require warrants? (Read the text carefully.) Is a search necessarily unreasonable if it lacks a warrant? Is a search necessarily reasonable if the police have a warrant?

What is a "search" in the first place? What is a "seizure"? How would you apply these terms, for example, to the requirement that all commercial airline passengers pass through metal detectors, empty their pockets, and remove their jackets and shoes? Is that a search or a seizure? Is there probable cause? Is a warrant required?

Does the Fourth Amendment protect only U.S. citizens, or does it apply to non-citizens as well? To whom does "[t]he right of the people" refer?

Does the Fourth Amendment apply to actions taken by government officials *abroad*? Actions directed against non-U.S. citizens abroad? Does it matter if the actions are taken for law enforcement purposes or for some other purpose (for example, the conduct of war)? Are U.S. armed forces engaged in military actions abroad limited by the provisions of the Fourth Amendment? Must a soldier have probable cause or a warrant in order to search or seize an enemy soldier? Cf. *United States v. Verdugo–Urquidez*, 494 U.S. 259 (1990) (Fourth Amendment protects the "right of the people" of the United States and does not apply to extraterritorial "searches" and "seizures" conducted abroad by U.S. officials, involving non-citizens).

What is the remedy if the Fourth Amendment's prohibitions are violated? The most widely used remedy is one that has been judicially developed. It is called the exclusionary rule—a court excludes from a criminal trial any evidence obtained by officers violating the amendment. Is this remedy consistent with the Fourth Amendment? Can Congress prescribe a different remedy, or is deciding the remedy for Fourth Amendment violations a question for the judiciary? And what should the remedy be for citizens who suffer an unreasonable search or seizure that produces no incriminating evidence whatsoever?

Kyllo v. United States

533 U.S. 27 (2001)

■ JUSTICE SCALIA delivered the opinion of the Court.

This case presents the question whether the use of a thermal-imaging device aimed at a private home from a public street to detect relative amounts of heat within the home constitutes a "search" within the meaning of the Fourth Amendment.

I

In 1991 Agent William Elliott of the United States Department of the Interior came to suspect that marijuana was being grown in the home belonging to petitioner Danny Kyllo. . . . Indoor marijuana growth typically requires high-intensity lamps. In order to determine whether an amount of heat was emanating from petitioner's home consistent with the use of such lamps, at 3:20 a.m. on January 16, 1992, Agent Elliott and Dan Haas used an Agema Thermovision 210 thermal imager to scan the triplex. Thermal imagers detect infrared radiation, which virtually all objects emit but which is not visible to the naked eye. . . . The scan of Kyllo's home took only a few minutes and was performed from the passenger seat of Agent Elliott's vehicle across the street from the front of the house and also from the street in back of the house. The scan showed that the roof over the garage and a side wall of petitioner's home were relatively hot compared to the rest of the home and substantially warmer than neighboring homes in the triplex. Agent Elliott concluded that petitioner was using halide lights to grow marijuana in his house, which indeed he was. Based on tips from informants, utility bills, and the thermal imaging, a Federal Magistrate Judge issued a warrant authorizing a search of petitioner's home, and the agents found an indoor growing operation involving more than 100 plants. Petitioner was indicted on one count of manufacturing marijuana, in violation of 21 U.S.C. § 841(a)(1). He unsuccessfully moved to suppress the evidence seized from his home and then entered a conditional guilty plea.

A divided Court of Appeals . . . affirmed. The court held that petitioner had shown no subjective expectation of privacy because he had made no attempt to conceal the heat escaping from his home, and even if he had, there was no objectively reasonable expectation of privacy because the imager "did not expose any intimate details of Kyllo's life," only "amorphous 'hot spots' on the roof and exterior wall[.]" We granted certiorari.

II

The Fourth Amendment provides that "[t]he right of the people to be secure in their persons, houses, papers, and effects, against unreasonable searches and seizures, shall not be violated." "At the very core" of the Fourth Amendment "stands the right of a man to retreat into his own home and there be free from unreasonable governmental intrusion." *Silverman v. United States*, 365 U.S. 505, 511 (1961). With few exceptions, the question whether a warrantless search of a home is reasonable and hence constitutional must be answered no.

On the other hand, the antecedent question whether or not a Fourth Amendment "search" has occurred is not so simple under our precedent. The permissibility of ordinary visual surveillance of a home used to be clear because, well into the 20th century, our Fourth Amendment jurisprudence was tied to common-law trespass. Visual surveillance was unquestionably lawful because "the eye cannot by the laws of England be guilty of a trespass." We have since decoupled violation of a person's Fourth Amendment rights from trespassory violation of his property, but the lawfulness of warrantless visual surveillance of a home has still been preserved. As we observed in *California v. Ciraolo*, 476 U.S. 207, 213 (1986), "[t]he Fourth Amendment protection of the home has never been extended to require law enforcement officers to shield their eyes when passing by a home on public thoroughfares."

One might think that the new validating rationale would be that examining the portion of a house that is in plain public view, while it is a "search"[1] despite the absence of trespass, is not an "unreasonable" one under the Fourth Amendment. But in fact we have held that visual observation is no "search" at all—perhaps in order to preserve somewhat more intact our doctrine that warrantless searches are presumptively unconstitutional. In assessing when a search is not a search, we have applied somewhat in reverse the principle first enunciated in *Katz* v. *United States,* 389 U. S. 347 (1967). *Katz* involved eavesdropping by means of an electronic listening device placed on the outside of a telephone booth—a location not within the catalog ("persons, houses, papers, and effects") that the Fourth Amendment protects against unreasonable searches. We held that the Fourth Amendment nonetheless protected Katz from the warrantless eavesdropping because he "justifiably relied" upon the privacy of the telephone booth. As Justice Harlan's oft-quoted concurrence described it, a Fourth Amendment search occurs when the government violates a subjective expectation of privacy that society recognizes as reasonable. See *id.,* at 361. We have subsequently applied this principle to hold that a Fourth Amendment search does *not* occur—even when the explicitly protected location of a *house* is concerned—unless "the individual manifested a subjective

---

[1] When the Fourth Amendment was adopted, as now, to "search" meant "[t]o look over or through for the purpose of finding something; to explore; to examine by inspection; as, to *search* the house for a book; to *search* the wood for a thief." N. Webster, An American Dictionary of the English Language 66 (1828) (reprint 6th ed. 1989).

expectation of privacy in the object of the challenged search," and "society [is] willing to recognize that expectation as reasonable." . . .

The present case involves officers on a public street engaged in more than naked-eye surveillance of a home. We have previously reserved judgment as to how much technological enhancement of ordinary perception from such a vantage point, if any, is too much. While we upheld enhanced aerial photography of an industrial complex in *Dow Chemical*, we noted that we found "it important that this is *not* an area immediately adjacent to a private home, where privacy expectations are most heightened."

III

It would be foolish to contend that the degree of privacy secured to citizens by the Fourth Amendment has been entirely unaffected by the advance of technology. For example, as the cases discussed above make clear, the technology enabling human flight has exposed to public view (and hence, we have said, to official observation) uncovered portions of the house and its curtilage that once were private. The question we confront today is what limits there are upon this power of technology to shrink the realm of guaranteed privacy.

The *Katz* test—whether the individual has an expectation of privacy that society is prepared to recognize as reasonable—has often been criticized as circular, and hence subjective and unpredictable. [I]n the case of the search of the interior of homes—the prototypical and hence most commonly litigated area of protected privacy—there is a ready criterion, with roots deep in the common law, of the minimal expectation of privacy that *exists,* and that is acknowledged to be *reasonable*. To withdraw protection of this minimum expectation would be to permit police technology to erode the privacy guaranteed by the Fourth Amendment. We think that obtaining by sense-enhancing technology any information regarding the interior of the home that could not otherwise have been obtained without physical "intrusion into a constitutionally protected area" constitutes a search—at least where (as here) the technology in question is not in general public use. This assures preservation of that degree of privacy against government that existed when the Fourth Amendment was adopted. On the basis of this criterion, the information obtained by the thermal imager in this case was the product of a search.

The Government maintains, however, that the thermal imaging must be upheld because it detected "only heat radiating from the external surface of the house." The dissent makes this its leading point, contending that there is a fundamental difference between what it calls "off-the-wall" observations and "through-the-wall surveillance." But just as a thermal imager captures only heat emanating from a house, so also a powerful directional microphone picks up only sound emanating from a house—and a satellite capable of scanning from many miles away would pick up only visible light emanating from a house. We rejected such a mechanical interpretation of the Fourth Amendment in *Katz,* where the eavesdropping device picked up only sound waves that reached the exterior of the phone booth. Reversing that approach would leave the homeowner at the mercy of advancing technology—including imaging technology that could discern all human activity in the home. . . .

The Government also contends that the thermal imaging was constitutional because it did not "detect private activities occurring in private areas." . . . Limiting the prohibition of thermal imaging to "intimate details" would not only be wrong in principle; it would be impractical in application, failing to provide "a workable accommodation between the needs of law enforcement and the interests protected by the Fourth Amendment," *Oliver v. United States*, 466 U.S. 170, 181 (1984). To begin with, there is no necessary connection between the sophistication of the surveillance equipment and the "intimacy" of the details that it observes—which means that one cannot say (and the police cannot be assured) that use of the relatively crude equipment at issue here will always be lawful. The Agema Thermovision 210 might disclose, for example, at what hour each night the lady of the house takes her daily sauna and bath—a detail that many would consider "intimate"; and a much more sophisticated system might detect nothing more intimate than the fact that someone left a closet light on. . . .

Where, as here, the Government uses a device that is not in general public use, to explore details of the home that would previously have been unknowable without physical intrusion, the surveillance is a "search" and is presumptively unreasonable without a warrant.

Since we hold the Thermovision imaging to have been an unlawful search, it will remain for the District Court to determine whether, without the evidence it provided, the search warrant issued in this case was supported by probable cause—and if not, whether there is any other basis for supporting admission of the evidence that the search pursuant to the warrant produced.

■ JUSTICE STEVENS, with whom THE CHIEF JUSTICE, JUSTICE O'CONNOR, and JUSTICE KENNEDY join, dissenting.

There is, in my judgment, a distinction of constitutional magnitude between "through-the-wall surveillance" that gives the observer or listener direct access to information in a private area, on the one hand, and the thought processes used to draw inferences from information in the public domain, on the other hand. . . .

I

There is no need for the Court to craft a new rule to decide this case, as it is controlled by established principles from our Fourth Amendment jurisprudence. One of those core principles, of course, is that "searches and seizures *inside a home* without a warrant are presumptively unreasonable." *Payton v. New York*, 445 U.S. 573, 586 (1980) (emphasis added). But it is equally well settled that searches and seizures of property in plain view are presumptively reasonable. Whether that property is residential or commercial, the basic principle is the same: "What a person knowingly exposes to the public, even in his own home or office, is not a subject of Fourth Amendment protection." That is the principle implicated here.

While the Court "take[s] the long view" and decides this case based largely on the potential of yet-to-be-developed technology that might allow "through-the-wall surveillance," this case involves nothing more than off-the-wall surveillance by law enforcement officers to gather information exposed to the general public from the outside of petitioner's home. . . . Unlike an x-ray scan, or other possible "through-the-wall" techniques, the detection of infrared radiation emanating from the home did not accomplish "an unauthorized physical penetration into the premises," nor did it "obtain information that it could not have obtained by observation from outside the curtilage of the house."

Indeed, the ordinary use of the senses might enable a neighbor or passerby to notice the heat emanating from a building, particularly if it is vented, as was the case here. . . . Such use of the senses would not convert into an unreasonable search if, instead, an adjoining neighbor allowed an officer onto her property to verify her perceptions with a sensitive thermometer. Nor, in my view, does such observation become an unreasonable search if made from a distance with the aid of a device that merely discloses that the exterior of one house, or one area of the house, is much warmer than another. Nothing more occurred in this case.

Thus, the notion that heat emissions from the outside of a dwelling are a private matter implicating the protections of the Fourth Amendment . . . is not only unprecedented but also quite difficult to take seriously. Heat waves, like aromas that are generated in a kitchen, or in a laboratory or opium den, enter the public domain if and when they leave a building. A subjective expectation that they would remain private is not only implausible but also surely not "one that society is prepared to recognize as 'reasonable.' " *Katz,* 389 U. S., at 361 (Harlan, J., concurring).

To be sure, the homeowner has a reasonable expectation of privacy concerning what takes place within the home, and the Fourth Amendment's protection against physical invasions of the home should apply to their functional equivalent. But the equipment in this case did not penetrate the walls of petitioner's home, and while it did pick up "details of the home" that were exposed to the public, it did not obtain "any information regarding the *interior* of the home." In the Court's own words, based on what the thermal imager "showed" regarding the outside of petitioner's home, the officers "concluded" that petitioner was engaging in illegal activity inside the home. It would be quite absurd to characterize their thought processes as "searches," regardless of whether they inferred (rightly) that petitioner was growing marijuana in his house, or (wrongly) that "the lady of the house [was taking] her daily sauna and bath." . . .

Notwithstanding the implications of today's decision, there is a strong public interest in avoiding constitutional litigation over the monitoring of emissions from homes, and over the inferences drawn from such monitoring. Just as "the police cannot reasonably be expected to avert their eyes from evidence of criminal activity that could have been observed by any member of the public," so too public officials should not have to avert their senses or their equipment from detecting emissions in the public domain such as excessive heat, traces of smoke, suspicious odors, odorless gases, airborne particulates, or radioactive emissions, any of which could identify hazards to the community. In my judgment, monitoring such emissions with "sense-enhancing technology," and drawing useful conclusions from such monitoring, is an entirely reasonable public service.

On the other hand, the countervailing privacy interest is at best trivial. . . . The interest in concealing the heat escaping from one's house pales in significance to "the chief evil against which the wording of the Fourth Amendment is directed," the "physical entry of the home," and it is hard to believe that it is an interest the Framers sought to protect in our Constitution. . . .

II

Instead of trying to answer the question whether the use of the thermal imager in this case was even arguably unreasonable, the Court has fashioned a rule that is intended to provide essential guidance for the day when "more sophisticated systems" gain the "ability to 'see' through walls and other opaque barriers." The newly minted rule encompasses "obtaining [1] by sense-enhancing technology [2] any information regarding the interior of the home [3] that could not otherwise have been obtained without physical intrusion into a constitutionally protected area . . . [4] at least where (as here) the technology in question is not in general public use." [Quoting majority opinion] In my judgment, the Court's new rule is at once too broad and too narrow, and is not justified by the Court's explanation for its adoption. As I have suggested, I would not erect a constitutional impediment to the use of sense-enhancing technology unless it provides its user with the functional equivalent of actual presence in the area being searched.

Despite the Court's attempt to draw a line that is "not only firm but also bright," the contours of its new rule are uncertain because its protection apparently dissipates as soon as the relevant technology is "in general public use[.]" Yet how much use is general public use is not even hinted at by the Court's opinion, which makes the somewhat doubtful assumption that the thermal imager used in this case does not satisfy that criterion. In any event, putting aside its lack of clarity, this criterion is somewhat perverse because it seems likely that the threat to privacy will grow, rather than recede, as the use of intrusive equipment becomes more readily available.

It is clear, however, that the category of "sense-enhancing technology" covered by the new rule is far too broad. It would, for example, embrace potential mechanical substitutes for dogs trained to react when they sniff narcotics. But in *United States v. Place*, 462 U.S. 696, 707 (1983), we held that a dog sniff that "discloses only the presence or absence of narcotics" does "not constitute a 'search' within the meaning of the Fourth Amendment," and it must follow that sense-enhancing equipment that identifies nothing but illegal activity is not a search either. Nevertheless, the use of such a device would be unconstitutional under the Court's rule, as would the use of other new devices that might detect the odor of deadly bacteria or chemicals for making a new type of high explosive, even if the devices (like the dog sniffs) are "so limited both in the manner in which" they obtain information and "in the content of the information" they reveal. . . .

The two reasons advanced by the Court as justifications for the adoption of its new rule are both unpersuasive. First, the Court suggests that its rule is compelled by our holding in *Katz*[.] . . . Yet there are critical differences between the cases. In *Katz*, the electronic listening device attached to the outside of the phone booth allowed the officers to pick up the content of the conversation inside the booth, making them the functional equivalent of intruders because they gathered information that was otherwise available only to someone inside the private area; it would be as if, in this case, the thermal imager presented a view of the heat-generating activity inside petitioner's home. . . .

Second, the Court argues that the permissibility of "through-the-wall surveillance" cannot depend on a distinction between observing "intimate details" such as "the lady of the house [taking] her daily sauna and bath," and noticing only "the nonintimate rug on the vestibule floor" or "objects no smaller than 36 by 36 inches." This entire argument assumes, of course, that the thermal imager in this case could or did perform "through-the-wall surveillance" that could identify any detail "that would previously have been unknowable without physical intrusion." . . . In fact, the device could not, and did not, enable its user to identify either the lady of the house, the rug on the vestibule floor, or anything else inside the house, whether smaller or larger than 36 by 36 inches. . . . But even if the device could reliably show extraordinary differences in the amounts of heat leaving his home, drawing the inference that there was something suspicious occurring inside the residence—a conclusion that officers far less gifted than Sherlock Holmes would readily draw—does not qualify as "through-the-wall surveillance," much less a Fourth Amendment violation. . . .

NOTES

1. *Kyllo* raises the question of what is a "search." It assumes that a search or seizure requires both probable cause and a warrant. Read the Fourth Amendment carefully. Do all searches and seizures require probable cause to be reasonable? Do all searches and seizures require warrants to be reasonable? Or is the text of the Fourth Amendment more naturally read to say that only warrants require probable cause? Why would this be so? Does it seem backwards? See generally Akhil R. Amar, THE CONSTITUTION AND CRIMINAL PROCEDURE: FIRST PRINCIPLES 1–45 (1997).

As you saw in *Kyllo*, the leading modern case on Fourth Amendment searches is *Katz v. United States*, 389 U.S. 347 (1967). Government agents attached a recording device to a public telephone booth, enabling them to learn of the defendant's illegal wagering activities—all without a warrant. Is such electronic surveillance of a public area a "search" covered by the Fourth Amendment? The Court said *yes*, and its analysis has framed all subsequent discussion of the threshold question of the scope of coverage of the Fourth Amendment's protections. In his majority opinion, Justice Stewart said:

> [T]he Fourth Amendment cannot be translated into a general constitutional 'right to privacy.' That Amendment protects individual privacy against certain kinds of governmental intrusion, but its protections go further, and often have nothing to do with privacy at all. Other provisions of the Constitution [i.e., the First, Third, and Fifth Amendments] protect personal privacy from other forms of governmental invasion. But the protection of a person's *general* right to privacy—his right to be let alone by other people—is, like the protection of his property and of is very life, left largely to the law of the individual States. . . .
>
> [T]he Fourth Amendment protects people, not places. What a person knowingly exposes to the public, even in his own home or office, is not a subject of Fourth Amendment protection. But what he seeks to preserve as private, even in an area accessible to the public, may be constitutionally protected. The Government stresses the fact that the telephone booth from which the petitioner made his calls was constructed partly of glass, so that he was as visible after he entered it as he would have been if he had remained outside. But what he sought to exclude when he entered the booth was not the intruding eye—it was the uninvited ear. He did not shed his right to do so simply because he made his calls from a place where he might be seen.

In a highly influential concurring opinion, Justice Harlan said:

> I join the opinion of the Court, which I read to hold only (a) that an enclosed telephone booth is an area where, like a home, and unlike a field, a person has a constitutionally protected reasonable expectation of privacy;

(b) that electronic as well as physical intrusion into a place that is in this sense private may constitute a violation of the Fourth Amendment; and (c) that the invasion of a constitutionally protected area by federal authorities is, as the Court has long held, presumptively unreasonable in the absence of a search warrant. . . .

My understanding of the rule that has emerged from prior decisions is that there is a twofold requirement, first, that a person have exhibited an actual (subjective) expectation of privacy and, second, that the expectation be one that society is prepared to recognize as "reasonable."

The *Katz* decision, especially the two-part formulation of Justice Harlan's concurrence, is central to how the Court has come to view the Fourth Amendment's requirements (but with many exceptions). Consider an example: if the police rummage through someone's garbage dumpster, is that a "search" covered by the Fourth Amendment? In *California v. Greenwood*, 486 U.S. 35 (1988), the Court held that while a person might have an actual, subjective expectation of privacy in the contents of his abandoned garbage, set outside in opaque bags for collection, it is not an expectation that society recognizes as reasonable. Accordingly, the police can rummage away without a warrant.

How do the two opinions in *Kyllo* apply *Katz*? What do you think the authors of each opinion consider to be the strengths and weaknesses of seeing the Fourth Amendment in terms of reasonable expectations of privacy?

2. How would you describe the approaches of the majority and the dissent to interpreting the Constitution?

3. As noted above, the most common remedy for a violation of the Fourth Amendment is the exclusion of the evidence that officers found by violating the Fourth Amendment. Assuming that the exclusionary rule is a proper remedy, how far should such exclusion reach? To answer this question the Court has developed the colorfully named "fruit of the poisonous tree" doctrine. The constitutional violation is the "poisonous tree," and the evidence it leads to is the "fruit." The doctrine applies to both Fourth and Fifth Amendment violations. But the Court has also developed exceptions to mitigate the harshness of excluding all of the "fruit" of a constitutional violation—exceptions having to do with whether the chain-of-causation from the initial violation was broken by some intervening event.

The fruit-of-the-poisonous-tree doctrine is discussed below in the notes after *Miranda v. Arizona*. Here consider how it would apply to a scene from the movie *Dirty Harry*, where the title character is played by Clint Eastwood. Harry is a San Francisco police detective. He climbs over a fence onto private property without a warrant, breaks into the quarters of a suspected serial killer (a caretaker's room deep inside a football stadium), finds a rifle, chases the suspect across the football field, shoots the suspect's legs out from under him, and threatens to kill the suspect, who screams for his lawyer. Harry demands to know where he has left his latest victim—a teenage girl who has been buried alive. The serial killer is coerced by torture into telling Harry where she is. But by the time the police reach the girl, she is dead. Assuming Harry has violated the suspect's Fourth and Fifth Amendment rights, what should be excluded from the evidence at trial? The rifle? The serial killer's confession? The girl's body? For more discussion, see Michael Stokes Paulsen, *Dirty Harry and the Real Constitution*, 64 U. Chi. L. Rev. 1457 (1997).

B. THE FIFTH AMENDMENT

Amendment V: No person shall be held to answer for a capital, or otherwise infamous crime, unless on a presentment or indictment of a Grand Jury, except in cases arising in the land or naval forces, or in the Militia, when in actual service in time of War or public danger; nor shall any person be subject for the same offence to be twice put in jeopardy of life or limb; nor shall be compelled in any criminal case to be a witness against himself, nor be deprived of life, liberty, or property, without due process of law; nor shall private property be taken for public use, without just compensation.

The Fifth Amendment is most well-known (at least in popular culture) for its right against compelled self-incrimination. But as you can see from reading it, that is only a part of what the amendment is about. More broadly, the Fifth Amendment is a compendium of criminal procedural protections, including the right to the screening process of a grand jury and the prohibition against "double jeopardy." It also guarantees the right to "due process of law," and the right not to have one's private property taken for public use without just compensation. (Due process is discussed in Chapter 7, and the Takings Clause is discussed later in this chapter.)

Consider the following case—one of the most famous in the history of the Supreme Court—as a case study in the interpretation of the Constitution:

Miranda v. Arizona

384 U.S. 436 (1966)

■ MR. CHIEF JUSTICE WARREN delivered the opinion of the Court.

The cases before us raise questions which go to the roots of our concepts of American criminal jurisprudence: the restraints society must observe consistent with the Federal Constitution in prosecuting individuals for crime. More specifically, we deal with the admissibility of statements obtained from an individual who is subjected to custodial police interrogation and the necessity for procedures which assure that the individual is accorded his privilege under the Fifth Amendment to the Constitution not to be compelled to incriminate himself. . . .

Our holding will be spelled out with some specificity in the pages which follow but briefly stated it is this: the prosecution may not use statements, whether exculpatory or inculpatory, stemming from custodial interrogation of the defendant unless it demonstrates the use of procedural safeguards effective to secure the privilege against self-incrimination. By custodial interrogation, we mean questioning initiated by law enforcement officers after a person has been taken into custody or otherwise deprived of his freedom of action in any significant way. As for the procedural safeguards to be employed, unless other fully effective means are devised to inform accused persons of their right of silence and to assure a continuous opportunity to exercise it, the following measures are required. Prior to any questioning, the person must be warned that he has a right to remain silent, that any statement he does make may be used as evidence against him, and that he has a right to the presence of an attorney, either retained or appointed. The defendant may waive effectuation of these rights, provided the waiver is made voluntarily, knowingly and intelligently. If, however, he indicates in any manner and at any stage of the process that he wishes to consult with an attorney before speaking there can be no questioning. Likewise, if the individual is alone and indicates in any manner that he does not wish to be interrogated, the police may not question him. The mere fact that he may have answered some questions or volunteered some statements on his own does not deprive him of the right to refrain from answering any further inquiries until he has consulted with an attorney and thereafter consents to be questioned.

I

The constitutional issue we decide in each of these cases is the admissibility of statements obtained from a defendant questioned while in custody or otherwise deprived of his freedom of action in any significant way. In each, the defendant was questioned by police officers, detectives, or a prosecuting attorney in a room in which he was cut off from the outside world. In none of these cases was the defendant given a full and effective warning of his rights at the outset of the interrogation process. In all the cases, the questioning elicited oral admissions, and in three of them, signed statements as well which were admitted at their trials. They all thus share salient features—incommunicado interrogation of individuals in a police-dominated atmosphere, resulting in self-incriminating statements without full warnings of constitutional rights.

An understanding of the nature and setting of this in-custody interrogation is essential to our decisions today. . . . [W]e stress that the modern practice of in-custody interrogation is psychologically rather than physically oriented. . . . The officers are told by the [police] manuals that the "principal psychological factor contributing to a successful interrogation is *privacy*—being alone with the person under interrogation." . . .

To highlight the isolation and unfamiliar surroundings, the manuals instruct the police to display an air of confidence in the suspect's guilt and from outward appearance to maintain only an interest in confirming certain details. The guilt of the subject is to be posited as a fact. The interrogator should direct his comments toward the reasons why the subject committed the act, rather than court failure by asking the subject whether he did it. Like other men, perhaps the subject has had a bad family life, had an unhappy childhood, had too much to drink, had an unrequited desire for women. The officers are instructed to minimize the moral seriousness of the offense, to cast blame on the victim or on society. These tactics are designed to put the subject in a psychological state where his story is but an elaboration of what the police purport to know already—that he is guilty. Explanations to the contrary are dismissed and discouraged. . . .

The interrogators sometimes are instructed to induce a confession out of trickery. The technique here is quite effective in crimes which require identification or which run in series. In the identification situation, the interrogator may take a break in his questioning to place the subject among a group of men in a line-up. "The witness or complainant (previously coached, if necessary) studies the line-up and confidently points out the subject as the guilty party." Then the questioning resumes "as though there were now no doubt about the guilt of the subject." A variation on this technique is called the "reverse line-up":

> The accused is placed in a line-up, but this time he is identified by several fictitious witnesses or victims who associated him with different offenses. It is expected that the subject will become desperate and con-

fess to the offense under investigation in order to escape from the false accusations.

The manuals also contain instructions for police on how to handle the individual who refuses to discuss the matter entirely, or who asks for an attorney or relatives. The examiner is to concede him the right to remain silent. "This usually has a very undermining effect. First of all, he is disappointed in his expectation of an unfavorable reaction on the part of the interrogator. Secondly, a concession of this right to remain silent impresses the subject with the apparent fairness of his interrogator." After this psychological conditioning, however, the officer is told to point out the incriminating significance of the suspect's refusal to talk:

> Joe, you have a right to remain silent. That's your privilege and I'm the last person in the world who'll try to take it away from you. If that's the way you want to leave this, O.K. But let me ask you this. Suppose you were in my shoes and I were in yours and you called me in to ask me about this and I told you, "I don't want to answer any of your questions." You'd think I had something to hide, and you'd probably be right in thinking that. That's exactly what I'll have to think about you, and so will everybody else. So let's sit here and talk this whole thing over.

Few will persist in their initial refusal to talk, it is said, if this monologue is employed correctly. In the event that the subject wishes to speak to a relative or an attorney, the following advice is tendered:

> [T]he interrogator should respond by suggesting that the subject first tell the truth to the interrogator himself rather than get anyone else involved in the matter. If the request is for an attorney, the interrogator may suggest that the subject save himself or his family the expense of any such professional service, particularly if he is innocent of the offense under investigation. The interrogator may also add, "Joe, I'm only looking for the truth, and if you're telling the truth, that's it. You can handle this by yourself."

From these representative samples of interrogation techniques, the setting prescribed by the manuals and observed in practice becomes clear. In essence, it is this: To be alone with the subject is essential to prevent distraction and to deprive him of any outside support. The aura of confidence in his guilt undermines his will to resist. He merely confirms the preconceived story the police seek to have him describe. Patience and persistence, at times relentless questioning, are employed. . . . The police then persuade, trick, or cajole him out of exercising his constitutional rights. . . .

In the cases before us today, given this background, we concern ourselves primarily with this interrogation atmosphere and the evils it can bring. . . . In these cases, we might not find the defendants' statements to have been involuntary in traditional terms. Our concern for adequate safeguards to protect precious Fifth Amendment rights is, of course, not lessened in the slightest. In each of the cases, the defendant was thrust into an unfamiliar atmosphere and run through menacing police interrogation procedures. The potentiality for compulsion is forcefully apparent, for example, in Miranda, where the indigent Mexican defendant was a seriously disturbed individual with pronounced sexual fantasies, and in Stewart, in which the defendant was an indigent Los Angeles Negro who had dropped out of school in the sixth grade. To be sure, the records do not evince overt physical coercion or patent psychological ploys. The fact remains that in

none of these cases did the officers undertake to afford appropriate safeguards at the outset of the interrogation to insure that the statements were
truly the product of free choice.

It is obvious that such an interrogation environment is created for no
purpose other than to subjugate the individual to the will of his examiner.
This atmosphere carries its own badge of intimidation. To be sure, this is
not physical intimidation, but it is equally destructive of human dignity. . . .

II

. . . The question in these cases is whether the privilege [against self-
incrimination] is fully applicable during a period of custodial interrogation.
In this Court, the privilege has consistently been accorded a liberal construction. We are satisfied that all the principles embodied in the privilege
apply to informal compulsion exerted by law-enforcement officers during in-
custody questioning. An individual swept from familiar surroundings into
police custody, surrounded by antagonistic forces, and subjected to the
techniques of persuasion de-scribed above cannot be otherwise than under
compulsion to speak. As a practical matter, the compulsion to speak in the
isolated setting of the police station may well be greater than in courts or
other official investigations, where there are often impartial observers to
guard against intimidation or trickery. . . .

III

Today, then, there can be no doubt that the Fifth Amendment privilege
is available outside of criminal court proceedings and serves to protect persons in all settings in which their freedom of action is curtailed in any significant way from being compelled to incriminate themselves. We have concluded that without proper safeguards the process of in-custody interrogation of persons suspected or accused of crime contains inherently compelling pressures which work to undermine the individual's will to resist and
to compel him to speak where he would not otherwise do so freely. In order
to combat these pressures and to permit a full opportunity to exercise the
privilege against self-incrimination, the accused must be adequately and
effectively apprised of his rights and the exercise of those rights must be
fully honored.

It is impossible for us to foresee the potential alternatives for protecting the privilege which might be devised by Congress or the States in the
exercise of their creative rule-making capacities. Therefore we cannot say
that the Constitution necessarily requires adherence to any particular solution for the inherent compulsions of the interrogation process as it is presently conducted. Our decision in no way creates a constitutional straitjacket which will handicap sound efforts at reform, nor is it intended to have
this effect. We encourage Congress and the States to continue their laudable search for increasingly effective ways of protecting the rights of the individual while promoting efficient enforcement of our criminal laws. However, unless we are shown other procedures which are at least as effective
in apprising accused persons of their right of silence and in assuring a continuous opportunity to exercise it, the following safeguards must be observed.

At the outset, if a person in custody is to be subjected to interrogation,
he must first be informed in clear and unequivocal terms that he has the
right to remain silent. For those unaware of the privilege, the warning is
needed simply to make them aware of it—the threshold requirement for an

intelligent decision as to its exercise. More important, such a warning is an absolute prerequisite in overcoming the inherent pressures of the interrogation atmosphere. . . . Further, the warning will show the individual that his interrogators are prepared to recognize his privilege should he choose to exercise it. . . .

The warning of the right to remain silent must be accompanied by the explanation that anything said can and will be used against the individual in court. This warning is needed in order to make him aware not only of the privilege, but also of the consequences of forgoing it. It is only through an awareness of these consequences that there can be any assurance of real understanding and intelligent exercise of the privilege. . . .

[T]he right to have counsel present at the interrogation is indispensable to the protection of the Fifth Amendment privilege under the system we delineate today. Our aim is to assure that the individual's right to choose between silence and speech remains unfettered throughout the interrogation process. . . . Thus, the need for counsel to protect the Fifth Amendment privilege comprehends not merely a right to consult with counsel prior to questioning, but also to have counsel present during any questioning if the defendant so desires. . . .

Accordingly we hold that an individual held for interrogation must be clearly informed that he has the right to consult with a lawyer and to have the lawyer with him during interrogation under the system for protecting the privilege we delineate today. As with the warnings of the right to remain silent and that anything stated can be used in evidence against him, this warning is an absolute prerequisite to interrogation. . . .

In order fully to apprise a person interrogated of the extent of his rights under this system then, it is necessary to warn him not only that he has the right to consult with an attorney, but also that if he is indigent a lawyer will be appointed to represent him. . . . Once warnings have been given, the subsequent procedure is clear. If the individual indicates in any manner, at any time prior to or during questioning, that he wishes to remain silent, the interrogation must cease. . . .

If the interrogation continues without the presence of an attorney and a statement is taken, a heavy burden rests on the government to demonstrate that the defendant knowingly and intelligently waived his privilege against self-incrimination and his right to retained or appointed counsel. This Court has always set high standards of proof for the waiver of constitutional rights, and we reassert these standards as applied to in custody interrogation. . . .

An express statement that the individual is willing to make a statement and does not want an attorney followed closely by a statement could constitute a waiver. But a valid waiver will not be presumed simply from the silence of the accused after warnings are given or simply from the fact that a confession was in fact eventually obtained. . . . The requirement of warnings and waiver of rights is a fundamental with respect to the Fifth Amendment privilege and not simply a preliminary ritual to existing methods of interrogation. . . .

■ [JUSTICE CLARK'S dissent is omitted.]

■ MR. JUSTICE HARLAN, whom MR. JUSTICE STEWART and MR. JUSTICE WHITE join, dissenting.

I believe the decision of the Court represents poor constitutional law and entails harmful consequences for the country at large.

At the outset, it is well to note exactly what is required by the Court's new constitutional code of rules for confessions. The foremost requirement, upon which later admissibility of a confession depends, is that a fourfold warning be given to a person in custody before he is questioned, namely, that he has a right to remain silent, that anything he says may be used against him, that he has a right to have present an attorney during the questioning, and that if indigent he has a right to a lawyer without charge. To forgo these rights, some affirmative statement of rejection is seemingly required, and threats, tricks, or cajolings to obtain this waiver are forbidden. If before or during questioning the suspect seeks to invoke his right to remain silent, interrogation must be forgone or cease; a request for counsel brings about the same result until a lawyer is procured. Finally, there are a miscellany of minor directives, for example, the burden of proof of waiver is on the State, admissions and exculpatory statements are treated just like confessions, withdrawal of a waiver is always permitted, and so forth.

While the fine points of this scheme are far less clear than the Court admits, the tenor is quite apparent. The new rules are not designed to guard against police brutality or other unmistakably banned forms of coercion. Those who use third-degree tactics and deny them in court are equally able and destined to lie as skillfully about warnings and waivers. Rather, the thrust of the new rules is to negate all pressures, to reinforce the nervous or ignorant suspect, and ultimately to discourage any confession at all. The aim in short is toward "voluntariness" in a utopian sense, or to view it from a different angle, voluntariness with a vengeance. . . .

The Court's opinion in my view reveals no adequate basis for extending the Fifth Amendment's privilege against self-incrimination to the police station. Far more important, it fails to show that the Court's new rules are well supported, let alone compelled, by Fifth Amendment precedents.

The Court's opening contention, that the Fifth Amendment governs police station confessions, is perhaps not an impermissible extension of the law but it has little to commend itself in the present circumstances. Historically, the privilege against self-incrimination did not bear at all on the use of extra-legal confessions, for which distinct standards evolved. . . .

The more important premise is that pressure on the suspect must be eliminated though it be only the subtle influence of the atmosphere and surroundings. The Fifth Amendment, however, has never been thought to forbid *all* pressure to incriminate one's self in the situations covered by it. . . . The Court appears similarly wrong in thinking that precise knowledge of one's rights is a settled prerequisite under the Fifth Amendment to the loss of its protections. . . .

How much harm this decision will inflict on law enforcement cannot fairly be predicted with accuracy. Evidence on the role of confessions is notoriously incomplete, and little is added by the Court's reference to the FBI experience and the resources believed wasted in interrogation. We do know that some crimes cannot be solved without confessions, that ample expert testimony attests to their importance in crime control, and that the Court is taking a real risk with society's welfare in imposing its new regime on the country. The social costs of crime are too great to call the new rules anything but a hazardous experimentation.

While passing over the costs and risks of its experiment, the Court portrays the evils of normal police questioning in terms which I think are exaggerated. Albeit stringently confined by the due process standards interrogation is no doubt often inconvenient and unpleasant for the suspect. However, it is no less so for a man to be arrested and jailed, to have his house searched, or to stand trial in court, yet all this may properly happen to the most innocent given probable cause, a warrant, or an indictment. Society has always paid a stiff price for law and order, and peaceful interrogation is not one of the dark moments of the law.

This brief statement of the competing considerations seems to me ample proof that the Court's preference is highly debatable at best and therefore not to be read into the Constitution. However, it may make the analysis more graphic to consider the actual facts of one of the four cases reversed by the Court. *Miranda v. Arizona* serves best, being neither the hardest nor easiest of the four under the Court's standards.

On March 3, 1963, an 18–year–old girl was kidnapped and forcibly raped near Phoenix, Arizona. Ten days later, on the morning of March 13, petitioner Miranda was arrested and taken to the police station. At this time Miranda was 23 years old, indigent, and educated to the extent of completing half the ninth grade. He had "an emotional illness" of the schizophrenic type, according to the doctor who eventually examined him; the doctor's report also stated that Miranda was "alert and oriented as to time, place, and person," intelligent within normal limits, competent to stand trial, and sane within the legal definition. At the police station, the victim picked Miranda out of a lineup, and two officers then took him into a separate room to interrogate him, starting about 11:30 a.m. Though at first denying his guilt, within a short time Miranda gave a detailed oral confession and then wrote out in his own hand and signed a brief statement admitting and describing the crime. All this was accomplished in two hours or less without any force, threats or promises and—I will assume this though the record is uncertain—without any effective warnings at all.

Miranda's oral and written confessions are now held inadmissible under the Court's new rules. One is entitled to feel astonished that the Constitution can be read to produce this result. These confessions were obtained during brief, daytime questioning conducted by two officers and unmarked by any of the traditional indicia of coercion. They assured a conviction for a brutal and unsettling crime, for which the police had and quite possibly could obtain little evidence other than the victim's identifications, evidence which is frequently unreliable. There was, in sum, a legitimate purpose, no perceptible unfairness, and certainly little risk of injustice in the interrogation. Yet the resulting confessions, and the responsible course of police practice they represent, are to be sacrificed to the Court's own finespun conception of fairness which I seriously doubt is shared by many thinking citizens in this country. . . .

In conclusion: Nothing in the letter or the spirit of the Constitution or in the precedents squares with the heavy-handed and one-sided action that is so precipitously taken by the Court in the name of fulfilling its constitutional responsibilities. The foray which the Court makes today brings to mind the wise and farsighted words of Mr. Justice Jackson in *Douglas v. Jeannette,* 319 U. S. 157, 181 (separate opinion): "This Court is forever adding new stories to the temples of constitutional law, and the temples have a way of collapsing when one story too many is added."

■ MR. JUSTICE WHITE, with whom MR. JUSTICE HARLAN and MR. JUSTICE STEWART join, dissenting.

... First, we may inquire what are the textual and factual bases of this new fundamental rule. To reach the result announced on the grounds it does, the Court must stay within the confines of the Fifth Amendment, which forbids self-incrimination only if *compelled*. Hence the core of the Court's opinion is that because of the "compulsion inherent in custodial surroundings, no statement obtained from (a) defendant (in custody) can truly be the product of his free choice," absent the use of adequate protective devices as described by the Court.... Insofar as appears from the Court's opinion, it has not examined a single transcript of any police interrogation, let alone the interrogation that took place in any one of these cases which it decides today. Judged by any of the standards for empirical investigation utilized in the social sciences the factual basis for the Court's premise is patently inadequate.

Although in the Court's view in-custody interrogation is inherently coercive, the Court says that the spontaneous product of the coercion of arrest and detention is still to be deemed voluntary. An accused, arrested on probable cause, may blurt out a confession which will be admissible despite the fact that he is alone and in custody, without any showing that he had any notion of his right to remain silent or of the consequences of his admission. Yet, under the Court's rule, if the police ask him a single question such as "Do you have anything to say?" or "Did you kill your wife?" his response, if there is one, has somehow been compelled, even if the accused has been clearly warned of his right to remain silent. Common sense informs us to the contrary. While one may say that the response was "involuntary" in the sense the question provoked or was the occasion for the response and thus the defendant was induced to speak out when he might have remained silent if not arrested and not questioned, it is patently unsound to say the response is compelled....

If the rule announced today were truly based on a conclusion that all confessions resulting from custodial interrogation are coerced, then it would simply have no rational foundation.... [E]ven if one assumed that there was an adequate factual basis for the conclusion that all confessions obtained during in-custody interrogation are the product of compulsion, the rule propounded by the Court will still be irrational, for, apparently, it is only if the accused is also warned of his right to counsel and waives both that right and the right against self-incrimination that the inherent compulsiveness of interrogation disappears. But if the defendant may not answer without a warning a question such as "Where were you last night?" without having his answer be a compelled one, how can the Court ever accept his negative answer to the question of whether he wants to consult his retained counsel or counsel whom the court will appoint? ...

All of this makes very little sense in terms of the compulsion which the Fifth Amendment proscribes. That amendment deals with compelling the accused himself. It is his free will that is involved. Confessions and incriminating admissions, as such, are not forbidden evidence; only those which are compelled are banned....

In sum, for all the Court's expounding on the menacing atmosphere of police interrogation procedures, it has failed to supply any foundation for the conclusions it draws or the measures it adopts.

Criticism of the Court's opinion, however, cannot stop with a demonstration that the factual and textual bases for the rule it propounds are, at best, less than compelling. Equally relevant is an assessment of the rule's consequences measured against community values. . . .

The most basic function of any government is to provide for the security of the individual and of his property. *Lanzetta v. State of New Jersey*, 306 U.S. 451, 455 (1939). These ends of society are served by the criminal laws which for the most part are aimed at the prevention of crime. Without the reasonably effective performance of the task of preventing private violence and retaliation, it is idle to talk about human dignity and civilized values. . . .

In some unknown number of cases the Court's rule will return a killer, a rapist or other criminal to the streets and to the environment which produced him, to repeat his crime whenever it pleases him. As a consequence, there will not be a gain, but a loss, in human dignity. The real concern is not the unfortunate consequences of this new decision on the criminal law as an abstract, disembodied series of authoritative proscriptions, but the impact on those who rely on the public authority for protection and who without it can only engage in violent self-help with guns, knives and the help of their neighbors similarly inclined. There is, of course, a saving factor: the next victims are uncertain, unnamed and unrepresented in this case. . . .

NOTES

1. Does the Fifth Amendment privilege against self-incrimination—"nor shall [any person] be compelled in any criminal case to be a witness against himself"—apply to compulsion in a sense other than being required, on pain of legal penalty, to testify against oneself? (That seems to be the sense in which compulsion is understood in the Sixth Amendment, which gives the accused the constitutional right "to have compulsory process for obtaining witnesses in his favor.") *Miranda* is about police interrogation—specifically "custodial" interrogation (a term that has generated its own issues of interpretation), when the suspect is not free to leave the police station or walk away from the officers. It is clear what the Court in *Miranda* was concerned about: the danger that custodial interrogation is where the true action is, and the constitutional right not to testify against oneself is of little value if one has already confessed to the police and signed a written statement of guilt.

Most scholars in this area appear to agree that the privilege was designed to spare the guilty person from the temptation to commit perjury, since a person who committed perjury was understood as evading punishment for the body but at the cost of endangering his soul. See, *e.g.*, Albert W. Alschuler, *A Peculiar Privilege in Historical Perspective: The Right to Remain Silent*, 94 Mich. L. Rev. 2625, 2641–42 (1996) ("The history of the privilege . . . is almost entirely a story of when and for what purposes people would be required to speak under oath."); Amar, THE CONSTITUTION AND CRIMINAL PROCEDURE 73 (1997) ("Those who framed the Fifth Amendment . . . believed that perjury was a mortal sin, resulting in eternal damnation: better to admit murder than commit perjury under oath.").

Does such an original understanding limit today's interpretation of the Fifth Amendment? *Miranda* was clearly an innovation, based on a perceived important public policy need to control police interrogation practices, in order to protect (some of) the *interests* protected by the Fifth Amendment. Is that justified? If so, what is the limit of what the Court could prescribe in order to protect Fifth Amendment interests?

2. Even on the narrower, historical reading, the Fifth Amendment is, at its core, a right to remain silent in court, in criminal cases—a right literally not to be compelled to be a witness against oneself in court. Of course, a defendant *may* testify. (Interestingly, for some of the same reasons the constitutional privilege was created, the common law of evidence for many years held that the accused in a criminal case *forbidden* to testify—the accused was disqualified from being a witness. Now, an individual is recognized as having a constitutional right, founded in notions of "due process of law" to testify in his or her own behalf, a right that might also be grounded in the accused's right to "compulsory process" to produce witnesses in his or her favor.) Given that the defendant may testify, if the defendant chooses not to, should the Fifth Amendment be understood to forbid the prosecution from commenting on the defendant's refusal to testify, and inviting the jury to draw what inferences it will from the defendant's choice? See *Griffin v. California*, 380 U.S. 609 (1965) (holding that the Fifth Amendment "forbids either comment by the prosecution on the accused's silence or instructions by the court that such silence is evidence of guilt").

3. Is the decision in *Miranda* really a constitutional decision? Put another way, does it actually say that the Fifth Amendment itself requires the system of warnings devised by the Court? Or is the case merely a prophylactic rule designed to protect the ability of suspects to make meaningful use of the Fifth Amendment privilege later on down the road? If it is a prophylactic rule rather than constitutionally required one, may Congress legislate a different rule, in effect repudiating *Miranda* by statute? One step further: Does a violation of *Miranda* that is not also a violation of the Fifth Amendment—imagine a purely voluntary confession by a suspect, following a failure of the police to read the defendant his rights—require exclusion of evidence as a remedy? If so, could Congress at least provide for a different remedy for violations of *Miranda*'s prophylactic rule?

These issues were presented in *United States v. Dickerson*, 530 U.S. 428 (2000). In the majority opinion, written by Chief Justice Rehnquist, the Court said:

> In *Miranda v. Arizona*, 384 U. S. 436 (1966), we held that certain warnings must be given before a suspect's statement made during custodial interrogation could be admitted in evidence. [Two years after] that decision, Congress enacted 18 U. S. C. § 3501, which in essence laid down a rule that the admissibility of such statements should turn only on whether or not they were voluntarily made. We hold that *Miranda*, being a constitutional decision of this Court, may not be in effect overruled by an Act of Congress, and we decline to overrule *Miranda* ourselves. We therefore hold that *Miranda* and its progeny in this Court govern the admissibility of statements made during custodial interrogation in both state and federal courts. . . .
>
> Congress may not legislatively supersede our decisions interpreting and applying the Constitution. This case therefore turns on whether the *Miranda* Court announced a constitutional rule or merely exercised its su-

pervisory authority to regulate evidence in the absence of congressional direction. . . .

The *Miranda* opinion itself begins by stating that the Court granted certiorari "to explore some facets of the problems of applying the privilege against self-incrimination to in-custody interrogation, *and to give concrete constitutional guidelines for law enforcement agencies and courts to follow.*" . . . Additional support for our conclusion that *Miranda* is constitutionally based is found in the *Miranda* Court's invitation for legislative action to protect the constitutional right against coerced self-incrimination. . . .

The dissent argues that it is judicial overreaching for this Court to hold § 3501 unconstitutional unless we hold that the *Miranda* warnings are required by the Constitution, in the sense that nothing else will suffice to satisfy constitutional requirements. But we need not go further than *Miranda* to decide this case. In *Miranda*, the Court noted that reliance on the traditional totality-of-the-circumstances test raised a risk of overlooking an involuntary custodial confession, [a] risk that the Court found unacceptably great when the confession is offered in the case in chief to prove guilt. The Court therefore concluded that something more than the totality test was necessary. . . . Section 3501 therefore cannot be sustained if *Miranda* is to remain the law.

Whether or not we would agree with *Miranda*'s reasoning and its resulting rule, were we addressing the issue in the first instance, the principles of *stare decisis* weigh heavily against overruling it now. We do not think there is such justification for overruling *Miranda*. *Miranda* has become embedded in routine police practice to the point where the warnings have become part of our national culture. While we have overruled our precedents when subsequent cases have undermined their doctrinal underpinnings, we do not believe that this has happened to the *Miranda* decision. If anything, our subsequent cases have reduced the impact of the *Miranda* rule on legitimate law enforcement while reaffirming the decision's core ruling that unwarned statements may not be used as evidence in the prosecution's case in chief. . . .

In sum, we conclude that *Miranda* announced a constitutional rule that Congress may not supersede legislatively. Following the rule of *stare decisis*, we decline to overrule *Miranda* ourselves.

Justice Scalia, joined by Justice Thomas, responded with a strongly worded dissent, including this passage:

Those to whom judicial decisions are an unconnected series of judgments that produce either favored or disfavored results will doubtless greet today's decision as a paragon of moderation, since it declines to overrule *Miranda*. Those who understand the judicial process will appreciate that today's decision is not a reaffirmation of *Miranda*, but a radical revision of the most significant element of *Miranda* (as of all cases): the rationale that gives it a permanent place in our jurisprudence. *Marbury v. Madison* held that an Act of Congress will not be enforced by the courts if what it prescribes violates the Constitution of the United States. That was the basis on which *Miranda* was decided. One will search today's opinion in vain, however, for a statement (surely simple enough to make) that what 18

U.S.C. § 3501 prescribes—the use at trial of a voluntary confession, even when a *Miranda* warning or its equivalent has failed to be given—violates the Constitution. The reason the statement does not appear is not only (and perhaps not so much) that it would be absurd, inasmuch as § 3501 excludes from trial precisely what the Constitution excludes from trial, viz., compelled confessions; but also that Justices whose votes are needed to compose today's majority are on record as believing that a violation of *Miranda* is *not* a violation of the Constitution. And so, to justify today's agreed-upon result, the Court must adopt a significant *new*, if not entirely comprehensible, principle of constitutional law. As the Court chooses to describe that principle, statutes of Congress can be disregarded, not only when what they prescribe violates the Constitution, but when what they prescribe contradicts a decision of this Court that "announced a constitutional rule". . . . [T]he only thing that can possibly mean in the context of this case is that this Court has the power, not merely to apply the Constitution but to expand it, imposing what it regards as useful "prophylactic" restrictions upon Congress and the States. That is an immense and frightening antidemocratic power, and it does not exist.

A NOTE ON *MIRANDA* AND THE *FRUIT OF THE POISONOUS TREE*

Miranda is more than a case about protecting Fifth Amendment rights to silence. It also requires that suspects be informed about their right to consult with an attorney. The Sixth Amendment protects the right to counsel: "In all criminal prosecutions, the accused shall enjoy the right to . . . have the Assistance of Counsel for his defence." Included here are excerpts from two cases that feature the interplay between the Fifth Amendment (the privilege against self-incrimination) and the Sixth Amendment (the right to counsel) in a custodial "interrogation."

The first case, *Brewer v. Williams*, 430 U.S. 387 (1977), is famous as the "Christian Burial Speech" case. Here we offer excerpts from two of the seven opinions in the case. Writing for the five justices in the majority, Justice Stewart described how Pamela Powers, a 10–year–old girl, disappeared when she and her family were visiting a YMCA in Des Moines, Iowa. Soon after her disappearance,

> Robert Williams, who had recently escaped from a mental hospital, . . . was seen in the YMCA lobby carrying some clothing and a large bundle wrapped in a blanket. He obtained help from a 14–year–old boy in opening the street door of the YMCA and the door to his automobile parked outside. When Williams placed the bundle in the front seat of his car the boy "saw two legs in it and they were skinny and white." Before anyone could see what was in the bundle Williams drove away. His abandoned car was found the following day in Davenport, Iowa, roughly 160 miles east of Des Moines. A warrant was then issued in Des Moines for his arrest on a charge of abduction.
>
> On the morning of December 26, a Des Moines lawyer named Henry McKnight went to the Des Moines police station and informed the officers present that he had just received a long-distance call from Williams, and that he had advised Williams to turn himself in to the Davenport police. Williams did surrender that morning to the police in Davenport, and they booked him on the charge specified in the arrest warrant and gave him the

warnings required by *Miranda.* . . . *[McKnight and Des Moines police of-ficers agreed that Williams would be brought from Davenport back to Des Moines, and that he would not be questioned during the trip. Detective Leaming and another police officer drove from Des Moines to pick up Williams. Before Williams left with the officers, he was reminded of his Miranda rights by a judge and by the officers, and he was instructed by another attorney not to make any statements until he arrived in Des Moines and talked with McKnight. This attorney "firmly stated that the agreement with McKnight was to be carried out that there was to be no interrogation of Williams during the automobile journey to Des Moines"; the attorney was denied permission to accompany Williams and the officers.—Editors]*

The two detectives, with Williams in their charge, then set out on the 160–mile drive. At no time during the trip did Williams express a willingness to be interrogated in the absence of an attorney. Instead, he stated several times that "[w]hen I get to Des Moines and see Mr. McKnight, I am going to tell you the whole story." Detective Leaming knew that Williams was a former mental patient, and knew also that he was deeply religious.

The detective and his prisoner soon embarked on a wide-ranging conversation covering a variety of topics, including the subject of religion. Then, not long after leaving Davenport and reaching the interstate highway, Detective Leaming delivered what has been referred to in the briefs and oral arguments as the "Christian burial speech." Addressing Williams as "Reverend," the detective said:

> I want to give you something to think about while we're traveling down the road. . . . Number one, I want you to observe the weather conditions, it's raining, it's sleeting, it's freezing, driving is very treacherous, visibility is poor, it's going to be dark early this evening. They are predicting several inches of snow for tonight, and I feel that you yourself are the only person that knows where this little girl's body is, that you yourself have only been there once, and if you get a snow on top of it you yourself may be unable to find it. And, since we will be going right past the area on the way into Des Moines, I feel that we could stop and locate the body, that the parents of this little girl should be entitled to a Christian burial for the little girl who was snatched away from them on Christmas [E]ve and murdered. And I feel we should stop and locate it on the way in rather than waiting until morning and trying to come back out after a snow storm and possibly not being able to find it at all.

Williams asked Detective Leaming why he thought their route to Des Moines would be taking them past the girl's body, and Leaming responded that he knew the body was in the area of Mitchellville a town they would be passing on the way to Des Moines. Leaming then stated: "I do not want you to answer me. I don't want to discuss it any further. Just think about it as we're riding down the road."

As the car approached Grinnell, a town approximately 100 miles west of Davenport, Williams asked whether the police had found the victim's shoes. When Detective Leaming replied that he was unsure, Williams directed the officers to a service station where he said he had left the shoes; a search for them proved unsuccessful. As they continued towards Des Moines, Williams asked whether the police had found the blanket, and directed the officers to a rest area where he said he had disposed of the blanket. Nothing was found. The car continued towards Des Moines, and as it approached Mitchellville, Williams said that he would show the officers where the body was. He then directed the police to the body of Pamela Powers. . . . Before [Williams's trial for murder], his counsel moved to suppress all evidence relating to or resulting from any statements Williams had made during the automobile ride from Davenport to Des Moines. . . .

There can be no doubt in the present case that judicial proceedings had been initiated against Williams before the start of the automobile ride from Davenport to Des Moines. A warrant had been issued for his arrest, he had been arraigned on that warrant before a judge in a Davenport courtroom, and he had been committed by the court to confinement in jail. . . . There can be no serious doubt, either, that Detective Leaming deliberately and designedly set out to elicit information from Williams just as surely as and perhaps more effectively than if he had formally interrogated him. Detective Leaming was fully aware before departing for Des Moines that Williams was being represented in Davenport by [one attorney] and in Des Moines by [another,] McKnight. Yet he purposely sought during Williams' isolation from his lawyers to obtain as much incriminating information as possible. . . .

Despite Williams' express and implicit assertions of his right to counsel, Detective Leaming proceeded to elicit incriminating statements from Williams. Leaming did not preface this effort by telling Williams that he had a right to the presence of a lawyer, and made no effort at all to ascertain whether Williams wished to relinquish that right. The circumstances of record in this case thus provide no reasonable basis for finding that Williams waived his right to the assistance of counsel. . . .

Although we do not lightly affirm the issuance of a writ of habeas corpus in this case, so clear a violation of the Sixth and Fourteenth Amendments as here occurred cannot be condoned. The pressures on state executive and judicial officers charged with the administration of the criminal law are great, especially when the crime is murder and the victim a small child. But it is precisely the predictability of those pressures that makes imperative a resolute loyalty to the guarantees that the Constitution extends to us all. . . .

One of the dissenters, Chief Justice Burger, said:

The result in this case ought to be intolerable in any society which purports to call itself an organized society. . . . Williams is guilty of the savage murder of a small child; no member of the Court contends he is not. While in custody, and after no fewer than five warnings of his rights to silence and to counsel, he led police to the concealed body of his victim. The Court concedes Williams was not threatened or coerced and that he spoke and acted voluntarily and with full awareness of his constitutional rights. In the face of all this, the Court now holds that because Williams was prompted by the detective's statement—not interrogation, but a statement—the jury must not be told how the police found the body.

Did the police violate the suspect's Fifth Amendment rights? Did the police violate *Miranda*? Does this case illustrate the necessity of the *Miranda* prophylactic rule, or does it illustrate how that rule frustrates good police work? Did the police violate the suspect's Sixth Amendment right to counsel by questioning him outside the presence of his lawyer and against his lawyer's explicit instructions? And if there was a violation, what was the appropriate remedy?

Seven years after *Brewer*, the Court decided a case arising from Williams's second trial. In *Nix v. Williams*, 467 U.S. 431 (1984), the Court created an "inevitable discovery" exception to the fruit-of-the-poisonous tree. At the second trial, the state trial court admitted evidence of the condition of the body of the murder victim, Pamela Powers, and it concluded "that the State had proved by a preponderance of the evidence that, if the search had not been suspended and Williams had not led the police to the victim, her body would have been discovered 'within a short time' in essentially the same condition as it was actually found." Williams was again convicted of first-degree murder. Williams challenged his conviction in habeas proceedings, but the Supreme Court denied relief. Chief Justice Burger wrote the opinion of the Court (for seven justices). Here is the heart of his argument:

> The core rationale consistently advanced by this Court for extending the exclusionary rule to evidence that is the fruit of unlawful police conduct has been that this admittedly drastic and socially costly course is needed to deter police from violations of constitutional and statutory protections. This Court has accepted the argument that the way to ensure such protections is to exclude evidence seized as a result of such violations notwithstanding the high social cost of letting persons obviously guilty go unpunished for their crimes. On this rationale, the prosecution is not to be put in a better position than it would have been in if no illegality had transpired.
>
> By contrast, the derivative evidence analysis ensures that the prosecution is not put in a worse position simply because of some earlier police error or misconduct. The independent source doctrine allows admission of evidence that has been discovered by means wholly independent of any constitutional violation. That doctrine, although closely related to the inevitable discovery doctrine, does not apply here; Williams' statements to Leaming indeed led police to the child's body, but that is not the whole story. The independent source doctrine teaches us that the interest of society in deterring unlawful police conduct and the public interest in having juries receive all probative evidence of a crime are properly balanced by putting the police in the same, not a worse, position that they would have been in if no police error or misconduct had occurred. When the challenged evidence has an independent source, exclusion of such evidence would put the police in a worse position than they would have been in absent any error or violation. There is a functional similarity between these two doctrines in that exclusion of evidence that would inevitably have been discovered would also put the government in a worse position, because the police would have obtained that evidence if no misconduct had taken place. Thus, while the independent source exception would not justify admission of evidence in this case, its rationale is wholly consistent with and justifies our adoption of the ultimate or inevitable discovery exception to the exclusionary rule. . . .
>
> Exclusion of physical evidence that would inevitably have been discovered adds nothing to either the integrity or fairness of a criminal tri-

al. . . . Nor would suppression ensure fairness on the theory that it tends to safeguard the adversary system of justice.

What do you think of the fruit-of-the-poisonous-tree doctrine? Is it required by the Constitution? If not—if it is a judicially crafted remedy for a constitutional violation—does that mean courts should be free to limit the remedy, as the Court did in *Nix v. Williams*? How should courts decide the scope of the doctrine?

Taking the Fifth (Apart): The Rest of the Amendment

The Fifth Amendment has much more to it (which can only be briefly summarized here):

1. *The Grand Jury Clause.* The institution of the grand jury was intended as a citizen-check on the exercise of civilian law-enforcement power by government officials to bring serious criminal charges against individuals. But it is a power to check, not to compel: a grand jury may indict a defendant, but it may not require the executive branch to continue the prosecution. *United States v. Cox*, 342 F.2d 167 (5th Cir. 1965). Grand juries are typically larger than the juries that decide criminal and civil trials (called "petit juries"), which are guaranteed by the Sixth and Seventh Amendments. The right to indictment by a grand jury has never been held by the Supreme Court to apply to the states through the Fourteenth Amendment.

2. *The Double Jeopardy Clause.* The Fifth Amendment next provides: "[N]or shall any person be subject for the same offence to be twice put in jeopardy of life or limb." The Double Jeopardy Clause might be thought of as constitutionalizing the law of judgments (i.e., claim and issue preclusion) as applied to criminal proceedings—the original meaning of the term-of-art "life or limb." The Double Jeopardy Clause thus bars a second prosecution for the same offense, following an acquittal in the first proceeding (or where the prosecution has provoked a mistrial). It also forbids a second prosecution for the same offense, following a *conviction* in the first proceeding—it thus forbids double punishment for the same crime. And it forbids retrial of any ultimate fact that was determined in the defendant's favor in a prior criminal proceeding.

But the Double Jeopardy Clause does not apply to non-penal civil proceedings or to successive criminal-civil proceedings. It thus does not bar private-party civil suits against a defendant for damages following acquittal of that person on criminal charges arising out of the same conduct. (Think of O.J. Simpson being sued for wrongful death, following his acquittal on criminal charges for murder.) Nor does the Double Jeopardy Clause bar successive prosecutions (or punishments) by two different governments (two different states, or a state and the federal government) for the same conduct, if each of them has legitimate jurisdiction over the criminal conduct in question, for the reason that they were not the same "party" that maintained the first prosecution (the "dual sovereign" doctrine). *Heath v. Alabama*, 474 U.S. 82 (1985).

Over the years, the Court has waffled over what is a criminal case covered by the Double Jeopardy Clause; fashioned tests for what constitutes the "same offense" within the meaning of the clause; and struggled with when "jeopardy" "attaches" and what the rules should be for appeals, erroneous jury verdicts, and mistrials.

3. *The Rest of the Fifth Amendment.* Next comes the Self–Incrimination Clause, which has already been considered. It is followed by the Due Process Clause, which is considered at length in Chapter 7, and the Takings Clause, which is considered at the conclusion of the materials on the Constitution and criminal procedure.

C. THE SIXTH AMENDMENT

Amendment VI: In all criminal prosecutions, the accused shall enjoy the right to a speedy and public trial, by an impartial jury of the State and district wherein the crime shall have been committed, which district shall have been previously ascertained by law, and to be informed of the nature and cause of the accusation; to be confronted with the witnesses against him; to have compulsory process for obtaining witnesses in his favor, and to have the Assistance of Counsel for his defense.

The Sixth Amendment protects important procedural trial rights of defendants in criminal cases: the right to trial by jury; the right to counsel; the right to confront the witnesses and evidence against the defendant; and the right to compel the attendance of witnesses supporting the defense. Each of these rights is designed to protect a criminal defendant against unjust conviction resulting from an unfair process. The right to a jury trial without delay, and within the community, was designed to protect the defendant against unjust or unfair prosecution. So too, the right to the assistance of counsel was an invaluable protection against unjust conviction as a result of unequal resources. Finally, the right of a defendant to confront the evidence and witnesses against him is rightly regarded as fundamental to the ability to defend oneself and refute unjust charges; the right of compulsory process is a corollary right to muster the evidence needed on one's own side of the case. That a defendant gets to challenge the evidence, and gets to present opposing evidence, is simply necessary to a fair process honestly directed to producing right outcomes. Uniting the Sixth Amendment's several protections is a concern for the integrity of the criminal trial process and the search for truth. Here we provide notes on the Sixth Amendment, emphasizing the right to counsel.

The note above on *Miranda* and the Fruit of the Poisonous Tree discussed *Brewer v. Williams*, a case decided on Sixth Amendment "right to counsel" grounds. The theory of the Court's decision was that the officer's "Christian Burial Speech" constituted interrogation in violation of the defendant's right to counsel because the defendant was already represented by counsel. *Brewer* (and other cases) are concerned with government interference with an existing attorney-client relationship.

When does the right to counsel exist—to what cases does it apply, and at what stage of proceedings? Is it a right *not to be prevented* from hiring counsel of one's choice, or is it a right to be *given* counsel if one cannot afford to hire an attorney? And when is an attorney so deficient that the defendant is effectively deprived of "the Assistance of Counsel"? The Court has considered these questions on numerous occasions.

In *Gideon v. Wainwright*, 372 U.S. 335 (1963), a man was charged with breaking and entering a poolroom with intent to commit a misdemeanor. He could not afford legal counsel and asked the court to appoint counsel for him, but under Florida law appointed counsel was available only in capital cases. The defendant represented himself and was convicted; he petitioned for habeas relief "on the ground that the trial court's refusal to appoint counsel for him denied him rights guaranteed by the Constitution and the Bill of Rights by the United States Government." Justice Black wrote the opinion of the Court:

> The Sixth Amendment provides, "In all criminal prosecutions, the accused shall enjoy the right . . . to have the Assistance of Counsel for his defence." We have construed this to mean that in federal courts counsel must be provided for defendants unable to employ counsel unless the right is competently and intelligently waived. [One of our prior cases] argued that this right is extended to indigent defendants in state courts by the Fourteenth Amendment. In response the Court stated that, while the Sixth Amendment laid down "no rule for the conduct of the states, the question recurs whether the constraint laid by the amendment upon the national courts expresses a rule so fundamental and essential to a fair trial, and so, to due process of law, that it is made obligatory upon the states by the Fourteenth Amendment." . . .
>
> The right of one charged with crime to counsel may not be deemed fundamental and essential to fair trials in some countries, but it is in ours. From the very beginning, our state and national constitutions and laws have laid great emphasis on procedural and substantive safeguards designed to assure fair trials before impartial tribunals in which every defendant stands equal before the law. This noble ideal cannot be realized if the poor man charged with crime has to face his accusers without a lawyer to assist him. A defendant's need for a lawyer is nowhere better stated than in the moving words of Mr. Justice Sutherland in *Powell v. Alabama*: "The right to be heard would be, in many cases, of little avail if it did not comprehend the right to be heard by counsel. Even the intelligent and educated layman . . . requires the guiding hand of counsel at every step in the proceedings against him. Without it, though he be not guilty, he faces the danger of conviction because he does not know how to establish his innocence."

Gideon is celebrated for its fulfillment of the Sixth Amendment's guarantee of the right "to have the Assistance of Counsel." But the provision of counsel might not be enough. Are there circumstances in which a defendant has an attorney, and yet the attorney is so bad that the defendant does not really have "Assistance of Counsel"? The Supreme Court has said *yes*. In *Strickland v. Washington*, 466 U.S. 668 (1984), the Court created the two-pronged modern test for ineffective-assistance-of-counsel claims. First, the defendant must prove that the lawyer was so incompetent as to not constitute the assistance of a lawyer at all; merely substandard performance by the lawyer does not violate the Sixth Amendment, as long as it falls within the broad range of professional competence. Second, the defendant must establish causation: the lawyer's ineptitude must have resulted in a miscarriage of justice. Thus defendants have a high burden of proof to establish a Sixth Amendment ineffective-assistance-of-counsel claim, though not an insurmountable one. E.g., *Burdine v. Johnson*, 262 F.3d 336 (5th Cir. 2001) (defendant successfully argued that he was denied the assistance of counsel when his lawyer slept through portions of his trial and death sentence hearing). Is the right to the effective assistance of counsel explicit in the Sixth Amendment? Is it a prophylactic rule?

A NOTE ON OTHER SIXTH AMENDMENT RIGHTS

1. *The Compulsory Process Clause.* Immediately preceding the Assistance of Counsel Clause is the clause that provides that the accused has the right to "compulsory process for obtaining witnesses in his favor." This right to compulsory process means also that the defendant has the power, enforced by the legal process, to subpoena and compel the attendance of witnesses. What if a witness refuses to testify—or invokes his own Fifth Amendment right against compelled self-incrimination? For a discussion of this problem, and analysis of the Supreme Court's cases concerning it, see Amar, THE CONSTITUTION AND CRIMINAL PROCEDURE: FIRST PRINCIPLES at 77–88.

2. *The Confrontation Clause.* This clause protects the right of the accused "to be confronted with the witnesses against him." The Supreme Court, after numerous doctrinal twists and turns, has finally settled on a reasonably straightforward reading of this provision, tied to its history: the Confrontation Clause "requires that a defendant have the opportunity to confront the witnesses who give testimony against him, except in cases where an exception to the confrontation right was recognized at the time of the founding." *Giles v. California*, 128 S. Ct. 2678, 2682 (2008). The central modern case interpreting the Confrontation Clause is *Crawford v. Washington*, 541 U.S. 36 (2004). *Crawford* painstakingly examined the language and history of the clause, and concluded that "the principal evil at which the Confrontation Clause was directed was the civil-law mode of criminal procedure, and particularly its use of *ex parte* examinations as evidence against the accused." It also concluded that "the Framers would not have allowed admission of testimonial statements of a witness who did not appear at trial unless he was unavailable to testify, and the defendant had had a prior opportunity for cross-examination." According to the Court, the Sixth Amendment did not create a balancing test or authorize courts create new exceptions to the confrontation right, but instead it "is most naturally read as a reference to the right of confrontation at common law, admitting only those exceptions established at the time of the founding."

3. *The Sixth Amendment Right to Trial By Jury.* In a recent series of cases the Court has held that the right to trial by jury means that every fact that forms an element of the offense, or that increases the penalty for a crime beyond what is specified in the statute defining the offense, must be submitted to a jury and proved beyond a reasonable doubt. *Apprendi v. New Jersey*, 530 U.S. 466 (2000). The *Apprendi* approach has upended prior precedents and practice, especially in the area of sentencing. In *Blakely v. Washington*, 542 U.S. 296 (2004), the Court invalidated state sentencing guidelines that required judges to enhance sentences on the basis of facts determined by the judge at sentencing and not by the jury at trial. In *United States v. Booker*, 543 U.S. 220 (2005), the Court invalidated the federal sentencing guidelines for similar reasons, but adopted a complex and confusing remedy for this Sixth Amendment violation.

A NOTE ON THE SEVENTH AMENDMENT RIGHT TO TRIAL BY JURY

Amendment VII: In Suits at common law, where the value in controversy shall exceed twenty dollars, the right of trial by jury shall be preserved, and no fact tried by a jury, shall be otherwise re-examined in any Court of the United States, than according to the rules of the common law.

1. *The Constitutional Convention.* The Seventh Amendment provides the right to jury trial in *civil* proceedings. Interestingly, it was the absence of a provision for civil jury trial that caught the attention of several delegates to the Constitutional Convention and led to the late-in-the-day proposal that the Constitution include a bill of rights. The Convention rejected the idea, leading some of the delegates—including George Mason of Virginia and Elbridge Gerry of Massachusetts—to decline to sign the proposed Constitution and become leading "Anti–Federalist" opponents in the ratification struggle, as discussed above in Chapter 1.

2. *"Suits at common law."* The traditional understanding of the phrase "Suits at common law" is that it refers to those types of civil lawsuits that would have been heard in the courts of "law"—rather than the courts of "equity" (or "chancery") or "admiralty"—in the division of judicial authority practiced in England and followed in the American states at the time the Seventh Amendment was adopted in 1791. Since the right to jury trial is "preserved" in such cases, the Supreme Court's interpretation and application of the amendment has followed a historical approach, asking whether a particular lawsuit is of the type that would have been heard in England's law courts in 1791 (even though today law and equity have merged in the federal system and most state systems).

3. *"Twenty dollars."* The amendment applies only to suits where "the value in controversy shall exceed twenty dollars." Is the Seventh Amendment indexed to inflation? See Note, *The Twenty Dollars Clause*, 118 Harv. L. Rev. 1665, 1672 (2005) (rejecting the notion that the "value" of "twenty dollars" permits inflation-adjustment over time).

4. *"The right of trial by jury."* Does this right include all the incidents of trial by jury as they existed in 1791? What were those features? Must a jury have twelve—and exactly twelve—members? May changes in procedure change the scope of the right—or is that exactly what the Seventh Amendment bars?

5. *"Shall be Preserved."* Does "preserved" necessarily mean, as noted above, that the right to civil jury trial must exist as it existed in 1791? Or, given that the Bill of Rights was designed to limit the power of only the *national* government, does "preserved" mean that if a jury trial right would have existed on some issue *in state court* that the fact that the case might have ended up in federal court (say, by virtue of diversity jurisdiction) should not alter the existence of a right to trial by jury? In other words, does "preserved" have a *historical* law-versus-equity meaning or a *federalism* meaning? An interesting consequence of the federalism reading of the Amendment is that it would make little sense to incorporate the Seventh Amendment as a limitation on state governments. (For discussion of a similar puzzle in the context of the Second Amendment, see the notes after *District of Columbia v. Heller.*) Notably, in the Court's "selective incorporation" approach to whether the Bill of Rights applies to the states, the Seventh Amendment is one of only a few provisions that the Court has not applied to the states.

6. *"And no fact ... re-examined."* The Amendment contains an anti-circumvention rule forbidding courts from re-examining facts found by a jury other than in accordance with the rules of the common law (which sometimes permitted judges to take cases from the jury, by directed verdict or judgment notwithstanding the verdict). Do "the rules of the common law" evolve—and

thus the meaning and scope of the no-re-examination rule potentially change? Or are they fixed by 1791 practice?

D. THE EIGHTH AMENDMENT

Amendment VIII: Excessive bail shall not be required, nor excessive fines imposed, nor cruel and unusual punishments inflicted.

By its terms, the Eighth Amendment appears to embrace general standards for punishments more than bright-line rules. It speaks of "excessive" bail, "excessive" fines, and "cruel and unusual" punishments. Does the use of such terms contemplate that the application of the Eighth Amendment will vary with changing general practices at different times and in different contexts? Is there any other way to measure what is excessive or unusual or cruel? Or is the better approach to look to historical practice at the time of the amendment's adoption and use that practice as a baseline for what is excessive or cruel? For example, if the death penalty, or putting someone in the stocks, or branding, was not regarded as a forbidden practice in 1791, should it be possible for such a practice later to be regarded as unconstitutional under the Eighth Amendment? Or should the question be what seemed excessive or cruel in 1868, when the Fourteenth Amendment was ratified? (Almost all so-called Eighth Amendment cases involve state laws.) If a court takes a more historical approach, how should it try to determine what was excessive or cruel in 1791 or 1868?

A number of the Court's Eighth Amendment cases have involved the death penalty. The capital punishment cases are a complicated and essentially unique area of practice. In *Furman v. Georgia*, 409 U.S. 902 (1972), the Supreme Court determined that the death penalty, as it was then applied, was random and unpredictable and therefore amounted to cruel and unusual punishment under the Eighth Amendment—"cruel and unusual in the same way that being struck by lightning is cruel and unusual." In *Gregg v. Georgia*, 428 U.S. 153 (1976), the Supreme Court lifted what had in effect been a moratorium on the death penalty. The Court upheld the use of the death penalty where the jury is required to find a statutorily prescribed aggravating factor and given guidance in the exercise of its discretion. Since *Furman* and *Gregg*, the Supreme Court has decided capital punishment cases by trying to assess "the evolving standards of decency that mark a maturing society." The Supreme Court often tallies state laws to see, for a particular category of cases, whether the death penalty is widely endorsed or is used in only a few states. And it sometimes considers how the death penalty is used outside the United States. See, e.g., *Roper v. Simmons*, 543 U.S. 551 (2005).

Reflect on the big-picture constitutional issue: What is the proper understanding of the term "cruel and unusual punishment"? Does it apply to punishment that is cruel but not unusual, or unusual but not cruel? Does "cruel" have an objective meaning? Should it be fixed by what the founding generation understood to be cruel? Or by what was considered cruel in 1868? Or is it inherently subjective? Does it require moral reasoning? If so, who should make the subjective determination and engage in the moral reasoning? Should it be legislatures, on the grounds that they reflect community judgments about what is or is not a cruel punishment? Or would that be an abdication by the courts of their constitutional duty to decide, in cases and controversies, whether a punishment is "cruel and unusual"? In short, how, and by whom, should the meaning of "cruel and unusual" be determined?

[*Assignment 58*]

V. THE TAKINGS CLAUSE

Amendment V: ... nor shall private property be taken for public use, without just compensation.

The original Constitution protected property rights in a number of ways. These included structural provisions designed to ensure the rule of law, such as representative government, separation of powers, and federalism. In addition, the Contracts Clause of Article I, Section 10 provided some protection against state interference with vested contractual obligations, an important safeguard of property.

Property rights gained additional protection against federal interference with the ratification of the Bill of Rights. The first ten amendments contain several provisions that pertain to property, including the Fourth Amendment and two provisions of the Fifth Amendment: the Due Process Clause, which is considered below in Chapter 7; and the Takings Clause, which is addressed here.

What Is a Taking of "Property" for a Public Use?

In its most classic sense, the Fifth Amendment requires the government to pay for property it acquires for public uses, such as post offices, roads, parks, office buildings, or military bases. Often these transactions are consensual in nature, and raise no constitutional issues at all. But when the government uses its power of eminent domain to take private property, the Fifth Amendment requires that the owner receive "just compensation." In such cases, the government files a "condemnation" action against the property holder, and the amount of compensation is determined by the fact finder, usually a jury.

In these classic cases of condemnation, the Fifth Amendment is essentially self-enforcing and rarely requires interpretation or judicial enforcement. But there are a number of contexts in which the government takes action short of condemnation that has the practical effect of converting private property to a public use. When this happens, the property owner is the one who files suit for compensation, and the case is called an "inverse condemnation" action. These cases raise the question of what is "property." As you may have learned in a first-year course on Property, the general rule is that "[p]roperty interests ... are not created by the Constitution. Rather, they are created and their dimensions are defined by existing rules or understandings that stem from an independent source such as state law." *Board of Regents v. Roth*, 408 U.S. 564, 577 (1972). But is there a fundamental constitutional core, which if not respected by the state, constitutes a taking? See Thomas W. Merrill, *The Landscape of Constitutional Property*, 86 Va. L. Rev. 885 (2000).

Consider these cases:

1. When there are competing claimants to a fund or other property, the conflict is often resolved by means of an interpleader action, in which the fund or property is deposited with the clerk of the court, and the court then determines who is the proper owner. Who owns the *interest* on the fund during the time it is deposited with the court? In *Webb's Fabulous Pharmacies v. Beckwith*, 449 U.S. 155 (1980), the state of Florida declared that the interest on interpleader accounts was "public money" because the court

clerk was under no legal obligation to invest the fund while it was under court control, and if the clerk did so, "the statute takes only what it creates." The Supreme Court reversed, holding:

> Neither the Florida Legislature by statute, nor the Florida courts by judicial decree, may accomplish the result the county seeks simply by recharacterizing the principal as "public money" because it is held temporarily by the court. The earnings of a fund are incidents of ownership of the fund itself and are property just as the fund itself is property. The state statute has the practical effect of appropriating for the county the value of the use of the fund for the period in which it is held in the registry.
>
> To put it another way: a State, by *ipse dixit*, may not transform private property into public property without compensation, even for the limited duration of the deposit in court. This is the very kind of thing that the Taking Clause of the Fifth Amendment was meant to prevent. That Clause stands as a shield against the arbitrary use of governmental power.

What is the difference between *ipse dixit* and ordinary common law adjudication? Is the principle that "[t]he earnings of a fund are incidents of ownership of the fund itself and are property just as the fund itself is property" a constitutional principle? If so, from what is it derived?

What if the state piles sand in front of a beach-front house as part of an erosion-reversal project? May the state legislature now "recharacterize" the ownership interests in the strip between dry beach and ocean to make it public property? How would that differ from the state statute in *Webb's*? May the same recharacterizing be done not by the legislature by the state supreme court? Does the answer depend on whether the state court decision applied the law or changed it? But doesn't a common law court have authority to change the common law? These questions were raised in *Stop the Beach Renourishment, Inc. v. Florida Department of Environmental Protection*, 130 S. Ct. 2592 (2010), though the Court chose not to decide whether a judicial decision can be a "taking" that requires the payment of compensation under the Takings Clause. (Four justices would have held that there can be judicial takings, but others did not think the question essential to the decision.)

2. The City of New York required owners of apartment buildings to permit cable television companies to install cables on their property. The cables occupied minimal space and were not harmful to the property. In *Loretto v. Teleprompter Manhattan CATV Corp.*, 458 U.S. 419 (1982), the Court held that this was a taking. The Court said that "a permanent physical occupation authorized by government is a taking without regard to the public interests that it may serve." Why might that be a sensible interpretation of the term "property"? Is the right to exclude the central feature of "property"? (Note that *Loretto* refers to "a *permanent* physical occupation": where the physical invasion is only temporary, the Court appears to use a balancing test.)

One of the more difficult questions about "property" in the Takings Clause is whether a taking occurs when the government insists that an owner transfer a property interest to the state as a condition of receiving regulatory permission to develop the property. This can also be understood as an example of an "unconstitutional conditions" question. Here is the Supreme Court's take:

Nollan v. California Coastal Commission

483 U.S. 825 (1987)

■ JUSTICE SCALIA delivered the opinion of the Court.

James and Marilyn Nollan appeal from a decision of the California Court of Appeal ruling that the California Coastal Commission could condition its grant of permission to rebuild their house on their transfer to the public of an easement across their beachfront property. . . .

I

The Nollans own a beachfront lot in Ventura County, California. A quarter-mile north of their property is Faria County Park, an oceanside public park with a public beach and recreation area. Another public beach area, known locally as "the Cove," lies 1,800 feet south of their lot. A concrete seawall approximately eight feet high separates the beach portion of the Nollans' property from the rest of the lot. The historic mean high tide line determines the lot's oceanside boundary. . . .

The Nollans' option to purchase was conditioned on their promise to demolish the bungalow and replace it. In order to do so, they were required to obtain a coastal development permit from the California Coastal Commission. On February 25, 1982, they submitted a permit application to the Commission in which they proposed to demolish the existing structure and replace it with a three-bedroom house in keeping with the rest of the neighborhood. . . .

[T]he Commission . . . granted the permit subject to their recordation of a deed restriction granting [an] easement. . . . *[The easement would allow the public to pass between Faria County Park and the Cove through a portion of their property between the seawall and the high tide line.— Editors]*

II

Had California simply required the Nollans to make an easement across their beachfront available to the public on a permanent basis in order to increase public access to the beach, rather than conditioning their permit to rebuild their house on their agreeing to do so, we have no doubt there would have been a taking. To say that the appropriation of a public easement across a landowner's premises does not constitute the taking of a property interest but rather (as Justice BRENNAN contends) "a mere restriction on its use" is to use words in a manner that deprives them of all their ordinary meaning. Indeed, one of the principal uses of the eminent domain power is to assure that the government be able to require conveyance of just such interests, so long as it pays for them. . . . We have repeatedly held that, as to property reserved by its owner for private use, "the right to exclude [others is] one of the most essential sticks in the bundle of rights that are commonly characterized as property." *Loretto v. Teleprompter Manhattan CATV Corp.,* 458 U.S. 419, 433 (1982). In *Loretto* we observed that where governmental action results in "[a] permanent physical occupation" of the property, by the government itself or by others, "our cases uniformly have found a taking to the extent of the occupation, without regard to whether the action achieves an important public benefit or has only minimal economic impact on the owner," *id.,* at 434–435. We think a "permanent physical occupation" has occurred, for purposes of that rule, where individuals are given a permanent and continuous right to pass to and fro, so that the real property may continuously be traversed, even though no particular individual is permitted to station himself permanently upon the premises. . . .

Given, then, that requiring uncompensated conveyance of the easement outright would violate the Fourteenth Amendment, the question becomes whether requiring it to be conveyed as a condition for issuing a land-use permit alters the outcome. We have long recognized that land-use regulation does not effect a taking if it "substantially advance[s] legitimate state interests" and does not "den[y] an owner economically viable use of his land," *Agins v. Tiburon,* 447 U.S. 255, 260 (1980). Our cases have not elaborated on the standards for determining what constitutes a "legitimate state interest" or what type of connection between the regulation and the state interest satisfies the requirement that the former "substantially advance" the latter. They have made clear, however, that a broad range of governmental purposes and regulations satisfies these requirements. The Commission argues that among these permissible purposes are protecting the public's ability to see the beach, assisting the public in overcoming the "psychological barrier" to using the beach created by a developed shorefront, and preventing congestion on the public beaches. We assume, without deciding, that this is so—in which case the Commission unquestionably would be able to deny the Nollans their permit outright if their new house (alone, or by reason of the cumulative impact produced in conjunction with other construction) would substantially impede these purposes, unless the denial would interfere so drastically with the Nollans' use of their property as to constitute a taking.

The Commission argues that a permit condition that serves the same legitimate police-power purpose as a refusal to issue the permit should not be found to be a taking if the refusal to issue the permit would not constitute a taking. We agree. Thus, if the Commission attached to the permit some condition that would have protected the public's ability to see the beach notwithstanding construction of the new house—for example, a height limitation, a width restriction, or a ban on fences—so long as the Commission could have exercised its police power (as we have assumed it could) to forbid construction of the house altogether, imposition of the condition would also be constitutional. Moreover (and here we come closer to the facts of the present case), the condition would be constitutional even if it consisted of the requirement that the Nollans provide a viewing spot on their property for passersby with whose sighting of the ocean their new house would interfere. Although such a requirement, constituting a permanent grant of continuous access to the property, would have to be considered a taking if it were not attached to a development permit, the Commission's assumed power to forbid construction of the house in order to protect the public's view of the beach must surely include the power to condition construction upon some concession by the owner, even a concession of property rights, that serves the same end. If a prohibition designed to accomplish that purpose would be a legitimate exercise of the police power rather than a taking, it would be strange to conclude that providing the owner an alternative to that prohibition which accomplishes the same purpose is not.

The evident constitutional propriety disappears, however, if the condition substituted for the prohibition utterly fails to further the end advanced as the justification for the prohibition. When that essential nexus is eliminated, the situation becomes the same as if California law forbade shouting fire in a crowded theater, but granted dispensations to those willing to contribute $100 to the state treasury. While a ban on shouting fire can be a core exercise of the State's police power to protect the public safety, and can thus meet even our stringent standards for regulation of speech, adding the unrelated condition alters the purpose to one which, while it may be legitimate, is inadequate to sustain the ban. . . . Similarly here, the lack of nexus between the condition and the original purpose of the building restriction converts that purpose to something other than what it was. The purpose then becomes, quite simply, the obtaining of an easement to serve some valid governmental purpose, but without payment of compensation. Whatever may be the outer limits of "legitimate state interests" in the takings and land-use context, this is not one of them. In short, unless the permit condition serves the same governmental purpose as the development ban, the building restriction is not a valid regulation of land use but "an out-and-out plan of extortion." *J.E.D. Associates, Inc. v. Atkinson*, 121 N.H. 581, 584 (1981).

III

. . . We are left, then, with the Commission's justification for the access requirement unrelated to land-use regulation: . . . "The access required as a condition of this permit is part of a comprehensive program to provide continuous public access along Faria Beach as the lots undergo development or redevelopment." That is simply an expression of the Commission's belief that the public interest will be served by a continuous strip of publicly accessible beach along the coast. The Commission may well be right that it is a good idea, but that does not establish that the Nollans (and other coastal residents) alone can be compelled to contribute to its realization. Rather, California is free to advance its "comprehensive program," if it wishes, by using its power of eminent domain for this "public purpose," see U.S. Const., Amdt. 5; but if it wants an easement across the Nollans' property, it must pay for it.

▪ [Dissenting opinions by Justices Brennan, Blackmun and Stevens are omitted.]

What Is a "Taking" of Property for Public Use?

In *Nollan*, the public gained use of the property in question. What if the government imposes restrictions that destroy all or part of the value of the property to its owner, but without giving the public any additional right to use it? These are generally called "regulatory takings." How does the Takings Clause apply to such actions? Consider the following major case.

Pennsylvania Coal Co. v. Mahon
260 U.S. 393 (1922)

▪ Mr. Justice Holmes delivered the opinion of the Court.

This is a bill in equity brought by the defendants in error to prevent the Pennsylvania Coal Company from mining under their property in such way as to remove the supports and cause a subsidence of the surface and of their house. The bill sets out a deed executed by the Coal Company in 1878, under which the plaintiffs claim. The deed conveys the surface but in express terms reserves the right to remove all the coal under the same and the grantee takes the premises with the risk and waives all claim for damages that may arise from mining out the coal. But the plaintiffs say that whatever may have been the Coal Company's rights, they were taken away by an Act of Pennsylvania, approved May 27, 1921 (P. L. 1198), commonly known there as the Kohler Act. . . .

The statute forbids the mining of anthracite coal in such way as to cause the subsidence of . . . any structure used as a human habitation, with certain exceptions, including among them land where the surface is owned by the owner of the underlying coal and is distant more than one hundred and fifty feet from any improved property belonging to any other person. As applied to this case the statute is admitted to destroy previously existing rights of property and contract. The question is whether the police power can be stretched so far.

Government hardly could go on if to some extent values incident to property could not be diminished without paying for every such change in the general law. As long recognized some values are enjoyed under an implied limitation and must yield to the police power. But obviously the implied limitation must have its limits or the contract and due process clauses are gone. One fact for consideration in determining such limits is the extent of the diminution. When it reaches a certain magnitude, in most if not in all cases there must be an exercise of eminent domain and compensation to sustain the act. So the question depends upon the particular facts. The greatest weight is given to the judgment of the legislature but it always is open to interested parties to contend that the legislature has gone beyond its constitutional power.

This is the case of a single private house. No doubt there is a public interest even in this, as there is in every purchase and sale and in all that happens within the commonwealth. Some existing rights may be modified even in such a case. But usually in ordinary private affairs the public interest does not warrant much of this kind of interference. A source of damage to such a house is not a public nuisance even if similar damage is inflicted on others in different places. The damage is not common or public. The extent of the public interest is shown by the statute to be limited, since the statute ordinarily does not apply to land when the surface is owned by the owner of the coal. Furthermore, it is not justified as a protection of personal safety. That could be provided for by notice. Indeed the very foundation of this bill is that the defendant gave timely notice of its intent to mine under the house. On the other hand the extent of the taking is great. It purports to abolish what is recognized in Pennsylvania as an estate in land—a very valuable estate—and what is declared by the Court below to be a contract hitherto binding the plaintiffs. If we were called upon to deal with the plaintiffs' position alone we should think it clear that the statute does not disclose a public interest sufficient to warrant so extensive a destruction of the defendant's constitutionally protected rights. . . .

The general rule at least is that while property may be regulated to a certain extent, if regulation goes too far it will be recognized as a taking. . . . In general it is not plain that a man's misfortunes or necessities will justify his shifting the damages to his neighbor's shoulders. We are in danger of forgetting that a strong public desire to improve the public condition is not enough to warrant achieving the desire by a shorter cut than the constitutional way of paying for the change. As we already have said this is a question of degree—and therefore cannot be disposed of by general propositions. But we regard this as going beyond any of the cases decided by this Court. . . .

We assume, of course, that the statute was passed upon the conviction that an exigency existed that would warrant it, and we assume that an exigency exists that would warrant the exercise of eminent domain. But the question at bottom is upon whom the loss of the changes desired should fall. So far as private persons or communities have seen fit to take the risk of acquiring only surface rights, we cannot see that the fact that their risk has become a danger warrants the giving to them greater rights than they bought.

■ MR. JUSTICE BRANDEIS dissenting.

. . . Coal in place is land, and the right of the owner to use his land is not absolute. He may not so use it as to create a public nuisance, and uses, once harmless, may, owing to changed conditions, seriously threaten the public welfare. Whenever they do, the Legislature has power to prohibit such uses without paying compensation; and the power to prohibit extends alike to the manner, the character and the purpose of the use. Are we justified in declaring that the Legislature of Pennsylvania has, in restricting the right to mine anthracite, exercised this power so arbitrarily as to violate the Fourteenth Amendment?

Every restriction upon the use of property imposed in the exercise of the police power deprives the owner of some right theretofore enjoyed, and is, in that sense, an abridgment by the state of rights in property without making compensation. But restriction imposed to protect the public health, safety or morals from dangers threatened is not a taking. The restriction here in question is merely the prohibition of a noxious use. The property so restricted remains in the possession of its owner. The state does not appropriate it or make any use of it. The state merely prevents the owner from making a use which interferes with paramount rights of the public. Whenever the use prohibited ceases to be noxious—as it may because of further change in local or social conditions—the restriction will have to be removed and the owner will again be free to enjoy his property as heretofore. . . .

It is said that one fact for consideration in determining whether the limits of the police power have been exceeded is the extent of the resulting diminution in value, and that here the restriction destroys existing rights of property and contract. But values are relative. If we are to consider the value of the coal kept in place by the restriction, we should compare it with the value of all other parts of the land. . . . But I suppose no one would contend that by selling his interest above 100 feet from the surface he could prevent the state from limiting, by the police power, the height of structures in a city. And why should a sale of underground rights bar the state's power? For aught that appears the value of the coal kept in place by the restriction may be negligible as compared with the value of the whole property, or even as compared with that part of it which is represented by the coal remaining in place and which may be extracted despite the statute. Ordinarily a police regulation, general in operation, will not be held void as to a particular property, although proof is offered that owing to conditions peculiar to it the restriction could not reasonably be applied. But even if the particular facts are to govern, the statute should, in my opinion be upheld in this case. For the defendant has failed to adduce any evidence from which it appears that to restrict its mining operations was an unreasonable exercise of the police power. . . .

NOTES

1. When the surface owner purchased the right to use and build upon the surface estate, the coal company explicitly reserved the right to mine all the

coal, and the surface owner assumed the risk from subsidence. Why should the state now deny the purchaser the benefit of the contract? Note that the Kohler Act is not a generally applicable environmental statute; it does not apply where surface rights and mineral rights are owned by the same person. Should this be framed as a case under the Takings Clause of the Fifth Amendment or under the Contracts Clause of Article I, Section 10?

2. What is the majority's test for when a regulation amounts to a regulatory taking? Is it when the regulation "goes too far"? In *Penn Central Transportation Co. v. City of New York*, 438 U.S. 104 (1978), the Court elaborated:

> The question of what constitutes a "taking" for purposes of the Fifth Amendment has proved to be a problem of considerable difficulty. While this Court has recognized that the "Fifth Amendment's guarantee . . . [is] designed to bar Government from forcing some people alone to bear public burdens which, in all fairness and justice, should be borne by the public as a whole," *Armstrong v. United States*, 364 U.S. 40, 49 (1960), this Court, quite simply, has been unable to develop any "set formula" for determining when "justice and fairness" require that economic injuries caused by public action be compensated by the government, rather than remain disproportionately concentrated on a few persons. Indeed, we have frequently observed that whether a particular restriction will be rendered invalid by the government's failure to pay for any losses proximately caused by it depends largely "upon the particular circumstances [in that] case." *United States v. Central Eureka Mining Co.*, 357 U.S. 155, 168 (1958).
>
> In engaging in these essentially ad hoc, factual inquiries, the Court's decisions have identified several factors that have particular significance. The economic impact of the regulation on the claimant and, particularly, the extent to which the regulation has interfered with distinct investment-backed expectations are, of course, relevant considerations. So, too, is the character of the governmental action. A "taking" may more readily be found when the interference with property can be characterized as a physical invasion by government, than when interference arises from some public program adjusting the benefits and burdens of economic life to promote the common good.

Id. at 123–24. Does this clarify when a regulatory taking exists?

In subsequent decisions, the Court has held that a regulation that deprives the owner of substantially all of the economic benefit of the property is a per se regulatory taking. Regulations depriving the owner of only a portion of the economic value, however, are subject to the deferential multi-factor test of *Penn Central*. This may appear to reduce the degree to which the inquiry is ad hoc, but it presents a daunting question: substantially all of what? If a property owner has a thousand-acre parcel, and the government requires him or her to maintain one hundred acres as a wetlands, should this be seen as taking "substantially" all the value of the one hundred acres, or as taking only ten percent of the entire parcel?

3. Justice Brandeis distinguishes between governmental actions that prevent a "noxious use" of property and those that "appropriate" or "make use" of the property on behalf of the public. Is that a tenable distinction? Under the state law in *Pennsylvania Coal*, was the public protected from the "harm" of subsidence, or was the public given the "use" and benefit of support? If a city

passes zoning rules to block additional development in an overcrowded area, should those rules be regarded as preventing the "harm" of future development, or seizing the "benefit" of open space for the public? Can you think of cases where the distinction is more clear-cut? For a defense of the harm-benefit distinction, see Jed Rubenfeld, *Usings*, 102 Yale L.J. 1077 (1993). Rubenfeld emphasizes that the Fifth Amendment requires compensation only for takings "for a public use" and not for actions that diminish value or prevent harm to others.

In *Lucas v. South Carolina Coastal Council*, 505 U.S. 1003 (1992), a divided Court rejected a generalized harm principle in favor of a narrower principle grounded in common law principles of nuisance. Because all property is held subject to the common law of nuisance, which prevents use of property in ways that harm others, state regulatory laws that do no more than enforce these nuisance principles (or make them explicit) do not "take" anything that the property holder ever really had. The prohibited use was "always unlawful." *Id.*, at 1027. Does this mean (should it mean?) the common law of nuisance as it existed in the nineteenth century, or as state courts may fashion it today? Why is it not true that owners hold their property subject to the possibility that the state will discover and prohibit new forms of harm? In *Mugler v. Kansas*, 123 U.S. 623 (1887), the legislature had outlawed the manufacture and sale of alcohol, substantially destroying the economic value of a brewery. Was the brewery owner entitled to compensation?

What Is a Taking of Private Property for a "Public Use"?

Does the Fifth Amendment also contain a restriction that private property may be taken *only* "for a public use"? May the government use the eminent domain power to take property from one person, for the benefit of another, presumably more politically "juiced," person or entity?

Kelo v. New London
545 U.S. 469 (2005)

■ JUSTICE STEVENS delivered the opinion of the Court.

In 2000, the city of New London approved a development plan that, in the words of the Supreme Court of Connecticut, was "projected to create in excess of 1,000 jobs, to increase tax and other revenues, and to revitalize an economically distressed city, including its downtown and waterfront areas." In assembling the land needed for this project, the city's development agent has purchased property from willing sellers and proposes to use the power of eminent domain to acquire the remainder of the property from unwilling owners in exchange for just compensation. The question presented is whether the city's proposed disposition of this property qualifies as a "public use" within the meaning of the Takings Clause of the Fifth Amendment to the Constitution.

I

The city of New London (hereinafter City) sits at the junction of the Thames River and the Long Island Sound in southeastern Connecticut. Decades of economic decline led a state agency in 1990 to designate the City a "distressed municipality." . . .

These conditions prompted state and local officials to target New London, and particularly its Fort Trumbull area, for economic revitalization. To this end, respondent New London Development Corporation (NLDC), a private nonprofit entity established some years earlier to assist the City in planning economic development, was reactivated. In January 1998, the State authorized a $5.35 million bond issue to support the NLDC's planning activities and a $10 million bond issue toward the creation of a Fort Trumbull State Park. In February, the pharmaceutical company Pfizer Inc. announced that it would build a $300 million research facility on a site immediately adjacent to Fort Trumbull; local planners hoped that Pfizer would draw new business to the area, thereby serving as a catalyst to the area's rejuvenation. . . .

The Fort Trumbull area is situated on a peninsula that juts into the Thames River. The area comprises approximately 115 privately owned properties, as well as the 32 acres of land formerly occupied by the naval facility (Trumbull State Park now occupies 18 of those 32 acres). The development plan encompasses seven parcels. Parcel 1 is designated for a waterfront conference hotel at the center of a "small urban village" that will include restaurants and shopping. This parcel will also have marinas for both recreational and commercial uses. A pedestrian "riverwalk" will originate here and continue down the coast, connecting the waterfront areas of the development. Parcel 2 will be the site of approximately 80 new residences organized into an urban neighborhood and linked by public walkway to the remainder of the development, including the state park. This parcel also includes space reserved for a new U.S. Coast Guard Museum. Parcel 3, which is located immediately north of the Pfizer facility, will contain at least 90,000 square feet of research and development office space. Parcel 4A is a 2.4–acre site that will be used either to support the adjacent state park, by providing parking or retail services for visitors, or to support the nearby marina. Parcel 4B will include a renovated marina, as well as the final stretch of the riverwalk. Parcels 5, 6, and 7 will provide land for office and retail space, parking, and water-dependent commercial uses.

The NLDC intended the development plan to capitalize on the arrival of the Pfizer facility and the new commerce it was expected to attract. In addition to creating jobs, generating tax revenue, and helping to "build momentum for the revitalization of downtown New London," the plan was also designed to make the City more attractive and to create leisure and recreational opportunities on the waterfront and in the park.

The city council approved the plan in January 2000, and designated the NLDC as its development agent in charge of implementation. The city council also authorized the NLDC to purchase property or to acquire property by exercising eminent domain in the City's name. The NLDC successfully negotiated the purchase of most of the real estate in the 90–acre area, but its negotiations with petitioners failed. As a consequence, in November 2000, the NLDC initiated the condemnation proceedings that gave rise to this case.

II

Petitioner Susette Kelo has lived in the Fort Trumbull area since 1997. She has made extensive improvements to her house, which she prizes for its water view. Petitioner Wilhelmina Dery was born in her Fort Trumbull house in 1918 and has lived there her entire life. Her husband Charles (also a petitioner) has lived in the house since they married some 60 years ago. In all, the nine petitioners own 15 properties in Fort Trumbull—4 in parcel 3 of the development plan and 11 in parcel 4A. Ten of the parcels are occupied by the owner or a family member; the other five are held as investment properties. There is no allegation that any of these properties is blighted or otherwise in poor condition; rather, they were condemned only because they happen to be located in the development area. . . .

III

Two polar propositions are perfectly clear. On the one hand, it has long been accepted that the sovereign may not take the property of *A* for the sole purpose of transferring it to another private party *B,* even though *A* is paid just compensation. On the other hand, it is equally clear that a State may transfer property from one private party to another if future "use by the public" is the purpose of the taking; the condemnation of land for a railroad with common-carrier duties is a familiar example. Neither of these propositions, however, determines the disposition of this case.

As for the first proposition, the City would no doubt be forbidden from taking petitioners' land for the purpose of conferring a private benefit on a particular private party. Nor would the City be allowed to take property under the mere pretext of a public purpose, when its actual purpose was to bestow a private benefit. The takings before us, however, would be executed pursuant to a "carefully considered" development plan. . . . [T]he City's development plan was not adopted "to benefit a particular class of identifiable individuals."

On the other hand, this is not a case in which the City is planning to open the condemned land—at least not in its entirety—to use by the general public. Nor will the private lessees of the land in any sense be required to operate like common carriers, making their services available to all comers. But although such a projected use would be sufficient to satisfy the public use requirement, this "Court long ago rejected any literal requirement that condemned property be put into use for the general public." Indeed, while many state courts in the mid–19th century endorsed "use by the public" as the proper definition of public use, that narrow view steadily eroded over time. Not only was the "use by the public" test difficult to administer (*e.g.,* what proportion of the public need have access to the property? at what price?), but it proved to be impractical given the diverse and always evolving needs of society. Accordingly, when this Court began applying the Fifth Amendment to the States at the close of the 19th century, it embraced the broader and more natural interpretation of public use as "public purpose." . . . Without exception, our cases have defined that concept broadly, reflecting our longstanding policy of deference to legislative judgments in this field.

In *Berman v. Parker,* 348 U.S. 26 (1954), this Court upheld a redevelopment plan targeting a blighted area of Washington, D. C., in which most of the housing for the area's 5,000 inhabitants was beyond repair. . . . The owner of a department store located in the area challenged the condemnation, pointing out that his store was not itself blighted and arguing that the creation of a "better balanced, more attractive community" was not a valid public use. Writing for a unanimous Court, Justice Douglas refused to evaluate this claim in isolation, deferring instead to the legislative and agency judgment that the area "must be planned as a whole" for the plan to be successful. . . .

In *Hawaii Housing Authority v. Midkiff,* 467 U.S. 229 (1984), the Court considered a Hawaii statute whereby fee title was taken from lessors and transferred to lessees (for just compensation) in order to reduce the concentration of land ownership. We unanimously upheld the statute and rejected the Ninth Circuit's view that it was "a naked attempt on the part of the state of Hawaii to take the property of A and transfer it to B solely for B's private use and benefit." Reaffirming *Berman*'s deferential approach to legislative judgments in this field, we concluded that the State's purpose of eliminating the "social and economic evils of a land oligopoly" qualified as a valid public use. Our opinion also rejected the contention that the mere fact that the State immediately transferred the properties to private individuals upon condemnation somehow diminished the public character of the taking. "[I]t is only the taking's purpose, and not its mechanics," we explained, that matters in determining public use. . . .

Viewed as a whole, our jurisprudence has recognized that the needs of society have varied between different parts of the Nation, just as they have evolved over time in response to changed circumstances. Our earliest cases in particular embodied a strong theme of federalism, emphasizing the "great respect" that we owe to state legislatures and state courts in discerning local public needs. For more than a century, our public use jurisprudence has wisely eschewed rigid formulas and intrusive scrutiny in favor of affording legislatures broad latitude in determining what public needs justify the use of the takings power.

IV

Those who govern the City were not confronted with the need to remove blight in the Fort Trumbull area, but their determination that the area was sufficiently distressed to justify a program of economic rejuvenation is entitled to our deference. The City has carefully formulated an economic development plan that it believes will provide appreciable benefits to the community, including—but by no means limited to—new jobs and increased tax revenue. . . . Given the comprehensive character of the plan, the thorough deliberation that preceded its adoption, and the limited scope of our review, it is appropriate for us, as it was in *Berman,* to resolve the challenges of the individual owners, not on a piecemeal basis, but rather in light of the entire plan. Because that plan unquestionably serves a public purpose, the takings challenged here satisfy the public use requirement of the Fifth Amendment. . . .

In affirming the City's authority to take petitioners' properties, we do not minimize the hardship that condemnations may entail, notwithstanding the payment of just compensation. We emphasize that nothing in our opinion precludes any State from placing further restrictions on its exercise of the takings power. Indeed, many States already impose "public use" requirements that are stricter than the federal baseline. Some of these requirements have been established as a matter of state constitutional law, while others are expressed in state eminent domain statutes that carefully limit the grounds upon which takings may be exercised. As the submissions of the parties and their *amici* make clear, the necessity and wisdom of using eminent domain to promote economic development are certainly matters of legitimate public debate. This Court's authority, however, extends only to determining whether the City's proposed condemnations are for a "public use" within the meaning of the Fifth Amendment to the Federal Constitution. Because over a century of our case law interpreting that provision dictates an affirmative answer to that question, we may not grant petitioners the relief that they seek. . . .

■ JUSTICE KENNEDY, concurring.

I join the opinion for the Court and add these further observations. . . .

A court applying rational-basis review under the Public Use Clause should strike down a taking that, by a clear showing, is intended to favor a particular private party, with only incidental or pretextual public benefits, just as a court applying rational-basis review under the Equal Protection Clause must strike down a government classification that is clearly intended to injure a particular class of private parties, with only incidental or pretextual public justifications. . . .

■ JUSTICE O'CONNOR, with whom THE CHIEF JUSTICE, JUSTICE SCALIA, and JUSTICE THOMAS join, dissenting.

Over two centuries ago, just after the Bill of Rights was ratified, Justice Chase wrote:

> An ACT of the Legislature (for I cannot call it a law) contrary to the great first principles of the social compact, cannot be considered a rightful exercise of legislative authority. . . . A few instances will suffice to explain what I mean. . . . [A] law that takes property from A. and gives it to B: It is against all reason and justice, for a people to entrust a Legislature with SUCH powers; and, therefore, it cannot be presumed that they have done it.

Calder v. Bull, 3 Dall. 386, 388 (1798) (emphasis deleted). Today the Court abandons this long-held, basic limitation on government power. Under the banner of economic development, all private property is now vulnerable to being taken and transferred to another private owner, so long as it might be upgraded—*i.e.,* given to an owner who will use it in a way that the legislature deems more beneficial to the public—in the process. To reason, as the Court does, that the incidental public benefits resulting from the subsequent ordinary use of private property render economic development takings "for public use" is to wash out any distinction between private and public use of property—and thereby effectively to delete the words "for public use" from the Takings Clause of the Fifth Amendment. Accordingly I respectfully dissent. . . .

While the Takings Clause presupposes that government can take private property without the owner's consent, the just compensation requirement spreads the cost of condemnations and thus "prevents the public from loading upon one individual more than his just share of the burdens of government." *Monongahela Nav. Co. v. United States,* 148 U.S. 312, 325 (1893). The public use requirement, in turn, imposes a more basic limitation, circumscribing the very scope of the eminent domain power: Government may compel an individual to forfeit her property for the *public's* use, but not for the benefit of another private person. . . . Where is the line between "public" and "private" property use? . . .

Our cases have generally identified three categories of takings that comply with the public use requirement, though it is in the nature of things that the boundaries between these categories are not always firm. Two are relatively straightforward and uncontroversial. First, the sovereign may transfer private property to public ownership—such as for a road, a hospital, or a military base. Second, the sovereign may transfer private property to private parties, often common carriers, who make the property available for the public's use—such as with a railroad, a public utility, or a stadium. But "public ownership" and "use-by-the-public" are sometimes too constricting and impractical ways to define the scope of the Public Use Clause. Thus we have allowed that, in certain circumstances and to meet certain exigencies, takings that serve a public purpose also satisfy the Constitution even if the property is destined for subsequent private use.

This case returns us for the first time in over 20 years to the hard question of when a purportedly "public purpose" taking meets the public use requirement. It presents an issue of first impression: Are economic development takings constitutional? I would hold that they are not. . . .

Here, in contrast [to *Berman* and *Midkiff*], New London does not claim that Susette Kelo's and Wilhelmina Dery's well-maintained homes are the source of any social harm. Indeed, it could not so claim without adopting the absurd argument that any single-family home that might be razed to make way for an apartment building, or any church that might be replaced with a retail store, or any small business that might be more lucrative if it were instead part of a national franchise, is inherently harmful to society and thus within the government's power to condemn. . . .

The Court protests that it does not sanction the bare transfer from A to B for B's benefit. It suggests two limitations on what can be taken after today's decision. First, it maintains a role for courts in ferreting out takings whose sole purpose is to bestow a benefit on the private transferee—without detailing how courts are to conduct that complicated inquiry. For his part, Justice KENNEDY suggests that courts may divine illicit purpose by a careful review of the record and the process by which a legislature arrived at the decision to take—without specifying what courts should look for in a case with different facts, how they will know if they have found it, and what to do if they do not. Whatever the details of Justice KENNEDY's as-yet-undisclosed test, it is difficult to envision anyone but the "stupid staff[er]" failing it. The trouble with economic development takings is that private benefit and incidental public benefit are, by definition, merged and mutually reinforcing. In this case, for example, any boon for Pfizer or the plan's developer is difficult to disaggregate from the promised public gains in taxes and jobs. . . .

Any property may now be taken for the benefit of another private party, but the fallout from this decision will not be random. The beneficiaries are likely to be those citizens with disproportionate influence and power in the political process, including large corporations and development firms. As for the victims, the government now has license to transfer property from those with fewer resources to those with more. The Founders cannot have intended this perverse result. "[T]hat alone is a *just* government," wrote James Madison, "which *impartially* secures to every man, whatever is his *own*." For the National Gazette, Property (Mar. 27, 1792), reprinted in 14 Papers of James Madison 266 (R. Rutland et al. eds.1983). . . .

■ JUSTICE THOMAS, dissenting.

Long ago, William Blackstone wrote that "the law of the land . . . postpone[s] even public necessity to the sacred and inviolable rights of private property." The Framers embodied that principle in the Constitution, allowing the government to take property not for "public necessity," but instead for "public use." Defying this understanding, the Court replaces the Public Use Clause with a "[P]ublic [P]urpose" Clause, . . . a restriction that is satisfied, the Court instructs, so long as the purpose is "legitimate" and the means "not irrational,". . . .

I cannot agree. If such "economic development" takings are for a "public use," any taking is, and the Court has erased the Public Use Clause from our Constitution . . . Today's decision is simply the latest in a string of our cases construing the Public Use Clause to be a virtual nullity, without the slightest nod to its original meaning. In my view, the Public Use Clause, originally understood, is a meaningful limit on the government's eminent domain power. Our cases have strayed from the Clause's original meaning, and I would reconsider them.

. . . Though one component of the protection provided by the Takings Clause is that the government can take private property only if it provides "just compensation" for the taking, the Takings Clause also prohibits the government from taking property except "for public use." Were it otherwise, the Takings Clause would either be meaningless or empty. If the Public Use Clause served no function other than to state that the government may take property through its eminent domain power—for public or private uses—then it would be surplusage. Alternatively, . . . the Clause would require the government to compensate for takings done "for public use," leaving it free to take property for purely private uses without the payment of compensation. This would contradict a bedrock principle well established by the time of the founding: that all takings required the payment of compensation. The Public Use Clause, like the Just Compensation Clause, is therefore an express limit on the government's power of eminent domain.

The most natural reading of the Clause is that it allows the government to take property only if the government owns, or the public has a legal right to use, the property, as opposed to taking it for any public purpose or necessity whatsoever. At the time of the founding, dictionaries primarily defined the noun "use" as "[t]he act of employing any thing to any purpose." 2 S. Johnson, A Dictionary of the English Language 2194 (4th ed. 1773) (hereinafter Johnson). The term "use," moreover, "is from the Latin *utor*, which means 'to use, make use of, avail one's self of, employ, apply, enjoy, etc.'" J. Lewis, Law of Eminent Domain § 165, p. 224, n. 4 (1888). When the government takes property and gives it to a private individual, and the public has no right to use the property, it strains language to say that the public is "employing" the property, regardless of the incidental benefits that might accrue to the public from the private use. The term "public use," then, means that either the government or its citizens as a whole must actually "employ" the taken property. See *id.*, at 223 (reviewing founding-era dictionaries). . . .

The consequences of today's decision are not difficult to predict, and promise to be harmful. So-called "urban renewal" programs provide some compensation for the properties they take, but no compensation is possible for the subjective value of these lands to the individuals displaced and the indignity inflicted by uprooting them from their homes. Allowing the government to take property solely for public purposes is bad enough, but extending the concept of public purpose to encompass any economically beneficial goal guarantees that these losses will fall disproportionately on poor communities. Those communities are not only systematically less likely to put their lands to the highest and best social use, but are also the least politically powerful. If ever there were justification for intrusive judicial review of constitutional provisions that protect "discrete and insular minorities," *United States v. Carolene Products Co.,* 304 U.S. 144, 152, n. 4 (1938), surely that principle would apply with great force to the powerless groups and individuals the Public Use Clause protects. The deferential standard this Court has adopted for the Public Use Clause is therefore deeply perverse. It encourages "those citizens with disproportionate influence and power in the political process, including large corporations and development firms," to victimize the weak.

Those incentives have made the legacy of this Court's "public purpose" test an unhappy one. In the 1950's, no doubt emboldened in part by the expansive understanding of "public use" this Court adopted in *Berman,* cities "rushed to draw plans" for downtown development. B. Frieden & L. Sagalyn, Downtown, Inc.: How America Rebuilds Cities 17 (1989). "Of all the families displaced by urban renewal from 1949 through 1963, 63 percent of those whose race was known were nonwhite, and of these families, 56 percent of nonwhites and 38 percent of whites had incomes low enough to qualify for public housing, which, however, was seldom available to them." Public works projects in the 1950's and 1960's destroyed predominantly minority communities in St. Paul, Minnesota, and Baltimore, Maryland. In 1981, urban planners in Detroit, Michigan, uprooted the largely "lower-income and elderly" Poletown neighborhood for the benefit of the General Motors Corporation. Urban renewal projects have long been associated with the displacement of blacks; "[i]n cities across the country, urban renewal came to be known as 'Negro removal.' " Over 97 percent of the individuals forcibly removed from their homes by the "slum-clearance" project upheld by this Court in *Berman* were black. Regrettably, the predictable consequence of the Court's decision will be to exacerbate these effects. . . .

NOTES

1. As a matter of legal doctrine, what is the difference between the position of the majority and that of Justice Kennedy? Between Justice Kennedy and Justice O'Connor? Between Justice O'Connor and Justice Thomas? Do any of them avoid the problem of judicial second-guessing of essentially economic issues?

2. If "public use" means "public purpose," should that mean that the courts must defer to any legislative judgment about the reasons for which private property has been taken away by the government? Is that a troubling proposition, or not necessarily so? Justify your answer. Justice Thomas says that "public use" means something like "use by the public." Is he right? Is this a constitutional principle, as opposed to a mere political preference? Does his position offer the possibility of a judicially manageable standard? In deciding what "public use" means, which types of constitutional argument, or modes of interpretation, are most helpful?

3. None of the opinions questions the presupposition that the Fifth Amendment forbids takings of property for anything other than "public use." But is that what the clause says? In form, doesn't the clause seem to say that *when* property is taken for public use, "just compensation" must be paid? Is it assumed that the government may not simply redistribute property from one private party to another? If so, where does this assumption find its roots in the law?

4. There was an intense political reaction to *Kelo,* and at least forty-three states adopted increased protections against takings, either by legislation or by ballot initiatives. Many of these were relatively small, symbolic changes, but some were much more significant, such as Nevada's prohibition on using eminent domain for land that would be taken from one private party and transferred to another (though with an exception for blight, which is defined broadly). For an overview, see Ilya Somin, *The Limits of Backlash: Assessing the Po-*

litical Response to Kelo, 93 Minn. L. Rev. 2100 (2009). Does the backlash to *Kelo* suggest that the Court's decision was wrong? Or does it suggest the opposite, that this is a question that can be resolved in the political branches?

5. In 2009, Pfizer announced its decision to begin vacating its New London campus. With Pfizer gone, "[i]t would leave behind the city's biggest office complex and an adjacent swath of barren land that was cleared of dozens of homes to make room for a hotel, stores and condominiums that were never built." Patrick McGeehan, *Pfizer to Leave City that Won Land-use Case*, N.Y. Times (Nov. 12, 2009). Where Susette Kelo's house once stood is now a wasteland.

VI. THE NINTH AND TENTH AMENDMENTS

> *Amendment IX: The enumeration in the Constitution, of certain rights, shall not be construed to deny or disparage others retained by the people.*
>
> *Amendment X: The powers not delegated to the United States by the Constitution, nor prohibited by it to the States, are reserved to the States respectively, or to the people.*

Completing the package of amendments comprising "the Bill of Rights" are two amendments that, unlike the others, do not appear to confer specific rights. Rather, the Ninth and Tenth Amendments appear to function as rules of interpretation concerning inferences *not* to be drawn from the proposal and adoption of the *other* amendments contained in the Bill of Rights. Both amendments address a problem inherent in enumeration: the Ninth Amendment addresses the fact that not all rights are enumerated in the Bill of Rights; the Tenth Amendment addresses the fact that not all possible powers are enumerated in Article One, Section Eight. The amendments adopt opposite rules of construction: the enumeration of rights does *not* mean that other rights do not exist, but the enumeration of powers *does* mean that Congress cannot exercise other powers.

The Ninth Amendment

The specification in the Constitution of certain rights—both in the original Constitution, and in the (then) newly adopted First through Eighth Amendments—does not operate to repeal or rescind ("deny or disparage") any and all other legal rights that individuals might have had by virtue of other sources of law, the Ninth Amendment proclaims. The people enjoy rights arising from longstanding custom and tradition, the common law, state constitutions, legislation, and other sources of law. The adoption of a necessarily incomplete national package of individual rights in the Bill of Rights does not work to extinguish other legal rights or assign control over all individual liberties into the hands of the national government. Nor should adoption of the Bill of Rights—the "enumeration in the Constitution of certain rights"—"be construed" even to "disparage" arguments in favor of other types of political or civil rights, or even natural law rights, within the realm of public and political debate. The Bill of Rights does not end the argument, or even end the discussion. It is a baseline; it is a statement that the Constitution itself protects these rights; it is not a statement that the corpus of the rights of humankind is now hereby deemed closed. Still less should it be understood as an implied repeal-by-negative-implication of *state* Bills of Rights, a pre-emption of the field as it were, by an act of national power.

The Ninth Amendment thus responded to concerns—expressed first by Federalist *opponents* of the idea of adding a Bill of Rights to the Constitution—that adding a list of rights might be taken to imply that all rights not so specified had been assigned into the hands of the new national government, thereby unwittingly enlarging its powers over individuals. Recall Alexander Hamilton's famous argument in *The Federalist No. 84* that a Bill of Rights was both unnecessary and affirmatively dangerous:

> I go further, and affirm that bills of rights, in the sense and to the extent in which they are contended for, are not only unnecessary in the proposed Constitution, but would even be dangerous. They would contain various exceptions to powers not granted; and, on this very account, would afford a colorable pretext to claim more than were granted. For why declare that things shall not be done which there is no power to do? Why, for instance, should it be said that the liberty of the press shall not be restrained, when no power is given by which restrictions may be imposed? I will not contend that such a provision would confer a regulating power; but it is evident that it would furnish, to men disposed to usurp, a plausible pretense for claiming that power. They might urge with a semblance of reason, that the Constitution ought not to be charged with the absurdity of providing against the abuse of an authority which was not given, and that the provision against restraining the liberty of the press afforded a clear implication, that a power to prescribe proper regulations concerning it was intended to be vested in the national government. This may serve as a specimen of the numerous handles which would be given to the doctrine of constructive powers, by the indulgence of an injudicious zeal for bills of rights.

James Madison, in a speech introducing his proposed Bill of Rights in the First Congress, raised this explanation for inclusion of the provision that eventually became the Ninth Amendment:

> It has been objected also against a bill of rights, that, by enumerating particular exceptions to the grant of power, it would disparage those rights which were not placed in that enumeration; and it might follow by implication, that those rights that were not placed in that enumeration, that those rights which were not singled out, were intended to be assigned into the hands of the General Government, and were consequently insecure. This is one of the most plausible arguments I have ever heard urged against the admission of a bill of rights into this system; but, I conceive, that it may be guarded against. I have attempted it, as gentlemen may see by turning to the last clause of the fourth resolution.

1 ANNALS OF CONG. 439 (1789). Madison's original proposal for what eventually became the Ninth and Tenth Amendments was as follows: "The exceptions here or elsewhere in the Constitution, made in favor of particular rights, shall not be so construed as to diminish the just importance of other rights retained by the people, or as to enlarge the powers delegated by the Constitution; but either as actual limitations of such powers, or as inserted merely for greater caution." *Id.*, at 435.

Justice Joseph Story, in his early and influential treatise on the Constitution, noted this political history as explaining the presence of the Ninth Amendment as a rule of construction designed to prevent an improper inference:

> This clause [the Ninth Amendment] was manifestly introduced to prevent any perverse, or ingenious misapplication of the well known maxim, that an affirmation in particular cases implies a negation in all others; and, *e converso*, that a negation in particular cases implies an affirmation in all others. The maxim, rightly understood, is perfectly sound and safe; but it has often been strangely forced from its natural meaning into the support of the most dangerous political heresies. The amendment was undoubtedly suggested by the reasoning of the Federalist on the subject of a general bill of rights.

3 Joseph Story, Commentaries on the Constitution of the United States, Section 1898, at 751–52 (1833).

Notwithstanding this historical evidence of original meaning and purpose, could the Ninth Amendment fairly be construed differently—say, as a "catch-all" provision designating *other (unspecified) federal constitutional rights*, to be discovered, invented, or adopted as time went on, presumably by courts? Otherwise, wouldn't the Ninth Amendment be a mere "truism," a simple rule of construction that does not add much to the Bill of Rights? (Is that really a problem, if that is what the amendment in fact means?) Doesn't the reference to "rights retained" imply that the Constitution should be understood as recognizing *other* constitutional rights?

But if so—if the Ninth Amendment creates to-be-named-later constitutional liberties—what are they? Is there a principled way to identify the content of those rights? Is the Ninth Amendment an invitation to courts to engage in natural law constitutional law-making, identifying new or evolving constitutional rights and enforcing them against democratic choices to the contrary? What would keep a willful judge from enacting his or her own policy preferences as constitutional law, under the rubric of the Ninth Amendment's supposed open-ended invitation to do so? (Wouldn't Chief Justice Taney, in *Dred Scott*, have loved such a suggestion? Why do you suppose he didn't invoke the Ninth Amendment in support of his invention of a right to property in slaves, immune from federal interference? Would that have been a more plausible textual hook on which to hang his atrocious invention than "due process of law"? Was it that Chief Justice Taney thought the Ninth Amendment was a less plausible argument than substantive due process?)

The suggestion that the Ninth Amendment creates additional, unspecified constitutional rights has long been a favorite of constitutional law scholars. See, e.g., The Rights Retained by the People: The Ninth Amendment and Constitutional Interpretation, Vols. I & II (Randy Barnett, ed. 1991, 1993) (collecting essays by scholars suggesting a wide range of ideas for giving further substantive content to the Ninth Amendment); see also Akhil Reed Amar, America's Constitution: A Biography 327–329 (2005); John Hart Ely, Democracy and Distrust 34–41 (1980).

But the suggestion has never been accepted by the Supreme Court. The closest the Court has come to relying on the Ninth Amendment are suggestions in a concurring opinion, joined by three justices, that the Ninth Amendment might reinforce a conclusion reached largely on other grounds, in *Griswold v. Connecticut*, 381 U.S. 479, 488–492 (1965) (Goldberg, J., concurring):

> The language and history of the Ninth Amendment reveal that the Framers of the Constitution believed that there are additional fundamental rights, protected from governmental infringement, which exist

alongside those fundamental rights specifically mentioned in the first eight constitutional amendments. . . . I do not mean to imply that the Ninth Amendment is applied against the States by the Fourteenth. Nor do I mean to state that the Ninth Amendment constitutes an independent source of rights protected from infringement by either the States or the Federal Government. Rather, the Ninth Amendment shows a belief of the Constitution's authors that fundamental rights exist that are not expressly enumerated in the first eight amendments and an intent that the list of rights included there not be deemed exhaustive.

For an argument that the Ninth Amendment leaves unenumerated natural rights in precisely the same legal status as they enjoyed prior to adoption of the Bill of Rights—not "denied or disparaged," but also not elevated to the level of enumerated, judicially enforceable overrides to otherwise lawful exercises of power—see Michael W. McConnell, *Natural Rights and the Ninth Amendment: How Does Lockean Legal Theory Assist in Interpretation?*, 5 NYU J. L. & Lib. 1 (2010). Prior to a written constitution, natural or conventional rights were protected via a kind of Blackstonian equitable interpretation: courts assumed that legislatures were aware of and did not intend to disturb natural rights, so they narrowly construed statutes to avoid doing so, on an as-applied basis. If the legislature passed legislation evincing a specific intention to abrogate such an unwritten right, however, the courts were not empowered to override that determination. Is that too weak of an interpretation of the Ninth Amendment? Is it too strong?

The Tenth Amendment

The Tenth Amendment is a companion provision to the Ninth Amendment: "The powers not delegated to the United States by the Constitution, nor prohibited by it to the States, are reserved to the States respectively, or to the people." Just as the Ninth Amendment is designed to prevent the conclusion that the addition of a Bill of Rights by negative implication assigned all other rights (in Madison's words) "into the hands of the General Government," the Tenth Amendment is designed to reinforce the conclusion that the enumeration of powers in Article I, Section 8 and elsewhere left all other powers in the hands of the states or the people.

In context, then, the Tenth Amendment appears not to introduce new, substantive restrictions on national government powers. Rather, the Tenth Amendment reaffirms—and emphasizes—the Constitution's original principle that the national government was to be one of limited, delegated powers only. It is, like the Ninth Amendment, a rule of construction. The Supreme Court has remarked that the Tenth Amendment thus states a "truism." *United States v. Darby*, 312 U.S. 100, 124 (1941). Indeed it does. It states that the powers not delegated to the national government are reserved to the states. But does it not subtly suggest something more: that it is important not to read the enumerated powers as a blank check for federal authority? Why have a Tenth Amendment if we interpret the enumerated powers, such as the Commerce Clause, so broadly that the federal government can do anything it wishes to do? See Gary Lawson, *A Truism with Attitude: The Tenth Amendment in Constitutional Context*, 83 Notre Dame L. Rev. 469 (2008).

Those who see the Tenth Amendment as a charter for strong states' rights must grapple, however, with its history. The Articles of Confederation contained a provision almost identical to the Tenth Amendment, with the difference that the powers not "expressly" delegated to the national government were left to the states. That makes a big difference. It prohibits anything other than a strict literal construction of Section 8. But the framers of the Tenth Amendment declined to use the word "expressly." Three times in the House and the Senate, anti-nationalists moved to amend the Tenth Amendment to add the word "expressly." Madison opposed the amendment, arguing that "because it was impossible to confine a Government to the exercise of express powers; there must necessarily be admitted powers by implication, unless the Constitution descended to recount every minutia." Even Roger Sherman, a principled advocate of state power, agreed. Accordingly, the motion lost, 17–32. Without the word "expressly," how potent is the Tenth Amendment's principle of construction?

The idea that the Tenth Amendment recognizes a residual "sovereignty" of sorts in the states was part of the reasoning of the Court in *New York v. United States,* 505 U.S. 144 (1992), presented in Chapter 4. The Court spoke of "the province of state sovereignty reserved by the Tenth Amendment." Conceding that the Amendment is "essentially a tautology" in terms of restraining the powers of Congress, the Court nonetheless concluded—as a matter of the logical structure of federalism—that Congress could not "commandeer" the legislative processes of state governments by directly compelling them to enact and enforce a federal law mandate. Does the rule of *New York* result from the text of the Tenth Amendment? Or does it result from structural principles and national-state relationships created by the document as a whole (to which the Tenth Amendment contributes)? Which mode of interpretation is doing the heavy lifting in such a case: Text? Structure? Historical purpose? Precedent? Policy?

A NOTE ON THE ELEVENTH AND TWELFTH AMENDMENTS

The Eleventh and Twelfth Amendments were not part of the "Bill of Rights," but they deserve mention before we proceed to the Reconstruction Amendments in the next chapter.

The Eleventh Amendment was adopted in 1795 as a direct response to the Supreme Court's decision in *Chisholm v. Georgia,* 2 U.S. (2 Dall.) 419 (1793), which was presented in Chapter 3. As you may remember, Chisholm, a citizen of South Carolina, had sued the state of Georgia in the Supreme Court's original jurisdiction, for alleged breach of a war-supplies contract. This was probably a proper invocation of federal court diversity jurisdiction, under Article III of the Constitution, and Congress had assigned such jurisdiction to the Supreme Court. But Georgia objected on grounds of "sovereign immunity" from suit and refused to show up to argue the case, instead filing a written protest to the Court's authority. As Akhil Amar notes, Georgia's objection may have led the Court's members to collapse two distinct issues into one—the question of *jurisdiction* and the question of the *merits of the sovereign immunity defense.* The Court ruled for Chisholm, finding jurisdiction and no immunity. Akhil Amar, AMERICA'S CONSTITUTION: A BIOGRAPHY 332–336 (2005).

Some were surprised and outraged at the idea that a "sovereign" state could be sued for damages without its consent—a departure from traditional understandings. More to the point, this appeared to be a departure from *Georgia state law*: a Georgian could not sue Georgia for damages, in Georgia state courts, without the state's consent to waive sovereign immunity. Why should the accident of diversity jurisdiction create a broader substantive right for a South Carolina citizen to sue Georgia without its consent in federal court? The Eleventh Amendment's solution was to repeal one category of Article III jurisdiction—suits against one state brought by citizens of another state: "The Judicial power of the United States shall not be construed to extend to any suit in law or equity, commenced or prosecuted against one of the United States by Citizens of another State, or by Citizens or Subjects of any Foreign State."

The Eleventh Amendment, by repealing one category of diversity jurisdiction, did not confer or embrace a substantive law right of state sovereign immunity as a matter of federal constitutional law. Nonetheless, in the case of *Hans v. Louisiana*, 134 U.S. 1 (1890), the Supreme Court held that the Eleventh Amendment conferred state sovereign immunity as a matter of substantive constitutional law, in diversity cases and in all others. *Hans* and the Eleventh Amendment acutely present the dilemma that arises whenever there is a conflict between the text of the Constitution and longstanding judicial precedent. For more discussion of *Chisholm* and *Hans,* see Chapter 3.

The Twelfth Amendment was a constitutional "fix" to the Electoral College enacted in 1804 that made two technical changes with potentially large structural significance. The original Article II directed electors for president to cast two votes. The highest vote-getter (assuming a majority) would be president, and the runner-up would be vice president. Importantly, electors did not designate which candidate they preferred for president and which for vice-president. This feature, combined with the fact that electors did not meet to deliberate in one location and indeed voted in different states at different times, made political competition for the presidency exceedingly difficult. Electors who wanted to choose one candidate for president and another for vice-president faced the choice of casting ballots for both persons—with the risk that the "presidential" and "vice-presidential" candidates would tie in the end—or throwing away the second vote, which risked allowing the other side's presidential candidate to become vice-president. The latter scenario came to pass in 1796, when Thomas Jefferson finished second to John Adams and thus became Adams's vice-president, despite the fact that they supported contending political agendas. The tie-vote scenario occurred in 1800, when Thomas Jefferson and his vice-presidential "running mate," Aaron Burr, received the same number of votes and the election devolved on the House of Representatives. Lame-duck Federalists in the House initially refused to vote for Jefferson as president, provoking the nation's first full-fledged constitutional crisis. (The Federalists relented after 35 ballots.)

None of this may have mattered particularly if the executive was not meant to be politically contested or otherwise reflect public opinion. And there is good evidence that the framers, or most of them, did not envision the presidency as a "political" office. But the Washington and Adams presidencies revealed the enormous political potential of the executive, and by 1800, partisans were not content to leave the choice of president to a group of cloistered electors. After the 1800 deadlock, the new Republican majorities in Congress pressed to change Article II to permit electors to designate which candidates they preferred for president and which for vice-president, and also to reduce the number of candidates referred to the House in the event of a disputed presidential election. President Jefferson backed the changes. The Republicans' stated goal: to make the executive the subject of political competition and by extension, the subject of popular choice.

The effect was to render the presidency more political, more populist, and potentially more powerful. See generally Joshua D. Hawley, *The Transformative Twelfth Amendment*, 54 Wm. & Mary L. Rev. (2013). Thomas Jefferson was the first president to claim that he was the representative of all the people with as much or greater claim than Congress to speak for the people's interests. He used this claim to justify an expansive legislative agenda, including the Louisiana Purchase. Every president since has followed his lead.

CHAPTER 7

THE RECONSTRUCTION AMENDMENTS

[*Assignment 59*]

I. TEXT, STRUCTURE, HISTORY, EARLY INTERPRETATION, AND ENFORCEMENT

The Civil War (1861–1865) and the Reconstruction period that followed it (1865–1876) produced a dramatic transformation in the American constitutional order. The War was, at one level, a struggle between visions of the Constitution—visions of the constitutional status of slavery, the authority of the Supreme Court, the location of sovereignty, and the nature of the Union. Did the Constitution protect a state's right to maintain the institution of slavery, immune from national interference? Did the Constitution protect the right to keep slaves in federal territories (as *Dred Scott* had held in 1857)? Did the Constitution exclude *all* black persons—slave and free—from U.S. and state citizenship and thus from the rights and privileges of citizenship (as *Dred Scott* also held)? Was the federal union a voluntary union of sovereign states, each of which could leave if it felt aggrieved? Or was the Union a nation with sovereign authority over the states, on matters so specified in the Constitution, and with no state entitled to defy the authority of the Union or to leave without the consent of the whole?

These were fundamental constitutional questions. They received their answers through what Lincoln called "this fiery trial" of civil war. The Union's victory in the Civil War resolved these longstanding constitutional arguments—by force. Not only that, it also produced changes to the text of the Constitution. The Thirteenth Amendment, adopted in 1865 as the War was drawing to a close, abolished slavery. The Fourteenth Amendment, adopted in 1868, designated a national citizenship, extended the rights of citizenship against state governments, and forbade states to deny anyone due process or the equal protection of the laws. It also broadly empowered Congress to effectuate these commands. The Fifteenth Amendment, adopted in 1870, forbade denial of the right to vote to the newly freed black citizens.

These amendments, and the Civil War, had a transformative effect:

> The Constitution we have today is in substantial measure the result of the single most decisive legal interpretive event of American history: the Civil War. The outcome of *Grant v. Lee* resolved the most important issue of antebellum constitutional dispute—the nature of the Union—in favor of the nationalist view of sovereignty and against the South's state-sovereignty view. It was a great Civil War, not a judicial opinion, that settled this issue. It was likewise the Civil War, not any correcting judicial decision, that reversed the most egregious error of the Supreme Court up to that point in our history—*Dred Scott*'s enshrinement of slavery as a fundamental constitutional property right

of (white) citizens, immune from federal interference as a matter of "due process" of law. And it was the War, not any judicial decision, that reversed the most egregious error of the framers in preserving and protecting slavery (to a considerable degree) in the first place.

Michael Stokes Paulsen, *The Civil War as Constitutional Interpretation*, 71 U. Chi. L. Rev. 691 (2004).

A. THE THIRTEENTH AMENDMENT

> *Section 1. Neither slavery nor involuntary servitude, except as a punishment for crime whereof the party shall have been duly convicted, shall exist within the United States, or any place subject to their jurisdiction.*
>
> *Section 2. Congress shall have power to enforce this article by appropriate legislation.*

The Thirteenth Amendment, passed by Congress in early 1865 and ratified that year by state legislatures (including some Reconstruction state legislatures in the South) abolished slavery throughout the nation. It is the only amendment to the Constitution that regulates not merely the powers of government but private conduct as well: no state may enforce slavery by law, and no private individual may hold another person as a slave. Slavery shall not "exist."

Section 2 of the Thirteenth Amendment gives Congress the power to enforce the slavery prohibition—a power to directly regulate the private actions of individuals toward other individuals. Did the Thirteenth Amendment's ban on slavery, coupled with Section 2's enforcement power, give Congress the power also to pass laws protecting the newly freed blacks from discrimination? By state and local laws? By the actions of private persons or businesses? How far did Congress's enforcement power reach?

It is part of the notorious history of the era that no sooner had slavery been constitutionally banned than states and localities in the South sought to replicate the prior subjugation, insofar as possible, by enacting "Black Codes." These restricted the rights of black citizens to own property, to engage in certain occupations, and to testify in court. They also imposed stringent labor requirements, such as a requirement that the contracts of black employees have a term of at least one year, with severe penalties for leaving employment before the contract term expired. Congress responded to the Black Codes with the Civil Rights Act of 1866. It prohibited discrimination—governmental and private—with respect to certain basic civil rights of contract, freedom to work, and capacity to use the courts. Section 1 of the Act provided:

> . . . That all persons born in the United States and not subject to any foreign power, excluding Indians not taxed, are hereby declared to be citizens of the United States; and such citizens, of every race and color, without regard to any previous condition of slavery or involuntary servitude, except as a punishment for crime whereof the party shall have been duly convicted, shall have the same right, in every State and Territory in the United States, to make and enforce contracts, to sue, be parties, and give evidence, to inherit, purchase, lease, sell, hold, and convey real and personal property, and to full and equal benefit of all laws and proceedings for the security of person and property, as is enjoyed by white citizens, and shall be subject to like punishment, pains,

and penalties, and to none other, any law, statute, ordinance, regulation, or custom, to the contrary notwithstanding.

In the preceding year, Congress had passed the Freedmen's Bureau Act, which authorized seizure of "abandoned" land and temporary assignment of it to newly freed slaves (rented with an option to buy after a period of years, if the United States could obtain valid title). For several years the Freedmen's Bureau also provided a considerable social welfare network, "staffed largely by Union Army officers[:] during its brief existence it distributed food to destitute blacks and whites, supervised the establishment of free-labor agriculture, and furnished much-needed financial assistance to set up schools for the ex-slaves." Peter Kolchin, AMERICAN SLAVERY 1619–1877 (2003).

Were these two statutes, the Civil Rights Act of 1866 and the Freedmen's Bureau Act of 1865, within the constitutional powers of Congress? Pursuant to what enumerated power? The war power? (The Freedmen's Bureau Act was adopted in March 1865, and Lee surrendered in April.) Or the Thirteenth Amendment, Section 2 enforcement power? (The Thirteenth Amendment was ratified by the requisite number of states in December 1865.) How long may enactments passed pursuant to the war power continue past the termination of military hostilities? Could the Thirteenth Amendment substitute for the war power as a justification for the Freedmen's Bureau Act? Or, put more generally, when may enactments passed pursuant to one constitutional power continue to operate pursuant to a later-enacted amendment's new constitutional power?

B. THE FOURTEENTH AMENDMENT

Section 1. All persons born or naturalized in the United States and subject to the jurisdiction thereof, are citizens of the United States and of the State wherein they reside. No State shall make or enforce any law which shall abridge the privileges or immunities of citizens of the United States; nor shall any State deprive any person of life, liberty, or property, without due process of law; nor deny to any person within its jurisdiction the equal protection of the laws. . . .

Section 5. The Congress shall have power to enforce, by appropriate legislation, the provisions of this article.

Concerns over whether Congress's enforcement power under Section 2 of the Thirteenth Amendment could fairly be construed to authorize such sweeping civil rights legislation was one of the primary reasons leaders of the Reconstruction Congress proposed the Fourteenth Amendment. Congressman John Bingham of Ohio, a member of the powerful Joint Committee on Reconstruction, was a driving force behind the move for what eventually became the Fourteenth Amendment. His initial proposal, submitted on behalf of the Committee in early 1866, read as follows:

The Congress shall have power to make all laws which shall be necessary and proper to secure to the citizens of each State all privileges and immunities of citizens in the several States; and to all persons in the several States equal protection in the rights of life, liberty, and property.

Congressional Globe, 39th Cong., 1st Sess. 1034 (1866).

In this proposal one can see the central elements of what became Section 1 of the Fourteenth Amendment: a protection for the "privileges and immunities" of citizens in the states; an idea of "equal protection" with respect to rights of "life, liberty, and property"; and a broad power for Congress to pass laws "necessary and proper" to achieve these protections.

Representative Bingham's "privileges and immunities" clause and "necessary and proper" clause reprised provisions in the original Constitution—the Privileges and Immunities Clause of Article IV and the Necessary and Proper Clause of Article I, Section 8. And, like Section 2 of the Thirteenth Amendment, it gave Congress power to legislate directly concerning the conduct of private individuals. Of course, Bingham's proposal was much broader than the Thirteenth Amendment: Congress could pass any law "necessary and proper" (presumably under the generous standard of *McCulloch*) to "secure" the "privileges and immunities of citizens of the several states" and to secure "to all persons" the equal protection of "life, liberty, and property."

The Fourteenth Amendment as eventually adopted has a somewhat different structure and logic, while retaining important elements of the Bingham proposal. The amendment divides the original Bingham proposal into two parts. The first is a prohibition on state government action, embodied in Section 1 of the amendment ("No State shall . . ."). The second is a legislative power of Congress to enforce that prohibition, embodied in Section 5 of the amendment ("The Congress shall have power to enforce, by appropriate legislation, the provisions of this article.").

Thus, the amendment as adopted is addressed to *state action*—action by a state government—that abridges privileges or immunities, denies equal protection, or lacks due process of law. And it gives Congress power to make laws "appropriate" (a term echoing Bingham's "necessary and proper" formulation) for enforcing those prohibitions on state action. Those prohibitions are cast in broad terms, just as in Bingham's original proposal. These changes and continuities—shifting from *a broad power to legislate with respect to civil rights* to *a broad prohibition of what states may do in abridging civil rights, with a power to enforce that prohibition*—have had significant consequences for American constitutional law.

What did the change mean in practical terms? Does Congress's legislative power under the Fourteenth Amendment include a power to regulate the actions of private individuals directly (such as discrimination by private persons, groups, or businesses)? May Congress determine that such legislation is "appropriate" to carrying into execution a prohibition on *state* action? If the answer is *No*, then the amendment as adopted is in that respect much narrower than the original Bingham proposal. Indeed, that appears (from the history) to have been one of the purposes of the change: "Moderate" Reconstruction Congress members feared that Bingham's proposal would give Congress too sweeping a power to legislate concerning local matters, thus upsetting the traditional federal-state balance of legislative power.

Another significant consequence of the restructuring of Bingham's proposal was to make the amendment more than just a grant of power to Congress to pass civil rights laws—laws that might be repealed by a subsequent Congress. Rather, because Section 1 of the Fourteenth Amendment is a direct prohibition, the amendment *itself* constrains state action denying citizens' privileges or immunities or denying persons due process of law or the equal protection of the laws. This entrenched the protection of civil rights in Section 1 against congressional backsliding in the future—a concern that some of the amendment's backers had about the original Bingham proposal. Representative (and future President) James Garfield expressed the concern this way:

> The civil rights bill is now a part of the law of the land. But every gentleman knows it will cease to be a part of the law whenever the sad moment arrives when [the Democratic] party comes into power. It is precisely for that reason that we propose to lift that great and good law above the reach of political strife, beyond the reach of the plots and machinations of any party, and fix it in the serene sky, in the eternal firmament of the Constitution, where no storm of passion can shake it and no cloud can obscure it.

Cong. Globe, 39th Cong., 1st Sess. 2462 (1866). The Fourteenth Amendment as finally adopted thus admits of direct judicial enforcement of the prohibitions contained in Section 1, with or without further implementing legislation by Congress pursuant to its powers under Section 5.

Which institution, then, should have primacy in interpreting and enforcing the Fourteenth Amendment—Congress or the courts? The history of the day suggests that Congress was expected to have the primary role. After all, one reason for the Fourteenth Amendment was the desire of members of Congress to provide a more secure constitutional basis for the civil rights legislation they had already passed, such as the Civil Rights Act of 1866. In addition, recent experience with the Supreme Court had not instilled confidence in its ability to faithfully interpret the Constitution and protect constitutional rights. Although the Court's membership had changed in the intervening years, the Fourteenth Amendment's drafters remembered *Dred Scott*. For these and other reasons, the members of Congress who originally proposed the Fourteenth Amendment expected that they, and not the courts, would be the primary expositors of the amendment's broad terms.

There is even a sense in which the Fourteenth Amendment explicitly repudiated the Supreme Court. The first sentence of the Fourteenth Amendment—an addition from Bingham's draft—reverses the first holding of *Dred Scott*: the outrageous proposition that even free blacks were not intended to be, and could not be, citizens of the United States and thus could not be citizens of any of the states within the meaning of Article IV's provision protecting the privileges and immunities of citizens of the several states and Article III's right to sue in federal courts under the Diversity Clause. (The Thirteenth Amendment had already repudiated the second holding of *Dred Scott*, which found a constitutional right to slavery and accordingly struck down Congress's prohibition of slavery in certain territories under the Missouri Compromise.)

Sandwiched between Section 1's prohibition and Section 5's enforcement power, several provisions of the Fourteenth Amendment addressed residual questions about slavery and the Civil War while also raising new questions about voting rights.

Section 2 repealed the notorious Three–Fifths Clause of the original Constitution. That section begins: "Representatives shall be apportioned among the several States according to their respective numbers, counting the whole number of persons in each State, excluding Indians not taxed." Thus, freed blacks were to be counted fully in a state's representation. By itself this provision would have perversely given the Southern states even more representation in Congress than they had before the War. But Section 2 further provided for a percentage deduction in representation if a state "denied to any of the male inhabitants of such State" over twenty-one years of age the right to vote in federal or state elections. Thus, if a state discriminated against blacks in the right to vote, their representation in Congress would be diminished commensurately. If a state denied blacks the right to vote entirely, it would receive *zero*-fifths representation for such persons (rather than the old three-fifths bonus).

Thus the Fourteenth Amendment did not actually require that states give the newly freed blacks the right to vote, but merely penalized them for not doing so. It was not until the adoption of the Fifteenth Amendment two years later, in 1870, that the Constitution provided: "The right of citizens of the United States to vote shall not be denied or abridged by the United States or by any State on account of race, color, or previous condition of servitude." (Like the Fourteenth Amendment, the Fifteenth granted Congress the "power to enforce" its provisions by "appropriate legislation.")

Section 3 of the Fourteenth Amendment addressed a divisive issue lingering from the Civil War: It disqualified from federal office anyone who had broken an oath of loyalty to support the Constitution of the United States by aiding in the rebellion, but it allowed Congress to remove the disability by a two-thirds vote of each house.

Section 4 of the Fourteenth Amendment provided that no slave-owner would be entitled to any "claim for the loss or emancipation of any slave." Section 4 also provided that the Union's Civil War debt "shall not be questioned." But any debt incurred "in aid of insurrection or rebellion against the United States" was repudiated. Section 4 prohibits the United States and any state from paying such debts.

Many members of the Reconstruction Congress that proposed the Fourteenth Amendment regarded its central features as the repeal of the Three–Fifths Clause with the representation penalty if a state denied voting rights to blacks (Section 2), and the disqualification from office of rebel oath-breakers (Section 3). Reconstruction Republicans feared the survival of the political order of the former Confederacy, including the prospect of former rebel leaders returning to Congress. And they saw the effect of the Black Codes in Southern states and the denial of the right to vote. Many questioned whether those states had actually been "reconstructed" at all.

Indeed, how could a state be thought to possess a "Republican Form of Government" if it denied the right to vote to a huge swath of its free male citizens? The United States had a constitutional obligation to guarantee genuinely republican regimes pursuant to the terms of the Republican Form of Government Clause (sometimes also called the Guarantee Clause) of Article IV of the Constitution. Denial of representation and the right to vote struck many Reconstruction politicians as unconstitutional. Thus, Congress steadfastly refused to seat representatives from states that refused (initially) to ratify the Fourteenth Amendment. When new Reconstruction state legislatures finally succumbed and voted to ratify the Fourteenth Amendment, then—and only then—did Congress decide that such states were worthy of re-admission to representation in Congress. Some historians and legal scholars have questioned whether Congress legitimately had the power to exclude the representatives of the Southern states. Some have gone further yet and questioned whether the ratification of the Fourteenth Amendment was constitutionally improper, under the Constitution's rules, set forth in Article V, for the amendment process. For representative arguments on either side, see Bruce Ackerman, WE THE PEOPLE: RECONSTRUCTION (VOL. II) (arguing that the adoption of the Fourteenth

Amendment was "illegal" under the rules of Article V governing constitutional amendments, but should therefore be taken as a precedent for "extra-textual" amendment of the Constitution); and John Harrison, *The Lawfulness of the Reconstruction Amendments*, 68 U. Chi. L. Rev. 375 (2001) (defending the amendments' validity).

Despite these other historically important provisions, most modern application of the Fourteenth Amendment has involved Section 1's second sentence—the modified language of Bingham's original proposal. The breadth and seeming ambiguity of some of Section 1's terms have given rise to enduring controversies in constitutional law. What are the "privileges or immunities" of citizens of the United States that states may not abridge? What is meant by "due process of law"? By the "equal protection of the laws"? In Bingham's original proposal, the broad language was essentially a delegation of power to Congress. But with the transformation of Bingham's proposal into a direct constitutional prohibition on state action, is the broad language now a similarly broad delegation to the judiciary? As you will see, the Fourteenth Amendment has become the basis for much of modern constitutional law—and for much of the controversy over the appropriate role of the judiciary in interpreting the Constitution.

The plan of this chapter is as follows: It begins with the *Slaughter–House Cases,* a famous collection of cases in which the Supreme Court first interpreted the Fourteenth Amendment, a paradigm for thinking about the meaning of the major provisions of Section 1. Next are several cases on the Fourteenth Amendment's structure and logic—on how it "works" in actual operation. These cases consider both the "state action" doctrine and the scope of Congress's Section 5 enforcement power. After that are the complicated and challenging modern doctrines surrounding the Equal Protection Clause: race discrimination, affirmative action, gender discrimination, and other possibly suspect classifications of persons. Finally, there is a lengthy consideration of the Due Process Clause. It begins with what is called procedural due process, and then traces the changing course of substantive due process, including famous cases such as *Lochner, Roe,* and *Lawrence.*

C. FORMATIVE JUDICIAL INTERPRETATION AND THE DEATH OF THE PRIVILEGES OR IMMUNITIES CLAUSE

Slaughter–House Cases
83 (16 Wall.) U.S. 36 (1873)

■ MR. JUSTICE MILLER delivered the opinion of the court.

These cases . . . arise out of the efforts of the butchers of New Orleans to resist the Crescent City Live–Stock Landing and Slaughter–House Company in the exercise of certain powers conferred by the charter which created it, and which was granted by the legislature of that State. . . .

The statute thus assailed as unconstitutional was passed March 8th, 1869, and is entitled "An act to protect the health of the city of New Orleans, to locate the stock-landings and slaughter-houses, and to incorporate the Crescent City Live–Stock Landing and Slaughter–House Company."

The first section forbids the landing or slaughtering of animals whose flesh is intended for food, within the city of New Orleans and other parishes and boundaries named and defined, or the keeping or establishing any slaughter-houses or *abattoirs* within those limits except by the corporation thereby created. . . .

The third and fourth sections authorize the company to establish and erect within certain territorial limits, therein defined, one or more stock-yards, stock-landings, and slaughter-houses, and imposes upon it the duty of erecting . . . one grand slaughter-house of sufficient capacity for slaughtering five hundred animals per day. . . . [T]he company . . . shall have the sole and exclusive privilege of conducting and carrying on the live-stock landing and slaughter-house business within the limits and privilege granted by the act, and that all such animals shall be landed at the stock-landings and slaughtered at the slaughter-houses of the company, and nowhere else. . . .

Section five orders the closing up of all other stock-landings and slaughter-houses. . . . These are the principal features of the statute, and are all that have any bearing upon the questions to be decided by us.

This statute is denounced not only as creating a monopoly and conferring odious and exclusive privileges upon a small number of persons at the expense of the great body of the community of New Orleans, but it is asserted that it deprives a large and meritorious class of citizens—the whole of the butchers of the city—of the right to exercise their trade, the business to which they have been trained and on which they depend for the support of themselves and their families; and that the unrestricted exercise of the business of butchering is necessary to the daily subsistence of the population of the city. . . .

The wisdom of the monopoly granted by the legislature may be open to question, but it is difficult to see a justification for the assertion that the butchers are deprived of the right to labor in their occupation, or the people in their daily service in preparing food, or how this statute, with the duties and guards imposed upon the company, can be said to destroy the business of the butcher, or seriously interfere with its pursuit.

The power here exercised by the legislature of Louisiana is, in its essential nature, one which has been, up to the present period in the constitutional history of this country, always conceded to belong to the States. . . .

"Unwholesome trades, slaughter-houses, operations offensive to the senses, the deposit of powder, the application of steam power to propel cars, the building with combustible materials, and the burial of the dead, may all," says Chancellor Kent, "be interdicted by law, in the midst of dense masses of population, on the general and rational principle, that every person ought so to use his property as not to injure his neighbors; and that private interests must be made subservient to the general interests of the community." This is called the police power. . . . The regulation of the place and manner of conducting the slaughtering of animals, and the business of butchering within a city, and the inspection of the animals to be killed for meat, and of the meat afterwards, are among the most necessary and frequent exercises of this power. . . .

In *Gibbons v. Ogden*, Chief Justice Marshall, speaking of inspection laws passed by the States, says: "They form a portion of that immense mass of legislation which controls everything within the territory of a State not surrendered to the General Government—all which can be most advantageously administered by the States themselves. Inspection laws, quarantine laws, health laws of every description, as well as laws for regulating the internal commerce of a State, and those which respect turnpike roads, ferries, & c., are component parts. No direct general power over these objects is granted to Congress; and consequently they remain subject to State legislation." . . .

It cannot be denied that the statute under consideration is aptly framed to remove from the more densely populated part of the city, the noxious slaughter-houses, and large and offensive collections of animals necessarily incident to the slaughtering business of a large city, and to locate them where the convenience, health, and comfort of the people require they shall be located. And it must be conceded that the means adopted by the act for this purpose are appropriate, are stringent, and effectual. . . .

It may . . . be considered as established, that the authority of the legislature of Louisiana to pass the present statute is ample, unless some restraint in the exercise of that power be found in the constitution of that State or in the amendments to the Constitution of the United States, adopted since the date of the decisions we have already cited. . . .

The plaintiffs . . . allege that the statute is a violation of the Constitution of the United States in these several particulars:

That it creates an involuntary servitude forbidden by the thirteenth article of amendment;

That it abridges the privileges and immunities of citizens of the United States;

That it denies to the plaintiffs the equal protection of the laws; and,

That it deprives them of their property without due process of law, contrary to the provisions of the first section of the fourteenth article of amendment.

This court is thus called upon for the first time to give construction to these articles.

We do not conceal from ourselves the great responsibility which this duty devolves upon us. No questions so far-reaching and pervading in their consequences, so profoundly interesting to the people of this country, and so important in their bearing upon the relations of the United States, and of the several States to each other and to the citizens of the States and of the United States, have been before this court during the official life of any of its present members. . . .

[W]ithin the last eight years three . . . articles of amendment of vast importance have been added by the voice of the people to [the Constitution].

The most cursory glance at these articles discloses a unity of purpose, when taken in connection with the history of the times, which cannot fail to have an important bearing on any question of doubt concerning their true meaning. Nor can such doubts, when any reasonably exist, be safely and rationally solved without a reference to that history; for in it is found the occasion and the necessity for recurring again to the great source of power in this country, the people of the States, for additional guarantees of human rights; additional powers to the Federal government; additional restraints upon those of the States. Fortunately that history is fresh within the memory of us all, and its leading features, as they bear upon the matter before us, free from doubt.

The institution of African slavery, as it existed in about half the States of the Union, and the contests pervading the public mind for many years, between those who desired its curtailment and ultimate extinction and those who desired additional safeguards for its security and perpetuation, culminated in the effort, on the part of most of the States in which slavery existed, to separate from the Federal government, and to resist its authority. This constituted the war of the rebellion, and whatever auxiliary causes may have contributed to bring about this war, undoubtedly the overshadowing and efficient cause was African slavery.

In that struggle slavery, as a legalized social relation, perished. It perished as a necessity of the bitterness and force of the conflict. When the armies of freedom found themselves upon the soil of slavery they could do nothing less than free the poor victims whose enforced servitude was the foundation of the quarrel. And when hard pressed in the contest these men (for they proved themselves men in that terrible crisis) offered their services and were accepted by thousands to aid in suppressing the unlawful rebellion, slavery was at an end wherever the Federal government succeeded in that purpose. The proclamation of President Lincoln expressed an accomplished fact as to a large portion of the insurrectionary districts, when he declared slavery abolished in them all. But the war being over, those who had succeeded in re-establishing the authority of the Federal government were not content to permit this great act of emancipation to rest on the actual results of the contest or the proclamation of the Executive, both of which might have been questioned in after times, and they determined to place this main and most valuable result in the Constitution of the restored Union as one of its fundamental articles. Hence the thirteenth article of amendment of that instrument. Its two short sections seem hardly to admit of construction, so vigorous is their expression and so appropriate to the purpose we have indicated.

1. Neither slavery nor involuntary servitude, except as a punishment for crime, whereof the party shall have been duly convicted, shall exist within the United States or any place subject to their jurisdiction.

2. Congress shall have power to enforce this article by appropriate legislation.

To withdraw the mind from the contemplation of this grand yet simple declaration of the personal freedom of all the human race within the jurisdiction of this government—a declaration designed to establish the freedom of four millions of slaves—and with a microscopic search endeavor to find in it a reference to servitudes, which may have been attached to property in certain localities, requires an effort, to say the least of it.

That a personal servitude was meant is proved by the use of the word "involuntary," which can only apply to human beings. The exception of servitude as a punishment for crime gives an idea of the class of servitude that is meant. The word servitude is of larger meaning than slavery, as the latter is popularly understood in this country, and the obvious purpose was to forbid all shades and conditions of African slavery. . . . And it is all that we deem necessary to say on the application of that article to the statute of Louisiana, now under consideration.

The process of restoring to their proper relations with the Federal government and with the other States those which had sided with the rebellion, undertaken under the proclamation of President Johnson in 1865, and before the assembling of Congress, developed the fact that, notwithstanding the formal recognition by those States of the abolition of slavery, the condition of the slave race would, without further protection of the Federal government, be almost as bad as it was before. Among the first acts of legislation adopted by several of the States in the legislative bodies which claimed to be in their normal relations with the Federal government, were laws which imposed upon the colored race onerous disabilities and burdens, and curtailed their rights in the pursuit of life, liberty, and property to such an extent that their freedom was of little value, while they had lost the protection which they had received from their former owners from motives both of interest and humanity.

They were in some States forbidden to appear in the towns in any other character than menial servants. They were required to reside on and cultivate the soil without the right to purchase or own it. They were excluded from many occupations of gain, and were not permitted to give testimony in the courts in any case where a white man was a party. It was said that their lives were at the mercy of bad men, either because the laws for their protection were insufficient or were not enforced.

These circumstances, whatever of falsehood or misconception may have been mingled with their presentation, forced upon the statesmen who had conducted the Federal government in safety through the crisis of the rebellion, and who supposed that by the thirteenth article of amendment they had secured the result of their labors, the conviction that something more was necessary in the way of constitutional protection to the unfortunate race who had suffered so much. They accordingly passed through Congress the proposition for the fourteenth amendment, and they declined to treat as restored to their full participation in the government of the Union the States which had been in insurrection, until they ratified that article. . . .

Before we proceed to examine more critically the provisions of this amendment, on which the plaintiffs in error rely, let us complete and dismiss the history of the recent amendments, as that history relates to the general purpose which pervades them all. A few years' experience satisfied the thoughtful men who had been the authors of the other two amendments that, notwithstanding the restraints of those articles on the States, and the laws passed under the additional powers granted to Congress, these were inadequate for the protection of life, liberty, and property, without which freedom to the slave was no boon. They were in all those States denied the right of suffrage. The laws were administered by the white man alone. It was urged that a race of men distinctively marked as was the negro, living in the midst of another and dominant race, could never be fully secured in their person and their property without the right of suffrage.

Hence the fifteenth amendment, which declares that "the right of a citizen of the United States to vote shall not be denied or abridged by any State on account of race, color, or previous condition of servitude." The negro having, by the fourteenth amendment, been declared to be a citizen of the United States, is thus made a voter in every State of the Union.

We repeat, then, in the light of this recapitulation of events, almost too recent to be called history, but which are familiar to us all; and on the most casual examination of the language of these amendments, no one can fail to be impressed with the one pervading purpose found in them all[:] . . . we mean the freedom of the slave race, the security and firm establishment of that freedom, and the protection of the newly-made freeman and citizen from the oppressions of those who had formerly exercised unlimited dominion over him. It is true that only the fifteenth amendment, in terms, mentions the negro by speaking of his color and his slavery. But it is just as true that each of the other articles was addressed to the grievances of that race, and designed to remedy them as the fifteenth.

We do not say that no one else but the negro can share in this protection. Both the language and spirit of these articles are to have their fair and just weight in any question of construction. Undoubtedly while negro slavery alone was in the mind of the Congress which proposed the thirteenth article, it forbids any other kind of slavery, now or hereafter. If Mexican peonage or the Chinese coolie labor system shall develop slavery of the Mexican or Chinese race within our territory, this amendment may safely be trusted to make it void. And so if other rights are assailed by the States which properly and necessarily fall within the protection of these articles, that protection will apply, though the party interested may not be of African descent. But what we do say, and what we wish to be understood is, that in any fair and just construction of any section or phrase of these amendments, it is necessary to look to the purpose which we have said was the pervading spirit of them all, the evil which they were designed to remedy, and the process of continued addition to the Constitution, until that purpose was supposed to be accomplished, as far as constitutional law can accomplish it.

The first section of the fourteenth article, to which our attention is more specially invited, opens with a definition of citizenship—not only citizenship of the United States, but citizenship of the States. No such definition was previously found in the Constitution, nor had any attempt been made to define it by act of Congress. It had been the occasion of much discussion in the courts, by the executive departments, and in the public journals. It had been said by eminent judges that no man was a citizen of the United States, except as he was a citizen of one of the States composing the Union. Those, therefore, who had been born and resided always in the District of Columbia or in the Territories, though within the United States, were not citizens. Whether this proposition was sound or not had never been judicially decided. But it had been held by this court, in the celebrated *Dred Scott* case, only a few years before the outbreak of the civil war, that a man of African descent, whether a slave or not, was not and could not be a citizen of a State or of the United States. This decision, while it met the condemnation of some of the ablest statesmen and constitutional lawyers of the country, had never been overruled; and if it was to be accepted as a constitutional limitation of the right of citizenship, then all the negro race who had recently been made freemen, were still, not only not citizens, but were incapable of becoming so by anything short of an amendment to the Constitution.

To remove this difficulty primarily, and to establish a clear and comprehensive definition of citizenship which should declare what should constitute citizenship of the United States, and also citizenship of a State, the first clause of the first section was framed.

All persons born or naturalized in the United States, and subject to the jurisdiction thereof, are citizens of the United States and of the State wherein they reside.

The first observation we have to make on this clause is, that it puts at rest both the questions which . . . have been the subject of differences of opinion. It declares that persons may be citizens of the United States without regard to their citizenship of a particular State, and it overturns the Dred Scott decision by making *all persons* born within the United States and subject to its jurisdiction citizens of the United States. That its main purpose was to establish the citizenship of the negro can admit of no doubt. . . .

The next observation . . . is, that the distinction between citizenship of the United States and citizenship of a State is clearly recognized and established. Not only may a man be a citizen of the United States without being a citizen of a State, but an important element is necessary to convert the former into the latter. He must reside within the State to make him a citizen of it, but it is only necessary that he should be born or naturalized in the United States to be a citizen of the Union.

It is quite clear, then, that there is a citizenship of the United States, and a citizenship of a State, which are distinct from each other, and which depend upon different characteristics or circumstances in the individual.

We think this distinction and its explicit recognition in this amendment of great weight in this argument, because the next paragraph of this same section . . . speaks only of privileges and immunities of citizens of the United States, and does not speak of those of citizens of the several States. The argument, however, in favor of the plaintiffs rests wholly on the assumption that the citizenship is the same, and the privileges and immunities guaranteed by the clause are the same.

The language is, "No State shall make or enforce any law which shall abridge the privileges or immunities of citizens of *the United States.*" It is a little remarkable, if this clause was intended as a protection to the citizen of a State against the legislative power of his own State, that the word citizen of the State should be left out when it is so carefully used, and used in contradistinction to citizens of the United States, in the very sentence which precedes it. It is too clear for argument that the change in phraseology was adopted understandingly and with a purpose.

Of the privileges and immunities of the citizen of the United States, and of the privileges and immunities of the citizen of the State, and what they respectively are, we will presently consider; but we wish to state here that it is only the former which are placed by this clause under the protection of the Federal Constitution, and that the latter, whatever they may be, are not intended to have any additional protection by this paragraph of the amendment.

If, then, there is a difference between the privileges and immunities belonging to a citizen of the United States as such, and those belonging to the citizen of the State as such the latter must rest for their security and protection where they have heretofore rested; for they are not embraced by this paragraph of the amendment.

The first occurrence of the words "privileges and immunities" in our constitutional history, is to be found in the fourth of the articles of the old Confederation. . . .

In the Constitution of the United States, which superseded the Articles of Confederation, the corresponding provision is found in section two of the fourth article, in the following words: "The citizens of each State shall be entitled to all the privileges and immunities of citizens of the several States."

There can be but little question that the purpose of both these provisions is the same, and that the privileges and immunities intended are the same in each. In the article of the Confederation we have some of these specifically mentioned, and enough perhaps to give some general idea of the class of civil rights meant by the phrase.

Fortunately we are not without judicial construction of this clause of the Constitution. The first and the leading case on the subject is that of *Corfield v. Coryell*, decided by Mr. Justice Washington in the Circuit Court for the District of Pennsylvania in 1823.

"The inquiry," he says, "is, what are the privileges and immunities of citizens of the several States? We feel no hesitation in confining these expressions to those privileges and immunities which are *fundamental*; which belong of right to the citizens of all free governments, and which have at all times been enjoyed by citizens of the several States which compose this Union, from the time of their becoming free, independent, and sovereign. What these fundamental principles are, it would be more tedious than difficult to enumerate. They may all, however, be comprehended under the following general heads: protection by the government, with the right to acquire and possess property of every kind, and to pursue and obtain happiness and safety, subject, nevertheless, to such restraints as the government may prescribe for the general good of the whole."

. . . The description, when taken to include others not named, but which are of the same general character, embraces nearly every civil right for the establishment and protection of which organized government is instituted. They are, in the language of Judge Washington, those rights which are fundamental. Throughout his opinion, they are spoken of as rights belonging to the individual as a citizen of a State. They are so spoken of in the constitutional provision which he was construing. And they have always been held to be the class of rights which the State governments were created to establish and secure. . . .

[The Privileges and Immunities Clause of Article IV] did not create those rights, which it called privileges and immunities of citizens of the States. It threw around them in that clause no security for the citizen of the State in which they were claimed or exercised. Nor did it profess to control the power of the State governments over the rights of its own citizens.

Its sole purpose was to declare to the several States, that whatever those rights, as you grant or establish them to your own citizens, or as you limit or qualify, or impose restrictions on their exercise, the same, neither more nor less, shall be the measure of the rights of citizens of other States within your jurisdiction.

. . . [There are] very few express limitations which the Federal Constitution imposed on the States—such, for instance, as the prohibition against ex post facto laws, bills of attainder, and laws impairing the obligation of contracts. But with the exception of these and a few other restrictions, the entire domain of the privileges and immunities of citizens of the States, as above defined, lay within the constitutional and legislative power of the States, and without that of the Federal government. Was it the purpose of the fourteenth amendment, by the simple declaration that no State should make or enforce any law which shall abridge the privileges and immunities of *citizens of the United States*, to transfer the security and protection of all the civil rights which we have mentioned, from the States to the Federal government? And where it is declared that Congress shall have the power to enforce that article, was it intended to bring within the power of Congress the entire domain of civil rights heretofore belonging exclusively to the States?

All this and more must follow, if the proposition of the plaintiffs in error be sound. For not only are these rights subject to the control of Congress whenever in its discretion any of them are supposed to be abridged by State legislation, but that body may also pass laws in advance, limiting and restricting the exercise of legislative power by the States, in their most ordinary and usual functions, as in its judgment it may think proper on all such subjects. And still further, such a construction . . . would constitute this court a perpetual censor upon all legislation of the States, on the civil rights of their own citizens, with authority to nullify such as it did not approve as consistent with those rights, as they existed at the time of the adoption of this amendment. The argument we admit is not always the most conclusive which is drawn from the consequences urged against the adoption of a particular construction of an instrument. But when, as in the case before us, these consequences are so serious, so far-reaching and pervading, so great a departure from the structure and spirit of our institutions; when the effect is to fetter and degrade the State governments by subjecting them to the control of Congress, in the exercise of powers heretofore universally conceded to them of the most ordinary and fundamental character; when in fact it radically changes the whole theory of the relations of the State and Federal governments to each other and of both these governments to the people; the argument has a force that is irresistible, in the absence of language which expresses such a purpose too clearly to admit of doubt.

We are convinced that no such results were intended by the Congress which proposed these amendments, nor by the legislatures of the States which ratified them.

Having shown that the privileges and immunities relied on in the argument are those which belong to citizens of the States as such, and that they are left to the State governments for security and protection, and not by this article placed under the special care of the Federal government, we may hold ourselves excused from defining the privileges and immunities of citizens of the United States which no State can abridge, until some case involving those privileges may make it necessary to do so.

But lest it should be said that no such privileges and immunities are to be found if those we have been considering are excluded, we venture to suggest some which owe their existence to the Federal government, its National character, its Constitution, or its laws.

One of these is well described in the case of *Crandall v. Nevada*. It is said to be the right of the citizen of this great country, protected by implied guarantees of its Constitution, "to come to the seat of government to assert any claim he may have upon that government, to transact any business he may have with it, to seek its protection, to share its offices, to engage in administering its functions. He has the right of free access to its seaports, through which all operations of foreign commerce are conducted, to the subtreasuries, land offices, and courts of justice in the several States." . . .

Another privilege of a citizen of the United States is to demand the care and protection of the Federal government over his life, liberty, and property when on the high seas or within the jurisdiction of a foreign government. . . . The right to peaceably assemble and petition for redress of grievances, the privilege of the writ of *habeas corpus*, are rights of the citizen guaranteed by the Federal Constitution. The right to use the navigable waters of the United States, . . . [and] all rights secured to our citizens by treaties with foreign nations, are dependent upon citizenship of the United

States, and not citizenship of a State. One of these privileges is conferred by the very article under consideration. It is that a citizen of the United States can ... become a citizen of any State of the Union by a *bona fide* residence therein, with the same rights as other citizens of that State. To these may be added the rights secured by the thirteenth and fifteenth articles of amendment, and by the other clause of the fourteenth, next to be considered.

But it is useless to pursue this branch of the inquiry, since we are of opinion that the rights claimed by these plaintiffs in error, if they have any existence, are not privileges and immunities of citizens of the United States within the meaning of the clause of the fourteenth amendment under consideration. ...

> All persons born or naturalized in the United States, and subject to the jurisdiction thereof, are citizens of the United States and of the State wherein they reside. No State shall make or enforce any law which shall abridge the privileges or immunities of citizens of the United States; nor shall any State deprive any person of life, liberty, or property without due process of law, nor deny to any person within its jurisdiction the equal protection of its laws.

The argument has not been much pressed in these cases that the defendant's charter deprives the plaintiffs of their property without due process of law, or that it denies to them the equal protection of the law. The first of these paragraphs has been in the Constitution since the adoption of the fifth amendment, as a restraint upon the Federal power. It is also to be found in some form of expression in the constitutions of nearly all the States, as a restraint upon the power of the States. This law then, has [not changed], except so far as the present amendment may place the restraining power over the States in this matter in the hands of the Federal government.

We are not without judicial interpretation, therefore, both State and National, of the meaning of this clause. And it is sufficient to say that under no construction of that provision that we have ever seen, or any that we deem admissible, can the restraint imposed by the State of Louisiana upon the exercise of their trade by the butchers of New Orleans be held to be a deprivation of property within the meaning of that provision.

> Nor shall any State deny to any person within its jurisdiction the equal protection of the laws.

In the light of the history of these amendments, and the pervading purpose of them, which we have already discussed, it is not difficult to give a meaning to this clause. The existence of laws in the States where the newly emancipated negroes resided, which discriminated with gross injustice and hardship against them as a class, was the evil to be remedied by this clause, and by it such laws are forbidden.

If, however, the States did not conform their laws to its requirements, then by the fifth section of the article of amendment Congress was authorized to enforce it by suitable legislation. We doubt very much whether any action of a State not directed by way of discrimination against the negroes as a class, or on account of their race, will ever be held to come within the purview of this provision. It is so clearly a provision for that race and that emergency, that a strong case would be necessary for its application to any other. But as it is a State that is to be dealt with, and not alone the validity of its laws, we may safely leave that matter until Congress shall have exercised its power, or some case of State oppression, by denial of equal justice in its courts, shall have claimed a decision at our hands. We find no such case in the one before us. . . .

In the early history of the organization of the government, its statesmen seem to have divided on the line which should separate the powers of the National government from those of the State governments, and though this line has never been very well defined in public opinion, such a division has continued from that day to this. . . .

Unquestionably [the war] has given great force to the argument, and added largely to the number of those who believe in the necessity of a strong National government.

But, however pervading this sentiment, and however it may have contributed to the adoption of the amendments we have been considering, we do not see in those amendments any purpose to destroy the main features of the general system. . . .

[W]hatever fluctuations may be seen in the history of public opinion on this subject during the period of our national existence, we think it will be found that this court, so far as its functions required, has always held with a steady and an even hand the balance between State and Federal power, and we trust that such may continue to be the history of its relation to that subject so long as it shall have duties to perform which demand of it a construction of the Constitution, or of any of its parts.

■ MR. JUSTICE FIELD, dissenting[, joined by the CHIEF JUSTICE, MR. JUSTICE SWAYNE, and MR. JUSTICE BRADLEY].

I am unable to agree with the majority of the courts in these cases, and will proceed to state the reasons of my dissent from their judgment. . . .

The substance of the averments of the plaintiffs in error is this: That prior to the passage of the act in question they were engaged in the lawful and necessary business of procuring and bringing to the parishes of Orleans, Jefferson, and St. Bernard, animals suitable for human food, and in preparing such food for market; that in the prosecution of this business they had provided in these parishes suitable establishments. . . . And they complain that the business of landing, yarding, and keeping, within the parishes named, cattle intended for sale or slaughter, which was lawful for them to pursue before the first day of June, 1869, is made by that act unlawful for any one except the corporation named; and that the business of slaughtering cattle and preparing animal food for market . . . is made by that act unlawful for them to pursue afterwards, except in the buildings of the company, and upon payment of certain prescribed fees, and a surrender of a valuable portion of each animal slaughtered. And they contend that the lawful business . . . cannot be thus taken from them and given over for a period of twenty-five years to the sole and exclusive enjoyment of a corporation of seventeen persons. . . .

No one will deny the abstract justice which lies in the position of the plaintiffs in error; and I shall endeavor to show that the position has some support in the fundamental law of the country.

It is contended in justification for the act in question that it was . . . the legitimate exercise of what is termed the police power of the State. That power undoubtedly extends to all regulations affecting the health, good order, morals, peace, and safety of society, and is exercised on a great variety of subjects, and in almost numberless ways. . . . But under the pretence of prescribing a police regulation the State cannot be permitted to encroach upon any of the just rights of the citizen, which the Constitution intended to secure against abridgment. . . .

The act of Louisiana presents the naked case, unaccompanied by any public considerations, where a right to pursue a lawful and necessary calling, previously enjoyed by every citizen, and in connection with which a thousand persons were daily employed, is taken away and vested exclusively for twenty-five years, for an extensive district and a large population, in a single corporation, or its exercise is for that period restricted to the establishments of the corporation, and there allowed only upon onerous conditions.

If exclusive privileges of this character can be granted to a corporation of seventeen persons, they may, in the discretion of the legislature, be equally granted to a single individual. If they may be granted for twenty-five years they may be equally granted for a century, and in perpetuity. . . . Indeed, upon the theory on which the exclusive privileges granted by the act in question are sustained, there is no monopoly, in the most odious form, which may not be upheld.

The question presented is, therefore, one of the gravest importance, not merely to the parties here, but to the whole country. It is nothing less than the question whether the recent amendments to the Federal Constitution protect the citizens of the United States against the deprivation of their common rights by State legislation. In my judgment the fourteenth amendment does afford such protection, and was so intended by the Congress which framed and the States which adopted it.

The counsel for the plaintiffs in error have contended, with great force, that the act in question is also inhibited by the thirteenth amendment.

That amendment prohibits slavery and involuntary servitude, except as a punishment for crime, but I have not supposed it was susceptible of a construction which would cover the enactment in question. I have been so accustomed to regard it as intended to meet that form of slavery which had previously prevailed in this country, and to which the recent civil war owed its existence, that I was not prepared, nor am I yet, to give to it the extent and force ascribed by counsel. Still it is evident that the language of the amendment is not used in a restrictive sense. It is not confined to African slavery alone. It is general and universal in its application. Slavery of white men as well as of black men is prohibited, and not merely slavery in the strict sense of the term, but involuntary servitude in every form.

The words "involuntary servitude" . . . include something more than slavery in the strict sense of the term; they include also serfage, vassalage, villenage, peonage, and all other forms of compulsory service for the mere benefit or pleasure of others. Nor is this the full import of the terms. The abolition of slavery and involuntary servitude was intended to make every one born in this country a freeman, and as such to give to him the right to pursue the ordinary avocations of life without other restraint than such as affects all others, and to enjoy equally with them the fruits of his labor. A prohibition to him to pursue certain callings, open to others of the same age, condition, and sex, or to reside in places where others are permitted to live, would so far deprive him of the rights of a freeman, and would place him, as respects others, in a condition of servitude. A person allowed to pursue only one trade or calling, and only in one locality of the country, would not be, in the strict sense of the term, in a condition of slavery, but probably none would deny that he would be in a condition of servitude. He certainly would not possess the liberties nor enjoy the privileges of a freeman. The compulsion which would force him to labor even for his own benefit only in one direction, or in one place, would be almost as oppressive and nearly as great an invasion of his liberty as the compulsion which would force him to labor for the benefit or pleasure of another, and would equally constitute an element of servitude. . . .

It is not necessary . . . to rest my objections to the act in question upon the terms and meaning of the thirteenth amendment. The provisions of the fourteenth amendment, which is properly a supplement to the thirteenth, cover, in my judgment, the case before us, and inhibit any legislation which confers special and exclusive privileges like these under consideration. The amendment was adopted to obviate objections which had been raised and pressed with great force to the validity of the Civil Rights Act, and to place the common rights of American citizens under the protection of the National government. . . .

The first clause of this amendment determines who are citizens of the United States, and how their citizenship is created. Before its enactment there was much diversity of opinion among jurists and statesmen whether there was any such citizenship independent of that of the State, and, if any existed, as to the manner in which it originated. . . .

The first clause of the fourteenth amendment changes this whole subject, and removes it from the region of discussion and doubt. It recognizes in express terms, if it does not create, citizens of the United States, and it makes their citizenship dependent upon the place of their birth, or the fact of their adoption, and not upon the constitution or laws of any State or the condition of their ancestry. . . .

The amendment does not attempt to confer any new privileges or immunities upon citizens, or to enumerate or define those already existing. It assumes that there are such privileges and immunities which belong of right to citizens as such, and ordains that they shall not be abridged by State legislation. If this inhibition . . . only refers, as held by the majority of the court in their opinion, to such privileges and immunities as were before its adoption specially designated in the Constitution or necessarily implied as belonging to citizens of the United States, it was a vain and idle enactment, which accomplished nothing, and most unnecessarily excited Congress and the people on its passage. With privileges and immunities thus designated or implied no State could ever have interfered by its laws, and no new constitutional provision was required to inhibit such interference. The supremacy of the Constitution and the laws of the United States always, controlled any State legislation of that character. But if the amendment refers to the natural and inalienable rights which belong to all citizens, the inhibition has a profound significance and consequence.

What, then, are the privileges and immunities which are secured against abridgment by State legislation?

In the first section of the Civil Rights Act Congress has given its interpretation to these terms, or at least has stated some of the rights which, in its judgment, these terms include; it has there declared that they include the right "to make and enforce contracts, to sue, be parties and give evidence, to inherit, purchase, lease, sell, hold, and convey real and personal property, and to full and equal benefit of all laws and proceedings for the security of person and property." . . .

The terms, privileges and immunities, are not new in the amendment; they were in the Constitution before the amendment was adopted. They are found in the second section of the fourth article, which declares that "the citizens of each State shall be entitled to all privileges and immunities of citizens in the several States," and they have been the subject of frequent consideration in judicial decisions. In *Corfield v. Coryell*, [the opinion of] Mr. Justice Washington . . . appears to me to be a sound construction of the clause in question. The privileges and immunities designated are those *which of right belong to the citizens of all free governments*. Clearly among these must be placed the right to pursue a lawful employment in a lawful manner, without other restraint than such as equally affects all persons. In the discussions in Congress upon the passage of the Civil Rights Act re- peated reference was made to this language of Mr. Justice Washington. . . .

The privileges and immunities designated in the second section of the fourth article of the Constitution are, then, according to the decision cited, those which of right belong to the citizens of all free governments, and they can be enjoyed under that clause by the citizens of each State in the several States upon the same terms and conditions as they are enjoyed by the citi- zens of the latter States. No discrimination can be made by one State against the citizens of the States in their enjoyment, nor can any greater imposition be levied than such as is laid upon its own citizens. It is a clause which insures equality in the enjoyment of these rights between citizens of the several States whilst in the same State. . . .

What the clause in question did for the protection of the citizens of one State against hostile and discriminating legislation of other States, the fourteenth amendment does for the protection of every citizen of the United States against hostile and discriminating legislation against him in favor of others, whether they reside in the same or in different States. If under the fourth article of the Constitution equality of privileges and immunities is secured between citizens of different States, under the fourteenth amend- ment the same equality is secured between citizens of the United States.

It will not be pretended that under the fourth article of the Constitu- tion any State could create a monopoly in any known trade or manufacture in favor of her own citizens, or any portion of them, which would exclude an equal participation in the trade or manufacture monopolized by citizens of other States. She could not confer, for example, upon any of her citizens the sole right to manufacture shoes, or boots, or silk, or the sole right to sell those articles in the State so as to exclude nonresident citizens from engag- ing in a similar manufacture or sale. The non-resident citizens could claim equality of privilege under the provisions of the fourth article with the citi- zens of the State exercising the monopoly as well as with others, and thus, as respects them, the monopoly would cease. . . .

Now, what the clause in question does for the protection of citizens of one State against the creation of monopolies in favor of citizens of other States, the fourteenth amendment does for the protection of every citizen of the United States against the creation of any monopoly whatever. The priv- ileges and immunities of citizens of the United States, of every one of them, is secured against abridgment in any form by any State. The fourteenth amendment places them under the guardianship of the National authori- ty. . . .

This equality of right, with exemption from all disparaging and partial enactments, in the lawful pursuits of life, throughout the whole country, is the distinguishing privilege of citizens of the United States. To them, everywhere, all pursuits, all professions, all avocations are open without other restrictions than such as are imposed equally upon all others of the same age, sex, and condition. The State may prescribe such regulations for every pursuit and calling of life as will promote the public health, secure the good order and advance the general prosperity of society, but when once prescribed, the pursuit or calling must be free to be followed by every citizen who is within the conditions designated, and will conform to the regulations. . . . The fourteenth amendment, in my judgment, makes it essential to the validity of the legislation of every State that this equality of right should be respected. How widely this equality has been departed from, how entirely rejected and trampled upon by the act of Louisiana, I have already shown. And it is to me a matter of profound regret that its validity is recognized by a majority of this court, for by it the right of free labor, one of the most sacred and imprescriptible rights of man, is violated. . . . [G]rants of exclusive privileges, such as is made by the act in question, are opposed to the whole theory of free government, and it requires no aid from any bill of rights to render them void. That only is a free government, in the American sense of the term, under which the inalienable right of every citizen to pursue his happiness is unrestrained, except by just, equal, and impartial laws.

■ MR. JUSTICE BRADLEY, also dissenting.

I concur in the opinion which has just been read by Mr. Justice FIELD; but desire to add a few observations for the purpose of more fully illustrating my views on the important question decided in these cases, and the special grounds on which they rest. . . .

It is contended that [the act in question] abridges the privileges and immunities of citizens of the United States, . . . and whether it does so or not is the simple question in this case. And the solution of this question depends upon the solution of two other questions, to wit:

First. Is it one of the rights and privileges of a citizen of the United States to pursue such civil employment as he may choose to adopt, subject to such reasonable regulations as may be prescribed by law?

Secondly. Is a monopoly, or exclusive right, given to one person to the exclusion of all others, to keep slaughter-houses, in a district of nearly twelve hundred square miles, for the supply of meat for a large city, a reasonable regulation of that employment which the legislature has a right to impose?

The first of these questions is one of vast importance, and lies at the very foundations of our government. . . .

If a State legislature should pass a law of caste, making all trades and professions, or certain enumerated trades and professions, hereditary, so that no one could follow any such trades or professions except that which was pursued by his father, would such a law violate the privileges and immunities of the people of that State as citizens of the United States, or only as citizens of the State? Would they have no redress but to appeal to the courts of that particular State? . . .

The right of a State to regulate the conduct of its citizens is undoubtedly a very broad and extensive one, and not to be lightly restricted. But there are certain fundamental rights which this right of regulation cannot infringe. It may prescribe the manner of their exercise, but it cannot subvert the rights themselves. I speak now of the rights of citizens of any free government. . . . In this free country, the people of which inherited certain traditionary rights and privileges from their ancestors, citizenship means something. . . .

The people of this country brought with them to its shores the rights of Englishmen; the rights which had been wrested from English sovereigns at various periods of the nation's history. One of these fundamental rights was expressed in these words, found in Magna Charta: "No freeman shall be taken or imprisoned, or be disseized of his freehold or liberties or free customs, or be outlawed or exiled, or any otherwise destroyed; nor will we pass upon him or condemn him but by lawful judgment of his peers or by the law of the land." English constitutional writers expound this article as rendering life, liberty, and property inviolable, except by due process of law. . . .

[T]he Declaration of Independence, which was the first political act of the American people in their independent sovereign capacity, lays the foundation of our National existence upon this broad proposition: "That all men are created equal; that they are endowed by their Creator with certain inalienable rights; that among these are life, liberty, and the pursuit of happiness." Here again we have the great threefold division of the rights of freemen, asserted as the rights of man. Rights to life, liberty, and the pursuit of happiness are equivalent to the rights of life, liberty, and property. These are the fundamental rights which can only be taken away by due process of law, and which can only be interfered with, or the enjoyment of which can only be modified, by lawful regulations necessary or proper for the mutual good of all; and these rights, I contend, belong to the citizens of every free government.

For the preservation, exercise, and enjoyment of these rights the individual citizen, as a necessity, must be left free to adopt such calling, profession, or trade as may seem to him most conducive to that end. Without this right he cannot be a freeman. This right to choose one's calling is an essential part of that liberty which it is the object of government to protect; and a calling, when chosen, is a man's property and right. Liberty and property are not protected where these rights are arbitrarily assailed. . . .

[E]ven if the Constitution were silent, the fundamental privileges and immunities of citizens, as such, would be no less real and no less inviolable than they now are. It was not necessary to say in words that the citizens of the United States should have and exercise all the privileges of citizens; the privilege of buying, selling, and enjoying property; the privilege of engaging in any lawful employment for a livelihood; the privilege of resorting to the laws for redress of injuries, and the like. Their very citizenship conferred these privileges. . . . [C]itizens of the United States [may] lay claim to every one of the privileges and immunities which have been enumerated; and among these none is more essential and fundamental than the right to follow such profession or employment as each one may choose, subject only to uniform regulations equally applicable to all. . . .

If my views are correct with regard to what are the privileges and immunities of citizens, it follows conclusively that any law which establishes a sheer monopoly, depriving a large class of citizens of the privilege of pursuing a lawful employment, does abridge the privileges of those citizens. . . .

[G]reat fears are expressed that this construction of the amendment will lead to enactments by Congress interfering with the internal affairs of the States, and establishing therein civil and criminal codes of law for the government of the citizens, and thus abolishing the State governments in everything but name; or else, that it will lead the Federal courts to draw to their cognizance the supervision of State tribunals on every subject of judicial inquiry, on the plea of ascertaining whether the privileges and immunities of citizens have not been abridged.

In my judgment no such practical inconveniences would arise. Very little, if any, legislation on the part of Congress would be required to carry the amendment into effect. Like the prohibition against passing a law impairing the obligation of a contract, it would execute itself. The point would be regularly raised, in a suit at law, and settled by final reference to the Federal court. As the privileges and immunities protected are only those fundamental ones which belong to every citizen, they would soon become so far defined as to cause but a slight accumulation of business in the Federal courts. Besides, the recognized existence of the law would prevent its frequent violation. But even if the business of the National courts should be increased, Congress could easily supply the remedy by increasing their number and efficiency. The great question is, What is the true construction of the amendment? When once we find that, we shall find the means of giving it effect. The argument from inconvenience ought not to have a very controlling influence in questions of this sort. The National will and National interest are of far greater importance. . . .

■ MR. JUSTICE SWAYNE, dissenting.

. . . The first section of the fourteenth amendment is alone involved in the consideration of these cases. No searching analysis is necessary to eliminate its meaning. Its language is intelligible and direct. Nothing can be more transparent. Every word employed has an established signification. There is no room for construction. There is nothing to construe. Elaboration may obscure, but cannot make clearer, the intent and purpose sought to be carried out. . . .

Life, liberty, and property are forbidden to be taken "without due process of law," and "equal protection of the laws" is guaranteed to all. . . . Property is everything which has an exchangeable value, and the right of property includes the power to dispose of it according to the will of the owner. Labor is property, and as such merits protection. The right to make it available is next in importance to the rights of life and liberty. It lies to a large extent at the foundation of most other forms of property, and of all solid individual and national prosperity. "Due process of law" is the application of the law as it exists in the fair and regular course of administrative procedure. "The equal protection of the laws" places all upon a footing of legal equality and gives the same protection to all for the preservation of life, liberty, and property, and the pursuit of happiness. . . .

The cases before us, therefore, present but two questions.

(1.) Does the act of the legislature creating the monopoly in question abridge the privileges and immunities of the plaintiffs in error as citizens of the United States?

(2.) Does it deprive them of liberty or property without due process of law, or deny them the equal protection of the laws of the State, they being *persons* "within its jurisdiction"?

. . . A more flagrant and indefensible invasion of the rights of many for the benefit of a few has not occurred in the legislative history of the country. The response to both inquiries should be in the affirmative. . . .

NOTES

1. *The Thirteenth Amendment.* The plaintiffs in *Slaughter–House* invoked several provisions in support of their claim that the city's grant of a monopoly was unconstitutional. Consider first the Court's discussion of the Thirteenth Amendment. How serious is the argument that the Thirteenth Amendment's prohibition on slavery and involuntary servitude reaches the grant of a business monopoly? If this were prohibited, what else might the Thirteenth Amendment forbid? Military conscription? Forcing parents to care for their children? Enforcement of personal service contracts? Cf. *Bailey v. State of Alabama*, 219 U.S. 219 (1911) (finding that Alabama peonage laws, which made breaking labor contracts a crime punishable by specific performance, violated the Thirteenth Amendment).

2. *The Due Process Clause.* What does the Court say about the claim that the city's grant of a monopoly deprived the plaintiffs of their life, liberty, or property "without due process of law"? Which of these three kinds of interests—life, liberty, and property—does the Court focus on? Why? Is Justice Swayne's definition of property persuasive? And note that the ordinance was duly enacted by the Louisiana legislature. Is that all that the Due Process Clause requires, or does it also constrain the kind of laws that may be passed?

3. *The Equal Protection Clause.* The Court describes the Equal Protection Clause as being motivated by "[t]he existence of laws in the States where the newly emancipated negroes resided, which discriminated with gross injustice and hardship against them as a class." In its review of the history leading to the enactment of the Fourteenth Amendment, the Court noted the oppressiveness of the Black Codes and the fact that the lives of the newly freed slaves "were at the mercy of bad men, *either because the laws for their protection were insufficient or were not enforced*" (emphasis added). The Court thus read the clause as a remedy for laws that were either substantively discriminatory against the newly freed slaves or not enforced on their behalf.

If the law at issue in *Slaughter–House* had restricted the operation of animal slaughterhouses to whites only—discriminating as to who may operate a business or engage in a trade or profession on the basis of race—would it have been unconstitutional under the Equal Protection Clause? Is the Equal Protection Clause limited to providing protection against state discrimination on the basis of race? Does the clause say "race"? One of the enduring questions of constitutional interpretation raised by the Fourteenth Amendment is how much its scope is determined by its broad language and how much by its specific historical purpose.

If the Equal Protection Clause does extend beyond its historical purpose, would it necessarily forbid every distinction or "discrimination" the government might make? After all, every law or regulation has some kind of distinction between the people or activities it applies to and the ones it does not apply to. If that is too far to go, then how would we decide which distinctions or classifications are permissible? What about asking if the distinction is a fair one? How would that apply to the regulation in *Slaughter–House*, which granted a monopoly to one business, essentially putting competitors out of business? Or does the idea of equal protection allow the government to make distinctions, even unfair ones, as long as it does not use race or similarly illegitimate criteria? *Slaughter–House*, as we shall see, anticipates modern doctrine on this point. The government may make distinctions in what it chooses to regulate and how—even regulations that will affect different persons differently, and sometimes seemingly unfairly—as long as government has not regulated on the basis of some illegitimate classification of persons, such as race, sex, or another immutable physical characteristic. Unless there is such a classification, the government needs only a mere "rational basis" for its legislative choices. See *Williamson v. Lee Optical Co.*, 348 U.S. 483 (1955).

4. *The Privileges or Immunities Clause and Incorporation.* Finally, we get to the major question in *Slaughter–House*: the meaning of the Privileges or Immunities Clause. What are "the privileges or immunities of citizens of the United States"?

One well-respected view is that this provision was a reasonably straightforward attempt to incorporate by reference the provisions of the Bill of Rights and other individual rights provisions of the original Constitution and to provide that "[n]o state shall abridge" these rights. In that sense, the Privileges or Immunities Clause could be seen as overruling another early case: *Barron v. Baltimore,* 32 U.S. 243 (1833) (presented in Chapter 1). That case had held (correctly at the time) that the provisions of the Bill of Rights limited the powers of the federal government only. The Fourteenth Amendment reversed that result going forward. See Akhil Reed Amar: THE BILL OF RIGHTS: CREATION AND RECONSTRUCTION 137–214 (1998); Michael Kent Curtis, NO STATE SHALL ABRIDGE: THE FOURTEENTH AMENDMENT AND THE BILL OF RIGHTS (1986).

Consider in support of this view the words of Senator Howard, a leading spokesman for what became the Fourteenth Amendment, as he presented and explained its language to the Senate (prior to this excerpt he had just read from *Corfield v. Coryell*, which is discussed further in the following note):

> Such is the character of the privileges and immunities spoken of in the second section of the fourth article of the Constitution. To these privileges and immunities, whatever they may be—for they are not and cannot be fully defined in their entire extent and precise nature—to these should be added the personal rights guaranteed and secured by the first eight amendments of the Constitution; such as the freedom of speech and of the press; the right of the people peaceably to assemble and petition the Government for a redress of grievances, a right appertaining to each and all the people; the right to keep and to bear arms; the right to be exempted from the quartering of soldiers in a house without the consent of the owner; the right to be exempt from unreasonable searches and seizures, and from any search or seizure except by virtue of a warrant issued upon a formal oath or affidavit; the right of an accused person to be informed of the nature of the accusation against him, and his right to be tried by an impartial jury of the vicinage; and also the right to be secure against excessive bail and against cruel and unusual punishments.
>
> Now, sir, here is a mass of privileges, immunities, and rights, some of them secured by the second section of the fourth article of the Constitution, which I have recited, some by the first eight amendments of the Constitution; and it is a fact well worthy of attention that the course of decision of our courts and the present settled doctrine is, that all these immunities, privileges, rights, thus guaranteed by the Constitution or recognized by it, are secured to the citizen solely as a citizen of the United States and as a party in their courts. They do not operate in the slightest

degree as a restraint or prohibition upon State legislation. *[Senator Howard is referring to Barron v. Baltimore.—Editors]*

... The great object of the first section of this amendment is, therefore, to restrain the power of the States and compel them at all times to respect these great fundamental guarantees.

Congressional Globe, 39th Cong., 1st Sess. 2765–66 (1866).

Does anything in the opinions in *Slaughterhouse* directly challenge this view? The conventional (though not unanimous) reading of *Slaughter–House* is that the majority opinion is inconsistent with the understanding that the Privileges or Immunities Clause incorporates the Bill of Rights against state governments. Indeed, it was because of this reading of *Slaughter–House* as foreclosing incorporation through that clause that the Court gradually turned to a different clause of the Fourteenth Amendment as the vehicle for incorporating most of the provisions of the Bill of Rights against the states: the Due Process Clause. (For more on incorporation, see "A Short History of the Bill of Rights" at the beginning of Chapter 6.)

5. *The Privileges or Immunities Clause and Corfield v. Coryell.* To win, the plaintiffs in *Slaughter–House* needed to persuade the Court that the Privileges or Immunities Clause did more than simply incorporate by reference the individual rights the original Constitution had guaranteed against interference from the national government. (The right to run a slaughterhouse is nowhere found in the Bill of Rights.) What arguments are there that the Privileges or Immunities Clause goes *beyond* incorporation of the Bill of Rights and the rights set forth in Article I, Section 9 of the Constitution? Senator Howard referred to the protections of Article IV, Section 2. Note that the Privileges *or* Immunities Clause of the Fourteenth Amendment was patterned on the language of the Privileges *and* Immunities Clause of Article IV. That clause in Article IV was designed to prohibit states from discriminating against citizens of other states, at least with respect to the fundamental rights of citizenship. What were those rights? And did they include a constitutional right to own and run a slaughterhouse?

The *Slaughter–House* opinions discuss the leading case on the Privileges and Immunities Clause of Article IV. That case, *Corfield v. Coryell*, 6 Fed. Cas. 546 (1823), was decided by Justice Bushrod Washington while sitting as a Circuit Judge. The case is discussed above in Chapter 4. A brief recap: New Jersey had enacted a law prohibiting out-of-staters from raking clams or gathering oysters in New Jersey coastal waters. A Pennsylvanian's boat was seized for violation of the law, and its owner sued to get his boat back, arguing that New Jersey's law conflicted with the Privileges and Immunities Clause. Justice Bushrod Washington wrote the opinion rejecting that constitutional argument, and setting forth what came to be regarded as the canonical description of what that clause embraced. (That description is quoted in the excerpt from *Corfield* in Chapter 4.)

What is the relevance of Justice Washington's interpretation of the Privileges and Immunities Clause of Article IV for understanding the Privileges or Immunities Clause of the Fourteenth Amendment? Whatever the original meaning of "privileges" and "immunities" in 1789 may have been, had those become legal terms of art, through established judicial interpretation, by 1868? Would that mean we should we see the drafters of the Fourteenth Amendment as reading in the dictum of *Corfield* when they said "privileges or immunities"? If so, what does *Corfield* mean? Did it establish an entirely open-ended meaning to "privileges" and "immunities" or did it constrain the types of privileges that a state must extend to citizens of other states? (Recall that Justice Washington ruled *against* the equal-rights-to-rake-clams claim.)

Corfield and the Article IV background suggest another way that the Privileges or Immunities Clause can be read: as a non-discrimination principle. Where the clause in Article IV forbade discrimination against out-of-staters with respect to certain rights, perhaps the clause in the Fourteenth Amendment forbade discrimination against *in-staters* with respect to those rights. In other words, the Privileges or Immunities Clause may have been originally understood as clarifying that the "privileges and immunities" guaranteed under Article IV also applied to the newly emancipated black citizens of the United States. For scholarly defenses of this reading of the Privileges or Immunities Clause, see Philip Hamburger, *Privileges or Immunities*, 105 Nw. U. L. Rev. 61 (2011) (providing a comprehensive history of the Privileges or Immunities Clause and arguing against the incorporation interpretation); John Harrison, *Reconstructing the Privileges or Immunities Clause*, 101 Yale L.J. 1385 (1992). If this anti-discrimination reading of the Privileges or Immunities Clause is right, would that clause have been understood as doing much of the work that today we usually associate with a different provision of the Fourteenth Amendment, the Equal Protection Clause? (One could also see the Privileges or Immunities Clause as protecting substantive rights *and* embodying an anti-discrimination command.)

On any of these ways of understanding the Privileges or Immunities Clause—as incorporating the Bill of Rights against the states, as providing a more ample set of *Corfield*-like substantive rights, as a non-discrimination principle, or as some combination of these disparate readings—one still needs to think about how this clause fits with the Equal Protection Clause. One of the ways of fitting them together, but hardly the only one, is to see the Privileges or Immunities Clause as targeting the problem of states *making* laws and the Equal Protection Clause as targeting the problem of states *failing to enforce* the laws that are already on the books.

6. *The Privileges or Immunities Clause and Congress.* A final possibility: The term "Privileges or Immunities" has no clear, determinate meaning beyond incorporation-by-reference of the Bill of Rights and other individual liberties explicitly recognized by the Constitution. But the clause admits of a broader range of meaning. Thus, Congress could legislate protection of civil rights extending beyond the core, pursuant to its "necessary and proper"-esque enforcement power in Section 5 of the amendment. This explanation fits the legislative history indicating that the framers of the Fourteenth Amendment wanted to validate the Civil Rights Act of 1866, which included protection of civil rights of contract, capacity to sue and be sued, employment, and use of public accommodations. Perhaps the judiciary could not enforce such understandings on its own, as a matter of the self-executing force of the Privileges or Immunities Clause of Section 1, but Congress could pursuant to its Section 5 power. (As you will see, the Court rejected at least one version of that argument in *The Civil Rights Cases*, decided ten years after *Slaughter–House*. By then, Reconstruction had effectively ended and the social, political, and legal landscape of the South was changing.)

[*Assignment 60*]

D. THE ORIGINAL MEANING AND EARLY INTERPRETATION OF "EQUAL PROTECTION OF THE LAWS"

Slaughter–House was the Supreme Court's first decision interpreting the Thirteenth Amendment and the Fourteenth Amendment's three main prohibitory ("No state shall") clauses—the Privileges or Immunities Clause, the Due Process Clause, and the Equal Protection Clause. The Court's primary focus was the Privileges or Immunities Clause. The day after its decision in *Slaughter–House*, the Court decided another case focused on the Privileges or Immunities Clause, *Bradwell v. Illinois*. But that case also offers a good introduction to the Equal Protection Clause.

Bradwell can be seen as raising (though not answering) central questions about the original meaning of the phrase "equal protection of the laws." Did it refer only to the equal *protection* of the laws—the right of all equally to receive the benefit of the enforcement of the laws for their protection (whatever the substance of those laws might be)? Or did it also imply that in *substance* state laws must not discriminate on illegitimate grounds in the provision of legal rights, privileges, and benefits—that is, that the substance of the laws must treat similarly situated persons equally? If so, what grounds of distinction are permissible? Clearly, the framers of the Fourteenth Amendment wanted to outlaw discrimination on the basis of race, and to empower Congress to legislate to effectuate that end. But the amendment is not worded in terms of race. If the Equal Protection Clause applies to more than just race discrimination, what other types of distinctions or classifications does it forbid states to make? For example, does it prohibit states from treating men and women differently, in terms of their privileges or immunities under the substantive law? If so, does that prohibition apply in every respect? What if it were clear that the framers of the Fourteenth Amendment were not concerned with providing equal treatment on the basis of sex—and indeed would not have intended such a result? Would their subjective intentions or expectations qualify—or even override—what would otherwise appear to be the meaning of the text? Are some or all of these determinations left to the judgment of Congress, as it exercises its enforcement power under Section 5 of the Fourteenth Amendment? Or is the scope of the Equal Protection Clause's prohibition a matter for the courts to decide?

Bradwell v. Illinois involved the refusal of the Illinois Supreme Court to admit a woman to the practice of law. The two cases that follow, *Minor v. Happersett* and *Strauder v. West Virginia*, are also early interpretations of the Equal Protection Clause.

Bradwell v. Illinois

83 (16 Wall.) U.S. 130 (1873)

■ MR. JUSTICE MILLER delivered the opinion of the court.

The record in this case is not very perfect, but it may be fairly taken that the plaintiff asserted her right to a license on the grounds, among others, that she was a citizen of the United States. . . .

In regard to [the fourteenth] amendment counsel for the plaintiff in this court truly says that there are certain privileges and immunities which belong to a citizen of the United States as such; otherwise it would be nonsense for the fourteenth amendment to prohibit a State from abridging them, and he proceeds to argue that admission to the bar of a State of a person who possesses the requisite learning and character is one of those which a State may not deny.

In this latter proposition we are not able to concur with counsel. We agree with him that there are privileges and immunities belonging to citizens of the United States, in that relation and character, and that it is these and these alone which a State is forbidden to abridge. But the right to admission to practice in the courts of a State is not one of them. This right in no sense depends on citizenship of the United States. It has not, as far as we know, ever been made in any State, or in any case, to depend on citizenship at all. Certainly many prominent and distinguished lawyers have been admitted to practice, both in the State and Federal courts, who were not citizens of the United States or of any State. But, on whatever basis this right may be placed, so far as it can have any relation to citizenship at all, it would seem that, as to the courts of a State, it would relate to citizenship of the State, and as to Federal courts, it would relate to citizenship of the United States.

The opinion just delivered in the *Slaughter–House Cases* renders elaborate argument in the present case unnecessary; for, unless we are wholly and radically mistaken in the principles on which those cases are decided, the right to control and regulate the granting of license to practice law in the courts of a State is one of those powers which are not transferred for its protection to the Federal government, and its exercise is in no manner governed or controlled by citizenship of the United States in the party seeking such license.

It is unnecessary to repeat the argument on which the judgment in those cases is founded. It is sufficient to say they are conclusive of the present case.

■ MR. JUSTICE BRADLEY [concurring, joined by MR. JUSTICE SWAYNE and MR. JUSTICE FIELD]:

I concur in the judgment of the court in this case, by which the judgment of the Supreme Court of Illinois is affirmed, but not for the reasons specified in the opinion just read. . . .

The claim of the plaintiff, who is a married woman, to be admitted to practice as an attorney and counsellor-at-law, is based upon the supposed right of every person, man or woman, to engage in any lawful employment for a livelihood. The Supreme Court of Illinois denied the application on the ground that, by the common law, which is the basis of the laws of Illinois, only men were admitted to the bar, and the legislature had not made any change in this respect, but had simply provided that no person should be admitted to practice as attorney or counsellor without having previously obtained a license for that purpose from two justices of the Supreme Court. . . . The court . . . regarded itself as bound by [the] limitation . . . that it should not admit any persons, or class of persons, not intended by the legislature to be admitted, even though not expressly excluded by statute. In view of this latter limitation the court felt compelled to deny the application of females to be admitted as members of the bar. Being contrary to the rules of the common law and the usages of Westminster Hall from time immemorial, it could not be supposed that the legislature had intended to adopt any different rule.

The claim that, under the fourteenth amendment of the Constitution, which declares that no State shall make or enforce any law which shall abridge the privileges and immunities of citizens of the United States, the statute law of Illinois, or the common law prevailing in that State, can no longer be set up as a barrier against the right of females to pursue any lawful employment for a livelihood (the practice of law included), assumes that it is one of the privileges and immunities of women as citizens to engage in any and every profession, occupation, or employment in civil life.

It certainly cannot be affirmed, as an historical fact, that this has ever been established as one of the fundamental privileges and immunities of the sex. On the contrary, the civil law, as well as nature herself, has always recognized a wide difference in the respective spheres and destinies of man and woman. Man is, or should be, woman's protector and defender. The natural and proper timidity and delicacy which belongs to the female sex evidently unfits it for many of the occupations of civil life. The constitution of the family organization, which is founded in the divine ordinance, as well as in the nature of things, indicates the domestic sphere as that which properly belongs to the domain and functions of womanhood. The harmony, not to say identity, of interest and views which belong, or should belong, to the family institution is repugnant to the idea of a woman adopting a distinct and independent career from that of her husband. So firmly fixed was this sentiment in the founders of the common law that it became a maxim of that system of jurisprudence that a woman had no legal existence separate from her husband, who was regarded as her head and representative in the social state; and, notwithstanding some recent modifications of this civil status, many of the special rules of law flowing from and dependent upon this cardinal principle still exist in full force in most States. One of these is, that a married woman is incapable, without her husband's consent, of making contracts which shall be binding on her or him. This very incapacity was one circumstance which the Supreme Court of Illinois deemed important in rendering a married woman incompetent fully to perform the duties and trusts that belong to the office of an attorney and counsellor.

It is true that many women are unmarried and not affected by any of the duties, complications, and incapacities arising out of the married state, but these are exceptions to the general rule. The paramount destiny and mission of woman are to fulfil the noble and benign offices of wife and mother. This is the law of the Creator. And the rules of civil society must be adapted to the general constitution of things, and cannot be based upon exceptional cases.

The humane movements of modern society, which have for their object the multiplication of avenues for woman's advancement, and of occupations adapted to her condition and sex, have my heartiest concurrence. But I am not prepared to say that it is one of her fundamental rights and privileges to be admitted into every office and position, including those which require highly special qualifications and demanding special responsibilities. In the nature of things it is not every citizen of every age, sex, and condition that is qualified for every calling and position. It is the prerogative of the legislator to prescribe regulations founded on nature, reason, and experience for the due admission of qualified persons to professions and callings demanding special skill and confidence. This fairly belongs to the police power of the State; and, in my opinion, in view of the peculiar characteristics, destiny, and mission of woman, it is within the province of the legislature to ordain what offices, positions, and callings shall be filled and discharged by men, and shall receive the benefit of those energies and responsibilities, and that decision and firmness which are presumed to predominate in the sterner sex.

For these reasons I think that the laws of Illinois now complained of are not obnoxious to the charge of abridging any of the privileges and immunities of citizens of the United States.

■ THE CHIEF JUSTICE [CHASE] dissented from the judgment of the court, and from all the opinions.

Minor v. Happersett

88 (21 Wall.) U.S. 162 (1875)

■ THE CHIEF JUSTICE [WAITE] delivered the opinion of the court.

The question is presented in this case, whether, since the adoption of the fourteenth amendment, a woman, who is a citizen of the United States and of the State of Missouri, is a voter in that State, notwithstanding the provision of the constitution and laws of the State, which confine the right of suffrage to men alone. . . .

It is contended that the provisions of the constitution and laws of the State of Missouri which confine the right of suffrage and registration therefor to men, are in violation of the Constitution of the United States, and therefore void. The argument is, that as a woman, born or naturalized in the United States and subject to the jurisdiction thereof, is a citizen of the United States and of the State in which she resides, she has the right of suffrage as one of the privileges and immunities of her citizenship, which the State cannot by its laws or constitution abridge.

There is no doubt that women may be citizens. They are persons, and by the fourteenth amendment "all persons born or naturalized in the United States and subject to the jurisdiction thereof" are expressly declared to be "citizens of the United States and of the State wherein they reside." But, in our opinion, it did not need this amendment to give them that position. . . .

[The Court shows at length that women were citizens prior to adoption of the Fourteenth Amendment, citing among other evidence that they could sue and be sued in federal court under diversity jurisdiction as "citizens of different states."—Editors]

Other proof of like character might be found, but certainly more cannot be necessary to establish the fact that sex has never been made one of the elements of citizenship in the United States. In this respect men have never had an advantage over women. The same laws precisely apply to both. The fourteenth amendment did not affect the citizenship of women any more than it did of men. In this particular, therefore, the rights of Mrs. Minor do not depend upon the amendment. She has always been a citizen from her birth, and entitled to all the privileges and immunities of citizenship. . . .

If the right of suffrage is one of the necessary privileges of a citizen of the United States, then the constitution and laws of Missouri confining it to men are in violation of the Constitution of the United States, as amended, and consequently void. The direct question is, therefore, presented whether all citizens are necessarily voters.

The Constitution does not define the privileges and immunities of citizens. For that definition we must look elsewhere. In this case we need not determine what they are, but only whether suffrage is necessarily one of them.

It certainly is nowhere made so in express terms. The United States has no voters in the States of its own creation. The elective officers of the United States are all elected directly or indirectly by State voters. The members of the House of Representatives are to be chosen by the people of the States, and the electors in each State must have the qualifications requisite for electors of the most numerous branch of the State legislature. Senators are to be chosen by the legislatures of the States, and necessarily the members of the legislature required to make the choice are elected by the voters of the State. Each State must appoint in such manner, as the legislature thereof may direct, the electors to elect the President and Vice-President. The times, places, and manner of holding elections for Senators and Representatives are to be prescribed in each State by the legislature thereof; but Congress may at any time, by law, make or alter such regulations, except as to the place of choosing Senators. It is not necessary to inquire whether this power of supervision thus given to Congress is sufficient to authorize any interference with the State laws prescribing the qualifications of voters, for no such interference has ever been attempted. The power of the State in this particular is certainly supreme until Congress acts.

The [fourteenth] amendment did not add to the privileges and immunities of a citizen. It simply furnished an additional guaranty for the protection of such as he already had. No new voters were necessarily made by it. Indirectly it may have had that effect, because it may have increased the number of citizens entitled to suffrage under the constitution and laws of the States, but it operates for this purpose, if at all, through the States and the State laws, and not directly upon the citizen.

It is clear, therefore, we think, that the Constitution has not added the right of suffrage to the privileges and immunities of citizenship as they existed at the time it was adopted. This makes it proper to inquire whether suffrage was coextensive with the citizenship of the States at the time of its adoption. If it was, then it may with force be argued that suffrage was one of the rights which belonged to citizenship, and in the enjoyment of which every citizen must be protected. But if it was not, the contrary may with propriety be assumed.

When the Federal Constitution was adopted, all the States, with the exception of Rhode Island and Connecticut, had constitutions of their own. These two continued to act under their charters from the Crown. Upon an examination of those constitutions we find that in no State were all citizens permitted to vote. Each State determined for itself who should have that power. . . . *[The Court proceeds to quote the suffrage qualifications of each of the 13 original states.—Editors]*

In this condition of the law in respect to suffrage in the several States it cannot for a moment be doubted that if it had been intended to make all citizens of the United States voters, the framers of the Constitution would not have left it to implication. So important a change in the condition of citizenship as it actually existed, if intended, would have been expressly declared.

But if further proof is necessary to show that no such change was intended, it can easily be found both in and out of the Constitution. By Article

4, section 2, it is provided that "the citizens of each State shall be entitled to all the privileges and immunities of citizens in the several States." If suffrage is necessarily a part of citizenship, then the citizens of each State must be entitled to vote in the several States precisely as their citizens are. This is more than asserting that they may change their residence and become citizens of the State and thus be voters. It goes to the extent of insisting that while retaining their original citizenship they may vote in any State. This, we think, has never been claimed. And again, by the very terms of the amendment we have been considering [the fourteenth], "Representatives shall be apportioned among the several States according to their respective numbers, counting the whole number of persons in each State, excluding Indians not taxed. But when the right to vote at any election for the choice of electors for President and Vice–President of the United States, representatives in Congress, the executive and judicial officers of a State, or the members of the legislature thereof, is denied to any of the male inhabitants of such State, being twenty-one years of age and citizens of the United States, or in any way abridged, except for participation in the rebellion, or other crimes, the basis of representation therein shall be reduced in the proportion which the number of such male citizens shall bear to the whole number of male citizens twenty-one years of age in such State." Why this, if it was not in the power of the legislature to deny the right of suffrage to some male inhabitants? And if suffrage was necessarily one of the absolute rights of citizenship, why confine the operation of the limitation to male inhabitants? Women and children are, as we have seen, "persons." They are counted in the enumeration upon which the apportionment is to be made, but if they were necessarily voters because of their citizenship unless clearly excluded, why inflict the penalty for the exclusion of males alone? Clearly, no such form of words would have been selected to express the idea here indicated if suffrage was the absolute right of all citizens.

And still again, after the adoption of the fourteenth amendment, it was deemed necessary to adopt a fifteenth, as follows: "The right of citizens of the United States to vote shall not be denied or abridged by the United States, or by any State, on account of race, color, or previous condition of servitude." The fourteenth amendment had already provided that no State should make or enforce any law which should abridge the privileges or immunities of citizens of the United States. If suffrage was one of these privileges or immunities, why amend the Constitution to prevent its being denied on account of race, & c.? Nothing is more evident than that the greater must include the less, and if all were already protected why go through with the form of amending the Constitution to protect a part?

It is true that the United States guarantees to every State a republican form of government. It is also true that no State can pass a bill of attainder, and that no person can be deprived of life, liberty, or property without due process of law. All these several provisions of the Constitution must be construed in connection with the other parts of the instrument, and in the light of the surrounding circumstances.

The guaranty is of a republican form of government. No particular government is designated as republican, neither is the exact form to be guaranteed, in any manner especially designated. Here, as in other parts of the instrument, we are compelled to resort elsewhere to ascertain what was intended.

The guaranty necessarily implies a duty on the part of the States themselves to provide such a government. All the States had governments when the Constitution was adopted. In all the people participated to some extent, through their representatives elected in the manner specially provided. These governments the Constitution did not change. They were accepted precisely as they were, and it is, therefore, to be presumed that they were such as it was the duty of the States to provide. Thus we have unmistakable evidence of what was republican in form, within the meaning of that term as employed in the Constitution. As has been seen, all the citizens of the States were not invested with the right of suffrage. In all, save perhaps New Jersey, this right was only bestowed upon men and not upon all of them. Under these circumstances it is certainly now too late to contend that a government is not republican, within the meaning of this guaranty in the Constitution, because women are not made voters.

The same may be said of the other provisions just quoted. Women were excluded from suffrage in nearly all the States by the express provision of their constitutions and laws. If that had been equivalent to a bill of attainder, certainly its abrogation would not have been left to implication. Nothing less than express language would have been employed to effect so radical a change. . . .

We have given this case the careful consideration its importance demands. If the law is wrong, it ought to be changed; but the power for that is not with us. The arguments addressed to us bearing upon such a view of the subject may perhaps be sufficient to induce those having the power, to make the alteration, but they ought not to be permitted to influence our judgment in determining the present rights of the parties now litigating before us. No argument as to woman's need of suffrage can be considered. We can only act upon her rights as they exist. It is not for us to look at the hardship of withholding. Our duty is at an end if we find it is within the power of a State to withhold.

Being unanimously of the opinion that the Constitution of the United States does not confer the right of suffrage upon any one, and that the constitutions and laws of the several States which commit that important trust to men alone are not necessarily void, we

AFFIRM THE JUDGMENT.

NOTES

1. Six justices in *Bradwell* took positions in line with the ones they had just taken in *Slaughter–House*. The five justices represented by the Opinion of the Court had been the majority in *Slaughter–House*, and for them the case was not difficult: just as there was no privilege to be a butcher in Louisiana, there was no privilege to be a lawyer in Illinois. Chief Justice Chase dissented in both cases. He supported women's professional advancement, and when he had been Lincoln's secretary of the treasury he had ensured that many women were hired by the Treasury Department. And in his political campaigns—he had been governor of Ohio, a U.S. senator, and a presidential candidate—one of his chief advisers was his daughter Kate. Unfortunately, Chase wrote no opinion in *Bradwell*, for he was in poor health and died less than a month after the decision was announced. But the remaining three justices—Bradley, Swayne, and Field—had dissented in *Slaughter–House*, and they needed to show why this case was different. Their attempt to do that was the infamous concurrence of Justice Bradley.

Was *Bradwell* rightly decided? If it was wrong, was it wrong only because *Slaughter–House* was wrong in its interpretation of the Privileges or Immunities Clause? Or was it wrong because of the injustice of the result? (Note how *Minor* argues, at the close of the opinion, that this should not be part of constitutional interpretation. Do you agree?)

2. Bradwell's counsel argued only on the basis of the Privileges or Immunities Clause. At the time it was not clear that the argument would be foreclosed, for *Bradwell* was argued a few months before the Court announced its decision in *Slaughter–House*. But would *Bradwell* have come out differently if it were considered under the Equal Protection Clause? (Recall *Slaughter–House*'s discussion of that clause.) How could the Court have overlooked its relevance to Myra Bradwell's claim? And how could her counsel have failed to advance that argument? One answer may lie in the identity of Bradwell's counsel, Matthew Hale Carpenter, a sitting U.S. senator and frequent advocate in the Supreme Court—who while representing Bradwell was also representing the state of Louisiana in *Slaughter–House*.

Imagine that Illinois had excluded its black citizens from the practice of law. Would that plainly have violated the Equal Protection Clause? If so, why would it not also violate the Equal Protection Clause to exclude women from the practice of law? Consider two possible responses (and their broader interpretive implications). One is that the Equal Protection Clause is concerned only with race, because its historical purpose was aimed at the repressive Black Codes and racial discrimination in law. The other is that the drafts*men* of the Fourteenth Amendment did not intend for the Equal Protection Clause to apply to discrimination against women. But these responses can be met with strong objections. The Equal Protection Clause does not use any terms that limit its scope to race—even though its drafters knew how to do this (compare the Fifteenth Amendment two years later, which did refer explicitly to race). And should the meaning of the amendment be limited by the subjective intentions of its drafters and their expectations about how it would be applied?

Or should *Bradwell* be considered rightly decided at the time because the social context of the day made it unthinkable that the amendment would provide equal legal status and privileges to women? Does the meaning of the language of the Constitution depend on changing social values? When courts interpret and apply the Constitution, should they take into account contemporary social norms that may tolerate discrimination?

3. Myra Bradwell had "read law" (apprenticed) with her husband, an Illinois attorney, and she then took the Illinois bar exam, passing with high honors. But she was denied admission by the Illinois Supreme Court on the ground "that when the legislature gave to this court the power of granting licenses to practice law, it was with not the slightest expectation that this privilege would be extended to women." Bradwell's biographer reports that by the time her case reached the U.S. Supreme Court the Illinois legislature had already passed a statute providing that "No person shall be precluded or debarred from any occupation, profession, or employment (except military) on account of sex." Jane M. Friedman, AMERICA'S FIRST WOMAN LAWYER 28 (1993). (Should that have made the case "moot"?) Bradwell never reapplied for admission, even after the U.S. Supreme Court's decision, having developed a career as a prominent legal journalist in Chicago. In 1890, the Illinois Supreme Court on its own reversed its prior action and admitted Bradwell to the Illinois bar. In 1892, the U.S. Su-

preme Court, on motion of the attorney general, retroactively granted Bradwell admission to the bar of that court as of the date of her original application in 1869.

4. *Bradwell* has been repudiated in the modern era by a series of Supreme Court decisions holding that the Equal Protection Clause forbids laws that make legal distinctions on the basis of sex, except in relatively narrow circumstances where a sex-based classification has an "exceedingly persuasive justification" closely tied to a real, biological difference between men and women and not merely a generalization or a socially constructed stereotype. See *United States v. Virginia*, 518 U.S. 515 (1996), and *Craig v. Boren*, 429 U.S. 190 (1976), both of which are included below.

5. On to *Minor*, which presents a different question: Is the right to vote in state and federal elections among the "privileges or immunities" of citizens of the United States? The Court's opinion in *Minor* was unanimous. Is there any good rebuttal to the argument that, given Section 2's language restricting representation in Congress if a state denied the right to vote on the basis of race, it would make no sense to read Section 1 as completely prohibiting denial of the right to vote on the basis of race (or, for that matter, sex)? And if voting were a "privilege or immunity" of citizens, then why would the Fifteenth Amendment have been necessary?

As you try to make sense of this, a distinction that may be helpful is the one between "civil rights" and "political rights," as those terms were generally used around the time of the Reconstruction amendments. Civil rights were the *Corfield*-style list of privileges and immunities—freedom to move, make contracts, own property, and so on. Political rights included the right to vote, serve on a jury, and hold political office. (There was not complete agreement, though, about what belonged in each category.) This distinction is particularly sensible in the context of Article IV—a state was not allowed to discriminate against out-of-state residents with respect to "privileges and immunities," meaning civil rights such as owning property, but it was allowed to prevent out-of-staters from voting and holding office. This distinction between civil rights and political rights helps explain how the Fourteenth Amendment was understood as requiring equality in civil rights, but the Fifteenth and Nineteenth Amendments were still needed in order to prohibit discrimination in voting. For more on the distinction between civil rights and political rights, see Akhil Reed Amar, *Women and the Constitution*, 18 Harv. J. L. & Pub. Pol'y 465 (1995); John Harrison, *Reconstructing the Privileges or Immunities Clause*, 101 Yale L.J. 1385 (1992).

6. The modern Supreme Court has interpreted the Equal Protection Clause of the Fourteenth Amendment as prohibiting certain forms of disparate treatment with respect to the right to vote. Indeed, these decisions have become central to our national politics and election process. See, e.g., *Baker v. Carr*, 369 U.S. 186 (1962) (Equal Protection Clause held to supply a judicially enforceable basis for challenging state election and representation arrangements); *Reynolds v. Sims*, 377 U.S. 533 (1964) (Equal Protection Clause held to create a one-person, one-vote standard for state election districts); *Harper v. Virginia Board of Elections*, 383 U.S. 663 (1966) (Equal Protection Clause held to forbid state poll tax of $1.50); *Bush v. Gore*, 531 U.S. 98 (2000) (Equal Protection Clause held to require that state-law vote recount rules and arrangements treat each voter's ballot consistently throughout the state). Cf. *Shaw v. Reno*, 509 U.S. 630

(1993) (Equal Protection Clause held to create a cause of action to challenge race-conscious drawing of election districts).

Can any of these modern decisions be justified on constitutional grounds other than the Fourteenth Amendment? (These cases—and that question—are addressed in Chapter 8.) One possibility, discussed by the Court in *Minor*, is that Article IV's Republican Form of Government Clause might supply a principle invalidating certain state rules or statutes pertaining to voting and vote-counting. If so, would the enforcement (and interpretation) of that principle be committed to Congress or to the courts? Recall the holding of *Luther v. Borden*, 48 U.S. 1 (1849) (presented in Chapter 3), that such issues are political questions for Congress and the president to decide. Isn't that the theory under which Congress refused to seat Southern states' representatives unless they agreed to ratify the Fourteenth Amendment—that Congress was the judge of what was or was not sufficient for a state's government to be "Republican" in "form"? Is the reasoning of *Minor* consistent with this view? Would it mean that the Reconstruction Congress could have passed legislation giving women the right to vote in all national and state elections? Pursuant to the Fourteenth Amendment or Article IV?

7. The outcome in *Minor* was eventually overturned by the adoption of Nineteenth Amendment in 1920, giving women the constitutional right to vote throughout the nation.

————

The Court's next major case interpreting the Fourteenth Amendment was *Strauder v. West Virginia*, involving that state's exclusion of black citizens from criminal juries. *Strauder* is a major early case interpreting the amendment, analyzing both the rights it protects and Congress's power under Section 5 to displace state law and procedure to enforce those rights.

Strauder v. West Virginia
100 U.S. 303 (1880)

■ MR. JUSTICE STRONG delivered the opinion of the Court.

The plaintiff in error, a colored man, was indicted for murder in the Circuit Court of Ohio County, in West Virginia, on the 20th of October, 1874, and upon trial was convicted and sentenced. The record was then removed to the Supreme Court of the State, and there the judgment of the Circuit Court was affirmed. The present case is a writ of error to that court, and it is now, in substance, averred that at the trial in the State court the defendant (now plaintiff in error) was denied rights to which he was entitled under the Constitution and laws of the United States.

In the Circuit Court of the State, before the trial of the indictment was commenced, the defendant presented his petition, verified by his oath, praying for a removal of the cause into the Circuit Court of the United States, assigning, as ground for the removal, that "by virtue of the laws of the State of West Virginia no colored man was eligible to be a member of the grand jury or to serve on a petit jury in the State; that white men are so eligible, and that by reason of his being a colored man and having been a slave, he had reason to believe, and did believe, he could not have the full and equal benefit of all laws and proceedings in the State of West Virginia for the security of his person as is enjoyed by white citizens, and that he had less chance of enforcing in the courts of the State his rights on the prosecution, as a citizen of the United States, and that the probabilities of a denial of them to him as such citizen on every trial which might take place on the indictment in the courts of the State were much more enhanced than if he was a white man." This petition was denied by the State court, and the cause was forced to trial. . . .

The law of the State . . . is as follows: "All white male persons who are twenty-one years of age and who are citizens of this State shall be liable to serve as jurors, except as herein provided." The persons excepted are State officials.

In this court, several errors have been assigned, and the controlling questions underlying them all are, first, whether, by the Constitution and laws of the United States, every citizen of the United States has a right to a trial of an indictment against him by a jury selected and impanelled without discrimination against his race or color, because of race or color; and, second, if he has such a right, and is denied its enjoyment by the State in which he is indicted, may he cause the case to be removed into the Circuit Court of the United States?

It is to be observed that the first of these questions is not whether a colored man, when an indictment has been preferred against him, has a right to a grand or a petit jury composed in whole or in part of persons of his own race or color, but it is whether, in the composition or selection of jurors by whom he is to be indicted or tried, all persons of his race or color may be excluded by law, solely because of their race or color, so that by no possibility can any colored man sit upon the jury.

The questions are important, for they demand a construction of the recent amendments of the Constitution. . . . The Fourteenth Amendment . . . is one of a series of constitutional provisions having a common purpose; namely, securing to a race recently emancipated, a race that through many generations had been held in slavery, all the civil rights that the superior race enjoy. The true spirit and meaning of the amendments, as we said in the *Slaughter–House Cases*, cannot be understood without keeping in view the history of the times when they were adopted, and the general objects they plainly sought to accomplish. At the time when they were incorporated into the Constitution, it required little knowledge of human nature to anticipate that those who had long been regarded as an inferior and subject race would, when suddenly raised to the rank of citizenship, be looked upon with jealousy and positive dislike, and that State laws might be enacted or enforced to perpetuate the distinctions that had before existed. Discriminations against them had been habitual. It was well known that in some States laws making such discriminations then existed, and others might well be expected. The colored race, as a race, was abject and ignorant, and in that condition was unfitted to command the respect of those who had superior intelligence. Their training had left them mere children, and as such they needed the protection which a wise government extends to those who are unable to protect themselves. They especially needed protection against unfriendly action in the States where they were resident. It was in view of these considerations the Fourteenth Amendment was framed and adopted. It was designed to assure to the colored race the enjoyment of all the civil rights that under the law are enjoyed by white persons, and to give to that race the protection of the general government, in that enjoyment, whenever it should be denied by the States. It not only gave citizenship and the privileges of citizenship to persons of color, but it denied to any State the power to withhold from them the equal protection of the laws, and authorized Congress to enforce its provisions by appropriate legislation. . . .

If this is the spirit and meaning of the amendment, whether it means more or not, it is to be construed liberally, to carry out the purposes of its framers. It ordains that no State shall make or enforce any laws which shall abridge the privileges or immunities of citizens of the United States (evidently referring to the newly made citizens, who, being citizens of the United States, are declared to be also citizens of the State in which they reside). It ordains that no State shall deprive any person of life, liberty, or property, without due process of law, or deny to any person within its jurisdiction the equal protection of the laws. What is this but declaring that the law in the States shall be the same for the black as for the white; that all persons, whether colored or white, shall stand equal before the laws of the States, and, in regard to the colored race, for whose protection the amendment was primarily designed, that no discrimination shall be made against them by law because of their color? The words of the amendment, it is true, are prohibitory, but they contain a necessary implication of a positive immunity, or right, most valuable to the colored race,—the right to exemption from unfriendly legislation against them distinctively as colored,— exemption from legal discriminations, implying inferiority in civil society, lessening the security of their enjoyment of the rights which others enjoy, and discriminations which are steps towards reducing them to the condition of a subject race.

That the West Virginia statute respecting juries—the statute that controlled the selection of the grand and petit jury in the case of the plaintiff in error—is such a discrimination ought not to be doubted. Nor would it be if the persons excluded by it were white men. If in those States where the colored people constitute a majority of the entire population a law should be enacted excluding all white men from jury service, thus denying to them the privilege of participating equally with the blacks in the administration of justice, we apprehend no one would be heard to claim that it would not be a denial to white men of the equal protection of the laws. Nor if a law should be passed excluding all naturalized Celtic Irishmen, would there by any doubt of its inconsistency with the spirit of the amendment. The very fact that colored people are singled out and expressly denied by a statute all right to participate in the administration of the law, as jurors, because of their color, though they are citizens, and may be in other respects fully qualified, is practically a brand upon them, affixed by the law, an assertion of their inferiority, and a stimulant to that race prejudice which is an impediment to securing to individuals of the race that equal justice which the law aims to secure to all others.

The right to a trial by jury is guaranteed to every citizen of West Virginia by the Constitution of that State, and the constitution of juries is a very essential part of the protection such a mode of trial is intended to secure. The very idea of a jury is a body of men composed of the peers or equals of the person whose rights it is selected or summoned to determine; that is, of his neighbors, fellows, associates, persons having the same legal status in society as that which he holds. Blackstone, in his Commentaries, says, "The right of trial by jury, or the country, is a trial by the peers of every Englishman, and is the grand bulwark of his liberties, and is secured to him by the Great Charter." . . . It is well known that prejudices often exist against particular classes in the community, which sway the judgment of jurors, and which, therefore, operate in some cases to deny to persons of those classes the full enjoyment of that protection which others enjoy. Prejudice in a local community is held to be a reason for a change of venue. The framers of the constitutional amendment must have known full well the existence of such prejudice and its likelihood to continue against the manumitted slaves and their race, and that knowledge was doubtless a motive that led to the amendment. By their manumission and citizenship the colored race became entitled to the equal protection of the laws of the States in which they resided; and the apprehension that through prejudice they might be denied that equal protection, that is, that there might be discrimination against them, was the inducement to bestow upon the national government the power to enforce the provision that no State shall deny to them the equal protection of the laws. Without the apprehended existence of prejudice that portion of the amendment would have been unnecessary, and it might have been left to the States to extend equality of protection.

In view of these considerations, it is hard to see why the statute of West Virginia should not be regarded as discriminating against a colored man when he is put upon trial for an alleged criminal offence against the State. It is not easy to comprehend how it can be said that while every white man is entitled to a trial by a jury selected from persons of his own race or color, or, rather, selected without discrimination against his color, and a negro is not, the latter is equally protected by the law with the former. Is not protection of life and liberty against race or color prejudice, a right, a legal right, under the constitutional amendment? And how can it be maintained that compelling a colored man to submit to a trial for his life by a jury drawn from a panel from which the State has expressly excluded every man of his race, because of color alone, however well qualified in other respects, is not a denial to him of equal legal protection?

We do not say that within the limits from which it is not excluded by the amendment a State may not prescribe the qualifications of its jurors, and in so doing make discriminations. It may confine the selection to males, to freeholders, to citizens, to persons within certain ages, or to persons having educational qualifications. We do not believe the Fourteenth Amendment was ever intended to prohibit this. Looking at its history, it is clear it had no such purpose. Its aim was against discrimination because of race or color. As we have said more than once, its design was to protect an emancipated race, and to strike down all possible legal discriminations against those who belong to it. To quote further from [the *Slaughter–House Cases*]: "In giving construction to any of these articles [amendments], it is necessary to keep the main purpose steadily in view." "It is so clearly a provision for that race and that emergency, that a strong case would be necessary for its application to any other." We are not now called upon to affirm or deny that it had other purposes.

The Fourteenth Amendment makes no attempt to enumerate the rights it designed to protect. It speaks in general terms, and those are as comprehensive as possible. Its language is prohibitory; but every prohibition implies the existence of rights and immunities, prominent among which is an immunity from inequality of legal protection, either for life, liberty, or property. Any State action that denies this immunity to a colored man is in conflict with the Constitution.

Concluding, therefore, that the statute of West Virginia, discriminating in the selection of jurors, as it does, against negroes because of their color, amounts to a denial of the equal protection of the laws to a colored man when he is put upon trial for an alleged offence against the State, it remains only to be considered whether the power of Congress to enforce the provisions of the Fourteenth Amendment by appropriate legislation is sufficient to justify the enactment of sect. 641 of the Revised Statutes.

A right or an immunity, whether created by the Constitution or only guaranteed by it, even without any express delegation of power, may be protected by Congress. *Prigg* v. *The Commonwealth of Pennsylvania*, 16 Pet. 539. . . . But there is express authority to protect the rights and immunities referred to in the Fourteenth Amendment, and to enforce observance of them by appropriate congressional legislation. And one very efficient and appropriate mode of extending such protection and securing to a party the enjoyment of the right or immunity, is a law providing for the removal of his case from a State court, in which the right is denied by the State law, into a Federal court, where it will be upheld. This is an ordinary mode of protecting rights and immunities conferred by the Federal Constitution and laws. Sect. 641 is such a provision. It enacts that "when any civil suit or criminal prosecution is commenced in any State court for any cause whatsoever against any person who is denied, or cannot enforce, in the judicial tribunals of the State, or in the part of the State where such prosecution is pending, any right secured to him by any law providing for the equal civil rights of citizens of the United States, or of all persons within the jurisdiction of the United States, such suit or prosecution may, upon the petition of such defendant, filed in said State court at any time before the trial, or final hearing of the case, stating the facts, and verified by oath, be removed before trial into the next Circuit Court of the United States to be held in the district where it is pending."

This act plainly has reference to sects. 1977 and 1978 of the statutes which partially enumerate the rights and immunities intended to be guaranteed by the Constitution, the first of which declares that "all persons within the jurisdiction of the United States shall have the same right in every State and Territory to make and enforce contracts, to sue, be parties, give evidence, and to the full and equal benefit of all laws and proceedings for the security of persons and property, as is enjoyed by white citizens, and shall be subject to like punishment, pains, penalties, taxes, licenses, and exactions of every kind, and to no other." This act puts in the form of a statute what had been substantially ordained by the constitutional amendment. It was a step towards enforcing the constitutional provisions. Sect. 641 was an advanced step, fully warranted, we think, by the fifth section of the Fourteenth Amendment. . . .

That the petition of the plaintiff in error, filed by him in the State court before the trial of his case, made a case for removal into the Federal Circuit Court, under sect. 641, is very plain, if, by the constitutional amendment and sect. 1977 of the Revised Statutes, he was entitled to immunity from discrimination against him in the selection of jurors, because of their color, as we have endeavored to show that he was. . . .

There was error, therefore, in proceeding to the trial of the indictment against him after his petition was filed. . . .

■ [MR. JUSTICE FIELD and MR. JUSTICE CLIFFORD dissented.]

NOTES

1. After *Strauder*'s proposition that "the law . . . shall be the same for the black as for the white" and that all races "shall stand equal before the laws of

the States," does anything else need to be said about the Equal Protection Clause and racial discrimination by the government? Alas, even great cases have their warts: we have deliberately not edited out *Strauder*'s racist language. Indeed, regrettable as it is, that language confirms the magnificence of *Strauder*'s declaration of legal principle: even a court steeped in cultural ideas of racial inferiority embraced the legal view that the Fourteenth Amendment rejected racial discrimination or segregation by government in any form. But as you will see, the Supreme Court soon retreated from *Strauder* with changes in the political and cultural sense of the times, upholding legally required segregation and validating schemes denying equal rights to black citizens.

2. Note the form in which the issue came to the Court in *Strauder*. Congress had passed a statute providing for federal court "removal" jurisdiction if a state's laws or procedures were not adequate to provide equal protection of the laws for blacks as well as whites. The West Virginia state courts had declined to permit removal. The Court found this a ground for reversal of Strauder's conviction, concluding that Congress had validly exercised its legislative power under Section 5 of the amendment. Keep *Strauder* in mind as you read the next set of cases, especially *The Civil Rights Cases*, on the scope of Congress's power under Section 5. Are *The Civil Rights Cases* consistent with *Strauder*?

[*Assignment 61*]

E. CONGRESS'S POWER TO ENFORCE THE RECONSTRUCTION AMENDMENTS

Central to the Reconstruction amendments—indeed, arguably their most important feature—was the grant of sweeping new legislative powers to Congress. Congress was given power to "enforce" the ban on slavery in the Thirteenth Amendment; to "enforce" with "appropriate" legislation the Fourteenth Amendment's broadly worded prohibitions on state denial of civil rights; and to "enforce" the Fifteenth Amendment's prohibition of racial discrimination in voting.

As noted above, the Reconstruction Congresses passed a series of important civil rights statutes pursuant to these powers, most of which remain in force today. The Civil Rights Act of 1866—passed after the Thirteenth Amendment was adopted but before the Fourteenth Amendment was proposed—provided that all persons born in the United States were citizens of the United States and listed rights and privileges of "such citizens, of every race and color, without regard to any previous condition of slavery." The law was aimed at the Black Codes enacted in several Southern states after slavery was banned.

Was the Civil Rights Act of 1866 within Congress's constitutional power to "enforce" the ban on slavery? President Johnson thought it exceeded Congress's constitutional power, and vetoed the Act. Congress passed it again over Johnson's veto, but constitutional doubts remained about whether the Thirteenth Amendment conferred power on Congress not only to punish slavery but also to prohibit discriminatory state laws. Those doubts were a substantial part of what motivated Congress to propose the Fourteenth Amendment, which was adopted in 1868, two years later. The Fourteenth Amendment explicitly granted power to Congress to enforce Section 1's prohibition on discriminatory state laws.

But did the Fourteenth Amendment enforcement power also reach purely private action—discrimination by private individuals or groups in matters of contract, employment, the provision of goods and services, or public accommodations? The text of the Fourteenth Amendment suggests that the answer is no: it appears to prohibit only state action, and the enforcement power is given to enforce that prohibition. Thus Congress possesses the power to enforce two quite different prohibitions: (1) the Thirteenth Amendment's prohibition of slavery and involuntary servitude, even by private actors; and (2) the Fourteenth Amendment's broader prohibition of discrimination in and denial of civil rights, but apparently only by state and local governments. The Thirteenth and Fourteenth Amendment enforcement powers thus leave a gap: Does either amendment grant Congress the power to forbid private discrimination in areas such as employment and public accommodations?

Enter the Civil Rights Act of 1875, in which Congress tried to push the outer limits of its legislative powers under the Thirteenth and Fourteenth Amendments. Section 1 provided that "all persons within the jurisdiction of the United States shall be entitled to the full and equal enjoyment of the accommodations, advantages, facilities, and privileges of inns, public conveyances on land or water, theatres, and other places of public amusement; subject only to the conditions and limitations established by law and applicable alike to citizens of every race and color, regardless of any condition of servitude." Section 2 provided criminal penalties and authorized civil suits for the award of monetary penalties.

The Supreme Court considered the act in *The Civil Rights Cases* (1883), made up of five consolidated cases, four involving criminal penalties and one civil liability. The Court held that the Civil Rights Act of 1875 was *not* within the scope of Congress's enforcement powers under the Thirteenth and Fourteenth Amendments. The Fourteenth Amendment enforcement power is limited to state action; and Congress's enforcement powers cannot be stretched to go beyond what the amendments actually prohibit. (It was not until the 1960s that such civil rights laws were again enacted—pursuant to the Commerce Clause power, rather than the power to enforce the provisions of the Fourteenth Amendment.)

The Civil Rights Cases is the foundational Supreme Court decision for two important questions of interpretation of the Fourteenth Amendment: first, the "state action" requirement; and second, the scope of Congress's enforcement power under Section 5 of the amendment. All subsequent interpretation of the amendment has followed the path marked out by that decision. But was the Court's analysis correct? Decide for yourself as you read *The Civil Rights Cases* and two modern cases illustrating how present doctrine carries forward the principles it established: *United States v. Morrison* (2000) (on state action) and *City of Boerne v. Flores* (1997) (on the Section 5 enforcement power).

The Civil Rights Cases

109 U.S. 3 (1883)

■ MR. JUSTICE BRADLEY delivered the opinion of the court. . . .

[T]he primary and important question in all the cases is the constitutionality of the law. . . . Its effect is to declare, that in all inns, public conveyances, and places of amusement, colored citizens, whether formerly slaves or not, and citizens of other races, shall have the same accommodations and privileges in all inns, public conveyances, and places of amusement, as are enjoyed by white citizens; and *vice versa*. The second section makes it a penal offense in any person to deny to any citizen of any race or color, regardless of previous servitude, any of the accommodations or privileges mentioned in the first section.

Has Congress constitutional power to make such a law? Of course, no one will contend that the power to pass it was contained in the Constitution before the adoption of the last three amendments. The power is sought, first, in the Fourteenth Amendment, and the views and arguments of distinguished Senators, advanced whilst the law was under consideration, claiming authority to pass it by virtue of that amendment, are the principal arguments adduced in favor of the power. We have carefully considered those arguments, as was due to the eminent ability of those who put them forward, and have felt, in all its force, the weight of authority which always invests a law that Congress deems itself competent to pass. But the responsibility of an independent judgment is now thrown upon this court; and we are bound to exercise it according to the best lights we have. . . .

It is State action of a particular character that is prohibited. Individual invasion of individual rights is not the subject-matter of the amendment. It has a deeper and broader scope. It nullifies and makes void all State legislation, and State action of every kind, which impairs the privileges and immunities of citizens of the United States, or which injures them in life, liberty, or property without due process of law, or which denies to any of them the equal protection of the laws. It not only does this, but, in order that the national will, thus declared, may not be a mere *brutum fulmen*, the last section of the amendment invests Congress with power to enforce it by appropriate legislation. To enforce what? To enforce the prohibition. To adopt appropriate legislation for correcting the effects of such prohibited State laws and State acts, and thus to render them effectually null, void, and innocuous. This is the legislative power conferred upon Congress, and this is the whole of it. It does not invest Congress with power to legislate upon subjects which are within the domain of State legislation; but to provide modes of relief against State legislation, or State action, of the kind referred to. It does not authorize Congress to create a code of municipal law for the regulation of private rights; but to provide modes of redress against the operation of State laws, and the action of State officers, executive or judicial, when these are subversive of the fundamental rights specified in the amendment. Positive rights and privileges are undoubtedly secured by the Fourteenth Amendment; but they are secured by way of prohibition against State laws and State proceedings affecting those rights and privileges, and by power given to Congress to legislate for the purpose of carrying such prohibition into effect; and such legislation must necessarily be predicated upon such supposed State laws or State proceedings, and be directed to the correction of their operation and effect. . . .

And so in the present case, until some State law has been passed, or some State action through its officers or agents has been taken, adverse to the rights of citizens sought to be protected by the Fourteenth Amendment, no legislation of the United States under said amendment, nor any proceeding under such legislation, can be called into activity, for the prohibitions of the amendment are against State laws and acts done under State authority. Of course, legislation may and should be provided in advance to meet the exigency when it arises, but it should be adapted to the mischief and wrong which the amendment was intended to provide against; and that is, State laws or State action of some kind adverse to the rights of the citizen secured by the amendment. Such legislation cannot properly cover the whole domain of rights appertaining to life, liberty, and property, defining them and providing for their vindication. That would be to establish a code of municipal law regulative of all private rights between man and man in society. It would be to make Congress take the place of the State legislatures and to supersede them. It is absurd to affirm that, because the rights of life, liberty, and property (which include all civil rights that men have) are by the amendment sought to be protected against invasion on the part of the State without due process of law, Congress may, therefore, provide due process of law for their vindication in every case; and that, because the denial by a State to any persons of the equal protection of the laws is prohibited by the amendment, therefore Congress may establish laws for their equal protection. In fine, the legislation which Congress is authorized to adopt in this behalf is not general legislation upon the rights of the citizen, but corrective legislation; that is, such as may be necessary and proper for counteracting such laws as the States may adopt or enforce, and which by the amendment they are prohibited from making or enforcing, or such acts and proceedings as the States may commit or take, and which by the amendment they are prohibited from committing or taking. It is not necessary for us to state, if we could, what legislation would be proper for Congress to adopt. It is sufficient for us to examine whether the law in question is of that character.

An inspection of the law [the Civil Rights Act of 1875] shows that it makes no reference whatever to any supposed or apprehended violation of the Fourteenth Amendment on the part of the States. It is not predicated on any such view. It proceeds *ex directo* to declare that certain acts committed by individuals shall be deemed offenses, and shall be prosecuted and punished by proceedings in the courts of the United States. It does not profess to be corrective of any constitutional wrong committed by the States; it does not make its operation to depend upon any such wrong committed. It applies equally to cases arising in States which have the justest laws respecting the personal rights of citizens, and whose authorities are ever ready to enforce such laws as to those which arise in States that may have violated the prohibition of the amendment. In other words, it steps into the domain of local jurisprudence, and lays down rules for the conduct of individuals in society towards each other, and imposes sanctions for the enforcement of those rules, without referring in any manner to any supposed action of the State or its authorities. *[The Court then contrasted provisions of the Civil Rights Act of 1875 with provisions of the Civil Rights Act of 1866.—Editors.]*

[The 1866 Act,] after declaring that all persons within the jurisdiction of the United States shall have the same right in every State and Territory to make and enforce contracts, to sue, be parties, give evidence, and to the full and equal benefit of all laws and proceedings for the security of persons and property as is enjoyed by white citizens, and shall be subject to like punishment, pains, penalties, taxes, licenses, and exactions of every kind, and none other, any law, statute, ordinance, regulation, or custom to the contrary notwithstanding, proceeds to . . . [prescribe punishments for violations committed by anyone who acts under color of state law.] This law is clearly corrective in its character, intended to counteract and furnish redress against State laws and proceedings, and customs having the force of law. . . .

In this connection, it is proper to state that civil rights, such as are guarantied by the Constitution against State aggression, cannot be impaired by the wrongful acts of individuals, unsupported by State authority in the shape of laws, customs, or judicial or executive proceedings. The wrongful act of an individual, unsupported by any such authority, is simply a private wrong, or a crime of that individual; an invasion of the rights of the injured party, it is true, whether they affect his person, his property, or his reputation; but if not sanctioned in some way by the State, or not done under State authority, his rights remain in full force, and may presumably be vindicated by resort to the laws of the State for redress. An individual cannot deprive a man of his right to vote, to hold property, to buy and to sell, to sue in the courts, or to be a witness or a juror; he may, by force or fraud, interfere with the enjoyment of the right in a particular case; he may commit an assault against the person, or commit murder, or use ruffian violence at the polls, or slander the good name of a fellow-citizen; but unless protected in these wrongful acts by some shield of State law or State authority, he cannot destroy or injure the right; he will only render himself amenable to satisfaction or punishment; and amenable therefore to the laws of the State where the wrongful acts are committed. . . .

The law in question [the Civil Rights Act of 1875], without any reference to adverse State legislation on the subject, declares that all persons shall be entitled to equal accommodation and privileges of inns, public conveyances, and places of public amusement, and imposes a penalty upon any individual who shall deny to any citizen such equal accommodations and privileges. This is not corrective legislation; it is primary and direct; it takes immediate and absolute possession of the subject of the right of admission to inns, public conveyances, and places of amusement. It supersedes and displaces State legislation on the same subject, or only allows it permissive force. It ignores such legislation, and assumes that the matter is one that belongs to the domain of national regulation. Whether it would not have been a more effective protection of the rights of citizens to have clothed Congress with plenary power over the whole subject, is not now the question. What we have to decide is, whether such plenary power has been conferred upon Congress by the Fourteenth Amendment; and, in our judgment, it has not.

We have discussed the question presented by the law on the assumption that a right to enjoy equal accommodations and privileges in all inns, public conveyances, and places of public amusement, is one of the essential rights of the citizen which no State can abridge or interfere with. Whether it is such a right or not is a different question, which, in the view we have taken of the validity of the law on the ground already stated, it is not necessary to examine. . . .

But the power of congress to adopt direct and primary, as distinguished from corrective, legislation on the subject in hand, is sought, in the second place, from the Thirteenth Amendment, which abolishes slavery. This amendment declares "that neither slavery, nor involuntary servitude, except as a punishment for crime, whereof the party shall have been duly convicted, shall exist within the United States, or any place subject to their jurisdiction;" and it gives Congress power to enforce the amendment by appropriate legislation. . . .

And such legislation may be primary and direct in its character; for the amendment is not a mere prohibition of State laws establishing or upholding slavery, but an absolute declaration that slavery or involuntary servitude shall not exist in any part of the United States. . . .

[I]t is assumed that the power vested in Congress to enforce the article by appropriate legislation, clothes Congress with power to pass all laws necessary and proper for abolishing all badges and incidents of slavery in the United States; and upon this assumption it is claimed that this is sufficient authority for declaring by law that all persons shall have equal accommodations and privileges in all inns, public conveyances, and places of public amusement; the argument being that the denial of such equal accommodations and privileges is in itself a subjection to a species of servitude within the meaning of the amendment. Conceding the major proposition to be true, that that Congress has a right to enact all necessary and proper laws for the obliteration and prevention of slavery, with all its badges and incidents, is the minor proposition also true, that the denial to any person of admission to the accommodations and privileges of an inn, a public conveyance, or a theater, does subject that person to any form of servitude, or tend to fasten upon him any badge of slavery? If it does not, then power to pass the law is not found in the Thirteenth Amendment. . . .

Congress, as we have seen, by the Civil Rights Bill of 1866, passed in view of the Thirteenth Amendment, before the Fourteenth was adopted, undertook to wipe out these burdens and disabilities, the necessary incidents of slavery, constituting its substance and visible form; and to secure to all citizens of every race and color, and without regard to previous servitude, those fundamental rights which are the essence of civil freedom, namely, the same right to make and enforce contracts, to sue, be parties, give evidence, and to inherit, purchase, lease, sell, and convey property, as is enjoyed by white citizens. Whether this legislation was fully authorized by the Thirteenth Amendment alone, without the support which it afterwards received from the Fourteenth Amendment, after the adoption of which it was re-enacted with some additions, it is not necessary to inquire. It is referred to for the purpose of showing that at that time (in 1866) Congress did not assume, under the authority given by the Thirteenth Amendment, to adjust what may be called the social rights of men and races in the community; but only to declare and vindicate those fundamental rights which appertain to the essence of citizenship, and the enjoyment or deprivation of which constitutes the essential distinction between freedom and slavery.

We must not forget that the province and scope of the Thirteenth and Fourteenth amendments are different: the former simply abolished slavery: the latter prohibited the States from abridging the privileges or immunities of citizens of the United States, from depriving them of life, liberty, or property without due process of law, and from denying to any the equal protection of the laws. The amendments are different, and the powers of Congress under them are different. What Congress has power to do under one, it may not have power to do under the other. Under the Thirteenth Amendment, it has only to do with slavery and its incidents. Under the Fourteenth Amendment, it has power to counteract and render nugatory all State laws and proceedings which have the effect to abridge any of the privileges or immunities of citizens of the United States, or to deprive them of life, liberty, or property without due process of law, or to deny to any of them the equal protection of the laws. Under the Thirteenth Amendment the legislation, so far as necessary or proper to eradicate all forms and incidents of slavery and involuntary servitude, may be direct and primary, operating upon the acts of individuals, whether sanctioned by State legislation or not; under the Fourteenth, as we have already shown, it must necessarily be, and can only be, corrective in its character, addressed to counteract and afford relief against State regulations or proceedings.

The only question under the present head, therefore, is, whether the refusal to any persons of the accommodations of an inn, or a public conveyance, or a place of public amusement, by an individual, and without any sanction or support from any State law or regulation, does inflict upon such persons any manner of servitude, or form of slavery, as those terms are understood in this country? Many wrongs may be obnoxious to the prohibitions of the Fourteenth Amendment which are not, in any just sense, incidents or elements of slavery. Such, for example, would be the taking of private property without due process of law; or allowing persons who have committed certain crimes (horse stealing, for example) to be seized and hung by the *posse comitatus* without regular trial; or denying to any person, or class of persons, the right to pursue any peaceful avocations allowed to others. What is called class legislation would belong to this category, and would be obnoxious to the prohibitions of the Fourteenth Amendment, but would not necessarily be so to the Thirteenth, when not involving the idea of any subjection of one man to another. The Thirteenth Amendment has respect, not to distinctions of race, or class, or color, but to slavery. The Fourteenth Amendment extends its protection to races and classes, and prohibits any state legislation which has the effect of denying to any race or class, or to any individual, the equal protection of the laws.

Now, conceding, for the sake of the argument, that the admission to an inn, a public conveyance, or a place of public amusement, on equal terms with all other citizens, is the right of every man and all classes of men, is it any more than one of those rights which the States by the Fourteenth Amendment are forbidden to deny to any person? and is the Constitution violated until the denial of the right has some State sanction or authority? Can the act of a mere individual, the owner of the inn, the public conveyance, or place of amusement, refusing the accommodation, be justly regarded as imposing any badge of slavery or servitude upon the applicant, or only as inflicting an ordinary civil injury, properly cognizable by the laws of the State, and presumably subject to redress by those laws until the contrary appears?

After giving to these questions all the consideration which their importance demands, we are forced to the conclusion that such an act of refusal has nothing to do with slavery or involuntary servitude, and that if it is violative of any right of the party, his redress is to be sought under the laws of the State; or, if those laws are adverse to his rights and do not protect him, his remedy will be found in the corrective legislation which Congress has adopted, or may adopt, for counteracting the effect of State laws, or State action, prohibited by the Fourteenth Amendment. It would be running the slavery argument into the ground to make it apply to every act of discrimination which a person may see fit to make as to the guests he will entertain, or as to the people he will take into his coach or cab or car, or admit to his concert or theater, or deal with in other matters of intercourse or business. Innkeepers and public carriers, by the laws of all the States, so far as we are aware, are bound, to the extent of their facilities, to furnish proper accommodation to all unobjectionable persons who in good faith apply for them. If the laws themselves make any unjust discrimination, amenable to the prohibitions of the Fourteenth Amendment, Congress has full power to afford a remedy under that amendment and in accordance with it.

When a man has emerged from slavery, and by the aid of beneficent legislation has shaken off the inseparable concomitants of that state, there must be some stage in the progress of his elevation when he takes the rank of a mere citizen, and ceases to be the special favorite of the laws, and when his rights as a citizen, or a man, are to be protected in the ordinary modes by which other men's rights are protected. There were thousands of free colored people in this country before the abolition of slavery, enjoying all the essential rights of life, liberty, and property the same as white citizens; yet no one, at that time, thought that it was any invasion of their personal status as freemen because they were not admitted to all the privileges enjoyed by white citizens, or because they were subjected to discriminations in the enjoyment of accommodations in inns, public conveyances, and places of amusement. Mere discriminations on account of race or color were not regarded as badges of slavery. If, since that time, the enjoyment of equal rights in all these respects has become established by constitutional enactment, it is not by force of the Thirteenth Amendment, (which merely abolishes slavery), but by force of the Fourteenth and Fifteenth Amendments.

On the whole, we are of opinion that no countenance of authority for the passage of the law in question can be found in either the Thirteenth or Fourteenth Amendment of the Constitution; and no other ground of authority for its passage being suggested, it must necessarily be declared void, at least so far as its operation in the several States is concerned.

This conclusion disposes of the cases now under consideration. In the cases of *United States v. Michael Ryan*, and of *Richard A. Robinson and Wife v. The Memphis & Charleston Railroad Company*, the judgments must be affirmed. In the other cases, the answer to be given will be, that the first and second sections of the act of congress of March 1, 1875, entitled "An Act to protect all citizens in their civil and legal rights," are unconstitutional and void, and that judgment should be rendered upon the several indictments in those cases accordingly.

■ MR. JUSTICE HARLAN, dissenting.

The opinion in these case proceeds, as it seems to me, upon grounds entirely too narrow and artificial. I cannot resist the conclusion that the substance and spirit of the recent amendments of the Constitution have been sacrificed by a subtle and ingenious verbal criticism. "It is not the words of the law but the internal sense of it that makes the law. The letter of the law is the body; the sense and reason of the law is the soul." Constitutional provisions, adopted in the interest of liberty, and for the purpose of securing, through national legislation, if need be, rights inhering in a state of freedom, and belonging to American citizenship, have been so construed as to defeat the ends the people desired to accomplish, which they attempted to accomplish, and which they supposed they had accomplished by changes in their fundamental law. By this I do not mean that the determination of these cases should have been materially controlled by considerations of mere expediency or policy. I mean only, in this form, to express an earnest conviction that the court has departed from the familiar rule requiring, in the interpretation of constitutional provisions, that full effect be given to the intent with which they were adopted. . . .

The Thirteenth Amendment, it is conceded, did something more than to prohibit slavery as an *institution*, resting upon distinctions of race, and upheld by positive law. My brethren admit that it established and decreed universal *civil freedom* throughout the United States. But did the freedom thus established involve nothing more than exemption from actual slavery? Was nothing more intended than to forbid one man from owning another as property? Was it the purpose of the nation simply to destroy the institution, and then remit the race, theretofore held in bondage, to the several States for such protection, in their civil rights, necessarily growing out of freedom, as those States, in their discretion, choose to provide? Were the States, against whose solemn protest the institution was destroyed, to be left perfectly free, so far as national interference was concerned, to make or allow discriminations against that race, as such, in the enjoyment of those fundamental rights which by universal concession, inhere in a state of freedom? . . .

That there are burdens and disabilities which constitute badges of slavery and servitude, and that the power to enforce by appropriate legislation the Thirteenth Amendment may be exerted by legislation of a direct and primary character, for the eradication, not simply of the institution, but of its badges and incidents, are propositions which ought to be deemed indisputable. They lie at the foundation of the Civil Rights Act of 1866. . . . [My brethren] admit . . . that Congress, by the act of 1866, passed in view of the Thirteenth Amendment, before the Fourteenth was adopted, undertook to remove certain burdens and disabilities, the necessary incidents of slavery, and to secure to all citizens of every race and color, and without regard to previous servitude, those fundamental rights which are the essence of civil freedom, namely, the same right to make and enforce contracts, to sue, be parties, give evidence, and to inherit, purchase, lease, sell, and convey property as is enjoyed by white citizens. . . . I do not contend that the Thirteenth Amendment invests Congress with authority, by legislation, to define and regulate the entire body of the civil rights which citizens enjoy, or may enjoy, in the several States. But I do hold that since slavery, as the court has repeatedly declared, *Slaughter-House Cases*, 16 Wall. 36; *Strauder v. West Virginia*, 100 U.S. 303, was the moving or principal cause of the adoption of that amendment, and since that institution rested wholly upon the inferiority, as a race, of those held in bondage, their freedom necessarily involved immunity from, and protection against, all discrimination against them, because of their race, in respect of such civil rights as belong to freemen of other races. Congress, therefore, under its express power to enforce that amendment, by appropriate legislation, may enact laws to protect that people against the deprivation, *on account of their race*, of any civil rights granted to other freemen in the same State; and such legislation may be of a direct and primary character, operating upon States, their officers and agents, and also, upon, at least, such individuals and corporations as exercise public functions and wield power and authority under the State. . . .

It remains now to inquire what are the legal rights of colored persons in respect of the accommodations, privileges and facilities of public conveyances, inns and places of public amusement?

First, as to public conveyances on land and water. . . . In *Olcott v. Supervisors*, 16 Wall. 694, it was ruled that railroads are public highways, established by authority of the State for the public use; that they are none the less public highways because controlled and owned by private corporations; that it is a part of the function of government to make and maintain highways for the convenience of the public; that no matter who is the agent, and what is the agency, the function performed is *that of the State*; [and] that although the owners may be private companies, they may be compelled to permit the public to use these works. . . .

Such being the relations these corporations hold to the public, it would seem that the right of a colored person to use an improved public highway, upon the terms accorded to freemen of other races, is as fundamental, in the state of freedom established in this country, as are any of the rights which my brethren concede to be so far fundamental as to be deemed the essence of civil freedom. "Personal liberty consists," says Blackstone, "in the power of locomotion, of changing situation, or removing one's person to whatever place one's own inclination may direct, without restraint, unless by due course of law." But of what value is this right of locomotion, if it may be clogged by such burdens as Congress intended by the act of 1875 to remove? They are burdens which lay at the very foundation of the institution of slavery as it once existed. . . .

Second, as to inns. The same general observations which have been made as to railroads are applicable to inns. . . . In *Rex v. Ivens*, [173 Eng. Rep. 94 (1835)], the court, speaking by Mr. Justice Coleridge, said:

> An indictment lies against an innkeeper who refuses to receive a guest, he having at the time room in his house; and either the price of the guest's entertainment being tendered to him, or such circumstances occurring as will dispense with that tender. This law is founded in good sense. The innkeeper is not to select his guests. He has no right to say to one, you shall come to my inn, and to another you shall not, as every one coming and conducting himself in a proper manner has a right to be received; and for this purpose innkeepers are a sort of public servants, they having in return a kind of privilege of entertaining travelers and supplying them with that they want.

These authorities are sufficient to show a keeper of an inn is in the exercise of a quasi public employment. The law gives him special privileges, and he is charged with certain duties and responsibilities to the public. The public nature of his employment forbids him from discriminating against any person asking admission as a guest on account of the race or color of that person.

Third. As to places of public amusement. . . . [The] places of public amusement, within the meaning of the act of 1875, are such as are established and maintained under direct license of the law. The authority to establish and maintain them comes from the public. The colored race is a part of that public. The local government granting the license represents them as well as all other races within its jurisdiction. A license from the public to establish a place of public amusement, imports, in law, equality of right, at such places, among all the members of that public. . . .

I am of the opinion that such discrimination practiced by corporations and individuals in the exercise of their public or quasi-public functions is a badge of servitude the imposition of which Congress may prevent under its power, by appropriate legislation, to enforce the Thirteenth Amendment; and consequently, without reference to its enlarged power under the Fourteenth Amendment, the act of March 1, 1875, is not, in my judgment, repugnant to the Constitution.

It remains now to consider these cases with reference to the power Congress has possessed since the adoption of the Fourteenth Amendment. . . .

The assumption that this amendment consists wholly of prohibitions upon State laws and State proceedings in hostility to its provisions, is unauthorized by its language. The first clause of the first section—"All persons born or naturalized in the United States, and subject to the jurisdiction thereof, are citizens of the United States, and of the State wherein they reside"—is of a distinctly affirmative character. . . .

It is, therefore, an essential inquiry what, if any, right, privilege or immunity was given, by the nation, to colored persons, when they were made citizens of the State in which they reside? . . . That they became entitled, upon the adoption of the Fourteenth Amendment, "to all privileges and immunities of citizens in the several States," within the meaning of section 2 of article 4 of the Constitution, no one, I suppose, will for a moment question. What are the privileges and immunities to which, by that clause of the Constitution, they became entitled? To this it may be answered, generally, upon the authority of the adjudged cases, that they are those which are fundamental in citizenship in a free republican government, such as are "common to the citizens in the latter States under their constitutions and laws by virtue of their being citizens." . . .

But what was secured to colored citizens of the United States—as between them and their respective States—by the grant to them of State citizenship? With what rights, privileges, or immunities did this grant invest them? There is one, if there be no others—exemption from race discrimination in respect of any civil right belonging to citizens of the white race in the same State. That, surely, is their constitutional privilege when within the jurisdiction of other States. And such must be their constitutional right, in their own State, unless the recent amendments be splendid baubles, thrown out to delude those who deserved fair and generous treatment at the hands of the nation. Citizenship in this country necessarily imports at least equality of civil rights among citizens of every race in the same State. . . .

If the grant to colored citizens of the United States of citizenship in their respective States, imports exemption from race discrimination, in their States, in respect of such civil rights as belong to citizenship, then, to hold that the amendment remits that right to the States for their protection, primarily, and stays the hands of the nation, until it is assailed by State laws or State proceedings, is to adjudge that the amendment, so far from enlarging the powers of Congress—as we have heretofore said it did—not only curtails them, but reverses the policy which the general government has pursued from its very organization. Such an interpretation of the amendment is a denial to Congress of the power, by appropriate legislation, to enforce one of its provisions. . . .

It was said of the case of *Dred Scott v. Sandford*, that this court, there overruled the action of two generations, virtually inserted a new clause in the Constitution, changed its character, and made a new departure in the workings of the federal government. I may be permitted to say that if the recent amendments are so construed that Congress may not, in its own discretion, and independently of the action or non-action of the States, provide, by legislation of a direct character, for the security of rights created by the national Constitution; . . . then, not only the foundations upon which the national supremacy has always securely rested will be materially disturbed, but we shall enter upon an era of constitutional law, when the rights of freedom and American citizenship cannot receive from the nation that efficient protection which heretofore was unhesitatingly accorded to slavery and the rights of the master.

But if it were conceded that the power of Congress could not be brought into activity until the rights specified in the act of 1875 had been abridged or denied by some State law or State action, I maintain that the decision of the court is erroneous. There has been adverse State action within the Fourteenth Amendment as heretofore interpreted by this court. . . .

In every material sense applicable to the practical enforcement of the Fourteenth Amendment, railroad corporations, keepers of inns, and managers of places of public amusement are agents and instrumentalities of the State, because they are charged with duties to the public, and are amenable, in respect of their duties and functions, to governmental regulation. It seems to me that, within the principle settled in *Ex parte Virginia*, a denial, by these instrumentalities of the State, to the citizen, because of his race, of that equality of civil rights secured to him by law, is a denial by the State, within the meaning of the Fourteenth Amendment. If it be not, then that race is left, in respect of the civil rights in question, practically at the mercy of corporations and individuals wielding power under the States.

But the court says that Congress did not, in the act of 1866, assume, under the authority given by the Thirteenth Amendment, to adjust what may be called the social rights of men and races in the community. I agree that government has nothing to do with social, as distinguished from technically legal, rights of individuals. No government ever has brought, or ever can bring, its people into social intercourse against their wishes. Whether one person will permit or maintain social relations with another is a matter with which government has no concern. I agree that if one citizen chooses not to hold social intercourse with another, he is not and cannot be made amenable to the law for his conduct in that regard; for even upon grounds of race, no legal right of a citizen is violated by the refusal of others to maintain merely social relations with him. What I affirm is that no State, nor the officers of any State, nor any corporation or individual wielding power under State authority for the public benefit or the public convenience, can, consistently either with the freedom established by the fundamental law, or with that equality of civil rights which now belongs to every citizen, discriminate against freemen or citizens, in those rights, because of their race, or because they once labored under the disabilities of slavery imposed upon them as a race. The rights which Congress, by the act of 1875, endeavored to secure and protect are legal, not social rights. The right, for instance, of a colored citizen to use the accommodations of a public highway upon the same terms as are permitted to white citizens, is no more a social right than his right, under the law, to use the public streets of a city or a town, or a turnpike road, or a public market, or a post-office, or his right to sit in a public building with others, of whatever race, for the purpose of hearing the political questions of the day discussed. . . .

The court, in its opinion, reserves the question whether Congress, in the exercise of its power to regulate commerce among the several States, might or might not pass a law regulating rights in public conveyances passing from one State to another. I beg to suggest that that precise question was substantially presented here in the only one of these cases relating to railroads—*Robinson and Wife v. Memphis & Charleston Railroad Company*. In that case it appears that Mrs. Robinson, a citizen of Mississippi, purchased a railroad ticket entitling her to be carried from Grand Junction,

Tennessee, to Lynchburg, Virginia. Might not the act of 1875 be maintained in that case, as applicable at least to commerce between the States, notwithstanding it does not, upon its face, profess to have been passed in pursuance of the power given to Congress to regulate commerce? Has it ever been held that the judiciary should overturn a statute because the legislative department did not accurately recite therein the particular provision of the Constitution authorizing its enactment? . . .

My brethren say, that when a man has emerged from slavery, and by the aid of beneficient legislation has shaken off the inseparable concomitants of that state, there must be some stage in the progress of his elevation when he takes the rank of a mere citizen, and ceases to be the special favorite of the laws, and when his rights as a citizen, or a man, are to be protected in the ordinary modes by which other men's rights are protected. It is, I submit, scarcely just to say that the colored race has been the special favorite of the laws. The statute of 1875, now adjudged to be unconstitutional, is for the benefit of citizens of every race and color. What the nation, through Congress, has sought to accomplish in reference to that race is—what had already been done in every State in the Union for the white race—to secure and protect rights belonging to them as freemen and citizens; nothing more. It was not deemed enough "to help the feeble up, but to support him after." The one underlying purpose of congressional legislation has been to enable the black race to take the rank of mere citizens. The difficulty has been to compel a recognition of the legal right of the black race to take the rank of citizens, and to secure the enjoyment of privileges belonging, under the law, to them as a component part of the people for whose welfare and happiness government is ordained. . . . Today it is the colored race which is denied, by corporations and individuals wielding public authority, rights fundamental in their freedom and citizenship. At some future time, it may be that some other race will fall under the ban of race discrimination. If the constitutional amendments be enforced, according to the intent with which, as I conceive, they were adopted, there cannot be, in this republic, any class of human beings in practical subjection to another class, with power in the latter to dole out to the former just such privileges as they may choose to grant. The supreme law of the land has decreed that no authority shall be exercised in this country upon the basis of discrimination, in respect of civil rights, against freemen and citizens because of their race, color, or previous condition of servitude. To that decree—for the due enforcement of which, by appropriate legislation, Congress has been invested with express power—every one must bow, whatever may have been, or whatever now are, his individual views as to the wisdom or policy, either of the recent changes in the fundamental law, or of the legislation which has been enacted to give them effect. . . .

NOTES

1. *The Thirteenth Amendment Enforcement Power.* The decision in *The Civil Rights Cases* has proved to be foundational for all subsequent interpretation of the scope of the Thirteenth and Fourteenth Amendments. But was it correct? Does the Thirteenth Amendment prohibit not only "slavery" but the "badges and incidents" of subordination, including private discrimination? Even if Section 1 of the amendment does not of its own force prohibit private discrimination, might Congress still legislate more broadly pursuant to its power under Section 2 to "enforce" the command that slavery no longer "exist"? If one accepts such a broad interpretation of either the self-executing effect of Section

1 or Congress's enforcement power under Section 2, would that mean that Congress could adopt and enforce a code of social relations operative within every state? This the majority thought untenable—more radical than the framers of the amendment envisaged. Was it? Isn't the necessary effect of the Thirteenth Amendment (and the Fourteenth) in fact a radical transfer of governing power from states to the national government in civil rights?

A century later the Supreme Court adopted a broader view of the Thirteenth Amendment enforcement clause powers of Congress, purporting to find that view supported by *The Civil Rights Cases*. In *Jones v. Alfred H. Mayer Co.*, 392 U.S. 409 (1968), the Court construed the Civil Rights Act of 1866 (reenacted in 1870, two years after ratification of the Fourteenth Amendment) to reach purely private racial discrimination in housing and sustained its constitutionality as an exercise of Congress's enforcement powers under the *Thirteenth* Amendment:

> Does the authority of Congress to enforce the 13th Amendment "by appropriate legislation" include the power to eliminate all racial barriers to the acquisition of real and personal property? We think the answer to that question is plainly yes. . . . Whether or not the Amendment *itself* did any more than [abolish slavery]—a question not involved in this case—it is at least clear that the Enabling Clause of that amendment empowered Congress to do much more. For that clause clothed "Congress with power to pass *all laws necessary and proper for abolishing all badges and incidents of slavery in the United States. [The Civil Rights Cases* (emphasis added)]. . . . Congress has the power under the Thirteenth Amendment rationally to determine what are the badges and incidents of slavery, and the authority to translate that determination into effective legislation. . . . [W]hatever else they may have encompassed, the badges and incidents of slavery—its "burdens and disabilities"—included restraints upon "those fundamental rights which are the essence of civil freedom, namely the same right [to] inherit, purchase, lease, sell and convey property, as is enjoyed by white citizens." [*Id.*] Just as the Black codes, enacted after the Civil War to restrict the free exercise of those rights, were substitutes for the slave system, so the exclusion of Negroes from white communities became a substitute for the Black Codes. And when racial discrimination herds men into ghettos and makes their ability to buy property turn on the color of their skin, then it too is a relic of slavery.

392 U.S., at 439–443. Subsequent cases have also held that parts of the Civil Rights Act of 1866 reach private commercial conduct of a discriminatory nature, but nonetheless fall within Congress's enforcement power under Section 2 of the Thirteenth Amendment. E.g., *Patterson v. McLean Credit Union*, 491 U.S. 164 (1989) (racial discrimination in making and enforcing contracts); *Runyon v. McCrary*, 427 U.S. 160 (1976) (racial discrimination in private schools). Are these cases right, as a matter of understanding the Thirteenth Amendment's enforcement power? Are they consistent with *The Civil Rights Cases*? On potential applications of the Thirteenth Amendment, see generally Symposium, *The Thirteenth Amendment: Meaning, Enforcement, and Contemporary Implications*, 112 Colum. L. Rev. 1447 (2012).

2. *The Fourteenth Amendment Enforcement Power.* Was the Court's decision that the Fourteenth Amendment is limited to "state action" correct? How else would one read the "No State shall" language of the amendment? Once

again, even if one thinks Section 1 invalidates of its own force only actions and laws of the state, is Congress's enforcement power under Section 5 broader? Might it be "appropriate" to "enforce" the prohibition on state denials of civil rights for Congress simply to take over and legislate directly the rights that state citizens have in economic, commercial, and social relations? Or would that be an improperly radical transformation of federalism, inconsistent with the Fourteenth Amendment's framers' design and the language they chose?

3. *What is "State Action"?* What do you make of Justice Harlan's dissenting argument that railroads, innkeepers, and operators of public amusements are state actors—by virtue either of performing some government function or of being licensed by government (or granted a corporate charter) to perform regulated activities? Is there "state action" in every regulated business?

The Court has often had to decide where the line is between state and private action. Consider the following cases. Is there state action if a private entity serves a "public function," as with a company town? *Marsh v. Alabama*, 326 U.S. 501 (1946) (finding state action in a company town's restrictions of free speech). What if a political party's primary performs a quasi-state function in selecting candidates for a general election to public office? The "white primary" cases found such to be state action for Fifteenth Amendment purposes. *Terry v. Adams*, 345 U.S. 461 (1953); *Smith v. Allwright*, 321 U.S. 649 (1944). Is state action present in judicial enforcement of some private contracts, such as racially restrictive covenants? *Shelley v. Kraemer*, 334 U.S. 1 (1948) (yes). In the award of damages for torts of defamation or intentional infliction of emotional distress? *New York Times Co. v. Sullivan*, 376 U.S. 254 (1964) (yes); *Hustler Magazine v. Falwell*, 485 U.S. 46 (1988) (yes). In permitting race-based peremptory strikes in jury selection? *Edmonson v. Leesville Concrete Co.*, 500 U.S. 614 (1991) (yes). Do the operations of a private restaurant, located within an off-street municipal automobile parking facility, constitute state action? *Burton v. Wilmington Parking Authority*, 365 U.S. 715 (1961) (yes). Which of these decisions strike you as correct? Why? Is there a principle running through these decisions?

Other cases have raised questions about when there is state action in state *inaction*. Is there state action when a state or local government delegates governing power to some private group? *Larkin v. Grendel's Den, Inc.*, 459 U.S. 116 (1982) (yes). When a statute authorizes discrimination by private parties? *Reitman v. Mulkey*, 387 U.S. 369 (1967) (yes: a 5–4 decision finding that intent of a referendum to repeal a fair housing law was to authorize private racial discrimination). If so, what about when a state permits racial discrimination or other tortious conduct by private parties, either by failing to enact adequate laws or by not enforcing the laws it already has? Is there a principled distinction between state action that simply fails to protect against certain harmful private conduct and state action that encourages, authorizes, or permits that private conduct? If state inaction could count as state action, would that mean the decision in *The Civil Rights Cases* was wrong?

4. *Equal Protection as a Duty of Protection?* Why not read the Equal Protection Clause as requiring states to *protect*, on an equal basis, all persons from private violence or similar wrongful acts by others? This reading finds support in the historical context, where there was a pervasive failure by Southern states to protect the newly freed slaves from violence by, among others, the Ku Klux Klan and lynching mobs. If the Equal Protection Clause does impose upon

the states a duty of protection, how far would that duty extend? Would it forbid states from knowingly (or recklessly?) looking the other way when harm was being done?

Consider the gruesome facts of two modern cases that were litigated not under the Equal Protection Clause (somewhat strangely, as a matter of the Fourteenth Amendment's text) but rather under the Due Process Clause. In *DeShaney v. Winnebago County Department of Social Services*, 489 U.S. 189 (1989), the court considered whether the Due Process Clause imposed a duty on the state to protect 4–year–old Joshua DeShaney from his abusive father. When Joshua was two years old the local Department of Social Services first learned that his father may have been abusing him. A caseworker was assigned, and for two years she made monthly visits to Joshua's home, observing and recording suspicious head injuries. Twice Joshua was taken to the emergency room with injuries indicating abuse, but the caseworker did not remove Joshua from his father's care. Then one day Joshua's father beat him so severely that he fell into a coma and suffered permanent brain damage. Joshua's mother sued the state, claiming that by failing to protect Joshua it had deprived him of "liberty" in violation of the Due Process Clause. That clause, the Court held, did not give a right to state protection from private actors. Rather, the Due Process Clause provides protection only from the state, and Joshua's relationship with the Department of Social Services did not place him in the state's custody.

In *Town of Castle Rock v. Gonzales*, 545 U.S. 748 (2005), the Court considered whether the plaintiff Jessica Gonzales had been deprived of a "property" right without due process when the police failed to enforce a restraining order that had been issued against her estranged husband. The restraining order forbade Ms. Gonzales' husband from going to the family home or having any unauthorized contact with their three daughters. One evening he took the three girls without permission while they were playing outside the house. Ms. Gonzales called the police, showed them a copy of the restraining order, and asked them to arrest her husband. They told her there was nothing they could do and told her to call again if the children weren't home by 10:00 PM. She reached her husband on his cell-phone, and he said that he had the children at an amusement park. She called the police and asked them to go to the amusement park and look for his car. Again she was told to wait until 10:00 PM. Shortly after 10:00 she called and was told to call again if they were not home by midnight. At midnight she called and told them her children were still missing. She then went to the station and made an incident report at 12:50 AM. In all this time nothing was done to enforce the restraining order or find her children. "At approximately 3:20 a.m., [Ms. Gonzales's] husband arrived at the police station and opened fire with a semiautomatic handgun he had purchased earlier that evening. Police shot back, killing him. Inside the cab of his pickup truck, they found the bodies of all three daughters, whom he had already murdered." In her suit against the state, Ms. Gonzales argued that she had been deprived of her "property interest" in enforcement of the restraining order without due process. But the Court held that there was no such property interest, because the police had discretion whether to arrest the violator of the restraining order. Therefore the benefit (the arrest of her husband) was not an absolute entitlement. And without a property interest, there was no violation of the Due Process Clause.

Both cases failed on due process grounds, but could these cases have been brought instead on a theory that the government had failed to provide the "equal protection of the laws"? If the state had made no effort to protect these plaintiffs because of their race, would that be a violation of both the literal meaning and historical purpose of the Equal Protection Clause? If so, can that be squared with the state-action doctrine in *The Civil Rights Cases*?

Note that European constitutional courts, under their differently worded fundamental documents, have sometimes ordered the enactment of a law protecting minority or individual rights. For example, the European Court of Human Rights held in *Von Hannover v. Germany*, Application Number 59320/00 (2004) that Germany had violated Princess Caroline of Monaco's right to privacy under Article 8 of the European Convention of Human Rights by failing to give her more effective tort remedies against the paparazzi who were intruding on her personal life. Or, to take another example, in 1975 and in 1993 the German Constitutional Court struck down as unconstitutional German national laws legalizing abortion on the grounds that they deprived the unborn of their right to life. See Vicki C. Jackson & Mark Tushnet, COMPARATIVE CONSTITUTIONAL LAW 110–140 (2d ed. 2006).

United States v. Morrison

529 U.S. 598 (2000)

■ CHIEF JUSTICE REHNQUIST delivered the opinion of the Court. . . .

In these cases we consider the constitutionality of 42 U.S.C. § 13981, [a provision of the Violence Against Women Act] which provides a federal civil remedy for the victims of gender-motivated violence. The United States Court of Appeals for the Fourth Circuit, sitting en banc, struck down § 13981 because it concluded that Congress lacked constitutional authority to enact the section's civil remedy. Believing that these cases are controlled by our decisions in *United States v. Lopez,* 514 U.S. 549 (1995), *United States v. Harris,* 106 U.S. 629 (1883), and the *In re Civil Rights Cases,* 109 U.S. 3 (1883), we affirm.

Petitioner Christy Brzonkala enrolled at Virginia Polytechnic Institute (Virginia Tech) in the fall of 1994. In September of that year, Brzonkala met respondents Antonio Morrison and James Crawford, who were both students at Virginia Tech and members of its varsity football team. Brzonkala alleges that, within 30 minutes of meeting Morrison and Crawford, they assaulted and repeatedly raped her. . . . Shortly after the rape Brzonkala stopped attending classes and withdrew from the university. . . . *[In a university administrative hearing, Morrison was given a two-semester suspension. This was eventually set aside on appeal within the university's administrative system.—Editors]*

In December 1995, Brzonkala sued Morrison, Crawford, and Virginia Tech. . . . Her complaint alleged that Morrison's and Crawford's attack violated § 13981 and that Virginia Tech's handling of her complaint violated Title IX of the Education Amendments of 1972. Morrison and Crawford moved to dismiss this complaint on the grounds that it failed to state a claim and that § 13981's civil remedy is unconstitutional. The United States . . . intervened to defend [the Act]'s constitutionality. . . .

Section 13981 was part of the Violence Against Women Act of 1994. It states that "[a]ll persons within the United States shall have the right to be free from crimes of violence motivated by gender." To enforce that right, [it] declares:

> A person (including a person who acts under color of any statute, ordinance, regulation, custom, or usage of any State) who commits a crime of violence motivated by gender and thus deprives another of the right declared in subsection (b) of this section shall be liable to the party injured, in an action for the recovery of compensatory and punitive damages, injunctive and declaratory relief, and such other relief as a court may deem appropriate.

... Every law enacted by Congress must be based on one or more of its powers enumerated in the Constitution. "The powers of the legislature are defined and limited; and that those limits may not be mistaken, or forgotten, the constitution is written." *Marbury v. Madison,* 1 Cranch 137, 176 (1803) (Marshall, C. J.). Congress explicitly identified the sources of federal authority on which it relied in enacting § 13981. It said that a "Federal civil rights cause of action" is established "[p]ursuant to the affirmative power of Congress . . . under section 5 of the Fourteenth Amendment to the Constitution, as well as under section 8 of Article I of the Constitution." ... *[The Court first held that the provision could not be supported as an exercise of Congress's power under the Commerce Clause.—Editors]*

The principles governing an analysis of congressional legislation under § 5 [of the Fourteenth Amendment] are well settled. Section 5 states that Congress may " 'enforce' by 'appropriate legislation' the constitutional guarantee that no State shall deprive any person of 'life, liberty, or property, without due process of law,' nor deny any person 'equal protection of the laws.' " *City of Boerne v. Flores*, 521 U.S. 507, 517 (1997). Section 5 is "a positive grant of legislative power," that includes authority to "prohibit conduct which is not itself unconstitutional and [to] intrud[e] into 'legislative spheres of autonomy previously reserved to the States.' " However, "[a]s broad as the congressional enforcement power is, it is not unlimited."

Petitioners' § 5 argument is founded on an assertion that there is pervasive bias in various state justice systems against victims of gender-motivated violence. This assertion is supported by a voluminous congressional record. Specifically, Congress received evidence that many participants in state justice systems are perpetuating an array of erroneous stereotypes and assumptions. Petitioners contend that this bias denies victims of gender-motivated violence the equal protection of the laws and that Congress therefore acted appropriately in enacting a private civil remedy against the perpetrators of gender-motivated violence to both remedy the States' bias and deter future instances of discrimination in the state courts.

As our cases have established, state-sponsored gender discrimination violates equal protection unless it "serves important governmental objectives and . . . the discriminatory means employed are substantially related to the achievement of those objectives." However, the language and purpose of the Fourteenth Amendment place certain limitations on the manner in which Congress may attack discriminatory conduct. These limitations are necessary to prevent the Fourteenth Amendment from obliterating the Framers' carefully crafted balance of power between the States and the National Government. Foremost among these limitations is the time-honored principle that the Fourteenth Amendment, by its very terms, prohibits only state action. "[T]he principle has become firmly embedded in our constitutional law that the action inhibited by the first section of the Fourteenth Amendment is only such action as may fairly be said to be that of the

States. That Amendment erects no shield against merely private conduct, however discriminatory or wrongful." *Shelley v. Kraemer*, 334 U.S. 1, 13, and n. 12 (1948).

Shortly after the Fourteenth Amendment was adopted, we decided two cases interpreting the Amendment's provisions, *United States v. Harris*, 106 U.S. 629 (1883), and the *Civil Rights Cases*, 109 U.S. 3 (1883). In *Harris*, the Court considered a challenge to Section 2 of the Civil Rights Act of 1871. That section sought to punish "private persons" for "conspiring to deprive any one of the equal protection of the laws enacted by the State." We concluded that this law exceeded Congress' Section 5 power because the law was "directed exclusively against the action of private persons, without reference to the laws of the State, or their administration by her officers." . . .

We reached a similar conclusion in the *Civil Rights Cases*. In those consolidated cases, we held that the public accommodation provisions of the Civil Rights Act of 1875, which applied to purely private conduct, were beyond the scope of the Section 5 enforcement power. 109 U.S., at 11 ("Individual invasion of individual rights is not the subject-matter of the [Fourteenth] [A]mendment"). See also, *e.g.*, *Romer v. Evans*, 517 U.S. 620, 628 (1996) ("[I]t was settled early that the Fourteenth Amendment did not give Congress a general power to prohibit discrimination in public accommodations").

The force of the doctrine of *stare decisis* behind these decisions stems not only from the length of time they have been on the books, but also from the insight attributable to the Members of the Court at that time. Every Member had been appointed by President Lincoln, Grant, Hayes, Garfield, or Arthur—and each of their judicial appointees obviously had intimate knowledge and familiarity with the events surrounding the adoption of the Fourteenth Amendment. . . .

Petitioners . . . argue that, unlike the situation in the *Civil Rights Cases*, here there has been gender-based disparate treatment by state authorities, whereas in those cases there was no indication of such state action. There is abundant evidence, however, to show that the Congresses that enacted the Civil Rights Acts of 1871 and 1875 had a purpose similar to that of Congress in enacting § 13981: There were state laws on the books bespeaking equality of treatment, but in the administration of these laws there was discrimination against newly freed slaves. . . .

But even if that distinction were valid, we do not believe it would save § 13981's civil remedy. For the remedy is simply not "corrective in its character, adapted to counteract and redress the operation of such prohibited [s]tate laws or proceedings of [s]tate officers." *Civil Right Cases*, at 18. Or, as we have phrased it in more recent cases, prophylactic legislation under § 5 must have a "congruence and proportionality between the injury to be prevented or remedied and the means adopted to that end." Section 13981 is not aimed at proscribing discrimination by officials which the Fourteenth Amendment might not itself proscribe; it is directed not at any State or state actor, but at individuals who have committed criminal acts motivated by gender bias.

In the present cases, for example, § 13981 visits no consequence whatever on any Virginia public official involved in investigating or prosecuting Brzonkala's assault. The section is, therefore, unlike any of the § 5 remedies that we have previously upheld. For example, in *Katzenbach v. Mor-*

gan, 384 U.S. 641 (1966), Congress prohibited New York from imposing literacy tests as a prerequisite for voting because it found that such a requirement disenfranchised thousands of Puerto Rican immigrants who had been educated in the Spanish language of their home territory. That law, which we upheld, was directed at New York officials who administered the State's election law and prohibited them from using a provision of that law. In *South Carolina v. Katzenbach*, 383 U.S. 301 (1966), Congress imposed voting rights requirements on States that, Congress found, had a history of discriminating against blacks in voting. The remedy was also directed at state officials in those States. Similarly, in *Ex parte Virginia*, 100 U.S. 339 (1879), Congress criminally punished state officials who intentionally discriminated in jury selection; again, the remedy was directed to the culpable state official.

Section 13981 is also different from these previously upheld remedies in that it applies uniformly throughout the Nation. Congress' findings indicate that the problem of discrimination against the victims of gender-motivated crimes does not exist in all States, or even most States. By contrast, the § 5 remedy upheld in *Katzenbach v. Morgan* was directed only to the State where the evil found by Congress existed, and in *South Carolina v. Katzenbach* the remedy was directed only to those States in which Congress found that there had been discrimination.

For these reasons, we conclude that Congress' power under § 5 does not extend to the enactment of § 13981.

Petitioner Brzonkala's complaint alleges that she was the victim of a brutal assault. But Congress' effort in § 13981 to provide a federal civil remedy can be sustained neither under the Commerce Clause nor under § 5 of the Fourteenth Amendment. If the allegations here are true, no civilized system of justice could fail to provide her a remedy for the conduct of respondent Morrison. But under our federal system that remedy must be provided by the Commonwealth of Virginia, and not by the United States.

■ JUSTICE SOUTER, with whom JUSTICE STEVENS, JUSTICE GINSBURG, and JUSTICE BREYER join, dissenting.

. . . Given my conclusion [that the provision is constitutional under the Commerce Clause], I need not consider Congress' authority under Section 5 of the Fourteenth Amendment. Nonetheless, I doubt the Court's reasoning rejecting that source of authority. The Court points out that in *United States v. Harris* and the *Civil Rights Cases*, the Court held that § 5 does not authorize Congress to use the Fourteenth Amendment as a source of power to remedy the conduct of *private persons*. That is certainly so. The Federal Government's argument, however, is that Congress used § 5 to remedy the actions of *state actors*, namely, those States which, through discriminatory design or the discriminatory conduct of their officials, failed to provide adequate (or any) state remedies for women injured by gender-motivated violence—a failure that the States, and Congress, documented in depth.

Neither *Harris* nor the *Civil Rights Cases* considered this kind of claim. The Court in *Harris* specifically said that it treated the federal laws in question as "directed *exclusively* against the action of private persons, without reference to the laws of the State or their administration by her officers." 106 U.S. at 640 (emphasis added); see also *Civil Rights Cases* at 14 (observing that the statute did "not profess to be corrective of any constitutional wrong committed by the States" and that it established "rules for

the conduct of individuals in society towards each other, . . . without referring in any manner to any supposed action of the State or its authorities").

The Court responds directly to the relevant "state actor" claim by finding that the present law lacks "congruence and proportionality" to the state
discrimination that it purports to remedy. That is because the law, unlike
federal laws prohibiting literacy tests for voting, imposing voting rights
requirements, or punishing state officials who intentionally discriminated
in jury selection is not "directed . . . at any State or state actor."

But why can Congress not provide a remedy against private actors?
Those private actors, of course, did not themselves violate the Constitution.
But this Court has held that Congress at least sometimes can enact remedial "[l]egislation . . . [that] prohibits conduct which is not itself unconstitutional." *Flores*, at 518; see also *Katzenbach v. Morgan*, at 651; *South Carolina v. Katzenbach*, at 308. The statutory remedy The statutory remedy
does not in any sense purport to "determine what constitutes a constitutional violation." . . . It restricts private actors only by imposing liability for
private conduct that is, in the main, already forbidden by state law. Why is
the remedy "disproportionate"? And given the relation between remedy and
violation—the creation of a federal remedy to substitute for constitutionally
inadequate state remedies—where is the lack of "congruence"?

The majority adds that Congress found that the problem of inadequacy
of state remedies "does not exist in all States, or even most States." But
Congress had before it the task force reports of at least 21 States documenting constitutional violations. And it made its own findings about pervasive
gender-based stereotypes hampering many state legal systems, sometimes
unconstitutionally so. The record nowhere reveals a congressional finding
that the problem "does not exist" elsewhere. Why can Congress not take the
evidence before it as evidence of a national problem? . . .

Despite my doubts about the majority's § 5 reasoning, I need not, and
do not, answer the § 5 question, which I would leave for more thorough
analysis if necessary on another occasion. . . .

■ [The concurring opinion of JUSTICE THOMAS and dissenting opinion of
JUSTICE BREYER are omitted.]

NOTES

1. Note the majority's (wooden?) reliance on the authority of *The Civil
Rights Cases* and the dissent's (strained?) attempt to distinguish that precedent. Is the real question whether Congress, pursuant to Section 5, may judge
for itself that state laws do not adequately protect women against private violence and directly provide that protection as a matter of federal law? Is that
question in *Morrison* different from the one presented in *The Civil Rights Cases*? Should the Court have reconsidered *The Civil Rights Cases*? Or should more
than one hundred years of accepting that precedent foreclose such inquiry?

2. The dissent in *Morrison* argued that the Violence Against Women Act's
regulation of private conduct could be a way of "enforcing" the Constitution as a
remedy. The dissent's discussion of whether such a "remedy" was a true remedy—in other words, whether it was proportional to curing an actual violation of
the Constitution—referenced the Court's decision three years earlier in *City of
Boerne v. Flores*, the next principal case.

The Court had already addressed questions concerning the scope of Congress's Section 5 enforcement power in previous cases. Most notably, in *Katzenbach v. Morgan*, 384 U.S. 641 (1966), the Court upheld Section 4(e) of the Voting Rights Act of 1965 as a valid exercise of Congress's Section 5 enforcement power. Section 4(e) prohibited states from denying the right to vote to anyone who had successfully completed sixth grade in an accredited school in Puerto Rico because of inability to read or write English. Several years earlier the Court had unanimously held that a state requirement that voters be able to read and write English did not violate Section 1 of the Fourteenth Amendment. Nevertheless, *Katzenbach* upheld Section 4(e) as a valid law to "enforce" the Fourteenth Amendment's prohibitions. The Court rejected that argument "that an exercise of congressional power under" Section 5 "can only be sustained if the judicial branch determines that the state law is prohibited by the provisions of the Amendment that Congress sought to enforce," since that would give Congress only an "insignificant role." Analogizing to the Necessary and Proper Clause and *McCulloch v. Maryland* (printed above in Chapter 3), the Court said the question was whether Section 4(e) was "plainly adapted" to enforce the Equal Protection Clause. The Court found that it was, because securing the right to vote for the Puerto Rican community in New York would enhance that group's political power, thereby helping it achieve "nondiscriminatory treatment in public services" and "perfect equality of civil rights and equal protection of the laws." It was enough that the Court could "perceive a basis upon which Congress might predicate a judgment" that the challenged provision either helped secure equal protection or remedied invidious discrimination.

That sweeping view of the enforcement power was tested by the Voting Rights Act Amendments of 1970. That statute abolished literacy tests for voting nationwide and provided the right to vote in federal and state elections for everyone over age 18. In *Oregon v. Mitchell*, 400 U.S. 112 (1970), the Court upheld the prohibition on literacy tests but divided over the eighteen-year-old vote requirement. Four justices would have upheld the provision under *Katzenbach*. Four justices would have struck it down as beyond Congress's powers under the Fourteenth Amendment. The decisive vote was Justice Black's. He considered the voting-age provision valid as applied to federal elections—as an exercise of Congress's Article I power to displace state law concerning the time, place, or manner of elections for federal office—but invalid as applied to elections for state office. Even under the reasoning of *Katzenbach*, he did not see the voting-age provision as enforcing the Fourteenth Amendment. (Shortly after *Mitchell* the Twenty–sixth Amendment was quickly proposed and ratified, ensuring that no state government could abridge the right to vote on account of age for persons "eighteen years of age or older.")

It was against this legal background—the sweeping view of the Section 5 power embraced in *Katzenbach* and the limitations suggested by *Mitchell*—that the Court took up the question of Congress's power to enact the Religious Freedom Restoration Act.

City of Boerne v. Flores

521 U.S. 507 (1997)

■ JUSTICE KENNEDY delivered the opinion of the Court.

A decision by local zoning authorities to deny a church a building permit was challenged under the Religious Freedom Restoration Act of 1993.

The case calls into question the authority of Congress to enact RFRA. We conclude the statute exceeds Congress' power.

I

Situated on a hill in the city of Boerne, Texas, some 28 miles northwest of San Antonio, is St. Peter Catholic Church. Built in 1923, the church's structure replicates the mission style of the region's earlier history. The church seats about 230 worshippers, a number too small for its growing parish. Some 40 to 60 parishioners cannot be accommodated at some Sunday masses. In order to meet the needs of the congregation the Archbishop of San Antonio gave permission to the parish to plan alterations to enlarge the building.

A few months later, the Boerne City Council passed an ordinance authorizing the city's Historic Landmark Commission to prepare a preservation plan with proposed historic landmarks and districts. Under the ordinance, the commission must preapprove construction affecting historic landmarks or buildings in a historic district.

Soon afterwards, the Archbishop applied for a building permit so construction to enlarge the church could proceed. City authorities, relying on the ordinance and the designation of a historic district (which, they argued, included the church), denied the application. The Archbishop brought this suit challenging the permit denial. . . . The Archbishop relied upon RFRA as one basis for relief from the refusal to issue the permit. The District Court concluded that by enacting RFRA Congress exceeded the scope of its enforcement power under § 5 of the Fourteenth Amendment. [The Fifth Circuit reversed.] . . .

II

Congress enacted RFRA in direct response to the Court's decision in *Employment Div., Dept. of Human Resources of Oregon v. Smith*, 494 U.S. 872 (1990). There we considered a Free Exercise Clause claim brought by members of the Native American Church who were denied unemployment benefits when they lost their jobs because they had used peyote. Their practice was to ingest peyote for sacramental purposes, and they challenged an Oregon statute of general applicability which made use of the drug criminal. In evaluating the claim, we declined to apply the balancing test set forth in *Sherbert v. Verner*, 374 U.S. 398 (1963), under which we would have asked whether Oregon's prohibition substantially burdened a religious practice and, if it did, whether the burden was justified by a compelling government interest. . . .

The application of the *Sherbert* test, the *Smith* decision explained, would have produced an anomaly in the law, a constitutional right to ignore neutral laws of general applicability. . . .

Four Members of the Court disagreed. They argued the law placed a substantial burden on the Native American Church members so that it could be upheld only if the law served a compelling state interest and was narrowly tailored to achieve that end. . . .

These points of constitutional interpretation were debated by Members of Congress in hearings and floor debates. Many criticized the Court's reasoning, and this disagreement resulted in the passage of RFRA. Congress announced:

(1) [T]he framers of the Constitution, recognizing free exercise of religion as an unalienable right, secured its protection in the First Amendment to the Constitution;

(2) laws 'neutral' toward religion may burden religious exercise as surely as laws intended to interfere with religious exercise;

(3) governments should not substantially burden religious exercise without compelling justification;

(4) in *Employment Division v. Smith*, 494 U.S. 872 (1990), the Supreme Court virtually eliminated the requirement that the government justify burdens on religious exercise imposed by laws neutral toward religion; and

(5) the compelling interest test as set forth in prior Federal court rulings is a workable test for striking sensible balances between religious liberty and competing prior governmental interests.

42 U.S.C. § 2000bb(a).

The Act's stated purposes are:

(1) to restore the compelling interest test as set forth in *Sherbert v. Verner*, and *Wisconsin v. Yoder*, and to guarantee its application in all cases where free exercise of religion is substantially burdened; and

(2) to provide a claim or defense to persons whose religious exercise is substantially burdened by government. § 2000bb(b).

RFRA prohibits "[g]overnment" from "substantially burden[ing]" a person's exercise of religion even if the burden results from a rule of general applicability unless the government can demonstrate the burden "(1) is in furtherance of a compelling governmental interest; and (2) is the least restrictive means of furthering that compelling governmental interest." The Act's mandate applies to any "branch, department, agency, instrumentality, and official (or other person acting under color of law) of the United States," as well as to any "State, or . . . subdivision of a State." The Act's universal coverage is confirmed in § 2000bb–3(a), under which RFRA "applies to all Federal and State law, and the implementation of that law, whether statutory or otherwise, and whether adopted before or after [RFRA's enactment]." In accordance with RFRA's usage of the term, we shall use "state law" to include local and municipal ordinances.

III

A

. . . Congress relied on its Fourteenth Amendment enforcement power in enacting the most far-reaching and substantial of RFRA's provisions, those which impose its requirements on the States. . . . The parties disagree over whether RFRA is a proper exercise of Congress' § 5 power "to enforce" by "appropriate legislation" the [Free Exercise Clause, as incorporated against the states by the Fourteenth Amendment.]

In defense of the Act, respondent the Archbishop contends, with support from the United States, that RFRA is permissible enforcement legislation. Congress, it is said, is only protecting by legislation one of the liberties guaranteed by the Fourteenth Amendment's Due Process Clause, the free exercise of religion, beyond what is necessary under *Smith*. It is said the congressional decision to dispense with proof of deliberate or overt discrimination and instead concentrate on a law's effects accords with the settled understanding that § 5 includes the power to enact legislation designed to prevent, as well as remedy, constitutional violations. It is further contended that Congress' § 5 power is not limited to remedial or preventive legislation.

All must acknowledge that § 5 is "a positive grant of legislative power" to Congress, *Katzenbach v. Morgan*, 384 U.S. 641, 651 (1966). In *Ex parte Virginia*, 100 U.S. 339, 345–346 (1879), we explained the scope of Congress' § 5 power in the following broad terms:

> Whatever legislation is appropriate, that is, adapted to carry out the objects the amendments have in view, whatever tends to enforce submission to the prohibitions they contain, and to secure to all persons the enjoyment of perfect equality of civil rights and the equal protection of the laws against State denial or invasion, if not prohibited, is brought within the domain of congressional power.

Legislation which deters or remedies constitutional violations can fall within the sweep of Congress' enforcement power even if in the process it prohibits conduct which is not itself unconstitutional and intrudes into "legislative spheres of autonomy previously reserved to the States." For example, the Court upheld a suspension of literacy tests and similar voting requirements under Congress' parallel power to enforce the provisions of the Fifteenth Amendment, as a measure to combat racial discrimination in voting, *South Carolina v. Katzenbach*, 383 U.S. 301, 308 (1966), despite the facial constitutionality of the tests [at the time]. We have also concluded that other measures protecting voting rights are within Congress' power to enforce the Fourteenth and Fifteenth Amendments, despite the burdens those measures placed on the States. *South Carolina v. Katzenbach*, supra (upholding several provisions of the Voting Rights Act of 1965); *Katzenbach v. Morgan*, supra (upholding ban on literacy tests that prohibited certain people schooled in Puerto Rico from voting); *Oregon v. Mitchell*, 400 U.S. 112 (1970) (upholding 5–year nationwide ban on literacy tests and similar voting requirements for registering to vote).

It is also true, however, that "[a]s broad as the congressional enforcement power is, it is not unlimited." In assessing the breadth of § 5's enforcement power, we begin with its text. Congress has been given the power "to enforce" the "provisions of this article." We agree with respondent, of course, that Congress can enact legislation under § 5 enforcing the constitutional right to the free exercise of religion. . . .

Congress' power under § 5, however, extends only to "enforc[ing]" the provisions of the Fourteenth Amendment. The Court has described this power as "remedial." The design of the Amendment and the text of § 5 are inconsistent with the suggestion that Congress has the power to decree the substance of the Fourteenth Amendment's restrictions on the States. Legislation which alters the meaning of the Free Exercise Clause cannot be said to be enforcing the Clause. Congress does not enforce a constitutional right by changing what the right is. It has been given the power "to enforce," not the power to determine what constitutes a constitutional violation. Were it not so, what Congress would be enforcing would no longer be, in any meaningful sense, the "provisions of [the Fourteenth Amendment]."

While the line between measures that remedy or prevent unconstitutional actions and measures that make a substantive change in the governing law is not easy to discern, and Congress must have wide latitude in determining where it lies, the distinction exists and must be observed. There must be a congruence and proportionality between the injury to be prevented or remedied and the means adopted to that end. Lacking such a connection, legislation may become substantive in operation and effect. History and our case law support drawing the distinction, one apparent from the text of the Amendment.

1

The Fourteenth Amendment's history confirms the remedial, rather than substantive, nature of the Enforcement Clause. The Joint Committee on Reconstruction of the 39th Congress began drafting what would become the Fourteenth Amendment in January 1866. The objections to the Committee's first draft of the Amendment, and the rejection of the draft, have a direct bearing on the central issue of defining Congress' enforcement power. In February, Republican Representative John Bingham of Ohio reported the following draft Amendment to the House of Representatives on behalf of the Joint Committee:

> The Congress shall have power to make all laws which shall be necessary and proper to secure to the citizens of each State all privileges and immunities of citizens in the several States, and to all persons in the several States equal protection in the rights of life, liberty, and property.

Cong. Globe, 39th Cong., 1st Sess., 1034 (1866).

The proposal encountered immediate opposition, which continued through three days of debate. Members of Congress from across the political spectrum criticized the Amendment, and the criticisms had a common theme: The proposed Amendment gave Congress too much legislative power at the expense of the existing constitutional structure. Democrats and conservative Republicans argued that the proposed Amendment would give Congress a power to intrude into traditional areas of state responsibility, a power inconsistent with the federal design central to the Constitution. . . .

As a result of these objections having been expressed from so many different quarters, the House voted to table the proposal until April. The Amendment in its early form was not again considered. Instead, the Joint Committee began drafting a new article of Amendment, which it reported to Congress on April 30, 1866.

Section 1 of the new draft Amendment imposed self-executing limits on the States. Section 5 prescribed that "[t]he Congress shall have power to enforce, by appropriate legislation, the provisions of this article." Under the revised Amendment, Congress' power was no longer plenary but remedial. Congress was granted the power to make the substantive constitutional prohibitions against the States effective. Representative Bingham said the new draft would give Congress "the power . . . to protect by national law the privileges and immunities of all the citizens of the Republic . . . whenever the same shall be abridged or denied by the unconstitutional acts of any State." Representative Stevens described the new draft Amendment as "allow[ing] Congress to correct the unjust legislation of the States." The revised Amendment proposal did not raise the concerns expressed earlier regarding broad congressional power to prescribe uniform national laws with respect to life, liberty, and property. . . .

The significance of the defeat of the Bingham proposal was apparent even then. During the debates over the Ku Klux Klan Act only a few years after the Amendment's ratification, Representative James Garfield argued there were limits on Congress' enforcement power, saying "unless we ignore both the history and the language of these clauses we cannot, by any reasonable interpretation, give to [§ 5] . . . the force and effect of the rejected [Bingham] clause." Scholars of successive generations have agreed with this assessment.

The design of the Fourteenth Amendment has proved significant also in maintaining the traditional separation of powers between Congress and the Judiciary. The first eight Amendments to the Constitution set forth self-executing prohibitions on governmental action, and this Court has had primary authority to interpret those prohibitions. The Bingham draft, some thought, departed from that tradition by vesting in Congress primary power to interpret and elaborate on the meaning of the new Amendment through legislation. . . . As enacted, the Fourteenth Amendment confers substantive rights against the States which, like the provisions of the Bill of Rights, are self-executing. The power to interpret the Constitution in a case or controversy remains in the Judiciary.

2

The remedial and preventive nature of Congress' enforcement power, and the limitation inherent in the power, were confirmed in our earliest cases on the Fourteenth Amendment. In the *Civil Rights Cases*, 109 U.S. 3 (1883), the Court invalidated sections of the Civil Rights Act of 1875 which prescribed criminal penalties for denying to any person "the full enjoyment of" public accommodations and conveyances, on the grounds that it exceeded Congress' power by seeking to regulate private conduct. The Enforcement Clause, the Court said, did not authorize Congress to pass "general legislation upon the rights of the citizen, but corrective legislation, that is, such as may be necessary and proper for counteracting such laws as the States may adopt or enforce, and which, by the amendment, they are prohibited from making or enforcing. . . ." The power to "legislate generally upon" life, liberty, and property, as opposed to the "power to provide modes of redress" against offensive state action, was "repugnant" to the Constitution. Although the specific holdings of these early cases might have been superseded or modified, their treatment of Congress' § 5 power as corrective or preventive, not definitional, has not been questioned.

Recent cases have continued to revolve around the question whether § 5 legislation can be considered remedial. . . .

3

Any suggestion that Congress has a substantive, non-remedial power under the Fourteenth Amendment is not supported by our case law. In *Oregon v. Mitchell*, a majority of the Court concluded Congress had exceeded its enforcement powers by enacting legislation lowering the minimum age of voters from 21 to 18 in state and local elections. The five Members of the Court who reached this conclusion explained that the legislation intruded into an area reserved by the Constitution to the States. . . .

There is language in our opinion in *Katzenbach v. Morgan*, 384 U.S. 641 (1966), which could be interpreted as acknowledging a power in Congress to enact legislation that expands the rights contained in § 1 of the Fourteenth Amendment. This is not a necessary interpretation, however, or even the best one. In *Morgan*, the Court considered the constitutionality of § 4(e) of the Voting Rights Act of 1965 . . . [and] perceived a factual basis on which Congress could have concluded that New York's literacy requirement "constituted an invidious discrimination in violation of the Equal Protection Clause." . . . As Justice Stewart explained in *Oregon v. Mitchell*, interpreting *Morgan* to give Congress the power to interpret the Constitution "would require an enormous extension of that decision's rationale."

If Congress could define its own powers by altering the Fourteenth Amendment's meaning, no longer would the Constitution be "superior paramount law, unchangeable by ordinary means." It would be "on a level with ordinary legislative acts, and, like other acts, ... alterable when the legislature shall please to alter it." *Marbury v. Madison*, at 177. Under this approach, it is difficult to conceive of a principle that would limit congressional power. Shifting legislative majorities could change the Constitution and effectively circumvent the difficult and detailed amendment process contained in Article V. We now turn to consider whether RFRA can be considered enforcement legislation under § 5 of the Fourteenth Amendment.

B

Respondent contends that RFRA is a proper exercise of Congress' remedial or preventive power. The Act, it is said, is a reasonable means of protecting the free exercise of religion as defined by *Smith*. It prevents and remedies laws which are enacted with the unconstitutional object of targeting religious beliefs and practices. ...

While preventive rules are sometimes appropriate remedial measures, there must be a congruence between the means used and the ends to be achieved. The appropriateness of remedial measures must be considered in light of the evil presented. ...

A comparison between RFRA and the Voting Rights Act is instructive. In contrast to the record which confronted Congress and the Judiciary in the voting rights cases, RFRA's legislative record lacks examples of modern instances of generally applicable laws passed because of religious bigotry. ... [T]he emphasis of the hearings was on laws of general applicability which place incidental burdens on religion. Much of the discussion centered upon anecdotal evidence of autopsies performed on Jewish individuals and Hmong immigrants in violation of their religious beliefs, and on zoning regulations and historic preservation laws (like the one at issue here), which, as an incident of their normal operation, have adverse effects on churches and synagogues. It is difficult to maintain that they are examples of legislation enacted or enforced due to animus or hostility to the burdened religious practices or that they indicate some widespread pattern of religious discrimination in this country. Congress' concern was with the incidental burdens imposed, not the object or purpose of the legislation. ...

Regardless of the state of the legislative record, RFRA cannot be considered remedial, preventive legislation, if those terms are to have any meaning. RFRA is so out of proportion to a supposed remedial or preventive object that it cannot be understood as responsive to, or designed to prevent, unconstitutional behavior. It appears, instead, to attempt a substantive change in constitutional protections. Preventive measures prohibiting certain types of laws may be appropriate when there is reason to believe that many of the laws affected by the congressional enactment have a significant likelihood of being unconstitutional. Remedial legislation under § 5 "should be adapted to the mischief and wrong which the [Fourteenth] amendment was intended to provide against." *Civil Rights Cases*, at 13.

RFRA is not so confined. Sweeping coverage ensures its intrusion at every level of government, displacing laws and prohibiting official actions of almost every description and regardless of subject matter. RFRA's restrictions apply to every agency and official of the Federal, State, and local

Governments. RFRA applies to all federal and state law, statutory or otherwise, whether adopted before or after its enactment. . . . Any law is subject to challenge at any time by any individual who alleges a substantial burden on his or her free exercise of religion. . . .

The stringent test RFRA demands of state laws reflects a lack of proportionality or congruence between the means adopted and the legitimate end to be achieved. If an objector can show a substantial burden on his free exercise, the State must demonstrate a compelling governmental interest and show that the law is the least restrictive means of furthering its interest. . . . Laws valid under *Smith* would fall under RFRA without regard to whether they had the object of stifling or punishing free exercise. We make these observations not to reargue the position of the majority in *Smith* but to illustrate the substantive alteration of its holding attempted by RFRA. . . .

When Congress acts within its sphere of power and responsibilities, it has not just the right but the duty to make its own informed judgment on the meaning and force of the Constitution. This has been clear from the early days of the Republic. In 1789, when a Member of the House of Representatives objected to a debate on the constitutionality of legislation based on the theory that "it would be officious" to consider the constitutionality of a measure that did not affect the House, James Madison explained that "it is incontrovertibly of as much importance to this branch of the Government as to any other, that the constitution should be preserved entire. It is our duty." 1 Annals of Congress 500 (1789). Were it otherwise, we would not afford Congress the presumption of validity its enactments now enjoy.

Our national experience teaches that the Constitution is preserved best when each part of the Government respects both the Constitution and the proper actions and determinations of the other branches. When the Court has interpreted the Constitution, it has acted within the province of the Judicial Branch, which embraces the duty to say what the law is. *Marbury v. Madison*. When the political branches of the Government act against the background of a judicial interpretation of the Constitution already issued, it must be understood that in later cases and controversies the Court will treat its precedents with the respect due them under settled principles, including *stare decisis,* and contrary expectations must be disappointed. RFRA was designed to control cases and controversies, such as the one before us; but as the provisions of the federal statute here invoked are beyond congressional authority, it is this Court's precedent, not RFRA, which must control. . . .

■ JUSTICE O'CONNOR, with whom JUSTICE BREYER joins . . . , dissenting.

I dissent from the Court's disposition of this case. I agree with the Court that the issue before us is whether the Religious Freedom Restoration Act of 1993 (RFRA) is a proper exercise of Congress' power to enforce § 5 of the Fourteenth Amendment. But as a yardstick for measuring the constitutionality of RFRA, the Court uses its holding in *Employment Div., Dept. of Human Resources of Oregon v. Smith*, 494 U.S. 872 (1990), the decision that prompted Congress to enact RFRA as a means of more rigorously enforcing the Free Exercise Clause. I remain of the view that *Smith* was wrongly decided, and I would use this case to reexamine the Court's holding there. Therefore, I would direct the parties to brief the question whether *Smith* represents the correct understanding of the Free Exercise Clause and set the case for reargument. If the Court were to correct the misinterpretation of the Free Exercise Clause set forth in *Smith*, it would simultaneously put our First Amendment jurisprudence back on course and allay the legitimate concerns of a majority in Congress who believed that *Smith* improperly restricted religious liberty. We would then be in a position to review RFRA in light of a proper interpretation of the Free Exercise Clause.

■ [The concurring opinions of JUSTICES STEVENS and SCALIA, and the dissenting opinion of JUSTICE SOUTER, are omitted.]

NOTES

1. What precisely was Congress doing when it enacted the Religious Freedom Restoration Act? Was it engaging in constitutional interpretation of the Free Exercise Clause and rejecting the Court's interpretation of that clause in *Employment Division v. Smith* (printed above in Chapter 6)? If so, is there anything wrong with that? Is Congress always bound by the Supreme Court's interpretations of the Constitution? Or as a coordinate branch of the national government may it independently interpret the Constitution? Is there some whiff of irritation in the Court's opinion in *City of Boerne*—some "how dare you question our interpretation of the Constitution"? If so, is that attitude appropriate? Necessary to vindicate the Court's authority? Was the Court right that RFRA's enactment was inconsistent with the Court's interpretive authority under *Marbury*?

2. When Congress legislates a broader prohibition under Section 5 of the Fourteenth Amendment, is there necessarily an assault on the Supreme Court's interpretation of Section 1? The argument has been made that

> when Congress interprets the provisions of the Bill of Rights for purposes of carrying out its enforcement authority under Section Five, it is not bound by the institutional constraints that in many cases lead the courts to adopt a less intrusive interpretation from among the textually and historically plausible meanings of the clause in question. Because these institutional constraints are predicated on the need to protect the discretionary judgments of representative institutions from uncabined judicial interference, there is no reason for Congress—the representatives of the people—to abide by them. Congress need not be concerned that its interpretations of the Bill of Rights will trench upon democratic prerogatives, because its actions *are* the expression of the democratic will of the people. Indeed, the same institutional constraints that lead the courts, in many cases, to adopt a reading of the Constitution that produces a more modest judicial role should have led the Court to be more respectful of the congressional decision represented by RFRA.

Michael W. McConnell, *The Supreme Court, 1996 Term, Comment: Institutions and Interpretation: A Critique of City of Boerne v. Flores,* 111 Harv. L. Rev. 153, 156 (1997). For a narrower reading of Section 5, see Steven G. Calabresi & Nicholas Stabile, *On Section Five of the Fourteenth Amendment,* 11 U. Pa. J. Const. L. 1431 (2009).

3. Could RFRA have been sustained on the ground that, even accepting the Court's decision in *Smith,* it was "appropriate" prophylactic legislation to prevent violations of the Free Exercise Clause as interpreted in *Smith*? The Court in *City of Boerne* adopted as a test whether the legislation was "congruent and proportional" to the violation asserted, and concluded that RFRA was wildly incongruent and disproportionate to *Smith*'s understanding of Free Ex-

ercise and so could not be understood as remedial or prophylactic legislation. How does this standard for judging the "appropriateness" of Congress's judgment compare with *McCulloch*'s standards for judging what laws are "proper" exercises of Congress's judgment under the Necessary and Proper Clause?

4. In a series of subsequent decisions, the Court has continued to hold that Congress's enforcement must be "congruent and proportional" with the Fourteenth Amendment *as construed by the Court*. But the Court's results are not easy to characterize:

a. In *Kimel v. Florida Board of Regents*, 528 U.S. 62 (2000), the Court held that Congress could not use the Section 5 power to authorize money damages suits against states for age discrimination—as Congress had done in the Age Discrimination in Employment Act—because the Court had earlier held that state government age classifications (in the form of mandatory retirement laws) do not violate the Equal Protection Clause. *Kimel* and the other cases in this note involved the Court's convoluted doctrine concerning state sovereign immunity from suits for damages. Under the Court's doctrine, the Eleventh Amendment gives states immunity from such suits (though its language does not say that) but Congress may abrogate that immunity pursuant to one of its post-Eleventh Amendment grants of legislative power. That in turn requires the Court to decide whether a given statute is within Congress's power under those post-Eleventh Amendment grants of legislative power, especially Section 5 of the Fourteenth Amendment.

b. In *Board of Trustees of University of Alabama v. Garrett*, 531 U.S. 356 (2001), the Court held that Congress could not authorize money damages suits against states for failing to accommodate persons with disabilities—as Congress had done in the Americans with Disabilities Act. "[I]t is the responsibility of this Court, not Congress, to define the substance of constitutional guarantees," the Court stated. The requirement of disability accommodation was not congruent and proportional to any violation or pattern of violation of the Equal Protection Clause. In *Tennessee v. Lane*, 541 U.S. 509 (2004), the Court tilted back in the other direction, finding that a different section of the same statute, applied so as to mandate physical access to a county courthouse for a paraplegic charged with a criminal offense, was within Congress's Section 5 power.

c. In *Nevada Department of Human Resources v. Hibbs*, 538 U.S. 721 (2003), the Court upheld Congress's power to apply the Family Medical Leave Act of 1993 to state governments, finding it permissible "prophylactic legislation" under Section 5. The statute gave employees twelve weeks of unpaid leave to care for ill relatives, and employers who violated it were subject to suits for damages. The Court concluded that Congress may enact "legislation that proscribes facially *constitutional* conduct" if it does so "in order to prevent and deter *unconstitutional* conduct" (emphases added), which Congress had done since the statute "aims to protect the right to be free from gender-based discrimination in the workplace." The Court distinguished *City of Boerne* on the ground that the Act was "narrowly targeted at the fault line between work and family—precisely where sex-based overgeneralization has been and remains strongest—and affects only one aspect of the employment relationship." *City of Boerne*, in contrast, "applied broadly to every aspect of state employers' operations." Is the distinction persuasive? Is *Hibbs* consistent with *United States v. Morrison?*

[*Assignment 62*]

II. THE EQUAL PROTECTION CLAUSE

A. THE SEGREGATION CASES

Does the anti-discrimination guarantee of Section 1 of the Fourteenth Amendment prohibit racial discrimination by state governments? The modern answer is an unequivocal *yes*. Today, such a prohibition is understood to be at the very core of the meaning of the Equal Protection Clause. Does legally enforced racial separation—segregation—violate this principle? Again, the modern answer is an unequivocal *yes*.

The earliest Supreme Court cases decided after the adoption of the Fourteenth Amendment are clear that the amendment forbids government racial discrimination of any kind—*Slaughter–House Cases* (1873) and *Strauder v. West Virginia* (1880) could not have been plainer on this point. But soon afterwards the Court began upholding segregation, discrimination, and Jim Crow—with a vengeance.

The history of judicial interpretation of the Equal Protection Clause on these core issues is not a pretty one. *Strauder* stands as an early, sound interpretation of the Fourteenth Amendment, to which the Court eventually returned in the landmark 1954 case of *Brown v. Board of Education*. But in between these bookends there is plenty of bad judicial history, raising important questions about constitutional interpretation.

Do the cases that follow suggest to you that it is inevitable for judicial decisions to be a product of the times in which the justices live—and not only inevitable but desirable? Or do they suggest quite the opposite—that courts should not allow contemporary social values to affect their interpretation of the Constitution, that doing so leads to the possibility of serious error, and that it is difficult for the legal system to work its way out of such errors without enormous strain? Or do the cases teach entirely different lessons: lessons about the strengths and weaknesses of looking to "original intent"? About the relationship between the intentions of drafters and the meaning of the language they adopted? This section begins with a seemingly minor statutory interpretation case from 1873, *Railroad Company v. Brown*, then proceeds with a series of decisions upholding legal segregation in various forms, often in the name of reflecting contemporary values— *Plessy v. Ferguson* (1896), *Cumming v. Board of Education* (1899), *Giles v. Harris* (1903), and *Berea College v. Kentucky* (1908).

Railroad Company v. Brown
84 U.S. 445 (1873)

In the year 1854, Congress authorized the Alexandria and Washington Railroad Company . . . to extend their road *into* the District of Columbia
. . . .

In 1863, the company got a further grant of power, authorizing it to extend its road northward, so as to connect itself with the Baltimore and Ohio

Railroad. This grant was, however, accompanied with a provision, "that no person shall be excluded from the cars on account of color." . . .

In this condition of things, one Catharine Brown, a colored woman, on the 8th of February, 1868, anterior to the adoption of the fourteenth and fifteenth amendments to the Constitution, bought a ticket to come from Alexandria to Washington. . . . No tickets were distinguished as for white persons or colored persons, nor for any particular sort or class of cars. All were exactly alike.

When the woman went to take her place in the cars there were standing there two cars, alike comfortable; the one, however, set apart for colored persons, and the other "for white ladies, and gentlemen accompanying them;" the regulation having been that in going down from Washington to Alexandria, the first should be occupied by the former, and the last by the latter; and that in coming back the use should be simply reversed. When about to get into one of the cars, a servant of the persons managing the road, stationed near the cars to direct passengers, told the woman not to get into the car into which she was about to enter, but to get into the one before it; that he had been instructed by persons in charge of the road not to permit colored persons to ride in the car in which she was getting, but to have them go in the other. The woman, however, persisted in going into the car appropriated for white ladies, and the man put her out with force, and as she alleged, some insult. She then got into the car into which she had been directed to get—the one assigned to colored people—was carried safely into Washington and got out there.

Hereupon she sued the *Washington, Alexandria, and Georgetown Railroad Company* in the Supreme Court of the District. . . .

The counsel of the company requested the court to instruct the jury: . . . That if by a standing regulation certain cars were appropriated and designated for the use of white persons, and certain others for the use of colored, and all the cars were equally safe, clean, and comfortable, and if this sort of regulation was one in force on the principal railroads of the country, and one which unless it has been adopted on this road, the travel on it would have been seriously injured and the receipts of the road decreased, and if the establishment of such a regulation itself increased the expenses of the road considerably—then, in case no insult nor greater force than was necessary had been used, and the plaintiff after taking a seat in the car appropriated for colored persons, was carried safely into Washington and got out there—that the plaintiff could not recover. The court refused to give any one of the instructions, and a verdict having been given in $1500 for the plaintiff and judgment entered on it, the company brought the case here, assigning as three causes of error the refusals to give the charges requested.

■ Mr. Justice Davis delivered the opinion of the court.

. . . The third and last assignment of error asserts the right of the company to make the regulation separating the colored from the white passengers.

If the defendant in error had the right to retain the seat she had first taken, it is conceded the verdict of the jury should not be disturbed. . . . This leads us to consider what Congress meant in directing that no person should be excluded from the cars of the company on account of color.

The plaintiff in error contends that it has literally obeyed the direction, because it has never excluded this class of persons from the cars, but on the contrary, has always provided accommodations for them.

This is an ingenious attempt to evade a compliance with the obvious meaning of the requirement. It is true the words taken literally might bear the interpretation put upon them by the plaintiff in error, but evidently Congress did not use them in any such limited sense. . . . It was the discrimination in the use of the cars on account of color, where slavery obtained, which was the subject of discussion at the time, and not the fact that the colored race could not ride in the cars at all. Congress, in the belief that this discrimination was unjust, acted. It told this company, in substance, that it could extend its road within the District as desired, but that this discrimination must cease, and the colored and white race, in the use of the cars, be placed on an equality. This condition it had the right to impose, and in the temper of Congress at the time, it is manifest the grant could not have been made without it. It was the privilege of the company to reject it, but to do this, it must reject the whole legislation with which it was connected. It cannot accept a part and repudiate the rest. Having, therefore, constructed its road as it was authorized to do, and in this way greatly added to the value of its property, it will be held to a faithful compliance with all the terms accompanying the grant by which it was enabled to secure this pecuniary advantage.

––––––––

We turn next to one of the most despised Supreme Court decisions of all time, *Plessy v. Ferguson,* which is representative of the Court's betrayal of the principles of the Equal Protection Clause as understood by its framers and as reflected in the Court's earliest decisions interpreting the clause.

Plessy v. Ferguson

163 U.S. 537 (1896)

■ MR. JUSTICE BROWN, after stating the case, delivered the opinion of the court.

. . . The constitutionality of this act is attacked upon the ground that it conflicts both with the Thirteenth Amendment of the Constitution, abolishing slavery, and the Fourteenth Amendment, which prohibits certain restrictive legislation on the part of the States.

1. That it does not conflict with the Thirteenth Amendment, which abolished slavery and involuntary servitude, except as a punishment for crime, is too clear for argument. Slavery implies involuntary servitude—a state of bondage; the ownership of mankind as a chattel, or at least the control of the labor and services of one man for the benefit of another, and the absence of a legal right to the disposal of his own person, property and services. . . .

A statute which implies merely a legal distinction between the white and colored races—a distinction which is founded in the color of the two races, and which must always exist so long as white men are distinguished from the other race by color—has no tendency to destroy the legal equality of the two races, or reëstablish a state of involuntary servitude. Indeed, we do not understand that the Thirteenth Amendment is strenuously relied upon by the plaintiff in error in this connection.

2. . . . The object of the [Fourteenth A]mendment was undoubtedly to enforce the absolute equality of the two races before the law, but in the nature of things it could not have been intended to abolish distinctions based upon color, or to enforce social, as distinguished from political equality, or a commingling of the two races upon terms unsatisfactory to either. Laws permitting, and even requiring, their separation in places where they are liable to be brought into contact do not necessarily imply the inferiority of either race to the other, and have been generally, if not universally, recognized as within the competency of the state legislatures in the exercise of their police power. The most common instance of this is connected with the establishment of separate schools for white and colored children, which have been held to be a valid exercise of the legislative power even by courts of States where the political rights of the colored race have been longest and most earnestly enforced. . . .

Laws forbidding the intermarriage of the two races may be said in a technical sense to interfere with the freedom of contract, and yet have been universally recognized as within the police power of the State.

The distinction between laws interfering with the political equality of the negro and those requiring the separation of the two races in schools, theatres, and railway carriages has been frequently drawn by this court. Thus, in *Strauder v. West Virginia*, 100 U.S. 303, it was held that a law of West Virginia limiting to white male persons, 21 years of age and citizens of the State, the right to sit upon juries, was a discrimination which implied a legal inferiority in civil society, which lessened the security of the right of the colored race, and was a step towards reducing them to a condition of servility. . . .

While we think the enforced separation of the races, as applied to the internal commerce of the State, neither abridges the privileges or immunities of the colored man, deprives him of his property without due process of law, nor denies him the equal protection of the laws, within the meaning of the Fourteenth Amendment, we are not prepared to say that the conductor, in assigning passengers to the coaches according to their race, does not act at his peril, or that the provision of the second section of the act, that denies to the passenger compensation in damages for a refusal to receive him into the coach in which he properly belongs, is a valid exercise of the legislative power. . . . [Here] the only issue made is as to the unconstitutionality of the act, so far as it requires the railway to provide separate accommodations, and the conductor to assign passengers according to their race.

It is claimed by the plaintiff in error that, in any mixed community, the reputation of belonging to the dominant race, in this instance the white race, is *property*, in the same sense that a right of action, or of inheritance, is property. Conceding this to be so, for the purposes of this case, we are unable to see how this statute deprives him of, or in any way affects his right to, such property. If he be a white man, and assigned to a colored coach, he may have his action for damages against the company for being deprived of his so called property. Upon the other hand, if he be a colored man and be so assigned, he has been deprived of no property, since he is not lawfully entitled to the reputation of being a white man.

In this connection, it is also suggested by the learned counsel for the plaintiff in error that the same argument that will justify the state legislature in requiring railways to provide separate accommodations for the two races will also authorize them to require separate cars to be provided for people whose hair is of a certain color, or who are aliens, or who belong to certain nationalities, or to enact laws requiring colored people to walk upon one side of the street, and white people upon the other, or requiring white men's houses to be painted white, and colored men's black, or their vehicles or business signs to be of different colors, upon the theory that one side of the street is as good as the other, or that a house or vehicle of one color is as good as one of another color. The reply to all this is that every exercise of the police power must be reasonable, and extend only to such laws as are enacted in good faith for the promotion of the public good, and not for the annoyance or oppression of a particular class. Thus, in *Yick Wo v. Hopkins*, 118 U.S. 356, it was held by this court that a municipal ordinance of the city of San Francisco, to regulate the carrying on of public laundries . . . without regard to the competency of the persons applying or the propriety of the places selected for the carrying on of the business . . . [was] a covert attempt on the part of the municipality to make an arbitrary and unjust discrimination against the Chinese race. . . .

So far, then, as a conflict with the Fourteenth Amendment is concerned, the case reduces itself to the question whether the statute of Louisiana is a reasonable regulation, and with respect to this there must necessarily be a large discretion on the part of the legislature. In determining the question of reasonableness it is at liberty to act with reference to the established usages, customs and traditions of the people, and with a view to the promotion of their comfort, and the preservation of the public peace and good order. Gauged by this standard, we cannot say that a law which authorizes or even requires the separation of the two races in public conveyances is unreasonable, or more obnoxious to the Fourteenth Amendment than the acts of Congress requiring separate schools for colored children in the District of Columbia, the constitutionality of which does not seem to have been questioned, or the corresponding acts of state legislatures.

We consider the underlying fallacy of the plaintiff's argument to consist in the assumption that the enforced separation of the two races stamps the colored race with a badge of inferiority. If this be so, it is not by reason of anything found in the act, but solely because the colored race chooses to put that construction upon it. The argument necessarily assumes that if, as has been more than once the case, and is not unlikely to be so again, the colored race should become the dominant power in the state legislature, and should enact a law in precisely similar terms, it would thereby relegate the white race to an inferior position. We imagine that the white race, at least, would not acquiesce in this assumption. The argument also assumes that social prejudices may be overcome by legislation, and that equal rights cannot be secured to the negro except by an enforced commingling of the two races. We cannot accept this proposition. If the two races are to meet upon terms of social equality, it must be the result of natural affinities, a mutual appreciation of each other's merits, and a voluntary consent of individuals. . . . Legislation is powerless to eradicate racial instincts, or to abolish distinctions based upon physical differences, and the attempt to do so can only result in accentuating the difficulties of the present situation. If the civil and political rights of both races be equal, one cannot be inferior to the other civilly or politically. If one race be inferior to the other socially, the Constitution of the United States cannot put them upon the same plane.

It is true that the question of the proportion of colored blood necessary to constitute a colored person, as distinguished from a white person, is one upon which there is a difference of opinion in the different States. . . . But these are questions to be determined under the laws of each State and are not properly put in issue in this case. Under the allegations of his petition it may undoubtedly become a question of importance whether, under the laws of Louisiana, the petitioner belongs to the white or colored race.

■ MR. JUSTICE HARLAN dissenting.

By the Louisiana statute, the validity of which is here involved, all railway companies (other than street railroad companies) carrying passengers in that State are required to have separate but equal accommodations for white and colored persons, "by providing two or more passenger coaches for each passenger train, *or* by dividing the passenger coaches by a *partition* so as to secure separate accommodations." . . . The managers of the railroad are not allowed to exercise any discretion in the premises, but are required to assign each passenger to some coach or compartment set apart for the exclusive use of his race. . . . Only "nurses attending children of the other race" are excepted from the operation of the statute. . . .

Thus, the state regulates the use of a public highway by citizens of the United States solely upon the basis of race.

However apparent the injustice of such legislation may be, we have only to consider whether it is consistent with the Constitution of the United States. . . .

In respect of civil rights, common to all citizens, the Constitution of the United States does not, I think, permit any public authority to know the race of those entitled to be protected in the enjoyment of such rights. Every true man has pride of race, and under appropriate circumstances, when the rights of others, his equals before the law, are not to be affected, it is his privilege to express such pride and to take such action based upon it as to him seems proper. But I deny that any legislative body or judicial tribunal may have regard to the race of citizens when the civil rights of those citizens are involved. . . .

It was said in argument that the statute of Louisiana does not discriminate against either race, but prescribes a rule applicable alike to white and colored citizens. But this argument does not meet the difficulty. Every one knows that the statute in question had its origin in the purpose, not so much to exclude white persons from railroad cars occupied by blacks, as to exclude colored people from coaches occupied by or assigned to white persons. . . . The thing to accomplish was, under the guise of giving equal accommodation for whites and blacks, to compel the latter to keep to themselves while traveling in railroad passenger coaches. No one would be so wanting in candor as to assert the contrary. The fundamental objection, therefore, to the statute, is that it interferes with the personal freedom of citizens. . . . If a white man and a black man choose to occupy the same public conveyance on a public highway, it is their right to do so, and no government, proceeding alone on grounds of race, can prevent it without infringing the personal liberty of each. . . .

If a State can prescribe, as a rule of civil conduct, that whites and blacks shall not travel as passengers in the same railroad coach, why may it not so regulate the use of the streets of its cities and towns as to compel white citizens to keep on one side of a street and black citizens to keep on the other? Why may it not, upon like grounds, punish whites and blacks who ride together in street cars or in open vehicles on a public road or street? Why may it not require sheriffs to assign whites to one side of a court-room and blacks to the other? And why may it not also prohibit the commingling of the two races in the galleries of legislative halls or in public assemblages convened for the consideration of the political questions of the day? Further, if this statute of Louisiana is consistent with the personal liberty of citizens, why may not the State require the separation in railroad coaches of native and naturalized citizens of the United States, or of Protestants and Roman Catholics?

The answer given at the argument to these questions was that regulations of the kind they suggest would be unreasonable, and could not, therefore, stand before the law. Is it meant that the determination of questions of legislative power depends upon the inquiry whether the statute whose validity is questioned is, in the judgment of the courts, a reasonable one, taking all the circumstances into consideration? A statute may be unreasonable merely because a sound public policy forbade its enactment. But I do not understand that the courts have anything to do with the policy or expediency of legislation. . . . There is a dangerous tendency in these latter days to enlarge the functions of the courts, by means of judicial interference with the will of the people as expressed by the legislature. Our institutions have the distinguishing characteristic that the three departments of government are coördinate and separate. Each much keep within the limits defined by the Constitution. And the courts best discharge their duty by executing the will of the law-making power, constitutionally expressed, leaving the results of legislation to be dealt with by the people through their representatives. . . .

The white race deems itself to be the dominant race in this country. And so it is, in prestige, in achievements, in education, in wealth, and in power. So, I doubt not, it will continue to be for all time, if it remains true to its great heritage and holds fast to the principles of constitutional liberty. But in view of the Constitution, in the eye of the law, there is in this country no superior, dominant, ruling class of citizens. There is no caste here. Our Constitution is color-blind, and neither knows nor tolerates classes among citizens. In respect of civil rights, all citizens are equal before the law. . . .

In my opinion, the judgment this day rendered will, in time, prove to be quite as pernicious as the decision made by this tribunal in the *Dred Scott case.* It was adjudged in that case that the descendants of Africans who were imported into this country, and sold as slaves, were not included nor intended to be included under the word "citizens" in the Constitution, and could not claim any of the rights and privileges which that instrument provided for and secured to citizens of the United States; that, at time of the adoption of the Constitution, they were "considered as a subordinate and inferior class of beings, who had been subjugated by the dominant race, and, whether emancipated or not, yet remained subject to their authority, and had no rights or privileges but such as those who held the power and the government might choose to grant them." The recent amendments of the Constitution, it was supposed, had eradicated these principles from our institutions. But it seems that we have yet, in some of the States, a dominant race—a superior class of citizens, which assumes to regulate the enjoyment of civil rights, common to all citizens, upon the basis of race. The present decision, it may well be apprehended, will not only stimulate aggressions, more or less brutal and irritating, upon the admitted rights of colored citizens, but will encourage the belief that it is possible, by means of state enactments, to defeat the beneficent purposes which the people of the United States had in view when they adopted the recent amendments of the Constitution, by one of which the blacks of this country were made citizens of the United States and of the States in which they respectively reside, and whose privileges and immunities, as citizens, the States are forbidden to abridge. Sixty millions of whites are in no danger from the presence here of eight millions of blacks. The destinies of the two races, in this country, are indissolubly linked together, and the interests of both require that the common government of all shall not permit the seeds of race hate to be planted under the sanction of law. What can more certainly arouse race hate, what more certainly create and perpetuate a feeling of distrust between these races, than state enactments which, in fact, proceed on the ground that colored citizens are so inferior and degraded that they cannot be allowed to sit in public coaches occupied by white citizens? That, as all will admit, is the real meaning of such legislation as was enacted in Louisiana.

The sure guarantee of the peace and security of each race is the clear, distinct, unconditional recognition by our governments, National and State, of every right that inheres in civil freedom, and of the equality before the law of all citizens of the United States, without regard to race. State enactments regulating the enjoyment of civil rights upon the basis of race, and cunningly devised to defeat legitimate results of the war, under the pretence of recognizing equality of rights, can have no other result than to render permanent peace impossible, and to keep alive a conflict of races, the continuance of which must do harm to all concerned. This question is not met by the suggestion that social equality cannot exist between the white and black races in this country. That argument, if it can be properly regarded as one, is scarcely worthy of consideration; for social equality no more exists between two races when traveling in a passenger coach or a public highway than when members of the same races sit by each other in a street car or in the jury box, or stand or sit with each other in a political assembly, or when they use in common the streets of a city or town, or when they are in the same room for the purpose of having their names placed on the registry of voters, or when they approach the ballot box in order to exercise the high privilege of voting. . . .

There is a race so different from our own that we do not permit those belonging to it to become citizens of the United States. Persons belonging to it are, with few exceptions, absolutely excluded from our country. I allude to the Chinese race. But by the statute in question, a Chinaman can ride in the same passenger coach with white citizens of the United States, while citizens of the black race in Louisiana, many of whom, perhaps, risked their lives for the preservation of the Union, who are entitled, by law, to participate in the political control of the State and nation, who are not excluded, by law or by reason of their race, from public stations of any kind, and who have all the legal rights that belong to white citizens, are yet declared to be criminals, liable to imprisonment, if they ride in a public coach occupied by citizens of the white race. It is scarcely just to say that a colored citizen should not object to occupying a public coach assigned to his own race. He does not object, nor, perhaps, would he object to separate coaches for his race if his rights under the law were recognized. But he does object, and he ought never to cease objecting to the proposition, that citizens of the white and black races can be adjudged criminals because they sit, or claim the right to sit, in the same public coach on a public highway.

The arbitrary separation of citizens, on the basis of race, while they are on a public highway, is a badge of servitude wholly inconsistent with the civil freedom and the equality before the law established by the Constitution. It cannot be justified upon any legal grounds.

If evils will result from the commingling of the two races upon public highways established for the benefit of all, they will be infinitely less than those that will surely come from state legislation regulating the enjoyment of civil rights upon the basis of race. We boast of the freedom enjoyed by our people above all other peoples. But it is difficult to reconcile that boast with a state of the law which, practically, puts the brand of servitude and degradation upon a large class of our fellow-citizens, our equals before the law. The thin disguise of "equal" accommodations for passengers in railroad coaches will not mislead any one, nor atone for the wrong this day done. . . .

For the reason stated, I am constrained to withhold my assent from the opinion and judgment of the majority.

NOTES

1. *Plessy* is the infamous case upholding racial segregation by law on the theory that "separate but equal" does not violate the Fourteenth Amendment's requirement of "equal protection of the laws." *Plessy*'s regime endured for 58 years, until the Court's decision in *Brown v. Board of Education* in 1954.

The Court purported not to be retreating from the principles announced in its prior cases. Is racial segregation consistent with *Strauder*'s view that the Fourteenth Amendment commands that "the law in the States shall be the same for the black as for the white; that all persons, whether colored or white, shall stand equal before the laws of the States, and, in regard to the colored race, for whose protection the amendment was primarily designed, that no discrimination shall be made against them by law because of their color"? If separate really were equal in a given situation—and in theory do adjacent train cars, arriving at the same time and at the same station, come about as close as possible?—would segregation *in and of itself* deprive someone of the "equal protection of the laws"?

The Court asserted that any "stigma" from segregation was a matter of one's own subjective perception, purely in the eye of the beholder. That very argument had been made by opponents of the Civil Rights Act of 1875 and soundly rejected by Congress. When the argument was revived by the Court in *Plessy*, Justice Harlan suggested it was deeply untruthful. It is hard to take seriously the majority's assertion. Yet even after one concludes that stigma is not wholly subjective, how should it be ascertained by a court? And is stigma alone a cognizable injury under the Equal Protection Clause? Is the Constitution, as Justice Harlan argues, "color blind"?

2. To support racial segregation in law, the Court appealed to "the established usages, customs, and traditions of the people . . . with a view to the promotion of their comfort, and the preservation of the public peace and good order." But Jim Crow laws were actually of recent vintage. It was only in 1877 that the political program of Reconstruction had been largely abandoned as a result of political compromises that resolved the extraordinarily close and hotly disputed Tilden–Hayes presidential election contest of 1876. And only following the end of Reconstruction was there widespread racial segregation in law:

The first major wave of segregation legislation did not occur until the 1880s. The first genuine Jim Crow law requiring segregation of all railroad facilities was passed by Florida in 1887, followed by Mississippi in 1888 and Texas in 1889. The Louisiana statute upheld in *Plessy v. Ferguson* was passed in 1890. By 1900, a rigid system of legally enforced segregation and subordination dominated all aspects of race relations throughout the South. The Compromise of 1877 marked not just a legal revolution, but a social revolution. It transformed the way the people of the South conducted their governments, exercised their legal rights, and lived their lives. It was accompanied by corroborating ideological shifts in science, literature, journalism, history, and religion. Far more than the Fourteenth Amendment, the Compromise of 1877 created a far-reaching and long-persisting constitutional regime: the regime of Jim Crow.

Michael W. McConnell, *The Forgotten Constitutional Moment*, 11 Const. Comm. 115, 132–133 (1994). It is difficult to discount the influence of this social, political, and cultural transformation as a factor explaining the difference between the spirit that animated the drafters of the Fourteenth Amendment, the Civil Rights Act of 1866, and the Civil Rights Act of 1875 and that animating *Plessy* in 1896. *Plessy*—and the laws it upheld—represented modern politics and the new social consensus.

3. We have not edited out the embarrassing features of Justice Harlan's (otherwise) celebrated dissent. Justice Harlan argues against the segregation of blacks and whites by appealing to racial prejudice against those of Chinese descent. He, too, appears to be a prisoner of the common social perceptions, the intuitions of his age. Does this affect how you think about constitutional interpretation? Should constitutional interpretation reflect the moral values of the justices—but those should just be better moral values than the ones of the majority in *Plessy*? Or is giving free play to moral intuitions just as likely to produce bad results as good ones? (Here is a question that is impossible to answer: which of your moral values are so conditioned by your social context that you do not even recognize how wrong they are?) Justice Harlan was the author of the majority opinion in the next case, decided three years after *Plessy*.

Cumming v. Board of Education

175 U.S. 528 (1899)

The plaintiffs in error, Cumming, Harper, and Ladeveze, citizens of Georgia and persons of color, suing on behalf of themselves and all others in like case joining with them, brought this action against the Board of Education of Richmond County. . . .

In the petition filed by them it was alleged . . . that they were persons of color and parents of children of school age lawfully entitled to the full benefit of any system of high schools organized or maintained by the Board; that up to the time of the said tax levy and for many years continuously prior thereto, the Board maintained a system of high schools in Richmond County in which the colored school population had the same educational advantages as the white school population, but on July 10, 1897, it withdrew from and denied to the colored school population any participation in the educational facilities of a high school system in the county, and had voted to continue to deny to that population any admission to or participation in such educational facilities; and that at the time of such withdrawal and denial the petitioners respectively had children attending the colored high school then existing, but who were now debarred from participation in the benefits of a public high school education though petitioners were being taxed therefor. . . .

■ MR. JUSTICE HARLAN, after stating the facts as above, delivered the opinion of the court.

This writ of error brings up for review a final order . . . in conformity to a judgment rendered in the Supreme Court of [Georgia]. That order, it is contended, deprived the plaintiffs in error of rights secured to them by the Fourteenth Amendment to the Constitution of the United States.

The Supreme Court of Georgia, after stating in its opinion that counsel for the petitioners did not point out in his brief what particular paragraph of the Fourteenth Amendment was violated, said: ". . . In our opinion, it is impracticable to distribute taxes equally. The appropriation of a portion of the taxes for a white girls' high school is not more discrimination against these colored plaintiffs than it is against many white people in the county. A taxpayer who has boys and no girls of a school age has as much right to complain of the unequal distribution of the taxes to a girls' high school as have these plaintiffs. The action of the Board appears to us to be more a discrimination as to sex than it does as to race. While the Board appropriates some money to assist a denominational school for white boys and girls, it has never established a high school for white boys, and, if the contention of these plaintiffs is correct, white parents who have boys old enough to attend a high school have as much right to complain as these plaintiffs, if they have not more. Without, therefore, going into an analysis of the different clauses of the Fourteenth Amendment of the Constitution of the United States, we content ourselves by saying that, in our opinion, the action of the Board did not violate any of the provisions of that amendment. It does not abridge the privileges or immunities of citizens of the United States, nor does it deprive any person of life, liberty, or property without due process of law, nor does it deny to any person within the state the equal protection of its laws."

The constitution of Georgia provides: "There shall be a thorough system of common schools for the education of children in the elementary branches of an English education only, as nearly uniform as practicable, the expenses of which shall be provided for by taxation, or otherwise. The schools shall be free to all children of the state, but separate schools shall be provided for the white and colored races." Art. 8, § 1.

It was said at the argument that the vice in the common school system of Georgia was the requirement that the white and colored children of the State be educated in separate schools. But we need not consider that question in this case. No such issue was made in the pleadings. Indeed, the plaintiffs distinctly state that they have no objection to the tax in question so far as levied for the support of primary, intermediate and grammar schools, in the management of which the rule as to the separation of races is enforced. We must dispose of the case as it is presented by the record.

The plaintiffs in error complain that the Board of Education used the funds in its hands to assist in maintaining a high school for white children without providing a similar school for colored children. The substantial relief asked is an injunction that would either impair the efficiency of the high school provided for white children or compel the Board to close it. But if that were done, the result would only be to take from white children educational privileges enjoyed by them, without giving to colored children additional opportunities for the education furnished in high schools. The colored school children of the county would not be advanced in the matter of their education by a decree compelling the defendant Board to cease giving support to a high school for white children. The Board had before it the question whether it should maintain, under its control, a high school for about sixty colored children or withhold the benefits of education in primary schools from three hundred children of the same race. It was impossible, the board believed, to give educational facilities to the three hundred colored children who were unprovided for, if it maintained a separate school for the sixty children who wished to have a high school education. Its decision was in the interest of the greater number of colored children, leaving the smaller number to obtain a high school education in existing private institutions at an expense not beyond that incurred in the high school discontinued by the Board.

We are not permitted by the evidence in the record to regard that decision as having been made with any desire or purpose on the part of the Board to discriminate against any of the colored school children of the county on account of their race. But if it be assumed that the Board erred in supposing that its duty was to provide educational facilities for the three hundred colored children who were without an opportunity in primary schools to learn the alphabet and to read and write, rather than to maintain a school for the benefit of the sixty colored children who wished to attend a high school, that was not an error which a court of equity should attempt to remedy by an injunction that would compel the board to withhold all assistance from the high school maintained for white children. If, in some appropriate proceeding instituted directly for that purpose, the plaintiffs had sought to compel the Board of Education, out of the funds in its hands or under its control, to establish and maintain a high school for colored children, and if it appeared that the Board's refusal to maintain such a school was in fact an abuse of its discretion and in hostility to the colored population because of their race, different questions might have arisen in the state court.

The state court did not deem the action of the Board of Education in suspending temporarily and for economic reasons the high school for colored children a sufficient reason why the defendant should be restrained by injunction from maintaining an existing high school for white children. It rejected the suggestion that the Board proceeded in bad faith or had abused the discretion with which it was invested by the statute under which it proceeded or had acted in hostility to the colored race. Under the circumstances disclosed, we cannot say that this action of the state court was, within the meaning of the Fourteenth Amendment, a denial by the State to the plaintiffs and to those associated with them of the equal protection of the laws or of any privileges belonging to them as citizens of the United States. We may add that while all admit that the benefits and burdens of public taxation must be shared by citizens without discrimination against any class on account of their race, the education of the people in schools maintained by state taxation is a matter belonging to the respective States, and any interference on the part of Federal authority with the management of such schools cannot be justified except in the case of a clear and unmistakable disregard of rights secured by the supreme law of the land. We have here no such case to be determined; and . . . this view disposes of the only question which this court has jurisdiction to review and decide.

NOTES

1. Does providing a high school education to (some) white children but not to any black children violate the Equal Protection Clause? Wouldn't that even violate the separate-but-equal rule of *Plessy*? If so, what is the appropriate remedy? If there were actually financial constraints on the board's ability to provide schools for all, should the Court have granted an injunction shutting down the all-white girls' high school? Wouldn't that have achieved equal treatment, at least? What does the majority see as wrong with that remedy?

2. Courts of equity have traditionally had broad discretion to fashion a remedy that is appropriate for the particular case. Equitable remedies include the one you are most familiar with, the injunction, but also include the appointment of a receiver to manage a complex organization (such as a hospital, prison, or school), the imposition of a constructive trust to ensure that a fund of money is used for its rightful beneficiaries, and even a writ of sequestration authorizing the seizure and sale of assets in order to comply with a court of equity's decree. What remedy should the Court have given here?

3. Does maintaining a high school for white girls but no high school for white *boys* violate the Equal Protection Clause? Imagine a different scenario: that the board had offered a high school education for all children but maintained separate-sex public high schools. Would that have violated the Equal Protection Clause? (Sex discrimination will be considered more later in this chapter.)

Giles v. Harris
189 U.S. 475 (1903)

■ MR. JUSTICE HOLMES delivered the opinion of the court:

This is a bill in equity brought by a colored man on behalf of himself "and on behalf of more than five thousand negroes, citizens of the county of Montgomery, Alabama, similarly situated and circumstanced as himself," against the board of registrars of that county. The prayer of the bill is in substance that the defendants may be required to enroll upon the voting lists the name of the plaintiff and of all other qualified members of his race who applied for registration before August 1, 1902, and were refused, and that certain sections of the Constitution of Alabama may be declared contrary to the 14th and 15th Amendments of the Constitution of the United States, and void.

The allegations of the bill may be summed up as follows: The plaintiff is subject to none of the disqualifications set forth in the Constitution of Alabama and is entitled to vote—entitled, as the bill plainly means, under the Constitution as it is. He applied in March, 1902, for registration as a voter, and was refused arbitrarily on the ground of his color, together with large numbers of other duly qualified negroes, while all white men were registered. The same thing was done all over the State. Under § 187 of article 8 of the Alabama Constitution, persons registered before January 1, 1903, remain electors for life unless they become disqualified by certain crimes, etc., while after that date severer tests come into play which would exclude, perhaps, a large part of the black race. Therefore by the refusal the plaintiff and the other negroes excluded were deprived, not only of their vote at an election which has taken place since the bill was filed, but of the permanent advantage incident to registration before 1903. The white men generally are registered for good under the easy test, and the black men are likely to be kept out in the future as in the past. This refusal to register the blacks was part of a general scheme to disfranchise them, to which the defendants and the State itself, according to the bill, were parties. The defendants accepted their office for the purpose of carrying out the scheme. The part taken by the State, that is, by the white population which framed the Constitution, consisted in shaping that instrument so as to give opportunity and effect to the wholesale fraud which has been practiced.

... By § 181, after January 1, 1903, only the following persons are entitled to register: First. Those who can read and write any article of the Constitution of the United States in the English language, and who either are physically unable to work or have been regularly engaged in some lawful business for the greater part of the last twelve months, and those who are unable to read and write solely because physically disabled. Second. Owners or husbands of owners of 40 acres of land in the state, upon which they reside, and owners or husbands of owners of real or personal estate in the state assessed for taxation at $300 or more, if the taxes have been paid, unless under contest. By § 183 only persons qualified as electors can take part in any method of party action. ... This, in brief, is the system which the plaintiff asks to have declared void.

Perhaps it should be added to the foregoing statement that the bill was filed in September, 1902, and alleged the plaintiff's desire to vote at an election coming off in November. This election has gone by, so that it is impossible to give specific relief with regard to that. But we are not prepared to dismiss the bill or the appeal on that ground, because to be enabled to cast a vote in that election is not ... the whole object of the bill. It is not even the principal object of the relief sought by the plaintiff. The principal object of that is to obtain the permanent advantages of registration as of a date before 1903. ...

It seems to us impossible to grant the equitable relief which is asked. ... The traditional limits of proceedings in equity have not embraced a remedy for political wrongs. But we cannot forget that we are dealing with a new and extraordinary situation, and we are unwilling to stop short of the final considerations which seem to us to dispose of the case.

The difficulties which we cannot overcome are two, and the first is this: The plaintiff alleges that the whole registration scheme of the Alabama Constitution is a fraud upon the Constitution of the United States, and asks us to declare it void. But, of course, he could not maintain a bill for a mere declaration in the air. He does not try to do so, but asks to be registered as a party qualified under the void instrument. If, then, we accept the conclusion which it is the chief purpose of the bill to maintain, how can we make the court a party to the unlawful scheme by accepting it and adding another voter to its fraudulent lists? If a white man came here on the same general allegations, admitting his sympathy with the plan, but alleging some special prejudice that had kept him off the list, we hardly should think it necessary to meet him with a reasoned answer. But the relief cannot be varied because we think that in the future the particular plaintiff is likely to try to overthrow the scheme. If we accept the plaintiff's allegations for the purposes of his case, he cannot complain. We must accept or reject them. It is impossible simply to shut our eyes, put the plaintiff on the lists, be they honest or fraudulent, and leave the determination of the fundamental question for the future. If we have an opinion that the bill is right on its face, or if we are undecided, we are not at liberty to assume it to be wrong for the purposes of decision. It seems to us that unless we are prepared to say that it is wrong, that all its principal allegations are immaterial, and that the registration plan of the Alabama Constitution is valid, we cannot order the plaintiff's name to be registered. It is not an answer to say that if all the blacks who are qualified according to the letter of the instrument were registered, the fraud would be cured. In the first place, there is no probability that any way now is open by which more than a few could be registered; but, if all could be, the difficulty would not be overcome. If the sections of the Constitution concerning registration were illegal in their inception, it would be a new doctrine in constitutional law that the original invalidity could be cured by an administration which defeated their intent. We express no opinion as to the alleged fact of their unconstitutionality beyond saying that we are not willing to assume that they are valid, in the face of the allegations and main object of the bill, for the purpose of granting the relief which it was necessary to pray in order that that object should be secured.

The other difficulty is of a different sort, and strikingly reinforces the argument that equity cannot undertake now, any more than it has in the past, to enforce political rights. . . . In determining whether a court of equity can take jurisdiction, one of the first questions is what it can do to enforce any order that it may make. This is alleged to be the conspiracy of a State, although the State is not and could not be made a party to the bill. The circuit court has no constitutional power to control its action by any direct means. And if we leave the state out of consideration, the court has as little practical power to deal with the people of the state in a body. The bill imports that the great mass of the white population intends to keep the blacks from voting. To meet such an intent something more than ordering the plaintiff's name to be inscribed upon the lists of 1902 will be needed. If the conspiracy and the intent exist, a name on a piece of paper will not defeat them. Unless we are prepared to supervise the voting in that State by officers of the court, it seems to us that all that the plaintiff could get from equity would be an empty form. Apart from damages to the individual, relief from a great political wrong, if done, as alleged, by the people of a state and the state itself, must be given by them or by the legislative and political department of the government of the United States.

■ [The dissenting opinions of JUSTICES HARLAN and BREWER are omitted.]

NOTES

1. Given the procedural posture of the case, the Court in *Giles* accepts the plaintiffs' allegations as true and proceeds on that premise. It denies relief on two grounds: first, that ordering the relief sought would merely further the alleged fraudulent overall scheme by increasing voter participation in it; and second, that the Court was essentially powerless to remedy the alleged fraud because of its size and the difficulty of fashioning relief without the courts essentially taking over the management of elections in Alabama. What arguments would you raise against these propositions? Can a fraud be "too big to fail" under the Constitution? Was the Court abdicating the enforcement of constitutional rights? The effect of the decision could hardly have been more momentous—as one scholar has put it, "*Giles* permit[ted] the virtual elimination of black citizens from political participation in the South." Richard H. Pildes, *Democracy, Anti–Democracy, and the Canon*, 17 Const. Comm. 295, 297 (2000).

What should the Court have done instead? What remedy should it have been willing to grant after trial? (Recall in this connection the equitable remedies mentioned in Note 2 after *Cumming v. Board of Education*.)

2. The author of *Giles* was Justice Oliver Wendell Holmes, Jr. You have read excerpts from a few opinions already in this book, including *Schenck* and *Debs*, which rejected First Amendment claims and upheld convictions for anti-war speeches. You will read more Holmes opinions later in this chapter, including not only his dissent in *Lochner* but also his opinion for the Court upholding the involuntary sterilization of the mentally retarded in *Buck v. Bell*. Holmes was undoubtedly a brilliant writer and aphorist, but given the content of his opinions, does he deserve his fame as one of the great Supreme Court justices of all time? For a reconsideration of Holmes's influence on the law, see Albert W. Alschuler, LAW WITHOUT VALUES: THE LIFE, WORK, AND LEGACY OF JUSTICE HOLMES (2002).

Berea College v. Kentucky
211 U.S. 45 (1908)

On October 8, 1904, the grand jury of Madison County, Kentucky, presented in the Circuit Court of that county an indictment, charging:

"The said Berea College, being a corporation duly incorporated under the laws of the state of Kentucky, and owning, maintaining, and operating a college, school, and institution of learning, known as 'Berea College,' located in the town of Berea, Madison county, Kentucky, did unlawfully and wilfully permit and receive both the white and negro races as pupils for instruction in said college, school, and institution of learning."

This indictment was found under an act of March 22, 1904, whose first section reads:

SEC. 1. That it shall be unlawful for any person, corporation, or association of persons to maintain or operate any college, school, or institution where persons of the white and negro races are both received as pupils for instruction, and any person or corporation who shall operate or maintain any such college, school, or institution shall be fined $1,000, and any person or corporation who may be convicted of violating the provisions of this act shall be fined $100 for each day they may operate said school, college, or institution after such conviction.

On a trial the defendant was found guilty and sentenced to pay a fine of one thousand dollars. . . .

■ MR. JUSTICE BREWER, after making the foregoing statement, delivered the opinion of the court.

There is no dispute as to the facts. That the act does not violate the Constitution of Kentucky is settled by the decision of its highest court, and the single question for our consideration is whether it conflicts with the Federal Constitution. . . .

In creating a corporation a State may withhold powers which may be exercised by and cannot be denied to an individual. It is under no obligation to treat both alike. In granting corporate powers the legislature may deem that the best interests of the State would be subserved by some restriction, and the corporation may not plead that, in spite of the restriction, it has more or greater powers because the citizen has. . . .

[I]t is unnecessary for us to consider anything more than the question of its validity as applied to corporations. The statute is clearly separable and may be valid as to one class while invalid as to another. Even if it were conceded that its assertion of power over individuals cannot be sustained, still it must be upheld so far as it restrains corporations.

There is no force in the suggestion that the statute, although clearly separable, must stand or fall as an entirety on the ground the legislature would not have enacted one part unless it could reach all. That the legislature of Kentucky desired to separate the teaching of white and colored children may be conceded; but it by no means follows that it would not have enforced the separation so far as it could do so, even though it could not make it effective under all circumstances. In other words, it is not at all unreasonable to believe that the legislature, although advised beforehand of the constitutional question, might have prohibited all organizations and corporations under its control from teaching white and colored children together. . . .

[The defendant] Berea College was organized under the authority of an act for the incorporation of voluntary associations. . . .

[I]t is settled "that a power reserved to the legislature to alter, amend, or repeal a charter authorizes it to make any alteration or amendment of a charter granted subject to it, which will not defeat or substantially impair the object of the grant, or any rights vested under it, and which the legislature may deem necessary to secure either that object or any public right."

Construing the statute, the Court of Appeals held that "if the same school taught the different races at different times, though at the same place, or at different times at the same place, it would not be unlawful." Now, an amendment to the original charter, which does not destroy the power of the college to furnish education to all persons, but which simply separates them by time or place of instruction, cannot be said to "defeat or substantially impair the object of the grant." The language of the statute is not in terms an amendment, yet its effect is an amendment, and it would be resting too much on mere form to hold that a statute which in effect works a change in the terms of the charter is not to be considered as an amendment, because not so designated. The act itself, being separable, is to be read as though it, in one section, prohibited any person, in another section any corporation and, in a third, any association of persons to do the acts named. Reading the statute as containing a separate prohibition on all corporations, at least, all state corporations, it substantially declares that any authority given by previous charters to instruct the two races at the same time and in the same place is forbidden, and that prohibition, being a departure from the terms of the original charter in this case, may properly be adjudged an amendment. . . .

We need concern ourselves only with the inquiry whether the first section can be upheld as coming within the power of a State over its own corporate creatures.

We are of opinion, for reasons stated, that it does come within that power.

■ MR. JUSTICE HOLMES and MR. JUSTICE MOODY concur in the judgment.

■ MR. JUSTICE HARLAN, dissenting:

This prosecution arises under the first section of an act of the General Assembly of Kentucky, approved March 22, 1904. The purpose and scope of the act is clearly indicated by its title. It is "An act to prohibit white and colored persons from attending the same school."

It is well to give here the entire statute, as follows:

SEC. 1. That it shall be unlawful for any person, corporation, or association of persons to maintain or operate any college, school, or institution where persons of the white and negro races are both received as pupils for instruction; and any person or corporation who shall operate or maintain any such college, school, or institution shall be fined $1,000, and any person or corporation who may be convicted of violating the provisions of this act shall be fined $100 for each day they may operate said school, college, or institution after such conviction.

SEC. 2. That any instructor who shall teach in any school, college, or institution where members of said two races are received as pupils for instruction shall be guilty of operating and maintaining same and fined as provided in the 1st section hereof.

SEC. 3. It shall be unlawful for any white person to attend any school or institution where negroes are received as pupils or receive instruction, and it shall be unlawful for any negro or colored person to attend any school or institution where white persons are received as pupils or receive instruction. Any person so offending shall be fined $50 for each day he attends such institution or school: *Provided*, That the provisions of this law shall not apply to any penal institution or house of reform.

SEC. 4. Nothing in this act shall be construed to prevent any private school, college, or institution of learning from maintaining a separate and distinct branch thereof, in a different locality, not less than 25 miles distant, for the education exclusively of one race or color.

SEC. 5. This act shall not take effect, or be in operation, before the 15th day of July, 1904.

The plaintiff in error, Berea College, is an incorporation, organized under the General Laws of Kentucky in 1859. Its original articles of incorporation set forth that the object of the founders was to establish and maintain an institution of learning, "in order to promote the cause of Christ." . . .

In 1904 the college was charged in a Kentucky state court with having unlawfully and willfully received both white and negro persons as pupils for instruction. . . . [A] trial was had which resulted in a verdict of guilty and the imposition of a fine of $1,000 on the college. The trial court refused an instruction asked by the defendant, to the effect that the statute was in violation of the Fourteenth Amendment of the Constitution of the United States. . . .

The state court . . . held it to be entirely competent for the State to adopt the policy of the separation of the races, even in private schools, and concluded its opinion in these words: "The right to teach white and negro children in a private school at the same time and place is not a property right." The state court (but without any discussion whatever) added, as if merely incidental to or a make-weight in the decision of the pivotal question, in this case, these words: "Besides, appellant, as a *corporation* created by this State, has no natural right to teach at all. Its right to teach is such as the State sees fit to give to it. The State may withhold it altogether or qualify it." It concluded: "We do not think the act is in conflict with the Federal Constitution."

Upon a review of the judgment below this court says that the statute is "clearly separable, and may be valid as to one class, while invalid as to another;" that "even if it were conceded that its assertion of power over individuals cannot be sustained, still the statute must be upheld so far as it restrains corporations." "It is unnecessary," this court says, "for us to consider anything more than the question of its validity *as applied to corporations. . . .* We need concern ourselves only with the inquiry whether the first section can be upheld as coming within the power of a State over its own *corporate* creatures." The judgment of the state court is now affirmed, and thereby left in full force, so far as Kentucky and its courts are concerned, although such judgment rests in part upon the ground that the statute is not, in any particular, in violation of any rights secured by the Federal Constitution. In so ruling, it must necessarily have been assumed by this court that the legislature may have regarded the teaching of white and colored pupils at the same time and in the same school or institution, when maintained by private individuals and associations, as wholly different in its results from such teaching when conducted by the same individuals acting under the authority of or representing a corporation. But, looking at the nature or subject of the legislation, it is inconceivable that the legislature consciously regarded the subject in that light. It is absolutely certain that the legislature had in mind to prohibit the teaching of the two races in the same private institution, at the same time, by whomsoever that institution was conducted. It is a reflection upon the common sense of legislators to suppose that they might have prohibited a private *corporation* from teaching by its agents, and yet left individuals and unincorporated associations entirely at liberty, by the same instructors, to teach the two races in the same institution at the same time. It was the teaching of pupils of the two races *together*, or in the same school, no matter by whom or under whose authority, which the legislature sought to prevent. The manifest purpose was to prevent the association of white and colored persons in the same school. That such was its intention is evident from the title of the act, which, as we have seen, was "to prohibit white and colored persons from attending the same school." . . .

Undoubtedly, the general rule is that one part of a statute may be stricken down as unconstitutional and another part, distinctly separable and valid, left in force. But that general rule cannot control the decision of this case. . . .

Now, can it for a moment be doubted that the legislature intended all the sections of the statute in question to be looked at, and that the purpose was to forbid the teaching of pupils of the two races together in the same institution, at the same time, *whether the teachers represented natural persons or corporations?* Can it be said that the legislature would have prohibited such teaching by corporations, and yet consciously permitted the teaching by private individuals or unincorporated associations? Are we to attribute such folly to legislators? Who can say that the legislature would have enacted one provision without the other? If not, then, in determining the intent of the legislature, the provisions of the statute relating to the teaching of the two races together by *corporations* cannot be separated in its operation from those in the same section that forbid such teaching by individuals and unincorporated associations. Therefore the court cannot, as I think, properly forbear to consider the validity of the provisions that refer

to teachers who do not represent corporations. If those provisions constitute, as, in my judgment, they, do, an essential part of the legislative
scheme or policy, and are invalid, then, under the authorities cited, the
whole act must fall. The provision as to corporations may be valid, and yet
the other clauses may be so inseparably connected with that provision and
the policy underlying it, that the validity of all the clauses necessary to effectuate the legislative intent must be considered. There is no magic in the
fact of incorporation which will so transform the act of teaching the two
races in the same school at the same time that such teaching can be
deemed lawful when conducted by private individuals, but unlawful when
conducted by the representatives of corporations.

There is another line of thought. The state court evidently regarded it
as necessary to consider the entire act; for it adjudged it to be competent for
the State to forbid *all* teaching of the two races together, in the same institution, at the same time, no matter by whom the teaching was done. The
reference at the close of its opinion, in the words above quoted, to the fact
that the defendant was a corporation, which could be controlled as the
State saw fit, was, as already suggested, only incidental to the main question determined by the court as to the extent to which the State could control the teaching of the two races in the same institution. The state court
upheld the authority of the State, under its general police power, to forbid
the association of the two races in the same institution of learning. . . .

In my judgment the court should directly meet and decide the broad
question presented by the statute. It should adjudge whether the statute,
as a whole, is or is not unconstitutional, in that it makes it a crime against
the State to maintain or operate a private institution of learning where
white and black pupils are received, at the same time, for instruction. In
the view which I have as to my duty I feel obliged to express my opinion as
to the validity of the act as a whole. I am of opinion that in its essential
parts the statute is an arbitrary invasion of the rights of liberty and property guaranteed by the Fourteenth Amendment against hostile state action
and is, therefore, void.

The capacity to impart instruction to others is given by the Almighty
for beneficent purposes and its use may not be forbidden or interfered with
by Government—certainly not, unless such instruction is, in its nature,
harmful to the public morals or imperils the public safety. The right to impart instruction . . . is, beyond question, part of one's liberty as guaranteed
against hostile state action by the Constitution of the United States. . . . If
pupils, of whatever race—certainly, if they be citizens—choose with the
consent of their parents or voluntarily to sit together in a private institution of learning while receiving instruction which is not in its nature harmful or dangerous to the public, no government, whether Federal or state,
can legally forbid their coming together, or being together temporarily, for
such an innocent purpose. If the Commonwealth of Kentucky can make it a
crime to teach white and colored children together at the same time, in a
private institution of learning, it is difficult to perceive why it may not forbid the assembling of white and colored children in the same Sabbath-
school, for the purpose of being instructed in the Word of God, although
such teaching may be done under the authority of the church to which the
school is attached as well as with the consent of the parents of the children.
So, if the state court be right, white and colored children may even be forbidden to sit together in a house of worship or at a communion table in the
same Christian church. In the cases supposed there would be the same as-

sociation of white and colored persons as would occur when pupils of the two races sit together in a private institution of learning for the purpose of receiving instruction in purely secular matters. Will it be said that the cases supposed and the case here in hand are different in that no government, in this country, can lay unholy hands on the religious faith of the people? The answer to this suggestion is that in the eye of the law the right to enjoy one's religious belief, unmolested by any human power, is no more sacred nor more fully or distinctly recognized than is the right to impart and receive instruction not harmful to the public. The denial of either right would be an infringement of the liberty inherent in the freedom secured by the fundamental law. . . . Have we become so inoculated with prejudice of race that an American government, professedly based on the principles of freedom, and charged with the protection of all citizens alike, can make distinctions between such citizens in the matter of their voluntary meeting for innocent purposes simply because of their respective races? Further, if the lower court be right, then a State may make it a crime for white and colored persons to frequent the same market places at the same time, or appear in an assemblage of citizens convened to consider questions of a public or political nature, in which all citizens, without regard to race, are equally interested. Many other illustrations might be given to show the mischievous, not to say cruel, character of the statute in question, and how inconsistent such legislation is with the great principle of the equality of citizens before the law.

Of course, what I have said has no reference to regulations prescribed for public schools, established at the pleasure of the State and maintained at the public expense. No such question is here presented and it need not be now discussed. My observations have reference to the case before the court, and only to the provision of the statute making it a crime for any person to impart harmless instruction to white and colored pupils together, at the same time, in the same private institution of learning. That provision is, in my opinion, made an essential element in the policy of the statute, and, if regard be had to the object and purpose of this legislation, it cannot be treated as separable nor intended to be separated from the provisions relating to corporations. The whole statute should therefore be held void; otherwise, it will be taken as the law of Kentucky, to be enforced by its courts, that the teaching of white and black pupils, at the same time, even in a *private* institution, is a crime against that Commonwealth, punishable by fine and imprisonment. . . .

■ MR. JUSTICE DAY also dissents.

NOTES

1. Take a moment to untangle the majority's rationale (and the dissent's objection) in *Berea College*: the Court upheld Kentucky's mandatory segregated-education law, as applied to private schools organized as "corporations," on the ground that states have plenary power to amend corporate charters they have granted. (Recall how Justice Harlan, in *The Civil Rights Cases*, considered that the grant of a corporate charter or license to operate a railroad, inn, or place of amusement made the grantee a state actor.) The *Berea College* majority purported not to address the application of the statute to individuals and "associations." In his blistering dissent, Justice Harlan thought that this was a ridiculous distinction and that, on the merits, the entire statute should be held unconstitutional.

2. What was Justice Harlan's argument on the merits? In his view, what provision of the Constitution did Kentucky's law violate? During the *Plessy* era, the Supreme Court had a tendency to view all issues of state regulation of businesses and other private activities through the lens of the Due Process Clause, asking whether the law at issue impaired rights of "liberty" or "property." The leading case in this now-discredited line was *Lochner v. New York*, 198 U.S. 45 (1905), which you will read later in this chapter. *Berea College* (1908) was decided just three years later, while the Court was still pursuing *Lochner*-style substantive due process. One can hear echoes of this in Justice Harlan's dissent in *Berea College*. But he appears to ground his objection more specifically in the themes of the First Amendment—the freedoms of religion, speech, and association. In 1908, the Court had not yet held that the Fourteenth Amendment made most of the provisions of the Bill of Rights applicable to state government action, and so his opinion speaks in the general "liberty" idiom of the day. Would his dissent be better understood today in terms of the proposition that the government cannot force a religious college to engage in racial segregation because of its First Amendment rights to free exercise of religion, freedom of speech, and freedom of association?

3. Assuming the applicability of the Bill of Rights to actions of state governments, how would you argue this case on behalf of Berea College?

4. Now turn the factual scenario inside out—always a good test of whether your legal argument is principled rather than result-driven. Imagine a religious college that practices not racial integration but racial *segregation* as a matter of asserted religious belief, but that the law now forbids racial segregation, even by private organizations. May the government prohibit, or punish, the college's practice? Or would that violate the college's rights to free exercise of religion, freedom of speech, and freedom of association? The case is drawn from a real one: *Bob Jones University v. United States*, 461 U.S. 574 (1983). The federal government withdrew the tax-exempt status of a religious university because of its racially discriminatory practices. In the Supreme Court, the religious university lost. Is this case different in any principled way from *Berea College*?

5. Did Kentucky's law violate the Equal Protection Clause? Whose equal protection rights were violated? The students'? Both white *and* black students? The school's? Should one party, in defense of its own legal position, have standing to raise someone else's asserted constitutional rights? See *Pierce v. Society of Sisters*, 268 U.S. 510 (1925) (allowing a private religious school to have standing to raise the asserted constitutional rights of its students and their parents, as well as its own rights). For more discussion of the doctrine of standing, see Chapter 3.

6. The racial attitudes the justices manifested in *Plessy, Cumming, Giles,* and *Berea College* can also be seen in other contemporaneous doctrines. For example, in *The Insular Cases*, 182 U.S. 1 (1901), the Court held that the Constitution does not apply, in all its particulars, to U.S. territories populated "by alien races, differing from us in religion, customs, laws, methods of taxation, and modes of thought." For critique, see Gary Lawson & Guy Seidman, THE CONSTITUTION OF EMPIRE: TERRITORIAL EXPANSION AND AMERICAN LEGAL HISTORY 194–201 (2004). In *Elk v. Wilkins*, 112 U.S. 94 (1884), the Court held that the members of "Indian tribes" were not covered by the Citizenship Clause of the Fourteenth Amendment, because they were "not subject to the jurisdiction" of the United States within the meaning of that clause. (Justice Harlan dis-

sented.) Yet only two years later the Court also held that Indian tribes were subject to the "plenary power" of Congress. *United States v. Kagama*, 118 U.S. 375 (1886). It was not until 1924 that Native American members of Indian tribes were granted U.S. citizenship by statute.

[Assignment 63]

B. THE DESEGREGATION CASES

In a deftly planned series of cases, the NAACP, led by Thurgood Marshall, took on *Plessy*'s "separate but equal" doctrine, eroding it in one context after another until it was eventually reconsidered by the Supreme Court in *Brown v. Board of Education*, 347 U.S. 483 (1954). *Brown* is without doubt one of the most significant decisions of U.S. constitutional history. It did not (quite) overrule *Plessy*, but it unanimously consigned *Plessy* to oblivion. It did not (quite) embrace the position of Justice Harlan's dissent in *Plessy*, but it came close to adopting a flat rule that the Equal Protection Clause forbids the government from classifying, segregating, or distinguishing persons—for any purpose—on the basis of their race. *Brown* declared "separate but equal" a violation of the Equal Protection Clause in one context, public education. In its wake, courts struck down racial segregation across the board in cases ranging from golf courses to transportation to swimming pools to marriage. In short, *Brown* restored the constitutional guarantee of equal protection of the laws to the place it had held at the close of Reconstruction, as illustrated by *Strauder*, and repudiated the era of betrayal of this constitutional vision exemplified by *Plessy, Giles,* and *Berea College*.

Here you will read *Brown*, as well as a companion case addressing segregation in the District of Columbia schools, *Bolling v. Sharpe*; the successor to *Brown* that considered the question of remedy, "*Brown II*"; and a lower court decision that anticipated *Brown*'s extension to segregated transportation, *Browder v. Gayle*. Next you will read an important decision a dozen years after *Brown, Loving v. Virginia,* invalidating state "antimiscegenation" laws forbidding marriage between blacks and whites—a variation on *Brown*'s theme that the Equal Protection Clause forbids segregation by law designed for racial subordination. Finally, you will read *Washington v. Davis*, which raises the question whether the clause forbids only laws that explicitly classify on the basis of race or also ones that produce a disparate impact along racial lines.

These cases present important questions not only about the substance of constitutional rights but also about the practice of constitutional interpretation: What is the meaning of the constitutional guarantee of "equal protection of the laws"? What was the original understanding about whether that guarantee forbade segregation in education? What place should that understanding have in constitutional interpretation? What criteria should a court use in interpreting open-ended or vague constitutional language? Does such language mean that the judiciary has more freedom to adopt what it considers the best understanding? Or does it suggest the opposite— that courts should defer to democratic choices unless the text gives a contrary rule with sufficient specificity? What place should be given in constitutional interpretation to longstanding judicial precedent and social practice? When there is a constitutional violation, what should courts consider when choosing and fashioning the remedy? And are the Supreme Court's interpretations of the Constitution supreme over those of all other political and governmental actors in our constitutional system?

Brown v. Board of Education (Brown I)

347 U.S. 483 (1954)

■ Mr. Chief Justice Warren delivered the opinion of the Court.

These cases come to us from the States of Kansas, South Carolina, Virginia, and Delaware. They are premised on different facts and different local conditions, but a common legal question justifies their consideration together in this consolidated opinion.

In each of the cases, minors of the Negro race, through their legal representatives, seek the aid of the courts in obtaining admission to the public schools of their community on a nonsegregated basis. In each instance, they have been denied admission to schools attended by white children under laws requiring or permitting segregation according to race. This segregation was alleged to deprive the plaintiffs of the equal protection of the laws under the Fourteenth Amendment. In each of the cases other than the Delaware case, a three-judge federal district court denied relief to the plaintiffs on the so-called "separate but equal" doctrine announced by this Court in *Plessy v. Ferguson*, 163 U.S. 537. Under that doctrine, equality of treatment is accorded when the races are provided substantially equal facilities, even though these facilities be separate. In the Delaware case, the Supreme Court of Delaware adhered to that doctrine, but ordered that the plaintiffs be admitted to the white schools because of their superiority to the Negro schools.

The plaintiffs contend that segregated public schools are not "equal" and cannot be made "equal," and that hence they are deprived of the equal protection of the laws. Because of the obvious importance of the question presented, the Court took jurisdiction. Argument was heard in the 1952 Term, and reargument was heard this Term on certain questions propounded by the Court.

Reargument was largely devoted to the circumstances surrounding the adoption of the Fourteenth Amendment in 1868. It covered exhaustively consideration of the Amendment in Congress, ratification by the states, then existing practices in racial segregation, and the views of proponents and opponents of the Amendment. This discussion and our own investigation convince us that, although these sources cast some light, it is not enough to resolve the problem with which we are faced. At best, they are inconclusive. The most avid proponents of the post-War Amendments undoubtedly intended them to remove all legal distinctions among "all persons born or naturalized in the United States." Their opponents, just as certainly, were antagonistic to both the letter and the spirit of the Amendments and wished them to have the most limited effect. What others in Congress and the state legislatures had in mind cannot be determined with any degree of certainty.

An additional reason for the inconclusive nature of the Amendment's history, with respect to segregated schools, is the status of public education at that time. In the South, the movement toward free common schools, supported by general taxation, had not yet taken hold. Education of white children was largely in the hands of private groups. Education of Negroes was almost nonexistent, and practically all of the race were illiterate. In fact, any education of Negroes was forbidden by law in some states. Today, in contrast, many Negroes have achieved outstanding success in the arts and sciences as well as in the business and professional world. It is true that public school education at the time of the Amendment had advanced further in the North, but the effect of the Amendment on Northern States was generally ignored in the congressional debates. Even in the North, the conditions of public education did not approximate those existing today. The curriculum was usually rudimentary; ungraded schools were common in rural areas; the school term was but three months a year in many states; and compulsory school attendance was virtually unknown. As a consequence, it is not surprising that there should be so little in the history of the Fourteenth Amendment relating to its intended effect on public education.

In the first cases in this Court construing the Fourteenth Amendment, decided shortly after its adoption, the Court interpreted it as proscribing all state-imposed discriminations against the Negro race. The doctrine of "separate but equal" did not make its appearance in this court until 1896 in the case of *Plessy v. Ferguson,* supra, involving not education but transportation. American courts have since labored with the doctrine for over half a century. In this Court, there have been six cases involving the "separate but equal" doctrine in the field of public education. In *Cumming v. Board of Education of Richmond County,* 175 U.S. 528, the validity of the doctrine itself was not challenged. In more recent cases, all on the graduate school level, inequality was found in that specific benefits enjoyed by white students were denied to Negro students of the same educational qualifications. [E.g.,] *Sweatt v. Painter,* 339 U.S. 629. In none of these cases was it necessary to re-examine the doctrine to grant relief to the Negro plaintiff. And in *Sweatt v. Painter,* the Court expressly reserved decision on the question whether *Plessy v. Ferguson* should be held inapplicable to public education.

In the instant cases, that question is directly presented. Here, unlike *Sweatt v. Painter,* there are findings below that the Negro and white schools involved have been equalized, or are being equalized, with respect to buildings, curricula, qualifications and salaries of teachers, and other "tangible" factors. Our decision, therefore, cannot turn on merely a comparison of these tangible factors in the Negro and white schools involved in each of the cases. We must look instead to the effect of segregation itself on public education.

In approaching this problem, we cannot turn the clock back to 1868 when the Amendment was adopted, or even to 1896 when *Plessy v. Ferguson* was written. We must consider public education in the light of its full development and its present place in American life throughout the Nation. Only in this way can it be determined if segregation in public schools deprives these plaintiffs of the equal protection of the laws.

Today, education is perhaps the most important function of state and local governments. Compulsory school attendance laws and the great expenditures for education both demonstrate our recognition of the importance of education to our democratic society. It is required in the performance of our most basic public responsibilities, even service in the armed forces. It is the very foundation of good citizenship. Today it is a principal instrument in awakening the child to cultural values, in preparing him for later professional training, and in helping him to adjust normally to his environment. In these days, it is doubtful that any child may reasonably be expected to succeed in life if he is denied the opportunity of an education. Such an opportunity, where the state has undertaken to provide it, is a right which must be made available to all on equal terms.

We come then to the question presented: Does segregation of children in public schools solely on the basis of race, even though the physical facilities and other "tangible" factors may be equal, deprive the children of the minority group of equal educational opportunities? We believe that it does.

In *Sweatt v. Painter*, in finding that a segregated law school for Negroes could not provide them equal educational opportunities, this Court relied in large part on "those qualities which are incapable of objective measurement but which make for greatness in a law school." In *McLaurin v. Oklahoma State Regents*, [339 U.S. 637,] the Court, in requiring that a Negro admitted to a white graduate school be treated like all other students, again resorted to intangible considerations: ". . . his ability to study, to engage in discussions and exchange views with other students, and, in general, to learn his profession." Such considerations apply with added force to children in grade and high schools. To separate them from others of similar age and qualifications solely because of their race generates a feeling of inferiority as to their status in the community that may affect their hearts and minds in a way unlikely ever to be undone. The effect of this separation on their educational opportunities was well stated by a finding in the Kansas case by a court which nevertheless felt compelled to rule against the Negro plaintiffs:

> Segregation of white and colored children in public schools has a detrimental effect upon the colored children. The impact is greater when it has the sanction of the law; for the policy of separating the races is usually interpreted as denoting the inferiority of the negro group. A sense of inferiority affects the motivation of a child to learn. Segregation with the sanction of law, therefore, has a tendency to [retard] the educational and mental development of Negro children and to deprive them of some of the benefits they would receive in a racial[ly] integrated school system.

Whatever may have been the extent of psychological knowledge at the time of *Plessy v. Ferguson*, this finding is amply supported by modern authority.[11] Any language in *Plessy v. Ferguson* contrary to this finding is rejected.

We conclude that in the field of public education the doctrine of "separate but equal" has no place. Separate educational facilities are inherently unequal. Therefore, we hold that the plaintiffs and others similarly situated for whom the actions have been brought are, by reason of the segregation complained of, deprived of the equal protection of the laws guaranteed by the Fourteenth Amendment. This disposition makes unnecessary any discussion whether such segregation also violates the Due Process Clause of the Fourteenth Amendment.[12]

Because these are class actions, because of the wide applicability of this decision, and because of the great variety of local conditions, the for-

---

[11] K. B. Clark, Effect of Prejudice and Discrimination on Personality Development (Midcentury White House Conference on Children and Youth, 1950); Witmer and Kotinsky, Personality in the Making (1952), c. VI; Deutscher and Chein, The Psychological Effects of Enforced Segregation: A Survey of Social Science Opinion, 26 J. Psychol. 259 (1948); Chein, What are the Psychological Effects of Segregation Under Conditions of Equal Facilities?, 3 Int. J. Opinion and Attitude Res. 229 (1949); Brameld, Educational Costs, in Discrimination and National Welfare (MacIver, ed., 1949), 44–48; Frazier, The Negro in the United States (1949), 674–681. And see generally Myrdal, An American Dilemma (1944).

[12] See *Bolling v. Sharpe* concerning the Due Process Clause of the Fifth Amendment.

mulation of decrees in these cases presents problems of considerable complexity. On reargument, the consideration of appropriate relief was necessarily subordinated to the primary question—the constitutionality of segregation in public education. We have now announced that such segregation is a denial of the equal protection of the laws. In order that we may have the full assistance of the parties in formulating decrees, the cases will be restored to the docket, and the parties are requested to present further argument on Questions 4 and 5 previously propounded by the Court for the reargument this Term.[13] The Attorney General of the United States is again invited to participate. The Attorneys General of the states requiring or permitting segregation in public education will also be permitted to appear as *amici curiae* upon request. . . .

Bolling v. Sharpe

347 U.S. 497 (1954)

■ MR. CHIEF JUSTICE WARREN delivered the opinion of the Court.

This case challenges the validity of segregation in the public schools of the District of Columbia. The petitioners, minors of the Negro race, allege that such segregation deprives them of due process of law under the Fifth Amendment. They were refused admission to a public school attended by white children solely because of their race. [We] have this day held that the Equal Protection Clause of the Fourteenth Amendment prohibits the states from maintaining racially segregated public schools. The legal problem in the District of Columbia is somewhat different, however. The Fifth Amendment, which is applicable in the District of Columbia, does not contain an equal protection clause as does the Fourteenth Amendment which applies only to the states. But the concepts of equal protection and due process, both stemming from our American ideal of fairness, are not mutually exclusive. The "equal protection of the laws" is a more explicit safeguard of prohibited unfairness than "due process of law," and, therefore, we do not imply that the two are always interchangeable phrases. But, as this Court has recognized, discrimination may be so unjustifiable as to be violative of due process.

Classifications based solely upon race must be scrutinized with particular care, since they are contrary to our traditions and hence constitutionally suspect. As long ago as 1896, this Court declared the principle "that the constitution of the United States, in its present form, forbids, so far as civil and political rights are concerned, discrimination by the general government, or by the states, against any citizen because of his race". And in

---

[13] "4. Assuming it is decided that segregation in public schools violates the Fourteenth Amendment *(a)* would a decree necessarily follow providing that, within the limits set by normal geographic school districting, Negro children should forthwith be admitted to schools of their choice, or *(b)* may this Court, in the exercise of its equity powers, permit an effective gradual adjustment to be brought about from existing segregated systems to a system not based on color distinctions?

"5. On the assumption on which questions 4 *(a)* and *(b)* are based, and assuming further that this Court will exercise its equity powers to the end described in question 4 *(b)*, *(a)* should this Court formulate detailed decrees in these cases; *(b)* if so, what specific issues should the decrees reach; *(c)* should this Court appoint a special master to hear evidence with a view to recommending specific terms for such decrees; *(d)* should this Court remand to the courts of first instance with directions to frame decrees in these cases, and if so what general directions should the decrees of this Court include and what procedures should the courts of first instance follow in arriving at the specific terms of more detailed decrees?"

Buchanan v. Warley, 245 U.S. 60, the Court held that a statute which limited the right of a property owner to convey his property to a person of another race was, as an unreasonable discrimination, a denial of due process of law.

Although the Court has not assumed to define "liberty" with any great precision, that term is not confined to mere freedom from bodily restraint. Liberty under law extends to the full range of conduct which the individual is free to pursue, and it cannot be restricted except for a proper governmental objective. Segregation in public education is not reasonably related to any proper governmental objective, and thus it imposes on Negro children of the District of Columbia a burden that constitutes an arbitrary deprivation of their liberty in violation of the Due Process Clause.

In view of our decision that the Constitution prohibits the states from maintaining racially segregated public schools, it would be unthinkable that the same Constitution would impose a lesser duty on the Federal Government. We hold that racial segregation in the public schools of the District of Columbia is a denial of the due process of law guaranteed by the Fifth Amendment to the Constitution.

Brown v. Board of Education (Brown II)
349 U.S. 294 (1955)

■ MR. CHIEF JUSTICE WARREN delivered the opinion of the Court.

These cases were decided on May 17, 1954. The opinions of that date, declaring the fundamental principle that racial discrimination in public education is unconstitutional, are incorporated herein by reference. All provisions of federal, state, or local law requiring or permitting such discrimination must yield to this principle. There remains for consideration the manner in which relief is to be accorded.

Because these cases arose under different local conditions and their disposition will involve a variety of local problems, we requested further argument on the question of relief. In view of the nationwide importance of the decision, we invited the Attorney General of the United States and the Attorneys General of all states requiring or permitting racial discrimination in public education to present their views on that question. The parties, the United States, and the States of Florida, North Carolina, Arkansas, Oklahoma, Maryland, and Texas filed briefs and participated in the oral argument.

These presentations were informative and helpful to the Court in its consideration of the complexities arising from the transition to a system of public education freed of racial discrimination. The presentations also demonstrated that substantial steps to eliminate racial discrimination in public schools have already been taken, not only in some of the communities in which these cases arose, but in some of the states appearing as *amici curiae*, and in other states as well.

Full implementation of these constitutional principles may require solution of varied local school problems. School authorities have the primary responsibility for elucidating, assessing, and solving these problems; courts will have to consider whether the action of school authorities constitutes good faith implementation of the governing constitutional principles. Because of their proximity to local conditions and the possible need for further hearings, the courts which originally heard these cases can best perform this judicial appraisal. Accordingly, we believe it appropriate to remand the cases to those courts.

In fashioning and effectuating the decrees, the courts will be guided by equitable principles. Traditionally, equity has been characterized by a practical flexibility in shaping its remedies and by a facility for adjusting and reconciling public and private needs. These cases call for the exercise of these traditional attributes of equity power. At stake is the personal interest of the plaintiffs in admission to public schools as soon as practicable on a nondiscriminatory basis. To effectuate this interest may call for elimination of a variety of obstacles in making the transition to school systems operated in accordance with the constitutional principles set forth in our May 17, 1954, decision. Courts of equity may properly take into account the public interest in the elimination of such obstacles in a systematic and effective manner. But it should go without saying that the vitality of these constitutional principles cannot be allowed to yield simply because of disagreement with them.

While giving weight to these public and private considerations, the courts will require that the defendants make a prompt and reasonable start toward full compliance with our May 17, 1954, ruling. Once such a start has been made, the courts may find that additional time is necessary to carry out the ruling in an effective manner. The burden rests upon the defendants to establish that such time is necessary in the public interest and is consistent with good faith compliance at the earliest practicable date. To that end, the courts may consider problems related to administration, arising from the physical condition of the school plant, the school transportation system, personnel, revision of school districts and attendance areas into compact units to achieve a system of determining admission to the public schools on a nonracial basis, and revision of local laws and regulations which may be necessary in solving the foregoing problems. They will also consider the adequacy of any plans the defendants may propose to meet these problems and to effectuate a transition to a racially nondiscriminatory school system. During this period of transition, the courts will retain jurisdiction of these cases.

The judgments below, except that in the Delaware case, are accordingly reversed and the cases are remanded to the District Courts to take such proceedings and enter such orders and decrees consistent with this opinion as are necessary and proper to admit to public schools on a racially nondiscriminatory basis with all deliberate speed the parties to these cases. The judgment in the Delaware case—ordering the immediate admission of the plaintiffs to schools previously attended only by white children—is affirmed on the basis of the principles stated in our May 17, 1954, opinion, but the case is remanded to the Supreme Court of Delaware for such further proceedings as that Court may deem necessary in light of this opinion.

NOTES

1. *Literature. Brown* is one of the most renowned and most discussed constitutional decisions in American history. The leading articles debating it at the time were Alexander M. Bickel, *The Original Understanding and the Segregation Decision*, 69 Harv. L. Rev. 1 (1955); Herbert Wechsler, *Toward Neutral Principles of Constitutional Law*, 73 Harv. L. Rev. 1 (1959); and Charles Black, *The Lawfulness of the Segregation Decisions*, 69 Yale L.J. 421 (1960). A more recent treatment of what the case means, with various scholars writing substi-

tute opinions for it, is WHAT *BROWN V. BOARD OF EDUCATION* SHOULD HAVE SAID: THE NATION'S TOP LEGAL EXPERTS REWRITE AMERICA'S LANDMARK CIVIL RIGHTS DECISION (Jack Balkin, ed. 2001).

2. *Rationale.* As famous as *Brown* is for the magnificent justness of its result and for its sound constitutional intuition about the meaning of "equal protection of the laws," the opinion is also noted for the opacity of some of its legal reasoning. What was the precise rationale of the *Brown* holding?

Is it that racial segregation is intrinsically discriminatory? This was the argument (in part) of Charles Black, in his article cited in the preceding note. The real-world "purpose and impact of segregation in the southern regional culture," he wrote, were "matters of common notoriety." If "a whole race of people finds itself confined within a system which is set up and continued for the very purpose of keeping it in an inferior race, and if the question is then solemnly propounded whether such a race is being treated 'equally,' I think we ought to exercise one of the sovereign prerogatives of philosophers—that of laughter."

Or is it that segregation was perceived as discriminatory? Note *Brown*'s discussion of social facts and realities, and its famous footnote invoking contemporary social science on the perception and psychological effects of segregation. Does the opinion depend on this line of thinking? Does the meaning of the Constitution's guarantee of "equal protection," as applied to segregation, depend on the most recent psychological or sociological studies? Imagine that a few years from now the latest social science studies conclude that separate single-race education is better for the emotional development and educational attainment of all children. Should the result be different? Harlan, dissenting in *Plessy,* would have said *no,* would he not?

Or does *Brown* depend on a judicial policy judgment, on the social facts and realities presented, that segregation is deeply harmful? If so, is that an appropriate basis for judicial decision-making, or at least an appropriate factor? If your answer is *yes,* then was it also appropriate for the Court to make a judicial policy judgment based on its assessment of social facts in *Plessy*? What are the strengths and limits of policy as a type of constitutional argument or mode of interpretation?

3. *Brown and Originalism. Brown* raises questions about history and the methodology of constitutional interpretation—in part because the Court's opinion at the outset disregards any historical evidence about original understanding. After the first oral argument in the case, in December 1952, the Court asked for further briefing and re-argument specifically addressed to the original understanding of the framers and ratifiers of the Fourteenth Amendment with respect to segregation. (In the interim, Chief Justice Fred Vinson died and Chief Justice Earl Warren was appointed.) The standard account in modern scholarship is that the Court did not rely on historical evidence of the framers' intent because the evidence did not support the Court's conclusion. For example, Alexander Bickel, who clerked for Justice Frankfurter when *Brown* was decided, wrote these words soon after the decision:

> The Court knew, of course, that its judgment would have an unparalleled impact on the daily lives of a very substantial portion of the population, and that the response of many of those affected would be in varying degrees hostile. It was necessary, therefore, if ever it had been, to exert to

the utmost the prestige, the oracular authority of the institution. To this end, it was desirable that the Court speak unanimously, with one voice from the deep. And the less said, the less chance of internal disagreement.... [These considerations] explain the brevity of the reference to the history of the fourteenth amendment's adoption and the briskness of the transition from an apparent assumption of that history's relevance to the statement that the clock cannot be turned back.

Beneath the brevity and beneath the briskness lies the pervasive problem of the weight to be accorded in constitutional adjudications to evidence of the framers' original understanding. Reliance on such evidence is subject to caveats applicable to the use of legislative history as an aid in statutory construction. What is more important, it may raise a fundamental question concerning the Court's function in construing the Constitution. The difficulty is best posed by quotation of two extreme judicial utterances, [one from Chief Justice Taney's opinion in *Dred Scott* and one from Justice Sutherland's dissent in *Blaisdell*,] both advocating meticulous adherence to original intent, so-called. . . .

Of course, such views, when they prevail, threaten disaster to government under a written constitution. . . . But it is a long way from rejection of the Taney–Sutherland doctrine to the proposition that the original understanding is simply not relevant. For arguments based on that understanding have a strong pull. They have decided cases for judges who held the views represented by the passages quoted. But the Court has also employed them without intentionally connoting, indeed while disavowing, such views. And they have been relied on by judges well aware that it was a constitution they are expounding.

The original understanding forms the starting link in the chain of continuity which is a source of the Court's authority, and it is not unnatural that appeals to it should recur as consistently as they do. Happily, finding the original understanding, like applying the Constitution itself, is, at best, "not a mechanical exercise but a function of statecraft" and of historical insight. And what is relevant is not alone the origin of constitutional provision, but also "the line of their growth," the further links in the chain of continuity. This being so and our law not being given to following hard and fast theoretical formulations on questions of the scope of this one, it is possible, in the Chief Justice's words, for historical materials to cast some light although they are inconclusive and although, in any event, the clock cannot be turned back.

Bickel, *The Original Understanding and the Segregation Decision*, 69 Harv. L. Rev. 1, 1–6 (1955). Bickel then discussed at length the adoption of the Fourteenth Amendment. He concluded that the history does not support the proposition that the framers of the amendment intended to abolish segregation, and that conclusion has been widely accepted in modern scholarship.

Whether Bickel was right about the history has been disputed, though. Michael McConnell has looked to a broader set of historical evidence: not only the debates when the Fourteenth Amendment was proposed but also the evidence of how Congress understood the amendment when exercising its powers under Section 5 to enact civil rights legislation, including the Civil Rights Act of 1875. Michael W. McConnell, *Originalism and the Desegregation Decisions*, 81 Va. L. Rev. 947 (1995). These post-enactment congressional debates show that "the belief that school segregation does in fact violate the Fourteenth Amendment was held during the years immediately following ratification by a substantial majority of political leaders who had supported the Amendment. In a large number of votes over a three and one half year period, between one-half and two-thirds of both houses of Congress voted in favor of school desegregation and against the principle of separate but equal." *Id.* at 953. Moreover, these debates in Congress "were conducted in explicitly constitutional terms," *id.*, and were consistent with judicial decisions of the time. Recall in this connection the Supreme Court's 1873 statutory interpretation decision, *Railroad Company v. Brown,* which noted that Congress of course intended to forbid segregated train cars in its nondiscrimination requirement enacted in 1863, since "in the temper of Congress at the time, it is manifest the grant could not have been made without" a condition prohibiting segregation. The argument that *Brown* is consistent with the original understanding of the Fourteenth Amendment has provoked sharp debate. For critiques, see Michael J. Klarman, *Brown, Originalism, and Constitutional Theory: A Response to Professor McConnell*, 81 Va. L. Rev. 1881 (1995); Earl M. Maltz, *Originalism and the Desegregation Decisions—A Response to Professor McConnell*, 13 Const. Comm. 223 (1996). For a justification of *Brown* that argues for an interaction between the Fourteenth Amendment and contemporaneous state constitutions, see Steven G. Calabresi & Sarah E. Agudo, *Individual Rights Under State Constitutions When the Fourteenth Amendment Was Ratified in 1868: What Rights Are Deeply Rooted in American History and Tradition?* 87 Tex. L. Rev. 7, 108–112 (2008) (noting that thirty-six of thirty-seven state constitutions in 1868 required the public provision of education, and concluding that education was a civil right protected under the Fourteenth Amendment).

Regardless of whether Bickel was right or wrong about the history, could he still have been right about the methodology? In other words, was he right to see original understanding as just the "starting link in the chain," because relying on it alone can lead to horrible outcomes such as *Dred Scott?* Since the publication of Bickel's article, *Dred Scott* has often been described as an example of what originalism can lead to. In evaluating that argument, does it matter why Chief Justice Taney advanced originalist arguments, or how persuasive they were? (His arguments in *Dred Scott* were rebutted by Justice Curtis's dissent.) More generally, how do we decide whether a type of argument is tainted by its use or misuse in the past? Does the invocation of originalist arguments by Chief Justice Taney discredit originalism? Does *Plessy's* attempt to "update" the Constitution in keeping with the times discredit that kind of approach? How should one decide?

4. *Precedent.* On the basis of the doctrine of *stare decisis*, should *Brown* have reaffirmed *Plessy?* That doctrine is meant to promote stability in the law and protect settled expectations. Were those purposes relevant for racial segregation by law, which had been in place since Reconstruction and around which considerable amounts of social practice had grown up? Or was the Court correct in casting aside decades of judicial precedents simply because they were wrong?

5. *Summing up the Constitutional Arguments.* Review the five types of constitutional argument, or modes of interpretation, discussed in Chapter 1: (1) text, (2) structure, (3) historical purpose, (4) practice and precedent, and (5) policy. In which direction does each of these cut in *Brown*, and how forcefully? How much weight should be given here to each type of argument? And what do the Court's decisions about race and the Equal Protection Clause—from

Strauder to *Plessy* to *Brown*—suggest are the strengths and limits of each of these types of constitutional argument?

6. *State and Federal?* In *Bolling v. Sharpe*, decided the same day as *Brown*, the Court decided to extend its ruling to the federal government. The constitutional basis for this is somewhat murky. The Fourteenth Amendment mentions no limit on the federal government: "No State shall. . . ." To the contrary, Section 5 of the amendment actually *empowers* the federal government. And if the Fourteenth Amendment's Equal Protection Clause did forbid the federal government to use race-based classifications, would that raise constitutional doubts about some Reconstruction statutes that aided the newly freed slaves, such as the Freedmen's Bureau Act? What is the Court's answer in *Bolling v. Sharpe*? Was it really unthinkable that the Reconstruction amendments would reflect a greater distrust of the states, barring state segregation in education but imposing no similar limit on the federal government with respect to the District of Columbia? The Court bases its decision on the Fifth Amendment's Due Process Clause, finding that the clause effects a kind of double-reverse-ricochet-incorporation of equal protection principles. Are you persuaded? Most commenters have not been kind to this reasoning. For example, John Hart Ely said, "I would have strained sorely to side with the Chief Justice had the language of the Fifth Amendment been able to bear his construction. It's hard to see how it can." John Hart Ely, DEMOCRACY AND DISTRUST: A THEORY OF JUDICIAL REVIEW 33 (1980); see also *id.* at 32 (calling the construction the Court gave to the Fifth Amendment in *Bolling* "gibberish both syntactically and historically"). Should this problem have been left to Congress? Is there another constitutional provision that can fairly be construed as invalidating federal racial segregation in education? In *Bolling*, what weight is the Court giving to each of the types of constitutional argument?

7. *Remedies.* Regardless of whether a court should consider social policy when it is interpreting the substantive requirements of the Constitution (a question raised above in Note 2), it is certainly traditional for courts to consider it when granting equitable remedies. Indeed, when a court of equity is deciding whether to grant an injunction, one traditional requirement (mentioned briefly in *Brown II*) is that the injunction must not disserve the public interest. After the remand in *Brown II*, what if it were clear to a lower court that forced integration would provoke massive resistance, disruption, and even violence? Would that mean the public interest would be disserved by an injunction that required immediate integration? Or would the public interest be disserved by any delay in obeying the mandate of the Constitution? In *Brown II*, the Court remanded to lower courts to actually fashion the relief, instructing them to act with "all deliberate speed." In giving the lower courts that instruction, was the Court wisely accommodating reality, or was it feebly tolerating the systematic violation of constitutional rights?

8. *Resistance.* There was in fact widespread resistance to *Brown* by pro-segregation elected officials in the South, and the next two decades would bring challenges to the Court's interpretive authority and even now that resistance raises questions about the power of the Court to effect social change. One example of the resistance came in Virginia, where the General Assembly passed laws that closed the integrated public schools, eliminated state funds for integrated schools, and provided tuition grants for use in private schools. (This and other examples of resistance are discussed in more detail below, in Note 4 after *Washington v. Davis*.)

Some segregationist officials in the South argued that *Brown* was wrong on the merits and that they were therefore not bound by it, echoing arguments of Thomas Jefferson and James Madison a century and a half earlier in the Virginia and Kentucky Resolutions. In response, in *Cooper v. Aaron*, 358 U.S. 1 (1958), the Court declared that since *Marbury* the supremacy of the judiciary has "been respected by this Court and the Country as a permanent and indispensable feature of our constitutional system." How would you distinguish the Southern segregationists' arguments from the ones made in the Virginia and Kentucky Resolutions and the ones made by Abraham Lincoln against *Dred Scott*? (The sources that are mentioned in this paragraph are all presented in Chapters 1 and 2.) Is the distinction that *Dred Scott* was wrong but *Brown* was right? Who decides which of the Court's decisions are wrong and which are right?

The history of resistance and judicial enforcement after *Brown* has provoked great controversy about the effectiveness of the judiciary as an instrument of social change. In a study of *Brown* and its aftermath, Gerald Rosenberg argued that what actually succeeded in rooting out segregation was action by Congress and the president, especially in passing and enforcing the Civil Rights Act of 1964. Rosenberg concludes:

> The use of the courts in the civil rights movement is considered the paradigm of a successful strategy for social change. . . . Yet, a closer examination reveals that before Congress and the executive branch acted, courts had virtually no direct effect on enforcing discrimination in the key fields of education, voting, transportation, accommodations and public places, and housing. Courageous and praiseworthy decisions were rendered, and nothing changed. Only when Congress and the executive branch acted in tandem with the courts did change occur in these fields. In terms of judicial effects, then, *Brown* and its progeny stand for the proposition that courts are impotent to produce significant social reform.

Gerald N. Rosenberg, THE HOLLOW HOPE: CAN COURTS BRING ABOUT SOCIAL CHANGE? 70–71 (2d. ed. 2008). For an alternative account that sees *Brown* as more consequential, though primarily in motivating both the supporters and the opponents of racial integration, see Michael J. Klarman, FROM JIM CROW TO CIVIL RIGHTS: THE SUPREME COURT AND THE STRUGGLE FOR RACIAL EQUALITY (2006). How should we decide whether *Brown* was a powerful force for social change?

9. *Extending Brown.* On its own terms, *Brown* was limited to segregation in public education. It did not directly overrule *Plessy*, other than to disapprove of it in that context. The Court extended *Brown* in a series of *per curiam* decisions requiring non-discrimination on the basis of race in public beaches and bathhouses, *Mayor and City Council of Baltimore City v. Dawson*, 350 U.S. 877 (1955); municipal golf courses, *Holmes v. Atlanta*, 350 U.S. 879 (1955); city parks, *New Orleans City Park Improvement Ass'n v. Detiege*, 358 U.S. 54 (1958); and municipal bus systems, *Gayle v. Browder*, 352 U.S. 903 (1956). Query: Were the lower courts bound to adhere to *Plessy* in these non-education contexts until the Supreme Court ruled separate-but-equal unconstitutional in these contexts as well? Consider the next case, in which a lower court declined to follow the "controlling" precedent of *Plessy*. Did the lower court act properly or improperly?

Browder v. Gayle

142 F. Supp. 707 (D.C. Ala. 1956)

■ RIVES, CIRCUIT JUDGE.

The purpose of this action is to test the constitutionality of both the statutes of the State of Alabama and the ordinances of the City of Montgomery which require the segregation of the white and colored races on the motor buses of the Montgomery City Lines, Inc., a common carrier of passengers in said City and its police jurisdiction. The plaintiffs are four Negro citizens who bring this action for themselves and on behalf of all other Negroes similarly situated. . . .

Each of the four named plaintiffs has either been required by a bus driver or by the police to comply with said segregation laws or has been arrested and fined for her refusal so to do. The plaintiffs, along with most other Negro citizens of the City of Montgomery, have since December 5, 1955, and up to the present time, refrained from making use of the transportation facilities provided by Montgomery City Lines, Inc. Plaintiffs and other Negroes desire and intend to resume the use of said buses if and when they can do so on a non-segregated basis without fear of arrest. . . .

The ultimate question is whether the statutes and ordinances requiring the segregation of the white and colored races on the common carrier motor buses in the City of Montgomery and its police jurisdiction are unconstitutional and invalid. . . .

The equal protection clause requires equality of treatment before the law for all persons without regard to race or color. See e.g., *Strauder v. West Virginia*, 100 U.S. 303.

In *Plessy v. Ferguson*, 163 U.S. 537, decided in 1896, the Supreme Court held as to intrastate commerce that a Louisiana statute requiring railway companies to provide equal but separate accommodations for the white and colored races was not in conflict with the provisions of the Fourteenth Amendment. That holding was repeatedly followed in later cases. . . .

In the *School Segregation Cases, Brown v. Board of Education of Topeka*, 347 U.S. 483 and *Bolling v. Sharpe*, 347 U.S. 497, the separate but equal doctrine was repudiated in the area where it first developed, i.e., in the field of public education. On the same day the Supreme Court made clear that its ruling was not limited to that field when it remanded "for consideration in the light of the *Segregation Cases* . . . and conditions that now prevail" a case involving the rights of Negroes to use the recreational facilities of city parks. *Muir v. Louisville Park Theatrical Association*, 347 U.S. 971 (1954).

Later the Fourth Circuit expressly repudiated the separate but equal doctrine as applied to recreational centers. Its judgment was affirmed by the Supreme Court. The doctrine has further been repudiated in [the Supreme Court's] holdings that the cities of Atlanta and of Miami cannot meet the test by furnishing the facilities of their municipal golf courses to Negroes on a segregated basis.

Even a statute can be repealed by implication. A fortiori, a judicial decision, which is simply evidence of the law and not the law itself, may be so impaired by later decisions as no longer to furnish any reliable evidence.[14]

We cannot in good conscience perform our duty as judges by blindly following the precedent of *Plessy v. Ferguson*, when our study leaves us in complete agreement with the Fourth Circuit's opinion in *Flemming v. South Carolina Electric & Gas Co.*, 224 F.2d 752, appeal dismissed April 23, 1956, 351 U.S. 901, that the separate but equal doctrine can no longer be safely followed as a correct statement of the law. In fact, we think that *Plessy v. Ferguson* has been impliedly, though not explicitly, overruled, and that, under the later decisions, there is now no rational basis upon which the separate but equal doctrine can be validly applied to public carrier transportation within the City of Montgomery and its police jurisdiction. The application of that doctrine cannot be justified as a proper execution of the state police power.

We hold that the statutes and ordinances requiring segregation of the white and colored races on the motor buses of a common carrier of passengers in the City of Montgomery and its police jurisdiction violate the due process and equal protection of the law clauses of the Fourteenth Amendment to the Constitution of the United States. ...

■ LYNNE, DISTRICT JUDGE (dissenting).

... For many years as a trial judge in the state and federal systems I have endeavored faithfully to understand and apply precedents established by the opinions of appellate courts. This was not a blind obedience to a legalistic formula embodied in the rule of stare decisis. It was the result of a simple belief that the laws which regulate the conduct, the affairs, and sometimes the emotions of our people should evidence not only the appearance but also the spirit of stability.

---

[14] ... [See] *Barnette v. West Virginia State Board of Education*, D.C., 47 F. Supp. 251:

> Ordinarily we would feel constrained to follow an unreversed decision of the Supreme Court of the United States, whether we agreed with it or not. It is true that decisions are but evidences of the law and not law itself; but the decisions of the Supreme Court must be accepted by the lower courts as binding upon them if any orderly administration of justice is to be attained. The developments with respect to the *Gobitis* case[,] however, are such that we do not feel that it is incumbent upon us to accept it as binding authority. Of the seven justices now members of the Supreme Court who participated in that decision, four have given public expression to the view that it is unsound, the present Chief Justice in his dissenting opinion rendered therein and three other justices in a special dissenting opinion in *Jones v. City of Opelika*. The majority of the court in *Jones*, moreover, thought it worth while to distinguish the decision in the *Gobitis* case, instead of relying upon it as supporting authority. Under such circumstances and believing, as we do, that the flag salute here required is violative of religious liberty when required of persons holding the religious views of plaintiffs, we feel that we would be recreant to our duty as judges, if through a blind following of a decision which the Supreme Court itself has thus impaired as an authority, we should deny protection to rights which we regard as among the most sacred of those protected by constitutional guaranties.

To like effect is the opinion of Judge Frank for the Second Circuit in *Perkins v. Endicott Johnson Corporation*, 128 F.2d 208:

> We would stultify ourselves and unnecessarily burden the Supreme Court if—adhering to the dogma, obviously fictional to any reader of its history, that alterations in that court's principles of decision never occur unless recorded in explicit statements that earlier decisions are overruled—we stubbornly and literally followed decisions which have been, but not too ostentatiously, modified. "The life of the law," as Mr. Justice Holmes said, "has been experience." Legal doctrines, as first enunciated, often prove to be inadequate under the impact of ensuing experience in their practical application. And when a lower court perceives a pronounced new doctrinal trend in Supreme Court decisions, it is its duty, cautiously to be sure, to follow not to resist it.

Judges of trial courts frequently find themselves in disagreement with the rationale of an old, but clearly controlling precedent. . . . But they are neither designed nor equipped to perform the legislative function of putting off the old and putting on the new. To arrogate to themselves this prerogative, in my humble opinion, would be the first, fatal step in making hollow the proud boast that ours is a "government of laws and not of men.". . . .

The majority recognize, it was conceded in oral arguments by counsel for plaintiffs, that *Plessy v. Ferguson*, is precisely in point, and that its holding has been repeatedly followed in later transportation cases. . . .

A comparatively new principle of pernicious implications has found its way into our jurisprudence. Lower courts may feel free to disregard the precise precedent of a Supreme Court opinion if they perceive a "pronounced new doctrinal trend" in its later decisions which would influence a cautious judge to prophesy that in due time and in a proper case such established precedent will be overturned explicitly. . . .

NOTES

1. Does a lower court judge have authority to "underrule" the Supreme Court this way? The Supreme Court has suggested that the answer is *no*. *Agostini v. Felton*, 521 U.S. 203, 237–238 (1997). For diverging answers from scholars, see Sanford Levinson, *On Positivism and Potted Plants: "Inferior" Judges and the Task of Constitutional Interpretation*, 25 Conn. L. Rev. 843 (1993) (yes); Michael Stokes Paulsen, *The Irrepressible Myth of* Marbury, 101 Mich. L. Rev. 2706, 2733–34 (2003) (yes); and Evan H. Caminker, *Why Must Inferior Courts Obey Superior Court Precedents?*, 46 Stan. L. Rev. 817 (1994) (no). Does underruling necessarily interfere with the supremacy of the Supreme Court, so long as the Court retains the power to review and reverse the lower court?

2. It took the Supreme Court more than a dozen years to extend the principle of *Brown* to marriage. It did so in the landmark decision which you will read next:

Loving v. Virginia
388 U.S. 1 (1967)

■ MR. CHIEF JUSTICE WARREN delivered the opinion of the Court.

This case presents a constitutional question never addressed by this Court: whether a statutory scheme adopted by the State of Virginia to prevent marriages between persons solely on the basis of racial classifications violates the Equal Protection and Due Process Clauses of the Fourteenth Amendment. For reasons which seem to us to reflect the central meaning of those constitutional commands, we conclude that these statutes cannot stand consistently with the Fourteenth Amendment.

In June 1958, two residents of Virginia, Mildred Jeter, a Negro woman, and Richard Loving, a white man, were married in the District of Columbia pursuant to its laws. Shortly after their marriage, the Lovings returned to Virginia and established their marital abode in Caroline County. At the October Term, 1958, of the Circuit Court of Caroline County, a grand jury issued an indictment charging the Lovings with violating Virginia's ban on interracial marriages. On January 6, 1959, the Lovings pleaded guilty to the charge and were sentenced to one year in jail; however, the trial judge suspended the sentence for a period of 25 years on the condition that the Lovings leave the State and not return to Virginia together for 25 years. He stated in an opinion that:

> Almighty God created the races white, black, yellow, malay and red, and he placed them on separate continents. And but for the interference with his arrangement there would be no cause for such marriages. The fact that he separated the races shows that he did not intend for the races to mix.

After their convictions, the Lovings took up residence in the District of Columbia. On November 6, 1963, they filed a motion in the state trial court to vacate the judgment and set aside the sentence on the ground that the statutes which they had violated were repugnant to the Fourteenth Amendment. . . . [The] state trial judge denied the motion to vacate the sentences, and the Lovings perfected an appeal to the Supreme Court of Appeals of Virginia. . . . The Supreme Court of Appeals upheld the constitutionality of the antimiscegenation statutes and, after modifying the sentence, affirmed the convictions.

The two statutes under which appellants were convicted and sentenced are part of a comprehensive statutory scheme aimed at prohibiting and punishing interracial marriages. The Lovings were convicted of violating § 20–58 of the Virginia Code:

> Leaving State to evade law.—If any white person and colored person shall go out of this State, for the purpose of being married, and with the intention of returning, and be married out of it, and afterwards return to and reside in it, cohabiting as man and wife, they shall be punished as provided in § 20–59, and the marriage shall be governed by the same law as if it had been solemnized in this State. The fact of their cohabitation here as man and wife shall be evidence of their marriage.

Section 20–59, which defines the penalty for miscegenation, provides:

> Punishment for marriage.—If any white person intermarry with a colored person, or any colored person intermarry with a white person, he shall be guilty of a felony and shall be punished by confinement in the penitentiary for not less than one nor more than five years.

Virginia is now one of 16 States which prohibit and punish marriages on the basis of racial classifications. Penalties for miscegenation arose as an incident to slavery and have been common in Virginia since the colonial period. The present statutory scheme dates from the adoption of the Racial Integrity Act of 1924, passed during the period of extreme nativism which followed the end of the First World War. The central features of this Act, and current Virginia law, are the absolute prohibition of a "white person" marrying other than another "white person, a prohibition against issuing marriage licenses until the issuing official is satisfied that the applicants" statements as to their race are correct, certificates of "racial composition" to be kept by both local and state registrars, and the carrying forward of earlier prohibitions against racial intermarriage.

I

In upholding the constitutionality of these provisions in the decision below, the Supreme Court of Appeals of Virginia referred to its 1955 decision in *Naim v. Naim*, 197 Va. 80, as stating the reasons supporting the validity of these laws. In *Naim*, the state court concluded that the State's legitimate purposes were "to preserve the racial integrity of its citizens," and to prevent "the corruption of blood," "a mongrel breed of citizens," and "the obliteration of racial pride," obviously an endorsement of the doctrine of White Supremacy. The court also reasoned that marriage has traditionally been subject to state regulation without federal intervention, and, consequently, the regulation of marriage should be left to exclusive state control by the Tenth Amendment.

. . . The State argues that the meaning of the Equal Protection Clause, as illuminated by the statements of the Framers, is only that state penal laws containing an interracial element as part of the definition of the offense must apply equally to whites and Negroes in the sense that members of each race are punished to the same degree. Thus, the State contends that, because its miscegenation statutes punish equally both the white and the Negro participants in an interracial marriage, these statutes, despite their reliance on racial classifications do not constitute an invidious discrimination based upon race. The second argument advanced by the State assumes the validity of its equal application theory. The argument is that, if the Equal Protection Clause does not outlaw miscegenation statutes because of their reliance on racial classifications, the question of constitutionality would thus become whether there was any rational basis for a State to treat interracial marriages differently from other marriages. On this question, the State argues, the scientific evidence is substantially in doubt and, consequently, this Court should defer to the wisdom of the state legislature in adopting its policy of discouraging interracial marriages.

Because we reject the notion that the mere "equal application" of a statute containing racial classifications is enough to remove the classifications from the Fourteenth Amendment's proscription of all invidious racial discriminations, we do not accept the State's contention that these statutes should be upheld if there is any possible basis for concluding that they serve a rational purpose. . . . [In] cases involving distinctions not drawn according to race, the Court has merely asked whether there is any rational foundation for the discriminations, and has deferred to the wisdom of the state legislatures. In the case at bar, however, we deal with statutes containing racial classifications, and the fact of equal application does not immunize the statute from the very heavy burden of justification which the Fourteenth Amendment has traditionally required of state statutes drawn according to race.

The State argues that statements in the Thirty-ninth Congress about the time of the passage of the Fourteenth Amendment indicate that the Framers did not intend the Amendment to make unconstitutional state miscegenation laws. Many of the statements alluded to by the State concern the debates over the Freedmen's Bureau Bill, which President Johnson vetoed, and the Civil Rights Act of 1866, enacted over his veto. While these statements have some relevance to the intention of Congress in submitting the Fourteenth Amendment, it must be understood that they pertained to the passage of specific statutes and not to the broader, organic purpose of a constitutional amendment. As for the various statements directly concerning the Fourteenth Amendment, we have said in connection with a related problem, that although these historical sources "cast some light" they are not sufficient to resolve the problem; "(a)t best, they are inconclusive. The most avid proponents of the post-War Amendments undoubtedly intended them to remove all legal distinctions among 'all persons born or naturalized in the United States.' Their opponents, just as certainly, were antagonistic to both the letter and the spirit of the Amendments and wished them to have the most limited effect." *Brown v. Board of Education*, 347 U.S. 483, 489 (1954). See also *Strauder v. State of West Virginia*, 100 U.S. 303, 310 (1880). We have rejected the proposition that the debates in the Thirty-ninth Congress or in the state legislatures which ratified the Fourteenth Amendment supported the theory advanced by the State, that the requirement of equal protection of the laws is satisfied by penal laws defining offenses based on racial classifications so long as white and Negro participants in the offense were similarly punished. *McLaughlin v. State of Florida*, 379 U.S. 184 (1964).

The State finds support for its "equal application" theory in the decision of the Court in *Pace v. State of Alabama*, 106 U.S. 583 (1883). In that case, the Court upheld a conviction under an Alabama statute forbidding adultery or fornication between a white person and a Negro which imposed a greater penalty than that of a statute proscribing similar conduct by members of the same race. The Court reasoned that the statute could not be said to discriminate against Negroes because the punishment for each participant in the offense was the same. However, as recently as the 1964 Term, in rejecting the reasoning of that case, we stated "*Pace* represents a limited view of the Equal Protection Clause which has not withstood analysis in the subsequent decisions of this Court." *McLaughlin v. Florida*, 379 U.S. at 188. As we there demonstrated, the Equal Protection Clause requires the consideration of whether the classifications drawn by any statute constitute an arbitrary and invidious discrimination. The clear and central purpose of the Fourteenth Amendment was to eliminate all official state sources of invidious racial discrimination in the States. *Slaughter–House Cases*, 16 Wall. 36, 71 (1873).

There can be no question but that Virginia's miscegenation statutes rest solely upon distinctions drawn according to race. The statutes proscribe generally accepted conduct if engaged in by members of different races.... At the very least, the Equal Protection Clause demands that racial classifications, especially suspect in criminal statutes, be subjected to the "most rigid scrutiny," *Korematsu v. United States*, 323 U.S. 214, 216 (1944), and, if they are ever to be upheld, they must be shown to be necessary to the accomplishment of some permissible state objective, independent of the racial discrimination which it was the object of the Fourteenth Amendment to eliminate.

There is patently no legitimate overriding purpose independent of invidious racial discrimination which justifies this classification. The fact that Virginia prohibits only interracial marriages involving white persons demonstrates that the racial classifications must stand on their own justification, as measures designed to maintain White Supremacy. We have consistently denied the constitutionality of measures which restrict the rights of citizens on account of race. There can be no doubt that restricting the freedom to marry solely because of racial classifications violates the central meaning of the Equal Protection Clause.

II

These statutes also deprive the Lovings of liberty without due process of law in violation of the Due Process Clause of the Fourteenth Amendment. The freedom to marry has long been recognized as one of the vital personal rights essential to the orderly pursuit of happiness by free men.

Marriage is one of the "basic civil rights of man," fundamental to our very existence and survival. *Skinner v. State of Oklahoma*, 316 U.S. 535, 541 (1942). To deny this fundamental freedom on so unsupportable a basis as the racial classifications embodied in these statutes, classifications so directly subversive of the principle of equality at the heart of the Fourteenth Amendment, is surely to deprive all the State's citizens of liberty without due process of law. The Fourteenth Amendment requires that the freedom of choice to marry not be restricted by invidious racial discriminations. Under our Constitution, the freedom to marry or not marry, a person of another race resides with the individual and cannot be infringed by the State. These convictions must be reversed.

■ [JUSTICE STEWART'S concurrence is omitted.]

NOTES

1. To be provocative: Where's the denial of *equal* protection of the laws in *Loving*? Are blacks and whites treated the same—according to the same rule? Neither blacks nor whites may marry outside of their race. Or does the Equal Protection Clause forbid all state *classifications* on the basis of race? Is the problem that this is a form of segregation? That it is a classification designed to subordinate a particular race? In other words, think of how you would state the combined principle of *Brown* and *Loving*. Is it no classifications based on race, ever? Is it no classifications that subjugate?

2. About eighty years earlier, in *Pace v. Alabama,* 106 U.S. 583 (1883), the Supreme Court had upheld an Alabama law prescribing a harsher sentence for cohabitating black and white couples than the sentence for cohabiting couples of the same race. The Court reasoned that because the law against interracial cohabitation was a distinct statute from the law penalizing same-race cohabitation, the disparate punishments were not a violation of equal protection. To the *Pace* court, the harsher punishment would only have been problematic if the same statute prescribed two different penalties for distinct classes of offenders. Does that make sense?

Pace survived until *McLaughlin v. Florida,* 379 U.S. 184 (1964), in which the Court reversed a criminal conviction for interracial cohabitation. The Court wrote that "we deal here with a classification based upon the race of the participants, which must be viewed in light of the historical fact that the central purpose of the Fourteenth Amendment was to eliminate racial discrimination emanating from official sources in the State." The state of Florida defended the law, citing *Pace* and arguing that the law did not violate equal protection because blacks and whites were punished equally if convicted. After citing a long string of cases that had undermined *Pace*'s holding, the *McLaughlin* Court rejected Florida's arguments and overruled *Pace* directly. The equal protection question was no longer whether the statute covered members of different races equally, but whether "there is an arbitrary or invidious discrimination between those classes covered by Florida's cohabitation law and those excluded." *McLaughlin* was cited by the Court in *Loving*, and it was treated as dispositive by Justice Stewart's concurrence in that case.

3. Although there has been scholarly debate over the historical purpose of the Fourteenth Amendment with respect to racial segregation (see Note 3 after *Brown*), there is a general consensus that the framers of the amendment did not intend it to constitutionalize a right to marry someone of a different race.

But cf. Steven A. Bank, Comment, *Anti–Miscegenation Laws and the Dilemma of Symmetry: The Understanding of Equality in the Civil Rights Act of 1875*, 2 U. Chi. L. Sch. Roundtable 303 (1995) (adducing evidence that some framers of the Fourteenth Amendment understood it to be inconsistent with anti-miscegenation laws). Thus one question that *Loving* poses, especially for originalists, is what to do if historical purpose diverges from other types of constitutional argument, such as text, precedent, and policy. Another way to put the question: how much weight should an interpreter give to the way the drafters of a constitutional provision expected that it would be applied? On the one hand, aren't the drafters' expected applications useful for informing our understanding of what highly general phrases in the Fourteenth Amendment mean? On the other hand, is there any serious reason in *Loving* to give the drafters' specific expectations more weight than all the other types of constitutional argument—including the text that was ratified as part of the Constitution, the exposition of that text in the central judicial precedent of *Brown*, and the powerful moral policy against the statute? For a critique of looking to the framers' expectations in *Loving*, see Steven G. Calabresi & Andrea Matthews, *Originalism and Loving v. Virginia*, 2012 BYU L. Rev. 1393 (2012). There is an abundant recent literature on the relationship between the text of a constitutional provision and its expected applications, and much of the literature examines the Equal Protection Clause of the Fourteenth Amendment. Good examples of the different views are Jack M. Balkin, LIVING ORIGINALISM (2011) and Christopher R. Green, *Originalism and the Sense-Reference Distinction*, 50 St. Louis U. L.J. 555 (2006).

4. *Palmore v. Sidoti*, 466 U.S. 429 (1984) involved a child custody battle following a divorce. The husband and the wife were white. The trial court awarded custody to the mother. But when she remarried a black man, the court awarded custody to the father, in "the best interest" of the child. "[D]espite the strides that had been made in bettering relations between the races in this country," the court held, it was inevitable that the daughter would "suffer from social stigmatization" resulting from the marriage. The Supreme Court unanimously reversed. It was absolutely clear, the Court said, "that the outcome would have been different" if the mother had remarried a white man. In the Court's words:

> A core purpose of the [Fourteenth Amendment] was to do away with all governmentally imposed discrimination based on race. Classifying persons according to their race is more likely to reflect racial prejudice than legitimate public concerns; the race, not the person, dictates the category. Such classifications are subject to the most exacting scrutiny. . . . The question . . . is whether the reality of private biases and the possible injury they might inflict are permissible considerations for removal of an infant child from the custody of its natural mother. We have little difficulty concluding that they are not. The Constitution cannot control such prejudices but neither can it tolerate them. Private biases may be outside the reach of the law, but the law cannot, directly or indirectly, give them effect.

What does *Palmore* imply for the practice of state or county adoption agencies matching (when possible) adoptive children and parents on the basis of race? Of granting prospective adoptive parents' preferences for a child of a specific race? Do such practices share the premises that the Court rejected so emphatically in *Palmore*? Are they inconsistent with the vision of *Loving*? For analysis of the problem, see Richard Banks, *The Color of Desire: Fulfilling*

Adoptive Parents' Racial Preferences Through Discriminatory State Action, 107 Yale L.J. 875 (1998).

5. In *Johnson v. California,* 543 U.S. 499 (2005), the Supreme Court considered the California Department of Corrections' unwritten policy of initially segregating prisoners according to race. Whenever new prisoners entered a correctional facility, the Department required them to be held in racially segregated double cells for up to sixty days. It claimed that the practice was necessary to prevent "violence caused by racial gangs." The Court held that strict scrutiny was appropriate in "every context" where racial classifications were used— including this one—and remanded the case. In its defense, the Department had argued that "[d]eference to the particular expertise of prison officials in the difficult task of managing daily prison operations requires a more relaxed standard of review for its segregation policy." Justices Scalia and Thomas adopted this position in their dissent, despite their usual commitment to a "colorblind Constitution." "The majority is concerned with sparing inmates the indignity and stigma of racial discrimination," Justice Thomas wrote. "California is concerned with their safety and saving their lives." What do you think?

[Assignment 64]

C. DISCRIMINATORY INTENT VERSUS DISPARATE IMPACT

In the area of race, does the Equal Protection Clause apply only to statutes that explicitly classify in racial terms? Or does it also apply to ones that have no explicit racial classifications but nevertheless affect different racial groups differently, i.e., that have a "disparate impact"? And in answering that question, if a statute has no explicit mention of race but does have a disparate impact on racial minorities, does it matter whether the legislators intended that disparate impact? These questions are central to the Court's decision in the next case.

Washington v. Davis
426 U.S. 229 (1976)

■ MR. JUSTICE WHITE delivered the opinion of the Court.

This case involves the validity of a qualifying test administered to applicants for positions as police officers in the District of Columbia Metropolitan Police Department. The test was sustained by the District Court but invalidated by the Court of Appeals. We are in agreement with the District Court and hence reverse the judgment of the Court of Appeals. . . .

[The amended complaint] alleged that the promotion policies of the Department were racially discriminatory and sought a declaratory judgment and an injunction. The respondents Harley and Sellers were permitted to intervene, their amended complaint asserting that their applications to become officers in the Department had been rejected, and that the Department's recruiting procedures discriminated on the basis of race against black applicants by a series of practices including, but not limited to, a written personnel test which excluded a disproportionately high number of Negro applicants. These practices were asserted to violate respondents' rights "under the due process clause of the Fifth Amendment to the United States Constitution."

According to the findings and conclusions of the District Court, to be accepted by the Department and to enter an intensive 17–week training program, the police recruit was required to satisfy certain physical and character standards, to be a high school graduate or its equivalent, and to receive a grade of at least 40 out of 80 on "Test 21," which is "an examination that is used generally throughout the federal service," which "was developed by the Civil Service Commission, not the Police Department," and which was "designed to test verbal ability, vocabulary, reading and comprehension."

The validity of Test 21 was the sole issue before the court on the motions for summary judgment. The District Court noted that there was no claim of "an intentional discrimination or purposeful discriminatory acts" but only a claim that Test 21 bore no relationship to job performance and "has a highly discriminatory impact in screening out black candidates." Respondents' evidence, the District Court said, warranted three conclusions: "(a) The number of black police officers, while substantial, is not proportionate to the population mix of the city. (b) A higher percentage of blacks fail the Test than whites. (c) The Test has not been validated to establish its reliability for measuring subsequent job performance." This showing was deemed sufficient to shift the burden of proof to the defendants in the action, petitioners here; but the court nevertheless concluded that on the undisputed facts respondents were not entitled to relief. The District Court relied on several factors. Since August 1969, 44% of new police force recruits had been black; that figure also represented the proportion of blacks on the total force and was roughly equivalent to 20–to–29–year–old blacks in the 50–mile radius in which the recruiting efforts of the Police Department had been concentrated. It was undisputed that the Department had systematically and affirmatively sought to enroll black officers many of whom passed the test but failed to report for duty. The District Court rejected the assertion that Test 21 was culturally slanted to favor whites and was "satisfied that the undisputable facts prove the test to be reasonably and directly related to the requirements of the police recruit training program and that it is neither so designed nor operates (sic) to discriminate against otherwise qualified blacks" It was thus not necessary to show that Test 21 was not only a useful indicator of training school performance but had also been validated in terms of job performance "The lack of job performance validation does not defeat the Test, given its direct relationship to recruiting and the valid part it plays in this process." The District Court ultimately concluded that "[t]he proof is wholly lacking that a police officer qualifies on the color of his skin rather than ability" and that the Department "should not be required on this showing to lower standards or to abandon efforts to achieve excellence." . . .

The Court of Appeals [reversed, declaring] that lack of discriminatory intent in designing and administering Test 21 was irrelevant; the critical fact was rather that a far greater proportion of blacks—four times as many—failed the test than did whites. This disproportionate impact, standing alone and without regard to whether it indicated a discriminatory purpose, was held sufficient to establish a constitutional violation, absent proof by petitioners that the test was an adequate measure of job performance in addition to being an indicator of probable success in the training program. . . .

The central purpose of the Equal Protection Clause of the Fourteenth Amendment is the prevention of official conduct discriminating on the basis of race. It is also true that the Due Process Clause of the Fifth Amendment contains an equal protection component prohibiting the United States from invidiously discriminating between individuals or groups. *Bolling v. Sharpe*, 347 U.S. 497 (1954). But our cases have not embraced the proposition that a law or other official act, without regard to whether it reflects a racially discriminatory purpose, is unconstitutional solely because it has a racially disproportionate impact.

Almost 100 years ago, *Strauder v. West Virginia*, 100 U.S. 303 (1880), established that the exclusion of Negroes from grand and petit juries in criminal proceedings violated the Equal Protection Clause, but the fact that a particular jury or a series of juries does not statistically reflect the racial composition of the community does not in itself make out an invidious discrimination forbidden by the Clause.

The school desegregation cases have also adhered to the basic equal protection principle that the invidious quality of a law claimed to be racially discriminatory must ultimately be traced to a racially discriminatory purpose. That there are both predominantly black and predominantly white schools in a community is not alone violative of the Equal Protection Clause. The essential element of de jure segregation is "a current condition of segregation resulting from intentional state action." *Keyes v. School Dist. No. 1*, 413 U.S. 189, 205 (1973). The differentiating factor between de jure segregation and so-called de facto segregation . . . is purpose or intent to segregate."

This is not to say that the necessary discriminatory racial purpose must be express or appear on the face of the statute, or that a law's disproportionate impact is irrelevant in cases involving Constitution-based claims of racial discrimination. A statute, otherwise neutral on its face, must not be applied so as invidiously to discriminate on the basis of race. *Yick Wo v. Hopkins*, 118 U.S. 356 (1886). It is also clear from the cases dealing with racial discrimination in the selection of juries that the systematic exclusion of Negroes is itself such an "unequal application of the law . . . as to show intentional discrimination." *Akins v. Texas, supra*, 325 U.S., at 404.

Necessarily, an invidious discriminatory purpose may often be inferred from the totality of the relevant facts, including the fact, if it is true, that the law bears more heavily on one race than another. [Nevertheless,] we have not held that a law, neutral on its face and serving ends otherwise within the power of government to pursue, is invalid under the Equal Protection Clause simply because it may affect a greater proportion of one race than of another. Disproportionate impact is not irrelevant, but it is not the sole touchstone of an invidious racial discrimination forbidden by the Constitution. Standing alone, it does not trigger the rule, *McLaughlin v. Florida*, 379 U.S. 184 (1964), that racial classifications are to be subjected to the strictest scrutiny and are justifiable only by the weightiest of considerations.

There are some indications to the contrary in our cases. In *Palmer v. Thompson*, 403 U.S. 217 (1971), the city of Jackson, Miss., following a court decree to this effect, desegregated all of its public facilities save five swimming pools which had been operated by the city and which, following the decree, were closed by ordinance pursuant to a determination by the city council that closure was necessary to preserve peace and order and that integrated pools could not be economically operated. Accepting the finding that the pools were closed to avoid violence and economic loss, this Court rejected the argument that the abandonment of this service was inconsistent with the outstanding desegregation decree and that the otherwise seemingly permissible ends served by the ordinance could be impeached by demonstrating that racially invidious motivations had prompted the city council's action. The holding was that the city was not overtly or covertly operating segregated pools and was extending identical treatment to both whites and Negroes. The opinion warned against grounding decision on legislative purpose or motivation, thereby lending support for the proposition that the operative effect of the law rather than its purpose is the paramount factor. But the holding of the case was that the legitimate purposes of the ordinance to preserve peace and avoid deficits were not open to impeachment by evidence that the councilmen were actually motivated by racial considerations. Whatever dicta the opinion may contain, the decision did not involve, much less invalidate, a statute or ordinance having neutral purposes but disproportionate racial consequences. . . .

[W]e have difficulty understanding how a law establishing a racially neutral qualification for employment is nevertheless racially discriminatory and denies "any person . . . equal protection of the laws" simply because a greater proportion of Negroes fail to qualify than members of other racial or ethnic groups. [Test 21,] which is administered generally to prospective Government employees, concededly seeks to ascertain whether those who take it have acquired a particular level of verbal skill; and it is untenable that the Constitution prevents the Government from seeking modestly to upgrade the communicative abilities of its employees rather than to be satisfied with some lower level of competence, particularly where the job requires special ability to communicate orally and in writing. Respondents, as Negroes, could no more successfully claim that the test denied them equal protection than could white applicants who also failed. The conclusion would not be different in the face of proof that more Negroes than whites had been disqualified by Test 21. That other Negroes also failed to score well would, alone, not demonstrate that respondents individually were being denied equal protection of the laws by the application of an otherwise valid qualifying test being administered to prospective police recruits.

Nor on the facts of the case before us would the disproportionate impact of Test 21 warrant the conclusion that it is a purposeful device to discriminate against Negroes and hence an infringement of the constitutional rights of respondents as well as other black applicants. As we have said, the test is neutral on its face and rationally may be said to serve a purpose the Government is constitutionally empowered to pursue. Even agreeing with the District Court that the differential racial effect of Test 21 called for further inquiry, we think the District Court correctly held that the affirmative efforts of the Metropolitan Police Department to recruit black officers, the changing racial composition of the recruit classes and of the force in general, and the relationship of the test to the training program negated any inference that the Department discriminated on the basis of race or that "a police officer qualifies on the color of his skin rather than ability." 348 F. Supp., at 18. . . .

■ [The concurring opinion of JUSTICE STEVENS is omitted.]

■ MR. JUSTICE BRENNAN, with whom MR. JUSTICE MARSHALL joins, dissenting.

The Court holds that the job qualification examination (Test 21) given by the District of Columbia Metropolitan Police Department does not unlawfully discriminate on the basis of race under either constitutional or statutory standards. [I] would affirm the Court of Appeals because petitioners have failed to prove that Test 21 satisfies the applicable statutory standards. . . .

[The bulk of the dissent focused on the asserted violation of the Title VII statute, which prohibits employment discrimination on the basis of race.— Editors]

Sound policy considerations support the view that, at a minimum, petitioners should have been required to prove that the police training examinations either measure job-related skills or predict job performance. Where employers try to validate written qualification tests by proving a correlation with written examinations in a training course, there is a substantial danger that people who have good verbal skills will achieve high scores on both tests due to verbal ability, rather than "job-specific ability." As a result, employers could validate any entrance examination that measures only verbal ability by giving another written test that measures verbal ability at the end of a training course. Any contention that the resulting correlation between examination scores would be evidence that the initial test is "job related" is plainly erroneous. It seems to me, however, that the Court's holding in this case can be read as endorsing this dubious proposition. . . .

I would hold that petitioners have not met their burden of proof and affirm the judgment of the Court of Appeals.

NOTES

1. *Analogies to the First Amendment.* Are you persuaded by the Court's reasoning? Does the Equal Protection Clause forbid state laws that have an unintended disproportionate effect on the basis of race? Is the clause about the use of racial classifications or about racial effects? Recall two cases from Chapter 6 that considered government motivation, both regarding clauses of the First Amendment: *United States v. O'Brien*, allowing the government to regulate expressive conduct but not when it does so *because* of the expressive content; and *Employment Division v. Smith*, reading the Free Exercise Clause as allowing many laws that have the effect of burdening religious exercise as long as they were not adopted for that reason. (These are general statements of those two cases; there are qualifications.) Is the test of *Washington v. Davis* similar to these tests? Is that a good approach for the Court to adopt in the context of racial discrimination? Why or why not?

2. *Bias in Administration.* In *Yick Wo v. Hopkins,* 118 U.S. 356 (1886), the Supreme Court held unconstitutional the detention of unlicensed Chinese laundry operators. San Francisco had passed ordinances requiring those who operated laundries in wooden buildings to obtain permits from the board of supervisors. Yick Wo had operated his laundry for twenty-two years and had recently passed a fire inspection when the board of supervisors chose not to renew his permit. After continuing to operate his laundry, Yick Wo was fined and then imprisoned for failure to pay the fine. Upon review, the Court discovered that while 80 wooden laundries operated by non-Chinese persons were granted renewals, 199 of the 200 Chinese-owned laundries were denied renewals. Though the ordinance was neutral on its face and was a legitimate exercise of local police power to protect the public from fire, the Court took issue with the unchecked discretion granted to the board of supervisors. The city acknowledged that discrimination had occurred and offered no justification for it, leaving the Court to find that "the conclusion cannot be resisted that no reason for

[the discrimination] exists except hostility to the race and nationality to which the petitioners belong, and which, in the eye of the law, is not justified."

3. *Evidence of Intent.* In *Gomillion v. Lightfoot,* 364 U.S. 339 (1960), the Supreme Court held that the redrawing of political boundaries to disenfranchise black voters could be challenged under the Fourteenth and Fifteenth Amendments. In 1957, the Alabama Legislature passed Local Act No. 140, which redrew the boundaries of the city of Tuskegee so as to remove "all save four or five of its 400 Negro voters while not removing a single white voter or resident." Tuskegee had been square-shaped, but the Act "transformed it into a strangely irregular twenty-eight-sided figure." When the plaintiffs—black Alabama citizens who were pushed outside of Tuskegee by the redistricting measure—challenged the Act, both the district court and court of appeals dismissed the case for failure to state a claim for which relief could be granted. Despite the plaintiffs' claims that the redistricting was racially discriminatory, the lower courts held that they had "no power to change any boundaries of municipal corporations fixed by a duly convened and elected legislative body, acting for the people in the State of Alabama." (Echoes of *Giles v. Harris*?) The Court rejected this conclusion, holding that while a state's authority to manage its own political subdivisions was substantial and deserved deference, it was not so absolute as to trump claims that constitutional rights had been violated. The plaintiffs had stated a valid claim and could go to trial. If the evidence "remained uncontradicted or unqualified, the conclusion would be irresistible, tantamount for all practical purposes to a mathematical demonstration, that the legislation is solely concerned with segregating white and colored voters by fencing Negro citizens out of town so as to deprive them of their preexisting municipal vote."

4. *Motive Matters.* Consider the extraordinary case of *Griffin v. County School Board of Prince Edward County,* 377 U.S. 218 (1964), which involved a Virginia county's determined resistance to school desegregation. After *Brown,* the Virginia legislature undertook a statewide effort to resist desegregation, closing integrated public schools and giving tuition grants for students to enroll in private schools. The Supreme Court of Appeals of Virginia struck down the legislation as a violation of the Virginia Constitution's requirement that the state provide a system of free public education. The legislature responded in April 1959 by adopting a so-called "freedom of choice" program, which included the repeal of the state's compulsory school attendance laws. Prince Edward County thereupon refused to levy school taxes for the 1959–1960 year, and its public schools did not open in the fall of 1959, even though the public schools of every other county in Virginia did. A group calling itself the Prince Edward School Foundation set up private schools exclusively for white children. And the public schools of the county remained closed for four years. In *Griffin,* the Supreme Court upheld a lower court's injunction against the Prince Edward County plan:

> [W]e agree with the District Court that, under the circumstances here, closing the Prince Edward County schools while public schools in all the other counties of Virginia were being maintained denied the petitioners and class of Negro students they represent the equal protection of the laws guaranteed by the Fourteenth Amendment. . . . [T]he record in the present case could not be clearer that Prince Edward's public schools were closed and private schools operated in their place with state and county assistance, for one reason, and one reason only: to ensure, through

measures taken by the county and the State, that white and colored children in Prince Edward County would not, under any circumstances, go to the same school. Whatever nonracial grounds might support a State's allowing a county to abandon public schools, the object must be a constitutional one, and grounds of race and opposition to desegregation do not qualify as constitutional."

Id. at 225, 231. Note that *Griffin* did not hold that "school choice" or "voucher" plans are *per se* unconstitutional, only that they are unconstitutional when designed and operated for purposes of accomplishing racial segregation. Likewise, in *Green v. County School Board,* 391 U.S. 430 (1968), the Supreme Court held that the "freedom of choice" school integration plan adopted by New Kent County, Virginia did not comply with the requirements of *Brown II.* Like Prince Edward County, New Kent County chose its own response to *Brown* following the Virginia legislature's failed anti-integration initiative. Unlike Prince Edward County, however, New Kent County only had two schools. Before *Brown,* the schools were segregated by law—New Kent for whites and George W. Watkins for blacks. The County's new "freedom of choice" plan gave students the option of attending either school. Students in the first and eighth grades chose which school they wanted to attend and were reassigned to the same school every year unless they applied for a change. From the plan's inception in 1961 until September 1964, not a single black student in the county applied to New Kent and not a single white student applied to George W. Watkins.

In striking down the New Kent County plan, the Court stated that "[w]e do not hold that a 'freedom-of-choice' plan might of itself be unconstitutional," but rather that New Kent's plan "cannot be accepted as a sufficient step to effectuate a transition to a unitary school system." It required the school board to "formulate a new plan and . . . fashion steps which promise realistically to convert promptly to a system without a 'white' school and a 'Negro' school, but just schools."

Clearly, *Griffin* and *Green* involved policies and practices designed to accomplish an impermissible goal of effectuating or maintaining racial segregation. They involved racially disparate impact *plus* the official intent to accomplish precisely that disparate impact. In each case, the official intent to discriminate could be clearly inferred from circumstances. (What if it were not? How does *Washington v. Davis* resolve this situation?)

In another case, *Palmer v. Thompson,* 403 U.S. 217 (1971), the Supreme Court found no equal protection violation where the city of Jackson, Mississippi closed its public pools following a district court ruling declaring the city's operation of segregated parks and other public facilities illegal. After the ruling, Jackson desegregated its "public parks, auditoriums, golf courses, and the city zoo," but decided to close its five public pools. In response, the plaintiffs—a group of black citizens of Jackson—filed suit, asking that the pools be reopened and desegregated. The plaintiffs argued that the pool closings were a violation of equal protection under the Fourteenth Amendment and one of the "badges and incidents" of slavery prohibited by the Thirteenth Amendment. The district court disagreed and "found that the closing was justified to preserve peace and order and because the pools could not be operated economically on an integrated basis." The court of appeals affirmed. In a 5–4 decision written by Justice Black, the Supreme Court affirmed as well, rejecting the plaintiff's reliance upon *Griffin* as precedent for their position.

Regarding *Griffin*, Justice Black wrote, "[the] case simply treated the school program for what it was—an operation of Prince Edward County schools under a thinly disguised 'private' school system actually planned and carried out by the State and the county to maintain segregated education with public funds." The pools were different, Justice Black argued, because the evidence showed that the city closed them indefinitely and had no intentions of reopening them as segregated private pools subsidized with state dollars. Do you find this reasoning persuasive? Would the Prince Edward County program really have survived judicial review if there had been no state subsidy component and the County had simply abandoned public education altogether? On the other hand, does the Equal Protection Clause impose a duty on the government to operate swimming pools? Was everyone treated equally, not "separate-but-equal" but "nobody-gets-a-public-pool" equal?

D. AFFIRMATIVE ACTION

The legacy of the landmark decisions in *Brown v. Board of Education* and *Loving v. Virginia* is the principle that the government may not discriminate, segregate, or otherwise invidiously classify on the basis of race—at least without an overwhelmingly "compelling" justification. Even then the government may classify on the basis of race only by "narrowly tailored" means that will precisely accomplish that justification. Does this principle mean that government also may not use race as an "affirmative" basis for granting benefits or privileges to minorities? Or should these more beneficent racial classifications be judged by a different, more lenient standard? Does it matter whether the government's stated objective is to atone for the nation's history of past discrimination? These questions are central to the debate over affirmative action, and they arise in many contexts, including government contracts, government employment, and state university admissions.

An Introductory Hypothetical (*Taxman v. Piscataway*)

Before considering the Supreme Court's cases in this area, reflect on the following hypothetical based on *Taxman v. Piscataway Township Board of Education*, 91 F.3d 1547 (3d Cir. 1996) (en banc)—a case that was almost decided by the Supreme Court. It settled after *certiorari* was granted.

In a public school district, two teachers—one a black woman, the other a white woman—are hired to teach at the same school. They have the same prior experience. They start on the same day. For budgetary reasons, the school needs to lay off one of them. The school board formally determines that the two are absolutely equal in terms of seniority, qualifications, and all other relevant considerations of merit. (Perhaps the board took this position to duck a difficult decision, avoiding the hard feelings that might come from evaluating the teachers' comparative merit. But no matter: those are the facts in the record.) The board decides to lay off the white teacher, solely on the basis of race. Otherwise its practice is to draw lots. The board's stated justification is the school district's affirmative action policy and its desire to promote racial diversity among its faculty.

Did the school district violate the Equal Protection Clause? Should affirmative action programs be governed by the same standard as other racial classifications? Or is there a difference between a benign race-based classification and an invidious one? If so, what is that difference? And is the school district's classification benign?

What justifications might the school district offer for its action that would persuade you that it should be upheld as constitutional? Consider the following options: (1) The need to remedy past societal discrimination against racial minorities? (2) The creation of more opportunities for minorities in a particular employment sector? (3) Greater diversity, in the sense of racial balance among teachers, as an independent value pursued for its own sake? (4) Promoting racial diversity where the school has a history of racial discrimination in employment? (5) Remedying the school district's past racial discrimination against this particular teacher? (6) Providing minority role models for minority students at the school? (7) None of the above?

Would your answers be different if the situation involved not school employment but rather admission to an elite state university? Or school assignment within a public school district where parents consider some schools better than others? Would your answers be different if the situation involved the consideration of race in bidding for government contracts? If you think through these questions systematically, you will have gone a long way toward understanding the constitutional debate over affirmative action and the Equal Protection Clause in the Supreme Court's decisions.

A NOTE ON THE MODERN HISTORY OF AFFIRMATIVE ACTION

It is impossible to understand the debate over affirmative action without a brief review of its history as a response to the nation's long practice of racial segregation and discrimination. As you have already seen, in the last months of the Civil War, Congress passed the Freedmen's Bureau Act. This act authorized the assignment of property to the newly freed slaves in the South. This was one of the first race-conscious federal programs to benefit a minority, and it was followed by several other statutes passed by Reconstruction Congresses, all in the wake of war and emancipation and against the backdrop of virulent hostility by many Southerners. You have also seen how the promise that the Fourteenth Amendment would ban invidious racial discrimination was initially honored by the Court in *Strauder v. West Virginia* (1880) but then denied in decisions such as *The Civil Rights Cases* (1883) and especially *Plessy v. Ferguson* (1896). Those later decisions, following the withdrawal of Union troops from the South in 1877, allowed Southern states and border states to experiment more and more boldly with laws establishing racial apartheid.

Eventually, Presidents Franklin Roosevelt and Harry Truman began acting to remove the structures of racial discrimination in federal employment and in the military. President Truman ordered the integration of the military in 1948. Six years later, *Brown v. Board of Education* struck a forceful blow against segregation. Almost a decade after that Congress passed the Civil Rights Act of 1964, prohibiting employment discrimination on the basis of race; and the Voting Rights Act of 1965, protecting black citizens' right to vote. Only during this "Second Reconstruction" did the structure of Jim Crow laws begin to crumble.

Two centuries of slavery and a century of Jim Crow had left black Americans disadvantaged in wealth, employment, education, and political power. To correct these deficits, the Kennedy, Johnson, and Nixon administrations each experimented with programs of "affirmative action" to achieve results commensurate with the promise of equality under law. The rationale was stated by

President Lyndon Johnson in a commencement address at Howard University in 1965:

> [F]reedom is not enough. You do not wipe away the scars of centuries by saying: Now you are free to go where you want, and do as you desire, and choose the leaders you please. You do not take a person who, for years, has been hobbled by chains and liberate him, bring him up to the starting line of a race and then say, "you are free to compete with all the others," and still justly believe that you have been completely fair. Thus it is not enough just to open the gates of opportunity. All our citizens must have the ability to walk through those gates. This is the next and the more profound stage of the battle for civil rights. We seek not just freedom but opportunity. We seek not just legal equity but human ability, not just equality as a right and a theory but equality as a fact and equality as a result.

In this modern form, affirmative action began as an effort to recruit minority students and employees. Over time, it evolved into more sweeping commitments to racial diversity in education and in the workplace. During the 1970s, affirmative action began to include minority "set asides" in federal contracting, in employment, and in university admissions. Some proponents of this type of affirmative action saw it as a down-payment on reparations owed by white Americans for slavery and segregation. Opponents criticized the new programs for undermining merit selection and fostering race-consciousness through quotas.

At roughly the same time, there were bitter struggles over mandatory busing as a way to integrate primary and secondary schools. After an uncertain start, the Supreme Court eventually settled on a policy of mandating busing only where there had been *de jure* segregation, i.e., segregation as a matter of law, and not where school districts were *de facto* segregated because of racial residential patterns.

In considering the constitutional issues surrounding affirmative action, presented in the cases that follow, think of several questions that flow from this brief history. First, does the anti-race-discrimination command of the Fourteenth Amendment even apply to discrimination that has benign motivations, as in affirmative-action programs? Second, does the American history of slavery, racial discrimination, and segregation justify racial preferences on a class-wide basis? Third, is there a difference between affirmative action in the form of seeking and recruiting qualified minority applicants and candidates and affirmative action in the form of giving preferences on the basis of race?

Racial Preferences in State University Admissions

As an entry point to the Supreme Court's cases on affirmative action, consider a case about racial preferences in state university admissions, *Grutter v. Bollinger*, 539 U.S. 306 (2003). In that case, the Court heard a challenge to a University of Michigan Law School program providing an unquantified racial preference in admissions in order to promote diversity in the entering class. It narrowly upheld (5–4) the Michigan Law School program. But in a companion case decided the same day, *Gratz v. Bollinger*, 539 U.S. 244 (2003), the Court narrowly struck down (6–3) the University of Michigan's *undergraduate* admissions racial preference program. That program gave a quantified racial preference—a bonus of twenty points for racial minority status on an applicant's admissions score. (There were one hundred possible points on the admissions score.) Only two justices agreed with the outcome in both cases. In other words, even though the Court treated the two cases differently for constitutional purposes, seven justices thought they should be treated the same way.

Grutter v. Bollinger

539 U.S. 306 (2003)

■ JUSTICE O'CONNOR delivered the opinion of the Court.

This case requires us to decide whether the use of race as a factor in student admissions by the University of Michigan Law School (Law School) is unlawful.

I–A

The Law School ranks among the Nation's top law schools. It receives more than 3,500 applications each year for a class of around 350 students. Seeking to "admit a group of students who individually and collectively are among the most capable," the Law School looks for individuals with "substantial promise for success in law school" and "a strong likelihood of succeeding in the practice of law and contributing in diverse ways to the well-being of others." More broadly, the Law School seeks "a mix of students with varying backgrounds and experiences who will respect and learn from each other." In 1992, the dean of the Law School charged a faculty committee with crafting a written admissions policy to implement these goals. . . .

The hallmark of that policy is its focus on academic ability coupled with a flexible assessment of applicants' talents, experiences, and potential "to contribute to the learning of those around them." The policy requires admissions officials to evaluate each applicant based on all the information available in the file, including a personal statement, letters of recommendation, and an essay describing the ways in which the applicant will contribute to the life and diversity of the Law School. In reviewing an applicant's file, admissions officials must consider the applicant's undergraduate grade point average (GPA) and Law School Admission Test (LSAT) score because they are important (if imperfect) predictors of academic success in law school. The policy stresses that "no applicant should be admitted unless we expect that applicant to do well enough to graduate with no serious academic problems."

The policy makes clear, however, that even the highest possible score does not guarantee admission to the Law School. Nor does a low score automatically disqualify an applicant. Rather, the policy requires admissions officials to look beyond grades and test scores to other criteria that are important to the Law School's educational objectives. . . .

The policy aspires to "achieve that diversity which has the potential to enrich everyone's education and thus make a law school class stronger than the sum of its parts." The policy . . . reaffirm[s] the Law School's longstanding commitment to . . . "racial and ethnic diversity with special reference to the inclusion of students from groups which have been historically discriminated against, like African–Americans, Hispanics and Native Americans, who without this commitment might not be represented in our student body in meaningful numbers." By enrolling a " 'critical mass' of [underrepresented] minority students," the Law School seeks to "ensur[e] their ability to make unique contributions to the character of the Law School."

The policy does not define diversity "solely in terms of racial and ethnic status."

B

Petitioner Barbara Grutter is a white Michigan resident who applied to the Law School in 1996 with a 3.8 GPA and 161 LSAT score. The Law School initially placed petitioner on a waiting list, but subsequently rejected her application. In December 1997, petitioner filed suit . . . [against the law school and its officers. She] alleged that her application was rejected because the Law School uses race as a "predominant" factor, giving applicants who belong to certain minority groups "a significantly greater chance of admission than students with similar credentials from disfavored racial groups." Petitioner also alleged that respondents "had no compelling interest to justify their use of race in the admissions process." Petitioner requested compensatory and punitive damages, an order requiring the Law School to offer her admission, and an injunction prohibiting the Law School from continuing to discriminate on the basis of race. . . .

During the 15–day bench trial, the parties introduced extensive evidence concerning the Law School's use of race in the admissions process. Dennis Shields, Director of Admissions when petitioner applied to the Law School, testified that he did not direct his staff to admit a particular percentage or number of minority students, but rather to consider an applicant's race along with all other factors. Shields testified that at the height of the admissions season, he would frequently consult the so-called "daily reports" that kept track of the racial and ethnic composition of the class (along with other information such as residency status and gender). This was done, Shields testified, to ensure that a critical mass of underrepresented minority students would be reached so as to realize the educational benefits of a diverse student body. Shields stressed, however, that he did not seek to admit any particular number or percentage of underrepresented minority students. . . .

In an attempt to quantify the extent to which the Law School actually considers race in making admissions decisions, the parties introduced voluminous evidence at trial. Relying on data obtained from the Law School, petitioner's expert, Dr. Kinley Larntz, generated and analyzed "admissions grids" for the years in question (1995–2000). These grids show the number of applicants and the number of admittees for all combinations of GPAs and LSAT scores. Dr. Larntz . . . concluded that membership in certain minority groups "is an extremely strong factor in the decision for acceptance," and that applicants from these minority groups "are given an extremely large allowance for admission" as compared to applicants who are members of nonfavored groups. Dr. Larntz conceded, however, that race is not the predominant factor in the Law School's admissions calculus.

Dr. Stephen Raudenbush, the Law School's expert, focused on the predicted effect of eliminating race as a factor in the Law School's admission process. In Dr. Raudenbush's view, a race-blind admissions system would have a "very dramatic," negative effect on underrepresented minority admissions. He testified that in 2000, 35 percent of underrepresented minority applicants were admitted. Dr. Raudenbush predicted that if race were not considered, only 10 percent of those applicants would have been admitted. Under this scenario, underrepresented minority students would have constituted 4 percent of the entering class in 2000 instead of the actual figure of 14.5 percent.

In the end, the District Court concluded that the Law School's use of race as a factor in admissions decisions was unlawful. . . . The District Court granted petitioner's request for declaratory relief and enjoined the Law School from using race as a factor in its admissions decisions. . . .

Sitting en banc, the Court of Appeals reversed the District Court's judgment and vacated the injunction. . . . We granted certiorari to resolve the disagreement among the Courts of Appeals on a question of national importance: Whether diversity is a compelling interest that can justify the narrowly tailored use of race in selecting applicants for admission to public universities.

II–A

We last addressed the use of race in public higher education over 25 years ago. In the landmark *Bakke* case, we reviewed a racial set-aside program that reserved 16 out of 100 seats in a medical school class for members of certain minority groups. The decision produced six separate opinions, none of which commanded a majority of the Court. Four Justices would have upheld the program against all attack on the ground that the government can use race to "remedy disadvantages cast on minorities by past racial prejudice." Four other Justices avoided the constitutional question altogether and struck down the program on statutory grounds. Justice Powell provided a fifth vote not only for invalidating the set-aside program, but also for reversing the state court's injunction against any use of race whatsoever. . . .

Since this Court's splintered decision in *Bakke,* Justice Powell's opinion announcing the judgment of the Court has served as the touchstone for constitutional analysis of race-conscious admissions policies. Public and private universities across the Nation have modeled their own admissions programs on Justice Powell's views on permissible race-conscious policies. . . .

Justice Powell began by stating that "[t]he guarantee of equal protection cannot mean one thing when applied to one individual and something else when applied to a person of another color. If both are not accorded the same protection, then it is not equal." *Bakke,* 438 U.S., at 289–290. In Justice Powell's view, when governmental decisions "touch upon an individual's race or ethnic background, he is entitled to a judicial determination that the burden he is asked to bear on that basis is precisely tailored to serve a compelling governmental interest." Under this exacting standard, only one of the interests asserted by the university survived Justice Powell's scrutiny.

First, Justice Powell rejected an interest in "reducing the historic deficit of traditionally disfavored minorities in medical schools and in the medical profession" as an unlawful interest in racial balancing. Second, Justice Powell rejected an interest in remedying societal discrimination because such measures would risk placing unnecessary burdens on innocent third parties "who bear no responsibility for whatever harm the beneficiaries of the special admissions program are thought to have suffered." Third, Justice Powell rejected an interest in "increasing the number of physicians who will practice in communities currently underserved," concluding that even if such an interest could be compelling in some circumstances the program under review was not "geared to promote that goal."

Justice Powell approved the university's use of race to further only one interest: "the attainment of a diverse student body." . . . Justice Powell was, however, careful to emphasize that in his view race "is only one element in a range of factors a university properly may consider in attaining the goal of a heterogeneous student body." . . .

In the wake of our fractured decision in *Bakke,* courts have struggled to discern whether Justice Powell's diversity rationale, set forth in part of the opinion joined by no other Justice, is nonetheless binding precedent. . . . We do not find it necessary to decide [this point. Rather,] for the reasons set out below, today we endorse Justice Powell's view that student body diversity is a compelling state interest that can justify the use of race in university admissions.

B

The Equal Protection Clause provides that no State shall "deny to any person within its jurisdiction the equal protection of the laws." Because the Fourteenth Amendment "protect[s] *persons,* not *groups,*" all "governmental action based on race—a *group* classification long recognized as in most circumstances irrelevant and therefore prohibited—should be subjected to detailed judicial inquiry to ensure that the *personal* right to equal protection of the laws has not been infringed." *Adarand Constructors, Inc. v. Peña,* 515 U.S. 200, 227 (1995). It follows from that principle that "government may treat people differently because of their race only for the most compelling reasons." *Id.*

We have held that all racial classifications imposed by government "must be analyzed by a reviewing court under strict scrutiny." This means that such classifications are constitutional only if they are narrowly tailored to further compelling governmental interests. "Absent searching judicial inquiry into the justification for such race-based measures," we have no way to determine what "classifications are 'benign' or 'remedial' and what classifications are in fact motivated by illegitimate notions of racial inferiority or simple racial politics." *Richmond v. J.A. Croson Co.,* 488 U.S. 469, 493 (1989) (plurality opinion). . . .

When race-based action is necessary to further a compelling governmental interest, such action does not violate the constitutional guarantee of equal protection so long as the narrow-tailoring requirement is also satisfied. . . .

III–A

With these principles in mind, we turn to the question whether the Law School's use of race is justified by a compelling state interest. Before this Court, as they have throughout this litigation, respondents assert only one justification for their use of race in the admissions process: obtaining "the educational benefits that flow from a diverse student body." . . .

It is true that some language in [our earlier affirmative action decisions] might be read to suggest that remedying past discrimination is the only permissible justification for race-based governmental action. See, *e.g., Richmond v. J.A. Croson Co.,* at 493 (plurality opinion) (stating that unless classifications based on race are "strictly reserved for remedial settings, they may in fact promote notions of racial inferiority and lead to a politics of racial hostility"). But we have never held that the only governmental use of race that can survive strict scrutiny is remedying past discrimination. Nor, since *Bakke,* have we directly addressed the use of race in the context of public higher education. Today, we hold that the Law School has a compelling interest in attaining a diverse student body.

The Law School's educational judgment that such diversity is essential to its educational mission is one to which we defer. The Law School's assessment that diversity will, in fact, yield educational benefits is substantiated by respondents and their *amici*. . . . Our holding today is in keeping with our tradition of giving a degree of deference to a university's academic decisions, within constitutionally prescribed limits. . . .

[T]he Law School's concept of critical mass is defined by reference to the educational benefits that diversity is designed to produce. These benefits are substantial. As the District Court emphasized, the Law School's admissions policy promotes "cross-racial understanding," helps to break down racial stereotypes, and "enables [students] to better understand persons of different races." These benefits are "important and laudable," because "classroom discussion is livelier, more spirited, and simply more enlightening and interesting" when the students have "the greatest possible variety of backgrounds."

The Law School's claim of a compelling interest is further bolstered by its *amici*, who point to the educational benefits that flow from student body diversity. In addition to the expert studies and reports entered into evidence at trial, numerous studies show that student body diversity promotes learning outcomes, and "better prepares students for an increasingly diverse workforce and society, and better prepares them as professionals." Brief for American Educational Research Association et al. as *Amici Curiae* 3.

These benefits are not theoretical but real, as major American businesses have made clear that the skills needed in today's increasingly global marketplace can only be developed through exposure to widely diverse people, cultures, ideas, and viewpoints. Brief for 3M et al. as *Amici Curiae* 5; Brief for General Motors Corp. as *Amicus Curiae* 3–4. What is more, high-ranking retired officers and civilian leaders of the United States military assert that, "[b]ased on [their] decades of experience," a "highly qualified, racially diverse officer corps . . . is essential to the military's ability to fulfill its principle mission to provide national security." Brief for Julius W. Becton, Jr., et al. as *Amici Curiae* 5. The primary sources for the Nation's officer corps are the service academies and the Reserve Officers Training Corps (ROTC), the latter comprising students already admitted to participating colleges and universities. At present, "the military cannot achieve an officer corps that is *both* highly qualified *and* racially diverse unless the service academies and the ROTC used limited race-conscious recruiting and admissions policies." *Ibid.* (emphasis in original). . . .

[T]he diffusion of knowledge and opportunity through public institutions of higher education must be accessible to all individuals regardless of race or ethnicity. . . . Moreover, universities, and in particular, law schools, represent the training ground for a large number of our Nation's leaders. Individuals with law degrees occupy roughly half the state governorships, more than half the seats in the United States Senate, and more than a third of the seats in the United States House of Representatives. . . .

The Law School has determined, based on its experience and expertise, that a "critical mass" of underrepresented minorities is necessary to further its compelling interest in securing the educational benefits of a diverse student body.

B

Even in the limited circumstance when drawing racial distinctions is permissible to further a compelling state interest, government is still "constrained in how it may pursue that end: [T]he means chosen to accomplish the [government's] asserted purpose must be specifically and narrowly framed to accomplish that purpose." *Shaw v. Hunt,* 517 U.S. 899, 908 (1996). . . .

To be narrowly tailored, a race-conscious admissions program cannot use a quota system. . . . Instead, a university may consider race or ethnicity only as a " 'plus' in a particular applicant's file," without "insulat[ing] the individual from comparison with all other candidates for the available seats." *Bakke* (Opinion of Powell, J.) at 317. . . .

We find that the Law School's admissions program bears the hallmarks of a narrowly tailored plan. . . . We are satisfied that the Law School's admissions program, like the Harvard plan described by Justice Powell, does not operate as a quota. Properly understood, a "quota" is a program in which a certain fixed number or proportion of opportunities are "reserved exclusively for certain minority groups." *Richmond v. J.A. Croson Co.,* at 496 (plurality opinion). . . . Justice Powell's distinction between the medical school's rigid 16–seat quota and Harvard's flexible use of race as a "plus" factor is instructive. . . . The Law School's goal of attaining a critical mass of underrepresented minority students does not transform its program into a quota. . . .

That a race-conscious admissions program does not operate as a quota does not, by itself, satisfy the requirement of individualized consideration. When using race as a "plus" factor in university admissions, a university's admissions program must remain flexible enough to ensure that each applicant is evaluated as an individual and not in a way that makes an applicant's race or ethnicity the defining feature of his or her application. . . .

Here, the Law School engages in a highly individualized, holistic review of each applicant's file, giving serious consideration to all the ways an applicant might contribute to a diverse educational environment. The Law School affords this individualized consideration to applicants of all races. There is no policy, either *de jure* or *de facto,* of automatic acceptance or rejection based on any single "soft" variable. Unlike the program at issue in *Gratz v. Bollinger,* 539 U.S. 244, the Law School awards no mechanical, predetermined diversity "bonuses" based on race or ethnicity. See 539 U.S., at 271–272 (distinguishing a race-conscious admissions program that automatically awards 20 points based on race from the Harvard plan, which considered race but "did not contemplate that any single characteristic automatically ensured a specific and identifiable contribution to a university's diversity"). . . .

We also find that, like the Harvard plan Justice Powell referenced in *Bakke,* the Law School's race-conscious admissions program adequately ensures that all factors that may contribute to student body diversity are meaningfully considered alongside race in admissions decisions. With respect to the use of race itself, all underrepresented minority students admitted by the Law School have been deemed qualified. . . . What is more, the Law School actually gives substantial weight to diversity factors besides race. . . .

Petitioner and the United States argue that the Law School's plan is not narrowly tailored because race-neutral means exist to obtain the educational benefits of student body diversity that the Law School seeks. We disagree. Narrow tailoring does not require exhaustion of every conceivable race-neutral alternative. Nor does it require a university to choose between maintaining a reputation for excellence or fulfilling a commitment to provide educational opportunities to members of all racial groups. . . .

The District Court took the Law School to task for failing to consider race-neutral alternatives such as "using a lottery system" or "decreasing the emphasis for all applicants on undergraduate GPA and LSAT scores." But these alternatives would require a dramatic sacrifice of diversity, the academic quality of all admitted students, or both. . . .

[I]n the context of its individualized inquiry into the possible diversity contributions of all applicants, the Law School's race-conscious admissions program does not unduly harm nonminority applicants.

We are mindful, however, that "[a] core purpose of the Fourteenth Amendment was to do away with all governmentally imposed discrimination based on race." *Palmore v. Sidoti,* 466 U.S. 429, 432 (1984). Accordingly, race-conscious admissions policies must be limited in time. This requirement reflects that racial classifications, however compelling their goals, are potentially so dangerous that they may be employed no more broadly than the interest demands. Enshrining a permanent justification for racial preferences would offend this fundamental equal protection principle. We see no reason to exempt race-conscious admissions programs from the requirement that all governmental use of race must have a logical end point. . . . In the context of higher education, the durational requirement can be met by sunset provisions in race-conscious admissions policies and periodic reviews to determine whether racial preferences are still necessary to achieve student body diversity. . . .

It has been 25 years since Justice Powell first approved the use of race to further an interest in student body diversity in the context of public higher education. . . . We expect that 25 years from now, the use of racial preferences will no longer be necessary to further the interest approved today. . . .

■ [JUSTICE GINSBURG'S concurrence is omitted.]

■ JUSTICE SCALIA, with whom JUSTICE THOMAS joins, concurring in part and dissenting in part.

I join the opinion of THE CHIEF JUSTICE. As he demonstrates, the University of Michigan Law School's mystical "critical mass" justification for its discrimination by race challenges even the most gullible mind. The admissions statistics show it to be a sham to cover a scheme of racially proportionate admissions.

I also join Parts I through VII of Justice THOMAS's opinion. I find particularly unanswerable his central point: that the allegedly "compelling state interest" at issue here is not the incremental "educational benefit" that emanates from the fabled "critical mass" of minority students, but rather Michigan's interest in maintaining a "prestige" law school whose normal admissions standards disproportionately exclude blacks and other minorities. If that is a compelling state interest, everything is. . . .

Unlike a clear constitutional holding that racial preferences in state educational institutions are impermissible, or even a clear anticonstitutional holding that racial preferences in state educational institutions are OK, today's *Grutter–Gratz* split double header seems perversely designed to prolong the controversy and the litigation. . . . I do not look forward to any of these cases. The Constitution proscribes government discrimination on the basis of race, and state-provided education is no exception.

■ JUSTICE THOMAS, with whom JUSTICE SCALIA joins as to Parts I–VII, concurring in part and dissenting in part.

Frederick Douglass, speaking to a group of abolitionists almost 140 years ago, delivered a message lost on today's majority:

> [I]n regard to the colored people, there is always more that is benevolent, I perceive, than just, manifested towards us. What I ask for the negro is not benevolence, not pity, not sympathy, but simply *justice*. The American people have always been anxious to know what they shall do with us. . . . I have had but one answer from the beginning. Do nothing with us! Your doing with us has already played the mischief with us. Do nothing with us! If the apples will not remain on the tree of their own strength, if they are worm-eaten at the core, if they are early ripe and disposed to fall, let them fall! . . . And if the negro cannot stand on his own legs, let him fall also. All I ask is, give him a chance to stand on his own legs! Let him alone! . . . [Y]our interference is doing him positive injury.

What the Black Man Wants: An Address Delivered in Boston, Massachusetts, on 26 January 1865, reprinted in 4 The Frederick Douglass Papers 59, 68 (J. Blassingame & J. McKivigan eds.1991) (emphasis in original).

Like Douglass, I believe blacks can achieve in every avenue of American life without the meddling of university administrators. Because I wish to see all students succeed whatever their color, I share, in some respect, the sympathies of those who sponsor the type of discrimination advanced by the University of Michigan Law School (Law School). The Constitution does not, however, tolerate institutional devotion to the status quo in admissions policies when such devotion ripens into racial discrimination. Nor does the Constitution countenance the unprecedented deference the Court gives to the Law School, an approach inconsistent with the very concept of "strict scrutiny."

No one would argue that a university could set up a lower general admissions standard and then impose heightened requirements only on black applicants. Similarly, a university may not maintain a high admissions standard and grant exemptions to favored races. The Law School, of its own choosing, and for its own purposes, maintains an exclusionary admissions system that it knows produces racially disproportionate results. Racial discrimination is not a permissible solution to the self-inflicted wounds of this elitist admissions policy.

The majority upholds the Law School's racial discrimination not by interpreting the people's Constitution, but by responding to a faddish slogan of the cognoscenti. Nevertheless, I concur in part in the Court's opinion. First, I agree with the Court insofar as its decision, which approves of only one racial classification, confirms that further use of race in admissions remains unlawful. Second, I agree with the Court's holding that racial discrimination in higher education admissions will be illegal in 25 years. I respectfully dissent from the remainder of the Court's opinion and the judgment, however, because I believe that the Law School's current use of race violates the Equal Protection Clause and that the Constitution means the same thing today as it will in 300 months.

I

. . . The Constitution abhors classifications based on race, not only because those classifications can harm favored races or are based on illegitimate motives, but also because every time the government places citizens on racial registers and makes race relevant to the provision of burdens or benefits, it demeans us all. "Purchased at the price of immeasurable human suffering, the equal protection principle reflects our Nation's understanding that such classifications ultimately have a destructive impact on the individual and our society." *Adarand Constructors, Inc. v. Peña,* 515 U.S. 200, 240 (1995) (THOMAS, J., concurring in part and concurring in judgment).

II

Unlike the majority, I seek to define with precision the interest being asserted by the Law School before determining whether that interest is so compelling as to justify racial discrimination. The Law School maintains that it wishes to obtain "educational benefits that flow from student body diversity." This statement must be evaluated carefully, because it implies that both "diversity" and "educational benefits" are components of the Law School's compelling state interest. Additionally, the Law School's refusal to entertain certain changes in its admissions process and status indicates that the compelling state interest it seeks to validate is actually broader than might appear at first glance.

Undoubtedly there are other ways to "better" the education of law students aside from ensuring that the student body contains a "critical mass" of underrepresented minority students. Attaining "diversity," whatever it means,[3] is the mechanism by which the Law School obtains educational benefits, not an end of itself. The Law School, however, apparently believes that only a racially mixed student body can lead to the educational benefits it seeks. How, then, is the Law School's interest in these allegedly unique educational "benefits" *not* simply the interest in "racial balancing" that the majority expressly rejects?

A distinction between these two ideas (unique educational benefits based on racial aesthetics and race for its own sake) is purely sophistic—so much so that the majority uses them interchangeably. The Law School's argument, as facile as it is, can only be understood in one way: Classroom aesthetics yields educational benefits, racially discriminatory admissions policies are required to achieve the right racial mix, and therefore the policies are required to achieve the educational benefits. It is the *educational benefits* that are the end, or allegedly compelling state interest, not "diversity."

One must also consider the Law School's refusal to entertain changes to its current admissions system that might produce the same educational benefits. The Law School adamantly disclaims any race-neutral alternative

---

[3] "[D]iversity," for all of its devotees, is more a fashionable catchphrase than it is a useful term, especially when something as serious as racial discrimination is at issue. Because the Equal Protection Clause renders the color of one's skin constitutionally irrelevant to the Law School's mission, I refer to the Law School's interest as an "aesthetic." That is, the Law School wants to have a certain appearance, from the shape of the desks and tables in its classrooms to the color of the students sitting at them.

I also use the term "aesthetic" because I believe it underlines the ineffectiveness of racially discriminatory admissions in actually helping those who are truly underprivileged. It must be remembered that the Law School's racial discrimination does nothing for those too poor or uneducated to participate in elite higher education and therefore presents only an illusory solution to the challenges facing our Nation.

that would reduce "academic selectivity," which would in turn "require the Law School to become a very different institution, and to sacrifice a core part of its educational mission." . . . In other words, the Law School seeks to improve marginally the education it offers without sacrificing too much of its exclusivity and elite status.

The proffered interest that the majority vindicates today, then, is not simply "diversity." Instead the Court upholds the use of racial discrimination as a tool to advance the Law School's interest in offering a marginally superior education while maintaining an elite institution. Unless each constituent part of this state interest is of pressing public necessity, the Law School's use of race is unconstitutional. I find each of them to fall far short of this standard.

III

A close reading of the Court's opinion reveals that all of its legal work is done through one conclusory statement: The Law School has a "compelling interest in securing the educational benefits of a diverse student body." . . . Under the proper standard, there is no pressing public necessity in maintaining a public law school at all and, it follows, certainly not an elite law school. Likewise, marginal improvements in legal education do not qualify as a compelling state interest.

While legal education at a public university may be good policy or otherwise laudable, it is obviously not a pressing public necessity. . . . Michigan has no compelling interest in having a law school at all, much less an *elite* one. . . . The only cognizable state interests vindicated by operating a public law school are, therefore, the education of that State's citizens and the training of that State's lawyers. . . . [But i]n 2002, graduates of the Law School made up less than 6% of applicants to the Michigan bar. Less than 16% of the Law School's graduated class elects to stay in Michigan after law school. . . .

In sum, the Law School trains few Michigan residents and overwhelmingly serves students, who, as lawyers, leave the State of Michigan. . . . It does not take a social scientist to conclude that it is precisely the Law School's status as an elite institution that causes it to be a waystation for the rest of the country's lawyers, rather than a training ground for those who will remain in Michigan. Again, the fact that few States choose to maintain elite law schools raises a strong inference that there is nothing compelling about elite status. . . .

IV

The interest in remaining elite and exclusive that the majority thinks so obviously critical requires the use of admissions "standards" that, in turn, create the Law School's "need" to discriminate on the basis of race. The Court validates these admissions standards by concluding that alternatives that would require "a dramatic sacrifice of . . . the academic quality of all admitted students," need not be considered before racial discrimination can be employed. . . . The Court never explicitly holds that the Law School's desire to retain the status quo in "academic selectivity" is itself a compelling state interest, and, as I have demonstrated, it is not. . . . [The] Law School should be forced to choose between its classroom aesthetic and its exclusionary admissions system—it cannot have it both ways.

With the adoption of different admissions methods, such as accepting all students who meet minimum qualifications, see Brief for United States as *Amicus Curiae* 13–14, the Law School could achieve its vision of the racially aesthetic student body without the use of racial discrimination. The Law School concedes this, but the Court holds, implicitly and under the guise of narrow tailoring, that the Law School has a compelling state interest in doing what it wants to do. I cannot agree. First, under strict scrutiny, the Law School's assessment of the benefits of racial discrimination and devotion to the admissions status quo are not entitled to any sort of deference, grounded in the First Amendment or anywhere else. Second, even if its "academic selectivity" must be maintained at all costs along with racial discrimination, the Court ignores the fact that other top law schools have succeeded in meeting their aesthetic demands without racial discrimination.

The Court bases its unprecedented deference to the Law School—a deference antithetical to strict scrutiny—on an idea of "educational autonomy" grounded in the First Amendment. In my view, there is no basis for a right of public universities to do what would otherwise violate the Equal Protection Clause. . . .

The Court's deference to the Law School's conclusion that its racial experimentation leads to educational benefits will, if adhered to, have serious collateral consequences. The Court relies heavily on social science evidence to justify its deference. . . . [B]ut see also Rothman, Lipset, & Nevitte, *Racial Diversity Reconsidered*, 151 Public Interest 25 (2003) (finding that the racial mix of a student body produced by racial discrimination of the type practiced by the Law School in fact hinders students' perception of academic quality). The Court never acknowledges, however, the growing evidence that racial (and other sorts) of heterogeneity actually impairs learning among black students. See, e.g., Flowers & Pascarella, *Cognitive Effects of College Racial Composition on African American Students After 3 Years of College*, 40 J. of College Student Development 669, 674 (1999) (concluding that black students experience superior cognitive development at Historically Black Colleges (HBCs) and that, even among blacks, "a substantial diversity moderates the cognitive effects of attending an HBC"); Allen, *The Color of Success: African–American College Student Outcomes at Predominantly White and Historically Black Public Colleges and Universities*, 62 Harv. Educ. Rev. 26, 35 (1992) (finding that black students attending HBCs report higher academic achievement than those attending predominantly white colleges). . . .

The majority grants deference to the Law School's "assessment that diversity will, in fact, yield educational benefits." It follows, therefore, that an HBC's assessment that racial homogeneity will yield educational benefits would similarly be given deference. An HBC's rejection of white applicants in order to maintain racial homogeneity seems permissible, therefore, under the majority's view of the Equal Protection Clause. Contained within today's majority opinion is the seed of a new constitutional justification for a concept I thought long and rightly rejected—racial segregation. . . .

[Moreover,] the majority ignores the "experience" of those institutions that have been forced to abandon explicit racial discrimination in admissions.

The sky has not fallen at Boalt Hall at the University of California, Berkeley, for example. Prior to Proposition 209's adoption of Cal. Const., Art. 1, § 31(a), which bars the State from "grant[ing] preferential treatment . . . on the basis of race . . . in the operation of . . . public education," Boalt Hall enrolled 20 blacks and 28 Hispanics in its first-year class for 1996. In 2002, without deploying express racial discrimination in admissions,

Boalt's entering class enrolled 14 blacks and 36 Hispanics. Total underrepresented minority student enrollment at Boalt Hall now exceeds 1996 levels. . . .

V

. . . [No] modern law school can claim ignorance of the poor performance of blacks, relatively speaking, on the Law School Admission Test (LSAT). Nevertheless, law schools continue to use the test and then attempt to "correct" for black underperformance by using racial discrimination in admissions so as to obtain their aesthetic student body. The Law School's continued adherence to measures it knows produce racially skewed results is not entitled to deference by this Court. . . .

Having decided to use the LSAT, the Law School must accept the constitutional burdens that come with this decision. The Law School may freely continue to employ the LSAT and other allegedly merit-based standards in whatever fashion it likes. What the Equal Protection Clause forbids, but the Court today allows, is the use of these standards hand-in-hand with racial discrimination. An infinite variety of admissions methods are available to the Law School. Considering all of the radical thinking that has historically occurred at this country's universities, the Law School's intractable approach toward admissions is striking.

The Court will not even deign to make the Law School try other methods, however, preferring instead to grant a 25–year license to violate the Constitution. And the same Court that had the courage to order the desegregation of all public schools in the South now fears, on the basis of platitudes rather than principle, to force the Law School to abandon a decidedly imperfect admissions regime that provides the basis for racial discrimination.

VI

. . . The Law School tantalizes unprepared students with the promise of a University of Michigan degree and all of the opportunities that it offers. These overmatched students take the bait, only to find that they cannot succeed in the cauldron of competition. And this mismatch crisis is not restricted to elite institutions. See T. Sowell, Race and Culture 176–177 (1994) ("Even if most minority students are able to meet the normal standards at the 'average' range of colleges and universities, the systematic mismatching of minority students begun at the top can mean that such students are generally overmatched throughout all levels of higher education"). Indeed, to cover the tracks of the aestheticists, this cruel farce of racial discrimination must continue—in selection for the Michigan Law Review, see University of Michigan Law School Student Handbook 2002–2003, pp. 39–40 (noting the presence of a "diversity plan" for admission to the review), and in hiring at law firms and for judicial clerkships—until the "beneficiaries" are no longer tolerated. While these students may graduate with law degrees, there is no evidence that they have received a qualitatively better legal education (or become better lawyers) than if they had gone to a less "elite" law school for which they were better prepared. And the aestheticists will never address the real problems facing "underrepresented minorities,"[11] instead continuing their social experiments on other people's children.

---

[11] For example, there is no recognition by the Law School in this case that even with their racial discrimination in place, black *men* are "underrepresented" at the Law School. See ABA–LSAC Guide 426 (reporting that the Law School has 46 black women and 28 black men). Why

Beyond the harm the Law School's racial discrimination visits upon its test subjects, no social science has disproved the notion that this discrimination "engender[s] attitudes of superiority or, alternatively, provoke[s] resentment among those who believe that they have been wronged by the government's use of race." *Adarand,* 515 U.S., at 241 (THOMAS, J., concurring in part and concurring in judgment). "These programs stamp minorities with a badge of inferiority and may cause them to develop dependencies or to adopt an attitude that they are 'entitled' to preferences." *Ibid.*

It is uncontested that each year, the Law School admits a handful of blacks who would be admitted in the absence of racial discrimination. Who can differentiate between those who belong and those who do not? The majority of blacks are admitted to the Law School because of discrimination, and because of this policy all are tarred as undeserving. This problem of stigma does not depend on determinacy as to whether those stigmatized are actually the "beneficiaries" of racial discrimination. When blacks take positions in the highest places of government, industry, or academia, it is an open question today whether their skin color played a part in their advancement. The question itself is the stigma—because either racial discrimination did play a role, in which case the person may be deemed "otherwise unqualified," or it did not, in which case asking the question itself unfairly marks those blacks who would succeed without discrimination. Is this what the Court means by "visibly open"? . . .

VII

. . . For the immediate future, however, the majority has placed its *imprimatur* on a practice that can only weaken the principle of equality embodied in the Declaration of Independence and the Equal Protection Clause. "Our Constitution is color-blind, and neither knows nor tolerates classes among citizens." *Plessy v. Ferguson,* 163 U.S. 537, 559 (1896) (HARLAN, J., dissenting). It has been nearly 140 years since Frederick Douglass asked the intellectual ancestors of the Law School to "[d]o nothing with us!" and the Nation adopted the Fourteenth Amendment. Now we must wait another 25 years to see this principle of equality vindicated. I therefore respectfully dissent from the remainder of the Court's opinion and the judgment.

■ [The dissenting opinions of CHIEF JUSTICE REHNQUIST and JUSTICE KENNEDY are omitted.]

NOTES

1. *DeFunis and Bakke. Grutter* was not the Court's first case involving racial preferences in state university admissions. In *DeFunis v. Odegaard,* 416 U.S. 312 (1974), Marco DeFunis, a white applicant who had been denied admission to the University of Washington School of Law brought suit to challenge the law school's consideration of race in admissions. The state trial court granted preliminary injunctive relief, ordering DeFunis admitted to law school while the case was pending. By the time the case reached the U.S. Supreme Court, DeFunis was nearing graduation. The law school acknowledged that it would allow him to complete his law school education no matter what the Court de-

---

does the Law School not also discriminate in favor of black men over black women, given this underrepresentation? The answer is, again, that all the Law School cares about is its own image among know-it-all elites, not solving real problems like the crisis of black male underperformance.

cided. The Court found the case moot and vacated the decisions below. Only Justice Douglas would have reached the merits; he would have ruled in DeFunis's favor, on the ground that the Equal Protection Clause requires "consideration of each applicant in a racially neutral way."

The issue returned to the Court in *Regents of the University of California v. Bakke*, 438 U.S. 265 (1978). The University of California–Davis Medical School set aside thirty of one hundred seats in its entering class for members of racial minority groups, with a separate admissions process for those thirty seats. A rejected white applicant sued. The California Supreme Court held the special admissions program unlawful and directed the trial court to order Bakke's admission.

The U.S. Supreme Court produced a famously divided outcome: Four justices voted to affirm, finding that consideration of race violated a federal civil rights law forbidding discrimination on the basis of race in any federally funded educational program (which presumably would also have meant an Equal Protection Clause violation). Four justices voted to reverse, concluding that the program was valid. *One* justice—Justice Powell—concluded that setting aside thirty seats was invalid but that it was in general permissible to consider race as one factor in admissions programs. That distinction was rejected by every other member of the Court. As Justice Brennan put it (in his opinion for the justices who would have upheld the program): "For purposes of constitutional adjudication, there is no difference between the two approaches. In any admissions program which accords special consideration to disadvantaged racial minorities, a determination of the degree of preference to be given is unavoidable, and any given preference that results in the exclusion of a white candidate is no more or less constitutionally acceptable than a program such as that at Davis." But even though Justice Powell's position was rejected by all the other justices, it determined the disposition of the case: five justices (including Justice Powell) held quotas and set-asides unlawful, and so Bakke himself won; five justices (including Justice Powell) held that race could be considered, and so reversed the California Supreme Court's order forbidding any consideration of race.

The split decision produced confusion for the next quarter century. But a majority in *Bakke* did embrace several propositions of law, which have continued as part of the Court's jurisprudence through and including *Grutter* and *Gratz*:

> a. *Strict scrutiny of minority racial preferences. Bakke* rejected a lesser standard of scrutiny for racial classifications that were not invidiously motivated: "Racial and ethnic distinctions of any sort are inherently suspect and thus call for the most exacting judicial examination."

> b. *No racial balancing for its own sake. Bakke* rejected racial balancing as a state interest that would be sufficiently compelling to justify a racial classification: "Preferring members of any one group for no reason other than race or ethnic origin is discrimination for its own sake. This the Constitution forbids."

> c. *Racial preferences not justified to remedy general societal discrimination. Bakke* considered general societal discrimination too "amorphous" to justify racial preferences: "We have never approved a classification that aids persons perceived as members of relatively victimized groups at the

expense of other innocent individuals in the absence of judicial, legislative, or administrative findings of constitutional or statutory violations."

d. *Racial preferences not justified by the existence of underserved communities.* *Bakke* found insufficient the evidence that those who benefitted from the racial preferences at issue would work in "underserved" communities—which was one theory advanced to justify them.

e. *Diversity a compelling government interest.* Justice Powell's opinion considered racial diversity in education a sufficiently compelling government interest to justify "flexible" consideration of race as a "plus," though it was not sufficiently compelling to justify a racial quota or set-aside. The four justices who thought minority race could be considered without limitation implicitly agreed that race could be considered *at least* as a "plus."

2. *Grutter and Gratz.* Fast-forward twenty-five years. *Grutter* carried forward some of *Bakke*'s propositions, but also some of its confusion. As mentioned in the opinions, on the same day the Court decided *Grutter* it also decided *Gratz v. Bollinger*, invalidating the same university's use of an automatic twenty-point bonus (out of one hundred possible points) for racial minority status in its undergraduate admissions program. The Court found that the use of a flat numerical preference—and one of so large a size—was unconstitutional. This distinguished the case from the unquantified preference in the law school admissions program upheld in *Grutter*. Does the distinction make sense? Is it principled? Should the undergraduate admissions office have simply copied the law school plan? Could it have done so?

Justices Breyer and O'Connor thought the distinction persuasive, but the other justices thought either that both programs should be upheld or that both should be struck down—a quantified preference was more explicit but was ultimately indistinguishable in principle and result from what was occurring in the law school program. Yet the two swing votes proved decisive, as did Justice Powell's vote in *Bakke*.

How does the doctrine of *stare decisis* apply in a situation like this? Should the doctrine apply? Was the Court right to treat Justice Powell's opinion in *Bakke* as the authoritative resolution of the Court twenty-five years earlier?

3. *Compelling Interest?* Is diversity in education a compelling state interest that justifies racial classification? The only other such interests the Court has found sufficiently "compelling" to permit race-based classification, besides diversity in higher education, are (1) the need to remedy identified discrimination against specific individuals (where accomplished by a narrowly tailored race-based remedy); and (2) the protection of national security. (The latter interest was found compelling in *Korematsu*, printed above in Chapter 3, which is the widely censured case justifying the Japanese–American internment program.) Is diversity of comparable importance? How should a court answer a question like that?

The dissenters argue that racial diversity is not the true interest at issue in *Grutter*. The University of Michigan could readily achieve such diversity with an admissions policy that used a lottery rather than competitive admissions. This would require lowering Michigan's selectivity. If the interest in diversity could be accomplished so readily, does that mean that Michigan's real interest is simply that of maintaining its selectivity—its elite status as a national law school? Is that a compelling interest? Are you persuaded by the dissent's argument? What is the majority's response?

In deciding that racial diversity in higher education is a compelling state interest, to what extent was the Court deferring to the expert judgment of education officials about what was needed in their contexts? Is this appropriate? If so, where else might it be appropriate—if education officials decided that separating students by sex was needed for a particular type of educational experience or environment? In thinking about deference to expert judgment, consider the amicus brief of retired military officers. (Reportedly, it was significant in the Court's decisionmaking.) Is deference to the judgment of military officials about the need for diversity, as a military matter, appropriate? If so, where else might that deference be invoked?

4. *Narrow Tailoring?* Assume that diversity is a compelling interest. There is still the question whether the use of racial preferences is sufficiently "narrowly tailored" to accomplish that interest. Should the university have been required to use race-neutral alternatives for producing diversity? (Is this just another way of asking the question posed above—whether selectivity, rather diversity, is the true interest involved?) What about using high school rank as a criterion, and not only college grades and scores? What do you think of the argument that use of race as a factor (rather than a hard quota) does not "unduly harm" non-minorities? Does its application to a specific form of state action change?

5. *Expiration Date?* What do you make of Justice O'Connor's suggestion—characterized by Justice Thomas's dissent as a 300–month "sunset" on the majority's holding—that programs like Michigan Law's might no longer be constitutional in twenty-five years (from 2003)? Is that a fair characterization of the majority's position? Does the meaning of the Constitution change with changed social circumstances? Does the meaning of the Constitution change with changed social circumstances? Does its application to a specific form of state action change?

6. *Race and Public School Assignment.* In *Parents Involved in Community Schools v. Seattle School District #1*, 551 U.S. 701 (2007), the Court was faced with the question "whether a public school that had not operated legally segregated schools or has been found to be unitary may choose to classify students by race and rely upon that classification in making school assignments." In a 5–4 opinion written by Chief Justice Roberts, the Court answered *no*. The classification was not justified as a remedy for past intentional discrimination, and could not be justified on grounds of seeking racial balance for its own sake. The Court distinguished *Grutter* as addressing the interest in "diversity in higher education" and involving a program in which race was only one consideration among many, not "*the* factor." The Court found no compelling interest justifying the school districts' practices: "the school districts have not carried their burden of showing that the ends they seek justify the particular extreme means they have chosen—classifying individual students on the basis of their race and discriminating among them on that basis." *Id.* at 745.

Is the distinction of *Grutter* persuasive? Was the Court too eagerly "tak[ing] the *Grutter* Court at its word" as to the limitations of its rationale? Four justices vigorously dissented, arguing that "the Equal Protection Clause permits local school boards to use race-conscious criteria to achieve positive race-related goals" and that plans like those at issue were warranted by the need to undo patterns of racial segregation and to vindicate the de-segregation vision of *Brown v. Board of Education.*

A NOTE ON AFFIRMATIVE ACTION OUTSIDE OF EDUCATION

1. *Contracting.* In *City of Richmond v. J.A. Croson Company*, 488 U.S. 469 (1989), the Supreme Court considered the constitutionality under the Equal Protection Clause of an ordinance adopted by the City Council of Richmond, Virginia. It specified that prime contractors to whom the city gave construction contracts must set aside 30% of all subcontracts for minority-owned businesses. These in turn were defined as being businesses that were at least 51% minority owned. Minority group members were defined as including "[c]itizens of the United States who are Blacks, Spanish-speaking, Orientals, Indians, Eskimos, or Aleuts." Although there was most certainly a history of discrimination against black citizens in Richmond, there was no proof of any prior discrimination against "Spanish-speakers, Orientals, Indians, Eskimos, or Aleuts." The Supreme Court held that the ordinance violated the anti-discrimination principles of the Fourteenth Amendment. Justice O'Connor's opinion striking down the ordinance did hold out the possibility that state and local governments might in some circumstances be able to discriminate on the basis of race to ameliorate the effects of past discrimination. Justice Scalia concurred separately, endorsing a color-blindness rule like the one championed by the first Justice Harlan in his dissent in *Plessy v. Ferguson.* Justice Marshall, whose dissent was joined by Justices Brennan and Blackmun, called the set-aside rule "a welcome symbol of racial progress [in] the former capital of the Confederacy."

Can *Grutter* and *Croson* be reconciled? Is the difference that one case involves state university admissions and the other set-asides or preferences in awarding government contracts? Is the difference that the admissions preferences upheld in *Grutter* were only one factor among several? Is a "plus" factor for race in admissions different in principle from awarding points in a competitive bid process for a government construction project? Or, if the two cases are inconsistent, which way should the inconsistency be resolved?

2. *State and Federal.* As a constitutional matter, are federal government affirmative action programs different from state programs? Recall that the text of the Equal Protection Clause limits only *state* governments. And recall *Bolling v. Sharpe* and the doctrinal acrobatics needed to extend the holding of *Brown v. Board of Education* to the federal government's authority over the District of Columbia schools.

The year after *Croson*, in *Metro Broadcasting, Inc. v. FCC*, 497 U.S. 547 (1990), a deeply divided Supreme Court upheld (5–4) minority preference programs in the federal government's awarding of certain broadcast licenses. The Court applied intermediate scrutiny (for the only time in this area of law) and found a sufficiently important government interest in diversity of programming, keyed to the race of station owners. Justice O'Connor's dissent argued that "only a compelling interest may support the Government's use of racial classifications" and that the Court's decisions up to that point had "recognized only one such interest: remedying the effects of racial discrimination." Justice Kennedy's dissent announced his "regret that after a century of judicial opinions we interpret the Constitution to do no more than move us from 'separate but equal' to 'unequal but benign.' "

Metro Broadcasting did not last long. In *Adarand Constructors, Inc. v. Pena*, 515 U.S. 200 (1995), the Supreme Court explicitly overruled *Metro Broadcasting* as inconsistent with the Court's previous cases, including *Croson*, in the course of striking down a minority preference in the awarding of federal contracts. *Adarand* was 5–4 in the opposite direction (the difference being Justice Thomas's appointment to the Court to replace Justice Marshall; Justice Souter voted in line with the justice he replaced, Justice Brennan). Justice O'Connor's majority opinion held that "strict scrutiny" applied and that racial preferences in contracting could not survive such scrutiny. Justice Scalia's concurrence argued that "government can never have a 'compelling interest' in discriminating on the basis of race in order to 'make up' for past racial discrimination in the opposite direction. Individuals who have been wronged by unlawful racial discrimination should be made whole; but under our Constitution there can be no such thing as either a creditor or a debtor race. . . . In the eyes of government, we are just one race here. It is American." One of the dissenters, Justice Stevens, argued that "[a]s a matter of constitutional and democratic principle, a decision by representatives of the majority to discriminate against the members of a minority race is fundamentally different from those same representatives' decision to impose incidental costs on the majority of their constituents in order to provide a benefit to a disadvantaged minority." "The former," he said "is virtually always repugnant to the principles of a free and democratic society, whereas the latter is, in some circumstances, entirely consistent with the ideal of equality." He faulted the majority for "obscur[ing] this essential dichotomy" through a "doctrinaire notion of 'consistency' in the standard applicable to all race-based governmental actions."

3. *Election Districts.* In *Shaw v. Reno* [*Shaw I*], 509 U.S. 630 (1993), the Supreme Court held that the Equal Protection Clause of the Fourteenth Amendment created a cause of action to challenge the creation of race-based election districts. In the post-Civil War South, drawing bizarrely shaped boundaries to alter the racial composition of election districts in favor of whites had been a common part of resisting Reconstruction. This time, however, the 1990 census granted North Carolina an additional twelfth seat in the House of Representatives and the state reapportioned its congressional districts in favor of black voters. In an effort to comply with the Voting Rights Act of 1965—which requires states to employ non-discriminatory voting practices—North Carolina created two new irregularly shaped congressional districts with a majority of black voters. The Court did not strike down the new districts directly, but ruled 5–4 that the reapportionment was "so irrational on its face that it can be understood only as an effort to segregate voters into separate voting districts because of their race, and that the separation lacks sufficient justification." The case was remanded for a determination of "whether the North Carolina plan is narrowly tailored to further a compelling governmental interest." Justice O'Connor wrote for the Court that "[r]acial classifications of any sort pose the risk of lasting harm to our society. They reinforce the belief, held by too many for too much of our history, that individuals should be judged by the color of their skin. Racial classifications with respect to voting carry particular dangers. Racial gerrymandering, even for remedial purposes, may balkanize us into competing factions; it threatens to carry us further from the goal of a political system in which race no longer . . . matters." Justice Stevens was again among the dissenters. He agreed that "[t]he existence of bizarre and uncouth district boundaries is powerful evidence of an ulterior purpose behind the shaping of those boundaries," but he considered that purpose to be both obvious and con-

stitutionally unproblematic. It was obvious that the district was drawn "to include a majority of African–American voters," and that purpose was unproblematic since it benefited "a group that lacks [political] power because it remains underrepresented in the state legislature." The case returned two more times to the Supreme Court. See *Shaw v. Hunt* [*Shaw II*], 517 U.S. 899 (1996); *Hunt v. Cromartie*, 526 U.S. 541 (1999).

[Assignment 65]

E. SEX DISCRIMINATION

In the *Slaughter–House Cases*, the Court said that the "one pervading purpose" of the Reconstruction amendments was "the freedom of the slave race, the security and firm establishment of that freedom, and the protection of the newly-made freeman and citizen from the oppressions of those who had formerly exercised unlimited dominion over him." 83 U.S. 36, 71 (1872). But does the Fourteenth Amendment's command that a state not "deny to any person within its jurisdiction the equal protection of the laws" apply only to denials of equal protection on the basis of race? Or does it include any other kind of government classifications of persons, such as state discrimination on the basis of sex?

The text of the Equal Protection Clause mentions no restriction to race. And by its own terms it protects every "person." But to say that the Equal Protection Clause does apply to more than just race only begins the inquiry. Exactly how, for example, would the Equal Protection Clause apply to government classifications predicated on sex or gender? Would the Equal Protection Clause invalidate all such legal distinctions, including "separate but equal" public restrooms? If not, why not? Are gender-based classifications exactly like race-based classifications? Is there a different Equal Protection Clause for each?

You have already seen one case where these questions might have been raised, *Bradwell v. Illinois*, 83 (16 Wall.) U.S. 130 (1873). Here are two modern cases in which the Court has worked out, and then re-worked, the standard of scrutiny it applies to sex-based classifications. The Court first adopted "intermediate scrutiny" as the standard of review in *Craig v. Boren* (1976). Twenty years later, in *United States v. Virginia* (1996), the Court interpreted that test to require an "exceedingly persuasive justification" for sex-based classifications—a formulation seemingly closer to the "strict scrutiny" that governs racial classifications.

The cases on sex discrimination portend a broader question, which will be taken up in the following set of materials: If the guarantee of equal protection of the laws forbids most government classifications on the basis of race and sex, then what other types of government classifications amount to a denial of equal protection of the laws? And what doctrinal test, or standard of scrutiny, should apply to them?

Craig v. Boren
429 U.S. 190 (1976)

■ MR. JUSTICE BRENNAN delivered the opinion of the Court.

The interaction of two sections of an Oklahoma statute prohibits the sale of "nonintoxicating" 3.2% beer to males under the age of 21 and to females under the age of 18. The question to be decided is whether such a gender-based differential constitutes a denial to males 18–20 years of age of the equal protection of the laws in violation of the Fourteenth Amendment. . . .

II–A

Before 1972, Oklahoma defined the commencement of civil majority at age 18 for females and age 21 for males. In contrast, females were held criminally responsible as adults at age 18 and males at age 16. After the Court of Appeals for the Tenth Circuit held in 1972, on the authority of *Reed v. Reed*, 404 U.S. 71 (1971) that the age distinction was unconstitutional for purposes of establishing criminal responsibility as adults, the Oklahoma Legislature fixed age 18 as applicable to both males and females. In 1972, 18 also was established as the age of majority for males and females in civil matters, except that [sections] of the 3.2% beer statute were simultaneously codified to create an exception to the gender-free rule.

Analysis may appropriately begin with the reminder that *Reed* emphasized that statutory classifications that distinguish between males and females are "subject to scrutiny under the Equal Protection Clause." To withstand constitutional challenge, previous cases establish that classifications by gender must serve important governmental objectives and must be substantially related to achievement of those objectives. Thus, in *Reed*, the objectives of "reducing the workload on probate courts," and "avoiding intrafamily controversy," were deemed of insufficient importance to sustain use of an overt gender criterion in the appointment of administrators of intestate decedents' estates. Decisions following *Reed* similarly have rejected administrative ease and convenience as sufficiently important objectives to justify gender-based classifications. And only two Terms ago, *Stanton v. Stanton*, expressly stating that *Reed v. Reed* was "controlling," held that *Reed* required invalidation of a Utah differential age-of-majority statute, notwithstanding the statute's coincidence with and furtherance of the State's purpose of fostering "old notions" of role typing and preparing boys for their expected performance in the economic and political worlds.

Reed v. Reed has also provided the underpinning for decisions that have invalidated statutes employing gender as an inaccurate proxy for other, more germane bases of classification. Hence, "archaic and overbroad" generalizations concerning the financial position of servicewomen and working women could not justify use of a gender line in determining eligibility for certain governmental entitlements. Similarly, increasingly outdated misconceptions concerning the role of females in the home rather than in the "marketplace and world of ideas" were rejected as loose-fitting characterizations incapable of supporting state statutory schemes that were premised upon their accuracy. In light of the weak congruence between gender and the characteristic or trait that gender purported to represent, it was necessary that the legislatures choose either to realign their substantive laws in a gender-neutral fashion, or to adopt procedures for identifying those instances where the sex-centered generalization actually comported with fact.

In this case, too, "*Reed*, we feel is controlling . . .," *Stanton v. Stanton*, at 13. We turn then to the question whether, under *Reed*, the difference between males and females with respect to the purchase of 3.2% beer warrants the differential in age drawn by the Oklahoma statute. We conclude that it does not.

B

The District Court recognized that *Reed v. Reed* was controlling. In applying the teachings of that case, the court found the requisite important governmental objective in the traffic-safety goal proffered by the Oklahoma Attorney General. It then concluded that the statistics introduced by the appellees established that the gender-based distinction was substantially related to achievement of that goal.

C

We accept for purposes of discussion the District Court's identification of the objective underlying [Sections] 241 and 245 as the enhancement of traffic safety. Clearly, the protection of public health and safety represents an important function of state and local governments. However, appellees' statistics in our view cannot support the conclusion that the gender-based distinction closely serves to achieve that objective and therefore the distinction cannot under Reed withstand equal protection challenge.

The appellees introduced a variety of statistical surveys. First, an analysis of arrest statistics for 1973 demonstrated that 18–20–year–old male arrests for "driving under the influence" and "drunkenness" substantially exceeded female arrests for that same age period. Similarly, youths aged 17–21 were found to be overrepresented among those killed or injured in traffic accidents, with males again numerically exceeding females in this regard. Third, a random roadside survey in Oklahoma City revealed that young males were more inclined to drive and drink beer than were their female counterparts. Fourth, Federal Bureau of Investigation nationwide statistics exhibited a notable increase in arrests for "driving under the influence." Finally, statistical evidence gathered in other jurisdictions, particularly Minnesota and Michigan, was offered to corroborate Oklahoma's experience by indicating the pervasiveness of youthful participation in motor vehicle accidents following the imbibing of alcohol. Conceding that "the case is not free from doubt," the District Court nonetheless concluded that this statistical showing substantiated "a rational basis for the legislative judgment underlying the challenged classification."

Even were this statistical evidence accepted as accurate, it nevertheless offers only a weak answer to the equal protection question presented here. The most focused and relevant of the statistical surveys, arrests of 18–20–year–olds for alcohol-related driving offenses, exemplifies the ultimate unpersuasiveness of this evidentiary record. Viewed in terms of the correlation between sex and the actual activity that Oklahoma seeks to regulate driving while under the influence of alcohol the statistics broadly establish that .18% of females and 2% of males in that age group were arrested for that offense. While such a disparity is not trivial in a statistical sense, it hardly can form the basis for employment of a gender line as a classifying device. Certainly if maleness is to serve as a proxy for drinking and driving, a correlation of 2% must be considered an unduly tenuous "fit." Indeed, prior cases have consistently rejected the use of sex as a decisionmaking factor even though the statutes in question certainly rested on far more predictive empirical relationships than this.

Moreover, the statistics exhibit a variety of other shortcomings that seriously impugn their value to equal protection analysis. Setting aside the obvious methodological problems,[14] the surveys do not adequately justify

---

[14] The very social stereotypes that find reflection in age-differential laws are likely substantially to distort the accuracy of these comparative statistics. Hence "reckless" young men

the salient features of Oklahoma's gender-based traffic-safety law. None purports to measure the use and dangerousness of 3.2% beer as opposed to alcohol generally, a detail that is of particular importance since, in light of its low alcohol level, Oklahoma apparently considers the 3.2% beverage to be "nonintoxicating." Moreover, many of the studies, while graphically documenting the unfortunate increase in driving while under the influence of alcohol, make no effort to relate their findings to age-sex differentials as involved here. Indeed, the only survey that explicitly centered its attention upon young drivers and their use of beer albeit apparently not of the diluted 3.2% variety reached results that hardly can be viewed as impressive in justifying either a gender or age classification.

There is no reason to belabor this line of analysis. It is unrealistic to expect either members of the judiciary or state officials to be well versed in the rigors of experimental or statistical technique. But this merely illustrates that proving broad sociological propositions by statistics is a dubious business, and one that inevitably is in tension with the normative philosophy that underlies the Equal Protection Clause. Suffice to say that the showing offered by the appellees does not satisfy us that sex represents a legitimate, accurate proxy for the regulation of drinking and driving. In fact, when it is further recognized that Oklahoma's statute prohibits only the selling of 3.2% beer to young males and not their drinking the beverage once acquired (even after purchase by their 18–20–year–old female companions), the relationship between gender and traffic safety becomes far too tenuous to satisfy *Reed*'s requirement that the gender-based difference be substantially related to achievement of the statutory objective.

We hold, therefore, that under *Reed*, Oklahoma's 3.2% beer statute invidiously discriminates against males 18–20 years of age. . . .

■ MR. JUSTICE POWELL, concurring.

I join the opinion of the Court as I am in general agreement with it. I do have reservations as to some of the discussion concerning the appropriate standard for equal protection analysis and the relevance of the statistical evidence. Accordingly, I add this concurring statement.

With respect to the equal protection standard, I agree that *Reed v. Reed* is the most relevant precedent. But I find it unnecessary, in deciding this case, to read that decision as broadly as some of the Court's language may imply. *Reed* and subsequent cases involving gender-based classifications make clear that the Court subjects such classifications to a more critical examination than is normally applied when "fundamental" constitutional rights and "suspect classes" are not present.[*]

---

who drink and drive are transformed into arrest statistics, whereas their female counterparts are chivalrously escorted home. Moreover, the Oklahoma surveys, gathered under a regime where the age-differential law in question has been in effect, are lacking in controls necessary for appraisal of the actual effectiveness of the male 3.2% beer prohibition. In this regard, the disproportionately high arrest statistics for young males and, indeed, the growing alcohol-related arrest figures for all ages and sexes simply may be taken to document the relative futility of controlling driving behavior by the 3.2% beer statute and like legislation, although we obviously have no means of estimating how many individuals, if any, actually were prevented from drinking by these laws.

[*] As is evident from our opinions, the Court has had difficulty in agreeing upon a standard of equal protection analysis that can be applied consistently to the wide variety of legislative classifications. There are valid reasons for dissatisfaction with the "two-tier" approach that has been prominent in the Court's decisions in the past decade. Although viewed by many as a result-oriented substitute for more critical analysis, that approach with its narrowly limited "upper-tier" now has substantial precedential support. As has been true of *Reed* and its

I view this as a relatively easy case. No one questions the legitimacy or importance of the asserted governmental objective: the promotion of highway safety. The decision of the case turns on whether the state legislature, by the classification it has chosen, had adopted a means that bears a "fair and substantial relation" to this objective. . . .

■ Mr. Justice Stevens, concurring.

There is only one Equal Protection Clause. It requires every State to govern impartially. It does not direct the courts to apply one standard of review in some cases and a different standard in other cases. . . .

I am inclined to believe that what has become known as the two-tiered analysis of equal protection claims does not describe a completely logical method of deciding cases, but rather is a method the Court has employed to explain decisions that actually apply a single standard in a reasonably consistent fashion. I also suspect that a careful explanation of the reasons motivating particular decisions may contribute more to an identification of that standard than an attempt to articulate it in all-encompassing terms. It may therefore be appropriate for me to state the principal reasons which persuaded me to join the Court's opinion.

In this case, the classification is not as obnoxious as some the Court has condemned, nor as inoffensive as some the Court has accepted. It is objectionable because it is based on an accident of birth, because it is a mere remnant of the now almost universally rejected tradition of discriminating against males in this age bracket, and because, to the extent it reflects any physical difference between males and females, it is actually perverse. The question then is whether the traffic safety justification put forward by the State is sufficient to make an otherwise offensive classification acceptable.

The classification is not totally irrational. For the evidence does indicate that there are more males than females in this age bracket who drive and also more who drink. Nevertheless, there are several reasons why I regard the justification as unacceptable. It is difficult to believe that the statute was actually intended to cope with the problem of traffic safety, since it has only a minimal effect on access to a not very intoxicating beverage and does not prohibit its consumption. Moreover, the empirical data submitted by the State accentuate the unfairness of treating all 18–21–year–old males as inferior to their female counterparts. The legislation imposes a restraint on 100% of the males in the class allegedly because about 2% of them have probably violated one or more laws relating to the consumption of alcoholic beverages. It is unlikely that this law will have a significant deterrent effect either on that 2% or on the law-abiding 98%. But even assuming some such slight benefit, it does not seem to me that an insult to all of the young men of the State can be justified by visiting the sins of the 2% on the 98%.

■ [The concurring opinion of Justice Blackmun and dissenting opinion of Chief Justice Burger are omitted.]

■ Mr. Justice Rehnquist, dissenting.

---

progeny, our decision today will be viewed by some as a "middle-tier" approach. While I would not endorse that characterization and would not welcome a further subdividing of equal protection analysis, candor compels the recognition that the relatively deferential "rational basis" standard of review normally applied takes on a sharper focus when we address a gender-based classification. So much is clear from our recent cases.

The Court's disposition of this case is objectionable on two grounds. First is its conclusion that men challenging a gender-based statute which treats them less favorably than women may invoke a more stringent standard of judicial review than pertains to most other types of classifications. Second is the Court's enunciation of this standard, without citation to any source, as being that "classifications by gender must serve important governmental objectives and must be substantially related to achievement of those objectives." The only redeeming feature of the Court's opinion, to my mind, is that it apparently signals a retreat by those who joined the plurality opinion in *Frontiero v. Richardson* from their view that sex is a "suspect" classification for purposes of equal protection analysis. I think the Oklahoma statute challenged here need pass only the "rational basis" equal protection analysis expounded in cases such as *McGowan v. Maryland* and *Williamson v. Lee Optical Co.*, and I believe that it is constitutional under that analysis.

I

. . . Most obviously unavailable to support any kind of special scrutiny in this case, is a history or pattern of past discrimination, such as was relied on by the plurality in *Frontiero* to support its invocation of strict scrutiny. There is no suggestion in the Court's opinion that males in this age group are in any way peculiarly disadvantaged, subject to systematic discriminatory treatment, or otherwise in need of special solicitude from the courts. . . .

It is true that a number of our opinions contain broadly phrased dicta implying that the same test should be applied to all classifications based on sex, whether affecting females or males. However, before today, no decision of this Court has applied an elevated level of scrutiny to invalidate a statutory discrimination harmful to males, except where the statute impaired an important personal interest protected by the Constitution. There being no such interest here, and there being no plausible argument that this is a discrimination against females, the Court's reliance on our previous sex-discrimination cases is ill-founded. It treats gender classification as a talisman which without regard to the rights involved or the persons affected calls into effect a heavier burden of judicial review.

The Court's conclusion that a law which treats males less favorably than females "must serve important governmental objectives and must be substantially related to achievement of those objectives" apparently comes out of thin air. The Equal Protection Clause contains no such language, and none of our previous cases adopt that standard. I would think we have had enough difficulty with the two standards of review which our cases have recognized the norm of "rational basis," and the "compelling state interest" required where a "suspect classification" is involved so as to counsel weightily against the insertion of still another "standard" between those two. How is this Court to divine what objectives are important? How is it to determine whether a particular law is "substantially" related to the achievement of such objective, rather than related in some other way to its achievement? Both of the phrases used are so diaphanous and elastic as to invite subjective judicial preferences or prejudices relating to particular types of legislation, masquerading as judgments whether such legislation is directed at "important" objectives or, whether the relationship to those objectives is "substantial" enough.

I would have thought that if this Court were to leave anything to decision by the popularly elected branches of the Government, where no constitutional claim other than that of equal protection is invoked, it would be the decision as to what governmental objectives to be achieved by law are "important," and which are not. As for the second part of the Court's new test, the Judicial Branch is probably in no worse position than the Legislative or Executive Branches to determine if there is any rational relationship between a classification and the purpose which it might be thought to serve. But the introduction of the adverb "substantially" requires courts to make subjective judgments as to operational effects, for which neither their expertise nor their access to data fits them. And even if we manage to avoid both confusion and the mirroring of our own preferences in the development of this new doctrine, the thousands of judges in other courts who must interpret the Equal Protection Clause may not be so fortunate.

II

The applicable rational-basis test is one which "permits the States a wide scope of discretion in enacting laws which affect some groups of citizens differently than others. The constitutional safeguard is offended only if the classification rests on grounds wholly irrelevant to the achievement of the State's objective. State legislatures are presumed to have acted within their constitutional power despite the fact that, in practice, their laws result in some inequality. A statutory discrimination will not be set aside if any state of facts reasonably may be conceived to justify it." *McGowan v. Maryland*, 366 U.S. at 425–426. . . .

I believe that a more traditional type of scrutiny is appropriate in this case, and I think that the Court would have done well here to heed its own warning that "[i]t is unrealistic to expect . . . members of the judiciary . . . to be well versed in the rigors of experimental or statistical technique." *Dandridge*, at 460. . . .

The Court's criticism of the statistics relied on by the District Court conveys the impression that a legislature in enacting a new law is to be subjected to the judicial equivalent of a doctoral examination in statistics. Legislatures are not held to any rules of evidence such as those which may govern courts or other administrative bodies, and are entitled to draw factual conclusions on the basis of the determination of probable cause which an arrest by a police officer normally represents. In this situation, they could reasonably infer that the incidence of drunk driving is a good deal higher than the incidence of arrest.

And while, as the Court observes, relying on a report to a Presidential Commission which it cites in a footnote, such statistics may be distorted as a result of stereotyping, the legislature is not required to prove before a court that its statistics are perfect. In any event, if stereotypes are as pervasive as the Court suggests, they may in turn influence the conduct of the men and women in question, and cause the young men to conform to the wild and reckless image which is their stereotype. . . .

Nor is it unreasonable to conclude from the expressed preference for beer by four-fifths of the age-group males that that beverage was a predominant source of their intoxication-related arrests. Taking that as the predicate, the State could reasonably bar those males from any purchases of alcoholic beer, including that of the 3.2% variety. This Court lacks the expertise or the data to evaluate the intoxicating properties of that beverage, and in that posture our only appropriate course is to defer to the reasonable inference supporting the statute that taken in sufficient quantity this beer has the same effect as any alcoholic beverage.

Quite apart from these alleged methodological deficiencies in the statistical evidence, the Court appears to hold that that evidence, on its face, fails to support the distinction drawn in the statute. The Court notes that only 2% of males (as against .18% of females) in the age group were arrested for drunk driving, and that this very low figure establishes "an unduly tenuous 'fit' " between maleness and drunk driving in the 18 to 20–year–old group. On this point the Court misconceives the nature of the equal protection inquiry.

The rationality of a statutory classification for equal protection purposes does not depend upon the statistical "fit" between the class and the trait sought to be singled out. It turns on whether there may be a sufficiently higher incidence of the trait within the included class than in the excluded class to justify different treatment. Therefore the present equal protection challenge to this gender-based discrimination poses only the question whether the incidence of drunk driving among young men is sufficiently greater than among young women to justify differential treatment. Notwithstanding the Court's critique of the statistical evidence, that evidence suggests clear differences between the drinking and driving habits of young men and women. Those differences are grounds enough for the State reasonably to conclude that young males pose by far the greater drunk-driving hazard, both in terms of sheer numbers and in terms of hazard on a per-driver basis. The gender-based difference in treatment in this case is therefore not irrational.

The Court's argument that a 2% correlation between maleness and drunk driving is constitutionally insufficient therefore does not pose an equal protection issue concerning discrimination between males and females. . . .

NOTES

1. *Defining Rights and Assessing Differences. Craig v. Boren* is an entertaining case but it frames serious issues. Begin by thinking carefully about the nature of the constitutional right being asserted. Is there a constitutional right to drink beer? Is there a constitutional right to drink beer if one is over eighteen years old? Peruse the Eighteenth and Twenty-first Amendments. If not, then the constitutional objection is that *women* between the ages of eighteen and twenty-one may drink 3.2% "beer" but *men* may not—thus the Equal Protection Clause claim in the case. Should men be able to invoke the clause to argue that they have been discriminated against by government on the basis of sex? Is discrimination on the basis of sex against men any different from discrimination on the basis of sex against women for legal purposes? Should they be governed by different standards? (One of the plaintiffs was a bar owner who invoked men's rights to be free of unconstitutional discrimination in order to be able to serve them beer.)

The classification in this case was explicitly based on sex. Was it based on a real difference between eighteen-year-old men and women? Was it based on differences in their patterns of behavior? Is the latter an allowable basis for state legislation—the real-world fact that young men were (at the time, in that place) more than ten times more likely to drink and drive than women? Is that kind of fact rooted in biology or is it entirely a function of social construction? Is it a stereotype? Why or why not?

2. *The Spectrum of Equal Protection.* As noted above, the Equal Protection Clause does not limit its coverage to government discrimination on the basis of race; that only begins the inquiry. But surely the "equal protection of the laws" does not mean that government may never make laws that affect different people differently. Is the idea that the law may treat different things differently, What sorts of differences matter? Are a person's intrinsic, permanent characteristics the ones that government may not take into account? If so, is the government never allowed to take those characteristics into account, or may they be taken into account as long as the government has a sufficiently good reason?

In modern legal doctrine, race is at one end of the spectrum for equal protection analysis. A racial classification treats similar things differently, and is presumptively invalid. The government can make rights and privileges, benefits and burdens, hinge on an individual's race only if it has a "compelling" justification and the racial classification is "narrowly tailored" to that justification. At the other end of the spectrum lies ordinary government regulation of conduct or behavior of various forms. Here the idea is that government is usually treating different things differently. At this end of the spectrum courts have applied a deferential "rational basis" test: a law is upheld as long as there is any conceivable basis for the distinctions and classifications that the government is drawing.

Where on this spectrum do sex-based classifications fall? How would the principle that like things must be treated alike apply—are men and women alike or different? One fairly obvious answer is that men and women are alike for many purposes, but different in meaningful respects for some other purposes. The task of applying "equal protection of the laws" to sex-based classifications, then, is to accurately sort out the respects in which men and women are alike from the respects in which they are truly, legitimately, necessarily different as a biological matter—and to tightly limit government sex-based classifications to the latter set of circumstances. (Easier said than done, as you will see presently.)

As you start thinking about what sex-based classifications fall into each category, consider this statement by Sylvia Law, *Rethinking Sex and the Constitution*, 132 U. Pa. L. Rev. 955, 965 (1984):

> There are . . . important points of difference between sex- and race-based discrimination. There is no reason to believe that black and white people are inherently different in any way that should ever be allowed to matter in the law. Men and women, by contrast, are different in significant sex-specific physical ways. Most differences between men and women are like differences between blacks and whites: statistical generalizations, which are more or less true in the aggregate but untrue in relation to particular individuals. Accurate statistical differences between men and women that are false in individual cases include weight, height, longevity, mathematical aptitude, aggression, capacity for nurturance, and physical strength. There are, however, other categorical differences between men and women that are not simply statistical generalizations, but rather sex-based physical differences relating to reproductive capacity. By categorical sex-based differences, what is meant, and *all that is meant*, is that most women and no men possess the capacity to reproduce the species.

3. *Generalizations and Norms.* Think back to the questions raised in Note 1 about whether in *Craig v. Boren* the state's generalization about the behavior

of men and women was accurate. When may governments legislate on the basis of true generalizations? Could a government-run life insurance program distinguish in premium rates based on the different statistical life expectancies of men and women? Could a government-run health insurance program distinguish in premium rates based on the different likelihood of different health maladies or diseases for men and women? On the basis of diseases and their occurrence rate that are specific to a particular sex (like breast cancer and testicular cancer)?

And consider activities and places where the sexes are separated. What about separate-sex bathrooms? Do social norms concerning privacy, modesty, and separation of the two sexes with respect to excretory functions reflect biological differences or improper stereotypes? What about single-sex state educational institutions?

4. *Pregnancy and Disparate Impact*. What about statutes that do not classify on the basis of sex but nonetheless have a disparate impact on the basis of sex? Recall the rule of *Washington v. Davis,* 426 U.S. 229 (1976), in the race context: disparate impact alone is not sufficient to establish a violation of the Equal Protection Clause. The Court has embraced the same rule in the context of sex. For example, classifications based on pregnancy are generally not treated as classifications on the basis of sex but are instead treated as classifications that have a disparate impact on women. See, e.g., *Geduldig v. Aiello*, 417 U.S. 484, 494–97 (1974) (upholding California disability compensation law that did not include pregnancy within its coverage of medical disabilities). Congress chose to address this situation in the Pregnancy Discrimination Act (an amendment to Title VII of the Civil Rights Act of 1964), forbidding the treatment of pregnancy-related illness less favorably than other medical conditions. The statute did not alter the *constitutional* holding of *Geduldig* that the Equal Protection Clause governs classifications based on sex itself and does not apply—absent evidence of intent to discriminate—to classifications that only have a disparate impact on men and women.

United States v. Virginia

518 U.S. 515 (1996)

■ JUSTICE GINSBURG delivered the opinion of the Court.

Virginia's public institutions of higher learning include an incomparable military college, Virginia Military Institute (VMI). The United States maintains that the Constitution's equal protection guarantee precludes Virginia from reserving exclusively to men the unique educational opportunities VMI affords. We agree.

I

Founded in 1839, VMI is today the sole single-sex school among Virginia's 15 public institutions of higher learning. VMI's distinctive mission is to produce "citizen-soldiers," men prepared for leadership in civilian life and in military service. VMI pursues this mission through pervasive training of a kind not available anywhere else in Virginia. Assigning prime place to character development, VMI uses an "adversative method" modeled on English public schools and once characteristic of military instruction. VMI constantly endeavors to instill physical and mental discipline in its cadets and impart to them a strong moral code. The school's graduates leave VMI with heightened comprehension of their capacity to deal with duress and stress, and a large sense of accomplishment for completing the hazardous course. . . .

Neither the goal of producing citizen-soldiers nor VMI's implementing methodology is inherently unsuitable to women. And the school's impressive record in producing leaders has made admission desirable to some women. Nevertheless, Virginia has elected to preserve exclusively for men the advantages and opportunities a VMI education affords.

II–A

. . . VMI today enrolls about 1,300 men as cadets. Its academic offerings in the liberal arts, sciences, and engineering are also available at other public colleges and universities in Virginia. But VMI's mission is special. It is the mission of the school:

> to produce educated and honorable men, prepared for the varied work of civil life, imbued with love of learning, confident in the functions and attitudes of leadership, possessing a high sense of public service, advocates of the American democracy and free enterprise system, and ready as citizen-soldiers to defend their country in time of national peril.

. . . VMI produces its "citizen-soldiers" through "an adversative, or doubting, model of education" which features "[p]hysical rigor, mental stress, absolute equality of treatment, absence of privacy, minute regulation of behavior, and indoctrination in desirable values." As one Commandant of Cadets described it, the adversative method "dissects the young student," and makes him aware of his "limits and capabilities," so that he knows "how far he can go with his anger, . . . how much he can take under stress, . . . exactly what he can do when he is physically exhausted."

VMI cadets live in spartan barracks where surveillance is constant and privacy nonexistent; they wear uniforms, eat together in the mess hall, and regularly participate in drills. Entering students are incessantly exposed to the rat line, "an extreme form of the adversative model," comparable in intensity to Marine Corps boot camp. Tormenting and punishing, the rat line bonds new cadets to their fellow sufferers and, when they have completed the seven-month experience, to their former tormentors. . . .

B

[Responding to a complaint by a female high-school student seeking admission to VMI, the United States sued Virginia and VMI, alleging that VMI's all-male admission policy violated the Equal Protection Clause. The District Court ruled for VMI. The Fourth Circuit reversed and suggested several remedies: admit women to VMI, establish parallel institutions or programs, or abandon state support and privatize the school.—Editors]

. . . In response to the Fourth Circuit's ruling, Virginia proposed a parallel program for women: Virginia Women's Institute for Leadership (VWIL). The four-year, state-sponsored undergraduate program would be located at Mary Baldwin College, a private liberal arts school for women . . .

Although VWIL would share VMI's mission—to produce "citizen-soldiers"—the VWIL program would differ . . . from VMI in academic offerings, methods of education, and financial resources. . . .

III

The cross-petitions in this suit present two ultimate issues. First, does Virginia's exclusion of women from the educational opportunities provided by VMI—extraordinary opportunities for military training and civilian leadership development—deny to women "capable of all of the individual activities required of VMI cadets" the equal protection of the laws guaranteed by the Fourteenth Amendment? Second, if VMI's "unique" situation—as Virginia's sole single-sex public institution of higher education—offends the Constitution's equal protection principle, what is the remedial requirement?

IV

We note, once again, the core instruction of this Court's pathmarking decisions in *J.E.B. v. Alabama*, 511 U.S. 127 (1994) and *Mississippi University for Women v. Hogan*, 458 U.S. 718 (1982): Parties who seek to defend gender-based government action must demonstrate an "exceedingly persuasive justification" for that action.

Today's skeptical scrutiny of official action denying rights or opportunities based on sex responds to volumes of history. As a plurality of this Court acknowledged a generation ago, "our Nation has had a long and unfortunate history of sex discrimination." *Frontiero v. Richardson*, 411 U.S. 677, 684 (1973). . . .

In 1971, for the first time in our Nation's history, this Court ruled in favor of a woman who complained that her State had denied her the equal protection of its laws. *Reed v. Reed* (holding unconstitutional Idaho Code prescription that, among "several persons claiming and equally entitled to administer [a decedent's estate], males must be preferred to females"). Since *Reed,* the Court has repeatedly recognized that neither federal nor state government acts compatibly with the equal protection principle when a law or official policy denies to women, simply because they are women, full citizenship stature-equal opportunity to aspire, achieve, participate in and contribute to society based on their individual talents and capacities.

Without equating gender classifications, for all purposes, to classifications based on race or national origin, the Court, in post-*Reed* decisions, has carefully inspected official action that closes a door or denies opportunity to women (or to men). To summarize the Court's current directions for cases of official classification based on gender: Focusing on the differential treatment or denial of opportunity for which relief is sought, the reviewing court must determine whether the proffered justification is "exceedingly persuasive." The burden of justification is demanding and it rests entirely on the State. The State must show "at least that the [challenged] classification serves 'important governmental objectives and that the discriminatory means employed' are 'substantially related to the achievement of those objectives." The justification must be genuine, not hypothesized or invented *post hoc* in response to litigation. And it must not rely on overbroad generalizations about the different talents, capacities, or preferences of males and females.

The heightened review standard our precedent establishes does not make sex a proscribed classification. Supposed "inherent differences" are no longer accepted as a ground for race or national origin classifications. Physical differences between men and women, however, are enduring: "[T]he two sexes are not fungible; a community made up exclusively of one [sex] is different from a community composed of both." *Ballard v. United States.*

"Inherent differences" between men and women, we have come to appreciate, remain cause for celebration, but not for denigration of the members of either sex or for artificial constraints on an individual's opportunity. Sex classifications may be used to compensate women "for particular economic disabilities [they have] suffered," *Califano v. Webster*, to advance full development of the talent and capacities of our Nation's people.[7] But such classifications may not be used, as they once were, to create or perpetuate the legal, social, and economic inferiority of women.

Measuring the record in this case against the review standard just described, we conclude that Virginia has shown no "exceedingly persuasive justification" for excluding all women from the citizen-soldier training afforded by VMI. We therefore affirm the Fourth Circuit's initial judgment, which held that Virginia had violated the Fourteenth Amendment's Equal Protection Clause. Because the remedy proffered by Virginia—the Mary Baldwin VWIL program—does not cure the constitutional violation, *i.e.*, it does not provide equal opportunity, we reverse the Fourth Circuit's final judgment in this case.

V

[Virginia advanced two justifications for VMI's exclusion of women: First, "single-sex education provides important educational benefits" and contributes to "diversity in educational approaches." Second, "the unique VMI method of character development and leadership training, the school's adversative approach, would have to be modified were VMI to admit women."—Editors]

A

Single-sex education affords pedagogical benefits to at least some students, Virginia emphasizes, and that reality is uncontested in this litigation. Similarly, it is not disputed that diversity among public educational institutions can serve the public good. But Virginia has not shown that VMI was established, or has been maintained, with a view to diversifying, by its categorical exclusion of women, educational opportunities within the Commonwealth. In cases of this genre, our precedent instructs that "benign" justifications proffered in defense of categorical exclusions will not be accepted automatically; a tenable justification must describe actual state purposes, not rationalizations for actions in fact differently grounded. . . .

Neither recent nor distant history bears out Virginia's alleged pursuit of diversity through single-sex educational options. In 1839, when the Commonwealth established VMI, a range of educational opportunities for men and women was scarcely contemplated. Higher education at the time was considered dangerous for women; reflecting widely held views about women's proper place, the Nation's first universities and colleges—for example, Harvard in Massachusetts, William and Mary in Virginia—admitted only men. VMI was not at all novel in this respect: In admitting

---

[7] Several *amici* have urged that diversity in educational opportunities is an altogether appropriate governmental pursuit and that single-sex schools can contribute importantly to such diversity. Indeed, it is the mission of some single-sex schools "to dissipate, rather than perpetuate, traditional gender classifications." See Brief for Twenty-six Private Women's Colleges as *Amici Curiae* 5. We do not question the Commonwealth's prerogative evenhandedly to support diverse educational opportunities. We address specifically and only an educational opportunity recognized by the District Court and the Court of Appeals as "unique," an opportunity available only at Virginia's premier military institute, the Commonwealth's sole single-sex public university or college.

no women, VMI followed the lead of the Commonwealth's flagship school, the University of Virginia, founded in 1819. . . .

Ultimately, in 1970, "the most prestigious institution of higher education in Virginia," the University of Virginia, introduced coeducation and, in 1972, began to admit women on an equal basis with men. . . .

Our 1982 decision in *Mississippi Univ. for Women* prompted VMI to reexamine its male-only admission policy. A Mission Study Committee, appointed by the VMI Board of Visitors, studied the problem from October 1983 until May 1986, and in that month counseled against "change of VMI status as a single-sex college." Whatever internal purpose the Mission Study Committee served—and however well meaning the framers of the report—we can hardly extract from that effort any Commonwealth policy evenhandedly to advance diverse educational options. . . .

In sum, we find no persuasive evidence in this record that VMI's male-only admission policy "is in furtherance of a state policy of 'diversity.' " . . . However "liberally" this plan serves the Commonwealth's sons, it makes no provision whatever for her daughters. That is not *equal* protection.

B

Virginia next argues that VMI's adversative method of training provides educational benefits that cannot be made available, unmodified, to women. Alterations to accommodate women would necessarily be "radical," so "drastic," Virginia asserts, as to transform, indeed "destroy," VMI's program. Neither sex would be favored by the transformation, Virginia maintains. . . .

The District Court forecast from expert witness testimony, and the Court of Appeals accepted, that coeducation would materially affect "at least these three aspects of VMI's program—physical training, the absence of privacy, and the adversative approach." And it is uncontested that women's admission would require accommodations, primarily in arranging housing assignments and physical training programs for female cadets. It is also undisputed, however, that "the VMI methodology could be used to educate women." . . .

It may be assumed, for purposes of this decision, that most women would not choose VMI's adversative method. As Fourth Circuit Judge Motz observed, however, in her dissent from the Court of Appeals' denial of rehearing en banc, it is also probable that "many men would not want to be educated in such an environment." . . . The issue, however, is not whether "women-or men-should be forced to attend VMI"; rather, the question is whether the Commonwealth can constitutionally deny to women who have the will and capacity, the training and attendant opportunities that VMI uniquely affords. . . .

[The Court found the generalizations about the preferences of women to reflect stereotypes.—Editors]

Virginia, in sum, "has fallen far short of establishing the 'exceedingly persuasive justification,' " *Mississippi Univ. for Women,* 458 U.S., at 731, that must be the solid base for any gender-defined classification.

VI

In the second phase of the litigation, Virginia presented its remedial plan-maintain VMI as a male-only college and create VWIL as a separate program for women. . . .

Virginia chose not to eliminate, but to leave untouched, VMI's exclusionary policy. . . . VWIL affords women no opportunity to experience the rigorous military training for which VMI is famed. Instead, the VWIL program "deemphasize[s]" military education and uses a "cooperative method" of education "which reinforces self-esteem." . . .

[The Court described the differences between the two programs at length. VWIL was not a "military institute," did not have the same faculty or course offerings, and did not enjoy the same long and prestigious tradition. Students did not live together in a "military-style residence," did not suffer the same physical rigor and mental stress, or enjoy the same "adversative training."—Editors]

As earlier stated, generalizations about "the way women are," estimates of what is appropriate for *most women,* no longer justify denying opportunity to women whose talent and capacity place them outside the average description. In contrast to the generalizations about women on which Virginia rests, we note again these dispositive realities: VMI's "implementing methodology" is not "inherently unsuitable to women;" "some women . . . do well under [the] adversative model;" "some women, at least, would want to attend [VMI] if they had the opportunity;" "some women are capable of all of the individual activities required of VMI cadets," and "can meet the physical standards [VMI] now impose[s] on men." It is on behalf of these women that the United States has instituted this suit, and it is for them that a remedy must be crafted, a remedy that will end their exclusion from a state-supplied educational opportunity for which they are fit, a decree that will "bar like discrimination in the future." . . .

For the reasons stated, the initial judgment of the Court of Appeals is affirmed, the final judgment of the Court of Appeals is reversed, and the case is remanded for further proceedings consistent with this opinion.

■ JUSTICE THOMAS took no part in the consideration or decision of these cases.

■ [CHIEF JUSTICE REHNQUIST's concurring opinion is omitted.]

■ JUSTICE SCALIA, dissenting.

Today the Court shuts down an institution that has served the people of the Commonwealth of Virginia with pride and distinction for over a century and a half. To achieve that desired result, it rejects (contrary to our established practice) the factual findings of two courts below, sweeps aside the precedents of this Court, and ignores the history of our people. As to facts: it explicitly rejects the finding that there exist "gender-based developmental differences" supporting Virginia's restriction of the "adversative" method to only a men's institution, and the finding that the all-male composition of the Virginia Military Institute (VMI) is essential to that institution's character. As to precedent: it drastically revises our established standards for reviewing sex-based classifications. And as to history: it counts for nothing the long tradition, enduring down to the present, of men's military colleges supported by both States and the Federal Government.

I

. . . I shall devote most of my analysis to evaluating the Court's opinion on the basis of our current equal protection jurisprudence, which regards this Court as free to evaluate everything under the sun by applying one of three tests: "rational basis" scrutiny, intermediate scrutiny, or strict scrutiny. . . .

I have no problem with a system of abstract tests such as rational basis, intermediate, and strict scrutiny (though I think we can do better than applying strict scrutiny and intermediate scrutiny whenever we feel like it). Such formulas are essential to evaluating whether the new restrictions that a changing society constantly imposes upon private conduct comport with that "equal protection" our society has always accorded in the past. But in my view the function of this Court is to *preserve* our society's values regarding (among other things) equal protection, not to *revise* them; to prevent backsliding from the degree of restriction the Constitution imposed upon democratic government, not to prescribe, on our own authority, progressively higher degrees. For that reason it is my view that, whatever abstract tests we may choose to devise, they cannot supersede—and indeed ought to be crafted *so as to reflect*—those constant and unbroken national traditions that embody the people's understanding of ambiguous constitutional texts. . . .

II

To reject the Court's disposition today, however, it is not necessary to accept my view that the Court's made-up tests cannot displace longstanding national traditions as the primary determinant of what the Constitution means. It is only necessary to apply honestly the test the Court has been applying to sex-based classifications for the past two decades. . . .

Only the amorphous "exceedingly persuasive justification" phrase, and not the standard elaboration of intermediate scrutiny, can be made to yield this conclusion that VMI's single-sex composition is unconstitutional because there exist several women (or, one would have to conclude under the Court's reasoning, a single woman) willing and able to undertake VMI's program. Intermediate scrutiny has never required a least-restrictive-means analysis, but only a "substantial relation" between the classification and the state interests that it serves. . . .

III

. . . It is beyond question that Virginia has an important state interest in providing effective college education for its citizens. That single-sex instruction is an approach substantially related to that interest should be evident enough from the long and continuing history in this country of men's and women's colleges. But beyond that, as the Court of Appeals here stated: "That single-gender education at the college level is beneficial to both sexes is a *fact established in this case*." (Emphasis added.)

. . . But besides its single-sex constitution, VMI is different from other colleges in another way. It employs a "distinctive educational method," sometimes referred to as the "adversative, or doubting, model of education." . . . A State's decision to maintain within its system one school that provides the adversative method is "substantially related" to its goal of good education. Moreover, it was uncontested that "if the state were to establish a women's VMI-type [*i.e.,* adversative] program, the program would attract an insufficient number of participants to make the program work;" and it was found by the District Court that if Virginia were to include women in VMI, the school "would eventually find it necessary to drop the adversative system altogether." Thus, Virginia's options were an adversative method that excludes women or no adversative method at all. Virginia's election to fund one public all-male institution and one on the adversative model—and to concentrate its resources in a single entity that serves both these interests in diversity—is substantially related to the Commonwealth's important educational interests. . . .

Under the constitutional principles announced and applied today, single-sex public education is unconstitutional. By going through the motions of applying a balancing test—asking whether the State has adduced an "exceedingly persuasive justification" for its sex-based classification—the Court creates the illusion that government officials in some future case will have a clear shot at justifying some sort of single-sex public education. . . .

[T]he rationale of today's decision is sweeping: for sex-based classifications, a redefinition of intermediate scrutiny that makes it indistinguishable from strict scrutiny. . . . [R]egardless of whether the Court's rationale leaves some small amount of room for lawyers to argue, it ensures that single-sex public education is functionally dead. The costs of litigating the constitutionality of a single-sex education program, and the risks of ultimately losing that litigation, are simply too high to be embraced by public officials. Any person with standing to challenge any sex-based classification can haul the State into federal court and compel it to establish by evidence (presumably in the form of expert testimony) that there is an "exceedingly persuasive justification" for the classification. . . . No state official in his right mind will buy such a high-cost, high-risk lawsuit by commencing a single-sex program. The enemies of single-sex education have won; by persuading only seven Justices (five would have been enough) that their view of the world is enshrined in the Constitution, they have effectively imposed that view on all 50 States.

This is especially regrettable because, as the District Court here determined, educational experts in recent years have increasingly come to "suppor[t] [the] view that substantial educational benefits flow from a single-gender environment, be it male or female, that cannot be replicated in a coeducational setting." 766 F. Supp., at 1415. "The evidence in th[is] case," for example, "is virtually uncontradicted" to that effect. *Ibid.* Until quite recently, some public officials have attempted to institute new single-sex programs, at least as experiments. In 1991, for example, the Detroit Board of Education announced a program to establish three boys-only schools for inner-city youth; it was met with a lawsuit, a preliminary injunction was swiftly entered by a District Court, and the Detroit Board of Education voted to abandon the litigation and thus abandon the plan. Today's opinion assures that no such experiment will be tried again. . . .

NOTES

1. What is the standard employed in *United States v. Virginia*, and is it the same as the one employed in *Craig v. Boren*? How is it distinguishable from "strict scrutiny"?

Under the standard in *United States v. Virginia*, may a state ever have a sufficient justification for single-sex higher education? Assume that a state (or a local school district) set up a diverse public school-choice program that included single-sex education options—a history distinguishable from VMI's. Would it necessarily be unconstitutional? Would the state's interest in diversity be sufficient to justify sex-segregated public education?

2. In *United States v. Virginia*, should the Supreme Court have deferred to the expert judgment of school officials about what was necessary to create their

desired educational environment, as it would seven years later in *Grutter v. Bollinger*?

3. By the time *United States v. Virginia* reached the Supreme Court, a generation of women had graduated from the federal military academies and only VMI and the Citadel, in South Carolina, continued to offer single-sex collegiate military training. Thus those institutions had become outliers from a national pattern of co-educational military training. Should this have had any effect on the justices? On the one hand, the federal precedent showed that gender stereotypes about women and the military had been in fact discriminatory and misguided. On the other hand, with West Point and Annapolis now co-ed, was there less harm in letting VMI and the Citadel stay the way they were? When is national uniformity desirable and when do we want diversity? Recall from Chapter 4 the discussion of how important national uniformity can be for protecting the civil rights of groups that have been the past victims of invidious discrimination.

4. Ohio State University has a renowned football team. Is the school obligated by the *VMI* decision to allow women to join the team?

5. In thinking about the implications of *United States v. Virginia*, consider the draft. Historically, compulsory military service has been limited to men only. Is a male-only draft unconstitutional?

In *Rostker v. Goldberg*, 453 U.S. 57 (1981), the Supreme Court, by vote of 6–3, upheld the exclusion of women from registration for the military draft. In 1980, responding to the Soviet invasion of Afghanistan, President Jimmy Carter sought to reactivate the dormant Military Selective Service Act in response to the invasion of Afghanistan by the Soviet Union. That statute allows the president to require male citizens to register for the draft, and though "Congress agreed that it was necessary to reactivate the registration process, and allocated funds for that purpose," it "did not allocate all the funds originally requested by the President, but only those necessary to register males. Although Congress considered the question at great length, it declined to amend the [act] to permit the registration of women." *Id.* at 61.

The underlying gender-based classification—exclusion of women from combat positions in the military (which was eventually repealed by executive action in 2013)—was not challenged in *Rostker*, and the majority concluded that Congress's registration plan satisfied *Craig v. Boren*'s requirement that gender-based classifications must be "substantially related to the achievement of an important governmental objective." The majority found it plain that Congress's interest in raising and supporting armies was important enough to justify the use of a gender-based classification. As a matter of policy, it was Congress's reasoned judgment to limit registration to males since the primary purpose of registration was to fill combat positions for which only males were eligible. The dissents in *Rostker* avoided challenging the exclusion of women from combat positions and focused their critiques on the majority's treatment of the legislative history and on the questionable nexus between registration for the draft and actual combat. Is *Rostker* consistent with *United States v. Virginia*?

[*Assignment 66*]

F. RACE, SEX, AND . . . WHAT ELSE? OTHER CLASSIFICATIONS UNDER THE EQUAL PROTECTION CLAUSE

The Equal Protection Clause cases we have read so far have focused on laws that classify on the basis of race or sex. As we have seen, racial discrimination by the government was at the very core of what the Fourteenth Amendment was meant to forbid. Accordingly, racial classifications are subject to "strict scrutiny" and treated as presumptively violating the Equal Protection Clause. Sex-based classifications, while perhaps not central to the Fourteenth Amendment's historical purposes (in the sense of the framers' subjective expectations and intentions) are nonetheless sufficiently analogous that they have, over time, come to be treated as quasi-suspect and subject to "intermediate scrutiny." (And some find additional support for heightened scrutiny for sex-based classifications in the Nineteenth Amendment, which prohibits government discrimination in voting "on account of sex.")

But should every type of government classification receive some level of heightened judicial scrutiny under the Equal Protection Clause? The courts have said *no*: legislatures generally need only some rational basis for their actions; the Equal Protection Clause is not a charter for the courts to supervise and scrutinize every policy choice made by elected officials. (Why then require even a "rational basis"? Does that invite judicial-policymaking, too?) As early as *Slaughter–House*, the Court adopted this view of the limited force of the Equal Protection Clause, holding that it does not justify judicial interference with the ordinary, debatable policy choices of legislatures.

If every classification does not receive heightened scrutiny under the Equal Protection Clause, but race and sex do, are there any other similar categories? Consider, for example, these categories: national origin, citizenship, age, disability, sexual orientation, and wealth. Should these categories receive heightened scrutiny, too? As you will see, for some of these the answer is *yes*, for some the answer is *no*, and for some the answer is unclear or in flux.

What is on your list of "suspect" or "quasi-suspect" bases for legal classification? What is the principled basis for your list? And how do you get to that list from the spare words of the Equal Protection Clause? Do subsequent constitutional amendments inform your list?

Once one has figured out what types of classifications are subject to the Equal Protection Clause, there remains the problem of how to decide when classifications actually deny persons "the equal protection of the laws." In doctrinal jargon: What should the level of judicial "scrutiny" be? Should it differ from category to category? Is there any principled standard for making such judgments?

These materials begin with a quick survey of the Court's doctrine outside the area of race and sex, and then offer two cases for thinking about the outer bounds of the Equal Protection Clause: *Buck v. Bell*, 274 U.S. 200 (1927), on physical and mental disabilities; and *Romer v. Evans,* 517 U.S. 620 (1996), on sexual orientation.

The General Rule of "Rational Basis"

The government makes classifications all the time. It is often perfectly sensible for the government to make distinctions in its policies based on its view that certain actions, persons, or situations are different from others. Usually those distinctions present no serious question of "equal protection." In doctrinal terms, the Supreme Court has adopted the term "rational basis" to describe the minimal degree of "scrutiny" applied to government classifications about ordinary things.

A classic case involving minimal scrutiny is *Railway Express Agency v. New York*, 336 U.S. 106 (1949), in which the Court upheld a New York City traffic regulation permitting delivery vehicles to display advertising so long as they were "engaged in the usual business or regular work of the owner," but prohibiting all vehicles "used merely or mainly for advertising." Plaintiffs challenged the regulation as a violation of the Equal Protection Clause. In the Court's words, the plaintiffs "point out that the regulation draws the line between advertisements of products sold by the owner of the truck and general advertisements. It is argued that unequal treatment on the basis of such a distinction is not justified by the aim and purpose of the regulation." The Court, however, rejected the argument: "We cannot say that the judgment is not an allowable one. . . . [T]he classification has relation to the purpose for which it is made and does not contain the kind of discrimination against which the Equal Protection Clause affords protection. . . . [T]he fact that New York City sees fit to eliminate from traffic this kind of distraction but does not touch what may be even greater ones in a different category, such as the vivid displays on Times Square, is immaterial. It is no requirement of equal protection that all evils of the same genus be eradicated or none at all."

Another standard illustration is *Williamson v. Lee Optical*, 348 U.S. 483 (1955). In *Lee Optical*, a group of Oklahoma opticians challenged a state law permitting only licensed optometrists and ophthalmologists to "fit lenses to a face." The Court held that treating opticians differently was valid under the Equal Protection Clause because there was a rational basis for doing so: "The District Court held that it violated the Equal Protection Clause of the Fourteenth Amendment to subject opticians to this regulatory system and to exempt . . . all sellers of ready-to-wear glasses. The problem of legislative classification is a perennial one, admitting of no doctrinaire definition. Evils in the same field may be of different dimensions and proportions, requiring different remedies. Or so the legislature may think. . . . Or the reform may take one step at a time, addressing itself to the phase of the problem which seems most acute to the legislative mind. . . . The legislature may select one phase of one field and apply a remedy there, neglecting the others. The prohibition of the Equal Protection Clause goes no further than the invidious discrimination."

(In both cases the Court also rejected challenges under the Due Process Clause. As it said in *Lee Optical*: "The day is gone when this Court uses the Due Process Clause of the Fourteenth Amendment to strike down state laws, regulatory of business and industrial conditions, because they may be unwise, improvident, or out of harmony with a particular school of thought." *Id.* at 488.)

It is important to note that in both *Railway Express* and *Lee Optical* the plaintiffs made strong objections to the laws they challenged. Both laws were riddled with inconsistencies and protected special interests against competition in the marketplace. For example, the law in *Lee Optical* has been aptly described as a "classic rent seeking statute," because "[e]ssentially all that this statute did was to generate business for eye doctors, thereby raising the price of duplicate lenses." Mark Tushnet, *Public Choice Constitutionalism and Economic Rights*, in LIBERTY, PROPERTY, AND THE FUTURE OF CONSTITUTIONAL DEVELOPMENT 23, 37 (Ellen Frankel Paul & Howard Dickman, eds. 1990). Nevertheless, the Court made clear that it was unwilling to strike down the laws under the Equal Protection Clause on these grounds, choosing instead to leave the policy questions to the legislatures.

The "Heightened Scrutiny" Exceptions

As you have seen, the Court's general deference to classifications made by legislatures stops when it comes to race and sex. Racial classifications are deemed "suspect" and are presumptively unconstitutional; sex-based classifications are deemed "quasi-suspect" (with all the imprecision that term entails) and are subject to a form of "intermediate" scrutiny. Each "tier" of scrutiny comes with its own test.

Beyond race and sex, the Court has had more difficulty in identifying what types of classifications should be treated as "suspect" or "quasi-suspect." One way courts have proceeded is by analogy—is the classification like race or sex? In trying to answer this question, some of the considerations they have looked to are whether: (1) there is a history of discrimination; (2) the classification concerns an immutable human characteristic, either an inherent biological condition or one attributable to the circumstances of one's birth; and (3) the classification disadvantages a "discrete and insular minority" excluded from the political process (the phrase "discrete and insular minority" comes from the famous footnote number four in *United States v. Carolene Products Co.*, 304 U.S. 144 (1938)). Which, if any, of these offer a principled basis for deciding which classifications are like race and sex? Consider how the Court has addressed the following candidates for heightened scrutiny:

Ethnicity. The Court has treated ethnicity or national origin as directly analogous to race, and as governed by the same standard. Indeed, the leading case for holding that racial classifications are subject to strict scrutiny was *Korematsu*, printed above in Chapter 3, which concerned the internment of Japanese Americans on the basis of nationality and race.

Birth to Unmarried Parents. In *Levy v. Louisiana*, 391 U.S. 68 (1968), the Court held that children born to unmarried parents could not be denied the right to recover in a wrongful death suit arising out of negligent medical care given to their mother. Because the Louisiana statute in question allowed similarly situated "legitimate" children to recover for their parents' wrongful death, the Court held that construing the statute to exclude "illegitimate" children was "invidious discrimination" in violation of the Equal Protection Clause. In the Court's words: "Legitimacy or illegitimacy of birth has no relation to the nature of the wrong allegedly inflicted on the mother. These children, though illegitimate, were dependent on her; she cared for them and nurtured them; they were indeed hers in the biological and in the spiritual sense; in her death they suffered wrong in the sense that any dependent would."

Alienage. Many statutes disadvantage aliens relative to citizens. Several times in the early 1970s the Court struck down state statutes that made distinctions on the basis of citizenship, such as by denying welfare benefits to lawful resident aliens or by requiring citizenship for civil service jobs or for the practice of law. Subsequent cases mostly went the other direction, allowing states to require citizenship for state troopers and public school teachers, though not for notaries public. In *Plyler v. Doe,* 457 U.S. 202 (1982), the Court expressly rejected the idea that illegal aliens are a suspect class: "Unlike most of the classifications that we have recognized as suspect," the Court said, "entry into this class, by virtue of entry into this country, is the product of voluntary action" and not "an absolutely immutable characteristic." *Id.* at 219 n. 19, 220. Nonetheless, the Court by a 5–4 vote, struck down a Texas statute excluding undocumented alien children from the state's public schools, because the restriction "is directed against children, and imposes its discriminatory burden on the basis of a legal characteristic over which children can have little control. It is thus difficult to conceive of a rational justification for penalizing these children for their presence within the United States."

Wealth and Poverty. Several times in the 1950s and '60s the Court hinted that classifications based on wealth should receive heightened scrutiny. For example, in *Griffin v. Illinois,* 351 U.S. 12 (1956), the Court said that "[i]n criminal trials a State can no more discriminate on account of poverty than on account of religion, race, or color." But a few years later, when considering the question more directly in *San Antonio Independent School District v. Rodriguez,* 411 U.S. 1 (1973), the Court by a 5–4 vote declined to apply heightened scrutiny to wealth classifications. In that case the Court upheld a state school-financing arrangement keyed to property tax values, which gave far more school funding to rich school districts than to poor ones.

These are not the only candidates for heightened scrutiny under the Equal Protection Clause, however. The following two cases raise questions about whether heightened scrutiny should also be given to statutes that classify on the basis of disability or sexual orientation.

Buck v. Bell

274 U.S. 200 (1927)

■ MR. JUSTICE HOLMES delivered the opinion of the Court.

This is a writ of error to review a judgment of the Supreme Court of Appeals of the State of Virginia, affirming a judgment of the Circuit Court of Amherst County, by which the defendant in error, the superintendent of the State Colony for Epileptics and Feeble Minded, was ordered to perform the operation of salpingectomy upon Carrie Buck, the plaintiff in error, for the purpose of making her sterile. The case comes here upon the contention that the statute authorizing the judgment is void under the Fourteenth Amendment as denying to the plaintiff in error due process of law and the equal protection of the laws.

Carrie Buck is a feeble-minded white woman who was committed to the State Colony above mentioned in due form. She is the daughter of a feeble-minded mother in the same institution, and the mother of an illegitimate feeble-minded child. She was eighteen years old at the time of the trial of her case in the Circuit Court in the latter part of 1924. An Act of Virginia approved March 20, 1924 recites that the health of the patient and the welfare of society may be promoted in certain cases by the sterilization of mental defectives, under careful safeguard, etc.; that the sterilization may be effected in males by vasectomy and in females by salpingectomy, without serious pain or substantial danger to life; that the Commonwealth is supporting in various institutions many defective persons who if now discharged would become a menace but if incapable of procreating might be discharged with safety and become self-supporting with benefit to themselves and to society; and that experience has shown that heredity plays an important part in the transmission of insanity, imbecility, etc. The statute then enacts that whenever the superintendent of certain institutions including the above named State Colony shall be of opinion that it is for the best interest of the patients and of society that an inmate under his care should be sexually sterilized, he may have the operation performed upon any patient afflicted with hereditary forms of insanity, imbecility, etc., on complying with the very careful provisions by which the act protects the patients from possible abuse.

The superintendent first presents a petition to the special board of directors of his hospital or colony, stating the facts and the grounds for his opinion, verified by affidavit. Notice of the petition and of the time and place of the hearing in the institution is to be served upon the inmate, and also upon his guardian, and if there is no guardian the superintendent is to apply to the Circuit Court of the County to appoint one. If the inmate is a minor notice also is to be given to his parents, if any, with a copy of the petition. The board is to see to it that the inmate may attend the hearings if desired by him or his guardian. The evidence is all to be reduced to writing, and after the board has made its order for or against the operation, the superintendent, or the inmate, or his guardian, may appeal to the Circuit Court of the County. The Circuit Court may consider the record of the board and the evidence before it and such other admissible evidence as may be offered, and may affirm, revise, or reverse the order of the board and enter such order as it deems just. Finally any party may apply to the Supreme Court of Appeals, which, if it grants the appeal, is to hear the case upon the record of the trial in the Circuit Court and may enter such order as it thinks the Circuit Court should have entered. There can be no doubt that so far as procedure is concerned the rights of the patient are most carefully considered, and as every step in this case was taken in scrupulous compliance with the statute and after months of observation, there is no doubt that in that respect the plaintiff in error has had due process at law.

The attack is not upon the procedure but upon the substantive law. It seems to be contended that in no circumstances could such an order be justified. It certainly is contended that the order cannot be justified upon the existing grounds. The judgment finds the facts that have been recited and that Carrie Buck "is the probable potential parent of socially inadequate offspring, likewise afflicted, that she may be sexually sterilized without detriment to her general health and that her welfare and that of society will be promoted by her sterilization," and thereupon makes the order. In view of the general declarations of the Legislature and the specific findings of the Court obviously we cannot say as matter of law that the grounds do not exist, and if they exist they justify the result. We have seen more than once that the public welfare may call upon the best citizens for their lives. It would be strange if it could not call upon those who already sap the strength of the State for these lesser sacrifices, often not felt to be such by those concerned, in order to prevent our being swamped with incompetence. It is better for all the world, if instead of waiting to execute degenerate offspring for crime, or to let them starve for their imbecility, society can prevent those who are manifestly unfit from continuing their kind. The principle that sustains compulsory vaccination is broad enough to cover cutting the Fallopian tubes. *Jacobson v. Massachusetts*, 197 U.S. 11. Three generations of imbeciles are enough.

But, it is said, however it might be if this reasoning were applied generally, it fails when it is confined to the small number who are in the institutions named and is not applied to the multitudes outside. It is the usual last resort of constitutional arguments to point out shortcomings of this sort. But the answer is that the law does all that is needed when it does all that it can, indicates a policy, applies it to all within the lines, and seeks to bring within the lines all similarly situated so far and so fast as its means allow. Of course so far as the operations enable those who otherwise must be kept confined to be returned to the world, and thus open the asylum to others, the equality aimed at will be more nearly reached.

■ Mr. Justice Butler dissents.

NOTES

1. *Buck* is a bracing decision for a reader today. "A mere five paragraphs long," the case has been described by Victoria Nourse as having "the highest ratio of injustice per word ever signed on to by eight Supreme Court Justices, progressive and conservative alike." Victoria Nourse, *Buck v. Bell: A Constitutional Tragedy from a Lost World*, 39 Pepp. L. Rev. 101, 102 (2011). The intellectual history and scientific opinion underlying the decision have been described this way:

> Early in the twentieth century, mainstream scientific opinion was won over by eugenics following the re-discovery of Mendel's genetic laws in 1900. . . . "More children from the fit, less from the unfit," became the motto for early twentieth century eugenicists. . . .
>
> By the 1920s, in an era when genetics was institutionalized at both state land-grant and private research universities, American geneticists enthusiastically embraced eugenics. Leading this scientific chorus, with support from the newly created Carnegie Institute of Washington, [was] the pioneering geneticist Charles Davenport. . . . America's two Nobel Prize winning geneticists of the era . . . added their support to the cause, as did the American Genetics Association and various state and regional medical societies. A larger circle of distinguished professionals, including [the presidents of Harvard University, Stanford University, and the University of Michigan, a number of leading biologists,] . . . American Museum of Natural History President Henry Fairfield Osborn, birth-control advocate Margaret Sanger, inventor Alexander Graham Bell, and the legendary California plant breeder Luther Burbank, also publicly backed eugenics. Even the era's most famous American with disabilities, Helen Keller, who became blind and deaf from a childhood illness, favored eugenic remedies for those born with severe disabilities. A wide range of American political leaders, including Presidents Theodore Roosevelt, William Howard Taft, Woodrow Wilson, and Calvin Coolidge, endorsed eugenic measures, and it was the Justices nominated by these four presidents who decided *Buck*. Wealthy philanthropists and foundations vied to support eugenics research and lawmaking. Indeed, the Virginia eugenics sterilization law upheld in *Buck* was based on a model statute drafted by the Harriman and Carnegie funded Eugenics Record Office. Advocates supported

by the New York-based Rockefeller and Russell Sage Foundations lobbied for enactment of eugenics legislation throughout the South. . . . Ultimately, by 1937, thirty-two states from California to Maine had enacted compulsory eugenic sterilization statutes and five more had sterilized citizens without passing a compulsory law. Many more states enacted measures to compel the sexual segregation of mentally ill or retarded persons.

Edward J. Larson, *Putting Buck v. Bell in Scientific and Historical Context: A Response to Victoria Nourse*, 39 Pepp. L. Rev. 119, 122–124 (2011). By the time of *Buck*, the practice of eugenic sterilization in the United States was waning, though it retained intellectual respectability. Even a decade later, a report of the American Neurological Association "denounced the sterilization of criminals" but "endorsed the procedure for certain mental conditions covered by Virginia's sterilization statute, such as schizophrenia, manic-depression, epilepsy, and so-called mental hereditary retardation." *Id.* at 127.

Given this context, even if the Court's decision would be wrong today, was it right in 1927? Should the tide of scientific opinion in favor of eugenics have affected how the Court interpreted the Constitution? More provocatively, is the holding in *Buck v. Bell* (outrageous rhetoric aside) actually correct as a matter of constitutional interpretation? Was the Court admirably exercising judicial restraint in the face of an ugly state statute that should never have been passed but which it had no basis for invalidating? Or was the Court failing in its constitutional duty to provide "equal protection of the laws" to a group that desperately needed it?

2. In considering Carrie Buck's claim under the Equal Protection Clause, today the starting point would be to determine the appropriate level of scrutiny. Is a disability classification like a classification on the basis of race or sex? For example, is there a history of discrimination against the mentally disabled? Is mental disability of the kind regulated by the statute at issue in *Buck* an immutable characteristic of birth? Are the mentally disabled a "discrete and insular minority," excluded from the political process? Or should the inquiry be whether the state classification treated like persons differently or different persons differently?

In *City of Cleburne v. Cleburne Living Center*, 473 U.S. 432 (1985), the Court struck down a zoning ordinance that excluded a group home for the mentally disabled, but the Court based its conclusion on improper motive and expressly held that no heightened scrutiny should be applied to a "mental retardation" classification.

In reaching the latter conclusion, the Court emphasized institutional competence, calling regulation in this area "a task for legislators guided by qualified professionals and not by the perhaps ill-informed opinions of the judiciary." The Court also noted that the passage of federal laws prohibiting discrimination against the mentally disabled. This "legislative response, which could hardly have occurred and survived without public support, negates any claim that the mentally retarded are politically powerless in the sense that they have no ability to attract the attention of the lawmakers. Any minority can be said to be powerless to assert direct control over the legislature, but if that were a criterion for higher level scrutiny by the courts, much economic and social legislation would now be suspect." Finally, the Court emphasized its concern about a limiting principle: "if the large and amorphous class of the mentally retarded were deemed quasi-suspect," then "it would be difficult to find a principled way to distinguish a variety of other groups who have perhaps immutable disabilities setting them off from others, who cannot themselves mandate the desired legislative responses, and who can claim some degree of prejudice from at least part of the public at large," such as "the aging . . . and the infirm."

In partial dissent, Justice Marshall noted that "the mentally retarded have been subject to a lengthy and tragic history," as "the rising tide of Social Darwinism" and "leading medical authorities" supported a "regime of state-mandated segregation and degradation . . . [that] rivaled . . . the worst excesses of Jim Crow." Are the majority's reasons not to give heightened scrutiny persuasive? Should the history of discrimination noted by the dissent be dispositive? And if the Court was willing to strike down the ordinance anyway under rational basis review, how much does the standard of scrutiny actually matter?

3. Does a failure to *accommodate* a disability deny equal protection of the laws to persons with that disability?

Romer v. Evans

517 U.S. 620 (1996)

■ JUSTICE KENNEDY delivered the opinion of the Court.

One century ago, the first Justice Harlan admonished this Court that the Constitution "neither knows nor tolerates classes among citizens." *Plessy v. Ferguson*, 163 U.S. 537, 559 (1896) (dissenting opinion). Unheeded then, those words now are understood to state a commitment to the law's neutrality where the rights of persons are at stake. The Equal Protection Clause enforces this principle and today requires us to hold invalid a provision of Colorado's Constitution.

I

The enactment challenged in this case is an amendment to the Constitution of the State of Colorado, adopted in a 1992 statewide referendum. The parties and the state courts refer to it as "Amendment 2," its designation when submitted to the voters. The impetus for the amendment and the contentious campaign that preceded its adoption came in large part from ordinances that had been passed in various Colorado municipalities. For example, the cities of Aspen and Boulder and the city and County of Denver each had enacted ordinances which banned discrimination in many transactions and activities, including housing, employment, education, public accommodations, and health and welfare services. What gave rise to the statewide controversy was the protection the ordinances afforded to persons discriminated against by reason of their sexual orientation. Amendment 2 repeals these ordinances to the extent they prohibit discrimination on the basis of "homosexual, lesbian or bisexual orientation, conduct, practices or relationships."

Yet Amendment 2, in explicit terms, does more than repeal or rescind these provisions. It prohibits all legislative, executive or judicial action at any level of state or local government designed to protect the named class, a class we shall refer to as homosexual persons or gays and lesbians. The amendment reads:

No Protected Status Based on Homosexual, Lesbian or Bisexual Orientation. Neither the State of Colorado, through any of its branches or departments, nor any of its agencies, political subdivisions, municipalities or school districts, shall enact, adopt or enforce any statute, regulation, ordinance or policy whereby homosexual, lesbian or bisexual orientation, conduct, practices or relationships shall constitute or otherwise be the basis of or entitle any person or class of persons to have or claim any minority status, quota preferences, protected status or claim of discrimination. This Section of the Constitution shall be in all respects self-executing.

Colo. Const., Art. II, § 30b.

... The State Supreme Court held that Amendment 2 was subject to strict scrutiny under the Fourteenth Amendment because it infringed the fundamental right of gays and lesbians to participate in the political process.... We granted certiorari, and now affirm the judgment, but on a rationale different from that adopted by the State Supreme Court.

II

The State's principal argument in defense of Amendment 2 is that it puts gays and lesbians in the same position as all other persons. So, the State says, the measure does no more than deny homosexuals special rights. This reading of the amendment's language is implausible. We rely not upon our own interpretation of the amendment but upon the authoritative construction of Colorado's Supreme Court ... as follows:

The immediate objective of Amendment 2 is, at a minimum, to repeal existing statutes, regulations, ordinances, and policies of state and local entities that barred discrimination based on sexual orientation ... and various provisions prohibiting discrimination based on sexual orientation at state colleges.

The "ultimate effect" of Amendment 2 is to prohibit any governmental entity from adopting similar, or more protective statutes, regulations, ordinances, or policies in the future unless the state constitution is first amended to permit such measures.

Sweeping and comprehensive is the change in legal status effected by this law. So much is evident from the ordinances the Colorado Supreme Court declared would be void by operation of Amendment 2. Homosexuals, by state decree, are put in a solitary class with respect to transactions and relations in both the private and governmental spheres. The amendment withdraws from homosexuals, but no others, specific legal protection from the injuries caused by discrimination, and it forbids reinstatement of these laws and policies.

The change Amendment 2 works in the legal status of gays and lesbians in the private sphere is far reaching, both on its own terms and when considered in light of the structure and operation of modern antidiscrimination laws. That structure is well illustrated by contemporary statutes and ordinances prohibiting discrimination by providers of public accommodations. "At common law, innkeepers, smiths, and others who 'made profession of a public employment,' were prohibited from refusing, without good reason, to serve a customer." *Hurley v. Irish–American Gay, Lesbian and Bisexual Group of Boston, Inc.*, 515 U.S. 557, 571 (1995). The duty was a general one and did not specify protection for particular groups. The common-law rules, however, proved insufficient in many instances, and it was settled early that the Fourteenth Amendment did not give Congress a general power to prohibit discrimination in public accommodations, *Civil Rights Cases*, 109 U.S. 3, 25 (1883). In consequence, most States have chosen to counter discrimination by enacting detailed statutory schemes.

Colorado's state and municipal laws typify this emerging tradition of statutory protection and follow a consistent pattern. The laws first enumerate the persons or entities subject to a duty not to discriminate. The list goes well beyond the entities covered by the common law. The Boulder ordinance, for example, has a comprehensive definition of entities deemed places of "public accommodation." They include "any place of business engaged in any sales to the general public and any place that offers services, facilities, privileges, or advantages to the general public or that receives financial support through solicitation of the general public or through governmental subsidy of any kind." The Denver ordinance is of similar breadth, applying, for example, to hotels, restaurants, hospitals, dental clinics, theaters, banks, common carriers, travel and insurance agencies, and "shops and stores dealing with goods or services of any kind."

These statutes and ordinances also depart from the common law by enumerating the groups or persons within their ambit of protection. Enumeration is the essential device used to make the duty not to discriminate concrete and to provide guidance for those who must comply. In following this approach, Colorado's state and local governments have not limited antidiscrimination laws to groups that have so far been given the protection of heightened equal protection scrutiny under our cases. Rather, they set forth an extensive catalog of traits which cannot be the basis for discrimination, including age, military status, marital status, pregnancy, parenthood, custody of a minor child, political affiliation, physical or mental disability of an individual or of his or her associates—and, in recent times, sexual orientation.

Amendment 2 bars homosexuals from securing protection against the injuries that these public-accommodations laws address. That in itself is a severe consequence, but there is more. Amendment 2, in addition, nullifies specific legal protections for this targeted class in all transactions in housing, sale of real estate, insurance, health and welfare services, private education, and employment. Aspen Municipal Code (1977); Boulder Rev. Code (1987); Denver Rev. Municipal Code (1991); Colo. Rev. Stat. (1988 and Supp. 1995).

Not confined to the private sphere, Amendment 2 also operates to repeal and forbid all laws or policies providing specific protection for gays or lesbians from discrimination by every level of Colorado government. The State Supreme Court cited two examples of protections in the governmental sphere that are now rescinded and may not be reintroduced. The first is Colorado Executive Order D0035 (1990), which forbids employment discrimination against " 'all state employees, classified and exempt' on the basis of sexual orientation." Also repealed, and now forbidden, are "various provisions prohibiting discrimination based on sexual orientation at state colleges." The repeal of these measures and the prohibition against their future reenactment demonstrate that Amendment 2 has the same force and effect in Colorado's governmental sector as it does elsewhere and that it applies to policies as well as ordinary legislation.

Amendment 2's reach may not be limited to specific laws passed for the benefit of gays and lesbians. It is a fair, if not necessary, inference from the broad language of the amendment that it deprives gays and lesbians even of the protection of general laws and policies that prohibit arbitrary discrimination in governmental and private settings. At some point in the systematic administration of these laws, an official must determine whether homosexuality is an arbitrary and, thus, forbidden basis for decision. Yet a decision to that effect would itself amount to a policy prohibiting discrimination on the basis of homosexuality, and so would appear to be no more valid under Amendment 2 than the specific prohibitions against discrimination the state court held invalid.

If this consequence follows from Amendment 2, as its broad language suggests, it would compound the constitutional difficulties the law creates. The state court did not decide whether the amendment has this effect, however, and neither need we. In the course of rejecting the argument that Amendment 2 is intended to conserve resources to fight discrimination against suspect classes, the Colorado Supreme Court made the limited observation that the amendment is not intended to affect many anti-discrimination laws protecting nonsuspect classes. In our view that does not resolve the issue. In any event, even if, as we doubt, homosexuals could find some safe harbor in laws of general application, we cannot accept the view that Amendment 2's prohibition on specific legal protections does no more than deprive homosexuals of special rights. To the contrary, the amendment imposes a special disability upon those persons alone. Homosexuals are forbidden the safeguards that others enjoy or may seek without constraint. They can obtain specific protection against discrimination only by enlisting the citizenry of Colorado to amend the State Constitution or perhaps, on the State's view, by trying to pass helpful laws of general applicability. This is so no matter how local or discrete the harm, no matter how public and widespread the injury. We find nothing special in the protections Amendment 2 withholds. These are protections taken for granted by most people either because they already have them or do not need them; these are protections against exclusion from an almost limitless number of transactions and endeavors that constitute ordinary civic life in a free society.

III

The Fourteenth Amendment's promise that no person shall be denied the equal protection of the laws must coexist with the practical necessity that most legislation classifies for one purpose or another, with resulting disadvantage to various groups or persons. We have attempted to reconcile the principle with the reality by stating that, if a law neither burdens a fundamental right nor targets a suspect class, we will uphold the legislative classification so long as it bears a rational relation to some legitimate end.

Amendment 2 fails, indeed defies, even this conventional inquiry. First, the amendment has the peculiar property of imposing a broad and undifferentiated disability on a single named group, an exceptional and, as we shall explain, invalid form of legislation. Second, its sheer breadth is so discontinuous with the reasons offered for it that the amendment seems inexplicable by anything but animus toward the class it affects; it lacks a rational relationship to legitimate state interests.

Taking the first point, even in the ordinary equal protection case calling for the most deferential of standards, we insist on knowing the relation between the classification adopted and the object to be attained. The search for the link between classification and objective gives substance to the Equal Protection Clause; it provides guidance and discipline for the legislature, which is entitled to know what sorts of laws it can pass; and it marks the limits of our own authority. In the ordinary case, a law will be sustained if it can be said to advance a legitimate government interest, even if the law seems unwise or works to the disadvantage of a particular group, or if the rationale for it seems tenuous. The laws challenged in the cases just cited were narrow enough in scope and grounded in a sufficient factual context for us to ascertain some relation between the classification and the purpose it served. By requiring that the classification bear a rational relationship to an independent and legitimate legislative end, we ensure that classifications are not drawn for the purpose of disadvantaging the group burdened by the law.

Amendment 2 confounds this normal process of judicial review. It is at once too narrow and too broad. It identifies persons by a single trait and then denies them protection across the board. The resulting disqualification of a class of persons from the right to seek specific protection from the law is unprecedented in our jurisprudence. The absence of precedent for Amendment 2 is itself instructive; "[d]iscriminations of an unusual character especially suggest careful consideration to determine whether they are obnoxious to the constitutional provision." *Louisville Gas & Elec. Co. v. Coleman*, 277 U.S. 32, 37–38 (1928).

It is not within our constitutional tradition to enact laws of this sort. Central both to the idea of the rule of law and to our own Constitution's guarantee of equal protection is the principle that government and each of its parts remain open on impartial terms to all who seek its assistance. . . . Respect for this principle explains why laws singling out a certain class of citizens for disfavored legal status or general hardships are rare. A law declaring that in general it shall be more difficult for one group of citizens than for all others to seek aid from the government is itself a denial of equal protection of the laws in the most literal sense. "The guaranty of 'equal protection of the laws is a pledge of the protection of equal laws.'" *Skinner v. Oklahoma ex rel. Williamson*, 316 U.S. 535, 541 (1942). . . .

A second and related point is that laws of the kind now before us raise the inevitable inference that the disadvantage imposed is born of animosity toward the class of persons affected. . . . "[I]f the constitutional conception of 'equal protection of the laws' means anything, it must at the very least mean that a bare . . . desire to harm a politically unpopular group cannot constitute a *legitimate* governmental interest." *Department of Agriculture v. Moreno*, 413 U.S. 528, 534 (1973). Even laws enacted for broad and ambitious purposes often can be explained by reference to legitimate public policies which justify the incidental disadvantages they impose on certain persons. Amendment 2, however, in making a general announcement that gays and lesbians shall not have any particular protections from the law, inflicts on them immediate, continuing, and real injuries that outrun and belie any legitimate justifications that may be claimed for it. We conclude that, in addition to the far-reaching deficiencies of Amendment 2 that we have noted, the principles it offends, in another sense, are conventional and venerable; a law must bear a rational relationship to a legitimate governmental purpose, and Amendment 2 does not.

The primary rationale the State offers for Amendment 2 is respect for other citizens' freedom of association, and in particular the liberties of landlords or employers who have personal or religious objections to homosexuality. Colorado also cites its interest in conserving resources to fight discrimination against other groups. The breadth of the amendment is so far removed from these particular justifications that we find it impossible to credit them. We cannot say that Amendment 2 is directed to any identifiable legitimate purpose or discrete objective. It is a status-based enactment divorced from any factual context from which we could discern a relationship to legitimate state interests; it is a classification of persons undertaken for its own sake, something the Equal Protection Clause does not permit. "[C]lass legislation . . . [is] obnoxious to the prohibitions of the Fourteenth Amendment. . . ." *Civil Rights Cases,* 109 U.S. at 24.

We must conclude that Amendment 2 classifies homosexuals not to further a proper legislative end but to make them unequal to everyone else. This Colorado cannot do. A State cannot so deem a class of persons a stranger to its laws. Amendment 2 violates the Equal Protection Clause.

■ JUSTICE SCALIA, with whom THE CHIEF JUSTICE and Justice THOMAS join, dissenting.

The Court has mistaken a Kulturkampf for a fit of spite. The constitutional amendment before us here is not the manifestation of a " 'bare . . . desire to harm' " homosexuals, but is rather a modest attempt by seemingly tolerant Coloradans to preserve traditional sexual mores against the efforts of a politically powerful minority to revise those mores through use of the laws. That objective, and the means chosen to achieve it, are not only unimpeachable under any constitutional doctrine hitherto pronounced (hence the opinion's heavy reliance upon principles of righteousness rather than judicial holdings); they have been specifically approved by the Congress of the United States and by this Court.

In holding that homosexuality cannot be singled out for disfavorable treatment, the Court contradicts a decision, unchallenged here, pronounced only 10 years ago, *see Bowers v. Hardwick,* 478 U.S. 186 (1986), and places the prestige of this institution behind the proposition that opposition to homosexuality is as reprehensible as racial or religious bias. Whether it is or not is *precisely* the cultural debate that gave rise to the Colorado constitutional amendment (and to the preferential laws against which the amendment was directed). Since the Constitution of the United States says nothing about this subject, it is left to be resolved by normal democratic means, including the democratic adoption of provisions in state constitutions. This Court has no business imposing upon all Americans the resolution favored by the elite class from which the Members of this institution are selected, pronouncing that "animosity" toward homosexuality is evil. I vigorously dissent.

I

. . . [T]he Court considers it unnecessary to decide the validity of the State's argument that Amendment 2 does not deprive homosexuals of the "protection [afforded by] general laws and policies that prohibit arbitrary discrimination in governmental and private settings." I agree that we need not resolve that dispute, because the Supreme Court of Colorado has resolved it for us . . .:

> [I]t is significant to note that Colorado law currently proscribes discrimination against persons who are not suspect classes, including discrimination based on age; marital or family status; veterans' status; and for any legal, off-duty conduct such as smoking tobacco, *Of course Amendment 2 is not intended to have any effect on this legislation, but seeks only to prevent the adoption of antidiscrimination laws intended to protect gays, lesbians, and bisexuals.*

The Court utterly fails to distinguish this portion of the Colorado court's opinion. . . . [T]he clear import of the Colorado [Supreme] court's conclusion . . . is that "general laws and policies that prohibit arbitrary discrimination" would continue to prohibit discrimination on the basis of homosexual conduct as well. This analysis, which is fully in accord with (indeed, follows inescapably from) the text of the constitutional provision, lays to rest such horribles, raised in the course of oral argument, as the prospect that assaults upon homosexuals could not be prosecuted. The amendment prohibits *special treatment* of homosexuals, and nothing more. It would not affect, for example, a requirement of state law that pensions be paid to all retiring state employees with a certain length of service; homosexual employees, as well as others, would be entitled to that benefit. But it would prevent the State or any municipality from making death-benefit payments to the "life partner" of a homosexual when it does not make such payments to the longtime roommate of a nonhomosexual employee. Or again, it does not affect the requirement of the State's general insurance laws that customers be afforded coverage without discrimination unrelated to anticipated risk. Thus, homosexuals could not be denied coverage, or charged a greater premium, with respect to auto collision insurance' but neither the State nor any municipality could require that distinctive health insurance risks associated with homosexuality (if there are any) be ignored.

Despite all of its hand wringing about the potential effect of Amendment 2 on general antidiscrimination laws, the Court's opinion ultimately does not dispute all this, but assumes it to be true. The only denial of equal treatment it contends homosexuals have suffered is this: They may not obtain *preferential* treatment without amending the State Constitution. That is to say, the principle underlying the Court's opinion is that one who is accorded equal treatment under the laws, but cannot as readily as others obtain *preferential* treatment under the laws, has been denied equal protection of the laws. If merely stating this alleged "equal protection" violation does not suffice to refute it, our constitutional jurisprudence has achieved terminal silliness.

The central thesis of the Court's reasoning is that any group is denied equal protection when, to obtain advantage (or, presumably, to avoid disadvantage), it must have recourse to a more general and hence more difficult level of political decisionmaking than others. The world has never heard of such a principle, which is why the Court's opinion is so long on emotive utterance and so short on relevant legal citation. And it seems to me most unlikely that any multilevel democracy can function under such a principle. For *whenever* a disadvantage is imposed, or conferral of a benefit is prohibited, at one of the higher levels of democratic decisionmaking (i.e., by the state legislature rather than local government, or by the people at large in the state constitution rather than the legislature), the affected group has (under this theory) been denied equal protection. To take the simplest of examples, consider a state law prohibiting the award of municipal contracts to relatives of mayors or city councilmen. Once such a law is passed, the group composed of such relatives must, in order to get the benefit of city contracts, persuade the state legislature-unlike all other citizens, who need only persuade the municipality. It is ridiculous to consider this a denial of equal protection, which is why the Court's theory is unheard of. . . .

III

[Justice Scalia next defends Amendment 2 as satisfying the "rational basis" test.—Editors]

The Colorado amendment does not, to speak entirely precisely, prohibit giving favored status to people who are *homosexuals;* they can be favored for many reasons—for example, because they are senior citizens or members of racial minorities. But it prohibits giving them favored status *be-*

cause of their homosexual conduct—that is, it prohibits favored status *for homosexuality.*

. . . [Amendment 2] put directly, to all the citizens of the State, the question: Should homosexuality be given special protection? They answered no. The Court today asserts that this most democratic of procedures is unconstitutional. Lacking any cases to establish that facially absurd proposition, it simply asserts that it *must* be unconstitutional, because it has never happened before. . . .

As I have noted above, this is proved false every time a state law prohibiting or disfavoring certain conduct is passed, because such a law prevents the adversely affected group—whether drug addicts, or smokers, or gun owners, or motorcyclists—from changing the policy thus established in "each of [the] parts" of the State. What the Court says is even demonstrably false at the constitutional level. The Eighteenth Amendment to the Federal Constitution, for example, deprived those who drank alcohol not only of the power to alter the policy of prohibition *locally* or through *state legislation,* but even of the power to alter it through *state constitutional amendment* or *federal legislation.* The Establishment Clause of the First Amendment prevents theocrats from having their way by converting their fellow citizens at the local, state, or federal statutory level; as does the Republican Form of Government Clause prevent monarchists.

But there is a much closer analogy, one that involves precisely the effort by the majority of citizens to preserve its view of sexual morality statewide, against the efforts of a geographically concentrated and politically powerful minority to undermine it. The Constitutions of the States of Arizona, Idaho, New Mexico, Oklahoma, and Utah *to this day* contain provisions stating that polygamy is "forever prohibited." Polygamists, and those who have a polygamous "orientation," have been "singled out" by these provisions for much more severe treatment than merely denial of favored status; and that treatment can only be changed by achieving amendment of the state constitutions. The Court's disposition today suggests that these provisions are unconstitutional, and that polygamy must be permitted in these States on a state-legislated, or perhaps even local-option, basis-unless, of course, polygamists for some reason have fewer constitutional rights than homosexuals.

The United States Congress, by the way, *required* the inclusion of these antipolygamy provisions in the Constitutions of Arizona, New Mexico, Oklahoma, and Utah, as a condition of their admission to statehood. . . . [T]his "singling out" of the sexual practices of a single group for statewide, democratic vote—so utterly alien to our constitutional system, the Court would have us believe—has not only happened, but has received the explicit approval of the United States Congress. . . . Has the Court concluded that the perceived social harm of polygamy is a "legitimate concern of government," and the perceived social harm of homosexuality is not?

IV

. . . Today's opinion has no foundation in American constitutional law, and barely pretends to. The people of Colorado have adopted an entirely reasonable provision which does not even disfavor homosexuals in any substantive sense, but merely denies them preferential treatment. Amendment 2 is designed to prevent piecemeal deterioration of the sexual morality favored by a majority of Coloradans, and is not only an appropriate means to that legitimate end, but a means that Americans have employed before.

Striking it down is an act, not of judicial judgment, but of political will. I dissent.

NOTES

1. A hypothetical: landlords and condominium associations in Denver have begun refusing apartments to lawyers (and law students!) on the ground that they tend to be litigious and just generally irascible. The lawyers strike back and succeed in having the city council pass an ordinance forbidding discrimination in housing on the basis of being a lawyer or law student. Outraged and offended at lawyers having written themselves into the city anti-discrimination ordinances as a protected class, the people of Colorado adopt a constitutional amendment forbidding the adoption by local governments of such lawyer-protection-from-discrimination ordinances. The lawyers (of course) bring a federal constitutional challenge under the Equal Protection Clause. What result?

2. The Colorado Supreme Court had determined that Amendment 2 constituted discrimination on the basis of sexual orientation and, as such, was subject to "strict scrutiny." The U.S. Supreme Court in *Romer* notes this argument, but declines to pursue it, instead deciding the case on an opaque variation of "rational basis." Why?

Consider the following hypotheticals and whether the Court's rational-basis analysis would reach the same result. Denver decided to repeal its specific sexual-orientation protection. Colorado Springs considered enacting an ordinance forbidding discrimination on the basis of sexual orientation, but decided not to. Grand Junction never thought about (and never enacted) an ordinance forbidding discrimination on the basis of sexual orientation. Which, if any, of these scenarios would violate the Equal Protection Clause?

3. Is a sexual-orientation-based classification like a classification on the basis of race or sex? In answering this, think of the questions courts often consider for this kind of analogy. Is there a history of discrimination against gays and lesbians in the United States? Are gays and lesbians a "discrete and insular minority," excluded from the political process? And—at the risk of provoking a free-for-all, but because the question is necessary for thinking about the legal doctrine—is sexual orientation an immutable characteristic of birth? How should courts determine whether it is an immutable characteristic? Should they look to the latest studies in biology or the social sciences? And what do those say? If the court makes a foray into the biological and social sciences and concludes that there is not just one answer—that some people may be immutably straight; others may be immutably gay; and still others may through some combination of situation, choice, and social conditioning be able to live in straight or gay relationships—how would that affect the constitutional analysis? And if future studies reach a different conclusion, from whatever conclusion they reach on the day you are reading this, should that change the answer to the constitutional question? Also, recall *Cleburne* and the reasons the Court gave for not applying heightened scrutiny. Are those applicable here, or are they distinguishable?

4. In dissent Justice Scalia raises the example of polygamy. Whatever answers you gave to the questions in the preceding note, consider whether you would you give the same ones if the questions were about polygamy. Is there a history of discrimination against polygamists in the United States? Are polygamists a "discrete and insular minority," excluded from the political process? If

there is such a thing as an orientation to multiple sexual partners, is that an immutable characteristic of birth? How should courts decide that question, and if they look to the biological and social sciences for the answers, what should they do if some day those answers change? And would the arguments against heightened scrutiny in *Cleburne* apply with equal force here?

5. Should some classifications that seem based on sexual orientation actually be considered classifications on the basis of sex? Consider again laws limiting marriage to opposite-sex couples, and the argument from *Loving v. Virginia*. That case struck down state laws banning interracial marriage on the ground that they classify on the basis of race—even though they purported to treat both blacks and whites the same way. So too, do laws banning same-sex marriage classify on the basis of sex—even though they purport to apply the same rule to members of both sexes (i.e., both males and females are permitted to marry only persons of the opposite sex). Just as the law at issue in *Loving* was subject to strict scrutiny as a racial classification, the argument would go, state laws allowing only opposite-sex marriage should be subject to "intermediate scrutiny" as sex-based classifications. Are you persuaded? Does it matter that the statute in *Loving* had a racially discriminatory purpose and effect—subordinating blacks to whites? Do state laws limiting marriage to opposite-sex couples have a sex-discriminatory purpose and effect, such as subordinating men to women or vice versa?

6. Would an affirmative action policy that gave preference in admission to a state university for gay and lesbian students violate the Equal Protection Clause?

7. In *Lawrence v. Texas*, 539 U.S. 558 (2003), printed later in this chapter, the Supreme Court struck down a Texas law forbidding certain homosexual sexual acts on the ground that the law violated the substantive due process liberty of the persons engaged in the acts. Justice Kennedy's majority opinion deliberately eschewed reliance on the Equal Protection Clause. Why? Was it because the law forbade conduct and was not addressed to orientation *per se*? Or was it to avoid any implication that the Constitution created a right to same-sex marriage? At the time this book went to press the Court had granted *certiorari* in but had not yet decided two cases that involve same-sex marriage and the Constitution: *United States v. Windsor* and *Hollingsworth v. Perry*.

A NOTE ON THE "FUNDAMENTAL INTERESTS" STRAND OF EQUAL PROTECTION DOCTRINE

Beginning in the 1960s, the Supreme Court suggested that heightened scrutiny may be appropriate not only when the classification is "suspect" but also when the interest at stake was sufficiently "fundamental." What classifications implicate a "fundamental interest"? At times the Court's answer seems to be those that disfavor the exercise of an express constitutional right. An example is *Police Department of Chicago v. Mosley*, 408 U.S. 92 (1972), in which the Court treated a law containing a content-based regulation of speech as being a problem "under the Equal Protection Clause, not to mention the First Amendment itself." In those cases, it might make more sense simply to ask whether the express constitutional right was violated.

But at other times the Court seems to think that "fundamental interests" are broader than express constitutional rights. Some of these cases concern familial interests, such as having children. See, e.g., *Skinner v. Oklahoma*, 316

U.S. 535 (1942). The big example, though, is the right to vote. Most of the Court's "fundamental interest" equal protection cases involve some aspect of asserted discrimination with respect to the exercise of the franchise. See, e.g., *Bush v. Gore*, 531 U.S. 98 (2000); *Harper v. Virginia*, 383 U.S. 663 (1966); *Baker v. Carr*, 369 U.S. 186 (1962). How the Constitution protects the right to vote is taken up in Chapter 8 of this book. There the question is considered not only under the Equal Protection Clause, which is the way the Court usually considers it, but also under the Republican Form of Government Clause in Article IV and under the four constitutional amendments protecting the right to vote against various forms of discrimination.

Final Thoughts on Equal Protection

There are many Supreme Court decisions over the years interpreting the Equal Protection Clause. The past several assignments of material have covered much ground—and much of it confusing. Here is a quick summary of the path traveled.

First, the introductory cases: *Slaughter–House* (1873), in addition to construing the Thirteenth Amendment and other clauses of the Fourteenth Amendment, was the Court's first interpretation of the Equal Protection Clause. The Court found that even a seemingly "unfair" business regulation—the grant of a monopoly, putting competitors out of business—was not a violation of the Equal Protection Clause, which was centrally concerned with prohibiting racial discrimination. *Bradwell v. Illinois* (1873) upheld Illinois's exclusion of women from the practice of law, applying *Slaughter–House*'s interpretation of the Privileges or Immunities Clause, but did not consider the application of the Equal Protection Clause. *Minor v. Happersett* (1875) held that the Fourteenth Amendment does not apply to voting rights.

On race: *Strauder v. West Virginia* (1880) held that the Fourteenth Amendment flatly forbids race-based differential treatment. *The Civil Rights Cases* (1883) adopted a narrow reading of Congress's enforcement power as not extending to private discrimination in public accommodations and began to mark the Court's retreat from a vigorous interpretation of the Equal Protection Clause to forbid racial discrimination. A major step in this retreat was *Plessy v. Ferguson* (1896), upholding separate-but-equal racial segregation. *Cumming v. Board of Education* (1899), *Giles v. Harris* (1903), and *Berea College v. Kentucky* (1908) also reflected the spirit of the times, each upholding mandatory segregation or otherwise refusing to enforce the anti-discrimination requirements of the Fourteenth and Fifteenth Amendments. *Brown v. Board of Education* (1954) and its successors marked a return to the spirit of *Strauder*, forbidding racial discrimination by the government and applying what has come to be known as "strict scrutiny." *Loving v. Virginia* (1967) finally struck down state laws mandating racial segregation in marriage. The modern debate over affirmative action is about whether the Equal Protection Clause requires that the government be color-blind or if instead minority preferences should be treated differently than majoritarian racial discrimination.

On sex: *Craig v. Boren* (1976) and *Virginia v. United States* (1996) erased *Bradwell* and replaced it with increasingly stronger forms of "intermediate scrutiny." The test is meant to capture the reality that men and women are alike for most purposes, but different for some.

Outside of race and sex, the general rule is that the Equal Protection Clause requires only a "rational basis" for the classifications the government is making. Some classifications have been considered possible exceptions—such as national origin, alienage, wealth and poverty, disability, and sexual orientation. But for most of these the Court has declined to give heightened scrutiny, though it has for national origin and the constitutional status of sexual orientation remains unsettled. In deciding which classifications receive heightened scrutiny, the courts look to considerations such as a history of discrimination, immutable characteristics, and exclusion from the political process.

In many ways, the doctrine captures reasonably well the original meaning of the text of the Equal Protection Clause. The clause forbids state governments to withdraw the protection of the laws from certain classes of individuals. The text makes no mention of race, but from the very beginning race has been the paradigm case for understanding its prohibition. By close analogy (especially after the Nineteenth Amendment), the clause has been widely understood as prohibiting discrimination on the basis of sex. Yet in other ways, the modern doctrine stands in sharp tension with the text of the amendment and its original understanding—especially on the question of which branch should be the central actor in interpreting and enforcing the amendment's prohibitions. Along the way, as the courts have interpreted the clause, there has been great injustice and great justice, from *Plessy* to *Brown*. But the modern doctrine, for all of its warts, its imprecision and its hyper-precision, its false starts and its tests and tiers, has at least reclaimed the central promise of the Equal Protection Clause, declared so long ago by the Supreme Court:

> What is this but declaring that the law in the States shall be the same for the black as for the white; that all persons, whether colored or white, shall stand equal before the laws of the States, and, in regard to the colored race, for whose protection the amendment was primarily designed, that no discrimination shall be made against them by law because of their color?

Strauder v. West Virginia, 100 U.S. 303, 307 (1880).

[*Assignment 67*]

III. DUE PROCESS OF LAW

There are two Due Process Clauses in the Constitution. Although their language is essentially identical, each one has a different context and constrains a different government. The Due Process Clause of the Fifth Amendment is surrounded by criminal procedure rights, and it limits the national government. It says: "[n]o person shall . . . be deprived of life, liberty, or property, without due process of law." The Due Process Clause of the Fourteenth Amendment, which was ratified during Reconstruction, extends that limitation to the states and is surrounded by the familiar guarantees of "privileges or immunities" and "equal protection." It says: "No State shall . . . deprive any person of life, liberty, or property, without due process of law."

Both clauses require something—"due process of law." But both require this only when the government is doing something—depriving someone of "life, liberty, or property." Out of these phrases come the two critical questions for interpreting and applying the Due Process Clauses. The first, threshold question is whether there has been a deprivation of "life, liberty, or property." If there has been, the second question is whether there was "due process of law."

Throughout the history of constitutional law in the United States, there has been great debate over whether "due process of law" imposes on the government only a requirement of *process* or also limits in some way the substance of what it may do. It is easy to imagine government action that takes life, liberty, or property without any process—for example, if the local sheriff, not acting pursuant to a statute or warrant or court order, went to your apartment and started taking away all of your furniture. In that case, you would be deprived of property, not only without "due process" but without any process at all. But imagine that a duly enacted statute, passed by a legislative majority, named you and said that all of your personal property now belonged to the sheriff. If the sheriff then took away your furniture, would you have received due process? And if that would be a violation of due process, what other constraints are there on the substance of the laws that the legislature might pass? For example, what if a statute, again meeting all the ordinary procedural requirements for legislation, established criminal penalties for anyone who possesses furniture? Or established criminal penalties for anyone who possesses alcohol? Or anyone who works more than ten hours a day? Which, if any, of these scenarios would deny someone "due process of law"? These kinds of questions all raise the central and highly contested issue of what, exactly, is required by the Due Process Clauses.

The materials in this section begin with the historical roots of due process, and the idea commonly known as "procedural due process." Next comes a lengthy consideration of the path the Court has charted in trying to develop and enforce a doctrine of "substantive due process." That path began with *Dred Scott*, where the Court read the Due Process Clause of the Fifth Amendment to prohibit Congress from making laws limiting a slaveholder's right to take slaves into the Territories (a case that is presented in Chapter 4). From there the path wound on to *Lochner* and other economic liberty cases in the early twentieth century, and then turned back as the Court retreated from substantive due process in the middle of that century. Then the path turned again, as the Court in the last third of the twentieth century revived substantive due process in cases involving contraception (*Griswold*), abortion (*Roe*), and sex (*Lawrence*).

A. DUE PROCESS AND SEPARATION OF POWERS

The Due Process Clauses in the Fifth and Fourteenth Amendments require "due process of law" before the state deprives a person of "life, liberty, or property." Consider first the threshold question of what counts as a deprivation of "life, liberty, or property." What do these terms mean? For the founders, *liberty* was the natural freedom that everyone was born with. It included the freedom to work, the freedom to worship, and what Blackstone called the freedom to "remov[e] one's person to whatsoever place one's own inclination may direct." *Property* was widely seen as a right to control a thing, such as land or a ship, deciding how it would be used and who would have access to it. For most of U.S. history, including when the Fifth Amendment and the Fourteenth Amendment were ratified, a property right was protected by the Due Process Clause only when the property interest became final, or "vested." A promise to sell land did not create a vested property right—the property vested when the sale was final. The scope of property was not deduced from natural rights, but was defined by and subject to statutes and judicial decisions. *Life* had its everyday meaning: it was what a person was deprived of through capital punishment.

Over time, the Court has recognized liberty and property interests that go beyond these traditional common law understandings. A prominent example of this "new property" is a claim to government benefits. In the landmark case of *Goldberg v. Kelly*, 397 U.S. 254 (1970), the Court concluded that the termination of welfare benefits was a deprivation of property, and that the government therefore had to provide "due process"—in the form of an evidentiary hearing—before there could be a termination.

Subsequent cases have considered how far *property* and *liberty* extend, though sometimes with inconsistent conclusions. Modern cases have found a liberty interest in one's personal reputation, *Wisconsin v. Constantineau*, 400 U.S. 433 (1971); or in the involuntary transfer of a state prisoner to a mental hospital, *Vitek v. Jones*, 445 U.S. 480 (1980). But other cases have emphasized limits. An untenured state university professor did not have a liberty or property interest in having his contract renewed, *Board of Regents v. Roth*, 408 U.S. 564 (1972); an individual labeled an "active shoplifter" by police flyers did not have a liberty or property interest in his reputation that required a hearing, *Paul v. Davis*, 424 U.S. 693 (1976); a child had no liberty interest in Social Services protecting him from an abusive father, *DeShaney v. Winnebago County Department of Social Services*, 489 U.S. 189 (1989); and a wife had no property interest in the enforcement of a restraining order against her abusive husband, *Town of Castle Rock v. Gonzales,* 545 U.S. 748 (2005). These cases address the outer boundaries of "liberty" and "property," but the core of those concepts remains well settled: property includes the control of things, such as land, books, and clothes; and liberty includes freedom from physical restraint.

When the government deprives someone of life, liberty, or property, the next question is whether the deprivation was made with *due process of law*. The Due Process Clauses stand in a long tradition of English and American procedural protections. These can be traced in English constitutional history back to Magna Carta (1215), which allowed the king to deprive a subject of liberty and property (and by implication life) only "by lawful judgment of his peers and by the law of the land."

The "law of the land" requirement came be to be understood as demanding a kind of procedural regularity: a person may be deprived of a right only upon trial under settled law. In English constitutional history, this was primarily a constraint on royal power. It was also an early form of what we would now call separation of powers, because it kept the executive (which in England was the king) from adjudicating cases. See Nathan S. Chapman & Michael W. McConnell, *Due Process as Separation of Powers*, 121 Yale L.J. 1672, 1682–1692 (2012). The king could deprive a person of rights *only* pursuant to some existing law (either common law or statute) and *only* after there had been a judgment from a common law court. According to Lord Coke, the greatest of the common law judges, what "the law of the land" required could thus be summed up as "due process."

In the United States, "law of the land" and "due process" were used for the most part interchangeably. Most state constitutions at the founding used the former phrase, though of course the U.S. Constitution used the latter. (That formulation was probably adopted in the U.S. Constitution to prevent confusion, because Article VI refers to the "supreme Law of the Land" in a different sense, describing the supremacy of federal law over state law.) In either formulation, these constitutional provisions were understood to prohibit the government from depriving someone of life, liberty, or property without application of general law by a court, according to traditional procedures.

As you read the following excerpts, ask yourself two questions. First, what counts as due process? Second, what if any requirement does "due process" impose on each branch of the national government—the legislature, the executive, and the judiciary?

St. George Tucker, View of the Constitution of the United States

From the Editor's Appendix, 1 Blackstone's Commentaries 203–206 (1803)

By the amendments to the constitution, no person shall be deprived of life, liberty, or property, without due process of law.

Due process of law as described by sir Edward Coke I, is by indictment or presentment of good and lawful men, where such deeds be done in due manner, or by writ original of the common law. Due process of law must then be had before a judicial court, or a judicial magistrate. The judicial power of the United States is vested in one supreme court, and such inferior tribunals, as congress may establish, and extends to all cases in law and equity, arising under the constitution, & c. . . .

In the distribution of the powers of government, the legislative powers were vested in congress . . . the executive powers (except in the instances particularly enumerated,) in the president and senate. The judicial powers (except in the cases particularly enumerated in the first article) in the courts: the word *the*, used in defining the powers of the executive, and of the judiciary, is, with these exceptions, co-extensive in it[s] signification with the word *all*: for all the powers granted by the constitution are either legislative, and executive, or judicial; to keep them for ever separate and distinct, except in the cases positively enumerated, has been uniformly the policy, and constitutes one of the fundamental principles of the American governments. . . .

It will be urged, perhaps, that the house of representatives of the United States is, like a British house of commons, a judicial court: to which the answer is, it is neither established as such by the constitution (except in respect to its own members,) nor has it been, nor can it be so established by authority of congress; for all the courts of the United States must be composed of judges commissioned by the president of the United States, and holding their offices during good behaviour, and not by the unstable tenure of biennial elections.

Joseph Story, Commentaries on the Constitution

Volume 3, § 1783 (1833)

The [Due Process Clause of the Fifth Amendment] is but an enlargement of the language of magna charta, *"nec super eum ibimus, nec super eum mittimus, nisi per legale judicium parium suorum, vel per legem terrae,"* neither will we pass upon him, or condemn him, but by the lawful judgment of his peers, or by the law of the land. Lord Coke says, that these latter words, *per legem terrae* (by the law of the land,) mean by due process of law, that is, without due presentment or indictment, and being brought in to answer thereto by due process of the common law. So that this clause in effect affirms the right of trial according to the process and proceedings of the common law.

Murray's Lessee v. Hoboken Land & Improvement Co.

59 U.S. 272 (1856)

. . . The words, "due process of law" were undoubtedly intended to convey the same meaning as the words "by the law of the land," in Magna Charta. Lord Coke, in his commentary on those words (2 Inst. 50), says they mean due process of law. The Constitutions which had been adopted by the several States before the formation of the federal Constitution, following the language of the great charter more closely, generally contained the words, "but by the judgment of his peers, or the law of the land." The ordinance of Congress of July 13, 1787, for the government of the territory of the United States northwest of the River Ohio, used the same words.

The Constitution of the United States, as adopted, contained the provision, that "the trial of all crimes, except in cases of impeachment, shall be by jury." When the fifth article of amendment containing the words now in question was made, the trial by jury in criminal cases had thus already been provided for. By the sixth and seventh articles of amendment, further special provisions were separately made for that mode of trial in civil and criminal cases. To have followed, as in the state constitutions, and in the ordinance of 1787, the words of Magna Charta, and declared that no person shall be deprived of his life, liberty, or property but by the judgment of his peers or the law of the land, would have been in part superfluous and inappropriate. To have taken the clause, "law of the land," without its immediate context, might possibly have given rise to doubts, which would be effectually dispelled by using those words which the great commentator on Magna Charta had declared to be the true meaning of the phrase, "law of the land," in that instrument, and which were undoubtedly then received as their true meaning.

That the warrant now in question [in this case] is legal process is not denied. It was issued in conformity with an act of Congress. But is it "due process of law"? The Constitution contains no description of those processes which it was intended to allow or forbid. It does not even declare what principles are to be applied to ascertain whether it be due process. It is manifest that it was not left to the legislative power to enact any process which might be devised. The article is a restraint on the legislative, as well as on the executive and judicial, powers of the government, and cannot be so construed as to leave Congress free to make any process "due process of law," by its mere will. To what principles, then, are we to resort to ascertain whether this process, enacted by Congress, is due process? To this the answer must be twofold. We must examine the Constitution itself to see whether this process be in conflict with any of its provisions. If not found to be so, we must look to those settled usages and modes of proceeding existing in the common and statute law of England, before the emigration of our ancestors, and which are shown not to have been unsuited to their civil and political condition by having been acted on by them after the settlement of this country. . . .

These were highly influential sources for American judges and lawyers between the founding and the Civil War, and they represent the standard view of what counted as "due process." It was not a kind of abstract procedural justice deduced from first principles, but rather it was the established and familiar processes of the common law courts known on both sides of the Atlantic. In the United States, the requirement of "due process" was explicitly understood as being rooted in the separation of powers established by the Constitution. See generally Chapman & McConnell, 121 Yale L.J. 1672 (2012). Courts could violate "due process" by failing to provide the established common law procedures. The executive could violate "due process" by circumventing the courts. And the legislature could violate "due process" by enacting legislation that circumvented the courts or abrogated their common law procedures. Thus each branch of the national government could violate the Due Process Clause of the Fifth Amendment: the judiciary by *not acting like a court should*, and the other two branches by acting *as if they were courts*.

This seems to have been the understanding of due process not only when the Fifth Amendment was ratified in 1791, but also when the Fourteenth Amendment was ratified in 1868. For example, in a debate in the House in 1866, Representative John Bingham said that the meaning of "due process" had been "settled long ago" by the courts," and members of Congress can "go and read their decisions." (Remember that Bingham proposed what eventually became the Fourteenth Amendment.)

Murray's Lessee offers a practical example of how the "due process" inquiry worked. In 1838 the Treasury Department audited the collector of customs for the port of New York, and found that he owed the government over $1.3 million (equivalent to more than $28 million today). Rather than using the ordinary judicial process and bringing a civil action, the solicitor of the Treasury issued a warrant for that amount, employing a summary procedure that Congress had authorized for recovering money owed to the government. By the time the case arrived in the Supreme Court, the key question was whether that summary procedure was "due process." (The threshold requirement was clearly met: taking back $1.3 million was a deprivation of property.) The Court noted that " 'due process of law' generally implies and includes" a number of established procedural protections that were missing in the summary procedure, such as "regular allegations, opportunity to answer, and a trial according to some settled course of judicial proceedings." And yet, the Court said, these requirements were "not universally true" under American law and "the law of England after Magna Charta." There were contexts where summary procedures had been traditionally allowed, and the Court identified one of those contexts as the recovery of money owed to the government. In reaching this conclusion the Court explored at length the procedures available in the English Court of Exchequer, as well as the text of the U.S. Constitution and subsequent practice. The bottom line was that the summary process given to the embezzling customs collector was in fact "due process." (Note that the author of the Court's opinion in *Murray's Lessee* was Justice Curtis, who a year later would be the Think of how you would apply the methodology of *Murray's Lessee* to other cases. In the excerpt from the case given above, the Court identifies two principles for determining whether "due process" has been violated. The first principle is examine the Constitution to see if the deprivation violates some *other* provision. The second principle is to look to the baseline of the established common law procedures in England as they have been received in the United States.

The second seems straightforward, but the first one may strike you as odd and circular. In deciding whether there is a violation of the Due Process Clause of the Fifth Amendment, why would it matter whether some other provision was violated? And if some other provision was in fact violated, wouldn't that make the Due Process Clause unnecessary? What is the Court saying? The key is to recognize the way the Due Process Clause is related to a host of other procedural protections in the original Constitution and the Bill of Rights. Many specific provisions of the Constitution require some kind of process that was well established at common law, such as the Sixth Amendment right to a jury trial in all criminal cases. And other specific provisions prevent either Congress or state legislatures from performing a quasi-judicial function, such as the prohibitions in Article I, Sections 9 and 10 on bills of attainder and ex post facto laws or the requirement of just compensation in the Takings Clause. These specific constitutional provisions overlap with the Due Process Clauses, often the very same government action could be considered both a violation of "due process" and a violation of some other provision. Not only do these more specific provisions overlap with "due process," they also show what it means. By what they require or forbid, they suggest the great central examples of what a violation of due process looks like. (The Article I, Section 9 and Section 10 restrictions are discussed above in Chapter 3, and the criminal procedure protections and the Takings Clause in Chapter 6.)

In more recent decisions, the Court has offered a somewhat different approach. It continues to focus on the specific situation or context in which a due process claim arises. However, instead of looking to what the traditional common law processes were in the relevant context, as the Court did *Murray's Lessee*, this approach uses a balancing test. On one side is the government's interest in the deprivation; and on the other side is the individual's interest in not suffering the deprivation. By weighing these interests against each other, the Court decides whether the process given amounted to "due process."

The following two cases illustrate these approaches. The first, *Calder v. Bull*, required the Court to decide whether a state legislature's order of a new trial in a probate case violated the Ex Post Facto Clause of the U.S. Constitution. While considering that question, the Court discusses many of the basic principles that are common to all of the more specific constitutional provisions that inform and illustrate "due process of law." The second case, *Matthews v. Eldridge*, is the central example of the Court's more recent balancing approach. As you read these cases, ask yourself what the strengths and weaknesses are of each approach.

Calder v. Bull

3 U.S. (3 Dall.) 386 (1798)

[On May 2, 1795, the Connecticut legislature passed a resolution or law ordering a new trial in a state probate case about the validity of a will. This set aside a decree of the probate court for Hartford, under which the Calders were set to inherit the estate in question. As a result, a state trial court held a new hearing in the probate case, at the end of which it ruled that the Bulls would inherit instead of the Calders. All available appeals within the Connecticut state courts were then taken, and the state courts all affirmed the judgment for the Bulls. The Calders appealed to the U.S. Supreme Court. They challenged the constitutionality of the Connecticut legislature's action,

arguing its retroactive operation violated Article I, Section 10's ban on ex post facto laws.—Editors]

In error from the State of *Connecticut*. The cause was argued at the last term, (in the absence of THE CHIEF JUSTICE) and now the court delivered their opinions *seriatim*.

■ CHASE, JUSTICE.

The Council for [the Calders] contend, that the said resolution or law of the *Legislature* of *Connecticut*, granting a *new hearing*, in the above case, is *an ex post facto law*, prohibited by the *Constitution of the United States*; that any law of the Federal government, or of any of the State governments, contrary to the *Constitution of the United States*, is *void*; and that this court possesses the power to declare *such* law *void*. . . .

Whether the Legislature of any of the States can revise and correct by law, a decision of any of its Courts of Justice, although not prohibited by the Constitution of the State, is a question of very great importance, and not necessary NOW to be determined; *because the resolution or law in question does not go so far.* I cannot subscribe to the *omnipotence* of a *State Legislature*, or that it is *absolute and without controul*; although its authority should not be *expressly* restrained by the *Constitution*, or *fundamental law*, of the State. The people of the *United States* erected their Constitutions, or forms of government, to establish justice, to promote the general welfare, to secure the blessings of liberty; and to protect their *persons* and *property* from violence. The purposes for which men enter into society will determine the *nature* and *terms* of the *social* compact; and as *they* are the foundation of the *legislative* power, *they* will decide what are the *proper* objects of it: The *nature*, and *ends* of *legislative* power will limit the *exercise* of it. . . . There are acts which the *Federal*, or *State*, Legislature cannot do, *without exceeding their authority*. There are certain *vital* principles in our *free Republican governments*, which will determine and over-rule an *apparent and flagrant* abuse of *legislative* power; as to authorize *manifest injustice by positive law*; or to take away that security for *personal liberty*, or private *property*, for the protection whereof of the government was established. An ACT of the Legislature (for I cannot call it a *law*) contrary to the *great first principles* of the *social compact*, cannot be considered a *rightful exercise* of *legislative* authority. . . .

A few instances will suffice to explain what I mean. A law that punished a citizen for an *innocent* action, or, in other words, for an act, which, when done, was in violation of no *existing* law; a law that destroys, or impairs, the *lawful private* contracts of citizens; a law that makes a man a *Judge in his own cause*; or a law that takes *property* from A. and gives it to B: It is against all reason and justice, for a people to entrust a Legislature with SUCH powers; and, therefore, it cannot be presumed that they have done it. . . .

ALL the restrictions contained in the Constitution of the *United States* on the power of the *State Legislatures*, were provided in favour of the authority of the *Federal* Government. The prohibition against their making *any ex post facto laws* was introduced for *greater* caution, and very probably arose from the knowledge, that *the Parliament of Great Britain* claimed and exercised a power to pass *such laws*, under the denomination of *bills of attainder*, or *bills of pains and penalties*; the *first* inflicting *capital*, and the other *less*, punishment. *These acts were legislative judgments; and an exercise of judicial power.* Sometimes [these acts of Parliament] respected the *crime*, by declaring acts to be treason, which were *not* treason, when committed; at other times, they violated the rules of evidence (to supply a deficiency of legal proof) by admitting *one* witness, when the *existing* law required *two*; by receiving evidence without *oath*; or the oath of the *wife* against the *husband*; or other testimony, which the courts of justice would not admit; at other times they inflicted *punishments*, where the party was not, by *law*, liable to *any punishment*; and in *other* cases, they inflicted *greater* punishment, than the law annexed to the offence.—The ground for the exercise of such *legislative* power was this, that the *safety* of the kingdom depended on the death, or other punishment, of the offender: as if traitors, when *discovered*, could be so formidable, or the government so insecure! With very few exceptions, the advocates of *such* laws were stimulated by ambition, or personal resentment, and vindictive malice. To prevent such, and similar, acts of violence and injustice, I believe, the Federal and State Legislatures, were prohibited from passing any bill of *attainder*; or any *ex post facto law*.

The Constitution of the *United States*, article 1, section 9, prohibits the Legislature of the *United States* from passing any *ex post facto law*; and, in section 10, lays several restrictions on the authority of the *Legislatures* of the several *states*; and, among them, "that no state shall pass any ex post facto law." . . .

I shall endeavour to show *what law* is to be considered an *ex post facto law*, within the words and meaning of the prohibition in the *Federal* Constitution. . . . [T]he plain and obvious meaning and intention of the prohibition is this; *that the Legislatures of the several states, shall not pass laws, after a fact done by a subject, or citizen, which shall have relation to such fact, and shall punish him for having done it.* The prohibition considered in this light, is an *additional* bulwark in favour of the personal security of the subject, to protect his person from *punishment by legislative acts*, having a retrospective operation. . . .

I will state *what laws* I consider *ex post facto laws*, within the *words* and the *intent* of the prohibition. 1st. Every law that makes an action, done before the passing of the law, and which was *innocent* when done, criminal; and punishes such action. 2d. Every law that *aggravates a crime*, or makes it *greater* than it was, when committed. 3d. Every law that *changes the punishment*, and inflicts a *greater punishment*, than the law annexed to the crime, when committed. 4th. Every law that alters the *legal* rules of *evidence*, and receives less, or different, testimony, than the law required at the time of the commission of the offence, *in order to convict the offender*. All these, and similar laws, are manifestly *unjust and oppressive*. . . .

The expressions "*ex post facto laws*," are *technical*, they had been in use long before the Revolution, and had acquired an appropriate meaning, by *Legislators, Lawyers*, and *Authors*. The celebrated and judicious *Sir William Blackstone*, in his commentaries, considers an *ex post facto law* precisely in the *same* light I have done. His opinion is confirmed by his successor, *Mr. Wooddeson*; and by the author of *the Federalist*, who I esteem superior to *both*, for his extensive and accurate knowledge of the *true principles of Government*.

I also rely greatly on the definition, or explanation of EX POST FACTO LAWS, as given by the Conventions of *Massachusetts, Maryland*, and *North Carolina*; in their several Constitutions, or forms of Government. . . .

[In the remainder of his opinion, Justice Chase argued that the Ex Post Facto Clause should be read as applying only to retroactive criminal laws, and that it should not be read in a way that would make unnecessary other provisions of the Constitution, such as the Contracts Clause of Article I, Section 10, and the Takings Clause of the Fifth Amendment. He also concluded that the action of the Connecticut legislature had not actually divested the Calders of any property, since their right to the property had not vested before the legislative action.—Editors]

■ PATERSON, JUSTICE.

The Constitution of *Connecticut* is made up of usages, and it appears that its Legislature have, from the beginning, exercised the power of granting new trials. . . . They [have twice] acted in a double capacity, as a house of legislation, with undefined authority, and also as a court of judicature in certain exigencies. . . . This usage makes up part of the Constitution of *Connecticut*, and we are bound to consider it as such, unless it be inconsistent with the Constitution of the United States. True it is, that the awarding of new trials falls properly within the province of the judiciary; but if the Legislature of Connecticut have been in the uninterrupted exercise of this authority, in certain cases, we must, in such cases, respect their decisions as flowing from a competent jurisdiction, or constitutional organ. . . . [Even] if the power, thus exercised, comes more properly within the description of a judicial than of a legislative power; . . . [if] the Legislature of that state acted in both capacities; then in the case now before us, it would be fair to consider the awarding of a new trial, as an act emanating from the judiciary side of the department. But as this view of the subject militates against [the Calders], their counsel has contended for a reversal of the judgment, on the ground, that the awarding of a new trial, was the effect of a legislative act, and that it is unconstitutional, because an *ex post facto law.* For the sake of ascertaining the meaning of these terms, I will consider the resolution of the General court of *Connecticut*, as the exercise of a legislative and not a judicial authority. The question, then, which arises on the pleadings in this cause, is, whether the resolution of the Legislature of *Connecticut*, be an *ex post facto law*, within the meaning of the Constitution of the *United States*? I am of opinion, that it is not.

The words, *ex post facto*, when applied to a law, have a technical meaning, and, in legal phraseology, refer to crimes, pains, and penalties. Judge *Blackstone's* description of the terms is clear and accurate. "There is, says he, a still more unreasonable method than this, which is called making of laws, *ex post facto*, when after an action, indifferent in itself, is committed, the Legislator, then, for the first time, declares it to have been a crime, and inflicts a punishment upon the person who has committed it. Here it is impossible, that the party could foresee that an action, innocent when it was done, should be afterwards converted to guilt by a subsequent law; he had, therefore, no cause to abstain from it; and all punishment for not abstaining, must, of consequence, be cruel and unjust." 1 *Bl. Com.* 46. Here the meaning, annexed to the terms *ex post facto laws*, unquestionably refers to crimes, and nothing else. The historic page abundantly evinces, that the power of passing such laws should be withheld from legislators; as it is a dangerous instrument in the hands of bold, unprincipled, aspiring, and party men, and has been [too] often used to effect the most detestable purposes.

On inspecting such of our state Constitutions, as take notice of laws made *ex post facto*, we shall find, that they are understood in the same sense. . . .

[E]x post facto laws have an appropriate signification; they extend to penal statutes, and no further; they are restricted in legal estimation to the creation, and, perhaps, enhancement of crimes, pains and penalties. The enhancement of a crime, or penalty, seems to come within the same mischief as the creation of a crime or penalty; and therefore they may be classed together. . . .

I had an ardent desire to have extended the provision in the Constitution to retrospective laws in general. *[Justice Paterson had been a delegate to the Constitutional Convention.—Editors]* There is neither policy nor safety in such laws; and, therefore, I have always had a strong aversion against them. It may, in general, be truly observed of retrospective laws of every description, that they neither accord with sound legislation, nor the fundamental principles of the social compact. But on full consideration, I am convinced, that *ex post facto laws* must be limited in the manner already expressed; they must be taken in their technical, which is also their common and general, acceptation, and are not to be understood in their literal sense.

■ IREDELL, JUSTICE.

Though I concur in the general result of the opinions, which have been delivered, I cannot entirely adopt the reasons that are assigned upon the occasion.

From the best information to be collected, relative to the Constitution of *Connecticut*, it appears, that the Legislature of that State has been in the uniform, uninterrupted, habit of exercising a general superintending power over its courts of law, by granting new trials. It may, indeed, appear strange to some of us. . . . [Yet it is not] altogether without some sanction for a Legislature to act as a court of justice. In *England*, we know, that one branch of the Parliament, the house of Lords, not only exercises a judicial power in cases of impeachment, and for the trial of its own members, but as the court of [last] resort, takes cognizance of many suits at law, and in equity: And that in construction of law, the jurisdiction there exercised is by the King in full Parliament; which shows that, in its origin, the causes were probably heard before the whole Parliament. When *Connecticut* was settled, the right of empowering her Legislature to superintend the Courts of Justice, was, I presume, early assumed. . . . The power, however, is judicial in its nature; and whenever it is exercised, as in the present instance, it is an exercise of judicial, not of legislative, authority.

But, let us, for a moment, suppose, that the resolution, granting a new trial, was a legislative act, it will by no means follow, that it is an act affected by the constitutional prohibition, that "no State shall pass any *ex post facto* law." . . .

If, then, a government, composed of Legislative, Executive and Judicial departments, were established, by a Constitution, which imposed no limits on the legislative power, the consequence would inevitably be, that whatever the legislative power chose to enact, would be lawfully enacted, and the judicial power could never interpose to pronounce it void. It is true, that some speculative jurists have held, that a legislative act against natural justice must, in itself, be void; but I cannot think that, under such a government, any Court of Justice would possess a power to declare it so. . . .

In order, therefore, to guard against so great an evil, it has been the policy of all the *American* states, which have, individually, framed their state constitutions since the revolution, and of the people of the *United States*, when they framed the Federal Constitution, to define with precision the objects of the legislative power, and to restrain its exercise within marked and settled boundaries. If any act of Congress, or of the Legislature of a state, violates those constitutional provisions, it is unquestionably void; though, I admit, that as the authority to declare it void is of a delicate and awful nature, the Court will never resort to that authority, but in a clear and urgent case. If, on the other hand, the Legislature of the Union, or the Legislature of any member of the Union, shall pass a law, within the general scope of their constitutional power, the Court cannot pronounce it to be void, merely because it is, in their judgment, contrary to the principles of natural justice. The ideas of natural justice are regulated by no fixed standard: the ablest and the purest men have differed upon the subject; and all that the Court could properly say, in such an event, would be, that the Legislature (possessed of an equal right of opinion) had passed an act which, in the opinion of the judges, was inconsistent with the abstract principles of natural justice. There are then but two lights, in which the subject can be viewed: 1st. If the Legislature pursue the authority delegated to them, their acts are valid. 2d. If they transgress the boundaries of that authority, their acts are invalid. In the former case, they exercise the discretion vested in them by the people, to whom alone they are responsible for the faithful discharge of their trust: but in the latter case, they violate a fundamental law, which must be our guide, whenever we are called upon as judges to determine the validity of a legislative act.

Still, however, in the present instance, the act or resolution of the Legislature of *Connecticut*, cannot be regarded as an *ex post facto* law; for, the true construction of the prohibition extends to criminal, not to civil, cases. It is only in criminal cases, indeed, in which the danger to be guarded against, is greatly to be apprehended. The history of every country in *Europe* will furnish flagrant instances of tyranny exercised under the pretext of penal dispensations. Rival factions, in their efforts to crush each other, have superseded all the forms, and suppressed all the sentiments, of justice; while attainders, on the principle of retaliation and proscription, have marked all the vicissitudes of party triumph. The temptation to such abuses of power is unfortunately too alluring for human virtue; and, therefore, the framers of the *American* Constitutions have wisely denied to the respective Legislatures, Federal as well as State, the possession of the power itself: They shall not pass any *ex post facto* law; or, in other words, they shall not inflict a punishment for any act, which was innocent at the time it was committed; nor increase the degree of punishment previously denounced for any specific offence.

The policy, the reason and humanity, of the prohibition, do not, I repeat, extend to civil cases, to cases that merely affect the private property of citizens. Some of the most necessary and important acts of Legislation are, on the contrary, founded upon the principle, that private rights must yield to public exigences. Highways are run through private grounds. Fortifications, Light-houses, and other public edifices, are necessarilly sometimes built upon the soil owned by individuals. In such, and similar cases, if the owners should refuse voluntarily to accommodate the public, they must be constrained, as far as the public necessities require; and justice is done, by allowing them a reasonable equivalent. Without the possession of this power the operations of Government would often be obstructed, and society itself would be endangered. It is not sufficient to urge, that the power may be abused, for, such is the nature of all power, such is the tendency of every human institution: and, it might as fairly be said, that the power of taxation, which is only circumscribed by the discretion of the Body, in which it is vested, ought not to be granted, because the Legislature, disregarding its true objects, might, for visionary and useless projects, impose a tax to the amount of nineteen shillings in the pound. We must be content to limit power where we can, and where we cannot, consistently with its use, we must be content to repose a salutary confidence. It is our consolation that there never existed a Government, in ancient or modern times, more free from danger in this respect, than the Governments of *America*.

Upon the whole, though there cannot be a case, in which an ex post facto law in criminal matters is requisite, or justifiable (for Providence never can intend to promote the prosperity of any country by bad means) yet, in the present instance the objection does not arise: Because, 1st. if the act of the Legislature of Connecticut was a judicial act, it is not within the words of the Constitution; and 2d. even if it was a legislative act, it is not within the meaning of the prohibition.

■ CUSHING, JUSTICE.

The case appears to me to be clear of all difficulty, taken either way. If the act is a judicial act, it is not touched by the Federal Constitution: and, if it is a legislative act, it is maintained and justified by the ancient and uniform practice of the state of *Connecticut*.

NOTES

1. Do the justices agree on the scope of the prohibition on *ex post facto* laws? What examples do the justices give of laws that would violate the Ex Post Facto Clause? Note that the Court did not consider whether the action of the Connecticut legislature violated the Due Process Clause, since that clause applies only to the national government (and of course the Fourteenth Amendment was decades in the future). But imagine exactly the same case but with one change: *Congress*, not the Connecticut legislature, had ordered a new trial in a probate case. Would that legislative action have violated the Due Process Clause of the Fifth Amendment? Would there have been a deprivation of property without due process, even though Congress was actually requiring *more* process, not less? Would there have been a lack of due process even though the statute was duly enacted and passed by majority vote? In such a case, would the problem with Congress's action be best characterized as a deficiency in "process" or "substance"? Or does that dichotomy not fully capture the problem with Congress making what is essentially a judicial decision? One more question about the hypothetical case in which Congress acts like the Connecticut legislature did in *Calder*: would that action violate any other provision of the U.S. Constitution?

2. What is the interpretive methodology in the opinions of Justice Chase and Justice Iredell? For each justice, what counts as legal authority to decide the case? Justice Chase's opinion is often cited as authority for courts being able to strike down statutes on the basis of natural law or unenumerated rights. If read more carefully, however, his opinion appears to suggest that principles of natural liberty and secure property operate as a canon of construction or background presumption: without a clear expression to the contrary the legislature would not be presumed to act in violation of these principles. But

even this invocation of natural justice was received skeptically by Justice Iredell, who noted with a degree of understatement that people often disagree about exactly what natural justice requires. How, if at all, should principles of natural justice affect the interpretation of the Constitution?

Matthews v. Eldridge
424 U.S. 319 (1975)

■ MR. JUSTICE POWELL delivered the opinion of the Court.

The issue in this case is whether the Due Process Clause of the Fifth Amendment requires that prior to the termination of Social Security disability benefit payments the recipient be afforded an opportunity for an evidentiary hearing. . . .

Respondent Eldridge was first awarded benefits in June 1968. In March 1972, he received a questionnaire from the state agency charged with monitoring his medical condition. Eldridge completed the questionnaire, indicating that his condition had not improved and identifying the medical sources, including physicians, from whom he had received treatment recently. The state agency then obtained reports from his physician and a psychiatric consultant. After considering these reports and other information in his file the agency informed Eldridge by letter that it had made a tentative determination that his disability had ceased in May 1972. The letter included a statement of reasons for the proposed termination of benefits, and advised Eldridge that he might request reasonable time in which to obtain and submit additional information pertaining to his condition.

In his written response, Eldridge disputed one characterization of his medical condition and indicated that the agency already had enough evidence to establish his disability. The state agency then made its final determination that he had ceased to be disabled in May 1972. This determination was accepted by the Social Security Administration (SSA), which notified Eldridge in July that his benefits would terminate after that month. The notification also advised him of his right to seek reconsideration by the state agency of this initial determination within six months.

Instead of requesting reconsideration Eldridge commenced this action challenging the constitutional validity of the administrative procedures established by the Secretary of Health, Education, and Welfare for assessing whether there exists a continuing disability. He sought an immediate reinstatement of benefits pending a hearing on the issue of his disability. The Secretary moved to dismiss on the grounds that Eldridge's benefits had been terminated in accordance with valid administrative regulations and procedures and that he had failed to exhaust available remedies. In support of his contention that due process requires a pretermination hearing, Eldridge relied exclusively upon this Court's decision in *Goldberg v. Kelly*, 397 U.S. 254 (1970), which established a right to an "evidentiary hearing" prior to termination of welfare benefits. The Secretary contended that *Goldberg* was not controlling since eligibility for disability benefits, unlike eligibility for welfare benefits, is not based on financial need and since issues of credibility and veracity do not play a significant role in the disability entitlement decision, which turns primarily on medical evidence. . . .

Procedural due process imposes constraints on governmental decisions which deprive individuals of "liberty" or "property" interests within the meaning of the Due Process Clause of the Fifth or Fourteenth Amendment. The Secretary does not contend that procedural due process is inapplicable to terminations of Social Security disability benefits. He recognizes, as has been implicit in our prior decisions, that the interest of an individual in continued receipt of these benefits is a statutorily created "property" interest protected by the Fifth Amendment. Rather, the Secretary contends that the existing administrative procedures, detailed below, provide all the process that is constitutionally due before a recipient can be deprived of that interest.

This Court consistently has held that some form of hearing is required before an individual is finally deprived of a property interest. The "right to be heard before being condemned to suffer grievous loss of any kind, even though it may not involve the stigma and hardships of a criminal conviction, is a principle basic to our society." *Joint Anti–Fascist Comm. v. McGrath*, 341 U.S. 123, 168 (1951) (Frankfurter, J., concurring). The fundamental requirement of due process is the opportunity to be heard "at a meaningful time and in a meaningful manner." Eldridge agrees that the review procedures available to a claimant before the initial determination of ineligibility becomes final would be adequate if disability benefits were not terminated until after the evidentiary hearing stage of the administrative process. The dispute centers upon what process is due prior to the initial termination of benefits, pending review.

In recent years this Court increasingly has had occasion to consider the extent to which due process requires an evidentiary hearing prior to the deprivation of some type of property interest even if such a hearing is provided thereafter. In only one case, *Goldberg v. Kelly*, 397 U.S., at 266–271, has the Court held that a hearing closely approximating a judicial trial is necessary. In other cases requiring some type of pretermination hearing as a matter of constitutional right the Court has spoken sparingly about the requisite procedures. *Sniadach v. Family Finance Corp.*, 395 U.S. 337 (1969), involving garnishment of wages, was entirely silent on the matter. In *Fuentes v. Shevin*, 407 U.S., the Court said only that in a replevin suit between two private parties the initial determination required something more than an *ex parte* proceeding before a court clerk. Similarly, *Bell v. Burson*, at 540, held, in the context of the revocation of a state-granted driver's license, that due process required only that the prerevocation hearing involve a probable-cause determination as to the fault of the licensee, noting that the hearing "need not take the form of a full adjudication of the question of liability." More recently, in *Arnett v. Kennedy*, we sustained the validity of procedures by which a federal employee could be dismissed for cause. They included notice of the action sought, a copy of the charge, reasonable time for filing a written response, and an opportunity for an oral appearance. Following dismissal, an evidentiary hearing was provided.

These decisions underscore the truism that "[d]ue process, unlike some legal rules, is not a technical conception with a fixed content unrelated to time, place and circumstances." "[D]ue process is flexible and calls for such procedural protections as the particular situation demands." Accordingly, resolution of the issue whether the administrative procedures provided here are constitutionally sufficient requires analysis of the governmental and private interests that are affected. More precisely, our prior decisions indicate that identification of the specific dictates of due process generally requires consideration of three distinct factors: First, the private interest that will be affected by the official action; second, the risk of an erroneous deprivation of such interest through the procedures used, and the probable value, if any, of additional or substitute procedural safeguards; and finally, the Government's interest, including the function involved and the fiscal and administrative burdens that the additional or substitute procedural requirement would entail. See, *e.g.*, *Goldberg v. Kelly*, 397 U.S., at 263–271.

We turn first to a description of the procedures for the termination of Social Security disability benefits and thereafter consider the factors bearing upon the constitutional adequacy of these procedures.

In order to establish initial and continued entitlement to disability benefits a worker must demonstrate that he is unable "to engage in any substantial gainful activity by reason of any medically determinable physical or mental impairment. . . ." To satisfy this test the worker bears a continuing burden of showing, by means of "medically acceptable clinical and laboratory diagnostic techniques," that he has a physical or mental impairment of such severity that "he is not only unable to do his previous work but cannot . . . engage in any other kind of substantial gainful work which exists in the national economy". . . . The continuing-eligibility investigation is made by a state agency acting through a "team" consisting of a physician and a nonmedical person trained in disability evaluation. The agency periodically communicates with the disabled worker, usually by mail in which case he is sent a detailed questionnaire or by telephone, and requests information concerning his present condition, including current medical restrictions and sources of treatment, and any additional information that he considers relevant to his continued entitlement to benefits.

Information regarding the recipient's current condition is also obtained from his sources of medical treatment. If there is a conflict between the information provided by the beneficiary and that obtained from medical sources such as his physician, or between two sources of treatment, the agency may arrange for an examination by an independent consulting physician. Whenever the agency's tentative assessment of the beneficiary's condition differs from his own assessment, the beneficiary is informed that benefits may be terminated, provided a summary of the evidence upon which the proposed determination to terminate is based, and afforded an opportunity to review the medical reports and other evidence in his case file. He also may respond in writing and submit additional evidence.

The state agency then makes its final determination, which is reviewed by an examiner in the SSA Bureau of Disability Insurance. . . . Upon acceptance by the SSA, benefits are terminated effective two months after the month in which medical recovery is found to have occurred.

If the recipient seeks reconsideration by the state agency and the determination is adverse, the SSA reviews the reconsideration determination and notifies the recipient of the decision. He then has a right to an evidentiary hearing before an SSA administrative law judge. The hearing is nonadversary, and the SSA is not represented by counsel. As at all prior and subsequent stages of the administrative process, however, the claimant may be represented by counsel or other spokesmen. If this hearing results in an adverse decision, the claimant is entitled to request discretionary review by the SSA Appeals Council, and finally may obtain judicial review.

Should it be determined at any point after termination of benefits, that the claimant's disability extended beyond the date of cessation initially established, the worker is entitled to retroactive payments. If, on the other hand, a beneficiary receives any payments to which he is later determined not to be entitled, the statute authorizes the Secretary to attempt to recoup these funds in specified circumstances.

Despite the elaborate character of the administrative procedures provided by the Secretary, the courts below held them to be constitutionally inadequate, concluding that due process requires an evidentiary hearing prior to termination. In light of the private and governmental interests at stake here and the nature of the existing procedures, we think this was error.

Since a recipient whose benefits are terminated is awarded full retroactive relief if he ultimately prevails, his sole interest is in the uninterrupted receipt of this source of income pending final administrative decision on his claim. His potential injury is thus similar in nature to that of the welfare recipient in *Goldberg*, the nonprobationary federal employee in *Arnett*, and the wage earner in *Sniadach*.

Only in *Goldberg* has the Court held that due process requires an evidentiary hearing prior to a temporary deprivation. It was emphasized there that welfare assistance is given to persons on the very margin of subsistence. . . . Eligibility for disability benefits, in contrast, is not based upon financial need. Indeed, it is wholly unrelated to the worker's income or support from many other sources, such as earnings of other family members, workmen's compensation awards, tort claims awards, savings, private insurance, public or private pensions, veterans' benefits, food stamps, public assistance, or the "many other important programs, both public and private, which contain provisions for disability payments affecting a substantial portion of the work force. . . ."

As *Goldberg* illustrates, the degree of potential deprivation that may be created by a particular decision is a factor to be considered in assessing the validity of any administrative decisionmaking process. The potential deprivation here is generally likely to be less than in *Goldberg*, although the degree of difference can be overstated. As the District Court emphasized, to remain eligible for benefits a recipient must be "unable to engage in substantial gainful activity." Thus, in contrast to the discharged federal employee in *Arnett*, there is little possibility that the terminated recipient will be able to find even temporary employment to ameliorate the interim loss.

As we recognized last Term, "the possible length of wrongful deprivation of . . . benefits [also] is an important factor in assessing the impact of official action on the private interests." The Secretary concedes that the delay between a request for a hearing before an administrative law judge and a decision on the claim is currently between 10 and 11 months. Since a terminated recipient must first obtain a reconsideration decision as a prerequisite to invoking his right to an evidentiary hearing, the delay between the actual cutoff of benefits and final decision after a hearing exceeds one year.

In view of the torpidity of this administrative review process, and the typically modest resources of the family unit of the physically disabled worker, the hardship imposed upon the erroneously terminated disability recipient may be significant. Still, the disabled worker's need is likely to be less than that of a welfare recipient. In addition to the possibility of access to private resources, other forms of government assistance will become available where the termination of disability benefits places a worker or his family below the subsistence level. In view of these potential sources of temporary income, there is less reason here than in *Goldberg* to depart from the ordinary principle, established by our decisions, that something less than an evidentiary hearing is sufficient prior to adverse administrative action.

An additional factor to be considered here is the fairness and reliability of the existing pretermination procedures, and the probable value, if any, of additional procedural safeguards. Central to the evaluation of any administrative process is the nature of the relevant inquiry. In order to remain eligible for benefits the disabled worker must demonstrate by means of "medically acceptable clinical and laboratory diagnostic techniques," that he is unable "to engage in any substantial gainful activity by reason of any *medically determinable* physical or mental impairment. . . ." (emphasis supplied). In short, a medical assessment of the worker's physical or mental condition is required. This is a more sharply focused and easily documented decision than the typical determination of welfare entitlement. In the latter case, a wide variety of information may be deemed relevant, and issues of witness credibility and veracity often are critical to the decisionmaking process. *Goldberg* noted that in such circumstances "written submissions are a wholly unsatisfactory basis for decision."

By contrast, the decision whether to discontinue disability benefits will turn, in most cases, upon "routine, standard, and unbiased medical reports by physician specialists," concerning a subject whom they have personally examined. . . . To be sure, credibility and veracity may be a factor in the ultimate disability assessment in some cases. But procedural due process rules are shaped by the risk of error inherent in the truthfinding process as applied to the generality of cases, not the rare exceptions. The potential value of an evidentiary hearing, or even oral presentation to the decisionmaker, is substantially less in this context than in *Goldberg*.

The decision in *Goldberg* also was based on the Court's conclusion that written submissions were an inadequate substitute for oral presentation because they did not provide an effective means for the recipient to communicate his case to the decisionmaker. Written submissions were viewed as an unrealistic option, for most recipients lacked the "educational attainment necessary to write effectively" and could not afford professional assistance. In addition, such submissions would not provide the "flexibility of oral presentations" or "permit the recipient to mold his argument to the issues the decision maker appears to regard as important." 397 U.S., at 269. In the context of the disability-benefits-entitlement assessment the administrative procedures under review here fully answer these objections. . . .

A further safeguard against mistake is the policy of allowing the disability recipient's representative full access to all information relied upon by the state agency. In addition, prior to the cutoff of benefits the agency informs the recipient of its tentative assessment, the reasons therefor, and provides a summary of the evidence that it considers most relevant. Opportunity is then afforded the recipient to submit additional evidence or arguments, enabling him to challenge directly the accuracy of information in his file as well as the correctness of the agency's tentative conclusions. These procedures, again as contrasted with those before the Court in *Goldberg*, enable the recipient to "mold" his argument to respond to the precise issues which the decisionmaker regards as crucial.

Despite these carefully structured procedures, amici point to the significant reversal rate for appealed cases as clear evidence that the current process is inadequate. Depending upon the base selected and the line of analysis followed, the relevant reversal rates urged by the contending parties vary from a high of 58.6% for appealed reconsideration decisions to an overall reversal rate of only 3.3%. Bare statistics rarely provide a satisfactory measure of the fairness of a decisionmaking process. Their adequacy is especially suspect here since the administrative review system is operated on an open-file basis. A recipient may always submit new evidence, and such submissions may result in additional medical examinations. Such fresh examinations were held in approximately 30% to 40% of the appealed cases, in fiscal 1973, either at the reconsideration or evidentiary hearing stage of the administrative process. In this context, the value of reversal rate statistics as one means of evaluating the adequacy of the pretermination process is diminished. Thus, although we view such information as relevant, it is certainly not controlling in this case.

In striking the appropriate due process balance the final factor to be assessed is the public interest. This includes the administrative burden and other societal costs that would be associated with requiring, as a matter of constitutional right, an evidentiary hearing upon demand in all cases prior to the termination of disability benefits. The most visible burden would be the incremental cost resulting from the increased number of hearings and the expense of providing benefits to ineligible recipients pending decision. No one can predict the extent of the increase, but the fact that full benefits would continue until after such hearings would assure the exhaustion in most cases of this attractive option. . . . We only need say that experience with the constitutionalizing of government procedures suggests that the ultimate additional cost in terms of money and administrative burden would not be insubstantial.

Financial cost alone is not a controlling weight in determining whether due process requires a particular procedural safeguard prior to some administrative decision. But the Government's interest, and hence that of the public, in conserving scarce fiscal and administrative resources is a factor that must be weighed. At some point the benefit of an additional safeguard to the individual affected by the administrative action and to society in terms of increased assurance that the action is just, may be outweighed by the cost. Significantly, the cost of protecting those whom the preliminary administrative process has identified as likely to be found undeserving may in the end come out of the pockets of the deserving since resources available for any particular program of social welfare are not unlimited.

But more is implicated in cases of this type than ad hoc weighing of fiscal and administrative burdens against the interests of a particular category of claimants. The ultimate balance involves a determination as to when, under our constitutional system, judicial-type procedures must be imposed upon administrative action to assure fairness. We reiterate the wise admonishment of Mr. Justice Frankfurter that differences in the origin and function of administrative agencies "preclude wholesale transplantation of the rules of procedure, trial and review which have evolved from the history and experience of courts." *FCC v. Pottsville Broadcasting Co.*, 309 U.S. 134, 143 (1940). The judicial model of an evidentiary hearing is neither a required, nor even the most effective, method of decisionmaking in all circumstances. The essence of due process is the requirement that "a person in jeopardy of serious loss [be given] notice of the case against him and opportunity to meet it." *Joint Anti–Fascist Comm. v. McGrath*, 341 U.S., at 171–172 (Frankfurter, J., concurring). All that is necessary is that the procedures be tailored, in light of the decision to be made, to "the capacities and circumstances of those who are to be heard," *Goldberg v. Kelly*, 397 U.S., at 268–269, to insure that they are given a meaningful opportunity to present their case. In assessing what process is due in this case, substantial weight must be given to the good-faith judgments of the individuals charged by Congress with the administration of social welfare programs that the procedures they have provided assure fair consideration of the entitlement claims of individuals. This is especially so where, as here, the prescribed procedures not only provide the claimant with an effective process for asserting his claim prior to any administrative action, but also assure a right to an evidentiary hearing, as well as to subsequent judicial review, before the denial of his claim becomes final.

We conclude that an evidentiary hearing is not required prior to the termination of disability benefits and that the present administrative procedures fully comport with due process.

■ MR. JUSTICE BRENNAN, with whom MR. JUSTICE MARSHALL concurs, dissenting.

For the reasons stated in my dissenting opinion in *Richardson v. Wright*, 405 U.S. 208, 212 (1972), I agree with the District Court and the Court of Appeals that, prior to termination of benefits, Eldridge must be afforded an evidentiary hearing of the type required for welfare beneficiaries under Title IV of the Social Security Act. I would add that the Court's consideration that a discontinuance of disability benefits may cause the recipient to suffer only a limited deprivation is no argument. It is speculative. Moreover, the very legislative determination to provide disability benefits, without any prerequisite determination of need in fact, presumes a need by the recipient which is not this Court's function to denigrate. Indeed, in the present case, it is indicated that because disability benefits were terminated there was a foreclosure upon the Eldridge home and the family's furniture was repossessed, forcing Eldridge, his wife, and their children to sleep in one bed. Tr. of Oral Arg. 39, 47–48. Finally, it is also no argument that a worker, who has been placed in the untenable position of having been denied disability benefits, may still seek other forms of public assistance.

■ MR. JUSTICE STEVENS took no part in the consideration or decision of this petition.

NOTES

1. Start with the threshold question for the Due Process Clauses: did Eldridge suffer a deprivation of life, liberty, or property? Next consider the Court's method for deciding whether "due process" has been given. What are the considerations that it weighs? In this case, in which direction does each consideration cut? Which considerations seem to you to be the most important? What happens if the interests strongly conflict? Are there other considerations the Court should have included?

2. How would *Calder v. Bull* have been decided under the *Matthews* test? How would *Matthews* have been decided using the approach outlined in *Murray's Lessee*?

3. Since *Matthews*, the Court has extended its analysis to many contexts. The most prominent example is *Hamdi v. Rumsfeld*, 542 U.S. 507 (2004), where the Court used the *Matthews* test to decide whether an enemy combatant being

held by the United States had received "due process." Hamdi was a U.S. citizen. He had been born in Louisiana, grew up in Saudi Arabia, and in 2001 was living in Afghanistan. During fighting in Afghanistan, he was captured by forces allied with the United States, and at the time of the Court's decision he was being held without trial in a naval brig off the coast of South Carolina. The Court found that the detention interfered with his "liberty interests," and that "the risk of erroneous deprivation of a citizen's liberty in the absence of sufficient process here is very real." "On the other side of the scale," the Court said, "are the weighty and sensitive governmental interests in ensuring that those who have in fact fought with the enemy during a war do not return to battle against the United States." Balancing these considerations, the Court concluded that Hamdi must receive "notice of the factual basis for his classification" as an enemy combatant, as well as "a fair opportunity to rebut the Government's factual assertions before a neutral decisionmaker." But the Court did not require an ordinary criminal trial, and it was explicit that there could be a presumption in favor of the government and that hearsay evidence could be introduced. Three justices strongly objected to the Court's use of the balancing test—two because it was insufficiently protective of individual rights (Justices Scalia and Stevens), and one because it was insufficiently protective of federal war powers (Justice Thomas). (A fuller excerpt from the case is presented above in Chapter 3.) Is the *Matthews* balancing test helpful in thinking through the interests involved in *Hamdi*? Given the interests that the Court was balancing, did it prescribe the right process? What are the strengths and weaknesses of applying a balancing test in this case? And how would the case have come out under the approach to due process found in *Murray's Lessee*?

[Assignment 68]

B. THE RISE AND FALL OF SUBSTANTIVE DUE PROCESS

One of the most persistent debates in constitutional law is whether "due process of law" imposes restrictions on the substantive content of laws enacted by Congress and state legislatures. On the one hand, some have argued that substantive due process is incoherent, a contradiction in terms. As one legal scholar famously put it, substantive due process is "like 'green pastel redness.' " John Hart Ely, DEMOCRACY AND DISTRUST: A THEORY OF JUDICIAL REVIEW 18 (1980); see also Akhil Amar, AMERICA'S CONSTITUTION 389 (2005) (stating that the formulation "verges on oxymoron"). On the other hand, as you will soon see, at times in its history the Supreme Court has embraced the notion that the Due Process Clauses allow it to weigh the substantive fairness of all laws that are passed by Congress and state legislatures.

The historical roots of due process discussed above suggest possible answers. Process *is* what the Due Process Clauses require. And the Due Process Clauses provide no absolute guarantee of life, liberty, or property, since it is expressly contemplated that each can be taken away as long as the requisite process is given. But each constitutional actor can act in a manner inconsistent with "due process of law"—including the legislature. Even when it enacts a law that complies with all the formalities of lawmaking, it can still violate due process if it is acting quasi-judicially. The classic example of such a quasi-judicial action, one that is insufficiently general and prospective, is recited in *Calder v. Bull* and scores of other cases: when a legislature takes from A to give to B. And on this view the constitutional prohibitions on bills of attainder, ex post facto laws, laws impairing the obligation of contracts, and takings without just compensation would all be addressed to specific ways that legislatures are especially likely to overstep their bounds by enacting laws that are legislative in form but quasi-judicial in substance.

But the modern doctrine of substantive due process is quite different, and it is not grounded in common law procedures and the separation of powers. Its first invocation came in *Dred Scott*, reprinted above in Chapter 4, where the Court located a right to own slaves in the Due Process Clause of the Fifth Amendment. Two decades later, after the ratification of the Fourteenth Amendment, the Court began to suggest that that amendment's Due Process Clause might supply a basis for a wide-ranging examination of the substance of state laws. In *Munn v. Illinois*, 94 U.S. 113 (1877), the Court hinted that "in private contracts, relating to matters in which the public has no interest, what is reasonable must be ascertained judicially." Within a decade, the Court had suggested several times that the power of the state to regulate business was subject to judicial scrutiny and limits. See, e.g., *Mugler v. Kansas*, 123 U.S. 623 (1887); *The Railroad Commission Cases*, 116 U.S. 307 (1886). By 1890, in *Chicago, M. & St. P. Ry. Co. v. Minnesota*, 134 U.S. 418 (1890), the Court had located this authority in the Due Process Clause of the Fourteenth Amendment, finding that a regulation of railroad rates violated due process requirements not only for its defective procedural protections, but also because rate regulation by administrative order would "in substance and effect" constitute a deprivation of property without due process. The reasonableness of the rates was "eminently a question for judicial investigation."

In *Allgeyer v. Louisiana*, 165 U.S. 578 (1897), the Court struck down a general and prospective Louisiana statute on grounds that are clearly identifiable in terms of modern substantive due process. The statute prohibited buying insurance from any company without an office or agent physically located in the state. The Court found that the prohibition "deprives the defendants of their liberty without due process of law." The Court stated: "The liberty mentioned in that amendment means not only the right of the citizen to be free from the mere physical restraint of his person, as by incarceration, but the term is deemed to embrace the right of the citizen to be free in the enjoyment of all his faculties; to be free to use them in all lawful ways; to live and work where he will; to earn his livelihood by any lawful calling; to pursue any livelihood or avocation, and for that purpose to enter into all contracts which may be proper, necessary and essential to his carrying out to a successful conclusion the purposes above mentioned." *Id.* at 589.

In this era where the Court adopted an expansively substantive conception of the Due Process Clauses, the most infamous case is *Lochner v. New York*, 198 U.S. 45 (1905). It is widely (though not universally) considered the epitome of the wrong way to interpret the Constitution. Why? Do you agree? Is it possible that the general approach of *Lochner* is correct, but the specific application was wrong? If so, how would a court know when a legislative act should be upheld and when it should instead be struck down as an excessive infringement on liberty? Or is the entire premise that a court may invalidate legislative acts in the absence of a reasonably clear constitutional text an invitation for judicial abuse?

Lochner v. New York

198 U.S. 45 (1905)

■ MR. JUSTICE PECKHAM . . . delivered the opinion of the court:

The indictment, it will be seen, charges that the plaintiff in error violated the labor law of the State of New York, in that he wrongfully and unlawfully required and permitted an employé working for him to work more than sixty hours in one week. . . . The mandate of the statute, that "no employé shall be required or permitted to work," is the substantial equivalent of an enactment that "no employé shall contract or agree to work," more than ten hours per day, and, as there is no provision for special emergencies, the statute is mandatory in all cases. It is not an act merely fixing the number of hours which shall constitute a legal day's work, but an absolute prohibition upon the employer permitting, under any circumstances, more than ten hours' work to be done in his establishment. The employé may desire to earn the extra money which would arise from his working more than the prescribed time, but this statute forbids the employer from permitting the employé to earn it.

The statute necessarily interferes with the right of contract between the employer and employés, concerning the number of hours in which the latter may labor in the bakery of the employer. The general right to make a contract in relation to his business is part of the liberty of the individual protected by the Fourteenth Amendment of the Federal Constitution. *Allgeyer* v. *Louisiana*, 165 U.S. 578. Under that provision no State can deprive any person of life, liberty or property without due process of law. The right to purchase or to sell labor is part of the liberty protected by this amendment, unless there are circumstances which exclude the right. There are, however, certain powers, existing in the sovereignty of each State in the Union, somewhat vaguely termed police powers, the exact description and limitation of which have not been attempted by the courts. Those powers, broadly stated, and without, at present, any attempt at a more specific limitation, relate to the safety, health, morals and general welfare of the public. Both property and liberty are held on such reasonable conditions as may be imposed by the governing power of the State in the exercise of those powers, and with such conditions the Fourteenth Amendment was not designed to interfere.

The State, therefore, has power to prevent the individual from making certain kinds of contracts, and in regard to them the Federal Constitution offers no protection. If the contract be one which the State, in the legitimate exercise of its police power, has the right to prohibit, it is not prevented from prohibiting it by the Fourteenth Amendment. Contracts in violation of a statute, either of the Federal or state government, or a contract to let one's property for immoral purposes, or to do any other unlawful act, could obtain no protection from the Federal Constitution, as coming under the liberty of person or of free contract. Therefore, when the State, by its legislature, in the assumed exercise of its police powers, has passed an act which seriously limits the right to labor or the right of contract in regard to their means of livelihood between persons who are *sui juris* (both employer and employé), it becomes of great importance to determine which shall prevail—the right of the individual to labor for such time as he may choose, or the right of the State to prevent the individual from laboring, or from entering into any contract to labor, beyond a certain time prescribed by the State.

This court has recognized the existence and upheld the exercise of the police powers of the States in many cases which might fairly be considered as border ones, and it has, in the course of its determination of questions regarding the asserted invalidity of such statutes, on the ground of their violation of the rights secured by the Federal Constitution, been guided by rules of a very liberal nature, the application of which has resulted, in numerous instances, in upholding the validity of state statutes thus assailed. . . .

It must, of course, be conceded that there is a limit to the valued exercise of the police power by the State. There is no dispute concerning this general proposition. Otherwise the Fourteenth Amendment would have no efficacy and the legislatures of the States would have unbounded power, and it would be enough to say that any piece of legislation was enacted to conserve the morals, the health or the safety of the people; such legislation would be valid, no matter how absolutely without foundation the claim might be. The claim of the police power would be a mere pretext—become another and delusive name for the supreme sovereignty of the State to be exercised free from constitutional restraint. This is not contended for. In every case that comes before this court, therefore, where legislation of this character is concerned, and where the protection of the Federal Constitution is sought, the question necessarily arises: Is this a fair, reasonable and appropriate exercise of the police power of the State, or is it an unreasonable, unnecessary and arbitrary interference with the right of the individual to his personal liberty or to enter into those contracts in relation to labor which may seem to him appropriate or necessary for the support of himself and his family? Of course the liberty of contract relating to labor includes both parties to it. The one has as much right to purchase as the other to sell labor.

This is not a question of substituting the judgment of the court for that of the legislature. If the act be within the power of the State it is valid, although the judgment of the court might be totally opposed to the enactment of such a law. But the question would still remain. Is it within the police power of the State? and that question must be answered by the court.

The question whether this act is valid as a labor law, pure and simple, may be dismissed in a few words. There is no reasonable ground for interfering with the liberty of person or the right of free contract, by determining the hours of labor, in the occupation of a baker. There is no contention that bakers as a class are not equal in intelligence and capacity to men in other trades or manual occupations, or that they are not able to assert their rights and care for themselves without the protecting arm of the State, interfering with their independence of judgment and of action. They are in no sense wards of the State. Viewed in the light of a purely labor law, with no reference whatever to the question of health, we think that a law like the one before us involves neither the safety, the morals nor the welfare of the public, and that the interest of the public is not in the slightest degree affected by such an act. The law must be upheld, if at all, as a law pertaining to the health of the individual engaged in the occupation of a baker. It does not affect any other portion of the public than those who are engaged in that occupation. Clean and wholesome bread does not depend upon whether the baker works but ten hours per day or only sixty hours a week. The limitation of the hours of labor does not come within the police power on that ground.

It is a question of which of two powers or rights shall prevail—the power of the State to legislate or the right of the individual to liberty of person and freedom of contract. The mere assertion that the subject relates, though but in a remote degree, to the public health, does not necessarily render the enactment valid. The act must have a more direct relation, as a means to an end, and the end itself must be appropriate and legitimate, before an act can be held to be valid which interferes with the general right of an individual to be free in his person and in his power to contract in relation to his own labor. . . .

We think the limit of the police power has been reached and passed in this case. There is, in our judgment, no reasonable foundation for holding this to be necessary or appropriate as a health law to safeguard the public health, or the health of the individuals who are following the trade of a baker. If this statute be valid . . . there would seem to be no length to which legislation of this nature might not go. . . .

We think that there can be no fair doubt that the trade of a baker, in and of itself, is not an unhealthy one to that degree which would authorize the legislature to interfere with the right to labor, and with the right of free contract on the part of the individual, either as employer or employé. In looking through the statistics regarding all trades and occupations, it may be true that the trade of a baker does not appear to be as healthy as some other trades, and is also vastly more healthy than still others. . . . There must be more than the mere fact of the possible existence of some small amount of unhealthiness to warrant legislative interference with liberty. It is unfortunately true that labor, even in any department, may possibly carry with it the seeds of unhealthiness. But are we all, on that account, at the mercy of legislative majorities? A printer, a tinsmith, a locksmith, a carpenter, a cabinetmaker, a dry goods clerk, a bank's, a lawyer's or a physician's clerk, or a clerk in almost any kind of business, would all come under the power of the legislature, on this assumption. No trade, no occupation, no mode of earning one's living, could escape this all-pervading power, and the acts of the legislature in limiting the hours of labor in all employments would be valid, although such limitation might seriously cripple the ability of the laborer to support himself and his family. In our large cities there are many buildings into which the sun penetrates for but a short time in each day, and these buildings are occupied by people carrying on the business of bankers, brokers, lawyers, real estate, and many other kinds of business, aided by many clerks, messengers, and other employés. Upon the assumption of the validity of this act under review, it is not possible to say that an act, prohibiting lawyers' or bank clerks, or others, from contracting to labor for their employers more than eight hours a day would be invalid. . . .

It is also urged, pursuing the same line of argument, that it is to the interest of the State that its population should be strong and robust, and therefore any legislation which may be said to tend to make people healthy must be valid as health laws, enacted under the police power. If this be a valid argument and a justification for this kind of legislation, it follows that the protection of the Federal Constitution from undue interference with liberty of person and freedom of contract is visionary, wherever the law is sought to be justified as a valid exercise of the police power. Scarcely any law but might find shelter under such assumptions, and conduct, properly so called, as well as contract, would come under the restrictive sway of the legislature. Not only the hours of employés, but the hours of employers, could be regulated, and doctors, lawyers, scientists, all professional men, as well as athletes and artisans, could be forbidden to fatigue their brains and bodies by prolonged hours of exercise, lest the fighting strength of the State be impaired. We mention these extreme cases because the contention is extreme. We do not believe in the soundness of the views which uphold this law. On the contrary, we think that such a law as this, although passed in the assumed exercise of the police power, and as relating to the public health, or the health of the employs named, is not within that power, and is invalid. The act is not, within any fair meaning of the term, a health law, but is an illegal interference with the rights of individuals, both employers and employs, to make contracts regarding labor upon such terms as they may think best, or which they may agree upon with the other parties to such contracts. Statutes of the nature of that under review, limiting the hours in which grown and intelligent men may labor to earn their living, are mere meddlesome interferences with the rights of the individual, and they are not saved from condemnation by the claim that they are passed in the exercise of the police power and upon the subject of the health of the individual whose rights are interfered with, unless there be some fair ground, reasonable in and of itself, to say that there is material danger to the public health, or to the health of the employés, if the hours of labor are not curtailed. . . .

This interference on the part of the legislatures of the Several states with the ordinary trades and occupations of the people seems to be on the increase. . . . It is impossible for us to shut our eyes to the fact that many of the laws of this character, while passed under what is claimed to be the police power for the purpose of protecting the public health or welfare, are, in reality, passed from other motives. We are justified in saying so when, from the character of the law and the subject upon which it legislates, it is apparent that the public health or welfare bears but the most remote relation to the law. . . .

It is manifest to us that the limitation of the hours of labor as provided for in this section of the statute under which the indictment was found, and the plaintiff in error convicted, has no such direct relation to, and no such substantial effect upon, the health of the employé, as to justify us in regarding the section as really a health law. It seems to us that the real object and purpose were simply to regulate the hours of labor between the master and his employés . . . in a private business, not dangerous in any degree to morals or in any real and substantial degree, to the health of the employés. Under such circumstances the freedom of master and employé to contract with each other in relation to their employment, and in defining the same, cannot be prohibited or interfered with, without violating the Federal Constitution. . . .

■ Mr. Justice Harlan, with whom Mr. Justice White and Mr. Justice Day concurred, dissenting.

While this court has not attempted to mark the precise boundaries of what is called the police power of the State, the existence of the power has been uniformly recognized, both by the Federal and state courts.

All the cases agree that this power extends at least to the protection of the lives, the health and the safety of the public against the injurious exercise by any citizen of his own rights. . . .

Speaking generally, the State, in the exercise of its powers, may not unduly interfere with the right of the citizen to enter into contracts that may be necessary and essential in the enjoyment of the inherent rights be-

longing to every one, among which rights is the right "to be free in the enjoyment of all his faculties, to be free to use them in all lawful ways, to live
and work where he will, to earn his livelihood by any lawful calling, to pursue any livelihood or avocation." This was declared in *Allgeyer* v. *Louisiana*,
165 U.S. 578, 589. But in the same case it was conceded that the right to
contract in relation to persons and property, or to do business, within a
State, may be "regulated, and sometimes prohibited, when the contracts or
business conflict with the policy of the State as contained in its statutes."
. . .

Granting, then, that there is a liberty of contract which cannot be violated even under the sanction of direct legislative enactment, but assuming, as according to settled law we may assume, that such liberty of contract is subject to such regulations as the State may reasonably prescribe
for the common good and the well-being of society, what, then, are the conditions under which the judiciary may declare such regulations to be in excess of legislative authority and void? Upon this point there is no room for
dispute, for the rule is universal that a legislative enactment, Federal or
state, is never to be disregarded or held invalid unless it be, beyond question, plainly and palpably in excess of legislative power. . . . If there be
doubt as to the validity of the statute, that doubt must therefore be resolved in favor of its validity, and the courts must keep their hands off,
leaving the legislature to meet the responsibility for unwise legislation. If
the end which the legislature seeks to accomplish be one to which its power
extends, and if the means employed to that end, although not the wisest or
best, are yet not plainly and palpably unauthorized by law, then the court
cannot interfere. In other words, when the validity of a statute is questioned, the burden of proof, so to speak, is upon those who assert it to be
unconstitutional. *McCulloch v. Maryland*, 4 Wheat. 316, 421.

Let these principles be applied to the present case. . . . It is plain that
this statute was enacted in order to protect the physical well-being of those
who work in bakery and confectionery establishments. . . . Whether or not
this be wise legislation it is not the province of the court to inquire. Under
our systems of government the courts are not concerned with the wisdom or
policy of legislation. So that in determining the question of power to interfere with liberty of contract, the court may inquire whether the means devised by the State are germane to an end which may be lawfully accomplished and have a real or substantial relation to the protection of health,
as involved in the daily work of the persons, male and female, engaged in
bakery and confectionery establishments. But when this inquiry is entered
upon I find it impossible, in view of common experience, to say that there is
here no real or substantial relation between the means employed by the
State and the end sought to be accomplished by its legislation. . . . Still less
can I say that the statute is, beyond question, a plain, palpable invasion of
rights secured by the fundamental law. Therefore I submit that this court
will transcend its functions if it assumes to annul the statute of New
York. . . .

Statistics show that the average daily working time among working-
men in different countries is, in Australia, 8 hours; in Great Britain, 9; in
the United States, 9¾; in Denmark, 9¾; in Norway, 10; Sweden, France,
and Switzerland, 10½; Germany, 10¼; Belgium, Italy, and Austria, 11; and
in Russia, 12 hours.

We judicially know that the question of the number of hours during
which a workman should continuously labor has been, for a long period,

and is yet, a subject of serious consideration among civilized peoples, and by those having special knowledge of the laws of health. Suppose the statute prohibited labor in bakery and confectionery establishments in excess of eighteen hours each day. No one, I take it, could dispute the power of the State to enact such a statute. But the statute before us does not embrace extreme or exceptional cases. It may be said to occupy a middle ground in respect of the hours of labor. What is the true ground for the State to take between legitimate protection, by legislation, of the public health and liberty of contract is not a question easily solved, nor one in respect of which there is or can be absolute certainty. . . .

I do not stop to consider whether any particular view of this economic question presents the sounder theory. . . . It is enough for the determination of this case, and it is enough for this court to know, that the question is one about which there is room for debate and for an honest difference of opinion. . . .

[T]he State is not amenable to the judiciary, in respect of its legislative enactments, unless such enactments are plainly, palpably, beyond all question, inconsistent with the Constitution of the United States. We are not to presume that the State of New York has acted in bad faith. Nor can we assume that its legislature acted without due deliberation, or that it did not determine this question upon the fullest attainable information and for the common good. We cannot say that the State has acted without reason, nor ought we to proceed upon the theory that its action is a mere sham. Our duty, I submit, is to sustain the statute as not being in conflict with the Federal Constitution, for the reason—and such is an all-sufficient reason—it is not shown to be plainly and palpably inconsistent with that instrument. Let the State alone in the management of its purely domestic affairs, so long as it does not appear beyond all question that it has violated the Federal Constitution. This view necessarily results from the principle that the health and safety of the people of a State are primarily for the State to guard and protect.

I take leave to say that the New York statute, in the particulars here involved, cannot be held to be in conflict with the Fourteenth Amendment, without enlarging the scope of the Amendment far beyond its original purpose, and without bringing under the supervision of this court matters which have been supposed to belong exclusively to the legislative departments of the several States when exerting their conceded power to guard the health and safety of their citizens by such regulations as they in their wisdom deem best. Health laws of every description constitute, said Chief Justice Marshall, a part of that mass of legislation which "embraces everything within the territory of a state, not surrendered to the general government; all which can be most advantageously exercised by the states themselves." *Gibbons v. Ogden*, 9 Wheat. 1, 203. A decision that the New York statute is void under the Fourteenth Amendment will, in my opinion, involve consequences of a far-reaching and mischievous character; for such a decision would seriously cripple the inherent power of the States to care for the lives, health and well-being of their citizens. Those are matters which can be best controlled by the States. The preservation of the just powers of the States is quite as vital as the preservation of the powers of the General Government. . . .

■ MR. JUSTICE HOLMES dissenting.

I regret sincerely that I am unable to agree with the judgment in this case, and that I think it my duty to express my dissent.

This case is decided upon an economic theory which a large part of the country does not entertain. If it were a question whether I agreed with that theory, I should desire to study it further and long before making up my mind. But I do not conceive that to be my duty, because I strongly believe that my agreement or disagreement has nothing to do with the right of a majority to embody their opinions in law. It is settled by various decisions of this court that state constitutions and state laws may regulate life in many ways which we as legislators might think as injudicious, or if you like as tyrannical, as this, and which, equally with this, interfere with the liberty to contract. Sunday laws and usury laws are ancient examples. A more modern one is the prohibition of lotteries. The liberty of the citizen to do as he likes so long as he does not interfere with the liberty of others to do the same, which has been a shibboleth for some well-known writers, is interfered with by school laws, by the Post Office, by every state or municipal institution which takes his money for purposes thought desirable, whether he likes it or not. The 14th Amendment does not enact Mr. Herbert Spencer's Social Statics. The other day we sustained the Massachusetts vaccination law. United States and state statutes and decisions cutting down the liberty to contract by way of combination are familiar to this court. Two years ago we upheld the prohibition of sales of stock on margins, or for future delivery, in the constitution of California. The decision sustaining an eight hour law for miners is still recent. Some of these laws embody convictions or prejudices which judges are likely to share. Some may not. But a constitution is not intended to embody a particular economic theory, whether of paternalism and the organic relation of the citizen to the State or of *laissez faire*. It is made for people of fundamentally differing views, and the accident of our finding certain opinions natural and familiar, or novel, and even shocking, ought not to conclude our judgment upon the question whether statutes embodying them conflict with the Constitution of the United States.

General propositions do not decide concrete cases. The decision will depend on a judgment or intuition more subtle than any articulate major premise. But I think that the proposition just stated, if it is accepted, will carry us far toward the end. Every opinion tends to become a law. I think that the word liberty in the Fourteenth Amendment is perverted when it is held to prevent the natural outcome of a dominant opinion, unless it can be said that a rational and fair man necessarily would admit that the statute proposed would infringe fundamental principles as they have been understood by the traditions of our people and our law. It does not need research to show that no such sweeping condemnation can be passed upon the statute before us. A reasonable man might think it a proper measure on the score of health. Men whom I certainly could not pronounce unreasonable would uphold it as a first instalment of a general regulation of the hours of work. Whether in the latter aspect it would be open to the charge of inequality I think it unnecessary to discuss.

NOTES

1. *Lochner* raises the fundamental question of what the Due Process Clause requires. Does it require only process—procedural regularity and the protection that comes from having authorized courts make decisions according to settled law? Or does it also restrict the substantive content of the laws that the state may enact? And if it does restrict the substance of the laws, what exactly are the restrictions? How does the Court in *Lochner* identify them?

If the due process argument for *Lochner* is weak, are there other ways to justify it? Could the result in *Lochner* be justified under the Equal Protection Clause—because the statute does not treat bakers who want to work overtime the same as bakers who do not? Or could the result be justified under the Privileges or Immunities Clause—because the statute infringes a privilege to work more than ten hours a day? Given *Slaughter–House*, how would the courts decide those questions? Or consider the Contracts Clause, found in Article I, Section 10, which forbids state laws that "impair[] the Obligation of Contracts." As discussed in Chapter 3, this clause prohibits states from *retroactively* impairing the vested obligations created by contracts. Should we extrapolate from the Contracts Clause and its preceding provisions (the prohibitions on bills of attainder and ex post facto laws), concluding that the Constitution contains a general principle of economic freedom? Would that kind of extrapolation justify what the Court was doing in *Lochner*? What are the strengths and weaknesses of that sort of extrapolation from particular textual provisions to of that sort of extrapolation from particular textual provisions to an abstract general principle?

2. The due process methodology of *Lochner* reigned for another three decades, roughly until the mid-1930s. During that time the Court struck down nearly two hundred laws and regulations on substantive due process grounds, though it also upheld many others. Every case of state regulation of business, commercial activity, labor, employment, and individual conduct seemed to present a constitutional question under *Lochner*. The Court would proceed this way. First it would consider whether the regulation interfered with "liberty" (which could be freedom of contract or some other liberty). If so, the Court would then ask whether the state's regulation was a legitimate exercise of the "police power" to regulate safety, health, morals, and general welfare of the public. Then the Court would weigh the intrusion upon liberty and the propriety of the legislature's choice. To use *Lochner*'s language: "In every case that comes before this court . . . the question necessarily arises: Is this a fair, reasonable and appropriate exercise of the police power of the State, or is it an unreasonable, unnecessary and arbitrary interference with the right of the individual to his personal liberty or to enter into those contracts in relation to labor which may seem to him appropriate . . . ?"

Lochner thus seemed to embrace pure policy balancing by courts, reviewing legislative policy choices, upholding some and rejecting others. Here are a few of the more famous decisions applying *Lochner*'s approach:

a. In *Muller v. Oregon*, 208 U.S. 412 (1908), the Court upheld an Oregon law prohibiting the employment of any woman for more than ten hours a day. The Court's reasoning was that the law was appropriate given the "physical structure" of women and the need to protect them "even when like legislation is not necessary for men and could not be sustained." But when Oregon passed a law establishing a ten-hour maximum work day for all factory workers, male and female, the Court upheld it in *Bunting v. Oregon*, 243 U.S. 426 (1917). (Is that consistent with the result in *Lochner*?)

b. In *Adair v. United States*, 208 U.S. 161 (1908), the Court struck down a federal law prohibiting railroads operating in interstate commerce from imposing "yellow dog" contracts on their employees. (These were contracts in which a worker agreed not to join a union.) Justice Harlan wrote the opinion, holding that the law violated the "right of a person to sell his labor upon such terms as he deems proper" and the "right of the purchaser of labor to prescribe the conditions" by contract. Employer and employee "have equality of right, and any legislation that disturbs that equality is an arbitrary interference with the liberty of contract."

c. In *Adkins v. Children's Hospital*, 261 U.S. 525 (1923), the Court struck down a District of Columbia law establishing a minimum wage for women, on the ground that this interfered with women's liberty of contract. Legislatures could impose maximum hours, but not minimum wages.

Do these holdings make sense? Is it possible to be consistent and principled in applying *Lochner*'s approach? If not, why not?

A NOTE ON WEST COAST HOTEL AND THE INTERRING OF LOCHNER

Beginning in the mid–1930s, the Court retreated from and then squarely repudiated the substantive due process approach of *Lochner*. There was no magic "*Lochner* is hereby overruled" proclamation, but the accumulated force of the decisions was precisely that. One of the most important of these decisions was *West Coast Hotel Co. v. Parrish*, 300 U.S. 379 (1937), which overruled *Adkins v. Children's Hospital*, 261 U.S. 525 (1923), the *Lochner*-era case that had struck down a minimum-wage law for women. Chief Justice Hughes's opinion for the Court rejected the idea that a similar minimum-wage law was a "deprivation of freedom of contract." He contended that the Court's precedent should be reconsidered because of "[t]he importance of the question, in which many States having similar laws are concerned, the close division by which the decision in the *Adkins* case was reached, and the economic conditions which have supervened." His argument proceeded this way:

> The constitutional provision invoked is the due process clause of the Fourteenth Amendment governing the States, as the due process clause invoked in the *Adkins* case governed Congress. In each case the violation alleged by those attacking minimum wage regulation for women is deprivation of freedom of contract. What is this freedom? The Constitution does not speak of freedom of contract. It speaks of liberty and prohibits the deprivation of liberty without due process of law. In prohibiting that deprivation the Constitution does not recognize an absolute and uncontrollable liberty. Liberty in each of its phases has its history and connotation. But the liberty safeguarded is liberty in a social organization which requires the protection of law against the evils which menace the health, safety, morals and welfare of the people. Liberty under the Constitution is thus necessarily subject to the restraints of due process, and regulation which is reasonable in relation to its subject and is adopted in the interest of the community is due process. . . .
>
> The legislature of the State was clearly entitled to consider the situation of women in employment, the fact that they are in the class receiving the least pay, that their bargaining power is relatively weak, and that they are the ready victims of those who would take advantage of their necessitous circumstances. . . . The legislature had the right to consider that its minimum wage requirements would be an important aid in carrying out its policy of protection. The adoption of similar requirements by many States evidences a deepseated conviction both as to the presence of the evil and as to the means adapted to check it. Legislative response to that conviction cannot be regarded as arbitrary or capricious, and that is all we

have to decide. Even if the wisdom of the policy be regarded as debatable and its effects uncertain, still the legislature is entitled to its judgment. . . .

Our conclusion is that the case of *Adkins v. Children's Hospital* should be, and it is, overruled.

Justice Sutherland, the author of the opinion of the Court in *Adkins*, dissented for himself and three other justices. He marshaled two main arguments. First, he argued that the proposition that the Due Process Clause of the Fourteenth Amendment "includes freedom of contract is so well settled as to be no longer open to question." In making this argument he strongly objected to one reason that Chief Justice Hughes gave for why that line of cases should be reconsidered, namely "because of 'the economic conditions which have supervened.'" In Justice Sutherland's words:

> [T]he meaning of the Constitution does not change with the ebb and flow of economic events. We frequently are told in more general words that the Constitution must be construed in the light of the present. If by that it is meant that the Constitution is made up of living words that apply to every new condition which they include, the statement is quite true. But to say, if that be intended, that the words of the Constitution mean today what they did not mean when written—that is, that they do not apply to a situation now to which they would have applied then—is to rob that instrument of the essential element which continues it in force as the people have made it until they, and not their official agents, have made it otherwise. . . .
>
> If the Constitution, intelligently and reasonably construed in the light of these principles, stands in the way of desirable legislation, the blame must rest upon that instrument, and not upon the court for enforcing it according to its terms. The remedy in that situation—and the only true remedy—is to amend the Constitution.

Justice Sutherland's second main argument was that the minimum-wage statute at issue was arbitrary in multiple ways:

> [It does not have] the slightest relation to the capacity or earning power of the employee, to the number of hours which constitute the day's work, the character of the place where the work is to be done, or the circumstances or surroundings of the employment. . . .
>
> [It] fixes minimum wages for adult women. Adult men and their employers are left free to bargain as they please; and it is a significant and an important fact that all state statutes to which our attention has been called are of like character. The common-law rules restricting the power of women to make contracts have, under our system, long since practically disappeared. Women today stand upon a legal and political equality with men. There is no longer any reason why they should be put in different classes in respect of their legal right to make contracts; nor should they be denied, in effect, the right to compete with men for work paying lower wages which men may be willing to accept. And it is an arbitrary exercise of the legislative power to do so. . . .
>
> An appeal to the principle that the legislature is free to recognize degrees of harm and confine its restrictions accordingly, is but to beg the question, which is—since the contractual rights of men and women are the

same, does the legislation here involved, by restricting only the rights of women to make contracts as to wages, create an arbitrary discrimination? We think it does. Difference of sex affords no reasonable ground for making a restriction applicable to the wage contracts of all working women from which like contracts of all working men are left free. Certainly a suggestion that the bargaining ability of the average woman is not equal to that of the average man would lack substance. The ability to make a fair bargain, as everyone knows, does not depend upon sex.

What do you make of these arguments? Was Chief Justice Hughes right that the Constitution says "liberty" not "freedom of contract"? Is that sufficient to decide the case? Why do you think he led the Court to retreat from its *Lochner*-style jurisprudence? And what do you make of Justice Sutherland's argument that even though the Constitution is applied to new circumstances, its meaning does not change? If so, would that support preserving the *Lochner* line of cases, as he argued? Or does it actually cut in the opposite direction? Was he right that the statute made arbitrary distinctions? Or should he have been more deferential to the legislature's policy judgment? Would his arguments have been stronger if the case had been argued under a different clause of the Fourteenth Amendment?

After *West Coast Hotel* it was certainly no longer true that due process protection of the freedom of contract was "well settled." In a succession of cases, the Court went from questioning *Lochner* to interring it. In *United States v. Carolene Products*, 304 U.S. 144 (1938), the Court rejected a substantive due process challenge to a federal prohibition of interstate shipment of "filled milk" (skim milk mixed with non-milk fats). It said that legislative judgments must be accepted where "any state of facts either known or which could reasonably be assumed, affords support for it." Along with its rejection of substantive due process, *Carolene Products* is well known for its fourth footnote, which left open the possibility of "more exacting judicial scrutiny" where legislation restricts the political processes available for redress of grievances, violates a specific prohibition of the Constitution ("such as those of the first ten amendments, which are deemed equally specific when held to be embraced within the Fourteenth"), or targets religious or racial minorities.

In *Railway Express Agency v. New York*, 336 U.S. 106 (1949) and *Williamson v. Lee Optical*, 348 U.S. 483 (1955), two cases that were discussed earlier in this chapter under "rational basis" review for equal protection analysis, the Court also rejected substantive due process claims. In *Railway Express Agency*, the Court said: "We do not sit to weigh evidence on the due process issue in order to determine whether the regulation is sound or appropriate; nor is it our function to pass judgment on its wisdom." In *Lee Optical* it said: "The day is gone when this Court uses the Due Process Clause of the Fourteenth Amendment to strike down state laws, regulatory of business and industrial conditions, because they may be unwise, improvident, or out of harmony with a particular school of thought."

About a decade later, in *Ferguson v. Skrupa*, 372 U.S. 726 (1963), the Court sustained a Kansas law prohibiting anyone from engaging in "the business of debt adjusting" except as part of the practice of law. The Court said Kansas "was free to decide for itself" what legislation to adopt. The Court noted that it had by now categorically rejected the *Lochner* approach of using "the 'vague contours' of the Due Process Clause to nullify laws which a majority of the Court believe[ ] to be economically unwise. . . . Unquestionably, there are arguments showing that the business of debt adjusting has social utility, but such arguments are properly addressed to the legislature, not to us. We refuse to sit as a 'super legislature to weigh the wisdom of legislation.' " Substantive Due Process was dead.

Until two years later, when the Supreme Court resurrected it: In *Griswold v. Connecticut*, 381 U.S. 479 (1965)—which you will read soon—the Court seemed to pick up just about where *Lochner* had left off. In doing so, the Court relied on, among other decisions, two *Lochner*-era cases that it had never repudiated. One of those, *Pierce v. Society of Sisters*, 268 U.S. 510 (1925), is printed here. The other was *Meyer v. Nebraska*, 262 U.S. 390 (1923), in which the Court reversed the criminal conviction of a parochial school teacher. The teacher had been prosecuted under a Nebraska statute prohibiting school instruction in any language other than English (through the eighth grade).

Pierce v. Society of Sisters

268 U.S. 510 (1925)

■ MR. JUSTICE MCREYNOLDS delivered the opinion of the Court.

These appeals are from decrees, based upon undenied allegations, which granted preliminary orders restraining appellants from threatening or attempting to enforce the Compulsory Education Act adopted November 7, 1922, under the initiative provision of her Constitution by the voters of Oregon. . . .

The challenged Act, effective September 1, 1926, requires every parent, guardian, or other person having control or charge or custody of a child between eight and sixteen years to send him "to a public school for the period of time a public school shall be held during the current year" in the district where the child resides; and failure so to do is declared a misdemeanor. . . . The manifest purpose is to compel general attendance at public schools by normal children, between eight and sixteen, who have not completed the eighth grade. . . .

Appellee the Society of Sisters is an Oregon corporation, organized in 1880, with power to care for orphans, educate and instruct the youth, establish and maintain academies or schools, and acquire necessary real and personal property. It has long devoted its property and effort to the secular and religious education and care of children, and has acquired the valuable good will of many parents and guardians. It conducts interdependent primary and high schools and junior colleges, and maintains orphanages for the custody and control of children between eight and sixteen. In its primary schools many children between those ages are taught the subjects usually pursued in Oregon public schools during the first eight years. Systematic religious instruction and moral training according to the tenets of the Roman Catholic Church are also regularly provided. . . . The business is remunerative—the annual income from primary schools exceeds thirty thousand dollars—and the successful conduct of this requires long time contracts with teachers and parents. The Compulsory Education Act of 1922 has already caused the withdrawal from its schools of children who would otherwise continue, and their income has steadily declined. The appellants, public officers, have proclaimed their purpose strictly to enforce the statute.

After setting out the above facts, the Society's bill alleges that the enactment conflicts with the right of parents to choose schools where their children will receive appropriate mental and religious training, the right of the child to influence the parents' choice of a school, the right of schools and teachers therein to engage in a useful business or profession, and is accordingly repugnant to the Constitution and void. And, further, that unless enforcement of the measure is enjoined the corporation's business and property will suffer irreparable injury.

Appellee Hill Military Academy is a private corporation organized in 1908 under the laws of Oregon, engaged in owning, operating, and conducting for profit an elementary, college preparatory, and military training school for boys between the ages of five and twenty-one years. The average attendance is one hundred, and the annual fees received for each student amount to some eight hundred dollars. . . . By reason of the statute and threat of enforcement appellee's business is being destroyed and its property depreciated; parents and guardians are refusing to make contracts for the future instruction of their sons, and some are being withdrawn. . . .

No question is raised concerning the power of the state reasonably to regulate all schools, to inspect, supervise and examine them, their teachers and pupils; to require that all children of proper age attend some school, that teachers shall be of good moral character and patriotic disposition, that certain studies plainly essential to good citizenship must be taught, and that nothing be taught which is manifestly inimical to the public welfare.

The inevitable practical result of enforcing the Act under consideration would be destruction of appellees' primary schools, and perhaps all other private primary schools for normal children within the state of Oregon. Appellees are engaged in a kind of undertaking not inherently harmful, but long regarded as useful and meritorious. Certainly there is nothing in the present records to indicate that they have failed to discharge their obligations to patrons, students, or the state. And there are no peculiar circumstances or present emergencies which demand extraordinary measures relative to primary education.

Under the doctrine of *Meyer v. Nebraska*, 262 U.S. 390, we think it entirely plain that the Act of 1922 unreasonably interferes with the liberty of parents and guardians to direct the upbringing and education of children under their control. As often heretofore pointed out, rights guaranteed by the Constitution may not be abridged by legislation which has no reasonable relation to some purpose within the competency of the state. The fundamental theory of liberty upon which all governments in this Union repose excludes any general power of the state to standardize its children by forcing them to accept instruction from public teachers only. The child is not the mere creature of the state; those who nurture him and direct his destiny have the right, coupled with the high duty, to recognize and prepare him for additional obligations.

Appellees are corporations and therefore, it is said, they cannot claim for themselves the liberty which the Fourteenth Amendment guarantees. Accepted in the proper sense, this is true. But they have business and property for which they claim protection. These are threatened with destruction through the unwarranted compulsion which appellants are exercising over present and prospective patrons of their schools. And this court has gone very far to protect against loss threatened by such action. . . .

NOTES

1. What kind of case is *Pierce*? Is it a case of *Lochner*-style substantive due process? Or is it a First Amendment case involving freedom of speech and free exercise of religion? Does it matter what the constitutional foundation is? In *Pierce* the Court did not explicitly rest its decision on the First Amendment, perhaps because it had not yet begun the process of incorporating the specific provisions of the Bill of Rights into the Fourteenth Amendment. Instead, the Court was in the habit of speaking of the Due Process Clause and of deprivations of "liberty" and "property." In later cases, including the next one you will read—*Griswold v. Connecticut*, 381 U.S. 479 (1965)—the Court characterized *Pierce* in terms of the rights protected by the First Amendment.

2. *Meyer* and *Pierce* have echoed in more recent Supreme Court decisions. For example, in *Wisconsin v. Yoder,* 406 U.S. 205 (1972), the Court held that the State of Wisconsin could not require members of the Old Order Amish to send their children to school beyond eighth grade, in violation of the Amish families' religious beliefs. The decision rested squarely on the Free Exercise Clause, but the Court noted the strongly supportive language of *Meyer* and *Pierce* concerning parents' rights to direct the upbringing and education of their children, including the choice of religious education, and the absence of a right of the state to seek to standardize children into a single mold. For further discussion of the parental rights involved in these cases, see Noa Ben–Asher, *The Lawmaking Family*, 90 Wash. U. L. Rev. (2012).

[*Assignment 69*]

C. SUBSTANTIVE DUE PROCESS REVIVED

Lochner was dead. As you read the following two cases, *Griswold v. Connecticut* and *Eisenstadt v. Baird*, ask yourself whether they brought *Lochner* back to life. Are they substantive due process decisions, the Ghost of *Lochner* Present? Or can they be justified on some alternative textual ground?

Griswold v. Connecticut

381 U.S. 479 (1965)

■ MR. JUSTICE DOUGLAS delivered the opinion of the Court.

Appellant Griswold is Executive Director of the Planned Parenthood League of Connecticut. Appellant Buxton is a licensed physician and a professor at the Yale Medical School who served as Medical Director for the League at its Center in New Haven. . . .

They gave information, instruction, and medical advice to *married persons* as to the means of preventing conception. They examined the wife and prescribed the best contraceptive device or material for her use. Fees were usually charged, although some couples were serviced free.

The statutes whose constitutionality is involved in this appeal provide[]:

> Any person who uses any drug, medicinal article or instrument for the purpose of preventing conception shall be fined not less than fifty dollars or imprisoned not less than sixty days nor more than one year or be both fined and imprisoned.

Any person who assists, abets, counsels, causes, hires or commands another to commit any offense may be prosecuted and punished as if he were the principal offender.

The appellants were found guilty as accessories and fined $100 each. . . .

We think that appellants have standing to raise the constitutional rights of the married people with whom they had a professional relationship. *Tileston v. Ullman*, 318 U.S. 44, is different, for there the plaintiff seeking to represent others asked for a declaratory judgment. In that situation we thought that the requirements of standing should be strict, lest the standards of "case or controversy" in Article III of the Constitution become blurred. Here those doubts are removed by reason of a criminal conviction for serving married couples in violation of an aiding-and-abetting statute. Certainly the accessory should have standing to assert that the offense which he is charged with assisting is not, or cannot constitutionally be, a crime.

This case is more akin to . . . *Pierce v. Society of Sisters*, where the owners of private schools were entitled to assert the rights of potential pupils and their parents. . . . The rights of husband and wife, pressed here, are likely to be diluted or adversely affected unless those rights are considered in a suit involving those who have this kind of confidential relation to them.

Coming to the merits, we are met with a wide range of questions that implicate the Due Process Clause of the Fourteenth Amendment. Overtones of some arguments suggest that *Lochner v. New York* should be our guide. But we decline that invitation as we did in *West Coast Hotel Co. v. Parrish*. We do not sit as a super-legislature to determine the wisdom, need, and propriety of laws that touch economic problems, business affairs, or social conditions. This law, however, operates directly on an intimate relation of husband and wife and their physician's role in one aspect of that relation.

The association of people is not mentioned in the Constitution nor in the Bill of Rights. The right to educate a child in a school of the parents' choice—whether public or private or parochial—is also not mentioned. Nor is the right to study any particular subject or any foreign language. Yet the First Amendment has been construed to include certain of those rights.

By *Pierce v. Society of Sisters*, the right to educate one's children as one chooses is made applicable to the States by the force of the First and Fourteenth Amendments. By *Meyer v. Nebraska*, the same dignity is given the right to study the German language in a private school. In other words, the State may not, consistently with the spirit of the First Amendment, contract the spectrum of available knowledge. The right of freedom of speech and press includes not only the right to utter or to print, but the right to distribute, the right to receive, the right to read (*Martin v. City of Struthers*, 319 U.S. 141) and freedom of inquiry, freedom of thought, and freedom to teach (see *Wieman v. Updegraff*, 344 U.S. 183)—indeed the freedom of the entire university community. *Sweezy v. New Hampshire*, 354 U.S. 234. Without those peripheral rights the specific rights would be less secure. And so we reaffirm the principle of the *Pierce* and the *Meyer* cases.

In *NAACP v. Alabama*, 357 U.S. 449, 462, we protected the "freedom to associate and privacy in one's associations," noting that freedom of association was a peripheral First Amendment right. Disclosure of membership lists of a constitutionally valid association, we held, was invalid "as entailing the likelihood of a substantial restraint upon the exercise by petitioner's members of their right to freedom of association." In other words, the First Amendment has a penumbra where privacy is protected from governmental intrusion. In like context, we have protected forms of "association" that are not political in the customary sense but pertain to the social, legal, and economic benefit of the members. In *Schware v. Board of Bar Examiners*, 353 U.S. 232, we held it not permissible to bar a lawyer from practice, because he had once been a member of the Communist Party. The man's "association with that Party" was not shown to be "anything more than a political faith in a political party" and was not action of a kind proving bad moral character.

Those cases involved more than the "right of assembly"—a right that extends to all irrespective of their race or ideology. The right of "association," like the right of belief (*Board of Education v. Barnette*, 319 U.S. 624), is more than the right to attend a meeting; it includes the right to express one's attitudes or philosophies by membership in a group or by affiliation with it or by other lawful means. Association in that context is a form of expression of opinion; and while it is not expressly included in the First Amendment its existence is necessary in making the express guarantees fully meaningful.

The foregoing cases suggest that specific guarantees in the Bill of Rights have penumbras, formed by emanations from those guarantees that help give them life and substance. See *Poe v. Ullman*, 367 U.S. 497, 516–522 (dissenting opinion [of Justice Harlan]).Various guarantees create zones of privacy. The right of association contained in the penumbra of the First Amendment is one, as we have seen. The Third Amendment in its prohibition against the quartering of soldiers "in any house" in time of peace without the consent of the owner is another facet of that privacy. The Fourth Amendment explicitly affirms the "right of the people to be secure in their persons, houses, papers, and effects, against unreasonable searches and seizures." The Fifth Amendment in its Self–Incrimination Clause enables the citizen to create a zone of privacy which government may not force him to surrender to his detriment. The Ninth Amendment provides: "The enumeration in the Constitution, of certain rights, shall not be construed to deny or disparage others retained by the people."

The Fourth and Fifth Amendments were described in *Boyd v. United States*, 116 U.S. 616, 630, as protection against all governmental invasions "of the sanctity of a man's home and the privacies of life." We recently referred in *Mapp v. Ohio*, 367 U.S. 643, 656, to the Fourth Amendment as creating a "right to privacy, no less important than any other right carefully and particularly reserved to the people."

We have had many controversies over these penumbral rights of "privacy and repose." See, *e.g.*, *Monroe v. Pape*, 365 U.S. 167; *Skinner v. Oklahoma*, 316 U.S. 535, 541. These cases bear witness that the right of privacy which presses for recognition here is a legitimate one.

The present case, then, concerns a relationship lying within the zone of privacy created by several fundamental constitutional guarantees. And it concerns a law which, in forbidding the *use* of contraceptives rather than regulating their manufacture or sale, seeks to achieve its goals by means having a maximum destructive impact upon that relationship. Such a law cannot stand in light of the familiar principle, so often applied by this Court, that a "governmental purpose to control or prevent activities constitutionally subject to state regulation may not be achieved by means which sweep unnecessarily broadly and thereby invade the area of protected freedoms." *NAACP v. Alabama*, 377 U.S. 288, 307. Would we allow the police to search the sacred precincts of marital bedrooms for telltale signs of the use of contraceptives? The very idea is repulsive to the notions of privacy surrounding the marriage relationship.

We deal with a right of privacy older than the Bill of Rights—older than our political parties, older than our school system. Marriage is a coming together for better or for worse, hopefully enduring, and intimate to the degree of being sacred. It is an association that promotes a way of life, not causes; a harmony in living, not political faiths; a bilateral loyalty, not commercial or social projects. Yet it is an association for as noble a purpose as any involved in our prior decisions.

■ MR. JUSTICE GOLDBERG, whom THE CHIEF JUSTICE and MR. JUSTICE BRENNAN join, concurring.

I agree with the Court that Connecticut's birth-control law unconstitutionally intrudes upon the right of marital privacy. . . . [T]he concept of liberty protects those personal rights that are fundamental, and is not confined to the specific terms of the Bill of Rights. My conclusion that the concept of liberty is not so restricted and that it embraces the right of marital privacy though that right is not mentioned explicitly in the Constitution is supported both by numerous decisions of this Court, referred to in the Court's opinion, and by the language and history of the Ninth Amendment. In reaching the conclusion that the right of marital privacy is protected, as being within the protected penumbra of specific guarantees of the Bill of Rights, the Court refers to the Ninth Amendment. I add these words to emphasize the relevance of that Amendment to the Court's holding. . . .

This Court, in a series of decisions, has held that the Fourteenth Amendment absorbs and applies to the States those specifics of the first eight amendments which express fundamental personal rights. The language and history of the Ninth Amendment reveal that the Framers of the Constitution believed that there are additional fundamental rights, protected from governmental infringement, which exist alongside those fundamental rights specifically mentioned in the first eight constitutional amendments.

The Ninth Amendment reads, "The enumeration in the Constitution, of certain rights, shall not be construed to deny or disparage others retained by the people." The Amendment is almost entirely the work of James Madison. It was introduced in Congress by him and passed the House and Senate with little or no debate and virtually no change in language. It was proffered to quiet expressed fears that a bill of specifically enumerated rights[3] could not be sufficiently broad to cover all essential rights and that the specific mention of certain rights would be interpreted as a denial that others were protected.[4]

In presenting the proposed Amendment, Madison said:

"It has been objected also against a bill of rights, that, by enumerating particular exceptions to the grant of power, it would disparage those

---

[3] Madison himself had previously pointed out the dangers of inaccuracy resulting from the fact that "no language is so copious as to supply words and phrases for every complex idea." The Federalist, No. 37.

rights which were not placed in that enumeration; and it might follow by implication, that those rights which were not singled out, were intended to be assigned into the hands of the General Government, and were consequently insecure. This is one of the most plausible arguments I have ever heard urged against the admission of a bill of rights into this system; but, I conceive, that it may be guarded against. I have attempted it, as gentlemen may see by turning to the last clause of the fourth resolution (the Ninth Amendment)." I Annals of Congress 439 (Gales and Seaton ed. 1834).

Mr. Justice Story wrote of this argument against a bill of rights and the meaning of the Ninth Amendment:

"In regard to . . . [a] suggestion, that the affirmance of certain rights might disparage others, or might lead to argumentative implications in favor of other powers, it might be sufficient to say that such a course of reasoning could never be sustained upon any solid basis. . . . But a conclusive answer is, that such an attempt may be interdicted (as it has been) by a positive declaration in such a bill of rights that the enumeration of certain rights shall not be construed to deny or disparage others retained by the people." II Story, Commentaries on the Constitution of the United States 626–627 (5th ed. 1891).

He further stated, referring to the Ninth Amendment:

"This clause was manifestly introduced to prevent any perverse or ingenious misapplication of the well known maxim, that an affirmation in particular cases implies a negation in all others; and, *e converso*, that a negation in particular cases implies an affirmation in all others." Id., at 651.

These statements of Madison and Story make clear that the Framers did not intend that the first eight amendments be construed to exhaust the basic and fundamental rights which the Constitution guaranteed to the people.[5]

. . . The Ninth Amendment to the Constitution may be regarded by some as a recent discovery and may be forgotten by others, but since 1791 it has been a basic part of the Constitution which we are sworn to uphold. To hold that a right so basic and fundamental and so deep-rooted in our society as the right of privacy in marriage may be infringed because that right is not guaranteed in so many words by the first eight amendments to the Constitution is to ignore the Ninth Amendment and to give it no effect whatsoever. Moreover, a judicial construction that this fundamental right is not protected by the Constitution because it is not mentioned in explicit terms by one of the first eight amendments or elsewhere in the Constitution would violate the Ninth Amendment, which specifically states that "[t]he enumeration in the Constitution, of certain rights shall not be *construed* to deny or disparage others retained by the people." (Emphasis added.)

A dissenting opinion suggests that my interpretation of the Ninth Amendment somehow "broaden[s] the powers of this Court." With all due respect, I believe that it misses the import of what I am saying. . . . I do not mean to imply that the Ninth Amendment is applied against the States by the Fourteenth. Nor do I mean to state that the Ninth Amendment consti-

---

[5] The Tenth Amendment similarly made clear that the States and the people retained all those powers not expressly delegated to the Federal Government.

tutes an independent source of rights protected from infringement by either the States or the Federal Government. Rather, the Ninth Amendment shows a belief of the Constitution's authors that fundamental rights exist that are not expressly enumerated in the first eight amendments and an intent that the list of rights included there not be deemed exhaustive. As any student of this Court's opinions knows, this Court has held, often unanimously, that the Fifth and Fourteenth Amendments protect certain fundamental personal liberties from abridgment by the Federal Government or the States. . . . The Ninth Amendment simply shows the intent of the Constitution's authors that other fundamental personal rights should not be denied such protection or disparaged in any other way simply because they are not specifically listed in the first eight constitutional amendments. I do not see how this broadens the authority of the Court; rather it serves to support what this Court has been doing in protecting fundamental rights.

Nor am I turning somersaults with history in arguing that the Ninth Amendment is relevant in a case dealing with a *State's* infringement of a fundamental right. While the Ninth Amendment—and indeed the entire Bill of Rights—originally concerned restrictions upon federal power, the subsequently enacted Fourteenth Amendment prohibits the States as well from abridging fundamental personal liberties. And, the Ninth Amendment, in indicating that not all such liberties are specifically mentioned in the first eight amendments, is surely relevant in showing the existence of other fundamental personal rights, now protected from state, as well as federal, infringement. In sum, the Ninth Amendment simply lends strong support to the view that the "liberty" protected by the Fifth And Fourteenth Amendments from infringement by the Federal Government or the States is not restricted to rights specifically mentioned in the first eight amendments.

In determining which rights are fundamental, judges are not left at large to decide cases in light of their personal and private notions. Rather, they must look to the "traditions and [collective] conscience of our people" to determine whether a principle is "so rooted [there] . . . as to be ranked as fundamental." *Snyder v. Com. of Massachusetts*, 291 U.S. 97, 105. The inquiry is whether a right involved "is of such a character that it cannot be denied without violating those 'fundamental principles of liberty and justice which lie at the base of all our civil and political institutions'. . . ." *Powell v. Alabama*, 287 U.S. 45, 67. "Liberty" also "gains content from the emanations of . . . specific [constitutional] guarantees" and "from experience with the requirements of a free society." *Poe v. Ullman*, 367 U.S. 497, 517 (dissenting opinion of MR. JUSTICE DOUGLAS).

I agree fully with the Court that, applying these tests, the right of privacy is a fundamental personal right, emanating "from the totality of the constitutional scheme under which we live." *Id.*, at 521. . . .

The Connecticut statutes here involved deal with a particularly important and sensitive area of privacy—that of the marital relation and the marital home. This Court recognized in *Meyer v. Nebraska* that the right "to marry, establish a home and bring up children" was an essential part of the liberty guaranteed by the Fourteenth Amendment. In *Pierce v. Society of Sisters*, the Court held unconstitutional an Oregon Act which forbade parents from sending their children to private schools because such an act "unreasonably interferes with the liberty of parents and guardians to direct the upbringing and education of children under their control." As this Court said, the *Meyer* and *Pierce* decisions "have respected the private realm of family life which the state cannot enter." . . .

The entire fabric of the Constitution and the purposes that clearly underlie its specific guarantees demonstrate that the rights to marital privacy and to marry and raise a family are of similar order and magnitude as the fundamental rights specifically protected.

Although the Constitution does not speak in so many words of the right of privacy in marriage, I cannot believe that it offers these fundamental rights no protection. The fact that no particular provision of the Constitution explicitly forbids the State from disrupting the traditional relation of the family—a relation as old and as fundamental as our entire civilization—surely does not show that the Government was meant to have the power to do so. Rather, as the Ninth Amendment expressly recognizes, there are fundamental personal rights such as this one, which are protected from abridgment by the Government though not specifically mentioned in the Constitution. . . .

The logic of the dissents would sanction federal or state legislation that seems to me even more plainly unconstitutional than the statute before us. Surely the Government, absent a showing of a compelling subordinating state interest, could not decree that all husbands and wives must be sterilized after two children have been born to them. Yet by their reasoning such an invasion of marital privacy would not be subject to constitutional challenge because, while it might be "silly," no provision of the Constitution specifically prevents the Government from curtailing the marital right to bear children and raise a family. While it may shock some of my Brethren that the Court today holds that the Constitution protects the right of marital privacy, in my view it is far more shocking to believe that the personal liberty guaranteed by the Constitution does not include protection against such totalitarian limitation of family size, which is at complete variance with our constitutional concepts. Yet, if upon a showing of a slender basis of rationality, a law outlawing voluntary birth control by married persons is valid, then, by the same reasoning, a law requiring compulsory birth control also would seem to be valid. In my view, however, both types of law would unjustifiably intrude upon rights of marital privacy which are constitutionally protected.

Although the Connecticut birth-control law obviously encroaches upon a fundamental personal liberty, the State does not show that the law serves any "subordinating [state] interest which is compelling" or that it is "necessary . . . to the accomplishment of a permissible state policy." The State, at most, argues that there is some rational relation between this statute and what is admittedly a legitimate subject of state concern—the discouraging of extra-marital relations. It says that preventing the use of birth-control devices by married persons helps prevent the indulgence by some in such extra-marital relations. The rationality of this justification is dubious, particularly in light of the admitted widespread availability to all persons in the State of Connecticut, unmarried as well as married, of birth-control devices for the prevention of disease, as distinguished from the prevention of conception. But, in any event, it is clear that the state interest in safeguarding marital fidelity can be served by a more discriminately tailored statute, which does not, like the present one, sweep unnecessarily broadly, reaching far beyond the evil sought to be dealt with and intruding upon the privacy of all married couples. . . . The State of Connecticut does have statutes, the constitutionality of which is beyond doubt, which prohibit adultery and fornication. These statutes demonstrate that means for achieving the same basic purpose of protecting marital fidelity are available to Connecticut without the need to "invade the area of protected freedoms." *NAACP v. Alabama*, at 307.

Finally, it should be said of the Court's holding today that it in no way interferes with a State's proper regulation of sexual promiscuity or misconduct. As my Brother HARLAN so well stated in his dissenting opinion in *Poe v. Ullman, supra*, 367 U.S. at 553:

Adultery, homosexuality and the like are sexual intimacies which the State forbids . . . but the intimacy of husband and wife is necessarily an essential and accepted feature of the institution of marriage, an institution which the State not only must allow, but which always and in every age it has fostered and protected. It is one thing when the State exerts its power either to forbid extra-marital sexuality . . . or to say who may marry, but it is quite another when, having acknowledged a marriage and the intimacies inherent in it, it undertakes to regulate by means of the criminal law the details of that intimacy.

In sum, I believe that the right of privacy in the marital relation is fundamental and basic—a personal right "retained by the people" within the meaning of the Ninth Amendment. Connecticut cannot constitutionally abridge this fundamental right, which is protected by the Fourteenth Amendment from infringement by the States. I agree with the Court that petitioners' convictions must therefore be reversed.

■ MR. JUSTICE HARLAN, concurring in the judgment.

I fully agree with the judgment of reversal, but find myself unable to join the Court's opinion. The reason is that it seems to me to evince an approach to this case very much like that taken by my Brothers BLACK and STEWART in dissent, namely: the Due Process Clause of the Fourteenth Amendment does not touch this Connecticut statute unless the enactment is found to violate some right assured by the letter or penumbra of the Bill of Rights.

In other words, what I find implicit in the Court's opinion is that the "incorporation" doctrine may be used to *restrict* the reach of Fourteenth Amendment Due Process. For me this is just as unacceptable constitutional doctrine as is the use of the "incorporation" approach to *impose* upon the States all the requirements of the Bill of Rights as found in the provisions of the first eight amendments and in the decisions of this Court interpreting them.

In my view, the proper constitutional inquiry in this case is whether this Connecticut statute infringes the Due Process Clause of the Fourteenth Amendment because the enactment violates basic values "implicit in the concept of ordered liberty," *Palko v. Connecticut*, 302 U.S. 319, 325. For reasons stated at length in my dissenting opinion in *Poe v. Ullman*, I believe that it does. While the relevant inquiry may be aided by resort to one or more of the provisions of the Bill of Rights, it is not dependent on them or any of their radiations. The Due Process Clause of the Fourteenth Amendment stands, in my opinion, on its own bottom. . . .

While I could not more heartily agree that judicial "self restraint" is an indispensable ingredient of sound constitutional adjudication, I do submit that the formula suggested for achieving it [by the dissent] is more hollow than real. "Specific" provisions of the Constitution, no less than "due process," lend themselves as readily to "personal" interpretations by judges whose constitutional outlook is simply to keep the Constitution in supposed "tune with the times." . . .

Judicial self-restraint will . . . be achieved in this area, as in other constitutional areas, only by continual insistence upon respect for the teachings of history, solid recognition of the basic values that underlie our society, and wise appreciation of the great roles that the doctrines of federalism and separation of powers have played in establishing and preserving American freedoms. Adherence to these principles will not, of course, obviate all constitutional differences of opinion among judges, nor should it. Their continued recognition will, however, go farther toward keeping most judges from roaming at large in the constitutional field than will the interpolation into the Constitution of an artificial and largely illusory restriction on the content of the Due Process Clause.

■ MR. JUSTICE WHITE, concurring in the judgment.

In my view this Connecticut law as applied to married couples deprives them of "liberty" without due process of law, as that concept is used in the Fourteenth Amendment. . . .

[T]his is not the first time this Court has had occasion to articulate that the liberty entitled to protection under the Fourteenth Amendment includes the right "to marry, establish a home and bring up children," *Meyer v. Nebraska*, and "the liberty . . . to direct the upbringing and education of children," *Pierce v. Society of Sisters*, and that these are among "the basic civil rights of man." *Skinner v. Oklahoma*. These decisions affirm that there is a "realm of family life which the state cannot enter" without substantial justification. *Prince v. Massachusetts*, 321 U.S. 158, 166. Surely the right invoked in this case, to be free of regulation of the intimacies of the marriage relationship, "come[s] to this Court with a momentum for respect lacking when appeal is made to liberties which derive merely from shifting economic arrangements." *Kovacs v. Cooper*, 336 U.S. 77, 95 (opinion of Frankfurter, J.). . . .

[T]he statute is said to serve the State's policy against all forms of promiscuous or illicit sexual relationships, be they premarital or extramarital, concededly a permissible and legitimate legislative goal. Without taking issue with the premise that the fear of conception operates as a deterrent to such relationships in addition to the criminal proscriptions Connecticut has against such conduct, I wholly fail to see how the ban on the use of contraceptives by married couples in any way reinforces the State's ban on illicit sexual relationships. . . . A statute limiting its prohibition on use to persons engaging in [a] prohibited relationship would serve the end posited by Connecticut in the same way, and with the same effectiveness, or ineffectiveness, as the broad anti-use statute under attack in this case. I find nothing in this record justifying the sweeping scope of this statute, with its telling effect on the freedoms of married persons, and therefore conclude that it deprives such persons of liberty without due process of law.

■ MR. JUSTICE BLACK, with whom MR. JUSTICE STEWART joins, dissenting.

I agree with my Brother STEWART'S dissenting opinion. And like him I do not to any extent whatever base my view that this Connecticut law is constitutional on a belief that the law is wise or that its policy is a good one. In order that there may be no room at all to doubt why I vote as I do, I feel constrained to add that the law is every bit as offensive to me as it is my Brethren of the majority and my Brothers HARLAN, WHITE and GOLDBERG who, reciting reasons why it is offensive to them, hold it unconstitutional.

There is no single one of the graphic and eloquent strictures and criticisms fired at the policy of this Connecticut law either by the Court's opinion or by those of my concurring Brethren to which I cannot subscribe—except their conclusion that the evil qualities they see in the law make it unconstitutional.

. . . The two defendants here were active participants in an organization which gave physical examinations to women, advised them what kind of contraceptive devices or medicines would most likely be satisfactory for them, and then supplied the devices themselves, all for a graduated scale of fees, based on the family income. Thus these defendants admittedly engaged with others in a planned course of conduct to help people violate the Connecticut law. Merely because some speech was used in carrying on the conduct—just as in ordinary life some speech accompanies most kinds of conduct—we are not in my view justified in holding that the First Amendment forbids the State to punish their conduct. Strongly as I desire to protect all First Amendment freedoms, I am unable to stretch the Amendment so as to afford protection to the conduct of these defendants in violating the Connecticut law. What would be the constitutional fate of the law if hereafter applied to punish nothing but speech is . . . quite another matter.

The Court talks about a constitutional "right of privacy" as though there is some constitutional provision or provisions forbidding any law ever to be passed which might abridge the "privacy" of individuals. But there is not. There are, of course, guarantees in certain specific constitutional provisions which are designed in part to protect privacy at certain times and places with respect to certain activities. Such, for example, is the Fourth Amendment's guarantee against "unreasonable searches and seizures." But I think it belittles that Amendment to talk about it as though it protects nothing but "privacy." To treat it that way is to give it a niggardly interpretation, not the kind of liberal reading I think any Bill of Rights provision should be given. The average man would very likely not have his feelings soothed any more by having his property seized openly than by having it seized privately and by stealth. He simply wants his property left alone. And a person can be just as much, if not more, irritated, annoyed and injured by an unceremonious public arrest by a policeman as he is by a seizure in the privacy of his office or home.

One of the most effective ways of diluting or expanding a constitutionally guaranteed right is to substitute for the crucial word or words of a constitutional guarantee another word or words, more or less flexible and more or less restricted in meaning. This fact is well illustrated by the use of the term "right of privacy" as a comprehensive substitute for the Fourth Amendment's guarantee against "unreasonable searches and seizures." "Privacy" is a broad, abstract and ambiguous concept which can easily be shrunken in meaning but which can also, on the other hand, easily be interpreted as a constitutional ban against many things other than searches and seizures. I have expressed the view many times that First Amendment freedoms, for example, have suffered from a failure of the courts to stick to the simple language of the First Amendment in construing it, instead of invoking multitudes of words substituted for those the Framers used. For these reasons I get nowhere in this case by talk about a constitutional "right of privacy" as an emanation from one or more constitutional provisions. I like my privacy as well as the next one, but I am nevertheless compelled to admit that government has a right to invade it unless prohibited by some specific constitutional provision. For these reasons I cannot agree with the Court's judgment and the reasons it gives for holding this Connecticut law unconstitutional.

This brings me to the arguments made by my Brothers HARLAN, WHITE, and GOLDBERG for invalidating the Connecticut law. Brothers HARLAN and WHITE would invalidate it by reliance on the Due Process Clause of the Fourteenth Amendment, but Brother GOLDBERG, while agreeing with Brother HARLAN, relies also on the Ninth Amendment.... I think that if properly construed neither the Due Process Clause nor the Ninth Amendment, nor both together, could under any circumstances be a proper basis for invalidating the Connecticut law. I discuss the due process and Ninth Amendment arguments together because on analysis they turn out to be the same thing—merely using different words to claim for this Court and the federal judiciary power to invalidate any legislative act which the judges find irrational, unreasonable or offensive.

The due process argument which my Brothers HARLAN and WHITE adopt here is based, as their opinions indicate, on the premise that this Court is vested with power to invalidate all state laws that it consider to be arbitrary, capricious, unreasonable, or oppressive, or this Court's belief that a particular state law under scrutiny has no "rational or justifying" purpose, or is offensive to a "sense of fairness and justice." If these formulas based on "natural justice," or others which mean the same thing, are to prevail, they require judges to determine what is or is not constitutional on the basis of their own appraisal of what laws are unwise or unnecessary. The power to make such decisions is of course that of a legislative body. Surely it has to be admitted that no provision of the Constitution specifically gives such blanket power to courts to exercise such a supervisory veto over the wisdom and value of legislative policies and to hold unconstitutional those laws which they believe unwise or dangerous.... While I completely sub-scribe to the holding of *Marbury v. Madison,* and subsequent cases, that our Court has constitutional power to strike down statutes, state or federal, that violate commands of the Federal Constitution, I do not believe that we are granted power by the Due Process Clause or any other constitutional provision or provisions to measure constitutionality by our belief that legislation is arbitrary, capricious or unreasonable, or accomplishes no justifiable purpose, or is offensive to our own notions of "civilized standards of conduct."[5] Such an appraisal of the wisdom of legislation is an attribute of the power to make laws, not of the power to interpret them. The use by federal courts of such a formula or doctrine or whatnot to veto federal or state laws simply takes away from Congress and States the power to make laws based on their own judgment of fairness and wisdom and transfers that power to this Court for ultimate determination—a power which was specifically denied to federal courts by the convention that framed the Constitution.

Of the cases on which my Brothers WHITE and GOLDBERG rely so heavily, undoubtedly the reasoning of two of them supports their result here—as would that of a number of others which they do not bother to name, e.g.,

---

[5] See Hand, The Bill of Rights (1958) 70:

"[J]udges are seldom content merely to annul the particular solution before them; they do not, indeed they may not, say that taking all things into consideration, the legislators' solution is too strong for the judicial stomach. On the contrary they wrap up their veto in a protective veil of adjectives such as 'arbitrary,' 'artificial,' 'normal,' 'reasonable,' 'inherent,' 'fundamental,' or 'essential,' whose office usually, though quite innocently, is to disguise what they are doing and impute to it a derivation far more impressive than their personal preferences, which are all that in fact lie behind the decision."

Lochner v. New York, Coppage v. Kansas, and *Adkins v. Children's Hospital*. The two they do cite and quote from, *Meyer v. Nebraska* and *Pierce v. Society of Sisters*, were both decided in opinions by Mr. Justice McReynolds which elaborated the same natural law due process philosophy found in *Lochner v. New York*, one of the cases on which he relied in *Meyer*. . . . Without expressing an opinion as to whether either of those cases reached a correct result in light of our later decisions applying the First Amendment to the States through the Fourteenth, I merely point out that the reasoning stated in *Meyer* and *Pierce* was the same natural law due process philosophy which many later opinions repudiated, and which I cannot accept. . . .

My Brother GOLDBERG has adopted the recent discovery that the Ninth Amendment as well as the Due Process Clause can be used by this Court as authority to strike down all state legislation which this Court thinks violates "fundamental principles of liberty and justice," or is contrary to the "traditions and [collective] conscience of our people." He also states, without proof satisfactory to me, that in making decisions on this basis judges will not consider "their personal and private notions." One may ask how they can avoid considering them. Our Court certainly has no machinery with which to take a Gallup Poll. And the scientific miracles of this age have not yet produced a gadget which the Court can use to determine what traditions are rooted in the "[collective] conscience of our people." Moreover one would certainly have to look far beyond the language of the Ninth Amendment to find that the Framers vested in this Court any such awesome veto powers over law-making, either by the States or by the Congress. Nor does anything in the history of the Amendment offer any support for such a shocking doctrine. The whole history of the adoption of the Constitution and Bill of Rights points the other way, and the very material quoted by my Brother GOLDBERG shows that the Ninth Amendment was intended to protect against the idea that "by enumerating particular exceptions to the grant of power" to the Federal Government, "those rights which were not singled out, were intended to be assigned into the hands of the General Government [the United States], and were consequently insecure." That Amendment was passed, not to broaden the powers of this Court or any other department of "the General Government," but, as every student of history knows, to assure the people that the Constitution in all its provisions was intended to limit the Federal Government to the powers granted expressly or by necessary implication. If any broad, unlimited power to hold laws unconstitutional because they offend what this Court conceives to be the "[collective] conscience of our people" is vested in this Court by the Ninth Amendment, the Fourteenth Amendment, or any other provision of the Constitution, it was not given by the Framers, but rather has been bestowed on the Court by the Court. This fact is perhaps responsible for the peculiar phenomenon that for a period of a century and a half no serious suggestion was ever made that the Ninth Amendment, enacted to protect state powers against federal invasion, could be used as a weapon of federal power to prevent state legislatures from passing laws they consider appropriate to govern local affairs. Use of any such broad, unbounded judicial authority would make of this Court's members a day-to-day constitutional convention.

I repeat so as not to be misunderstood that this Court does have power, which it should exercise, to hold laws unconstitutional where they are forbidden by the Federal Constitution. My point is that there is no provision of the Constitution which either expressly or impliedly vests power in this Court to sit as a supervisory agency over acts of duly constituted legislative bodies and set aside their laws because of the Court's belief that the legislative policies adopted are unreasonable, unwise, arbitrary, capricious or irrational. The adoption of such a loose, flexible, uncontrolled standard for holding laws unconstitutional, if ever it is finally achieved, will amount to a great unconstitutional shift of power to the courts which I believe and am constrained to say will be bad for the courts and worse for the country. Subjecting federal and state laws to such an unrestrained and unrestrainable judicial control as to the wisdom of legislative enactments would, I fear, jeopardize the separation of governmental powers that the Framers set up and at the same time threaten to take away much of the power of States to govern themselves which the Constitution plainly intended them to have.

I realize that many good and able men have eloquently spoken and written, sometimes in rhapsodical strains, about the duty of this Court to keep the Constitution in tune with the times. The idea is that the Constitution must be changed from time to time and that this Court is charged with a duty to make those changes. For myself, I must with all deference reject that philosophy. The Constitution makers knew the need for change and provided for it. Amendments suggested by the people's elected representatives can be submitted to the people or their selected agents for ratification. That method of change was good for our Fathers, and being somewhat old fashioned I must add it is good enough for me. And so, I cannot rely on the Due Process Clause or the Ninth Amendment or any mysterious and uncertain natural law concept as a reason for striking down this state law. The Due Process Clause with an "arbitrary and capricious" or "shocking to the conscience" formula was liberally used by this Court to strike down economic legislation in the early decades of this century, threatening, many people thought, the tranquility and stability of the Nation. See, e.g., *Lochner v. New York*, 198 U.S. 45. That formula, based on subjective considerations of "natural justice," is no less dangerous when used to enforce this Court's views about personal rights than those about economic rights. I had thought that we had laid that formula, as a means for striking down state legislation, to rest once and for all in cases like *West Coast Hotel Co. v. Parrish*, 300 U.S. 379, and many other opinions. See also *Lochner v. New York*, 198 U.S. 45, 74 (Holmes, J., dissenting).

In *Ferguson v. Skrupa*, 372 U.S. 726, 730, this Court two years ago said in an opinion joined by all the Justices but one that

> The doctrine that prevailed in *Lochner, Coppage, Adkins, Burns*, and like cases—that due process authorizes courts to hold laws unconstitutional when they believe the legislature has acted unwisely—has long since been discarded. We have returned to the original constitutional proposition that courts do not substitute their social and economic beliefs for the judgment of legislative bodies, who are elected to pass laws.

. . . In 1798, when this Court was asked to hold another Connecticut law unconstitutional, Justice Iredell said:

> ". . . [If] the Legislature of the Union, or the Legislature of any member of the Union, shall pass a law, within the general scope of their constitutional power, the Court cannot pronounce it to be void, merely because it is, in their judgment, contrary to the principles of natural justice. The ideas of natural justice are regulated by no fixed standard: the ablest and the purest men have differed upon the subject; and all that the Court could properly say, in such an event, would

be, that the Legislature (possessed of an equal right of opinion) had passed an act which, in the opinion of the judges, was inconsistent with the abstract principles of natural justice." *Calder v. Bull*, 3 Dall. 386, 399.

. . . So far as I am concerned, Connecticut's law as applied here is not forbidden by any provision of the Federal Constitution as that Constitution was written, and I would therefore affirm.

■ MR. JUSTICE STEWART, whom MR. JUSTICE BLACK joins, dissenting.

Since 1879 Connecticut has had on its books a law which forbids the use of contraceptives by anyone. I think this is an uncommonly silly law. As a practical matter, the law is obviously unenforceable, except in the oblique context of the present case. As a philosophical matter, I believe the use of contraceptives in the relationship of marriage should be left to personal and private choice, based upon each individual's moral, ethical, and religious beliefs. As a matter of social policy, I think professional counsel about methods of birth control should be available to all, so that each individual's choice can be meaningfully made. But we are not asked in this case to say whether we think this law is unwise, or even asinine. We are asked to hold that it violates the United States Constitution. And that I cannot do.

In the course of its opinion the Court refers to no less than six Amendments to the Constitution: the First, the Third, the Fourth, the Fifth, the Ninth, and the Fourteenth. But the Court does not say which of these Amendments, if any, it thinks is infringed by this Connecticut law.

We *are* told that the Due Process Clause of the Fourteenth Amendment is not, as such, the "guide" in this case. With that much I agree. There is no claim that this law, duly enacted by the Connecticut Legislature, is unconstitutionally vague. There is no claim that the appellants were denied any of the elements of procedural due process at their trial, so as to make their convictions constitutionally invalid. And, as the Court says, the day has long passed since the Due Process Clause was regarded as a proper instrument for determining "the wisdom, need, and propriety" of state laws. Compare *Lochner v. New York*, 198 U.S. 45, with *Ferguson v. Skrupa*, 372 U.S. 726. . . .

As to the First, Third, Fourth, and Fifth Amendments, I can find nothing in any of them to invalidate this Connecticut law. . . . [U]nless the solemn process of constitutional adjudication is to descend to the level of a play on words, there is not involved here any abridgment of "the freedom of speech, or of the press; or the right of the people peaceably to assemble, and to petition the Government for a redress of grievances." No soldier has been quartered in any house. There has been no search, and no seizure. Nobody has been compelled to be a witness against himself.

The Court also quotes the Ninth Amendment, and my Brother GOLDBERG'S concurring opinion relies heavily upon it. But to say that the Ninth Amendment has anything to do with this case is to turn somersaults with history. The Ninth Amendment, like its companion the Tenth, which this Court held "states but a truism that all is retained which has not been surrendered," *United States v. Darby*, 312 U.S. 100, 124, was framed by James Madison and adopted by the States simply to make clear that the adoption of the Bill of Rights did not alter the plan that the *Federal* Government was to be a government of express and limited powers, and that all rights and powers not delegated to it were retained by the people and the individual States. Until today no member of this Court has ever suggested that the Ninth Amendment meant anything else, and the idea that a federal court could ever use the Ninth Amendment to annul a law passed by the elected representatives of the people of the State of Connecticut would have caused James Madison no little wonder.

What provision of the Constitution, then, does make this state law invalid? The Court says it is the right of privacy "created by several fundamental constitutional guarantees." With all deference, I can find no such general right of privacy in the Bill of Rights, in any other part of the Constitution, or in any case ever before decided by this Court.

At the oral argument in this case we were told that the Connecticut law does not "conform to current community standards." But it is not the function of this Court to decide cases on the basis of community standards. We are here to decide cases "agreeably to the Constitution and laws of the United States." It is the essence of judicial duty to subordinate our own personal views, our own ideas of what legislation is wise and what is not. If, as I should surely hope, the law before us does not reflect the standards of the people of Connecticut, the people of Connecticut can freely exercise their true Ninth and Tenth Amendment rights to persuade their elected representatives to repeal it. That is the constitutional way to take this law off the books.[8]

NOTES

1. What is the constitutional interpretive methodology in *Griswold?* How would you describe the Court's approach? Is it textual interpretation? Historical evidence of original meaning? Is the result supported by inferential reasoning from precedent? Is the method one of extrapolating from specific constitutional texts and precedents to a more abstract principle? If the liberties expressly protected by the Bill of Rights are starting points, what are the stopping points that the Court identifies? How does the majority respond to the dissenting justices' arguments that they are merely imposing their own personal views on the legislature?

2. The majority mentions, but does not greatly rely on, the Ninth Amendment. But Justice Goldberg makes it central to his concurrence, and he draws a stinging rebuttal from Justice Black. Which of them has the better of the argument? What is the function of the Ninth Amendment in the Bill of Rights? If it does provide the basis for striking down the Connecticut law, what other statutes should be struck down on its authority? What principles should courts use in deciding its scope? (For more discussion of the Ninth Amendment, see Chapter 6.)

3. What do you think of Justice Harlan's argument that the majority's rationale is *too narrow*, and that federal courts have the duty to identify and protect, in a restrained manner, the values "implicit in the concept of ordered liberty"? Justice Harlan cites his famous dissent in *Poe v. Ullman,* 367 U.S. 497 (1961), a case in which the Court had found an earlier challenge to Connecticut's birth control law to be non-justiciable. In that dissent, Justice Harlan spoke of the Fourteenth Amendment as protecting a tradition of liberty, rooted in the past and continuing to grow:

---

[8] The Connecticut House of Representatives recently passed a bill repealing the birth control law. The State Senate has apparently not yet acted on the measure, and today is relieved, of that responsibility by the Court.

Were due process merely a procedural safeguard, it would fail to reach those situations where the deprivation of life, liberty or property was accomplished by legislation which by operating in the future could, given even the fairest possible procedure in application to individuals, nevertheless destroy the enjoyment of all three. Thus the guaranties of due process, though having their roots in Magna Carta's "*per legem terrae*" and considered as procedural safeguards "against executive usurpation and tyranny," have in this country "become bulwarks also against arbitrary legislation."
. . .

Due process has not been reduced to any formula; its content cannot be determined by reference to any code. The best that can be said is that, through the course of this Court's decisions, it has represented the balance which our Nation, built upon postulates of respect for the liberty of the individual, has struck between that liberty and the demands of organized society. If the supplying of content to this constitutional concept has of necessity been a rational process, it certainly has not been one where judges have felt free to roam where unguided speculation might take them. The balance of which I speak is the balance struck by this country, having regard to what history teaches are the traditions from which it developed as well as the traditions from which it broke. That tradition is a living thing. A decision of this Court which radically departs from it could not long survive, while a decision which builds on what has survived is likely to be sound. No formula could serve as a substitute, in this area, for judgment sand restraint.

. . . This "liberty" is not a series of isolated points pricked out in terms of the taking of property; the freedom of speech, press, and religion; the right to keep and bear arms; the freedom from unreasonable searches and seizures; and so on. It is a rational continuum which, broadly speaking, includes a freedom from all substantial arbitrary impositions and purposeless restraints, and which also recognizes, what a reasonable and sensitive judgment must, that certain interests require particularly careful scrutiny of the state needs asserted to justify their abridgment.

Id. at 541–543 (Harlan, J., dissenting). Justice Harlan proceeded to apply this approach to the Connecticut statute. He found that our legal tradition included "the category of morality among state concerns." *Id.* at 545. Accordingly, he considered it unobjectionable for a state to have "laws forbidding adultery, fornication and homosexual practices," since legal restrictions "confining sexuality to lawful marriage[] form a pattern so deeply pressed into the substance of our social life that any constitutional doctrine in this area must build upon that basis." *Id.* at 546. Nevertheless, he contended that the Connecticut statute was different because it regulated sex within marriage. In Justice Harlan's words, quoted later in *Griswold,* "It is one thing when the State exerts its power either to forbid extramarital sexuality altogether, or to say who may marry, but it is quite another when, having acknowledged a marriage and the intimacies inherent in it, it undertakes to regulate by means of the criminal law the details of that intimacy." *Id.* at 553. And Justice Harlan emphasized the statute's "utter novelty," for although other state and federal laws had restricted the distribution of contraceptives, none of these had criminally punished their use. *Id.* at 554.

How is Justice Harlan's approach (in his *Poe* dissent and *Griswold* concurrence) different from the approach taken by the majority in *Griswold*? Would it have provided a stronger or weaker answer to the critique of the *Griswold* dissenters? What are its strengths and vulnerabilities as an approach to interpreting the Constitution?

4. Is the majority's reasoning limited to marriage, or can *Griswold* be understood on its own terms as recognizing a general constitutional right to "privacy" in matters of sexual conduct or contraception? (Do some of the opinions explicitly deny such a general right?) Consider, for example, whether under *Griswold* there is a constitutional right to engage in premarital sex or adultery. Could such rights be extrapolated from *Griswold*'s reasoning? Or would that be performing a *Griswold* on *Griswold* itself—and is there anything wrong with that?

5. If you think *Griswold* is a strained reading of the Constitution's text, then consider the hypothetical suggested by Justice Goldberg: A state requires sterilization after a married couple has had two children (for the stated compelling interest of population control). Or make the hypothetical worse yet: after two live births, compulsory abortion of subsequent pregnancies. Would that be constitutional? If not, why not? What provision of the Constitution invalidates it? How would Justice Black answer this parade of horribles?

6. An exercise: If you were to write a constitutional amendment explicitly granting a constitutional right to privacy, what would it say? Try it. But be careful: would the text of your proposed amendment be capable of being interpreted as conferring a constitutional right to torture puppies in your basement? To have a meth lab in your kitchen? Would you need to make any changes to your privacy amendment to achieve the popular support needed for ratification? How closely does the language of your amendment track any provision of the current Constitution?

Eisenstadt v. Baird

405 U.S. 438 (1972)

■ Mr. Justice Brennan delivered the opinion of the Court.

Appellee William Baird was convicted at a bench trial in the Massachusetts Superior Court under Massachusetts General Laws Ann., c. 272, § 21, first, for exhibiting contraceptive articles in the course of delivering a lecture on contraception to a group of students at Boston University and, second, for giving a young woman a package of Emko vaginal foam at the close of his address. The Massachusetts Supreme Judicial Court unanimously set aside the conviction for exhibiting contraceptives on the ground that it violated Baird's First Amendment rights, but by a four-to-three vote sustained the conviction for giving away the foam. Baird subsequently filed a petition for a federal writ of habeas corpus, which the District Court dismissed. On appeal, however, the Court of Appeals for the First Circuit vacated the dismissal. . . . We affirm.

Massachusetts General Laws Ann., c. 272, § 21, under which Baird was convicted, provides a maximum five-year term of imprisonment for "whoever . . . gives away . . . any drug, medicine, instrument or article whatever for the prevention of conception," except as authorized in § 21A. Under § 21A, "[a] registered physician may administer to or prescribe for any married person drugs or articles intended for the prevention of pregnancy or conception." . . . The statutory scheme distinguishes among three distinct classes of distributees—*first*, married persons may obtain contraceptives to prevent pregnancy, but only from doctors or druggists on prescription; *second*, single persons may not obtain contraceptives from anyone to prevent pregnancy; and, *third*, married or single persons may obtain contraceptives from anyone to prevent, not pregnancy, but the spread of disease. . . .

The legislative purposes that the statute is meant to serve are not altogether clear. . . . The Court of Appeals, for reasons that will appear, did not consider the promotion of health or the protection of morals through the deterrence of fornication to be the legislative aim. Instead the court concluded that the statutory goal was to limit contraception in and of itself—a purpose that the court held conflicted "with fundamental human rights" under *Griswold v. Connecticut*, 381 U.S. 479 (1965), where this Court struck down Connecticut's prohibition against the use of contraceptives as an unconstitutional infringement of the right of marital privacy.

We agree that the goals of deterring premarital sex and regulating the distribution of potentially harmful articles cannot reasonably be regarded as legislative aims of §§ 21 and 21A. And we hold that the statute, viewed as a prohibition on contraception *per se*, violates the rights of single persons under the Equal Protection Clause of the Fourteenth Amendment. . . .

[The Court first held that Baird had standing "to assert the rights of unmarried persons denied access to contraceptives."—Editors]

The question for our determination in this case is whether there is some ground of difference that rationally explains the different treatment accorded married and unmarried persons under §§ 21 and 21A. For the reasons that follow, we conclude that no such ground exists.

First. Section 21 stems from [an earlier statute] which prohibited without exception, distribution of articles intended to be used as contraceptives. [T]he Massachusetts Supreme Judicial Court [has] explained that the law's "plain purpose is to protect purity, to preserve chastity, to encourage continence and self restraint, to defend the sanctity of the home, and thus to engender in the State and nation a virile and virtuous race of men and women." Although the State clearly abandoned that purpose with the enactment of § 21A, at least insofar as the illicit sexual activities of married persons are concerned, the court [has] reiterated that the object of the legislation is to discourage premarital sexual intercourse. Conceding that the State could, consistently with the Equal Protection Clause, regard the problems of extramarital and premarital sexual relations as "[e]vils . . . of different dimensions and proportions, requiring different remedies," *Williamson v. Lee Optical Co.*, 348 U.S. 483, 489 (1955), we cannot agree that the deterrence of premarital sex may reasonably be regarded as the purpose of the Massachusetts law.

It would be plainly unreasonable to assume that Massachusetts has prescribed pregnancy and the birth of an unwanted child as punishment for fornication, which is a misdemeanor under Massachusetts [law]. Aside from the scheme of values that assumption would attribute to the State, it is abundantly clear that the effect of the ban on distribution of contraceptives to unmarried persons has at best a marginal relation to the proffered objective. What Mr. Justice Goldberg said in *Griswold v. Connecticut*, 381 U.S., at 498 (concurring opinion), concerning the effect of Connecticut's prohibition on the use of contraceptives in discouraging extramarital sexual relations, is equally applicable here. "The rationality of this justification is dubious, particularly in light of the admitted widespread availability to all persons in the State of Connecticut, unmarried as well as married, of birth-control devices for the prevention of disease, as distinguished from the prevention of conception." Like Connecticut's laws, §§ 21 and 21A do not at all regulate the distribution of contraceptives when they are to be used to prevent, not pregnancy, but the spread of disease. Nor, in making contraceptives available to married persons without regard to their intended use, does Massachusetts attempt to deter married persons from engaging in illicit sexual relations with unmarried persons. Even on the assumption that the fear of pregnancy operates as a deterrent to fornication, the Massachusetts statute is thus so riddled with exceptions that deterrence of premarital sex cannot reasonably be regarded as its aim.

Moreover, §§ 21 and 21A on their face have a dubious relation to the State's criminal prohibition on fornication. As the Court of Appeals explained, "Fornication is a misdemeanor [in Massachusetts], entailing a thirty dollar fine, or three months in jail. Violation of the present statute is a felony, punishable by five years in prison. We find it hard to believe that the legislature adopted a statute carrying a five-year penalty for its possible, obviously by no means fully effective, deterrence of the commission of a ninety-day misdemeanor." Even conceding the legislature a full measure of discretion in fashioning means to prevent fornication, and recognizing that the State may seek to deter prohibited conduct by punishing more severely those who facilitate than those who actually engage in its commission, we, like the Court of Appeals, cannot believe that in this instance Massachusetts has chosen to expose the aider and abetter who simply *gives away* a contraceptive to *20* times the *90–day* sentence of the offender himself. The very terms of the State's criminal statutes, coupled with the *de minimis* effect of §§ 21 and 21A in deterring fornication, thus compel the conclusion that such deterrence cannot reasonably be taken as the purpose of the ban on distribution of contraceptives to unmarried persons.

Second. Section 21A was added to the Massachusetts General Laws by Stat. 1966, c. 265, § 1. The Supreme Judicial Court [has] held that the purpose of the amendment was to serve the health needs of the community by regulating the distribution of potentially harmful articles. It is plain that Massachusetts had no such purpose in mind before the enactment of § 21A. As the Court of Appeals remarked, "Consistent with the fact that the statute was contained in a chapter dealing with 'Crimes Against Chastity, Morality, Decency and Good Order,' it was cast only in terms of morals." . . . Nor did the Court of Appeals "believe that the legislature [in enacting § 21A] suddenly reversed its field and developed an interest in health. Rather, it merely made what it thought to be the precise accommodation necessary to escape the *Griswold* ruling."

Again, we must agree with the Court of Appeals. If health were the rationale of § 21A, the statute would be both discriminatory and overbroad. . . . [I]f the Massachusetts statute were a health measure, it would not only invidiously discriminate against the unmarried, but also be overbroad with respect to the married. . . . We conclude, accordingly, that, despite the statute's superficial earmarks as a health measure, health, on the face of the statute, may no more reasonably be regarded as its purpose than the deterrence of premarital sexual relations.

Third. If the Massachusetts statute cannot be upheld as a deterrent to fornication or as a health measure, may it, nevertheless, be sustained simply as a prohibition on contraception? . . . The Court of Appeals [held]:

To say that contraceptives are immoral as such, and are to be forbidden to unmarried persons who will nevertheless persist in having intercourse, means that such persons must risk for themselves an unwanted pregnancy, for the child, illegitimacy, and for society, a possible obligation of support. Such a view of morality is not only the very mirror image of sensible legislation; we consider that it conflicts with fundamental human rights. In the absence of demonstrated harm, we hold it is beyond the competency of the state.

We need not and do not, however, decide that important question in this case because, whatever the rights of the individual to access to contraceptives may be, the rights must be the same for the unmarried and the married alike.

If under *Griswold* the distribution of contraceptives to married persons cannot be prohibited, a ban on distribution to unmarried persons would be equally impermissible. It is true that in *Griswold* the right of privacy in question inhered in the marital relationship. Yet the marital couple is not an independent entity with a mind and heart of its own, but an association of two individuals each with a separate intellectual and emotional makeup. If the right of privacy means anything, it is the right of the *individual*, married or single, to be free from unwarranted governmental intrusion into matters so fundamentally affecting a person as the decision whether to bear or beget a child.

On the other hand, if *Griswold* is no bar to a prohibition on the distribution of contraceptives, the State could not, consistently with the Equal Protection Clause, outlaw distribution to unmarried but not to married persons. In each case the evil, as perceived by the State, would be identical, and the underinclusion would be invidious. . . .

We hold that by providing dissimilar treatment for married and unmarried persons who are similarly situated, Massachusetts General Laws Ann., c. 272, §§ 21 and 21A, violate the Equal Protection Clause.

■ MR. JUSTICE POWELL and MR. JUSTICE REHNQUIST took no part in the consideration or decision of this case.

■ MR. JUSTICE DOUGLAS, concurring.

While I join the opinion of the Court, there is for me a narrower ground for affirming the Court of Appeals. This to me is a simple First Amendment case, that amendment being applicable to the States by reason of the Fourteenth. . . .

Baird gave an hour's lecture on birth control and as an aid to understanding the ideas which he was propagating he handed out one sample of one of the devices whose use he was endorsing. A person giving a lecture on coyote-getters would certainly improve his teaching technique if he passed one out to the audience; and he would be protected in doing so unless of course the device was loaded and ready to explode, killing or injuring people. The same holds true in my mind for mouse-traps, spray guns, or any other article not dangerous *per se* on which speakers give educational lectures. . . .

Handing an article under discussion to a member of the audience is a technique known to all teachers and is commonly used. . . . I do not see how we can have a Society of the Dialogue, which the First Amendment envisages, if time-honored teaching techniques are barred to those who give educational lectures.

■ MR. JUSTICE WHITE, with whom MR. JUSTICE BLACKMUN joins, concurring in the result.

In *Griswold v. Connecticut*, 381 U.S. 479 (1965), we reversed criminal convictions for advising married persons with respect to the use of contraceptives. . . . Our general reluctance to question a State's judgment on matters of public health must give way where, as here, the restriction at issue burdens the constitutional rights of married persons to use contraceptives. In these circumstances we may not accept on faith the State's classification of a particular contraceptive as dangerous to health. Due regard for protecting constitutional rights requires that the record contain evidence that a restriction on distribution of vaginal foam is essential to achieve the statutory purpose, or the relevant facts concerning the product must be such as to fall within the range of judicial notice.

Neither requirement is met here. . . . That Baird could not be convicted for distributing Emko to a married person disposes of this case. Assuming, *arguendo*, that the result would be otherwise had the recipient been unmarried, nothing has been placed in the record to indicate her marital status. The State has maintained that marital status is irrelevant because an unlicensed person cannot legally dispense vaginal foam either to married or unmarried persons. This approach is plainly erroneous and requires the reversal of Baird's conviction; for on the facts of this case, it deprives us of knowing whether Baird was in fact convicted for making a constitutionally protected distribution of Emko to a married person. . . .

Because this case can be disposed of on the basis of settled constitutional doctrine, I perceive no reason for reaching the novel constitutional question whether a State may restrict or forbid the distribution of contraceptives to the unmarried.

■ MR. CHIEF JUSTICE BURGER, dissenting.

The judgment of the Supreme Judicial Court of Massachusetts in sustaining appellee's conviction for dispensing medicinal material without a license seems eminently correct to me and I would not disturb it. It is undisputed that appellee is not a physician or pharmacist and was prohibited under Massachusetts law from dispensing contraceptives to anyone, regardless of marital status. To my mind the validity of this restriction on dispensing medicinal substances is the only issue before the Court, and appellee has no standing to challenge that part of the statute restricting the persons to whom contraceptives are available. There is no need to labor this point, however, for everyone seems to agree that if Massachusetts has validly required, as a health measure, that all contraceptives be dispensed by a physician or pursuant to a physician's prescription, then the statutory distinction based on marital status has no bearing on this case.

The opinion of the Court today brushes aside appellee's status as an unlicensed layman by concluding that the Massachusetts Legislature was not really concerned with the protection of health when it passed this statute. . . . I am puzzled by [MR. JUSTICE DOUGLAS'S] characterization of the case. If the suggestion is that appellee was merely displaying the contraceptive material without relinquishing his ownership of it, then the argument must be that the prosecution failed to prove that appellee had "given away" the contraceptive material. But appellee does not challenge the sufficiency of the evidence, and himself summarizes the record as showing that "at the close of his lecture he invited members of the audience . . . to come and help themselves." . . .

My disagreement with the opinion of the Court and that of MR. JUSTICE WHITE goes far beyond mere puzzlement, however, for these opinions seriously invade the constitutional prerogatives of the States and regrettably hark back to the heyday of substantive due process.

In affirming appellee's conviction, the highest tribunal in Massachusetts held that the statutory requirement that contraceptives be dispensed only through medical channels served the legitimate interest of the State in protecting the health of its citizens. The Court today blithely hurdles this authoritative state pronouncement and concludes that the statute has no such purpose. [The argument is advanced that] since the distribution of contraceptives was prohibited as a moral matter in Massachusetts prior to 1966, it is impossible to believe that the legislature was concerned with health when it lifted the complete ban but insisted on medical supervision. I fail to see why the historical predominance of an unacceptable legislative purpose makes incredible the emergence of a new and valid one. . . .

MR. JUSTICE WHITE, while acknowledging a valid legislative purpose of protecting health, concludes that the State lacks power to regulate the distribution of the contraceptive involved in this case as a means of protecting health. . . . [His] opinion invokes *Griswold* v. *Connecticut,* and puts the statutory classification to an unprecedented test: either the record must contain evidence supporting the classification or the health hazards of the particular contraceptive must be judicially noticeable. This is indeed a novel constitutional doctrine and not surprisingly no authority is cited for it. . . .

I cannot believe that unanimity of expert opinion is a prerequisite to a State's exercise of its police power, no matter what the subject matter of the regulation. Even assuming no present dispute among medical authorities, we cannot ignore that it has become commonplace for a drug or food additive to be universally regarded as harmless on one day and to be condemned as perilous on the next. . . .

Even if it were conclusively established once and for all that the product dispensed by appellee is not actually or potentially dangerous in the somatic sense, I would still be unable to agree that the restriction on dispensing it falls outside the State's power to regulate in the area of health. The choice of a means of birth control, although a highly personal matter, is also a health matter in a very real sense, and I see nothing arbitrary in a requirement of medical supervision. . . .

It is revealing, I think, that those portions of the majority and concurring opinions rejecting the statutory limitation on distributors rely on no particular provision of the Constitution. I see nothing in the Fourteenth Amendment or any other part of the Constitution that even vaguely suggests that these medicinal forms of contraceptives must be available in the open market. I do not challenge *Griswold v. Connecticut,* despite its tenuous moorings to the text of the Constitution, but I cannot view it as controlling authority for this case. The Court was there confronted with a statute flatly prohibiting the use of contraceptives, not one regulating their distribution. I simply cannot believe that the limitation on the class of lawful distributors has significantly impaired the right to use contraceptives in Massachusetts. By relying on *Griswold* in the present context, the Court has passed beyond the penumbras of the specific guarantees into the uncircumscribed area of personal predilections. . . .

NOTES

1. *Eisenstadt* is a key transition case between the *Griswold* decision in 1965 and *Roe v. Wade*, which was decided the year after *Eisenstadt*. The key passage is as follows: "It is true that in *Griswold* the right of privacy in question inhered in the marital relationship. Yet . . . [i]f the right of privacy means anything, it is the right of the individual, married or single, to be free from unwarranted governmental intrusion into matters so fundamentally affecting a person as the decision whether to bear or beget a child." The passage made two important moves. First, it took *Griswold,* a case emphasizing the sanctity of marriage, and turned it into a right "of the individual, married or single." Second, it cast *Griswold*'s privacy right as "the decision to bear or beget a child" rather than a right to be free of criminal punishment in a private relationship. Was *Eisenstadt*'s reasoning a warranted or unwarranted extension of the reasoning of *Griswold*'s?

2. *Eisenstadt* is presented as a case under the Equal Protection Clause. But what exactly is the "suspect classification" in the statute? Marriage? Is it irrational to treat the married and unmarried differently? After *Eisenstadt* is marital status a suspect classification? As you answer that question, remember the questions that courts often ask when deciding whether a classification is sufficiently analogous to race and sex to receive heightened scrutiny: Is there a history of discrimination against the unmarried? Is not being married an immutable characteristic? Are the unmarried a "discrete and insular minority" excluded from the political process? If marital status is not a suspect classification after *Eisenstadt*, does that mean the case is less about equal protection than about substantive due process?

3. Does *Eisenstadt* transform the right to privacy into a right to control sexual activity and reproduction? If so, does that mean that laws against incest, polygamy, and prostitution are also unconstitutional? Or is the privacy right in *Eisenstadt* better characterized as a right to control one's own body? If so, would compulsory vaccination laws be vulnerable to constitutional challenge? Laws against suicide? Laws requiring people, in certain circumstances, to take breathalyzer tests?

[*Assignment 70*]

D. ABORTION

The next substantive due process case almost needs no introduction: *Roe v. Wade*. Does the Constitution create a right to abortion of a human fetus?

Roe v. Wade

410 U.S. 113 (1973)

■ MR. JUSTICE BLACKMUN delivered the opinion of the Court.

This Texas federal appeal and its Georgia companion, *Doe v. Bolton*, 410 U.S. 179, present constitutional challenges to state criminal abortion legislation. The Texas statutes under attack here are typical of those that have been in effect in many States for approximately a century. The Georgia statutes, in contrast, have a modern cast and are a legislative product that, to an extent at least, obviously reflects the influences of recent attitudinal change, of advancing medical knowledge and techniques, and of new thinking about an old issue.

We forthwith acknowledge our awareness of the sensitive and emotional nature of the abortion controversy, of the vigorous opposing views, even among physicians, and of the deep and seemingly absolute convictions that the subject inspires. One's philosophy, one's experiences, one's exposure to the raw edges of human existence, one's religious training, one's attitudes toward life and family and their values, and the moral standards one establishes and seeks to observe, are all likely to influence and to color one's thinking and conclusions about abortion.

In addition, population growth, pollution, poverty, and racial overtones tend to complicate and not to simplify the problem.

Our task, of course, is to resolve the issue by constitutional measurement, free of emotion and of predilection. . . . We bear in mind[] Mr. Justice Holmes' admonition in his now-vindicated dissent in *Lochner v. New York*, 198 U.S. 45, 76 (1905):

[The Constitution] is made for people of fundamentally differing views, and the accident of our finding certain opinions natural and familiar or novel and even shocking ought not to conclude our judgment upon the question whether statutes embodying them conflict with the Constitution of the United States.

I

The Texas statutes that concern us here . . . make it a crime to "procure an abortion," as therein defined, or to attempt one, except with respect to "an abortion procured or attempted by medical advice for the purpose of saving the life of the mother." Similar statutes are in existence in a majority of the States.

Texas first enacted a criminal abortion statute in 1854. This was soon modified into language that has remained substantially unchanged to the present time. . . .

II

Jane Roe [pseudonym], a single woman who was residing in Dallas County, Texas, instituted this federal action in March 1970 against the District Attorney of the county. She sought a declaratory judgment that the Texas criminal abortion statutes were unconstitutional on their face, and an injunction restraining the defendant from enforcing the statutes.

Roe alleged that she was unmarried and pregnant; that she wished to terminate her pregnancy by an abortion "performed by a competent, licensed physician, under safe, clinical conditions"; that she was unable to get a "legal" abortion in Texas because her life did not appear to be threatened by the continuation of her pregnancy; and that she could not afford to travel to another jurisdiction in order to secure a legal abortion under safe conditions. She claimed that the Texas statutes were unconstitutionally vague and that they abridged her right of personal privacy, protected by the First, Fourth, Fifth, Ninth, and Fourteenth Amendments. By an amendment to her complaint Roe purported to sue "on behalf of herself and all other women similarly situated."

James Hubert Hallford, a licensed physician, sought and was granted leave to intervene in Roe's action. In his complaint he alleged that he had been arrested previously for violations of the Texas abortion statutes and that two such prosecutions were pending against him. . . .

On the merits, the District Court held that the "fundamental right of single women and married persons to choose where to have children is protected by the Ninth Amendment, through the Fourteenth Amendment," and that the Texas criminal abortion statutes were void on their face because they were both unconstitutionally vague and constituted an overbroad infringement of the plaintiffs' Ninth Amendment rights. . . .

[In Parts III and IV the Court addressed the procedural posture and justiciability of the case, concluding that the case was properly before it.— Editors]

V

The principal thrust of appellant's attack on the Texas statutes is that they improperly invade a right, said to be possessed by the pregnant woman, to choose to terminate her pregnancy. Appellant would discover this right in the concept of personal "liberty" embodied in the Fourteenth Amendment's Due Process Clause; or in personal marital, familial, and sexual privacy said to be protected by the Bill of Rights or its penumbras, see *Griswold v. Connecticut*, 381 U.S. 479 (1965); *Eisenstadt v. Baird*, 405 U.S. 438 (1972); or among those rights reserved to the people by the Ninth Amendment, *Griswold v. Connecticut*, 381 U.S., at 486 (Goldberg, J., concurring). Before addressing this claim, we feel it desirable briefly to survey, in several aspects, the history of abortion, for such insight as that history may afford us, and then to examine the state purposes and interests behind the criminal abortion laws.

VI

[Here Justice Blackmun offered a legal and cultural history of abortion. He noted the abortifacients of the Persian Empire, the practices of Greece and Rome, the opinion of the ancient Ephesian gynecologist Soranos, the condemnation of abortion in the Hippocratic Oath, the views of the Pythagoreans, the status of the fetus at common law, the history of statutes restricting abortion in England and America, the position of the American Medical Association, and a recent vote of the American Bar Association's House of Delegates.—Editors]

VII

Three reasons have been advanced to explain historically the enactment of criminal abortion laws in the 19th century and to justify their continued existence.

It has been argued occasionally that these laws were the product of a Victorian social concern to discourage illicit sexual conduct. Texas, however, does not advance this justification in the present case. . . .

A second reason is concerned with abortion as a medical procedure. When most criminal abortion laws were first enacted, the procedure was a hazardous one for the woman. . . . [I]t has been argued that a State's real concern in enacting a criminal abortion law was to protect the pregnant woman, that is, to restrain her from submitting to a procedure that placed her life in serious jeopardy.

Modern medical techniques have altered this situation. . . . Consequently, any interest of the State in protecting the woman from an inherently hazardous procedure, except when it would be equally dangerous for her to forgo it, has largely disappeared. Of course, important state interests in the areas of health and medical standards do remain. The State has a legitimate interest in seeing to it that abortion, like any other medical procedure, is performed under circumstances that insure maximum safety for the patient. . . . [T]he risk to the woman increases as her pregnancy continues. Thus, the State retains a definite interest in protecting the woman's own health and safety when an abortion is proposed at a late stage of pregnancy.

The third reason is the State's interest—some phrase it in terms of duty—in protecting prenatal life. Some of the argument for this justification rests on the theory that a new human life is present from the moment of conception. The State's interest and general obligation to protect life then extends, it is argued, to prenatal life. Only when the life of the pregnant mother herself is at stake, balanced against the life she carries within her, should the interest of the embryo or fetus not prevail. Logically, of course, a legitimate state interest in this area need not stand or fall on acceptance of the belief that life begins at conception or at some other point prior to life birth. In assessing the State's interest, recognition may be given to the less rigid claim that as long as at least *potential* life is involved, the State may assert interests beyond the protection of the pregnant woman alone. . . .

It is with these interests, and the weight to be attached to them, that this case is concerned.

VIII

The Constitution does not explicitly mention any right of privacy. In a line of decisions, however, . . . the Court has recognized that a right of personal privacy, or a guarantee of certain areas or zones of privacy, does exist under the Constitution. In varying contexts, the Court or individual Justices have, indeed, found at least the roots of that right in the First Amendment, *Stanley v. Georgia*, 394 U.S. 557, 564 (1969); in the Fourth and Fifth Amendments, *Terry v. Ohio*, 392 U.S. 1, 8–9 (1968), *Katz v. United States*, 389 U.S. 347, 350 (1967), *Boyd v. United States*, 116 U.S. 616 (1886); in the penumbras of the Bill of Rights, *Griswold v. Connecticut*, 381 U.S., at 484–485; in the Ninth Amendment, *id.*, at 486 (Goldberg, J., concurring); or in the concept of liberty guaranteed by the first section of the Fourteenth Amendment, see *Meyer v. Nebraska*, 262 U.S. 390, 399 (1923). These decisions make it clear that only personal rights that can be deemed "fundamental" or "implicit in the concept of ordered liberty," *Palko v. Connecticut*, 302 U.S. 319, 325 (1937), are included in this guarantee of personal privacy. They also make it clear that the right has some extension to activities relating to marriage, *Loving v. Virginia*, 388 U.S. 1, 12 (1967); procreation, *Skinner v. Oklahoma*, 316 U.S. 535, 541–542 (1942); contraception, *Eisenstadt v. Baird*, 405 U.S., at 453–454; family relationships, *Prince v. Massachusetts*, 321 U.S. 158, 166 (1944); and child rearing and education, *Pierce v. Society of Sisters*, 268 U.S. 510, 535 (1925).

This right of privacy, whether it be founded in the Fourteenth Amendment's concept of personal liberty and restrictions upon state action, as we feel it is, or, as the District Court determined, in the Ninth Amendment's reservation of rights to the people, is broad enough to encompass a woman's decision whether or not to terminate her pregnancy. The detriment that the State would impose upon the pregnant woman by denying this choice altogether is apparent. Specific and direct harm medically diagnosable even in early pregnancy may be involved. Maternity, or additional offspring, may force upon the woman a distressful life and future. Psychological harm may be imminent. Mental and physical health may be taxed by child care. There is also the distress, for all concerned, associated with the unwanted child, and there is the problem of bringing a child into a family already unable, psychologically and otherwise, to care for it. In other cases, as in this one, the additional difficulties and continuing stigma of unwed motherhood may be involved. All these are factors the woman and her responsible physician necessarily will consider in consultation.

On the basis of elements such as these, appellant and some *amici* argue that the woman's right is absolute and that she is entitled to terminate her pregnancy at whatever time, in whatever way, and for whatever reason she alone chooses. With this we do not agree. Appellant's arguments that Texas either has no valid interest at all in regulating the abortion decision, or no interest strong enough to support any limitation upon the woman's sole determination, are unpersuasive. The Court's decisions recognizing a right of privacy also acknowledge that some state regulation in areas protected by that right is appropriate. As noted above, a State may properly assert important interests in safeguarding health, in maintaining medical standards, and in protecting potential life. At some point in pregnancy, these respective interests become sufficiently compelling to sustain regulation of the factors that govern the abortion decision. The privacy right involved, therefore, cannot be said to be absolute. . . .

We, therefore, conclude that the right of personal privacy includes the abortion decision, but that this right is not unqualified and must be considered against important state interests in regulation. . . .

Where certain 'fundamental rights' are involved, the Court has held that regulation limiting these rights may be justified only by a "compelling state interest," and that legislative enactments must be narrowly drawn to express only the legitimate state interests at stake.

In the recent abortion cases, courts have recognized these principles. Those striking down state laws have generally scrutinized the State's interests in protecting health and potential life, and have concluded that neither interest justified broad limitations on the reasons for which a physician and his pregnant patient might decide that she should have an abortion in the early stages of pregnancy. Courts sustaining state laws have held that the State's determinations to protect health or prenatal life are dominant and constitutionally justifiable.

IX

The District Court held that the appellee failed to meet his burden of demonstrating that the Texas statute's infringement upon Roe's rights was necessary to support a compelling state interest, and that, although the appellee presented "several compelling justifications for state presence in the area of abortions," the statutes outstripped these justifications and swept "far beyond any areas of compelling state interest." Appellant and appellee both contest that holding. Appellant, as has been indicated, claims an absolute right that bars any state imposition of criminal penalties in the area. Appellee argues that the State's determination to recognize and protect prenatal life from and after conception constitutes a compelling state interest. As noted above, we do not agree fully with either formulation.

A. The appellee and certain *amici* argue that the fetus is a "person" within the language and meaning of the Fourteenth Amendment. In support of this, they outline at length and in detail the well-known facts of fetal development. If this suggestion of personhood is established, the appellant's case, of course, collapses, for the fetus' right to life would then be guaranteed specifically by the Amendment. . . . [Yet] no case could be cited that holds that a fetus is a person within the meaning of the Fourteenth Amendment.

The Constitution does not define "person" in so many words. Section 1 of the Fourteenth Amendment contains three references to "person." The first, in defining "citizens," speaks of "persons born or naturalized in the United States." The word also appears both in the Due Process Clause and in the Equal Protection Clause. "Person" is used in other places in the Constitution: in the listing of qualifications for Representatives and Senators, Art. I, § 2, cl. 2, and § 3, cl. 3; in the Apportionment Clause, Art. I, § 2, cl. 3; in the Migration and Importation provision, Art. I, § 9, cl. 1; in the Emolument Clause, Art, I, § 9, cl. 8; in the Electors provisions, Art. II, § 1, cl. 2, and the superseded cl. 3; in the provision outlining qualifications for the office of President, Art. II, § 1, cl. 5; in the Extradition provisions, Art. IV, § 2, cl. 2, and the superseded Fugitive Slave Clause 3; and in the Fifth, Twelfth, and Twenty-second Amendments, as well as in §§ 2 and 3 of the Fourteenth Amendment. But in nearly all these instances, the use of the word is such that it has application only postnatally. None indicates, with any assurance, that it has any possible prenatal application.[54]

All this, together with our observation that throughout the major portion of the 19th century prevailing legal abortion practices were far freer than they are today, persuades us that the word "person," as used in the Fourteenth Amendment, does not include the unborn. This is in accord with the results reached in those few cases where the issue has been squarely presented. . . .

This conclusion, however, does not of itself fully answer the contentions raised by Texas, and we pass on to other considerations.

B. The pregnant woman cannot be isolated in her privacy. She carries an embryo and, later, a fetus, if one accepts the medical definitions of the developing young in the human uterus. The situation therefore is inherently different from marital intimacy, or bedroom possession of obscene material, or marriage, or procreation, or education, with which *Eisenstadt* and *Griswold, Stanley, Loving, Skinner* and *Pierce* and *Meyer* were respectively concerned. As we have intimated above, it is reasonable and appropriate for a State to decide that at some point in time another interest, that of health of the mother or that of potential human life, becomes significantly involved. The woman's privacy is no longer sole and any right of privacy she possesses must be measured accordingly.

Texas urges that, apart from the Fourteenth Amendment, life begins at conception and is present throughout pregnancy, and that, therefore, the State has a compelling interest in protecting that life from and after conception. We need not resolve the difficult question of when life begins. When those trained in the respective disciplines of medicine, philosophy, and theology are unable to arrive at any consensus, the judiciary, at this

---

[54] When Texas urges that a fetus is entitled to Fourteenth Amendment protection as a person, it faces a dilemma. Neither in Texas nor in any other State are all abortions prohibited. Despite broad proscription, an exception always exists. The exception [in the Texas statute], for an abortion procured or attempted by medical advice for the purpose of saving the life of the mother, is typical. But if the fetus is a person who is not to be deprived of life without due process of law, and if the mother's condition is the sole determinant, does not the Texas exception appear to be out of line with the Amendment's command? . . .

point in the development of man's knowledge, is not in a position to speculate as to the answer. . . .

In areas other than criminal abortion, the law has been reluctant to
endorse any theory that life, as we recognize it, begins before life birth or to
accord legal rights to the unborn except in narrowly defined situations and
except when the rights are contingent upon life birth. For example, the traditional rule of tort law denied recovery for prenatal injuries even though
the child was born alive. That rule has been changed in almost every jurisdiction. . . . In short, the unborn have never been recognized in the law as
persons in the whole sense.

X

In view of all this, we do not agree that, by adopting one theory of life,
Texas may override the rights of the pregnant woman that are at stake. We
repeat, however, that the State does have an important and legitimate interest in preserving and protecting the health of the pregnant woman,
whether she be a resident of the State or a non-resident who seeks medical
consultation and treatment there, and that it has still *another* important
and legitimate interest in protecting the potentiality of human life. These
interests are separate and distinct. Each grows in substantiality as the
woman approaches term and, at a point during pregnancy, each becomes
"compelling."

With respect to the State's important and legitimate interest in the
health of the mother, the "compelling" point, in the light of present medical
knowledge, is at approximately the end of the first trimester. This is so because of the now-established medical fact that until the end of the first trimester mortality in abortion may be less than mortality in normal childbirth. It follows that, from and after this point, a State may regulate the
abortion procedure to the extent that the regulation reasonably relates to
the preservation and protection of maternal health. Examples of permissible state regulation in this area are requirements as to the qualifications of
the person who is to perform the abortion; as to the licensure of that person; as to the facility in which the procedure is to be performed, that is,
whether it must be a hospital or may be a clinic or some other place of less-
than-hospital status; as to the licensing of the facility; and the like.

This means, on the other hand, that, for the period of pregnancy prior
to this "compelling" point, the attending physician, in consultation with his
patient, is free to determine, without regulation by the State, that, in his
medical judgment, the patient's pregnancy should be terminated. If that
decision is reached, the judgment may be effectuated by an abortion free of
interference by the State.

With respect to the State's important and legitimate interest in potential life, the "compelling" point is at viability. This is so because the fetus
then presumably has the capability of meaningful life outside the mother's
womb. State regulation protective of fetal life after viability thus has both
logical and biological justifications. If the State is interested in protecting
fetal life after viability, it may go so far as to proscribe abortion during that
period, except when it is necessary to preserve the life or health of the
mother.

Measured against these standards, [the Texas statute], in restricting
legal abortions to those "procured or attempted by medical advice for the
purpose of saving the life of the mother," sweeps too broadly. The statute
makes no distinction between abortions performed early in pregnancy and

those performed later, and it limits to a single reason, "saving" the mother's life, the legal justification for the procedure. The statute, therefore, cannot survive the constitutional attack made upon it here. . . .

XI

To summarize and to repeat:

1. A state criminal abortion statute of the current Texas type, that excepts from criminality only a *life-saving* procedure on behalf of the mother, without regard to pregnancy stage and without recognition of the other interests involved, is violative of the Due Process Clause of the Fourteenth Amendment.

(a) For the stage prior to approximately the end of the first trimester, the abortion decision and its effectuation must be left to the medical judgment of the pregnant woman's attending physician.

(b) For the stage subsequent to approximately the end of the first trimester, the State, in promoting its interest in the health of the mother, may, if it chooses, regulate the abortion procedure in ways that are reasonably related to maternal health.

(c) For the stage subsequent to viability, the State in promoting its interest in the potentiality of human life may, if it chooses, regulate, and even proscribe, abortion except where it is necessary, in appropriate medical judgment, for the preservation of the life or health of the mother.

2. The State may define the term "physician," as it has been employed in the preceding paragraphs of this Part XI of this opinion, to mean only a physician currently licensed by the State, and may proscribe any abortion by a person who is not a physician as so defined.

In *Doe v. Bolton*, procedural requirements contained in one of the modern abortion statutes are considered. That opinion and this one, of course, are to be read together.[67]

This holding, we feel, is consistent with the relative weights of the respective interests involved, with the lessons and examples of medical and legal history, with the lenity of the common law, and with the demands of the profound problems of the present day. The decision leaves the State free to place increasing restrictions on abortion as the period of pregnancy lengthens, so long as those restrictions are tailored to the recognized state interests. The decision vindicates the right of the physician to administer medical treatment according to his professional judgment up to the points where important state interests provide compelling justifications for intervention. Up to those points, the abortion decision in all its aspects is inherently, and primarily, a medical decision, and basic responsibility for it must rest with the physician. If an individual practitioner abuses the privilege of exercising proper medical judgment, the usual remedies, judicial and intra-professional, are available. . . .

---

[67] Neither in this opinion nor in *Doe v. Bolton*, 410 U.S. 179, do we discuss the father's rights, if any exist in the constitutional context, in the abortion decision. No paternal right has been asserted in either of the cases, and the Texas and the Georgia statutes on their face take no cognizance of the father. We are aware that some statutes recognize the father under certain circumstances. North Carolina, for example, requires written permission for the abortion from the husband when the woman is a married minor, that is, when she is less than 18 years of age; if the woman is an unmarried minor, written permission from the parents is required. We need not now decide whether provisions of this kind are constitutional.

■ [Concurring opinions by CHIEF JUSTICE BURGER and JUSTICE DOUGLAS are omitted.]

■ MR. JUSTICE STEWART, concurring.

In 1963, this Court, in *Ferguson v. Skrupa*, 372 U.S. 726, purported to sound the death knell for the doctrine of substantive due process, a doctrine under which many state laws had in the past been held to violate the Fourteenth Amendment. As Mr. Justice Black's opinion for the Court in *Skrupa* put it: "We have returned to the original constitutional proposition that courts do not substitute their social and economic beliefs for the judgment of legislative bodies, who are elected to pass laws." *Id.*, at 730.

Barely two years later, in *Griswold v. Connecticut*, 381 U.S. 479, the Court held a Connecticut birth control law unconstitutional. In view of what had been so recently said in *Skrupa*, the Court's opinion in *Griswold* understandably did its best to avoid reliance on the Due Process Clause of the Fourteenth Amendment as the ground for decision. Yet, the Connecticut law did not violate any provision of the Bill of Rights, nor any other specific provision of the Constitution. So it was clear to me then, and it is equally clear to me now, that the *Griswold* decision can be rationally understood only as a holding that the Connecticut statute substantively invaded the "liberty" that is protected by the Due Process Clause of the Fourteenth Amendment. As so understood, *Griswold* stands as one in a long line of pre-*Skrupa* cases decided under the doctrine of substantive due process, and I now accept it as such. . . .

The asserted state interests are protection of the health and safety of the pregnant woman, and protection of the potential future human life within her. These are legitimate objectives . . . [but] I think the Court today has thoroughly demonstrated that these state interests cannot constitutionally support the broad abridgment of personal liberty worked by the existing Texas law. Accordingly, I join the Court's opinion holding that that law is invalid under the Due Process Clause of the Fourteenth Amendment.

■ MR. JUSTICE REHNQUIST, dissenting.

. . . I would reach a conclusion opposite to that reached by the Court. I have difficulty in concluding, as the Court does, that the right of "privacy" is involved in this case. Texas, by the statute here challenged, bars the performance of a medical abortion by a licensed physician on a plaintiff such as Roe. A transaction resulting in an operation such as this is not "private" in the ordinary usage of that word. Nor is the "privacy" that the Court finds here even a distant relative of the freedom from searches and seizures protected by the Fourth Amendment to the Constitution, which the Court has referred to as embodying a right to privacy. *Katz v. United States*, 389 U.S. 347 (1967).

If the Court means by the term "privacy" no more than that the claim of a person to be free from unwanted state regulation of consensual transactions may be a form of "liberty" protected by the Fourteenth Amendment, there is no doubt that similar claims have been upheld in our earlier decisions on the basis of that liberty. . . . The test traditionally applied in the area of social and economic legislation is whether or not a law such as that challenged has a rational relation to a valid state objective. *Williamson v. Lee Optical Co.*, 348 U.S. 483, 491 (1955). The Due Process Clause of the Fourteenth Amendment undoubtedly does place a limit, albeit a broad one, on legislative power to enact laws such as this. If the Texas statute were to prohibit an abortion even where the mother's life is in jeopardy, I have little doubt that such a statute would lack a rational relation to a valid state objective under the test stated in *Williamson*. But the Court's sweeping invalidation of any restrictions on abortion during the first trimester is impossible to justify under that standard, and the conscious weighing of competing factors that the Court's opinion apparently substitutes for the established test is far more appropriate to a legislative judgment than to a judicial one. . . .

While the Court's opinion quotes from the dissent of Mr. Justice Holmes in *Lochner v. New York*, 198 U.S. 45, 74 (1905), the result it reaches is more closely attuned to the majority opinion of Mr. Justice Peckham in that case. As in *Lochner* and similar cases applying substantive due process standards to economic and social welfare legislation, the adoption of the compelling state interest standard will inevitably require this Court to examine the legislative policies and pass on the wisdom of these policies in the very process of deciding whether a particular state interest put forward may or may not be "compelling." The decision here to break pregnancy into three distinct terms and to outline the permissible restrictions the State may impose in each one, for example, partakes more of judicial legislation than it does of a determination of the intent of the drafters of the Fourteenth Amendment.

The fact that a majority of the States reflecting, after all the majority sentiment in those States, have had restrictions on abortions for at least a century is a strong indication, it seems to me, that the asserted right to an abortion is not "so rooted in the traditions and conscience of our people as to be ranked as fundamental," *Snyder v. Massachusetts*, 291 U.S. 97, 105 (1934). Even today, when society's views on abortion are changing, the very existence of the debate is evidence that the "right" to an abortion is not so universally accepted as the appellant would have us believe.

To reach its result, the Court necessarily has had to find within the scope of the Fourteenth Amendment a right that was apparently completely unknown to the drafters of the Amendment. As early as 1821, the first state law dealing directly with abortion was enacted by the Connecticut Legislature. By the time of the adoption of the Fourteenth Amendment in 1868, there were at least 36 laws enacted by state or territorial legislatures limiting abortion. While many States have amended or updated their laws, 21 of the laws on the books in 1868 remain in effect today. Indeed, the Texas statute struck down today was, as the majority notes, first enacted in 1857 and "has remained substantially unchanged to the present time."

There apparently was no question concerning the validity of this provision or of any of the other state statutes when the Fourteenth Amendment was adopted. The only conclusion possible from this history is that the drafters did not intend to have the Fourteenth Amendment withdraw from the States the power to legislate with respect to this matter. . . .

■ MR. JUSTICE WHITE, with whom MR. JUSTICE REHNQUIST joins, dissenting.

At the heart of the controversy in these cases are those recurring pregnancies that pose no danger whatsoever to the life or health of the mother but are, nevertheless, unwanted for any one or more of a variety of reasons—convenience, family planning, economics, dislike of children, the embarrassment of illegitimacy, etc. The common claim before us is that for any one of such reasons, or for no reason at all, and without asserting or claiming any threat to life or health, any woman is entitled to an abortion at her request if she is able to find a medical advisor willing to undertake the procedure. . . .

With all due respect, I dissent. I find nothing in the language or history of the Constitution to support the Court's judgments. The Court simply fashions and announces a new constitutional right for pregnant women and, with scarcely any reason or authority for its action, invests that right with sufficient substance to override most existing state abortion statutes. The upshot is that the people and the legislatures of the 50 States are constitutionally disentitled to weigh the relative importance of the continued existence and development of the fetus, on the one hand, against a spectrum of possible impacts on the mother, on the other hand. As an exercise of raw judicial power, the Court perhaps has authority to do what it does today; but in my view its judgment is an improvident and extravagant exercise of the power of judicial review that the Constitution extends to this Court.

The Court apparently values the convenience of the pregnant woman more than the continued existence and development of the life or potential life that she carries. Whether or not I might agree with that marshaling of values, I can in no event join the Court's judgment because I find no constitutional warrant for imposing such an order of priorities on the people and legislatures of the States. In a sensitive area such as this, involving as it does issues over which reasonable men may easily and heatedly differ, I cannot accept the Court's exercise of its clear power of choice by interposing a constitutional barrier to state efforts to protect human life and by investing women and doctors with the constitutionally protected right to exterminate it. This issue, for the most part, should be left with the people and to the political processes the people have devised to govern their affairs. . . .

NOTES

1. *Personhood and the Fourteenth Amendment. Roe v. Wade* is, of course, one of the most controversial Supreme Court decisions of all time. The case spurs heated, emotional arguments. Start, however, with a *legal* analysis of the case. (There will be plenty of time for passionate argument once the holdings of the case have been established.)

An initial question the Court faced was whether an unborn human fetus is a "person" within the meaning of Section One of the Fourteenth Amendment: "[N]or shall any State deprive any *person* of life, liberty, or property, without due process of law; nor deny to any *person* within its jurisdiction the equal protection of the laws." The Court acknowledged the importance of this question, and at least one pre-*Roe* court had held that any claimed right to abortion must yield to the right to life of the unborn child and to the state's obligation to safeguard that life. *Steinberg v. Brown*, 321 F. Supp. 741 (N.D. Ohio 1970) ("Once human life has commenced"—which the court found as a matter of biology occurs at conception—"the constitutional protections found in the Fifth and Fourteenth Amendments impose upon the state the *duty* of safeguarding it.").

What is the proper interpretive method for ascertaining the meaning of the word "person" as used in the amendment? Is the question decided by the *text*? Is there an intrinsic meaning of the word "person"? Does it refer to all human beings—all members of the species *homo sapiens*—and if so does that include living but not yet born human fetuses? Does the answer depend on the commonplace usage of the term "person" at the time the Fourteenth Amendment was adopted? Or should the question be decided by making inferences from the Constitution's *structure* and other provisions? As Justice Blackmun notes, the other constitutional provisions that refer to "persons" are in contexts where a limitation to *born* persons is clearly contemplated. Or should the question be decided by looking to the *purpose* of the framers of the Fourteenth Amendment and whether they specifically intended that the term "person" embrace fetal human life? Is it relevant that, as Justice Rehnquist notes, in 1868 thirty-six state and territorial legislatures prohibited abortion in most situations? Does it matter that the framers of the amendment did not specifically address this issue? Is the Court free to address it in whatever way it thinks is best as a matter of *policy*? If so, as the justices resolve that policy question, what kinds of evidence should they consider—their own moral judgments about abortion? Their perceptions of societal norms? Their perceptions of scientific knowledge?

2. *Roe's Holding.* What is the scope of the abortion right recognized in *Roe*? The Court's holding requires careful parsing. First, the Court identified a substantive due process liberty of a woman to have an abortion, based in part on earlier decisions concerning the right of privacy in marriage, procreation, contraception, and the raising of children. This "right of privacy" flowed from the Fourteenth Amendment's "concept of personal liberty" and was "broad enough to encompass a woman's decision whether or not to terminate her pregnancy."

Next, the Court divided pregnancy into trimesters, based on the Court's understanding of the stages of fetal development and the ability to live independently outside of the mother's womb. The Court then crafted somewhat different rules for each trimester, based on its balancing of the mother's liberty interest against the state interest in protecting fetal human life. (That state interest, the Court held, becomes theoretically stronger, even "compelling," as pregnancy progresses.)

a. In the first trimester, the right to abortion is plenary and may be exercised for any reason the woman chooses.

b. In the second trimester, the Court permits regulations designed to protect "maternal health" but not to protect the fetus. The right to abortion in the second trimester remains plenary.

c. In the third trimester—which the Court identified as roughly the point of "viability" when the child could survive outside the mother's womb—the state interest in protecting fetal human life becomes "compelling," *but* the state nonetheless must permit abortion during this time for reasons related to the mother's health. Thus, the third trimester *exception* to the plenary right to abortion is itself made subject to a health exception.

3. *Roe's Health Exception and Doe v. Bolton.* Is the health exception narrow—in which case most late-term abortions could be prohibited? Or broad—in which case it means that a woman could almost always have an abortion, even in the eighth or ninth month of pregnancy? The answer depends on what considerations are included in "health" and who has the discretion to decide how serious a health impairment must be in order to justify a third-trimester abortion. What if carrying a child to term would delay for six months the ability of the mother to receive radiation treatment for cancer, with increased risk of death? Most everyone would agree that this is a serious risk to health—perhaps

even to life. Similarly, what if a woman is unlikely to die from the pregnancy or childbirth, but might suffer from gestational diabetes, with potentially detrimental health effects for the rest of her life? But proceed down the slope further and it becomes increasingly less obvious that the health exception should apply: How serious must the detrimental health effects be? Would the prospect of temporary but debilitating hip pain be sufficient to permit a late-term abortion? What if having a child would be a psychological burden? What if having a child would be emotionally troubling (and what sort of things should count in this category)? What if having a child would be financially difficult? An obstacle to career plans? A social embarrassment? A hateful reminder of a despised former boyfriend? What if one feels one already has too many children?

Which of these things fall within the health exception? In *Roe*'s companion case, *Doe v. Bolton*, the Court adopted a broad definition of "health" for satisfying *Roe*'s requirements and vested broad discretion in a woman and her doctor to decide whether the exception should apply. In *Doe*, the Court was considering whether Georgia's statute permitting abortions where a doctor determines that "an abortion is necessary" was too restrictive of the right to abortion recognized in *Roe*. The Court found the Georgia statute constitutional because it construed it to allow doctors to consider anything that might relate, directly or indirectly, to a woman's health: "[T]he medical judgment [of the physician] may be exercised in light of all factors—physical, emotional, psychological, familial, and the woman's age—relevant to the well-being of the patient. All these factors may relate to health." *Doe v. Bolton*, 410 U.S. at 192. How do each of the hypotheticals in the preceding paragraph come out under the Court's standard in *Doe*? Are there some reasons for having an abortion that could never fit within the health exception? Or is the consequence of *Roe*, combined with *Doe*'s elaboration of health considerations, that the Court created a constitutional right to abortion for essentially any reason, throughout all nine months of pregnancy, up to the point of birth?

4. *Constitutional Basis.* Now consider the constitutional legitimacy of *Roe* by pondering two sets of questions, each of which will provoke one side in the debate:

      a. Is there any plausible textual, structural, or historical basis for the substantive due process reasoning of *Roe*? Do the substantive due process precedents, such as *Griswold* and *Eisenstadt*, even support it? Is there anything about *Roe*'s approach to constitutional law that could not, in principle, be deployed to create a constitutional right to freedom of contract (*à la Lochner*) or a constitutional right to own slaves as property (*à la Dred Scott*)? Is there any defense to the charge that this is judicial activism?

      b. If there is no substantive due process right protecting childbirth decisions, what would prevent the government from passing and enforcing a law mandating abortions, say, when a family already has two children? From mandating forced sterilization of women who have given birth to more than two children? From mandating abortion when prenatal tests show evidence that the child would be born with Down Syndrome or a similar disability? If the Due Process Clauses do not confer substantive rights, what constitutional check is there on Congress and state legislatures enacting these laws?

5. *Alternative Grounds.* The methodology and reasoning of *Roe* have been widely criticized, both by supporters and opponents of the result that it

reached. John Hart Ely famously said that *Roe* was "*not* constitutional law and gives almost no sense of an obligation to try to be," for "*before* the Court can get to the 'balancing' stage, *before* it can worry about the next case and the case after that (or even about its institutional position) it is under an obligation to trace its premises to the charter from which it derives its authority." John Hart Ely, *The Wages of Crying Wolf: A Comment on Roe v. Wade*, 82 Yale L.J. 920, 947, 949 (1973). In response to these critiques, a number of alternative grounds for the decision have been advanced. See, e.g., WHAT *ROE V. WADE* SHOULD HAVE SAID (Jack M. Balkin, ed. 2005). Consider and evaluate the following:

a. Do laws prohibiting or restricting abortion constitute discrimination on the basis of sex, because only women become pregnant, and thus deny women the "equal protection of the laws"? For arguments in favor of this alternative ground for *Roe*, see Ruth Bader Ginsburg, *Some Thoughts on Autonomy and Equality in Relation to* Roe v. Wade, 63 N.C. L. Rev. 375 (1985); Sylvia A. Law, *Rethinking Sex and the Constitution*, 132 U. Pa. L. Rev. 855, 963 (1984); Catharine A. MacKinnon, *Reflections on Sex Equality Under Law*, 100 Yale L.J. 1281, 1311 (1991). As discussed earlier in this chapter, however, the courts have generally treated classifications keyed to pregnancy as having a disparate impact on women but not as classifications on the basis of sex. E.g., *Geduldig v. Aiello*, 417 U.S. 484, 494–97 (1974). And courts generally uphold laws that have only a disparate impact against a protected class unless there is an intent to discriminate. Would the Equal Protection Clause argument be stronger if the Court had ruled the other way in *Geduldig* (or in *Washington v. Davis*, the pivotal disparate-impact case for race)? Should those cases be overruled—should it be sufficient to establish a violation of equal protection that a law or regulation produces a disparate impact on the basis of race or sex? And would the sex-discrimination grounds for *Roe* be vitiated if a state were to hold a referendum on abortion restrictions in which only women could vote? One more question about sex discrimination and abortion: under *Roe*, may states prohibit sex-selection abortion?

b. Do abortion restrictions violate the Ninth Amendment? Note that the Court in *Roe* brushed aside this basis for its decision, even though the court below had invoked it. What are the strengths and vulnerabilities of grounding *Roe* in the Ninth Amendment? If the Ninth Amendment contains a right to abortion, what else does it contain? Is that basis for the decision less vulnerable to the charge that courts can reach whatever result they like?

c. Is the right to abortion protected by the Fourteenth Amendment's Privileges or Immunities Clause? For an argument that it is a privilege of citizenship to protect one's bodily integrity and to decide whether to become a parent, see Jack Balkin, *Abortion and Original Meaning*, 24 Const. Comm., 291, 328–336 (2007). Recall that in *Slaughter–House* the Court declined to read that clause as a font of substantive rights not tightly related to *federal* citizenship, but what if that case was wrong? If the Court were to read "the privileges or immunities of citizens of the United States" at a level of generality sufficiently high to include a right to abortion, would that provide a better basis for *Roe*? Would it provide a stronger defense to the objection that there is no constraint on what the courts can decide is a constitutional right?

d. Do abortion restrictions violate the Thirteenth Amendment by requiring the "involuntary servitude" of childbearing? For an argument in the affirmative, see Andrew Koppelman, *Forced Labor: A Thirteenth Amendment Defense of Abortion*, 84 Nw. U. L. Rev. 480 (1990). Does this stretch the language of the Thirteenth Amendment too far? Does it trivialize the Constitution's ban on true slavery? If the argument were accepted, would all legal requirements on parents be invalidated?

e. Although not an alternative ground for the result in *Roe*, an alternative approach is suggested by a draft legal opinion of the widely respected late Judge Henry Friendly of the Second Circuit in an abortion case three years before *Roe* was decided. (That case became moot before a decision on the merits.) Judge Friendly concluded that "the decision what to do about abortion is for the elected representatives of the people, not for three, or even nine, appointed judges." And he specifically rejected the plaintiffs' appeal to *Griswold*: "The type of abortion the plaintiffs particularly wish to protect against governmental sanction is the antithesis of privacy. The woman consents to intervention in the uterus by a physician, with the usual retinue of assistants, nurses, and other paramedical personnel, indeed the condition calling for such intervention may very likely have been established by clinical tests. While *Griswold* may well mean that the state cannot compel a woman to submit to an abortion, but see *Buck v. Bell*, it is exceedingly hard to read it as supporting a conclusion that the state may not prohibit other persons from committing one or even her doing so herself." The entire draft opinion is reprinted in A. Raymond Randolph, *Before Roe v. Wade: Judge Friendly's Draft Abortion Opinion*, 29 Harv. J.L. & Pub. Pol'y 1035 (2006). If Judge Friendly is right that *Griswold* cannot be extended to cover *Roe*, is there any constraint on what the state can require or restrict in relation to childbearing? Is he right that *Griswold* can be read to prohibit compelled abortion?

6. *Comparative Constitutional Law: The Decision of the German Constitutional Court.* In 1975, just two years after *Roe*, the West German Constitutional Court held that a recently enacted statute legalizing abortion during the first twelve weeks after conception violated that nation's Basic Law. See 39 BVerfGE 1 (1975). Article 2, Paragraph 2, Sentence 1 of the Basic Law provides that "Everyone [*Jeder*] has a right to life." According to the Constitutional Court, " 'Everyone' in the sense of [this provision] is 'everyone living'; expressed in another way: every life possessing human individuality; 'everyone' also includes the yet unborn human being." The court held that the "duty of the state to protect [life] is comprehensive. It forbids not only—self-evidently—direct state attacks on the life developing itself but also requires the state to take a position protecting and promoting this life, that is to say, it must, above all, preserve it even against illegal attacks by others. . . . Human life represented, within the order of the Basic Law, an ultimate value, the particulars of which need not be established; it is the living foundation of human dignity and prerequisite for all other fundamental rights." Yet the court recognized exceptions. One exception covered the first fourteen days from conception (roughly the point prior to implantation); another was a prohibition on punishing a woman for obtaining an abortion when pregnancy presents "a danger for her life or the danger of a grave impairment of her condition of health"; and another was the court's permission for the legislature to "leave the interruption of pregnancy free of punishment" in "the cases of the eugenic, ethical (criminological), and of

the social or emergency indication for abortion." The two dissenting justices did not dispute that unborn life is protected by the Basic Law, but invoked the "requirement of judicial restraint," arguing that the nature of protection to be given unborn life must be determined by the legislature. The decision of the Constitutional Court was reaffirmed following reunification of Germany in 1991, but subsequently modified to permit the legislature in certain circumstances not to prescribe punishment for first trimester abortions—notwithstanding the Court's reaffirmation that the German constitution protected the right to life of the unborn.

What accounts for the difference between the U.S. and German decisions? The decisions occurred at about the same time. Opposition to abortion is sometimes attributed to religion, but religious practice is more pervasive in the United States than in Germany. Is the German constitutional term "everyone" more comprehensive than the U.S. constitutional term "person"? Is the unqualified "right to life" under the German Basic Law different from the right of every U.S. person against deprivation of "life . . . without due process of law" and to "the equal protection of the laws"? For a translation of the German case, see 9 J. Marshall J. Prac. & Proc. 605 (1976) (R. Jonas & J. Gorby, trans). For a fuller discussion of the case, as well as a 1988 Canadian case striking down (on procedural grounds) a national law limiting abortions, see Vicki C. Jackson & Mark Tushnet, COMPARATIVE CONSTITUTIONAL LAW 74–136 (2d. ed. 2006).

7. *From Roe to Casey. Roe* led to many more cases, some arising from state laws testing the decision's limits or seeking to have it overruled or modified. Here is a brief survey of the abortion decisions between *Roe* and the next principal case, *Planned Parenthood v. Casey*, 505 U.S. 833 (1992):

a. *Fathers.* The Court struck down a state law requiring the father's consent to abortion, holding that the abortion choice belongs to the woman exclusively. *Planned Parenthood of Central Missouri v. Danforth,* 428 U.S. 52 (1976).

b. *Minors.* In a series of cases, the Court considered state laws providing for parental consent or notice in the case of a minor daughter's abortion. The Court struck down a flat requirement of parental consent, upheld parental consent if there is a "judicial bypass" alternative for a "mature" minor, and upheld some but not all forms of parental-notice (as opposed to consent) requirements. E.g., *Bellotti v. Baird,* 428 U.S. 132 (1976); *Planned Parenthood of Kansas City v. Ashcroft,* 462 U.S. 476 (1983).

c. *Funding.* The Court has upheld state and federal actions declining to fund abortion, sustaining the government's prerogative to subsidize childbirth but not abortion with Medicaid benefits. *Maher v. Roe,* 432 U.S. 464 (1977); *Harris v. McRae,* 448 U.S. 297 (1980).

d. *Regulation.* The Court invalidated state laws requiring informed consent, a waiting period, the performance of certain abortions in hospitals, the use of a particular abortion technique most likely in post-viability abortions to protect the life of the fetus, and the presence of a second physician. *Akron v. Akron Center for Reproductive Health,* 462 U.S. 416 (1983); *Thornburgh v. American College of Obstetricians & Gynecologists,* 476 U.S. 747 (1986). (Note that both cases were partially overruled in *Planned Parenthood v. Casey.*)

Then, in *Webster v. Reproductive Health Services*, 492 U.S. 490 (1989), the Court upheld a Missouri law that stated in its preamble that "the life of each human being begins at conception," that forbade most abortions at state hospitals, and that required physicians to determine if an unborn child of twenty weeks' gestational age or greater might be able to live outside the mother's womb. The decision in *Webster* led many observers to speculate that the Court was on the verge of overruling *Roe*. Five justices had voted to uphold all of the provisions of the Missouri law, though without a majority opinion or controlling rationale. And after *Webster*, two supporters of *Roe*—Justice Brennan and Justice Marshall—were replaced by justices thought to oppose it, Justice Souter and Justice Thomas. As you will soon see, though, *Webster* did not augur a total reversal of the Court's jurisprudence on abortion.

[*Assignment 71*]

The next case, *Planned Parenthood v. Casey*, 505 U.S. 833 (1992), is one of the most significant Supreme Court decisions of all time, both practically and jurisprudentially. It explicitly reaffirmed *Roe*'s embrace of a constitutional right to abortion, at a time when most observers thought that *Roe* was destined to undergo a slow, *Lochner*-style decline. Moreover, *Casey* reaffirmed a constitutional right to abortion even though a majority of the justices appear to have thought *Roe* was wrongly decided. It embraced a dramatic view of the significance of precedent and *stare decisis* in constitutional adjudication—arguably the first full-blown theory of precedent in the Court's more than two-century history. And it collated and appeared to embrace, in some form, the Court's previous substantive due process decisions.

Planned Parenthood v. Casey

505 U.S. 833 (1992)

■ JUSTICE O'CONNOR, JUSTICE KENNEDY, and JUSTICE SOUTER announced the judgment of the Court and delivered the opinion of the Court with respect to Parts I, II, III, V–A, V–C, and VI, an opinion with respect to Part V–E, in which JUSTICE STEVENS joins, and an opinion with respect to Parts IV, V–B, and V–D.

I

Liberty finds no refuge in a jurisprudence of doubt. Yet 19 years after our holding that the Constitution protects a woman's right to terminate her pregnancy in its early stages, *Roe v. Wade*, 410 U.S. 113 (1973), that definition of liberty is still questioned. Joining the respondents as amicus curiae, the United States, as it has done in five other cases in the last decade, again asks us to overrule *Roe*.

At issue in these cases are five provisions of the Pennsylvania Abortion Control Act of 1982, as amended in 1988 and 1989. The Act requires that a woman seeking an abortion give her informed consent prior to the abortion procedure, and specifies that she be provided with certain information at least 24 hours before the abortion is performed. § 3205. For a minor to obtain an abortion, the Act requires the informed consent of one of her parents, but provides for a judicial bypass option if the minor does not wish to or cannot obtain a parent's consent. § 3206. Another provision of the Act requires that, unless certain exceptions apply, a married woman seeking an abortion must sign a statement indicating that she has notified her husband of her intended abortion. § 3209. The Act exempts compliance with these three requirements in the event of a "medical emergency". . . . In addition to the above provisions regulating the performance of abortions, the Act imposes certain reporting requirements on facilities that provide abortion services. . . .

After considering the fundamental constitutional questions resolved by *Roe*, principles of institutional integrity, and the rule of *stare decisis*, we are led to conclude this: the essential holding of *Roe v. Wade* should be retained and once again reaffirmed.

It must be stated at the outset and with clarity that *Roe*'s essential holding, the holding we reaffirm, has three parts. First is a recognition of the right of the woman to choose to have an abortion before viability and to obtain it without undue interference from the State. Before viability, the State's interests are not strong enough to support a prohibition of abortion or the imposition of a substantial obstacle to the woman's effective right to elect the procedure. Second is a confirmation of the State's power to restrict abortions after fetal viability, if the law contains exceptions for pregnancies which endanger the woman's life or health.

And third is the principle that the State has legitimate interests from the outset of the pregnancy in protecting the health of the woman and the life of the fetus that may become a child. These principles do not contradict one another; and we adhere to each.

II

Constitutional protection of the woman's decision to terminate her pregnancy derives from the Due Process Clause of the Fourteenth Amendment. It declares that no State shall "deprive any person of life, liberty, or property, without due process of law." The controlling word in the cases before us is "liberty." Although a literal reading of the Clause might suggest that it governs only the procedures by which a State may deprive persons of liberty, for at least 105 years, the Clause has been understood to contain a substantive component as well, one "barring certain government actions regardless of the fairness of the procedures used to implement them." *Daniels v. Williams*, 474 U.S. 327, 331 (1986).

It is . . . tempting . . . to suppose that the Due Process Clause protects only those practices, defined at the most specific level, that were protected against government interference by other rules of law when the Fourteenth Amendment was ratified. But such a view would be inconsistent with our law. It is a promise of the Constitution that there is a realm of personal liberty which the government may not enter. We have vindicated this principle before. Marriage is mentioned nowhere in the Bill of Rights and interracial marriage was illegal in most States in the 19th century, but the Court was no doubt correct in finding it to be an aspect of liberty protected against state interference by the substantive component of the Due Process Clause in *Loving v. Virginia*, 388 U.S. 1, 12 (1967) (relying, in an opinion for eight Justices, on the Due Process Clause).

Neither the Bill of Rights nor the specific practices of States at the time of the adoption of the Fourteenth Amendment marks the outer limits of the substantive sphere of liberty which the Fourteenth Amendment protects. See U.S. Const., Amdt. 9. As the second Justice Harlan recognized:

> [T]he full scope of the liberty guaranteed by the Due Process Clause cannot be found in or limited by the precise terms of the specific guarantees elsewhere provided in the Constitution. This 'liberty' is not a series of isolated points pricked out in terms of the taking of property;

the freedom of speech, press, and religion; the right to keep and bear arms; the freedom from unreasonable searches and seizures; and so on. It is a rational continuum which, broadly speaking, includes a freedom from all substantial arbitrary impositions and purposeless restraints, . . . and which also recognizes, what a reasonable and sensitive judgment must, that certain interests require particularly careful scrutiny of the state needs asserted to justify their abridgment.

Poe v. Ullman, 367 U.S., at 543 (opinion dissenting from dismissal on jurisdictional grounds). . . .

The inescapable fact is that adjudication of substantive due process claims may call upon the Court in interpreting the Constitution to exercise that same capacity which by tradition courts always have exercised: reasoned judgment. Its boundaries are not susceptible of expression as a simple rule. That does not mean we are free to invalidate state policy choices with which we disagree; yet neither does it permit us to shrink from the duties of our office. . . .

Men and women of good conscience can disagree, and we suppose some always shall disagree, about the profound moral and spiritual implications of terminating a pregnancy, even in its earliest stage. Some of us as individuals find abortion offensive to our most basic principles of morality, but that cannot control our decision. Our obligation is to define the liberty of all, not to mandate our own moral code. The underlying constitutional issue is whether the State can resolve these philosophic questions in such a definitive way that a woman lacks all choice in the matter, except perhaps in those rare circumstances in which the pregnancy is itself a danger to her own life or health, or is the result of rape or incest.

It is conventional constitutional doctrine that where reasonable people disagree the government can adopt one position or the other. That theorem, however, assumes a state of affairs in which the choice does not intrude upon a protected liberty. . . .

Our law affords constitutional protection to personal decisions relating to marriage, procreation, contraception, family relationships, child rearing, and education. Our cases recognize "the right of the individual, married or single, to be free from unwarranted governmental intrusion into matters so fundamentally affecting a person as the decision whether to bear or beget a child." Our precedents "have respected the private realm of family life which the state cannot enter." These matters, involving the most intimate and personal choices a person may make in a lifetime, choices central to personal dignity and autonomy, are central to the liberty protected by the Fourteenth Amendment. At the heart of liberty is the right to define one's own concept of existence, of meaning, of the universe, and of the mystery of human life. Beliefs about these matters could not define the attributes of personhood were they formed under compulsion of the State.

These considerations begin our analysis of the woman's interest in terminating her pregnancy but cannot end it, for this reason: though the abortion decision may originate within the zone of conscience and belief, it is more than a philosophic exercise. Abortion is a unique act. It is an act fraught with consequences for others: for the woman who must live with the implications of her decision; for the persons who perform and assist in the procedure; for the spouse, family, and society which must confront the knowledge that these procedures exist, procedures some deem nothing short of an act of violence against innocent human life; and, depending on one's beliefs, for the life or potential life that is aborted. Though abortion is conduct, it does not follow that the State is entitled to proscribe it in all instances. That is because the liberty of the woman is at stake in a sense unique to the human condition and so unique to the law. The mother who carries a child to full term is subject to anxieties, to physical constraints, to pain that only she must bear. That these sacrifices have from the beginning of the human race been endured by woman with a pride that ennobles her in the eyes of others and gives to the infant a bond of love cannot alone be grounds for the State to insist she make the sacrifice. Her suffering is too intimate and personal for the State to insist, without more, upon its own vision of the woman's role, however dominant that vision has been in the course of our history and our culture. The destiny of the woman must be shaped to a large extent on her own conception of her spiritual imperatives and her place in society.

It should be recognized, moreover, that in some critical respects the abortion decision is of the same character as the decision to use contraception, to which *Griswold v. Connecticut*, *Eisenstadt v. Baird*, and *Carey v. Population Services International* afford constitutional protection. We have no doubt as to the correctness of those decisions. They support the reasoning in *Roe* relating to the woman's liberty because they involve personal decisions concerning not only the meaning of procreation but also human responsibility and respect for it. . . .

It was this dimension of personal liberty that *Roe* sought to protect, and its holding invoked the reasoning and the tradition of the precedents we have discussed, granting protection to substantive liberties of the person. *Roe* was, of course, an extension of those cases and, as the decision itself indicated, the separate States could act in some degree to further their own legitimate interests in protecting prenatal life. The extent to which the legislatures of the States might act to outweigh the interests of the woman in choosing to terminate her pregnancy was a subject of debate both in *Roe* itself and in decisions following it.

While we appreciate the weight of the arguments made on behalf of the State in the cases before us, arguments which in their ultimate formulation conclude that *Roe* should be overruled, the reservations any of us may have in reaffirming the central holding of *Roe* are outweighed by the explication of individual liberty we have given combined with the force of *stare decisis*.

We turn now to that doctrine.

III–A

The obligation to follow precedent begins with necessity, and a contrary necessity marks its outer limit. With Cardozo, we recognize that no judicial system could do society's work if it eyed each issue afresh in every case that raised it. See B. Cardozo, THE NATURE OF THE JUDICIAL PROCESS 149 (1921). Indeed, the very concept of the rule of law underlying our own Constitution requires such continuity over time that a respect for precedent is, by definition, indispensable. At the other extreme, a different necessity would make itself felt if a prior judicial ruling should come to be seen so clearly as error that its enforcement was for that very reason doomed.

Even when the decision to overrule a prior case is not, as in the rare, latter instance, virtually foreordained, it is common wisdom that the rule of *stare decisis* is not an "inexorable command," and certainly it is not such in every constitutional case. Rather, when this Court reexamines a prior holding, its judgment is customarily informed by a series of prudential and pragmatic considerations designed to test the consistency of overruling a prior decision with the ideal of the rule of law, and to gauge the respective costs of reaffirming and overruling a prior case. Thus, for example, we may ask whether the rule has proven to be intolerable simply in defying practical workability; whether the rule is subject to a kind of reliance that would lend a special hardship to the consequences of overruling and add inequity to the cost of repudiation; whether related principles of law have so far developed as to have left the old rule no more than a remnant of abandoned doctrine; or whether facts have so changed, or come to be seen so differently, as to have robbed the old rule of significant application or justification.

So in this case we may enquire whether *Roe*'s central rule has been found unworkable; whether the rule's limitation on state power could be removed without serious inequity to those who have relied upon it or significant damage to the stability of the society governed by it; whether the law's growth in the intervening years has left *Roe*'s central rule a doctrinal anachronism discounted by society; and whether *Roe*'s premises of fact have so far changed in the ensuing two decades as to render its central holding somehow irrelevant or unjustifiable in dealing with the issue it addressed.

1

Although *Roe* has engendered opposition, it has in no sense proven "unworkable," representing as it does a simple limitation beyond which a state law is unenforceable. While *Roe* has, of course, required judicial assessment of state laws affecting the exercise of the choice guaranteed against government infringement, and although the need for such review will remain as a consequence of today's decision, the required determinations fall within judicial competence.

2

The inquiry into reliance counts the cost of a rule's repudiation as it would fall on those who have relied reasonably on the rule's continued application. Since the classic case for weighing reliance heavily in favor of following the earlier rule occurs in the commercial context, where advance planning of great precision is most obviously a necessity, it is no cause for surprise that some would find no reliance worthy of consideration in support of *Roe*.

While neither respondents nor their *amici* in so many words deny that the abortion right invites some reliance prior to its actual exercise, one can readily imagine an argument stressing the dissimilarity of this case to one involving property or contract. . . . This argument would be premised on the hypothesis that reproductive planning could take virtually immediate account of any sudden restoration of state authority to ban abortions.

To eliminate the issue of reliance that easily, however, one would need to limit cognizable reliance to specific instances of sexual activity. But to do this would be simply to refuse to face the fact that for two decades of economic and social developments, people have organized intimate relationships and made choices that define their views of themselves and their places in society, in reliance on the availability of abortion in the event that contraception should fail. The ability of women to participate equally in the economic and social life of the Nation has been facilitated by their ability to control their reproductive lives. The Constitution serves human values, and while the effect of reliance on *Roe* cannot be exactly measured, neither can the certain cost of overruling *Roe* for people who have ordered their thinking and living around that case be dismissed.

3

No evolution of legal principle has left *Roe*'s doctrinal footings weaker than they were in 1973. No development of constitutional law since the case was decided has implicitly or explicitly left *Roe* behind as a mere survivor of obsolete constitutional thinking.

It will be recognized, of course, that *Roe* stands at an intersection of two lines of decisions, but in whichever doctrinal category one reads the case, the result for present purposes will be the same. The *Roe* Court itself placed its holding in the succession of cases most prominently exemplified by *Griswold v. Connecticut*, 381 U.S. 479 (1965). When it is so seen, *Roe* is clearly in no jeopardy, since subsequent constitutional developments have neither disturbed, nor do they threaten to diminish, the scope of recognized protection accorded to the liberty relating to intimate relationships, the family, and decisions about whether or not to beget or bear a child.

Roe, however, may be seen not only as an exemplar of *Griswold* liberty but as a rule (whether or not mistaken) of personal autonomy and bodily integrity, with doctrinal affinity to cases recognizing limits on governmental power to mandate medical treatment or to bar its rejection. If so, our cases since *Roe* accord with *Roe*'s view that a State's interest in the protection of life falls short of justifying any plenary override of individual liberty claims. *Cruzan v. Director, Mo. Dept. of Health*, 497 U.S. 261, 278 (1990). . . .

4

We have seen how time has overtaken some of *Roe*'s factual assumptions: advances in maternal health care allow for abortions safe to the mother later in pregnancy than was true in 1973, and advances in neonatal care have advanced viability to a point somewhat earlier. But these facts go only to the scheme of time limits on the realization of competing interests, and the divergences from the factual premises of 1973 have no bearing on the validity of *Roe*'s central holding, that viability marks the earliest point at which the State's interest in fetal life is constitutionally adequate to justify a legislative ban on nontherapeutic abortions. The soundness or unsoundness of that constitutional judgment in no sense turns on whether viability occurs at approximately 28 weeks, as was usual at the time of *Roe*, at 23 to 24 weeks, as it sometimes does today, or at some moment even slightly earlier in pregnancy, as it may if fetal respiratory capacity can somehow be enhanced in the future. Whenever it may occur, the attainment of viability may continue to serve as the critical fact, just as it has done since *Roe* was decided; which is to say that no change in *Roe*'s factual underpinning has left its central holding obsolete, and none supports an argument for overruling it.

5

The sum of the precedential enquiry to this point shows *Roe*'s underpinnings unweakened in any way affecting its central holding. While it has engendered disapproval, it has not been unworkable. An entire generation has come of age free to assume *Roe*'s concept of liberty in defining the capacity of women to act in society, and to make reproductive decisions; no erosion of principle going to liberty or personal autonomy has left *Roe*'s central holding a doctrinal remnant; *Roe* portends no developments at odds with other precedent for the analysis of personal liberty; and no changes of fact have rendered viability more or less appropriate as the point at which the balance of interests tips. Within the bounds of normal *stare decisis* analysis, then, and subject to the considerations on which it customarily turns, the stronger argument is for affirming *Roe*'s central holding, with whatever degree of personal reluctance any of us may have, not for overruling it.

B

In a less significant case, *stare decisis* analysis could, and would, stop at the point we have reached. But the sustained and widespread debate *Roe* has provoked calls for some comparison between that case and others of comparable dimension that have responded to national controversies and taken on the impress of the controversies addressed. Only two such decisional lines from the past century present themselves for examination, and in each instance the result reached by the Court accorded with the principles we apply today.

The first example is that line of cases identified with *Lochner v. New York*, 198 U.S. 45 (1905), which imposed substantive limitations on legislation limiting economic autonomy in favor of health and welfare regulation, adopting, in Justice Holmes's view, the theory of laissez-faire. *Id.*, at 75 (dissenting opinion). The *Lochner* decisions were exemplified by *Adkins v. Children's Hospital of District of Columbia*, 261 U.S. 525 (1923), in which this Court held it to be an infringement of constitutionally protected liberty of contract to require the employers of adult women to satisfy minimum wage standards. Fourteen years later, *West Coast Hotel Co. v. Parrish*, 300 U.S. 379 (1937), signaled the demise of *Lochner* by overruling *Adkins*. . . .

The second comparison that 20th century history invites is with the cases employing the separate-but-equal rule for applying the Fourteenth Amendment's equal protection guarantee. They began with *Plessy v. Ferguson*, 163 U.S. 537 (1896), holding that legislatively mandated racial segregation in public transportation works no denial of equal protection, rejecting the argument that racial separation enforced by the legal machinery of American society treats the black race as inferior. . . .

West Coast Hotel and *Brown* each rested on facts, or an understanding of facts, changed from those which furnished the claimed justifications for the earlier constitutional resolutions. Each case was comprehensible as the Court's response to facts that the country could understand, or had come to understand already, but which the Court of an earlier day, as its own declarations disclosed, had not been able to perceive. As the decisions were thus comprehensible they were also defensible, not merely as the victories of one doctrinal school over another by dint of numbers (victories though they were), but as applications of constitutional principle to facts as they had not been seen by the Court before. In constitutional adjudication as elsewhere in life, changed circumstances may impose new obligations, and the thoughtful part of the Nation could accept each decision to overrule a prior case as a response to the Court's constitutional duty.

Because the cases before us present no such occasion it could be seen as no such response. Because neither the factual underpinnings of *Roe*'s central holding nor our understanding of it has changed (and because no other indication of weakened precedent has been shown), the Court could not pretend to be reexamining the prior law with any justification beyond a present doctrinal disposition to come out differently from the Court of 1973. To overrule prior law for no other reason than that would run counter to the view repeated in our cases, that a decision to overrule should rest on some special reason over and above the belief that a prior case was wrongly decided.

C

The examination of the conditions justifying the repudiation of *Adkins* by *West Coast Hotel* and *Plessy* by *Brown* is enough to suggest the terrible price that would have been paid if the Court had not overruled as it did. In the present cases, however, as our analysis to this point makes clear, the terrible price would be paid for overruling. Our analysis would not be complete, however, without explaining why overruling *Roe*'s central holding would not only reach an unjustifiable result under principles of *stare decisis*, but would seriously weaken the Court's capacity to exercise the judicial power and to function as the Supreme Court of a Nation dedicated to the rule of law. To understand why this would be so it is necessary to understand the source of this Court's authority, the conditions necessary for its preservation, and its relationship to the country's understanding of itself as a constitutional Republic.

The root of American governmental power is revealed most clearly in the instance of the power conferred by the Constitution upon the Judiciary of the United States and specifically upon this Court. As Americans of each succeeding generation are rightly told, the Court cannot buy support for its decisions by spending money and, except to a minor degree, it cannot independently coerce obedience to its decrees. The Court's power lies, rather, in its legitimacy, a product of substance and perception that shows itself in the people's acceptance of the Judiciary as fit to determine what the Nation's law means and to declare what it demands.

. . . Where, in the performance of its judicial duties, the Court decides a case in such a way as to resolve the sort of intensely divisive controversy reflected in *Roe* and those rare, comparable cases, its decision has a dimension that the resolution of the normal case does not carry. It is the dimension present whenever the Court's interpretation of the Constitution calls the contending sides of a national controversy to end their national division by accepting a common mandate rooted in the Constitution.

The Court is not asked to do this very often, having thus addressed the Nation only twice in our lifetime, in the decisions of *Brown* and *Roe*. But when the Court does act in this way, its decision requires an equally rare precedential force to counter the inevitable efforts to overturn it and to thwart its implementation. Some of those efforts may be mere unprincipled emotional reactions; others may proceed from principles worthy of profound respect. But whatever the premises of opposition may be, only the most convincing justification under accepted standards of precedent could suffice to demonstrate that a later decision overruling the first was anything but a surrender to political pressure, and an unjustified repudiation of the principle on which the Court staked its authority in the first instance. So to overrule under fire in the absence of the most compelling reason to reexamine a watershed decision would subvert the Court's legitimacy beyond any serious question. . . .

The Court's duty in the present cases is clear. In 1973, it confronted the already-divisive issue of governmental power to limit personal choice to undergo abortion, for which it provided a new resolution based on the due process guaranteed by the Fourteenth Amendment. Whether or not a new social consensus is developing on that issue, its divisiveness is no less today than in 1973, and pressure to overrule the decision, like pressure to retain it, has grown only more intense. A decision to overrule *Roe*'s essential holding under the existing circumstances would address error, if error there was, at the cost of both profound and unnecessary damage to the Court's legitimacy, and to the Nation's commitment to the rule of law. It is therefore imperative to adhere to the essence of *Roe*'s original decision, and we do so today.

IV

From what we have said so far it follows that it is a constitutional liberty of the woman to have some freedom to terminate her pregnancy. We conclude that the basic decision in *Roe* was based on a constitutional analysis which we cannot now repudiate. The woman's liberty is not so unlimited, however, that from the outset the State cannot show its concern for the life of the unborn, and at a later point in fetal development the State's interest in life has sufficient force so that the right of the woman to terminate the pregnancy can be restricted.

That brings us, of course, to the point where much criticism has been directed at *Roe*, a criticism that always inheres when the Court draws a specific rule from what in the Constitution is but a general standard. We conclude, however, that the urgent claims of the woman to retain the ultimate control over her destiny and her body, claims implicit in the meaning of liberty, require us to perform that function. Liberty must not be extinguished for want of a line that is clear. And it falls to us to give some real substance to the woman's liberty to determine whether to carry her pregnancy to full term.

We conclude the line should be drawn at viability, so that before that time the woman has a right to choose to terminate her pregnancy. We adhere to this principle for two reasons. First, as we have said, is the doctrine of *stare decisis*. Any judicial act of line-drawing may seem somewhat arbitrary, but *Roe* was a reasoned statement, elaborated with great care. We have twice reaffirmed it in the face of great opposition. Although we must overrule those parts of *Thornburgh* and *Akron I* which, in our view, are inconsistent with *Roe*'s statement that the State has a legitimate interest in promoting the life or potential life of the unborn, the central premise of those cases represents an unbroken commitment by this Court to the essential holding of *Roe*. It is that premise which we reaffirm today.

The second reason is that the concept of viability, as we noted in *Roe*, is the time at which there is a realistic possibility of maintaining and nourishing a life outside the womb, so that the independent existence of the second life can in reason and all fairness be the object of state protection that now overrides the rights of the woman. Consistent with other constitutional norms, legislatures may draw lines which appear arbitrary without the necessity of offering a justification. But courts may not. We must justify the lines we draw. And there is no line other than viability which is more workable. To be sure, as we have said, there may be some medical developments that affect the precise point of viability, but this is an imprecision within tolerable limits given that the medical community and all those who must apply its discoveries will continue to explore the matter. The viability line also has, as a practical matter, an element of fairness. In some broad sense it might be said that a woman who fails to act before viability has consented to the State's intervention on behalf of the developing child.

The woman's right to terminate her pregnancy before viability is the most central principle of *Roe* v. Wade. It is a rule of law and a component of liberty we cannot renounce.

On the other side of the equation is the interest of the State in the protection of potential life. The *Roe* Court recognized the State's "important and legitimate interest in protecting the potentiality of human life." The weight to be given this state interest, not the strength of the woman's interest, was the difficult question faced in *Roe*. We do not need to say whether each of us, had we been Members of the Court when the valuation of the state interest came before it as an original matter, would have concluded, as the *Roe* Court did, that its weight is insufficient to justify a ban on abortions prior to viability even when it is subject to certain exceptions. The matter is not before us in the first instance, and coming as it does after nearly 20 years of litigation in *Roe*'s wake we are satisfied that the immediate question is not the soundness of *Roe*'s resolution of the issue, but the precedential force that must be accorded to its holding. And we have concluded that the essential holding of *Roe* should be reaffirmed.

Yet it must be remembered that *Roe v. Wade* speaks with clarity in establishing not only the woman's liberty but also the State's "important and legitimate interest in potential life." That portion of the decision in *Roe* has been given too little acknowledgment and implementation by the Court in its subsequent cases. Those cases decided that any regulation touching upon the abortion decision must survive strict scrutiny, to be sustained only if drawn in narrow terms to further a compelling state interest. See, *e.g.*, *Akron I*, *supra*, 462 U.S., at 427. Not all of the cases decided under that formulation can be reconciled with the holding in *Roe* itself that the State has legitimate interests in the health of the woman and in protecting the potential life within her. In resolving this tension, we choose to rely upon *Roe*, as against the later cases.

Roe established a trimester framework to govern abortion regulations. Under this elaborate but rigid construct, almost no regulation at all is permitted during the first trimester of pregnancy; regulations designed to protect the woman's health, but not to further the State's interest in potential life, are permitted during the second trimester; and during the third trimester, when the fetus is viable, prohibitions are permitted provided the life or health of the mother is not at stake. Most of our cases since *Roe* have involved the application of rules derived from the trimester framework.

The trimester framework no doubt was erected to ensure that the woman's right to choose not become so subordinate to the State's interest in promoting fetal life that her choice exists in theory but not in fact. We do not agree, however, that the trimester approach is necessary to accomplish this objective. A framework of this rigidity was unnecessary and in its later interpretation sometimes contradicted the State's permissible exercise of its powers.

Though the woman has a right to choose to terminate or continue her pregnancy before viability, it does not at all follow that the State is prohibited from taking steps to ensure that this choice is thoughtful and informed. Even in the earliest stages of pregnancy, the State may enact rules and regulations designed to encourage her to know that there are philosophic and social arguments of great weight that can be brought to bear in favor of continuing the pregnancy to full term and that there are procedures and institutions to allow adoption of unwanted children as well as a certain degree of state assistance if the mother chooses to raise the child herself. "[T]he Constitution does not forbid a State or city, pursuant to democratic processes, from expressing a preference for normal childbirth." *Webster v. Reproductive Health Services*, 492 U. S., at 511 (opinion of the Court). It follows that States are free to enact laws to provide a reasonable framework for a woman to make a decision that has such profound and lasting meaning. This, too, we find consistent with *Roe*'s central premises, and indeed the inevitable consequence of our holding that the State has an interest in protecting the life of the unborn.

We reject the trimester framework, which we do not consider to be part of the essential holding of *Roe*. Measures aimed at ensuring that a woman's choice contemplates the consequences for the fetus do not necessarily interfere with the right recognized in *Roe*, although those measures have been found to be inconsistent with the rigid trimester framework announced in that case. A logical reading of the central holding in *Roe* itself, and a necessary reconciliation of the liberty of the woman and the interest of the State in promoting prenatal life, require, in our view, that we abandon the trimester framework as a rigid prohibition on all previability regulation aimed at the protection of fetal life. The trimester framework suffers from these basic flaws: in its formulation it misconceives the nature of the pregnant woman's interest; and in practice it undervalues the State's interest in potential life, as recognized in *Roe*.

As our jurisprudence relating to all liberties save perhaps abortion has recognized, not every law which makes a right more difficult to exercise is, *ipso facto*, an infringement of that right. . . . Numerous forms of state regulation might have the incidental effect of increasing the cost or decreasing the availability of medical care, whether for abortion or any other medical procedure. The fact that a law which serves a valid purpose, one not designed to strike at the right itself, has the incidental effect of making it more difficult or more expensive to procure an abortion cannot be enough to invalidate it. Only where state regulation imposes an undue burden on a woman's ability to make this decision does the power of the State reach into the heart of the liberty protected by the Due Process Clause. . . .

These considerations of the nature of the abortion right illustrate that it is an overstatement to describe it as a right to decide whether to have an abortion "without interference from the State." All abortion regulations interfere to some degree with a woman's ability to decide whether to terminate her pregnancy. It is, as a consequence, not surprising that despite the protestations contained in the original *Roe* opinion to the effect that the Court was not recognizing an absolute right, the Court's experience applying the trimester framework has led to the striking down of some abortion regulations which in no real sense deprived women of the ultimate decision. Those decisions went too far because the right recognized by *Roe* is a right "to be free from unwarranted governmental intrusion into matters so fundamentally affecting a person as the decision whether to bear or beget a child." Not all governmental intrusion is of necessity unwarranted; and that brings us to the other basic flaw in the trimester framework: even in *Roe*'s terms, in practice it undervalues the State's interest in the potential life within the woman.

Roe v. Wade was express in its recognition of the State's "important and legitimate interest[s] in preserving and protecting the health of the pregnant woman [and] in protecting the potentiality of human life." The trimester framework, however, does not fulfill *Roe*'s own promise that the State has an interest in protecting fetal life or potential life. *Roe* began the contradiction by using the trimester framework to forbid any regulation of abortion designed to advance that interest before viability. Before viability, *Roe* and subsequent cases treat all governmental attempts to influence a woman's decision on behalf of the potential life within her as unwarranted. This treatment is, in our judgment, incompatible with the recognition that there is a substantial state interest in potential life throughout pregnancy.

The very notion that the State has a substantial interest in potential life leads to the conclusion that not all regulations must be deemed unwarranted. Not all burdens on the right to decide whether to terminate a pregnancy will be undue. In our view, the undue burden standard is the appropriate means of reconciling the State's interest with the woman's constitutionally protected liberty. . . .

A finding of an undue burden is a shorthand for the conclusion that a state regulation has the purpose or effect of placing a substantial obstacle in the path of a woman seeking an abortion of a nonviable fetus. A statute with this purpose is invalid because the means chosen by the State to further the interest in potential life must be calculated to inform the woman's free choice, not hinder it. And a statute which, while furthering the interest in potential life or some other valid state interest, has the effect of placing a substantial obstacle in the path of a woman's choice cannot be considered a permissible means of serving its legitimate ends. To the extent that the opinions of the Court or of individual Justices use the undue burden standard in a manner that is inconsistent with this analysis, we set out what in our view should be the controlling standard. In our considered judgment, an undue burden is an unconstitutional burden. Understood another way, we answer the question . . . whether a law designed to further the State's interest in fetal life which imposes an undue burden on the woman's decision before fetal viability could be constitutional. The answer is no.

Some guiding principles should emerge. What is at stake is the woman's right to make the ultimate decision, not a right to be insulated from all others in doing so. Regulations which do no more than create a structural mechanism by which the State, or the parent or guardian of a minor, may express profound respect for the life of the unborn are permitted, if they are not a substantial obstacle to the woman's exercise of the right to choose. Unless it has that effect on her right of choice, a state measure designed to persuade her to choose childbirth over abortion will be upheld if reasonably related to that goal. Regulations designed to foster the health of a woman seeking an abortion are valid if they do not constitute an undue burden.

Even when jurists reason from shared premises, some disagreement is inevitable. That is to be expected in the application of any legal standard which must accommodate life's complexity. We do not expect it to be otherwise with respect to the undue burden standard. We give this summary:

(a) To protect the central right recognized by *Roe v. Wade* while at the same time accommodating the State's profound interest in potential life, we will employ the undue burden analysis as explained in this opinion. An undue burden exists, and therefore a provision of law is invalid, if its purpose or effect is to place a substantial obstacle in the path of a woman seeking an abortion before the fetus attains viability.

(b) We reject the rigid trimester framework of *Roe v. Wade*. To promote the State's profound interest in potential life, throughout pregnancy the State may take measures to ensure that the woman's choice is informed, and measures designed to advance this interest will not be invalidated as long as their purpose is to persuade the woman to choose childbirth over abortion. These measures must not be an undue burden on the right.

(c) As with any medical procedure, the State may enact regulations to further the health or safety of a woman seeking an abortion. Unnecessary health regulations that have the purpose or effect of presenting a substantial obstacle to a woman seeking an abortion impose an undue burden on the right.

(d) Our adoption of the undue burden analysis does not disturb the central holding of *Roe* v. Wade, and we reaffirm that holding. Regardless of whether exceptions are made for particular circumstances, a State may not prohibit any woman from making the ultimate decision to terminate her pregnancy before viability.

(e) We also reaffirm *Roe*'s holding that "subsequent to viability, the State in promoting its interest in the potentiality of human life may, if it chooses, regulate, and even proscribe, abortion except where it is necessary, in appropriate medical judgment, for the preservation of the life or health of the mother."

These principles control our assessment of the Pennsylvania statute, and we now turn to the issue of the validity of its challenged provisions.

V

The Court of Appeals applied what it believed to be the undue burden standard and upheld each of the provisions except for the husband notification requirement. We agree generally with this conclusion, but refine the undue burden analysis in accordance with the principles articulated above. We now consider the separate statutory sections at issue. . . .

A

Because it is central to the operation of various other requirements, we begin with the statute's definition of medical emergency. Under the statute, a medical emergency is "[t]hat condition which, on the basis of the physician's good faith clinical judgment, so complicates the medical condition of a pregnant woman as to necessitate the immediate abortion of her pregnancy to avert her death or for which a delay will create serious risk of substantial and irreversible impairment of a major bodily function."

Petitioners argue that the definition is too narrow, contending that it forecloses the possibility of an immediate abortion despite some significant health risks. . . .

The District Court found that there were three serious conditions which would not be covered by the statute: preeclampsia, inevitable abortion, and premature ruptured membrane. Yet, as the Court of Appeals observed, it is undisputed that under some circumstances each of these conditions could lead to an illness with substantial and irreversible consequences. While the definition could be interpreted in an unconstitutional manner, the Court of Appeals construed the phrase "serious risk" to include those circumstances. . . . [We] conclude that, as construed by the Court of Appeals, the medical emergency definition imposes no undue burden on a woman's abortion right.

B

We next consider the informed consent requirement. Except in a medical emergency, the statute requires that at least 24 hours before performing an abortion a physician inform the woman of the nature of the procedure, the health risks of the abortion and of childbirth, and the "probable gestational age of the unborn child." The physician or a qualified nonphysician must inform the woman of the availability of printed materials published by the State describing the fetus and providing information about medical assistance for childbirth, information about child support from the father, and a list of agencies which provide adoption and other services as alternatives to abortion. An abortion may not be performed unless the woman certifies in writing that she has been informed of the availability of these printed materials and has been provided them if she chooses to view them.

Our prior decisions establish that as with any medical procedure, the State may require a woman to give her written informed consent to an abortion. In this respect, the statute is unexceptional. Petitioners challenge the statute's definition of informed consent because it includes the provision of specific information by the doctor and the mandatory 24–hour waiting period. The conclusions reached by a majority of the Justices in the separate opinions filed today and the undue burden standard adopted in this opinion require us to overrule in part some of the Court's past decisions, decisions driven by the trimester framework's prohibition of all previability regulations designed to further the State's interest in fetal life.

In *Akron I*, 462 U.S. 416, we invalidated an ordinance which required that a woman seeking an abortion be provided by her physician with specific information "designed to influence the woman's informed choice between abortion or childbirth." As we later described the *Akron I* holding in *Thornburgh v. American College of Obstetricians and Gynecologists*, 476 U.S., at 762, there were two purported flaws in the Akron ordinance: the information was designed to dissuade the woman from having an abortion and the ordinance imposed "a rigid requirement that a specific body of information be given in all cases, irrespective of the particular needs of the patient. . . ."

To the extent *Akron I* and *Thornburgh* find a constitutional violation when the government requires, as it does here, the giving of truthful, nonmisleading information about the nature of the procedure, the attendant health risks and those of childbirth, and the "probable gestational age" of the fetus, those cases go too far, are inconsistent with *Roe*'s acknowledgment of an important interest in potential life, and are overruled. This is clear even on the very terms of *Akron I* and *Thornburgh*. Those decisions, along with *Danforth*, recognize a substantial government interest justifying a requirement that a woman be apprised of the health risks of abortion and childbirth. It cannot be questioned that psychological well-being is a facet of health. Nor can it be doubted that most women considering an abortion would deem the impact on the fetus relevant, if not dispositive, to the decision. In attempting to ensure that a woman apprehend the full consequences of her decision, the State furthers the legitimate purpose of reducing the risk that a woman may elect an abortion, only to discover later, with devastating psychological consequences, that her decision was not fully informed. If the information the State requires to be made available to the woman is truthful and not misleading, the requirement may be permissible.

We also see no reason why the State may not require doctors to inform a woman seeking an abortion of the availability of materials relating to the consequences to the fetus, even when those consequences have no direct relation to her health. An example illustrates the point. We would think it constitutional for the State to require that in order for there to be informed consent to a kidney transplant operation the recipient must be supplied with information about risks to the donor as well as risks to himself or herself. A requirement that the physician make available information similar to that mandated by the statute here was described in *Thornburgh* as "an outright attempt to wedge the Commonwealth's message discouraging abortion into the privacy of the informed-consent dialogue between the woman and her physician." We conclude, however, that informed choice need not be defined in such narrow terms that all considerations of the effect on the fetus are made irrelevant. As we have made clear, we depart from the holdings of *Akron I* and *Thornburgh* to the extent that we permit a State to further its legitimate goal of protecting the life of the unborn by enacting legislation aimed at ensuring a decision that is mature and informed, even when in so doing the State expresses a preference for childbirth over abortion. In short, requiring that the woman be informed of the availability of information relating to fetal development and the assistance available should she decide to carry the pregnancy to full term is a reasonable measure to ensure an informed choice, one which might cause the woman to choose childbirth over abortion. This requirement cannot be considered a substantial obstacle to obtaining an abortion, and, it follows, there is no undue burden.

Our prior cases also suggest that the "straitjacket" of particular information which must be given in each case interferes with a constitutional right of privacy between a pregnant woman and her physician. As a preliminary matter, it is worth noting that the statute now before us does not require a physician to comply with the informed consent provisions "if he or she can demonstrate by a preponderance of the evidence, that he or she reasonably believed that furnishing the information would have resulted in a severely adverse effect on the physical or mental health of the patient." In this respect, the statute does not prevent the physician from exercising his or her medical judgment.

Whatever constitutional status the doctor-patient relation may have as a general matter, in the present context it is derivative of the woman's position. The doctor-patient relation does not underlie or override the two more general rights under which the abortion right is justified: the right to make family decisions and the right to physical autonomy. On its own, the doctor-patient relation here is entitled to the same solicitude it receives in other contexts. Thus, a requirement that a doctor give a woman certain information as part of obtaining her consent to an abortion is, for constitutional purposes, no different from a requirement that a doctor give certain specific information about any medical procedure.

All that is left of petitioners' argument is an asserted First Amendment right of a physician not to provide information about the risks of abortion, and childbirth, in a manner mandated by the State. To be sure, the physician's First Amendment rights not to speak are implicated, but only as part of the practice of medicine, subject to reasonable licensing and regulation by the State. We see no constitutional infirmity in the requirement that the physician provide the information mandated by the State here.

The Pennsylvania statute also requires us to reconsider the holding in *Akron I* that the State may not require that a physician, as opposed to a qualified assistant, provide information relevant to a woman's informed consent. Since there is no evidence on this record that requiring a doctor to give the information as provided by the statute would amount in practical terms to a substantial obstacle to a woman seeking an abortion, we conclude that it is not an undue burden. . . .

Our analysis of Pennsylvania's 24–hour waiting period between the provision of the information deemed necessary to informed consent and the performance of an abortion under the undue burden standard requires us to reconsider the premise behind the decision in *Akron I* invalidating a parallel requirement. In *Akron I* we said: "Nor are we convinced that the State's legitimate concern that the woman's decision be informed is reasonably served by requiring a 24–hour delay as a matter of course." We consider that conclusion to be wrong. The idea that important decisions will be more informed and deliberate if they follow some period of reflection does not strike us as unreasonable, particularly where the statute directs that important information become part of the background of the decision. The statute, as construed by the Court of Appeals, permits avoidance of the waiting period in the event of a medical emergency and the record evidence shows that in the vast majority of cases, a 24–hour delay does not create any appreciable health risk. In theory, at least, the waiting period is a reasonable measure to implement the State's interest in protecting the life of the unborn, a measure that does not amount to an undue burden.

Whether the mandatory 24–hour waiting period is nonetheless invalid because in practice it is a substantial obstacle to a woman's choice to terminate her pregnancy is a closer question. The findings of fact by the District Court indicate that because of the distances many women must travel to reach an abortion provider, the practical effect will often be a delay of much more than a day because the waiting period requires that a woman seeking an abortion make at least two visits to the doctor. The District Court also found that in many instances this will increase the exposure of women seeking abortions to "the harassment and hostility of anti-abortion protestors demonstrating outside a clinic." As a result, the District Court found that for those women who have the fewest financial resources, those who must travel long distances, and those who have difficulty explaining their whereabouts to husbands, employers, or others, the 24–hour waiting period will be "particularly burdensome."

These findings are troubling in some respects, but they do not demonstrate that the waiting period constitutes an undue burden. We do not doubt that, as the District Court held, the waiting period has the effect of "increasing the cost and risk of delay of abortions," but the District Court did not conclude that the increased costs and potential delays amount to substantial obstacles. . . . Yet, as we have stated, under the undue burden standard a State is permitted to enact persuasive measures which favor childbirth over abortion, even if those measures do not further a health interest. And while the waiting period does limit a physician's discretion, that is not, standing alone, a reason to invalidate it. In light of the construction given the statute's definition of medical emergency by the Court of Appeals, and the District Court's findings, we cannot say that the waiting period imposes a real health risk.

We also disagree with the District Court's conclusion that the "particularly burdensome" effects of the waiting period on some women require its invalidation. A particular burden is not of necessity a substantial obstacle. Whether a burden falls on a particular group is a distinct inquiry from whether it is a substantial obstacle even as to the women in that group. And the District Court did not conclude that the waiting period is such an obstacle even for the women who are most burdened by it. Hence, on the record before us, and in the context of this facial challenge, we are not convinced that the 24–hour waiting period constitutes an undue burden.

We are left with the argument that the various aspects of the informed consent requirement are unconstitutional because they place barriers in the way of abortion on demand. Even the broadest reading of *Roe,* however, has not suggested that there is a constitutional right to abortion on demand. Rather, the right protected by *Roe* is a right to decide to terminate a pregnancy free of undue interference by the State. Because the informed consent requirement facilitates the wise exercise of that right, it cannot be classified as an interference with the right *Roe* protects. The informed consent requirement is not an undue burden on that right.

C

Section 3209 of Pennsylvania's abortion law provides, except in cases of medical emergency, that no physician shall perform an abortion on a married woman without receiving a signed statement from the woman that she has notified her spouse that she is about to undergo an abortion. The woman has the option of providing an alternative signed statement certifying that her husband is not the man who impregnated her; that her husband could not be located; that the pregnancy is the result of spousal sexual assault which she has reported; or that the woman believes that notifying her husband will cause him or someone else to inflict bodily injury upon her. A physician who performs an abortion on a married woman without receiving the appropriate signed statement will have his or her license revoked, and is liable to the husband for damages.

. . . In well-functioning marriages, spouses discuss important intimate decisions such as whether to bear a child. But there are millions of women in this country who are the victims of regular physical and psychological abuse at the hands of their husbands. Should these women become pregnant, they may have very good reasons for not wishing to inform their husbands of their decision to obtain an abortion. Many may have justifiable fears of physical abuse, but may be no less fearful of the consequences of reporting prior abuse to the Commonwealth of Pennsylvania. Many may have a reasonable fear that notifying their husbands will provoke further instances of child abuse; these women are not exempt from § 3209's notification requirement. Many may fear devastating forms of psychological abuse from their husbands, including verbal harassment, threats of future violence, the destruction of possessions, physical confinement to the home, the withdrawal of financial support, or the disclosure of the abortion to family and friends. These methods of psychological abuse may act as even more of a deterrent to notification than the possibility of physical violence, but women who are the victims of the abuse are not exempt from § 3209's notification requirement. And many women who are pregnant as a result of sexual assaults by their husbands will be unable to avail themselves of the exception for spousal sexual assault, § 3209(b)(3), because the exception requires that the woman have notified law enforcement authorities within 90 days of the assault, and her husband will be notified of her report once an investigation begins, § 3128(c). If anything in this field is certain, it is that victims of spousal sexual assault are extremely reluctant to report the abuse to the government; hence, a great many spousal rape victims will not be exempt from the notification requirement imposed by § 3209.

The spousal notification requirement is thus likely to prevent a significant number of women from obtaining an abortion. It does not merely make abortions a little more difficult or expensive to obtain; for many women, it will impose a substantial obstacle. We must not blind ourselves to the fact that the significant number of women who fear for their safety and the safety of their children are likely to be deterred from procuring an abortion as surely as if the Commonwealth had outlawed abortion in all cases.

Respondents attempt to avoid the conclusion that § 3209 is invalid by pointing out that it imposes almost no burden at all for the vast majority of women seeking abortions. They begin by noting that only about 20 percent of the women who obtain abortions are married. They then note that of these women about 95 percent notify their husbands of their own volition. Thus, respondents argue, the effects of § 3209 are felt by only one percent of the women who obtain abortions. . . . The analysis does not end with the one percent of women upon whom the statute operates; it begins there. . . . The proper focus of constitutional inquiry is the group for whom the law is a restriction, not the group for whom the law is irrelevant. . . . The unfortunate yet persisting conditions we document above will mean that in a large fraction of the cases in which § 3209 is relevant, it will operate as a substantial obstacle to a woman's choice to undergo an abortion. It is an undue burden, and therefore invalid.

This conclusion is in no way inconsistent with our decisions upholding parental notification or consent requirements. Those enactments, and our judgment that they are constitutional, are based on the quite reasonable assumption that minors will benefit from consultation with their parents and that children will often not realize that their parents have their best interests at heart. We cannot adopt a parallel assumption about adult women. . . .

Section 3209 embodies a view of marriage . . . repugnant to our present understanding of marriage and of the nature of the rights secured by the Constitution. Women do not lose their constitutionally protected liberty when they marry. The Constitution protects all individuals, male or female, married or unmarried, from the abuse of governmental power, even where that power is employed for the supposed benefit of a member of the individual's family. These considerations confirm our conclusion that § 3209 is invalid.

D

We next consider the parental consent provision. Except in a medical emergency, an unemancipated young woman under 18 may not obtain an abortion unless she and one of her parents (or guardian) provides informed consent as defined above. If neither a parent nor a guardian provides consent, a court may authorize the performance of an abortion upon a determination that the young woman is mature and capable of giving informed consent and has in fact given her informed consent, or that an abortion would be in her best interests.

We . . . reaffirm today, that a State may require a minor seeking an abortion to obtain the consent of a parent or guardian, provided that there is an adequate judicial bypass procedure. . . .

E

Under the recordkeeping and reporting requirements of the statute, every facility which performs abortions is required to file a report stating its name and address as well as the name and address of any related entity, such as a controlling or subsidiary organization. In the case of state-funded institutions, the information becomes public.

For each abortion performed, a report must be filed identifying: [information respecting the physician, facility, patient, and abortion procedure]. Every abortion facility must also file quarterly reports showing the number of abortions performed broken down by trimester. In all events, the identity of each woman who has had an abortion remains confidential.

In *Danforth,* 428 U.S., at 80, we held that recordkeeping and reporting provisions "that are reasonably directed to the preservation of maternal health and that properly respect a patient's confidentiality and privacy are permissible." We think that under this standard, all the provisions at issue here, except that relating to spousal notice, are constitutional. Although they do not relate to the State's interest in informing the woman's choice, they do relate to health. The collection of information with respect to actual patients is a vital element of medical research, and so it cannot be said that the requirements serve no purpose other than to make abortions more difficult. Nor do we find that the requirements impose a substantial obstacle to a woman's choice. At most they might increase the cost of some abortions by a slight amount. While at some point increased cost could become a substantial obstacle, there is no such showing on the record before us. . . .

VI

Our Constitution is a covenant running from the first generation of Americans to us and then to future generations. It is a coherent succession. Each generation must learn anew that the Constitution's written terms embody ideas and aspirations that must survive more ages than one. We accept our responsibility not to retreat from interpreting the full meaning of the covenant in light of all of our precedents. We invoke it once again to define the freedom guaranteed by the Constitution's own promise, the promise of liberty. . . .

■ JUSTICE STEVENS, concurring in part and dissenting in part.

. . . The Court is unquestionably correct in concluding that the doctrine of *stare decisis* has controlling significance in a case of this kind, notwithstanding an individual Justice's concerns about the merits. The central holding of *Roe v. Wade,* 410 U.S. 113 (1973), has been a "part of our law" for almost two decades. It was a natural sequel to the protection of individual liberty established in *Griswold v. Connecticut,* 381 U.S. 479 (1965). The societal costs of overruling *Roe* at this late date would be enormous. *Roe* is an integral part of a correct understanding of both the concept of liberty and the basic equality of men and women. . . .

■ JUSTICE BLACKMUN, concurring in part, concurring in the judgment in part, and dissenting in part.

. . . Three years ago, in *Webster v. Reproductive Health Services,* 492 U.S. 490 (1989), four Members of this Court appeared poised to "cas[t] into darkness the hopes and visions of every woman in this country" who had come to believe that the Constitution guaranteed her the right to reproductive choice. All that remained between the promise of *Roe* and the darkness of the plurality was a single, flickering flame. Decisions since *Webster* gave little reason to hope that this flame would cast much light. But now, just when so many expected the darkness to fall, the flame has grown bright. I do not underestimate the significance of today's joint opinion. Yet I remain steadfast in my belief that the right to reproductive choice is entitled to the full protection afforded by this Court before *Webster.* And I fear for the darkness as four Justices anxiously await the single vote necessary to extinguish the light.

Make no mistake, the joint opinion of Justices O'CONNOR, KENNEDY, and SOUTER is an act of personal courage and constitutional principle.... The Court's reaffirmation of *Roe*'s central holding is also based on the force of *stare decisis*.... In the 19 years since *Roe* was decided, that case has shaped more than reproductive planning—"[a]n entire generation has come of age free to assume *Roe*'s concept of liberty in defining the capacity of women to act in society, and to make reproductive decisions." The Court understands that, having "call[ed] the contending sides ... to end their national division by accepting a common mandate rooted in the Constitution," a decision to overrule *Roe* "would seriously weaken the Court's capacity to exercise the judicial power and to function as the Supreme Court of a Nation dedicated to the rule of law." What has happened today should serve as a model for future Justices and a warning to all who have tried to turn this Court into yet another political branch....

In one sense, the Court's approach is worlds apart from that of THE CHIEF JUSTICE and Justice SCALIA. And yet, in another sense, the distance between the two approaches is short—the distance is but a single vote.

I am 83 years old. I cannot remain on this Court forever, and when I do step down, the confirmation process for my successor well may focus on the issue before us today. That, I regret, may be exactly where the choice between the two worlds will be made.

■ CHIEF JUSTICE REHNQUIST, with whom JUSTICE WHITE, JUSTICE SCALIA, and JUSTICE THOMAS join, concurring in the judgment in part and dissenting in part.

The joint opinion, following its newly minted variation on *stare decisis*, retains the outer shell of *Roe v. Wade*, 410 U.S. 113 (1973), but beats a wholesale retreat from the substance of that case. We believe that *Roe* was wrongly decided, and that it can and should be overruled consistently with our traditional approach to *stare decisis* in constitutional cases. We would adopt the approach of the plurality in *Webster v. Reproductive Health Services*, 492 U.S. 490 (1989), and uphold the challenged provisions of the Pennsylvania statute in their entirety....

We have held that a liberty interest protected under the Due Process Clause of the Fourteenth Amendment will be deemed fundamental if it is "implicit in the concept of ordered liberty." *Palko v. Connecticut*, 302 U.S. 319, 325 (1937). Three years earlier we referred to a "principle of justice so rooted in the traditions and conscience of our people as to be ranked as fundamental." These expressions are admittedly not precise, but our decisions implementing this notion of "fundamental" rights do not afford any more elaborate basis on which to base such a classification.

In construing the phrase "liberty" incorporated in the Due Process Clause of the Fourteenth Amendment, we have recognized that its meaning extends beyond freedom from physical restraint. In *Pierce v. Society of Sisters*, 268 U.S. 510 (1925), we held that it included a parent's right to send a child to private school; in *Meyer v. Nebraska*, 262 U.S. 390 (1923), we held that it included a right to teach a foreign language in a parochial school. Building on these cases, we have held that the term "liberty" includes a right to marry, *Loving v. Virginia*, 388 U.S. 1 (1967); a right to procreate, *Skinner v. Oklahoma ex rel. Williamson*, 316 U.S. 535 (1942); and a right to use contraceptives, *Griswold v. Connecticut*, 381 U.S. 479 (1965); *Eisenstadt v. Baird*, 405 U.S. 438 (1972). But a reading of these opinions makes clear that they do not endorse any all-encompassing "right of privacy."

In *Roe v. Wade*, the Court recognized a "guarantee of personal privacy" which "is broad enough to encompass a woman's decision whether or not to terminate her pregnancy." We are now of the view that, in terming this right fundamental, the Court in *Roe* read the earlier opinions upon which it based its decision much too broadly. Unlike marriage, procreation, and contraception, abortion "involves the purposeful termination of a potential life." The abortion decision must therefore "be recognized as *sui generis*, different in kind from the others that the Court has protected under the rubric of personal or family privacy and autonomy." One cannot ignore the fact that a woman is not isolated in her pregnancy, and that the decision to abort necessarily involves the destruction of a fetus.

Nor do the historical traditions of the American people support the view that the right to terminate one's pregnancy is "fundamental." The common law which we inherited from England made abortion after "quickening" an offense. At the time of the adoption of the Fourteenth Amendment, statutory prohibitions or restrictions on abortion were commonplace; in 1868, at least 28 of the then–37 States and 8 Territories had statutes banning or limiting abortion. By the turn of the century virtually every State had a law prohibiting or restricting abortion on its books. . . . On this record, it can scarcely be said that any deeply rooted tradition of relatively unrestricted abortion in our history supported the classification of the right to abortion as "fundamental" under the Due Process Clause of the Fourteenth Amendment.

We think, therefore, both in view of this history and of our decided cases dealing with substantive liberty under the Due Process Clause, that the Court was mistaken in *Roe* when it classified a woman's decision to terminate her pregnancy as a "fundamental right" that could be abridged only in a manner which withstood "strict scrutiny." . . . The Court in *Roe* reached too far when it analogized the right to abort a fetus to the rights involved in *Pierce, Meyer, Loving*, and *Griswold*, and thereby deemed the right to abortion fundamental.

The joint opinion of Justices O'CONNOR, KENNEDY, and SOUTER cannot bring itself to say that *Roe* was correct as an original matter, but the authors are of the view that "the immediate question is not the soundness of *Roe*'s resolution of the issue, but the precedential force that must be accorded to its holding." Instead of claiming that *Roe* was correct as a matter of original constitutional interpretation, the opinion therefore contains an elaborate discussion of *stare decisis*. . . . *Roe* analyzed abortion regulation under a rigid trimester framework, a framework which has guided this Court's decisionmaking for 19 years. The joint opinion rejects that framework.

Stare decisis is defined in Black's Law Dictionary as meaning "to abide by, or adhere to, decided cases." Whatever the "central holding" of *Roe* that is left after the joint opinion finishes dissecting it is surely not the result of that principle. While purporting to adhere to precedent, the joint opinion instead revises it. *Roe* continues to exist, but only in the way a storefront on a western movie set exists: a mere facade to give the illusion of reality. Decisions following *Roe*, such as *Akron* and *Thornburgh*, are frankly overruled in part under the "undue burden" standard expounded in the joint opinion.

In our view, authentic principles of *stare decisis* do not require that any portion of the reasoning in *Roe* be kept intact. "*Stare decisis* is not . . . a universal, inexorable command," especially in cases involving the interpretation of the Federal Constitution. Erroneous decisions in such constitutional cases are uniquely durable, because correction through legislative action, save for constitutional amendment, is impossible. It is therefore our duty to reconsider constitutional interpretations that "depar[t] from a proper understanding" of the Constitution. Our constitutional watch does not cease merely because we have spoken before on an issue; when it becomes clear that a prior constitutional interpretation is unsound we are obliged to reexamine the question. See, *e.g.*, *West Virginia Bd. of Ed. v. Barnette*, 319 U.S. 624, 642 (1943); *Erie R. Co. v. Tompkins*, 304 U.S. 64, 74–78 (1938).

The joint opinion discusses several *stare decisis* factors which, it asserts, point toward retaining a portion of *Roe*. Two of these factors are that the main "factual underpinning" of *Roe* has remained the same, and that its doctrinal foundation is no weaker now than it was in 1973. Of course, what might be called the basic facts which gave rise to *Roe* have remained the same—women become pregnant, there is a point somewhere, depending on medical technology, where a fetus becomes viable, and women give birth to children. But this is only to say that the same facts which gave rise to *Roe* will continue to give rise to similar cases. It is not a reason, in and of itself, why those cases must be decided in the same incorrect manner as was the first case to deal with the question. And surely there is no requirement, in considering whether to depart from *stare decisis* in a constitutional case, that a decision be more wrong now than it was at the time it was rendered. If that were true, the most outlandish constitutional decision could survive forever, based simply on the fact that it was no more outlandish later than it was when originally rendered.

The joint opinion also points to the reliance interests involved in this context in its effort to explain why precedent must be followed for precedent's sake. . . . But, as the joint opinion apparently agrees, any traditional notion of reliance is not applicable here. The Court today cuts back on the protection afforded by *Roe,* and no one claims that this action defeats any reliance interest in the disavowed trimester framework. Similarly, reliance interests would not be diminished were the Court to go further and acknowledge the full error of *Roe,* as "reproductive planning could take virtually immediate account of" this action. . . .

In the end, having failed to put forth any evidence to prove any true reliance, the joint opinion's argument is based solely on generalized assertions about the national psyche, on a belief that the people of this country have grown accustomed to the *Roe* decision over the last 19 years and have "ordered their thinking and living around" it. . . . [A]t various points in the past, the same could have been said about this Court's erroneous decisions that the Constitution allowed "separate but equal" treatment of minorities, see *Plessy v. Ferguson*, 163 U.S. 537 (1896), or that "liberty" under the Due Process Clause protected "freedom of contract," see *Adkins v. Children's Hospital of District of Columbia*, 261 U.S. 525 (1923); *Lochner v. New York*, 198 U.S. 45 (1905). The "separate but equal" doctrine lasted 58 years after *Plessy*, and *Lochner*'s protection of contractual freedom lasted 32 years. However, the simple fact that a generation or more had grown used to these major decisions did not prevent the Court from correcting its errors in those cases, nor should it prevent us from correctly interpreting the Constitution here.

Apparently realizing that conventional *stare decisis* principles do not support its position, the joint opinion advances a belief that retaining a portion of *Roe* is necessary to protect the "legitimacy" of this Court. . . . But the joint opinion goes on to state that when the Court "resolve[s] the sort of intensely divisive controversy reflected in *Roe* and those rare, comparable cases," its decision is exempt from reconsideration under established principles of *stare decisis* in constitutional cases. This is so, the joint opinion contends, because in those "intensely divisive" cases the Court has "call[ed] the contending sides of a national controversy to end their national division by accepting a common mandate rooted in the Constitution," and must therefore take special care not to be perceived as "surrender[ing] to political pressure" and continued opposition. This is a truly novel principle, one which is contrary to both the Court's historical practice and to the Court's traditional willingness to tolerate criticism of its opinions. Under this principle, when the Court has ruled on a divisive issue, it is apparently prevented from overruling that decision for the sole reason that it was incorrect, *unless opposition to the original decision has died away.*

The first difficulty with this principle lies in its assumption that cases that are "intensely divisive" can be readily distinguished from those that are not. The question of whether a particular issue is "intensely divisive" enough to qualify for special protection is entirely subjective and dependent on the individual assumptions of the Members of this Court. In addition, because the Court's duty is to ignore public opinion and criticism on issues that come before it, its Members are in perhaps the worst position to judge whether a decision divides the Nation deeply enough to justify such uncommon protection. Although many of the Court's decisions divide the populace to a large degree, we have not previously on that account shied away from applying normal rules of *stare decisis* when urged to reconsider earlier decisions. Over the past 21 years, for example, the Court has overruled in whole or in part 34 of its previous constitutional decisions.

The joint opinion picks out and discusses two prior Court rulings that it believes are of the "intensely divisive" variety, and concludes that they are of comparable dimension to *Roe.* It appears to us very odd indeed that the joint opinion chooses as benchmarks two cases in which the Court chose not to adhere to erroneous constitutional precedent, but instead enhanced its stature by acknowledging and correcting its error, apparently in violation of the joint opinion's "legitimacy" principle. See *West Coast Hotel Co. v. Parrish*; *Brown v. Board of Education.* One might also wonder how it is that the joint opinion puts these, and not others, in the "intensely divisive" category, and how it assumes that these are the only two lines of cases of comparable dimension to *Roe.* . . .

There are other reasons why the joint opinion's discussion of legitimacy is unconvincing as well. In assuming that the Court is perceived as "surrender[ing] to political pressure" when it overrules a controversial decision, the joint opinion forgets that there are two sides to any controversy. The joint opinion asserts that, in order to protect its legitimacy, the Court must refrain from overruling a controversial decision lest it be viewed as favoring those who oppose the decision. But a decision to *adhere* to prior precedent is subject to the same criticism, for in such a case one can easily argue that the Court is responding to those who have demonstrated in favor of the original decision. . . . But this perceived dilemma arises only if one assumes, as the joint opinion does, that the Court should make its decisions with a view toward speculative public perceptions. If one assumes instead, as the Court surely did in both *Brown* and *West Coast Hotel*, that the Court's legitimacy is enhanced by faithful interpretation of the Constitution irrespective of public opposition, such self-engendered difficulties may be put to one side. . . .

■ JUSTICE SCALIA, with whom THE CHIEF JUSTICE, JUSTICE WHITE, and JUSTICE THOMAS join, concurring in the judgment in part and dissenting in part.

. . . The Court's reliance upon *stare decisis* can best be described as contrived. It insists upon the necessity of adhering not to all of *Roe*, but only to what it calls the "central holding." It seems to me that *stare decisis* ought to be applied even to the doctrine of *stare decisis*, and I confess never to have heard of this new, keep-what-you-want-and-throw-away-the-rest version. . . .

The Imperial Judiciary lives. It is instructive to compare [the joint opinion's] Nietzschean vision of us unelected, life-tenured judges—leading a Volk who will be "tested by following," and whose very "belief in themselves" is mystically bound up in their "understanding" of a Court that "speak[s] before all others for their constitutional ideals"—with the somewhat more modest role envisioned for these lawyers by the Founders.

"The judiciary . . . has . . . no direction either of the strength or of the wealth of the society, and can take no active resolution whatever. It may truly be said to have neither Force nor Will, but merely judgment. . . ." The Federalist No. 78.

. . . It is particularly difficult, in the circumstances of the present decision, to sit still for the Court's lengthy lecture upon the virtues of "constancy," of "remain[ing] steadfast," and adhering to "principle." Among the five justices who purportedly adhere to *Roe*, at most three agree upon the *principle* that constitutes adherence (the joint opinion's "undue burden" standard)—and that principle is inconsistent with *Roe*. To make matters worse, two of the three, in order thus to remain steadfast, had to abandon previously stated positions. . . . The only principle the Court "adheres" to, it seems to me, is the principle that the Court must be seen as standing by *Roe*. . . .

I cannot agree with, indeed I am appalled by, the Court's suggestion that the decision whether to stand by an erroneous constitutional decision must be strongly influenced—against overruling, no less—by the substantial and continuing public opposition the decision has generated. The Court's judgment that any other course would "subvert the Court's legitimacy" must be another consequence of reading the error-filled history book that described the deeply divided country brought together by *Roe*. In my history book, the Court was covered with dishonor and deprived of legitimacy by *Dred Scott v. Sandford*, 19 How. 393 (1857), an erroneous (and widely opposed) opinion that it did not abandon, rather than by *West Coast Hotel Co. v. Parrish*, 300 U.S. 379 (1937), which produced the famous "switch in time" from the Court's erroneous (and widely opposed) constitutional opposition to the social measures of the New Deal. (Both *Dred Scott* and one line of the cases resisting the New Deal rested upon the concept of "substantive due process" that the Court praises and employs today.) Indeed, *Dred Scott* was "very possibly the first application of substantive due process in the Supreme Court, the original precedent for *Lochner v. New York* and *Roe v. Wade*." D. Currie, The Constitution in the Supreme Court 271 (1985). . . .

There is a poignant aspect to today's opinion. Its length, and what might be called its epic tone, suggest that its authors believe they are bringing to an end a troublesome era in the history of our Nation and of our Court. "It is the dimension" of authority, they say, to "cal[l] the contending sides of national controversy to end their national division by accepting a common mandate rooted in the Constitution."

There comes vividly to mind a portrait by Emanuel Leutze that hangs in the Harvard Law School: Roger Brooke Taney, painted in 1859, the 82d year of his life, the 24th of his Chief Justiceship, the second after his opinion in *Dred Scott*. He is all in black, sitting in a shadowed red armchair, left hand resting upon a pad of paper in his lap, right hand hanging limply, almost lifelessly, beside the inner arm of the chair. He sits facing the viewer and staring straight out. There seems to be on his face, and in his deep-set eyes, an expression of profound sadness and disillusionment. Perhaps he always looked that way, even when dwelling upon the happiest of thoughts. But those of us who know how the lustre of his great Chief Justiceship came to be eclipsed by *Dred Scott* cannot help believing that he had that case—its already apparent consequences for the Court and its soon-to-be-played-out consequences for the Nation—burning on his mind. I expect that two years earlier he, too, had thought himself "call[ing] the contending sides of national controversy to end their national division by accepting a common mandate rooted in the Constitution."

It is no more realistic for us in this litigation, than it was for him in that, to think that an issue of the sort they both involved—an issue involving life and death, freedom and subjugation—can be "speedily and finally settled" by the Supreme Court, as President James Buchanan in his inaugural address said the issue of slavery in the territories would be. Quite to the contrary, by foreclosing all democratic outlet for the deep passions this issue arouses, by banishing the issue from the political forum that gives all participants, even the losers, the satisfaction of a fair hearing and an honest fight, by continuing the imposition of a rigid national rule instead of allowing for regional differences, the Court merely prolongs and intensifies the anguish.

We should get out of this area, where we have no right to be, and where we do neither ourselves nor the country any good by remaining.

NOTES

1. *Casey* is a massively important case, arguably even more significant—at least in some respects—than the case it reaffirmed, *Roe v. Wade*:

a. *Abortion*. *Casey*'s reaffirming of what the Joint Opinion called the "central holding" of *Roe* was a judicial act of enormous consequence. *Roe* had been the rule for nineteen years, from 1973 to 1992. *Casey* could have overruled *Roe* but instead reaffirmed it. *Casey*, rather than *Roe*, accounts for the constitutional law of abortion since 1992. Under any view, the decision affects millions of lives every year. For supporters, the decision vindicated the freedom of millions of women, indeed of all women, to have an abortion—a right regarded by many (and by the opinion) as central to women's identity and freedom. For opponents, the decision consigned more than a million innocent unborn lives to death every year. No matter one's view of the merits, the stakes are huge.

The decision in *Casey* came as a bit of a surprise. Based on votes in earlier cases, one could have reasonably predicted that as many as seven justices might have voted to uphold all of the provisions of Pennsylvania's law, and either overrule or seriously undercut *Roe*. Justice O'Connor and Justice Kennedy had been on record as sharply critical of *Roe,* and both had voted to uphold all aspects of the Missouri law at issue in *Webster* in 1989. Justice Souter also had been predicted by some to be a vote against *Roe*. Nevertheless, *Casey* did not reverse *Roe*. Instead, the Joint Opinion reaffirmed it, but it also replaced its trimester framework with a new "undue burden" test.

b. *Substantive Due Process.* Part II of the Joint Opinion, which commanded a majority of the Court, reaffirmed the judicial practice of reviewing and invalidating laws based on substantive due process (albeit less on grounds that the approach is correct than on grounds of *stare decisis*). This was a significant doctrinal development, and it has had an enduring impact not only in abortion law but also in the Court's assisted-suicide and sexual-privacy cases.

c. *Stare Decisis.* Part III of the Joint Opinion sets forth a full-blown judicial theory of *stare decisis*—somewhat surprisingly, for the first time in the Court's history—and appears to make that theory the centerpiece of the decision. The Joint Opinion repeatedly implies that at least some of the justices forming the majority would not have thought *Roe* correct as an original matter, and that the outcome of *Casey* is attributable to the force of precedent. Is there any other case where the Court has reached a result in a major constitutional case contrary to what a majority thought the Constitution actually requires or permits for the stated reason of following precedent?

d. *Judicial Supremacy.* Part of the Court's explanation for adhering to *Roe* was that overruling a case on which it had "staked its authority" would "seriously weaken the Court's capacity to exercise the judicial power and to function as the Supreme Court of a nation dedicated to the rule of law." What do you make of this? Is the Court's legitimacy a legitimate consideration? Should the justices seek to preserve their political capital as they are deciding cases? Is the Court right that it is—and needs to be perceived as—the ultimate authority in understanding the Constitution? Whatever one's answer to these questions, *Casey* is a major declaration about the role of the Supreme Court in constitutional interpretation.

2. The Supreme Court has never said that *stare decisis* is absolute, and it has overruled hundreds of its prior constitutional decisions. The Court in *Casey* cited several factors relevant to deciding whether to overrule or adhere to a prior decision: "workability," "reliance," whether a precedent is a mere "remnant of abandoned doctrine," whether there have been "changed facts," and public perceptions of "judicial integrity" and the maintenance of the Court's institutional prestige and power. Evaluate each consideration. Which ones are you persuaded of? Which of these considerations (if any) trump the importance of deciding a constitutional question correctly? Or are these considerations part of what it actually means to decide a constitutional question correctly? How would these criteria, faithfully applied, decide a case like *Brown*, in light of decades of contrary precedent since *Plessy*? Or *West Coast Hotel*, after the decades of *Lochner*-style substantive due process decisions? Are you persuaded by

Casey's explanation of why those precedents were rightly overruled? Can the *Casey* standard for adherence to precedent be squared with *Casey*'s own over-ruling of two prior abortion decisions (*Akron* and *Thornburgh*)? After you have considered how this standard would apply to *Brown*, *West Coast Hotel*, and *Casey* itself, think again about the criteria for when the Court should follow prec-edent. Can these factors be applied in a principled manner, or are they inher-ently subject to manipulation?

Interestingly, the Court did not assert that *stare decisis* is constitutionally required but only that it was a doctrine of judicial policy. If the doctrine is one of mere policy, can it be abrogated by Congress? Indeed, taking the reasoning one step further, if adherence to precedent is a matter of judicial policy, is it proper for the Court as a general matter to reach outcomes for policy reasons that it would otherwise conclude are contrary to the Constitution? Is it proper for the other branches to depart from the Constitution for policy reasons? Or would such a departure by any of the branches be inconsistent with *Marbury*'s rule that the Constitution is supreme? If so, what—if anything—makes such a policy-driven approach appropriate for the judiciary? See generally Michael Stokes Paulsen, *Abrogating Stare Decisis by Statute: May Congress Remove the Precedential Effect of* Roe *and* Casey?, 109 Yale L.J. 1535 (2000).

3. In what ways does *Casey* change abortion law? First, consider the re-placement of *Roe*'s trimester framework with a straight pre-/post-viability line. Does this change alter the circumstances in which the state could prohibit or limit the availability of abortion? (Note that *Casey* retains the requirement of a health exception that would permit aborting even viable fetuses in some cir-cumstances.) Are there any abortions that states may prohibit under *Casey* that they could not prohibit under *Roe*? Are there any abortions that states may prohibit under either *Roe* or *Casey*?

Next, consider *Casey*'s embrace of Justice O'Connor's preferred "undue burden" standard for pre-viability abortions. Under *Roe*, any law affecting the choice of abortion prior to viability was subject to "strict scrutiny" because it violated the fundamental right to privacy; the state needed a compelling inter-est to justify the restriction. Under *Casey*, only laws that impose an "undue burden" on the choice to abort (before viability) receive strict scrutiny. What is an "undue burden"? The Court spoke in terms of whether a state regulation "has the purpose or effect of placing a substantial obstacle in the path of a woman seeking an abortion of a nonviable fetus." A state must choose means "calculated to inform the woman's free choice, not hinder it." But as long as the state does not impose an undue burden it can "create a structural mechanism" that "express[es] profound respect for the life of the unborn," or adopt measures that are "designed to persuade" a woman "to choose childbirth over abortion" or "to foster [her] health." What does this mean in practice? What clues are af-forded by the regulations the Court upheld (with the Joint Opinion constituting only a plurality view): twenty-four-hour waiting periods and informed consent requirements? What clues are afforded by the regulations the Court struck down: the spousal notification requirements? Under *Casey*'s "undue burden" standard, is there any type of pre-viability abortion that a state may ban en-tirely? Could it ban sex-selection abortions? Under *Casey*'s "undue burden" standard, may a state require that an ultrasound of the human fetus be taken and shown to the mother, along with information about the stage of fetal devel-opment? Could a state require abortion providers to give pregnant women a leaflet stating that abortion "is the killing of your baby, an independent living human being"?

In all, what do you think of the "undue burden" standard? Does it preserve the essence of *Roe*? Does it gut *Roe*? Does it have a more plausible basis in the text, structure, logic, and history of the Constitution?

4. Does *Casey* essentially claim in Part 2 that the advance of women's economic and social equality over the past generation has been attributable, at least in part, to the ready availability of abortion as a back-up method of birth control? What is your reaction to this? Is it offensive and demeaning to women? Is it descriptively accurate? Is the availability of abortion essential to women's equality? Was sex equality the unarticulated true premise of the Court's decision in *Casey* in a way that differed from the reasoning of *Roe*? Is it instructive that the one provision of the Pennsylvania law not upheld by the Joint Opinion was the one requiring spousal notification? What do you think of the Court's reasoning on that point?

5. What do you think of Justice Blackmun's partial concurrence and its invocation of the "light" and the "darkness"? What was he alluding to? Perhaps it was J.R.R. Tolkien, who wrote for a character in *The Fellowship of the Ring*: "Torment in the dark was the danger that I feared, and it did not hold me back. But I would not have come, had I known the danger of light and joy." Or perhaps it was the first chapter of the Gospel of John, which says: "In him was life, and the life was the light of men. The light shines in the darkness, and the darkness has not overcome it." Did Justice Blackmun, the author of *Roe*, see himself as "the light" and his opponents as forces of "darkness"? Did he see himself as a martyr for the cause of *Roe*? Is Justice Blackmun's opinion—noting his age—almost an invitation to make the issue of abortion and *Roe* a subject of the then-upcoming presidential campaign of 1992 and of judicial confirmation hearings concerning his successor? Is that appropriate?

6. Chief Justice Rehnquist's dissent states that the majority has abandoned *Roe* and merely left its outer shell. What do you think? Did he miss the import of *Casey* entirely? Is he trying to "spin" the consequences of the majority's holding? Is there evidence in the style and writing of the first part of his dissent that it may at one time have been a draft *majority* opinion going the other way? What is your assessment of his criticisms of the majority's reliance on *stare decisis*? In what ways do the dissent of Chief Justice Rehnquist and the dissent of Justice Scalia diverge?

7. Since *Casey*, the Court has decided two momentous abortion cases: *Stenberg v. Carhart*, 530 U.S. 914 (2000) (*Carhart I*), and *Gonzales v. Carhart*, 550 U.S. 124 (2007) (*Carhart II*). These cases present nearly identical issues of whether government may ban a particular *manner* of late-term abortion colloquially referred to as "partial-birth" abortion but known in medical terms as "dilation and extraction" or "D & X" abortion. A warning: the clinical descriptions of the procedures in the following paragraph—and even more so in the Court's opinions in these cases—are graphic.

Because of the typically late stage of pregnancy at which the procedure is performed, the fetus cannot be suctioned out of the womb whole by vacuum tube (as is typical in a "dilation and evacuation," or "D & E," abortion). Accordingly, in a D & X abortion, the doctor first dilates the woman's cervix, induces labor, and delivers the fetus, except for the head (which is too large). The doctor then punctures the skull with a scissors or another sharp surgical tool, suctions out the mostly born fetus's brain matter with a vacuum tube, collapses the skull, and proceeds to deliver the head, completing the abortion.

In *Carhart I*, Nebraska purported to prohibit this manner of abortion procedure. Why? What difference does it make *how* an abortion is performed? Was the prohibition intended to make a political or moral point, with no material effect on the number of abortions? Is this a legitimate purpose for an abortion restriction? Does it constitute an "undue burden" on the abortion choice under *Casey*? In *Carhart I*, a 5–4 majority struck down Nebraska's law on the grounds that (1) the law was vague and might be construed to prohibit even (more common) D & E abortions, thus creating an "undue burden" on the choice of abortion, as that term was used in *Casey*; and (2) the law lacked a health-of-the-mother exception, as required by *Roe*, *Doe*, and *Casey,* and thus could not be applied even to prohibit D & X abortions after the point of viability.

In *Carhart II*, decided seven years later, the Court (again in a 5–4 ruling) upheld Congress's slightly different partial-birth prohibition, distinguishing but not overruling *Carhart I*. (The difference is explained by the retirement and replacement of one of the justices in the *Carhart I* majority.) The Court found the federal statute not to be vague because it was, the Court said, clearly limited only to D & X abortion procedures and could not be construed to prohibit the alternative D & E method. To what extent, then, does the Court's decision rest on the fact that the federal law does not place an "undue burden" on the right to abortion *because there is always another available method of abortion*? Is that consistent with *Casey*? Is it a logical extension of *Casey*?

[*Assignment 72*]

E. SUBSTANTIVE DUE PROCESS AND CONSTITUTIONAL INTERPRETATION

The next three cases raise in especially acute ways the methodology of substantive due process. As you read them, think of the following questions: If the Supreme Court is going to be in the business of invalidating laws as violations of substantive due process, what principles should it use? How should it decide which liberties to protect? Should it look primarily to the past, the present, or the future? What answers are most consistent with the powers, limits, and duties that the Constitution gives to Congress, the president, and the courts? And consider this always-useful thought experiment: How would you answer these questions if you knew that the Court was entirely composed of people who disagreed with all of your most strongly held values and beliefs?

Washington v. Glucksberg
521 U.S. 702 (1997)

■ CHIEF JUSTICE REHNQUIST delivered the opinion of the Court.

The question presented in this case is whether Washington's prohibition against "caus[ing]" or "aid[ing]" a suicide offends the Fourteenth Amendment to the United States Constitution. We hold that it does not.

It has always been a crime to assist a suicide in the State of Washington. In 1854, Washington's first Territorial Legislature outlawed "assisting another in the commission of self-murder." Today, Washington law provides: "A person is guilty of promoting a suicide attempt when he knowingly causes or aids another person to attempt suicide." "Promoting a suicide attempt" is a felony, punishable by up to five years' imprisonment and up to a $10,000 fine. At the same time, Washington's Natural Death Act, enacted in 1979, states that the "withholding or withdrawal of life-sustaining treatment" at a patient's direction "shall not, for any purpose, constitute a suicide."

Petitioners in this case are the State of Washington and its Attorney General. Respondents . . . are physicians who practice in Washington. These doctors occasionally treat terminally ill, suffering patients, and declare that they would assist these patients in ending their lives if not for Washington's assisted-suicide ban[, which they argue] . . . is, on its face, unconstitutional.

The plaintiffs asserted "the existence of a liberty interest protected by the Fourteenth Amendment which extends to a personal choice by a mentally competent, terminally ill adult to commit physician-assisted suicide." . . .

We begin, as we do in all due process cases, by examining our Nation's history, legal traditions, and practices. See, *e.g.*, *Casey*, at 849–850; *Moore v. East Cleveland*, 431 U.S. 494, 503 (1977) (plurality opinion) (noting importance of "careful 'respect for the teachings of history' "). In almost every State—indeed, in almost every western democracy—it is a crime to assist a suicide. The States' assisted-suicide bans are not innovations. Rather, they are longstanding expressions of the States' commitment to the protection and preservation of all human life. . . .

More specifically, for over 700 years, the Anglo–American common-law tradition has punished or otherwise disapproved of both suicide and assisting suicide. . . . Sir William Blackstone, whose Commentaries on the Laws of England not only provided a definitive summary of the common law but was also a primary legal authority for 18th– and 19th–century American lawyers, referred to suicide as "self-murder" and "the pretended heroism, but real cowardice, of the Stoic philosophers, who destroyed themselves to avoid those ills which they had not the fortitude to endure. . . ." Blackstone emphasized that "the law has . . . ranked [suicide] among the highest crimes," although, anticipating later developments, he conceded that the harsh and shameful punishments imposed for suicide "borde[r] a little upon severity."

For the most part, the early American Colonies adopted the common-law approach. . . . [For example,] Virginia . . . required ignominious burial for suicides, and their estates were forfeit to the Crown.

Over time, however, the American Colonies abolished these harsh common-law penalties. . . . [T]he movement away from the common law's harsh sanctions did not represent an acceptance of suicide; rather, . . . this change reflected the growing consensus that it was unfair to punish the suicide's family for his wrongdoing. Nonetheless, although States moved away from Blackstone's treatment of suicide, courts continued to condemn it as a grave public wrong.

That suicide remained a grievous, though nonfelonious, wrong is confirmed by the fact that colonial and early state legislatures and courts did not retreat from prohibiting assisting suicide. . . . The earliest American statute explicitly to outlaw assisting suicide was enacted in New York in

1828, and many of the new States and Territories followed New York's example.... By the time the Fourteenth Amendment was ratified, it was a crime in most States to assist a suicide....

The Washington statute at issue in this case was enacted in 1975 as part of a revision of that State's criminal code. Four years later, Washington passed its Natural Death Act, which specifically stated that the "withholding or withdrawal of life-sustaining treatment ... shall not, for any purpose, constitute a suicide" and that "[n]othing in this chapter shall be construed to condone, authorize, or approve mercy killing...." In 1991, Washington voters rejected a ballot initiative which, had it passed, would have permitted a form of physician-assisted suicide. Washington then added a provision to the Natural Death Act expressly excluding physician-assisted suicide.

... [M]any proposals to legalize assisted-suicide have been and continue to be introduced in the States' legislatures, but none has been enacted.... [T]he States are currently engaged in serious, thoughtful examinations of physician-assisted suicide and other similar issues....

Attitudes toward suicide itself have changed ... but our laws have consistently condemned, and continue to prohibit, assisting suicide. Despite changes in medical technology and notwithstanding an increased emphasis on the importance of end-of-life decisionmaking, we have not retreated from this prohibition. Against this backdrop of history, tradition, and practice, we now turn to respondents' constitutional claim.

The Due Process Clause guarantees more than fair process, and the "liberty" it protects includes more than the absence of physical restraint. The Clause also provides heightened protection against government interference with certain fundamental rights and liberty interests. In a long line of cases, we have held that, in addition to the specific freedoms protected by the Bill of Rights, the "liberty" specially protected by the Due Process Clause includes the rights to marry; to have children; to direct the education and upbringing of one's children; to marital privacy; to use contraception; to bodily integrity; and to abortion. We have also assumed, and strongly suggested, that the Due Process Clause protects the traditional right to refuse unwanted lifesaving medical treatment.

But we "ha[ve] always been reluctant to expand the concept of substantive due process because guideposts for responsible decisionmaking in this unchartered area are scarce and open-ended." By extending constitutional protection to an asserted right or liberty interest, we, to a great extent, place the matter outside the arena of public debate and legislative action. We must therefore "exercise the utmost care whenever we are asked to break new ground in this field," lest the liberty protected by the Due Process Clause be subtly transformed into the policy preferences of the Members of this Court.

Our established method of substantive-due-process analysis has two primary features: First, we have regularly observed that the Due Process Clause specially protects those fundamental rights and liberties which are, objectively, "deeply rooted in this Nation's history and tradition," [*Moore v. East Cleveland,* 431 U.S. 494, 503 (1977) (plurality opinion)], and "implicit in the concept of ordered liberty," such that "neither liberty nor justice would exist if they were sacrificed," *Palko v. Connecticut,* 302 U.S. 319, 325, 326 (1937). Second, we have required in substantive-due-process cases a "careful description" of the asserted fundamental liberty interest. Our Nation's history, legal traditions, and practices thus provide the crucial "guideposts for responsible decisionmaking," that direct and restrain our exposition of the Due Process Clause. . . .

Justice SOUTER, relying on Justice Harlan's dissenting opinion in *Poe v. Ullman,* would largely abandon this restrained methodology, and instead ask "whether [Washington's] statute sets up one of those 'arbitrary impositions' or 'purposeless restraints' at odds with the Due Process Clause of the Fourteenth Amendment." In our view, however, the development of this Court's substantive-due-process jurisprudence has been a process whereby the outlines of the "liberty" specially protected by the Fourteenth Amendment—never fully clarified, to be sure, and perhaps not capable of being fully clarified—have at least been carefully refined by concrete examples involving fundamental rights found to be deeply rooted in our legal tradition. This approach tends to rein in the subjective elements that are necessarily present in due-process judicial review. In addition, by establishing a threshold requirement—that a challenged state action implicate a fundamental right before requiring more than a reasonable relation to a legitimate state interest to justify the action, it avoids the need for complex balancing of competing interests in every case.

Turning to the claim at issue here, the Court of Appeals stated that "[p]roperly analyzed, the first issue to be resolved is whether there is a liberty interest in determining the time and manner of one's death," or, in other words, "[i]s there a right to die?" Similarly, respondents assert a "liberty to choose how to die" and a right to "control of one's final days," and describe the asserted liberty as "the right to choose a humane, dignified death," and "the liberty to shape death." As noted above, we have a tradition of carefully formulating the interest at stake in substantive-due-process cases. For example, although *Cruzan v. Missouri Dep't of Health,* 497 U.S. 261 (1990), is often described as a "right to die" case, we were, in fact, more precise: We assumed that the Constitution granted competent persons a "constitutionally protected right to refuse lifesaving hydration and nutrition." The Washington statute at issue in this case prohibits "aid[ing] another person to attempt suicide," and, thus, the question before us is whether the "liberty" specially protected by the Due Process Clause includes a right to commit suicide which itself includes a right to assistance in doing so.

We now inquire whether this asserted right has any place in our Nation's traditions. Here, as discussed, we are confronted with a consistent and almost universal tradition that has long rejected the asserted right, and continues explicitly to reject it today, even for terminally ill, mentally competent adults. To hold for respondents, we would have to reverse centuries of legal doctrine and practice, and strike down the considered policy choice of almost every State.

Respondents contend, however, that the liberty interest they assert *is* consistent with this Court's substantive-due-process line of cases, if not with this Nation's history and practice. Pointing to *Casey* and *Cruzan,* respondents read our jurisprudence in this area as reflecting a general tradition of "self-sovereignty," and as teaching that the "liberty" protected by the Due Process Clause includes "basic and intimate exercises of personal autonomy." According to respondents, our liberty jurisprudence, and the broad, individualistic principles it reflects, protects the "liberty of competent, terminally ill adults to make end-of-life decisions free of undue government interference." The question presented in this case, however, is whether the protections of the Due Process Clause include a right to commit suicide with another's assistance. With this "careful description" of respondents' claim in mind, we turn to *Casey* and *Cruzan.*

In *Cruzan,* we considered whether Nancy Beth Cruzan, who had been severely injured in an automobile accident and was in a persistive vegetative state, "ha[d] a right under the United States Constitution which would require the hospital to withdraw life-sustaining treatment" at her parents' request. . . . After reviewing a long line of relevant state cases, we concluded that "the common-law doctrine of informed consent is viewed as generally encompassing the right of a competent individual to refuse medical treatment." Next, we reviewed our own cases on the subject, and stated that "[t]he principle that a competent person has a constitutionally protected liberty interest in refusing unwanted medical treatment may be inferred from our prior decisions." Therefore, "for purposes of [that] case, we assume[d] that the United States Constitution would grant a competent person a constitutionally protected right to refuse lifesaving hydration and nutrition." We concluded that, notwithstanding this right, the Constitution permitted Missouri to require clear and convincing evidence of an incompetent patient's wishes concerning the withdrawal of life-sustaining treatment.

Respondents contend that in *Cruzan* we "acknowledged that competent, dying persons have the right to direct the removal of life-sustaining medical treatment and thus hasten death," and that "the constitutional principle behind recognizing the patient's liberty to direct the withdrawal of artificial life support applies at least as strongly to the choice to hasten impending death by consuming lethal medication." . . .

The right assumed in *Cruzan,* however, was not simply deduced from abstract concepts of personal autonomy. Given the common-law rule that forced medication was a battery, and the long legal tradition protecting the decision to refuse unwanted medical treatment, our assumption was entirely consistent with this Nation's history and constitutional traditions. The decision to commit suicide with the assistance of another may be just as personal and profound as the decision to refuse unwanted medical treatment, but it has never enjoyed similar legal protection. Indeed, the two acts are widely and reasonably regarded as quite distinct. In *Cruzan* itself, we recognized that most States outlawed assisted suicide—and even more do today—and we certainly gave no intimation that the right to refuse unwanted medical treatment could be somehow transmuted into a right to assistance in committing suicide.

Respondents also rely on *Casey.* . . . The Court of Appeals, like the District Court, found *Casey* "highly instructive" and "almost prescriptive" for determining "what liberty interest may inhere in a terminally ill person's choice to commit suicide": "Like the decision of whether or not to have an abortion, the decision how and when to die is one of the most intimate and personal choices a person may make in a lifetime, a choice central to personal dignity and autonomy."

Similarly, respondents emphasize the statement in *Casey* that: "At the heart of liberty is the right to define one's own concept of existence, of meaning, of the universe, and of the mystery of human life. Beliefs about these matters could not define the attributes of personhood were they formed under compulsion of the State." By choosing this language, the Court's opinion in *Casey* described, in a general way and in light of our prior cases, those personal activities and decisions that this Court has identified as so deeply rooted in our history and traditions, or so fundamental to our concept of constitutionally ordered liberty, that they are protected by the Fourteenth Amendment. . . . That many of the rights and liberties protected by the Due Process Clause sound in personal autonomy does not warrant the sweeping conclusion that any and all important, intimate, and personal decisions are so protected, and *Casey* did not suggest otherwise.

The history of the law's treatment of assisted suicide in this country has been and continues to be one of the rejection of nearly all efforts to permit it. That being the case, our decisions lead us to conclude that the asserted "right" to assistance in committing suicide is not a fundamental liberty interest protected by the Due Process Clause. The Constitution also requires, however, that Washington's assisted-suicide ban be rationally related to legitimate government interests. This requirement is unquestionably met here. As the court below recognized,[20] Washington's assisted-suicide ban implicates a number of state interests. . . .

We therefore hold that [the Washington statute] does not violate the Fourteenth Amendment, either on its face or "as applied to competent, terminally ill adults who wish to hasten their deaths by obtaining medication prescribed by their doctors." . . .

Throughout the Nation, Americans are engaged in an earnest and profound debate about the morality, legality, and practicality of physician-assisted suicide. Our holding permits this debate to continue, as it should in a democratic society. The decision of the en banc Court of Appeals is reversed, and the case is remanded for further proceedings consistent with this opinion.

■ JUSTICE SOUTER, concurring in the judgment.

. . . The question is whether the statute sets up one of those "arbitrary impositions" or "purposeless restraints" at odds with the Due Process Clause of the Fourteenth Amendment. *Poe v. Ullman,* 367 U.S. 497 (1961) (Harlan, J., dissenting). I conclude that the statute's application to the doctors has not been shown to be unconstitutional, but I write separately to give my reasons for analyzing the substantive due process claims as I do, and for rejecting this one. . . .

[Here Justice Souter offered a lengthy history of due process, including Magna Carta's guarantee of "the law of the land," U.S. federal and state constitutional provisions, and the development of substantive due process in the Supreme Court. Among the Court decisions discussed are Dred Scott; the substantive due process decisions of the Lochner era, which he called "the echo of Dred Scott"; and the modern substantive due process doctrine reflected in Griswold, Roe, and Casey. Justice Souter approved of the second Justice Harlan's dissent in Poe v. Ullman as the legitimate judicial approach to substantive due process. That dissent is quoted at length earlier in this chapter in the notes following Griswold.—Editors]

This enduring tradition of American constitutional practice is, in Justice Harlan's view, nothing more than what is required by the judicial authority and obligation to construe constitutional text and review legislation for conformity to that text. Like many judges who preceded him and many who followed, he found it impossible to construe the text of due process

---

[20] The court identified and discussed six state interests: (1) preserving life; (2) preventing suicide; (3) avoiding the involvement of third parties and use of arbitrary, unfair, or undue influence; (4) protecting family members and loved ones; (5) protecting the integrity of the medical profession; and (6) avoiding future movement toward euthanasia and other abuses.

without recognizing substantive, and not merely procedural, limitations. "Were due process merely a procedural safeguard it would fail to reach those situations where the deprivation of life, liberty or property was accomplished by legislation which by operating in the future could, given even the fairest possible procedure in application to individuals, nevertheless destroy the enjoyment of all three." The text of the Due Process Clause thus imposes nothing less than an obligation to give substantive content to the words "liberty" and "due process of law." . . .

My understanding of unenumerated rights in the wake of the *Poe* dissent and subsequent cases avoids the absolutist failing of many older cases without embracing the opposite pole of equating reasonableness with past practice described at a very specific level. See *Planned Parenthood v. Casey*, 505 U.S., at 847–849. That understanding begins with a concept of "ordered liberty," *Poe*, 367 U.S., at 549 (Harlan, J., dissenting), comprising a continuum of rights to be free from "arbitrary impositions and purposeless restraints," *id.* at 543. . . .

This approach calls for a court to assess the relative "weights" or dignities of the contending interests, and to this extent the judicial method is familiar to the common law. Common-law method is subject, however, to two important constraints in the hands of a court engaged in substantive due process review. First, such a court is bound to confine the values that it recognizes to those truly deserving constitutional stature, either to those expressed in constitutional text, or those exemplified by "the traditions from which [the Nation] developed," or revealed by contrast with "the traditions from which it broke." *Id.* at 542. . . .

The second constraint, again, simply reflects the fact that constitutional review, not judicial lawmaking, is a court's business here. The weighing or valuing of contending interests in this sphere is only the first step, forming the basis for determining whether the statute in question falls inside or outside the zone of what is reasonable in the way it resolves the conflict between the interests of state and individual. It is no justification for judicial intervention merely to identify a reasonable resolution of contending values that differs from the terms of the legislation under review. It is only when the legislation's justifying principle, critically valued, is so far from being commensurate with the individual interest as to be arbitrarily or pointlessly applied that the statute must give way. Only if this standard points against the statute can the individual claimant be said to have a constitutional right. . . .

Just as results in substantive due process cases are tied to the selections of statements of the competing interests, the acceptability of the results is a function of the good reasons for the selections made. It is here that the value of common-law method becomes apparent, for the usual thinking of the common law is suspicious of the all-or-nothing analysis that tends to produce legal petrification instead of an evolving boundary between the domains of old principles. Common-law method tends to pay respect instead to detail, seeking to understand old principles afresh by new examples and new counterexamples. The "tradition is a living thing," *id.* at 542, albeit one that moves by moderate steps carefully taken. . . . Exact analysis and characterization of any due process claim are critical to the method and to the result. . . .

In my judgment, the importance of the individual interest here, as within that class of "certain interests" demanding careful scrutiny of the State's contrary claim cannot be gainsaid. Whether that interest might in some circumstances, or at some time, be seen as "fundamental" to the degree entitled to prevail is not, however, a conclusion that I need draw here, for I am satisfied that the State's interests described in the following section are sufficiently serious to defeat the present claim that its law is arbitrary or purposeless.

The State has put forward several interests to justify the Washington law as applied to physicians treating terminally ill patients, even those competent to make responsible choices: protecting life generally, discouraging suicide even if knowing and voluntary, and protecting terminally ill patients from involuntary suicide and euthanasia, both voluntary and nonvoluntary. . . . [T]he third is dispositive for me. . . . The State claims interests in protecting patients from mistakenly and involuntarily deciding to end their lives, and in guarding against both voluntary and involuntary euthanasia. . . .

The experimentation that should be out of the question in constitutional adjudication displacing legislative judgments is entirely proper, as well as highly desirable, when the legislative power addresses an emerging issue like assisted suicide. The Court should accordingly stay its hand to allow reasonable legislative consideration. While I do not decide for all time that respondents' claim should not be recognized, I acknowledge the legislative institutional competence as the better one to deal with that claim at this time.

■ [The concurring opinion of JUSTICE O'CONNOR, and the opinions concurring in the judgment of JUSTICES STEVENS and BREYER, are omitted.]

NOTES

1. The Supreme Court had previously addressed "right to die" questions in *Cruzan v. Missouri Department of Health*, 497 U.S. 261 (1990). In that case, the Court had assumed, but did not hold, that there may exist a "liberty interest" of the individual to refuse medical care, but it ultimately found that such an interest would not be violated by a state law requiring "clear and convincing" evidence that a comatose patient actually would have wished to refuse treatment. In *Glucksberg* the Court returned to this contested area. Did the majority in *Glucksberg* recognize a constitutional right either to die or to refuse medical treatment? What was the holding?

2. In the movie *The Incredibles*, superhero Mr. Incredible (and apparently the government) is sued for saving the life of an attempted suicide:

Oliver Sansweet's Lawyer: Mr. Sansweet didn't ask to be saved. Mr. Sansweet didn't want to be saved. And the injuries received from Mr. Incredible's "actions," so-called, causes him daily pain.

Mr. Incredible, lunging towards Sansweet: Hey, I saved your life!

Oliver Sansweet: You didn't save my life, you ruined my death, that's what you did!

Who was right, Mr. Incredible or Oliver Sansweet?

3. What is the methodology established by *Glucksberg* for adjudicating claims of new substantive due process rights? Identify the relevant passage in Chief Justice Rehnquist's opinion. Does this proposition command a majority of the Court? Contrast that position with that of Justice Souter in his concurring opinion. How do the positions differ? Are both positions faithful to the text of

the Constitution? (Is neither one faithful to the text?) What do you make of
Justice Souter's view that the adjudication of "substantive due process" claims
is essentially an invitation for judges to apply a "common law" method to discovering constitutional rights?

Consider what would happen if you were to apply the *Glucksberg* test to
some of the preceding cases: *Lochner, Pierce, Griswold, Roe,* and *Casey*? In
each, was there a right, identified at its most specific level, that was "objectively, deeply rooted" in the nation's history and its traditions of liberty?

4. Under the standard adopted by Chief Justice Rehnquist's majority opinion, is there any plausible argument that a claim to physician-assisted suicide
is "objectively, deeply rooted" in the nation's history and traditions as an essential part of ordered liberty? Does that history and tradition preclude a claim
that there is a substantive due process right to physician-assisted suicide?
Have cultural norms and understandings changed—and, if so, does that mean
our understanding of the Constitution should also change?

––––––––––

As you read the following two cases, *Bowers v. Hardwick*, 478 U.S. 186
(1986), and *Lawrence v. Texas,* 539 U.S. 558 (2003), note their contrasting
interpretive approaches. One resembles *Glucksberg* in its interpretive
methodology, declining to accept new substantive due process rights not
closely tied to history and tradition, while the other takes a markedly different approach. Although these two cases are presented together because
of the similar questions raised, you should note carefully how they fit into
the chronology of the more recent substantive due process cases: *Roe*
(1973), *Bowers* (1986), *Casey* (1992), *Glucksberg* (1997), and finally *Lawrence* (2003). In each of these cases, did the Court consistently and faithfully apply the reasoning and methodology of the substantive due process case
that immediately preceded it? If so, does that mean that the Court's approach has been largely consistent and principled? If not, does that suggest
that in recent decades the Court has had as much difficulty in consistently
applying substantive due process as it did in the *Lochner* era?

Bowers v. Hardwick
478 U.S. 186 (1986)

■ JUSTICE WHITE delivered the opinion of the Court.

In August 1982, respondent Hardwick was charged with violating the
Georgia statute criminalizing sodomy by committing that act with another
adult male in the bedroom of respondent's home. After a preliminary hearing, the District Attorney decided not to present the matter to the grand
jury unless further evidence developed.

Respondent then brought suit in the Federal District Court, challenging the constitutionality of the statute insofar as it criminalized consensual
sodomy. He asserted that he was a practicing homosexual, that the Georgia
sodomy statute, as administered by the defendants, placed him in imminent danger of arrest, and that the statute for several reasons violates the
Federal Constitution. . . .

The only claim properly before the Court, therefore, is Hardwick's
challenge to the Georgia statute as applied to consensual homosexual sod-

omy. We express no opinion on the constitutionality of the Georgia statute as applied to other acts of sodomy. . . . The issue presented is whether the Federal Constitution confers a fundamental right upon homosexuals to engage in sodomy and hence invalidates the laws of the many States that still make such conduct illegal and have done so for a very long time. The case also calls for some judgment about the limits of the Court's role in carrying out its constitutional mandate.

We first register our disagreement with the Court of Appeals and with respondent that the Court's prior cases have construed the Constitution to confer a right of privacy that extends to homosexual sodomy and for all intents and purposes have decided this case. . . . [W]e think it evident that none of the rights announced in those cases bears any resemblance to the claimed constitutional right of homosexuals to engage in acts of sodomy that is asserted in this case. No connection between family, marriage, or procreation on the one hand and homosexual activity on the other has been demonstrated, either by the Court of Appeals or by respondent. Moreover, any claim that these cases nevertheless stand for the proposition that any kind of private sexual conduct between consenting adults is constitutionally insulated from state proscription is unsupportable.

. . . [R]espondent would have us announce, as the Court of Appeals did, a fundamental right to engage in homosexual sodomy. This we are quite unwilling to do. It is true that despite the language of the Due Process Clauses of the Fifth and Fourteenth Amendments, which appears to focus only on the processes by which life, liberty, or property is taken, the cases are legion in which those Clauses have been interpreted to have substantive content, subsuming rights that to a great extent are immune from federal or state regulation or proscription. Among such cases are those recognizing rights that have little or no textual support in the constitutional language. *Meyer*, *Prince*, and *Pierce* fall in this category, as do the privacy cases from *Griswold* to *Carey*.

Striving to assure itself and the public that announcing rights not readily identifiable in the Constitution's text involves much more than the imposition of the Justices' own choice of values on the States and the Federal Government, the Court has sought to identify the nature of the rights qualifying for heightened judicial protection. In *Palko v. Connecticut*, 302 U.S. 319, 325, 326 (1937), it was said that this category includes those fundamental liberties that are "implicit in the concept of ordered liberty," such that "neither liberty nor justice would exist if [they] were sacrificed." A different description of fundamental liberties appeared in *Moore v. East Cleveland*, 431 U.S. 494, 503 (1977) (opinion of POWELL, J.), where they are characterized as those liberties that are "deeply rooted in this Nation's history and tradition."

It is obvious to us that neither of these formulations would extend a fundamental right to homosexuals to engage in acts of consensual sodomy. Proscriptions against that conduct have ancient roots. See generally Survey on the Constitutional Right to Privacy in the Context of Homosexual Activity, 40 U. Miami L. Rev. 521, 525 (1986). Sodomy was a criminal offense at common law and was forbidden by the laws of the original 13 States when they ratified the Bill of Rights. In 1868, when the Fourteenth Amendment was ratified, all but 5 of the 37 States in the Union had criminal sodomy laws. In fact, until 1961, all 50 States outlawed sodomy, and today, 24 States and the District of Columbia continue to provide criminal penalties for sodomy performed in private and between consenting adults. Against this background, to claim that a right to engage in such conduct is "deeply rooted in this Nation's history and tradition" or "implicit in the concept of ordered liberty" is, at best, facetious.

Nor are we inclined to take a more expansive view of our authority to discover new fundamental rights imbedded in the Due Process Clause. The Court is most vulnerable and comes nearest to illegitimacy when it deals with judge-made constitutional law having little or no cognizable roots in the language or design of the Constitution.

That this is so was painfully demonstrated by the face-off between the Executive and the Court in the 1930's, which resulted in the repudiation of much of the substantive gloss that the Court had placed on the Due Process Clauses of the Fifth and Fourteenth Amendments. There should be, therefore, great resistance to expand the substantive reach of those Clauses, particularly if it requires redefining the category of rights deemed to be fundamental. Otherwise, the Judiciary necessarily takes to itself further authority to govern the country without express constitutional authority. The claimed right pressed on us today falls far short of overcoming this resistance.

Respondent, however, asserts that the result should be different where the homosexual conduct occurs in the privacy of the home. He relies on *Stanley v. Georgia*, 394 U.S. 557 (1969), where the Court held that the First Amendment prevents conviction for possessing and reading obscene material in the privacy of one's home: "If the First Amendment means anything, it means that a State has no business telling a man, sitting alone in his house, what books he may read or what films he may watch."

Stanley did protect conduct that would not have been protected outside the home, and it partially prevented the enforcement of state obscenity laws; but the decision was firmly grounded in the First Amendment. The right pressed upon us here has no similar support in the text of the Constitution, and it does not qualify for recognition under the prevailing principles for construing the Fourteenth Amendment. Its limits are also difficult to discern. Plainly enough, otherwise illegal conduct is not always immunized whenever it occurs in the home. Victimless crimes, such as the possession and use of illegal drugs, do not escape the law where they are committed at home. *Stanley* itself recognized that its holding offered no protection for the possession in the home of drugs, firearms, or stolen goods. And if respondent's submission is limited to the voluntary sexual conduct between consenting adults, it would be difficult, except by fiat, to limit the claimed right to homosexual conduct while leaving exposed to prosecution adultery, incest, and other sexual crimes even though they are committed in the home. We are unwilling to start down that road.

Even if the conduct at issue here is not a fundamental right, respondent asserts that there must be a rational basis for the law and that there is none in this case other than the presumed belief of a majority of the electorate in Georgia that homosexual sodomy is immoral and unacceptable. This is said to be an inadequate rationale to support the law. The law, however, is constantly based on notions of morality, and if all laws representing essentially moral choices are to be invalidated under the Due Process Clause, the courts will be very busy indeed. Even respondent makes no such claim, but insists that majority sentiments about the morality of homosexuality should be declared inadequate. We do not agree, and are unpersuaded that the sodomy laws of some 25 States should be invalidated on this basis.

■ CHIEF JUSTICE BURGER, concurring.

I join the Court's opinion, but I write separately to underscore my view that in constitutional terms there is no such thing as a fundamental right to commit homosexual sodomy.

As the Court notes, the proscriptions against sodomy have very "ancient roots." Decisions of individuals relating to homosexual conduct have been subject to state intervention throughout the history of Western civilization. . . . To hold that the act of homosexual sodomy is somehow protected as a fundamental right would be to cast aside millennia of moral teaching.

This is essentially not a question of personal "preferences" but rather of the legislative authority of the State. I find nothing in the Constitution depriving a State of the power to enact the statute challenged here.

■ JUSTICE POWELL, concurring.

I join the opinion of the Court. . . . This is not to suggest, however, that respondent may not be protected by the Eighth Amendment of the Constitution. The Georgia statute at issue in this case authorizes a court to imprison a person for up to 20 years for a single private, consensual act of sodomy. In my view, a prison sentence for such conduct—certainly a sentence of long duration—would create a serious Eighth Amendment issue. . . .

In this case, however, respondent has not been tried, much less convicted and sentenced. Moreover, respondent has not raised the Eighth Amendment issue below. For these reasons this constitutional argument is not before us.

■ JUSTICE BLACKMUN, with whom JUSTICE BRENNAN, JUSTICE MARSHALL, and JUSTICE STEVENS join, dissenting.

This case is no more about "a fundamental right to engage in homosexual sodomy," as the Court purports to declare, than *Stanley v. Georgia*, 394 U.S. 557 (1969), was about a fundamental right to watch obscene movies, or *Katz v. United States*, 389 U.S. 347 (1967), was about a fundamental right to place interstate bets from a telephone booth. Rather, this case is about "the most comprehensive of rights and the right most valued by civilized men," namely, "the right to be let alone." *Olmstead v. United States*, 277 U.S. 438, 478 (1928) (Brandeis, J., dissenting).

The statute at issue denies individuals the right to decide for themselves whether to engage in particular forms of private, consensual sexual activity. . . . Like Justice Holmes, I believe that "[i]t is revolting to have no better reason for a rule of law than that so it was laid down in the time of Henry IV. It is still more revolting if the grounds upon which it was laid down have vanished long since, and the rule simply persists from blind imitation of the past." Holmes, The Path of the Law, 10 Harv. L. Rev. 457, 469 (1897). I believe we must analyze Hardwick's claim in the light of the values that underlie the constitutional right to privacy. . . .

[T]he Court's almost obsessive focus on homosexual activity is particularly hard to justify in light of the broad language Georgia has used. . . . The sex or status of the persons who engage in the act is irrelevant as a matter of state law. In fact, to the extent I can discern a legislative purpose for Georgia's 1968 enactment of [the statute], that purpose seems to have been to broaden the coverage of the law to reach heterosexual as well as homosexual activity. . . .

In construing the right to privacy, the Court has proceeded along two somewhat distinct, albeit complementary, lines. First, it has recognized a privacy interest with reference to certain decisions that are properly for the individual to make. Second, it has recognized a privacy interest with reference to certain places without regard for the particular activities in which the individuals who occupy them are engaged. The case before us implicates both the decisional and the spatial aspects of the right to privacy.

The Court concludes today that none of our prior cases dealing with various decisions that individuals are entitled to make free of governmental interference "bears any resemblance to the claimed constitutional right of homosexuals to engage in acts of sodomy that is asserted in this case." While it is true that these cases may be characterized by their connection to protection of the family, the Court's conclusion that they extend no further than this boundary ignores the warning in *Moore v. East Cleveland*, 431 U.S. 494, 501 (1977) (plurality opinion), against "clos[ing] our eyes to the basic reasons why certain rights associated with the family have been accorded shelter under the Fourteenth Amendment's Due Process Clause." We protect those rights not because they contribute, in some direct and material way, to the general public welfare, but because they form so central a part of an individual's life. . . .

Only the most willful blindness could obscure the fact that sexual intimacy is "a sensitive, key relationship of human existence, central to family life, community welfare, and the development of human personality," *Paris Adult Theatre I v. Slaton*, 413 U.S. 49, 63 (1973). The fact that individuals define themselves in a significant way through their intimate sexual relationships with others suggests, in a Nation as diverse as ours, that there may be many "right" ways of conducting those relationships, and that much of the richness of a relationship will come from the freedom an individual has to choose the form and nature of these intensely personal bonds. . . . The Court claims that its decision today merely refuses to recognize a fundamental right to engage in homosexual sodomy; what the Court really has refused to recognize is the fundamental interest all individuals have in controlling the nature of their intimate associations with others.

The behavior for which Hardwick faces prosecution occurred in his own home, a place to which the Fourth Amendment attaches special significance. The Court's treatment of this aspect of the case is symptomatic of its overall refusal to consider the broad principles that have informed our treatment of privacy in specific cases. Just as the right to privacy is more than the mere aggregation of a number of entitlements to engage in specific behavior, so too, protecting the physical integrity of the home is more than merely a means of protecting specific activities that often take place there. . . .

The Court's interpretation of the pivotal case of *Stanley v. Georgia*, 394 U.S. 557 (1969), is entirely unconvincing. Stanley held that Georgia's undoubted power to punish the public distribution of constitutionally unprotected, obscene material did not permit the State to punish the private possession of such material. According to the majority here, Stanley relied entirely on the First Amendment, and thus, it is claimed, sheds no light on cases not involving printed materials. But that is not what *Stanley* said. Rather, the *Stanley* Court anchored its holding in the Fourth Amendment's special protection for the individual in his home. . . .

"The right of the people to be secure in their . . . houses," expressly guaranteed by the Fourth Amendment, is perhaps the most "textual" of the various constitutional provisions that inform our understanding of the right to privacy, and thus I cannot agree with the Court's statement that "[t]he right pressed upon us here has no . . . support in the text of the Constitution." Indeed, the right of an individual to conduct intimate relationships in the intimacy of his or her own home seems to me to be the heart of the Constitution's protection of privacy. . . .

Essentially, petitioner argues, and the Court agrees, that the fact that the acts described in [the statute] "for hundreds of years, if not thousands, have been uniformly condemned as immoral" is a sufficient reason to permit a State to ban them today.

I cannot agree that either the length of time a majority has held its convictions or the passions with which it defends them can withdraw legislation from this Court's scrutiny. See, *e.g.*, *Roe v. Wade*, 410 U.S. 113 (1973); *Loving v. Virginia*, 388 U.S. 1 (1967); *Brown v. Board of Education*, 347 U.S. 483 (1954).[5] . . . It is precisely because the issue raised by this case touches the heart of what makes individuals what they are that we should be especially sensitive to the rights of those whose choices upset the majority.

The assertion that "traditional Judeo–Christian values proscribe" the conduct involved cannot provide an adequate justification. . . . A State can no more punish private behavior because of religious intolerance than it can punish such behavior because of racial animus. . . .

■ [JUSTICE STEVENS'S dissenting opinion is omitted.]

Lawrence v. Texas

539 U.S. 558 (2003)

■ JUSTICE KENNEDY delivered the opinion of the Court.

Liberty protects the person from unwarranted government intrusions into a dwelling or other private places. In our tradition the State is not omnipresent in the home. And there are other spheres of our lives and existence, outside the home, where the State should not be a dominant presence. Freedom extends beyond spatial bounds. Liberty presumes an autonomy of self that includes freedom of thought, belief, expression, and certain intimate conduct. The instant case involves liberty of the person both in its spatial and in its more transcendent dimensions.

I

The question before the Court is the validity of a Texas statute making it a crime for two persons of the same sex to engage in certain intimate sexual conduct.

---

[5] The parallel between *Loving* and this case is almost uncanny. There, too, the State relied on a religious justification for its law. There, too, defenders of the challenged statute relied heavily on the fact that when the Fourteenth Amendment was ratified, most of the States had similar prohibitions. There, too, at the time the case came before the Court, many of the States still had criminal statutes concerning the conduct at issue. Yet the Court held, not only that the invidious racism of Virginia's law violated the Equal Protection Clause, but also that the law deprived the Lovings of due process by denying them the "freedom of choice to marry" that had "long been recognized as one of the vital personal rights essential to the orderly pursuit of happiness by free men."

In Houston, Texas, officers of the Harris County Police Department were dispatched to a private residence in response to a reported weapons disturbance. They entered an apartment where one of the petitioners, John Geddes Lawrence, resided. The right of the police to enter does not seem to have been questioned. The officers observed Lawrence and another man, Tyron Garner, engaging in a sexual act. The two petitioners were arrested, held in custody overnight, and charged and convicted before a Justice of the Peace.

The complaints described their crime as "deviate sexual intercourse, namely anal sex, with a member of the same sex (man)." . . . The petitioners, having entered a plea of *nolo contendere*, were each fined $200 and assessed court costs of $141.25. . . .

We granted certiorari to consider three questions:

1. Whether petitioners' criminal convictions under the Texas "Homosexual Conduct" law—which criminalizes sexual intimacy by same-sex couples, but not identical behavior by different-sex couples—violate the Fourteenth Amendment guarantee of equal protection of the laws.

2. Whether petitioners' criminal convictions for adult consensual sexual intimacy in the home violate their vital interests in liberty and privacy protected by the Due Process Clause of the Fourteenth Amendment.

3. Whether *Bowers v. Hardwick* should be overruled. . . .

II

We conclude the case should be resolved by determining whether the petitioners were free as adults to engage in the private conduct in the exercise of their liberty under the Due Process Clause of the Fourteenth Amendment to the Constitution. For this inquiry we deem it necessary to reconsider the Court's holding in *Bowers*.

There are broad statements of the substantive reach of liberty under the Due Process Clause in earlier cases, but the most pertinent beginning point is our decision in *Griswold v. Connecticut*, 381 U.S. 479 (1965).

In *Griswold* the Court invalidated a state law prohibiting the use of drugs or devices of contraception and counseling or aiding and abetting the use of contraceptives. The Court described the protected interest as a right to privacy and placed emphasis on the marriage relation and the protected space of the marital bedroom.

After *Griswold* it was established that the right to make certain decisions regarding sexual conduct extends beyond the marital relationship. In *Eisenstadt v. Baird*, 405 U.S. 438 (1972), the Court invalidated a law prohibiting the distribution of contraceptives to unmarried persons. The case was decided under the Equal Protection Clause; but with respect to unmarried persons, the Court went on to state the fundamental proposition that the law impaired the exercise of their personal rights. . . .

The opinions in *Griswold* and *Eisenstadt* were part of the background for the decision in *Roe v. Wade*, 410 U.S. 113 (1973)[, which] . . . recognized the right of a woman to make certain fundamental decisions affecting her destiny and confirmed once more that the protection of liberty under the Due Process Clause has a substantive dimension of fundamental significance in defining the rights of the person. . . . [T]he holding and rationale in *Roe*[] confirmed that the reasoning of *Griswold* could not be confined to the protection of rights of married adults. This was the state of the law with respect to some of the most relevant cases when the Court considered *Bowers v. Hardwick.*

The facts in *Bowers* had some similarities to the instant case. A police officer, whose right to enter seems not to have been in question, observed Hardwick, in his own bedroom, engaging in intimate sexual conduct with another adult male. The conduct was in violation of a Georgia statute making it a criminal offense to engage in sodomy. One difference between the two cases is that the Georgia statute prohibited the conduct whether or not the participants were of the same sex, while the Texas statute, as we have seen, applies only to participants of the same sex. . . .

The Court began its substantive discussion in *Bowers* as follows: "The issue presented is whether the Federal Constitution confers a fundamental right upon homosexuals to engage in sodomy and hence invalidates the laws of the many States that still make such conduct illegal and have done so for a very long time." That statement, we now conclude, discloses the Court's own failure to appreciate the extent of the liberty at stake. To say that the issue in *Bowers* was simply the right to engage in certain sexual conduct demeans the claim the individual put forward, just as it would demean a married couple were it to be said marriage is simply about the right to have sexual intercourse. The laws involved in *Bowers* and here are, to be sure, statutes that purport to do no more than prohibit a particular sexual act. Their penalties and purposes, though, have more far-reaching consequences, touching upon the most private human conduct, sexual behavior, and in the most private of places, the home. The statutes do seek to control a personal relationship that, whether or not entitled to formal recognition in the law, is within the liberty of persons to choose without being punished as criminals.

This, as a general rule, should counsel against attempts by the State, or a court, to define the meaning of the relationship or to set its boundaries absent injury to a person or abuse of an institution the law protects. It suffices for us to acknowledge that adults may choose to enter upon this relationship in the confines of their homes and their own private lives and still retain their dignity as free persons. When sexuality finds overt expression in intimate conduct with another person, the conduct can be but one element in a personal bond that is more enduring. The liberty protected by the Constitution allows homosexual persons the right to make this choice.

Having misapprehended the claim of liberty there presented to it, and thus stating the claim to be whether there is a fundamental right to engage in consensual sodomy, the *Bowers* Court said: "Proscriptions against that conduct have ancient roots." . . . [T]he following considerations counsel against adopting the definitive conclusions upon which *Bowers* placed such reliance.

At the outset it should be noted that there is no longstanding history in this country of laws directed at homosexual conduct as a distinct matter. Beginning in colonial times there were prohibitions of sodomy derived from the English criminal laws passed in the first instance by the Reformation Parliament of 1533. The English prohibition was understood to include relations between men and women as well as relations between men and men. Nineteenth-century commentators similarly read American sodomy, buggery, and crime-against-nature statutes as criminalizing certain relations between men and women and between men and men. The absence of legal prohibitions focusing on homosexual conduct may be explained in part by noting that according to some scholars the concept of the homosexual as a distinct category of person did not emerge until the late 19th century. Thus early American sodomy laws were not directed at homosexuals as such but instead sought to prohibit nonprocreative sexual activity more generally. This does not suggest approval of homosexual conduct. It does tend to show that this particular form of conduct was not thought of as a separate category from like conduct between heterosexual persons.

Laws prohibiting sodomy do not seem to have been enforced against consenting adults acting in private. . . . Instead of targeting relations between consenting adults in private, 19th–century sodomy prosecutions typically involved relations between men and minor girls or minor boys, relations between adults involving force, relations between adults implicating disparity in status, or relations between men and animals. . . .

[T]he infrequency of these prosecutions . . . makes it difficult to say that society approved of a rigorous and systematic punishment of the consensual acts committed in private and by adults. The longstanding criminal prohibition of homosexual sodomy upon which the *Bowers* decision placed such reliance is as consistent with a general condemnation of nonprocreative sex as it is with an established tradition of prosecuting acts because of their homosexual character. . . .

It was not until the 1970's that any State singled out same-sex relations for criminal prosecution, and only nine States have done so. Post–*Bowers* even some of these States did not adhere to the policy of suppressing homosexual conduct. Over the course of the last decades, States with same-sex prohibitions have moved toward abolishing them.

In summary, the historical grounds relied upon in *Bowers* are more complex than the majority opinion and the concurring opinion by Chief Justice Burger indicate. Their historical premises are not without doubt and, at the very least, are overstated.

It must be acknowledged, of course, that the Court in *Bowers* was making the broader point that for centuries there have been powerful voices to condemn homosexual conduct as immoral. The condemnation has been shaped by religious beliefs, conceptions of right and acceptable behavior, and respect for the traditional family. For many persons these are not trivial concerns but profound and deep convictions accepted as ethical and moral principles to which they aspire and which thus determine the course of their lives. These considerations do not answer the question before us, however. The issue is whether the majority may use the power of the State to enforce these views on the whole society through operation of the criminal law. "Our obligation is to define the liberty of all, not to mandate our own moral code." *Planned Parenthood v. Casey*, 505 U.S. 833, 850 (1992).

. . . [W]e think that our laws and traditions in the past half century are of most relevance here. These references show an emerging awareness that liberty gives substantial protection to adult persons in deciding how to conduct their private lives in matters pertaining to sex. "[H]istory and tradition are the starting point but not in all cases the ending point of the substantive due process inquiry." *County of Sacramento v. Lewis*, 523 U.S. 833, 857 (1998) (KENNEDY, J., concurring).

This emerging recognition should have been apparent when *Bowers* was decided. In 1955 the American Law Institute promulgated the Model Penal Code and made clear that it did not recommend or provide for "criminal penalties for consensual sexual relations conducted in private." . . .

In *Bowers* the Court referred to the fact that before 1961 all 50 States had outlawed sodomy, and that at the time of the Court's decision 24 States and the District of Columbia had sodomy laws. Justice Powell pointed out that these prohibitions often were being ignored, however. Georgia, for instance, had not sought to enforce its law for decades.

The sweeping references by Chief Justice Burger to the history of Western civilization and to Judeo–Christian moral and ethical standards did not take account of other authorities pointing in an opposite direction. A committee advising the British Parliament recommended in 1957 repeal of laws punishing homosexual conduct. Parliament enacted the substance of those recommendations 10 years later.

Of even more importance, almost five years before *Bowers* was decided the European Court of Human Rights considered a case with parallels to *Bowers* and to today's case. An adult male resident in Northern Ireland alleged he was a practicing homosexual who desired to engage in consensual homosexual conduct. The laws of Northern Ireland forbade him that right. He alleged that he had been questioned, his home had been searched, and he feared criminal prosecution. The court held that the laws proscribing the conduct were invalid under the European Convention on Human Rights. Authoritative in all countries that are members of the Council of Europe (21 nations then, 45 nations now), the decision is at odds with the premise in *Bowers* that the claim put forward was insubstantial in our Western civilization.

In our own constitutional system the deficiencies in *Bowers* became even more apparent in the years following its announcement. The 25 States with laws prohibiting the relevant conduct referenced in the *Bowers* decision are reduced now to 13, of which 4 enforce their laws only against homosexual conduct. In those States where sodomy is still proscribed, whether for same-sex or heterosexual conduct, there is a pattern of nonenforcement with respect to consenting adults acting in private. The State of Texas admitted in 1994 that as of that date it had not prosecuted anyone under those circumstances.

Two principal cases decided after *Bowers* cast its holding into even more doubt. In *Planned Parenthood v. Casey*, 505 U.S. 833 (1992), the Court reaffirmed the substantive force of the liberty protected by the Due Process Clause. The *Casey* decision again confirmed that our laws and tradition afford constitutional protection to personal decisions relating to marriage, procreation, contraception, family relationships, child rearing, and education. In explaining the respect the Constitution demands for the autonomy of the person in making these choices, we stated as follows:

> These matters, involving the most intimate and personal choices a person may make in a lifetime, choices central to personal dignity and autonomy, are central to the liberty protected by the Fourteenth Amendment. At the heart of liberty is the right to define one's own concept of existence, of meaning, of the universe, and of the mystery of human life. Beliefs about these matters could not define the attributes of personhood were they formed under compulsion of the State.

Persons in a homosexual relationship may seek autonomy for these purposes, just as heterosexual persons do. The decision in *Bowers* would deny them this right.

The second post-*Bowers* case of principal relevance is *Romer v. Evans*, 517 U.S. 620 (1996). There the Court struck down class-based legislation directed at homosexuals as a violation of the Equal Protection Clause. *Romer* invalidated an amendment to Colorado's Constitution which named as a solitary class persons who were homosexuals, lesbians, or bisexual either by "orientation, conduct, practices or relationships," and deprived them of protection under state antidiscrimination laws. We concluded that the provision was "born of animosity toward the class of persons affected" and further that it had no rational relation to a legitimate governmental purpose.

As an alternative argument in this case, counsel for the petitioners and some *amici* contend that *Romer* provides the basis for declaring the Texas statute invalid under the Equal Protection Clause. That is a tenable argument, but we conclude the instant case requires us to address whether *Bowers* itself has continuing validity. Were we to hold the statute invalid under the Equal Protection Clause some might question whether a prohibition would be valid if drawn differently, say, to prohibit the conduct both between same-sex and different-sex participants.

Equality of treatment and the due process right to demand respect for conduct protected by the substantive guarantee of liberty are linked in important respects, and a decision on the latter point advances both interests. If protected conduct is made criminal and the law which does so remains unexamined for its substantive validity, its stigma might remain even if it were not enforceable as drawn for equal protection reasons. When homosexual conduct is made criminal by the law of the State, that declaration in and of itself is an invitation to subject homosexual persons to discrimination both in the public and in the private spheres. The central holding of *Bowers* has been brought in question by this case, and it should be addressed. Its continuance as precedent demeans the lives of homosexual persons.

The stigma this criminal statute imposes, moreover, is not trivial. The offense, to be sure, is but a class C misdemeanor, a minor offense in the Texas legal system. Still, it remains a criminal offense with all that imports for the dignity of the persons charged. The petitioners will bear on their record the history of their criminal convictions. . . .

The foundations of *Bowers* have sustained serious erosion from our recent decisions in *Casey* and *Romer*. When our precedent has been thus weakened, criticism from other sources is of greater significance. In the United States criticism of *Bowers* has been substantial and continuing, disapproving of its reasoning in all respects, not just as to its historical assumptions. See, *e.g.*, C. Fried, Order and Law: Arguing the Reagan Revolution—A First-hand Account 81–84 (1991); R. Posner, Sex and Reason 341–350 (1992). The courts of five different States have declined to follow it in interpreting provisions in their own state constitutions parallel to the Due Process Clause of the Fourteenth Amendment.

To the extent *Bowers* relied on values we share with a wider civilization, it should be noted that the reasoning and holding in *Bowers* have been rejected elsewhere. The European Court of Human Rights has [not followed] *Bowers*. . . . Other nations, too, have taken action consistent with an affirmation of the protected right of homosexual adults to engage in intimate, consensual conduct. The right the petitioners seek in this case has been accepted as an integral part of human freedom in many other countries. There has been no showing that in this country the governmental interest in circumscribing personal choice is somehow more legitimate or urgent.

The doctrine of *stare decisis* is essential to the respect accorded to the judgments of the Court and to the stability of the law. It is not, however, an inexorable command. In *Casey* we noted that when a court is asked to overrule a precedent recognizing a constitutional liberty interest, individual or societal reliance on the existence of that liberty cautions with particular strength against reversing course. The holding in *Bowers*, however, has not induced detrimental reliance comparable to some instances where recognized individual rights are involved. Indeed, there has been no individual or societal reliance on *Bowers* of the sort that could counsel against overturning its holding once there are compelling reasons to do so. *Bowers* itself causes uncertainty, for the precedents before and after its issuance contradict its central holding. . . .

Bowers was not correct when it was decided, and it is not correct today. It ought not to remain binding precedent. *Bowers v. Hardwick* should be and now is overruled.

The present case does not involve minors. It does not involve persons who might be injured or coerced or who are situated in relationships where consent might not easily be refused. It does not involve public conduct or prostitution. It does not involve whether the government must give formal recognition to any relationship that homosexual persons seek to enter. The case does involve two adults who, with full and mutual consent from each other, engaged in sexual practices common to a homosexual lifestyle. The petitioners are entitled to respect for their private lives. The State cannot demean their existence or control their destiny by making their private sexual conduct a crime. Their right to liberty under the Due Process Clause gives them the full right to engage in their conduct without intervention of the government. "It is a promise of the Constitution that there is a realm of personal liberty which the government may not enter." *Casey, supra,* at 847. The Texas statute furthers no legitimate state interest which can justify its intrusion into the personal and private life of the individual.

Had those who drew and ratified the Due Process Clauses of the Fifth Amendment or the Fourteenth Amendment known the components of liberty in its manifold possibilities, they might have been more specific. They did not presume to have this insight. They knew times can blind us to certain truths and later generations can see that laws once thought necessary and proper in fact serve only to oppress. As the Constitution endures, persons in every generation can invoke its principles in their own search for greater freedom. . . .

■ JUSTICE O'CONNOR, concurring in the judgment.

The Court today overrules *Bowers v. Hardwick*, 478 U.S. 186 (1986). I joined *Bowers*, and do not join the Court in overruling it. Nevertheless, I agree with the Court that Texas' statute banning same-sex sodomy is unconstitutional. Rather than relying on the substantive component of the Fourteenth Amendment's Due Process Clause, as the Court does, I base my conclusion on the Fourteenth Amendment's Equal Protection Clause.

The Equal Protection Clause of the Fourteenth Amendment "is essentially a direction that all persons similarly situated should be treated alike." *Cleburne* v. *Cleburne Living Center,* 473 U.S. 432, 439 (1985). Under our rational basis standard of review, "legislation is presumed to be valid and will be sustained if the classification drawn by the statute is rationally related to a legitimate state interest." *Id.* at 440. . . .

The statute at issue here makes sodomy a crime only if a person "engages in deviate sexual intercourse with another individual of the same sex." Sodomy between opposite-sex partners, however, is not a crime in Texas. That is, Texas treats the same conduct differently based solely on the participants. Those harmed by this law are people who have a same-sex sexual orientation and thus are more likely to engage in behavior prohibited by [the statute]. . . .

And the effect of Texas' sodomy law is not just limited to the threat of prosecution or consequence of conviction. Texas' sodomy law brands all homosexuals as criminals, thereby making it more difficult for homosexuals to be treated in the same manner as everyone else. . . .

The only question in front of the Court in *Bowers* was whether the substantive component of the Due Process Clause protected a right to engage in homosexual sodomy. *Bowers* did not hold that moral disapproval of a group is a rational basis under the Equal Protection Clause to criminalize homosexual sodomy when heterosexual sodomy is not punished.

This case raises a different issue than *Bowers*: whether, under the Equal Protection Clause, moral disapproval is a legitimate state interest to justify by itself a statute that bans homosexual sodomy, but not heterosexual sodomy. It is not. Moral disapproval of this group, like a bare desire to harm the group, is an interest that is insufficient to satisfy rational basis review under the Equal Protection Clause. See, *e.g.*, *Romer v. Evans*, 517 U.S., at 634–635. Indeed, we have never held that moral disapproval, without any other asserted state interest, is a sufficient rationale under the Equal Protection Clause to justify a law that discriminates among groups of persons.

Moral disapproval of a group cannot be a legitimate governmental interest under the Equal Protection Clause because legal classifications must not be "drawn for the purpose of disadvantaging the group burdened by the law." *Id.*, at 633. Texas' invocation of moral disapproval as a legitimate state interest proves nothing more than Texas' desire to criminalize homosexual sodomy. But the Equal Protection Clause prevents a State from creating "a classification of persons undertaken for its own sake." *Id.*, at 635. . . .

Texas argues, however, that the sodomy law does not discriminate against homosexual persons. Instead, the State maintains that the law discriminates only against homosexual conduct. While it is true that the law applies only to conduct, the conduct targeted by this law is conduct that is closely correlated with being homosexual. Under such circumstances, Texas' sodomy law is targeted at more than conduct. It is instead directed toward gay persons as a class. . . .

[T]he State cannot single out one identifiable class of citizens for punishment that does not apply to everyone else, with moral disapproval as the only asserted state interest for the law. . . .

Whether a sodomy law that is neutral both in effect and application, see *Yick Wo v. Hopkins*, 118 U.S. 356 (1886), would violate the substantive component of the Due Process Clause is an issue that need not be decided today. I am confident, however, that so long as the Equal Protection Clause requires a sodomy law to apply equally to the private consensual conduct of homosexuals and heterosexuals alike, such a law would not long stand in our democratic society. . . .

That this law as applied to private, consensual conduct is unconstitutional under the Equal Protection Clause does not mean that other laws distinguishing between heterosexuals and homosexuals would similarly fail under rational basis review. Texas cannot assert any legitimate state interest here, such as national security or preserving the traditional institution of marriage. Unlike the moral disapproval of same-sex relations—the asserted state interest in this case—other reasons exist to promote the institution of marriage beyond mere moral disapproval of an excluded group. . . .

■ JUSTICE SCALIA, with whom THE CHIEF JUSTICE and JUSTICE THOMAS join, dissenting.

"Liberty finds no refuge in a jurisprudence of doubt." *Planned Parenthood v. Casey*, 505 U.S. 833, 844 (1992). That was the Court's sententious response, barely more than a decade ago, to those seeking to overrule *Roe v. Wade*, 410 U.S. 113 (1973). The Court's response today, to those who have engaged in a 17–year crusade to overrule *Bowers v. Hardwick*, 478 U.S. 186 (1986), is very different. The need for stability and certainty presents no barrier.

Most of the rest of today's opinion has no relevance to its actual holding—that the Texas statute "furthers no legitimate state interest which can justify" its application to petitioners under rational-basis review. Though there is discussion of "fundamental proposition[s]" and "fundamental decisions," nowhere does the Court's opinion declare that homosexual sodomy is a "fundamental right" under the Due Process Clause; nor does it subject the Texas law to the standard of review that would be appropriate (strict scrutiny) if homosexual sodomy *were* a "fundamental right." Thus, while overruling the *outcome* of *Bowers*, the Court leaves strangely untouched its central legal conclusion: "[R]espondent would have us announce . . . a fundamental right to engage in homosexual sodomy. This we are quite unwilling to do." Instead the Court simply describes petitioners' conduct as "an exercise of their liberty"—which it undoubtedly is—and proceeds to apply an unheard-of form of rational-basis review that will have far-reaching implications beyond this case.

I

I begin with the Court's surprising readiness to reconsider a decision rendered a mere 17 years ago in *Bowers v. Hardwick*. I do not myself believe in rigid adherence to *stare decisis* in constitutional cases; but I do believe that we should be consistent rather than manipulative in invoking the doctrine. Today's opinions in support of reversal do not bother to distinguish—or indeed, even bother to mention—the paean to *stare decisis* coauthored by three Members of today's majority in *Planned Parenthood v. Casey*. There, when *stare decisis* meant preservation of judicially invented abortion rights, the widespread criticism of *Roe* was strong reason to *reaffirm* it:

> Where, in the performance of its judicial duties, the Court decides a case in such a way as to resolve the sort of intensely divisive controversy reflected in *Roe*[,] . . . its decision has a dimension that the resolution of the normal case does not carry. . . . [T]o overrule under fire in the absence of the most compelling reason . . . would subvert the Court's legitimacy beyond any serious question.

505 U.S., at 866–867. Today, however, the widespread opposition to *Bowers*, a decision resolving an issue as "intensely divisive" as the issue in *Roe*,

is offered as a reason in favor of *overruling* it. Gone, too, is any "enquiry" (of the sort conducted in *Casey*) into whether the decision sought to be overruled has "proven unworkable," *id.*, at 855.

Today's approach to *stare decisis* invites us to overrule an erroneously decided precedent (including an "intensely divisive" decision) *if*: (1) its foundations have been "ero[ded]" by subsequent decisions; (2) it has been subject to "substantial and continuing" criticism; and (3) it has not induced "individual or societal reliance" that counsels against overturning. The problem is that *Roe* itself—which today's majority surely has no disposition to overrule—satisfies these conditions to at least the same degree as *Bowers*.

(1) A preliminary digressive observation with regard to the first factor: The Court's claim that *Planned Parenthood v. Casey* "casts some doubt" upon the holding in *Bowers* (or any other case, for that matter) does not withstand analysis. As far as its holding is concerned, *Casey* provided a *less* expansive right to abortion than did *Roe, which was already on the books when* Bowers *was decided.* And if the Court is referring not to the holding of Casey, but to the dictum of its famed sweet-mystery-of-life passage ("At the heart of liberty is the right to define one's own concept of existence, of meaning, of the universe, and of the mystery of human life"): That "casts some doubt" upon either the totality of our jurisprudence or else (presumably the right answer) nothing at all. I have never heard of a law that attempted to restrict one's "right to define" certain concepts; and if the passage calls into question the government's power to regulate *actions based on* one's self-defined "concept of existence, etc.," it is the passage that ate the rule of law.

I do not quarrel with the Court's claim that *Romer* "eroded" the "foundations" of *Bowers*' rational-basis holding. But *Roe* and *Casey* have been equally "eroded" by *Washington v. Glucksberg*, 521 U.S. 702, 721 (1997), which held that *only* fundamental rights which are "deeply rooted in this Nation's history and tradition" qualify for anything other than rational-basis scrutiny under the doctrine of "substantive due process." . . .

(2) *Bowers*, the Court says, has been subject to "substantial and continuing [criticism], disapproving of its reasoning in all respects, not just as to its historical assumptions." . . . [T]he Court [cites] two books. See *ibid.* (citing C. Fried, Order and Law; R. Posner, Sex and Reason). Of course, *Roe* too (and by extension *Casey)* had been (and still is) subject to unrelenting criticism, including criticism from the two commentators cited by the Court today. See Fried, at 75 ("*Roe* was a prime example of twisted judging"); Posner, at 337 ("[The Court's] opinion in *Roe* . . . fails to measure up to professional expectations regarding judicial opinions"); Posner, Judicial Opinion Writing, 62 U. Chi. L. Rev. 1421, 1434 (1995) (describing the opinion in *Roe* as an "embarrassing performance[e]").

(3) That leaves, to distinguish the rock-solid, unamendable disposition of *Roe* from the readily overrulable *Bowers*, only the third factor [i.e., societal reliance]. . . . It seems to me that the "societal reliance" on the principles confirmed in *Bowers* and discarded today has been overwhelming. Countless judicial decisions and legislative enactments have relied on the ancient proposition that a governing majority's belief that certain sexual behavior is "immoral and unacceptable" constitutes a rational basis for regulation. *[Here Justice Scalia cites state and federal cases relying on Bowers to uphold restrictions on the sale of sex toys, military service by those who engage in homosexual conduct, fornication, adultery, and public inde-*

cency.—Editors] State laws against bigamy, same-sex marriage, adult incest, prostitution, masturbation, adultery, fornication, bestiality, and obscenity are likewise sustainable only in light of *Bowers'* validation of laws based on moral choices. Every single one of these laws is called into question by today's decision; the Court makes no effort to cabin the scope of its decision to exclude them from its holding. The impossibility of distinguishing homosexuality from other traditional "morals" offenses is precisely why *Bowers* rejected the rational-basis challenge. "The law," it said, "is constantly based on notions of morality, and if all laws representing essentially moral choices are to be invalidated under the Due Process Clause, the courts will be very busy indeed."

What a massive disruption of the current social order, therefore, the overruling of *Bowers* entails. Not so the overruling of *Roe*, which would simply have restored the regime that existed for centuries before 1973, in which the permissibility of, and restrictions upon, abortion were determined legislatively State by State. . . .

To tell the truth, it does not surprise me, and should surprise no one, that the Court has chosen today to revise the standards of *stare decisis* set forth in *Casey*. It has thereby exposed *Casey's* extraordinary deference to precedent for the result-oriented expedient that it is.

II

Having decided that it need not adhere to *stare decisis*, the Court still must establish that *Bowers* was wrongly decided and that the Texas statute, as applied to petitioners, is unconstitutional.

[The Texas statute] undoubtedly imposes constraints on liberty. So do laws prohibiting prostitution, recreational use of heroin, and, for that matter, working more than 60 hours per week in a bakery. But there is no right to "liberty" under the Due Process Clause, though today's opinion repeatedly makes that claim. The Fourteenth Amendment *expressly allows* States to deprive their citizens of "liberty," *so long as "due process of law" is provided.* . . .

Our opinions applying the doctrine known as "substantive due process" hold that the Due Process Clause prohibits States from infringing *fundamental* liberty interests, unless the infringement is narrowly tailored to serve a compelling state interest. *Washington v. Glucksberg*, 521 U.S., at 721. We have held repeatedly, in cases the Court today does not overrule, that *only* fundamental rights qualify for this so-called "heightened scrutiny" protection—that is, rights which are "deeply rooted in this Nation's history and tradition." All other liberty interests may be abridged or abrogated pursuant to a validly enacted state law if that law is rationally related to a legitimate state interest.

Bowers held, first, that criminal prohibitions of homosexual sodomy are not subject to heightened scrutiny because they do not implicate a "fundamental right" under the Due Process Clause. . . .

The Court today does not overrule this holding. Not once does it describe homosexual sodomy as a "fundamental right" or a "fundamental liberty interest," nor does it subject the Texas statute to strict scrutiny. Instead, having failed to establish that the right to homosexual sodomy is "deeply rooted in this Nation's history and tradition," the Court concludes that the application of Texas's statute to petitioners' conduct fails the rational-basis test, and overrules *Bowers'* holding to the contrary. "The Texas statute furthers no legitimate state interest which can justify its intrusion into the personal and private life of the individual." . . .

[Part III reviews the Court's substantive due process and fundamental rights jurisprudence and argues that Bowers rightly rejected the claim that homosexual conduct was a fundamental right "deeply rooted in the Nation's history and tradition," and therefore so clearly "implicit in the concept of ordered liberty" that "neither liberty nor justice would exist if it were sacrificed."—Editors]

IV

I turn now to the ground on which the Court squarely rests its holding: the contention that there is no rational basis for the law here under attack. This proposition is so out of accord with our jurisprudence—indeed, with the jurisprudence of any society we know—that it requires little discussion.

The Texas statute undeniably seeks to further the belief of its citizens that certain forms of sexual behavior are "immoral and unacceptable," *Bowers*, at 196—the same interest furthered by criminal laws against fornication, bigamy, adultery, adult incest, bestiality, and obscenity. *Bowers* held that this *was* a legitimate state interest. The Court today reaches the opposite conclusion. The Texas statute, it says, "furthers *no legitimate state interest* which can justify its intrusion into the personal and private life of the individual" (emphasis added). The Court embraces instead Justice Stevens' declaration in his *Bowers* dissent, that "the fact that a governing majority in a State has traditionally viewed a particular practice as immoral is not a sufficient reason for upholding a law prohibiting the practice." . . . This effectively decrees the end of all morals legislation. If, as the Court asserts, the promotion of majoritarian sexual morality is not even a *legitimate* state interest, none of the above-mentioned laws can survive rational-basis review.

V

Finally, I turn to petitioners' equal-protection challenge, which no Member of the Court save Justice O'Connor embraces: On its face [the statute] applies equally to all persons. Men and women, heterosexuals and homosexuals, are all subject to its prohibition of deviate sexual intercourse with someone of the same sex. To be sure, [it] does distinguish between the sexes insofar as concerns the partner with whom the sexual acts are performed: men can violate the law only with other men, and women only with other women. But this cannot itself be a denial of equal protection, since it is precisely the same distinction regarding partner that is drawn in state laws prohibiting marriage with someone of the same sex while permitting marriage with someone of the opposite sex.

The objection is made, however, that the antimiscegenation laws invalidated in *Loving v. Virginia*, 388 U.S. 1, 8 (1967), similarly were applicable to whites and blacks alike, and only distinguished between the races insofar as the *partner* was concerned. In *Loving*, however, we correctly applied heightened scrutiny, rather than the usual rational-basis review, because the Virginia statute was "designed to maintain White Supremacy." A racially discriminatory purpose is always sufficient to subject a law to strict scrutiny, even a facially neutral law that makes no mention of race. See *Washington v. Davis*, 426 U.S. 229, 241–242 (1976). No purpose to discriminate against men or women as a class can be gleaned from the Texas law, so rational-basis review applies. That review is readily satisfied here by the same rational basis that satisfied it in *Bowers*—society's belief that certain forms of sexual behavior are "immoral and unacceptable," 478 U.S., at 196. This is the same justification that supports many other laws regulating sexual behavior that make a distinction based upon the identity of the partner—for example, laws against adultery, fornication, and adult incest, and laws refusing to recognize homosexual marriage.

JUSTICE O'CONNOR argues that the discrimination in this law which must be justified is not its discrimination with regard to the sex of the partner but its discrimination with regard to the sexual proclivity of the principal actor.... Of course the same could be said of any law. A law against public nudity targets "the conduct that is closely correlated with being a nudist," and hence "is targeted at more than conduct"; it is "directed toward nudists as a class." But be that as it may. Even if the Texas law *does* deny equal protection to "homosexuals as a class," that denial *still* does not need to be justified by anything more than a rational basis, which our cases show is satisfied by the enforcement of traditional notions of sexual morality.

JUSTICE O'CONNOR simply decrees application of "a more searching form of rational basis review" to the Texas statute. The cases she cites do not recognize such a standard, and reach their conclusions only after finding, as required by conventional rational-basis analysis, that no conceivable legitimate state interest supports the classification at issue. Nor does JUSTICE O'CONNOR explain precisely what her "more searching form" of rational-basis review consists of. It must at least mean, however, that laws exhibiting "a desire to harm a politically unpopular group" are invalid *even though* there may be a conceivable rational basis to support them.

This reasoning leaves on pretty shaky grounds state laws limiting marriage to opposite-sex couples. JUSTICE O'CONNOR seeks to preserve them by the conclusory statement that "preserving the traditional institution of marriage" is a legitimate state interest. But "preserving the traditional institution of marriage" is just a kinder way of describing the State's *moral disapproval* of same-sex couples. Texas's interest in [the statute] could be recast in similarly euphemistic terms: "preserving the traditional sexual mores of our society." In the jurisprudence JUSTICE O'CONNOR has seemingly created, judges can validate laws by characterizing them as "preserving the traditions of society" (good); or invalidate them by characterizing them as "expressing moral disapproval" (bad). . . .

Let me be clear that I have nothing against homosexuals, or any other group, promoting their agenda through normal democratic means. Social perceptions of sexual and other morality change over time, and every group has the right to persuade its fellow citizens that its view of such matters is the best. That homosexuals have achieved some success in that enterprise is attested to by the fact that Texas is one of the few remaining States that criminalize private, consensual homosexual acts. But persuading one's fellow citizens is one thing, and imposing one's views in absence of democratic majority will is something else. I would no more require a State to criminalize homosexual acts—or, for that matter, display *any* moral disapprobation of them—than I would *forbid* it to do so. What Texas has chosen to do is well within the range of traditional democratic action, and its hand should not be stayed through the invention of a brand-new "constitutional right" by a Court that is impatient of democratic change. It is indeed true that "later generations can see that laws once thought necessary and proper in fact serve only to oppress"; and when that happens, later generations can repeal those laws. But it is the premise of our system that those judgments are to be made by the people, and not imposed by a governing caste that knows best.

One of the benefits of leaving regulation of this matter to the people rather than to the courts is that the people, unlike judges, need not carry things to their logical conclusion. The people may feel that their disapprobation of homosexual conduct is strong enough to disallow homosexual marriage, but not strong enough to criminalize private homosexual acts—and may legislate accordingly. The Court today pretends that it possesses a similar freedom of action, so that we need not fear judicial imposition of homosexual marriage, as has recently occurred in Canada (in a decision that the Canadian Government has chosen not to appeal). At the end of its opinion—after having laid waste the foundations of our rational-basis jurisprudence—the Court says that the present case "does not involve whether the government must give formal recognition to any relationship that homosexual persons seek to enter." Do not believe it. More illuminating than this bald, unreasoned disclaimer is the progression of thought displayed by an earlier passage in the Court's opinion, which notes the constitutional protections afforded to "personal decisions relating to *marriage, procreation, contraception, family relationships, child rearing, and education*" (emphasis added), and then declares that "[p]ersons in a homosexual relationship may seek autonomy for these purposes, just as heterosexual persons do." Today's opinion dismantles the structure of constitutional law that has permitted a distinction to be made between heterosexual and homosexual unions, insofar as formal recognition in marriage is concerned. If moral disapprobation of homosexual conduct is "no legitimate state interest" for purposes of proscribing that conduct; and if, as the Court coos (casting aside all pretense of neutrality), "[w]hen sexuality finds overt expression in intimate conduct with another person, the conduct can be but one element in a personal bond that is more enduring"; what justification could there possibly be for denying the benefits of marriage to homosexual couples exercising "[t]he liberty protected by the Constitution"? Surely not the encouragement of procreation, since the sterile and the elderly are allowed to marry. This case "does not involve" the issue of homosexual marriage only if one entertains the belief that principle and logic have nothing to do with the decisions of this Court. Many will hope that, as the Court comfortingly assures us, this is so.

The matters appropriate for this Court's resolution are only three: Texas's prohibition of sodomy neither infringes a "fundamental right" (which the Court does not dispute), nor is unsupported by a rational relation to what the Constitution considers a legitimate state interest, nor denies the equal protection of the laws. I dissent.

■ JUSTICE THOMAS, dissenting.

I join JUSTICE SCALIA'S dissenting opinion. I write separately to note that the law before the Court today "is . . . uncommonly silly." *Griswold v. Connecticut,* 381 U.S. 479, 527 (1965) (Stewart, J., dissenting). If I were a member of the Texas Legislature, I would vote to repeal it. Punishing someone for expressing his sexual preference through noncommercial consensual conduct with another adult does not appear to be a worthy way to expend valuable law enforcement resources.

Notwithstanding this, I recognize that as a Member of this Court I am not empowered to help petitioners and others similarly situated. My duty, rather, is to "decide cases agreeably to the Constitution and laws of the United States." *Id.,* at 530. And, just like Justice Stewart, I "can find [neither in the Bill of Rights nor any other part of the Constitution a] general right of privacy," *ibid.,* or as the Court terms it today, the "liberty of the person both in its spatial and more transcendent dimensions."

NOTES

1. *Bowers* and *Lawrence* employed quite different methodology for substantive due process. First, consider the methodology of *Bowers*. Was it similar to the approach taken in *Glucksberg*—invalidating a statute under substantive due process only where a claimed liberty is, taken at its most specific level, "deeply rooted" in the nation's history and its traditions of liberty? Is it true, as *Bowers* asserts, that the Court comes closest to illegitimacy when it creates new, non-textual rights? Next, consider the methodology of *Lawrence*. The majority opinion begins with a sweeping statement of principle: "Liberty presumes an autonomy of self that includes freedom of thought, belief, expression, and certain intimate conduct. The instant case involves liberty of the person both in its spatial and in its more transcendent dimensions." How does the Court connect that principle to the holding in the case? What is the methodology from *Lawrence* that the Court can use in future cases? How is it different from the methodology of Justice Souter in his *Glucksberg* concurrence? How would *Glucksberg* have been decided if the Court had instead used *Lawrence*'s methodology? How would *Lochner* have been decided?

2. What is the difference in effect between the reasoning of the *Lawrence* majority and that of Justice O'Connor's concurrence? Is the Equal Protection Clause argument embraced by Justice O'Connor broader or narrower in its implications than the majority's Due Process Clause argument? Which argument for *Lawrence*'s result—an argument based in the Equal Protection Clause or in the Due Process Clause—is easier to ground in the line of cases beginning with *Griswold*? Which is easier to anchor in the text and structure of the Constitution? Do the two arguments have different implications for whether the Court should invalidate laws that allow marriage only for opposite-sex couples? (As this book went to press, the Court was considering two cases involving, in one way or another, constitutional claims to same-sex marriage: *United States v. Windsor* and *Hollingsworth v. Perry*.)

3. What do you make of Justice Scalia's *stare decisis* point? What, exactly, is he dissenting from? The holding in *Lawrence*? Or is his real target the holding in *Casey*? Is he objecting to the Court's inconsistent application of *stare decisis*, or is he objecting to the doctrine itself? Is *Lawrence* consistent with the criteria for overruling precedent that *Casey* establishes? If the Court is inconsistent in its approach to *stare decisis*, what should it do—adhere more strictly to past decisions, or abandon any pretense of relying on precedent and decide each constitutional case on its own merits? Recall that Justice O'Connor had been in the majority in *Bowers*, and that she would not have overruled it in *Lawrence*. Should individual justices apply some version of the doctrine of *stare decisis* to their own past opinions and votes?

4. Is Justice Scalia right that *Lawrence* holds that moral views cannot be a rational basis for law? Is that the only way to read the majority decision? Is it the best way? Is Justice Scalia right that there is no way to distinguish "preserving the traditions of society" from "expressing moral disapproval"? After *Lawrence*, can either of those characterizations support a statutory classifica-

tion? Does it depend on the kind of interest involved? How does the Court specify and characterize the interest at stake in *Lawrence*?

Looking Back at Substantive Due Process

This chapter has presented a number of due process cases. Some are straightforwardly about procedural due process (*Calder* and *Eldridge*). Some are part of the Court's shift to substantive due process at the start of the twentieth century (*Lochner* and *Pierce*). Some are major steps in the evolution of the Court's modern substantive due process jurisprudence (*Griswold*, *Eisenstadt*, *Roe*, and *Casey*). And some are cases that acutely represent the Court's struggle over the methodology of substantive due process (*Glucksberg*, *Bowers*, and *Lawrence*).

As you think back over these cases, consider again the basic questions of constitutional interpretation they raise. Which cases are most easily traced to the text, structure, and history of the Constitution? If you are generally inclined to accept the Court's modern substantive due process jurisprudence, how do you respond to the charge that the justices are imposing their own moral and political views on the people, as in *Dred Scott* and *Lochner*? Which of the cases you have read are most vulnerable to this argument? If you are generally inclined to reject the Court's modern substantive due process jurisprudence, how do you respond to the argument that substantive due process is necessary to protect against severe and intrusive legislative restrictions? Which of the cases involve laws that most squarely raise this concern?

More generally, what do you take away from these cases about how to interpret the Constitution? What is the proper method? However you answer that question, how would you justify your choice of method to someone who was critical of it? Would you advise that it be used for every constitution, or is it specific to the U.S. Constitution? What are the demands it makes on judges, in the sense of what does it require them to be good at? What are the method's strengths and weaknesses? Does it lead to any constitutional results you think are dangerous or unwise? If so, are those results a reason to reject your approach? If not—if your constitutional analysis would mirror what you think is good policy—is *that* a reason to reject your approach?

CHAPTER 8

REPRESENTATION, VOTING, AND REPUBLICANISM

[Assignment 73]

How democratic is the Constitution? How representative is America's ostensibly representative government? What does the Constitution say about voting? This chapter addresses these questions, and it takes up a theme that pervades the entire Constitution and is reflected in a number of specific provisions: "republicanism."

I. REPUBLICANISM AND ELECTORAL STRUCTURES

If you were to ask people what kind of regime the United States has, most would answer: a democracy. The founders would have been more likely to answer: a republic. By "democracy" the founders understood government directly by the people through something like town meetings or even through mobs. In *The Federalist No. 39*, James Madison defined a "republic" as "a government which derives all its powers directly or indirectly from the great body of the people, and is administered by persons holding their offices during pleasure for a limited period, or during good behavior." In other words, a republic is a government in which the people rule indirectly, through representatives—what today might be called a representative democracy.

Much of the constitutional text sets forth the structure of representative government at the federal level, but it says nothing about the structure of government at the state or local level, leaving this to be determined by the various state constitutions. The only federal constitutional constraint on the politics or governing structures of the states in the original Constitution is the Republican Form of Government Clause (also called the Guarantee Clause), which provides that "the United States shall guarantee to every State in this Union a Republican Form of Government." Art. IV, Sec. 4. The logic of this provision is clear: much as the European Union has insisted that no country can be considered for entry unless it is a liberal democracy, our founders believed that a Union could not be established if some of its elements were monarchies, aristocracies, or dictatorships. This leaves much latitude to state constitutional law, but what are the limits? How is the Republican Form of Government Clause to be enforced? As noted earlier, the Supreme Court, in *Luther v. Borden*, 48 U.S. 1 (1849), found this a political judgment committed to Congress and the president, and not independently to be determined by the federal courts. Is this an effective way of enforcing the Guarantee Clause's "guarantee"?

Members of the House of Representatives are elected by "the People" of "the several States," and (until the Seventeenth Amendment) senators were elected by the state legislatures. Art. I, Secs. 2–3. House members are allotted among the states according to population, and each state is entitled to two senators. The president is elected indirectly, by "Electors" chosen by each state "in such Manner as the Legislature thereof may direct." Art. II,

Sec. 1. Each state is allotted a number of electors equal to the number of its representatives plus its senators, thus giving a slight edge to the smaller states. Nothing in the Constitution requires that electors be chosen by popular election, and for the first several decades, it was common for legislatures themselves to elect the electors. (This had a tendency to convert state legislative elections into a kind of national referendum.) Since 1824, all states have chosen electors by popular vote, usually on a state-wide basis.

The original constitutional text had little to say about the machinery of elections. Article I, Section 3 provides that "The Time, Places and Manner of holding Elections for Senators and Representatives, shall be prescribed in each State by the Legislature thereof; but the Congress may at any time by Law make or alter such Regulations, except as to the Places of chusing Senators." This gives state legislatures the authority to determine how elections will be conducted for state offices, and allows them to control elections for Congress in the first instance. But it allows Congress, when it wishes, to override state law and make its own regulations for congressional elections. Congress has exercised this power from time to time, such as by requiring single-member districting for elections to the House. It is notable, given how important electoral structure is in constitutional design, that so little of it was addressed by the original Constitution.

It may not be surprising, then, that voting qualifications and electoral structure have predominated in subsequent amendments. Since 1789, the Constitution has been amended eighteen times, for a total of twenty-seven amendments. Twelve of those amendments pertain to selection of representatives or executive officers. Read all of the amendments, and identify those that fall in this category. Think about what they accomplish, and why. Seven of the amendments expanded the suffrage. Probably the most significant of the others was the Seventeenth Amendment, adopted in 1913. It provides for the election of senators by popular vote rather than by the state legislatures, thus reversing one of the major structural compromises of the Constitutional Convention. Although justified largely on the ground that popular election of senators would make government more democratic, it had the effect of eliminating the representation of states as states in the national legislature, thus removing the Constitution's main structural safeguard for federalism. Before the Seventeenth Amendment, every federal law required the approval not only of representatives of a majority of Americans, but also representatives of the state governments—a powerful protection for the balance of power between federal and state governments. After the Seventeenth Amendment, only the self-restraint of Congress and the (sporadic) intervention of the courts remained to check aggrandizement of federal power at the expense of the states.

In this chapter, we will explore three of the most important constitutional questions arising from the Constitution's provisions about voting and elections: Who can vote? How are districts drawn? How are disputed elections decided?

A. WHO CAN VOTE?

Article I, Section 2 provides that the House of Representatives is chosen biannually "by the People of the several States." Who are "the People"? What are the "several States?" Does the latter term include the District of Columbia? Does the former term include all citizens? The Constitution further provides that for both House and Senate elections, voters "in each State shall have the Qualifications requisite for Electors of the most numerous Branch of the State Legislature." Art. I, Sec. 2 (representatives); Amend. XVII (senators). At the time the Constitution was proposed and ratified, every state but one limited the franchise to male voters (the exception, New Jersey, subsequently repealed women's suffrage in 1807). All states excluded slaves (and most excluded free blacks) from voting. And all imposed property qualifications. A few allowed aliens to vote. This was the broadest franchise in history, but even so, far fewer than half of adults could vote. In what sense, then, were members of Congress elected by "the People"? In *The Federalist No. 39*, Madison explained that, to be "republican," power must be "derived from the great body of the society, not from an inconsiderable proportion or a favored class of it." Otherwise, he explained, "a handful of tyrannical nobles, exercising their oppressions by a delegation of their powers," could be called a republic. Universal suffrage was not required, yet at some point a too-restrictive franchise would be unrepublican. The only test of when this point would be reached was that voting qualifications for federal office must be the same ones used for elections to the most numerous branch of the state legislature. The founders evidently thought this was democracy enough.

Under the notorious Three–Fifths Compromise, slaves were counted as three-fifths of a person for purposes of allocating congressional seats, although they were not allowed to vote. This permitted the voting population of the slave states, who were often slave owners, to exercise political power greater than their share of the citizen population. As we have already seen, this tipped the 1800 election in favor of the Southern slave-owning candidate, Thomas Jefferson, and may have been responsible for the fact that every president until Lincoln, with the sole exception of the two one-term Adamses, was either a slaveholder or a Northern slavery sympathizer.

During the early nineteenth century, the states abolished property qualifications, leading to universal suffrage for white males. This change was a tenet of Jacksonian Democracy, and it occurred without any involvement of federal constitutional law.

The last state to abolish property qualifications was Rhode Island. It was governed according to a revised royal charter dating back to 1663, which confined voting to property owners. By 1840, only a minority of the adult male population could vote. Because any change required the support of the privileged minority (who liked their power) there seemed to be no peaceful means of empowering the majority. Explicitly invoking the right of revolution under the Declaration of Independence, an unauthorized "People's Convention" met under the leadership of Thomas Dorr, drew up a new constitution, held elections, and established a shadow government in competition with the government under the charter. Violence ensued, called "Dorr's Rebellion." The Dorrites attempted to capture the state's arsenal but were not successful; the rebellion was put down by force and Dorr was arrested and prosecuted for treason against the state. Soon after, however, the charter government liberalized the franchise. In a lawsuit arising from the incident, the Supreme Court declined to decide which one of the competing governments was legitimate, declaring this a "political question." (This case, *Luther v. Borden*, is printed in Chapter 3.)

The Thirteenth Amendment (1865), adopted after the Civil War, abolished slavery and thus implicitly repealed the Three–Fifths Clause. The amendment gave former slaves their freedom but it did not give them the vote. The ironic result was to increase the political power of the defeated Southern states, which gained an estimated sixteen seats in the House (out of 243) and the same number of Electoral College votes. The Republican Party, representing the victorious North, responded with the Fourteenth Amendment (1868), Section Two of which provided that when the right to vote "is denied to any of the male inhabitants of such State, being twenty-one years of age, and citizens of the United States, or in any way abridged, except for participation in rebellion, or other crime, the basis of representation therein shall be reduced in the proportion which the number of such male citizens shall bear to the whole number of male citizens twenty-one years of age in such State." Thus, states denying former slaves the right to vote would lose representation based on those inhabitants. This had its greatest effect in Southern states with numerous former slaves. Northern states could deny the vote to their much smaller black populations at little representational cost.

Note the wording of Section Two. It was highly controversial at the time of its adoption, because it introduced the word "male"—and hence express sex discrimination—into the Constitution for the first time. It also appears to bless the exclusion of felons from the franchise. Today, an estimated 5.85 million Americans have been convicted of felonies, and many have permanently lost their right to vote. In *Richardson v. Ramirez*, 418 U.S. 24 (1974), the Supreme Court upheld the exclusion of felons from the franchise largely because Section Two demonstrates that the original understanding of the Fourteenth Amendment permitted such exclusion.

Next came the Fifteenth Amendment, ratified in 1870. It provided that the right to vote "shall not be denied or abridged by the United States or by any State on account of race, color, or previous condition of servitude." Like Section Two of the Fourteenth Amendment, the Fifteenth drove a wedge between two wings of the civil rights movement: those primarily concerned with the rights of the former slaves, and those equally committed to sex equality and women's suffrage. The Fifteenth Amendment, enforced by acts of Congress, was successful at first. Black Southerners voted in large numbers throughout the 1870s and into the 1880s, providing a well of supporters for the Republican Party. But after a disputed presidential election was resolved with the Compromise of 1877, U.S. troops were withdrawn from the South and federal enforcement virtually ceased. White Southerners used increasingly devious means of disenfranchisement, and by 1900 virtually no black citizens could vote in the states of the former Confederacy. In *Giles v. Harris*, 189 U.S. 475 (1903) (printed in Chapter 7), in an opinion by Justice Oliver Wendell Holmes, the Supreme Court effectively rendered the Fifteenth Amendment a dead letter. Not until Congress enacted the Voting Rights Act in 1965 were black Americans again able to exercise their constitutional right to vote.

Apart from Section Two, did the Fourteenth Amendment affect the authority of the states to restrict the franchise through voting qualifications? As discussed in Chapter 7, the Court, in one of its earliest interpretations of the Fourteenth Amendment, *Minor v. Happersett*, 88 U.S. 162 (1875), rejected a constitutional challenge alleging that Missouri's limitation of the right to vote to men violated the Fourteenth Amendment. (If you have not read this case—or even if you have—this would be an opportune time to consider it.) The plaintiff in the case argued that the right to vote was protected by the Privileges or Immunities Clause of the Fourteenth Amendment. The Court rejected that argument, pointing to the express sex-based distinction of Section Two of the Fourteenth Amendment; the negative implication of the Fifteenth Amendment, which forbade suffrage discrimination for race but not sex; and the traditional understanding that the amendment was addressed to "civil rights" rather than to "political rights" such as the right to vote.

The remedy for sex discrimination in voting was eventually a constitutional amendment. The Constitution was amended several times in the twentieth century to extend the franchise, with women's suffrage leading the way. The Nineteenth Amendment (1920) forbids discrimination of the basis of sex, thus reversing the outcome of *Minor v. Happersett*; the Twenty-third (1961) gives inhabitants of the District of Columbia the right to choose electors for president; the Twenty-fourth (1964) forbids imposition of poll taxes in federal elections, and the Twenty-sixth (1971) forbids denial of the vote based on age for persons older than seventeen.

Do these amendments, along with the Fifteenth and Section Two of the Fourteenth, cast any light on what it means to say, in Article I, Section 2, and the Seventeenth Amendment, that members of Congress will be elected by "the People"? Does this reference to "the People" create a constitutional right to vote in federal elections that does not also apply to state elections? The Constitution gives the states authority to determine voting qualifications, while forbidding them to employ certain criteria (race, sex, age) in doing so. What is the constitutional status of restrictions not covered by one of these amendments?

Harper v. Virginia State Board of Elections
383 U.S. 663 (1966)

■ JUSTICE DOUGLAS delivered the opinion of the Court:

[This case involved a $1.50 poll tax imposed as a condition to voting in state elections. The Twenty-fourth Amendment, which was ratified in 1964, forbids poll taxes in federal elections.—Editors]

. . . While the right to vote in federal elections is conferred by Art. I, § 2, of the Constitution, the right to vote in state elections is nowhere expressly mentioned. . . .

We conclude that a State violates the Equal Protection Clause of the Fourteenth Amendment whenever it makes the affluence of the voter or payment of any fee an electoral standard. Voter qualifications have no relation to wealth nor to paying or not paying this or any other tax. Our cases demonstrate that the Equal Protection Clause of the Fourteenth Amendment restrains the States from fixing voter qualifications which invidiously discriminate. . . .

Long ago in *Yick Wo v. Hopkins*, 118 U.S. 356, 370 [(1886),] the Court referred to "the political franchise of voting" as a "fundamental political right, because preservative of all rights." Recently in *Reynolds v. Sims*, 377 U.S. 533, 561–562, we said, "Undoubtedly, the right of suffrage is a fundamental matter in a free and democratic society. Especially since the right to exercise the franchise in a free and unimpaired manner is preservative of other basic civil and political rights, any alleged infringement of the right of citizens to vote must be carefully and meticulously scrutinized." . . .

We say the same whether the citizen, otherwise qualified to vote, has $1.50 in his pocket or nothing at all, pays the fee or fails to pay it. The principle that denies the State the right to dilute a citizen's vote on account of his economic status or other such factors by analogy bars a system which excludes those unable to pay a fee to vote or who fail to pay.

It is argued that a State may exact fees from citizens for many different kinds of licenses; that if it can demand from all an equal fee for a driver's license, it can demand from all an equal poll tax for voting. But we must remember that the interest of the State, when it comes to voting, is limited to the power to fix qualifications. Wealth, like race, creed, or color, is not germane to one's ability to participate intelligently in the electoral process. Lines drawn on the basis of wealth or property, like those of race (*Korematsu v. United States*, 323 U.S. 214, 216), are traditionally disfavored. To introduce wealth or payment of a fee as a measure of a voter's qualifications is to introduce a capricious or irrelevant factor. The degree of the discrimination is irrelevant. In this context—that is, as a condition of obtaining a ballot—the requirement of fee paying causes an "invidious" discrimination (*Skinner v. State of Oklahoma*, 316 U.S. 535, 514) that runs afoul of the Equal Protection Clause. Levy "by the poll," as stated in Breedlove v. Suttles, 302 U.S. at 281, is an old familiar form of taxation; and we say nothing to impair its validity so long as it is not made a condition to the exercise of the franchise. Breedlove v. Suttles sanctioned its use as "a prerequisite of voting." Id., at 283. To that extent the *Breedlove* case is overruled.

We agree, of course, with Mr. Justice Holmes that the Due Process Clause of the Fourteenth Amendment "does not enact Mr. Herbert Spencer's Social Statics" (*Lochner v. People of State of New York*, 198 U.S. 45, 75). Likewise, the Equal Protection Clause is not shackled to the political theory of a particular era. In determining what lines are unconstitutionally discriminatory, we have never been confined to historic notions of equality, any more than we have restricted due process to a fixed catalogue of what was at a given time deemed to be the limits of fundamental rights. See *Malloy v. Hogan*, 378 U.S. 1, 5–6. Notions of what constitutes equal treatment for purposes of the Equal Protection Clause do change. . . .

In a recent searching re-examination of the Equal Protection Clause, we held, as already noted, that "the opportunity for equal participation by all voters in the election of state legislators" is required. *Reynolds v. Sims,* supra, 377 U.S. at 566. We decline to qualify that principle by sustaining this poll tax. Our conclusion, like that in *Reynolds v. Sims*, is founded not on what we think governmental policy should be, but on what the Equal Protection Clause requires.

We have long been mindful that where fundamental rights and liberties are asserted under the Equal Protection Clause, classifications which might invade or restrain them must be closely scrutinized and carefully confined. Those principles apply here. For to repeat, wealth or fee paying has, in our view, no relation to voting qualifications; the right to vote is too precious, too fundamental to be so burdened or conditioned.

■ Mr. Justice Black, dissenting.

In *Breedlove v. Suttles*, 302 U.S. 277, decided December 6, 1937, . . . we unanimously upheld the right of the State of Georgia to make payment of its state poll tax a prerequisite to voting in state elections. We rejected at that time contentions that the state law violated the Equal Protection Clause of the Fourteenth Amendment because it put an unequal burden on different groups of people according to their age, sex, and ability to pay. . . .

Later, May 28, 1951, I joined the Court's judgment in *Butler v. Thompson*, 341 U.S. 937, upholding, over the dissent of Mr. Justice Douglas, the Virginia state poll tax law challenged here against the same equal protection challenges. Since the *Breedlove* and *Butler* cases were decided the Federal Constitution has not been amended in the only way it could constitutionally have been, that is, as provided in Article V of the Constitution. I would adhere to the holding of those cases. The Court, however, overrules *Breedlove* in part, but its opinion reveals that it does so not by using its limited power to interpret the original meaning of the Equal Protection Clause, but by giving that clause a new meaning which it believes represents a better governmental policy. . . .

I think the interpretation that this Court gave the Equal Protection Clause in *Breedlove* was correct. The mere fact that a law results in treating some groups differently from others does not, of course, automatically amount to a violation of the Equal Protection Clause. To bar a State from drawing any distinctions in the application of its laws would practically paralyze the regulatory power of legislative bodies. Consequently "[t]he constitutional command for a state to afford 'equal protection of the laws' sets a goal not attainable by the invention and application of a precise formula." Voting laws are no exception to this principle. All voting laws treat some persons differently from others in some respects. . . .

A study of our cases shows that this Court has refused to use the general language of the Equal Protection Clause as though it provided a handy instrument to strike down state laws which the Court feels are based on bad governmental policy. The equal protection cases carefully analyzed boil down to the principle that distinctions drawn and even discriminations imposed by state laws do not violate the Equal Protection Clause so long as these distinctions and discriminations are not "irrational," "irrelevant," "unreasonable," "arbitrary," or "invidious." These vague and indefinite terms do not, of course, provide a precise formula or an automatic mechanism for deciding cases arising under the Equal Protection Clause. The restrictive connotations of these terms, however (which in other contexts have been used to expand the Court's power inordinately) are a plain recognition of the fact that under a proper interpretation of the Equal Protection Clause States are to have the broadest kind of leeway in areas where they have a general constitutional competence to act. In view of the purpose of the terms to restrain the courts from a wholesale invalidation of state laws under the Equal Protection Clause it would be difficult to say that the poll tax requirement is "irrational" or "arbitrary" or works "invidious discriminations." State poll tax legislation can "reasonably," "rationally" and without an "invidious" or evil purpose to injure anyone be found to rest on a number of state policies including (1) the State's desire to collect its revenue, and (2) its belief that voters who pay a poll tax will be interested in furthering the State's welfare when they vote. . . . Although I join the Court in disliking the policy of the poll tax, this is not in my judgment a justifiable reason for holding this poll tax law unconstitutional. Such a holding on my part would, in my judgment, be an exercise of power which the Constitution does not confer upon me.

. . . The Court gives no reason at all to discredit the long-standing beliefs that making the payment of a tax a prerequisite to voting is an effective way of collecting revenue and that people who pay their taxes are likely to have a far greater interest in their government. The Court's failure to give any reasons to show that these purposes of the poll tax are "irrational," "unreasonable," "arbitrary," or "invidious" is a pretty clear indication to me that none exist. I can only conclude that the primary, controlling, predominate, if not the exclusive reason for declaring the Virginia law unconstitutional is the Court's deep-seated hostility and antagonism, which I share, to making payment of a tax a prerequisite to voting.

The Court's justification for consulting its own notions rather than following the original meaning of the Constitution, as I would, apparently is based on the belief of the majority of the Court that for this Court to be bound by the original meaning of the Constitution is an intolerable and debilitating evil; that our Constitution should not be "shackled to the political theory of a particular era," and that to save the country from the original Constitution the Court must have constant power to renew it and keep it abreast of this Court's more enlightening theories of what is best for our society. It seems to me that this is an attack not only on the great value of our Constitution itself but also on the concept of a written constitution which is to survive through the years as originally written unless changed through the amendment process which the Framers wisely provided. Moreover, when a "political theory" embodied in our Constitution becomes outdated, it seems to me that a majority of the nine members of this Court are not only without constitutional power but are far less qualified to choose a new constitutional political theory than the people of this country proceeding in the manner provided by Article V. . . .

■ [The dissent of JUSTICE HARLAN, joined by JUSTICE STEWART, is omitted.]

NOTES

1. On August 27, 1962, Congress proposed the Twenty-fourth Amendment, which was ratified by the requisite three-quarters of the states on January 23, 1964. This amendment abolished the poll tax, but only for federal elections. It was only two years later, in the case you just read, that the Supreme Court struck down poll taxes as applied to all elections, state as well as federal. Should the *expressio unius* canon be applied to constitutional amendments? Imagine that the Constitution were a statute, and you were asked whether the section of the statute containing the words of our Fourteenth Amendment had made poll taxes unconstitutional. Would the existence of the section of the statute containing the words of our Twenty-fourth Amendment affect your interpretation? Does the fact that, even after the Fourteenth Amendment, the People have amended the Constitution four times to eliminate particular restrictions on the franchise (race, sex, age, and poll taxes in federal elections) influence your interpretation? Were those amendments unnecessary?

2. What constitutional standard did the Court apply in *Harper*? Did it conclude that poll taxes are wholly arbitrary and unrelated to a legitimate purpose? Or did it conclude that restrictions on the fundamental right to vote require especially strong justifications? In later cases, the Supreme Court explicitly applied strict scrutiny to restrictions on the franchise, which means that the restriction must be necessary for the achievement of a compelling governmental purpose. As noted in Chapter 7, the Court has applied this standard, under the Equal Protection Clause, both to "suspect classifications" of persons and—in a more strained reading of the text—to restrictions on "fundamental rights." Is voting a "fundamental right"? Does it matter that, as Justice Douglas notes in his *Harper* majority opinion, "the right to vote in state elections is nowhere expressly mentioned" in the Constitution?

3. Why didn't the Court treat the poll tax as a *Fifteenth* Amendment issue? After all, there is substantial historical evidence that poll taxes were explicitly adopted for the purpose of disenfranchising black (and sometimes poor white) voters. See J. Morgan Kousser, THE SHAPING OF SOUTHERN POLITICS: SUFFRAGE RESTRICTIONS AND THE ESTABLISHMENT OF THE ONE–PARTY SOUTH, 1880–1910 (1974).

4. Since *Harper*, only one constitutional amendment expanding the franchise has been adopted (the Twenty–sixth Amendment forbidding denial of the right to vote on the basis of age for persons eighteen or older), but the Supreme Court has declared many other voting restrictions unconstitutional. These include:

- Exclusion of voters who were unable to explain provisions of the federal or state constitution (*Louisiana v. United States*, 380 U.S. 145 (1965))

- Literacy tests (*Gaston County v. United States*, 395 U.S. 285 (1969))

- Property qualifications in bond approval referenda (*Cipriano v. City of Houma*, 395 U.S. 701 (1969); *City of Phoenix v. Kolodziejski*, 399 U.S. 204 (1970); *Hill v. Stone*, 421 U.S. 289 (1975))

- Limiting the franchise in school district elections to parents of children in school and those liable to pay school property taxes (*Kramer v. Union Free School Dist. No. 15*, 395 U.S. 621 (1969))

- Exclusion of persons living in federal enclaves from voting in state elections (*Evans v. Cornman*, 398 U.S. 419 (1970))

- One-year residency requirement (*Dunn v. Blumstein*, 405 U.S. 330 (1972))

- Prohibiting voting in a primary by anyone who had voted in the other party's primary within 23 months (*Kusper v. Pontikes*, 414 U.S. 51 (1973))

- Restricting the franchise for trustees of the Office of Hawaiian Affairs to persons of "Hawaiian ancestry" (*Rice v. Cayetano*, 528 U.S. 495 (2000) (Fifteenth Amendment))

On the other hand, the Court has upheld some voter restrictions:

- Twenty-one year voting age (*Oregon v. Mitchell*, 400 U.S. 112 (1970) (holding that Congress lacked the power to lower the voting age in state elections because this was beyond the scope of enforcing the Fourteenth Amendment))—a restriction superseded by the Twenty–sixth Amendment

- Disenfranchisement of felons (*Richardson v. Ramirez*, 418 U.S. 24 (1974))

- Weighting votes for directors of an agricultural and power district according to extent of land ownership (*Ball v. James*, 451 U.S. 355 (1981))

- The Court's most recent relevant decision came on the highly controversial subject of state requirements that voters show photo identification—requirements that supporters say will reduce voter fraud, but which critics say will suppress the vote of poor, elderly, and minority voters. In *Crawford v. Marion County Election Bd.*, 553 U.S. 181

(2008), the Court upheld such a requirement. The lack of evidence on the record for either side played an important part in the decision. The state presented no evidence that in-person voter fraud had ever occurred in Indiana, and the plaintiffs presented no evidence that any person would be unable to vote as a result of the requirement. Three justices (Stevens, Roberts, and Kennedy) held only that in light of this record, the plaintiffs had not met their burden of showing that the law was facially unconstitutional. They explained:

> [U]nder the standard applied in *Harper,* even rational restrictions on the right to vote are invidious if they are unrelated to voter qualifications. In *Anderson v. Celebrezze,* 460 U.S. 780 (1983), however, we confirmed the general rule that "evenhanded restrictions that protect the integrity and reliability of the electoral process itself" are not invidious and satisfy the standard set forth in *Harper,* 460 U.S., at 788, n. 9. Rather than applying any "litmus test" that would neatly separate valid from invalid restrictions, we concluded that a court must identify and evaluate the interests put forward by the State as justifications for the burden imposed by its rule, and then make the "hard judgment" that our adversary system demands.

Is that a "judicially manageable standard"? Three justices (Scalia, Thomas, and Alito) reasoned that "universally applicable" requirements are subject only to "a deferential 'important regulatory interest' standard" unless they impose a "severe burden on the right to vote." Two justices (Souter and Ginsburg) dissented on the ground that the burden on poor, old, and disabled voters, while not "severe," was substantial enough to outweigh the largely abstract and unsupported state interest in preventing in-person vote fraud. They reasoned:

> If the Court's decision in *Harper v. Virginia Bd. of Elections* stands for anything, it is that being poor has nothing to do with being qualified to vote. *Harper* made clear that "[t]o introduce wealth or payment of a fee as a measure of a voter's qualifications is to introduce a capricious or irrelevant factor." The State's requirements here, that people without cars travel to a motor vehicle registry and that the poor who fail to do that get to their county seats within 10 days of every election, likewise translate into unjustified economic burdens uncomfortably close to the outright $1.50 fee we struck down 42 years ago. Like that fee, the onus of the Indiana law is illegitimate just because it correlates with no state interest so well as it does with the object of deterring poorer residents from exercising the franchise.

Justice Breyer also dissented, largely on the ground that the Indiana law is one of the most restrictive in the country, and the record "nowhere provides a convincing reason" for these increased burdens.

B. ONE PERSON, ONE VOTE

Determining who can vote is just the first step. The shape, size, and contours of electoral districts can have profound effects on the allocation of political power. For most of our history, these decisions were made by state legislatures without federal judicial interference. In many states, legislatures failed or refused to draw new maps in response to changes in the distribution of population. This coincided with a time of relative decline in rural populations and the dramatic growth of suburbs. The effect was preserve rural and agricultural political dominance even after these areas ceased to have a majority of the population. In *Colegrove v. Green*, 328 U.S. 549 (1946), plaintiffs challenged an Illinois congressional districting plan that was largely unchanged from that created after the census of 1900. The Supreme Court held that a suit challenging the congressional districting scheme for the State of Illinois was not justiciable in federal court. The Court stated: "To sustain this action would cut very deep into the very being of Congress. Courts ought not to enter this political thicket. The remedy for unfairness in districting is to secure State legislatures that will apportion properly, or to invoke the ample powers of Congress."

That changed in the 1960s, with *Baker v. Carr*, a challenge to state legislative districting in Tennessee. Despite a state constitutional requirement that state legislative districts be drawn according to population, which lacked any procedure for state judicial enforcement, the legislature left existing legislative boundaries in place from 1901 to 1963. As a result, the suburbs and cities were grossly underrepresented. For example, rural Moore County, Tennessee, had a single representative for 2,340 voters, whereas urban Shelby County was allotted only eight representatives for its over 312,000 voters—roughly 44,000 voters per representative. Voters in rural districts having only 40% of the voting population elected 63 of the 99 members of the state House of Representatives—almost a two-thirds majority. Districts having only 37% of the voting population elected 20 of the 33 senators—a 61% majority. Moreover, the urban and suburban majority had no peaceful political means for redressing the electoral balance. The state supreme court held that it had no power to order reapportionment, and Tennessee had no mechanism for bypassing the legislature to achieve constitutional reform. No matter how loudly the people of Nashville, Memphis, Chattanooga, and the suburbs complained, the rural legislators had no incentive to respond. They were in control. Why would they give up power when they did not have to?

Baker v. Carr

369 U.S. 186 (1962)

■ MR. JUSTICE BRENNAN delivered the opinion of the Court.

. . . The complaint, alleging that by means of a 1901 statute of Tennessee apportioning the members of the General Assembly among the State's 95 counties, "these plaintiffs and others similarly situated, are denied the equal protection of the laws accorded them by the Fourteenth Amendment to the Constitution of the United States by virtue of the debasement of their votes," was dismissed by a three-judge court convened under 28 U.S.C. § 2281 in the Middle District of Tennessee. The court held that it lacked jurisdiction of the subject matter and also that no claim was stated upon which relief could be granted. . . . We hold that the dismissal was error, and remand the cause to the District Court for trial and further proceedings consistent with this opinion.

. . . We understand the District Court to have read the cited cases as compelling the conclusion that since the appellants sought to have a legislative apportionment held unconstitutional, their suit presented a "political question" and was therefore nonjusticiable. We hold that this challenge to an apportionment presents no nonjusticiable "political question." . . .

Of course the mere fact that the suit seeks protection of a political right does not mean it presents a political question. Such an objection "is little more than a play upon words." *Nixon v. Herndon*, 273 U.S. 536. Rather, it is argued that apportionment cases, whatever the actual wording of the complaint, can involve no federal constitutional right except one resting on the guaranty of a republican form of government, and that complaints based on that clause have been held to present political questions which are nonjusticiable.

We hold that the claim pleaded here neither rests upon nor implicates the Guaranty Clause and that its justiciability is therefore not foreclosed by our decisions of cases involving that clause. . . . Appellants' claim that they are being denied equal protection is justiciable, and if "discrimination is sufficiently shown, the right to relief under the equal protection clause is not diminished by the fact that the discrimination relates to political rights." *Snowden v. Hughes*, 321 U.S. 1, 11. . . .

Our discussion . . . requires review of a number of political question cases . . . That review reveals that in the Guaranty Clause cases and in the other "political question" cases, it is the relationship between the judiciary and the coordinate branches of the Federal Government, and not the federal judiciary's relationship to the States, which gives rise to the "political question." . . .

Prominent on the surface of any case held to involve a political question is found a textually demonstrable constitutional commitment of the issue to a coordinate political department; or a lack of judicially discoverable and manageable standards for resolving it; or the impossibility of deciding without an initial policy determination of a kind clearly for nonjudicial discretion; or the impossibility of a court's undertaking independent resolution without expressing lack of the respect due coordinate branches of government; or an unusual need for unquestioning adherence to a political decision already made; or the potentiality of embarrassment from multifarious pronouncements by various departments on one question.

Unless one of these formulations is inextricable from the case at bar, there should be no dismissal for non-justiciability on the ground of a political question's presence. . . .

But it is argued that this case shares the characteristics of decisions that constitute a category not yet considered, cases concerning the Constitution's guaranty, in Art. IV, § 4, of a republican form of government. . . . Guaranty Clause claims involve those elements which define a "political question," and for that reason and no other, they are nonjusticiable. In particular, we shall discover that the nonjusticiability of such claims has nothing to do with their touching upon matters of state governmental organization. . . .

Clearly, several factors were thought by the Court in Luther [v. Borden] to make the question there "political": the commitment to the other branches of the decision as to which is the lawful state government; the unambiguous action by the president, in recognizing the charter government as the lawful authority; the need for finality in the executive's decision; and the lack of criteria by which a court could determine which form of government was republican.

But the only significance that Luther could have for our immediate purposes is in its holding that the Guaranty Clause is not a repository of judicially manageable standards which a court could utilize independently in order to identify a State's lawful government. The Court has since refused to resort to the Guaranty Clause—which alone had been invoked for the purpose—as the source of a constitutional standard for invalidating state action.

Just as the Court has consistently held that a challenge to state action based on the Guaranty Clause presents no justiciable question so has it held, and for the same reasons, that challenges to congressional action on the ground of inconsistency with that clause present no justiciable question. . . .

We come, finally, to the ultimate inquiry whether our precedents as to what constitutes a nonjusticiable "political question" bring the case before us under the umbrella of that doctrine. A natural beginning is to note whether any of the common characteristics which we have been able to identify and label descriptively are present. We find none: The question here is the consistency of state action with the Federal Constitution. We have no question decided, or to be decided, by a political branch of government coequal with this Court. Nor do we risk embarrassment of our government abroad, or grave disturbance at home if we take issue with Tennessee as to the constitutionality of her action here challenged. Nor need the appellants, in order to succeed in this action, ask the Court to enter upon policy determinations for which judicially manageable standards are lacking. Judicial standards under the Equal Protection Clause are well developed and familiar, and it has been open to courts since the enactment of the Fourteenth Amendment to determine, if on the particular facts they must, that a discrimination reflects no policy, but simply arbitrary and capricious action.

This case does, in one sense, involve the allocation of political power within a State, and the appellants might conceivably have added a claim under the Guaranty Clause. Of course, as we have seen, any reliance on that clause would be futile. But because any reliance on the Guaranty Clause could not have succeeded it does not follow that appellants may not be heard on the equal protection claim which in fact they tender. True, it must be clear that the Fourteenth Amendment claim is not so enmeshed with those political question elements which render Guaranty Clause claims nonjusticiable as actually to present a political question itself. But we have found that not to be the case here. . . .

We conclude that the complaint's allegations of a denial of equal protection present a justiciable constitutional cause of action upon which appellants are entitled to a trial and a decision. The right asserted is within the reach of judicial protection under the Fourteenth Amendment. . . .

■ MR. JUSTICE FRANKFURTER, whom MR. JUSTICE HARLAN joins, dissenting.

The Court today reverses a uniform course of decision established by a dozen cases, including one by which the very claim now sustained was unanimously rejected only five years ago. The impressive body of rulings thus cast aside reflected the equally uniform course of our political history regarding the relationship between population and legislative representation—a wholly different matter from denial of the franchise to individuals because of race, color, religion or sex. Such a massive repudiation of the experience of our whole past in asserting destructively novel judicial power demands a detailed analysis of the role of this Court in our constitutional scheme. Disregard of inherent limits in the effective exercise of the Court's "judicial Power" not only presages the futility of judicial intervention in the essentially political conflict of forces by which the relation between population and representation has time out of mind been and now is determined. It may well impair the Court's position as the ultimate organ of "the supreme Law of the Land" in that vast range of legal problems, often strongly entangled in popular feeling, on which this Court must pronounce. The Court's authority—possessed of neither the purse nor the sword—ultimately rests on sustained public confidence in its moral sanction. Such feeling must be nourished by the Court's complete detachment, in fact and in appearance, from political entanglements and by abstention from injecting itself into the clash of political forces in political settlements. . . .

The present case involves all of the elements that have made the Guarantee Clause cases non-justiciable. It is, in effect, a Guarantee Clause claim masquerading under a different label. But it cannot make the case more fit for judicial action that appellants invoke the Fourteenth Amendment rather than Art. IV, § 4, where, in fact, the gist of their complaint is the same—unless it can be found that the Fourteenth Amendment speaks with greater particularity to their situation. . . . Of course, if a controversy falls within judicial power, it depends "on how he (the plaintiff) casts his action," whether he brings himself within a jurisdictional statute. But where judicial competence is wanting, it cannot be created by invoking one clause of the Constitution rather than another. . . .

To find such a political conception legally enforceable in the broad and unspecific guarantee of equal protection is to rewrite the Constitution. See *Luther v. Borden, supra.* Certainly, "equal protection" is no more secure a foundation for judicial judgment of the permissibility of varying forms of representative government than is "Republican Form." Indeed since "equal protection of the laws" can only mean an equality of persons standing in the same relation to whatever governmental action is challenged, the determination whether treatment is equal presupposes a determination concerning the nature of the relationship. This, with respect to apportionment, means an inquiry into the theoretic base of representation in an acceptably republican state. For a court could not determine the equal-protection issue without in fact first determining the Republican–Form issue, simply because what is reasonable for equal-protection purposes will depend upon what frame of government, basically, is allowed. To divorce "equal protection" from "Republican Form" is to talk about half a question.

The notion that representation proportioned to the geographic spread of population is so universally accepted as a necessary element of equality between man and man that it must be taken to be the standard of a political equality preserved by the Fourteenth Amendment—that it is, in appellants' words "the basic principle of representative government"—is, to put it bluntly, not true. However desirable and however desired by some among the great political thinkers and framers of our government, it has never been generally practiced, today or in the past. It was not the English system, it was not the colonial system, it was not the system chosen for the national government by the Constitution, it was not the system exclusively or even predominantly practiced by the States at the time of adoption of the Fourteenth Amendment, it is not predominantly practiced by the States today. . . .

Manifestly, the Equal Protection Clause supplies no clearer guide for judicial examination of apportionment methods than would the Guarantee Clause itself. Apportionment, by its character, is a subject of extraordinary complexity, involving—even after the fundamental theoretical issues concerning what is to be represented in a representative legislature have been fought out or compromised—considerations of geography, demography, electoral convenience, economic and social cohesions or divergencies among particular local groups, communications, the practical effects of political institutions like the lobby and the city machine, ancient traditions and ties of settled usage, respect for proven incumbents of long experience and senior status, mathematical mechanics, censuses compiling relevant data, and a host of others. Legislative responses throughout the country to the reapportionment demands of the 1960 Census have glaringly confirmed that these are not factors that lend themselves to evaluations of a nature that are the staple of judicial determinations or for which judges are equipped to adjudicate by legal training or experience or native wit. And this is the more so true because in every strand of this complicated, intricate web of values meet the contending forces of partisan politics. The practical significance of apportionment is that the next election results may differ because of it. Apportionment battles are overwhelmingly party or intra-party contests. It will add a virulent source of friction and tension in federal-state relations to embroil the federal judiciary in them. . . .

NOTES

1. Note the deep similarity between *Baker* and *Luther v. Borden* (discussed in Chapter 3). In both cases, as a result of state electoral rules, a minority held political control over a state, and there was nothing the majority could do about it. Does this violate the Republican Form of Government Clause? If so, how is the "Guarantee" to be made effective?

2. The Court seems to offer two grounds for distinguishing prior cases that held that apportionment issues were non-justiciable. The first was that the "political question" doctrine does not apply to cases involving state governments rather than "coordinate branches" of the federal government. Why does that matter? Does that distinguish *Luther*? Does that distinguish *Colegrove*? Is vertical comity less important than horizontal comity? If there are no "judicially manageable standards" for deciding a controversy, or if some non-judicial body has been entrusted with a constitutional decision, why does it matter that the defendant is a state? The Court's second ground is that the plaintiff proceeded under the Equal Protection Clause, not the Republican Form of Government Clause. Why might that matter? Would a standard be any more judicially manageable if it were advanced under the heading of the Equal Protection Clause instead of the Republican Form of Government Clause?

3. What is Justice Frankfurter worried about? Is there really a "political thicket" here? To be sure, if the federal courts were asked to make subjective judgments about political matters like districting, they would appear to be partisan and might lose the public's confidence. But is "one person, one vote" a subjective or malleable standard? Does its application give the appearance of partisanship? Note that at the time *Baker* was decided, "one person, one vote" was only one possible approach to the merits. Many observers thought that other rational considerations could be taken into account—and many of those considerations would have had predictable partisan consequences. Did the conclusion

that there were "judicially manageable standards" to decide the controversy depend, in advance, on resolution of the merits? Can a court determine that the constitutional standard applicable to a case is "judicially manageable" without first deciding, on the merits, exactly which standard is applicable?

Reynolds v. Sims
377 U.S. 533 (1964)

■ CHIEF JUSTICE WARREN delivered the opinion of the Court:

. . . Legislators represent people, not trees or acres. Legislators are elected by voters, not farms or cities or economic interests. As long as ours is a representative form of government, and our legislatures are those instruments of government elected directly by and directly representative of the people, the right to elect legislators in a free and unimpaired fashion is a bedrock of our political system. It could hardly be gainsaid that a constitutional claim had been asserted by an allegation that certain otherwise qualified voters had been entirely prohibited from voting for members of their state legislature. And, if a State should provide that the votes of citizens in one part of the State should be given two times, or five times, or 10 times the weight of votes of citizens in another part of the State, it could hardly be contended that the right to vote of those residing in the disfavored areas had not been effectively diluted. . . . Weighting the votes of citizens differently, by any method or means, merely because of where they happen to reside, hardly seems justifiable. . . .

[T]he concept of equal protection has been traditionally viewed as requiring the uniform treatment of persons standing in the same relation to the governmental action questioned or challenged. With respect to the allocation of legislative representation, all voters, as citizens of a State, stand in the same relation regardless of where they live. Any suggested criteria for the differentiation of citizens are insufficient to justify any discrimination, as to the weight of their votes, unless relevant to the permissible purposes of legislative apportionment. Since the achieving of fair and effective representation for all citizens is concededly the basic aim of legislative apportionment, we conclude that the Equal Protection Clause guarantees the opportunity for equal participation by all voters in the election of state legislators. Diluting the weight of votes because of place of residence impairs basic constitutional rights under the Fourteenth Amendment just as much as invidious discriminations based upon factors such as race, or economic status. Our constitutional system amply provides for the protection of minorities by means other than giving them majority control of state legislatures. . . .

We are told that the matter of apportioning representation in a state legislature is a complex and many-faceted one. We are advised that States can rationally consider factors other than population in apportioning legislative representation. We are admonished not to restrict the power of the States to impose differing views as to political philosophy on their citizens. We are cautioned about the dangers of entering into political thickets and mathematical quagmires. Our answer is this: a denial of constitutionally protected rights demands judicial protection; our oath and our office require no less of us. . . .

We hold that, as a basic constitutional standard, the Equal Protection Clause requires that the seats in both houses of a bicameral state legislature must be apportioned on a population basis. Simply stated, an individual's right to vote for state legislators is unconstitutionally impaired when its weight is in a substantial fashion diluted when compared with votes of citizens living on other parts of the State. . . .

Since neither of the houses of the Alabama Legislature, under any of the three plans considered by the District Court, was apportioned on a population basis, we would be justified in proceeding no further. However, one of the proposed plans, that contained in the so-called 67–Senator Amendment, at least superficially resembles the scheme of legislative representation followed in the Federal Congress. . . .

Much has been written since our decision in *Baker v. Carr* about the applicability of the so-called federal analogy to state legislative apportionment arrangements. After considering the matter, the court below concluded that no conceivable analogy could be drawn between the federal scheme and the apportionment of seats in the Alabama Legislature under the proposed constitutional amendment. We agree. . . . Attempted reliance on the federal analogy appears often to be little more than an after-the-fact rationalization offered in defense of maladjusted state apportionment arrangements. The original constitutions of 36 of our States provided that representation in both houses of the state legislatures would be based completely, or predominantly, on population. And the Founding Fathers clearly had no intention of establishing a pattern or model for the apportionment of seats in state legislatures when the system of representation in the Federal Congress was adopted. Demonstrative of this is the fact that the Northwest Ordinance, adopted in the same year, 1787, as the Federal Constitution, provided for the apportionment of seats in territorial legislatures solely on the basis of population.

The system of representation in the two Houses of the Federal Congress is one ingrained in our Constitution, as part of the law of the land. It is one conceived out of compromise and concession indispensable to the establishment of our federal republic. Arising from unique historical circumstances, it is based on the consideration that in establishing our type of federalism a group of formerly independent States bound themselves together under one national government. . . . [A]t the time of the inception of the system of representation in the Federal Congress, a compromise between the larger and smaller States on this matter averted a deadlock in the Constitutional Convention which had threatened to abort the birth of our Nation. . . .

Political subdivisions of States—counties, cities, or whatever—never were and never have been considered as sovereign entities. Rather, they have been traditionally regarded as subordinate governmental instrumentalities created by the State to assist in the carrying out of state governmental functions. . . . The relationship of the States to the Federal Government could hardly be less analogous. . . .

■ [The dissent of JUSTICE HARLAN and the concurrence of JUSTICE CLARK are omitted.]

NOTES

1. *Reynolds* involved state legislative districts. It was preceded by *Wesberry v. Sanders*, 376 U.S. 1 (1964), which involved federal congressional districts. The outcomes were analytically indistinguishable: *Reynolds* required "substantial" equality for state legislative districts; *Wesberry* required that fed-

eral congressional districts be equal "as nearly as is practicable." But they were decided under different provisions of the Constitution. *Reynolds* was an interpretation of the Equal Protection Clause, while *Wesberry* rested on the command of Art. I, Section 2, Clause 1, that Representatives be chosen "by the People of the several States." Is either rationale more persuasive? What might be the differences?

2. *Wesberry* and *Reynolds* were among the most transformative decisions in the history of the Supreme Court. Unlike de jure segregation, the phenomenon of unequal districts was not confined to any one region. Nearly every state was out of compliance with the new standard. In fully 37 of the 45 states entitled to more than one representative, the difference between the largest and the smallest House district exceeded 100,000 persons—making the boundaries of 398 of the 435 House districts unconstitutional. Disparities among state legislative districts were even more extreme: a dozen states had districts with five times the population of another district.

For most of its history, the United States was predominantly rural. But by the 1960, almost two-thirds of Americans lived in metropolitan areas (cities or suburbs). Yet at the time of *Wesberry* and *Reynolds*, 214 congressional districts still had a rural majority. After the redistricting forced by these decisions, this number fell to 155 in 1968 and 130 in 1972. What policy changes would you expect to see from this shift in political power?

3. If Article I, Section 2, Clause 1 (*Wesberry*) or the Fourteenth Amendment (*Reynolds*) required equipopulous districts, no one seemed to notice it at the time. In the first election after adoption of the original Constitution, every state with multiple single-member districts drew lines with substantial population disparities. The smallest district in Georgia comprised 19,273 people (13,261 of whom were slaves), while the largest comprised 37,946 (including 8,801 slaves). In Massachusetts, the smallest comprised 39,594 and the largest 89,972. The largest disparity within a state was in New York. New York's First District comprised 40,784 people (5,598 of them slaves), while the Sixth District comprised 105,659 people (including 4,523 slaves). Much the same was true after ratification of the Fourteenth Amendment. For example, districts in Iowa ranged from 46,733 to 138,032. See Samuel B. Parsons et al., UNITED STATES CONGRESSIONAL DISTRICTS, 1788–1841 (1978) and UNITED STATES CONGRESSIONAL DISTRICTS, 1843–1883 (1978).

4. The degree of malapportionment in *Baker* and *Reynolds* screamed out for remedy. In these states, disparities were both systematic and self-perpetuating: a rural minority controlled state government, and there was no constitutional or peaceful mechanism for reform. What of less dramatic inequality, or cases where there is a democratic remedy? In *Lucas v. Forty–Fourth General Assembly of the State of Colorado*, 377 U.S. 713 (1964), decided the same day as *Reynolds*, the Court considered the constitutionality of a districting scheme for the State of Colorado. Just two years previously, in 1962, the voters of Colorado were presented with two alternative districting schemes: one based representation in both houses of the state legislation almost exclusively on population, and the other created somewhat smaller districts for sparsely populated areas of the state (leaving the metropolitan areas with a majority of the legislators, but a smaller majority than they would be entitled to as a matter of sheer population). The voters overwhelmingly chose the second plan; it

carried a majority in every county. How should this case have been decided? How would you articulate the proper standard?

Unlike *Reynolds*, which was an 8–1 decision, there were three dissenters in *Lucas*. The majority held that the Colorado map violated the one person, one vote rule. Justice Stewart argued in dissent that the Equal Protection Clause "demands but two basic attributes of any plan of state legislative apportionment." First, it must be rational. Second, it "must be such as not to permit the systematic frustration of the will of a majority of the electorate of the State." How is such a standard derived from the Equal Protection Clause? Would it be more persuasively derived from the Republican Form of Government Clause?

5. *Reynolds* and *Wesberry* seemed to allow some flexibility: "Mathematical exactness or precision is hardly a workable constitutional requirement." *Reynolds*, 377 U.S. at 577. By 1969, however, the Court would hold that the one person, one vote rule "permits only the limited population variances which are unavoidable despite a good-faith effort to achieve absolute equality, or for which justification is shown." *Kirkpatrick v. Preisler*, 394 U.S. 526, 531 (1969). That case involved a maximum deviation of 3.13 percent between the largest district and the mathematical ideal, and the Court rejected a number of rationales for deviations set forth by the state, including: geographical compactness; following existing county, municipal, or other jurisdictional boundaries; avoiding fragmentation of areas with distinctive economic or social interests; compensating for large numbers of persons ineligible to vote; and anticipating population shifts. Since then precise mathematical equality has become possible, but the Court has varied in how aggressively it polices minute differences in district size. Compare *Karcher v. Daggett*, 462 U.S. 725 (1983) (striking down federal congressional districting scheme on account of a deviation of 0.69%), with *Tennant v. Jefferson County Commission*, 567 U.S. ___ (2012) (per curiam) (upholding, for purposes of federal constitutional law, a federal congressional districting scheme in which the deviation was .79%, even though that deviation could have been completely eliminated, because of deference to state interests such as "avoiding contests between incumbents and not splitting political subdivisions").

For purposes of state legislative districting, the Court has allowed a variance of 10 percent between the largest and smallest districts. The Court grounded this distinction in part on the difference between the Equal Protection Clause and Article I, Section 2. Is that persuasive? Is it perhaps backwards? Does a rule of precise mathematical equality have any untoward consequences?

6. How can *Reynolds* and *Wesberry* be squared with the requirement of Article I, Section 2, Clause 3, that representatives "be apportioned among the several States . . . according to their respective Numbers," which has generally been interpreted as meaning total population? See e.g., *Kalson v. Paterson*, 542 F.3d 281, 289 n.16 (2d Cir. 2008). Total population includes people not eligible to vote, such as aliens and children, who are not evenly distributed across districts. A vote cast in a district with relatively large numbers of aliens or children thus is weighted more heavily than a vote cast in other districts. These effects can been quite large. For example, in one case, federal congressional districts of nearly equal population in a state ranged from 282,000 to 429,000 in voting age population. *Karcher*, 462 U.S. at 772 n.6 (White, J., dissenting). This disparity far exceeds what would be tolerated under one person, one vote. Does

it suggest that voting power should be apportioned among districts according to some other measure, such as voting age citizen population? Does it make sense for the Court to create a standard that cannot be achieved in light of Article I, Section 2, Clause 3?

7. Lovers of historical irony may appreciate the fact that the United States Constitution would likely not have been ratified if the one person, one vote rule had prevailed at the time of selection of delegates to the state ratifying conventions. In Virginia, the largest state, the Constitution was ratified by a slim majority of 89–79 (88–80 on a key procedural motion). At its ratifying convention, each county was authorized two delegates, regardless of population. This favored ratification, because the tidewater counties, which tended to support the Constitution, were less populous than the piedmont counties, which tended to oppose it. Jean Edward Smith, JOHN MARSHALL: DEFINER OF A NATION 119 (1996).

[*Assignment 74*]

C. GERRYMANDERING

Even assuming districts are equal in population, district boundaries can have profound effects on the outcomes of elections. The process of drawing lines for the purpose of affecting outcomes is called "gerrymandering." The practice is as old as the republic. Its name derives from Elbridge Gerry, a delegate to the Constitutional Convention and later vice president under James Madison. A political cartoonist depicted a districting map devised under Gerry's governorship as looking like a salamander—hence a the word "gerrymander." As long as legislatures were free to use districts that were unequal in population, there was not as much occasion for cartographic creativity. In recent decades, however, gerrymandering has become a more prevalent, and more precise, phenomenon, for two primary reasons. First, the advent of computer districting programs has enabled mapmakers to manipulate election data with surgical precision. Second, the precise mathematical equality rule forced mapmakers to deviate substantially from traditional jurisdictional boundaries, such as counties and municipalities; adherence to these boundaries had been the main constraint against gerrymandering.

Gerrymandering comes in three flavors: partisan, incumbency protection, and racial. A partisan gerrymander seeks to maximize the number of legislative seats that will likely be won by the party that controls the districting. An incumbency-protection gerrymander protects the seats of incumbent legislators of both parties. A racial gerrymander seeks to achieve certain results along racial lines. In earlier times, this often took the form of attempts to reduce the political influence of racial minorities. Since passage of the Voting Rights Act, it has become more common for mapmakers to create districts likely to elect minority legislators. Because racial minorities have historically had lower percentages of voting-age population, and within that population a lower percentage of registered voters, it was thought necessary to have a supermajority of minority voters to assure political victory. Creating such a district reduces the numbers and influence of minority voters in other districts.

If Democrats and Republicans were evenly distributed throughout the state it would not be possible to gerrymander by party. But residential patterns are not uniform. Rural areas and suburbs tend to be more Republican, and urban areas more Democratic. The two principal techniques of gerrymandering are called "packing" and "cracking." Packing is the most effective. This involves packing the largest possible numbers of the other party into a single district. Since every vote in excess of a majority is "wasted," it serves the interest of the party in power to create districts with 70, 80, or 90 percent of voters of the other party. Cracking involves dividing voters of the other party into two or more districts, rendering them a minority in each.

What do the critics of gerrymandering say is wrong with it? It makes the legislature less responsive and accountable to the public. Changes in popular opinion are less likely to be translated into changes in political outcomes. The creation of racially or politically homogeneous districts may cause politics to become more divisive—more racially polarized or more partisan. Most fundamentally, it allows those in power at the time of districting to determine (within limits) the probable outcome of future elections. This seems undemocratic (and unrepublican): in a democratic republic, the electorate chooses its representatives, rather than having the representatives choose their electorates. And in extreme cases, gerrymandering may allow a party to cling to control even if it no longer represents the majority of voters.

In response, supporters of gerrymandering argue that the drawing of districts is an inherently political activity. It can never really be non-partisan—regardless of whether it is done by legislatures, by courts, or by citizen commissions. Given that it is a quintessentially political decision, these supporters say, there is no reason not to allow these decisions to be made by the body that makes most of our political decisions, namely the legislature.

You might ask yourself what provisions of the Constitution, if any, have purposes or values that are implicated by gerrymanders. Equal Protection? The requirement that representatives and senators be chosen by "the People"? The Republican Form of Government Clause? Are the same constitutional values implicated by racial gerrymandering as by partisan gerrymandering or incumbency protection? What, if anything, is the judicial role in all of this?

Shaw v. Reno

509 U.S. 630 (1993)

■ JUSTICE O'CONNOR delivered the opinion of the Court.

This case involves two of the most complex and sensitive issues this Court has faced in recent years: the meaning of the constitutional "right" to vote, and the propriety of race-based state legislation designed to benefit members of historically disadvantaged racial minority groups. As a result of the 1990 census, North Carolina ... enacted a reapportionment plan that included one majority-black congressional district. After the Attorney General of the United States objected to the plan, the General Assembly passed new legislation creating a second majority-black district. Appellants allege that the revised plan ... constitutes an unconstitutional racial gerrymander. The question before us is whether appellants have stated a cognizable claim.

I

The voting age population of North Carolina is approximately 78% white, 20% black, and 1% Native American; the remaining 1% is predominantly Asian. The black population is relatively dispersed; blacks constitute a majority of the general population in only 5 of the State's 100 counties. . . .

The first of the two majority-black districts contained in the revised plan, District 1, is somewhat hook shaped. . . . District 1 has been compared to a "Rorschach ink-blot test," and a "bug splattered on a windshield."

The second majority-black district, District 12, is even more unusually shaped. It is approximately 160 miles long and, for much of its length, no wider than the I–85 corridor. It winds in snakelike fashion through tobacco country, financial centers, and manufacturing areas "until it gobbles in enough enclaves of black neighborhoods." . . . Of the 10 counties through which District 12 passes, 5 are cut into 3 different districts; even towns are divided. At one point the district remains contiguous only because it intersects at a single point with two other districts before crossing over them. . . .

Appellants contended that the General Assembly's revised reapportionment plan violated several provisions of the United States Constitution, including the Fourteenth Amendment. They alleged that the General Assembly deliberately "create[d] two Congressional Districts in which a majority of black voters was concentrated arbitrarily—without regard to any other considerations, such as compactness, contiguousness, geographical boundaries, or political subdivisions" with the purpose "to create Congressional Districts along racial lines" and to assure the election of two black representatives to Congress. . . .

The three-judge District Court . . . first took judicial notice of a fact omitted from appellants' complaint: that appellants are white. It rejected the argument that race-conscious redistricting to benefit minority voters is *per se* unconstitutional. The majority also rejected appellants' claim that North Carolina's reapportionment plan was impermissible. . . .

II

. . . Our focus is on appellants' claim that the State engaged in unconstitutional racial gerrymandering. That argument strikes a powerful historical chord: It is unsettling how closely the North Carolina plan resembles the most egregious racial gerrymanders of the past. . . .

[A]ppellants' complaint alleged that the deliberate segregation of voters into separate districts on the basis of race violated their constitutional right to participate in a "color-blind" electoral process.

. . . This Court never has held that race-conscious state decisionmaking is impermissible in *all* circumstances. What appellants object to is redistricting legislation that is so extremely irregular on its face that it rationally can be viewed only as an effort to segregate the races for purposes of voting, without regard for traditional districting principles and without sufficiently compelling justification. For the reasons that follow, we conclude that appellants have stated a claim upon which relief can be granted under the Equal Protection Clause.

III–A

The Equal Protection Clause['s] . . . central purpose is to prevent the States from purposefully discriminating between individuals on the basis of race. *Washington v. Davis*, 426 U.S. 229, 239 (1976). Laws that explicitly distinguish between individuals on racial grounds fall within the core of that prohibition. . . .

Classifications of citizens solely on the basis of race "are by their very nature odious to a free people whose institutions are founded upon the doctrine of equality." They threaten to stigmatize individuals by reason of their membership in a racial group and to incite racial hostility. Accordingly, we have held that the Fourteenth Amendment requires state legislation that expressly distinguishes among citizens because of their race to be narrowly tailored to further a compelling governmental interest.

These principles apply not only to legislation that contains explicit racial distinctions, but also to those "rare" statutes that, although race neutral, are, on their face, "unexplainable on grounds other than race." *Arlington Heights v. Metropolitan Housing Development Corp.*, 429 U.S. 252, 266 (1977). . . .

B

Appellants contend that redistricting legislation that is so bizarre on its face that it is "unexplainable on grounds other than race," *Arlington Heights*, 429 U.S., at 266, demands the same close scrutiny that we give other state laws that classify citizens by race. . . .

Put differently, we believe that reapportionment is one area in which appearances do matter. A reapportionment plan that includes in one district individuals who belong to the same race, but who are otherwise widely separated by geographical and political boundaries, and who may have little in common with one another but the color of their skin, bears an uncomfortable resemblance to political apartheid. It reinforces the perception that members of the same racial group—regardless of their age, education, economic status, or the community in which they live—think alike, share the same political interests, and will prefer the same candidates at the polls. We have rejected such perceptions elsewhere as impermissible racial stereotypes. By perpetuating such notions, a racial gerrymander may exacerbate the very patterns of racial bloc voting that majority-minority districting is sometimes said to counteract.

The message that such districting sends to elected representatives is equally pernicious. . . . [E]lected officials are more likely to believe that their primary obligation is to represent only the members of that group, rather than their constituency as a whole. This is altogether antithetical to our system of representative democracy. . . .

For these reasons, we conclude that a plaintiff challenging a reapportionment statute under the Equal Protection Clause may state a claim by alleging that the legislation, though race-neutral on its face, rationally cannot be understood as anything other than an effort to separate voters into different districts on the basis of race, and that the separation lacks sufficient justification. . . . [W]e express no view as to whether "the intentional creation of majority-minority districts, without more," always gives rise to an equal protection claim. *Post* (WHITE, J., dissenting). We hold only that, on the facts of this case, appellants have stated a claim sufficient to defeat the state appellees' motion to dismiss. . . .

■ JUSTICE WHITE, with whom JUSTICE BLACKMUN and JUSTICE STEVENS join, dissenting.

. . . The grounds for my disagreement with the majority are simply stated: Appellants have not presented a cognizable claim, because they have not alleged a cognizable injury. To date, we have held that only two types of state voting practices could give rise to a constitutional claim. The first involves direct and outright deprivation of the right to vote, for example by means of a poll tax or literacy test. Plainly, this variety is not implicated by appellants' allegations and need not detain us further. The second type of unconstitutional practice is that which "affects the political strength of various groups," *Mobile v. Bolden*, 446 U.S. 55, 83 (1980) (STEVENS, J., concurring in judgment), in violation of the Equal Protection Clause. As for this latter category, we have insisted that members of the political or racial group demonstrate that the challenged action have the intent and effect of unduly diminishing their influence on the political process. . . .

The central explanation has to do with the nature of the redistricting process. As the majority recognizes, "redistricting differs from other kinds of state decision-making in that the legislature always is *aware* of race when it draws district lines, just as it is aware of age, economic status, religious and political persuasion, and a variety of other demographic factors." . . .

Redistricting plans also reflect group interests and inevitably are conceived with partisan aims in mind. To allow judicial interference whenever this occurs would be to invite constant and unmanageable intrusion. Moreover, a group's power to affect the political process does not automatically dissipate by virtue of an electoral loss. Accordingly, we have asked that an identifiable group demonstrate more than mere lack of success at the polls to make out a successful gerrymandering claim. . . .

Because districting inevitably is the expression of interest group politics, . . . the question in gerrymandering cases is "whether a particular group has been unconstitutionally denied its chance to effectively influence the political process." . . .

To distinguish a claim that alleges that the redistricting scheme has discriminatory intent and effect from one that does not has nothing to do with dividing racial classifications between the "benign" and the malicious—an enterprise which, as the majority notes, the Court has treated with skepticism. Rather, the issue is whether the classification based on race discriminates against *anyone* by denying equal access to the political process. . . .

Racial gerrymanders come in various shades: At-large voting schemes; the fragmentation of a minority group among various districts "so that it is a majority in none," otherwise known as "cracking"; the "stacking" of "a large minority population concentration . . . with a larger white population"; and, finally, the "concentration of [minority voters] into districts where they constitute an excessive majority," also called "packing." In each instance, race is consciously utilized by the legislature for electoral purposes; in each instance, we have put the plaintiff challenging the district lines to the burden of demonstrating that the plan was meant to, and did in fact, exclude an identifiable racial group from participation in the political process.

Not so, apparently, when the districting "segregates" by drawing odd-shaped lines. In that case, we are told, such proof no longer is needed. Instead, it is the *State* that must rebut the allegation that race was taken into account, a fact that, together with the legislators' consideration of ethnic, religious, and other group characteristics, I had thought we practically took for granted . . .

The consideration of race in "segregation" cases is no different than in other race-conscious districting; from the standpoint of the affected groups, moreover, the line-drawings all act in similar fashion. A plan that "segregates" being functionally indistinguishable from any of the other varieties of gerrymandering, we should be consistent in what we require from a claimant: proof of discriminatory purpose and effect. . . .

■ JUSTICE STEVENS, dissenting.

For the reasons stated by Justice WHITE, the decision of the District Court should be affirmed. I add these comments to emphasize that the two critical facts in this case are undisputed: First, the shape of District 12 is so bizarre that it must have been drawn for the purpose of either advantaging or disadvantaging a cognizable group of voters; and, second, regardless of that shape, it *was* drawn for the purpose of facilitating the election of a second black representative from North Carolina.

These unarguable facts, which the Court devotes most of its opinion to proving, give rise to three constitutional questions: Does the Constitution impose a requirement of contiguity or compactness on how the States may draw their electoral districts? Does the Equal Protection Clause prevent a State from drawing district boundaries for the purpose of facilitating the election of a member of an identifiable group of voters? And, finally, if the answer to the second question is generally "No," should it be different when the favored group is defined by race? Since I have already written at length about these questions, my negative answer to each can be briefly explained.

The first question is easy. There is no independent constitutional requirement of compactness or contiguity, and the Court's opinion does not suggest otherwise. The existence of bizarre and uncouth district boundaries is powerful evidence of an ulterior purpose. . . . Such evidence will always be useful in cases that lack other evidence of invidious intent. In this case, however, we know what the legislators' purpose was: The North Carolina Legislature drew District 12 to include a majority of African–American voters. . . . Evidence of the district's shape is therefore . . . irrelevant.

As for the second question, I believe that the Equal Protection Clause is violated when the State creates . . . uncouth district boundaries . . . for the sole purpose of making it more difficult for members of a minority group to win an election. The duty to govern impartially is abused when a group with power over the electoral process defines electoral boundaries solely to enhance its own political strength at the expense of any weaker group. That duty, however, is not violated when the majority acts to facilitate the election of a member of a group that lacks such power. . . . The difference between constitutional and unconstitutional gerrymanders has nothing to do with whether they are based on assumptions about the groups they affect, but whether their purpose is . . . to strengthen the unequal distribution of electoral power. . . .

Finally, we must ask whether otherwise permissible redistricting to benefit an underrepresented minority group becomes impermissible when the minority group is defined by its race. The Court today answers this question in the affirmative, and its answer is wrong. If it is permissible to draw boundaries to provide adequate representation for rural voters, for union members, for Hasidic Jews, for Polish Americans, or for Republicans, it necessarily follows that it is permissible to do the same thing for members of the very minority group whose history in the United States gave birth to the Equal Protection Clause. A contrary conclusion could only be described as perverse.

■ [The dissent of JUSTICE SOUTER and the dissent of JUSTICE BLACKMUN are omitted.]

Vieth v. Jubelirer

541 U.S. 267 (2004)

■ JUSTICE SCALIA announced the judgment of the Court and delivered an opinion, in which THE CHIEF JUSTICE, JUSTICE O'CONNOR, and JUSTICE THOMAS join. . . .

I

The facts, as alleged by the plaintiffs, are as follows. The population figures derived from the 2000 census showed that Pennsylvania was entitled to only 19 Representatives in Congress, a decrease in 2 from the Commonwealth's previous delegation. Pennsylvania's General Assembly took up the task of drawing a new districting map. At the time, the Republican Party controlled a majority of both state Houses and held the Governor's office. . . . On January 3, 2002, the General Assembly passed [a plan creating 13 seats with a Republican advantage], which was signed into law by Governor Schweiker.

Plaintiffs, registered Democrats who vote in Pennsylvania, brought suit. . . .

II

Political gerrymanders are not new to the American scene. One scholar traces them back to the Colony of Pennsylvania at the beginning of the 18th century. . . .

It is significant that the Framers provided a remedy for such practices in the Constitution. Article I, § 4, while leaving in state legislatures the initial power to draw districts for federal elections, permitted Congress to "make or alter" those districts if it wished. Many objected to the congressional oversight established by this provision. In the course of the debates in the Constitutional Convention, Charles Pinckney and John Rutledge moved to strike the relevant language. James Madison responded in defense of the provision that Congress must be given the power to check partisan manipulation of the election process by the States:

> Whenever the State Legislatures had a favorite measure to carry, they would take care so to mould their regulations as to favor the candidates they wished to succeed. Besides, the inequality of the Representation in the Legislatures of particular States, would produce a like inequality in their representation in the Natl. Legislature, as it was presumable that the Counties having the power in the former case would secure it to themselves in the latter. What danger could there be in giving a controuling power to the Natl. Legislature?

2 Records of the Federal Convention of 1787, pp. 240–241 (M. Farrand ed.1911).

Although the motion of Pinckney and Rutledge failed, opposition to the "make or alter" provision of Article I, § 4 and the defense that it was needed to prevent political gerrymandering continued to be voiced in the state ratifying debates. . . .

The power bestowed on Congress to regulate elections, and in particular to restrain the practice of political gerrymandering, has not lain dormant. In the Apportionment Act of 1842, Congress provided that Representatives must be elected from single-member districts "composed of contiguous territory." Congress . . . in 1872 further required that districts "contai[n] as nearly as practicable an equal number of inhabitants." In the Apportionment Act of 1901, Congress imposed a compactness requirement. 31 Stat. 733. The requirements of contiguity, compactness, and equality of population were repeated in the 1911 apportionment legislation, but were not thereafter continued. Today, only the single-member-district-requirement remains. See 2 U.S.C. § 2c. Recent history, however, attests to Congress's awareness of the sort of districting practices appellants protest, and of its power under Article I, § 4, to control them. Since 1980, no fewer than five bills have been introduced to regulate gerrymandering in congressional districting.

Eighteen years ago, we held that the Equal Protection Clause grants judges the power-and duty-to control political gerrymandering, see *Davis v. Bandemer*, 478 U.S. 109 (1986). It is to consideration of this precedent that we now turn.

III

. . . Over the dissent of three Justices, the Court held in *Davis v. Bandemer* that, since it was "not persuaded that there are no judicially discernible and manageable standards by which political gerrymander cases are to be decided," 478 U.S., at 123, such cases *were* justiciable. The clumsy shifting of the burden of proof for the premise (the Court was "not persuaded" that standards do not exist, rather than "persuaded" that they do) was necessitated by the uncomfortable fact that the six-Justice majority could not discern what the judicially discernable standards might be. . . . The lower courts have lived with that assurance of a standard (or more precisely, lack of assurance that there is no standard), coupled with that inability to specify a standard, for the past 18 years. . . .

Nor can it be said that the lower courts have, over 18 years, succeeded in shaping the standard that this Court was initially unable to enunciate. They have simply applied the standard set forth in *Bandemer*'s four-Justice plurality opinion. This might be thought to prove that the four-Justice plurality standard has met the test of time—but for the fact that its application has almost invariably produced the same result (except for the incurring of attorney's fees) as would have obtained if the question were nonjusticiable: Judicial intervention has been refused. . . . To think that [the lower court in the one case in which relief was provided] has brought forth "judicially discernible and manageable standards" would be fantasy.

Eighteen years of judicial effort with virtually nothing to show for it justify us in revisiting the question whether the standard promised by *Bandemer* exists. As the following discussion reveals, no judicially discernible and manageable standards for adjudicating political gerrymandering claims have emerged. Lacking them, we must conclude that political gerrymandering claims are nonjusticiable and that *Bandemer* was wrongly decided.

A

We begin our review of possible standards with that proposed by Justice White's plurality opinion in *Bandemer* because, as the narrowest ground for our decision in that case, it has been the standard employed by the lower courts. The plurality concluded that a political gerrymandering claim could succeed only where plaintiffs showed "both intentional discrimination against an identifiable political group and an actual discriminatory effect on that group." 478 U.S., at 127. As to the intent element, the plurality acknowledged that "[a]s long as redistricting is done by a legislature, it should not be very difficult to prove that the likely political consequences of the reapportionment were intended." However, the effects prong was significantly harder to satisfy. Relief could not be based merely upon the fact that a group of persons banded together for political purposes had failed to achieve representation commensurate with its numbers, or that the apportionment scheme made its winning of elections more difficult. Rather, it would have to be shown that, taking into account a variety of historic factors and projected election results, the group had been "denied its chance to effectively influence the political process" as a whole, which could be achieved even without electing a candidate. It would not be enough to establish, for example, that Democrats had been "placed in a district with a supermajority of other Democratic voters" or that the district "departs from pre-existing political boundaries." Rather, in a challenge to an individual district the inquiry would focus "on the opportunity of members of the group to participate in party deliberations in the slating and nomination of candidates, their opportunity to register and vote, and hence their chance to directly influence the election returns and to secure the attention of the winning candidate." A statewide challenge, by contrast, would involve an analysis of "the voters' direct *or indirect* influence on the elections of the state legislature as a whole." *Ibid.* (emphasis added). With what has proved to be a gross understatement, the plurality acknowledged this was "of necessity a difficult inquiry." . . .

In the lower courts, the legacy of the plurality's test is one long record of puzzlement and consternation. . . . Because this standard was misguided when proposed, has not been improved in subsequent application, and is not even defended before us today by the appellants, we decline to affirm it as a constitutional requirement.

B

Appellants take a run at enunciating their own workable standard based on Article I, § 2, and the Equal Protection Clause. We consider it at length not only because it reflects the litigant's view as to the best that can be derived from 18 years of experience, but also because it shares many features with other proposed standards, so that what is said of it may be said of them as well. Appellants' proposed standard retains the two-pronged framework of the *Bandemer* plurality—intent plus effect—but modifies the type of showing sufficient to satisfy each.

To satisfy appellants' intent standard, a plaintiff must "show that the mapmakers acted with a *predominant intent* to achieve partisan advantage," which can be shown "by direct evidence or by circumstantial evidence that other neutral and legitimate redistricting criteria were subordinated to the goal of achieving partisan advantage." Brief for Appellants 19 (emphasis added). As compared with the *Bandemer* plurality's test of mere intent to disadvantage the plaintiff's group, this proposal seemingly makes the standard more difficult to meet—but only at the expense of making the standard more indeterminate.

"Predominant intent" to disadvantage the plaintiff's political group refers to the relative importance of that goal as compared with all the other goals that the map seeks to pursue-contiguity of districts, compactness of districts, observance of the lines of political subdivision, protection of incumbents of all parties, cohesion of natural racial and ethnic neighborhoods, compliance with requirements of the Voting Rights Act of 1965 regarding racial distribution, etc. Appellants contend that their intent test *must* be discernible and manageable because it has been borrowed from our racial gerrymandering cases. . . .

[A]pplying a "predominant intent" test to *racial* gerrymandering is easier and less disruptive. The Constitution clearly contemplates districting by political entities, see Article I, § 4, and unsurprisingly that turns out to be root-and-branch a matter of politics. By contrast, the purpose of segregating voters on the basis of race is not a lawful one, and is much more rarely encountered. Determining whether the shape of a particular district is so substantially affected by the presence of a rare and constitutionally suspect motive as to invalidate it is quite different from determining whether it is so substantially affected by the excess of an ordinary and lawful motive as to invalidate it. Moreover, the fact that partisan districting is a lawful and common practice means that there is almost *always* room for an election-impeding lawsuit contending that partisan advantage was the predominant motivation; not so for claims of racial gerrymandering. Finally, courts might be justified in accepting a modest degree of unmanageability to enforce a constitutional command which (like the Fourteenth Amendment obligation to refrain from racial discrimination) is clear; whereas they are not justified in inferring a judicially enforceable constitutional obligation (the obligation not to apply *too much* partisanship in districting) which is both dubious and severely unmanageable. For these reasons, to the extent that our racial gerrymandering cases represent a model of discernible and manageable standards, they provide no comfort here.

The effects prong of appellants' proposal replaces the *Bandemer* plurality's vague test of "denied its chance to effectively influence the political process," with criteria that are seemingly more specific. The requisite effect is established when "(1) the plaintiffs show that the districts systematically 'pack' and 'crack' the rival party's voters, *and* (2) the court's examination of the 'totality of circumstances' confirms that the map can thwart the plaintiffs' ability to translate a majority of votes into a majority of seats." Brief for Appellants 20. This test is loosely based on our cases applying § 2 of the Voting Rights Act of 1965, to discrimination by race. But a person's politics is rarely as readily discernible—and *never* as permanently discernible—as a person's race. Political affiliation is not an immutable characteristic, but may shift from one election to the next; and even within a given election, not all voters follow the party line. . . . These facts make it impossible to assess the effects of partisan gerrymandering, to fashion a standard for evaluating a violation, and finally to craft a remedy.

Assuming, however, that the effects of partisan gerrymandering can be determined, appellants' test would invalidate the districting only when it prevents a majority of the electorate from electing a majority of representatives. . . . [T]his standard rests upon the principle that groups (or at least political-action groups) have a right to proportional representation. But the Constitution contains no such principle. It guarantees equal protection of the law to persons, not equal representation in government to equivalently sized groups. . . .

Our one-person, one-vote cases have no bearing upon this question, neither in principle nor in practicality. Not in principle, because to say that each individual must have an equal say in the selection of representatives, and hence that a majority of individuals must have a majority say, is not at all to say that each discernible group, whether farmers or urban dwellers or political parties, must have representation equivalent to its numbers. And not in practicality, because the easily administrable standard of population equality adopted by *Wesberry* and *Reynolds* enables judges to decide whether a violation has occurred (and to remedy it) essentially on the basis of three readily determined factors where the plaintiff lives, how many voters are in his district, and how many voters are in other districts; whereas requiring judges to decide whether a districting system will produce a statewide majority for a majority party casts them forth upon a sea of imponderables, and asks them to make determinations that not even election experts can agree upon.

For these reasons, we find appellants' proposed standards neither discernible nor manageable. . . .

IV

We turn next to consideration of the standards proposed by today's dissenters. We preface it with the observation that the mere fact that these four dissenters come up with three different standards—all of them different from the two proposed in *Bandemer* and the one proposed here by appellants—goes a long way to establishing that there is no constitutionally discernible standard.

A

. . . Justice STEVENS's confidence that what courts have done with racial gerrymandering can be done with political gerrymandering rests in part upon his belief that "the same standards should apply." But in fact the standards are quite different. A purpose to discriminate on the basis of race receives the strictest scrutiny under the Equal Protection Clause, while a similar purpose to discriminate on the basis of politics does not. . . .

Justice STEVENS relies on *First Amendment cases* to suggest that politically discriminatory gerrymanders are subject to strict scrutiny under the *Equal Protection Clause*. It is elementary that scrutiny levels are claim specific. An action that triggers a heightened level of scrutiny for one claim may receive a very different level of scrutiny for a different claim because the underlying rights, and consequently constitutional harms, are not comparable. To say that suppression of political speech (a claimed First Amendment violation) triggers strict scrutiny is not to say that failure to give political groups equal representation (a claimed equal protection violation) triggers strict scrutiny. . . .

B

. . . Under Justice SOUTER's proposed standard, in order to challenge a particular district, a plaintiff must show (1) that he is a member of a "cohesive political group"; (2) "that the district of his residence . . . paid little or no heed" to traditional districting principles; (3) that there were "specific correlations between the district's deviations from traditional districting principles and the distribution of the population of his group"; (4) that a hypothetical district exists which includes the plaintiff's residence, remedies the packing or cracking of the plaintiff's group, and deviates less from traditional districting principles; and (5) that "the defendants acted intentionally to manipulate the shape of the district in order to pack or crack his group." When those showings have been made, the burden would shift to the defendants to justify the district "by reference to objectives other than naked partisan advantage."

While this five-part test seems eminently scientific, upon analysis one finds that each of the last four steps requires a quantifying judgment that is unguided and ill suited to the development of judicial standards. . . . What is a lower court to do when, as will often be the case, the district adheres to some traditional criteria but not others? Justice SOUTER's only response to this question is to evade it: "It is not necessary now to say exactly how a district court would balance a good showing on one of these indices against a poor showing on another, for that sort of detail is best worked out case by case." But the devil lurks precisely in such detail. The central problem is determining when political gerrymandering has gone too far. . . .

Justice SOUTER's proposal is doomed to failure for a more basic reason: No test—yea, not even a five-part test—can possibly be successful unless one knows what he is testing *for*. In the present context, the test ought to identify deprivation of that minimal degree of representation or influence to which a political group is constitutionally entitled. . . . Justice SOUTER avoids the difficulties of those formulations by never telling us what his test is looking for, other than the utterly unhelpful "extremity of unfairness." . . .

C

. . . The criterion Justice BREYER proposes is nothing more precise than "the *unjustified* use of political factors to entrench a minority in power." While he invokes in passing the Equal Protection Clause, it should be clear to any reader that what constitutes *unjustified* entrenchment depends on his own theory of "effective government." . . .

Justice BREYER provides no real guidance for the journey. Despite his promise to do so, he never tells us what he is testing for, beyond the unhelpful "*unjustified* entrenchment." Instead, he "set[s] forth several sets of circumstances that lay out the indicia of abuse," "along a continuum," proceeding (presumably) from the most clearly unconstitutional to the possibly unconstitutional. . . . In sum, we neither know precisely what Justice BREYER is testing for, nor precisely what fails the test.

V

Justice KENNEDY recognizes that we have "demonstrat[ed] the shortcomings of the other standards that have been considered to date." He acknowledges, moreover, that we "lack . . . comprehensive and neutral principles for drawing electoral boundaries"; and that there is an "absence of rules to limit and confine judicial intervention." From these premises, one might think that Justice KENNEDY would reach the conclusion that political gerrymandering claims are nonjusticiable. Instead, however, he concludes that courts should continue to adjudicate such claims because a standard *may* one day be discovered. . . .

VI

We conclude that neither Article I, § 2, nor the Equal Protection Clause, nor (what appellants only fleetingly invoke) Article I, § 4, provides a judicially enforceable limit on the political considerations that the States and Congress may take into account when districting.

Considerations of *stare decisis* do not compel us to allow *Bandemer* to stand. That case involved an interpretation of the Constitution, and the claims of *stare decisis* are at their weakest in that field, where our mistakes cannot be corrected by Congress. See *Payne v. Tennessee,* 501 U.S. 808, 828 (1991). . . .

While we do not lightly overturn one of our own holdings, "when governing decisions are unworkable or are badly reasoned, this Court has never felt constrained to follow precedent." 501 U.S., at 827. Eighteen years of essentially pointless litigation have persuaded us that *Bandemer* is incapable of principled application. We would therefore overrule that case, and decline to adjudicate these political gerrymandering claims. . . .

■ JUSTICE KENNEDY, concurring in the judgment.

. . . While agreeing with the plurality that the complaint the appellants filed in the District Court must be dismissed, and while understanding that great caution is necessary when approaching this subject, I would not foreclose all possibility of judicial relief if some limited and precise rationale were found to correct an established violation of the Constitution in some redistricting cases.

When presented with a claim of injury from partisan gerrymandering, courts confront two obstacles. First is the lack of comprehensive and neutral principles for drawing electoral boundaries. No substantive definition of fairness in districting seems to command general assent. Second is the absence of rules to limit and confine judicial intervention. With uncertain limits, intervening courts—even when proceeding with best intentions— would risk assuming political, not legal, responsibility for a process that often produces ill will and distrust.

That courts can grant relief in districting cases where race is involved does not answer our need for fairness principles here. Those controversies implicate a different inquiry. They involve sorting permissible classifications in the redistricting context from impermissible ones. Race is an impermissible classification. . . . Politics is quite a different matter. . . . Because there are yet no agreed upon substantive principles of fairness in districting, we have no basis on which to define clear, manageable, and politically neutral standards for measuring the particular burden a given partisan classification imposes on representational rights. . . .

Because, in the case before us, we have no standard by which to measure the burden appellants claim has been imposed on their representational rights, appellants cannot establish that the alleged political classifications burden those same rights. . . . As a consequence, appellants' complaint alleges no impermissible use of political classifications and so states no valid claim on which relief may be granted. . . .

The plurality thinks I resolve this case with reference to no standard, but that is wrong. The Fourteenth Amendment standard governs; and there is no doubt of that. My analysis only notes that if a subsidiary standard could show how an otherwise permissible classification, as applied, burdens representational rights, we could conclude that appellants' evidence states a provable claim under the Fourteenth Amendment standard.

. . . [T]he complaint in this case also alleged a violation of First Amendment rights. The First Amendment may be the more relevant constitutional provision in future cases that allege unconstitutional partisan gerrymandering. After all, these allegations involve the First Amendment interest of not burdening or penalizing citizens because of their participation in the electoral process, their voting history, their association with a political party, or their expression of political views. See *Elrod v. Burns*, 427 U.S. 347 (1976) (plurality opinion). Under general First Amendment principles those burdens in other contexts are unconstitutional absent a compelling government interest. . . . First Amendment concerns arise where a State enacts a law that has the purpose and effect of subjecting a group of voters or their party to disfavored treatment by reason of their views. In the context of partisan gerrymandering, that means that First Amendment concerns arise where an apportionment has the purpose and effect of burdening a group of voters' representational rights.

Where it is alleged that a gerrymander had the purpose and effect of imposing burdens on a disfavored party and its voters, the First Amendment may offer a sounder and more prudential basis for intervention than does the Equal Protection Clause. The equal protection analysis puts its emphasis on the permissibility of an enactment's classifications. This works where race is involved since classifying by race is almost never permissible. It presents a more complicated question when the inquiry is whether a generally permissible classification has been used for an impermissible purpose. That question can only be answered in the affirmative by the subsidiary showing that the classification as applied imposes unlawful burdens. The First Amendment analysis concentrates on whether the legislation burdens the representational rights of the complaining party's voters for reasons of ideology, beliefs, or political association. . . .

■ JUSTICE STEVENS, dissenting.

. . . The concept of equal justice under law requires the State to govern impartially. Today's plurality opinion would exempt governing officials from that duty in the context of legislative redistricting and would give license, for the first time, to partisan gerrymanders that are devoid of any rational justification. In my view, when partisanship is the legislature's sole motivation—when any pretense of neutrality is forsaken unabashedly and all traditional districting criteria are subverted for partisan advantage—the governing body cannot be said to have acted impartially. . . .

The judicial standards applicable to gerrymandering claims are deeply rooted in decisions that long preceded *Bandemer* and have been refined in later cases. Among those well-settled principles is the understanding that a district's peculiar shape might be a symptom of an illicit purpose in the line-drawing process. . . . [Our] decisions . . . have also considered the process by which the districting schemes were enacted, looked to other evidence demonstrating that purely improper considerations motivated the decision, and included maps illustrating outlandish district shapes.

Given this clear line of precedents, I should have thought the question of justiciability in cases such as this—where a set of plaintiffs argues that a single motivation resulted in a districting scheme with discriminatory effects—to be well settled. The plurality's contrary conclusion cannot be squared with our long history of voting rights decisions. Especially perplexing is the plurality's *ipse dixit* distinction of our racial gerrymandering cases. . . .

To begin with, the plurality errs in assuming that politics is "an ordinary and lawful motive." We have squarely rejected the notion that a "purpose to discriminate on the basis of politics" is never subject to strict scrutiny. On the contrary, "political belief and association constitute the core of those activities protected by the First Amendment," *Elrod v. Burns*, 427 U.S. 347, 356 (1976) (plurality opinion), and discriminatory governmental decisions that burden fundamental First Amendment interests are subject to strict scrutiny. Thus, unless party affiliation is an appropriate requirement for the position in question, government officials may not base a decision to hire, promote, transfer, recall, discharge, or retaliate against an employee, or to terminate a contract, on the individual's partisan affiliation or speech. It follows that political affiliation is not an appropriate standard for excluding voters from a congressional district. . . .

[O]ur recent racial gerrymandering cases have examined the shape of the district and the purpose of the districting body to determine whether race, above all other criteria, predominated in the line-drawing process. . . . Under the *Shaw* cases, then, the use of race as a criterion in redistricting is not *per se* impermissible, . . . but when race is elevated to paramount status—when it is the be-all and end-all of the redistricting process—the legislature has gone too far. . . .

Just as irrational shape can serve as an objective indicator of an impermissible legislative purpose, other objective features of a districting map can save the plan from invalidation. We have explained that "traditional districting principles," which include "compactness, contiguity, and respect for political subdivisions," are "important not because they are constitutionally required . . . but because they are objective factors that may serve to defeat a claim that a district has been gerrymandered on racial lines." . . .

In my view, the same standards should apply to claims of political gerrymandering, for the essence of a gerrymander is the same regardless of whether the group is identified as political or racial. Gerrymandering always involves the drawing of district boundaries to maximize the voting strength of the dominant political faction and to minimize the strength of one or more groups of opponents. In seeking the desired result, legislators necessarily make judgments about the probability that the members of identifiable groups—whether economic, religious, ethnic, or racial—will vote in a certain way. The overriding purpose of those predictions is political. It follows that the standards that enable courts to identify and redress a racial gerrymander could also perform the same function for other species of gerrymanders. . . .

The plurality reasons that the standards for evaluating racial gerrymanders are not workable in cases such as this because partisan considerations, unlike racial ones, are perfectly legitimate. Until today, however, there has not been the slightest intimation in any opinion written by any Member of this Court that a naked purpose to disadvantage a political minority would provide a rational basis for drawing a district line. On the contrary, our opinions referring to political gerrymanders have consistently assumed that they were at least undesirable, and we always have indicated that political considerations are among those factors that may not dominate districting decisions. Purely partisan motives are "rational" in a literal sense, but there must be a limiting principle. . . . The rational basis for government decisions must satisfy a standard of legitimacy and neutrality; an acceptable rational basis can be neither purely personal nor purely partisan. . . .

In sum, in evaluating a challenge to a specific district, I would apply the standard set forth in the *Shaw* cases and ask whether the legislature allowed partisan considerations to dominate and control the lines drawn, forsaking all neutral principles. Under my analysis, if no neutral criterion can be identified to justify the lines drawn, and if the only possible explanation for a district's bizarre shape is a naked desire to increase partisan strength, then no rational basis exists to save the district from an equal protection challenge. Such a narrow test would cover only a few meritorious claims, but it would preclude extreme abuses, . . . and it would perhaps shorten the time period in which the pernicious effects of such a gerrymander are felt. This test would mitigate the current trend under which partisan considerations are becoming the be-all and end-all in apportioning representatives. . . .

■ JUSTICE SOUTER, with whom JUSTICE GINSBURG joins, dissenting.

The Constitution guarantees both formal and substantial equality among voters. For 40 years, we have recognized that lines dividing a State into voting districts must produce divisions with equal populations: one person, one vote. . . .

Creating unequally populous districts is not, however, the only way to skew political results by setting district lines. . . . However equal districts may be in population as a formal matter, the consequence of a vote cast can be minimized or maximized, and if unfairness is sufficiently demonstrable, the guarantee of equal protection condemns it as a denial of substantial equality . . .

Since this Court has created the problem no one else has been able to solve, it is up to us to make a fresh start. There are a good many voices saying it is high time that we did, for in the years since *Davis*, the increasing efficiency of partisan redistricting has damaged the democratic process to a degree that our predecessors only began to imagine. *[Lengthy citation to scholarly commentary omitted.—Editors]*

I would therefore preserve *Davis's* holding that political gerrymandering is a justiciable issue, but otherwise start anew. I would adopt a political gerrymandering test analogous to the summary judgment standard crafted in *McDonnell Douglas Corp. v. Green*, 411 U.S. 792 (1973), calling for a plaintiff to satisfy elements of a prima facie cause of action, at which point the State would have the opportunity not only to rebut the evidence supporting the plaintiff's case, but to offer an affirmative justification for the districting choices, even assuming the proof of the plaintiff's allegations. My own judgment is that we would have better luck at devising a workable prima facie case if we concentrated as much as possible on suspect characteristics of individual districts instead of statewide patterns. . . . Finally, in the same interest of threshold simplicity, I would stick to problems of single-member districts; if we could not devise a workable scheme for dealing with claims about these, we would have to forget the complications posed by multimember districts.

For a claim based on a specific single-member district, I would require the plaintiff to make out a prima facie case with five elements. First, the resident plaintiff would identify a cohesive political group to which he belonged . . .

Second, a plaintiff would need to show that the district of his residence paid little or no heed to those traditional districting principles whose disregard can be shown straightforwardly: contiguity, compactness, respect for political subdivisions, and conformity with geographic features like rivers and mountains. . . .

Indeed, although compactness is at first blush the least likely of these principles to yield precision, it can be measured quantitatively in terms of dispersion, perimeter, and population ratios, and the development of standards would thus be possible. It is not necessary now to say exactly how a district court would balance a good showing on one of these indices against a poor showing on another, for that sort of detail is best worked out case by case.

Third, the plaintiff would need to establish specific correlations between the district's deviations from traditional districting principles and the distribution of the population of his group. . . . To make their claim stick, they would need to point to specific protuberances on the Draconian shape that reach out to include Democrats, or fissures in it that squirm away from Republicans. . . . That would begin, but not complete, the plaintiff's case that the defendant had chosen either to pack the group (drawn a district in order to include a uselessly high number of the group) or to crack it (drawn it so as to include fatally few), the ordinary methods of vote dilution in single-member district systems.

Fourth, a plaintiff would need to present the court with a hypothetical district including his residence, one in which the proportion of the plaintiff's group was lower (in a packing claim) or higher (in a cracking one) and which at the same time deviated less from traditional districting principles than the actual district. . . .

Fifth, and finally, the plaintiff would have to show that the defendants acted intentionally to manipulate the shape of the district in order to pack or crack his group. I would, however, treat any showing of intent in a major-party case as too equivocal to count unless the entire legislature were controlled by the governor's party (or the dominant legislative party were vetoproof). . . .

A plaintiff who got this far would have shown that his State intentionally acted to dilute his vote, having ignored reasonable alternatives consistent with traditional districting principles. I would then shift the burden to the defendants to justify their decision by reference to objectives other than naked partisan advantage. They might show by rebuttal evidence that districting objectives could not be served by the plaintiff's hypothetical district better than by the district as drawn, or they might affirmatively establish legitimate objectives better served by the lines drawn than by the plaintiff's hypothetical. . . .

■ JUSTICE BREYER, dissenting.

. . . [Consideration of the fundamentals of democratic governance] can help identify at least one circumstance where use of purely political boundary-drawing factors can amount to a serious, and remediable, abuse, namely, the *unjustified* use of political factors to entrench a minority in power. By entrenchment I mean a situation in which a party that enjoys only minority support among the populace has nonetheless contrived to take, and hold, legislative power. By *unjustified* entrenchment I mean that the minority's hold on power is purely the result of partisan manipulation and not other factors. These "other" factors that could lead to "justified" (albeit temporary) minority entrenchment include sheer happenstance, the existence of more than two major parties, the unique constitutional requirements of certain representational bodies such as the Senate, or reliance on traditional (geographic, communities of interest, etc.) districting criteria.

The democratic harm of unjustified entrenchment is obvious. . . . Where unjustified entrenchment takes place, voters find it far more difficult to remove those responsible for a government they do not want; and these democratic values are dishonored.

. . . Unless some other justification can be found in particular circumstances, political gerrymandering that so entrenches a minority party in power violates basic democratic norms and lacks countervailing justification. For this reason, whether political gerrymandering does, or does not, violate the Constitution in other instances, gerrymandering that leads to entrenchment amounts to an abuse that violates the Constitution's Equal Protection Clause. . . .

I do not claim that the problem of identification and separation is easily solved, even in extreme instances. But courts can identify a number of strong indicia of abuse. The presence of actual entrenchment, while not always unjustified (being perhaps a chance occurrence), is such a sign, particularly when accompanied by the use of partisan boundary-drawing criteria in the way that Justice STEVENS describes, *i.e.*, a use that both departs from traditional criteria and cannot be explained other than by efforts to achieve partisan advantage. . . .

In the case before us, there is a strong likelihood that the plaintiffs' complaint could be amended readily to assert circumstances consistent with those I have set forth as appropriate for judicial intervention. For that reason, I would authorize the plaintiffs to proceed; and I dissent from the majority's contrary determination.

NOTES

1. Because Justice Kennedy dissented from the conclusion that political gerrymandering claims are non-justiciable, but concurred with the dismissal of the complaint on the ground the plaintiff had set forth no constitutional standard that had been violated, his opinion is the narrowest, and therefore the controlling opinion. What does it mean? What is the point of holding such cases justiciable if there is no available constitutional theory on which plaintiffs might succeed?

At the time of *Baker v. Carr*, the Court had not yet hit upon a judicially manageable standard for cases of unequal district size. Justices Frankfurter and Harlan, among others, thought that because there were many possible legitimate criteria for districting, the courts could not interfere without appearing partisan and political. The one person, one vote standard answered that objection: it could be applied unflinchingly in all cases, and it did not systematically favor one political party over the other. Of course, adoption of this standard came at the cost of a more nuanced system, such as that advocated by the dissenters in *Lucas*, the Colorado case. Is there a comparable standard for gerrymandering cases?

2. The dissenters rely on different constitutional theories. Justice Souter rests on Equal Protection. Justice Stevens invokes the First Amendment. Justice Breyer does not mention the Republican Form of Government Clause, but his concern about "minority entrenchment" sounds like a claim that the government is unrepublican. Interestingly, none of the justices invokes the provi-

sion of Article I, Section Two, Clause 1 that representatives must be chosen by "the People," even though this case involves federal congressional districts and that Clause had previously been the textual peg for challenges to congressional districting (e.g., *Wesberry*). Are these seemingly quite different constitutional principles interchangeable in the context of partisan gerrymandering cases?

3. Why, precisely, does the plurality maintain that racial gerrymandering presents a different question from partisan gerrymandering? There are three main reasons. First, race is more discernible and immutable than political allegiance. But is it true, as the plurality asserts, that these facts "make it impossible to assess the effects of partisan gerrymandering"? Professional politicians seem capable of assessing these effects; why can't courts? Second, racial discrimination entails strict scrutiny, while discrimination on the basis of political allegiance does not (except sometimes). But Justice Stevens's argument is that discrimination on the basis of politics, at least in this context, *should* receive strict scrutiny. Is he right? The plurality says that partisan districting is "common" and "lawful." But so was unequal districting before *Baker*. Why not venture again into the political thicket? Third, the Constitution explicitly condemns discrimination on the basis of race and does not mention partisan gerrymandering. But is it so clear that the intentional creation of a majority-minority district violates this principle, assuming that the non-minority population is not deprived of its "fair share" of political influence? And the Constitution does mention, and "guarantee," a republican form of government. Why does the plurality avoid that principle?

But maybe the racial gerrymandering cases cut the other way. As we have seen, the Court set out on a path of disapproving districts that were drawn predominantly on racial lines, but it never embraced the usual constitutional principle that race is a forbidden consideration altogether. *Miller v. Johnson*, 515 U.S. 900, 928–29 (1995) (O'Connor, J., concurring). In later cases, the Court seemingly relaxed its scrutiny. E.g., *Easley v. Cromartie*, 532 U.S. 234 (2001). At this point, does the race analogy offer judicially manageable standards for partisan gerrymandering?

4. If we think of the Equal Protection Clause, the plurality's assumption that the Constitution speaks more directly to racial gerrymandering than to partisan gerrymandering seems right. But is the same true of the Republican Form of Government Clause? Partisan gerrymandering, at least in its extreme form (as described by Justice Breyer) allows a minority to entrench itself, which arguably goes to the heart of republicanism. Racial gerrymandering involves a decision by the majority to allow a minority to exercise a greater degree of political power. Is that unrepublican?

5. Two means of controlling gerrymandering are computer programs and commissions. When politicians draw lines personally, no one can say what their real motives are, but computers take into account only the factors they are programmed to take into account. What would you think of a computer program that takes into account only population, compactness, contiguity, and established political boundaries? Another possibility is having a nonpartisan commission draw districting lines, as is done in about a dozen states. One question to consider is how a reliably nonpartisan commission could be selected, without effectively empowering incumbents and political insiders. Another questions is whether federal actors could require the more extensive use of such commissions. Could Congress require commission-based districting for federal elections

under its Article I, Section 4, Clause 1 power to "make or alter" state regulations governing the "Times, Places, and Manner of holding Elections for Senators and Representatives"? Could Congress require commission-based districting for state elections under its Fourteenth Amendment, Section Five enforcement power? Or could a federal court require commission-based districting as a remedy for partisan gerrymandering?

A NOTE ON INCUMBENCY–PROTECTION GERRYMANDERS

The Supreme Court has never entertained a square challenge to a gerrymander designed to protect incumbents, but in a number of decisions it refers to this as a legitimate districting purpose. Why is that? In his dissent in *Easley v. Cromartie*, 532 U.S. 234 (2001), Justice Thomas stated that he was willing to "assume, because the District Court did, that the goal of protecting incumbents is legitimate," but he called this assumption "questionable." Is it? Who would have standing to contest an incumbency-protection gerrymander?

[*Assignment 75*]

II. CASE STUDY: THE PRESIDENTIAL ELECTION PROCESS

Article II provides an elaborate process for electing the president: "Each State shall appoint, in such Manner as the Legislature thereof may direct, a Number of Electors, equal to the whole Number of Senators and Representatives to which the State may be entitled in the Congress." Art. II, Sec. 1. No senator, representative, or anyone else holding a federal office may serve as an elector. This system is today colloquially referred to as the "Electoral College."

The Electoral College reflects both of the major compromises over representation at the founding: the Three–Fifths Compromise over slavery, and the "Great Compromise" between small and large states. Many Northern representatives favored direct popular election, but James Madison and others noted that this would deny to Southern states the representation-enhancing power attributable to the holding of large numbers of slaves. (A direct election would have excluded slaves.) By instead adopting the Electoral College and granting electors based on representation in the House of Representatives, the Convention built into the system of electing the president the Three–Fifths Compromise's (slavery-rewarding) representation rule for the House. The Electoral College also built into the system of presidential election the compromise that produced the Senate, with equal representation of each state regardless of whether it was small or large.

Unsurprisingly, prior to the Civil War, this weighted over-representation of slaveholding states, and to a lesser extent smaller states, helped make four of the nation's first five presidents Southerners (all Virginians—Washington, Jefferson, Madison, Monroe), collectively holding the presidency for 32 of the nation's first 36 years under the Constitution. The over-representation also tended to produce mostly slavery-sympathetic or slavery-accommodating presidents, even when coming from a Northern state—until the election of an anti-slavery Northerner, Abraham Lincoln, in 1860. For an excellent general history of the political effects of the Electoral College, see Akhil Amar, AMERICA'S CONSTITUTION: A BIOGRAPHY 148–159 (2005).

Under Article II, Section 1, the electors meet in their respective states—separated from each other, to guard against collaboration, cabal, or conspiracy—on a common designated day. The electors then cast two votes. In the original Constitution, these two votes were for two candidates for president, one of whom could not be from the same state as the elector. The candidate receiving the most votes became president; the runner-up became vice president (assuming they each received a majority of the electors' votes). In the event no candidate received a majority, or if there was a tie, the House of Representatives would choose the president from among the top five vote-getters. At this tie-breaking stage of the process, each state's delegation of representatives would get one vote, as a unit—a rule of equal representation of the states. Because the House of Representatives would be the departing, "lame-duck" House, the system permitted ousted representatives to choose the new president.

The election of 1800 revealed some of the problems with this system. The Democratic–Republicans' two candidates, Thomas Jefferson and Aaron Burr, running as a "ticket" (the plan had been for Jefferson to be president and Burr the vice president), *tied* in the Electoral College, producing a long deadlock in the House of Representatives, which was finally broken when the (largely defeated) Federalist House of Representatives agreed to Jefferson as the lesser of two evils. The Twelfth Amendment, adopted in 1804, changed the two-vote process, to account for the emergence of political parties, tickets, and the strategic voting that had produced the debacle of 1800 (and that had nearly done the same thing in 1796). With the Twelfth Amendment, the Constitution now provides that electors cast separate ballots for president and for vice president (still with requirement that one of those votes be for an out-of-stater). If no candidate receives a majority, the House of Representatives chooses (one-state, one-vote, as before) from the top five presidential candidates.

As noted earlier, nothing in the Constitution limits a state legislature's choice as to how that state will choose its electors. The legislature could choose the electors itself. Or it could use any other method. Over time, states came to choose systems in which electors favoring a specific candidate were selected based on state-wide popular votes, with most states opting for a winner-of-the-state-gets-all-the-electors system. But state legislatures need not keep such systems. They could provide for proportional representation of electors, based on candidates' popular vote percentages. They could provide for elections of electors based on House districts. They could even decide that electors will be chosen by a state university's constitutional law professors.

An advantage (or is it one?) of the Electoral College system is that it permits a candidate who has received only a plurality of the nation-wide popular vote nonetheless to obtain a clear majority in the Electoral College. Lincoln won only 40% of the national popular vote—the most of the candidates, but far short of a majority of the nation—yet pretty much swept the Northern states and thereby received 180 electoral votes, well over the necessary 152 to make a majority. It is often said that the Electoral College requires candidates to address a wide range of differing constituencies, throughout the nation, and not be limited to merely regional support, however strong. But the election of Lincoln is a counter-example.

One disadvantage (or is it one?) of the Electoral College system is that it permits a candidate who has *lost* the popular vote to another candidate still to win a majority in the Electoral College and become president. This has happened four times in our nation's history. In 1876, Rutherford B. Hayes defeated Samuel Tilden, although Tilden won the popular vote. In 1888, Benjamin Harrison ousted President Grover Cleveland, although Cleveland won the popular vote. (Cleveland was re-elected in 1892, the only president to serve non-consecutive terms.) In 1860, John F. Kennedy defeated Richard Nixon in the Electoral College, although by some calculations Richard Nixon narrowly bested him in the popular vote. (That result depends on how one interprets the popular votes of Alabama, which adopted a bizarre system requiring voters to cast eleven different votes for president—one for each of Alabama's eleven electors.) And in 2000, George W. Bush defeated Al Gore, Jr., despite Gore having won the popular vote.

The Presidential Election Cases, involving the 2000 election contest between then-Texas Governor Bush and then-Vice President Gore, raised a series of fascinating constitutional controversies. In the end, Bush defeated Gore in the popular vote in the state of Florida by the extraordinarily narrow margin of 537 votes (2,912,790 votes for Bush to 2,912,253 votes for Gore), also giving him an extraordinarily narrow victory in the Electoral College: 271 Electoral College votes for Bush, 266 Electoral College votes for Gore (one of Washington D.C.'s electors abstained).

Litigation over the standards for the state-law recount and "contest" produced the most famous recent application of the equal protection principles of *Baker v. Carr* and *Reynolds v. Sims*. In *Bush v. Palm Beach County Canvassing Bd.*, 531 U.S. 70 (2000), the Court held that uneven and inconsistent standards used in the recount of votes cast for presidential electors in Florida violated the Equal Protection Clause. More controversially, the Court held there was insufficient time for the state to conduct a new recount in compliance with these mandates, and it thus rejected Vice President's Gore's challenge to the earlier count, effectively awarding the presidency to Governor Bush.

Was this a step into Justice Frankfurter's feared "political thicket"? Was it the inevitable result of the process of constitutionalization of U.S. elections begun in *Baker v. Carr*? Should the Court have held the case nonjusticiable? If so, should the Florida state court decision have been allowed to stand (even if it contained constitutional flaws)? If the proper outcome of the election was a "political question," who should have decided it?

The 2000 presidential election dispute actually produced *two* Supreme Court decisions. We start with the less famous one, *Bush v. Palm Beach County Canvassing Board*, which set the stage for the round of appeals culminating in *Bush v. Gore*.

Bush v. Palm Beach County Canvassing Board

531 U.S. 70 (2000)

■ The Court delivered a PER CURIAM opinion.

The Supreme Court of the State of Florida interpreted its elections statutes in proceedings brought to require manual recounts of ballots, and the certification of the recount results, for votes cast in the quadrennial Presidential election held on November 7, 2000. Governor George W. Bush, Republican candidate for the Presidency, filed a petition for certiorari to review the Florida Supreme Court decision. We granted certiorari on two of the questions presented by petitioner: whether the decision of the Florida Supreme Court, by effectively changing the State's elector appointment procedures after election day, violated the Due Process Clause or 3 U.S.C. § 5, and whether the decision of that court changed the manner in which the State's electors are to be selected, in violation of the legislature's power to designate the manner for selection under Art. II, § 1, cl. 2, of the United States Constitution.

On November 8, 2000, the day following the Presidential election, the Florida Division of Elections reported that Governor Bush had received 2,909,135 votes, and respondent Democrat Vice President Albert Gore, Jr., had received 2,907,351, a margin of 1,784 in Governor Bush's favor. [An automatic machine recount] resulted in a much smaller margin of victory for Governor Bush. Vice President Gore then exercised his statutory right to submit written requests for manual recounts to the canvassing board of any county. He requested recounts in four counties: Volusia, Palm Beach, Broward, and Miami–Dade.

The parties urged conflicting interpretations of the Florida Election Code respecting the authority of the canvassing boards, the Secretary of State (hereinafter Secretary), and the Elections Canvassing Commission. On November 14, in an action brought by Volusia County, and joined by the Palm Beach County Canvassing Board, Vice President Gore, and the Florida Democratic Party, the Florida Circuit Court ruled that the statutory 7–day deadline was mandatory, but that the Volusia [County] board could amend its returns at a later date. . . . *[The Secretary of State set a deadline and criteria for submission of late returns.—Editors]*

[T]he Florida Democratic Party and Vice President Gore . . . argue[d] that the Secretary had acted arbitrarily and in contempt of the court's earlier ruling. The following day, the court denied the motion, ruling that the Secretary had not acted arbitrarily and had exercised her discretion in a reasonable manner consistent with the court's earlier ruling. The Democratic Party and Vice President Gore appealed . . .

The [Florida] Supreme Court, with the expedition requisite for the controversy, issued its decision on November 21. *Palm Beach County Canvassing Bd. v. Harris*, 772 So.2d 1220 (2000). . . .

[The majority opinion next describes how the Florida Supreme Court held that under state election law "a discrepancy between a sample manual recount and machine returns due to the way in which a ballot was punched or marked did constitute an 'error in vote tabulation' sufficient to trigger the statutory provisions for a full manual recount." The court also found a conflict between provisions of state law as to whether the Secretary of State was required to ignore late manual recounts or merely had discretion to do so.— Editors] The court thus imposed a deadline of November 26, at 5 p.m., for a return of ballot counts. The 7–day deadline of § 102.111, assuming it would have applied, was effectively extended by 12 days. The court further directed the Secretary to accept manual counts submitted prior to that deadline.

As a general rule, this Court defers to a state court's interpretation of a state statute. But in the case of a law enacted by a state legislature applicable not only to elections to state offices, but also to the selection of Presidential electors, the legislature is not acting solely under the authority given it by the people of the State, but by virtue of a direct grant of authority made under Art. II, § 1, cl. 2, of the United States Constitution. That provision reads: "Each State shall appoint, in such Manner as the Legislature thereof may direct, a Number of Electors, equal to the whole Number of

Senators and Representatives to which the State may be entitled in the Congress. . . ."

Although we did not address the same question petitioner raises here, in *McPherson v. Blacker*, 146 U.S. 1, 25 (1892), we said:

> [Art. II, § 1, cl. 2] does not read that the people or the citizens shall appoint, but that "each State shall"; and if the words "in such manner as the legislature thereof may direct," had been omitted, it would seem that the legislative power of appointment could not have been successfully questioned in the absence of any provision in the state constitution in that regard. Hence the insertion of those words, while operating as a limitation upon the State in respect of any attempt to circumscribe the legislative power, cannot be held to operate as a limitation on that power itself.

There are expressions in the opinion of the Supreme Court of Florida that may be read to indicate that it construed the Florida Election Code without regard to the extent to which the Florida Constitution could, consistent with Art. II, § 1, cl. 2, "circumscribe the legislative power." The opinion states, for example, that "[t]o the extent that the Legislature may enact laws regulating the electoral process, those laws are valid only if they impose no 'unreasonable or unnecessary' restraints on the right of suffrage" guaranteed by the State Constitution. 772 So.2d, at 1236. The opinion also states that "[b]ecause election laws are intended to facilitate the right of suffrage, such laws must be liberally construed in favor of the citizens' right to vote. . . ." *Id.* at 1237.

In addition, 3 U.S.C. § 5 provides in pertinent part:

> If any State shall have provided, by laws enacted prior to the day fixed for the appointment of the electors, for its final determination of any controversy or contest concerning the appointment of all or any of the electors of such State, by judicial or other methods or procedures, and such determination shall have been made at least six days before the time fixed for the meeting of the electors, such determination made pursuant to such law so existing on said day, and made at least six days prior to said time of meeting of the electors, shall be conclusive, and shall govern in the counting of the electoral votes as provided in the Constitution, and as hereinafter regulated, so far as the ascertainment of the electors appointed by such State is concerned.

The parties before us agree that whatever else may be the effect of this section, it creates a "safe harbor" for a State insofar as congressional consideration of its electoral votes is concerned. . . . Since § 5 contains a principle of federal law that would assure finality of the State's determination if made pursuant to a state law in effect before the election, a legislative wish to take advantage of the "safe harbor" would counsel against any construction of the Election Code that Congress might deem to be a change in the law.

After reviewing the opinion of the Florida Supreme Court, we find "that there is considerable uncertainty as to the precise grounds for the decision." *Minnesota v. National Tea Co.*, 309 U.S. 551, 555 (1940). This is sufficient reason for us to decline at this time to review the federal questions asserted to be present.

> It is fundamental that state courts be left free and unfettered by us in interpreting their state constitutions. But it is equally important that ambiguous or obscure adjudications by state courts do not stand as

barriers to a determination by this Court of the validity under the federal constitution of state action. Intelligent exercise of our appellate powers compels us to ask for the elimination of the obscurities and ambiguities from the opinions in such cases.

Id., at 557.

Specifically, we are unclear as to the extent to which the Florida Supreme Court saw the Florida Constitution as circumscribing the legislature's authority under Art. II, § 1, cl. 2. We are also unclear as to the consideration the Florida Supreme Court accorded to 3 U.S.C. § 5. The judgment of the Supreme Court of Florida is therefore vacated, and the case is remanded for further proceedings not inconsistent with this opinion.

Bush v. Gore

531 U.S. 98 (2000)

■ The Court delivered a PER CURIAM opinion.

I

On December 8, 2000, the Supreme Court of Florida ordered that the Circuit Court of Leon County tabulate by hand 9,000 ballots in Miami–Dade County. It also ordered the inclusion in the certified vote totals of 215 votes identified in Palm Beach County and 168 votes identified in Miami–Dade County for Vice President Albert Gore, Jr., and Senator Joseph Lieberman, Democratic candidates for President and Vice President. The State Supreme Court noted that petitioner George W. Bush asserted that the net gain for Vice President Gore in Palm Beach County was 176 votes, and directed the Circuit Court to resolve that dispute on remand. *Gore v. Harris*, 772 So.2d 1243, 1248, n. 6. The court further held that relief would require manual recounts in all Florida counties where so-called "undervotes" had not been subject to manual tabulation. The court ordered all manual recounts to begin at once. Governor Bush and Richard Cheney, Republican candidates for President and Vice President, filed an emergency application for a stay of this mandate. On December 9, we granted the application, treated the application as a petition for a writ of certiorari, and granted certiorari. . . .

The proceedings leading to the present controversy are discussed in some detail in our opinion in *Bush v. Palm Beach County Canvassing Bd.*, 531 U.S. 70 (2000) *(per curiam) (Bush I)*. . . . On November 26, the Florida Elections Canvassing Commission certified the results of the election and declared Governor Bush the winner of Florida's 25 electoral votes. On November 27, Vice President Gore, pursuant to Florida's contest provisions, filed a complaint in Leon County Circuit Court contesting the certification. . . . The Circuit Court denied relief, stating that Vice President Gore failed to meet his burden of proof. . . .

[T]he Florida Supreme Court affirmed in part and reversed in part. . . . [It] held that Vice President Gore had satisfied his burden of proof . . . with respect to his challenge to Miami–Dade County's failure to tabulate, by manual count, 9,000 ballots on which the machines had failed to detect a vote for President ("undervotes"). Noting the closeness of the election, the court explained that "[o]n this record, there can be no question that there are legal votes within the 9,000 uncounted votes sufficient to place the results of this election in doubt." A "legal vote," as determined by the Supreme Court, is "one in which there is a 'clear indication of the intent of the voter.' " The court therefore ordered a hand recount of the 9,000 ballots in Miami–Dade County. Observing that the contest provisions vest broad discretion in the circuit judge to "provide any relief appropriate under such circumstances," § 102.168(8), the Supreme Court further held that the Circuit Court could order "the Supervisor of Elections and the Canvassing Boards, as well as the necessary public officials, in all counties that have not conducted a manual recount or tabulation of the undervotes . . . to do so forthwith, said tabulation to take place in the individual counties where the ballots are located."

The Supreme Court also determined that both Palm Beach County and Miami–Dade County, in their earlier manual recounts, had identified a net gain of 215 and 168 legal votes for Vice President Gore. Rejecting the Circuit Court's conclusion that Palm Beach County lacked the authority to include the 215 net votes submitted past the November 26 deadline, the Supreme Court explained that the deadline was not intended to exclude votes identified after that date through ongoing manual recounts. As to Miami–Dade County, the court concluded that although the 168 votes identified were the result of a partial recount, they were "legal votes [that] could change the outcome of the election." The Supreme Court therefore directed the Circuit Court to include those totals in the certified results, subject to resolution of the actual vote total from the Miami–Dade partial recount.

The petition presents the following questions: whether the Florida Supreme Court established new standards for resolving Presidential election contests, thereby violating Art. II, § 1, cl. 2, of the United States Constitution and failing to comply with 3 U.S.C. § 5, and whether the use of standardless manual recounts violates the Equal Protection and Due Process Clauses. With respect to the equal protection question, we find a violation of the Equal Protection Clause.

II–A

The closeness of this election, and the multitude of legal challenges which have followed in its wake, have brought into sharp focus a common, if heretofore unnoticed, phenomenon. Nationwide statistics reveal that an estimated 2% of ballots cast do not register a vote for President for whatever reason, including deliberately choosing no candidate at all or some voter error, such as voting for two candidates or insufficiently marking a ballot. In certifying election results, the votes eligible for inclusion in the certification are the votes meeting the properly established legal requirements.

This case has shown that punchcard balloting machines can produce an unfortunate number of ballots which are not punched in a clean, complete way by the voter. After the current counting, it is likely legislative bodies nationwide will examine ways to improve the mechanisms and machinery for voting.

B

The individual citizen has no federal constitutional right to vote for electors for the President of the United States unless and until the state legislature chooses a statewide election as the means to implement its power to appoint members of the electoral college. U.S. Const., Art. II, § 1. This is the source for the statement in *McPherson v. Blacker*, 146 U.S. 1, 35 (1892), that the state legislature's power to select the manner for appointing electors is plenary; it may, if it so chooses, select the electors itself, which indeed was the manner used by state legislatures in several States for many years after the framing of our Constitution. History has now favored the voter, and in each of the several States the citizens themselves vote for Presidential electors. When the state legislature vests the right to vote for President in its people, the right to vote as the legislature has prescribed is fundamental; and one source of its fundamental nature lies in the equal weight accorded to each vote and the equal dignity owed to each voter. The State, of course, after granting the franchise in the special context of Article II, can take back the power to appoint electors.

The right to vote is protected in more than the initial allocation of the franchise. Equal protection applies as well to the manner of its exercise. Having once granted the right to vote on equal terms, the State may not, by later arbitrary and disparate treatment, value one person's vote over that of another. See, *e.g.*, *Harper v. Virginia Bd. of Elections*, 383 U.S. 663, 665 (1966) ("[O]nce the franchise is granted to the electorate, lines may not be drawn which are inconsistent with the Equal Protection Clause of the Fourteenth Amendment"). It must be remembered that "the right of suffrage can be denied by a debasement or dilution of the weight of a citizen's vote just as effectively as by wholly prohibiting the free exercise of the franchise." *Reynolds v. Sims*, 377 U.S. 533, 555 (1964).

There is no difference between the two sides of the present controversy on these basic propositions. Respondents say that the very purpose of vindicating the right to vote justifies the recount procedures now at issue. The question before us, however, is whether the recount procedures the Florida Supreme Court has adopted are consistent with its obligation to avoid arbitrary and disparate treatment of the members of its electorate.

Much of the controversy seems to revolve around ballot cards designed to be perforated by a stylus but which, either through error or deliberate omission, have not been perforated with sufficient precision for a machine to register the perforations. In some cases a piece of the card—a chad—is hanging, say, by two corners. In other cases there is no separation at all, just an indentation.

The Florida Supreme Court has ordered that the intent of the voter be discerned from such ballots. For purposes of resolving the equal protection challenge, it is not necessary to decide whether the Florida Supreme Court had the authority under the legislative scheme for resolving election disputes to define what a legal vote is and to mandate a manual recount implementing that definition. The recount mechanisms implemented in response to the decisions of the Florida Supreme Court do not satisfy the minimum requirement for nonarbitrary treatment of voters necessary to secure the fundamental right. Florida's basic command for the count of legally cast votes is to consider the "intent of the voter." This is unobjectionable as an abstract proposition and a starting principle. The problem inheres in the absence of specific standards to ensure its equal application. The formulation of uniform rules to determine intent based on these recurring circumstances is practicable and, we conclude, necessary.

The law does not refrain from searching for the intent of the actor in a multitude of circumstances; and in some cases the general command to ascertain intent is not susceptible to much further refinement. In this instance, however, the question is not whether to believe a witness but how to interpret the marks or holes or scratches on an inanimate object, a piece of cardboard or paper which, it is said, might not have registered as a vote during the machine count. The factfinder confronts a thing, not a person. The search for intent can be confined by specific rules designed to ensure uniform treatment.

The want of those rules here has led to unequal evaluation of ballots in various respects. See *id.* at 1267 (Wells, C.J., dissenting) ("Should a county canvassing board count or not count a 'dimpled chad' where the voter is able to successfully dislodge the chad in every other contest on that ballot? Here, the county canvassing boards disagree"). As seems to have been acknowledged at oral argument, the standards for accepting or rejecting contested ballots might vary not only from county to county but indeed within a single county from one recount team to another.

The record provides some examples. A monitor in Miami–Dade County testified at trial that he observed that three members of the county canvassing board applied different standards in defining a legal vote. And testimony at trial also revealed that at least one county changed its evaluative standards during the counting process. Palm Beach County, for example, began the process with a 1990 guideline which precluded counting completely attached chads, switched to a rule that considered vote to be legal if any light could be seen through a chad, changed back to the 1990 rule, and then abandoned any pretense of a *per se* rule, only to have a court order that the county consider dimpled chads legal. This is not a process with sufficient guarantees of equal treatment.

An early case in our one-person, one-vote jurisprudence arose when a State accorded arbitrary and disparate treatment to voters in its different counties. *Gray v. Sanders*, 372 U.S. 368 (1963). The Court found a constitutional violation. We relied on these principles in the context of the Presidential selection process in *Moore v. Ogilvie*, 394 U.S. 814 (1969), where we invalidated a county-based procedure that diluted the influence of citizens in larger counties in the nominating process. There we observed that "[t]he idea that one group can be granted greater voting strength than another is hostile to the one man, one vote basis of our representative government."

The State Supreme Court ratified this uneven treatment. It mandated that the recount totals from two counties, Miami–Dade and Palm Beach, be included in the certified total. The court also appeared to hold *sub silentio* that the recount totals from Broward County, which were not completed until after the original November 14 certification by the Secretary, were to be considered part of the new certified vote totals even though the county certification was not contested by Vice President Gore. Yet each of the counties used varying standards to determine what was a legal vote. Broward County used a more forgiving standard than Palm Beach County, and uncovered almost three times as many new votes, a result markedly disproportionate to the difference in population between the counties.

In addition, the recounts in these three counties were not limited to so-called undervotes but extended to all of the ballots. The distinction has real consequences. A manual recount of all ballots identifies not only those ballots which show no vote but also those which contain more than one, the so-called overvotes. Neither category will be counted by the machine. This is not a trivial concern. At oral argument, respondents estimated there are as many as 110,000 overvotes statewide. As a result, the citizen whose ballot was not read by a machine because he failed to vote for a candidate in a way readable by a machine may still have his vote counted in a manual recount; on the other hand, the citizen who marks two candidates in a way discernible by the machine will not have the same opportunity to have his vote count, even if a manual examination of the ballot would reveal the requisite indicia of intent. Furthermore, the citizen who marks two candidates, only one of which is discernible by the machine, will have his vote counted even though it should have been read as an invalid ballot. The State Supreme Court's inclusion of vote counts based on these variant standards exemplifies concerns with the remedial processes that were under way.

That brings the analysis to yet a further equal protection problem. The votes certified by the court included a partial total from one county, Miami–Dade. The Florida Supreme Court's decision thus gives no assurance that the recounts included in a final certification must be complete. Indeed, it is respondents' submission that it would be consistent with the rules of the recount procedures to include whatever partial counts are done by the time of final certification, and we interpret the Florida Supreme Court's decision to permit this. See 772 So.2d, at 1261–1262, n. 21 (noting "practical difficulties" may control outcome of election, but certifying partial Miami–Dade total nonetheless). This accommodation no doubt results from the truncated contest period established by the Florida Supreme Court in *Palm Beach County Canvassing Bd. v. Harris*, at respondents' own urging. The press of time does not diminish the constitutional concern. A desire for speed is not a general excuse for ignoring equal protection guarantees.

In addition to these difficulties the actual process by which the votes were to be counted under the Florida Supreme Court's decision raises further concerns. That order did not specify who would recount the ballots. The county canvassing boards were forced to pull together ad hoc teams of judges from various Circuits who had no previous training in handling and interpreting ballots. Furthermore, while others were permitted to observe, they were prohibited from objecting during the recount.

The recount process, in its features here described, is inconsistent with the minimum procedures necessary to protect the fundamental right of each voter in the special instance of a statewide recount under the authority of a single state judicial officer. Our consideration is limited to the present circumstances, for the problem of equal protection in election processes generally presents many complexities.

The question before the Court is not whether local entities, in the exercise of their expertise, may develop different systems for implementing elections. Instead, we are presented with a situation where a state court with the power to assure uniformity has ordered a statewide recount with minimal procedural safeguards. When a court orders a statewide remedy, there must be at least some assurance that the rudimentary requirements of equal treatment and fundamental fairness are satisfied.

Given the Court's assessment that the recount process underway was probably being conducted in an unconstitutional manner, the Court stayed the order directing the recount so it could hear this case and render an expedited decision. The contest provision, as it was mandated by the State Supreme Court, is not well calculated to sustain the confidence that all citizens must have in the outcome of elections. The State has not shown that its procedures include the necessary safeguards. The problem, for instance, of the estimated 110,000 overvotes has not been addressed, although Chief Justice Wells called attention to the concern in his dissenting opinion.

Upon due consideration of the difficulties identified to this point, it is obvious that the recount cannot be conducted in compliance with the requirements of equal protection and due process without substantial additional work. It would require not only the adoption (after opportunity for argument) of adequate statewide standards for determining what is a legal vote, and practicable procedures to implement them, but also orderly judicial review of any disputed matters that might arise. In addition, the Secretary has advised that the recount of only a portion of the ballots requires that the vote tabulation equipment be used to screen out undervotes, a function for which the machines were not designed. If a recount of overvotes were also required, perhaps even a second screening would be necessary. Use of the equipment for this purpose, and any new software developed for it, would have to be evaluated for accuracy by the Secretary, as required by Fla. Stat. Ann. § 101.015 (Supp.2001).

The Supreme Court of Florida has said that the legislature intended the State's electors to "participat[e] fully in the federal electoral process," as provided in 3 U.S.C. § 5. 772 So.2d, at 1289; see also *Palm Beach County Canvassing Bd. v. Harris*, 772 So.2d 1220, 1237 (Fla.2000). That statute, in turn, requires that any controversy or contest that is designed to lead to a conclusive selection of electors be completed by December 12. That date is upon us, and there is no recount procedure in place under the State Supreme Court's order that comports with minimal constitutional standards. Because it is evident that any recount seeking to meet the December 12 date will be unconstitutional for the reasons we have discussed, we reverse the judgment of the Supreme Court of Florida ordering a recount to proceed.

Seven Justices of the Court agree that there are constitutional problems with the recount ordered by the Florida Supreme Court that demand a remedy. See *post* (SOUTER, J., dissenting); *post* (BREYER, J., dissenting). The only disagreement is as to the remedy. Because the Florida Supreme Court has said that the Florida Legislature intended to obtain the safe-harbor benefits of 3 U.S.C. § 5, Justice BREYER's proposed remedy—remanding to the Florida Supreme Court for its ordering of a constitutionally proper contest until December 18—contemplates action in violation of the Florida Election Code. . . .

None are more conscious of the vital limits on judicial authority than are the Members of this Court, and none stand more in admiration of the Constitution's design to leave the selection of the President to the people, through their legislatures, and to the political sphere. When contending parties invoke the process of the courts, however, it becomes our unsought responsibility to resolve the federal and constitutional issues the judicial system has been forced to confront. The judgment of the Supreme Court of Florida is reversed, and the case is remanded for further proceedings not inconsistent with this opinion. . . .

■ CHIEF JUSTICE REHNQUIST, with whom JUSTICE SCALIA and JUSTICE THOMAS join, concurring.

We join the per curiam opinion. We write separately because we believe there are additional grounds that require us to reverse the Florida Supreme Court's decision.

I

. . . In most cases, comity and respect for federalism compel us to defer to the decisions of state courts on issues of state law. That practice reflects our understanding that the decisions of state courts are definitive pronouncements of the will of the States as sovereigns. Cf. *Erie R. Co. v. Tompkins*, 304 U.S. 64 (1938). Of course, in ordinary cases, the distribution of powers among the branches of a State's government raises no questions of federal constitutional law, subject to the requirement that the government be republican in character. See U.S. Const., Art. IV, § 4. But there are a few exceptional cases in which the Constitution imposes a duty or confers a power on a particular branch of a State's government. This is one of them. Article II, § 1, cl. 2, provides that "[e]ach State shall appoint, in such Manner as the *Legislature* thereof may direct," electors for President and Vice President. (Emphasis added.) Thus, the text of the election law itself, and not just its interpretation by the courts of the States, takes on independent significance.

In *McPherson v. Blacker*, 146 U.S. 1 (1892), we explained that Art. II, § 1, cl. 2, "convey[s] the broadest power of determination" and "leaves it to the legislature exclusively to define the method" of appointment. A significant departure from the legislative scheme for appointing Presidential electors presents a federal constitutional question. Title 3 U.S.C. § 5 informs our application of Art. II, § 1, cl. 2, to the Florida statutory scheme, which, as the Florida Supreme Court acknowledged, took that statute into account. Section 5 provides that the State's selection of electors "shall be conclusive, and shall govern in the counting of the electoral votes" if the electors are chosen under laws enacted prior to election day, and if the selection process is completed six days prior to the meeting of the electoral college. As we noted in *Bush v. Palm Beach County Canvassing Bd.*:

> Since § 5 contains a principle of federal law that would assure finality of the State's determination if made pursuant to a state law in effect before the election, a legislative wish to take advantage of the 'safe harbor' would counsel against any construction of the Election Code that Congress might deem to be a change in the law.

If we are to respect the legislature's Article II powers, therefore, we must ensure that postelection state-court actions do not frustrate the legislative desire to attain the "safe harbor" provided by § 5.

In Florida, the legislature has chosen to hold statewide elections to appoint the State's 25 electors. Importantly, the legislature has delegated the authority to run the elections and to oversee election disputes to the Secretary of State and to state circuit courts. Isolated sections of the code may well admit of more than one interpretation, but the general coherence of the legislative scheme may not be altered by judicial interpretation so as to wholly change the statutorily provided apportionment of responsibility among these various bodies. In any election but a Presidential election, the Florida Supreme Court can give as little or as much deference to Florida's executives as it chooses, so far as Article II is concerned, and this Court will have no cause to question the court's actions. But, with respect to a Presidential election, the court must be both mindful of the legislature's role under Article II in choosing the manner of appointing electors and deferential to those bodies expressly empowered by the legislature to carry out its constitutional mandate.

In order to determine whether a state court has infringed upon the legislature's authority, we necessarily must examine the law of the State as it existed prior to the action of the court. Though we generally defer to state courts on the interpretation of state law ... there are of course areas in which the Constitution requires this Court to undertake an independent, if still deferential, analysis of state law.... This inquiry does not imply a disrespect for state *courts* but rather a respect for the constitutionally prescribed role of state *legislatures*. To attach definitive weight to the pronouncement of a state court, when the very question at issue is whether the court has actually departed from the statutory meaning, would be to abdicate our responsibility to enforce the explicit requirements of Article II.

II

Acting pursuant to its constitutional grant of authority, the Florida Legislature has created a detailed, if not perfectly crafted, statutory scheme that provides for appointment of Presidential electors by direct election. . . .

In its first decision, the Florida Supreme Court extended the 7–day statutory certification deadline established by the legislature. This modification of the code, by lengthening the protest period, necessarily shortened the contest period for Presidential elections. Underlying the extension of the certification deadline and the shortchanging of the contest period was, presumably, the clear implication that certification was a matter of significance: The certified winner would enjoy presumptive validity, making a contest proceeding by the losing candidate an uphill battle. In its latest opinion, however, the court empties certification of virtually all legal consequence during the contest, and in doing so departs from the provisions enacted by the Florida Legislature.

The court determined that canvassing boards' decisions regarding whether to recount ballots past the certification deadline . . . are to be reviewed de novo, although the Election Code clearly vests discretion whether to recount in the boards, and sets strict deadlines subject to the Secretary's rejection of late tallies and monetary fines for tardiness. Moreover, the Florida court held that all late vote tallies arriving during the contest period should be automatically included in the certification regardless of the certification deadline . . ., thus virtually eliminating both the deadline and the Secretary's discretion to disregard recounts that violate it.

Moreover, the court's interpretation of "legal vote," and hence its decision to order a contest-period recount, plainly departed from the legislative scheme. Florida statutory law cannot reasonably be thought to *require* the counting of improperly marked ballots. . . .

[A]s we indicated in our remand of the earlier case, in a Presidential election the clearly expressed intent of the legislature must prevail. And there is no basis for reading the Florida statutes as requiring the counting of improperly marked ballots, as an examination of the Florida Supreme Court's textual analysis shows. We will not parse that analysis here, except to note that the principal provision of the Election Code on which it relied, § 101.5614(5), was, as Chief Justice Wells pointed out in his dissent in *Gore v. Harris*, 772 So.2d 1243, 1267 (2000) (*Harris II*), entirely irrelevant. The State's Attorney General (who was supporting the Gore challenge) confirmed in oral argument here that never before the present election had a manual recount been conducted on the basis of the contention that "undervotes" should have been examined to determine voter intent. For the court to step away from this established practice, prescribed by the Secretary, the state official charged by the legislature with "responsibility to . . . [o]btain and maintain uniformity in the application, operation, and interpretation of the election laws," was to depart from the legislative scheme.

III

The scope and nature of the remedy ordered by the Florida Supreme Court jeopardizes the "legislative wish" to take advantage of the safe harbor provided by 3 U.S.C. § 5. December 12, 2000, is the last date for a final determination of the Florida electors that will satisfy § 5. Yet in the late afternoon of December 8th—four days before this deadline—the Supreme Court of Florida ordered recounts of tens of thousands of so-called "undervotes" spread through 64 of the State's 67 counties. . . .

Surely when the Florida Legislature empowered the courts of the State to grant "appropriate" relief, it must have meant relief that would have become final by the cutoff date of 3 U.S.C. § 5. In light of the inevitable legal challenges and ensuing appeals to the Supreme Court of Florida and petitions for certiorari to this Court, the entire recounting process could not possibly be completed by that date. Whereas the majority in the Supreme Court of Florida stated its confidence that "the remaining undervotes in these counties can be [counted] within the required time frame," it made no assertion that the seemingly inevitable appeals could be disposed of in that time. . . .

As the dissent noted:

In [the four days remaining], all questionable ballots must be reviewed by the judicial officer appointed to discern the intent of the voter in a process open to the public. Fairness dictates that a provision be made for either party to object to how a particular ballot is counted. Additionally, this short time period must allow for judicial review. I respectfully submit this cannot be completed without taking Florida's presidential electors outside the safe harbor provision, creating the very real possibility of disenfranchising those nearly six million voters who are able to correctly cast their ballots on election day."

772 So.2d, at 1269 (opinion of Wells, C.J.) (footnote omitted).

The other dissenters echoed this concern: "[T]he majority is departing from the essential requirements of the law by providing a remedy which is impossible to achieve and which will ultimately lead to chaos." *Id.*, at 1273 (Harding, J., dissenting, jointed by Shaw, J.).

Given all these factors, and in light of the legislative intent identified by the Florida Supreme Court to bring Florida within the "safe harbor" provision of 3 U.S.C. § 5, the remedy prescribed by the Supreme Court of Florida cannot be deemed an "appropriate" one as of December 8. It significantly departed from the statutory framework in place on November 7, and authorized open-ended further proceedings which could not be completed by December 12, thereby preventing a final determination by that date.

For these reasons, in addition to those given in the *per curiam* opinion, we would reverse.

■ JUSTICE STEVENS, with whom JUSTICE GINSBURG and JUSTICE BREYER join, dissenting.

The Constitution assigns to the States the primary responsibility for determining the manner of selecting the Presidential electors. See Art. II, § 1, cl. 2. When questions arise about the meaning of state laws, including election laws, it is our settled practice to accept the opinions of the highest courts of the States as providing the final answers. On rare occasions, however, either federal statutes or the Federal Constitution may require federal judicial intervention in state elections. This is not such an occasion.

The federal questions that ultimately emerged in this case are not substantial. Article II provides that "[e]ach *State* shall appoint, in such Manner as the Legislature *thereof* may direct, a Number of Electors." It does not create state legislatures out of whole cloth, but rather takes them as they come—as creatures born of, and constrained by, their state constitutions. Lest there be any doubt, we stated over 100 years ago in *McPherson v. Blacker*, 146 U.S. 1, 25 (1892), that "[w]hat is forbidden or required to be done by a State" in the Article II context "is forbidden or required of the legislative power under state constitutions as they exist." In the same vein, we also observed that "[t]he [State's] legislative power is the supreme authority except as limited by the constitution of the State." *Ibid.* The legislative power in Florida is subject to judicial review pursuant to Article V of the Florida Constitution, and nothing in Article II of the Federal Constitution frees the state legislature from the constraints in the State Constitution that created it. Moreover, the Florida Legislature's own decision to employ a unitary code for all elections indicates that it intended the Florida Supreme Court to play the same role in Presidential elections that it has historically played in resolving electoral disputes. The Florida Supreme Court's exercise of appellate jurisdiction therefore was wholly consistent with, and indeed contemplated by, the grant of authority in Article II. . . .

Even assuming that aspects of the remedial scheme might ultimately be found to violate the Equal Protection Clause, I could not subscribe to the majority's disposition of the case. As the majority explicitly holds, once a state legislature determines to select electors through a popular vote, the right to have one's vote counted is of constitutional stature. As the majority further acknowledges, Florida law holds that all ballots that reveal the intent of the voter constitute valid votes. Recognizing these principles, the majority nonetheless orders the termination of the contest proceeding before all such votes have been tabulated. Under their own reasoning, the appropriate course of action would be to remand to allow more specific procedures for implementing the legislature's uniform general standard to be established.

In the interest of finality, however, the majority effectively orders the disenfranchisement of an unknown number of voters whose ballots reveal their intent—and are therefore legal votes under state law—but were for some reason rejected by ballot-counting machines. It does so on the basis of the deadlines set forth in Title 3 of the United States Code. But, as I have already noted, those provisions merely provide rules of decision for Congress to follow when selecting among conflicting slates of electors. They do not prohibit a State from counting what the majority concedes to be legal votes until a bona fide winner is determined. . . . Thus, nothing prevents the majority, even if it properly found an equal protection violation, from ordering relief appropriate to remedy that violation without depriving Florida voters of their right to have their votes counted. As the majority notes, "[a] desire for speed is not a general excuse for ignoring equal protection guarantees."

Finally, neither in this case, nor in its earlier opinion in *Palm Beach County Canvassing Bd. v. Harris*, 772 So.2d 1220 (2000), did the Florida Supreme Court make any substantive change in Florida electoral law. Its decisions were rooted in long-established precedent and were consistent with the relevant statutory provisions, taken as a whole. It did what courts do—it decided the case before it in light of the legislature's intent to leave no legally cast vote uncounted. In so doing, it relied on the sufficiency of the general "intent of the voter" standard articulated by the state legislature, coupled with a procedure for ultimate review by an impartial judge, to resolve the concern about disparate evaluations of contested ballots. If we assume—as I do—that the members of that court and the judges who would have carried out its mandate are impartial, its decision does not even raise a colorable federal question.

What must underlie petitioners' entire federal assault on the Florida election procedures is an unstated lack of confidence in the impartiality and capacity of the state judges who would make the critical decisions if the vote count were to proceed. Otherwise, their position is wholly without merit. The endorsement of that position by the majority of this Court can only lend credence to the most cynical appraisal of the work of judges throughout the land. It is confidence in the men and women who administer the judicial system that is the true backbone of the rule of law. Time will one day heal the wound to that confidence that will be inflicted by today's decision. One thing, however, is certain. Although we may never know with complete certainty the identity of the winner of this year's Presidential election, the identity of the loser is perfectly clear. It is the Nation's confidence in the judge as an impartial guardian of the rule of law.

■ JUSTICE SOUTER, with whom JUSTICE BREYER joins, and with whom JUSTICE STEVENS and JUSTICE GINSBURG join as to all but Part III, dissenting.

The Court should not have reviewed either *Bush v. Palm Beach County Canvassing Bd.* or this case, and should not have stopped Florida's attempt to recount all undervote ballots, by issuing a stay of the Florida Supreme Court's orders during the period of this review. If this Court had allowed the State to follow the course indicated by the opinions of its own Supreme Court, it is entirely possible that there would ultimately have been no issue requiring our review, and political tension could have worked itself out in the Congress following the procedure provided in 3 U.S.C. § 15. The case being before us, however, its resolution by the majority is another erroneous decision. . . .

There are three issues: whether the State Supreme Court's interpretation of the statute providing for a contest of the state election results somehow violates 3 U.S.C. § 5; whether that court's construction of the state statutory provisions governing contests impermissibly changes a state law from what the State's legislature has provided, in violation of Article II, § 1, cl. 2, of the National Constitution; and whether the manner of interpreting markings on disputed ballots failing to cause machines to register votes for President (the undervote ballots) violates the equal protection or due process guaranteed by the Fourteenth Amendment. None of these issues is difficult to describe or to resolve. . . .

It is only on the third issue before us that there is a meritorious argument for relief, as this Court's *per curiam* opinion recognizes. It is an issue that might well have been dealt with adequately by the Florida courts if the state proceedings had not been interrupted, and if not disposed of at the state level it could have been considered by the Congress in any electoral vote dispute. But because the course of state proceedings has been interrupted, time is short, and the issue is before us, I think it sensible for the Court to address it.

Petitioners have raised an equal protection claim (or, alternatively, a due process claim), in the charge that unjustifiably disparate standards are applied in different electoral jurisdictions to otherwise identical facts. . . . I can conceive of no legitimate state interest served by these differing treatments of the expressions of voters' fundamental rights. The differences appear wholly arbitrary.

In deciding what to do about this, we should take account of the fact that electoral votes are due to be cast in six days. I would therefore remand the case to the courts of Florida with instructions to establish uniform standards for evaluating the several types of ballots that have prompted differing treatments, to be applied within and among counties when passing on such identical ballots in any further recounting (or successive recounting) that the courts might order.

Unlike the majority, I see no warrant for this Court to assume that Florida could not possibly comply with this requirement before the date set for the meeting of electors, December 18. . . .

■ [JUSTICE GINSBURG's dissenting opinion is omitted.]

■ JUSTICE BREYER, with whom JUSTICE STEVENS and JUSTICE GINSBURG join except as to Part I–A–1, and with whom JUSTICE SOUTER joins as to Part I, dissenting.

The Court was wrong to take this case. It was wrong to grant a stay. It should now vacate that stay and permit the Florida Supreme Court to decide whether the recount should resume.

I

The political implications of this case for the country are momentous. But the federal legal questions presented, with one exception, are insubstantial.

A–1

The majority raises three equal protection problems with the Florida Supreme Court's recount order: first, the failure to include overvotes in the manual recount; second, the fact that *all* ballots, rather than simply the undervotes, were recounted in some, but not all, counties; and third, the absence of a uniform, specific standard to guide the recounts. . . .

The majority's third concern does implicate principles of fundamental fairness. The majority concludes that the Equal Protection Clause requires that a manual recount be governed not only by the uniform general standard of the "clear intent of the voter," but also by uniform subsidiary standards (for example, a uniform determination whether indented, but not perforated, "undervotes" should count). The opinion points out that the Florida Supreme Court ordered the inclusion of Broward County's undercounted "legal votes" even though those votes included ballots that were not perforated but simply "dimpled," while newly recounted ballots from other counties will likely include only votes determined to be "legal" on the basis of a stricter standard. In light of our previous remand, the Florida Supreme Court may have been reluctant to adopt a more specific standard than that provided for by the legislature for fear of exceeding its authority under Article II. However, since the use of different standards could favor one or the other of the candidates, since time was, and is, too short to permit the lower courts to iron out significant differences through ordinary judicial review, and since the relevant distinction was embodied in the order of the State's highest court, I agree that, in these very special circumstances, basic principles of fairness may well have counseled the adoption of a uniform standard to address the problem. . . .

2

Nonetheless, there is no justification for the majority's remedy, which is simply to reverse the lower court and halt the recount entirely. An appropriate remedy would be, instead, to remand this case with instructions that, even at this late date, would permit the Florida Supreme Court to require recounting *all* undercounted votes in Florida . . . whether or not previously recounted prior to the end of the protest period, and to do so in accordance with a single uniform standard.

The majority justifies stopping the recount entirely on the ground that there is no more time. . . . But the majority reaches this conclusion in the absence of *any* record evidence that the recount could not have been completed in the time allowed by the Florida Supreme Court. . . . Of course, it is too late for any such recount to take place by December 12, the date by which election disputes must be decided if a State is to take advantage of the safe harbor provisions of 3 U.S.C. § 5. Whether there is time to conduct a recount prior to December 18, when the electors are scheduled to meet, is a matter for the state courts to determine. . . .

By halting the manual recount, and thus ensuring that the uncounted legal votes will not be counted under any standard, this Court crafts a remedy out of proportion to the asserted harm. And that remedy harms the very fairness interests the Court is attempting to protect . . . . .

B

. . . I cannot agree that The Chief Justice's unusual review of state law in this case is justified by reference either to Art. II, § 1, or to 3 U.S.C. § 5. Moreover, even were such review proper, the conclusion that the Florida Supreme Court's decision contravenes federal law is untenable. . . .

II

Despite the reminder that this case involves "an election for the President of the United States," *ante,* at 533 (Rehnquist, C. J., concurring), no preeminent legal concern, or practical concern related to legal questions, required this Court to hear this case, let alone to issue a stay that stopped Florida's recount process in its tracks. With one exception, petitioners' claims do not ask us to vindicate a constitutional provision designed to protect a basic human right. Petitioners invoke fundamental fairness, namely, the need for procedural fairness, including finality. But with the one "equal protection" exception, they rely upon law that focuses, not upon that basic need, but upon the constitutional allocation of power. . . .

Of course, the selection of the President is of fundamental national importance. But that importance is political, not legal. And this Court should resist the temptation unnecessarily to resolve tangential legal disputes, where doing so threatens to determine the outcome of the election. The Constitution and federal statutes themselves make clear that restraint is appropriate. . . .

[T]he Twelfth Amendment commits to Congress the authority and responsibility to count electoral votes. A federal statute, the Electoral Count Act, enacted after the close 1876 Hayes–Tilden Presidential election, specifies that, after States have tried to resolve disputes (through "judicial" or other means), Congress is the body primarily authorized to resolve remaining disputes . . . . .

Given this detailed, comprehensive scheme for counting electoral votes, there is no reason to believe that federal law either foresees or requires resolution of such a political issue by this Court. Nor, for that matter, is there any reason to think that the Constitution's Framers would have reached a different conclusion. Madison, at least, believed that allowing the judiciary to choose the Presidential electors "was out of the question." Madison, July 25, 1787 (reprinted in 5 Elliot's Debates on the Federal Constitution 363 (2d ed. 1876)).

The decision by both the Constitution's Framers and the 1886 Congress to minimize this Court's role in resolving close federal Presidential elections is as wise as it is clear. However awkward or difficult it may be for Congress to resolve difficult electoral disputes, Congress, being a political body, expresses the people's will far more accurately than does an unelected Court. And the people's will is what elections are about.

Moreover, Congress was fully aware of the danger that would arise should it ask judges, unarmed with appropriate legal standards, to resolve a hotly contested Presidential election contest. Just after the 1876 Presidential election, Florida, South Carolina, and Louisiana each sent two slates of electors to Washington. Without these States, Tilden, the Democrat, had 184 electoral votes, one short of the number required to win the Presidency. With those States, Hayes, his Republican opponent, would have had 185. In order to choose between the two slates of electors, Congress decided to appoint an electoral commission composed of five senators, five representatives, and five Supreme Court justices. Initially the Commission was to be evenly divided between Republicans and Democrats, with Justice David Davis, an Independent, to possess the decisive vote. However, when at the last minute the Illinois Legislature elected Justice Davis to the United States Senate, the final position on the Commission was filled by Supreme Court Justice Joseph P. Bradley.

The Commission divided along partisan lines, and the responsibility to cast the deciding vote fell to Justice Bradley. He decided to accept the votes by the Republican electors, and thereby awarded the Presidency to Hayes.

Justice Bradley immediately became the subject of vociferous attacks. Bradley was accused of accepting bribes, of being captured by railroad interests, and of an eleventh-hour change in position after a night in which his house "was surrounded by the carriages" of Republican partisans and railroad officials. C. Woodward, Reunion and Reaction 159–160 (1966). Many years later, Professor Bickel concluded that Bradley was honest and impartial. He thought that "the great question for Bradley was, in fact, whether Congress was entitled to go behind election returns or had to accept them as certified by state authorities," an "issue of principle." The Least Dangerous Branch 185 (1962). Nonetheless, Bickel points out, the legal question upon which Justice Bradley's decision turned was not very important in the contemporaneous political context. He says that "in the circumstances the issue of principle was trivial, it was overwhelmed by all that hung in the balance, and it should not have been decisive." *Ibid.*

For present purposes, the relevance of this history lies in the fact that the participation in the work of the electoral commission by five Justices, including Justice Bradley, did not lend that process legitimacy. Nor did it assure the public that the process had worked fairly, guided by the law. Rather, it simply embroiled Members of the Court in partisan conflict, thereby undermining respect for the judicial process. And the Congress that later enacted the Electoral Count Act knew it.

This history may help to explain why I think it not only legally wrong, but also most unfortunate, for the Court simply to have terminated the Florida recount. Those who caution judicial restraint in resolving political disputes have described the quintessential case for that restraint as a case marked, among other things, by the "strangeness of the issue," its "intractability to principled resolution," its "sheer momentousness, . . . which tends to unbalance judicial judgment," and "the inner vulnerability, the self-doubt of an institution which is electorally irresponsible and has no earth to draw strength from." *Id.*, at 184. Those characteristics mark this case.

At the same time, as I have said, the Court is not acting to vindicate a fundamental constitutional principle, such as the need to protect a basic human liberty. No other strong reason to act is present. Congressional statutes tend to obviate the need. And, above all, in this highly politicized matter, the appearance of a split decision runs the risk of undermining the public's confidence in the Court itself. That confidence is a public treasure. It has been built slowly over many years, some of which were marked by a Civil War and the tragedy of segregation. It is a vitally necessary ingredient of any successful effort to protect basic liberty and, indeed, the rule of law itself. We run no risk of returning to the days when a President (responding to this Court's efforts to protect the Cherokee Indians) might have said, "John Marshall has made his decision; now let him enforce it!" D. Loth, Chief Justice: John Marshall and The Growth of the American Republic 365 (1948). But we do risk a self-inflicted wound—a wound that may harm not just the Court, but the Nation.

. . . Justice Brandeis once said of the Court, "The most important thing we do is not doing." Bickel, at 71. What it does today, the Court should have left undone. I would repair the damage done as best we now can, by permitting the Florida recount to continue under uniform standards. . . .

NOTES

1. What is the scope of authority the Constitution gives to states to prescribe how electors are chosen? Could a state constitutionally choose to let the state governor choose that state's presidential electors? Could the state legislature appoint electors itself? Is the choice of procedure entirely at the whim of the state legislature? Or is it the choice of the state legislature, but subject to the interpretations of state courts and the limitations of that state's constitution? What if the judiciary's interpretation of the state constitution essentially rewrites the legislature's statute? What does *Bush v. Palm Beach County Canvassing Commission* say about this issue? What does *Bush v. Gore* say? If Article II of the Constitution commits the decision to the state legislatures, does that constrain—as a matter of federal constitutional law—the presumed usual power of state courts to exercise state constitutional law judicial review of state legislative acts? Does this render state judicial interpretations of state law subject to *federal* judicial review to decide whether the state courts have improperly usurped the province of the state legislatures?

Or could a state legislature decide that electors should be chosen by a state election procedure, but then prescribe that only the votes of persons in one racial group would be counted? Why not—if the state's choice of methods is entirely up to the state legislature's discretion? Is it because, whatever procedure is chosen, that procedure may not violate some *other* constitutional provision? If a state may not adopt a racially discriminatory vote-counting procedure for choosing electors, may it adopt a procedure that weights votes differently from different parts of the state? Or would that violate *Baker v. Carr* and *Reynolds v. Sims?* Is the (successful) claim made by the Bush side, in *Bush v. Gore,* that a recount that treats ballots differently in different counties very much different? If so, in what ways? At the time, many commentators argued that the Court's decision was "political" (i.e., partisan) and therefore improper. Do you agree? If the places of the two presidential candidates had been reversed, would the Court's decision have been the same? That is, imagine that Gore had had more votes and that the Bush team had succeeded in persuading a seemingly partisan (Republican, rather than Democrat) Florida Supreme Court to order a selective recount and include late returns from the Bush side's "best" counties. Would the U.S. Supreme Court have found this a violation of the Equal Protection principles of *Baker* and *Reynolds*? Is the Equal Protection Clause holding of *Bush v. Gore* right if and only if *Baker* and *Reynolds* are right? Is *Bush v. Gore* wrong on the Equal Protection Clause holding, even if *Baker* and *Reynolds* are right?

2. What do you make of the concurrence's argument that an additional reason for the outcome is that the Florida Supreme Court's decisions violated Article II of the Constitution, by usurping the federal constitutional discretion of the state legislature? Does this argument seem more appropriate for *Bush v. Palm Beach County Canvassing Commission*?

3. In *Bush v. Gore* seven justices found that Florida's actions violated the Equal Protection clause (the five justices in the majority, as well as Justices Souter and Breyer). But those seven justices divided sharply over the remedy. The majority's remedy was to invalidate the recount and not permit a re-recount; Justices Souter and Breyer disagreed. What is your assessment of the remedy adopted? Was time really up? Should the Court have remanded to the Florida Supreme Court to try a third time? Should the majority have agreed to this position in order to present a more unified face on its disposition? Is it appropriate for the Court to take public perceptions and public reactions into account in deciding how to resolve a high-stakes public controversy of this sort? Should the Court simply have denied certiorari and let the Florida Supreme Court decision stand?

4. Should the Court have treated the constitutional questions presented as nonjusticiable "political questions"? If so, what body should have decided these issues? The Florida secretary of state? The Florida Supreme Court? Its legislature? Congress? What was the position of the dissenters on these questions?

5. *Bush v. Gore* raises—yet one more time—the question of the proper role of the Supreme Court in our constitutional system. Should the Court exercise an "active" role or a "restrained" role? What principles should govern the Court in its interpretation of the Constitution and in the exercise of the judicial power? What is the appropriate role of other actors in our constitutional system— including elected officials, federal and state—in interpreting the Constitution? To what extent should courts defer to political resolutions of constitutional issues? Or should everyone who swears an oath to support the Constitution of the United States exercise an independent responsibility to interpret and apply the Constitution faithfully—not deferring to anyone else's interpretation? And of course: what does it mean to interpret and apply the Constitution faithfully? Does faithful interpretation of the Constitution mean something different from a search for results that match one's own personal policy preferences? Is constitutional law more than politics?

THE ARTICLES OF CONFEDERATION

Preamble

To all to whom these Presents shall come, we the undersigned Delegates of the States affixed to our Names send greeting.

Articles of Confederation and perpetual Union between the States of New Hampshire, Massachusetts bay, Rhode Island and Providence Plantations, Connecticut, New York, New Jersey, Pennsylvania, Delaware, Maryland, Virginia, North Carolina, South Carolina and Georgia.

Article I

The Stile of this Confederacy shall be "The United States of America."

Article II

Each state retains its sovereignty, freedom, and independence, and every power, jurisdiction, and right, which is not by this Confederation expressly delegated to the United States, in Congress assembled.

Article III

The said States hereby severally enter into a firm league of friendship with each other, for their common defense, the security of their liberties, and their mutual and general welfare, binding themselves to assist each other, against all force offered to, or attacks made upon them, or any of them, on account of religion, sovereignty, trade, or any other pretense whatever.

Article IV

The better to secure and perpetuate mutual friendship and intercourse among the people of the different States in this Union, the free inhabitants of each of these States, paupers, vagabonds, and fugitives from justice excepted, shall be entitled to all privileges and immunities of free citizens in the several States; and the people of each State shall free ingress and regress to and from any other State, and shall enjoy therein all the privileges of trade and commerce, subject to the same duties, impositions, and restrictions as the inhabitants thereof respectively, provided that such restrictions shall not extend so far as to prevent the removal of property imported into any State, to any other State, of which the owner is an inhabitant; provided also that no imposition, duties or restriction shall be laid by any State, on the property of the United States, or either of them.

If any person guilty of, or charged with, treason, felony, or other high misdemeanor in any State, shall flee from justice, and be found in any of the United States, he shall, upon demand of the Governor or executive power of the State from which he fled, be delivered up and removed to the State having jurisdiction of his offense.

Full faith and credit shall be given in each of these States to the records, acts, and judicial proceedings of the courts and magistrates of every other State.

Article V

For the most convenient management of the general interests of the United States, delegates shall be annually appointed in such manner as the legislatures of each State shall direct, to meet in Congress on the first Monday in November, in every year, with a power reserved to each State to recall its delegates, or any of them, at any time within the year, and to send others in their stead for the remainder of the year.

No State shall be represented in Congress by less than two, nor more than seven members; and no person shall be capable of being a delegate for more than three years in any term of six years; nor shall any person, being a delegate, be capable of holding any office under the United States, for which he, or another for his benefit, receives any salary, fees or emolument of any kind.

Each State shall maintain its own delegates in a meeting of the States, and while they act as members of the committee of the States.

In determining questions in the United States in Congress assembled, each State shall have one vote.

Freedom of speech and debate in Congress shall not be impeached or questioned in any court or place out of Congress, and the members of Congress shall be protected in their persons from arrests or imprisonments, during the time of their going to and from, and attendance on Congress, except for treason, felony, or breach of the peace.

Article VI

No State, without the consent of the United States in Congress assembled, shall send any embassy to, or receive any embassy from, or enter into any conference, agreement, alliance or treaty with any King, Prince or State; nor shall any person holding any office of profit or trust under the United States, or any of them, accept any present, emolument, office or title of any kind whatever from any King, Prince or foreign State; nor shall the United States in Congress assembled, or any of them, grant any title of nobility.

No two or more States shall enter into any treaty, confederation or alliance whatever between them, without the consent of the United States in Congress assembled, specifying accurately the purposes for which the same is to be entered into, and how long it shall continue.

No State shall lay any imposts or duties, which may interfere with any stipulations in treaties, entered into by the United States in Congress assembled, with any King, Prince or State, in pursuance of any treaties already proposed by Congress, to the courts of France and Spain.

No vessel of war shall be kept up in time of peace by any State, except such number only, as shall be deemed necessary by the United States in Congress assembled, for the defense of such State, or its trade; nor shall any body of forces be kept up by any State in time of peace, except such number only, as in the judgement of the United States in Congress assembled, shall be deemed requisite to garrison the forts necessary for the defense of such State; but every State shall always keep up a well-regulated and disciplined militia, sufficiently armed and accoutered, and shall provide and constantly have ready for use, in public stores, a due number of filed pieces and tents, and a proper quantity of arms, ammunition and camp equipage.

No State shall engage in any war without the consent of the United States in Congress assembled, unless such State be actually invaded by enemies, or shall have received certain advice of a resolution being formed by some nation of Indians to invade such State, and the danger is so imminent as not to admit of a delay till the United States in Congress assembled can be consulted; nor shall any State grant commissions to any ships or vessels of war, nor letters of marque or reprisal, except it be after a declaration of war by the United States in Congress assembled, and then only against the Kingdom or State and the subjects thereof, against which war has been so declared, and under such regulations as shall be established by the United States in Congress assembled, unless such State be infested by pirates, in which case vessels of war may be fitted out for that occasion, and kept so long as the danger shall continue, or until the United States in Congress assembled shall determine otherwise.

Article VII

When land forces are raised by any State for the common defense, all officers of or under the rank of colonel, shall be appointed by the legislature of each State respectively, by whom such forces shall be raised, or in such manner as such State shall direct, and all vacancies shall be filled up by the State which first made the appointment.

Article VIII

All charges of war, and all other expenses that shall be incurred for the common defense or general welfare, and allowed by the United States in Congress assembled, shall be defrayed out of a common treasury, which shall be supplied by the several States in proportion to the value of all land within each State, granted or surveyed for any person, as such land and the buildings and improvements thereon shall be estimated according to such mode as the United States in Congress assembled, shall from time to time direct and appoint.

The taxes for paying that proportion shall be laid and levied by the authority and direction of the legislatures of the several States within the time agreed upon by the United States in Congress assembled.

Article IX

The United States in Congress assembled, shall have the sole and exclusive right and power of determining on peace and war, except in the cases mentioned in the sixth article—of sending and receiving ambassadors—entering into treaties and alliances, provided that no treaty of commerce shall be made whereby the legislative power of the respective States shall be restrained from imposing such imposts and duties on foreigners, as their own people are subjected to, or from prohibiting the exportation or importation of any species of goods or commodities whatsoever—of establishing rules for deciding in all cases, what captures on land or water shall be legal, and in what manner prizes taken by land or naval forces in the service of the United States shall be divided or appropriated—of granting letters of marque and reprisal in times of peace—appointing courts for the trial of piracies and felonies committed on the high seas and establishing courts for receiving and determining finally appeals in all cases of captures, provided that no member of Congress shall be appointed a judge of any of the said courts.

The United States in Congress assembled shall also be the last resort on appeal in all disputes and differences now subsisting or that hereafter may arise between two or more States concerning boundary, jurisdiction or any other causes whatever; which authority shall always be exercised in the manner following. Whenever the legislative or executive authority or lawful agent of any State in controversy with another shall present a petition to Congress stating the matter in question and praying for a hearing, notice thereof shall be given by order of Congress to the legislative or executive authority of the other State in controversy, and a day assigned for the appearance of the parties by their lawful agents, who shall then be directed to appoint by joint consent, commissioners or judges to constitute a court for hearing and determining the matter in question: but if they cannot agree, Congress shall name three persons out of each of the United States, and from the list of such persons each party shall alternately strike out one, the petitioners beginning, until the number shall be reduced to thirteen; and from that number not less than seven, nor more than nine names as Congress shall direct, shall in the presence of Congress be drawn out by lot, and the persons whose names shall be so drawn or any five of them, shall be commissioners or judges, to hear and finally determine the controversy, so always as a major part of the judges who shall hear the cause shall agree in the determination: and if either party shall neglect to attend at the day appointed, without showing reasons, which Congress shall judge sufficient, or being present shall refuse to strike, the Congress shall proceed to nominate three persons out of each State, and the secretary of Congress shall strike in behalf of such party absent or refusing; and the judgement and sentence of the court to be appointed, in the manner before prescribed, shall be final and conclusive; and if any of the parties shall refuse to submit to the authority of such court, or to appear or defend their claim or cause, the court shall nevertheless proceed to pronounce sentence, or judgement, which shall in like manner be final and decisive, the judgement or sentence and other proceedings being in either case transmitted to Congress, and lodged among the acts of Congress for the security of the parties concerned: provided that every commissioner, before he sits in judgement, shall take an oath to be administered by one of the judges of the supreme or superior court of the State, where the cause shall be tried, "well and truly to hear and determine the matter in question, according to the best of his judgement, without favor, affection or hope of reward": provided also, that no State shall be deprived of territory for the benefit of the United States.

All controversies concerning the private right of soil claimed under different grants of two or more States, whose jurisdictions as they may respect such lands, and the States which passed such grants are adjusted, the said grants or either of them being at the same time claimed to have originated antecedent to such settlement of jurisdiction, shall on the petition of either party to the Congress of the United States, be finally determined as near as may be in the same manner as is before prescribed for deciding disputes respecting territorial jurisdiction between different States.

The United States in Congress assembled shall also have the sole and exclusive right and power of regulating the alloy and value of coin struck by their own authority, or by that of the respective States—fixing the standards of weights and measures throughout the United States—regulating the trade and managing all affairs with the Indians, not members of any of the States, provided that the legislative right of any State within its own limits be not infringed or violated—establishing or regulating post offices from one State to another, throughout all the United States, and exacting such postage on the papers passing through the same as may be requisite to defray the expenses of the said office—appointing all officers of the land forces, in the service of the United States, excepting regimental officers—

appointing all the officers of the naval forces, and commissioning all officers whatever in the service of the United States—making rules for the government and regulation of the said land and naval forces, and directing their operations.

The United States in Congress assembled shall have authority to appoint a committee, to sit in the recess of Congress, to be denominated "A Committee of the States", and to consist of one delegate from each State; and to appoint such other committees and civil officers as may be necessary for managing the general affairs of the United States under their direction—to appoint one of their members to preside, provided that no person be allowed to serve in the office of president more than one year in any term of three years; to ascertain the necessary sums of money to be raised for the service of the United States, and to appropriate and apply the same for defraying the public expenses—to borrow money, or emit bills on the credit of the United States, transmitting every half-year to the respective States an account of the sums of money so borrowed or emitted—to build and equip a navy—to agree upon the number of land forces, and to make requisitions from each State for its quota, in proportion to the number of white inhabitants in such State; which requisition shall be binding, and thereupon the legislature of each State shall appoint the regimental officers, raise the men and cloath, arm and equip them in a solid-like manner, at the expense of the United States; and the officers and men so cloathed, armed and equipped shall march to the place appointed, and within the time agreed on by the United States in Congress assembled. But if the United States in Congress assembled shall, on consideration of circumstances judge proper that any State should not raise men, or should raise a smaller number of men than the quota thereof, such extra number shall be raised, officered, cloathed, armed and equipped in the same manner as the quota of each State, unless the legislature of such State shall judge that such extra number cannot be safely spread out in the same, in which case they shall raise, officer, cloath, arm and equip as many of such extra number as they judge can be safely spared. And the officers and men so cloathed, armed, and equipped, shall march to the place appointed, and within the time agreed on by the United States in Congress assembled.

The United States in Congress assembled shall never engage in a war, nor grant letters of marque or reprisal in time of peace, nor enter into any treaties or alliances, nor coin money, nor regulate the value thereof, nor ascertain the sums and expenses necessary for the defense and welfare of the United States, or any of them, nor emit bills, nor borrow money on the credit of the United States, nor appropriate money, nor agree upon the number of vessels of war, to be built or purchased, or the number of land or sea forces to be raised, nor appoint a commander in chief of the army or navy, unless nine States assent to the same: nor shall a question on any other point, except for adjourning from day to day be determined, unless by the votes of the majority of the United States in Congress assembled.

The Congress of the United States shall have power to adjourn to any time within the year, and to any place within the United States, so that no period of adjournment be for a longer duration than the space of six months, and shall publish the journal of their proceedings monthly, except such parts thereof relating to treaties, alliances or military operations, as in their judgement require secrecy; and the yeas and nays of the delegates of each State on any question shall be entered on the journal, when it is desired by any delegates of a State, or any of them, at his or their request shall be furnished with a transcript of the said journal, except such parts as are above excepted, to lay before the legislatures of the several States.

Article X

The Committee of the States, or any nine of them, shall be authorized to execute, in the recess of Congress, such of the powers of Congress as the United States in Congress assembled, by the consent of the nine States, shall from time to time think expedient to vest them with; provided that no power be delegated to the said Committee, for the exercise of which, by the Articles of Confederation, the voice of nine States in the Congress of the United States assembled be requisite.

Article XI

Canada acceding to this confederation, and adjoining in the measures of the United States, shall be admitted into, and entitled to all the advantages of this Union; but no other colony shall be admitted into the same, unless such admission be agreed to by nine States.

Article XII

All bills of credit emitted, monies borrowed, and debts contracted by, or under the authority of Congress, before the assembling of the United States, in pursuance of the present confederation, shall be deemed and considered as a charge against the United States, for payment and satisfaction whereof the said United States, and the public faith are hereby solemnly pledged.

Article XIII

Every State shall abide by the determination of the United States in Congress assembled, on all questions which by this confederation are submitted to them. And the Articles of this Confederation shall be inviolably observed by every State, and the Union shall be perpetual; nor shall any alteration at any time hereafter be made in any of them; unless such alteration be agreed to in a Congress of the United States, and be afterwards confirmed by the legislatures of every State.

And Whereas it hath pleased the Great Governor of the World to incline the hearts of the legislatures we respectively represent in Congress, to approve of, and to authorize us to ratify the said Articles of Confederation and perpetual Union. Know Ye that we the undersigned delegates, by virtue of the power and authority to us given for that purpose, do by these presents, in the name and in behalf of our respective constituents, fully and entirely ratify and confirm each and every of the said Articles of Confederation and perpetual Union, and all and singular the matters and things therein contained: And we do further solemnly plight and engage the faith of our respective constituents, that they shall abide by the determinations of the United States in Congress assembled, on all questions, which by the said Confederation are submitted to them. And that the Articles thereof shall be inviolably observed by the States we respectively represent, and that the Union shall be perpetual.

In Witness whereof we have hereunto set our hands in Congress. Done at Philadelphia in the State of Pennsylvania the ninth day of July in the Year of our Lord One Thousand Seven Hundred and Seventy–Eight, and in the Third Year of the independence of America.

TABLE OF CASES

The principal cases are in bold type.

INDEX

References are to pages